CLC Cumulative Title Index

Vols. 1-117

"A" (Cummings) 15:160, 162
"A" (Merrill) 8:383-84, 386; 13:377
"A" (Zukofsky) 1:385; 2:487; 4:599; 11:581; 18:558-61
"A, a, a, Domine Deus" (Jones) 42:245, 249
"A André Masson" (Cabral de Melo Neto) 76:156
A Antonio Mairena, cantador ("To A. M., a Flamenco Singer") (Cabral de Melo Neto) 76:164
"'A' Bomb in Wardour Street" (Weller) 26:444
A caso (Landolfi) 49:213-14
A ciascuno il suo (*A Man's Blessing*) (Sciascia) 9:474-75; 41:388-90, 392-94
"A. D." (Burgess) 40:126
"A extraordinária senhorita do país do Sonho" (Dourado) 23:151
À haute flamme (*At Full Flame*) (Tzara) 47:390, 395
"A la recherche d'un nouveau mode d'expression" (de Man) 55:422
"Á la santé du serpent" (Char) 9:166; 11:118; 14:128
"A la Víbora de la mar" ("To the Sea Serpent"; "To the Snake of the Sea") (Fuentes) 113:236
A lume spento (Pound) 1:276; 2:343; 10:407; 48:288; 112:329-31
"A. M." (Strand) 71:280, 288
"A qué hora venderemos todo" ("At What Time Will We Sell Everything?") (Zamora) 89:368, 384
"'A Story' by John V. Marsh" (Wolfe) 25:472
"A un pauvre écoeuré" (Reverdy) 53:286
À une sérénité crispée (*To a Tensed Serenity*) (Char) 9:162; 11:115; 55:288
Aa Went the Blaydon Races (Taylor) 27:441, 443
"Aaron" (Theriault) 79:408, 416
Aaron (Theriault) 79:399-401, 405-06, 408, 413, 418, 419
"Abacus" (Seifert) 93:317, 340
Abaddón, el exterminador (*Abaddon, the Exterminator*) (Sabato) 10:446; 23:381
Abaddon, the Exterminator (Sabato)
    See *Abaddón, el exterminador*
Abahn Sabana David (Duras) 68:94
"Abalone Soup" (Seth) 90:338
"The Abandoned" (Abse) 29:15, 17-18
"The Abandoned British Cemetery at Balasore, India" (Mahapatra) 33:284
The Abandoned Men (Duhamel)
    See *Les hommes abandonnés*
The Abandoned Woman (Condon) 8:150
'Abath al aqdar (Mahfuz) 52:292-93
"Abat-Jour" (Reverdy) 53:281

ABBA ABBA (Burgess) 15:103-04; 22:78; 81:303, 307, 94:60
L'abbé C (Bataille) 29:45
The Abbess of Crewe: A Modern Morality Tale (Spark) 5:398-400; 8:493-95; 40:394-95; 94:353
Abbey Road (Lennon and McCartney) 12:364, 376-77, 380; 35:278, 281-82,289-90
"Abbeyforde" (Davie) 8:164
Abbey's Road (Abbey) 36:18-19; 59:238, 241
"The Abbot" (Brown) 48:57
"Abby, This Is Your Father" (Perelman) 49:258
"ABC" (Bowering) 47:31
"ABC" (Justice) 102:250, 265-66
ABC de Castro Alves (Amado) 40:34
The ABC Murders (Christie) 6:108; 8:142; 12:113-14, 117, 119, 122-23; 48:72-3; 110:112, 122, 124
ABC of Economics (Pound) 7:333
ABC of Reading (Pound) 4:417
ABC: The Alpha Beth Book (Nichol) 18:367, 369
ABCD (Slavitt) 5:392
ABCDEFGHIJKLMNOPQRSTUVWXYZ (Disch) 36:126-27
The ABC's of Astronomy: An Illustrated Dictionary (Gallant) 17:127
The ABC's of Chemistry: An Illustrated Dictionary (Gallant) 17:128
The ABC's of Cinema (Cendrars) 106:194
"The Abduction from the Seraglio" (Barthelme) 23:48
"Abduction of the Endursky Enigma" (Iskander)
    See "Umykanie, ili Zagadka Endurtsev"
"The Abduction; or, The Mystery of the Endurtsies" (Iskander)
    See "Umykanie, ili Zagadka Endurtsev"
"Abdul and Ebenezer" (Kesey) 46:224
Abe Lincoln Grows Up (Sandburg) 35:357
Los abel (Matute) 11:363-64
"Abel's Bride" (Levertov) 66:238
"Abencaján el Bojarí, muerto en su laberinto" ("Abenjacán the Bojarí, Dead in His Labyrinth") (Borges) 19:47
Abend mit Goldrand: Eine Märchen Posse. 55 Bilder aus der Lä/endlichkeit fur Gönner der VerschreibKunst (*Evening Edged in Gold: A FairytalefArse. 55 Scenes from the Countryside for Patrons of Errata*) (Schmidt) 56:397-400, 402, 404
"Abenjacán the Bojarí, Dead in His Labyrinth" (Borges)
    See "Abencaján el Bojarí, muerto en su laberinto"
"Das Abenteuer" (Boell) 72:71, 77
Abenteuer eines Brotbeutels, und andere

Geschichten (Boell) 15:70; 27:58
Aber auch diese Sonne ist heimatlos (Sachs) 98:321
"Abercrombie Station" (Vance) 35:420
"Aberdarcy: The Chaucer Road" (Amis) 40:41
"Aberdeen" (Smith) 64:395-96
"Aberporth" (Fuller) 62:186
Aberration of Starlight (Sorrentino) 22:394-96; 40:385, 391
"Abertackle" (Powys) 46:325
Abgelegene Gehöfte (Eich) 15:204
Abhijan (Ray) 16:483
"The Abiding Vision" (West) 31:454
"Abigail Adams: Peper-dulse Seaweed and Fever Talk, 1786" (Dubie) 36:135
"Abiku" (Clark) 38:117, 125, 128-29
"Abiku" (Soyinka) 36:409
Abingdon Square (Fornes) 61:138, 142-43
Abinger Harvest (Forster) 1:104; 2:135; 15:226, 229; 45:132, 144
Abismos de pasion (*Wuthering Heights*) (Bunuel) 80:24, 28, 30, 47
"Ablazione de duodeno per ulcera" (Gadda) 11:211
"Able, Baker, Charlie, Dog" (Vaughn) 62:456-57, 459
Able Was I Ere I Saw Elba: Selected Poems (Hoffman) 13:286-87
"Abnegation" (Rich) 36:371
The Abolition (Schell) 35:369-70
The Abolition of Man (Lewis) 6:311; 27:269
The Abolitionist of Clark Gable Place (Webb) 7:516
The Abominable Man (Wahloo)
    See *Den vedervaerdige mannen fraan saeffle*
"The Abomination" (Murray) 40:335-36
"Abomunist Manifesto" (Kaufman) 49:203-04
"Aborigine" (Williams) 42:440
"Abortion" (Ai) 69:16
"Abortion" (Selzer) 74:270-72
"The Abortion" (Walker) 27:448; 103:411
The Abortion: An Historical Romance, 1966 (Brautigan) 3:86-9; 5:71; 9:124; 12:60-3, 69-70; 34:314-15, 317; 42:50, 56-7, 60, 62
"abortion cycle #1" (Shange) 25:402, 404
"Abortive Joy" (Tchicaya) 101:347
"About a New Anthology Again..." (Avison) 97:114
"About Atlanta" (Shange) 38:394
About Centennial: Some Notes on the Novel (Michener) 5:289
About Chinese Women 65:328
About Chinese Women (Kristeva)
    See *Des chinoises*

1

"About Effie" (Findley)   **102**:97, 105, 107-08, 111, 116
About Face (Fo)
   See *Clascon trombette e penacchi*
About Fiction: Reverent Reflections on the Nature of Fiction with Irreverent Observations on Writers, Readers, and Other Abuses (Morris)   **7**:245, 247; **18**:351
About Harry Towns (Friedman)   **5**:126-27; **56**:106-07, 109
"About Infinity and the Lenesdorf Pools" (Dubie)   **36**:130
About Looking (Berger)   **19**:40
"About Love and Money" (Cooper)   **56**:71
"About Marriage" (Levertov)   **66**:237
"About Money" (Ignatow)   **40**:258
"About Religion" (Lorde)   **71**:232
"About That Mile" (Smith)   **64**:397
"About That Similarity" (Aksyonov)   **101**:22
"About the House" (Auden)   **1**:9; **3**:22, 24, 29; **6**:19; **9**:57
"About the Writer's Work" (Ehrenburg)   **62**:178
"About These Germans" (Blunden)   **56**:30
About Three Bricks Shy of a Load: A Highly Irregular Lowdown on the Year the Pittsburgh Steelers Were Super But Missed the Bowl (Blount)   **38**:44-5
About Tilly Beamis (Elliott)   **38**:182
"Above Calgary" (Bowering)   **47**:20
"Above Dalton" (Mott)   **15**:380
"Above Everything" (Ignatow)   **40**:259
Above Suspicion (MacInnes)   **27**:278-79; **39**:349-51
Above the Barriers (Pasternak)
   See *Poverkh barierov*
"Above the City" (Laughlin)   **49**:220
"Above the Gods" (Murdoch)   **51**:291-92
Abra (Barfoot)   **18**:35
"Abracadabra" (Livesay)   **79**:332
"Abracadastra" (Connell)   **45**:113
"Abraham and Orpheus" (Schwartz)   **10**:464
"Abraham Darby's Bridge" (Fisher)   **25**:161
Abraham in the Fire (Shamlu)   **10**:470
"Abraham Lincoln and the Art of the World" (Moore)   **47**:268
"Abraham Lincoln in Cleveland" (Crase)   **58**:163, 165
"Abraham Lincoln of Rock Spring Farm" (Tolson)   **105**:233
Abraham Lincoln: The Prairie Years (Sandburg)   **10**:451; **35**:343-44, 350, 357
Abraham Lincoln: The War Years (Sandburg)   **10**:451; **35**:348-51
"Abraham's Knife" (Garrett)   **51**:144
Abraham's Knife and Other Poems (Garrett)   **3**:192; **51**:144-45
Abram in the Salt (Sachs)   **98**:322
Abraxas (Audiberti)   **38**:22, 34
Abrégé de la nuit (Tzara)   **47**:385
Abroad (Weller)
   See *Split*
Abroad: British Literary Traveling between the Wars (Fussell)   **74**:124, 128, 137, 146-47
"Abrupt Daylight Sadness" (Coles)   **46**:113
Absalom, Absalom! (Faulkner)   **3**:149, 153, 155-57; **6**:176-78, 180-81; **8**:207, 210-11; **9**:200-01; **11**:197, 202, 206-07; **14**:168-72, 176, 178-79; **18**:143-44, 147-50; **28**:138, 140, 143, 145-6; **52**:106-47
Absalom in the Tree (Mathias)   **45**:237
"Abschied" (Boell)   **72**:70, 73
Abschied von den Eltern: Erzählung (The Leavetaking) (Weiss)   **15**:563; **51**:389

"An Absence" (Ginzburg)
   See "Un assenza"
"Absence" (McAuley)   **45**:254
"Absence" (Thomas)   **48**:381
An Absence (Johnson)   **40**:263
"An Absence of Slaves" (Jacobsen)   **102**:239
Absence of Unicorns, Presence of Lions (Mott)   **15**:380
"Absences" (Justice)   **19**:234; **102**:252, 264
"Absences" (Larkin)   **18**:295; **64**:260, 262, 266
"Absences" (MacEwen)   **55**:168
Absences (Tate)   **2**:431-32; **25**:429
Absent and Present (Kallman)   **2**:221
Absent Friends (Ayckbourn)   **5**:35-6; **8**:34; **18**:28; **33**:47-9; **74**:8, 19, 22
Absent in the Spring (Christie)   **12**:114; **48**:78
"L'Absente" (Senghor)   **54**:408
"Absentia animi" (Ekeloef)   **27**:117
Absolute Beginners (Griffiths)   **52**:182-83
Absolute Beginners (MacInnes)   **4**:314; **23**:282-87
"The Absolute Dance" (MacEwen)   **13**:357
"The Absolute Ghost" (Redgrove)   **41**:351
An Absolute Hero (Humphreys)   **47**:190-91
"Absolute Zero" (Parra)   **102**:351-53
Absolutely Free (Zappa)   **17**:584, 588-89, 591
Absolutely Live (Morrison)   **17**:289-91, 295
Absolutely Nothing to Get Alarmed About (Wright)   **49**:430-31
"An Absolutely Ordinary Rainbow" (Murray)   **40**:340
"Absolution" (Sassoon)   **36**:389
"Absolution" (Thomas)   **6**:534; **48**:374, 380
"The Absorbed" (Avison)   **97**:77-8
Der Abstecher (The Detour) (Walser)   **27**:462
"Abstinence Makes the Heart Grow Fonder" (Ammons)   **57**:53
"The Abstract Calorie" (Ciardi)   **40**:162
Absurd Person Singular (Ayckbourn)   **5**:35-7; **8**:34; **18**:28; **33**:42, 47-9; **74**:3, 7-8, 18, 31, 34
"Absurd Prayer" (Cohen)   **38**:131
"El abuelo" ("The Grandfather") (Guillen)   **79**:244, 248-49
"Abundance" (Ciardi)   **40**:155
"Abundance" (Kunene)   **85**:165
"Abundance" (Moore)   **47**:265
"The Abundant Dreamer" (Brodkey)   **56**:62, 64, 67
"The Abused: Hansel and Gretel" (Smith)   **42**:351
"The Abyss" (Roethke)   **3**:433; **8**:456-57; **101**:290, 309
The Abyss (Yourcenar)
   See *L'oeuvre au noir*
Abyss: Two Novellas (Wilhelm)   **7**:537
"Abyssinia" (Sillitoe)   **6**:500
"Abzählreime" (Celan)   **82**:52
"Acaba" (Aleixandre)   **9**:14
Academia Nuts (Larson)   **31**:239
Academic Squaw: Reports to the World from the Ivory Tower (Rose)   **85**:312, 314
Academic Year (Enright)   **31**:148, 151-52
L'Acadie pour quasiment rien (Maillet)   **54**:304, 310
Acan (p'Bitek)   **96**:300
"Acana" (Guillen)   **48**:162; **79**:240
Acastos: Two Platonic Dialogues (Murdoch)   **51**:291-92
"Accattone" (Pasolini)   **20**:258-59; **37**:347
Accattone (Pasolini)   **106**:206, 208-09, 219, 221-22, 225-26, 248, 251, 253, 263, 273

"The Accent of a Coming Foot" (Williams)   **45**:454
"Accents of Death" (Farrell)   **66**:112
Acceptable Losses (Shaw)   **34**:369
"Acceptance" (Hughes)   **108**:297
"Acceptance of Spring" (Tzara)
   See "Acceptation du printemps"
The Acceptance World (Powell)   **3**:400, 402; **9**:436; **10**:413
"Acceptation du printemps" ("Acceptance of Spring") (Tzara)   **47**:390, 395
"Access to the Children" (Trevor)   **71**:324
"The Accident" (Lem)   **40**:295, 297
"Accident" (Munro)   **95**:305, 308-09
"An Accident" (Narayan)   **28**:293
"The Accident" (Strand)   **18**:516, 518; **41**:437; **71**:283
Accident (Mosley)   **43**:312-16, 319, 321
Accident (Pinter)   **11**:443; **27**:391
The Accident (Wiesel)
   See *Le jour*
Accident: A Day's News (Wolf)   **58**:436-39
"Accident Zone" (Campbell)   **42**:89
"Accidental Bird Murder" (Hillis)   **66**:193
Accidental Death of an Anarchist (Fo)
   See *Morte accidentale di un anarchico*
An Accidental Man (Murdoch)   **1**:237; **2**:297-98; **3**:347; **15**:388-89
The Accidental Tourist (Tyler)   **44**:311-15, 317-21; **59**:201-08, 210; **103**:226-27, 244, 247-48, 250, 255-56, 260, 266, 271, 272, 275
"Accidentally on Purpose" (Frost)   **9**:221; **13**:230
"Accidents Will Happen" (Costello)   **21**:71
"An Accompanist" (Desai)   **97**:150
"The Accompanist" (Pritchett)   **15**:442
The Accomplice (Duerrenmatt)
   See *Der Mitmacher*
Les accomplices (Simenon)   **2**:398
"Accomplished Desires" (Oates)   **19**:351
"Accomplishments" (Macdonald)   **13**:356
"According to the Old Bards" (Padilla)   **38**:349
"Account" (Milosz)   **82**:298
"Account of the Journey by the Capibaribe River from Its Source to the City of Recife" (Cabral de Melo Neto)   **76**:167
"Account Rendered" (Brittain)   **23**:91
Account Unsettled (Simenon)   **2**:399
"The Accountant's House" (Seth)   **43**:388
"Accumulation" (Updike)   **43**:436
"The Accursed Huntsman" (Garrett)   **51**:140
"The Accusation" (Mahapatra)   **33**:284
"The Accuser" (Milosz)   **22**:306; **31**:262
"Ace in the Hole" (Simon)   **17**:467
"Ace in the Hole" (Updike)   **23**:473
Ace in the Hole (Wilder)   **20**:456-57, 463
Ace of Clubs (Coward)   **1**:65; **29**:139
"An Ace of Hearts" (Nemerov)   **36**:306, 308
Ace of Pentacles (Wieners)   **7**:535-36
"El acercamiento a Almotásim" ("The Approach to al Mu'tasim"; "The Approach to Almotasim") (Borges)   **1**:38; **3**:77; **8**:96; **48**:35, 45; **83**:164
"The Ache of Marriage" (Levertov)   **66**:237, 250
"The Achieve of, the Mastery of the Thing" (Colwin)   **23**:130; **84**:149
Achievement in American Poetry, 1900-1950 (Bogan)   **39**:388; **46**:81; **93**:64, 100
"The Achill Woman " (Boland)   **113**:73, 90, 99, 111, 116-17, 126
"Achilles" (Harris)   **25**:212

"Achilles' Last Stand" (Page and Plant) 12:480, 483

Achimoona (Campbell) 85:18

"Achronos" (Blunden) 56:39

Achterloo (Duerrenmatt) 102:69

"The Achziv Poems" (Amichai) 9:24; 22:30; 57:37

The Achziv Poems (Amichai) 116:97

"Acid" (Kelman) 58:295

"Acid" (Oliver) 98:278

O acidente (Migueis) 10:341

Acis in Oxford and Other Poems (Finch) 18:154

"Acknowledgements and Dedication, Sort Of" (Berrigan) 4:58

Ackroyd (Feiffer) 8:217; 64:151-52, 157-58, 162

"The Acolyte" (Levertov) 66:237

The Acolyte (Astley) 41:47-9

"Acon" (H. D.) 73:115, 139

"Acorn, Yom Kippur" (Nemerov) 36:306

El acoso (Carpentier) 11:97; 38:92; 110:48-9

"Acquaintance with Time in Early Autumn" (Warren) 39:258

"Acquainted with the Night" (Frost) 1:110; 3:170; 9:219; 10:194-95, 198; 15:250; 26:125

Acquainted with the Night (Boell)
   See *Und Sagte kein einziges Wort*

Acque e terre (Quasimodo) 10:427

Acquired Tastes: A Beginner's Guide to Serious Pleasures (Mayle)
   See *Expensive Habits*

An Acre of Grass (Stewart) 7:465

"An Acre of Land" (Thomas) 6:530; 13:542

Acres and Pains (Perelman) 9:415; 49:266

"The Acrobat" (Hirsch) 31:215

Acrobats (Horovitz) 56:150-51

The Acrobats (Richler) 5:371-74; 13:482-83, 485

The Acrophile (Kaniuk) 19:238-39

"Across a Crowded Room" (Pym) 111:245

Across the Bitter Sea (Dillon) 17:98-100

Across the Black Waters (Anand) 23:14, 19; 93:24, 31, 43

Across the Board on Tomorrow Morning (Saroyan) 10:453

"Across the Bridge" (Boell)
   See "An der Brücke"

"Across the Lines" (Price) 63:327

Across the Pacific (Huston) 20:164

Across the River and into the Trees (*The Things That I Know*) (Hemingway) 3:231, 234, 242-43; 6:225, 227, 231; 8:283, 291; 13:275, 278; 19:218; 39:399-400, 403, 428, 430-32, 434-35; 41:197, 202, 205, 207; 50:427; 61:226; 80:112, 117-18, 145-46

Across the Sea of Suns (Benford) 52:69-71, 77

Across the Sea Wall (Koch) 42:259-65

"Across the Street and into the Grill" (White) 10:530

"Across the Wide Missouri" (Wideman) 34:298

"Across the World the Beholder Come" (Gustafson) 36:220

"The Act and Place of Poetry" (Bonnefoy)
   See "L'acte et le lieu de la poésie"

The Act of Creation (Koestler) 33:236-37

Act of Darkness (King) 53:209-10, 212-13

"Act of Faith" (Shaw) 7:411

Act of Faith and Other Stories (Shaw) 23:396

"An Act of God" (Nemerov) 36:309

The Act of Life (Cousteau) 30:105-07

"The Act of Love" (Creeley) 2:108

"Act of Love" (Scannell) 49:327, 331

"The Act of Love: Poetry and Personality" ("Poetry and Personality") (Carruth) 84:115, 117

"An Act of Prostitution" (McPherson) 77:361, 365

An Act of Terror (Brink) 106:117-18, 133, 137

"Act of Union" (Heaney) 25:245; 74:157, 162

Act One (Stow) 23:436

Act One: An Autobiography (*Un Homme de Broadway*) (Hart) 66:180-82, 188, 191

Act without Words II (Beckett) 6:46; 18:41

Act without Words I
   See *Actes sans paroles I*

Acta sanctorum (Lengyel) 7:202

Acte (Durrell) 1:86; 4:145; 13:184

"L'acte et le lieu de la poésie" ("The Act and Place of Poetry") (Bonnefoy) 58:45, 50, 59

Actes sans paroles I (*Act without Words I*) (Beckett) 1:20; 3:47; 6:46; 11:42; 18:41; 83:117

"Actfive" (MacLeish) 8:362

Actfive, and Other Poems (MacLeish) 8:362; 68:290

"Action" (Bukowski) 82:27

"Action" (Levertov) 66:250

"The Action" (Murray) 40:336

The Action (King) 53:213

Action (Shepard) 6:496-97; 17:448; 41:410

"Action and Epilogue" (Ciardi) 40:156

L'action de la justice est éteinte (Char) 14:126

Active Antology (Pound) 112:337

The Activists Papers (Bond) 23:71

"The Actor" (Williams) 42:440

"The Actor to the Audience" (Turner) 48:399

The Actor's Nightmare (Durang) 27:91-3

An Actor's Revenge (Ichikawa)
   See *Yukinojo henge*

"An Actor's War" (Williams) 42:445

"Acts of God" (Boyle) 90:63

The Acts of King Arthur and His Noble Knights: From the Winchester Manuscripts of Thomas Malory and Other Sources (Steinbeck) 13:535; 21:387

"Acts of Love" (McCarthy) 39:487

Acts of Love (Kazan) 63:220-21

Acts of Theft (Cohen) 31:93-4

"Actue Crisis Identity" (Royko) 109:405

"Acuérdate" ("Remember") (Rulfo) 80:200, 216

"Acute Triangle" (Raphael) 14:438

"Ad Castitatem" (Bogan) 93:66

Ad horef, 1974 (Yehoshua) 31:470

"Ad Libitum" (Elytis) 100:179, 181

Ad m'avet (*Late Love; Unto Death*) (Oz) 8:436; 54:352

Ada; or, Ardor: A Family Chronicle (Nabokov) 1:244-46; 2:300-01, 304-05; 3:352-53, 345-55; 4:2497; 6:352, 354-55, 357-58; 8:407-16, 418; 11:391-93, 395; 15:393-94, 396; 44:465-69, 473; 64:348, 350-51

"Adagio" (Seth) 90:350

L'adalgisa, disegni milanesi (Gadda) 11:211

"Adam" (Tomlinson) 45:393-94

"Adam and Eve" (Shapiro) 8:486; 53:330, 334

"Adam and the Sacred Nine" (Hughes) 37:174, 177-78

Adam by Adam: The Autobiography of Clayton Powell, Jr. (Powell) 89:210-11

Adam, Eve, and the Serpent (Pagels) 104:212-17, 229, 234

Adam in Moonshine (Priestley) 34:361, 364

"Adam Kadmon" (Nye) 42:308-09

"Adam, One Afternoon" (Calvino) 33:101

Adam, One Afternoon, and Other Stories (Calvino)
   See *L'entrada en guerra*

"Adam Raised a Cain" (Springsteen) 17:483, 490

Adam Resurrected (Kaniuk) 19:239, 241

"Adam Snow" (Ashbery) 77:68-69

Adam, Where Art Thou? (Boell)
   See *Wo warst du, Adam?*

"Adam Yankev" (Simpson) 7:429

"The Adamant" (Roethke) 8:460

Adame miroir (Genet) 44:390

"Adam's Bride" (Jolley) 46:213

Adam's Dream (Belitt) 22:54, 52

"Adam's Legacy" (MacNeice) 53:233

Adam's Rest (Millin) 49:246

"Adam's Song to Heaven" (Bowers) 9:122

Adam's Task: Calling Animals by Name (Hearne) 56:128-32, 134

The Adaptable Man (Frame) 22:144, 146; 96:168-69, 190, 196-97, 211-12, 216-17

Addams and Evil (Addams) 30:12

"Added Weight" (Bissett) 18:58

"Addendum to 'The Block'" (Van Duyn) 116:422, 427

"The Adder" (Chappell) 78:116-17

Addictions (Enright) 4:155; 8:203

Addictions (Hyde) 21:178-79

The Adding Machine (Rice) 7:359-64; 49:292-94, 299, 301-02, 304-05

The Adding Machine: Collected Essays (Burroughs) 42:76-7

"Addio" (Ciardi) 40:161

"Addio" (Gilliatt) 53:146

Additional Dialogue (Trumbo) 19:445

"Address for a Prize-Day" (Auden) 11:18

"Address to Existence" (Wheelock) 14:571

"An Address to the Literary Philosophical Society" (Wain) 46:411

"Address to the Lord" (Berryman) 62:45

"The Address to the Parents" (Bell) 31:47

"Adelaide's Dream" (Middleton) 13:389

"Adélia" (Conde) 92:106

"Aden" (Hall) 51:170

The Adept (McClure) 6:316, 319

Adept's Gambit (Leiber) 25:301

"Adiere" ("Breeze") (Arghezi) 80:9

"L'adieu" (Butor) 15:117

"Adieu" (Endo) 99:307

"Adieu á Charlot" ("Second Populist Manifesto") (Ferlinghetti) 27:137, 139

"Adieu, Mlle. Veronique" (Brodsky) 6:96

"Adieu, New-York!" ("Good-Bye, New York") (Morand) 41:301

"Adieu to Norman, Bon Jour to Joan and Jean-Paul" (O'Hara) 78:335

"Un adieu, un salut" (Char) 9:167

Adieux: A Farewell to Sartre (Beauvoir)
   See *La céremonie des adieux: Suivi de entretiens avec Jean-Paul Sartre*

"Adios carnero" (Ulibarri) 83:416

Adios, Mr. Moxley (Jacobsen) 48:196, 198-99

Los adioses (*The Goodbyes*) (Onetti) 10:376

"Adivinanzas" (Guillen) 48:166

Admass (Priestley) 2:347

An Admirable Woman (Cohen) 31:94-5

"The Admiral and the Nuns" (Tuohy) 37:427, 433

The Admiral and the Nuns with Other Stories (Tuohy) 37:426-27, 430

Admiral Hornblower in the West Indies (Forester) 35:171

Admiral of the Ocean Sea: A Life of Christopher Columbus (Morison) 70:331, 335, 342, 344, 346, 350, 353

The Admiral on the Wheel (Thurber) 25:440

"The Admiralty Spire" (Nabokov) 6:358

"The Admirer" (Singer) 6:511; 9:487

"Admiring the Scenery" (O'Faolain) 14:406

Admission to the Feast (Beckman)
    See *Tillträde till festen*

"Adolescence" (Dove) 81:134

"Adolescence of Day" (Elytis) 49:114

"Adolescence—III" (Dove) 81:137

Un adolescent d'autrefois (Mauriac) 9:369; 56:216

The Adolescent Savenko (Limonov) 67:180

"Adolfo Miller" (Ulibarri) 83:415

"Adolpho's Disappeared and We Haven't a Clue Where to Find Him" (Rooke) 25:392

"Adonis" (H. D.) 73:119

"La adoración de los magos" (Cernuda) 54:47

"Adoration" (Gilchrist) 48:119, 121

"Adoration" (Moure) 88:227

"Adore Her" (Robison) 98:307

"Adowe: We Return Thanks" (Kenny) 87:240

The Adrian Mole Diaries
    See *The Secret Diary of Adrian Mole, Aged 13 3/4*

The Adrian Mole Diaries
    See *The Growing Pains of Adrian Mole*

"The Adriatic" (Prokosch) 48:309

Adrienne Mesurat (Green) 77:266-69, 274, 289-90, 294

Adrift in Soho (Wilson) 3:537; 14:588

"Adrift Just Off the Islets of Langerhans: Latitude 38 54'N, Longitude 00'13" " (Ellison) 13:207; 42:128-29

"Adult Art" (Gurganus) 70:191, 194, 196

"Adult Bookstore" (Shapiro) 8:486; 15:477-78

"Adult Grief" (Gluck) 44:217, 222

"The Adult Holiday" (Spencer) 22:406

The Adult Life of Toulouse Lautrec (Acker) 45:14-15; 111:11, 21, 23, 25, 32-33, 37, 42

"The Adulterous Woman" (Camus)
    See "La femme adultère"

"Adultery" (Banks) 72:5, 9

"Adultery" (Dickey) 15:174

"Adultery" (Dubus) 36:143-46; 97:199-202, 218-21, 226-27, 229

"Adultery" (Gunn) 32:214

Adultery, and Other Choices (Dubus) 13:184; 36:143-44, 146-48; 97:197-99, 207-09, 219, 231, 235

"Adulthood" (Giovanni) 19:190; 64:185

"Adulthood (For Claudia)" (Giovanni) 117:195

"Adults Only" (Stafford) 29:382

"Advancing Luna—and Ida B. Wells" (Walker) 27:448; 103:407, 409, 411-12

Advancing Paul Newman (Bergstein) 4:55

"Advent" (Grass) 32:198-99

"Advent" (H. D.) 73:136, 138

"Advent" (Merton) 83:392

"Advent" (Rexroth) 112:405

"Advent, 1966" (Levertov) 5:248; 28:239

"Advent Calendar" (Schnackenberg) 40:382

"The Adventure" (Lagerkvist)
    See "Äventyret"

"Adventure in a Room" (Green) 97:292

"Adventure in an Antique Shop" (Akhmadulina)
    See "Prikliuchenie v antikvarnom magazine"

Adventure in Baltimore (Isherwood) 44:397

Adventure in Grey (Buero Vallejo)
    See *Aventura en lo gris*

"The Adventure of a Bather" (Calvino) 33:101-02

"The Adventure of a Clerk" (Calvino) 39:314

"The Adventure of a Poet" (Calvino) 39:314

"The Adventure of a Reader" (Calvino) 33:102

"The Adventure of Ricoletti of the Clubfoot" (Derleth) 31:137

"The Adventure of the Bearded Lady" (Queen) 3:422

"The Adventure of the Cheap Flat" (Christie) 110:111

"The Adventure of the Glass-Domed Clock" (Queen) 11:461

"The Adventure of the Late Mr. Faversham" (Derleth) 31:137

"The Adventure of the Norcross Riddle" (Derleth) 31:137

The Adventure of the Unique Dickensians (Derleth) 31:138

The Adventurer (Zweig) 34:378; 42:466-67

The Adventurers (Robbins) 5:380

"Adventures" (Urdang) 47:400

Adventures in Everyday Life (Oe)
    See *Nichijoseikatsu no boken*

Adventures in the Alaskan Skin Trade (Hawkes) 49:156-60

"Adventures in the Bohemian Jungle" (Kavanagh) 22:240, 243

Adventures of a Columnist (Berton) 104:47

"Adventures of a Haversack" (Boell) 72:100

The Adventures of a Photographer in La Plata (Bioy Casares)
    See *La aventura de un fotógraf en La Plata*

Adventures of a Young Man (Dos Passos) 4:137; 11:156; 15:183, 187; 34:420; 82:72

The Adventures of Augie March (Bellow) 1:27-30, 33; 2:49-53; 3:48-51, 60-2; 6:53-8, 61; 8:75-6; 10:37, 44; 13:69-73; 15:47-50, 53, 52-6; 25:85; 33:65-6, 69, 71; 34:545; 63:28, 32-5, 37, 41; 79:61-2, 76, 83-4

The Adventures of Ellery Queen (Queen) 3:422

The Adventures of Fathead, Smallhead, and Squarehead (Sanchez) 116:301, 309

The Adventures of Gerard (Skolimowski) 20:350, 354

"The Adventures of God in His Search for the Black Girl" (Brophy) 6:99; 105:6, 8, 12, 31

The Adventures of God in His Search for the Black Girl (Brophy) 6:98-100

The Adventures of Gurudeva (Naipaul) 39:356

"The Adventures of My Seven Uncles" (Cendrars)
    See "Le Panama ou les aventures de mes sept oncles"

The Adventures of Robina, by Herself (Tennant) 52:404-06

The Adventures of Solar Pons (Derleth) 31:139

The Adventures of Strong Vanya (Preussler) 17:375

Adventures of the Letter I (Simpson) 4:500; 7:428-29; 9:486; 32:379

The Adventures of the Stainless Steel Rat (Harrison) 42:204

The Adventures of Una Persson and Catherine Cornelius in the Twentieth Century (Moorcock) 27:349; 58:354-55

The Adventures of Wesley Jackson (Saroyan) 8:467

The Adventures of William Saroyan (Saroyan) 8:467

"The Adventuress" (O'Connor) 23:331

The Adversary (Ray)
    See *Pratidwandi*

Advertisements for Myself (Mailer) 1:189-90, 192; 2:258, 264-65; 3:311-13, 315; 4:323; 8:366, 368-72; 11:339-40, 343; 28:255-57; 39:416, 423, 425; 74:203-04, 207, 212, 225; 111:95, 104, 107, 118-20, 135, 137

"Advertising=Poetry" (Cendrars) 106:179

"Advice" (Milosz) 56:234

"Advice" (Singer) 69:305

"Advice on Reading the Confessional Poet" (Kuzma) 7:196

"Advice to a Discarded Lover" (Adcock) 41:13

Advice to a God (Van Duyn) 63:436

"Advice to a Lady" (Padilla) 38:352

"Advice to a Prophet" (Wilbur) 3:531; 6:568; 53:404; 110:351, 359-60, 378

Advice to a Prophet and Other Poems (Wilbur) 3:532; 6:568; 53:396, 398-99, 405, 410; 110:352, 384

"'Advice' to a Young Poet" (Kunene) 85:176

"Advice to King Lear" (Cassity) 42:99

"Advice to My Friends" (Kroetsch) 57:292-94

Advice to My Friends (Kroetsch) 57:292-93

"Advice to the Old (Including Myself)" (Boyle) 58:75-6

Advise and Consent (Drury) 37:98-100, 102-08, 111

Aeducação pela pedra (*Education by Stone*) (Cabral de Melo Neto) 76:153-54, 156, 158-59, 163

"The Aegean" (Squires) 51:381

"Aegean Route" (Elytis) 100:179

"Aegeis" (Elytis) 49:110

"Aegeodrome" (Elytis) 100:187

Aegypt (Crowley) 57:162-64

"Aeneas at Washington" (Tate) 2:429; 11:525

Aeneid (Day Lewis) 6:127

The Aerial Letter (Brossard)
    See *La lettre aérienne*

"Aerial Ways" ("Vozdushnye puti") (Pasternak) 7:293; 18:386

"Aerialist" (Plath) 51:342

The Aerodrome: A Love Story (Warner) 45:432-35, 437-41

"The Aeroplanes at Brescia" (Davenport) 6:123; 14:140; 38:140

"El aeroplano" (Guillen) 48:159

"Aesculapian Notes" (Redgrove) 41:355

"Aesthetic" (Tomlinson) 13:546; 45:402

"Aesthetics" (MacCaig) 36:285

Aesthetics (Olson) 28:344

"Aesthetics after War" (Eberhart) 56:91

The Aesthetics of Chaosmos (Eco) 60:125

"Aesthetics of the Shah" (Olds) 85:291

"Aet Beran Byrg" (Grigson) 7:136

"Aether" (Ginsberg) 36:183

"Los afanes" (Bioy Casares) 88:94

"Afar a Bird" (Beckett) 29:57

"Affabulazione" (Pasolini) 37:347

"The Affair" (Bell) 8:65-6

"An Affair" (Ezekiel) 61:104

The Affair (Snow) 1:316; 4:502; 6:516; 13:512; 19:427

"An Affair, Edited" (Gaitskill) 69:203

"An Affair of Honor" (Nabokov) 3:354

"The Affair of the Bungalow" (Christie) 110:130, 144-46
"An Affair of the Heart" (Hope) 52:208
"An Affair of the Heart" (Sargeson) 31:364
An Affair with the Moon (White) 49:399
Une affaire de viol (*A Case of Rape*) (Himes) 2:195; 18:249; 108:229
L'affaire Saint Fiacre (Simenon) 3:451-52
Affairs in a Tent (Ayckbourn) 74:20
L'affamée (Leduc) 22:264
"Affection" (Barthelme) 46:43; 59:249-51
"Affinities" (Hersey) 81:330
Affinities (Watkins) 43:444, 447, 452-53
"Affinities II" (Blackburn) 9:100
"Affinity" (Thomas) 48:380
"Affirmation" (Allen) 84:5
"Affirmation" (Wheelock) 14:571
"Affirmations" (Pound) 7:326
"Affirmative Action Berkeley, 1977" (Rose) 85:316
Affliction (Banks) 72:11-19, 22
An Afghanistan Picture Show: Or, How I Saved the World (Vollmann) 89:285-87, 290-92, 297098, 301, 307
"Afin qu'il n'y soit rien changè" (Char) 9:163
"Afloat" (Beattie) 40:64, 66; 63:2, 17, 19
"Africa" (Giovanni) 117:197
"Africa Emergent" (Gordimer) 33:183
"Africa I" (Giovanni) 117:196
"The African Ambassador" (Kallman) 2:221
African Calliope (Hoagland) 28:184-85
The African Child (Laye)
See *L'enfant noir*
"African China" (Tolson) 105:240
An African Elegy (Okri) 87:323
African Firebrand: Jomo Kenyatta (Archer) 12:17
African Horse (Pownall) 10:419
The African Image (Mphahlele) 25:332-33, 335, 341
African Laughter (Lessing) 94:266-68
"The African Magician" (Gordimer) 33:180
The African Queen (Forester) 35:159-61, 165-66, 169-70, 172, 174
The African Queen (Huston) 20:161, 165-66
"African Question Mark" (Hughes) 15:295
African Religions in Western Scholarship (p'Bitek) 96:291, 294
African Songs of Love, War, Grief and Abuse (Damas)
See *Poèmes nègres sur des airs africains*
African Stories (Lessing) 2:239; 3:288; 22:279; 94:280
"African Tea Ceremony" (Hope) 52:209
"The African Trilogy" (Diamond) 30:110-11
African Trio (Simenon) 18:487
African-American (Shange) 74:298
African-American Baseline Essays 70:406
Africanus Instructus (Foreman) 50:163, 165, 171
Africa's Cultural Revolution (p'Bitek) 96:299, 310
L'Afrique fantôme de Dakar a Djibouti, 1931-1933 (Leiris) 61:341, 352
"L'Afrique, un continent difficile" (Conde) 92:112-13
"Afro-American" (Dumas) 62:151
Afro-American Literature in the Twentieth Century: The Achievement of Intimacy 65:365
Afro-American Literature: The Reconstruction of Instruction 65:364, 379, 381, 386
The Afrocentric Idea (Asante) 70:389-90
Afrocentricity: The Theory of Social Change

(Asante) 70:390
"After" (Angelou) 77:28
"After" (Lane) 25:288
"After 37 Years My Mother apologizes for My Childhood" (Olds) 85:295, 304
"After a Death" (Stevenson) 33:379
"After a Death" (Tomlinson) 13:548
"After a Departure" (Abse) 7:1; 29:15
"After a Fifteenth-Century Miniature Showing King Mark Stabbing Tristram in the Presence of Ysolt" (Dacey) 51:79
"After a Flight" (Montale) 7:231; 9:388
"After a Flight" (Montefiore)
See "Dopa una fuga"
"After a Journey" (Brodsky) 100:61
"After a Nightmare" (Davison) 28:99-100
"After a Phrase Abandoned by Wallace Stevens" (Justice) 102:270, 277, 279-80, 283
"After All" (Bowie) 17:57, 59
"After an Attack" (Transtroemer) 52:410; 65:219, 228
"After Apple-Picking" (Frost) 1:110; 3:170; 15:245, 248; 26:112, 115-16, 123, 128
"After Auschwitz" (Sexton) 6:494
After Babel (Steiner) 24:434, 437
After Candlemas (Arthur) 12:27, 29
"After Cavafy" (Mahon) 27:286-88
"After Christmas" (Mathias) 45:236
"After Consulting My Yellow Pages" (Wagoner) 3:508
"After Dark" (Rich) 3:428; 7:365, 368
After Dark (Wellman) 49:389-90, 394, 396
After Dark, My Sweet (Thompson) 69:378, 387, 389
"After Death" (Aleixandre) 36:29
"After Douglas" (Merwin) 88:211
"After Drinking All Night with a Friend" (Bly) 10:57
"After Eden" (Simmons) 43:412, 414
After Every Green Thing (Abse) 29:12-14, 16-17
"After Exile" (Brutus) 43:88
After Experience: Poems and Translations (Snodgrass) 2:405-06; 6:513-14; 18:491, 494; 68:383, 388, 391, 393, 397
"After Feydeau" (Schuyler)
See "What to Do? A Problem Play"
"After Ford" (Burgess) 94:76
"After Frost" (Creeley) 78:160
"After Grief" (Plumly) 33:313
"After He Left" (Ding Ling)
See "Ta zou hou"
After Hours (Campion) 95:6
After Hours (Scorsese) 89:240-42, 260, 265-68
"After I Have Voted" (Jensen) 37:187
"After Illness in Childhood" (Urdang) 47:400
"After I'm Gone" ("Da Da Da Da Da") (McGrath) 28:280
"After Images: Autobiographical Sketches" (Snodgrass) 68:394
After Julius (Howard) 29:244-46
"After Keats" (Levine)
See "Having Been Asked 'What Is a Man?' I Answer"
"after Kent State" (Clifton) 66:65, 67
After Lazarus: A Filmscript (Coover) 46:121-22
After Leaving Mr. Mackenzie (Rhys) 2:372-73; 4:445; 6:453-55; 14:446, 450-51; 51:357-59, 368, 370
After Lorca (Spicer) 8:497; 18:507, 512; 72:348, 352-57, 359-65

After Lydia (Rattigan) 7:355
"After Magritte" (Stoppard) 3:470; 4:524, 527; 8:502-03; 29:399-401; 91:189
After Many a Summer Dies the Swan (Huxley) 1:150-52; 4:238-40, 243; 8:304; 35:243-44; 79:306, 328
After Martial (Porter) 5:347
"After Mecca" (Brooks) 49:28
"After Melville" (Rukeyser) 10:442; 27:411
After Moondog (Shapiro) 76:114-18
"After My Fashion" (Powys) 46:323-24
"After Nerval" (Mahon) 27:287, 289-90
"After Paradise" (Milosz) 56:246; 82:290
"After Pasternak" (Creeley) 78:160
"After Rain" (Page) 7:291; 18:379
"After Rain" (Trevor) 116:394
After Rain (Trevor) 116:394-96
"After Reading *Mickey in the Night Kitchen* for the Third Time before Bed" (Dove) 81:150
"After Rilke" (Schwartz)
See "Late Autumn in Venice"
"After Saturday Night Comes Sunday" (Sanchez) 116:306, 313
"After School" (Merwin) 88:206
"After Soweto" (Brink) 36:68
"After Spring Snow, What They Saw" (Dubie) 36:137
After Strange Gods: A Primer of Modern Heresy (Eliot) 6:165-66; 24:162-63, 182-83; 34:394, 403; 41:156-59
After Such Knowledge (Blish) 14:87
After Such Pleasures (Parker) 15:414; 68:325
"After Terror" (Oates) 33:294
After the Act (Graham) 23:193-94
"After the Alphabets" (Merwin) 88:197, 206
"After the April Festivals" (Disch) 36:127
After the Armies Have Passed (Kessler) 4:270
"After the Ball" (Colter) 58:146-47
"After the Ball" (McCartney) 35:286
After the Ball (Coward) 29:140
After the Banquet (Mishima) 4:357-58; 9:382; 27:336
"After the Big Parade" (Ginsberg) 109:318
After the Bombing and Other Short Poems (Blunden) 56:29, 34-5, 39, 41, 45, 47
"After the Crash" (MacNeice) 10:323, 325
"After the Cries of the Birds" (Ferlinghetti) 27:139; 111:65
"After the Dance" (Gaye) 26:132
"After the Death of Mdabuli, Son of Mhawu" (Kunene) 85:176
"After the Defeat" (Ritsos) 6:464
"After the Denim" (Carver) 22:102
"After the Dinner Party" (Warren) 39:265; 59:298
After the Fairy Tale (Aitmatov)
See *Belyj parokhod*
"After the Faith Healings" (Appleman) 51:17
After the Fall (Kazan) 63:226, 235
After the Fall (Miller) 1:216-18; 2:279-80; 6:326-33, 336; 10:342-43; 15:373-74, 376; 26:322, 324, 327; 47:254-56, 258; 78:318-19, 325
After the First Death (Cormier) 30:81-3, 85-6, 88-91
After the Funeral (*Funerals Are Fatal*) (Christie) 12:124; 48:72, 76
"After the Game" (Dubus) 97:213, 216, 229
"After the Gold Rush" (Young) 17:583
After the Gold Rush (Young) 17:569-70, 572-73, 577-79
"After the 'I Ching'" (Spacks) 14:511

"After the Last Dynasty" (Kunitz) 6:287
"After the Lecture" (Thomas) 48:375
After the New Criticism (Lentricchia) 34:574
"After the Persian" (Bogan) 4:69; 39:387, 393; 46:90; 93:65
After the Prize (Weldon) 36:444-45
"After the Quarrel" (Rukeyser) 27:411
"After the Rain" (Mahapatra) 33:284
"After the Rats" (Purdy) 6:428
After the Rehearsal (Bergman) 72:59, 61
"After the Riots" (Enright) 31:150
"After the Sex Bomb" (Ewart) 13:208
"After the Sirens" (Hood) 28:187
"After the Storm" (Hemingway) 8:285, 287; 30:192
"After the Storm" (Santos) 22:364
"After the Storm" (Simon) 26:409
"After the Street Fighting" (Ciardi) 40:155
After the Stroke (Sarton) 91:244, 246
"After the Sun Has Risen" (Farrell) 66:129
After the Sundown (Jordan) 37:195
"After the Surgery" (Bottoms) 53:30
"After the Surprising Conversions" (Lowell) 4:295; 15:344
After the Tale (Aitmatov)
  See *Belyj parokhod*
"After the War" (Smith) 64:388
"After Thomas Hardy" (McFadden) 48:244
"After Three Photographs of Brassai" (Dubie) 36:134
"After Thunder" (Johnston) 51:240, 250-52
"After Two Years of Analysis: Reactions" (Dickey) 28:119
"After Whistler" (Plumly) 33:316
"After Winter" (Brown) 59:266
"After Wyatt" (O'Hara) 5:325
"After You, My Dear Alphonse" (Jackson) 60:229
"After You've Gone" (Adams) 65:348
After You've Gone (Adams) 65:348-49
"After-Image" (Caldwell) 1:51
"Afterimages" (Lorde) 71:235
"Afterimages" (MacEwen) 55:163-64, 169
Afterlife (Monette) 82:324, 326-28, 331
"Afterlives" (Mahon) 27:290
"The Afterlives of Count Zeppelin" (Cassity) 42:99
"Aftermath" (Plath) 14:426
Aftermath (Jagger and Richard) 17:237, 239
"Afternoon" (Ellison) 11:183; 114:131
"Afternoon and Evening at Ohrid" (Wright) 5:519
"An Afternoon at the Beach" (Bowers) 9:121
"Afternoon Dancing" (Trevor) 7:478; 116:377
"Afternoon Happiness" (Kizer) 80:182
Afternoon Men (Powell) 1:277; 3:400; 7:339; 10:409-11; 31:319, 322
"Afternoon Nap" (Cortazar) 5:109
"The Afternoon of a Faun" (Ferber) 93:145, 180
Afternoon of a Faun (Hearon) 63:163
Afternoon of a Pawnbroker (Fearing) 51:110-11
"Afternoon of an American Boy" (White) 34:430
An Afternoon of Pocket Billiards (Taylor) 44:301
Afternoon of the Unreal (Salinas) 90:326, 330
Afternoon Off (Bennett) 77:86-9
"Afternoon on Elba" (O'Faolain) 47:325
"The Afternoon Sun" (Durrell) 13:188
"Afternoon Sun" (Willingham) 51:403
"Afternoon Walk" (Miles) 34:245

Afternoons in Mid-America (Caldwell) 8:123; 14:95
"Afterthought" (Lowell) 37:240
"Afterthought" (Musgrave) 13:401
"After-Thoughts" (MacEwen) 55:163-64, 167, 169
"Afterthoughts of Donna Elvira" (Kizer) 80:173
"Afterthoughts on the Rosenbergs" (Fiedler) 4:163
Aftertones (Ian) 21:186
"Afterward" (Appleman) 51:15
"An Afterward" (Heaney) 14:246; 74:160, 164, 167; 91:115
"Afterward" (Warren) 39:257, 262
"Afterwards" (Davison) 28:101
"Afterwards" (Muske) 90:312
Afterwards (Benet)
  See *Despuúes*
"An Afterword: For Gwen Brooks" (Madhubuti) 73:215
"Afterword on Rupert Brooke" (Prince) 22:339-40
"An Afterword to 'Lolita'" (Nabokov) 64:348
"An Afterword to My Father" (Bell) 8:65; 31:47
"Afterwords" (Gass) 15:255
Afterworlds (MacEwen) 55:163-69
Aftonland (*Evening Land*) (Lagerkvist) 10:313; 13:330, 332-33
Agaguk (Theriault) 79:399, 401, 403, 406-408, 410, 412, 415, 417-18, 420
"Again" (Raine) 103:190
"Again, Again, Again" (Robison) 98:306, 308
"Again at Waldheim" (Rexroth) 49:277
Again Calls the Owl (Craven) 17:80
"Again *El cante flamenco*" (Cabral de Melo Neto)
  See "Ainda *El cante flamenco*"
Again to the North (Mackenzie) 18:313
Against a Darkening Sky (Lewis) 41:253, 256-57, 263
Against a League of Liars (Acorn) 15:10
"Against Botticelli" (Hass) 18:213
"Against Confidences" (Davie) 31:109
"Against Coupling" (Adcock) 41:15, 18
"Against Destiny" (Tchicaya) 101:347
"Against Dryness: A Polemical Sketch" (Murdoch) 2:297; 3:346; 6:347-48
"Against Dullness" (Szirtes) 46:393
"Against Elegies" (Hacker) 91:110-11
Against Emptiness (Zweig) 34:378; 42:465-67
Against Entropy (Frayn) 3:164; 7:106
"Against Extremity" (Tomlinson) 13:548; 45:402
Against Forgetting: Twentieth-Century Poetry of Witness (Forche) 86:142, 144
"Against Illuminations" (MacLeish) 68:286
Against Infinity (Benford) 52:68-9, 71-2, 77
"Against Interpretation" (Sontag) 105:207-08
Against Interpretation and Other Essays (Sontag) 1:322; 10:484; 31:405-06, 416-18; 105:209, 215-18, 225
"Against Memory" (Bunting) 47:44
"Against Romanticism" (Amis) 40:39, 44
"Against San Francisco" (Cassity) 42:95
"Against Silence" (Hacker) 72:191
"Against Stupidity" (Asimov) 19:26
"Against the Age" (Simpson) 7:426
Against the Circle (Ghiselin) 23:169
Against the Fall of Night (Clarke) 1:59; 13:153;

35:121-22, 127
Against the Grain: Selected Essays, 1975-1985 (Eagleton) 63:106-07
Against the Silences (Blackburn) 43:66-8
"Against the Silences to Come" (Loewinsohn) 52:283-84
"Against the Wind" (Seger) 35:384, 387
Against the Wind (Seger) 35:384-87
"Against Your Beliefs" (Snodgrass) 68:389
"Agamemnon" (Ritsos) 13:488
Agamemnon (Berkoff) 56:12
Agantuk (*The Stranger; The Visitor*) (Ray) 76:360, 366
Agatha (Colegate) 36:110-11, 113
Agatha (Duras) 68:85, 92; 100:143
Agatha Christie: A Biography (Morgan) 39:436, 438-39, 441-43
"Agbor Dancer" (Clark) 38:117, 121, 128
"Age" (Breton) 9:126
"An Age" (Jensen) 37:190
"Age" (Larkin) 64:262
"Age" (Thomas) 48:376
An Age (*Cryptozoic*) (Aldiss) 14:13
L'âge de discrétion (*The Age of Discretion*) (Beauvoir) 14:70; 31:45; 44:345
L'âge de raison (*The Age of Reason*) (Sartre) 1:304-05; 44:493; 50:383
L'age d'homme (*Manhood: A Journey from Childhood into the Fierce Order of Virility*) (Leiris) 61:341-54, 357-58, 360
L'age d'or (*The Golden Age*) (Bunuel) 16:145-6; 80:19-20, 27-34, 36-8, 40-1, 44-5, 47, 50, 56-7
"The Age of a Wart" (White) 69:413-14
The Age of Amazement (Appelfeld)
  See *Tor Ha-pela'ot*
The Age of Anxiety: A Baroque Eclogue (Auden) 1:9-10; 2:23-4; 3:26-7; 4:33; 11:19; 14:31; 43:15, 20, 26-7
Age of Aquarius: You and Astrology (Branley) 21:23-4
Age of Assassins: The Story of Prisoner No. 1234 (Soupault)
  See *Le temps des assassins*
The Age of Defeat (Wilson) 14:586
"The Age of Desire" (Barker) 52:52-3, 55
The Age of Discretion (Beauvoir)
  See *L'âge de discrétion*
"The Age of Dogma"
  See "Eonul dogmatic"
Age of Eternal Peace (Haavikko)
  See *Ikuisen rauhau aika*
The Age of Grief (Smiley) 53:347-50; 76:230, 233, 235
The Age of Happy Problems (Gold) 7:122; 42:189
"The Age of Herbert and Vaughan" (Blunden) 56:39
"The Age of Innocence" (Hope) 51:221
The Age of Innocence (Scorsese) 89:268-70
"The Age of Iron" (Haavikko) 34:175, 177-79
Age of Iron (Coetzee) 66:101-04, 106-07; 117:59-61, 75, 79-82, 85, 87-90, 92, 102
The Age of Jackson (Schlesinger) 84:347-48, 352, 370-71, 375, 377, 379, 382, 384
"The Age of Kaie" (Harris) 25:217
"The Age of Lead" (Atwood) 84:96, 98
The Age of Longing (Koestler) 3:271; 33:234, 241-42
The Age of Rainmakers (Harris) 25:217
The Age of Reason (Hope) 51:226
The Age of Reason (Koestler) 3:271

The Age of Reason (Sartre)
  See *L'âge de raison*
The Age of Roosevelt (Schlesinger)   **84**:375, 378
The Age of Scandal (White)   **30**:449
The Age of Suspicion: Essays on the Novel (Sarraute)
  See *L'ere du soupçon: Essais sur le roman*
Age of Thunder (Prokosch)   **4**:420; **48**:312, 314
The Age of Wonders (Appelfeld)
  See *Tor Ha-pela'ot*
"Age, Race, Class and Sex: Women Redefining Difference" (Lorde)   **71**:244-45
"Age to Youth" (Wright)   **53**:424
"The Aged" (Kuzma)   **7**:196
"Aged Man Surveys the Past Time" (Warren)   **13**:573
"The Ageing Lovers" (Dickey)   **3**:127
The Agency (Fearing)   **51**:110
"The Agency of the Letter in the Unconscious; or, Reason Since Freud" (Lacan)
  See "L'instance de la lettre"
"The Agent" (Jones)   **42**:242-43
"The Agent" (Wilbur)   **6**:568; **53**:398
Agent (Hinde)   **6**:242
Agent in Place (MacInnes)   **27**:282
Agents and Patients (Powell)   **10**:411-12
Agents and Witnesses (Newby)   **2**:311; **13**:408, 410
Un agenzia matrimoniale (Fellini)   **16**:276
L'aggrandissement (Mauriac)   **9**:363
"Aggressivitly in Psychoanalysis" (Lacan)   **75**:280, 294
"Aghwee the Sky Monster" (Oe)
  See "Sora no kaibutsu Aguwee"
"Aging Female Reads Little Magazines" (Atwood)   **84**:69
"Aging Into Death: Petrify then Dissolve" (Rose)   **85**:314
"The Agnes Cleves Papers" (Avison)   **97**:69-71, 76-7, 80-1, 84, 91, 105, 110, 127
Agoak, l'héritage d'Agaguk (*Agoak: The Legacy of Agaguk*) (Theriault)   **79**:407
Agoak: The Legacy of Agaguk (Theriault)
  See *Agoak, l'héritage d'Agaguk*
Agon: Towards a Theory of Revisionism (Bloom)   **24**:81; **103**:20-1, 23-5, 30, 33-4, 37, 47-8, 54
"Agonia" ("Agony") (Ungaretti)   **11**:556
"Agonie" (Tchicaya)   **101**:350
"Agonist of the Acceleration Lane" (Fulton)   **52**:158-59
"Agony" (Ungaretti)
  See "Agonia"
The Agony and the Ecstasy (Stone)   **7**:469, 471
"An Agony. As Now" (Baraka)   **10**:20
The Agony of Flies (Canetti)
  See *Die Fliegenpein*
The Agony of the American Left (Lasch)   **102**:293
"Agoraphobia" (Prager)   **56**:276
"Agosta the Winged Man and Rasha the Black Dove" (Dove)   **81**:137
Agostino (Moravia)   **7**:240, 244; **18**:343
"Agosto" (Aleixandre)   **9**:12
Agrestes (Cabral de Melo Neto)   **76**:160-61, 163-64, 166, 168
Agricola and the Fox (Haavikko)
  See *Agricola ja kettu*
Agricola ja kettu (*Agricola and the Fox*) (Haavikko)   **18**:208; **34**:173

"Agricultural Caress" (Betjeman)   **43**:43
Agrippina (Neihardt)   **32**:331
Agua (Arguedas)   **10**:8; **18**:5-6
"Agua sexual" ("Sexual Water") (Neruda)   **1**:247
Água viva (Lispector)   **43**:265-66
"As águas do Recife" (Cabral de Melo Neto)   **76**:169
"El águila" (Cernuda)   **54**:47-8
Aguirre, the Wrath of God (Herzog)   **16**:322-25, 331, 333-35
"Agulhas" ("Needles") (Cabral de Melo Neto)   **76**:168-69
The Agunah (Grade)   **10**:246
"Agunot: A Tale" (Agnon)   **14**:2
Ah! Ah! (*Ha! Ha!*) (Ducharme)   **74**:61, 65-8
Ah, but Your Land Is Beautiful (Paton)   **25**:362-63; **55**:311; **106**:294-95, 298, 300
"Ah Life, This Lowgrade Infection" (Honig)   **33**:213
"Ah, mon bon château.?.?." (Yourcenar)   **38**:462
"Ah, Nonny, Nonny" (Kherdian)   **9**:318
Ah Pook Is Here and Other Texts (Burroughs)   **15**:112
"Ah, Woe Is Me" (Gordimer)   **70**:178
"Ahasuerus" (Nemerov)   **36**:301
Ahasverus död (*The Death of Ahasuerus*) (Lagerkvist)   **7**:199; **10**:311-12; **13**:332; **54**:280-83, 285
"Ahavnu Kan" ("We Loved Here") (Amichai)   **116**:109
"Ahead" (Aldiss)
  See "The Failed Men"
"Ahmet Ertegun" ("Within That Context, One Style: Eclectic, Reminiscent, Amused, Fickle, Perverse") (Trow)   **52**:421-22
"El ahogado más hermoso del mundo" ("The Handsomest Drowned Man in the World: A Tale for Children") (Garcia Marquez)   **2**:149; **27**:148, 154; **47**:148, 151
Ai no barei (*Empire of Passion*) (Oshima)   **20**:256-57
Ai no megane wa irogarasu (*The Eyeglass of Love Is Colored Glass*) (Abe)   **81**:286
Ai-ch'ing ti san-pu ch u (*Love: A Trilogy*) (Pa Chin)   **18**:372-73
"Aïda in the Mirror" (Shamlu)   **10**:470
"Aide-Memoire" (Forche)
  See "El Salvador: An Aide Memoire"
AIDS and Its Metaphors (Sontag)   **105**:206, 215, 219, 227
"Aigeltinger" (Williams)   **42**:450
L'aigle à deux têtes (*The Eagle Has Two Heads*) (Cocteau)   **8**:148-49; **16**:223, 225; **43**:105, 112
"Aile" (Reverdy)   **53**:289
Aimé Césaire: Profil d'une oeuvre (Conde)   **92**:100
Aimé Césaire: The Collected Poetry (Cesaire)   **32**:112-13; **112**:8
The Aimer Gate (Garner)   **17**:150-51
Aimez-vous Brahms? (Sagan)   **17**:421-22, 425
"The Aims of Education" (Eliot)   **41**:155
The Aims of Interpretation (Hirsch)   **79**:255, 257-58, 260-62
"Ainda *El cante flamenco*" ("Again *El cante flamenco*") (Cabral de Melo Neto)   **76**:162
L'aîné des Fercheaux (Simenon)   **47**:379
Ain't I a Woman: Black Women and Feminism (hooks)   **94**:132-40, 144, 154, 159-60
"Ain't It Strange" (Smith)   **12**:539
"Ain't Nature Wonderful!" (Ferber)   **93**:142, 145

"Ain't No Crime" (Joel)   **26**:213
"Ain't No Love in These Streets" (Milner)   **56**:225
"Ain't No Man Righteous, No Not One" (Dylan)   **77**:186
Ain't Supposed to Die a Natural Death (Van Peebles)   **2**:447-48
"Ain't That Peculiar" (Robinson)   **21**:347
"Air" (Reverdy)   **53**:289
"Air" (Walcott)   **25**:451
"The Air" (Zappa)   **17**:586
Air and Angels (Hill)   **113**:318
"The Air and the Wind" (Galeano)   **72**:139
"Air and Variations" (Daryush)   **19**:122
Air Apparent (Gardner)   **30**:153
L'air de l'eau (Breton)   **54**:30; **9**:127-28, 132; **15**:91
"Air Hostess" (Amichai)   **57**:38
Air Indien (Morand)   **41**:304
"The Air of June Sings" (Dorn)   **10**:159
"Air Raid" (Achebe)   **7**:6; **11**:3; **26**:21
Air Raid (MacLeish)   **68**:286
Air Surgeon (Slaughter)   **29**:373
An Air That Kills (King)   **53**:204
The Air We Breathe (Josipovici)   **43**:222-23
Airborn (Paz)
  See *Hijos del aire*
Airborn/Hijos del aire (Tomlinson)   **45**:398, 400
The Air-Conditioned Nightmare (Miller)   **4**:351
The Air-Line to Seattle (Lynn)   **50**:426
"Airman's Virtue" (Meredith)   **4**:348
"The Airport" (Lowell)   **9**:335
Airport (Hailey)   **5**:156-57
Airs above the Ground (Stewart)   **7**:467; **35**:391
"The Airship Boys in Africa" (Cassity)   **42**:99
Airships (Hannah)   **23**:209, 211-12; **38**:232-35; **90**:126, 128-31, 138-39, 141, 143-48, 159-61, 163
Airshipwreck (Deighton)   **46**:128
Airways (Pasternak)   **63**:290
Airways, Inc. (Dos Passos)   **4**:134; **15**:184; **25**:144
"The Airy Tomb" (Thomas)   **6**:534; **48**:378
"Aisling" (Heaney)   **74**:162
"Aix-en-Provence" (Rexroth)   **49**:283
"Aja" (Becker and Fagen)   **26**:84
Aja (Becker and Fagen)   **26**:83-4
Ajaiyi and His Inherited Poverty (Tutuola)   **29**:435, 442-43
"Ajanta" (Rukeyser)   **6**:478; **27**:407-08, 410-11, 414
"Ajax" (Ritsos)   **13**:488
"Um ajuste de contas" ("A Score Settled") (Dourado)   **60**:85
"Akai mayu" ("The Red Cocoon") (Abe)   **8**:1; **81**:292
Akallabêth (Tolkien)   **3**:481
"Akanishi Kakita" (Shiga)   **33**:366
Aké: The Years of Childhood (Soyinka)   **36**:413-14
Akhshav bara'ash (Amichai)   **116**:123
Akhshav Uveyamim (*Now and In Other Days*) (Amichai)   **116**:125
"Akiba" (Rukeyser)   **15**:457
Akillesovo serdtse (*My Achilles Heart*) (Voznesensky)   **57**:414-15, 418
"Akkayya" (Rao)   **56**:312
"An Akoulina of the Irish Midlands" (Lavin)   **4**:282; **18**:304
Aku-Aku: The Secret of Easter Island (Heyerdahl)   **26**:191, 193
"Akueke" (Achebe)   **75**:15-16

"Akuma" ("The Devil"; "Satan") (Tanizaki) 8:509

"Al amor" (Aleixandre) 9:15

"Al azar" (Otero) 11:427

Al cielo se sube a pie (*To Heaven One Climbs on Foot*) (Ulibarri) 83:407, 412, 416

"Al Denny" (Keillor) 115:286

Al pie de la letra (*Starting from Scratch*) (Castellanos) 66:45, 47, 52

Al que quiere! (Williams) 13:603; 42:450, 459

"Alabama" (Young) 17:570, 572-73, 582

"Alabama Poem" (Giovanni) 19:192; 117:195

"Alabama Song" (Morrison) 17:286-87

Aladdin Sane (Bowie) 17:59-62, 64, 66-7

"The Alamo Plaza" (Rooke) 25:390

Alan and the Animal Kingdom (Holland) 21:150, 154

Alan Mendelsohn, the Boy from Mars (Pinkwater) 35:317-20

Alanna Autumnal (Barker) 48:9-10, 22

"Alan's Psychedelic Breakfast" (Pink Floyd) 35:305, 311

"The Alarming Revenge of a Domestic Pet" (Buzzati) 36:92

Alarms and Diversions (Thurber) 11:532

"Alas, Poor Richard" (Baldwin) 17:38

Alaska (Michener) 60:258-62; 109:376-77, 381, 386

"Alaska Passage" (Birney) 11:51

"Alaskan Meander" (Richards) 14:453

"Alatus" (Wilbur) 53:405; 110:360

"Alba" (Spicer) 72:364

"Alba after Six Years" (Middleton) 13:387

El alba del alhelí (Alberti) 7:8

"Alba innominata" (Pound) 10:407

"The Albanian Virgin" (Munro) 95:319, 322, 324

"The Albatross" (Hill) 113:281-82, 312

The Albatross and Other Stories (Hill) 4:228; 113:281, 291, 293, 297, 303, 310, 312, 325

Albatross Two (Thiele)
   See *Fight against Albatross Two*

"Albergo Empedocle" (Forster) 13:220

Albergo Empedocle, and Other Writings (Forster) 4:166

Albert Angelo (Johnson) 6:263; 9:300, 302

"Albert des capitales" ("Albert of the Capitals") (Duras) 40:118; 68:75-6, 78, 80, 83, 90, 94

"Albert Giacometti (On a Postage Stamp or Medallion)" (Leiris) 61:361

"Albert of the Capitals" (Duras)
   See "Albert des capitales"

"Alberta Bound" (Lightfoot) 26:278-79

Albertine in Five Times (Tremblay) 102:378-79

"Albert's Bridge" (Stoppard) 4:524; 15:519; 29:394, 397

"Albino" (Komunyakaa) 94:246

"Albino Pheasants" (Lane) 25:286-87

Albino Pheasants (Lane) 25:285, 288

"The Album" (Day Lewis) 10:131

"Album" (Miles) 34:245

Album de familia (Castellanos) 66:58

Albúm familiar (*Family Album: Three Novellas*) (Alegria) 75:44, 51-3

Album of Destiny (Stuart) 8:507; 11:509

"Album of Dreams" (Milosz) 31:269; 56:236, 240-41

The Album of the Soundtrack of the Trailer of the Film "Monty Python and the Holy Grail" (Monty Python) 21:226

"Albuquerque" (Tomlinson) 45:397

"Albuquerque" (Young) 17:574

"Albuquerque Back Again, 12/6/74" (Ortiz) 45:305

"Alcatraz" (Olds) 85:296

"Alceste" (Hecht) 8:266

"Alceste in the Wilderness" (Hecht) 8:267, 269; 13:269

The Alcestiad (Wilder) 1:364; 6:577; 10:536; 82:377

"Alcestis and the Poet" (Porter) 33:321

"Alcestis on the Poetry Circuit" (Jong) 83:290

"The Alchemist" (Bogan) 4:68; 46:83-4, 89; 93:64, 66, 69, 81, 93

"The Alchemist" (Pound) 10:406

"The Alchemist Lost to Human Gifts" (Lerman) 9:329

"Alcide 'Slow Drag' Pavageau" (Matthews) 40:321

"Alcohol" (Carver) 36:100

"Alcohol" (Davies) 21:92

"Alcohol" (Duras) 68:100

"The Alcoholic Love Poems" (Alexie) 96:8

The Alcoholics (Thompson) 69:384, 386-87

Alcoholism (Silverstein and Silverstein) 17:454

"Aldarion and Erendis" (Tolkien) 38:432

"Alder Catkin" (Yevtushenko) 26:468

"The Alderman's Day in the City" (Johnston) 51:244

"Aldershot Crematorium" (Betjeman) 10:52; 43:47

"The Ale House Poems" (Blackburn) 43:62

"Alec" (O'Connor) 23:329

Aleck Maury, Sportsman (Gordon) 6:204; 13:242; 29:186, 188-90; 83:228-29, 233, 240, 242, 247, 253-54, 257, 260

Alehouse Sonnets (Dubie) 36:129, 135, 139

"Aleluja" (Pasolini) 106:233

"El aleph" ("The Aleph") (Borges) 2:72, 76; 4:73; 13:108-09; 44:353; 48:33, 35, 39-40, 42, 45; 83:166, 183, 185-86, 189

"The Aleph" (Borges)
   See "El aleph"

El aleph (*The Aleph, and Other Stories, 1933-1969*) (Borges) 2:72, 74, 76-7; 4:74; 9:118, 120; 13:105; 44:356, 363, 368; 48:33-5; 83:156, 158, 160-61, 164, 171, 185, 189

The Aleph, and Other Stories, 1933-1969 (Borges)
   See *El aleph*

"Alerted" (Heaney) 74:169

"Alethia" (Johnson) 51:236

"Alewives Pool" (Kinnell) 5:216

"Alexander" (Bates) 46:49-50, 67

Alexander Pope (Sitwell) 2:404

Alexandra (Martin) 89:107-09, 116, 125-26, 129

Alexandre Chenevert (*The Cashier*) (Roy) 10:441; 14:465-66, 469

"Alexandria" (Shapiro) 15:476

"Alexandria, 641 A.D." (Borges) 83:169

Alexandria: A History and a Guide (Forster) 13:221; 45:134

"Alexandria and Henrietta" (Barthelme) 46:42

The Alexandria Quartet (Durrell) 1:83-7; 4:144-47; 6:151-53; 8:190-93; 13:185-88; 27:95-8, 100

Alexis; ou, Le traité du vain combat (Yourcenar) 38:460-61, 464; 50:362-65; 87:383-84, 394-97, 399-400

"The Alfano Ending" (Cassity) 42:99

"Alfansa" (Forche) 25:170

De Alfonce Tennis (Donleavy) 45:126-27

Alfred and Guinevere (Schuyler) 23:387-88

Alfred Dies (Horovitz) 56:155-56

"Alfred Jarry in Boston" (Donnell) 34:159

Alfred the Great (Gustafson) 36:216

Alfred the Great (Horovitz) 56:152, 155-56

"Algebra" (Theroux) 28:425

"Algebra and Fire" (Barth) 51:24

"Algera" (Pastan) 27:369

The Algiers Motel Incident (Hersey) 81:332, 334, 337

"Alguien desordena estas rosas" ("Someone Has Disturbed the Roses") (Garcia Marquez) 3:181-82

"Alguien que anda por ahí" ("Someone Walking Around") (Cortazar) 33:125,34:333

Alguma poesia (Andrade) 18:4

"Algunos aspectos del cuento" (Cortazar) 92:159

"Ali" (Merwin) 45:274-75

Ali dagli occhi azzurri (Pasolini) 37:346-47

Alianza y condena (Rodriguez) 10:439-40

"L'alias du 'Non' et du néant" ("The Alias of the 'NO' and Nothingness") (Ferron) 94:121, 129

"The Alias of the 'NO' and Nothingness" (Ferron)
   See "L'alias du 'Non' et du néant"

Alibi (Kroetsch) 57:284-87

"Alibis" (Longley) 29:293, 296

"Alibis and Lullabies" (Peacock) 60:292

"Alicante Lullaby" (Plath) 111:201

"Alice" (Barthelme) 115:71

"Alice" (Creeley) 11:139

Alice Doesn't Live Here Any More (Scorsese) 20:362-27, 329, 334, 338-39; 89:221-22, 232, 240-41, 243, 245, 256, 260, 263, 266-67

"Alice, Falling" (Millhauser) 109:157-58, 160-61

Alice Fell (Tennant) 52:398-99, 406

Alice in Bed (Sontag) 105:214, 223-25

"Alice Is Gone" (Auden) 43:17

Alice K's Guide to Life (Knapp) 99:52

"Alice Long's Dachsunds" (Spark) 8:493; 40:402

"Alice's Last Adventure" (Ligotti) 44:54

"Alicia Who Sees Mice" (Cisneros) 69:146

The Alien (Mitchell) 25:322

"The Alien Corn" (Maugham) 67:219

"An Alien Craft" (Akhmadulina)
   See "Chuzhoe remeslo"

An Alien Heat (Moorcock) 5:294; 27:348-49; 58:347-48

The Alien Intelligence (Williamson) 29:454

"Alien Territory" (Atwood) 84:105

"Alienation and Affection" (Sadoff) 9:467

" Alienation: Two Bees" (Ferlinghetti) 111:60

"The Alienations of Mr. Cogito" (Herbert) 9:275

The Alienist (Carr) 86:41-9

"The Aliens" (Auden) 9:59

"Aliens" (Leavitt) 34:78-9

"The Aliens" (McCullers) 12:433

"Alighieri's Dream" (Baraka)
   See "A Chase"

"Alinsky No in Their League" (Royko) 109:408

Alinsky's Diamond (McHale) 5:281-83

"Alison" (Costello) 21:66-7

"Alive" (Appleman) 51:14

Alive (Read) 4:445; 10:435; 25:377

"Alive and Dead" (Fuller) **62**:185

"Alive and Well on a Friendless Voyage" (Ellison) **42**:130

"Alive for an Instant" (Koch) **44**:251

Alive: Poems, 1971-1972 (Wright) **11**:578; **53**:429-30, 432

"Alive Together" (Mueller) **13**:400

"Alkmene" (Dinesen) **29**:159, 163; **95**:35, 47, 59

All (Campbell) **32**:80

"All about and to a Female Artist" (Delaney) **29**:146

"All About—And Back Again" (Knight) **40**:283-86

All against All (Adamov)
   See *Tous contre tous*

"All along the Watchtower" (Dylan) **12**:185

"All Around the Mulberry Tree" (Hunter) **35**:226

"All at One Point" (Calvino) **8**:127

"All Attempts Will End in Failure" (Berriault) **54**:4

"All Avoidable Talk" (Narayan) **47**:305

All Bleeding (Barker) **37**:37

All Creatures Great and Small (Herriot) **12**:282

"All Day and All of the Night" (Davies) **21**:88

"all day i have seen you" (Young Bear) **94**:366, 369

All Day on the Sands (Bennett) **77**:86, 88, 93

"All Day Sucker" (Wonder) **12**:660

All Dressed Up and Nowhere to Go; or, The Poor Man's Guide to the Affluent Society (Bradbury) **32**:55; **61**:41

All Fires the Fire, and Other Stories (Cortazar)
   See *Todos los fuegos el fuego*

"All Fools' Eve" (Avison) **97**:70

"All Generations Before Me" (Amichai) **116**:127

All God's Children Need Traveling Shoes (Angelou) **64**:35-8; **77**:7, 13-15, 20, 22, 27-8, 31

All Good Men (Fleming) **37**:119-21

All Good Men (Griffiths) **52**:173, 181-84

"All Grass Is Flesh" (L'Heureux) **52**:272

"All Hallows" (Gluck) **7**:119

"All He Needs Is Feet" (Himes) **7**:160; **108**:227, 235

All Heaven in a Rage (Duffy) **37**:116

All Her Children (Wakefield) **7**:503

All I Could Never Be (Yezierska) **46**:444-45, 447

"All I Gotta Do" (Giovanni) **19**:192; **64**:187-88

"All I Need Is a Girl" (Sondheim) **30**:377

"All I Really Want to Do" (Dylan) **77**:176

"All in Green Went My Love Riding" (Cummings) **68**:46

All in the Family (Lear) **12**:326-32, 336, 338

All in the Family (O'Connor) **14**:392-93

"All in the Streets" (Baraka) **5**:48

All Is But a Beginning (Neihardt) **32**:336

"All Is Mine" (Guillen)
   See "Tengo"

All Is Mine (Guillen)
   See *Tengo*

"All Kinds of Caresses" (Ashbery) **77**:46

"All Legendary Obstacles" (Montague) **46**:264-66, 275-76

All Love (Seifert)
   See *Samá láska*

"All Lovers Love the Spring" (Gordon) **83**:231

All Men Are Enemies (Aldington) **49**:14, 18

All Men Are Mortal (Beauvoir)

   See *Tous les hommes sont mortels*

All Mod Cons (Weller) **26**:444-45

All My Children (Nixon) **21**:242-48; 250-53

All My Friends Are Going to Be Strangers (McMurtry) **2**:272; **3**:333; **7**:214-15; **11**:371; **27**:329-31; **44**:255

"All My Friends Died" (Carroll) **35**:79

All My Little Ones (Ewart) **46**:150

"All My Pretty Ones" (Sexton) **53**:318, 320, 322

All My Pretty Ones (Sexton) **4**:482-83; **8**:482-83; **15**:471-72; **53**:312, 316-18, 320-21, 324

All My Relations: An Anthology of Contemporary Native Fiction (King) **89**:92

"All My Sins" (Fuentes)
   See "Todos mis pecados"

All My Sins Remembered (Haldeman) **61**:177, 182-83

All My Sons (Kazan) **63**:234

All My Sons (Miller) **1**:216, 218-19; **6**:327, 329-32; **10**:342, 344; **15**:371-74; **26**:321-22; **47**:251, 254-56; **78**:293, 301-02, 306, 312, 318, 324

"All Night, All Night" (Schwartz) **45**:355-56

All Night Long (Caldwell) **60**:50

"All of Which Isn't Singing Is Mere Talking" (Cummings) **15**:164

All or Nothing (Powys) **46**:323, 325

All Our Yesterdays (Ginzburg)
   See *Tutti i nostri ieri*

All Over (Albee) **2**:1-4; **5**:13-14; **9**:6, 9; **11**:12; **13**:4-5; **25**:36, 38, 40; **53**:21; **113**:15, 17, 22-3. 28

All Over Town (Schisgal) **6**:490-91

All Quiet on the Western Front (Remarque)
   See *Im Westen nichts Neues*

"All Revelation" (Frost) **13**:225, 230; **26**:118

All Roads at Once (Corn) **33**:113-14

All Said and Done (Beauvoir)
   See *Tout compte fait*

All Screwed Up (Wertmueller)
   See *Everything's in Place, Nothing's in Order*

"All Set About with Fever Trees" (Durban) **39**:44-6

All Set About with Fever Trees (Durban) **39**:44-6

"All Shook Up" (Boyle) **36**:63

All Shot Up (Himes) **18**:246; **58**:264, 267

"All Sorts of Impossible Things" (McGahern) **48**:264

All Soul's Day (Konwicki)
   See *Zaduszki*

"All Souls Night" (Day Lewis) **6**:129

All Souls' Rising (Bell) **102**:20-23

"All Strange Away" (Beckett) **29**:59

"All Summer Long" (Anderson) **23**:29-30, 33

"All Systems Break Down" (Bottoms) **53**:29

"All Systems Tower and Collapse" (Bottoms) **53**:29

All That Fall (Beckett) **6**:42, 44-5, 47; **10**:30; **11**:34; **14**:79; **18**:42; **29**:63; **57**:79; **59**:255

All That Glitters (Lear) **12**:337-38

"All That Is" (Wilbur) **53**:412; **110**:357

"All That Is Lovely in Men" (Creeley) **78**:136

"All That Is Perfect in Woman" (Williams) **42**:456

All That Jazz (Fosse) **20**:126-27

"All That Lies Buried" (Dobyns) **37**:80

All That Rises Must Converge (O'Connor)
   See *Everything That Rises Must Converge*

"All That Time" (Swenson) **106**:337

"All the Animal inside Us" (Bottoms) **53**:31

All the Assholes in the World and Mine (Bukowski) **41**:69

All the Beauty of the World (Seifert) **93**:326

All the Best People (Wilson) **32**:447

"All the Birds Come Home to Roost" (Ellison) **42**:130

"All the Blood within Me" (Amis) **40**:43, 45

All the Brave Promises (Settle) **19**:410; **61**:371

All: The Collected Short Poems, 1923-1958 (Zukofsky) **1**:385; **4**:599

All the Conspirators (Isherwood) **1**:155-56; **9**:292-93; **11**:295, 298-300; **14**:280-81, 285; **44**:396-97, 400-01

"All the Critics Love U in New York" (Prince) **35**:326-27

"All the Days of Our Lives" (Smith) **25**:410; **73**:357

"All the Dead Dears" (Plath) **11**:445; **51**:344

"All the Earth, All the Air" (Roethke) **101**:328, 332

"All the Fine Young Horses" (MacEwen) **13**:357

"All the Fruits Had Fallen" (Schwartz) **45**:361

"All the Kinds of Yes" (Tiptree) **48**:388; **50**:357

All the King's Men (Warren) **1**:352-56; **4**:577, 580-83; **6**:555-56; **8**:536, 539-40, 543; **10**:518; **13**:574, 579; **39**:264, 266; **53**:359-67, 369, 372-85; **59**:296, 298-300, 303

"All the Lies That Are My Life" (Ellison) **42**:129-30

All the Little Live Things (Stegner) **9**:508-09; **49**:353; **81**:340, 348, 352

"All the Lonely People" (McPherson) **77**:359-60

"All the Lovely Ladies" (Lightfoot) **26**:281

All the News That's Fit to Sing (Ochs) **17**:329, 331-32

All the Nice People (Leonard)
   See *Mick and Mick*

All the President's Men (Goldman) **48**:128

All the Pretty Horses (McCarthy) **101**:164-65, 168-69, 171, 173, 176, 180, 182-92, 194-97, 199-200, 202-05

"All the Pussy We Want" (Bukowski) **41**:68

All the Rest Have Died (Gunn) **5**:152

"All the Sounds of the Rainbow" (Spinrad) **46**:384

All the Strange Hours: The Excavation of a Life (Eiseley) **7**:92-3

"All the Strength We Got" (Cliff) **21**:65

All the Summer Voices (Corcoran) **17**:72

"All the Time in the World" (Dubus) **97**:236-37

All the Time in the World (Williams) **42**:440-41

"All the Universe in a Mason Jar" (Haldeman) **61**:174, 176

"All the Way" (Gaye) **26**:132

"All the Way in Flagstaff, Arizona" (Bausch) **51**:55-7

All the Way to Bantry Bay (Kiely) **23**:265

"All the Young Punks" ("New Boots and Contracts") (Clash) **30**:43-4

All These Women (Bergman)
   See *For att ente tala om alla dessa kvinnor*

"All Things Are Water" (Mathews) **6**:315

All Things Bright and Beautiful (Herriot) **12**:283

All Things Bright and Beautiful (Waterhouse) **47**:417

All Things Considered (Baker) **31**:27

All Things Nice (Billington) **43**:53-4

All Things Wise and Wonderful (Herriot) **12**:283

"All This Review" (Dodson) **79**:193

All Times, All Peoples: A World History of Slavery (Meltzer) **26**:307

All Together Now (Bridgers) **26**:91-3

"All Tomorrow's Parties" (Reed) **21**:303, 314

"All Too Clearly" (Ferlinghetti) **27**:139

All Us Come Cross the Water (Clifton) **66**:67, 86-7

"All Wars Are Holy" (Codrescu) **46**:102

All We Need of Hell (Crews) **49**:76-9

All What Jazz: A Record Diary, 1961-68 (Larkin) **33**:262, 268; **39**:334, 340, 343-44

"All Winter" (Hogan) **73**:159

All Women Are Fatal (Mauriac)
   See *Toutes les femmes sont fatales*

"All Worlds Have Halfsight, Seeing Either With" (Cummings) **15**:164

"All You Can Hold for Five Bucks" (Mitchell) **98**:169, 184

"All You Need Is Love" (Lennon and McCartney) **35**:287

"All You Wanna Do Is Dance" (Joel) **26**:215, 220

"All You Who Sleep Tonight" (Seth) **90**:351

All You Who Sleep Tonight (Seth) **90**:350-1, 353, 361

"All You Zombies" (Heinlein) **14**:253; **26**:165, 174, 178

"Alla noia" (Ungaretti) **11**:555; **15**:536-37

"Alla Tha's All Right, but" (Jordan) **114**:145

"Allal" (Bowles) **19**:59, 61; **53**:37

All-American (Tunis) **12**:593-94, 598

All-Bright Court (Porter) **70**:96-101

"Alle" ("Everything") (Bachmann) **69**:35, 37

"Alle Tage" (Bachmann) **69**:38

"Allegiance" (Taylor) **37**:407-08, 412; **44**:305-06

Allegiances (Stafford) **4**:520-21; **7**:460

"The Allegorical Method" (Warner) **45**:434, 439

Allegories of Reading (de Man) **55**:384, 386, 391, 400, 406, 409-10, 415

"Allegory for Seafaring Black Mother" (Dodson) **79**:196

The Allegory of Love: A Study in Medieval Tradition (Lewis) **6**:308; **14**:321-22; **27**:259

"An Allegory of Man's Fate" (Hood) **28**:193

"Allegory of the Adolescent and the Adult" (Barker) **48**:21

"Allegre" (Walcott) **25**:448; **76**:279

L'allegria (Ungaretti) **7**:481-82, 484; **11**:556-60; **15**:536-39

"Allegro" (Transtroemer) **52**:410; **65**:224, 235

Allegro Postillions (Keates) **34**:201-03

Allen Verbatim (Ginsberg) **6**:201

"Allentown" (Joel) **26**:222-23

"Aller et retour" (Barnes) **29**:27, 30

"Aller et retour" (Sartre) **24**:416-17

Allergies (Silverstein and Silverstein) **17**:456

Allergy (Taylor) **27**:440, 443

Alley Jaggers (West) **7**:522-25; **96**:375, 380

The Alleys of Eden (Butler) **81**:123, 127

"Allhallows Eve" (Gustafson) **36**:219

"Allie" (Graves) **45**:166

The Alligation (Ferlinghetti) **2**:134; **111**:63

"The Alligator Bride" (Hall) **37**:142, 147

The Alligator Bride: Poems Selected and New (Hall) **1**:137; **37**:141-42; **59**:156

The Alligator Groom (Hall) **1**:137

The Alligator Report (Kinsella) **43**:257-58

"Alligators and Paris and North America" (Dickey) **28**:119

All-Night Visitors (Major) **19**:291-92, 294-95; **48**:212, 215, 217

"All-Nite Donuts" (Goldbarth) **38**:205

"Allons Mes Enfants" (Hannah) **90**:158

Allophanes (Bowering) **15**:84; **47**:22-3, 28-9, 32

"Allotments" (Harrison) **43**:175

"Alma" (Chappell) **78**:116

"Almanac" (Swenson) **14**:520; **61**:390

Almanac of the Dead: A Novel (Silko) **74**:331, 350-52; **114**:330-31, 334-37, 340-43

"Almeyer's Mother" (Findley) **102**:111

"The Almond of the World" (Elytis) **100**:179

"The Almond Trees" (Walcott) **25**:451

Almost a Fairy Tale (Buero Vallejo) **15**:100-02

Almost a Life (Friedman) **7**:109

"Almost an Elegy" (Brodsky)
   See "Pochti elegiia"

Almost April (Sherburne) **30**:360

Almost at the End (Yevtushenko) **51**:431-33

"Almost Aubade" (Hacker) **72**:184

Almost By Chance A Woman: Elizabeth (Fo)
   See *Elisabetta: Quasi per Caso una Donna*

Almost Cinderella (Potter) **86**:346

"Almost Grown" (Berry) **17**:54

"Almost in Iowa" (Irving) **112**:172, 175

"Almost Noon" (Galvin) **38**:198

Almost Paradise (Isaacs) **32**:255-56

Alms for Oblivion (Dahlberg) **7**:68-70; **14**:136

Alms for Oblivion (Raven) **14**:440-43

"Almswomen" (Blunden) **56**:27-8, 32, 37, 48, 52

"El almuerzo" ("The Lunch") (Cortazar) **34**:332

Alnilam (Dickey) **47**:98-101; **109**:236, 240, 241, 257

Aloes (Fugard)
   See *A Lesson from Aloes*

"Alone" (Angelou) **77**:29

"Alone" (Singer) **23**:418

L'alone grigio (Ortese) **89**:192

"Alone in Africa" (Rush) **44**:92, 94-5

"Alone in the Lumber Business" (Ashbery) **77**:62-3

Alone of All Her Sex (Warner) **59**:217

Alone on the Pacific (Ichikawa) **20**:179, 182

Alone with America (Howard) **7**:166

Aloneness (Brooks) **49**:35, 37

"Along Lake Michigan" (Leithauser) **27**:240-42

"Along the Edges" (McGahern) **48**:264

"Along the Road" (Van Duyn) **116**:405

Along the Road: Notes and Essays of a Tourist (Huxley) **3**:256; **11**:287; **18**:269

"Along the Scenic Route" (Ellison) **13**:203; **42**:127

"Along These Lines" (Williams) **42**:443

Along with Youth: Hemingway, the Early Years (Griffin) **39**:398-403

"L'alouette" (Char) **9**:161

L'alouette (*The Lark*) (Anouilh) **1**:7; **3**:11; **13**:17-18, 21-2; **40**:53, 56-7, 61; **50**:278-80

"O alpendre no canavial" ("A Veranda on the Cane Field") (Cabral de Melo Neto) **76**:169

"Alpha" (Tolson) **105**:241, 247-48, 253, 263-64, 283-84

Alpha Alpha (Barker) **37**:32, 37

Alpha Beta (Whitehead) **5**:488-89

"The Alphabet Begins with AAA" (Derleth) **31**:133

An Alphabet for Gourmets (Fisher) **76**:341-42; **87**:119-20

Alphabet for the Lost Years (Schaeffer) **11**:491

The Alphabet of Grace (Buechner) **2**:82

"Alphabetical Africa" (Abish) **22**:16, 18, 22

Alphabetical Order (Frayn) **7**:107-08

"Alphabets" (Heaney) **74**:161-62, 175-77, 190, 193

Alphabets (Perec) **116**:251

Alphaville (Godard) **20**:133-34, 137, 149

Alpine (Oppen) **34**:359

"The Alpine Christ" (Jeffers) **54**:250-51

"An Alpine Idyll" (Hemingway) **3**:240-41; **13**:273; **30**:181, 184

Alpýdubókin (*The Atom Station; Atómstödin*) (Laxness) **25**:295, 298, 300

"Already One" (Young) **17**:580

"Als der Krieg ausbrach" (*Enter and Exit; When the War Began; When the War Started*) (Boell) **27**:62-3, 67; **72**:79

Als der Krieg zu Ende war (*When the War Ended; When the War Was Over*) (Boell) **27**:67; **72**:78, 80

Als der Krieg zu Ende war (*When the War Was Over*) (Frisch) **9**:217; **14**:182-83; **18**:160-62; **44**:196, 199

"Alta niña de caña y amapola" (Guillen) **79**:241

Altanima (Audiberti) **38**:23

"Altar Boy" (Fante) **60**:133

The Altar Steps (Mackenzie) **18**:314

"Die Alte Frau, die alte Marshallin" (Dickey) **28**:119

Alte Meister (*Old Masters*) (Bernhard) **61**:22

"Altele" (Singer) **6**:509

The Alteration (Amis) **8**:11-12; **13**:13-14; **40**:42

Altered States (Chayefsky) **23**:119-20

An Alternate Life (Duncan) **55**:295

Alternating Current (Paz)
   See *Corriente alterna*

"The Alternative" (Baraka) **33**:55

"Alternative Commencement Address at Dartmouth College" (Jordan) **114**:153

The Alternative Society: Essays from the Other World (Rexroth) **2**:371; **49**:277

"Altitudes" (Wilbur) **53**:410; **110**:348, 353

"Alto do Trapuá" ("The Heights of Trapua") (Cabral de Melo Neto) **76**:167

"L'alto veliero" ("The Tall Sailing Ship") (Quasimodo) **10**:428

Altogether: The Collected Stories of W. Somerset Maugham (Maugham)
   See *East and West: The Collected Short Stories of W. Somerset Maugham*

Alturas de Macchu Picchu (*The Heights of Macchu Picchu; Macchu Picchu*) (Neruda) **1**:247; **5**:301, 303-04; **7**:260; **28**:307-08, 314; **62**:325, 328

"The Alumnae Bulletin" (Prager) **56**:276-78

"Aluroid" (Birney) **6**:78

"The Alvordton Spa and Sweat Shop" (Kauffman) **42**:251

"Always" (Strand) **71**:280

Always Coming Home (Le Guin) **45**:219-21

"Always for the First Time" (Breton) **54**:30

Always on Sale (Aksyonov)
   See *Vsegda v prodaze*

"Always the Effort to Gather It All" (Coles) **46**:108-09

Always the Young Strangers (Sandburg) **10**:451; **35**:353-54, 357, 360

Always Young and Fair (Richter)　30:319-21, 325

"Am I an Irishwoman?" (Brophy)　105:12

"Am I Blue" (Henley)　23:217

"Am I Blue?" (Walker)　58:408

"Am I My Neighbor's Keeper?" (Eberhart)　3:133; 11:177; 19:140-42

"Am Ortler" (Bernhard)　32:20

"Am Strande von Tanger" (Salter)　52:367, 369; 59:195-96, 198

Am ungenauen Ort (Wellershoff)　46:435

Am Ziel (*At One's Goal*) (Bernhard)　61:26

Amadeus (Shaffer)　18:477-78; 37:382-89

Amado mio (Pasolini)　106:254-55

"Amahl and the Night Visitors: A Guide to the Tenor of Love" (Moore)　39:85; 45:279-80

"Amalfi" (Aldington)　49:17

Amalgamemnon (Brooke-Rose)　40:110-11

"Amana Grass" (Silkin)　6:498

Amana Grass (Silkin)　2:396; 6:498; 43:404

"Amanda" (Waldman)　7:509

"Amanda Dreams She Has Died and Gone to the Elysian Fields" (Kumin)　13:327

Amanda/Miranda (Peck)　21:300-01

Amanda's Choice (Holland)　21:147-48

"L'amande croyable au lendemain neuf" (Char)　9:162

"Amandine" (Tournier)　95:383-86

Amandine ou les deux jardins (Tournier)　95:367-68, 383

L'amant (*The Lover*) (Duras)　34:162-63; 40:185-87; 68:73-4, 76-7, 79-85, 87, 90-5, 98-9; 100:119-22, 126, 128-32, 134, 136, 138-39, 141-49

L'Amant de la Chine du Nord (Duras)　100:121, 123, 131-33, 136, 138-42, 144-45, 149

La amante (Alberti)　7:8-9

L'amante anglaise (*The Lovers of Viorne*) (Duras)　6:149; 11:166; 40:175-76, 181-83; 68:89

Amantes (*Lovhers*) (Brossard)　115:105, 107, 110-11, 114-18, 121-23, 132-36, 140

"Los amantes viejos" ("The Old Lovers") (Aleixandre)　9:17

Les amants puérils (*The Puerile Lovers*) (Crommelynck)　75:150, 153, 155-56, 162-63, 166, 168

"Amanuensis" (Godwin)　31:197

"Amao guniang" ("Miss Amao") (Ding Ling)　68:56

Amarcord (*I Remember*) (Fellini)　16:288-90, 294-97, 299-300; 85:51, 59-60, 63-4, 66, 69-71, 74-8, 81-2

"Amargura para tres sonámbulos" ("Bitter Sorrow for Three Sleepwalkers"; "Bitterness for Three Sleepwalkers") (Garcia Marquez)　3:181; 47:148

"The Amateur" (Gustafson)　36:220

The Amateur (Littell)　42:276-77

Amateurs (Barthelme)　8:52-3; 13:61; 46:35-6; 59:247; 115:71

"An Amateur's Guide to the Night" (Robison)　42:342-43

An Amateur's Guide to the Night (Robison)　42:342-43; 98:306, 318

"Amazed and Confused" (Diamond)　30:113

"Amazement" (Milosz)　22:308

"Amazing" (Fuller)　62:199, 204

"Amazing Grace" (Mueller)　13:399

"Amazing Grace in the Back Country" (Warren)　18:536-37

"Amazing Journey" (Townshend)　17:526, 538

"Amazing Perfume Offer" (Redgrove)　41:354

The Amazing Spider Man (Lee)　17:259-60

"Amazonka" (Bagryana)　10:12

"The Amazons" (Barker)　48:9, 12, 20

"Amazons" (Selzer)　74:273

Amazons: An Intimate Memoir by the First Woman Ever to Play in the National Hockey League (DeLillo)　27:79-80

"The Ambassador" (Reid)　33:350

The Ambassador (Brink)　106:105-06, 124, 136

"The Amber Witch" (Nye)　42:304

"Ambergris" (Graham)　48:146

"Amberjack" (Tiptree)　48:396

"Amberose Triste" (Broumas)　73:17

The Amberstone Exit (Feinstein)　36:168

"Ambience" (Graves)　45:166

Ambit (Aleixandre)
　See *Ambito*

"The Ambition Bird" (Sexton)　4:483; 53:313

Ambito (*Ambit*; *Space*) (Aleixandre)　9:10, 12, 15; 36:23, 25, 28-9

Le ambizioni sbagliate (*Mistaken Ambitions*) (Moravia)　7:240; 46:281

"Àmbroise, la baleine et Gabrielle" (Theriault)　79:408

"Ambrose His Mark" (Barth)　9:66, 69; 89:3, 7-8, 14, 16, 19, 22, 40-1, 43, 49, 54, 58-9

"Ambrose Syme" (McGrath)　55:74, 76

"Ambroso" (Isherwood)　14:284

"Ambulance Blues" (Young)　17:573, 581-82

"Ambulances" (Larkin)　8:332; 13:337; 18:298-99; 33:260; 39:342; 64:266

"Ambush" (O'Brien)　103:143

Ambush (Read)　4:439

Ambush at Tether's End (Walker)　61:424

Amédée; or, How to Get Rid of It (Ionesco)
　See *Amédée; ou, Comment s'en débarrasser*

Amédée; ou, Comment s'en débarrasser (*Amédée; or, How to Get Rid of It*) (Ionesco)　4:251; 6:247-50, 253-54; 9:287; 41:227, 230; 86:332-34

L'amélanchier (*The Juneberry Tree*) (Ferron)　94:104, 106-7, 109, 111, 113-15, 124, 126-27

"Amelia" (Mitchell)　12:442

"Amelia Earheart" (Smith)　12:535

"Amen" (Hogan)　73:154

Amen (Amichai)　9:25; 22:30; 116:89-90, 92

"Amen and Out" (Aldiss)　14:15

The Amen Corner (Baldwin)　5:40; 17:31, 34, 37; 50:283, 294; 67:8

"Amena Karanova" (Ulibarri)　83:417

L'Amer (*These Our Mothers, or The Disintegrating Chapter*) (Brossard)　115:105, 107, 114-15, 119, 123-24, 127-29, 133, 136, 155-56

Amer Eldorado (Federman)　47:122, 127

"America" (Angelou)　77:29

"America" (Diamond)　30:113-14

"America" (Ginsberg)　6:199; 13:239-41; 36:180, 187, 192; 69:211, 215; 109:337, 355

"America" (Prince)　35:332

"America" (Simon)　17:462-63

"America" (Sondheim)　30:387

America (Baudrillard)
　See *Amérique*

America a Prophecy: A New Reading of American Poetry from Pre-Columbian Times to the Present (Rothenberg)　57:382

"America! America!" (Plath)　11:451

"America! America!" (Schwartz)　10:462, 466; 45:353-55; 87:334-36, 342, 43

America, America (Kazan)　6:273; 16:367-68, 370-71; 63:213-15, 221-22, 233, 235

America at Last (White)　30:449

"America Began in Houses" (Crase)　58:159, 164

"America Competes" (Gurganus)　70:190-91, 195-96

America Day by Day (Beauvoir)　44:343

"America Drinks" (Zappa)　17:588

"America Drinks and Goes Home" (Zappa)　17:585, 588

América, fábula de fábulas, y otros ensayos (Asturias)　13:39

America Hurrah (van Itallie)　3:492-93

America in 1492 (Josephy)　70:352

America Invulnerable (Carr)　86:47

America Is Hard to Find (Berrigan)　4:56

America, My Wilderness (Prokosch)　4:422; 48:317

"America, Seen through Photographs, Darkly" (Sontag)　10:486

"America the Beautiful" (Leiber)　25:304

America, Their America (Clark)　38:117, 127-28

"America: Toward Yavneh" (Ozick)　28:348

America Was Promises (MacLeish)　8:362; 14:338; 68:286, 289-90, 293

The American (Fast)　23:157

"An American Adventure" (Oates)　3:360

American Appetites (Oates)　108:374, 381, 386, 388

"American Art and Non-American Art" (O'Hara)　78:375

"The American Background" (Williams)　67:420-21

"The American Bakery" (Apple)　33:21

"American Beauty" (Canin)　55:36, 38-9

American Beauty (Ferber)　93:156-59, 164, 171-72, 189-90

The American Bicentennial Series (Jakes)　29:248-49

"American Blood" (DeLillo)　54:87

American Buffalo (Mamet)　9:360-61; 15:356, 357-58; 34:218, 220-22, 224; 46:246, 248-50, 252, 254-55

"American Buttons" (Voznesensky)　57:421, 428

"The American Cancer Society or There Is More Than One Way to Skin a Coon" (Lorde)　71:249-50

The American Caravan (Mitchell)　98:

"American Change" (Ginsberg)　3:195; 4:181; 109:364

American Characteristics, and Other Essays (Wilder)　15:575-76; 82:378, 386

An American Childhood (Dillard)　60:77-81; 115:179, 181, 189, 197, 200-01

"American Citizen" (Boyle)　58:69

The American Communist Party: A Critical History (Howe)　85:119-20

"The American Couple" (Butler)　81:122-23, 127-29

American Dad (Janowitz)　43:209-10

American Days (Poliakoff)　38:382-84

The American Drama Since 1918 (Krutch)　24:285

The American Dream (Albee)　1:4-5; 2:2-4; 3:6; 5:10-11; 9:2, 4-5, 9-10; 13:7; 25:35, 40; 53:22, 24, 27; 86:120, 125; 113:3-5, 9, 15, 18, 26, 31, 34-5, 40, 47-8, 54

An American Dream (Mailer)　1:190-93; 2:258-

59, 261, 263; **3**:312-13, 317-18; **4**:321, 323; **5**:268; **8**:364-66, 369, 372-73; **11**:340-43; **14**:350-52; **28**:256-57, 261; **39**:421; **74**:203-07, 209, 224, 226, 233-34, 236, 245; **111**:95, 98-9, 108, 117-18, 120-21, 141, 148-49

"American Dreams" (Carey)   **40**:127-29, 133; **96**:24, 27-8, 30, 37, 66-7

American Dreams (Sapphire)   **99**:80-2, 84, 87-8

American Dreams, American Nightmares (Madden)   **5**:265

American Dreams: Lost and Found (Terkel)   **38**:425-26, 428

American Earth (Caldwell)   **14**:93, 96; **50**:299-300; **60**:44, 46, 48

The American Earthquake (Wilson)   **2**:478

American Energies (Birkerts)   **116**:152-53, 157

"American Express" (Salter)   **52**:368; **59**:194, 196-97

American Expression (Lezama Lima)   See *La expresión americana*

American Fictions, 1940-1980: A Comprehensive History and Critical Evaluation (Karl)   **34**:551-54

"The American Flag" (Miles)   **14**:370

American Folksong (Guthrie)   **35**:184, 192

"American/French Poems" (Laughlin)   **49**:224

American Gigolo (Schrader)   **26**:394-96, 398-99

American Girl (Tunis)   **12**:592-93

American Gothic (Bloch)   **33**:84

American Graffiti (Lucas)   **16**:408-11, 416-17

The American Gun Mystery (Queen)   **11**:460

The American Health System (Ehrenreich)   **110**:152-53, 177

American Heritage Picture History of the Civil War (Catton)   **35**:90

"The American Hotel" (Brautigan)   **12**:57

American Hunger (Wright)   **9**:585-86; **74**:378-83, 388-89

An American in Washington (Baker)   **31**:25-6

American Indian Fiction (Larson)   **31**:239-40

"American Indian Songs" (Rexroth)   **112**:377

American Indians in the Pacific: The Theory behind the Kon-Tiki Expedition (Heyerdahl)   **26**:190-91

The American Jitters (Wilson)   **24**:486

"American Journal" (Hayden)   **37**:159

American Journal (Hayden)   **14**:240-41; **37**:153-58, 160

The American Kaleidoscope: Race, Ethnicity, and the Civil Culture (Fuchs)   **70**:376, 382, 385, 410

American Landscape (Rice)   **7**:360-61; **49**:298, 300, 302-03, 305

"American Landscapes" (Montague)   **46**:265

"American Letter" (MacLeish)   **68**:273, 287-88, 292

The American Liberals and the Russian Revolution (Lasch)   **102**:292, 318

"American Light: A Hopper Perspective" (Sissman)   **18**:488

"The American Loneliness" (Wilder)   **82**:357

American Madness (Capra)   **16**:163-64

"American Mantras and Songs" (Ferlinghetti)   **6**:184; **27**:139

"An American Marriage" (Klein)   **30**:236

An American Marriage (Masters)   **48**:220

An American Memory (Larsen)   **55**:69-72

An American Millionaire (Schisgal)   **6**:490

American Mischief (Lelchuk)   **5**:240-43, 245

"American Muse" (Walcott)   **67**:348

The American Newness: Culture and Politics in the Age of Emerson (Howe)   **85**:142-45, 150

"An American Nightingale" (Yevtushenko)   **26**:463-64

American Outpost: A Book of Reminiscences (Sinclair)   **63**:346, 349

"American Plastic: The Matter of Fiction" (Vidal)   **8**:527-28; **10**:504

"American Poetry" (Simpson)   **7**:427

"American Poetry and American Life" (Pinsky)   **94**:301-2

American Poetry in the Twentieth Century (Rexroth)   **49**:279; **112**:386

"American Poets" (Bell)   **8**:66

American Pop (Bakshi)   **26**:74-6

"American Portrait, Old Style" (Warren)   **13**:582; **18**:534; **39**:260, 264

An American Prayer (Morrison)   **17**:292-96

"American Primitive" (Smith)   **6**:513

American Primitive (Oliver)   **34**:246-49; **98**:258-50, 269, 272-73, 275-77, 279, 290, 295-96, 298, 300-02

An American Procession (Kazin)   **34**:555-64

American Psycho (Ellis)   **71**:143-74; **117**:132-35, 138, 140-41, 143, 145-51, 153-61

"American Radio Company" (Keillor)   **115**:296

"American Rhapsodies" (Fearing)   **51**:106

"American Rhapsody" ("5") (Fearing)   **51**:106; **51**:108

An American Romance (Casey)   **59**:119-20, 122

"American Scenes (1904-1905)" (Justice)   **102**:274, 285

American Scenes and Other Poems (Tomlinson)   **2**:436-37; **4**:543-44, 546, 548; **13**:545, 547-48; **45**:401

American Scrapbook (Charyn)   **5**:104

"American Sexual Reference: Black Male" (Baraka)   **115**:47, 49

"American Sketches" (Justice)   **102**:260-61, 270

The American Soldier (Fassbinder)   See *Der Amerikanische Soldat*

American Stars 'n Bars (Young)   **17**:576, 579

"An American Student in Paris" (Farrell)   **66**:131

"American Suite" (Urdang)   **47**:400

"The American Sun" (Kaufman)   **49**:205

An American Takes a Walk (Whittemore)   **4**:588

"American Tune" (Simon)   **17**:466

"American Twilights, 1957" (Wright)   **3**:543; **5**:519

The American University: How It Runs, Where It Is Going (Barzun)   **51**:40-1

The American Way (Hart and Kaufman)   **38**:261-62, 266; **66**:175, 189

The American Way in Sport (Tunis)   **12**:597

"The American Way of Life" (Alegria)   **75**:

An American Werewolf in London (Landis)   **26**:276-77

"Americana" (Rakosi)   **47**:344, 347

Americana (DeLillo)   **10**:134-35; **13**:175-76, 178; **27**:76-9, 81; **39**:117, 125; **76**:182

The Americanization of Emily (Chayefsky)   **23**:117

"Americans" (Riding)   **7**:374

The Americans (Jakes)   **29**:249

"America's Color Blind: The Modeling of Minorities" (Reed)   **60**:310

America's Coming of Age (Brooks)   **29**:78, 81-3, 87

Amérika (Alegria)   **57**:11

Amerika (Klima)   164, 170

Der Amerikanische Soldat (*The American Soldier*) (Fassbinder)   **20**:107, 116

Amérique (*America*) (Baudrillard)   **60**:24-5

Amers (*Seamarks*) (Perse)   **4**:399-401; **11**:433, 435-36; **46**:306, 308

Les ames fortes (Giono)   **4**:184

The Amethyst Ring (O'Dell)   **30**:277-78

Le amiche (Antonioni)   **20**:19, 21-2, 24-5, 29

"Amid Mounting Evidence" (Ashbery)   **77**:66

"Amigo Acres" (Jensen)   **37**:186

"Amigos de corazon" (Middleton)   **13**:387

"Amithaine" (Smith)   **43**:420

"Amitié du prince" (Perse)   **11**:434; **46**:301, 307

"Amities" (Scannell)   **49**:330

Amnesia (Cooper)   **86**:50-60

"Amnesiac" (Plath)   **51**:340; **111**:160, 163

"Amo, amas, amat, amamus, amatis, Enough" (Perelman)   **49**:265

Amok Time (Sturgeon)   **39**:364

"Among All These" (Blunden)   **56**:48

"Among Artisans' Houses" (Davie)   **31**:124

"Among Bells" (Merwin)   **88**:208-09, 211

Among Friends (Fisher)   **76**:339-40; **87**:123, 125, 130

Among Friends (Wright)   **44**:334

"Among Murderers and Madmen" (Bachmann)   See "Unter Mördern und Irren"

"Among Ourselves" (Lorde)   **71**:244

"Among School Children" (Van Duyn)   **116**:401

Among the Beasts/Parmi les monstres (Federman)   **47**:128

Among the Believers: An Islamic Journey (Naipaul)   **37**:319, 321-24, 328; **105**:155, 176

"Among the Bumble Bees" (Plath)   **11**:451

Among the Dangs (Elliott)   **2**:131

"Among the Gods" (Kunitz)   **6**:287

"Among the Impressionists" (Wiggins)   **57**:433

"Among the Massagetae" (Hesse)   **25**:259

"Among the Narcissi" (Plath)   **51**:349; **111**:203-04, 214

"Among the Ordained" (Zamora)   **89**:369

"Among the Paths to Eden" (Capote)   **3**:99; **13**:134-36

"Among the Roses" (Lessing)   **94**:272, 275

"Among the Ruins" (Friel)   **115**:216, 218-20

Amongst Thistles and Thorns (Clarke)   **8**:143; **53**:85-7, 92

"Amongst Those Left Are You" (Johnson)   **6**:265; **9**:301

"El amor iracundo" (Aleixandre)   **9**:15

"Amor loci" (Auden)   **14**:30

Amor mundo y todos los cuentos (Arguedas)   **10**:9

"El amor no es relieve" (Aleixandre)   **36**:31

"El amor padecido" (Aleixandre)   **9**:15

De amor y de sombra (*Of Love and Shadows*) (Allende)   **57**:17, 19, 23, 25-9, 33; **97**:4, 19, 25, 27, 40, 42, 57, 59, 62

Amor y Ecuador (Ulibarri)   **83**:412, 416

"The Amoralists" (Colter)   **58**:147

The Amoralists and Other Tales (Colter)   **58**:146-47

"Amorality Tale" (Bova)   **45**:75

"Amore" (Moure)   **88**:227

Un amore (*A Love Affair*) (Buzzati)   **36**:87-90, 94-6

L'amore coniugale, e altri racconti (Moravia)   **2**:293; **7**:244

Gli amori difficili (*Difficult Loves*) (Calvino)   **11**:90; **33**:100-02; **39**:306, 310, 314-17;

73:42

"Amorosa anticipación" (Borges) 6:88

L'amorosa menzogna (Antonioni) 20:28

"An Amorous Debate" (Gunn) 18:202

"L'amour" ("Love") (Char) 9:165

L'amour (*Love*) (Duras) 3:129; 40:178, 180, 185; 68:91

Amour au goût de mer (Theriault) 79:401, 415-16, 419

L'amour au temps des solitudes (Gallo) 95:99

L'amour fou (Breton) 9:127-28, 130; 54:21, 26-7, 31

L'ampélour (Audiberti) 38:23

The Ampersand Papers (Stewart) 32:420

Amphitryon Thirty-Eight (Behrman) 40:88

"Amplitude" (Gallagher) 63:123, 125

Amplitude: New and Selected Poems (Gallagher) 63:122-26

Amputations (Macdonald) 13:355-56; 19:291

"The Amputee" (Dacey) 51:79

Amras (Bernhard) 32:17-18; 61:9, 21

Amrita (*To Whom She Will*) (Jhabvala) 29:252-53, 255, 260; 94:167, 169-70, 176, 180, 200

"Am-traking to the Adirondacks" (Kenny) 87:247

Amulet (Rakosi) 47:343, 346

"Amusing Our Daughters" (Kizer) 80:174, 178, 180, 183-84

"Amy Son" (Bennett) 28:29

"An den Wassern Babels" ("By the Waters of Babylon") (Celan) 82:55

"An der Angel" (Boell) 72:70-1

"An der Brücke" ("Across the Bridge") (Boell) 72:69

"L'an trentiesme de mon eage" (MacLeish) 68:273, 285, 291

L'an V de la révolution algérienne (*A Dying Colonialism; Sociologie d'une révolution; Studies in a Dying Colonialism; Year Five of the Algerian Revolution*) (Fanon) 74:71-2, 74, 80

"Ana María" (Donoso) 32:156, 158

"Ana María" (Guillen) 79:229, 241

The Anabaptists (Duerrenmatt) 102:55, 58, 60

The Anabaptists (Durrenmatt)
  See *Die Wiedertäufer*

Anabase (*Anabasis*) (Perse) 4:399-400; 11:433-34; 46:298-302, 305-09

"Anabasis" (Merwin) 45:270

Anabasis (Perse)
  See *Anabase*

"Anabasis I" (Merwin) 45:270

"Anabasis II" (Merwin) 45:270

"Anacleto morones" (Rulfo) 80:200

"Anacreontic" (Winters) 32:470

"Anadyomene" (Walcott) 67:352

"The Anagogic Man" (Macpherson) 14:346

"An Anagram of Ideas on Art, Form, and Film" (Deren) 102:38, 47

Anagrams (Moore) 45:280-84; 68:296, 298-99

Anagrams (Slavitt) 5:391-92; 14:490

"Anahorish" (Heaney) 7:148; 14:243; 25:245, 249; 74:157

Anaïs Nin Reader (Nin) 4:378-79

Analecta del reloj (*Clock Analect*) (Lezama Lima) 4:288; 101:110

Anales de los Xahil (Asturias) 13:37

"L'analyse structurale en linguistique et en anthropologie" (Levi-Strauss) 38:300

"Analysis" (Livesay) 79:348

"Analysis of Baseball" (Swenson) 106:331, 339

"The Analytical Language of John Wilkins" (Borges) 83:193

Ananke (Lem) 40:291, 295

"Anaphora" (Bishop) 32:29, 34

"L'anapo" (Quasimodo) 10:428

Anarchism (Forman) 21:120

"Anarchism and the Religious Impulse" (Rexroth) 112:402

Anarchism Is Not Enough (Riding) 3:431

The Anarchist's Convention (Sayles) 14:483-84

"Anarchy" (MacEwen) 55:163, 168

"Anarchy and Authority in American Literature" (Howe) 85:152

"The Anasazi Woman" (Lewis) 41:260-61

Anastomòsi (Gadda) 11:211

"Anathema" (Voznesensky) 15:554

The Anathemata: Fragments of an Attempted Writing (Jones) 2:216-19; 4:259-62; 7:187-91; 13:307-12; 42:237-44, 246-48

"Anatole France" (Howard) 47:170

The Anatolian (Kazan) 63:221-22, 233

Anatolian Tales (Kemal) 29:265

"Anatomy" (Sorrentino) 40:384

Anatomy and Solidary: Interviews with Jürgen Habermas (Habermas) 104:76-7, 87

"Anatomy Lab" (Ciardi) 40:154

"The Anatomy Lesson" (Connell) 45:106

The Anatomy Lesson (Roth) 31:340-47; 47:357-59, 362; 86:256

The Anatomy Lesson and Other Stories (Connell) 45:106-07, 109

"The Anatomy of Bliss" (L'Heureux) 52:279

Anatomy of Criticism (Frye) 24:208-09, 211, 213, 215, 217, 219, 222-23, 229, 231; 70:271, 273-77

"The Anatomy of Mind" (Gass) 39:480

The Anatomy of Nonsense (Winters) 8:552; 32:458

An Anatomy of Reticence (Havel) 58:244

"Anbarlulu" (Mahfuz) 52:292

"The Ancestors" (Wright) 53:419

The Ancestors and the Sacred Mountain (Kunene) 85:171, 175, 177

Ancestral Vices (Sharpe) 36:402

The Anchor Tree (Humphreys) 47:182-83

Anchors Aweigh: The Story of David Glasgow Farragut (Latham) 12:324

Ancia (Otero) 11:425

Les anciennes odeurs (*Remember Me*) (Tremblay) 29:427; 102:372, 374, 377-78

"Ancient Amphitheater" (Ritsos) 31:325

The Ancient Child (Momaday) 85:270-71, 273-74

Ancient Evenings (Mailer) 28:257-63; 39:416, 421, 423; 74:205, 207, 224, 231, 233, 237; 111:116-18, 120, 135, 141

"An Ancient Goddess: Two Pictures" (Blunden) 56:47

"The Ancient Heroes and the Bomber Pilot" (Hughes) 9:285

"Ancient History" (Bausch) 51:55

Ancient History: A Paraphase (McElroy) 5:279; 47:238-39, 241-42, 244-45

Ancient Light (Lightman) 81:78

"Ancient Lights" (Clarke) 6:113; 9:168

Ancient Lights: Poems and Satires, First Series (Clarke) 6:113; 9:167, 169

The Ancient Ones (Lewis) 41:260-61

"The Ancient Ones: Betátakin" (Lewis) 41:260-61

"The Ancient Rain" (Kaufman) 49:205-07

The Ancient Rain: Poems, 1956-1978 (Kaufman) 49:204-06

"Ancient Rites and Mysteries" (Williams) 39:101

"Ancient Signs" (Hirsch) 50:197

"Ancient Slang" (MacEwen) 55:163, 167

"Ancient Sorceries" (Blackwood) 71:86

"The Ancient Woman" (Mueller) 51:279

"The Ancre at Hamel: Afterwards" (Blunden) 56:43

"And" (Creeley) 11:138

"And" (Gass) 39:481-82

"And" (Goldbarth) 38:207

& (And) (Cummings) 8:156; 15:155, 160; 68:35

And (Cummings)
  See *&*

"And a Few Negroes Too" (Madhubuti)
  See "A Message All Blackpeople Can Dig (& A Few Negroes Too)"

And a Nightingale Sang (Taylor) 27:442, 444

And a Threefold Cord (La Guma) 19:272-73, 276

And Again? (O'Faolain) 14:407; 70:319-21

And All Between (Snyder) 17:473-75

"And All Flows Past" (Zamora) 89:392

And All the Stars a Stage (Blish) 14:83

"And Another One" (Ortiz) 45:306

"And Another Thing" (Giovanni) 4:189

And Both Were Young (L'Engle) 12:345

"And Call Me Conrad" (Zelazny) 21:467

And Chaos Died (Russ) 15:461

And Dangerous to Know (Daly) 52:91

And Death White as Words (Breytenbach) 23:84

"And Forty-second Street" (MacLeish) 68:273

"And Give Us Our Trespasses" (Livesay) 79:337, 350

And Grieve, Lesbia: Poems (Kenny) 87:245

"And I Am Driftwood" (Brutus) 43:97

"And I Awoke and Found Me Here on the Cold Hill's Side" (Tiptree) 48:385; 50:357

"And I Dreamt I Was a Tree" (Alegria) 75:49

"And I Have Come upon This Place by Lost Ways" (Tiptree) 48:389

"And I Moved" (Townshend) 17:541

"And I Will Be Heard" (Beecher) 6:48

"And in My Heart" (Cassill) 4:95; 23:106

And in the Human Heart (Aiken) 1:4; 52:20, 26

...And Ladies of the Club (Santmyer) 33:358-62

"And Leave the Driving to Us" (Kenny) 87:249

And Live Apart (Peacock) 60:291, 295, 297

"And Men Decay" (Santos) 22:364

"...And Mr. Ferritt" (Wright) 53:428

"... And My Fear is Great" (Sturgeon) 39:361

"And Narrating Them..." (Ritsos) 6:464

And Never Said a Word (Boell)
  See *Und Sagte kein einziges Wort*

And No Birds Sang (Mowat) 26:345-47

And No One Knows Where to Go (Sachs)
  See *Und Niemand weiss weiter*

"And Not in Utter Nakedness" (Yurick) 6:583

And Now for Something Completely Different (Monty Python) 21:223, 225

"And Now, Goodbye" (Seifert) 44:422

And Now Here's Johnny (Ephron) 17:110

...And Now Miguel (Krumgold) 12:316-17, 319-21

"...And Now You Don't" (Asimov) 26:60

"And of Clay Are We Created" (Allende) **97**:4, 63

And on the Eighth Day (Queen) **11**:461

"And Once More like the Lights of the Open-Hearth Furnace" (Akhmadulina) **53**:9

And One Day Lasts Longer than an Age (Aitmatov)

See *I dol'she veka dlitsia den'*

"And One for My Dame" (Sexton) **53**:316, 322

And Quiet Flows the Don (Sholokhov) **7**:418

"And Sarah Laughed" (Greenberg) **30**:162

"And Say of What You Saw in the Dark" (Lane) **25**:286

...And Searching Mind (Williamson) **29**:455-56

"And So Goodbye to Cities" (Merton) **83**:395

"And So I Go" (Grace) **56**:120

"And So I Grew up to Be Nineteen and to Murder" (Oates) **3**:359

"And So Today" (Sandburg) **35**:342

"And Some of His Enemies" (Fenton)

See "The Fruit-Grower in War-Time"

"And Son" (Bell) **8**:67

"And Still I Rise" (Angelou) **35**:30; **77**:30

And Still I Rise (Angelou) **12**:14; **35**:29-30, 32; **64**:32; **77**:15, 22, 30

And Summer Nights (Wilson)

See *Summer Days*

"And That Night" (Ignatow) **7**:182

And That's the Truth (Tomlin) **17**:517

And the Air Didn't Answer (Kerr) **55**:377-80; **59**:400

And the Band Played On: Politics, People, and the AIDS Epidemic (Shilts) **85**:322, 324-29, 331, 339, 341-44

"And the Child Lied" (Nakos) **29**:322

"And the Children of Birmingham" (Merton) **83**:393

"And the Crooked Shall Become Straight" (Agnon)

See "Vehaya he'akov lemishor"

And the Day Lasts Longer Than a Century (Aitmatov)

See *I dol'she veka dlitsia den'*

"And the Moon Be Still as Bright" (Bradbury) **42**:38

"And the Rain Came Down!" (Ngugi wa Thiong'o) **36**:317

And the Ship Sails On (Fellini)

See *E la nave va*

"And the Singer Sings His Songs" (Diamond) **30**:111

"And the Trains Go On" (Levine) **14**:315-16, 318-19

"And the Wave Sings because It Is Moving" (Larkin) **64**:282

And the Wife Ran Away (*The Fat Woman's Joke*) (Weldon) **11**:565; **36**:445, 448

"And Then" (Barthelme) **115**:69-70

And Then I Told the President (Buchwald) **33**:90-1

And Then I Wrote (Nelson) **17**:305

And Then There Were None (*Ten Little Indians*; *Ten Little Niggers*) (Christie) **1**:58; **6**:108; **8**:142; **12**:113-14, 120, 122-23, 125; **48**:73; **110**:112, 116, 122-23, 138

And Then There Were None (Clair) **20**:71

"And Then There Were Three" (Shaw) **7**:412; **34**:370

And Then We Heard Thunder (Killens) **10**:300

And Then We Moved to Rossenarra or The Art of Emigrating (Condon) **100**:102, 110

"And There Is Always One More Story" (Ortiz) **45**:304, 306

And They Put Handcuffs on the Flowers (Arrabal)

See *Et ils passèrent des menottes aux fleurs*

And Things That Go Bump in the Night (McNally) **7**:216-18; **41**:292; **91**:157

"And Ut Pictura Poesis Is Her Name" (Ashbery) **15**:30; **77**:61

"And Wanton Optics Roll the Melting Eye" (Huxley) **5**:192

"And What About the Children" (Lorde) **71**:259

And Where Were You, Adam? (Boell)

See *Wo warst du, Adam?*

"And Why Should Not Old Men Be Mad?" (O'Faolain) **47**:331

And Yet (Neruda) **28**:315

"And Yet They Are Knocking at Your Door" (Buzzati) **36**:94

"And You Know" (Ashbery) **77**:58

And You, Thoreau! (Derleth) **31**:136

And You, Too (Endo)

See *Nanji mo mata*

"And You Were a Baby Girl" (Peacock) **60**:293

An Andalusian Dog (Bunuel)

See *Un chien andalou*

"Andar" (Otero) **11**:427

Der andere Prozeß: Kafkas Briefe an Felice (*Kafka's Other Trial: The Letters to Felice*; *The Other Trial*) (Canetti) **25**:111, 113; **75**:139; **86**:301, 303

"The Anderson Boy" (Hansen) **38**:240

The Anderson Tapes (Sanders) **41**:376-78, 381-82

Andersonville (Kantor) **7**:194-96

Andorra (Frisch) **3**:167; **9**:217-18; **14**:182-83; **18**:163; **32**:188, 191, 195; **44**:181-83, 193, 196-98, 200, 207

André Breton (Gracq) **48**:133-35

"Andrea" (O'Hara) **42**:319

"Andrée Rexroth" (Rexroth) **49**:281-82; **112**:391

Andrei Rublev (Tarkovsky) **75**:370-72, 374-76, 379, 382-86, 388-89, 396, 401-03, 407, 410, 412

"Andrew" (Bowles) **68**:9

"Andrew Marvell" (Eliot) **24**:171, 178

"Andrina" (Brown) **48**:60-1; **100**:84, 86

Andrina and Other Stories (Brown) **48**:59, 61; **100**:84

Androgyne, mon amour (Williams) **39**:452; **45**:443-45

"The Android and the Human" (Dick) **72**:107

Android at Arms (Norton) **12**:463

"Andromache" (Dubus) **36**:144-45; **97**:208

"Andromeda Chained to Her Rock the Great Nebula in her Heart" (Rexroth) **112**:375

The Andromeda Strain (Crichton) **2**:108; **6**:119; **54**:63-5, 67, 69-70, 72, 74, 76; **90**:69-71, 82, 89

"Andrum juli" (Transtroemer) **52**:409

Andy (Nichol) **18**:370

"Andy Warhol" (Bowie) **17**:58

"Aneas and Dido" (Brodsky) **50**:121-23

"The Anecdotes" (Durrell) **27**:97

Anecdotes of Destiny (Dinesen) **10**:149; **29**:156; **95**:37, 53

"Der Anfang von etwas" (Lenz) **27**:245

Ange (Woolrich) **77**:392

"L'ange heurtebise" ("The Angel Heurtebise") (Cocteau) **8**:146-47

"Das angebrochene Jahr" (Celan) **82**:51

"Angel" (Brodkey) **56**:57-9, 61-2, 68

"The Angel" (McFadden) **48**:246

"The Angel" (McGrath) **55**:73-75

"The Angel" (Springsteen) **17**:487

Angel (*Danny Boy*) (Jordan) **110**:268-76, 278

Angel (Taylor) **2**:432; **29**:408

"Angel and Man" (Watkins) **43**:452

Angel Arms (Fearing) **51**:103-05, 107-11, 117, 122

An Angel at My Table (Campion) **95**:5-8, 12, 14, 18, 25-26

An Angel at My Table (Frame) **66**:143-45, 150; **96**:174, 193-94, 196, 201-03, 208, 217-18, 220

"Angel Butcher" (Levine) **4**:288; **5**:252; **14**:318

Angel City (Shepard) **17**:445, 447-49; **41**:409, 412

"Angel Come Home" (Wilson) **12**:654

An Angel Comes to Babylon (Duerrenmatt)

See *Ein Engel kommt nach Babylon*

An Angel Comes to Babylon (Durrenmatt)

See *Ein Engel kommt nach Babylon*

El ángel exterminador (*Exterminating Angel*) (Bunuel) **16**:133-34, 139, 141, 148; **80**:34-8

Angel Eyes (Estleman) **48**:103-04, 107

"Angel Face" (Woolrich) **77**:400

Angel Fire (Oates) **3**:361

"Angel Fix" (Tiptree) **48**:389, 393

"The Angel Heurtebise" (Cocteau)

See "L'ange heurtebise"

Angel in Heavy Shoes (Weber) **12**:634

"The Angel in the Alcove" (Williams) **45**:452

Angel in the Forest: A Fairy Tale of Two Utopias (Young) **82**:397-98, 400, 404-06, 408-414

Angel in the Parlor: Five Stories and Eight Essays (Willard) **37**:463-64

Angel Landing (Hoffman) **51**:202-03

"Angel Levine" (Malamud) **1**:201; **11**:346-48; **27**:299, 306; **44**:412-13, 417, 420; **85**:191

The Angel of History (Forche) **86**:137-45

Angel of Light (Oates) **33**:286-88; **52**:331, 339; **108**:352

"The Angel of the Bridge" (Cheever) **15**:130; **64**:57, 61-3, 65

"The Angel of the Church" (Phillips) **28**:362

Angel on Skis (Cavanna) **12**:100

Angel Pavement (Priestley) **34**:361, 363-65

"The Angel Poem" (Stern) **40**:410-11

"An Angel Sat on a Tomb-Stone Top ..." (Levi) **41**:243

Angel Street: A Victorian Thriller (Hamilton)

See *Gaslight: A Victorian Thriller*

The Angel That Troubled the Waters, and Other Plays (Wilder) **5**:496; **10**:531, 533; **15**:569; **82**:362, 384

"Angela" (Lennon) **35**:264

"Angela" (Mukherjee) **53**:266, 270

Angela Davis (*An Autobiography*) (Davis) **77**:111, 113-14, 116, 128

Angela's Ashes (McCourt) **109**:146-55

The Angelic Avengers (Dinesen) **10**:152; **29**:154-56; **95**:37, 48, 68

"The Angelic Imagination: Poe as God" (Tate) **2**:429; **6**:527; **14**:528

"Angelica" (Blackwood) **100**:15

Angelici dolori (Ortese) **89**:195, 197-98

"Angelita's Utility" (Zamora) **89**:394

"L'angelo nero" ("The Black Angel") (Montale) **7**:225

"The Angels" (Kundera) **19**:269

"The Angels" (Updike) **3**:485

Angels (Johnson) **52**:234-35, 237-41

"Angels and Ministers of Grace" (O'Faolain) **14**:406

Angels and Other Strangers: Family Christmas Stories (Paterson) **30**:282-83

Angels Are So Few (Potter) **58**:391

"Angels at the Ritz" (Trevor) **71**:323; **116**:374, 377

Angels at the Ritz, and Other Stories (Trevor) **7**:477-78; **9**:529; **25**:446; **71**:324; **116**:333, 374, 377

Angels Can't Do Better (De Vries) **28**:114-15

Angels Fall (Wilson) **36**:461-64

Angels Falling (Elliott) **47**:105-07

"The Angel's Gift" (Bova) **45**:75

Angels in America: A Gay Fantasia on National Themes (Kushner) **81**:197-99, 201-04, 206-13

Angels of Darkness (Woolrich) **77**:400

"The Angels of Detroit" (Levine) **2**:244; **4**:286

"Angels of the Love Affair" (Sexton) **53**:321

Angels on Toast (Powell) **66**:356, 358-59, 363, 370, 375-76

"The Angels Wanna Wear My Red Shoes" (Costello) **21**:67

The Angels Weep (Smith) **33**:378

"Angelus Domini" (Moure) **88**:227

"Anger" (Creeley) **78**:137

"Anger" (Dobyns) **37**:77-8

Anger (Sarton) **49**:315-16; **91**:251

"Anger Lay by Me" (Daryush) **19**:120

Les anges du péché (Bresson) **16**:102-03

Les anges noirs (Mauriac) **56**:211-13

Angest (Anguish) (Lagerkvist) **13**:334; **54**:274

"Angie" (Jagger and Richard) **17**:228-29, 232, 240

L'anglais décrit dans le château fermé (Mandiargues) **41**:278-79

Angle of Ascent (Hayden) **9**:270; **14**:240; **37**:153, 157, 160

"Angle of Geese" (Momaday) **85**:230-31, 248-49, 262-63, 266-67, 280

Angle of Geese, and Other Poems (Momaday) **85**:247, 262, 281

Angle of Repose (Stegner) **9**:510; **49**:354-56, 360; **81**:344, 347-52

The Angled Road (Levine) **54**:291-92, 297

"An Angler at Heart" (Frazier) **46**:165

Angles and Circles (Grigson) **7**:136

"Anglo-Mongrels and the Rose" (Loy) **28**:249

Anglo-Saxon Attitudes (Wilson) **2**:471-74; **3**:535; **5**:514; **25**:463-64

"Anglosaxon Street" (Birney) **6**:72, 78

L'angoisse du Roi Salomon (Gary) **25**:191

Angry Abolitionist: William Lloyd Garrison (Archer) **12**:17

The Angry Exile (Krotkov) **19**:264

The Angry Hills (Uris) **32**:431, 433

The Angry Ones (Williams) **5**:497

"Angry Young Man" (Joel) **26**:215-16, 219

"The Angry Young Men" (Barthelme) **5**:55; **115**:85

"The Angry-Year" (Godwin) **31**:197-98

Angst (Cixous) **92**:53, 56

Angst essen Seele auf (Fear Eats Up Souls) (Fassbinder) **20**:106-07

Anguish (Lagerkvist) See *Angest*

"The Anguish of an Alien" (Endo) **99**:307

Ani maamin: A Song Lost and Found Again (Wiesel) **5**:493

Ania Malina (Osborne) **50**:70-2

Aniara (Martinson) **14**:356

Anicet (Aragon) **22**:42

Anihtá hártia (Open Book) (Elytis) **49**:117, 119; **100**:187

"Anima" (Eberhart) **56**:87

"Animal" (Jensen) **37**:188

"Animal Behavior" (Colwin) **5**:108; **84**:146, 149

Animal Clocks and Compasses (Hyde) **21**:173

Animal Crackers (Kaufman) **38**:265

"Animal Crossing" (Squires) **51**:383

"Animal de luz" ("Animal of Light") (Neruda) **28**:309

Animal Dreams (Kingsolver) **81**:191, 194

The Animal Game (Tuohy) **37**:425-26, 428, 431

"Animal Hospital" (Moss) **7**:247

The Animal Inside (Jacobsen) **48**:190-91, 195, 197; **102**:236

"Animal Lover" (Donaldson) **46**:142-43

Animal Magnetism (Prose) **45**:324-25

"Animal of Light" (Neruda) See "Animal de luz"

Animal Spirits: Stories to Live By (McFadden) **48**:256-57

"The Animal That Drank Up Sound" (Stafford) **7**:461

The Animal, the Vegetable, and John D. Jones (Byars) **35**:74

"The Animal Trainer" (Berryman) **62**:71

"Animal, Vegetable, and Mineral" (Bogan) **46**:90

Animal, Vegetable, Mineral (Deutsch) **18**:118

The Animal-Lover's Book of Beastly Murder (Highsmith) **14**:260; **42**:214; **102**:197

"Animals" (Byrne) **26**:97-8

Animals (Pink Floyd) **35**:309-13, 315

"Animals All Around" (Soto) **80**:284

"Animals Are Passing from Our Lives" (Levine) **4**:287; **9**:332; **14**:317; **33**:273

The Animals' Arrival (Jennings) **14**:292

"The Animals at the Adelaide Zoo" (Ewart) **46**:152

"The Animals' Christmas" (Dacey) **51**:79

The Animals in That Country (Atwood) **2**:19; **8**:30, 32; **13**:44; **25**:63, 67

"Animula" (Eliot) **13**:201; **15**:217

"Animula" (Merwin) **1**:213; **88**:193

Anishinabe Adisokan (Vizenor) See *Summer in the Spring: Ojibwe Lyric Poems and Tribal Songs*

Anishinabe Nagamon (Vizenor) **103**:296

"Ankor Wat" (Ginsberg) **6**:198

Ann Lee's and Other Stories (Bowen) **22**:67

"Anna" (Dinesen) **10**:149-50

"Anna" (Dubus) **97**:223, 228

Anna (Almedingen) **12**:7

"Anna Fierling" (Shange) See "How I Moved Anna Fierling to the Southwest Territories, or My Personal Victory over the Armies of Western Civilization"

Anna Hastings: The Story of a Washington Newspaperwoman (Drury) **37**:109

Anna Karenina and Other Essays (Leavis) **24**:305, 308

"Anna Liffey" (Boland) **113**:87, 89, 91, 94-5, 100-01, 111, 120, 127-28

"Anna Lisa's Nose" (Berriault) **54**:3; **109**:96

"Anna, Part I" (Gilchrist) **48**:120, 122

Anna Sophie Hedvig (Abell) **15**:1, 4

"Anna, soror" (Yourcenar) **87**:433

Anna, soror (Yourcenar) **87**:405, 412

"Anna Swanton" (Durcan) **43**:115

The Annals of Brekkukot (Laxness) See *Brekkukotsannáll*

Annals of Innocence and Experience (Read) **4**:437

Annals of the Five Senses (MacDiarmid) **63**:251

"Anna's Song" (Gaye) **26**:133

"Anne" (Beauvoir) **31**:42

"Anne at the Symphony" (Shields) **113**:441

"Anne Boleyn's Song" (Sitwell) **67**:323

"Anne Frank Huis" (Motion) **47**:287, 294

"Anne Rey" (Kaplan) **50**:55-6

Anne Sexton: A Self-Portrait in Letters (Sexton) **10**:468-69; **15**:473; **53**:312-13

"Anne, Sylvia, Virginia, Adrienne" (Broumas) **10**:76

Les anneaux de Bicêtre (The Bells of Bicêtre) (Simenon) **1**:309; **47**:379

L'annee derniére a Marienbad (Last Year at Marienbad) (Resnais) **16**:498, 500-11

L'année dernière à Marienbad (Last Year at Marienbad) (Robbe-Grillet) **1**:286-87; **2**:374, 376; **4**:449; **6**:465-66; **8**:453-54; **14**:455-56, 462; **43**:360, 366

Annerton Pit (Dickinson) **12**:176-77

Annette (Caldwell) **14**:95

Anni mirabiles, 1921-1925 (Blackmur) **24**:65

"The Anniad" (Brooks) **49**:27

Annie Allen (Brooks) **1**:46; **5**:74-6; **15**:93; **49**:22, 26-7, 31-2, 35

"Annie Christian" (Prince) **35**:325-26, 328

Annie Hall (Allen) **16**:7-8, 10-11, 13-15, 17-18; **52**:38-40, 45-6, 48-50

Annie John (Kincaid) **43**:249-51; **68**:205-12, 216-18, 220-28

"Annie She" (Lane) **25**:289

"Annie Upside Down" (Fuller) **62**:196-97, 204

The Annihilation of Mylos (Ritsos) **6**:463

Annika and the Wolves (Zoline) **62**:462

"Anniversaries" (Dunn) **40**:172

"Anniversaries" (Justice) **102**:270

"Anniversaries" (Motion) **47**:286, 289, 292-93

Anniversaries (Coles) **46**:108-09

Anniversaries: From the Life of Gesine Cresspahl (Johnson) See *Jahrestage: Aus dem Leben von Gesine Cresspahl IV*

Anniversaries: From the Life of Gesine Cresspahl (Johnson) See *Jahrestage: Aus dem Leben von Gesine Cresspahl III*

"An Anniversary" (Berry) **27**:34

"Anniversary" (Ciardi) **40**:156

"Anniversary" (Elytis) **49**:114; **100**:189

"Anniversary" (Jong) **83**:289

The Anniversary (Ray) See *Pratidwandi*

"Anniversary Project" (Haldeman) **61**:176

"The Anniversary Song" (Kherdian) **9**:318

"Anno Domini" (Barker) **48**:24

"Anno Domini" (Brodsky) **13**:115; **50**:123, 131

"Anno Domini" (Raine) **103**:180, 189

Anno Domini (Barker) **48**:21-2

Anno Domini (Raine) **32**:349

Anno Domini MCMXXI (Akhmatova) **25**:24, 27; **64**:5, 10

"Annointed with Oils" (Nowlan) **15**:399

"An Annotated Exequy" (Sissman) **9**:490

"Annotations of Auschwitz" (Porter) **33**:322

"Annotations of Giant's Town" (Fuller) 62:194

"Annual" (Swenson) 106:347

"The Annual Heron" (Price) 43:351

"Annunciation" (Livesay) 79:334, 336

"Annunciation" (Morgan) 2:294

"The Annunciation" (Mueller) 51:281

"Annunciation" (Sarton) 14:482

The Annunciation (Gilchrist) 34:164-65; 48:116-18, 120

"Annunciations" (Hill) 8:295; 45:178-79, 184, 187

"Annus Mirabilis" (Larkin) 8:333; 9:323-24; 64:282

"Annus Mirabilis, 1961" (Montague) 46:271

"Anodyne" (Mac Laverty) 31:253-54

"Anoint the Ariston" (Elytis) 100:187

"Anon" (Boland) 40:98

"Anonymiad" (Barth) 3:41; 5:51-2; 9:68, 70-1; 51:23; 89:6-11, 15-19, 21-4, 29-30, 32, 34, 36, 45-6, 48, 51, 55-6, 58-9, 63-4

"Anonymity" (Forster) 3:160

"An Anonymous Affair" (Williams) 42:440

The Anonymous Lover (Logan) 5:254-55

"Anonymous Signature" (MacLeish) 68:273

"Anonymous Sins" (Oates) 6:367

Anonymous Sins and Other Poems (Oates) 1:251; 3:359; 6:367

"The Anonymous Telephone Caller" (MacEwen) 55:168

"Anorexic" (Boland) 40:99-100; 67:44, 46; 113:58, 60-61, 109, 123

"Another and Another and..." (Weiss) 14:557

"Another Animal" (Swenson) 106:347

Another Animal (Swenson) 4:533-34; 61:390, 398-99; 106:317, 324, 331, 336, 340, 345-46

Another Antigone (Gurney) 50:180, 184; 54:219-20, 223

"Another April" (Stuart) 11:514

"Another Brick in the Wall" (Pink Floyd) 35:313

"Another Christmas" (Avison) 97:72, 111

"Another Christmas" (Trevor) 14:536; 71:326, 337; 116:338, 345-47, 360

Another Country (Baldwin) 1:14-16; 2:31; 3:32; 4:40-2; 5:41-2; 13:48-50, 52; 15:42; 17:23-4, 28-32, 34, 36-7, 44-5; 42:14, 18; 50:283-84, 289, 293, 296; 67:14; 90:5, 31-2

"Another Day" 99:176

"Another Day Another Dollar" (Selby) 8:475-76

"Another Day, Another Night" (McAuley) 45:255

"Another Dog's Death" (Updike) 43:436

"Another Fragment" (Laughlin) 49:220

"Another Hanging" (Stuart) 11:512

Another Heaven and Earth (Haavikko)
See *Toinen taivas ja maa*

"Another Hundred People" (Sondheim) 30:391, 395

"Another Journey" (Livesay) 79:337

"Another Journey from Béthune to Cuinchy" (Blunden) 56:43

Another Kind (West) 50:360

"Another Life" (Bidart) 33:74

"Another Life" (Levine) 9:332; 14:316, 318

Another Life (Walcott) 4:574-76; 9:556; 14:549, 551; 25:452; 42:418-23; 67:342-44, 348-51, 354-55, 357-58; 76:270, 272, 274-76, 278, 280, 282-85

Another Life. The House on the Embankment: Three Novellas (Trifonov)
See *Drugaia zhizn'*

"Another Little Boy" (Aldiss) 5:15

Another Marvelous Thing (Colwin) 84:141-43, 150, 153

"Another Merry Widow" (Klappert) 57:66

Another Monty Python Record (Monty Python) 21:224, 226

"Another Pair of Hands" (Spark) 40:403

Another Part of the Forest (Hellman) 2:187; 14:258; 18:221-22; 34:349; 52:191

Another Part of the Wood (Bainbridge) 18:32-5; 22:44; 62:23-4, 30

Another Passenger (Simon) 26:410-12

"Another Place" (Merwin) 88:212-13

Another Place (Priestley) 2:347

"Another Poem for Me—After Recovering from an O.D." (Knight) 40:286

"Another River: The Ebro" (Cabral de Melo Neto)
See "Otro rio: O Ebro"

Another Roadside Attraction (Robbins) 9:453; 32:366, 368-74; 64:371-73, 376-78, 382

Another Side of Bob Dylan (Dylan) 12:185, 198; 77:167

"Another Snowstorm" (Zaturenska) 11:580

Another Song (Cage) 41:86

"Another Sorrowing Woman" (Belitt) 22:52

"Another Space" (Page) 7:292; 18:379

"Another Star" (Wonder) 12:662

"Another State" (Loewinsohn) 52:285

"Another Suitcase in Another Hall" (Rice and Webber) 21:432

"Another Sunday Morning" (Mahon) 27:293

"Another Tempest" (Van Duyn) 116:427

"Another Time" (Auden) 3:22; 6:23; 11:14; 14:26

"Another Time" (O'Brien) 65:167, 169, 172

Another Time in Fragments (Eigner) 9:180

"Another Try at It" (Bowering) 47:19

"Another Unhappy Love Song" (Cryer) 21:81

"Another Voice" (Wilbur) 3:531

Another War, Another Peace (Glasser) 37:134

Another World (Hanley) 5:167-68

Another World (Nixon) 21:242

"Anothering" (Plumly) 33:313

"Anoukis et plus tard Jeanne" (Char) 11:116

Anpao: An American Indian Odyssey (Highwater) 12:286-87

Anrufung des Grossen Bären (Bachmann) 69:41

"Anschluss" (Boyle) 58:70

"Ansell" (Forster) 2:136

"Anseo" (Muldoon) 72:266

Ansichten eines Clowns (*The Clown*) (Boell) 2:68; 3:74-5; 6:83; 9:102, 106-09; 11:52-3, 55-6, 58; 27:61, 67; 39:292-96; 72:68, 73

"Ansiedad para el día" (Aleixandre) 9:15

Ansikte mot ansikte (*Face to Face*) (Bergman) 16:77-8, 81; 72:53-7, 59, 61

Ansiktet (*The Face*; *The Magician*) (Bergman) 16:47-9, 52, 62, 64-7, 81-2; 72:31, 33, 40-1, 50

"Answer" (Achebe) 11:4; 26:22

"An Answer" (Bowers) 9:122

"Answer" (Capote) 13:137

"The Answer" (Jeffers) 54:249-50

"The Answer" (Montague) 46:268

The Answer (Lee) 105:85

The Answer (Wylie) 43:468

Answer as a Man (Caldwell) 28:68-9; 39:302-03

An Answer from Limbo (Moore) 1:225; 5:295-96; 7:235; 19:331; 32:313; 90;238-41, 243-44, 247-48, 250-54, 261, 272, 277, 280-2,288

"Answer in the Affirmative" (Fisher) 87:124

"An Answer to Some Questions on How I Write" (Giovanni) 64:196; 117:189, 204

Answer Yes or No (Mortimer) 28:281

"Answering a Question in the Mountains" (Ashbery) 25:58

"Answering the Deer: Genocide and Continuance in the Poetry of American Indian Women" (Allen) 84:15, 36, 39, 41

"Answers in Progress" (Baraka) 5:48; 33:55

"Ant Trap" (Kennedy) 42:255

"Antaeus" (Heaney) 74:158, 162

The Antagonists (Gann) 23:167

Antarctic Fugue (Cendrars)
See *Le plan de l'aiguille*

Antarctic Traveller (Pollitt) 28:367-68

"Antecedents" (Tomlinson) 45:396

Antechamber and Other Poems (McClure) 10:334

"Antelación de amor" (Borges) 19:45

"Antelope Standing, Some Lying" (Smith) 22:387

"Antennae" (Gascoyne) 45:148

Anteroom to Paradise (Zinoviev) 19:488

"Antheap" (Breytenbach) 23:86-7

Antheil and the Treatise on Harmony (Pound) 48:292

"Anthem" (Auden) 2:28

Anthem (Rand) 30:297, 300-01, 304-05; 79:369, 372-73, 378, 392-94

"Anthem of the Decades" (Kunene) 85:162, 164-65

Anthem of the Decades: A Zulu Epic (Kunene) 85:163-64, 171-72, 175, 178

"Anthem Sprinters" (Bradbury) 42:35

"Anthem to Peacefulness" (Kunene) 85:175, 177

Anthills of the Savannah (Achebe) 51:7-10; 75:2, 4-8, 12-13, 17-27

Anthologie de la nouvelle poésie nègre et malgache de langue Française (*Anthology of the New Black and Madagascan Poetry*) (Senghor) 54:400, 404

Anthologie Nègre (Cendrars) 106:149, 185

Anthology of the New Black and Madagascan Poetry (Senghor)
See *Anthologie de la nouvelle poésie nègre et malgache de langue Française*

Anthony Rose (Feiffer) 64:163

"Anthony's Song" (Joel)
See "Movin' Out"

"Anthracite Country" (Parini) 54:360

Anthropologie structurale (*Structural Anthropology*) (Levi-Strauss) 38:294-98

An Anthropologist at Work (Mead) 37:280

"An Anthropologist's Confession" (Porter) 33:323

"The Anthropology Convention" (Rose) 85:314

"Anthropology: What Is Lost in Rotation" (Wilson) 49:416

"Anthropomorphosis" (Szirtes) 46:391

The Anthropos-Specter-Beast (Konwicki)
See *Zwierzoczlekoupiór*

"Antibes: Variations on a Theme" (Jones) 10:286, 289

Antic Hay (Huxley) 1:151-52; 4:238-40, 243-44; 5:192-94; 8:304; 11:281-82, 284, 288;

18:265, 267-69; 35:232, 235, 244; 79:304, 306, 312, 328

"Anticipation" (Schuyler) 23:391

"Anticipation" (Simon) 26:407, 410

The Anti-Death League (Amis) 2:6, 8-9; 3:8-9; 5:23; 8:12; 13:12-13, 15; 40:42

"Anti-Father" (Dove) 81:138

"The Antifeminist Woman" (Rich) 18:447

Anti-Galaxie Nebulae (Ludlam) 50:344

Antigone (Anouilh) 3:11; 8:22; 13:16-17, 19, 20-1; 40:51-3, 56-8, 60; 50:278-80

Antigone (Cocteau) 8:144, 147; 43:109, 111

"Antigone, This Is It" (Reed) 60:313

"Antigua" (Soto) 80:276

Antigua, Penny, Puce (Graves) 44:476

The Antigua Stamp (Graves} 45:171

The Antihead (Tzara)
   See *L'antitête*

Anti-Man (Koontz) 78:200

Antimémoirs (Malraux) 57:306, 308, 311, 318-19, 322-24

Anti-Memoirs (Malraux) 1:203; 13:366-69

Antimiry (*Antiworlds*) (Voznesensky) 1:349; 15:553-55; 57:413-16, 420, 425-26

"L'antimonio" ("Fire-Damp") (Sciascia) 8:473; 41:392

"Antinoüs: The Diaries" (Rich) 11:475-76; 36:366

Antiode (Cabral de Melo Neto) 76:152

"The Antiphon" (Levertov) 66:245

The Antiphon (Barnes) 3:36; 4:43-4; 8:48; 29:26-32

L'antiphonaire (Aquin) 15:17

Anti-Platon (Bonnefoy) 58:57, 59

"Antipodes" (Soupault) 68:405

"Anti-Poem" (Ewart) 46:148

Antipoems: New and Selected (Parra) 102:348

Antipolitics (Konrad) 73:184-87

"The Antiquary" (Reaney) 13:473

"Antique Father" (Kizer) 39:171

"Antique Harvesters" (Ransom) 4:431; 11:471

"Antiquity" (Dickey) 28:118

Anti-Semite and Jew (Sartre) 52:380

"The Anti-Soviet Soviet Union" (Voinovich) 49:382-83

L'antitête (*The Antihead*) (Tzara) 47:385, 389-91, 394

Antitheses (Berryman) 25:95

Antiworlds (Voznesensky)
   See *Antimiry*

Antoine et Colette (Truffaut) 20:399-400; 101:398, 410-11

"Antoine et l'orpheline" (Truffaut) 101:398-400

Antología clásica de la literatura Argentina (Borges) 44:363

Antología de la literatura fantástica (*The Book of Fantasy*) (Bioy Casares) 8:94; 83:176; 88:92, 95

Antología personal (*Personal Anthology*) (Borges) 48:46; 83:159

Anton Pan 75:65

Antonietta (Hersey) 81:330-32, 334

Antonio Azorín (Azorín) 11:27

"Antony in Behalf of the Play" (Burke) 24:128

"Antonyin's" (Hill) 113:330-31

"Antrim to the Boyne" (Boland) 113:110

Antrobus Complete (Durrell) 41:139

"The Ants" (Empson) 19:155

"Antwerp, 1984" (Durcan) 70:153

"The Anvil of Jove" (Benford) 52:63

"Anxiety" (Paley) 37:334-35

Anxiety (Rozewicz)

   See *Niepokój*

"Anxiety and Ashes" (Jensen) 37:188

Anxiety and Ashes (Jensen) 37:187

The Anxiety of Influence (Bloom) 24:72, 74-6, 79; 103:2, 4-6, 9, 11-13, 20, 22-6, 28, 33, 41, 44-6, 49-51, 53-4

Any Cold Jordan (Bottoms) 53:33

"Any Day Now" (Derleth) 31:131-33

Any Day of Your Life (Kherdian) 9:317-18

Any God Will Do (Condon) 45:94, 97; 100:113

"Any Major Dude Will Tell You" (Becker and Fagen) 26:79

Any Man's Death (Estleman) 48:106-07

Any Minute I Can Split (Rossner) 6:468; 9:456-57

Any Old Iron (Burgess) 62:133-39

Any Shape or Form (Daly) 52:89

"Any Size We Please" (Frost) 9:223

"Any Time" (Dunn) 36:153

"Any Time" (Stafford) 29:384

"Any Time at All" (Lennon and McCartney) 12:375; 35:274

"Any Vacation" (Stafford) 29:384

Any Woman's Blues (Jong) 83:316-17, 321

"Any World" (Becker and Fagen) 26:80, 84

Anya (Schaeffer) 6:488; 11:492

Anya Koro (*A Dark Night's Passing*) (Shiga) 33:365, 369-71, 373

"Anybody Else like Me?" (Miller) 30:264

Anybody's Woman (Arzner) 98:70-1

Anyone Can Whistle (Sondheim) 30:378-80, 385, 387, 392, 395-97, 400

"anyone lived in a pretty how town" (Cummings) 3:119; 15:162; 68:48, 51

"Anything" (Dorris) 109:307

"Anything Long and Thin" (Zweig) 34:379

Anything on Its Side (Eigner) 9:181

"Anything Rather than the Angel" (Herbert) 9:275

"Anything to Declare?" (Forster) 45:134

"Anyway, Anyhow, Anywhere" (Townshend) 17:525, 528, 530, 532

Anywhere but Here (Simpson) 44:97-102

"Apa mare" ("In Deep Waters") (Arghezi) 80:13

"Apacalipsis de Solentiname" ("Apocalypse at Solentiname") (Cortazar) 33:124

"Apache Love" (Ortiz) 45:311

Aparajito (*The Unconquered*) (Ray) 16:474-78, 482-83, 485-86, 491; 76:356, 360, 366

El apartamiento (Marques) 96:253, 260

Apartheid and the Archbishop: The Life and Times of Geoffrey Clayton, Archbishop of Cape Town (Paton) 25:363

Apartment in Athens (Wescott) 13:592

"The Apartment Next to the War" (Disch) 36:127

"The Apathetic Bookie Joint" (Fuchs) 22:157, 161

The Apathetic Bookie Joint (Fuchs) 22:156, 160-61

Ape and Essence (Huxley) 1:150-52; 4:239, 243; 5:193; 8:303; 35:234-35, 241; 79:300

The Ape Inside Me (Platt) 26:354, 356

"The Ape Judges" (Arghezi)
   See "Maimutoii judecatori"

"The Ape Lady in Retirement" (Boyle) 90:45

"Apellesova cherta" (Pasternak)
   See "Il tratto di Apelle"

"El apellido" ("The Family Name"; "The Surname") (Guillen) 48:163; 79:233, 237

Apel'siny iz Marokko (Aksyonov)
   See *Oranges from Morocco*

"Apeman" (Davies) 21:91

"Apeneck Sweeney" (Eliot) 13:202

"The Apes of God Revisited" (Sorrentino) 7:451

"The Apex Animal" (Avison) 97:88-9, 110, 122, 124

"Aphrodissia, the Widow" (Yourcenar)
   See "La veuve Aphrodissia"

"Aplauso humano" (Cernuda) 54:59

Apo-33 Bulletin A Metabolic Regulator (Burroughs) 109:184

"Apocalipsis" ("Apocalypse"; "Apocalypse") (Cardenal) 31:75

"Apocalypse"
   See "Apocalipsis"

"Apocalypse"
   See "Apocalipsis"

"Apocalypse" (MacEwen) 55:163-64, 167-69

"Apocalypse at Solentiname" (Cortazar)
   See "Apacalipsis de Solentiname"

"Apocalypse at the Plaza" (Klein) 30:235-36

"Apocalypse, For Spencer" (Moure) 88:217

Apocalypse Now (Coppola) 16:245-49

"The Apocalypse of John" (Samarakis) 5:382

"Apocalypse: Umbrian Master, about 1490" (Enzensberger) 43:153

"Apocalyptics" (Avison) 97:76, 90-1, 127

"Apocryphal Doubts of Marianne Moore" (Cabral de Melo Neto)
   See "Dúvidas apócrifas de Marianne Moore"

L'apocryphe (Pinget) 37:362-63

"Apollo and Daphne" (Rodgers) 7:378

"Apollo and Marsyas" (Herbert) 9:272; 43:184, 188, 190, 194

Apollo and the Whores (Fuentes) 113:263

"An Apollonian Elegy" (Duncan) 7:88

Apollonius of Tyana (Olson) 11:420

"Apologia" (Hirsch) 31:215

"Apologia" (McGinley) 14:367

"Apologies" (Piercy) 27:376

"Apologies to All the People in Lebanon" (Jordan) 114:147, 150

Apologies to the Iroquois (Wilson) 2:475; 24:487

"Apologue" (Gustafson) 36:218

"The Apology" (Barthelme) 46:37-8

"Apology" (Mueller) 51:280

"The Apology" (Voigt) 54:431

"Apology for Apostasy?" (Knight) 40:282

"Apology for Bad Dreams" (Jeffers) 2:212; 11:307, 312

Apology for Heroism (Anand) 93:38-9, 43-4

"An Apology for Not Invoking the Muse" (Ciardi) 44:383

"An Apology for the Revival of Christian Architecture in England" (Hill) 45:178, 181-82, 190

"Apology of Genius" (Loy) 28:246, 248, 251

"Apostasy" (Robison) 42:338

"The Apostate" (Kizer) 80:172

"Apostle Birds" (Wright) 53:423

Apostles of Light (Douglas) 73:68-70, 72-5, 83, 85, 95

"Apostrophe to a Nephew" (McGinley) 14:365

"An Apostrophe to One of the Landed Gentry" (Betjeman) 43:32

The Apothecary's Shop (Enright) 31:145-46

"Apotheosis" (Ekelof) 27:117

"Apotheosis of an Unhappy Hypocrite" (Waugh) 107:371

"The Apotheosis of Myra" (Tevis)   **42**:372, 377

"The Apotheosis of Tins" (Mahon)   **27**:288-90

Appalachian Wilderness (Abbey)   **59**:244

"The Apparition" (Roethke)   **101**:331

The Apparition (Eberhart)   **56**:88

"Apparition d'aerea" (Char)   **14**:127

"Apparitions" (Merwin)   **45**:274-75

"An Appearance" (Plath)   **111**:203, 214

"The Appearance of Metaphor and the Meaning of Culture"
    See "Geneza metaforei si sensul culturii"

"Appearances" (Mahapatra)   **33**:279

"Appearances" (Swenson)   **106**:345

Appearances Are Deceiving (Bernhard)
    See *Der Schein trügt*

Appearing Nightly (Tomlin)   **17**:518, 520, 523

"L'appendice aux confitures de coing" ("Appendix to 'Quince Jam'") (Ferron)   **94**:125-26

"Appendix to 'Quince Jam'" (Ferron)
    See "L'appendice aux confitures de coing"

"L'Appennino" (Pasolini)   **106**:265

"Applause" (Muske)   **90**:317

Applause (Mamoulian)   **16**:418-20, 422-24

"The Apple" (Kinnell)   **29**:284-85, 289

"Apple" (Peck)   **3**:377

"The Apple" (Roddenberry)   **17**:412-13

The Apple (Gelber)   **6**:196; **79**:208-09, 211-15, 217, 221-24

"Apple and Mole" (Davidson)   **19**:126

Apple Bough (Streatfeild)   **21**:403

The Apple Broadcast and Other New Poems (Redgrove)   **41**:358

An Apple from One's Lap (Seifert)
    See *Jablko z klína*

An Apple From the Lap (Seifert)
    See *Jablko z klína*

An Apple from Your Lap (Seifert)
    See *Jablko z klína*

The Apple in the Dark (Lispector)
    See *A maçã no escuro*

Apple of the Eye (Middleton)   **38**:330

The Apple of the Eye (Wescott)   **13**:590-92

"The Apple Tree" (Dunn)   **40**:169

The Apple Tree: A Short Novel and Some Stories (Kiss Me Again, Stranger: A Collection of Eight Stories, Long and Short) (du Maurier)   **59**:286

"The Apple Trees" (Gluck)   **7**:119-20; **22**:174

"The Apple Trees at Olema" (Hass)   **99**:143

Appleby and Honeybath (Stewart)   **32**:422-23

"Apple-Doors" (Dacey)   **51**:80

"Apples" (Bowering)   **47**:22

"Apples" (Hartley)   **22**:216

"Apples" (Merwin)   **18**:336; **88**:203

"Apples and Pears" (Davenport)   **38**:146-48

Apples and Pears, and Other Stories (Davenport)   **38**:146-48

"Apples and Water" (Graves)   **45**:166-67

"The Applicant" (Plath)   **9**:428; **14**:423; **17**:348; **51**:346; **62**:396, 415; **111**:159, 172-74, 181-86, 203

"The Applicant" (Swados)   **12**:557-58

"Applicaton of Terminology" (Burke)   **24**:118

"The Appointment" (Kumin)   **28**:220

Appointment in Samarra (O'Hara)   **1**:260-62; **2**:324-25; **3**:371; **6**:384; **42**:311-18, 320-21, 323-24

Appointment with Death (Christie)   **12**:125; **48**:74; **110**:114

"Apprehension" (Van Doren)   **10**:496

"Apprehensions" (Duncan)   **15**:190; **41**:128-29

"Apprehensions" (Hecht)   **13**:269; **19**:207

"Apprehensions" (Plath)   **3**:390

"The Apprentice" (Bambara)   **88**:22-23, 28, 43, 52-54

"The Apprentice" (Brown)   **73**:24

"The Apprentice" (Dybek)   **114**:62, 64-5, 71, 74

"The Apprentice Psychiatrist" (Green)   **77**:263-64

The Apprentices (Garfield)   **12**:233, 238-39

The Apprentices (Strugatskii and Strugatskii)   **27**:433

The Apprenticeship of Duddy Kravitz (Richler)   **5**:373-75, 377-78; **9**:451-52; **13**:481, 486; **18**:453, 455-56; **46**:347-48, 350-51; **70**:220, 223, 232

"The Approach to al Mu'tasim" (Borges)
    See "El acercamiento a Almotásim"

"The Approach to Almotasim" (Borges)
    See "El acercamiento a Almotásim"

An Approach to Literature (Brooks)   **110**:20, 29-30, 33

"The Approach to Montego Bay" (Lezama Lima)
    See "Para llegar a Montego Bay"

"The Approaches" (Merwin)   **13**:386

"Approaches to How They Behave" (Graham)   **29**:198

"Approaches to T.S. Eliot" (Leavis)   **24**:310

Approaching Oblivion: Road Signs on the Treadmill Toward Tomorrow (Ellison)   **13**:203

"The Approaching Obsolescence of Housework: A Working Class Perspective" (Davis)   **77**:123

"Approaching Prayer" (Dickey)   **109**:237, 273

Approaching Simone (Terry)   **19**:440

"L'Approche de Clarice Lispector" (Cixous)   **92**:74, 80-2

Approximate Man (Tzara)
    See *L'homme approximatif*

"The Approximate Size of My Favorite Tumor" (Alexie)   **96**:12

"Approximations" (Hayden)   **9**:270; **37**:159

"Appunti per un poema popolari" (Pasolini)   **37**:346

L'après-midi de Monsieur Andesmas (Duras)   **40**:180; **100**:146

"April"   **75**:71

April (Gascoyne)   **45**:158

"April 5, 1974" (Wilbur)   **9**:570

"April 7, 1969" (Brautigan)   **12**:72

"April 25th, as Usual" (Ferber)   **93**:139

"April Fool's Day" (Shapcott)   **38**:400

"April Fugue" (Shapcott)   **38**:402

April Galleons (Ashbery)   **77**:62-6, 68-70

"The April Hill" (Lewis)   **41**:254-55

"April Inventory" (Snodgrass)   **2**:404; **18**:491; **68**:390, 396

April, June, and November (Raphael)   **2**:367; **14**:436

"April Kinney" (Derleth)   **31**:138

"April Rise" (Lee)   **90**:191

April Snow (Linney)   **51**:263-64

"An April Sunday" (Larkin)   **64**:258

"The April Witch" (Bradbury)   **42**:32

"April Woods: Morning" (Berry)   **4**:59

"Aprille" (Keillor)   **115**:267, 287-93

Apt Pupil (King)   **26**:240-42; **61**:327, 331; **113**:338, 352

"Apuntes para una declaración de fe" (Castellanos)   **66**:44, 49-51

Apur sansar (The World of Apu) (Ray)   **16**:475-78, 480, 482, 485-86, 490-491; **76**:356, 358, 360, 366

"Aqua del recuerdo" (Guillen)   **79**:240

"Aquafuerte" (Guillen)   **79**:240

Aquarium (Soupault)   **68**:404

"Aquarius" (Thomas)   **13**:539; **37**:417; **107**:332

"The Aquatic Uncle" (Calvino)
    See "Lo zio acquativo"

Aquí pasan cosas raras (Valenzuela)   **31**:438; **104**:355, 370, 388

The Aquitaine Progression (Ludlum)   **43**:276-77

Arabes et Israeliens (Arabs and Israelis: A Dialogue) (Friedlander)   **90**:109

Arabeskot (Arabesques) (Shammas)   **55**:85-91

Arabesques (Shammas)
    See *Arabeskot*

Arabian Days (O'Brien)   **13**:415

The Arabian Nights (Pasolini)
    See *Il fiore della Mille e una notte*

The Arabian Nights Murder (Carr)   **3**:101

Arabs and Israelis: A Dialogue (Friedlander)
    See *Arabes et Israeliens*

"The Arabs of Palestine" (Gellhorn)   **60**:196

"Arachne" (Empson)   **3**:147; **19**:155; **33**:141

"Arachne, Astonished" (Jacobsen)   **48**:194

Aracoeli (Morante)   **47**:280-84

Les Araignées (Lang)   **103**:88

"Araki Thomas" (Endo)   **99**:289-90, 293, 295

"La araña" ("The Spider") (Cortazar)   **92**:172

Aranyer dín ratri (Days and Nights in the Forest) (Ray)   **16**:483, 485-89, 493; **76**:360, 362, 367

Ararat (Gluck)   **81**:166, 168, 171

Ararat (Thomas)   **31**:431-35

"Arawak Horizon" (Harris)   **25**:217

Die Arbeit des Lebens: Autobiographische Texte (Wellershoff)   **46**:438

La arboleda perdida (Alberti)   **7**:9

Los árboles mueren de pie (Casona)   **49**:42-3, 45, 49

"Arbor" (Willard)   **37**:464

"L'arbre" (Theriault)   **79**:407

"Arbre de décision" (Bowering)   **47**:29

L'arbre de guernica (Guernica) (Arrabal)   **9**:33, 37, 41; **18**:19, 23; **58**:4, 7, 9, 12, 16, 24-5

L'arbre des voyageurs (Traveler's Tree) (Tzara)   **47**:390, 393

"L'arbre, la lampe" (Bonnefoy)   **15**:74

"The Arc Inside and Out" (Ammons)   **5**:29; **25**:44; **108**:16-7, 54

Arc Musical (Bow Harp) (Tchicaya)   **101**:348, 353

Arcadia (Reid)   **33**:348-51

Arcadia (Stoppard)   **91**:182-93

Arcadio (Goyen)   **40**:215-16, 218

Arcady and Other Places (Buckley)   **57**:126, 130-33

Arcane 17 (Breton)   **9**:127; **15**:87; **54**:21, 26, 28

L'arc-en-ciel, Journal 1981-1984 (Green)   **77**:282, 284

"The Arch of Triumph" (Canetti)   **75**:132

Arch of Triumph (Remarque)   **21**:329-32

"The Archaelogy of Knowledge" (Foucault)   **31**:177

"The Archaeologist" (Mahon)   **27**:288

"The Archaeologist" (Simmons)   **43**:414

Archaeologist of Morning (Olson)   **5**:328; **9**:412; **29**:329

The Archaeology of Knowledge (Foucault)
  See *L'archéologie du savoir*
"Archaeology of Snow" (Purdy) **6**:428; **14**:430; **50**:236, 244
"The Archangel of the Suburb" (Ferron) **94**:103
"Archangel Returning Home" **75**:77
Archangels Don't Play Pinball (Fo) **109**:118-19, 121
L'archéologie du savoir (*The Archaeology of Knowledge*) (Foucault) **31**:177-79, 185; **34**:339, 341; **69**:170, 186
"Archeology" (Pollitt) **28**:367
"The Archer" (Smith) **15**:513
Archer in Hollywood (Macdonald) **41**:267
"Archetypal Criticism: Theory of Myths" (Frye) **24**:208
"Archetype and Signature: A Study of the Relationship between Biography and Poetry" (Fiedler) **4**:163; **13**:211; **24**:203
"The Archetypes" (Frye) **24**:216
Archibald of the Cross (Bunuel)
  See *Ensayo de un crimen*
Archibaldo de la Cruz (Bunuel)
  See *Ensayo de un crimen*
"Archipelago" (Gluck) **7**:120
"Archistichs" (Voznesensky) **57**:425
The Architect (Haavikko)
  See *Arkkitehti*
The Architect and the Emperor of Assyria (Arrabal)
  See *L'Architecte et l'Empereur d'Assyria*
L'Architecte et l'Empereur d'Assyria (*The Architect and the Emperor of Assyria*) (Arrabal) **2**:15-16; **9**:33, 38, 41; **18**:20-1; **58**:7, 9-11, 14-15, 17-19, 22
"Architecture" (Barthelme) **117**:5
"The Architecture of California" (Vaughn) **62**:457-58
Archives de ma tour d'ivoire (Cendrars) **106**:170
Archives du nord (Yourcenar) **19**:484; **87**:389, 396, 412, 417, 433
"Archways" (Oates) **6**:370
"Arco invisible de Viñales" ("The Invisible Arch of Viñales") (Lezama Lima) **101**:121
El arco y la lira: El poema. la revelación poética, poesia,e historia (*The Bow and the Lyre: The Poem, the Poetic Revelation, and History*) (Paz) **3**:375; **4**:396-97; **6**:396-98; **10**:390; **51**:324, 326-27, 331, 336; **65**:176-77
"L'arcs" (Butor) **15**:114
Arctic Grail (Berton) **104**:50-1, 53-6
"Arctic Rhododendrons" (Purdy) **50**:245
Arctic Summer, and Other Fiction (Forster) **22**:136-37; **45**:131-33
"Arctic Syndrome: Dream Fox" (Atwood) **8**:32
"Arcturus" (Connell) **45**:106-07, 109
Ardabiola (Yevtushenko) **51**:427, 430-31
Ardele; or, The Daisy (Anouilh)
  See *Ardèle; ou, La marguerite*
Ardèle; ou, La marguerite (*Ardele; or, The Daisy*) (Anouilh) **13**:21; **50**:280
The Ardent Slingsman (Neruda)
  See *El hondero entusiasta, 1923-1924*
Les ardoises du toit (Reverdy) **53**:288
"Ardor/Awe/Atrocity" (Abish) **22**:17, 19, 22
"Are Canadians Politically Naive?" (Skvorecky) **69**:335-36
"Are Flowers Whores?" (Smart) **54**:421
"Are These Actual Miles?" (Carver) **53**:65
"Are You a Doctor?" (Carver) **22**:99
Are You in the House Alone? (Peck) **21**:298-99

"Are You Listening?" (Ellison) **42**:127
"Are You Ready" (Dylan) **77**:190
"Are You Ready for the Country" (Young) **17**:571
Are You Ready for the Country (Jennings) **21**:203-04
"Are You Ready to Rock?" (Sapphire) **99**:81
"Are You Still There" (Harjo) **83**:278-79
"Are You the Right Size?" (Powell) **89**:207
Are You There God? It's Me, Margaret (Blume) **12**:44-7; **30**:20-3
"Are You Ticklish" (Simon) **26**:409
"Are You with Me?" (Swados) **12**:557
Are Your Teeth White? Then Laugh! (p'Bitek)
  See *Lak tar miyo kinyero wi lobo*
"An Area in the Cerebral Hemisphere" (Major) **19**:298
An Area of Darkness (Naipaul) **4**:371, 373-74; **7**:253-54; **13**:406-07; **18**:363; **37**:319, 321; **105**:133-34, 151, 155, 159, 161, 171, 180
"Arena" (Rodriguez) **10**:440
Aren't You Rather Young to be Writing Your Memoirs? (Johnson) **6**:263; **9**:303
Aretheus (Krleza) **114**:177
Arfive (Guthrie) **23**:199
L'argent de la poche (*Small Change*) (Truffaut) **20**:404; **101**:384-87, 400, 403-04,407
"The Argentine Ant" (Calvino)
  See *La formica Argentina*
"The Argentine Writer and Tradition" (Borges)
  See "El escritor argentino y la tradición"
"Argon" (Levi) **37**:223, 227
"Argonaut" (Seferis) **11**:495
The Argot Merchant Disaster: Poems New and Selected (Starbuck) **53**:354-56
"Argument" (Auden) **11**:18
"Argument" (Char) **11**:111
"The Argument for the Benevolent God" (Ewart) **46**:150
Argument of Kings (Scannell) **49**:333-34
"Argyle Street" (Mathias) **45**:235
"Argyria" (Aldington) **49**:6
"Aria" (Barthelme) **23**:47
"Ariadne" (Simic) **49**:337
Ariadne: Le chemin de Créte (Marcel) **15**:361
"Ariel" (Plath) **5**:339-345; **9**:433; **14**:424, 428; **17**:351, 353, 360-61, 363, 365-66; **50**:446; **51**:342-43, 352; **111**:161, 175-76, 178, 199
Ariel (Plath) **1**:269-70; **2**:335-38; **3**:388-91; **5**:339-40, 342-43, 345-46; **9**:424-25, 432-33; **11**:445-49; **14**:422-26; **17**:345-50, 352-53, 355-56, 361-64, 366-69; **50**:441, 444; **62**:386, 425; **111**:158, 160, 164, 167-69, 176-82, 185-86, 210, 216
Ariel Poems (Eliot) **1**:89; **2**:128; **15**:213-14
Arigato (Condon) **6**:115; **8**:150; **10**:111
Arilla Sun Down (Hamilton) **26**:151-52, 154-55
"Arion" (Herbert) **43**:183
The Aristocrat (Richter) **30**:325
Aristocrats (Friel) **42**:174; **59**:145-49; **115**:224-25, 227-29, 234, 236, 241-42, 247
Aristofaniana s ljugaškami (*Aristophaniana with Frogs*) (Aksyonov) **37**:12
Aristophaniana with Frogs (Aksyonov)
  See *Aristofaniana s ljugaškami*
The Aristos: A Self-Portrait in Ideas (Fowles) **2**:138; **4**:170-71; **6**:185; **9**:210-11, 213, 216; **10**:184, 189; **15**:233; **33**:160, 164, 166-67, 171, 173; **87**:141-42, 159, 175-

77, 182, 186
"Arizona Highways" (Welch) **52**:429-30
The Ark (Benary-Isbert) **12**:30-2, 35
"Ark of Bones" (Dumas) **6**:145; **62**:150, 153, 155, 161-64
Ark of Bones (Dumas) **6**:145; **62**:150-52, 158-60
The Ark Sakura (Abe)
  See *Hakobune sakura maru*
"The Arkansas Testament" (Walcott) **67**:359, 361; **76**:275
The Arkansas Testament (Walcott) **67**:342, 358-63; **76**:288
Arkhipelag GULag, 1918-1956: Op' bit khudozhestvennopo issledovaniia (*The Gulag Archipelago, 1918-1956: An Experiment in Literary Investigation*) (Solzhenitsyn) **4**:512-516; **7**:436-41, 443, 445-47; **10**:478-79; **34**:484-85, 489, 491, 493; **78**:386-87, 389, 401, 403-06, 410-11, 423-24, 426-27
Arkkitehti (*The Architect*) (Haavikko) **34**:170
"An Arles, an Arles for My Hiring" (Bunting) **39**:300
Arlette (Freeling) **38**:187
The Arm and the Darkness (Caldwell) **28**:57-8; **39**:303
The Arm and the Flame (Seifert)
  See *Ruka a plamen*
The Arm of Flesh (Salter) **52**:358-59, 363
The Arm of the Starfish (L'Engle) **12**:347, 351
Arm Yourself or Harm Yourself: A One-Act Play: A Message of Self-Defense to Black Men (Baraka) **115**:36
An Armada of Thirty Whales (Hoffman) **6**:243; **13**:286-87; **23**:237-38
"The Armadillo" (Bishop) **9**:93; **13**:88-9; **32**:37, 43
Armadillo in the Grass (Hearon) **63**:160, 166
"Armageddon" (Ransom) **4**:435
"Armageddon" (Scott) **22**:372
Armageddon (Uris) **7**:491; **32**:431-32, 434
"Armageddon, Armageddon" (Muldoon) **32**:318-19; **72**:265-66
Armageddon?: Essays 1983-1987 (*At Home: Essays*) (Vidal) **72**:398, 400
"Armageddon News" (Bissett) **18**:58
"Armaja Das" (Haldeman) **61**:174, 176-78
"Las armas secretas" ("Secret Weapons") (Cortazar) **10**:113; **13**:164; **33**:126; **34**:329
Armas y coraçoes (Dourado) **23**:151
Armed Forces (Costello) **21**:71-2
Armed Love (Lerman) **9**:328-31
"Les armes miraculeuses" ("Miraculous Weapons") (Cesaire) **32**:113; **112**:10, 12, 29
An Armful of Warm Girl (Spackman) **46**:376-78, 380-81
The Armies of the Moon (MacEwen) **13**:358; **55**:163, 166
The Armies of the Night: History as a Novel, the Novel as History (Mailer) **1**:191, 193; **2**:259-60, 263-65; **3**:312-15, 317, 319; **4**:321-23; **8**:367-73; **11**:340-41, 343-44; **14**:349-50, 352-53; **28**:256-57, 262; **39**:425; **74**:204-06, 213-17, 225, 231; **111**:103, 106-08, 110, 113-15, 120, 125-26, 131, 133, 148, 151
"Armistice" (Bowering) **32**:47
"Armistice Day" (Simon) **17**:461
L'armoireà glace un beau soir (Aragon) **22**:41
Les armoires vides (*Cleaned Out; Empty Cupboards*) (Ernaux) **88**:98-101, 105-06,

108, 114-15, 120

Armored Cav (Clancy)   112:77

"Armor's Undermining Modesty" (Moore)   8:401; 10:350

The Armourer's House (Sutcliff)   26:428, 433, 435, 439

"Arms" (Beer)   58:32, 36

The Arms of Venus (The Hands of Venus; Ruce Venušiny) (Seifert)   34:256; 93:306, 315, 318, 335, 341

Armstrong's Last Goodnight (Arden)   6:7-8, 11; 13:24-5, 29; 15:18, 25

"Army of Occupation" (Boyle)   58:81-2

Arna Bontemps-Langston Hughes Letters, 1925-67 (Bontemps)   18:65-6

"The Arno at Rovezzano" (Montale)   9:387

Arnold and Degener, One Chase Manhattan Plaza (Auchincloss)   18:24

"Arnold and Pater" (Eliot)   24:166

Arnold Bennett (Drabble)   5:117

Arnold Bennett (Wain)   2:458

"The Arnold Crombeck Story" (McGrath)   55:76

"Arnold Stone" (O'Hara)   42:319

Arnoumai (Samarakis)   5:381; 5:381

Aromates chasseurs (Aromatic Hunters) (Char)   55:285, 288

Aromatic Hunters (Char)
See *Aromates chasseurs*

"Aromos" (Parra)   102:340

"Around Pastor Bonhoeffer" (Kunitz)   6:287

"Around the Bend in Eighty Days" (Perelman)   5:338

"Around the Corner from Francis Bacon" (Durcan)   43:118

Around the Day in Eighty Worlds (Cortazar)
See *La vuelta al día en ochenta mundos*

Around the Dead Sea (Endo)   99:308

"Around the Dear Ruin" (Berriault)   54:3

"Around the Dial" (Davies)   21:107

"Around the Light House" (Durcan)   70:151-52

Around the Mountain: Scenes from Montreal Life (Hood)   15:284; 28:188

"Around the World" (Graver)   70:49, 52-3

Around the World in 80 Days (Welles)   80:380, 386

Around the World in a Day (Prince)   35:331-32

Around the World in Eighty Days (Perelman)   23:335; 44:500-02; 49:269-70

El arpa y la sombra (The Harp and the Shadow) (Carpentier)   70:347, 351; 110:69, 74, 78

Arrabal celebrando la ceremonia de la confusión (Arrabal Celebrating the Ceremony of Confusion) (Arrabal)   18:18; 58:6

Arrabal Celebrating the Ceremony of Confusion (Arrabal)
See *Arrabal celebrando la ceremonia de la confusión*

The Arrangement (Kazan)   6:273; 16:368, 370-71; 63:215, 221, 223, 229, 233-34

"Arrangement in Black and White" (Parker)   15:415; 68:326, 330, 334, 336

"Arras" (Page)   7:292; 18:380

"The Arrest of Oscar Wilde at the Cadogan Hotel" (Betjeman)   43:32, 42

L'arrestation (Anouilh)   8:24

"Arrests" (Samarakis)   5:382

L'arrière-pays (Bonnefoy)   9:112; 58:51-4, 60

"Arrival" (Celan)   19:95

"Arrival" (Guillen)   48:164, 166; 79:230

"The Arrival" (Merwin)   88:202

Arrival and Departure (Koestler)   15:310-11; 33:229-30, 233, 238, 240-41, 243-44

"Arrival at Santos" (Bishop)   13:88, 93; 32:37

"Arrival of My Cousin" (Jacobsen)   48:191

"The Arrival of the Bee Box" (Plath)   9:429, 431; 14:425; 51:342

Arrival of the Gods (Buero Vallejo)
See *Llegada de los dioes*

"Arrivals, Departures" (Larkin)   33:256; 64:262, 266

"Arrivals Wolfville" (Birney)   6:74, 77

The Arrivants: A New World Trilogy (Brathwaite)   11:67

"Arriving" (Piercy)   27:376

"Arriving at the Point of Departure" (Plumly)   33:311

"Arriving in the Country Again" (Wright)   3:540

"Arriving Late for a Movie" (Dacey)   51:82

The Arrivistes: Poems, 1940-1949 (Simpson)   4:498; 32:378

"Arrogant" (Matthews)   40:325

Arrogant Beggar (Yezierska)   46:444

"Arrow" (Dove)   81:152

Arrow in the Blue (Koestler)   15:311-12; 33:234-35, 243

An Arrow in the Wall: Selected Poetry and Prose (Voznesensky)   57:426-28

Arrow of God (Achebe)   1:1; 3:1-3; 5:1, 3; 7:3-4, 6-7; 11:1-5; 26:13-20, 25, 27; 51:2-3, 5, 7; 75:3-4, 6, 8-10

Arrow Pointing Nowhere (Daly)   52:89

Arrowroot (Tanizaki)
See *Yoshinokuzu*

Arrowsmith (Ford)   16:303

Ars amandi (Arrabal)   9:35; 18:22

Ars longa, vita brevis (Arden)   15:21

"Ars poetica" (Davie)   31:118

"Ars poetica" (Dove)   81:140, 150-51

"Ars poetica" (Dunn)   6:148

"Ars poetica" (Kennedy)   42:256

"Ars poetica" (Longley)   29:296

"Ars Poetica" (MacLeish)   8:360-61, 363; 14:337-38; 68:273, 284, 287, 290-91, 293-94

"Ars poetica?" (Milosz)   22:308, 310; 56:238, 242; 82:303

"Ars poetica" (Richards)   14:455

"Ars poetica" (Tomlinson)   4:548

Ars Poetica: In the American Grain (Williams)
See *In the American Grain*

"Ars Poetica: Or; Who Lives in the Ivory Tower?" (McGrath)   59:178, 181

"Ars poetica. Scrisori unei fetite" (Arghezi)   80:11

"Arse poetica" (Jong)   6:267

Arse poetica: A Monologue by an Arsehole (Breytenbach)   23:87

"Arsehole" (Raine)   103:186, 190-91, 199, 209

Arsenal (Char)   11:114; 55:287

"Arsenal by Night" (Neruda)
See "Maestranzas de noche"

Arsenic and Old Lace (Kesselring)   45:207-10

"Arsenio" (Montale)   7:222; 9:387; 18:342

"Art" (Levertov)   15:337

"Art" (Major)   19:297

Art and Ardor (Ozick)   28:351-55; 62:347

"Art and Democracy" (Jones)   7:190

"Art and Eros" (Murdoch)   51:291-92

"Art and Extinction" (Harrison)   43:180

"Art and Fortune" (Trilling)   9:531; 11:542; 24:450-53, 461

"Art and Life" (Johnston)   51:244

"Art and Mr. Mahoney" (McCullers)   12:433

"Art and Neurosis" (Trilling)   24:452, 456

Art and Outrage (Miller)   84:250

"Art and Politics: The Editorship of Blast'" (Williams)   22:464

"Art and Responsibility" (Bakhtin)   83:36

Art and Revolution (Berger)   2:54; 19:37

"Art and Sacrament" (Jones)   7:188-90; 42:244

"Art and the Obvious" (Huxley)   79:310

"Art and the Ravens" (Watkins)   43:442

"Art and the Underground" (Sukenick)   48:368, 370

Art and Value
See *Arta si valoare*

Art as Second Nature: Occasional Pieces, 1950-74 (Hamburger)   14:234

Art Buchwald's Paris (Buchwald)   33:87

Art Chronicles, 1954-1966 (O'Hara)   5:325; 13:423; 78:359

"Art for Art's Sake" (Forster)   4:166; 77:216

"Art History" (Gurganus)   70:190-91, 194, 196

Art in Anchorage (Gray)   49:147

"Art Lecture" (Ezekiel)   61:97, 101, 103

An Art Lover's Collection (Perec)
See *Un cabinet d'amateur*

"Art Notes" (Pound)   112:351

"The Art of Bergotte" (Bowen)   15:78

"The Art of Biography" (Lively)   32:276

The Art of Birds (Neruda)
See *Arte de pájaros*

"The Art of Courtly Love" (Garrett)   51:140

The Art of Darkness (McFadden)   48:257-58

The Art of Dining (Howe)   48:173-75

The Art of Easter Island (Heyerdahl)   26:193

The Art of Eating: Five Gastronomical Works (Fisher)   76:337, 339, 341-42; 87:120, 122, 125

"The Art of Fiction: An Interview" (Ellison)   114:91, 102

The Art of Fiction: Notes on Craft for Young Writers (Gardner)   34:547-50

"The Art of Literature and Commonsense" (Nabokov)   23:315

"The Art of Living" (Gardner)   28:161

The Art of Living, and Other Stories (Gardner)   28:161-63

"The Art of Love" (Fuller)   62:186-87, 193

"The Art of Love" (Koch)   44:244-45, 249-50

The Art of Love (Koch)   8:323; 44:246, 249, 251

"The Art of Needles and Sins" (Okudzhava)   59:378-79

"Art of Poetry" (Ammons)   5:29

"Art of Poetry" (Bonnefoy)
See "Art poétique"

"The Art of Poetry" (Koch)   8:323; 44:249, 251

"The Art of Response" (Lorde)   71:260

The Art of Salad Gardening (Okudzhava)   81:275

The Art of Seeing (Huxley)   3:253

"The Art of the Film" (Carpenter)   41:103

The Art of the Novel: Vladislav Vancura's Search for the Great Epic (Kundera)
See *Unemi románu: Cesta Vladislava Vancuryza velkou epikou*

"The Art of the Octopus" (Levertov)   28:243

"Art of the Possible" (Lowell)   37:238

The Art of the Self (Kosinski)　53:221, 225
Art of the Sonnet (Orlovitz)　22:334, 336
"The Art of the Word and the Culture of Folk Humor (Rabelais and Gogol)" (Bakhtin)　83:24
The Art of War (Walker)
　See *The Power Plays*
The Art of Worldly Wisdom (Rexroth)　6:450; 22:344, 347; 49:274, 279, 284; 112:365, 374-76, 384
Art on My Mind (hooks)　94:159
"Art poétique" ("Art of Poetry") (Bonnefoy)　58:42, 51
"Art Review" (Fearing)　51:111, 116
Eine Art Schadensabwicklung (Habermas)　104:87
"Art School" (Weller)　26:443
"Art Student" (Spender)　5:401
Arta si valoare (*Art and Value*)　75:80
Arte de pájaros (*The Art of Birds*) (Neruda)　28:312-14; 62:331
"El arte narrativo y la magia" ("Narrative Art and Magic") (Borges)　13:108; 48:47; 83:163
Artefactos (*Artifacts*) (Parra)　102:334, 355-56
"Artemis" (Broumas)　73:2, 4, 6, 9
"Artemis" (Williams)　56:427
Artemis Hates Romance (Thesen)　56:414-15, 417, 421
"Arthur" (Hellman)　52:192
Arthur (Davies)　21:91, 93, 100
"Arthur at Ampelos" (Forster)　45:133
"Arthur Bond" (Goyen)　40:216, 218
Arthur Dimmesdale (Larson)　31:241
Arthur Miller's Collected Plays (Miller)　4:2369, 2373; 6:334; 15:371; 26:319, 321-22; 78:309, 311, 314, 316, 319, 324
Arthur Rex: A Legendary Novel (Berger)　11:46-8; 18:57-8; 38:39
"Arthur Rimbaud" (Char)　11:115
"Arthur Snatchfold" (Forster)　22:135
Articles of Faith (Harwood)　32:224-25
Articulate Energy: An Inquiry into the Syntax of English Poetry (Davie)　8:162, 167
Articulation of Sound Forms in Time (Howe)　72:202-05, 207, 209
"Artifact" (Rukeyser)　10:442
Artifact (Benford)　52:73-4
Artifacts (Parra)
　See *Artefactos*
"Artifax in Extremis" (Davie)　31:123-24
"Artificer" (Kennedy)　42:255
"Artificer" (Milosz)　56:247
"Artificial Illuminations" (Urdang)　47:399-400
The Artificial Jungle (Ludlam)　46:244; 50:342-44
The Artificial Kid (Sterling)　72:372
"The Artificial Nigger" (O'Connor)　3:365-66; 6:381; 13:419; 15:410; 21:256-57, 263-64; 104:117, 123, 135, 190, 192
An Artificial Nigger (O'Connor)
　See *A Good Man Is Hard to Find and Other Stories*
"Artificial Roses" (Garcia Marquez)　47:151
An Artificial Wilderness: Essays on Twentieth Century Literature (Birkerts)　116:147-52
De Artificiali Perspectiva or Anamorphosis (The Brothers Quay)　95:347
"The Artist" (Avison)　97:76, 80, 84
"The Artist" (Heaney)　37:165; 74:169
"An Artist" (Jeffers)　54:236

"The Artist" (Koch)　5:219; 8:322; 44:243, 247-48
"The Artist as Housewife/The Housewife as Artist" (Jong)　83:298
"Artist at Home" (Faulkner)　3:155-56; 18:145-47
"The Artist at Work" (Camus)
　See "Jonas ou l'artiste au travail"
Artist Descending a Staircase (Stoppard)　15:519; 29:397, 401, 404
An Artist in the Family (Millin)　49:243-46
"An Artist in the North" (Transtroemer)　65:236
An Artist of the Floating World (Ishiguro)　56:158-61; 59:159, 161, 163-65, 167; 110:220, 222-26, 228, 231-34, 243-44, 246, 257-59, 261-62
"An Artist Waiting in a Country House" (Dunn)　40:168
"Artists" (Smith)　25:409-10; 73:358
"The Artists' and Models' Ball" (Brooks)　49:32
Artists in Crime (Marsh)　53:249
"Artist's Model One" (Lowell)　11:330
"Artists Only" (Byrne)　26:96
"Artists, Providers, Places to Go" (Fisher)　25:159
"Art-Luck-Risk" (Elytis)　100:190
"Arts et métiers" (Butor)　15:114
An Arts of the Difficult World (Roberts)　76:209, 212-13, 215, 219
Artsot hatan (*Where the Jackals Howl and Other Stories*) (Oz)　8:436; 27:358-61; 54:352
Arturo's Island (Morante)
　See *L'isola di Arturo*
"An Arundel Tomb" (Larkin)　8:332; 18:300; 33:258, 261, 263; 39:335, 344-45; 64:263, 277, 279
Arztliche seelsorge (*The Doctor and the Soul: An Introduction to Logotherapy*) (Frankl)　93:209-10, 214, 216, 218-19, 223
"As" (Wonder)　12:662
"As a Comment on Romans 1:10" (Avison)　97:121
"As Birds Bring Forth the Sun" (MacLeod)　56:198-99
As Birds Bring Forth the Sun and Other Stories (MacLeod)　56:197-200
"As Breathing and Consciousness Return" (Solzhenitsyn)
　See "Dykhanie"
"As Children Together" (Forche)　25:172
"As Evening Lays Dying" (Salinas)　90:332
As Ever: The Collected Correspondence of Allen Ginsberg and Neal Cassady (Ginsberg)　36:185
"As Expected" (Gunn)　32:214
"As facas Pernambucanas" ("Knives of Pernambuco") (Cabral de Melo Neto)　76:165
"As Fast As You Can" (Feldman)　7:103
As for Me and My House (Ross)　13:490, 492-94
"As Freedom Is a Breakfast-Food" (Cummings)　15:162
"As He Came Near Death" (Fisher)　25:159
"As I Came from the Holy Land" (Ashbery)　6:12; 25:58
"As I Grow Older" (Hughes)　108:283
As I Lay Dying (Faulkner)　1:98, 102; 3:153; 6:179-80; 8:207; 9:198-200; 11:202, 204-06; 14:173, 175, 178; 28:140-43; 52:107, 113, 138; 68:109
"As I Step over the Puddle" (Wright)　3:541,

543; 28:466
"As I Walked Out One Evening" (Betjeman)　43:40
As I Walked Out One Midsummer Morning (Lee)　90:188-91, 202-4, 206-7, 209-10
"As I Was Going Up the Stairs" (Chester)　49:55-6
"As I Was Saying" (Parra)　102:353-54
"As I Went Out One Morning" (Dylan)　12:185
As If by Magic (Wilson)　3:535-36; 5:514-15; 25:458-59, 461, 463-64
As If: Poems New and Selected (Ciardi)　40:154, 156, 162; 44:375, 379, 381
As imaginações pecaminosas (*Sinful Minds*) (Dourado)　60:85
"As in a Dream I Would Yet Remain" (Lerman)　9:329
As Is (Hoffman)　40:254-56
"As It Should Be" (Mahon)　27:288
"As It Was in the Beginning" (Richter)　30:319
"As John to Patmos" (Walcott)　76:278
"As Mortes e o Triunfo de Rosalinda" ("The Deaths and the Victory of Rosalinda") (Amado)　106:74, 77
"As of July 6, I Am Responsible for No Other Debts than My Own" (Jones)　81:65
"As Old as the Century" (Pritchett)　41:332
"As on a Darkling Plain" (Taylor)　44:302
"As One Put Drunk into the Packet Boat" (Ashbery)　13:31; 15:28
As Sad as She Is (Onetti)
　See *Tan triste como ella*
"Às seis e meia no largo do carmo" (Dourado)　23:151
As sete portas du Bahia (Amado)　106:62
"As Sparks Fly Upward" (Hollander)　2:197
As Ten, as Twenty (Page)　7:291
As Testimony (Duncan)　55:293
"As the 'Billy World Turns" (Jennings)　21:204-05
"As the Dead Prey upon Us" (Olson)　29:334
"As the Manatees Go to Drink at the Source" (Senghor)　54:408
"As the Mist Leaves No Scar" (Cohen)　38:132
"As the Night Goes" (Jiles)　58:272
"As the Window Darkens" (Jensen)　37:189
As the World Turns (Nixon)　21:242, 246
As They Reveled (Wylie)　43:462
As They Were (Fisher)　76:340; 87:122, 128
As Thousands Cheer (Hart)　66:176, 178, 185, 190
As We Are Now (Sarton)　4:471-72; 14:480-81; 49:322; 91:240, 246-50
"As We Know" (Ashbery)　15:33-4
As We Know (Ashbery)　15:33-6; 25:52-3, 58-9; 41:38, 41
"As We Like It" (Auden)　14:26
"As You Came from the Holy Land" (Ashbery)　6:12; 15:26; 77:51-2
"As You Leave Me" (Knight)　40:279, 286
Asakusa Kurenaidan (Kawabata)　107:105, 107
"Ascending Image" (Donnell)　34:156
"Ascension" (Levine)　33:275
"Ascension" (Thomas)　107:338, 340, 342, 346
Ascension (Konwicki)
　See *Wniebowstapienie*
"The Ascent" (Kennedy)　42:255
"Ascent" (Merwin)　88:194
"Ascent into Hell" (Hope)　51:214, 224
Ascent into Hell (Greeley)　28:177-78
The Ascent of F6 (Auden)　1:9; 3:26; 11:18; 14:30-1; 43:21

The Ascent of F6 (Isherwood) **44**:396. 399

The Ascent of Mount Fuji (Aitmatov)
   See *Voskhozhdenie na Fudzhiamu*

Ascent to Dmai (Harris) **25**:209-10. 216

Ascent to Orbit (Clarke) **35**:128

The Ascent to the Truth (Merton) **83**:403

"El asesino desinteresado Bill Harrigan" ("The
   Disinterested Killer Bill Harrigan")
   (Borges) **83**:165

Ash (Walker) **14**:552

Ash on a Young Man's Sleeve (Abse) **29**:11.
   18. 20

"Ash Wednesday" (Seifert) **93**:332

Ashani sanket (*Distant Thunder*) (Ray) **16**:488-
   89, 493-94; **76**:357. 360. 362. 367

Ashenden; or, The British Agent (Maugham)
   67:210

"Ashes" (Peterkin) **31**:308

Ashes (Levine) **14**:320-21; **33**:270-72

Ashes (Rudkin) **14**:470-71

Ashes and Diamonds (Wajda) **16**:577-79, 581-
   82, 584

"Ashes and Wrath" (L'Heureux) **52**:272

"The Ashes of a Poet" (Solzhenitsyn) **7**:432

The Ashes of Gramsci (Pasolini)
   See *Le ceneri di Gramsci*

Ashes of Izalco (Alegria)
   See *Cenizas de Izalco*

"Ashikari" (Tanizaki) **8**:510; **28**:414. 416.
   418

Ashini (Theriault) **79**:399, 401, 406, 411-
   412, 416-418

"The Ashplant" (Heaney) **91**:125

"The Ashtray" (Carver) **36**:107

"Ashurnatsirpal III" (Sandburg) **15**:466

Ash-Wednesday (Eliot) **1**:90-2; **2**:128-29;
   3:137-39, 141; **6**:163. 165-66; **9**:183-84,
   186-89; **10**:167-68. 170; **13**:194, 200-02;
   15:208, 213-17; **34**:524-25, 529-31;
   41:148, 151, 154-56, 162; **55**:350, 362,
   371; **57**:179, 181, 186, 213

Asi en la paz como en la guerra (*In Peace as in
   War*) (Cabrera Infante) **5**:96

Asian Figures (Merwin) **5**:287; **45**:273

The Asian Journal of Thomas Merton (Merton)
   3:337

"The Asian Shore: A Tale of Possession" (Disch)
   7:86

"The Asians Dying" (Merwin) **13**:385; **88**:206

The Asiatics (Prokosch) **4**:421; **48**:302-04,
   307, 309, 312-15

"An Aside" (Blunden) **56**:48

Asimov on Science Fiction (Asimov) **26**:57

Asimov's Guide to Shakespeare (Asimov)
   76:312

*Asimov's Guide to the Bible, Volume I: The Old
   Testament* (*The Old Testament*) (Asimov)
   76:312

*Asimov's Guide to the Bible, Volume II: The
   New Testament* (*The New Testament*)
   (Asimov) **76**:312

Asimov's Mysteries (Asimov) **26**:37

Asimov's New Guide to Science (Asimov)
   76:313

Asinamali! (Ngema) **57**:339-44

Ask Again (Johnston) **51**:248-49, 254

"Ask Him" (Carver) **53**:61

Ask Me No Questions (Schlee) **35**:374

Ask Me Now (Young) **19**:480

*Ask Me Tomorrow, or The Pleasant Comedy of
   Young Fortunatus* (Cozzens) **92**:203

Ask Me Tomorrrow (Cozzens) **11**:126, 128,
   131; **92**:178, 180-82, 184-86, 194, 203-
   06. 208

Ask the Dust (Fante) **60**:129-30. 132-34

"Ask the Roses" (Levine) **14**:318

Ask Your Mama: 12 Moods for Jazz (Hughes)
   10:279; **15**:294; **35**:216. 218, 220;
   108:283-84, 335

Aslan Norval (Traven) **11**:537

"Asleep?" (Silkin) **6**:498

Asleep in the Sun (Bioy Casares)
   See *Dormir al sol*

"Asleep: With Still Hands" (Ellison) **42**:127

Asmodée (Mauriac) **56**:212. 214-15

"Asmodeus" (Hill) **8**:294

"An Aspect of Love, Alive in the Fire and Ice"
   (Brooks) **49**:28

"Aspects" (MacCaig) **36**:288

"Aspects of a Play" (Bentley) **24**:47

Aspects of Eve (Pastan) **27**:369

Aspects of Feeling (Vansittart) **42**:398-401

"Aspects of God" (Broumas) **10**:76

"Aspects of Lilacs" (Moss) **45**:287

Aspects of the Dying Process (Wilding) **73**:398

Aspects of the Novel (Forster) **3**:160; **4**:165;
   9:208-09; **13**:219; **15**:224, 227; **45**:136,
   138, 140, 143-44; **77**:205, 214-15, 222

Aspects of the Present (Mead) **37**:282

*Aspects of the Presidency: Truman and Ford in
   Office* (Hersey) **81**:332, 335

"Aspen Tree" (Celan) **82**:37-8, 47

"Aspen's Song" (Winters) **32**:469

Os ásperos tempos (Amado) **106**:59

Asphalt Georgics (Carruth) **84**:135

The Asphalt Jungle (Huston) **20**:160, 162,
   165

"The Asphalt Orangery" (Aksyonov) **101**:22

"Asphodel" (Welty) **14**:562

"Asphodel. That Greeny Flower" (Williams)
   9:572-73, 575; **22**:465, 467-68; **42**:463-
   64

An Aspidistra in Babylon: Four Novellas (*The
   Grapes of Paradise: Four Short Novels*)
   (Bates) **46**:65

"Asra" (Muldoon) **72**:281

"Ass" (Salinas) **90**:326

"Assassin" (Mahapatra) **33**:277, 283

"Assassin" (Tomlinson) **4**:544; **13**:548-49;
   45:393. 404

The Assassin (O'Flaherty) **5**:321

The Assassin (Shaw) **23**:396

"Assassination Raga" (Ferlinghetti) **6**:184;
   27:137, 139

"The Assassins" (Epstein) **7**:97

"The Assassins" (Prokosch) **48**:304, 306

"Assassins" (Szirtes) **46**:393

The Assassins (Camus)
   See *Les justes*

The Assassins (Kazan) **6**:273; **63**:216-18

Assassins (Mosley) **43**:313-14; **70**:204

The Assassins (Prokosch) **48**:302-04, 306-10

The Assassins: A Book of Hours (Oates) **6**:374;
   9:402-05; **19**:350, 353-54; **33**:289;
   52:338; **108**:386, 391

The Assault (Mulisch) **42**:289-92

Assault with Intent (Kienzle) **25**:276

"Assaut de la pitié" (Malraux) **13**:367

"Assay of the Infinite Man" (Neruda)
   See *Tentativa del hombre infinito*

Assays (Rexroth) **22**:346

"The Assembly" (Borges)
   See *El congreso*

"The Assembly" (Gallant) **38**:195

"Un assenza" ("An Absence") (Ginzburg)
   54:198; **70**:283

Assez (*Enough*) (Beckett) **6**:36, 38, 42; **18**:51-
   2

"Assia" (Trevor) **116**:388

The Assignation (Oates) **108**:374-76

"Assignment" (Carruth) **84**:136

The Assignment (Duerrenmatt) **102**:83, 85-
   90

Assignment in Brittany (MacInnes) **27**:279;
   39:349-51

Assignment: Sports (Lipsyte) **21**:208

"Assisi" (Celan) **19**:88

"The Assistance" (Blackburn) **43**:61

The Assistant (Malamud) **1**:195-98, 200-01;
   2:265-69; **3**:320-21, 323-24; **5**:269-70;
   8:374, 376; **9**:341-42, 346-50; **11**:345-46,
   348-54; **18**:319, 321; **27**:295-98, 301;
   44:411-18, 420; **78**:247-86; **85**:200

Assorted Prose (Updike) **13**:557; **23**:463, 473;
   34:285-86

The Assumption of the Rogues and Rascals
   (Smart) **54**:413-14, 419-22, 425-26

Assumptions (Hacker) **72**:182-84, 189-90

"Assunta" (Chatwin) **57**:153

"Assunta 2" (Chatwin) **57**:153

Assured Survival (Bova) **45**:74, 76

The Assyrian, and Other Stories (Saroyan)
   29:361

"Asteroids" (Tallent) **45**:387

Ästhetik (Lukacs) **24**:332, 335

Die Ästhetik des Widerstands, Vol. 1 (Weiss)
   51:387-91, 395

Die Ästhetik des Widerstands, Vol. 2 (Weiss)
   51:388-91

Die Ästhetik des Widerstands, Vol. 3 (Weiss)
   51:388-91

El astillero (Onetti) **10**:374-76

The Astonished Man (Cendrars)
   See *L'homme foudroyé*

The Astral Mirror (Bova) **45**:75

Astral Weeks (Morrison) **21**:231-32, 236-37,
   240

"An Astrologer's Day" (Narayan) **28**:293

An Astrologer's Day and Other Stories
   (Narayan) **28**:293, 301, 303

Astrology: Sense or Nonsense? (Gallant) **17**:130

Astrology: Wisdom of the Stars (Kettelkamp)
   12:306

"Astrometaphysical" (Frost) **26**:118

"Astronauts" (Hayden) **37**:157

The Astronauts (Lem) **40**:289-90

"The Astronomer" (Schevill) **7**:400

The Astronomer and Other Stories (Betts) **3**:73;
   28:34

"The Astronomer Poems" (Wakoski) **9**:554

The Astronomers (Bowers) **9**:121

"The Astronomers at Mont Blanc" (Bowers)
   9:121

"Astronomical Riddles" (Leithauser) **27**:242

Astronomy (Branley) **21**:21-2

"Astronomy Domine" (Pink Floyd) **35**:307

Astyanax (Mandiargues) **41**:275

"Asunto de prinicpio" ("A Matter of Origin")
   (Zamora) **89**:386

The Asutra (Vance) **35**:421

"The Asylum" (Carruth) **4**:94; **84**:119, 128

Asylum Piece (Kavan) **82**:116-17, 119-20

"At a Bach Concert" (Rich) **7**:371; **73**:323

"At a Cathedral Service" (Blunden) **56**:39

"At a Difficult Time" (Ghose) **42**:179

"At a Funeral" (Brutus) **43**:91

"At a Party" (Bogan) **46**:83-4, 90; **93**:64

"At a Poetry Conference, Expo '67" (Wright)
   53:428

"At a Potato Digging" (Heaney)　5:171;
　14:243; 25:251; 74:158
"At a Public Dinner" (Wright)　53:429
"At a Ritual Worship on a Saturday Afternoon"
　(Mahapatra)　33:282
"At a Slight Angle to the Universe" (Raine)
　103:205
"At a Yorkshire Bus Stop" (Dunn)　40:165-66
"At Akitio" (Baxter)　14:62
"At Assissi" (McAuley)　45:254
"At Auden's Grave" (Shapiro)　53:334
At Bertram's Hotel (Christie)　6:108; 12:116-
　17; 110:116, 134-35, 137
"At Bickford's" (Stern)　40:410
"At Bluebeard's Castle" (Howard)　10:277
"At Breakfast" (Swenson)　106:318-19
"At Briggflatts Meeting House" (Bunting)
　47:53
"At Brown Crane Pavilion" (Kennedy)　42:256
"At Carnoy" (Sassoon)　36:385, 392
"At Cove on the Crooked River" (Stafford)
　29:380
"at creation" (Clifton)　66:83
"At Dawn" (Rulfo)
　See "En la madrugada"
"At Dawn, Sitting in My Father's House"
　(Cook-Lynn)　93:116
"At Daybreak" (Rulfo)
　See "En la madrugada"
"At Delft" (Tomlinson)　45:399
"At East River" (Swenson)　61:399; 106:325
"At Evergreen Cemetary" (Purdy)　6:428
"At Every Gas Station There Are Mechanics"
　(Dunn)　36:151
At Fever Pitch (Caute)　29:108-09
"At First Sight" (Adams)　46:17
"At First Sight" (Campbell)　42:84
"At Ford's Theater" (Voznesensky)　59:378
At Freddie's (Fitzgerald)　51:123-25; 61:117-
　18
At Full Flame (Tzara)
　See *À haute flamme*
"at gettysburg" (Clifton)　66:82-3
"At Grass" (Larkin)　5:227; 8:339; 39:336,
　339, 342, 345; 64:260, 262, 266, 269-
　70, 279
"At Hand" (Zamora)　89:387
At Heaven's Gate (Warren)　4:578, 580, 582-
　83; 10:519; 13:574; 39:266; 53:359, 361,
　376
"At Holwell Farm" (Tomlinson)　13:549
"At Home" (Merwin)　88:195
"At Home" (Reading)　47:352
At Home (Weller)
　See *Split*
At Home: Essays (Vidal)
　See *Armageddon?: Essays 1983-1987*
"At Home with Ron Padgett" (Schuyler)　23:388
"At Hotel Berlin" (Voznesensky)　57:426
"At Jeanneret's Beach" (McAuley)　45:254
"at jonestown" (Clifton)　66:82
"At Karl Weilink's Exhibition" ("Na vystavke
　Karla Veilinka") (Brodsky)　100:55
"At Kinosaki" (Shiga)
　See "Kinosaki nite"
At Lady Molly's (Powell)　3:400
At Land (Deren)　16:251-53; 102:28, 31, 37-
　40, 42, 44, 47-8
"At Last" (Kincaid)　43:248; 68:208
"At Last" (Montague)　46:272, 277
"At Last" (Walcott)　9:557; 76:280, 285
"At Least I Have Made a Woman of Her"
　(Oates)　108:348

"At Lemmons" (Day Lewis)　10:131
"At Luca Signorelli's Resurrection of the Body"
　(Graham)　48:148
"At Lunch with the Rock Critic Establishment"
　(Trow)　52:419
"At Majority" (Rich)　7:364
"At Martha's Deli" (Muldoon)　32:319
"At Midsummer" (Dubie)　36:142
"At Millstreet" (Buckley)　57:134
"At Mitylene" (Aldington)　49:6
"At Mrs. Preston's" (White)　49:408
"At Muzat" (Sarton)　14:482
At My Father's Wedding　70:422
At My Heart's Core (Davies)　42:104
"at nagasaki" (Clifton)　66:82
"At Night" (Dubus)　97:235
At Night All Cats Are Grey (Boyle)　19:67
"At Nightfall" (Silkin)　43:404
"At No Distance" (Fisher)　25:158
"At North Farm" (Ashbery)　41:33, 35, 37;
　77:69
"At Once" (Fisher)　25:159
At One's Goal (Bernhard)
　See *Am Ziel*
"At Osborne House" (Hooker)　43:202
At Paradise Gate (Smiley)　53:345-46
"At Paso Rojo" (Bowles)　53:36, 49
"At Pentre Ifan" (Walker)　13:566
"At Père Lachaise" (Van Duyn)　63:443
At Play in the Fields of the Lord (Matthiessen)
　5:274; 7:210, 212; 11:360; 32:287-88,
　290; 64:302-04, 307, 309, 311, 321, 327-
　28
"At Pleasure Bay" (Pinsky)　94:307
"At Porthcothan" (Middleton)　13:387
"At Risk" (Momaday)　85:282
"At Roblin Lake" (Purdy)　6:428
"At Rugmer" (Blunden)　56:30, 44
"At Sallygap" (Lavin)　18:302-03
"At Sea" (Hemingway)　6:232; 8:285
"At Sechelt" (Livesay)　79:336
"At Seventeen" (Ian)　21:185
At Seventy, Journal of a Solitude (Sarton)
　91:246-47, 250-51
"At Stoke" (Tomlinson)　6:536; 13:548;
　45:396
At Swim-Two-Birds (O'Brien)　1:252; 4:383;
　5:314-15, 317; 7:268-70; 10:362-64;
　47:311-17, 319-23
At Swords' Points (Norton)　12:456
At Terror Street and Agony Way (Bukowski)
　5:81; 41:67; 108:112
At Terror Street and Agony Way (Bukowski)
　108:113
"At That Time; or, The History of a Joke"
　(Paley)　37:333
"At the All-Night Cafe" (Soto)　80:301
"At the Athenian Market" (Purdy)　50:238
"At the Bar, 1948" (Sissman)　18:490
"At the Beach" (Adams)　46:17
"At the Beach" (Friedman)　56:105
"At the Birth of an Age" (Jeffers)　54:238;
　11:306, 310
"At the Bodega" (Ferlinghetti)　111:65
"At the Bomb Testing Site" (Stafford)　29:382
"At the Bottom of the River" (Kincaid)
　68:210-11
At the Bottom of the River (Kincaid)　43:247-
　51; 68:207-11, 217-18, 220, 225
At the Building Site (Konwicki)
　See *Przy budowie*
"At the Burning Ground" (Mahapatra)　33:280
"At the Cafe" (Moss)　45:287

"At the Cemetery" (Harper)　7:139
"At the Center" (Gunn)　3:216
"At the Cinema" (Young)　82:396
"At the Country Club" (Hope)　52:208-09
"At the Court of Yearning"　75:74
At the Court of Yearning
　See *La curtile dorului*
"At the Crossroads" (Connell)　45:109
At the Crossroads (Connell)　45:109-12
"At the Dressing Table" (Szirtes)　46:391
"At the Drug Store" (Taylor)　18:527; 37:409
"At the Edge" (Tomlinson)　45:400
At the Edge of the Body (Jong)　18:278
"At the Edge of the Jungle" (Lane)　25:285,
　287
"At the End of a Caboose" (Jensen)
　See "To a Stranger"
At the End of the Open Road (Simpson)　4:498-
　500; 7:427-29; 32:376-77, 379
"At the End of the Open Road, 1963"
　(Simpson)　32:378
"At the Executed Murderer's Grave" (Wright)
　3:543; 5:519; 10:545; 28:470
"At the Fair" (Smith)　64:391-92
"At the Fall of an Age" (Jeffers)　54:237, 246;
　11:305, 310
"At the Fishhouses" (Bishop)　9:95; 13:92-3;
　15:59; 32:37-9, 41
"At the Foot of the Hill, Birdie's School"
　(Hodgins)　23:230
"At the Frick" (Hecht)　8:266
At the Front Door of the Atlantic (Kerrigan)
　4:269; 6:275-76
"At the Funeral of Great-Aunt Mary" (Bly)
　38:56
"At the Gate of the Valley" (Herbert)　9:271,
　273; 43:188
At the Gates of Pompeii (Faludy)　42:139-40
"At the German Writers Conference in
　Munich" (Dove)　81:137
"At the Glass Factory in Cavan Town" (Boland)
　113:92
"At the Grave of Henry James" (Auden)　43:27
"At the Grave of Marianne Moore" (Hirsch)
　31:215
"At the Grave of My Brother" (Stafford)
　29:379
"At the Grave of Virgil Campbell" (Chappell)
　40:145
"At the Grave of Wallace Stevens" (Corn)
　33:117
"At the Hungarian Border" (Faludy)　42:141
"At the Ice Cream Parlor" (Parini)　54:363-64
"At the Indian Killer's Grave" (Lowell)　4:302;
　8:350-51
At the Jerusalem (Bailey)　45:39-40, 42, 44,
　46, 48-9
"At the Jewish Museum" (Pastan)　27:368
"At the Landing" (Welty)　22:460
"At the Masseurs's's" (Moss)　7:249-50
At the Moon's Inn (Lytle)　22:299
"At the Movies: Virginia, 1956" (Voigt)
　54:433-34
"At the National Gallery" (Forster)　45:133
"At the Night Court" (Simic)　49:343
"At the Point of No Return" (Wagoner)　15:560
"At the Portal" (Narayan)　47:304
"At the Post Office" (Simmons)　43:412
At the Rendezvous of Victory (James)　33:223
"At the River" (Grace)　56:111, 118
"At the Sale" (Smith)　64:395
"At the San Francisco Airport" (Winters)
　4:591; 32:468

"At the Screen Door" (Komunyakaa) **86**:193;
    94:242
"At the Seashore" **75**:76
At the Shores (Rogers) **57**:367-68
"At the Sight of Last Night's Fire" (Davison)
    28:100
"At the Sink" (Szirtes) **46**:391
At the Speed of Sound (McCartney) **35**:283-
    86
"At the Springs of Orlu" (Le Guin) **45**:219
"At the Summary of a Passion" (Tchicaya)
    See "Au Sommaire d'une Passion"
"At the Swings" (Taylor) **44**:301
"At the Tolstoy Museum" (Barthelme) **3**:43;
    6:30; **46**:36, 40; **115**:56, 67-69, 80
"At the Tomb of the Czech Kings" (Seifert)
    93:335
"At the Typewriter" (Thesen) **56**:417
"At the Villa Madeira" (Ewart) **46**:150
At the Water Divide
    See *La cumpana apelor*
At the Watershed
    See *La cumpana apelor*
"At the Well" (Piercy) **27**:376
At the White Monument and Other Poems
    (Redgrove) **41**:347, 349
"At The Zoo" (Simon) **17**:459, 463
"At Thirteen" (Stevenson) **7**:462
"At This Moment of Time" (Schwartz) **45**:355
"At Thurgarton Church" (Barker) **48**:22
"At Times in Flight" (Roth) **104**:249, 251
"At Usk" (Norris) **14**:388
"At Walden Pond" (Skelton) **13**:506
At War with the U.S. (Bowering) **15**:84; **47**:28-
    9
At Weddings and Wakes (McDonald) **90**:236-
    34
*At West Point: The Men and Times of the United
    States Military Academy* (Fleming)
    37:122-23
"At What Time Will We Sell Everything?"
    (Zamora)
    See "A qué hora venderemos todo"
"At Will Rogers Beach" (Steele) **45**:366
"At Woodward's Garden: Resourcefulness Is
    More Than Understanding" (Frost) **4**:174
Atame! (*Tie Me Up, Tie Me Down*) (Almodovar)
    114:26, 32, 37, 55
Atarashii hito yo mezameyo (Oe) **36**:350
Der Atem (*The Breath*) (Bernhard) **32**:25;
    61:11
Atemwende (*Breath-Turning*) (Celan) **10**:101;
    19:90; **53**:72, 74, 76-7, 79-80, 82; **82**:32
El atentado (Ibarguengoitia) **37**:182-83
Athabasca (MacLean) **50**:348
"Athene's Song" (Boland) **67**:46; **113**:96, 109
"Athens Apartment" (Purdy) **6**:429
"Athens, Florence" (Thomas) **13**:544
Atheological Summa (Bataille)
    See *Somme athéologique*
"The Athlone Years" (Durcan) **43**:117
"At-Homeness in the Self" (Gregor) **9**:255
"The Atlantic" (Tomlinson) **45**:399
The Atlantic Abomination (Brunner) **8**:105
Atlantic City (Guare) **29**:205-06, 208; **67**:79,
    81, 86
"Atlantic Coast Reggae" (Jordan) **114**:161-62
"Atlantic Crossing" (Gustafson) **36**:216
Atlantic High (Buckley) **37**:61
Atlantis (Dudek) **11**:159-60; **19**:138
Atlantis (Powys) **7**:348-49; **46**:322-23
"Atlantis and the Department Store" (Avison)
    97:76, 89

Atlas (Borges) **44**:360; **48**:48
*An Atlas of the Difficult World: Poems. 1988-
    1991* (Rich) **73**:333-34, 336-37; **76**:208-
    20
Atlas Shrugged (Rand) **3**:423; **30**:293-303;
    44:448, 450-54; **79**:358-62, 365, 367,
    369-75, 389, 391-96
"Atmosphere Anthrax" (Rakosi) **47**:344
"Atmosphere in Weird Fiction" (Smith) **43**:421
Atom (Asimov) **76**:317
"Atom Heart Mother" (Pink Floyd) **35**:307
Atom Heart Mother (Pink Floyd) **35**:305-07,
    311
The Atom Station (Laxness)
    See *Alpýdubókin*
"Atomic Power" (Campbell) **32**:74
Atoms Today and Tomorrow (Hyde) **21**:172,
    175
Atómstödin (Laxness)
    See *Alpýdubókin*
"Atonal Blues" (Hope) **52**:209
The Atrocity Exhibition (*Love and Napalm:
    Export USA*) (Ballard) **3**:34; **6**:27; **14**:40-
    1; **36**:35-6, 46
"Atrophied Preface" (Burroughs) **15**:112
"Atsvut vesimha" ("Sadness and Joy")
    (Amichai) **116**:122
Attachments (Rossner) **9**:457-58; **29**:356
The Attack on Literature and Other Essays
    (Wellek) **28**:453-54
"An Attempt at an Explanation" (Sargeson)
    31:365
"An Attempt at Jealousy" (Raine) **103**:188,
    190
"An Attempt at Self-Criticism" (Castellanos)
    66:56
"An Attempt to Hold Back History" (Amichai)
    116:97
An Attempted Escape (Strugatskii and
    Strugatskii)
    See *Popytka k begstvu*
The Attempted Rescue: An Autobiography
    (Aickman) **57**:2
Attention (Moravia)
    See *L'attenzione*
L'attenzione (*Attention*; *The Lie*) (Moravia)
    2:292, 294; **7**:240-42, 244; **11**:383;
    46:284-85
Atti impuri (Pasolini) **106**:254-55
Attic (Dunn) **71**:132-35
"Attic Red-Figure Calyx, Revelling in Progress,
    circa 510 B.C." (Howard) **47**:170-71
"Attica State" (Lennon) **35**:264
"Attis; or, Something Missing" (Bunting)
    10:83-4; **47**:45, 52, 54
"Attitude" (Broumas) **73**:15-15
"Attitude" (Davies) **21**:105
"Attitude" (Keillor) **40**:274
"Attitude Dancing" (Simon) **26**:409-10
"Les attitudes spectrales" (Breton) **9**:127
"Attitudes toward Henry James" (Rahv) **24**:359
Attitudes toward History (Burke) **24**:125-27,
    133
"Attracta" (Trevor) **14**:536; **71**:327; **116**:338-
    39, 342, 360, 376, 383
"Attractive Modern Homes" (Bowen) **22**:67
"Au" (Lennon) **35**:265
Au bout du rouleau (Simenon) **47**:379
Au château d'Argol (Gracq) **11**:244-45;
    48:133-37, 140-42
*Au commencement était l'amour: Psychanalyse
    et foi* (*In the Beginning Was Love: Psy-
    choanalysis and Faith*) (Kristeva) **77**:314

Au hasard, Balthazar (Bresson) **16**:110-12,
    114
"Au Sommaire d'une Passion" ("At the Sum-
    mary of a Passion") (Tchicaya) **101**:351
"Au tombeau de Charles Fourier" (Davenport)
    38:140
"Au vieux jardin" (Aldington) **49**:16
"Aubade" (Empson) **8**:202; **19**:159; **34**:336
"Aubade" (Hoffman) **6**:243
"Aubade" (Larkin) **33**:262; **39**:335, 337, 339,
    341-44, 348; **64**:259-60, 263, 266-67,
    272, 280, 285
"Aubade" (MacNeice) **53**:234, 239
"Aubade: Harlem" (Merton) **83**:392
"Aubade: Lake Erie" (Merton) **83**:392
"Aubades" (Shapcott) **38**:400
"Aubade—The Annunciation" (Merton)
    83:391
L'aube (*Dawn*) (Wiesel) **3**:530; **5**:491
Aube à la saison (Brossard) **115**:102
"L'aube fille des larmes" (Bonnefoy) **58**:45
"Auckland" (Baxter) **14**:62
"Audacity" (Scott) **22**:373
"Audacity of the Lower Gods" (Komunyakaa)
    94:247
"Audenesque for an Initiation" (Ewart) **13**:208;
    46:153
"Auden's Funeral" (Spender) **41**:427-28
"The Audible Reading of Poetry" (Winters)
    4:592
"Audience" ("Interview") (Havel) **58**:237-38,
    240, 243
The Audience (Havel) **25**:224-25, 227, 230;
    65:413, 439-40
"Audience Dispersed" (Avison) **97**:128
"Audiencia privada" ("Private Audience") (Roa
    Bastos) **45**:346
Audrey Hepburn's Neck **99**:37-41
Audubon, A Vision (Warren) **6**:557-58; **8**:539;
    10:520-21; **13**:574, 576-77, 581-82;
    18:533, 536; **39**:259, 264, 266-68; **59**:296,
    298
Audun and the Polar Bear (Haavikko)
    See *Audun ja jääkarhu*
Audun ja jääkarhu (*Audun and the Polar Bear*)
    (Haavikko) **34**:170, 173
Auélien (Aragon) **22**:37
"Auf dass die Verfolgten nicht die Verfolger
    werden" (Sachs) **98**:328, 350
Auf dem Turm (*The Spectacle at the Tower*)
    (Hofmann) **54**:225-26, 228
Auf der Mantuleasa-Strasse (Eliade) **19**:147
"Aufenthalt in X" ("Sojourn in X") (Boell)
    72:69, 79
Aufsätze zur Literatur (Grass) **22**:195
*Der Auftrag oder Vom Beobachten des
    Beobachters der Beobachter: Novelle in
    vierundzwanzig Sätzen* (Duerrenmatt)
    102:80
Aufzeichnungen, 1942-48 (*Notes*) (Canetti)
    14:121-24; **25**:107-10, 114; **75**:127, 130-
    32, 134-35
"Die Augenbinde" (Lenz) **27**:257
Das Augenspiel: Lebensgeschichte 1931-1937
    (*The Play of the Eyes*) (Canetti) **75**:140,
    143-44, 146; **86**:297-99, 301-02
L'augmentation (Perec) **56**:257
"Auguiano Religious Articles Rosaries Statues"
    (Cisneros) **69**:153
"Auguries" (Livesay) **79**:338
"Augury" (Heaney) **7**:148
"August" (Carruth) **84**:136
"August" (Oliver) **34**:249; **98**:290, 298

"August" (Pasternak)   63:313
"August" (Rich)   3:429
"August" (Walker)   13:566
August (Rossner)   29:355-57
"August 19, Pad 19" (Swenson)   61:392
"August 22, 1939" (Rexroth)   22:345; 49:284;
   112:396
"August, 1914" (Masefield)   11:357-58;
   47:227, 233
August 1914 (Solzhenitsyn)
   See *Avgust chetyrnadtsatogo*
"August, 1940" (Fuller)   28:158
"August, 1968" (Auden)   3:29
"August 1974: A Tapestry" (Muske)   90:317
"August Afternoon" (Caldwell)   14:96
August August August (Kohout)   13:324
"August Eschenburg" (Millhauser)   54:324-25,
   327
"August for the People" (Auden)   43:16
August Is a Wicked Month (O'Brien)   5:313;
   116:178-79, 183, 185, 192-93, 227
"August Journal" (Hacker)   91:110-11
"August Moon" (Warren)   39:273
"August Night" (Swenson)   106:347
"August Saturday" (Trevor)   71:348
August Snow (Price)   63:325
"Augusta née Hoffman" (Suknaski)   19:434
"Augustine's Concubine" (Updike)   15:546
Augustus (MacLennan)   92:306
Aujourd'hui Michelet (Barthes)   24:32
Aún es de día (*Still It Is the Day*) (Delibes)
   18:111
"Aunt Creasy, on Work" (Williams)   13:600
Aunt Dan and Lemon (Shawn)   41:399-403
"Aunt Helen" (Eliot)   41:150
"Aunt Jennifer's Tigers" (Rich)   11:477; 18:445
Aunt Julia and the Scriptwriter (Vargas Llosa)
   See *La tiá Julia y el escribidor*
"Aunt Justina" (Cheever)   3:108
"Aunt Maggie, the Strong One" (Friel)   5:128
"Aunt Maria and the Gourds" (Davidson)
   13:170
"Aunt Mary" (Oliver)   98:266
"Aunt Rectita's Good Friday" (Kennedy)
   42:257
Aunts Aren't Gentlemen (Wodehouse)   5:517
The Aunt's Story (White)   3:522-23; 4:583-
   85; 5:486-87; 7:531; 18:544-45, 547;
   65:275-80, 282; 69:392-97, 399-401,
   405-08, 410-11
Aura (Fuentes)   8:222-23; 41:167, 169, 171-
   72; 60:158, 162; 113:242, 253
"Auras on the Interstate" (Vizenor)   103:301
"Aurelia Paris" (Duras)   68:90
Aurélia Steiner (Duras)
   See *Aurélia Steiner, dite Aurélia Vancouver*
Aurélia Steiner (Duras)
   See *Aurélia Steiner, dite Aurélia Melbourne*
Aurélia Steiner, dite Aurélia Melbourne (*Aurélia
   Steiner*) (Duras)   68:91-2, 96
Aurélia Steiner, dite Aurélia Vancouver (*Aurélia
   Steiner*) (Duras)   68:91-2, 96-7
"The Aurelian" (Nabokov)   1:242
The Aurochs
   See *Zubr*
"Aurora" (Morand)   41:295, 297, 308
Aurora (Fornes)   61:129, 132
Aurora (Leiris)   61:341
"Aurora Borealis" (Dove)   50:153, 157; 81:139
"Aurora Borealis" (Faludy)   42:140
Aurora Dawn (Wouk)   38:444-47
L'aurte par lui-même (Baudrillard)   60:24-5
Aus dem Leben der Marionetten (*From the Life*

of the Marionettes) (Bergman)   72:59, 61
Aus dem Leben eines Fauns: Kurzroman
   (*Scenes from the Life of a Faun*) (Schmidt)
   56:390-91, 403-05
Aus dem Tagebuch einer Schnecke (*From the
   Diary of a Snail*) (Grass)   2:174; 4:205-
   07; 6:208-09; 11:250; 15:262-63; 32:202;
   49:137, 140
"Aus dem Zweiten Reich" (Bunting)   10:83-4;
   47:45, 54
Aus der Fremde: Spredchoper in 7 szenen
   (Jandl)   34:196-97, 199-200
"Aus meinem Tagebuch" (Hildesheimer)   49:174
Auschwitz (Barnes)
   See *Laughter!*
Ausgefragt (*Cross-Examined*) (Grass)   32:198-
   200
Ausgewählte Gedichte (*Collected Poems*)
   (Eich)   15:204
Ausgewählte Gedichte (*Selected Poems*) (Sachs)
   98:322
"The Auspice of Jewels" (Riding)   7:375
"Auspicious Occasion" (Mistry)   71:270-71,
   273
Une aussi longue absence (Duras)   68:94
"Austerities" (Simic)   49:336; 68:373
Austerities (Simic)   49:335-37, 341, 343
"Australia" (Hope)   51:216, 221, 226
"An Australian Garden" (Porter)   33:320
Aut tunc aut Nunguam (Durrell)   13:185
"Author and Director: A Delicate Situation"
   (Williams)   45:446
"An Author and His Work" (Mauriac)   56:219
"The Author and the Hero in Aesthetic Activ-
   ity" (Bakhtin)   83:12
"The Author Apologizes to His Readers"
   (Barth)   14:50
Author from a Savage People (Pesetsky)
   28:359
"The Author in Truth" (Cixous)   92:81-2
"The Author of Christine" (Howard)   7:165
"The Author of the Acacia Seeds and Other
   Extracts from the 'Journal of the Asso-
   ciation of Therolinguistics'" (Le Guin)
   45:213, 216
"The Author to His Body on Their Fifteenth
   Birthday, 29 ii 80" (Nemerov)   36:306
"Authors and Writers" (Barthes)
   See "Écrivains et écrivants"
"The Author's Last Words to His Students"
   (Blunden)   56:40, 42
Auto da fé (Montale)   7:223, 228; 9:387
Auto do frade (*The Friar*; *The Friar's Way*)
   (Cabral de Melo Neto)   76:155-56, 160-
   62, 168
"Auto Wreck" (Shapiro)   15:476-77; 53:330,
   334
"Autobiografia in tempo di guerra" (Vittorini)
   9:549
"The Autobiographer as *Torero*" (Leiris)
   61:344
"Autobiographia literaria" (O'Hara)   13:424,
   427; 78:345-46, 365
"An Autobiographical Essay" (Borges)   48:33,
   35; 83:180
Autobiographical Fragment (Yglesias)   22:492
An Autobiographical Novel (Rexroth)   11:473;
   22:343-44; 49:276, 280, 289; 112:377,
   380, 386-87, 389, 400, 402, 404
Autobiographical Writings (Hesse)   2:190-91;
   17:216
Autobiographies (O'Casey)   15:405
"Autobiography" (Ferlinghetti)   6:184; 10:176-

77
"Autobiography" (Gunn)   18:199, 204; 81:177
"Autobiography" (Harjo)   83:272, 274
"Autobiography" (MacLeish)   8:362
"Autobiography" (MacNeice)   53:232
"Autobiography" (Seifert)   93:324
"Autobiography" (Steele)   45:362
An Autobiography (Brooks)   29:85
An Autobiography (Christie)   12:125; 39:439,
   443; 48:78; 110:125-26, 128
Autobiography (*Future Indefinite*) (Coward)
   51:76
An Autobiography (Davis)
   See *Angela Davis*
Autobiography (Frame)   96:219-20
Autobiography (Powys)   7:349; 9:439-40;
   15:433; 46:322
Autobiography (Trilling)   11:540
Autobiography (Zukofsky)   11:581-82; 18:557
Autobiography: A Novel (Rechy)   107:259
"Autobiography: A Self-Recorded Fiction"
   (Barth)   3:41; 9:66, 69; 51:23; 89:4-5, 8,
   11-12, 15-16, 19, 27-30, 32-3, 43, 50-2,
   57, 59, 61
"The Autobiography of a Dog" (Stuart)   34:376
The Autobiography of a Gorgon (Hall)   51:171
Autobiography of a Princess (Jhabvala)
   29:259-60; 94:187, 194
The Autobiography of LeRoi Jones (Baraka)
   115:10, 39
*The Autobiography of LeRoi Jones/Amiri
   Baraka* (Baraka)   33:60-2
The Autobiography of Malcolm X (Haley)
   8:259; 12:243-46; 76:345, 347-49, 352
The Autobiography of Malcolm X (Malcolm X)
   82:171, 173-76, 188-193, 195-201, 203-
   08, 210-14, 217-23, 226; 117:295, 299,
   301, 308, 317-18, 326-31, 340-41, 345-
   46, 350, 353-57, 359-61
The Autobiography of Miss Jane Pittman (*Miss
   Jane Pittman*) (Gaines)   3:179; 11:218;
   18:165, 167; 86:171, 173, 175-78
The Autobiography of My Mother (Brown)
   32:64-6, 68-9
"An Autobiography of Religious Development"
   (King)   83:338
The Autobiography of W. E. B. Du Bois (Du
   Bois)   96:138-39, 146-51
The Autobiography of William Carlos Williams
   (Williams)   22:465, 468-69; 42:452, 454,
   460-61
Autobiology (Bowering)   15:83; 47:23
"Autocar" (Roberts)   14:463
"Autocrítica" (Cabral de Melo Neto)   76:158
Auto-da-Fé (Canetti)
   See *Die Blendung*
"Automatic" (Prince)   35:328
Automatic Pilot (Ritter)   52:353-55, 357
"Automation Song" (Ochs)   17:333
The Automobile Graveyard (Arrabal)
   See *Le cimetière des voitures*
"The Automobile That Wouldn't Run"
   (Caldwell)   14:96
O automobilista Infundioso ("The *ndioso*
   Driver") (Cabral de Melo Neto)   76:168
Los autonautas de la cosmopista (*The
   Autonauts of the Cosmohighway*)
   (Cortazar)   34:329, 331
The Autonauts of the Cosmohighway (Cortazar)
   See *Los autonautas de la cosmopista*
"Autonomy" (Ammons)   57:53
"La autopista del sur" ("The Southern Thru-
   way") (Cortazar)   5:110; 13:158

"The Autopsy" (Elytis)   **49**:107, 113; **100**:156, 175, 192

"Autopsy Report 86-13504:" (Sapphire)   **99**:81

"The Autopsy Room" (Carver)   **55**:276

"Autorengespräch" (Hofmann)   **54**:225

Un autoritratto (Buzzati)   **36**:97

"Autorretrato" ("Self Portrait") (Castellanos)   **66**:53, 61

Autour de Mortin (Pinget)   **13**:442

L'autre (Chedid)   **47**:85

L'autre (*The Other One*) (Green)   **3**:205

L'autre (Green)   **77**:277-78

L'autre (Loewinsohn)   **52**:284-85

"Autre Fois" (Soupault)   **68**:406

L'autre sommeil (Green)   **11**:260; **77**:269, 276, 277

"Autres" (Guillevic)   **33**:194

Autres: Poèmes, 1969-1979 (Guillevic)   **33**:194

"Autumn" (Fugard)   **48**:109

"Autumn" (Ignatow)   **7**:182; **14**:275

"Autumn" (Landolfi)   **11**:321

"Autumn" (Larkin)   **64**:258

"Autumn" (Livesay)   **79**:333, 340

"Autumn" (Morrison)   **10**:354

"Autumn" (Neruda)
    See "Otoño"

"Autumn" (Pasternak)   **63**:313

"Autumn" (Shapcott)   **38**:402

"Autumn" (Voznesensky)   **57**:413, 415

Autumn (Mojtabai)   **29**:318-20

"Autumn 1980" (Hacker)   **72**:183-84

"Autumn Afternoon" (Farrell)   **66**:129, 131

An Autumn Afternoon (Ozu)   **16**:447-51, 454, 456

"Autumn Again" (Levine)   **14**:316

"Autumn Begins in Martins Ferry, Ohio" (Wright)   **3**:540; **28**:465

"The Autumn Bleat of the Weathervane Trombone" (Chappell)   **40**:144; **78**:91

"Autumn Chapter in a Novel" (Gunn)   **81**:185

"Autumn Chill"   **75**:76

Autumn Day (Pa Chin)
    See *Ch'iu*

"The Autumn Dog" (Theroux)   **11**:528

"Autumn Equinox" (Rich)   **6**:459

"Autumn Evening" (Merwin)   **88**:203

The Autumn Garden (Hellman)   **2**:187; **8**:281; **14**:255-60; **18**:221, 223-24; **34**:349, 351

"Autumn in California" (Rexroth)   **49**:277, 284; **112**:397

"Autumn in Florida" (Tremain)   **42**:385-86

An Autumn in Italy (O'Faolain)   **70**:315

"Autumn in Sigulda" (Voznesensky)   **57**:420

"Autumn in the Skerries" (Transtroemer)
    See "Höstlig skärgård"

Autumn Journal (MacNeice)   **1**:186; **4**:315-18; **10**:327; **53**:232-33, 235-37, 239-40, 243-44

Autumn Landscape (Cummings)   **15**:157

"Autumn Leaves" (Ginsberg)   **109**:329

"Autumn Madrigal" (Shapcott)   **38**:401

"Autumn Meadow" (Kis)   **57**:246

"Autumn of a Dormouse" (Gilliatt)   **53**:147

The Autumn of the Patriarch (Garcia Marquez)   **8**:232-33; **10**:215-17; **15**:254; **27**:147-48, 150-51, 153, 155-57; **47**:146-47, 151; **55**:139, 144-47

"Autumn on Nan-Yueh" (Empson)   **8**:202; **19**:152, 159

"An Autumn Park" (Gascoyne)   **45**:158

An Autumn Penitent (Callaghan)   **41**:89

The Autumn People (Arthur)   **12**:27, 29

Autumn Quail (Mahfuz)   **55**:181; **52**:304

"Autumn Scene" (Snodgrass)   **68**:397

"Autumn Sequel" (MacNeice)   **1**:186; **4**:317

Autumn Sequel: A Rhetorical Poem (MacNeice)   **1**:186; **4**:317; **10**:325; **53**:232-33, 240

"Autumn Shade" (Bowers)   **9**:121-22

Autumn Sonata (Bergman)
    See *Höstsonaten*

"Autumn Song" (Morrison)   **21**:234

"Autumn Song" (Watkins)   **43**:450

"Autumn Sunshine" (Trevor)   **71**:325; **116**:338, 342-43, 345, 385

Autumn Testament (Baxter)   **14**:66

Autumn to Autumn (Alvarez)   **13**:9

"Autumnal" (Scott)   **22**:372

"Autumnal Equinox on Mediterranean Beach" (Warren)   **13**:573

"Autumnal Sunset"   **75**:76

"Aux arbres" (Bonnefoy)   **58**:43

"Aux premiers âges" (Damas)   **84**:179

Available Light (Booth)   **23**:76

Available Light (Currie)   **44**:39-43

Available Light (Piercy)   **62**:377-79

Avalanche (Boyle)   **19**:62; **58**:64, 73, 75-6

Avalanche Express (Polonsky)   **92**:415

L'avalée des avalés (*The Swallower Swallowed*) (Ducharme)   **74**:56-7, 60-1

"Avalon" (Davidson)   **13**:168

Avanti (Wilder)   **20**:464-65

Avarice House (Green)
    See *Mont-Cinère*

The Avatar (Anderson)   **15**:15

"Avatars" (MacEwen)   **55**:163-64, 167, 169

"Avatars of the Tortoise" (Borges)   **10**:64; **83**:156, 160, 162

"Ave Luna, Morituri Te Salutant" (Faludy)   **42**:137, 140, 142

"Ave Maria" (O'Hara)   **78**:333, 354

"Ave Maria" (Tanizaki)   **28**:419

Ave Maria (Linney)   **51**:263

"Ave Regina Coelorum" (Hill)   **45**:180

L'avea (Adamov)   **25**:16

"Avelino Arredondo" (Borges)   **48**:41

L'avenir dure longtemps (*The Future Lasts a Long Time; The Future Lasts Forever*) (Althusser)   **106**:12, 16-17, 28, 31-2, 37-40, 42

l'Avenir est dans les oeufs (*The Future Is in Eggs*) (Ionesco)   **4**:251; **6**:248

La aventura de un fotógraf en La Plata (*The Adventures of a Photographer in La Plata*) (Bioy Casares)   **88**:91

Aventura en lo gris (*Adventure in Grey*) (Buero Vallejo)   **15**:101-03; **46**:98

Las aventuras de Robinson Crusoe (*Robinson Crusoe*) (Bunuel)   **16**:128-29, 148; **80**:23, 25, 28-9, 36

Aventuras sigilosas (*Quiet Adventures*) (Lezama Lima)   **101**:121

Les aventures d'Ori d'Or (Theriault)   **79**:412

"Äventyret" ("The Adventure") (Lagerkvist)   **54**:286

"The Avenue" (Muldoon)   **32**:320

"The Avenue Bearing the Initial of Christ into the New World" (Kinnell)   **5**:215-17; **13**:320, 322; **29**:280-82, 284, 289-90

The Avenue Bearing the Initial of Christ into the New World: Poems, 1946-1964 (Kinnell)   **5**:217-18; **13**:320-22; **29**:286

"The Avenue of Poplars" (Williams)   **42**:463

An Avenue of Stone (Johnson)   **1**:161; **27**:215-16

"Avenue of the Americas" (Simic)   **49**:343

"The Average Egyptian Faces Death" (Updike)   **23**:475

"Average Person" (McCartney)   **35**:292

"Averroes's Search" (Borges)
    See "La busca de Averroes"

"Avey" (Toomer)   **1**:341; **22**:425

Avgust chetyrnadtsatogo (*August 1914; Krasnoe koleso: Povestvovanie v otmerennykh srokakh. Uzel I, Avgust chetyrnadtsatogo; The Red Wheel, Knot I: August 1914*) (Solzhenitsyn)   **1**:321; **2**:408-13; **4**:508-12, 514-15; **7**:432-34, 436, 438, 442-45; **9**:503; **10**:479; **18**:498; **33**:483, 489-91; **34**:489; **59**:372-77; **78**:282, 398-99, 401, 413-21, 423

"Aviation" (Fulton)   **52**:160

The Aviator (Gann)   **23**:167-68

"Avie Loves Ric Forever" (Mazer)   **26**:295

"Avila" (West)   **96**:383

L'Aviva (Brossard)   **115**:120

"Avocado Lake" (Soto)   **80**:288

Avram Iancu   **75**:64-5, 67

Avril brisé (Kadare)
    See *Prilli i thyer*

Avsked till Hamlet (*Farewell to Hamlet*) (Johnson)   **14**:294

L'avventura (Antonioni)   **20**:19-21, 26, 31

The Awaited Sign (Buero Vallejo)
    See *La señal que se espera*

"Awaiting His Execution" (Ritsos)   **6**:464

"Awake" (Harrison)   **6**:223

Awake! and Other Wartime Poems (Rodgers)   **7**:377-78

Awake and Sing! (Odets)   **2**:318-19; **28**:323-30, 332-40; **98**:190, 193-95, 198-210, 212, 215-18, 220-25, 227-31, 234-40, 242, 245, 250, 252

Awake for Mourning (Kops)   **4**:274

Awake in Spain (O'Hara)   **78**:368-69

Awake in th Red Desert (Bissett)   **18**:60

Awaken, Bells Falling: Poems, 1959-1967 (Turco)   **11**:549-50; **63**:429-30

"Awakened before I Meant" (Corn)   **33**:116

"Awakening" (Borges)
    See "El despertar"

"Awakening" (Kunene)   **85**:175

"The Awakening" (Miller)   **14**:373

The Awakening Land (Richter)   **30**:324, 328

The Awakening of George Darroch (Jenkins)   **52**:230

"The Awakening of the Mummy" (Mahfuz)
    See "Yaqzat al mumya'"

"Awakening to Song Over Rooftops" (Transtroemer)   **65**:222-23

Awakenings (Sacks)   **67**:285, 287-91, 295-96, 298-99, 304

"Awatobi" (Lewis)   **41**:260-62

"Away!" (Frost)   **13**:227

"Away" (Miles)   **34**:245; **39**:354

Away (Creeley)   **36**:118

Away (Urquhart)   **90**:394-9, 402

"Away from It All" (Heaney)   **37**:169; **91**:118-19

"Away from the Numbers" (Weller)   **26**:443-44

Away from the Vicarage (Streatfeild)   **21**:408

"Away from Water" (Broumas)   **73**:9

"Away in Airdrie" (Kelman)   **58**:295

"Away, Melancholy" (Smith)   **25**:422-23

"The Away-Bound Train" (Murray)   **40**:340

"Awe and Devastation of Solomos" (Elytis)   **100**:189

"A-W-F Unlimited" (Herbert)   **44**:394

"Awful Music" (Merton)   **83**:384

The Awful Rowing Toward God (Sexton)
6:492-94; 8:484; 53:312, 319, 322

An Awfully Big Adventure (Bainbridge) 62:38-40

An Awkward Lie (Stewart) 14:512

Awlad haretna (*The Children of Gabalawi*; *Children of Our Neighborhood*) (Mahfuz)
52:294-95, 300-01; 55:171-76, 178, 183, 185

"Ax" (Simic) 49:339; 68:364

The Axe (Vaculik) 7:494-95

Axe Handles (Snyder) 32:395, 397, 400

Axe Time, Sword Time (Corcoran) 17:76-7

"Axel" (Nye) 42:304

Axel's Castle: A Study in the Imaginative Literature of 1870-1930 (Wilson) 1:372-73; 2:475; 3:538; 8:550; 24:464-70, 472-74, 478-81, 483-86

The Axe's Edge (Gunnars) 69:264

"The Ax-Helve" (Frost) 10:197; 26:112

The Axion Esti (*Worthy It Is*) (Elytis) 49:114; 100:155-56, 158-63, 165, 167, 170, 175, 181, 183-84, 187-88, 190, 192

"Axis" (Paz) 51:334-35

"Axolotl" (Cortazar) 33:123, 131-32; 34:331-32

"Ay negra, si tu supiera" ("Aye, Black Lover, If You Only Knew"; "If You Only Knew..."; "Si tú supiera") (Guillen) 48:161; 79:245-46

"Aye, and Gomorrah" (Delany) 38:154

"Aye, Black Lover, If You Only Knew" (Guillen)
See "Ay negra, si tu supiera"

"Ayer me dijeron negro" ("Yesterday I Was Called Nigger") (Guillen) 48:161

The Aylwin's (Stewart) 7:466

Ázma iroikó ke pénthimo yia ton haméno anthipolohaghó tis Alvanías (*Heroic and Elegiac Song for the Lost Second Lieutenant of the Alb nian Campaign*) (Elytis) 49:106-07, 114-15

Azrael (*Twelve Poems*) (Warner) 19:460

"Aztec" (McIntyre) 18:327

"Aztec Angel" (Salinas) 90:324, 327

"The Azure Steppe" (Sholokhov) 7:417

"B" (Merrill) 8:383-84

B (Figes) 31:163

"B/ Betty Boop/ Boop-boop-a-doop/ Babel/ Bable" (Sorrentino) 7:449

"B. C." (Moss) 7:250

"B Negative" (Kennedy) 42:254

"B. W., 1916-1979" (Cage) 41:86

Baal Babylone (Arrabal) 9:33; 18:18; 58:4, 6-7, 9-11

Der Baal tshuve (Singer)
See *Der Bal-tshuve*

Baalbec, a Stain (Benet)
See *Baalbec, una mancha*

Baalbec, una mancha (*Baalbec, a Stain*) (Benet) 28:23

Baba Goya (*Nourish the Beast*) (Tesich) 40:418-19, 421-22

"Baba O'Reilly" (Townshend) 17:532, 535

"Las babas del diablo" ("Blow-Up"; "The Devil's Spittle") (Cortazar) 2:103; 3:115; 13:158; 15:146, 148; 33:125, 132-34, 136; 92:149

Babble (Baumbach) 23:55

Babbling April (Greene) 70:292

Babe (Wiggins) 57:430, 439

"Babe I'm Gonna Leave You" (Page and Plant) 12:482

"Babel" (Simon) 39:209

Babel (Smith) 12:541-42

Babel to Byzantium (Dickey) 7:79; 47:97; 109:245

Babel-17 (Delany) 14:146; 38:149-50, 153-54, 160-62

"Babelogue" (Smith) 12:543

"Babel's Children" (Barker) 52:55

Babes and Sucklings (Wylie) 43:460, 469

The Babe's Bed (Wescott) 13:592

"Babette's Feast" (Dinesen) 10:150

"Babi Yar" (Yevtushenko) 3:547; 13:620; 26:461, 464; 51:428, 431

"Babies" (Fulton) 52:161

"The Babies" (Strand) 18:519; 41:431; 71:283

"Babocka" ("The Butterfly") (Brodsky) 13:117; 36:76, 78; 50:124-25, 131

"Baboons in the Perennial Bed" (Piercy) 62:378

"Baby" (Barthelme) 59:250

"Baby" (Campbell) 42:88-9

"Baby" (Sontag) 13:517

"Baby Blue" (O'Brien) 13:416; 116:208, 210

Baby Breakdown (Waldman) 7:507

Baby, Come on Inside (Wagoner) 3:508

"Baby Department" (Redgrove) 41:354

"Baby Doll" (Berry) 17:54

Baby Doll (Kazan) 16:366, 368, 373-74; 63:233, 235

Baby Doll (Williams) 39:446

"Baby Driver" (Simon) 17:460-61, 465

"Baby Face" (Reed) 21:309

"Baby I" (Armatrading) 17:10

"Baby I'm a Star" (Prince) 35:329

The Baby in the Icebox and Other Short Fiction (Cain) 28:54

Baby Is Three (Sturgeon) 22:410; 39:361, 364-66

Baby, It's Cold Inside (Perelman) 3:382; 5:337; 23:337; 49:269, 272

Baby Love (Edgar) 42:116, 124

Baby Love (Maynard) 23:289-91

"Baby Pictures" (Giles) 39:64-5

"Baby Pictures of Famous Dictators" (Simic) 68:378

"Baby Sister" (Himes) 4:229; 18:249

Baby Snakes (Zappa) 17:594

Baby, the Rain Must Fall (Foote) 51:131

"Baby V" (Levine)
See "Baby Villon"

"Baby Villon" ("Baby V") (Levine) 4:287; 5:252; 9:332; 33:273

Baby with the Bathwater (Durang) 38:170-74

"Baby You're a Rich Man" (Lennon and McCartney) 12:360

Babycakes (Maupin) 95:192, 194-97, 199, 201, 203, 208

"Babylon" (Herbert) 43:191

"Babylon" (Simic) 68:377

"Babylon" (Tolson) 105:288

Babylon by Bus (Marley) 17:272

"The Babylon Lottery" (Borges)
See "La lotería en Babilonia"

"Babylon Revisited" (Baraka) 5:48

"Babylon Sisters" (Becker and Fagen) 26:85

"Babylonish Dialects" (Raine) 103:197

"A Baby's Mouth" (Peterkin) 31:306-08

"The Babysitter" (Coover) 7:58

"The Babysitters" (Klappert) 57:256-59, 265

"The Babysitters" (Plath) 5:345; 51:344

"Baby-Sitting" (Clarke) 61:73-4

"Baccalaureate" (MacLeish) 8:362

The Bacchae of Euripides: A Communion Rite (Soyinka) 36:412; 44:298

"Bacchus" (Empson) 3:147; 8:202; 19:156; 33:142

Bacchus (Cocteau) 15:134; 43:104-06, 112

"Bachanale" (Hayden) 37:156

"The Bachelor" (O'Brien) 36:336; 116:186

Bachelor Girls (Wasserstein) 90:429-30, 432, 435, 437

The Bachelor of Arts (Narayan) 7:255; 28:291, 299

Bachelorhood: Tales of the Metropolis (Lopate) 29:300-02

"Bachelors" (Williams) 42:443

The Bachelors (Montherlant) 19:324-25

The Bachelors (Spark) 2:417; 3:466; 13:520-522; 18:501; 40:398, 400; 94:326, 328-29, 332

Bachelors Anonymous (Wodehouse) 5:516-17

"The Bachelor's Dilemma" (Gold) 42:189

Back (Green) 2:178; 13:252, 255; 97:243, 245-47, 249, 254-55, 257, 270, 279, 282-83, 288-90, 293

"Back Again, Home" (Madhubuti) 6:313; 73:194, 199, 207

Back Bog Beast Bait (Shepard) 4:489-90; 17:443

The Back Country (Snyder) 1:318; 2:406; 5:393-95; 9:500; 32:387-88, 391-92, 396, 399

"Back Door Man" (Morrison) 17:287, 292

"Back Down to Earth" (Simon) 26:411

"Back from Australia" (Betjeman) 43:46

"Back from Java" (Aldiss) 40:19

"Back from teh Market" (Boland) 113:96

"Back Gate" (Cabral de Melo Neto)
See "Postigo"

"Back Home" (Berry) 17:51

"Back Home in Pompeii" (Ciardi) 40:158; 44:382

"Back in '72" (Seger) 35:379

Back in '72 (Seger) 35:379-80

"Back in the U.S.S.R." (Lennon and McCartney) 12:379

Back in the World (Wolff) 64:450-54, 456-57

The Back of the North Wind (Freeling) 38:187-88

"Back Seat of My Car" (McCartney) 12:372; 35:279

"Back Street Girl" (Jagger and Richard) 17:230, 234-35, 238

Back Talk (Weidman) 7:517

"Back Then" (Komunyakaa) 94:246-47

"Back to Africa" (Bennett) 28:26-7, 29

Back to Barter 81:275

"Back to China" (Fiedler) 4:160

"Back to Kentucky" (Ferron) 94:103

"Back to Life" (Gunn) 32:208

"Back to Tahiti" (Honig) 33:213

"Back to the Basics of Love" (Jennings)
See "Luckenbach, Texas"

"Back to the Beast" (Wellman) 49:391

Back to the Egg (McCartney) 35:286-88

"Back to the Land" (Davis) 49:91

Back to the Night (Armatrading) 17:7

"Back to Val d'Or" (Ferron) 94:103

"Backatcha" (Robinson) 21:346

"Backcasting" (Ammons) 57:53

"Background, Casually" (Ezekiel) 61:107

Background in Tennessee (Scott) 43:382-85

Background to Danger (Ambler) 4:18; 6:2, 3; 9:19

Background with Chorus (Swinnerton) 31:426

"Background with Revolutionaries" (MacLeish)

68:281

"Backlands" (Dorfman) **77**:141-45

"The Backlash Blues" (Hughes) **15**:292

"Backside to the Wind" (Durcan) **43**:114

"Backstreets" (Springsteen) **17**:480, 484, 489

"Backsweep/Black" (Blackburn) **43**:65

Backtrack (Hansen) **38**:239

"The Backward Look" (Heaney) **7**:148

"The Backward Look" (Nemerov) **9**:395

The Backward Look (O'Connor) **14**:397

A Backward Place (Jhabvala) **4**:258; **29**:253, 255-57, 259-60; **94**:166, 169-70, 176-70, 181, 203

The Backward Shadow (Banks) **23**:41

"Backwards Traveller" (McCartney) **35**:288

"Backwaters" (Dunn) **40**:167

"Backyard Dramas with Mamas" (Loewinsohn) **52**:285

"Bad" (Matthews) **40**:324-25

Bad Apple (Bograd) **35**:63-4

Bad Attitudes (Carr) **86**:47

Bad Behavior (Gaitskill) **69**:198-206

Bad Blood (Tchicaya)
  See *Le Mauvais Sang*

"Bad Boats" (Jensen) **37**:190

Bad Boats (Jensen) **37**:186-92

Bad Boy (Thompson) **69**:383-84, 388

Bad Boys (Cisneros) **69**:151

"Bad Characters" (Stafford) **19**:431; **68**:423, 437

Bad Characters (Stafford) **68**:431, 435

"Bad Company" (Gallagher) **63**:121

Bad Connections (Johnson) **58**:283-855

A Bad Day for Sales (Leiber) **25**:301

Bad Debts (Wolff) **41**:454-55, 457, 460

"Bad Dogs" (Sayles) **14**:483

"Bad Dreams" (Taylor) **18**:523; **37**:409, 411

"A Bad Example" (Maugham) **67**:220

"The Bad Girl" (Vollmann) **89**:296

Bad Habits (McNally) **4**:347; **7**:218-19; **41**:292

"A Bad Heart" (Rendell) **28**:384

The Bad Infinity (Wellman) **65**:242

Bad Luck under the Roof (Kohout) **13**:325

A Bad Man (Elkin) **4**:153-54; **6**:169; **9**:190; **27**:122-23; **51**:85, 88, 100; **91**:213

"A Bad Memory Block" (Moravia) **46**:286

"The Bad Music" (Jarrell) **13**:299

"Bad News" (Atwood) **84**:104

"A Bad Night: A Lexical Exercise" (Auden) **6**:19; **43**:27

"The Bad Old Days" (Rexroth) **112**:400

BAD: or, the Dumbing of America (Fussell) **74**:140-41, 143, 145-47

Bad Penny (Wellman) **65**:239, 241-42

The Bad Place (Koontz) **78**:218

The Bad Sister (Tennant) **13**:537; **52**:397

The Bad Sleep Well (Kurosawa) **16**:399, 401-03

"Bad Vision at the Skagit" (Hugo) **32**:242

Badenheim, 1939 (Appelfeld) **23**:35-7; **47**:2-4, 6-7

"The Badgers" (Heaney) **14**:246; **25**:247

"The Badgers" (Heaney) **74**:159

The Badgers (Leonov)
  See *Barsuki*

"Badlands" (Springsteen) **17**:483-86

Badlands (Kroetsch) **23**:271; **57**:282-84, 288-91

Badly Sings the Nightingale (Seifert) **34**:259

Badon Parchments (Masefield) **11**:357

The Bag (Yurick) **6**:583

Baga (Pinget) **13**:442; **37**:360

"La bagarede" (Kinnell) **5**:216

"Bagatelles" (Spender) **5**:401

"Bagatelles" (Tomlinson) **45**:393

Bagatelles pour un massacre (*Trifles for a Massacre*) (Celine) **47**:79

Bagdad Saloon (Walker) **61**:424-28

"The Bagel" (Ignatow) **7**:178

"Bagel Shop Jazz" (Kaufman) **49**:203

"The Bagful of Dreams" (Vance) **35**:428

"Baggs" (Blackburn) **43**:65, 69

The Bagman (Arden) **15**:21

"Bagpipe Music" (MacNeice) **53**:235

"Bagpipe Music" (Simmons) **43**:409

"The Bagpiping People" (Dunn) **40**:171

"Bahia, Brazil" (Carver) **53**:61

Bahia de todos os santos (Amado) **106**:57, 62

La Baie des anges (Gallo) **95**:98

Uma bailadora Sevilhana (Cabral de Melo Neto) **76**:161

"A bailarina" ("The Dancer") (Cabral de Melo Neto) **76**:151

"The Bailbondsman" (Elkin) **6**:169; **14**:157-58; **27**:122; **51**:101

The Bailbondsman (Elkin) **91**:216

Bailegangaire (Murphy) **51**:307-08

"Le baiser" (Char) **9**:163

Le baiser au lépreux (*The Kiss to the Leper*) (Mauriac) **4**:341; **9**:367-68; **56**:204-06, 214, 217, 219

Baisers volés (*Stolen Kisses*) (Truffaut) **20**:385, 391-92, 397, 399; **101**:382, 386, 388, 390, 396, 398, 400, 410-11, 413

"Bait" (Heaney) **14**:243

"Baja" (Stern) **40**:414

"Baked Potatoes" (Urdang) **47**:399

Baker Street at Sunset (Steele) **45**:362

The Baker, the Baker's Wife, and the Little Baker's Boy (Anouilh)
  See *Le boulanger, la boulangère, et le petit mitron*

"The Bakery Poems" (Blackburn) **43**:62-3

Bakunin: Eine Invention (Bienek) **11**:48

Le bal des voleurs (*Thieves' Carnival*) (Anouilh) **3**:11; **8**:24; **13**:16; **40**:54, 57; **50**:279

"La balada azul" (Guillen) **79**:251

Balada de Atta Troll (Casona) **49**:40

"Balada de los dos abuelos" ("Ballad of the Two Grandfathers") (Guillen) **48**:162, 168; **79**:230, 232, 237, 248-49

"Balada del güje" ("Ballad of the Güije"; "Ballad of the River Spirit") (Guillen) **79**:231, 237, 248

Balade Petrice Kerempuha (*The Ballads of Petrica Kerempuh*) (Krleza) **114**:167, 176, 185-86

"Balakirevs dröm" (Transtroemer) **52**:409

"Balalaika" (Dubie) **36**:130

"The Balance" (Sherwin) **7**:415

"The Balance" (Waugh) **107**:392-93

"Balance His, Swing Yours" (Stegner) **81**:346

Balance of Terror (Shaffer) **14**:484

"Balances" (Giovanni) **19**:191

Balancing Acts (Schwartz) **31**:389-90

Balancing Acts: Contemporary Stories by Russian Women (Goscilo) **59**:370-71, 379

"Balboa, The Entertainer" (Baraka) **115**:40

Le balcon (*The Balcony*) (Genet) **1**:115; **2**:157-58; **5**:136-37; **10**:224-25, 227; **14**:198, 203, 205; **44**:385-90; **46**:172-73

Un balcon en forêt (Gracq) **11**:245; **48**:136, 139-41

"Balcony" (Bromell) **5**:74

The Balcony (Genet)
  See *Le balcon*

"The Bald Primaqueera" (O'Casey) **88**:260, 262

The Bald Soprano (Ionesco)
  See *La cantatrice chauve*

Baldur's Gate (Clark) **19**:105-06

"La baleine" (Theriault) **79**:408

"The Balek Scales" (Boell)
  See "Die Waage der Baleks"

Balkan Trilogy (Manning) **5**:271; **19**:301, 304

A Ball of Malt and Madame Butterfly: A Dozen Stories (Kiely) **23**:260; **43**:239

"Ballad" (Ammons) **8**:14; **9**:29; **108**:12

"Ballad" (Cohen) **38**:131

The Ballad and the Source (Lehmann) **5**:235, 238

La ballad du grand macabre (Ghelderode) **11**:226

A Ballad for Hogskin Hill (Forman) **21**:122

"Ballad from Childhood" (Lorde) **71**:251

"Ballad of a Marriage" (Simmons) **43**:406, 413-14

Ballad of a Stonepicker (Ryga) **14**:472-73

"Ballad of a Sweet Dream of Peace" (Warren) **13**:575

"Ballad of a Thin Man" (Dylan) **77**:174-76, 179-81

"The Ballad of Barnaby" (Auden) **6**:18, 21

"A Ballad of Beauty and Time" (Boland) **113**:124

The Ballad of Benny Perhaps (Brinsmead) **21**:33

"The Ballad of Billie Potts" (Warren) **4**:578-80; **8**:539; **13**:573-76; **39**:264; **59**:298-99

"The Ballad of Billy the Kid" (Joel) **26**:213, 218

"The Ballad of Birmingham" (Randall) **1**:283

"The Ballad of Blossom" (Van Duyn) **116**:410

The Ballad of Cable Hogue (Peckinpah) **20**:275-79, 282-84

"The Ballad of Chocolate Mabbie" (Brooks) **49**:22

"A Ballad of Despair" (Skelton) **13**:507

The Ballad of Dingus Magee (Markson) **67**:191-92, 194, 197

"Ballad of Donald White" (Dylan) **77**:166

"The Ballad of Erse O. Reilly" (Ewart) **46**:151

"The Ballad of Gerry Kelly: Newsagent" (Simmons) **43**:411-12

"Ballad of Henry, Bridegroom" (Jacobsen) **48**:190

"Ballad of Hollis Brown" (Dylan) **12**:180; **77**:166

"A Ballad of Home" (Boland) **113**:108

"Ballad of Jarvis Street" (Johnston) **51**:243

"The Ballad of Jesse Neighbors" (Humphrey) **45**:203-04

"The Ballad of Jimmy Governor" (Murray) **40**:336, 340

"Ballad of John Cable and Three Gentlemen" (Merwin) **88**:205

"A Ballad of Johnnie Question" (Skelton) **13**:507

"Ballad of Ladies Lost and Found" (Hacker) **72**:182-85, 190

"Ballad of Longwood Glen" (Nabokov) **8**:407

"The Ballad of Lord Timbal" (Fuller) **62**:184, 185

"Ballad of Mary's Son" (Hughes) **108**:299

"Ballad of Me" (Livesay) **79**:338, 341, 350

"Ballad of Mister Dutcher and the Last Lynching in Gupton" (Warren) **6**:556; **8**:537

"Ballad of Mr. Chubb" (Birney) **6**:75

"The Ballad of Nat Turner" (Hayden) **5**:168; **9**:270; **37**:155

"A Ballad of Nuggets" (Yevtushenko) **26**:464

"Ballad of Oedipus Sex" (Abse) **29**:16

"A Ballad of Oyo" (Mphahlele) **25**:339

"Ballad of Pearl May Lee" (Brooks) **49**:22

The Ballad of Peckham Rye (Spark) **2**:414, 416; **3**:466; **8**:493; **13**:521, 523; **18**:501; **40**:393; **94**:326-28, 331-33

A Ballad of Remembrance (Hayden) **5**:168; **14**:241; **37**:156-57, 159-60

"Ballad of Simón Caraballo" (Guillen) **48**:164, 166

The Ballad of Soapy Smith (Weller) **53**:391-92

"The Ballad of Sue Ellen Westerfield" (Hayden) **14**:240

"Ballad of Sweeney Todd" (Sondheim) **30**:394, 397-98

"The Ballad of the Black Cloud" (Grass) **32**:200

"Ballad of the Carpenter" (Ochs) **17**:331

"The Ballad of the Children of the Czar" (Schwartz) **10**:465; **87**:336

"Ballad of the Crucified Rose" (MacDiarmid) **63**:252

"Ballad of the Despairing Husband" (Creeley) **36**:122

"The Ballad of the Flint" (Christie) **110**:127

"Ballad of the Full Stop" (Voznesensky) **57**:413

Ballad of the Ghost Train (*Ballad of the Phantom Train*) (Arrabal) **58**:23, 27

"Ballad of the Girl Whose Name Is Mud" (Hughes) **108**:330

"A Ballad of the Good Lord Baden-Powell" (Ewart) **46**:151

"Ballad of the Güije" (Guillen)
See "Balada del güje"

"The Ballad of the Hell Hound" (Faludy) **42**:141

"Ballad of the Hoppy Toad" (Walker) **1**:351

"Ballad of the Icondic" (Ciardi) **44**:383

"A Ballad of the Investiture, 1969" (Betjeman) **10**:53

"Ballad of the Landlord" (Hughes) **35**:222

"Ballad of the Lord and Columbus" (McGinley) **14**:366

"Ballad of the Mari Lwyd" (Watkins) **43**:441, 445-46, 450-51, 454-56

Ballad of the Mari Lwyd and Other Poems (Watkins) **43**:440-43, 448-49, 453-54, 457

"Ballad of the Outer Dark" (Watkins) **43**:454-56

Ballad of the Outer Dark and Other Poems (Watkins) **43**:457

Ballad of the Phantom Train (Arrabal)
See *Ballad of the Ghost Train*

"Ballad of the Rattlesnake" (Tolson) **36**:427; **105**:231, 260

"Ballad of the River Spirit" (Guillen)
See "Balada del güje"

The Ballad of the Sad Café (Albee) **2**:2; **5**:13; **9**:5; **13**:5; **25**:38; **86**:120

The Ballad of the Sad Café (McCullers) **100**:245-46, 249-50, 252, 254-56, 259-64

The Ballad of the Sad Cafe: The Novels and Stories of Carson McCullers (McCullers) **1**:207-09; **4**:345-46; **10**:338-39; **12**:412-13, 415-16, 418, 421, 424, 426-29, 431-32; **48**:235, 241; **100**:260

"Ballad of the Two Grandfathers" (Guillen)
See "Balada de los dos abuelos"

"The Ballad of the Wall" (Ratushinskaya) **54**:385

"Ballad of the World Extinct" (Celan)
See "Ballade von der erloschenen Welt"

The Ballad of Typhoid Mary (Federspiel) **42**:143-44, 146

"The Ballad of U.S. Steel" (Ochs) **17**:333

"The Ballad of William Worthy" (Ochs) **17**:324-30

"Ballad of Your Puzzlement" (Warren) **18**:539

"The Ballad of Yucca Flats" (Barker) **48**:18

"The Ballad Trap" (Murray) **40**:335

Ballada raboty (Voznesensky) **15**:555-56

"Ballade for Braque" (Deutsch) **18**:120

"A Ballade for Mr. Rhodes" (Cassity) **42**:95

"Ballade for the Duke of Orleans" (Wilbur) **53**:405

"Ballade of Lost Objects" (McGinley) **14**:367

"Ballade of the Sayings" (Merwin) **88**:205

"Ballade un peu banale" (Smith) **15**:515

"Ballade vom Auszug der drei" (Celan) **82**:54

"Ballade von der erloschenen Welt" ("Ballad of the World Extinct") (Celan) **82**:52-3

Ballads and Poems (Masefield) **47**:227

The Ballads of Petrica Kerempuh (Krleza)
See *Balade Petrice Kerempuha*

The Ballads of Villon (Faludy) **42**:139

"The Ballast Hole" (Blunden) **56**:52

Ballet Fever (Cavanna)
See *Take a Call, Topsy*

The Ballet or the Bullet (Malcolm X) **82**:228; **117**:354

Ballet Shoes (Streatfeild) **21**:396-97, 403, 405-07, 412-13, 416

Ballets sans musique, sans personne, sans rien (Celine) **47**:72

"The Balloon" (Barthelme) **13**:55; **46**:35

Balloon (Colum) **28**:88-9

"Balloon over the Rhondda" (Mathias) **45**:235

The Balloonist (Harris) **9**:261

"Balloons" (Plath) **9**:426, 428; **17**:360; **51**:342; **111**:167, 175

"The Ballroom at Sandover" (Merrill) **34**:229

"Ballroom Dancing" (McCartney) **35**:290-91, 293

"The Ballroom of Romance" (Trevor) **71**:339; **116**:332, 357, 363, 372, 376, 385

The Ballroom of Romance, and Other Stories (Trevor) **7**:476-77; **71**:322, 324; **116**:331-32, 374

"Balls-Up" (Epstein) **39**:465

Balm in Gilead (Wilson) **36**:465-66

Balthazar (Durrell) **1**:87; **4**:144, 146; **8**:191-92; **13**:185-86; **41**:136

"Balthazar's Marvelous Afternoon" (Garcia Marquez)
See "La prodigiosa tarde de Baltazar"

The Balthus Poems (Dobyns) **37**:79-81

"The Baltic Night" (Morand) **41**:297

"Baltics" (Transtroemer) **65**:224, 237

Baltics (Transtroemer)
See *Österjöar*

The Baltimore Waltz (Vogel) **76**:262-69

Der Bal-tshuve (*Der Baal tshuve*; *The Penitent*) (Singer) **38**:410-12; **69**:306-07, 315

Balún-Canán (*The Nine Guardians*) (Castellanos) **66**:43, 48-9, 60-1

"Balzac" (Carver) **36**:100

Balzac's Horse (Hofmann) **54**:229

La Bamba (Valdez) **84**:403-04, 407-08, 415

Bambi (Prince) **35**:323

I bambini ci guardano (De Sica) **20**:89, 91-2

"Bambini della creazione" (Ortese) **89**:194

"Bananafish" (Salinger)
See "Bananafish"

Bananas (Allen) **16**:2-5, 15-17; **52**:45

"Bananas-Slide" (Asturias) **8**:25

"Band Concert" (Sandburg) **10**:450

"Band Music" (Fuller) **62**:184

Band of Angels (Warren) **4**:581; **8**:540; **53**:366; **59**:298

"The Band of Hope" (Kelman) **58**:302

Band of Outsiders (Godard)
See *Bande à part*

"Band on the Run" (McCartney) **35**:282-84

Band on the Run (McCartney) **12**:377, 380; **35**:282-86, 291

The Band Rotunda (Baxter) **14**:65

Bande à part (*Band of Outsiders*) (Godard) **20**:131, 138

Bandicoot (Condon) **10**:111

Bandido! (Valdez) **84**:414, 416-17

Bandits (Leonard) **71**:214-17, 219-21, 223, 225

Bandits (Taylor) **27**:441, 444

"Bandit's Wives" (Jiles) **58**:276-77

"Bandung Conference" (Malcolm X) **117**:354

"Banff: An Exercise in Political Astronomy" (Avison) **97**:76

"Bang" (Muldoon) **32**:319

Bang the Drum Slowly (Harris) **19**:200, 203

"Bang-Bang You're Dead" (Spark) **8**:493; **40**:402

"Banging on My Drum" (Reed) **21**:312-13

Banished Children of Eve: A Novel of Civil War in New York (Quinn) **91**:72-85

"The Banished Gods" (Mahon) **27**:287-88

"The Banished One" (Agnon)
See "Ha nidah"

"Bank Holiday" (McGahern) **48**:273

Bank Shot (Westlake) **7**:528; **33**:438-40

Banker (Francis) **42**:151-52, 155; **102**:131, 160

Banket u Blitvi (*Banquet in Blithuania*) (Krleza) **8**:329; **114**:168, 176-77, 186

"Banking Potatoes" (Komunyakaa) **94**:241

"Bankrobber" (Clash) **30**:47-8

"Banks of a Stream Where Creatures Bathe" (Merrill) **13**:381

Le Banlieue de Paris (Cendrars) **106**:167, 173

"Banneker" (Dove) **81**:133, 137

Banners (Deutsch) **18**:118

The Banners (Krleza)
See *Zastave*

The Banquet (Slaughter) **56**:411

Banquet in Blithuania (Krleza)
See *Banket u Blitvi*

"The Banquet of Crow" (Parker) **68**:335

"Bans o' Killing" (Bennett) **28**:29-30

"Banyan" (Swenson) **61**:403

"The Banyan Tree, Old Year's Night" (Walcott) **76**:286

"A Baobab Tree in Recife" (Cabral de Melo Neto)
See "Um boabá no Recife"

"The Baptism" (Bishop) **32**:40

The Baptism (Baraka) **33**:59

Baptismal (Tesich) **40**:421

"Baptizing" (Munro) **95**:294, 304

"Bar Italia" (Williams) **42**:443

"Bar Mitzvah" (Goldemberg) **52**:165

Barabbas (Lagerkvist) **54**:271, 275, 278-83, 285; **7**:198-99, 201; **10**:311-12; **13**:330

"Baraka pet be" ("Hut Five B") (Krleza) **114**:167

"Barbados" (Marshall) **27**:311-12; **72**:227, 248

"Barbara" (Prevert)   15:438
"Barbara Ann" (Wilson)   12:647
Un barbare en Asie (*A Barbarian in Asia*) (Michaux)   8:392
The Barbarian and the Geisha (Huston)   20:163
A Barbarian in Asia (Michaux)
   See *Un barbare en Asie*
Barbarian in the Garden (Herbert)
   See *Barbarzynca w ogrodzie*
"Barbarian Pastorals" (Dunn)   40:168
"The Barbarians" (Highsmith)   102:203
Barbarians (Dunn)   40:167-68, 171
The Barbarous Coast (Macdonald)   14:333; 41:267, 272
Barbarous Knowledge (Hoffman)   6:242; 23:240
The Barbary Light (Newby)   2:310
Barbary Shore (Mailer)   1:187-92; 2:258, 263; 3:311, 315; 4:319, 323; 8:364, 368-69, 373; 11:342-43; 28:256-57; 74:203-04, 206-07, 221-22, 224; 111:94, 101, 108, 113, 136
Barbarzynca w ogrodzie (*Barbarian in the Garden*) (Herbert)   9:275; 43:184, 189-90, 192-94
La barbe de François Hertel (Ferron)   94:114
Barbe-Bleue (Tournier)   95:379, 381
"The Barbecue" (Dixon)   52:98
Barbedor (Tournier)   95:369
"The Barber" (O'Connor)   3:366
"The Barber" (Raine)   103:186
"The Barber of Bariga" (Mphahlele)   25:339
"The Barber Whose Uncle Had His Head Bitten Off by a Circus Tiger" (Saroyan)   29:363
The Barber's Trade Union and Other Stories (Anand)   93:57
"Barbie" (Soto)   80:298
"Barbie-Q" (Cisneros)   69:153, 155
A barca dos homens (*The Ship of Men*) (Dourado)   23:150; 60:85-9, 91-2
La barca sin pescador (Casona)   49:44, 46-8
Barcarole (Neruda)   28:313-15
The Barclay Family Theatre (Hodgins)   23:235
"Bardon Bus" (Munro)   95:305-06, 315, 318, 325
"The Bare Arms in Packing Cases" (Mahapatra)   33:277
"Barefoot and Pregnant" (Armatrading)   17:10
"Barefoot and Pregnant in Des Moines" (Kinsella)   43:253, 255-56
Barefoot in the Head: A European Fantasia (Aldiss)   14:12-14
Barefoot in the Park (Simon)   6:502-03; 11:495; 31:393, 396, 403; 39:218; 70:238, 240-41
Barely and Widely, 1956-1958 (Zukofsky)   4:599
Barfly (Bukowski)   82:23-6; 108:88, 91, 94
"Bargain" (Guthrie)   23:199
"The Bargain Sale" (Johnston)   51:243
A Bargain with God (Savage)   40:370
The Bark Tree (Queneau)
   See *Le chiendent*
"The Barking" (Bachmann)   69:47
"Barking Man" (Bell)   102:7
Barking Man and Other Stories (Bell)   102:5-7
"The Barn" (Blunden)   56:37
Barn Blind (Smiley)   53:344-45
"Barn Burning" (Faulkner)   6:179; 11:199
"The Barn Cuts Off the View" (Ferber)   93:180
Barn Fever and Other Poems (Davison)   28:104

Bárnabo delle montagne (*Barnabo of the Mountains*) (Buzzati)   36:83, 91-2, 95
Barnabo of the Mountains (Buzzati)
   See *Bárnabo delle montagne*
"The Barney Game" (Friel)   42:166
"Barnum Museum" (Millhauser)   109:158, 161
The Barnum Museum (Millhauser)   109:157-60, 165, 167, 169-70, 174
Barometer Rising (MacLennan)   2:257; 14:339, 342, 344; 92:298, 300-02, 304-14, 316-17, 321-22, 326, 340-42, 346
The Baron in the Trees (Calvino)
   See *Il barone rampante*
Il barone rampante (*The Baron in the Trees*) (Calvino)   5:97; 8:129-30; 11:89, 91; 22:87, 89-90; 33:97; 39:306-08, 314, 316-17; 73:35, 54, 58
"Baroque Comment" (Bogan)   39:388; 46:81, 86; 93:65, 79-81
Baroque 'n' Roll (Brophy)   105:19-20, 29
"A Baroque Wall-Fountain in the Villa Sciarra" (Wilbur)   3:530; 53:398; 110:356, 362, 374, 383, 387
"Barra de Navidad: Envoi" (Muske)   90:318
"Barrack Room Fiddle Tune" (Ross)   13:496
The Barracks (McGahern)   5:280; 9:370-71, 374; 48:261-63, 267, 269, 271-72
"Barracks Apt. Fourteen" (Weiss)   3:516
The Barracks Thief (Wolff)   39:283-86
The Barracks Thief, and Selected Stories (Wolff)   64:451, 454, 456-57
Barrage against the Pacific (Duras)
   See *Un barrage contre le Pacifique*
Un barrage contre le Pacifique (*Barrage against the Pacific*; *The Sea Wall*) (Duras)   6:149; 40:176, 178-79, 185, 187; 68:77, 82-3, 85, 91-2, 95-6, 98, 100; 100:118, 129, 138, 140-41, 144-46
Barren Terrain (Neruda)   28:315
"Barren Woman" (Plath)   51:340
"Barricade Smith: His Speeches" (Klein)   19:259
"The Barrie Cooke Show, May 1988" (Durcan)   70:152
Barrier (Skolimowski)   20:348-49, 351-54
Barrier Island (MacDonald)   44:407
Barroco (Sarduy)   97:374, 376-78, 405, 412, 414
"Bar-Room Matins" (MacNeice)   4:318
Barry Lyndon (Kubrick)   16:390-92
"Barrytown" (Becker and Fagen)   26:79
"Bars" (Guillen)   79:229
"Barstool Blues" (Young)   17:579
Barsuki (*The Badgers*) (Leonov)   92:236-38, 242-43, 247-48, 253, 257, 259, 266, 270, 275-78
"Bart and Helene at Annie and Fred's" (Gold)   42:197
Bartleby (Albee)   113:4
"Bartok and the Geraniums" (Livesay)   79:345-46
Barton Fink (The Coen Brothers)   108:147, 149, 151-64, 166-67, 169-71
"Barua a Soldani" (Dinesen)   95:46
"Baruch" (Simpson)   9:485
Les bas fonds (Renoir)   20:288, 303
Base Case (Rathbone)   41:342-43
"Base Details" (Sassoon)   36:391, 397
"Baseball" (Bowering)   47:21
Baseball: A Poem in the Magic Number Nine (Bowering)   15:83
"Baseball and the Meaning of Life" (Hall)   37:149
"Baseball and Writing" (Moore)   47:261, 263

Baseball in April, and Other Stories (Soto)   80:298, 300
"The Baseball Spur" (Kinsella)   43:253, 256-57
"Basement" (Bambara)   88:48
"The Basement" (Lagerkvist)   54:288
The Basement (Pinter)   11:443; 15:423; 27:387, 394-95
The Basement: Meditations on a Human Sacrifice (Millett)   67:254-57
"The Basement Room" (Greene)   3:215; 70:293-94
The Basement Tapes (Dylan)   77:182
The Basement Window (Buero Vallejo)
   See *El tragaluz*
"Básezn nejpokornejší" ("The Most Humble Poem") (Seifert)   93:338
"A Bash in the Tunnel" (O'Brien)   7:270; 10:362
Basi and Co. (Saro-Wiwa)   114:258, 261, 267, 274-75
Basic English (Richards)   24:395
Basic Movements (Gregor)   9:254
Basic Training (Wiseman)   20:473-74
The Basic Training of Pavlo Hummel (Rabe)   4:425-28; 8:449-51; 33:341-44
"The Basilica at Vezelay" (Matthews)   40:324
"Basilisk" (Ellison)   13:206
Basin and Range (McPhee)   36:298-99
"A Basin of Eggs" (Swenson)   4:532
"Basis from Her Garden" (Barthelme)   115:81
Basket Case (Peck)   17:342
The Basketball Diaries (Carroll)   35:78-80
"Baskets" (Gluck)   44:217, 222
"Baskets" (Jensen)   37:188
"The Basket-Weaver's Companion" (Char)
   See "La compagne du vannier"
"The Basque and Bijou" (Nin)   60:276
The Bass Saxophone (Skvorecky)
   See *Legenda emöke*
The Bassarids, Opera Seria with Intermezzo in One Act (Auden)   4:34
"The Bastard" (Caldwell)   14:93
The Bastard (Caldwell)   50:299-300
The Bastard (Jakes)   29:248-49
"The Bastard Bannerman" (Spillane)   13:528
The Bastard King (Hibbert)   7:156
Bastard Out of Carolina   78:3-6, 8-9, 11, 13
"Bastille Day on 25th Street" (Dybek)   114:61, 66
"El bastón" (Marques)   96:233, 244
"De Bat He Fly in Me Face" (Simon)   26:411
"A Bat in the Monastery" (L'Heureux)   52:272, 274
"A Bat on the Road" (Heaney)   74:167
La bataille de Pharsale (*The Battle of Pharsalus*) (Simon)   4:496-97; 9:483; 15:493-94, 496-97; 39:203, 205-11, 214-15
Batailles dans la montagne (Giono)   4:184-85; 11:234
La bâtarde (Leduc)   22:260-61
"The Bath" (Carver)   36:101, 104
"The Bath" (Snyder)   5:395
"Bath after Sailing" (Updike)   23:476
"The Bath House" (Gunn)   18:200
"Bathers" (Prokosch)   48:309
"Bathing at Glymenopoulo" (Motion)   47:292-94
"Bathing Beauty" (Garrett)   3:192
"Bathing in Diabolic Acid" (McFadden)   48:246-48
"Bath-Sheba" (Shapiro)   53:330

"De Bathsuit and de Cow" (Bennett) 28:27
Batman: The Ultimate Evil (Vachss) 106:366-67
Batman's Beachhead (Buzo) 61:53-4
Bâtons, chiffres, et lettres (Queneau) 5:360-61
The Bat-Poet (Jarrell) 2:210; 13:303
"Bats" (Jarrell) 9:295
Bats Out of Hell (Hannah) 90:158-60, 162-63
"Bats Out of Hell Division" (Hannah) 90:161, 163-64
"Battaglia notturna alla biennale di Venezia" (Buzzati) 36:86
"Battered" (Souster) 5:395
"The Battered Wife" (Davie) 31:124
"The Battery" (Kinsella) 43:255
"Battery Park: High Noon" (Belitt) 22:48-9
"The Battle" (Simpson) 7:426
"The Battle Continues" (MacDiarmid) 19:289
Battle Cry (Uris) 7:490; 32:430-31, 433
"The Battle for the Hill" (Amichai) 22:30; 57:38; 116:106-07
"The Battle in the Hills" (Brown) 48:61
The Battle Lost and Won (Manning) 19:302-04
Battle of Angels (Williams) 5:502; 11:572, 575; 45:452; 71:263-65, 367; 111:424
"The Battle of Aughrim" (Murphy) 41:312-13, 317-19
The Battle of Aughrim (Murphy) 41:312, 314-16
"The Battle of Britain Dinner, New York, 1963" (Coward) 29:135
The Battle of Bubble and Squeak (Pearce) 21:291, 293
"The Battle of Evermore" (Page and Plant) 12:475, 477, 481-82
The Battle of Little Bighorn (Sandoz) 28:404
A Battle of Nerves (*Maigret's War of Nerves*) (Simenon) 47:370, 374, 376, 383
The Battle of Pharsalus (Simon)
    See *La bataille de Pharsale*
The Battle of San Pietro (Huston) 20:158, 165
The Battle of Shrivings (*Shrivings*) (Shaffer) 5:387-88; 14:486; 18:475-77
"The Battle of the Trees" (Graves) 6:210
The Battle of the Villa Fiorita (Godden) 53:159-60
"A Battle of Wills Disguised" (Piercy) 27:376
"Battle Piece" (Belitt) 22:50
Battle Surgeon (Slaughter) 29:373
The Battlefield (Mayne) 12:390-91, 393, 407
Battlefield Earth: A Saga of the Year 3000 (Hubbard) 43:204-08
Battlefield President: Dwight D. Eisenhower (Archer) 12:15
"Battlefields" (Scannell) 49:330
"The Battler" (Hemingway) 13:273; 30:184, 189-90, 196; 39:402
Battling Butler (Keaton) 20:190, 196
Bau einer Laube (Wellershoff) 46:435
"Baudelaire" (Eliot) 57:182
Baudelaire (Sartre) 24:404-06, 410; 50:373, 383
"Baudelaire as Art Critic" (Paz) 51:332
Baumgartner's Bombay (Desai) 97:165-66, 168, 170, 172, 181-82, 185, 190, 192
Die Baumwollpflücker (Traven)
    See *Der Wobbly*
"Bavaria" (Schnackenberg) 40:378
"The Bay" (Baxter) 14:62
The Bay at Nice (Hare) 58:230-31
"Bay Days" (Moss) 45:292
The Bay Is Not Naples (Ortese)

    See *Il mare non bagna Napoli*
Bay of Noon (Hazzard) 18:214-18
The Bay Psalm Book Murder (Harriss) 34:192-93
Bayn al-Qasrayn (Mahfuz) 52:293, 295, 300; 55:171
Bayou Backwaters (Eckert) 17:106
Bazaar and Rummage 61:409-10
"Bazaar, Five P.M." (Mahapatra) 33:284
"Be" (Diamond) 30:111
Be a Farmer's Boy (Taylor) 27:442
Be Angry at the Sun and Other Poems (Jeffers) 54:246; 11:309, 311
"Be Cool, Be Calm, and Keep Yourself Together" (Wonder) 12:655
"Be Grave, Woman" (Riding) 7:374
"Be Here in the Morning" (Wilson) 12:641
"Be My Girl-Sally" (Police, The) 26:363
Be My Guest! (Ewart) 13:209
"Be Still" (Wilson) 12:641
"Be with Me" (Simon) 26:410
Be Yourself (Connelly) 7:56
The Beach Boys Love You (Wilson) 12:651-52
The Beach Boys Party Album (Wilson) 12:643, 651
The Beach Boys Today! (Wilson) 12:643, 650
"Beach Burial" (Slessor) 14:493, 498
"Beach Glass" (Clampitt) 32:115, 118
"The Beach Murders" (Ballard) 36:38
"The Beach Party" (Grau) 9:240
Beach Plovers (Kawabata)
    See *Hamachidori*
"Beach Squatter" (Davis) 49:91, 94-5
Beach Towels (Sachs) 35:335
"The Beach Umbrella" (Colter) 58:138, 140
The Beach Umbrella (Colter) 58:138-40, 143, 146
The Beach Waifs (Amado)
    See *Capitães da areia*
"Beach with White Cloud" (Gustafson) 36:217
"Beachcombers" (Williams) 42:442
"The Beachhead" (Gunn) 18:203; 32:207
"Beachmaster" (Norris) 14:388
The Beachmasters (Astley) 41:49-50
"Beachworld" (King) 37:207
"The Beacon" (Wilbur) 6:570; 53:405, 410; 110:348, 353
"The Beaded Pear" (Simpson) 32:377-78
"Beagling" (Smith) 42:356
An Béal Bocht (*The Poor Mouth: A Bad Story about the Hard Life*) (O'Brien) 4:385; 5:314-17; 7:269; 47:316-17
Beale Street Sundown (Lee) 52:270
Beale Street: Where the Blues Began (Lee) 52:265-69
"Beam Us Home" (Tiptree) 48:385-86
"Beams" (Lorde) 71:255, 260
The Bean Eaters (Brooks) 1:46; 5:75; 15:93-4; 49:22, 27, 30-2, 35-6
"Bean Spasms" (Berrigan) 37:46
Bean Spasms (Berrigan) 37:42-3
The Bean Trees (Kingsolver) 55:64-8; 81:191, 193-95
"Beans" (Grace) 56:116-18, 121
Beans: All about Them (Silverstein and Silverstein) 17:455
The Beans of Egypt, Maine (Chute) 39:37-43
"Beans with Garlic" (Bukowski) 5:81; 108:112
Beany and the Beckoning Road (Weber) 12:632
Beany Has a Secret Life (Weber) 12:633, 635
Beany Malone (Weber) 12:632

"The Bear" (Faulkner) 1:101; 6:174, 176; 8:211; 11:201; 18:149; 28:143
"The Bear" (Frost) 10:193-94, 196-97
"Bear" (Gunnars) 69:257
"The Bear" (Kinnell) 2:230; 3:268-69; 5:216; 13:318-20, 322; 29:284, 288
"The Bear" (Momaday) 85:224-25, 231, 248, 262-64
"Bear" (Nowlan) 15:398
Bear (Engel) 36:159-62
"A Bear and a Love" (Ulibarri)
    See "Un oso y un amor"
"The Bear and the Kiss" (Dinesen) 10:148-50; 95:61
"A Bear Hunt" (Faulkner) 6:179
Bear Island (MacLean) 3:309; 13:359, 361-63
"Bear News" (Frazier) 46:165
"The Bear on the Delhi Road" (Birney) 6:75, 78
"Bear Paw" (Hugo) 32:240-41
Die Bearbeitung der mütze (Jandl) 34:196, 198, 200
The Beard (McClure) 6:317, 320; 10:331-32
Bearded Ladies (Grenville) 61:151-52, 154-56, 159, 161-62
"Bearded Lady" (Zamora) 89:384-85, 387
"The Bearded Lady Tells Her Story Late at Night While Drunk in the Bar" (Moure) 88:219
"Bearded Oaks" (Warren) 8:539; 39:264; 59:301-02
"The Bearded Woman, by Ribera" (Muldoon) 32:318
The Beardless Warriors (Matheson) 37:244-45
Beard's Roman Women (Burgess) 8:113; 15:103; 81:303
Beardsley and His World (Brophy) 105:16
Bearheart—the Heirship Chronicles (Vizenor) 103:311, 340
Bearing an Hourglass (Anthony) 35:40-1
The Bear's Famous Invasion of Sicily (Buzzati) 36:82-4
"The Beast" (Plath) 11:448; 111:159, 164
"The Beast" (Roethke) 46:363; 101:311
The Beast (Wilson) 33:460-61, 463, 465
The Beast in Me, and Other Animals: A New Collection of Pieces and Drawings about Human Beings and Less Alarming Creatures (Thurber) 5:439
Beast in View (Rukeyser) 27:407-08, 410
The Beast Master (Norton) 12:456-57, 461, 468
The Beast Must Die (Day Lewis) 6:129
"Beast of Burden" (Jagger and Richard) 17:239-40
A Beast Story (Kennedy) 66:205-08
"The Beast That Etcetera" (Ellison)
    See "The Beast That Shouted Love at the Heart of the World"
"The Beast That Shouted Love at the Heart of the World" ("The Beast That Etcetera") (Ellison) 13:206
The Beast That Shouted Love at the Heart of the World (Ellison) 42:127
The Beastly Beatitudes of Balthazar B (Donleavy) 1:76; 4:123-25; 6:139, 141-42; 10:153-54; 45:125
"Beastly Manhattan" (Baker) 31:31
Beastly Tales from Here and There (Seth) 90:353
"Beasts" (Wilbur) 14:578-79; 53:411; 110:355, 376

Beasts (Crowley)   57:156-57, 162

Beasts of the Southern Wild and Other Stories (Betts)   3:73; 6:69

"The Beat" (Costello)   21:68

The Beat Boys (Holmes)
   See *Go*

Beat of the City (Brinsmead)   21:26-8

Beat the Devil (Capote)   34:322

Beat the Devil (Huston)   20:163, 165

Beat the Last Drum: The Siege of Yorktown, 1781 (Fleming)   37:120

Beat to Quarters (*The Happy Return*) (Forester)   35:161-63, 166, 169-70

"The Beaters" (Gunn)   32:207

"The Beating of a Drum" (Eliot)   15:208

"Beating That Boy" (Ellison)   54:141

Beating the Bushes: Selected Essays, 1941-1970 (Ransom)   4:437

"Beatitude" (Moure)   88:227

The Beatles (Lennon and McCartney)   12:364

The Beatles VI (Lennon and McCartney)   35:274

"Beatrice and Dante" (Graves)   45:169

"Beatrice Passes" (Christie)   110:126

"Beatrice Trueblood's Story" (Stafford)   19:430; 68:434

"The Beau Monde of Mrs. Bridge" (Connell)   45:107, 109

Le beau serge (Chabrol)   16:168, 170, 173-74, 178, 180-81, 183

Un beau ténébreux (Gracq)   11:245; 48:136-41

The Beaubourg Effect (Baudrillard)   60:36

"Beaufort Tides" (Beecher)   6:49

La beauté du diable (Clair)   20:64, 71

The Beauties and the Furies (Stead)   5:403; 32:411, 413-15; 80:307, 317-18, 347, 349

Beautiful (Billington)   43:55

"The Beautiful Amanita Muscaria" (Wakoski)   7:505

"The Beautiful American Word, Sure" (Schwartz)   87:347

"Beautiful and Cruel" (Cisneros)   69:150

"The Beautiful and the Sublime" (Sterling)   72:372

"Beautiful Black Men (with compliments and apologies to all not mentioned by name)" (Giovanni)   19:191; 64:185, 187

"Beautiful Boy" ("Darling Boy") (Lennon)   35:272-74

"The Beautiful Changes" (Wilbur)   9:569; 53:399, 408

The Beautiful Changes and Other Poems (Wilbur)   3:531; 6:568; 9:569; 14:576; 53:396-97, 401, 403-04, 406-07, 409-10; 110:352, 380

Beautiful City (Walker)
   See *The East End Plays*

"The Beautiful Comrade Furazhkin" (Aksyonov)   101:10-11

A Beautiful Day (Wellershoff)
   See *Ein schöner Tag*

The Beautiful Empire (Ghose)   42:180-81

Beautiful Feathers (Ekwensi)   4:151-52

The Beautiful Friend and Other Stories (Stolz)   12:551-52

Beautiful Girl (Adams)   13:2-3; 46:16-17, 22

The Beautiful Inventions (Fuller)   62:198-99, 201-02, 204

"Beautiful Loser" (Seger)   35:380-81, 383

Beautiful Loser (Seger)   35:380-81, 383

Beautiful Losers (Cohen)   3:109; 38:135, 137

"Beautiful Noise" (Diamond)   30:112

Beautiful Noise (Diamond)   30:112-13

The Beautiful People (Saroyan)   10:454; 56:376

"The Beautiful Poem" (Brautigan)   3:87

The Beautiful Room is Empty (White)   110:321. 323-32, 337, 339, 342-43

"Beautiful Speech" (Boland)   113:100

"Beautiful Streamers" (Rabe)   8:451

"Beautiful Thing" (Williams)   22:466

The Beautiful Visit (Howard)   29:242

Beautiful Women: Ugly Scenes (Bryan)   29:105-06

The Beautiful Words (Jones)   52:250-51, 254

"Beauty" (Christie)   110:125

"The Beauty" (Ekelof)   27:119

"Beauty" (Huxley)   11:283-84

Beauty and Sadness (Kawabata)   107:102-03, 108

"Beauty and the Beast" (Broumas)   73:5

"Beauty and the Beast" (Dove)   81:137

Beauty and the Beast (Cocteau)
   See *La belle et la bête*

Beauty and the Beast (Hunter)   31:226-27

Beauty and the Beast (Page)   40:355

"The Beauty of the Head" (Swenson)   61:402; 106:329, 344

The Beauty Part (Perelman)   44:503, 505

"A Beauty that Rages" (Honig)   33:211

The Beautyful Ones Are Not Yet Born (Armah)   5:31; 33:23-5, 27-9, 31-2

Les beaux draps (*Fine Mess*) (Celine)   47:79

Les beaux quartiers (*Residential Quarter*) (Aragon)   22:35, 37

The Beaver Men (Sandoz)   28:407

"Beaver Tears" (Tiptree)   48:389

"Beaverbank" (Hugo)   32:243

"The Beavers of Renfrew" (Purdy)   50:240-41, 246

"Bebop Boys" (Hughes)   35:222

"Becalmed on Strange Waters" (Ashbery)   77:67

"Because" (Pastan)   27:369

"Because I Never Learned" (Lane)   25:287

Because I Was Flesh (Dahlberg)   7:63, 67, 69; 14:135-38

Because I Was Invited (Wright)   11:578

Because It Is Bitter and Because It Is My Heart (Oates)   108:374-75, 378, 386, 388, 390

"Because My Father Always Said He Was the Only Indian Who Saw Jimi Hendrix Play 'The Star-Spangled Banner' at Woodstock" (Alexie)   96:5, 13

Because of Love (Skelton)   13:508

Because of Madeline (Stolz)   12:550, 552-53

"Because of Me, Because of You" (Jarrell)   2:209

Because of the Cats (Freeling)   38:184

"Because One Is Always Forgotten" (Forche)   25:172; 83:214

"Because the Night" (Smith)   12:543

"Because You Asked about the Line between Prose and Poetry" (Nemerov)   36:306

Bech: A Book (Updike)   1:345; 2:440-41; 5:456, 459-460; 9:541; 13:559; 43:430-31

Bech Is Back (Updike)   43:430-32

"Bech Third Worlds It" (Updike)   43:430

"Bech Wed" (Updike)   43:430, 432

"Bechbretha" (Muldoon)   72:273

The Becker Wives and Other Stories (Lavin)   18:303; 99:312

Becket; or, The Honor of God (Anouilh)
   See *Becket; ou, L'honneur de Dieu*

Becket; ou, L'honneur de Dieu (*Becket: or, The Honor of God*) (Anouilh)   1:7; 3:12; 13:17-18, 21-2; 40:56-8, 61; 50:278-80

"Beckoned" (Pearce)   21:292

Beckonings (Brooks)   15:93-4; 49:23, 29, 35-8

"Becky" (Toomer)   1:341; 13:552

Becky Sharp (Mamoulian)   16:421-22, 424, 427

Becky Swan's Book (Musgrave)   54:333

Becoming a Man: Half a Life Story (Monette)   82:328-30

"The Bed" (Berry)   27:35

"The Bed" (Gunn)   81:178

"Bed among the Lentils" (Bennett)   77:101

Bed and Board (Truffaut)
   See *Domicile conjugal*

"Bed & Breakfast" (Raine)   103:179

A Bed by the Sea (Gregor)   9:254

"A Bed for the Night" (Yezierska)   46:443

A Bed of Feathers (Davies)   23:144

A Bed of Flowers (Waugh)   7:514

The Bed Sitting Room (Lester)   20:226, 228-29

Bed/Time/Story (Robinson)   10:439

"Bedfordshire" (Davie)   31:112, 116

"The Bedfordshire Clanger" (Bates)   46:62

"The Bedroom Eyes of Mrs. Vansittart" (Trevor)   25:445; 71:326, 347

Bedroom Farce (Ayckbourn)   18:28-30; 33:41, 49; 74:3, 7, 19, 29, 31, 34

"Bedroom of Music" (Williams)   42:442

"Beds and Boards" (Chester)   49:56

Beds in the East (Burgess)   4:82; 22:74; 81:301

"The Bed's Too Big Without You" (Police, The)   26:364

Bedside Manners (Valenzuela)   104:390-92

"Bed-Time" (Johnston)   51:243

"Bedtime" (Levertov)   66:237

Bedtime Stories (Van Duyn)   3:491-92; 63:442-43; 116:408, 417-18, 426

"Bedtime Story" (Abse)   29:20

"Bedtime Story" (Simic)   22:383

"A Bedtime Story for My Son" (Redgrove)   6:445

"A Bedtime Story for My Wife" (Leyner)   92:281

"The Bee Hive" ("An Elegy to the Guevara") (Rosenblatt)   15:446

"The Bee Meeting" (Plath)   11:450; 14:429; 17:360; 111:176, 179

"The Bee of Words" (Dudek)   19:136

Bee Tree and Other Stuff (Peck)   17:339-40

"Beech Buds" (Clarke)   61:73

"The Beech Tree" (Hoffman)   23:238

The Beekeepers (Redgrove)   41:356-57

"The Beekeeper's Daughter" (Plath)   9:431; 111:178

Been Down So Long It Looks Like Up to Me (Farina)   9:195

"Been on a Train" (Nyro)   17:313, 316, 318

"Beer at the Corner Bar" (Bukowski)   41:73

"The Beer was Spilled on the Barroom Floor" (Keillor)   115:277

"Bees Stopped" (Ammons)   25:44

The Beet Queen (Erdrich)   54:166-72

"Beethoven" (Herbert)   9:275; 43:187

"Beethoven Attends the C Minor Seminar" (Tomlinson)   6:536

"Beethoven Opus 111" (Clampitt)   32:116

"Beethoven Triumphant" (Berryman)   3:68, 70; 6:64; 8:91, 93; 25:96

"Beethoven's Death Mask" (Spender)   41:418,

428

The Beetle Leg (Hawkes)   2:183; 3:221, 223; 4:215, 218; 7:140, 142, 144, 146; 14:237; 15:270-71; 27:191, 199; 49:161

Beetlecreek (Demby)   53:99-101, 103-06, 109-15

Der Befehl (Hochwalder)   36:235-38

"Before a Cashier's Window in a Department Store" (Wright)   10:544

"Before an Old Painting of the Crucifixion" (Momaday)   85:225, 248, 266-67

"Before Dark" (Berry)   4:59

Before Dawn (Rattigan)   7:355

"Before Death" (Ali)   69:31

"Before Disaster" (Winters)   4:593; 32:468, 470

"Before Hanging" (Simmons)   43:408

"Before His Time" (Oz)   27:360-62

"before leaving me, the poem: eagle butte and black river falls" (Young Bear)   94:363

"Before March" (MacLeish)   68:286

Before My Time (Howard)   5:188-89; 14:267; 46:187

"Before Pentecost" (Buckley)   57:130

Before Retirement (Bernhard)
    See *Vor dem Ruhestand*

"Before Sex" (Gerstler)   70:159

Before She Met Me (Barnes)   42:26-8

Before Sleep (Booth)   23:77

"Before Spring" (Boland)   67:45; 113:108

"Before the Anaesthetic" (Betjeman)   34:309; 43:36

"Before the Big Storm" (Stafford)   29:380

Before the Blackout (Soyinka)   44:286

Before the Brave (Patchen)   18:392

"Before the Celtic Yoke" (Durcan)   43:113

"Before the Deluge" (Browne)   21:36-7, 40

Before the Flood (Dylan)   77:175

"Before the Judgement" (Duncan)   41:128, 130

"Before the Party" (Maugham)   67:206

Before the Revolution (Bertolucci)   16:83-8, 92-5, 99-100

"Before the Storm" (Campbell)   42:92

"Before the Story" (Cohen)   38:132

Before You Say "Hello" (Calvino)   39:306

Die Befristeten (*The Deadlined*; *Life-Terms*; *The Numbered*; *Their Days Are Numbered*) (Canetti)   14:121-22; 75:124, 127, 129-30, 134, 146-47; 86:303

"Beg, Sl Tog, Inc, Cont, Rep" (Hempel)   39:67, 69-70

The Beggar (Mahfuz)   55:181; 52:300

A Beggar in Jerusalem (Wiesel)   3:527, 529; 37:455

"Beggar in the Snow" (Baxter)   78:28

"The Beggar Is King" (Harris)   25:212

The Beggar Maid: Stories of Flo and Rose (Munro)
    See *Who Do You Think You Are?*

Beggar on Horseback (Connelly)   7:56

Beggar on Horseback (Kaufman)   38:257, 264-66

The Beggar Queen (Alexander)   35:28

"Beggars Banquet" (Jagger and Richard)   17:222-23, 226, 229, 233, 237, 240-41

"Beggars Would Ride" (Bainbridge)   62:36-7

"Begging the Dialect" (Skelton)   13:507

Begin with Walking (Shapcott)   38:401

The Beginners (Jacobson)   4:253, 255; 14:290

"Beginner's Guide" (Nemerov)   36:301

Beginner's Love (Klein)   30:243

"The Beginning" (Van Duyn)   116:422

"Beginning" (Wright)   3:540; 28:465

A Beginning and an End (Mahfuz)
    See *Bidaya wa-nihaya*

"Beginning. and End" (Nichol)   18:366

"The Beginning Is Also the End" (Burroughs)   109:196

"The Beginning Is Zero" (Giovanni)   64:183

The Beginning of an Unknown Century (*In That Dawn*) (Paustovsky)   40:368

"The Beginning of April" (Williams)   33:443

"The Beginning of September" (Hass)   99:151

"The Beginning of Something" (Dixon)   52:100

The Beginning of Spring (Fitzgerald)   61:119-23

"The Beginning of the End" (Achebe)   26:22

The Beginning of the Long Dash (Thesen)   56:420, 422

The Beginning Place (*Threshold*) (Le Guin)   22:274-75; 45:215-16, 221

"Beginning to Say No" (Gallagher)   63:123

"Beginning to See the Light" (Reed)   21:318-19

Beginning with My Streets: Essays and Recollections (Milosz)   82:308, 311

Beginning with O (Broumas)   10:76-7; 73:2, 4-13, 16

"Beginnings" (Adcock)   41:16

"Beginnings" (Coover)   7:58; 32:127

"Beginnings" (Frame)   96:189, 191

"Beginnings" (Haines)   58:217

"Beginnings" (Hayden)   37:153

"The Beginnings of a Fortune" (Lispector)   43:267, 269

"The Beginnings of a Sin" (Mac Laverty)   31:255

"Beginnings of Conservative Thought" (Barrett)   27:23

Begleitumstände: Frankfurter Vorlesungen (Johnson)   40:265, 270

"Begotten of the Spleen" (Simic)   22:383; 68:379

Begstvo Mistera Mak-Kinli (*The Flight of Mr. MacKinley*; *Mr. MacKinley's Flight*; *Mr. McKinley Runs Away*) (Leonov)   92:252, 278-79

Begstvo Sandukova (Leonov)
    See *Volk*

"Beguiled" (Abe)   81:297

"Behaving like a Jew" (Stern)   40:406

"Behaviorism" (Faludy)   42:138

"The Behaviour of Dogs" (Raine)   103:180

"Behemoth" (Huxley)   11:283

"Behind a Shut Door" (MacCaig)   36:285

Behind All This There's Great Happiness Hiding (Amichai)   22:30; 116:137

"Behind the Blue Curtain" (Millhauser)   109:157, 160

"Behind the Curtained World (1942)" (O'Casey)   88:267

Behind the Door (Bassani)   9:76

Behind the Green Curtains (O'Casey)   5:318; 9:407; 88:272-74

Behind the Lines: Gender and the Two World Wars   65:327

Behind the Log (Pratt)   19:376, 380, 383-84

Behind the Makeup (Arzner)   98:69

"Behind the Mirror" (Gunn)   18:201

"Behind the North Wind" (Davie)   10:123

Behind the Scenes at the Museum (Atkinson)   99:97-103

Behind the Trail of Broken Treaties: An Indian Declaration of Independence (Deloria)   21:112-14

"Behold Goliath" (Chester)   49:55-7

Behold Goliath (Chester)   49:54-6

"Behold the Husband in His Perfect Agony" (Hannah)   38:234; 90:148, 150

"Behold the Lilies of the Field" (Hecht)   8:268; 13:269

Behold the Man (Moorcock)   27:347-48; 58:349, 352, 357

"Behührung" (Wolf)   58:426

"Being a Lutheran Boy-God in Minnesota" (Bly)   38:58

"Being a Man" (Theroux)   46:401

"Being a Woman" (Urdang)   47:400

"Being Adults" (Thesen)   56:420, 423

"Being Alive" (Sondheim)   30:392, 395, 400, 403

Being Alive: Poems, 1958-78 (Purdy)   14:435; 50:246

Being and Having (Marcel)   15:359, 364

Being and Nothingness: An Essay on Phenomenological Ontology (Sartre)
    See *L'être et le néant: Essai d'ontologie phénoménologique*

Being and Time (Heidegger)
    See *Sein und Zeit*

"Being Blind" (Adcock)   41:14

"Being Country Bred" (Oliver)   98:291

"Being for the Benefit of Mr. Kite" (Lennon and McCartney)   12:358

Being Geniuses Together (Boyle)   58:75, 77

Being Here: Poetry, 1977-80 (Warren)   18:539; 39:255-59, 264-66, 270-73

"Being Kind to Titina" (White)   69:398

"Being Left" (Piercy)   62:367-68

"Being Lost, As Usual" (Thesen)   56:418

"Being of Hope and Rain" (Aleixandre)   36:29

"Being of Three Minds" (Nemerov)   6:362

"Being Stolen From" (Trevor)   25:446; 71:326, 347

Being There (Kosinski)   1:172; 2:231-33; 3:272-73; 6:282-84; 10:307; 15:313-14; 53:219-20, 222, 226, 228; 70:297-98, 301, 306

Being Two Isn't Easy (Ichikawa)   20:181, 186

Being with Children (Lopate)   29:298-300

Being with You (Robinson)   21:350-51

The Bejeweled Boy (Asturias)   13:40

"Bela" (Stern)   100:333

Bela Lugosi's White Christmas (West)   7:524; 96:380

"Belagerung" (Eich)   15:202

Belaia staia (Akhmatova)
    See *Belaya staya*

Belaia staja (Akhmatova)
    See *Belaya staya*

Belaya staya (*Belaia staia*; *Belaia staja*; *White Flock*) (Akhmatova)   25:24-7; 64:3-4, 8-9

"Belderg" (Heaney)   14:244; 25:245

"Belfast" (Heaney)   25:249

"Belfast" (MacNeice)   4:316; 53:238

"Belfast vs. Dublin" (Boland)   113:114

Belfry (Ritsos)   13:487

"Believable Linden, Pumpkin, Cherry, Etc." (Bell)   31:46

Believe Them (Robison)   98:306-09, 318

"Believers" (Updike)   15:546

Believing   65:444-48

"Belize" (Gilchrist)   48:119

The Bell (Murdoch)   1:234-36; 2:295-96, 298; 3:345, 347-48; 6:343, 345, 348; 15:385; 22:327; 51:291-92

The Bell (O'Connor)   14:398

"Bell Birds" (Wright)   53:423

"Bell Boy" (Townshend)   17:532

"Bell Buoy" (Merwin)   5:288

"Bell Call" (Ashton-Warner)   19:22

The Bell Family (Family Shoes) (Streatfeild)
   21:401, 405, 411

A Bell for Adano (Hersey)   1:144; 7:153;
   40:226-27, 238-39, 241; 81:332-37;
   97:297-98, 301-02, 304-06, 324

The Bell Jar (Plath)   1:270; 2:336-37; 3:390-
   91; 5:342-44; 9:423-24, 432; 11:450-51;
   17:345, 350-54, 356-58, 361, 364-65,
   368; 50:439-42, 446, 448; 51:343, 350-
   51; 62:385-401, 404-429; 111:157-59,
   161, 163-64, 166, 168, 178, 184, 187-
   95, 197-99, 213, 215

"Bella dama sin piedad" (Castellanos)   66:53

"Bella Fleace Gave a Party" (Waugh)   27:477

"The Bella Lingua" (Cheever)   11:121

The Bellarosa Connection (Bellow)   63:40-3

"Belle" (Simenon)   2:399

La belle bête (Mad Shadows) (Blais)   2:63;
   4:67; 6:81; 13:96-7

La belle captive (Robbe-Grillet)   8:454; 43:367

Belle de jour (Bunuel)   16:141; 80:50-2, 56-7

"La belle époque" (Milosz)   82:297, 310

La belle et la bête (Beauty and the Beast)
   (Cocteau)   8:145, 148; 15:134; 16:222,
   225-26, 228-29

"Belle Isle, 1949" (Levine)   9:333

"Belle Starr" (Guthrie)   35:193

Bellefleur (Oates)   19:354-56; 33:289, 291-
   92, 295-96; 52:331, 339; 108:348, 371,
   374-75, 378, 385, 391

"Bellerophoniad" (Barth)   5:51-2; 14:53, 55

Les belles images (The Pretty Pictures)
   (Beauvoir)   14:68; 71:48, 51-3

The Belles Lettres Papers (Simmons)   57:408-
   10

Belles on Their Toes (Gilbreth and Carey)
   17:153-54, 156

Les belles-de-nuit (Clair)   20:63, 71

Les belles-soeurs (Tremblay)   29:419-20, 423,
   426; 102:360-63, 369, 371-72, 374-76,
   381, 383-87

Bellisima (Visconti)   16:564, 575

"Bellow Ellijay" (Dickey)   7:80

The Bells (Reed)   21:316-17

"Bells for John Whiteside's Daughter" (Ransom)   5:365

"Bells in Winter" ("Bells of Winter") (Milosz)
   31:262-63

Bells in Winter (Milosz)   22:308-10; 31:262,
   267, 269; 56:239, 242; 82:297-98

The Bells of Agony (Dourado)   60:94

The Bells of Basel (Aragon)
   See Les cloches de bâle

The Bells of Bicêtre (Simenon)
   See Les anneaux de Bicêtre

"The Bells of Britany" (Christie)   110:127

"Bells of the Evening" (Lightfoot)   26:281

"Bells of Winter" (Milosz)
   See "Bells in Winter"

"Bells on the Breeze" (Blunden)   56:49

"The Belly" (Selzer)   74:279

The Belly (Tchicaya)
   See Le Ventre

"Belly Dancer at the Hotel Jerome" (Dunn)
   36:153-55

"Belly Song" (Knight)   40:287

Belly Song and Other Poems (Knight)   40:283,
   285

"The Belonging Kind" (Gibson)   63:130

Beloved (Morrison)   55:195-213; 81:231-32,
   234-35, 237-40, 242, 244, 247, 252-53,
   255-56, 258-63, 265-66, 268-69, 272;
   87:262-309

The Beloved Bandit (The Hold-Up Man) (Hart)
   66:176, 180

"Below" (Berry)   46:72

"Below" (Celan)   82:46

"Below Freezing on Pinelog Mountain" (Bottoms)   53:30

Below Grass Roots (Waters)   88:328, 334, 337,
   339, 345, 349, 360, 362

"Below the Ridge" (Hemingway)   80:105

Below the Root (Snyder)   17:473

Below the Salt (Costain)   30:98

"Belsen, Day of Liberation" (Hayden)   37:159

The Belting Inheritance (Symons)   14:523

Le belvédère (Mandiargues)   41:275, 278

Belyi dozhd (White Rain) (Aitmatov)   71:7,
   14-15

Belyj parokhod (After the Fairy Tale; After the
   Tale; Posle skazki (Belyj parokhod); The
   White Ship (After the Fairy Tale); The White
   Steamer; The White Steamship)
   (Aitmatov)   71:4, 7, 10-11, 13-15, 18-
   19, 21, 23

"Ben Jonson" (Eliot)   24:176

Ben Preserve Us (Bermant)   40:90

"The Bench" (Dixon)   52:99, 101

Bench of Desolation (Chabrol)   16:178

"Benchmark" (Raphael)   14:438

"Bend Down Low" (Marley)   17:269

A Bend in the River (Naipaul)   13:407; 18:359-
   61, 363-64; 37:321-22, 324, 328-29;
   105:158, 161-62, 170, 176, 181

Bend Sinister (Nabokov)   1:240; 2:300; 3:353,
   355; 6:352, 355, 357; 8:412, 415, 418;
   15:391, 396; 23:312

The Bender (Scott)   9:476-77

Bending the Bow (Duncan)   2:122; 4:141; 7:89;
   15:190; 41:129-30; 55:293, 295

Bendingo Shafter (L'Amour)   25:281

"Beneath My Hands" (Cohen)   38:132

Beneath the Fortinaria (Bukowski)   108:110

Beneath the Shadow of the Mountain (Ritsos)
   13:488

Beneath the Stone (Tabori)   19:435

Beneath the Wheel (Hesse)
   See Unterm Rad

"Benediction" (Kaufman)   49:203

"Benedictory" (Riding)   7:374

The Benefactor (Sontag)   1:322; 13:515;
   31:417-18; 105:197, 207, 215, 225

Benefactors (Frayn)   47:136-40

"Beneficiaries" (Gallagher)   63:121

"The Benefit Concert" (Davies)   23:142

Benefits (Fairbairns)   32:162-63

"Benerci kendini nicin öldürdü" ("Why Did
   Benerjee Kill Himself?") (Hikmet)
   40:244-45

Benighted (The Old Dark House) (Priestley)
   34:361, 363

Benito Cereno (Lowell)   4:299; 8:352, 354-55;
   11:324-25

Benjy (O'Connor)   14:393

"Bennie" (Cook-Lynn)   93:126

"Ben's Last Fight" (Merton)   83:397

"Benson's Visitor" (Kelman)   58:298

Bent (Miles)   39:354

Bent (Sherman)   19:415-16

"Bent Water in the Tasmanian Highlands"
   (Murray)   40:341, 343

"Benzedrine" (Bowering)   47:19

"Beowulf: The Monsters and the Critics"
   (Tolkien)   38:439, 442

"Berck-Plage" (Plath)   9:425, 428; 11:450;
   17:348-49; 51:341; 111:168, 177

"The Bereaved" (Abse)   29:18

"Bereavement" (Beer)   58:37

"Berechnungen I" ("Calculations I") (Schmidt)
   56:391-92, 404

"Bereft" (Frost)   13:223; 26:121, 124-25

"Bereft" (Reading)   47:351

Bereitschaftsdienst Bericht uber die Epidemie
   (Nossack)   6:365

Bérénice d'Egypte (Chedid)   47:82, 87

Berenike (Rexroth)   11:473

Berg (Quin)   6:441

Berichte zur Gesinnungslage der Nation (Reports on the Ideological Situation of the
   Nation) (Boell)   72:85

"The Berkeley Concert" (Bruce)   21:48

"Berkeley Eclogue" (Hass)   99:142

"Berkeley House" (Adams)   46:17

"Berkshire" (Davie)   31:120

"The Berkshire Kennet" (Aldington)   49:10

Berl Make Tea (Bermant)   40:89-90

"Berlin" (Ferlinghetti)   27:139

Berlin (Haviaras)   33:202

Berlin (Reed)   21:304, 306-07, 312

The Berlin Antigone (Hochhuth)   18:253

"Berlin, Border of the Divided World" (Johnson)
   15:304

Berlin Days (Poliakoff)   38:380, 385

The Berlin Ending (Hunt)   3:251

Berlin Game (Deighton)   46:129-32

"Berlin Is Hard on Colored Girls" (Lorde)
   71:262

Berlin Solstice (Fraser)   64:178

The Berlin Stories (Isherwood)   14:282-85;
   44:396-97, 400

The Berlin Wall Café (Durcan)   43:117-18;
   70:150

The Berlin Warning (Guild)   33:189

Bernabé (Valdez)   84:404-07, 413

"Bernadette" (Gallant)   18:172

Bernard Clare (Farrell)   66:124-26

Bernard Shaw (Bentley)   24:46

Bernice Bobs Her Hair (Silver)   20:344

Beröringen (The Touch) (Bergman)   16:71;
   72:47, 50, 53-5, 57, 59

Berries Goodman (Neville)   12:449-52

Berro Dágua (Amado)
   See "A Morte e a morte de Quincas Berro
      Dágua"

"A Berry Feast" (Snyder)   32:387

"Berry Picking" (Layton)   15:322

"The Berry Stain" (L'Heureux)   52:275

Berryman's Sonnets (Sonnets to Chris)
   (Berryman)   1:33; 2:56; 3:65; 4:63; 6:62-
   5; 8:89-91; 10:49-50; 13:78-9; 25:93-5;
   62:43, 47, 50-2, 54, 56, 71, 75-6

Bert Breen's Barn (Edmonds)   35:154, 156

Bertha and Other Plays (Koch)   5:219; 44:241

Berthe (Tremblay)   102:364-66

Bertie and May (Norton)   12:460

Bertie Makes a Break (Felsen)   17:121

Bertie Takes Care (Felsen)   17:120

Der Beruf des Dichters (Canetti)   25:109

Die Berühmten (Celebrities) (Bernhard)   61:20

"Beryl" (Metcalf)   37:299

Beryll Gazes into the Night, or the Lost and
   Refound Alphabet (Sachs)
   See Beryll sieht in der Nacht

Beryll Sees in the Night (Sachs)
   See Beryll sieht in der Nacht

Beryll sieht in der Nacht (*Beryll Gazes into the Night, or the Lost and Refound Alphabet; Beryll Sees in the Night*) (Sachs) **98**:322, 351
"Beseda" (Aksyonov) **101**:35
Det besegrade livet (*Life Vanquished*) (Lagerkvist) **54**:274-75
Beside a Norman Tower (de la Roche) **14**:150
Beside the Ocean of Time (Brown) **100**:79-82, 84, 87
"Beside the Sea" (Johnston) **51**:243
"Beside the Seashore" (Betjeman) **43**:34, 40-2
"Beside the Seaside" (Smith) **25**:420-21
"Besides a Dinosaur, Whatta Ya Wanna Be When You Grow Up?" (Bradbury) **42**:42
"Besieged" (O Hehir) **41**:324
El beso de la mujer araña (*Kiss of the Spider Woman*) (Puig) **28**:371-72, 374; **65**:262, 269-72
Eine bessere Welt (*Ergo*) (Lind) **4**:293; **82**:137-40, 142, 145
"Bessie Smith at Roy Thomson Hall" (Ondaatje) **51**:315
"Best" (Tate) **2**:432
The Best and the Last of Edwin O'Connor (O'Connor) **14**:392
The Best Christmas (Kingman) **17**:243
"The Best Dog" (Govier) **51**:166-67
The Best Hour of the Night (Simpson) **32**:378-82, 384
The Best Man (Vidal) **4**:552, 559; **8**:528; **22**:438
The Best Man to Die (Rendell) **28**:383, 385
The Best Of (Cliff) **21**:63
"Best of All Possible Worlds" (Kristofferson) **26**:266
The Best of Antrobus (Durrell) **41**:139
The Best of Arthur C. Clarke (Clarke) **18**:106
The Best of Carly Simon (Simon) **26**:410
The Best of Friends (Humphreys) **47**:182, 184, 190
The Best of Fritz Leiber (Leiber) **23**:303-04
The Best of H. E. Bates (Bates) **46**:59
The Best of Harry Harrison (Harrison) **42**:203
The Best of Henry Miller (Miller) **84**:241
The Best of Jack Vance (Vance) **35**:419
The Best of John W. Campbell (Campbell) **32**:77-8, 80
The Best of Myles: A Selection from "Cruiskeen Lawn" (O'Brien) **47**:312
The Best of Rhys Davies (Davies) **23**:148
The Best of S. J. Perelman (Perelman) **49**:265
The Best of Simple (Hughes) **10**:278
The Best of Willie Nelson (Nelson) **17**:305
Best Science Fiction Stories (Aldiss) **5**:15
"The Best Shod" ("Los mejor calzados") (Valenzuela) **104**:364, 388
The Best Short Stories of J.G. Ballard (Ballard) **14**:39; **36**:41
"Best Society" (Larkin) **64**:258, 263
The Best Times: An Informal Memoir (Dos Passos) **82**:108
Bestialitéérotique (Arrabal) **58**:18
Le bestiaries (*The Matador*) (Montherlant) **8**:393
"Bestiario" (Cortazar) **10**:113; **13**:164
"Bestiario" (Neruda) **28**:312
Bestiario (*Bestiary*) (Cortazar) **2**:104; **10**:118; **33**:125, 128; **34**:329, 332
"Bestiary" (Olds) **39**:187
Bestiary (Cortazar)
    See *Bestiario*
A Bestiary (Wilbur) **14**:577

"A Bestiary for My Daughters Mary and Katharine" (Rexroth) **112**:400
"A Bestiary of the Garden for Children Who Should Have Known Better" (Gotlieb) **18**:191
Bestie del '900 (Palazzeschi) **11**:432
The Best-Loved Short Stories of Jesse Stuart (Stuart) **34**:376
Der Besuch der alten Dame (Duerrenmatt) **102**:69, 76-7
Der Besuch der alten Dame (*The Visit: A Tragi-Comedy*) (Durrenmatt) **1**:81; **4**:138; **8**:194, 197; **11**:168, 170; **15**:195-96, 200-01; **43**:120-21, 123-26, 128
"The Bet" (Abe) **81**:298
"Bet hakravot hatsva'i habriti behar hatsofim" ("The British Military Cemetery on Tsofim Mountain") (Amichai) **116**:110
"Beta" (Tolson) **105**:242, 254, 265, 272
La Bêté humaine (Lang) **103**:85
La bête humaine (*The Human Beast*) (Renoir) **20**:287
La bête noire (Audiberti)
    See *La fête noire*
"Les bêtes" (Gascar) **11**:220-22
"Bêtes" (Reverdy) **53**:289-90
Les bêtes (Gascar) **11**:220-22
"Beth Brant, 1981: Letter & Post Card" (Kenny) **87**:255
"Bethe" (Hellman) **52**:192
Beton (*Concrete*) (Bernhard) **32**:26-7; **61**:14-17, 19-20, 22-3, 29
The Betrayal (Hartley) **2**:182
Betrayal (Pinter) **15**:425-26; **27**:388-92, 395-96; **58**:373, 376, 384-85; **73**:276
Betrayed by F. Scott Fitzgerald (Carlson) **54**:35-6
Betrayed by Rita Hayworth (Puig)
    See *La traicion de Rita Hayworth*
"The Betrayer of Israel" (Singer) **38**:407; **69**:320
"Betrothed" (Agnon) **14**:1
"Betrothed" (Bogan) **93**:65, 78, 82
Betsey Brown (Shange) **38**:395-96
The Betsy (Robbins) **5**:378-79
A Better Class of Person (Osborne) **45**:317-19
"Better Homes & Gardens" (Loewinsohn) **52**:284
Better Living (Walker)
    See *The East End Plays*
"A Better Mousetrap" (Brunner) **8**:107
"The Better Part of Wisdom" (Bradbury) **42**:35
"Better Than Counting Sheep" (Warren) **39**:274
Better Than Sex (Thompson) **104**:345-47
"Better Things" (Davies) **21**:107
"Betty" (Moure) **88**:224
"Betty Lou's Gettin' Out Tonight" (Seger) **35**:384-85
"Betty's Ball Blues" (Reed) **13**:478
Le betullenane (Yevtushenko) **13**:620
"Between" (Johnston) **51**:253
Between (Brooke-Rose) **40**:105, 111
"Between Earth and Sky" (Grace) **56**:116, 119-20
Between Existenialism and Marxism (Sartre) **18**:472-73
Between Facts and Norms: Contributions to a Discourse Theory of Law and Democracy (Habermas)
    See *Faktizität und Geltung: Beiträge zur Diskurstheorie des Techts und des*

demokratischen Rechtsstaats
Between Famine and Agape (Pinget)
    See *Entre fantoine et agapa*
"Between Friends" (Musgrave) **54**:334
Between Here and Now (Thomas) **48**:381
"Between March and April Is the Cruelest Month" (Padilla) **38**:349, 352
"Between Men" (Lessing) **22**:278
Between Men (Govier) **51**:167-68
Between Mouthfuls (Ayckbourn) **33**:40
"Between Myself and Death" (Rexroth) **49**:284
"Between Our Selves" (Lorde) **71**:235, 259
Between Our Selves (Lorde) **71**:257
Between Past and Future (Arendt) **98**:6-9, 11, 26
Between Planets (Heinlein) **3**:225; **26**:171, 176; **55**:302
"Between Points" (Soto) **80**:291
Between Right and Right (Yehoshua) **31**:474
Between Sartre and Camus (Vargas Llosa) **42**:408
Between Silences (Jin) **109**:52-3
"Between Tears and Laughter" (Anand) **93**:57
Between Tears and Laughter (Anand) **93**:57
"Between the Bridges" (Hugo) **32**:247
Between the Buttons (Jagger and Richard) **17**:224, 232, 235, 237, 239
"Between the Lines" (Pinter) **1**:267
"Between the Lines" (Smith) **25**:410; **73**:359
Between the Lines (Ian) **21**:184-85
Between the Lines (Silver) **20**:343-45
Between the Lines (Wakefield) **7**:502
"Between the Living and the Dead" (Ignatow) **40**:259
Between the Numen and the Moha (Blackmur) **24**:59, 65-6
"Between the Pool and the Gardenias" (Danticat) **94**:98-9
"Between the Porch and the Altar" (Lowell) **4**:295; **8**:358
"Between the Porch and the Altar" (Stafford) **4**:518
"Between the Sheets" (Bowering) **47**:28-9
Between Time and Timbuktu; or, Prometheus-Five, a Space Fantasy (Vonnegut) **12**:625-26
Between Two Lives (Turner) **48**:398-99
"Between Two Nights" (Arghezi)
    See "Între doua nopti"
"Between Two Nowheres" (MacCaig) **36**:285
"Between Two Prisoners" (Dickey) **109**:238
Between Two Rivers: Selected Poems 1956-1984 (Kenny) **87**:244, 248-49
"Between Two Seas" (Broumas) **73**:16
"Between Two Shores" (Mac Laverty) **31**:252, 254
"Between Two Texts" (Porter) **33**:324
Between Two Tides (FitzGerald) **19**:176, 180
Between Two Worlds (Rice) **7**:360; **49**:300, 303-05
Between Two Worlds (Schwarz-Bart)
    See *Ti Jean l'horizon*
"Between What I See and What I Say" (Paz) **51**:335; **65**:190
"Between Zero and One" (Gallant) **38**:194
Beulah Land (Davis) **49**:85-6, 89-90, 97
The Beulah Quintet (Settle) **61**:369-74, 376, 378-79, 387
"Beverly Hills, Chicago" (Brooks) **49**:27
"A Bevy of Aunts" (Lavin) **99**:321-22
"Beware" (Fearing) **51**:110

"Beware" (Knight) **40**:279
"Beware My Love" (McCartney) **35**:284
Beware of the Trains (Crispin) **22**:110
"Beware, Soul Brother" (Achebe) **26**:22, 24
Beware, Soul Brother and Other Poems
  (Achebe) **7**:6; **11**:3-4
Beware the Months of Fire (Lane) **25**:284-85,
  288
"Beware...The Vibes of Marx" (Raine) **103**:180
"Bewitched" (Edmonds) **35**:146
The Bewitched (Barnes) **5**:49-50; **56**:5-9
"The Bewlay Brothers" (Bowie) **17**:58
Bewusstseins-Industrie (*The Consciousness In-
  dustry: On Literature, Politics, and the
  Media*) (Enzensberger) **43**:147-48, 154
"Beyond" (Faulkner) **3**:152
"Beyond" (Sa-Carniero)
  See "Beyond"
Beyond (Richards) **24**:401
Beyond a Boundary (James) **33**:219, 222-25
Beyond a Reasonable Doubt (Lang) **20**:208,
  216; **103**:89
Beyond All This Fiddle (Alvarez) **5**:17
Beyond Another Door (Levitin) **17**:265-66
Beyond Apollo (Malzberg) **7**:208
Beyond Criticism (Shapiro) **4**:485, 487
Beyond Culture (Trilling) **9**:530; **11**:546;
  24:458-59, 462-63
Beyond Dark Hills (Stuart) **14**:514; **34**:373,
  375
*Beyond Earth: The Search for Extraterrestrial
  Life* (Gallant) **17**:131-32
*Beyond Feminist Aesthetics: Feminist Litera-
  ture and Social Change* **65**:340
Beyond Formalism: Literary Essays, 1958-1970
  (Hartman) **27**:179-80, 182-84, 187
"Beyond Harm" (Olds) **85**:306
"Beyond Howth Head" (Mahon) **27**:286-87,
  290-91
"Beyond Lies the Wub" ("The Wub") (Dick)
  72:113
Beyond Mozambique (Walker) **61**:426-27, 432
"Beyond Power" (Rosenthal) **28**:394
Beyond Power: A Sequence (Rosenthal)
  28:391-92, 394-95
Beyond Power: On Women, Men, and Morals
  (French) **60**:138-40, 142-47
"Beyond Sargasso" (Heaney) **14**:243
"Beyond Survival" (Levi) **50**:337
"Beyond the Alps" (Lowell) **8**:349; **15**:345-
  48
Beyond the Bedroom Wall: A Family Album
  (Woiwode) **6**:578-79; **10**:540-41
Beyond the Blue Event Horizon (Pohl) **18**:413
Beyond the Curve (Abe) **81**:296, 298
Beyond the Dead Reef (Tiptree) **48**:394-95
Beyond the Dragon's Mouth (Naipaul) **39**:355-
  58
"Beyond the End" (Barnes)
  See "Spillway"
"Beyond the Eyelids" (Redgrove) **41**:352
Beyond the Fringe (*Fringe*) (Bennett) **45**:54-
  6; **77**:83, 85-6, 92-5, 98-9, 102, 104
"Beyond the Gentility Principle" (Alvarez)
  5:17
"Beyond the Glass Mountain" (Stegner) **49**:350
*Beyond the Hundredth Meridian: John Wesley
  Powell and the Second Opening of the
  West* (Stegner) **81**:347, 349, 351-52
"Beyond the Hunting Woods" (Justice) **102**:262
Beyond the Law (Mailer) **74**:217
Beyond the Limit (Ratushinskaya) **54**:381-82
"Beyond the Liss" (Montague) **46**:266, 268

"Beyond the Mexique Bay" (Huxley) **3**:255;
  18:269; **79**:310
Beyond the Mountains (Rexroth) **112**:373
Beyond the Mountains (Rexroth) **11**:472;
  22:345, 347; **49**:279-80; **112**:372, 376,
  387
"Beyond the Novel" (Cioran) **64**:82, 84, 97
"Beyond the Pale" (Trevor) **25**:445-46;
  71:323, 326, 327, 337, 339, 342, 347;
  116:360, 367, 371-72, 376, 383, 385
Beyond the Pale, and Other Stories (Trevor)
  25:445-47; **71**:325, 346; **116**:348
Beyond the Palisade (Baxter) **14**:59-60
"Beyond the Peacock: The Reconstruction of
  Flannery O'Connor" (Walker) **58**:405
"Beyond the Pleasure Principle" (Nemerov)
  2:307
"Beyond the Red River" (McGrath) **59**:180
*Beyond the Revolution: My Life and Times Since
  "Famous Long Ago"* (Mungo) **72**:292
"Beyond the Snow Belt" (Oliver) **98**:266
Beyond the Vicarage (Streatfeild) **21**:411-12
Beyond the Wall (Abbey) **36**:20; **59**:238, 242
"Beyond the Zero" (Pynchon) **11**:452
Beyond Therapy (Durang) **27**:90, 92-3; **38**:171,
  174
Beyond This Horizon (Heinlein) **3**:224-26;
  14:247, 249; **55**:304
Beyond This Place (Cronin) **32**:137-38
"The B-Flat Sonata" (Johnston) **51**:254
B.F.'s Daughter (Marquand) **10**:329
The Biafra Story (Forsyth) **36**:174
"Bialik's Hint" (Ozick) **62**:344, 349, 351
"Bianca's Hands" (Sturgeon) **39**:361, 366
The Bible (Huston) **20**:170
The Bible of the Beasts of the Little Field
  (Schaeffer) **22**:369-70
"Bibliographical Note" (Yourcenar) **87**:411
*A Bibliography of the King's Book or, Eikon
  Basilike* (Howe) **72**:208
"La biblioteca de Babel" ("The Library of Ba-
  bel") (Borges) **1**:39; **2**:72, 77; **8**:96, 98,
  101-02; **9**:116, 118; **13**:108-09; **19**:46;
  44:358, 362, 368; **48**:45-6; **83**:156-57,
  164, 177-78, 183
"Bicentennial Man" (Asimov) **26**:50, 56, 58
The Bicentennial Man, and Other Stories
  (Asimov) **26**:39, 50, 53-6; **92**:7, 9
Les biches (Chabrol) **16**:170-74, 180-81, 183
Les biches (Cocteau) **15**:134
Bicicletone (Pasolini) **106**:222, 224
"Bicultural" (Johnston) **51**:240, 242, 252
Bicycle Days (Schwartz) **59**:83-8
The Bicycle Thief (De Sica)
  See *Ladri di biciclette*
"Bicycles" (Ritter) **52**:355
"Bicycles, Muscles, Cigarettes" (Carver) **53**:64
La bicyclette du condamné (*The Condemned
  Man's Bicycle*) (Arrabal) **9**:35, 38; **58**:4,
  6, 8, 17, 26-7
"The Bicyclist" (Schnackenberg) **40**:379
"A Bid" (Corn) **33**:117
Bid Me to Live (A Madrigal) (*A Madrigal*) (H.
  D.) **8**:258; **14**:223, 229; **31**:203, 207,
  211; **34**:444; **73**:122-25, 127-33, 135
Bid Time Return (Matheson) **37**:247
Bidaya wa-nihaya (*A Beginning and an End*)
  (Mahfuz) **52**:292-93, 300, 304; **55**:173-
  74, 181-82
"A Bidding Grace" (Hope) **51**:215
Il bidone (*The Swindle*) (Fellini) **16**:274, 276,
  298; **85**:59
Biedermann und die Brandstifter: Ein Lehrstück

ohne Lehre (*The Firebugs: A Learning Play
  without a Lesson*) (Frisch) **3**:166-68;
  9:217; **14**:182; **18**:161, 163; **32**:188, 191,
  195; **44**:181-83, 196-97, 199-200
"Bien Pretty" (Cisneros) **69**:154-55
"Biens équaux" (Char) **9**:163
"Bientôt" (Damas) **84**:167, 169, 174, 177-
  78, 182
"Bienvenue" (Char) **14**:126
"Bière de pécheur" (Landolfi) **49**:214, 217
"Biesiada u hrabiny Kotlubaj" ("The Feast at
  Countess Fritter's") (Gombrowicz) **49**:127
The Bievres Desert (Duhamel) **8**:189
Biffures (Leiris) **61**:341-43, 347, 351-53, 355-
  57, 359
Big and Little (Strauss)
  See *Gross und Klein*
Big as Life (Doctorow) **113**:152, 176
Big Bad Love (Brown) **73**:22-3
Big Bang (Sarduy) **97**:417
  See *Big Bang*
The Big Barn (Edmonds) **35**:145, 148-49, 151,
  156
"Big Barn Bed" (McCartney) **35**:281
"Big Bessie Throws Her Son into the Street"
  (Brooks) **49**:27-8
"Big Black Good Man" (Wright) **21**:438, 443
"Big Blonde" (Parker) **15**:414-15; **68**:326,
  329, 332, 334-35
The Big Bounce (Leonard) **71**:224
"Big Boy Leaves Home" (Wright) **1**:380;
  14:596; **21**:444, 453
The Big Brass Ring (Welles) **80**:413
"Big Brother" (Wonder) **12**:657, 663
"Big Brother, Little Sister" (Ihimaera) **46**:200
"Big Business" (Guillevic) **33**:191
"The Big Cats" (Reading) **47**:352
"The Big Circus" (Bagryana) **10**:14
The Big City (Ray)
  See *Mahanagar*
The Big Clock (Fearing) **51**:112-13, 115-16,
  119-22
"The Big Country" (Byrne) **25**:96-8
Big David, Little David (Hinton) **111**:90
"A Big Day at Big House" (Iskander)
  See "Bol'shoiden' Bol'shogo Doma"
The Big Dipper (Billington) **43**:53-4
"Big Elegy" (Brodský)
  See "The Great Elegy for John Donne"
"The Big Flash" (Spinrad) **46**:383
"Big Fleas and Little Fleas" (White) **49**:407
Big Fleas and Little Fleas (White) **49**:407
The Big Four (Christie) **6**:108; **48**:74; **110**:111
"The Big Front Yard" (Simak) **55**:320
*The Big Funk: A Casual Play or Talk around
  the Polis* (Shanley) **75**:331-32
"Big Game" (Boyle) **90**:62-3
"The Big Garage" (Boyle) **36**:57
The Big Gold Dream (Himes) **58**:267
The Big Green Book (Graves) **39**:325
"The Big Heart" (Sexton) **6**:492
The Big Heart (Anand) **23**:12, 14-16; **93**:24,
  30-2, 41-3, 50
The Big Heat (Lang) **20**:205, 207, 208; **103**:99
"The Big House" (Muldoon) **32**:319; **72**:264-
  65
The Big House (Behan) **79**:25, 27
"The Big Hunger" (Miller) **30**:262-63, 265
"The Big It" (Guthrie) **23**:199
The Big It (Guthrie) **23**:198
*A Big Jewish Book: Poems and Other Visions of
  the Jews from Tribal Times to Present*
  (Rothenberg) **57**:382

"Big Joe and the Nth Generation" (Miller) 30:262, 264-65

"Big Jules" (Callaghan)　41:98

The Big Kill (Spillane)　3:468; 13:526

The Big Knife (Odets)　2:318, 320; 28:330-34, 339-40; 98:201, 216-17, 224, 228, 235-36, 242, 244-48, 251-52

The Big Knives (Lancaster)　36:245

"The Big Knockover" (Hammett)　47:161

The Big Knockover: Selected Stories and Short Novels (Hammett)　5:161-62

The Big Laugh (O'Hara)　42:319, 322

"Big Leaguer" (Fante)　60:133

"The Big Leagues" (Bowering)　47:24

"Big Liz" (Muldoon)　32:318

"Big Machine" (Hillis)　66:195-200

Big Mama's Funeral (Garcia Marquez)
　See *Los funerales de la Mamá Grande*

The Big Man (McIlvanney)　42:285

"Big Meadows in March" (Brosman)　9:135

"Big Meeting" (Hughes)　108:298

"Big Momma" (Madhubuti)　73:213

The Big Money (Dos Passos)　1:77; 4:131-33, 135, 137; 11:157; 15:182-83; 34:419, 422, 424; 82:65-8, 71-5, 79, 82, 89, 91-2, 95, 97-103, 105, 107-10, 112

"Big My Secret, But It's Bandaged" (Swenson) 106:341

The Big Nickel (Willingham)　5:512; 51:410-11

Big Night (Powell)　66:366

"Big Numbers" (Szymborska)　99:192

"The Big Outside World" (Beattie)　63:14

Big Planet (Vance)　35:423, 425-26

"The Big Plum" (Colwin)　5:107; 84:150

"The Big Pot Game" (Bukowski)　41:68

Big River (Buzo)　61:64-6

The Big Rock Candy Mountain (Stegner) 49:348, 357, 360; 81:339-40, 343, 347-50, 352

"The Big Rock-Candy Mountain" (Sissman) 9:491

"Big Sam Was My Friend" (Ellison)　42:126

The Big Sea: An Autobiography (Hughes) 10:279; 15:293; 44:511; 108:284, 290, 292, 295-96, 311-12, 314, 317, 323

The Big Sell (Berton)　104:47

The Big Sell (Berton)　104:45, 47

The Big Shave (Scorsese)　20:326

"The Big Shot" (Faulkner)　18:148

"Big Shot" (Joel)　26:216-17, 220-21

"Big Sister's Clothes" (Costello)　21:76

"Big Sky" (Davies)　21:90

The Big Sky (Guthrie)　23:195-96, 198-201

"The Big Space Fuck" (Vonnegut)　22:451

A Big Storm Knocked It Over (Colwin)　84:153

Big Sur (Kerouac)　14:305; 29:271-72; 61:296, 308-09

Big Sur and the Oranges of Hieronymous Bosch (Miller)　14:374; 84:243, 258

The Big Time (Leiber)　25:302-03, 305, 309, 311

The Big Time (Scannell)　49:327

Big Time: Scenes from a Service Economy (Reddin)　67:269-70

Big Toys (Buzo)　61:62

"The Big Trip Up Yonder" (Vonnegut)　12:617

"Big Two-Hearted River" (Hemingway)　3:238, 240; 6:234; 8:289; 10:268; 13:270-71, 273, 278-79; 30:180-81, 183-84, 190-95, 197-98, 200-02; 39:401-02; 41:197; 50:412, 415, 421-22, 424, 427; 61:194, 197, 203, 207, 214, 228; 80:151

"Big Valley Vineyard" (Saroyan)　1:301

"Big Wheels: A Tale of the Laundry Game" ("Milkman 2") (King)　37:207

"Big Wind" (Roethke)　101:287, 294-95

The Big Woods (Faulkner)　18:149

Big World (Andrade)
　See *Mundo grande*

"Big Yellow Taxi" (Mitchell)　12:442

A Bigamist's Daughter (*That Night*) (McDonald) 90:214-17, 221-22, 227-28, 230, 233

"Bigfoot" (Muldoon)　72:270

Bigfoot Dreams (Prose)　45:326-28

"Big-Foot Sal" (Edmonds)　35:157

"Bigfoot Stole My Wife" (Carlson)　54:39

The Bigger Light (Clarke)　8:143; 53:90, 93-5

"The Bight" (Bishop)　9:95; 13:93; 32:34, 37

Bijou (Madden)　5:265-66; 15:350

"Bike" (Pink Floyd)　35:307

"The Bike" (Sillitoe)　57:392

"The Bike" (Soto)　80:301

"The Bilal's Fourth Wife" (Ousmane)　66:347, 350

"Bildnis eines Dichters" (Hildesheimer) 49:173-74

Bilete de papagal (Arghezi)　80:3

"Biletul" ("The Note") (Arghezi)　80:11

Bilgewater (Gardam)　43:167-68

"Bilingual Sestina" (Alvarez)　93:17

"Bilking the Statues" (Ashbery)　77:67

"Bill" (Masefield)　11:358

"Bill" (Powers)　57:349, 357-58

"Bill Boston" (Dickinson)　49:104

"Bill Brand" (Griffiths)　52:174, 182-84

"Bill of Fare" (Enzensberger)　43:144

A Bill of Rites, a Bill of Wrongs, a Bill of Goods (Morris)　7:247; 37:313

Bill, the Galactic Hero (Harrison)　42:199-200, 205-06

Billard um halbzehn (*Billiards at Half-past Nine*) (Boell)　2:67; 3:74; 6:83; 9:102-04, 106, 108-10; 11:52, 55-56, 58; 27:60; 39:292-95; 72:68, 72-3, 85

"Billboards" (Ondaatje)　51:316

"Billboards Build Freedom of Choice" (Birney) 6:75

"Billennium" (Ballard)　14:41; 36:36, 41

Billiards at Half-past Nine (Boell)
　See *Billard um halbzehn*

"Billings and Cooings from 'The Berkeley Barb'" (Van Duyn)　63:437, 439; 116:408

The Billion Dollar Brain (Deighton)　4:119; 7:75; 46:125

Billion Dollar Brain (Russell)　16:541, 548

The Billion Dollar Sure Thing (Erdman) 25:153-54

A Billion for Boris (Rodgers)　12:494

Billion Year Spree: The History of Science Fiction (Aldiss)　14:14; 40:16

A Billionaire (Ichikawa)　20:181-82

"Billons" (Glissant)　68:181

Billy (French)　86:61-7

Billy Bathgate (Doctorow)　65:134-39, 141-45; 113:158, 161, 166, 168-70, 176-78

"Billy Boy" (Keillor)　115:277

Billy Buck (*The Visitor*) (Poole)　17:372

"Billy Dee" (Kristofferson)　26:267

"Billy Ducks among the Pharoahs" (De Marinis) 54:100

"Billy Hunt" (Weller)　26:444

Billy Liar (Waterhouse)　47:415-16, 418, 420-21

Billy Liar on the Moon (Waterhouse)　47:420-21

Billy Phelan's Greatest Game (Kennedy) 28:204-06; 34:206-09; 53:190, 192-94

Billy the Kid (Spicer)　8:498; 18:508-09

"Billy the Mountain" (Zappa)　17:588

Biloxi Blues (Simon)　39:216-19; 70:236, 240, 243

Bilvav yamim (*In the Heart of the Seas*) (Agnon) 4:12; 8:8

"Bimini" (Hemingway)　6:232; 8:285

Bin; oder, Die Reise nach Peking (Frisch)　3:167; 44:193-95, 200

"Bin'arenu uvizkenenu" ("With Our Youth and with Our Aged") (Agnon)　14:3

Binary (Crichton)　54:68

"Binding the Dragon" (Sarton)　91:254

Bing (*Ping*) (Beckett)　2:48; 6:38; 9:83; 11:40-1; 14:78; 18:50; 29:57, 59

Bingo (Brown)　79:167

Bingo: Scenes of Money and Death (Bond) 4:70; 6:84-6; 13:102; 23:64

Binstead's Safari (Ingalls)　42:232-33

Bio (Berry)　17:53

Bio of a Space Tyrant (Anthony)　35:39-40

Biochemistry and Human Metabolism (Asimov)　76:315

"Biografía de Tadeo Isidoro Cruz" ("Biography of Tadeo Isidoro Cruz"; "The Life of Tadeo Isidoro Cruz") (Borges)　13:104-5

Biografie: Ein Spiel (*Biography: A Game*; *Biography: A Play*) (Frisch)　3:167; 14:181-82; 18:161-62; 32:191; 44:189, 193-96, 198-200, 203-04

Biograph (Dylan)　77:186, 188, 190

Biographia literaria (Brooks)　24:104

"Biography"　75:63, 70, 77

"A Biography" (Bell)　8:66

"Biography" (Ciardi)　40:157

"Biography" (Gustafson)　36:214

"Biography" (Herbert)　43:183

"Biography" (Masefield)　47:229-30

"Biography" (Ondaatje)　51:310

"Biography" (Tomlinson)　45:393

Biography (Behrman)　40:74-6, 80, 82

Biography: A Game (Frisch)
　See *Biografie: Ein Spiel*

Biography: A Play (Frisch)
　See *Biografie: Ein Spiel*

"Biography in the First Person" (Dunn)　36:152

Biography of a Buick (Morris)　76:
　See *Motor City*

"Biography of a Story" (Jackson)　87:234

"Biography of Tadeo Isidoro Cruz" (Borges)
　See "Biografía de Tadeo Isidoro Cruz"

Biography of T.H. White (Warner)　19:460

Bionics: Man Copies Nature's Machines (Silverstein and Silverstein)　17:452

"Bio-poetics Sketch" (Harjo)　83:270

"Biotherm (for Bill Berkson)" (O'Hara)　2:323; 13:431; 78:359-64

"Bip Bop" (McCartney)　35:280

"Birch Bark" (Ondaatje)　51:318

"The Birch Tree of Iron" (Padilla)　38:351

"Birches" (Frost)　3:170; 4:174; 9:219, 229; 15:242, 244-45, 248; 26:111-12, 116, 122, 125

"Birches" (Leithauser)　27:240-42

"The Birchwood" (Daryush)　19:121

Birchwood (Banville)　46:26-7, 32

The Birch-Wood (Wajda)　16:582-83

"Bird" (Harjo)　83:280

"Bird" (Hesse)　25:259

"The Bird" (Lane)　25:284

"Bird?" (Lowell)　11:329

"The Bird" (Simic)   9:481; 22:383
"The Bird" (Smith)   15:514
Bird (Hinde)   6:241
Bird Alone (O'Faolain)   14:402; 70:316-17, 320-21
"Bird and the Muse" (Zaturenska)   6:586
Bird at My Window (Guy)   26:140-41
"The Bird Frau" (Dove)   81:137
Bird in the Bush (Rexroth)   22:346; 112:371, 390
A Bird in the House (Laurence)   3:278; 50:314-15, 319-20, 322; 62:267-68, 270-72, 278, 280, 282, 293, 296, 305-06
"Bird in the Lighted Hall" (Brown)   48:60
"Bird Lament" (Swados)   12:557
"Bird Life" (Willingham)   51:403
The Bird of Dawning (Masefield)   11:357
"The Bird of Jesus" (Colum)   28:90
"The Bird of Night" (Jarrell)   13:303
The Bird of Night (Hill)   4:227-28; 113:278-80, 282, 287, 292-93, 297, 301, 303-05, 322, 330
A Bird of Paper: Poems of Vicente Aleixandre (Aleixandre)   36:32
"The Bird of Paradise" (Laing)   95:127, 136
"Bird Song" (Kogawa)   78:167
"The Bird Watcher" (Kotzwinkle)   35:254
"Bird Watching" (Ciardi)   44:382
"The Bird with the Dark Plumes" (Jeffers)   54:237
"Birdbrain!" (Ginsberg)   36:196
"Birdie" (Merwin)   88:195
"Birdland" (Smith)   12:537
"Birdland's Golden Age" (Stuart)   11:510-11
"The Birdnesters" (Szirtes)   46:392, 395
"The Birds" (Blackburn)   43:64
"The Birds" (du Maurier)   59:285, 287
"The Birds" (Jacobsen)   48:190
"Birds" (Kenny)   87:242
"The Birds" (Turner)   48:398-99
The Birds (Hitchcock)   16:343-44, 348, 350, 353, 359
Birds (Perse)
   See *Oiseaux*
The Birds (Vesaas)   48:407-10
Birds (Wright)   53:423-24, 428, 431
"Birds/Amsterdam" (Blackburn)   9:100
"The Birds Complain" (Szirtes)   46:395
"The Birds Do Thus" (Frost)   10:199; 15:246
The Birds Fall Down (West)   7:525-26; 9:560; 50:394, 405, 408
"Birds in Winter" (Ignatow)   14:275
"A Bird's Life" (Swenson)   14:518
The Bird's Nest (Jackson)   60:211-12, 216-17, 219-20, 229, 231
"A Bird's Nest Made of White Reed Fiber" (Bly)   15:63
"Birds of a Feather" (Humphrey)   45:205
"Birds of a Feather" (Lamming)   66:220
Birds of America (McCarthy)   3:328-29; 5:276; 14:363; 59:291
The Birds of Paradise (Scott)   9:476-77; 60:328, 340
Birds of Passage (Rubens)   31:351
The Birds of Pompeii (Ciardi)   44:382
"Birds of Prey" (White)   49:408
Birds of Prey (White)   49:408
The Birds of the Air (Ellis)   40:190-91, 193
"The Birds of Vietnam" (Carruth)   7:41; 84:134
"The Birds Poised to Fly" (Highsmith)   102:203
The Birds Too Are Gone (Kemal)
   See *Kuslar da gitti*
"Birds Who Nest in the Garage" (Bell)   31:50

"Birdwatching" (Livesay)   79:338
"Bird-Witted" (Moore)   8:398
Birdy (Wharton)   18:542-44; 37:436-37, 439-43
"Birmingham" (MacNeice)   1:186; 4:316; 53:231, 238
"Birmingham Sunday" (Hughes)   15:295
"Birth" (Anand)   23:18
"Birth" (Clarke)   61:73
"Birth" (Hooker)   43:197
"Birth" (MacBeth)   5:265
"Birth" (Nin)   60:267
"Birth Day" (Avison)   97:92
"The Birth in a Narrow Room" (Brooks)   49:26, 31
"Birth of a Coachman" (Durcan)   43:114
The Birth of a Grandfather (Sarton)   14:482; 49:312-13
Birth of a Hero (Gold)   42:188, 191-92
The Birth of a New Republic (Williamson)   29:454
"Birth of a Notion" (Asimov)   26:50
"Birth of a Salesman" (Tiptree)   48:385; 50:356
The Birth of a Story (Paustovsky)   40:368
"The Birth of Black Boy" (Wright)   74:389
The Birth of David (Robbe-Grillet)   14:462
"Birth of Love" (Warren)   6:556, 558; 8:542-43; 39:266
The Birth of the Christ (Endo)   99:285, 287
The Birth of the Clinic: An Archaeology of Medical Perception (Foucault)
   See *Naissance de la clinique: Une archéologie du regard médical*
"The Birth of the Poet" (Acker)   111:46
"Birth of the Virgin" (Swenson)   106:349
"The Birth of Tragedy" (Oates)   6:371
"The Birth of Venus" (Williams)   42:456
Birth Rate (Rozewicz)   9:464
"Birthday" (Ciardi)   40:153
"Birthday" (Fuller)
   See "Lines for a 21st Birthday"
"Birthday" (Louie)   70:79
"A Birthday Card" (Beer)   58:36
The Birthday Gift (Shapcott)   38:404
The Birthday Murderer (Bennett)   35:44
"Birthday on the Acropolis" (Sarton)   49:320
"The Birthday Party" (Berriault)   54:3
"The Birthday Party" (Jackson)   60:228
The Birthday Party (Pinter)   3:386; 6:407-08, 411, 413-14, 416-18, 420; 9:420; 11:437-38, 440-41, 444; 15:422, 426; 27:384-85, 387-89, 392-94, 396; 58:371-72, 375-76, 384-85; 73:249, 251-52, 256, 266, 276, 281
"Birthday Poem" (Simmons)   43:411
"Birthday Poem" (Whalen)   29:447
"Birthday Poem" (Young)   19:477
"Birthday Poem (For Clifford Sealy)" (Lamming)   66:220
"A Birthday Present" (Plath)   9:426-27; 11:447; 14:423, 425; 17:347-48, 366-67; 51:345; 111:168-69, 178
"Birthday Sestina" (Voigt)   54:429
"Birthday Star Atlas" (Simic)   49:341
"Birthday Thirty-Five: Diary Entry" (Chappell)   40:143-44; 78:92
The Birthgrave (Lee)   46:233
"The Birthmark" (Ellison)   11:182; 114:93
"The Birthplace" (Heaney)   37:168; 74:168
Birthplace (Haavikko)
   See *Synnyinmaa*
Birthplace: Moving into Nearness (Wilson)

49:416-18
"Birthplace Revisited" (Corso)   11:123
Birthright (Stribling)   23:439, 445, 447-48
Births (Saroyan)   29:363
"Birthstone" (Musgrave)   54:341
Birthstone (Thomas)   22:418
"Birthstones" (Van Duyn)   63:443
"Bishop" (Barthelme)   23:47
"Bishop Berkeley of Cloyne" (Young)   82:396-397
"Bishop Erik Grave's Grave" (Gustafson)   36:218
"Bishop of Cork Murders His Wife" (Durcan)   43:114-15
The Bishop's Bonfire: A Sad Play within the Tune of a Polka (O'Casey)   5:318, 320; 9:407; 11:409; 88:257-58, 262-63, 270, 272-73
Bishop's Progress (Mano)   2:270; 10:327-28
"Bishopston Stream" (Watkins)   43:444
Bison
   See *Zubr*
"Bison Crossing Near Mt. Rushmore" (Swenson)   61:397
The Bit between My Teeth: A Literary Chronicle of 1950-1965 (Wilson)   8:550; 24:479, 481
A Bit of Singing and Dancing (Hill)   4:227-28; 113:281, 293, 297, 310, 312, 325, 330
"Bitch" (Dahl)   6:121; 79:183
"Bitch" (Jagger and Richard)   17:224, 226, 229, 236
"Bitch" (Kizer)   80:185
Bitches and Sad Ladies: An Anthology of Fiction by and about Women   65:347, 350
"The Bite" (Stern)   40:414
"Bite the Bullet" (Young)   17:576
"Bite-Me-Not; or, Fleur de Fur" (Lee)   46:234
"Bitka kod Bistrice Lesne" (Krleza)   114:167
"Bits and Pieces of Our Land" (Bell)   31:49
Bitter Angel (Gerstler)   70:155-59
The Bitter Box (Clark)   19:104-05
"A Bitter Farce" (Schwartz)   10:462; 87:334
"Bitter Fruit of the Tree" (Brown)   59:265
The Bitter Glass (Dillon)   17:94
The Bitter Heritage: Vietnam and American Democracy, 1941-1966 (Schlesinger)   84:361, 373
Bitter Lemons (Durrell)   8:193; 13:188
"The Bitter Moon" (Winters)   32:468
"The Bitter River" (Hughes)   108:283
"Bitter Sorrow for Three Sleepwalkers" (Garcia Marquez)
   See "Amargura para tres sonámbulos"
Bitter Sweet (Coward)   1:64; 29:132, 137
The Bitter Tears of Petra von Kant (Fassbinder)   20:106-09
"Bitter Thought in Exile" (Kunene)   85:175
"Bitterness for Three Sleepwalkers" (Garcia Marquez)
   See "Amargura para tres sonámbulos"
Bivouac (Lopez y Fuentes)
   See *Campamento*
Bizarre Behavior (Innaurato)   60:200-01
Bizou (Klein)   30:244
Den blaa Pekingeser (The Blue Pekinese) (Abell)   15:2, 7
"Blacamán el bueno vendedor de milagros" (Garcia Marquez)
   See "Blacamán the Good, Vendor of Miracles"
"Blacamán the Good, Vendor of Miracles" ("Blacamán el bueno vendedor de milagros") (Garcia Marquez)   27:147;

47:151
The Black Aesthetic (Gayle) **65**:364
Black African Poems (Cendrars) **106**:190
Black Alibi (Woolrich) **77**:389, 400, 404
Black Amber (Whitney) **42**:433
Black and Blue (Jagger and Richard) **17**:236, 238, 242
Black and Blue Magic (Snyder) **17**:470
"Black and Tan" (Bell) **102**:5-6
"The Black and White" (Pinter) **27**:387
Black and White (Brophy) **105**:16
Black and White (*Journey to Nowhere: A New World Tragedy*) (Naipaul) **32**:326-28; **39**:355-57
Black and White (Sorrentino) **7**:449
Black and White Keys (Hood) **28**:195-96
Black and White Minstrels (Taylor) **27**:443
"The Black Angel" (Montale)
See "L'angelo nero"
Black Angel (Cristofer) **28**:97
The Black Angel (Woolrich) **77**:389, 390-92, 394-95, 397-98, 400-01, 403-05
"Black Angels" (Friedman) **56**:97
Black Angels: Stories (Friedman) **3**:165
Black April (Peterkin) **31**:302-06, 309-12
"Black Art" (Baraka) **5**:48; **115**:39
"The Black Art" (Sexton) **10**:468; **53**:316, 319-20, 324
Black as He's Painted (Marsh) **53**:247, 249, 254
"Black as Ink" (Lee) **46**:234
Black Athena: The Afroasiatic Roots of Classical Civilization, Volume 1—The Fabrication of Ancient Greece, 1785-1985 (Bernal) **70**:363, 371, 387
Black Bagatelles (Hall) **51**:174-75
"The Black Ball" (Ellison) **114**:127
"Black Bart" (Dickinson) **49**:102-03
The Black BC's (Clifton) **66**:67, 86-7
The Black Beast (Audiberti)
See *La fête noire*
Black Beech and Honeydew: An Autobiography (Marsh) **53**:248, 257
Black Betty (Mosley) **97**:347-48, 350-54, 358, 361
"The Black Bird" (Ngugi wa Thiong'o) **36**:317
Black Body Blues (Edwards) **43**:138-39
"The Black Book" (Smith) **43**:422
The Black Book (Durrell) **1**:84-5; **4**:147; **6**:154; **8**:192; **13**:184-85; **41**:136, 138
The Black Book (Morrison) **87**:264, 277-78
"The Black Box" (Ewart) **46**:154
Black Box (Oz) **54**:352-57
The Black Boxer (Bates) **46**:51
"Black Boy" (Boyle) **58**:66
Black Boy: A Record of Childhood and Youth (Wright) **1**:379-80; **3**:545; **4**:594, 597; **9**:583-86; **14**:596-98; **21**:434-35, 442-44, 448-49, 457; **74**:355-96
"The Black Boy Looks at the White Boy" (Baldwin) **13**:52; **42**:18; **50**:293
"Black Cargo Ships of War" (Ferron) **94**:103
The Black Cat Tavern (Mahfuz)
See *Khammarat al-qitt al-aswad*
The Black Cauldron (Alexander) **35**:23, 25
"The Black Christ" (Madhubuti) **73**:208-09
Black Cloud, White Cloud: Two Novellas and Two Stories (Douglas) **73**:65-7, 69, 73-5, 80-3, 87, 93, 95
Black Coach (Jordan) **37**:193
Black Coffee (Christie) **39**:437
Black Comedy (Shaffer) **5**:386-89; **14**:486; **18**:475

"The Black Cottage" (Frost) **10**:198
"Black Cow" (Becker and Fagen) **26**:84
"Black Crow" (Mitchell) **12**:443
The Black Curtain (Woolrich) **77**:389-90, 394, 397-98, 400, 404
"BLACK DADA NIHILISMUS" (Baraka) **5**:45, 48; **10**:19; **115**:39
"Black Dog" (Page and Plant) **12**:475, 480, 482
Black Dog, Red Dog (Dobyns) **37**:80-2
"Black Dominion" (Senghor)
See "Domaine noir"
Black Dougal (Walker) **14**:552
The Black Dudley Murder (Allingham)
See *The Crime at Black Dudley*
Black Eagle Child: The Facepaint Narratives (Young Bear) **94**:373-78
Black Easter (Blish) **14**:83, 87
"Black Edge" (Lee) **90**:177
Black Elk Speaks (Neihardt) **32**:335-36
Black Faces, White Faces (*The Pineapple Bay Hotel*) (Gardam) **43**:166-67, 170
The Black Feast (Audiberti)
See *La fête noire*
Black Feeling, Black Talk (Giovanni) **117**:178, 190, 194
Black Feeling, Black Talk, Black Judgement (Giovanni) **19**:190-91; **64**:182, 185-86, 188, 190-91, 195; **117**:181-82, 185, 191
"The Black Ferris" (Bradbury) **42**:36
"The Black Filly" (Lane) **25**:285
Black Fire (Jones and Neal) **65**:371
"Black Flakes" (Celan)
See "Schwarze Flocken"
The Black Flame (Du Bois) **64**:117, 119; **96**:133
"Black for Dinner" (Colter) **58**:143
"Black Friday" (Becker and Fagen) **26**:80
Black Gangster (Goines) **80**:92, 95-7
The Black Gate (Arghezi)
See *Poarta neagra*
Black Genesis: Fortress of Evil (Hubbard) **43**:207
The Black Girl (Ousmane)
See *La Noire de...*
Black Girl Lost (Goines) **80**:93
"Black Goblet" (Pasternak) **7**:298
"Black Hair" (Soto) **80**:289
Black Hair (Soto) **80**:282-83, 288-89
"The Black Hand of the Raj" (McGrath) **55**:73
Black Hearts in Battersea (Aiken) **35**:17, 20
"The Black Helmet" (Glassco) **9**:237
The Black Hermit (Ngugi wa Thiong'o) **7**:266; **36**:320
"The Black Hills" (Everson) **5**:123
"Black Hills Survival Gathering, 1980" (Hogan) **73**:148, 150
"Black Hole" (Swan) **69**:362-63
The Black Hole (Mowat) **26**:336
Black Holes and Baby Universes and Other Essays (Hawking) **105**:69, 71
"Black Holes Aren't Black" (Hawking) **105**:67
Black Holes, Black Stockings (Broumas) **73**:11-15
Black Holes, White Dwarfs, and Superstars (Branley) **21**:22
The Black Horses (Vesaas)
See *Dei svarte hestane*
Black Hosts (Senghor)
See *Hosties noires*
"The Black House" (Highsmith) **42**:215
The Black House (Highsmith) **42**:214; **102**:199

The Black House (Theroux) **5**:427-28; **8**:512; **11**:531; **28**:425-26; **46**:405
Black in America (Jackson) **12**:291
The Black Interpreters (Gordimer) **33**:183; **70**:163, 172
"Black Is My Favorite Color" (Malamud) **2**:266; **44**:416, 419
Black Is the Color of the Cosmos: Essays on Afro-American Literature and Culture, 1942-1981 (Davis) **65**:397
Black Island Memorial (Neruda)
See *Memorial de Isla Negra*
Black Jack (Garfield) **12**:217-18, 224-26, 230, 232, 234-35, 237, 240
"Black Jackets" (Gunn) **32**:208
The Black Jacobins: Toussaint L'Ouverture and the San Domingo Revolution (James) **33**:218-19, 221-22, 225
"The Black Jewel" (Merwin) **45**:275; **88**:205
The Black Joke (Mowat) **26**:339, 341-43
Black Judgement (Giovanni) **19**:191; **117**:178, 190, 195, 198
"Black Kettle Raises the Stars and Stripes" (Simpson) **7**:429
Black Lamb and Grey Falcon (West) **7**:525-26; **9**:561-63; **31**:455-56, 458, 460; **50**:394, 396, 398-402, 404-09
"Black Liberation/Socialist Revolution" (Baraka) **14**:49
Black Light (Kinnell) **3**:270; **5**:215
"The Black Lights" (Jones) **81**:62, 65, 67
Black Like Me (Griffin) **68**:202-03
Black Literature and Literary Theory **65**:365, 378, 380, 398
Black Looks: Race and Representation (hooks) **94**:150, 152-53, 156, 159-60
"Black Love" (Madhubuti) **73**:211
"The Black Madonna" (Lessing) **22**:279
"The Black Madonna" (Spark) **13**:522; **40**:401, 404
"Black Magic" (Sanchez) **116**:277-78, 294
Black Magic (Morand)
See *Magie noire*
"The Black Magic of Barney Haller" (Thurber) **5**:429, 438
Black Magic: Sabotage, Target Study, Black Art; Collected Poetry, 1961-1967 (Baraka) **5**:46-8; **14**:45; **115**:10, 38-9
Black Magnificence (Walker) **19**:454
"Black Man" (Wonder) **12**:659-60, 662-63
"A Black Man Sings in New York City" (Guillen) **79**:230
"A Black Man Talks of Reaping" (Bontemps) **18**:65
"Black Man with a Horn" (Klein) **34**:71
"The Black Man's Lament" (Damas)
See "La complainte du nère"
"Black Maps" (Strand) **71**:285
Black Marina (Tennant) **52**:402-04
Black Marsden (Harris) **25**:210, 216
A Black Mass (Baraka) **5**:47-8; **115**:34, 36, 40-4
Black Mass (Bond) **23**:66
"The Black Mesa" (Merrill) **13**:381
"Black Messiah" (Davies) **21**:103-04
Black Mischief (Waugh) **1**:359; **3**:512; **13**:584-87; **27**:470, 477; **107**:357, 362, 370-71, 383, 393, 396
Black Misery (Hughes) **35**:219; **108**:336
"Black Money" (Gallagher) **18**:169
Black Money (Macdonald) **2**:255; **14**:334-35; **41**:266, 270
The Black Moon (Graham) **23**:194

"Black Mother Praying in the Summer of 1943" (Dodson)   **79**:191

"Black Mother Woman" (Lorde)   **71**:232, 245

Black Mountain Breakdown (Smith)   **25**:407-08, 410-11; **73**:340-41, 343, 348, 358

"Black Mountain Side" (Page and Plant)   **12**:479, 482

Black Music (Baraka)   **14**:45; **33**:62; **115**:28, 39

Black Narcissus (Godden)   **53**:150-53, 155-56, 160, 163-64

"Black Night" (Seger)   **35**:380

Black Night Window (Newlove)   **14**:377

Black Novel (with Argentines) (Valenzuela)
  See *Novela negra con arentinos*

"A Black November Turkey" (Wilbur)   **3**:530

"Black Nude" (Tomlinson)   **13**:546

The Black Obelisk (Remarque)   **21**:332

Black on Black: Baby Sister and Selected Writings (Himes)   **4**:229; **7**:159; **18**:249; **108**:227

Black Opal (Prichard)   **46**:330-32, 335-36, 338-41

Black Orpheus and Other Love Poems (Komunyakaa)   **94**:223

The Black Path of Fear (Woolrich)   **77**:404

The Black Pearl (O'Dell)   **30**:270, 273

"The Black Pen" (Donnell)   **34**:159

"The Black Pentecostal Fire" (Brown)   **5**:78

"Black People!" (Baraka)   **5**:48

Black Picture Show (Gunn)   **5**:152-53

"The Black Pig" (Montague)   **46**:277

"Black Poems, Poseurs and Power" (Giovanni)   **19**:192; **64**:183; **117**:183

"Black Poetics/for the many to come" (Madhubuti)   **73**:198

"Black Pony Eating Grass" (Bly)   **15**:68

Black Power (Wright)   **4**:596; **14**:597

Black Pride (Madhubuti)   **2**:238; **73**:191, 205, 207-10, 214-15

The Black Prince (Murdoch)   **3**:347-49; **4**:368, 370; **6**:343, 345, 348-49; **11**:384; **31**:287-88, 290; **51**:287-89, 291

The Black Prince, and Other Stories (Grau)   **4**:207, 210

"The Black Rabbit" (White)   **30**:452

Black Rain (Ibuse)
  See *Kuroi ame*

Black Reconstruction: An Essay toward a History of the Part Which Black Folk Played in the Attempt to Reconstruct Democracy in America, 1860-1880 (Du Bois)   **13**:180-81; **64**:105-07, 116; **96**:146, 149, 160

The Black Rider (Burroughs)   **109**:182

"Black River" (Kenny)   **87**:248

Black Robe (Moore)   **90**:263-69, 272-76, 283-89, 296, 298

"Black Rook in Rainy Weather" (Plath)   **11**:447; **51**:344; **111**:202

The Black Rose (Costain)   **30**:93, 95-8

Black Sea (Paustovsky)   **40**:368

"The Black Sheep" (Boell)
  See "Die schwarzen schafe"

Black Sheep (Rice)   **7**:360; **49**:305

Black Ship to Hell (Brophy)   **29**:92; **105**:3, 7, 9, 12, 30, 34

The Black Shrike (MacLean)   **50**:348-49

"Black Shroud" (Ginsberg)   **109**:364

"Black Shylock" (Auchincloss)   **45**:30

"Black Silk" (Gallagher)   **63**:116, 119

"Black Sketches" (Madhubuti)   **73**:206

Black Skins and White Masks (Fanon)
  See *Peau noire, masques blancs*

Black Skins, White Masks (Fanon)
  See *Peau noire, masques blancs*

"Black Snakes" (Oliver)   **98**:261, 265

Black Snow (Aquin)
  See *Neige noir*

"Black Song" (Guillen)
  See "Canto negro"

The Black Soul (O'Flaherty)   **5**:321

The Black Spaniel Mystery (Cavanna)   **12**:97

"The Black Spear" (Hayden)   **5**:168-69

The Black Spectacles (Carr)
  See *The Problem of the Green Capsule*

Black Spring (Miller)   **4**:351; **14**:375; **43**:298-99; **84**:234-36, 239, 241, 243, 262

"The Black Stag" (Char)   **9**:166

The Black Stallion (Farley)   **17**:115

The Black Stallion and Satan (Farley)   **17**:116

The Black Stallion and the Girl (Farley)   **17**:118

The Black Stallion Mystery (Farley)   **17**:117

The Black Stallion Returns (Farley)   **17**:115

The Black Stallion Revolts (Farley)   **17**:117

The Black Stallion's Filly (Farley)   **17**:116-17

The Black Stallion's Ghost (Farley)   **17**:118

The Black Stallion's Sulky Colt (Farley)   **17**:117

The Black Star Passes (Campbell)   **32**:73, 76, 80

Black Sun (Abbey)   **36**:17-19; **59**:242

Black Sun: Depression and Melancholia (Kristeva)
  See *Soleil noir: Dépression et melancholie*

Black Sun: The Brief Transit and Violent Eclipse of Harry Crosby (Wolff)   **41**:457-58

"The Black Swan" (Merrill)   **13**:379; **91**:238

Black Swan (Hope)   **52**:216

The Black Swan (Walser)
  See *Der schwarze Schwan*

"Black Swans" (McAuley)   **45**:254

Black Thunder (Bontemps)   **1**:37; **18**:63-5

Black Tickets (Phillips)   **15**:419-21; **33**:305-08

"Black Tie" (Barthelme)   **117**:6

The Black Tower (James)   **18**:273; **46**:205-09

"The Black Tsar" (Morand)
  See "Le tsar noir"

"Black Tuesday" (Swenson)   **106**:321

"The Black Unicorn" (Lorde)   **18**:309

The Black Unicorn (Lorde)   **18**:309; **71**:231-36, 240-41, 243, 246, 252, 254, 257-58, 260, 262

Black Venus (Saints and Strangers) (Carter)   **41**:121-22

The Black Venus (Davies)   **23**:143, 145

"The Black Virginity" (Loy)   **28**:246, 253

Black Voices from Prison (Knight)   **40**:281, 283, 285

Black Water (Oates)   **108**:374, 395-96

"The Black Wedding" (Singer)   **9**:487; **15**:504; **69**:306; **111**:305

"A Black Wedding Song" (Brooks)   **15**:94; **49**:36

The Black Wine (Bennett)   **5**:58-9

Black Wolf (Edmonds)   **35**:146

The Black Woman: An Anthology (Bambara)   **88**:5

"Black Women and Feminism" (hooks)   **94**:144

"The Black Writer and the Southern Experience" (Walker)   **103**:413

"A Black Writer's Burden" (Achebe)   **26**:18

"Black Xmas" (Monette)   **82**:333

"Blackberries" (Komunyakaa)   **94**:241

"Blackberries" (Oliver)   **98**:256

Blackberries (McClure)   **10**:333

"Blackberry Winter" (Warren)   **1**:353; **4**:579

Blackberry Winter: My Earlier Years (Mead)   **37**:279-80

"Blackberrying" (Plath)   **3**:389; **9**:425; **51**:353; **111**:214

"Blackberry-Picking" (Heaney)   **91**:119

"Blackbird" (Lennon and McCartney)   **35**:279

"Blackbird Bye Bye" (Bernard)   **59**:45-6

Blackbird Bye Bye (Bernard)   **59**:43-45

"Blackbird in a Bramble Bough" (Kiely)   **43**:239, 244

"Blackbird in a Sunset Bush" (MacCaig)   **36**:285

"Blackbird Pie" (Carver)   **53**:62, 65; **55**:273, 275, 284

"A Blackbird Singing" (Thomas)   **48**:379

The Blackboard Jungle (Hunter)   **31**:217-18, 220-22, 225-26

"The Blackened Pot" (Ritsos)   **31**:326, 328

The Blackened Pot (Ritsos)   **13**:488

"Blackerchief Dick" (Allingham)   **19**:11

Blackeyes (Potter)   **58**:393-94, 397-98, 400; **86**:346, 352

"Blackgirl Learning" (Madhubuti)   **73**:213

The Blackheath Poisonings: A Victorian Murder Mystery (Symons)   **14**:523-24; **32**:428

"Blackie, the Electric Rembrandt" (Gunn)   **3**:215

The Blacking Factory (Sheed)   **2**:392-94; **10**:473; **53**:339

Black-Label (Damas)   **84**:156-57, 159-164, 167, 176-78, 180, 182, 186

"Blackleaf Swamp" (Oliver)   **19**:362; **98**:266

Blackmail (Hitchcock)   **16**:352

The Blackmailer (Colegate)   **36**:113-14

"Blackman/An Unfinished History" (Madhubuti)   **73**:196, 212, 214

"Blackness" (Kincaid)   **68**:208, 210-11

"The Blackness of Blackness: A Critique on the Sign and the Signifying Monkey" (Gates)   **65**:382, 393, 397, 399

Blackrobe: Isaac Jogues, b. March 11, 1607, d. October 18, 1646 (Kenny)   **87**:241-43, 245, 252-53, 258

The Blacks: A Clown Show (Genet)
  See *Les nègres: Clownerie*

"Black-Shouldered Kite" (Wright)   **53**:423

"Blacksnake" (Jiles)   **58**:273, 281

"The Blackstone Rangers" (Brooks)   **49**:30

"Blackstudies" (Lorde)   **71**:232, 250

"The Blackthorn Bush in Spring" (Blunden)   **56**:34

"Blackwater Mountain" (Wright)   **6**:580

"Blackwater Wood" (Oliver)   **98**:257, 267

Blade of Light (Carpenter)   **41**:102-03

Blade on a Feather (Potter)   **86**:346-47

"Blaen Crwt" (Clarke)   **61**:73, 79-80

Blake and Tradition (Raine)   **7**:352

Blake's Apocalypse (Bloom)   **103**:11, 13, 19

"Blake's Bible" (Frye)   **70**:274

"Blake's Sunflower" (Smart)   **54**:421

"Blame It on the Stones" (Kristofferson)   **26**:266

Blaming (Taylor)   **29**:409-12

Blanche ou l'oubli (Aragon)   **3**:14

"Blanchi" ("Whitewash") (Damas)   **84**:171, 176-77

Blanco (Paz)   **3**:376; **6**:398; **10**:389, 391; **51**:327, 333-34; **65**:182-84, 196, 198-200

Les blancs (Hansberry)   **17**:189-90, 192-93; **62**:242

"Blancura" (Aleixandre)   **9**:14

Bland Beginning (Symons)   **14**:523

"Blank ..." (Ellison)   **42**:131

"A Blank" (Gunn)   **81**:180-81

"The Blank Page" (Dinesen)   **10**:145, 152,

95:55
"Blank Thought" (Paz)
  See "El pensamiento en blanco"
The Blanket Word (Arundel) **17**:18
"Blankets" (La Guma) **19**:272
"Blanks" (Wittlin) **25**:469
"The Blasphemer" (Singer) **6**:509
"Blast Off" (Grenville) **61**:154
Blasts and Benedictions (O'Casey) **15**:406; **88**:260, 267
Blätter aus dem Brotsack (Frisch) **44**:190-91, 193, 195
Blaubart (*Bluebeard*) (Frisch) **32**:193-95; **44**:206-07
Blaze of Noon (Gann) **23**:162-63
The Blaze of Noon (Heppenstall) **10**:271-72
Blazing Saddles (Brooks) **12**:76-82
The Bleaching Ground (Vesaas)
  See *Bleikeplassen*
The Bleaching Place (Vesaas)
  See *Bleikeplassen*
The Bleaching Yard (Vesaas)
  See *Bleikeplassen*
"Bleating" (Zamora) **89**:394
Die Blechtrommel (*The Tin Drum*) (Grass) **1**:125-26; **2**:171-73; **4**:201-04, 206; **6**:207-08; **11**:247-48, 251-52; **15**:259-60; **22**:189, 191; **32**:197-98, 200, 203-04; **49**:140, 142-43; **88**:134-82
"Bleecker Street, Summer" (Walcott) **42**:423; **67**:353
"Bleeding" (Swenson) **14**:519-21; **61**:393, 401; **106**:328, 349
"The Bleeding Heart" (Stafford) **68**:449
The Bleeding Heart (French) **18**:158-60; **60**:147
"Bleed-Through" (Harjo) **83**:268
Bleikeplassen (*The Bleaching Ground*; *The Bleaching Place*; *The Bleaching Yard*) (Vesaas) **48**:404, 406-07, 413
"Bleistein-Chicago Semite Viennese" (Eliot) **13**:202
Die Blendung (*Auto-da-Fé*; *The Blinding*; *The Deception*; *The Delusion*; *The Tower of Babel*) (Canetti) **3**:98; **14**:119-21; **25**:107-14; **75**:120-21, 123-31, 134-37, 140, 142-44; **86**:293-95, 297-98, 301-03
"Bless Me, Father" (Dubus) **36**:147; **97**:211
Bless Me, Ultima (Anaya) **23**:22-5
Bless the Beasts and the Children (Swarthout) **35**:402-03
"Bless You" (Lennon) **35**:268
Blessed above Women (Johnson) **27**:213
"Blessed Are Those Who Mourn" (Maitland) **49**:235
Blessed Art Thou (Ingalls) **42**:232-35
"Blessed Assurance" (Hughes) **108**:329
Blessed Assurance: A Moral Tale (Gurganus) **70**:190-92, 194, 196
"Blessed Is the Man" (Moore) **47**:264
"Blessed Is the Name of the Lord Forever" (Dylan) **77**:186
"The Blessed Mary Fogarty" (Simmons) **43**:411
"The Blessed Virgin Mary Compared to a Window" ("A Window") (Merton) **83**:378, 389
"Blessing" (Hogan) **73**:149
"The Blessing" (Kizer) **39**:169
"A Blessing" (Wright) **3**:540, 543; **5**:521; **10**:543
The Blessing (Mitford) **44**:484, 489-92
The Blessing Way (Hillerman) **62**:256, 259-60
"Blessings" (Dubus) **97**:213, 236-37

Le bleu du ciel (*Sky Blue*) (Bataille) **29**:39
"Bleue maison" (Blunden) **56**:41
Des bleus à l'âame (*Scars on the Soul*) (Sagan) **6**:481-82; **17**:427
"Blickwechsel" (Wolf) **29**:464
"Blight" (Dybek) **114**:70-1, 76, 81-2
"Blighters" (Sassoon) **36**:385-86, 391, 397
The Blind Beauty (Pasternak) **10**:382
The Blind Bow-Boy (Van Vechten) **33**:386-89, 392, 394-95, 397-98
Blind Date (Foote) **51**:135
Blind Date (Kosinski) **10**:307-09; **15**:315-17; **53**:216-17, 219, 221, 223, 226-27; **70**:298, 303, 306
"Blind Dog" (Narayan) **28**:302
"Blind Euchre" (De Marinis) **54**:100
Blind Eye (Edmonds) **35**:147
Blind Fireworks (MacNeice) **4**:317; **10**:324; **53**:233-34
"The Blind Leading the Blind" (Lowell) **8**:350
"The Blind Leading the Blind" (Mueller) **51**:279
The Blind Lion (Allen) **84**:9, 37
"Blind Love" (Pritchett) **13**:467-68; **41**:330, 333
"The Blind Man" (Wright) **53**:417-19, 428
The Blind Man (Duerrenmatt)
  See *Der Blinde*
The Blind Man (Durrenmatt)
  See *Der Blinde*
"A Blind Man at the Museum" (Nemerov) **36**:309
Blind Man with a Pistol (*Hot Day, Hot Night*) (Himes) **2**:194-95; **18**:246; **58**:258, 266-68, 270; **108**:234, 237-40, 242, 247, 249-52, 265, 268-72, 277, 278-79
"Blind Man's Buff" (Fuller) **62**:196, 201
Blind Man's Holiday (Everson) **27**:133-34
"A Blind Man's Tale" (Tanizaki)
  See "Momoku monogatari"
The Blind Mice (Friel) **42**:163
"A Blind Negro Singer" (Smith) **64**:398
Blind Photographer (Rosenblatt) **15**:447
"Blind School" (Buckley) **57**:136
"The Blind Seer of Ambon" (Merwin) **88**:209
"Blind Singer in a Train" (Mahapatra) **33**:282
Blind Understanding (Middleton) **38**:333-34
Der Blinde (*The Blind Man*) (Duerrenmatt) **102**:53
Der Blinde (*The Blind Man*) (Durrenmatt) **8**:194; **11**:168-69; **15**:194-95, 199
"Der blinde junge" (Loy) **28**:246, 248, 251
"Blinded by the Light" (Springsteen) **17**:477, 487
Blinded by the Light (Brancato) **35**:66-9
Blindenschrift (Enzensberger) **43**:146, 151
Der Blindensturz (*The Parable of the Blind*) (Hofmann) **54**:226, 227-28, 230
"Blinder" (Gordimer) **33**:185
The Blindfold (Hustvedt) **76**:56-63
Blindfolded (Saura)
  See *Los ojos vendados*
The Blinding (Canetti)
  See *Die Blendung*
"Blindness" (Borges) **48**:47
"Blindness" (Campbell) **32**:74, 78, 80
Blindness (Green) **13**:251, 254; **97**:242, 247, 251-57, 259-60, 262-64, 266, 287, 292
Blindness and Insight (de Man) **55**:384, 386, 396, 400-01, 409, 413-14
"Bliss" (Johnston) **51**:241, 243
Bliss (Carey) **40**:129-30, 132-33; **55**:114, 117; **96**:21-6, 28-31, 35-6, 39-43, 50, 52-5,

57, 59, 63, 65, 70, 72, 80-1
Blithe Spirit: An Improbable Farce (Coward) **29**:135, 137-39; **51**:70, 73, 77
Blitzkrieg (Deighton) **22**:117
Bliznets v tuchakh (*The Twin In the Clouds*) (Pasternak) **10**:387; **18**:381; **63**:289
"The Blizzard" (Dacey) **51**:81
The Blizzard (Leonov)
  See *Metel*
"Blk/Rhetoric" (Sanchez) **116**:272, 295, 327
"blk / wooooomen / chant" (Sanchez) **116**:295
"Block" (Carruth) **84**:136
"The Block" (Kelman) **58**:295
"The Block" (Van Duyn) **63**:445; **116**:413
Block-notes de un regista (*A Director's Notebook*; *Fellini: A Director's Notebook*) (Fellini) **16**:299; **85**:63-4, 73
Blomskryf: Uit die gedigte van Breyten Breytenbach en Jan Blom (Breytenbach) **23**:83
The Blond Baboon (van de Wetering) **47**:407
"Blonde in the Bleachers" (Mitchell) **12**:437
Blonde on Blonde (Dylan) **4**:149; **6**:157; **12**:182, 184, 191, 199; **77**:168-69, 173, 177, 190
Blonde Venus (Sternberg) **20**:372
"Blood" (Murray) **40**:335-36, 340
"Blood" (Singer) **3**:458; **15**:504; **111**:296, 319
Blood and Grits (Crews) **23**:136; **49**:72-4, 76-7
Blood and Guts in High School Plus Two (Acker) **45**:15-19; **111**:5-6, 9-10, 18, 20, 24-5, 31, 34, 37-40, 42, 44-5
"Blood and Its Relationship to Water" (Carlson) **54**:39
Blood and Sand (Mamoulian) **16**:424, 426-28
"Blood and Water" (McGrath) **55**:73-4, 76
Blood and Water and Other Tales (McGrath) **55**:73-7
"Blood Bank" (Miller) **30**:263-64
The Blood Bay Colt (Farley) **17**:116
Blood, Bread, and Poetry: Selected Prose, 1979-1985 (Rich) **73**:319-22; **76**:215, 219
"Blood, Bread, and Poetry: The Location of the Poet" (Rich) **73**:323-24
Blood Brothers (Price) **12**:490-91
Blood Brothers (Shaffer) **60**:318, 320, 322
"Blood Disease" (McGrath) **55**:73, 75
Blood Feud (Sutcliff) **26**:437
Blood Feud (Wertmueller) **16**:599-600
Blood for a Stranger (Jarrell) **2**:207-10; **6**:260; **13**:298-300
Blood for Blood (Gloag) **40**:212
The Blood Knot (Fugard) **5**:130; **9**:230, 232-34; **14**:190; **25**:175; **40**:196-97, 200-01, 203-04; **80**:61-6, 68-72, 74, 79-80, 83, 86
Blood Meridian, or, The Evening Redness in the West (McCarthy) **57**:337-38; **101**:142-46, 152-53, 157, 164-65, 168-70, 176-82, 186, 195-96, 198-99, 201-05
The Blood of a Poet (Cocteau)
  See *Le sang d'un poète*
The Blood of Others (Beauvoir)
  See *Le sang des autres*
Blood of Requited Love (Puig)
  See *Sangre de amor correspondido*
"The Blood of Strangers" (Garrett) **3**:191
The Blood of the Bambergs (Osborne) **45**:313-14, 316
"Blood of the Conquistadores" (Alvarez) **93**:7

The Blood of the Lamb (De Vries) 1:73; 2:114;
    7:77; 28:106, 109; 46:134-35, 137
"Blood of Tyrants" (Bova) 45:73
Blood on the Forge (Attaway) 92:26-46
Blood on the Tracks (Dylan) 6:157; 12:191;
    77:172, 178
The Blood Oranges (Hawkes) 1:139; 2:185;
    3:223; 4:214-19; 7:140-46; 9:268-69;
    27:190-92, 194-96, 199; 49:161-64
The Blood Red Game (Moorcock)
    See *The Sundered Worlds*
Blood Red, Sister Rose (Keneally) 5:210-12;
    10:298; 19:245-46; 43:236; 117:215, 217,
    227-30, 234, 248
Blood Relations (Dillon) 17:100
Blood Relations (Pollock) 50:224-26
"Blood Relatives" (Apple) 33:20-2
Blood Relatives (Chabrol) 16:184
"Blood River Day" (Brutus) 43:92, 96
"Blood, Sea" (Calvino)
    See "Il sangue, il mare"
Blood Simple (The Coen Brothers) 108:120-
    30, 133, 135-40, 142, 145-47, 149, 151-
    52, 157-62, 165-70
"Blood Sisters" (Haldeman) 61:181
Blood Sisters (De Palma)
    See *Sisters*
Blood Sisters: An Examination of Conscience
    (Miner) 40:326-28
"Blood Son" (Matheson) 37:246
"Blood Soup" (Dybek) 114:64-5, 71, 73-6
Blood Sport (Francis) 22:151-52; 42:148-50,
    154-58; 102:127, 131, 147
Blood Sport (Jones) 7:192-93
"Blood, Taint, Flaw, Degeneration" (Coetzee)
    66:99, 101
"Blood Test" (Swenson) 61:405
Blood Tie (Settle) 19:410; 61:373, 378, 385,
    387-88
Blood Ties (Richards) 59:187
"Bloodbirth" (Lorde) 71:232
"Blood-Burning Moon" (Toomer) 13:552;
    22:426
"Bloodfall" (Boyle) 90:56
"Bloodfire" (Chappell) 78:96
Bloodfire: A Poem (Chappell) 40:142, 144-
    45, 147; 78:91-2, 96, 111
"Bloodfire in the Garden" (Chappell) 78:92
The Bloodletters (Greenberg) 57:226-28
Bloodline (Gaines) 3:179; 18:167; 86:173,
    177
Bloodlines (Wright) 6:581; 13:612, 614;
    28:456-57, 460
"Bloodshed" (Ozick) 7:288; 62:341-42, 353-
    54
Bloodshed and Three Novellas (Ozick) 7:288-
    89, 290; 28:349-51, 355; 62:350
"Bloodsmiles" (Madhubuti) 73:206
A Bloodsmoor Romance (Oates) 33:290-91,
    293, 295-96; 52:329, 331, 339; 108:348,
    375, 385, 391
"The Bloodstained Bridal Gown; or, Xavier
    Kilgarvan's Last Case" (Oates) 108:349-
    51, 353
"The Bloodstained Pavement" (Christie)
    48:72; 110:130, 141, 145
Bloodstone (Ivask)
    See *Verikivi*
"Bloodstream" (Brunner) 8:110
"The Bloody Chamber" (Carter) 41:118
The Bloody Chamber, and Other Stories
    (Carter) 41:116-18, 121-22; 76:326, 330
The Bloody Country (Collier and Collier)

    30:71-2
Bloody Marvellous (Rathbone) 41:338
Bloody Murder (Symons) 32:425
The Bloody Sun (Bradley) 30:29
The Bloom of Candles: Verse from a Poet's Year
    (Lee) 90:182
The Bloomingdale Papers (Carruth) 7:41;
    10:100; 18:87; 84:119
"The Blooms of Dublin" (Burgess) 40:119-20
Bloomsbury (Luke) 38:317-18
Bloomsbury: A House of Lions (Edel) 29:173-
    75
"The Bloomsbury Group Live at the Apollo"
    (Frazier) 46:163-64
"Blor" (Mitford) 44:489
Blosch (*Cow*) (Sterchi) 65:100-04
"Blossom" (Oliver) 98:
"Blossom" (Plumly) 33:315
Blossom (Vachss) 106:361-62
"Blossoms" (Oliver) 34:247, 249; 98:257, 296
"Blots" (Hollander) 5:186
Blott on the Landscape (Sharpe) 36:400
"The Blouse" (Hersey) 81:329
"The Blow" (Neruda)
    See "El golpe"
"Blow and Counterblow" (Montale)
    See "Botta e riposta"
Blow Job (Warhol) 20:415, 421
Blow Out (De Palma) 20:83
"Blow, West Wind" (Warren) 10:525
Blow Wind, Come Wrack (Child) 19:103
Blow, Wind of Fruitfulness (Baxter) 14:60-1
Blow Your House Down (Barker) 32:14; 94:2,
    5, 7, 9, 11, 13, 15
"Blowin' in the Wind" (Dylan) 4:149; 12:183;
    77:161, 166-67
"Blowing Eggs" (Muldoon) 32:317; 72:265
The Blowing of the Seed (Everson) 5:122
Blow-Job (Wilson) 33:460, 463-64
Blown Away (Sukenick) 48:370
Blown Figures (Thomas) 7:472-73; 13:538,
    540; 37:417, 423-24; 107:316, 318-19,
    333-36, 340-41, 344-45, 348, 351
"Blow-Up" (Cortazar)
    See "Las babas del diablo"
Blow-Up (Antonioni) 20:30-3, 35-7
Blow-Up, and Other Stories (Cortazar)
    See *Blow-Up, and Other Stories*
"Blowups Happen" (Heinlein) 55:302
Blubber (Blume) 12:47
"Blue" (Hillis) 66:195-99
"Blue" (Swenson) 106:344
Blue (Mitchell) 12:436-37, 443
Blue above the Trees (Clark) 12:129-30
Blue Adept (Anthony) 35:36-8
"Blue Africa" (Levertov) 66:240
"The Blue Angel" (Ginsberg) 36:182; 109:358
The Blue Angel (Sternberg) 20:369-73
"Blue Arab" (Wright) 53:427
"The Blue Background" (Aldiss) 40:21
Blue Belle (Vachss) 106:355-61
"Blue Blood" (Ferber) 93:153
The Blue Boat (Mayne) 12:388-89, 395
"Blue Boom Ceremonial" (Vizenor) 103:293
Blue Boy on Skates (Rosenthal) 28:391, 394
"Blue Bug" (Moore) 13:396
"The Blue Car" (Valenzuela) 104:382
"Blue Chair in a Sunny Day" (MacCaig) 36:281
Blue Chicory (Niedecker) 10:361; 42:296
A Blue Child for that Shadow (Marques)
    See *Un niño azul para esa sombra*
Blue City (Macdonald) 3:307; 14:333; 34:416;
    41:271

Blue Collar (Schrader) 26:389-93, 395, 399
Blue Day (Lustig) 56:188-89
"Blue Dive" (Chappell) 40:142; 78:95
"Blue Dodge" (Leyner) 92:281
"The Blue Dress" (Olds) 85:294
"The Blue Dress" (Trevor) 116:385
The Blue Estuaries: Poems, 1923-1968 (Bogan)
    4:68; 39:387-88, 390-93, 396; 46:86-90;
    93:71, 102
Blue Eyes (Charyn) 5:105; 8:135-36
Blue Eyes, Black Hair (Duras)
    See *Les yeux bleux, cheveux noir*
"The Blue Feather" (Bates) 46:63
Blue Fin (Thiele) 17:494
Blue Fire (Whitney) 42:433
"Blue Flames" (Lustig) 56:182
The Blue Garden (Howes) 15:289
Blue Gardenia (Lang) · 20:216; 103:87, 96,
    99, 101
"The Blue Geranium" (Christie) 110:140, 143-
    44
"The Blue Ghazals" (Rich) 7:366; 11:476;
    18:446; 36:366
"Blue Girls" (Ransom) 4:431
"Blue Glass" (Adcock) 41:17-18
The Blue Hammer (Macdonald) 14:328;
    34:417; 41:270
The Blue Hawk (Dickinson) 12:174-76
"Blue Heron" (Oliver) 98:303
Blue Highways: A Journey into America (Heat-
    Moon) 29:222-26
"The Blue Hour" (Graver) 70:52, 54
"The Blue House" (Transtroemer) 65:228
"Blue Island" (Powers) 1:282
"Blue Island Intersection" (Sandburg) 10:450
Blue Jacket: War Chief of the Shawnees (Eckert)
    17:106
The Blue Knight (Wambaugh) 3:508-09;
    18:532
"The Blue Lake" (Gustafson) 36:212
The Blue Light (Riefenstahl) 16:520-22, 525-
    26
The Blue Machines of Night (Hillis) 66:193-
    94
The Blue Macushla (Murphy) 51:305
The Blue Man (Platt) 26:348
"The Blue Meridian" (Toomer) 22:424, 427-
    28
*Blue Meridian: The Search for the Great White
    Shark* (Matthiessen) 5:273; 7:210;
    32:292; 64:305-06, 309
"Blue Moles" (Plath) 11:446-47; 111:203
Blue Monday (Wakoski) 9:554
"Blue Motel Room" (Mitchell) 12:442
The Blue Mountains of China (Wiebe) 11:567-
    69; 14:572-74
Blue Movie (Southern) 7:454
Blue Movie (*Viva and Louis*) (Warhol) 20:419
"The Blue Nap" (Matthews) 40:322
Blue of Noon (Bataille) 29:48
Blue Pastoral (Sorrentino) 40:387-89
The Blue Pekinese (Abell)
    See *Den blaa Pekingeser*
"Blue Poles" (Crase) 58:164-65
"Blue Red and Grey" (Townshend) 17:536
Blue Remembered Hills (Potter) 58:392;
    86:345-46, 348-49, 351
"Blue Ridge" (Voigt) 54:430, 432
"The Blue Rim of Memory" (Levertov) 15:339
The Blue Room (Simenon) 1:309; 18:486;
    47:375
The Blue Rose (Straub) 107:304
The Blue Rose Trilogy (Straub) 107:302

"Blue Serge" (Ferber) 93:140

"Blue Skies Motel" (Creeley) 78:142

Blue Skies, No Candy (Greene) 8:252

"Blue Skies, White Breasts, Green Trees" (Stern) 40:407

The Blue Sky (Donnell) 34:156-58

"Blue Sonata" (Ashbery) 77:45

"Blue Spanish Eyes" (Thomas) 107:339-40, 346

"The Blue Stones" (Carver) 36:100

"Blue Suburban" (Nemerov) 6:361

"Blue Suede Shoes" (Ai) 69:9-10, 17

"The Blue Swallows" (Nemerov) 36:302

The Blue Swallows (Nemerov) 2:306-08; 9:394; 36:302

"The Blue Swan: An Essay on Music in Poetry" (Wakoski) 40:454-55

Blue Thunder (Green) 25:199-200

"The Blue Tick Pig" (Stuart) 14:514

"Blue Toboggans" (Morgan) 31:275

Blue Velvet (Lynch) 66:261, 263-69, 271

Blue Voyage (Aiken) 10:3; 52:25

"The Blue Water Man" (Valenzuela)
   See "El fontanero azul"

"Blue Window" (Pollitt) 28:367-68

Blue Window (Lucas) 64:288-89, 292, 295-96

Blue Wine (Hollander) 14:265-66

A Blue Wing Tilts at the Edge of the Sea (Hall) 13:259

"The Blue Yonder: A Tale of Cleanliness" (Vollmann) 89:277-78, 302

"Bluebeard" (Barthelme) 59:251; 115:81

Bluebeard (Frisch)
   See *Blaubart*

Bluebeard (Ludlam) 46:239-42, 244; 50:343-45

Bluebeard (Vonnegut) 111:361

Bluebeard and After (Heppenstall) 10:272

"Bluebeard's Egg" (Atwood) 84:67-8

Bluebeard's Egg (Atwood) 84:67, 96, 105

"Bluebell Meadow" (Kiely) 23:266; 43:245

"Bluebird" (McCartney) 35:282

"Bluebirdbluebirdthrumywindow" (Sanchez) 116:302

"The Blue-Eyed Buddhist" (Gilchrist) 48:121

"Blue-Eyed Giant" (Hikmet) 40:244

"The Blueprint" (Blunden) 56:34

"Blueprint for a Monument of War" (Klein) 19:259

"Blueprint for Negro Writing" (Wright) 14:597; 21:451, 456

"Blues" (Damas)
   See "Limbé"

"Blues" (Hughes) 35:214

"Blues" (Sanchez) 116:303-04, 328

Blues (Hersey) 81:335, 337

"Blues Ain't No Mockin Bird" (Bambara) 88:21, 27

Blues and Roots/Rue and Bluets (Williams) 13:600

A Blues Book for Blue Black Magical Women (Sanchez) 116:272, 274, 280-81, 299, 301-02, 309-11, 313, 316, 321

The Blues Brothers (Landis) 26:274-76

"Blues des projets" (Butor) 3:93

"Blues for a Melodeon" (McGinley) 14:364

"Blues for Benny Kid Paret" (Smith) 22:386

"Blues/for J. C. " (Broumas) 73:2

"Blues for John Coltrane" (Matthews) 40:318

"Blues for Men" (Hughes) 15:291

Blues for Mister Charlie (Baldwin) 2:32; 4:40; 5:40; 17:27, 31, 33-4, 37, 40; 50:282-83, 290

"Blues for Warren" (McGrath) 59:175

Blues, Ideology, and Afro-American Literature: A Vernacular Theory (Baker) 65:365, 382, 385

"Blues I'm Playing" (Hughes) 108:313, 315

"Blues Montage" (Hughes) 108:335

Blues People: Negro Music in White America (Baraka) 10:19; 14:46; 33:54, 58, 60, 62; 115:5-7, 9-10, 28, 32, 39

"The Blues Roots of Contemporary African-American Poetry" (Williams) 89:348, 355

"Blues Song for the Phoenix Bus Depot Derelict" (Ortiz) 45:303

"Blues Songs" (Dumas) 62:155

The Bluest Eye (Morrison) 4:366; 10:354-55; 22:314-15, 318-19; 55:196, 200, 205, 207-09; 81:217-20, 225-29, 233-39, 254, 256, 260, 262, 267-68; 87:263, 291-92, 294, 304

"Bluetit and Wren" (Clarke) 61:82

"Blume" (Celan) 10:103; 19:92

The Blunderer (Highsmith) 2:193; 4:225; 42:211; 102:170, 172, 185, 188, 211

"A Blunt Instrument" (Brown) 63:56

The Blush (Taylor) 2:432

Bo ni natta otako (*The Man Who Turned into a Stick*) (Abe) 8:1; 81:291

"The Boa" (Duras) 40:176, 184

"Um boabá no Recife" ("A Baobab Tree in Recife") (Cabral de Melo Neto) 76:167

"Board of Selection" (Enright) 31:150

"The Boarder" (Simpson) 7:426

"The Boarding House" (Trevor) 71:322

The Boarding House (Trevor) 7:475; 25:443; 71:345; 116:331, 334-35, 348, 374, 377

Boarding House Rules (Farrell) 66:131

The Boardinghouse Keeper (Audiberti)
   See *La logeuse*

"The Boat" (Bowering) 15:82

"The Boat" (MacLeod) 56:192-96, 198, 200

The Boat (Buchheim) 6:100-02

The Boat (Hartley) 22:213

The Boat (Keaton) 20:193

"Boat Animals" (Aldiss) 40:19

The Boat in the Evening (Vesaas) 48:411-13

A Boat Load of Home Folk (Astley) 41:46, 48

"Boat Ride" (Gallagher) 63:116, 118, 120

The Boat Who Wouldn't Float (Mowat) 26:337, 347

Boating for Beginners (Winterson) 64:427-29, 432-34

The Boatman (Macpherson) 14:345-47

"Boats" (Dunn) 36:153

"Boats" (Montague) 46:269

Boaz and Ruth (Young) 5:524

"Bob, a Dog" (Smith) 73:353, 356-58

"Bob and Bing Visit Saskatchewan" (Hillis) 66:194

Bob Dylan (Dylan) 77:166

Bob Dylan at Budokan (Dylan) 77:173, 175

Bob the Gambler (Barthelme) 117:27

"Bobby Brown" (Zappa) 17:592

"bobby hutton" (Sanchez) 116:294

"Bobby's Room" (Dunn) 40:171

"Bobo's Metamorphosis" (Milosz) 56:236

"La bocca della verità" (Davison) 28:103

"Boccaccio: The Plague Years" (Dove) 81:137

Bochkotara (Aksyonov)
   See *The Tare of Barrels*

The Bodach (*The Walking Stones*) (Hunter) 21:157-58

Bodalsia telenok s dubom (*The Oak and the Calf*) (Solzhenitsyn) 18:497-500; 34:481, 484, 487; 78:394, 407

Bödeln (Lagerkvist) 13:333; 54:267-68, 274-76, 286, 288, 290

Bodicea's Chariot: The Warrior Queens (Fraser) 107:153, 155-59, 161

"Bodies" (Oates) 6:370-71; 19:348

Bodies and Souls (Rechy) 107:256, 259

"Bodies like Flowers" (Cernuda) 54:58

"Bodies of Work" (Acker) 111:46

Bodies of Work (Acker) 111:46

Bodily Harm (Atwood) 25:66, 68-70; 84:80-1, 85, 97

"Bodily Secrets" (Trevor) 71:333

"Body" (Broumas) 73:9

"Body" (Jiles) 58:280

The Body (Benedikt) 4:54

The Body (King) 26:240-42; 61:331, 333; 113:390-91

The Body (Sansom) 2:383

"Body and Soul" (Broumas) 73:8-9

Body and Soul (Polonsky) 92:377-81, 383, 386, 393, 402, 404-05, 414-15

"The Body and the Earth" (Berry) 46:75

The Body as Language: Outline of a "New Left" Theology (Eagleton) 63:101

"Body Icons" (Phillips) 28:363

"The Body in Grant's Tomb" (Woolrich) 77:390

The Body in the Library (Christie) 12:120; 48:77

The Body Is the Hero (Glasser) 37:133

The Body Lovers (Spillane) 13:528

"A Body Not Yet Born" (Bly) 15:68

"The Body of Romulus" (Dobyns) 37:78

"Body of Summer" (Elytis) 15:218; 49:106

Body of Summer (Elytis) 15:218, 221

Body of This Death (Bogan) 39:384, 390; 46:77-80, 83, 85, 89; 93:85, 90-1, 96, 105

Body of Waking (Rukeyser) 27:408, 411

"The Body Opulent" (Fulton) 52:161

"The Body Politic" (Barker) 52:53-5

Body Rags (Kinnell) 1:168; 2:230; 3:268-70; 5:216, 218; 13:320; 29:283-84, 288, 290

"The Body Shop" (Graver) 70:53-4

"The Body Upstairs" (Woolrich) 77:403

"Boeing Crossing" (Clark) 38:129

"The Boeotian Count" (Murray) 40:336

Boesman and Lena (Fugard) 5:130; 9:230, 232-34; 14:189-91; 25:175; 40:197, 200, 203; 80:62, 68-70, 74, 83-4, 86-7

Boetian Earth (Nakos) 29:322-23

"Le boeuf sur le toit" (O'Hara) 13:424

"The Bofors A A Gun" (Ewart) 46:154

"Bog Man" (Atwood) 84:98

"Bog Oak" (Heaney) 5:171; 14:243; 25:245

"The Bog People" (Heaney) 25:250

"Bog Queen" (Heaney) 5:172; 14:244; 25:243, 251

"Bogan, Louise, a Poetess" (Schwartz) 45:361

The Bogey Man (Plimpton) 36:354, 356

"Bogey Music" (Garner) 35:288

"The Bogeyman" (Buzzati) 36:94

"Bogland" (Heaney) 7:148; 14:243, 245; 25:243, 245-46

"Bogland" (Heaney) 74:154

Bogmail (McGinley) 41:281-83

Bogue's Fortune (Symons) 14:523

"Bogyman" (Adcock) 41:14

Bohemia (Azorin) 11:24

Bohin Manor (Konwicki) 117:267, 275, 280,

291
O boi (Andrade) 18:3
"The Boiling Water" (Koch) 44:246
"Le bois de l'epte" (Char) 9:159
Boises (Glissant) 68:180
"A Boisterous Poem about Poetry" (Wain) 11:563
The Bold and Magnificent Dream (Catton) 35:95
The Bold Cavaliers (Brown) 47:37
Bold John Henebry (Dillon) 17:96
"Bolezn'" ("Sickness") (Akhmadulina) 53:12
"A Boll of Roses" (Dumas) 6:145; 62:150, 152, 155, 162-63
The Bollo Caper (Buchwald) 33:94
"Bol'shoiden' Bol'shogo Doma" ("A Big Day at Big House") (Iskander) 47:198
Bolt (Francis) 102:126-28
Bomarzo (Mujica Lainez) 31:279-84
"Bomb" (Corso) 1:63
"The Bomb Shop" (O'Faolain) 70:313-14
"Bombay Arrival" (Lee) 90:182
Bombay Talkie (Jhabvala) 94:192
Bomber: Events Relating to the Last Flight of an R.A.F. Bomber over Germany on the Night of June 31, 1943 (Deighton) 4:119; 22:115; 46:127-28
"Bombers" (Day Lewis) 10:133
"Bombinations of a Chimera" (MacDiarmid) 63:244
"Bombing Casualties in Spain" (Read) 4:439
"The Bombs" (Redgrove) 41:357
Bombs Away: The Story of a Bomber Team (Steinbeck) 34:405
"Bon Voyage" (Coward) 51:74
"Bona and Paul" (Toomer) 4:549; 13:551, 556
"Bona Dea" (Scannell) 49:334
Bona, l'amour et la peinture (Mandiargues) 41:278
The Bonadventure: A Random Journal of an Atlantic Holiday (Blunden) 56:33, 51
"Bonaventure" (Gallant) 38:194
Bonchi (Ichikawa) 20:182, 185
"The Bond" (Waddington) 28:439
"Bond and Free" (Frost) 26:113
A Bond Honoured (Osborne) 5:332; 11:421; 45:313-14, 316
"Bone" (Selzer) 74:283
Bone (Ng) 81:81-8
"Bone Courts: The Natural Rights of Tribal Bones" (Vizenor)
    See "Bone Courts: The Rights and Narrative Representations of Tribal Bones"
"Bone Courts: The Rights and Narrative Representations of Tribal Bones" ("Bone Courts: The Natural Rights of Tribal Bones") (Vizenor) 103:312
"Bone Dance: New and Selected Poems, 1965-1993" (Rose) 85:317
"Bone Dreams" (Heaney) 14:244
The Bone People (Hulme) 39:158-67
"Bone Poem" (Oliver) 98:265, 274
"Bone Thoughts" (Starbuck) 53:352
Bone Thoughts (Starbuck) 53:352-53
Bonecrack (Francis) 2:142-43; 22:152; 42:148-50, 155, 158; 102:132
"Bones" (Aldington) 49:12
"The Bones" (Merwin) 5:288
"Bones of Contention" (O'Connor) 14:398
Bones of Contention (O'Connor) 14:398, 400; 23:327
"The Bones of My Father" (Knight) 40:283,

286
Bones of the Cuttlefish (Montale)
    See *Ossi di seppia*
"The Bones Speak" (Wright) 53:418
"Bonfire" (Gallagher) 63:124
"Bonfire" (p'Bitek) 96:272
"Bonfire" (Walker) 13:565
A Bonfire (Johnson) 27:222-23
The Bonfire of the Vanities (Wolfe) 35:467; 51:413-18, 420-23
"Bongo Song" (Guillen)
    See "La canción del bongo"
Le bonheur (Varda) 16:555-59
"Le bonheur de Bolinka" (Gascar)
    See "Les femmes"
Bonheur d'occasion (*The Tin Flute*) (Roy) 10:441; 14:465-66, 468-69
Bonjour, là, bonjour (Tremblay) 29:419, 421, 423; 102:362, 372, 374-75
Bonjour tristesse (Sagan) 6:481-82; 9:468; 17:416-17; 36:380, 382-83
"Bonn Diary" (Boell)
    See "Hauptstädtisches Journal"
"Bonnard: A Novel" (Howard) 7:165; 10:277
La bonne moitié (Gary) 25:189
Les bonnes (*The Maids*) (Genet) 2:157-58, 160; 5:136; 10:225; 14:197; 44:385-90; 46:172-73, 182
Les bonnes femmes (Chabrol) 16:170, 173-74, 177, 181
"The Bonnie Broukit Bairn" (MacDiarmid) 11:336; 19:289; 63:252
"Bonny Chung" (Jenkins) 52:226
Les bons débarreas (Ducharme) 74:67
"Bonsai Poems" (Kaufman) 49:207
"Bonus" (Ammons) 25:42
A Bonus (Smart) 54:421, 426
"Bonus for a Salesman" (Deighton) 46:127
The Boo (Conroy) 74:47, 49-51
"The Booby and the Noddy" (Appleman) 51:17
"Boogey on Reggae Woman" (Wonder) 12:661
"Boogie 1 a.m." (Hughes) 108:299-304
"Boogie with Stu" (Page and Plant) 12:477
Boogie Woogie Landscapes (Shange) 74:294, 307-10
A Book (Barnes) 29:26-7
A Book (Brossard)
    See *Un Livre*
The Book and the Brotherhood (Murdoch) 51:293-94, 296-97
The Book as World (French) 18:157
The Book Class (Auchincloss) 45:33-4
"Book Codes: II" (Forche) 86:144-45
"Book Codes: III" (Forche) 86:142
"Book Ends" (Harrison) 43:175
"A Book from Venice" (Watkins) 43:442
"The Book I Read" (Byrne) 26:95
"A Book in the Ruins" (Milosz) 56:245
The Book Lovers (Garfield) 12:234
The Book of Absent People (Modarressi) 44:82-5
"Book of Ancestors" (Atwood) 13:44
"Book of Ayres" (Loewinsohn) 52:285
"The Book of Balaam's Ass" (Jones) 7:187, 191; 42:242-43
A Book of Beasts (*The Broken Ark*) (Ondaatje) 51:316
The Book of Beasts (White) 30:449
"The Book of Black Arts" (Brown) 48:55
A Book of Canadian Poetry (Smith) 15:514
A Book of Change (Morgan) 23:296-97
The Book of Changes (Dillard) 5:116
"A Book of Charms" (Livesay) 79:339, 351

A Book of Common Prayer (Didion) 8:174-77; 14:151, 154-55; 32:143, 145, 148
The Book of Daniel (Doctorow) 6:131-36; 11:140, 142-43; 37:84, 87, 90-4; 44:167-68, 170, 172-76, 179; 65:135; 113:132-34, 137-39, 141, 143-45, 150-52, 156, 158-59, 165-66, 168-70, 172, 176-78, 180
The Book of Deeds (Agnon)
    See *Sefer ha-Maasim*
Book of Dreams (Kerouac) 29:270; 61:296
The Book of Dreams (Vance) 35:427
The Book of Ebenezer Le Page (Edwards) 25:149-52
The Book of Embraces (Galeano) 72:138-41, 143-44
"The Book of Ephraim" (Merrill) 8:381-84, 386-88; 13:376-77, 381-82; 18:328-31; 34:226-31, 234-36, 238, 240; 91:235-237
Book of Fables (Agnon)
    See *Sefer ha-Maasim*
The Book of Fantasy (Bioy Casares)
    See *Antología de la literatura fantástica*
The Book of Flights (Le Clezio) 31:246-47, 249
The Book of Folly (Sexton) 2:392; 4:482-83; 6:491-92, 494; 15:471; 53:312, 321-22
The Book of Forms: A Handbook of Poetics (Turco) 63:430-31
Book of Friends: A Tribute to Friends of Long Ago (Miller) 43:297-98
The Book of Fritz Leiber (Leiber) 25:307
The Book of Fub (Frayn) 31:189; 47:135
"The Book of Galahad" (Spicer) 18:513
"The Book of Gawain" (Spicer) 18:513
The Book of Giuliano Sansevero (Giovene)
    See *The Book of Sansevero*
The Book of Gods and Devils (Simic) 68:375-77
The Book of Guys (Keillor) 115:285-86, 293-95
"The Book of Gwenivere" (Spicer) 18:513
The Book of Imaginary Beings (Borges) 2:70-2; 8:96, 99; 83:176
The Book of J (Bloom and Rosenberg) 65:290-311
The Book of Jamaica (Banks) 37:25; 72:4, 14
The Book of Jessica: A Theatrical Transformation (Campbell) 85:19, 25-8
A Book of Jesus (Goyen) 8:251; 14:213; 40:218
"The Book of Juniper" (Paulin) 37:355
"The Book of Kings and Fools" (Kis) 57:252-54
"The Book of Knowledge" (Nemerov) 36:301
"The Book of Lancelot" (Spicer) 18:513
The Book of Laughter and Forgetting (Kundera)
    See *Le livre du rire et de l'oubli*
The Book of Lights (Potok) 26:374-76; 112:261-62, 266-67, 293
The Book of Lost Tales, Part I (Tolkien) 38:441-43
The Book of Lost Tales, Part II (Tolkien) 38:442
A Book of Lyrics (Krleza)
    See *Knjiga lirike*
Book of Magazine Verse (Spicer) 8:499; 18:507; 72:345-46, 351, 358
Book of Mercy (Cohen) 38:137-38
"The Book of Merlin" (Spicer) 18:513
The Book of Merlyn (White) 30:449-51
Book of Moments (Burke) 2:87

The Book of Mrs. Noah (Roberts)   48:343-44
A Book of Music (Spicer)   8:498
The Book of Newfoundland Verse (Pratt)   19:376, 378, 381-82
The Book of Nightmares (Kinnell)   1:168; 2:229-30; 3:268-70; 5:218; 13:318, 320-22; 29:282, 284-85, 288-90
A Book of Nonsense (Peake)   54:373; 7:301
The Book of Phoebe (Smith)   39:97-9
"The Book of Pins" (Findley)   102:108
Book of Questions (Neruda)
    See *Libro de las preguntas*
The Book of Repulsive Women (Barnes)   29:28
The Book of Saints (Ricci)
    See *Lives of the Saints*
"The Book of Sand" (Borges)   48:38, 41
The Book of Sand (Borges)   9:117; 13:110; 19:52; 44:356, 365; 48:37-41; 83:189-90
The Book of Sansevero (*The Book of Giuliano Sansevero*) (Giovene)   7:117
The Book of Sinera (Espriu)   9:193
A Book of Spells (Maitland)   49:236
The Book of Splendors (Foreman)   50:169
The Book of the Body (Bidart)   33:76-81
The Book of the Crime (Daly)   52:92
"The Book of the Dead" (Rukeyser)   15:457-59; 27:404, 410
The Book of the Dead (Daly)   52:89
"The Book of the Death of Arthur" (Spicer)   18:513
Book of the Hopi (Waters)   88:343, 347, 355-56, 363-65
The Book of the Lion (Daly)   52:90
"The Book of the Market" (Raine)   103:179
A Book of the Milky Way Galaxy for You (Branley)   21:18
The Book of the New Sun (Wolfe)   25:474-79
The Book of the Night (Lerman)   56:179-80
A Book of the Planet Earth for You (Branley)   21:21-2
The Book of Three (Alexander)   35:23-6
A Book of Toys (Arghezi)
    See *Cartea cujucarii*
Book of Vagaries (Neruda)
    See *Extravagario*
A Book of Venus for You (Branley)   21:18
Book That Doesn't Bite (Valenzuela)
    See *Libro que no muerde*
"Book Titles" (Lopate)   29:302
"The Bookcase" (Transtroemer)   52:410
Bookends (Simon)   17:459-60, 464, 466
Booker T. Washington: The Making of a Black Leader, 1856-1901 (Harlan)   34:184, 186, 189-91
Booker T. Washington: The Wizard of Tuskegee, 1901-1915 (Harlan)   34:183-91
"Bookkeeping" (Brodkey)   56:60, 64
"Books" (McFadden)   48:244
"Books" (Phillips)   28:363
"Books Are Bombs" (Breytenbach)   23:84
Books Do Furnish a Room (Powell)   3:402; 7:339, 343; 9:435, 437; 10:416
The Books in Fred Hampton's Apartment (Stern)   4:522
"Books Which Have Influenced Me" (Rao)   56:296
The Bookshop (Fitzgerald)   19:172-73; 61:115, 117, 120
"A Bookshop Idyll" (Amis)   40:40, 44
"Bookworm" (Morrissy)   99:78
"Boom!" (Nemerov)   6:361
The Boom in Spanish American Literature: A Personal History (Donoso)

    See *Historia personal del 'boom'*
"Boom Town" (Stafford)   29:381
Boomerang (Hannah)   90:139-45, 147, 159, 160
Boomerang! (Kazan)   63:225
The Boomerang Clue (Christie)
    See *Why Didn't They Ask Evans?*
"Boomtown Blues" (Seger)   35:386-87
"Boon" (Muldoon)   32:319
"A Boor" (Bukowski)   82:14
"Boots" (Hood)   28:193
Boots (Yevtushenko)   26:466
"The Boot's Tale" (McGrath)   55:74
"Booze, Cars, and College Girls" (Gray)   49:148-49, 152
"Bop Bop against That Curtain" (Bukowski)   108:87
Bopha! (Mtwa)   47:297-99
Boquitas pintadas, folletín (*Heartbreak Tango*) (Puig)   3:407; 5:354-56; 10:420; 28:369-71; 65:266, 271-73
"Bora Ring" (Wright)   53:418, 427, 431
"Bordeaux in My Pirough" (Berry)   17:52
The Bordelais Natives (Audiberti)
    See *Les naturels du Bordelais*
The Border (Feinstein)   36:172-73
Border Hawk (Alexander)   35:22
"Border Lord" (Kristofferson)   26:267
Border Lord (Kristofferson)   26:267
Borderline (Hospital)   42:221-23
Borderliners (Hoeg)   95:111-15, 117-19
"Borders" (King)   89:98-9, 102
Borders (Nichol)   18:369
"Borealis" (Morand)   41:308
Borges: A Reader (Borges)   48:44-7; 83:162
"Borges and American Violence" (Dorfman)   77:155
"Borges and I" (Borges)
    See "Borges y yo"
Borges en/y/sobre cine (*Borges In/And/On Film*) (Borges)   83:166
Borges In/And/On Film (Borges)
    See *Borges en/y/sobre cine*
"Borges ou le voyant" (Yourcenar)   87:424
"Borges y yo" ("Borges and I") (Borges)   13:113; 48:34-5, 45; 83:157, 191
Ilborghese stregato (Buzzati)   36:84
Borghesia (Ginzburg)   11:230; 54:198-99, 208
A Boring Afternoon (Hrabal)   67:125
"Born 1925" (Brittain)   23:91
"Born Bad" (Cisneros)   69:147
Born Bad (Vachss)   106:364
The Born Dancer (Olson)   11:420
Born Free (Adamson)   17:1-5
"A Born Genius" (O'Faolain)   1:259; 14:402
Born in Captivity (*Hurry on Down*) (Wain)   2:457; 15:561-62; 46:407-09, 419
"Born in the Fifties" (Police, The)   26:363-64
Born in the Gardens (Nichols)   36:328-29
"Born in Time" (Dylan)   77:185
Born Indian (Kinsella)   27:238-39; 43:260
Born of a Woman: New and Selected Poems (Knight)   40:282-87
Born on the Fourth of July (Stone)   73:377-79, 381-82, 385
"Born to Run" (Springsteen)   17:479, 489
Born to Run (Springsteen)   17:478-86, 488-90
"Born to Win" (Cliff)   21:60
Born to Win (Guthrie)   35:185-88, 192, 194
"Born Yesterday" (Larkin)   13:339; 64:282
Born Yesterday (Kanin)   22:229
Borom Sarret (Ousmane)   66:334
Borrowed Time: An AIDS Memoir (Monette)

    82:316-22, 324-31
"Borrowed Tune" (Young)   17:573
"Borrowing of Trees" (Buckley)   57:131
Borstal Boy (Behan)   1:26; 8:64; 11:44; 15:44; 79:24-7, 29, 34-5, 39-40, 47, 49-51, 55-8
Bosnian Chronicle (Andric)   8:19
Bosoms and Neglect (Guare)   14:221-22; 29:206, 209; 67:79, 84-5, 88
The Boss Dog (Fisher)   76:333, 335-36, 339, 341
Boss: Richard J. Daley of Chicago (Royko)   109:399, 401-02, 404
Boston: A Documentary Novel of the Sacco-Vanzetti Case (Sinclair)   11:498; 63:346-47, 349, 351-53, 359-60, 362, 371-76
Boston Adventure (Stafford)   7:455, 458; 19:430; 68:420-21, 423-24, 430, 434, 444, 446-49
The Boston Book (Forbes)   12:208
"Boston Common" (Berryman)   3:70
"The Boston Evening Transcript" (Eliot)   41:160
"The Bostonians" (Stafford)   4:517
The Bostonians (Jhabvala)   94:185, 187
Boswell: A Modern Comedy (Elkin)   4:154; 6:170; 9:190-91; 27:120-21; 51:85-90, 99; 91:213-15
"The Botanic Gardens" (Freeman)   55:55, 57
"Botanical Nomenclature" (Clampitt)   32:118
"Botany" (Longley)   29:295
"Botany Bay; or, The Rights of Women" (Hope)   51:226
"Botella al mar" (Cortazar)   34:333
"Both Sides Now" (Diamond)   30:111
"Both Sides Now" (Mitchell)   12:436, 438, 441
Die Botschaft ("Breaking the News"; "The Message") (Boell)   72:69, 73, 78
"Botta e riposta" ("Blow and Counterblow"; "Thrust and Riposte") (Montale)   7:224; 9:387
"Bottle Caps" (Dybek)   114:68
The Bottle Factory Outing (Bainbridge)   5:40; 8:36-7; 10:16-17; 18:33-4; 22:45; 62:24-5, 29, 33, 36
"The Bottle Garden" (Boland)   67:39-40; 113:84
"Bottle Pickers" (Lane)   25:285
"Bottleneck Blues" (Hillis)   66:194
"The Bottles Become New, Too" (Wilbur)   53:405
"Bottles of Beaujolais" (Louie)   70:79, 81
Bottom Dogs (Dahlberg)   7:61, 63, 65-6, 71; 14:135, 137-38
"The Bottom Line" (Elkin)   14:158
The Bottom of the Bottle (Simenon)   1:309
"The Bottom of the Harbor" (Mitchell)   98:182
The Bottom of the Harbor (Mitchell)   98:159-61, 166-69, 171-73, 175, 177, 180-83, 187
Bottom: On Shakespeare (Zukofsky)   2:488; 4:599
Le boucher (Chabrol)   16:177, 182-83
Les bouches inutiles (*The Useless Mouths; Who Shall Die?*) (Beauvoir)   8:59; 31:40-1; 44:343
"Bouclez-la" (Damas)   84:178
Bouddha vivant (*The Living Buddha*) (Morand)   41:299-300, 304, 306-07
Boudu sauvé des eaux (Renoir)   20:291-94, 296, 301, 310
"Bought" (O'Faolain)   47:328

Bought and Sold (Moravia)
   See *Bought and Sold*
*Le boulanger, la boulangère, et le petit mitron
   (The Baker, the Baker's Wife, and the Little
   Baker's Boy)* (Anouilh)   13:21; 40:58-9
"Boulevard" (Browne)   21:42
Le boulevards de ceinture (Ring Roads)
   (Modiano)   18:337-38
Bound for Glory (Guthrie)   35:182-84, 186-
   88, 190, 192, 194
*Bound for the Rio Grande: The Mexican
   Struggle, 1845-1850* (Meltzer)   26:302-
   03
"Boundaries" (Fuller)   62:192
"Boundaries of Utopia" (Huxley)   79:327
"The Boundary" (Berry)   46:74
"The Boundary Commission" (Muldoon)
   72:268
"Bouquet in Dog Time" (Carruth)   84:131
"A Bouquet of Ten Roses" (Bly)   38:54
Bourgeois Anonymous (Philipson)   53:274
Le bourgeois avant-garde (Ludlam)   46:243;
   50:342, 344
Le Bourgeois Gentilhomme (The Brothers
   Quay)   95:349-50
Le bourgeois gentleman (Maillet)   54:309, 313
"Bourgeois Poem" (Dacey)   51:83
The Bourgeois Poet (Shapiro)   4:485-86; 8:485-
   86; 15:478-79; 53:329-34
Bourlinguer (Planus) (Cendrars)   106:167, 173,
   181-84, 186-87, 190
"Bourn" (Ammons)   108:21
The Bourne Identity (Ludlum)   22:291; 43:277-
   78
The Bourne Supremacy (Ludlum)   43:277-78
A bout de souffle (Breathless) (Godard)   20:128-
   29, 135, 143, 148
La boutique obscure (The Dark Store) (Perec)
   116:234, 246
Les bouts de bois de Dieu (God's Bits of Wood)
   (Ousmane)   66:333, 337-38, 343, 346,
   349
*The Bow and the Lyre: The Poem, the Poetic
   Revelation, and History* (Paz)
   See *El arco y la lira: El poema. la revelación
   poetica, poesia,e historia*
"Bow Down" (Barnes)   11:30
Bow Harp (Tchicaya)
   See *Arc Musical*
Bowen's Court (Bowen)   11:61-3
"Bowery" (Ignatow)   40:258
"Bowery Phoenix" (Miller)   14:373-74
"The Bowl of Blood" (Jeffers)   11:306; 54:252
"Bowls" (Moore)   10:348; 13:396; 47:260
"The Bowmen" (Haavikko)   34:168, 175
"The Bowmen of Shu" (Davenport)   38:146-
   47
"Box" (Creeley)   36:122; 78:141
"The Box" (Endo)   99:296-98, 307
Box (Albee)   2:2-4; 5:13-14; 9:6-9; 13:5; 25:38;
   53:22, 26; 113:8-9, 22-3
"A Box for Tom" (Tate)   25:428
The Box Garden (Shields)   113:405-06, 408,
   410, 412-13, 424, 437-38, 442-43, 445
The Box in Which Something Rattles
   (Aksyonov)   101:22
The Box Man (Abe)
   See *Hako otoko*
*The Box of Delights; or, When the Wolves Were
   Running* (Masefield)   11:356
"Box Seat" (Toomer)   4:550; 13:551, 554;
   22:425
"Box Step" (Barthelme)   117:14-15, 17-18

Boxcar Bertha (Scorsese)   20:337; 89:219, 221,
   236, 239, 267
"The Boxer" (Simon)   17:460-61, 463, 465
Der Boxer (Becker)   19:35
"A Boxer's Fate" (Yevtushenko)   26:463
"Boxes" (Carver)   53:62, 65, 67; 55:274, 277
"A Boy" (Ashbery)   77:58
"Boy" (Ciardi)   40:160; 44:380-81
"The Boy" (O'Connor)   14:392
"Boy" (Sargeson)   31:362
"The Boy" (Tanizaki)   14:527
"Boy" (Voznesensky)   15:555
Boy (Fry)   2:144
Boy (Hanley)   5:167
Boy (Oshima)   20:245-46, 248, 253
"Boy and Dog" (Brown)   73:20
A Boy and His Dog (Ellison)   13:203; 42:127
Boy and Tarzan Appear in a Clearing! (Baraka)
   115:29-30
"The Boy and the Coyote" (Ortiz)   45:305
The Boy and the Monkey (Garfield)   12:235
"The Boy and the Sea" (Lamming)   66:220
"A Boy Asks a Question of a Lady" (Barnes)
   29:27
Boy at the Window (Dodson)   79:188-91, 199
"Boy by a River" (Walker)   13:566
"Boy 'Carrying-In' Bottles in Glass Works"
   (Ryan)   65:214-15
"The Boy Cried Wolf" (Woolrich)   77:400
"The Boy Died in My Alley" (Brooks)   15:94;
   49:23, 36, 38
"A Boy, Dreaming" (Hillis)   66:193
The Boy Friend (Russell)   16:543, 546, 548
"The Boy from Kingsburg" (Saroyan)   29:363
Boy Gets Car (Felsen)   17:123
"A Boy Grows Older" (Callaghan)   41:98
"A Boy in Church" (Graves)   45:166
Boy in Darkness (Peake)   54:366, 373, 376-77
"Boy in Rome" (Cheever)   7:49; 15:131
The Boy in the Basement (Inge)   19:230
"The Boy in the Green Hat" (Klein)   30:235-
   36
"The Boy Knows the Truth" (Singer)   15:507
"The Boy Made of Meat" (Snodgrass)   68:388
The Boy on the Straightback Chair (Tavel)
   6:529
"The Boy on the Waggon" (Blunden)   56:39
*The Boy Scout Handbook, and Other Observa-
   tions* (Fussell)   74:124-26, 129, 137
"The Boy Stood on the Burning Deck" (For-
   ester)   35:173
Boy: Tales of Childhood (Dahl)   79:182
The Boy under the Bed (Dacey)   51:80-1
"Boy Walking Back to Find His Father's Cattle"
   (Klappert)   57:259-60, 266
The Boy Who Could Make Himself Disappear
   (Platt)   26:349-50, 356
"The Boy Who Fell Forty Feet" (Graver)
   70:49, 51
The Boy Who Followed Ripley (Highsmith)
   42:213-14; 102:170, 173, 179, 182, 193,
   195, 209, 220
"The Boy Who Talked with Animals" (Dahl)
   79:181
The Boy Who Waterskied to Forever (Tiptree)
   48:395
The Boy with a Cart (Fry)   10:200
The Boy with a Trumpet (Davies)   23:145-46
"Boy with Book of Knowledge" (Nemerov)
   9:395
"Boy with His Hair Cut Short" (Rukeyser)
   27:404, 406, 410
"Boy with Pigeons" (Dobyns)   37:81

The Boyds of Black River (Edmonds)   35:156
"The Boyfriend" (Oates)   108:382
"Boyhood" (Farrell)   66:129
Boyhood (Coetzee)   117:102
"Boyhood in Tobacco Country" (Warren)
   39:264
"The Boyish Lover" (Colwin)   84:146, 149
"Boys and Girls" (Farrell)   66:129
"Boys and Girls" (Munro)   95:298
Boys and Girls Come out to Play (Dennis)   8:173
Boys and Girls Together (Goldman)   48:124-
   25, 127-28
"Boys at a Picnic" (Oates)   6:370
"Boys. Black." (Brooks)   49:29, 36
"A Boy's Calendar" (Brown)   100:82-3
"Boys in Dresses" (Komunyakaa)   94:234, 241
"The Boys in the Back Room" (O'Hara)   3:371
*The Boys in the Back Room: Notes on Califor-
   nia Novelists* (Wilson)   24:473
The Boys in the Island (Koch)   42:259-62
Boys in the Trees (Simon)   26:411-12
The Boys of Summer (Kahn)   30:230-33
The Boys of Winter (Sheed)   53:340-43
"The Boys on Their Bikes" (Brodkey)   56:60-
   1
A Boy's Own Story (White)   27:481-82;
   110:315-16, 318, 321, 323, 325, 327-29,
   331, 336-37, 339, 341, 343
"Boys! Raise Giant Mushrooms in Your Cel-
   lar!" (Bradbury)   15:86; 42:33
"Boy's Room" (Oppen)   7:281
The Boys Who Stole the Funeral (Murray)
   40:339
A Boy's Will (Frost)   4:176; 10:195-96; 13:224;
   15:239, 246; 26:116-19, 124, 128
Bozena Nemcová's Fan (Seifert)
   See *Vejír Bozeny Nemcové*
BP (Nichol)   18:369
"Bracken Hills in Autumn" (MacDiarmid)
   19:289
"Bradshaw On: The Family"   70:419, 422
"Bragg and Minna" (Findley)   102:110
Braided Lives (Piercy)   27:377-81; 62:376
Brain 2000 (Gann)   23:167
"Brain Damage" (Barthelme)   6:30; 46:36, 40
"Brain Damage" (Pink Floyd)   35:306, 309
"Brain Dust" (Cohen)   19:113
"Brain Stealers of Mars" (Campbell)   32:75
Brainchild (Saul)   46:368-69
The Brain's the Target (Acorn)   15:8, 10
"Brainstorm" (Nemerov)   36:305
"Brainsy" (O'Faolain)   32:342
*Brainwashing and Other Forms of Mind Con-
   trol* (Hyde)   21:178
"Braly Street" (Soto)   80:287-88, 293-94
"Bran" (Muldoon)   32:320
"The Branch Line" (Beer)   58:31
"The Branch Line" (Blunden)   56:44
A Branch of the Blue Nile (Walcott)   67:347;
   76:275
The Branch Will Not Break (Wright)   3:540-
   44; 5:518-21; 10:543-46; 28:463-66,
   468-71
"Branches" (Avison)   97:78, 93
Branches of the Trees (Ray)
   See *Shakha Proshakha*
The Brand (Olson)   28:343
"Brand New Cadillac" (Clash)   30:47
Brand New Morning (Seger)   35:379
*Brandbilen som foerwann (The Fire Engine
   That Disappeared)* (Wahloo)   7:502
"A Brand-New Approach" (Bioy Casares)
   88:78

Brand's Heide: Zwei Erzählungen (Schmidt) **56**:390, 405

Brandstetter and Others (Hansen) **38**:240

"Brasilia" (Plath) **9**:427; **51**:340, 345

"The Brass Atlas" (Jiles) **58**:275-76

The Brass Butterfly (Golding) **17**:160, 169, 174

The Brass Check: A Study of American Journalism (Sinclair) **11**:497; **15**:499, 502; **63**:346-47

The Brass Cupcake (MacDonald) **44**:407

"Brass Knuckles" (Dybek) **114**:61-2

Brass Knuckles (Dybek) **114**:61-3, 65, 72, 77, 81

"The Brass Ring" (Carver) **55**:279

"Brass Spittoons" (Hughes) **1**:149

Brassneck (Brenton) **31**:62, 67

Brassneck (Hare) **29**:214

Bratsk Hydroelectric Station (Yevtushenko) See *The Bratsk Station*

The Bratsk Station (*Bratsk Hydroelectric Station*) (Yevtushenko) **13**:619; **26**:462, 465-66

"Bravado" (Frost) **26**:118

The Brave African Huntress (Tutuola) **5**:443; **14**:539; **29**:438

Brave Are My People: Indian Heroes Not Forgotten (Waters) **88**:370-71

The Brave Coward (Buchwald) **33**:87-8

The Brave Cowboy (Abbey) **36**:11, 13-15, 18; **59**:239, 241-42

The Brave Free Men (Vance) **35**:421

Brave New World (Huxley) **1**:151-52; **3**:255-56; **4**:237-40, 243-44; **5**:192-94; **8**:304-06; **18**:265-66, 268; **35**:232-41, 243-45; **79**:283-329

Brave New World Revisited (Huxley) **4**:239-241; **5**:194; **18**:266; **35**:235-37, 242-43; **79**:324

"Brave People" (Kunene) **85**:175

"Brave Strangers" (Seger) **35**:384

"Brave Words for a Startling Occasion" (Ellison) **114**:117

"Braveries" (Pinsky) **19**:372

A Bravery of Earth (Eberhart) **3**:134; **11**:178; **19**:143; **56**:74, 81, 86

Braving the Elements (Merrill) **2**:275; **3**:334-35; **6**:323; **8**:388; **13**:376, 381; **18**:331; **91**:228, 231

Bravo (Ferber) **93**:180-81

Bravoure (*Gothic Romance*) (Carrere) **89**:69, 71-73

"Bravura Passage" (Reid) **33**:350

"The Brawler in Who's Who" (Pratt) **19**:380

The Brazen Head (Powys) **7**:349; **46**:322-23

Brazen Prison (Middleton) **38**:330

"Brazil" (Marshall) **27**:311-12; **72**:230

"Brazil, January 1, 1502" (Bishop) **13**:89, 93-4; **32**:37

"Brazil-Copacabana" (Guillen) **79**:230

Brazzaville Beach (Boyd) **70**:132-45

"The Breach" (Murray) **40**:337

"Bread" (Brand) **7**:30

Bread (Hunter) **31**:223

Bread and a Stone (Bessie) **23**:59-60, 62

Bread and a Sword (Scott) **43**:381-82, 384

Bread and Butter (Taylor) **27**:440, 443, 446

"Bread and Butter Smith" (Bainbridge) **62**:35

Bread and Jam for Frances (Hoban) **25**:266

Bread and Wine (Silone) **4**:492, 494

"Bread from Stones" (Garrett) **51**:152

Bread Givers (Yezierska) **46**:443-44, 446, 448

"The Bread God" (Montague) **46**:265

Bread in the Wilderness (Merton) **83**:387, 401

"The Bread of the World; Praises III" (McGrath) **59**:181, 183

The Bread of Those Early Years (Boell) See *Das Brot der frühen Jahre*

The Bread of Time to Come (Malouf) See *Fly Away Peter*

The Bread of Truth (Thomas) **48**:374, 380

Bread Rather Than Blossoms (Enright) **31**:148-49

Bread upon the Waters (Shaw) **23**:399-401; **34**:369

Bread, Wine, and Salt (Nowlan) **15**:398

Bread—and Roses: The Struggle of American Labor, 1865-1915 (Meltzer) **26**:298-99

The Breadfruit Lotteries (Elman) **19**:151

The Breadwinner (Maugham) **1**:204; **67**:225-26

Break a Leg, Betsy Maybe (Kingman) **17**:246-47

Break In (Francis) **42**:160-61; **102**:128, 148

Break in Harvest and Other Poems (Mathias) **45**:235-36

"Break of Day" (Avison) **97**:75

"Break On Through" (Jones) **81**:62, 65, 67

"Break on Through" (Morrison) **17**:295

Break the News (Clair) **20**:70

"Breakdancing" (Graham) **48**:151

The Breakdown (Duerrenmatt) See *Die Panne*

"Breakfast" (Bowen) **22**:65-6

"Breakfast" (Williams) **31**:464

Breakfast at Tiffany's (Capote) **1**:55; **3**:99-100; **13**:134, 136-37; **19**:81-2, 85-7; **34**:320, 324-25; **38**:78, 82, 84, 87; **58**:120

A Breakfast for Barbarians (MacEwen) **13**:358

Breakfast in the Ruins (Moorcock) **5**:294

Breakfast of Champions; or, Goodbye, Blue Monday! (Vonnegut) **3**:501-04; **4**:568, 570; **5**:465-66, 468-70; **8**:530, 532-35; **12**:608-09, 613-14, 616-17, 619-20, 624-29; **40**:445-48; **60**:417, 432, 434; **111**:359-61, 363, 366, 371

Breakfast with the Nikolides (Godden) **53**:152-53, 157, 161

Breakheart Pass (MacLean) **13**:359, 361, 363; **50**:348

"The Break-In" (Adams) **46**:16-17

Breaking and Entering (Kennedy) **42**:255

Breaking Away (Tesich) **40**:421-23; **69**:368, 370-71, 373

Breaking Bread: Insurgent Black Intellectual Life (hooks) **94**:150, 155-56

"Breaking Camp" (Piercy) **18**:406; **27**:374

Breaking Camp (Piercy) **3**:384; **6**:401-02; **18**:405; **27**:374; **62**:376

"Breaking Glass" (Bowie) **17**:65

"Breaking Ground" (Gunn) **18**:199

Breaking Ice (McMillan) **112**:224-25, 228, 236

"The Breaking Mold" (Davidson) **19**:128

The Breaking of Bumbo (Sinclair) **2**:401

"The Breaking of the Day" (Davison) **28**:99

The Breaking of the Day (Davison) **28**:99-100

The Breaking of the Vessels (*Vessels*) (Bloom) **24**:82; **103**:23-4, 31, 35, 37

"Breaking Open" (Rukeyser) **27**:413

Breaking Open (Rukeyser) **6**:478-80; **10**:442; **15**:458; **27**:410-12

"Breaking Out" (Ammons) **108**:56

"Breaking Out the Shovel" (Alexie) **96**:13

The Breaking Point (du Maurier) **59**:286

"Breaking the Ice with Poorer People" (Lebowitz) **36**:248

"Breaking the News" (Boell) See "Die Botschaft"

"Breaking the News to Doll" (Kauffman) **42**:252

Breaking the Silence (Poliakoff) **38**:385

Breaking Up (Klein) **30**:241-42

"The Breaking Up of the Winships" (Thurber) **5**:431

"Breaking Us" (Silkin) **43**:403

Break-Neck (Celine) See *Casse-pipe*

"The Breakthrough" (Aickman) **57**:3

Breakthrough Fictioneers (Kostelanetz) **28**:213, 219

The Breakthrough of Petushikhino (Leonov) See *Petushikhinsky Prolom*

Breakthroughs in Science (Asimov) **26**:36-7

Breaktime (Chambers) **35**:98-9

"The Break-Up" (Klein) **19**:259

The Breast (Roth) **2**:379-80; **3**:436-38; **4**:453, 455-57, 459; **6**:475-76; **9**:461-62; **15**:449, 452; **22**:353, 356; **47**:363; **66**:417; **86**:254

"Breast Milky" (Pink Floyd) **35**:311

The Breast of Peace See *Brestkii mir*

"Breasts" (Gallagher) **18**:170

"Breasts" (Simic) **9**:479, 481; **68**:365

"Breath" (Jacobsen) **48**:192

"Breath" (Levine) **5**:251

Breath (Beckett) **4**:51; **6**:36, 38-9, 43, 45; **9**:83; **10**:36; **29**:65

The Breath (Bernhard) See *Der Atem*

Breath, Eyes, Memory (Danticat) **94**:90-2, 94-6, 98

"Breath from the Sky" (McCullers) **12**:432

A Breath of Air (Godden) **53**:156

The Breath of Clowns and Kings (Weiss) **8**:547

A Breath of Fresh Air (Cavanna) **12**:101

"A Breath of Lucifer" (Narayan) **28**:295

"Breathe" (Pink Floyd) **35**:307

Breathe upon These Slain (Scott) **43**:380-81, 384

Breathin' My Name with a Sigh (Wah) **44**:324, 326, 328

"Breathing" (Howes) **15**:289

"Breathing" (Solzhenitsyn) See "Dykhanie"

"Breathing Is Key: Sarah, 1985" (McNally) **82**:262

"Breathing Jesus" (Hempel) **39**:70

Breathing Lessons (Tyler) **59**:199-210; **103**:249-50, 252-53, 255-56, 260, 265-67, 275

The Breathing Method (King) **26**:240, 242; **113**:343

"Breathing Room: July" (Transtroemer) **65**:223

"Breathing Room: Something About My Brother" (Gurganus) **70**:191, 195

"The Breathing, the Endless News" (Dove) **81**:151

Breathing the Water (Levertov) **66**:250-53

Breathing Tokens (Sandburg) **15**:470; **35**:358

"Breathing Trouble" (Busch) **10**:91-2

Breathing Trouble and Other Stories (Busch) **7**:38; **10**:91-2

Breathless (Godard) See *A bout de souffle*

Breath-Turning (Celan) See *Atemwende*

Brébeuf and His Brethren (Pratt) **19**:376-81,

383-84

"Brechfa Chapel" (Mathias) **45**:237

The Breed to Come (Norton) **12**:464-65

"The Breeder" (Highsmith) **102**:186, 197

"Breeders" (Thomas) **107**:340, 342-43

"Breeze" (Arghezi)
See "Adiere"

Breezeblock Park (Russell) **60**:317, 319-20

Brekkukotsannáll (*The Annals of Brekkukot; The Fish Can Sing*) (Laxness) **25**:292, 300

Bremen Speech (Celan)
See *Speech on the Occasion of Receiving the Literature Prize of the Free Hanseatic City of Bremen*

Brendan Behan's Island (Behan) **79**:25-7, 37

Brendan Behan's New York (Behan) **79**:25, 52

"Brennbar's Rant" (Irving) **112**:173

"Brennende liebe, 1904" (Gluck) **7**:120; **22**:174

"Brent's Deus ex machina" (Deighton) **46**:127

Brestkii mir (*The Breast of Peace*) **59**:359-62

"Breughel's Two Monkeys" (Szymborska) **99**:195, 199

Breve for Afrika, 1914-34 (Dinesen) **95**:62

Una breve vacanza (*A Brief Vacation*) (De Sica) **20**:96-7

"Brewed and Filled by ..." (Bukowski) **41**:68

Brewster McCloud (Altman) **16**:21, 25, 28-9, 35, 38, 40-1, 43; **116**:3-5, 7, 11, 14, 21, 46, 59, 66

"The Briar Patch" (Warren) **53**:359; **59**:298

Briarpatch (Thomas) **39**:246-47, 249

"The Bribe" (Borges) **48**:39

The Brickfield (Hartley) **2**:182

"The Bricklayers' Lunch Hour" (Ginsberg) **109**:353

Bricks to Babel (Koestler) **33**:243-44

The Bridal Canopy (Agnon)
See *Hakhnasat kalah*

"The Bridal Night" (O'Connor) **14**:399; **23**:332

"Bridal Photo, 1906" (Ciardi) **40**:156

"Bridal Piece" (Gluck) **7**:119

"Bridal Suite" (Raphael) **14**:438

"Bride" (Broumas) **73**:9

"Bride and Groom Lie Hidden for Three Days" (Hughes) **37**:178

The Bride of Glomdale (Dreyer) **16**:259-62

"The Bride of Innisfallen" (Welty) **105**:324

The Bride of Innisfallen (Welty) **2**:461; **5**:479; **22**:461-62; **105**:307, 327, 335

The Bride Price (Emecheta) **14**:159; **48**:97, 99, 101

The Bride Wore Black (Truffaut)
See *La mariée etait en noir*

The Bride Wore Black (Woolrich) **77**:389-90, 400, 403

The Bride Wore Red (Arzner) **98**:87, 91-2, 94

"The Bridegroom" (Gordimer) **33**:179-80

"The Bridegroom" (Smith) **15**:514, 516

A Bridegroom for Marcela (Klima) **56**:167-68

"The Bridegroom's Body" (Boyle) **19**:64-5; **58**:64, 67

"The Brides" (Hope) **3**:250; **51**:211, 214

The Bride's House (Powell) **66**:366

Brides of Reason (Davie) **5**:115; **8**:162; **10**:123, 125

Brideshead Revisited: The Sacred and Profane Memories of Captain Charles Ryder (Waugh) **1**:357-58, 360; **3**:510-14; **8**:543-44; **13**:585; **19**:461, 465; **27**:469-74, 476-77; **107**:357-58, 360-62, 368-70,

376, 385-86, 388-90, 400-01

"Bridge" (Ammons) **8**:16-18; **9**:30; **108**:28

"The Bridge" (Blaise) **29**:75

"The Bridge" (Ferron) **94**:103, 124

"Bridge" (Okigbo) **84**:301, 305-06, 308

"The Bridge" (Walcott) **14**:550

"The Bridge" (Young) **17**:571

The Bridge (Mano) **10**:328

The Bridge (Talese) **37**:391, 403

The Bridge at Andau (Michener) **109**:375, 378-79, 382

"The Bridge at Arta" (Stewart) **32**:421

The Bridge at Arta and Other Stories (Stewart) **32**:420-21

The Bridge Builders (Sutcliff) **26**:430

The Bridge in the Jungle (Traven) **8**:519-20; **11**:536

The Bridge of Beyond (Schwarz-Bart)
See *Pluie et vent sur Télumée Miracle*

Bridge of Birds (Hughart) **39**:155-57

"The Bridge of Dreams" (Tanizaki)
See "Yume no ukihashi"

"Bridge of Music, River of Sand" (Goyen) **8**:250; **14**:212; **40**:216-17

The Bridge of San Luis Rey (Wilder) **1**:364-66; **6**:573-74, 576-78; **10**:536; **15**:572, 574; **35**:442; **82**:338-40, 344-45, 348, 350, 352-53, 355, 365, 367-68, 371-72, 376-77, 379, 382

The Bridge of Water (Berry) **46**:73

The Bridge of Years (Sarton) **49**:309-10; **91**:245

"Bridge over Troubled Waters" (Simon) **17**:464

Bridge over Troubled Waters (Simon) **17**:459-60, 464

"The Bridge, Palm Sunday, 1973" (Corn) **33**:114

"The Bridge Players" (Simmons) **43**:408

"Bridge through My Window" (Lorde) **71**:235, 252

Bridge to Terabithia (Paterson) **12**:485; **30**:282-87

A Bridge Too Far (Ryan) **7**:385

Bridgeport Bus (Howard) **5**:188, 190; **14**:267; **46**:186

"Bridges" (Tallent) **45**:388

Bridges (Haavikko)
See "Sillat"

The Bridges (Vesaas) **48**:409-10

The Bridges of Toko-Ri (Michener) **29**:311; **109**:376, 378-79, 382

Bridges-Go-Round (Clarke) **16**:215

"Bridging" (Apple) **30**:20-1

"The Bridle" (Carver) **36**:101, 104

Bridle the Wind (Aiken) **35**:21

Brief an einen jungen Katholiken (Boell) **9**:106; **11**:54

Brief Diversions (Priestley) **34**:361

"Brief Encounter" (Coward) **29**:142

"A Brief Essay on the Subject of Celebrity: With Numerous Digressions and Particular Attention to the Actress Rita Hayworth" (Connell) **45**:115

"Brief for a Future Defense" (Belitt) **22**:49

"A Brief History of *A Brief History*" (Hawking) **105**:72

A Brief History of Time: From the Big Bang to Black Holes (Hawking) **63**:143-44, 151-52, 154-55; **105**:56-8, 61-3, 65-6, 69-72

A Brief Life (Onetti)
See *La vida breve*

Brief Moment (Behrman) **40**:74-6, 78

"Brief Reflection on Two Hot Shots" (Baraka) **115**:41

A Brief Vacation (De Sica)
See *Una breve vacanza*

"The Briefcase" (Muldoon) **72**:281

"The Briefcase" (Singer) **6**:509; **9**:486

The Briefcase (Abe) **81**:284, 286

Briefing for a Descent into Hell (Lessing) **2**:239-42; **3**:284-85, 289-91; **6**:295-97, 299, 303-04; **10**:313-15; **15**:334; **94**:253, 258, 261, 264, 270, 282, 284, 286, 288, 293, 295-96

Briefings: Poems Small and Easy (Ammons) **2**:12-14; **5**:26-7; **9**:26-7, 29; **25**:45; **57**:55, 58-9

"Brigade de cuisine" (McPhee) **36**:298

"Brigade-Leader Kiazym" (Iskander)
See "Brigadir Kiazym"

"Brigadier" (Smith) **15**:514

"The Brigadier and the Golf Widow" (Cheever) **64**:57

The Brigadier and the Golf Widow (Cheever) **3**:106-07; **64**:60, 62

"Brigadir Kiazym" ("Brigade-Leader Kiazym") (Iskander) **47**:198

Briggflatts (Bunting) **10**:83-4, 86; **39**:297-300; **47**:46, 48-56

"Bright" (Cummings) **15**:157

"Bright and Morning Star" (Wright) **1**:380; **14**:597; **21**:444, 453-55; **74**:390

Bright Angel **99**:106

Bright Book of Life (Kazin) **34**:561; **38**:277-78, 281-82

Bright Center of Heaven (Maxwell) **19**:304-05

"A Bright Day" (Montague) **46**:275-76

The Bright Day (Hocking) **13**:285

Bright Day (Priestley) **5**:351

"Bright Day in Boston" (Lowell) **11**:330; **37**:233

"The Bright Field" (Walcott) **14**:549

Bright Flows the River (Caldwell) **28**:68

Bright Journey (Derleth) **31**:133-34, 138

Bright Land (Ferber) **93**:178

"Bright Leaf" (Voigt) **54**:433

Bright Lights, Big City (McInerney) **34**:81-4; **112**:179-88, 196-97, 199-200, 202-04, 206, 208, 211, 215-17

"Bright New Day" (Mphahlele) **25**:340

Bright New Universe (Williamson) **29**:457-60

Bright Orange for the Shroud (MacDonald) **27**:275; **44**:408

"Bright Phoenix" (Bradbury) **98**:121

A Bright Room Called Day (Kushner) **81**:197, 206, 208, 210, 212

Bright Shadow (Priestley) **34**:362

Bright Shadow (Thomas) **35**:406-07

"The Bright Side" (Ammons) **57**:50

Bright Skin (Peterkin) **31**:304-06, 309-11

A Bright Star Falls (Weber) **12**:633

"The Bright Void of the Wind" (Le Guin) **45**:219

"Bright-Cut Irish Silver" (Boland) **113**:69

Brighten the Corner Where You Are (Chappell) **78**:101

The Brightfount Diaries (Aldiss) **14**:14

"Brightness as a Poignant Light" (Ignatow) **14**:275

Brightness Falls (McInerney) **112**:197-203, 212-13, 215, 218

Brightness Falls from the Air (Tiptree) **48**:392-94; **50**:355, 357

Brighton Beach Memoirs (Simon) **31**:400-02; **39**:216-17, 219; **70**:236, 238, 240-43

The Brighton Belle and Other Stories (King)

53:208
Brighton Rock (Greene) 1:131-33, 135; 3:207, 209-10, 212-14; 6:213, 215, 217-19; 14:216-19; 18:197; 27:173, 175-76; 37:140; 70:287, 290-91, 293; 72:149-51, 155, 157-59, 161-63, 165, 178
Brighton Rock (Skvorecky) 15:512
La brigitta (Audiberti) 38:31
Brill Among the Ruins (Bourjaily) 62:99-101, 104
"The Brilliant Leaves" (Gordon) 6:203; 29:189; 83:231, 238
"Brimmer" (Cheever) 15:131
Brimstone and Treacle (Potter) 58:392, 400; 86:346, 348, 350
"Brimstone Yellow" (Szirtes) 46:393
"Brindis" ("Cheers!") (Guillen) 48:162
"Bring Down the Beams" (Bukowski) 41:64
Bring Forth the Body (Raven) 14:442
Bring Larks and Heroes (Keneally) 5:210-11; 8:318; 10:298; 19:243, 245, 247; 117:209-11, 214-17, 221, 225, 227, 229-30, 232-34, 243-45, 248
Bring Me a Unicorn: Diaries and Letters of Anne Morrow Lindbergh, 1922-1928 (Lindbergh) 82:150
"Bring Me My Bride" (Sondheim) 30:378
Bring Me Sunshine (Taylor) 27:443-45
Bring Me the Head of Alfredo Garcia (Peckinpah) 20:279-82
"Bring Me the Sunflower" (Montale) 9:388
Bring On the Bad Guys (Lee) 17:261
"Bring on the Lucie" ("Freda People") (Lennon) 35:267
"Bring the Day" (Roethke) 101:273, 279, 298, 335, 340
The Bringer of Water (Berry) 8:85
Bringing It All Back Home (Dylan) 6:155-57; 12:181-82, 184, 199; 77:168, 170, 188
"Bringing to Light" (Gunn) 18:201, 204
"Brink of Darkness" (Winters) 8:552
The Brink of Darkness (Winters) 8:552; 32:467
Brink of Life (Bergman)
  See *Nära livet*
Brisées: Broken Branches (Leiris) 61:361-62
"Bristol and Clifton" (Betjeman) 6:68; 43:32
The British Dramatists (Greene) 72:153
"British Guiana" (Marshall) 27:311-12; 72:229
"British Migraine Association Poetry Competition" (Musgrave) 54:335
"The British Military Cemetery on Tsofim Mountain" (Amichai)
  See "Bet hakravot hatsva'i habriti behar hatsofim"
The British Museum Is Falling Down (Lodge) 36:269-70
British Sounds (Godard) 20:150
The Broad Back of the Angel (Rooke) 25:391-92
"The Broad Bean Sermon" (Murray) 40:336, 341
"Broadcast" (Larkin) 33:256; 39:345; 64:263
"Broadway Baby" (Sondheim) 30:401
Broadway Bound (Simon) 70:236-37, 240-43
Broadway, Broadway (McNally) 41:292
"Broadway to Buenos Aires" (Ferber) 93:141-42
"Broagh" (Heaney) 7:148; 14:242-43; 74:157
Broca's Brain (Sagan) 30:336-38, 343
"Brock" (Muldoon) 72:273
"Broderie anglaise" (Gilliatt) 53:146
Brogg's Brain (Platt) 26:356

The Broken Ark (Ondaatje)
  See *A Book of Beasts*
"Broken Arrow" (Young) 17:569, 572, 577-78
"Broken Blossoms" (Chappell) 40:142
Broken Canes (Vansittart) 42:390, 399
"Broken Chain" (Soto) 80:300
"Broken Column" (Hollander) 5:186
The Broken Connection: On Death and the Continuity of Life (Lifton) 67:142, 152-55
"Broken Connections" (Oates) 9:403
The Broken Cord: A Family's Ongoing Struggle with Fetal Alcohol Syndrome (Dorris) 109:296-99, 304-05, 307-08, 310-11, 313
"Broken Field Running" (Bambara) 19:34; 88:22, 28, 37, 53-55
"Broken Flag" (Smith) 12:544
"Broken Freedom Song" (Kristofferson) 26:268
The Broken Ground (Berry) 27:34; 46:69
"Broken Hearts Are for Assholes" (Zappa) 17:592
"The Broken Home" (Merrill) 6:323; 13:380-81; 91:229
"Broken Homes" (Trevor) 14:536; 71:326
"Broken Jar" (Paz)
  See "El cántaro roto"
A Broken Journey (Callaghan) 14:100; 41:91
Broken Laws (Hoffman) 6:243; 13:286-87
"Broken Merchandise" (Bukowski) 41:73
"The Broken Ones" (MacBeth) 5:265
Broken Patterns (Jordan) 37:194
The Broken Penny (Symons) 14:523
"The Broken Pitcher" (Paz)
  See "El cántaro roto"
The Broken Places (Shaara) 15:474
The Broken Places (MacBeth) 5:264
"Broken Promise" (MacLeish) 68:286
"Broken Routine" (Archer) 28:14
"The Broken Sandal" (Levertov) 5:249
"The Broken Sea" (Watkins) 43:441
Broken Soil (Colum)
  See *The Fiddler's House*
The Broken Sword (Anderson) 15:12
Broken Vessels (Dubus) 97:231-33, 236
The Broken Wheel: Chung Kuo II (Wingrove) 68:453, 456-57
"A Broken World" (O'Faolain) 1:259; 32:343
"Bromios" (Aldington) 49:4
The Bronc People (Eastlake) 8:198, 200
Brontë Wilde (Howe) 47:174
The Bronx is Next (Sanchez) 116:282, 301
El Bronx Remembered: A Novella and Stories (Mohr) 12:446-47
"Bron-yr-aur" (Page and Plant) 12:477, 479, 482
"Bronze" (Walcott) 76:279
"A Bronzeville Mother Loiters in Mississippi. Meanwhile a Mississippi Mother Burns Bacon" (Brooks) 15:92; 49:27, 32-3, 36
"Bronzeville Woman in a Red Hat" (Brooks) 15:93
"The Brooch" (Hill) 113:330-31
"Brooding" (Ignatow) 40:258
"The Brook" (Blunden) 56:44
"The Brook" (Davis) 49:92
"Brooklyn" (Marshall) 27:311-12
The Brooklyn Bridge (Miller) 84:293
"Brooklyn from Clinton Hill" (Moore) 47:270
"Brooklyn, Iowa, and West" (Miles) 14:369
"Brooklyn Is My Neighborhood" (McCullers)

100:260
"Brooklyn Pigeon" (Kenny) 87:247
Brooklyn-Manhattan Transit: A Bouquet for Flatbush (Blackburn) 43:63, 66
The Broom of the System (Wallace) 50:92-6; 114:347-51, 358-59, 361-62, 364, 367-68, 372
"Brooms" (Simic) 9:479; 49:337, 339; 68:370, 379
Brosok na yug (*Southern Adventure*; *A Throw to the South*) (Paustovsky) 40:366, 368
Das Brot der frühen Jahre (*The Bread of Those Early Years*) (Boell) 2:68; 9:109-11; 11:54, 57; 27:57-8; 39:294
"Brothel-Going" (Faludy) 42:140
"The Brother" (Coover) 7:58; 15:145
"Brother" (Davies) 21:102
"Brother" (O'Brien) 65:167-69; 116:204
"The Brother" (Walcott) 76:285
"Brother Alvin" (Lorde) 71:247
"Brother and Sisters" (Wright) 53:425, 427
"Brother André, Père Lamarche and My Grandmother Eugenie Blagdon" (Hood) 28:189
Brother Cain (Raven) 14:439
Brother, Can You Spare a Dime? The Great Depression, 1929-1933 (Meltzer) 26:299, 305
Brother Dusty-Feet (Sutcliff) 26:428, 433, 435
"Brother Fire" (MacNeice) 4:315, 318
"Brother Jordan's Fox" (L'Heureux) 52:275
"Brother Love's Traveling Salvation Show" (Diamond) 30:111
Brother, My Brother (Santos) 22:362, 365
"Brother of the Mount of Olives" (Monette) 82:333-34
"The Brother Poems" (Urdang) 47:399
Brother to Dragons (Warren) 1:352; 4:578-80; 10:517-18; 13:574-77, 581; 18:535-38; 39:260, 266; 59:298
"Brother to Methusalem" (Still) 49:366
Brotherhood (Ward) 19:458
"Brotherhood in Pain" (Warren) 13:578
"The Brotherhood Movement" (Bioy Casares) 88:78
"The Brotherhood of Men" (Eberhart) 56:80, 88
The Brotherhood of the Grape (Fante) 60:132, 136
The Brotherhood of the Red Poppy (Troyat) 23:460
Brotherly Love (Hoffman) 23:241-43
"Brothers" (Cohen) 19:113
"The Brothers" (King) 8:322
"Brothers" (Merwin) 8:390
"The Brothers" (Smith) 64:391
The Brothers (Barthelme) 117:12-14, 19, 22-6
Brothers (Goldman) 48:131
Brothers (Rubens) 31:352
Brothers and Keepers (Wideman) 36:456-57; 67:370, 374-75, 379-82, 388
Brothers and Sisters (Compton-Burnett) 15:135, 138; 34:495-96, 499-500
The Brothers and Sisters of the Toda Family (Ozu) 16:451
Brothers, I Loved You All: Poems, 1969-1977 (Carruth) 18:87-9; 84:119-20, 122-23, 130-31, 135
Brothers Keepers (Westlake) 7:529
Brothers of Earth (Cherryh) 35:103-04
"Brothers of No Kin" (Richter) 30:309
Brothers of No Kin and Other Stories (Richter)

30:309, 323

The Brothers Rico (Simenon) 1:309; 2:399

"Brought Up to Be Timid" (Buckley) 57:133

"Broward Dowdy" (Blaise) 29:70-1

"Brown America in Jail: Kilby" (Hughes) 108:318

"The Brown Book of the Hitler Terror" (Read) 4:439

"Brown Dog" (Harrison) 66:167-70

"Brown Earth" (Nyro) 17:313

Brown Girl, Brownstones (Marshall) 27:308-09, 311-12, 314-16; 72:212, 222-23, 226-27, 231-32, 243, 248-50, 252, 254-55

"The Brown Menace or Poem to the Survival of Roaches" (Lorde) 71:248

Brown on Resolution (Forester) 35:158, 165, 170, 174

"Brown Sugar" (Jagger and Richard) 17:224, 226, 229-30, 235-38, 242

"Brown Tish" (Bowering) 47:31

"Browning in Venice" (Watkins) 43:452

The Browning Version (Rattigan) 7:355-56

"The Browns" (Barthelme) 117:15, 17-18

"Brown's Descent" (Frost) 15:248

"Brownshoes" (Sturgeon) 22:411

"Brownstone" (Adler) 8:6

Brownstone Eclogues and Other Poems (Aiken) 52:21, 26

The Brownsville Raid (Fuller) 25:180-81

A Browser's Dictionary and Native's Guide to the Unknown American Language (Ciardi) 44:378-79, 383

Le bruissement de la langue (*The Rustle of Language*) (Barthes) 83:88

"Un bruit de soie" (Hebert) 29:228

"Brujerías o tonterías" ("Sorcery or Foolishness") (Ulibarri) 83:415

"El brujo postergado" ("The Sorcerer Postponed") (Borges) 13:106

Brumby Innes (Prichard) 46:337

"Bruno" (Warner) 7:513

Bruno's Dream (Murdoch) 1:236; 3:345, 349; 6:344, 349; 31:293; 51:288

"Bruns" (Rush) 44:91-3, 95

"Brunswick Avenue" (Govier) 51:166

"Brush Fire" (Rooke) 25:390-91

Brush Fire (Tchicaya)
See *Brush Fire*

Brustein's Window (Hansberry)
See *The Sign in Sydney Brustein's Window*

The Brute (Bunuel)
See *El bruto*

El bruto (*The Brute*) (Bunuel) 16:147; 80:23

Brutus's Orchard (Fuller) 28:148, 153, 157, 159

"Bubba" (Sanchez) 116:302, 306, 313

The Bubble (Anand) 93:52-53, 55-57

"Bubbs Creek Haircut" (Snyder) 32:387

"Bubnovy valet" ("The Knave of Diamonds") (Leonov) 92:262

"The Bubus" (Cendrars) 106:159

Bucarest (*Bucharest*) (Morand) 41:304

Buchanan Dying (Updike) 5:455-57; 15:543; 23:476-77; 43:431

"Buchanan's Fancy" (Simmons) 43:410

Bucharest (Morand)
See *Bucarest*

The Buchwald Stops Here (Buchwald) 33:94

"The Buck" (Oates) 108:383

Buck and the Preacher (Poitier) 26:357-58, 360

"Buck Duke and Mama" (Taylor) 5:426

"Buck in the Bottoms" (Derleth) 31:132

"Buck Moon—From the Field Guide to Insects" (Oliver) 98:

Buck Private (Valdez)
See *Soldado razo*

Buckdancer's Choice (Dickey) 2:115; 4:122; 7:79-80; 47:93, 95; 109:243-44

The Bucket of Blood (O'Hara) 42:319

The Bucket Shop (*Everything Must Go*) (Waterhouse) 47:419

"Buckeye" (Rose) 85:312

"Buckley at Mons" (Hemingway) 39:398

Buckthorn (Akhmatova)
See *Podorozhnik*

Bucolic Comedies (Sitwell) 67:312

"Bucolics" (Auden) 3:23; 14:29

"Bud" (Fuller) 62:206

"Bud and Tom" (Kinsella) 43:256

"The Buddha" (Soto) 80:298

The Buddha of Suburbia (Kureishi) 64:249-53

"The Buddha's Last Instruction" (Oliver) 98:280-81

"Buddhism" (Borges) 48:47, 49

"The Buddhist" (Ferron) 94:103, 125

The Buddhist Car and Other Characters (Schevill) 7:401

Buddies (Kenny) 87:249

Budding Prospects: A Pastoral (Boyle) 36:60-3; 55:106, 111; 90:43-4, 47, 49

Buddy and the Old Pro (Tunis) 12:597

"Buddy the Leper" (Keillor) 115:295

"Budgie" (MacNeice) 4:318

"Budilnikut" (Bagryana) 10:13

Las buenas consciencias (*The Good Conscience*) (Fuentes) 22:164; 113:230, 253

The Buenos Aires Affair (Puig) 5:354-56; 10:420; 28:369-71; 65:265-66, 269, 271-72

"Buenos Dias" (Broumas) 73:9

La bufera e altro (*The Storm and Other Things*; *The Storm and Other Things*) (Montale) 7:222-26, 228-30, 232; 9:387; 18:340

Buff (Fuller) 28:151, 153

"Buffalo" (Peacock) 60:298

"Buffalo. 12.7.41" (Howe) 72:202

Buffalo Bill and the Indians; or, Sitting Bull's History Lesson (Altman) 16:36, 41, 43; 116:18-20, 26-8, 30-1, 35, 59, 72

"Buffalo Bill's Defunct" (Cummings) 8:154; 12:151

"Buffalo Climbs out of Cellar" (Willard) 7:539

The Buffalo Hunter (Straub) 107:306-07

The Buffalo Hunters (Sandoz) 28:403-04, 407

The Buffalo Shoot (Kuzma) 7:197

Buffalo Springfield (Young) 17:568

"Buffalo Story" (Silko) 74:334-35, 338

"Buffs" (Pownall) 10:419

Bug Jack Barron (Spinrad) 46:383, 386

"Bugle Song" (Stegner) 81:345-46

The Bugles Blowing (Freeling)
See *What Are the Bugles Blowing For?*

"Bugs in the Bug" (Royko) 109:406

"Buick" (Shapiro) 53:330, 334

"Build Soil: A Political Pastoral" (Frost) 3:170; 10:193; 44:460, 462

"The Builder and the Dream" (Stuart) 11:510

"The Building" (Larkin) 5:225-26, 230; 8:332, 337; 9:323; 13:335; 18:297-98; 33:260, 262-63; 39:341; 64:266, 280, 282

"Building a Person" (Dunn) 36:154

"Building a Teaching Community" (hooks) 94:156-57

"Building Houses" (Smith) 42:351

"The Building of the Prison" (Saro-Wiwa) 114:254

"The Building Site" (Duras) 40:184-85

The Build-Up (Williams) 5:510

"Bujah and the Strong Force" (Amis) 62:6-8, 10

The Bukowski/Purdy Letters: A Decade of Dialogue, 1964-1974 (Bukowski) 108:81, 114-15

"The Bulahdelah-Taree Holiday Song Cycle" (Murray) 40:338-40

"The Bulgarian Poetess" (Updike) 15:543

"The Bulge" (Johnston) 51:245

"The Bull" (Wright) 53:418-19

The Bull and the Spear (Moorcock) 5:294

"The Bull Calf" (Frame) 96:218

Bull Fire (Harris) 9:261

The Bull from the Sea (Renault) 3:425; 17:394-97, 400-01

Bull Island (Smith) 22:384-85

"The Bull Moose" (Nowlan) 15:399

"The Bull Moses" (Hughes) 37:176

"Bull of Bandylaw" ("The Bull of Bendylaw") (Plath) 17:348, 366

"The Bull of Bendylaw" (Plath)
See "Bull of Bandylaw"

"The Bullaun" (Adcock) 41:17-18

"The Bulldozer" (Francis) 15:239

Bullet Park (Cheever) 3:107, 109; 7:50; 8:138-39; 11:120, 123; 25:116-18; 64:49-50, 57-9

"Bulletin" (Fearing) 51:106

"Le bulletin des baux" (Char) 9:164, 166

"Bulletin from the Writer's Colony" (Jacobsen) 48:192

"The Bullets of Camden, North Carolina" (Smith) 22:385

The Bullfighters (Montherlant) 19:322

Bullies (Trow) 52:419-20, 424

Bullivant and the Lambs (Compton-Burnett)
See *Manservant and Maidservant*

"Bullocky" (Wright) 53:416, 423, 427, 430

"Bull-Ring: Plaza Mexico" (Belitt) 22:49

The Bull's Hide (Espriu) 9:193

"The Bully" (Reaney) 13:473

"Bum Prayer" (Carrier) 78:83

Bumazhnyi peizazh (*The Paper Landscape*) (Aksyonov) 37:13

Bumblebee Dithyramb (Rosenblatt) 15:447

The Bumblebee Flies Anyway (Cormier) 30:90-1

"Bumblebees" (Mason) 82:244, 256

The Bundle (Bond) 23:65, 67, 70

A Bundle of Myrrh (Neihardt) 32:330

A Bundle of Nerves (Aiken) 35:17

"The Bungalows" (Plomer) 4:407

The Bungalows (Ashbery) 3:16

"Bunkhouse North" (Lane) 25:284

Le buono figlie (Buzzati) 36:84

Burannyi polustanok (Aitmatov)
See *I dol'she veka dlitsia den'*

"Burbank with a Baedeker: Bleistein with a Cigar" (Eliot) 13:193; 34:394, 403; 41:151; 55:346-48, 355, 364-66, 370-71

"Burchfield's World" (Phillips) 28:364

"Burden" (Eberhart) 11:178

"A Burden for Critics" (Blackmur) 24:61

"The Burden of Black Women" (Du Bois) 64:114, 116

"Burden of Freedom" (Kristofferson) 26:267

The Burden of Our Time (Arendt)
See *The Origins of Totalitarianism*

"The Burdened Man" (Paley) 4:392

Burger's Daughter (Gordimer) **18**:187-88; **51**:157-59, 161; **70**:163-64, 166-67, 170-76, 181, 186-88
The Burglar (Brophy) **105**:8-10, 30
"The Burglar of Babylon" (Bishop) **13**:89; **32**:38, 42
"Burglary" (Matthews) **40**:324
"A Burglary" (Ryan) **65**:209-12, 214-16
"Burial" (Lowell) **11**:331
"Burial" (Walker) **58**:405
"Burial at Sea" (Singer) **69**:311
"Burial by Salt" (Piercy) **62**:379
"The Burial of Saint Brendan" (Colum) **28**:90
"The Burial of the Dead" (Eliot) **2**:130; **6**:165; **9**:188; **10**:168; **15**:212; **113**:216
The Burial of the Sardine (Arrabal)
    See *L'enterrement de la sardine*
"Burial Party" (Masefield) **11**:358
"Buried Although" (Johnson) **6**:265; **9**:301
Buried Child (Shepard) **17**:449; **34**:265, 267, 269; **41**:408-09, 411, 415-16; **44**:264-66, 268-69
Buried City (Moss) **7**:249-50; **14**:375-76; **45**:286
The Buried Day (Day Lewis) **6**:126; **10**:126
Buried for Pleasure (Crispin) **22**:109
"Buried in a Blue Suit" (Vizenor) **103**:297
"The Buried Lake" (Tate) **2**:429; **4**:451; **11**:525, 527; **14**:529
The Buried Mirror (Fuentes) **113**:255-56, 262
"The Buried Port" (Ungaretti) **7**:484; **11**:559
"Buriga" (Leonov)
    See "Buryga"
"Burl" (Mosher) **62**:312
Burma Rifles: A Story of Merrill's Marauders (Bonham) **12**:54
The Burmese Harp (Ichikawa) **20**:176, 181
The Burn (Aksyonov)
    See *Ozhog*
"Burn and burn and burn" (Bukowski) **108**:113
"Burn Center" (Olds) **39**:189
The Burn Ward (Glasser) **37**:130
"Burnin' and Lootin'" (Marley) **17**:269, 271-72
"The Burning" (Momaday) **85**:269
"The Burning" (Welty) **22**:457
Burning (Johnson) **5**:198
"The Burning Babe" (Duncan) **41**:130
The Burning Book (Gee) **57**:219-22
The Burning Boys (Fuller) **62**:207-08
"Burning Brambles" (Mathias) **45**:238
Burning Brambles: Selected Poems, 1944-1979 (Mathias) **45**:236-37
Burning Bright: A Play in Story Form (Steinbeck) **1**:325; **13**:534; **21**:382; **34**:409; **45**:372, 374, 378
"The Burning Bush" (Turco) **63**:429-30
The Burning Cactus (Spender) **91**:261
"The Burning Child" (Clampitt) **32**:115
"Burning Chrome" (Gibson) **39**:139; **63**:129, 132, 134, 139
Burning Chrome (Gibson) **63**:139
The Burning Court (Carr) **3**:101
"The Burning Eyes" (Gordon) **29**:187; **83**:231
The Burning Flames, and Other Stories (Rulfo)
    See *El llano en llamas, y otros cuentos*
The Burning Glass (Behrman) **40**:85-6
Burning Grass (Ekwensi) **4**:151-52
"Burning Hills" (Ondaatje) **51**:311-12, 315, 317
The Burning Hills (L'Amour) **25**:278; **55**:306, 308
"The Burning House" (Beattie) **40**:66; **63**:9,
12, 19
The Burning House (Beattie) **40**:63-6; **63**:2-3, 5, 9, 11-13, 15, 17
Burning in Water Drowning in Flame: Selected Poems 1955-1973 (Bukowski) **108**:110
The Burning Library (White) **110**:332, 334-35, 337-38,340
"Burning Love Letters" (Moss) **7**:247; **50**:353
The Burning Man (Millin) **49**:250
The Burning Mystery of Anna in 1951 (Koch) **44**:246, 248
"The Burning of Paper Instead of Children" (Rich) **6**:458; **36**:373
"The Burning of the Waters" (Still) **49**:368
"Burning Oneself In" (Rich) **3**:428; **11**:477
"Burning Oneself Out" (Rich) **3**:428; **7**:367; **11**:477
The Burning Perch (MacNeice) **4**:315-17; **10**:325; **53**:240, 242
The Burning Plain, and Other Stories (Rulfo)
    See *El llano en llamas, y otros cuentos*
Burning Questions (Shulman) **10**:475-76
"Burning Sky" (Weller) **26**:446
"Burning the Cat" (Merwin) **5**:285
"Burning the Effects" (Buckley) **57**:126, 131
"Burning the Frankenstein Monster: Elegiac Letter to Richard Dillard" (Chappell) **78**:91
Burning the Ivy (Walker) **13**:566-67
"Burning the Letters" (Jarrell) **2**:210
"Burning the Letters" (Plath) **51**:340
"Burning the News" (Turco) **11**:549-50; **63**:429-30
"Burning the Small Dead" (Snyder) **32**:391
"Burning the Tomato Worms" (Forche) **25**:168, 170; **83**:207
Burning Water (Bowering) **47**:26, 29, 31, 34
"The Burning Wheel" (Huxley) **11**:282
The Burning Wheel (Huxley) **4**:243; **11**:282-84
The Burning Wind (Krleza)
    See *Plameni vjetar*
The Burning Women of Far Cry (De Marinis) **54**:99-100
Burnish Me Bright (Cunningham) **12**:165
"Burnished" (Stevenson) **33**:382
"Burns Unit" (Blackwood) **100**:2
"The Burnt Bridge" (MacNeice) **53**:242
"Burnt Norton" (Eliot) **1**:92; **2**:125; **3**:139; **6**:165; **9**:184; **10**:171; **13**:194; **15**:210-11, 215-16; **24**:174; **34**:399, 401, 527, 529-32; **41**:146, 152, 154-55, 160-61; **55**:367-68, 374; **57**:186; **113**:192
The Burnt Ones (White) **5**:486-87; **7**:532-33; **69**:397-98
Burnt Weenie Sandwich (Zappa) **17**:586-87
A Burnt-Out Case (Greene) **1**:130, 134-35; **3**:209, 213; **6**:213-16, 220; **14**:219; **27**:173, 175-76; **37**:137; **70**:289, 293; **72**:177
Burr (Vidal) **4**:553-54, 556-57; **6**:548-50; **8**:525-26, 528; **10**:504; **33**:406-07, 409-11; **72**:377, 379-80, 382, 384-85, 387, 389, 391-92, 394-95, 398, 400-02, 404
Burr Oaks (Eberhart) **11**:178; **56**:79
"Burr Oaks: The Barn" (Eberhart) **56**:86
Bursting into Song (Purdy) **50**:248
"Bursting Rapture" (Frost) **9**:223
Bury My Heart at Wounded Knee: An Indian History of the American West (Brown) **18**:70-2; **47**:38-9
Bury the Dead (Shaw) **7**:411-12; **23**:394-95, 397; **34**:369

"Buryga" ("Buriga") (Leonov) **92**:237, 242, 255, 261, 266, 275
"Burying an Enemy" (Wittlin) **25**:468
"Burying the Babies" (Macdonald) **19**:290
"The Bus" (Singer) **23**:421-22; **38**:410
The Bus Conductor Hines (Kelman) **58**:295-96, 299, 302; **86**:185
Bus Riley's Back in Town (Inge) **8**:310
Bus Stop (Inge) **1**:153; **8**:308; **19**:226, 228-29
"Bus Stop in Nevada" (Montague) **46**:265
"Bus Stop: Or, Fear and Loneliness on Potrero Hill" (Justice) **102**:283
"La busca de Averroes" ("Averroes's Search") (Borges) **6**:90; **19**:46-7, 52; **83**:164, 183
"Búscate plata" ("Git Dough"; "Go and Look for Bread"; "Go Get Money") (Guillen) **48**:161, 168; **79**:245
"Bush" (Jacobsen) **48**:198
"Bush Christmas Eve" (Jacobsen) **48**:191; **102**:236
The Bush Garden (Frye) **70**:275
"A Bush League Hero" (Ferber) **93**:140
Bushuko hiwa (*The Secret History of the Lord of Musashi*; *The Secret Life of the Lord of Musashi*; *Secret Stories of the Lord of Musashi*; *The Secret Tales of the Lord of Musashi*; "Secrets of Lord Bushu") (Tanizaki) **28**:418-21
The Bushwhacked Piano (McGuane) **3**:329-31; **7**:213; **18**:323, 325; **45**:258, 262
"Business as Usual" (Reid) **33**:351
"Business Girls" (Betjeman) **43**:41
"Business Is Business" (Boell)
    See "Geschäft ist Geschäft"
"Business Is Business" (Friedman) **56**:107
"The Business Man of Alicante" (Levine) **4**:287
"The Business of Fancydancing" (Alexie) **96**:2
The Business of Fancydancing (Alexie) **96**:2-5, 7-8, 13, 16-17
The Business of Good Government (Arden) **6**:10; **13**:29; **15**:20
Business of Killing (Leiber) **25**:302
"Business Personals" (Ashbery) **15**:30;**77**:45
"Business Talk" (Apple) **33**:22
"A Business Trip Home" **59**:370
The Businessman (Disch) **36**:127-28
"Busride" (Cortazar)
    See "Omnibus"
"Buster's Hand" (Masters) **48**:224
Bustin' Loose (Pryor) **26**:380
"Busy about the Tree of Life" (Zoline) **62**:462, 464
Busy about the Tree of Life (*The Heat Death of the Universe, and Other Stories*) (Zoline) **62**:461-64
"Busy Body under a Cherry Tree" (Enright) **31**:149
"Busy Doin' Nothin'" (Wilson) **12**:641, 650
"A Busy Man" (Nabokov) **15**:394
"The Busy Man Speaks" (Bly) **10**:57; **38**:58
"But" (MacEwen) **55**:164-66
"But Alas Edgar" (Lamming) **66**:224
"But at Last" (Blunden) **56**:39
"But at the Stroke of Midnight" (Warner) **7**:513
"But Before" (Yevtushenko) **26**:467
But Do Blondes Prefer Gentlemen? (Burgess)
    See *Homage to QWERT YUIOP, and Other Writings*
But for Bunter (Hughes) **48**:187-88
But for Whom Charlie (Behrman) **40**:88
"But He Was Cool; or, He Even Stopped for Green Lights" (Madhubuti) **6**:313; **73**:199, 210

"But in a Thousand Other Worlds" (Grayson) **38**:210

"But It Still Goes On" (Graves) **45**:171

But Not to Keep (Kahn) **30**:233-34

"But That Is Another Story" (Justice) **102**:261

But We Are Exiles (Kroetsch) **5**:220-21; **23**:269; **57**:282, 288

"But We Are Hungry" (Marley)
See "Them Belly Full"

"But What Is the Reader to Make of This?" (Ashbery) **41**:36

But Who Wakes the Bugler (De Vries) **28**:112-13

Butch and Sundance: The Early Days (Lester) **20**:231-32

Butch Cassidy and the Sundance Kid (Goldman) **48**:126-28

Butch Cassidy and the Sundance Kid (Hill) **26**:196-97, 199-201, 203-05, 207-08, 211

"The Butcher" (Raine) **103**:186

"The Butcher" (Williams) **42**:440

"Butcher Shop" (Simic) **49**:342; **68**:364

Butcher's Dozen: A Lesson for the Octave of Widgery (Kinsella) **4**:271; **19**:251-52, 257

Butcher's Moon (Westlake) **33**:437

"The Butcher's Wife" (Erdrich) **54**:165

"Buteo Regalis" (Momaday) **85**:225, 231, 262, 264, 268

Butley (Gray) **9**:240-42; **36**:201-05, 207, 210

Der Butt (*The Flounder*) (Grass) **11**:250-54; **32**:202, 204; **49**:140, 142-43

"A Buttefly on F Street" (Jones) **76**:65

The Butter and Egg Man (Kaufman) **38**:265-66

The Buttercup Chain (Elliott) **47**:103, 107

"Buttercups" (Lowell) **8**:358

Buttered Side Down (Ferber) **93**:140, 147

Butterfield Eight (O'Hara) **6**:384-86; **42**:311-12, 320-21, 324

"Butterflies" (Dickey) **15**:177

"Butterflies" (Grace) **56**:123

"Butterflies" (Kinsella) **27**:237

"The Butterfly" (Avison) **97**:68, 70-72, 75

"The Butterfly" (Brodsky)
See "Babocka"

"The Butterfly" (Giovanni) **64**:187

The Butterfly (Cain) **3**:96-7; **11**:84; **28**:47-8, 51, 53

"Butterfly Bones; or Sonnet Against Sonnets" (Avison) **97**:76, 85, 99, 104, 123, 129, 134-37

"The Butterfly Boy" (Vollmann) **89**:304, 313

"The Butterfly Collector of Corofin" (Durcan) **43**:114

"The Butterfly Farm" (McGuckian) **48**:277

The Butterfly Hunter (van de Wetering) **47**:409

Butterfly on Rock (Jones) **10**:286, 289

The Butterfly Plague (Findley) **27**:141; **102**:99-100, 104-05, 114

Butterfly Stories: A Novel (Vollmann) **89**:286, 304-05, 307-08, 311, 313, 315-16

The Button (McClure) **6**:317

"The Button Maker's Tale" (Szirtes) **46**:395

"Les buveurs d'horizons" (Reverdy) **53**:281

Buy Jupiter, and Other Stories (Asimov) **26**:50

Buy Me Blue Ribbons (Elliott) **38**:176

A Buyer's Market (Powell) **1**:277; **3**:400; **9**:438; **10**:412, 414-15; **31**:320-21

Buying Time (Haldeman) **61**:185-86

"Buzzard" (Clarke) **61**:82

"By a Frozen River" (Levine) **54**:297-98, 300-01

"By Al Liebowitz's Pool" (Nemerov) **36**:306-08

By Any Means Necessary (Lee) **105**:112

By Any Means Necessary (Malcolm X) **117**:319

By Avon River (H. D.) **8**:258; **31**:202, 204, 208; **73**:115-17, 139

"By Candlelight" (Plath) **5**:345; **51**:353

By Cheating the Heart (Tchicaya)
See *A Triche-coeur*

"By Comparison" (MacCaig) **36**:279

"By Daylight and in Dream" (Wheelock) **14**:570

By Daylight and in Dream: New and Selected Poems (Wheelock) **14**:570

"By Destiny Denied" (Allen) **52**:42

"By Ferry to the Island" (Smith) **64**:388, 393, 398

By Grand Central Station I Sat Down and Wept (Smart) **54**:411-15, 417-23, 425-26

"By Himself" (Cocteau) **8**:146

"By His Bootstraps" (Heinlein) **26**:163; **55**:302

By Love Possessed (Cozzens) **1**:65-6; **4**:111, 113-16; **11**:126-27, 131-32; **92**:177-82, 184-86, 189-90, 193-94, 211

"By Means of a Reciprocal Correspondence" ("By Way of Private Correspondence") (Voinovich) **10**:506

"By Morning" (Swenson) **106**:319

By Night Unstarred: An Autobiographical Novel (Kavanagh) **22**:244

"By No Means Native" (Rich) **36**:365

"By Special Request" (Waugh) **27**:476

"By the Belgian Frontier" (Blunden) **56**:45

"By the Burn" (Kelman) **86**:185

"By the Falls" (Harrison) **42**:203

"By the Flooded Canal" (Ashbery) **77**:67

By the Highway Home (Stolz) **12**:554

"By the Lake" (Sitwell) **67**:335

"By the Light of an Apple" (Cixous) **92**:81

"By the North Gate" (Oates) **6**:370

By the North Gate (Oates) **6**:369-70; **108**:341, 368

By the Pricking of My Thumbs (Christie) **12**:117; **48**:71-2, 75

"By the Riverside" (Kizer) **80**:173, 185

"By the Road to the Air Base" (Winters) **32**:468

"By the Sea" (Adams) **46**:17

"By the Sea" (Gellhorn) **60**:189, 192

"By the Sea" (Smith) **64**:390, 393

"By the Sea" (Sondheim) **30**:394

By the Seashore (Akhmatova) **64**:11

"By the Snake River" (Stafford) **29**:382

"By the Waters of Babylon" (Celan)
See "An den Wassern Babels"

By the Waters of Manhattan (Reznikoff) **9**:450

By the Waters of Whitechapel (Kops) **4**:274

"By Way of Private Correspondence" (Voinovich) **49**:373, 376

"By Way of Private Correspondence" (Voinovich)
See "By Means of a Reciprocal Correspondence"

"By What Means" (Klappert) **57**:257

"Bye, Bye Love" (Simon) **17**:460, 465

Bye-Bye, Black Bird (Desai) **37**:66-7, 70-1; **97**:149, 160

"Bye-Child" (Heaney) **5**:170; **7**:148

"Byl letnii polden" (Trifonov) **45**:408

The By-Pass Control (Spillane) **13**:528

"Bypassing Rue Descartes" (Milosz) **56**:244; **82**:301

"Byre" (MacCaig) **36**:282

"The Byrnies" (Gunn) **18**:203; **32**:208

"The Bystander" (Berriault) **54**:4-5; **109**:96

"Bystanders" (Matthews) **40**:323

Býti básníkem (*To Be a Poet*) (Seifert) **44**:423, 426; **93**:308, 322, 331-32, 335-37

"Byzantium" (Thesen) **56**:422

Byzantium Endures (Moorcock) **27**:351-52; **58**:349, 352-59

"C" (Merrill) **8**:385-86

C (Reading) **47**:352-54

"C Major" (Transtroemer) **52**:410

"C Minor" (Wilbur) **53**:399

"C. Musonius Rufus" (Davenport) **38**:140

A Cab at the Door (Pritchett) **5**:352-53; **13**:465-66

Cab Calloway Stands In for the Moon (Reed) **60**:306-07

"Cabal" (Swenson) **106**:331

The Cabala (Wilder) **1**:366; **6**:576; **15**:571-74; **82**:339-40, 342, 344-45, 356, 362, 369-72, 376, 379, 382

"The Cabalist of East Broadway" (Singer) **6**:510; **38**:407

Caballo de copas (*My Horse Gonzalez*) (Alegria) **57**:10, 13-14

Cabaret (Fosse) **20**:122-23

Cabbagetown (Garner) **13**:236

"The Cabdriver's Smile" (Levertov) **15**:339

El cabellero inactual (Azorin) **11**:27

La cabeza de la hidra (*The Hydra Head*) (Fuentes) **13**:231-32; **41**:167-68, 171; **60**:153, 170

"The Cabin" (Carver) **53**:67

"A Cabin in the Clearing" (Frost) **9**:224

The Cabin: Reminiscence and Diversions (Mamet) **91**:144, 146-47, 150

Cabin the in the Sky (Corcoran) **17**:76

Un cabinet d'amateur (*An Art Lover's Collection*) (Perec) **116**:238, 247, 250

"The Cabinet Maker" (Sayles) **14**:483

"The Cabinet of Edgar Allan Poe" (Carter) **41**:122

The Cabinet of Jan Svankmajer (The Brothers Quay) **95**:335, 341, 344-45, 348, 351, 353

"A Cabinet of Seeds Displayed" (Nemerov) **9**:394-95

Cab-Intersec (Walker) **14**:552

Cabiria (Fellini)
See *Le notti di Cabiria*

Cables to Rage (Lorde) **71**:260

"Cables to Rage, or I've Been Talking on This Street Corner a Hell of a Long Time" (Lorde) **71**:232

"Cables to the Ace" (Merton) **83**:384

Cables to the Ace; or, Familiar Liturgies of Misunderstanding (Merton) **1**:211; **3**:336; **83**:388-89, 397, 404

"Caboose Thoughts" (Sandburg) **35**:352

Cabot Wright Begins (Purdy) **2**:348-49; **4**:422-23; **10**:421, 423-24; **52**:343, 345, 347

"Cabras" (Blackburn) **43**:68

Cacao (Amado)
See *Cacáu*

Cacáu (*Cacao*) (Amado) **40**:24-7; **106**:71

"The Cachalot" (Pratt) **19**:377-79, 382-83

"Los cachorros" ("The Cubs") (Vargas Llosa) **31**:443-44

Los cachorros (*The Cubs, and Other Stories*) (Vargas Llosa) **10**:498; **31**:443-45; **85**:352

"El cacique Cruzto" ("Cruzto, Indian Chief") (Ulibarri) **83**:417

Cactus Country (Abbey) **36**:16-17

Cadastre (Cesaire) **112**:15, 18
"Cadence" (Bowering) **15**:82
"Cadence" (Dubus) **36**:144; **97**:229
Cadente (Arghezi) **80**:6, 8
"Cadenza" (Hughes) **9**:280
"Cadieu" (Ferron) **94**:103, 120
The Cadillac Cowboys (Swarthout) **35**:400-01
"Cadillac Flambé" (Ellison) **86**:318; **114**:100
Cadillac Jack (McMurtry) **27**:332-34; **44**:254, 258
Le cadran lunaire (Mandiargues) **41**:275, 278-79
Cae la noche tropical (*Tropical Night Falling; A Tropical Nightfall*) (Puig) **65**:269, 272
"Caer Arianrhod" (Fuller) **62**:192
"Caesar's Platter" (White) **49**:408
Caesar's Wife (Maugham) **1**:204; **11**:368; **15**:366; **67**:223
"Café" (Bowering) **32**:46
"Café" (Milosz) **31**:260
"Café: 3 A.M." (Hughes) **108**:329-30
"The Café Filtre" (Blackburn) **43**:63
Café Myriam (*The Sweetshoppe Myriam*) (Klima) **56**:166-68
"Cafe on the Left Bank" (McCartney) **35**:285
"Cafe Society" (Vanderhaeghe) **41**:450, 452
"Café Tableau" (Swenson) **106**:338
"The Cafeteria" (Singer) **38**:409; **69**:320
"Cafeteria in Boston" (Gunn) **81**:176, 178, 187
"The Cage" (Montague) **46**:266-67, 277
The Cage (Cheever) **48**:64-5
"Cage, 1974" (Rozewicz) **23**:362
La cage aux folles (Fierstein) **33**:156-57
La cage de verre (Simenon) **2**:398
A Cage for Lovers (Powell) **66**:362-63
"The Cage of Sand" (Ballard) **14**:40
A Cage of Spines (Swenson) **61**:390, 399; **106**:314-16, 319, 325,340, 347
Cage without Grievance (Graham) **29**:193-94, 198
"Caged Bird" (Angelou) **77**:31
"Cages" (Vanderhaeghe) **41**:448-50
Cahena: A Dream of the Past (Wellman) **49**:397-98
Cahier d'un retour au pays natal ("Notebook of a Return to the Native Land"; *Return to My Native Land*) (Cesaire) **19**:95, 97-8; **32**:110, 113; **112**:6, 8-12, 21-4, 26-9, 31-3, 35-9
Cahiers pour une morale (Sartre) **50**:379, 382
Cahoot's Macbeth (Stoppard) **29**:395-97; **91**:190
"Cailleach" (Jones) **42**:242
Caimán (Buero Vallejo) **46**:98-100
"Cain Rose Up" (King) **61**:331
Cain, Where Is Your Brother? (Mauriac) **56**:219
Cain x Three (Cain) **28**:52
The Caine Mutiny Court Martial (Altman) **116**:59
The Caine Mutiny Court-Martial (Wouk) **1**:375-77; **9**:579-80; **38**:444-48, 452
"Caino" (Ungaretti) **11**:555
The Cairo Trilogy (Mahfuz)
    See *al-Thulatthiyya*
Caitaani mutharaba-ini (*Devil on the Cross*) (Ngugi wa Thiong'o) **36**:319-20, 322-24
Cajetan et la taupe (Theriault) **79**:412
Cakes and Ale; or, The Skeleton in the Cupboard (Maugham) **1**:204; **11**:370; **15**:367; **67**:206, 210-15, 218-19, 229-30; **93**:257, 263
"Cakewalk" (Smith) **25**:409

Cakewalk (Smith) **25**:409-10; **73**:340, 355, 357-59
Cal (Mac Laverty) **31**:255-57
Cal y canto (Alberti) **7**:9
"El calamar opta por su tinta" (Bioy Casares) **88**:94
"Calamiterror" (Barker) **8**:46; **48**:10, 12, 17
Calamity Town (Queen) **11**:458
"Calamus" (Sandburg) **4**:463
A Calander and an Hourglass (Konwicki)
    See *Kalendarz i klepsydra*
"The Calculation of Probability" (Landolfi) **49**:212
"Calculations I" (Schmidt)
    See "Berechnungen I"
Calderón and the Seizures of Honor (Honig) **33**:213-14
Caldicott Place (*The Family at Caldicott Place*) (Streatfeild) **21**:409-10
"Cale frînta" ("Tortuous Road") (Arghezi) **80**:8
Cale sèche (Reverdy) **53**:282-83
Calendar of an Invisible April (Elytis) **49**:118-19
"A Calendar of Love" (Brown) **48**:52, 57
A Calendar of Love and Other Stories (Brown) **48**:51-2, 54, 57; **100**:84
A Calendar of Sin: American Melodramas (Scott) **43**:377-79, 385
"calendrier lagunaire" (Cesaire) **112**:31
"Caliban Remembers" (Weiss) **8**:545; **14**:553, 556-57
"Caliban über Setebos" (Schmidt) **56**:391
Caliban's Fillibuster (West) **7**:523-24; **96**:375, 377, 384, 386
"Calico Shoes" (Farrell) **66**:129
Calico Shoes and Other Stories (Farrell) **66**:129-30
"California" (Mitchell) **12**:443
"California" (Zamora) **89**:370, 372-73, 376, 392-93
The California Feeling: A Personal View (Beagle) **104**:5-7
"California Girls" (Wilson) **12**:644, 647, 649
California Split (Altman) **16**:30-1, 33-5; **116**:14, 16, 21-2, 48, 67
California Suite (Simon) **11**:496; **31**:403-04
"California, This is Minnesota Speaking" (Dunn) **36**:153
California Time (Raphael) **14**:437
Californians (Jeffers) **11**:305; **54**:233, 235-36, 244, 250
"Caligula" (Lowell) **4**:299; **8**:350-51, 355
Caligula (Camus) **1**:52; **2**:100; **9**:139, 141-42, 145-46, 152; **11**:93, 95; **14**:108, 114-15; **32**:84-6, 88-90, 92-3, 96, 98, 100-01; **63**:76-7; **69**:109
Caligula, and Three Other Plays (Camus) **32**:84
"Ca'line's prayer" (Clifton) **66**:73
"Call" (Bagryana)
    See "Zov"
"Call" (Lorde) **71**:255, 260-61
"The Call" (O'Brien) **36**:340
The Call: An American Missionary in China (Hersey) **40**:240-42; **81**:335; **97**:324
"Call Any Vegetable" (Zappa) **17**:588
"Call at Corazón" (Bowles) **53**:37, 39, 49
Call at Corazón and Other Stories (Bowles) **53**:49
"Call First" (Campbell) **42**:87, 89
Call for a Miracle (Kiely) **23**:262; **43**:245
"A Call for Militant Resistance" (hooks) **94**:145
A Call for Nixonicide and Glory to the Chilean

Revolution (Neruda)
    See *Incitación al Nixonicidio y alabanza de la revolución Chilena*
Call for the Dead (le Carre) **3**:281; **5**:233-34; **15**:325
A Call in the Midst of a Crowd (Corn) **33**:114-16, 118
"Call It a Good Marriage" (Graves) **45**:169
"Call It a Loan" (Browne) **21**:42
Call It Experience: The Years of Learning How to Write (Caldwell) **50**:299-300
"Call It Fear" (Harjo) **83**:266
Call It Sleep (Roth) **2**:377-78; **6**:470-74; **11**:487-90; **104**:238-58, 262-65, 268-70, 273-75, 277-79, 281-91, 294-300, 304, 306, 311-13, 315, 317-30
Call Me a Liar (Mortimer) **28**:283, 285
Call Me Charley (Jackson) **12**:289-91
"Call Me Comrade" (Clark) **5**:107
Call Me Ishmael: A Study of Melville (Olson) **5**:326-27; **29**:326-27, 332
Call Me Ishtar (Lerman) **56**:175-76, 178
"Call Me Lightning" (Townshend) **17**:530
Call Me Ruth (Sachs) **35**:334
Call My People Home (Livesay) **79**:345-46
"The Call of Nature" (Harrison) **43**:180
The Call of Service: A Witness to Idealism (Coles) **108**:207, 209
The Call of Stories (Coles) **108**:193, 201
"The Call of the Sea" (Neruda)
    See "Llama el océano"
"The Call of the Wild" (Scott) **22**:372
"A Call on Mrs. Forrester" (Thurber) **11**:533
A Call to Order (Cocteau) **43**:99-100
"The Call Up" (Clash) **30**:47-9
"Callaghan Revisited" (Avison) **97**:108
"Calle Sierpes" ("Sierpes Street") (Cabral de Melo Neto) **76**:167
"Called" (O Hehir) **41**:324
"Called Home" (Beer) **58**:38
The Callender Papers (Voigt) **30**:419-20
"The Caller" (Scannell) **49**:327
Caller Anonymous (Hamilton) **51**:193
The Call-Girls (Koestler) **3**:271
"Calling Card" (Campbell)
    See "First Foot"
Calling for Help (*Cries for Help*) (Handke) **8**:262; **15**:266-67
Calling Myself Home (Hogan) **73**:149, 155-57
"The Calling of Names" (Angelou) **64**:32
Calling Out to Yeti (Szymborska) **99**:194, 199, 203, 207, 211
"Calling Sister Midnight" (Bowie) **17**:66
"Calling to the Badger" (Bly) **10**:59
"Callings" (Galeano) **72**:139
"The Calm" (Carver) **53**:64
"The Calm" (Gallagher) **63**:118
"Calm" (Hass) **99**:143
"A Calm Rain" (Blunden) **56**:39
"Le Calmant" ("The Calmative") (Beckett) **4**:51; **10**:34, 36; **18**:49; **29**:63
"The Calmative" (Beckett)
    See "Le Calmant"
"Calming Kali" (Clifton) **66**:80
"Calvin in the Casino" (Cassity) **42**:97
"Calypso" (Broumas) **73**:2
Calypso (Hunter) **31**:224
"The Camaldolese Come to Big Sur" (Beecher) **6**:49
"Camarillo Brillo" (Zappa) **17**:589
"Camberley" (Betjeman) **43**:40
"The Camberwell Beauty" (Pritchett) **5**:354; **13**:465, 467-68; **41**:332

The Camberwell Beauty, and Other Stories (Pritchett) **5**:352-54; **13**:465

Cambio de armas (*Other Weapons*) (Valenzuela) **31**:438-39; **104**:363, 370-72, 376-77, 385, 392

Cambio de piel (*A Change of Skin*) (Fuentes) **3**:175-76; **8**:223; **22**:165-67; **41**:167, 169, 171; **60**:152-55, 164, 171; **113**:230-31, 233-34

Cambridge (Phillips) **96**:329-33, 342-52, 354-55, 357

" Cambridge Elegy" (Olds) **85**:295

"Camden Town" (Dickey) **47**:92

"Came Away with Betjeman..." (Ewart) **46**:154

"Came the Terrible Dark Lords" (Sherwin) **7**:415

"Camelot" (Watkins) **43**:443

The Camel's Eye (Aitmatov)
   See *Verbliuzhii glaz*

The Camera Always Lies (Hood) **15**:283; **28**:188, 190, 195

Camera Lucida: Reflections on Photography (Barthes)
   See *La chambre claire: Note sur la photographie*

The Cameraman (Keaton) **20**:196

"Camilla" (Robison) **42**:339

Camilla Dickinson (L'Engle) **12**:345

Camille: A Tear-Jerker (Ludlam) **46**:240-42; **50**:342-44, 346

"Caminado" (Guillen) **48**:162

El camino (*The Path*) (Delibes) **18**:109-10, 112-13, 117

"Camino de amor" (Laughlin) **49**:224

"El Camino de Santiago" (Carpentier) **110**:48, 54, 57

Camino Real (*Ten Blocks on the Camino Real*) (Williams) **2**:465; **5**:498-500; **7**:543; **11**:571-73; **15**:581; **45**:446-47; **71**:269, 384, 386, 405; **111**:379-83, 388

"El camino verde" (Blackburn) **43**:64

Le camion: Suivi de entretien avec Michelle Porte (*The Truck*) (Duras) **20**:101-03; **40**:178, 183; **68**:90, 96

La camisa de fuerza (Parra) **102**:334, 343

"Camouflage" (Longley) **29**:292

Camouflage (Muske) **90**:310, 312

"Camouflaging the Chimera" (Komunyakaa) **94**:228-30, 240

"The Camp" (Davis) **49**:92

"Camp Cataract" (Bowles) **68**:6-7, 9, 11-14, 16, 19-21

Camp Concentration (Disch) **36**:123-24

"A Camp in the Prussian Forrest" (Jarrell) **6**:261

"The Camp in the Wood (Somme Battle, 1916)" (Blunden) **56**:44

"Camp Rose" (Freeman) **55**:56-7

The Campaign (Fuentes) **113**:252-54

"Campaigner" (Young) **17**:577

"Campaigning" (Steinem) **63**:384

Campamento (*Bivouac*) (Lopez y Fuentes) **32**:279-81

The Campfire Reflection (*The Fire's Reflection*) (Trifonov) **45**:420-21

"Camping at Split Rock" (Wright) **53**:425

"Camping in Madera Canyon" (Swenson) **106**:351

"Camping in the Valley" (Tate) **25**:427

"Camping Out" (Empson) **8**:201; **19**:155, 157

"Campo dei Fiori" (Milosz) **56**:247-48; **82**:278, 299

Campos de Níjar (Goytisolo) **23**:185

Campus Ethnoviolence and the Policy of Options (Ehrlich) **70**:378

"The Campus on the Hill" (Snodgrass) **2**:404; **18**:491; **68**:388

"Can a Woman Be a Shit?" (Ewart) **46**:154

Can Ethics Be Christian? (Gustafson) **100**:201, 229

"Can Graham Greene Write English?" (Fussell) **74**:125

"Can I Get A Witness" (Jordan) **114**:151

"Can I See Arcturus from Where I Stand?" (Warren) **8**:539; **13**:573, 577-78

Can You Do It Until You Need Glasses? The Different Drug Book (Felsen) **17**:124-25

Can You Find Me (Fry) **14**:188-89

Can You Hear Me at the Back? (Clark) **29**:128-29

"'Can You Remember?'" (Blunden) **56**:30

Can You See Me Yet? (Findley) **102**:96-7, 103, 105

Can You Sue Your Parents for Malpractice? (Danziger) **21**:84-5

"Caña" (Guillen) **48**:163; **79**:240

"Canada: Case History, 1945" (Birney) **6**:76; **11**:49

"The Canada Council Poet" (Bowering) **47**:31

Canada Made Me (Levine) **54**:292, 294, 298-300

"The Canada of Myth and Reality" (Davies) **25**:132

Canada udner Siege (Berton) **104**:58

"The Canadian Authors Meet" (Scott) **22**:372, 376

"Canadian Experience" (Clarke) **53**:97

"The Canadian Prairies View of Literature" (Donnell) **34**:155, 157-59

"The Canadian Social Register" (Scott) **22**:372

Canadian Sunset (McFadden) **48**:258-59

"Canal Bank Walk" (Kavanagh) **22**:243

"The Canal Garden" (Seifert) **93**:337

Canal Zone (Wiseman) **20**:477

"Canaletto in the National Gallery of Ireland" (Boland) **113**:108

"Canals" (Sillitoe) **57**:388

"A Canary for One" (Hemingway) **6**:231

Canary in a Cat House (Vonnegut) **3**:500; **111**:351

"Canary in Bloom" (Dove) **50**:153, 155, 157

"O canavial e o mar" (Cabral de Melo Neto) **76**:168

Can-Can (Linney) **51**:263

Canção de berço (*Cradle Song*) (Andrade) **18**:4

Cancer (Silverstein and Silverstein) **17**:453-54

Cancer (*Moonchildren*) (Weller) **10**:525-26; **53**:386-93

"Cancer: A Dream" (Sissman) **18**:488, 490

"The Cancer Cells" (Eberhart) **19**:144

The Cancer Journals (Lorde) **71**:237, 243, 248, 252-53

Cancer Lab (Berger) **12**:40

The Cancer Ward (Solzhenitsyn)
   See *Rakovyi korpus*

"Cancerqueen" (Landolfi)
   See "Cancroregina"

Cancerqueen and Other Stories (Landolfi) **11**:321; **49**:210-13

"Canción" (Parra) **102**:339

"Una canción de amor" (Neruda) **28**:309-10

Canción de gesta (*Chanson de geste*) (Neruda) **28**:312, 314

"La canción del bongo" ("Bongo Song"; "The Song of the Bongo") (Guillen) **48**:162; **79**:233, 250

"La canción del oeste" (Cernuda) **54**:57

Canciones rusas (Parra) **102**:340, 356

Les cancrelats (*The Roaches*) (Tchicaya) **101**:354-55, 357-58, 362-65

"Cancroregina" ("Cancerqueen") (Landolfi) **49**:209-10, 212

"The Candidate" (Tuohy) **37**:432

Candidate (Fuller) **25**:180

Candide (Hellman) **52**:201

Candido; or, A Dream Dreamed in Sicily (Sciascia) **41**:385, 387, 394

Candle (Akhmadulina) **53**:15

A Candle at Dusk (Almedingen) **12**:4

"The Candle Flame" (Lewis) **41**:255, 263

"A Candle for Pasch" (Gustafson) **36**:218

A Candle for St. Jude (Godden) **53**:155-56, 161

"A Candle in a Gale Wind" (Childress) **96**:114-15, 118

A Candle in Her Room (Arthur) **12**:24-6, 29

Candle in the Wind (Solzhenitsyn)
   See *Svecha na vetru*

The Candle in the Wind (White) **30**:444-46

Candle of the Wicked (Wellman) **49**:388

"Candle Poems" (MacNeice) **53**:233

"Candles" (Plath) **5**:345; **11**:449; **111**:181

Candles in Babylon (Levertov) **28**:243; **66**:237-39, 250

"The Candles of Your Eyes" (Purdy) **52**:350

The Candles of Your Eyes (Purdy) **52**:349-50

Candy (*Lollipop*) (Southern) **7**:453-54

The Candy Factory (Fraser) **64**:167-69, 171-75

"Candy Says" (Reed) **21**:314, 317, 322-23

"Candy Seller" (Bennett) **28**:26

"Candy Store Rock" (Page and Plant) **12**:480

"Candy-Man Beechum" (Caldwell) **1**:51; **60**:50, 67

"Candy's Room" (Springsteen) **17**:483, 485

Cane (Toomer) **1**:341; **4**:548-50; **13**:550-52, 556; **22**:423, 425-26, 429

"The Cane in the Corridor" (Thurber) **5**:432

"Canecutter's Song" (Dabydeen) **34**:148

"Canis Major" (Frost) **26**:118

"Canje" (Harris) **25**:212

"The Cannas" (Fugard) **48**:109

Cannery Row (Steinbeck) **1**:325; **9**:514, 517-18, 520; **21**:382, 391; **34**:405, 410, 412-14; **45**:370, 373; **59**:350-51; **75**:350

"Cannery Row Revisited " (Naipaul) **105**:155

The Cannibal (Hawkes) **1**:138; **2**:183; **3**:221, 223; **4**:212-14; **7**:141-42, 145-46; **14**:238; **15**:270-71, 273; **27**:190-91, 195-96, 199; **49**:155-56, 161, 164

The Cannibal Galaxy (Ozick) **28**:354-56; **62**:341, 343, 346-47, 351-55, 357-58

The Cannibals (Tabori) **19**:437-38

Cannibals and Christians (Mailer) **1**:189-90, 192; **2**:258, 264; **3**:313, 320; **28**:256; **74**:212; **111**:95, 100

"Cannibals and Missionaries" (Fuller) **62**:186

Cannibals and Missionaries (Fuller) **62**:186-87, 194, 197, 201, 203

Cannibals and Missionaries (McCarthy) **14**:359-64; **39**:488; **59**:289

"Canoeing at Night" (Leithauser) **27**:242

"The Canoes" (Dunn) **40**:170-71

"The Canonization" (Brutus) **43**:91

"Canons of Christianity" (Ochs) **17**:331

Canopus in Argos: Archives (Lessing) **15**:333-34; **22**:285-86; **40**:303-04, 306-07, 309,

315-16; **94**:252, 258, 261, 282, 286-87

"Canopus, Vega, Rigel, Aldeban" (Dickey) **3**:127

Can't Buy a Thrill (Becker and Fagen) **26**:79, 81

"Can't Depend on Love" (Lightfoot) **26**:279

Can't Pay? Won't Pay! (Fo) **32**:174; **109**:143

Can't Quit You, Baby (Douglas) **73**:90-2, 98-9

"Can't Stand Losing You" (Police, The) **26**:363-64

Cantares Mexicanos I (Cardenal) **31**:73

Cantares Mexicanos II (Cardenal) **31**:73

"El cántaro roto" ("Broken Jar"; "The Broken Pitcher") (Paz) **65**:190-91

La cantatrice chauve (*The Bald Soprano*) (Ionesco) **1**:154; **4**:250-52; **6**:248, 252-54; **9**:286; **11**:290; **15**:298; **41**:224-25, 229-30, 232; **86**:331-33, 339

The Canterbury Tales (Pasolini)
     See *I racconti di Canterbury*

Canti Barocchi (Piccolo) **13**:441

"Canticle" (Berry) **46**:70

"Canticle" (McAuley) **45**:250

"Canticle" (Nowlan) **15**:399

"Canticle for Good Friday" (Hill) **45**:189

A Canticle for Leibowitz (Miller) **4**:352-53; **30**:253-58, 260-63, 265-66

"Canticle of St. John" (Smith) **15**:515

Cántico (Guillen) **11**:262-63

La cantidad hechizada (Lezama Lima) **4**:288

La cantidad hechizada (*The Enchanted Quantity*) (Lezama Lima) **101**:121

"The Cantina" (Soto) **80**:276

"Cantina Music" (Walcott) **25**:456

"Canto I" (Pound) **48**:282; **112**:334, 336, 345, 350, 354, 356-57

"Canto II" (Pound) **112**:323-25, 336

"Canto IV" (Pound) **10**:400; **112**:310-12

"Canto VII" (Pound) **48**:283; **112**:310, 312

"Canto VIII" (Pound) **10**:402; **112**:318, 337

"Canto IX" (Pound) **10**:402

"Canto XI" (Pound) **112**:337

"Canto XIII" (Pound) **48**:293; **112**:336-37

"Canto XXV" (Pound) **7**:327

"Canto XXXVI" (Pound) **48**:282

"Canto XXXIX" (Pound) **7**:328

"Canto XLII" (Pound) **112**:302

"Canto XLIV" (Pound) **112**:302

"Canto XLV" (Pound) **7**:330; **112**:357

"Canto XLVII" (Pound) **7**:328; **13**:462

"Canto XLIX' (Pound) **112**:343

"Canto LII" (Pound) **7**:327; **112**:332, 335

"Canto LXI" (Pound) **112**:332

"Canto LXII" (Pound) **112**:332

"Canto LXXI" (Pound) **112**:332, 335

"Canto LXXII" (Pound) **112**:335

"Canto LXXIV" (Pound) **1**:277; **7**:328; **48**:287; **112**:301-08, 322, 326, 337, 339, 350, 355

"Canto LXXVI" (Pound) **112**:304, 355, 357

"Canto LXXX" (Pound) **7**:326; **112**:355-57

"Canto LXXXI" (Pound) **7**:326, 328, 335; **48**:290

"Canto LXXXIV" (Pound) **48**:285; **112**:339

"Canto LXXXVII" (Pound) **112**:357

"Canto LXXXIX" (Pound) **48**:294

"Canto XCIX" (Pound) **48**:286

"Canto CXVI" (Pound) **7**:329

"Canto CXVII" (Pound) **112**:335

"Canto a las madres de los milicianos muertos" ("Song for the Mothers of Dead Militiamen"; "To the Mothers of the Dead Militia") (Neruda) **62**:323

"Canto a Stalingrado" (Neruda) **62**:336

"Canto amor" (Berryman) **3**:70

"A canto da Andaluzia" (Cabral de Melo Neto) **76**:163

Canto for a Gypsy (Smith) **25**:412-13

Canto general de Chile (*General Song*) (Neruda) **2**:309; **5**:301-04; **7**:258-59, 261-62; **9**:396-97; **28**:309-14; **62**:327, 329, 332-33

"Canto nacional" ("Nicaraguan canto") (Cardenal) **31**:77

"Canto negro" ("Black Song") (Guillen) **48**:168; **79**:233

Cantos (Pound) **1**:274-76; **2**:339-45; **3**:394-99; **4**:407-18; **5**:348-49; **7**:323, 325-36, 338; **10**:400-03, 406-08; **13**:454, 456-57, 459, 461-62; **18**:422-23, 425-27; **34**:507, 509-1; **112**:30106, 308, 320-24, 327-29, 331-40, 343, 357

"Cantos LII-LXXXI" (Pound) **18**:423

Cantos ceremoniales (Neruda) **28**:314

Cantos para soldados y sones para turistas (*Songs for Soldiers and Tunes for Tourists*) (Guillen) **48**:158-60, 162, 164; **79**:229, 251

"Canute" (Davies) **23**:148

"Canzon: Of Incense" (Pound) **10**:407

"Canzon: The Yearly Slain" (Pound) **10**:407

"Canzone" (Ashbery) **13**:35

"Canzone" (Ungaretti) **7**:481-82, 485; **11**:556

"La canzone clandestina della Grande Opera" (Morante) **47**:281

"Canzones" (Okigbo)
     See "Four Canzones (1957-1961)"

Canzoni (Pound) **2**:343

O cão sem plumas (*The Featherless Dog*) (Cabral de Melo Neto) **76**:152-53, 156-57, 168

Cap of Darkness (Wakoski) **40**:452, 455-57

Capable of Honor (Drury) **37**:102-03, 105

The Cape (Eliade)
     See *Die Pelerine*

"Cape Alava" (Hugo) **32**:237

"Cape Breton" (Bishop) **9**:95; **32**:31, 34, 42-3

"Cape Cod" (Brodsky)
     See "A Cape Cod Lullaby"

"Cape Cod Autumn" (Starbuck) **53**:352

"A Cape Cod Lullaby" (Brodsky)
     See "A Cape Cod Lullaby"

"A Cape Cod Lullaby" ("Cape Cod"; "A Cape Cod Lullaby"; "Kolbel'naya treskovogo mysa") (Brodsky) **13**:117; **36**:75-78, 80; **50**:124-25, 128, 132; **100**:43, 48, 50, 54

"Cape Dread" (Merwin) **5**:288; **13**:383

Cape Drives (Hope) **52**:208

Cape Fear (MacDonald)
     See *The Executioners*

Cape Fear (Scorsese) **89**:258, 261-63, 265-67, 269

"The Cape of Good Hope" (Morgan) **31**:277

Cape of Storms (Brink) **106**:126-33

"The Capibaribe Valley" (Cabral de Melo Neto)
     See "Valo do Capibaribe"

Capitães da areia (*The Beach Waifs*) (Amado) **40**:26-7; **106**:60

"The Capital" (Auden) **43**:22

Capital (Duffy) **37**:117

Capital City (Sandoz) **28**:402, 406-07

"Capital, Just Capital" (Starbuck) **53**:354

"The Capital of the World" (Hemingway) **6**:229

"Capital Punishment" (Vizenor) **103**:311

"Capitalism, Modernism and Postmodernism" (Eagleton) **63**:107

Capitalism: The Unknown Ideal (Rand) **30**:304

"The Capitalist's Love Letter" (Dunn) **36**:154

Capitol (Card) **50**:143

"Capitol Air" (Ginsberg) **36**:196

"Capitol Radio" (Clash) **30**:43

Capitol: The Worthing Chronicle (Card) **47**:66-8

"Caplja" (Aksyonov)
     See "The Heron"

Caplja (*Heron*) (Aksyonov) **37**:12

Le caporal epinglé (Renoir) **20**:292-93, 297-98, 307

Cappella (Horovitz) **56**:151

Caprice (Bowering) **47**:33-4

"Caprichos" (Transtroemer) **52**:410

The Capricorn Bracelet (Sutcliff) **26**:437

"Caprilarología" ("Carillariology") (Asturias) **8**:25

"The Captain" (Dubus) **36**:147

"The Captain" (Hersey) **81**:330

"The Captain" (Michaels) **6**:325

The Captain (de Hartog) **19**:131

"Captain Ahab, A Novel by the White Whale" (West) **96**:375

The Captain and the Enemy (Greene) **70**:292, 294; **72**:177

Captain Blackman (Williams) **5**:496-97

"Captain Blood" (Barthelme) **46**:43

"Captain Carpenter" (Ransom) **2**:363; **4**:431; **5**:365

Captain Cook (MacLean) **50**:350

"Captain Dobbin" (Slessor) **14**:496-97

The Captain from Connecticut (Forester) **35**:164-65

"Captain Haddock" (Szirtes) **46**:393

"Captain Hendrik's Story" (Ingalls) **42**:234

"Captain Holm" (Swenson) **61**:402; **106**:329

Captain Horatio Hornblower (Forester) **35**:161, 163, 170

"Captain Jack" (Joel) **26**:213, 218-19, 222, 215

Captain Maximus (Hannah) **38**:233-35; **90**:137-39, 144, 147, 159, 160

"Captain Nicholas Strong" (Ciardi) **40**:155-56

The Captain of Köpenick: A German Fairytale in Four Acts (Zuckmayer) **18**:553-56

Captain of the Discovery: The Story of Captain George Vancouver (Haig-Brown) **21**:139-41

Captain Pantoja and the Special Service (Vargas Llosa)
     See *Pantaleón y las visitadoras*

Captain Quiros (McAuley) **45**:248-52, 254

"Captain Scuttle" (Scannell) **49**:331

Captain Shigemoto's Mother (Tanizaki)
     See *Shosho Shigemoto no haha*

Captain Slaughterboard Drops Anchor (Peake) **54**:369, 372-74

Captain S.O.S. (Simenon) **47**:374

The Captain with the Whiskers (Kiely) **23**:263; **43**:245

Captains and the Kings (Caldwell) **2**:95; **28**:65-6; **39**:302-03

The Captains and the Kings (Johnston) **7**:185-86

"The Captain's Gift" (Stafford) **4**:518; **19**:431

"The Captain's Son" (Taylor) **18**:527; **50**:251; **71**:304, 308, 315, 317

The Captain's Verses (Neruda)
     See *Versos del capitán*

The Captain's Watch (Garfield) 12:235

"Captation" (Damas) 84:159

Un captif amoureux (Genet) 46:183

"The Captive" (Borges) 1:39

"The Captive" (Gordon) 29:187, 189; 83:231

"The Captive" (Singer) 9:486

The Captive (O'Dell) 30:275-78

The Captive Mind (Milosz)
See *Zniewolony umysl*

The Captive of Kensington Palace (Hibbert) 7:155

"The Captive Speaking" (Carroll) 38:102-03

Captive Universe (Harrison) 42:200, 205-06

"Captives of the Flame" (Delany) 14:144

"Captivity" (Alexie) 96:12

"Captivity Captive" (Hall) 51:179-81

The Captivity of Pixie Shedman (Linney) 51:261

"Captivity of the Fly" (MacLeish) 8:362

The Capture of Detroit (Berton) 104:60

"The Captured Woman" (Barthelme) 46:36; 115:65

"The Capuchin from Toutes Aides" (Roy) 14:467

"The Car" (Crews) 49:73

Car (Crews) 6:118; 23:133, 138; 49:67, 71-3, 76-7, 79

The Car Cemetery (Arrabal)
See *Le cimetière des voitures*

"Car Crazy Cutie" (Wilson) 12:643

"Car Jamming" (Clash) 30:50-2

"Car Journeys" (Abse) 29:18

"Car Talk" (Bernard) 59:46

La cara de la desgracia (The Face of Misfortune; The Image of Misfortune) (Onetti) 10:377

Les carabiniers (Godard) 20:144, 149

"Les carabosses" (Hacker) 72:188

Caracole (White) 110:316-21, 323, 328, 337

"Caravan" (Longley) 29:296

"Caravan of Silence" (Eberhart) 56:76-7

The Caravan Passes (Tabori) 19:436

Caravan to Vaccares (MacLean) 13:359

"La caravane des férédjes" (Kadare) 52:261

Caravans (Michener) 1:214; 29:311; 109:376, 378-79, 382

"Carbon" (Levi) 37:223, 227

"The Carcass" (Wagoner) 3:508

"The Card Cheat" (Clash) 30:46-7

The Card File (Rozewicz) 9:464-65

"The Card Players" (Larkin) 5:228; 8:337; 13:337, 341; 33:261; 64:275

"The Cardinal" (O'Connor) 14:392-94

"A Cardinal" (Snodgrass) 2:404; 18:491; 68:388

The Cardinal of the Kremlin (Clancy) 112:52, 55-6, 62-3, 66, 69, 74-5, 77, 84, 88

The Cardinal Sins (Greeley) 28:175-76

"The Cardinal's First Tale" (Dinesen) 10:145, 152; 29:153; 95:49, 51-2, 55, 64

"The Cardinal's Third Tale" (Dinesen) 10:152

"Cards" (Beattie) 63:18

The Cards Face Down (Buero Vallejo)
See *Las cartas boca abajo*

Cards of Identity (Dennis) 8:172-73

The Cards of the Gambler (Kiely) 23:260, 262; 43:245

Cards on the Table (Christie) 12:113, 117, 122; 110:111, 130

"Care" (Robison) 42:339

"Care by Women" (Pesetsky) 28:358

c/o Arnold's Corners (Newton) 35:300-01

The Care of the Self: The History of Sexuality,

Vol. 3 (Foucault)
See *Histoire de la sexualité, Vol. 3: Le souci de soi*

"A Career" (Narayan) 47:305

Career in C Major (Cain) 28:45-6, 52-3

"Career Opportunities" (Clash) 30:44-5, 49

"Carefree" (Byrne) 26:94

"Careful" (Carver) 36:100, 102

Careful, He Might Hear You (Elliott) 38:176-77, 181

"A Careful Passion" (Walcott) 25:449; 76:280

"Careful with That Ax, Eugene" (Pink Floyd) 35:305

Careless Love (Adams) 13:2

"Careless Talk" (Bowen) 22:65

"Carentan O Carentan" (Simpson) 7:426; 32:383

The Caretaker (Pinter) 1:266-67; 3:385-86; 6:404-05, 407-08, 411, 413, 415, 417, 420; 9:419-20; 11:438-39, 441-43; 15:422, 426; 27:385, 387-88, 394, 396; 58:373-74, 376, 380, 384; 73:249, 256-58, 266, 281

The Carfitt Crisis and Two Other Stories (Priestley) 9:441

Cargo of Eagles (Allingham) 19:13

"Cargo Rap" (Phillips) 96:322-23, 326, 343

"Cargoes" (Masefield) 47:229, 233

"The Caribbean" (Guillen) 48:159

Caribbean (Michener) 60:262-63; 109:377, 382, 386

Caribbean: Culture or Mimicry? ("Culture or Mimicry") (Walcott) 76:276-77, 281, 285, 287

Caribbean Discourse: Selected Essays (Glissant)
See *Le discours antillais*

A Caribbean Mystery (Christie) 6:109; 48:72

"The Caribbean Provedor" (Connell) 45:114

"The Cariboo Horses" (Purdy) 50:238

The Cariboo Horses (Purdy) 6:428; 50:237, 246

"Cariboo Winter" (Lane) 25:284

La cariciamás profunda (Cortazar) 10:114

"Carillariology" (Asturias)
See "Caprilarología"

"Carillon" (Transtroemer) 65:236

Carine ou la jeune fille folle de son âme (Crommelynck) 75:153, 155-56, 169

"Caring" (Scott) 22:372

"Caring for Animals" (Silkin) 43:399, 401

"Caring for Surfaces" (Van Duyn) 116:428

"Carioca Song" (Guillen) 79:230

Caritas (Broumas) 73:5, 7, 13-14, 16

Caritas (Wesker) 42:429-30

"Caritas #2" (Broumas) 73:7

"Caritas #3" (Broumas) 73:7

Carl and the Passions—So Tough (Wilson) 12:646, 650

Carl Rakosi: Collected Prose (Rakosi) 47:348

"A Carlos Pena Filho" ("For C. P. F.") (Cabral de Melo Neto) 76:163

Carlota (O'Dell) 30:274

"Carlow Village Schoolhouse" (Murphy) 41:321

Carly Simon (Simon) 26:406-07, 410

"Carlyle and German Romanticism, 1929" (Wellek) 28:446

"Carmel Point" (Jeffers) 54:243

"Carmella, Adelina, and Florry" (Mazer) 26:295

Carnac (Guillevic) 33:191-92, 194

Carnage (Audiberti) 38:31, 33

The Carnal and the Crane (Hine) 15:280, 282

The Carnal Island (Fuller) 28:153-54

"Carnal Knowledge" (White) 49:409

Carnal Knowledge (Feiffer) 8:216; 64:149-50, 159, 161, 163-64

The Carnal Myth (Dahlberg) 1:72; 7:64-8

"Carnal World" (Ritsos) 31:332

"The Carnation" (Mansfield) 9:303

"The Carnation" (Ponge) 18:415

"Carnation" (Weller) 26:447

The Carnation Gang (Poliakoff) 38:374-75, 377, 379-80, 385

"Carnations" (Roethke) 101:296

Carnaval afuera, carnaval adentro (Carnival Outside, Carnival Inside) (Marques) 96:241-42

"Carnaval de maiz" (Ferlinghetti) 6:183

"Carnegie, Oklahoma, 1919" (Momaday) 85:281

Carnets (Notebooks) (Camus) 1:53; 4:92; 9:149; 32:97; 63:62-3; 69:138

"Carnets de notes 1942-1948" (Yourcenar) 87:412

Carnets II (Camus) 63:74

"Carnival" (Dinesen) 10:149-51; 95:61-9

Carnival (Everson) 27:135

Carnival (Mackenzie) 18:312, 314-15

The Carnival (Prokosch) 48:306-07, 309-10

Carnival! (Rathbone) 41:339

Carnival Country (Amado)
See *O país do carnaval*

"The Carnival Dog, the Buyer of Diamonds" (Canin) 55:36

Carnival for the Gods (Swan) 69:355-60, 363

The Carnival in My Mind (Wersba) 30:434-35

Carnival Land (Amado)
See *O país do carnaval*

"The Carnival Man" (Lane) 25:283

Carnival of Longing (Gunnars) 69:265-68

"Carnival of Turtles" (Brosman) 9:135

Carnival Outside, Carnival Inside (Marques)
See *Carnaval afuera, carnaval adentro*

A Carnival Story (Amado)
See "História do Carnaval"

Carnivals: Entertainments and Posthumous Tales (Dinesen) 10:148-50, 152-53; 95:68, 71

Caro Michele (No Way) (Ginzburg) 5:141; 54:196-200, 202-03, 205, 207-12

"Carol" 75:77

"Carol" (Brown) 5:77

Carol (Highsmith) 102:210-11, 218

"Carol with Variations, 1936" (McGinley) 14:366

Caroline (Maugham) 67:223

Caroline England (Streatfeild) 21:396-97

"Caroline Naked: A Husband to His Wife" (Dacey) 51:80

"Caroline, No" (Wilson) 12:646, 649-50

"Caroline's Wedding" (Danticat) 94:93, 95-6, 98-9

Le carosse d'or (The Golden Coach) (Renoir) 20:288-89, 297, 302, 305

La carpa de los raquachis (Valdez) 84:398, 413-14

The Carpathians (Frame) 66:146-49; 96:186, 208-09, 212-13, 215-17

"Carpe Noctem, If You Can" (Thurber) 5:433

"The Carpenter" (Lane) 25:288

The Carpenter at the Asylum (Monette) 82:314

Carpenter of the Sun (Willard) 7:539-40; 37:462

The Carpenter Years (Cohen) 7:52; 31:91-3

The Carpentered Hen and Other Tame Crea-

tures (*Hoping for a Hoopoe*) (Updike) 23:472-76
"Carpenters" (Cassity) 42:97
"Carpenters" (Salinger)
    See "Raise High the Roofbeam, Carpenters"
The Carpenters (Tesich) 40:416-17, 422-23
Carpenter's Gothic (Gaddis) 43:156-60, 162-63; 86:148-49, 153, 155, 157-58, 164-67
"A Carpet Not Bought" (Merrill) 2:273
The Carpetbaggers (Robbins) 5:380
"Los Carpincheros" ("The Carpincho Hunters") (Roa Bastos) 45:345
"The Carpincho Hunters" (Roa Bastos)
    See "Los Carpincheros"
La carreta (Marques) 96:224-25, 228, 233, 240-44, 250, 253-54, 256
"Carrickfergus" (MacNeice) 53:231, 242
Carrie (King) 12:309; 26:234-37, 239, 242; 37:199, 202, 204-07; 61:321, 323, 326, 331, 335; 113:335-36, 341, 343, 347, 355-56, 360-61, 368-69, 383-84, 386-89, 391
Carrie (De Palma) 20:77-83
"Carried Away" (Munro) 95:319, 321-22, 324
"Carrier" (Meredith) 55:192
The Carrier of Ladders (Merwin) 1:213; 2:277; 5:288; 13:384-86; 18:332; 45:273-74, 276-77; 88:192-94, 197, 200, 205
The Carrier Pigeon (Seifert)
    See *Poštovní holub*
"Carriers of the Dream Wheel" (Momaday) 85:268
"Carrigskeewaun" (Longley) 29:293
"The Carrion Spring" (MacLeish) 8:360
"Carrion Spring" (Stegner) 81:340, 352
"Carrots, Noses, Snow, Rose, Roses" (Gass) 15:258
Carry On, Mr. Bowditch (Latham) 12:322, 325
"Cars Go By Outside, One after Another" (O Hehir) 41:324
The Cars that Ate Paris (Weir) 20:424-25
The Cart (Ferron)
    See *La Charrette*
Cart and Cwidder (Jones) 26:225-29
"A Cart with Apples" (Middleton) 13:388
"Carta a un senorita en París" ("Carta a un srta. en París"; "Letter to a Young Lady in Paris") (Cortazar) 5:109; 10:114, 118; 33:129; 34:331-32
"Carta a un srta. en París" (Cortazar)
    See "Carta a un senorita en París"
"Carta abierta" (Alberti) 7:9
"Carta de creencia" (Paz) 65:198
"Cartagena de Indias" (Birney) 6:75, 78
"Cartas a una desconocida" (Parra) 102:340-41
Las cartas boca abajo (*The Cards Face Down*) (Buero Vallejo) 15:98-9, 101-02
"Carte postale" (Reading) 47:352
La carte postale: De Socrate à Freud et au-delà (*The Post Card: From Socrates to Freud and Beyond*) (Derrida) 87:93, 96, 104, 106-08
Cartea cujucarii (*A Book of Toys*) (Arghezi) 80:6, 13
"Carter Fell" (Bowering) 47:29
"Les cartes postales" (Carrier) 78:59
Carticica de seara (*Little Book of Evening*) (Arghezi) 80:6, 8, 11
"The Cartographer of Meadows" (Ciardi) 44:382

"Cartographies of Silence" (Rich) 11:477
"Cartography" (Bogan) 46:83; 93:64
"Cartography Is an Inexact Science" (Cassity) 42:97
"Cartoon" (Coover) 46:121-22
Cartridge Music (Cage) 41:78
"The Cartridges" (Levine) 4:287
Carving a Statue (Greene) 70:294
"The Caryatids" (Dinesen) 10:152; 29:155, 163; 95:69
"Caryl Chessman Interviews the P.T.A...." (Kaufman) 49:205
Un cas intéressant (Camus) 32:100
"Casa al mare" (Ginzburg) 11:229; 54:198
"La casa de Asterión" ("The House of Asterión") (Borges) 4:73; 48:38
Casa de campo (*A House in the Country*) (Donoso) 32:161; 99:217, 219-20, 222, 231, 241, 267-68, 270-71
La casa de los espíritus (*The House of the Spirits*) (Allende) 39:28-36; 57:16-23, 25-33; 97:4-6, 8-10, 17-20, 23-5, 27, 33, 36-7, 42, 44-8, 50-52, 55-7, 59, 62-3
"La casa dei doganieri" ("The Customs-Officer's House") (Montale) 9:387
"La casa del bosco" ("The House in the Woods") (Ortese) 89:198
"Casa sul mare" ("House by the Sea") (Montale) 7:228
"Casa tomada" ("The House Taken Over") (Cortazar) 10:118; 33:128, 332; 34:332
"La casa vacía" (Castellanos) 66:50
La casa verde (*The Green House*) (Vargas Llosa) 3:493-94; 6:544, 546-47; 9:544, 546; 10:498, 501; 15:550-52; 31:444-45, 447 449; 42:408; 85:352, 354, 356, 365, 370-71, 373-75, 381, 389, 392
"Casabianca" (Bishop) 32:29, 37, 39
"Casablanca, Summer, 1940" (Faludy) 42:142
Casanova (Fellini)
    See *Casanova di Federico Fellini*
"Casanova and the Extra" (Hofmann) 54:229
Casanova di Federico Fellini (*Casanova*; *Fellini's Casanova*) (Fellini) 16:297-98, 300; 85:51, 53, 60, 69-70, 74, 78, 81
Casanova's Chinese Restaurant (Powell) 3:400; 7:340, 345; 9:435; 10:408, 418
"Casarola" (Tomlinson) 13:548; 45:393
"The Casbah" (Faludy) 42:140
"Cascadilla Falls" (Ammons) 5:28; 25:42; 57:51, 59
"Cascando" (Beckett) 6:43, 45, 47; 29:62; 57:99
"Cascob" (Mathias) 45:235
La case du commandeur (Glissant) 68:174-80, 184
"Case in Point" (Jordan) 114:146
"The Case of Claus von Bulow" (Amis) 62:2, 5
"A Case of Coincidence" (Rendell) 48:320
"A Case of Conscience" (O'Connor) 23:331
A Case of Conscience (Blish) 14:83, 86
The Case of Lena Smith (Sternberg) 20:369, 371
The Case of Lucy Bending (Sanders) 41:381
"The Case of Motorman Seventeen" (Davidson) 13:170
"A Case of Murder" (Scannell) 49:327
A Case of Need (Crichton) 54:63
A Case of Rape (Himes)
    See *Une affaire de viol*

A Case of Samples: Poems, 1946-1956 (Amis) 2:5; 40:40
"The Case of The" (Van Duyn) 116:410
The Case of the Gilded Fly (Crispin) 22:108, 110
The Case of the Late Pig (Allingham) 19:15
The Case of the Midwife Toad (Koestler) 8:325
The Case of the One-Penny Orange (Fast) 23:160
The Case of the Poisoned Eclairs (Fast) 23:161
The Case of the Russian Diplomat (Fast) 23:160
The Case of the Workers' Plane (Edgar) 42:116
"Case Study" (Ezekiel) 61:92, 100
The Case Worker (Konrad)
    See *A látogató*
A Casebook of Murder (Wilson) 14:589
The Casement (Swinnerton) 31:423
"Casey's Last Ride" (Kristofferson) 26:266, 270
"Cash on Delivery" (Crispin) 22:111
"The Cashier" (Voznesensky) 57:414
The Cashier (Roy)
    See *Alexandre Chenevert*
Casing the Promised Land (Carr) 86:47
Casino Royale (Fleming) 3:159; 30:130-33, 136, 138-39, 145, 147, 149
Un caso clinico (*A Clinical Case*) (Buzzati) 36:85, 93
El caso sabato (Sabato) 23:378
"Cass and Me" (Muldoon) 32:318; 72:272
"Cassandra" (Barnard) 48:26
"Cassandra" (Bogan) 39:387, 392; 46:83; 93:64, 85, 87-88, 90, 92
Cassandra: A Novel and Four Essays (Wolf)
    See *Voraussetzungen einer Erzählung: Kassandra*
"Cassation" ("A Little Girl Tells a Story to a Lady") (Barnes) 3:37; 29:27, 30-1
Casse-pipe (*Break-Neck*) (Celine) 47:79
Cast a Cold Eye (McCarthy) 3:326; 39:491; 59:289
"Cast and Cast Again" (Humphrey) 45:205
"Cast reci" ("A Part of Speech") (Brodsky) 13:116; 36:74-81; 50:121, 124, 131, 137; 100:52
Cast reci (*Chast' rechi*; *A Part of Speech*) (Brodsky) 13:116-17; 36:74-5, 77-81; 50:121, 124, 131, 137; 100:48-50, 52-5, 58, 61
Cast the First Stone (Himes) 2:195; 4:229; 18:247-48; 58:255-56, 263-64; 108:228-29, 231, 259
"The Castaway" (Walcott) 25:450; 67:345, 357; 76:280-81
Castaway (Cozzens) 1:66-7; 4:111; 11:125, 128, 131; 92:183-85, 189, 199-200
The Castaway, and Other Poems (Walcott) 25:449-50, 452; 42:421-22; 67:346, 357, 360; 76:274
Caste Marks: Style and Status in the U.S.A. (Fussell)
    See *Class: A Guide through the American Class System*
"Castiliane" (Walcott) 25:450
Castilla (Azorin) 11:25
The Casting of Bells (Seifert)
    See *Odlévání zvonu*
The Casting of the Bells (Seifert)
    See *Odlévání zvonu*
Casting the Bells (Seifert)
    See *Odlévání zvonu*
"The Castle" (Ali) 69:31

"The Castle" (Prokosch) 48:307
The Castle (Gold) 4:192
The Castle (Klima) 56:163, 166, 168, 170
Castle Conquer (Colum) 28:87-8, 92
Castle in Sweden (Sagan)
    See *Château en Suède*
Castle in the Air (Westlake) 33:438-39
The Castle in the Sea (O'Dell) 30:278
The Castle of Crossed Destinies (Calvino)
    See *Illl castello dei destini incrociati*
"The Castle of Glubbdubdrib" (Slessor) 14:494
The Castle of Llyr (Alexander) 35:23-5
"The Castle of Purity" (Paz) 19:365
Castle on the Border (Benary-Isbert) 12:32
Castle Roogna (Anthony) 35:37
Castle to Castle (Celine)
    See *D'un château l'autre*
Castle Tzingal (Chappell) 40:146-47, 149;
    78:97, 102, 106-08
"Castles and Distances" (Wilbur) 6:570
"Castration or Decapitation?" ("Le Sexe ou la
    tête?") (Cixous) 92:57-8, 69, 72-3
"The Castrato Singer" (Squires) 51:380
A Casual Affair: A Modern Fairytale (Fraser)
    64:169-71
Casual Condemnations (Wesker) 3:519
"A Casual Encounter" (Plomer) 8:446
"A Casual Incident" (Farrell) 66:130
"The Casualties" (Clark) 38:129
Casualties and Peace (O'Brien) 116:179, 181,
    183, 185, 192, 227
Casualties: Poems (Clark) 38:125, 129
"Casualty" (Heaney) 25:247; 74:163-64
"Casualty" (Longley) 29:292-93, 297
The Casuarina Tree (Maugham) 11:370
"The Cat" (Turco) 11:551
A Cat, a Man, and Two Women (Tanizaki)
    See *The Cat, Shozo, and Two Women*
Cat among the Pigeons (Christie) 12:116;
    48:73-5
Cat and Mouse (Grass)
    See *Katz und Maus*
The Cat and Shakespeare: A Tale of India (Rao)
    25:366-68, 370-73; 56:289-90, 294, 298,
    301, 306-07, 312
The Cat and the Blackbird (Duncan) 55:293
"The Cat and the Casino" (Sagan) 36:382
The Cat and the King (Auchincloss) 45:31
"The Cat and the Saxophone" (Hughes) 35:220
The Cat Ate My Gymsuit (Danziger) 21:83-4
Cat Chaser (Leonard) 28:236; 71:213, 216-
    17, 221-23
"Cat in an Empty Apartment" (Szymborska)
    99:197, 208, 211
"The Cat in the Attic" (Martin) 89:111-12,
    116
"Cat in the Garden" (Hall) 51:170
"The Cat in the Hat for President" (Coover)
    32:122; 87:25, 58
Cat in the Mirror (Stolz) 12:555
"Cat in the Rain" (Hemingway) 6:233; 19:211,
    218; 30:189, 191; 39:433; 50:426
The Cat Inside (Burroughs) 109:182
"The Cat Jumps" (Bowen) 11:65; 22:65, 67
The Cat Jumps and Other Stories (Bowen)
    11:66
Cat Man (Hoagland) 28:179-80
Cat of Many Tails (Queen) 11:462-63
Cat on a Hot Tin Roof (Kazan) 63:222, 234
Cat on a Hot Tin Roof (Williams) 1:368; 2:465;
    5:499-501, 503-04; 7:542-43, 545; 8:547;
    11:572, 574, 576; 19:472; 30:466; 39:446;
    45:444-46, 452-53, 455; 71:268, 371,

380; 111:377-78, 380, 384, 386, 388, 394,
    408, 419, 422-24
Cat People (Schrader) 26:398-99
"Cat Poem" (Zamora)
    See "Gata Poem"
The Cat, Shozo, and Two Women (*A Cat, a Man,
    and Two Women*) (Tanizaki) 28:414
"The Cat Song" (Nyro) 17:318-19
"Cat Spring" (Frame) 96:201
The Cat Who Walks Through Walls (Heinlein)
    55:301, 303
The Cat Who Wished to Be a Man (Alexander)
    35:25-6, 28
"Cat Within" (Narayan) 28:301
"The Cat Woman" (Dybek) 114:62, 73, 75
"Cat Wood" (Amado) 40:31
"Cataclysm" (Powys) 46:325
The Catacombs (Demby) 53:100-15
"The Catalan Night" (Morand)
    See "La nuit Catalane"
Catalina (Maugham) 1:204; 15:368
"Catalina Parra" (Parra) 102:340
"The Catalogue of Charms" (Wakoski) 4:572
"The Catalogues of Memory" (MacEwen)
    13:357
"the Catalonian Night" (Morand)
    See "La nuit Catalane"
"Catalyst" (Ammons) 108:6
"Cataract" (Baxter) 78:17
"Catastrophe" (Buzzati)
    See "Qualcosa era successo"
Catastrophe (Beckett) 29:65-6; 59:255, 258
Catastrophe Practice (Mosley) 43:317-20,
    322; 70:199, 202-03, 205
*Catastrophe: The Strange Stories of Dino
    Buzzati* (Buzzati) 36:88, 92, 94
"The Catbird Seat" (Thurber) 5:432, 442;
    11:533
"the catch" (Bukowski) 108:114
"The Catch" (Gordimer) 18:186; 33:176
"catch" (Sanchez) 116:295
The Catch (Bowering) 47:23
The Catch (Oe)
    See *Shiiku*
The Catch (Oshima) 20:247, 251
The Catch (Weiss) 14:553, 556
Catch a Falling Spy (Deighton)
    See *Twinkle, Twinkle, Little Spy*
"Catch a Fire" (Marley) 17:270, 272
Catch as Catch Can (*La foire d'empoigne*)
    (Anouilh) 13:22
Catch as Catch Can (Anouilh)
    See *La foire d'empoigne*
Catch as Catch Can (Poole) 17:371-72
"Catch Me Now I'm Falling" (Davies) 21:105
"Catch That Rabbit" (Asimov) 92:4
"Catch That Zeppelin" (Leiber) 25:307
Catch-22 (Heller) 1:139-40; 3:228-30; 5:173-
    82; 8:275-80; 11:265-68; 36:224-31;
    63:172-209
The Catcher in the Rye (Salinger) 1:295-99;
    3:444-45; 8:464-65; 12:496-97, 502,505,
    514, 516-18; 56:319-65
"Catcher in the Rye-and-Water" (Ritter)
    52:355
"Catching Geese" (McGuckian) 48:278
Catchpenny Street (Cavanna) 12:98
"Catechism for Cape Malays" (Cassity) 42:96
"Categories" (Ekelof)
    See "Kategorier"
"Categories" (Giovanni) 64:186-87; 117:199,
    202
"Category Z" (Abbott) 48:6

"Catering" (Gilliatt) 10:230; 13:237; 53:147
A Caterpillar Anthology (Eshleman) 7:98
"A Caterpillar on the Desk" (Bly) 15:63
"The Catfish" (Bottoms) 53:29
The Catfish Man (Charyn) 18:100
"Cathay" (Millhauser) 54:325-27, 329-30
Cathay (Pound) 10:400; 34:507; 48:282, 284,
    289, 293; 112:340-46, 348-49
"Cathedral" (Carver) 36:103-04, 53:65,
    55:274, 276, 278, 281-82
Cathedral (Carver) 36:100-05; 53:60, 62-3
"The Cathedral Chair" (Silkin) 43:402
Cathedral Wednesday (Mayne) 12:388, 390,
    403
Cathedrals in Space (Blish) 14:86
Catherine Carmier (Gaines) 18:165-66;
    86:173, 178
Catherine Carter (Johnson) 27:216, 223
"Catherine of Alexandria" (Dove) 81:135,
    137
"Catherine of Siena" (Dove) 81:135, 137
Catherine the Great (Troyat) 23:462
The Catherine Wheel (Byrne) 26:99
The Catherine Wheel (Stafford) 7:455-58;
    19:430; 68:421, 424, 434, 448-49
"Cathleen Sweeping" (Johnston) 51:239, 250,
    252
Catholic Boy (Carroll) 35:79-80
The Catholic Experience (Greeley) 28:169
"Catholic Girls" (Zappa) 17:593
"The Catholic Novelist in the Protestant South"
    (O'Connor) 13:419
Catholics (Moore) 3:341; 5:294, 297; 7:236-
    37, 239; 8:394; 19:331-33; 32:310-12;
    90:250, 255-56, 262, 264, 267, 269-70,
    272-73, 289
"Pamphlet contre les catholiques de France"
    (Green) 77:244, 278, 280-81, 289
La catira (Cela) 4:96
"Catman" (Ellison) 13:207
The Cat-Nappers (Wodehouse) 5:517
"Cato" (Bioy Casares) 88:94
Cato Street (Shaw) 5:390
Cat-O-Nine-Deaths (Valenzuela)
    See *El gato eficaz*
"Catrin" (Clarke) 61:73
Cats and Bats and Things with Wings (Aiken)
    52:27
"Cats and Students, Bubbles and Abysses" (Bass)
    79:5-6, 11
"Cat's Cradle" (Leiber) 25:307
Cat's Cradle (Vonnegut) 1:348; 2:453-55;
    3:495, 497-503, 505-06; 4:561-63, 566-
    67, 569; 5:466-69; 8:530-35; 12:601-04,
    607, 609-11, 613-14, 617-19, 622-23,
    625; 22:445; 40:44; 60:416-17, 421, 432,
    440; 111:351, 355, 358-59, 363, 366, 368
Cat's Eye (Atwood) 84:69-72, 78-9, 86, 88-9,
    98-9, 104-08
Cat's Eye (King) 37:206
"Cat's in the Well" (Dylan) 77:182, 184-85
"The Cats of St. Nicholas" (Seferis) 11:493
The Cat's Pajamas (De Vries) 28:106
*The Cat's Pajamas and Witch's Milk: Two Nov-
    els* (De Vries) 1:73; 2:113; 28:106-07
"Cats Pyre" (Dybek) 114:61
Catseye (Norton) 12:469
"Cat-Tails" (Lightfoot) 26:278
"Cattle Dream" (Raine) 45:341
"Cattle Egret" (p'Bitek) 96:286
The Cattlemen (Sandoz) 28:404, 407
Catullus (Zukofsky) 4:580; 11:580-81; 18:560
"Catullus on Friendship" (Davie) 31:123

Caught (Green)   2:178; 13:252-53, 255; 97:243, 245-48, 254, 257, 268-70, 275-76, 280, 282-83, 288-91, 293
Caught on a Train (Poliakoff)   38:385-86
"The Cauliflower" (Haines)   58:216
"A Cauliflower in Her Hair" (Jackson)   60:214
The Cause (Bernhard)
    See *Die Ursache*
Cause for Alarm (Ambler)   6:2; 9:19
Cause for Wonder (Morris)   1:233; 37:312-13
"Causerie" (Tate)   2:428; 4:535; 11:523; 14:528
The Cautious Heart (Sansom)   2:383
Cavalcade (Coward)   1:64; 29:132, 135, 138; 51:69
Cavalcanti (Pound)   13:462
The Cavalier Case (Fraser)   107:59
Il cavaliere inesistente (*The Invisible Knight; The Nonexistent Knight*) (Calvino)   5:97; 8:128-30; 11:91; 22:87, 89-90; 33:97; 39:307, 314, 317; 73:37, 58
Le cavaliseul (Audiberti)   38:32
"Cavar un foso" (Bioy Casares)   88:94
"The Cave" (Laughlin)   49:221-23
"The Cave" (Turner)   48:399
"The Cave" (Williams)   33:445
The Cave and the Spring: Essays on Poetry (Hope)   51:218-19, 222
Cave Birds: An Alchemical Cave Drama (Hughes)   9:281; 14:272; 37:172-73, 175-76, 178
"Cave Call" (Clark)   38:128
The Cave Dwellers (Saroyan)   10:454
"The Cave of Night" (Montague)   46:271, 273-74, 276
Cave with Echoes (Elliott)   47:103
"Caveat Emptor" (Stafford)   19:431
The Cavern (Anouilh)   50:280
The Caves of Steel (Asimov)   9:50; 19:26, 28; 26:39-43, 46-8, 53, 56, 58, 63; 76:314; 92:13
"Caviar and Bread Again" (Williams)   9:571
Caviar and Cabbage (Tolson)   36:432; 105:281
"Caviare at the Funeral" (Simpson)   32:378
Caviare at the Funeral (Simpson)   32:376-79, 381
"Cawdor" (Jeffers)   54:233, 237-38, 248
Cawdor, and Other Poems (Jeffers)   11:305; 54:233, 236
"The Caxangá Driver" (Cabral de Melo Neto)
    See "O motorneiro de Caxangá"
"Cayuga Lake in Winter" (Matthews)   40:319
La caza (*The Hunt*) (Saura)   20:314-15, 317
"C.B. and Q." (Dorn)   10:160-61
"C-dur" ("C-Minor") (Transtroemer)   65:235
Ce formidable bordel! (Ionesco)   11:292-94; 86:341
Ce qui était perdu (Mauriac)   56:207, 212
Ce qu'il faut d'amour àL'homme (Green)   77:284
Ce qu'ils disent ou rien (Ernaux)   88:100
"Ce soir" (Char)   14:127
Ce-ai cu mine, vîntule? (*Why are Cross With Me, oh, Wind?; Wind, What Do You Want of Me?*) (Arghezi)   80:6, 11, 13
"Ceasing Upon the Midnight" (Seth)   90:338
"Cecie" (Thomas)   13:542
Cecil (Mujica Lainez)   31:283
Cecile among Us (Duhamel)   8:189
Cécile; ou, L'école des pères (Anouilh)   1:7; 13:17
"Cecilia" (Simon)   17:460
Cecily (Holland)   21:147-48
Cedartown, Georgia (Jennings)   21:201

"Ceil" (Brodkey)   56:57-60
"Cel ce gîndeste singur" ("The One Who Thinks Alone") (Arghezi)   80:8
Cela s'appelle l'aurore (*Men Call It Dawn*) (Bunuel)   16:143, 147; 80:25, 30, 40
The Celebrants (Feinstein)   36:169
"Celebration" (Cohen)   38:132
"The Celebration" (Dickey)   47:95
"Celebration" (McGrath)   59:183
Celebration (Settle)   61:377-79, 385, 387-88
Celebration (Swados)   5:420-23
Celebration (Waterhouse)   47:416
"Celebration for June 24" (McGrath)   59:181
"A Celebration for Northrop Frye" (Johnston)   51:249
Célébration hasidique: Portraits et legendes (*Souls on Fire: Portraits and Legends of Hasidic Masters*) (Wiesel)   11:570; 37:456-57, 459
"The Celebration of the Lizard" (Morrison)   17:290-92
"Celebrations" (Sarton)   49:310
Celebrations (Plomer)   4:406
Celebrations after the Death of John Brennan (Kennedy)   8:320
Celebrations and Attacks: Thirty Years of Literary and Cultural Commentary (Howe)   85:137
Celebrities (Bernhard)
    See *Die Berühmten*
The Celebrity (Hobson)   25:271-72
La céleste bicyclette (*The Celestial Bicycle*) (Carrier)   78:65
The Celestial Bicycle (Carrier)
    See *La céleste bicyclette*
"Celestial Globe" (Nemerov)   36:303
Celestial Navigation (Jiles)   58:271-72, 275, 277-80
Celestial Navigation (Tyler)   7:479-80; 18:530; 28:434; 44:321; 59:202, 204, 206; 103:235, 237-39, 241, 243-45, 259, 261, 273
"The Celestial Omnibus" (Forster)   45:136
The Celestial Omnibus (Forster)   15:223
"The Celestial Plot" (Bioy Casares)   88:59
The Celestial Plot (Bioy Casares)
    See *La trama celeste*
Celestino antes del alba (*Singing from the Well*) (Arenas)   41:25-7
"Celia" (Baker)   8:40
"Celia" (Brown)   48:52
"Celia Is Back" (Hempel)   39:68-70
"Celibacy" (Clarke)   9:168
Les célibataires (Montherlant)   8:393
The Cell (Bienek)   7:28-9
"Cell Song" (Knight)   40:281
"The Cellar" (Roth)   2:378
"The Cellar" (Soto)   32:403
The Cellar (Bernhard)
    See *Der Keller*
"The Cellars" (Campbell)   42:84, 92
"Celles" (Hacker)   72:192
Cellophane (Wellman)   65:242
The Cells of Love (Buckler)
    See *The Cruelest Month*
"Celluloid Heroes" (Davies)   21:94, 97
Celluloid Heroes (Williamson)   56:439
"Cement" (Bova)   45:75
The Cement Garden (McEwan)   13:370-72; 66:275-80, 282-83, 290, 294
El cementario de automóviles (Arrabal)
    See *Le cimetière des voitures*
El cementerio de automóviles (Arrabal)

See *Le cimetière des voitures*
"Cemetary in Alagoas" (Cabral de Melo Neto)
    See "Cemitério Alagoano"
"Cemetary in Paraiba" (Cabral de Melo Neto)
    See "Cemitério Parabiano"
"Cemetary in Pernambucano" (Cabral de Melo Neto)
    See "Cemitério Pernambucano (Floresta do navio)"
The Cemetery of Annunciations (Arghezi)
    See *Cimitirul Buna-Vestire*
"Cemetery of Whales" (Yevtushenko)
    See "The Whales' Graveyard"
"Cemitério Alagoano" ("Cemetary in Alagoas") (Cabral de Melo Neto)   76:168
"Cemitério Parabiano" ("Cemetary in Paraiba") (Cabral de Melo Neto)   76:154, 168
"Cemitério Pernambucano (Floresta do navio)" ("Cemetary in Pernambucano") (Cabral de Melo Neto)   76:168
"Cenas da vida de Joaquim Cardozo" ("Scenes of J. C.'s Life") (Cabral de Melo Neto)   76:165
"Le ceneri di Gramscí" (Pasolini)   37:348; 106:244-45, 253
Le ceneri di Gramsci (*The Ashes of Gramsci*) (Pasolini)   37:348; 106:220, 232, 241, 243-44, 250, 262-63, 267
Cenizas de Izalco (*Ashes of Izalco*) (Alegria)   75:45, 47, 49-51
"The Censor" (Tanizaki)   28:415
"The Censors" (Valenzuela)   104:382
"Censorship" (Ciardi)   40:162
"Censorship" (Simmons)   43:408
"Censorship and Literature" (Brink)   36:68; 106:119
"Censorship From Left and Right" (hooks)   94:158
"Census Taker" (Oates)   6:370
Cent ans dans les bois (Maillet)   54:310-12
Cent jours (Audiberti)   38:32
"The Centaur" (Swenson)   106:316, 344, 346
The Centaur (Updike)   1:344-45; 2:440, 442; 3:485-86, 488; 5:450-53, 458-60; 7:487-88; 9:537-38, 541; 13:557-59, 561; 23:463, 465, 467-69, 476; 43:433; 70:249, 253
Centaur Aisle (Anthony)   35:37
"The Centaur Overhead" (Bowers)   9:122
"Centaur Song" (H. D.)   73:119
"The Centaurs" (Longley)   29:295
"The Centaurs" (Muldoon)   32:318-19
"A Centenary Ode: Inscribed to Little Crow, Leader of the Sioux Rebellion in Minnesota, 1862" (Wright)   10:544
Centennial (Michener)   5:289-91; 11:375; 29:311, 315; 109:375, 377-79, 381, 383
Centennial Food Guide (Berton)   104:47
The Centennial History of the Civil War (Catton)   35:92-4
"Center" (Ammons)   5:27; 25:44
"Center" (Miles)   34:245
"The Center of Attention" (Hoffman)   6:243
The Center of Attention (Hoffman)   6:242-44; 13:286
"The Centerpiece" (Matthiessen)   64:321, 323-24
"Cento Virgilianus" (Strand)   71:287-88
The Centogenarian (Eliade)
    See *Der Hundertjärige*
El central (Arenas)   41:28-9
"Central Heating System" (Spender)   5:401
The Central Motion (Dickey)   47:95-6, 98;

109:245
"Central Park South" (Souster)   5:396
"The Centre" (Silkin)   43:400
Le Centre blanc (Brossard)   115:103-04, 110-11, 121
"Centre Court" (McPhee)   36:296
"The Centre of the Universe" (Durcan)   70:151
"Century Oaks" (Williams)   42:442
A Century of Hero-Worship (Bentley)   24:43-5, 50
A Century of Sonnets (Michener)   109:380
"Century Poem" (Morgan)   23:299
The Century's Daughter (Barker)   94:2, 9, 16
"The Century's Decline" (Szymborska)   99:194, 200, 211
Century's Ebb (Dos Passos)   4:138; 8:181-82; 25:146
Cenzura transcendenta (_Transcendent Censorship_)   75:80
"Ceol-Bag for James McAuley" (Buckley)   57:134
"Cephalus" (Strand)   41:439-40
Cerberus (Dudek)   19:136
Cere perse (Bufalino)   74:39
"Cereals for Roughage" (Bowering)   47:23
"Cerebral Cortex" (Klappert)   57:260
Cerebro y corazón (_Head and Heart_) (Guillen)   48:157, 159, 165; 79:240
Ceremonia de la confusión (Arrabal)   58:7
Cérémonial de la violence (Chedid)   47:82, 87
"The Ceremonial Motion of Indian Time: Long Ago, So Far" (Allen)   84:14, 36
"Ceremonias de rechazo" ("Rituals of Rejection") (Valenzuela)   104:372, 375-76
La cérémonie des adieux: Suivi de entretiens avec Jean-Paul Sartre (_Adieux: A Farewell to Sartre; The Ceremony of Farewells_) (Beauvoir)   31:43-5; 44:342, 345, 349-51; 71:83
Cérémonie pour un noir assassiné (_Ceremony for a Murdered Black_) (Arrabal)   58:11, 17
"Ceremonies" (Oates)   6:370
The Ceremonies (Klein)   34:70-2
"Ceremony" (Mahapatra)   33:277, 282
"Ceremony" (Wilbur)   110:388
The Ceremony (Oshima)   20:249-51, 254
Ceremony (Parker)   27:367
Ceremony (Silko)   23:406-08, 412; 74:318, 320, 323, 329, 342-43, 347-48, 351; 114:283-84, 286-89, 291, 293, 295, 297, 301-07, 309, 320, 322, 324, 326-27, 330, 335-36
Ceremony, and Other Poems (Wilbur)   6:568; 14:576-77; 53:396-99, 404-07, 410; 110:380
"Ceremony and Vision" (Berryman)   62:71
Ceremony for a Murdered Black (Arrabal)
   See _Cérémonie pour un noir assassiné_
"Ceremony for Any Beginning" (Pinsky)   38:359
"Ceremony for Cedar, in an Old House" (Shapcott)   38:399-400, 403
Ceremony in Lone Tree (Morris)   1:231-33; 3:342-43; 18:349-52, 354; 37:310-13
The Ceremony of Farewells (Beauvoir)
   See _La cérémonie des adieux: Suivi de entretiens avec Jean-Paul Sartre_
Ceremony of Innocence (Forman)   21:118, 123
The Ceremony of Innocence (Ribman)   7:358
Ceremony of the Innocent (Caldwell)   28:67
Les cerfs-volants (Gary)   25:190-91
A Certain Distance (Francis)   15:238

"Certain Distant Suns" (Greenberg)   30:166
Certain Honorable Men (Serling)   30:357
A Certain Lucas (Cortazar)
   See _Un tal Lucas_
"Certain Mercies" (Graves)   2:176; 44:478
Certain Noble Plays of Japan (Pound)   48:289
A Certain Plume (Michaux)
   See _Un certain plume_
Un certain plume (_A Certain Plume_) (Michaux)   8:392; 19:311
"A Certain Refrain" (Mahapatra)   33:281, 284
"A Certain Silence" (Middleton)   13:389
A Certain Smile (Sagan)   17:417-21
"Certain Words, A Garden" (Moure)   88:228
A Certain World: A Commonplace Book (Auden)   2:26; 3:22; 6:16
Certaines choses naturelles (Laughlin)   49:220
"Certainties" (Ciardi)   40:155
"Certified Life" (Fearing)   51:111
"Certs" (Lane)   25:289
Cervantes; o, La crítica de la lectura ("Cervantes, or The Criticism of Reading") (Fuentes)   10:208; 60:164
"Cervantes, or The Criticism of Reading" (Fuentes)
   See _Cervantes; o, La crítica de la lectura_
Ces enfants de ma vie (_Children of My Heart_) (Roy)   14:469-70
Ces fruits si doux de l'arbre à pain (Tchicaya)   101:355
César and Augusta (Harwood)   32:225-26
Césarée (Duras)   68:92, 96
C'est beau (_It's Beautiful_) (Sarraute)   8:470-71; 80:241
Cet obscure objet du désir (_That Obscure Object of Desire_) (Bunuel)   16:151-52; 80:52-3, 56
"C'était toi" (Joel)   26:220-21
"Cette émotion appelée poésie" (Reverdy)   53:284
Cette voix (Pinget)   13:444
Cetyre temperamenta (Aksyonov)   37:12
Ceux de la soif (Simenon)   3:450
"Cezanne at Aix" (Tomlinson)   45:392-93
"Chablis" (Barthelme)   59:250-51
"Chac Mool" (Fuentes)   22:170-71; 41:166
Chacun pour soi (Crommelynck)   75:152
Chad Hanna (Edmonds)   35:150-53, 156-57
"Chaddeleys and Flemings" (Munro)   95:302
"Chagall's 'Les Plumes en Fleur'" (Van Duyn)   116:427
Chagrins précoces (Kis)
   See _Rani jadi_
"Chain" (Lorde)   71:233
"The Chain of Aforgomon" (Smith)   43:423, 425
The Chain of Chance (Lem)   15:329-30; 40:292, 296
"A Chain of Love" (Price)   3:406
A Chain of Voices (Brink)   36:65-9, 73; 106:123-24, 126-27
Chain Reaction (Guild)   33:188-89
Chaining the Lady (Anthony)   35:37-8
"The Chair" (Davenport)   38:146-48
"A Chair" (Popa)   19:373
The Chair (Lieber)   6:311
La chair et le sang (Mauriac)   56:203-04, 206
"Chair Gallows" (Komunyakaa)   94:246
"The Chair of Tears" (Vizenor)   103:293, 297
The Chairs (Clarke)   16:217
The Chairs (Ionesco)
   See _Les chaises_
Les chaises (_The Chairs_) (Ionesco)   4:251-52;

6:248, 251-53, 255-57; 9:286; 11:290; 41:222-26, 229-30; 86:331, 333-34, 340
"Chaka" (Prince)   22:339
"Chaka" (Senghor)   54:391-94, 400
"Chalk" (Abse)   29:16
The Chalk Garden (Bagnold)   25:75-8
The Chalk Giants (Roberts)   14:463-64
"Chalk Pebble" (Clarke)   61:80
"The Challenge" (Borges)   13:104; 48:33
"The Challenge" (Vargas Llosa)   31:443
"The Challenge of Fear" (Paton)   25:364
"The Challenge of Our Time" (Forster)   9:204
"A Challenge to Churches and Synagogues" (King)   83:348
Challenge to the Learned Doctors (Arguedas)   18:8
La chamade (Sagan)   17:424-25
The Chamber (Grisham)   84:199-201
Chamber Music (Grumbach)   13:257-58; 64:198-200
Chamber Music (Kopit)   18:287-88; 33:248-50
"Chamber of Commerce Tour" (Lieberman)   36:264
"The Chamber of Poetry" (Brown)   48:59
"La chambre" (Bonnefoy)   15:74
"La chambre" (Carrier)   78:59
"La chambre" ("The Room") (Sartre)   52:381
La chambre claire: Note sur la photographie (_Camera Lucida: Reflections on Photography_) (Barthes)   83:89-90
"La chambre nuptiale" (Carrier)   78:68
La chambre rouge (Mallet-Joris)   11:355
La chambre verte (_The Green Room_) (Truffaut)   20:405-07; 101:396-97, 407, 410
Les chambres de bois (_The Silent Rooms_) (Hebert)   4:219; 29:231-32, 236-38, 240-41
"The Champ" (Boyle)   36:57-8
Un champ d'îles (Glissant)   68:179, 181
"Champagne Barn" (Levine)   54:297, 301
"Champagne on the Terraces" (Townshend)   42:379-80
"The Champion of the World" (Dahl)   79:176, 178, 183
Champion's Choice (Tunis)   12:593
Champions du monde (Morand)   41:303-04, 306
"Champs Elysees of Broadway" (Hacker)   91:110
Les champs magnétiques (_The Magnetic Fields_) (Breton and Soupault)   2:81; 9:132; 54:25, 28, 31-2; 68:404, 408, 410-13
La chanca (Goytisolo)   23:185, 189
"The Chance" (Carey)   55:114; 96:28, 39, 53, 55, 68
"Chance" (H. D.)   73:119
A Chance Child (Walsh)   35:432-33
"Chance Encounters" (Yevtushenko)   26:468
Chance, Luck, and Destiny (Dickinson)   12:174-75
"A Chance Meeting" (Colter)   58:146
Chance Meetings (Saroyan)   10:456-57
"The Chance to Love Everything" (Oliver)   98:258-59
The Chancellor Manuscript (Ludlum)   22:289; 43:275
A Chancer (Kelman)   58:296-97, 299, 301; 86:185
"The Chances of Rhyme" (Tomlinson)   45:393
"Chances R" (Ginsberg)   109:364
"Chandeliers and Shadows" (Pinter)   27:387
"Chanel" (Durrell)   27:96

The Chaneysville Incident (Bradley)   23:80-2
"The Change" (Berry)   4:59
A Change for the Better (Hill)   113:288-90, 293, 297-99, 305, 309-11, 320-21, 325
"Change Is Not Always Progress" (Madhubuti)   73:213
"The Change: Kyoto-Tokyo Express" (Ginsberg)   36:184
"A Change of Air" (Auden)   9:59
A Change of Heart (Butor)
   See *La modification*
A Change of Heart (Humphreys)   47:187
"A Change of Life Style" (Aksyonov)   101:9
A Change of Light, and Other Stories (Cortazar)   33:123-24; 34:329
A Change of Season (Ehrenburg)
   See *The Thaw*
A Change of Skin (Fuentes)
   See *Cambio de piel*
"A Change of Weather" (MacDiarmid)   63:243
A Change of World (Rich)   3:427; 7:367, 370; 18:445-46; 36:365-66, 370, 372, 374, 378; 73:314, 323, 325
Change!: Seventy-One Glimpses of the Future (Asimov)   26:57
The Change War (Leiber)   25:308
Change Your Bedding! (O'Hara)   78:365-66
"Changed from Martial's Epigrams" (Porter)   33:318
"Changeling" (Gunnars)   69:260-61
The Changeling (Jenkins)   52:223, 225-28
The Changeling (Snyder)   17:471, 473-74
The Changeling (Williams)   31:463-64
Changeling (Zelazny)   21:478-79
"The Changeover" (Fisher)   87:126
"Changes" (Bowie)   17:58, 61
"Changes" (Heaney)   37:165, 169
"Changes" (Kunene)   85:175
"Changes" (Ochs)   17:330-31, 333
"Changes of Name" (Parra)
   See "Name Changes"
"Changes; or, Reveries at a Window Overlooking a Country Road with Two Women Talking Blues in the Kitchen" (Komunyakaa)   94:247-49
Change-Up: New Poems (Souster)   14:504
"Changing" (Cryer)   21:81
"Changing a Way of Life" (Aksyonov)   101:15
Changing Appearance (Olson)   28:342-43
Changing Centuries: Selected Poems (Alegria)   57:14
The Changing Forest: Life in the Forest of Dean Today (Potter)   86:346
Changing Heaven (Urquhart)   90:387, 389, 391-3, 395-6, 398, 402
The Changing Land (Zelazny)   21:479
The Changing Light at Sandover (Merrill)   34:226-32, 234-42; 91:2228 232, 234-36, 238
Changing Mind (Aiken)   52:28
"Changing Names" (Szirtes)   46:395
The Changing of the Guard (Ehle)   27:105
Changing Places (Lodge)   36:271, 273, 277
The Changing Room (Storey)   2:425-26; 4:528; 5:414-16
"Changing Season"   75:78
"Changing the Children" (Kumin)   28:224
"Changing the Subject" (Enright)   31:149
Changing Woman (Sainte-Marie)   17:431
"Channels of Grace: A View of the Earlier Novels of Emyr Humphreys" (Mathias)   45:238
Chanson de geste (Neruda)

See *Canción de gesta*
"Chanson de l'oiseleur" (Prevert)   15:437
"Chanson Juive" (Celan)   82:55-6
"Chanson of a Lady in the Shade" (Celan)   82:37
"Chanson pathetique" (Barnard)   48:27
"Chanson philosophique" (Steele)   45:365
"Chanson un peu naïve" (Bogan)   4:68; 46:77-8, 81
Chansons (Soupault)   68:408
"Le chant d l'homme" (Roumain)   19:344
"Chant de l'initié" (Senghor)   54:410
Le chant du monde (Giono)   4:184, 186
Le chant du styréne (Resnais)   16:496, 502-03, 506
Un chant ecarlate (*Scarlet Song*) (Ba)
Une chant et l'autre pas (*One Sings, the Other Doesn't*) (Varda)   16:559-60
"A Chant for Young/Brothas and Sistuhs" (Sanchez)   116:295
The Chant of Jimmie Blacksmith (Keneally)   5:210-11; 8:319; 10:298; 14:301; 19:242-46; 43:233, 236; 117:215, 217, 224, 229-31, 240, 243, 247-48
Chant of Saints: A Gathering of Afro-American Literature   65:364
"Chant of Seasons" (Turco)   63:429
"Chant to Be Used in Processions around a Site with Furnaces" (Merton)   83:384
"Chantal" (Beauvoir)   31:42
Chants de la balandrane (Char)   14:130; 55:288
Chants d'ombre ("Songs of the Shade") (Senghor)   54:390-91, 407, 410
Chants pour naëtt (*Chants pour signare*; *Songs for Naëtt*) (Senghor)   54:390, 396, 407-09
Chants pour signare (Senghor)
   See *Chants pour naëtt*
Chaos (Lagerkvist)
   See *Kaos*
Chaos and Night (Montherlant)
   See *Le chaos et la nuit*
Le chaos et la nuit (*Chaos and Night*) (Montherlant)   8:393; 19:326
Le chapeau de Paille (Clair)   20:61
La chapelle ardente (Marcel)   15:363
The Chapman of Rhymes (Priestley)   34:362
The Chapman Report (Wallace)   7:509; 13:567-68
"Chapter 7" (Swenson)   61:405
"Chapter 30" (Klappert)   57:259-60
Chapter Two (Simon)   11:496; 31:398-99, 401, 403-04; 39:217; 70:238
Chapterhouse, Dune (Herbert)   44:393-94
Chapters: My Growth as a Writer (Duncan)   26:108
Chaque homme dans sa nuit (*Each Man in His Darkness*) (Green)   77:270-71, 276-78, 290
"A Character Must Have a Name" (Barnard)   48:27
"The Character of Our Addiction" (Young Bear)   94:364
"The Character of Washington" (Goodman)   4:197
"Characteristics of G. F." (Faludy)   42:138
"Charades" (Fuller)   62:196-97, 201
Charades and Celebrations (Urdang)   47:397-98
The Charcoal Burners (Musgrave)   54:335-37, 340
"The Charge of History" (Hearne)   56:126

Chariot of Wrath (Leonov)
   See *Vziatie Velikoshumska*
The Charioteer (Renault)   11:472; 17:393
Chariots of the Gods? (von Daniken)   30:421-27
"Charity" (Dybek)   114:64-5
"Charity" (Nissenson)   4:381
Charivari (Hawkes)   4:212; 7:140, 145; 9:263-64; 14:239-40; 15:272; 27:191; 49:161
"Charles Baudelaire" (Dubie)   36:130
Charles Darwin: A Scientific Biography (Gallant)   17:129
Charles Darwin and the Origin of the Species (Gallant)   17:129
Charles Darwin: The Making of a Scientist (Gallant)   17:129
Charles Lonceville's Fate (Paustovsky)   40:367
"Charles Olson" (Bowering)   15:83
Charles Olson Reading at Berkeley (Olson)   6:387
"Charles River" (Lowell)   4:304
Charles Ryder's Schooldays and Other Stories (Waugh)   27:476-77
"Charles Simic" (Simic)   49:342
"Charles White" (Giovanni)   117:202
"Charleston" (Donoso)   4:127; 8:180; 32:158
"Charleston" (Morand)   41:301
Charleston and Other Stories (Donoso)
   See *Cuentos*
Charley Starts from Scratch (Jackson)   12:290
"Charlie" (Nowlan)   15:398
Charlie and the Chocolate Factory (Dahl)   79:177, 179
Charlie and the Great Glass Elevator: The Further Adventures of Charlie Bucket and Willy Wonka, Chocolate-Maker Extraordinary (Dahl)   79:177
"A Charlie Brown Thanksgiving" (Schulz)   12:531
Charlie Brown's Second Super Book of Questions and Answers: About the Earth and Space...from Plants to Planets! (Schulz)   12:533
"Charlie Don't Surf" (Clash)   30:49
"Charlie Freak" (Becker and Fagen)   26:79, 82
Charlie in the House of Rue (Coover)   32:122-25; 46:116, 121-22
Charlie the Tramp (Hoban)   7:162; 25:266
"Charlie's Girl" (Reed)   21:311
"Charlie's Greek" (O'Faolain)   32:341, 344
"Charlotte Corday" (Tomlinson)   13:550; 45:401
"Charlotte Esmond" (Bates)   46:51
Charlotte's Row (Bates)   46:53
Charlotte's Web (White)   34:425-28, 430, 432; 39:369-70, 372-73, 375-77, 380
"Charlottetown Harbour" (Acorn)   15:9
"The Charm" (Creeley)   36:118; 78:162
"A Charm against the Toothache" (Weiss)   8:546; 14:557
The Charm: Early and Uncollected Poems (Creeley)   2:106-07; 8:153
Le charme discret de la bourgeoisie (Bunuel)   16:137, 141-43, 149, 152; 80:49, 54, 56
Charmed Life (Jones)   26:227-28, 230
A Charmed Life (McCarthy)   3:326-27; 14:357, 360, 363; 59:289, 291, 293
"Charming" (Matthews)   40:325
Charms for the Easy Life (Gibbons)   88:132-33
"Charnel Ground" (Ginsberg)   109:329
"Charnel House, Rothwell Church" (Scannell)   49:329-30
The Charnel Rose, Senlin: A Biography, and

Other Poems (Aiken) 52:20, 28
"Charon" (MacNeice) 4:316; 10:325; 53:243
Charon's Cosmology (Simic) 22:380; 49:340
La Charrette (*The Cart*) (Ferron) 94:113, 117, 120, 124-26
"The Chart" (Merwin) 8:390
Charulata (Ray) 16:480-87, 490, 492, 494-95; 76:360, 362, 365-67
"Charwoman" (Belitt) 22:48, 52
The Chas Addams Mother Goose (Addams) 30:15-16
Chas Addams's Monster Rally (Addams) 30:13
"A Chase" ("Alighieri's Dream") (Baraka) 33:55
"The Chase" (Calvino) 5:99; 73:31-2
The Chase (Foote) 51:130-31
Chase the Game (Jordan) 37:195
"Chasing the Paper-Shaman" (Rose) 85:313
"Chasms" (Squires) 51:380, 382
"Chassidische Schriften" (Sachs) 98:364-65
Chast' rechi (Brodsky)
   See *Cast reci*
Chat Show (White) 49:410-11
"La châtaigne et le fruit à pain" (Conde) 92:104
The Chateau (Maxwell) 19:307
"Chateau d'If" (Vance) 35:427
Château en Suède (*Castle in Sweden*) (Sagan) 6:481-82; 17:422-23, 426; 6:481-82
"Chateau Hardware" (Ashbery) 2:18
Chatsky; or, The Importance of Being Stupid (Burgess) 81:302
"Chattanooga" (Reed) 5:368; 6:448
"Chattanooga-Choo-Choo" (Donoso) 8:179-80; 32:159; 99:241
Chatter on the Nile (Mahfuz)
   See *Tharthara fawq al-Nil*
Chatterton (Ackroyd) 52:9-10, 12-16
Chatting on the Nile (Mahfuz)
   See *Tharthara fawq al-Nil*
"Chatting with the Tide at Jaqueira" (Cabral de Melo Neto)
   See "Prosas da maré na Jaqueira"
"Chaucerian" (Sargeson) 31:370
Chaud et froid ou l'idée de Monsieur Dom (*Hot and Cold*) (Crommelynck) 75:154, 156, 159, 162-64, 166, 169
Che Guevara Speaks: Selected Speeches and Writings (Guevara) 87:199-201
"Che Guevara's Cigars" (Berrigan) 37:44
"Che vuoi pastore d'aria" (Quasimodo) 10:428
"Cheap Thrills" ("In the Back of My Car") (Zappa) 17:585
Cheaper by the Dozen (Gilbreth and Carey) 17:152-54, 156
"Cheapskate" (Clash) 30:44
The Cheat (Jordan) 37:195-96
Check (Barker) 37:31, 34
Checkmate (Behan) 79:27
Checkmates (Milner) 56:227-28
"Checkpoint Charlie" (Durcan) 43:118
"Cheepnis" (Zappa) 17:591
The Cheer (Meredith) 22:303; 55:193
The Cheer Leader (McCorkle) 51:273-76
"Cheerful-By Request" (Ferber) 93:138
Cheerful—By Request (Ferber) 93:138, 141-42
"Cheers!" (Guillen)
   See "Brindis"
"Cheers" (Phillips) 15:419
"A Cheery Soul" (White) 5:486; 7:532; 69:398
"Cheesecake" (Muldoon) 32:318-19
"Chefs and Spoons" (Grass) 15:260

"Chef's House" (Carver) 36:100, 104; 53:67
"Chekhov" (Moss) 7:250
"Chekhov on Sakhalin" (Heaney) 74:175
"Chekhov on the West Heath" (Levertov) 15:338
Chekhov's Grandmother (McClure) 6:317
The Chelsea Girls (Warhol) 20:416-18, 422
"Chelsea in Winter" (Ewart) 46:148, 150
"Chelsea Morning" (Mitchell) 12:435
The Chemicals We Eat and Drink (Silverstein and Silverstein) 17:454, 456
"Chemin de fer" (Bishop) 32:34, 36, 39
Le chemin des écoliers (Ayme) 11:22
"Les chemins" (Bonnefoy) 15:74
Les chemins de la liberté (*The Roads of Freedom*) (Sartre) 1:303-06; 7:390, 398; 24:411-12; 44:494, 497; 50:377, 380, 383; 52:382, 388
Les chemins de la mer (Mauriac) 9:368; 56:212
"Chemistry" (Swift) 41:443
"chemotherapy" (Clifton) 66:84
Les chênes qu'on abat... (Malraux) 57:307
The Chequer Board (Shute) 30:374
Cher Antoine; ou, L'amour raté (*Dear Antoine; or, The Love That Failed*) (Anouilh) 13:20-2; 40:59-61
Cherche tes mots, cherche tes pas (*Look for Your Words, Look for Your Steps*) (Carrier) 78:65
"Cherish" (Moure) 88:227-28
"Cherish the Ladies" (Muldoon) 32:322
Chernowitz! (Arrick) 30:18-19
"Cherokee Bend" (Lightfoot) 26:283
The Cherokee Trail (L'Amour) 25:282
"Cherry Cherry" (Diamond) 30:111
"Cherry Saplings" (Snodgrass) 68:399
"The Cherry Stone" (Olesha) 8:430, 432
The Cherry Stone (Olesha)
   See *Vishnevaya kostochka*
"The Cherry Tree" (Gunn) 18:199, 201
"Cherrylog Road" (Dickey) 7:80, 84
Chers Zoiseaux (Anouilh) 40:60
Chesapeake (Michener) 11:374-76; 29:311, 315; 60:260; 109:375, 377, 379, 381, 388
"Cheshire" (Betjeman) 43:51
"Chesnut Tree—Three Storeys Up" (Avison) 97:111
"The Chess Match" (Hood) 28:192
The Chess Players (Ray)
   See *Shatranj Ke Khilari*
The Chessmaster and His Moves (Rao) 56:306-11
"The Chevalier of the Place Blanche" (Rhys) 14:446
Les chevaliers de la table ronde (*The Knights of the Round Table*) (Cocteau) 16:220; 43:106, 111
"Les chevaux" (Gascar) 11:220
La chevelure de Bérénice (Simon) 39:215
"Chévere" (Guillen) 48:161-63
Une chèvre sur un nuage (*A Goat on a Cloud*) (Arrabal) 18:21
Cheyenne Autumn (Ford) 16:309, 311-12, 319-20
Cheyenne Autumn (Sandoz) 28:403-04, 407
Chez Charlotte and Emily (Baumbach) 23:55
"Chez Jane" (O'Hara) 13:426-27
Chez nous (Nichols) 5:305-06, 309; 36:329
"Chi" (Tolson) 105:253, 276-77
Ho Chi Minh: Legend of Hanoi (Archer) 12:19
Chia (*Family*) (Pa Chin) 18:371, 373
Chiaroscuro (*Morning*) (Horovitz) 56:148-49, 152

La chiave a stella (*The Monkey's Wrench; The Wrench*) (Levi) 50:332-36, 339
"Chicago" (Sandburg) 4:463; 10:448-49; 15:466, 469; 35:347, 358
Chicago (Shepard) 4:490; 6:497; 17:434-35, 439-40, 444
Chicago: City on the Make (Algren) 10:6
"The *Chicago Defender* Sends a Man to Little Rock" (Brooks) 15:94-5; 49:36
"The Chicago Picasso" (Brooks) 49:28
Chicago Poems (Sandburg) 4:463; 10:447, 449-51; 15:466-67; 35:338-43, 347, 352, 358
The Chicago Race Riots, July, 1919 (Sandburg) 35:355
The Chicano Soldier (Valdez)
   See *Soldado razo*
Chicanos (Coles) 108:194
"The Chicken" (Lispector) 43:269-70
"Chicken" (Sillitoe) 57:388
"Chicken Fate" (Landolfi) 49:217
Chicken Inspector No. 23 (Perelman) 23:337
The Chicken Run (Chambers) 35:97
Chicken Soup with Barley (Wesker) 3:518-19; 5:482, 484; 42:427, 430
"The Chicken without a Head" (Simic) 68:379
"Chickens" (Ferber) 93:136, 141
"The Chicken's Egg" (Cabral de Melo Neto)
   See "O ovo da galinha"
"Chickens the Weasel Killed" (Stafford) 29:380-81
"Chico King Popular Singer" (Rogin) 18:457
Los chicos (Matute) 11:363
Chief (Bonham) 12:52-3, 55
Chief Joseph of the Nez Perce (Warren) 39:262-64
"Chief Justice Burger, Teen Idol" (Grayson) 38:210
Un chien andalou (*An Andalusian Dog*) (Bunuel) 16:133-34, 138, 140-41, 149-50, 152; 80:19-21, 25-6, 28, 31, 35, 37-8, 51, 55-6
Le chien couchant (*Salad Days*) (Sagan) 36:383
Le chien de coeur (Char) 9:163
Le chiendent (*The Bark Tree*) (Queneau) 2:359; 5:359-62; 10:430; 42:332-33
La chienne (Renoir) 20:292-93, 301, 305-08, 310
"Chijin no ai" ("A Fool's Love"; "An Idiot's Love") (Tanizaki) 8:509; 28:414, 418
"Chike's School Days" (Achebe) 75:13-14
"The Child" (Dudek) 11:159
"The Child" (Eberhart) 56:77
"The Child" (Ferron) 94:103, 119
"Child" (Plath) 3:391; 9:434; 51:345; 111:167, 199, 206
"The Child" (Silkin) 43:400
"The Child" (Wright) 53:417
"The Child and the Madman" (Wiesel) 5:490
"The Child and the Shadow" (Le Guin) 71:195-97, 199, 200
"Child and Wattle Tree" (Wright) 53:417
"Child Asleep" (Clark) 38:125
"The Child Asleep" (Rukeyser) 27:404
"Child Beater" (Ai) 69:4, 16
The Child Buyer (Hersey) 1:144; 2:188; 40:232-34, 239-40; 81:335; 97:302
Child by Fever (Foote) 75:230-31, 239, 243
"A Child Ill" (Betjeman) 43:34, 41-2
The Child in Chains (Mauriac)
   See *L'enfant chargé de chaînes*
The Child in Time (McEwan) 66:286-94
"The Child Is the Meaning of This Life"

(Schwartz)　**4**:478; **10**:462, 466; **45**:353-54; **87**:337
"The Child Looks Out" (Livesay)　**79**:332
"A Child: Marginalia on an Epigraph" (Avison)　**97**:78, 113
"Child Naming Flowers" (Hass)　**18**:213
"The Child of Civilization" (Brodsky)　**50**:134
"Child of Europe" (Milosz)　**56**:237, 247-48
Child of Fire (O'Dell)　**30**:270-71, 275
Child of Fortune (Spinrad)　**46**:388-89
Child of God (McCarthy)　**4**:341-43; **57**:330-33; **101**:134-35, 144, 146-47, 149-54, 159-61, 163-64, 167, 176-77, 179, 183, 185, 195, 197-98, 201-04
"Child of Our Time" (Boland)　**40**:99; **67**:43; **113**:96
Child of Our Time (del Castillo)　**38**:163-64, 166-67
A Child of Queen Victoria (Plomer)　**4**:406
Child of Rage (Thompson)　**69**:384
A Child of the Century (Hecht)　**8**:269, 272
Child of the Owl (Yep)　**35**:469-71
"Child on Top of a Greenhouse" (Roethke)　**3**:432; **101**:262, 295
Child o'War (Garfield)　**12**:226-27, 230, 238
"The Child Screams and Looks Back at You" (Banks)　**72**:4
"The Child/The Ring/The Road" (Willard)　**37**:464
"Child Trapped in a Barber Shop" (Levine)　**33**:273
"The Child Who Favored Daughter" (Walker)　**19**:453; **58**:404, 406; **103**:359-64, 368, 407, 410-12
Childe Byron (Linney)　**51**:261-62
"Childe Horvald to the Dark Tower Came" (Ciardi)　**40**:154, 157
"Childe Roland" (Howard)　**7**:168
The Childhod of Ivan (Tarkovsky)
　See *Ivanovo Detstvo*
"Childhood" (Aldington)　**49**:6, 9, 16
"Childhood" (Justice)　**19**:235; **102**:251, 275, 277
"Childhood" (Walker)　**6**:554
Childhood (Sarraute)
　See *Enfance*
Childhood (Wilder)　**1**:366; **82**:363
"Childhood and Interruption" (Smith)　**25**:421
Childhood and Other Neighborhoods (Dybek)　**114**:62, 64, 67, 70-3, 75, 77-8
A Childhood in Agram (Krleza)
　See *Djetinjstvo u Agramu, 1902-1903*
Childhood Is Not Forever (Farrell)　**66**:129, 132
The Childhood of an Equestrian (Edson)　**13**:190
"The Childhood of Hölderlin" (Watkins)　**43**:452
"The Childhood of Luvers" (Pasternak)　**7**:293; **10**:383; **18**:385-87; **63**:290
"The Childhood of Luvers" (Pasternak)
　See "Detstvo Luvers"
Childhood of the Magician (Willard)　**7**:539-40
"The Childhood of William Blake" (Padilla)　**38**:349, 351-53
"The Childhood of Zhenya Luvers" (Pasternak)
　See "Detstvo Luvers"
A Childhood: The Biography of a Place (Crews)　**23**:134-37; **49**:68-71, 73-4, 76-7, 79
Childhood's End (Clarke)　**1**:59; **4**:104-05; **13**:152-55; **18**:103-06; **35**:120, 122-27
"A Childish Prank" (Hughes)　**4**:236

"Childless Woman" (Plath)　**3**:391; **5**:345; **9**:427; **14**:424; **62**:404; **111**:168, 210
"Childlessness" (Merrill)　**13**:379-81
The Childlike Life of the Black Tarantula (Acker)　**45**:14-15; **111**:15-18, 21, 25, 32, 36
"The Child-Martyr" (Oates)　**9**:403
"The Children" (Bell)　**8**:67
"The Children" (Cheever)　**15**:127
"Children" (Kizer)　**39**:169
"The Children" (Lustig)　**56**:182
"The Children" (Sexton)　**6**:492
"Children" (Tanizaki)
　See "Shonen"
Children　**59**:399
Children (Gurney)　**32**:217-19; **50**:176-77
The Children (de Hartog)　**19**:132
"Children and Art" (Sondheim)　**30**:403; **39**:175
Children and Others (Cozzens)　**92**:189
"Children Are Bored on Sunday" (Stafford)　**7**:457; **19**:431; **68**:422
Children Are Bored on Sunday (Stafford)　**68**:421
Children Are Civilians, Too (Boell)　**27**:66-7; **72**:73
Children at the Gate (Banks)　**23**:40
The Children at the Gate (Wallant)　**5**:477; **10**:512-16
"Children Children" (McCartney)　**35**:286
"Children, Dogs, and Desperate Men" (Colwin)　**84**:150
Children from Their Games (Shaw)　**23**:398
"Children in Exile" (Fenton)　**32**:170
Children in Exile: Poems, 1965-1984 (Fenton)　**32**:169
Children Is All (Purdy)　**2**:348-49; **4**:422; **10**:421; **28**:378-79; **52**:350
Children of a Lesser God (Medoff)　**23**:292-95
Children of Crisis (Coles)　**108**:186-88, 193-94, 203-05, 210, 214
"Children of Darkness" (Wilbur)　**14**:579; **53**:398
Children of Dune (Herbert)　**12**:277-78; **23**:221-24, 227; **35**:199, 201-02, 205, 207-09; **44**:393-94; **85**:88-9, 93-6, 100
The Children of Dynmouth (Trevor)　**9**:528-29; **14**:535; **25**:444; **71**:326, 340, 346; **116**:334, 375, 377, 381-83
The Children of Gabalawi (Mahfuz)
　See *Awlad haretna*
Children of God (Fisher)　**7**:103
The Children of Ham (Brown)　**30**:38-41
"Children of Light" (Lowell)　**4**:297; **8**:350; **11**:326, 329; **37**:237
Children of Light (Stone)　**42**:359-64
"The Children of Lir" (Durcan)　**70**:150
"Children of Loneliness" (Yezierska)　**46**:442, 449
Children of Loneliness (Yezierska)　**46**:442-43
Children of Men (Vesaas)
　See *Menneskebonn*
Children of My Heart (Roy)
　See *Ces enfants de ma vie*
"Children of Old Somebody" (Goyen)　**14**:214; **40**:217-18
"Children of Our Age" (Szymborska)　**99**:204
Children of Our Neighborhood (Mahfuz)
　See *Awlad haretna*
Children of Power (Shreve)　**23**:403-04
Children of Primrose Lane (Streatfeild)　**21**:412, 414
Children of Segu (Conde)
　See *Ségou: La terre en miettes*

"Children of Strikers" (Chappell)　**40**:142
Children of the Albatross (Nin)　**1**:249; **4**:376, 379
Children of the Arbat (Rybakov)　**53**:295-302; **59**:368, 381-82, 387-89, 391, 393
Children of the Black Sabbath (Hebert)
　See *Les infants du sabat*
"Children of the Corn" (King)　**61**:331, 333-34; **113**:336-38, 380
The Children of the Dream (Bettelheim)　**79**:109
Children of the Game (Cocteau)
　See *Les enfants terribles*
"Children of the Headmaster" (Trevor)　**71**:342; **116**:375
Children of the Holocaust (Lustig)　**56**:186
The Children of the House (Pearce)　**21**:282-84, 287, 291
"Children of the Kingdom" (Klein)　**34**:71
The Children of the Man in the Moon (Carrier)
　See *Les enfants du bonhomme dans la lune*
Children of the Mire: Modern Poetry from Romanticism to the Avant-Garde (Paz)
　See *Los hijos del limo: Del romanticismo a la vanguardia*
"Children of the Mississippi" (Brown)　**1**:47; **23**:96; **59**:266
"Children of the Moon" (Du Bois)　**64**:110-11
Children of the Revolution: A Yankee Teacher in the Cuban Schools (Kozol)　**17**:254-55
Children of the Rose (Feinstein)　**36**:169
"Children of the Sea" (Danticat)　**94**:93, 95-100
Children of Violence (Lessing)　**1**:173-75; **2**:239-41; **3**:282-83, 286, 289, 290-91; **6**:290, 292, 295-96, 298, 300, 304; **22**:280-81, 283-86
"Children of Wealth in Your Warm Nursery" (Daryush)　**19**:121-22
The Children on the Top Floor (Streatfeild)　**21**:404, 407-08
"Children on Their Birthdays" (Capote)　**1**:55; **3**:99; **13**:134, 139-40; **19**:79, 86; **58**:98
"Children Passing" (Blunden)　**56**:47
"The Children: Proemio" (Berryman)　**8**:93
"Children Walking Home from School through Good Neighborhood" (Justice)　**102**:284
A Children's Biography of Langston Hughes (Walker)　**103**:357
"The Children's Campaign" (Lagerkvist)
　See "Det lilla fälttåget"
"Children's Court" (Hochman)　**8**:297
"The Children's Crusade" (Levine)　**14**:318
The Children's Crusade　**75**:64-6
Children's Day (Waterhouse)　**47**:419
"The Children's Game" (Stafford)　**68**:422
The Children's Hell (Nakos)
　See *The Children's Inferno*
The Children's Hour (Hellman)　**2**:187; **8**:281; **14**:256, 258-60; **18**:220-21, 225; **34**:347-49; **44**:528-29, 532; **52**:191, 202, 205
The Children's Inferno (*The Children's Hell*) (Nakos)　**29**:321, 323
"The Children's Orchard" (Rukeyser)　**15**:458
"Children's Rhymes" (Hughes)　**10**:281
"Children's Story" (Handke)
　See "Child's Story"
The Children's Story (Clavell)　**25**:127-28; **87**:2-4, 19
"A Child's Calendar" (Brown)　**48**:53-4, 57
A Child's Garden of Curses (Perelman)　**49**:272
"The Child's Grave" (Blunden)　**56**:39
"Child's Guide to Parents" (Nash)　**23**:322

A Child's History (Newman) 8:419

"A Child's Nightmare" (Wright) 53:424

"Child's Park Stones" (Plath) 111:200

"Child's Play" (Malouf) 28:268-69

Child's Play (Slavitt) 5:392

Child's Play (Walser)
See *Ein Kinderspiel*

"A Child's Prayer" (Sassoon) 36:385

"Child's Story" ("Children's Story") (Handke) 38:225, 228-29

"Childsong" (Diamond) 30:110

Childwold (Oates) 9:404-05; 19:349-50, 353; 33:289; 52:338; 108:386, 391

"Childybawn" (O'Faolain) 32:341, 344; 70:318

"Chile" (Lane) 25:286

The Chilean Spring (Alegria)
See *El Paso de los Gansos*

"Chiliastic Sapphics" (Hacker) 91:109

Chi-liu (*Turbulent Stream*) (Pa Chin) 18:371-72, 374

The Chill (Macdonald) 1:185; 2:256; 14:332, 334-35; 41:268

Chills and Fever (Ransom) 4:436; 5:365

Chills and Other Poems (*Fever and Other New Poems*) (Akhmadulina) 53:15

Chilly Scenes of Winter (Beattie) 8:54-7; 13:64-5; 40:66; 63:3-4, 7-9, 13, 22

"Chimera" (Howes) 15:290

Chimera (Barth) 2:37-9; 3:42; 5:51; 7:22-5; 9:74; 10:24; 14:52-4, 56; 27:28; 51:20-3, 26, 29; 89:10-11, 24-5, 31-2, 39, 45, 47, 63

Chimes at Midnight (*Falstaff*) (Welles) 20:439-40, 443, 445, 448, 450-51; 80:367-69, 373, 377, 391, 393, 409-12, 414

Chimes at Midnight (White) 49:408

"Chimes for Yahya" (Merrill) 8:381

"The Chimney" (Campbell) 42:88-9

"Chimney Bluff" (Crase) 58:163, 166

"Chimneys" (Cummings) 15:159

"China" (Donoso) 8:178; 11:146; 32:156

"China" (Johnson) 51:234, 236

China Court: The Hours of a Country House (Godden) 53:158-59, 161

China Diary (Spender) 91:263

China Gold (Buck) 11:77

China in the Twentieth Century (Archer) 12:21

China Men (Kingston) 19:249-51; 58:308-17, 327

"China Poems" (Lane) 25:289

China Poems (Brutus) 43:89

China Trace (Wright) 13:614-15; 28:457-58

The Chinaberry Tree: A Novel of American Life (Fauset) 54:169-71, 175, 177,179-80, 182, 187, 189-90

Chinatown (Polanski) 16:470-73

Chinatown (Towne) 87:353-54, 359, 361-66, 369-70, 373-78

The Chinese Agent (Moorcock)
See *Somewhere in the Night*

The Chinese Americans (Meltzer) 26:307-08

The Chinese and the Americans (Archer) 12:22

"The Chinese Banyan" (Meredith) 22:302

Chinese Dynasty Cantos (Pound) 112:351, 358

"Chinese Food" (Jong) 4:264

"The Chinese Geomancer" (Chatwin) 57:153

The Chinese Girl (Godard)
See *La Chinoise*

"The Chinese Insomniacs" (Jacobsen) 48:194

The Chinese Insomniacs (Jacobsen) 48:192-93, 195

"The Chinese Novel" (Buck) 7:32

The Chinese Orange Mystery (Queen) 3:422

"Chinese Poem" (Smith) 64:400

The Chinese Prime Minister (Bagnold) 25:76-8

"The Chinese Restaurant in Portrush" (Mahon) 27:292

Chinese Roulette (Fassbinder) 20:117

"The Chinese Statue" (Archer) 28:14

"Chinese Tallow" (Plumly) 33:315

The Chinese Wall (Frisch)
See *Die chinesische Mauer: Eine Farce*

Die chinesische Mauer: Eine Farce (*The Chinese Wall; Der chinesische Mauer: Eine Farce*) (Frisch) 3:166-67; 9:217; 14:181-83; 18:160; 44:181, 195-97, 203

Der chinesische Mauer: Eine Farce (Frisch)
See *Die chinesische Mauer: Eine Farce*

"The Chink" (Stegner) 81:346

Chinmoku (*Silence*) (Endo) 7:95-6; 14:160, 162; 19:160-61; 54:152-55, 157, 159-60, 162; 99:282-95, 298-300, 302, 305, 307-09

La Chinoise (*The Chinese Girl*) (Godard) 20:138, 143

"Chinoiserie" (Fuller) 4:178; 28:151

"Chinoiserie" (Wright) 6:581

"Chinook" (Muldoon) 72:275

The Chip-Chip Gatherers (Naipaul) 32:324-25, 327; 39:355-56, 358

"Chipping Away at Death" (Dunn) 36:151

"Chips" (Durcan) 70:149, 153

Chips with Everything (Wesker) 3:517-18; 5:482-83; 42:425-28, 430

"Chirico" (Fisher) 25:158

Chirundo (Mphahlele) 25:340, 345-46

Chiryo-to (*Towers of Healing*) (Oe) 86:244

"The Chiseller" (Callaghan) 41:98

The Chisholms (Hunter) 11:280; 31:224

Chit-Chat on the Nile (Mahfuz)
See *Tharthara fawq al-Nil*

Ch'iu (*Autumn Day*) (Pa Chin) 18:371-72

Ch'i-yüan (*Garden of Rest; Leisure Garden*) (Pa Chin) 18:373, 375

Chloe in the Afternoon (Rohmer) 16:532, 534-35

Chloris and the Creeps (Platt) 26:351-53

Chloris and the Freaks (Platt) 26:351-53

Chloris and the Weirdos (Platt) 26:352-53

"Choc Bay" (Walcott) 76:278-79

Chocky (Wyndham) 19:475

"Chocolate Footballs" (Giles) 39:64

"Chocolate Pudding" (Mazer) 26:291

A Chocolate Soldier (Colter) 58:146

The Chocolate War (Cormier) 12:134-38; 30:181-91

"Chocolates" (Simpson) 32:377-78

"Choice" (Ammons) 25:44

"A Choice" (Christie) 110:126

The Choice (Schell) 35:366-67

"A Choice of Butchers" (Trevor) 71:348

A Choice of Enemies (Richler) 5:371-74; 13:484-85; 46:349

A Choice of Gods (Simak) 55:320

"A Choice of Profession" (Malamud) 44:420

A Choice of Shelley's Verse (Spender) 91:263

"Choices" (Cunningham) 31:102, 104

"The Choir and Music of Solitude and Silence" (Schwartz) 45:355

The Choirboys (Wambaugh) 18:532-33

"Le choix" (Theriault) 79:407

"Cholera" (Dove) 81:137

"Chomei at Toyama" (Bunting) 10:83-4; 39:299; 47:44-5, 52, 55

"The Chomsky File" (Stewart) 32:421

"Choose Something like a Star" (Frost) 9:222

"Choosing a Homesite" (Booth) 23:74-5

Choosing Equality: The Case for Democratic Schooling 70:366

"Chopin in Winter" (Dybek) 114:69-70, 72, 74-5, 81-2

"Chor der Stern" ("Chorus of Stars") (Sachs) 98:327, 349, 355

"Chor der Ungeborenen" ("Chorus of the Unborn") (Sachs) 14:475; 98:327, 349

"Chor der Waisen" ("Chorus of Orphans") (Sachs) 98:327, 349

"Chorale" (Hope) 51:212, 216

"Chorale" (McAuley) 45:246, 248

"A Chorale of Cherokee Night Music as Heard through an Open Window Long Ago" (Williams) 13:600

"Chord" (Merwin) 88:206

"Chords of Fame" (Ochs) 17:333-35

"Chöre nach Mitternacht" ("Choruses After Midnight") (Sachs) 98:325, 327, 355

"Choricos" (Aldington) 49:2-4, 6, 9, 12, 16

Chorister's Cake (Mayne) 12:387-88, 390, 403

"Choros Sequence from Morpheus" (H. D.) 73:114

"Choros Translations" (H. D.) 73:121

"Chorus" (Ciardi) 40:157

"Chorus" (Lorde) 71:248

"Chorus for the Untenured Personnel" (Bowers) 9:122

A Chorus Line (Kirkwood) 9:319-20

"Chorus of Clouds" (Sachs) 98:327

A Chorus of Disapproval (Ayckbourn) 74:7, 15, 21, 23, 31, 34-5

"Chorus of Furies—Overheard—guarda, mi disse, le feroce Erine" (Bunting) 47:44

"Chorus of Invisible Things" (Sachs) 98:327

"Chorus of Orphans" (Sachs)
See "Chor der Waisen"

"Chorus of Shades" (Sachs) 98:327

"Chorus of Stars" (Sachs)
See "Chor der Stern"

"Chorus of Stones" (Sachs) 98:327

"Chorus of the Saved" (Sachs) 98:327

"Chorus of the Unborn" (Sachs) 14:475
See "Chor der Ungeborenen"

"Chorus of Things Left Behind" (Sachs) 98:327

"Chorus of Trees" (Sachs) 98:327

"Chorus of Wanderers" (Sachs) 98:327

"Choruses After Midnight" (Sachs)
See "Chöre nach Mitternacht"

"Choruses Describing the States of Mind of Dido" (Ungaretti)
See "Cori descrittivi d'anima di Didone"

"The Chosen" (Voigt) 54:433

The Chosen (Potok) 2:338-39; 7:321; 26:367-72, 374, 376; 112:256-61, 263-64, 266-67, 269-75, 277-80, 282-83, 289-91, 293, 295

Chosen Country (Dos Passos) 15:186; 25:140-41, 146; 34:422; 82:76

Chosen Defects (Neruda)
See *Defectos escogidos: 2000*

A Chosen Light (Montague) 13:391; 46:264, 266-68, 271-72, 275, 278

"The Chosen One" (Davies) 23:147-48

The Chosen One and Other Stories (Davies) 23:146

The Chosen Place, the Timeless People (Marshall) 27:309-13, 315; 72:212-13, 216, 219, 231, 233, 235, 247-48, 250-51, 254

Chosen Poems: Old and New (Lorde) 71:235, 246, 260

Les Choses: A Story of the Sixties (Perec)
  See *Les choses: Une histoire des années soixante*

Choses et autres (Prevert) 15:440

Les choses: Une histoire des années soixante (Les Choses: A Story of the Sixties) (Perec) 56:253-54, 260, 268; 116:231-322, 236, 242, 245, 252-53, 261

"Chosun" (Fenton) 32:166, 169

"Choteau" (Bass) 79:3-6, 17

Chou En-Lai (Archer) 12:20

"Choughs" (Clarke) 61:79, 82

Chris Axelson, Blacksmith (Ringwood) 48:330, 334-36

"Chris's Last Party" (Highsmith) 42:216

Christ and the Moral Life (Gustafson) 100:220, 229

"Christ Climbed Down" (Ferlinghetti) 111:64

"Christ in Alabama" (Hughes) 1:147; 10:279; 35:218; 108:298, 328

Christabel (Potter) 58:399-400; 86:346, 352-53

Christian Behavior (Lewis) 27:260-61

"The Christian in the Diaspora" (Merton) 83:383

"Christian Island" (Lightfoot) 26:278-79

"Christianity and I" (Endo) 54:158

"Christianity and Revolution" (Arendt) 98:51

"Christians" (Scott) 43:370

"The Christian's Year in Miniature" (Avison) 97:86

Christie in Love (Brenton) 31:56-7, 59, 62, 65-6, 69

Christie Malry's Own Double-Entry (Johnson) 6:263; 9:301-02

A Christina Stead Reader (Stead) 32:411

"Christine" (Green) 77:266

Christine (King) 26:244; 37:206; 61:325, 328, 336; 113:336, 344, 347, 388, 391

Christine, and Other Stories (Green)
  See *Le voyageur sur la terre*

"Christmas" (Betjeman) 6:69; 43:45, 51

"Christmas" (McGahern) 48:263

Christmas (Durrenmatt)
  See *Weihnacht*

Christmas and the Beads of Sweat (Nyro) 17:313-14, 317, 319-20

Christmas at Fontaigne's (Kotzwinkle) 35:256-58

"Christmas at Rillingham's" (Wain) 46:411

"Christmas at the End of a Decade" (Squires) 51:378, 381

"A Christmas Ballad" (Brodsky) 4:77

"Christmas Ballad" (Wright) 53:426

"Christmas Beaches" (Voznesensky) 57:421

A Christmas Birthday Story (Laurence) 50:314

"A Christmas Card" (Merton) 83:392

"A Christmas Card after the Assassinations" (Van Duyn) 7:498

"A Christmas Carol" (Ciardi) 40:157

"Christmas Cold" (Buckley) 57:133

"A Christmas Conspiracy Tale" (Klima) 56:171

"Christmas Eve" (Ammons) 108:51, 53, 58

"Christmas Eve" (Ciardi) 40:157

"Christmas Eve" (Morgan) 31:275

Christmas Eve (Brennan) 5:72-3

"Christmas Eve at Johnson's Drugs N Goods" (Bambara) 88:22, 28

"Christmas Eve Service at Midnight at St. Michael's" (Bly) 15:63; 38:57

"Christmas Every Day" (Boell)
  See "Nicht nur zur Weihnachtzeit"

"Christmas from Summertime Seen" (Avison) 97:117-18

"Christmas Gift" (Himes) 7:160; 108;235

"A Christmas Greeting" (Wright) 5:520

A Christmas Holiday (Maugham) 1:204

"A Christmas Hymn" (Wilbur) 53:405, 411; 110:356, 385

"Christmas in Biafra" (Achebe) 7:6; 11:3-4; 26:21

Christmas in Biafra and Other Poems (Achebe) 7:6; 26:20-21, 24

"Christmas in My Soul" (Nyro) 17:316, 318

"Christmas Is Coming" (Hecht) 8:267; 13:269

"A Christmas Letter from Ted and Jean Just to Catch Up and Let You All Know How We All Are ... Doing" (Gray) 49:147

"A Christmas Memory" (Capote) 13:134-36; 19:82, 87; 34:321-22; 38:84, 87

"A Christmas Memory" (Giovanni) 117:192

"Christmas Morning" (O'Connor) 14:399

"Christmas Poem" (O'Hara) 6:385

"Christmas Poem, 1965" (Ondaatje) 14:407

"Christmas Present for a Poet" (Van Duyn) 116:425

Christmas Pudding (Mitford) 44:492

"A Christmas Recalled" (Porter) 33:317

"The Christmas Robin" (Graves) 45:169

"Christmas Roses" (O'Brien) 36:341

"Christmas Sermon" (Levi) 41:245, 248

"Christmas Shopping" (MacNeice) 53:231

The Christmas Sky (Branley) 21:17

"Christmas Star" (Pasternak) 63:312-13, 315, 317

"A Christmas Storm" (Nemerov) 36:306-08

"Christmas Story" (Naipaul) 105:150

"A Christmas Thought" (Hannah) 90:158

"A Christmas Tragedy" (Christie) 110:141-42, 144-45

"Christmas Tree" (Weldon) 36:444

"Christmas Trees" (Frost) 15:246, 248

"The Christmas Virgin" (Derleth) 31:138

"Christmas with Two Children's Stories" (Hesse) 25:260-61

Christopher and His Kind, 1929-1939 (Isherwood) 14:286; 44:397-401

Christopher Blake (Hart) 66:178, 182-83, 189-90

Christopher Columbus 70:351

Christopher Columbus, Mariner (Morison) 70:351

Christopher Columbus: Master of the Atlantic (Thomas) 70:338

Christopher Strong (Arzner) 98:62-6, 70-1, 74, 81, 85-7

Christopher Unborn (Fuentes)
  See *Cristóbal nonato*

"Christo's" ("Cristo's") (Muldoon) 72:273-74, 277

Chroma (Barthelme) 117:5-6

"A Chromatic Passing-Note" (Amis) 40:41

"Chromium" (Levi) 37:223

Chromos (Alfau) 66:8-13

"Chronic" (Avison) 97:76, 128

"Chronic" (Ezekiel) 61:108

"A Chronic Condition" (Wilbur) 3:534; 110:351

The Chronicle and the Chant of the Ages 75:61

Chronicle in Stone (Kadare) 52:261-63

Chronicle of a Death Foretold (Garcia Marquez)
  See *Crónica de una muerte anunciada*

"Chronicle of a Decade" (Elytis) 100:190-91

"Chronicle of a Demise" (Williams) 15:579

"Chronicle of Anse Saint-Roch" (Ferron) 94:124-25

Chronicle of Dawn (Sender)
  See *Crónica del alba*

Chronicle of Early Youth (Sender)
  See *Crónica del alba*

A Chronicle of Love Affairs (Konwicki)
  See *Kronika wypadków miłosnych*

A Chronicle of Love Events (Konwicki)
  See *Kronika wypadków miłosnych*

Chronicle of Our Time (Ehrenburg) 62:179

"A Chronicle of the Coming of the New Ice Age" (Haavikko) 34:178

Chronicle of Youth (Brittain) 23:93

"Chronicler's Notice" (Arghezi)
  See "Tableta de cronicar"

Chronicles of Bustos Domecq (Bioy Casares)
  See *Crónicas de Bustos Domecq*

Chronicles of Our Peaceful Kitchen (Tanizaki) 28:414

Chronicles of Prydain (Alexander) 35:26, 28

The Chronicles of Robin Hood (Sutcliff) 26:428, 433, 435

Chronicles of Solar Pons (Derleth) 31:138

The Chronicles of Thomas Covenant, the Unbeliever (Donaldson) 46:140, 142, 144

Chronique (Perse) 4:400; 46:308

Chronique de la ville de pierre (Kadare) 52:261

Chronique des Pasquier (Duhamel) 8:186

Chroniques (Giono) 4:184

Chroniques du plateau Mont-Royal (Tremblay) 29:424, 427

Chroniques du XXme siècle (Morand) 41:305

Chroniques romanesques (Giono) 4:187

"Chronologues" (Goldbarth) 38:205-06

The Chrysalids (Wyndham) 19:475-76

"Chrysallis" (Montale) 9:386

"Chrysanthemum Show" (Day Lewis) 10:131

"Chrysanthemum Tea" (Sondheim) 30:397

"The Chrysanthemums" (Steinbeck) 9:516, 519; 21:391-92; 34:415; 45:382

Chrysothemis (Ritsos) 13:488

"The Chuck Show of Television" (Keillor) 115:286, 295

"Chun" (Le Guin) 45:213

Ch'un (Spring) (Pa Chin) 18:371

Chung Kuo (Antonioni) 20:38

Chung Kuo: The Middle Kingdom, Book One (Wingrove) 68:451-57

Chunga's Revenge (Zappa) 17:587

"The Chuppah" (Piercy) 62:371

The Church as Moral Decision Maker (Gustafson) 100:195

"Church Going" (Larkin) 3:277; 5:223, 230; 8:332, 335, 337-38, 339; 13:335-36, 340; 18:294, 297; 33:256, 259-60, 263; 39:340-42, 345; 64:261, 265, 269-70, 277, 282-83

"The Church in High Street" (Campbell) 42:83, 92

"Church of England: Thoughts Occasioned by Hearing the Bells of Magdalen Tower from the Botanic Garden, Oxford on St. Mary Magdalen's Day" (Betjeman) 43:50

Church Poems (Betjeman) 34:306, 309; 43:49-50

Churchill Barriers (Brown) 100:85

The Churchill Play (Brenton) 31:58, 62-7

"Churn Milk Joan" (Hughes) 14:273

"Churning Day" (Heaney) 25:244; 91:119

"The Chute" (Olds) 85:298

La chute (The Fall) (Camus) 1:52-4; 2:97-8;

4:91-2; 9:144-46, 150; 11:95; 14:107, 110, 113-14; 32:86-7, 91; 63:63, 68, 71, 75, 77, 83-90; 69:135

La chute dans le temps (The Fall into Time) (Cioran) 64:82-5, 87-8, 92

"Chuy" (Soto) 80:278, 291-92, 296

"Chuzhoe remeslo" ("An Alien Craft") (Akhmadulina) 53:11

"Ciant da li ciampanis" (Pasolini) 106:233

"Ciants di muart" (Pasolini) 106:233

A ciascuno il suo (A Man's Blessing) (Sciascia) 9:474; 41:389-90

"Cicada" (Ihimaera) 46:200

Cicada (Haines) 58:217-19, 221

"Cicada Queen" (Sterling) 72:368

"Cicadeas" (Mueller) 51:281

Le Cid maghané (Ducharme) 74:63-7

A cidade sitiada (Lispector) 43:261, 265

"Cider Hill" (Williams) 45:445

The Cider House Rules (Irving) 38:251-55; 112:154-58, 165

Cider with Rosie (The Edge of Day) (Lee) 90:182-85, 187-88, 190-92, 195-96, 198-99, 201, 204, 207, 209

Le Ciel de Québec (The Penniless Redeemer) (Ferron) 94:108, 112-17, 122, 124-25, 127

La Ciel et la merde (Arrabal) 58:18

Cien años de soledad (One Hundred Years of Solitude) (Garcia Marquez) 2:148-50; 3:179-83; 8:230, 232-33; 10:214-17; 15:254; 27:147-55; 47:143-44, 146-51, 153-54; 55:134, 136, 138-39, 144-47; 68:139-168

Cien sonetos de amor (One Hundred Love Sonnets) (Neruda) 28:313-14; 62:334

Cigarettes (Mathews) 52:311-12, 316-18

Cimarron (Ferber) 18:151; 93:153-56, 159, 164, 171, 174, 176, 179, 181, 185-87, 189-90

Le cimetière des voitures (The Automobile Graveyard; The Car Cemetery; El cementario de automóviles; El cementerio de automóviles) (Arrabal) 9:34, 38; 18:19; 58:3-4, 7-8, 11, 16-17, 21, 24-6

Cimitirul Buna-Vestire (The Cemetery of Annunciations) (Arghezi) 80:6

"Cina" ("Dinner") (Arghezi) 80:7

"Cîntatre omului" ("Ode to Man") (Arghezi) 80:4

Cinco horas con Mario (Five Hours with Mario) (Delibes) 8:169; 18:113

5 narraciones y 2 fábulas (5 Tales and 2 Fables) (Benet) 28:25

Cinder (De Marinis) 54:97-8

"Cinderella" (Jarrell) 13:302

"Cinderella and the Mob" (Woolrich) 77:390

"The Cinderella Waltz" (Beattie) 40:66; 63:19

"The Cinema" (Salter) 52:369

"Cinema and Ballad of the Great Depression" (Justice) 102:285

"Cinema as an Art Form" (Deren) 102:43

"Cinema of a Man" (MacLeish) 68:273

"Cinematography: The Creative Use of Reality" (Deren) 102:43-4

Cingiz Ajtmatov: Povesti i rasskazy (Aitmatov)
See *Povestri i rasskazy*

A cinkos (The Loser) (Konrad) 73:175-84

"The Cinnamon Peeler" (Ondaatje) 51:318

Cinnamon Skin (MacDonald) 27:275-76

Cinque romanzi brevi (Ginzburg) 11:229

"Cinquevalli" (Morgan) 31:276

Cîntare omului (Arghezi) 80:6, 8

Cintece noi (New Songs) (Arghezi) 80:6

La ciociara (Two Women) (Moravia) 7:240-41; 11:382; 18:344, 349

La ciociara (Two Women) (De Sica) 20:89-90, 94

CIOPW (Cummings) 12:146; 68:35

"Cipango's Hinder Door" (Dahlberg) 7:63

Cipango's Hinder Door (Dahlberg) 7:63

The Cipher (Borges) 44:356

Cipher (Mosley) 43:317

Los cipreses creen en Dios (The Cypresses Believe in God) (Gironella) 11:234, 237

Circa 1492: Art in the Age of Exploration 70:355

"Circe" (Auden) 6:18

"Circe" (Broumas) 10:77; 73:8

"Circe" (H. D.) 73:105

"Circe" (Hope) 51:212, 220

"Circe" (Miller) 14:373

"Circle" (Moss) 14:376

"The Circle" (Nabokov) 3:354

The Circle (Feinstein) 36:167-68

The Circle (Maugham) 1:204; 11:368-70; 67:223-25, 227; 93:244

"The Circle Game" (Atwood) 4:27

"The Circle Game" (Mitchell) 12:436

The Circle Game (Atwood) 4:24, 26-27; 8:30; 13:42; 15:37; 25:63-4, 66-7; 84:68

The Circle Game (Lieber) 6:311

The Circle Home (Hoagland) 28:180

"The Circle Is Small" (Lightfoot) 26:282

"A Circle of Fire" (O'Connor) 1:257; 15:412; 21:256-57

"A Circle of Friends" (Voinovich) 49:376-77

"Circle of Prayer" (Munro) 50:211, 215-16, 218, 220

A Circle of Quiet (L'Engle) 12:349-50

The Circle of Reason (Ghosh) 44:44-8

"Circle of Steel" (Lightfoot) 26:280, 283

"Circle One" (Dodson) 79:193

"A Circle Tour of the Rockies" (Dudek) 11:161

"Circle Two" (Dodson) 79:193

"Circles" (Van Doren) 6:541

Circles on the Water (Piercy) 27:380-81; 62:373

"The Circling Hand" (Kincaid) 43:249

El circo (Goytisolo) 23:186

"Circolo della caccia" (Davison) 28:103

"Circonstances de la poésie" (Reverdy) 53:283

"The Circuit" (Avison) 97:115

Circuit by the Moon and Color (Tzara)
See *Circuit par la lune et par la couleur*

Circuit par la lune et par la couleur (Circuit by the Moon and Color) (Tzara) 47:390

"Circular from America" (Barker) 48:18

"The Circular Ruins" (Borges)
See "Las ruinas circulares"

Circular Stairs, Distress in the Mirrors (Klappert) 57:259-60, 264

"The Circular Valley" (Bowles) 19:61; 53:37, 42

"Circulation of the Song" (Duncan) 41:127, 130; 55:298-99

Circulatory Systems: The Rivers Within (Silverstein and Silverstein) 17:451

"The Circus" (Gustafson) 36:220

"The Circus" (Koch) 8:323; 44:249, 251

"Circus" (MacNeice) 53:231

"The Circus" (Porter) 7:317; 15:429

The Circus (Chaplin) 16:187-89, 199-201, 204

Circus (MacLean) 13:363; 63:265

"The Circus Animals' Desertion" (Van Duyn) 116:401, 417, 426

"The Circus at Luxor" (Naipaul) 105:157

The Circus in the Attic, and Other Stories (Warren) 1:353

"Circus in Three Rings" (Plath) 17:362; 111:178

The Circus Is Coming (Circus Shoes) (Streatfeild) 21:398, 402, 404-06, 414, 416

A Circus of Needs (Dunn) 36:153-55

Circus Shoes (Streatfeild)
See *The Circus Is Coming*

"Cirque d'hiver" (Bishop) 9:92, 94-6

"Ciruelo silvestre" (Rodriguez) 10:440

Cistercian Contemplatives (Merton) 34:465

Cistercian Life (Merton) 34:465

"Cistercians in Germany" (Lowell) 4:302

The Cistern (Seferis) 5:384

"Citadel" (Jagger and Richard) 17:221

"The Citadel" (L'Heureux) 52:274

The Citadel (Cronin) 32:133-36, 138, 140

The Citadel of the Autarch (Wolfe) 25:477-79

La cité dans l'oeuf (Tremblay) 29:425-26; 102:372

La cité fertile (Chedid) 47:85-6

"Citez-m'en" (Damas) 84:160

"Cities" (Byrne) 26:97

"The Cities" (H. D.) 73:105

The Cities (Blackburn) 9:100; 43:61-3, 65

Cities Burning (Randall) 1:283

Cities in Bezique (Kennedy) 66:205, 208-09

Cities in Flight (Blish) 14:82

Cities of the Interior (Nin) 1:248; 4:376-77; 14:382-84, 386; 60:275-76, 278, 280

"The Cities of the Plain" (Van Duyn) 63:439; 116:404, 430

Cities of the Red Night: A Boys' Book (Burroughs) 22:84-6; 42:73, 80

"Cities, Plains and People" (Durrell) 27:97

"Citified" (Ammons) 57:53

Citizen Kane (Welles) 20:431-36, 438-54; 80:371-72, 374, 378, 382, 386, 391, 393, 396, 402-04, 406-09, 411, 413-17, 419-23

Citizen of the Galaxy (Heinlein) 3:225; 14:247; 26:161, 165-66, 173, 177

"CITIZEN RESPONSIBILITY (Hey! I'm Running for Office!)" (Giovanni) 117:204

"Citizen Ship" (Smith) 12:544

Citizen Tom Paine (Fast) 23:155

Citizens (Levin) 7:204

Citizens of Ohio (Edmonds) 35:146

La città delle donne (City of Women) (Fellini) 85:53, 60, 66, 70, 74, 76, 79-81

La città e la casa (The City and the House) (Ginzburg) 54:201-02, 205, 209-13; 70:280

Le città invisibili (Invisible Cities) (Calvino) 5:99-101; 8:126-27, 129, 131-32; 11:92; 22:89, 93; 33:98-101; 39:306-07, 309-10, 314-17; 73:41, 48, 51-2, 57-8

"City" (Fisher) 25:157-59, 161

"The City" (Wright) 53:426

City (Simak) 55:319-21

"City Afternoon" (Ashbery) 15:32

The City and the Dogs (Vargas Llosa)
See *La ciudad y los perros*

The City and the House (Ginzburg)
See *La città e la casa*

The City and the Island (Davison) 28:100

The City and the Pillar (Vidal) 2:449; 4:557-58; 6:550; 22:432-33; 33:406; 72:378, 387

The City and the Stars (Clarke) 4:105; 35:121-

22, 127
"City Boy" (Michaels)　25:315-16
The City Boy (Wouk)　38:445-47
The City Builder (Konrad)
　See A városalapító
A City for Lincoln (Tunis)　12:595, 598
"A City Garden in April" (Swenson)　61:400;
　106:326
The City in Tears (Seifert)
　See Město v slzách
The City in the Mist (Trow)　52:422-24
"The City Is in Total Darkness" (Shaw)　7:412
"City Life" (Barthelme)　13:55; 46:40; 115:63,
　70
City Life (Barthelme)　1:18; 3:43; 6:28-30;
　8:50, 52-3; 13:55; 46:35-6; 40; 59:247,
　249; 115:56, 60, 63, 68
"City Lights" (Reed)　21:317
City Lights (Chaplin)　16:188-89, 195, 198-
　201, 203-04
"The City Limits" (Ammons)　5:27; 9:27;
　25:43; 108:11
"The City Lost in the Snow" (Calvino)　33:100
"City of a Thousand Suns" (Delany)　14:144
"The City of Acknowledgement" (Shapcott)
　38:400-01
City of Angels (Gelbart)　61:147-50
City of Darkness (Bova)　45:68-9
"City of Fire" (Harjo)　83:283
City of Glass (Auster)　47:12-16
City of Illusions (Le Guin)　13:345, 348, 351;
　22:265; 45:218, 222
City of Night (Rechy)　7:356-57; 14:443-45;
　107:223-39, 243, 254, 256-58, 260
The City of Satisfactions (Hoffman)　6:243;
　13:287
"The City of Silence" (Matthews)　40:320
City of Spades (MacInnes)　4:314; 23:281-87
City of Splintered Gods (Faludy)
　See Karoton
City of the Chasch (Vance)　35:422, 424
"A City of the Dead, a City of the Living"
　(Gordimer)　33:185
"The City of the End of Things" (Thesen)
　56:417
"A City of the Living" (Gordimer)　33:185
"The City of the Living" (Stegner)　49:351;
　81:346
The City of the Living, and Other Stories
　(Stegner)　49:351; 81:346
The City of the Olesha Fruit (Dubie)　36:133-
　34, 140, 142
City of the Seven Serpents (O'Dell)　30:276
"The City of the Singing Flame" (Smith)
　43:420-22, 424-25
The City of Trembling Leaves (Clark)　28:77,
　80-3
City of Women (Fellini)
　See La città delle donne
A City on a Hill (Higgins)　7:157-58
"City on Fire" (Sondheim)　30:394, 398
City Primeval: High Noon in Detroit (Leonard)
　28:234, 236; 71:207, 219, 222, 224
"City Seasons" (Denby)　48:84
"City Song" (Gustafson)　36:216
City Streets (Mamoulian)　16:420-21, 423-24
City Sugar (Poliakoff)　38:375, 378, 380-83,
　385-86
A City Winter (O'Hara)　13:427
"City without a Name" (Milosz)　11:377;
　56:249
"City without Smoke" (Denby)　48:81, 84
"City without Walls" (Auden)　11:17; 14:27

City without Walls and Other Poems (Auden)
　2:25-6; 3:22, 24, 29; 4:33; 6:17-19; 14:27;
　43:18
"CITYCity-city" (Kerouac)　29:271
"A City's Death by Fire" (Walcott)　25:450;
　76:273, 280
"The City's Life" (Waddington)　28:437
"Ciudad ajena" ("The Foreign City")
　(Valenzuela)　104:355, 386
Ciudad Real (Castellanos)　66:60
La ciudad y los perros (The City and the Dogs;
　The Time of the Hero) (Vargas Llosa)
　3:493; 6:545-46; 10:498-500; 31:445,
　447, 449; 42:409; 85:352, 358, 364, 366,
　370-71, 375, 389
"Ciudades" (Otero)　11:427
Ciugrena (Arrabal)　18:19; 58:7-8
"Civil Disobedience" (Arendt)　98:12
"Civil Peace" (Achebe)　26:23; 75:15
"Civil Rights Poem" (Baraka)　5:48
Civil to Stangers (Pym)　111:284, 287
"Civil War" (O'Flaherty)　34:356
The Civil War: A Narrative (Foote)　75:232,
　240, 243-248, 251, 257-60, 262-63
Civil Wars (Brown)　32:68-70
Civil Wars (Jordan)　23:256-57; 114:152-53
"Civilian and Soldier" (Soyinka)　36:409
La civilisation du bossale (Conde)　92:100
"The Civilisation of Iron" (Kunene)　85:166
"Civilities of Lamplight" (Tomlinson)　45:392
"Civility a Bogey" (Avison)　97:72, 109
"Civilization" (Summers)　10:494
"Civilization and Its Discontents" (Ashbery)
　9:43; 41:40
"Civilization and Its Discontents" (Matthews)
　40:324
"Civilization and Its Discontents" (Roth)
　66:386
Clad in Light (Seifert)　34:257
Clad in Light (Seifert)
　See Svetlem odená
"Claiming Kin" (Voigt)　54:429-30
Clair de femme (Gary)　25:191
"Clair de terre" (Breton)　9:126
Claire de Lune (Linney)　51:263
Claire de terre (Breton)　54:17, 29-30, 32-3
Claire's Knee (Rohmer)
　See Le genou de Claire
"Clairvoyance" (Gerstler)　70:157
"The Clairvoyant" (Gass)　8:242; 15:255
"The Clam Digger" (Bowering)　47:29-30
The Clam Shell (Settle)　61:374, 385
The Clam Theater (Edson)　13:190
Clamor (Guillen)　11:262
"Clampdown" (Clash)　30:46
Le clan des Ostendais (Simenon)　18:482
The Clan of the Cave Bear (Auel)　31:22-3;
　107:3-5, 7-9, 11-16, 18,21-24
"Clancy" ("Nowadays Clancy Can't Even Sing")
　(Young)　17:568-69
"Clancy in the Tower of Babel" (Cheever)
　64:65
The Clang Birds (L'Heureux)　52:276-77, 279
Clans of the Alphane Moon (Dick)　30:123,
　125; 72:109, 121
"Clap Hands, Here Comes Charlie" (Bainbridge)
　62:37
"Clapp's Pond" (Oliver)　34:247; 98:256
"Clara" (O'Brien)　13:416
Clara (Valenzuela)　104:376-77, 382
Clara's Ole Man (Bullins)　5:82-3
"Clarendon Whatmough" (Adcock)　41:14
"Clarice Lispector: The Approach" (Cixous)

　See "Clarice Lispector: The Approach"
"Clarifications for Robert Jacoby" (Matthias)
　9:362
The Clarinet and Saxophone Book (Berger)
　12:40
"Clarisa" (Allende)　97:11
"Clarissa" (Morand)　41:295, 297, 308
Clark Gifford's Body (Fearing)　51:109-10, 121
Claro enigma (Andrade)　18:5
"Clartés terrestres" (Reverdy)　53:290
Clascon trombette e penacchi (About Face;
　Trumpets and Rasperrries) (Fo)　32:176;
　109:109-11, 119-20, 136-37, 139, 143,
　146
The Clash (Clash)　30:43-6
Clash by Night (Lang)　20:207
Clash by Night (Odets)　2:320; 28:329-30,
　332-33; 98:197-99, 229, 237, 241, 244
"Clash City Rockers" (Clash)　30:43-4
"Class" (Bukowski)　41:74; 108:85-6
"Class" (Tomlinson)　6:535
Class: A Guide through the American Class
　System (Caste Marks: Style and Status in
　the U.S.A.) (Fussell)　74:127-28, 137, 142,
　146-47
The Class of '49 (Carpenter)　41:107-08
"Class of 1949" (Levine)　54:298-99
Class Pictures (Sachs)　35:334
"The Class Reunion" (Amichai)　116:107
"Classic" (Ammons)　2:14
"Classic Ballroom Dances" (Simic)　49:338
Classic Ballroom Dances (Simic)　22:381, 383,
　49:341; 68:369
Classic, Romantic, and Modern (Barzun)
　See Romanticism and the Modern Ego
"A Classic Waits for Me" (White)　10:528
"Classical Portrait" (Gustafson)　36:220
Classics and Commercials: A Literary Chronicle
　of the Forties (Wilson)　3:538; 8:550;
　24:479, 481, 487
"The Classics and the Man of Letters" (Eliot)
　41:155
Classics Revisited (Rexroth)　22:346; 49:286;
　112:387
"Classified" (Ferber)　93:153
"Classroom Windmills" (Vizenor)　103:288
"Claude Emerson, Reporter" (O'Hara)　42:319
"Claude Gauvreau" (Ferron)　94:126
"Claude Glass" (Ondaatje)　51:313
"The Claude Glass" (Szirtes)　46:393-94
"Claudius' Diary" (Shiga)
　See "Kurodiasu no nikki"
"Claudius' Journal" (Shiga)
　See "Kurodiasu no nikki"
Claudius the God and His Wife Messalina
　(Graves)　1:128; 6:211; 39:322-23, 325;
　45:173
"Claud's Dog" (Dahl)　79:178
"Claudy" (Simmons)　43:411
"Claus Von Stauffenberg" (Gunn)　18:201;
　32:208
Claw (Barker)　37:32, 34-5, 37
The Claw of the Conciliator (Wolfe)　25:474-
　78
The Clay and the Wheel (Vesaas)
　See Leiret og hjulet
"Clay Bertrand Is Alive and in Camelot"
　(Cassity)　42:95
Clay's Ark (Butler)　38:66
Clea (Durrell)　1:87; 4:144; 8:190-92; 13:185-
　86, 188
Clea and Zeus Divorce (Prager)　56:278-81
"A Clean Quiet House" (Fuchs)　22:157

"A Clean, Well-Lighted Place" (Hemingway) 6:231; 8:285; 10:268, 270; 13:272, 279; 30:192; 34:478; 41:198; 61:203

Cleaned Out (Ernaux)
See *Les armoires vides*

"Cleaning the Well" (Chappell)   78:96

"Cleanup Time" (Lennon)   35:272-74

Clear and Present Danger (Clancy)   112:53-6, 65, 77, 84, 90

"Clear Autumn" (Rexroth)   49:283

A Clear Introduction to Later History (Haavikko)
See *Selvä johdatus myöhempään historiaan*

Clear Light of Day (Desai)   19:134-35; 37:70-2; 97:139-40, 14549, 166, 168, 178-80

"Clear Morning" (Gluck)   81:167, 170, 173

"Clear Night" (Paz)
See "Noche en claro"

Clear Pictures: First Loves, First Guides (Price)   63:337-38

"Clearances" (Heaney)   74:160-62, 174-75, 191, 194

"The Clearest Day" (Cook-Lynn)   93:124

"Clearfield" (Freeman)   55:57-8

"The Clearing" (Baraka)   14:42

"The Clearing" (Slavitt)   14:491

"The Clearing" (Thomas)   31:430

Clearing (Berry)   27:35-6

Clearing in the Sky and Other Stories (Stuart)   34:373, 376

"Clearing the Air" (Willard)   37:463

"Clearness" (Wilbur)   6:570; 9:569

"Les clefs de la mort" ("The Keys of Death") (Green)   77:264-66

"The Cleggan Disaster" (Murphy)   41:311-12, 314, 316

Clem Anderson (Cassill)   4:95; 23:102-04

"Clem Maverick" (Vliet)   22:441

Clemmons (Masters)   48:222-24

"Clenched Fist" (Ihimaera)   46:200

The Clenched Fist (Lagerkvist)
See *Den knutna näven*

Cléo de 5 à 7 (*Cleo from Five to Seven*) (Varda)   16:554, 557-59

Cleo from Five to Seven (Varda)
See *Cléo de 5 à 7*

"Cleopatra" (Akhmatova)   64:16

"Clepsydra" (Ashbery)   2:19; 41:40-1; 77:60-1

"The Cleric" (Heaney)   74:169

The Clerk's Journal: Being the Diary of a Queer Man (Aiken)   52:21-2

"The Cleveland Wrecking Yard" (Brautigan)   12:59, 63-4

"The Clever One" (Gellhorn)   60:187

Clever Soldiers (Poliakoff)   38:375-77, 380, 385

The Clewiston Test (Wilhelm)   7:538

"A Client" (Rao)   56:291, 293

The Client (Grisham)   84:195-99

"The Cliff" (Baxter)   78:17

"Cliff and Wave" (Graves)   45:169

The Cliff of Time (Abe)   81:291

"Cliffdwellers" (Gilliatt)   53:146

Cliffs of Fall and Other Stories (Hazzard)   18:213, 215-18

"The Cliff-Temple" (H. D.)   73:104, 139

The Climate of Eden (Hart)   66:178-79, 182, 189-90

"The Climate of Insomnia" (Shaw)   7:412

"Climbers" (Wild)   14:581

"Climbing Alone" (Wagoner)   15:560

The Climbing Frame (Hocking)   13:285

Climbing into the Roots (Saner)   9:468-69

"Climbing Katahdin" (Hoffman)   6:243

"Climbing Milestone Mountain" (Rexroth)   112:383

"Climbing the Chagrin River" (Oliver)   34:249

"Climbing the Streets of Worcester, Mass." (Harjo)   83:281-82

"Climbing the Tower" (Crews)   49:68, 75

"Climbing This Hill Again" (Stern)   40:406

"Clinamen; or, Poetic Misprision" (Bloom)   24:77

Clinging to the Wreckage: A Part of Life (Mortimer)   28:288-89; 43:308

A Clinical Case (Buzzati)
See *Un caso clinico*

"Clio" (Barthelme)   117:5

Clio and the Doctors: Psycho-History, Quanto-History, and History (Barzun)   51:43, 45-6

Clive Barker's Books of Blood, Vols. I-III (Barker)   52:51-4, 56-7

Clive Barker's Books of Blood, Vols. IV-VI (Barker)   52:52-3, 56-7

"C.L.M." (Masefield)   47:233

Cloak and Dagger (Lang)   20:207, 216

"Cloak of Aesir" (Campbell)   32:75-6, 78, 80

Cloak of Darkness (MacInnes)   27:284-85

A Cloak of Light (Morris)   37:316-17

"Clochard" (Szymborska)   99:200

"Un clochard m'a demandé dix sous'" (Damas)   84:177

"Un clochard m'a demandé dix sous" (Damas)   84:177

Les cloches de bâle (*The Bells of Basel*) (Aragon)   3:13; 22:34, 37

Les cloches sur le coeur (Char)   11:113

"The Clock" (Abse)   29:13

"The Clock" (Beer)   58:38

Clock Analect (Lezama Lima)
See *Analecta del reloj*

"Clock and Heart" (Wright)   53:426

"A Clock in the Square" (Rich)   36:365

"Clock Invention" (Goldbarth)   38:200

The Clock Winder (Tyler)   11:552; 28:431; 103:237-38, 243-44, 259, 263-65, 267-69, 273

"A Clock with No Hands" (Nemerov)   36:303

Clock without Hands (McCullers)   1:209-10; 4:346; 10:335, 338; 12:418-21, 424-25, 427, 430; 48:232, 234; 100:251-52, 255-56

Clockers (Lee)   105:120-21, 127, 129

The Clocks (Christie)   12:122; 48:74-5

The Clocks (Hildesheimer)
See *Die Uhren*

A Clockwork Orange (Burgess)   2:85-7; 4:80-1, 84-5; 5:87-8, 90-1; 8:112; 10:86-8, 90; 13:124-128; 15:104, 106-07; 22:69-70, 74, 76-8; 40:114-17, 125; 62:127-32, 138; 81:300-02, 305-06, 310; 94:23-88

A Clockwork Orange (Kubrick)   16:383-84, 386, 388-91

A Clockwork Orange 2004 (Burgess)   94:81

A Clockwork Orange: A Play with Music (Burgess)   94:80, 82-85

The Clockwork Testament; or, Enderby's End (Burgess)   4:84; 5:88-91; 8:112-13; 40:115, 122-23; 62:125, 130, 132; 94:57, 65, 69-70, 84

"The Cloister of the Lilies" (Wiebe)   14:575

"Cloistered" (Heaney)   74:193

"Clone" (Cortazar)   33:126-30

The Cloning (Wild)   14:581

Clonk Clonk (Golding)   2:169; 17:177; 81:325

Clope au dossier (Pinget)   13:442; 37:363

Close Encounters of the Third Kind (Spielberg)   20:360-62, 364-67

Close Harmony (Rice)   7:360

"Close Listening" (Birkerts)   116:164, 167

Close of Play (Gray)   14:215; 36:205, 207

Close of Play (Raven)   14:440, 443

Close Quarters (Golding)   81:317-18, 320, 324-26

Close Quarters (Heinemann)   50:187, 191

Close Relations (Isaacs)   32:254-55

Close Sesame (Farah)   53:134-35, 138-39

Close the Sky, Ten by Ten (Mahapatra)   33:281, 284

"Close to the Borderline" (Joel)   26:220

Close to the Sun Again (Callaghan)   41:88-90, 94-5

Closed All Night (Morand)
See *Fermé la nuit*

The Closed Chaplet (Riding)   3:432

"The Closed Door" (Donoso)
See "La puerta cerrada"

The Closed Garden (Green)   77:262, 264, 270

The Closed Garden (Green)   77:262, 264, 270

The Closed Harbour (Hanley)   3:220

Closely Observed Trains (Hrabal)
See *Ostre sledované vlaky*

Closely Watched Trains (Hrabal)
See *Ostre sledované vlaky*

The Closest of Strangers: Liberalism and the Politics of Race in New York (Sleeper)   70:374

"Closets" (Shange)   25:399

"Close-Up" (Ammons)   108:21

Close-Up (Deighton)   46:126-27

"Closing"   75:78

"The Closing Down of Summmer" (MacLeod)   56:196-200

"Closing in New Haven" (Klappert)   57:259

The Closing of the American Mind: How Higher Education Has Failed Democracy and Impoverished Souls of Today's Students (Bloom)   70:364, 400

"Closing the Time-Lid" (Card)   47:67

"Cloteel" (Brown)   59:265

"Clothe the Naked" (Parker)   15:415; 68:327, 334-35, 340

Clothed in Light (Seifert)
See *Svetlem odená*

"Clothes" (Szymborska)   99:196

Clothes for a Summer Hotel: A Ghost Play (Williams)   19:473; 45:447, 449, 455

"Clothes Make the Man" (Matheson)   37:246

"The Clothes Pit" (Dunn)   40:166

"Clotheslines" (Jones)   10:285

"Clothespin" (Dybek)   114:61

"La clôture" (Perec)   56:254

La clôture et autres poémes (Perec)   56:254-55

"The Cloud" (Elytis)   49:110

"The Cloud" (Fowles)   6:187-89; 15:232; 87:157, 163

"The Cloud" (Walcott)   14:549

The Cloud Catchers (Holden)   18:258

Cloud Chamber (Dorris)   109:296-300, 311-13

The Cloud Forest; A Chronicle of the South American Wilderness (Matthiessen)   11:360; 32:286, 290

Cloud Handkerchief (Tzara)
See *Mouchoir de nuages*

Cloud Nine (Churchill)   31:84-9; 55:122

A Cloud on Sand (De Ferrari) 65:42-6
"The Cloud Parade" (Jensen) 37:187, 190
Cloud, Stone, Sun, and Vine (Sarton) 91:241
"The Cloud-Gatherer" (Elytis) 49:110
"Clouds" (Ashbery) 77:54
"Clouds" (Jacobsen) 48:198
"The Clouds" (Williams) 9:572; 42:450
The Clouds (Cernuda)
  See *Las nubes*
Clouds (Frayn) 31:191
Clouds (Mitchell) 12:435-36
"The Clouds Go Soft" (O'Hara) 13:430
The Clouds over Metapontion (Johnson)
  See *Molnen över Metapontion*
"Cloudy" (Simon) 17:459
The Cloven Viscount (Calvino)
  See *Il visconte dimezzato*
"Clown" (Michaux) 8:391
"The Clown" (Tanizaki) 28:414
The Clown (Boell)
  See *Ansichten eines Clowns*
The Clown (Corcoran) 17:74-5 ·
I clowns (*The Clowns*) (Fellini) 16:284-86,
  299; 85:55, 59, 64-6, 69, 74, 76, 78-81
The Clowns (Fellini)
  See *I clowns*
Clown's Houses (Sitwell) 67:312
Les clowns lyriques (Gary) 25:190
The Clowns of God (West) 33:432-33
The Club (Players) (Williamson) 56:435, 437,
  442-43
"Club Dread" (Ritter) 52:355
"Clubland" (Costello) 21:75
"Clues" (Rukeyser) 15:459
Clues of the Caribbees (Stribling) 23:445
Clunie (Peck) 17:343
Cluster (Anthony) 35:37
"Clusters Traveling Out" (Graham) 29:196
Clutch of Constables (Marsh) 53:247, 250-51,
  253
A Clyack-Sheaf (MacDiarmid) 4:313
"Clywedog" (Clarke) 61:80
"C-Minor" (Transtroemer)
  See "C-dur"
"Coach" (Robison) 42:342; 98:306
"Coal" (Lorde) 71:232
Coal (Lorde) 18:309; 71:235, 248, 251-52,
  262
"Coal and Fire" (MacNeice) 10:324; 53:233
"Coal Train" (Parini) 54:362
"The Coalman" (Williams) 42:440
The Coast of Chicago (Dybek) 114:68, 70, 72-
  3, 77, 79-81
The Coast of Illyria (Parker) 68:340-41
"Coast of Texas" (Sorrentino) 40:386
"Coast of Trees" (Ammons) 108:56
A Coast of Trees (Ammons) 25:45; 57:51, 59;
  108:24, 55
Coastal Disturbances (Howe) 48:176-79
"The Coast-Range Christ" (Jeffers) 11:309
"The Coasts of Cerigo" (Hope) 3:250; 51:223
The Coat (Fugard) 80:66
"The Coat of Arms" (Bell) 31:46
A Coat of Varnish (Snow) 19:427-30
"The Coats" (Gallagher) 63:124
"Cobbler" (Carroll) 38:103
"The Cobbler and the Machine" (Anand) 23:18
Cobra (Sarduy) 6:485-87; 97:367-69, 372-
  78, 380-81, 393-95, 397, 399-403, 406,
  409-17
"Cobra amor" (Aleixandre) 9:14
The Cobweb (Gibson) 23:173
"Cocaine" (Browne) 21:40

Cochise (Wild) 14:580-81
"Cock Crow" (Gordon) 83:250, 259
Cock Pit (Cozzens) 11:131; 92:196-98
Cock Robin (Rice) 49:301
Cock Robin; or, A Fight for Male Survival
  (Billington) 43:54
Cock-a-Doodle Dandy (O'Casey) 5:318, 320;
  9:409, 411; 11:408-09; 15:404-05;
  88:257-58, 260, 262, 269-71
"Cockadoodledoo" (Singer) 9:487
"The Cockatoos" (White) 7:533
The Cockatoos (White) 4:587; 5:485-87;
  7:533; 65:275
"Cockfight" (Beagle) 104:5
"Cockles and Mussels" (Hill) 113:291
Cockpit (Kosinski) 6:285; 10:305-07, 309;
  15:313-14, 316-17; 53:216-17, 220-23,
  226-27; 70:298, 304, 306
"Cocks" (Hirsch) 31:214, 216
*Cocksfoot, Crested Dog's Tail, Sweet Vernal
  Grass* (Norris) 14:388
Cocksure (Richler) 5:375-76, 378; 13:481,
  484, 486; 18:451-52, 455; 46:347-50;
  70:232
The Cocktail Hour (Gurney) 54:221-23
"Cocktail Party" (Warren) 39:256, 273
The Cocktail Party (Eliot) 2:126, 129; 3:140;
  6:164, 167; 9:186; 13:194-95; 15:208-09;
  24:172; 34:394; 41:143-46; 55:346, 352-
  53, 360, 367
"Cocktails at Doney's" (Trevor) 71:340
"Cocktails at the Mausoleum" (Musgrave)
  54:341
"The Cocky Walkers" (Peake) 54:372
The Cocoanuts (Kaufman) 38:265
"Cocu et content" (Damas) 84:179
Le cocu magnifique (*The Magnanimous Cuck-
  old; The Magnificent Cuckold*)
  (Crommelynck) 75:150-53, 156, 159,
  161-63, 168-69
Cocuyo (Sarduy) 97:417
"Coda" (Allen) 84:37
"Coda" (Bernard) 59:46
"Coda" (Robbe-Grillet) 8:454; 14:462
"coda for innocent persons" (Moure) 88:229
"Coda: The Faustian Pact" (Birkerts) 116:167
"The Code" (Frost) 26:111-12
"Code Book Lost" (Warren) 13:582; 39:270
Code Name Valkyrie (Forman) 21:119-20
"Codes" (Howard) 47:169
"Codex" (Transtroemer) 65:237
"Codger" (Coles) 46:108
Il codice di Perela (Palazzeschi) 11:432
"Codicil" (Walcott) 42:418; 67:357, 360
"Cod'ine" (Sainte-Marie) 17:430
"Coed Anghred" (Mathias) 45:235
Coeur à cuir (Audiberti) 38:30
Le coeur des autres (Marcel) 15:363
"Le coeur écartelé" (Reverdy) 53:281
"Le coeur, l'eau non troublée" (Bonnefoy)
  15:74
"Coffee" (Brautigan) 12:65
"Coffee" (Moure) 88:219
"Coffee with Oliver" (Trevor) 71:342, 349
The Coffer Dams (Markandaya) 38:324
A Coffin for Dimitrios (Ambler)
  See *The Mask of Dimitrios*
"Cofiant" (Clarke) 61:84
Cogan's Trade (Higgins) 4:224-25; 7:158
La cognizione del dolore (Gadda) 11:209, 211,
  213-15
"Cohen on the Telephone" (Hollander) 8:299
"Cohorts" (Gold) 42:198

Coils (Eshleman) 7:98-9
"A Coin for the Ferryman" (MacEwen) 55:169
A Coin in Nine Hands (Yourcenar)
  See *Denier du rêve*
Coins and Coffins (Wakoski) 7:507; 40:454,
  457
"Coisas de cabeceira, Recife" ("Reveries on a
  pillow, Recife") (Cabral de Melo Neto)
  76:168
"Coisas de cabeceira, Sevilha" ("Reveries on a
  Pillow, Seville") (Cabral de Melo Neto)
  76:168
"The Cokboy" (Rothenberg) 57:374
Cola de lagartija (*The Lizard's Tail*) (Valenzuela)
  31:438-39; 104:364-65, 380, 382, 388,
  390, 392
"A Cold and Married War" (Piercy) 27:374
Cold Chills (Bloch) 33:84
The Cold Country and Other Plays for Radio
  (Hill) 113:283-84, 295
"Cold Didn't Keep the Stuff" (Ammons) 57:57
Cold Fire (Koontz) 78:218
Cold Gradations (Middleton) 38:331, 333
The Cold Green Element (Layton) 15:318
"Cold Ground Was My Bed Last Night"
  (Garrett) 51:147
Cold Ground Was My Bed Last Night (Garrett)
  51:146-47
Cold Hand in Mine: Strange Stories (Aickman)
  57:3
Cold Heaven (Moore) 32:311-14; 90:259-60,
  263, 265, 268, 273-75, 289-90, 292-3
"Cold Journey" (Haines) 58:220
Cold Lazarus (Potter) 86:343-46, 348
Cold Morning Sky (Zaturenska) 11:579
Cold Mountain (Frazier) 109:48-51
Cold Nights (Pa Chin) 18:373, 375
Cold on the Shoulder (Lightfoot) 26:280-81
"Cold Poem" (Oliver) 98:266, 273
"Cold Print" (Campbell) 42:83-5, 92
Cold Print (Campbell) 42:91-2
"Cold Rains" (Salinas) 90:322-23
A Cold Red Sunrise (Kaminsky) 59:170-72
"Cold Rheum" (Ammons) 108:61
"Cold Spell" (Scannell) 49:329-30
"A Cold Spring" (Bishop) 4:65; 13:91; 32:38,
  41
"The Cold Spring" (Levertov) 28:239
Cold Spring Harbor (Joel) 26:217
"Cold Turkey" (Lennon) 35:265, 270-71
The Cold War and the Income Tax (Wilson)
  24:487
"The Cold Wind and the Warm" (Bradbury)
  42:34
The Cold Wind and the Warm (Behrman) 40:84
"Cold Wind in August" (Morrison) 21:237
"Cold-Blooded" (Atwood) 84:105
"The Cold-Blooded Romantics" (Huxley) 8:305
"The Colder the Air" (Bishop) 32:43
"Coldness" (Montague) 46:272
"The Coldness" (Silkin) 43:399-400
"Coldwater Morning" (Diamond) 30:111
"Coleraine, 1977" (Simmons) 43:413-14
"Coleridge Crossing the Plain of Jars, 1833"
  (Dubie) 36:135, 139
Coleridge on the Imagination (Richards)
  24:387, 389, 393-94, 400-01
Colibrí (Sarduy) 97:404-07, 409-10
Collaborators (Kauffman) 42:252-53
"Collage" (Brooks) 4:78
Collages (Nin) 4:378; 14:381, 383; 60:281
Colleagues (*Kollegi*) (Aksyonov) 101:6, 9,
  13-15, 17, 29

Collect Your Hand Baggage (Mortimer) 28:283-86

Collected and New Poems, 1924-1963 (Van Doren) 6:541-42

The Collected Books of Jack Spicer (Spicer) 8:497; 18:506; 72:345, 348, 352

Collected Earlier Poems (Williams) 42:450, 452

Collected Earlier Poems 1940 to 1960 (Levertov) 28:241-42; 66:251

Collected Early Poems of Ezra Pound (Pound) 10:407

Collected Essays (Greene) 6:217

Collected Essays (Huxley) 35:242

Collected Essays (Schwartz) 87:335

The Collected Essays and Occasional Writings of Katherine Anne Porter (Porter) 1:274; 101:223-24, 237

The Collected Essays of J.V. Cunningham (Cunningham) 31:103, 105

The Collected Essays of Leslie Fiedler (Fiedler) 4:161-63

The Collected Essays of Ralph Ellison (Ellison) 114:122-23, 131

The Collected Essays of Robert Creeley (Creeley) 78:160

The Collected Ewart, 1933-1980 (Ewart) 46:147, 149-52

The Collected Greed, Parts 1-13 (Wakoski) 40:457

Collected Impressions (Bowen) 3:84

Collected Later Poems (Clarke) 6:110-11; 9:167

Collected Later Poems (Williams) 42:450, 455-56

The Collected Letters of a Nobody (Waterhouse) 47:424

The Collected Longer Poems of Kenneth Rexroth (Rexroth) 2:371; 6:451; 22:347-48; 112:364, 369, 386, 395

"Collected Novels" (Hollander) 14:264

Collected Plays (Maugham) 67:225

Collected Plays (Soyinka) 44:286

The Collected Plays of Gwen Pharis Ringwood (Ringwood) 48:338-39

Collected Poems (Aiken) 3:5; 52:19, 21

Collected Poems (Aldington) 49:6-9, 14-15

The Collected Poems (Ammons) 108:24, 28, 55

Collected Poems (Auden) 6:24; 9:56-8; 11:21; 14:33-4; 43:15-17, 19, 26

Collected Poems (Barker) 48:23-4

Collected Poems (Barnard) 48:25-8

Collected Poems (Beecher) 6:49

Collected Poems (Beer) 58:38

Collected Poems (Betjeman) 6:65-6, 68; 34:305; 43:34-5, 41, 43-4, 46

The Collected Poems (Bishop) 4:66; 9:93

Collected Poems (Boyle) 19:64; 58:69

Collected Poems (Brown) 63:57

Collected Poems (Bunting) 39:298; 47:50-1, 53, 55

Collected Poems (Clarke) 6:110-12; 9:167

Collected Poems (Cummings) 3:116; 12:144; 15:162; 68:29, 35, 39, 49

Collected Poems (Daryush) 19:120-22

Collected Poems (Denby) 48:82-4

Collected Poems (Dugan) 2:121; 6:144

Collected Poems (Eberhart) 3:135; 19:143

Collected Poems (Eich)
   See *Ausgewählte Gedichte*

Collected Poems (Empson) 8:202; 34:335-36

Collected Poems (Enright) 31:153-55

Collected Poems (Faludy) 42:141

Collected Poems (Frost) 10:198; 44:457

Collected Poems (Gascoyne) 45:149-52, 154

Collected Poems (Goodman) 4:197; 7:128

Collected Poems (Grass)
   See *Gesammelte Gedichte*

Collected Poems (Haavikko) 34:174

Collected Poems (Hayden)
   See *Robert Hayden: Collected Poems*

Collected Poems (Hill) 45:189-90

Collected Poems (Jarrell) 6:261; 9:295

Collected Poems (Jennings) 5:197; 14:292

Collected Poems (Kavanagh) 22:235, 240

Collected Poems (Koch) 44:248

Collected Poems (Larkin) 64:256-87

Collected Poems (Layton) 15:321

Collected Poems (MacDiarmid) 2:253; 4:309, 313; 11:334; 63:244, 246, 256

Collected Poems (Milosz)
   See *Czeslaw Milosz: The Collected Poems, 1931-1987*

Collected Poems (Moore) 8:398; 19:339, 342; 47:264-65

Collected Poems (Neihardt) 32:330-31

Collected Poems (Oppen) 7:285-86; 13:434; 34:358-59

Collected Poems (Pasternak) 63:289-90

The Collected Poems (Patchen) 18:394

The Collected Poems (Plath) 51:339-45, 350-53

Collected Poems (Plomer) 8:446-47

Collected Poems (Popa) 19:375

Collected Poems (Porter) 33:320-26

Collected Poems (Pound) 7:335

Collected Poems (Prince) 22:339

Collected Poems (Read) 4:440

Collected Poems (Riding) 7:373, 375

Collected Poems (Rodgers) 7:377-78

Collected Poems (Sandburg) 15:468

Collected Poems (Sarton) 91:243

Collected Poems (Sitwell) 67:317, 355

Collected Poems (Smith) 15:513-15

Collected Poems (Spender) 91:264

Collected Poems (Tomlinson) 45:404-05

Collected Poems (Transtroemer) 65:226

Collected Poems (Van Doren) 6:542

Collected Poems (Winters) 32:467-69

Collected Poems (Wright) 3:541-42; 5:520; 10:542, 544; 28:463, 465, 471-72

Collected Poems (Young) 5:526

Collected Poems (Zaturenska) 6:585; 11:579-80

Collected Poems, 1938 (Graves) 45:163, 165

Collected Poems, 1954 (Day Lewis) 6:128

Collected Poems, 1955 (Graves) 1:127, 127; 2:174; 6:212

Collected Poems, 1959 (Graves) 39:328; 45:163

Collected Poems, 1965 (Graves) 45:166

Collected Poems, 1968 (Fisher) 25:157-59

Collected Poems, 1919-62 (Deutsch) 18:119-20

Collected Poems, 1930-83 (Miles) 34:243-45; 39:352-54

Collected Poems, 1908-1956 (Sassoon) 36:388, 391

Collected Poems, 1909-1935 (Eliot) 15:206, 211-12; 41:155

Collected Poems, 1917-1952 (MacLeish) 68:288-89, 293

Collected Poems, 1919-1976 (Tate) 11:526-27; 14:530

Collected Poems, 1923-1953 (Bogan) 39:390; 46:82-3, 85, 87; 93:87

Collected Poems, 1924-1962 (Grigson) 7:135; 39:330

Collected Poems, 1928-1953 (Spender) 5:401; 41:418, 420, 427-29; 91:264

Collected Poems, 1930-1955 (Barker) 48:17

Collected Poems, 1930-1960 (Eberhart) 56:84, 87-8

Collected Poems, 1930-1965 (Barker) 8:46

Collected Poems, 1930-1965 (Hope) 3:250; 51:218

Collected Poems, 1930-1973 (Sarton) 4:472; 14:480; 49:314

Collected Poems, 1930-1976 (Eberhart) 11:178

Collected Poems (1930-1993) (Sarton) 91:253

Collected Poems, 1931-1974 (Durrell) 27:96-7

Collected Poems, 1935-1980 (Raine) 45:340-41

Collected Poems, 1936-1960 (Fuller) 4:177; 28:149-51, 158-59

Collected Poems, 1936-1970 (McAuley) 45:250, 252-53

Collected Poems, 1937-1971 (Berryman) 62:71, 75

Collected Poems, 1940-1978 (Shapiro) 15:477-79

Collected Poems, 1942-1970 (Wright) 53:426, 428-29, 432

Collected Poems, 1942-1977 (Graham) 29:197-99

Collected Poems, 1944-1979 (Amis) 40:39-40, 44

Collected Poems, 1947-1980 (Ginsberg) 36:193-99; 109:331, 338, 352, 356, 358, 364

Collected Poems, 1948-1976 (Abse) 29:17-19

Collected Poems, 1948-1984 (Walcott) 42:418-21, 423; 67:349, 352, 354, 357-58; 76:296

Collected Poems, 1950-1970 (Davie) 5:114-16; 8:166; 10:123, 125; 31:117

Collected Poems, 1951-1971 (Ammons) 2:13-14; 3:10-11; 5:28-9, 31; 8:14, 17, 19; 9:27; 25:42-4, 48; 57:49, 58; 108:5-6, 8-9, 24, 27

Collected Poems, 1951-1975 (Causley) 7:41-2

Collected Poems, 1955-1975 (Levi) 41:246-48

The Collected Poems, 1956-1974 (Dorn) 10:156-57; 18:129

Collected Poems, 1957-1982 (Berry) 46:72-3

Collected Poems, 1958-1970 (MacBeth) 2:251-52; 5:263

Collected Poems, 1963-1980 (Grigson) 39:330

Collected Poems, 1970-1983 (Davie) 31:123-24

Collected Poems and Epigrams (Cunningham) 3:122; 31:102

Collected Poems and Selected Translations (Sisson) 8:491

The Collected Poems of Al Purdy (Purdy) 50:235, 243-48

The Collected Poems of A.M. Klein (Klein) 19:260

The Collected Poems of Carl Rakosi (Rakosi) 47:347-48

The Collected Poems of E. J. Pratt (Pratt) 19:376

The Collected Poems of Earle Birney (Birney)

11:49, 51

The Collected Poems of Frank O'Hara (O'Hara)   **2**:322-23; **5**:323, 325; **13**:430; **78**:339

The Collected Poems of George Garrett (Garrett)   **51**:151

Collected Poems of H. D. (H. D.)   **8**:257; **14**:223; **31**:201, 208; **73**:109, 115, 117, 119

The Collected Poems of Howard Nemerov (Nemerov)   **36**:300-04

The Collected Poems of Kathleen Raine (Raine)   **45**:332-34, 336-37, 340-41

Collected Poems of Kenneth Fearing (Fearing)   **51**:108-09, 111

The Collected Poems of Langston Hughes (Hughes)   **108**:334-35

The Collected Poems of Louis MacNeice (MacNeice)   **1**:186; **4**:316; **53**:238, 243-44

Collected Poems of Lucio Piccolo (Piccolo)   **13**:440-41

The Collected Poems of Muriel Rukeyser (Rukeyser)   **15**:456-58, 460

The Collected Poems of Octavio Paz, 1957-1987 (Paz)   **51**:332, 334, 336; **65**:195-201

Collected Poems of Padraic Colum (Colum)   **28**:90

The Collected Poems of Paul Blackburn (Blackburn)   **43**:68-9

The Collected Poems of Robert Creeley, 1945-1975 (Creeley)   **36**:116-17, 119-21; **78**:135

The Collected Poems of Sterling A. Brown (Brown)   **23**:100-01; **59**:265-69

The Collected Poems of Stevie Smith (Smith)   **8**:491; **25**:417-18, 422

The Collected Poems of Theodore Roethke (Roethke)   **1**:291; **3**:433; **8**:457, 460; **101**:271, 273

The Collected Poems of Thomas Merton (Merton)   **11**:374; **83**:384-85, 397

Collected Poems: The Two Seasons (Livesay)   **4**:294; **79**:340-41

Collected Poetry (Dudek)   **11**:160; **19**:138

The Collected Poetry of Aldous Huxley (Huxley)   **5**:192

The Collected Poetry of W. H. Auden, 1945 (Auden)   **2**:23; **11**:20

The Collected Prose (Bishop)   **32**:40, 43-4

Collected Prose (Celan)   **53**:82-3

Collected Prose (Hayden)   **37**:159

The Collected Prose of Robert Creeley (Creeley)   **36**:122

Collected Short Stories (Amis)   **40**:43-5

The Collected Short Stories (Dahl)   **79**:183

Collected Short Stories (Forster)   **45**:132

Collected Short Stories (Huxley)   **35**:242

The Collected Short Stories of Julia Peterkin (Peterkin)   **31**:306-07

The Collected Short Stories, Volume 2 (Coward)   **51**:74

Collected Shorter Poems (Auden)   **6**:21

Collected Shorter Poems, 1930-1944 (Auden)   **43**:26

Collected Shorter Poems, 1946-1991 (Carruth)   **84**:134, 136

The Collected Shorter Poems of Kenneth Rexroth (Rexroth)   **2**:369; **22**:347; **49**:277, 280; **112**:364-65, 369, 376, 386, 395, 398

The Collected Stories (Boyle)   **90**:61

Collected Stories (Garcia Marquez)   **47**:145-48, 150-51

Collected Stories (Greene)   **3**:211-13

Collected Stories (Malamud)
  See *The Stories of Bernard Malamud*

Collected Stories (Pritchett)   **41**:331-33, 335

Collected Stories (Sargeson)   **31**:364-65

The Collected Stories (Trevor)   **116**:362-63, 371, 394

Collected Stories (Williams)   **45**:452-56

Collected Stories: 1939-1976 (Bowles)   **19**:60-1

The Collected Stories of Caroline Gordon (Gordon)   **29**:187-90

The Collected Stories of Chester Himes (Himes)   **108**:227-28, 234-35, 241

The Collected Stories of Elizabeth Bowen (Bowen)   **22**:64-5, 67-8

The Collected Stories of Eudora Welty (Welty)   **22**:458; **105**:297-300

The Collected Stories of Frank Tuohy (Tuohy)   **37**:432-33

The Collected Stories of Hortense Calisher (Calisher)   **8**:124-25

The Collected Stories of Isaac Bashevis Singer (Singer)   **38**:407-10; **69**:306

The Collected Stories of Jean Stafford (Stafford)   **4**:517; **19**:430-31; **68**:422, 424, 430, 433-35, 449

Collected Stories of John O'Hara (O'Hara)   **42**:325-27

The Collected Stories of Katherine Anne Porter (Porter)   **3**:393

The Collected Stories of Noël Coward (Coward)   **29**:141; **51**:74

The Collected Stories of Peter Taylor (Taylor)   **4**:542; **18**:523-24, 526; **37**:411-13; **44**:305; **71**:299, 308

The Collected Stories Of Seán O'Faoláin (O'Faolain)   **70**:320-21

The Collected Stories of Seán O'Faoláin, Volume 2 (O'Faolain)   **32**:340

The Collected Stories of Seán O'Faoláin, Volume 3 (O'Faolain)   **32**:341-44

Collected Stories of Wallace Stegner (Stegner)   **81**:339, 346-47

Collected Stories of William Faulkner (Faulkner)   **6**:179-80; **18**:148-49

The Collected Stories of William Goyen (Goyen)   **8**:250; **14**:211, 213-14; **40**:215

The Collected Stories of William Humphrey (Humphrey)   **45**:203-04

The Collected Stories of Wolfgang Hildesheimer (Hildesheimer)   **49**:179-80

The Collected Tales of E. M. Forster (Forster)   **22**:129

Collected Verse (Smith)   **15**:515

Collected Verse Translations (Gascoyne)   **45**:153

Collected Works (Pa Chin)   **18**:373

Collected Works (Tanizaki)   **28**:421

The Collected Works of Billy the Kid (Nichol)   **18**:366

The Collected Works of Billy the Kid: Left Handed Poems (Ondaatje)   **14**:408-10; **29**:339-42; **51**:310-13, 317-19; **76**:204

The Collected Works of Jane Bowles (Bowles)   **68**:4-5, 7

The Collected Works of John Masefield (Masefield)   **47**:230

"Collecting Pictures" (Coles)   **46**:113

The Collection (Pinter)   **3**:385-86; **6**:413; **11**:441; **15**:423; **27**:385-86, 394-95; **58**:373, 376; **73**:251, 257

A Collection of Great Dance Songs (Pink Floyd)   **35**:313

A Collection of Sand (Calvino)
  See *Collezïone di sabbia*

La collectionneuse (Rohmer)   **16**:529-31, 533-34

"Collective Dawns" (Ashbery)   **13**:36; **77**:45

"The Collector" (Redgrove)   **41**:351

The Collector (Fowles)   **1**:109; **2**:138-39; **3**:163; **4**:171; **6**:184, 186-89; **9**:213-15; **10**:184, 187-88; **15**:234; **33**:159-67, 169-75; **87**:147-48, 154, 159-62, 175, 178, 181, 184, 187

The Collector and Other Poems (Redgrove)   **41**:347-48, 351

"The Collector of Treasures" (Head)   **67**:93-5, 98, 107

The Collector of Treasures (Head)   **25**:237; **67**:96-8, 111

"Collectors" (Carver)   **22**:96, 99; **55**:281

"The Collectors" (Mistry)   **71**:270, 272

"Collector's Item" (Brodsky)   **100**:70

College (Keaton)   **20**:189, 191, 193, 196

"The College Ghost" (Fuller)   **62**:200, 204

"College of Religious Misunderstandings" (Montague)   **46**:274

Collezïone di sabbia (*A Collection of Sand*) (Calvino)   **39**:315

Collin (Heym)   **41**:218-19

Colline (Giono)   **4**:186; **11**:232

"Collision" (Shields)   **113**:404, 408, 413, 432

Collision (Tiptree)   **48**:394-95

Collision Orbit (Williamson)   **29**:455

Collisions (Caute)   **29**:118-19, 122

"Colloquy" (Jackson)   **60**:211, 217

Colloquy for the States (MacLeish)   **14**:338

"Colloquy in Black Rock" (Lowell)   **4**:303; **8**:348; **15**:346

Colmain (Gray)   **36**:200

La colmena (*The Hive*) (Cela)   **4**:96-7, 98; **13**:145-47; **59**:126-27, 129, 134-44

Colombe (*Mademoiselle Colombe*) (Anouilh)   **1**:7; **3**:11; **8**:24; **13**:17; **40**:54, 59-60

Il colombre (Buzzati)   **36**:97

"A Colonel" (Blunden)   **56**:43

"The Colonel" (Forche)   **25**:171-72; **83**:197, 201, 212, 214, 216, 221, 223; **86**:140

"Colonel Fantock" (Sitwell)   **67**:335

The Colonel Has No One to Write Him (Garcia Marquez)
  See *El colonel no tiene quien le escribe*

Colonel Mint (Mano)   **10**:328

Colonel Mint (West)   **7**:524-25; **14**:568; **96**:374

El colonel no tiene quien le escribe (*The Colonel Has No One to Write Him; No One Writes to the Colonel*) (Garcia Marquez)   **2**:148, 150; **3**:183; **10**:216; **27**:147, 155; **47**:145-46, 149, 153; **55**:140; **68**:140, 145, 151, 153

"Colonel Shaw and the Massachusetts' Fifty-Fourth" (Lowell)   **8**:350

Colonel Sun: A James Bond Adventure (Amis)   **2**:8, 10; **3**:9

"The Colonel's Daughter" (Tremain)   **42**:386

The Colonel's Daughter (Aldington)   **49**:11

The Colonel's Daughter and Other Stories (Tremain)   **42**:385-86

"The Colonel's Hash Resettled" (Munro)   **95**:295

"The Colonel's Wife" (Dubus)   **97**:234, 236, 238

The Colonial Harem   **65**:329

"Colonialist Criticism" (Achebe)   **75**:2

"Colonisation in Reverse" (Bennett)   **28**:28

"Colonoscope Nite" (Leyner) **92**:283

"Colony" (Dick) **72**:108

"The Colony" (Singer) **3**:454

Colony (Bova) **45**:70, 72

The Color Curtain (Wright) **4**:596; **21**:449

"Color Me Real" (Cooper) **56**:70

Color of Darkness (Purdy) **2**:348-49; **10**:421; **28**:376-79; **52**:350

The Color of Light (Goldman) **48**:129-30

The Color of Money (Scorsese) **89**:242-43, 249, 260

The Color of Money (Tevis) **42**:377

"The Color of Time" (Williams) **33**:449

The Color Purple (Walker) **27**:449-51, 454; **46**:424-25, 427-32; **58**:405-15; **103**:366-68, 372, 374-76, 380, 383, 385, 387-89, 391-93, 395-98, 405, 411, 417, 419, 422, 428

Color Struck! (Hurston) **30**:223

"Colorado" (Beattie) **13**:64

"Colorado" (Cernuda) **54**:55

"Colorado" (Van Duyn) **116**:400

The Colorado (Waters) **88**:331-36, 341, 351, 360, 362-64, 366

The Colored Museum (Wolfe) **49**:419-24

"Colored Spade" (Ragni and Rado) **17**:385

The Colorist (Daitch) **103**:62-4, 66-78

"The Colors" (Disch) **7**:87

"The Colors of Night" (Momaday) **85**:268

"The Colors of Our Age: Pink and Black" (Smith) **42**:353

"Colors of the Sun" (Browne) **21**:37

"Colors without Objects" (Swenson) **61**:392; **106**:331

"Colossus" (Plath) **111**:178

The Colossus, and Other Poems (Plath) **1**:270; **2**:335-37; **3**:391; **5**:339, 343, 345; **9**:425, 432-33; **11**:445-47; **14**:422-25; **17**:344-45, 347-50, 352, 366-68; **50**:442, 449; **51**:340,343-44, 347; **62**:386, 389; **111**:159, 164-65, 167, 177-78, 185

The Colossus of Maroussi (Miller) **1**:223-24; **9**:381; **14**:374

"Colour Bar" (Bennett) **28**:29

The Colour of Blood (Moore) **90**:268-70, 272, 274-75, 289-90

The Colour of the Times (Souster) **14**:502

Colour Scheme (Marsh) **53**:249-51, 253, 255-56, 258-59

Colour the Flesh the Colour of Dust (Cook) **58**:150-51, 153-58

"The Colour-Machine" (Gunn) **32**:208

Colours in the Dark (Reaney) **13**:472, 475

The Colours of the Day (Gary) **25**:184

The Colours of War (Cohen) **19**:112-13, 115

La Colpa è sempre del diavolo (Fo) **109**:115

"The Colt" (Stegner) **81**:346

"A Coltrane Poem" (Sanchez) **116**:296

Columba (Slaughter) **56**:408, 411

Columbella (Whitney) **42**:433-34

Columbia and Beyond: The Story of the Space Shuttle (Branley) **21**:23

The Columbia: Power House of North America (Latham) **12**:324

Columbus **70**:338, 346, 354

Columbus and the Age of Discovery **70**:343

"Columbus and the Fat Lady" (Cohen) **19**:113

The Columbus Encyclopedia (Bedini) **70**:341

Columbus: For Gold, God, and Glory **70**:343

Columbus: His Enterprise (Koningsberger) **70**:339

"Columbus in Chains" (Kincaid) **43**:249

The Columbus Myth: Did Men of Bristol Reach America Before Columbus? (Wilson) **70**:338

The Columbus Papers (Obregon) **70**:331

Columbus: The Great Adventure—His Life, His Times, and His Voyages **70**:331, 340, 351, 353

"Columns and Caryatids" (Kizer) **80**:177

Coma (Cook) **14**:131

Coma (Crichton) **54**:71; **90**:69

The Comb (The Brothers Quay)
 See *The Comb from the Museum of Sleep*

The Comb from the Museum of Sleep (*The Comb*) (The Brothers Quay) **95**:347-49, 351, 353-55

"The Combat" (Thomas) **48**:379

"Combat" (Williams) **33**:447

"Combat Cultural" (Moore) **47**:263

"Combat Pay for Jodie" (Komunyakaa) **94**:226, 233

Combat Rock (Clash) **30**:50-2

"The Combine" (Weller) **26**:443

"Combustion" **75**:62

"Come Again Tomorrow" (Gordimer) **70**:166

Come Alive at 505 (Brancato) **35**:68-9

"Come Along, Marjorie" (Spark) **8**:493

Come Along with Me (Jackson) **60**:213-214, 217, 233, 235

"Come and Buy My Toys" (Bowie) **17**:65

Come and Get It (Ferber) **93**:163-64, 171

"Come as You Are" (Bernard) **59**:45

Come As You Are (Mortimer) **28**:286

"Come Away, Death" (Pratt) **19**:385

"Come Back" (Merwin) **45**:278

Come Back, Dr. Caligari (Barthelme) **2**:39, 41; **3**:43; **6**:31; **8**:49-50, 53; **23**:44, 47; **46**:35, 39-40; **59**:247, 249; **115**:56-7, 65

Come Back, Little Sheba (Inge) **1**:153; **8**:308; **19**:226-30

Come Back to Erin (O'Faolain) **7**:275; **14**:402, 404; **70**:312, 317, 321

Come Back to the Fiva and Dime, Jimmy Dean, Jimmy Dean (Altman) **116**:39, 47, 59, 67, 73

"Come Back to the Raft Ag'in Huck Honey!" (Fiedler) **4**:163; **13**:211; **24**:195, 203

Come Back Wherever You Are (Weber) **12**:634

"Come before His Countenance with a Joyful Leaping" (Wagoner) **5**:474

Come Blow Your Horn (Simon) **6**:502; **31**:396-97, 400, 403; **70**:238, 240

"Come Break with Time" (Bogan) **46**:77, 89-90; **93**:65, 96

Come Dance with Kitty Stobling (Kavanagh) **22**:235

Come Gentle Spring (Stuart) **34**:376

Come Home Early, Child (Dodson) **79**:198

"Come In" (Frost) **10**:194; **26**:118, 123

"Come Inside" (Waugh) **107**:369

"Come into Animal Presence" (Levertov) **15**:337

"Come into My Cellar" (Bradbury) **15**:86; **42**:33-4

"Come into My Parlour" (Muldoon) **72**:267

"Come, Lady Death" (Beagle) **104**:5, 25

"Come Live with Me Angel" (Gaye) **26**:132

Come Nineveh, Come Tyre (Drury) **37**:106-07

"Come on a Coming" (Dixon) **52**:100

"Come On Back" (Gardner) **28**:161-62

"Come On, My Lucky Lads" (Blunden) **56**:38, 43

"Come On, Ye Sons of Art" (Paley) **37**:337

"Come Out the Wilderness" (Baldwin) **17**:33

Come Out to Play (Comfort) **7**:54

"Come Round Here" (Robinson)
 See "If You Wanna Make Love"

"'Come Sleep . . .'" (Bogan) **39**:391, 393; **93**:67

Come Softly to My Wake: The Poems of Christy Brown (Brown) **63**:51

Come, Tell Me How You Live (Christie) **6**:110; **48**:78

Come, the Restorer (Goyen) **5**:149; **8**:250-51; **14**:212, 214; **40**:218

Come the Sweet By and By (Lerman) **9**:329-31

"Come Then to Prayers" (Larkin) **64**:282

"Come Thunder" ("Thunder Can Break") (Okigbo) **25**:354, 356; **84**:316

"Come to My Merry Grave" (Yevtushenko) **51**:432

Come to the Edge (Cunningham) **12**:166

"Come Together" (Lennon and McCartney) **12**:364, 380

Come Unto These Yellow Sands (Carter) **76**:329

"Come Upstairs" (Simon) **26**:413

Come Upstairs (Simon) **26**:413

Come Wind, Come Weather (du Maurier) **59**:286

Come Winter (Hunter) **11**:279

"Come with Me" (Bly) **5**:64

"Comeback" (Scannell) **49**:329-31

Comeback (Francis) **102**:142-43, 158

The Comedians (Greene) **1**:134; **3**:207, 210, 212-14; **9**:246-51; **18**:194; **27**:173, 175-76; **37**:136; **70**:289-90, 293; **72**:156-57, 163, 165

Comedians (Griffiths) **13**:256-57; **52**:174-79, 185

Comedy: American Style (Fauset) **19**:170-71; **54**:177, 187-90

"Comedy Cop" (Farrell) **66**:131

"Comedy Events You Can Do" (Martin) **30**:248

Comedy Is Not Pretty (Martin) **30**:249

The Comedy of Neil Simon (Simon) **31**:396

"The Comedy of the White Dog" (Gray) **41**:181, 183

Comedy of Vanity (Canetti)
 See *Die Komödie der Eitelkeit*

Comedy of Vanity & Life-Terms (Canetti) **75**:145

"Comedy Tonight" (Sondheim) **30**:378

"Comemos sombra" (Aleixandre) **9**:12

"The Come-On" (Dunn) **40**:168

"Comes a Time" (Young) **17**:583

Comes a Time (Young) **17**:579-80

Comes the Blind Fury (Saul) **46**:366, 369

"Comes Winter: The Sea Hunting" (Dubie) **36**:135, 141-42

"The Comet" (Aleixandre) **36**:28

"Comet Watch on Indian Key" (Swenson) **61**:403

The Cometeers (Williamson) **29**:455, 458-59

Comets, Meteoroids, and Asteroids (Branley) **21**:20

"Comfort" (Kaplan) **50**:55-7

Comfort (Kaplan) **50**:55-7

"Comfort at Fifty" (Levi) **41**:248

Comfort Me with Apples (De Vries) **1**:73; **28**:106, 108, 112

The Comfort of Strangers (McEwan) **66**:282-85, 288, 292-94

Comfort Woman (Keller) **109**:63-6

The Comfortable Pew (Berton) **104**:44, 47, 57

The Comforters (Spark) **2**:414-18; **3**:465-66; **5**:400; **8**:496; **13**:520, 522-23; **18**:501; **40**:393, 395, 398-400; **94**:326, 328,k 330-334, 336, 350, 353-54

"The Comforts of Home" (O'Connor) **6**:377, 382; **15**:410; **21**:263-64, 269, 276;**104**:107-08, 110, 115, 123-24, 135-36, 155, 179-80, 184, 194-96

The Comic (Glanville) **6**:202

"Comic at the Palladium" (Bruce) **21**:48, 53-4

"Comin' Down Again" (Jagger and Richard) **17**:228-29

"Comin' Home" (Seger) **35**:386-87

"The Coming" (Ciardi) **40**:157

"Coming" (Larkin) **5**:227; **8**:333; **33**:256, 259-60; **64**:262, 266, 274

"Coming Apart" (Walker) **27**:448, 450; **103**:366, 407-08, 411-12, 423

"Coming Attraction" (Leiber) **25**:301-04

"Coming Attractions" (Wolff) **64**:450, 452-54

Coming Attractions (Tally) **42**:366-67

"Coming Back in Spring" (Merwin) **45**:274

"Coming Close to Donna" (Hannah) **90**:145, 146

"Coming Down from the Acropolis" (Snodgrass) **68**:399

Coming Down from Wa (Thomas) **107**:350-52

"Coming Down through Somerset" (Hughes) **37**:175

"Coming Events" (Montague) **46**:269

The Coming Forth by Day of Osiris Jones (Aiken) **52**:20, 26-7

The Coming Fury (Catton) **35**:89-94

"Coming Home" (Gallagher) **18**:168

"Coming Home" (Hecht) **13**:269

Coming Home (Jones) **52**:255

"Coming Home on the 5:22" (Ciardi) **44**:381

"Coming in for Supper" (Bly) **10**:62

"Coming in from the Cold" (Marley) **17**:273

"Coming in from the Cold" (Walker) **58**:409

Coming into Eighty (Sarton) **91**:245

"Coming into His Kingdom" (McGahern) **48**:267

Coming into the Country (McPhee) **36**:296-99

"Coming into Town, Cold" (Musgrave) **54**:341

"Coming of Age" (Musgrave) **54**:338

The Coming of Age (Beauvoir)
See *La vieillesse*

Coming of Age in Samoa (Mead) **37**:268-71, 275, 277, 281, 283-85

Coming of Age in SoHo (Innaurato) **60**:201-04, 206-07

Coming of Age: New and Selected Poems (Deutsch) **18**:119

"The Coming of Kali" (Clifton) **66**:80

"The Coming of Light" (Strand) **18**:521; **41**:432

"The Coming of Spring" (Behan) **79**:39

The Coming of Stork (Williamson) **56**:431-33, 435

"The Coming of the Cat" (Beer) **58**:32

"The Coming of the Eagles" (Dumas) **62**:155

The Coming of the Lord (Millin) **49**:244-46, 252

The Coming of the New Deal (Schlesinger) **84**:352-55, 382

"The Coming of War" (MacNeice) **53**:237

The Coming of Winter (Richards) **59**:187, 189, 192

"Coming Over Coldwater" (Muske) **90**:313

"Coming Round" (Ammons) **57**:57

"Coming Round" (Hope) **52**:209

Coming through Slaughter (Ondaatje) **14**:410; **29**:339-40, 342-43; **51**:314, 317-20; **76**:204

"Coming to Canada" (Shields) **113**:442

Coming to Canada (Shields) **113**:441-42

"Coming to Get You" (Simon) **26**:413

"Coming to Summer" (Ammons) **108**:19

"Coming to Terms" (Mohr) **12**:447

Coming to Terms (Miles) **34**:244

"Coming to This" (Strand) **71**:285

"Coming to Writing" (Cixous) **92**:80-3, 95

"Coming to Writing" and Other Essays (Cixous) **92**:80-1, 83, 95

"The Coming Triumph of the Free World" (De Marinis) **54**:101

"Coming Up" (McCartney) **35**:287-88

"Comings and Goings" (Tallent) **45**:387

Comings and Goings (Terry) **19**:440

Comings Back: A Sequence of Poems (Goldbarth) **38**:200-01, 203

Command, and I Will Obey You (Moravia)
See *Command, and I Will Obey You*

"Command Performance" (Miller) **30**:263-64

Command the Morning (Buck) **11**:77

The Commandant (Anderson) **37**:19

"Commander Lowell 1887-1950" (Lowell) **3**:300

"Commands of Love" (Peacock) **60**:298

La commare secca (The Grim Reaper) (Bertolucci) **16**:84-5

La commare secca (The Grim Reaper) (Bertolucci) **16**:84-85

Comme l'eau qui coule (Two Lives and a Dream) (Yourcenar) **50**:363-64; **87**:396-97, 399, 404

Comme nous avons été (Adamov) **25**:12

"Commemoration" (Elytis) **49**:114

"The Commencement" (Dickey) **3**:127

"A Commencement Address" (Brodsky) **50**:132, 136

"Commencement, Pingree School" (Updike) **43**:430

"A Comment" (Ezekiel) **61**:107

Comment ca va (Godard) **20**:153

Comment c'est (How It Is) (Beckett) **1**:22; **3**:44; **6**:36, 41; **9**:78, 83-4, 88; **10**:27, 29, 31-4; **11**:32, 34, 37, 39-40; **14**:70, 74, 77, 79-80; **18**:42, 52; **29**:56-7, 59, 65-6

"Commentary" (Auden) **43**:18

Commentary on a Falling Star (Kommentar till ett stjärnfall) (Johnson) **14**:294

"Commercial" (Updike) **15**:546

"Commercialization" (Cliff) **21**:60-1

Les commettants de Caridad (Theriault) **79**:401, 408, 417

"A Commination" (Hope) **51**:215, 221

"La commission des fêtes" (Kadare) **52**:261

"Commitment" (Ezekiel) **61**:92, 100

The Commitments (Doyle) **81**:158-61

"Committee of the Whole" (Herbert) **44**:394

The Commodore (Forester)
See *Commodore Hornblower*

Commodore Hornblower (The Commodore) (Forester) **35**:165-67, 170

The Common Asphodel: Collected Essays on Poetry, 1922-1949 (Graves) **45**:174

The Common Chord (O'Connor) **14**:399

"The Common Fate of Objects" (Lerman) **9**:331

The Common Glory (Green) **25**:197

A Common Grace (MacCaig) **36**:280, 288

The Common Heart (Horgan) **53**:175-76

"The Common Man" (Smith) **15**:517

"Common Mannerism" (Davie) **10**:124

Common One (Morrison) **21**:239-40

The Common Pasture (Masters) **48**:219

The Common Pursuit (Gray) **36**:209-10

The Common Pursuit (Leavis) **24**:295, 297-98, 308

A Common Room, Essays 1954-1987 (Price) **63**:323, 326-28, 333-35

"Common Words in Uncommon Orders" (Williams) **13**:601

Commonplace Book (Forster) **45**:134, 143-44

"The Commonwealth Air Training Plan" (Johnston) **51**:253

Communalism: From Its Origins to the Twentieth Century (Rexroth) **11**:473

"Commune présence" (Char) **14**:126

The Communicants (Bergman)
See *Nattvardsgästerna*

The Communication Cord (Friel) **42**:173; **115**:221-23, 230-31, 239, 241-42, 245

"Communication in White" (Madhubuti) **73**:209

"Communications Breakdown" (Page and Plant) **12**:473, 475, 477-78

"Communion" (Ignatow) **7**:177, 179

"The Communion" (Levertov) **15**:337

"Communion" (Tchicaya) **101**:353

La communion solonelle (First Communion; First Holy Communion; The Solemn Communion) (Arrabal) **9**:39; **18**:21; **58**:10, 16-18, 22

"Communionism" (Snyder) **32**:392

"Communism and Christianity" (Cowley) **39**:461

Communism and the French Intellectuals, 1914-1960 (Caute) **29**:109-10

"Communist" (Ford) **46**:161

"Communist Cardinal Visits Dublin" (Durcan) **43**:115

"Communist Mentalities" (Scott) **43**:385

"The Communist Party to Youth" (Pasolini) **106**:225

"Communist Women" (Davis) **77**:120-21

Les communistes (Aragon) **3**:13; **22**:37

"Les Communistes et la paix" *(The Communists and the Peace)* (Sartre) **50**:374

The Communists and the Peace (Sartre)
See "Les Communistes et la paix"

"Community" (Clarke) **61**:73

"Community" (Piercy) **27**:375

"Community" (Silkin) **43**:397

"Commuters" (Hirsch) **50**:198

"Como el viento" (Cernuda) **54**:59

Como en la guerra (He Who Searches) (Valenzuela) **31**:436-39; **104**:354, 356-58, 360, 370, 374, 377-79, 388

"Como lavoro" (Gadda) **11**:211

"Como les iba diciendo" (Parra) **102**:342

"De como o Mulato Porciúncula Descarregou seu Defunto" ("How the Mulatto Porciúncula Got the Corpse Off His Back"; "Porciúncula") (Amado) **106**:74-76

Como quien espera el alba (Cernuda) **54**:45, 53, 61

"Comp Lit 101: Walt Grows Up" (Shields) **97**:430

"The Compact: At Volterra" (Tomlinson) **45**:392

"La compagne du vannier" ("The Basket-Weaver's Companion") (Char) **9**:164

"Compagnie de l'écolière" (Char) **14**:127

"Le compagnon de la dernière heure" (Chedid)

47:87

Les compagnons dans le jardin (Char)   9:159
"The Companion" (Campbell)   42:86, 89
"The Companion" (Christie)   110:141-42, 145
"The Companions" (Nemerov)   2:307
"Companions" (Rao)   56:291
Companions of the Day and Night (Harris)   25:210, 216
Companions of the Left Hand (Tabori)   19:435
"Company" (Dove)   81:139, 146
"Company" (Longley)   29:296
"The Company" (Raine)   45:333, 338
Company (Beckett)   29:57-62, 67; 59:255, 260
The Company (Creeley)   78:160
Company (Sondheim)   30:380-92, 395-97, 399-402; 39:175
"The Company I Keep" (Ezekiel)   61:95
The Company I've Kept (MacDiarmid)   63:255
Company Limited (Ray)
   See *Simabaddha*
The Company of Children (Spacks)   14:510
The Company of Eagles (Gann)   23:166-67
"A Company of Laughing Faces" (Gordimer)   33:180-81
"The Company of Lovers" (Wright)   11:578; 53:423, 427, 430-31
The Company of Men (Gary)   25:183-85
"The Company of Wolves" (Carter)   41:117, 119
The Company of Wolves (Carter)   76:324
The Company of Wolves (Jordan)   110:275-76, 278, 280-82
The Company of Women (Gordon)   22:184-86
The Company She Keeps (McCarthy)   1:206; 3:326-28; 14:360, 363; 24:342; 59:289-91, 293
"Comparatives" (Momaday)   85:248, 263
"Comparing X-Rays" (Spacks)   14:510
"Comparison" (Nowlan)   15:399
"A Comparison" (Plath)   11:451
"A Comparison of the Conceptions of God in the Thinking of Paul Tillich and Henry Nelson Wieman" (King)   83:339
Compartiment tueurs (*The Sleeping Car Murders; The 10:30 from Marseilles*) (Japrisot)   90:167-69
"The Compartment" (Carver)   36:104
The Compass Flower (Merwin)   8:389-90; 13:383; 18:334-37; 45:274, 277-78; 88:194, 197, 200, 202-03, 205
The Compass Rose (Le Guin)   45:216-17
"A Compassionate Leave" (Yates)   23:483
"Complaint" (Wright)   28:470
"The Complaint of the Morpethshire Farmer" (Bunting)   39:300; 47:45
"La complainte de nègre" (Damas)   84:176
"La complainte du nère" ("The Black Man's Lament") (Damas)   84:176
"The Complaisant Husband" (Simmons)   43:408
The Complaisant Lover (Greene)   3:211; 6:213-15; 70:292, 294
A Completa verdade sobre as discutides aventuras do comandante Vasco Moscoso d'Aragão (Amado)   106:57
The Complete Bolivian Diaries of Che Guevara, and Other Captured Documents (Guevara)
   See *El diario de Che en Bolivia: noviembre 7, 1966, a octubre 7, 1967*
"Complete Control" (Clash)   30:43-5, 47
The Complete Knowledge of Sally Fry (Murphy)   34:91-2

Complete Plays (Behan)   79:58
The Complete Poems (Bishop)   4:66; 13:95; 15:59-61; 32:33, 35, 38, 41
Complete Poems (Cendrars)   106:188
Complete Poems (Cummings)   3:119
The Complete Poems (Denby)   48:84-5
Complete Poems (Jarrell)   6:259; 9:296
Complete Poems (Sandburg)   15:466; 35:351-52, 359
The Complete Poems (Sexton)   53:312-14, 316, 320-23
Complete Poems, 1910-1962 (Cummings)   68:52
Complete Poems, 1920-1976 (MacDiarmid)   19:289
Complete Poems, 1923-1962 (Cummings)   68:42
The Complete Poems, 1927-1979 (Bishop)   32:36-9, 43, 45
The Complete Poems and Plays, 1909-1950 (Eliot)   34:392
The Complete Poems of Anna Akhmatova (Akhmatova)   64:17-20
The Complete Poems of Marianne Moore (Moore)   8:399; 19:340, 342-43; 47:260-61, 270
The Complete Poems of Richard Aldington (Aldington)   49:16
Complete Poems of Robert Frost (Frost)   13:225; 26:114, 117
The Complete Prose of Marianne Moore (Moore)   47:267-69, 271
The Complete Robot (Asimov)   26:58
The Complete Short Stories of L.P. Hartley (Hartley)   22:215-16
A Complete State of Death (Gardner)   30:152-53
The Complete Stories (O'Connor)   2:318; 3:366
The Complete Stories of Alice Walker (Walker)   103:422
The Complete Stories of Erskine Caldwell (Caldwell)   14:96
"The Complete Works" (Berrigan)   37:43
Complete Works (Aleixandre)
   See *Obras completas*
"Completed" (Williams)   5:502; 45:453
"Complex Autumnal" (Kizer)   80:172
"Compleynte, Etc." (Rosenthal)   28:395
"A Complicated Nature" (Trevor)   71:326
Complicity (Cooke)   55:46-8
Complimentaries: Uncollected Essays (Richards)   14:454; 24:401
"Compline" (Berryman)   3:71
"The Composer's Winter Dream" (Dubie)   36:135
"Composition in Black and White" (Pollitt)   28:367
"Composition in Retrospect" (Cage)   41:86
The Composition Reader (Tanizaki)   28:414
"The Compost Heap" (Watkins)   43:450
Comprador (Cudlip)   34:38-9
"Compression" (Thomas)   107:340-41, 346
Compromising Positions (Isaacs)   32:253-54
Compulsion (Levin)   7:203-04, 205
"Compulsive Qualifications" (Howard)   10:275-76
"Compulsory Heterosexuality and Lesbian Existence" (Rich)   73:320, 323
The Computer That Went on Strike (Asimov)   19:25
"The Computer's First Christmas Card" (Morgan)   31:275-76
"Comrade" (Soupault)   68:406

Comrade Jacob (Caute)   29:108, 121
Comrade Kirillov (Rao)   56:298, 314-16
"Comrade Past and Mister Present" (Codrescu)   46:105
Comrade Past and Mister Present (Codrescu)   46:105
"Comrade Smart-hat" (Aksyonov)   101:18
Comstock Lode (L'Amour)   25:281-82
"Con la señora du gast" (Azorin)   11:24
Con las horas contadas (*Your Hours Are Numbered*) (Cernuda)   54:58, 60
"Con los ojos cerrados" (*With Closed Eyes*) (Arenas)   41:28
"Con Quevedo en primavera" ("With Quevedo during Spring") (Neruda)   28:310; 62:334
"Con Sequences" (Livesay)   79:340
Concealed Enemies (Whitemore)   37:445-47
Conceived in Liberty (Fast)   23:154, 157
"The Concentration City" (Ballard)   36:36, 41
"Concentration Moon" (Zappa)   17:589, 593
Concentric Circles (Bowering)   47:25
"The Concept in Fiction" (Gass)   2:155
"The Concept of Baroque in Literary Scholarship" (Wellek)   28:445
"The Concept of Character in Fiction" (Gass)   15:258
The Concept of Nation and the African View of Socialism (Senghor)
   See *Nation et voie africaine du socialisme*
"The Concept of Time in Historiography" (Heidegger)   24:279
"Conception" (Sarton)   49:309
Concepts of Criticism (Wellek)   28:445-46, 449, 454
"Concerning My Neighbors the Hittites" (Simic)   68:378
"Concerning Nature" (Ashbery)   77:63
"Concerning the Bodyguard" (Barthelme)   13:59; 59:250-51
"Concerning the Greek Tyrant" (Carey)   96:35
"Concert" (Wideman)   67:385
"Concert at Long Melford Church" (Beer)   58:31, 36
The Concert at Saint Ovide (Buero Vallejo)
   See *El concierto de San Ovidio*
Concert dans oeuf (Arrabal)   9:33; 58:9, 11
"The Concert of Hyacinths" (Elytis)   49:111
Concert on the Island (Seifert)
   See *Koncert na ostrove*
"The Concert: Oratorio for a Season of Wrath" (L'Heureux)   52:273
"Concert Party: Busseboom" (Blunden)   56:52
Concerto in B Goode (Berry)   17:51
"The Concession" (Thomas)   48:375
"The Concessions" (Ondaatje)   51:315
"Conch-Shell" (Wright)   53:418
Concierto barroco (Carpentier)   11:102, 107; 110:57-8, 69-70, 72-4
El concierto de San Ovidio (*The Concert at Saint Ovide*) (Buero Vallejo)   15:98, 101-02; 46:95-8
Concluding (Green)   2:178; 13:252-53, 255; 97:243-51, 254-57, 267, 270, 272, 279-82, 288-90, 293
"Conclusion" (Leffland)   19:280
"The Conclusion" (Yehoshua)   31:472
Conclusive Evidence: A Memoir (Nabokov)
   See *Speak, Memory: An Autobiography Revisited*
"Concord" (Lowell)   4:300
"Concord" (Paz)   65:182
Concrete (Bernhard)

See *Beton*
Concrete Island (Ballard) 6:28; 14:39, 41
The Concrete Island (Bowering) 15:83; 47:22
"Concrete Jungle" (Marley) 17:271-72
"Concrete Relations with Others" (Sartre) 13:498, 501
"The Concrete Universal" (Ransom) 2:364; 5:367
Concurring Beasts (Dobyns) 37:74-8
"Concussion" (Campbell) 42:84, 92
"Concussion" (MacLennan) 92:340
"Le condamnéa mort" (Genet) 44:389-90
Un condamné a mort s'est echappé (Bresson) 16:105, 107-08, 111
"The Condemned" (Allen) 52:42
"Condemned Door" (Cortazar) 5:109
The Condemned Man's Bicycle (Arrabal)
See *La bicyclette du condamné*
The Condemned of Altona (Sartre)
See *Les séquestrés d'Altona*
The Condemned of Altona (De Sica)
See *Les séquestrés d'Altona*
"Condemned Site" (Van Duyn) 116:411
"The Condemned Well" (Brown) 5:78; 48:57
Condenados a vivir (Gironella) 11:237
"The Condensed Shorter Testament" (Mahon) 27:291
"The Condiment" (Corman) 9:169
"La condition botanique" (Hecht) 8:266
La condition humaine (*Man's Fate*) (Malraux) 1:203; 4:324-25, 327-31, 333-36; 9:353-55, 358; 13:365-69; 15:351-53; 57:300-02, 304-05, 307, 309-17, 321, 324
The Condition of Muzak (Moorcock) 27:349-50; 58:348-49, 357
"The Condition of the Working Classes, 1970" (Bly) 10:59
"The Condition We Call Exile" (Brodsky) 100:69
"Conditional" (Richards) 14:455
Conditionally Human (Miller) 30:260, 262-64
"The Conditioned Reflex" (Lem) 40:291
"Conditions for Leaving" (Jordan) 5:203
"The Condolence" (Pound) 112:309
"Condolence Visit" (Mistry) 71:272
"Condolences to Every One of Us" (Gurganus) 70:190, 192, 195
"The Condominium" (Elkin) 4:154; 6:169; 27:122; 51:99-100
Condominium (MacDonald) 44:407-09
"The Condor" (Jeffers) 54:234
"El cóndor" (Ulibarri) 83:417
El cóndor, and Other Stories (Ulibarri) 83:418
The Condor and the Cows (Isherwood) 14:279; 44:397-98
"El condor pasa" (Simon) 17:461
A Condor Passes (Grau) 4:208-09
Conduct Unbecoming: Lesbians and Gays in the U.S. Military, Vietnam to the Persian Gulf (Shilts) 85:329-32, 334-38, 342-43
Conducting Bodies (Simon)
See *Les corps conducteurs*
The Cone-Gatherers (Jenkins) 52:220, 225-27, 229
"El conejo pionero" (Ulibarri) 83:416
"The Coney" (Muldoon) 72:273, 277
"Coney Island" (Beattie) 63:14, 18
"Coney Island Baby" (Reed) 21:311-12, 314, 316
Coney Island Baby (Reed) 21:310-13, 315
A Coney Island of the Mind (Ferlinghetti) 6:183; 10:174-77; 27:137-39; 111:50-1,

53-8, 60, 64, 72
Confabulations: Poems for Malcolm Lowry (Thesen) 56:415-16, 419-22
The Confederacy (Green) 25:198
A Confederacy of Dunces (Toole) 19:441-43; 64:404-24
A Confederate General from Big Sur (Brautigan) 3:87-9; 5:71; 12:57, 59, 62, 66-8, 70; 34:315-16; 42:50, 57, 60, 62-3, 65
Confederates (Keneally) 14:302-03; 19:247-49; 27:232; 43:230, 234; 117:225, 227, 229, 231, 241
"The Conference" (Singer) 69:306
La conférence inachevée (Ferron) 94:128-29
Conference of Victims (Berriault) 54:2; 109:90
Las confesiones de un pequeño filósofo (Azorin) 11:27
"Confession" (Arghezi)
See "Duhovniceasca"
"The Confession" (Justice) 102:251, 265
"The Confession" (Nyro) 17:312, 319
The Confession (Adamov) 25:20
The Confession of a Child of the Century by Samuel Heather (Rogers) 57:364-67
Confession of a Lover (Anand) 93:32-34, 36, 56
"The Confession of the Flesh" (Foucault) 69:184
"Confession Overheard in a Subway" (Fearing) 51:110
The Confession Stone (Dodson) 79:199
"The Confessional" (Bidart) 33:78-81
"The Confessional" (O'Faolain) 32:341
The Confessional (Simenon) 8:487
Confessional (Williams) 2:465-66; 5:502; 45:448
"Confessional Poem" (Scannell) 49:328, 330
The Confessional Poets (Phillips) 28:362
Les confessions de Dan Yack (*Dan Yack*) (Cendrars) 18:95, 97; 106:169, 183, 185-86, 190
Confessions from Left Field: A Baseball Pilgrimage (Mungo) 72:291-92
Confessions of a Bad Girl (Pesetsky) 65:349-50
"Confessions of a Former Anti-Semite" (Baraka) 115:10
Confessions of a Knife (Selzer) 74:279, 281
Confessions of a Mask (Mishima)
See *Kamen no kokuhaku*
Confessions of a Native-Alien (Ghose) 42:177
"Confessions of a Pornographer's Shroud" (Barker) 52:54
Confessions of a Spent Youth (Bourjaily) 62:90-3, 95-6, 98, 104, 107
Confessions of a Teenage Baboon (Zindel) 26:474-75, 480
Confessions of a Toe-Hanger (Harris) 12:262
Confessions of an Irish Rebel (Behan) 79:28, 34
The Confessions of Edward Dahlberg (Dahlberg) 7:68-9
The Confessions of Josef Baisz (Jacobson) 14:290-91
The Confessions of Nat Turner (Styron) 1:331; 3:473-74; 5:418-20; 11:515-16, 518-19, 521; 15:526; 60:392-93, 398, 400
"The Confessions of St. Jim-Ralph: Our Patron of Falling Short, Who Became a Prayer" (Johnson) 52:234
Confessions of Summer (Lopate) 29:300
"A Confessor's Words" (Arghezi)
See "Cuvinte duhovnicesti"

The Confidence Course (Potter) 58:400
The Confidence Man (Garfield) 12:241
The Confident Years (Brooks) 29:84, 89
The Confidential Agent (Greene) 1:131; 3:212; 9:250; 18:194; 27:175; 37:140; 72:148, 151, 155, 169, 171-72, 176, 179
The Confidential Clerk (Eliot) 1:90; 13:194-95; 15:209; 34:389; 41:143, 145
"Confidential Report" (Laughlin) 49:220
Confidential Report (Welles)
See *Mr. Arkadin*
Confieso que he vivido: memorias (*Memoirs*) (Neruda) 9:389-99; 28:310; 62:327, 329, 332
"Configurations" (Ammons) 108:11, 23
Configurations (Paz) 4:398; 6:397-98
Confirmation: An Anthology of African-American Women (Baraka) 115:10
Les confitures de coings (Ferron)
See *La nuit*
Conflagration (Ichikawa)
See *Enjo*
"The Conflict" (Day Lewis) 10:128
"Conflict" (Scott) 22:372, 374
Conflicts of Spring (Gustafson) 36:222
The Conformist (Bertolucci) 16:85-8, 90, 92-5, 97-8, 100
The Conformist (Duerrenmatt) 102:58, 60
The Conformist (Moravia)
See *Il conformista*
Il conformista (*The Conformist*) (Moravia) 7:243; 11:383; 27:356; 46:282-83
"Confrontation" (Sillitoe) 57:391, 396
The Confrontation (Caute) 29:114
Confrontation (Lengyel) 7:202
Confrontations: Studies in the Intellectual and Literary Relations betweenGermany, England, and the United States during the Nineteenth Century (Wellek) 28:446-47
"Confused" (Singer) 69:306, 308-09
"Confusion" (Cozzens) 11:124, 128, 131; 92:196-97, 201
"Confusion and Poetry" (Tate) 24:445
"Confusion in Language" (Shapiro) 53:327
"The Confusion of Belief" (Shapiro) 53:327
"Confusion of the Senses" (Rexroth) 112:404
La confusione degle stili (Pasolini) 37:344
"La confusione degli stili" (Pasolini) 106:245
Confusions (Ayckbourn) 18:28; 33:40-1
"Congenital" (Wright) 6:579, 581
Congo (Senghor) 54:410
Congo (Crichton) 54:72-3; 90:93
"Congratulations" (Simon) 17:461
Congratulations! You're Not Pregnant: An Illustrated Guide to Birth Control (Mayle)
See *We're Not Pregnant: An Illustrated Guide to Birth Control*
"Congregation of the Story-Tellers at a Funeral of Soweto Children" (Kunene) 85:175
El congreso ("The Assembly"; *The Congress*) (Borges) 2:72; 9:117; 13:110; 48:37-41
"The Congress" (Borges) 83:189-90
The Congress (Borges)
See *El congreso*
The Congressman Who Loved Flaubert and Other Washington Stories (Just) 4:265-67
"Coniagui Women" (Lorde) 18:309; 71:232, 247, 254
Conjectures of a Guilty Bystander (Merton) 83:402-03
Conjugal Love (Moravia)
See *Conjugal Love*

"A Conjugation" (Ezekiel) 61:93

Conjunciones y disyunciones (Conjunctions and Disjunctions) (Paz) 4:396-397; 10:390; 51:331; 65:181-82, 184

Conjunctions and Disjunctions (Paz)
See *Conjunciones y disyunciones*

Los conjurados (The Conspirators) (Borges) 44:353

"Conjuration" (Wilbur) 53:405

Conjure: Selected Poems, 1963-1970 (Reed) 2:369; 3:424; 5:368-370; 6:448; 13:478

Conjure Wife (Leiber) 25:301, 305-06, 310

Conjuros (Rodriguez) 10:439

"A Connacht Doctor Dreams of an African Woman" (Durcan) 43:115

Connaissance par les gouffres (Knowledge from the Abyss) (Michaux) 8:393; 19:312-13

Connecting Times: The Sixties in Afro-American Fiction 65:379

"Connection" (Gaitskill) 69:199

"Connection" (Jagger and Richard) 17:232

"Connection" (Munro) 95:306

"Connection" (Transtroemer) 65:223

The Connection (Clarke) 16:215-18

The Connection (Gelber) 1:114; 6:196-97; 79:202-08, 210, 212-25

"Connections" (Simmons) 43:406

"The Conning Tower" (Parker) 15:417

"A Connoisseur" (Blunden) 56:47

The Connoisseur (Connell) 4:110; 6:115-17; 45:112

"The Connoisseur of Jews" (Rothenberg) 57:374

"The Connoisseuse of Slugs" (Olds) 85:289

"The Connor Girls" (O'Brien) 36:339, 341; 116:186

"Conon in Exile" (Durrell) 27:97

Les conquérants (The Conquerors) (Malraux) 4:324-25, 327, 329-31, 335; 9:353-54, 356; 13:364-66, 368; 15:352; 57:300-05, 311

The Conquering Hero (Gelbart) 21:124-25

"The Conqueror Worm" (Donaldson) 46:143

The Conquerors (Costain) 30:95, 97, 99

The Conquerors (Eckert) 17:107

The Conquerors (Malraux)
See *Les conquérants*

"The Conquest" (Murray) 40:336

"The Conquest" (Samarakis) 5:382

"Conquest of Dawn" (Kunene) 85:166

Conquest of Eden 1493-1515: The Other Voyages of Columbus (Paiewonsky) 70:331, 355

The Conquest of Mt. Everest (Kopit) 33:249-50

The Conquest of Paradise: Christopher Columbus and the Columbian Legacy (Sale) 68:354-58, 360

The Conquest of Paradise: Christopher Columbus and the Columbian Legacy (Sale) 70:331, 345, 349, 351, 353

Conquest of the Universe (When Queens Collide) (Ludlam) 46:239; 50:342, 344

"Conquistador" (Hope) 3:250; 51:216, 221

Conquistador (MacLeish) 8:361-63; 14:336-37; 68:275-79, 284-90, 292

"Conrad in Twilight" (Ransom) 11:466

"Conrad Martins in 1850" (Shapcott) 38:404

"Conrad's Darkness" (Naipaul) 37:321; 105:155

"Conrad's Journey" (Berryman) 10:46; 13:76

La consagración de la primavera (Carpentier) 110:74-5, 77

"Conscience" (Williams) 56:429

The Conscience (Fuentes) 60:156-57, 160

The Conscience of the Rich (Snow) 1:317; 6:516; 13:508-10; 19:426

The Conscience of Words (Canetti)
See *Das Gewissen der Worte*

"Les consciences atténuantes" (Tzara) 47:394

"Consciousness" (Milosz)
See "Swiadomosc"

The Consciousness Industry: On Literature, Politics, and the Media (Enzensberger)
See *Bewusstseins-Industrie*

"The Conscript" (MacNeice) 4:318

"A Consecration" (Masefield) 11:358; 47:230

"The Consent" (Nemerov) 9:394-95

Consenting Adult (Hobson) 7:163-64

Consenting Adults; or, The Duchess Will Be Furious (De Vries) 28:105-08, 111

"Consequences" (Meredith) 13:375

Consequently I Rejoice (Jennings) 14:293

"The Conservation of Races" (Du Bois) 96:154, 160

The Conservationist (Gordimer) 5:145-48; 7:131-32; 10:239-40; 33:183; 51:156, 158, 161; 70:163-65, 167, 170, 172, 182-83

Conservatism: From John Adams to Churchill (Viereck) 4:560

Conservatism Revisited (Viereck) 4:560

"Conservatory" (Barthelme) 115:81

"Conserving the Magnitude of Uselessness" (Ammons) 108:28

"Consider" (Auden) 43:21

"Consider the Lilies" (Ferber) 93:153

Consider the Lilies (Hill) 113:285-86

Consider the Lilies (Smith) 64:389, 393

Consider the Lillies (Waugh) 7:514

Consider the Oyster (Fisher) 76:337-38, 340-41; 87:118, 120

"Consider This and In Our Time" (Auden) 14:32; 43:15

"A Considerable Speck" (Frost) 10:196-97

A Considerable Town (Fisher) 76:341; 87:120-21

"Considering the Snail" (Gunn) 32:209

Il consiglio d'Egitto (The Council of Egypt) (Sciascia) 8:474; 9:474; 41:389, 393

"The Consolation of Nature" (Martin) 89:118

The Consolation of Nature, and Other Stories (Martin) 89:110-13, 116, 118, 121, 125, 128-29, 137

"Consolations of Age" (Aldiss) 40:21

"The Consolations of Horror" (Ligotti) 44:53

"Consolations of Philosophy" (L'Heureux) 52:279

"Consolations of Philosophy" (Mahon) 27:288, 290-91

"A Consolatory Tale" (Dinesen) 29:159, 161-62; 95:35, 51

"Consorting with Angels" (Sexton) 53:321

"The Conspiracy" (Spinrad) 46:384

"The Conspiracy" (Tomlinson) 45:398

The Conspiracy (Hersey) 2:188; 7:154; 40:240

The Conspiracy of Equals (Ehrenburg) 62:176

Conspiracy of Knaves (Brown) 47:40-2

Conspirator (Benson) 17:49

"The Conspirators" (Burke) 2:87

"The Conspirators" (Prokosch) 48:309

The Conspirators (Borges)
See *Los conjurados*

The Conspirators (Havel) 25:224-27, 229

The Conspirators (Prokosch) 4:420; 48:311-12

Conspirators and Poets (Enright) 31:147-48

"A Constable Calls" (Heaney) 7:149; 74:167

Constance Markievicz (O'Faolain) 70:316-17

Constance; or, Solitary Practices (Durrell) 27:97-100; 41:134-38

"Constancia" (Fuentes) 113:242-43

"The Constant Symbol" (Frost) 1:111; 26:119

The Constant Wife (Arzner) 98:69

The Constant Wife (Maugham) 67:223-27

Constantly Singing (Simmons) 43:412-14

Constellations (Breton) 54:29-30; 9:132-34; 15:91

The Constellations: How They Came to Be (Gallant) 17:133

"The Constipated Frenchman" (Singh) 11:505

"Constituents of a Theory of the Media" (Enzensberger) 43:149

"Construction" (Barthelme) 115:81

Constructions (Frayn) 7:107

The Consul's Daughter (Schlee) 35:372

The Consul's File (Theroux) 11:528-29; 15:533; 28:428

"Consultation" (Dorfman) 77:142

"The Consumer Bulletin Annual" (Barthelme) 5:54

Consumer Society (Baudrillard)
See *La société de consommation*

"A Consumer's Report" (Porter) 33:319

"The Consuming Fire" (Callaghan) 41:98

"The Consumptive, Belsen, 1945" (Peake) 54:375

"Contact" (Dunn) 36:154

"Contam de Clarice Lispector" ("What They Say about C. L.") (Cabral de Melo Neto) 76:163

The Contaminated Man (Keyes)
See *The Touch*

"The Contemplative Soul" (Huxley) 11:283

The Contemporaneity Game (Oe)
See *Dojidai gemu*

Contemporaries (Kazin) 38:274-75, 279

"A Contemporary" (Merwin) 88:204

"A Contemporary Film of Lancasters in Action" (Ewart) 46:153

Contemporary Realism (Lukacs) 24:319

Contemporary Scottish Studies (MacDiarmid) 19:287

"Contemporary Trends in French Literature" (de Man) 55:421

Contempt (Godard)
See *Le mépris*

"Contend in Vain" (Asimov) 19:26

"The Contender" (Davies) 21:91

"The Contender" (Hughes) 9:284; 37:177

"The Contender" (Santos) 22:365

The Contender (Lipsyte) 21:207-09

The Contenders (Wain) 2:457; 46:408-09

"Content" (Ignatow) 14:275

"Content" (Townshend) 17:528

Contes anglais et autres (Ferron) 94:108, 123-24

Contes du chat perché (Ayme) 11:22

Contes du pays incertain (Contes: Tales from the Uncertain Country; Tales from the Uncertain Country) (Ferron) 94:103-4, 106, 110, 123-24

Contes inédits (Ferron) 94:123-24

Contes pour buveurs attardés (Tremblay) 29:426

Contes pour milles oreilles (Carrier) 78:59, 63, 67

Contes pour un homme seul (Theriault) 79:400, 410-12

Contes: Tales from the Uncertain Country (Ferron)
  See *Contes du pays incertain*
"The Contest" (Paley) 37:337
"Contest of the Bards" (Ginsberg) 36:191, 196
Il contesto (Equal Danger) (Sciascia) 8:474; 9:475; 41:388-91, 393-94
"context" (Plath) 111:217, 220
"Contexts" (Monette) 82:315
Contexts of Poetry: Interviews 1960-1970 (Creeley) 78:120
"The Continent as the Letter M" (Crase) 58:160, 162
"Continent of Strangers" (Blaise) 29:75
"The Continental College of Beauty" (Strand) 71:287
Continental Drift (Banks) 37:28-30; 72:2-5, 7, 9, 11-12, 14, 16-18, 22
The Continental Op (Hammett) 5:160-62
"Continent's End" (Jeffers) 54:236, 244
"Contingencies" (Dobyns) 37:75
"Continuación" (Alonso) 14:26
"Continue by Waking" (Dobyns) 37:75
"La continuidad histórica" (Azorin) 11:24
"Continuing" (Ammons) 25:45
A Continuing Journey (MacLeish) 14:338
"Continuing to Live" (Larkin) 39:340
Continuities in Cultural Evolution (Mead) 37:274
"Continuity" (Levine) 54:299
"The Continuity of Norman Mailer" (Oe) 86:214
Continuous: Fifty Sonnets from "The School of Eloquence" (Harrison) 43:177-80
A Continuous Harmony (Berry) 27:33, 36
"The Continuous Life" (Strand) 71:288
The Continuous Life (Strand) 71:278, 286-90
"Continuous Performance" (Fearing) 51:119
"Continuum" (Kumin) 28:224
"Contra mortem" (Carruth) 4:94
Contra Mortem (Carruth) 84:119
"Contra naturam" (Howard) 10:274
"Contra prudentium" (Ekelof) 27:110
Contraataque (Sender) 8:478
"A Contract" (Baraka) 5:45
The Contract (Carlisle) 33:103
Contract with the World (Rule) 27:421-22
The Contractor (Storey) 2:424-25; 4:529-30; 5:414-17; 8:505
The Contradictions (Ghose) 42:177-78
Contraries (Oates) 108:388
The Contrary Experience: Autobiographies (Read) 4:440-41
Contrasto for a Solo Voice (Fo) 32:176
"Contrasts" (Cendrars) 106:180
"Contrasts" (Smith) 64:396
Contre la mélancolie: Célébration hassidique II (Four Hasidic Masters and Their Struggle against Melancholy) (Wiesel) 37:451, 455-56
"Contre notre amour qui ne voulait rien d'autre" (Damas) 84:186
Le contrebandière (Maillet) 54:311
Contre-Jour: A Triptych after Pierre Bonnard (Josipovici) 43:227-28
"Contrition" (Bausch) 51:55-7
"Contrition" (Dubus) 97:211
Control (Goldman) 48:129
"Controversy" (Prince) 35:324
Controversy (Prince) 35:324-28, 331-32
"Contusion" (Plath) 9:426-27; 14:424; 51:341; 62:406; 111:163, 199

"Contusion" (Wonder) 12:660, 662
"Convalescence" (Dybek) 114:67
"Convalescing" (Oates) 19:348
"Convenience" (Murphy) 41:320
La convention belzébir (Ayme) 11:22
"The Conventional Wisdom" (Elkin) 14:157-58
"Converging City" (Okri) 87:314
"Conversa de Sevilhana" (Cabral de Melo Neto) 76:161
Conversación en la catedral (Conversation in the Cathedral) (Vargas Llosa) 6:544-48; 9:542-44; 10:496-98, 501; 15:549-52; 31:444-45; 42:404, 409; 85:350, 352-56, 358-60, 362, 364, 395
"Conversación galante" (Parra) 102:341
"Conversation" (Ai) 69:9
"Conversation" (Giovanni) 4:189
The Conversation (Coppola) 16:237-39, 242, 244-45, 249
"A Conversation about Balzac's Horse" (Hofmann) 54:229
"Conversation at Tea" (Kinnell) 13:321
"Conversation et sous-conversation" (Sarraute) 2:385
"Conversation Galante" (Eliot) 1:92
"Conversation in a Bedroom" (Davidson) 19:128
"A Conversation in Rome" (Voznesensky) 57:427
Conversation in the Cathedral (Vargas Llosa)
  See *Conversación en la catedral*
"Conversation in the Mountains" (Celan)
  See "Gespräch im Gebirge"
"Conversation in the Park" (Hacker) 72:188
The Conversation of the Three Walking Men (Weiss) 15:563
"Conversation on a Country Path about Thinking" (Heidegger) 24:266-69
"Conversation on V" (Dodson) 79:194
"Conversation Piece" (Ewart) 46:151
Conversation Piece (Point-to-Point) (Keane) 31:232-33
Conversation Piece (Visconti) 16:573, 575-76
La conversation souveraine (Char) 11:113
"Conversation with a Fireman from Brooklyn" (Gallagher) 63:118
Conversation with Calliope (Hope) 51:217
"Conversation With Death" (Seifert) 93:342
"Conversation with Langston Hughes" (Guillen) 48:167
"A Conversation with My Father" (Paley) 4:392; 6:392-93; 37:332
"Conversation with My Uncle" (Sargeson) 31:363, 373
Conversation with My Uncle (Sargeson) 31:364, 369
"A Conversation with Myself" (Knight) 40:282
Conversations (Rothenberg) 6:477
Conversations in Another Room (Josipovici) 43:226
Conversations in Bloomsbury (Anand) 93:35, 44
Conversations in Sicily (Vittorini)
  See *Conversazione in Sicilia*
"Conversations of the Tide at Jaqueira" (Cabral de Melo Neto)
  See "Prosas da maré na Jaqueira"
Conversations on a Homecoming (Murphy)
  See *The White House*
Conversations with Algren (Algren) 33:12
Conversations with Children (Laing) 95:157

"Conversations with Goethe" (Barthelme) 46:39, 42
"Conversations with Helmholtz" (Allen) 52:35
Conversations with Isaac Bashevis Singer (Singer) 69:308
"Conversations with Jan" (Wakoski) 4:572
Conversations with Professor Y (Celine)
  See *Entretiens avec le Professeur Y*
"Conversations with Unicorns" (Carey) 40:128; 96:25
Conversazione in Sicilia (Conversations in Sicily; In Sicily) (Vittorini) 6:551; 9:546-52; 14:543-47
"Converse at Night in Copenhagen" (Dinesen) 10:152; 95:50
"Conversió i mort d'en quim federal" (Espriu) 9:192
"The Conversion" (Banks) 37:24
"Conversion" (Toomer) 22:426
"The Conversion of William Kirkwood" (McGahern) 48:272-73
The Conversions (Mathews) 6:314-16; 52:307-10, 315-18
"The Convert" (Ciardi) 40:157
"The Convert" (Shapiro) 4:486
The Converts: A Novel of Early Christianity (Warner) 45:440-41
The Convict Bird (Vollmann) 89:304
Convict Thirteen (Keaton) 20:192
"Conviction" (Smith) 44:444
"Los convidados de agosto" (Castellanos) 66:48
Los convidados de agosto (The Guests of August) (Castellanos) 66:48
"Convocation Address: Queen's University, 29/5/71" (Johnston) 51:245, 253
Convoy (Altman) 16:43
Convoy (Peckinpah) 20:282
"Conway Burying Ground" (MacLeish) 8:363
"The Cooboo" (Prichard) 46:333, 345
"The Cook" (Young Bear) 94:361, 366
"Cook County" (MacLeish) 68:285, 288
"Cook of the House" (McCartney) 35:285
"Cookie" (Taylor) 18:522; 37:409
"A Cooking Egg" (Eliot) 15:210-11
"The Cooking Lesson" (Castellanos) 66:60-1
The Cooking of Provincial France (Fisher) 76:342
Cooking Together: Recipes and Recollections (Hellman) 34:347
"The Cook's Lesson" (Fuller) 62:185, 194-95
Cool Cat (Bonham) 12:52-3
Cool Country (Barnard) 48:26-7
The Cool Crazy Committed World of the '60s (Berton) 104:47
"Cool Dark Ode" (Justice) 102:258
Cool Memories 1980-1985 (Baudrillard) 60:24
Cool Repentance (Fraser) 32:186
"Cool Tombs" (Sandburg) 10:448-49; 35:352
"The Cool Web" (Graves) 1:128; 45:169-70, 173
The Cool World (Clarke) 16:217-19
Cool Zebras of Light (Peters) 7:303
Coolie (Anand) 23:13, 15; 93:24, 29, 31-32, 42, 50
"Coon Song" (Ammons) 25:43; 108:5, 8, 30
Coonardoo: The Well in the Shadow (Prichard) 46:328-29, 331-32, 334-38, 341, 343-45
"Cooney on World Affairs" (Carpenter) 41:108
Coonskin (Bakshi) 26:70-5
Co-Op (Sinclair) 15:498
"Cooped Up" (Baker) 31:28
Cooper (Masters) 48:224-25

"Cootchie" (Bishop) **32**:38, 42

Cop Hater (Hunter) **31**:224

Cop Killer (Wahloo)
  See *Polismördaren*

Cop Out (Queen) **11**:464

Copacetic (Komunyakaa) **94**:217-20, 224, 246-47

"Copacetic Mingus" (Komunyakaa) **94**:247

"Copenhagen Season" (Dinesen) **10**:152; **95**:52

"Copla" (Alonso)
  See *Oscura noticia*

Cop-Out (Guare) **29**:203-05

"Cop-Out Session" (Knight) **40**:287

"The Copper Beech" (Hine) **15**:282

"The Copperhead" (Bottoms) **53**:33

"Coppersmith" (Murphy) **41**:317

Coppia aperta (Fo) **109**:109

Coprolites (Goldbarth) **5**:143

Cops (Keaton) **20**:192, 195

Cops and Robbers (Westlake) **7**:528

"Cops of the World" (Ochs) **17**:330

"Coq au vin" (Ciardi) **40**:159

Le coq de bruyère (*The Woodcock*) (Tournier) **23**:452-53; **36**:440; **95**:361-62, 367-68, 377-78, 382-83

"le coq pondeur" (Theriault) **79**:408

Coquette (Swinnerton) **31**:422-23

Cora Fry (Brown) **32**:66-7

"Coral Sea, 1945" (Muske) **90**:309-10

Coralie Lansdowne Says No (Buzo) **61**:52-6, 58-9, 61-6, 68-9

"Coralles 1948" (Honig) **33**:211

El corazón amarillo (*The Yellow Heart*) (Neruda) **28**:310; **62**:333-34, 336

"Le Corbillard" ("The Hearse") (Tchicaya) **101**:351

La corde et les souris (Malraux) **57**:306

La corde raide (Simon) **39**:206, 209, 211

Cordélia (Mallet-Joris) **11**:355

"Cordelia's Song" (Zaturenska) **11**:580

Les cordes-de-bois (Maillet) **54**:303-04, 306-08, 311

A Cordiall Water: A Garland of Odd & Old Recipes to Assuage the Ills of Man or Beast (Fisher) **76**:338, 342; **87**:123, 125-26

"Cori descrittivi d'anima di Didone" ("Choruses Describing the States of Mind of Dido") (Ungaretti) **7**:481, 485; **15**:537

The Coriander (Dillon) **17**:95

"Coriolan" (Eliot) **41**:161

Coriolanus (Berkoff) **56**:20-3

"Coriolanus and His Mother" (Schwartz) **10**:464-65

"Coriolanus Leaves Home" (Beer) **58**:38

"Corkscrew" (Hammett) **47**:161

"Corky's Car Keys" (Ashbery) **25**:54

Corn (Ludlam) **46**:240-41

"Corn Close" (Creeley) **78**:150-51

"Corn Flakes" (Phillips) **28**:364

The Corn Is Green (Williams) **15**:576-77

Cornelius (Priestley) **2**:346

"The Corner" (Capote) **13**:137

"The Corner of the Eye" (Warren) **39**:259

The Corner That Held Them (Warner) **7**:511; **19**:460

The Cornerman (Gardner) **30**:154

Corners in the Glass (Gustafson) **36**:217-19, 222

"Cornet at Night" (Ross) **13**:493-94

The Cornet Player Who Betrayed Ireland (O'Connor) **23**:330-31

"Cornet Solo" (Day Lewis) **10**:131

"Cornfields" (Watkins) **43**:450

Cornhuskers (Sandburg) **10**:448-49, 451; **15**:466; **35**:339-41, 343, 352

Cornish Trilogy (Davies) **91**:201, 204

"Cornwall" (Corn) **33**:117

"Cornwall" (Davie) **8**:165

"Corona" (Celan) **19**:89; **53**:71

"Corona" (Delany) **38**:154

Corona de amor y muerte (Casona) **49**:49

Coronación (*Coronation*) (Donoso) **4**:126-27; **8**:178-79; **11**:145-46; **32**:151-54, 158; **99**:216, 218-19, 221-23, 232, 239, 263

"Coronary Thrombosis" (Oates) **15**:402

The Coronation (Arrabal)
  See *Le couronnement*

Coronation (Donoso)
  See *Coronación*

The Coronation Murder Mystery (O'Hara) **78**:364

Coroner's Pidgin (*Pearls before Swine*) (Allingham) **19**:17

Coronis (Booth) **13**:103

Corpo de baile or grande sertao: Veredas (*The Devil to Pay in the Backlands*) (Rosa) **23**:348-50, 353, 355-57

"The Corporal" (Gunn) **18**:199

"Corporate Entity" (MacLeish) **68**:270, 290

"The Corporation Gardener's Prologue" (Raine) **103**:180

Les corps conducteurs (*Conducting Bodies*) (Simon) **4**:497; **9**:482; **15**:493-95; **39**:205-06, 208-11

"Corps d'Energie/Rituels d'Ecriture" (Brossard) **115**:126

Les corps etrangers (Cayrol) **11**:107

Corps perdu (Cesaire) **112**:13, 15, 29

The Corpse on the Dike (van de Wetering) **47**:405-06, 412

"The Corpses at Zinderneuf" (Cassity) **42**:96

Correction (Bernhard)
  See *Korrektur*

"Corrections: Executive Suite" (Moure) **88**:232

"Corrections to the Saints: Transubstantial" (Moure) **88**:232

Corregidora (Jones) **6**:265-66; **9**:307

"Correspondence" (McCullers) **12**:433

The Correspondence of Thomas Percy and Richard Farmer (Brooks) **110**:31

"The Correspondence School Instructor Says Goodbye to His Poetry Students" (Kinnell) **29**:290

"Correspondences" (Rukeyser) **27**:411

Correspondences: A Family History in Letters (Stevenson) **7**:462-64

The Corrida at San Feliu (Scott) **9**:476; **60**:329, 340

"The Corridor" (Gunn) **18**:201

Corridor and Stairs (Ritsos) **31**:327

Corridors of Power (Snow) **1**:317; **4**:500, 502; **9**:496-97; **19**:427

Corridos (Valdez) **84**:403-04, 406, 410, 414-15

Corriente alterna (*Alternating Current*) (Paz) **3**:375, 377; **4**:396-97; **6**:396-98; **10**:390; **51**:331; **65**:182

Corrigan (Blackwood) **100**:7, 9-10, 15, 28

Corrosive Sublimate (Sorrentino) **3**:461; **7**:448, 451

"Corruption" (Lively) **32**:277

Corruption (Mosley) **43**:311, 319, 321

"The Corset" (Connell) **45**:110

"Corson's Inlet" (Ammons) **5**:26-7, 29; **8**:16-19; **9**:26, 30; **25**:43, 47-8; **108**:10, 14-17, 28, 45

Corson's Inlet (Ammons) **2**:12; **5**:25-6, 28; **8**:15; **108**:5, 24, 46, 60

Le cortège des vainqueurs (*With the Victors*) (Gallo) **95**:96-8

"Cortés and Montezuma" (Barthelme) **13**:59; **46**:35

"Cortez the Killer" (Young) **17**:575, 579, 583

"Corymba" (Davidson) **13**:168; **19**:129

Una cosa è una cosa (Moravia) **18**:346

The Cosmic Carnival of Stanislaw Lem (Lem) **40**:296

The Cosmic Connection (Sagan) **30**:331-33, 343; **112**:413, 416

The Cosmic Engineers (Simak) **55**:319

The Cosmic Express (Williamson) **29**:454

Cosmic Profit: How to Make Money without Doing Time (Mungo) **72**:291

The Cosmic Rape (Sturgeon) **22**:413; **39**:361

"Cosmic Sleepwalker" (Ekelof) **27**:117

Le cosmicomiche (*Cosmicomics*) (Calvino) **5**:99, 101; **8**:127, 129-31; **11**:89, 91-2; **22**:89, 93; **33**:98-9; **39**:306-07, 309, 313-15, 317; **73**:40-4, 47-8, 54, 57-8

Cosmicomics (Calvino)
  See *Le cosmicomiche*

"Cosmogony" (Borges) **44**:354

The Cosmological Eye (Miller) **43**:298; **84**:252

"The Cosmology of Finding Your Place" (Dorn) **10**:159

Cosmopolatain Greetings (Ginsberg) **109**:316, 318, 329

The Cosmopolitan Girl (Drexler) **6**:142-43

"Cosmopolitan Lady" (Coward) **29**:139

Cosmos (Gombrowicz)
  See *Kosmos*

Cosmos (Sagan) **30**:338-39, 340, 342-44; **112**:409-15, 418-19, 423-30, 433, 437, 442

"The Cost" (Hecht) **13**:270

"The Cost of Seriousness" (Porter) **33**:320

The Cost of Seriousness (Porter) **13**:452-53; **33**:320-21, 323, 325

"The Costa San Giorgio" (Loy) **28**:249

"La Côte Basque, 1965" (Capote) **8**:133; **34**:321, 323

Cotnoir (*Dr. Cotnoir*) (Ferron) **94**:106-07, 118, 120, 124, 126-27

"Cottage for Sale" (Murphy) **41**:319

"The Cottage Hospital" (Betjeman) **43**:36

"Cottage Street, 1953" (Wilbur) **14**:579; **110**:361-62, 369, 385-86

Cotter's England (Stead)
  See *Dark Places of the Heart*

"Cotton Avenue" (Mitchell) **12**:443

"Cotton Candy" (Giovanni) **64**:195

Cotton Candy on a Rainy Day (Giovanni) **64**:188, 191, 194-95; **117**:184, 186, 192-93, 197-98, 205

The Cotton Club (Puzo) **107**:213

The Cotton Club: New Poems (Major) **19**:293

Cotton Comes to Harlem (Himes) **4**:229; **7**:159; **18**:246; **58**:258, 267; **108**:233, 239, 256, 269, 276-77

"Cotton Gonna Kill Me Yet" (Himes) **7**:159

"Cotton Jenny" (Lightfoot) **26**:283

The Cotton Pickers (Traven) **11**:536

"Cottonfields" (Wilson) **12**:645

"Cottonwood: Part I" (Silko) **114**:314

"Cottonwood: Part II Buffalo Man" (Silko) **74**:345; **114**:314

Couch (Warhol) **20**:415

"Cougar Meat" (Gallagher) **63**:125

"Could Have" (Szymborska) **99**:200
Could Have (Szymborska) **99**:199
"Could I Leave You?" (Sondheim) **30**:382
"Could You Be Loved" (Marley) **17**:273
The Council of Egypt (Sciascia)
    See *Il consiglio d'Egitto*
"Counsel" (Bukowski) **41**:66
Counsellor-at-Law (Rice) **7**:359-63; **49**:298-300, 302
"Counsels" (Milosz) **5**:293
Count Belisarius (Graves) **39**:322; **45**:172
Count Bruga (Hecht) **8**:269
"Count Fersen to the Queen" (Christie) **110**:126
Count Julian (Goytisolo)
    See *La reivindicación del Conde Don Julián*
"Count Lothar's Heart" (Boyle) **58**:66
Count Öderland (Frisch)
    See *Graf Öderland*
"Count the Clock That Tells the Time" (Ellison) **42**:130
Count Zero (Gibson) **39**:143; **63**:129-32, 134-39
Countdown (Altman) **16**:19, 41; **116**:11, 35, 47
Countdown (Slaughter) **29**:377
Countdown to Ecstasy (Becker and Fagen) **26**:79-80
"Countee Cullen" (Dodson) **79**:193
Counter-Attack and Other Poems (Sassoon) **36**:385-86, 390-93
Counterblast (McLuhan) **83**:366
CounterBlasts No. 9: Mr. Bevan's Dream **61**:421
Counter-Clock World (Dick) **30**:115, 117, 124; **72**:121-22
Counterfeit Nazi: The Ambiguity of Good (Friedlander)
    See *Kurt Gerstein ou l'ambiguité du bien*
A Counterfeit of Silence (Stow) **23**:436
"Counter-Hegemonic Art: Do the Right Thing" (hooks) **94**:145
"Countering" (Ammons) **9**:27
The Counterlife (Roth) **47**:360-67; **86**:248, 250, 253, 255-57, 259-63
"Counterparts" (Dobyns) **37**:75
Counterparts (Fuller) **28**:153, 159
"Counterpoint" (Haldeman) **61**:174, 176
Counterpoint (Holland) **21**:154
Counter-Statement (Burke) **24**:118-20, 127-28, 132
Countess from Hong Kong (Chaplin) **16**:203
"The Countess of Pembroke's Dream" (Hope) **51**:222
Counties of Contention (Kiely) **43**:245
"Counting" (Larkin) **64**:262
"Counting Coup" (Plumly) **33**:312
"The Counting Game" (Graver) **70**:52, 54
"The Counting Houses" (Merwin) **18**:334
"Counting Months" (Leavitt) **34**:78-9
Counting My Steps: An Autobiography (Lind) **2**:245; **4**:293; **27**:271, 273; **82**:140-43
"Counting the Mad" (Justice) **102**:278-79
Counting the Ways: A Vaudeville (Albee) **9**:10; **11**:13; **53**:21-2; **86**:121; **113**:24, 31
Country (Griffiths) **52**:179-80
The Country (Plante) **23**:345-47; **38**:365-67, 370-71
The Country Ahead of Us, the Country Behind (Guterson) **91**:104
"Country & Western I" (Hacker) **72**:192
"Country & Western II" (Hacker) **72**:192
"Country Bedroom" (MacCaig) **36**:281
The Country between Us (Forche) **25**:170-72;

83:198, 207, 210-14, 219, 221; **86**:138-39, 141-42, 144
"Country Burial" (Lewis) **41**:254, 263
"Country Church" (Thomas) **13**:543
"Country Churchyard" (Warner) **19**:460
"The Country Clergy" (Thomas) **13**:544; **48**:379
"The Country Club" (Muldoon) **32**:319; **72**:265
Country Cooking and Other Stories (Mathews) **52**:307-08
"Country Cooking from Central France: Roast Boned Rolled Stuffed Shoulder of Lamb" ("Farce Double") (Mathews) **52**:307, 313
The Country Cousin (Auchincloss) **18**:24-5
"Country Dance" (MacCaig) **36**:285
"A Country Festival" (Mahapatra) **33**:283
"The Country Fiddler" (Montague) **46**:266
"Country Full of Swedes" (Caldwell) **1**:51; **60**:49-50
"Country Girl" (Brown) **48**:57
"Country Girl" (Young) **17**:569-70
The Country Girl (Odets) **2**:319-20; **28**:334, 339-40; **98**:195-96, 198-99, 209, 211-12, 215-17, 228, 230-32, 236-37, 251-52
Country Girls (O'Brien) **3**:365; **5**:313; **36**:337; **116**:182, 187, 190-93, 205-06, 214
The Country Girls Trilogy (O'Brien) **65**:170, 172; **116**:189, 195-96, 226-27
"A Country God" (Blunden) **56**:37-8, 41
Country Growth (Derleth) **31**:132-33
"The Country Houses" (Prokosch) **48**:310
"The Country Husband" (Cheever) **64**:53-4
"Country Junction" (Garrigue) **8**:240
"A Country Life" (Jarrell) **2**:209
"A Country Love Story" (Stafford) **4**:518; **68**:449
"Country Matters" (Montague) **46**:267, 275
"The Country Mouse" (Bishop) **32**:40-1, 43
"Country Mouse, City Mouse" (Price) **63**:336
"Country Music" (Cohen) **19**:115-16
Country Music (Wright) **28**:460
"Country Night" (Ondaatje) **51**:317
"The Country North of Belleville" (Purdy) **14**:433; **50**:237
The Country of a Thousand Years of Peace and Other Poems (Merrill) **2**:272; **13**:379; **91**:228
The Country of Her Dreams (Elliott) **47**:113-14
The Country of Marriage (Berry) **6**:61; **27**:33-4, 36
The Country of Purple Clouds (Strugatskii and Strugatskii) **27**:432
A Country of Strangers (Richter) **30**:322-23
The Country of the Heart (Wersba) **30**:431-32
Country of the Minotaur (Ghiselin) **23**:169-72
Country of the Open Heart (McFadden) **48**:257-58
"Country Pie" (Dylan) **12**:186
"A Country Place" (Bitov) **57**:119
Country Place (Petry) **1**:266; **7**:305; **18**:403-04
Country Places (Andrade) **18**:4
"Country Pleasures" (Grenville) **61**:152
Country Pleasures (Brammer) **31**:53-4
Country Poems (Derleth) **31**:138
"The Country Ride" (Slessor) **14**:493
"Country Road H" (Baxter) **78**:25
The Country Scene (Masefield) **11**:357
Country Sentiment (Graves) **6**:210; **45**:163, 166
"Country Station" (Adcock) **41**:14
"A Country Tale" (Dinesen) **10**:152

"Country Town" (Buckley) **57**:129
"Country Town" (Wright) **11**:578; **53**:427
"Country Towns" (Slessor) **14**:496
"A Country Walk" (Kinsella) **4**:271; **19**:251, 255
Country without Maps (Garrigue) **2**:153-54; **8**:239
Country You Can't Walk In (Kelly) **55**:159
"Countrymen" (Kennedy) **8**:320
"County" (Betjeman) **43**:47
"The County Engineer" (Durcan) **43**:114-15
"County Fair" (Ryan) **65**:211, 215
"County Ward" (Soto) **80**:286
"The Coup" (Archer) **28**:14
"The Coup" (Chatwin) **59**:279
The Coup (Updike) **13**:559-63; **15**:544, 548; **23**:470; **34**:289; **43**:431; **70**:249
Le coup de grâce (*Coup de Grâce*) (Yourcenar) **19**:482; **38**:454, 456, 464; **50**:363, 365; **87**:387, 390-91, 394, 396-98, 413-17, 419, 421
Coup de Grâce (Yourcenar)
    See *Le coup de grâce*
Le coupable (*The Guilty*) (Bataille) **29**:38-9
"Couperin-Le-Grand in Turkey" (Gustafson) **36**:213
"A Coupla Scalped Indians" (Ellison) **114**:93, 94, 126, 138
"The Couple" (Strand) **71**:286, 288
"A Couple" (Swenson) **106**:337
"The Couple" (Voigt) **54**:431
A Couple of Comedians (Carpenter) **41**:105-08
"A Couple of Fools" (Bates) **46**:67
Couples (Updike) **1**:343-45; **2**:440, 442-44; **3**:488; **5**:449-52, 456, 458-59; **7**:485, 489-90; **9**:537-38; **13**:557-59, 561-62; **15**:541, 545; **23**:456-67, 471, 477; **34**:284, 286, 293; **70**:249, 252
Couplings and Groupings (Terry) **19**:441
"Coups de couteaux" ("Knife Blows") (Mauriac) **56**:206
"Courage" (Akhmatova) **25**:25; **64**:15
Courage (Akhmatova) **25**:29-30
"Courage Means Running" (Empson) **34**:540
"The Courage of Shutting Up" (Plath) **51**:340, 344
The Courage of Turtles (Hoagland) **28**:180-81, 186
"The Courage to See" (Solzhenitsyn) **78**:405
"La courageuse" (Theriault) **79**:408
"The Couriers" (Plath) **111**:204
Le couronnement (*The Coronation*) (Arrabal) **9**:34, 38; **18**:20; **58**:11
"A Course in Filmmaking" (Mailer) **1**:193
Court and Spark (Mitchell) **12**:438, 440, 442
The Court and the Castle (West) **7**:526; **9**:562; **31**:458
"Court Day" (Still) **49**:362
"The Court Historian (A Satirical Composition)" (MacNeice) **53**:233
"Court Martial" (Warren) **39**:268
Court of Appeal (Richards) **14**:453
Court of Chaos (Zelazny) **21**:471-73
"The Court of Divine Justice" (Klappert) **57**:266
"Court of Inquiry" (Amis) **40**:43, 45
"Courtesies of the Interregnum" (Gunn) **81**:187
"Courting Disaster" (Roth) **4**:459
The Courting of Marie Jenvrin (Ringwood) **48**:329-30, 335, 337-39
"Courtly Vision" (Mukherjee) **53**:267, 269
"Courts-circuits" (Simon) **15**:497

"Courtship" (Dove) **50**:156-57
"Courtship" (O'Brien) **116**:186
"Courtship" (Strand) **18**:519; **41**:438; **71**:285
"Courtship, Diligence" (Dove) **50**:156
The Courtyard **59**:368
"The Courtyards" (Szirtes) **46**:395-96
Courtyards in Delft (Mahon) **27**:292
Cousin Angélica (Saura)
    See *La prima Angélica*
"Cousin Harriet" (Eliot) **13**:202
"Cousin Larry" (Parker) **68**:334, 336
Cousin Rosamund (West) **50**:397
"Cousins" (Bellow) **33**:67-8; **63**:42
"Cousins" (Ihimaera) **46**:200
Les cousins (Chabrol) **16**:167-68, 173-74, 180, 183
"Couvade" (Harris) **25**:217
The Covenant (Michener) **29**:311-14; **109**:375, 379, 381, 386
"Covenant Woman" (Dylan) **77**:185-87, 190
"Coventry" (Heinlein) **55**:302
Cover Charge (Woolrich) **77**:387
Cover Her Face (James) **18**:272; **46**:205, 207, 210
"Cover Note" (Merwin) **88**:209
"Covered Bridge" (Warren) **39**:265
The Covered Wagon (Ford) **16**:302
"The Covering of Light" (Strand) **18**:518
"The Covert" (Blunden) **56**:48
"The Cow" (Ciardi) **40**:157
"The Cow" (Prichard) **46**:332-33, 343, 345
Cow (Sterchi)
    See *Blosch*
"The Cow in Apple-Time" (Frost) **26**:112
"Cow in Calf" (Heaney) **14**:243
A Cow in the House and Other Stories (Kiely) **23**:265
The Cow Jumped over the Moon (Birney) **6**:79
"The Cow of the Barricades" (Rao) **56**:291, 312, 314
The Cow of the Barricades and Other Stories (Rao) **56**:287, 291, 294, 296, 306
"The Cow That Swam Lake Ontario" (McFadden) **48**:257
"Coward" (Avison) **97**:80
Coward Plays (Coward) **29**:137
The Cowards (Skvorecky)
    See *Zbabelci*
"Cowards from the Colleges" (Hughes) **108**:319
"Cowboy" (Steele) **45**:362
Cowboy Mouth (Shepard) **6**:495; **17**:441, 443-45
Cowboy Mouth (Smith) **12**:534
"Cowboys" (Williams) **56**:427
Cowboys #2 (Shepard) **17**:440-41; **41**:409, 412
"Cowboys and Indians" (Stafford) **4**:517
"Cowgirl in the Sand" (Young) **17**:569
"Cowpats" (Sargeson) **31**:362, 370
"Cows" (Plumly) **33**:313
"Cows: A Vision" (Gallagher) **18**:169
"The Cows at Night" (Carruth) **7**:40; **84**:132
"Cows in Trouble" (Martin) **30**:248
"The Cowshed Blues" (Carruth) **84**:129
"The Cowslip Field" (Bates) **46**:67
"Cowtown" (Simon) **26**:410
"Coyote" (Mitchell) **12**:441-42
"Coyote and the Stro'ro'ka Dancers" (Silko) **74**:348
A Coyote Columbus Story (King) **89**:92, 94, 97-8, 101
"Coyote Holds a Full House in His Hand" (Silko) **23**:411; **74**:349

"Coyotes" (Mason) **82**:244
Coyote's Daylight Trip (Allen) **84**:3, 11, 38
"Crab" (Adcock) **41**:18
"A Crab" (Gunn) **18**:200
"Crab" (Smith) **42**:347-48
Crab Apple Jelly (O'Connor) **14**:395, 398-400
"Crab Boil" (Dove) **81**:147
"Crab Crack" (Updike) **43**:436
"The Crab Feast" (Malouf) **28**:268
"Crabs" (Carey) **96**:27-8, 30, 36, 67
"Crabs" (Piercy) **27**:375
"The Crabs Are Crazy" (Ochs) **17**:335
Crache-à-pic (The Devil Is Loose!) (Maillet) **54**:317-18
The Crack in Space (Dick) **72**:121
Crack Steppin' (Milner) **56**:225
"Cracked Actor" (Bowie) **17**:60
"The Cracked Looking-Glass" (Porter) **101**:211
Crackers: This Whole Many-Angled Thing of Jimmy, More Carters, Ominous Little Animals, Sad Singing Women, My Daddy and Me (Blount) **38**:45-8
A Cracking of Thorns (Hollander) **8**:298
"Cracklin' Rose" (Diamond) **30**:110-11, 113-14
"The Cracks" (Creeley) **78**:143
Cracks (Purdy) **4**:422; **10**:421; **28**:378-79
The Crackwalker (Thompson) **39**:253
"Cradle Song" (Chester) **49**:55
Cradle Song (Andrade)
    See *Canção de berço*
Craft Slices (Bowering) **47**:30-1
The Crafte So Longe to Lerne (Purdy) **3**:408; **6**:428
Craig's Wife (Arzner) **98**:63, 71, 74, 81-3, 86
Crampton Hodnet (Pym) **37**:378-79; **111**:263, 268, 270, 275, 277-78, 283-85
"The Crane" (Watkins) **43**:444
"A Cranefly in September" (Hughes) **37**:180
The Cranes Fly Early (Aitmatov)
    See *Rannie zhuravli*
"The Crank" (Baxter) **45**:52; **78**:17
"The Crank That Made the Revolution" (Gray) **41**:183
"Craps" (Oates) **108**:384
Crash (Ballard) **3**:34-5; **6**:27-8; **14**:41
Crash Club (Felsen) **17**:122-23
The Crash of '79 (Erdman) **25**:154-55
Les crasseux (Maillet) **54**:305-07, 310-11, 313-17
"Crate" (Sturgeon) **22**:411
"Crátion du Monde" (Crase) **58**:164
Craven House (Hamilton) **51**:183, 190, 194
"A Craving for Innocence" (Gary) **25**:186
A Craving for Swan (Codrescu) **46**:105
Crawl (Williams) **33**:444
Crawling Arnold (Feiffer) **64**:159-60
"Crawling Out at Parties" (Bottoms) **53**:29, 31
"Crazy" (Olson) **28**:343
"Crazy Carlson's Meadow" (Bly) **38**:55, 57
Crazy Cock (Miller) **84**:261
"Crazy, Crazy, Now Showing Everywhere" (Gilchrist) **34**:165
"Crazy Gypsy" (Salinas) **90**:322, 324, 327
Crazy Gypsy (Salinas) **90**:323-24, 326, 330, 332
"Crazy Horse names his daughter" (Clifton) **66**:82
Crazy Horse: The Strange Man of Oglalas (Sandoz) **28**:402-03, 407

"The Crazy Hunter" (Boyle) **19**:64-5; **58**:67
Crazy in Berlin (Berger) **3**:63; **5**:60; **8**:83; **18**:53-4, 57; **38**:36-8
"Crazy in the Stir" (Himes) **58**:265, 267; **108**:227
The Crazy Kill (Himes) **18**:245; **58**:257, 261, 265, 267
Crazy Like a Fox (Perelman) **23**:334, 339; **49**:264
"The Crazy Old Man" (Nissenson) **4**:381
"Crazy Pigeon" (Knight) **40**:279
The Crazy Ray (Clair)
    See *Paris qui dort*
Crazy Salad (Ephron) **17**:111-13; **31**:159
"Crazy Times" (Waddington) **28**:440
Cream in My Coffee (Potter) **86**:346
Creamy and Delicious: Eat My Words (In Other Words) (Katz) **47**:216, 218, 222
"La créance" ("Credit Due") (Ferron) **94**:126
"Creating a Personal Mythology" (Wakoski) **40**:454
"Creation" (Harris) **25**:212
"Creation" (Tanizaki) **28**:415
"The Creation" (Van Duyn) **63**:441; **116**:402, 408, 429
Creation (Vidal) **22**:436-40; **33**:407; **72**:385, 387
"The Creation, according to Coyote" (Ortiz) **45**:306
La création culturelle dans la société moderne (Cultural Creation) (Goldmann) **24**:242, 250
La Création de Monde (Cendrars) **106**:190
"Creation of Anguish" (Nemerov) **2**:306-07
"The Creation of the Animals" (Tillinghast) **29**:415
The Creation of the World and Other Business (Miller) **2**:280; **15**:373
The Creative Element: A Study of Vision, Despair and Orthodoxy Among Some Modern Writers (Spender) **91**:261
Creative Fidelity (Marcel) **15**:359
"The Creative Impulse" (Maugham) **67**:219
"The Creative Instinct" (Maugham) **67**:205
"Creative Jive" (Codrescu) **46**:104
Creative Mythology (Campbell)
    See *The Masks of God: Creative Mythology*
The Creative Writer (Birney) **11**:50
"The Creator and the Commissars" (Heym) **41**:217
Creature Comforts (Addams) **30**:16
"The Creature from the Black Lagoon" (Jensen) **37**:192
"Creatures" (Jacobsen) **48**:198
Creatures (Colum) **28**:91
Les creátures (Varda) **16**:558
"The Creature's Claim" (Johnston) **51**:243, 245, 247, 252
Creatures in an Alphabet (Barnes) **29**:32
Creatures of Light and Darkness (Zelazny) **21**:464
"Credences of Summer" (Ashbery) **77**:65-66
Credentials of a Sympathiser (Barker) **37**:37
"Credit Due" (Ferron)
    See "La créance"
"Credo" (Cohen) **38**:131
"Credo" (McAuley) **45**:253
A Creed for the Third Millennium (McCullough) **107**:139-40, 154
Creek Mary's Blood (Brown) **18**:70-2; **47**:40
Creepshow (King) **26**:239-40, 243-44; **37**:206
"Creon's Mouse" (Davie) **10**:121-22
"Crepe Myrtle" (Aiken) **52**:24

Crépusale (Gallo)   95:98

Crepúscularia (*The Twilight Book*) (Neruda) 28:312-13; 62:322-23

Le crépuscule des dieux de la steppe (Kadare) 52:259

Crépuscules (Soupault)   68:408

"Crescent Moon like a Canoe" (Piercy) 27:376, 381

Cress Delahanty (West)   7:521; 17:545-48, 551

Cressida (Baxter)   14:62

The Crest on the Silver: An Autobiography (Grigson)   39:331

"The Cretan Woman" (Jeffers)   54:242

The Cretan Woman (Jeffers)   11:306

"Crevasse" (Faulkner)   8:213

"Crevasses" (Cesaire)   112:20, 22-3, 25

"Crèvecoeur" (Niedecker)   42:299

"Crèvecoeur" (Reverdy)   53:283

Le crève-coeur (*Heartbreak*) (Aragon) 22:37

"Crew" (Willard)   37:463

"Crew-Cuts" (Hall)   37:142

Cria! (*Cria cuervos*) (Saura)   20:316-20

Cria cuervos (Saura)
  See *Cria!*

Cría ojos (*My House Is on Fire*) (Dorfman) 77:141-44

The Cricket beneath the Waterfall and Other Stories (Krleza)   8:330; 114:185

Cricket Country (Blunden)   56:34, 48

"Cricket Master" (Betjeman)   43:43

"Crickets" (Butler)   81:129

"Criers and Kibitzers, Kibitzers and Criers" (Elkin)   51:98

Criers and Kibitzers, Kibitzers and Criers (Elkin) 4:152, 154; 51:88, 98-9;91:213-14

Cries and Whispers (Bergman)
  See *Viskningar och rop*

Cries for Help (Handke)
  See *Calling for Help*

Crime and Justice in Our Time (Hyde) 21:180

"Crime & Punishment" (Dybek)   114:61

"Crime and the Law" (MacInnes)   23:286

The Crime at Black Dudley (*The Black Dudley Murder*) (Allingham)   19:13

The Crime at Lock 14 (Simenon)   47:369

"Crime at the Tennis Club" (Moravia)
  See "Crime at the Tennis Club"

Le crime de M. Lange (*The Crime of Monsieur Lange*) (Renoir)   20:291, 294, 296-98, 306, 309-10

"Le crime de Suzana" (Kadare)   52:261

A Crime in Holland (Simenon)   47:370

Crime na Calle Relator (*Crime on Relator Street*) (Cabral de Melo Neto)   76:161

The Crime of Monsieur Lange (Renoir)
  See *Le crime de M. Lange*

"The Crime of S. Karma" (Abe)
  See "S. Karuma-shi no hanzai"

The Crime of S. Karma (Abe)
  See *S. Karuma-shi no hanzai*

"The Crime of the Mathematics Professor" (Lispector)   43:269

Crime on Relator Street (Cabral de Melo Neto)
  See *Crime na Calle Relator*

Crime Partners (Goines)   80:94, 96

Crime Passionel (Sartre)
  See *Les mains sales*

"Crimes of Conscience" (Gordimer)   33:184

Crimes of Passion (Orton)   43:330

Crimes of the Heart (Henley)   23:214-17

Crimes Times Three: Cover Her Face. A Mind to Murder. Shroud for a Nightingale

(James)   18:273

"The Criminal" (Tanizaki)   28:417

The Criminal (Thompson)   69:386

"A Criminal Act" (Harrison)   42:203

"Criminal Ballad" (Hughes)   9:284

"The Criminal Child" (Genet)   14:197

Criminal Conversation (Freeling)   38:184-85

The Criminal Life of Archilbaldo de la Cruz (Bunuel)
  See *Ensayo de un crimen*

Criminals in Love (Walker)
  See *The East End Plays*

The Crimson Gang of Asakusa (Lacey)
  See *The Crimson Gang of Asakusa*

Crimson Ramblers (West)   7:521; 17:550

"Crinkle, Near Birr" (Durcan)   70:147

"The Crinoid" (Watkins)   43:450

"A Crippen Case in Japan" (Tanizaki)   14:527

"Cripple Creek Ferry" (Young)   17:569-71, 582

"Crippled Inside" (Lennon)   35:263-64

"Crise de coeur" (Hollander)   5:186

Crises of the Republic (Arendt)   98:11

"The Crisis" (Barthelme)   13:59; 46:41

"Crisis" (Berryman)   62:58

"Crisis" (Marley)   17:271

Crisis (Bergman)
  See *Kris*

Crisis in the Church: A Study of Religion in America (Greeley)   28:174

"The Crisis of Man" (Camus)   69:104

The Crisis of the Old Order: 1919-1933 (Schlesinger)   84:351, 380, 382

Crisis: Pages from a Diary (Hesse)
  See *Krisis: Ein Stuck Tagebuch*

"Crisscross" (Sommer)   25:425

Cristóbal nonato (*Christopher Unborn*) (Fuentes)   60:161, 168-69, 171-73; 113:251-53

"Cristo's" (Muldoon)
  See "Christo's"

Cristoval Colon (Krleza)
  See *Kristofor Kolombo*

"Criteria for Negro Art" (Du Bois)   64:120, 123; 96:146

"The Critic" (O'Hara)   13:427; 78:356

The Critic (Brooks)   12:76

"The Critic as Clown" (Eagleton)   63:107

"La critica" (Ginzburg)   54:207

"Critical Can-Opener" (Brautigan)   3:89

Critical Essays (Barthes)
  See *Essais critiques*

Critical Essays (Enzensberger)   43:153-54

"Critical Languages" (Acker)   111:47

"The Critical Method of R. P. Blackmur" (Schwartz)   10:462

The Critical Path (Frye)   24:231; 70:277

Critical Understanding: The Powers and Limits of Pluralism (Booth)   24:97-9

Critical Writings, 1953-1978 (de Man)   55:413-14

"Criticism and Crisis" (de Man)   55:397

Criticism and Ideology: A Study in Marxist Literary Theory (Eagleton)   63:94, 96-7, 101-04, 112-13

Criticism and Social Change (Lentricchia) 34:571-75

Criticism and Truth (Barthes)
  See *Critique et vérité*

"Criticism as Pure Speculation" (Ransom) 4:434

"Criticism, History, and Critical Relativism" (Brooks)   110:9, 35

"Criticism in the Jungle" (Gates)   65:366, 378, 398

Criticism in the Wilderness: The Study of Literature Today (Hartman)   27:185-88

"Criticism, Inc." (Ransom)   24:368

"Il critico d'arte" (Buzzati)   36:86

"Critics" (Busch)   47:62

"Critics and Connoisseurs" (Moore)   47:262

Critics and Criticism (Crane)   27:71

"Critics and Thinkers" (Birkerts)   116:148

"Critics Can Bleed" (Fisher)   25:160

"A Critic's Job of Work" (Blackmur)   24:56-7, 62

Critique de la raison dialectique, Volume I: Théorie des ensembles pratiques (*Critique of Dialectical Reason: Theory of Practical Ensembles*) (Sartre)   4:474; 7:390-91, 393-94, 397; 9:470; 24:410, 412, 421; 44:494-95, 498; 50:382-84; 52:373, 380, 384-85, 388-89

"Critique de la vie quotidienne" (Barthelme) 3:43-4; 13:55-6; 23:49; 115:60

Critique et vérité (*Criticism and Truth*) (Barthes) 24:37; 83:77-8, 80, 89

Critique of Dialectical Reason: Theory of Practical Ensembles (Sartre)
  See *Critique de la raison dialectique, Volume I: Théorie des ensembles pratiques*

"A Critique of Political Ecology" (Enzensberger)   43:149-50, 154

The Croatian God Mars (Krleza)
  See *Hrvatski bog Mars*

"Croatoan" (Ellison)   13:207

"The Crocodile and the Monkey" (Seth)   90:353

"The Crocodiles of Yamoussoukro" (Naipaul) 37:325, 327-29

The Crofter and the Laird (McPhee)   36:294

Croissez et multipliez (Marcel)   15:360

Il crollo della baliverna (Buzzati)   36:91

Crome Yellow (Huxley)   1:150-51; 4:238-44; 5:194; 8:304; 11:281-82, 284, 288; 18:265, 267-69; 35:235, 240, 243; 79:287, 306, 309, 326-28

Cromedeyre-le-viel (Romains)   7:381

Cromwell (Storey)   4:529; 5:416

Cromwell: Our Chief of Men (*Cromwell: The Lord Protector*) (Fraser)   32:180-83, 185; 107:35-38

Cromwell: The Lord Protector (Fraser)
  See *Cromwell: Our Chief of Men*

Cronaca di un amore (Antonioni)   20:19, 21-2, 24, 28

Crónica de una muerte anunciada (*Chronicle of a Death Foretold*) (Garcia Marquez) 27:148-53, 156-58; 47:146-48, 151, 153-54; 55:134; 68:158, 161

Crónica del alba (*Chronicle of Dawn; Chronicle of Early Youth*) (Sender)   8:478, 481

Crónicas de Bustos Domecq (*Chronicles of Bustos Domecq*) (Bioy Casares)   88:64, 78

Crónicas reales (*Royal Chronicles*) (Mujica Lainez)   31:281

"Cronkhite Beach" (Tomlinson)   45:400

Cronopios and Famas (Cortazar)
  See *Historia de cronopios y de famas*

Crooked House (Christie)   12:117, 120; 48:74-5; 110:137

The Crooked Lines of God: Poems, 1949-54 (Everson)   1:96; 14:166

"The Crooked Made Straight" (Agnon)
  See "Vehaya he'akov lemishor"

"A Crooked Prayer" (Okri)   87:314

Crooklyn (Lee)   105:115-20, 127-28, 130

"Crop Campers" (Davis)   49:93

Cropper's Cabin (Thompson)   69:384

"Cross" (Hughes)   10:280; 108:314, 334-35

"The Cross" (Tate)   2:430; 4:536; 6:525

Cross Country (MacLennan)   92:304, 306, 330, 341, 346, 349

"Cross Cut" (Davison)   28:103

"Cross Examination" (Sukenick)   48:369

"Cross My Heart" (Ochs)   17:334

Cross of Iron (Peckinpah)   20:282-83

Cross Purpose (Camus)
   See *Le malentendu*

"Cross Ties" (Kennedy)   42:256-57

Cross Ties: Selected Poems (Kennedy)   42:255-58

Cross Town (Kesselring)   45:207

Crossbloods: Bone Courts, Bingo, and Other Reports (Vizenor)   103:311-12

"Crossbones" (Michaels)   25:314

"Cross-Country Snow" (Hemingway)   1:143; 10:269; 30:181, 191, 197-98

"The Crossed Apple" (Bogan)   39:393; 46:78, 83, 86; 93:64, 96

Cross-Examined (Grass)
   See *Ausgefragt*

"The Crossing" (Dumas)   6:145

The Crossing (McCarthy)   101:183-85, 187-89, 191-97, 199-205

"Crossing a River" (Wagoner)   15:560

"Crossing into Eden" (Stegner)   81:347

Crossing Over (Elman)   19:151

"Crossing the Border" (Hillis)   66:194

Crossing the Border (Oates)   11:403-04

"Crossing the Great Void" (Abish)   22:19

"Crossing the Line" (Muldoon)   72:273

Crossing the Mangrove (Conde)
   See *Traversée de la mangrove*

"Crossing the Mississippi" (Hemingway)   30:197

Crossing the River (Phillips)   96:350-55, 357

Crossing the River Twice (Haviaras)   33:202

"Crossing the Rubicon" (Thomas)   37:419-21; 107:327-28, 330-31, 349-50

"Crossing the Swamps" (Oliver)   34:247; 98:274, 297

"Crossing the Water" (Plath)   51:349; 111:210, 214-15

Crossing the Water: Transitional Poems (Plath)   1:270-71; 2:337-38; 3:389, 391; 5:339, 343, 345; 9:433; 11:447-49; 14:424-26; 17:352-54, 362-64; 62:389; 111:158, 166-67, 180-81, 185

Crossing to Safety (Stegner)   49:360-61; 81:345, 349-50

"Crossing Water" (Harjo)   83:282

"Crossings" (Dorfman)   77:142, 144

"Crossings" (Heaney)   74:188-89

Crossings (Rovit)   7:383-84

The Crossroad Murders (*Maigret at the Crossroads*) (Simenon)   47:369, 379

"Crossroads" (Dobyns)   37:77

"Crossroads" (Gunn)   32:212

"Crossroads" (Hemingway)   39:399, 401-02

"Crossroads Inn" (Ryan)   65:213, 215

"The Crossroads of the World, Etc." (Merwin)   5:288

The Crossroads of Time (Norton)   12:467, 470-71

"Cross-Stitch" (Graham)   48:145

Crosstime Agent (Norton)   12:469

"Crotch Lake" (Sanders)   53:304

"Crow" (Carroll)   35:80

"Crow" (Ezekiel)   61:109

"Crow" (Hogan)   73:154

Crow (Booth)   13:103

The Crow and the Heart (Carruth)   4:93; 84:128, 135

"the crow children walking circles in the snow" (Young Bear)   94:363

Crow: From the Life and Songs of the Crow (Hughes)   2:199-205; 4:235-37; 9:280-81, 283; 14:272-73; 37:171-72, 174-81

"Crow Jane in High Society" (Baraka)   115:39

Crowbar (Wellman)   65:240-41

"The Crowd Punk Season Drew" (Hannah)   90:127, 130

Crowds and Power (Canetti)
   See *Masse und Macht*

"Crowing-Hen Blues" (Hughes)   15:292

The Crown and the Cross (Slaughter)   29:376

"Crown Fire" (Caldwell)   60:48

The Crown of Columbus (Dorris)   109:296-98, 307-09

The Crown of Columbus (Dorris and Erdrich)   70:332, 348, 355

A Crown of Feathers, and Other Stories (Singer)   3:457-59; 6:509-11; 9:486-87; 11:499; 15:507; 23:422

"The Crown of Frogs" (Ryan)   65:209-10, 215-16

"Crown of Thorns" (Celan)
   See "Dornenkranz"

"Crown Point Pensioners" (Hughes)   37:172

The Crown Princess and Other Stories (Brophy)   29:90-1; 105:8, 15, 30

Crowned Heads (Tryon)   11:548-49

"Crowned Out" (Celan)   82:37

Crownfire (Caldwell)   50:301

"The Crowning" (Broumas)   73:16

"Crows" (Carroll)   38:103

"The Crows" (Ezekiel)   61:104

"Crows" (Mahapatra)   33:283

"Crows" (Simic)   49:336-37

Crows (Dickinson)   49:101-03

"Crow's Account of St. George" (Hughes)   4:236; 9:284

"Crow's Account of the Battle" (Hughes)   4:236

"Crows at Paestum" (Garrett)   11:219; 51:147

"Crow's First Lesson" (Hughes)   2:200-01

"Crow's Theology" (Hughes)   2:204; 4:236

"Crowson" (Nye)   42:304

"Croydon" (Betjeman)   43:52

The Crozart Story (Fearing)   51:119

Le cru et le cuit (*The Raw and the Cooked*) (Levi-Strauss)   38:297-301, 304, 306, 309

Crucial Conversations (Sarton)   14:480-81; 91:245

The Crucible (Miller)   1:216-17, 219; 2:278, 280; 6:326, 328-32; 10:342, 346; 15:372-73; 26:312-15, 319, 324-25, 327; 47:251, 254, 256; 78:287-329

Crucible of Power (Williamson)   29:455

"The Crucifix" (Read)   4:439

Crucifix in a Deathhand: New Poems, 1963-1965 (Bukowski)   5:80-1; 41:67; 82:15; 108:81, 110

"The Crucifixion" (Akhmatova)   64:12

"Crucifixion" (Ochs)   17:333, 335

"Crucifixions" (Walker)   9:558

"Crucifixus etiam" (Miller)   30:262-65

"The Cruel Falcon" (Jeffers)   54:244

"Cruel Shoes" (Martin)   30:246

Cruel Shoes (Martin)   30:248

"The Cruel Suitor" (Oates)   108:350-51

The Cruelest Month (*The Cells of Love*) (Buckler)   13:121-22

Cruelty (Ai)   4:16; 14:7-8; 69:3-6, 8, 11-13, 16-17

"The Cruise" (Rukeyser)   27:404

"Cruise (Letters from a Young Lady of Leisure)" (Waugh)   27:477

The Cruise of "The Breadwinner" (Bates)   46:61, 63-5

The Cruise of the Cashalot (Edmonds)   35:147

The Cruise of the Santa Maria (Dillon)   17:97

"The Cruising Auk" (Johnston)   51:239, 249-51

The Cruising Auk (Johnston)   51:238-45, 247-52

"Cruising for Burgers" (Zappa)   17:585

Cruising Speed (Buckley)   7:34; 37:61

Cruising with Reuben and the Jets (Zappa)   17:585, 589

Crump's Terms (Ghose)   42:181

"The Crunge" (Page and Plant)   12:477, 482

"Crusade" (Oz)   5:335; 8:436-37

The Crusaders (Heym)   41:212-13, 216

"A Crusader's Christmas" (Brown)   100:83

"The Crushed Nettle" (Duras)   68:90

"Crushing a Butterfly" (McCarthy)   24:346

"Crusoe in England" (Bishop)   9:96-7; 13:89-91, 94-5; 15:61; 32:31, 33, 37, 39

Crusoe's Daughter (Gardam)   43:172-73

"Crusoe's Island" (Walcott)   25:451-52; 76:274, 280

"Crusoe's Journal" (Walcott)   76:281

Crust (Popa)   19:373

"La cruz" (Parra)   102:343

"Cruz Alta" (Soupault)   68:407

"Cruzto, Indian Chief" (Ulibarri)
   See "El cacique Cruzto"

"Cry" (Bagryana)
   See "Vik"

"A Cry" (Oe)   86:241

"The Cry" (Smith)   64:392

"Cry Ararat!" (Page)   7:291; 18:377

"Cry Baby Cry" (Lennon and McCartney)   35:274

Cry Evil (Rooke)   25:392-93

"Cry for Me" (Kelley)   22:247

The Cry for the Dead (Wright)   53:432

Cry for the Strangers (Saul)   46:366

"The Cry Going Out over Pastures" (Bly)   10:62

A Cry of Absence (Jones)   4:263

A Cry of Angels (Montgomery)   7:233

"Cry of Birth" (Clark)   38:126-27

A Cry of Players (Gibson)   23:179-80

The Cry of the Crow (George)   35:178-79

The Cry of the Halidon (Ludlum)   43:274-75

The Cry of the Owl (Highsmith)   2:192-93; 102:170, 172

A Cry of Whiteness (Fleming)   37:122

Cry Softly! The Story of Child Abuse (Hyde)   21:180

Cry, the Beloved Country: A Story of Comfort in Desolation (Paton)   4:395; 10:387; 25:357-62; 55:310-14; 106:278-79, 281-83, 288, 293-94, 297-300, 304-06, 311

Cry, the Peacock (Desai)   37:64-70; 97:142, 149, 151-52, 154, 160-62

Cry to Heaven (Rice)   41:364-65

"Cry to Me" (Marley)   17:269

Cry Wolf (Smith)   33:375-76

Cryer and Ford: You Know My Music (Cryer)   21:80

The Crying Game (Braine)   1:43

The Crying Game (Jordan) **110**:282-89, 291-93, 295-309

Crying in the Wilderness: The Struggle for Justice in South Africa (Tutu) **80**:356-57

The Crying of Lot 49 (Pynchon) **2**:354-55, 357; **3**:409-12, 414-15, 417-20; **6**:434-36, 438-39; **9**:444-45; **11**:452, 455-57; **18**:429-34, 436-37; **33**:327-31, 333-35, 338; **62**:432-33, 436, 439, 443, 445-46, 448-49, 451, 453; **72**:294-342

The Cryptogram (Mamet) **91**:144-54

Cryptozoic (Aldiss)
   See *An Age*

"The Crystal" (Aiken) **52**:24, 26-7

Crystal and Fox (Friel) **5**:128-29; **42**:168; **115**:229, 241

The Crystal Cave (Stewart) **7**:462; **35**:391, 393-96; **117**:368-69, 376, 385-86, 390-92, 394

Crystal Express (Sterling) **72**:372

"The Crystal Fantasy" (Kawabata) **9**:311
   See "Suisho Genso"

The Crystal Garden (Feinstein)
   See *The Glass Alembic*

The Crystal Gryphon (Norton) **12**:463, 465

"The Crystal Interior of a Filthy Man" (Rozewicz) **23**:362

"Crystal Lake" (Harjo) **83**:276

The Crystal Lithium (Schuyler) **5**:383

"Crystal Night" (Levertov) **66**:239

"A Crystal Principle" (Young) **82**:396, 412

"The Crystal Ship" (Vinge) **30**:410

"The Crystal Skull" (Raine) **45**:337

Crystal Vision (Sorrentino) **40**:384-87, 389

The Crystal World (Aldington) **49**:15, 18

The Crystal World (Ballard) **6**:27-8; **14**:41; **36**:35-7, 45

C'tà ton tour Laura Cadieux (Tremblay) **102**:375

"Ctesiphon" (Christie) **110**:127

Cuaderno de bitácora de 'Rayuela' (Cortazar) **92**:169, 171-73

Cuaderno San Martín (*San Martín Copybook*) (Borges) **19**:45; **44**:367

"Cualquier tiempo pasado fue peor" (Guillen) **48**:159

"Cuarta versión" ("Fourth Version") (Valenzuela) **31**:438, 440; **104**:372, 377-78

Cuatro para Delfina (*Four for Delfina*) (Donoso) **99**:242

"Cuba" (Hemingway) **6**:232; **8**:285

"Cuba" (Muldoon) **32**:321; **72**:266

Cuba (Lester) **20**:232

"Cuba, 1962" (Ai) **69**:3-4, 8, 11, 13

Cuba and His Teddy Bear (Povod) **44**:86-90

"Cuba Confrontation" (Clark) **38**:129

"Cuba libre" (Baraka) **14**:48

"Cuba: Púeblo y poesía" (Guillen) **79**:238

"Cuba Revisited" (Gellhorn) **60**:191

Cuba, Yes? (Caute) **29**:119

The Cuban Thing (Gelber) **1**:114

The Cube Root of Uncertainty (Silverberg) **7**:425

"The Cubs" (Vargas Llosa)
   See "Los cachorros"

The Cubs, and Other Stories (Vargas Llosa)
   See *Los cachorros*

Cuchama and Sacred Mountains (Waters) **88**:365

"El cuchillo y la piedra" (Marques) **96**:227, 244

"Cuckold's Song" (Cohen) **38**:131

"Cuckoo Corn" (Muldoon) **72**:265

The Cuckoo Tree (Aiken) **35**:17

"The Cuckoo-Spit" (Lavin) **4**:281; **99**:321-22

Cuckooz Countrey (Slessor) **14**:492, 495

Cue for Passion (Rice) **7**:363; **49**:301-02

"Cuento de dos jardines" ("Story of Two Gardens"; "A Tale of Two Gardens") (Paz) **65**:183, 198

Cuentos (*Charleston and Other Stories*) (Donoso) **4**:127; **8**:180; **99**:223

Cuentos breves y extraordinarios (*Extraordinary Tales*) (Bioy Casares) **88**:64

Cuentos puertorriqueños de hoy (Marques) **96**:229

Cugel's Saga (Vance) **35**:428

"The Cuirassiers of the Frontier" (Graves) **45**:162

Cuisine Novella (Laurent) **50**:59-61

Cujo (King) **26**:238-42; **37**:203, 208; **61**:319, 321, 331; **113**:335, 342-45, 347, 355-56, 358-59, 369, 388, 390

"Cul De Sac Valley" (Walcott) **67**:360

"Culag Pier" (MacCaig) **36**:282

Cul-de-sac (Polanski) **16**:463-68, 471-72

Cul-de-sac (*Kesten and Cul-de-sac*) (Theriault) **79**:400, 403, 412

"Cullen" (Page) **18**:377

"Culloden and After" (Smith) **64**:394

"The Cult of Experience in American Writing" (Rahv) **24**:352, 355-56

"The Cult of Power" (Warner) **45**:435

The Cult of Power (Warner) **45**:433-34, 441

"The Cultivated Man" (Phillips) **28**:362-63

"The Cultivation of Christmas Trees" (Eliot) **41**:152

"El culto de los libros" (Borges) **83**:169

"Cultural Center" (Montague) **46**:266

Cultural Creation (Goldmann)
   See *La création culturelle dans la société moderne*

"Cultural Directives" (Szirtes) **46**:395

"A Cultural Exchange" (Godwin) **31**:198

"Cultural Exchange" (Hughes) **35**:218

"Cultural Exchanges" (Hacker) **72**:192

"Cultural Freedom" (Enright) **31**:150, 155

"Cultural Literacy" (Hirsch) **79**:267

Cultural Literacy (Hirsch) **79**:265, 270-71, 273-77, 279-80

"'Cultural Literacy' Does Not Mean 'Core Curriculum'" (Hirsch) **79**:267

"Cultural Man" (Mead) **37**:280

"Cultural Notes" (Fearing) **51**:117

"Culture and Anarchy" (Rich) **36**:376

Culture and Commitment: A Study of the Generation Gap (Mead) **37**:275-77

Culture and Environment (Leavis) **24**:301

"Culture Now: Some Animadversions, Some Laughs" (Bellow) **8**:74

The Culture of Narcissism (Lasch) **102**:289-90, 293-94, 301, 319

"Culture or Mimicry" (Walcott)
   See "Caribbean: Culture or Mimicry"

"Culture, Self, and Style" (Gass) **39**:482

"Culture: The Antinomy of the Scientific Method" (Percy) **6**:401

"Cumberland Station" (Smith) **22**:385-86

Cumberland Station (Smith) **22**:384-87, 389; **42**:346, 348, 350, 352-53

"Cummings" (Davenport) **38**:141

La cumpana apelor (*At the Water Divide*; *At the Watershed*; *On the Great Water Divide*) **75**:77-8

Cumpleaños (Fuentes) **41**:167; **60**:158; **113**:253

The Cunning Man (Davies) **91**:198, 200-3, 207, 209, 210

"Cunt and Kant and a Happy Home" (Bukowski) **41**:68

"El cuòr su l'agua" (Pasolini) **106**:260

Cup of Gold: A Life of Henry Morgan, Buccaneer, with Occasional References to History (Steinbeck) **1**:325-26; **5**:407; **9**:512; **21**:380, 390; **34**:409, 411; **45**:374; **59**:322, 333; **75**:349-50

The Cupboard (Tremain) **42**:384-85

"Cupid and Psyche" (Elytis) **100**:189

"The Cupola" (Bogan) **93**:90-2, 96, 102-03, 105

"Cups with Broken Handles" (Ashbery) **41**:37

"Cura pastoralis" (Hood) **28**:189, 193

"The Curable Romantic" (Fuller) **62**:206

"The Cure" (King) **8**:321

"Cure" (Moure) **88**:224

"The Cure" (Simic) **22**:380

The Cure (Foreman) **50**:160-62, 164-65, 168-69

The Cure at Troy: A Version of Sophocles' Philoctetes (Heaney) **74**:195-96; **91**:124

A Cure for Cancer (Moorcock) **27**:349-50; **58**:347-49

A Cure for Dreams (Gibbons) **88**:127-28, 131-32

"The Cure for Warts" (Muldoon) **32**:315

Curfew (Donoso)
   See *Lá Desesperanza*

Curious (Bowering) **15**:83; **47**:22, 28

"The Curious Child" (Matheson) **37**:246

"Curlew" (Clarke) **61**:82

"The Curlew" (Watkins) **43**:454

"Curls and a Quiet Country Face" (Bowles) **68**:9

"The Current" (Merwin) **88**:202

"Current Account" (Tremain) **42**:386

"Current Status 1/22/87" (Monette) **82**:321, 332

The Currents of Space (Asimov) **19**:25; **26**:48, 64

A Curriculum of Inclusion: Report of the Commissioner's Task Force on Minorities **70**:371, 374, 378

"Curriculum vitae" (Hirsch) **50**:196

Curries and Other Indian Dishes (Anand) **93**:23-4

"A Curse" (Morrissy) **99**:78

"The Curse" (Prichard) **46**:332, 343, 345

"The Curse of Eve" (Atwood) **84**:89

The Curse of Lono (Thompson) **40**:430-31

"Curse of the Earth Magician" (Piercy) **14**:406; **27**:375

Curse of the Starving Class (Shepard) **17**:446-47; **34**:267, 269, 271; **41**:409-11, 413-14, 416; **44**:264-66, 268-69

The Curse of the Viking Grave (Mowat) **26**:336-37, 342-43

"The Cursed Play" (Tanizaki) **28**:417

"The Curtain" (Wright) **53**:426

Curtain (Christie) **6**:108, 110; **8**:140-42; **12**:120-22; **48**:71, 77-8; **110**:120-21, 123

"A Curtain of Green" (Welty) **105**:368

A Curtain of Green and Other Stories (Welty) **1**:362; **14**:561-62; **22**:458-59; **33**:414; **105**:298

Curtain Up (Streatfeild) **21**:407, 416

La curtile dorului (*At the Court of Yearning*; *In the Court of Yearning*; *In the Courtyard of Yearning*) **75**:67, 78

Curtmantle (Fry)   2:143-44; 10:200-01; 14:186
"Curva minore" (Quasimodo)   10:427
"Curve of Binding Energy" (McPhee)   36:295, 297
"Cushendun" (MacNeice)   53:237
"Cuss-Cuss" (Bennett)   28:29
"The Custard Heart" (Parker)   68:327, 334-35, 340
"Custard Pie" (Page and Plant)   12:477
Custer Died for Your Sins: An Indian Manifesto (Deloria)   21:108-11
"The Custodian" (Hill)   113:281, 294, 297, 310
The Custom House (King)   53:205-07
"Customers" (Lively)   32:277
The Customs Collector in Baggy Pants (Ferlinghetti)   111:63
"Customs of the Country" (Bell)   102:6
"The Customs-Officer's House" (Montale)
    See "La casa dei doganieri"
"Cut" (Dixon)   52:95, 97
"Cut" (Plath)   9:426-27; 17:348, 351, 359; 51:340, 342-43; 111:160-63, 182, 185, 203
"Cut Flower" (Peacock)   60:293
"Cut Glass" (Barthelme)   117:5
"Cut Grass" (Larkin)   5:229-30; 8:333, 339; 39:333, 345; 64:282
"Cut of Mind" (Broumas)   73:9
The Cut Pages (Fisher)   25:160, 162
"Cut the Grass" (Ammons)   9:27; 25:44
"Cut Worm" (Fisher)   25:160
"Cute Chick!" (Kelman)   58:301-02
The Cut-Rate Kingdom (Keneally)   43:233-34; 117:225
Cuts (Bradbury)   61:40-2, 44-7
"The Cutter-Off of Water" (Duras)   68:100-02
"Cuttin Down to Size" (Dumas)   6:145
"The Cutting Edge" (Levine)   4:286
The Cutting Edge (Gilliatt)   13:238-39
"Cutting Greens" (Clifton)   66:88
Cutting Lisa (Everett)   57:217
Cutting Timber (Bernhard)
    See *Holzfällen: Eine Erregung*
"Cuttings" (Roethke)   11:485; 19:397; 11:485
"Cuttings (Later)" (Roethke)   101:293, 334
Cuttlefish Bones (Montale)
    See *Ossi di seppia*
"Cuvinte duhovnicesti" ("A Confessor's Words") (Arghezi)   80:3
Cuvinte potrivite (*Fitting Words; Words Made to Measure*) (Arghezi)   80:6-11
"Cy" (Dixon)   52:98, 100
Cybele (Oates)   33:289
Cyberiad: Fables for the Cybernetic Age (Lem)   8:344; 15:327-28; 40:296
"Cybernetics and Ghosts" (Calvino)   73:45, 48
"The Cycads" (Wright)   53:418
"Cyclamen" (Thomas)   48:380
"Cycle" (Kunene)   85:165
"The Cycle" (Roethke)   19:397; 46:362
"Cycle Number Twenty-Two" (Nichol)   18:369
Cycle of the Werewolf (King)   37:205; 61:331; 113:361, 365, 388
A Cycle of the West (Neihardt)   32:334-35, 337-38
Cycle Smash (Chambers)   35:98
"The Cycles of American History" (Schlesinger)   84:379
The Cycles of American History (Schlesinger)   84:379-81, 383, 385-86
"The Cycles of American Politics" (Schlesinger)

84:385
"Cycling in the Lake District" (Murray)   40:336
"A Cyclist" (Goodman)   4:197
"The Cyclone" (Hesse)   6:237
The Cyclone (*Strong Wind*) (Asturias)   3:18; 8:27-8
"Cynddylan on a Tractor" (Thomas)   48:375
"Cynic Song" (Eberhart)   56:75
"Cynthia" (Simpson)   7:429
"Cynthis in California" (Laughlin)   49:221
Cypress and Acacia (Watkins)   43:442-43, 451-52, 456
The Cypresses Believe in God (Gironella)
    See *Los cipreses creen en Dios*
Cyrano (Burgess)   81:301
"Cyril" (Willingham)   51:403
Cyrion (Lee)   46:232
Cyrion in Stone (Lee)   46:232
"Cyrion in Wax" (Lee)   46:231
"The Czar's Last Christmas Letter: A Barn in the Urals" (Dubie)   36:132
Czerwona rekawiczka (*The Red Glove*) (Rozewicz)   23:358
Czeslaw Milosz: The Collected Poems, 1931-1987 (*Collected Poems*) (Milosz)   56:246, 249, 251; 82:290, 296-99, 303, 309-11
"D" (Cummings)   15:160
"D" (Merrill)   8:383-85
"D. D. Byrde Callyng Jennie Wren" (Snodgrass)   68:399
D. H. Lawrence (West)   50:360
D. H. Lawrence: An Unprofessional Study (Nin)   4:379
D. H. Lawrence, Novelist, Poet, Prophet (Spender)   91:263
Da (Leonard)   19:281, 283
"Da Da Da Da Da" (McGrath)
    See "After I'm Gone"
Da Silva da Silva's Cultivated Wilderness (Harris)   25:211, 216
Da Vinci's Bicycle (Davenport)   14:142; 38:139, 148
"The Dacey Players...." (Dacey)   51:83
Dad (Wharton)   37:435-38, 441-43
"Dada" (Boyle)   36:57
"Daddy" (Clifton)   66:74
"Daddy" (Plath)   2:336; 3:390; 5:341, 343; 9:424-26, 430; 11:445-50; 14:423-26, 428; 17:346-48, 350, 353, 356, 359, 363, 369; 50:440; 51:342-45, 353; 62:404-05, 415; 111:159, 166, 173-76, 178-79, 181-82, 208-09, 211, 216-19, 221
"Daddy" (Tevis)   42:372, 377
Daddy Boy (Cameron)   59:47-51
Daddy Cool (Goines)   80:93, 98
Daddy, Daddy (Durcan)   70:146-54
"Daddy Don't Live in That New York City No More" (Becker and Fagen)   26:79-80
"Daddy Garbage" (Wideman)   36:455
"Daddy Wolf" (Purdy)   28:378-79
Daddyji (Mehta)   37:292, 294-95
Daddy's Girl (Savage)   40:372-73
"Daddy's Song" (Kristofferson)   26:270
"Daddy's Tune" (Browne)   21:39
Dador (*Giver*) (Lezama Lima)   101:121
"Daedalus" (Barker)   48:9
"Daedalus" (Squires)   51:380
Daedalus (Squires)   51:378
"Daedalus Broods on the Equestrian Olympic Trials" (Hearne)   56:127
"The Daemon" (Bogan)   46:81; 93:65
"The Daemon Lover" (Jackson)   60:212, 235
The Daffodil Fields (Masefield)   11:357;

47:226-28, 230
The Daffodil Murderer (Sassoon)   36:389
"Daffodildo" (Swenson)   106:341
"Daffodils" (Brown)   100:87
"Daffy Duck in Hollywood" (Ashbery)   15:30; 77:46, 48, 61
Dage paa en sky (*Days on a Cloud*) (Abell)   15:1, 6
Dagger of the Mind (Fearing)   51:109, 112, 116
Daggers and Javelins: Essays, 1974-1979 (Baraka)   33:61-2; 115:14, 30
Dago Red (Fante)   60:130-31, 133
Dagon (Chappell)   40:138-40; 78:97-100, 110, 112, 114, 116
"Daguerreotypes" (Dinesen)   95:61
Daguerreotypes (Varda)   16:559
Daguerreotypes, and Other Essays (Dinesen)   95:58, 61
The Dahomean (Yerby)   22:490
"Dahomey" (Lorde)   71:232
The Daily Round (Lopate)   29:299
The Dain Curse (Hammett)   3:218-19; 10:252; 19:193, 195-96; 47:156, 159-61
The Dainty Monsters (Ondaatje)   14:407-08; 29:341; 51:310, 316
"Daisy" (Johnston)   51:243
"Daisy" (Maugham)   67:220
"Daisy's Valentine" (Gaitskill)   69:199
Daiyon kampyoki (*Inter Ice Age 4*) (Abe)   22:12; 53:5-6; 81:285, 290
Dal fondo delle comagne (Luzi)   13:352
"Dal laboratorio" (Pasolini)   106:247
The Dalkey Archive (O'Brien)   1:252; 4:383, 385; 7:270; 10:362-63; 47:313-14, 316, 318-20
Dal'she...Dal'she...Dal'she! (*Further...Further...Further!*)   59:358, 361-62
Dalva (Harrison)   66:159-60, 163-66, 168-69, 171
"Dam Neck, Virginia" (Eberhart)   19:144; 56:79
La dama del alba (Casona)   49:42-6, 49-52
Damage (Hart)   70:59-64
Damaged Goods: The Great Play "Les avariés" by Brieux, Novelized with the Approval of the Author (Sinclair)   63:348
The Damages (Howard)   7:165, 168; 10:276; 47:167-68
"Damals in Odessa" ("That Time in Odessa") (Boell)   72:69, 79
The Damask Drum (Mishima)   27:343-45
"Damastes z przydomkiem Prokustes mówi" (Herbert)   43:186
Damballah (Wideman)   34:298, 300; 36:454-55; 67:374, 380
Dam-Burst of Dreams (Nolan)   58:361-62, 366
La dame dans l'auto avec des lunettes et un fusil (*The Lady in the Car with Glasses and a Gun*) (Japrisot)   90:168, 170
"Dame of the British Empire, BBC" (Gilliatt)   53:145
La dame qui avait des chaines aux chevilles (*Lady with Chains*) (Carrier)   78:73
Les dames du Bois de Boulogne (Bresson)   16:103, 107-09, 111
"Dämmerung" (Celan)   82:52
"The Damnation" (Kizer)   80:173
"Damnation Alley" (Zelazny)   21:479
Damnation Alley (Zelazny)   21:464-65, 479
The Damnation Game (Barker)   52:52, 55-7
"Damnation of Vancouver" (Birney)   6:74-5

"Damned" (Berryman)   10:51; 62:74
The Damned (Fanon)
   See Les damnés de la terre
The Damned (Visconti)   16:568-70, 574-75
Damnée Manon, sacrée Sandra (Tremblay)   29:419, 422-25, 427; 102:375
Les damnés de la terre (The Damned; The Wretched of the Earth) (Fanon)   74:71-2, 74-86
"Damoetas" (Hollander)   5:186
"Der Dampfkessel-Effekt" ("The Steam Boiler Effect") (Grass)   32:199
Dan Yack (Cendrars)
   See Les confessions de Dan Yack
"Danae" (Le Guin)   45:212
"Danae" (Howes)   15:289
"The Dance" (Duncan)   15:192
"Dance" (Kenny)   87:240
"The Dance" (Larkin)   64:258, 260, 263-64, 280-81
"The Dance" (Strand)   71:285
"The Dance" (Thomas)   107:333
The Dance and the Railroad (Hwang)   55:151-52
"The Dance Called David" (Weiss)   14:556
"Dance, Dance" (Shapcott)   38:399, 401
"Dance, Dance, Dance" (Wilson)   12:644, 647, 651
Dance, Girl, Dance (Arzner)   98:63-4, 73-8, 81, 84, 86-7, 90-1
"Dance Hall" (Miller)   14:373
Dance Hall of the Dead (Hillerman)   62:251-54, 256-57, 259
Dance in the Desert (L'Engle)   12:348-49
A Dance in the Sun (Jacobson)   4:255-56
The Dance Is One (Scott)   22:376
Dance Lessons for Adult and Advanced Pupils (Hrabal)
   See Tanecni hodiny pro starsi a pokrocilé
Dance Me Outside (Kinsella)   27:235-37; 43:258, 260
"Dance: Nicaragua" (Jordan)   114:146
Dance Night (Powell)   66:366
The Dance of Death (Auden)   11:18; 14:30-1; 43:15-16, 18, 29
"The Dance of Death and Human Inequality" (Milosz)   56:232
The Dance of Genghis Cohn (Gary)   25:186
A Dance of the Forests (Soyinka)   3:462; 5:396; 14:506-07; 36:410; 44:279-83, 285, 287
"Dance of the Girls' Chemises" (Seifert)   93:333
"Dance of the Happy Shades" (Munro)   95:284, 287
Dance of the Happy Shades and Other Stories (Munro)   6:341-42; 10:357; 19:343-44; 50:210; 95:284, 295-97, 300, 302, 312-13
"The Dance of the Solids" (Updike)   23:475
Dance of the Years (The Galantrys) (Allingham)   19:12
"Dance of Words" (Graves)   11:256
Dance on My Grave (Chambers)   35:100-01
Dance on the Earth (Laurence)   50:314, 320; 62:304-08
"Dance Piece" (Belitt)   22:49
"Dance Script with Electric Ballerina" (Fulton)   52:159
Dance Script with Electric Ballerina (Fulton)   52:157-61
Dance the Eagle to Sleep (Piercy)   3:383-84; 62:362-65, 381
"Dance the Night Away" (Carroll)   35:81

Dance: The Ritual of Experience (Highwater)   12:287-88
A Dance to Still Music (Corcoran)   17:73-4
A Dance to the Music of Time (Powell)   1:277-78; 3:400-04; 7:338-46; 9:435-39; 10:408-18; 31:314, 316-23
A Dance, with Some Many Words (Olson)   11:420
"The Dancer" (Cabral de Melo Neto)
   See "A bailarina"
"The Dancer" (Govier)   51:166
"The Dancer" (Swados)   5:420
The Dancer (Kawabata)
   See Maihime
The Dancer from Atlantis (Anderson)   15:15
Dancer from the Dance (Holleran)   38:245-47
Dancer with One Leg (Dobyns)   37:79
Dancers at Night (Richards)   59:187, 189
"Dancers at the End of Time" (Moorcock)   5:294
"Dancers at the Moy" (Muldoon)   72:264
Dancers, Buildings, and People in the Streets (Denby)   48:82
"Dancers Exercising" (Clampitt)   32:116
Dancers in Mourning (Allingham)   19:15
Dancers in the Scalp House (Eastlake)   8:200
Dancers on the Shore (Kelley)   22:246, 250
Dances of Death (Tindall)   7:474
"Dancey" (Brown)   100:82-3
Dancin' (Fosse)   20:126
"Dancin' with Mr. D" (Jagger and Richard)   17:228, 238
"The Dancing" (Stern)   40:413-14
Dancing (Young)   19:477, 480
Dancing After Hours (Dubus)   97:234-38
Dancing at Lughnasa (Friel)   115:233, 236-39, 241, 245, 250
Dancing Aztecs (Westlake)   33:437-38
Dancing Back Strong the Nation (Kenny)   87:238-41
"Dancing Barefoot" (Smith)   12:544
"Dancing Bear" (Vanderhaeghe)   41:449
The Dancing Bear (Dickinson)   12:170-71, 174-75
The Dancing Bears (Merwin)   1:212; 2:276; 5:284; 8:389; 13:384; 45:268; 88:205
The Dancing Chicken (Musgrave)   54:341-42
"Dancing Days" (Page and Plant)   12:476, 482
"The Dancing Girls" (Ferber)   93:139
Dancing Girls, and Other Stories (Atwood)   13:44-46; 25:61-2, 70; 84:70, 96
"Dancing on Park Avenue" (Dunn)   36:151-52
Dancing on the Grave of a Son of a Bitch (Wakoski)   4:574; 9:554; 40:455
"Dancing Sam" (Browne)   21:41
Dancing Shoes (Streatfeild)
   See Wintle's Wonders
"Dancing with Poets" (Voigt)   54:432
Dandelion on the Acropolis (Stuart)   34:375
Dandelion Wine (Bradbury)   1:42; 10:68-70; 15:84; 42:36, 42, 44; 98:111, 144
"Dandelions" (Silkin)   43:398
"Dandy; or, Astride the Funky Finger of Lust" (Bullins)   7:37
"The Dane's Place" (Donoso)   32:158
The Danger (Francis)   42:152-53; 102:162
"The Danger at Funny Junction" (Bell)   8:65
Danger: Memory! (I Can't Remember Anything) (Miller)   47:255-58
Danger Signal (Samarakis)
   See Sima kindynou

The Danger Tree (Manning)   19:302, 304
Dangerous Corner (Priestley)   2:346; 5:351; 34:361, 363-64
Dangerous Crossings (Donnell)   34:156, 158
"Dangerous Dads" (Leyner)   92:293-94
Dangerous French Mistress, and Other Stories (Colwin)
   See Passion and Affect
"The Dangerous Gift" (Graves)   1:129
"A Dangerous Man" (Faulkner)   18:149
"Dangerous Play" (Motion)   47:293-94
Dangerous Play: Poems, 1974-1984 (Motion)   47:290-93
"A Dangerous Remedy" (Davies)   23:142
Dangerous Spring (Benary-Isbert)   12:33, 35
The Dangerous Summer (Hemingway)   6:226; 41:201-04
Dangerous Visions (Ellison)   13:203
"Dangerous Woman" (Rooke)   25:391
"The Dangling Conversations" (Simon)   17:458-59, 464-66
Dangling in the Tournefortia (Bukowski)   41:69-70; 82:5, 13
Dangling Man (Bellow)   1:28-32; 2:49, 51, 53; 3:48-52, 55; 6:56-7, 60; 8:69-71, 74, 78; 10:39, 43; 13:71-2; 15:47-50, 52-56; 25:80, 85; 33:65-6; 63:31-2; 79:76, 80, 82
The Dangling Witness (Bennett)   35:44-5
Daniel Come to Judgement (Hocking)   13:285
Daniel Martin (Fowles)   9:213-16; 10:188-90; 15:232-33; 33:164, 166, 171-75; 87:141, 148, 158, 161-62, 164, 167-70, 172, 178-84
Danny and the Deep Blue Sea: An Apache Dance (Shanley)   75:320, 328
Danny Boy (Jordan)
   See Angel
Danny Hill (King)   53:213
"Danny in Transit" (Leavitt)   34:77
Danny O'Neill (Farrell)   11:195
"Danny's Girls" (Mukherjee)   115:363
"Dans la marche" (Char)   9:164
Dans la pluie giboyeuse (Char)   14:126
Dans le labyrinthe (In the Labyrinth) (Robbe-Grillet)   1:286, 289-90; 2:374; 4:447-48, 450; 6:465-68; 8:451-52; 10:437; 14:456-57, 461; 43:360, 362
Dans le leurre du seuil (In the Illusion of the Threshhold; In the Lure of the Threshold) (Bonnefoy)   9:114; 15:73; 58:50-1, 54, 56-7, 60-1
"Dans le restaurant" (Eliot)   57:206
"Dans les années profondes" (Jouve)   47:204
Dans les années sordides (Mandiargues)   41:275
"Danse Macabre" (Faludy)   42:139, 142
"Danse Macabre" (Raine)   32:349
Danse Macabre (King)   113:336, 338, 355, 366, 390, 392
"Dante" (Akhmatova)   64:16
Dante (Baraka)
   See The Eighth Ditch
Dante (Eliot)   24:182-83
"Dante and the Lobster" (Beckett)   10:29
"Dante... Bruno. Vico.. Joyce" (Beckett)   11:34; 29:67; 59:260
"Dante Etudes" (Duncan)   41:128-30; 55:298
The Danzig Trilogy (Danziger Trilogie) (Grass)   15:259; 22:193; 88:175
Danziger Trilogie (Grass)
   See The Danzig Trilogy
"Daphne with Her Thighs in Bark" (Boland)   40:100; 113:70-1, 124

Dar (*The Gift*) (Nabokov) 1:242; 2:299-300, 305; 3:355; 6:355; 8:415, 417-18; 11:392; 23:309; 44:467, 469; 46:291; 64:366

Darconville's Cat (Theroux) 25:432-34

D'arcs de cycle la dérive (Brossard) 115:121

"Darfsteller" (Miller) 30:260, 262, 265

Daria 75:65-6

"Darien" (Graves) 2:175

"The Daring Young Man on the Flying Trapeze" (Saroyan) 1:301; 8:468; 29:361; 34:457; 56:374-75

"The Dark" (Jones) 76:65

"The Dark" (Oates) 6:367

The Dark (McGahern) 5:280; 9:371-72; 48:260-63, 269-72

Dark Adaptation (Transtroemer)
     See *Mörkerseende*

"Dark Ages" (Reid) 33:350

The Dark Ages (Asimov) 76:312

The Dark and Feeling: Black American Writers and Their Work (Major) 19:293, 295

The Dark and the Light (Vittorini) 6:551; 14:544

The Dark Arena (Puzo) 1:282; 2:352; 6:429; 36:358, 362; 107:174-76, 199, 212, 215

"Dark Arm, Hanging over the Edge of Infinity" (Williams) 45:443-44

"Dark around Light" (Bowering) 47:19

The Dark at the Top of the Stairs (Inge) 1:153; 8:307-08; 19:226-30

The Dark at the Top of the Stairs (Kazan) 63:234

"Dark Benediction" (Miller) 30:263-64

"The Dark Brain of Piranesi" (Yourcenar) 38:461

The Dark Brain of Piranesi, and Other Essays (Yourcenar)
     See *Sous bénéfice d'inventaire*

Dark Bridwell (Fisher) 7:105

Dark Brown (McClure) 6:320

The Dark Canoe (O'Dell) 30:268-70

The Dark Child (Laye)
     See *L'enfant noir*

Dark Companions (Campbell) 42:90-1

Dark Conceit: The Making of Allegory (Honig) 33:209-10

"Dark Continent" (Reading) 47:352

"A Dark Country" (Mahon) 27:288

The Dark Crusader (MacLean) 50:349-50

The Dark Dancer (Prokosch) 48:315

The Dark Daughters (Davies) 23:142-43

Dark Entries (Aickman) 57:2

The Dark Eye in Africa (van der Post) 5:463

"Dark Eye in September" (Celan) 82:36

The Dark Frontier (Ambler) 4:19

"Dark Gift" (Wright) 53:428

"Dark Glasses" (Longley) 29:293

Dark Glasses (Hood) 28:191-92

The Dark Glasses (King) 53:204-05

Dark Green, Bright Red (Vidal) 33:406

Dark Habits (Almodovar)
     See *Entre Tinieblas*

The Dark Half (King) 61:337; 113:388, 390-92

Dark Harvest (Ringwood) 48:329-30, 334-39

Dark Horse (Knebel) 14:309

"Dark Horse of Darran" (Prichard) 46:333

"Dark House" (Plath) 11:446, 448; 111:164, 167, 179

"Dark Houses" (Davison) 28:102

The Dark Is Light Enough (Fry) 2:143-44; 10:200-02; 14:186-87

The Dark Is Not So Dark (Everson) 27:134

Dark Is the Sun (Farmer) 19:168

The Dark Journey (Green)
     See *L'eviathan*

The Dark Kingdom (Patchen) 1:265

The Dark Labyrinth (Durrell) 1:85

The Dark Lady (Auchincloss) 9:55

"Dark Lagoon" (Reaney) 13:473

"The Dark Men" (Dubus) 97:204-05

The Dark Night of Resistance (Berrigan) 4:57

A Dark Night's Passing (Shiga)
     See *Anya Koro*

"Dark O' the Moon" (Brown) 59:262

"Dark Odyssey of Soosie" (Mowat) 26:344-45

Dark of the Woods (Koontz) 78:199

"Dark Pines under Water" (MacEwen) 13:358

Dark Piper (Norton) 12:458, 461, 464, 467

"The Dark Place Inside" (Potok) 112:280

Dark Places of the Heart (*Cotter's England*) (Stead) 2:421-22; 5:403; 32:408-09, 412, 414; 80:305, 307, 311-12, 316, 331, 339, 341, 345

Dark Pony (Mamet) 15:358; 46:250-51

Dark Princess (Du Bois) 64:113-14, 117-18

"Dark Prophecy: I Sing of Shine" (Knight) 40:284

Dark Quartet (Banks) 23:42

"Dark Rings" (Levine) 4:286

The Dark River (Millin) 49:238-39, 243, 246

"Dark Room" (H. D.) 31:213

"The Dark Room" (Williams) 45:454

The Dark Room (Narayan) 28:299

The Dark Root of a Scream (Valdez) 84:397-98, 406, 413

"Dark Sheila" (Christie) 110:126, 128

The Dark Side of Genius: The Life of Alfred Hitchcock (Spoto) 39:445, 451-52

"The Dark Side of the Earth" (Zweig) 42:467

The Dark Side of the Earth (Zweig) 34:378; 42:466-67

The Dark Side of the Moon (Pink Floyd) 35:306-13, 315

"The Dark Smoke" (Dorris) 109:309-10

"Dark Song" (Ammons) 108:8

"The Dark Song" (Shamlu) 10:471

The Dark Store (Perec)
     See *La boutique obscure*

"Dark Summer" (Bogan) 93:95

Dark Summer (Bogan) 39:390; 46:77-80, 89-90; 93:90, 92-4, 96, 103

"The Dark Sun" (Hirsch) 31:215

"Dark Symphony" (Tolson) 36:424-25, 427; 105:239, 260, 282, 288

The Dark Symphony (Koontz) 78:197

Dark Symphony (Tolson) 105:282

Dark Testament (Abrahams) 4:1

"Dark They Were, and Golden-Eyed" ("The Naming of Names") (Bradbury) 42:32

The Dark Tower (MacNeice) 53:239-40

The Dark Tower: The Gunslinger (King) 61:337; 113:381-82, 388-89, 393

The Dark Tunnel (Macdonald) 14:332-33; 34:416; 41:265

"A Dark Walk" (Taylor) 18:526-27

"Dark Waters of the Beginning" (Okigbo) 84:312

"Dark Ways We Lead Each Other" (Livesay) 79:344

Dark Wedding (Sender)
     See *Epitalamio del prieto Trinidad*

"Dark Well" (Thomas) 48:380

"Dark Wild Honey" (Swenson) 106:339

The Dark Wind (Hillerman) 62:255-56, 258

A Dark-Adapted Eye (Rendell) 48:326-27

A Dark-Adapted Eye (Vine) 50:263-64

"Darkening Hotel Room" (Corn) 33:115

"The Darkening Moon" (Stafford) 68:434

"Darker" (Strand) 41:438

"Darker Ends" (Nye) 42:305

Darker Ends (Nye) 13:412; 42:304-05

Darker: Poems (Strand) 6:521-22; 18:515, 517-19; 41:436; 71:278, 284-86

The Darker Proof (White) 110:324-26

Darker Than Amber (MacDonald) 27:275; 44:408

Darker than You Think (Williamson) 29:455-56, 459-60

Darkfall (Koontz) 78:197, 202-03, 206-07, 209-17

"Darkmotherscream" (Voznesensky) 57:421

"The Darkness" (Purdy) 50:240-41

"Darkness" (Wain) 46:415

Darkness (Brink)
     See *Kennis van die Aand*

Darkness (Mukherjee) 53:265-68, 270-71; 115:365, 386

Darkness and Day (Compton-Burnett) 34:500

"Darkness and Light" (Spender) 10:492

The Darkness and the Dawn (Costain) 30:99

Darkness at Noon (Kingsley) 44:235-36, 238

Darkness at Noon (Koestler) 1:170; 3:270-71; 6:281; 8:324-25; 15:310, 312; 33:227-30, 233-35, 239-44

Darkness at Noon (Solzhenitsyn) 78:380

Darkness Casts No Shadow (Lustig) 56:184-85

A Darkness in My Soul (Koontz) 78:199, 203

Darkness in Saint Louis Bearheart (Vizenor) 103:284-85, 288, 294-96, 298, 304, 310, 314-19, 323-25, 327-28, 330, 332-33, 348-52

"The Darkness of Practical Reason" (Murdoch) 6:349

The Darkness of the Body (Plante) 7:307; 23:344

Darkness on the Edge of Town (Springsteen) 17:482, 484-86, 490

"The Darkness Out There" (Lively) 32:277

The Darkness Surrounds Us (Sorrentino) 7:449; 22:391

"Darkness 'til Dawn" (Simon) 26:410

"Darkness under the Trees" (Salinas) 90:332

Darkness under the Trees/Walking behind the Spanish (Salinas) 90:331

Darkness Visible (Golding) 17:178-81; 27:161-64, 166-67, 169; 81:317-20, 323, 325

Darkover (Bradley) 30:26-7, 29, 32

Darkover Landfall (Bradley) 30:26, 28, 30

"Darkroom" (McCartney) 35:288

"The Darkwater Hall Mystery" (Amis) 40:43-5

Darkwater: Voices from within the Veil (Du Bois) 64:104, 116; 96:138

"Darlin'" (Wilson) 12:643, 645, 651

"Darling" (Dixon) 52:100

Darling (Raphael) 14:436-37

"Darling Boy" (Lennon)
     See "Beautiful Boy"

The Darling Buds of May (Bates) 46:58-60

"Darling, It's Frightening! When a Poet Loves ..." (Pasternak) 10:383

"Darling Nikki" (Prince) 35:331-32

Darrell (Montgomery) 7:232

"Darryl and the Moose" (McFadden) 48:243

The D'Arthez Case (Nossack)
     See *Der Fall d'Arthez*

"Dartmoor" (Christie)   **110**:127

"Darwin" (Niedecker)   **42**:296, 300

"Darwin in 1881" (Schnackenberg)   **40**:378-80

Darwin, Marx, Wagner: Critique of a Heritage (Barzun)   **51**:35, 50

"Darwin's Ark" (Appleman)   **51**:17

Darwin's Ark (Appleman)   **51**:16-17

"Darwin's Bestiary" (Appleman)   **51**:17

"Darwin's Rubber Plant" (Faludy)   **42**:137, 140

"Dash It" (Dillard)   **115**:210

Dashiell Hammett: A Life (Johnson)   **48**:203-04

Dasma (*The Wedding*) (Kadare)   **52**:258-59

A Date for Diane (Cavanna)   **12**:97-9

"Date with a Bird" (Tolstaya)   **59**:371

"Dates: Penkhull New Road" (Tomlinson)   **6**:536

"Dating Your Mom" (Frazier)   **46**:163-65

Dating Your Mom (Frazier)   **46**:163-65

"Dative Haruspices" (Rexroth)   **112**:397

Dauber (Masefield)   **11**:357-58; **47**:225-31, 233

"Daughter" (Caldwell)   **60**:60

"Daughter" (Fuller)   **62**:206

"Daughter" (Voigt)   **54**:430

Daughter Buffalo (Frame)   **2**:142; **3**:164; **6**:190; **22**:145-46; **66**:145; **96**:179, 181-82, 184-86, 191-92, 194, 197, 199, 217

"The Daughter Finds Her Father Dead" (Durcan)   **43**:118

"Daughter in the House" (Kennedy)   **42**:257

"Daughter, Last Glimpses Of" (Updike)   **15**:547

"Daughter of Invention" (Alvarez)   **93**:9

Daughter of Jerusalem (*The Languages of Love*) (Maitland)   **49**:230-31, 234

Daughter of Regals and Other Tales (Donaldson)   **46**:142-43

Daughter of Silence (West)   **33**:427-28

Daughter of the Legend (Stuart)   **11**:514; **34**:377

Daughters (Marshall)   **72**:254-60

A Daughter's a Daughter (Christie)   **1**:58; **39**:442

Daughters and Sons (Compton-Burnett)   **15**:137-38, 141; **34**:500

A Daughter's Geography (Shange)   **38**:394

Daughters, I Love You (Hogan)   **73**:148, 150, 152, 156

"The Daughters of Blossom Street" (Plath)   **3**:390; **11**:450

Daughters of Earth (Enright)   **31**:150

Daughters of Eve (Duncan)   **26**:106-07

"The Daughters of Mama Sea" (Shamlu)   **10**:471

Daughters of Men (Orton)   **13**:437

"Daughters of Passion" (O'Faolain)   **47**:328

Daughters of Passion (O'Faolain)   **47**:327-28, 331

"Daughters of the Vieux Carré" (Rooke)   **25**:390

"Daumier" (Barthelme)   **46**:36, 41; **115**:65, 70, 89

"Dauntless Little John" (Calvino)   **22**:90

"D'autres chants" (Senghor)   **54**:409

"Dave Loves Macker 14.2.83" (Durcan)   **43**:117

Dave Sulkin Cares (Knebel)   **14**:309

Davey Logan, Intern (Felsen)   **17**:121

"David" (Birney)   **6**:72, 74-6, 79; **11**:51

"David" (Pasolini)   **106**:228

"David" (Pastan)   **27**:369

David and Broccoli (Mortimer)   **28**:283-85

David and Other Poems (Birney)   **6**:72

David Bowie (*Love You till Tuesday*) (Bowie)   **17**:67

David Knudsen (Elliott)   **2**:130-31

David Live (Bowie)   **17**:63-4, 68

"David Lynch Keeps His Head" (Wallace)   **114**:388

"David Riesman Reconsidered" (Mailer)   **111**:104

The David Show (Gurney)   **50**:175, 184

David Starr, Space Ranger (Asimov)   **26**:35, 41

David Sterne (Blais)   **4**:67; **6**:82

"David Watts" (Davies)   **21**:91

Davita's Harp (Potok)   **112**:266-67, 269, 293

Davor (*Max: A Play; Therefore; Uptight*) (Grass)   **2**:173; **4**:204; **11**:248; **49**:139

"Dawn" (Dudek)   **19**:136

"Dawn" (Lowell)   **4**:304

"Dawn" (Mahapatra)   **33**:277-78, 282

"Dawn" (Powers)   **1**:280

Dawn (Buero Vallejo)
See *Madrugada*

Dawn (Wiesel)
See *L'aube*

"Dawn at Puri" (Mahapatra)   **33**:283

Dawn Ginsbergh's Revenge (Perelman)   **5**:337; **23**:334-35, 337; **44**:501-02; **49**:257-59, 261, 264, 270

"The Dawn in Erewhon" (Davenport)   **6**:125; **14**:139; **38**:140, 147-48

"The Dawn of Phallocentrism" (Cixous)   **92**:85, 87

Dawn of Remembered Spring (Stuart)   **34**:376

Dawn O'Hara (Ferber)   **93**:135, 140, 146, 172

Dawn to the West: Japanese Literature of the Modern Era (Keene)   **34**:566-70

"Dawn Travellers" (Miller)   **14**:373

"Dawn Walk" (Hirsch)   **50**:197

Dawn Wind (Sutcliff)   **26**:429-31, 433-36, 439

"Dawnings" (Livesay)   **79**:348

"Dawns" (Milosz)   **82**:297-98

"The Daws" (Thurber)   **5**:435

"The Day" (Fuller)   **28**:149

"The Day" (Lowell)   **9**:336

"Day" (Tomlinson)   **45**:398, 400-01

"A Day" (Trevor)   **116**:395

"The Day After" (Soto)   **80**:290

"Day after Chasing Porcupines" (Welch)   **52**:428

Day after Day (Quasimodo)
See *Giorno dopo giorno*

The Day after Judgment (Blish)   **14**:83, 87

"The Day after My Friends became Godly and Great" (Mahapatra)   **33**:284

The Day after Sunday (Summers)   **10**:493-94

"The Day After Superman Died" (Kesey)   **46**:224-26, 228

"Day and Night" (Cesaire)   **32**:111

Day and Night (Livesay)   **15**:339, 341; **79**:332, 342, 345-46

The Day and the Way We Met (Stolz)   **12**:549-50

"a day at the oak tree meet" (Bukowski)   **108**:75

"The Day Bed" (Eberhart)   **11**:178

"The Day Before" (Endo)   **54**:161

"The Day Before" (Spencer)   **22**:402

"The Day before the Revolution" (Le Guin)   **13**:348

The Day before Tomorrow (Hikmet)   **40**:248

A Day Book (Creeley)   **2**:108; **4**:118; **8**:153; **11**:138; **15**:151; **78**:128-30, 133

Day by Day (Lowell)   **8**:357; **9**:336, 339; **11**:330-31; **15**:344; **37**:232, 236, 238-39

Day by Night (Lee)   **46**:231

"Day Dream" (Thesen)   **56**:421

"Day Falcon" (Gotlieb)   **18**:191

"A Day for Anne Frank" (Williams)   **33**:441-43

Day for Night (Truffaut)
See *La nuit américaine*

"The Day He Died" (Hughes)   **37**:176

"The Day He Himself Shall Wipe My Tears Away" (Oe)
See "Mizu kara waga namida o nuguitamo hi"

"The Day I Don't Remember" (Rule)   **27**:423

The Day I Met a Lion (Kantor)   **7**:195

"The Day I Was Conceived" (Rose)   **85**:313

"A Day in Africa" (Du Bois)   **64**:114, 117

"A Day in Late October" (Van Duyn)   **7**:498; **63**:439; **116**:402-03

"A Day in Salamanca" (Squires)   **51**:379, 381-82

The Day in Shadow (Sahgal)   **41**:371

"A Day in the Country" (Millhauser)   **54**:324-27

"A Day in the Dark" (Bowen)   **22**:65-6

A Day in the Death of Joe Egg (Nichols)   **5**:305-08; **36**:326-27, 329-34; **65**:161-62, 164

"A Day in the Jungle" (Jackson)   **60**:213

"A Day in the Life" (Lennon and McCartney)   **12**:357-58, 368, 374; **35**:264

"A Day in the Life of a Doe" (Allen)   **52**:35

"A Day in the Open" (Bowles)   **68**:6-7

The Day Is Dark (Blais)
See *Le jour est noir*

"The Day Itself" (Merwin)   **88**:210, 212

"The Day Lady Died" (O'Hara)   **5**:325; **78**:337-38, 344, 349, 376

The Day Lasts More than a Century (Aitmatov)
See *I dol'she veka dlitsia den'*

The Day Lasts More than a Hundred Years (Aitmatov)
See *I dol'she veka dlitsia den'*

"A Day Like Rousseau's *Dream*" (Swenson)   **61**:405

A Day Marked X (Heym)
See *Five Days in June*

A Day No Pigs Would Die (Peck)   **17**:336-39, 341

Day of Absence (Ward)   **19**:456-58

"The Day of Forever" (Ballard)   **3**:33

Day of Freedom—Our Armed Forces (Riefenstahl)   **16**:522, 525

"A Day of Old Age" (Le Clezio)   **31**:243

A Day of Pleasure: Stories of a Boy Growing Up in Warsaw (Singer)   **111**:311

"A Day of Rain" (Mahapatra)   **33**:281, 284

"Day of Success" (Plath)   **11**:450

The Day of the Burning (Malzberg)   **7**:209

"Day of the Butterfly" (Munro)   **95**:291

The Day of the Dog (Frayn)   **31**:188; **47**:135

"The Day of the Dying Rabbit" (Updike)   **2**:445

The Day of the Jackal (Forsyth)   **2**:136-37; **5**:125; **36**:174-75, 177

The Day of the Owl (Sciascia)
See *Il giorno della civetta*

"Day of the Rat" (Sondheim)   **30**:390

The Day of the Scorpion (Scott)
See *The Raj Quartet*

"The Day of the Small Winds" (Souster)   **14**:505

"The Day of the Starter" (Durcan)   **43**:114

The Day of the Triffids (Wyndham)   **19**:474-76

"The Day of Treachery" (Kunene)   **85**:162

"Day of Wrath" (Davison)   **28**:103

"Day of Wrath" (Jhabvala)   **94**:173

Day of Wrath (Child)   **19**:100

Day of Wrath (Dreyer)   16:256-61, 263-66, 269

"The Day Off" (Sondheim)   39:174

"A Day on the Big Branch" (Nemerov)   36:303, 305

The Day Room (DeLillo)   54:85

"The Day Slats Fell for a Girl" (Royko)   109:407

"The Day Stalin Died" (Lessing)   22:277

"The Day That Beaumont Became Aquainted with His Pain" (Le Clezio)   31:243-44

"The Day the Buffalo Danced" (Martin)   30:248

The Day the Call Came (Hinde)   6:239, 241

"The Day the Dancers Came" (Santos)   22:365-66

"The Day the Pig Fell into the Well" (Cheever)   7:49

The Day the Whales Shall be Annihilated (Oe)
    See *Kujira no shimetsu suru hi*

The Day the Whores Came Out to Play Tennis (Kopit)   18:286-87, 289; 33:248, 250

"The Day They Burned the Books" (Rhys)   14:447; 51:370, 375

The Day They Came to Arrest the Book (Hentoff)   26:187-88

"The Day We Got Drunk on Cake" (Trevor)   116:384

The Day We Got Drunk on Cake, and Other Stories (Trevor)   7:475; 71:324; 116:332

"Day without Night" (Gluck)   44:215, 222-23

"Daybreak" (Aldington)   49:7

"Daybreak" (Leithauser)   27:242

"Daybreak" (Pasternak)   63:312-13

"Daybreak" (Soto)   80:286-87

Daybreak (Slaughter)   29:376

"Daybreak at Pisa" (Findley)   102:108

"Daybreak at the Maternity Ward" (Everson)   27:133

"Daybreak in Alabama" (Hughes)   108:332-33

The Daybreakers (L'Amour)   25:280

Daydream Mechanics (Brossard)
    See *Mécanique jongleuse*

"Daydreams" (O'Connor)   23:325

Daylight (Milosz)   82:298

"Daylight Katy" (Lightfoot)   26:282

"Daynights" (MacEwen)   55:164

"Days" (Davies)   21:107

"Days" (Larkin)   8:332; 39:344; 64:268-69, 271, 285

Days (Figes)   31:163-64

Days (Robison)   42:338-43; 98:318

"Day's Affirmation" (Read)   4:439

"Days and Nights" (Koch)   44:248-49

Days and Nights (Koch)   44:248

Days and Nights in Calcutta (Blaise)   29:71

Days and Nights in Calcutta (Mukherjee)   115:386

Days and Nights in the Forest (Ray)
    See *Aranyer din ratri*

Days and Nights of Love and War (Galeano)   72:129-31, 143-44

Days and Occasions (Paz)
    See *Días hábiles*

The Days Before (Porter)   13:447; 101:223

Days between Stations (Erickson)   64:137-40, 142, 144

"Day's End" (Bates)   46:49

Day's End and Other Stories (Bates)   46:49, 53

"Days of 1935" (Merrill)   2:275; 6:323

"Days of 1992" (Hacker)   91:110

Days of 1945-1951: A Poet's Journal (George Seferis: A Poet's Journal) (Seferis)   5:385;
11:493-94

The Days of Awe (Agnon)   8:9

Days of Grass (Lee)   46:232

Days of Man (Bitov)
    See *Dni cheloveka*

"The Days of Nietzsche" (Stern)   40:406, 408

"Days of the Dancing" (McKuen)   3:332

Days of the Year (Johnson)
    See *Jahrestage: Aus dem Leben von Gesine Cresspahl*

Days of Thunder (Towne)   87:374

Days of Wine and Neuroses (Mull)   17:299

Days of Wrath (Malraux)
    See *Le temps du mépris*

Days on a Cloud (Abell)
    See *Dage paa en sky*

The Days Run Away Like Wild Horses over the Hills (Bukowski)   82:4, 15; 108:81

"Days through Starch and Bluing" (Fulton)   52:161

Days to Come (Hellman)   2:187; 14:258-59; 18:221, 226; 34:348; 52:191

"A Day's Wait" (Hemingway)   6:231

"A Day's Work" (Capote)   19:85

The Daysman (Middleton)   38:334-35

"Daystar" (Dove)   50:154; 81:139

"Daytona" (Cernuda)   54:55

"Dazed and Confused" (Page and Plant)   12:478

"Dazzle" (Capote)   19:85

Un de baumugnes (Giono)   4:186; 11:233

"The de Cats Family" (Dinesen)   10:149-50; 95:67

"La dea cieca e veggente" (Landolfi)   49:214

"The Deacon" (Updike)   7:488

"Deacon Blues" (Becker and Fagen)   26:84

"The Deacon's Tale" (Rooke)   25:392-93

"The Dead" (Dudek)   11:158

"The Dead" (Oates)   108:354, 368, 370-71

The Dead and the Living (Olds)   32:346-47; 39:186-93; 85:287-88, 291-92, 300, 305

"Dead as They Come" (McEwan)   66:275, 279, 280-81

Dead Babies (Amis)   9:26; 38:11-13; 62:5, 7, 12, 17; 101:59-63, 86-89

"Dead Baby" (Dobyns)   37:82

The Dead Beat (Bloch)   33:83

"A Dead Boche" (Graves)   45:166

Dead Cert (Francis)   2:142-43; 22:154; 42:148-49, 153; 102:131-32, 140-41, 144-47, 153, 159-60

"The Dead Cow in the Canyon" (Ferron)   94:128

"Dead Dog" (Scannell)   49:326

"Dead Elms by a River" (Leithauser)   27:241-42

Dead End (Kingsley)   44:231-34, 237-38

"Dead End Street" (Davies)   21:97

"Dead Every Enormous Piece" (Cummings)   15:162

The Dead Father (Barthelme)   6:31; 8:49-52, 54; 13:58; 46:35, 45; 59:247, 249; 115:63-5, 67, 78-9, 81, 87, 92-6, 98-9

Dead Fingers Talk (Burroughs)   75:93

"Dead Flowers" (Jagger and Richard)   17:230

"Dead Gallop" (Neruda)
    See "Galope muerto"

The Dead Girls (Ibarguengoitia)
    See *Las muertas*

The Dead House (Ritsos)   13:488-89

"The Dead in Korea" (Dybek)   114:74

"The Dead in Melanesia" (Jarrell)   9:298

The Dead Kingdom (Montague)   46:277, 279

"The Dead Lad" (Pasolini)   106:260

"Dead Lakes" (Waddington)   28:438

Dead Languages (Shields)   97:421-34

"A Dead Leaf" (Moss)   45:292

"Dead Leaf in May" (Aiken)   52:28

Dead Leaves (Garcia Marquez)
    See *La hojarasca*

The Dead Lecturer (Baraka)   3:35; 5:44-6; 10:20; 115:31, 38-9

"Dead Letters" (Blunden)   56:40

Dead Letters Sent, and Other Poems (Kenny)   87:245

"The Dead Man" (Borges)
    See "El muerto"

"Dead Man" (McPherson)
    See "The Story of a Dead Man"

Dead Man Blues (Woolrich)   77:400

A Dead Man in Deptford (Burgess)   81:303, 312-13

Dead Man Leading (Pritchett)   41:335

"Dead Man's Folly" (Christie)   12:124

"Dead Man's Path" (Achebe)   26:21-3

"The Dead Man's Room" (Logan)   5:255

Dead Men Don't Wear Plaid (Martin)   30:251-52

"Dead Men's Fingers" (Longley)   29:294

The Dead of the House (Greenberg)   3:202

"Dead on Her Feet" (Woolrich)   77:403

"The Dead Poet" (Purdy)   50:248

"The Dead Poets of Vancouver" (Bowering)   47:33

The Dead Priestess Speaks (H. D.)   31:208

"Dead Reckoning" (Shacochis)   39:199-200

Dead Reckoning (Fearing)   51:106-07, 110

"Dead Roses" (White)   69:398

"Dead Roses" (Woolrich)   77:389, 398

The Dead Sea Scrolls (Wilson)   2:477

The Dead Seagull (Barker)   8:43; 48:21

"The Dead Seal near McClure's Beach" (Bly)   15:63

Dead Snowmen (Foreman)   50:169

"Dead Soldiers" (Chappell)   40:145; 78:91, 95

"Dead Soldiers" (Fenton)   32:166, 169

Dead Star Station (Williamson)   29:454

"Dead Still" (Voznesensky)   57:414

"The Dead Time" (Ballard)   36:47

Dead Voices: Natural Agonies in the New World (Vizenor)   103:312, 320, 334-37, 340

Dead Water (Marsh)   53:250-51

"The Dead Wingman" (Jarrell)   9:299; 13:300

The Dead Without Burial (Sartre)
    See *Morts sans sépulture*

Dead Yesterdays (Ginzburg)
    See *Tutti i nostri ieri*

The Dead Zone (King)   26:234, 237-39, 242; 37:201-02, 204; 61:319, 329; 113:336, 342, 344-45, 347, 360, 363, 388, 390

Dead-End Werther (Fiedler)   24:188

Deadeye Dick (Vonnegut)   40:441-46

The Deadline (Duerrenmatt)
    See *Die Frist*

Deadline at Dawn (Odets)   98:197, 245-46

Deadline at Dawn (Woolrich)   77:389-91, 393-94, 396, 398-99, 404-05

The Deadlined (Canetti)
    See *Die Befristeten*

The Deadly Companions (Peckinpah)   20:272, 283

The Deadly Gift (Bennett)   35:42-3

Deadly Hall (Carr)   3:101

"Deadly Leap" (Alegria)   75:49

Deadly Nightshade (Daly)   52:87

A Deadly Shade of Gold (MacDonald)   44:408

Deafman Glance (Wilson)   7:549

"Deaf-Mutes at the Ballgame" (Jacobsen) 48:190, 195; 102:237

Dealing in Futures (Haldeman) 61:181-82

Dealing; or, The Berkeley-to-Boston Forty-Brick Lost-Bag Blues (Crichton) 54:66

"Dealing with the Mystics" (Cioran) 64:79, 82

"Dean of Men" (Taylor) 18:523; 50:251

The Dean's December (Bellow) 25:81-6; 33:67, 70-1; 34:546; 63:32-4

"Dear Alexandros" (Updike) 23:473

Dear and Glorious Physician (Caldwell) 28:61-2; 39:302-03

Dear Antoine; or, The Love That Failed (Anouilh)
See *Cher Antoine; ou, L'amour raté*

Dear Bill, Remember Me? and Other Stories (Mazer) 26:291, 295

Dear Carolyn: Letters to Carolyn Cassady (Kerouac) 29:278

The Dear Deceit (Brooke-Rose) 40:103-04

Dear Departed (Yourcenar)
See *Souvenirs pieux*

Dear Digby (Muske) 90:315-17

"Dear Dorothy" (Creeley) 78:141

"Dear Elizabeth" (Swenson) 106:321

"Dear Freud" (Major) 19:297

"Dear Friend" (McCartney) 12:372; 35:280

"Dear Helen" (Simic) 49:341, 343

"Dear Illusion" (Amis) 40:43-5

"Dear John" (Kaufman) 49:203

Dear John, Dear Coltrane (Harper) 22:207

"Dear Jool, I Miss You in Saint-Saturnin" (Hacker) 72:192

"Dear Judas" (Jeffers) 54:237; 11:310

Dear Judas and Other Poems (Jeffers) 54:237; 11:305, 310-11

"The Dear Ladies of Cincinnati" (Stevenson) 7:463

"Dear Landlord" (Dylan) 12:185

"Dear Mama" (Sanchez) 116:307, 311

"Dear Masoch" (Codrescu) 46:106

"Dear Men and Women" (Wheelock) 14:571

"Dear Mother" (Cliff) 21:63

Dear Mr. Capote (Lish) 45:225-31

"Dear Mr. President" (Whalen) 6:566

"The Dear Old Village" (Betjeman) 6:68; 43:37

"Dear Paul: Four Versions" (Niedecker) 42:299

"Dear People" (Kaufman) 49:207

"Dear Phil Donahue" (Smith) 25:409; 73:357

"Dear Pop" (Carroll) 38:102-03

"Dear Pope" (Schwartz) 45:361

Dear Rat (Cunningham) 12:164

Dear Shadows: Portraits from Memory (Wain) 46:420

Dear Summer Sister (Oshima) 20:251

"Dear Yoko" (Lennon) 35:272, 274

Dearly Beloved (Lindbergh) 82:166-67

"A Death" (Creeley) 11:136

"Death" (Mailer) 111:96

Death (Allen) 52:37, 43

"Death II" (Mphahlele) 25:336

"Death Alone" (Neruda)
See "Sola la muerte"

Death along the Wabash (Saroyan) 10:453-54

"Death and Co." (Plath) 2:336; 11:445; 14:424; 17:347-48; 51:342, 345-46; 111:203

Death and Friends (Anderson) 9:31

Death and Letters (Daly) 52:91-2

Death and Life of a Severino (Cabral de Melo Neto)
See *Morte e vida severina e outraos poemas*

em voz alta

The Death and Life of Harry Goth (Mano) 2:270; 10:328

Death and Resurrection of Konstandinos Paleologhos (Elytis) 49:108; 100:175

Death and Taxes (Parker) 68:325

Death and the Children (Horgan) 9:278

"Death and the Compass" (Borges)
See "La muerte y la brújula"

Death and the Dancing Footman (Marsh) 53:249-51

"Death and the Good Life" (Hugo) 32:241-42

Death and the King's Horseman (Soyinka) 36:411; 44:287-90

"Death and the Maiden" (Lowell) 4:304

"Death and the Maiden" (Nemerov) 9:394; 36:305

Death and the Maiden (Dorfman) 77:154-55

"Death at a Great Distance" (Oliver) 98:292

Death at an Early Age (Kozol) 17:249-51, 254

Death at Crane's Court (Dillon) 17:95

"Death at Dawn" (Soyinka) 36:410; 44:280

Death at Sea (Prokosch) 48:308-10

Death at the Bar (Marsh) 53:250

Death at the President's Lodging (Stewart)
See *Seven Suspects*

"The Death Baby" (Sexton) 53:322-23

"Death Ballad" (Berryman) 62:74

"Death Be Not Proud" (Simmons) 43:411

Death before Bedtime (Vidal) 22:434

"Death behind Bars" (Crispin) 22:111

"The Death Bell" (Watkins) 43:446, 451

The Death Bell: Poems and Ballads (Watkins) 43:442, 447, 449

"Death by Drowning" (Christie) 110:141, 143

"Death by Drowning" (Eberhart) 11:177

Death by Hanging (Oshima)
See *Koshikei*

"Death by Landscape" (Atwood) 84:95, 98

"Death by Rarity" (Young) 82:397

"Death by Water" (Eliot) 15:214

"Death by Water" (Smith) 12:535

"Death Chant for Mr. Johnson's America" (Souster) 14:504

Death Claims (Hansen) 38:236-37

Death Comes as the End (Christie) 6:109; 8:142; 12:114-15; 48:74-5

"Death Constant beyond Love" (Garcia Marquez)
See "Muerte constante más allá der amor"

"The Death Dance" (Madhubuti) 73:208

The Death Dealers (Spillane) 13:528

"Death, etc." (Hogan) 73:157

Death Flight (Hunter) 31:228

"Death Fugue" (Celan)
See "Todesfuge"

"Death Goes to a Party" (Martin) 89:110, 112-13, 118

"Death, Great Smoothener" (Swenson) 106:350

Death in a Tenured Position (*A Death in the Faculty*) (Heilbrun) 25:256-57

Death in a White Tie (Marsh) 53:249-50

Death in April (Greeley) 28:175

Death in Don Mills (Garner) 13:237

"Death in Dreams: The Interpretation of Nightmares" (Leet) 11:323

Death in Ecstasy (Marsh) 7:209; 53:250, 254

"Death in January" (Buckley) 57:131

"Death in Jerusalem" (Trevor) 116:363

"Death in Leamington" (Betjeman) 43:32, 40, 52

Death in Life: Survivors of Hiroshima (Lifton) 67:137-40, 142, 153-54

"Death in Mexico" (Levertov) 66:253

"Death in Miami Beach" (Gold) 42:195

Death in Midsummer, and Other Stories (Mishima) 6:338-39

"Death in Spring" (Bates) 46:51

Death in the Afternoon (Hemingway) 1:141; 3:235, 241; 6:226, 228, 230; 8:283, 290; 13:271; 19:218; 30:179, 189-90; 34:477-79; 39:400, 403, 430, 433; 41:199, 201, 203; 50:422, 429; 61:225; 80:137, 150

Death in the Air (*Death in the Clouds*) (Christie) 12:122; 39:439; 48:72

"A Death in the Aquarium" (Hugo) 32:252

Death in the Clouds (Christie)
See *Death in the Air*

A Death in the Faculty (Heilbrun)
See *Death in a Tenured Position*

Death in the Fifth Position (Vidal) 22:434

"Death in the Lounge Bar" (Scannell) 49:328

"A Death in the North" (MacBeth) 5:265

Death in This Garden (Bunuel)
See *La mort en ce jardin*

Death in Venice (Visconti) 16:569-73, 575

"Death in Vietnam" (Salinas)
See "Death of Vietnam"

"Death Invited" (Swenson) 106:350

Death Is a Lonely Business (Bradbury) 42:45-6; 98:144

"Death Is the Star" (Clash) 30:51-2

Death Kit (Sontag) 1:322; 2:413-14; 13:515; 31:418; 105:197, 207, 225

Death Likes It Hot (Vidal) 22:434

Death List (Bullins) 1:47

Death List (Goines) 80:91, 94

"Death Mother" (Morgan) 23:301

Death Mother and Other Poems (Morgan) 23:299-301

The Death Notebooks (Sexton) 4:483-84; 6:492, 494; 8:483; 15:472; 53:322

"Death of a Bird" (Silkin) 43:399-400

"Death of a Bomber" (Ciardi) 40:152

Death of a Career Girl (Lang) 20:212

"Death of a Chieftain" (Montague) 46:264

Death of a Chieftain and Other Stories (Montague) 46:264, 278

"Death of a Chleuch Dancer" (Faludy) 42:138, 140

"Death of a Critic" (Lowell) 11:331; 37:238

"Death of a Favorite" (Powers) 57:356

Death of a Fool (Marsh) 53:249-51

"Death of a Friend" (Cohen) 19:113

"Death of a Ghost" (Allingham) 19:11, 14

"The Death of a Good Man" (Phillips) 28:362

Death of a Harbour Master (Simenon) 18:481; 47:372

Death of a Hawker (van de Wetering) 47:406-07, 411-12

Death of a Hero (Aldington) 49:9, 11

Death of a Hero (Anand) 23:18

Death of a Huntsman (Bates) 46:61

"The Death of a Kinsman" (Taylor) 37:408, 411; 44:305; 50:260; 71:295

Death of a Lady's Man (Cohen) 38:136-37

"Death of a Lesser Man" (Berriault) 54:3, 5

"Death of a Man" (L'Heureux) 52:272

Death of a Man (Boyle) 58:64

"The Death of a Mormon Elder" (Freeman) 55:57-8

"Death of a Naturalist" (Heaney) 25:241

Death of a Naturalist (Heaney) 5:171-72; 7:147, 149-50; 14:242-43, 245; 25:241-

42, 244, 246, 248, 250; **37**:165; **74**:156-57, 163, 167, 170, 188, 192, 194; **91**:121, 123, 125, 127

"Death of a Peasant" (Thomas) **6**:534; **13**:543

Death of a Peer (*Surfeit of Lampreys*) (Marsh) **7**:210; **53**:251-52, 254, 258

"Death of a Pig" (White) **34**:430

"Death of a Poet in Battle-Dress" (Simmons) **43**:407

Death of a Politician (Condon) **45**:98-9; **100**:100, 110, 113

"Death of a Public Servant" (Kizer) **80**:172, 185

Death of a Salesman (Kazan) **63**:222, 231, 234

Death of a Salesman (*The Inside of His Head*) (Miller) **1**:216-19; **2**:278-80; **6**:326-37; **10**:342-44; **15**:370-74, 376; **26**:310-24, 327; **47**:250-51, 253-55; **78**:288-90, 293, 295, 297-99, 301-02, 305-06, 309, 311-13, 318, 324-25, 328

"Death of a Son" (Silkin) **6**:498; **43**:398, 400-01, 404

"Death of a Spaceman" (Miller) **30**:263-65

"The Death of a Toad" (Wilbur) **6**:569

"The Death of a Traveling Salesman" (Welty) **2**:462; **14**:561; **33**:414, 424; **105**:306-07, 325

"Death of a Vermont Farm Woman" (Howes) **15**:290

Death of a Young, Young Man (Russell) **60**:320

The Death of Ahasuerus (Lagerkvist) See *Ahasverus död*

"Death of an Actor" (Williams) **42**:445

Death of an Expert Witness (James) **18**:273; **46**:205-06

"Death of an Explorer" (Gascoyne) **45**:158

"Death of an Old Lady" (MacNeice) **53**:238

The Death of Artemio Cruz (Fuentes) See *La muerte de Artemio Cruz*

"The Death of Assia G." (Amichai) See "Mota Shel Assia G."

"The Death of Aunt Alice" (Abse) **29**:18

The Death of Bessie Smith (Albee) **2**:4; **5**:10; **9**:2-3, 5; **25**:33; **113**:3-6, 43

"The Death of Celan" (Amichai) See "Moto Shel Celan"

"Death of Childhood Beliefs" (Blunden) **56**:49

"The Death of Cock Robin" (Snodgrass) **68**:398

The Death of Cock Robin (Snodgrass) **68**:388, 393-94

"The Death of Crazy Horse" (Clifton) **66**:82

The Death of Dickey Draper and Nine Other Stories (Weidman) **7**:517

"The Death of Don Quixote" (Glassco) **9**:237

"The Death of Edward Lear" (Barthelme) **13**:59, 63; **46**:35

"The Death of Egorushka" (Leonov) See "Ghibel' Egorushki"

"The Death of Elsa Baskoleit" (Boell) See "Der Tod der Elsa Baskoleit"

"The Death of Emmit Till" (Dylan) **77**:166

"The Death of Francisco Pizarro" (Ai) **69**:8

"The Death of Fred Clifton" (Clifton) **66**:82

The Death of Jim Loney (Welch) **52**:426, 430-36, 438

"The Death of Justina" (Cheever) **15**:127, 130; **25**:120

"The Death of Keats" (Watkins) **43**:452

"Death of King George V" (Betjeman) **2**:60; **34**:306

"The Death of Kropotkin" (Read) **4**:442

"The Death of Leon Trotsky" (Goodman)

4:197

"Death of Little Boys" (Tate) **2**:429

The Death of Malcolm X (Sanchez) **116**:301

"The Death of Marilyn Monroe" (Olds) **39**:190

"The Death of Mary Queen of Scots" (Monty Python) **21**:227

"The Death of Me" (Malamud) **9**:348; **44**:419

The Death of Methusaleh, and Other Stories (Singer) **69**:309-11, 313-14, 316

"The Death of Methuselah" (Singer) **69**:310, 312-14

The Death of Mr. Baltisberger (Hrabal) **13**:290-91; **67**:121, 126

"The Death of Myth-Making" (Plath) **9**:432

"Death of Narcissus" (Lezama Lima) See "Muerte de Narciso"

"The Death of Pan" **75**:76

"The Death of Picasso" (Davenport) **38**:144-45

"The Death of Randall Jarrell" (Shapiro) **53**:328

"The Death of Reason" (Boland) **113**:110, 126

"The Death of Robert Browning" (Urquhart) **90**:384-5

The Death of Robin Hood (Vansittart) **42**:397-98

"The Death of Saint Narcissus" (Eliot) **57**:204

The Death of Seneca (Hine) **15**:282

"The Death of St. Catherine of Siena" (Buckley) **57**:129

"The Death of the Author" (Barthes) See "La mort de l'auteur"

"The Death of the Author" (Gass) **39**:481-82

"The Death of the Ayatollah Khomenei" (Durcan) **70**:147

"The Death of the Ball Turret Gunner" (Jarrell) **2**:211; **9**:298; **13**:300, 302-03; **49**:201

"Death of the Band" (Katz) **47**:220, 222

"The Death of the Bird" (Hope) **51**:216, 221

"Death of the Creative Process" (Olsen) **4**:386

"The Death of the Fathers" (Sexton) **4**:483; **6**:495; **15**:472; **53**:314, 321-23

Death of the Fox (Garrett) **3**:189-90, 193; **11**:220; **51**:148-49, 151, 153

The Death of the Heart (Bowen) **1**:39-41; **3**:82-3; **6**:94-5; **11**:59-62, 64; **15**:78-9

Death of the Hind Legs and Other Stories (Wain) **46**:415

"The Death of the Hired Man" (Frost) **3**:170; **9**:218; **13**:230; **15**:246-47; **26**:112-13, 123, 127-28

Death of the Inquisitor (Sciascia) See *La morte dell'inquisitore*

"Death of the Kapowsin Tavern" (Hugo) **32**:246-47

Death of the Kapowsin Tavern (Hugo) **32**:234-35, 237-38, 244, 247, 249

"The Death of the King of France" (Landolfi) **49**:209-10

"Death of the Miners or the Widows of the Earth" (Kunene) **85**:176

"Death of the Nazarene" (Shamlu) **10**:471

The Death of the Novel and Other Stories (Sukenick) **3**:475; **4**:531

"The Death of the Old Man" (Yehoshua) **31**:472

The Death of the Old Man (Yehoshua) **13**:617; **31**:468, 472

"The Death of the Old Men" (Fiedler) **24**:194

"The Death of the Pythia" (Duerrenmatt) See "Das Sterben der Pythia"

"The Death of the Right Fielder" (Dybek) **114**:68, 83

"The Death of the Small Commune" (Piercy)

18:406; **27**:375

The Death of Tragedy (Steiner) **24**:425-27

"The Death of Uncle Silas" (Bates) **46**:52

"Death of Vietnam" ("Death in Vietnam") (Salinas) **90**:324, 327

The Death of Virgil (Skvorecky) **15**:511

The Death of William Posters (Sillitoe) **3**:448; **6**:500; **19**:421

"Death of Women" (Coles) **46**:108

"Death on All Fronts" (Ginsberg) **36**:185

"A Death on the East Side" (Gold) **42**:193

Death on the Installment Plan (Celine) See *Mort à crédit*

Death on the Nile (Christie) **12**:113-14, 117; 122-23; **39**:438; **48**:72, 74, 76-7; **110**:121-22

"Death or Glory" (Clash) **30**:46-7

"Death or the Waiting Room" (Aleixandre) **36**:29

"A Death Road for the Condor" (Macdonald) **41**:270

Death Shall Not Enter the Palace (Marques) See *La muerte no entrará en palacio*

The Death Ship (Traven) See *Das Totenschiff*

"Death Sits in the Dentist's Chair" (Woolrich) **77**:401

Death, Sleep, and the Traveler (Hawkes) **4**:215-19; **7**:140-46; **9**:269; **27**:190-91, 194-96, 199; **49**:162-64

Death Suite (Rooke) **25**:393-95

Death to the French (Forester) See *Rifleman Dodd*

"A Death to Us" (Silkin) **43**:400-01

"Death to Van Gogh's Ear!" (Ginsberg) **6**:199; **13**:239-40

"Death Valley" (Oates) **108**:384

"Death Valley Scotty" (Guthrie) **35**:193

Death Wears a Red Hat (Kienzle) **25**:275

"The Deathbird" (Ellison) **13**:207; **42**:128-29

Deathbird Stories: A Pantheon of Modern Gods (Ellison) **13**:203, 206, 208; **42**:128

"The Death-in-Life of Benjamin Reid" (Styron) **60**:393

"The Deathmaker at San Quentin" (Bowering) **47**:33

Deathman, Do Not Follow Me (Bennett) **35**:42, 45

"Deaths" (Swenson) **106**:350

"The Deaths about You When You Stir in Sleep" (Ciardi) **40**:157-58

"The Deaths and the Victory of Rosalinda" (Amado) See "As Mortes e o Triunfo de Rosalinda"

"Deaths at Sea" (Dubus) **97**:214, 216, 218

Death's Deputy (Hubbard) **43**:203-04

"Death's Door" (Gunn) **81**:180, 187

"Death's Echo" (Auden) **6**:21

"Death's Head" (Gotlieb) **18**:193

"Death's Head Revisited" (Serling) **30**:358

Death's Master (Lee) **46**:231-34

"The Deaths of Uncles" (Kumin) **13**:327

Deathwatch (Genet) See *Haute surveillance*

The Deathworld Trilogy (Harrison) **42**:205

"Debates" (Corn) **33**:116

"Debbie Go Home" (Paton) **25**:360

"Debout" ("On Your Feet") (Tchicaya) **101**:350

Debridement (Harper) **7**:139; **22**:207-08

"Debriefing" (Sontag) **13**:516-17

The Debriefing (Littell) **42**:276

"Debris" (Ammons) **57**:49

"Débris" (Cesaire)　19:98
"Debris" (Fearing)　51:106
Debt of Honor (Clancy)　112:76-80, 82, 84, 90
"A Debt of Honour" (Pritchett)　41:333
The Debt to Pleasure (Lanchester)　99:54-61
"Debtors' Lane" (Okigbo)　25:350; 84:328, 330-31
"Debts" (Paley)　37:337
"Debut" (Hunter)　35:226
The Debut (Brookner)
　See *A Start in Life*
Debutante Hill (Duncan)　26:100
Decade (Young)　17:577-80, 582
"Decades" (Howard)　7:170; 10:275-76
The Decameron (Pasolini)
　See *Il Decamerone*
Il Decamerone (*The Decameron*) (Pasolini)　20:266-68; 106:224, 226
The Decay of the Angel (*Five Signs of God's Decay*) (Mishima)　4:356-58; 6:337; 27:341-42
"December" (Akhmadulina)　53:11
"December" (Oliver)　98:303
"December" (Simic)　49:341
"December 6th" (Forester)　35:173
"December 29, 1890: Wounded Knee Creek" (Momaday)　85:281
"December 1920" (Seifert)　93:339
"December Evening 1972" (Transtroemer)　65:221, 230
"December in Florence" ("Dekabr' vo Florentsii") (Brodsky)　13:117; 50:125; 100:52
"December of My Springs" (Giovanni)　64:191
"December Thirty-one St. Silvester" (Warner)　19:461
A Decent Birth, a Happy Funeral (Saroyan)　8:467
"Deception" (Corn)　33:116
The Deception (Canetti)
　See *Die Blendung*
Deception (Roth)　86:248-49, 252-53
"Deception Bay" (Malouf)　28:268
"Deceptions" (Larkin)　8:332, 340; 18:294; 33:261; 39:336; 64:262, 266, 268, 270
Deceptive Distinctions (Epstein)　65:325
The Deceptive Grin (Ewart)　13:209
Decider (Francis)　102:150-52
"Deciduous Branch" (Kunitz)　14:312-13
"Decipherings" (Levertov)　66:240
The Decision (Drury)　37:111-12
Decision at Delphi (MacInnes)　27:281; 39:350
Decision at Doona (McCaffrey)　17:280
"Decision on King Street" (Souster)　5:396
"Decisions to Disappear" (Dunn)　36:151
"Declaration" (Lessing)　3:292; 6:295
"A Declaration for 1955" (Boyle)　58:74
"Declaration, July 4" (Corn)　33:116
Declarations of War (*Eleven Declarations of War*) (Deighton)　4:119; 46:127
Declensions of a Refrain (Gregor)　9:254
"Decline and Fall" (Swan)　69:361-62
Decline and Fall (Waugh)　1:357-59; 3:510-13; 8:543-44; 13:584-85; 19:461; 44:520; 107:357, 362-64, 370-71, 378, 383, 385, 393, 397, 399, 401, 406
"The Decline and Fall of Frankie Buller" (Sillitoe)　6:501; 57:387
"The Decline of the Argo" (Ritsos)　6:464
Decline of the New (Howe)　85:121-22
The Decline of the West (Caute)　29:111-14, 121-22
"The Decolonization of American Literature"

(Shapiro)　53:328
Deconstruction and Criticism (Bloom)　103:20, 25, 28
"Decoration" (Bogan)　46:85-6
Découvertes (Ionesco)　41:229
"Decoy" (Ashbery)　25:58; 77:48, 57
"Decreator" (Redgrove)　6:445; 41:351, 353
Dedans (Cixous)　92:90
Dedica (Pasolini)　106:233
"Dedicated" (Leavitt)　34:78-9
"Dedicated Follower of Fashion" (Davies)　21:97, 103
A Dedicated Man (Taylor)　2:432
"Dedication" (Boland)　40:100
"A Dedication" (Merrill)　34:239
"Dedication" (Milosz)　31:259; 56:233; 82:289, 296
Dedication (Ekeloef)　27:109-11
"Dedication for a Plot of Ground" (Williams)　42:452
"Dedication: The Other Woman and the Novelist" (Boland)　113:115
"Dedication to a Poet" (Kunene)　85:166
"Dedication to Hunger" (Gluck)　22:175; 44:216; 81:173
"Dedications" (Rich)　73:336-37; 76:218
Dedications and Other Darkhorses (Komunyakaa)　94:218, 230, 239, 246
"Dedicatory Epistle" (Fuller)　28:158
"Dedicatory Stanzas" (Day Lewis)　10:134
"Deductible Yacht" (Auchincloss)　9:52
Deenie (Blume)　12:47; 30:20, 23
The Deep (Benchley)　8:82
The Deep (Crowley)　57:156, 162, 164
The Deep (Spillane)　13:527-28
"Deep Analysis" (Larkin)　64:282
The Deep Blue Goodbye (MacDonald)　3:307; 44:407-08
The Deep Blue Sea (Rattigan)　7:355
"A Deep Breath at Dawn" (Hecht)　8:268
"The Deep End" (Mac Laverty)　31:253
Deep End (Skolimowski)　20:349, 352-54
"Deep Forbidden Lake" (Young)　17:577
The Deep Has Many Voices (Ringwood)　48:330-31, 334-37, 339
Deep River (Endo)　99:284, 288, 297, 299-310
"The Deep River: A Story oF Ancient Tribal Migration" (Head)　67:98
Deep Rivers (Arguedas)
　See *Los ríos profundos*
The Deep Sleep (Morris)　1:233; 3:343; 18:352; 37:311
"The Deep Supermarket" (Durcan)　70:147
The Deep Tangled Wildwood (Connelly)　7:56
The Deep Tangled Wildwood (Kaufman)　38:257
Deep Torrent, Dark River (Yourcenar)
　See *Fleuve profond, sombre rivière*
Deep Water (Highsmith)　2:193; 42:211, 215; 102:170, 172-73, 201-02, 204
"Deep Woods" (Nemerov)　36:305
"The Deeper Friendship" (Blunden)　56:38
"The Deeper Lesson" (Carroll)　10:98
Deeper than the Darkness (*The Stars in Shroud*) (Benford)　52:60, 65
Deeper than the Darkness (Benford)
　See *The Stars in Shroud*
"The Deeps" (Roberts)　14:464
"Deep-Sea Fish" (Turner)　48:399
"Deer among Cattle" (Dickey)　7:81
The Deer at Our House (Caldwell)　50:302
"Deer Dance/For Your Return" (Silko)　74:330, 347; 114:316

"Deer Dancer" (Harjo)　83:272, 274, 280-81
"Deer Dancers at Santo Domingo" (Lewis)　41:260-61
"Deer Ghost" (Harjo)　83:273, 282
The Deer Hunter (Cimino)　16:209-14
"The Deer of Providencia" (Dillard)　60:74-5; 115:197
"Deer on the High Hills" ("Deer on the High Hills—A Meditation") (Smith)　64:388, 394, 396, 398
"Deer on the High Hills—A Meditation" (Smith)
　See "Deer on the High Hills"
The Deer Park (Mailer)　1:187-90, 192-93; 2:258-59, 263; 3:311, 313, 318; 4:319, 321-23; 5:268; 8:364, 366, 370, 373; 11:339-40, 342-43, 345; 14:348, 352; 28:257; 74:203, 206, 222-24, 233; 111:94-5, 98, 100, 103, 108, 120, 130, 133, 135, 148
The Deer Pasture (Bass)　79:2, 10, 15-18
"Deer Song" (Silko)　74:330; 114:316
"Deer Trails in Tzityonyana" (Rooke)　25:394
"Deerslayer's Campfire Talk" (Stafford)　4:520
"De-Evolution" (Livesay)　79:338, 350
"Defeat" (Aldington)　49:7
"Defeat" (Boyle)　58:66
"The Defeat of Youth" (Huxley)　11:282, 284
The Defeat of Youth, and Other Poems (Huxley)　11:282, 284
"The Defeated" (Gordimer)　18:185; 33:177
"The Defeated" (Kavanagh)　22:243
"Defection of a Favorite" (Powers)　57:356
The Defection of A. J. Lewinter (Littell)　42:274-76
"Defective Story" (Raine)　103:180
Defectos escogidos: 2000 (*Chosen Defects; Selected Failings*) (Neruda)　28:310; 62:333-34, 336
"Defence" (Silkin)　43:397, 400
The Defendant (Mahfuz)　52:298
"Defender of the Faith" (Roth)　2:380; 22:357; 31:335
"Defender of the Little Falaya" (Gilchrist)　34:164
Defending Ancient Springs (Raine)　7:351
Defenestration of Prague (Howe)　72:195, 197-98, 208
"Defensa de Violeta Parra" (Parra)　102:340
The Defense (Nabokov)　1:241-43; 2:303; 3:352, 355; 8:418; 11:393; 15:396; 46:295; 64:348, 366
The Defense of Granada (Brandys)　62:112
The Defense of the Sugar Islands: A Recruiting Post (Cassity)　42:96-7
"The Defenseman" (Banks)　72:4
"Defensio in extremis" (Berryman)　25:96
The Defiant Agents (Norton)　12:467
"Define This Word" (Fisher)　76:338
"Defining the Poet" (Turco)　11:551
Definitely Maybe (Strugatskii and Strugatskii)　27:435-37
"Definition" (Dodson)　79:194
"definition for blk / children" (Sanchez)　116:295
"Definition in the Face of Unnamed Fury" (Dove)　81:139
Definition of Blue (Ashbery)　13:33
"Definitions" (Wright)　6:580
"Definitions of Poetry" (Sandburg)　35:352
"Definitive Dialogue" (Ali)　69:32
The Deflowered One (Nakos)
　See *Le livre de mon pierrot*
"Defrauded Woman" (Scannell)　49:331

Defy the Wilderness (Banks)   23:42

"Degas's Laundresses" (Boland)   40:101; 113:109, 123

Le degré zéro de l'écriture (Writing Degree Zero; Zero Degree Writing) (Barthes)   24:22, 25-7, 30-1, 33, 37, 39-41; 83:67-9, 83, 85, 90, 100

Degree of Trust (Voinovich) See *Stepen' doveriia*

"Degrees" (Thomas)   37:423; 107:320-21, 333

Degrees (Butor) See *Degrés*

Degrees of Freedom (Byatt)   65:131

"Degrees of Gray in Philipsburg" (Hugo)   32:240, 248, 250

Degrés (Degrees) (Butor)   3:92-3; 8:116-18, 120-21; 11:79-80; 15:115, 117-19

"Dehorning" (Hughes)   37:175

Dei svarte hestane (The Black Horses) (Vesaas)   48:404-05, 407

Dei ukjende mennene (The Unknown Men) (Vesaas)   48:405

"Dein Leib im Rauch durch die Luft" (Sachs)   98:327

"Dein Schimmer" (Celan)   82:51-3

"Deities" (Montague)   46:277

"Deja vu" (Urdang)   47:400

Déjà vu (Young)   17:569-70

"Déjeuner sur l'herbe" (Thomas)   37:421; 107:328

Le déjeuner sur l'herbe (Picnic on the Grass) (Renoir)   20:290-93, 297, 303-04

"Dekabr' vo Florentsii" (Brodsky) See "December in Florence"

Dekachto lianotragouda tes pikres patridas (Eighteen Short Songs of the Bitter Motherland) (Ritsos)   6:463; 13:487

Del Corso's Gallery (Caputo)   32:106

Del pozo y del Numa: Un ensayo y una leyenda (Of the Well and Numa: An Essay and a Legend) (Benet)   28:23-4

Delano: The Story of the California Grape Strike (Dunne)   28:120-21, 125

"El delator" (Marques)   229

The Delay (Hildesheimer) See *Die Verspätung*

The Delectable Mountains (Malone)   43:281

"The Delegate" (Porter)   13:452-53; 33:322-23

"The Delhi Division" (Moorcock)   58:347

"Delia's Father" (Colwin)   84:146, 150

A Deliberate Policy (Schell)   35:369

A Delicate Balance (Albee)   1:4-5; 2:1, 3-4; 3:6-7; 5:11, 13; 9:4-6, 9; 11:13; 13:3, 5, 7; 25:35-8, 40; 53:20-1, 24; 86:119-20, 124-25; 113:9-10, 12-15, 17, 21-2, 28, 40

"The Delicate Bird Who Is Flying Up Our Asses" (Bell)   8:65-6

"Delicate Criss-Crossing Beetle Trails Left in the Sand" (Snyder)   32:395

"The Delicate Prey" (Bowles)   53:36, 43, 46

A Delicate Prey and Other Stories (Bowles)   1:41-2; 2:79; 19:56; 53:37-40

"Delight" (Warren)   13:577

"The Delight Song of Tsoai-talee" (Momaday)   85:247, 265

"Delights of Winter at the Shore" (Whalen)   29:445

Delinquent Chacha (Mehta)   37:290

The Delinquents (Altman)   16:41; 116:12-13, 46

"Delirious" (Prince)   35:327

Delirium's Mistress (Lee)   46:234

"Delitto al circolo di tennis" (Moravia)   7:240

"Deliverance" (Graves)   45:166, 168

Deliverance (Dickey)   1:73-4; 2:116; 4:121-23; 7:81, 84-6; 10:139-40, 142-43; 15:176-77; 47:91, 93, 98-100; 109:243, 245, 257-63, 276-77, 279-80, 282-83, 285-86

"Delivering" (Dubus)   36:145-46; 97:202, 208, 223

"The Delivery" (Smith)   22:385

"The Delivery" (Van Duyn)   116:421, 427

"Della's Modesty" (Gerstler)   70:156, 159

"Delphi: Commentary" (Kroetsch)   57:292-93

"Delphine" (Morand)   41:295, 297, 308

"Delta" (Tolson)   105:274

The Delta Decision (Smith)   33:377

The Delta Factor (Spillane)   13:528

Delta of Venus (Nin)   8:425; 11:398; 14:387; 60:269, 274-77

Delta Wedding (Welty)   1:361; 2:462-63; 5:478; 14:561; 22:457, 461; 33:421-24; 105:303, 316, 325, 336-38, 340, 360, 382, 389

"The Deltoid Pumpkin Seed" (McPhee)   36:295, 297

Le déluge (The Flood) (Le Clezio)   31:243, 245-46, 249

"The Deluge at Norderney" (Dinesen)   10:146; 29:162; 95:35-6, 48, 50-2, 64, 67

The Delusion (Canetti) See *Die Blendung*

"Delusion for a Dragon Slayer" (Ellison)   42:126, 128-29

Delusions, Etc. of John Berryman (Berryman)   2:57-9; 3:66-71; 4:62-3; 6:63-4; 8:91-2; 10:51; 13:82-3; 25:91-2, 95-7; 62:45-6, 74-5

Delusion's Master (Lee)   46:231, 234

Dem (Kelley)   22:247-49

Dem unbekannten Sieger (To the Unknown Hero) (Nossack)   6:364-66

Demain matin, Montréal m'attend (Tremblay)   29:419, 425; 102:372, 374, 376

"Demands of the Muse" (Watkins)   43:452-53

"Demands of the Poet" (Watkins)   43:452-53

The deMaury Papers (Holland)   21:151

Demelza (Graham)   23:191

"Le déménagement" (Roy)   10:440

Le déménagement (Simenon)   47:379

Dementia Thirteen (Coppola)   16:231, 244, 249

"Demeter" (Broumas)   73:2

"Demeter" (H. D.)   73:105, 128

Demian (Hesse)   1:145-47; 2:189-90; 3:245, 248; 6:236-37; 11:270, 272; 17:195, 198, 201-02, 204-06, 211-12, 217-18; 25:261; 69:272, 287, 289, 294, 296

"The Demiurge" (Cioran)   64:80, 89, 94

"Demiurges" (Sherwood)   81:102

"The Demiurge's Laugh" (Frost)   26:117

"Demo against the Vietnam War, 1968" (Abse)   7:2; 29:18-19

Democracy (Didion)   32:146-50

Democracy and Esther (Linney)   51:259, 265

Democracy and Poetry (Warren)   10:520; 13:582

"Democracy in America" (Oates)   6:371

"Democratic Party Poem" (Williams)   13:604

"A Democratic School" (Cozzens)   92:201

"Demolition with Tobacco Speck" (Raine)   103:186

"A Demon" (O'Brien)   65:170, 172; 116:203

The Demon (Selby)   8:477

Demon Box (Kesey)   46:224-29

A Demon in My View (Rendell)   28:384; 48:320-21

A Demon in My View (Vine)   50:264

"The Demon Love" (Rich)   73:328

"The Demon Lover" (Bowen)   15:77-8; 22:65

"The Demon Lover" (Rich)   6:458; 7:366

The Demon Lover and Other Stories (Ivy Gripped the Steps) (Bowen)   11:63; 15:77; 22:63-4, 68

The Demon of Scattery (Anderson)   15:15

Demon Princes (Vance)   35:421, 423, 426-27

Demon Seed (Koontz)   78:199, 203

The Demon-Haunted World (Sagan)   112:437-38, 440, 443

"Demons" (Oates)   6:367

Demons by Daylight (Campbell)   42:83-4, 87-90

The Demonstration (Caute)   29:113-15, 122

"The Demonstrators" (Welty)   105:299, 311-13

"Dendrocacalia" (Abe)   81:297

"Denial" (Gustafson)   36:211

Denier du rêve (A Coin in Nine Hands) (Yourcenar)   38:457-60, 464-65; 50:363-64; 87:383, 390, 404

"Denis le boiteux" (Theriault)   79:408

"Denouement" (Fearing)   51:105, 117

"The Deodand" (Hecht)   19:207-10

Le départ (Skolimowski)   20:347-49, 352-53

"The Departed" (Davie)   31:117

"Departing Song" (Young)   82:411

The Department (Williamson)   56:434-35, 441

"Department of Public Monuments" (Simic)   49:343

"Departmental" (Frost)   10:196; 34:475

"Departure" (Fast)   23:156

"The Departure" (Olds)   39:189-90; 85:289

"Departure" (Plath)   111:201

"Departure" (Scott)   22:376

"Departure" (Tomlinson)   45:394

Departure and Other Stories (Fast)   23:156

"Departure from the Bush" (Atwood)   8:32

"Departure in Middle Age" (Mathias)   45:238

"Departure in the Dark" (Day Lewis)   6:127; 10:131

"Departures" (Barthelme)   115:65, 68-9

"Departures" (L'Heureux)   52:279

Departures (Justice)   6:271-72; 19:233; 102:249-50, 261, 264, 270, 277, 280-81, 283

Dependencies (Mueller)   51:279-81

Depends: A Poet's Notebook (Montale) See *Quaderno de quattro anni*

Le dépeupleur (The Lost Ones) (Beckett)   2:47-8; 3:45; 4:50, 52; 6:36, 38, 40, 42; 9:83; 11:39-40; 18:49-51; 29:57, 59-60, 62, 67

"Deposition: Testimony Concerning a Sickness" (Burroughs)   15:111

"Depot Bay" (Levine)   33:275

The Depraved Sleepers (Ruyslinck) See *De ontaarde slapers*

"Depravity: Two Sermons" (Davie)   31:116

"The Depreciated Legacy of Cervantes" ("The Novel and Europe") (Kundera)   68:242; 115:321

"Depressed by a Book of Bad Poetry" (Wright)   3:540

"Depression" (Bly)   5:63; 10:56

The Deptford Trilogy (Davies)   42:101-03, 106-07, 109; 75:180, 184, 190, 192, 199, 214; 91:201-04

Depth of Field (Heyen) **13**:281; **18**:230
"The Depths" (Levertov) **5**:246
"Depths" (Silkin) **43**:396, 400, 404
The Deputy (Hochhuth)
  See *Der Stellvertreter*
"Derbyshire" (Davie) **31**:120
"Derelict" (Day Lewis) **6**:128; **10**:131
"Dereliction" (Achebe) **11**:4
"The Derelicts of Ganymede" (Campbell)
  32:73
Dereva detstva (*The Tree of Childhood*)
  (Iskander) **47**:199
"Dereviannaia koroleva" ("The Wooden
  Queen") (Leonov) **92**:237, 242, 256,
  262-63
Derivations (Duncan) **2**:123; **15**:187-8; **55**:294
"Derm Fool" (Sturgeon) **22**:410
Le dernier havre (Theriault) **79**:415
Le dernier milliardaire (*The Last Billionaire*)
  (Clair) **20**:61-2, 70
La dernier reveillon (Renoir) **20**:300
Le dernier tableau ou le portrait de Dieu
  (Cixous)
  See "The Last Painting or the Portrait of
  God"
"Dernières cartouches" (Soupault) **68**:407
Les dernières nuits de Paris (*Last Nights of
  Paris*) (Soupault) **68**:416
Les dernières paroles d'un impie (Pasolini)
  106:254-55
Les derniers jours (Queneau) **5**:360; **42**:335-
  36
Les derniers rois mages (*The Last Magi*)
  (Conde) **92**:125-26, 131-34
Des chinoises (*About Chinese Women*)
  (Kristeva) **77**:303-05, 312
Des Clefs et des serrures (Tournier) **95**:361,
  365, 381
Des journées entières dans les arbres (*Whole
  Days in the Trees*) (Duras) **6**:149; **40**:175,
  184; **68**:92; **100**:145
Des mois (Landolfi) **49**:215
Des Teufels General (*The Devil's General*)
  (Zuckmayer) **18**:553-54, 556-57
Des tonnes de semence (Audiberti) **38**:21
Des traces de pas (Simenon) **8**:488
A Descant for Gossips (Astley) **41**:43-4, 48-9
Descant on Rawley's Madrigal (Bunting)
  39:298
"Descartes and the Stove" (Tomlinson) **45**:392
Descending Figure (Gluck) **22**:175-77; **44**:214,
  216, 221-22, 224; **81**:173
"Descent" (Ritsos) **31**:330
"Descent" (Weiss) **14**:556
"The Descent" (Williams) **42**:452
The Descent (Berriault) **54**:1; **109**:90
"The Descent Beckons" (Williams) **13**:604
"Descent in a Parachute" (Belitt) **22**:49
"Descent of Man" (Boyle) **36**:57-8
Descent of Man, and Other Stories (Boyle)
  36:56-9, 61, 63; **90**:45, 49-50
The Descent of Winter (Williams) **2**:468-69;
  42:462
*Descent to the Dead: Poems Written in Ireland
  and Great Britain* (Jeffers) **54**:237, 244,
  246
"Descoberta da literatura" ("Discovering Lit-
  erature") (Cabral de Melo Neto) **76**:164
A Descoberta de América pelos Turcos (Amado)
  106:91
"Description of a Masque" (Ashbery) **41**:34,
  37-40
"Description of a Pain in the Solar Plexus"

  (Akhmadulina) **53**:12
"Description of a View" (Empson) **19**:157
Description of San Marco (Butor) **8**:118;
  15:117-18
"A Description of Some Confederate Soldiers"
  (Jarrell) **2**:209
"Descriptive Passages" (Matthews) **40**:324
"La Desdichada" (Fuentes) **113**:242-43
"Desecration" (Jhabvala) **8**:313
"The Desert" (Faludy) **42**:140
"Desert" (Hogan) **73**:151
Désert (Le Clezio) **31**:251
"The Desert as Garden of Paradise" (Rich)
  73:331
"Desert Breakdown, 1968" (Wolff) **64**:450-
  51, 454
Le désert de l'amour (*The Desert of Love*)
  (Mauriac) **4**:338-41; **9**:368; **56**:204-07,
  214, 216
Desert Drum (Schlee) **35**:372
"Desert Elm" (Bowering) **47**:23
A Desert Incident (Buck) **11**:77; **18**:80
"Desert Island Discs" (Townshend) **17**:533
Desert Love (Montherlant)
  See *La rose de sable*
*L   e
  de indexhung indexhung indexhung indexhung set
  mauve* (*Mauve Desert*) (Brossard)
  115:119-20, 122-23, 135-36, 155
"The Desert Music" (Williams) **9**:575; **22**:465-
  66; **42**:455, 463
The Desert Music, and Other Poems (Williams)
  22:465; **42**:451, 454, 463
The Desert of Love (Mauriac)
  See *Le désert de l'amour*
The Desert of the Heart (Rule) **27**:416-17, 421
"Desert Places" (Frost) **1**:110; **9**:227-28;
  13:225; **15**:244; **26**:121
"Desert Places" (Haines) **58**:214
The Desert Rose (McMurtry) **44**:259
Desert Solitaire: A Season in the Wilderness
  (Abbey) **36**:12-13, 16, 18-19, 21;
  59:238-45
The Desert Year (Krutch) **24**:290
"Desertion" (Simak) **55**:320
"Desertions" (Honig) **33**:212
"Desertmartin" (Paulin) **37**:355
Il deserto dei tartari (*The Tartar Steppe*)
  (Buzzati) **36**:83-9, 91-5
Il deserto rosso (*The Red Desert*) (Antonioni)
  20:29-31, 34-5
Les désespéranto (*The Despairing*) (Tzara)
  47:385, 387, 390, 394
La Desesperanza (*Curfew; Despair; Despera-
  tion; Hopelessness*) (Donoso) **99**:217, 219,
  222-23, 232, 242, 256-69
"Desespoir d'un volontaire libre" (Senghor)
  54:410
"Deshoras" (Cortazar) **33**:134; **34**:333
"Design" (Frost) **1**:110; **3**:174; **9**:221, 228;
  13:228; **15**:250; **26**:124-25
Design for Living (Coward) **1**:64; **29**:132-33,
  135-36, 138; **51**:69-73, 75, 77
"Design in Living Colors" (Rich) **36**:365
The Designated Heir (Kumin) **5**:222
"Desire" (Beattie) **40**:66; **63**:2, 9
"Desire" (Hughes) **108**:332
"Desire" (Peacock) **60**:293-94, 297
"Desire" (Raine) **45**:337
"Desire" (Wilson) **49**:416
Desire (Dylan) **12**:192; **77**:178
"Desire and the Black Masseur" (Williams)
  15:579-80; **45**:453-54, 456; **71**:363;

  111:419, 419
*Desire in Language: A Semiotic Approach to
  Literature and Art* (Kristeva) **77**:309-10,
  312, 320
"Desire in November" (Calvino) **33**:102
"Desire Is a World by Night" (Berryman) **62**:56
"Desire on Domino Island" (Smith) **73**:357
Desires (L'Heureux) **52**:279
Desmonde (Cronin) **32**:141
Desolación de la quimera (Cernuda) **54**:58,
  60
"A Desolation" (Ginsberg) **36**:182
Desolation Angels (Kerouac) **3**:264; **29**:270,
  272
"Desolation Row" (Dylan) **3**:130; **4**:149;
  6:156; **12**:181; **77**:161-62, 164, 187
*Le désordre de la mémoire: Entretiens avec
  Francine Mallet* (Mandiargues) **41**:278
"Despair" (Berryman) **25**:95-6
Despair (Crumb) **17**:84
Despair (Donoso)
  See *La Desesperanza*
Despair (Fassbinder) **20**:117
Despair (Nabokov) **1**:242-43; **2**:302; **6**:359;
  8:412; **11**:394; **15**:396; **44**:465, 467;
  46:292, 294; **64**:351, 366
*Despair and Orthodoxy Among Some Modern
  Writers* (Spender) **91**:261
"Despair in Being Tedious" (Duncan) **41**:128,
  130
The Despairing (Tzara)
  See *Les désespéranto*
"Desperadoes: Missouri 1861-1882 (or The
  James Gang and Their Relations)" (Jiles)
  58:276-77
Desperate Characters (Fox) **2**:139-40; **8**:217-
  18
"Desperate Measures" (Gallagher) **63**:121-22
"Desperate Measures" (Starbuck) **53**:353
Desperate Measures (Starbuck) **53**:353-54
The Desperate People (Mowat) **26**:334
"A Desperate Vitality" (Pasolini)
  See "Una Disperata Vitalita"
Desperation (Donoso)
  See *La Desesperanza*
"El despertar" ("Awakening") (Borges) **3**:80
"The Despicable Bastard" (Endo) **54**:157, 161
Despierta, mi bien, despierta (Alegria) **75**:46
"Despisals" (Rukeyser) **15**:458; **27**:412-13
"Despondency and Madness: On Lowell's
  'Skunk Hour'" (Berryman) **13**:76
"Despues de la muerte" (Aleixandre) **9**:16
Despuíes (*Afterwards*) (Benet) **28**:23-4
Dessa Rose (Williams) **89**:324-28, 330-36,
  338, 340-45, 348, 350, 358
"Destierro" (Castellanos) **66**:50
Le destin (Tchicaya) **101**:365
"Le destin de la Flandre" (de Man) **55**:423
*Le destin glorieux du Maréchal Nnikon Nniku,
  prince qu'on sort* (*The Glorious Destiny
  of Marshal Nnikon Nniku*) (Tchicaya)
  101:365
Destination Biafra (Emecheta) **48**:97-8
Destination Moon (Heinlein) **55**:304
Destination Unknown (Christie) **110**:113
Destination: Void (Herbert) **23**:219-20, 224,
  226; **35**:197-98, 209; **44**:393-94
"Destinies" (Schaeffer) **22**:368-69
Destinies (Mauriac)
  See *Destins*
The Destinies of Darcy Dancer, Gentleman
  (Donleavy) **10**:154-55; **45**:123, 125
"Destino" (Castellanos) **66**:50

"Destino de la carne" (Aleixandre) 9:16; 36:27

"Destino trágico" (Aleixandre) 9:16

Destins (*Destinies*; *Lines of Life*) (Mauriac) 4:341; 56:206, 212

Destiny (Edgar) 42:112-13, 115-17, 121-24

Destiny (Lang) 20:200, 203

Destiny Express (Rodman) 65:89-94

Destiny Times Three (Leiber) 25:301-03

Deštník z Piccadilly (*Piccadilly*; *Umbrella from Piccadilly*; *The Umbrella from Piccadilly*; *An Umbrella from Piccadilly*) (Seifert) 93:308-09, 320-25, 330-31, 337, 344

Destroy, She Said (Duras)
    See *Détruire, dit-elle*

La destrucción o el amor (*Destruction or Love*) (Aleixandre) 9:11, 15; 36:23-30

Destruction (Pa Chin) 18:373

"The Destruction of Kreshev" (Singer) 6:508; 9:488; 38:408; 69:310-11; 111:305-06

"The Destruction of Pompeii" (Aksyonov) 101:41

The Destruction of Reason (Lukacs) 24:319-20

"The Destruction of the Goetheanum" (Salter) 52:367, 369

Destruction or Love (Aleixandre)
    See *La destrucción o el amor*

The Destructive Element: A Study of Modern Writers and Beliefs (Spender) 10:490; 91:261, 264

Details (Enzensberger)
    See *Einzelheiten*

Details of a Sunset, and Other Stories (Nabokov) 8:417; 15:393

Detained: A Writer's Prison Diary (Ngugi wa Thiong'o) 36:318-19

The Detainee (Soyinka) 44:285

"The Detective" (Ai) 69:17

"The Detective" (Plath) 3:390; 11:449; 51:340; 111:169, 203

Detective Story (Kingsley) 44:234-35, 238

The Detling Secret (Symons) 32:428

Detour (Brodsky) 19:69-70

The Detour (Walser)
    See *Der Abstecher*

"Detroit Abe" (Friedman) 56:107

"Detroit Conference of Unity and Art" (Giovanni) 64:194

"Detroit Skyline, 1949" (Mason) 43:288; 82:254-55

Détruire, dit-elle (*Destroy, She Said*) (Duras) 6:150; 20:98-101; 40:179; 68:87, 98; 100:146

"Detstvo Luvers" ("The Childhood of Luvers"; "The Childhood of Zhenya Luvers"; "Zhenia's Childhood") (Pasternak) 7:293; 10:383; 18:385-87; 63:290

The Deuce (Butler) 81:123, 126

Deus Irae (Dick) 10:138; 72:108

Deus irae (Zelazny) 21:470

"Deutsch Durch Freud" (Jarrell) 9:296

"Deutsches Requiem" (Borges) 1:39; 19:45, 47; 83:157

Deutschland, Deutschland unter anderm (*Germany, Germany among Other Things*) (Enzensberger) 43:154

Deutschstunde (*The German Lesson*) (Lenz) 27:246-52

Deux Anglaises et le continent (*Two English Girls*) (Truffaut) 20:392, 394-96; 101:380, 382-84, 396-97

Les deux bourreaux (*Los dos verdugos*; *The Executioners*; *The Two Executioners*)

(Arrabal) 9:33-37; 18:17-18; 58:3-7, 10, 12, 16, 21, 24-6

"Les deux critiques" (Barthes) 24:26

Deux hommes (Duhamel) 8:186

"Les deux lys" (Ferron) 94:129

"Les deux mains" (Hebert) 29:227

Deux ou trois choses que je sais d'elle (*Two or Three Things I Know about Her*) (Godard) 20:140, 144, 146-48

Deux sous de violettes (Anouilh) 50:279

Les deux timides (Clair) 20:61, 66, 69

Deuxième bélvèdere (Mandiargues) 41:278

Le deuxième sexe (*The Second Sex*) (Beauvoir) 1:19; 2:43-4; 4:45-9; 8:58, 60-1; 31:33-9, 41-3; 44:341-51; 50:387-92; 71:37-43, 45-50, 53-4, 56-61, 63-5, 67, 72-8, 83-7

Le deux-millième étage (*They Won't Demolish Me!*) (Carrier) 13:143-44; 78:50-1, 57-8, 60, 62, 67-70

Dévadé (Ducharme) 74:68

DeValera (O'Faolain) 70:317

Devi (*The Goddess*) (Ray) 16:479-80, 483, 486, 491, 493; 76:357

"The Devil" (Tanizaki)
    See "Akuma"

"The Devil and Irv Cherniske" (Boyle) 90:45

The Devil and the Good Lord (Sartre)
    See *Le diable et le bon Dieu*

The Devil at the Long Bridge (Bacchelli)
    See *Diavolo al pontelungo*

The Devil Came from Dublin (Carroll) 10:97-100

"Devil Car" (Zelazny) 21:465

The Devil Doll (Browning) 16:121

The Devil Finds Work (Baldwin) 8:40-2; 17:40-1; 42:16, 18-19, 22; 90:31

Devil in a Blue Dress (Mosley) 97:327-35, 337-44, 347-48, 351-54, 358-60

The Devil in a Forest (Wolfe) 25:473

A Devil in Paradise (Miller) 2:281

The Devil in the Desert (Horgan) 53:176-77

The Devil Is a Woman (Sternberg) 20:371-73, 378

The Devil Is Loose! (Maillet)
    See *Crache-à-pic*

Devil of a State (Burgess) 2:85; 4:81; 22:77; 40:113-15; 81:301; 94:23-24, 40

Devil on the Cross (Ngugi)
    See *Caitaani mutharaba-ini*

The Devil on the Road (Westall) 17:558-60

The Devil Rides Outside (Griffin) 68:194-201

The Devil Soldier (Carr) 86:42, 47

The Devil to Pay (Queen) 11:458

The Devil to Pay in the Backlands (Rosa)
    See *Corpo de baile or grande sertao: Veredas*

The Devil Tree (Kosinski) 2:232-33; 3:272-74; 6:283-84; 10:307; 15:313-14, 316; 53:219-20, 225-26, 228; 70:298, 306

Devil with Boobs (Fo) 109:143

Devilhorn (Bonham) 12:55

Devil-in-the-Fog (Garfield) 12:216-17, 224-25, 227-28, 230, 234-36, 240

The Devils (Russell) 16:543-44, 546-50

"The Devil's Advice to Poets" (Kennedy) 42:256

The Devil's Advocate (Caldwell) 28:60; 39:303

The Devil's Advocate (West) 6:564; 33:427-29, 431-33

The Devil's Alternative (Forsyth) 36:175-76

The Devils and Canon Barham (Wilson) 3:540

The Devil's Children (Dickinson) 12:169-70, 172

The Devil's Eye (Bergman)

    See *Djävulens öga*

The Devil's General (Zuckmayer)
    See *Des Teufels General*

"Devil's Half-Acre; or, The Mystery of the 'Cruel Suitor'" (Oates) 108:349

The Devil's Mode (Burgess) 62:139

The Devils of Loudun (Huxley) 3:253; 4:240, 243; 5:195; 35:239

The Devil's Picture Book (Hine) 15:281, 283

"The Devil's Spittle" (Cortazar)
    See "Las babas del diablo"

The Devil's Stocking (Algren) 33:17

"Devils Talk in Broad Daylight" (Tanizaki) 28:414

The Devil's Wanton (Bergman)
    See *Fängelse*

"Devonshire" (Davie) 8:165-66

"Devonshire Street, W. 1" (Betjeman) 43:34, 50

"The Devoted" (Howard) 7:165

Devoted Ladies (Keane) 31:232-33

"Devoted Son" (Desai) 97:150

Devotion (Strauss)
    See *Die Widmung*

"Devotion: That It Flow; That There Be Concentration" (Gallagher) 63:118-20, 126

"Devyatsat pyaty god" ("The Year 1905") (Pasternak) 18:382; 63:288-89, 293, 308

D.H. Lawrence, Novelist (Leavis) 24:297, 300, 305, 308-10

Dhalgren (Delany) 8:168-69; 14:144; 38:151-54, 159, 161-62

The Dharma Bums (Kerouac) 1:166; 2:226-27, 229; 3:263-65; 14:303-07; 61:286, 293, 296, 306-09

Dhiádhromos ke skála (Ritsos) 6:463

"D.H.S.S." (Lessing) 94:265

Di Familie Moskat (*The Family Moskat*) (Singer) 1:312-13; 3:455-56; 6:507; 11:501; 15:503-06; 23:414, 417-20; 111:293-94, 305, 340

Un dia en la vida (*One Day of the Life*) (Argueta) 31:19-21

"Diabetes" (Dickey) 47:96

Le diable et le bon Dieu (*The Devil and the Good Lord*; *Lucifer and the Lord*) (Sartre) 4:476; 7:392; 9:471; 13:498-99, 502; 18:470; 50:381, 385

Le diable, probablement (Bresson) 16:119

Diadème (Jouve) 47:206

Diadia Sandro i konets kozlotura (*Uncle Sandro and the End of the Goatibex*) (Iskander) 47:197, 200

"Diagrams" (Goldbarth) 38:205

Dial M for Murder (Hitchcock) 16:341, 346

"The Dialect of the Tribe" (Mathews) 52:308, 313-14

"Dialectics" (Vollmann) 89:284

"The Dialectics of Love" (McGrath) 28:275, 279; 59:177

"Dialectics of Rationalization" (Habermas) 104:87

"Dialing for Dollars" (Mull) 17:300

The Dialogic Imagination (Bakhtin)
    See *Voprosy literatury i estetiki*

"Diálogo" (Cabral de Melo Neto) 76:158

"Diàlogo" (Fuentes) 113:244

Dialogo dei massimi sistemi (Landolfi) 49:215

"Diálogo del espejo" ("Dialogue in a Mirror") (Garcia Marquez) 3:181; 15:252

"El diálogo y el ruido" ("Dialogue and Noise") (Paz) 65:190

Diálogos con los hombres más honrados

(Castellanos)　66:53
Diálogos del conocimiento (*Dialogues of Knowledge*) (Aleixandre)　9:17; 36:27, 30-2
"Dialogue" (Dickey)　28:118
"Dialogue" (Garrigue)　8:240
"Dialogue" (Scott)　22:374
"Dialogue III" (Barker)　8:47
"Dialogue and Noise" (Paz)
　See "El diálogo y el ruido"
"Dialogue at Three in the Morning" (Parker)　15:417
Dialogue de Rome (Duras)　68:92
"Dialogue in a Mirror" (Garcia Marquez)
　See "Diálogo del espejo"
"Dialogue in the Stoneworks" (Ciardi)　40:156
A Dialogue: James Baldwin and Nikki Giovanni (Giovanni)　117:183-84, 192
"Dialogue of the Greater Systems" (Landolfi)　49:215, 217
"A Dialogue of Watching" (Rexroth)　112:400
"Dialogue on the Art of Composition" (Kundera)　68:247-49; 115:321
"Dialogue on the Art of the Novel" (Kundera)　115:321
"Dialogue on the Greater Harmonies" (Landolfi)　49:210
Dialogue with Death (Koestler)　15:309; 33:229
"Dialogues des règnes" (Butor)　3:93
Dialogues, Etc. (Barker)　8:47; 48:24
"Dialogues of Gog and Magog" (Barker)　48:24
Dialogues of Knowledge (Aleixandre)
　See *Diálogos del conocimiento*
Dialogues with the Devil (Caldwell)　28:65; 39:303
Diamantes y pedernales (Arguedas)　10:8
"The Diameter of the Bomb" (Amichai)　57:46
"Diamond Body" (MacDiarmid)　4:310
"The Diamond Cutters" (Rich)　7:373
The Diamond Cutters, and Other Poems (Rich)　7:368, 370; 18:446, 449; 36:366, 372, 374, 378; 73:325, 328, 330; 76:211
Diamond Dogs (Bowie)　17:61-3, 65-8
"A Diamond Guitar" (Capote)　13:134; 19:82
Diamond Head (Waters)　88:362
The Diamond Hunters (Smith)　33:374
"The Diamond Merchant" (Wakoski)　9:554-55
The Diamond Smugglers (Fleming)　30:131
Diamonds Are Forever (Fleming)　30:131-32, 136, 142, 147-49
Diamonds Bid (Rathbone)　41:337
Diamonds of the Night (Lustig)　56:185-86
"Diana and Actaeon" (Porter)　33:319, 324
Diana: The Goddess Who Hunts Alone (Fuentes)　113:269
"The Dianas" ("The Huntress") (Stead)　32:408; 80:305
Diane (Isherwood)　44:397
La diane Française (*French Reveille*) (Aragon)　22:37
"Diaper" (Birney)　6:75
·*Diaries* (Guevara)
　See *El diario de Che en Bolivia: noviembre 7, 1966, a octubre 7, 1967*
The Diaries of Evelyn Waugh (Waugh)　27:475; 44:520, 524-25
The Diaries of Jane Somers (Lessing)　40:316; 94:258-60, 272
"Diario" (Otero)　11:427
El diario de Che en Bolivia: noviembre 7, 1966, a octubre 7, 1967 (*The Complete Boliv-*

ian Diaries of Che Guevara, and Other Captured Documents; Diaries; The Diary of Che Guerara; Bolivia: November 7, 1966—October 7, 1967) (Guevara)　87:206, 210
Diario de la guerra del cerdo (*Diary of the War of the Pig*) (Bioy Casares)　4:63-4; 13:84-5; 88:60, 90, 92
Diario de un cazador (*Diary of a Hunter*) (Delibes)　18:113
Diario de un enfermo (Azorin)　11:27
Diario del '71 e del '72 (*Diary of '71 and '72*) (Montale)　7:231; 9:387; 18:340
Diario in pubblico (Vittorini)　9:551; 14:543
"Diario para un cuento" (Cortazar)　33:135; 34:333
El diario que a diario (Guillen)　48:160
Diario: Una sua bella biografia (Ungaretti)　7:482
"The Diarrhea Gardens of El Camino Real" (Martin)　30:248
"Diarrhea of a Writer" (Grayson)　38:211
"Diary" (Stern)　100:345
Diary (Gombrowicz)
　See *Dziennik*
Diary (Nin)　1:247-48; 4:377-78; 8:424; 11:396-99; 14:384-85
Diary 1928-1957 (Green)　77:270
"Diary: Audience, 1966" (Cage)　41:78
Diary: How to Improve the World (*You Will Only Make Matters Worse*) (Cage)　41:77-8, 80, 82, 85
Diary of '71 and '72 (Montale)
　See *Diario del '71 e del '72*
Diary of a Chambermaid (Bunuel)
　See *Le journal d'une femme de chambre*
The Diary of a Chambermaid (Renoir)　20:303-04
Diary of a Country Priest (Bresson)
　See *Journal d'un curé de campagne*
The Diary of a Good Neighbour (Lessing)　40:308-10, 315; 94:258, 261
Diary of a Hunter (Delibes)
　See *Diario de un cazador*
Diary of a Mad Housewife (Kaufman)　3:263; 8:317
Diary of a Mad Old Man (Tanizaki)
　See *Futen rojin nikki*
"Diary of a Naturalist" (Milosz)　31:261-62; 82:295
"Diary of a New York Apartment Hunter" (Lebowitz)　36:249
The Diary of a Rapist (Connell)　4:109; 45:110-11
The Diary of a Seducer (Rothenberg)　6:477
Diary of a Shinjuku Thief (Oshima)　20:246, 248-49, 251, 254
Diary of a Yunbogi Boy (Oshima)　20:250
Diary of a Yuppie (Auchincloss)　45:36-7
"The Diary of Abraham Segal, Poet" (Klein)　19:258
The Diary of Alexander Patience (Orlovitz)　22:332
"The Diary of an African Nun" (Walker)　19:450; 103:406-07, 410-11
"Diary of an Invisible April" (Elytis)　100:175, 182-83, 185-86
Diary of an Old Man (Bermant)　40:90-2
The Diary of Anaïs Nin, 1931-1934, Vol. 1 (Nin)　8:423; 11:397, 399; 14:384
The Diary of Anaïs Nin, 1934-1939, Vol. 2 (Nin)　4:380; 11:397; 14:384
The Diary of Anaïs Nin, 1939-1944, Vol. 3

(Nin)　8:425; 11:397; 14:384
The Diary of Anaïs Nin, 1944-1947, Vol. 4 (Nin)　4:377; 11:397-98; 14:384-85
The Diary of Anaïs Nin, 1947-1955, Vol. 5 (Nin)　4:379-80; 11:398; 14:385
The Diary of Anaïs Nin, 1955-1966, Vol. 6 (Nin)　8:423; 11:398; 14:385
The Diary of Anaïs Nin: Vols. I-VII (Nin)　60:275, 277-78
The Diary of Che Guerara; Bolivia: November 7, 1966—October 7, 1967 (Guevara)
　See *El diario de Che en Bolivia: noviembre 7, 1966, a octubre 7, 1967*
The Diary of Dr. Eric Zero (Orlovitz)　22:332
"The Diary of K. W." (Berriault)　54:3-5; 109:96-7
"The Diary of Miss Sophie" (Ding Ling)
　See "Shafei nüshi de riji"
The Diary of Samuel Marchbanks (Davies)　13:173; 25:129; 42:103, 105; 75:182-83
"The Diary of the Rose" (Le Guin)　45:213, 216-17
Diary of the War of the Pig (Bioy Casares)
　See *Diario de la guerra del cerdo*
A Diary without Dates (Bagnold)　25:72-3
Días hábiles (*Days and Occasions*) (Paz)　65:181
"Los días y los temas" (Otero)　11:427
"Diaspora" (Lorde)　71:258, 260
Diavolo al pontelungo (*The Devil at the Long Bridge*) (Bacchelli)　19:30
The (Diblos) Notebook (Merrill)　2:275; 91:234
The Dice of War (Giovene)　7:117
Diceria dell'untore (*The Plague-Sower*; *The Plague-Sower*) (Bufalino)　74:38-9
Dicey's Song (Voigt)　30:418-20
"Dichtung und Wahrheit" (Hecht)　8:269
The Dick (Friedman)　3:165; 5:127; 56:99-102, 107
Dick Deterred (Edgar)　42:111-12, 116, 121
"Dick Donnelly" (Buckley)　57:135
The Dick Francis Treasury of Great Horseracing Stories (Francis)　102:141
The Dick Gibson Show (Elkin)　4:154; 6:169; 9:190-91; 14:158; 27:122-23, 125; 51:85, 89, 91, 96-7; 91:213
"Dickens Digested" (Davies)　42:103
"The Dickies" (Gardam)　43:169
"Dictated But Not Read" (Ferber)　93:
The Dictators (Archer)　12:16
Dictatorship of the Conscience
　See *Diktatura sovesti*
The Dictionary of Cultural Literacy: What Every American Needs To Know (Hirsch)　70:363, 396
Dictionary of the Khazars: A Lexicon Novel in 100,000 Words (Pavic)
　See *Hazarski recnik*
"Dictum: For a Masque of Deluge" (Merwin)　8:388; 88:207
"Did I Say" (Stern)　100:344
"Did She Mention My Name?" (Lightfoot)　26:278
Did She Mention My Name? (Lightfoot)　26:278
"Did You Say the War Is Over?" (McKuen)　3:333
"Didactic Piece" (Bogan)　93:65, 67, 69, 90-91
"Didn't He Ramble" (Simmons)　43:410
"Dido's Lament" (Castellanos)
　See "Lamentación de Dido"
"Didymus" (MacNeice)　4:316

"An die Sonne" ("To the Sun") (Bachmann) 69:42

Died in the Wool (Marsh) 53:250-51, 255-56, 259-60

Died on a Rainy Sunday (Aiken) 35:16-17

Dien cai dau (Komunyakaa) 86:191; 94:225-26, 228-29, 231-34, 236, 240

"Dienstag, den 27. September" (Wolf) 29:464

"Dies irae" (Lowell) 1:182

"Dies irae" (Morgan) 31:276

"Diese Kette von Rätseln" (Sachs) 98:341

Le Dieu bleu (Cocteau) 15:134

Le Dieu caché (*The Hidden God; This Hidden God*) (Goldmann) 24:234, 236, 238-39, 241, 243, 245, 247, 251, 254

Dieu nous l'a donné (Conde) 52:79-81; 92:99-100

Dieu tenté par les mathematiques (Arrabal) 9:35

"Difference" (Aldiss) 14:15

"Difference" (Derrida) 24:145

The Difference Engine (Sterling) 72:372-73

A Difference of Design (Spackman) 46:378-80

The Difference Within: Feminism and Critical Theory (Meese and Parker) 65:338

"The Differences" (Gunn) 81:178

A Different Drummer (Kelley) 22:248, 250

A Different Face (Manning) 19:300

"Different Finger" (Costello) 21:76

Different Fleshes (Goldbarth) 38:202-04

A Different Kind of Christmas (Haley) 76:347

"Different Kinds of Plays" (Bentley) 24:47

A Different Person (Merrill) 91:227-28 230, 236

Different Seasons (King) 26:240-43; 37:207; 61:327-28; 113:338, 343, 351-52

A Different World (Ghose) 42:181-82

"Differently" (Munro) 95:310-11, 314-15

The Difficult Hour (Lagerkvist) 54:277

Difficult Loves (Calvino)
  See *Gli amori difficili*

The Difficult Ones (Frisch)
  See *Die Schwierigen; oder, J'adore ce qui me brûle*

Difficult Women: A Portrait of Three (Plante) 38:368-72

Dig a Grave and Let Us Bury Our Mother (Smart) 54:425-26

"Dig, He Said, Dig" (Musgrave) 54:335

Dig the New Breed (Weller) 26:447

The Digestive System: How Living Creatures Use Food (Silverstein and Silverstein) 17:451

The Digger's Game (Higgins) 4:222-24; 7:158; 10:274

"Digging" (Hall) 37:142

"Digging" (Heaney) 25:244, 248, 250-51; 74:150-51, 155, 163, 165, 180

"Digging for China" (Wilbur) 53:410; 110:348, 353

"Digging In" (Piercy) 62:367

Digging Out (Roiphe) 3:435

"The Digging Skeleton (after Baudelaire)" (Heaney) 74:158

Dijalekticki antibarbarus (Krleza) 114:174

Diktatura sovesti (*Dictatorship of the Conscience*) 59:358, 360-1, 364

"The Dileas" (MacLean) 63:270

The Dilemma of Love (Giovene) 7:117

The Dilemma of the Contemporary Novelist (Wilson) 34:580-81

"Díles que no me maten!" ("Tell Them Not to Kill Me") (Rulfo) 80:201, 222

"Dili" (Pasolini) 106:228

"Diligence Is to Magic As Progress Is to Flight" (Moore) 19:341

Dilli ki Sham (Ali) 69:25

"Dilton Marsh Halt" (Betjeman) 43:46

Le dimanche de la vie (*The Sunday of Life*) (Queneau) 2:359; 5:358-59, 362; 10:432; 42:332, 334

Dimanche m'attend (Audiberti) 38:32

Die Dimension des Autors: Essays und Aufsätzes, Reden und Gespräche (Wolf) 58:430-31

"The Dimensions of a Tiger" (MacEwen) 13:357

Dimetos (Fugard) 9:232-33; 80:62, 68-9

"Dimitri" (Theriault) 79:408

Dinah and the Green Fat Kingdom (Holland) 21:153

Le diner en ville (*The Dinner Party*) (Mauriac) 9:363-64

Dingley Falls (Malone) 43:281-82, 284

"Dining from a Treed Condition: An Historical Survey" (Harper) 22:209

The Dining Room (Gurney) 32:218-20; 50:177-79, 183-84; 54:216-22

Dinky Hocker Shoots Smack! (Kerr) 12:296-98, 301; 35:250

"Dinner" (Arghezi)
  See "Cina"

"The Dinner" (Lispector) 43:269

"Dinner Along the Amazon" (Findley) 102:107-08

Dinner Along the Amazon (Findley) 102:107, 109-11

Dinner at Eight (Ferber) 93:159-61, 165

Dinner at Eight (Kaufman) 38:259

Dinner at the Homesick Restaurant (Tyler) 28:432-35; 44:313, 315, 321; 59:202-08, 210; 103:217-18, 220-21, 223-30, 233-35, 238-44, 247-48, 260-61, 263-64, 268-71, 275

"Dinner for One" (Tremain) 42:386

"Dinner in Audoghast" (Sterling) 72:372

The Dinner Party (Mauriac)
  See *Le diner en ville*

Dinny and the Witches (Gibson) 23:177, 180

Dinosaur Planet (McCaffrey) 17:283

Dinosaur Tales (Bradbury) 42:42

Dintr-un foisor (*From a Watch Tower*) (Arghezi) 80:13

The Dionne Years: A Thirties Melodrama (Berton) 104:46-7, 57

Dionysus in '69 (De Palma) 20:78

"El dios de los toros" (Bioy Casares) 88:67-8

De dioses, hombrecitos, y policias (*The Gods, the Little Guys, and the Police*) (Costantini) 49:61-2

Dioses y hombres de huarochiri (Arguedas) 10:9

"Diplomacy: The Father" (Snodgrass) 68:381-82

"Diplomatic Relations" (Theroux) 11:528

Diplopic (Reading) 47:352-53

"Diptych: Jesus and the Stone" (Baxter) 78:28

"Diptych with Votive Tablet" (Paz)
  See "Preparatory Exercise (Dyptych with Votive Tablet)"

The Dirdir (Vance) 35:422, 424

Dire Coasts (Holmes) 56:145

"Direadh" (MacDiarmid) 4:309; 11:333

Le directeur de l'opéra (Anouilh) 40:57, 59

"Direction" (Macdonald) 13:356

The Direction of the March (Adamov)
  See *Le sens de la marche*

"The Direction of the Treatment and the Principles of its Power" (Lacan) 75:295

"Directions to a Rebel" (Rodgers) 7:378

Directionscore: Selected and New Poems (Madhubuti) 73:205, 215

"Directive" (Frost) 1:110; 4:176; 9:221, 228; 15:245, 250; 26:119-20, 124, 126

"Directive" (Haines) 58:214

"Directive" (Redgrove) 41:352

"Director of Alienation" (Ferlinghetti) 27:137; 111:59

A Director's Notebook (Fellini)
  See *Block-notes de un regista*

Direption (Booth) 13:103

"Dirge" (Dylan) 4:150

"Dirge" (Eliot) 55:366

"Dirge" (Fearing) 51:117

"Dirge for a Penny Whistle" (Gustafson) 36:216

"Dirge for the New Sunrise (August 6, 1945)" (Sitwell) 67:333, 336

"Dirge Notes" (Huddle) 49:183

"Dirge of the Palm Race" (Kunene) 85:166

"Dirge over a Pot of Pâté de Foie Grass" (McGinley) 14:366

Dirk Gently's Holistic Detective Agency (Adams) 60:3-6

"Dirt" (Salter) 52:369; 59:197

"The Dirty Hand" (Strand) 71:284

Dirty Hands (Sartre)
  See *Les mains sales*

Dirty Hearts (Sanchez) 116:301

Dirty Linen (Stoppard) 8:503-04; 29:397, 400

"Dirty Mind" (Prince) 35:323, 328

Dirty Mind (Prince) 35:323-25, 327-28, 330

Dirty Story (Ambler) 4:19; 9:19

Dirty Tricks; or, Nick Noxin's Natural Nobility 7:407

"The Dirty Word" (Shapiro) 53:332

Dirty Work (Brown) 73:20-3, 27

Los dís enmascarados (*The Masked Days*) (Fuentes) 8:223; 41:166, 171

A Disaffection (Kelman) 58:302-05; 86:181, 185, 188-89

The Disappearance (Guy) 26:144-45

The Disappearance (Perec)
  See *La disparition*

The Disappearance (Trifonov) 59:382

The Disappearance (Wylie) 43:466-67, 470, 472

"The Disappearance of the Fireflies" (Pasolini) 106:251

"Disappearances" (Hogan) 73:152

Disappearances (Mosher) 62:310-15

"The Disappeared" (Baxter) 78:25-27, 30

Disappearing Acts (McMillan) 61:364-67; 112:222, 225-28, 230, 234, 236, 239-41, 243, 246-48, 250, 252

"The Disappearing Island" (Heaney) 74:190

"Disappointment" (Newlove) 14:378

"A Disaster" (Hughes) 2:205

Disaster (O'Brien) 17:324

"Disasters" (Fuller) 4:178

"Disasters of the Sun" (Livesay) 79:351-52

The Discarded Image: An Introduction to Medieval and Renaissance Literature (Lewis) 3:296; 6:308

"The Disciple of Bacon" (Epstein) 27:128

"A Discipline" (Berry) 27:34

"Discipline" (Brown) 73:23

"The Discipline" (Clarke) 53:91

"Discipline and Honor" (Berry) 46:75

"Discipline and Hope" (Berry) **27**:38-9

Discipline and Punish: The Birth of the Prison (Foucault)

See *Surveiller et punir: Naissance de la prison*

Disclosure (Crichton) **90**:88-95, 97

"Disco Apocalypse" (Browne) **21**:42

"Disco Mystic" (Reed) **21**:317

Le discours antillais (Caribbean Discourse: Selected Essays) (Glissant) **68**:175, 178-80, 184-87, 189-90

Discours de la méthode (Ionesco) **6**:252

"Discours de Rome" (Lacan)

See "Fonction et champ de la parole et du langage en psychanalyse"

Discours sur le colonialisme (Discourse on Colonialism) (Cesaire) **112**:6-7, 20, 39

"Discourse" (Thesen) **56**:415

"A Discourse concerning Temptation" (Hecht) **8**:267

"Discourse Ethics, Law and Sittlichkeit" (Habermas) **104**:87

"Discourse in Life and Discourse in Art" (Bakhtin) **83**:14, 28

"Discourse in the Novel" (Bakhtin) **83**:11, 14, 25, 44-6, 58-9

"The Discourse of the Good Thief" (Parra) **102**:353-54

The Discourse of the Great Sleep (Cocteau) **8**:146

"Discourse on Beauty" (Elytis) **49**:110

Discourse on Colonialism (Cesaire)

See *Discours sur le colonialisme*

"The Discourse on Language" (Foucault) **31**:177

The Discourse on Language (Foucault)

See *L'orare du discours*

"Discourse on Poetry" (Quasimodo) **10**:427

Discourse on Thinking (Heidegger) **24**:266

Discourse on Vietnam (Weiss)

See *Viet Nam Diskurs*

"Discoveries, Trade Names, Genitals, and Ancient Instruments" (Rakosi) **47**:348

"Discovering Literature" (Cabral de Melo Neto)

See "Descoberta da literatura"

"Discovering Obscenities on Her Wall" (Smith) **42**:346

"The Discovery" (Barthelme) **115**:71

"The Discovery" (MacEwen) **13**:358

"Discovery of Chile" (Neruda) **1**:247

"The Discovery of Mexico" (Fuentes) **113**:256

"A Discreet Miracle" (Allende) **97**:9, 11

Discrepancies and Apparitions (Wakoski) **7**:507; **40**:454

Discrete Series (Oppen) **7**:283, 285; **34**:389-59

Discriminations (Wellek) **28**:451-52

"The Discriminator" (Scannell) **49**:330

"The Discursive Mode" (Hope) **51**:215, 217-18, 222

Discusión (Borges) **83**:162-63, 165-66

"Disdain" (Aldington) **49**:4, 7

"Disease" (Tate) **25**:428

Disease and the Novel (Meyers) **39**:433

Disease Detectives (Berger) **12**:42

"The Diseases of Costume" (Barthes) **83**:70

"The Disembodied Lady" (Sacks) **67**:301

The Disenchanted (Schulberg) **7**:402-03; **48**:347-50, 352-53

Disent les imbéciles (Fools Say) (Sarraute) **8**:472-73; **10**:460; **31**:386; **80**:257-58

"Disfiguration" (Ghose) **42**:179

"The Disgrace of Jim Scarfedale" (Sillitoe) **57**:388, 392, 394

"Disguise" (Singer) **69**:313

"Disguised Zenith" (Ashbery) **77**:68

"Disguises" (Townshend) **17**:529

"Dishonest Modesty" (Simon) **26**:410

Dishonored (Sternberg) **20**:369-70, 372, 378-79

"The Disincarnation" (Sisson) **8**:491

"The Disinherited" (Bowen) **22**:62-3, 66-7

The Disinherited (Cohen) **19**:112-14, 116

The Disinherited (del Castillo) **38**:165-67

"Disintegration" (Kostelanetz) **28**:218

"The Disinterested Killer Bill Harrigan" (Borges)

See "El asesino desinteresado Bill Harrigan"

Disjecta: Miscellaneous Writings and a Dramatic Fragment (Beckett) **29**:67

Disjointed Fictions (Grayson) **38**:208-09, 211-12

"Disloyal to Civilzation: Feminism, Racism, Gynephobia" (Rich) **73**:323

"Dismantling the Silence" (Simic) **9**:480

Dismantling the Silence (Simic) **6**:502; **9**:478-79, 481; **22**:379-80, 382; **68**:368, 379

"Disneyad" (Apple) **33**:19

"Disobedience" (Moravia) **46**:282

Disobedience (Moravia)

See *La disubbidienza*

"Disobedience and Women's Studies" (Rich) **73**:322

"Disparities" (Okri) **87**:315

La disparition (The Disappearance; A Void) (Perec) **56**:254-56, 258, 260-63, 265, 268-72; **116**:233-34, 240, 243, 245-46, 248, 250-52, 254, 262-67, 269-70

La disparition d'Odile (Simenon) **2**:399

Dispatches (Swados) **12**:560-62

"Una Disperata Vitalita" ("A Desperate Vitality") (Pasolini) **106**:220, 239, 241, 249, 253, 264

"The Dispersal" (Avison) **97**:128

"Dispersed Titles" (Avison) **97**:76, 83, 88, 94, 96, 98, 109, 111, 122-23, 125, 127-29, 131-32

"Displaced Person" (Murphy) **41**:319

"The Displaced Person" (O'Connor) **1**:255, 257; **3**:366; **13**:419; **15**:410, 412; **21**:256, 261-62, 266-67, 269-71, 278; **104**:105, 124, 137, 179

"Displacement" (Allen) **84**:5

"Displacement" (Louie) **70**:78

"Disposal" (Snodgrass) **68**:382

"The Dispossessed" (Berryman) **10**:50; **13**:78

The Dispossessed (Berryman) **2**:56; **3**:70; **8**:91; **10**:48; **13**:75, 77-8; **25**:89; **62**:71, 75-6

The Dispossessed: An Ambiguous Utopia (Le Guin) **8**:341-43; **13**:348, 350-51; **22**:268-69; **45**:213-15, 217, 220-23

Disputed Questions (Merton) **83**:403

"Le disque de Caruso" (Theriault) **79**:407

"The Disquieted Muses" (Plath)

See "The Disquieting Muses"

"The Disquieting Muses" ("The Disquieted Muses") (Plath) **2**:336; **17**:360; **51**:344

"The Dissecting Table" (Szirtes) **46**:392

La dissémination (Dissemination) (Derrida) **24**:141, 155; **87**:72, 88-9, 91-2, 103

Dissemination (Derrida)

See *La dissémination*

Dissentient Voice: The Ward-Phillips Lectures for 1980 with Some Related Pieces (Davie) **31**:120-22

"Dissertation by Wax Light" (Eberhart) **56**:80

"Disseverings, Divorces" (Nemerov) **36**:309

"The Dissolving Fabric" (Blackburn) **43**:69

The Dissolving Fabric (Blackburn) **43**:63

"Distance" (Boland) **113**:94

"Distance" ("Everything Stuck to Him") (Carver) **53**:64

"A Distance" (Merwin) **88**:212

The Distance (Seger) **35**:386-87

"Distance and a Certain Light" (Swenson) **61**:397, 400; **106**:326

The Distance and the Dark (White) **49**:404-05

The Distance Anywhere (Hanson) **13**:264

"A Distance of Half a Kilometer" (Voinovich) **10**:505

"Distances" (Alexie) **96**:4

"The Distances" (Carroll) **35**:78

"The Distances" (Cortazar)

See "Lejana"

"Distances" (Goldbarth) **38**:205

"Distances" (Hugo) **32**:252

"Distances" (Okigbo) **84**:302, 307, 312, 314-22, 324-27, 329, 332-33, 336, 341-42

Distances (Okigbo) **25**:349, 352, 356

The Distances (Olson) **2**:326; **11**:415

"Distancia del amigo" (Castellanos) **66**:50

"The Distant" (Ritsos) **31**:331

The Distant, 1975 (Ritsos) **31**:328-30

"Distant Chirping Birds" (Matthews) **40**:324

"A Distant Episode" (Bowles) **19**:57, 60

"Distant Fingers" (Smith) **12**:539

The Distant Lands (Green)

See *Les pays lointains*

A Distant Likeness (Bailey) **45**:41-2, 44, 46

"Distant Lover" (Gaye) **26**:133

"Distant Music" (Beattie) **13**:65

The Distant Music (Davis) **49**:91-2, 97

"The Distant Past" (Trevor) **7**:478; **116**:338-39, 359

Distant Relations (Fuentes)

See *Una familia lejana*

The Distant Shore (de Hartog) **19**:130

Distant Stars (Delany) **38**:154

Distant Thunder (Ray)

See *Ashani sanket*

A Distant Trumpet (Horgan) **53**:177-79, 181

Distant Years (Paustovsky) **40**:368

"Dístico español" (Cernuda) **54**:46

"Distinctions" (Tomlinson) **45**:399

Distinctions (Wesker) **42**:429-30

"The Distinguished Elephant" (Keates) **34**:202-03

Distortions (Beattie) **8**:54-7; **13**:65; **40**:63, 66; **63**:3, 9-12, 15, 17-19

Distractions (Middleton) **7**:220-21

"The Distractions; the Music" (Loewinsohn) **52**:285

"Distractions of a Fiction Writer" (Bellow) **8**:74; **25**:87

"Los distraídos" (Castellanos) **66**:52

"Distress Sale" (Carver) **36**:107; **55**:273

"A District in the City" (Hugo) **32**:236

District of Columbia (Dos Passos) **4**:133, 137; **25**:145-46; **34**:420, 422; **82**:76, 85

Disturbances (Bernhard)

See *Verstörung*

Disturbances in the Field (Schwartz) **31**:390-92

Disturbing the Peace (Yates) **7**:555-56; **8**:555-56

Disturbing the Peace: A Conversation with Karel Hvízdala (Havel) **65**:433-38, 441-43

La disubbidienza (Disobedience) (Moravia) **7**:244; **18**:343; **27**:354

The Disuniting of America: Reflections on a Multicultural Society (Schlesinger) 70:405; 84:387, 389, 391

"A Disused Shed in Co. Wexford" (Mahon) 27:287-89, 291-93

"Dit du péégrin" (Guillevic) 33:193-94

Dita Sax (Lustig) 56:182

"The Ditch" (Ryan) 65:216

The Ditch: A Spiritual Trial (Voznesensky) 57:425

"Dithyramb" (Ekeloef) 27:110

"The Diver" (Hayden) 5:169; 37:155, 158

"The Diver" (Pritchett) 13:468; 41:331

"Divergence" (Char) 11:116

"The Diver's Vision" (Merwin) 88:198

"The Diverse Causes" (Ondaatje) 14:407

Diversifications (Ammons) 8:14, 17; 9:29-30; 25:44; 108:12, 24, 55

"Diversions" (Fisher) 25:161

The Diversions of Purley and Other Poems (Ackroyd) 52:9

Diversity and Depth in Fiction: Selected Critical Writings of Angus Wilson (Wilson) 34:579-83

"The Divestment of Beauty" (Riding) 7:375

"The Divided Life Re-Lived" (Fuller) 28:153

A Divided People (Lynn) 50:426

The Divided Self: A Study of Sanity and Madness (Laing) 95:124, 129-35, 137-41, 144, 153-54, 156, 166, 168-74, 177, 179, 181-82, 184-86, 188

Divided Soul: The Life of Gogol (Troyat) 23:461

"Dividends" (O'Faolain) 14:405; 70:319

The Dividing Night (Scannell) 49:325-26

The Dividing Stream (King) 53:203-04

Divina commedia (MacDiarmid) 4:310; 11:334

"Divination by a Cat" (Hecht) 8:266

"The Divine Claudius" (Herbert) 43:191

Divine Comedies: Poems (Merrill) 8:380-81, 384, 386, 388; 13:376-78, 381-82; 18:328; 34:226-27, 231; 91:228, 232

"The Divine Comedy" (Borges) 48:47, 49

"Divine Comedy" (Dodson) 79:193

Divine Comedy (Dodson) 79:188, 193, 197

Divine Disobedience: Profiles in Catholic Radicalism (Gray) 22:199-200

The Divine Enchantment (Neihardt) 32:332-33

Divine Horsemen: The Living Gods of Haiti (*The Voodoo Gods*) (Deren) 16:254; 102:26-7, 31, 36-8, 44-9

The Divine Invasion (Dick) 72:113, 119-20

The Divine Mimesis (Pasolini) 106:265

The Divine Pilgrim (Aiken) 52:22, 26

"The Diviner" (Heaney) 25:244; 74:153, 167

The Diviners (Laurence) 6:289-90; 13:342; 50:312-15, 319-22; 62:266-84, 287-88, 290, 293-308

Diving for Sunken Treasure (Cousteau) 30:105

"Diving into the Wreck" (Rich) 3:428; 6:459; 7:371, 373; 11:475-77; 36:374; 76:210-11

Diving into the Wreck: Poems, 1971-1972 (Rich) 3:427-29; 6:459; 7:367-69, 371-73; 11:476, 478; 18:447; 36:368, 372-73, 375, 377; 73:314, 325-27, 331; 76:217

A Diving Rock on the Hudson (Roth) 104:324-26, 329-30

"Divinità in incognito" (Montale) 9:386

"Divinities" (Merwin) 88:191

"Division" (Bogan) 46:90; 93:81, 90-2, 98

"Division" (Merwin) 3:339

A Division of the Spoils (Scott)
See *The Raj Quartet*

Division Street (Tesich) 40:421-23; 69:368, 370-71, 373

Division Street: America (Terkel) 38:418-23, 425

"Divisions" (Silkin) 43:404

Divisions on a Ground (Frye) 70:275

Divisions on a Ground (Nye) 42:305

"Divorce" (Jong) 83:289

"The Divorce" (Smith) 22:384

Divorce American Style (Lear) 12:326

"Divorce as a Moral Act" (Gold) 42:189

"Divorce of Lovers" (Sarton) 91:254

"The Divorce Papers" (Sexton) 15:473

"Divorced Child" (Coles) 46:113

Diwan (Ekeloef)
See *Diwan över fursten av Emigón*

Diwan över fursten av Emigón (*Diwan*) (Ekeloef) 27:116-17

Dix heures et demie du soir en été (*Ten-Thirty on a Summer Night*) (Duras) 6:149; 11:166; 40:179-81; 68:74, 85

Dixiana Moon (Fox) 22:141-42

Dix-neuf poèmes élastiques (*Nineteen Elastic Poems*) (Cendrars) 18:94; 106:163, 177, 181, 185-86, 190-91, 197-98

"D.J." (Bowie) 17:66

"Django" (Ellison) 42:129

Djävulens öga (*The Devil's Eye*) (Bergman) 72:40

Djetinjstvo u Agramu, 1902-1903 (*A Childhood in Agram*) (Krleza) 8:330; 114:166, 171

Djinn (*Le rendez-vous*) (Robbe-Grillet) 43:362-64

Dlia pol'zy dela (*For the Good of the Cause*) (Solzhenitsyn) 4:507; 7:432

"D.M.S.R." (Prince) 35:327-28

"The DNA Molecule Is the Nude Descending a Staircase" (Swenson) 14:521

Dni cheloveka (*Days of Man*) (Bitov) 57:115

"Do" (Tolson) 105:262-63, 283

Do Androids Dream of Electric Sheep? (Dick) 30:123, 125-28; 72:104, 108, 110, 113, 117-24

Do Black Patent Leather Shoes Really Reflect Up? (Powers) 66:380-83

"De Do Do Do, De Da Da Da" (Police, The) 26:365-66

"Do I Hear a Waltz?" (Sondheim) 30:379

Do I Hear a Waltz? (Sondheim) 30:379, 385, 387, 389, 392, 395

"Do It Again" (Becker and Fagen) 26:79-81

"Do It Again" (Wilson) 12:650

"Do It All Night" (Prince) 35:323

Do, Lord, Remember Me (Garrett) 3:190; 11:219; 51:147

"Do Me a Favour" (Hill) 113:288-90, 309-10, 320

"Do Me Baby" (Prince) 35:324-26

"Do Not Touch" (Pasternak) 63:280

"Do polityka" (Milosz) 56:238

"Do Re Mi" (Guthrie) 35:193

Do Re Mi (Kanin) 22:230

"Do Right to Me Baby (Do unto Others)" (Dylan) 77:186

"Do the Dead Sing?" (King)
See "The Reach"

"Do the Dog" (Mull) 17:299

Do the Right Thing (Lee) 105:84-89, 93, 95, 98, 101-03, 106, 108-09, 111, 113, 123-24, 126, 128, 129

Do These Bones Live (Dahlberg) 7:67, 69-70; 14:134, 137

Do What You Will (Huxley) 4:238; 35:241; 79:310

Do with Me What You Will (Oates) 3:362-64; 6:368-69, 373; 9:405; 14:401; 19:351-52; 52:338; 108:344, 391

"Do You Believe in Cabeza de Vaca?" (Swan) 69:363-65

Do You Believe in Cabeza de Vaca? (Swan) 69:363

Do You Hear Them? (Sarraute)
See *Vous les entendez?*

"Do You Love Me?" (Carey) 96:21, 38-9

Do You Love Me? An Entertainment in Conversation and Verse (Laing) 95:155

"Do You Really Think It's Fair?" (Mazer) 26:295

"Do You Think..." (Creeley) 2:108; 4:117

La doble historia del Doctor Valmy (*The Double Case History of Doctor Valmy*) (Buero Vallejo) 15:101; 46:95-6

Doc (Pollock) 50:223-27

"Doc For Doc" (McPherson)
See "A Solo Song: For Doc"

"Doc Mahoney and the Laughter of War" (Klappert) 57:268

"Doc Rivers" (Williams)
See "Old Doc Rivers"

"Las doce figuras del mundo" (Bioy Casares) 88:68

Docherty (McIlvanney) 42:283-86

The Docile Puerto Rican (Marques) 96:233

The Dock Brief (Mortimer) 28:282-84, 286

Dock Ellis in the Country of Baseball (Hall) 37:143, 149

"Docker" (Heaney) 74:167

Le docker noir (Ousmane) 66:334

"Dockery and Son" (Larkin) 5:227; 8:332, 339; 18:294, 298-99; 33:256-57; 39:335, 341; 64:260, 264, 266, 268

Docking at Palermo (Hugo) 32:236

"The Dock-Witch" (Ozick) 7:287-88; 62:350-51

"Dockyards at Night" (Neruda)
See "Maestranzas de noche"

"Doc's Story" (Wideman) 67:379-81, 384

Docteur Popaul (Chabrol) 16:182

"The Doctor" (Dubus) 97:195, 204-05

"Doctor" (Ignatow) 7:182

Doctor Anaconda's Solar Fun Club (Rosenblatt) 15:448

"The Doctor and the Doctor's Wife" (Hemingway) 10:269; 30:186-87, 190, 192, 196, 199, 201-02

The Doctor and the Soul: An Introduction to Logotherapy (Frankl)
See *Arztliche seelsorge*

"Doctor Blanke's First Command" (Forester) 35:173

Doctor Brodie's Report (Borges)
See *El informe de Brodie*

Doctor Cobb's Game (Cassill) 4:95; 23:108

Doctor Copernicus (Banville) 46:28

"Doctor Crombie" (Greene) 3:213

Doctor DeMarr (Theroux) 46:399-401

Doctor Detroit (Friedman) 56:108

Doctor Fischer of Geneva; or, The Bomb Party (Greene) 18:195-98; 27:177; 70:294

Doctor Frigo (Ambler) 6:3-4

"Doctor Havel after Ten Years" ("Doctor Havel Ten Years Later"; "Doctor Havel ten years later") (Kundera) 32:260

"Doctor Havel Ten Years Later" (Kundera)
See "Doctor Havel after Ten Years"
"Doctor Havel ten years later" (Kundera)
See "Doctor Havel after Ten Years"
The Doctor Is Sick (Burgess) 22:69, 74; 40:115;
94:52
Doctor Mirabilis (Blish) 14:83, 87
"Doctor My Eyes" (Browne) 21:35
"The Doctor of Starlight" (Levine) 33:275
"The Doctor of the Heart" (Sexton) 4:483
Doctor Rat (Kotzwinkle) 14:309-10; 35:255-
56, 258
Doctor Sax: Faust Part Three (Kerouac) 1:167;
2:228; 3:264; 14:307; 29:270; 61:299,
308-10, 314
Doctor Slaughter (Theroux)
See *Half Moon Street*
Doctor Sleep (Bell) 102:8-10
The Doctor Stories (Williams) 42:457-58
"The Doctor Will See You Now" (Fearing)
51:108
"Doctor Wu" (Becker and Fagen) 26:80
Doctor Zhivago (Pasternak)
See *Dr. Zhivago*
"The Doctors" (Barnes) 3:37; 11:30
Doctors and Women (Cheever) 48:67-8
Doctors at Risk (Slaughter) 29:378
"The Doctor's House" (Collins) 44:37
"A Doctor's Journal Entry for August 6, 1945"
(Seth) 90:351
Doctors of Philosophy (Spark) 3:467
"The Doctor's Son" (O'Hara) 42:312
"The Doctor's Son" (Stewart) 32:422
The Doctor's Son, and Other Stories (O'Hara)
42:320
Doctors Wear Scarlet (Raven) 14:440
The Doctor's Wife (Moore) 8:394-96; 32:310-
11, 313; 90:251, 257, 259, 268, 277-8,
281-2, 304
The Doctor's Wife Comes to Stay (Swinnerton)
31:426
"Doctrinal Point" (Empson) 19:157
"The Doctrine of the Leather-Stocking Jesus"
(Willard) 37:464
"Docu-fiction" (Birkerts) 116:148
Documentaires (Cendrars)
See *Kodak*
"Documentary" (Alegria) 75:49
"A Documentary from America" (Stafford)
29:382
*Documents Relating to the Sentimental Agents
in the Volyen Empire* (Lessing) 40:305-
07, 309, 312-15
Dodes'ka-den (Kurosawa) 16:404
Dodesukaden (West) 96:
"Dodging Apples" (Price) 43:346
"Doe Season" (Kaplan) 50:55-7
"Does a High Wind Make Me Reel?"
(Voznesensky) 57:427
"Does Daniel Believe in Order?" (Klappert)
57:268
"Does It Matter?" (Sassoon) 36:391
Does This School Have Capital Punishment?
(Hentoff) 26:185-86
"The Dog" (Durrenmatt)
See "Der Hund"
"Dog" (Ferlinghetti) 111:64
"The Dog" (Newlove) 14:378
"The Dog" (Williams) 33:448
"A Dog after Love" (Amichai) 22:33
The Dog beneath the Skin (Isherwood) 44:396,
399
The Dog beneath the Skin; or, Where Is Francis?

(Auden) 1:9; 6:23; 11:18; 14:32; 43:16,
21
"Dog Breath" (Zappa) 17:585, 588
"The Dog Carla" (Szirtes) 46:393
"Dog Creek Mainline" (Wright) 6:580-81
Dog Days (Gray) 36:202
"Dog Dream" (Smith) 12:535
"Dog Explosion" (Hood) 28:189
"Dog Heaven" (Vaughn) 62:456, 458
"Dog Life" (Strand) 41:439-41
"A Dog Lover's Confession" (Van Duyn)
116:420
"Dog Prospectus" (Redgrove) 41:354
A Dog So Small (Pearce) 21:282, 284-87
Dog Soldiers (Stone) 5:409-11; 23:426, 428-
31; 42:358-63
"Dog Star" (Musgrave) 54:341
The Dog Who Wouldn't Be (Mowat) 26:333,
335-36, 338-39, 343-44
"The Dog with the Wooden Leg" (Woolrich)
77:389-90
Dog Years (Grass)
See *Hundejahre*
"The Dog-Days" (Cunningham) 31:97-9, 101
"Dogfight" (Gibson) 63:134
"Dogfish" (Oliver) 98:259
Dogg's Hamlet (Stoppard) 15:520; 29:395-
98
Dogg's Hamlet, Cahoot's Macbeth (Stoppard)
29:396-97
"Dogg's Our Pet" (Stoppard) 29:395
"The Dogg's Troupe 'Hamlet'" (Stoppard)
29:397
"Dogs" (Pink Floyd) 35:311
"Dogs" (Townshend) 17:529-30
"Dogs and Books" (Kis)
See "Psi i knjige"
"Dogs Are Shakespearean, Children Are Strang-
ers" (Schwartz) 87:347
*The Dogs Bark: Public People and Private
Places* (Capote) 3:100; 8:132-33; 34:320;
38:85
"Dog's Death" (Updike) 3:485
Dogs Enjoy the Morning (Kiely) 23:259-60,
263-64; 43:245
"Dogs in My Nose" (Martin) 30:248
"The Dogs in the Great Glen" (Kiely) 23:267-
68; 43:244
A Dog's Life (Mayle) 89:154
The Dogs of Paradise (Stone) 70:335, 351
The Dogs of Pavlov (Abse) 7:2
The Dogs of War (Forsyth) 5:125; 36:175,
177
A Dog's Ransom (Highsmith) 2:194; 42:213;
102:185, 209
Dogsbody (Jones) 26:226-27, 230
Dogtown (Bonham) 12:51-2
The Dogtown Tourist Agency (Vance) 35:422
"The Dogwood Tree" (Updike) 23:463
"Doing It Differently" (Piercy) 27:375
"Doing Lennon" (Benford) 52:75-6
"Doing Right" (Clarke) 53:97
"Doing the Twist on Nails" (Yevtushenko)
3:547
"Dois castelhanos em Sevilha" ("Two Castilians
in Seville") (Cabral de Melo Neto) 76:163
Dois palamentos (*Two Voices*) (Cabral de Melo
Neto) 76:158, 169
Dojidai gemu (*The Contemporaneity Game; A
Game of Simultaneity*) (Oe) 36:350;
86:226, 228, 230, 232, 234, 239-41, 244
"Dojoji" (Mishima) 27:341
"Doke to saisei e no sozoryku" ("Toward the

Imagination of Buffoonery and Regeneration") (Oe) 86:215, 223
*Doktor Murkes gesammeltes Schweigen, und
andere Satiren* (*Dr. Murke's Collected Silences; Murke's Collected Silences*) (Boell)
15:70; 27:59, 61, 64; 39:296; 72:72, 73,
80, 101
La dolce vita (Fellini) 16:272-74, 276-82,
284, 287, 290-91, 293-94, 298, 300;
85:51, 58-60, 64, 67, 69, 71, 73-6, 78-82
Dolgoe proshchanie (*The Long Farewell*)
(Trifonov) 45:408, 417, 423
Dolina Issy (*The Issa Valley*) (Konwicki)
117:283
Dolina Issy (*The Issa Valley; The Valley of Issa*)
(Milosz) 11:378; 22:305-07, 312-13;
31:260-61, 264, 270; 82:280-81, 285, 289
"The Doll" (O'Brien) 36:336, 339; 116:201-
03
"The Doll" (Summers) 10:493
"The Doll House" (McGinley) 14:364
"The Doll Queen" (Fuentes)
See "La muñeca reina"
"The Doll That Does Everything" (Matheson)
37:246
The Doll Who Ate His Mother (Campbell)
42:86-7, 90, 92-3
The $ Value of Man (Wilson) 7:551
The Dollmaker (Arnow) 2:14; 7:15-16; 18:11-
16
The Dolls (Haavikko)
See *Nuket*
"Dolls, Dolls, Dolls, Dolls" (Shields) 113:430
"The Dolls Museum in Dublin" (Boland) 113:92-
3
"Dolor" (Roethke) 19:397, 401; 46:356;
101:263, 291
Il dolore (*The Grief*) (Ungaretti) 7:481-82,
485; 11:556
Dolores (Compton-Burnett) 3:112; 10:110;
15:135, 138; 34:495, 499
Dolores Claiborne (King) 113:384-85, 388,
392-93
The Dolphin (Lowell) 3:302-06; 4:301, 304;
5:257-59; 8:355-58; 9:336; 11:328, 330-
31; 37:236-38
"A Dolphin in the Forest, a Wild Board on the
Waves" (Newman) 8:419
Dolphins (Cousteau) 30:106
The Dolphins (Spender) 91:262, 264, 269
"The Dolt" (Barthelme) 115:56, 69, 94
Dom na naberezhnoi (*The House on the Em-
bankment*) (Trifonov) 45:408-11, 413-
14, 416-19, 421-23; 59:383
"Dom tvorchestva" ("House of Creation")
(Akhmadulina) 53:12
"Domaine noir" ("Black Dominion") (Senghor)
54:401
"Domaine Public" (Hill) 45:178
"Dome of Sunday" (Shapiro) 15:476-77
"The Dome Poem" (Smith) 22:385
"La Domenica Uliva" (Pasolini) 106:233
"Domesday Book" (Lowell) 11:331; 37:238
"Domestic" (Johnston) 51:244-45
"Domestic and Personal" (Simmons) 43:414
A Domestic Animal (King) 53:208
Domestic Arrangements (Klein) 30:242
"A Domestic Dilemma" (McCullers) 12:413,
425, 433; 100:246
Domestic Fuel (Moure) 88:219-23, 227, 229-
30
"Domestic Interior" (Boland) 113:71-2, 92,
94, 98, 109, 124

"Domestic Life in America" (Updike) **15**:545-46

Domestic Particulars (Busch) **10**:91-3

Domestic Relations: Short Stories (O'Connor) **23**:325

Domicile conjugal (*Bed and Board*) (Truffaut) **20**:389, 392, 399-401; **101**:382, 386, 396, 398, 411, 413

"Dominant Margins" (Ammons) **57**:53, 57

"Dominican Shoe Tinkers" (Lieberman) **36**:262

"The Dominicans" (Brodsky) **36**:77

"Dominion Square" (Souster) **5**:396

"Domino" (Morrison) **21**:232-33

Domino (Whitney) **42**:436

Le dompteur d'ours (Theriault) **79**:399-400, 402, 408, 412

"Don" (Dixon) **52**:100

Don Bueno (Ghose) **42**:184

Don de la ebriedad (Rodriguez) **10**:439

Don Fernando (Maugham) **67**:216, 219, 222

"Don Giovanni" (Keillor) **115**:294

"Don Gustano" (Padilla) **38**:349

Don Juan (Camus) **32**:91

Don Juan; oder, Die Liebe zur Geometrie (*Don Juan; or, The Love of Geometry*) (Frisch) **3**:167; **9**:217; **14**:182; **18**:161; **32**:195; **44**:182-83, 197-98

Don Juan; or, The Love of Geometry (Frisch)
  See *Don Juan; oder, Die Liebe zur Geometrie*

"Don Juan y el diablo" (Casona) **49**:47

"Don Juan's Reckless Daughter" (Mitchell) **12**:443

Don Juan's Reckless Daughter (Mitchell) **12**:443-44

Don Julián (Goytisolo)
  See *La reivindicación del Conde Don Julián*

"A Don Looks at His Fellows" (Betjeman) **43**:32

Don l'Orignal (Maillet) **54**:303-08

"Don Marquis" (White) **10**:528

"Don Nicomedes" (Ulibarri) **83**:415

Don Q (Lopez Portillo) **46**:235-37

Don Quixote (Acker) **45**:18-20; **111**:3-4, 6-8, 11-12, 18-19, 21-2, 25-6, 28, 31-3, 34-5, 37-9

Don Quixote (Lightfoot) **26**:278-79

Don Quixote (Welles) **80**:367, 371, 413

The Don Tales (Sholokhov)
  See *Donskie rasskazy*

"Don: The True Story of a Young Person" (Keillor) **40**:274

"Don Tómas Vernes" (Ulibarri) **83**:415

Dona Flor and Her Two Husbands (Amado)
  See *Dona Flor e seus dois maridos*

Dona Flor e seus dois maridos (*Dona Flor and Her Two Husbands*) (Amado) **13**:11; **40**:32-5; **106**:54-5, 57, 61, 65, 73, 78-9, 81, 84, 86

Doña inés (Azorin) **11**:25

Donadieu (Hochwalder) **36**:235-38

A Donald Justice Reader (Justice) **102**:277, 283

"Donat" (Ortese)
  See "Le sei della sera"

"La doncella y la muerte" (Parra) **102**:342

Donde esta la casa de Dios (Shange)
  See *Sanctuary*

Donde habite el olvido (Cernuda) **54**:41, 55, 60

De donde son los cantantes (*From Cuba with a Song*) (Sarduy) **6**:486; **97**:366-67, 369, 372, 376, 384, 386-92, 395-98, 409-10, 415, 417

Donde viven las águilas (*Up Among the Eagles*) (Valenzuela) **104**:376-77

"Done Too Soon" (Diamond) **30**:111

Donna mi prega (Pound) **4**:418

"Donne ch'avete intelletto d'amore" (Ciardi) **44**:383

Le donne di Messina (*Women of Messina*) (Vittorini) **6**:551-52; **9**:548; **14**:547

"Donnerbach mühle" (Char) **9**:165

The Do-Nothing Bar (Cocteau) **8**:148

Donovan's Reef (Ford) **16**:312-13, 319

Don's Party (Williamson) **56**:431-32, 435, 439, 443

Donskie rasskazy (*The Don Tales*) (Sholokhov) **7**:416, 420; **15**:483-85

"Don't" (Williams) **33**:441

Don't Ask (Levine) **33**:273

"Don't Ask Me Why" (Joel) **26**:221

"Don't Be Denied" (Young) **17**:571-72, 582

Don't Bite the Sun (Lee) **46**:230

"Don't Bring Me Oscars" ("When Its Shoesies That I Need") (Perelman) **5**:338

Don't Call Me Katie Rose (Weber) **12**:633

"Don't Cry, Darling, It's Blood All Right" (Nash) **23**:322

"Don't Cry for Me, Argentina" (Rice and Webber) **21**:431

"Don't Cry, Old Man" (Ian) **21**:186

Don't Cry, Scream (Madhubuti) **2**:238; **73**:193, 195, 198, 205, 207, 209-15

Don't Drink the Water (Allen) **52**:48

Don't Forget to Write (Buchwald) **33**:89

Don't Gag On It ... Goof On It (Crumb) **17**:84

Don't Get God Started (Milner) **56**:226-27

Don't Go Away Mad (Saroyan) **8**:467

Don't Go Gentle (*The Last Pad*) (Inge) **8**:308

Don't Grow Old (Ginsberg) **109**:338

"Don't Have a Baby Till You Read This" (Giovanni) **19**:192; **64**:183; **117**:191

"Don't Interrupt the Sorrow" (Mitchell) **12**:439

"Don't Leave Me Now" (Pink Floyd) **35**:311

"Don't Let It Bring You Down" (McCartney) **35**:285-86

"Don't Let It Bring You Down" (Young) **17**:569-70

"Don't Let Me Down" (Lennon and McCartney) **35**:274

Don't Look and It Won't Hurt (Peck) **21**:295

Don't Look Back (Dylan) **77**:161

Don't Look Now (du Maurier)
  See *Not after Midnight*

"Don't Make Me Hate You!" (Ewart) **46**:154

Don't Never Forget: Collected Views and Reviews (Brophy) **29**:94; **105**:5, 8

Don't Play Dead before You Have To (Wojciechowska) **26**:455

Don't Play Us Cheap (Van Peebles) **2**:448

Don't Sit under the Apple Tree (Brancato) **35**:65, 67

Don't Slam the Door When You Go (Corcoran) **17**:72

"Don't Stand So Close to Me" (Police, The) **26**:365

Don't Stop the Carnival (Wouk) **38**:449

"The Don't Swear Man" (Mitchell) **98**:186

"Don't Take Me Alive" (Becker and Fagen) **26**:82-3

Don't Take Teddy (Friis-Baastad) **12**:213-14

"Don't Talk" ("Put Your Head on My Shoulder") (Wilson) **12**:646

Don't Tell Alfred (Mitford) **44**:490-92

"Don't Tell Me You Don't Know" **78**:3

"Don't Think Twice, It's All Right" (Dylan) **77**:173

"Don't Think...Feel" (Diamond) **30**:112

Don't Tread on Me: The Selected Letters of S. J. Perelman (Perelman) **49**:269-70

"Don't Wanna Be" (Sanchez) **116**:301

"Don't Worry about the Government" (Byrne) **26**:94-5, 98

"Don't Worry Baby" (Wilson) **12**:644, 649

"Don't Worry Kyoko" (Lennon) **35**:265

"Don't Write about the Storm" (Akhmadulina)
  See "Ne pisat' o groze"

"Don't You Ever Wash That Thing" (Zappa) **17**:591

"Don't You Hear the Dogs Barking?" (Rulfo)
  See "No oyes ladrar los perros"

"Don't you talk about My Momma" (Jordan) **114**:152

Don't You Turn Back (Hughes) **35**:219

Don't You Want to Be Free? (Hughes) **108**:295

"Don't You Worry 'bout a Thing" (Wonder) **12**:657

"Doo Doo Doo Doo Doo" ("Heartbreaker") (Jagger and Richard) **17**:229

"Doodle Bugs" (Harrison) **43**:176

Doom (Gerhardie) **5**:140

"Doom Is Dark and Deeper than Any Sea Dingle" (Auden) **3**:24; **6**:20

"The Doom of Antarion" (Smith) **43**:419

Doomed (Kurosawa)
  See *Ikiru*

"The Doomed in Their Sinking" (Gass) **15**:258

The Doomsday Gang (Platt) **26**:352-53

The Doomsters (Macdonald) **14**:334; **41**:272

Doonesbury (Trudeau) **12**:588-91

The Doonesbury Chronicles (Trudeau) **12**:590

"The Door" (Barthelme) **13**:63

"The Door" (Bitov) **57**:114-15

"The Door" (Creeley) **8**:153; **15**:149; **78**:124, 130, 132

"Door" (Hoffman) **6**:244

"A Door" (Merwin) **5**:286

"The Door" (Strand) **18**:516; **41**:431; **71**:283

"The Door" (Turco) **11**:551

"The Door: A Prologue of Sorts" (Coover) **7**:58; **15**:145; **32**:121

The Door Between (Queen) **11**:461-63

The Door into Summer (Heinlein) **1**:139; **26**:165

Door into the Dark (Heaney) **5**:170-72; **7**:146-48, 150; **14**:242-43, 245; **25**:243-46; **37**:165; **74**:153-54, 156-57, 162, 170-71, 179, 193; **91**:117, 121, 123, 128

The Door of Life (Bagnold) **25**:73-4

"The Door Prohibited" (Dacey) **51**:81

The Doors (Morrison) **17**:287, 291, 295-96

The Doors (Stone) **73**:380-83

"The Doors of His Face, the Lamps of His Mouth" (Zelazny) **21**:468

The Doors of His Face, the Lamps of His Mouth and Other Stories (Zelazny) **21**:465, 468, 474-75

The Doors of Perception (Huxley) **4**:239, 241; **5**:194; **8**:303; **18**:270; **35**:241, 243

The Doors of Stone (Prince) **22**:338

"The Doorway" (Gluck) **81**:164, 167

"Doorways" (McGahern) **48**:263-64, 271

Doorways in the Sand (Zelazny) **21**:469-70

"Dopa una fuga" ("After a Flight") (Montale) **7**:228

Dopefiend: The Story of a Black Junkie (Goines) **80**:92, 95

"Der Doppelgänger" ("The Double")

(Durrenmatt) **15**:195

"Dordogne" (Ekelof) **27**:118-19

Doris and Doreen (Bennett) **77**:86, 88

"Dorking Thigh" (Plomer) **4**:407

Dormir al sol (*Asleep in the Sun*; *Sleeping in the Sun*) (Bioy Casares) **13**:84; **88**:64-5

"Dornenkranz" ("Crown of Thorns") (Celan) **82**:56-7

Doroga na okean (*Road to the Ocean*; *Way to the Ocean*) (Leonov) **92**:240, 246-47, 249-55, 259, 261, 276-77

"Dorot ba'arets" (Amichai) **116**:117

Dorothea Lange: A Photographer's Life (Meltzer) **26**:305-06

Dorothy and Me (Ayckbourn) **33**:44

Dorp Dead (Cunningham) **12**:163-65

"Dorset" (Davie) **8**:167-68

"Dos, caddy d'aisselles" (Perec) **56**:258

Las dos caras del patroncito (*The Two Faces of the Boss*) (Valdez) **84**:395

"Dos cartas" (Donoso) **32**:156, 158

Dos crímenes (*Two Crimes*) (Ibarguengoitia) **37**:183-85

"Las dos Elenas" ("The Two Elenas") (Fuentes) **8**:222; **22**:167-68; **113**:236

Dos españoles del siglo de oro (Alonso) **14**:20

"Dos niños" ("Two Children") (Guillen) **79**:250

Dos Passos: A Life (Carr) **34**:419-23

"Dos poemas" (Castellanos) **66**:50

Los dos verdugos (Arrabal)
See *Les deux bourreaux*

"Dos vidas" (Aleixandre) **9**:17

The Dosadi Experiment (Herbert) **12**:279; **23**:219, 221; **35**:209; **44**:393-94

"Dossy" (Frame) **96**:185

Dostoevsky
See *Problemy tvorcestva Dostoevskogo*

"Dostoievski and the Collapse of Liberalism" (Warner) **45**:433-34

Doting (Green) **2**:178; **13**:252, 254; **97**:245, 248, 250, 254, 257, 276, 278-79, 283, 286, 290-91, 293

"The Dotted Line of Progress" (Aksyonov) **101**:20

"The Double" (Durrenmatt)
See "Der Doppelgänger"

The Double Agent (Blackmur) **24**:53, 56-7

The Double Axe and Other Poems (Jeffers) **2**:212; **3**:260; **11**:305, 311; **15**:301; **54**:240-41, 246

"Double Bird" (Ignatow) **14**:276-77

The Double Case History of Doctor Valmy (Buero Vallejo)
See *La doble historia del Doctor Valmy*

"Double Charley" (Stern) **39**:244

"The Double Corner" (Stegner) **49**:350

Double Dare (Potter) **58**:391

The Double Dealer (Faulkner) **9**:201

"Double Derivation, Association, and Cliché: From the Great Tournament Roll of Westminster" (Matthias) **9**:362

"Double Dialogue: Homage to Robert Frost" (Rukeyser) **15**:457

Double, Double (Queen) **11**:463

The Double Dream of Spring (Ashbery) **2**:17-19; **4**:21-4; **9**:41, 44; **13**:30-1, 33; **15**:26-7, 31-3; **25**:58; **41**:40; **77**:47, 50, 52, 54

"Double Exposure" (Swenson) **106**:332

Double Exposure (Plath) **50**:450

Double Fantasy (Lennon) **35**:270, 272-76

"Double Feature" (Hayden) **37**:156

"Double Feature" (Roethke) **19**:397

Double Honeymoon (Connell) **45**:112

"The Double Horror" (Ezekiel) **61**:104

"The Double Image" (Sexton) **15**:472; **53**:312, 316, 318, 320

The Double Image (Levertov) **28**:241-42; **66**:251

The Double Image (MacInnes) **27**:281-82; **39**:351

Double Indemnity (Cain) **3**:96; **28**:45-7, 49-53

Double Indemnity (Wilder) **20**:456, 460

"Double Jeopardy: Making Sense of AIDS" (Amis) **62**:2, 4, 6

"The Double Life of Robertson Davies" (Davies) **75**:183

"The Double Looking Glass" (Hope) **51**:224

"Double Monologue" (Rich) **36**:374

"Double Nigger" (Dumas) **6**:145; **62**:153-54

Double or Nothing (Federman) **6**:181; **47**:119-24, 127-29, 131-32

Double Persephone (Atwood) **25**:64-5; **84**:89

The Double Room (Klima) **56**:168-69

"The Double Session" (Derrida) **87**:89

A Double Shadow (Turner) **48**:400

The Double Shadow and Other Fantasies (Smith) **43**:417

"The Double Shame" (Spender) **41**:428; **91**:269

Double Solitaire (Anderson) **23**:33

"Double Sonnet for Minimalists" (Van Duyn) **116**:415

Double Star (Heinlein) **1**:139; **14**:254; **26**:163, 165; **55**:300, 303

"The Double Thumb" (Bates) **46**:62

The Double Tree: Selected Poems, 1942-1976 (Wright) **11**:578; **53**:430

Double Vision: American Thoughts Abroad (Knowles) **26**:258-59

The Double Witness (Belitt) **22**:54-6

Double Yoke (Emecheta) **48**:98-100

"Doubled Mirrors" (Rexroth) **112**:399

The Doubleman (Koch) **42**:266-68

"Doubles" (Hood) **28**:195

"Doubling" (Daitch) **103**:77

Doubling the Point (Coetzee) **117**:68-9, 73

"Doubt" (Aldington) **49**:7

"Doubt" (Dobyns) **37**:76

"Doubt" (Gerstler) **70**:156-57

Doubtfire (Nye) **13**:412; **42**:302-04

"The Doubtful Passage" (Cardenal)
See "El estrecho dudoso"

"The Doughty Oaks" (Piercy) **27**:376

"The Dougtful Passage"
See "El estrecho dudoso"

"The Doukhubor" (Newlove) **14**:378

"La douleur" ("The War") (Duras) **68**:76, 80-2, 90; **100**:120-21, 126, 135, 149

La douleur (*The War: A Memoir*) (Duras) **68**:73-82, 84-5, 90-5, 99

The Dove (Beagle) **104**:5

"A Dove in Santiago" (Yevtushenko) **26**:469

Dove Inside (Neruda)
See *Paloma por dentro*

Dov'è la mia patria (Pasolini) **106**:232

The Dove of Popular Flight—Elegies (Guillen)
See *La paloma de vuelo popular: Elegiás*

A Dove of the East and Other Stories (Helprin) **7**:152; **10**:260, 262; **22**:222

"Dove sta memoria" (Tomlinson) **45**:402

"Dover" (Auden) **43**:16

"Dover Beach" (Jarrell) **13**:298

"Dover Beach" (Van Duyn) **116**:417

Dover Beach (Betjeman) **10**:52

"Dover Beach—A Note to That Poem" (MacLeish) **8**:363; **68**:288

The Doves of Venus (Manning) **19**:300

"Dowager" (Montague) **46**:274

"The Dower Chest" (Richter) **30**:329

"Down" (Graves) **1**:128; **45**:167

Down a Dark Hall (Duncan) **26**:103-05

Down All the Days (Brown) **63**:48-56

"Down along the Cove" (Dylan) **12**:185

Down among the Women (Weldon) **6**:562; **11**:565; **19**:466-67; **36**:447

Down and In (Sukenick) **48**:370-72

"Down and Out" (Hughes) **35**:221

"Down at the Cross" (Baldwin) **13**:52; **42**:14

"Down at the Dinghy" (Salinger) **12**:499; **56**:329

"Down at the Docks" (Koch) **5**:219

Down by the River (Adler) **35**:11-12

Down by the River (O'Brien) **116**:225-28

"Down by the Riverside" (Wright) **21**:442, 444, 453-54

"Down by the Seaside" (Page and Plant) **12**:477, 479

"Down by the Station, Early in the Morning" (Ashbery) **41**:37, 40

"Down Cemetery Road" (Porter) **33**:324

"Down East" (Laurence) **62**:280

"Down from Another Planet They Have Settled to Mend" (Miles) **14**:369

Down From the Hill (Sillitoe) **57**:398-99

"Down From Troy" (Selzer) **74**:263, 279

"Down Here on Greene Street" (Mazer) **26**:296

"Down in a Tube Station at Midnight" (Weller) **26**:444-46

"Down in the Dump" (White) **69**:398

"Down in the Wood" (Christie) **110**:126, 128

Down in the Zero (Vachss) **106**:364-65

"Down on the Funny Farm" (Raine) **32**:350, 353

"Down Our Way" (Wain) **46**:415

"Down, Satan!" (Barker) **52**:53

Down Second Avenue (Mphahlele) **25**:333, 336-37, 341, 343

"Down the Line with the Annual" (Barthelme) **6**:29

Down the Long Table (Birney) **6**:70-2; **11**:49-50

Down the River (Abbey) **36**:19-20; **59**:238, 242

"Down the River with Henry Thoreau" (Abbey) **36**:21

Down the Seine and up the Potomac with Art Buchwald (Buchwald) **33**:94-5

"Down Then by Derry" (Kiely) **43**:244-45

"Down There" (Campbell) **42**:87, 89

Down There on a Visit (Isherwood) **1**:155; **9**:294; **11**:296-98, 300; **14**:278, 280, 282-84, 286; **44**:397-98, 402

Down These Mean Streets (Thomas) **17**:497-502

"Down to the Wire" (Young) **17**:577

"Down to You" (Mitchell) **12**:438

"Down to Zero" (Armatrading) **17**:10

"Down, Wanton, Down!" (Graves) **45**:161, 169

Down Where the Moon Is Small (Llewellyn) **7**:207

"Down with the Restoration!" (Perelman) **49**:258

"Down-and-Out" (Queneau) **42**:337

Downbelow Station (Cherryh) **35**:106-07, 109, 113

Downerstag (Hochwalder) **36**:236-38

"The Downfall of Fascism in Black Ankle County" (Mitchell)　**98**:187

"Downhill" (Beattie)　**63**:17, 19

Downriver; or, The Vessels of Wrath (Sinclair)　**76**:221-28

"Downstairs at Fitzgerald's" (Trevor)　**25**:446

"Downstream" (Kinsella)　**4**:271; **19**:255

"Downtown, America" (Montague)　**46**:265, 270

"Downward" (Swenson)　**61**:391

"Downward" (Williams)　**33**:441

"The Downward Path to Wisdom" (Porter)　**7**:311; **27**:399; **101**:210-12

"The Dowser" (Redgrove)　**41**:357

"Dowson and Company" (Mahon)　**27**:290

"Doxology" (Ammons)　**108**:19

"Dr. Beeber" (Singer)　**3**:453

Dr. Bloodmoney, or How We Got Along After the Bomb (Dick)　**30**:124-25, 127; **72**:107, 110, 114, 121

"Dr. Cooper's Story" (Reading)　**47**:350

Dr. Cotnoir (Ferron)
　　See *Cotnoir*

"Dr. Faust's Sea-Spiral Spirit" (Redgrove)　**41**:353

Dr. Faust's Sea-Spiral Spirit and Other Poems (Redgrove)　**41**:349, 351-52

Dr. Futurity (Dick)　**72**:120

Dr. Golf (Fox)　**22**:140

Dr. Gruber's Daughter (Elliott)　**47**:115-17

"Dr. Hachiyas Tagebuch aus Hiroschima" (Canetti)　**75**:129

Dr. Heart: A Novella and Other Stories (Clark)　**5**:105-07

Dr. Hero (Horovitz)　**56**:151-52

Dr. Jekyll and Mr. Holmes (Estleman)　**48**:103

Dr. Jekyll and Mr. Hyde (Mamoulian)　**16**:420-21, 423-25

Dr. Kane of the Arctic Seas (Berton)　**104**:60

Dr. Kheal (Fornes)　**39**:138; **61**:130-31, 137

Dr. Mabuse the Gambler (Lang)　**20**:202; **103**:85

Dr. Murke's Collected Silences (Boell)
　　See *Doktor Murkes gesammeltes Schweigen, und andere Satiren*

Dr. No (Fleming)　**30**:133-34, 139, 149-50

"Dr. Perelman, I Presume; or, Small Bore in Africa" (Perelman)　**23**:336

Dr. Strangelove; or, How I Learned to Stop Worrying and Love the Bomb (Kubrick)　**16**:378-89, 391

"Dr. Voke and Mr. Veech" (Ligotti)　**44**:53-4

"Dr. Woolacott" (Forster)　**3**:161; **15**:231; **45**:140, 143

Dr. Zhivago (*Doctor Zhivago*) (Pasternak)　**7**:293-301; **10**:383-85, 387; **18**:382-85, 388-89; **59**:382, 384, 388, 391; **63**:282-83, 286-87, 289, 292-96, 299, 301, 304, 306-13, 318

"Draco, Draco" (Lee)　**46**:232

Dracula (Browning)　**16**:121-22, 124-26

Dracula (Welles)　**80**:379

Dracula, Go Home! (Platt)　**26**:353-54, 356

"Draft Dodger Rag" (Ochs)　**17**:331, 333, 339

A Draft of XVI Cantos (Pound)　**4**:412; **112**:332

A Draft of XXX Cantos (Pound)　**10**:400; **50**:437

A Draft of Shadows (Paz)
　　See *Pasado en claro*

Drafts and Fragments of Cantos CX to CXVII (Pound)　**2**:343; **4**:413-14; **13**:463; **34**:505; **48**:282-85, 299

"Dragged Fighting from His Tomb" (Hannah)　**90**:130, 148, 150

"Dragger Captain" (Mitchell)　**98**:160-61, 182

"The Dragon" (Barthelme)　**115**:65, 68-9

"The Dragon" (Govier)　**51**:166

"Dragon" (Ondaatje)　**51**:310, 316

"The Dragon" (Spark)　**40**:402

"The Dragon and the Unicorn" (Rexroth)　**49**:276-77, 279-80, 282, 285; **112**:386, 394, 402-04

The Dragon and the Unicorn (Rexroth)　**6**:450-51; **22**:346-47; **49**:277; **112**:373, 376-77, 387

The Dragon Can't Dance (Lovelace)　**51**:267-68, 271

Dragon Country (Williams)　**45**:450-51

Dragon, Dragon and Other Tales (Gardner)　**8**:238

Dragon Harvest (Sinclair)　**63**:358

"Dragon Head" (Jin)　**109**:52, 54

The Dragon in the Sea (Herbert)
　　See *Twenty-First Century Sub*

Dragon Magic (Norton)　**12**:462

The Dragon Masters (Vance)　**35**:417-19, 423, 426

Dragon of the Lost Sea (Yep)　**35**:473

Dragon on a Pedestal (Anthony)　**35**:39-40

Dragon Seed (Buck)　**11**:75-7

Dragon Summer (Arthur)　**12**:24, 28

Dragon Tears (Koontz)　**78**:219

Dragondrums (McCaffrey)　**17**:283-84

Dragonflight (McCaffrey)　**17**:280-81, 283

"Dragonfly" (Bogan)　**46**:90-1; **93**:65

"The Dragonfly-Mother" (Levertov)　**66**:240

Dragonquest: Being the Further Adventures of the Dragonriders of Pern (McCaffrey)　**17**:281, 283

The Dragonriders of Pern (McCaffrey)　**17**:281

Dragons in the Waters (L'Engle)　**12**:351

Dragon's Island (Williamson)　**29**:450, 459-60

The Dragons of Eden: Speculations on the Evolution of Human Intelligence (Sagan)　**30**:333-36, 343-44; **112**:413, 419, 431

"Dragon's Seed" (Bell)　**102**:5, 7

"The Dragon's Teeth" (Gordon)
　　See "One against Thebes"

The Dragon's Teeth (Queen)　**11**:458

Dragon's Teeth (Sinclair)　**11**:497; **15**:500; **63**:355-56, 359, 376

Dragon's Teeth: Literature in the English Revolution (Wilding)　**73**:399

Dragonsinger (McCaffrey)　**17**:282-84

Dragonsong (McCaffrey)　**17**:282-83

Dragonwings (Yep)　**35**:468, 470-71

Drake, The Man They Called a Pirate (Latham)　**12**:323

"Drama o puerta cerrada" (Cernuda)　**54**:56

"Dramas" (O'Brien)　**65**:167, 171

"Dramaturgie des Labyrinths" (Duerrenmatt)　**102**:61-2

"Drame Bourgeoise" (Ashbery)　**13**:36

Dramen (Canetti)　**86**:303

Dramen (Hochwalder)　**36**:235

Dramouss (*A Dream of Africa*) (Laye)　**4**:284-85; **38**:285, 288-91

"The Draped Mirrors" (Borges)　**8**:99

"The Drawer" (Klappert)　**57**:258, 266

"Drawing Lessons" (Nemerov)　**36**:304

"The Drawing Master" (Urquhart)　**90**:384, 386

"Drawing Names" (Mason)　**82**:234

The Drawing of the Three (King)　**113**:382

"Drawing Room" (Ezekiel)　**61**:104

"Drawing the Triangle" (Simic)　**49**:337

"Drawing Wildflowers" (Graham)　**48**:145, 147

"Drawings by Children" (Mueller)　**51**:282

Drawn and Quartered (Addams)　**30**:11-12

Drawn and Quartered (Cioran)
　　See *Écartèlement*

"Dread" (Barker)　**52**:51, 53

Dread Companion (Norton)　**12**:459, 462-63, 467

"The Dread Redeemer Lazarus Morrell" (Borges)
　　See "El espantoso redentor Lazarus Morell"

"Dreaded Hell" (Onetti)
　　See "El infierno tan temido"

"The Dreadful Day of Judgement" (Rendell)　**48**:320

The Dreadful Lemon Sky (MacDonald)　**27**:275

"The Dream" (Bogan)　**46**:81-4; **93**:64, 67-8, 81

"The Dream" (Bowers)　**9**:122

"A Dream" (Ciardi)　**40**:156

"The Dream" (Ekelof)　**27**:110, 114

"Dream" (Livesay)　**79**:338, 341, 343

"The Dream" (Roethke)　**46**:363; **101**:315, 328

"Dream" (Sarton)　**91**:254

"Dream" (Thomas)　**13**:541-42

"Dream" (Wright)　**53**:419

The Dream (Montherlant)
　　See *Le songe*

The Dream (Smith)　**64**:401-02

"The Dream, 1863" (Hayden)　**9**:270; **14**:240; **37**:157

"Dream after Nanook" (Swenson)　**61**:398

Dream and the Leg (Michaux)
　　See *Les rêves et la jambe*

"The Dream and the Triumph" (Buckler)　**13**:119

A Dream Awake (Dodson)　**79**:190

"Dream: Bluejay or Archeopteryx" (Atwood)　**8**:31

"Dream Boogie" (Hughes)　**108**:299-300, 302-04

"Dream Boogie: Variation" (Hughes)　**108**:299, 301, 303-04

"Dream Children" (Godwin)　**8**:248-49

Dream Children (Godwin)　**8**:248-49; **22**:180; **31**:195; **69**:232-33, 243, 247

Dream Craters (Rosenblatt)　**15**:447-48

"A Dream Deferred" (Hughes)　**35**:218, 221

The Dream Department (Perelman)　**49**:258-59

"Dream Dogs" (Codrescu)　**46**:102

"Dream Flight" (Smith)　**42**:348

Dream Flights (Smith)　**42**:346-51, 353

A Dream Fulfilled, and Other Stories (Onetti)
　　See *Un sueño realizado y otros cuentos*

Dream Girl (Rice)　**7**:361, 363; **49**:299-300

"The Dream Habitues" (Jacobsen)　**48**:194

"Dream III" (Jiles)　**58**:279

A Dream in the Luxembourg (Aldington)　**49**:11-15, 18

"A Dream in the Woods of Virginia" (Simpson)　**7**:427

A Dream Journey (Hanley)　**8**:265-66; **13**:261

"Dream Journeys" (Hesse)　**3**:248

"The Dream Keeper" (Hughes)　**35**:214

The Dream Keeper and Other Poems (Hughes)　**35**:214; **108**:283

A Dream Like Mine (Kelly)　**55**:156-61

The Dream Master (Zelazny)　**21**:463, 470

"Dream Objects" (Updike)　**3**:485

The Dream of a Beast (Jordan)　**110**:274-75, 278

*The Dream of a Common Language: Poems,
   1974-1977* (Rich)   **11**:478-79; **18**:448-
   51; **36**:368, 373-74, 376; **73**:315, 317,
   326, 332; **76**:217
"The Dream of a House" (Price)   **43**:351
"Dream of a Large Lady" (Kizer)   **39**:169
"Dream of a Mannikin; or, The Third Person"
   (Ligotti)   **44**:53-5
A Dream of Africa (Laye)
   See *Dramouss*
"A Dream of Beauty" (Smith)   **43**:424
Dream of Dark Harbor (Kotzwinkle)   **35**:255
Dream of Fair to Middling Women (Beckett)
   29:67
"A Dream of Fair Women" (Amis)   **40**:39-40,
   44
A Dream of Ghosts (Bonham)   **12**:54
A Dream of Governors (Simpson)   **4**:499; **7**:426-
   428; **32**:378
The Dream of Heroes (Bioy Casares)
   See *El sueño de los héroes*
"A Dream of Jealousy" (Heaney)   **14**:246;
   74:164
"Dream of Judgement" (Dunn)   **40**:167
"The Dream of Lee" (Price)   **43**:350-51
Dream of Orchids (Whitney)   **42**:437
"Dream of Pairing" (Shange)   **74**:311
"Dream of Planets" (Kunene)   **85**:175
"The Dream of Private Clitus" (Jones)   **7**:191
"The Dream of South" (Williams)   **39**:101
The Dream of Success (Lynn)   **50**:426
"Dream of the Butterflies" (Danticat)   **94**:100
"Dream of the Future" (Jeffers)   **54**:235
"The Dream of the Gods" (Hesse)   **25**:260
"The Dream of the Islanders of Thomas Mann"
   (Dubie)   **36**:136
"A Dream of Whitman Paraphrased, Recog-
   nized, and Made More Vivid by Renoir"
   (Schwartz)   **45**:355
"Dream of Winter" (Brown)   **48**:51
"A Dream of Winter" (Lehmann)   **5**:240
Dream on Monkey Mountain (Walcott)   **76**:276-
   77, 282, 286
*The Dream on Monkey Mountain, and Other
   Plays* (Walcott)   **2**:459-60; **4**:574; **9**:556;
   25:451-52, 454-55; **67**:347, 350, 352
"A Dream Pang" (Frost)   **26**:116-17
"Dream Record: June 1955" (Ginsberg)
   109:358
"The Dream Sleepers" (Grace)   **56**:116
The Dream Sleepers and Other Stories (Grace)
   56:116-17, 119, 123
"Dream Song 2" (Berryman)   **62**:60
"Dream Song 3" (Berryman)   **62**:69
"Dream Song 4" (Berryman)   **62**:54
"Dream Song 13" (Berryman)   **62**:62
"Dream Song 15" (Berryman)   **62**:73
"Dream Song 20" (Berryman)   **62**:44
"Dream Song 23" ("The Lay of Ike")
   (Berryman)   **62**:63, 73
"Dream Song 25" (Berryman)   **62**:61, 65
"Dream Song 26" (Berryman)   **62**:61, 65
"Dream Song 27" (Berryman)   **62**:45, 61
"Dream Song 29" (Berryman)   **62**:48, 62
"Dream Song 36" (Berryman)   **62**:65
"Dream Song 50" (Berryman)   **62**:61-2
"Dream Song 53" (Berryman)   **62**:70
"Dream Song 56" (Berryman)   **62**:45
"Dream Song 66" (Berryman)   **62**:48, 69
"Dream Song 69" (Berryman)   **62**:61, 63
"Dream Song 71" (Berryman)   **62**:63
"Dream Song 75" (Berryman)   **62**:63
"Dream Song 76" ("Henry's Confession")
   (Berryman)   **62**:61-2
"Dream Song 78" (Berryman)   **62**:66, 68-9
"Dream Song 81" (Berryman)   **62**:66
"Dream Song 82" (Berryman)   **62**:66
"Dream Song 85" (Berryman)   **62**:66
"Dream Song 86" (Berryman)   **62**:65-6
"Dream Song 97" (Berryman)   **62**:57
"Dream Song 100" (Berryman)   **62**:58
"Dream Song 159" (Berryman)   **62**:74
"Dream Song 162" (Berryman)   **62**:70
"Dream Song 163" (Berryman)   **62**:70
"Dream Song 171" (Berryman)   **62**:64
"Dream Song 175" (Berryman)   **62**:64
"Dream Song 180" (Berryman)   **62**:70
"Dream Song 181" (Berryman)   **62**:70
"Dream Song 185" (Berryman)   **62**:74
"Dream Song 191" (Berryman)   **62**:48
"Dream Song 219" ("So Long? Stevens")
   (Berryman)   **62**:59
"Dream Song 242" (Berryman)   **62**:58
"Dream Song 256" (Berryman)   **62**:65
"Dream Song 258" (Berryman)   **62**:48
"Dream Song 303" (Berryman)   **62**:44
"Dream Song 319" (Berryman)   **62**:65
"Dream Song 373" (Berryman)   **62**:63
"Dream Song 384" (Berryman)   **62**:62, 65
The Dream Songs (Berryman)   **1**:33-4; **2**:56-
   9; **3**:66-72; **4**:60-3; **6**:63-5; **8**:87-92;
   10:45-52; **13**:76, 78-9, 81-3; **25**:89-99;
   62:43-50, 54-7, 59-61, 63-74, 76-7
"The Dream Spinners" (Christie)   **110**:125
Dream Street Rose (Lightfoot)   **26**:282
The Dream Team (McGinniss)   **32**:300-01
"Dream Variations" (Hughes)   **108**:296, 300
"The Dream Vendor's August" (Okri)   **87**:314-
   15
The Dream Watcher (Wersba)   **30**:429-31, 433
The Dream Weaver (Buero Vallejo)   **15**:100-02
"A Dream with No Stump Roots in It" (Huddle)
   49:181-2
Dream Work (Oliver)   **98**:259-61, 267, 272,
   276-77, 282, 286, 302
A Dreambook for Our Time (Konwicki)
   See *Sennik współczesny*
Dreamchild (Potter)   **58**:391-92; **86**:346, 353
"The Dreamer" (Fante)   **60**:133
"The Dreamer" (Soyinka)   **36**:411
The Dreamer (Green)
   See *Le visionnaire*
"The Dreamer and the Watcher" (Gluck)
   44:220
*The Dreamer Examines His Pillow: A Hetero-
   sexual Homily* (Shanley)   **75**:321
A Dreamer for a People (Buero Vallejo)
   See *Un soñador para un pueblo*
"Dreamer in a Dead Language" (Paley)   **37**:336,
   339
"The Dreamers" ("Drømmerne") (Dinesen)
   29:157-58, 164; **95**:42-4, 47, 55, 64, 73
"Dreamers" (Smith)   **73**:353, 356
"Dreamers of the Absolute, Part I: Pamphlets
   and Bombs" (Enzensberger)   **43**:150
"Dreamers of the Absolute, Part II: The Beau-
   tiful Souls of Terror" (Enzensberger)
   43:150
Dreamhouse (Grenville)   **61**:155-63
"The Dreaming Child" (Dinesen)   **29**:159;
   95:35
"Dreaming Crew" (Swan)   **69**:365
"Dreaming from the Waist" (Townshend)
   17:536
Dreaming in Bronze (Thomas)   **31**:430
Dreaming in Cuban (Garcia)   **76**:39-45
"Dreaming in Daylight" (Warren)   **39**:274
The Dreaming Jewels (Sturgeon)   **39**:361, 364
Dreaming My Dreams (Jennings)   **21**:202, 204,
   206
*Dreaming of Babylon: A Private Eye Novel,
   1942* (Brautigan)   **9**:124-25; **12**:74; **42**:56-
   7, 60-1
"Dreaming of Horses" (Jensen)   **37**:190
"Dreaming of Immortality in a Thatched Hut"
   (Stevenson)   **33**:379
"Dreaming of You" (Monette)   **82**:323, 332
"Dreaming Winter" (Welch)   **52**:428
"Dreamland" (Lightfoot)   **26**:282
"Dreamland" (Mitchell)   **12**:443
Dreamland (Higgins)   **10**:273-74
Dreamland Lake (Peck)   **21**:296
"Dreams" (Creeley)   **36**:121
"Dreams" (Findley)   **102**:111
"Dreams" (Galeano)   **72**:130
"Dreams" (Giovanni)   **64**:185
"Dreams" (Oliver)   **98**:265, 268, 271, 276
Dreams (Bergman)
   See *Kvinnodröm*
Dreams (Eich)
   See *Träume*
Dreams (Kettelkamp)   **12**:305
"Dreams and Dollars" (Yezierska)   **46**:443
Dreams from Bunker Hill (Fante)   **60**:133-34
"Dreams Must Explain Themselves" (Le Guin)
   13:347; **71**:188, 199
Dreams of a Summer Night (Barker)   **48**:18,
   21-2
"Dreams of Adulthood" (Ashbery)   **77**:65-6
*Dreams of Dark and Light: The Great Fiction
   of Tanith Lee* (Lee)   **46**:234
Dreams of Glory (Fleming)   **37**:128-29
Dreams of Leaving (Hare)   **29**:215
Dreams of Roses and Fire (Johnson)
   See *Drömmar om rosor och eld*
Dreams of Sleep (Humphreys)   **34**:63-6;
   57:234-36, 238
"Dreams of the Animals" (Atwood)   **84**:68
Dreams of the Kalahari (Slaughter)   **56**:409-
   10
"Dreams of Water" (Justice)   **102**:263
Dreamsnake (McIntyre)   **18**:326
The Dreamstone (Cherryh)   **35**:112-13
"Dreamtigers" (Borges)   **3**:81; **13**:107
Dreamtigers (Borges)
   See *El hacedor*
Die drei Grazien (*The Three Graces*) (Eliade)
   19:148
"Dreiser's *Sister Carrie*" (Farrell)   **66**:139
"Das dreissigste Jahr" ("The Thirtieth Year")
   (Bachmann)   **69**:37
Das dreissigste Jahr (*The Thirtieth Year*)
   (Bachmann)   **69**:35, 37, 44
"Drenched in Light" (Hurston)   **7**:172; **30**:211
The Dresden Green (Freeling)   **38**:184
"The Dress" (Creeley)   **78**:126
"The Dress" (Strand)   **71**:278, 285-86
Dress Her in Indigo (MacDonald)   **44**:408
"Dress Me Up as a Robber" (McCartney)
   35:289-91
Dressed in Light (Seifert)
   See *Svetlem odená*
"Dressed Like Summer Leaves" (Dubus)
   97:214, 216
Dressed to Kill (De Palma)   **20**:81-2
"Dressed Up" (Hughes)   **1**:148
The Dresser (Harwood)   **32**:227-28
A Dressing of Diamond (Freeling)   **38**:186-87
"Dressing Up for the Carnival" (Shields)

113:408
Dressing Up: Transvestism and Drag, the History of an Obsession (Ackroyd) 52:5, 14
The Dressmaker (*The Secret Glass*) (Bainbridge) 4:39; 5:39-40; 8:37; 10:16; 18:33; 22:46; 62:24, 29, 38
Dried Hand (Tchicaya)
  See *La main sèche*
The Drifters (Michener) 109:375, 378-79
"The Drifter's Escape" (Dylan) 12:185
Driftglass (Delany) 14:147; 38:154, 160-61
"The Drifting" (Bell) 8:66
"Drifting" (Grace) 56:116
Drifting Home (Berton) 104:47
Drifting into War (Bissett) 18:59
"Drifting Off" (Heaney) 74:169
"Driftwood" (Wilbur) 6:570; 110:383
"A Drink in the Passage" (Paton) 25:359-60
"A Drink of Water" (Heaney) 7:151
"Drink to Me Only with Labyrinthine Eyes" (Ligotti) 44:54
"Drink Ye All of It" (Wiebe) 14:574
"The Drinker" (Lowell) 1:181
Drinking: A Love Story (Knapp) 99:47-53
Drinking Companion (Ayckbourn) 33:40
"Drinking From a Helmet" (Dickey) 109:237
The Drinking Gourd (Hansberry) 17:191-93
Drinking in America (Bogosian) 45:62-4
Drinking Sapphire Wine (Lee) 46:230
"Drinking Song" (Hecht) 8:267; 13:269
Drinks before Dinner (Doctorow) 15:179-80; 37:91; 113:149, 176
"Drinks with X" (Moss) 45:292
Das Dritte Buch über Achim (*The Third Book about Achim*) (Johnson) 5:200-01; 10:283-84; 15:304-06; 40:268
"The Drive" (Bullins) 7:37
"Drive Back" (Young) 17:575
"The Drive Home" (Banks) 37:23
"The Drive Home" (Merwin) 18:334; 88:205
"A Drive in the Country/Henri Toulouse-Lautrec" (Middleton) 13:388
"Drive My Car" (Lennon and McCartney) 35:268
"A Drive through Hell" (Bukowski) 82:23
"A Drive through Spring" (Ciardi) 40:157
"Driven to Tears" (Police, The) 26:365
"Driver" (Barthelme) 117:5, 7
"The Driver" (Voznesensky) 57:427
The Driver's Seat (Spark) 2:416-19; 3:464-65; 5:400; 8:495; 13:524; 40:395, 397, 399-400
"Drivin'" (Davies) 21:91
"Driving across the American Desert and Thinking of the Sahara" (Ciardi) 40:161
"Driving across the Prairie" (Dorn) 10:161
"Driving Back from the Funeral" (Collins) 44:38
Driving Force (Francis) 102:143-44, 149
"Driving Home" (Waddington) 28:438
Driving Home (Waddington) 28:437-38
"Driving Home in Breaking Season" (Smith) 22:387
"Driving in from Muskoka Slow Rain Blues" (Donnell) 34:159
Driving Miss Daisy (Uhry) 55:264-67
"Driving My Parents Home at Christmas" (Bly) 15:68; 38:57
"Driving on the A 30" (Williams) 42:443
"Driving Through" (Ammons) 108:19
"Driving through Ohio" (Bly) 5:61
"Driving Through Oregon" (Haines) 58:222
"Driving through Sawmill Towns" (Murray)

40:340-41
Driving Today and Tomorrow (Hyde) 21:171-72
"Driving Toward Boston I Run Across One of Robert Bly's Old Poems" (McGrath) 59:179-81
"Driving toward the Lac Qui Parle River" (Bly) 5:61
"Driving toward the Moon" (Kinsella) 43:253, 255-56
"Driving West" (Beer) 58:33, 38
Driving West (Beer) 58:32-3, 36, 39
"Drogo" (Strand) 41:440
Les drôlatiques, horrifiques, et épouvantables aventures de Panurge, ami de Pantagruel, d'aprés Rabelais (Maillet) 54:313, 317
Drôle de baraque (Kennedy)
  See *Funnyhouse of a Negro*
Drôles de journal (Rakosi) 47:347
Drömmar om rosor och eld (*Dreams of Roses and Fire*) (Johnson) 14:295
"Drømmerne" (Dinesen)
  See "The Dreamers"
A Drop of Patience (Kelley) 22:247-48, 251
"A Drop of Pure Liquid" (Willingham) 51:403
"Dropping Dance" (Grenville) 61:162
The Drought (Ballard) 6:28; 14:41; 36:33-6
"A Drover" (Colum) 28:90
"Drover's Song" (Mathias) 45:235
"The Drowned" (Bottoms) 53:32
Drowned Ammet (Jones) 26:227-29
The Drowned and the Saved (Levi)
  See *I sommersi e i salvati*
"The Drowned Child" (Gluck) 44:214
"The Drowned Giant" (Ballard) 3:33; 14:41; 36:36, 39-41
"The Drowned Man: Death between Two Rivers" (McGrath) 28:275
The Drowned World (Ballard) 3:32-4; 6:27; 14:41; 36:35-6, 42, 45
"Drowning" (Boyle) 36:57-8
"Drowning" (Olds) 32:346
"Drowning 1954" (Keillor) 40:275
The Drowning of Wasyl Nemitchuk; or, A Fine Colored Easter Egg (Ringwood) 48:334-36, 339
The Drowning Pool (Macdonald) 2:256; 14:334; 41:265, 271
"Drowning Puppies" (Simmons) 43:408
The Drowning Season (Hoffman) 51:201-02, 207
Drowning with Others (Dickey) 7:80, 82-3; 109:244-45
"The Drowning Young Man" (Rukeyser) 27:404
"Drüben auf den Inseln" (Lenz) 27:245
"Drug Store" (Shapiro) 4:486; 15:476
Drugaia zhizn' (*Another Life. The House on the Embankment: Three Novellas*)(Trifonov) 45:408-10, 416-20
"Drugged" (Hall) 51:172
"Drugoe" ("Something Else") (Akhmadulina) 53:12
"Drugs" (Byrne) 26:97
"Drug-Stabbing Time" (Clash) 30:43
"A Drugstore in Winter" (Ozick) 28:353-54
The Druid's Rest (Williams) 15:577
"The Drum" (Bogan) 93:90
"Drum" (Voznesensky) 57:424
"Drummer" (Vanderhaeghe) 41:448-50
The Drummer (Fugard) 80:80
The Drummer Boy (Garfield) 12:218, 221, 223-27, 235, 237
"The Drummer of All the World" (Laurence)

62:274
"Drums" (Kenny) 87:240
"Drums" (Okigbo) 84:315
Drums along the Mohawk (Edmonds) 35:147-51, 153, 155-56
Drums along the Mohawk (Ford) 16:304, 310
Drums and Colours: An Epic Drama (Walcott) 25:453-54
Drums at Dusk (Bontemps) 1:37; 18:63, 65
Drums Beneath the Window (O'Casey)
  See *Drums Under the Window*
"Drums in Scotland" (Hugo) 32:242
The Drums of Father Ned (*Father Ned*) (O'Casey) 5:318; 11:406-07, 409-10; 15:405; 88:241-42, 270, 273-75
Drums, Rattles, and Bells (Kettelkamp) 12:304
Drums Under the Window (*Drums Beneath the Window*) (O'Casey) 88:239
"Drumtochty Castle School" (Barker) 48:19
"Drunk" (Plumly) 33:312
"The Drunk Hunter" (Bottoms) 53:29-30
The Drunk in the Furnace (Merwin) 1:212-13; 2:276; 5:288; 8:388-89; 13:383; 18:333, 335; 45:268, 270, 276-77; 88:186, 205-06
A Drunk Man Looks at the Thistle (MacDiarmid) 2:254; 4:309-13; 11:333-38; 19:288-90; 63:239, 241-42, 244, 249
"Drunk with Love" (Gilchrist) 48:119, 121
Drunk with Love (Gilchrist) 48:119-22
"Drunk with the Buddha" (Bukowski) 82:27
"The Drunkard" (O'Connor) 14:398
"The Drunkard's Sunday" (Keillor) 40:274
Drunken Angel (Kurosawa) 16:402-03
"The Drunken Fisherman" (Lowell) 1:181; 4:303
"The Drunken Poet" (Nowlan) 15:399
The Drunken Sisters (Wilder) 10:536
"Drunks" (Smith) 22:386
The Drunks (Newlove)
  See *Leo and Theodore*
"Drunks in the Bass Boat" (Bottoms) 53:32
Drury Lane's Last Case (Queen) 11:460
Dry Dreams (Carroll) 35:80
"Dry Foot Bwoy" (Bennett) 28:26, 30
The Dry Heart (Ginzburg)
  See *E stato così*
Dry Lips Oughta Move to Kapuskasing (Highway) 92:218-20, 224-25, 227-32
"The Dry Prophet" (Watkins) 43:454, 457
"The Dry Salvages" (Eliot) 1:92; 6:164-65; 13:194; 15:215-16; 24:174; 34:525, 529-30; 41:152; 55:347, 362; 57:206, 211
"Dry September" (Faulkner) 3:156; 18:147; 52:142
Dry Summer in Provence (Brand) 7:29
Dry Sun, Dry Wind (Wagoner) 3:508; 5:473
Dry Victories (Jordan) 11:312
A Dry White Season (Brink) 18:69-70; 36:65, 67; 106:98-9, 104, 119, 124, 130, 133, 137, 139, 142, 143, 145
"Dry Your Eyes" (Diamond) 30:112
"Dryad" (Davidson) 13:168; 19:124, 129
"The Dryad War" (Paz) 65:200
Drypoints of the Hasidim (Prince) 22:338-39
"DTNB" (Weller) 26:448
Du domaine (Guillevic) 33:192-94
The Du Mauriers (du Maurier) 59:286
Du mouvement et de l'immobilité de Douve (*On the Motion and Immobility of Douve*) (Bonnefoy) 9:112, 114; 58:41-54, 57-60
Du surréalisme en ses oeuvres vives et

d'ephemerides surréalistes (*Of Surrealism in Its Living Works*) (Breton) 54:16, 28

"Du wanxiang" (Ding Ling) 68:67-9

"Duality" (Abse) 29:16

Duas aguas (*Two Waters*) (Cabral de Melo Neto) 76:153

"Dubieties" (Cassity) 6:107

Dubin's Lives (Malamud) 18:319-22; 27:302; 44:413, 415, 419-20

Dubious Honors (Fisher) 76:341

"Dublin" (MacNeice) 53:237

Dubliners (Swinnerton) 31:421

"Dublinesque" (Larkin) 5:227; 8:333

Ducdame (Powys) 7:348; 46:314-15, 324

"The Duchess" (Cheever) 11:121

"The Duchess' Red Shoes" (Schwartz) 10:462

La duchesse de Langeais (Tremblay) 29:419-20, 425; 102:362-65, 370, 376

La duchesse et le roturier (Tremblay) 29:424, 427-28; 102:370

"Duck Blind" (Hass) 99:141

Duck Song (Mercer) 5:284

The Duck Variations (Mamet) 15:356-58; 46:247, 249-50

"Duck-Chasing" (Kinnell) 5:217

"The Ducking Stool" (Muldoon) 32:319; 72:265

"The Ducks" (Carver) 22:96; 36:106

"Ducks On the Wall" (Davies) 21:99

"Duck's Yas Yas" (Crumb) 17:83

"Duckweed" (Leithauser) 27:240, 242

Dude (Ragni and Rado) 17:386

Due East (Sayers) 50:82-7

"Due Process" (Musgrave) 54:334

"The Duel" (Belitt) 22:48

"The Duel" (Borges)
  See "El duelo"

Duel (Spielberg) 20:357-58

"Duel in Pernambucan Fashion" (Cabral de Melo Neto)
  See "Duelo à pernambucana"

The Dueling Machine (Bova) 45:66

"El duelo" ("The Duel") (Borges) 10:67; 13:105; 83:189

Duelo (Benet) 28:23

"Duelo à pernambucana" ("Duel in Pernambucan Fashion") (Cabral de Melo Neto) 76:165

Duelo en el paraíso (Goytisolo) 23:186

"The Duet" (Auden) 14:28

"Duet" (Oates) 6:367

Duet for Cannibals (Sontag) 31:409

"Duffy's Circus" (Muldoon) 32:319; 72:275

"The Dufluflu Bird" (Johnston) 51:239

Dúfnaveislan rónika (Laxness) 25:300

"The Dugong" (Wright) 53:425

"Duhovniceasca" ("Confession") (Arghezi) 80:2, 6

Duishen (Aitmatov)
  See *Pervyi uchitel'*

Duke Decides (Tunis) 12:594

"The Duke Imlach Story" (Faust) 8:215

The Duke in Darkness (Hamilton) 51:189

"The Duke in His Domain" (Capote) 8:132; 13:139

The Duke of Deception: Memories of My Father (Wolff) 41:459-61

Dulcy (Connelly) 7:55

Dulcy (Kaufman) 38:257-58, 264-66

"Dull Tale" (Faulkner) 18:148

"Dulse" (Munro) 95:302, 306, 315, 318

The Duluoz Legend (Kerouac) 61:309-10

Duluth (Vidal) 33:408-09; 72:384-87, 389

"La dumaiu: kak ia byla glupa" ("I Think: How Stupid I Have Been") (Akhmadulina) 53:12

"The Dumb Dutchman" (Forester) 35:173

"Dumb Show" (Aldiss) 14:10

"Dumb Waiter" (Miller) 30:261

The Dumb Waiter (Altman) 116:59

The Dumb Waiter (Pinter) 6:407-08, 411, 413, 416-18, 420; 11:437-38, 441; 15:422; 27:385, 387-88, 393; 73:276

Dumb Witness (Christie) 48:73

"The Dumbfounding" (Avison) 97:85, 87, 121

The Dumbfounding (Avison) 2:29; 4:36; 97:73, 77, 79-86, 88, 92-3, 99-100, 104-05, 108, 110-17, 128

"The Dummy" (Sontag) 13:518

"The Dummy in the Window" (Walker) 58:409

"The Dump: A Dream Come True" (Sissman) 9:491

"Dump Gull" (Howe) 47:173-74

The Dumplings (Lear) 12:334

D'un château l'autre (*Castle to Castle*) (Celine) 3:103-05; 4:98, 100, 102-03; 7:45; 9:158; 47:74-5, 77-9

"The Dun Cow and the Hag" (Dubie) 36:134

"The Dun Dakotas" (Roth) 104:250-51

"Duncan" (Simon) 17:461, 466

"Duncan Spoke of a Process" (Baraka) 5:45

Dunciad Minimus (Hope)
  See *Dunciad Minor: An Heroick Poem*

Dunciad Minor: An Heroick Poem (*Dunciad Minimus*) (Hope) 51:211, 215, 217, 226

Dune (Herbert) 12:270-81; 23:221-27; 35:196, 198-208, 210; 44:392-95; 85:85-112

Dune (Lynch) 66:264, 269, 271

"D'une jeunesse européenne" (Malraux) 57:301-02

Dune Messiah (Herbert) 12:271-73, 276-77; 23:221-24, 226-27; 35:196, 199, 201, 207-08; 44:393-94; 85:88-9, 93-6, 110-11

Dunelawn (McNally) 4:347; 7:218

"Dunes" (Ammons) 25:43-4; 108:23

Dunfords Travels Everywheres (Kelley) 22:249, 251-52

Dunkirk (Pratt) 19:385

The Dunne Family (Farrell) 8:205; 11:194-95

Dunnigan's Daughter (Behrman) 40:83

"Dunyazadiad" (Barth) 5:51; 14:52; 51:22; 89:10

The Duplex: A Black Love Fable in Four Movements (Bullins) 5:82-3; 7:36

Duplicate Keys (Smiley) 53:346-47

The Duplications (Koch) 8:324; 44:246, 248, 250

A Durable Fire (Sarton) 4:471

"Durango" (Cernuda) 54:55

Durango Street (Bonham) 12:49, 53

Durdane (Vance) 35:427

"Durham" (Harrison) 43:175

"During a Solar Eclipse" (Nemerov) 36:306

"During Days of Horror, Despair, and World Change" (Parker) 68:334

"During Fever" (Lowell) 37:243

"Dusie" (Barnes) 3:37

"Dusk" (Harrison) 33:198

"Dusk" (Ritsos) 13:488

"Dusk" (Salter) 59:196

Dusk and Other Stories (Salter) 52:368-69; 59:194-98

"Dusk before Fireworks" (Parker) 68:326, 335, 337, 339

"Dusk: Elegy for the Dark Sun" (Hirsch) 31:215

Dusk of Dawn (Du Bois) 64:127; 96:138, 146, 148

A Dusk of Idols (Blish) 14:86

"Dusk on the Bay" (Birney) 6:74

"Dusk Shows Us What We Are and Hardly Mean" (Schwartz) 87:347

Dusklands (Coetzee) 23:121-22; 66:90-2, 95, 99; 117:32-5, 38-9, 44-5, 47, 65, 67, 79-81, 83, 85

"Dust" (Johnston) 51:244-45

"Dust" (Williams) 42:442

"Dust" (Wright) 11:578

Dust Bowl Ballads (Guthrie) 35:184

Dust on the Paw (Jenkins) 52:219-22, 225-27

"Dust on the Pearls" (Daly) 17:91

Dust Tracks on a Road (Hurston) 30:213-14, 226; 61:256-57, 267, 269, 275

The Dust within the Rock (Waters) 88:328-29, 335, 337-40, 345, 360-62

"Dusting" (Dove) 50:153, 158; 81:139

Dustland (Hamilton) 26:155-56

Dusty Answer (Lehmann) 5:235, 239

Dutch Interior (O'Connor) 14:397; 23:328-29

Dutch Shea, Jr. (Dunne) 28:125-29

The Dutch Shoe Mystery (Queen) 3:421

Dutch Uncle (Gray) 9:241; 36:201-04, 207

Dutchman (Baraka) 1:163; 2:35; 3:35-6; 5:44-7; 14:43-4, 46, 49; 33:54, 57-60, 62; 115:10, 32-3, 37-8, 44-50

"Duties of a Black Revolutionary Artist" (Walker) 103:376

A Dutiful Daughter (Keneally) 5:209-11; 8:319; 14:302; 19:245; 117:215, 226-27

"Duty" (Ritsos) 31:325

Duveen (Behrman) 40:83, 85, 88

"Dúvidas apócrifas de Marianne Moore" ("Apocryphal Doubts of Marianne Moore") (Cabral de Melo Neto) 76:160, 166

"Duwamish Head" (Hugo) 32:237-38, 247

"Duwamish No. Two" (Hugo) 32:242

"Duzo spiè" ("A Magic Mountain") (Milosz) 56:244

"Dva tovarishcha" ("Two Comrades"; "Two Friends") (Voinovich) 10:506-07; 49:373

Dvärgen (*The Dwarf*) (Lagerkvist) 10:311; 13:334; 54:270-71, 275, 278, 288

"Dvojnik" (Coles) 67:179

Dvorák in Love (Skvorecky)
  See *Scherzo capriccioso*

The Dwarf (Lagerkvist)
  See *Dvärgen*

"The Dwarf and the Doll" (Boell)
  See "Der Zwerg und die Puppe"

The Dwarfs (Pinter) 6:411; 11:438; 15:423; 27:385-86; 73:249

Dwell in the Wilderness (Bessie) 23:58-9, 61

"The Dweller in the Gulf" (Smith) 43:420

"Dweller in the Martian Depths" (Smith) 43:422

Dwellers in the Land: The Bioregional Vision (Sale) 68:352-54

"The Dwelling" (Ammons) 57:53, 55

"The Dwelling House" (Turco) 11:550-51

The Dwelling Places of God (Vesaas)
  See *Guds bustader*

"Dwellings" (Guillevic) 33:192

"Dyâli" (Cesaire) 112:19

"D'yer Maker" (Page and Plant) 12:476, 482

The Dyer's Hand and Other Essays (Auden) 2:22, 24-5; 3:24-5; 4:34; 6:16; 14:27, 31

"Dying" (Oates)   6:370

"Dying" (Stern)   39:237

"Dying: An Introduction" (Sissman)   9:492

Dying: An Introduction (Sissman)   9:489-90, 492; 18:488

"A Dying Art" (Mahon)   27:290

A Dying Colonialism (Fanon)
   See *L'an V de la révolution algérienne*

The Dying Earth (Vance)   35:417-23, 425-28

"Dying for Love" (Shields)   113:408, 426, 429-30

"Dying for Survival" (Cousteau)   30:106

"The Dying Garden" (Nemerov)   36:306

The Dying Gaul and Other Writings (Jones)   13:312; 42:238-39

"The Dying Goddess" (Kizer)   15:309; 39:169; 80:184

Dying, in Other Words (Gee)   57:218-21

Dying Inside (Silverberg)   7:425

"The Dying Man" (Roethke)   8:455, 460; 101:286

"The Dying Miner" (Guthrie)   35:193

"The Dying Night" (Asimov)   26:44-5

"A Dying Race" (Motion)   47:286, 293

Dying Young (Leimbach)   65:63-6

"Dykhanie" ("As Breathing and Consciousness Return"; "Breathing") (Solzhenitsyn)   78:403-04

Dylan Thomas: No Man More Magical (Sinclair)   14:488

Dymer (Lewis)   27:258, 265

Dymkov's View of the Universe (Leonov)   92:278

"Dynamite" (Smiley)   53:348-49

Dynamite Voices I: Black Poets of the 1960's (Madhubuti)   73:196, 202-04, 207

"The Dynasts" (Blunden)   56:38

Dynasty of Death (Caldwell)   28:55-7, 59-60, 65, 67; 39:302-03

"Dyslexia" (Pesetsky)   28:358

Dzhamilia (Aitmatov)   71:3, 6, 10, 13, 16

Dziennik (*Diary*) (Gombrowicz)   7:124; 49:122-23, 131

Dziura w niebe (Konwicki)   117:285

Dziura w niebie (*A Hole in the Sky*) (Konwicki)   8:326; 117:257, 284

"E" (Merrill)   8:384-85

"E & O E" (Tolson)   105:265, 271, 284

E la nave va (*And the Ship Sails On*; *The Ship Sails On*) (Fellini)   85:51, 60, 71, 75, 78, 81-2

E. M. Forster: The New Collected Short Stories (Forster)   45:140

"E muet mutant" (Brossard)   115:141

"E se" (Buzzati)   36:97

E stato cosi (*The Dry Heart*) (Ginzburg)   11:228-29; 54:193, 198, 206; 70:281, 283

"E Unibus Plurnam: Television and U. S. Fiction" (Wallace)   114:388

"Each Bird Walking" (Gallagher)   63:117

"Each Dawn" (Levine)   33:275

"Each Day of Summer" (Swenson)   106:339

Each Man in His Darkness (Green)
   See *Chaque homme dans sa nuit*

Each Man's Son (MacLennan)   2:257; 14:340, 342; 92:322, 326-27, 341-42, 347

"Each Night" (Ignatow)   40:258

"Each Other" (Lessing)   22:278

"The Eagle" (Castellanos)   66:60

"The Eagle" (Tate)   14:532

The Eagle and the Iron Cross (Swarthout)   35:401, 403

The Eagle and the Raven (Michener)   109:326

"Eagle Descending" (Warren)   39:274

Eagle Eye (Calisher)   4:87-8

"Eagle Flies on Friday; Greyhound Runs at Dawn" (Hillis)   66:197

Eagle Fur (Peck)   17:343

The Eagle Has Two Heads (Cocteau)
   See *L'aigle à deux têtes*

Eagle in the Sky (Smith)   33:375

The Eagle of the Ninth (Sutcliff)   26:425-30, 432-35, 437, 439-40

The Eagle on the Coin (Cassill)   23:102

Eagle or Sun? (Paz)   3:375; 6:398

"Eagle Poem" (Harjo)   83:286

"Eagle Squadron" (Forester)   35:173

"The Eagles" (Guillen)   48:159

Eagles and Traces (Transtroemer)
   See *Klanger och spår*

The Eagles Gather (Caldwell)   28:56-7; 39:302-03

"The Eagle's Mile" (Dickey)   109:246-47, 251, 273

The Eagle's Mile (Dickey)   109:236, 245-46, 264

Eagle's Nest (Kavan)   13:316

"Eaglet Tricks" (Musgrave)   54:341

Ealdwood (Cherryh)   35:113

"The Ear" (Ayrton)   7:18

An Ear in Bartram's Tree: Selected Poems, 1957-1967 (Williams)   13:600

"Ear of Corn" (Lowell)   11:331

The Ear of the Other (Derrida)
   See *L'oreille de l'autre*

"Ear To the Ground" (Sillitoe)   57:396

"Earl Casillis's Lady" (Warner)   19:461

"Earl Grey" (Keillor)   115:295

"Earliest Recollection" (Ammons)   57:54

"Early Americana" (Richter)   30:329

Early Americana and Other Stories (Richter)   30:306-07, 311, 314-15, 319, 323

The Early Asimov; or, Eleven Years of Trying (Asimov)   3:16; 26:38

Early Autumn (Parker)   27:367

The Early Ayn Rand (Rand)   79:373

"Early Copper" (Sandburg)   35:356

The Early Cranes (Aitmatov)
   See *Rannie zhuravli*

"Early Dark" (Price)   43:347; 63:325

"Early Darkness" (Gluck)   81:167, 170

Early Elkin (Elkin)   51:96

"Early Evening Algebra" (Simic)   49:343; 68:378

"Early Evening Quarrel" (Hughes)   15:292

"Early Frost" (Norris)   14:387

"Early Grave" (Major)   19:298

"Early Harvest" (Santos)   22:363

"Early in the Morning" (Lustig)   56:185-86

"Early in the Summer of 1970" (Yehoshua)   13:617; 31:471, 473

Early in the Summer of 1970 (Yehoshua)   13:617-18; 31:471

Early Man and the Ocean: A Search for the Beginnings of Navigation and Seaborne Civilizations (Heyerdahl)   26:194

"Early Marriage" (Richter)   30:307

"Early Mondrian" (O'Hara)   78:344

Early Moon (Sandburg)   35:357

Early Morning (Bond)   4:69-70; 6:86; 13:98, 102; 23:66

"Early Morning: Cape Cod" (Swenson)   106:339

"Early Morning Feed" (Redgrove)   6:445

"Early Morning in Early April" (Ammons)   57:58-9

"Early Morning Rain" (Lightfoot)   26:279

"Early Noon" (Bachmann)
   See "Früher Mittag"

"Early Poems" (Tate)   14:532

Early Poems, 1935-1955 (Paz)   4:397; 6:398; 10:390; 51:333; 65:197

"Early Pompeian" (Walcott)   25:456; 42:423

"The Early Purges" (Heaney)   25:244

Early Selected y mas: Poems, 1949-1966 (Blackburn)   43:62-4

The Early Spanish Main (Sauer)   70:331, 351

Early Spring (Ozu)   16:448, 450, 455

Early Summer (Ozu)   16:449, 451

"Early Waking" (Zweig)   34:379

"Early Walk" (Pastan)   27:368

The Early Williamson (Williamson)   29:456-57

The Early Years (Derleth)   31:126

"Earnest Money" (Dorris)   109:307, 310

The Earp Brothers of Tombstone: The Story of Mrs. Virgil Earp (Waters)   88:359-60

"The Earring" (Woolrich)   77:389

"The Ears of Johnny Bear" ("Johnny Bear") (Steinbeck)   13:530

"Earth" (Creeley)   78:154

"The Earth" (Pasternak)   63:312

"Earth" (Redgrove)   6:445

"The Earth" (Sexton)   6:494

"Earth" (Voznesensky)   57:419

"Earth" (Walcott)   9:557

"Earth and I Give You Turquoise" (Momaday)   85:231, 262

The Earth Compels (MacNeice)   10:326; 53:231, 234-35

"Earth Dweller" (Stafford)   29:383

"The Earth Eats Everything" (Smith)   64:393

Earth Erect (Popa)
   See *Uspravna zemlja*

"The Earth from this Distance" (Dobyns)   37:82

Earth House Hold: Technical Notes and Queries to Fellow Dharma Revolutionaries (Snyder)   5:393; 32:389, 391, 394, 396, 399

Earth Is Room Enough: Science Fiction Tales of Our Own Planet (Asimov)   26:40

The Earth Is the Lord's (Caldwell)   28:57; 39:302-03

"The Earth Lover" (Prichard)   46:337

The Earth Lover and Other Verses (Prichard)   46:337

"The Earth Men" (Bradbury)   42:38

"Earth, Moon" (Boyle)   36:58

"The Earth of July" (Mahapatra)   33:279

The Earth: Planet Number Three (Branley)   21:17-18

"Earth Psalm" (Levertov)   15:337

Earth Stopped (White)   30:449

"The Earth That Falls Away" (Avison)   97:79, 84, 93

Earth upon Earth (Tzara)
   See *Terre sur terre*

"Earth Walk" (Meredith)   13:375

Earth Walk: New and Selected Poems (Meredith)   4:347-49; 13:375; 55:193

Earth Worms (Innaurato)   21:193-94

"Earth Your Dancing Place" (Swenson)   106:346

The Earth-Bound, 1924-1944 (Lewis)   41:254

"Earth-Bread" (Still)   49:365

Earthdivers (Vizenor)   103:285, 288-89, 292-93, 296-98, 310, 327

Earthfasts (Mayne)   12:392-93, 396, 398, 401-02, 404-06

Earthlight (Clarke)   **13**:155; **35**:121
Earthlight (MacEwen)   **55**:163
Earthly Bread (Mewshaw)   **9**:376-77
Earthly Possessions (Tyler)   **11**:553-54; **18**:529-
   30; **28**:432; **44**:315; **59**:202; **103**:216-17,
   222-25, 228, 235, 237, 240-44, 256, 259,
   270, 273
Earthly Powers (Burgess)   **22**:75-9; **40**:119,
   122, 124; **62**:124-25, 127, 132-33, 136;
   81:303-04, 307, 310
Earthman, Come Home (Blish)   **14**:85
"Earth-Numb" (Hughes)   **37**:177-78
Earthquake (Puzo)   **107**:211, 213
An Earthquake in My Family (Federspiel)
   42:145-46
Earth's Changing Climate (Gallant)   **17**:132-
   33
Earth's Children (Auel)   **31**:23
Earthsea Trilogy (Le Guin)   **13**:347, 350; **22**:270
"Earthset and the Evening Star" (Asimov)
   19:28
Earthsleep: A Poem (Chappell)   **40**:143-45;
   78:91-3, 96, 111
"Earth-Visitors" (Slessor)   **14**:497
Earth-Visitors (Slessor)   **14**:495-96
"The Earthwoman and the Waterwoman"
   (Levertov)   **66**:238
Earthworks (Aldiss)   **14**:12-13
Earthworks: Poems, 1960-1970 (Hochman)
   3:250; **8**:297
Earthworms (Innaurato)   **60**:201
*Earthy Delights, Unearthly Adornments: Ameri-
   can Writers as Image Makers* (Morris)
   18:353; **37**:316
"Earwigs" (Carver)   **55**:276
Earwitness: Fifty Characters (Canetti)
   See *Der Ohrenzeuge: Fünfzig Charaktere*
"East" (Hoffman)   **6**:244; **13**:289
East and West (Buck)   **7**:34
*East and West: Selected Poems of George
   Faludy* (Faludy)   **42**:136-41
*East and West: The Collected Short Stories of W.
   Somerset Maugham (Altogether: The Col-
   lected Stories of W. Somerset Maugham)*
   (Maugham)   **1**:204; **67**:205, 209
"East Coast Journey" (Baxter)   **14**:63
"East Coker" (Eliot)   **1**:92; **3**:139; **6**:165;
   10:168; **13**:201-02; **15**:215-16; **34**:527,
   530; **55**:374
*East: Elegy for the East End and Its Energetic
   Waste* (Berkoff)   **56**:12-14, 16
*The East End Plays (Beautiful City; Better Liv-
   ing; Criminals in Love)* (Walker)   **44**:329-
   33; **61**:431-33
"East European Cooking" (Simic)   **49**:335-36
East India and Company (Morand)   **41**:298-
   99
East Is East (Boyle)   **90**:49-61
East of Eden (Kazan)   **16**:364-69; **63**:226-27,
   233
East of Eden (Steinbeck)   **1**:325-27; **5**:407;
   9:512-15, 517-20; **21**:367, 371, 374-75,
   378, 382-83, 385-86, 391; **34**:405-07,
   409-10, 413-15; **45**:369-85; **59**:350-51,
   353
The East of Eden Letters (Steinbeck)   **59**:348
East of Farewell (Hunt)   **3**:252
East of Suez (Maugham)   **11**:369
East of the City (Dudek)   **11**:159; **19**:136
"East of the Sun and West of the Moon"
   (Merwin)   **8**:389; **88**:205
East Side General (Slaughter)   **29**:375
"East Side Story" (Seger)   **35**:380, 382

East Slope (Paz)
   See *Ladera este*
"East Texas Red" (Guthrie)   **35**:190-91, 193
East, West (Rushdie)   **100**:287, 290, 293, 315
East Wind: West Wind (Buck)   **11**:70-2, 76
"Eastbourne" (Montale)   **9**:387-88
"Easter" (Avison)   **97**:90
"Easter" (Broumas)   **73**:8
"Easter" (Kinnell)   **5**:217
"Easter" (Nemerov)   **36**:306
"Easter" (O'Hara)   **2**:323; **13**:426; **78**:355
Easter (Smith)   **12**:543
"Easter 1918" (Christie)   **110**:125, 127
"An Easter Carol" (Clarke)   **53**:95
The Easter Egg (Reaney)   **13**:472, 475
"Easter Hymn" (Hope)   **51**:211, 220-21
Easter in New York (Cendrars)
   See *Les pâques*
"Easter in Pittsburgh" (Laughlin)   **49**:220, 225
"Easter Island" (Kristofferson)   **26**:269
Easter Island (Kristofferson)   **26**:269
"The Easter Lilies" (Gardam)   **43**:171
"Easter Morning" (Ammons)   **25**:46; **57**:49,
   51; **108**:56-7
"Easter Morning" (Clampitt)   **32**:114
Easter Parade (Yates)   **8**:555-56
"Easter Rising" (MacDiarmid)   **11**:336
"Easter Sunday" (Ginsberg)   **36**:185
"Easter Sunday" (Souster)   **14**:503
Eastern Slope (Paz)
   See *Ladera este*
Eastern Standard (Greenberg)   **57**:229-32
"The Eastmill Reception Centre" (Metcalf)
   37:306
Eastward Ha! (Perelman)   **9**:415-16; **15**:417-
   18
"Easy Boogie" (Hughes)   **108**:299-304
"The Easy House" (Dickey)   **28**:118
"Easy in the Islands" (Shacochis)   **39**:198-200
Easy in the Islands (Shacochis)   **39**:198-201
"Easy Knowledge" (Fuller)   **62**:193
"Easy Morning" (Lightfoot)   **26**:279
"An Easy One" (Weidman)   **7**:516
"Easy Rider" (Brautigan)   **12**:64, 67
"Easy Skanking" (Marley)   **17**:270-71
"Easy to Be Hard" (Ragni and Rado)   **17**:385
Easy to Kill (Christie)   **110**:112
Easy Travel to Other Planets (Mooney)   **25**:329-
   30
Easy Virtue (Coward)   **29**:131, 137, 139; **51**:69,
   77
"Eat" (Sapphire)   **99**:80
Eat (Warhol)   **20**:415-16
"Eat at Home" (McCartney)   **35**:279
The Eaten Heart (Aldington)   **49**:8, 10-13, 18
*Eaters of the Dead: The Manuscript of Ibn
   Fadlan, Relating His Experience with the
   Northmen in A.D. 922* (Crichton)   **54**:70;
   90:91
"Eating Alone in Restaurants" (Friedman)
   56:105
Eating at Arby's (Grayson)   **38**:211-12
"Eating Fish" (Johnston)   **51**:239, 246
"The Eating Match" (Bates)   **46**:62
"Eating Out" (Michaels)   **6**:324
"Eating Out the Angel of Death" (Simic)   **9**:481
Eating People Is Wrong (Bradbury)   **32**:49-51,
   53; **61**:34, 39-40, 42, 45
"Eating Poetry" (Strand)   **18**:516, 518; **41**:438;
   71:284, 286
"Eating Sparrows" (Gallagher)   **63**:120
"Eating the Other" (hooks)   **94**:150
"Eating the Pig" (Hall)   **13**:259

"Eating the Placenta" (Dixon)   **52**:100
"L'eau de Pâques" (Theriault)   **79**:407
L'eau vive (Giono)   **11**:232
"Eaux-meres" (Char)   **55**:289
"Eavesdropper" (Plath)   **51**:343; **111**:215
E.B. White: A Biography (Elledge)   **34**:425-32
"Ebano real" ("Royal Ebony") (Guillen)
   48:162; **79**:234, 240
"Ebb at Evening" (Everson)   **5**:123
Ebony and Crystal (Smith)   **43**:417
"Ebony and Ivory" (McCartney)   **35**:289-92
"Ebony Eyes" (Wonder)   **12**:660, 662
The Ebony Tower (Fowles)   **6**:186-89; **9**:213,
   216; **10**:188; **15**:23-32; **33**:171,173-74;
   87:147, 151-52, 158, 162-63, 177-78
"éboulis" (Cesaire)   **112**:30
Écartèlement (Drawn and Quartered) (Cioran)
   64:94-6
"Ecce homo" (Berryman)   **6**:64
"Ecce homo" (Corso)   **11**:123
"Ecce homo" (Gascoyne)   **45**:147-49, 157-58
"Ecce homo" (Raine)   **45**:330
"Ecce Tempus"   **75**:79
"Eccentric Motion" (Rukeyser)   **27**:405
The Eccentricities of a Nightingale (Williams)
   8:548-49
Ecclesiastes (Mahon)   **27**:287-88
*L'échange symbolique et la mort (Symbolic
   Exchange and Death)* (Baudrillard)   **60**:12-
   15, 18, 24, 33
Echec à la reine (Chedid)   **47**:82-3
"Echec et mât" (Damas)   **84**:179
"Echo" (Barth)   **3**:41; **9**:67, 70; **51**:23-4; **89**:4-
   5, 9-10, 12, 16, 19-20, 22-3, 26-7, 34,
   43-4, 48, 50, 54, 61, 63
"The Echo" (Bowles)   **19**:60; **53**:46, 49
"The Echo and the Nemesis" (Stafford)   **7**:459;
   19:430; **68**:422, 434, 449
The Echo at Coole (Clarke)   **6**:112; **9**:167
The Echo Chamber (Josipovici)   **43**:221-22
"Echo for the Promise of Georg Trakl's Life"
   (Wright)   **5**:520
The Echo Gate (Longley)   **29**:294-96
"Echo Of" (Creeley)   **36**:121
"Echo Tree" (Dumas)   **6**:145; **62**:153, 155,
   162
"Echoes" (Creeley)   **36**:121; **78**:140, 161
"Echoes" (Dinesen)   **10**:152; **95**:47-8
"Echoes" (Pink Floyd)   **35**:306, 311
Echoes (Creeley)   **36**:121
Echoes and Traces (Transtroemer)
   See *Klanger och spår*
"Echoes from the Great War" (Blunden)   **56**:44
Echoes Inside the Labyrinth (McGrath)   **59**:175
The Echoing Green: Three Elegies (Levi)
   41:249
The Echoing Grove (Lehmann)   **5**:235, 238
"Echo's Bones" (Beckett)   **9**:81
Echo's Bones and Other Precipitates (Beckett)
   9:80-1; **14**:78
"Une eclaircie" (Reverdy)   **53**:290
"Eclipse" (Fuller)   **28**:149
"Eclipse" (Pink Floyd)   **35**:306-07
The Eclipse (Antonioni)
   See *L'eclisse*
Eclipse (Hogan)   **73**:149-50, 154
The Eclipse (Oates)   **108**:376
Eclipse (Trumbo)   **19**:446-47
"Eclipse Calypso" (Thesen)   **56**:420
"Eclipse Morning" (Swenson)   **61**:405
Eclipse of Stars (Sachs)
   See *Sternverdunkelung*
"Eclipses" (Breton)   **54**:28

L'eclisse (The Eclipse) (Antonioni) 20:23, 26-8, 30-2

"Eclogue" (Ashbery) 77:43

"Eclogue" (Hall) 59:151, 153, 155-56

"Eclogue" (Ransom) 11:470

"Eclogue between the Motherless" (MacNeice) 53:231

"An Eclogue for Christmas" (MacNeice) 4:315; 10:324; 53:231, 233

"Eclogue from Iceland" (MacNeice) 53:231, 234

"Eclogue IV: Winter" ("Ekloga 4-aya: Zimnyaya") (Brodsky) 100:43-4, 49-50

Eclogues (Davenport) 38:144-45, 148

Eclogues (MacNeice) 4:317

Eclogues (Read) 4:442

L'école des cadavres (Celine) 3:104; 47:79

"Ecologue" (Ginsberg) 3:195; 36:185; 109:364

"Economía doméstica" ("Home Economics") (Castellanos) 66:61

"Economics" (Auden) 6:18

"The Economist's Song" (Kunitz) 6:287

Ecopoemas (Ecopoems) (Parra) 102:347, 355

Ecopoems (Parra)
   See Ecopoemas

"Ecossaise, Berceuse, Polonaise" (Fuchs) 22:159

Ecrire (Duras) 100:134-35, 148

Ecrits (Écrits: A Selection) (Lacan) 75:280, 284, 288, 290, 298, 314-15

Écrits: A Selection (Lacan)
   See Ecrits

L'écriture et la différence (Writing and Difference) (Derrida) 24:153; 87:72, 88, 104

"Écrivains et écrivants" ("Authors and Writers") (Barthes) 24:34; 83:98

"Ecstasy" (hooks) 94:157

"Ecstasy" (Olds) 39:187, 189

The Ecstasy Business (Condon) 45:94-5, 97

"Ecstasy of a Song" (Kunene) 85:175

The Ecstasy of Communication (Baudrillard) 60:36

The Ecstasy of Dr. Miriam Garner (Feinstein) 36:170

The Ecstasy of Matter (Le Clezio)
   See L'extase matérielle

The Ecstasy of Rita Joe (Ryga) 14:472

"Ecstatic" (Johnston) 51:254

Ecuador (Michaux) 8:392

Ecue-yamba-ó! (Carpentier) 11:102-04; 38:95-6, 98; 110:69, 75-7

"Ed è subito sera" (Quasimodo) 10:427

Ed è subito sera (Quasimodo) 10:428-29

"Eddie, Are You Kidding" (Zappa) 17:588

"Eddie Mac" (McGahern) 48:272

"Eddie the Eunuch" (Kristofferson) 26:269

"Eddy" (Musgrave) 54:334

The Eddy Duchin Story (Hart) 66:182

"Eden" (Scott) 22:372, 375

Eden (Lem) 40:290

Eden and After (Robbe-Grillet)
   See L'Eden et après

L'éden cinéma (Eden Cinema) (Duras) 40:176-78; 69:92, 95-6

Eden Cinema (Duras)
   See L'éden cinéma

"Eden, Eden" (MacEwen) 13:357

Eden End (Priestley) 2:346; 5:350-51; 34:365

L'Eden et après (Eden and After) (Robbe-Grillet) 1:289; 4:449; 43:367

Eden: Graphics and Poetry (Tomlinson) 45:394, 404-05

Edens Lost (Elliott) 38:178-79, 181

Edgar Allan Poe: A Study in Genius (Krutch) 24:286-87

Edgar Allen (Neufeld) 17:307-08, 311

"The Edgar Era" (Keillor)
   See "WLT"

"Edgar Jené and the Dream about the Dream" (Celan)
   See "Edgar Jené und der Traum vom Traume"

"Edgar Jené und der Traum vom Traume" ("Edgar Jené and the Dream about the Dream") (Celan) 19:89; 82:53

"Edgar Poe's Tradition" (McLuhan) 83:360

"Edge" (Gunnars) 69:260

"The Edge" (Komunyakaa) 94:230

"Edge" (Montague) 46:275-76

"The Edge" (Narayan) 28:301

"Edge" (Plath) 5:344; 9:427, 433-34; 14:424, 426; 17:360, 366; 62:406; 111:168, 206

The Edge (Francis) 102:131, 133-36, 139, 147-48, 158

An Edge in My Voice (Ellison) 42:133

The Edge of Being (Spender) 2:420; 5:401

Edge of Being: Poems (Spender) 91:261

The Edge of Darkness (Chase) 2:101

The Edge of Day (Lee)
   See Cider with Rosie

The Edge of Impossibility: Tragic Forms in Literature (Oates) 3:361

The Edge of Next Year (Stolz) 12:554-55

The Edge of Sadness (O'Connor) 14:389-90, 392-94

The Edge of the Alphabet (Frame) 6:190; 22:145-46, 148; 96:167, 174-76, 178-79, 182, 190-91, 195-96, 203, 217

"The Edge of the Forest" (Murray) 40:336-37

The Edge of the Paper (Tindall) 7:473

The Edge of the Sea (Carson) 71:94, 101-09

"The Edge of the World" (Cheever) 64:66

The Edible Woman (Atwood) 2:19-20; 3:19; 4:26, 28; 8:30-1, 34; 13:42, 44, 46; 15:37, 39; 25:63-4, 68; 44:146-47, 152-53; 84:50-2, 71, 78-9, 86, 90, 99, 107

Edipo Re (Oedipus Rex) (Pasolini) 20:260-61, 263-65, 267, 269; 106:226, 256

Edisto (Powell) 34:97-101

Edith Jackson (Guy) 26:143-45

Edith's Diary (Highsmith) 14:260; 42:215; 102:172-73, 190-91, 209

"Editorial" (Reading) 47:352

Edmond (Mamet) 46:252-55

Edmund Campion (Waugh) 107:358, 361

Edmund Husserl's "Origin of Geometry": An Introduction (Derrida)
   See Traduction et introduction à l'origine de la géométrie d'Edmund Husserl

"Edmund to Gloucester" (Snodgrass) 68:397

Edsel (Shapiro) 4:487; 53:333

"Eduard Munch" (Mahon) 27:286, 288

"A educão pela pedra" (Cabral de Melo Neto) 76:160, 164, 168

The Educated Imagination (Frye) 24:214, 226; 70:278

Educating Rita (Russell) 60:317-25

"Education" (Davies) 21:101

"Education" (Madhubuti) 73:207

"An Education" (Ozick) 7:288; 62:353-54

Education and the University (Leavis) 24:308

"Education by Poetry" (Frost) 9:221

Education by Stone (Cabral de Melo Neto)
   See Aeducacão pela pedra

L'éducation des filles (Mauriac) 9:369

Education Européenne (A European Educa-tion) (Gary) 25:184-86

An Education in Blood (Elman) 19:150

"Education of a Novelist" (Rich) 73:330

"The Education of Mingo" (Johnson) 51:234-36

The Education of Patrick Silver (Charyn) 8:136

The Education of Skinny Spew (Brenton) 31:57

Education through Art (Read) 4:443

"The Educational Experience" (Barthelme) 8:53; 115:80

"Edward" (Hughes) 4:236

"Edward and God" (Kundera) 32:260; 68:241, 261

The Edward Dahlberg Reader (Dahlberg) 7:63-4

The Edward Hoagland Reader (Hoagland) 28:183-85

"Edward the Conqueror" (Dahl) 79:176

Edward: The Final Days (Barker) 37:34

"Edward Weston in Mexico City" (Dacey) 51:80

Edwin (Mortimer) 43:308

Edwin Arlington Robinson (Winters) 32:460

Edwin Mullhouse: The Life and Death of an American Writer, 1943-1954, by Jeffrey Cartwright (Millhauser) 54:319-28, 330-31; 21:215-19; 109:161-62, 165-70, 173-74

"The Eel" (Montale)
   See "L'anguilla"

"The Eel Teller" (Shapcott) 38:404

"The Eemis Stane" (MacDiarmid) 19:285-86, 288; 63:252

"Eena Wales" (Bennett) 28:29

The Effect of Gamma Rays on Man-in-the-Moon Marigolds (Gamma Rays; Marigolds; Moon Marigolds) (Zindel) 6:586; 26:472-73

"L'effet du réel" (Barthes) 83:90

L'effet Glapion (The Glapion Effect) (Audiberti) 38:23

Effi Briest (Fassbinder) 20:108-09, 113-14, 116

The Efficient Cat (Valenzuela)
   See El gato eficaz

Effluences from the Sacred Cave: More Selected Essays and Reviews (Carruth) 84:125, 127, 129

"Effort at Speech" (Meredith) 4:348; 13:375

"Effort at Speech between Two People" (Rukeyser) 27:404-05

"Efforts of Affection" (Bishop) 32:44

"Efforts of Affection" (Moore) 1:230; 19:340; 47:264

L'effroi la joie (Char) 14:124

Efuru (Nwapa) 65:329-33

"Egg" (Hoffman) 6:244

"The Egg" (Snyder) 5:395

"The Egg and the Hen" (Lispector)
   See "O ovo e a galinha"

"The Egg and the Machine" (Frost) 10:193

"The Egg Boiler" (Brooks) 49:32

"An Egg for the Major" (Forester) 35:173

"The Egg Race" (Updike) 15:547-48

"Egg-Head" (Hughes) 14:270

The Egghead Republic: A Short Novel from the Horse Latitudes (Schmidt)
   See Die Gelehrtenrepublik: Kurzroman aus den Rossbreiten

"The Eggplant Epithalamion" (Jong) 6:267

"Eggs" (Olds) 85:289

Eggs (Howe) 47:174

"The Eggs Speak Up" (Arendt)   **98**:55
L'église (Celine)   **3**:104-05; **7**:43; **9**:154
The Ego and the Centaur (Garrigue)   **2**:153
"Ego Confessions" (Ginsberg)   **109**:333
"The Ego Is Always at the Wheel" (Schwartz)   **87**:348
The Ego Is Always at the Wheel: Bagatelles (Schwartz)   **45**:359-60; **87**:344, 348
"Ego Tripping" (Giovanni)   **64**:195; **117**:184, 197, 200
"The Egoist" (Neruda)
   See "El egoísta"
"The Egoist" (Nowlan)   **15**:398
"El egoísta" ("The Egoist"; "The Selfish One") (Neruda)   **62**:335
"The Egoist's Prayer" (Ezekiel)   **61**:108
"Egorushka's Destruction" (Leonov)
   See "Ghibel' Egorushki"
"Egorushka's Undoing" (Leonov)
   See "Ghibel' Egorushki"
Ego-Tripping and Other Poems for Young People (Giovanni)   **117**:168, 184, 191
"The Egret" (Oliver)   **98**:289
"Egrets" (Oliver)   **34**:247; **98**:257
"Egypt" (H. D.)   **73**:105
"Egypt from My Inside" (Golding)   **3**:199; **27**:169
The Egypt Game (Snyder)   **17**:470-72
"Egypt, Tobago" (Walcott)   **42**:423
An Egyptian Bondage and Other Stories (Kessler)   **4**:269
The Egyptian Cross Mystery (Queen)   **11**:460
"Egyptian Gold" (Garrett)   **3**:192; **11**:219; **51**:148
An Egyptian Journal (Golding)   **81**:323-24
"An Egyptian Passage" (Weiss)   **14**:556
The Egyptians (Asimov)   **76**:312
Egyptology (Foreman)   **50**:163, 168
Eh Joe (Beckett)   **6**:39, 45; **9**:83-4; **18**:42-3
Die Ehe des Herrn Mississippi (*The Marriage of Mr. Mississippi*) (Duerrenmatt)   **102**:53, 56-7, 74, 76-8, 80
Die Ehe des Herrn Mississippi (*Fools Are Passing Through*; *The Marriage of Mr. Mississippi*) (Durrenmatt)   **4**:140; **8**:194; **11**:168-69; **15**:194-95, 198; **43**:125
Die Ehen in Philippsburg (*Marriage in Philippsburg*) (Walser)   **27**:456-60, 467
"Ehrengard" (Dinesen)   **10**:145; **29**:156; **95**:52-4
Eiche und Angora (*The Rabbit Race*) (Walser)   **27**:455, 461-62, 465
Eichmann in Jerusalem: A Report on the Banality of Evil (Arendt)   **66**:26-7, 31; **98**:6, 11, 18, 27, 30-1, 34, 43, 48-9, 53, 55
"Eidolon" (H. D.)   **31**:207
"Eidolon (Phantom) Parade" (Scannell)   **49**:331
"The Eiffel Tower" (Buzzati)   **36**:94
The Eiger Sanction (Trevanian)   **29**:429-32
"VIII" (Kinnell)   **3**:268; **13**:322
8 1/2 (Fellini)
   See *Otto e Mezzo*
"Eight Aspects of Melissa" (Durrell)   **27**:97
Eight Days (Seifert)
   See *Osm dnu*
"Eight Days a Week" (Lennon and McCartney)   **35**:275
Eight Days of Luke (Jones)   **26**:225, 230
"Eight for Ornette's Music" (Rexroth)   **22**:346
"Eight Games of Strategy" (Morgan)   **2**:295
Eight Hours Don't Make a Day (Fassbinder)   **20**:106
Eight Hundred Rubles (Neihardt)   **32**:331

Eight Men (Wright)   **3**:545; **9**:584-85; **14**:596, 598; **21**:437; **74**:382, 390
8 Million Ways to Die (Stone)   **73**:382
Eight Mortal Ladies Possessed (Williams)   **5**:502-03; **7**:544
"Eight O'Clock One Morning" (Grau)   **9**:240
"Eight People on a Golf Course and One Bird of Freedom Flying Over" (Ferlinghetti)   **111**:66
"Eight Plus" (Creeley)   **78**:161
Eight Plus One (Cormier)   **30**:87
"Eight Poems on Portraits of the Foot" (Logan)   **5**:253
"Eighteen Days without You" (Sexton)   **6**:492
1876: A Novel (Vidal)   **8**:525-26; **33**:407, 409-11; **72**:377, 382-85, 387, 389, 391-93, 395-96, 399-402, 404
Eighteen Short Songs of the Bitter Motherland (Ritsos)
   See *Dekachto lianotragouda tes pikres patridas*
18 Stories (Boell)   **27**:63; **72**:67, 73
"Eighteen West Eleventh Street" (Merrill)   **6**:323
"1889 and the Devil's Mode" (Burgess)   **62**:139
Eighteenth-Century Women Poets: An Oxford Anthology   **65**:316-17, 343
"1830" (Davenport)   **6**:125
An Eighteen-Year-Old Looks Back on Life (Maynard)   **23**:289
"Eighth Air Force" (Jarrell)   **9**:299; **13**:300, 302-03; **49**:193
The Eighth Day (Wilder)   **1**:366; **6**:576-78; **10**:533, 535; **15**:575; **82**:354-56, 367-68, 375, 378
"The Eighth Ditch" (Baraka)   **115**:17
The Eighth Ditch (*Dante*) (Baraka)   **33**:59; **115**:10, 17
"The Eighth Voyage of Sinbad" (Millhauser)   **109**:157-59, 161
"Eighty" (Berryman)   **13**:81
"Eighty Acres" (Wright)   **53**:425
"The Eighty Yard Run" (Shaw)   **34**:369-70
Eighty-Eight Poems (Hemingway)   **19**:219
The Eighty-Minute Hour: A Space Opera (Aldiss)   **5**:15-16; **14**:14
Eighty-Seventh Precinct Series (Hunter)   **31**:225
Eighty-Sixed (Feinberg)   **59**:59-62
"Eileann Chanaidh" (Raine)   **45**:341
Eimi (Cummings)   **1**:68; **12**:142-43, 145, 161; **15**:161; **68**:32, 35, 38-9, 48-50
Einer fur alle, alle fur einen (Fo)   **32**:172
Einführung in die Metaphysik (Heidegger)   **24**:264
Das Einhorn (*The Unicorn*) (Walser)   **27**:456, 459-61, 464, 467
Einladung an alle (Wellershoff)   **46**:435-36
"Der Einsame" (Celan)   **10**:104
"Einstein" (MacLeish)   **8**:359; **14**:337; **68**:271, 273-76, 286, 289-90
The Einstein Intersection (Delany)   **8**:168-69; **14**:146; **38**:149-50, 152, 154, 160-61
Einstein on the Beach (Wilson)   **9**:577
Einstein überquert die Elbe bei Hamburg (Lenz)   **27**:251-52
"Einstein's Bathrobe" (Moss)   **45**:289
Einstein's Dreams (Lightman)   **81**:71-80
Einstein's Monsters (Amis)   **62**:6-11, 15-16
"Einundzwanzig Punkte du zen *Physikern*" ("Twenty-One Points about The *Physicists*") (Durrenmatt)   **15**:196
Einzelheiten (*Details*; *Odds and Ends*) (Enzensberger)   **43**:154

Eirei no koe (Mishima)   **27**:342
"Eisenheim the Illusionist" (Millhauser)   **109**:157-58, 161, 171
Eisenhower, My Eisenhower (Charyn)   **5**:104
"Eisenhower's Visit to Franco, 1959" (Wright)   **3**:540
"The Ejection Seat" (Aksyonov)   **101**:15
"Ekloga 4-aya: Zimnyaya" (Brodsky)
   See "Eclogue IV: Winter"
El (*This Strange Passion*) (Bunuel)   **16**:135, 147, 150-51; **80**:23-4, 27-31, 34, 47, 50
"El Greco" (Dubie)   **36**:130, 137
"El Greco: Espolio" (Birney)   **6**:77; **11**:50
El hermano (Linney)   **51**:260
"Elaboration" (Carruth)   **84**:129
"Elaine in a Bikini" (Johnston)   **51**:240, 245-46
Elämä ja aurinko (*Life and Sun*) (Sillanpaa)   **19**:417-19
"L'élan vital" (Montale)   **9**:388
"Elbow Room" (McPherson)   **77**:357-59, 362-63, 372-73, 375, 377-78, 382-85
Elbow Room (McPherson)   **19**:310; **77**:355-57, 362, 364, 366, 374, 378, 382, 384
Elbowing the Seducer (Gertler)   **34**:49-53
"The Elder Gods" (Campbell)   **32**:75
"The Elder Lady" (Borges)   **10**:67
The Elder Sister (Swinnerton)   **31**:423
The Elder Statesman (Eliot)   **1**:91; **6**:168; **13**:195; **15**:209-10; **41**:143, 145-46, 148, 152
"Elderly Politicians" (Hughes)   **10**:279
Elders and Betters (Compton-Burnett)   **15**:140; **34**:496
"The Eldest" (Ferber)   **93**:138, 141
"The Eldest of Things" (Abbott)   **48**:4, 7
Eldorado Red (Goines)   **80**:96
Eleanor (Lerman)   **56**:178-79
"Eleanor on the Cliff" (Wakoski)   **40**:456
"Eleanor Rigby" (Lennon and McCartney)   **35**:293
The Elected Member (Rubens)   **19**:402; **31**:351-52
Elected Silence: The Autobiography of Thomas Merton (Merton)   **3**:336
"Election Day" (Hansen)   **38**:240
"Elective Affinities" (Jacobsen)   **48**:192, 194
"Electra on Azalea Path" (Plath)   **17**:360; **50**:448; **51**:344; **111**:178, 219, 221
"Electric Aunt Jemima" (Zappa)   **17**:586
"An Electric Blanket" (Frame)   **96**:215
Electric City and Other Stories (Grace)   **56**:122-23
"Electric Guitar" (Byrne)   **26**:98
The Electric Kool-Aid Acid Test (Wolfe)   **2**:482; **9**:578; **35**:451-56, 459-66; **51**:419-20
The Electric Life (Birkerts)   **116**:152, 157
"An Electric Sign Goes Dark" (Sandburg)   **35**:341
"Electrical Storm" (Hayden)   **37**:151
The Electrification of the Soviet Union (Raine)   **103**:196-97, 199
The Electromagnetic Spectrum: Key to the Universe (Branley)   **21**:23
The Electronic Nigger (Bullins)   **1**:47; **5**:82
"The Electronic Siege" (Campbell)   **32**:73
"Elegi" ("Elegy") (Transtroemer)   **65**:235-36
"Elegía" (Castellanos)   **66**:50-1
Elegia (*Elegy*) (Neruda)   **28**:310; **62**:333, 336
"Elegía para cantar" ("Elegy for Singing") (Neruda)   **62**:336
"Elegiac Calculation" (Szymborska)   **99**:200
Elegiac Feelings American (Corso)   **1**:64

"Elegiac Stanzas for Alban Berg" (Gascoyne)
  See "Strophes elegiaque: A la memoire
  d'Alban Berg"
"Elegías del amado fantasma" (Castellanos)
  66:50
"Elegie" (Smith)   12:537
"Elégie des circoncis" ("Elegy of the Circum-
  cised") (Senghor)   54:391
"Elegies" (Ekelof)   27:110
"Elegies" (Levertov)   5:249
"Elegies" (Rukeyser)   27:408
Elegies (Dunn)   40:170-72
Elegies (Endo)   54:160
Elegies (Rukeyser)   27:407
"Elegies for Paradise Valley" (Hayden)   14:241;
  37:154, 156, 158
"Elegies for the Ochre Deer on the Walls at
  Lascaux" (Dubie)   36:139-40, 142
"The Elegies of Jutting Rock" (Elytis)   100:190
"Elegy" (Auden)   4:33
"Elegy" (Berry)   46:71-3
"Elegy" (Bidart)   33:76
"Elegy" (Broumas)   73:8
"Elegy" (Brown)   5:77
"Elegy" (Cohen)   38:131
"Elegy" (Ekeloef)
  See *En Mölna-elegi*
"Elegy" (Forche)   86:139, 142
"Elegy" (Gunn)   32:214
"Elegy" (Heaney)   25:245; 74:159
"The Elegy" ("Variations on a Theme of the
  Seventeenth Century") (Hope)   51:217,
  221
"Elegy" (Johnston)   51:249
"Elegy" (Kunene)   85:160, 162
"Elegy" (Morgan)   2:295
"Elegy" (Roethke)   101:269, 271
"Elegy" (Simic)   22:381
"Elegy" (Stafford)   29:385
"Elegy" (Transtroemer)
  See "Elegi"
"Elegy" (Walcott)   42:421; 76:279-82
"Elegy" (Young)   19:480
Elegy (Neruda)
  See *Elegía*
Elegy (West)   9:562
"Elegy 1969" (Strand)   71:284
An Elegy and Other Poems (Blunden)   56:47
"Elegy Anticipating Death" (Barker)   48:9
"Elegy Asking That It Be the Last" (Dubie)
  36:130
"Elegy at the Year's End" (Baxter)   14:62
"Elegy for a Cricket" (Cunningham)   31:98
"Elegy for a Dead Soldier" (Shapiro)   15:475,
  478
"Elegy for a Freelance" (Carter)   5:103
Elegy for a Lady (Miller)   47:253
"Elegy for a Warbler" (Pack)   13:439
"Elegy for a Youth Changed to a Swan" (Boland)
  67:43
"Elegy for Alto" (Okigbo)   25:353, 356;
  84:312, 316, 321, 331-32
"Elegy for Camagüey" (Guillen)   79:230
"Elegy for Dead Animals" (Martin)   89:111,
  118
"Elegy for Father Stephen" (Merton)   83:395
"An Elegy for Five Old Ladies" (Merton)
  83:395
"Elegy for Jane" (Roethke)   8:455; 11:483;
  46:363; 101:269, 304, 327, 329-30, 333
"Elegy for John Donne" (Brodsky)
  See "The Great Elegy for John Donne"
"Elegy for Margaret" (Spender)   41:426, 428;

91:261
"Elegy for Mitch Stuart" (Stuart)   34:375
"Elegy for Msizi" (Kunene)   85:165-66
"Elegy for My Father" (Moss)   7:247; 45:290,
  292; 50:353
"Elegy for My Father" (Strand)   6:521-22;
  18:519; 71:279
"Elegy for My Friend E. Galo" (Kunene)
  85:165
"Elegy for My Sister" (Moss)   45:286, 289,
  292; 50:353
"Elegy for Sam" (Ciardi)   40:154
"Elegy for Singing" (Neruda)
  See "Elegía para cantar"
"Elegy for Slit-Drum" (Okigbo)   25:354, 356;
  84:314, 316, 321
"Elegy for Sylvia Plath" (Schaeffer)   6:489
"Elegy for the Gas Dowsers" (MacBeth)   9:340
"Elegy for the Giant Tortoises" (Atwood)
  15:37
"Elegy for the Labouring Poor" (Hooker)
  43:196-97, 199-200
"Elegy for the Lost Parish" (Dunn)   40:168
"Elegy for the Monastery Barn" (Merton)
  83:394
"An Elegy for the Unknown Man Nicknamed
  Donda" (Kunene)   85:165
"Elegy for Thelonious" (Komunyakaa)   86:191
"Elegy for Wesley Wells" (Hall)   37:143
"Elegy for Y. Z." (Milosz)   82:299, 304
"Elegy in a Botanic Garden" (Slessor)   14:492
"Elegy in a Kensington Churchyard" (Spark)
  40:393
"Elegy in a Rainbow" (Brooks)   49:36, 38
"Elegy in an Abandoned Boatyard" (Smith)
  42:349, 353-54
"Elegy Just in Case" (Ciardi)   40:157; 44:381,
  383
"Elegy of Fortinbras" (Herbert)
  See "Tren Fortynbrasa"
"Elegy of Midnight" (Senghor)   54:391
"Elegy of the Circumcised" (Senghor)
  See "Elégie des circoncis"
"Elegy of the Waters" (Senghor)   54:391
"Elegy of the Wind" (Okigbo)   25:354; 84:316
Elegy on Dead Fashion (Sitwell)   9:493-96
"Elegy on Spain" (Barker)   48:10-11, 15, 20,
  23
"Elegy on the Closing of the French Brothels"
  (Durrell)   27:97
"An Elegy on the Death of Kenneth Patchen"
  (Ferlinghetti)   6:184; 111:65
"Elegy on the Lost Child" (Amichai)   22:29
"The Elegy on the Lost Child" (Amichai)   57:44
"An Elegy: R. R. 1916-1941" (Gascoyne)
  45:157
"Elegy to Emmett Till" (Guillen)   48:164;
  79:230
Elegy to John Donne and Other Poems
  (Brodsky)   100:58-9
"An Elegy to the Guevera" (Rosenblatt)
  See "The Bee Hive"
"Elegy to the Pulley of Superior Oblique"
  (Dubie)   36:133
"Elegy to the Sioux" (Dubie)   36:133
"Elegy—The Streets" (Denby)   48:82
"The Element" (Merwin)   8:390
"Element" (Page)   18:379
The Elemental Odes (Neruda)
  See *Odas elementales*
"Elementary Attitudes" (Van Duyn)   63:440;
  116:420
"Elementary Cosmogony" (Simic)   9:478;

68:373
Elementary Odes (Neruda)
  See *Odas elementales*
"An Elementary School Classroom" (Spender)
  91:263
The Elements (Hooker)   43:196-97
"Elements constitutifs d'une civilisation
  d'inspiration négro-af ricaine" (Senghor)
  54:409
Eléments de sémiologie (*Elements of Semiol-
  ogy*) (Barthes)   24:26, 42; 83:85, 94
"Elements of Immortality" (Rudnik)   7:384
The Elements of Poetry (FitzGerald)   19:178
The Elements of San Joaquin (Soto)   32:401-
  02, 404-05; 80:277-79, 281-83, 285,
  292-95, 298
Elements of Semiology (Barthes)
  See *Eléments de sémiologie*
The Elements of Style (White)   10:528; 34:425,
  428; 39:369-71, 373, 377, 379
"Elephant" (Carver)   53:62, 64-7; 55:278
"Elephant" (Neruda)   7:260
Elephant, and Other Stories (Carver)   53:62,
  66-7
The Elephant and the Kangaroo (White)
  30:442, 449
Elephant Bangs Train (Kotzwinkle)   5:220;
  14:309; 35:253-54
"Elephant Hunt" (Cendrars)   106:158
The Elephant Man (Lynch)   66:257, 259-60,
  269, 271
The Elephant Man (Pomerance)   13:444-46
"The Elephant Shooter" (Paton)   25:360
"The Elephant-Man" (Hill)   113:281
Elephants Can Remember (Christie)   48:72;
  110:123
"Elethia" (Walker)   103:410-12, 423
Eleuthéria (Beckett)   57:99; 59:254; 83:115
"The Elevator" (Bowering)   47:22
"Eleven" (MacLeish)   68:285
Eleven (Highsmith)   102:172
"Eleven Addresses to the Lord" (Berryman)
  3:68, 70; 6:64; 25:92, 95; 62:44, 66, 74-
  5
Eleven Declarations of War (Deighton)
  See *Declarations of War*
Eleven Kinds of Loneliness (Yates)   7:554;
  23:481-82
"Eleven O'Clock at Night" (Bly)   38:54
"Eleven Poems of Exhaustion" (L'Heureux)
  52:273
Eleven Poems on the Same Theme (Warren)
  4:579; 13:573-77
"Eleven Political Poems" (Buckley)   57:126,
  131
Eleven Stained-Glass Segments (Endo)   54:160
"11Outlined Epitaphs" (Dylan)   6:157; 77:178
"Eleventh Avenue Racket" (Sandburg)   35:352
"The Eleventh Floor" (Baxter)   45:53; 78:18
"11th R. S. R." (Blunden)   56:41, 43
The Eleventh Summer (Gebler)   39:60-2
"El-Hajj Malik El-Shabazz" (Hayden)   37:155
Eli: A Mystery Play on the Sufferings of Israel
  (Sachs)   14:475; 98:322, 332, 334-36,
  344-45
Eli and the Thirteenth Confession (Nyro)
  17:312-13, 315, 317-21
"Eli the Fanatic" (Roth)   66:418
Elia Kazan: A Life (Kazan)   63:223-33
"Elias Schneebaum" (Kaplan)   50:55, 57
Elidor (Garner)   17:134-40, 142-44, 149, 151
Eliduc (Fowles)   87:150, 153
Eligible Men (Elkin)

See *Searches and Seizures*
The Eligible Men (Elkin)　6:169
"El eliglia" (Cernuda)　54:48
"Elimination" (Campbell)　32:78, 80
Elimination Dance (Ondaatje)　51:317
"Eli's Comin'" (Nyro)　17:318
"Elisa and Mary" (Musgrave)　54:334
"Elisabetta, Carlotta, Catherine" ("Raising the Demon") (Kaplan)　50:55, 57
Elisabetta: Quasi per Caso una Donna (*Almost By Chance A Woman: Elizabeth*) (Fo)　109:101, 116, 119, 140
"Elite 6" (Wah)　44:327
"Elite 9" (Wah)　44:324
"The Elite Viewer" (Colwin)　84:150
"Elixir" (Murphy)　41:319
"Elizabeth" (Adams)　46:21
"Elizabeth" (Hill)　113:330-31
"Elizabeth" (Jackson)　60:211, 235
"Elizabeth" (Muldoon)　72:265-66
"Elizabeth" (Ondaatje)　14:408
Elizabeth Alone (Trevor)　7:477; 9:529; 71:326, 345-46; 116:334-35, 338
Elizabeth Appleton (O'Hara)　42:319, 322-24
"Elizabeth of England" (Christie)　110:127
Elizabethan Essays (Eliot)　24:181
"Elizabeth's War with the Christmas Bear, 1601" (Dubie)　36:133
"The Elk Song" (Hogan)　73:158
Elle est là (Sarraute)　31:381
"Elle est pour moi" (Theriault)　79:408
"Elle est trois," ("La mort") (Lee)　46:234
"Elle me force sans jamais répit" (Senghor)　54:396
Ellen (Almedingen)　12:5-7
Ellen Foster (Gibbons)　50:46-9; 88:123-24, 126, 128-30, 132
Ellen Rogers (Farrell)　66:128-29
"Ellen Terhune" (Wilson)　8:551
"Ellen West" (Bidart)　33:76
Elliot Loves (Feiffer)　64:163-64
"Ellis Island" (Helprin)　22:220-23
Ellis Island and Other Stories (Helprin)　22:221-22; 32:229-30, 232
"Elm" (Plath)　1:270; 9:427; 50:446; 51:344; 111:159, 203, 213-15
"Elm Buds" (Sandburg)　35:356
The Elm Street Lot (Pearce)　21:291
"Elms" (Gluck)　44:218, 222
"Elms" (Williams)　56:425
Éloges (Perse)　11:433; 46:298, 300, 302-10
"Elogio de la madrastra" (*In Praise of the Step-mother*) (Vargas Llosa)　85:379, 385-86
Elogio de la sombra ("In Praise of Darkness"; *In Praise of Darkness*; *In Praise of Darkness*) (Borges)　3:82; 4:75; 6:89-90, 92-3; 8:103; 9:120
"Elohim merakhem al yaldey hagan" ("God Has Mercy on Kindergarten Children"; "God Has Pity on the Kindergarten Children"; "God Pities the Kindergarten Children") (Amichai)　22:30; 57:40-1, 46; 116:111
"Else a Great Prince in Prisons Lies" (Levertov)　66:250
"Elsewhen" (Heinlein)　26:165
"Elsewhere" (Bishop)　13:89
"Elsewhere" (Walcott)　67:359, 361
Elsewhere, Perhaps (Oz)
　See *Makom aher*
"Elsewheres" (Justice)　102:258
"Elvis Presley: He Did It His Way" (Amis)　62:5
"Elysian Fields" (Hacker)　91:110
"Em" (Dixon)　52:97

"The Emancipator" (Gilchrist)　48:119-22
"The Emasculation of Ted Roper" (Lively)　32:277
"The Embalmer's Art" (Musgrave)　54:338
Embarkation (Salamanca)　4:462; 15:463-65
Embers (Beckett)　6:45, 47; 18:42; 29:61; 57:89
The Embezzler (Auchincloss)　4:29-30; 9:53
The Embezzler (Cain)　3:96; 28:45-6, 54
"Emblem of a Virtuous Woman" (Castellanos)
　See "Emblema de la virtuosa"
"Emblema de la virtuosa" ("Emblem of a Virtuous Woman") (Castellanos)　66:46
"Emblems" (Tate)　14:529
Emblems of a Season of Fury (Merton)　83:394
"Emblems of Exile" (McGrath)　59:178, 180
"Emblems of Passion" (Causley)　7:42
The Embodiment of Knowledge (Williams)　42:453
"The Embrace" (Bell)　8:66
"The Embrace" (Gluck)　44:214, 222-23
"Embrace Me You Child" (Simon)　26:408
"Embracing Change" (hooks)　94:156
"Embryos" (Piercy)　27:375
"The Emerald" (Merrill)　13:381
Emerald (Whitney)　42:436-37
Emerald City (Williamson)　56:443-44
The Emerald City of Oz (Thurber)　25:438
"The Emerald Essay" (Wakoski)　7:504; 40:453
"Emergancy Room" (Van Duyn)　116:421
The Emergence of African Fiction (Larson)　31:237-38
"Emergence of Ernest Hemingway" (Wilson)　24:481
The Emergence of Metaphor and the Meaning of Culture
　See *Geneza metaforei si sensul culturii*
Emergences—Résurgences (Michaux)　19:314, 317
"Emergency Commission" (Clark)　38:125
Emergency Exit (Major)　19:295; 48:211-16
Emergency Exit (Silone)　4:493
"Emergency Haying" (Carruth)　7:41
Emergency Poems (Parra)　2:331; 102:334, 342, 353-56
"Emerging" (Thomas)　48:379, 381, 383
"Emerson and German Philosophy, 1943" (Wellek)　28:446
"Emerson and the Essay" (Gass)　39:477, 480, 482
"The Emigrant Irish" (Boland)　113:82
"The Emigrants" (Brand)　7:30
The Emigrants (Lamming)　2:235; 4:279; 66:218, 221, 223, 227-30
"The Emigre" (Ai)　69:9-10
"Emigre" (Merwin)　88:195
Emilia Galotti (Duerrenmatt)　102:61
"Emily" (Benson)　17:47
Emily (Benson)　17:47
"Emily Dickinson" (Pastan)　27:369
"Emily Dickinson" (Tate)　4:537
"Emily Dickinson in Southern California" (Kennedy)　42:257-58
"Emily Dickinson's Horses" (Donnell)　34:159
Emily L. (Duras)　68:91, 97-9, 101-02; 100:136, 144
Emily Stone (Redmon)　22:341-42
Emlyn: An Early Autobiography (Williams)　15:578
"Emma, Flaubert and the Pleasure Principle" (Vargas Llosa)　85:366
Emma in Love (Arundel)　17:14, 16
Emma McChesney and Co. (Ferber)　93:137, 140-42

Emma McChesney Stories (Ferber)　93:185
Emma Tupper's Diary (Dickinson)　12:169-70
"Emma Zunz" (Borges)　2:70; 6:88; 19:49-50; 83:186, 188
"Emmanuele! Emmanuele!" (Gordon)　13:245; 29:187-90
Emma's Island (Arundel)　17:14, 18
Emmeline (Rossner)　29:352-55
Emmène-moi au bout du monde! (*To the End of the World*) (Cendrars)　18:97; 106:176, 178, 187
"Emmy Moore's Journal" (Bowles)　68:9
Emotional Rescue (Jagger and Richard)　17:242
"Empedoklean Reveries" (Duncan)　41:130
The Emperor Alexander I (Almedingen)　12:2
Emperor of America (Condon)　100:95-102, 111
The Emperor of Ice-Cream (Moore)　1:225; 3:341; 5:296; 7:235-36, 239; 19:331, 334-35; 90:243-5, 247-8, 250-1, 253-5, 258, 263, 273, 277-8
"Emperor of the Air" (Canin)　55:35-6, 38
Emperor of the Earth: Modes of Eccentric Vision (Milosz)　56:250; 82:281
Emperor Shaka the Great: A Zulu Epic (Kunene)　85:164, 166, 168-72, 174-75, 179-80, 182-84, 187
"The Emperor with the Golden Hands" (Bunting)　47:49
The Emperors (Forsyth)　36:177
The Emperor's Clothes (Tabori)　19:437
"Emperors of the Island" (Abse)　29:16
The Emperor's Snuff Box (Carr)　3:101
The Emperor's Virgin (Fraser)　64:170
Emphyrio (Vance)　35:427
Empire (Vidal)　72:391-404
Empire (Warhol)　20:416-17, 421
"Empire Builders" (MacLeish)　68:290
L'empire céleste (Mallet-Joris)　11:355
The Empire City (Goodman)　1:123; 4:197-98; 7:128
L'empire de sens (*In the Realm of the Senses*) (Oshima)　20:251-53, 255-56
L'empire des signes (*Empire of Signs*) (Barthes)　24:36; 83:78
"L'empire et la trappe" (Audiberti)　38:21
"Empire of Dreams" (Simic)　49:337, 339
Empire of Passion (Oshima)
　See *Ai no barei*
Empire of Signs (Barthes)
　See *L'empire des signes*
"The Empire of the Necromancers" (Smith)　43:424
Empire of the Senseless (Acker)　111:9-11, 16-17, 20, 25, 32-4, 37-40
Empire of the Sun (Ballard)　36:47-8
Empire Star (Delany)　8:169; 38:150-54, 161
Empire, York Street (Moure)　88:216, 219, 227, 229
"Empires" (Williams)　42:442
The Empire's Old Clothes: What the Lone Ranger, Babar, and Other Innocent Heroes Do to Our Minds (Dorfman)
　See *Reader's nuestro que estás en la tierra: Ensayos sobre el imperialismo cultural*
"Empiricists of Crimson" (Dubie)　36:139
Empirismo eretico (Pasolini)　106:224-25, 235, 245-47
L'emploi du temps (*Passing Time*) (Butor)　3:92; 8:114-19; 11:78-82; 15:114-17
"Employment for the Castes in Abeyance" (Murray)　40:338
"Empress" (Livesay)　79:337

"Empson Lieder" (Sissman) 9:491
The Empty Canvas (Moravia)
   See La noia
"An Empty Chair" (Blunden) 56:40
The Empty Copper Sea (MacDonald) 27:275
Empty Cupboards (Ernaux)
   See Les armoires vides
"The Empty Day" (Laughlin) 49:220
The Empty Fortress: Infantile Autism and the
   Birth of the Self (Bettelheim) 79:111,
   124
"Empty Glass" (Townshend) 17:542
Empty Glass (Townshend) 17:540-42
"The Empty Hills" (Winters) 32:469
Empty Mirror (Ginsberg) 1:119; 3:194; 4:182-
   83; 36:181-85, 195; 109:340, 353, 371
The Empty Mirror: Experiences in a Japanese
   Zen Monastery (van de Wetering) 47:402-
   05
"Empty Provinces" (Prokosch) 48:309
"Empty Rooms" (Sorrentino) 7:449
Empty Swings (Vizenor) 103:296
"An Empty Threat" (Frost) 13:225
"Empty Vessel" (MacDiarmid) 11:337; 63:252
"Empty Water" (Merwin) 88:206
"Empty White Blotch on Map of Universe: A
   Possible View" (Warren) 18:539
"Empty Words" (Cage) 41:84
Empty Words: Writings, '73-'78 (Cage) 41:82-
   4, 86
En attendant Godot (Waiting for Godot)
   (Beckett) 1:20-4; 2:44-7; 3:44, 46-7;
   4:49-52; 6:33, 35, 37-40, 42-7; 9:78, 81,
   83-5, 87; 10:25, 29-30, 33; 11:32-3, 37-
   8, 42-3; 14:70, 73, 75, 78-9; 18:41-4, 48-
   9; 57:62-112; 59:252-58, 260;
   83:108-09, 111-13, 115-17, 129-30, 132-
   35, 142-44, 147, 150-51
En castellano (Otero) 11:425
"En el día de los difuntos" (Alonso) 14:25
En esta tierra (Matute) 11:364
En etrange pays dans mon pays lui-même
   (Aragon) 22:42
"En face" (Reverdy) 53:289
"En file indienne" (Damas) 84:176
En la ardiente oscuridad (In the Burning Dark-
   ness) (Buero Vallejo) 15:100; 46:93, 95
En la cuerda floja (On the High Wire; On the
   Wire) (Arrabal) 58:17, 27-8
"En la madrugada" ("At Dawn"; "At Day-
   break") (Rulfo) 80:200
"En la popa hay un cuerpo reclinado" (Marques)
   96:229, 241, 244
En la tierra de en medio (Castellanos) 66:53
En lektion i kärlek (A Lesson in Love) (Bergman)
   16:60-1; 72:40-1, 48, 52, 62
"En medio de la multitud" (Cernuda) 54:52
En México (Dudek) 11:159-61; 19:137-38
En mi jardín pastan los héroes (Heroes Are
   Grazing in My Garden) (Padilla) 38:350-
   51, 354
"En Mi-Careme" (Walcott) 25:450
En Passion (A Passion; The Passion of Anna)
   (Bergman) 16:63-4, 68-9, 74-5; 72:49-
   50, 53, 57, 59
En pèlerin et en étranger (Yourcenar) 87:412,
   419, 424
En pièces détachées (Tremblay) 29:419-20,
   422; 102:361-62, 364-65, 371-72, 374-
   77
"En roulant ma boute, roulant" (McNickle)
   89:183
En un vasto dominio (In a Vast Dominion)

(Aleixandre) 9:12, 17; 36:24, 26
"En una ciudad llamada San Juan" (Marques)
   96:227
En vrac: Notes (Reverdy) 53:286
"An Encampment at Morning" (Merwin)
   13:383
The Enchaféd Flood; or, The Romantic Ico-
   nography of the Sea (Auden) 14:27
The Enchanted Echo (Purdy) 50:235-36
"An Enchanted Garden" (Calvino)
   See "Un giardino incantato"
"The Enchanted Nurse" (Goyen) 14:211-12
The Enchanted Pig (Ludlam) 46:241-42;
   50:342, 344
The Enchanted Pimp (Callaghan) 41:90-2,
   97-8
The Enchanted Quantity (Lezama Lima)
   See La cantidad hechizada
The Enchanter (Nabokov)
   See Volshebnik
Enchantment (Merkin) 44:62-6
Enciklopedia mrtvih (The Encyclopedia of the
   Dead; Encyclopedie des morts) (Kis)
   57:249, 251-54
The Enclosure (Hill) 113:287-88, 291, 295,
   309, 320
"Encontro com um poeta" ("Encounter With
   a Poet") (Cabral de Melo Neto) 76:163
"Encore" (Purdy) 28:378-79
Encore (Lacan)
   See Séminaire XX
Encore: A Journal of the 80th Year (Sarton)
   91:245-46, 252-53
"An Encounter" (Auden) 6:18; 43:18
"An Encounter" (Coover) 32:127
"An Encounter" (Frost) 26:117, 122
"The Encounter" (Howard) 7:165
"Encounter" (Milosz) 82:293
"Encounter" (Olds) 32:346
"An Encounter" (Prichard) 46:333
"Encounter" (Yevtushenko) 1:382
Encounter in April (Sarton) 49:307, 320;
   91:245
"Encounter in Buffalo" (Barnard) 48:27
"Encounter With a Poet" (Cabral de Melo Neto)
   See "Encontro com um poeta"
"Encounter with a Red Circle" (Cortazar)
   33:124
"Encounter with Silence" (Gascoyne) 45:151
"Encounter with the Ancestors" (Kunene)
   85:175-77
Encounters (Berrigan) 4:56
Encounters (Bowen) 22:67
Encounters (Ringwood) 48:331
"Encounters with Suicide" (Cioran) 64:89, 94
Encounters with the Archdruid (McPhee)
   36:295
The Encyclopaedist (Mortimer) 28:284
An Encyclopedia of Murder (Wilson) 14:589
"The Encyclopedia of the Dead" (Kis)
   See "L'encyclopedie des morts"
The Encyclopedia of the Dead (Kis)
   See Enciklopedia mrtvih
Encyclopédie de la pléiade (Queneau) 5:360
"L'encyclopedie des morts" ("The Encyclope-
   dia of the Dead") (Kis) 57:249, 251,
   253-54
Encyclopedie des morts (Kis)
   See Enciklopedia mrtvih
"The Encyclopedists" (Asimov) 19:26; 26:63
"The End" (Beckett)
   See "La Fin"
"The End" (Lennon and McCartney) 35:278

"The End" (Morrison) 17:285-86, 289, 292,
   295
"The End" (Neruda) 28:312
"The End" (Smith) 12:539
"The End" (Strand) 71:288-89
The End and the Beginning (Szymborska)
   99:194, 199, 203, 208, 211
"The End" Appendix (Kostelanetz) 28:218
End as a Man (Willingham) 51:399-408, 410
"The End" Essentials (Kostelanetz) 28:218
"The End of 1968" (Montale)
   See "Fine del '68"
"End of a Beginning" (Kelman) 58:301
"The End of a Career" (Stafford) 7:459;
   19:430; 68:434
The End of a Fine Epoch (Brodsky)
   See Konets prekrasnoy epokhi
"The End of a Good Man" (O'Faolain) 32:341
The End of a Little Man (Leonov)
   See Konets melkogo cheloveka
End of a Mission (Boell)
   See Ende einer Dienstfahrt
The End of a Petty Man (Leonov)
   See Konets melkogo cheloveka
The End of a Primitive (Himes) 108:230, 232
"End of a Season" (Scannell) 49:329
"End of a Summer's Day" (Campbell) 42:85-6
The End of a Trivial Man (Leonov)
   See Konets melkogo cheloveka
"The End of a War" (Read) 4:439
"End of a World" (Rodgers) 7:378
The End of an Insignificant Man (Leonov)
   See Konets melkogo cheloveka
The End of Beauty (Graham) 48:150-55
The End of Eternity (Asimov) 9:50; 19:26-7;
   26:48, 64
End of Exile (Bova) 45:68
"The End of Fiction" (Hildesheimer) 49:173,
   175
"The End of Grief" (Abbott) 48:6
The End of Intelligent Writing (Kostelanetz)
   28:213, 215-18
The End of Lieutenant Boruvka (Skvorecky)
   69:333, 345-47
"The End of Love" (Raine) 45:338
"End of Magna" (Dixon) 52:99
"The End of March" (Bishop) 9:97-8; 13:95;
   32:30, 37
The End of Me Old Cigar (Osborne) 5:333-34;
   45:319
The End of Modernity (McAuley) 45:250-51
The End of My Life (Bourjaily) 8:103; 62:80-
   5, 88-9, 92-5, 98-9, 103, 107
"End of Play" (Graves) 45:165
"End of Play" (Taylor) 18:526
"The End of Romance" (Brown) 73:20
"The End of Science Fiction" (Mueller) 51:281
The End of Solomon Grundy (Symons) 14:523
"The End of Something" (Hemingway) 3:242;
   10:269; 30:186-87, 189-90, 192, 195-98
"End of Summer" (Gluck) 81:167-68
"The End of Summer" (Haines) 58:213
End of Summer (Behrman) 40:78-80, 82, 87
The End of Summer (Hill) 113:295
The End of Summer (Ozu) 16:454, 456
The End of the Affair (Greene) 1:131-32, 134;
   3:207, 209-11, 213-14; 6:213-16, 220;
   9:251; 14:217-19; 27:173; 70:289;
   72:155, 167, 169, 177-78
"The End of the Avant-Garde" (Pasolini)
   106:258
"The End of the Axletree" (Gray) 41:181,
   183

"The End of the Beginning" (O'Casey) 11:405
"The End of the Book and the Beginning of Writing" (Derrida) 24:147
The End of the Dream (Wylie) 43:472
"The End of the Duel" (Borges) 4:75; 10:67; 44:353
End of the Game (Cortazar)
  See *Final del juego*
End of the Game, and Other Stories (Cortazar) 92:139
"The End of the Indian Poems" (Plumly) 33:313
The End of the Night (Mauriac)
  See *La fin de la nuit*
"The End of the Owls" (Enzensberger) 43:144-45
"The End of the Party" (Greene) 3:215
"The End of the Rainbow" (Jarrell) 9:296
The End of the Ring (Llewellyn) 7:207
The End of the Road (Barth) 1:17-18; 2:36; 3:38-9, 42; 5:51; 7:23; 9:68, 72; 14:49, 51, 56; 27:26, 29; 51:20-1, 29; 89:9, 17, 24
The End of the Row (Green) 25:192
"The End of the Story" (Smith) 43:420, 424-25
"The End of the Towpath" (Edmonds) 35:155
"The End of the World" (Branley) 21:20
"The End of the World" (Gluck) 44:222
"The End of the World" (Hildesheimer)
  See "Das Ende einer Welt"
"The End of the World" (MacLeish) 14:338; 68:291, 294
"The End of the World" (McGrath) 28:280
End of the World (Kopit) 33:252-54
The End of the World (Valdez)
  See *El fin del mundo*
"The End of the World, 1843" (Schnackenberg) 40:380
The End of the World Filmed by the Angel of Notre Dame (Cendrars) 106:191
The End of the World in Our Usual Bed in a Night Full of Rain (Wertmueller) 16:597-99
The End of the World News (Burgess) 40:120-21, 123; 62:130-33; 81:304
The End of White World Supremacy (Malcolm X) 117:320, 341
"End of Winter" (Gluck) 81:167
"The End of Your Life" (Levine) 14:320
An End to Innocence (Fiedler) 4:163; 13:211; 24:188, 203
"End to Laughter" (Santos) 22:364
An End to Perfect (Newton) 35:303
End to Torment: A Memoir of Ezra Pound (H. D.) 31:207-08, 212; 73:135-37, 139, 141, 143-44
End Zone (DeLillo) 8:171-72; 10:134-35; 13:175-79; 27:76-80, 82, 84, 86; 39:116-17, 125; 54:79-83, 85; 76:171, 180, 182
"The Endangered Roots of a Person" (Rose) 85:314
Das Ende der Fiktionen: Reden aus fünfundzwanzig Jahren (Hildesheimer) 49:179
Ende einer Dienstfahrt (*End of a Mission*) (Boell) 6:83-4; 11:58; 39:294; 72:89, 93
"Das Ende einer Welt" ("The End of the World") (Hildesheimer) 49:174, 179
"Ende eines Sommers" (Eich) 15:202
Endeavors of Infinite Man (Neruda)
  See *Tentativa del hombre infinito*
Endecott and the Red Cross (Lowell) 8:352;

11:324-25
Enderby (Burgess) 2:86; 4:80-1; 5:88, 90-1; 10:87-8; 13:127; 22:71, 78; 40:114, 116-18; 81:302; 94:40
Enderby Outside (Burgess) 5:85, 88-9; 8:112; 40:114, 118, 123; 62:130
Enderby's Dark Lady; or, No End to Enderby (Burgess) 40:122-23; 62:130, 132
Ender's Game (Card) 44:163-65; 47:69; 50:142-45, 147-51
"Endfray of the Ofay" (Leiber) 25:307
Endgame (Beckett)
  See *Fin de partie*
Endgame: A Journal of the Seventy-ninth Year (Sarton) 91:251-52
"Ending" (Swenson) 61:395; 106:335
Ending (Wolitzer) 17:561-62
Ending Up (Amis) 5:21-4; 8:10-11; 13:13-14; 44:135, 139, 142, 144
"Endings" (Adcock) 41:16
"Endings" (Boland) 67:45-6
"Endings" (Van Duyn) 116:422
"Endings" (Walcott) 14:549
"Endless" (Rukeyser) 27:409
"Endless Life" (Ferlinghetti) 27:139
Endless Life: Selected Poems (Ferlinghetti) 27:136-37, 139
Endless Love (Spencer) 30:405-08
Endless Night (Christie) 1:58; 48:71-2; 110:132
Endless Race (Holden) 18:257
The Endless Short Story (Sukenick) 48:370
"Endless Wire" (Lightfoot) 26:282
"The Endochronic Properties of Resublimated Thiotimoline" (Asimov) 9:50
"Ends" (Beckett) 9:84
Ends and Means (Huxley) 11:286; 18:269; 79:286
Ends and Means (Middleton) 38:331
Ends and Odds (Beckett) 9:83-4; 14:74; 18:43; 29:61
"Endure No Conflict: Crosses Are Keepsakes" (Graham) 29:193
"The Enduring Chill" (O'Connor) 6:382; 10:365-66; 13:419-20; 15:412; 21:257, 263, 267, 272; 104:107, 110, 115, 124, 135-36, 152, 179, 183-84, 188, 194
"Eneboerne" ("Familien de Cats") (Dinesen) 95:69-71
"The Enemies" (Gordon) 29:187; 83:231
"Enemies" (O'Brien) 103:140
The Enemies (Broner) 19:70
Enemies: A Love Story (Singer)
  See *Sonim, di Geschichte fun a Liebe*
Enemies of the System: A Tale of Homo Uniformis (Aldiss) 14:14
Enemigo rumor (*Hostile Murmurs*) (Lezama Lima) 101:121
"The Enemy" (Rosenthal) 28:394
"The Enemy" (Singer) 69:305
The Enemy (Garfield) 12:241
The Enemy (Green)
  See *L'ennemi*
The Enemy Camp (Weidman) 7:516
The Enemy in the Blanket (Burgess) 22:73; 81:300
The Enemy Joy (Belitt) 22:49-50, 52
"An Enemy of the People" (Callaghan) 41:98
An Enemy of the People (Miller) 78:308, 322
An Enemy of the People (Ray)
  See *Ganashatru*
The Enemy Sea (Polonsky) 92:374
The Enemy Stars (Anderson) 15:11
"Enemy Territory" (Kelley) 22:250, 252

The Enemy Within (Friel) 42:173-74; 115:246, 249
"Energies" (Boland) 113:72
The Energies of Art (Barzun) 51:39
"The Energized Man" (Dickey) 109:249
Energy for the Twenty-First Century (Branley) 21:21-2
The Energy of Slaves (Cohen) 3:110; 38:137
Energy to Burn (Simmons) 43:408-09, 413
Enfance (*Childhood*) (Sarraute) 31:384-86; 80:243, 245, 255, 257
L'enfance d'un chef (Sartre) 7:395-96; 9:472
L'enfant chargé de chaines (*The Child in Chains; Young Man in Chains*) (Mauriac) 9:368; 56:203, 206
L'enfant noir (*The African Child; The Dark Child*) (Laye) 4:282, 284-85; 38:284-91
L'enfant sauvage (*The Wild Child*) (Truffaut) 20:386, 389, 393, 397; 101:375, 381-82, 384, 386, 395-97, 400, 407, 411, 413
"L'enfantillage" (Mandiargues) 41:278
Les enfantômes (Ducharme) 74:59-61, 68
Les enfants (Duras) 68:96
Les enfants du bonhomme dans la lune (*The Children of the Man in the Moon; The Hockey Sweater, and Other Stories*) (Carrier) 78:62-7, 72, 77
Les enfants terribles (*Children of the Game; The Holy Terrors*) (Cocteau) 1:59; 8:145, 147; 15:132-33; 43:102-05, 111
El enfermo (Azorin) 11:27
Engaged in Writing (Spender) 41:418
"Engagements" (Janowitz) 43:212
Ein Engel kommt nach Babylon (*An Angel Comes to Babylon*) (Duerrenmatt) 102:55, 57, 74, 77, 79, 83
Ein Engel kommt nach Babylon (*An Angel Comes to Babylon*) (Durrenmatt) 8:194; 11:168-69, 171-72; 15:196
"L'engendrement de la formule" (Kristeva) 77:301
O engenheiro (*The Engineer*) (Cabral de Melo Neto) 76:150, 152-54, 156-57, 159, 169
"Engführung" ("The Straitening") (Celan) 10:102; 19:90, 95; 53:77; 82:42, 45
"Enghcantment" (Christie) 110:125
"The Engine at Heartspring's Center" (Zelazny) 21:479
Engine Summer (Crowley) 57:157-62
Engine Trouble (Narayan) 28:296
The Engineer (Cabral de Melo Neto)
  See *O engenheiro*
The Engineer of Human Souls: An Entertainment of the Old Themes of Life, Women, Fate, Dreams, the Working Class, Secret Agents, Love, and Death (Skvorecky)
  See *Příběh inženýra lidských duší*
"Engineer-Private Paul Klee Misplaces an Aircraft between Milbertschofen and Cambrai, March 1916" (Barthelme) 3:44; 13:57; 59:251; 115:69
"England" (Davie) 5:114; 8:165, 167
"England" (Stevenson) 7:462
"England: Eulogy and Lament" (Ginzburg) 54:202
England Have My Bones (White) 30:449
England Made Me (Greene) 3:209; 27:173, 175; 72:148, 150-51, 161
England, Our England (Waterhouse) 47:417
"England versus England" (Lessing) 22:278
"Englands of the Mind" (Heaney) 25:249-50
The English (Priestley) 5:350
"English and the Afrikaans Writer" (Brink)

36:69

"English and Welsh" (Tolkien)   38:442

The English Assassin: A Romance of Entropy (Moorcock)   27:349-50; 58:347-48

The English Auden: Poems, Essays, and Dramatic Writings, 1927-1939 (Auden)   14:31-4; 43:14-17

"English Civil War" (Clash)   30:43, 46

The English Comic Characters (Priestley)   34:361-62

"The English Fiction of Samuel Beckett: An Essay in Stylistic Analysis" (Coetzee)   117:48

"The English Garden" (Abish)   22:17, 19

"An English Garden in Austria" (Jarrell)   9:297

The English Gentleman (Raven)   14:439, 442

"The English Girl" (Levine)   54:294

English Journey (Priestley)   34:361, 363-64, 366

English Journey: or, The Road to Milton Keynes (Bainbridge)   62:25-8

"The English Language of the South" (Brooks)   86:279

"The English Lesson" (Mohr)   12:447

"English Lessons" (Pasternak)   10:383

"English Literature and the Small Coterie" (Kelman)   86:186

English Literature in Our Time and the University (Leavis)   24:306, 308

English Literature in the Sixteenth Century, Excluding Drama (Lewis)   6:308; 27:261-62

English Made Plain (Burgess)
See *Language Made Plain*

The English Novel (Priestley)   34:362

"The English Novel of the Future" (Green)   97:260

English Novelists (Bowen)   11:62

"English Now" (Paulin)   37:356-57

"The English Orphan's Monologue" (Reaney)   13:473

English Pastoral Poetry (Empson)
See *Some Versions of Pastoral*

The English Patient (Ondaatje)   76:196-207

English Poems (Blunden)   2:65; 56:36-7, 47

"English Rose" (Weller)   26:444

English Subtitles (Porter)   33:320-21, 325

The English Teacher (*Grateful to Life and Death*) (Narayan)   7:254-55; 28:291-92, 294, 297, 299

"English Threnody and American Tragedy" (Spender)   5:402

An Englishman Abroad (Bennett)   77:90, 95, 97, 100

"An Englishman in Texas" (Middleton)   13:388

"Englishman's Road" (Hooker)   43:198, 200

Englishman's Road (Hooker)   43:198-201

Englishmen (Hope)   52:213-14

"An English-Speaking Quebecker Looks at Quebec" (MacLennan)   92:306

"The Englishwoman" (Jhabvala)   29:259

Enid Bagnold's Autobiography (Bagnold)   25:77

"The Enigma" (Camus)   14:110

"The Enigma" (Fowles)   6:189; 33:174; 87:151, 155, 157-58, 176-77

"Enigma" (Thomas)   48:376

The Enigma of Arrival (Naipaul)   105:159-61, 173, 178-79, 181-82

"The Enigma of Edward FitzGerald" (Borges)   83:161

The Enigma of Stonehenge (Fowles)   87:176-77

"The Enigma: Rilke" (Hirsch)   31:216

Enjo (*Conflagration*) (Ichikawa)   20:177, 179, 186

Enjoy (Bennett)   45:58

Enjoying Opera (Streatfeild)   21:408

Enken i spejlet (Abell)   15:1

Det enkla och det svåra (Martinson)   14:355

Enlarging the Change: The Princeton Seminars in Literary Criticism, 1949-1951 (Fitzgerald)   39:318, 471-73, 475

"Enlightenment" (Miles)   34:245

L'ennemi (*The Enemy*) (Green)   77:271, 277

"Uma enorme rès deitada" ("A Huge Cow Lying Down") (Cabral de Melo Neto)   76:164

Enormous Changes at the Last Minute (Paley)   4:391-94; 18:391-93; 37:332, 334-35, 337-38

"The Enormous Gas Bill at the Dwarf Factory. A Horror Movie to Be Shot with Eyes." (Kaufman)   49:205

"The Enormous Radio" (Cheever)   3:107; 11:120; 15:127-29; 64:65

The Enormous Radio, and Other Stories (Cheever)   7:49; 15:127

The Enormous Room (Cummings)   1:68; 8:158-60; 12:139, 142-46, 156-57, 161; 15:158; 68:25, 35, 38, 43, 50

"Enough" (Creeley)   15:151

Enough (Beckett)
See *Assez*

Enough! (Westlake)   33:438

"Enough for You" (Kristofferson)   26:268

Enough of Green (Stevenson)   33:380-81

Enough Rope (Parker)   68:324

Enough Said: Poems, 1974-1979 (Whalen)   29:447

Enquiry (Francis)   42:148, 155

"An Enquiry into Two Inches of Ivory" (Raine)   103:179, 182, 186

Ensayo de un crimen (*Archibald of the Cross; Archibaldo de la Cruz; The Criminal Life of Archilbaldo de la Cruz*) (Bunuel)   16:129, 136, 139; 80:22, 24, 26-9, 34, 36, 47

Ensayos (Marques)   96:242, 245

"Enshroud" (Roethke)   11:486

Enslaved (Masefield)   11:357

"Enslavement: Three American Cases" (Berryman)   8:90

Enter a Free Man (Stoppard)   5:413-14; 15:518; 29:394, 397-99

Enter a Murderer (Marsh)   53:247, 249

Enter and Exit (Boell)
See "Als der Krieg ausbrach"

Enter Solly Gold (Kops)   4:274

"Enter Your Garden" (Tillinghast)   29:414

"Entering the Kingdom" (Oliver)   19:363; 98:266, 287, 290, 294

"Entering the Temple in Nimes" (Wright)   28:467

"Enterprise" (Ezekiel)   61:91

"Enterprise" (Montague)   46:270

L'enterrement de la sardine (*The Burial of the Sardine*) (Arrabal)   9:39; 18:17-18

"The Entertainer" (Joel)   26:214, 219

The Entertainer (Osborne)   1:263; 2:327-28; 5:333; 11:422, 424; 45:313-16, 321

"Entertaining God" (Walker)   103:410-12

Entertaining Mr. Sloane (Orton)   4:387-88; 13:435-36; 43:326-29, 331-34

Entertaining Strangers (Gurney)   32:218

An Entertainment (Williams)
See *This Is*

"The Entertainment of the Senses" (Auden)   6:19

"The Entertainment of War" (Fisher)   25:158

Entfernung von der Truppe (Boell)   2:68; 3:75; 11:53-5, 58; 27:61-2; 39:294; 72:68, 93

"The Enthusiast" (Leet)   11:323

"Enthusiastic Fires" (Keates)   34:202-03

The Enthusiastic Slinger (Neruda)
See *El hondero entusiasta, 1923-1924*

El entierro de la sardina (Arrabal)
See *L'Eterrement de la sardine*

The Entire Son (Guillen)
See *El son entero*

"Entitled Story" (Lish)   45:230

"The Entombment" (Hine)   15:280

"Entomology" (Longley)   29:295

Entr'acte (Clair)   20:57, 61, 69

L'entrada en guerra (*Adam, One Afternoon, and Other Stories*) (Calvino)   33:98-9; 39:314; 73:42

"Entrance" (Elytis)   100:187

Entrance of the Celebrant (Musgrave)   13:400; 54:341

"The Entrance of Winifred into Valhalla" (Cassity)   42:97

The Entrance to Porlock (Buechner)   4:79

"Entranceways" (Ammons)   57:57

"Entrapped and Abondoned" (Sommer)   25:425

"Entre·chiens et loups" (Gascar)   11:221, 223

Entre fantoine et agapa (*Between Famine and Agape*) (Pinget)   37:359, 364-66

Entre la vie et la mort (*Between Life and Death*) (Sarraute)   2:386; 4:466-70; 8:472; 31:378-80, 382-83; 80:238, 240, 245-47, 250

Entre l'écriture (Cixous)   92:90, 96

Entre Tinieblas (*Dark Habits; Sisters of Darkness*) (Almodovar)   114:4-5, 11-14, 17-8, 22-3, 25

"L'entrée" (Butor)   15:117

El entremés del mancebo que casó con mujer brava (Casona)   49:40

Entretiens avec le Professeur Y (*Conversations with Professor Y*) (Celine)   9:152; 47:77, 79-80

Entretiens sur la poésie (Bonnefoy)   58:60

"Entries" (Tate)   2:432

"Entropy" (Mahon)   27:287-88, 290-91

"Entropy" (Pynchon)   6:430, 432, 434-35; 11:452; 33:329, 334, 338-40; 62:433, 446, 450; 72:302-04

"Entropy at Hartburn" (Silkin)   43:400

"Entry" (Elytis)   100:170

Entry into Jerusalem (Middleton)   38:334

Die Entscheidung (Seghers)   7:408

"Enueg I" (Beckett)   9:80

"L'envers du monde" (Hebert)   29:228

L'envers et l'endroit (Camus)   9:145; 14:107, 111, 114, 116; 32:86, 88, 96; 69:112, 117

"Envidia" (Azorin)   11:24

"Envies and Identifications: Dante and the Modern Poet" (Heaney)   74:181

"The Environmental Revolution" (Hughes)   37:173

"Envoi" (Boland)   67:40, 46; 113:82, 85-86, 106-08

"Envoi" (Pound)   112:309-14

"Envoi: The Search for Beauty" (Montague)   46:274

Envoy Extraordinary (Golding)   2:169; 17:177; 81:325

"Envoy from D'Aubigné" (Merwin)   1:213; 88:194

The Envoy from Mirror City (Frame) **66**:146, 150; **96**:194, 202-03, 217-20

"The Envoy of Mr. Cogito" (Herbert) **9**:276; **43**:189

"Envoys Are Going to Lenin" (Yevtushenko) **26**:462

"Envy" (Yevtushenko) **26**:461

Envy (Olesha)
    See *Zavist'*

"Envy: or, Yiddish in America" (Ozick) **7**:287-88; **28**:347-48; **62**:345, 353-54, 357

Enzymes in Action (Berger) **12**:39

"Eonul dogmatic" ("The Age of Dogma") **75**:80

"L'epaule" (Bonnefoy) **15**:74

Epaves (*The Strange River*) (Green) **11**:261; **77**:267-68

Eperons: Les styles de Nietzsche (*Spurs: Nietzsche's Styles*) (Derrida) **24**:151; **87**:92

"The Epic and the Novel" (Bakhtin) **83**:5, 14, 16, 18, 34, 60-1

"The Epic Love of Elmii Banderii" (Laurence) **62**:280

The Epic of Gilgamesh (The Brothers Quay)
    See *Little Songs of the Chief Officer of Hunar Louse, or This Unnameable Little Broom*

"The Epic of Sheik Bedreddin" (Hikmet)
    See "Seyh Bedreddin destani"

The Epic of Sheik Bedreddin and Other Poems (Hikmet) **40**:247-48, 250

"Epic of the War of Liberation" (Hikmet) **40**:244

"Epic Theatre and Dramatic Theatre" (Sartre) **52**:373

Epics of the West (Neihardt) **32**:330-31

"The Epidemic" (Buzzati) **36**:92

Epidemic! (Slaughter) **29**:377

Epidemic! The Story of the Disease Detectives (Archer) **12**:23

"Epidermal Macabre" (Roethke) **46**:357

"Epigram" (Lowell) **8**:350

"Epigram Eight" (Cunningham) **31**:102

"Epigram Forty-Three" (Cunningham) **31**:104

Epigramas (*Epigrams*) (Cardenal) **31**:71

"Epigrams" (H. D.) **73**:108

Epigrams (Cardenal)
    See *Epigramas*

"Epigraph" (Atwood) **84**:106

"Epigraphs Written on Air" (Sachs)
    See "Grabschriften in die Luft geschrieben"

"Epilog" (Rose) **85**:312-13

"Epilog" ("Epilogue") (Transtroemer) **65**:222, 224, 233, 235

"Epilog to Stifters 'Nachsommer'" (Boell)
    See "Epilog zu Stifters 'Nachsommer'"

"Epilog zu Stifters 'Nachsommer'" ("Epilog to Stifters 'Nachsommer'") (Boell) **6**:83; **72**:77

"Epilogue" (Akhmatova) **25**:28

"Epilogue" (Aldington) **49**:3-4, 7, 18

"Epilogue" (Ciardi) **44**:381

"Epilogue" (Gascoyne) **45**:148

"Epilogue" (Ignatow) **14**:277

"Epilogue" (Lowell) **8**:358; **11**:331; **37**:232, 239

"Epilogue" (MacNeice) **53**:231

"Epilogue" (Silkin) **43**:401

"The Epilogue" (Tomlinson) **45**:397, 403

"Epilogue" (Transtroemer)
    See "Epilog"

"Epilogue from a New Home: For Tony Barkan" (Matthias) **9**:362

Epilogue III (Graves) **45**:165

"Epilogue: Romanticism in 1960" (Barzun) **51**:39

"Epilogue: The Photographer" (Munro) **95**:304

"Epilogue: Women Like Us" (Danticat) **94**:99

"Epiphany" (Moure) **88**:227, 229

"Epiphany" (Sondheim) **30**:398

"An Epiphany" (Stafford) **29**:382

"An Epiphany Tale" (Brown) **48**:59

"Episode" (Durrell) **27**:96

"Episode at Gastein" (Sansom) **2**:383; **6**:484

Episode in Palmetto (Caldwell) **60**:53

"Episode in the Life of an Ancestor" (Boyle) **19**:62

"An Episode in the Life of Professor Brooke" (Wolff) **64**:446-47, 449-50

An Episode of Sparrows (Godden) **53**:157, 161

"Episode, Scene, Speech, and Word: The Madness of Lear" (Maclean) **78**:235

Episodes of the Revolutionary War (Guevara)
    See *Pasajes de la guerra revolucionaria*

"Epistemology" (Wilbur) **53**:404-05; **110**:350

"Epistle" (Cardenal) **31**:77

"An Epistle: Edward Sackville to Venetia Digby" (Hope) **51**:213, 215, 217-18, 220

"An Epistle from Holofernes" (Hope) **3**:250; **51**:215, 217-18, 220-21

"Epistle to a Godson" (Auden) **14**:27

Epistle to a Godson and Other Poems (Auden) **2**:27-8; **3**:22-4, 29; **6**:16-19; **43**:18, 27

"An Epistle to a Patron" (Prince) **22**:338, 340

"Epistle to Angus Macintyre" (Fuller) **62**:203

"Epistle To Be Left in the Earth" (MacLeish) **68**:294

"Epistle to His Verses" (Brodsky)
    See "Poslanie k stikham"

"Epistle to Sabin Dragoi" (Arghezi)
    See "Epistola lui Sabin Dragoi"

Epistles to Several Persons (Fuller) **62**:188-91, 194-95, 197, 201-03

"Epistola lui Sabin Dragoi" ("Epistle to Sabin Dragoi") (Arghezi) **80**:3

Epitalamio del prieto Trinidad (*Dark Wedding*) (Sender) **8**:478

"Epitaph" **75**:78

"Epitaph" (Alegria) **75**:46

"Epitaph" (H. D.) **73**:119

"Epitaph" (O'Brien) **65**:167-69, 171-2

"Epitaph" (Parra) **102**:345

"Epitaph" (Pound) **2**:343

"Epitaph" (Smith) **15**:514

"The Epitaph" (Thomas) **6**:530

Epitaph for a Dead Beat (Markson) **67**:191

"Epitaph for a Lady's Man" (Wagoner) **3**:508

"Epitaph for a Negro Woman" (Dodson) **79**:187, 191

Epitaph for a Spy (Ambler) **6**:4; **9**:18

Epitaph for a Tramp (Markson) **67**:191

"Epitaph for an Old Woman" (Paz) **51**:335

"Epitaph for Anton Schmidt" (Gunn) **18**:203

"Epitaph for Biafra" (Saro-Wiwa) **114**:253

"Epitaph for Fire and Flower" (Plath) **17**:368

"Epitaph for Flann O'Brien" (Mahon) **27**:287, 290

Epitaph for George Dillon (Osborne) **5**:331-33; **45**:313-15, 317

Epitaph for the Young: A Poem in XII Cantos (Walcott) **25**:452; **76**:273, 284

"Epitaph in a Country Churchyard" (Beer) **58**:36

"Epitaph on a Tyrant" (Auden) **43**:22

"Epitaph: 'The Man with the Golden Arm'" (Algren) **33**:15

Epitáphios (Ritsos) **13**:428; **31**:324, 328

"Epitaphs" (Matthews) **40**:324

Epitaphs and Occasions (Fuller) **28**:147-48, 152-53, 158

Epitaphs for Our Times: The Letters of Edward Dahlberg (Dahlberg) **7**:64

"Epithalamion" (Abse) **29**:14, 19

"Epithalamion" (Cummings) **12**:146; **15**:159

"Epithalamion" (Kizer) **80**:174

"Epithalamion" (Longley) **29**:296

"Epithalamion" (Raine) **32**:349

"Epithalamion" (Wright) **6**:580

"Epithalamion after a War" (Ciardi) **44**:380

"Epithalamium" (Reading) **47**:352

Epithalamium in Time of War (Gustafson) **36**:216

Epithets of War (Scannell) **49**:327-28, 331

Epitomé (Tchicaya) **101**:345-48, 350-53, 358-60

Epitome/Epigraphs for the Summary of a Passion (Tchicaya)
    See *Epitomé/Les Mots de Tête pour le Sommaire d'une Passion*

Epitomé/Les Mots de Tête pour le Sommaire d'une Passion (*Epitome/Epigraphs for the Summary of a Passion*) (Tchicaya) **101**:351

"Epîtres à la Princesse" (Senghor) **54**:390-91, 396, 410

Epoch and Artist: Selected Writings (Jones) **4**:259, 262; **7**:187-88, 190; **13**:309, 312; **42**:238, 243, 245, 247

"Epode: The New Bus Terminal" (Goodman) **4**:198

Épreuves du vivant (Chedid) **47**:82

"Epsilon" (Tolson) **105**:241, 269, 274

Epsom Downs (Brenton) **31**:65, 67

"Epstein" (Roth) **15**:449-50

Equal Danger (Sciascia)
    See *Il contesto*

"Equal in Paris" (Baldwin) **42**:18

"Equal Opportunity" (Lorde) **71**:260

"Equal, That Is, to the Real Itself" (Olson) **29**:338

"The Equaliser" (Clash) **30**:48-9

The Equalizer (Williamson) **29**:452, 455

"Equals" (Seth) **90**:350

"Equanimity" (Murray) **40**:342-43

The Equations of Love (Wilson) **13**:607-08, 611

Equator (Aldiss) **14**:12

"Equilibrist" (Swenson) **106**:336-37, 347

"The Equilibrists" (Ransom) **2**:363; **4**:431, 435; **5**:365; **11**:467

Equinox (Figes) **31**:161-62

Equinox Flower (Ozu) **16**:451, 453

L'équinoxe de Septembre (Montherlant) **8**:394

"Equinoxiale" (Tchicaya) **101**:350

Equus (Shaffer) **5**:386-90; **14**:486-87; **18**:475-78; **37**:383-84; **60**:355-81

"Er kam als Bierfahrer" (Boell) **72**:77

"Era proibito" (Buzzati) **36**:86

Erään elämän Sotoa (*The Harvest of a Life*) (Sillanpaa) **19**:419

Eras and Modes in English Poetry (Miles) **2**:278

Eraserhead (Lynch) **66**:257, 259-61, 263-65, 268-71

The Erasers (Robbe-Grillet)
    See *Les gommes*

Erasmus of Rotterdam (Faludy) **42**:139-40

"Erasure" (Simic) **49**:337

"Ercole the Butcher" (Turco) 11:552
L'ere du soupçon: Essais sur le roman (The Age of Suspicion: Essays on the Novel) (Sarraute) 2:384, 386; 4:465; 8:469; 31:377, 385-86; 80:229, 236, 239-40, 242, 244-45, 248, 250, 254
"Erect" (Tchicaya) 101:346
Erections, Ejaculations, Exhibitions, and General Tales of Ordinary Madness (Bukowski)
See Life and Death in the Charity Ward
"Das Ereignis" ("The Event") (Heidegger) 24:276
Ere-Voice (Rakosi) 47:344-45
"Erfurt 1970 and 1891" (Grass) 49:137
Ergo (Lind)
See Eine bessere Welt
Erica (Vittorini) 9:549
Erie Water (Edmonds) 35:146, 149, 151, 156-57
"Erige Cor Tuum ad Me in Coelum" (H. D.) 73:118
Erik Dorn (Hecht) 8:269, 272-73
Erkenntnis und Interesse (Knowledge and Human Interests) (Habermas) 104:69, 75
"Erlanger Rede über das absurde Theater" (Hildesheimer) 49:167-68
Erläuterungen zu Hölderlins Dichtung (Heidegger) 24:260
"Erlinda and Mr. Coffin" (Vidal) 33:407
The Erlking (Tournier)
See Le roi des Aulnes
The Ermine (Anouilh)
See L'hermine
Die Ermittlung: Oratorium in Elf Gesëngen (The Investigation) (Weiss) 3:515; 15:564, 566; 51:387-88, 391, 394, 396
Ernest Hemingway and His World (Burgess) 13:125
Ernest Hemingway: Selected Letters, 1917-1961 (Selected Letters, 1917-1961) (Hemingway) 30:201; 41:203
Ernest K. Gann's Flying Circus (Gann) 23:167
"Eroded Hills" ("Inheritor") (Wright) 53:419
"Eros" (Broumas) 73:17
"Eros" (Oppen) 7:281
"Eros absconditus" (Gascoyne) 45:147
"Eros and Agape" (Auden) 4:35
"Eros and Psyche" (Aldington) 49:16
Eros at Breakfast, and Other Plays (Davies) 42:104
"Eros at Temple Stream" (Levertov) 28:239
"Eros at the World Kite Pageant" (Lieberman) 36:262-63
Eros at the World Kite Pageant: Poems, 1979-82 (Lieberman) 36:262-65
Eros e Priapo (Gadda) 11:213
"Eros, Eroticism, and the Pedagogical Process" (hooks) 94:157
Eros in Dogma (Barker) 48:16, 20
"Éros suspendu" (Char) 14:128
"Eros to Howard Nemerov" (Van Duyn) 63:437, 439
"Eros Turannos" (Walker) 103:410
"Erosion" (Graham) 48:148-49
Erosion (Graham) 48:147-54
"Erosion: Transkei" (Brutus) 43:92
"The E(rot)ic Potato" (McGrath) 55:73-4
Erotic Tales (Moravia) 46:285-87
"Erotica" (Creeley) 78:141
Erotica (Ritsos) 31:332
"Erotica vs. Pornography" (Steinem) 63:381
Eroticism (Bataille)
See L'erotisme

L'erotisme (Eroticism) (Bataille) 29:43, 45
The Erpingham Camp (Orton) 43:326-27, 330, 332-34
"Errand" (Carver) 53:65-7; 55:278, 283
"Errata" (Queneau) 42:333
"The Errigal Road" (Montague) 46:274-75
"Error" (Singer) 9:487
An Error of Judgement (Johnson) 27:219-20, 224
"The Errors" (Goldbarth) 38:201, 205-06
"Erschaffung der eva" (Jandl) 34:198
Az értlemiség utja az oszatályhatalomhoz (The Intellectuals on the Road to Class Power: A Sociological Study of the Role the Intelligentsia in Socialism) (Konrad) 73:167-68, 171-72, 174, 176, 187
"Eruntics" (Lem) 40:298
"Eruption" (Van Duyn) 116:422
Erzählungen, 1950-1970 (Boell) 72:76
"Es olvido" (Parra) 102:340
"Es que somos muy pobres" ("We Are Very Poor"; "We're Very Poor") (Rulfo) 80:200-01, 216
Es steht geschrieben (Duerrenmatt) 102:76
Es steht geschrieben (It Is Written) (Durrenmatt) 4:140; 8:194; 11:168-71; 15:194
"Es tan corto el amor, y es tan largo el olvido" ("Love Is So Short, Forgetting Is So Long") (Neruda) 7:257
"Es wird etwas geschehen" (Boell) 15:69-70; 72:72
L'Escadron blindé (The Tank Corps; Tankový prapor) (Skvorecky) 69:336, 340-43
"The Escapade" (Ignatow) 7:173
Escapade (Scott) 43:372-73, 383-85
Escapade (Warner) 45:438-39
"Escape" (Asimov) 92:4, 12
"Escape" (Blunden) 56:43
"Escape" (Bova) 45:73
"The Escape" (Campbell) 32:74
"Escape" (Huxley) 11:282
"Escape" (Johnston) 51:243
"The Escape" (Saro-Wiwa) 114:253
Escape! (Bova) 45:67
The Escape Artist (Wagoner) 3:507; 5:474
Escape Attempt (Strugatskii and Strugatskii)
See Popytka k begstvu
Escape from the Evil Prophecy (Kingman) 17:246
"Escape from the Planet of the Humanoids" (Grayson) 38:212
The Escape into You (Bell) 8:66-67; 31:46-9
Escape Plus (Bova) 45:73
"Escape the Close Circle" (Major) 19:298
"Escaping Again" (Dobyns) 37:76-7
"Escapist—Never" (Frost) 9:224
Escarmouches (Ferron) 94:126, 128
"Escarpment" (Ondaatje) 51:315
"A escola das facas" ("School of Knives") (Cabral de Melo Neto) 76:160
A escola das facas (The School of Knives) (Cabral de Melo Neto) 76:153, 155,158, 160, 163, 165
"Escrito en el agua" (Cernuda) 54:47
Escrito sobre un cuerpo (Writing on a Body) (Sarduy) 6:486; 97:367, 393, 405
El escritor (Azorin) 11:27
"El escritor argentino y la tradición" ("The Argentine Writer and Tradition") (Borges) 48:44; 83:192-93
"La escritura del Dios" ("The God's Script") (Borges) 8:98-9; 9:116; 44:353-54; 83:166

"Escuela de noche" (Cortazar) 33:135
La esfera (The Sphere) (Sender) 8:478, 480-82
"Eskimo" (Munro) 50:210, 216, 219
"Eskimo Love" (Apple) 33:22
"The Eskimo Motor in the Detention Cell" (West) 96:395
"Eskimo Pie" (Hollander) 2:197
"Esmé" (Salinger)
See "For Esmé—with Love and Squalor"
Esmond in India (Jhabvala) 4:258; 29:255-58; 94:169-70, 176-77, 180-81, 184, 189-91, 193, 200
El esoritor y sus fantasmas (Sabato) 10:446; 23:379
La espada encendida (Neruda) 7:257
Espadas como labios (Swords Like Lips) (Aleixandre) 9:11, 13; 36:23, 25-6, 30
"Espagne" ("Spain") (Cocteau) 8:145
The Espalier (Warner) 19:460
España en el corazón: himno a las glorias del pueblo en la guerra (1936-1937) (Spain at Heart; Spain in My Heart; Spain in the Heart) (Neruda) 7:258-59; 28:314; 62:323
España: Poema en cuatro angustias y una esperanza (Spain: A Poem in Four Anguishes and a Hope) (Guillen) 48:158; 79:229
"Un español habla de su tierra" (Cernuda) 54:61
"El espantoso redentor Lazarus Morell" ("The Dread Redeemer Lazarus Morell"; "The Terrible Redeemer Lazarus Morell") (Borges) 48:36; 83:166
Espèces d'espaces (Species of Spaces) (Perec) 116:234
An Especially Tricky People (Trudeau) 12:590
Un especie de memoria (Alegria) 57:14
"Los espejos" ("Mirrors") (Borges) 3:81
"Espérance, o savanes" (Tchicaya) 101:349
"Esperimento di magia" (Buzzati) 36:86
"L'espion des pouilles" (Mandiargues) 41:279
Les Espions (Lang) 103:88
"The Esplanade" (Zweig) 34:379; 42:469
L'espoir ("Les paysans") (Malraux) 9:356
L'espoir (Man's Hope) (Malraux) 1:203; 4:325-29, 333, 335-36; 9:354, 356-58; 13:366-69; 15:352; 57:303-04, 306, 308-10, 321, 323-24
"Espresso" (Transtroemer) 65:224
Ésprit de corps: Sketches from Diplomatic Life (Durrell) 41:139
"L'esprit de l'escalier" (Murray) 40:337
Essai sur la situation de la poésie (Tzara) 47:395
Essais (Camus) 63:75
Essais critiques (Critical Essays) (Barthes) 24:27, 41; 83:67, 70, 73-4, 78, 88
"An Essay at War" (Duncan) 41:128
"An Essay on Criticism" (Van Duyn) 63:438
"Essay on Death" (Carruth) 84:136
"Essay on Memory" (FitzGerald) 19:178-79, 181-82
An Essay on Morals (Wylie) 43:465, 472
"Essay on Poetics" (Ammons) 2:13; 8:14-16, 18-19; 9:28-9; 25:44-5, 47; 57:57, 59; 108:11, 32-3, 35-6, 40, 43, 46
"Essay on Psychiatrists" (Pinsky) 9:417; 38:360, 362
Essay on Rime (Shapiro) 53:326-30, 332
"Essay on Sanity" (Dunn) 36:154-55
"Essay on Stone" (Carruth) 18:89

"Essay on Style" (O'Hara)　**78**:350, 356, 360
Essay on the Essay (Lukacs)　**24**:326
Essay on Tragedy (Lukacs)　**24**:326
Essays in Craft and Elucidation (Blackmur)　**24**:56
Essays in Poetry: Mainly Australian (Buckley)　**57**:132
Essays in Self-Criticism (Althusser)　**106**:41
Essays in Understanding, 1930-1954 (Arendt)　**98**:51, 54
Essays of E. B. White (White)　**10**:531; **39**:370, 377
Essays of Four Decades (Tate)　**14**:531
Essays on Contemporary Issues (Oe)
　See *Oe Kenzaburo dojidai ronshu*
Essays on Culture and Politics (Fiedler)　**24**:203
Essays on Literature and Politics, 1932-1972 (Rahv)　**24**:356-57, 360-61
Essays on Realism (Lukacs)　**24**:339
Essays on Rime (Shapiro)　**4**:486
"Esse" (Milosz)　**82**:298
"Esse est percipi" (Bioy Casares)　**88**:78
Essene (Wiseman)　**20**:473-74, 477
"Die Essenholer" (Boell)　**72**:69
"Essential Beauty" (Larkin)　**8**:332, 340; **64**:269
The Essential Gesture (Gordimer)　**70**:168-71, 186
The Essential Haiku (Hass)　**99**:150, 155, 157
The Essential Lenny Bruce (Bruce)　**21**:51
Essential Reading (Reading)　**47**:354
"Essentialism and Experience" (hooks)　**94**:157
"Essentials of Spontaneous Prose" (Kerouac)　**29**:273-74; **61**:309, 312
"Essex" (Davie)　**8**:165; **31**:117
Essex Poems, 1963-1967 (Davie)　**5**:113-14; **8**:162, 165-66; **31**:117
"Esta muy caliente" (Bowering)　**47**:28
The Establishment (Fast)　**23**:161
The Establishment Is Alive and Well in Washington (Buchwald)　**33**:92-3
"La estampa antigua" (Aleixandre)　**9**:17
The Estate (Singer)　**3**:454-56; **6**:511; **9**:488; **15**:505
"Estatura del vino" ("A Statute of Wine") (Neruda)　**7**:258
Este Domingo (*This Sunday*) (Donoso)　**4**:126-28; **8**:178; **11**:145-46; **32**:152-54, 156, 158; **99**:216, 239
"Estelí" (Alegria)　**75**:34
"Esther" (Toomer)　**13**:552; **22**:426
Esther (Hochwalder)　**36**:235, 238
"Esther's Tomcat" (Hughes)　**9**:280
"Esthetics and Loss" (White)　**110**:333, 341
"Estienne Redivivus" (Klappert)　**57**:268
"Estoy cansado" (Cernuda)　**54**:55
"Estoy-eh-muut and the Kunideeyahs" (Silko)　**74**:347
"The Estrangement" (Blunden)　**56**:41
"El estrecho dudoso" ("The Doubtful Passage"; "The Dougtful Passage") (Cardenal)　**31**:74-6
"La estrella" ("The Star") (Neruda)　**62**:335
"The Estuary" (Beer)　**58**:31-2
"Estuary" (MacCaig)　**36**:283
"Estuary" (Merwin)　**18**:335
The Estuary (Beer)　**58**:31-2, 36
"Estudos para uma bailadora andaluza" ("Studies for an Andalusian Dancer") (Cabral de Melo Neto)　**76**:161
"Et caetera" ("Et Cetera") (Damas)　**84**:177-78
"Et Cetera" (Damas)
　See "Et caetera"

Et ils passerent des menottes aux fleurs (*And They Put Handcuffs on the Flowers*; *Y pondrán esposas a las flores*) (Arrabal)　**2**:15; **9**:36; **58**:12, 15-17, 23, 26-7
"Et in arcadia ego" (Rozewicz)　**23**:358
Et les chiens se taisaient: Tragédie (Cesaire)　**112**:21, 26-30
"Et maintenant" (Damas)　**84**:180
E.T.: The Book of the Green Planet (Kotzwinkle)　**35**:258-59
E.T., the Extra-Terrestrial in His Adventure on Earth (Kotzwinkle)　**35**:256-58
Et Tu, Babe (Leyner)　**92**:284-94
"Eta" (Tolson)　**105**:272, 284
"Etape" (Reverdy)　**53**:289
L'état de siège (*The State of Siege*) (Camus)　**1**:54; **9**:146; **14**:114-15; **32**:84-8, 90-1, 94, 96-8, 100-01; **63**:63
Les états-généraux (Breton)　**9**:126
"Etcetera" (Borges)　**48**:36
L'été (*Summer*) (Camus)　**1**:53; **14**:111; **32**:86
L'ete meurtrier (*One Deadly Summer*) (Japrisot)　**90**:168-70
"Eterna" (Lavin)　**99**:320
"Eternal Contemporaries" (Durrell)　**27**:97
Eternal Curse on the Reader of These Pages (Puig)　**28**:373-74; **65**:268, 271
The Eternal Day of Michel de Ghelderode (The Brothers Quay)　**95**:330, 340-41, 353
"The Eternal Feminine" (Castellanos)
　See *El eterno femenino*
Eternal Fire (Willingham)　**5**:511-12; **51**:407-08, 410
"The Eternal Kansas City" (Morrison)　**21**:237
"The Eternal Moment" (Forster)　**3**:162; **45**:132
"The Eternal Province" (Landolfi)　**49**:216-17
"The Eternal Rectangle" (Willingham)　**51**:403
The Eternal Return (Cocteau)
　See *L'éternel retour*
The Eternal Smile and Other Stories (Lagerkvist)　**54**:276; **7**:199, 201
"Eternal Snow" (Govier)　**51**:165-67
"The Eternal Wager" (Elytis)　**49**:109-10, 118
"Eternal Woman" (Ferlinghetti)　**111**:65
Eternal Worry (Dabrowska)
　See *Wieczne zmartwiene*
"Eternamente" (Aleixandre)　**9**:17
L'éternel retour (*The Eternal Return*) (Cocteau)　**16**:229; **43**:107
Eternity to Season (Harris)　**25**:204, 212-13
"Eternity's Woods" (Zweig)　**42**:470
Eternity's Woods (Zweig)　**34**:379-80; **42**:469
El eterno femenino ("The Eternal Feminine") (Castellanos)　**66**:47, 59-61
L'Eterrement de la sardine (*El entierro de la sardina*) (Arrabal)　**58**:4-6
"Ether" (Ginsberg)　**109**:325
"The Ether Breather" (Sturgeon)　**22**:410; **39**:361, 366
"The Ethic of Care for the Self as a Practice of Freedom" (Foucault)　**69**:192
"Ethical Criticism: Theory of Symbols" (Frye)　**24**:230
Ethics from a Theocentric Perspective (Gustafson)　**100**:199-201, 205-07, 212-14, 216, 222-23, 229, 232, 235
The Ethics of Ambiguity (Beauvoir)　**1**:19
"The Ethics of Linguistics" (Kristeva)　**77**:312-14
"The Ethics of Living Jim Crow" (Wright)　**9**:584; **21**:453; **74**:380, 388, 390, 393

Éthiopiques (Senghor)　**54**:390, 407-09
Ethnic Identity: The Transformation of White America (Alba)　**70**:379, 410
Ethnic Options: Choosing Ethnic Identities in America　**70**:381
Ethnic Radio (Murray)　**40**:338
"The Ethnographer Faced with Colonialism" (Leiris)　**61**:361
Étier: Poèmes, 1965-1975 (Guillevic)　**33**:193-94
"Les etiquettes jaunes" (O'Hara)　**13**:427
Eto ja—Edichka (*It's Me, Eddie*) (Coles)　**67**:168-73, 175-82
"L'etoile" (Wilbur)　**53**:407
Les ètoiles du sud (*The Stars of the South*) (Green)　**77**:293-94
"Eton Rifles" (Weller)　**26**:445-46
"L'Etrange Agonie" (Tchicaya)　**101**:350
L'étranger (*The Outsider*; *The Stranger*) (Camus)　**1**:52-4; **2**:97-9; **4**:90; **9**:139-41, 144-50, 152; **11**:93-5; **14**:104-08, 110-14, 116-18; **32**:86, 88-90, 96, 100; **63**:60-2, 64-6, 68, 71-3, 75-83; **69**:103-41
Etrangers à nous-mêmes (*Strangers to Ourselves*) (Kristeva)　**77**:323, 325-26, 330, 332, 336
L'être et le néant: Essai d'ontologie phénoménologique (*Being and Nothingness: An Essay on Phenomenological Ontology*) (Sartre)　**1**:303-05; **4**:473-75, 477; **7**:389, 396; **9**:470; **13**:498; **18**:473; **24**:406, 409, 412-14; **44**:494-95, 497; **50**:375, 378-80, 382-83; **52**:373, 376-79, 381, 383-84, 388
L'etreinte de Vénus (Theriault)　**79**:415
"An Étude for Emma" (Ferber)　**93**:140
"Etude in F" (Jandl)　**34**:197
"L'Eubage" (Cendrars)　**106**:170
"Eucharist" (Buckley)　**57**:129
"Euclidians" (Guillevic)
　See "Euclidiennes"
"Euclidiennes" ("Euclidians") (Guillevic)　**33**:192, 194
Eugene Onegin (Nabokov)　**1**:244; **3**:351; **8**:412, 417
"Eugene Thornton" (Johnston)　**51**:253
"Eulogy" (Pryor)　**26**:378
Eulogy for a Small Time Thief (Pinero)　**55**:316-18
"Eulogy for Alvin Frost" (Lorde)　**71**:323-33, 247
"Eulogy on Vladimír Holan" (Seifert)
　See "Pocta Vladimíru Holanovi"
"Eumenides" (Aldington)　**49**:7
Eunuchs of the Forbidden City (Ludlam)　**46**:239-40; **50**:342
"The Euphemisms" (Reading)　**47**:351
"Euphoria" (Ekeloef)　**27**:113-14, 119
"Eurasian Girl My Love" (Kerrigan)　**6**:276
The Euro-Killers (Rathbone)　**41**:341, 343
"Europa" (Walcott)　**42**:423
Europa (Gary)　**25**:189
Europa and the Bull (Rodgers)　**7**:377-78
Europa's Lover (Dunn)　**40**:169-70
"Europe" (Ashbery)　**2**:18; **4**:23; **9**:43; **25**:49-50, 58; **77**:42
"Europe" (Ehrenburg)　**62**:170
"Europe" (Kunene)　**85**:166, 177
Europe (Dudek)　**11**:158-60; **19**:136, 138
"Europe and America" (Ignatow)　**40**:258
Europe at Love (Morand)
　See *L'Europe galante*
L'Europe galante (*Europe at Love*) (Morand)

41:302-05

The Europe of Trusts (Howe)   72:208

Europe; or, Up and Down with Baggish and Schreiber (Stern)
See *Europe; or, Up and Down with Schreiber and Baggish*

Europe; or, Up and Down with Schreiber and Baggish (*Europe; or, Up and Down with Baggish and Schreiber*) (Stern)   4:523; 39:236

Europe without Baedeker (Wilson)   8:550; 24:487

A European Education (Gary)
See *Education Européenne*

"The European Scene" (Phillips)   28:363

"European Son" (Reed)   21:304, 323

The European Tribe (Phillips)   96:319-20, 322, 328, 330, 332, 335, 352, 354, 356

European Witness (Spender)   41:422-23; 91:261

The Europeans (Jhabvala)   94:185, 187

"Euryclea's Tale" (Rich)   11:475-76; 36:366

"Eurydice" (H. D.)   73:104

"Eurydice" (Sitwell)   67:324

Eurydice (Anouilh)   8:22; 13:16-17; 40:50, 52, 55-7; 50:278-80

"Eurydice in Darkness" (Davison)   28:100

"Eurydice in the Underworld" (Acker)   111:46-7

Eurydice in the Underworld (Acker)   111:46

"Eustace" (Malouf)   28:269

Eustace and Hilda (Hartley)   22:213, 217

Eustace Chisholm and the Works (Purdy)   2:349; 10:424; 28:380; 52:344, 347

Eva (Levin)   7:204-05

Eva aftjener sin barnepligt (Abell)   15:1

"Eva está dentro de su gato" ("Eva Inside Her Cat") (Garcia Marquez)   3:181; 47:150

Eva Gay: A Romantic Novel (Scott)   43:379-80, 384-85

"Eva Inside Her Cat" (Garcia Marquez)
See "Eva está dentro de su gato"

Eva Luna (Allende)   57:33-4; 97:2, 4, 9-11, 13, 17-18, 20, 23, 25, 27-8, 42, 51-2, 55-7, 59

Eva Trout; or, Changing Scenes (Bowen)   6:94; 11:59-61, 63-4

"Evaluation of an Unwritten Poem" (Szymborska)
See "Unwritten Poem Review"

"An Evaluation under a Pine Tree, Lying on Pine Needles" (Eberhart)   11:178

"Evangeline" (Faulkner)   18:148-50

Evangéline deusse (Maillet)   54:304, 309, 312, 314-16

"Evangelist" (Davie)   5:113

"The Evans Country" (Amis)   2:6

Evaristo Carriego (Borges)   44:363; 83:165-66

Eva's Man (Jones)   9:306-08

"Eve" (Livesay)   79:337

The Eve of Manhood (Marques)
See *La víspera del hombre*

Eve of Retirement (Bernhard)
See *Vor dem Ruhestand*

The Eve of St. Venus (Burgess)   2:86; 22:71; 40:115-17

The Eve of the Green Grass (Dowell)   60:99

"Eve the Fox" (Allen)   84:24

Evelyn Brown (Fornes)   39:138; 61:137

Evelyn Waugh: The Early Years, 1903-39 (Stannard)   44:520-22

Even Cowgirls Get the Blues (Robbins)   9:454; 32:366-74; 64:371-73, 377-80, 382-83

Even Dwarfs Started Small (Herzog)   16:322-23, 325, 327, 331-32

"Even Greenland" (Hannah)   38:234-35; 90:138

Even If I Could (Williams)   33:442

"Even in Communal Pitches" (Kelman)   58:301

"Even Now" (Seger)   35:386-87

"The Even Sea" (Swenson)   106:315

"Even Song" (Sissman)   9:491

"Even The Devil Can't Save the World" (Moravia)   46:286-87

Even the Fist Once Was an Open Hand and Fingers (Amichai)
See *Gam ha'egrof haya pa'am yad ptuba ve'etsba'ot*

"Even Then" (Steele)   45:362

Even Tide (Woiwode)   10:542

"Even Venus Turns Over" (Barker)   8:47

"Evenin' Air Blues" (Hughes)   35:221

"Evening" (Merton)   83:392

"Evening" (Prokosch)   48:309

Evening (Akhmatova)
See *Vecher*

"Evening, after the Auction" (Steele)   45:362

"An Evening Alone at Bunyah" (Murray)   40:334, 337

Evening at Grinde (Vesaas)
See *Grinde-kveld; eller, Den gode engelen*

"Evening at Wolf Trap" (Taylor)   44:302

Evening Dawns (Konwicki)
See *Zorze wieczorne*

Evening Edged in Gold: A FairytalefArse. 55 Scenes from the Countryside for Patrons of Errata (Schmidt)
See *Abend mit Goldrand: Eine Märchen Posse. 55 Bilder aus der Lä/endlichkeit fur Gönner der VerschreibKunst*

"The Evening Grass" (Boyle)   58:69

"Evening Hawk" (Warren)   8:540; 13:578; 18:536; 39:266

Evening in Byzantium (Shaw)   7:413

"Evening in Connecticut" (Tuohy)   37:432

Evening in Spring (Derleth)   31:127, 135

"Evening in the Country" (Ashbery)   2:17; 4:23; 15:30; 41:40

"Evening in the Sanitarium" (Bogan)   46:83, 90; 93:64, 78

"The Evening Journey of Yatir" ("The Tropville Evening Express") (Yehoshua)   31:467, 470

Evening Land (Lagerkvist)
See *Aftonland*

"The Evening of Ants" (Soto)   80:287-88

"An Evening of Russian Poetry" (Nabokov)   8:407

The Evening of the Holiday (Hazzard)   18:214, 217-18

"The Evening of the Mind" (Justice)   19:233

"The Evening of the Second Day" (Chappell)   40:147

"Evening of the Visitation" (Merton)   83:391

An Evening Performance: New and Selected Short Stories (Garrett)   51:151-52

"The Evening Primrose" (Parker)   68:325

Evening Primrose (Sondheim)   30:389

"Evening Signs at Gallt-y-Celliog" (Fuller)   62:192

"Evening Song" (Toomer)   22:426

"Evening Star" (McFadden)   48:246, 248

Evening Star (Sherburne)   30:361

"Evening Talk" (Simic)   68:377

Evening Verses (Arghezi)   80:10

"Evening Walk" (Soto)   80:301

An Evening with Dead Essex (Kennedy)   66:214

"An Evening with Jackie Kennedy, or, The Wild West of the East" (Mailer)   111:106-07

"An Evening with John Joe Dempsey" (Trevor)   71:322; 116:333, 358-59, 363-64

An Evening with Richard Nixon and ... (Vidal)   2:449-50

"The Evening's at Seven" (Thurber)   5:430

An Evening's Frost (Frost)   1:110

"The Event" (Dove)   50:153, 155, 157-58; 81:138

"Event" (Ezekiel)   61:92, 97

"The Event" (Heidegger)
See "Das Ereignis"

"Event" (Plath)   3:390; 51:340, 346; 111:203

"An Event" (Wilbur)   14:577; 53:408, 410, 412; 110:351, 353, 357, 383

Eventail de fer (Montherlant)   19:325

Events and Celebrations (Vliet)   22:441

Events and Signals (Scott)   22:371

Events and Wisdoms: Poems, 1957-1963 (Davie)   5:114; 8:164; 10:123

"Events at Drimaghleen" (Trevor)   71:341, 343, 348; 116:379-80

"The Events at Poroth Farm" (Klein)   34:71

Events following the Closure of a Motorcycle Factory (Edgar)   42:116

"Eventual Proteus" (Atwood)   4:27; 8:32

"Eventually the Poem for Keewaydin" (Ondaatje)   51:310

"Ever After" (Gallagher)   18:170

Ever After (Swift)   88:313-18, 320-23

Ever the Winds of Chance (Sandburg)   35:360

The Everest Hotel (Wilson)   33:461, 464

"Evergreen Cemetery" (Purdy)   50:245

The Everlasting Mercy (Masefield)   11:357-58; 47:225-31, 233

The Everlasting Sky: New Voices from the People Named the Chippewa (Vizenor)   103:296-97

The Everlastings (Dubie)   36:134-35, 137-38, 141

"Every Breath You Take" (Police, The)   26:366

Every Brilliant Eye (Estleman)   48:106-07

"Every Bullet Has Its Billet" (Bates)   46:56

"Every Day a Little Death" (Sondheim)   30:389, 400

Every Day Except Christmas (Anderson)   20:11, 16-17

Every Day Is Saturday (White)   10:528-29

"Every Day of His Life" (Hodgins)   23:230

"Every Evening When the Sun Goes Down" (Ashbery)   25:59

Every Form of Refuge Has Its Price (Pinero)   55:316-18

Every Good Boy Deserves Favour: A Piece for Actors and Orchestra (Stoppard)   15:518; 29:395-97, 402, 404; 34:272; 91:190

"Every Little Hurricane" (Alexie)   96:4

"Every Little Thing" (Lennon and McCartney)   35:274

"Every Little Thing She Does Is Magic" (Police, The)   26:365-66

Every Man for Himself (Godard)
See *Sauve qui peut (La vie)*

Every Man for Himself and God against All (The Mystery of Kaspar Hauser) (Herzog)   16:324-26, 329-32, 334

"Every Man His Own Critic" (Crane)   27:74

"Every Night" (McCartney)   35:278-79

Every Night's a Bullfight (Gardner)
See *Every Night's a Festival*

Every Night's a Festival (Every Night's a Bull-fight) (Gardner) **30**:153
"Every Other Thursday" (Ferber) **93**:153, 180
"Every Traveler Has One Vermont Poem" (Lorde) **71**:258
"Everybody Has a Dream" (Joel) **26**:215
"Everybody, I Love You" (Young) **17**:569-70
Everybody Knows This Is Nowhere (Young) **17**:569-70, 572, 579
"Everybody Loves You Now" (Joel) **26**:217, 222
"Everybody Ought to Have a Maid" (Sondheim) **30**:378
"Everybody Says Don't" (Sondheim) **30**:379
"Everybody's a Star" (Davies) **21**:99
"Everybody's Gonna Be Happy" (Davies) **21**:89
Everybody's in Showbiz (Davies) **21**:94-5
"Everybody's Lib" (Brophy) **105**:13
"Everybody's Protest Novel" (Baldwin) **4**:40-2; **15**:42; **17**:33; **42**:14; **50**:291; **67**:5, 14
"Everyday Use" (Walker) **103**:361, 407
"The Everydayness of the Soul" (Herbert) **9**:275
"Everyone Knows the World Is Ending" (Fulton) **52**:161
"Everyone Knows Whom the Saved Envy" (Galvin) **38**:198
Everyone Sang (Sassoon) **36**:391
"Everyone's Gone to the Movies" (Becker and Fagen) **26**:80
Everyone's Trash Problem (Hyde) **21**:179-80
"Everything" (Bachmann)
 See "Alle"
"Everything" (Levine) **14**:321
"Everything and Nothing" (Borges) **1**:39; **2**:75; **83**:172
"Everything: Eloy, Arizona, 1956" (Ai) **69**:11
Everything for Sale (Wajda) **16**:579-80
Everything in the Garden (Albee) **3**:7; **5**:13; **13**:5; **25**:38
"Everything is Green" (Wallace) **114**:347, 349
"Everything Is Nice" (Bowles) **68**:6, 8, 11
Everything Must Go (Waterhouse)
 See *The Bucket Shop*
"Everything Stuck to Him" (Carver)
 See "Distance"
"Everything That Acts Is Actual" (Levertov) **15**:337
Everything That Moves (Schulberg) **48**:350-51
"Everything That Rises Must Converge" (O'Connor) **13**:419; **15**:410, 413; **21**:269, 276; **104**:112, 115, 126-29, 131, 133, 135, 137, 143, 145, 148, 151, 162-63, 168-69, 171-80, 182-84, 186, 190, 199, 200-02
Everything That Rises Must Converge (All That Rises Must Converge) (O'Connor) **3**:369; **6**:377; **21**:262, 264, 267, 276; **104**:102-03, 106-07, 113, 116, 125, 127, 135, 138, 161, 165, 178-79, 187-90
Everything to Live For (Horgan) **53**:182-83, 185
"Everything Went Still" (Van Doren) **10**:496
Everything You Always Wanted to Know about Sex (Allen) **16**:4-5; **52**:38-9, 45
"Everything You Did" (Becker and Fagen) **26**:83
Everything You've Heard Is True (Sherwood) **81**:102, 109
"Everything's All Right" (Rice and Webber) **21**:426
"Everything's Alright" (Wonder)
 See "Uptight"

"Everything's Coming Up Roses" (Sondheim) **30**:377, 395
"Everything's Foreseeable" (Simic) **68**:379
Everything's in Place, Nothing's in Order (All Screwed Up) (Wertmueller) **16**:591, 595, 598
"Everywhere" (Matthews) **40**:322, 324
Eves (Ehrenburg) **62**:175
Evgenia Ivanova (Leonov) **92**:253, 261, 265, 268-69, 278
L'eviathan (The Dark Journey) (Green) **77**:262-65, 267, 269-71, 290
"Evidence" (Asimov) **26**:50, 54, 56; **92**:4, 8, 12
"The Evidence" (Jong) **6**:268
Evidence of Love (Grau) **9**:240
Evidence of Love (Jacobson) **4**:255; **14**:289
The Evidence of Things Not Seen (Baldwin) **42**:15-16, 18, 20-3; **50**:283, 293, 297
Evidence of Things Seen (Daly) **52**:88-9
The Evidence That Wasn't There (Adler) **35**:12-13
Det eviga leendet (Lagerkvist) **13**:333; **54**:266-68, 274, 286, 288-89
"Evil" (Wonder) **12**:656, 663
"Evil and the English Novel" (Wilson) **34**:582
"The Evil Angel" (Lagerkvist)
 See "Den onda ängeln"
"Evil Days" (Pasternak) **63**:313
The Evil Demon of Images (Baudrillard) **60**:36
"The Evil Eye" (Ciardi) **40**:154
The Evil Hour (Garcia Marquez)
 See *La mala hora*
Evil Is Abroad (Audiberti)
 See *Le mal court*
The Evil Runs (Audiberti)
 See *Le mal court*
Evil Sagas (Lagerkvist)
 See *Onda sagor*
Evil Tales (Lagerkvist)
 See *Onda sagor*
Evil under the Sun (Christie) **6**:110; **12**:123; **48**:72-3, 75; **110**:114
Evita (Rice and Webber) **21**:431-33
"The Evitable Conflict" (Asimov) **26**:54, 56, 64; **92**:4, 8-9, 12, 19
"Evocation" (Thesen) **56**:418
"Evolution" (Swenson) **106**:314, 337, 346, 348-49
"Evolution" (Townshend) **17**:528, 531
Evolution and Genetics: The Code of Life (Silverstein and Silverstein) **17**:453, 456
"Évolution de rêve, rêve et révolution: Réalité" (Prevert) **15**:440
"Evolution in Light and Water" (Hogan) **73**:150
"The Evolution of Birds of Paradise" (Tallent) **45**:387-88
"Evolutionary Poem No. 1" (Knight) **40**:285
"Evolutionary Poem No. 2" (Knight) **40**:285
"Evolutions" (Arghezi) **80**:2
The Ewings (O'Hara) **2**:324-25; **42**:324
Ex cathedra (Connelly) **7**:56
Ex Cranium, Night (Rakosi) **47**:345-46
"Ex Nihilo" (Chappell) **78**:96
"Ex ponto" (Ekeloef) **27**:119
"The Exact Location of the Soul" (Selzer) **74**:264, 271
The Exact Name (Ezekiel) **61**:91, 93-4, 96, 100-01, 103
"The Exact Nature of Plot" (Schaeffer) **22**:369-70
"The Exacting Ghost" (Watkins) **43**:452

The Exaggerations of Peter Prince (Katz) **47**:215-17
"Das Examen" (Lenz) **27**:252
"Examen de la obra de Herbert Quain" ("An Examination of the Work of Herbert Quain") (Borges) **3**:77; **83**:164, 180
"The Examination" (Snodgrass) **6**:514; **68**:388, 397
The Examination (Pinter) **27**:388
"Examination at the Womb-Door" (Hughes) **2**:203; **9**:281
"An Examination of the Work of Herbert Quain" (Borges)
 See "Examen de la obra de Herbert Quain"
"Examiner" (Scott) **22**:377
"Examples" (Hollander) **8**:299
"Exaugeral Address" (Baraka) **14**:43
"Ex-Basketball Player" (Updike) **23**:473
"La excavación" ("The Excavation") (Roa Bastos) **45**:345-47
"The Excavation" (Roa Bastos)
 See "La excavación"
Excavations (Van Vechten) **33**:390
"Excellence and the Pleasure Principle" (Stegner) **49**:359
"The Excellent Irony" (Blunden) **56**:47
Excellent Women (Pym) **13**:469-71; **37**:370, 375-76; **111**:225-27, 229, 232, 234-39, 243, 245-48, 263-65, 269-70, 273, 278-79, 281-87
"Excelsior! We're Going to the Moon! Excelsior!" (Vonnegut) **12**:610
Except for Me and Thee (West) **7**:521; **17**:550-53
"Except That She Smokes, Drinks Booze and Talks Rough, Miss Mazie Is a Nun" ("Mazie") (Mitchell) **98**:154, 164, 177, 180
"Excerpt from a Letter" (Seifert)
 See "Úryvek z dopisu"
"Excerpt from Work in Progress..." (Avison) **97**:70-1
Excerpts from a Life (Buckler) **13**:120
"Excerpts from a Poem for Samuel Beckett" (Boyle) **58**:76
Excerpts from the Real World: A Prose Poem in Ten Parts (Kroetsch) **57**:296-98
Excerpts from Visions of Cody (Kerouac) **29**:274
"Exchange" (Cixous) **92**:78-9
The Exchange (Trifonov)
 See *Obmen*
"An Exchange between the Fingers and the Toes" (Fuller) **62**:185
"An Exchange of Views" (Fussell) **74**:140
"Exchange Value" (Johnson) **51**:235-36
"Exchanges" (Dickey) **15**:178; **47**:92-3, 95, 98
"Excitement in Ergo" (Willingham) **51**:403
"Exclamación" (Paz) **10**:392; **51**:327
"El excluido" (Castellanos) **66**:52
The Exclusions of a Rhyme (Cunningham) **31**:97-9, 106
"Exclusive" (Olds) **32**:347
"The Excruciating Final Days of Dr. Jekyll, Englishman" (Ligotti) **44**:54
"Excursion" (Garrett) **51**:148
"Excursion in Reality" (Waugh) **27**:477
"The Excursionists" (Santos) **22**:364
Excursions in the Real World (Trevor) **116**:378, 386
"Excursions, Incursions" (Piercy) **27**:376
Excuses, Excuses (Edgar) **42**:116
"Execution" (Guillen) **79**:229

"The Execution" (Nowlan) **15**:399

"L'exécution de Maski" ("The Execution of Maski") (Ferron) **94**:118, 121, 127

Execution Eve (Buckley) **7**:34

"The Execution of Clemmie Lake" (Nowlan) **15**:398

"The Execution of Cornelius Vane" (Read) **4**:437, 439

"The Execution of Imre Nagy" (Faludy) **42**:138

The Execution of Justice (Duerrenmatt) **102**:83-4

"The Execution of Maski" (Ferron)
   See "L'exécution de Maski"

"The Execution of Stenka Razin" (Yevtushenko) **26**:462

The Executioner (Bennett) **35**:45

The Executioner (Lagerkvist) **54**:271

The Executioner Waits (Herbst) **34**:449, 451, 455

The Executioners (Arrabal)
   See *Les deux bourreaux*

The Executioners (*Cape Fear*) (MacDonald) **44**:408

The Executioner's Block (Aitmatov)
   See *Plakha*

The Executioner's Song (Mailer) **14**:351-54; **28**:260, 262; **39**:416, 419; **74**:202, 205-06, 210, 225, 228-31, 237; **111**:118, 120-21, 123-35, 148-49

"Executive" (Betjeman) **34**:306; **43**:47

Executive Orders (Clancy) **112**:80-6

Exécutoire (Guillevic) **33**:191, 194

"The Executor" (Spark) **40**:403

An Exemplary Life (Lenz)
   See *Das Vorbild*

"An Exequy" (Porter) **13**:453; **33**:321-25

Exercices de style (*Exercises in Style*) (Queneau) **2**:359; **5**:359, 361; **10**:429-30; **42**:331, 333-34

"The Exercise" (Mac Laverty) **31**:252, 254

"Exercise on a Sphere" (Hope) **51**:222

Exercises in Style (Perec) **56**:267

Exercises in Style (Queneau)
   See *Exercices de style*

"Exhaustion" (Barth)
   See "The Literature of Exhaustion"

"Exhaustion Now Is a More Frequent Guest" (Brodsky) **36**:81

"The Exhibition" (Stevenson) **33**:381

"Exhibitionist" (Boland) **113**:60, 62-3

"Exhortation" (Bogan) **46**:83; **93**:64

"The Exhortation" (Gustafson) **36**:214

"Exil" ("Exile") (Perse) **46**:304

L'exil (Laye) **38**:292

L'exil (Montherlant) **19**:328

Exil (*Exile and Other Poems*) (Perse) **4**:399-400; **11**:433-34; **46**:302-05, 307-09

L'Exil de James Joyce ou l'art du remplacement (Cixous) **92**:50, 70

L'éxil et le royaume (*Exile and the Kingdom*) (Camus) **1**:52; **9**:144-45, 150-51; **14**:107, 110, 114; **63**:71, 77

"Exile" (Aldington) **49**:9

"Exile" (Feinstein) **36**:168

"Exile" (Gellhorn) **60**:183-84

"Exile" (Guillen) **79**:229

"Exile" (Lane) **25**:286

"Exile" (Perse)
   See "Exil"

The Exile (Buck) **7**:32; **11**:74-5

An Exile (Jones) **4**:262

Exile (Weiss) **3**:514

Exile and Other Poems (Aldington) **49**:5, 10,
17

Exile and Other Poems (Perse)
   See *Exil*

Exile and the Kingdom (Camus)
   See *L'éxil et le royaume*

Exile Ends in Glory: The Life of a Trappestine, Mother M. Berchmans (Merton) **34**:465

The Exile of James Joyce or the Art of Replacement (Cixous)
   See *The Exile of James Joyce or the Art of Replacement*

Exile on Main Street (Jagger and Richard) **17**:224-25, 228-29, 232-33, 235-36

"Exile Prolonged by Real Reasons" (Murray) **40**:344

Exiled from Earth (Bova) **45**:67

"The Exiles" (Auden) **11**:16

"The Exiles" (Bradbury) **98**:111

"Exiles" (Strand) **18**:518, 520; **41**:434

Exiles and Emigres: Studies in Modern Literature (Eagleton) **63**:93, 101-02

Exiles and Marriages (Hall) **59**:154

"Exiles from Their Land, History Their Domicile" (Spender) **41**:427

"The Exiles Letter" (Pound) **2**:343; **112**:343, 345

Exiles of the Stars (Norton) **12**:460, 462, 469

"The Exile's Return" (Lowell) **9**:335; **11**:325

Exile's Return (Cowley) **39**:458, 461

The Existence and Discovery of Beauty (Kawabata) **107**:108, 110

The Existential Background of Human Dignity (Marcel) **15**:364

Existential Errands (Mailer) **2**:263-64; **111**:126

The Existential Vacuum: A Challenge to Psychiatry (Frankl) **93**:208

"L'existentialisme" (Behan) **79**:39-40

L'existentialisme et la sagesse des nations (Beauvoir) **44**:344

"The Exit" (Elytis) **100**:171, 187

Exit Lady Masham (Auchincloss) **45**:33

"Exit Line" (Ciardi) **44**:381

"Exit Molloy" (Mahon) **27**:290

Exit the King (Ionesco)
   See *Le roi se meurt*

"Ex-Judge at the Bar" (Tolson) **105**:259

"Exodo" (Castellanos) **66**:50

"Exodus" (Cohen) **38**:131

"Exodus" (Kizer) **39**:170

Exodus (Marley) **17**:269-72

Exodus (Uris) **7**:490-91; **32**:433, 435-38

"Exorcised" (Blunden) **56**:45

"Exorcising Ghosts and Ancestors" (Shapcott) **38**:404

"The Exorcism" (Roethke) **19**:399; **101**:263, 265

"The Exorcism" (Smith) **64**:391

Exorcismos de esti(l)o (Cabrera Infante) **25**:102

The Exorcist (Blatty) **2**:63-4

"Exotic Nile" (Barthelme) **117**:17

"The Exotic Nouns" (Reid) **33**:350

"Exotic Pleasures" (Carey) **40**:133; **96**:27, 39

Exotic Pleasures (Carey) **96**:36

Expanded Universe: The New Worlds of Robert A. Heinlein (Heinlein) **55**:301, 303

"An Expanded Want Ad" (Leithauser) **27**:242

"The Expansion of the Universe" (Gilchrist) **48**:119

"The Expatriate" (Forche) **25**:171

"The Expatriates" (Williams) **42**:442

The Expatriates (Jenkins) **52**:224-25, 228

"The Expatriates' Party" (Vanderhaeghe) **41**:449-50, 453

L'expatrié (Green) **77**:293

"Expectation of Life" (Watkins) **43**:444

"Expecting to Fly" (Young) **17**:569, 577

"The Expedition" (Barthelme) **46**:36

"'An Expedition at the Pole'" (Dillard)
   See "An Expedition to the Pole"

"An Expedition to the Pole" ("'An Expedition at the Pole'") (Dillard) **60**:74-5; **115**:198, 206

"The Expelled" (Beckett)
   See "L'Expulsé"

"Expelled" (Cheever) **64**:66

The Expense of Greatness (Blackmur) **24**:54-5, 61, 66

"The Expense of Spint" (Oates) **6**:370; **108**:368, 370-71

"The Expense of Spirit in a Waste of Shame" (Mueller) **51**:280

Expensive Habits (Howard) **46**:188-91

Expensive Habits (*Acquired Tastes: A Beginner's Guide to Serious Pleasures*)(Mayle) **89**:147-48, 150

"The Expensive Moment" (Paley) **37**:333, 336, 338

Expensive People (Oates) **1**:251; **2**:314-16; **3**:359-60; **6**:368, 371; **11**:402; **15**:400; **19**:349-51; **52**:338; **108**:343, 385, 391

An Expensive Place to Die (Deighton) **46**:126

"Experience" (Simmons) **43**:412

Experience and Art (Krutch) **24**:283, 289

"Experience and Fiction" (Jackson) **60**:213

Experience and Religion: A Lay Essay in Theology (Mosley) **43**:321

"Experience and the Objects of Knowledge in the Philosophy of F. H. Bradley" (*Knowledge and Experience in the Philosophy of F. H. Bradley*) (Eliot) **24**:172; **113**:205, 207, 209-10

"Experience by Battle" (Hersey) **97**:304-05

"Experience Evoked" (Eberhart) **56**:78

L'expérience intérieure (*The Inner Experience*) (Bataille) **29**:38, 44, 48-9

"An Experience of India" (Jhabvala) **94**:181-82, 185

An Experience of India (Jhabvala) **4**:257-58; **29**:258

The Experience of Literature (Trilling) **9**:532

"The experience of Poetry in a Scientific Age" (Swenson) **106**:334

"Experience of the Theatre" (Ionesco) **86**:331

"Experiences with Images" (MacNeice) **10**:324

"Experiment" (Kogawa) **78**:167

"Experiment" (Szymborska) **99**:192

An Experiment in Criticism (Lewis) **3**:295; **27**:264

"The Experiment That Failed" (Logan) **5**:253

"Experimental" (Kavan) **82**:120

"Experimental Death Unit #1" (Baraka) **115**:35-6

Experimental Death Unit #1 (Baraka) **5**:46

Experimenting with an Amen (Thomas) **48**:383

Experiments in Optical Illusions (Branley) **21**:16

Experiments in Science (Branley) **21**:15

Experiments in Sky Watching (Branley) **21**:17

Experiments with a Microscope (Branley) **21**:16

Experiments with Atomics (Branley) **21**:16

Experiments with Electricity (Branley) **21**:15

Experts Are Puzzled (Riding) **3**:431

"Expiation" (Jhabvala) **94**:209

"Explaining a Few Things" (Neruda)
   See "Explico algunas cosas"

"The Explanation" (Barthelme) **59**:251; **115**:56

"Explanation" (Enright) **31**:154

"Explanation" (Livesay) **79**:341

"Explanation" (Pasternak) **63**:313

"Explanation of a Map" (Graham) **29**:198

An Explanation of America (Pinsky) **19**:370-72; **38**:356, 360-62, **94**:299, 305, 308,311, 322

"Explico algunas cosas" ("Explaining a Few Things"; "I Explain a Few Things") (Neruda) **62**:336

An Exploded View (Longley) **29**:292-94, 296

The Exploration of Space (Clarke) **35**:117, 121

Exploration of the Moon (Branley) **21**:17

"Exploration over the Rim" (Dickey) **28**:117

The Explorer (Maugham) **15**:365; **93**:230

"The Explorers" (Hope) **51**:214

"Explorers" (Simic) **22**:380

"The Explorers" (Weidman) **7**:516

Explorers of the Atom (Gallant) **17**:130

Exploring by Astronaut: The Story of Project Mercury (Branley) **21**:17

Exploring Chemistry (Gallant) **17**:127

Exploring Mars (Gallant) **17**:126

Exploring the Brain (Silverstein and Silverstein) **17**:454, 456

Exploring the Earth and the Cosmos (Asimov) **26**:58-9

Exploring the Moon (Gallant) **17**:126

Exploring the Planets (Gallant) **17**:127-28

Exploring the Sun (Gallant) **17**:127

Exploring the Universe (Gallant) **17**:126

Exploring the Weather (Gallant) **17**:126

Exploring under the Earth (Gallant) **17**:127

"The Explosion" (Aleixandre) **36**:28

"The Explosion" (Larkin) **5**:230; **8**:332-33, 339; **13**:335; **18**:300-01; **39**:336; **64**:266, 280, 285

Explosion in the Cathedral (Carpentier)
See *El siglo de las luces*

"The Explosion of Black Poetry" (Major) **19**:293

Exposition of the Orthodox Faith (John)
See "Isolt of Brittany"

"Exposure" (Heaney) **7**:151; **25**:246; **74**:159-60, 163-64, 167, 169, 180, 184

"Exposure" (Musgrave) **13**:400

"Exposures" (Benford) **52**:76

La expresión americana (*American Expression*) (Lezama Lima) **101**:121-22

"Expression" (Gunn) **32**:214

Expressions of Sea Level (Ammons) **2**:12; **5**:25-6; **25**:43, 48; **108**:2, 5, 7, 26, 46

"L'Expulsé" ("The Expelled") (Beckett) **3**:45; **10**:34-5

"The Expulsion" (Stern) **40**:412-13

"The Ex-Queen among the Astronomers" (Adcock) **41**:15, 17-18

The Exquisite Corpse (Chester) **49**:57-60

L'extase matérielle (*The Ecstasy of Matter*) (Le Clezio) **31**:247, 249

"Extelopedia" (Lem) **40**:298-99

Extending upon the Kingdom (Booth) **13**:104

Exterminating Angel (Bunuel)
See *El ángel exterminador*

"The Extermination of the Jews" (Bell) **8**:65

The Exterminator (*Exterminator!*) (Burroughs) **2**:93; **5**:92-3; **22**:86; **42**:75, 79-80; **75**:93

Exterminator! (Burroughs)
See *The Exterminator*

"Extinct Birds" (Wright) **53**:428

"The Extinction Tales" (Boyle) **36**:57-8

"Extra Gang" (Davis) **49**:91, 94, 97

Extra Innings: New Poems (Souster) **14**:504-05

"An Extra Joyful Chorus for Those Who Have Read This Far" (Bly) **10**:61

"Extractions and Contractions" (Blaise) **29**:70, 75

"Extracts from a Private Life" (Rakosi) **47**:343

"Extracts from Addresses to the Academy of Fine Ideas" (Pinsky) **38**:357

"Extracts from the Journal of Elisa Lynch" (Stanton) **9**:507

The Extraordinary Adventures of Julio Jurenito and His Disciples (*Julio Jurenito; The Unusual Adventures of Julio Jurenito and His Disciples*) (Ehrenburg) **18**:130, 134, 136; **34**:435-39; **62**:174-75, 178-80

"The Extraordinary Patience of Things" (Zamora) **89**:393

Extraordinary Tales (Bioy Casares)
See *Cuentos breves y extraordinarios*

Extraordinary Women (Mackenzie) **18**:314

Extraterrestrial Civilizations (Asimov) **26**:50-1

"Extraterrestrial Relays" (Clarke) **35**:118

Extraterritorial (Steiner) **24**:432-33

"An Extravagance of Laughter" (Ellison) **114**:125

"An Extravagance of Laughter" (Ellison) **114**:125

"The Extravagance of the Dead" (Oe)
See "Shisha no ogori"

Extravagario (*Book of Vagaries*) (Neruda) **1**:247; **2**:309; **5**:303-05; **7**:261; **28**:310-15

Extreme Magic (Calisher) **8**:125; **38**:70-1

"Extremes and Moderations" (Ammons) **2**:13; **8**:16, 18; **9**:29-30; **57**:59; **108**:9, 11, 38, 44

The Extremists: Gadflies of American Society (Archer) **12**:17

The Extremities (Mastrosimone) **36**:289-92

Exultate! Jubilate! (Kotzwinkle) **5**:220

Exultations (Pound) **2**:343

"An Ex-Voto in an Old Roman Town" (Kerrigan) **6**:276

"The Eye" (Hillis) **66**:194, 197, 199

"The Eye" (Olds) **32**:347; **39**:187

"The Eye" (Powers) **1**:280, 282; **4**:419

"The Eye" (Tate) **11**:528; **14**:530

"The Eye" (Wilbur) **9**:568

The Eye (Nabokov) **1**:242; **2**:302; **15**:396; **64**:348

"The Eye Altering" (Le Guin) **45**:213

Eye among the Blind (Holdstock) **39**:152

"Eye and Tooth" (Lowell) **8**:351; **11**:327

The Eye in the Door (Barker) **94**:15, 17-19

The Eye in the Pyramid (Wilson) **9**:576

Eye in the Sky (Dick) **30**:116; **72**:104, 108, 120, 122

The Eye of a Needle (Scott) **22**:371

The Eye of Conscience: Photographers and Social Change (Meltzer) **26**:302

"The Eye of Innocence: Some Notes on the Role of the Child in Literature" (Fiedler) **24**:203

"Eye of the Beholder" (Brunner) **8**:109

The Eye of the Camel (Aitmatov)
See *Verbliuzhii glaz*

The Eye of the Heron (Le Guin) **45**:214-15, 217-18

"The Eye of the Hurricane" (Brown) **48**:52

Eye of the Monster (Norton) **12**:467

Eye of the Needle (Follett) **18**:155-56

The Eye of the Scarecrow (Harris) **25**:204, 215

The Eye of the Storm (White) **3**:521-25; **4**:584-87; **5**:484-88; **7**:532; **9**:567; **65**:274-77, 279, 282; **69**:401-02, 405, 411

The Eye of the Story (Welty) **14**:565-67; **33**:423

The Eye of the Tiger (Smith) **33**:375

"Eye to Eye" (Lorde) **71**:244

"The Eye-Beaters" (Dickey) **2**:117; **10**:142; **15**:174; **109**:267-68, 273, 292

The Eye-Beaters, Blood, Victory, Madness, Buckhead, and Mercy (Dickey) **2**:116-17; **4**:120-21; **10**:141; **47**:92, 95-6; **109**:245, 264, 267-69, 272

The Eyeglass of Love Is Colored Glass (Abe)
See *Ai no megane wa irogarasu*

Eyeless in Gaza (Huxley) **1**:151; **4**:237-40, 243-44; **5**:194; **8**:304-05; **11**:281-82, 286; **18**:265, 267; **35**:240-41, 243-44; **79**:327-28

"The Eyeless Saying Yes" (Santos) **22**:361

"The Eye-Mote" (Plath) **5**:345; **17**:348; **111**:160

"Eyes" (Amichai) **116**:98

"Eyes" (Blaise) **29**:70

Eyes and Memory (Aragon)
See *Les yeux et la memoire*

Eyes at the Back of Our Heads (Levertov)
See *With Eyes at the Back of Our Heads*

Eyes, Etc. (Clark) **19**:107

"Eyes Fastened with Pins" (Simic) **68**:379

Eyes in the Fishbowl (Snyder) **17**:470-71

Eyes of a Blue Dog (Garcia Marquez) **47**:147

Eyes of Amber (Vinge) **30**:415

"Eyes of Amber" and Other Stories (Vinge) **30**:410

"The Eyes of Children at the Brink of the Sea's Grasp" (Jacobsen) **102**:240

The Eyes of Darkness (Koontz) **78**:200-01

"Eyes of Dust" (Ellison) **42**:126

The Eyes of Heisenberg (Herbert) **23**:226-27; **35**:196-98; **44**:393-94

"Eyes of Night Time" (Rukeyser) **27**:408

The Eyes of Reason (Heym) **41**:213-16

The Eyes of the Dragon (King) **113**:366, 381

"The Eyes of the Drowned Watch Keels Going Over" (Merwin) **5**:285

The Eyes of the Interred (Asturias) **3**:18; **8**:27-8

The Eyes of the Madonna (Arghezi)
See *Ochii Maicii Domnului*

The Eyes of the Overworld (Vance) **35**:417-20, 423, 427-28

"The Eyes of the World" (Beer) **58**:31, 36

"Eyes of Zapata" (Cisneros) **69**:153

Eyes on the Harem (Fornes) **39**:138; **61**:128-29

"Eyes Only" (Pastan) **27**:371

"Eyes That Last I Saw in Tears" (Eliot) **15**:213

"Eyes That Open" (Bowering) **15**:82

"Eyes to See" (Cozzens) **92**:189

"Eyes to Wonder" (Bachmann) **69**:47

"Eyesight" (Ammons) **2**:14; **25**:42

Eyewitness (Hall) **51**:170

"Eyze min adam" ("What Kind of Man") (Amichai) **116**:122

"Ezra Pound" (MacDiarmid) **63**:256

Ezra Pound and His World (Ackroyd) **52**:5

"Ezra Pound and the Great Style" (Carruth) **84**:124

Ezra Pound: Poet as Sculptor (Davie) **31**:109-

13

Ezra Pound: The Solitary Volcano (Tytell) 50:434-35, 437-38

"F" (Merrill)   8:384

F for Fake (Welles)   20:452-53; 80:391, 396-97, 413, 416

"F. H. Underhill, 1889-1971" (Johnston)   51:253

"F. Scott Fitzgerald" (Wilson)   24:481

"Fa" (Tolson)   105:262

Faabeleita vuodelta 1965 (*Fables from the Year 1965*) (Haavikko)   34:170

"The Fabbri Tape" (Auchincloss)   45:33

"A Faber Melancholy" (Dunn)   40:167

"Fable" (Golding)   58:194, 199; 81:315-16, 319

"Fable" (Ponge)   18:417

"A Fable" (Walker)   103:366, 411

"A Fable" (Wilbur)   53:412; 110:357, 371

Fable (Cabral de Melo Neto)
   See *Fabúe Anfion*

A Fable (Faulkner)   3:153; 9:203; 11:202; 14:171, 175; 28:140

Fable (Pinget)   7:305; 37:361, 363

Fable (Taylor)   27:439, 441

"Fable from the Cayoosh Country" (Barnard)   48:25

The Fable of Amphion (Cabral de Melo Neto)
   See *Fabúe Anfion*

"The Fable of Anfion" (Cabral de Melo Neto)
   See "Fábula de Anfion"

"A Fable of Joan Miro" (Paz)   65:200

"Fables about Error" (Meredith)   13:375; 21:302

Fables for Our Time and Famous Poems Illustrated (Thurber)   5:430, 432-35, 442; 25:437

Fables from the Year 1965 (Haavikko)
   See *Faabeleita vuodelta 1965*

Fables of Brunswick Avenue (Govier)   51:165-67

Fables of Identity (Frye)   24:216; 70:275

The Fables of La Fontaine (Moore)   4:359, 363

Fabrications (Ayrton)   7:18, 20

La fabrique du pré (Ponge)   18:417

"Fabrizio's: Criticism and Response" (Allen)   52:41-2, 48

Fabúe Anfion (*Fable*; *The Fable of Amphion*) (Cabral de Melo Neto)   76:152, 157, 162, 168

"Fábula de Anfion" ("The Fable of Anfion") (Cabral de Melo Neto)   76:152

Fabulazzo Osceno (Fo)   109:101, 109

"The Fabulous Eddie Brewster" (Blaise)   29:70

The Fabulous Invalid (Hart and Kaufman)   38:266; 66:175, 182, 188-89

The Fabulous Miss Marie (Bullins)   5:82-3; 7:36

The Fabulous Riverboat (Farmer)   19:165-67

Uma faca só lâmina (*A Knife All Blade*) (Cabral de Melo Neto)   76:153, 156, 158, 160, 165, 167

"La façade" (Butor)   15:117

"Façade" (Reverdy)   53:281

Façade (Sitwell)   9:493; 67:312, 324, 335, 337

"The Face" (Jarrell)   13:302

"A Face" (Moore)   8:397; 10:350

"The Face" (Smith)   15:517

The Face (Bergman)
   See *Ansiktet*

Face (Pineda)   39:94-6

The Face (Vance)   35:426

Face à ce qui se dérobe (*Facing What Is Disappearing*) (Michaux)   19:316-17

"The Face and the Image" (Agnon)
   See "Ha-panim la-panim"

The Face behind the Face (Yevtushenko)   26:466-68

The Face beside the Fire (van der Post)   5:463

A Face for a Clue (Simenon)   47:370

"The Face in the Bar Room Mirror" (Fearing)   51:119

"A Face in the Crowd" (Davies)   21:99

A Face in the Crowd (Kazan)   16:367-69; 63:226-27, 229, 233, 235

A Face in the Crowd (Schulberg)   7:403

"The Face in the Mirror" (Graves)   39:321; 45:169

"A Face in the Trash" (Benedikt)   14:82

La face intérieure (Tzara)   47:388

"Face Lift" (Plath)   17:365-66; 111:210

Face of a Fighter (Nelson)   17:305

The Face of Another (Abe)
   See *Tanin no kao*

The Face of England in a Series of Occasional Sketches (Blunden)   56:38

The Face of Fear (Koontz)   78:203

"The Face of Hate" (Lavin)   99:321-22

"The Face of Helen" (Christie)   110:112

The Face of Innocence (Sansom)   6:483

The Face of Misfortune (Onetti)
   See *La cara de la desgracia*

The Face of the Enemy (Scannell)   49:325

"The Face of the Waters'" (FitzGerald)   19:175-77, 179, 182-83

The Face of Trespass (Rendell)   28:384; 48:321

The Face of War (Gellhorn)   60:185-86, 190, 193-95

A Face of War (Maysles and Maysles)   16:440

The Face That Must Die (Campbell)   42:87, 90-1, 93

Face the Music (Hart)   66:176, 182

"Face to Face" (Rich)   11:475-76

"Face to Face" (Wolff)   64:446, 449

Face to face (Aitmatov)
   See *Litsom k litsu*

Face to Face (Bergman)
   See *Ansikte mot ansikte*

Face to Face (Davies)   21:88-9

Face to Face (Mehta)   37:287-88, 292, 294

Face to Face (Queen)   11:464

Faceache (Barker)   37:32

The Faceless Man (Vance)   35:421

"Face-Lift" (Mueller)   51:284

"Faces" (Koch)   44:243

Faces (Cassavetes)   20:45, 47

"The Faces at Pine Dunes" (Campbell)   42:92

"The Faces I Love" (Stern)   100:338

Faces in My Time: The Memoirs of Anthony Powell (Powell)   31:317-20, 322

Faces in the Water (Frame)   2:141; 6:190; 22:146; 66:143-46; 96:166-67, 174-75, 178-79, 190-92, 195, 202, 209, 218, 220

"Faces of an Age"   75:75

Faces of Anxiety (Rozewicz)   9:463; 23:358

The Faces of Blood Kindred: A Novella and Ten Stories (Goyen)   14:210; 40:218

"The Faces of the Medal" (Cortazar)   33:123-25

Les fâcheux (Cocteau)   15:134

Facial Justice (Hartley)   22:212

The Facilitators; or, Mister Hole-in-the-Day (Redgrove)   41:357-58

"Facing" (Swenson)   106:348-49

"Facing It" (Komunyakaa)   86:191; 94:226-27, 230, 233

Facing It (Brancato)   35:70

Facing Nature (Updike)   43:435-36

"Facing Shadows" (Jin)   109:53

Facing the Chair: Story of the Americanization of Two Foreignborn Workmen (Dos Passos)   25:140; 82:108

"Facing the Forests" ("The Lover") (Yehoshua)   31:474

Facing the Forests (*Opposite the Forests*) (Yehoshua)   31:467, 469-70, 472-73

"Facing the Funerals" (Nemerov)   36:309

Facing the Lions (Wicker)   7:533-34

Facing the Music (Brown)   73:20, 22

Facing the Tree (Ignatow)   7:178-79, 181-82; 14:275-76

Facing What Is Disappearing (Michaux)
   See *Face à ce qui se dérobe*

Facism (Forman)   21:120

Die Fackel im Ohr: Lebensgeschichte 1921-1931 (*The Torch in My Ear*) (Canetti)   25:113-14; 75:141-42, 144; 86:294, 297, 300-02

"Fackelzug" ("Torch Procession") (Celan)   82:54-5

Façons d'endormi, façons d'éveillé (*Ways of a Sleeping Man, Ways of a Waking Man*) (Michaux)   8:392

"The Fact in Fiction" (McCarthy)   14:360

The Fact of a Doorframe: Poems Selected and New, 1950-1984 (Rich)   36:366, 378-79; 73:325-26, 330

"Facteur Cheval" ("Postman Cheval") (Breton)   54:27

"Factoring" (Avison)   97:70-2

"The Factory" (Springsteen)   17:483-84

Factotum (Bukowski)   9:137; 41:68, 70-1; 82:10-13, 17-19, 22-28; 108:72, 97-8, 103-04, 106, 108

"The Facts" (Althusser)   106:32, 37

"Facts" (L'Heureux)   52:275

The Facts (Althusser)   106:40-1

The Facts: A Novelist's Autobiography (Roth)   86:249-50, 257

Facts about Sex: A Basic Guide (Gordon)   26:136-37, 139

Facts about Sex for Today's Youth (Gordon)   26:137, 139

Facts about Veneral Disease for Today's Youth (Gordon)   26:137, 139

"The Facts and Issues" (Berryman)   13:82; 25:92; 62:45

The Facts in the Case of E.A. Poe (Sinclair)   14:489-90

"The Facts of Life" (Kumin)   28:222

"Facts of Life" (Raine)   103:182

Facts of Life (Howard)   14:268; 46:185, 187-90

The Facts of Life: An Essay in Feelings, Facts, and Fantasy (Laing)   95:154, 169

The Facts of Life and Other Fictions (Nye)   42:308-09

The Faded Sun: Kesrith (Cherryh)   35:105-06, 111

The Faded Sun: Kutath (Cherryh)   35:106, 111

The Faded Sun: Shon'jir (Cherryh)   35:105-06, 111

Fadensonnen (*Thread-Suns*) (Celan)   10:101; 19:91; 53:70, 73, 76, 79; 82:34

Fadeout (Hansen)   38:236-37, 239

Fading, My Parmacheene Belle (Scott)   50:88-

90
"A Fading Phantom" (Blunden)   56:47
"Fafnir" (Hope)   3:250
Faggots (Kramer)   42:269-70
"Fah" (Abse)   29:16
Fahrenheit 451 (Bradbury)   10:68, 70; 42:35-6, 40-2; 98:103-05, 107-13, 115-18, 120-29, 133, 136-38, 141-48
Fahrenheit 451 (Truffaut)   20:384, 387, 390-91; 101:375, 377-79, 383, 386, 391, 395-97, 406-07, 412
Fahrt ins Staublose (*Journey into the Beyond*) (Sachs)   98:322-24, 328
"The Failed Men" ("Ahead") (Aldiss)   14:10-11
"Failing Perspective" (Young)   82:412
"A Failure" (Day Lewis)   6:127
"The Failure" (Kelman)   58:298
"Failure" (Pollitt)   28:367-68
Failure to Zigzag (Vandenburgh)   59:100-04
"The Faint" (Updike)   15:547
"Faint Music" (Hass)   99:155
"Faint Praise" (Williams)   33:442
"Fair" (Brunner)   8:105
Fair and Tender Ladies (Smith)   73:350-52, 354-59
Fair Blows the Wind (L'Amour)   25:281
"Fair Exchange" (Santos)   22:361
"Fair Exchange" (White)   49:408
Fair Game (Johnson)   5:198; 48:201
"The Fair in St. Giles" (Raine)   103:186
"The Fair in the Woods" (Gunn)   3:216
The Fair Sister (Goyen)   5:149; 14:210-12, 214; 40:218
Fair Slaughter (Barker)   37:33-4, 41
Fair Stood the Wind for France (Bates)   46:57-61
"Fair Warning" (Brunner)   8:108
"Fair Weather" (Parker)   68:324
"Fairbanks Under the Solstice" (Haines)   58:222
"The Fairground" (Longley)   29:293, 296
"Fairground Music" (Fuller)   62:184
Fairground Music (Fuller)   62:184-86, 200
"The Fairies" (Enright)   31:148
"The Fairies" (Shamlu)   10:470-71
Fairies and Fusiliers (Graves)   45:166
A Fairly Conventional Woman (Shields)   113:401, 403, 405-06, 410, 411, 414, 438, 446
A Fairly Good Time (Gallant)   7:110-11; 38:194
"Fairly High Assimilation Rag" (Ammons)   57:49
A Fairly Honourable Defeat (Murdoch)   2:297; 3:347; 31:289, 293
"Fairweather Father" (Simon)   26:410
"Fairy Flood" (Hughes)   37:180
"A Fairy Story" (Smith)   25:419
"Fairy Tale" (Brunner)   8:107
"Fairy Tale" (Butler)   81:122, 127
"Fairy Tale" (Fuller)   62:184-85
"A Fairy Tale" (Pasternak)
    See "Skazka"
A Fairy Tale of New York (Donleavy)   4:123, 125-26; 6:140-41; 10:153; 45:128
"A Fairytale about the Rain" ("A Tale about Rain in Several Episodes") (Akhmadulina)   53:10-15
Faites vos jeux (*Place Your Bets*) (Tzara)   47:390
"The Faith" (Mahapatra)   33:282-83
Faith and the Good Thing (Johnson)   7:183; 51:228-29, 233; 65:152, 156-57
Faith and Treason: The Story of the Gunpow-

der Plot (Fraser)   107:66-67
Faith Healer (Friel)   42:169-70, 174-75; 59:149; 115:224-26, 228-29, 231, 234-35, 241-42, 244, 248
"The Faith Healer Come to Rabun County" (Bottoms)   53:29
"Faith Healing" (Larkin)   8:332; 18:294; 33:258; 39:334
"Faith, Hope, and Charity" (McGahern)   48:264, 271
"Faith in the Afternoon" (Paley)   4:392; 37:332, 337-38
"Faith Is a Concrete Object" (Gustafson)   36:215
The Faith of Graffiti (Mailer)   4:322; 14:351
"The Faith That Illuminates" (Eliot)   24:177
"The Faithful" (Enright)   31:155
"The Faithful" (Jacobsen)   102:236
"The Faithful" (McPherson)   19:310; 77:359, 365-66
Faithful Are the Wounds (Sarton)   49:312, 322; 91:242
"The Faithful Mouse" (Seth)   90:353
The Faithful Ruslan (Vladimov)   59:384, 388
"Faithful to Thee, Terra, in Our Fashion" (Tiptree)   48:385
"The Faithful Wife" (Beer)   58:31-2
"The Faithless Wife" (O'Faolain)   14:406
Les Faits (Althusser)   106:12
The Fake Fish (Abe)   81:284, 286, 289
"A Fake Novel about the Life of Rimbaud" (Spicer)   18:510
"Fakin' It" (Simon)   17:459, 461
Faktizität und Geltung: Beiträge zur Diskurstheorie des Techts und des demokratischen Rechtsstaats (*Between Facts and Norms: Contributions to a Discourse Theory of Law and Democracy*) (Habermas)   104:83-4, 86-7, 92, 94, 96-7
"The Falcon and the Dove" (Read)   4:439
A Falcon Flies (*Flight of the Falcon*) (Smith)   33:376-78
Falconer (Cheever)   8:136-40; 11:120, 123; 15:129; 25:118-21; 64:49-51, 57, 59, 65-8
"A Fall" (Moss)   45:287
"The Fall" (Mueller)   51:280
"The Fall" (Murphy)   41:314
"Fall" (Neruda)
    See "Otoño"
"The Fall" (Raine)   45:337
"The Fall" (Smith)   64:390
The Fall (Camus)
    See *La chute*
The Fall (Duerrenmatt)   102:54
"Fall 1961" (Lowell)   11:327
Fall and Rise (Dixon)   52:101-02
"The Fall and Rise of Mrs. Habgood" (Gellhorn)   60:187
"Fall Comes in Back-Country Vermont" (Warren)   13:573
Der Fall d'Arthez (*The D'Arthez Case*) (Nossack)   6:365
Der Fall Franza (*The Franza Case*) (Bachmann)   69:36, 47-8, 59-60
"A Fall from Grace" (Maitland)   49:236
The Fall into Time (Cioran)
    See *La chute dans le temps*
"Fall of a City" (Spender)   41:419
"Fall of a House" (Honig)   33:211
The Fall of America: Poems of These States 1965-1971 (Ginsberg)   3:195; 4:181-82;

6:200-01; 36:181, 184-85, 188, 191, 194, 196; 109:357, 362
"The Fall of Edward Barnard" (Maugham)   15:370
The Fall of Kelvin Walker: A Fable of the Sixties (Gray)   41:183-84
"The Fall of Literary History" (Wellek)   28:453
A Fall of Moondust (Clarke)   35:124, 127
"The Fall of Night" (Merton)   83:392
The Fall of Paris (Ehrenburg)   18:131; 62:169, 177-80
"The Fall of Rome" (Auden)   43:20
The Fall of the City (MacLeish)   68:286
The Fall of the Dream Machine (Koontz)   78:201, 203
The Fall of the House of Usher (Berkoff)   56:15
The Fall of the Towers (Delany)   38:150
"Fall Pageant" (Ashbery)   77:65
"The Fall River Axe Murders" (Carter)   41:122
"Fall, Sierra Nevada" (Rexroth)   49:280-81; 112:390
"Fall Song" (Oliver)   34:249; 98:256
Die Falle (Duerrenmatt)
    See *Der Nihilist*
"Fallen Angel" (Van Duyn)   116:422
Fallen Angels (Coward)   1:64; 51:69, 77
Fallen Asleep While Young (*The Maid Silja*) (Sillanpaa)   19:417-18
The Fallen Curtain (Rendell)   28:384
"The Fallen, Fallen World" (Avison)   97:89, 109
The Fallen House (Baxter)   14:60-1
The Fallen Idol (Greene)   70:289, 294; 72:165
"Fallgesetze" (Lenz)   27:252
"Falling" (Dickey)   2:115, 117; 7:82; 10:141; 15:177; 109:246-48, 250-52, 254-56, 266, 283, 293
Falling (Dickey)   47:95
Falling (Schaeffer)   6:488; 11:492; 22:367
"Falling Asleep over Scott" (Starbuck)   53:354
"Falling Asleep over the 'Aeneid'" (Lowell)   4:301; 8:349, 356; 9:336
The Falling Astronauts (Malzberg)   7:208
Falling Bodies (Kaufman)   3:263; 8:317
"The Falling Dog" (Barthelme)   46:35; 115:60
"The Falling Girl" (Buzzati)   36:94
"Falling in Love" (Dubus)   97:235
"Falling in Love Again" (Gaye)   26:134
"Falling in Love at Sixty-Five" (Van Duyn)   63:445; 116:411, 423
Falling in Place (Beattie)   18:37-40; 40:66, 63:4-5, 7-9, 13
The Falling of the Grain (Everson)   14:165
"Falling of the Rain" (Joel)   26:217-18
"Falling; or, On the Vertical and Horizontal Elements in the Life of Contemporary Man" (Rozewicz)
    See "Spadanie czyli; o, Elementach wertykalnych i horyzontalnych w zyciu czlowieka wspolczesnego"
"Falling out of Love" (Brown)   73:23
"Falling Rocks, Narrowing Road, Cul-de-sac, Stop" (O'Faolain)   70:314
"The Falling Sky" (Levine)   14:316
The Fallow Land (Bates)   46:50-1, 53, 56
"Falls" (Van Duyn)   116:422, 426, 431
"The Falls of Love" (Moss)   50:353
"Falsche Schönheit" ("Wrong Beauty") (Grass)   32:199
The False and True Green (Quasimodo)
    See *Il falso e vero verde*
"The False Bride's Story" (Mueller)   51:282
False Coin (Swados)   5:420, 422

False Country of the Zoo (Garrigue)   8:239
"False Documents" (Doctorow)   113:156
False Entry (Calisher)   2:96; 4:88; 38:68-9, 74
"False Leads" (Komunyakaa)   94:239
"False Lights" (Godwin)   8:249
"False Notes" (Reverdy)
   See "Fausses notes"
"False Shuffles" (Urquhart)   90:373-5, 381
False Shuffles (Urquhart)   90:398
"A False Spring" (Boland)   113:89
A False Spring (Jordan)   37:194-95
The False Start (Mahapatra)   33:280, 284
"False Youth, Autumn, Clothes of the Age"
   (Dickey)   15:177; 47:91-2, 95
Il falso e vero verde (*The False and True Green*)
   (Quasimodo)   10:428
Falstaff (Nye)   13:413; 42:305-06, 308
Falstaff (Welles)
   See *Chimes at Midnight*
FAM and YAM: An Imaginary Interview (Albee)
   113:32
"Fame" (Bowie)   17:62
"Fame" (Miller)   47:250
"Fame" (Walker)   27:449; 103:366, 407-08,
   410, 412, 423
Fame and Love in New York (Sanders)   53:308-
   09
Fame and Obscurity (Talese)   37:393, 403
*Fame Became of Him: Hemingway as Public
   Writer* (Raeburn)   34:477-78
Famiglia (*Family*) (Ginzburg)   11:230; 54:198-
   200, 208; 70:279
La famiglia Manzoni (*The Manzoni Family*)
   (Ginzburg)   54:200-02, 209-13; 70:280
"La familia" (Cernuda)   54:61
La familia de Pascual Duarte (*The Family of
   Pascual Duarte*; *Pascual Duarte's Fam-
   ily*) (Cela)   4:96-8; 13:145-47; 59:126-
   29, 132-34, 141-44
La familia del héroe (Cela)   4:96
Una familia lejana (*Distant Relations*) (Fuentes)
   41:164-68, 171; 60:155, 170; 113:262
"Una familia para Clotilde" ("A Family for
   Clotilde") (Valenzuela)   104:357
"Familiär" ("Family Matters") (Grass)   32:198
"Familiar Poem" (Chappell)   78:111
"Familien de Cats" (Dinesen)
   See "Eneboerne"
"Families" (Reed)   21:317, 320-21
Families and Survivors (Adams)   6:1-2; 13:1-
   2; 46:13-14
The Families of Schizophrenics (Laing)
   See *Sanity, Madness and the Family*
"La Famille Adam" (Tournier)   95:362
"The Family" (Boyle)   58:74
"Family" (Miles)   14:369; 34:245
"Family" (Oates)   108:384-85
"The Family" (Oliver)   19:362
Family (Donovan)   35:142-43
Family (Ginzburg)
   See *Famiglia*
A Family (Harwood)   32:226-27
Family (Hill)   113:327
Family (Pa Chin)
   See *Chia*
The Family (Plante)   23:343-47; 38:365-67,
   370-71
Family: A Novel in the Form of a Memoir (Gold)
   42:195, 197
"A Family Affair" (L'Heureux)   52:278
A Family Affair (Mehta)   37:296
A Family Affair (Stewart)   14:512
"Family Affairs" (Angelou)   35:32

Family Affairs (L'Heureux)   52:277-78
"Family Album" (Fearing)   51:117
"Family Album" (Harjo)   83:286
"Family Album" (Porter)   13:452
Family Album: Three Novellas (Alegria)
   See *Albúm familiar*
A Family and a Fortune (Compton-Burnett)
   3:111; 10:110; 15:137; 34:495
Family and Friends (Brookner)   51:59-60,
   62-4
The Family Arsenal (Theroux)   8:513-14;
   11:529, 531-32; 28:425-26; 46:399, 405
The Family at Caldicott Place (Streatfeild)
   See *Caldicott Place*
"Family Attractions" (Freeman)   55:55
"A Family Chat" (Landolfi)   49:212
"Family Circle" (Dorfman)   77:141-43
Family Circle (Hocking)   13:285
Family Circles (Ayckbourn)   33:41-2
"Family Conference" (Montague)   46:267, 277
"The Family Cycle" (Kis)   57:249
"Family Dancing" (Leavitt)   34:78
Family Dancing (Leavitt)   34:77-9
Family Devotions (Hwang)   55:151-52
"A Family Discourse (Or, John Constable's
   Painting 'The Valley Farm')" (Blunden)
   56:37-8
A Family Failing (Arundel)   17:16, 18-19
Family Feeling (Yglesias)   7:558-59; 22:493
"A Family for Clotilde" (Valenzuela)
   See "Una familia para Clotilde"
A Family Gathering (Broughton)   19:72-4
"Family Happiness" (Colwin)   84:146-47, 150
Family Happiness (Colwin)   84:139-41, 143,
   146-47, 150, 153
The Family Idiot: Gustave Flaubert, 1821-1857
   (Sartre)
   See *L'idiot de la famille: Gustave Flaubert
   de 1821 à 1857*
"The Family in Modern Drama" (Miller)
   10:345; 15:373
"The Family Jewels" (Blount)   38:46
Family Letters of Robert and Elinor Frost (Frost)
   44:459
The Family Lie (Simenon)   18:486
"Family Life" (Urdang)   47:399
Family Life (Altman)   16:24
Family Life (Banks)   37:23; 72:14
"A Family Likeness" (Lavin)   99:322-23
A Family Likeness (Lavin)   99:321-22
Family Linen (Smith)   73:343-44, 350, 352,
   357-58
A Family Madness (Keneally)   43:234-37;
   117:224-26, 231, 234-36, 243
"A Family Man" (Pritchett)   15:443
"Family Matters" (Grass)
   See "Familiär"
The Family Moskat (Singer)
   See *Di Familie Moskat*
"The Family Name" (Guillen)
   See "El apellido"
"The Family Novel" (Jiles)   58:272, 279, 281
A Family of Foxes (Dillon)   17:95-6, 101
"The Family of Love" (McAuley)   45:249
The Family of Pascual Duarte (Cela)
   See *La familia de Pascual Duarte*
Family Pictures (Brooks)   15:92-3; 49:23, 28-
   30, 35, 37
Family Plot (Hitchcock)   16:353-54, 359
"Family Portrait" (Alexie)   96:9
"The Family Reunion" (Eliot)   1:90; 13:194-
   95; 15:207-09; 24:172; 34:397, 529, 531;
   41:143-46, 152; 55:346, 356

"Family Reunion" (Steele)   45:362
A Family Reunion (Albee)   25:36
Family Reunion (Nash)   23:321
Family Sayings (Ginzburg)
   See *Lessico famigliare*
"Family Seat" (Murphy)   41:320
"Family Secrets" (Shields)   113:411, 432
Family Shoes (Streatfeild)
   See *The Bell Family*
"Family Sins" (Trevor)   71:341-2, 348-50
Family Sins, and Other Stories (Trevor)
   71:341; 116:347-48, 378-79
"A Family Supper" (Ishiguro)   110:224
"The Family Sweetheart" (Dourado)
   See "Queridinha da familia"
*The Family: The Story of Charles Manson's
   Dune Buggy Attack Battalion* (Sanders)
   53:304-07, 310
"Family Ties" (Lispector)   43:268-69
Family Ties (Lispector)
   See *Laços de familia*
Family Trade (Carroll)   38:107-08
"The Family Tree" (Boland)   40:96
A Family Trust (Just)   27:228
Family Voices (Pinter)   27:393, 396; 58:369-
   70, 372, 374-75, 381-84; 73:277
"Family Walls" (Brennan)   5:73
A Family's Affairs (Douglas)   73:63-6, 73-5,
   79-85, 92-3
The Famine (Creasey)   11:134
Famine (Murphy)   51:305
Famine (O'Flaherty)   34:355-57
"The Famine Road" (Boland)   40:96; 67:46;
   113:122
The Famished Road (Okri)   87:323-26, 328-
   31
Famous All Over Town (Santiago)   33:352-54
Famous American Negroes (Hughes)   108:286
"The Famous Final Scene" (Seger)   35:383
"Famous Groupies" (McCartney)   35:285-86
Famous Last Words (Findley)   27:144-45;
   102:109-10, 114-18
*Famous Long Ago: My Life and Hard Times
   with Liberation News Service* (Mungo)
   72:285-89, 291
Famous Men of Modern Biology (Berger)   12:37
Famous Negro Heroes of America (Hughes)
   108:286
Famous Negro Music Makers (Hughes)   108:283
The Famous Ones (Bernhard)   61:12
"Famous Poet" (Hughes)   9:280
The Famous Stanley Kidnapping Case (Snyder)
   17:475
Famous Young Rebels (Archer)   12:20
The Fan Club (Wallace)   7:510; 13:568-69
The Fan Man (Kotzwinkle)   5:219-20; 35:257
The Fanatic (Levin)   7:205
*A Fanatic Heart: Selected Stories of Edna
   O'Brien* (O'Brien)   36:338-41; 116:186-
   87, 195, 208-09
"Fancy" (Cunningham)   31:97, 102
"Fancy" (Davies)   21:88
"Fancy and Memory" (Blunden)   56:44
The Fancy Dress Party (Moravia)   7:244;
   46:282-83
"Fancy Flights" (Beattie)   8:57; 63:17
Fancy Goods (Morand)
   See *Tendres stocks*
Fancy Goods. Open All Night (Morand)
   41:307-08
Fancy Meeting You Again (Kaufman)   38:267
Fancy Strut (Smith)   25:406-07, 410
"The Fancy Woman" (Taylor)   18:523; 37:407,

409
Fando and Lis (Arrabal)
  See *Fando et Lis*
Fando et Lis (*Fando and Lis*; *Fando y Lis*)
  (Arrabal) **58**:3, 7-9, 10, 18-19, 21
Fando y Lis (Arrabal)
  See *Fando et Lis*
"Fan-Fare" (Waugh) **107**:399
Fanfare for Elizabeth (Sitwell) **67**:325-27
Fängelse (*The Devil's Wanton*; *Prison*)
  (Bergman) **72**:39, 52
Fanny (Almedingen) **12**:5-7
Fanny and Alexander (Bergman)
  See *Fanny och Alexander*
*Fanny: Being the True History of the Adven-
  tures of Fanny Hackabout-Jones* (Jong)
  18:278-79; **83**:307-08, 311, 315, 321
Fanny Herself (Ferber) **18**:150, 153; **93**:137-
  38, 147, 171
Fanny och Alexander (*Fanny and Alexander*)
  (Bergman) **72**:57-61
Fanny Otcott (Wilder) **82**:384
Fanny Peculiar (Waterhouse) **47**:422
"Fans" (Hannah) **38**:234; **90**:138
A Fan's Notes (Exley) **6**:170-72; **11**:186-87
Fanshen (Hare) **29**:212-14
"Fantasia" (Livesay) **79**:342
"Fantasia on 'The Nut-Brown Maid'" (Ashbery)
  13:30, 35; **15**:29-30, 32, 34; **41**:37, 40;
  77:44-5, 68
"Fantasia on the Seventies" (White) **110**:332,
  341-42
Los fantasmos de mi cerebo (*Phantoms of My
  Brain*) (Gironella) **11**:236
The Fantastic Four (Lee) **17**:257-58
Fantastic Mr. Fox (Dahl) **79**:177
"Fantastic Voyage" (Bowie) **17**:66
Fantastic Voyage (Asimov) **76**:315
"Fantastic World's End" (Moure) **88**:218
Fantastyka i futurologia (Lem) **40**:300
"Fantasy" (O'Hara) **78**:333
Fantasy and Fugue (Fuller) **4**:178; **28**:148
The Fantasy Poets: Philip Larkin (Larkin)
  64:257
Fantomas against the Multinational Vampires
  (Cortazar)
  See *Fantomas contra los vampiros
  multinacionales*
Fantomas contra los vampiros multinacionales
  (*Fantomas against the Multinational
  Vampires*) (Cortazar) **10**:117-18; **33**:123
Le fantôme de la liberté (*Phantom of Liberty*)
  (Bunuel) **16**:144, 148, 152; **80**:57
Le fantôme de Marseille (Cocteau) **43**:107
"Les fantômes du temps des feuilles mortes"
  (Carrier) **78**:69
"Far and Scattered Are the Tribes that Industri-
  alization Has Left Behind" (Jiles) **58**:281
"Far Away" ("Long Ago") (Durrell) **13**:188
Far Away from Anywhere Else (Le Guin)
  See *Very Far Away from Anywhere Else*
"Far Cry" (Gaye) **26**:135
"The Far Cry" (Yevtushenko) **26**:462
Far Cry (MacCaig) **36**:284
A Far Cry (Rovit) **7**:383
"A Far Cry after a Close Call" (Howard) **7**:165;
  10:277; **47**:167
"A Far Cry from Africa" (Walcott) **25**:451-
  52; **42**:418, 421; **67**:347, 352, 354; **76**:273
"A Far Cry from Bowmore" (Jenkins) **52**:226
"The Far Field" (Roethke) **8**:460; **11**:484-85;
  19:396, 398, 400; **46**:364; **101**:289, 304-
  05, 307, 319-20, 326

The Far Field (Roethke) **1**:291; **3**:432-34;
  8:455, 457; **11**:485; **19**:396, 398; **46**:355,
  357, 361, 364; **101**:267, 286-90, 296,
  304, 310, 327, 330, 332-33
"Far Floridas" (Mott) **15**:381
Far from Cibola (Horgan) **53**:174
Far from Home (Sebestyen) **30**:346-47, 349-
  51
Far from Home (Tevis) **42**:372, 377
Far from Shore (Major) **26**:286-88
"Far from the City" (Santos) **22**:364
Far from the City of Class and Other Stories
  (Friedman) **3**:165; **56**:95-6
"Far from the Opposite Shore" (Steinem)
  63:379
Far from the Sea (Hunter) **31**:226
Far in the Day (Cunningham) **12**:166
Far Journey of Oudin (Harris) **25**:203, 205,
  214
"Far Off" (Guillen) **79**:230
"Far Out" (Larkin) **64**:258
The Far Pavilions (Kaye) **28**:198-202
Far Rainbow (Strugatskii and Strugatskii)
  27:434, 437
Far Side of the Dollar (Macdonald) **2**:256;
  3:308; **14**:334-35; **41**:266, 270
The Far Side of Victory (Greenberg) **30**:167-
  68
Far to Go (Streatfeild) **21**:413, 416
Far Tortuga (Matthiessen) **5**:274-75; **7**:210-
  12; **11**:359-60; **32**:290, 297; **64**:307, 309,
  311-14, 316, 320, 324-25, 327-28
Far Voyager: The Story of James Cook
  (Latham) **12**:325
"Far West" (Cendrars) **106**:175
"Far West" (Smith) **15**:516-17
"Faraway Image" (Cortazar)
  See "Lejana"
The Faraway Island (Corcoran) **17**:76
"Far-Away Meadow" (Frost) **4**:175
"Farce Double" (Mathews)
  See "Country Cooking from Central France:
  Roast Boned Rolled Stuffed Shoulder of
  Lamb"
"The Farcical History of Richard Greenow"
  (Huxley) **79**:326
"Fare Well" (Berryman) **62**:71, 75
"The Farenheit Man" (Frame) **96**:189
"Farewell" (Amichai) **116**:138
"Farewell" (Dybek) **114**:72
"Farewell" (Powers) **8**:448; **57**:349
"Farewell at the Station" (Young) **82**:396
"Farewell Blues" (Amis) **40**:41
Farewell, Gul'sary! (Aitmatov)
  See *Proschai, Gul'sary!*
Farewell Happy Fields (Raine) **7**:353
"Farewell, My Lovely!" (White) **10**:527;
  34:426
"The Farewell Party" (Desai) **97**:150, 152-53
The Farewell Party (Kundera)
  See *La valse aux adieux*
"Farewell Rehearsed" (Tate) **14**:531
Farewell, Spring! (Seifert)
  See *Jaro sbohem*
"A Farewell Thing While Breathing"
  (Bukowski) **41**:66
"Farewell to Annabel" (Lightfoot) **26**:279
A Farewell to Arms (Hemingway) **1**:141, 143-
  44; **3**:231, 234-35, 239-40; **6**:225-27,
  230, 234; **8**:283, 290-91; **10**:266-67, 271;
  13:271, 273-75, 277-79; **19**:218; **30**:179,
  181, 195, 198-99; **34**:477-79; **61**:196,
  201, 218; **80**:104, 113, 115, 117-18, 128,

  134, 136-37, 142, 146-49
"Farewell to Earth" (Clarke) **35**:122
Farewell to Greatness! (Carroll) **10**:97-8
Farewell to Hamlet (Johnson)
  See *Avsked till Hamlet*
"A Farewell to Omsk" (Perelman) **15**:417;
  49:265
"Farewell to September" (Herbert) **43**:183
Farewell to the Sea: A Novel of Cuba (Arenas)
  See *Otra vez el mar*
*A Farewell to the Twentieth Century: A Com-
  pendium of the Absurd* (Berton) **104**:62
Farewell Victoria (White) **30**:449
"Farewells" (Alegria) **75**:49
La farfalla di Dinard (Montale) **7**:223, 226
Fargo (The Coen Brothers) **108**:165-71
"The Faring" (Davidson) **13**:169
"The Farm" (Hall) **37**:142
"The Farm" (MacLeish) **68**:286-87, 292
The Farm (Storey) **4**:529; **5**:415
The Farm at Grinde (*Grindegard: Morgonen*)
  (Vesaas) **48**:405, 411
"Farm behind Battle Zone" (Blunden) **56**:44
"Farm Country" (Oliver) **98**:266
"Farm Implements and Rutabagas in a Land-
  scape" (Ashbery) **15**:32
"The Farm Novels of C. M. van den Heever"
  (Coetzee) **66**:99
"The Farm on the Great Plains" (Stafford)
  29:380
"Farm Wife" (Thomas) **48**:379
Farmer (Harrison) **14**:235; **33**:199-201;
  66:154-56, 158, 160-61, 163
Farmer Giles of Ham (Tolkien) **12**:574
"Farmer in the Dell" (Ferber) **93**:139
Farmer in the Sky (Heinlein) **3**:226; **26**:171,
  175-76; **55**:302
Farmer of the Clouds and Poetry until Now
  (Andrade)
  See *Fazendeira do ar y poesia até agora*
The Farmer Takes a Wife (Connelly) **7**:57
"The Farmers" (Bottoms) **53**:31
"Farmers" (Lane) **25**:288
"The Farmer's Children" (Bishop) **32**:40
The Farmers Hotel (O'Hara) **2**:325
"The Farmer's Wife" (Sexton) **53**:317
Farming: A Handbook (Berry) **6**:61; **8**:85;
  27:32-3, 36; **46**:73
Farmstead of Time (Celan)
  See *Zeitgehöft*
Farmyard (Kroetz)
  See *Stallerhof*
Farnham's Freehold (Heinlein) **14**:254;
  26:172; **55**:303
A Far-Off Place (van der Post) **5**:463-64
Farragan's Retreat (McHale) **3**:332; **5**:281-
  82
Far-Ranging Beetleology (Neruda) **62**:327
Fars reise (*Father's Journey*) (Vesaas) **48**:405
Farther Off from Heaven (Humphrey) **45**:199-
  200, 202-03, 205
"Farther On" (Browne) **21**:40
The Farthest Shore (Le Guin) **13**:347; **22**:266,
  271; **71**:180-82, 186-88, 190-91, 194-96,
  198, 200, 203-04
Farthest Star (Williamson) **29**:462
"Fascinating Fascism" (Sontag) **105**:197, 216-
  19
"Fascination" (Schuyler) **23**:391
"Fascinations" (Bowie) **17**:62
"Fascist Honeymoon" (Dybek) **114**:67
"Las fases de Severo" ("Severo's Phases")
  (Cortazar) **13**:164; **33**:124

The Fashion in Shrouds (Allingham) 19:12, 16

"Fashion in the 70's" (Swenson) 106:330

The Fashion System (Barthes)
See *Système de la mode*

Fashions for Women (Arzner) 98:62-3, 69, 74

"The Fast" (Singer) 15:504; 111:295

"Fast Break" (Hirsch) 50:195, 198

"The Fast Bus" (Strand) 71:283

Fast, Fast Relief (Berton) 104:47

"Fast Forward" (Cameron) 44:33

Fast Sam, Cool Clyde, and Stuff (Myers) 35:295-96

"Fast Speaking Woman" (Waldman) 7:508

Fast Speaking Woman (Waldman) 7:508

Fastes d'enfer (Ghelderode) 11:226

"The Fastest Runner on Sixty-First Street" (Farrell) 66:131

"Fastitocalon" (Borges) 8:96

"Fat" (Carver) 53:65

The Fat and the Lean (Polanski) 16:468, 471

Fat City (Huston) 20:172

"The Fat Girl" (Dubus) 36:144-45; 97:198, 204, 207, 216, 221

The Fat Girl (Sachs) 35:335-36

"The Fat Lady" (Carruth) 84:135

"Fat Lip" (Guillen)
See "Negro bembón"

"The Fat Man" (Dinesen) 10:152

"The Fat Man" (Newlove) 14:378

"The Fat Man in History" (Carey) 96:25, 28, 36, 38, 67

The Fat Man in History (Carey) 40:127-30, 134; 96:22, 24, 36-8, 53-4, 63-4, 68, 70

Fat Man Poems (Wild) 14:580

The Fat Man: Selected Poems, 1962-1972 (Newlove) 14:378

Fat Men from Space (Pinkwater) 35:320

"Fat Molly" (Durcan) 43:114

"The Fat of the Land" (Yezierska) 46:441, 449

Fat Woman (Rooke) 25:392-94; 34:251, 254

The Fat Woman Next Door Is Pregnant (Tremblay)
See *La grosse femme d'à côté est enciente*

The Fat Woman's Joke (Weldon)
See *And the Wife Ran Away*

Fata Morgana (Breton) 54:30

Fata Morgana (Herzog) 16:321-23, 327

Fata Morgana (Kotzwinkle) 14:311; 35:255-57

"Fatal Interview: Penthesilea and Achilles" (Warren) 13:573

A Fatal Inversion (Rendell) 48:326-27

Fatal Strategies (Baudrillard)
See *Les stratégies fatales*

Fatal Vision (McGinniss) 32:304-06

The Fatal Woman (Glassco) 9:237

"Fate" (Olds) 39:191; 85:288

Fate (Ai) 69:18

Fate Is the Hunter (Gann) 23:166

"The Fate of Flesh" (Aleixandre) 36:27

The Fate of Mary Rose (Blackwood) 100:2-4, 9, 13-14, 27, 31

"The Fate of Pleasure" (Trilling) 24:462

The Fate of Reading and Other Essays (Hartman) 27:180, 182-84

The Fate of the Earth (Schell) 35:365-70

Fates Worse than Death (Vonnegut) 111:368-70, 373

"The Father" (Carver) 22:99; 55:275

"The Father" (Cassill) 4:95; 23:105

"A Father" (Mukherjee) 53:270

"Father" (Plath) 51:348

"Father" (Soto) 80:284

"Father" (Walker) 58:409

The Father (Olds) 85:305-08

"Father and Daughter" (Eberhart) 11:177

"Father and Daughter" (Sanchez) 116:278-79, 281, 301

A Father and His Fate (Compton-Burnett) 34:500

"A Father and His Son" (Wiesel) 37:450

"Father and I" (Lagerkvist) 54:276

The Father and Other Stories (Cassill) 23:106

"Father and Son" (Ai) 69:7

"Father and Son" (Buckley) 57:130

"Father and Son" (Eberhart) 11:177

"Father and Son" (Hughes) 108:315, 317, 327

"Father and Son" (Santos) 22:361

Father and Son (Compton-Burnett) 10:109

Father and Son (Farrell) 66:114, 116-17

"A Father at His Son's Baptism" (Gerstler) 70:158

"Father Ch., Many Years Later" (Milosz) 56:240; 82:303, 306

"Father Christmas" (Davies) 21:103

The Father Christmas Letters (Tolkien) 8:515

Father Figure (Peck) 21:299

"Father Guzman" (Stern) 100:333

"Father in the Library" (Milosz) 56:232

Father Is a Pillow Tied to a Broom (Soto) 80:277

"Father Mat" (Kavanagh) 22:240

Father Melancholy's Daughter (Godwin) 69:252-55

"Father/Mother Haibun #9" (Wah) 44:327

Father Ned (O'Casey)
See *The Drums of Father Ned*

"The Father of My Country" (Wakoski) 7:506; 40:454

"A Father out Walking on the Lawn" (Dove) 81:138

"Father Philip" (Dabrowska) 15:169

"Father Son, and Holy Ghost" (Lorde) 71:245

Father Stafford (Hope) 83:170

"Father, the Cavalier" (Davie) 31:116

"The Father to His Children" (Simmons) 43:414

"Father to Sons" (Day Lewis) 10:130

"Fatherhood" (Wilson) 49:415-16

"Fathering" (Mukherjee) 53:270-71

Fathering (Delbanco) 6:129-30

"The Fathers" (Rothenberg) 57:374

The Fathers (Tate) 2:427; 4:537; 6:527; 9:523, 525; 11:522, 526-27; 14:530-31, 533; 24:442

Fathers: A Novel in the Form of a Memoir (Gold) 4:192; 7:120, 122; 42:192, 194-95, 197-98

"Fathers and Bridges over Hell: Deep Rivers" (Dorfman) 77:156

Fathers and Crows (Vollmann) 89:283, 285-86, 288, 291-97, 300, 306, 309-13

"Fathers and Sons" (Hemingway) 10:270; 30:181, 194, 197, 199

"Father's Bedroom" (Lowell) 37:243

"The Fathers' Daughters" (Spark) 40:401

"Father's Day" (Shields) 97:433

Father's Day (Goldman) 48:125, 128

"A Father's Ear" (Yevtushenko) 26:468

A Father's Hours (Mahapatra) 33:277, 281, 283

Father's Journey (Vesaas)
See *Fars reise*

Fathers Playing Catch with Sons: Essays on Sport (Mostly Baseball) (Hall) 37:148-49

"A Father's Son" (Yevtushenko) 26:467

"A Father's Story" (Dubus) 36:147-48; 97:199-200, 218, 222, 224, 226, 228-29, 233

A Father's Words (Stern) 39:245

"The Fatigue" (Jones) 4:259; 7:191

"Fatty" (Gunn) 81:185

Fatu-Hiva (Heyerdahl) 26:193

"Faulkner and the Fugitive-Agrarians" (Brooks) 86:288

"The Fault" (Montague) 46:270

Fault Lines (Carroll) 38:106-08

The Fault of Angels (Horgan) 53:169-71, 176

"Fauna of Mirrors" (Borges) 8:99

"Fausse porte ou portrait" (Reverdy) 53:290

"Fausses notes" ("False Notes") (Reverdy) 53:291

Faust (Nye) 42:306-08

"Faust: A Skit" (Justice) 102:254

A Faust Book (Enright) 31:153-55

"The Faustian Pact" (Birkerts) 116:157, 163

"Faustian Sketches" (Fuller) 28:150

"Faustina; or, Rock Roses" (Bishop) 32:33, 38, 42

Faustrecht der Freiheit (Fassbinder) 20:108

"Faustus Kelly" (O'Brien) 7:270; 10:362

"The Fauve" (Humphrey) 45:193, 203

The Favor (Guild) 33:187-88

The Favorite (Wright) 44:334

Favorite Haunts (Addams) 30:16

"The Favourite" (O'Brien) 5:311-12

The Favourite Game (Cohen) 3:109; 38:132-34

Favourite Nights (Poliakoff) 38:384, 386

"A Favourite Scene (Recalled on Looking at Birket Foster's Landscape)" (Blunden) 56:37

Favours (Rubens) 19:404-05

"Fawn" (Davison) 28:104

"Fawn" (Kinsella) 27:237

"The Fawn" (Oliver) 98:266

Fawn (Peck) 17:338-39

Fay's Circus (Prichard)
See *Haxby's Circus: The Lightest, Brightest Little Show on Earth*

Fazendeira do ar y poesia até agora (*Farmer of the Clouds and Poetry until Now*) (Andrade) 18:5

FBI (Berger) 12:41

"Fear" (Carver) 36:107

"Fear" (Dobyns) 37:76-7

"The Fear" (Frost) 1:110; 15:240; 26:119

"Fear" (Merwin) 88:200

"Fear" (Read) 4:439

"The Fear" (Tanizaki)
See "Kyofu"

Fear (Hubbard) 43:203, 205, 207

The Fear (Keneally) 5:210; 19:245-46; 117:210, 213-15

Fear and Desire (Kubrick) 16:376, 380, 385-86, 388-89

Fear and Hope of the Federal Republic of Germany (Kroetz) 41:240

Fear and Loathing in Las Vegas: A Savage Journey to the Heart of the American Dream (Thompson) 9:526-27; 17:504-05, 510, 514-15; 40:426-31; 104:334-35, 338, 340, 343, 345-51

The Fear and Loathing Letters, Vol. 1 (Thompson) 104:348, 350

Fear and Loathing: on the Campaign Trail, '72 (Thompson) 9:527-28; 17:505, 507-

09, 511-12; **40**:427-28; **104**:334-36, 338, 340, 345, 347
"Fear and Trembling" (Warren)   **39**:257, 259, 262
Fear Eats Up Souls (Fassbinder)
   See *Angst essen Seele auf*
"Fear: Four Examples" (Lish)   **45**:228-30
Fear Is the Key (MacLean)   **13**:361; **50**:348-50
"The Fear of Bo-talee" (Momaday)   **85**:247
"The Fear of Burial" (Gluck)   **22**:175-177
"Fear of Death" (Ashbery)   **15**:28; **25**:52
Fear of Falling (Ehrenreich)   **110**:164, 166-67, 169, 173, 176, 178-81
Fear of Fear (Fassbinder)   **20**:114
Fear of Fifty (Jong)   **83**:319
"The Fear of Flying" (Van Duyn)   **63**:438-39; **116**:407
Fear of Flying (Jong)   **4**:263-65; **6**:267, 269-70; **8**:313-15; **83**:290-91, 296-97, 300-04, 307-11, 316-20
Fear of Heaven (Mortimer)   **43**:307
"Fear of Math" (Cameron)   **44**:33, 35
Fear of Music (Byrne)   **26**:97-8
"The Fearful" (Plath)   **14**:424; **51**:341; **111**:168, 204
"Fearful Rock" (Wellman)   **49**:388, 395
Fearful Symmetry: A Study of William Blake (Frye)   **24**:207, 231; **70**:273, 275-76
"Fearless" (Pink Floyd)   **35**:306
The Fearless Treasure (Streatfeild)   **21**:401, 411
The Fearless Vampire Killers; or, Pardon Me, But Your Teeth Are In My Neck (Polanski)   **16**:464, 466-67, 473
"Fears" (Collins)   **44**:38
"The Feast at Countess Fritter's" (Gombrowicz)
   See "Biesiada u hrabiny Kotlubaj"
"The Feast at Paplay" (Brown)   **48**:60
"Feast Day" (Voigt)   **54**:433
A Feast for Boris (Bernhard)
   See *Eine Fest für Boris*
The Feast of All Saints (Rice)   **41**:363-64
Feast of Friends (Morrison)   **17**:288
The Feast of Lupercal (Moore)   **1**:225; **3**:341; **5**:295-96; **19**:330, 334; **32**:314; **90**:238-40, 246, 251-4, 262, 288
A Feast of Snakes (Crews)   **23**:132, 134, 139; **49**:68-72, 74, 76-9
Feast of Stephen (Davies)   **75**:209
Feast of Victors (Solzhenitsyn)   **10**:479
Feast or Famine? The Energy Future (Branley)   **21**:24
A Feast Unknown (Farmer)   **19**:164, 167
Feather Crowns (Mason)   **82**:258-60
Feather Woman of the Jungle (Tutuola)   **14**:540, 542
"A Feather-Bed for Critics" (Blackmur)   **24**:56-7
The Feathered Serpent (O'Dell)   **30**:276-78
The Featherless Dog (Cabral de Melo Neto)
   See *O cão sem plumas*
"Featherly" (Cummings)   **68**:37
"Feathers" (Carver)   **53**:65; **36**:103, 106; **55**:278
"Feathers" (Kinsella)   **27**:236
"Feathers" (Ortiz)   **45**:310
"Feathers from the Hill" (Merwin)   **45**:273
Feathers from the Hill (Merwin)   **18**:336-37
The Feathers of Death (Raven)   **14**:439, 443
"Februar" (Eich)   **15**:204
"February" (Merwin)   **88**:192
"February" (Simic)   **49**:337
February Dragon (Thiele)   **17**:493, 495

"February Ground" (Dahlberg)   **7**:63
"February Seventeenth" (Hughes)   **37**:174-76, 180
"February the 20th Street" (Williams)   **42**:441
"February: The Boy Breughel" (Dubie)   **36**:131, 136
"February's Full Moon" (Akhmadulina)   **53**:15
"The Fecund Complain They Are Not Honored" (Piercy)   **62**:378
Federico Fellini's intervista (*Intervista*) (Fellini)   **85**:59-60, 66, 73-6, 78-82
Fedora (Wilder)   **20**:466
"Feeders" (Barthelme)   **117**:14
"Feeding Ducks" (MacCaig)   **36**:283
"Feeding Time" (Kumin)   **28**:224
"Feel All My Love Inside" (Gaye)   **26**:132
"Feel Like a Number" (Seger)   **35**:383-84
"Feel Like Fucking" (Smith)   **12**:541
"Feel Me" (Swenson)   **4**:534; **14**:518; **61**:393; **106**:344-45
"The Feel of a Face" (Plumly)   **33**:311
"The Feel of Hands" (Gunn)   **6**:220
"The Feel of the Trigger" (Westlake)   **33**:440
"Feeling and Precision" (Moore)   **47**:270, 272
"Feeling for Life" (Cooper)   **56**:71
"Feeling Fucked Up" (Knight)   **40**:283, 286-87
"Feeling Groovy" (Simon)   **17**:458-59, 464, 466
"Feeling into Words" (Heaney)   **25**:249; **74**:156, 179
"Feeling Old" (Ortiz)   **45**:310
"Feeling Sorry for Yourself" (Peacock)   **60**:298
Feeling You're Behind (Nichols)   **33**:332
Féerie pour une autre fois (Celine)   **1**:56; **4**:102; **47**:76-7
Féerie pour une autre fois II: Normance (Celine)   **4**:102; **47**:76-7
Feet in Chains (Roberts)
   See *Traed mewn cyffion*
"Feet on the Ground" (Wakoski)   **2**:459
Fefu and Her Friends (Fornes)   **39**:138; **61**:126-29, 133-38, 141
Feiffer: Jules Feiffer's America from Eisenhower to Reagan (Feiffer)   **64**:156
Feiffer on Civil Rights (Feiffer)   **64**:153
Feiffer on Nixon: The Cartoon Presidency (Feiffer)   **64**:153
Feiffer's Album (Feiffer)   **64**:158
Feiffer's Marriage Manual (Feiffer)   **64**:158
Felicia's Journey (Trevor)   **116**:389-93
"Felicity in Turin" (Durcan)   **70**:152-53
"Felis Catus" (Berriault)   **54**:3; **109**:96
"Felix" (Aleixandre)   **36**:26
"The Fell of Dark" (Skelton)   **13**:507
Fell Purpose (Derleth)   **31**:138
"Fellatio" (Updike)   **3**:485
Fellini: A Director's Notebook (Fellini)
   See *Block-notes de un regista*
"Fellini on Fellini" (Fellini)   **85**:82
Fellini Roma (Fellini)
   See *Roma*
Fellini's Casanova (Fellini)
   See *Casanova di Federico Fellini*
Fellini's Roma (Fellini)
   See *Roma*
Fellini's Satyricon (Fellini)
   See *Satyricon*
Fellow Feelings (Howard)   **7**:169; **10**:275-76; **47**:168
The Fellowship of the Ring (Tolkien)   **12**:563-65; **38**:431
The Fellow-Travellers (Caute)   **29**:116-18

"Fem strofer till Thoreau" ("Five Stanzas to Thoreau") (Transtroemer)   **52**:410; **65**:222-23
"female" (Clifton)   **66**:87
"Female" (Smith)   **12**:534
Female Friends (Weldon)   **6**:562-63; **9**:559-60; **11**:565; **19**:466-69; **36**:446-47
The Female Man (Russ)   **15**:461-62
Female Parts (Fo)   **32**:175
"Feminine Intuition" (Asimov)   **19**:25; **26**:50, 56
"The Feminine Landscape in Leslie Marmon Silko's *Ceremony*" (Allen)   **84**:31
The Feminine Mystique (Friedan)   **74**:90-3, 96-9, 102-03, 105-08, 110-11
"The Feminine Note in Literature" (Forster)   **45**:132
Feminine Wiles (Bowles)   **68**:9
Feminism/Postmodernism   **65**:342-43
Feminism Unmodified: Discourses on Life and Law (MacKinnon)   **65**:324
"A Feminist Challenge" (hooks)   **94**:152
"feminist scholarship: ethical questions" (hooks)   **94**:143
Feminist Theory: From Margin to Center (hooks)   **94**:140-42, 144
Une femme (*A Woman's Story*) (Ernaux)   **88**:98-100, 106-12, 115-17
"La femme adultère" ("The Adulterous Woman") (Camus)   **9**:144; **14**:114; **63**:71, 77
"La femme Anna" (Theriault)   **79**:408
La femme Anna, et autres contes (Theriault)   **79**:407-08
Une femme douce (Bresson)   **16**:115
La femme du Gange (*Woman of the Ganges*) (Duras)   **20**:99-101; **40**:178; **68**:91
Une femme est une femme (Godard)   **20**:130, 140, 148
"Femme Fatale" (Reed)   **21**:303, 314, 319, 321
La femme gelée (*A Frozen Woman*) (Ernaux)   **88**:100, 120
Le femme infidele (Chabrol)   **16**:172-75, 179
Une femme mariée (*The Married Woman: Fragments of a Film Made in 1964*) (Godard)   **20**:131, 133, 136, 149
Une femme qu'a le coeur trop petit (*A Woman Whose Heart Is Too Small*) (Crommelynck)   **75**:154, 161, 169
La femme rompue (*The Woman Destroyed*) (Beauvoir)   **2**:43; **8**:63; **14**:70; **31**:43; **44**:343, 350-51; **71**:48-53
La Femme sur la Lune (Lang)
   See *Die Frau im Mond*
"Les femmes" ("Le bonheur de Bolinka") (Gascar)   **11**:220-21
Les femmes (Gascar)   **11**:221-22
Femmes (Simon)   **39**:208, 215
Les femmes du boeuf (Audiberti)   **38**:22-3, 28
Fen (Churchill)   **31**:88-9; **55**:126
Fen Country (Crispin)   **22**:111
Fences (Wilson)   **50**:267-71; **63**:447-49, 451, 453-54, 456-58
The Fencing Master and Other Stories (Rogin)   **18**:457
Fenêtres dormantes et porte sur la toit (Char)   **55**:288
Feng (Wain)   **11**:561; **15**:561
"Fenstad's Mother" (Baxter)   **78**:26-30
Fer-de-lance (Stout)   **3**:471
Ferdinand (Zukofsky)   **2**:487
Ferdydurke (Gombrowicz)   **4**:193, 195; **7**:122-

26; **11**:241; **49**:121-23, 126-29, 133
Fergus (Moore)   **1**:225-26; **3**:340; **5**:296-97;
   7:238; **19**:331-32, 334; **32**:311, 313-14;
   90:243, 247, 249-51, 254-5, 272-3, 277,
   281
"Fergus Falling" (Kinnell)   **29**:285
Fergus Lamont (Jenkins)   **52**:229
The Ferguson Affair (Macdonald)   **14**:334
The Ferlie (Hunter)   **21**:157
Fermé la nuit (*Closed All Night*) (Morand)
   41:298, 303, 306
"Fern" (Hughes)   **14**:271
"Fern" (Toomer)   **1**:341; **22**:426
"Fern Beds in Hampshire County" (Wilbur)
   53:407; **110**:359
"Fern Dying" (Moss)   **14**:376; **45**:292
Fernwood 2-Night (Lear)   **12**:337-38; **17**:300-
   01
Ferraille (Reverdy)   **53**:279, 281, 285
Ferrements (*Shackles*) (Cesaire)   **19**:95; **32**:112-
   13; **112**:29
"The Ferris Wheel" (Van Duyn)   **116**:412, 415
"The Ferry; or, Another Trip to Venice"
   (Cortazar)   **33**:123-25
"Ferry Port" (Merwin)   **88**:194
Ferryman's Song (Ekelof)   **27**:110
Fertig (Yurick)   **6**:584
"Fertilizing the Continent" (Oates)   **33**:294
Fervor de Buenos Aires (*Fervor of Buenos
   Aires*) (Borges)   **6**:88; **8**:95; **19**:44, 49;
   44:361, 367
Fervor of Buenos Aires (Borges)
   See *Fervor de Buenos Aires*
Fest der Schoneit (*Festival of Beauty*)
   (Riefenstahl)   **16**:521
Fest der Volker (*Festival of the People*)
   (Riefenstahl)   **16**:521
Eine Fest für Boris (*A Feast for Boris*) (Bernhard)
   32:24; **61**:12
Festianus, Martyrer (Eich)   **15**:203
"Festival" (Beer)   **58**:36
"Festival" (Berry)   **17**:52
Festival at Farbridge (Priestley)   **34**:361
Festival of Beauty (Riefenstahl)
   See *Fest der Schoneit*
"The Festival of the Dead" (King)   **53**:212
Festival of the People (Riefenstahl)
   See *Fest der Volker*
"A Festive Day" (Seifert)
   See "Slavnostní den"
The Festivity (Haavikko)
   See *Juhlat*
"The Festubert Shrine" (Blunden)   **56**:41
"Festubert: The Old German Line" (Blunden)
   56:41
"Die Festung" (Lenz)   **27**:245
"The Fetch" (Aickman)   **57**:6-7
"Fête des arbres et du chasseur" (Char)   **11**:116
La fête noire (*La bête noire*; *The Black Beast*;
   The Black Feast) (Audiberti)   **38**:22, 24,
   26-30, 32
Les fetes galantes (Clair)   **20**:66
"Le Fétischiste" (Tournier)   **95**:361, 383
Fetish (Harris)   **25**:212
"Fetishes" (Selzer)   **74**:273
The Fetishist and Other Stories (Tournier)
   36:438
"Fetus" (Lowell)   **37**:234
Feu de braise (Mandiargues)   **41**:278
Feu de Brousse (Tchicaya)   **101**:346-47
Feu froid (Breytenbach)   **23**:83
Le feu sur la terre (Mauriac)   **56**:215
"Feud" (Roethke)   **19**:397

The Feud (Berger)   **38**:38-42
"Feuer-Nacht" (Bogan)   **46**:86; **93**:92-3, 95
Feuilles de route (Cendrars)   **18**:95; **106**:185,
   198
Feuilles de température (Morand)   **41**:303
Feuillets d'Hypnos (*Leaves of Hypnos*) (Char)
   9:159-60; **14**:127; **55**:287-89
Feux (*Fires*) (Yourcenar)   **38**:455-57, 459, 461,
   464; **50**:363-64; **87**:383, 385-87, 390, 399
"Fever" (Akhmadulina)
   See "Oznob"
"Fever" (Boland)   **113**:82, 84, 92
"Fever" (Carver)   **36**:103-04
"Fever" (Le Clezio)   **31**:243
"Fever" (Hirsch)   **50**:195, 197
"Fever" (Updike)   **23**:474
"Fever" (Wideman)   **67**:379-83, 385
Fever (Le Clezio)
   See *Le fièvre*
"Fever 103°" (Plath)   **2**:336; **3**:390; **9**:425,
   428, 433; **14**:428; **17**:355, 365-66;
   51:342, 345; **111**:160, 163, 176-78, 181,
   199, 209, 219
"Fever and Chills" (Elliott)   **2**:131
Fever and Other New Poems (Akhmadulina)
   See *Chills and Other Poems*
"Fever Dream" (Bradbury)   **15**:85-6; **42**:35
"The Fever Monument" (Brautigan)   **12**:59
Fever Pitch (Waters)   **88**:326, 359
"The Fever Toy" (Wright)   **6**:580
"The Fever Tree" (Rendell)   **48**:320
The Fever Tree and Other Stories (Rendell)
   48:320
Fever: Twelve Stories (Wideman)   **67**:378, 380-
   82, 384-85, 388, 390
"Fever-Chills" (Masefield)   **11**:358
"Feverish" (Adcock)   **41**:15
"Das Feverschiff" ("The Lightship") (Lenz)
   27:249, 252-54
"A Few Day's War Which One is Not Certain
   Happened" (Konwicki)
   See "Kilka dni wojny o ktorej nie wiadomo,
   czy byla"
"A Few Don'ts by an Imagiste" (Pound)   **4**:410;
   13:457; **48**:289
"A Few Drinks with Alcock and Brown" (Wain)
   46:411
A Few Enquiries (Sackler)   **14**:479
A Few Fair Days (Gardam)   **43**:165-66
A Few Green Leaves (Pym)   **19**:387-88;
   37:376-77; **111**:227-29, 234, 236, 238,
   240, 242-48, 263-66, 270-71, 273, 281-
   82, 287-88
A Few Hours of Sunlight (*Sunlight on Cold
   Water*) (Sagan)   **17**:426
A Few Late Chrysanthemums (Betjeman)
   34:306, 309; **43**:33-4
"A Few Minutes" (Transtroemer)   **65**:222
"A Few Notes about Aunt Gwen" (Fisher)
   87:131
"A Few Notes of Poetry" (Thesen)   **56**:421
A Few Poems (Barnard)   **48**:26
"A Few Words about Fascism" (Levi)   **41**:246
"The Fez" (Becker and Fagen)   **26**:83
Fiabe Italiene (*Italian Folktales*) (Calvino)
   11:91; **22**:89-90, 92; **33**:100; **39**:306-07,
   309, 314; **73**:42, 53-4
"Fiammetta Breaks Her Peace" (Dove)   **81**:137
"The Fiancés" (Kis)   **57**:246
"Fiat homo" (Miller)   **30**:254, 259
"Fiat lux" (Miller)   **30**:254
"Fiat voluntas tua" (Miller)   **30**:254
Fibrilles (Leiris)   **61**:343-44, 347, 350-51, 356

Ficciones, 1935-1944 (*Fictions*) (Borges)   **2**:72,
   75-7; **3**:77; **4**:74; **6**:93-4; **8**:99, 101-02;
   9:118-19; **13**:105; **19**:49; **44**:356, 363,
   368; **48**:37, 42, 44, 46; **83**:156, 158, 160-
   61, 184
"Fiction" (Nemerov)   **9**:395
"Fiction" (Strand)   **71**:280
Fiction (Reading)   **47**:350, 354
"Fiction: A Lens on Life" (Stegner)   **49**:359
Fiction and the Colonial Experience (Meyers)
   39:433
"Fiction and the Criticism of Fiction" (Rahv)
   24:354, 361
Fiction and the Figures of Life (Gass)   **2**:155;
   8:240; **11**:225; **15**:255; **39**:477
Fiction and Wisdom (McCarthy)   **59**:290
"Fiction for Teenagers" (Hentoff)   **26**:184
"Fiction Today; or, The Pursuit of Non-Knowl-
   edge" (Federman)   **47**:126
"The Fiction Writer" (Jacobsen)   **48**:195
"The Fiction Writer and his Country"
   (O'Connor)   **21**:262
Fictions (Borges)
   See *Ficciones, 1935-1944*
"Fictions of the Feminine" (Fulton)   **52**:161
Fictive Certainties (Duncan)   **55**:294-95
"The Fiddle" (Sillitoe)   **57**:391, 396
"The Fiddle and the Drum" (Mitchell)   **12**:435
The Fiddler (Millin)   **49**:245-46
"Fiddler Crabs" (Brosman)   **9**:135
"The Fiddler on Twenty-Third Street"
   (Callaghan)   **41**:98
Fiddler's Green (Gann)   **23**:163
The Fiddler's House (*Broken Soil*) (Colum)
   28:86-7
Fidelities (Watkins)   **43**:449-50, 453
"Field" (Abse)   **29**:15
"Field" (Broumas)   **73**:15, 17
"Field" (Soto)   **80**:286, 294
"A Field by the River" (Davis)   **49**:93
"Field Flowers" (Gluck)   **81**:167-68
The Field God (Green)   **25**:193, 199-200
Field Guide (Hass)   **18**:208-13; **99**:139-141,
   148-150, 154-55, 157
"Field Guide to the Western Birds" (Stegner)
   49:351
Field Guide to the Western Birds (Stegner)
   81:345-46
"Field Hospital" (Jarrell)   **9**:299
"The Field Hospital" (Muldoon)   **32**:317
"Field Music" (Smith)   **42**:356
Field Notes (Kroetsch)   **23**:273-75; **57**:292-94
"Field of Battle" (Trevor)   **116**:378, 387
"The Field of Blue Children" (Williams)   **5**:502;
   45:447, 452-54
"A Field of Carnations" (Enzensberger)   **43**:145
"A Field of Light" (Roethke)   **11**:480, 485;
   46:362; **101**:274, 283, 324, 335-37, 339
"Field of Opportunity" (Young)   **17**:580
"The Field of Roses" (Simmons)   **43**:408
"A Field of Snow on a Slope of the Rosenberg"
   (Davenport)   **38**:140
"The Field of Vision" (Le Guin)   **8**:343
"Field of Vision" (Heaney)   **74**:192
The Field of Vision (Morris)   **1**:231, 233; **3**:342-
   43; **7**:246; **18**:350, 352, 354; **37**:310-12
"A Field of Wheat" (Ross)   **13**:492-93
"Field Poem" (Soto)   **32**:404; **80**:279, 287,
   294
"The Field Trip" (Voigt)   **54**:433
"Field Work" (Heaney)   **74**:164
Field Work (Heaney)   **14**:244-46; **25**:242-44,
   246-51; **37**:162, 164-67; **74**:157, 159-60,

162-67, 171-73, 175, 177, 188, 190, 193, 197; **91**:115, 117-18, 122-23

Fielding Gray (Raven)　**14**:441

"Fields" (Johnston)　**51**:243

"The Fields" (Merwin)　**45**:274, 276

The Fields (Richter)　**30**:310-15, 318-19, 324-25

"Fields at Dusk" (Salter)　**59**:194

Fields of Fire (Webb)　**22**:453-55

Fields of Grace (Eberhart)　**3**:135

Fields of Peace (Brand)　**7**:30

"The Fiend" (Dickey)　**15**:173

"Fiend's Weather" (Bogan)　**46**:78; **93**:93

The Fierce Dispute (Santmyer)　**33**:356-57

"Fierce Girl Playing Hopscotch" (Fulton)　**52**:162

The Fiery Hunt (Olson)　**11**:420

The Fiery Hunt, and Other Plays (Olson)　**11**:420

"Fiesta" (Pasolini)　**106**:230

Fiesta (Hemingway)
See *The Sun Also Rises*

Fiesta al noroeste (Matute)　**11**:362-64

"Fiesta en grande" (Donoso)　**11**:145; **32**:158

Fiestas (Goytisolo)　**23**:186

"Las fiestas en el campo" (Azorin)　**11**:24

Le fièvre (*Fever*) (Le Clezio)　**31**:243-45

La fièvre monte à El Pao (Bunuel)　**80**:36, 40, 42-4, 52

"Fifine Answers" (Pound)　**48**:288

Fifteen Big Ones (Wilson)　**12**:648, 650-52

"15 Flower World Variations" (Rothenberg)　**57**:381

"The Fifteen-Dollar Eagle" (Plath)　**3**:390; **11**:451; **62**:395

"Fifteenth Farewell" (Bogan)　**4**:68; **46**:78

"Fifth Avenue, Uptown" (Baldwin)　**42**:16

Fifth Business (Davies)　**2**:113; **7**:72-4; **13**:173-74; **25**:131, 133-35; **42**:101-03, 105-07, 109; **75**:178, 180-81, 184-85, 187, 190, 192, 199, 204-05, 211-12, 214-16, 224; **91**:198, 200-2, 204, 206

The Fifth Child (Lessing)　**94**:287

Fifth Chinese Daughter (Wong)　**17**:565-67

The Fifth Column (Hemingway)　**13**:274, 278; **80**:101, 105, 121, 149

"Fifth Commandment" (Brunner)　**8**:107

"Fifth Day" (FitzGerald)　**19**:177, 179

"The Fifth Day" (Matthiessen)　**64**:321, 323-24

Fifth Decad of Cantos (Pound)　**48**:284

"The Fifth Gospel" (Morgan)　**31**:275

"The Fifth Head of Cereberus" (Wolfe)　**25**:472

The Fifth Head of Cereberus (Wolfe)　**25**:472-74, 476

The Fifth of July (Wilson)　**14**:590-92; **36**:459-61, 463-65

The Fifth Sally (Keyes)　**80**:165

"The Fifth Sense" (Beer)　**58**:38

The Fifth Son (Wiesel)　**37**:458-59

Fifth Sunday (Dove)　**81**:140-41, 146

"Fifty Dollars" (Elkin)　**51**:96

"Fifty Grand" (Hemingway)　**3**:233; **30**:179; **80**:104

"Fifty Males Sitting Together" (Bly)　**38**:57

Fifty Poems (Cummings)　**8**:154; **12**:154-53; **15**:162; **68**:35, 48

Fifty Poems Fifty (Whittemore)　**4**:588

Fifty Roads to Turn (Hamner)　**12**:257

Fifty Stories (Boyle)　**19**:66; **58**:74, 76

"Fifty Ways to Leave Your Lover" (Simon)　**17**:465-66

Fifty Works of English Literature We Could Do

Without (Brophy)　**6**:99; **29**:95-6; **105**:5-6, 29-30

"A Fifty Year Old Man" (Endo)　**99**:288, 297, 301

"Fifty-Fifty" (Sandburg)　**35**:356

"Fifty-Fifty" (Zappa)　**17**:590

"59x: A True Tale" (Nye)　**42**:309

"The Fifty-Ninth Bear" (Plath)　**3**:390

"The Fifty-Ninth Street Bridge Song" (Simon)　**17**:461, 464, 466

Fifty-Second Street (Joel)　**26**:216-17, 220-21

"Fifty-Seven Views of Fujiyama" (Davenport)　**38**:145-47

53 Days (Perec)
See *53 Jours*

53 Jours (*53 Days*) (Perec)　**116**:238, 254-55

52 Pick-Up (Klappert)　**57**:64

Fifty-two Pickup (Leonard)　**28**:233; **71**:223

"The Fifty-Yard Dash" (Saroyan)　**8**:468

"The Fig Tree" (Porter)　**27**:402

"The Fig Tree" (Pritchett)　**15**:443

"Fight" (Bukowski)　**82**:14

The Fight (Mailer)　**11**:344; **14**:351; **28**:259

Fight against Albatross Two (*Albatross Two*) (Thiele)　**17**:495

Fight Back: For the Sake of the People, for the Sake of the Land (Ortiz)　**45**:308-10

Fight for Freedom (Hughes)　**108**:284, 286

Fight Night on a Sweet Saturday (Settle)　**19**:409-10; **61**:373-74, 376, 383

"The Fighter" (Kristofferson)　**26**:269

Fighter (Deighton)　**22**:117

Fightin': New and Collected Stories (Ortiz)　**45**:309-11

Fighting Angel (Buck)　**7**:32; **11**:74-5

The Fighting Cock (Anouilh)　**50**:278

"Fighting Depression, I Take My Family on a Picnic" (Baxter)　**78**:25

"Fighting for the Rebound" (Mukherjee)　**115**:364

The Fighting Indians of the West (Brown)　**47**:37

Fighting International Fat (Reynolds)　**38**:390-91

Fighting Terms: A Selection (Gunn)　**3**:215; **18**:200; **32**:207, 210-11; **81**:177, 183, 185

"Fighting the Bureaucracy" (Appleman)　**51**:15

"The Fights" (Acorn)　**15**:8-9

Figleafing through History: The Dynamics of Dress (Harris)　**12**:263

"La figlia che piange" (Eliot)　**1**:90; **9**:187, 189; **13**:201; **15**:213; **41**:146, 150-51

"Figure" (Summers)　**10**:494

"The Figure a Poem Makes" (Frost)　**4**:177

"Figure in a Landscape" (Gascoyne)　**45**:148

"The Figure in the Carpet" (Hollander)　**5**:186

"The Figure in the Carpet" (Stevenson)　**33**:382

Figure in the Door (Gregor)　**9**:253

"The Figure in the Doorway" (Frost)　**9**:228

A Figure of Speech (Mazer)　**26**:289-90, 292, 296

"Figure over the Town" (Goyen)　**40**:216-17

"The Figured Wheel" (Pinsky)　**38**:355, 361; **94**:299, 306, 308; **94**:299, 306, 308

"The Figurehead" (Shapiro)　**53**:331

Figures Capable of Imagination (Bloom)　**103**:4, 14, 24-5

Figures for an Apocalypse (Merton)　**83**:400

Figures in Black: Words, Signs and the 'Racial' Self (Gates)　**65**:379, 381-82, 393-94, 398

Figures in Bright Air (Plante)　**7**:308; **23**:344

Figures in Modern Literature (Priestley)　**34**:361

Figures in the Foreground (Swinnerton)

31:426

Figures of Enchantment (Ghose)　**42**:185

"Figures of Space" (Young)　**82**:412

Figures of Speech (Enright)　**31**:146-47, 152

Figures of the Human (Ignatow)　**7**:174-76; **14**:276; **40**:258

Figures of Thought: Speculations on the Meaning of Poetry and Other Essays (Nemerov)　**36**:303-04

Figures of Time (Hayden)　**37**:156, 160

Figuro in the Night (O'Casey)　**5**:318; **88**:268

La fijeza (*Fixity*) (Lezama Lima)　**101**:121

File on a Diplomat (*An Instant in the Wind*) (Brink)　**18**:67-8; **36**:67, 69; **106**:99, 124, 126-27, 136-37

The File on Stanley Patton Buchta (Faust)　**8**:215

Files on Parade (O'Hara)　**42**:312, 320

"Filet" (Montague)　**46**:270

La fille de Christophe Colomb (Ducharme)　**74**:57

La fille de l'eau (Renoir)　**20**:291, 301

"La fille Eva" (Theriault)　**79**:407

La fille laide (Theriault)　**79**:400, 408, 411-12, 419

"La fille noire" (Theriault)　**79**:408

"Filling Night with the Name: Funeral as Local Color" (Warren)　**39**:256, 272

"Filling Station" (Bishop)　**9**:92; **32**:33, 38-9

"Filling the Boxes of Joseph Cornell" (Wakoski)　**4**:571

"Filling the Forms" (Hoffman)　**6**:243; **13**:289

Fillmore East (Zappa)　**17**:587, 593

"A Film" (Barthelme)　**115**:65

Film (Beckett)　**6**:36; **9**:82, 84; **18**:43, 47; **59**:253, 255

Un film comme les autres (*A Film Like Any Other*) (Godard)　**20**:150

"Film Digression" (Sukenick)　**48**:370

Film Is Evil: Radio Is Good (Foreman)　**50**:160, 164-71, 173

A Film Like Any Other (Godard)
See *Un film comme les autres*

"Film Preview in the Morning" (Shiga)　**33**:366

The Films in My Life (Truffaut)　**101**:407

"Filo del amor" (Aleixandre)　**9**:15

Fils de personne (Montherlant)　**19**:327

Filthy Lucre: or, The Tragedy of Andrew Ledwhistle and Richard Soleway (Bainbridge)　**62**:36

Filthy Rich (Walker)
See *The Power Plays*

"Filthy with Things" (Boyle)　**90**:62-3

"La Fin" ("The End") (Beckett)　**4**:51; **10**:34, 36

Fin de fiesta (Goytisolo)
See *The Party's Over*

La fin de la nuit (*The End of the Night*) (Mauriac)　**56**:207-09

Fin de mundo (Neruda)　**7**:257; **28**:310, 312

Fin de partie (*Endgame*) (Beckett)　**1**:20, 24; **2**:44-6; **3**:44, 46-7; **4**:51; **6**:39-43, 47; **9**:84-5, 87; **10**:26, 30-1; **11**:37, 42-3; **14**:79; **18**:45, 47; **29**:54, 61, 65, 67; **59**:252-55, 257-59; **83**:108-51

El fin del mundo (*The End of the World*) (Valdez)　**84**:400, 406

El fin del viaje (*Journey's End*) (Neruda)　**62**:336

"Fin du monde" (Hebert)　**29**:237

"Final" (Neruda)　**28**:310

The Final Addiction (Condon)　**100**:102-05

The Final Adventures of the Robber Hotzenplotz (Preussler)　**17**:377

Final Analysis (Gould) 4:200-01; **10**:241
Final Blackout (Hubbard) 43:203-04, 206
"The Final Choruses for the Promised Land" (Ungaretti) 7:485
The Final Circle of Paradise (Strugatskii and Strugatskii) 27:435
Final Concrete Testament (Nichol) **18**:369
Final Curtain (Marsh) 53:247, 254
The Final Cut (Pink Floyd) 35:314-16
Final del juego (*End of the Game*) (Cortazar) 2:103-04; **13**::157; 33:123, 126, 130; 34:329, 332
"Final Dwarf" (Roth) 104:284, 311
The Final Folly of Captain Dancy (Evans) 70:332
The Final Hour (Caldwell) 28:63; 39:303
"The Final Martyrs" (Endo) 99:298
The Final Martyrs (Endo) 99:284, 288, 298, 300-01, 306-07
"Final Meeting" (Kizer) 80:183
"The Final Night" (Faludy) 42:140
"Final Notations" (Rich) 76:212, 214, 218
The Final Opus of Leon Solomon (Badanes) 59:38-42
The Final Passage (Phillips) 96:315-17, 323-24, 329-30, 332, 335, 338, 341, 343, 352, 354
Final Payments (Gordon) 13:249-50; 22:185, 187-88
The Final Programme (Moorcock) 27:349-50; 58:347-48, 357
"The Final Proof of Fate and Circumstance" (Abbott) 48:5, 7
"the final solution" (Sanchez) 116:278, 294
Final Solutions (Seidel) 18:474-75
"A Final Sonnet" (Berrigan) 37:42
"Final Trophy" (Ellison) 42:131
"Finale: Presto" (Davison) 28:100
"Finale/Your Eyes" 99:180
"Finally" (Jacobsen) 48:193
"Finally I See Your Skin" (Lerman) 9:329
The Financial Expert (Narayan) 7:255; 28:291, 299; 47:301, 304, 307
"Financial Statement" (Slavitt) 14:491
"The Financial World" (Brophy) 29:91
"Financially the Paper..." (Barthelme) 46:42
Find a Victim (Macdonald) 41:265, 268, 272
Find My Killer (Wellman) 49:387, 391
Find the Changeling (Benford) 52:67
Find Your Way Home (Hopkins) 4:233-34
"The Finder" (Spencer) 22:405
Finders (Friel)
  See *Winners*
"Finding" (Davenport) 38:141
"Finding a Girl in America" (Dubus) 36:145-47; 97:199, 201, 220, 226
Finding a Girl in America (Dubus) 36:146, 148; 97:198, 205, 208-09, 220, 231, 235
"Finding a Poem" (Snodgrass) 68:384
"Finding a Remedy" (Longley) 29:295
"Finding a Voice" (Welty) 105:320-22, 378, 382
"Finding an Old Ant Mansion" (Bly) 38:54-5, 58-60
Finding Gold (Norris) 14:387
Finding Losses (Bronk) 10:75
"Finding Natasha" (Bell) 102:6, 8
"The Finding of the Way" (MacLennan) 92:344
Finding the Centre (Naipaul) 37:325-29; 105:172-73, 179
"Finding the Haystack in the Needle" (Jordan) 114:153
Finding the Islands (Merwin) 45:273, 278;

88:194-95
Finding the Sun (Albee) 53:23-4; 86:120-21, 124
Finding Them Lost, and Other Poems (Moss) 45:292; 50:353
Findings (Berry) 8:85; 46:69-70
Findings (Howard) 7:166, 168; 10:276; 47:168
A Fine and Private Place (Beagle) 7:25-6; 104:2-7, 10, 24-5
A Fine and Private Place (Callaghan) 14:102; 41:88-90, 94-6; 65:245, 248-50, 253
A Fine and Private Place (Queen) 11:465
"Fine As Fine Can Be" (Lightfoot) 26:281
Fine Clothes to the Jew (Hughes) 1:147; 10:279; 44:508, 511; 108:293-94, 310, 319, 323
A Fine Day (Vesaas)
  See *Ein vakker dag*
"Fine del '68" ("The End of 1968") (Montale) 9:387
A Fine Madness (Baker) 8:38-9
"Fine Memory" (Seger) 35:380
Fine Mess (Celine)
  See *Les beaux draps*
"A Fine Old Firm" (Jackson) 60:229
A Fine Red Rain (Kaminsky) 59:171
A Fine Romance (Seton) 27:425-29
A Fine, Soft Day (Forman) 21:122
"A Fine Son" (Dahl)
  See "Genesis and Catastrophe"
"Fine Western Land: Cloud-Light" (Buckley) 57:136
Finest Short Stories of Seán O'Faoláin (*The Stories of Seán O'Faoláin*) (O'Faolain) 31:340:70:318
"The Finger" (Creeley) 36:121
Finger of Fire (Braine) 41:60
"Finger Prints" (Seifert) 93:325, 331
"Finger Wet, Finger Dry" (Bates) 46:62
"Fingernail Sunrise" (Watkins) 43:450
"Fingers and Toes" (Michaels) 25:315
Fingers at Air: Experimental Poems, 1969 (Shapcott) 38:399-401
Fingers in the Door (Tuohy) 37:428-30, 432
Fingers of Hermes (Squires) 51:377, 381
Finian's Rainbow (Coppola) 16:232, 244
"Finis Not Tragedy" (Smith) 64:399
The Finished Man (Garrett) 3:190; 11:220; 51:141-42, 145-46
The Finishing School (Godwin) 69:236-39, 243, 246, 252
"Finishing the Hat" (Sondheim) 30:403
The Finishing Touch (Brophy) 29:92-4; 105:7-8, 12, 30, 38-9, 41-2
Finishing Touches (Kerr) 22:257-58
"Finisterre" (Plath) 111:214
Finisterre (Montale) 7:221-22, 226
Finn and Hengest: The Fragment and the Episode (Tolkien) 38:440, 442
Finnegan's Funeral Parlor and Ice Cream Shoppe (Kerr) 59:400-02
"Finnish Rhapsody" (Ashbery) 77:69-70
A Finnish Suite (Haavikko)
  See *Suomalainen sarja*
Finnley Wren (Wylie) 43:461-63, 469-71
"Fiona the First" (Kinsella) 27:237
Il fiore della Mille e una notte (*The Arabian Nights*) (Pasolini) 20:270; 106:226, 241, 248, 250, 266, 270
"Fire" (Creeley) 78:135
"The Fire" (Dickinson) 49:102
"The Fire" (Duncan) 15:190-91; 41:124, 130
"Fire" (Hoffman) 6:244
"Fire" (Hughes) 108:297

"Fire" (Ryan) 65:216
Fire (Pa Chin) 18:374
"Fire and Cloud" (Wright) 14:596-97; 21:444, 453-54
Fire and Ice (Stegner) 49:347
The Fire and the Anvil (Baxter) 14:60, 62-3
The Fire and the Sun: Why Plato Banished the Artists (Murdoch) 51:289, 291
"Fire and the Tide" (Stevenson) 33:381
"The Fire Autumn" (Murray) 40:334-36
"The Fire Balloons" (Bradbury) 10:71
"The Fire Down Below" (Seger) 35:382, 386
Fire Down Below (Golding) 81:317-18, 320, 325-26
"The Fire Eaters" (Bates) 46:63
The Fire Engine That Disappeared (Wahloo)
  See *Brandbilen som foerwann*
"Fire Escape" (Woolrich) 77:390
Fire from Heaven (Renault) 3:426; 17:400
"The Fire i' the Flint" (Heaney) 74:178
Fire in the Basement (Kohout) 13:325
Fire in the Belly: On Being a Man (Keen) 70:420, 422-23, 425-26, 458
"Fire in the Hole" (Becker and Fagen) 26:84
Fire in the Morning (Spencer) 22:398-400, 403
Fire in the Stone (Thiele) 17:494-95
"Fire in the Vineyards" (Boyle) 58:71
"Fire Island" (Swenson) 14:519; 106:349-50
"Fire Lake" (Seger) 35:384-86
"The Fire Next Time" ("Letter from a Region in My Mind") (Baldwin) 42:15-17, 19; 50:284
The Fire Next Time (Baldwin) 2:32-3; 3:31; 4:41; 5:41; 8:41-2; 13:52-3; 15:42-3; 17:25, 28, 34, 36, 38, 42; 42:14-19, 22-3; 50:282, 291-93, 295; 67:8, 27
"Fire Now Wakening on the River" (Chappell) 78:96
"The Fire of Despair Has Been Our Saviour" (Bly) 38:60
"Fire on Belmont Street" (Davidson) 19:127
"Fire on Greenstone" (Ihimaera) 46:195
Fire on Stone (Gustafson) 36:215-18
Fire on the Mountain (Abbey) 36:13, 15-16; 59:241
Fire on the Mountain (Desai) 19:133; 37:70, 72; 97:144, 149-50, 159, 161-63, 168-69, 171, 177, 180, 186
The Fire Screen (Merrill) 2:274-75; 6:323; 13:380-82; 91:228, 230
Fire Sequence (Winters) 32:468
"The Fire Sermon" (Eliot) 9:183; 10:169; 15:212; 41:155-56; 113:223
Fire Sermon (Morris) 3:343; 7:245-46; 37:313
"Fire Station" (Bukowski) 82:14, 17, 22
"Fire Storm" (Alexie) 96:10
"Fire: The People" (Corn) 33:116
"A Fire Truck" (Wilbur) 53:410; 110:353, 384
"The Firebombing" (Dickey) 1:73; 2:115; 7:80-1, 84; 47:93; 109:238, 244, 266, 272, 281-82
Firebrand (Troyat) 23:457
"The Firebug" (Sillitoe) 57:388
The Firebugs: A Learning Play without a Lesson (Frisch)
  See *Biedermann und die Brandstifter: Ein Lehrstück ohne Lehre*
Firecrackers (Van Vechten) 33:388, 397-98
"Fire-Damp" (Sciascia)
  See "L'antimonio"
The Fire-Dwellers (Laurence) 3:281; 50:312,

314-15, 319, 321; **62**:269-72, 279, 282, 284-86, 291-92, 306

The Fire-Eaters (MacEwen)   **13**:358; **55**:164

Firefall (Van Duyn)   **116**:417-18, 420-23, 426-27

"The Firefighter" (Kinsella)   **43**:256-57

"Fireflies" (Hollander)   **2**:197

"Fireflies" (Muske)   **90**:309-10, 312

Fireflies (Naipaul)   **32**:323-25, 327; **39**:355-56, 358

Fireflood, and Other Stories (McIntyre)   **18**:327

Firekeeper (Medoff)   **23**:294

"The Fireman" (Bradbury)   **98**:108-09, 111, 114-15, 144

Fireman Flower and Other Stories (Sansom)   **2**:383

"Fires" (Carver)   **36**:103, 107; **55**:283

"The Fires" (Shiga)   **33**:367

Fires (Yourcenar)
    See *Feux*

Fires: Essays, Poems, Stories, 1966-1982 (Carver)   **39**:99, 106; **53**:66

Fires in th tempul OR th jinx ship nd othr trips (Bissett)   **18**:60

Fires in the Mirror: Crown Heights, Brooklyn and Other Identities (Smith)   **86**:266, 268-72

Fires in the Sky: The Birth and Death of Stars (Gallant)   **17**:132

Fires of Azeroth (Cherryh)   **35**:106, 112

The Fires of Spring (Michener)   **29**:309-11; **109**:377

"Fires on Llyrn" (Clarke)   **61**:79-81

Fires on the Plain (Ichikawa)
    See *Nobi*

The Fire's Reflection (Trifonov)
    See *The Campfire Reflection*

Fireship (Vinge)   **30**:409-10

Fireship and Mother and Child (Vinge)   **30**:409

Firestarter (King)   **26**:236-37, 241; **37**:199, 201, 203, 205; **61**:319, 331; **113**:335-36, 338, 343, 345, 347, 369-70, 388, 391

"Firewater" (Chappell)   **40**:145

Fireweed (Walsh)   **35**:430, 433

Fireweeds (Weiss)   **8**:546; **14**:553-54, 556-57

"Firewood" (Banks)   **72**:5

"Firewood" (Chappell)   **40**:144

"Firewood" (McPhee)   **36**:296

"Fireworks" (Shapiro)   **15**:475

Fireworks (Thompson)   **69**:388

Fireworks: A History and Celebration (Plimpton)   **36**:357

Fireworks: Nine Profane Pieces (Carter)   **5**:101-03; **41**:121

The Firm (Grisham)   **84**:190-97, 199

Firm Beliefs of William Faulkner (Brooks)
    See *On the Prejudices, Predilections, and Firm Beliefs of William Faulkner*

Firozsha Baag (Mistry)
    See *Tales from Firozsha Baag*

"First" (Avison)   **97**:82

"The First" (Soto)   **80**:277

"The First Adam" (Gardam)   **43**:171

"First Advertisements for Myself" (Mailer)   **111**:120

"First American Ode" (Barker)   **48**:13

"A First American Views His Land" (Momaday)   **85**:265, 268

First and Last Loves (Betjeman)   **6**:67; **34**:311; **43**:38

First and Last Words (Chappell)   **78**:98

First and Vital Candle (Wiebe)   **14**:574

First Blues: Rags, Ballads, and Harmonium Songs (Ginsberg)   **36**:196

The First Book of Ballet (Streatfeild)   **21**:401

The First Book of Jazz (Hughes)   **108**:300

The First Book of Negroes (Hughes)   **108**:291-92

First Book of Odes (Bunting)   **39**:297

The First Born Son (Buckler)   **13**:120

"First Boyfriend" (Olds)   **85**:294

The First Circle (Solzhenitsyn)
    See *V kruge pervom*

The First Cities (Lorde)   **18**:307; **71**:240, 257

First Comes Courage (Arzner)   **98**:69, 73-4, 87, 93-5

"First Communion" (Fante)   **60**:133

"First Communion" (Kinnell)   **5**:217

"The First Communion" (Suknaski)   **19**:432

First Communion (Arrabal)
    See *La communion solonelle*

"First Confession" (Kennedy)   **42**:255

"First Conjugation" (O'Faolain)   **47**:325

"First Dark" (Spencer)   **22**:405-06

"The First Day" (Jones)   **76**:64-5, 67

"The First Day" (Nemerov)   **36**:304

"First Day after the War" (Kunene)   **85**:175

"First Day of School" (Squires)   **51**:381, 383

"The First Day of Summer" (Saroyan)   **29**:362

"First Day of Winter" (Pancake)   **29**:348, 350

"The First Day Out from Troy" (Squires)   **51**:381

The First Deadly Sin (Sanders)   **41**:377-79

"First Death" (Justice)   **102**:269, 285

"First Death in Nova Scotia" (Bishop)   **9**:91; **32**:33-4, 37-8

The First Decade (Duncan)   **15**:187-88; **55**:294

"The First Declension" (Gardam)   **43**:167

"First Draft of Cantos I-III" (Pound)   **10**:400

"First Dream" (Guillen)
    See "Primero sueño"

"First Encounter" (Clarke)   **35**:122

First Encounter (Dos Passos)
    See *One Man's Initiation—1917*

First Encounters (Ulibarri)
    See *Primeros encuentros/First Encounters*

"First Essay on Interest" (Murray)   **40**:343

"First Exercise" (Ryan)   **65**:209

"First Fall" (Bernard)   **59**:44

The First Fast Draw (L'Amour)   **25**:280

"First Fight. Then Fiddle" (Brooks)   **5**:76

"The First Flight" (Heaney)   **91**:117

"First Flight" (Van Duyn)   **7**:498; **63**:436; **116**:402, 406, 412

"First Foot" ("Calling Card") (Campbell)   **42**:89

The First Four (Merwin)   **88**:205

The First Freedom: The Tumultuous History of Free Speech in America (Hentoff)   **26**:185-87

"First Frost" (Simic)   **49**:341

"First Frost" (Voznesensky)   **57**:414-15

"First Goodbye" (Gluck)   **44**:216

"First Heat" (Taylor)   **71**:309-11, 313-15

"First Hippy Revolution" (Garnett)   **3**:189

First Holy Communion (Arrabal)
    See *La communion solonelle*

"First Hymn to Lenin" (MacDiarmid)   **2**:255; **19**:289; **63**:245

"A 'First Impression' (Tokyo)" (Blunden)   **56**:39, 46

First Indian on the Moon (Alexie)   **96**:5, 7-12, 17

"The First Invasion of Ireland" (Montague)   **46**:266

"The First Kingdom" (Heaney)   **74**:169

First Lady (Endo)   **99**:285

"First Lesson" (Willard)   **37**:463

First Lesson (White)   **30**:449

"First Lesson about Man" (Merton)   **83**:396-97

First Light (Baxter)   **78**:19-21, 25-26, 30-32

"The First Line" (Moss)   **45**:287-88, 293

"First Love" (Olds)   **85**:295

"First Love" (Welty)   **1**:361; **105**:298, 385

First Love (Beckett)
    See *Premier amour*

"First Love and Other Sorrows" (Brodkey)   **56**:55-6, 63

First Love, and Other Stories (Beckett)   **3**:47; **6**:38-9; **29**:56

First Love, Last Rites (McEwan)   **13**:369-71; **66**:275-76, 280, 292, 294

First Lover, and Other Stories (Boyle)   **58**:64

"The First Madam" (Schaeffer)   **11**:491

The First Man in Rome: Marius (McCullough)   **107**:153, 155-58, 163-66

"First Manhattans" (Gilchrist)   **48**:120

First Manifesto (McGrath)   **59**:177

First Marriage (Howe)   **47**:175

"First Meditation" (Roethke)   **101**:312

"First Meeting with Ivan Shark" (Dobyns)   **37**:77

"The First Men on Mercury" (Morgan)   **31**:275

"First Names and Empty Pockets" (Kinsella)   **27**:237

"First Night" (Olds)   **32**:346; **85**:286

"The First Night of Fall and Falling Rain" (Schwartz)   **45**:355

First Papers (Hobson)   **25**:272

First Person Singular (Maugham)   **67**:209

First Poems (Merrill)   **2**:272, 274-75; **3**:335; **13**:379; **91**:228, 230

First Poems (Turco)   **11**:550; **63**:428, 430

First Poems, 1946-1954 (Kinnell)   **13**:321

"First Prayer" (Atwood)   **13**:44

"First Principal" (Guthrie)   **23**:199

"The First Report of the Shipwrecked Foreigner to the Kadanh of Derb" (Le Guin)   **45**:213

"The First Seven Years" (Malamud)   **27**:306; **44**:412

"First Sex" (Olds)   **85**:297

"The First Shot" (Achebe)   **7**:6; **11**:3; **26**:24

"First Sight" (Larkin)   **5**:227; **39**:336

"First Snow" (Mosher)   **62**:313

"First Snow" (Nemerov)   **36**:304

"First Snow" (Oliver)   **34**:246

"First Snow" (Sarton)   **49**:320

"The First Snow in Alsace" (Wilbur)   **6**:570; **53**:397; **110**:381

"First Sonata for Karlen Paula" (Sandburg)   **35**:356

The First Songs (*More Than a New Discovery*) (Nyro)   **17**:313

"First South and Cambridge" (Hugo)   **32**:236

"The First Spade in the West" (Fiedler)   **13**:214

"The First Sunday"   **75**:62

The First Teacher (Aitmatov)
    See *Pervyi uchitel'*

"The First Thing the Baby Did Wrong..." (Barthelme)   **46**:42

"First Things, and Last" (Nemerov)   **36**:308

"First Things First" (Elytis)   **100**:191

First Things Last (Malouf)   **28**:268

"The First Time" (Creeley)   **78**:135

"First Trip through the Automatic Carwash" (Van Duyn)   **63**:444-45; **116**:413

First Will and Testament (Patchen)   **18**:392

"The First Year of My Life" (Spark)   **40**:403

"Firstborn" (Wright) 6:580
The Firstborn (Fry) 2:144; 10:200-01; 14:186, 188
Firstborn (Gluck) 7:118-19; 22:173-76; 44:216
"Firsts" (Ciardi) 40:162
"The Fish" (Banks) 72:3, 5
"Fish" (Barthelme) 117:18
"The Fish" (Bishop) 1:34-5; 4:66; 32:29, 32, 37-8, 42-3
"The Fish" (Clark) 5:105
"The Fish" (Dinesen) 29:159
"The Fish" (Moore) 2:291; 4:362; 10:353; 47:260, 262, 266
"The Fish" (Oliver) 34:249; 98:257, 272, 290, 297
"The Fish Are All Sick" (Stevenson) 33:383
"Fish Bones" (Oliver) 98:283
The Fish Can Sing (Laxness)
   See *Brekkukotsannáll*
"The Fish Counter at Bonneville" (Stafford) 29:381
"Fish Crier" (Sandburg) 15:468; 35:355
"The Fish of His Woman" (Dacey) 51:80
"Fish Shop" (Townshend) 42:379-81
Fish, Sweet Giraffe, the Lion Snake and Owl (Dacey) 51:78
Fish Tales (Jones) 34:67-9
"Fish, Tomatoes, Mama, and Book" (Major) 19:298
"The Fish Who Could Close His Eyes" (Clark) 28:79
"The Fisherman" (Banks) 37:26
"Fisherman" (Dunn) 40:170
"The Fisherman" (O'Brien) 103:146, 148
"Fisherman" (Watkins) 43:450
The Fisherman and His Wife (De Marinis) 54:98
"The Fisherman from Chihuahua" (Connell) 45:114
Fisherman's Spring (Haig-Brown) 21:137
Fisherman's Summer (Haig-Brown) 21:138, 142
The Fisherman's Whore (Smith) 22:384-85, 387, 389; 42:352, 356
Fisherman's Winter (Haig-Brown) 21:137-38
"The Fishermen at South Head" (Murray) 40:343
"The Fishermen of the Seine" (Humphrey) 45:205
Fishermen with Ploughs: A Poem Cycle (Brown) 5:76-8; 48:53-4, 57; 100:84
"The Fisher's Wish" (Goldbarth) 5:144
"The Fish-Hawk" (Wheelock) 14:571
"Fishing" (Nye) 42:305
"Fishing" (Thomas) 13:545
Fishing (Weller) 10:525-26; 53:389-90, 392
"Fishing Fever" (Davis) 49:92
"Fishing for Albacore" (Smith) 6:513
"The Fishing Lake" (Spencer) 22:406
"Fishing Off Nova Scotia" (Olds) 32:346
"The Fishing Pole of the Drowned Man" (Carver) 36:107
"Fishing the White Water" (Lorde) 71:257
"The Fishing-Boat Picture" (Sillitoe) 57:388
"Fishnet" (Lowell) 8:355
Fiskadoro (Johnson) 52:235-41
"Fission" (Sayles) 14:483
"The Fist" (Walcott) 14:549; 42:422; 76:285
The Fist Too Was Once the Palm of an Open Hand and Fingers (Amichai)
   See *Gam ha'egrof haya pa'am yad ptuba ve'etsba'ot*
Die Fistelstimme (Hofmann) 54:224

Le fiston (*Monsieur Levert*) (Pinget) 7:305; 13:442
"A Fit against the Country" (Wright) 28:462
"Fits" (Munro) 50:208, 210, 214-16, 218, 220
"Fitter's Night" (Miller) 47:249-50
"The Fitting" (Barnard) 48:25-6
Fitting Words (Arghezi)
   See *Cuvinte potrivite*
"Five" (Cummings) 15:161
"5" (Fearing)
   See "American Rhapsody"
5 (Reading) 47:352-54
"Five Accounts of a Monogamous Man" (Meredith) 13:375; 22:302; 55:191
Five Acre Virgin, and Other Stories (Jolley) 46:214
Five Ages (Levi) 41:247-48
"Five Ages of a Poet" (Levi) 41:248
Five Alone (Derleth) 31:127-28
"Five A.M." (Fearing) 51:119
"Five A.M. in the Pine Woods" (Oliver) 98:283, 292
"Five American Sonnets" (Simmons) 43:412, 414
"Five Bells" (Slessor) 14:493-95, 498
Five Bells (Slessor) 14:495-96
Five Biblical Portraits (Wiesel) 37:455, 457
Five Boyhoods (Updike) 23:463
"Five Chinese Songs" (Guillen) 79:229
Five Corners (Shanley) 75:322-23, 326-28, 330, 332
Five Days in June (*A Day Marked X*) (Heym) 41:216-18
Five Decades (Shaw) 34:369
Five Decades, a Selection: Poems, 1925-1970 (Neruda) 5:303; 7:260
"Five Domestic Interiors" (Scannell) 49:330
"The Five Faces of Pity" (Barker) 8:46; 48:14
Five Finger Exercise (Shaffer) 5:386, 388-89; 14:484-86; 18:475-76
"Five Flights Up" (Bishop) 32:37
Five for Sorrow, Ten for Joy (Godden) 53:162
Five Gates to Hell (Clavell) 87:18
"Five Generations" (Porter) 33:318
"The Five Gold Bands" (Vance) 35:419
"Five Green Waves" (Brown) 48:52
"Five Highways" (Moure) 88:221, 227
Five Hours with Mario (Delibes)
   See *Cinco horas con Mario*
Five Hundred Scorpions (Hearon) 63:166-68
"Five Letters from an Eastern Empire" (Gray) 41:179, 183
Five Little Pigs (Christie)
   See *Murder in Retrospect*
"The Five Master Terms" (Burke) 24:127
Five Masters: A Study in the Mutation of the Novel (Krutch) 24:281
"Five Meals" (Hacker) 72:192
"Five Men" (Herbert) 43:190
"Five Men against the Theme, 'My Name is Red Hot. Yo Name ain Doodley Squat'" ("My Name Is Red Hot. Yo Name Ain Doodley Squat") (Brooks) 49:36, 38
"Five O'Clock Shadow" (Betjeman) 6:69
Five Patients (Crichton) 2:108
"Five Pedantic Pieces" (Ashbery) 15:34
Five Plays (Mortimer) 28:286
Five Plays (Shepard) 4:489; 17:436
Five Plays of Langston Hughes (Hughes) 35:217
"Five Poems" (Avison) 97:67
"Five Poems about Poetry" (Oppen) 7:281
"Five Poems from Japanese Paintings" (Pollitt)

28:367-68
"Five Poems on Film Directors" (Morgan) 31:276
"Five Points" (Munro) 95:307, 310, 314
Five Seasons (Angell) 26:30-2
"Five Senses" (Wright) 53:424, 428-29
"The Five Senses: A Bestiary" (Dacey) 51:79
Five Senses: Selected Poems (Wright) 53:423-25, 431
"Five Short Moral Poems" (Levi) 41:248
Five Signs of God's Decay (Mishima)
   See *The Decay of the Angel*
The Five Stages of Grief: Poems (Pastan) 27:369-70
"Five Stanzas to Thoreau" (Transtroemer)
   See "Fem strofer till Thoreau"
Five Stories of Ferrara (Bassani) 9:76
5 Tales and 2 Fables (Benet)
   See *5 narraciones y 2 fábulas*
"Five Visions of Captain Cook" (Slessor) 14:492, 494-95
"The Five Voyages of Arnor" (Brown) 48:57
"Five Walks on the Edge" (Viereck) 4:559
"Five Ways of Facing the Deep" (Booth) 23:75
A Five Year Sentence (Rubens) 19:404
"Five Years" (Bowie) 17:59
Five Years (Goodman) 2:171; 4:196-97
Five Years (Levinson) 49:226-27
The Five-Fold Mesh (Belitt) 22:48, 52
"The Five-Forty-Eight" (Cheever) 15:130; 64:48, 65
Fives (Dacey) 51:82
"The Five-Thousandth Baritone" (Newman) 8:419
"Five-Twenty" (White) 5:487; 7:533
"Fixed" (Dunn) 40:166
"Fixed Ideas" ("Fixed Opinions") (Slessor) 14:493
"Fixed Opinions" (Slessor)
   See "Fixed Ideas"
The Fixer (Malamud) 1:198-99; 2:266, 268-69; 3:321-23; 5:269-70; 9:348-49; 11:348-51, 354; 18:319-20; 27:295-98, 301-02; 44:411, 413, 415, 417, 419; 78:271; 85:200
"Fixing a Hole" (Lennon and McCartney) 12:359
Fixity (Lezama Lima)
   See *La fijeza*
Fizzles (Beckett)
   See *Foirades*
A Flag for Sunrise (Stone) 23:426-31; 42:359-63
A Flag on the Island: A Fantasy for a Small Screen (Naipaul) 13:404-05; 105:157
"The Flag Rave" (Murray) 40:338
Flagons and Apples (Jeffers) 54:233-35, 244, 250; 11:305
"Flags" (Moure) 88:217
Flags in the Dust (Faulkner)
   See *Sartoris*
"Flake" (Morgan) 31:275
"Flakes" (Zappa) 17:593
"The Flame" (Pound) 48:288
Flame into Being (Burgess) 40:124
The Flame of Life (Sillitoe) 6:500
The Flame of New Orleans (Clair) 20:70
The Flames (Ali)
   See *Sholay*
Flames Across the Border: The Canadian-American Tragedy, 1813-1814 (Berton) 104:42-3, 46, 59
Flames Going Out (Platt) 26:354-56

Flaming Bodies (Wilson) 33:463-64

"Flaming Eternity" (p'Bitek) 96:287

The Flaming Sword (Neruda) 28:314

Flamingo Feather (van der Post) 5:463

"Flamingos Fly" (Morrison) 21:237

"Flamingos of the Soda Lakes" (Lieberman) 36:261

The Flanders Road (Simon)
See *La route des Flandres*

A Flann O'Brien Reader (O'Brien) 47:317

Flannery O'Connor's South (Coles) 108:179, 180, 183

Flare Path (Rattigan) 7:354

Flash and Filigree (Southern) 7:452

"Flash Flood" (Snodgrass) 68:397

A Flash of Green (MacDonald) 44:408

"A Flashing Cliff" (Rukeyser) 27:406

"The Flashing Pigeons as They Wheel" (Goodman) 4:197

The Flashman Papers (Fraser) 7:106

"A Flat One" (Snodgrass) 68:388

Flats (Wurlitzer) 2:482-84; 4:597-98; 15:588-89

"The Flats Road" (Munro) 95:300, 303

"Flatted Fifth" (Hughes) 35:222

"Flattery" (Lopate) 29:302

"Flaubert in Egypt" (Warren) 6:555; 8:538

Flaubert y "Madame Bovary" (Vargas Llosa)
See *La orgía perpetua: Flaubert y "Madame Bovary"*

"Flaubert's Early Prose" (Creeley) 78:141

Flaubert's Parrot (Barnes) 42:27-30

Flavio (Parks) 16:460

The Flavor of Green Tea over Rice (Ozu) 16:450

"The Flaw" (Lowell) 8:354

The Flaw (Samarakis) 5:381-82

"Flawless Play Restored: The Masque of Fungo" (Sorrentino) 14:500

Flaws in the Glass (White) 65:274, 276; 69:406-07, 410

The Flea Circus (Brammer) 31:53-4

A Flea in Her Ear (The Brothers Quay) 95:347, 350

The Flea of Sodom (Dahlberg) 7:67; 14:137

Flèche d'Orient (Morand) 41:304

"Flee on Your Donkey" (Sexton) 6:493; 10:468

"Fleecing" (Gilliatt) 10:230

"Fleeting Friendships" (Castellanos) 66:60-1

"Fleetwood Cafe" (Baxter) 78:28

"Flemish Rain" (Szirtes) 46:393, 395

The Flemish Shop (Simenon) 47:371

"Flesh" (Wright) 53:420, 424

Flesh (Brophy) 6:100; 11:68; 29:92, 97-8; 105:10, 29-30, 32-33

Flesh (Farmer) 19:164

Flesh and Blood (Hamill) 10:251

Flesh and Blood (Humphreys) 47:181-82, 184, 187, 190

Flesh and Blood (Williams) 56:425-29

"Flesh and the Mirror" (Carter) 5:103

The Flesh in the Furnace (Koontz) 78:199-200

"Fleshing-out the Season" (Komunyakaa) 94:234

"La fleur qui disait amour" (Theriault) 79:408

"Les fleurs" (Ligotti) 44:54

Les fleurs bleues (Queneau) 10:430-32

Fleuve profond, sombre rivière (*Deep Torrent, Dark River*) (Yourcenar) 50:364; 87:401

Le fleuvre de feu (Mauriac) 56:204, 206

"Flexion" (Zamora) 89:363

Die Fliegenpein (*The Agony of Flies*) (Canetti) 86:301

Ein fliehendes Pferd (Walser) 27:463-64

"Flies" (Grace) 56:122

The Flies (Sartre)
See *Les mouches*

"Flight" (Johnston) 51:239, 244, 251

"Flight" (Kenny) 87:255

"Flight" (McGuane) 45:266

"The Flight" (Neruda) 62:332

"The Flight" (Roethke) 11:481

"Flight" (Steinbeck) 21:369, 381, 389, 391-92

"Flight" (Swan) 69:360-61, 363-64

Flight 115 (O'Hara) 78:364

"Flight from Byzantium" (Brodsky) 50:132

Flight from Fiesta (Waters) 88:358

The Flight from the Enchanter (Murdoch) 1:233-34, 236; 2:295; 3:345, 347; 6:345-48; 11:386-87; 15:381-84; 31:293, 295

Flight into Camden (Storey) 2:423; 4:528

"Flight into Darkness" (Gustafson) 36:211, 214, 216, 218

"The Flight Into Egypt" (Buckley) 57:129

"The Flight into Egypt" (Merton) 83:378

"Flight into Super-Time" (Smith) 43:422

Flight of Exiles (Bova) 45:67

The Flight of Icarus (Queneau)
See *Le vol d'Icare*

The Flight of Mr. MacKinley (Leonov)
See *Begstvo Mistera Mak-Kinli*

"The Flight of Pigeons from the Palace" (Barthelme) 46:36; 115:80

"A Flight of Ravens" (Bradbury) 42:33

The Flight of Sandukov (Leonov)
See *Volk*

"The Flight of the Earls" (Boland) 67:46

The Flight of the Falcon (du Maurier) 59:280-81, 284

Flight of the Falcon (Smith)
See *A Falcon Flies*

The Flight of the Wild Gander: Explorations in the Mythological Dimension (Campbell) 69:76

"Flight Pattern" (Greenberg) 30:166

Flight to Africa (Clarke) 6:110-11; 9:167

Flight to Canada (Reed) 13:479-80; 32:355-56, 358-59, 364; 60:302, 313

Flight to the West (Rice) 7:360-61; 49:300, 302, 304

Flight Today and Tomorrow (Hyde) 21:171, 175

"Flighting for Duck" (Empson) 19:158

Flightpoint (Weiss)
See *Fluchtpunkt*

Flights (King) 8:321

Flights (Shepard) 36:405-07

"Flights of Fancy" (Trevor) 14:537

"Fling" (Hersey) 81:329

Fling, and Other Stories (Hersey) 81:329-30, 332

The Flint Anchor (Warner) 7:511-12; 19:460

"The Flitting" (McGuckian) 48:276

Floaters (Ezekiel) 34:46-8

"Floating" (Rexroth) 112:398

Floating Bear (Baraka) 115:3

"The Floating Bridge of Dreams" (Tanizaki)
See "Yume no ukihashi"

Floating Dragon (Straub) 28:411; 107:265, 267-68, 271, 274-78, 280-83, 285, 288-90, 302, 304-10

"The Floating Feathers Shield" (Momaday) 85:280

The Floating Light Bulb (Allen) 52:44-5

The Floating Opera (Barth) 2:36; 3:38, 42; 7:23; 9:68, 72; 10:21-2; 14:49-51, 56; 27:26-7, 29; 51:20-1; 89:8-9, 17, 27, 47-8

"The Floating Poem, Unnumbered" (Rich) 73:331

"The Floating Truth" (Paley) 37:337

The Floating World 59:63-69

The Floating World (Michener) 109:376, 379, 382

"The Flock" (Walcott) 42:422

"A Flock of Trouble" (Davis) 49:94

"The Flood" (Clark) 38:129

"The Flood" (Richter) 30:329

"The Flood" (Tomlinson) 45:397-98, 400-01, 403

"The Flood" (Wright) 53:417

The Flood (Le Clezio)
See *Le déluge*

Flood (Grass) 4:202; 15:260

Flood (Matthews) 40:322, 324

The Flood (Tomlinson) 45:396-98, 400-04

Flood (Vachss) 106:354, 357-59, 361, 365

Flood (Warren) 59:302

Flood: A Romance of Our Time (Warren) 1:356; 4:578; 8:540

"Flood Burial" (Foote) 75:230-31

"Flood Light" (Matthews) 40:322

"Flood Plain" (Matthews) 40:324

"Flood Tide" (Yehoshua) 31:468-69

The Flood unto my Soul (Oe)
See *Kozui wa waga tamashii ni oyobi*

"Flooded Meadows" (Gunn) 3:216

"The Flooded Valley" (Mathias) 45:235, 238

The Flooded Valley (Mathias) 45:234-35

"Floods" (Raine) 103:194

"Floods of Florence" (Ochs) 17:332

"Floodtide" (Bova) 45:73

Floodtide (Yerby) 1:381

"Floor" (Williams) 33:448

"Flophouse" (Fearing) 51:106

"Una flor amarilla" ("A Yellow Flower") (Cortazar) 34:332

La flor de mi secreto (*The Flower of My Secret*) (Almodovar) 114:55, 58

Floralie, où es-tu? (*Floralie, Where Are You?*) (Carrier) 13:140-41, 143-44; 78:38-40, 45-6, 49, 53-6, 59-61, 63, 67-71, 79, 82-3

Floralie, Where Are You? (Carrier)
See *Floralie, où es-tu?*

"Florence" (Denby) 48:84

Florence (Childress) 86:309, 311, 314; 96:88, 103-04, 109, 112

"Florence Green is 81" (Barthelme) 3:43; 5:57; 46:35; 115:66

"Florence Nightingale" (Longley) 29:297

The Florence Poems (Olson) 28:344

"Florentines" (Hill) 18:239

Flores del volcán/Flowers from the Volcano (*Flowers from the Volcano*) (Alegria) 75:35-8, 40-2, 46, 49, 53

Flori de mucigai (*Flowers of Mildew; Flowers of Mold*) (Arghezi) 80:6-7, 9-10

"Florida" (Bishop) 4:65; 9:94; 13:92-3; 32:38

Florida Frenzy (Crews) 49:73-4, 77

"Florizel's Complaint" (Fuller) 62:184

Flotsam (Remarque) 21:328, 330

The Flounder (Grass)
See *Der Butt*

Flow Chart (Ashbery) 77:70-6

Flow My Tears, the Policeman Said (Dick) 30:123, 125; 72:104, 106

"The Flower" (Creeley) 36:118; 78:144
"The Flower" (Warren) 13:578
The Flower and the Leaf: A Contemporary Record of American Writing since 1941 (Cowley) 39:457-62
The Flower and the Nettle: Diaries and Letters of Anne Morrow Lindbergh, 1936-1939 (Lindbergh) 82:153, 155, 160
"Flower Bulbs" (Dudek) 11:160
"Flower Dump" (Roethke) 3:432; 11:481; 101:296
Flower, Fist, and Bestial Wail (Bukowski) 41:63; 82:15; 108:81
"The Flower Garden" (Jackson) 60:211, 229
Flower Herding on Mount Monadnock (Kinnell) 3:269; 5:216; 13:321; 29:283
"Flower Herding on the Mountain" (Kinnell) 5:216; 29:280
"Flower Lady" (Ochs) 17:333
The Flower Master (McGuckian) 48:275-77, 279
"Flower Music" (Livesay) 15:340; 79:338
"The Flower of Coleridge" (Borges) 83:160
"The Flower of Kiltymore" (Friel) 115:252-53
The Flower of My Secret (Almodovar)
   See *La flor de mi secreto*
"The Flower Piece" (Bates) 46:51
"Flower Poems" (Silkin) 2:396; 43:397, 404
"Flower Punk" (Zappa) 17:591
Flower Wreath Hill: Later Poems (Rexroth) 112:392, 395
"The Flower-Cart and the Butcher" (Klappert) 57:264
"The Flower-Gatherers" (Blunden) 56:37
"Flower-Gathering" (Frost) 26:113
The Flowering and Subsequent Deflowering of New England (Angell) 26:29
Flowering Cactus (Hamburger) 5:158
Flowering Cherry (Bolt) 14:87-9
"Flowering Death" (Ashbery) 15:33-4
"The Flowering Dream: Notes on Writing" (McCullers) 4:345; 10:335; 12:427; 100:262
"Flowering Eucalypt in Autumn" (Murray) 40:343
"Flowering Judas" (Porter) 3:393; 7:310, 315, 320; 10:396, 399; 13:448-49; 15:432; 27:401; 101:209-10, 212, 224-28, 235-39, 242, 253
Flowering Judas, and Other Stories (Porter) 1:272; 13:447; 101:209-10, 212, 215, 222, 249, 255
The Flowering of New England (Brooks) 29:81-2, 88
Flowering of the Cumberland (Arnow) 7:15-16; 18:12
"The Flowering of the Rod" (H. D.) 8:255, 257-58; 14:223, 225, 227; 31:201-03,208; 34:445
The Flowering Peach (Odets) 2:320; 28:334-35, 339-40; 98:198-200, 210-13, 217, 228-31, 234-37, 241, 252-53
"Flowering Plum" (Gluck) 22:174
"Flowering Quince" (Ciardi) 40:157
"Flowering Sudden" (L'Heureux) 52:272
The Flowering Suns (Ferron)
   See *Les grands soleils*
"Flowers" (Akhmadulina)
   See "Tsvety"
"The Flowers" (Walker) 103:406, 411-12
Flowers and Shadows (Okri) 87:313-14, 322, 325

Flowers for Algernon (Keyes) 80:162-68
Flowers for Hitler (Cohen) 38:132, 134-37
Flowers for the Judge (Allingham) 19:15
"Flowers for the Void" (Snyder) 32:388
"Flowers from the Volcano" (Alegria) 75:34, 39, 41, 53
Flowers from the Volcano (Alegria)
   See *Flores del volcán/Flowers from the Volcano*
"The Flowers Grow High" (Guillen) 79:229-30
"Flowers in the Interval" (MacNeice) 4:316
"The Flowers of Boredom" (De Marinis) 54:101
Flowers of Darkness (Cohen) 19:116
"Flowers of Edo" (Sterling) 72:372
Flowers of Mildew (Arghezi)
   See *Flori de mucigai*
Flowers of Mold (Arghezi)
   See *Flori de mucigai*
"The Flowers That Bloom in Spring" (Metcalf) 37:300
"The Flower-Women" (Smith) 43:422
Flucht und Verwandlung (Sachs) 98:322, 324
Der Flüchtling (Hochwalder) 36:234-36
Fluchtpunkt (Flightpoint) (Weiss) 15:563; 51:389
Fluff (Olson) 11:420
Ein Flugzeug über dem Haus (Walser) 27:456-57
"The Flume" (Bogan) 46:78-9; 93:90, 94-5, 97
The Flute Book (Berger) 12:39-40
"Flute Maker's Story" (Cook-Lynn) 93:116
"The Flute Player of Brindaban" (Ezekiel) 61:104
The Flute-Player (Thomas) 22:417-18; 31:435
The Flutes of Autumn (Levi) 41:248
"Fly" (Merwin) 88:206
"The Fly" (Shapiro) 15:475, 478; 53:334
"Fly" (Weller) 26:444
The Fly (Clavell) 87:18
Fly (Lennon) 35:267
Fly and the Fly-Bottle: Encounters with British Intellectuals (Mehta) 37:289-90
Fly Away Home (Piercy) 62:366-69, 373
Fly Away Home (Tindall) 7:473-74
Fly Away Peter (The Bread of Time to Come) (Malouf) 28:268-70
Fly Free (Adler) 35:14-15
A Fly Hunt (Hunting Flies) (Wajda) 16:580
"The Fly in the Coffin" (Caldwell) 14:96
A Fly on the Wall (Hillerman) 62:251, 262-63
"Fly Paper" (Hammett) 47:159
Flycatcher and Other Stories (Bowering) 47:22
"Flying" (Mahon) 27:288
Flying (Millett) 67:241-53, 256, 258
"Flying a Red Kite" (Hood) 28:187, 193
Flying a Red Kite (Hood) 15:284; 28:187, 190
The Flying Boy: Healing the Wounded Man 70:421, 423
"The Flying Bum" (Plomer) 4:407
"The Flying Change" (Taylor) 44:302-03
The Flying Change (Taylor) 44:300, 302-03
Flying Colours (Forester) 35:163, 166, 170
Flying Correspondent (Felsen) 17:120
"Flying Crooked" (Graves) 45:174
Flying Finish (Francis) 42:148-50, 155, 158; 102:131, 144, 154-55
"The Flying Goat" (Bates) 46:55
The Flying Goat (Bates) 46:55-6
Flying Hero Class (Keneally) 117:239
"Flying Home" (Ellison) 86:324; 114:94, 95,

102, 108, 131
"Flying Home" (Kinnell) 29:285
Flying Home and Other Stories (Ellison) 114:124, 126, 130, 137-38
"Flying House" (Swenson) 4:533
Flying Inland (Spivack) 6:520-21
"Flying on the Ground" (Young) 17:568
"Flying out of It" (Ferlinghetti) 10:175
The Flying Swans (Colum) 28:89, 92-3
"Flying Switch" (Davis) 49:91, 94
"Flying to Belfast, 1977" (Raine) 32:351; 103:181, 184
Flying to Nowhere (Fuller) 62:199-200, 202-05
"Flying Underground" (Giovanni) 117:198
The Flying Wasp (O'Casey) 88:260
"The Flynch Cows" (Nowlan) 15:398
F.M. (Linney) 51:262
"Foal" (Watkins) 43:453
"Foam" (Enzensberger) 43:145-46
FOB (Hwang) 55:152
Foco novo (Pomerance) 13:444
Focus (Miller) 47:248-49
"Fodder" (Heaney) 5:172
Fodor's Indian America (Highwater) 12:285
Foe (Coetzee) 66:90-6, 98-9, 106; 117:34, 46-7, 49-50, 59-60, 67, 75-6, 80-1, 86-7, 102
"Foetal Song" (Oates) 6:367
"Fog" (Kavan) 5:206; 82:120
"Fog" (Sandburg) 10:449, 15:468
"Fog" (Soto) 80:287, 294
"Fog" (Warren) 10:521
Fog (Wu) (Pa Chin) 18:372-73
The Fog Comes on Little Pig Feet (Wells) 12:637-38
"Fog Envelops the Animals" (Dickey) 7:83
"The Fog Horn" (Bradbury) 42:35, 42; 98:115
"The Fog Man" (Boyle) 90:64
"Fog Report" (Lorde) 71:234, 252
Fogarty (Neville) 12:451-52
Foggage (McGinley) 41:284-86
"The Foggy Lane" (Simpson) 7:428-29
"Foggy Street" (Voznesensky) 57:419
"Foghorn in Horror" (Rukeyser) 15:459
The Foibles and Fables of an Abstract Man (Honig) 33:216
"Le foin de Martial" (Theriault) 79:408
Foirades (Fizzles; For to end yet again and Other Fizzles; Pour finir encour et Autres Foirades) (Beckett) 9:83-4; 14:74, 80; 29:61
La foire d'empoigne (Catch as Catch Can) (Anouilh) 1:7; 13:21-2; 40:56-7
La foire d'empoigne (Anouilh)
   See *Catch as Catch Can*
The Folded Leaf (Maxwell) 19:305-06
"Folding a Shirt" (Levertov) 5:246
The Folding Screens (Genet)
   See *Les paravents*
The Folding Star (Hollinghurst) 91:132-42
"Folie à deux" (Adcock) 41:15
La folie en tête (Mad in Pursuit) (Leduc) 22:262
Folie et déraison: Histoire de la folie à l'âge classique (Madness and Civilization: A History of Insanity in the Age of Reason) (Foucault) 31:171, 173, 176, 178, 184-85; 34:340-42, 345; 69:158, 165, 169-70
The Folk of the Air (Beagle) 104:23-5, 27, 32, 34
"Folk Tale" (Jiles) 58:277
"Folk Tale" (Pastan) 27:369
"Folksong" (Hogan) 73:150, 153

Follies (Sondheim)　**30**:381-91, 396-97, 399-402; **39**:175
"Follow Me, Comrades"　**75**:69
Follow Me Down (Foote)　**75**:230-31, 237, 243, 251
Follow My Mind (Cliff)　**21**:63
"Follow the Eagle" (Kotzwinkle)　**35**:254
Follow the Footprints (Mayne)　**12**:388, 397
"Follow the Leader" (Reed)　**21**:312-13
Follow the Yellow Brick Road (Potter)　**58**:391-92
The Followed Man (Williams)　**14**:583
"Follower" (Heaney)　**74**:180, 194
Following a Lark (Brown)　**100**:84, 87-8
"Der Folterknecht" ("The Torturer") (Durrenmatt)　**8**:195; **15**:193
Fombombo (Stribling)　**23**:445
"Fon" (Dumas)　**6**:145; **62**:155, 160, 162
"Fonction et champ de la parole et du langage en psychanalyse" ("Discours de Rome"; "The Function and Field of Speech and Language in Psychoanalysis"; "The Language of the Self"; "The Rome Discourse") (Lacan)　**75**:284, 293, 295, 300
"Fond Farewell to the 'Chicago Quarterly'" (Whalen)　**29**:446
"Fond Memory" (Boland)　**67**:39; **113**:108
"Fondo con figuras" (Aleixandre)　**36**:31
Fong and the Indians (Theroux)　**8**:513
La Fontaine des innocents (Gallo)　**95**:98-9
La fontaine narrative (Char)　**14**:125
Fontamara (Silone)　**4**:492, 494
"Fontan" (Brodsky)　**13**:115
"El fontanero azul" ("The Blue Water Man") (Valenzuela)　**104**:388
"La fonte" (Alonso)　**14**:25
"Food" (Jacobsen)　**48**:194, 199
Food for Centaurs (Graves)　**11**:254
"Food for Love" (Kizer)　**39**:169-70
"Food for Thought" (Robinson)　**21**:350-51
"The Food of Love" (Dickey)　**28**:119
"The Food Thief" (Olds)　**85**:293, 301
"The Fool" (MacDiarmid)　**63**:251
The Fool (Bond)　**13**:103
The Fool (Garfield)　**12**:235, 238
The Fool and the Madman (Bernhard)
　　See *Der Ignorant und der Wahnsinnige*
Fool for Love (Altman)　**116**:49, 59, 73
Fool for Love (Shepard)　**34**:265-71; **41**:412, 414-16; **44**:264-65, 268-70
A Fool i' the Forest: A Phantasmagoria (Aldington)　**49**:5-6, 8-11, 13, 15-17
"The Fool on the Hill" (Lennon and McCartney)　**12**:362
"A Fool Too Fast" (Ciardi)　**40**:161
The Fooleen: A Crucial Week in the Life of a Grocer's Assistant (Murphy)　**51**:306-07
"Fooling Marie" (Bukowski)　**41**:73
"Foolish" (Spacks)　**14**:511
"Foolish Pride" (Cliff)　**21**:63
"The Foolish Wing" (Ciardi)　**40**:151
Fools (Simon)　**31**:399-400, 403-04; **39**:219; **70**:235
Fools Are Passing Through (Durrenmatt)
　　See *Die Ehe des Herrn Mississippi*
Fools Crow (Welch)　**52**:435-38
Fools Die (Puzo)　**36**:359-62; **107**:193, 213
"Fool's Education" (Price)　**6**:423; **43**:345
"A Fool's Love" (Tanizaki)
　　See "Chijin no ai"
Fools of Fortune (Trevor)　**71**:321, 323-25, 327, 329, 340, 342, 346, 349-350; **116**:348, 351-52, 365, 367-72, 376-77,

382-83
Fools of Time (Frye)　**70**:277
The Fool's Progress (Abbey)　**59**:238-39, 242
Fools Say (Sarraute)
　　See *Disent les imbéciles*
"A Foot in the Door" (Friedman)　**56**:96
"Foot Notes" (Phillips)　**28**:363
The Football Game of the First Year of Manen (Oe)
　　See *Man'en gan'nen no futtoboru*
Footfalls (Beckett)　**9**:84; **11**:43; **14**:74, 78; **18**:46; **29**:63-4; **59**:253
"Foothold" (Bowen)　**22**:64
Footmen's Quartet (Coward)　**29**:138
"Footnote" (Rosenthal)　**28**:394
"A Footnote on Monasticism: Dingle Peninsula" (Montague)　**46**:265
"Footnote to a Laundry List" (Santos)　**22**:365
"Footnote to a Pretentious Book" (Baraka)　**5**:45
"Footnote to Howl" (Ginsberg)　**69**:212, 214, 219, 221, 223, 225-26; **109**:347, 350, 359, 370
"Footnote to Wisdom" (Santos)　**22**:361
Footprints (Levertov)　**3**:292-93; **66**:251
"Footprints in the Jungle" (Maugham)　**67**:206
The Footprints of the Prophet
　　See *Pasii profetului*
"Footsteps" (Dobyns)　**37**:79
"Footsteps in the Dark" (Nowlan)　**15**:398
"Footsteps in the Footprints" (Cortazar)　**33**:123
Footsteps of the Hawk (Vachss)　**106**:365-66
Footsteps on the Stairs (Adler)　**35**:12
"The Foot-Washing" (Ammons)　**108**:51
"For A" (Bowering)　**15**:82; **47**:19
"For a Birthday" (Plath)　**11**:446
"For a Birthday" (Wright)　**53**:428
"For a Bitter Season" (Garrett)　**3**:192
For a Bitter Season: New and Selected Poems (Garrett)　**11**:219, 219; **51**:147-48
"for a black prostitute" (Sanchez)　**116**:307, 322
"For a Breath I Tarry" (Zelazny)　**21**:466-67, 479
"For a Brother in Asia" (Celan)　**82**:34
"For a Child Pronounced Mentally Defective" (Silkin)　**43**:398
"For a Coming Extinction" (Merwin)　**13**:385; **88**:202, 206
For a Critique of the Political Economy of the Sign (Baudrillard)
　　See *Pour une critique de l'économie politique du signe*
"For a Dancer" (Browne)　**21**:36-7, 39, 41
"For a Dead African" (Brutus)　**43**:96
"For a Fatherless Son" (Plath)　**3**:391; **51**:345
"For a few Hopi Ancestors" (Rose)　**85**:312
"For a Five-Year-Old" (Adcock)　**41**:13, 18
"For a Friend" (Ignatow)　**7**:180
"For a Friend Who Was Killed in the War" (Kunene)　**85**:166
"For a Lamb" (Eberhart)　**56**:84
"For a Man Your Age" (Dixon)　**52**:99
"For a Mexican Painter" (Rukeyser)　**27**:408
For a Nameless Tomb (Onetti)
　　See *Para una tumba sin nombre*
For a New Novel (Robbe-Grillet)　**1**:287; **2**:375; **14**:462; **43**:360
"For a Poet I Know" (Giovanni)　**19**:190
"For a Russian Poet" (Rich)　**6**:458
"For a Singer" (Acorn)　**15**:9
"For a Young Artist" (Hayden)　**9**:270; **37**:160

"For Abe Klein: Poet" (Livesay)　**79**:351
"For Adrian" (Walcott)　**67**:361
For All That I Found There (Blackwood)　**6**:79-80
For All the Seasons of Your Mind (Ian)　**21**:182
For All the Wrong Reasons (Neufeld)　**17**:310
"For an Unmarked Grave" (Mathias)　**45**:238
"For Andrew" (Adcock)　**41**:13, 18
"For Angus MacLeod" (Smith)　**64**:389
"For Anna Akmatova" (Lowell)　**1**:182
"For Anna Mae Pictou Aquash, Whose Spirit Is Present Here and in the Dappled Stars (For We Remember the Story and Tell It Again So that We May All Live)" (Harjo)　**83**:274, 281-82
"For Anne" (Cohen)　**38**:132
"For Any Member of the Security Police" (Jacobsen)　**48**:190
For att ente tala om alla dessa kvinnor (*All These Women; Now about These Women*) (Bergman)　**16**:55-6, 70; **72**:40
"For Better for Worse" (Gellhorn)　**14**:195; **60**:184
"for Black history month/February 1986" (Sanchez)　**116**:318
"For Black People" (Madhubuti)　**73**:214-15
"For Black Poets Who Think of Suicide" (Knight)　**40**:285
"For Bonfires" (Morgan)　**31**:275
"For Brigid" (Buckley)　**57**:131
"For C" (Whalen)　**29**:446
"For C. P. F." (Cabral de Melo Neto)
　　See "A Carlos Pena Filho"
"For Charlie Beaulieu in Yellowknife" (Musgrave)　**54**:338
"For Chekhov" (Hass)　**18**:212
for colored girls who have considered suicide/ when the rainbow is enuf: A Choreopoem (Shange)　**8**:484-85; **25**:396-99, 401-05; **38**:393, 395; **74**:291, 293-99, 302, 307-11, 313
For Continuity (Leavis)　**24**:308
"For Danton" (Tomlinson)　**13**:550
"For David Emmanuel" (Silkin)　**6**:498
"For David Kalstone" (Van Duyn)　**116**:411
"For David St. John Who's Written a Poem" (Dubie)　**36**:130
"For Dear Life" (Gordimer)　**18**:189
"For deLawd" (Clifton)　**66**:73
"For Denise Levertov" (Kinnell)　**29**:288
"for domestic workers in the african diaspora" (Sanchez)　**116**:307
"For Dudley" (Wilbur)　**53**:406, 413; **110**:384, 386
"For Each of You" (Lorde)　**71**:254
"For Eleanor and Bill Monahan" (Williams)　**22**:465
"For Eli Jacobsen" (Rexroth)　**49**:285
"For Ellen" (Wilbur)　**53**:412; **110**:357
"For Emily, Whenever I May Find Her" (Simon)　**17**:461
"For Eric Dolphy" (Knight)　**40**:284
"For Esmé—with Love and Squalor" ("Esmé") (Salinger)　**1**:298; **12**:497, 510
"For Ever and Ever, Amen" (Smith)　**15**:517
For Everyman (Browne)　**21**:35, 37, 40
"For Everyone" (Neruda)　**7**:261
"For Fear of Little Men" (Wellman)　**49**:393
"For Françoise Adnet" (Jones)　**10**:287
"For Freckle-Faced Gerald" (Knight)　**40**:286
"For Free" (Mitchell)　**12**:442
"For/From Lew" (Snyder)　**32**:400
"For Futures" (Miles)　**39**:354

"For George Lamming" (Birney) 6:76
"For George Santayana" (Lowell) 8:349
"For Good Measure" (Elytis) 100:190
For Good Measure: The Story of Modern Measurement (Berger) 12:37-8
"For Granny" ("From Hospital") (Clark) 38:117, 121, 126-27
"For Harold Bloom" (Ammons) 25:44; 108:17
"For Helen" (Hecht) 19:208
"For Her" (Strand) 18:518; 41:432
"For Her First Exhibition with Love" (Cage) 41:86
For Her Own Good: One Hundred Fifty Years of Experts' Advice to Women (Ehrenreich) 110:177-78
"For His Father" (Meredith) 4:347
For Instance (Ciardi) 40:162
"For James Dean" (O'Hara) 13:423
"For Jan, In Bar Maria" (Kizer) 80:175, 180, 182
"For Jenny and Roger" (Garrigue) 8:240
"For Jeromé—With Love and Kisses" (Lish) 45:228-30
"For Jessica, My Daughter" (Strand) 18:518, 521; 41:438
"For John, after His Visit: Suffolk, Fall" (Matthias) 9:362
"For John Berryman" (Ignatow) 14:275
"For John Berryman" (Lowell) 11:330
"For John, Who Begs Me Not to Enquire Further" (Sexton) 53:320
"For Johnny Pole on the Forgotten Beach" (Sexton) 10:469
"For Julia Li Qiu" (Van Duyn) 116:422
"For K. J., Leaving and Coming Back" (Hacker) 72:192
"For Keats" (Smith) 64:399
For Kicks (Francis) 22:150, 152-53; 42:149-50, 153, 156, 158; 102:154
"For L. G.: Unseen for Twenty Years" (Rich) 6:459
For Lancelot Andrewes: Essays on Style and Order (Eliot) 24:182; 57:213
"For Langston Hughes" (Knight) 40:279
För levande och döda (For Living and Dead) (Transtroemer) 65:229, 233, 237
"For Lil' Bit" (Jordan) 114:146
For Living and Dead (Transtroemer)
   See *För levande och döda*
For Lizzie and Harriet (Lowell) 3:302-04, 306; 4:301; 5:257, 259; 8:358; 9:336; 11:328; 15:344
"For Love" (Creeley) 36:119-20; 78:162
For Love Alone (Stead) 2:422-23; 32:406-09, 411-12, 414-15; 80:307-08, 317-19, 324-27, 330-33, 336, 342, 346, 348
"For Love of Eleanor" (Rooke) 25:391
"For Love of Gomez" (Rooke) 25:391-92
For Love of Imabelle (A Rage in Harlem) (Himes) 58:257-58, 262, 266-70; 108:232, 241, 264; 108:232, 236-39, 241, 264, 267-70, 275
"For Love of Madeline" (Rooke) 25:391
For Love: Poems, 1950-1960 (Creeley) 1:67; 2:106-07; 8:151-53; 11:137-38; 15:150-51; 36:119-20; 78:124-26, 134-38, 143-44, 147
"For Lucy" (Mueller) 51:280
"For Ma" (Dabydeen) 34:150
"For Malcolm, a Year After" (Knight) 40:279, 284
"For Marguerite, Real Love" (Codrescu) 46:102

"For Marianne Moore" (Ignatow) 14:275
"For marilyn m" (Bukowski) 108:111
For Marx (Althusser)
   See *Pour Marx*
"For Mary Ann Youngren" (Bidart) 33:80
For Mary, with Love (Savage) 40:376-77
"For May Swenson" (Van Duyn) 116:427
"For Miriam" (Tomlinson) 45:397-98, 400-01, 403
"For My American Family" (Jordan) 114:151
"For My Brother Reported Missing in Action, 1943" (Merton) 83:379, 393
"For My Daughter" (Ignatow) 7:178
"For My Daughter" (Wright) 53:424, 431
"For My Daughter, Now Seven Years Old" (Coles) 46:107, 113
"For My Father" (Kherdian) 6:281
"For My Father" (Whalen) 6:565
For My Great Folly (Costain) 30:92
"For My Husband" (Voigt) 54:431
"For My Lady" (Sanchez) 116:295
"For My Mother" (Creeley) 8:153
"For My Mother" ("To My Mother") (Smith) 64:389, 393, 396
"For My Mother" (Steele) 45:363
"For My Mother" (Voigt) 54:431
"For My People" (Walker) 6:554
"For My Sister Molly Who in the Fifties" (Walker) 19:453
"For My Son" (Rukeyser) 15:458
"For My Son Noah, Ten Years Old" (Bly) 38:58
"For My Son When He Can Read" (Zukofsky) 18:560
"For My Sons" (Garrett) 51:144
"For Neruda" (Galvin)
   See "Lemon Ode"
"For New England" (Wright) 53:427
For No Good Reason (Sarraute) 80:244-45
"For Norman Mailer" (Lowell) 5:256
"For Old Times' Sake" (Simon) 26:412
"For Once in My Life" (Wonder) 12:661
"For Once, Then, Something" (Frost) 10:198; 15:245
"For One Moment" (Ignatow) 40:258
"For Our Brothers: Blue Jay, Gold Finch, Flicker, Squirrel" (Ortiz) 45:307
"For P. da C." (Cabral de Melo Neto)
   See "A Pereira da Costa"
"For Paul" (Niedecker) 42:299-300
"(For Peppe, Who Will Ultimately Judge Our Efforts)" (Giovanni) 117:194
"For Peter Taylor" (Lowell) 5:302
For Pollution Fighters Only (Hyde) 21:175
"For Precision" (Wright) 53:420
"For Real" (Robison) 98:307-08
"For Realism" (Fisher) 25:157
"For Richer for Poorer" (Gellhorn) 14:195; 60:184-85
"For Robert Frost" (Kinnell) 29:281, 283, 287-88
"For Robert Frost" (Levi) 41:242
"For Rupert—With No Promises" (Lish) 45:229
"For Sale" (Lowell) 37:243
"For Sarah" (Codrescu) 46:102
"For Saundra" (Giovanni) 64:182, 193-94; 117:195
"For Saying that It Won't Matter" (Merwin) 88:193
For Services Rendered (Maugham) 1:204; 15:366; 67:225-26
"For Seurat, 1859-1891" (Plumly) 33:311
"For Sidney Bechet" (Larkin) 33:259

"For Someone" (Weller)
   See "I Need You"
For Special Services (Gardner) 30:157-58
"For Strong Women" (Piercy) 27:377
"For Such a Bird He Had No Convenient Cage" (Garrigue) 8:239
"For Sydney Bechet" (Larkin) 64:278
"For Sylvia or Amina (Ballad Air & Fire)" (Baraka) 115:38
"For the Altarpiece of the Roseau Vally Church" (Walcott) 76:285-86
"For the Anniversary of My Death" (Merwin) 88:191, 206
For the Birds (Cage) 41:83
"For the Chinese New Year and for Bill Berkson" (O'Hara) 2:323
"For the Concerned" (Bukowski) 82:23
"For the Conjunction of Two Planets" (Rich) 36:365
"For the Dead" (Rich) 3:427
"For the Death of Lombardi" (Dickey) 15:177-78; 47:91-2, 98; 109:245
For the Defense (Rice) 49:302
"For the Fallen" (Levine) 9:333; 14:316, 318-19
"For the Father of Sandro Gulotta" (Lewis) 41:261-62
For the Good of the Cause (Solzhenitsyn)
   See *Dlia pol'zy dela*
"For the Good Times" (Kristofferson) 26:266
"For the Inmost Lost" (Graham) 29:194
For the Just Cause (Grossman) 41:188, 193
"For the Lost Generation" (Kinnell) 29:288
For the Municipality's Elderly (Reading) 47:349-51
"For the New Year" (Creeley) 78:135
"For the Poet Who Said Poets Are Struck by Lightning Only Two or Three Times" (Klappert) 57:258
"For the Previous Owner" (McGuckian) 48:278
"For the Rain in March: The Blackened Hearts of Herons" (Young Bear) 94:361-63, 371
"For the Record" (Lorde) 71:260
"For the Roses" (Mitchell) 12:440
For the Roses (Mitchell) 12:437, 440, 442
"For the Running of the New York Marathon" (Dickey) 15:177; 47:92
For the Sleepwalkers (Hirsch) 31:214-16; 50:195-97
"For the Stranger" (Forche) 83:209
"For the Student Strikers" (Wilbur) 110:382
"For the Tears in Your Eyes" (Prince) 35:332
For the Time Being (Auden) 1:9; 2:23-4; 3:27; 4:33; 9:55; 11:19-20; 14:31; 43:15
"For the Turnstiles" (Young) 17:573, 581
For the Unfallen: Poems, 1952-1958 (Hill) 8:293-94, 296; 45:178-79, 181, 184, 186-87
"For the Union Dead" (Lowell) 1:179-82, 184; 2:246-49; 3:300-02; 4:297-98, 301-03; 5:257-58; 8:350-51, 353, 357; 9:336-37; 11:325-27; 15:343-44, 347-48; 37:234, 236-37, 240
For the Union Dead (Lowell) 1:179-82, 184; 2:247-49; 3:300-02; 4:297-98, 301-03; 5:257-58; 8:350-51, 353, 357; 11:325, 327-28; 15:343-44, 347-48; 37:234
"For the Unknown Seamen of the 1939-45 War Buried in Iona Churchyard" (Smith) 64:388, 393
"For the Year" (Merwin) 88:211
"For There Is No Help in Them" (Blunden) 56:46

"For Theresa" (Giovanni)   19:190

"For Thomas Moore" (Simmons)   43:411

"For Tinkers Who Travel on Foot" (Avison)
   97:93

For to end yet again and Other Fizzles (Beckett)
   See *Foirades*

For to End Yet Again, and Other Fizzles
   (Beckett)   29:57, 59

"For Unborn Malcolms" (Sanchez)   116:277,
   294

For Us the Living (Lancaster)   36:242-43

"For W. C. W." (Creeley)   15:152; 78:125,
   137

"For WCW" (Bowering)   15:82

For Whom the Bell Tolls (Hemingway)   1:141,
   143; 3:236-37, 239-40; 6:225, 229-31,
   234; 8:283-84, 286, 288, 292-93; 10:266;
   13:271, 275, 277-79; 19:220-21, 224;
   30:179, 183; 34:479; 39:430; 61:194, 201,
   215; 80:101-59

"For William Carlos Williams" (Kinnell)
   29:288

"For You" (Prince)   35:323

"For You" (Springsteen)   17:484, 487

For You (Prince)   35:323-24, 330

For You Departed (Paton)
   See *Kontakion for You Departed*

For You: Poems (Carruth)   4:94; 7:40; 84:119,
   131

"For You, Who Didn't Know" (Willard)   37:464

"For Your Information" (O'Hara)   13:431

"For Your Life" (Page and Plant)   12:480

"For Your Viewing Entertainment" (Friedman)
   3:166

"El forastero gentil/The Gallant Stranger"
   (Ulibarrí)   83:415

"The Forbidden" (Barker)   52:55

Forbidden Colors (Mishima)   2:286, 288;
   9:382-83; 27:337, 343

"Forbidden Dances" (Urquhart)   90:384-5

Forbidden Disappointments (Carroll)   38:102-
   03

The Forbidden Forest (Eliade)
   See *Forêt interdite*

Forbidden Frontier (Harris)   12:262-64, 267

Forbidden Fruit, and Other Stories (Iskander)
   See *Trinadtsaty podvig Gerakla*

"Forbidden Love" (Daryush)   19:120

Forbidden Pleasures (Cernuda)
   See *Los placeres prohibidos*

The Forbidden Tower (Bradley)   30:27-9

"Force" (Walcott)   9:557

The Force and Other Poems (Redgrove)   6:445;
   41:348-49, 351-52

La force de l'âge (*The Prime of Life*) (Beauvoir)
   1:19; 31:42; 44:345, 349-50; 50:390;
   71:56, 60, 76, 78, 80

La force des choses (*Force of Circumstance*)
   (Beauvoir)   4:47; 8:62; 14:67; 31:34;
   44:343, 345, 349-50; 50:388, 390; 71:56,
   67, 72-4, 78, 81-2

Force of Circumstance (Beauvoir)
   See *La force des choses*

Force of Evil (Polonsky)   92:375, 377-83,
   387-88, 391, 393-406, 408-15

The Force of Habit (Bernhard)
   See *Die Macht der Gewohnheit*

Force of Light (Celan)
   See *Lichtzwang*

Force Ten from Navarone (MacLean)   50:348-
   49; 63:264-65

"Forced Retirement" (Giovanni)   64:191

The Forces of Plenty (Voigt)   54:430-32, 434

"Forcing House" (Roethke)   3:432; 101:293-
   94

"Forcing the End" (Nissenson)   4:381

"Fordie" (Brophy)   29:91; 105:8

"Foreboding" (Ashbery)   15:28

"Forefathers" (Blunden)   56:32, 51

A Foreign Affair (Hunt)   3:252

A Foreign Affair (Wilder)   20:455-56, 460,
   465

Foreign Affairs (Lurie)   39:177-85

Foreign Affairs, and Other Stories (O'Faolain)
   7:273-74, 276; 32:343; 70:314, 319

Foreign Bodies (Aldiss)   40:19

"The Foreign City" (Valenzuela)
   See "Ciudad ajena"

Foreign Correspondent (Hitchcock)   16:359

Foreign Devils (Enright)   31:150

Foreign Devils (Faust)   8:214-15

"The Foreign Lands" (Jacobsen)   48:191

"The Foreign Legation" (Doctorow)   37:91,
   93-4; 113:153

The Foreign Legion (Lispector)   43:272

"Foreign Shores" (Salter)   52:368; 59:196

Foreign Studies (Endo)   99:285, 289-90, 293-
   96

"The Foreigner" (Nowlan)   15:399

"Foreigner" (Page)   7:291

"The Foreigner" (Urdang)   47:399

The Foreigner (Plante)   38:371-73

The Foreigner (Shue)   52:390-93

"The Foreman" (Peterkin)   31:306, 308

"The Foreman Kyazym" (Iskander)   47:196

Forensic and the Navigators (Shepard)   17:437-
   38, 440, 444

Forerunner Foray (Norton)   12:465

"The Forest" (Bitov)   57:114-15

"Forest" (Simic)   9:480

"Forest" (Swenson)   14:521; 106:334

"The Forest" (Wright)   53:429

"The Forest beyond the Glass" (Turco)   11:551

"The Forest Hit by Modern Use" (Murray)
   40:343

A Forest in Flower (Mishima)
   See *Hanazakari no mori*

The Forest in Full Bloom (Mishima)
   See *Hanazakari no mori*

"Forest Mould" (Richter)   30:323

"Forest of Europe" (Walcott)   67:357

A Forest of Flowers (Saro-Wiwa)   114:252

"The Forest of Men" (Elytis)   49:110

"The Forest of the South" (Gordon)   83:231,
   234, 239

The Forest of the South (Gordon)   13:247;
   29:189; 83:230, 232, 242, 251

"The Forest Path" (Wright)   53:419

Forestilling om det Tyvende Århundrede (*The
   History of Danish Dreams*) (Hoeg)   95:116,
   118-19

"The Forests" (Davis)   49:92

The Forests of Lithuania (Davie)   5:114; 8:163,
   167; 10:123

Forêt interdite (*The Forbidden Forest*) (Eliade)
   19:144-45

Foretaste of Glory (Stuart)   11:512; 34:377

"Foretelling the Future" (Atwood)   25:69

"The Forethought" (Du Bois)   64:132

Forever (Blume)   12:44-6; 30:21-5

Forever and a Day (Isherwood)   44:397

"Forever and the Earth" (Bradbury)   42:35

Forever Fernwood (Lear)   12:338

Forever Flowing (Grossman)   41:186-89

Forever Free (Adamson)   17:4

"Forever Hold Your Peace" (Cheever)   15:127

Forever Morning (Davison)   15:170

"Forever My Love" (Simon)   26:409

"Forever O'Clock" (Warren)   8:536

Forever Panting (De Vries)   3:125-26; 28:110

"Forever to a Hudson Bay Blanket" (Tiptree)
   50:357

The Forever War (Haldeman)   61:170-71, 173-
   75, 177, 181-85

"Forever Young" (Dylan)   4:150

"Forevermore" (Agnon)   4:12

"Foreword" (Merwin)   88:192

"Foreword" (Pinsky)   94:302

"Foreword to the Reader of (Some) General
   Culture" (Ciardi)   44:375

"A Foreword to Three Pieces" (Shange)
   74:308-09

Forewords and Afterwords (Auden)   3:23-5;
   6:17; 14:31

Forfeit (Francis)   22:150; 42:148-51, 153, 157-
   58; 102:128, 132

"The Forge" (Heaney)   25:241; 91:121

"La forge" (Theriault)   79:407

The Forge (Stribling)   23:440, 442, 444, 449

"Forgers of Myth" (Sartre)   13:502

Forget Foucault (Baudrillard)
   See *Oublier Foucault*

"Forget What Did" (Larkin)   8:333; 64:282

"Forgetfulness" (Campbell)   32:75, 78, 80

Forget-Me-Not Lane (Nichols)   5:305-07;
   36:329-30, 333; 65:161

"Forgetting" (O'Brien)   116:193

"Forgetting" (Williams)   56:429

Forgetting Elena (White)   27:478-80, 482;
   110:316, 318, 320, 327-28, 336

"Forgetting This World" (Sadoff)   9:466

"Forgetting to Mention Allende" (Kelman)
   58:298

"(Forgive Me) My Little Flower Princess"
   (Lennon)   35:275-76

"Forgiven" (Brautigan)   3:88; 12:65

"Forgiveness in Families" (Munro)   10:357;
   95:287

"The Forgotten Captain" (Transtroemer)
   65:237

The Forgotten Man (Hikmet)
   See *Unutulan adam*

"Forgotten Sex" (Ashbery)   77:62-3, 69

"Forgotten Song" (Ashbery)   77:65, 67

*The Forgotten Victory: The Battle for New Jer-
   sey, 1780* (Fleming)   37:125

"Fork" (Simic)   22:383; 49:337, 339, 341-42;
   68:370-71, 374, 379

The Fork River Space Project (Morris)   18:351

*Forked Tongue: the Politics of Bilingual Edu-
   cation* (Porter)   70:377-78, 384

"The Forks" (Powers)   1:282; 57:358

"Forks with Points Up" (Ignatow)   7:180

"Forlesen" (Wolfe)   25:475

Den förlorade jaguaren (Martinson)   14:355

*The Forlorn Demon: Didactic and Critical Es-
   says* (Tate)   24:442-43

Form and Fable in American Fiction (Hoffman)
   23:240

"The Form and Function of the Novel"
   (Goldbarth)   38:206

"Form, Ideology and 'The Secret Agent'"
   (Eagleton)   63:107

The Form of Loss (Bowers)   9:121

A Form of Women (Creeley)   2:106; 15:149

"Form Rejection Letter" (Dacey)   51:79

"La forma de la espada" ("The Shape of the
   Sword") (Borges)   10:66; 19:47

A Formal Feeling (Oneal)   30:280-81

The Formal Method in Literary Scholarship (Bakhtin)
  See *Formal'nyj metod v literaturovedenii*
Formal'nyj metod v literaturovedenii (*The Formal Method in Literary Scholarship*) (Bakhtin)   83:3, 6-7, 21-2, 26-7, 31-4, 45
La formica Argentina ("The Argentine Ant") (Calvino)   5:98; 11:89, 91; 39:315
"Forms and Citizens" (Ransom)   5:364
Forms of Discovery (Winters)   4:591-92; 32:463-64, 466
Forms of Exile (Montague)   13:390; 46:265-66, 278
"Forms of the Earth at Abiquiu" (Momaday)   85:269-70
"Forms of Time and Chronotope in the Novel" (Bakhtin)   83:5, 15, 34, 60, 62
"Formulation" (Raine)   45:335
"Fornalutx" (Layton)   15:322
"The Forsaken" (Livesay)   79:340
Forsaking All Others (Breslin)   43:74-6, 78
Fort Apache (Ford)   16:311, 315
Fort Everglades (Slaughter)   29:374
The Fort of Gold (Dillon)   17:94-5
"Fort Sill: Set-angia" (Momaday)   85:281
"Fortitude" (Vonnegut)   12:611
Fortællinger om Natten (*Night Dreams*) (Hoeg)   95:116
"The Fortress" (Gluck)   7:119
"The Fortress" (Sexton)   53:319
Fortress Besieged (Ch'ien Chung-shu)   22:105-07
"Fortuna lo que ha querido" ("Fortune Always has Her Way"; "What Destiny Wanted") (Fuentes)   113:237
A Fortunate Madness (Shreve)   23:402
A Fortunate Man (Berger)   19:37
The Fortunate Pilgrim (Puzo)   2:352; 36:358-60, 362; 107:174-76, 182, 199, 207, 212, 215
"The Fortunate Traveller" (Walcott)   25:456-57; 42:423; 76:275, 297
The Fortunate Traveller (Walcott)   25:455-57; 42:418-19, 421-22; 67:348, 355-56, 358, 360, 362
"Fortune Always has Her Way" (Fuentes)
  See "Fortuna lo que ha querido"
The Fortune Cookie (*Meet Whiplash Willie*) (Wilder)   20:461
Fortune Heights (Dos Passos)   4:134; 15:185; 25:144-45
Fortune Is a Woman (Graham)   23:191
Fortune, My Foe (Davies)   42:104
"The Fortune Teller" (Spark)   40:402
"Fortunes" (Waddington)   28:438
Fortune's Daughter (Hoffman)   51:204-08
Fortune's Favorites (McCullough)   107:164-66
Fortunes of a Fool (Megged)   9:375
Forty Beads on a Hangman's Rope (Hall)   51:170-71, 175
"Forty Something" (Hass)   99:154
Forty Stories (Barthelme)   59:250-51; 115:80-1
Forty Thousand in Gehenna (Cherryh)   35:113-14
"Forty Whacks" (Howe)   47:172-74
Forty Whacks (Howe)   47:172-74
"Forty Years On" (Auden)   6:18
Forty Years On (Bennett)   45:55-6, 58; 77:84, 96, 99
Forty Years On. Getting On. Habeas Corpus

(Bennett)   45:58; 77:99
"Forty-Five a Month" (Narayan)   28:293
Forty-Five Mercy Street (Sexton)   8:483-84; 10:467; 15:473; 53:313
.44 (Breslin)   43:73-4
XLI Poems (Cummings)   8:156; 12:139, 156; 15:160; 68:35, 45
The 42nd Parallel (Dos Passos)   1:77; 8:181; 11:152, 157; 34:419, 424; 82:61-2, 64-8, 71, 73, 83-5, 89, 91-2, 95, 97-8, 100-03, 107-11
"47 Beds" (Gray)   49:152; 112:111
"The Forty-Seventh Saturday" (Trevor)   116:338, 385
"A Forty-Year-Old Man" (Endo)   54:157
Forward from Liberalism (Spender)   10:491; 91:261, 263, 265-66
Forward in Time (Bova)   45:69
Forward the Foundation (Asimov)   76:313-14
"Forward to the Reader" (Parra)   102:345
"Fossil, 1975" (Lewis)   41:263
"Fossil Gathering" (Porter)   5:346
"Fossil Inscription" (Ekelof)   27:110
"Fossils" (McGuckian)   48:276
"Fosterage" (Heaney)   25:246
"Fosterling" (Heaney)   74:190, 194; 91:125
"Fotografia do engenho Timbó" ("Photo of the Timbó Plantation") (Cabral de Melo Neto)   76:169
Foucault's Pendulum (Eco)   60:114-15
"Foul Shots: A Clinic" (Matthews)   40:322
"Found a Job" (Byrne)   26:96-7
Found a Peanut (Margulies)   76:194
"The Found Boat" (Munro)   95:302
"Found in the Cabbage Patch" (Mueller)   51:282
Found in the Street (Highsmith)   42:216; 102:197-201, 209
Found, Lost, Found: The English Way of Life (Priestley)   9:442
"Found Paradise" (Keillor)   40:274
"The Found Picture" (Graham)   29:199
"Foundation" (Asimov)   26:60-2
"Foundation" (Masters)   48:223
"Foundation" (Redgrove)   6:445
Foundation (Asimov)   76:313-14, 316-17; 92:18, 20-2
The Foundation (Buero Vallejo)
  See *La fundación*
Foundation and Earth (Asimov)   76:313; 92:18
Foundation and Empire (Asimov)   3:17; 19:26; 26:46; 76:313-14; 92:21-2
The Foundation Trilogy: Three Classics of Science Fiction (Asimov)   1:8; 3:17; 19:26, 28; 26:38-9, 45-6, 48, 50, 59-64; 76:313, 316, 318
Foundation's Edge (Asimov)   26:58-9, 63-5; 76:313
The Foundations of Aesthetics (Richards)   24:389, 397
"The Foundations of American Industry" (Hall)   37:142
Founder Member (Gardner)   30:152
The Founders (Green)   25:198
Founder's Praise (Greenberg)   30:165
The Founding of Montreal (Scott)   22:371
"A Foundling" (Atwood)   25:67
The Foundling and Other Tales of Prydain (Alexander)   35:26
"The Foundry House" (Friel)   5:128; 42:163; 115:216, 218
"The Fountain of Arethusa" (Davie)   31:119,

124
"The Fountain of Cyanë" (Davie)   31:119, 124
The Fountain of Youth (Welles)   20:447
The Fountain Overflows (West)   7:525, 528; 9:562; 31:456-58; 50:394-95, 397, 399, 408
"Fountain Piece" (Swenson)   4:533; 61:399; 106:325
"Fountainebleau" (Young)   17:576
The Fountainhead (Rand)   30:292-95, 297-98, 300-03; 44:448, 450-52, 454; 79:357-58, 361-65, 369, 371-75, 378-83, 389-95
"The Fountains of Aix" (Swenson)   106:320-21, 349-50
The Fountains of Paradise (Clarke)   13:155; 18:107; 35:124, 126-27
"Four" (Cummings)   15:161
4 (Cage)   41:79
"4 A.M." (Fearing)   51:114
"4 A.M. Traffic" (Ghose)   42:179
"The Four Apples" (Apple)   33:21
"Four Archetypes" (Soyinka)   36:415, 417; 44:285
"Four Auguries" (Atwood)   15:37
"The Four Beauties" (Bates)   46:61
"Four California Deaths" (Bowering)   47:29
"Four Canzones (1957-1961)" ("Canzones") (Okigbo)   25:350-51, 354; 84:310, 324-25, 328-29, 331-32, 336
"Four Cycles of Love Poems" (Barker)   8:46
Four Days (Buell)   10:82-3
"Four Dead Beats to a Bar" (Scannell)   49:332
Four Dubliners: Wilde, Yeats, Joyce, and Beckett (Ellmann)   50:306-07
"Four Exposures: Light Meter" (Eberhart)   11:178
"Four Eyes" (Ondaatje)   14:407; 51:310, 312, 316
Four for Delfina (Donoso)
  See *Cuatro para Delfina*
"Four for Sir John Davies" (Roethke)   46:363; 101:286, 289, 304
Four for Tomorrow (Zelazny)   21:468
Four Friends (Tesich)   69:371
The Four Fundamental Concepts of Psychoanaylsis (Lacan)   75:290, 293-94, 298
Four Hasidic Masters and Their Struggle against Melancholy (Wiesel)
  See *Contre la mélancolie: Célébration hassidique II*
"Four Horsemen" (Clash)   30:46-7
The 400 Blows (Truffaut)
  See *Les quatre cents coups*
The 400 Eels of Sigmund Freud (Mojtabai)   9:385-86; 15:379
"Four in Blue" (Robinson)   21:343
"Four Introductions" (Giovanni)   64:196
Four Kings and a Queen (Sturgeon)   39:365
"Four Lakes' Days" (Eberhart)   56:75, 80, 87-8
The Four Loves (Lewis)   3:296; 6:308
"Four Men" (Harmon)   38:243
The Four Musketeers (Lester)   20:230
Four Nights of a Dreamer (Bresson)   16:117-18
"Four Notions of Love and Marriage" (Momaday)   85:247
The Four of Hearts (Queen)   11:461-62
Four Past Midnight (King)   113:366, 385
"Four Penny" (Cohen)   38:131
"Four Personal Lectures" (Snodgrass)   10:477-78

Four Plays (Inge) 19:226-27
"Four Poems" (Bishop) 13:88
"Four Poems of Departure" (Pound) 112:343
"Four Preludes on Playthings of the Wind"
(Sandburg) 10:448; 35:352
The Four Quartets (Eliot) 1:89-92; 2:125,
129; 3:137-39; 6:160-64, 166, 168; 9:184,
186, 188; 10:168-70; 13:191-94, 200-02;
15:210, 213-17; 24:181; 34:387-88, 390,
392, 395, 39; 55:346, 350, 353, 360, 362,
374; 57:201, 208-09; 113:207-225
"Four Quartz Crystal Clocks" (Moore) 2:291
Four Reforms (Buckley) 37:59
Four Screenplays of Ingmar Bergman
(Bergman) 72:31, 33, 35
"The Four Seasons" (Shields) 113:442
The Four Seasons (Wesker) 5:483; 42:427,
429
The Four Seasons of Success (Schulberg)
48:349-50
"Four Sketches for Herbert Read" (Spender)
5:401
"Four Soldiers" (Nemerov) 36:308
"Four Songs" (Livesay) 79:337, 343, 351
"4 Songs of Life" (Young Bear) 94:362, 364
"Four Spells" (Beer) 58:38
Four Spot (Cabral de Melo Neto)
See *Quaderna*
Four Springs (Honig) 33:213-14, 216
"Four Stations in His Circle" (Clarke) 53:87
"Four Sticks" (Page and Plant) 12:475, 477,
481
"The Four Suspects" (Christie) 110:140, 142-
43
"The Four Temperaments" (Aksyonov)
101:41
"The Four Temperaments" (Transtroemer)
65:223, 226
Four Twelves Are Forty-eight (Kesselring)
45:208-09
"Four Walks in the Country near Saint Brieve"
(Mahon) 27:290
"Four Ways of Knowledge" (Bly) 38:55
The Four Winds of Love (Mackenzie) 18:313,
315-16
The Four Wise Men (*Gaspard, Melchior, et
Balthazar*) (Tournier) 36:433-37, 440;
95:361-64, 368-71, 381-82
"A Four Years' Harvest" (MacDiarmid) 63:251
The Four Years' Notebook (Montale)
See *Quaderno de quattro anni*
Fourbis (Leiris) 61:341-43, 347, 351, 356-57
The Four-Chambered Heart (Nin) 4:376;
14:386; 60:279
The Four-Dimensional Nightmare (Ballard)
3:33
Four-Fifty from Paddington (Christie) 12:117
The Four-Gated City (Lessing) 1:175; 2:239-
42; 3:282-83, 285, 287, 289-90, 292;
6:291-92, 295-97, 302-04; 10:314-15;
15:332, 334; 22:281, 284; 40:303-04, 312;
94:253, 257, 282, 284, 286
The Fourposter (de Hartog) 19:130
Fourskin (Vizenor) 103:288
The Foursome (Whitehead) 5:488
"Fourteen" (Hacker) 72:182
Fourteen (Sachs) 35:335
Fourteen Hundred Thousand (Shepard)
17:435-36, 439; 41:409
"Fourteen Minutes to Go" (Voinovich) 49:375
"Fourteen Rulers" (Haavikko) 34:175
14 Stories (Dixon) 52:95-9, 101
1492: The Decline of Medievalism and the Rise

of the Modern Age (Litvinoff)
See *1492: The Year and the Era*
*1492: The Life and Times of Juan Cabezón of
Castille* (Aridjis)
See *1492: Vida y tiempas de Juan Cabeóz de
Castilla*
1492: The Year and the Era (*1492: The De-
cline of Medievalism and the Rise of the
Modern Age*) (Litvinoff) 70:338, 344,
353
1492: Vida y tiempas de Juan Cabeóz de Castilla
(*1492: The Life and Times of Juan
Cabezón of Castille*) (Aridjis) 70:339,
347, 359
The Fourteenth Cadillac (Jackson) 12:290-91
The Fourteenth Chronicle (Dos Passos) 4:136-
38; 8:181
"The Fourteenth Street Poem" (Simic) 68:376
The Fourth (Puzo) 107:204, 213
"Fourth Act" (Jeffers) 54:242
The Fourth Angel (Rechy) 7:356; 107:225,
228, 239, 256
"The Fourth Day Out from Santa Cruz" (Bowles)
19:60
The Fourth Deadly Sin (Sanders) 41:382
*The Fourth Dimension: Selected Poems of
Yannis Ritsos* (Ritsos) 13:488; 31:326-
28, 331
"The Fourth Month of the Landscape Artist"
(Rich) 7:369
"Fourth of July" (Snodgrass) 68:382, 389
"The Fourth of July" (Wilbur) 9:571; 53:405
"Fourth of July at Santa Ynez" (Haines) 58:218
"Fourth of July in Maine" (Lowell) 1:181;
9:337; 15:343
"Fourth Poem from Niceragua Libre: Report
from the Frontier" (Jordan) 114:162
The Fourth Protocol (Forsyth) 36:177-78
"Fourth Psalm" (Merwin) 88:194
Fourth Quarter and Other Poems (Wright)
53:432; 11:578
The Fourth Side of the Triangle (Queen) 11:464
"The Fourth Sparrow" (Ozick) 62:351
Fourth Street East (Weidman) 7:517
"Fourth Version" (Valenzuela)
See "Cuarta versión"
"Fourth Voice: The Grandmother" (Davison)
28:101
"The Fourth Wonder of the World" (Shields)
97:431
"Four-Word Lines" (Swenson) 106:337
Les fous de Bassan (Hebert) 29:239
"The Fox" (Clarke) 61:73
"The Fox" (Day Lewis) 10:131
"The Fox" (Jeffers) 54:234
"The Fox" (Levine) 33:275
"The Fox" (Muldoon) 72:276
"Fox" (Robbins) 21:340
"The Fox" (Tomlinson) 13:549
Fox and His Friends (Fassbinder) 20:108
The Fox and the Camellias (Silone) 4:493
"Fox Hunters" (Pancake) 29:346, 348-49
The Fox in the Attic (Hughes) 1:149; 11:278
"The Fox of Peapack" (White) 39:377
The Fox of Peapack and Other Poems (White)
10:529
Fox on a Barn Door (Walker) 13:565
Fox Prints (McGinley) 41:284, 286-87
"The Foxes" (Bates) 46:62-3
"Foxes" (Findley) 102:111
"The Foxes" (Oliver) 98:292
"Foxes' Moon" (Tomlinson) 13:548
The Foxes of Harrow (Yerby) 1:381; 7:556-

57; 22:487-88
Foxfire: Confessions of a Girl Gang (Oates)
108:393
The Foxglove Saga (Waugh) 7:513-14
"Foxhunt" (Hughes) 37:172
Foxybaby (Jolley) 46:218-19, 221
"fPot-au-Feu" (Van Duyn) 116:429
"Fragment" (Ashbery) 77:44, 50-1
"Fragment" (Ortiz) 45:307
"A Fragment" (Winters) 32:468
"Fragment" (Zweig) 34:379
Fragment (Ashbery) 2:19; 3:16; 4:24; 13:30,
33; 15:32; 41:40
"fragment 3" (Sanchez) 116:307
"Fragment from Public Secret" (Kaufman)
49:207
"Fragment of a Letter" (Seifert) 93:324
"Fragment of Autobiography" (Brophy)
105:22
"Fragment Thirty-Six" (H. D.) 31:201
"Fragment: To a Mirror" (Justice) 19:235;
102:249-50, 256
The Fragmented Life of Don Jacobo Lerner
(Goldemberg) 52:163-65, 167-69
Fragmentos a su imán (*Magnet Fragments*)
(Lezama Lima) 101:121
"Fragments" (Creeley) 11:138
"Fragments" (Dobyns) 37:78
"The Fragments" (Lagerkvist) 54:287
Fragments (Armah) 5:31; 33:25, 27, 29, 31-
2, 36-8
Fragments: A Concerto Grosso (Albee) 86:124
Fragments d'un déluge (Giono) 4:188
Fragments d'un discours amoureux (*A Lover's
Discourse: Fragments*) (Barthes) 24:35-
6; 83:80-5, 89, 102, 104
Fragments d'un paradis (Giono) 4:188
"Fragments from a Parable" (Jordan) 114:149
"Fragments from Italy" (Ciardi) 40:158
"Fragments from the Deluge" (Okigbo) 25:350,
352; 84:301, 309, 312, 314, 322, 326,
328, 331, 334, 341-42
"Fragments of a Hologram Rose" (Gibson)
63:129
Fragments of a Journal (Ionesco) 6:253;
11:290; 86:332
"Fragments of a Liquidation" (Howe) 72:195
"Fragments towards a Religio Poetae"
(Gascoyne) 45:147, 149
Fragola e panna (Ginzburg) 54:207
"The Frame" (Dixon) 52:98, 100
"Frame" (Rich) 36:370; 73:330
"Frame-Tale" (Barth) 3:41; 9:66; 51:23; 89:4,
7, 10, 15, 18, 22-23, 30, 32, 34, 38-9, 41,
43, 47, 49, 54-5, 59, 61
The Fran Lebowitz High Stress Diet (Lebowitz)
36:249
France-la-doulce (Morand) 41:304, 306
The Frances Ann Lebowitz Collection
(Lebowitz) 36:250
The Franchise (Gent) 29:182-83
The Franchiser (Elkin) 9:190-92; 14:159;
27:122-23; 51:85, 88-9, 95-6, 99-101;
91:213, 223
"Francis" (Nowlan) 15:399
"Franciso, I'll Bring You Red Carnations"
(Levine) 14:320; 33:274
The Francoeur Novels (Plante) 38:371
François Truffaut: Correspondence 1945-1984
(Truffaut) 101:404
"Frank and Billy" (Colwin) 84:141
Frank and Maisie: A Memoir with Parents
(Sheed) 53:338-40, 342

Frank and Stein and Me (Platt)   26:356
Frank der Fünfte (*Frank V*) (Durrenmatt) 15:195-96, 199
"Frank Sinatra or Carleton Carpenter" (Lish) 45:229-30
Frank V (Duerrenmatt)   102:54-5
Frank V (Durrenmatt)
  See *Frank der Fünfte*
"Frank Worley, D.C.M., July, 1954" (Blunden) 56:40
Frankenstein Unbound (Aldiss)   5:15; 14:14
"Frankforter Poetic-Vorlesungen" (Bachmann) 69:58
"The Frankfurt *Hauptbahnhof*" (Kroetsch) 57:292-93
Frankie and Johnny in the Clair de Lune (McNally)   91:159
The Franklin Scare (Charyn)   18:98
"The Franklin Stove" (Dixon)   52:97
"Franny" (Salinger)   1:299; 12:512-13
Franny and Zooey (Salinger)   1:298; 8:463; 12:512, 518; 56:342, 348
Frantz Fanon (Caute)   29:113
"Franz, a Goose" (Sarton)   14:482
The Franza Case (Bachmann)
  See *Der Fall Franza*
Fraternité de la parole (Chedid)   47:81
A Fratricide/Ein Brudermord (The Brothers Quay)   95:330, 333, 339-40
"Frau Bauman, Frau Schmidt, and Frau Schwartze" (Roethke)   101:269-70, 286, 295
Die Frau im Mond (*La Femme sur la Lune*; *The Girl in the Moon*; *The Woman in the Moon*) (Lang)   20:204, 211; 103:88-9, 95
"Fraulein" (Ferber)   93:162
"Fraying Paradise"   75:68
"The Freak" (Wojciechowska)   26:457
The Freak Mamma (Fo)   32:176
Freak Out (Zappa)   17:588-91, 593
"The Freak Show" (Willard)   7:540
Freaks (Browning)   16:122, 124-26
Freaks (Fiedler)   13:214
Freaky Deaky (Leonard)   71:217-18, 221-23, 225-26
Freaky Friday (Rodgers)   12:493-95
The Fred Chappell Reader (Chappell)   78:116
"Freda People" (Lennon)
  See "Bring on the Lucie"
Freddy's Book (Gardner)   18:180-84; 28:166-68; 34:550
Freddy's Book (Neufeld)   17:309-10
"Freddy's Store" (Carroll)   35:81
"Frederick" (Smith)   12:543
"Frederick Douglass" (Hayden)   5:168; 37:153, 155, 157
Frederick the Great (Mitford)   44:485
"Fredericksted Dusk" (Walcott)   76:285
"Frederiksted Nights" (Walcott)   14:551; 76:285
Fredi and Shirl and the Kids (Elman)   19:150-51
"The Free" (Merwin)   13:385
"Free" (Prince)   35:328
Free Agents (Apple)   33:20-2
"The Free and the Caged" (Cooper)   56:70
Free at Last (Bontemps)   18:64
Free Fall (Golding)   1:121-22; 2:166-68; 3:196, 198-200; 10:232-33, 237; 17:161, 163, 166, 172, 174, 177-78, 180; 27:162-64, 167; 58:184-85; 81:317, 323
"Free Fantasia: Tiger Flowers" (Hayden) 37:158

"Free Flight" (Jordan)   114:156
"Free Life" (Diamond)   30:111
The Free Man (Richter)   30:308, 310-12, 319-21
The Free Men (Ehle)   27:103
"Free Money" (Smith)   12:535, 538
Free Schools (Kozol)   17:251-52
Free to Be Muhammad Ali (Lipsyte)   21:212-13
"A Free Translation" (Raine)   103:186, 188
A Free Translation (Raine)   32:353-54; 103:184
"Free Translation Of Reverdy" (Cabral de Melo Neto)
  See "Paráfrase de reverdy"
"Free Will and the Commendatore" (Borges) 48:43
"Free Women" (Lessing)   6:292-93
"Freedman" (Heaney)   37:162
Freedom Comes to Mississippi: The Story of Reconstruction (Meltzer)   26:299-300
The Freedom Drum (*Young Martin Luther King*) (Childress)   86:309
"The Freedom Kick" (Foote)   75:230-31
"Freedom, New Hampshire—Three" (Kinnell) 29:281, 289
Freedom of Action (Michaux)
  See *Liberté d'action*
The Freedom of the City (Friel)   5:129-30; 42:168-69, 173-74; 115:231, 234-36, 242, 244, 246, 248, 250, 256-57
The Freedom of the Poet (Berryman)   8:87, 90-1; 10:45-6; 13:76; 62:59
Freedom Road (Fast)   23:155
Freedom Road (Forman)
  See *Freedom's Blood*
Freedom under Parole (Paz)
  See *Libertad bajo palabra*
Freedom's Blood (*Freedom Road*) (Forman) 21:122-23
"Freedom's Last Stand" (Bochco and Kozoll) 35:58
"Freedom's Plow" (Hughes)   10:282; 108:283
The Freeing of the Dust (Levertov)   8:348; 66:238, 243
The Free-Lance Pallbearers (Reed)   2:368-69; 3:424; 5:368-70; 6:448-50; 13:476-77; 32:363; 60:300, 305, 307, 311
Freely Espousing (Schuyler)   23:388, 391
The Freeway (Nichols)   5:306-09; 36:329
The Freewheelin' Bob Dylan (Dylan)   4:149; 12:184, 198; 77:168
Freewheeling Frank (McClure)   10:332
"The Freeze" (Kuzma)   7:196
"The Freeze" (Martin)   89:111, 118
"Freezing to death" (Muske)   90:308
Freidizm: Kriticheskii ocherk (*Freudianism: A Marxist Critique*; *Freudism*) (Bakhtin) 83:3, 7, 13, 23, 25, 29-30
"Freies Hörspiel" (Jandl)   34:200
"The Freighters" (Lewis)   41:261
"Freitzke's Turn" (Vance)   35:422
Frêle bruit (Leiris)   61:349, 351
French Cancan (Renoir)   20:288-89
French Connections: Voices from the Women's Movement in France   65:325
French Dressing (Russell)   16:541
French Girls Are Vicious and Other Stories (Farrell)   66:130
"French Intellectuals, 1946" (Faludy)   42:140
French Kiss (Brossard)   115:103-08, 110-11, 117-18, 148, 150-51, 154
"French Kissing" (Johnston)   51:240-41, 245
"French Lessons" (Rasputin)   59:379

"French Letters: Theories of the New Novel" (Vidal)   8:527
The French Lieutenant's Woman (Fowles) 1:109; 2:137-39; 3:163; 4:170, 172-73; 6:184-89; 9:213-16; 10:184, 186-90; 15:234; 33:166, 169, 171-75; 87:138, 142-44, 147, 149-50, 156, 158, 161-62, 173-74, 176, 178-83
The French Lieutenant's Woman (Pinter) 27:391
"The French Master" (Abse)   29:15-16
French Persian Cats Having a Ball (Morgan) 31:272
"A French Poem" (Merton)   83:384
French Postcards (Klein)   30:241
The French Powder Mystery (Queen)   3:422
French Reveille (Aragon)
  See *La diane Française*
French without Tears (Rattigan)   7:354-55
A Frenchman Must Die (Boyle)   58:64
Frenchman's Creek (du Maurier)   6:147; 11:162; 59:280-84, 286-87
"Freneau, Whitman, and Williams" (Pinsky) 94:301, 303
Frenzy (Bergman)
  See *Hets*
Frenzy (Hitchcock)   16:350-54
Frequencies (Thomas)   13:544-45; 48:380-82
Frequent Hearses (Crispin)   22:109
Frère bois (Tzara)   47:396
Frère François (*God's Fool: The Life and Times of Francis of Assisi*) (Green)   77:282-83
"Fresco: Departure for an Imperialist War" (McGrath)   59:181
"Frescoes for Mr. Rockefeller's City" (MacLeish)   68:288
Frescoes for Mr. Rockefeller's City (MacLeish) 8:362; 14:338; 68:279, 281-82, 284-85, 288-89, 292
"Frescoes of the New World II" (Walcott) 76:274
"Fresh" (Pearce)   21:289
"Fresh Air" (Koch)   8:322; 44:241, 243, 245-47, 249-51
The Fresh Air (Shamlu)   10:470
"Fresh Spring in Whose Deep Woods I Sought" (Daryush)   19:123
Fresh Water, Sea Water (Levi)   41:244
"The Fresh-Ploughed Hill" (Nowlan)   15:398
"Freshwater West" (Mathias)   45:235
Freud (*The Secret Passion*) (Huston)   20:168-69, 173
"Freud and Literature" (Trilling)   24:454, 456
Freud and Man's Soul (Bettelheim)   79:134
"Freud and the Analysis of Poetry" (Burke) 24:127, 130
"Freud and the Crisis of Our Culture" (Trilling) 24:457
The Freud Scenario (Sartre)   52:385
Freudianism: A Marxist Critique (Bakhtin)
  See *Freidizm: Kriticheskii ocherk*
Freudism (Bakhtin)
  See *Freidizm: Kriticheskii ocherk*
The Friar (Cabral de Melo Neto)
  See *Auto do frade*
The Friar's Way (Cabral de Melo Neto)
  See *Auto do frade*
"Friday" (Grass)   32:200
Friday (Heinlein)   26:178-79; 55:303
The Friday Book; or, Book-Titles Should Be Straightforward and Subtitles Avoided: Essays and Other Nonfiction (Barth) 51:24-6, 29; 89:57

"Friday Morning: The Orderly's Tale" (Klima) 56:170

"Friday Night" (Hogan) 73:150

"Friday Night in the Royal Station Hotel" (Larkin) 8:332, 337; 64:266

Friday; or, The Other Island (Tournier) See *Vendredi; ou, La vie sauvage*

Friday the Rabbi Slept Late (Kemelman) 2:225

"Friday the Thirteenth" (Ginsberg) 36:185

"Friday's Child" (Livesay) 79:348

"Friday's Child" (Pastan) 27:371

"Friday's Footprint" (Gordimer) 33:180

Friday's Footprint (Gordimer) 18:185; 33:179-80; 70:162

Friday's Hiding (Arden) 15:21

"A Friend and Protector" (Taylor) 18:522; 37:411-13; 44:305, 310; 50:260; 71:295

A Friend from England (Brookner) 51:63-6

"A Friend of Kafka" (Singer) 23:419

A Friend of Kafka, and Other Stories (Singer) 3:453, 455; 6:509; 9:488; 23:419

"Friend of My Youth" (Munro) 95:310, 315

Friend of My Youth (Munro) 95:306-09, 311, 313, 318, 320, 322, 324

"A Friend of Ours Who Knits" (Shields) 113:441

"A Friend of the Earth" (Thurber) 5:432

"Friend of the Family" (Boyle) 19:63

"A Friend of the Family" (Dybek) 114:67

"A Friend of the Family" (Simpson) 7:429

"The Friend of the Fourth Decade" (Merrill) 6:323; 13:380-81

Friendly Fire (Bryan) 29:102-04

The Friendly Persuasion (West) 7:519-21; 17:543-48, 550-52

The Friendly Young Ladies (Renault) 17:390-91

"Friends" (Ian) 21:183

"Friends" (O'Brien) 103:140

"Friends" (Page and Plant) 12:475

"Friends" (Paley) 37:334, 336, 339

"Friends" (Wilson) 12:641

Friends (Abe) See *Tomodachi, enemoto takekai*

The Friends (Guy) 26:141-45

The Friends (Wesker) 3:519-20; 42:426-30

Friends (Wilson) 12:641-42, 644, 649-50, 652

Friends and Heroes (Manning) 19:301

Friends and Lovers (MacInnes) 27:280

"Friends and Occasions" (Johnston) 51:248-49, 254

Friends and Relations (Bowen) 3:84; 11:62; 15:78

Friends in Low Places (Raven) 14:441

The Friends of Eddie Coyle (Higgins) 4:222-24; 7:158; 10:273-74; 18:233-35

The Friends of God (Vansittart) See *The Siege*

"Friends of Miss Reece" (Hill) 113:291, 310, 312, 325

"The Friends of Plonk" (Amis) 40:43

"The Friends of the Family" (Barthelme) 115:86

The Friends of the Loony Lake Monster (Bonham) 12:53

"Friendship" (Katz) 47:220, 223

"Friendship and Poverty" (Rooke) 25:392

"Friendship on Visit" (Riding) 7:374

A Friendship: The Letters of Dan Rowan and John D. MacDonald (MacDonald) 44:408-09

"The Frightened Man" (Bogan) 46:77; 93:65

"Frightening Civil Servants" (Priestley) 34:362

Fringe (Bennett) See *Beyond the Fringe*

A Fringe of Leaves (White) 9:566-68; 65:275-76, 278-79, 282; 69:405

Die Frist (*The Deadline*) (Duerrenmatt) 102:61, 64

"Fritz" (Stern) 40:413, 415

"Fritz Bugs Out" (Crumb) 17:82

Fritz the Cat (Bakshi) 26:66-70, 73-5

Fritz the Cat (Crumb) 17:82

"The Frivolous Cake" (Peake) 54:369

"Frog Autumn" (Plath) 11:447; 111:185, 200

"The Frog Hunters" (Colter) 58:147

"Frog Pond" (Muske) 90:318

"Frog Trouncin' Contest" (Stuart) 11:512

"Frogfather" (Wellman) 49:393

The Frogs (Sondheim) 30:389, 402

"Frog's Woman" (Bowering) 32:47

"The Frolic" (Ligotti) 44:53

A Frolic of His Own (Gaddis) 86:146-69

Der Fröliche Weinberg (*The Gay Vineyards*; *The Merry Vineyard*) (Zuckmayer) 18:553-55

"From a Berkeley Notebook" (Johnson) 52:232

"From a Certain Protocol" (Tanizaki) 28:415

From a Crooked Rib (Farah) 53:132-33, 135-36

"From a Daybook" (Swenson) 106:333

"From a Diary" (Voznesensky) 57:421

"From a Distance" (Bell) 8:67

"From a Forthcoming Blue Book" (Forster) 45:134

"From a Grown-Up to a Child" (Christie) 110:125

From a Land Where Other People Live (Lorde) 18:307-08; 71:231, 254

"From a Litany" (Strand) 6:522; 18:515-16; 71:285

"From a Long Distance" (Ezekiel) 61:104

"From a Lost Diary" (Strand) 71:286

"From a Notebook" (Justice) 6:271

"From a Notebook, October '68—May '69" ("Notebook") (Levertov) 5:249; 28:240

"From a Provincial" (Avison) 97:74-5, 80, 123

"From a Refugee's Notebook" (Ozick) 28:350-51; 62:351

From a Seaside Town (Levine) 54:293-95, 297, 300

"From a Suburban Window" (Abse) 29:16

"From a Survivor" (Rich) 3:427, 429; 36:366

"From a Traveller" (Seth) 43:388

From a View to a Death (Powell) 3:404; 10:411-12; 31:320

From a Watch Tower (Arghezi) See *Dintr-un foisor*

"From a Window" (Olson) 28:343

"From a Writer's Notebook" (Cisneros) 69:145

"From Action to Image: Theories of the Lyric in the Eighteenth Century" (Maclean) 78:235-36

"From Allegories to Novels" (Borges) 83:161

From an Abandoned Work (Beckett) 6:38, 42; 11:39-40; 29:56

"From an Airplane" (Cabral de Melo Neto) See "De um avião"

"From an Almanac" (Baraka) 5:45

"From an Exchange of Letters" (Voinovich) 49:376-77

"From an Old House in America" (Rich) 6:459; 7:372; 11:475; 36:366, 375; 73:328;

76:218

"From Athens County, Ohio" (Plumly) 33:311

From Bauhaus to Our House (Wolfe) 35:460, 464; 51:416, 420

From Beginning to End (Lengyel) 7:202

From Behind the Veil (Stepto) 65:379, 381

From Bondage (Roth) 104:327-31

From Bourgeois Land (Smith) 64:390, 395, 398-99

From Cliché to Archetype (McLuhan) 83:366

From Cuba with a Song (Sarduy) See *De donde son los cantantes*

"From Dawn 'til Dusk" (Aksyonov) 101:9

From Death-Camp to Existentialism: A Psychiatrist's Path to a New Therapy (Frankl) See *Ein psycholog erlebt das konzentrationslager*

From Desire to Desire (Yevtushenko) 13:620

"From Don Giovanni" (Thomas) 31:434

From Doon with Death (Rendell) 28:385, 387; 48:319

"From: Elephant" (Neruda) 28:307

"From Elfland to Poughkeepsie" (Le Guin) 13:347; 22:274

"From Em, Me" (Johnson) 6:264

From Every Chink of the Ark and Other New Poems (Redgrove) 41:354-55

From Fear Set Free (Sahgal) 41:370

From Feathers to Iron (Day Lewis) 6:128; 10:126-27, 131-32

From Flushing to Calvary (Dahlberg) 7:66, 68; 14:135-37

"From Gloucester Out" (Dorn) 10:159

From Heaven Lake: Travels through Sinkiang and Tibet (Seth) 43:386-87; 90:335-36, 349, 356-7

From Here to Eternity (Jones) 1:161-62; 3:260-62; 10:290-94; 39:405-10, 412-15

"From His Dream" (Young Bear) 94:362

"From Hospital" (Clark) See "For Granny"

"From Huesca with Love and Kisses" (O'Faolain) 32:341

"From Humaweepi: Warrior Priest" (Silko) 23:408

From Lexington to Liberty (Lancaster) 36:244-45

"From Memory" (Forche) 25:169

From Morn to Midnight (Rice) 7:359

"From My Window" (Williams) 33:448

"From Okra to Greens: A Different Kinda Love Story" (Shange) 38:394

"From One Identity to Another" (Kristeva) 77:320

"From Orient Point" (Hacker) 72:192

"From P Forward" (Pesetsky) 28:357

From Plan to Planet (Madhubuti) 65:403

"From Poe to Valéry" (Eliot) 113:194-211

"From Proust to Dada" (Gold) 42:197

"From *Raven's Road*" (Allen) 84:28

"From Realism to Reality" (Robbe-Grillet) 43:360

From Rockaway (Eisenstadt) 50:38-42

From Russia, with Love (Fleming) 3:15; 30:131, 132, 137, 142, 148-50

From Sand Creek: Rising in This Heart Which Is Our America (Ortiz) 45:308

"From Shannon" (Brutus) 43:90

"From Silver Lake" (Browne) 21:34, 37

From Sleep Unbound (Chedid) See *Le sommeil délivré*

From Snow and Rock, from Chaos: Poems,

1965-1972 (Carruth)   4:94; 7:40-1; 84:119

"From Someone to Nobody" (Borges)   83:162

"From Spiralling Ecstatically This" (Cummings)   68:41

From Submarines to Satellites (Hyde)   21:172

"From Superstition" ("Out of Superstition") (Pasternak)   10:382; 63:280

"From the African Diary" (Transtroemer) See "Ur en afrikansk dagbok"

"From the Arsonist" (Muske)   95:314

"From the Attic" (Davies)   75:197

"From the Babur-Nama" (Seth)   43:388

From the Berkeley Hills (Elliott)   2:131

"From the Canton of Expectation" (Heaney)   74:161, 174-75, 177

"From the Cave" (Lorde)   71:262

"From the Childhood of Jesus" (Pinsky)   94:306, 308, 312

"From 'The Chronicles of Knarn'" (Nichol)   18:368

"From the Crypts of Memory" (Smith)   43:424

"From the Cupola" (Merrill)   2:273; 13:376, 381

"From the Depth"   75:61

"From the Diary of a New York Lady" ("New York Lady") (Parker)   68:334

From the Diary of a Snail (Grass) See *Aus dem Tagebuch einer Schnecke*

"From the Diary of a Young Lady" (Parker)   68:330

"From the Dressing Room" (McGuckian)   48:277

From the Fifteenth District (Gallant)   18:172-73

From the First Nine (Merrill)   34:235

"From the Flying-Boat" (Blunden)   56:49

"From the Foundry of the Soul" (Ekelof)   27:110

"From the Frontier of Writing" (Heaney)   74:162, 172

"From the Hazel Bough" (Birney)   6:75

From the Heart of the Country (Coetzee) See *In the Heart of the Country*

"From the Hot Hills" (Lane)   25:288

"From the House of Yemanjá" (Lorde)   71:233, 250-51

"From the Image Flow—Summer of 1986" (Levertov)   66:251

"From the Imperial" (Motion)   47:289

From the Irish (Simmons)   43:414-15

"From the Irish of Pangur Ban" (Boland)   67:43

"From the Japanese" (Gluck)   44:216, 222

"From the Joke Shop" (Fuller)   28:157

From the Joke Shop (Fuller)   28:154-55, 159

"From the Journal of a Leper" (Updike)   15:544, 546-47

"From the Journals of a Poet" (Bogan)   39:394

From the Life of the Marionettes (Bergman) See *Aus dem Leben der Marionetten*

"From the Masque Hyacinth" (H. D.)   73:108

"From the Painting 'Back from the Market'" (Boland)   40:100; 113:89, 93, 109

"From the Phoenix to the Unnamable, Impossibly Beautiful Wild Bird" (Chester)   49:55-6

"From the Pillar" (Huxley)   11:284

"From the Prehistory of Novelistic Discourse" ("From the Prehistory of the Novel-Word") (Bakhtin)   83:5, 59, 61

"From the Prehistory of the Novel-Word" (Bakhtin) See "From the Prehistory of Novelistic Discourse"

course" "From the Questions to Mary" (Redgrove)   41:352

"From the Ravages of Life We Create" (Kunene)   85:165

From the Realm of Morpheus (Millhauser)   54:329-331; 109:157, 170, 174

"From the Reflections of Mr. Glass" (Redgrove)   41:352

"From the Republic of Conscience" (Heaney)   74:174

"From the Rising of the Sun" (Milosz) See "From Where the Sun Rises"

From the River's Edge (Cook-Lynn)   93:124-30, 132

"From the Roof" (Levertov)   66:236, 250

"From the Rooftops" (Haines)   58:216

From "The School of Eloquence" and Other Poems (Harrison)   43:175-77, 180-81

"From the Secret Notebook of Fellow-Traveler Sand" (Olesha)   8:430

"From the Song of Ullikummi" (Olson)   11:416

From the Terrace (O'Hara)   2:324-25; 6:385; 42:313, 316-18, 322

"From the Testament of Tourmaline: Variations of Themes of 'The Tao Teh Ching'" (Stow)   23:436

"From the Town Guide" (Fisher)   25:161

"From the Very First Coming Down" (Auden)   14:32; 43:15

"From the Vestibule" (Zamora)   89:369

From the Wilderness (MacLean)   50:349

"From the Winter of 1947" (Transtroemer)   52:417; 65:230

From This Condensery: The Complete Writings of Lorine Niedecker (Niedecker)   42:297-300

From Threshold to Threshold (Celan) See *Von Schwelle zu Schwelle*

From Time to Time (Ciardi)   40:153-54; 44:378, 382

"From 'Twelfth Night'" (Burke) See "Trial Translation"

From under the Rubble (*Rubble*) (Solzhenitsyn)   34:486; 78:403, 405-06, 427-28

"From Where the Sun Rises" ("From the Rising of the Sun"; "The Rising of the Sun") (Milosz)   11:377, 380-81; 22:308, 310; 56:237; 82:293-95, 297, 304-06, 309

"From William Tyndale to John Frith" (Bowers)   9:122

"From Work to Text" (Barthes)   83:88

"From Yellow Lake: An Interview" (Van Duyn)   116:415

"A Front" (Jarrell)   13:300

"Front de la rose" (Char)   14:125

The Front Page (Hecht)   8:270

"A Front Page Story" (Farrell)   66:112

The Front Room Boys (Buzo)   61:53-61, 64, 67-9

"Front Seat" (Rendell)   48:320

"Front Tooth Crowned with Gold" (Simic)   49:337

Frontier Wolf (Sutcliff)   26:437

"Frontier Woman" (Richter)   30:307

"Frontiers" (Aldiss)   40:19

"The Frontiers of Criticism" (Eliot)   24:178

"Frontiers of Writing" (Heaney)   91:129

"The Frontiersman" (Turner)   48:398

"Frontispiece" (Swenson)   106:315

"Frontispoem" (Rose)   85:313

Frontline General: Douglas MacArthur (Archer)   12:15

Frossia (Almedingen)   12:7

"Frost" (Johnston)   51:249

Frost (Bernhard)   32:17-20, 27; 61:9, 21

Frost: A Literary Life Reconsidered (Pritchard)   34:468-74

Frost on the Sun (Jones)   10:285, 288

"Frost Still in the Ground" (Bly)   15:68

"Frosty Night" (Graves)   45:167

"The Frozen Fields" (Bowles)   2:79; 53:46, 48-9

"Frozen Jap" (McCartney)   35:289

Frozen Music (King)   53:212-13

"The Frozen Wedding Party" (Kadare)   52:263

A Frozen Woman (Ernaux) See *La femme gelée*

"Früh die Meere" (Sachs)   98:359

"Früher Mittag" ("Early Noon") (Bachmann)   69:39, 54

Das Frühwerk (Celan)   82:48

"Fruit" (Ezekiel)   61:101

"The Fruit" (Urdang)   47:399

Fruit (Brenton)   31:56-7, 60

"The Fruit Man, the Meat Man, and the Manager" (Hood)   28:193

The Fruit Man, the Meat Man, and the Manager (Hood)   28:188-90

"Fruit on a Straight-Sided Tray" (Boland)   40:101; 67:45

Le fruit permis (*Permitted Fruit*) (Tzara)   47:390

"The Fruit-Grower in War-Time" ("And Some of His Enemies") (Fenton)   32:164, 166

"Fruition at Forty" (Narayan)   28:293

Fruits and Vegetables (Jong)   4:263; 6:267; 8:313-15; 18:277; 83:291, 299

Les fruits d'or (*The Golden Fruits*) (Sarraute)   2:384-86; 4:464-70; 8:469, 472; 31:379, 383, 386; 80:236, 238, 240, 252

Früjesång (Ekelof)   27:112, 114

Frunze (Arghezi)   80:6, 8

"Frutta" (Viereck)   4:559

"The Fuck Machine" (Bukowski)   41:68, 75; 108:85

Fucking Martin (Peck) See *Martin and John*

"Fudano-Tsuji" (Endo)   54:161; 99:301

"Fuego fatuo" (Ulibarri)   83:412

"Fuel for the Fire" (Shields)   113:408, 432

"Fuel Stoppage on Gladesville Road Bridge in the Year 1980" (Murray)   40:343

Fuera del juego (*Sent off the Field*) (Padilla)   38:353

"Fuga a caballo" (Aleixandre)   9:13

Le fugitif (Gascar)   11:222-23

"Fugitive" (Fulton)   52:160

The Fugitive (Ford)   16:312-13

Fugitive (Montgomery)   7:233-34

Fugitive Kind (Williams)   111:424

The Fugitive Pigeon (Westlake)   7:528

"Fugitives Return" (Warren)   13:581

"Los fugitivos" (Carpentier)   110:76

"Fugue" (O'Faolain)   32:340, 343; 70:314-15

"La Fugue du petit Poucet" (Tournier)   95:367, 378, 383-87, 389

Fugue in a Nursery (Fierstein)   33:152-53

A Fugue in Time (Godden) See *Take Three Tenses*

"The Führer Bunker" (Snodgrass)   68:388

The Führer Bunker: A Cycle of Poems in Progress (Snodgrass)   10:478; 18:492, 494-95; 68:383-86, 391, 398

"Fuku" (Yevtushenko)   51:431-33

"Fulani Cattle" (Clark)   38:121, 126, 128

"The Fulfilled Destiny of Electra" (Glassco) 9:237

Fulfillingness' First Finale (Wonder) 12:657

"Fulfillment" (Hughes) 108:332

"The Fulfillment" (Schwartz) 45:361

"Fulfilment" (Blunden) 56:48

Fulgor y muerte de Joaquín Murieta (*Splendor and Death of Joaquín Murieta*) (Neruda) 5:301, 305; 28:312

"The Full Belly" (White) 5:487; 7:532

Full Disclosure (Safire) 10:446-47

"Full Fathom Five" (Plath) 9:425; 17:360; 51:344; 111:178, 209

Full House (Keane) 31:232

"Full Moon" (Davies) 21:102

Full of Life (Fante) 60:131-36

Full of Lust and Good Usage (Dunn) 36:152-53, 155

"Full Sail" (Wilson) 12:654

Full Term (Stewart) 14:512

Fully Empowered (Neruda) 7:260-62; 9:398; 28:314

"The Fully-Licensed Whore" (Highsmith) 102:186, 197

The Fume of Poppies (Kozol) 17:248-49

"Fumiko no ashi" ("Fumiko's Feet") (Tanizaki) 8:509

"Fumiko's Feet" (Tanizaki)
   See "Fumiko no ashi"

"Fun" (Johnston) 51:244

"Fun and Games" (Major) 19:298

"Fun, Fun, Fun" (Wilson) 12:646, 649-50, 653

Fun in a Chinese Laundry (Sternberg) 20:375

The Fun of It: A Love Story (Neufeld) 17:310-11

"The Function and Field of Speech and Language in Psychoanalysis" (Lacan)
   See "Fonction et champ de la parole et du langage en psychanalyse"

"Function of Blizzard" (Warren) 39:273

"The Function of Criticism" (Eliot) 113:207

The Function of Criticism (Winters) 32:462-63

The Function of Criticism: From 'The Spectator' to Post-Structuralism (Eagleton) 63:98-9

"The Function of the Poet in Society" (Rexroth) 49:287

"Functional Poetry: A Proposal" (Dudek) 11:159; 19:137

La fundación (*The Foundation*) (Buero Vallejo) 46:94, 98-100

"Fundamental Disagreement with Two Contemporaries" (Rexroth) 49:278; 112:372

"The Funeral" (Matheson) 37:246

"The Funeral" (Redgrove) 41:359

"The Funeral" (Spender) 41:427-28

Funeral Games (Orton) 13:435; 43:326, 330, 332, 335

Funeral Games (Scannell) 49:334

Funeral in Berlin (Deighton) 7:74-5; 22:114; 46:125-26, 128-30

A Funeral in Teresienburg (Krleza) 8:329

"Funeral Music" (Hill) 8:295; 45:178-80, 185-87, 189

"Funeral na Inglaterra" (Cabral de Melo Neto) 76:161

"The Funeral of Ally Flett" (Brown) 5:77

"The Funeral of Bobo" (Brodsky) 36:79-80

The Funeral of Mama Grand (Garcia Marquez)
   See *Los funerales de la Mamá Grande*

"Funeral Prayer" (Carrier) 78:83

"Funeral Rites" (Heaney) 7:148, 151; 14:242, 244; 25:246; 74:162; 91:116

Funeral Rites (Genet)
   See *Pompes funèbres*

Los funerales de la Mamá Grande (*Big Mama's Funeral; The Funeral of Mama Grand; Mama Grande's Funeral*) (Garcia Marquez) 2:148; 3:183; 27:151; 47:148, 150; 68:141, 150-51, 153

Funerals Are Fatal (Christie)
   See *After the Funeral*

"Funes el memorioso" ("Funes the Memorious") (Borges) 1:39; 2:71-2; 6:90; 8:97; 48:42, 45-6; 83:157, 168-69, 183

"Funes the Memorious" (Borges)
   See "Funes el memorioso"

"Fun-Fair of Words" (Rodgers) 7:378

"Funhouse" (Barth)
   See "Lost in the Funhouse"

Funhouse (Barth)
   See *Lost in the Funhouse: Fiction for Print, Tape, Live Voice*

Funhouse (Bogosian) 45:61-2

The Funhouse (Koontz) 78:202

"Funky Dung" (Pink Floyd) 35:311

"A Funky Space Reincarnation" (Gaye) 26:134

"Funland" (Oates) 33:296

Funland and Other Poems (Abse) 7:1-2; 29:18-19

Funny Girl (Wasserstein) 59:223

The Funny Man (Chaplin) 16:200

"Funny Papers by Hiram Handspring" (Laughlin) 49:224

"A Funny Thing" (Bates) 46:55-6, 62

A Funny Thing Happened on the Way to the Forum (Gelbart) 21:125-26; 61:147-49

A Funny Thing Happened on the Way to the Forum (Lester) 20:223, 226

A Funny Thing Happened on the Way to the Forum (Sondheim) 30:378, 383, 385, 395, 401-02

Funnyhouse of a Negro (*Drôle de baraque*) (Kennedy) 66:205, 209-10, 212-14

"The Fur Coat" (O'Faolain) 32:343

Fureur et mystère (Char) 9:163; 11:115; 14:127

El furgón de cola (Goytisolo) 23:185, 187

"Las furias y las penas" ("The Furies and the Pains") (Neruda) 62:329-31

Die Furie des Verschwindens (Enzensberger) 43:151

"The Furies" (Sexton) 53:320, 322-23

"The Furies" (Zelazny) 21:468

The Furies (Jakes) 29:248

The Furies (Ringwood) 48:339

"The Furies and the Pains" (Neruda)
   See "Las furias y las penas"

Furious (Moure) 88:223-26, 231

"The Furious Seasons" (Carver) 55:275

Furious Seasons, and Other Stories (Carver) 22:97; 55:275

"The Furlough" (Tolson) 105:282

"Furnished Lives" (Silkin) 43:398-400

"Furnished Room" (Corso) 11:123

"Furry Sings the Blues" (Mitchell) 12:441

Fürsorgliche Belagerung (*The Safety Net*) (Boell) 27:67-9; 39:293

The Further Adventures of Huckleberry Finn (Matthews) 45:240-44

The Further Adventures of the Robber Hotzenplotz (Preussler) 17:375-76

Further Fables for Our Time (Thurber) 5:430-32, 434, 442

"The Further Off from England" (McGinley) 14:365

A Further Range (Frost) 3:174; 4:174; 9:220, 228; 10:196; 26:117, 119; 34:475

"Further Recollections" (Lem) 40:294

Further Sightings (Rothenberg) 6:477

Further Tales of the City (Maupin) 95:191-92, 194-95, 197, 199, 203

Further...Further...Further!
   See *Dal'she...Dal'she...Dal'she!*

"Fury" (Theroux) 46:398

Fury (Lang) 20:206, 216; 103:85

The Fury (De Palma) 20:79-80

"The Fury of Aerial Bombardment" (Eberhart) 11:176, 178; 19:140, 144; 56:88-9, 91

"The Fury of Rain" (Harjo) 83:274, 276, 283

"The Fuse" (Browne) 21:39

Le fusil-harpon et autres nouvelles (*The Harpoon Gun and Other Stories*) (Vassilikos) 4:552

Futen rojin nikki (*Diary of a Mad Old Man*) (Tanizaki) 14:526-27; 28:414-15, 418

Futility (Gerhardie) 5:139-40

"The Future" (Ignatow) 7:178; 14:275

"The Future" (Murray) 40:341

"A Future for the Novel" (Robbe-Grillet) 43:360

"Future Green" (Jacobsen) 48:191

Future History (Heinlein) 26:164

The Future in the Present: Selected Writings (James) 33:221-22

Future Indefinite (Coward)
   See *Autobiography*

The Future Is in Eggs (Ionesco)
   See *l'Avenir est dans les oeufs*

The Future Is Ours, Comrade: Conversations with the Russians (Kosinski) 2:232; 53:220; 70:298, 300, 305

The Future Lasts a Long Time (Althusser)
   See *L'avenir dure longtemps*

The Future Lasts Forever (Althusser)
   See *L'avenir dure longtemps*

"Future Legend" (Bowie) 17:68

"The Future of Music" (Cage) 41:84

"The Future of Poetry" (Ransom) 4:436; 5:365

"The Future of Science: Prometheus, Apollo, Athena" (Bova) 45:75

The Future of Social Studies (Michener) 109:376

"The Future of the Novel as an Art Form" (MacLennan) 92:306

Futures (Hochman) 8:297

The Futurological Congress (Lem) 15:327-28; 40:289, 296

Futz (Owens) 8:434

"G" (Berger) 2:54; 19:38, 40

"G" (Merrill) 8:385

"Gabon" (Kinsella) 43:258

"Gabor" (Swift) 41:443

"Gabriel and the Water Shortage" (Olds) 85:297

"Gabriel García Márquez and the Invention of America" (Fuentes) 60:162

Gabriel García Márquez: Historia de un deicidio (Vargas Llosa) 10:500; 85:355, 378

The Gabriel Hounds (Stewart) 35:391

Gabriela, Clove and Cinnamon (Amado)
   See *Gabriela, cravo e canela*

Gabriela, cravo e canela (*Gabriela, Clove and Cinnamon*) (Amado) 13:11-12; 40:28-9, 31-5; 106:54-5, 57, 60-2, 65, 73, 77-8, 84-6, 89

Gabriel's Lament (Bailey) 45:47-9

"The Gadget Lover" (McLuhan) **83**:367

"Gaeltacht" (Buckley) **57**:134, 136

Gagner (Guillevic) **33**:191-92, 194

Le gai savoir (Godard) **20**:140

"Gaiety" (Sitwell) **67**:312

Gai-jin (Clavell) **87**:7, 16-18

Gaily, Gaily (Hecht) **8**:273

"Gaily Teetering on the Bath's Edge" (Brutus) **43**:91

"Gain" (Montague) **46**:270, 274

"Gaines Mill" (Mott) **15**:380-81

Gaining Ground (Barfoot) **18**:36

Gala (West) **14**:568-69; **96**:368, 373, 375

"Galactic Consumer Reports" (Brunner) **8**:108

Galactic Derelict (Norton) **12**:463, 467

Galactic Effectuator (Vance) **35**:422

Galactic Pot-Healer (Dick) **30**:125; **72**:121

"Galán" (MacLeish) **68**:290

"Galanta" (O'Hara) **78**:333

The Galantrys (Allingham)
     See *Dance of the Years*

Galápagos (Vonnegut) **40**:446-50; **111**:361

Galas: A Modern Tragedy (Ludlam) **46**:242; **50**:342-44

"Galatea" (Thomas) **37**:419-20; **107**:328

Galatea (Cain) **28**:48-9, 51, 53-4

Galatea 2.2 (Powers) **93**:295, 297-302

Galaxies like Grains of Sand (Aldiss) **14**:11

"Gale in April" (Jeffers) **54**:236

"Galician Nights, or, a Novel in Progress" (Rothenberg) **57**:383

The Galileans (Slaughter) **29**:375

The Galilee Hitch-Hiker (Brautigan) **12**:57, 61

"Galileo Galilei" (Smith) **6**:513

"The Gallery" (Murray) **40**:338

"The Gallery" (Transtroemer) **52**:414

A Gallery of Harlem Portraits (Tolson) **36**:429-30; **105**:237-40, 249, 256, 258-63, 281, 283-84

"Gallery Walk: Art and Nature" (Moss) **45**:290

"Galley Slave" (Asimov) **76**:320; **92**:13-4

Gallipoli (Masefield) **11**:358

Gallipoli (Williamson) **56**:437

Die Gallistl'sche Krankheit (Walser) **27**:460-61, 464, 466

"A Gallon of Gas" (Davies) **21**:104

"Galloping Foxley" (Dahl) **79**:178, 180

"Gallows Pole" (Page and Plant) **12**:475

Gallows Songs (Snodgrass) **6**:514

Galoots (Sandburg) **35**:340

"Galop" (Davison) **28**:100

"Galope muerto" ("Dead Gallop") (Neruda) **62**:322

The Galton Case (Macdonald) **1**:185; **2**:255; **14**:333-34; **34**:416; **41**:268-69, 271-72

The Galvanized Yankees (Brown) **47**:37

"Galway" (MacNeice) **53**:237

Gam ha'egrof haya pa'am yad ptuba ve'etsba'ot (*Even the Fist Once Was an Open Hand and Fingers; The Fist Too Was Once the Palm of an Open Hand and Fingers*) (Amichai) **116**:121

The Gambler (Alvarez) **13**:9

"The Gambler: A Ballet with Words" (Kavanagh) **22**:240

"The Gambler, the Nun, and the Radio" (Hemingway) **30**:179, 185; **80**:110

"The Gamblers" (Stoppard) **15**:518

"The Game" (Abse) **29**:16-17

"A Game" (Adcock) **41**:14

"The Game" (Barthelme) **8**:50; **23**:45; **115**:76

"The Game" (Gluck) **22**:173

"The Game" (Kis) **57**:246

The Game (Byatt) **19**:75

The Game and the Ground (Vansittart) **42**:389-90, 400

"A Game at Salzburg" (Jarrell) **13**:298

Game Crossing (Kroetz) **41**:239

A Game for the Living (Highsmith) **2**:193

Game in Heaven with Tussy Marx (Read) **4**:444; **25**:375

A Game Men Play (Bourjaily) **62**:104-06

"The Game of Blood and Dust" (Zelazny) **21**:479

"The Game of Chess" (Borges) **19**:46; **83**:177

"A Game of Chess" (Eliot) **6**:164; **15**:212; **34**:401; **41**:155

"A Game of Clue" (Millhauser) **109**:158, 160

A Game of Dark (Mayne) **12**:395, 398-99, 401-03

A Game of Football (Oe)
     See *Man'en gan'nen no futtoboru*

A Game of Hide and Seek (Sargeson) **31**:367, 374

A Game of Hide and Seek (Taylor) **29**:410

A Game of Patience (King) **8**:321

A Game of Simultaneity (Oe)
     See *Dojidai gemu*

A Game of Touch (Hood) **28**:187, 190

"A Game of Truth" (Klima)
     See "Hra na pravdu"

"Games" (Fowles) **15**:232

Games (Klima) **56**:168-70

Games (Popa)
     See *Igre*

"Games Are the Enemies of Beauty, Truth, and Sleep, Amanda Said" (Barthelme) **13**:56

"Games at Sunlight" (Desai) **97**:153

"Games at Twilight" (Desai) **19**:134; **97**:149, 151, 171, 176

Games of Chance (Gunn) **32**:214

Games of Chance (Hinde) **6**:239

Games of Choice (Gee) **29**:177

Gamma Rays (Zindel)
     See *The Effect of Gamma Rays on Man-in-the-Moon Marigolds*

"The Gamut" (Angelou) **77**:28

Ganashatru (*An Enemy of the People*) (Ray) **76**:356, 360, 362

"Gandhi" (Mahapatra) **33**:281

"Gandy Dancing" (Wiggins) **57**:433-34

The Gang That Couldn't Shoot Straight (Breslin) **4**:76; **43**:70-1, 74, 76, 78

"The Ganges" (Dubie) **36**:136-37

"Gangrene" (Levine) **5**:251; **14**:316-17

The Gangs of Kosmos (Bowering) **15**:82

"A Gangsterdom of the Spirit" (Doctorow) **113**:177

Le gant de crin (Reverdy) **53**:280, 283-86, 290-91

"The Gap" (Tomlinson) **13**:548

"The Gap in the Hedge" (Thomas) **6**:534

Gapi (Maillet) **54**:306, 315-16

Gapi et Sullivan (Maillet) **54**:314

Garage Sale (Ringwood) **48**:339

"Garageland" (Clash) **30**:45

Garbage (Ammons) **108**:46-9, 59, 60-1

The Garbage Man (Dos Passos)
     See *The Moon Is a Gong*

"The Garbageman Is Drunk" (Acorn) **15**:10

García Lorca (Honig) **33**:208-09

Les garçons (Montherlant) **8**:393

"The Garden" (Bitov) **57**:114-15

"The Garden" (Dunn) **40**:166

"The Garden" (Gluck) **22**:175, 77

"The Garden" (Govier) **51**:166

"Garden" ("Heat") (H. D.) **14**:223; **31**:205, 207; **34**:445; **73**:118, 121

"The Garden" (Oliver) **98**:265

"A Garden" (Peacock) **60**:295

"Garden" (Sherwin) **7**:415

"The Garden" (Simon) **26**:407

"The Garden" (Stevenson) **33**:383

"The Garden" (Strand) **18**:520; **41**:432

"The Garden" (Thomas) **48**:376

"The Garden" (Warren) **13**:573

The Garden (Summers) **10**:493

Garden, Ashes **57**:239, 242-49

"The Garden at St. John's" (Swenson) **106**:317

"The Garden House" (L'Heureux) **52**:272

"Garden in the Wind" (Roy) **14**:469

Garden in the Wind (Roy) **14**:469

The Garden Next Door (Donoso)
     See *El jardín de al lado*

The Garden of Adonis (Gordon) **6**:203-04; **13**:242; **29**:186; **83**:233-34, 243, 247, 252-54

Garden of Broken Glass (Neville) **12**:453-54

"The Garden of Delight" (Hass) **18**:211

The Garden of Delights (Carrier)
     See *Le jardin des délices*

The Garden of Delights (Saura) **20**:314, 317, 320, 322

"The Garden of Earthly Delights" (Milosz) **56**:251

"Garden of Earthly Delights" (Oe) **86**:231

"The Garden of Earthly Delights" (Porter) **33**:321

"The Garden of Earthly Delights" (Simic) **6**:502

The Garden of Earthly Delights (Arrabal)
     See *Le jardin des délices*

A Garden of Earthly Delights (Oates) **1**:252; **2**:314; **3**:359; **6**:368; **9**:406; **19**:353; **33**:291; **52**:336, 338; **108**:341-42, 391

The Garden of Eden (Hemingway) **6**:230; **8**:285; **41**:204-08; **50**:412-14, 417, 419, 422, 426-29, 431; **80**:146, 150-51, 153, 156

"The Garden of Eros" (Squires) **51**:383

The Garden of Forking Paths (Borges)
     See *El jardín de senderos que se bifurcan*

"The Garden of Gethsemane" (Pasternak) **7**:294

"The Garden of Hecate" (Squires) **51**:383

"The Garden of Love" (Livesay) **79**:340-41

"The Garden of Maia" (Squires) **51**:383

"The Garden of Medusa" (Squires) **51**:382-83

"The Garden of Niobe" (Squires) **51**:382

"The Garden of Prometheus" (Squires) **51**:382

Garden of Rest (Pa Chin)
     See *Ch'i-yüan*

"The Garden of Stubborn Cats" (Calvino) **33**:100

The Garden of the Finzi-Continis (Bassani) **9**:74-7

The Garden of the Finzi-Continis (De Sica) **20**:95

"The Garden of the Forking Paths" (Borges)
     See "El jardín de senderos que se bifurcan"

"The Garden of the Gods" (Gunn) **18**:200; **32**:208

The Garden of the Savage Beasts (Duhamel) **8**:188-89

Garden of Time (Dodson) **79**:186

The Garden of Weapons (Gardner) **30**:156

"The Garden Party" (Davie) **5**:114; **8**:164; **10**:125

The Garden Party (Havel) **25**:219-26, 228-29; **58**:240, 242; **65**:420, 429, 431-32, 435, 438

"The Garden Sees" (Elytis) **100**:179

"The Garden Shukkei-en" (Forche) **86**:139-41, 143

Garden Spot, U.S.A. (Garrett) **51**:145-46

"Garden State" (Ginsberg) **36**:192

"The Gardener" (Haines) **58**:214

"The Gardener" (Raine) **32**:351-52

"The Gardener" (Wheelock) **14**:571

"The Gardener to His God" (Van Duyn) **116**:403

The Gardener's Song (McCarthy) **101**:202

Gardenia (Guare) **29**:207-08; **67**:78-81

"The Gardens" (Oliver) **34**:247, 249; **98**:273, 299-300

"The Gardens of the Villa d'Este" (Hecht) **8**:266-67

Gardens of the World (Squires) **51**:381-83

"Gare du midi" (Auden) **43**:22

"Gargantua" (Calisher) **38**:76

Gargoyle Cartoons (McClure) **6**:320

Gargoyles (Bernhard)
    See *Verstörung*

La Garibaldina (Vittorini) **9**:549

The Garish Day (Billington) **43**:58

Garito de hospicianos (Cela) **4**:96

"A Garland for Christopher Smart" (Van Duyn) **116**:403, 418

A Garland for the Appalachians (Williams) **13**:600

"A Garland for Thomas Eakins" (Tomlinson) **13**:546

"Garland for You" (Warren) **13**:575

A Garland of Love (Bioy Casares)
    See *Guirnalda con amores*

The Garnett Family (Heilbrun) **25**:252

Il garofano rosso (Vittorini) **9**:548-49

"The Garret" (Hildesheimer) **49**:180

The Garrick Year (Drabble) **2**:118; **5**:117; **8**:184; **22**:120; **53**:117-18, 121

Garrochés en paradis (Maillet) **54**:304

"Gas" (Adcock) **41**:14

Gas House McGinty (Farrell) **4**:157; **66**:114, 116, 122, 127, 135

"Gases" (Bernard) **59**:44

Gaslight: A Victorian Thriller (Angel Street: A Victorian Thriller) (Hamilton) **51**:187, 189-90, 192-94, 196-98

Gasoline (Corso) **1**:64; **11**:123

"Gaspard de la nuit" (Donoso) **99**:241

Gaspard de la nuit (Donoso) **8**:180; **32**:160

Gaspard, Melchior, et Balthazar (Tournier)
    See *The Four Wise Men*

Gäst hos verkligheten (Guest of Reality) (Lagerkvist) **13**:330; **54**:267-68, 271-72, 274, 276, 286, 288-89

The Gastronomical Me (Fisher) **76**:335-36, 338-41; **87**:120, 122-23, 125, 129

"Gata Poem" ("Cat Poem") (Zamora) **89**:370, 373-76, 386, 389, 394

The Gate (Day Lewis) **10**:128-29, 131

"The Gate at the Center" (Olson) **11**:419

"The Gate in His Head" (Ondaatje) **51**:311-12, 315

"The Gate of a Great Mansion" (Sillitoe) **57**:396

Gate of Ivrel (Cherryh) **35**:102-04, 112

"The Gate of Morning" (Milosz) **11**:380

"The Gates" (Rukeyser) **10**:443

The Gates (Johnston) **7**:185-86

The Gates (Rukeyser) **10**:442

"Gates of Eden" (Dylan) **6**:155

The Gates of Hell (Willingham) **51**:403, 410-11

The Gates of November (Potok) **112**:295-96

"The Gates of the Arsenal" (Milosz) **82**:297

The Gates of the Forest (Wiesel)
    See *Les portes de la forêt*

"Gates of the West" (Clash) **30**:45

The Gates of Wrath: Rhymed Poems, 1948-1952 (Ginsberg) **6**:199-201; **36**:181; **69**:223, 225; **109**:352-53

"The Gateway" (Hope) **51**:224

"The Gateway" (Wright) **53**:419, 431

Gateway (Pohl) **18**:411-13

The Gateway (Wright) **53**:419-20, 423, 428, 431

Gather, Darkness! (Leiber) **25**:301-02, 305, 310

Gather Together in My Name (Angelou) **12**:11-12; **35**:30-1; **64**:24, 27, 29-30, 34, 36, 38-9; **77**:4-15, 22-4

A Gathered Church: The Literature of the English Dissenting Interest, 1700-1930 (Davie) **31**:113-14, 117, 120-21

"Gathering" (Voigt) **54**:429

The Gathering (Hamilton) **26**:156-57

Gathering Evidence: A Memoir (Bernhard) **61**:19-22, 30

"Gathering Mushrooms" ("Mushroom Gathering") (Muldoon) **32**:321-22; **72**:282

"The Gathering of Californians" (Brautigan) **3**:90; **12**:65

"A Gathering of Men" (Moyers) **70**:416, 418-20, 423, 429-30, 435, 457

A Gathering of Old Men (Gaines) **86**:176-77

"Gathering of Shields" (Momaday) **85**:280

"The Gathering of the Whakapapa" (Ihimaera) **46**:201

The Gathering Storm (Empson) **19**:152, 156-57; **33**:141-42; **34**:335

Gathering the Tribes (Forche) **25**:168-71; **83**:206, 210-12; **86**:139, 142

"Gatineau" (Avison) **97**:71-4

El gato eficaz (Cat-O-Nine-Deaths; The Efficient Cat) (Valenzuela) **31**:439-40; **104**:354-61, 366-70, 377-79, 387

"GATSBY'S THEORY OF AESTHETICS" (Baraka) **115**:38-9

La gauche divine (Baudrillard) **60**:33

"Gaucho" (Becker and Fagen) **26**:85

Gaucho (Becker and Fagen) **26**:84-5

"The Gauchos" (Borges) **8**:103

Gaudete (Hughes) **9**:282; **14**:272-73; **37**:171-72, 174-76, 178-79

Gaudier-Brzeska: A Memoir (Pound) **10**:401; **13**:458

The Gaudy (Stewart) **7**:466

The Gaudy Place (Chappell) **40**:140-41; **78**:97

"Gaugin" (Walcott) **67**:360

"Gauguin" (Raine) **103**:186, 188

Gauguin (Resnais) **16**:505

"The Gauzy Edge of Paradise" (Gilchrist) **34**:164-65

The Gavin Ewart Show: Selected Poems, 1939-1985 (Ewart) **13**:209; **46**:148, 153-54

"Gay Chaps at the Bar" (Brooks) **49**:35-6

The Gay Desperado (Mamoulian) **16**:423-24

"The Gay Old Dog" (Ferber) **93**:138, 141, 146-47, 180

"Gay Paree" (Bennett) **28**:27, 29

"The Gay Philosopher" (White) **110**:332, 336, 341

The Gay Place (Brammer) **31**:53-5

"Gay Talese: Sex Affirmative" (Amis) **62**:5

The Gay Vineyards (Zuckmayer)
    See *Der Fröliche Weinberg*

The Gayden Chronicles (Cook) **58**:154

The Gazabos: Forty-One Poems (Honig) **33**:210-11, 213, 215

The Gaze (Marques)
    See *La Mirada*

"Gazebo" (Carver) **55**:275

"Gde, vysokaya, tvoy tsyganyonok" ("Where, Tall Girl, Is Your Gypsy Babe") (Akhmatova) **64**:9

"Le géant blanc lépreux du paysage" (Tzara) **47**:394-95

"Gebete für den toten Bräutigam" (Sachs) **98**:325, 327, 347, 353

Gedichte 1938-1944 (Celan) **82**:48-49, 52, 57

Gee, Officer Krupke (Sondheim) **30**:376, 387

The Geek (Nova) **31**:296-97, 299

Geek Love (Dunn) **71**:133-40

"Geese" (Dobyns) **37**:79

"The Geese" (Graham) **48**:145, 154

Das Geheimherz der Uhr: Aufzeichnungen 1973-1985 (The Secret Heart of the Clock: Notes, Aphorisms, Fragments, 1973-1985) (Canetti) **75**:144-45; **86**:296-97, 300-01

Gehen (Bernhard) **61**:9

"Geisenhausen" (Eich) **15**:203

Geisterbahn (Kroetz) **41**:234

Gelassenheit (Heidegger) **24**:277

Der Gelbe hund (Jandl) **34**:198-200

Die Gelehrtenrepublik: Kurzroman aus den Rossbreiten (The Egghead Republic: A Short Novel from the Horse Latitudes) (Schmidt) **56**:393, 396-97, 399-402, 404-405

"Gemcrack" (Phillips) **15**:420-21

Gemini (Innaurato) **21**:191-92, 196-97; **60**:199-206

Gemini (Tournier) **23**:453-56; **36**:437, 441; **95**:371-73, 381

Gemini: An Extended Autobiographical Statement on My First Twenty-Five Years of Being a Black Poet (Giovanni) **2**:164-65; **19**:191; **64**:183-85, 187-89, 191-92; **117**:167-68, 181-84, 186, 191, 194, 201

The Gemini Contenders (Ludlum) **22**:289

"Gemini—A Prolonged Autobiographical Statement on Why" (Giovanni) **64**:184; **117**:183

"Gemistus Pletho" (Forster) **45**:132

"Gemona-del-friuli, 1961-1976" (Davie) **31**:117

Gender and the Politics of History **65**:327

Gene Green—The Untouchable (Aksyonov) **101**:22

Gene Wolfe's Book of Days (Wolfe) **25**:475-76

"The General" (Asimov) **26**:61, 63

"The General" (Head) **67**:111

"The General" (Sassoon) **36**:388, 391, 393

"General" (Strand) **18**:516

The General (Forester) **35**:160-63, 166, 170, 174

The General (Keaton) **20**:189, 191-92, 194-97

The General (Sillitoe) **1**:307; **3**:448

The General and the President (Schlesinger) **84**:373

General Confession (Davies) **7**:73

The General Danced at Dawn (Fraser) **7**:106

Le général de l'armée morte (Kadare)

See *Gjenerali i ushtrisë së vdekur*
The General Died at Dawn (Odets)   **28**:337;
   98:207, 242-44
"General Electric" (Scott)   **22**:373
General Ludd (Metcalf)   **37**:303-07
"The General Nature of Ritual" (Burke)   **24**:126
General Relativity: An Einstein Centenary Survey (Hawking)   **105**:46-7
The General Returns from One Place to Another (O'Hara)   **13**:431; **78**:364, 370-71
General Song (Neruda)
   See *Canto general de Chile*
Generalerna (*The Generals*) (Wahloo)   **7**:501-02
Generally a Virgin (Hinde)   **6**:241-42
The Generals (Wahloo)
   See *Generalerna*
"The General's Day" (Trevor)   **71**:322, 324, 339; **116**:332
The General's Lady (Forbes)   **12**:204
The General's Wife (Straub)   **107**:304-05
A Generation (Wajda)   **16**:578, 581
"Generation III" (Lorde)   **71**:262
"Generation Gap" (Ciardi)   **40**:161
"Generation of '45" (Cabral de Melo Neto)
   See "A geração de '45"
Generation of Swine (Thompson)   **104**:335-36, 347
Generation of Vipers (Wylie)   **43**:463-66, 471-72
Generation without Farewell (Boyle)   **58**:68, 70
Generation X: Tales for an Accelerated Culture (Coupland)   **85**:30-41
"Generations" (Kenny)   **87**:252, 254
"Generations" (Sanchez)   **116**:315
"Generations" (Stevenson)   **7**:462
Generations (Pollock)   **50**:224
Generations: A Memoir (Clifton)   **19**:110-11; **66**:66-7, 74, 78, 80, 84-6
The Generations of Men (Wright)   **53**:421-22
Generations of Winter (*Pokolenie zimy*) (Aksyonov)   **101**:47-53, 55
"Générique" (Simon)   **15**:496-97
The Generous Days (Spender)   **2**:419-20; **5**:401; **91**:264
The Generous Heart (Fearing)   **51**:116, 121
A Generous Man (Price)   **3**:405-06; **43**:342-44, 346; **50**:231-32; **63**:341
"Genesis" (Elytis)   **100**:156, 159, 161, 163-64, 166
"Genesis" (Hill)   **8**:294; **45**:184, 186-87, 189
Genesis (Stegner)   **81**:340, 345-46
"Genesis 2" (MacEwen)   **55**:167
"Genesis 1-2: 4" (Bidart)   **33**:80
"Genesis and Catastrophe" ("A Fine Son") (Dahl)   **79**:181
Genesis, Book II (Schwartz)   **87**:344, 347
Genesis: Book One (Schwartz)   **4**:479; **10**:464-65; **45**:358-59; **87**:334, 347
Genesis of the Clowns (Harris)   **25**:211
"The Genesis of the Metaphor and the Sense of Culture"
   See "Geneza metaforei si sensul culturii"
"Genesis on an Endless Mosaic" (Dumas)   **62**:155
"Genessee Falls" (Crase)   **58**:162-63, 165
"Genetic Expedition" (Dove)   **81**:141, 151
"Genetics" (Alexie)   **96**:10
The Genetics Explosion (Silverstein and Silverstein)   **17**:457
Genève (Bowering)   **15**:83; **47**:21
"Genevieve" (Lorde)   **71**:260

"Geneza metaforei si sensul culturii" ("The Appearance of Metaphor and the Meaning of Culture"; "The Genesis of the Metaphor and the Sense of Culture")   **75**:59, 63, 74
Geneza metaforei si sensul culturii (*The Emergence of Metaphor and the Meaning of Culture*)   **75**:80
Gengoedelsens veje (Dinesen)   **95**:68
Génie (Jouve)   **47**:206
Le génie de lieu (Butor)   **8**:116; **15**:118
"Genie's Prayer under the Kitchen Sink" (Dove)   **81**:152
Génitrix (Mauriac)   **4**:339-40; **9**:367-68; **56**:204-06, 214, 217, 219
"The Genius" (Barthelme)   **3**:43-4; **59**:250
"Genius" (Levine)   **33**:272
"The Genius" (MacLeish)   **8**:362
The Genius (Brenton)   **31**:69
Genius and Lust (Mailer)   **74**:225-27
The Genius and the Goddess (Huxley)   **4**:243; **5**:195; **35**:242
"The Genius Freaks" (McIntyre)   **18**:327
"The Genius of Smalltown America" (Williams)   **39**:100
Geniuses (Reynolds)   **38**:387-91
Geniusz sierocy (*The Orphan Genius*) (Dabrowska)   **15**:169
The Genoa Ferry (Harwood)   **32**:225-26
The Genocidal Mentality: Nazi Holocaust and Nuclear Threat (Lifton)   **67**:162-65
Genocide in Nigeria (Saro-Wiwa)   **114**:261
The Genocides (Disch)   **36**:123
A Genoese Fancy (Hughes)   **48**:184
Le genou de Claire (*Claire's Knee*) (Rohmer)   **16**:531-34, 536, 540
Genshuku natsunawatari (*Solemn Tightrope Walking*; *Solemnly Walking the Tightrope*) (Oe)   **36**:349; **86**:215, 224, 226-27
Gente del po (Antonioni)   **20**:24
"Gentians" (McGuckian)   **48**:276
"The Gentle Art" (Gordimer)   **18**:185
"Gentle as Flowers Make the Stories" (Metcalf)   **37**:299, 301
The Gentle Barbarian: The Life and Work of Turgenev (Pritchett)   **13**:467-69
A Gentle Creature (Bresson)   **16**:113-14
The Gentle Insurrection (Betts)   **28**:32-4
The Gentle Island (Friel)   **5**:129; **42**:173-74
A Gentle Occupation (Bogarde)   **19**:43
"The Gentle People" (Shaw)   **23**:395
"Gentle Reader" (Jacobsen)   **48**:195
"Gentle Reader" (Loewinsohn)   **52**:284
"The Gentle Sex" (Ewart)   **13**:210; **46**:149, 153
"The Gentle Snorer" (Van Duyn)   **116**:399, 406, 429
The Gentle Tamers: Women of the Old Wild West (Brown)   **47**:36
The Gentle Weight Lifter (Ignatow)   **7**:173-75; **14**:276; **40**:258
Gentlehands (Kerr)   **12**:300-01, 303; **35**:250-51
Gentleman and Ladies (Hill)   **113**:288-90, 297-98, 303, 305, 308-10, 320
"The Gentleman Arms" (Wiggins)   **57**:433-34, 436
The Gentleman Caller (Bullins)   **1**:47
The Gentleman Caller (Williams)   **71**:364, 373
"The Gentleman from Cracow" (Singer)   **3**:453; **38**:410; **69**:306
"The Gentleman from Shallot" ("The Gentleman of Shallot") (Bishop)   **9**:96; **32**:29,

44-5
"The Gentleman of Shallot" (Bishop)
   See "The Gentleman from Shallot"
"Gentleman without Company" (Neruda)   **1**:247
Gentleman's Agreement (Hobson)   **7**:163-64; **25**:269-71
Gentleman's Agreement (Kazan)   **63**:223, 225, 229, 234
Gentlemen, I Address You Privately (Boyle)   **19**:64; **58**:64-5
Les génts (*The Giants*) (Le Clezio)   **31**:248-49
"Genuine and Poignant" (Hearne)   **56**:125
"Geographer" (Hacker)   **91**:109
"Geography" (Olds)   **32**:346
Geography III (Bishop)   **9**:97; **13**:89-91, 94-5; **15**:60-1; **32**:29-31, 33, 35, 37-9, 41-2
Geography of a Horsedreamer (Shepard)   **4**:491-92; **6**:495, 497; **17**:443-44
The Geography of Lograire (Merton)   **3**:335-36; **11**:372; **83**:398, 404
"The Geography of the House" (Auden)   **14**:29
The Geography of the Imagination (Davenport)   **38**:140-46
Geography of the Near Past (Young)   **19**:480
"Geometaphysics" (Avison)   **97**:67-8, 70, 72, 111
"The Geometry of Love" (Cheever)   **64**:46-8
"Georg Heym—przygoda prawie metafizyczna" ("Georg Heym—The Almost Metaphysical Adventure") (Herbert)   **9**:275; **43**:187
"Georg Heym—The Almost Metaphysical Adventure" (Herbert)
   See "Georg Heym—przygoda prawie metafizyczna"
Georg Trakl (Heidegger)   **24**:255
"George" (Stead)
   See "The Girl from the Beach"
George: An Early Autobiography (Williams)   **15**:578
"George and the Seraph" (Brooke-Rose)   **40**:106
"George Bowering" (McFadden)   **48**:244
"George Bush" (Keillor)   **115**:295
"George Eliot and Radical Evil" (Howe)   **85**:153
"George Meredith, 1861" (Day Lewis)   **10**:131
George Mills (Elkin)   **27**:124-26; **51**:93, 98, 101; **91**:213-14, 223-24
"George Oppen" (Bowering)   **47**:28
George Seferis: A Poet's Journal (Seferis)
   See *Days of 1945-1951: A Poet's Journal*
George, Vancouver: A Discovery Poem (Bowering)   **15**:83; **47**:23, 28
George Washington Crossing the Delaware (Koch)   **5**:218
"George Washington Meets the King of Spain" ("On the Magellanic Clouds") (Wakoski)   **9**:555
The George Washington Poems (Wakoski)   **2**:459; **4**:572; **7**:505; **9**:555; **40**:454
George Washington September, Sir! (Harwood)   **32**:222
George Washington Slept Here (Hart and Kaufman)   **38**:265; **66**:175, 182-86
Georges Bataille's Bathrobe (Foreman)   **50**:171
Georgia (Soupault)   **68**:404-07
Georgia Boy (Caldwell)   **14**:96; **50**:300, 302; **60**:49, 55
"Georgia Dusk" (Toomer)   **13**:551; **22**:423, 426
Georgia, Georgia (Angelou)   **77**:15, 18, 21
"A Georgia Song" (Angelou)   **77**:31
The Georgian House: A Tale in Four Parts (Swinnerton)   **31**:424
The Georgian Literary Scene: A Panorama (*The*

Georgian Scene: A Literary Panorama) (Swinnerton) **31**:424-25, 428

The Georgian Scene: A Literary Panorama (Swinnerton)

See *The Georgian Literary Scene: A Panorama*

Georgics (Day Lewis) **6**:127; **10**:134

"Georgie and Fenwick" (Nowlan) **15**:398

."Georgie Grimes" (Brown) **59**:265

Georgina and the Dragon (Kingman) **17**:246

Les géorgiques (Simon) **39**:212

Georgy Girl (Nichols) **65**:162

"A geração de '45" ("Generation of '45") (Cabral de Melo Neto) **76**:157

"Gerald" (Lane) **25**:284

Gerald: A Portrait (du Maurier) **59**:286

Geraldine Bradshaw (Willingham) **51**:401-05, 407-09, 411

Gerald's Party (Coover) **46**:116-22; **87**:41-2, 58-61, 63-4

"The Geranium" (Grace) **56**:122-23

"The Geranium" (O'Connor) **3**:366:**6**:382, 21:277; **104**:188

"Geraniums" (Hogan) **73**:158-59

"Gerard" (Spacks) **14**:511

Gerard Manley Hopkins Meets Walt Whitman in Heaven and Other Poems (Dacey) **51**:82

Gerard's Game (King) **113**:388-89, 392-93

"Gerbil Funeral" (Olds) **85**:295-96

"The Gerbil That Ate Los Angeles" (Kinsella) **43**:258

Gerbils: All about Them (Silverstein and Silverstein) **17**:455

"Gerda in the Eyrie" (Hacker) **72**:182

Die gerettete Zunge: Geschichte einer Jugend (*The Tongue Set Free: Remembrance of a European Childhood*) (Canetti) **25**:110-14; **75**:130, 133, 141, 144; **86**:294-95, 297, 301-02

"Geriatrics" (Enright) **8**:203

"German and English Romanticism: A Confrontation, 1963" (Wellek) **28**:447

"A German Idyll" (Bates) **46**:52

The German Lesson (Lenz)

See *Deutschstunde*

A German Love Story (Hochhuth)

See *Eine Liebe in Deutschland*

"The German Refugee" ("The Jewish Refugee") (Malamud) **8**:375; **44**:415

"A German Requiem" (Fenton) **32**:166-67, 170

"The Germanic Day" (Ewart) **46**:152-53

Germany, Germany among Other Things (Enzensberger)

See *Deutschland, Deutschland unter anderm*

Germfree Life: A New Field in Biological Research (Silverstein and Silverstein) **17**:451

"Germinal" (Hogan) **73**:159

"The Gernsback Continuum" (Gibson) **63**:129-30, 132

Geronimo Rex (Hannah) **23**:207-08, 211; **38**:232-34; **90**:126-28, 130, 134, 136, 139-40, 143-44, 152, 155-59

"A Geronimo Story" (Silko) **74**:349; **114**:317-18

"Gerontion" (Eliot) **3**:137; **6**:160-62, 167; **10**:167-68; **13**:192-93, 195-96, 199-201; **15**:213, 217; **24**:163; **34**:393-94, 529; **41**:151-52, 154-55; **55**:346, 348, 351-52, 355, 364-65, 371, 374; **57**:174-75, 190, 202, 208, 210; **113**:219

Gerpla (*The Happy Warriors*) (Laxness) **25**:293, 298, 300

"Gershwin's Second Prelude" (Baxter) **78**:16

Gertrud (Dreyer) **16**:262-65, 269

Gertrude (*Gertrude and I*) (Hesse) **17**:195, 202, 216

Gertrude and I (Hesse)

See *Gertrude*

"Gertrude Stein and the Geography of the Sentence" (Gass) **15**:258

Gesammelte Erzählungen (Wolf) **29**:464

Gesammelte Gedichte (*Collected Poems*) (Grass) **2**:173; **32**:200

Gesammelte Werke (Celan) **53**:81; **82**:52

Gesang vom lusitanischen Popanz (*Song of the Lusitanian Bogey*; *Song of the Lusitanian Bogeyman*) (Weiss) **15**:565; **51**:387, 391-92, 394

"Geschäft ist Geschäft" ("Business Is Business") (Boell) **27**:58; **72**:70, 101

"Geshem bisdeh hakrav" ("Rain on the Battlefield") (Amichai) **116**:110

"Gespräch im Gebirge" ("Conversation in the Mountains") (Celan) **53**:81, 83

"Gespräch mit Horst Bienek" (Canetti) **86**:295

"Gespräch mit Joachim Schickel" (Canetti) **86**:295

Gespräch über Balzac's Pferd: Vier Novellen (Hofmann) **54**:224

"Gestalt at Sixty" (Sarton) **14**:482

Gestalt Therapy (Goodman) **4**:197-98

"Gestes, ponctuation, et langage poétique" (Tzara) **47**:386

"Gesthemane" (Pasternak) **63**:313

Die gestohlene Melodie (*The Stolen Melody*) (Nossack) **6**:364

Gestos (*Gestures*) (Sarduy) **6**:486; **97**:365, 367, 372, 390, 417

Die gestundete Zeit (Bachmann) **69**:36-9, 41

"The Gesture" (McClure) **6**:319

"Gestures" (Hoffman) **6**:243

Gestures (Sarduy)

See *Gestos*

Gestures and Other Poems (Ritsos) **31**:326

"Get a Seeing-Eyed Dog" (Hemingway) **30**:182

Get Happy!! (Costello) **21**:74

Get Home Free (Holmes) **56**:137-38

"Get It" (McCartney) **35**:289-91

"Get Off My Cloud" (Jagger and Richard) **17**:226, 234-35

Get Off the Unicorn (McCaffrey) **17**:282-83

Get on the Bus (Lee) **105**:127-30

"Get on the Right Thing" (McCartney) **35**:281

"Get Ready" (Robinson) **21**:348

Get Ready for Battle (Jhabvala) **29**:253-55; **94**:166-70, 181

Get Shorty (Leonard) **71**:223-24

Get to Know Your Rabbit (De Palma) **20**:74

"Get Up" (Davies) **21**:103-04

"Get Up in The Morning" (Jiles) **58**:271

Get Your Man (Arzner) **98**:63, 87

The Getaway (Peckinpah) **20**:276-80, 282

The Getaway (Thompson) **69**:378-81, 383, 386, 389

Der geteilte Himmel (Wolf) **14**:593; **58**:432

"Die geteilte Zukunft" (Canetti) **86**:295

"Gethsemane" (Raine) **103**:179

"Gettin' By High and Strange" (Kristofferson) **26**:267

"Gettin' Hungry" (Wilson) **12**:643

"Getting an Education" (Swan) **69**:360

"Getting around Town" (Dobyns) **37**:77

"Getting Away from Already Being Pretty Much Away from It All" (Wallace) **114**:388

"Getting Away from It All" (Dobyns) **37**:76-7

"Getting Better" (Lennon and McCartney) **12**:358

"Getting Closer" (McCartney) **35**:286-87

Getting Even (Allen) **52**:35-6, 40, 45, 47

Getting High in Government Circles (Buchwald) **33**:93

"Getting in the Wood" (Snyder) **32**:397

"Getting into Death" (Disch) **7**:86

Getting into Death and Other Stories (Disch) **7**:86-7; **36**:123

Getting It Right (Howard) **29**:246-47

"Getting Married Today" (Sondheim) **30**:386

Getting Off (Carpenter) **41**:104

Getting On (Bennett) **45**:58; **77**:98

Getting Out (Norman) **28**:317-21

"Getting Outside" (Kelman) **58**:298

"Getting Ready" (Hannah) **38**:233-35; **90**:137

"Getting There" (Plath) **5**:345; **9**:433; **14**:428; **17**:366; **51**:345; **111**:204, 221

"Getting There" (Wagoner) **15**:560

"Getting Things Straight" (Welch) **52**:429

Getting Through (McGahern) **48**:263-64, 271

"Getting Through Sunday Somehow" (Bradbury) **42**:35

"Getting Through to the End" (Dobyns) **37**:76

"Getting Through Winter" (Dobyns) **37**:78-9

"Getting to Know All about You" (Oates) **108**:384

Getting to Know the General (Greene) **37**:137-38; **72**:177

"Getting to the End" (Macdonald) **13**:356

"Getting to Williamstown" (Hood) **28**:193

"Getting Up" (Dobyns) **37**:80

"Getting Used to It" (Dunn) **40**:171

"Gettysburg" (Coupland) **85**:36

Das Gewissen der Worte (*The Conscience of Words*) (Canetti) **25**:114; **75**:129-30, 132, 142; **86**:293, 301

"Der Gewöhnliche Rilke" (Jandl) **34**:196

"The Geysers" (Gunn) **18**:199-201; **32**:209, 211; **81**:179

"Ghalib, Two Years after the Mutiny" (Seth) **90**:351

Ghare Bahire (*The Home and the World*) (Ray) **76**:360, 362

"Ghastly Good Taste" (Betjeman) **43**:43

"Ghazal at Full Moon" (Jordan) **114**:150

"Ghazals" (Harrison) **33**:198

"Ghazals" (Rich) **6**:458; **18**:446

"The Ghetto" (Ehrenburg) **62**:171

Ghetto (Sobol) **60**:382-90

"Ghetto Defendant" (Clash) **30**:50-2

"Ghetto Funeral" (Reznikoff) **9**:450

"Ghibel' Egorushki" ("The Death of Egorushka"; "Egorushka's Destruction"; "Egorushka's Undoing") (Leonov) **92**:237, 263

Ghláfkos thrassákis (Vassilikos) **8**:524

"The Ghost" (Peacock) **60**:297-98

"The Ghost" (Slessor) **14**:497

"Ghost and Flesh" (Goyen) **40**:216

Ghost and Flesh: Stories and Tales (Goyen) **14**:212; **40**:218

A Ghost at Noon (Moravia) **7**:244

The Ghost Belonged to Me (Peck) **21**:297, 299

"Ghost Dance" (Smith) **12**:543

Ghost Dance (Maso) **44**:57-61

The Ghost Downstairs (Garfield) **12**:226-27, 232, 234-35, 237

The Ghost Front (Bonham) **12**:50

"A Ghost Garden" (Tuohy) **37**:431

The Ghost Goes West (Clair) **20**:62

"The Ghost Hammer" (Pinsky)   **94**:308, 312
"The Ghost Horses" (Dinesen)   **10**:148-49
The Ghost in the Machine (Koestler)   **1**:169; **33**:237-38, 240, 242
Ghost in the Machine (Police, The)   **26**:365-66
A Ghost in the Music (Nichols)   **38**:343
Ghost in the Wheels (Birney)   **11**:51
"A Ghost May Come" (Ginsberg)   **36**:182
Ghost of a Chance (Burroughs)   **109**:182
"The Ghost of a Flea" (Lively)   **32**:276
"The Ghost of a Ghost" (Leithauser)   **27**:240, 242
Ghost of Ballyhooly (Cavanna)   **12**:101
The Ghost of Hellsfire Street (Platt)   **26**:354-55
The Ghost of Henry James (Plante)   **23**:341-42, 344
"The Ghost of Magnetism" (Vollmann)   **89**:296
The Ghost of Monsieur Scarron (Lewis)   **41**:255-59, 262
The Ghost Road (Barker)   **94**:17-20
"The Ghost Ship" (Strand)   **71**:283
"A Ghost Story" (Butler)   **81**:129
Ghost Story (Straub)   **28**:410-11; **107**:265-66, 268, 271, 274, 276, 278, 280-82, 287, 288, 291, 302, 304-10
Ghost Tantras (McClure)   **6**:319-20
"Ghost Town" (Longley)   **29**:296
Ghost Trio (Beckett)   **9**:84
"Ghost Village" (Fuller)   **62**:186, 193, 203
"Ghost Voice" (Fuller)   **28**:157
The Ghost Way (Hillerman)   **62**:258-59
"The Ghost Who Vanished by Degrees" (Davies)   **42**:103
The Ghost Writer (Roth)   **15**:450-55; **22**:354-56, 360; **31**:337-41, 345, 347-49; **47**:357-59, 366; **86**:250, 253, 261-63
"Ghosts" (O'Brien)   **36**:336, 341
"Ghosts" (O'Connor)   **23**:331
"Ghosts" (Oliver)   **34**:249; **98**:257, 272, 274, 287
"Ghosts" (Weller)   **26**:447-48
Ghosts (Auster)   **47**:13-16
Ghosts (Hunter)   **31**:224
The Ghosts (Perec)
   See *Les revenentes*
The Ghosts Call You Poor (Suknaski)   **19**:433-34
Ghosts I Have Been (Peck)   **21**:299-300
"Ghosts in England" (Jeffers)   **54**:246
"The Ghost's Leave-taking" (Plath)   **2**:335; **51**:340; **111**:178
"Ghosts of Cape Horn" (Lightfoot)   **26**:283
The Ghosts of Forever (Bradbury)   **42**:41
The Ghosts of Glencoe (Hunter)   **21**:156, 162, 167
The Ghosts of Stone Hollow (Snyder)   **17**:475
"Ghosts of the Missionaries" (Starbuck)   **53**:352
"Ghosts: Some Words before Breakfast" (Harrison)   **43**:175
"The Ghoul" (Smith)   **43**:422
"Giacometti's Race" (Phillips)   **28**:364
An Giall (*The Hostage*) (Behan)   **1**:26; **8**:63-4; **11**:44-5; **15**:45-6; **79**:25-7, 29-31, 33-4, 40-2, 44, 47-9, 52, 54-5, 58
Giant (Ferber)   **18**:151; **93**:181-83, 185, 187-88, 190
Giant in Gray: A Biography of Wade Hampton of South Carolina (Wellman)   **49**:392
"The Giant on Giant-Killing" (Howard)   **10**:275-76
"The Giant Puff Ball" (Blunden)   **56**:26

"Giant Snail" (Bishop)   **32**:42
"A Giant Step for Mankind" (Allen)   **52**:41
"Giant Streak Snarls Race" (Willard)   **7**:539
"Giant Toad" (Bishop)   **32**:42
"Giant Tortoise" (Leithauser)   **27**:240, 242
The Giants (Le Clezio)
   See *Les génts*
Giant's Bread (Christie)   **12**:112
Giants from Eternity (Wellman)   **49**:387
Giants of Jazz (Terkel)   **38**:418
"Un giardino incantato" ("An Enchanted Garden") (Calvino)   **33**:99, 101
"The Gibber" (Roethke)   **11**:481; **46**:362
"Gibson Street" (Nyro)   **17**:316, 318
Gideon (Chayefsky)   **23**:114, 117
Gideon's Fire (Creasey)   **11**:134
Gideon's Power (Creasey)   **11**:134
"The Gift" (Carver)   **55**:273
"The Gift" (Ciardi)   **10**:107; **40**:155
"The Gift" (Creeley)   **36**:118
"The Gift" (Daly)   **17**:91
"The Gift" (Gluck)   **22**:176
"The Gift" (L'Heureux)   **52**:275
"Gift" (Merwin)   **3**:339
"Gift" (Milosz)   **5**:293; **56**:248
"The Gift" (Oliver)   **98**:284
"The Gift" (Raine)   **103**:189
"The Gift" (Steinbeck)   **9**:515
"The Gift" (Swan)   **69**:365
"Gift" (Urquhart)   **90**:386
The Gift (Dickinson)   **12**:171-72, 174
The Gift (H. D.)   **31**:208, 212-13
The Gift (Hamill)   **10**:251
The Gift (Humphreys)   **47**:180, 186, 188-89
The Gift (Nabokov)
   See *Dar*
The Gift (Weller)   **26**:447
"Gift for a Believer" (Levine)   **14**:318
A Gift from Nessus (McIlvanney)   **42**:281
A Gift from the Boys (Buchwald)   **33**:88
Gift from the Sea (Lindbergh)   **82**:154-55, 158-60, 163-67
"Gift from the Stars" (Clarke)   **35**:122
The Gift of Asher Lev (Potok)   **112**:290-93
"The Gift of Fire" (Mueller)   **13**:399
The Gift of Good Land (Berry)   **27**:37-9
"Gift of Grass" (Adams)   **13**:2
"A Gift of Great Value" (Creeley)   **78**:162
"The Gift of Laughter" (Fauset)   **54**:181
"A Gift of Light" (Belitt)   **22**:50
A Gift of Magic (Duncan)   **26**:102
"A Gift of Mercy" (Findley)   **102**:110
"The Gift of the Prodigal" (Taylor)   **37**:411-13; **44**:305-06; **50**:251; **71**:304, 306
"The Gift of the Second Snow" (Smith)   **22**:385
A Gift of Time (Kanin)   **22**:230-31
"The Gift of Wilderness" (Stegner)   **49**:359
A Gift of Wings (Bach)   **14**:35
"The Gift Outright" (Frost)   **1**:110; **44**:459, 462
The Gift to Be Simple: A Garland for Ann Lee (Peters)   **7**:303-04
"The Gifts of Iban" (Steinbeck)   **21**:390
"Gifts of Rain" (Heaney)   **5**:172; **14**:243; **37**:169; **74**:157
"Gifts without Recipients" (Kunene)   **85**:162
"Gigamesh" (Lem)   **15**:330
The Gigli Concert (Murphy)   **51**:303-06
"Gigolo" (Ferber)   **93**:145-46
"Gigolo" (Plath)   **5**:342; **111**:206
"The Gigolo" (Sagan)   **17**:428
"Gila Flambé" (Barthelme)   **36**:52; **117**:7, 14, 18

"Gilbert's Mother" (Trevor)   **116**:376, 395
"The Gilded Man" (Ai)   **14**:8; **69**:4-6, 11-12, 17
"The Gilded Six-Bits" (Hurston)   **7**:172; **30**:211, 215, 219, 223; **61**:263
Gilden-Fire (Donaldson)   **46**:141, 143
Giles Goat-Boy; or, The Revised New Syllabus (Barth)   **1**:17-18; **2**:36-9; **3**:39-40, 42; **7**:22-3; **9**:61-3, 65, 68-9, 71; **10**:22-4; **14**:49-51, 55-6; **51**:20-1, 23, 25-6, 28; **89**:7, 11, 14, 17, 27
"Gilgamesh and Friend" (Purdy)   **6**:428; **50**:236
Gilles et Jeanne: Récit (Tournier)   **36**:438; **95**:372, 374-75, 390-91, 395
"Gills" (Moure)   **88**:220
"Gimme Shelter" (Jagger and Richard)   **17**:226
Gimme Shelter (Maysles and Maysles)   **16**:440-43
"Gimme Some Truth" (Lennon)   **12**:367; **35**:263-64, 267
"Gimpel Tam" ("Gimpel the Fool") (Singer)   **1**:310, 312; **3**:452-53, 455, 458-59; **6**:508; **11**:500; **23**:414, 418, 422; **38**:407; **69**:306, 309, 311, 320; **111**:292, 294, 296, 312-13, 344-46
Gimpel Tam und andere Dertseylungen (*Gimpel the Fool, and Other Stories*) (Singer)   **3**:453; **11**:502
"Gimpel the Fool" (Singer)
   See "Gimpel Tam"
Gimpel the Fool, and Other Stories (Singer)
   See *Gimpel Tam und andere Dertseylungen*
"Gin" (Blackburn)   **9**:100
The Gin Game (Coburn)   **10**:107-08
"Gin the Goodwife Stint" (Bunting)   **47**:45, 49
Ginger and Fred (Fellini)
   See *Ginger e Fred*
Ginger Coffey (Moore)
   See *The Luck of Ginger Coffey*
Ginger e Fred (*Ginger and Fred*) (Fellini)   **85**:53-7, 60, 66, 71-2, 76, 81-2
"Ginger from Next Door" (Aksyonov)   **101**:18
The Ginger Horse (Daly)   **17**:91
The Ginger Man (Donleavy)   **1**:75-6; **4**:123-26; **6**:139-42; **10**:153-55; **45**:123-25, 128-29
Ginger, You're Barmy (Lodge)   **36**:266-67
"The Gingerbread House" (Coover)   **7**:58; **15**:145
The Gingerbread Lady (Simon)   **6**:505; **11**:495; **31**:395-96, 400, 403; **70**:244
"Ginger's Friday" (Harrison)   **43**:175
The Gingham Dog (Wilson)   **7**:547
Il gioco segreto (Morante)   **47**:279
"Gioconda and Si-Ya-U" (Hikmet)
   See "Jokund ile Si-Ya-U"
The Gioconda Smile (Huxley)   **5**:195
La giornata d'uno scruttatore (*The Watcher, and Other Stories*) (Calvino)   **5**:98, 99, 101; **8**:127, 129-30; **11**:89, 91; **39**:308, 314-16
Il giorno della civetta (*The Day of the Owl; Mafia Vendetta*) (Sciascia)   **8**:474; **9**:475; **41**:388-89, 393
Giorno dopo giorno (*Day after Day*) (Quasimodo)   **10**:428-29
Giorno per giorno dal 1922 al 1966 (Bacchelli)   **19**:32
"Giotto's Joy" (Kristeva)   **77**:312
"Giovanni and His Wife" (Landolfi)   **49**:210
"Giovanni Franchi" (Loy)   **28**:251, 253
Giovanni Pisano, Sculptor (Ayrton)   **7**:18
Giovanni's Room (Baldwin)   **1**:13-14, 16; **2**:32;

3:32; 4:40-1; 5:41-3; 13:51-2; 15:41-2; 17:21, 29-30, 32, 36, 41, 44-5; 42:21; 50:283, 293-94, 296; 90:5, 31-2
"Gipsies Revisited" (Mahon)   27:288, 290
"Giraffe" (Plumly)   33:312
"Giraffe" (Swenson)   61:405
"The Giraffe" (Young)   82:412
Giraffe: Poems by Stanley Plumly (Plumly)   33:311-13
"Girl" (Kincaid)   43:247-48, 250
"The Girl" (Olds)   85:293
Girl 6 (Lee)   105:122-23, 127-28
"The Girl across the Room" (Adams)   46:17
"The Girl and the Train" (Cabral de Melo Neto)   76:169
"Girl at the Piano" (Graham)   48:145
"Girl at the Seaside" (Murphy)   41:312
"Girl Bathing" (Clark)   38:117, 127-28
"Girl Beatnik" (Yevtushenko)   26:463-64
The Girl beneath the Lion (Mandiargues)   41:273-74, 276
"Girl Blue" (Wonder)   12:656
A Girl Can Dream (Cavanna)   12:98-9
"Girl Don't Tell Me" (Wilson)   12:647
"Girl Friend" (Colter)   58:140
"The Girl from California" (O'Hara)   42:326
The Girl from Mars (Williamson)   29:456
"The Girl from the Beach" ("George") (Stead)   32:409; 80:306
The Girl Green as Elderflower (Stow)   23:437-38; 48:358-61
The Girl Hunters (Spillane)   13:526, 528
The Girl I Left Behind (The Woman I Abandoned) (Endo)   99:285-86, 299-300, 305-06
"A Girl in a Library" (Jarrell)   9:297; 13:298; 49:197, 201
The Girl in a Swing (Adams)   18:2
"A Girl in a Window" (Wright)   28:462
The Girl in Blue (Wodehouse)   10:537
Girl in Gingham (Metcalf)   37:301-03, 305
The Girl in Melanie Klein (Harwood)   32:223
"The Girl in the Field" (Monette)   82:315
The Girl in the Grove (Duncan)   26:103
Girl in the Mirror (Sherburne)   30:362
The Girl in the Moon (Lang)
   See Die Frau im Mond
The Girl in the Opposite Bed (Arundel)   17:14, 17
The Girl in the Plain Brown Wrapper (MacDonald)   44:408
"Girl in Time Lost" (Derleth)   31:132
"Girl in White" (Dobyns)   37:81
A Girl in Winter (Larkin)   5:223-24, 229; 8:337-38; 9:324; 13:335, 337-38; 33:263, 265-66; 39:334, 340, 347; 64:260, 280
"The Girl Next Door" (Levine)   54:298, 301
A Girl of Forty (Gold)   42:198
"The Girl of My Dreams" (Malamud)   8:375; 44:419
"Girl of My Dreams" (Matheson)   37:245
"Girl of my Dreams" (Okudzhava)   59:378-79
"Girl of the North Country" (Dylan)   4:149; 12:186; 77:172-73
"Girl on the Beach" (Williams)   42:440
"A Girl Sewing" (Szirtes)   46:393-94
"A Girl Skating" (Colwin)   23:129; 84:150
The Girl That He Marries (Lerman)   56:176-78
"Girl Trouble" (Smith)   12:535
Girl, Twenty (Amis)   1:6; 2:10-11; 3:7-8; 5:22; 8:12; 40:42
Girl Waiting in the Shade (Davies)   23:147

"A Girl Walking into a Shadow" (Wright)   3:542
"The Girl Who Approached the Fire" (Kawabata)   107:107
The Girl Who Knew Tomorrow (Sherburne)   30:362
"The Girl Who Knew What They Meant" (Sturgeon)   22:411
"The Girl Who Raised Pigeons" (Jones)   76:65, 69
"The Girl Who Sang" (Aldiss)   40:21
The Girl Who Wanted a Boy (Zindel)   26:481
The Girl Who Was Plugged In (Tiptree)   48:388-89, 395
"The Girl Who Went to Mexico" (Nowlan)   15:399
Girl with a Monkey (Astley)   41:43-4, 48-9
"Girl with Coffee Tray" (Fuller)   62:197
"Girl with Curious Hair" (Wallace)   114:348, 352
Girl with Curious Hair (Wallace)   114:349-52, 359, 361, 368
The Girl with Green Eyes (O'Brien)   3:364; 116:182
"The Girl with Harlequin Glasses" (Colwin)   5:108
"The Girl with the Hungry Eyes" (Leiber)   25:303
The Girl with the Incredible Feeling (Swados)   12:558, 560
The Girl with the Scar (Lustig)   56:188-89
"The Girl with the Silver Eyes" (Hammett)   47:164
"Girlfriend Is Better" (Byrne)   26:99
"Girlhood of Jane Harrison" (Levertov)   66:238
"The Girls" (Elytis)   100:191
"Girls" (Gallagher)   63:121
The Girls (Ferber)   93:142, 144-45, 147-48, 164, 180
Girls Are Girls and Boys Are Boys: So What's the Difference? (Gordon)   26:137
Girls at Play (Theroux)   8:512; 28:423-24
"The Girls at the Sphinx" (Farrell)   66:131
"Girls at War" (Achebe)   26:23; 75:14, 16
Girls at War, and Other Stories (Achebe)   3:2; 7:6; 26:20-2; 75:14, 17
"Girls Bathing, Galway, 1965" (Heaney)   25:245
"Girls Fighting Broadway" (Shapiro)   53:330
Girls in Their Married Bliss (O'Brien)   5:313; 116:182-83, 193, 197, 199
"The Girls in Their Summer Dresses" (Shaw)   7:412; 23:395; 34:368, 370
The Girls of Slender Means (Spark)   2:415; 3:463, 467; 13:524-25; 18:501-02; 40:394, 396, 399-400; 94:350, 353
"The Girls of Summer" (Sondheim)   30:398
"Girls on the Beach" (Wilson)   12:644
A Girl's Own Story (Campion)   95:2, 6, 11
"Girl's Song" (Bogan)   46:81; 93:92, 98
"A Girl's Story" (Bambara)   88:8, 22, 28, 42
Girls Turn Wives (Klein)   30:239
"The Girls Want to Be with the Girls" (Byrne)   26:96
"Girovago" (Ungaretti)   11:555
Le gisant mis en lumiere (Char)   55:288-89
"Git Dough" (Guillen)
   See "Búscate plata"
"Giulia Lazzari" (Maugham)   67:216
Giulietta degli spiriti (Juliet of the Spirits) (Fellini)   16:278-80, 286-87, 293, 299; 85:51, 54, 59, 62-3, 68, 74, 76, 79-82
La giullarata (Fo)   109:114-15
Il giusto della vita (Luzi)   13:352

Give Birth to Brightness: A Thematic Study in Neo-Black Literature (Williams)   89:319, 323, 340
Give 'Em Enough Rope (Clash)   30:43, 45-6, 51
"Give Ireland Back to the Irish" (McCartney)   35:292
"Give It Time to Be Tender" (Kristofferson)   26:268
"Give Me a Body You Mountains"   75:69
Give Me One Good Reason (Klein)   30:237-38
"Give Me Time and I'll Tell You" (Buckley)   57:133
Give My Regards to Broad Street (McCartney)   35:293
"Give Peace a Chance" (Lennon)   35:261, 267, 270-71
Give Thankx (Cliff)   21:65
Give the Boys a Great Big Hand (Hunter)   31:220
Give the People What They Want (Davies)   21:107
"Give to the Rich" (Jacobsen)   48:190
"Give Us Our Peace" (Hughes)   108:334
"Give Us This Day" (Kogawa)   78:167
"Give Way, Ye Gates" (Roethke)   8:455; 101:262, 273, 277, 280-81, 335, 340
"Give Your Heart to the Hawks" (Jeffers)   54:237-38, 245-46
Give Your Heart to the Hawks and Other Poems (Jeffers)   11:307; 54:237, 245
The Giveaway (Jellicoe)   27:210
"A Given Grace" (Tomlinson)   2:437; 6:536
"The Given Note" (Heaney)   25:249
Giver (Lezama Lima)
   See Dador
Giving Back Diamonds (Bowering)   32:48
"Giving Birth" (Atwood)   13:46-7
Giving Good Weight (McPhee)   36:298
"Giving It Up" (Williams)   33:441
Giving Offense: Essays on Censorship (Coetzee)   117:93-4, 96, 101
"Givings" (Ammons)   108:56
Gjenerali i ushtrisë së vdekur (Le général de l'armée morte) (Kadare)   52:257, 261
"Gkragkâta" (Ritsos)   6:463
The Glad Hand (Wilson)   33:462-64
"Glad Heart at the Supermarket" (Van Duyn)   116:411, 413
Gladiator (Wylie)   43:460, 462
"Gladiators" (La Guma)   19:272
The Gladiators (Koestler)   1:170; 3:270; 15:309-10; 33:227, 239-40, 243
"Gladness and Madness" (Hall)   37:145
"Glamour" (Ferber)   93:161
"Glamour Profession" (Becker and Fagen)   26:84
A Glance Away (Wideman)   36:450-53, 455
"A Glance from the Bridge" (Wilbur)   53:413; 110:382
"Glanmore Revisited" (Heaney)   74:188, 190, 193, 195, 197
"Glanmore Sonnets" (Heaney)   14:246; 25:247-48; 74:175, 190, 195
The Glapion Effect (Audiberti)
   See L'effet Glapion
Glas (Derrida)   24:153-55; 87:72, 93, 96-7, 103-10
Glasgow is Like the Sea (MacDiarmid)   63:248
"Glasgow Schoolboys, Running Backwards" (Dunn)   40:168
Glasgow Sonnets (Morgan)   31:273, 275-77
Glasnost in Action: Cultural Renaissance in

Russia (Nove) 59:396
Das Glasperlenspiel (The Glass Bead Game; Magister Ludi) (Hesse) 1:146-47; 2:190-92; 3:243-47; 6:237-38; 11:270-72; 17:195, 197-98, 204-07, 216-18; 25:259, 261, 69:278-83, 287, 290-92
"Glass" (Kawabata) 107:107
The Glass Alembic (The Crystal Garden) (Feinstein) 36:169
The Glass Bead Game (Hesse)
   See *Das Glasperlenspiel*
The Glass Blowers (du Maurier) 6:146
The Glass Cage (Wilson) 3:537
The Glass Cell (Highsmith) 42:212; 102:170, 172-73, 202-04, 209
The Glass Cottage: A Nautical Romance (Redgrove) 41:353
A Glass Face in the Rain (Stafford) 29:387-88
The Glass Flame (Whitney) 42:436
"The Glass Floor" (King) 37:202
"Glass Grain" (Tomlinson) 4:543
The Glass Highway (Estleman) 48:104, 107
Glass Houses (Joel) 26:220-22
The Glass Key (Hammett) 3:218-20; 5:162; 19:193-95; 47:156-57, 162-65
The Glass Key (Welles) 80:380
"The Glass King" (Boland) 67:46; 113:86, 98
The Glass Menagerie (Williams) 1:367, 369; 2:465-66; 5:498-99, 501, 503-04; 7:540-41, 543, 545; 8:547, 549; 11:571-76; 15:580; 19:470, 473-74; 30:455-58, 461, 464-66, 469-70; 39:446; 71:354-406; 111:379-80, 388-89, 391, 393, 395, 397, 404, 408, 414, 417-24
"The Glass Mountain" (Barthelme) 1:18; 6:29; 13:57; 46:35, 40, 45; 115:65, 68-9, 77
A Glass of Blessings (Pym) 13:469-70; 19:387; 37:373; 111:227-28, 230-31, 239, 243-48, 258, 263-64, 266, 269, 271, 278, 283-85
"The Glass of Madeira" (Rakosi) 47:348
"The Glass of Pure Water" (MacDiarmid) 4:312
"A Glass of Tea" (White) 5:486
"A Glass of Wine" (La Guma) 19:274
The Glass on the Table of Claudius Civilis's Conspirers (Haavikko)
   See *Lasi Claudius Civiliksen salaliittolaisten pöydällä*
Glass People (Godwin) 5:142; 8:248; 22:182-83; 69:247
The Glass Teat: Essays of Opinion on the Subject of Television (Ellison) 13:205
The Glass Trumpet (Waddington) 28:437
The Glass Village (Queen) 11:464
"The Glassblowers" (Peake) 54:366, 369
The Glassblowers (du Maurier) 59:286
The Glass-Sided Ants' Nest (Skin Deep) (Dickinson) 12:168, 171; 35:130-31, 133, 137
The Glassy Sea (Engel) 36:162-63
"A Glastonbury Cricket Match" (Ewart) 46:152
A Glastonbury Romance (Powys) 7:348-50; 9:440-41; 15:433, 436; 46:316-18, 320-22, 324
"Glazunoviana" (Ashbery) 77:58
"The Gleaner" (Bates) 46:52-3, 61
"Gleaning" (Blunden) 56:37
"Gleanings from Snow Country" (Kawabata) 107:104, 107-08
Gleisdreieck (Triangle Junction) (Grass) 15:263; 32:198, 200-01
Gleiwitzer Kindheit: Gedicte aus zwanzig Jahren

(Bienek) 11:48
Glembajevi (The Glembays) (Krleza) 8:329; 114:167, 175
The Glembays (Krleza)
   See *Glembajevi*
"Glen Albyn" (MacDiarmid) 63:242
"Glencull Waterside" (Montague) 46:274
Glenda (Cortazar)
   See *Queremos tanto a Glenda*
"Glendower" (Nye) 42:309
Glengarry Glen Ross (Mamet) 34:218-24; 46:254-55
"Glengormley" (Mahon) 27:288, 291
"Glenna—A Child of the 60's" (Tomlin) 17:522-23
"Glenthorne Poems" (Fisher) 25:160
"Glenway Wescott's War Work" (Wilson) 24:481
"Glimmerings" (Schaeffer) 11:491
"Glimpse at a Jockey" (Miller) 47:250
A Glimpse of Nothingness: Experiences in an American Zen Community (van de Wetering) 47:404
The Glimpses of the Moon (Crispin) 22:110
Glissements progressifs du plaisir (Robbe-Grillet) 8:454; 43:367
"Glitter: A Memory" (Carpenter) 41:107-08
The Glittering Clouds (Paustovsky) 40:367
The Glittering Coffin (Potter) 86:345, 349
"Glittering Pie" (Miller) 43:298
The Glittering Prizes (Raphael) 14:437-38
Glitz (Leonard) 71:208-10, 212-18, 221-24, 226-27
Global Dumping Ground: The International Traffic in Hazardous Waste (Moyers) 74:257
"The Global Fidget" (Dunn) 6:148-49
"The Globe" (Olson) 28:343
"La gloire des rois" ("The Glory of Kings") (Perse) 46:300-01
"The Gloomy Tune" (Paley) 4:392; 37:337
"Gloria" (Elytis) 100:156, 159, 161, 163-64, 166
Gloria (Cassavetes) 20:55-6
Gloria mundi (Clark) 19:107-08
Gloria Star (Tremblay) 102:365-66
"Gloria Steinem and the Feminist Utopia" (Amis) 62:2
Gloriana; or, The Unfulfill'd Queen (Moorcock) 27:351; 58:349
La glorie de Dina (del Castillo) 38:169
The Glorious Destiny of Marshal Nnikon Nniku (Tchicaya)
   See *Le destin glorieux du Maréchal Nnikon Nniku, prince qu'on sort*
The Glorious Ones (Prose) 45:323-24, 326
A Glorious Third (Seton) 27:427-29
"Glory"
   See "One Song Glory"
"The Glory" (Ciardi) 44:381
"Glory" (Komunyakaa) 94:237, 241
Glory (Romantic Times) (Nabokov) 1:246; 2:301-02, 304; 11:393-94; 15:396; 44:469
The Glory and the Dream (Hilliard) 15:280
Glory and the Lightning (Caldwell) 28:67
The Glory Girl (Byars) 35:75-6
"Glory in the Daytime" (Parker) 68:326, 334, 337
The Glory of Hera (Gordon) 6:206; 29:190; 83:258, 261
"The Glory of Kings" (Perse)
   See "La gloire des rois"

The Glory of the Hummingbird (De Vries) 7:76-7
Glory Road (Catton) 35:85-6
Glory Road (Heinlein) 14:251; 26:165; 55:303
"The Glory Trumpeter" (Walcott) 25:449; 67:353-54
"Gloss Gimel" (Klein) 19:262
"Glossolalia" (Barth) 9:68; 51:23; 89:5-7, 9, 15, 21, 44, 61-2
"Gloucestershire" (Davie) 8:166
"The Glove" (Dinesen) 10:152
"The Gloves" (Middleton) 13:389
Gloves to the Hangman (Walker) 13:566
"Glow Girl" (Townshend) 17:534
"Glowing Enigmas" (Sachs) 14:476
   See *Glühende Rätsel*
"A Glowing Future" (Rendell) 48:320
"Glowing Riddles" (Sachs)
   See *Glühende Rätsel*
"A Glowworm Illuminates the Night" (Ritsos) 31:324
"Gloze" (Corn) 33:117
"Glubokim golosom proroka" ("With the Deep Voice of a Prophet") (Akhmadulina) 53:11
Glühende Rätsel ("Glowing Enigmas"; "Glowing Riddles") (Sachs) 14:476-77; 98:324, 328, 334-35
"La Glutton, in Suburb" (Shapcott) 38:400
"Gluttony" (Dobyns) 37:76
The Gnädiges Fräulein (The Mutilated; Slapstick Tragedy) (Williams) 2:465; 5:502, 504; 15:580; 19:471-72; 30:470; 45:450-51
"Gnat-Psalm" (Hughes) 37:179
"Gnome" (Pink Floyd) 35:307
Gnomes and Occasions (Nemerov) 6:362-63; 9:395; 36:302
"Gnomic Variations for Kenneth Burke" (Nemerov) 36:309
The Gnomobile (Sinclair) 11:497
The Gnostic Gospels (Pagels) 104:205-08, 210-11, 214, 217, 220-21, 224, 229, 234
Go (The Beat Boys) (Holmes) 56:136, 138-42, 145
"Go and Look for Bread" (Guillen)
   See "Búscate plata"
Go Back for Murder (Christie) 12:125
"Go Cry on Somebody Else's Shoulder" (Zappa) 15:588
"Go Down Matthew" (Barnes) 11:31
Go Down, Moses and Other Stories (Faulkner) 1:102; 3:151-52; 6:174; 8:210-14; 14:172, 175, 179; 18:149; 28:140, 143, 145; 68:129
"Go Get Money" (Guillen)
   See "Búscate plata"
Go in Beauty (Eastlake) 8:198, 200
"Go like This" (Moore) 39:82-4; 45:279
"Go, Lovely Rose" (Eberhart) 56:84
"Go Not to Lethe Celebrates Its Twenty-Seventh Anniversary: A Soap Opera Journal Special" (Grayson) 38:209
Go Saddle the Sea (Aiken) 35:18, 21
Go, Team, Go! (Tunis) 12:597
Go Tell It on the Mountain (Baldwin) 1:13-14, 16; 2:31-2; 3:31-2; 4:40-1; 5:40-1, 43; 8:41; 13:51-2; 15:41; 17:20, 29, 31-2, 36-7, 42-4; 42:14, 17-18; 50:283-84, 293-95; 67:3-30; 90:5, 10, 12, 31
Go Tell the Lemming (Rubens) 19:403
Go to the Widow-Maker (Jones) 1:162; 3:261; 10:292; 39:406-07, 409

"Go Wake Jessie Up. We Are Going to the Beach!" (Gray)　**49**:147

Go West (Keaton)　**20**:188

"Go West Young Man" (Laughlin)　**49**:220

Go When You See the Green Man Walking (Brooke-Rose)　**40**:106

The Goalie's Anxiety at the Penalty Kick (Handke)　**5**:164-67; **10**:255-56, 258; **15**:268; **38**:216, 218-20, 223

The Goat (Keaton)　**20**:194

Goat Dances: Poems and Prose (Loewinsohn)　**52**:285

"A Goat for Azazel" (Porter)　**101**:223

A Goat on a Cloud (Arrabal)
See *Une chèvre sur un nuage*

Goat Song (Yerby)　**22**:488-89

Goatfoot, Milktongue, Twinbird (Hall)　**37**:145-47

"A Goatherd at Luncheon" (Calvino)　**39**:314

The Goatibex Constellation (Iskander)
See *Sozvezdie Kozlotura*

"Goats and Monkeys" ("Of Goats and Monkeys") (Walcott)　**25**:449; **42**:423; **67**:350, 352-53; **76**:270

Goat's Head Soup (Jagger and Richard)　**17**:228-29, 232-33, 236, 238

"The Go-Away Bird" (Spark)　**8**:493; **13**:520; **40**:401, 404

The Go-Away Bird, and Other Stories (Spark)　**13**:519

"El gobernador Glu Glu" (Ulibarri)　**83**:416

The Go-Between (Hartley)　**2**:181-82; **22**:211, 213-14, 217-19

The Go-Between (Pinter)　**27**:391; **58**:376

Goblin Reservation (Simak)　**55**:320

"Una goccia" (Buzzati)　**36**:96-7

"The God" (H. D.)　**73**:120

"God" (Lennon)　**35**:261-62, 266

"God" (Prince)　**35**:331

"God" (Swenson)　**61**:400; **106**:316, 327, 345-46, 350

God (Allen)　**52**:36-7, 43-4, 48

God: A Biography (Miles)　**100**:275-83

A God against the Gods (Drury)　**37**:108-09

"God and Gods" (Endo)　**54**:158; **99**:285

A God and His Gifts (Compton-Burnett)　**3**:111-12; **15**:140

God and Mammon (Mauriac)　**56**:218

God and Man at Yale (Buckley)　**37**:53, 55-7, 61

"God and the Article Writer" (Berriault)　**109**:92-3, 95

"God and the Cobbler" (Narayan)　**28**:301

The God beneath the Sea (Garfield)　**12**:219, 222, 229-30, 235

God Bless (Feiffer)　**8**:216; **64**:149-50

"God Bless America" (Fuller)　**62**:186, 193

God Bless the Child (Hunter)　**35**:223-27

God Bless You, Mr. Rosewater; or, Pearls before Swine (Vonnegut)　**1**:347; **2**:453, 455; **3**:495, 497, 499-500, 505-06; **4**:561-64, 567; **5**:466, 469; **8**:531-32; **12**:601-02, 604-05, 607, 614, 618-19, 623; **40**:446-47; **60**:417, 424, 427, 431; **111**:351, 354, 359, 371

God Emperor of Dune (Herbert)　**23**:221-23; **35**:199, 201-03, 206-09; **44**:393-94; **85**:93-6

"God Full of Mercy" (Amichai)　**116**:100, 128

"God Has Manifested Himself unto Us As Canadian Tire" (Hood)　**28**:194

"God Has Mercy on Kindergarten Children" (Amichai)
See "Elohim merakhem al yaldey hagan"

"God Has Pity on the Kindergarten Children" (Amichai)
See "Elohim merakhem al yaldey hagan"

"God Hunger" (Ryan)　**65**:211

God Hunger (Ryan)　**65**:208-16

"A God in the Garden" (Sturgeon)　**22**:410; **39**:360, 366

"God Is" (Mathias)　**45**:238

"God Is a Helicopter with a Big Searchlight" (Wild)　**14**:580

"God Is Love" (Gaye)　**26**:130

God Is Red (Deloria)　**21**:111-12

"God Knows" (Dylan)　**77**:183-84

God Knows (Heller)　**36**:228-31

God Made Alaska for the Indians (Reed)　**32**:361-62

The God Makers (Herbert)　**12**:272; **35**:209; **44**:394; **85**:88

"The God of Dostoyevsky" (Richards)　**24**:395

"The God of Flowers" (Levertov)　**66**:241

The God of Glass (Redgrove)　**41**:355-56

The God of Small Things (Roy)　**109**:68-78

The God of Tarot (Anthony)　**35**:35

"The God of the Bulls" (Borges)　**48**:42

God of the Labyrinth (Wilson)　**14**:584

God on the Rocks (Gardam)　**43**:168-69

"God Only Knows" (Wilson)　**12**:643

God Perkins (Pownall)　**10**:419-20

"God Pities the Kindergarten Children" (Amichai)
See "Elohim merakhem al yaldey hagan"

The God Project (Saul)　**46**:367

"God Rest Ye Merry, Gentleman: Part II" (Walcott)　**67**:359

"God Rest You Merry, Gentlemen" (Hemingway)　**3**:242; **19**:219

God Save the Child (Parker)　**27**:363, 365-67

"God Save You, Future Humanity" (Asturias)　**8**:26

God Sends Sunday (Bontemps)　**1**:37; **18**:62-3

The God That Failed (Koestler)　**33**:238

The God That Failed (Wright)　**74**:382

"God, The" (McFadden)　**48**:249

"The God Who Eats Corn" (Murphy)　**41**:312-13, 317-18

God without Thunder: An Unorthodox Defense of Orthodoxy (Ransom)　**2**:362; **4**:433-34, 436-37; **5**:363-64

Godbody (Sturgeon)　**39**:361

"Goddamn Pussycats" (Thurber)　**25**:436

Godded and Codded (O'Faolain)　**47**:325-26, 330; **108**:399, 425

"The Goddess" (Levertov)　**66**:238, 245

The Goddess (Chayefsky)　**23**:113

The Goddess (Ray)
See *Devi*

The Goddess and Other Women (Oates)　**6**:373; **19**:353; **108**:372

Le godelureaux (Chabrol)　**16**:183

"Godfather" (Dorfman)　**77**:141, 143

The Godfather (Coppola)　**16**:233-42, 244, 248-49

The Godfather (Puzo)　**2**:351-52; **6**:429-30; **36**:359-63; **107**:175-76, 178-203, 205-16, 218

The Godfather Papers and Other Confessions (Puzo)　**2**:352; **36**:360; **107**:175, 189, 213

The Godfather, Part II (Coppola)　**16**:240-45, 249

The Godfather: Part II (Puzo)　**107**:202, 213

The Godfather: Part III (Puzo)　**107**:193, 208, 213

"Godmother" (Parker)　**68**:340

The Godmother (Elliott)　**47**:104

"Gods" (Sexton)　**6**:494

God's Bits of Wood (Ousmane)
See *Les bouts de bois de Dieu*

God's Country and My People (Morris)　**7**:247; **37**:312-13

Gods, Demons, and Others (Narayan)　**28**:299, 302

God's Ear (Lerman)　**56**:180

God's Favorite (Simon)　**6**:505-06; **11**:496

God's Fool: The Life and Times of Francis of Assisi (Green)
See *Frère François*

Gods from Outer Space (von Daniken)　**30**:423-24

God's Grace (Malamud)　**27**:298-302; **44**:413, 416, 419

God's Images (Dickey)　**10**:142

"The Gods in Flight" (Aldiss)　**40**:21

God's Little Acre (Caldwell)　**14**:95, 97-9; **50**:298-303; **60**:44-8, 50, 54, 58-60, 64-5

God's Measurements (Lieberman)　**36**:261-64

God's Mistress (Galvin)　**38**:198-99

"The Gods of the Earth Beneath" (Blunden)　**56**:48

Gods of the Plague (Fassbinder)　**20**:113, 116

God's Pocket (Dexter)　**34**:43-5

God's Radar (Arrick)　**30**:19

"The God's Script" (Borges)
See "La escritura del Dios"

God's Snake (Spanidou)　**44**:104-10

God's Sparrows (Child)　**19**:100, 103

God's Stepchildren (Millin)　**49**:240-41, 243, 245-46, 249, 251-55

The Gods, the Little Guys, and the Police (Costantini)
See *De dioses, hombrecitos, y policias*

"The Gods Themselves" (Asimov)　**19**:26

The Gods Themselves (Asimov)　**19**:26, 28; **26**:37-40, 47-50, 63; **76**:313

"God's Typhoon" (Hersey)　**81**:329

God's Warrior (Slaughter)　**29**:377

God's World (Mahfuz)　**55**:183, 188

The Godstone and the Blackymor (White)　**30**:449

The Godwulf Manuscript (Parker)　**27**:363-65

Gog (Sinclair)　**2**:400-02; **14**:488

"Gog II and III" (Hughes)　**37**:173

Gogo no eiko (The Sailor Who Fell from Grace with the Sea) (Mishima)　**2**:286; **4**:354, 357; **27**:337, 340-41, 343

"Gogol's Wife" (Landolfi)　**49**:209-11

Gogol's Wife and Other Stories (Landolfi)　**11**:321; **49**:209-10, 212

"Gogo's Late Wife Tranquilla" (Durcan)　**43**:114

Goin a Buffalo (Bullins)　**7**:36

"Goin' Down This Road" (Guthrie)　**35**:184

"Goin' Home" (Smith)　**12**:539

"Goin' to Town" (Storm)
See "Going to Town"

"Going" (Larkin)　**64**:257, 259, 261, 274

Going (Elliott)　**38**:180

"Going After Cacciato" (O'Brien)　**103**:144, 146

Going After Cacciato (O'Brien)　**19**:356-59; **40**:345-48; **103**:131-39, 141, 143-49, 152, 159-60, 163-64, 166, 168-69, 172-75

Going All the Way (Wakefield) 7:502-03

"Going Away" (Nemerov) **36**:305

Going Away: A Report, a Memoir (Sigal) 7:424-25

"Going Back" (Stanton) 9:508

"Going Back to Cape de Santo Agostinho" (Cabral de Melo Neto)
   See "De volta ao Cabro de Santo Agostinho"

"Going Back to Sleep" (Sadoff) 9:466

Going Back to the River (Hacker) **72**:191-92

"Going Back West" (Cliff) 21:62

Going Down (Markson) **67**:185-86, 191-94

Going Down Fast (Piercy) 3:384; **27**:372; **62**:362-63, 365, 369

"Going Down on Love" (Lennon) **35**:268

Going Down Slow (Metcalf) **37**:298-300, 304

"Going Dutch" (Moss) 7:249

"Going for the Bread" (Grace) **56**:122

Going for the Rain (Ortiz) **45**:300-02, 304-08

"Going for Water" (Frost) **26**:116

"Going, Going" (Larkin) 5:226; 8:333, 340; **18**:294, 298-99; **33**:261, 269; **39**:346; **64**:266, 274

"Going, Going, Gone" (Dylan) **77**:182

"Going Home" (Kenny) **87**:248

"Going Home" (Trevor) **116**:375

Going Home (Lessing) **94**:266, 276

"Going Home: Ben's Church, Virginia" (Smith) **42**:350

"Going Home to Mayo, Winter, 1949" (Durcan) **43**:114-15

"Going Home to Russia" (Durcan) **70**:152

"Going Mad" (Cliff) 21:63

"Going North" (Salinas) **90**:325

Going on Sixteen (Cavanna) **12**:97, 99

"Going Out as a Ghost" (Hood) **28**:192

"Going Out to Sea" (Freeman) **55**:55, 58

"Going Places" (Michaels) **25**:314, 316-17

Going Places (Michaels) 6:324; **25**:314-16

Going Solo (Dahl) **79**:182-83

Going through the Motions (Govier) **51**:164-66

Going thru Changes (Wesley) 7:518

"Going to California" (Page and Plant) **12**:475

"Going to Church" (Jiles) **58**:275-76

"Going to Europe" (Govier) **51**:166

Going to Extremes (McGinniss) **32**:303-04

"Going to Headquarters" (Calvino) **33**:99

"Going to India" (Blaise) **29**:73

Going to Jerusalem (Charyn) 5:103

"Going to Massachusetts" (Bowles) **68**:9-10, 18

"Going to Meet the Man" (Baldwin) 8:40

Going to Meet the Man (Baldwin) 8:40; **17**:33; **50**:296; **90**:2, 19, 33

"Going to Naples" (Welty) **105**:299

"Going to Russia" (Vanderhaeghe) **41**:449

"Going to School" (McNickle) **89**:180

Going to School: The African-American Experience **70**:375-76

"Going to See the Leaves" (Collins) **44**:37

Going to See the Leaves (Collins) **44**:36-8

"Going to Sleep in the Country" (Moss) **45**:291

"Going to the Bakery" (Bishop) 9:93; **32**:37

Going to the Sun (George) **35**:178

Going to the Territory (Ellison) **86**:319, 323, 326; **114**:123, 128

"Going to Town" ("Goin' to Town") (Stegner) **81**:346

Going to War with All My Relations: New and Selected Poems (Rose) **85**:317

"Going Under" (Dubus) **97**:200, 202, 209, 218

"Going West Alone" (Holmes) **56**:143

"Going with the Current" (Transtroemer) **65**:229

"The Going-Away Clothes" (Pownall) **10**:419

"Gold" (Brown) **32**:64

"Gold" (Hall) **37**:142

"Gold" (Muldoon) **72**:272

Gold (Cendrars)
   See *L'or*

Gold (Diamond) **30**:111

"Gold and Silver" (Tanizaki) **28**:417

Gold and Silver Waltz (Linney) **51**:263

Gold and Work (Pound) **112**:357

"The Gold Bride" (Stead) **80**:334

The Gold Bug Variations (Powers) **93**:282, 286-99, 301

The Gold Cell (Olds) **85**:291-93, 296, 298-300, 302, 305, 308

"Gold Coast" (McPherson) **77**:351-52, 358, 360, 373-74, 377

"Gold Coast Customs" (Sitwell) **67**:317, 322, 335

"The Gold Diggers" (Creeley) **11**:136; **36**:122

The Gold Diggers (Creeley) 4:118; 8:151; **11**:136-37; **78**:126, 128, 130, 144, 147

The Gold Diggers (Monette) **82**:315-16, 328

Gold from Crete (Forester) **35**:173

The Gold in the Sea (Friel) **42**:164-65; **115**:216, 252

"The Gold Lily" (Gluck) **81**:172

Gold Mine (Smith) **33**:374

"Gold Nuggets" (Brown) **73**:23

The Gold of the Gods (von Daniken) **30**:424

The Gold of the Tigers: Selected Later Poems (Borges)
   See *El oro de los tigres*

"The Gold of Tomas Vargas" (Allende) **97**:12, 31-2

The Gold Rush (Chaplin) **16**:187, 189, 198-201, 206-07

Gold through the Trees (Childress) **86**:309, 311, 314; **96**:103, 109-10

"The Gold Watch" (Anand) **23**:21

"The Gold Watch" (McGahern) **48**:273

The Golden Age (Bunuel)
   See *L'age d'or*

The Golden Age (Gurney) **32**:221

"Golden Apple" (Kundera)
   See "The Golden Apple of Eternal Desire"

"The Golden Apple" (Kundera)
   See "The Golden Apple of Eternal Desire"

The Golden Apple (Wilson) 9:576

"The Golden Apple of Desire" (Kundera)
   See "The Golden Apple of Eternal Desire"

"The Golden Apple of Eternal Desire" ("Golden Apple"; "The Golden Apple"; "The Golden Apple of Desire") (Kundera) 4:278; **32**:260

"The Golden Apples" (Welty) 1:361; 2:463; 5:479-80; **14**:562, 565; **22**:458, 461; **33**:419-20

The Golden Apples (Welty) **105**:299, 303, 319, 321, 325, 327, 333, 336, 338, 340, 349, 383-86

The Golden Apples of the Sun (Bradbury) **10**:70; **42**:32

The Golden Barge (Moorcock) **58**:350-51

The Golden Bees of Tulami (Bonham) **12**:54

"The Golden Bird" (Brown) **100**:81

The Golden Bird: Two Orkney Stories (Brown) **48**:61

"The Golden Bough" (Heaney) **74**:194

"The Golden Bough" (Mahon) **27**:291

Golden Boy (Gibson) **23**:179

Golden Boy (Odets) 2:318, 320; **28**:326-27, 330, 332-33, 336, 340-41; **98**:196, 198-202, 205, 208-10, 229, 235, 237, 241, 243-44, 251-52

The Golden Breath: Studies in Five Poets of the New India (Anand) **93**:24

"Golden Builders" (Buckley) **57**:132-33

Golden Builders and Other Poems (Buckley) **57**:132-33

The Golden Chains (Barker) **48**:19, 21, 24

The Golden Chalice (Gustafson) **36**:217

The Golden Child (Fitzgerald) **19**:172; **61**:115, 117

The Golden Coach (Leonov)
   See *Zolotaya kareta*

The Golden Coach (Renoir)
   See *Le carosse d'or*

The Golden Country (Endo) **54**:151; **99**:285, 297

The Golden Door (Scott) **43**:373-74

The Golden Droplet (Tournier)
   See *La Goutte d'or*

Golden Earring (Polonsky) **92**:378, 383, 416

The Golden Evening (Middleton) **38**:330

The Golden Fleece (Gurney) **50**:183

The Golden Fortress (Ray)
   See *Sonar Kella*

The Golden Fruits (Sarraute)
   See *Les fruits d'or*

The Golden Gate (MacLean) **13**:359, 363; **63**:266

The Golden Gate (Seth) **43**:388-94; **90**:336, 338-41, 343-50, 353-8, 361, 365,367-71

"The Golden Gift of Grey" (MacLeod) **56**:194

Golden Girls (Page) **40**:352-55

The Golden Gizmo (Thompson) **69**:383, 386-87

"Golden Gloves" (Oates) **52**:332

The Golden Harvest (Amado) **106**:86, 89

The Golden Hawk (Yerby) 7:556

The Golden Helix (Sturgeon) **39**:364

The Golden Honeycomb (Markandaya) 8:377-78

"The Golden Horseshoe" (Hammett) **10**:252

"The Golden Idol" (Kristofferson) **26**:269

The Golden Isle (Slaughter) **29**:374

"The Golden Mean" (Ammons) **108**:22

Golden Miles (Prichard) **46**:334, 338, 342-43

The Golden Notebook (Lessing) 1:173-75; 2:239-41; 3:282-90, 292; **6**:290, 292-300, 302-03; **10**:314-15; **15**:331, 334-35; **22**:280-81; **40**:314-15; **94**:252-53, 257, 260, 262, 265, 272, 277, 282-84, 286-91, 293

Golden Ophelia (Ruyslinck) **14**:471-72

The Golden Rendezvous (MacLean) **13**:361

"Golden Retriever" (Muske) **90**:308

The Golden Rose: Literature in the Making (Paustovsky) **40**:359, 368

Golden Sardine (Kaufman) **49**:203, 205

The Golden Shadow (Garfield) **12**:229-30, 235

The Golden Spur (Powell) **66**:362-64, 368, 372-73, 375-76

"Golden State" (Bidart) **33**:75

"Golden State" (Sayles) **14**:483

Golden State (Bidart) **33**:73-7, 79-81

Golden States (Cunningham) **34**:40-2

"The Golden Treasury of Knowledge" (McFadden) **48**:246

Golden Tripe (Crommelynck)
   See *Tripes d'or*

The Golden Unicorn (Whitney)   42:435
"Golden Wasp" (Transtroemer)
   See "Guldstekel"
"The Golden West" (Fuchs)   22:156
"Golden Years" (Bowie)   17:63
Goldengrove (Walsh)   35:430-33
"Goldenrod" (Oliver)   98:287
Goldfinger (Fleming)   30:137, 146, 149
The Goldfish (Anouilh)
   See *Les poissons rouges; ou, Mon père, ce
      héros*
Goldilocks (Hunter)   11:280; 31:226-27
Goldilocks (Kerr)   22:255
"The Gold-Rimmed Eyeglasses" (Bassani)   9:77
"The Golem" (Borges)   19:46
The Golem (Singer)   69:306
The Golem (Wiesel)   37:457
The Golf Omnibus (Wodehouse)   5:516
"Golgotha" (Kennedy)   42:255
"Golgotha Is a Mountain" (Bontemps)   18:65
"Goliath and David" (Graves)   45:166
Golk (Stern)   4:523; 39:235-36.
"El golpe" ("The Blow") (Neruda)   7:261
Les gommes (*The Erasers*) (Robbe-Grillet)
   1:287-90; 2:373-74; 6:465-66; 8:453;
   10:437; 14:455, 458-62; 43:360, 364, 366
"Gondwanaland" (Purdy)   50:247
"Gone" (Sandburg)   15:468; 35:358
"Gone at Last" (Simon)   17:466
"Gone Away" (Levertov)   66:239
"Gone Away Blues" (McGrath)   28:277
"Gone Clear" (Cliff)   21:65
Gone Fishin' (Mosley)   97:352
Gone in January (Abse)   29:21
"Gone in October" (Holmes)   56:143-44
*Gone in October: Last Reflections on Jack
   Kerouac* (Holmes)   56:143-44
Gone Indian (Kroetsch)   5:221; 23:273;
   57:283, 288, 294-96
"Gone Three Days" (Hood)   28:195
Gone to Ground (White)   30:449
Gone to Soldiers (Piercy)   62:372-77
"The Gong of Time" (Sandburg)   35:356
"Gonna change My Way of Thinking" (Dylan)
   77:186
"Gonna Roll the Bones" (Leiber)   25:304, 307
Gonna Take a Miracle (Nyro)   17:316-17
"Good" (Matthews)   40:324-25
Good (Taylor)   27:443-47
Good and Bad at Games (Boyd)
   See *School Ties: Good and Bad at Games,
      and Dutch Girls*
"Good and Bad Dreams" (Price)   6:423; 43:345
The Good and Faithful Servant (Orton)
   43:326, 329, 332-33
The Good Apprentice (Murdoch)   51:287-90,
   292, 296-97
Good As Gold (Heller)   11:268-69; 36:223-28,
   230-31
"The Good Author" (Kizer)   80:185
Good Behaviour (Keane)   31:233-35
Good Bones (Atwood)   84:104-05
"A Good Boy" (Sargeson)
   See "Sketch from Life"
"Good Brothers" (Cohen)   38:131
"Good Bye to All That" (Scott)   22:373
"A Good Chance" (Cook-Lynn)   93:124, 126
The Good Companions (Priestley)   2:346-47;
   34:361-66
The Good Conscience (Fuentes)
   See *Las buenas consciencias*
"Good Copy" (Rand)   79:374
"Good Country People" (O'Connor)   1:257;

2:317; 13:421; 15:408, 412; 21:255-56,
   262-64, 266, 272; 66:310; 104:106, 124,
   135, 173
"A Good Daughter" (Moravia)   7:244
"Good Day Sunshine" (Lennon and McCartney)
   35:293
A Good Day to Die (Harrison)   6:225; 33:200;
   66:153, 155, 158
The Good Doctor (Simon)   6:504; 31:399, 403;
   70:238
The Good Earth (Buck)   7:32-3; 11:70-4, 76-
   7; 18:76-80
*A Good Enough Parent: A Book on Child Rear-
   ing* (Bettelheim)   79:142
The Good European (Blackmur)   2:61
The Good Fellow (Kaufman)   38:265
"Good for Me" (Seger)   35:384
"Good Form" (O'Brien)   103:139, 143, 174
"Good Frend" (H. D.)   31:204; 73:116, 139
"Good Friday" (Clampitt)   32:114-15
"Good Friday" (Dybek)   114:75
"Good Friday" (Smith)   15:515
"Good Friday" (Watkins)   43:447
"Good Friday 1971. Riding Westward"
   (Muldoon)   72:264-65
Good Friday and Other Poems (Masefield)
   11:358; 47:227, 229
A Good Girl Is Hard to Find (Baraka)   33:59
The Good God of Manhattan (Bachmann)
   See *Der gute Gott von Manhattan*
Good Hearts (Price)   63:323-25, 327-33, 335-
   36, 339, 341
"The Good Herdsman" (Davison)   15:170
"Good Hours" (Frost)   15:248
Good Intentions (Nash)   23:319
A Good Journey (Ortiz)   45:301, 304-08, 311
"The Good Life" (Lowell)   4:304
"The Good Life" (Strand)   71:285
The Good Listener (Johnson)   7:184-85; 27:224
Good Luck in Cracked Italian (Hugo)   32:235,
   238, 242, 244-45
Good Luck, Miss Wyckoff (Inge)   8:309
"The Good Man" (Van Duyn)   116:403
A Good Man in Africa (Boyd)   28:37-42; 53:50-
   1, 53, 55-6; 70:132, 134-35, 138, 140-42
"A Good Man Is Hard to Find" (O'Connor)
   1:255, 257; 2:317; 3:366, 368; 6:381;
   10:368; 15:408, 412; 21:256, 263, 270,
   272; 66:313, 330; 104:105, 117, 128, 138,
   173, 175
A Good Man Is Hard to Find and Other Stories
   (*An Artificial Nigger*) (O'Connor)   10:367;
   13:417; 15:408; 21:256-57, 262, 266;
   104:108, 120, 137, 165, 179, 190
"Good Mirrors Are Not Cheap" (Lorde)   71:232
"Good Morning" (Codrescu)   46:103
"Good Morning" (Schuyler)   23:391
"Good Morning" (Van Doren)   6:542
Good Morning (Ozu)
   See *Ohayo*
Good Morning America (Sandburg)   15:466;
   35:345-46, 352
*Good Morning Blues: The Autobiography of
   Count Basie* (Murray)   73:242
"Good Morning, Good Morning" (Lennon and
   McCartney)   12:357-58; 35:276
Good Morning: Last Poems (Van Doren)   6:541-
   43; 10:496
Good Morning, Midnight (Rhys)   2:371-73;
   6:453-55, 457; 14:446-47, 449-51;
   19:393-94; 51:360-61, 366-70, 375
"Good Morning Revolution" (Hughes)
   108:294, 296

*Good Morning, Revolution: Uncollected So-
   cial Protest Writings* (Hughes)   5:191;
   108:318-21
The Good Mother (Miller)   44:67-76
"Good Neighbors" (Richter)   30:320
"The Good New Days" (Leiber)   25:304
"Good News" (Kuzma)   7:197
"Good News" (Voigt)   54:433
Good News (Abbey)   59:238, 242
Good News About the Earth (Clifton)   19:109;
   66:64-5, 67, 79-81, 84-6
Good News of Death and Other Poems
   (Simpson)   4:498; 7:427; 32:378
Good News: Poems (Kuzma)   7:196-97
"A Good Night" (Montague)   46:270, 274
"Good Night Mr. James" (Simak)   55:320
Good Night Sweet Ladies (Blackwood)   100:4
Good Night, Sweetheart (Tiptree)   48:394-95
"Good Night, Willie Lee, I'll See You in the
   Morning" (Walker)   103:382
Good Old James (Donovan)   35:142
The Good Parts (Horovitz)   56:155
"Good Samaritan" (O'Hara)   6:385
"The Good Samaritan" (Sargeson)   31:363
Good Samaritan, and Other Stories (O'Hara)
   6:384-85
A Good Scent from a Strange Mountain (But-
   ler)   81:121-130
A Good School (Yates)   23:480, 482
The Good Shepherd (Fleming)   37:124-25
The Good Shepherd (Forester)   35:171, 174
"The Good Shepherd: Atlanta, 1981" (Ai)
   69:9, 15
"Good Ships" (Ransom)   4:431
The Good Son (Nova)   31:298-300
The Good Spirit of Laurel Ridge (Stuart)
   11:511; 14:517
"Good Taste" (Asimov)   19:28
"The Good Tenor Man" (Hood)   28:193
The Good Terrorist (Lessing)   40:310-17;
   94:258, 286
"The Good Thing" (Byrne)   25:96
"Good Tidings for the Blooming Apple"   75:77
"Good times" (Clifton)   19:108-09; 66:66-8,
   75, 80-1, 84-5
Good Times/Bad Times (Kirkwood)   9:319
"Good Timin'" (Wilson)   12:653
"Good Vibes" (Porter)   13:451
"Good Vibrations" (Wilson)   12:642-45
"The Good Virgin, Then...by Crivelli" (Kerrigan)
   6:276
*"The Good War": An Oral History of World War
   II* (Terkel)   38:426-29
"Good Wars" (De Marinis)   54:100
Good Will (Smiley)   76:236, 238
*Good Woman: Poems and a Memoir, 1969-
   1980* (Clifton)   66:81, 84-6
"The Good Women" (Sillitoe)   57:392
The Good Word and Other Words (Sheed)
   53:336-38
Good Work (Schumacher)   80:269-70
"Goodby and Keep Cold" (Frost)   10:195
Good-By My Shadow (Stolz)   12:550, 553
"Good-Bye" (Betjeman)   6:69
"Goodbye" (Miles)   34:245
"A Goodbye" (Van Duyn)   116:408
Goodbye (Sansom)   6:484
"Goodbye and Good Luck" (Paley)   37:331,
   337
Goodbye California (MacLean)   13:364; 50:348
Goodbye, Chicken Little (Byars)   35:73
"Goodbye Christ" (Hughes)   1:147; 44:511-
   12; 108:294, 297, 320

Goodbye, Columbus (Roth)   1:292-93; 2:378-80; 3:435-38, 440; 4:451-52, 454-57, 459; 6:474-76; 9:459, 462; 15:449, 452-53, 455; 22:350; 31:334-35, 342, 346; 86:250, 252, 254

Goodbye, Columbus, and Five Short Stories (Roth)   47:364; 66:386, 389, 421

"Goodbye Cruel World" (Pink Floyd)   35:312

Goodbye Earth (Richards)   14:452, 455

"A Goodbye for Evadne Winterbottom" (Bradbury)   32:53

The Goodbye Girl (Simon)   70:237-38, 240

"Goodbye, Goldeneye" (Swenson)   61:403

"Goodbye, Goodbye, Be Always Kind and True" (Garrett)   3:191

Goodbye Harold, Good Luck (Thomas)   107:333,337

Goodbye, Howard (Linney)   51:262

The Goodbye Look (Macdonald)   2:256; 14:335-36; 41:267, 269

"Goodbye Marcus, Goodbye Rose" (Rhys)   14:446; 19:390-91; 51:370

"Goodbye Margery" (Derleth)   31:132-33

Goodbye, Mickey Mouse (Deighton)   46:128-29

"Goodbye Morbid Bear" (Stern)   100:329

"Goodbye, My Brother" (Cheever)   15:127; 64:53, 65

"Good-Bye, New York" (Morand)
   See "Adieu, New-York!"

"Goodbye Party for Miss Pushpa T. S." (Ezekiel)   61:95, 110

The Goodbye People (Gardner)   44:210

"Goodbye, Shirley Temple" (Mitchell)   98:157

"Good-bye, Son" (Lewis)   41:254

Good-bye, Son and Other Stories (Lewis)   41:253

Goodbye Spring (Seifert)
   See *Jaro sbohem*

"Goodbye, Sweetwater" (Dumas)   62:159, 162

Goodbye, Sweetwater (Dumas)   62:157, 159, 161, 163-64

Good-Bye to All That (Graves)   2:177; 39:322-28; 44:477, 479-80; 45:170-74

Goodbye to Berlin (Isherwood)   1:156; 9:291, 293; 11:298-300; 14:283, 286; 44:396-97, 400, 402-04

"Goodbye to Goodbye" (Dixon)   52:100

"Goodbye to London" (MacNeice)   53:239

"Goodbye to the Flowerclock" (Haines)   58:217

"Goodbye to the Garden" (Fuller)   62:185

"Good-bye to the Mezzogiorno" (Auden)   6:20

Goodbye to the Summer (Carroll)   10:97-8

Goodbye, Wisconsin (Wescott)   13:591-92

Goodbye without Leaving (Colwin)   84:143-47, 150-52

The Goodbyes (Onetti)
   See *Los adioses*

Goodfellas (Scorsese)   89:254-59, 261-63, 265, 267

A Goodly Fellowship (Chase)   2:101

A Goodly Heritage (Chase)   2:100

"Goodman Jacksin and the Angel" (Barker)   8:46; 48:15, 24

"Goodness and Mercy" (Munro)   95:310, 314

"The Goodnight" (Simpson)   7:428

"Goodnight" (Smith)   25:420; 44:440

"Goodnight Ladies" (Reed)   21:304-05

"Goodnight, Old Daisy" (Wain)   46:415

"Goodnight Saigon" (Joel)   26:222-23

"Goodnight Sweetheart" (Purdy)   28:378

"Goodnight Tonight" (McCartney)   35:287-89

Goodnight Willie Lee, I'll See You in the Morning (Walker)   19:452; 58:405; 103:357, 371

"Goodwill to Men" (Gellhorn)   60:179-81

"Goodwood Comes Back" (Warren)   39:260

Goopy gyne bagha byne (Ray)
   See *Goupi gyne bagha*

Goose and Tomtom (Rabe)   33:342-43, 346

"The Goose Fish" (Nemerov)   36:305

"Goose Moon" (Kinsella)   27:236

The Goose on the Grave (Hawkes)   2:183, 185; 3:221, 223; 4:212-13; 7:141; 15:270, 273; 27:190; 49:161, 164

Goosefoot (McGinley)   41:282-84, 286

The Goose-Step: A Study of American Education (Sinclair)   15:499; 63:346-47

The Goosesteppers (Alegria)
   See *El Paso de los Gansos*

Gor Saga (Duffy)   37:116

"Gorboduc" (Ashbery)   77:64, 68

"Gorbunov and Gorchakov" (Brodsky)   4:78; 36:81; 50:122, 125; 100:51

Gord's Gold (Lightfoot)   26:281

Gore and Igor (Levin)   7:206

"The Gorge" (Belitt)   22:50

A Gorgeous Bird like Me (*Such a Gorgeous Kid Like Me*) (Truffaut)   20:393; 101:379-84, 396, 410

The Gorgon and Other Beastly Tales (Lee)   46:232

"The Gorilla Girl" (Motion)   47:292

"Gorilla, My Love" (Bambara)   88:3, 8, 12, 17, 20-1, 39, 42, 46

Gorilla, My Love (Bambara)   19:32; 88:3, 11-12, 18-20, 22, 27-28, 41-42, 49

Gorilla Queen (Tavel)   6:529

"Gorillas" (Ondaatje)   51:310

Le gorille roi (Simenon)   47:374

Gorky (Tesich)   40:419-21

Gorky Park (Potter)   86:346

Gorky Park (Smith)   25:412-15

The Gorky Poems (Rothenberg)   6:477; 57:376

Gormenghast (Peake)   54:366-68, 370-72, 374-75, 377-78

The Gormenghast Trilogy (Peake)   7:302

"Gornyy rodnichok" (Voznesensky)   57:417

Gosforth's Fête (Ayckbourn)   33:41

The Goshawk (White)   30:442-43, 449

"Goshawk, Antelope" (Smith)   22:389

Goshawk, Antelope (Smith)   22:387-90; 42:345-49, 352-53, 357

"Gospel" (Dove)   50:155; 81:144

"Gospel" (Jones)   76:65-6

"Gospel" (Pinero)   55:317

The Gospel according to Chegem (Iskander)
   See *Sandro iz Chegema*

The Gospel according to Joe (Gurney)   32:217

"The Gospel according to Mark" (Borges)   10:66; 83:193

The Gospel according to St. Matthew (Pasolini)
   See *Il vangelo secondo Matteo*

The Gospel According to Steiner (Tarkovsky)   75:399

"Gospel Birds and Other Stories of Lake Wobegon" (Keillor)   115:296

The Gospel Singer (Crews)   6:117-18; 23:131, 134, 138; 49:68-73, 77

The Goss Women (Cassill)   4:95; 23:108-09

"The Gossamers" (Tomlinson)   4:545

Gossip (Walker)
   See *The Power Plays*

Gossip from the Forest (Keneally)   8:318-19; 10:298; 14:303; 19:246; 43:230, 233,

236; 117:215, 224-25, 231-35

"Got to Be Free" (Davies)   21:92

"Got to Begin Again" (Joel)   26:218

"Got to Have Will Power" (Guillen)
   See "Hay que tené boluntá"

"The Gothic Dusk" (Prokosch)   48:309

Gothic Romance (Carrere)
   See *Bravoure*

Gothic Tales (Dinesen)   95:49

"Gotta Broken Heart Again" (Prince)   35:323-24

"Gotta Get to Boston" (Guthrie)   35:183

"Gotta Serve Somebody" (Dylan)   77:186, 190

Goupi gyne bagha (*Goopy gyne bagha byne*) (Ray)   16:492

"The Gourd Dancer" (Momaday)   85:268

The Gourd Dancer (Momaday)   19:318; 85:256, 262-67, 269-70, 281

La Goutte d'or (*The Golden Droplet*) (Tournier)   95:374-75, 377, 382

Government (Traven)   8:520

"The Government Bears" (Bass)   79:6, 12

The Government of Egypt (Forster)   77:238

The Government of the Tongue: Selected Prose, 1978-1987 (Heaney)   74:183-84, 189-90; 91:223-24

"Governmentality" (Foucault)   69:179

"Governor" (Guillen)   79:229

"The Governor's Ball" (Carlson)   54:37

The Governor's Bridge Is Closed (Hood)   28:192

The Goy (Harris)   19:201-02, 204

"Goya's 'Two Old People Eating Soup'" (Van Duyn)   116:410

Gozos de la vista (Alonso)   14:17, 23

Graal Flibuste (Pinget)   7:305; 13:442

The Grabber (Ehrenburg)
   See *Rvach*

"Grabschriften in die Luft geschrieben" ("Epigraphs Written on Air") (Sachs)   98:325, 327, 354

"Grace" (Arghezi)   80:10

"The Grace" (Creeley)   4:118

"Grace" (Harjo)   83:271-72

"Grace" (Wilbur)   53:397, 409

"Grace" (Wright)   53:429

Grace (Gee)   57:223-25

La grâce (Marcel)   15:360, 363

"Grace Abounding" (Ammons)   25:46; 57:52; 108:57

Grace Abounding (Howard)   46:185-87

Grace after Meat (Ransom)   4:436

"Grace and Faigel" (Levine)   54:297

"Grace at World's End" (Buckley)   57:131

Grace before Ploughing (Masefield)   11:357

"Grace before Song" (Pound)   48:288

The Grace Divorce (Swinnerton)   31:427

"Grace Notes" (Smith)   64:397

Grace Notes (Dove)   81:140, 147, 149-51

"The Graceless Years" (Lerman)   9:328

"Grace's House" (Merton)   83:392-93

Gracias Haus (Merton)   83:393

"Gracie" (Fisher)   87:131

"A Gracious Rain" (Tilghman)   65:106, 108-09, 111-12

"Grackles, Goodbye" (Warren)   39:272

Gradations of Grandeur (Gustafson)   36:221

"Gradual of the Northern Summer" (Davidson)   2:113

The Graduate (Webb)   7:514-16

The Graduate (Willingham)   5:512

"Graduate School" (Lerman)   9:328

The Graduate Wife (Raphael)   2:367

"Graduation" (Dubus)   36:144-45

"Graduation Nite" (Shange)   25:402
Graf Öderland (Count Öderland) (Frisch)
    3:167; 9:217; 14:182-83; 44:181, 194,
    196-97, 199-200
"Graffiti" (Cortazar)   33:130, 132
"Graffiti" (Nemerov)   36:309
Graffiti (Damas)   84:156, 159-60, 179
"Graffiti from the Gare Saint-Manqué" (Hacker)
    72:182-84, 190
"Grafton Street" (Behan)   79:38
Graham Greene on Film: Collected Film Criti-
    cism, 1935-1940 (Greene)
    See The Pleasure-Dome: The Collected Film
    Criticism, 1935-40
"Grail" (Ellison)   42:131
"The Grail Mass" (Jones)   42:242
Le grain de la voix: Entretiens 1962-1980 (The
    Grain of the Voice: Interviews, 1962-1980)
    (Barthes)   83:88-90
"Grain de sel" (Damas)   84:179
"The Grain Kings" (Roberts)   14:464
A Grain of Mustard Seed (Sarton)   49:314,
    91:244
"A Grain of Rice" (Scott)   22:376
The Grain of the Voice: Interviews, 1962-1980
    (Barthes)
    See Le grain de la voix: Entretiens 1962-
    1980
A Grain of Wheat (Ngugi wa Thiong'o)   3:358;
    7:263-66; 36:310, 312-17, 321, 323
La graine (Gascar)   11:222
Grains et issues (Seeds and Bran) (Tzara)
    47:389-91
"Graiul noptii" ("The Voice of Night")
    (Arghezi)   80:2
A Grammar of Metaphor (Brooke-Rose)
    40:103
A Grammar of Motives (Burke)   24:124, 127-
    28, 134
The Grammar of the Real: Selected Prose,
    1959-1974 (McAuley)   45:253
The Grammelot of Zanni (Fo)   109:102
Gran Casino (Bunuel)   16:149; 80:21
El gran serafin (Bioy Casares)   13:84
El gran zoo (Patria o muerte! The Great Zoo,
    and Other Poems by Nicolás Guillén)
    (Guillen)   48:156, 158-59; 79:229
"Granate" (Guillen)   79:240
Grand Canary (Cronin)   32:131-32
Le grand cerémonial (The Grand Ceremony;
    The Great Ceremony) (Arrabal)   9:33;
    18:20; 58:9-10, 17-18
The Grand Ceremony (Arrabal)
    See Le grand cerémonial
"Grand Coulee Dam" (Guthrie)   35:193
"The Grand Dance" (MacEwen)   55:165
The Grand Design (Dos Passos)   4:133; 11:156;
    15:187; 34:420
Le grand écart (Cocteau)   15:132; 43:102-03
"Grand Entrance" (Dybek)   114:67
"Grand Galop" (Ashbery)   13:34; 15:28; 41:40;
    77:60
"Grand Illusion" (Dubie)   36:135
The Grand Illusion (Renoir)
    See La grande illusion
Grand Manoeuvres (Ellis)   7:93-5
Grand National (Tunis)   12:599
"Grand Prairie: So Far from Poland" (Moure)
    88:217
The Grand Tarot (Ludlam)   46:239; 50:346
Le grand théâtre (Giono)   11:230
The Grand Tour (Rice)   49:300-01
Le grand troupeau (Giono)   4:184, 186

"The Grand View" (Abse)   7:1; 29:15
The Grand Wazoo (Zappa)   17:590
La grande Claudine (Hebert)   4:219; 13:267
La grande et la petite manoeuvre (The Maneu-
    ver) (Adamov)   25:12, 14, 17-19
La grande gaieté (Great Fun) (Aragon)   3:15;
    22:37, 41
La grande illusion (The Grand Illusion)
    (Renoir)   20:287-90, 292-93, 295, 297,
    300, 302-03, 307-08
"The Grande Malade" ("The Little Girl Con-
    tinues") (Barnes)   3:37; 29:27
"La grande mélancolie d'une avenue" (Soupault)
    68:404
Il grande ritratto (Larger than Life) (Buzzati)
    36:86-91, 96-7
Les grandes épreuves de l'esprit (The Great
    Ordeals of the Mind) (Michaux)   8:392;
    19:312
Les grandes manoeuvres (Clair)   20:64
"The Grandfather" (Guillen)
    See "El abuelo"
"Grandfather" (Mahon)   27:290
"The Grandfather" (Soto)   80:298, 301
"Grandfather and Grandson" (Singer)   3:457;
    6:511; 38:408
"The Grandfather Poem" (Dobyns)   37:77
"The Grandfathers" (Justice)   102:277, 282-
    83
The Grandfathers (Richter)   30:318-19, 321,
    325
"A Grandfather's Last Letter" (Dubie)   36:142
"Grandma" (Adcock)   41:14
"Grandma's Man" (Welch)   14:559
"Grandmother" (Allen)   84:6, 30
"Grandmother" (McIlvanney)   42:282
"grandmother" (Young Bear)   94:363, 371
"Grandmother Dying" (Merwin)   45:277
"Grandmother in the Garden" (Gluck)   22:173
"Grandmother Watching at Her Window"
    (Merwin)   88:205
"The Grandmothers" (Rothenberg)   57:373
The Grandmothers: A Family Portrait
    (Wescott)   13:590-92
Grandmothers of the Light: A Medicine Woman's
    Sourcebook (Allen)   84:45-6
"Grandparents: Can They Love Too Much?"
    (Coles)   108:194
"Grand-père n'avait peur de rien ni de personne"
    (Carrier)   78:63
Les grands chemins (Giono)   4:186, 188
Les grands soleils (The Flowering Suns)
    (Ferron)   94:110, 114, 120, 124-25
"The Grange" (Smith)   25:419
"La grange d'Emilien" (Theriault)   79:408
"Granite and Cypress" (Jeffers)   54:233, 244
"Granite and Steel" (Moore)   47:263
Granite Lady (Schaeffer)   6:489; 11:491
The Granite Pail: The Selected Poems of Lorine
    Niedecker (Niedecker)   42:296-99
"Granma" (Sargeson)   31:362
Granny (Poliakoff)   38:379
Granny Reardun (Garner)   17:149-50
Grant Moves South (Catton)   35:88-9
"Grantchester Meadows" (Pink Floyd)   35:305
"Grantchester Meadows" (Plath)   17:350
"Grape Sherbet" (Dove)   81:135, 138
"The Grapes" (Hecht)   19:207-10
The Grapes and the Wind (Neruda)
    See Las uvas y el viento
The Grapes of Paradise: Four Short Novels
    (Bates)
    See An Aspidistra in Babylon: Four Novellas

The Grapes of Wrath (Ford)   16:304, 313-14
The Grapes of Wrath (Steinbeck)   1:324-26;
    5:405-08; 9:512-20; 13:529-34; 21:367-
    69, 371-74, 376, 381-84, 386, 390-91;
    34:404-05, 407-15; 45:369-71, 373-77,
    382-83; 59:315-33, 335-37, 339-54;
    75:341, 343, 350, 357
"Grapette" (Barthelme)   117:14, 16, 18
"The Graph" (Ciardi)   10:106; 44:381
"Grasp the Sparrow's Tail" (Wah)   44:326
"The Grass" (Bowering)   47:20
"Grass" (Corn)   33:117, 120
"Grass" (Sandburg)   4:463; 10:448-49
The Grass (Simon)
    See L'herbe
The Grass Crown (McCullough)   107:155, 163-
    66
The Grass Dancer (Power)   91:67-71
The Grass Dies (Dowell)
    See One of the Children Is Crying
"Grass Fires" (Lowell)   37:238
The Grass Harp (Capote)   1:55; 8:133; 13:134-
    35, 137, 139; 19:80-1, 86-7; 34:320-22;
    38:78-9, 84, 87; 58:86
The Grass Is Singing (Lessing)   1:173; 3:283,
    290-91; 6:292, 294, 298, 303-04; 22:280;
    40:310, 315; 94:253, 255-56, 266-67,
    277, 280-81, 284-86
A Grass Rope (Mayne)   12:387-89, 392, 398,
    400, 407
"The Grass Still Grows, the River Still Flows"
    (Dorris)   109:310
"The Grass Was Gone for Miles around Where
    Lil's White Arse Had Bumped the Ground"
    (Cummings)   68:29
"The Grass Widows" (Trevor)   116:333, 338,
    375
Grasse (Delbanco)   6:130
"La grasse matinée" (Prevert)   15:439
"Grasse: The Olive Trees" (Wilbur)   53:413
"The Grassfire Stanzas" (Murray)   40:343
"Grasshoppers" (Jolley)   46:213
Grateful to Life and Death (Narayan)
    See The English Teacher
"Gratified Desires" (Davison)   28:103
"Gratitude" (Gluck)   7:120
"Gratitude, Need, and Gladness" (Davie)   31:124
"The Grauballe Man" (Heaney)   14:242;
    25:242-43, 250-51; 74:158
"The Grave" (Gardner)   18:178
"A Grave" (Moore)   4:362; 19:340; 47:267
"The Grave" (Porter)   7:315-16, 320; 10:397;
    15:430
"The Grave Dwellers" (Oates)   3:359
"The Grave of Lost Stories" (Vollmann)
    89:283, 302
"Grave of Signor Casanova" (Seifert)   34:261
"The Grave of the Famous Poet" (Atwood)
    25:62
"The Grave of the Right Hand" (Wright)   6:580
The Grave of the Right Hand (Wright)   6:579-
    81; 13:612, 614
"The Grave Rubbings" (Lieberman)   36:262
"A Grave Unvisited" (Thomas)   48:375
Grave Witness (Levi)   41:250
Gravedigger (Hansen)   38:239
"Grave-Dirt" (Musgrave)   13:401
Grave-Dirt and Selected Strawberries
    (Musgrave)   54:341; 13:400-01
"Gravel" (Moss)   45:286-87
"The Gravel Ponds" (Levi)   41:242-43
The Gravel Ponds (Levi)   41:242-43, 246
"Gravelly Run" (Ammons)   8:16; 9:30; 108:20

"The Gravel-Pit Field" (Gascoyne)   45:147, 153-54, 157-59

Graven Images (Thomas)   107:342-45, 351

Graves and Resurrections (Scannell)   49:332

"Graveyard Day" (Mason)   28:271

"The Graveyard Heart" (Zelazny)   21:468

"Graveyard in Norfolk" (Warner)   19:460-61

"The Graveyard Shift" (King)   113:336

"Gravity" (Beattie)   40:64; 63:19

"Gravity" (Montague)   46:277

Gravity's Rainbow (Pynchon)   2:354-58; 3:412-20; 6:432-39; 9:443-47; 11:452, 454-55; 18:430-41; 33:330-40; 62:432, 435-40, 443, 445-48, 451, 453; 72:332, 335-36, 340

"The Gray Heron" (Kinnell)   29:285

"Gray Matter" (King)   26:237

Gray Soldiers (Smith)   42:354

Gray's Anatomy (Gray)   112:127, 132-36

The Graywolf Annual Five: Multi-Cultural Literacy   70:363

"Grazing Locomotives" (MacLeish)   68:290

Grease (Jacobs and Casey)   12:292-95

"Greaseball" (McFadden)   48:258

"Greasy Lake" (Boyle)   90:61-3

Greasy Lake, & Other Stories (Boyle)   90:44-6, 49, 57

The Great American Fourth of July Parade: A Verse Play for Radio (MacLeish)   14:338

The Great American Jackpot (Gold)   4:192; 14:208; 42:192

The Great American Novel (Roth)   3:436-40; 4:457, 459; 6:474-75; 9:461; 15:449, 452; 22:352-53; 31:334-35; 47:363

The Great American Novel (Williams)   2:468-69; 5:509; 9:572; 42:454

"The Great American Novel: Winter, 1927" (Dubie)   36:132

The Great Auk (Eckert)   17:103-05

"The Great Automatic Grammatisator" (Dahl)   79:175, 183

"The Great Bear Cult" (Gray)   41:181, 183

"The Great Blackberry Pick" (Pearce)   21:289

"The Great Blue Heron" (Kizer)   80:171-72, 181-82

The Great Canadian Sonnet (McFadden)   48:249

"The Great Carbuncle" (Plath)   111:202

The Great Ceremony (Arrabal)
   See *Le grand cerémonial*

The Great Chain of Life (Krutch)   24:290

"The Great Chinese Dragon" (Ferlinghetti)   111:64

Great Circle (Aiken)   5:9; 10:3; 52:31

Great Climate (Wilding)   73:404

The Great Cloak (Montague)   13:392; 46:272-73, 275, 277, 279

The Great Code: The Bible and Literature (Frye)   24:231; 70:271-73, 275-77

"The Great Dam Disaster, a Ballad" (Starbuck)   53:354

"A Great Day" (Sargeson)   31:365, 370

"A Great Day for a Bananafish" (Salinger)
   See "A Perfect Day for Bananafish"

"Great Days" (Barthelme)   46:41

Great Days (Barthelme)   13:59-64; 23:51; 46:35, 37-8, 41; 59:247; 115:64

The Great Days (Dos Passos)   4:132, 135; 15:186; 25:140-41, 145-46; 34:422

"The Great Deception" (Morrison)   21:234-35

The Great Depression, 1929 to 1939 (Berton)   104:56-8

The Great Dethriffe (Bryan)   29:101-02

The Great Dictator (Chaplin)   16:192, 195-96, 201, 203-04

"The Great Difference" (Singh)   11:505

The Great Divorce (Lewis)   3:299; 27:261, 266

The Great Divorce (Martin)   89:135, 137-38

"The Great Duck" (Middleton)   13:389

"The Great Elegy for John Donne" ("Big Elegy"; "Elegy for John Donne") (Brodsky)   50:121, 123, 128

The Great Escape (Clavell)   87:18

The Great Exhibition (Hare)   29:213-14

"Great Expectations" (Ritter)   52:356

Great Expectations (Acker)   45:14-17, 19-20; 111:3, 5-6, 8-9, 21, 25, 31-5, 41

The Great Fake Book (Bourjaily)   62:106-08

The Great Fear: The Anti-Communist Purge under Truman and Eisenhower (Caute)   29:119-20

"Great Fennville Swamp" (Crase)   58:159, 162-63, 166

"The Great Feud" (Pratt)   19:377-78, 382, 385

"The Great Fillmore Street Buffalo Drive" (Momaday)   85:281

"The Great Fire" (Bradbury)   42:32

The Great Fire of London (Ackroyd)   52:2-4, 6-7, 15-16

The Great Fortune (Manning)   19:300-01

Great Fun (Aragon)
   See *La grande gaieté*

The Great Game (Vesaas)
   See *Det store spelet*

"A Great Generation" (Kunene)   85:166

"The Great Genius" (Berrigan)   37:44

"The Great Gig in the Sky" (Pink Floyd)   35:306

The Great Gilly Hopkins (Paterson)   12:486-87; 30:283, 285, 287

"The Great Godalmighty Bird" (Dowell)   60:107, 109

"A Great God's Angel Standing" (Kiely)   23:260; 43:239

Great Goodness of Life (A Coon Show) (Baraka)   115:35

"The Great, Grand, Soap-Water Kick" (Gardam)   43:169

Great Granny Webster (Blackwood)   100:2, 9, 14, 19

"The Great Horned Owl" (Piercy)   27:379

"The Great Horned Owl" (Simic)   49:336

"Great House" (Walcott)
   See "Ruins of a Great House"

"The Great Hug" (Barthelme)   8:52

The Great Hunger (Kavanagh)   22:234-35, 237-38, 242

Great Ideas in Physics (Lightman)   81:78

Great Ideas of Science (Asimov)   26:37

The Great Indian Novel (Tharoor)   70:103-12

"Great Infirmities" (Simic)   22:382; 49:338; 68:369

Great Jones Street (DeLillo)   54:80-2; 8:172; 10:134-35; 13:175-76, 178-79; 27:77-9; 39:117, 119, 123, 125; 76:180, 182, 185

The Great Letter E (Schor)   65:95-9

Great Lion of God (Caldwell)   2:95; 39:302-03

The Great Lost Kinks Album (Davies)   21:94-5

"The Great Man" (Motion)   47:288, 294

"The Great Mountains" (Steinbeck)   9:515-16

"The Great Music Robbery" (Baraka)   115:12

"Great Nights Returning" (Watkins)   43:447, 454

The Great Occasion (Colegate)   36:108-09, 113-14

The Great O'Neill (O'Faolain)   14:402, 404; 70:321

The Great Ordeals of the Mind (Michaux)
   See *Les grandes épreuves de l'esprit*

"The Great Palace of Versailles" (Dove)   50:154; 81:139

The Great Passage
   See *În marea trecere*

"Great Poets Die in Steaming Pots of Shit" (Bukowski)   41:68, 75; 108:85

"Great Praises" (Eberhart)   56:84, 87

The Great Quillow (Thurber)   5:430, 438, 442; 25:437

The Great Railway Bazaar: By Train through Asia (Theroux)   8:512-13; 15:533-35; 28:425; 46:402

"The Great Rememberer" (Holmes)   56:143-44

Great River: The Rio Grande in North American History (Horgan)   9:279; 53:178

"The Great Rubble Lady Speaks" (Grass)   32:200

The Great Santini (Conroy)   30:77-8, 80; 74:44-52

The Great Shark Hunt: Strange Tales from a Strange Time (Thompson)   17:513-15; 40:426-27, 431; 104:347

The Great Sinner (Isherwood)   44:397

Great Sky River (Benford)   52:76-7

"The Great Slow Kings" (Zelazny)   21:465-66

"The Great Society" (Bly)   10:55

Great Son (Ferber)   93:176-77, 179, 187-88, 190

"The Great Suburban Showdown" (Joel)   26:214, 217-18

"The Great Switcheroo" (Dahl)   6:121

The Great Tradition (Leavis)   24:294, 297-98, 300, 303, 308, 313

The Great Train Robbery (Crichton)   6:119; 54:68-71, 76; 90:69, 71

"Great Tranquillity" (Amichai)   57:38

Great Tranquillity: Questions and Answers (Amichai)   57:37-8; 116:97-8

The Great Transfer (Yanovsky)   18:551-52

"Great Uncle Crow" (Bates)   46:59-60, 67

"Great Unexpectations" (Atwood)   84:92

The Great Victorian Collection (Moore)   5:297-98; 7:236-39; 8:394; 19:331-33; 32:309, 311, 313-14; 90:250, 255-6, 263, 265, 269, 272, 289

The Great Waldo Pepper (Hill)   26:203-05, 207-08, 211

"The Great War" (Scannell)   49:326

The Great War and Modern Memory (Fussell)   74:120-23, 125, 128, 133-34, 137, 139-40, 143-44

"The Great Wave" (Levertov)   28:243

The Great Wave, and Other Stories (Lavin)   18:302, 307

The Great White Hope (Sackler)   14:478-80

The Great Winter (Kadare)   52:262

The Great World (Malouf)   86:207

The Great World and Timothy Colt (Auchincloss)   4:28; 9:54; 45:26-7, 29, 37

Great World Circus (Kotzwinkle)   35:257

The Greater Apollo (FitzGerald)   19:176, 181

"The Greater Festival of Masks" (Ligotti)   44:53-4

"The Greater Music" (Weiss)   14:556

"The Greater Whiteness" (Swenson)   4:533

The Greatest Battle (Glasser)   37:133

The Greatest Crime (Wilson)   32:449

Greatest Hits Volume Two (Dylan) 77:172
"The Greatest Living Patagonian" (Shapiro)
    8:486
"The Greatest Man in the World" (Thurber)
    11:533
"The Greatest People in the World" (Bates)
    46:57
"The Greatest Poet Writing in English Today"
    (Bogan) 93:105
"El Greco" (Peake) 54:369
"Greece" (Ekeloef) 27:119
"Greed" (Williams) 56:425
Greed (Wakoski) 7:506
"Greed and Aggression" (Olds) 39:193; 85:292,
    297
"Greed Park" (Wiggins) 57:434
Greed, Part 9 (Wakoski) 4:573; 7:504
Greed, Parts 8, 9, 11 (Wakoski) 4:573
Greed, Parts 5-7 (Wakoski) 4:572
"The Greed to Be Fulfilled" (Wakoski) 40:457
Greek (Berkoff) 56:16-17, 19-20
The Greek (Nova) 7:267
The Greek Coffin Mystery (Queen) 3:421;
    11:460-61
Greek Fire (Graham) 23:192
The Greek Islands (Durrell) 13:188-89
Greek Man Seeks Greek Maiden (Duerrenmatt)
    102:59
The Greek Myths (Graves) 1:128; 6:211;
    11:255, 257
"Greek Portrait" (Milosz) 56:237
"The Greek Pothole" (Howard) 47:171
The Greek Treasure (Stone) 7:471
The Greeks (Asimov) 76:312
"Green: An Epistle" (Hecht) 13:269
"Green Atom Number Five" (Donoso) 8:179-
    80; 32:160
The Green Brain (Herbert) 23:221, 226;
    44:393-94
"Green Breeks" (Dunn) 40:169
"Green Candles" (Kinsella) 43:253
Green Cars Go East (Carroll) 10:98
"Green Categories" (Thomas) 6:534
Green Centuries (Gordon) 6:203-06; 29:185,
    189; 83:230, 233-34, 242-43, 251-54,
    258-59, 261
"The Green Chapel" (Mathias) 45:238
The Green Child (Read) 4:438, 440-44
The Green Cow (O'Casey) 88:260
"Green Days in Brunei" (Sterling) 72:372
"Green Earrings" (Becker and Fagen) 26:83
Green Eyes (Shepard) 34:108-10
"Green Fingers" (Fuller) 62:185
"Green Flows the River of Lethe-O" (Sitwell)
    67:317
The Green Fool (Kavanagh) 22:234, 242
The Green Gene (Dickinson) 35:131, 133-34
The Green Girl (Williamson) 29:454
Green Grass, Blue Sky, White House (Morris)
    7:247
Green Grass, Running Water (King) 89:91-7,
    99-101
"The Green Grave and the Black Grave" (Lavin)
    18:302
Green, Green My Valley Now (Llewellyn) 7:207
"Green Hell" (Boyle) 36:56-7
The Green Hills of Africa (Hemingway) 1:141;
    3:234, 239, 241; 6:226, 228; 8:283-84;
    10:267; 13:281; 19:219; 34:477-78;
    39:430, 433; 41:198, 203; 80:101, 140,
    143
"The Green Hills of Earth" (Heinlein) 55:301-
    02

The Green House (Vargas Llosa)
    See *La casa verde*
"Green Lampshade" (Simic) 22:383
"The Green Lanes" (Kiely) 23:260
"Green Lantern's Solo" (Baraka) 5:45
"Green Light" (Fearing) 51:117, 119, 122
"Green Magic" (Vance) 35:427
The Green Man (Amis) 2:8-9; 3:9; 5:22; 8:12;
    13:12-13; 40:42-3
The Green Man (Young) 5:524
The Green Mare (Ayme)
    See *La jument verte*
"Green Memory" (Hughes) 35:222
The Green Millennium (Leiber) 25:301, 303
"Green Mountain, Black Mountain"
    (Stevenson) 33:382-83
The Green Pastures (Connelly) 7:55
Green Pitcher (Livesay) 15:339, 341; 79:332,
    340
"A Green Place" (Smith) 6:513
The Green Pope (Asturias) 3:18; 8:27-8
"Green Rain" (Livesay) 79:353
The Green Ripper (MacDonald) 44:408
The Green Room (Truffaut)
    See *La chambre verte*
"The Green Shepherd" (Simpson) 7:426
Green Shoots (Morand)
    See *Tendres stocks*
"Green Song" (Sitwell) 2:402; 67:320, 324
Green Song (Sitwell) 67:317
"Green Stain" (MacCaig) 36:284
"Green Stakes for the Garden" (Thomas)
    13:540
"The Green Step" (Koch) 44:248
Green Street (Arundel) 17:12, 17
"Green Thursday" (Peterkin) 31:308
Green Thursday (Peterkin) 31:301, 303, 306-
    08, 310-11
"The Green Torso" (Warner) 7:512
"The Green Twig and the Black Trunk" (Rahv)
    24:359
The Green Wall (Wright) 3:540-43; 5:519;
    10:542, 545; 28:461, 468, 470
Green Water, Green Sky (Gallant) 18:171
"Green Water Tower" (Merwin) 45:276
The Green Wave (Rukeyser) 6:478; 27:408,
    410
Green with Beasts (Merwin) 1:213; 2:276;
    5:285; 8:389; 13:384; 45:268-70, 276;
    88:205-06
"The Green Woods of Unrest" (Graves) 45:169
Green World (Waddington) 28:436, 438-39
"Green World One" (Waddington) 28:438-39
The Green Years (Cronin) 32:136, 139
"The Greenest Island" (Theroux) 28:425
The Greengage Summer (Godden) 53:158,
    163
A Greenish Man (Wilson) 33:464
The Greenlanders (Smiley) 53:349-51; 76:235,
    237-38
"Greenleaf" (O'Connor) 1:257; 15:412-13;
    21:267, 269, 271, 276; 104:103, 109, 115,
    124, 135-36, 154, 166, 173, 179-80, 182-
    84, 191-92, 195
"Greenstone" (Ashton-Warner) 19:22
"The Greenstone Patu" (Ihimaera) 46:201
Greenvoe (Brown) 5:77; 48:53-4, 57-8, 60;
    100:80-1, 83, 86
"Greenwich Time" (Beattie) 63:3, 8
"Greenwich Village: A Memory" (Dunn)
    36:154-55
"Greenwich Village Saturday Night" (Feldman)
    7:102

Greetings (De Palma) 20:72-5, 78
Greetings from Ashbury Park, NJ (Springsteen)
    17:477-78, 480, 484, 486-87
"Greggery Peccary" (Zappa) 17:592
"Grenada Revisited: An Interim Report" (Lorde)
    71:245
Grendel (Gardner) 2:151-53; 3:184, 187; 5:131,
    133-35; 7:112-15; 8:233-34, 236-238;
    10:218-22; 18:173-183; 28:162-63, 166-
    67
Grenelle (Holland) 21:150
Ein grenzloser Nachmittag (Walser) 27:462
"Ein Grenzfall" (Lenz) 27:252
The Grey Among the Green (Fuller) 62:206
"The Grey and the Green" (Fuller) 62:206
"The Grey Boy" (Raine) 103:190
Grey Eminence (Huxley) 1:150; 3:253; 4:240,
    243; 5:193; 8:303
Grey Gardens (Maysles and Maysles) 16:444
"Grey Heat" (Hamburger) 5:159
"The Grey Horse" (Prichard) 46:332-33, 345
Grey Is the Color of Hope (Ratushinskaya)
    54:382-83, 386-87
"Grey John" (Lane) 25:285
"The Grey Land" (Stevenson) 33:380
"The Grey Ones" (Priestley) 2:347
Greybeard (Aldiss) 14:12
"Greyday" (Angelou) 77:29
"The Grey-Eyed King" (Akhmatova) 25:25
"Greyhound for Breakfast" (Kelman) 58:299-
    303
Greyhound for Breakfast, and Other Stories
    (Kelman) 58:297-302; 86:189
"Greyhound People" (Adams) 46:16
"Greyhounding" (Kenny) 87:247
*Greystoke: The Legend of Tarzan, Lord of the
    Apes* (Towne) 87:369-70, 374
The Grid of Language (Celan)
    See *Sprachgitter*
Il grido (*The Outcry*) (Antonioni) 20:20, 22,
    25
Un grido e paesaggi (Ungaretti) 7:483; 11:556
Grieche sucht Griechin (Duerrenmatt) 102:62
Grieche sucht Griechin (*Once a Greek...*)
    (Durrenmatt) 1:81; 4:140; 8:195-96;
    43:120-21, 128
"Grief" (Dobyns) 37:76
"Grief" (Muldoon) 72:267, 269
The Grief (Ungaretti)
    See *Il dolore*
Grief and Stars (Ekelof) 27:110
"The Grief of Men" (Bly) 38:57-8
"Griefs of the Sea" (Watkins) 43:441, 447
"Grieg on a Stolen Piano" (Mphahlele) 25:339
Grierson's Raid (Brown) 47:35, 37
"Grieve For the Dear Departed" (Moore)
    90:277-8
Griever: An American Monkey King in China
    (Vizenor) 103:300, 309-12, 328-29, 332-
    33, 340
"Griff" (Clarke) 53:89, 91
Griffin's Way (Yerby) 7:557
"Griffon" (Dobyns) 37:77
Griffon (Dobyns) 37:76-8
The Grifters (Thompson) 69:385
The Grim Reaper (Bertolucci)
    See *La commare secca*
The Grim Reaper (Bertolucci)
    See *La commare secca*
"Grimoire" (Dobyns) 37:76-7
Grimus (Rushdie) 23:364; 55:216, 218
Grindegard: Morgonen (Vesaas)
    See *The Farm at Grinde*

Grinde-kveld; eller, Den gode engelen (Evening at Grinde) (Vesaas) **48**:411

Grindekveld; eller, Den gode engelen (Vesaas) **48**:405, 411

El gringo viejo (The Old Gringo) (Fuentes) **41**:172-75; **60**:155-60, 165, 170; **113**:239-42, 251, 265, 267-68

"The Grip of the Geraghty's" (O'Connor) **23**:330

"Gristmill" (Komunyakaa) **94**:241

"Gritty" (Ewart) **46**:152

"Grizzly Cowboys" (Bass) **79**:17

The Groaning Board (Addams) **30**:15

Die Große Wut de Philipp Hotz (Frisch) **14**:182-83

"Groom" (Dybek) **114**:67

"Groping" (Thomas) **48**:382

Groping for Words **61**:409-10

"Gros Islet" (Walcott) **67**:360; **76**:299

"Le Gros Sang" (Tchicaya) **101**:349

Gros-câlin (Gary) **25**:188

Gross und Klein (Big and Little) (Strauss) **22**:408

La grosse femme d'à côté est enciente (The Fat Woman Next Door Is Pregnant) (Tremblay) **29**:419, 423-25, 427; **102**:370, 373-75, 377, 379

"La grosse fifi" (Rhys) **51**:355

"Grosse Landschaft bei Wien" (Bachmann) **69**:40

"Der Grosse Lübbe-See" (Eich) **15**:202

"Der Grosse Wildenberg" (Lenz) **27**:245

"Grosses Geburtstagsblaublau mit Reimzeug und Assonanz" (Celan) **82**:52

"Grotesques" (Strand) **71**:286-89

"La grotte" (Mandiargues) **41**:278

La grotte (Anouilh) **40**:58-9

"Ground" (Davison) **28**:103

The Ground We Stand On (Dos Passos) **15**:183; **25**:137, 145

Ground Work: Before the War (Duncan) **41**:127-31; **55**:290-91, 293, 295, 298

Ground Work II: In the Dark (Duncan) **55**:293-95

"The Groundhog" (Eberhart) **11**:177; **19**:140, 143; **56**:76-7, 79-80, 87, 90

The Group (McCarthy) **1**:205-06; **3**:326-29; **5**:276; **14**:357-58, 360, 363; **24**:349; **59**:289, 291-93

"Group Life: Letchworth" (Betjeman) **6**:68; **43**:36-7

"Group of Progressive Catholics" (Boell) **9**:108

Group Portrait with Lady (Boell)
    See *Gruppenbild mit Dame*

Group Therapy (Hearon) **63**:164-67

"Groups and Series" (Denby) **48**:83

"Grove and Building" (Bowers) **9**:122

"Grove of Academe" (H. D.) **14**:224

The Grove of Eagles (Graham) **23**:193

"Groves of Academe" (Hacker) **91**:111

The Groves of Academe (McCarthy) **1**:206; **3**:326; **5**:275; **14**:357, 363; **39**:486

"Grow Old Along with Me: The Best Is Yet to Be" (Lively) **32**:277

"Grow Old with Me" (Lennon) **35**:275-76

"Growin' Up" (Springsteen) **17**:487

"Growing Boys" (Aickman) **57**:6-7

Growing into Love (Kennedy) **8**:319-20; **42**:255

Growing Pains (du Maurier) **11**:164; **59**:285-88

The Growing Pains of Adrian Mole (The Adrian Mole Diaries) **61**:410-16, 418-21

Growing Points (Jennings) **14**:292-93

"The Growing Stone" (Camus)
    See "La pierre qui pousse"

The Growing Summer (Streatfeild)
    See *The Magic Summer*

"Growing Up" (Boland) **113**:77

Growing Up (Baker) **31**:30-1

Growing Up Absurd (Goodman) **2**:171; **4**:195, 198; **7**:129-30, 131

"Growing Up Female" (Bettelheim) **79**:125

Growing Up in New Guinea (Mead) **37**:270-71

Growing Up in Public (Reed) **21**:319-21

Growing Up Stupid under the Union Jack (Clarke) **53**:89-91, 93, 95

"Growltiger's Last Stand" (Eliot) **55**:347

Grown Ups (Feiffer) **64**:155-56, 161-64

"Grownup" (Simon) **26**:409

Grown-ups and Other Problems: Help for Small People in a Big World (Mayle) **89**:143

"The Gruagach" (Montague) **46**:267-68

"Grumootvodite" (Bagryana) **10**:13

"Gruppa 'Konkret'" (Coles) **67**:174

Gruppenbild mit Dame (Group Portrait with Lady) (Boell) **2**:66-7; **3**:73-6; **6**:84; **11**:55-6, 58; **27**:64; **39**:292-93, 295-96; **72**:78, 85, 89, 100

"Gruzinskiye beryozy" (Voznesensky) **57**:417

"Gruzinskiye dorogi" (Voznesensky) **15**:555

"Guadalajara Hospital" (Ai) **69**:6, 14

Guadeloupe (Conde) **92**:132

"Guadeloupe, W.I." (Guillen) **48**:157, 166

"The Guanajuato Mummies" (Belitt) **22**:54

"Guard Duty" (Transtroemer) **52**:410; **65**:223-24

Guard of Honor (Cozzens) **1**:67; **4**:112, 114-16; **11**:124, 127, 132-33; **92**:176, 178, 181-82, 184, 186-89, 194, 212

"The Guardian Angel" (Soto) **80**:300

"Guardian Angel" (Willingham) **51**:403

The Guardian Angel (Havel) **25**:224

"Guardian Dragon" (Humphrey) **45**:205

The Guardian of the Word (Laye)
    See *Le maitre de la parole: Kouma lafôlô kouma*

"The Guardians" (Merwin) **18**:335; **88**:200

The Guardians (Stewart) **7**:464

Guatemala: Occupied Country (Galeano) **72**:129

"A Guatemalan Idyll" (Bowles) **68**:6-7, 12

"Guayaquil" (Borges) **4**:75; **10**:67

Gudgekin the Thistle Girl and Other Tales (Gardner) **8**:238

Guds bustader (The Dwelling Places of God) (Vesaas) **48**:411

"Le gué dans le torrent" (Theriault) **79**:407

"La güera" (Ulibarri) **83**:415

Guerillas (Naipaul) **7**:252-54; **9**:391-93; **13**:407; **18**:359, 361, 363-65; **37**:324; **105**:139-42, 157, 161-71, 176, 181

Les guerillères (Wittig) **22**:473-77

Guernica (Arrabal)
    See *L'arbre de guernica*

Guernica (Resnais) **16**:502, 505-06

"El güero" ("The Güero") (Donoso) **4**:127; **8**:178; **32**:158

"The Güero" (Donoso)
    See "El güero"

La guerra de guerrillas (Guerrilla Warfare; On Guerrilla Warfare) (Guevara) **87**:199, 201, 203, 207, 212

La guerra del fin del mundo (The War of the End of the World) (Vargas Llosa) **31**:448-49; **42**:403-07, 409, 411; **85**:350, 352-53, 355, 362-63, 379-80, 382-83, 389-95

Guerra del tiempo (The War of Time) (Carpentier) **11**:100; **38**:92, 94-5; **110**:48, 53

La guerre est finie (Resnais) **16**:504-06, 509-13

La guerre, Yes Sir! (Carrier) **13**:140-44; **78**:37-41, 44-9, 51-2, 54-7, 60-1, 67-71, 73, 79-80, 82-4, 87-9

Guerrilla Warfare (Guevara)
    See *La guerra de guerrillas*

"Guerrilla Warfare: A Method" (Guevara) **87**:212

Guerrillas (Hochhuth) **18**:254

"Guess" (Pearce) **21**:292

"Guess Whose Loving Hands" (Mazer) **26**:291

"Guessers" (Sandburg) **35**:358

"The Guest" (Camus)
    See "L'hôte"

"Guest" (Enright) **31**:154

"The Guest" (Middleton) **13**:387

"The Guest" (Watkins) **43**:450, 453

A Guest and His Going (Newby) **2**:311; **13**:407-08

"A Guest at the Spa" (Hesse) **2**:191; **11**:270; **17**:216

A Guest for the Night (Agnon)
    See *Ore'ah natah lalun*

A Guest of Honour (An Honoured Guest) (Gordimer) **3**:201; **5**:145, 147; **7**:132; **10**:239; **18**:187; **33**:182-83; **51**:161; **70**:163, 165, 170, 184

Guest of Reality (Lagerkvist)
    See *Gäst hos verkligheten*

Guests (Dorris) **109**:309

The Guests (Harwood) **32**:224

"Guests in the Promised Land" (Hunter) **35**:226

Guests in the Promised Land (Hunter) **35**:226-27

The Guests of August (Castellanos)
    See *Los convidados de agosto*

"Guests of the Nation" (O'Connor) **23**:328, 330

Guests of the Nation (O'Connor) **14**:398, 400-01; **23**:327, 329, 332

Guests of War (Jenkins) **52**:223, 225, 227-28

"Guevara" (Salinas) **90**:322, 324, 329

Guevle de Pierre (Queneau) **5**:360-61

Guiana Quartet (Harris) **25**:203, 213

"Guide" (Ammons) **5**:27; **8**:16; **9**:30; **108**:21, 50

The Guide (Narayan) **7**:255; **28**:292, 295, 300; **47**:304

"Guide Book" (Coles) **46**:108-09

"Guide for the Misfortune Hunter" (Lebowitz) **36**:250

A Guide for the Perplexed (Levi) **76**:71-6

A Guide for the Perplexed (Schumacher) **80**:265-66, 268, 273

"Guide through the Aegean" (Elytis) **100**:171

"A Guide to Berlin" (Nabokov) **15**:393

Guide to Kulchur (Pound) **4**:414; **7**:334; **13**:461; **112**:321, 328, 332

"A Guide to Poetry" (Ciardi) **10**:107; **40**:152, 157

"A Guide to Some of the Lesser Ballets" (Allen) **52**:35

Guide to the Ruins (Nemerov) **6**:361; **36**:304

"A Guided Tour through the Zoo" (Ignatow) **40**:258

The Guiding Light (Nixon) **21**:242

"The Guiding Miss Gowd" (Ferber)　93:142
"Guido the Ice House Man" (Turco)　11:552
Guignol's band (Celine)　1:56; 4:101; 9:152, 154; 47:71-2, 74
"Guíl an rannaire" (Behan)　79:38-9
"The Guild" (Olds)　39:193
"Guillaume de Lorris" (Pound)　7:337
Guillevic (Guillevic)　33:191, 193
"Guillotine" (Woolrich)　77:403
"Guilt" (Betjeman)　43:51
"Guilt" (Lish)　45:229
"Guilt" (Oates)　15:402
"Guilt" (Ritter)　52:355-56
"Guilt Gems" (Updike)　15:546-47
The Guilt Merchants (Harwood)　32:223
"Guiltiness" (Marley)　17:269
The Guilty (Bataille)
　　See *Le coupable*
Guilty Pleasures (Barthelme)　5:54-5; 6:29; 46:36; 59:247; 115:63, 68
A Guilty Thing Surprised (Rendell)　28:385, 387
"The Guinea Pig Lady" (Banks)　37:26
The Guinea Pigs (Vaculik)
　　See *Sekrya*
The "Guinguette" by the Seine (Simenon)　47:371
Guirnalda con amores (*A Garland of Love*) (Bioy Casares)　13:84, 86; 88:94
"The Guitar" (Bottoms)　53:34
"Guitar" (Dodson)　79:191
"Guitar or Moon" (Aleixandre)　36:30
"Guitar Recitivos" (Ammons)　5:29
The Gulag Archipelago, 1918-1956: An Experiment in Literary Investigation (Solzhenitsyn)
　　See *Arkhipelag GULag, 1918-1956: Op' bit khudozhestvennopo issledovaniia*
Gulag Archipelago Three (Solzhenitsyn)　78:385
"Guldstekel" ("Golden Wasp") (Transtroemer)　65:233
"Gulf" (Heinlein)　3:226; 26:165; 55:302-03
"The Gulf" (Walcott)　25:451; 67:354; 76:274, 281
The Gulf, and Other Poems (Walcott)　2:460; 14:549, 551; 25:450-52; 42:421; 67:346
"The Gulf Between" (Calisher)　38:71
Los gulfos (Saura)　20:313
"Gulfport" (Smith)　25:410
Gull Number 737 (George)　35:176
"Gull on a Post" (Hooker)　43:197
The Gull Wall (Eshleman)　7:100
Gullah (Childress)
　　See *Sea Island Song*
"Gulliver" (Plath)　9:428
"Gulliver" (Slessor)　14:494
"Gulliver" (Soyinka)　36:415-17; 44:285
Gulliver (Simon)　4:495; 9:483-84; 15:490-92; 39:203-06, 209, 211
"Gulls" (Guillevic)　33:191
"The Gulls" (Livesay)　79:341
"The Gulls at Longbird Island" (Bronk)　10:75
"Gulls from a Fantail" (Ciardi)　40:157
"The Gully" (Banks)　72:5
"The Gum Forest" (Murray)　40:338
"Gum-Trees Stripping" (Wright)　53:431
"The Gun" (Dobyns)　37:81
The Gun (Forester)　35:159, 161-62, 168, 170
Gun before Butter (*Question of Loyalty*) (Freeling)　38:183
A Gun for Sale (*This Gun for Hire*) (Greene)　1:130; 3:213; 27:173; 70:290; 72:148

"Gun in the Grass at Your Feet" (Shields)　97:433
"Gun Law at Vermilion: Anna, 1988" (McNally)　82:262
"The Gun Shop" (Updike)　15:545
"Gun, White Castle" (Klappert)　57:259
The Gunman (O'Casey)
　　See *The Shadow of a Gunman*
"The Gunner's Dream" (Pink Floyd)　35:315
"Gunners' Passage" (Shaw)　7:411; 23:396
"Gunpowder Morning in a Gray Room" (Crase)　58:165
"Gunpowder Plot" (Scannell)　49:324, 328, 331-32
Guns in the Afternoon (Peckinpah)
　　See *Ride the High Country*
The Guns of Avalon (Zelazny)　21:466, 473
"Guns of Brixton" (Clash)　30:46, 50
Guns of Burgoyne (Lancaster)　36:241-44
The Guns of Darkness (Schlee)　35:372
The Guns of Navarone (MacLean)　13:360-62; 50:347, 349; 63:261-62, 264-70
"Guns of the Enemy" (Cozzens)　92:201
Guns on the Roof (Clash)　30:43-4, 46
Gunsight (Weiss)　3:516; 8:545; 14:556-57
Gunslinger (Dorn)　10:155-59; 18:128
Gunslinger, Book II (Dorn)　10:158
"Gura vetrei" ("The Hearth") (Arghezi)　80:5-6
Gurney (Silkin)　43:405
The Guru (Jhabvala)　29:259; 94:189
Gus and Al (Innaurato)　60:205-08
"De Gustibus Ain't What Dey Used to Be" (Perelman)　44:505
Der gute Gott von Manhattan (*The Good God of Manhattan*) (Bachmann)　69:48-50
The Gutenberg Elegies: The Fate of Reading in an Electronic Age (Birkerts)　116:154-58, 161-64, 167, 173
The Gutenberg Galaxy: The Making of Typographic Man (McLuhan)　37:253-57, 259-63; 83:359-60, 362-63, 373-74
"The Gutting of Couffignal" (Hammett)　47:156, 159, 164
"The Guttural Muse" (Heaney)　25:244
"The Gut-Wrenching Machine" (Bukowski)　41:75; 108:85
"The Guy with the Crutch" (Kelman)　58:301
"Guzman, Go Home" (Sillitoe)　57:388-89
Guzman, Go Home and Other Stories (Sillitoe)　57:388, 392
"Gwen" (Kincaid)　43:249
"Gwendolyn" (Bishop)　32:40
Gwiazda zaranna (*Morning Star*) (Dabrowska)　15:166, 170
"Gwilan's Harp" (Le Guin)　45:213, 216
Gycklarnas afton (*The Naked Night*; *Sawdust and Tinsel*; *The Sunset of a Clown*) (Bergman)　16:46, 49, 51, 53, 61, 66, 70, 73, 81; 72:29-30, 40-1, 48, 62
"The Gymnast" (Voigt)　54:431-32
"The Gymnosophist" (Ekeloef)　27:119
Gyn/Ecology (Sarton)　91:246
Gypsy (Sondheim)　30:376-78, 385, 387, 389, 390, 395, 400
"The Gypsy Girl" (Davis)　49:83, 93
Gypsy, Gypsy (Godden)　53:151-52
Gypsy in Amber (Smith)　25:412-13
The Gypsy's Curse (Crews)　6:118-19; 49:71-2, 76-7
"The Gyroscope" (Rukeyser)　27:408
The Gyrth Chalice Mystery (*Look to the Lady*) (Allingham)　19:14
"H" (Merrill)　8:384

H. G. Wells: Aspects of a Life (West)　50:359-60
H siao-jen, h siao shih (*Little People, Little Things*) (Pa Chin)　18:374
"The H Street Sledding Record" (Carlson)　54:39
"Ha chi je na I Am Coming" (Forche)　25:170
Ha! Ha! (Ducharme)
　　See *Ah! Ah!*
"Haarlem" (Corso)　11:123
Ha-atalef (Megged)　9:375
The HAB Theory (Eckert)　17:108
La Habana para un infante difunto (*Infante's Inferno*) (Cabrera Infante)　25:104; 45:78-83
Habeas Corpus (Bennett)　45:57-8; 77:87
The Habit of Being: Letters of Flannery O'Connor (O'Connor)　13:421-22; 15:413; 21:278
The Habit of Empire (Horgan)　53:178
"The Habit of Loving" (Lessing)　6:298; 10:316; 22:277
"Les habitants du continent des chas sans aiguilles" (Arp)　5:34
"Habitar o tempo" ("To Dwell in Time") (Cabral de Melo Neto)　76:168
"Habitations of the Word" (Gass)　39:480
Habitations of the Word (Gass)　39:477-82
"Habits" (Giovanni)　64:195
"The Habits" (MacNeice)　10:324
El hablador (*The Storyteller*) (Vargas Llosa)　85:376, 395-98
"Hablar y decir" (Paz)　65:177
Háblenme de Funes (*Talk to Me about Funes*) (Costantini)　49:61
"El hacedor" ("The Maker") (Borges)　6:93; 8:101; 9:120; 84:158
El hacedor (*Dreamtigers*; *The Maker*) (Borges)　2:71-2; 3:77; 8:101; 13:106-07; 44:356; 83:158-59, 171, 191
"Hacienda" (Porter)　7:311; 13:449; 27:402; 101:214
Hacienda (Porter)　101:215
The Hack (Sheed)　4:487
"Hack Wednesday" (Atwood)　84:95, 97
Hackenfeller's Ape (Brophy)　11:67-8; 29:91-3, 97-8; 105:7-8, 11, 29-30
"Had I a Hundred Mouths" (Goyen)　40:217-18
Had I a Hundred Mouths: New and Selected Stories, 1947-1983 (Goyen)　40:218-19
"Had to Phone Ya" (Wilson)　12:648
"Hades and Euclid" (Martinson)　14:357
Hadrian VII (Luke)　38:313-18
Hadrian's Memoirs (Yourcenar)
　　See *Mémoires d'Hadrien*
"Haecity" (Cunningham)　31:98
"The Hag of Beare" (Montague)　46:268-69
Hagakure nyumon (Mishima)　9:385; 27:342
"Hagibor ha'amiti shel ha'agedah" ("The Real Hero of the Agedah") (Amichai)　116:112-13
"Haha no kouru ki" ("Longing for Mother"; "A Record of Longing for Mother"; "Reminiscence of My Beloved Mother"; "Yearning for My Mother") (Tanizaki)　28:420
Haï (Le Clezio)　31:251
"Haibun" (Ashbery)　41:34
"Haig" (Smith)　64:388
"Haiku" (Sanchez)　116:302, 328
"Hail Mary" (Fante)　60:133
Hail to the Chief (Hunter)　11:279
"Hailstones" (Heaney)　74:162, 174, 191

La haine de la poésie (Bataille)   29:39

"Haines" (Soupault)   68:405

"Hair" (Bly)   10:55

"Hair" (Olson)   28:343

Hair (Ragni and Rado)   17:378-88

Hair (Weller)   53:393

"Hair Jewellery" (Atwood)   13:45

The Hair of Harold Roux (Williams)   14:582-83

"Hairball" (Atwood)   84:96-7

"A Haircut" (Carver)   55:273

Haircut (Warhol)   20:416, 421

The Haircutting (Hrabal)
   See *Postriziny*

"The Hairless Mexican" (Maugham)   67:219

"A Hairline Fracture" (Clampitt)   32:115-16

"A Hairpin Turn above Reading, Jamaica" (Matthews)   40:321

The Hairs of My Grandfather's Head (Laughlin)   49:220

"Hairy Belly" (Ammons)   57:57

"Haitian Divorce" (Becker and Fagen)   26:83

Haitian Earth (Walcott)   67:342

The Haj (Uris)   32:436-37

Hakai (*The Sin*) (Ichikawa)   20:182

Hakhnasat kalah (*The Bridal Canopy*) (Agnon)   4:11-12; 8:8; 14:3

Hako otoko (*The Box Man*) (Abe)   8:1-2; 53:2, 5-6; 81:285, 287, 293

Hakobune sakura maru (*The Ark Sakura*) (Abe)   53:2-7; 81:294-95

Halbzeit (*Half Time*) (Walser)   27:456-61, 465, 467

"Halcyon" (H. D.)   73:121

"Halcyon" (Ihimaera)   46:199

"Hale Hardy and the Amazing Animal Woman" (Beattie)   8:55; 63:3, 17

"Half a Mile Away" (Joel)   26:217

"Half an Hour Before He Died" (Kelman)   58:298

"Half Life" (Carlson)   54:37

"Half Life" (Monette)   82:320, 322, 332

"Half Light" (Szirtes)   46:391

Half Moon Street (*Doctor Slaughter*) (Theroux)   46:398-401, 404

Half Portions (Ferber)   93:139, 142, 147

Half Remembered (Davison)   28:101-02

Half Sun Half Sleep (Swenson)   4:533; 14:518; 61:392; 106:320-21, 348-49

Half Time (Walser)
   See *Halbzeit*

"Half-Breed" (Asimov)   26:39

Halfbreed (Campbell)   85:2-5, 8-9, 11-2, 14, 17, 20-5

"Half-Breeds on Venus" (Asimov)   26:39

"Half-Caste Girl" (Wright)   53:427

"Half-Deity" (Moore)   10:350

The Half-Finished Heaven (Transtroemer)
   See *Den halvfärdiga himlen*

"A Half-Grown Porcupine" (Bly)   15:63

"Halfjack" (Zelazny)   21:479

Half-Lives (Jong)   4:263-64; 6:267-68; 8:313-15; 18:277; 83:289, 291, 299-300

The Half-Made Heaven (Transtroemer)
   See *Den halvfärdiga himlen*

"The Half-Moon Blackbird" (Durcan)   70:151-52

The Half-Mother (Tennant)
   See *Woman Beware Woman*

"A Half-Private Letter on Poetry" (Milosz)   56:237

The Half-Ready Sky (Transtroemer)
   See *Den halvfärdiga himlen*

"Half-Scissors" (Redgrove)   41:352

The Half-Sisters (Seton)   27:425-27

"Hälfte des Lebens" (Hildesheimer)   49:179

"Halfway" (Ammons)   108:24

Halfway Down the Coast (Blackburn)   43:64-5

Halfway Home (Monette)   82:327-28, 331

"Halfway House" (Silverberg)   7:425

Halfway House (Queen)   11:458, 461

Halfway House: A Miscellany of New Poems (Blunden)   56:44, 48

Halfway to Silence (Sarton)   49:314

"Halfway to the Moon" (Aksyonov)   101:9-10, 15, 20, 30

"A Hall of Mirrors" (Rosenblatt)   15:446

A Hall of Mirrors (Stone)   5:409-10; 23:424-26, 429-30; 42:358-63

"Les halles d'Ypres" (Blunden)   56:41

Halleyova kometa (Seifert)
   See *Halleyová kometa*

Halleyová kometa (*Halleyova kometa*; *Halley's Comet*) (Seifert)   34:257; 93:319, 336-37, 343

Halley's Comet (Seifert)
   See *Halleyová kometa*

"Halloran's Child" (Hill)   113:282

Halloran's Little Boat (Keneally)   117:213

"Hallow Eve with Spaces for Ghosts" (Piercy)   27:374

"Hallowe'en" (Aiken)   10:4; 52:26

Hallowe'en (Christie)   48:74; 110:137

"Halloween Delight" (Smith)   42:353

"Halloween Poem" (Cohen)   38:131

"Hallowind" (Chappell)   78:96

Hallucinations (Arenas)
   See *El mundo alucinante: Una novela de aventuras*

"Haloes" (Abse)   29:18

"The Halt" (Miles)   14:369

"A Halt in the Desert" (Brodsky)
   See "Ostanovka v pustyne"

Halt in the Wilderness (Brodsky)   13:114

"The Halted Battalion" (Blunden)   56:45

Den halvfärdiga himlen (*The Half-Finished Heaven*; *The Half-Made Heaven*; *The Half-Ready Sky*) (Transtroemer)   52:409-10, 412, 415; 65:222-23, 225, 229, 233, 236

The Ham Funeral (White)   7:532

Ham on Rye (Bukowski)   41:70-3; 82:6, 8-10, 28; 108:88, 102

Hamachidori (*Beach Plovers*) (Kawabata)   107:121

"Hamari Gali" ("Our Lane") (Ali)   69:25

"Hamatsa" (Bowering)   15:82

"A Hambledon Sequence" (Hooker)   43:199

"The Hambone and the Heart" (Sitwell)   67:313, 325

Hamilton County (Kantor)   7:196

Hamilton Stark (Banks)   37:23-4, 26-7; 72:4-5

"Hamlen Brook" (Wilbur)   110:361

"Hamlet" (Honig)   33:215-16

"Hamlet" (Pasternak)   63:312-13

"Hamlet" (Soyinka)   36:416-17; 44:285

The Hamlet (Faulkner)   1:101-02; 3:149, 151-52, 156; 6:174, 179; 8:211; 11:197, 203-04; 14:178-79; 18:148-49; 28:138, 140, 145; 52:114, 139

Hamlet (Olivier)   20:234-37, 242-43

"Hamlet and His Problems" (Eliot)   24:172, 176

Hamlet in Autumn (Smith)   64:399

The Hamlet of A. MacLeish (MacLeish)   3:310; 14:336; 68:271-73, 275, 284, 286, 289-90

The Hamlet of Stepney Green (Kops)   4:274

Hamlet, Revenge! (Stewart)   14:511

Hamlet's Mother and Other Women (Heilbrun)   65:344

"Hamlets of the World" (Shaw)   23:396

Hamlet's Twin (Aquin)
   See *Neige noir*

"A Hammer" (Guillevic)   33:191

"The Hammer Man" (Bambara)   19:33; 88:16

The Hammerhead Light (Thiele)   17:496

Hammertown Tales (Masters)   48:223-24

"Hammond, England" (Blunden)   56:37

"Hamnavoe Market" (Brown)   48:57, 60

Hamnstad (*Port of Call*) (Bergman)   16:46-7, 50-1, 60; 72:52, 62

"Hampshire" (Davie)   8:165

"Hampstead: The Horse Chestnut Trees" (Gunn)   18:199, 202

"Hamrick's Polar Bear" (Caldwell)   60:50

Hams al-junun (*The Whisper of Madness*) (Mahfuz)   55:174, 176

"Ham's Departure" (Leonov)
   See "Ukhod Khama"

"Ham's Gift" (Dowell)   60:107-08

Hamsters (Silverstein and Silverstein)   17:456

"Hamuel Gutterman" (Tolson)   105:237

"Han no hanza" ("Han's Crime") (Shiga)   33:366

Han som fik leva om sitt liv (*He Who Lived His Life Over Again*; *The Man Who Lived His Life Over Again*; *The Man Who Was Given His Life to Live Again*) (Lagerkvist)   54:269-70, 272, 275, 278

Hanazakari no mori (*A Forest in Flower*; *The Forest in Full Bloom*) (Mishima)   2:286; 27:338

"The Hand" (Thomas)   48:379

The Hand (Stone)   73:363-64, 382

Hand in Glove (Marsh)   53:248

"Hand in Hand" (Costello)   21:68

"Hand of a Wanker" (McGrath)   55:73, 75

The Hand of Oberon (Zelazny)   21:470-71, 473

"Hand of the Mind" (Spacks)   14:511

Hand Out (Rathbone)   41:337

"Hand Poem" (Phillips)   28:363

"The Hand That Cradles the Rock" (Perelman)   49:263

The Hand That Cradles the Rock (Brown)   79:153

A Handbook For Drowning (Shields)   97:428-34

A Handbook for Visitors from Outer Space (Kramer)   34:74-6

A Handbook of Practical Morality (Arghezi)
   See *Manual de morala practica*

"Handcarved Coffins: A Nonfiction Account of an American Crime" (Capote)   19:84-5

"The Handcuff Manual" (Vollmann)   89:283, 296

A Handful of Dust (Waugh)   1:357-60; 3:509-13; 8:544-45; 13:585-88; 19:462-64; 27:470-71, 476-77; 44:524; 107:360-62, 364, 366, 370-71, 378, 380, 398, 400-01

A Handful of Rice (Markandaya)   38:323

"The Handgun" (De Marinis)   54:101-02

"The Handing Down" (Berry)   46:70

Handkerchief of Clouds (Tzara)
   See *Mouchoir de nuages*

"The Handkerchief of Ghost Tree" (Thomas)

31:430

Handling Sin (Malone) 43:282-85

The Handmaid's Tale (Atwood) 44:146-51, 153-62; 84:67, 69, 71, 79, 86, 97-104, 107

The Hand-Reared Boy (Aldiss) 5:14; 14:14

"Hand-Rolled Cigarettes" (Kunitz) 6:287

"Hands" (Birney) 6:74

"Hands" (Brautigan) 3:86

"The Hands" (Campbell) 93:95

"Hands" (Landolfi) 11:321; 49:212

"Hands" (Purdy) 50:246

Hands across the Sea (Coward) 51:70

"The Hands around the Neck" (Moravia) 46:286

The Hands of Day (Neruda)
  See *Las manos del día*

The Hands of Venus (Seifert)
  See *The Arms of Venus*

"Hands Off, Foreign Devil" (Enright) 31:155

"Hands over Head" (Clark) 38:125

Hands Up! (Skolimowski) 20:352-53

The Handsome Heart (De Vries) 28:113-14

"Handsome Is as Handsome Does" (Pritchett) 41:333

A Handsome Man (Cheever) 48:63-4

"The Handsomest Drowned Man in the World: A Tale for Children" (Garcia Marquez)
  See "El ahogado más hermoso del mundo"

"Handsworth Liberties" (Fisher) 25:160-61

"Handwritten News" (Char) 55:289

"Handy Dandy" (Dylan) 77:182

"Hanefesh" ("The Soul") (Amichai) 116:122

Hang for Treason (Peck) 17:340-41

"Hang of It" (Salinger) 12:498

The Hang of the Gaol (Barker) 37:37, 39

"Hang On to the Good Times" (Cryer) 21:81

"Hang On to Yourself" (Bowie) 17:59, 65

"Hangdog Hotel Room" (Lightfoot) 26:282

"The Hanged Man" (Cohen) 19:113

"The Hanged Man's Prayer" (Carrier) 78:83

"Hangin' Round" (Reed) 21:305

"Hanging Fire" (Lorde) 71:232, 247

"The Hanging Judge" (Boland) 40:96; 113:122

"The Hanging Man" (Davison) 28:103

"The Hanging Man" (Plath) 9:427-28

"Hanging Out in America" (Allen) 84:5

"Hanging Out with the Magi" (Rooke) 25:394

The Hanging Stones (Wellman) 49:393, 396

"Hangman" (Ai) 69:11

Hangmen Also Die (Lang) 20:207, 216

The Hangover (Sargeson) 31:365-67, 374

Hangover Square; or, The Man with Two Minds: A Story of Darkest Earl's Court in the Year 1939 (Hamilton) 51:187-88, 190, 193-94, 196-98

Hangsaman (Jackson) 60:216-20, 229-31, 234

"Hanka" (Singer) 6:511; 11:499

Hanky Panky (Poitier) 26:362

Hannah Arendt—Karl Jaspers: Correspondence, 1926-1969 (Arendt) 98:47

Hannah's House (Hearon) 63:159-60, 162

"Hannes" (Hesse) 25:262

Hanoi (McCarthy) 14:358-59

"Hanoi Hannah" (Komunyakaa) 94:226, 232, 245

"Han's Crime" (Shiga)
  See "Han no hanza"

Hans Feet in Love (Sansom) 2:383; 6:482-84

Hans nådes tid (*His Grace's Days*) (Johnson) 14:296

"Hänsel to Gretel" (Monette) 82:314

"Ha-panim la-panim" ("The Face and the Im-

age") (Agnon) 8:8

"Hapax" (Rexroth) 112:395, 400, 402

"Ha'penny" (Paton) 25:359; 55:313

"Hapless Dancer" (Townshend) 17:532

"Happening" (Ezekiel) 61:109

"Happening" (Honig) 33:216

"Happenings" (Phillips) 28:364

Happenstance (Shields) 113:401, 404-08, 410, 412, 424, 431, 437-39, 441, 445-46

"The Happier Life" (Dunn) 40:166

The Happier Life (Dunn) 6:148; 40:165-67

"The Happiest I've Been" (Updike) 34:291

"Happiness" (Ciardi) 44:381

"Happiness" (Gluck) 22:177

"Happiness" (Lavin) 18:305; 99:312-15, 319, 322

"Happiness" (Oliver) 34:246, 249; 98:299-300

"Happiness" (Prichard) 46:332, 345

"Happiness" (Sandburg) 35:355

"Happiness" (Warner) 7:512

Happiness (Lavin) 99:322

"Happiness Does Not Come in Colors" (Cooper) 56:70

"Happiness in Herat" (Paz) 65:200

"Happiness Is..." (Jones) 52:250

Happiness Is Too Much Trouble (Hochman) 8:298

Happiness: Selected Short Stories (Prichard) 46:345

"Happy" (Beattie) 40:65-6

Happy All the Time (Colwin) 13:156-57; 84:139-40, 142, 146-47, 149-53

Happy As Larry (Hinde) 6:238-39

"Happy August the Tenth" (Williams) 5:502-03; 45:452

"The Happy Autumn Fields" (Bowen) 22:64-6, 68

"Happy Birthday" (Bambara) 88:12, 15, 46

"Happy Birthday" (Bidart) 33:76

"Happy Birthday" (Lispector) 43:268-69

Happy Birthday, Wanda June (Vonnegut)
  See *Penelope*

A Happy Childhood (Matthews) 40:323-25

"Happy Day" (Byrne) 26:95

Happy Days (Beckett) 3:45; 4:51; 6:36, 39, 43, 46-7; 9:83, 85; 10:29-34; 11:33, 37-8; 14:70-1, 80; 18:43, 47-8; 57:78-9, 109; 59:252, 255; 83:138

Happy Days (Marshall) 17:275-78

Happy Days (Nash) 23:317

Happy Days Are Here Again (Taylor) 27:439-40

A Happy Death (Camus)
  See *La mort heureuse*

"Happy Ending" (Beer) 58:31

Happy Ending (Ward) 19:456-57

Happy Endings Are All Alike (Scoppettone) 26:402-03

"Happy Enough" (Johnston) 51:245-46, 248, 253-54

Happy Enough: Poems, 1935-1972 (Johnston) 51:245-48, 250, 252-54

Happy Families (Maloff) 5:270-71

"A Happy Family" (Trevor) 116:361, 371

The Happy Family (Swinnerton) 31:423

"The Happy Farmer" (Thomas) 107:338, 340, 342

"Happy Feet" (Martin) 30:246

Happy for the Child (Jenkins) 52:219-20, 222, 225

The Happy Foreigner (Bagnold) 25:71-2

"A Happy Ghost" (Johnston) 51:240

The Happy Girls (Vollmann) 89:302, 304

The Happy Haven (Arden) 6:4-6, 8-9; 13:23, 29

"The Happy Highway" (Phillips) 28:362

Happy Homecoming (Conde)
  See *Hérémakhonon: On doit attendre le bonheur*

The Happy Island (Powell) 66:354-55, 369

Happy Jack (Townshend) 17:530, 534

The Happy Journey to Trenton and Camden (Wilder) 6:577; 10:531-32; 35:441, 446; 82:352, 363-64, 387

Happy Lies (Taylor) 27:445

The Happy Man (Hall) 59:152-54

The Happy Marriage, and Other Poems (MacLeish) 8:359; 68:270, 272, 277

"Happy New Year" (Auden) 43:16

"The Happy Onion" (Oates) 6:370

The Happy Return (Forester)
  See *Beat to Quarters*

"The Happy Three" (Roethke) 46:364; 101:332-33

Happy to Be Here: Stories and Comic Pieces (Keillor) 40:273-74

"Happy Together" (Weller) 26:447

Happy Valley (White) 5:486; 7:530-32; 65:275, 277, 279; 69:392-96, 399, 407

"A Happy View" (Day Lewis) 10:131

"The Happy Warrior" (Read) 4:439

The Happy Warriors (Laxness)
  See *Gerpla*

"The Happy Worrier" (Simmons) 43:413

"Happy Xmas" ("War Is Over") (Lennon) 35:270-71

"Hapworth 16, 1924" (Salinger) 8:463; 12:518

Harald (Haavikko) 34:173

The Harangues (Walker) 19:454-55

"The Harbor at Seattle" (Hass) 99:141

"The Harbour" (Walcott) 76:278, 280

"The Harbour in the Evening" (Paulin) 37:353

"Hard and Soft" (Laughlin) 49:220, 222-23

The Hard Blue Sky (Grau) 4:207

Hard Candy (Vachss) 106:359-61, 365

Hard Candy: A Book of Stories (Williams) 45:447

"The Hard Core of Beauty" (Williams) 42:456

"The Hard Core of Love" (Livesay) 79:347

"Hard Daddy" (Hughes) 108:329

A Hard Day's Night (Lennon and McCartney) 12:356, 359, 375; 35:293

A Hard Day's Night (Lester) 20:218-19, 228

"A Hard Death" (Sarton) 91:244

Hard Facts: Excerpts (Baraka) 10:21; 33:58; 115:27, 39

Hard Feelings (King) 8:322

Hard Freight (Wright) 6:579-81; 13:612, 614

The Hard Hours (Hecht) 8:268; 13:269; 19:207-08

The Hard Life: An Exegesis of Squalor (O'Brien) 1:252; 4:383; 7:270; 10:364; 47:313-14, 316, 320

Hard Lines (Nash) 23:316-17

Hard Loving (Piercy) 3:384; 18:406; 27:375; 62:376

Hard Nose the Highway (Morrison) 21:234, 236, 238

Hard Rain (Dorfman)
  See *Moros en la costa*

Hard Rain (van de Wetering) 47:412-13

Hard Rain Falling (Carpenter) 41:100-03

"A Hard Rain's A-Gonna Fall" (Dylan) 4:149; 12:189; 77:164, 184, 187

"Hard Riding" (McNickle) 89:182-83

"Hard Road to Travel" (Cliff) **21**:60

"Hard Rock Returns to Prison" (Knight) **40**:286

"A Hard Row to Hoe" (Garrett) **51**:140

"Hard Sell" (Boyle) **90**:45, 48

"Hard Time" (Piercy) **62**:378

Hard Times: An Oral History of the Great Depression (Terkel) **38**:420-25, 428

Hard to Be a God (Strugatskii and Strugatskii) **27**:432-37

"Hard Traveling" (Guthrie) **35**:185, 190, 193

A Hard Winter (Queneau)
See *Un rude hiver*

Hard Words, and Other Poems (Le Guin) **45**:212-13, 216

"Hardcastle Crags" (Plath) **11**:446; **17**:367; **111**:200, 202, 206

Hardcore (Schrader) **26**:392-96, 398-99

Hardcore (Thompson) **69**:382-83

Hardcover (Shammas) **55**:86

The Harder They Come (Cliff) **21**:61, 63-4

The Harder They Come (Thelwell) **22**:415-16

The Harder They Fall (Schulberg) **7**:402; **48**:350

"Hardest It Is" (Scott) **22**:372

"Hardfhip aboard American Sloop the Peggy, 1765" (Reading) **47**:351

"Hardham" (Blunden) **56**:49

"Hard-Luck Stories" (Munro) **95**:315-19

"Hardly Ever" (Boyd) **28**:38

Hardwater Country (Busch) **18**:84-5

"Hardweed Path Going" (Ammons) **108**:4

"Hardy and the Hag" (Fowles) **87**:178-80

"The Hardys" (Humphrey) **45**:203

"Hare" (Clarke) **61**:79

Hare and Hornbill (p'Bitek) **96**:278, 301

"The Hare and the Tortoise" (Seth) **90**:353

"Harlem" (Hughes) **108**:333

"Harlem" (Tolson) **105**:281

The Harlem Book of the Dead (Dodson) **79**:196

Harlem Gallery: Book I, The Curator (Tolson) **36**:426-28, 430-31; **105**:234-35, 240-42, 244-45, 247-50, 253-58, 262-66, 269-72, 274-77, 279-88, 290, 292, 294

"A Harlem Game" (Dumas) **6**:145; **62**:150, 154, 161

"The Harlem Ghetto" (Baldwin) **2**:32; **42**:16, 20-2

"The Harlem Group of Negro Writers" (Tolson) **105**:280

"Harlem Hopscotch" (Angelou) **77**:28-9

"Harlem Montana: Just Off the Reservation" (Welch) **52**:429

"A Harlequin" (Tanizaki)
See "Hokan"

Harlequin (Fo) **109**:129-34

Harlequin (West) **6**:564-65

"The Harlequin Tea Set" (Christie) **110**:128

"Harlequinette" (Tournier) **95**:379

"Harlequin's Lane" (Christie) **110**:128

Harlequin's Stick—Charlie's Cane (Madden) **15**:350

"Harley Talking" (Hood) **28**:189

Harlot's Ghost (Mailer) **74**:231, 233-34, 236-37, 240, 242-43, 245-46; **111**:134-38

L'harmattan (Ousmane) **66**:334

"Harmony" (Kauffman) **42**:251-52

"Harmony of the World" (Baxter) **45**:50-2

Harmony of the World (Baxter) **45**:50-2; **78**:16-17, 19, 21-22, 25-7, 32

Harm's Way (Wellman) **65**:242

"The Harness" (Steinbeck) **45**:382

Harold Muggins Is a Martyr (Arden) **15**:21

Harold of Orange (Vizenor) **103**:298, 302, 321, 341

Harold Urey: The Man Who Explored from Earth to Moon (Silverstein and Silverstein) **17**:452

Harold's Leap (Smith) **25**:420

Haroun and the Sea of Stories (Rushdie) **100**:287, 301, 315

The Harp and the Shadow (Carpentier)
See *El arpa y la sombra*

"Harp, Anvil, Oar" (Graves) **39**:326

Harp of a Thousand Strings (Davis) **49**:83-5, 89-90, 96-7

"The Harp of Wales" (Williams) **45**:443

"Harper's Bazaar" (Findley) **102**:97

"Harpers Ferry" (Rich) **73**:330-32

The Harpoon Gun and Other Stories (Vassilikos)
See *Le fusil-harpon et autres nouvelles*

"Harriet" (Lorde) **71**:241

Harriet (Kazan) **63**:225, 234

Harriet Hume (West) **31**:454, 457, 459

Harriet Said (Bainbridge) **4**:39; **5**:39-40; **8**:37; **10**:16; **18**:34; **22**:44-5; **62**:24, 30

"Harrison Bergeron" (Vonnegut) **12**:617

Harrison, Texas (Foote) **51**:130

Harris's Requiem (Middleton) **38**:332

"The Harrow" (Davie) **31**:116

"Harrow Street at Linden" (Oates) **52**:331

"Harry" (Newlove) **14**:378

"Harry and Barney" (Farrell) **66**:127

"Harry and Violet" (Thomas) **37**:419, 422; **107**:327

Harry Dernier: A Play for Radio Production (Walcott) **25**:453

Harry, Noon and Night (Ribman) **7**:357

"Harry's Death" (Carver) **36**:106

"Harsh Climate" (Simic) **22**:383

The Harsh Voice (West) **31**:453-54, 457; **50**:405-06

"Hart Crane" (Creeley) **36**:120

"The Hartford Girl" (Selzer) **74**:261

"The Hartleys" (Cheever) **15**:129

Hart's Hope (Card) **47**:68-9

Haruka/Love Poems (Jordan) **114**:153-55

"Harv Is Plowing Now" (Updike) **15**:543

Harvard Diaries (Coles) **108**:194

"Harvard Yard in April: April in Harvard Yard" (Richards) **14**:453-54

"Harvest" (Blunden) **56**:38

"Harvest" (Fowles) **15**:232

"Harvest" (Matthews) **40**:321

"Harvest" (p'Bitek) **96**:299

"Harvest" (Sitwell) **67**:319

"Harvest" (Soto) **80**:286

"Harvest" (Voigt) **54**:428

"Harvest" (Young) **17**:582

Harvest (Young) **17**:570, 572, 574, 577-80, 583

"Harvest at Mynachlog" (Clarke) **61**:74, 79, 81-3

"The Harvest Bow" ("The Harvest Knot") (Heaney) **14**:246; **25**:243-44, 246-47, 250; **37**:164; **74**:165, 177, 195

Harvest Comedy (Swinnerton) **31**:426

"Harvest Home" (Baxter) **78**:25

Harvest Home (Tryon) **3**:483-84; **11**:548

"Harvest Hymn" (Betjeman) **43**:45-6

"The Harvest Knot" (Heaney)
See "The Harvest Bow"

The Harvest of a Life (Sillanpaa)
See *Erään elämän Sotoa*

Harvest of Youth (Stuart) **8**:507; **34**:373, 375-76

Harvest on the Don (Sholokhov) **7**:418

"Harvest Song" (Toomer) **4**:549-50; **22**:424

"Has Pinochle Lost Its Whack?" (Royko) **109**:406

"The Hashish-Eater; or, The Apocalypse of Evil" (Smith) **43**:416, 418

"Hasidic Tales" (Allen) **52**:35, 45

"Haskell's Mill" (Davison) **28**:103

"Hassan in England" (Forster) **45**:133

"The Hat Act" (Coover) **3**:113; **7**:58; **15**:145; **46**:116

"The Hat Factory" (Durcan) **43**:113

"Hate and War" (Clash) **30**:44

"Hate Blows a Bubble of Despair into" (Cummings) **68**:44

"Hateful" (Clash) **30**:46-7

Hatfield, the Rainmaker (*The Rainmaker*) (Ringwood) **48**:329-30, 333, 335-38

Hath Not a Jew (Klein) **19**:260-61

"Hatred of Men with Black Hair" (Bly) **10**:55

Hatter's Castle (Cronin) **32**:128-33, 140

The Hatter's Phantoms (Simenon) **8**:487

"A Haul" (Heaney) **74**:197

"The Haulier's Wife" (Durcan) **43**:118

"The Haunted Armchair" (Redgrove) **41**:348, 351

"The Haunted Boy" (McCullers) **12**:433

The Haunted Earth (Koontz) **78**:200

"Haunted House" (Graves) **45**:166-67

Haunted Houses (Kettelkamp) **12**:305

The Haunted Land (Stow) **23**:432

"Haunted Landscape" (Ashbery) **15**:34; **25**:53

The Haunted Mesa (L'Amour) **55**:307-08

The Haunted Mountain (Hunter) **21**:159, 162

"Haunting" (Simon) **26**:411

The Haunting of Hill House (Jackson) **11**:302; **60**:211, 216-17, 220, 229, 234-35

The Haunting of Julia (Straub) **107**:288

"Hauptstädtisches Journal" ("Bonn Diary") (Boell) **72**:68, 72

"Ein Haus aus lauter Liebe" (Lenz) **27**:245

Haus ohne Hüter (*Tomorrow and Yesterday*; *The Unguarded House*) (Boell) **6**:83; **11**:52, 57-8; **72**:72

Der Hausierer (Handke) **5**:163

Hausipungo (Arguedas) **18**:7

Hausmusik (Neruda) **2**:309

Haussuchung (Lenz) **27**:246

Haute surveillance (*Deathwatch*) (Genet) **2**:158; **10**:225; **14**:198, 201; **44**:385-87, 390; **46**:173

"Havana Dreams" (Hughes) **108**:324

The Havana Inquiry (Enzensberger)
See *Das Verhör von Habana*

"Havana Moon" (Berry) **17**:56

Havana Treatises (Lezama Lima)
See *Tratados en la habana*

"Have a Cigar" (Pink Floyd) **35**:307-08

"Have a Cuppa Tea" (Davies) **21**:92

"Have a Good Rest" (Nagy) **7**:251

"Have a Good Time" (Simon) **17**:465

"Have a Talk with God" (Wonder) **12**:660, 664

"H'ave Caesar; or, Boadicea's Revenge" (Nash) **23**:323

Have I Ever Lied to You? (Buchwald) **33**:92

"Have I Got a Chocolate Bar for You!" (Bradbury) **42**:35

"Have I Outgrown You?" (Miles) **14**:369

"Have Mercy Judge" (Berry) **17**:55

Have Space Suit—Will Travel (Heinlein) **3**:225; **14**:249-51; **26**:161-62, 165, 173, 177

"have you ever kissed a panther" (Bukowski)

108:74
"Have You Forgotten" (Moss)   45:289
"Have You Seen Me?" (Graver)   70:49, 52-3
"Have You Seen Me?" (Van Duyn)   116:430-31
Have You Seen Me? (Graver)   70:48-54
"Have You Seen Your Mother, Baby" (Jagger and Richard)   17:235
Haven in a Heartless World (Lasch)   102:293, 301, 327
Haven's End (Marquand)   10:330
"Haven't Got Time for the Pain" (Simon)   26:408-09, 411
"Having Been Asked 'What Is a Man?' I Answer" ("After Keats") (Levine)   33:273-74
"Having Fallen into Place" (Fisher)   87:122
"Having No Ear" (Davie)   31:124-25
"Having Replaced Love with Food and Drink: A Poem for Those Who've Reached Forty" (Wakoski)   40:455
"Having the Human Thing of Joy" (Abbott)   48:5, 7
"The Haw Lantern" (Heaney)   74:176-77
The Haw Lantern (Heaney)   74:160-62, 172-75, 183, 186, 189-92, 194; 91:122, 124
Hawaii (Michener)   5:289-90; 11:375; 29:311; 60:260-61; 109:375-81, 383, 385-86, 388
Hawaii: The Sugar-Coated Fortress (Gray)   22:201
"The Hawk" (Ciardi)   40:157
"Hawk" (Oliver)   98:288
"The Hawk in the Rain" (Hughes)   14:270
The Hawk in the Rain (Hughes)   2:197-98, 201-02; 4:235-37; 9:281-82, 284-85; 14:269-70; 37:171, 175
The Hawk Is Dying (Crews)   6:118; 23:133, 138; 49:73, 76, 79
"The Hawk Is Flying" (Crews)   49:73
"The Hawk Is Hungry" (McNickle)   89:183
The Hawk Is Hungry, and Other Stories (McNickle)   89:179
Hawk Moon (Shepard)   4:490
"Hawk on the Wind" (Derleth)   31:130-31, 133
"Hawk Roosting" (Hughes)   4:235
The Hawk that Dare Not Hunt by Day (O'Dell)   30:273
"Hawkfall" (Brown)   48:55, 60
Hawkfall and Other Stories (Brown)   48:55; 100:84
The Hawkline Monster: A Gothic Western (Brautigan)   5:70-2; 12:70; 34:315, 317; 42:50, 56-8, 60
Hawkmistress! (Bradley)   30:29, 32
The Hawks and the Sparrows (Pasolini)
   See *Uccellacci e uccellini*
"The Hawk's Cry in Autumn" (Brodsky)   100:43-4, 67
"A Hawk's Cry in Winter" (Brodsky)   100:47
Hawks, Doves, and the Eagle (Archer)   12:17
"Hawk's Shadow" (Gluck)   44:216, 218
Hawksmoor (Ackroyd)   52:6-15
"The Hawthorn Hedge" (Wright)   53:416, 427
"The Hawthorn Tree" (Gluck)   81:168
"Hawthorn Trees in Spring: A Lament of Women" (Christie)   110:127
"Hawthorne" (Lowell)   8:351
"Hawthorne in Our Time" (Trilling)   11:547
Haxby's Circus: The Lightest, Brightest Little Show on Earth (*Fay's Circus*) (Prichard)   46:329-32, 337, 341
"Hay Fever" (Hope)   51:227

Hay Fever (Coward)   1:64; 9:172; 29:131, 133, 135, 137, 139; 51:69-70, 73-5, 77
Hay que sonreír (Valenzuela)   31:438-40; 104:356, 387
"Hay que tené boluntá" ("Got to Have Will Power"; "One Must Have Willpower") (Guillen)   79:246
Haydn and the Valve Trumpet (Raine)   103:202-04
Hayduke Lives (Abbey)   59:238, 245
"The Hayfield" (Bowering)   47:24
"Hayfork Point" (Murray)   40:335
"Haying before Storm" (Rukeyser)   27:408
The Hazard and the Gift (McAuley)   45:253
Hazard, the Painter (Meredith)   13:372-73; 22:303; 55:193
"Hazardous Occupations" (Sandburg)   10:450
The Hazards of Holiness (Everson)   5:121; 14:166
"Hazard's Optimism" (Meredith)   13:373; 55:192
Hazarski recnik (*Dictionary of the Khazars: A Lexicon Novel in 100,000 Words*) (Pavic)   60:282-90
"Haze" (Sandburg)   35:352
"Hazel" (Shields)   113:408
"A Hazel Stick for Catherine Ann" (Heaney)   37:165; 74:167
"A Hazy Shade of Winter" (Simon)   17:463
"H.D." (Duncan)   41:128
H.D. Book (Duncan)   55:291
"He" (Ashbery)   15:27
"He" (Ferlinghetti)   10:175; 111:65
"He" (Porter)   7:317; 101:209-10
"He and I" (Ginzburg)   54:208
"He and It" (Stevenson)   33:382-83
"He and the Cat" (Mphahlele)   25:344
"He Beats His Women" (Bukowski)   108:84
"He 'Digesteth Harde Yron'" (Moore)   10:347; 47:262, 267
"He Don't Plant Cotton" (Powers)   1:282
"He Held Radical Light" (Ammons)   9:27; 57:59
"He Is a Strange Biological Phenomenon" (Atwood)   25:67
"He Is Last Seen" (Atwood)   25:67
"He Kept on Burning" (Ai)   69:7
"He Knew" (Himes)   58:265
"He Loves Me, He Loves Me Not" (Achebe)   26:21
"He na tye Woman" (Allen)   84:4
"He of the Assembly" (Bowles)   53:41
"He Reappears" (Atwood)   25:67
"He Resigns" (Berryman)   8:93; 13:83; 25:95-6; 62:46
"He Sees Through Stone" (Knight)   40:279, 281, 286
He/She (Gold)   42:193-94
"He Shuttles" (Sturgeon)   22:410
"He Tears Easily . . ." (Rozewicz)   9:465
"He that None could Capture" (Swenson)   106:337
"He Was Such a Nice Chap—Why Did He Do It?" (Brunner)   8:110
He Who Hunted Birds in His Father's Village: The Dimensions of a Haida Myth (Snyder)   32:393
He Who Lived His Life Over Again (Lagerkvist)
   See *Han som fik leva om sitt liv*
He Who Must Die (Capra)   16:157
He Who Searches (Valenzuela)
   See *Como en la guerra*
"He Who Shapes" (Zelazny)   21:467, 479

"he wrote in lovely blood" (Bukowski)   108:75
"The Head" (Phillips)   28:363-64
"Head" (Prince)   35:323-25
Head above Water (Emecheta)   48:101
Head and Heart (Guillen)
   See *Cerebro y corazón*
Head Comix (Crumb)   17:82
The Head, Guts and Soundbone Dance (Cook)   58:149-50, 154-58
"Head Hewn with an Axe" (Tomlinson)   13:546
Head in the Clouds (Troyat)   23:461
The Head in the Soup (Levi)   41:246
Head o' W-Hollow (Stuart)   14:513; 34:373, 376
"Head of a Girl, at the Met" (Updike)   43:436
"The Head of Babylon" (Barnes)   29:32
"The Head of the Bed" (Hollander)   5:187; 8:300, 302; 14:264
"The Head on the Pole" (Neruda)   1:247
Head over Heels (Silver)   20:345-46
Head over Wheels (Kingman)   17:247
Head to Toe (Orton)   43:325, 328, 330
"The Head Transplant" (Durcan)   43:113
Headbirths; or, The Germans Are Dying Out (Grass)   32:202-05; 49:142
Headhunter (Findley)   102:117-18, 121
"Heading for Nandi" (Updike)   23:476
"Heading Home" (Campbell)   93:106
"Heading Home" (Endo)   99:297, 307
Heading West (Betts)   28:35-6
The Headless Cupid (Snyder)   17:471-72
"The Headless Hawk" (Capote)   13:133-34, 136, 140; 38:81; 58:86
Headman (Platt)   26:351-52, 355
"The Headmaster" (McPhee)   36:296-97
"The Head-Rape" (Thomas)   13:541
Heads (Brenton)   31:57
"Heads Float about Me" (Peake)   54:369
"Heads in the Women's Ward" (Larkin)   64:264
"Heads of Houses" (Taylor)   37:413
The Heads of the Town up to the Aether (Spicer)   8:498; 18:510; 72:348, 350, 357
Heads You Win, Tails I Lose (Holland)   21:148
"Headwaiter" (Himes)   108:235, 241
"Headwaters" (Momaday)   85:233, 266, 277
Healer (Dickinson)   35:136, 138
The Healer (Slaughter)   29:375
The Healers (Armah)   33:29, 32-4
"Healing Animal" (Harjo)   83:275
The Healing Art (Wilson)   33:452
The Healing Arts (Kettelkamp)   12:308
"The Healing of Mis" (Clarke)   6:112
"Healing Our Wounds: Liberatory Mental Health Care" (hooks)   94:159
Health (Altman)   116:59
"The Health of the Sick" (Cortazar)   5:110
A Health unto His Majesty (Hibbert)   7:156
"The Healthiest Girl in Town" (Stafford)   7:457; 68:423, 431, 449
"Healthy Kate" (Markson)   67:193
Hear and Forgive (Humphreys)   47:178, 185, 187
Hear, My Country, My Affliction (Arrabal)
   See *Oye, patria, mi aflicción*
Hear That Lonesome Whistle Blow: Railroads of the West (Brown)   47:38-9
"Hear the Dogs Barking" (Rulfo)
   See "No oyes ladrar los perros"
"Hear the Voice of the Bard" (Ewart)   46:153
Hear the Wind Blow! (Beecher)   6:48
"Heard by a Girl" (Bogan)   46:83; 93:64
"Hearing" (Merwin)   45:274
Hearing (Page)   40:350-51

"Hearing of the End of the War" (Tillinghast) 29:416

Hearing Secret Harmonies (Powell) 7:338-41, 343-45; 9:435-38; 10:416-17; 31:320

"Hearing Steps" (Simic) 68:364

"The Hearse" (Tchicaya)
See "Le Corbillard"

"The Heart" (Merwin) 88:205

"Heart" (Seth) 90:350

The Heart (Ichikawa) 20:181-82

"Heart and Mind" (Sitwell) 67:320

"Heart and Soul" (Giles) 39:64

"Heart Believes with Blows" (Broumas) 73:9

Heart Disease (Silverstein and Silverstein) 17:455

A Heart for the Gods of Mexico (Aiken) 52:25

The Heart Hears Songs of Home (Vesaas)
See *Hjarta høyrer sine heimlandstonar*

The Heart Is a Lonely Hunter (McCullers) 1:207-09; 4:345-46; 10:335-36, 338-40; 12:408-09, 412-14, 422-28, 430, 432; 48:230-31, 234-35, 237-38, 240; 100:240-41, 245-49, 251, 254, 256, 258-60, 264, 268, 272

"The Heart Never Fits Its Wanting" (Abbott) 48:3

The Heart Never Fits Its Wanting (Abbott) 48:3

"Heart of a Champion" (Boyle) 36:57; 90:63

"Heart of a Dybbuk" (Shields) 97:431, 433

"The Heart of a King" (Plomer) 4:406

Heart of a Stranger (Laurence) 278-81

The Heart of a Woman (Angelou) 35:30-2; 64:24-5, 27, 33, 36, 39; 77:4-7, 13-15, 18, 22, 26-7

The Heart of Another (Gellhorn) 60:179-181, 191

"Heart of Autumn" (Warren) 13:582; 18:534; 39:258, 266; 59:297

Heart of Aztlan (Anaya) 23:25-6

Heart of Glass (Herzog) 16:328, 331, 333

"Heart of Gold" (Lavin) 99:321

"Heart of Gold" (Young) 17:571

"The Heart of Hialmar" (Walker) 13:566

"Heart of the Backlog" (Warren) 18:537

Heart of the Comet (Benford) 52:74-7

"Heart of the Country" (McCartney) 35:279

Heart of the Country (Matthews) 45:243-44

The Heart of the Country (Weldon) 59:229-34

The Heart of the Matter (Greene) 1:131-33, 135; 3:206, 209-10, 213-14; 6:213,216-20; 9:244, 250-51; 14:216-18; 27:173; 37:136, 140; 70:289-91, 293-95; 72:148-49, 151-52, 155, 177-78

Heart of the River (Slaughter) 56:410

"The Heart of Thomas Hardy" (Betjeman) 43:34, 44

"The Heart on the Water" (Pasolini) 106:260

Heart Songs, and Other Stories 81:275

"Heart to Hang Onto" (Townshend) 17:537

"Heartache" (Townshend) 17:528, 531

"Heartbeat" (Harjo) 83:271

Heartbreak (Aragon)
See *Le crève-coeur*

The Heartbreak Kid (May) 16:432-37

Heartbreak Tango (Puig)
See *Boquitas pintadas, folletín*

"Heartbreaker" (Jagger and Richard)
See "Doo Doo Doo Doo Doo"

"Heartbreaker" (Page and Plant) 12:474

Heartbreaks along the Road (Carrier)
See *De l'amour dans la ferraille*

"Heartburn" (Calisher) 38:67

"Heartburn" (Taylor) 44:302

Heartburn (Ephron) 31:157-59

"The Hearth" (Arghezi)
See "Gura vetrei"

The Heartkeeper (Sagan) 17:425-26

"Heartland" (Hogan) 73:150

"Heartland" (Phillips) 96:321-22, 326

Heartland (Harris) 25:204, 214

Heartland (Maloff) 5:271

Heartlight (Diamond) 30:114

"The Hearts" (Pinsky) 94:306, 310

"The Heart's Advantage" (Shacochis) 39:199

"The Heart's Garden/The Garden's Heart" (Rexroth) 49:276, 279; 112:386, 402

The Heart's Garden/The Garden's Heart (Rexroth) 2:370; 6:450; 22:347-49; 49:278; 112:372-73, 387

The Heart's Journey (Sassoon) 36:392

"Heart's Needle" (Snodgrass) 6:514; 18:494; 68:383, 388, 390, 395-96

Heart's Needle (Snodgrass) 2:404-06; 6:513-14; 18:490-92; 68:382-83, 387-88, 390-92, 395-98

The Hearts of Men: American Dreams and the Flight from Commitment (Ehrenreich) 110:156, 161, 165, 176-77

"Hearts of Oak and Bellies of Brass" (McGahern) 48:263, 266-68

"Hearts Together" (Betjeman) 43:48

Heartsease (Dickinson) 12:168, 170, 172-74

Heart-Shape in the Dust (Hayden) 37:155-56, 160

Heartstones (Rendell) 48:327

Heartway Guide (Tzara)
See *Indicateur des chemins de coeur*

"Heat" (H. D.)
See "Garden"

"Heat" (Johnson) 52:232, 234

"Heat" (Moure) 88:230

Heat (Goldman) 48:130

Heat (Hunter) 31:226

"Heat 2" (Moure) 88:230

"Heat 3" (Moure) 88:230

Heat and Dust (Jhabvala) 8:311-12; 29:259-60, 262-63; 94:171, 174, 179, 183-89, 193-94, 196-99, 201-6, 212

Heat and Other Stories (Oates) 108:374, 379, 383, 385

Heat Death (Dobyns) 37:78-9

"The Heat Death of the Universe" (Zoline) 62:460-64

The Heat Death of the Universe, and Other Stories (Zoline)
See *Busy about the Tree of Life*

"Heat Lightning" (Jiles) 58:279

"Heat Lightning" (Smith) 25:411

The Heat of the Day (Bowen) 1:39; 3:82; 11:62-4; 15:79-80

The Heat of the Sun: Stories and Tales (O'Faolain) 14:404; 32:340; 70:319

"The Heat Rises in Gusts" (Stern) 40:414

"Heat Wave Breaks" (Warren) 13:582

"The Heathen" (Marley) 17:269-70

Heathen Valley (Linney) 51:257

The Heat's On (Himes) 18:246; 58:258, 267; 108:233, 236, 238-39, 268

"Heatwave/St. Louis" (Jiles) 58:272, 280

"Heaven" (Byrne) 26:98

"Heaven" (Gaitskill) 69:199-200, 203

"Heaven" (Levine) 14:317

Heaven (Barker) 37:39

Heaven and Crap (Arrabal) 58:17

"Heaven and Earth" (Gluck) 81:167

Heaven and Hell (Huxley) 4:239, 241; 18:270; 35:241

"Heaven as Anus" (Kumin) 13:326; 28:224

"Heaven Help the Devil" (Lightfoot) 26:283

"Heaven, in a Way" (Hall) 51:173

Heaven, in a Way (Hall) 51:172-73

"Heaven Is Ten Zillion Light Years Away" (Wonder) 12:657

Heaven Knows Where (Enright) 31:151-52

The Heaven Makers (Herbert) 12:278; 35:196, 198-99; 44:393-94

"The Heaven of Animals" (Dickey) 1:73; 7:83

"Heaven on a Summer Night" (Beattie) 63:18

Heaven on Earth (Elliott) 47:108-10

"The Heavenly Animal" (Phillips) 15:421

"Heavenly City, Earthly City" (Duncan) 7:88

The Heavenly Ladder (Mackenzie) 18:314

Heaven's My Destination (Wilder) 1:364, 366; 5:496; 6:575-77; 15:572-73, 575; 82:342-43, 345, 349, 365, 373-74, 376, 378

Heaven's Secret (Lagerkvist)
See *Himlens hemlighet*

Heavensgate (Okigbo) 25:347, 349, 351, 354-55; 84:299-302, 304, 306-07, 309, 313, 317-18, 321-22, 327, 330, 336-37

"The Heaviness of Clay" (Seifert) 93:337

"The Heaviness of His Wisdom" (Berry) 46:70

"The Heavy" (Ferlinghetti) 111:65

"The Heavy Bear That Goes with Me" (Schwartz) 10:462, 465; 45:356

"Heavy Breathing" (Hughes) 108:331

Heavy Breathing (Whalen) 29:447

"Heavy Connection" (Morrison) 21:237

Heavy Laden (Wylie) 43:459-60, 462, 469

"Heavy Music" (Seger) 35:378-81, 383, 386

Heavy Sand (Rybakov)
See *Heavy Sands*

Heavy Sands (Heavy Sand) (Rybakov) 23:370-74; 53:295

"The Heavy Sugar" (Woolrich) 77:402

Heavy Traffic (Bakshi) 26:68-70, 73-5

"Heavy Women" (Plath) 5:340; 111:167

"The Hebrides" (Longley) 29:293, 296

Hécate (Jouve) 47:203

Hechima kun (Mr. Gourd) (Endo) 54:159

The Heckler (Hunter) 31:220

"Hector and Freddie" (Wilding) 73:395, 398

"The Hector Quesadilla Story" (Boyle) 36:63

"Hedge Tutor" (Fuller) 62:203

"The Hedgeapple" (Bell) 31:51

"The Hedgehog Killed on the Road" (Blunden) 56:41

"Hedges in Winter" (Muldoon) 32:317

Hedy (Warhol) 20:422

Hedylus (H. D.) 31:207-08, 210; 73:112-13, 122-23, 131-33

Heed the Thunder (Thompson) 69:383

The Heel of Achilles: Essays, 1968-1973 (Koestler) 6:281

"Heemskerck Shoals" (FitzGerald) 19:175, 179

The Heidi Chronicles (Wasserstein) 59:218-27

The Heidi Chronicles, and Other Plays (Wasserstein) 90:424-25, 427, 430-37, 439

"Heigh-Ho on a Winter Afternoon" (Davie) 5:114

The Height of the Scream (Campbell) 42:86, 88-90

"Heights of Folly" (Simic) 68:377

The Heights of Macchu Picchu (Neruda)
See *Alturas de Macchu Picchu*

"The Heights of Trapua" (Cabral de Melo Neto)
See "Alto do Trapuá"

Das Heilige Experiment (*The Strong Are Lonely*) (Hochwalder)   36:232-40
Heimatmuseum (*The Heritage*) (Lenz)   27:254-56
Heimsljós (*World Light*) (Laxness)   25:293, 296, 299
Heine's Germany (Faludy)   42:139
"The Heiress" (Akhmatova)   64:13
"The Heiress of All the Ages" (Rahv)   24:354
"Heirloom" (Spinrad)   46:384
The Heirs of Columbus (Vizenor)   70:348; 103:312, 319-20, 334, 340
Heirs of Darkness (Snyder)   17:475
"The Heirs of Stalin" (Yevtushenko)
   See "Stalin's Heirs"
"Heirs of the Living Body" (Munro)   95:300
"Hejira" (Mitchell)   12:442
Hejira (Mitchell)   12:440, 443
"Hélas" (Creeley)   78:134
Hélas (Simenon)   47:374
"Heldensagen" (Hope)   51:211
Held's Angels (Gilbreth and Carey)   17:154
"Helen" (Elytis)   49:110; 100:172
"Helen" (Gustafson)   36:222
"Helen" (H. D.)   73:118
"Helen" (Hellman)   52:201-02
"Helen" (Jeffers)   11:305
"Helen" (Lowell)   1:182
"Helen" (Wilbur)   14:577; 110:348
Helen (Ritsos)   13:488
"Helen Grown Old" (Lewis)   41:255
"Helen, I Love You" (Farrell)   66:131
Helen in Egypt (H. D.)   3:217; 8:258; 14:223, 230; 31:204, 206-08, 211-12; 34:442; 73:121, 123-27, 139-41, 143
Helen of Troy, N.Y. (Connelly)   7:56
"Helen, Thy Beauty Is to Me—" (Fante)   60:133
"Helen Wheels" (McCartney)   35:282
Helena (Waugh)   27:470, 472; 44:522-23; 107:360, 367, 369-70
"Helen's Exile" (Camus)   2:99
"Helicinas, Mollusles, and Wentletraps" (Dubie)   36:135
"A Helicopter View of Terrestrial Stars" (Murray)   40:336
Det heliga landet (Lagerkvist)   10:312; 13:332-33
"Heliodora" (H. D.)   31:201; 73:107, 120
Heliodora, and Other Poems (H. D.)   31:208; 73:107-10, 113, 120
"Heliogabalus" (Squires)   51:379
"Hell" (Graves)   45:165
"Hell" (Justice)   102:281
"The Hell Cantos" (Pound)   112:350-51, 356-57
Hell Has No Limits (Donoso)
   See *El lugar sin límites*
Hell House (Matheson)   37:247
A Hell of a Woman (Thompson)   69:379, 381, 383, 387, 389
Hell on Ice (Welles)   80:379-80
"The Hell Poem" (Berryman)   62:58
"Hellas Is Florida" (Benford)   52:62
The Hellenic Secret (Strugatskii and Strugatskii)   27:432
Heller in Pink Tights (L'Amour)   55:306
"Hell-Fire" (Asimov)   26:40
Hellfire (Saul)   46:369
The Hellfire Club (Straub)   107:301-04
Helliconia Spring (Aldiss)   40:18-22
Helliconia Summer (Aldiss)   40:19-22
Helliconia Winter (Aldiss)   40:21-2

"Hello" (Corso)   11:123
Hello (*Hello: A Journal, February 29-May 3, 1976*) (Creeley)   11:139; 78:140, 147
Hello: A Journal, February 29-May 3, 1976 (Creeley)
   See *Hello*
"Hello Again" (Diamond)   30:113
Hello America (Ballard)   36:42
Hello and Goodbye (Fugard)   5:130; 9:232-34; 14:189; 40:197, 201; 80:62, 69, 74
"Hello Cheeverland, Goodbye" (Findley)   102:100, 104, 108
Hello, Darkness (Sissman)   18:487, 489
"Hello, I Love You" (Morrison)   17:290-91, 295
Hello, I'm Erica Jong (Acker)   111:17
"Hello Mr. Soul" ("Mr. Soul") (Young)   17:569, 577-78
"Hello, Mrs. Newman" (Levine)   54:297
Hello, My Love, Goodbye (Weber)   12:634
"Hello, Operator? I Don't Want a Policeman" (Perelman)   49:258
Hello Out There (Saroyan)   10:453; 56:376
Hello...Wrong Number (Sachs)   35:334
Hell's Angels: A Strange and Terrible Saga (Thompson)   9:526; 17:503-05, 510-11; 40:426; 104:337, 339, 343, 347-50
Hellstrom's Hive (Herbert)   12:275-76; 35:196; 44:394
Helmet of Clay (*A Helmetful of Earth*; *Prilba hliny*) (Seifert)   34:257; 93:306, 319, 335, 343, 346
A Helmetful of Earth (Seifert)
   See *Helmet of Clay*
Helmets (Dickey)   2:117; 7:80-1, 83-4; 109:244
Helmets and Wasps (Mott)   15:379
"The Helmsman" (Cunningham)   31:97, 100, 102, 104
"The Helmsman" (H. D.)   73:109
The Helmsman (Cunningham)   31:96, 99
"The Helmsmen" (Merwin)   18:334; 45:277-78
Hèloïse (Hebert)   29:239-41
"Help" (Lennon and McCartney)   35:270, 274
"Help" (Tiptree)   48:385
Help! (Lester)   20:219-22
"Help, I'm a Rock" (Zappa)   17:588
"Help Me, Rhonda" (Wilson)   12:644, 647, 653
Help Stamp Out Marriage (Waterhouse)
   See *Say Who You Are*
"Help Thou Mine Unbelief" (MacLennan)   92:308, 330, 346
Help Wanted (Kroetz)   41:241
"Help Your Child to Wonder" (Carson)   71:104-05
"Helpful O'Malley" (Bainbridge)   62:35-6, 38
"A Helping Hand" (Sansom)   6:483
"Helpless" (Young)   17:570, 574
Hemingway (Lynn)   50:412-16, 418-20, 422-30
Hemingway: A Biography (Meyers)   39:427-34
Hemingway at Midnight (Cowley)   39:460
"Hemingway in Space" (Amis)   40:43
Hemingway's First War (Reynolds)   44:516-17
Hemligheter på vägen (*Secrets on the Road*; *Secrets on the Way*) (Transtroemer)   52:409-10, 412; 65:226, 229, 233-34, 236
"Hemlock" (Williams)   42:442
Hemlock and After (Wilson)   2:471, 473-74; 3:535; 5:513-14; 25:459, 464; 34:581
"Hemlocks" (Dorn)   10:159

Hemmet och stjärnan (*The Home and the Star*) (Lagerkvist)   54:275
"The Hen" (Voigt)   54:429
"The Hen Flower" (Kinnell)   3:269; 29:282
"The Hen House" (Montague)   46:267
"Henceforth, from the Mind" (Bogan)   46:84, 86-7, 89; 93:61, 67, 69, 76, 81
Henceforward (Ayckbourn)   74:19-20, 25, 31, 34-5
Henderson the Rain King (Bellow)   1:28-31; 2:49, 51, 53-4; 3:48, 50, 53-9; 6:53-5, 58, 60; 8:69, 73-7, 79; 10:44; 13:71-3; 15:47-9, 52, 54-5, 57; 25:80-1, 85; 33:66, 71; 34:545; 63:28, 32; 79:76, 83
Hengest's Tale (Walsh)   35:429
Henri Christophe: A Chronicle in Seven Scenes (Walcott)   25:453
Henri Matisse (Aragon)   22:39
"Henrietta and Alexandra" (Barthelme)   46:42
Henry Adams (Blackmur)   24:66
Henry and Cato (Murdoch)   8:405-06; 11:384-85, 389-90; 31:294
"Henry Bech Redux" (Updike)   5:454
"Henry by Night" (Berryman)   13:83; 25:92
Henry Geldzahler (Warhol)   20:415
"Henry James" (Nye)   42:305
Henry James (West)   7:525; 9:560; 31:450
"Henry James and His Cult" (Rahv)   24:359
"Henry James as a Characteristic American" (Moore)   47:268, 270
"Henry James by the Pacific" (Justice)   102:277
Henry James: The Conquest of London, 1870-1881 (Edel)   29:168-69
Henry James: The Master, 1901-1916 (Edel)   29:171
Henry James: The Middle Years, 1882-1895 (Edel)   29:168-69
Henry James: The Treacherous Years, 1895-1901 (Edel)   29:169-70, 172
Henry James: The Untried Years, 1843-1870 (Edel)   29:167
Henry Miller: Letters to Anaïs Nin (Miller)   84:249
"Henry the Navigator" (McAuley)   45:248
Henry Three (Krumgold)   12:318-20
Henry V (Olivier)   20:234-35, 237, 242-43
"Henry's Confession" (Berryman)
   See "Dream Song 76"
"Henry's Fate" (Berryman)   8:93
Henry's Fate and Other Poems, 1967-1972 (Berryman)   10:46-8; 13:83; 62:43, 70, 74
"Henry's Understanding" (Berryman)   13:83; 25:92, 96
"A Hepcat May Look at a King" (Perelman)   49:262
"Hephaestus" (Wilbur)   6:570
"Heptonstall" (Hughes)   37:178
"Heptonstall Graveyard, 22 October 1989" (Durcan)   70:151-52
"Her" (Lessing)   94:265
Her (Ferlinghetti)   2:133; 10:175, 177-78; 111:59-66
Her (H. D.)
   See *HERmione*
"Her and It" (Berryman)   25:92
Her Brother (Ichikawa)   20:182
"Her Dream House" (Bell)   8:66
"Her Early Work" (Swenson)   106:340-41
"Her Girls" (Ferber)   93:162
"Her Hand" (Honig)   33:213
"Her Hand Given Over" (Aleixandre)   36:30
"Her Kind" (Sexton)   10:468; 53:314, 316,

318, 320, 324

"Her Longing" (Roethke) **101**:331

"Her Morning Dreams" (Fuller) **62**:187, 203

Her Mothers (Broner) **19**:71

Her Mother's Daughter (French) **60**:147-50

"Her Quaint Honor" (Gordon) **13**:248; **83**:231

"Her Report" (Ryan) **65**:215

"Her Reticence" (Roethke) **101**:331

"Her Second Career" (Rand) **79**:374

"Her Sense of Timing" (Elkin) **91**:217-19, 223

Her Side of It (Savage) **40**:376

"Her Smoke Rises Up Forever" (Tiptree) **48**:390, 392

"Her Strut" (Seger) **35**:384

"Her Sweet Jerome" (Walker) **58**:404; **103**:398, 406-07

"Her Table Spread" (Bowen) **3**:84; **22**:64-5

"Her Three Days" (Ousmane) **66**:349

"Her Throat" (Wakoski) **2**:459

"Her Time" (Roethke) **101**:331

Her Victory (Sillitoe) **57**:396

"Her Voice Could Not Be Softer" (Clarke) **9**:168

"Her Whole Existence" (Himes) **108**:227

"Her Wisdom" (Merwin) **45**:269

"Her Words" (Roethke) **101**:331

"Her Wrath" (Roethke) **101**:266, 332-33

"Hera, Hung from the Sky" (Kizer) **80**:171, 184

"Heraclitus by the Lake" **75**:69

"Heraclitus on Rivers" (Mahon) **27**:292

"Herakleitos" (Davenport) **14**:140

Herakles (MacLeish) **3**:310; **8**:362; **14**:336-37

"The Herb of Death" (Christie) **110**:144-45

L'herbe (*The Grass*) (Simon) **4**:495; **9**:482; **15**:485-86, 490-94; **39**:204-05, 207-10

Die Herberge (Hochwalder) **36**:238

"Herbert White" (Bidart) **33**:74, 76, 78

"Herbier de Bretagne" (Guillevic) **33**:193

Herbs and Apples (Santmyer) **33**:355-56

"Herbstmanöver" (Bachmann) **69**:38

"Herbsttag" (Hildesheimer) **49**:179

Hercule Poirot's Christmas (Christie) **48**:71, 73

"Hercules and Antaeus" (Heaney) **74**:158, 162

Hercules, My Shipmate (Graves) **39**:322

A Herd of Deer (Dillon) **17**:98, 101

"The Herds" (Merwin) **88**:202

"Here" (Abse) **7**:2

"Here" (Creeley) **36**:121

"Here" (Larkin) **8**:332, 339; **9**:325; **18**:296-97, 301; **33**:260; **39**:341; **64**:266, 276, 279

"Here" (Monette) **82**:323

"Here and Elsewhere" (Walcott) **76**:275

"Here and Now" (Levine) **14**:321

Here and Now (Levertov) **28**:242; **66**:237-38

"Here and There" (Dunn) **36**:155

"Here and There" (Montale) **9**:387

"Here and There" (Wallace) **114**:347

"Here at Cubist College" (Grayson) **38**:210

"Here Be Dragons" (Baldwin) **42**:21

"Here Be Dragons" (Stevenson) **7**:463

"Here, but Unable to Answer" (Hugo) **32**:250

"Here Come the Clowns—Didn't They?" (McGinley) **14**:367

"Here Come Those Tears Again" (Browne) **21**:38

Here Comes, and Other Poems (Jong) **6**:270; **83**:298

Here Comes Everybody: An Introduction to

James Joyce for the Ordinary Reader (*Re Joyce*) (Burgess) **10**:86; **40**:122

Here Comes the Groom (Capra) **16**:160

"Here Comes the Maples" (Updike) **15**:546

"Here Comes the Night" (Wilson) **12**:653-54

"Here Comes the Weekend" (Weller) **26**:443-44

Here Comes There Goes (Saroyan) **56**:385

"Here Comes Yet Another Day" (Davies) **21**:94

"Here, Daphne!" (Masters) **48**:224

Here Endeth the Lesson (Bermant) **40**:92

"Here in the Night" (Jensen) **37**:186, 189

Here Is a Ghost (Abe)

   See *Yurei wa koko ni iru*

"here is another bone to pick with you" (Clifton) **66**:83

Here Is Einbaum (Morris) **3**:344; **7**:247

"Here Is New York" (White) **39**:370, 377

"Here It Is" (Ignatow) **40**:260

"Here Lies a Lady" (Ransom) **4**:431

Here Lies Our Sovereign Lord (Hibbert) **7**:156

Here Lies: The Collected Stories of Dorothy Parker (Parker) **68**:327

Here, My Dear (Gaye) **26**:133-34

"Here Next the Chair I Was When Winter Went" (Graham) **29**:198

"Here on a Darkling Plain" (Derleth) **31**:133

"Here She Comes Now" (Reed) **21**:319

"Here the Legions Halted, Here the Ranks Were Broken" (Masefield) **47**:233

"Here There Be Tygers" (King) **37**:207; **61**:331

"Here to Learn" (Bowles) **53**:39-40, 44

Here to Stay: Studies in Human Tenacity (Hersey) **97**:305

"Here to Yonder" (Hughes) **108**:321

"Here Today" (Carruth) **84**:127

"Here Today" (McCartney) **35**:289-91, 293

"Here Today" (Wilson) **12**:646

"Here We Are a Point of Sanity" (Kogawa) **78**:167

"Here We Loved" (Amichai) **116**:95

"Heredity" (Harrison) **43**:179

Hérémakhonon: On doit attendre le bonheur (*Happy Homecoming*) (Conde) **52**:85; **52**:79-82, 85; **92**:99-100, 102, 104-05, 107-09, 111-12, 126, 130-31

"Here's Ronnie" (Amis) **62**:5

"Here's to the State of Mississippi" (Ochs) **17**:331

"Here's to the State of Richard Nixon" (Ochs) **17**:334

"The Heresy of Paraphrase" (Brooks) **110**:35

The Heresy of Self-Love: A Study of Subversive Individualism (Zweig) **34**:378

"The Heretical Cricket" (Momaday) **85**:274

Los heréticos (*The Heretics*) (Valenzuela) **31**:438; **104**:355-57, 376-77

The Heretics (Valenzuela)

   See *Los heréticos*

Heretics of Dune (Herbert) **35**:206-08; **44**:393-94

"Herida en cuatro tiempos" (Rodriguez) **10**:440

"Heritage" (Christie) **110**:127

"Heritage" (Still) **49**:363, 365

The Heritage (Lenz)

   See *Heimatmuseum*

Heritage (West) **50**:359-60

A Heritage and Its History (Compton-Burnett) **1**:61

Heritage of Hastur (Bradley) **30**:27, 29-31

"A Heritage of Liberation" (Kunene) **85**:175

A Heritage of Stars (Simak) **55**:320

Herkules und der Stall des Augias (Duerrenmatt) **102**:61-2, 70, 76

Herkules und der Stall des Augias (Durrenmatt) **15**:196

"Herlinda Leaves" (Castellanos) **66**:55-6

Hermaios (Rexroth) **11**:473; **22**:345

Herman and Alice (Mohr) **12**:446

Hermann Lauscher (Hesse) **17**:198

   See *Hinterlassene Schriften und Gedichte von Hermann Lauscher*

"El hermano mayor" (Castellanos) **66**:50

Hermes 3000 (Kotzwinkle) **35**:254

Hermes, Dog and Star (Herbert)

   See *Hermes, pies i gwiazda*

"Hermes of The Ways" (H. D.) **73**:105, 115, 139

Hermes, pies i gwiazda (*Hermes, Dog and Star*) (Herbert) **43**:183, 192

"Hermetic Definition" (H. D.) **8**:258; **14**:224; **31**:204-05, 208, 211; **73**:143-44

Hermetic Definition (H. D.) **73**:136, 139, 143

"Hermetiques ouvriers" (Char) **11**:116

L'hermine (*The Ermine*) (Anouilh) **13**:16, 19, 21; **40**:55; **50**:279

HERmione (*Her*) (H. D.) **14**:229, 231; **31**:209-12; **73**:135

"A Hermit" (Mahon) **27**:288

"The Hermit" (Smith) **64**:391

The Hermit (Ionesco)

   See *Le solitaire*

The Hermit and Other Stories (Smith) **64**:391

"The Hermit at Outermost House" (Plath) **11**:446

"The Hermit Cackleberry Brown, on Human Vanity" (Williams) **13**:600

The Hermit of 69th Street: The Working Papers of Norbert Kosky (Kosinski) **53**:227-29; **70**:298, 302, 307-09

"The Hermit of Hudson Pond" (Van Duyn) **116**:410

"Hermonax" (H. D.) **31**:213

"Hero" (Creeley) **78**:140

"The Hero" (Friedman) **56**:97

"Hero" (Madhubuti) **73**:211

"The Hero" (Moore) **10**:350; **47**:270

"The Hero" (Neruda)

   See "El héroe"

"The Hero" (Sassoon) **36**:385, 392

The Hero (Kopit) **33**:249-50

The Hero (Maugham) **15**:365, 370

A Hero Ain't Nothin but a Sandwich (Childress) **12**:106-08; **86**:306, 308, 312; **96**:91, 100, 108

The Hero and the Blues (Murray) **73**:230, 236, 238, 240, 243

"The Hero and the Hydra" (McAuley) **45**:246, 250-51, 254

A Hero in His Time (Cohen) **7**:51-2; **31**:93

"Hero Negative" (Coles) **67**:181

"The Hero of Currie Road" (Paton) **10**:388

"Hero of Our Time" (Megged) **9**:375

The Hero Rises Up (Arden) **6**:10; **15**:21-2, 25

The Hero with a Thousand Faces (Campbell) **69**:67-9, 72, 74, 76, 80-4, 88-91, 93, 95, 97, 99

The Hero with the Private Parts (Lytle) **22**:293

"Hero Worship" (Parker) **68**:336

Herod and Mariamne (Lagerkvist)

   See *Mariamne*

"El héroe" ("The Hero") (Neruda) **28**:315

"The Heroes" (Simpson) **32**:382

Heroes (Bowie) **17**:65-7

Heroes (McGinniss) **32**:301-02

Heroes (Poliakoff) **38**:377, 380, 385

Heroes (Shields) **97**:420, 423-24, 429, 432-33

"Heroes and Villains" (Wilson) **12**:645

Heroes and Villains (Carter) **5**:102; **41**:113; **76**:329

"Heroes Are Gang Leaders" (Baraka) **33**:55; **115**:15-6

Heroes Are Grazing in My Garden (Padilla)
   See *En mi jardín pastan los héroes*

"Heroes are Made in Childhood" (Greene) **72**:151

"Heroes Die but Once" (Spinrad) **46**:384

"Heroes/Elders" (Creeley) **78**:160

"The Heroes in the Dark House" (Kiely) **23**:268; **43**:244

The Heroic Age (Haviaras) **33**:205-07

Heroic and Elegiac Song for the Lost Second Lieutenant of the Alb nian Campaign (Elytis)
   See *Ázma iroikó ke pénthimo yia ton haméno anthipolohaghó tis Alvanías*

"Heroic and Elegiac Song for the Lost Second Lieutenant of the Albanian Campaign" (Elytis) **100**:155, 175, 190, 192

"Heroic Simile" (Hass) **18**:209, 211, 213

"The Heroics of Realism" (Hartman) **27**:179

"Heroin" (Reed) **21**:302, 307-08, 314, 316, 318-20, 322

"Heroine" (Dinesen) **10**:151; **29**:159; **95**:42

"The Heroine" (Highsmith) **102**:205, 220

"Heroines" (Rich) **36**:370

"The Heron" ("Caplja") (Aksyonov) **101**:28, 41-2

"Heron" (Plumly) **33**:312

"The Heron" (Watkins) **43**:454

Heron (Aksyonov)
   See *Caplja*

The Heron (Bassani) **9**:75-6

"The Heron and the Astronaut" (Lindbergh) **82**:166

"Heron at Port Talbot" (Clarke) **61**:82

Les Héros de mon enfance (Tremblay) **102**:372

"A Hero's Death" (Lagerkvist) **54**:276

"The Hero's Kitchen" (Johnston) **51**:243

"Hero's Return" (Hunter) **35**:226

Herovit's World (Malzberg) **7**:208

Herr Nightingale and the Satin Woman (Kotzwinkle) **35**:255

The Herr Witch Doctor (Millin) **49**:250, 252

Hers (Alvarez) **5**:19-20

Herself (Calisher) **2**:96-7; **4**:87

Herself Defined: The Poet H.D. and Her World (Guest) **34**:441-45, 447

"Herself in Love" (Wiggins) **57**:433-34, 436

Herself in Love (Wiggins) **57**:433-36, 438-40

Herzog (Bellow) **1**:31-3; **2**:50-1, 53; **3**:48-51, 53-6, 58, 60-1; **6**:50, 52, 54-5, 58, 60-1; **8**:68-9, 73-7; **10**:42; **13**:66-7, 69, 73; **15**:46-7, 49-50, 54-6, 58; **25**:80-1, 84-6; **33**:65-6, 69-71; **34**:545; **63**:27, 30-2, 35, 38-9, 41; **79**:76, 79, 83

"He's a Real Gone Guy: A Short Requiem for Percival Angleman" (McGrath) **59**:175

"He's Misstra Know-It-All" (Wonder) **12**:657

He's My Boy (Gilbreth and Carey) **17**:156

"An Hesitation on the Bank of the Delaware" (Barthelme) **5**:54

"Hesperides" (Prokosch) **48**:307

The Hessian (Fast) **23**:159

"The Hessian Prisoner" (Bates) **46**:51

Hester Street (Silver) **20**:341-44

"Heterosexism and Dancing" (Blount) **38**:45

Hets (*Frenzy*; *Torment*) (Bergman) **16**:46; **72**:51, 61

Hetty Dorval (Wilson) **13**:607-09

"Hetty Sleeping" (Gardam) **43**:169

"He-Who-Came-Forth" (Levertov) **66**:237

"Hey Babe" (Young) **17**:576

Hey, Big Spender (Bonham) **12**:53-4

Hey, Dummy (Platt) **26**:350-51

"Hey, Have You Got a Cig, the Time, the News, My Face?" (Hannah) **90**:158, 160

"Hey Hey" (McCartney) **35**:291-92

"Hey Hey, My My" ("Into the Black") (Young) **17**:581, 583

Hey Jack! (Hannah) **90**:135-37, 145-46

"Hey Jude" (Lennon and McCartney) **35**:278, 294

Hey Little Walter **65**:444-48

"Hey Nineteen" (Becker and Fagen) **26**:85

"Hey Sailor, What Ship?" (Olsen) **13**:433; **114**:192, 194, 198, 222-23, 232-35

"Hey, Taxi!" (Ferber) **93**:162

Hey, That's My Soul You're Stomping On (Corcoran) **17**:77

"Hey You" (Lightfoot) **26**:282

Heyday (Spackman) **46**:375-76, 378

"Heyfitz" (Cohen) **19**:113

H.G. Wells: Critic of Progress (Williamson) **29**:457

Hi Johnny (Hunter) **21**:161

Hi, Mom! (De Palma) **20**:74

"HIALOG (any number can play)" (Avison) **97**:114

"Hiatus" (Avison) **97**:69, 74

"Hibernaculum" (Ammons) **2**:13-14; **3**:11; **5**:29, 31; **8**:16, 18; **9**:27-30; **25**:47; **57**:58-9; **108**:33-4, 36, 42, 45, 53

Hibernaculum (Ammons) **108**:60

"Hibernation" (Blackburn) **9**:100

"Hiccups" (Damas)
   See "Hoquet"

"Hickman Arrives" (Ellison) **86**:329; **114**:99, 102, 102

Hickory, Dickory, Dock (Christie) **110**:121

"Hid Life" (Avison) **97**:117

"The Hidden Bole" (FitzGerald) **19**:179, 181

The Hidden Canyon (Abbey) **59**:238

"Hidden Door" (Ferlinghetti) **2**:134; **111**:65

The Hidden Fortress (Kurosawa) **16**:397

The Hidden God (Brooks) **24**:107, 109, 114; **86**:278, 287; **110**:10, 12, 28-9

The Hidden God (Goldmann)
   See *Le Dieu caché*

The Hidden Ground of Love (Merton) **83**:404

"A Hidden History" (Okri) **87**:315

A Hidden Life (Dourado)
   See *Uma vida em segredo*

The Hidden Mountain (Roy)
   See *La montagne secrète*

"Hidden Name, Complex Fate" (Ellison) **54**:141; **114**:116

The Hidden Target (MacInnes) **27**:283-84

The Hidden Waterfall (Zaturenska) **6**:585; **11**:579-80

The Hidden Wound (Berry) **27**:32-3

"Hide and Seek" (Gunn) **32**:213

"Hide and Seek" (Scannell) **49**:328

Hide and Seek (Potter) **58**:388-89, 391; **86**:346

Hide and Seek (West) **17**:552

"Hideout" (Hugo) **32**:247-48

Hiding (Klein) **30**:240

"Hiding in Poems" (Nagy)
   See "Versben bujdosó"

Hiding in Poems (Nagy)
   See *Versben bujdosó*

"Hiding Man" (Barthelme) **115**:65-6, 71

Hiding Place (Wideman) **34**:298; **36**:454-55; **67**:374

"Hier ist Tibten" ("This Is Tibet!") (Boell) **72**:72

Hier régnant désert (Bonnefoy) **58**:43-5, 47-54, 57-9

"The Hieroglyphic Monad" (Leiris) **61**:361

"Hieroglyphics" (Harjo) **83**:284

High (Hinde) **6**:240-41

"High and Dry" (Lightfoot) **26**:280

High and Low (Betjeman) **10**:52; **43**:42-3, 46

High and Low (Kurosawa) **16**:402-04

The High and the Mighty (Gann) **23**:163-64

The High Cost of Living (Piercy) **14**:420-21; **18**:409; **62**:362, 365, 376

High Cotton (Pinckney) **76**:98-113

High Crimes and Misdemeanors (Greenberg) **30**:165-66

"High Dive" (Empson) **3**:147; **19**:154, 157

"High Gannet" (Parini) **54**:360-61

Th High Green Hill (Bissett) **18**:61-2

"High Ground" (McGahern) **48**:272-73

High Ground (McGahern) **48**:272-73

High Hearts (Brown) **43**:85-6; **79**:169

High Heels (Almodovar)
   See *Tacones lejanos*

The High House (Arundel) **17**:12-14, 16, 18

High in Vietnam Hot Damn (Pomerance) **13**:444

"High Island" (Murphy) **41**:318

High Island (Murphy) **41**:313-15, 317-20

"High John Is Risen Again" (Hamilton) **26**:152-53

The High King (Alexander) **35**:24

"The High Malady" (Pasternak)
   See "Vysokaya bolesn"

"High Plains Rag" (Galvin) **38**:198

The High Road (O'Brien) **116**:199-200

"The High Road of St. James" (Carpentier) **11**:101; **38**:95

"High School" (Beattie) **63**:18

High School (Wiseman) **20**:468-74, 476

"High Speed Car Wash" (Durcan) **43**:118

High Spirits (Davies) **42**:103; **75**:184

High Spirits (Jordan) **110**:275

High Stakes (Francis) **22**:152; **42**:149, 156

"A High Subjectivity" (Young) **82**:396, 412

"High Tension Lines across a Landscape" (Ciardi) **40**:154

High Tide in the Garden (Adcock) **41**:14-15, 17

High Time along the Wabash (Saroyan) **10**:454

"High to Low" (Hughes) **35**:222

High Towers (Costain) **30**:94-5

"High Water" (Mosher) **62**:312

High Water (Highsmith) **102**:205

The High White Wall (Sherburne) **30**:360-61

High, Wide, and Handsome (Mamoulian) **16**:423-24, 426

High Wind in Jamaica (Hughes) **1**:149

"High Windows" (Larkin) **5**:230-31; **8**:332, 339; **13**:339-40; **18**:301; **33**:261; **39**:346; **64**:265, 269, 272, 282, 284

High Windows (Larkin) **5**:225-31; **8**:332-33, 336-41; **9**:323; **13**:337-38, 340-41; **18**:297, 300-01; **33**:256, 259-62, 269; **39**:333-34, 338-39, 341, 344, 64:259, 263-64, 270-72, 275, 277-78, 280, 285

"Higher Arguments in Favor of Discipline..."

(Milosz) **82**:297

"Higher Ground" (Wonder) **12**:657, 661

Higher Ground (Phillips) **96**:321-24, 326-33, 335, 337, 339, 341, 343, 350, 354

"The Higher Keys" (Merrill) **34**:229, 236

Highest Standard of Living (Reddin) **67**:268-69

Highgate Road (Ammons) **25**:45

Highland Fling (Mitford) **44**:489, 492

"Highland Games" (MacCaig) **36**:287

"A Highland Girl Studying Poetry" (Smith)
   See "A Young Highland Girl Studying Poetry"

"Highland Portrait" (Smith) **64**:394

Highpockets (Tunis) **12**:596

High-Rise (Ballard) **14**:41; **36**:38

"High-Water Railers" (Hannah) **90**:158, 160

"The Highway" (Bradbury) **10**:71

"Highway" (Moure) **88**:230

"Highway 5" (Moure) **88**:230

"Highway 6" (Moure) **88**:230

Highway 61 Revisited (Dylan) **4**:149; **6**:155; **12**:181, 184, 199; **77**:162, 168, 170, 174, 179-80

"Highway 66" (Laughlin) **49**:222

"Highway in April" (Avison) **97**:112

"Highway: Michigan" (Roethke) **46**:356

"Hi-Ho the Ambulance-O" (Nash) **23**:322

La hija de Rappaccini (Paz) **10**:391-92

La hija del engaño (Bunuel) **80**:23

"El hijo de Andrés Aparicio" (Fuentes) **113**:22:171; **60**:165; **113**:257-58
   See "The Son of Andrés Aparicio"

Hijo de hombre (*Son of Man*) (Roa Bastos) **45**:343-47

"El hijo de Karmaria" ("The Son of Karmaria") (Valenzuela) **104**:387

El hijo pródigo (Paz) **65**:176

Hijos de la ira (Alonso) **14**:16, 22

Hijos del aire (*Airborn*) (Paz) **19**:368

Los hijos del limo: Del romanticismo a la vanguardia (*Children of the Mire: Modern Poetry from Romanticism to the Avant-Garde*) (Paz) **4**:398; **6**:398; **10**:391, 393; **51**:336; **65**:176, 178, 180, 188

Los hijos muertos (Matute) **11**:362-65

Hikaya bila bidaya wala nihaya (Mahfuz) **52**:292

"Hiking on the Coast Range" (Rexroth) **49**:277; **112**:398

Hilaire Belloc (Wilson) **33**:457-58

"Hilda" (Ransom) **4**:431

"The Hill" (Creeley) **15**:149

"A Hill" (Hecht) **8**:268

"The Hill" (Ritsos) **31**:325

"The Hill" (Strand) **71**:285-86

"Hill Burial" (Winters) **32**:468-69

"Hill Field" (Montague) **46**:267

The Hill of Devi, and Other Writings (Forster) **45**:138; **77**:213, 217-18, 226, 228-29

"The Hill of Evening" (Merwin) **88**:212

The Hill of Evil Counsel (Oz) **54**:347, 352; **11**:428-29; **27**:359; **33**:302

The Hill of Summer (Drury) **37**:110-11

The Hill Road (Mayne) **12**:392

Hill Street Blues (Bochco and Kozoll) **35**:49-61

"The Hill Wife" (Frost) **10**:193, 198; **26**:113

"The Hillies" (Updike) **9**:537

"The Hills" (Brodsky) **13**:114

"Hills Like White Elephants" (Hemingway) **3**:234; **19**:211; **50**:413, 415

"Hills of Tuscany" (Lee) **90**:199

"Hilmar Enick" (Tolson) **36**:429

Him (Cummings) **8**:160; **12**:144, 146, 153; **68**:35, 47

Him She Loves? (Kerr) **35**:250

"Him with His Foot in His Mouth" (Bellow) **33**:68; **63**:28, 39

Him with His Foot in His Mouth, and Other Stories (Bellow) **33**:67-71

Der Himbeerpflücker (*The Raspberry Picker*) (Hochwalder) **36**:235, 237-39, 241

Himlens hemlighet (*Heaven's Secret; The Secret of Heaven*) (Lagerkvist) **54**:268, 271, 274, 277

Himmo (Kaniuk) **19**:239

"Himno entre ruinas" ("Hymn among the Ruins") (Paz) **4**:396

Himnusz minden időben (*Hymn for Anytime*) (Nagy) **7**:252

Hind's Kidnap: A Pastoral on Familiar Airs (McElroy) **5**:279; **47**:237-39, 241-42, 244-45

Hindsight (Dickinson) **35**:136-38

The Hindsight Saga (Perelman) **23**:338; **44**:503

"A Hindu Sage at the Sorbonne" (Asturias) **8**:26

The Hindu View of Art (Anand) **93**:44

"Hindus" (Mukherjee) **53**:270

"The Hinge" (Gilliatt) **53**:146

"The Hint of an Explanation" (Greene) **72**:148

"Hinterland" (Shields) **113**:414

"Hinterlands" (Gibson) **63**:129-30

Hinterlassene Schriften und Gedichte von Hermann Lauscher (*Hermann Lauscher; The Posthumous Writings and Poems of Hermann Lauscher*) (Hesse) **69**:198, 287

"Hints from Ariosto" (Porter) **33**:325

"Hiob" (Sachs) **98**:356

Hipogrifo violento (Sender) **8**:479

"Hipparchia" (H. D.) **73**:112

"A Hippocratic Oath for the Pluralist" (Booth) **24**:98

The Hippodrome (Colter) **58**:139-40, 143-44, 146

Hippolytus (Rexroth) **11**:472

Hippolytus Temporizes (H. D.) **31**:208; **73**:111, 117

"The Hippopotamus" (Eliot) **15**:216; **41**:151

"Hips" (Cisneros) **69**:144

The Hired Man (Bragg) **10**:71-2

"Hiroshima" (Lowell) **15**:343

Hiroshima (Hersey) **1**:144; **7**:153; **40**:234, 239, 241; **81**:332-37; **97**:298-301, 303-07, 312, 315-22, 324

"Hiroshima Mon Amour" (Duras) **100**:124, 149

Hiroshima, mon amour (Duras) **34**:162; **40**:180-81, 185-86; **68**:74, 76-7, 81, 85, 87-9, 91, 94, 98; **100**:119, 130-31

Hiroshima, mon amour (Resnais) **16**:496-503, 505-07, 509-13, 517

Hiroshima Notes (Oe)
   See *Hiroshima noto*

Hiroshima noto (*Hiroshima Notes*) (Oe) **36**:347; **86**:213, 236, 238, 241

Hiroshima Poems (Purdy) **3**:408; **14**:432; **50**:246

"Hiroshima: The Aftermath" (Hersey) **81**:335; **97**:309-14

"Hiroshima, Watts, My Lai" (Hayden) **37**:153

"His Animal Is Finally a Kind of Ape" (Stern) **40**:408

"His Ashes" (Olds) **85**:306

His Band and the Street Choir (Morrison) **21**:232

His Butler's Story (Coles) **67**:180

"His Dog" (Prichard) **46**:345

His Enemy, His Friend (Tunis) **12**:598-99

"His Excellency" (Maugham) **67**:210

"His Excellency the Masquerader" (Clark) **38**:125

His Father's Hands (Kinsella) **19**:254

"His First Real Snow" (Shapcott) **38**:404

"His Foreboding" (Roethke) **101**:332

His Grace's Days (Johnson)
   See *Hans nådes tid*

His Head (Ferlinghetti) **111**:64

His Human Majesty (Boyle) **19**:63; **58**:64

"His Last Day" (Himes) **108**:227, 258

"His Manner of Returning" (Williams) **45**:444

His Master's Voice (Lem) **40**:291, 297-98, 300

"His Middle-Class Blues" (Enzensberger) **43**:145

"His Night of Sadness" (Kunene) **85**:176

His Own Man (Gellhorn) **14**:195; **60**:186-87, 193

"His Plans for Old Age" (Meredith) **13**:373

His Present Discontents (Rosenthal) **28**:392, 394-95

"His Shining Helmet: Its Horsehair Crest" (Gallagher) **63**:125

"His Smell" (Olds) **85**:306-7

"His Son, in His Arms, in Light, Aloft" (Brodkey) **56**:60

"His Stillness" (Olds) **85**:308

His Toy, His Dream, His Rest: 308 Dream Songs (Berryman) **1**:34; **2**:56-7; **3**:67, 70; **8**:87; **13**:75, 80, 83; **25**:89-91, 93-4; **62**:43, 68

"His Wife Survived Him" (Brophy) **29**:91

The Hispanic Americans (Meltzer) **26**:308

"Hisperica Famina" (Spicer) **72**:357-58

"Hissen som gick ner i helvete" ("The Lift That Went Down into Hell") (Lagerkvist) **54**:287

The Hissing of Summer Lawns (Mitchell) **12**:438-40, 442-43

Hissing Tales (Gary) **25**:186

Histoire (Simon) **4**:495, 497; **9**:482, 484; **15**:488, 492-94; **39**:203, 205-07, 209-11

L'histoire d'Adele H. (*The Story of Adele H.*) (Truffaut) **20**:397-98; **101**:396-97, 410-11

Histoire de la sexualité, Vol. 1: La volonté de savoir (*The History of Sexuality, Vol. 1: An Introduction; La volonté de savoir; The Will to Power*) (Foucault) **31**:181-82, 185; **34**:339-42, 344; **69**:161-62, 165-69, 173-77, 179, 181, 183-84, 186, 189

Histoire de la sexualité, Vol. 2: L'usage des plaisirs (*L'usage des plaisirs; The Use of Pleasure: The History of Sexuality, Vol. 2*) (Foucault) **34**:342-43; **69**:166-68, 171-73, 176-77, 181, 187, 189, 191-92

Histoire de la sexualité, Vol. 3: Le souci de soi (*The Care of the Self: The History of Sexuality, Vol. 3; Le souci de soi*) (Foucault) **34**:342-43; **69**:166-68, 171, 177, 181, 189

"Histoire de lipogramme" (Perec) **56**:256

Histoire de l'oeil (*Story of the Eye*) (Bataille) **29**:39-42, 45, 48

"Histoire de lunes" (Carpentier) **11**:102-03; **110**:75-7

"Histoire de rats" (Bataille) **29**:38-9

Histoire d'une maison (Cayrol) **11**:110

Histoire et psychanalyse: Essai sur les possibilites et les limites de la psychohistoire (*History and Psychoanalysis: An Inquiry into the Possibilities and Limits of Psychohistory*) (Friedlander) **90**:112

Histoire et utopie (*History and Utopia*) (Cioran) **64**:97-9

Histoire extraordinaire (Butor) **8**:117

Histoires d'amour (*Tales of Love*) (Kristeva) **77**:324

"Historia" (Kadare) **52**:259

Historia de cronopios y de famas (*Cronopios and Famas*) (Cortazar) **2**:103; **10**:118; **13**:164; **33**:135; **34**:329, 331-32; **92**:147-48

Historia de la eternidad (*A History of Eternity*) (Borges) **44**:363, 368; **83**:163, 171

La historia de Mayta (*Mayta; The Real Life of Alejandro Mayta; The Real Story of Alejandro Mayta; The Real Story of Alejandro Mayta*) (Vargas Llosa) **42**:408-13; **85**:350, 352, 355, 362, 364, 366-68, 379, 383, 386-87, 389, 391, 395-96

Historia de una escalera (*Story of a Staircase; Story of a Stairway*) (Buero Vallejo) **15**:97; **46**:93

Historia del corazón (*The History of the Heart; The Story of the Heart*) (Aleixandre) **9**:18

"Historia del guerrero y de la cautiva" ("History of the Warrior and the Captive"; "Story of the Warrior and the Captive") (Borges) **13**:104; **83**:161

"História do Carnaval" (*A Carnival Story*) (Amado) **106**:74-5

"Historia Minotaura" (Herbert) **43**:187

Historia personal del 'boom' (*The Boom in Spanish American Literature: A Personal History; A Personal History of the "Boom"*) (Donoso) **8**:179-80; **32**:154; **99**:216, 218, 220-21, 230

Historia secreta de una novella (Vargas Llosa) **10**:500

Historia universal de la infamia (*History of Infamy; A Universal History of Infamy*) (Borges) **2**:77; **4**:74; **13**:106; **44**:362-63, 365, 368; **48**:35-6; **83**:163-66, 171

"Historial de un libro" (Cernuda) **54**:50

The Historian (Fuller) **28**:151

Historias de la Artámila (Matute) **11**:363

Historias desaforados (Bioy Casares) **88**:88

Historias fingidas y verdaderas (Otero) **11**:425-27

"Historical Afterword" (Berger) **19**:39, 41

"A Historical Approach to the Media" (McLuhan) **83**:367

The Historical Atlas of World Mythology (*The Way of the Animal Powers; The Way of the Seeded Earth*) (Campbell) **69**:82-3, 95

"Historical Criticism: Theory of Modes" (Frye) **24**:230

Historical Evidence and the Reading of Seventeenth-Century Poetry (Brooks) **86**:288-89; **110**:16-17, 31, 38

"A Historical Footnote to Consider Only When All Else Fails" (Giovanni) **64**:191

"The Historical Interpretation of Literature" (Wilson) **24**:470

The Historical Novel (Lukacs) **24**:318-20, 334

"Historical Process" (Enzensberger) **43**:146

"Histories" (Tomlinson) **45**:393

"History" (Berry) **27**:36

"History" (Hall) **59**:151, 155-56

"History" (Muldoon) **32**:320

"History" (Sherwood) **81**:102

"History" (Simic) **49**:342

"History" (Soto) **80**:280, 287

History (Lowell) **3**:302-05; **4**:301, 304; **5**:256-59; **8**:353-55, 357; **9**:334, 339; **11**:328-29, 331; **15**:344; **37**:235-38, 240

"History: 13" (Olds) **85**:296, 298

History: A Novel (Morante)
See *La storia*

"History: A Story Has Only a Few Good Years" (Wilson) **49**:416

History and Class-Consciousness (Lukacs) **24**:320, 324, 327, 338

History and Human Survival: Essays on the Young and Old, Survivors and the Dead, Peace and War, and on Contemporary Psychohistory (Lifton) **67**:142-43

History and Psychoanalysis: An Inquiry into the Possibilities and Limits of Psychohistory (Friedlander)
See *Histoire et psychanalyse: Essai sur les possibilites et les limites de la psychohistoire*

"History and the New American Novel" (Alter) **34**:515

History and Tradition in Afro-American Culture **65**:379

History and Utopia (Cioran)
See *Histoire et utopie*

"History as Apple Tree" (Harper) **7**:139

"History as Poetry" (Hill) **8**:295; **45**:185

"A History: for colored girls who have considered suicide/ when therainbow is enuf" (Shange) **74**:308-09

History Is Your Own Heartbeat (Harper) **7**:138-39

"History Lesson" (Simic) **68**:378-79

"History Lessons" (Komunyakaa) **94**:234

The History Man (Bradbury) **32**:52-3, 55-6; **61**:34-5, 37-40, 42, 44

"The History of a Contraoctave" (Pasternak)
See "The Story of Counter-Octave"

"A History of Bitic Literature" (Lem) **40**:298

"The History of Crome Manor" (Huxley) **79**:304

The History of Danish Dreams (Hoeg)
See *Forestilling om det Tyvende Århundrede*

"History of Eternity" (Borges) **83**:163-64

A History of Eternity (Borges)
See *Historia de la eternidad*

"The History of Fire" (Hogan) **73**:158

"The History of Galadriel and Celeborn" (Tolkien) **38**:431

History of Humanism (Faludy) **42**:140

History of Infamy (Borges)
See *Historia universal de la infamia*

A History of Modern Criticism, 1750-1950: Vol. 4, The Later Nineteenth Century (Wellek) **28**:443-44, 446-49, 451-52, 454, 447, 447, 450, 450

"History of My Heart" (Pinsky) **38**:355, 357-58, 362-63; **94**:298-99, 307, 309

History of My Heart (Pinsky) **38**:355-56, 358-59, 361-63; **94**:298-99, 305-6, 309, 322

A History of Pan-African Revolt (James) **33**:219

The History of Polish Literature (Milosz) **31**:261-62

"The History of Sexuality" (Foucault) **69**:193

The History of Sexuality, Vol. I: An Introduction (Foucault)
See *Histoire de la sexualité, Vol. 1: La volonté de savoir*

A History of the American Film (Durang) **27**:88-90

The History of the Growth of Heaven (Codrescu) **46**:102-03

The History of the Heart (Aleixandre)
See *Historia del corazón*

"History of the Poet as a Whore" (Madhubuti) **73**:199

"History of the Targo" (Borges) **48**:45

"History of the Warrior and the Captive" (Borges)
See "Historia del guerrero y de la cautiva"

History: the Home Movie (Raine) **103**:205-07, 210-13

"A Hit Album" (Sorrentino) **40**:386

"The Hitch Hiker" (Williams) **42**:440

Hitchhike (Holland) **21**:151

The Hitchhiker (Simenon) **2**:399

"The Hitch-Hikers" (Welty) **33**:415; **105**:307

The Hitchhiker's Guide to the Galaxy (Adams) **27**:11-15; **60**:2-7

"The Hitchhiking Game" (Kundera) **9**:321; **32**:260; **115**:308, 346

"Hitherto Uncollected" (Moore) **47**:263

"Hitler, According to Speer" (Canetti) **86**:295

"The Hitler Diaries" (Hugo) **32**:249

Hitler er les États-Unis (1939-1941) (*Prelude to Downfall: Hitler and the United States 1939-1941*) (Friedlander) **90**:104, 112

The Hitleriad (Klein) **19**:263

"The Hitlerian Spring" (Montale)
See "La primavera Hitleriana"

"Hitler's Daughter" (Federspiel) **42**:145

"Hitler's First Photograph" (Szymborska) **99**:198, 201

Hitting Town (Poliakoff) **38**:375-78, 380, 383, 386

The Hive (Cela)
See *La colmena*

Hiver Caraïbe (Morand) **41**:304

L'hiver de force (Ducharme) **74**:57, 68

"Hi-Way Songs" (Lightfoot) **26**:279

Hjarta høyrer sine heimlandstonar (*The Heart Hears Songs of Home*) (Vesaas) **48**:405-06

Hjärtats sånger (*Songs of the Heart*) (Lagerkvist) **54**:275

H'm (Thomas) **6**:530, 532; **48**:380-82

H.M. Pulham, Esquire (Marquand) **10**:329-31

H.M.S. Ulysses (MacLean) **3**:309; **13**:359-61; **50**:347-50; **63**:259-64, 267-68

"Hoantteniate" (Kenny) **87**:258

Hob taht al-Matar (Mahfuz) **52**:296-97

The Hobbit; or, There and Back Again (Tolkien) **1**:336, 338, 340; **2**:435; **3**:477, 480-81; **8**:515-16; **12**:563-64, 566-70, 577-80, 583-85; **38**:431-32, 435, 438-42

"The Hobbyist" (Pesetsky) **28**:357

"The Hobo" (Wild) **14**:581

The Hoboken Chicken Emergency (Pinkwater) **35**:317, 320

Die Hochzeit (*The Wedding; The Wedding Feast*) (Canetti) **14**:121; **75**:127; **86**:298, 301, 303

"The Hockey Hero" (Bowering) **47**:19

"The Hockey Poem" (Bly) **15**:63

The Hockey Sweater, and Other Stories (Carrier)
See *Les enfants du bonhomme dans la lune*

Hocus Pocus (Vonnegut) 351-52, 354-58, 361-68

"Hoeing" (Soto) **80**:286, 288

"Hoffmeier's Antelope" (Swift) **41**:446

Hofmeyr (Paton) **25**:363

"Hofstedt and Jean—and Others" (Brodkey)

56:60, 64

Hog Butcher (Fair)   18:139, 141

"Hog Heaven" (Williams)   33:446

"A Hog Loves Its Life: Something About My Grandfather" (Gurganus)   70:191, 193, 195-96

"Hoist High the Roof Beam, Carpenters" (Salinger)

See "Raise High the Roofbeam, Carpenters"

La hojarasca (*Dead Leaves*; *Leaf Storm*) (Garcia Marquez)   2:148; 3:180; 47:145, 149-50, 153; 2:149; 3:180-81; 10:216; 15:254; 27:147-48, 155; 47:145; 55:138; 68:141, 145, 153, 156

Hojas de Parra (*Pages from Parra*) (Parra)   102:332-33

Hojo no umi (*The Sea of Fertility: A Cycle of Novels*) (Mishima)   2:287; 4:355-58; 6:337-38; 9:383-84; 27:341-43

"Hojoki" (Rexroth)   112:405

"Hokan" ("A Harlequin") (Tanizaki)   28:417

"Hokuro no tegami" (Kawabata)   107:71, 104

"Hola Migvelin!" (Levine)   14:317

The Holcroft Covenant (Ludlum)   22:289

Hold April (Stuart)   11:510

"Hold Back the Tears" (Young)   17:576-77

Hold Fast (Major)   26:284-88

Hold Me! (Feiffer)   64:151, 159, 164

"Hold Me Fast, Don't Let Me Pass" (Munro)   95:310, 315

Hold On (Douglas)   73:65-7, 81, 94

"Hold On, Hold Out" (Browne)   21:41-2

"Hold On John" (Lennon)   35:262

Hold Out (Browne)   21:41-2

Hold Your Hour and Have Another (Behan)   79:24-5, 27

Hold Zero! (George)   35:176

The Holder of the World (Mukherjee)   115:371-73

"Hölderlin" (Hamburger)   5:159

Hölderlin (Weiss)   51:386-87, 391, 393, 395, 397

"Hölderlin und das Wesen der Dichtung" (Heidegger)   24:259

Hölderlin's Madness (Gascoyne)   45:148, 152-54

"Holding Course" (Heaney)   74:162

"Holding in the Sky" (Stafford)   29:380

Holding On (Jones)   52:246-48, 254

"Holding the Great Blind Man by the Hand" ("Holding the Great Blind Man's Hand")   75:62, 77

"Holding the Great Blind Man's Hand"

See "Holding the Great Blind Man by the Hand"

Holding the Pose (Thesen)   56:414-16, 421

"Holding the Towel" (Swenson)   106:337

"Holding Together" (Bell)   102:5, 7

"Hold-Up" (MacNeice)   10:325

The Hold-Up Man (Hart)

See *The Beloved Bandit*

"The Hole" (Dixon)   52:99-100

"The Hole" (Hood)   28:192

The Hole (Simpson)   29:365-69

"The Hole/Birth Catalogue" (Ozick)   28:352

"Hole in the Day" (Tilghman)   65:106-07, 109-12

"A Hole in the Floor" (Wilbur)   3:530; 6:570; 53:399, 405; 110:351

A Hole in the Head (Capra)   16:156, 160

"The Hole in the Sea" (Bell)   8:66; 31:46

A Hole in the Sky (Konwicki)

See *Dziura w niebie*

"The Hole That Jack Dug" (Sargeson)   31:362, 365, 370-71

"Holiday" (Ferber)   93:153

"Holiday" (Grace)   56:112

"Holiday" (Porter)   101:256

"Holiday" (Sitwell)   67:319-20, 336

"The Holiday" (Smith)   44:436, 440

Holiday (Middleton)   7:219-21; 38:333

The Holiday (Smith)   25:416-17, 422-23; 44:439

A Holiday for Murder (Christie)   48:77

"A Holiday for Three" (Derleth)   31:132

The Holiday Friend (Johnson)   27:224

"A Holiday from Strict Reality" (Reid)   33:351

"Holiday in Waikiki" (Davies)   21:88-9

"Holiday Inn Blues" (Ferlinghetti)   111:60

"Holidays" (Williams)   42:443

Holland (Wilson)   12:646, 654

"The Holland of the Mind" (Zoline)   62:462-64

Holland's Glory (de Hartog)   19:133

"Hollow" (L'Heureux)   52:273

"Hollow" (Pancake)   29:346-50

The Hollow (*Murder After Hours*) (Christie)   6:108; 12:125; 48:70-1, 73-6; 110:135

"The Hollow Herring" (Aksyonov)   101:42

The Hollow Hills (Stewart)   7:468; 35:393-96; 117:369, 372, 376, 385

The Hollow Land (Gardam)   43:170

The Hollow Lands (Moorcock)   5:294; 58:347-48

The Hollow Man (Carr)   3:101

The Hollow Men (Eliot)   1:90, 92; 2:128-29; 6:163; 9:188; 10:170; 13:196-97; 15:214, 216-17; 34:525, 530; 41:147, 151, 154, 161; 55:346, 350-51, 373; 57:187

"A Hollow Stone" (Oz)   27:360

"A Hollow Tree" (Bly)   15:63

"Holloway Jail" (Davies)   21:92

"Holly" (Heaney)   37:165; 74:169

"The Holly and the Ivy" (Stevenson)   33:383

Holly from the Bongs (Garner)   17:135, 147

"Holly, Holly" (Diamond)   30:112

"Hollywood" (Kaufman)   49:202-03

Hollywood (Bukowski)   82:23-6, 28; 108:88-9, 91

Hollywood (Cendrars)   106:190, 193-94

Hollywood (Kanin)   22:231

Hollywood: A Novel of America in the 1920s (Vidal)   72:400-04, 406

"Hollywood and Vine" (Montague)   46:265

"A Hollywood Diary" (Fuchs)   22:159, 161

The Hollywood Kid (Wojciechowska)   26:452-53

"Hollywood Nights" (Seger)   35:383, 385

"Hollywood State of Mind" (Joel)   26:214-15

Hollywood's Canada (Berton)   104:46-7, 57

"The Holmes-Laski Correspondence" (Wilson)   24:481

Holocaust (Reznikoff)   9:449

"The Holy Bird"   75:68

"The Holy Child's Song" (Merton)   83:378, 392

"Holy Day" (Bissett)   18:58

Holy Disorders (Crispin)   22:110

"The Holy Earth" (Wheelock)   14:571

Holy Europe (Adamov)

See *Sainte-Europe*

"Holy Face" (Huxley)   35:241

The Holy Ghostly (Shepard)   17:443

Holy Ghosts (Linney)   51:259-60, 264

The Holy Grail (Spicer)   18:507, 512, 514; 72:351

"The Holy Land" (Updike)   43:431

The Holy Land (Lagerkvist)   54:281-85

"The Holy Man" (Hood)   28:189

"Holy Moon" (MacCaig)   36:283

"holy night" (Clifton)   66:81

Holy Place (Fuentes)

See *Zona sagrada*

"Holy Saturday" (Oates)   15:402

"Holy Satyr" (H. D.)   73:109

"The Holy Shroud" (Raine)   45:334

Holy Smoke (Cabrera Infante)   45:81-4

Holy Smoke (Howe)   47:175-77

"Holy Sonnet" (Sherwin)   7:415

Holy Stones (Weldon)   36:445

The Holy Terrors (Cocteau)

See *Les enfants terribles*

Holy the Firm (Dillard)   9:178-79; 60:70; 115:168-75, 182-85, 187-88, 197, 199-207, 209

"Holy Thursday" (Hill)   45:186

"Holy Thursday" (Muldoon)   72:275

The Holy Tree (Jenkins)   52:224, 226-27

"Holy Trinity" (Betjeman)   43:41-2

"Holy Week" (Pasternak)   63:313

Holy Week (Aragon)

See *La semaine sainte*

"The Holy Words of Tristan Tzara" (Rothenberg)   57:381

Holzfällen: Eine Erregung (*Cutting Timber*; *Woodcutters*) (Bernhard)   61:29-31

Holzwege (Heidegger)   24:264, 277

Homage and Desecrations (Paz)   51:336

"Homage to a Government" (Larkin)   5:226; 8:340; 33:261; 64:274

Homage to Adana (Kherdian)   6:280-81; 9:317

"Homage to Back to Methuselah" (Brophy)   105:6

Homage to Blenholt (Fuchs)   8:220-22; 22:155, 158

"Homage to César Paladíon" (Borges)   19:48; 48:37

"Homage to Cézanne" (Wright)   28:457-60

"Homage to Clichés" (MacNeice)   10:324; 53:235

Homage to Clio (Auden)   3:29

"Homage to Clotho: A Hospital Suite" (Sissman)   9:492; 18:488, 490

Homage to Creely (Spicer)   8:499; 18:510

Homage to Daniel Shays: Collected Essays, 1952-1972 (Vidal)   2:450-51; 4:553; 6:550; 8:528

"Homage to Dashiell Hammett" (Macdonald)   41:270

"Homage to Duke Ellington on His Birthday" (Ellison)   86:327

Homage to Edgar Allan Poe (Smith)   42:346, 350, 353, 357

"Homage to Emerson, on Night Flight to New York" (Warren)   8:539; 18:536; 39:267

"Homage to Ezra Pound" (Wright)   6:579

"Homage to Horace" (MacNeice)   53:242

Homage to John Dryden: Three Essays on Poetry of the Seventeenth Century (Eliot)   24:158, 167, 169, 171, 182

"Homage to Lorca" (Ciardi)   40:156

"Homage to L.S. Lowry" (Longley)   29:294

"Homage to Lucille, Dr. Lord-Heinstein" (Piercy)   62:371

"Homage to Lucretius" (Whalen)   29:446

"Homage to Marcus Aurelius" (Brodsky)   100:61, 69, 74

"Homage to Matthew Arnold" (Rosenthal)   28:391

"homage to mine" (Clifton)   66:80

Homage to Mistress Bradstreet (Berryman)
2:56, 58; 3:65-8, 70; 4:61-2; 6:64-5; 8:86-
7, 91-3; 10:47, 49-5; 13:78-9, 81-2; 25:89,
91, 94, 97-8; 62:43-4, 46, 56, 72, 74, 76

"homage to my hair" (Clifton)   66:69, 88

"homage to my hips" (Clifton)   66:88

"Homage to Nadar" (Howard)   47:169

"Homage to Paul Robeson" (Hayden)   37:158

"Homage to Pavese" (Levertov)   15:338

"Homage to Postman Cheval" (Szirtes)   46:393

*Homage to QWERT YUIOP, and Other Writings
(But Do Blondes Prefer Gentlemen?)* (Burgess)   62:124; 94:76

"Homage to Sextus Propertius" (Pound)   2:342,
344; 3:396; 4:408; 7:335-36; 13:459, 462;
48:282, 284:112:309-12, 340

"Homage to Shakespeare" (Cheever)   64:66

"Homage to Switzerland" (Hemingway)   30:192

"Homage to the Chinese" (Haines)   58:221

"Homage to the Empress of the Blues"
(Hayden)   37:155, 160

"Homage to the Memory of Wallace Stevens"
(Justice)   102:264, 283-84

"Homage to the Weather" (Hamburger)   14:234

"Homage to Theodore Dreiser" (Warren)
6:555; 8:537; 39:270

"Homage to William Cowper" (Davie)   5:115

"Homage to Winter" (Rich)   73:315

"Homage to Yalta" (Brodsky)   36:80

"Hombre" (Purdy)   14:435

"El hombre" ("The Man") (Rulfo)   80:200,
213, 215

Un hombre (Where the Soul Was Shallow)
(Gironella)   11:234-35, 238

Hombre (Leonard)   71:208, 211, 219-21, 225

"Un hombre anda bajo la luna" ("A Man Walks
beneath the Moon") (Neruda)   62:322

"Hombre de la esquina rosada" ("Hombres de
las orillas"; "Man on the Pink Corner";
"The Pink Corner Man"; "Streetcorner
Man") (Borges)   13:104; 48:33, 35-6;
83:166

Hombre de paso/Just Passing Through
(Goldemberg)   52:165, 168

El hombre junto al mar (Padilla)   38:351

Hombre y Dios (Man and God) (Alonso)   14:17,
23

El hombre y sus sueños (Marques)   96:224,
243

"El hombrecito" (Donoso)   8:178; 11:146

"Hombres de las orillas" (Borges)
See "Hombre de la esquina rosada"

Hombres de maíz (Men of Maize) (Asturias)
8:28; 13:37, 39-40

"Los hombres XIX" ("The Men XIX") (Neruda)
62:334

Hombres y engranajes (Sabato)   10:446; 23:379

"Home" (Beer)   58:32

"Home" (Creeley)   78:141

"Home" (Gordimer)   70:178, 180

"Home" (Hughes)   108:315

"Home" (King)   53:212

"Home" (Lorde)   71:258

"Home" (Lowell)   37:238

"Home" (O Hehir)   41:324

"Home" (Phillips)   15:419-21

"Home" (Shields)   113:425

"Home" (Updike)   15:540

Home (Olson)   28:343

Home (Storey)   2:424-25; 4:528-29; 5:415,
417; 8:505

"Home Address" (Bronk)   10:75

"Home after Three Months Away" (Lowell)
15:347

"Home Again" (Johnston)   51:240, 244

"Home Again" (Montague)   46:270

Home Again (Montague)   46:266

Home and Colonial (Coward)   29:140

Home and Exile (Nkosi)   45:294

The Home and the Star (Lagerkvist)
See *Hemmet och stjärnan*

The Home and the World (Ray)
See *Ghare Bahire*

"Home at Last" (Becker and Fagen)   26:84

Home Before Dark (Bridgers)   26:90-2

*Home before Dark: A Biographical Memoir of
John Cheever by His Daughter* (Cheever)
48:65-8

Home before Night (Leonard)   19:282-83

The Home Book (Schuyler)   23:388

"Home Burial" (Frost)   1:110; 9:227; 26:111,
113, 119

"Home Burial" (Kennedy)   42:256

Home Chat (If It Must Be So) (Buck)   18:80

Home Chat (Coward)   29:131

Home Cooking: A Writer in the Kitchen (Colwin)
84:142-43

Home Course in Religion (Soto)   80:302

"Home Economics" (Castellanos)
See "Economía doméstica"

Home Fires (Guare)   29:203

"Home for a Couple of Days" (Kelman)   58:298

"Home for Thanksgiving" (Merwin)   88:205

"Home for the Elderly" (Raine)   32:349;
103:186

A Home for the Heart (Bettelheim)   79:111

"Home for Wayfarers" (Sayles)   14:483

"Home Free" (Johnston)   51:243, 245, 252

Home Free (Johnston)   51:240-49, 251-52

"Home from Greece" (Stern)   40:407

"Home from Hiroshima" (Clark)   38:129

Home from the Hill (Humphrey)   45:193-99,
201-02

*Home from the War: Vietnam Veterans—Neither
Victims nor Executioners* (Lifton)   67:143,
145, 150, 154

"The Home Front" (Stafford)   68:422

Home Front Memo (Sandburg)   35:354

Home Game (Quarrington)   65:203

"Home Girl" (Ferber)   93:145

"Home Ground" (Longley)   29:295

"Home Home Home" (Ferlinghetti)   27:139

"Home Is a Wounded Heart" (Diamond)   30:112

"Home Is So Sad" (Larkin)   5:227; 64:266

"Home Is the Hangman" (Zelazny)   21:474

Home Is the Sailor (Amado)
See *Os velhos marinheiros*

"Home Is Where You Hang Yourself" (Richler)
46:352

"Home Movie" (Rule)   27:423

"Home Movies" (Broumas)   73:9

Home Movies (De Palma)   20:80

"The Home of the Human Race" (Saroyan)
8:468

"Home Paddock" (Shapcott)   38:398

The Home Place (Morris)   1:232; 37:313, 316

"Home Revisited: Midnight and Thursday"
(Ciardi)   40:154

"Home Run" (Bukowski)   41:73

Home: Social Essays (Baraka)   5:45; 14:48;
33:53-4, 63; 115:10, 45, 47-9

"Home Sweet Home" (Carroll)   10:96-7

Home Sweet Home (Richler)   46:351-53

"Home Thoughts" (Turco)   11:552

"Home Town" (Snodgrass)   68:388

"Home Town" (Waterhouse)   47:417

Home Truths: Selected Canadian Stories (Gallant)   38:189-91, 193-94

Homeage to the American Indians
See *Homenaje a los indios americanos*

Homeboy (Morgan)   65:75-80

"Homecoming" (Alvarez)   93:6

"Homecoming" (Lowell)   37:238

"Homecoming" (Sanchez)   116:276, 293

Homecoming (Alvarez)   93:2, 6, 8-10

The Homecoming (Hamner)   12:258

The Homecoming (Pinter)   3:385-88; 6:404,
410-14, 416-17, 420; 9:420; 11:442-45;
15:422-23, 426; 27:385, 392-95; 58:369-
71, 373, 375, 383-84; 73:247-81

Homecoming (Sanchez)   116:272, 274-76, 278,
282, 293-94, 301-02, 308-09, 313-14,
324

Homecoming (Homecomings) (Snow)   4:501;
13:508-09, 511; 19:425, 427

Homecoming (Voigt)   30:417-19

*Homecoming: Essays of African and Carib-
bean Literature, Culture, and Politics*
(Ngugi wa Thiong'o)   36:310-12, 318

"Homecoming in Late March" (Steele)   45:363

"Homecoming of Emma Lazarus" (Kinnell)
29:287

*Homecoming: Reclaiming and Championing
Your Inner Child*   70:425

"Homecomings" (Heaney)   25:243, 247

Homecomings (Snow)
See *Homecoming*

Homefront (Walser)
See *Zimmerschlacht*

Homegirls and Hand Grenades (Sanchez)
116:287, 289, 299, 302-07, 309, 313, 317,
324

"Homegrown" (Young)   17:576

Homeland, and Other Stories (Kingsolver)
81:191

"The Homeless" (Merwin)   13:386

"Homeless" (Seth)   43:388

"Home-longing" (Atwood)   84:105

"The Homely Heroine" (Ferber)   93:140, 146

"Homemade" (McEwan)   66:277-79

"Home-Made Beer" (Purdy)   14:431; 50:247

Homemade Love (Cooper)   56:70-2

"Homenagem renovada a Marianne Moore"
("Renewed Homage to Marianne Moore")
(Cabral de Melo Neto)   76:160, 165

"Homenaje" (Cernuda)   54:47

*Homenaje a los indios americanos (Homeage
to the American Indians)* (Cardenal)
31:71-2

"Homeplace" (hooks)   94:145

"Homer" (Katz)   47:216

Homer's Daughter (Graves)   45:172

"Homes" (Montague)   46:274

"Homesickness" (Bennett)   28:27

"Home-Sickness...from the Town" (Huxley)
11:282-83

Homespun of Oatmeal Gray (Goodman)   2:169,
171

"Homestead, 1914" (Suknaski)   19:432

"The Homestead Called Damascus" (Rexroth)
22:344, 347; 49:274-75, 279,284-85;
112:373-75, 379-80

"The Homestead Orchard" (Davis)   49:91, 94,
97

"Hometown Piece for Messers Alston and
Reese" (Moore)   47:261, 263

"Homeward Bound" (Simon)   17:465-66

The Homeward Bounders (Jones)   26:231

Homeward to America (Ciardi) **40**:151, 153, 156-57; **44**:378

"Homewards" (Transtroemer) **52**:418

The Homewood Trilogy (Wideman) **67**:371, 374-75, 384

"Homework" (Van Duyn) **7**:498; **63**:437, 440; **116**:402, 420, 428

"Homework Assignment on the Subject of Angels" (Rozewicz) **23**:363

Homeworld (Harrison) **42**:206-07

"Hommage à Bournonville" (Hoeg) **95**:116-17

"Hommage à Cezanne" (Durcan) **70**:151-52

"Hommage et famine" (Char) **9**:164

"Hommage to a Young Witch" (Cortazar) **10**:117

"Hommage to Malcolm Lowry" (Mahon) **27**:287

"Hommage to the British Museum" (Empson) **8**:202

L'homme approximatif (*Approximate Man*) (Tzara) **47**:386-91, 393-95

L'homme assis dans le couloir (Duras) **68**:91

L'homme atlantique (Duras) **40**:181, 183-84; **68**:96

L'homme au petit chien (Simenon) **18**:483

L'homme aux valises (*Man with Bags*) (Ionesco) **9**:287-90; **11**:294; **41**:230; **86**:332, 341

Un homme comme un autre (Simenon) **8**:488

Un Homme de Broadway (Hart)
   See *Act One: An Autobiography*

Un homme de Dieu (Marcel) **15**:363

"L'homme du parc Monceau" (Mandiargues) **41**:277

"L'homme et la bête" (Levine) **14**:317

"L'homme et la bête" (Senghor) **54**:410

"L'homme et les choses" (Sartre) **24**:418

L'homme foudroyé (*The Astonished Man*) (Cendrars) **18**:93, 96, 98; **106**:167, 169, 172-73, 179, 182-83, 185, 187-88, 190, 192

"L'homme ligoté" (Sartre) **24**:417

L'homme nu (Levi-Strauss) **38**:304, 306, 308

Un homme paisible (Michaux) **19**:311

Un homme qui dort (*A Man Asleep*) (Perec) **56**:256-58; **116**:232-33, 235, 237-38, 246-48, 252-53, 261

L'homme qui ment (Robbe-Grillet) **4**:449; **8**:454; **14**:457; **43**:366

L'homme révolté (*The Rebel*) (Camus) **2**:97, 99; **4**:89, 91-2; **9**:143; **11**:95; **14**:107-09, 111-12, 115, 117; **32**:90, 97; **63**:62-3, 69, 71-3, 75, 82, 86, 117, 127, 133-36; **69**:117, 127, 133-36

Les hommes abandonnés (*The Abandoned Men*) (Duhamel) **8**:187

Les hommes de bonne volonté (*Men of Good Will*) (Romains) **7**:379-82

Les Hommes naissent tous le même jour (Gallo) **95**:98

"Hommunculus" (Bogan) **46**:86

Homo Faber: A Report (Frisch) **3**:167; **18**:163; **32**:188-90, 192, 194; **44**:183-85, 187-90, 199

Homo sexualis (Oe) **36**:347; **86**:225

Homo viator (Marcel) **15**:359

"The Homosexual Villain" (Mailer) **111**:104

Homosexuality and Literature, 1890-1930 (Meyers) **39**:433

"Homosexuality in Robert Duncan's Poetry" (Gunn) **32**:212

El hondero entusiasta, 1923-1924 (*The Ardent Slingsman*; *The Enthusiastic Slinger*; *Man with a Sling*) (Neruda) **28**:312; **62**:323

Hondo (L'Amour) **25**:279; **55**:306-08

Honest Confession of a Literary Sin (Stuart) **34**:375

"Honest Confrontation" (Ritsos) **31**:325

The Honest-to-God Schnozzola (Horovitz) **56**:149

"Honesty" (Joel) **26**:216-17

"Honey" (Johnston) **51**:243

"Honey" (Wright) **28**:469

Honey and Bread (Davies) **23**:141

Honey and Salt (Sandburg) **4**:463; **10**:449, 452; **15**:467; **35**:356

"Honey and Tobacco" (Silkin) **43**:401

"Honey at the Table" (Oliver) **34**:249; **98**:298

Honey for the Bears (Burgess) **13**:124; **22**:69, 78; **40**:115-16; **81**:301; **94**:25, 52, 64-5

Honey in the Horn (Davis) **49**:80-5, 89-90, 94, 97-8

Honey out of the Rock (Deutsch) **18**:118

Honey Seems Bitter (Kiely) **23**:262; **43**:245

"The Honey Tree" (Oliver) **98**:299-300

The Honey Tree (Elliott) **47**:110-11

"Honey, We'll Be Brave" (Farrell) **66**:112, 131

Honeybath's Haven (Stewart) **14**:512

Honeybuzzard (Carter)
   See *Shadow Dance*

Honeycomb (Saura) **20**:315

"The Honeyed Peace" (Gellhorn) **60**:183-84

The Honeyed Peace (Gellhorn) **60**:183-84

The Honeyman Festival (Engel) **36**:158-59, 162, 165

"Honeymoon" (O'Brien) **5**:311

"Honeymoon" (Seifert) **93**:333

"The Honeymoon" (Simmons) **43**:414

Honeymoon (Seifert) **34**:256

"Honeymoon at Tramore" (Trevor) **71**:341; **116**:347, 363

The Honeymoon Voyage (Thomas) **13**:542; **31**:430

A Hong Kong House: Poems, 1951-1961 (Blunden) **56**:35-6, 40, 45, 47, 50

Honky Tonk Heroes (Jennings) **21**:202, 205

"Honky Tonk in Cleveland" (Sandburg) **35**:352

"Honkytonk" (Shapiro) **15**:476

"Honneurs funèbres" (Kis) **57**:249

"Honolulu" (Dickey) **28**:119

"Honolulu" (Maugham) **67**:206

Honor Among Lovers (Arzner) **98**:69-70, 87

Honor, Power, Riches, Fame, and the Love of Women (Just) **27**:229

Honor Thy Father (Talese) **37**:393-94, 404

Honorable Men (Auchincloss) **45**:34-6

The Honorary Consul (Greene) **3**:212-15; **6**:219-20; **14**:219; **18**:197-98; **27**:173, 175-76; **37**:137; **70**:289, 292-93

"The Honored Dead" (Pancake) **29**:347, 350

"Honourable Estate" (Brittain) **23**:90

The Honourable Schoolboy (le Carre) **9**:326-27; **15**:324-26

"The Hon. Sec." (Betjeman) **2**:60; **43**:43

An Honoured Guest (Gordimer)
   See *A Guest of Honour*

The Honours Board (Johnson) **27**:221, 223-24

"Hoodlums" (Sandburg) **35**:341

"Hoodoo Valley" (Roy) **14**:469

"The Hoofer" (Miller) **30**:264-65

"Hook" (Clark) **28**:78-9

"The Hook" (Weiss) **3**:517; **14**:556

Hook a Fish, Catch a Mountain: An Ecological Spy Story (George) **35**:177

"Hooks" (Williams) **56**:425

"Hoop Dancer" (Allen) **84**:39-40, 43

Hoops (Myers) **35**:298

Hooters (Tally) **42**:367

Hop Signor! (Ghelderode) **11**:226

"Hope" (Avison) **97**:115

"Hope" (Hughes) **108**:336

"The Hope" (Ignatow) **4**:247

"Hope" (Lustig) **56**:182

"Hope" (Milosz) **31**:266

"Hope" (Mueller) **13**:399-400

"Hope" (Warren) **39**:270

Hope (Moravia)
   See *La speranza*

Hope and Suffering: Sermons and Speeches (Tutu) **80**:357-59

"Hope Atherton's Wanderings" (Howe) **72**:204

"The Hope Chest" (Stafford) **7**:457

A Hope for Poetry (Day Lewis) **10**:128, 133

Hope of Heaven (O'Hara) **42**:312, 320-21

"Hope Springs" (Loewinsohn) **52**:285

"Hope Stories" (Moure) **88**:232

Hopeful Monsters (Mosley) **70**:199-206

Hopelessness (Donoso)
   See *La Desesperanza*

"Hopes Rise" (Boyle) **90**:62-3

"Hopi Overlay" (Rose) **85**:312

Hoping for a Hoopoe (Updike)
   See *The Carpentered Hen and Other Tame Creatures*

"Hopkins to Whitman" (Dacey) **51**:83

"Hopper: The Loneliness Factor" (Strand) **71**:278

Hopscotch (Cortazar)
   See *Rayuela*

Hopscotch (Horovitz) **56**:155

"Hoquet" ("Hiccups") (Damas) **84**:168, 177-78, 180

"La hora cero" (Cardenal)
   See "La hora O"

A hora da estrela (*The Hour of the Star*) (Lispector) **43**:263-67, 271

"La hora O" ("La hora cero"; "Zero Hour") (Cardenal) **31**:71, 75-7

"Horace and Margaret's Fifty-Second" (Baxter) **45**:51; **78**:17

"Horae Canonicae" (Auden) **14**:29

"The Horatians" (Auden) **4**:33; **11**:17

Hore (*Rounds*) (Arghezi) **80**:6, 8

Horeb's Stone (Duhamel) **8**:187

"Horizon" (Soupault) **68**:405

Horizon (MacInnes) **27**:279-80

L'horizon (Marcel) **15**:363

"Horizon and Style"
   See "Orizont si stil"

"Horizons West" (Gregor) **9**:253

"The Horizontal Bop" (Seger) **35**:384-85

The Horn (Holmes) **56**:136-37, 140

Horn (Mano) **2**:270; **10**:328

"Horn Came" (Beckett) **29**:57

Horn of Africa (Caputo) **32**:104-06

Horn of My Love (p'Bitek) **96**:276-78, 291-92, 294, 299, 301-02, 306-07, 311

"Horn of Plenty" (Gordimer) **33**:179

Hornblower and the "Atropas" (Forester) **35**:170

Hornblower and the Crisis (Forester)
   See *Hornblower during the Crisis*

The Hornblower Companion (Forester) **35**:172

Hornblower during the Crisis (*Hornblower and the Crisis*) (Forester) **35**:171

"The Hornet's House" (Belitt) **22**:50-1

"Horns" (Haines) **58**:215, 219

"Horoscope" (Clark)   38:127

Les horreurs de la guerre (Perec)   56:264

"Horror Movie" (Dybek)   114:64, 70

"Horror Movie" (Moss)   14:375-76

"Horror Stories" (Jiles)   58:271, 275, 277-78, 281

"Hors livre" (Derrida)   24:156

"Horse" (Gluck)   44:217-18, 221-22

"The Horse" (Merwin)   8:390; 18:334

"The Horse" (Raine)   32:349; 103:186

"The Horse" (Wright)   28:462

"Horse and Swan Feeding" (Swenson)   61:398-99; 106:313, 324-25, 340

"A Horse and Two Goats" (Narayan)   47:304-06

A Horse and Two Goats, and Other Stories (Narayan)   28:295

"The Horse Chestnut Tree" (Eberhart)   19:144

"The Horse Fair" (Brown)   100:81

Horse Feathers (Perelman)   44:501-02, 504-05; 49:270

"The Horse in the Cage" (Plumly)   33:313

"Horse Latitudes" (Matthiessen)   64:321, 324

"Horse Latitudes" (Morrison)   17:291-92

The Horse Latitudes (Ferrigno)   65:47-50

The Horse Show at Midnight (Taylor)   44:301

The Horse Tamer (Farley)   17:117-18

"The Horse That Died of Shame" (Momaday)   85:247, 279

Horse under Water (Deighton)   7:75; 22:114-15

"Horseback" (Kizer)   80:183

"Horseback in the Rain" (Still)   49:363

The Horsehair Sofa (Hughes)   48:181

"Horseman" (Zelazny)   21:479

The Horseman (Haavikko)   34:173, 175, 177-79

"The Horseman of Agawa" (Purdy)   50:246-47

The Horseman on the Roof (Giono)
   See *Le hussard sur le toit*

Horseman, Pass By (McMurtry)   2:272; 7:213-15; 11:371; 27:324-31; 44:256

"Horses" (Hughes)   4:235; 9:281; 14:270

"Horses" (Neruda)   7:260

"Horses" (Smith)   12:536

"Horses" (Smith)   73:357

Horses (Harjo)
   See *She Had Some Horses*

Horses (Smith)   12:535-40, 543

"Horses at Valley Store" (Silko)   74:347

Horses Don't Bet on People and Neither Do I (Bukowski)   82:13-14

"Horses Graze" (Brooks)   15:93; 49:36

A Horse's Head (Hunter)   31:221

Horses Make a Landscape Look More Beautiful (Walker)   58:407, 409

Horse's Neck (Townshend)   42:378-81

Horses of Anger (Forman)   21:116

"Horsie" (Parker)   68:326, 334, 337

"Hortatory" (Dacey)   51:80

Hosanna (Tremblay)   29:418-19, 421; 102:360-61, 364, 372, 374

"Hosanna Heysanna" (Rice and Webber)   21:426

"Hose and Iron" (Kuzma)   7:197

"The Hospice" (Aickman)   57:3

"Hospital" (Bowering)   47:19

"The Hospital" (Kavanagh)   22:243

The Hospital (Chayefsky)   23:116, 118

The Hospital (Fearing)   51:107-08, 121-22

Hospital (Wiseman)   20:469-70, 472

"A Hospital Christmas Eve" (McCullers)   4:345

"The Hospital in Winter" (Fisher)   25:159

The Hospital Play (Shawn)   41:400

"Hospital / poem (for etheridge 9/26/69)" (Sanchez)   116:295

Hospital Zone (Stolz)   12:549-50

"Hostage" (Oates)   108:384

The Hostage (Behan)
   See *An Giall*

Hostage (Household)   11:277

The Hostage Towers (MacLean)   50:348

"Hostages" (Banks)   72:3, 5

"Hostages" (Wideman)   67:379, 384

Hostages (Heym)   41:210-11, 213, 215

Hostages to Fortune (Humphrey)   45:201-02

Hosties noires (*Black Hosts*) (Senghor)   54:390-91, 399-400, 407, 410

Hostile Murmurs (Lezama Lima)
   See *Enemigo rumor*

"Höstlig skärgård" ("Autumn in the Skerries") (Transtroemer)   52:418; 65:233

Höstsonaten (*Autumn Sonata*) (Bergman)   16:80-1; 72:57, 59

"Hot" (Bukowski)   108:113

Hot and Cold (Crommelynck)
   See *Chaud et froid ou l'idée de Monsieur Dom*

"Hot as Sun Glasses" (McCartney)   35:278-79

"Hot Ashes" (Arghezi)   80:10

Hot August Night (Diamond)   30:113

"Hot Broth" (Barnard)   48:27

Hot Cars (Hunter)   31:228

"Hot Coils" (McFadden)   48:244

A Hot Country (*Love and Death in a Hot Country*) (Naipaul)   32:327-28; 39:355-57

Hot Day, Hot Night (Himes)
   See *Blind Man with a Pistol*

"Hot Day on the Gold Coast" (Shacochis)   39:199-200

"Hot Dog" (Stern)   100:345

The Hot Gates, and Other Occasional Pieces (Golding)   3:199; 17:169-70; 27:164, 167, 169; 58:190, 192-94; 81:318

"Hot Ice" (Dybek)   114:70-1, 74-7, 83

Hot Ice (Ludlam)   46:240

The Hot Iron (Green)   25:193

"Hot June" (Avison)   97:77-8, 83

The Hot l Baltimore (Wilson)   7:548; 14:590, 592; 36:465-66

Hot Money (Francis)   102:128, 130-32, 148, 158

"Hot Night on Water Street" (Simpson)   7:426

Hot Rats (Zappa)   17:586, 590

The Hot Rock (Westlake)   7:528; 33:436, 438-40

Hot Rocks (Jagger and Richard)   17:226

Hot Rod (Felsen)   17:121-22

Hot Sleep: The Worthing Chronicle (Card)   47:67-8

"Hot Spell" (Jensen)   37:192

Hot Water Music (Bukowski)   41:72-3

Hotcakes (Simon)   26:408-09

"L'hôte" ("The Guest") (Camus)   9:144-45; 14:114; 63:71; 69:135

"Hotel" (Creeley)   78:154

"Hotel" (Dobyns)   37:75

"Hotel" (Merwin)   45:272

"The Hotel" (Singer)   69:311-12

The Hotel (Bowen)   11:62; 15:78

Hotel (Hailey)   5:157-58

"Hotel Behind the Lines" (Boyle)   58:81

Hotel de Dream (Tennant)   13:536-37; 52:398

Hôtel du Commerce (Hochwalder)   36:235

Hotel du Lac (Brookner)   34:136-43; 51:59, 61-3, 65

The Hotel in Amsterdam (Osborne)   2:328; 5:333; 11:421; 45:313-16

Hotel Lautreamont (Ashbery)   77:77

The Hotel New Hampshire (Irving)   23:247-54; 38:250-52; 112:139-41, 154-58, 164-65

"The Hotel Normandie Pool" (Walcott)   25:455-57; 76:275

"The Hotel of the Idle Moon" (Trevor)   71:326; 116:371

"The Hotel of the Total Stranger" (White)   39:375

Hotel Pastis: A Novel of Provence (Mayle)   89:150-53

The Hotel Play (Shawn)   41:399

Hotel "To the Lost Climber" (Strugatskii and Strugatskii)   27:434

The Hotel Wentley Poems (Wieners)   7:535-37

Hôtes de passage (Malraux)   9:358; 57:307, 320

Hothouse (Aldiss)
   See *The Long Afternoon of Earth*

The Hothouse (Pinter)   27:388, 392, 394; 58:371, 385

Hothouse (Terry)   19:441

The Hothouse by the East River (Spark)   3:465-66; 5:400; 8:495; 13:524-25; 94:353

Hotline (Hyde)   21:177

"Hots On for Nowhere" (Page and Plant)   12:480

The Hottentot Room (Hope)   52:214-17

"Houdini" (Weidman)   7:517

"Houdini's Picnic" (Mitchell)   98:180

"Hound" (Donnell)   34:158

"The Hound" (Faulkner)   18:149

The Hound of Earth (Bourjaily)   62:84-9, 93

The Hound of Ulster (Sutcliff)   26:433

Hounds on the Mountain (Still)   49:362-63, 365

"The Hour" (Dunn)   40:165

"An Hour" (Milosz)   22:308; 82:298

"The Hour and the Years" (Gordimer)   33:177

An Hour Beyond Midnight (Hesse)
   See *Eine Stunde hinter Mitternacht*

Hour of Gold, Hour of Lead: Diaries and Letters of Anne Morrow Lindbergh, 1929-1932 (Lindbergh)   82:151

"The Hour of Letdown" (White)   10:527

"The Hour of Not Quite Rain" (Young)   17:569

The Hour of the Star (Lispector)
   See *A hora da estrela*

The Hour of the Wolf (Bergman)
   See *Vargtimmen*

Hourglass (Kis)
   See *Pescanik*

Hourra l'oural (Aragon)   3:15

"The Hours" (Dubie)   36:133

"An Hour's Restless Sleep" (McFadden)   48:244

"The House" (Adcock)   41:13

"The House" (Coles)   46:107

"The House" (Hogan)   73:158

"The House" (Merwin)   45:274

"House" (O Hehir)   41:323-24

"The House" (Olson)   28:343

"The House" (Sexton)   15:472

"House" (Tomlinson)   45:398, 400-01

"The House" (Zweig)   42:470

A House and Its Head (Compton-Burnett)   15:135, 138, 141

"The House at Sagg" (Crase)   58:161, 165

"House behind a House" (Seger)   35:386

House, Bridge, Fountain, Gate (Kumin)   13:326

"House by the Sea" (Montale)

See "Casa sul mare"
The House by the Sea: A Journal (Sarton) 14:482; 49:317-18. 322
A House by the Shore (Neruda)   28:313-14
"House Dick" (Hammett)   47:156
A House Divided (Buck)   7:31-2; 11:71, 73, 76-7; 18:80
A House for Mr. Biswas (Naipaul)   4:371-75; 7:252-54; 9:392-93; 13:403-06; 18:359-61, 363; 37:323-25, 327, 329; 105:140, 147, 149, 151-52, 154-56, 160, 170, 180-81
"The House Friend" (Singer)   69:311-12
"The House Growing" (Updike)   23:476
"House Guest" (Bishop)   32:39
"House Hunting" (Oates)   108:381
The House in Blind Alley (Rice)   7:364; 49:305
The House in Clewe Street (Lavin)   18:304; 99:312
The House in Cornwall (Streatfeild)
   See *The Secret of the Lodge*
The House in Darkness (Vesaas)
   See *Huset i mørkret*
"A House in Festubert" (Blunden)   56:30, 38, 44
"The House in French Village" (Strand)   41:434
A House in Order (Dennis)   8:173
The House in Paris (Bowen)   1:39; 3:82-3; 11:59-60, 62-4; 15:78-9
"The House in the Acorn" (Redgrove)   41:348
"House in the Country" (Davies)   21:97
A House in the Country (Donoso)
   See *Casa de campo*
The House in the Dark (Vesaas)
   See *Huset i mørkret*
A House in the Middle of the Highway (Popa)
   See *Kucá nasred druma*
A House in the Uplands (Caldwell)   14:99; 60:53
"House in the Wind" (Stuart)   34:375
"The House in the Woods" (Ortese)
   See "La casa del bosco"
"House in Toas" (Hughes)   108:310
"The House in Turk Street" (Hammett)   47:164
"House Is an Enigma" (Jensen)   37:189-90
"House Lie, Believe the Lying Sea" (Hugo)   32:247
House Made of Dawn (Momaday)   2:289-90; 19:318-21; 85:226-30, 232-33, 238, 241, 245-48, 250-51, 255-57, 262, 270-73; 95:214-81
"The House Martins" (Hamburger)   5:159
House Mother Normal: A Geriatric Comedy (Johnson)   6:262-63; 9:300-02
"The House Next Door" (Dunn)   6:149
A House Not Meant to Stand (Williams)   45:455
"House o' Law" (Bennett)   28:29
The House of a Thousand Lanterns (Hibbert)   7:156
House of All Nations (Stead)   2:420, 423; 5:403-05; 8:500; 32:411-12, 415; 80:307, 326, 329, 334, 336, 338, 341, 349
"The House of an Old Woman" (Kelman)   58:295
The House of Assignation (Robbe-Grillet)
   See *La maison de rendez-vous*
"The House of Asterión" (Borges)
   See "La casa de Asterión"
The House of Blue Leaves (Guare)   8:253; 14:220; 29:204-05, 208; 67:78-9, 82-6, 88
The House of Brass (Queen)   11:465
The House of Breath (Goyen)   5:148-49; 8:250;

14:209-11, 214; 40:215, 218
"House of Chirundo" (Mphahlele)   25:340
The House of Connelly (Green)   25:194, 196, 198-99
The House of Cornwall (Streatfeild)
   See *The Secret of the Lodge*
House of Cowards (Abse)   29:21-2
"House of Creation" (Akhmadulina)
   See "Dom tvorchestva"
"The House of Darkstones" (Peake)   54:372
The House of Dies Drear (Hamilton)   26:147-48, 153-54
The House of Dust: A Symphony (Aiken)   52:22, 28
House of Earth (Buck)   11:73, 75
The House of Fiction: An Anthology of the Short Story, with Commentary (Gordon)   6:203; 13:245; 83:232, 235, 251
The House of Five Talents (Auchincloss)   4:29; 45:27-8
House of Flowers (Capote)   13:134-35; 19:81-2; 34:322; 38:82
"The House of God" (Hope)   51:221
The House of Hanover: England in the Eighteenth Century (Garfield)   12:232-34
"House of Haunts" (Queen)   11:461
The House of Hospitalities (Tennant)   52:405-06
House of Incest (Nin)   4:378-79; 8:425; 14:381, 383-84; 60:279, 281
The House of Intellect (Barzun)   51:36-8
"The House of Lamplight Alley" (Aksenov)   22:27
House of Liars (Morante)
   See *Menzogna e sortilegio*
House of Light (Oliver)   98:276-80, 282-85, 290, 293-94, 302
The House of Mirth (Auchincloss)   9:55
"The House of My Dreams" (O'Brien)   5:311-12; 8:429; 36:341; 116:194-95
"A House of My Own" (Cisneros)   69:148
"The House of Okumura VII" (Eshleman)   7:99
"The House of Oliver Ames" (McGinley)   14:366
"House of Rest" (Betjeman)   43:50
The House of Roses (Endo)   99:285-86
"House of Shade" (Kaye)   28:198
The House of Sleep (*Sleep Has His House*) (Kavan)   13:315; 82:118-19, 126
House of Splendid Isolation (O'Brien)   116:211, 213-15, 226
House of the Blue Horse (Kingman)   17:244
"The House of the Heart" (Wakoski)   9:554
"The House of the Injured" (Haines)   58:215
The House of the Prophet (Auchincloss)   18:25-7
"House of the Sleeping Beauties" (Kawabata)
   See "Nemureru bijo"
House of the Sleeping Beauties, and Other Stories (Kawabata)
   See *Nemureru bijo*
The House of the Solitary Maggot (Purdy)   10:424; 52:342-43, 347
The House of the Spirits (Allende)
   See *La casa de los espíritus*
The House of Thunder (Koontz)   78:200
The House of Women (Bermant)   40:95
"House on a Cliff" (MacNeice)   53:238
The House on Coliseum Street (Grau)   4:207
"The House on Kings Road" (Monette)   82:323
"The House on Lamplight Alley" (Aksyonov)   101:19
The House On Mango Street (*Mango Street*)

(Cisneros)   69:144-45, 148-56
The House on Marshland (Gluck)   7:118-19; 22:174-76; 44:215-16, 221, 224
The House on Quai Notre Dame (Simenon)   8:486
"The House on Tenth" (Bowering)   47:24
The House on the Bluff (Douglas)   73:65-7, 74-5, 86, 94
House on the Corner (Dove)
   See *The Yellow House on the Corner*
The House on the Embankment (Trifonov)
   See *Dom na naberezhnoi*
"A House on the Heights" (Capote)   38:84
The House on the Mound (Derleth)   31:138
The House on the Shore (Dillon)   17:93
The House on the Strand (du Maurier)   6:147; 59:287
House Party: A Soulful Happening (Bullins)   5:82; 7:36
"House Party to Celebrate the Destruction of the Roman Catholic Church in Ireland" (Kavanagh)   22:240
"The House Taken Over" (Cortazar)
   See "Casa tomada"
"The House That Jack Built" (Davenport)   38:143
"The House Through" (Motion)   47:288-89, 293
"A House to Let" (Lavin)   99:321-22
"The House Where I Was Born" (Day Lewis)   10:131
The House without the Door (Daly)   52:88
"Houseboat Days" (Ashbery)   25:52
Houseboat Days (Ashbery)   13:30, 35-6; 15:29, 31-5; 25:52-3, 58; 41:35-6, 38, 40-1; 77:44-5, 54-5
"The Housebreaker of Shady Hill" (Cheever)   64:48
The Housebreaker of Shady Hill, and Other Stories (Cheever)   7:49; 15:127; 64:54
"Housecleaning" (Giovanni)   117:196
"Household" (Jensen)   37:189
Household Hints (Longley)   29:295
Household Saints (Prose)   45:325
Household Tales of Moon and Water (Willard)   37:463-64
The Householder (Jhabvala)   29:254-56; 94:167-68, 170, 176, 181, 184-85, 189-93, 205
"The Housekeeper" (Bishop)   32:40
Housekeeping (Robinson)   25:386-89
"Houseplants" (McFadden)   48:250
"Houses" (Merwin)   88:195
Houses and Travellers (Merwin)   8:389-90; 18:334; 88:194
"Houses in North Oxford" (Raine)   103:179, 186
The Houses of Children: Collected Stories (Dowell)   60:107-109
"The Houses of Iszm" (Vance)   35:420
"The Houses of the City" (Berriault)   109:96
"Houses of the Holy" (Page and Plant)   12:477, 482
Houses of the Holy (Page and Plant)   12:476, 479-80, 482
Houses without Doors (Straub)   107:284, 304
"The Housewarming" (Day Lewis)   10:131
"Housewife" (Schaeffer)   11:491
"Housewife" (Sexton)   8:483; 53:316
Housewives (Page)   40:351
"Houston and History" (Steinem)   63:381
"Houston, Houston, Do You Read?" (Tiptree)   48:388-90, 395

"How?" (Lennon)   35:264-65, 267
"How" (Moore)   39:84-5; 45:279-80
"How about This?" (Carver)   36:106
"How Beautiful Is Youth" (Hesse)   17:218
"How 'Bigger' Was Born" (Wright)   21:450; 48:423, 428
"How Bozo the Button Buster Busted All His Buttons when a Mouse Came" (Sandburg)   15:468
"How Claeys Died" (Sansom)   6:484
"How Close" (Ortiz)   45:303, 305
"How Crime Keeps America Healthy" (Puzo)   2:352
"How Did I Get Away with Killing One of the Biggest Lawyers in the State? It Was Easy" (Walker)   103:407, 410
"How Distant" (Larkin)   5:223; 8:333; 13:335; 18:300; 64:282
"How Divine Is Forgiving" (Piercy)   62:379
"How Do I Feel" (Fearing)   51:117
"How Do I Love You?" (Shapiro)
   See "Sonnet VIII"
"How Do You Do, Dr. Berryman, Sir?" (Berryman)   3:66
"How Do You Sleep?" (Lennon)   12:367, 381; 35:263-64, 268
"How Do You Think It Feels" (Reed)   21:306
"How Duke Valentine Contrived" (Bunting)   47:45, 49
"How Everything Happens (Based on a Study of the Wave)" (Swenson)   61:393; 106:335, 339, 351
How Far Can You Go? (Lodge)   36:273-74
How Far It Is From Here, How Near (Konwicki)
   See *Jak daleko stad, jak blisko*
"How Gentle" (Oates)   6:367; 33:294
How German Is It (Abish)   22:20-3
How Green Was My Valley (Ford)   16:305, 316
How Green Was My Valley (Llewellyn)   7:207; 80:188-96
"How Hard It Is to Keep from Being King When It's in You and in the Situation" (Frost)   9:229
How I Became a Holy Mother (Jhabvala)   8:312-13; 29:259; 94:183-85, 187
"How I Came to Be a Graduate Student" (Rose)   85:311
"How I Came to Understand Irving Layton" (McFadden)   48:248, 256
"How I Come to You" (Peacock)   60:298
"How I Contemplated the World from the Detroit House of Correction and Began My Life Over Again" (Oates)   11:400; 52:338; 108:367-68
"How I Escaped from the Labyrinth" (Dacey)   51:79
How I Escaped from the Labyrinth, and Other Poems (Dacey)   51:79-81
"How I Finally Lost My Heart" (Lessing)   10:316; 22:278
"How I Found America" (Yezierska)   46:441
"How I Got My Nickname" (Kinsella)   43:256
How I Got That Story (Gray)   29:200-01
How I Got to Be Perfect (Kerr)   22:258
How I Grew (McCarthy)   59:290-91
"How I Joined the Seal Herd" (Kroetsch)   23:273
How I Met My Husband (Munro)   6:341; 10:357
"How I Missed the Million Dollar Round Table" (Kinsella)   43:258
"How I Moved Anna Fierling to the Southwest Territories, or My Personal Victory over the Armies of Western Civilization" ("Anna Fierling") (Shange)   74:308

"How I Run Away and Make My Mother Toe the Line" (Mazer)   26:295
"How I See Things" (Komunyakaa)   86:192; 94:224
How I Spent My Summer Holidays (Mitchell)   25:327-28
"How I Started to Write" (Fuentes)   113:256
How I Won the War (Lester)   20:224-26
"How I Write" (Eberhart)   56:89
"How I Write" (Welty)   105:328, 333, 335
"How I Write My" ("Plays: Self") (Foreman)   50:167
"How I Wrote One of My Books" (Fuentes)   60:162
"How It Goes On" (Kumin)   13:328; 28:225
How It Is (Beckett)
   See *Comment c'est*
"How It Was" (Milosz)   11:380
How Late It Was, How Late (Kelman)   86:180-89
How Life Began: Creation versus Evolution (Gallant)   17:131
How Long Is Always (Weber)   12:634
"How Long Will I Be Able To..." (Ashbery)   77:42
"How Lousy Is Your Marriage: A 10-Minute Quiz That Could Help You Improve It" (Keillor)   115:286
"How Many Friends" (Townshend)   17:535-36
"How Many Goodly Creatures" (Fuller)   62:199, 202
"How Many Heavens" (Sitwell)   67:320
"How Many Midnights" (Bowles)   19:60; 53:37
How Many Miles to Babylon? (Fox)   2:139
How Many Miles to Babylon? (Johnston)   7:185-86
"How Many More Times" (Page and Plant)   12:473
"How Many Nights" (Kinnell)   29:282
"How Mice Make Love" (Rosenblatt)   15:446
"How Modern Christians Should Think about Man" (King)   83:339
"How Morning Glories Could Bloom at Dusk" (Graham)   48:145
"How Much" (Dybek)   114:67
"How Much Earth" (Levine)   33:271
How Much Is That in Dollars? (Buchwald)   33:89-90
"How Not to Rate a Poet" (Carruth)   84:127
"How Not to Write a Novel" (Grayson)   38:211
"How Now We Talk" (Riding)   7:374
"How Shall We Tell the Children" (Grass)
   See "Wie sagen wir es den Kindern?"
How She Died (Yglesias)   7:557-58; 22:493
"How soon can I leave?" (Hill)   113:293
How Stella Got Her Groove Back (McMillan)   112:238, 240-46
"How Still the Hawk" (Tomlinson)   45:392
"How 'Studs Lonigan' Was Written" (Farrell)   66:134
"How Such a Lady" (Van Doren)   6:541
"How Sweet and Proper It Is" (Dobyns)   37:78
How Sweet It Is (Marshall)   17:274-75
"How Sweet to Be an Idiot" (Monty Python)   21:226
How the Dead Count (Sherwin)   15:480
How the Fishes Live (Lieber)   6:311
How the Garcia Girls Lost Their Accents (Alvarez)   93:2-5, 8-11, 13-8
"How the Last War Ended" (Garrett)   51:140
"How the Mulatto Porciúncula Got the Corpse Off His Back" (Amado)

See "De como o Mulato Porciúncula Descarregou seu Defunto"
"How the Old Man Died" (Ferron)   94:103, 119
How the Other Half Loves (Ayckbourn)   5:35; 18:29; 33:42, 45, 47; 74:3, 18-19, 29, 31, 33-5
"How the Piano Came to Be Prepared" (Cage)   41:84
"How the Plains Indians Got Horses" (Plumly)   33:312
"How the Story Ends" (Vanderhaeghe)   41:450
How the West Was Won (L'Amour)   55:308
How to Be a Father (Gilbreth and Carey)   17:155
"How to Be an Other Woman" (Moore)   39:84; 45:279-80; 68:296
"How to Be Old" (Swenson)   106:319
"How to Become a Writer" (Moore)   39:84; 45:279-80
"How to Build a Balcony" (Selzer)   74:274
"How to Build a Slaughter-house" (Selzer)   74:274
How to Cook a Wolf (Fisher)   76:339, 341; 87:118-20, 122
"How to Cover the Ground" (MacCaig)   36:288
"How To Disembark from a Lark" (Benedikt)   14:81
"How to Enter a Big City" (Merton)   83:395
"How to Fill In a Crossword Puzzle" (Scannell)   49:324
"How to Fry Chicken" (Colwin)   84:142
"How to Get On in Society" (Betjeman)   6:69; 43:40
"How to Get There" (O'Hara)   78:343
"How to Get to Green Springs" (Smith)   22:386
"How to Grow a Wisteria" (O'Brien)   5:313
"How to Hypnotize" (Gerstler)   70:158
"How to Make a Universe" (Barth)   89:57-8
How to Make an American Quilt (Otto)   70:91-5
"How to Make Stew in the Pinacate Desert" (Snyder)   5:393
"How to Play Championship Tennis" (Muldoon)   32:318-19; 72:265
"How to Read" (Pound)   4:411; 10:402
"How to Read a Book" (Brodsky)   100:70
How to Read a Novel (Gordon)   83:251
How to Read a Page (Richards)   24:395, 401
How to Read Donald Duck: Imperialist Ideology in the Disney Comic (Dorfman)
   See *Para leer al Pato Donald*
How to Save Your Own Life (Jong)   8:314-15; 83:302, 304-05, 307, 310-11, 313, 318-19
How to See Deer (Booth)   23:77
"How to Stuff a Pepper" (Willard)   7:539; 37:464
"How to Swing Those Obbligatos Around" (Fulton)   52:158
"How to Take a Successful Nap" (Friedman)   56:105
How to Talk Dirty and Influence People (Bruce)   21:47
"How to Talk to Your Mother" ("Notes") (Moore)   39:83-4; 45:279-80
"How to Tell a True War Story" (O'Brien)   103:137, 139-40, 161, 166, 174
"How to Win" (Brown)   32:63-4
"How to Write a Novel" (Lish)   45:228, 230
How to Write a Play (Ludlam)   50:342
"How to Write a Poem" (Lish)   45:229-30
"How to Write a Poem about the Sky" (Silko)

23:412; 74:347

"How to Write a Short Story" (O'Faolain) 14:406

"How to Write Like Someone Else" (Roethke) 46:361

"How Truth—Leaps (Stumbles) Across Stage" (Foreman) 50:164

"How Wang-Fo Was Saved" (Yourcenar) 38:463; 87:402-03

"How We Are Flowers" (Oates) 6:367

"How Yesterday Looked" (Sandburg) 35:352

"How You Get Born" (Jong) 83:289

Howards End (Forster) 1:103, 106-07; 2:134-36; 3:160; 4:165, 167-69; 9:204-08; 10:180-81; 13:215-20; 15:223-25, 231; 22:131-32, 136-37; 45:132-33, 135-38, 140, 142-43; 77;196, 216-17, 221, 223, 229-30, 234, 241

"Howard's Way" (Howard) 10:275-76

Howbah Indians (Ortiz) 45:301

"However Much I Booze" (Townshend) 17:536

"Howl" (Ginsberg) 2:162-63; 3:194; 4:181, 183; 6:199; 13:239-41; 36:180-85, 192, 195-97; 69:211-28; 109:316-17, 323-28, 332-33, 335-37, 347-52, 355, 358, 369-72

Howl, and Other Poems (Ginsberg) 1:118-19; 2:162-64; 3:193, 195; 6:199, 201-02; 13:239-41; 36:183-84, 187-89, 191, 193-96, 198; 69:211-12, 214, 219, 222; 109:334, 337-42, 344, 350, 352-54, 356, 362, 363

"Howling for Love" (Scannell) 49:332

Howrah Bridge, and Other Poems (Baxter) 14:65

"How's the Night Life on Cissalda?" (Ellison) 42:129-30

Hoy es fiesta (*Today's a Holiday*) (Buero Vallejo) 15:98, 101

Hoyt's Child (Cassill) 23:109

HPSCHD (Cage) 41:83

"Hra na pravdu" ("A Game of Truth"; "The Truth Game") (Klima) 56:172-73

"Hríšné mesto" ("Sinful City") (Seifert) 93:339

Hrvatska rapsodija (Krleza) 114:167, 170, 173

Hrvatski bog Mars (*The Croatian God Mars*) (Krleza) 114:167, 176-77

"Hub Fans Bid Kid Adieu" (Updike) 23:463, 473

"The Hubbub" (Ammons) 57:53

"Huckleberry Finn and the Hero" (Oe) 86:226

"Huckleberry Woman" (Merwin) 13:387

Hud (McMurtry) 2:272; 7:213-15

"Hudson Street" (Bronk) 10:75

"The Hudsonian Curlew" (Snyder) 5:395

Hudsucker Proxy (The Coen Brothers) 108:155-61, 166, 169

"Hue and Cry" (McPherson) 77:358-59, 373, 375, 377

Hue and Cry (McPherson) 19:309; 77:350-52, 364-66, 374

Huelgistas (*The Strikers*) (Valdez) 84:395

Huey, the Engineer (Stuart) 14:514

"The Hug" (Gunn) 81:177, 180-81, 184, 187

"A Huge Cow Lying Down" (Cabral de Melo Neto)
  See "Uma enorme rês deitada"

The Huge Season (Morris) 1:231-33; 37:310-12

Hugging the Shore: Essays and Criticism (Updike) 34:284-87, 289-95

The Hugh MacDiarmid Anthology

(MacDiarmid) 4:313; 19:288

Hugh Selwyn Mauberley (Pound) 2:340-42; 3:395-96; 4:412; 7:332, 335; 10:400, 404; 13:456, 462; 18:427-28; 34:507; 48:282-85, 287, 289, 290, 298-300; 50:437; 112:308-14

"Hughie" (O'Connor) 23:331

"Hugo" (Mac Laverty) 31:254

Hugo le terrible (Conde) 92:132

Hugoliad; or, The Grotesque and Tragic Life of Victor Hugo (Ionesco) 86:336-37

"Huhediblu" (Celan) 82:52

Huis clos (*No Exit*) (Sartre) 4:476; 9:470; 13:501-02; 18:470; 50:370, 380, 382-84; 52:376-77, 381, 383, 388

Hula (Shea) 86:98-105

"Huleikat—the Third Poem about Dicky" (Amichai) 116:130

"Hulk Couture" (Leyner) 92:293

"The Hull Sit-In" (Dunn) 40:166

Hullabaloo over Georgie and Bonnie's Pictrues (Jhabvala) 94:171-72

Hulme's Investigations into the Bogart Script (Ghose) 42:182-83

The Human Beast (Renoir)
  See *La bête humaine*

"The Human Being and the Dinosaur" (Thurber) 5:434

"The Human Bomb" (Lieberman) 36:261

The Human Climate (Jacobsen) 48:190

The Human Comedy (Saroyan) 8:466; 56:373-74

"A Human Condition" (Davies) 23:145

"Human Condition" (Gunn) 18:199

The Human Condition (Arendt) 66:21-2, 24, 26, 36; 98:3, 7-8, 14, 19-22, 27, 48, 52, 54

Human Desire (Lang) 20:205, 216; 103:88, 99

"The Human Element" (Maugham) 67:211

The Human Factor (Greene) 9:250-51; 14:219-20; 18:193-94, 197-98; 27:175-77; 37:138; 70:289, 292-93; 72:177

"The Human Fly" (Boyle) 90:45

"Human Highway" (Young) 17:580

Human Landscapes (Hikmet)
  See *Memleketimden insan manzaralari*

Human Landscapes from My Land (Hikmet)
  See *Memleketimden insan manzaralari*

Human Nature and the Human Condition (Krutch) 24:290

The Human Predicament (Hughes) 11:278

The Human Province (Canetti)
  See *Die Provinz des Menschen: Aufzeichnungen, 1942-1972*

"Human Relationships" (Ginzburg) 54:201, 209

The Human Rights Book (Meltzer) 26:306

Human Scale (Sale) 68:350-53, 359

The Human Season (Wallant) 5:477; 10:511-13, 515-16

The Human Season: Selected Poems, 1926-1972 (MacLeish) 3:311; 68:293

"Human Sheep" (Oe) 86:224, 227

"The Human Situation" (Spender) 10:492

"Human Torso Gives Birth" (Sapphire) 99:80

"The Human Universe" (Olson) 11:417-19; 29:327, 329, 334

The Human Voice (Cocteau) 43:110

Human Voices (Fitzgerald) 19:174-75; 51:124; 61:116-17

Human Wishes (Hass) 99:139-43, 145-50, 154-55, 157

"Humanism and Naturalism" (Tate) 24:439

"The Humanism of Irving Babbitt" (Eliot) 57:183

"The Humanist" (Cunningham) 31:104

"The Humanist" (Eberhart) 56:77

"The Humanist" (Hill) 8:295

"The Humanist's Tragedy" (Jeffers) 2:212

Humanities in America: Report to the President, the Congress, and the American People 70:362

"Humano ardor" (Aleixandre) 9:15

The Humanoid Touch (Williamson) 29:461

The Humanoids (Williamson) 29:449, 452, 455-60

Humanscapes from My Land (Hikmet)
  See *Memleketimden insan manzaralari*

"Humaweepi" (Silko) 74:328

The Humble Administrator's Garden (Seth) 43:387-88; 90:337-8, 353, 361

The Humble Cemetery 59:363, 381

"The Humble Dollar" (Baker) 31:29

"A Humble Protest" (Dos Passos) 82:105

The Humbler Creation (Johnson) 1:161; 27:219-20, 223

Humboldt's Gift (Bellow) 6:55-61; 8:69-71, 80-1; 10:44; 13:73-5; 15:54-5; 25:82-6; 33:71; 34:545-46; 63:27, 31, 33-5, 37, 39

"Hume" (Smith) 64:398

"The Humiliation" (Friedman) 56:97

"Humiliation with Honor" (Brittain) 23:91

"Humility" (Chappell) 40:149

"Humility, Concentration, and Gusto" (Moore) 10:353; 47:268, 270, 272

"The Hummingbird" (Paz) 51:335

"The Hummingbird Comes Home" (Woolrich) 77:389

"Hummingbirds" (Oliver) 98:304

Humoresque (Odets) 98:245

Humorous and/or Not So Humourous (Kenny) 87:252

Humors of Blood and Skin: A John Hawkes Reader (Hawkes) 49:155

"Hump" (Feldman) 7:103

"Humpbacks" (Oliver) 98:257, 271-72, 297-98

Humpty Dumpty (Hecht) 8:270-73

Humulus le muet (Anouilh) 40:57

"Hun" (Burgess) 62:139

"The Hunch" (Dunn) 40:165

"Hunchback Girl: She Thinks of Heaven" (Brooks) 49:26

"The Hunchback of Dugbe" (Soyinka) 36:409

"Hunchback on the Buga Road" (Musgrave) 54:341

"Der Hund" ("The Dog") (Durrenmatt) 15:194

Hundejahre (*Dog Years*) (Grass) 1:125-26; 2:171-73; 4:201-04, 206; 6:207-08; 11:247; 15:261, 263; 22:190; 32:201; 88:136, 139, 143-45, 159

Der Hundertjährige (Eliade)
  See *Der Hundertjärige*

Der Hundertjärige (*The Centogenarian*; *Der Hundertjährige*) (Eliade) 19:148

A Hundred Camels in the Courtyard (Bowles) 53:41

"A Hundred Collars" (Frost) 15:240

The Hundred Islands (Clark) 12:132

"A Hundred Years from Now" (Stern) 100:340

Hundreds of Fireflies (Leithauser) 27:240-43

"The Hungarian Insurrection" (Elytis) 49:110

"The Hungarian Night" (Morand)
  See "La nuit Hongroise"

"The Hungarian Professor" (Archer)　28:14
"Hunger" (Haines)　58:220
"Hunger" (Mahapatra)　33:279, 283, 276
"Hunger" (Rhys)　6:454-55; 51:356
"Hunger" (Rich)　36:374
"Hunger" (Shacochis)　39:201
Hunger (Lessing)　22:279; 94:268
"Hunger and Cold" (Sandburg)　35:356
Hunger and Thirst (Ionesco)
　See *La soif et la faim*
The Hungered One: Early Writings (Bullins)
　7:37
"Hungerfield" (Jeffers)　54:242, 245
Hungerfield and Other Poems (Jeffers)　54:242;
　11:306-07
"Hungering" (Jong)　8:314
Hungry as the Sea (Smith)　33:376
"A Hungry Fighter" (Raine)　103:186, 189
"Hungry for You" (Police, The)　26:365
The Hungry Ghosts (Oates)　6:371
Hungry Hearts (Prose)　45:325-26
Hungry Hearts (Yezierska)　46:441, 446
The Hungry Hill (du Maurier)　59:286
Hungry Hills (Ryga)　14:472-73
"Hunktown" (Mason)　82:244
Hunky Dory (Bowie)　17:58-9, 61-2, 64, 67
"Hunt" (Dumas)　6:146
"The Hunt" (Jones)　7:189, 191; 13:311; 42:241
"The Hunt" (Lem)　8:345; 40:295, 297
Hunt (Alvarez)　13:8-10
The Hunt (Saura)
　See *La caza*
The Hunt by Night (Mahon)　27:293
The Hunt for Red October (Clancy)　45:85-90;
　112:49-52, 54-66, 69, 72-4, 76-8, 81, 83-
　4, 88, 90
"Hunt the Thimble" (Abse)　7:1; 29:16, 18
The Hunted (Leonard)　28:234; 71:223
*Hunted like a Wolf: The Study of the Seminole
　War* (Meltzer)　26:301-02
"The Hunter" (Doctorow)　37:91, 93-4;
　113:152-52, 156
"The Hunter" (Ignatow)　7:177
"A Hunter" (Kelman)　58:301
"The Hunter after Roots" (Neruda)　62:327
Hunter of Worlds (Cherryh)　35:103-05, 110
The Hunters (Salter)　52:359, 363
Hunter's Green (Whitney)　42:434
Hunter's Horn (Arnow)　7:15-16; 18:10, 12,
　16
"Hunters in the Snow" (Wolff)　64:449, 451
Hunters in the Snow (Wolff)
　See *In the Garden of the North American
　Martyrs*
"A Hunter's Moon" (Thomas)　107:337-38,
　340
The Hunter's Year (Milosz)
　See *Rok mysliwego*
"Hunting" (Head)　67:98
"Hunting a Hare" (Voznesensky)　57:414, 427
"A Hunting Accident" (Gordimer)　18:190
"Hunting Civil War Relics at Nimblewill Creek"
　(Dickey)　4:120
The Hunting Dark (Skelton)　13:507
Hunting Flies (Wajda)
　See *A Fly Hunt*
"Hunting Ivan Shark" (Dobyns)　37:76
"The Hunting of Death: The Unicorn" (Lee)
　46:232
"Hunting on Sweetwater Creek" (Bottoms)
　53:31
The Hunting Party (Bernhard)
　See *Die Jagdgesellschaft*

"Hunting Pheasants in a Cornfield" (Bly)　5:61
"A Hunting Story" (Silko)　74:347; 114:316
Hunting Stuart (Davies)　7:73
Hunting the Fairies (Mackenzie)　18:316
"Hunting the Phoenix" (Levertov)　66:251
*Hunting the Wild Pineapple and Other Related
　Stories* (Astley)　41:47, 49
Hunting Tigers under Glass (Richler)　5:376-
　77; 13:481
"The Huntress" (Johnston)　51:243
"The Huntress" (Stead)
　See "The Dianas"
"The Huntsman's Apology" (Montague)
　13:391; 46:269
Las Hurdes—Tierra sin pan (*Land without
　Bread*; *Tierra sin pan*) (Bunuel)　80:19,
　21, 28, 30, 36, 38-9, 42, 49, 51
"Huria's Rock" (Grace)　56:111
L'hurluberlu; ou, Le réactionnaire amoureux
　(Anouilh)　13:17; 40:57-8, 60-1
Hurlyburly (Rabe)　33:344-47
Hurrah for Anything (Patchen)　18:395
"Hurrah for Freedom" (Lind)　82:129-30
"Hurrah for Thunder" (Okigbo)　25:354, 356;
　84:316, 323
"A Hurricane at Sea" (Swenson)　61:400;
　106:326
Hurricane Lamp (Cassity)　42:99
Hurry Home (Wideman)　5:489; 36:451-54;
　67:371
Hurry on Down (Wain)
　See *Born in Captivity*
Hurry Sundown (Foote)　51:131
"Hurry Up Please It's Time" (Sexton)　15:472
"Hurrying Away from the Earth" (Bly)　10:58
"The Hurrying Brook" (Blunden)　56:29
Hurskas kurjuus (Sillanpaa)　19:419-20
"Hurt" (Nowlan)　15:398
"Hurt Hawks" (Jeffers)　54:244
"The Hurt Trees" (Bell)　8:67; 31:48
"Husband and Wife with Newspaper" (Hall)
　51:172
"The Husband I Bought" (Rand)　79:373-74
"Husband to Wife" (Simmons)　43:407
Husbands (Cassavetes)　20:46-7
"A Husband's Return" (Trevor)　71:341, 343,
　348
Huset i mørkret (*The House in Darkness*; *The
　House in the Dark*) (Vesaas)　48:404, 406-
　07, 413
Huskuld the Herald (Vesaas)
　See *Sendemann Huskuld*
The Hussar (Rezzori)　25:381
Le hussard sur le toit (*The Horseman on the
　Roof*) (Giono)　4:184, 187-88; 11:231
"The Hustler" (Lane)　25:286
The Hustler (Tevis)　42:369-70, 372, 374-75,
　377
"Hut" (Pinsky)　94:309
"Hut Five B" (Krleza)
　See "Baraka pet be"
Huui, Huui (Burr)　6:103-04
"Huxley Hall" (Betjeman)　6:68; 43:35-7
"Huzza!" (Stern)　40:413
Hvezdy nad rajskou zahradou (*Stars over Para-
　dise Garden*) (Seifert)　44:426
"Hyacinth" (Gluck)　44:217, 222
"Hyacinth" (H. D.)　73:120
"The Hyacinth" (Raine)　45:330
"A Hyacinth for Edith" (Smith)　15:513
"The Hyacinth Symphony" (Elytis)　100:172
"Hyacinths with Brevity" (Gustafson)　36:218
"Hybrids of Plants and of Ghosts" (Graham)

48:145
Hybrids of Plants and of Ghosts (Graham)
　48:144-47, 150-54
The Hydra Head (Fuentes)
　See *La cabeza de la hidra*
"Hydraulics" (Meredith)　4:349
Hydrogen Box (Ginsberg)　109:356
"Hyla Brook" (Frost)　26:122
"The Hyland Family" (Farrell)　66:129
"Hymen" (H. D.)　8:258; 31:201, 205, 208;
　73:119-20
Hymen (H. D.)　73:105-07, 128
"Hymeneal" (O'Faolain)　32:343
"Hymie's Bull" (Ellison)　114:131, 138
"Hymn" (Ammons)　5:26-7; 8:13; 25:48;
　57:52; 108:50-1, 54, 57-8
"Hymn" (Ginsberg)　3:194; 36:182, 187, 195
"Hymn" (Ian)　21:186
"Hymn" (Milosz)　56:240
"Hymn" (Reading)　47:350
"Hymn" (Smith)　12:544
"Hymn" (Warner)　45:429
"Hymn among the Ruins" (Paz)
　See "Himno entre ruinas"
Hymn and Lament for Cyprus (Ritsos)　13:487
"Hymn before Action" (Forster)　15:228;
　45:132
Hymn for Anytime (Nagy)
　See *Himnusz minden időben*
"Hymn in Two Dimensions" (Elytis)　49:109
"Hymn IV" (Ammons)　5:27
"Hymn of Fire" (Wittlin)　25:468
"Hymn of Not Much Praise for New York City"
　(Merton)　83:395
"A Hymn of Restlessness, Madness, and Bore-
　dom" (Wittlin)　25:468
Hymn of the Pearl (Milosz)　82:310
"Hymn to a Spoonful of Soup" (Wittlin)
　25:467-68
"Hymn to Dispel Hatred at Midnight" (Win-
　ters)　32:468
"Hymn to Ham" (Blount)　38:47
"Hymn to Lanie Poo" (Baraka)　5:45; 14:45
Hymn to Life (Schuyler)　5:383
"Hymn to Maria Neféli" (Elytis)　49:110
"Hymn to Nessa" (Durcan)　43:113
"Hymn to Ra" (Christie)　110:128
"Hymn to the New Omagh Road" (Montague)
　46:270, 273
Hymn to the Rising Sun (Green)　25:198
Hymne (Jouve)　47:206, 212
Hymns (Wittlin)　25:467-68
Hymns in Darkness (Ezekiel)　61:107, 109
Hymns to St. Geryon (McClure)　6:319
Hypnos Walking (Char)　55:287
Hypnosis: The Wakeful Sleep (Kettelkamp)
　12:306-07
"Hypochondriac" (Swift)　41:443
"Hypochondriac Logic" (Davie)　10:121
"Hypocrite Swift" (Bogan)　39:385; 46:81;
　93:61
"Hypocrite Woman" (Levertov)　66:238, 250
"Hysteria" (Eliot)　1:90; 41:150, 160
"I" (Merrill)　8:386-87
I, a Man (Warhol)　20:419
"I Accuse" (Neruda)
　See "Yo acuso"
"I Ain't Got No Home in This World Any-
　more" (Guthrie)　35:184, 191
I Ain't Marching Any More (Ochs)　17:330-34
"I Always Wanted You to Admire My Fasting;
　or, Looking at Kafka" (Roth)　15:449,
　451

"I Am" (Riding)   7:375

"I Am 21" (Robison)   42:342-43

I Am a Camera (Isherwood)   44:397

I Am a Cat (Ichikawa)   20:187

"I Am a Child" (Young)   17:572, 578, 583

"I Am a Child in These Hills" (Browne)   21:35, 37

"I Am a Dangerous Woman" (Harjo)   83:279

"I Am a Lonesome Hobo" (Dylan)   12:185

"I Am a Rock" (Simon)   17:459, 461, 463, 466

"I Am a Sioux Brave, He Said in Minneapolis" (Wright)   5:520

"I Am a Victim of Telephone" (Ginsberg)   36:188

"I Am a Woman" (Brown)   79:154

"I Am Alive" (Momaday)   95:243

"I Am an Animal" (Townshend)   17:541

"I Am Bigfoot" (Carlson)   54:39

"I Am Dreaming of a White Christmas: The Natural History of a Vision" (Warren)   6:558; 8:537; 10:525; 13:577

I Am Elijah Thrush (Purdy)   2:350-51; 4:423; 10:424-25; 52:343

"I Am Fourteen" (Voznesensky)   57:426-27

I Am from Moscow (Krotkov)   19:264

"I Am Goya" (Voznesensky)   57:414-15, 423, 425-27

"I Am, I Said" (Diamond)   30:112

"I Am in Danger—Sir—" (Rich)   76:218

"I Am It and It Is I" (Campbell)   42:90

I am Joaquin (Valdez)   84:396

I Am Lazarus (Kavan)   13:317

I Am Legend (Matheson)   37:246-50

I Am Mary Dunne (Moore)   1:225; 3:341; 5:296-97; 7:237, 239; 8:395; 19:331; 32:313; 90:238, 240-2, 247, 249-51, 254-55, 265, 272, 304

"I Am No Son of the Fact" ("I Am Not a Son of Deed")   75:62, 78

"I Am Not a Son of Deed"   See "I Am No Son of the Fact"

"I Am Not Done Yet" (Clifton)   66:72, 85

"I Am Not Myself" (Bates)   46:55-6

"I Am Not Now, Nor Have I Ever Been, a Matrix of Lean Meat" (Perelman)   49:265

I Am One of You Forever (Chappell)   40:146-48; 78:95, 98, 101, 114, 115

"I Am Peter" (Turco)   11:549

"I Am Shaking to Death" (Hannah)   38:234; 90:137-38, 143

"I Am She" (Giovanni)   117:199

"I Am That Face About Which Fire Fell" (Barker)   48:9

I Am the Beautiful Stranger (Drexler)   2:119-20; 6:142

I Am the Bitter Name (Williams)   33:443-45

I Am the Cheese (Cormier)   12:136-38; 30:81-3, 85, 87-9, 91

I Am the Clay (Potok)   112:293-94

I Am the Doorway (King)   37:205

I Am the Living (Cliff)   21:65

"I Am the People, the Mob" (Sandburg)   35:353

"I Am the Sun" (Hoffman)   6:243

"I Am the Sun" ("Sun") (Kenny)   87:240-41, 245

"I Am the Walrus" (Lennon and McCartney)   12:360, 362; 35:261-62, 268

I Am the World (Vansittart)   42:399

"I Am Vertical" (Plath)   9:433; 11:447; 51:340, 345

I Am Walking in the Garden of His Imaginary Palace (Urquhart)   90:375, 377, 390,

398

"I am You" (Ferlinghetti)   111:65

"I Am Your Singer" (McCartney)   35:280

I and My True Love (MacInnes)   27:280

"I and Your Eyes" (Knight)   40:284-85, 287

"I Apologize" (Komunyakaa)   94:235-36

I Apologize for the Eyes in My Head (Komunyakaa)   94:218, 224, 230, 235, 240, 247

"I Ask Her" (Bowering)   15:82

"I Believe in Love" (Reed)   21:312-13

"I Believe in You" (Dylan)   77:176, 186-87

"I Believe in You" (Young)   17:582

"I Blame It All on Mama" (Mitchell)   98:187

"I Bought a Little City" (Barthelme)   46:36

"I Bought a Palm-Tree" (Peake)   54:372

I Brake for Delmore Schwartz (Grayson)   38:211-13

"I Break the Sky" (Dodson)   79:193

"I Build an Orange Church" (Smith)   64:394

"I Came from Yonder Mountain" (Connell)   45:107

"I Came on a Slaveship" (Guillen)   79:230

"I Came out of the Mother Naked" (Bly)   10:57, 62; 38:52

I Can Get It for You Wholesale (Polonsky)   92:378, 405

I Can Get It for You Wholesale (Weidman)   7:516-18

"I Can Hear Music" (Wilson)   12:645

"I Can See for Miles" (Townshend)   17:530, 538

"I Can Still Picture the Caribou" (Young Bear)   94:364

I, Candidate for Governor and How I Got Licked (Sinclair)   11:497; 15:498

"I Cannot Forget the Woman in the Mirror" (Olds)   85:295

"I Cannot Place the Face" (Deren)   102:38

"I Cannot Stand Tears" (Bukowski)   41:63, 66

"I Can't Explain" (Townshend)   17:530, 539

I Can't Imagine Tomorrow (Williams)   45:451

"I Can't Let My Heaven Walk Away" (Wonder)   12:656

"I Can't Quit You Baby" (Page and Plant)   12:479

"I Can't Reach You" (Townshend)   17:529, 531

I Can't Remember Anything (Miller)   See *Danger: Memory!*

"I Can't See Your Face in My Mind" (Morrison)   17:295

I Can't Stay Long (Lee)   90:192, 198-99, 201

I Ching (Tillinghast)   29:415

I, Claudius (Graves)   1:128; 6:211; 39:321-24, 326-28; 45:172-73

I Come as a Thief (Auchincloss)   4:29-30; 6:15

I Confess (Hitchcock)   16:343, 351

"I Could Give All to Time" (Frost)   9:225

"I Could Not Be Here at All" (Ammons)   57:49-50

"I Could See the Smallest Things" (Carver)   22:102

I Crossed the Minch (MacNeice)   10:326; 53:234-35

"I Cry, Love! Love!" (Roethke)   101:274, 335, 339-41

"I Declare Myself an Impure Man" (Guillen)   48:159

"I Declare, Under Penalty of Milkshake" (Perelman)   23:336

I den tiden (*In That Time*) (Lagerkvist)   54:286

"I Did It to Attract Women" (Musgrave)

54:334

"I Did Not Learn Their Names" (Ellison)   114:131

"I didn't want to" (Bukowski)   108:106

"I Do/Dig Everything Swinging" (Williams)   13:600

"I Do It for Your Love" (Simon)   17:466

"I Do Not Know" (Musgrave)   54:341

I Do Remember the Fall (Kelly)   55:159

I dol'she veka dlitsia den' (*And One Day Lasts Longer than an Age*; *And the Day Lasts Longer Than a Century*; *Burannyi polustanok*; *The Day Lasts More than a Century*; *The Day Lasts More than a Hundred Years*) (Aitmatov)   71:7-9, 18-19, 21, 26-7, 30, 33

"I Don't Believe You" (Dylan)   77:173

"I Don't Blame You At All" (Robinson)   21:343, 345

I Don't Have to Show You No Stinking Badges (Valdez)   84:403-05, 407-08, 410, 413, 415, 417

"I Don't Know" (Carroll)   35:77

"I Don't Know" (McFadden)   48:252

I Don't Know (McFadden)   48:251-52, 255

"I Don't Know How to Love Him" (Rice and Webber)   21:424-25

"I Don't Know Why You Think" (Guillen)   See "No sé por qué piensas tú"

"I Don't Need a Bedsheet with Slits for Eyes to Kill You" (Bukowski)   82:26

"I Don't Need You Any More" (Miller)   6:333; 10:345; 47:249-50

I Don't Need You Any More (Miller)   47:249

"I Don't Wanna Be a Soldier, I Don't Wanna Die" (Lennon)   35:263-65, 267

"I Don't Wanna Face It" (Lennon)   35:275

"I Don't Want to Be Alone" (Joel)   26:220

"I Don't Want to Die" (Himes)   108:227

"I Don't Want to Go to Chelsea" (Costello)   21:68, 75

I Don't Want to Know Anyone Too Well, and Other Stories (Levine)   54:293, 295, 299

"I Dream I'm the Death of Orpheus" (Rich)   7:366; 11:478

"I Dreamed I Saw St. Augustine" (Dylan)   12:185

"I Dreamed That in a City Dark As Paris" (Simpson)   7:426; 9:486

"I, Dreamer" (Miller)   30:263

I Dreamt I Was a Nymphomaniac: Imagining (Acker)   45:14; 111:25, 32, 36

"I, Eliza Custis" (Grayson)   38:210

"I Envy You Your Great Adventure" (Dowell)   60:109

I, Etcetera (Sontag)   13:516-19; 31:411; 105:197, 206

"I Expand My Horizons" (Trow)   52:420

"I Expected to Spend My Time" (Alegria)   75:34

"I Explain a Few Things" (Neruda)   See "Explico algunas cosas"

"I feel good in my trousers" (Amichai)   116:98

"I Feel Pretty" (Sondheim)   30:378, 387, 395

"I Feel, Therefore I Exist" (Voznesensky)   57:425

"I Felt" (Ignatow)   7:179

"I Find You" (Ignatow)   40:261

"fiumi" (Ungaretti)   11:555

"Fled Paris" (Butor)   11:80

"I Fly in Dream" (Cocteau)   8:146

I for One (Sargeson)   31:364, 367

"I Found a Dead Fox" (Oliver)   98:303

"I Found Out" (Lennon)   **35**:262, 266
"I Gather the Limbs of Osiris" (Pound)   **13**:454; **48**:288-89
I Gave at the Office (Westlake)   **33**:436
"I Gave Up before Birth" (Beckett)   **29**:57
"I Get Around" (Wilson)   **12**:646, 649, 651, 653
"I Get By" (Robison)   **98**:317
"I Get Wild/Wild Gravity" (Byrne)   **26**:99
"I Give You Back" (Harjo)   **83**:266
"I Go Back to May 1937" (Olds)   **85**:292-93, 305
"I Got a Little Flat off Third and Yen" (Tate)   **25**:430
"I Got By in Time" (Weller)   **26**:443
"I Got Life" (Ragni and Rado)   **17**:385
"I Got Plenty" (Carroll)   **35**:77
"I Got the Blues" (Jagger and Richard)   **17**:229, 242
"I Got the News" (Becker and Fagen)   **26**:84
"I Had a King" (Mitchell)   **12**:440
"I Had a Strange Dream" (Ratushinskaya)   **54**:385
I Hardly Knew You (O'Brien)
   See *Johnny, I Hardly Knew You*
"I Hate Paris" (Butor)   **11**:80
"I Have" (Guillen)
   See "Tengo"
I Have (Guillen)
   See *Tengo*
"I Have a Dream" (King)   **83**:343-46, 349
I Have Been Here Before (Priestley)   **34**:361, 365
"I Have Been in You" (Zappa)   **17**:592-93
"I Have Kept My Vigil" (Harrison)   **42**:203
I Have Killed (Cendrars)   **106**:191
"I Have No Mouth and I Must Scream" (Ellison)   **42**:126
"I Have Nothing to Declare but My Genius" (Perelman)   **5**:338
I Hear America Swinging (De Vries)   **7**:78; **10**:136, 138; **28**:107
"I Hear the Oriole's Voice" (Akhmatova)   **64**:16
"I Hear You, Doc" (Reed)   **13**:480
"I Heard Her Call My Name" (Reed)   **21**:314
I Heard My Sister Speak My Name (Savage)   **40**:374-75
I Heard the Owl Call My Name (Craven)   **17**:79-81
"I Heard Wild Geese" (Ekeloef)   **27**:119
I, Judas (Caldwell)   **28**:67; **39**:302
"I Just Love Carrie Lee" (Douglas)   **73**:65-7, 82
"I Just Wasn't Made for These Times" (Wilson)   **12**:646
"I Kill, Therefore I Am" (Ochs)   **17**:332
I Knew a Phoenix: Sketches for an Autobiography (Sarton)   **49**:316; **91**:245-48
"I Knew a Woman" (Roethke)   **8**:460; **19**:401; **46**:363; **101**:328-29
I Knock at the Door: Swift Glances Back at Things That Made Me (O'Casey)   **5**:320; **88**:237-38, 240
"I Know" (Berryman)   **62**:58
"I Know a Man" (Creeley)   **15**:153; **36**:121; **78**:120, 135, 137
"I Know I Remember, but How Can I Help You?" (Carruth)   **7**:41
I Know What You Did Last Summer (Duncan)   **26**:103-06, 108
"I Know What You Mean, Erdupps MacChurbbs: Autobiographical Myths and Metaphors"

(Vizenor)   **103**:281, 299
I Know Why the Caged Bird Sings (Angelou)   **12**:9; **35**:30-3; **64**:24-5, 27-30, 34-9; **77**:2-13, 15-17, 19, 21-3, 31-3, 35
I, Laminarian (Cesaire)
   See *Moi, Laminaire*
I Lay My Cards on the Table (Aragon)
   See *J'abats mon jeu*
I Like It Here (Amis)   **1**:5; **2**:4, 9
"I Like My Body" (Cummings)   **3**:118
"I Live among the Shadows" (Salinas)   **90**:332
I Live in Fear (Kurosawa)   **16**:403
"I Live on Your Visits" (Parker)   **68**:337
I Live under a Black Sun (Sitwell)   **67**:314-15
I Lock My Door upon Myself (Oates)   **108**:379-81, 385
"I Long for People through Whom the Past" (Coles)   **46**:112
"I Look at My Hand" (Swenson)   **106**:344
"I Look Out for Ed Wolfe" (Elkin)   **51**:98
"I Love Every Little Thing about You" (Wonder)   **12**:663
I Love Liberty (Brown)   **79**:169
"I Love My Friend" (Hughes)   **35**:214; **108**:331
"I Love My Rooster" (Still)   **49**:366
I Love Myself When I Am Laughing....A Zora Neale Hurston Reader (Walker)   **103**:357, 372
"I Love Someone" (Stafford)   **19**:431
"I Love You" (Creeley)   **78**:141
"I Love You Dear" (Robinson)   **21**:343
I Married a Dead Man (Woolrich)   **77**:389-91, 393-98, 400, 402-05
I Married a Witch (Clair)   **20**:70
I Married You for the Fun of It (Ginzburg)   **70**:282
I Marry You: A Sheaf of Love Poems (Ciardi)   **40**:155-56, 163; **44**:380, 382
"I Maureen" (Spencer)   **22**:406
I May Be Wrong, But I Doubt It (Royko)   **109**:404
"I May Have Sung with Jerry Jeff" (Blount)   **38**:46
"I May, I Might, I Must" (Moore)   **8**:401; **47**:261
"I May Smoke Too Much" (Kristofferson)   **26**:269
"I Meet Time" (Ali)   **69**:32
"I, Mencius, Pupil of the Master ..." (Olson)   **11**:416
I Met a Boy I Used to Know (Weber)   **12**:634
"I Met a Little Girl" (Gaye)   **26**:133-34
"I Must Have You" (Oates)   **19**:352
I Myself Am a Woman (Ding Ling)   **68**:66-7, 69
"I Need Help" (Hirsch)   **50**:195, 198-99
"I Need Help from the Philosophers" (Stern)   **40**:408; **100**:337
"I Need, I Need" (Roethke)   273, 279, 335, 340
"I Need You" ("For Someone") (Weller)   **26**:443
"I Need You Baby" (Berry)   **17**:56
I Never Danced at the White House (Buchwald)   **33**:93
I Never Loved Your Mind (Zindel)   **6**:586; **26**:471-73, 475, 479-80
I Never Promised You a Rose Garden (Greenberg)   **7**:135; **30**:161-66
I Never Said I Loved You (Bennett)   **35**:46
I Never Sang for My Father (Anderson)   **23**:32
"I Never Saw Morning" (Tyler)   **103**:258
"I Nildeltat" (Transtroemer)   **52**:409
"I No More Real than Evil in My Roof" (Graham)   **29**:193

I, Olli, and Orvokki (Salama)
   See *Minä, Olli ja Orvokki*
I On Feminine Culture (Castellanos)
   See *Sobre cultura femenina*
"I Only Am Escaped Alone to Tell Thee" (Nemerov)   **36**:305
I Ought to Be in Pictures (Simon)   **31**:398-99, 403
"I, Ozymandias" (Ihimaera)   **46**:200
I Passed This Way (Ashton-Warner)   **19**:23-4
"I Peer Through Ugliness" (Nolan)   **58**:366
"I, Pierre Rivière, Having Slaughtered My Mother, My Sister, and My Brother" (Foucault)
   See "*Moi, Pierre Rivière, ayant égurgé ma mer, ma soeur, et mon frère*"
"I Pity the Poor Immigrant" (Dylan)   **12**:185
"I Pity the Wind" (Stern)   **40**:414
"I Plant Geraniums" (Giovanni)   **117**:200
"I Play Chess with an Arab Professor" (Faludy)   **42**:141
"I Pressed My Hands Together..." (Akhmatova)   **64**:8
"I Put a Name in an Envelope..." (Barthelme)   **46**:42
"I Put My Blue Genes On" (Card)   **47**:67
"I, Quiyumucon" (Harris)   **25**:217
I raconti accoppiamenti giudiziosi (Gadda)   **11**:211
"I Remember" (Boland)   **67**:39; **113**:82, 108
I Remember (Fellini)
   See *Amarcord*
I Remember (Pasternak)   **7**:295
I Remember (Perec)
   See *Je me souviens*
"I Remember Babylon" (Clarke)   **13**:148
"I Remember, I Remember" (Larkin)   **5**:227; **8**:332; **18**:294, 301; **33**:256; **39**:336; **64**:266
"I Remember! I Remember!" (O'Faolain)   **14**:406
I Remember! I Remember! (O'Faolain)   **7**:275; **32**:340-41; **70**:319
I Remember Petersburg (Almedingen)
   See *My Saint Petersburg*
"I Ride My High Bicycle" (Adcock)   **41**:18
I, Robot (Asimov)   **9**:50; **19**:27; **26**:35, 37, 46-7, 53; **76**:313-14, 318-20; **92**:1-23
"I Said 'My Name Is "Ozzy" Manders, Dean of Kings'" (Frayn)   **47**:135
"I Save Your Coat, but You Lose It Later" (Gallagher)   **63**:117, 126
"I Saw Eternity" (Bogan)   **46**:78, 81, 83; **93**:64-5
"I Saw Her Dancing" (Piercy)   **62**:379
"I Saw Her Standing There" (Lennon and McCartney)   **12**:374
I Saw in My Dream (Sargeson)   **31**:364, 367-68, 371-73
"I Saw One Walking" (Avison)   **97**:69, 75
"I Second That Emotion" (Robinson)   **21**:342
"I See" (Redgrove)   **6**:445; **41**:351
I See a Long Journey (*Three of a Kind*) (Ingalls)   **42**:232-35
I See By My Outfit (Beagle)   **104**:4-5
"I See, Said the Blind Man, As He Put Down His Hammer and Saw" (Ashbery)   **41**:39
"I seek the word" (Szymborska)   **99**:202
I Sent a Letter to My Love (Rubens)   **19**:403-04
I Served the King of England (Hrabal)
   See *Obsluhoval jsem anglického krále*
"I Set It My Task" (Ammons)   **108**:19
"I Shall Laugh Purely" (Jeffers)   **11**:306

"I Shall Marry the Miller's Son" (Sondheim) **30**:384, 392

I Shall Not Be Moved (Angelou) **64**:40

I Shall Not Hear the Nightingale (Singh) **11**:504, 506-07

"I Shot the Sheriff" (Marley) **17**:267-69

"I Should Tell You" **99**:169

"I Shout Love" (Acorn) **15**:9

"I Sing of Olaf Glad and Big" (Cummings) **3**:118

"I Sing the Body Electric!" (Bradbury) **42**:37

I Sing the Body Electric! (Bradbury) **42**:34, 39

"I Sit by the Window" (Brodsky) **36**:78, 81; **100**:52

"I Sit in One of the Dives/On Fifty-Second Street" (Auden) **43**:22

i: Six Nonlectures (Cummings) **3**:117-18; **8**:155; **68**:46

"I Sleep a Lot" (Milosz) **82**:297

"I Smell Esther Williams" (Leyner) **92**:281

I Smell Esther Williams (Leyner) **92**:281, 285, 292-93

I sommersi e i salvati (*The Drowned and the Saved*) (Levi) **50**:330, 332, 336, 338-40

I Speak of Africa (Plomer) **4**:406

"I Speak of the City" (Paz) **51**:335; **65**:190

I Spy (Mortimer) **28**:283-84

"I Spy a Stranger" (Rhys) **51**:376

"I Spy Strangers" (Amis) **40**:43-5

"I Stand Here Ironing" (Olsen) **13**:432; **114**:192, 194, 197-98, 202, 207, 210, 212, 214, 221, 223, 231-35, 245

"I Stood with the Dead" (Sassoon) **36**:385

"I Substitute for the Dead Lecturer" (Baraka) **5**:45

"I Surrender in the March of My Bones" (Salinas) **90**:332

"I Swear" (Akhmadulina) **53**:14

"I Take Back Everything I've Said" (Parra) **102**:349-50, 352-53

"I Taste the Ashes of Your Death" (Bukowski) **41**:66

"I, Tekonwatonti" (Kenny) **87**:254

"i thank You God for most this amazing" (Cummings) **15**:163

I That Was Born in Wales (Watkins) **43**:453-55

I, the Jury (Spillane) **3**:468-69; **13**:526-27

I, the Supreme (Roa Bastos)
  See *Yo, el supremo*

"I Think: How Stupid I Have Been" (Akhmadulina)
  See "La dumaiu: kak ia byla glupa"

"I Think It Rains" (Soyinka) **44**:277

"I Think of All Soft Limbs" (Gustafson) **36**:222

"I Thought I Was a Child" (Browne) **21**:35, 37

I Thought of Daisy (Wilson) **1**:373; **2**:474-75; **24**:468-69

I, Tituba, Sorceress, Black Woman of Salem (Conde)
  See *Moi, Tituba, sorcière, noire de Salem*

"I Told You I Like Indians" (Ortiz) **45**:301

"I, Too, Sing America" (Hughes) **5**:191; **108**:283, 314, 324

"I Too Will End" (Barker) **48**:12

"I Tried to Be a Communist" (Wright) **21**:455-56

"I Understand the Sin That Weighs upon My House" **75**:62, 69, 78

"I Used to Live Here Once" (Rhys) **19**:390-91

"I Useta Live in the World (But Then I Moved to Harlem)" (Shange) **25**:402

"I Visited the Poet..." (Akhmatova) **64**:20

I Waited on the King of England (Hrabal)
  See *Obsluhoval jsem anglického krále*

"I Walked Out to the Graveyard" (Eberhart) **19**:143

"I Walked over the Grave of Henry James" (Eberhart) **56**:81

"I Walked the Boulevard" (Cummings) **68**:51

"I Wanna Be Black" (Reed) **21**:316

"I Wanna Be Your Lover" (Prince) **35**:323-24, 328

"I Wanna Pick You Up" (Wilson) **12**:652

"I Wanna Woman" (O'Casey) **11**:406

"I Want a Sunday Kind of Love" (Gold) **42**:192

"I Want, I Want" (Plath) **111**:164

I Want It Now (Amis) **2**:7, 9; **13**:12

"I Want to Ask a Terrifying Question" (Kaufman) **49**:207

I Want to Be Honest (Voinovich)
  See *Kochu byt' chestnym*

"I Want to Be Your Love" (Robinson) **21**:348-49

"I Want to Boogie with You" (Reed) **21**:317, 321

"I Want to Dance" **75**:76

I Want to Go to Moscow (Duffy) **37**:116

"I Want to Live!" (Jones) **81**:63, 65, 69

"I Want to Play" **75**:69

"I Want to Sing" (Giovanni) **64**:191

"I Want You" (Dylan) **12**:182

I Want You (Gaye) **26**:132-33

"I Want You Women Up North to Know" (Olsen) **114**:221

"I Want You—She's So Heavy" (Lennon and McCartney) **12**:380

I Wanted a Year without Fall (Busch) **10**:91-2

"I Wanted to be There When My Father Died" (Olds) **85**:308

"I Wanted to Overthrow the Government but All I Brought Down Was Somebody's Wife" (Bukowski) **41**:67

I Wanted to Write a Poem: The Autobiography of the Works of a Poet (Williams) **22**:467-68; **42**:449

"I Wanted You to Know" (Levine) **33**:274

"I Was a Playboy Bunny" (Steinem) **63**:378, 380, 383

I Was Amelia Earhart (Mendelsohn) **99**:63-71

I Was Born But... (Ozu) **16**:447-48, 453

"I Was Born in Lucerne" (Levine) **33**:274-75

"I Was Born in Náchod..." (Skvorecky) **69**:335-36

I Was Dancing (O'Connor) **14**:394

"I Was in Love" (Oates) **19**:348-49

"I Was Made to Love Her" (Wonder) **12**:655

"I Was Writing" (Rozewicz) **9**:463

"I Watched a Bird" (Souster) **14**:501

"I Watched a Snake" (Graham) **48**:148

"I Went Out in the Sun" (Ammons) **108**:18

I Went to Russia (O'Flaherty) **34**:356-57

"I Went to See Irving Babbitt" (Eberhart) **56**:76

"I Will" (Spacks) **14**:511

I Will Call It Georgie's Blues (Newton) **35**:302

I Will Fear No Evil (Heinlein) **14**:252, 254-55; **26**:163, 165-66; **55**:303

"I Will Keep Her Company" (Davies) **23**:148

"I Will Lie Down" (Swenson) **106**:350

"I Will Live and Survive" (Ratushinskaya) **54**:385

I Will Marry When I Want (Ngugi wa Thiong'o)
  See *Ngaahika Ndeenda*

"I Will Not Crush the World's Corolla of Wonders" **75**:76

"I Will Sing You One-O" (Frost) **9**:220

"I Will Teach You about Murder" (Lerman) **9**:329

"I Wish" (Wonder) **12**:660, 662

I Wish This War Were Over (O Hehir) **41**:324-26

I Wonder As I Wander: An Autobiographical Journey (Hughes) **10**:279; **108**:284, 290-91, 298, 318, 324

"I Wore My New Canary Suit" (Christie) **110**:126

"I Would Die 4 U" (Prince) **35**:329, 331-32

"I Would Have Been a Trumpet Player If I Hadn't Gone to College" (Baraka) **115**:28

I Would Have Saved Them If I Could (Michaels) **6**:324-26; **25**:316

"I Would Like" (Yevtushenko) **51**:432

"I Would Like to Dance" (Ian) **21**:186

"I Would Like to Describe" (Herbert) **43**:188

I Would Steal Horses (Alexie) **96**:5, 8

"I Wouldn't Be in Your Shoes" (Woolrich) **77**:401, 403

I Write Your Name (Carroll) **35**:81

"I Wrote a Good Omelet" (Giovanni) **117**:177

"Iambic Feet Considered as Honorable Scars" (Meredith) **4**:348

"Ibadan" (Clark) **38**:117, 120, 126, 128

"Ibadan Dawn—After Pied Beauty" (Clark) **38**:128

Iberia: Spanish Travels and Reflections (Michener) **29**:311; **60**:256-57

"Ibn Gabirol" (Amichai) **116**:84

"Icarium Mare" (Wilbur) **110**:361

"Icarus" (Kaufman) **8**:317

"Icarus Descending" (Benford) **52**:64

Icarus's Mother (Shepard) **17**:436, 439, 445; **41**:407

"Ice" (Ai) **14**:8; **69**:6-7

"Ice" (Oliver) **98**:265

"Ice" (Tallent) **45**:387

Ice (Cristofer) **28**:97

Ice (Hunter) **31**:227

Ice (Kavan) **5**:205-06; **13**:316; **82**:122-26

"The Ice Age" (Gerstler) **70**:158

The Ice Age (Drabble) **10**:163-66; **53**:121-22, 124

Ice Age (Livesay) **79**:344-45, 349

Ice and Fire (Dworkin) **43**:135

"Ice at Last" (Johnston) **51**:251

"Ice Block" (Voznesensky) **57**:421

Ice Brothers (Wilson) **32**:449

Ice Cod Bell or Stone (Birney) **6**:72, 78

"Ice Cream" (Creeley) **78**:140

"The Ice Cream Man" (Raine) **103**:179, 186

Ice Crown (Norton) **12**:459-60, 467

"Ice Cube Culture: A Shared Passion for Speaking Truth: bell hooks and Ice Cube in Dialogue" (hooks) **94**:158

"The Ice House Gang" (Rooke) **25**:390-91

The Ice in the Bedroom (Wodehouse) **2**:480

Ice Palace (Ferber) **18**:152; **93**:183-85, 188, 190

The Ice Palace (*Palace of Ice*) (Vesaas) **48**:407-09

The Ice Saints (Tuohy) **37**:427-28, 431

Ice Station Zebra (MacLean) **13**:361-62; **50**:348-50; **63**:264-65, 269

"The Ice Storm" (Ashbery) **77**:65, 67

"The Ice Wagon Going down the Street" (Gallant) **38**:194

Icebreaker (Gardner) **30**:158

An Ice-Cream War: A Tale of the Empire (Boyd) **28**:39-42; **53**:50-1, 53, 55-6; **70**:132, 138, 140, 142

"Icehouse" (Matthews) **40**:322

"The Icehouse, Pointe au Baril, Ontario"

(Matthews) **40**:320

"Iceland" (MacNeice) **53**:231

The Ice-Shirt (Vollmann) **89**:279-86, 290-92, 294-301, 309-11, 313

"Ich schreibe für Leser" (Frisch) **44**:189

"Ich schreibe kein Buch über Kafka" (Hildesheimer) **49**:174

Ici et ailleurs (Godard) **20**:153

Ici et maintenant (Adamov) **25**:19

The Icicle, and Other Stories (Sinyavsky) **8**:488

"Icicles" (Gass) **2**:154; **8**:244

"Icicles" (Pinsky) **94**:308-9

Icoane de lemn (*Icons on Wood*; *Wooden Icons*) (Arghezi) **80**:3, 6, 11

"Icon" (Piercy) **27**:373

L'iconoclaste (Marcel) **15**:361, 363

"The Iconoclasts" (Avison) **97**:68, 71, 80, 111

Iconographs (Swenson) **4**:534; **14**:519; **61**:392-94, 397, 400-01; **106**:320-21, 325, 327-28, 338, 342, 344, 349-50

"Icons" (Waddington) **28**:438

Icons on Wood (Arghezi)
See *Icoane de lemn*

I'd Rather Be Right (Hart and Kaufman) **38**:261, 265; **66**:175, 185

"Idaho" (Ashbery) **77**:42

"Idaho" (Hannah) **38**:233-35; **90**:138-39, 147

"Idaho Falls, 1961" (Hogan) **73**:148

"Idaho Out" (Dorn) **10**:159-61

"Idanre" (Soyinka) **36**:409; **44**:278

Idanre and Other Poems (Soyinka) **36**:409; **44**:277, 279

"The Idea" (Carver) **22**:97

"The Idea" (Strand) **71**:287-88

"An Idea for Film" (Hannah)
See "Power and Light (An Idea for Film)"

The Idea of a Christian Society (Eliot) **6**:166; **9**:185

"The Idea of Ancestry" (Knight) **40**:279-81, 283-84, 286

"The Idea of Entropy at Maenporth Beach" (Redgrove) **41**:348, 352

"The Idea of Perfection" (Murdoch) **3**:346; **15**:388

"The Idea of the Good" (Wright) **28**:465

The Idea of the Humanities (Crane) **27**:72-4

"The Idea of the Modern" (Howe) **85**:149, 151

"The Idea of Trust" (Gunn) **18**:202

"Ideal Landscape" (Rich) **18**:446

"The Idealism of American Criticism" (Eagleton) **63**:106

"The Idealists" (Campbell) **32**:75

Ideals: A Book of Farce and Comedy (Scott) **43**:375-76

Ideas and the Novel (McCarthy) **24**:347-50; **59**:292

"Une idée fondamentale de phénoménologie de Husserl" (Sartre) **7**:391

Identification Marks: None (Skolimowski)
See *Rysopis*

Identität und Differenz (*Identity and Difference*) (Heidegger) **24**:277

"Identities" (Muldoon) **72**:265

"Identity" (Ammons) **25**:43

"Identity" (Avison) **97**:76

"Identity and Argument for Prayer" (Warren) **13**:582

Identity and Difference (Heidegger)
See *Identität und Differenz*

"Identity Check" (Enzensberger) **43**:152

The Identity of Yeats (Ellmann) **50**:309

"Ideographs" (Olds) **39**:188

The Ideology of the Aesthetic (Eagleton) **63**:110-14

"The Ides of March" (Fuller) **28**:149

The Ides of March (Wilder) **1**:364, 366; **5**:494, 496; **6**:572-73, 575-78; **15**:573; **82**:348, 353, 374, 376-77, 379

An Idiom of Night (Jouve) **47**:209

"The Idiom of the Argentines" (Borges) **44**:357

El idioma de los Argentinos (Borges) **44**:363

"Idiosyncrasy and Technique" (Moore) **47**:268, 270

The Idiot (Kurosawa) **16**:401, 403-05

L'idiot de la famille: Gustave Flaubert de 1821 à 1857 (*The Family Idiot: Gustave Flaubert, 1821-1857*) (Sartre) **7**:397; **24**:421-22; **50**:382; **52**:373, 380, 385-87, 389

The Idiot Princess of the Last Dynasty (Klappert) **57**:261-66, 269-70

Idiotiki Odos (Elytis) **100**:187-88

"Idiots First" (Malamud) **18**:317-18; **27**:299, 306-07; **44**:412-13, 415; **85**:217

Idiots First (Malamud) **1**:198; **3**:321; **5**:269; **9**:346, 348; **18**:318; **27**:298, 301; **44**:413

The Idiots Karamazov (Durang) **27**:87-8

The Idiots Karamazov (Innaurato) **60**:201

"An Idiot's Love" (Tanizaki)
See "Chijin no ai"

The Idle Class (Chaplin) **16**:191

"An Idle Visitation" (Dorn) **10**:158

"Idleness in South Africa" (Coetzee) **66**:99, 105; **117**:51

"The Idler" (Bitov) **57**:114-15

"Ido and Enam" (Agnon) **4**:12

"The Idol House of Astarte" (Christie) **110**:143

The Idol Hunter (Unsworth)
See *Pascali's Island*

"The Idol of the Cyclades" (Cortazar)
See "El ídolo de las cícladas"

"El ídolo de las cícladas" ("The Idol of the Cyclades") (Cortazar) **10**:114; **33**:129; **34**:332

The Idols of the Cave (Prokosch) **4**:420; **48**:312-14

"Idoto" (Okigbo) **25**:355

Idut belye snegi (Yevtushenko) **26**:462

"Idyll for a Fool" (Gustafson) **36**:214, 216

"Idylle" (Damas) **84**:179

"Idylls of Dugan and Strunk" (Stern) **39**:239

"If" (Hogan) **73**:149

"If" (Warren) **39**:258

If (Anderson) **20**:13-16, 18

"If All Men Were Brothers Would You Let One Marry Your Sister?" (Sturgeon) **39**:361-62

"If Anyone Had Told Me" (Aleixandre)
See "If Someone Could Have Told Me"

"If Anything Will Level with You Water Will" (Ammons) **108**:28

If Beale Street Could Talk (Baldwin) **4**:41-3; **5**:42-4; **15**:42; **17**:39, 45; **50**:297; **90**:31

"If Beggars Were Horses" (Dowell) **60**:104-05, 109

If Birds Build with Your Hair (Snodgrass) **68**:387-88

"If Blood Were Not as Powerful as It Is" (Gallagher) **63**:126

"If Dogs Run Free" (Dylan) **77**:161

"If Ever You Go to Dublin Town" (Kavanagh) **22**:238

"If Everything Happens That Can't Be Done" (Cummings) **15**:163

If He Hollers Let Him Go (Himes) **2**:195; **4**:229; **7**:159; **58**:251, 254-55, 259, 261-63, 265-66; **108**:228, 231, 236, 253-55, 267, 271, 274

"If Hitler Had Invaded England" (Forester) **35**:173

"If I Could Only Live at the Pitch That Is Near Madness" (Eberhart) **19**:143; **56**:86

If I Die in a Combat Zone, Box Me Up and Ship Me Home (O'Brien) **7**:271; **19**:357; **40**:348; **103**:132, 134, 136, 143, 149-50, 157, 169-76

"If I Fell" (Lennon and McCartney) **35**:268

"If I Forget Thee Jerusalem" (Amichai) **116**:128

"If I Had Children" (Swenson) **106**:342

"If I Had My Way" (Creeley) **15**:153

"if i have made, my lady, intricate" (Cummings) **3**:117; **15**:161

If I Love You, Am I Trapped Forever? (Kerr) **12**:297-98

"If I Only Had the Words" (Joel) **26**:218

"If I only knew" (Sachs)
See "Wenn ich nur wusste"

"If I Should Ever Travel!" (Ferber) **93**:146

"If I Should Open My Mouth" (Bowles) **53**:36-7

"If I Think of You Again It Will Be the Fifty-third Monday of Next Year" (Harjo) **83**:273, 275

"If I Were Sixteen Today" (Moore) **1**:227; **47**:267

"If Into Love The Image Burdens" (Baraka) **5**:45

If It Be Not I (Van Duyn) **116**:418-19, 423, 427

If It Must Be So (Buck)
See *Home Chat*

"If It Were Not for You" (Carruth) **7**:40

"If It Were You" (Page) **18**:379

"If It's Magic" (Wonder) **12**:659

"If Love Were All" (Coward) **29**:138

"If Men Could Menstruate" (Steinem) **63**:382, 384

"If Momma Was Married" (Sondheim) **30**:377, 387

"If Money" (Fearing) **51**:106

If Morning Ever Comes (Tyler) **18**:531; **28**:429-32; **44**:315; **59**:203; **103**:227, 235, 244, 258, 263-65, 269

If Mountains Die: A New Mexico Memoir (Nichols) **38**:342-44

"If Music Could Talk" (Clash) **30**:49

"If, My Darling" (Larkin) **33**:258; **64**:260, 262, 266

"If Never Again" (Gallagher) **18**:170

"If Not for You" (Dylan) **6**:156

If Not Now, When? (Levi)
See *Se non ora, quando?*

"If Not Poetry, Then What?" (Castellanos) **66**:56

"An 'If' of History" (Achebe) **26**:21, 24

If on a Winter's Night a Traveler (Calvino)
See *Se una notte d'inverno un viaggiatore*

"If Once in Silence" (Dunn) **36**:154

"If One Green Bottle. . ." (Thomas) **13**:539; **37**:420; **107**:318, 320, 334-36, 347-48

"If Poetry Were Not a Morality" (Gallagher) **63**:126

"If Someone Could Have Told Me" ("If Anyone Had Told Me") (Aleixandre) **36**:30

If Summer Should Return (Adamov) **25**:20

"If the Cap Fits" (Simmons) **43**:411

If the Earth Falls In (Clark)   12:131

"If the Impressionists Were Dentists" (Allen)   52:37

If the Old Could ... (Lessing)   40:308-09, 315; 94:258

"If the Owl Calls Again" (Haines)   58:215

"If the Pope Doesn't Break with the U.S.A." (Parra)   102:354

"If the River Was Whiskey" (Boyle)   90:46-7, 50, 62

If the River Was Whiskey (Boyle)   90:45-8

If the Stars Are Gods (Benford)   52:59, 61

If the Sun Dies (Fallaci)
   See *Se il sole muore*

"If There's a Reason" (Lightfoot)   26:282

If They Come in the Morning: Voices of Resistance (Davis)   77:108-10

"If They Knew Yvonne" (Dubus)   97:197, 217, 228-29

"If This Goes On" (Heinlein)   55:302, 304

"If We Had Bacon" (Roth)   6:473

"If We Take All Gold" (Bogan)   39:387; 93:90

"If You" (Creeley)   36:118

"If You Are About to Die Now" (Smith)   64:393

If You Believe the Pythagoreans (Grossman)   41:187-88

If You Call This Cry a Song (Carruth)   84:128-31

"If You Could Read My Mind" (Lightfoot)   26:281

If You Could Read My Mind (Lightfoot)   26:278

If You Could See Me Now (Straub)   28:409-10; 107:266, 268, 274-78, 280-81, 302, 304-10

"If You Don't Like Hank Williams" (Kristofferson)   26:269

"If You Forget the Germans" (Stern)   40:406

"If You Know What I Mean" (Diamond)   30:112

"If You Love the Body" (Tillinghast)   29:415

"If You Only Knew..." (Guillen)
   See "Ay negra, si tu supiera"

If You Please (Breton and Soupault)
   See *S'il vous plaît*

"If You Saw a Negro Lady" (Jordan)   114:145

"If You See Her, Say Hello" (Dylan)   77:172-73

"If You Touched My Heart" (Allende)   97:37

"If You Wanna Make Love" ("Come Round Here") (Robinson)   21:350-51

"If You're Dying, Choose a Mausoleum" (Miller)   14:373

"If You're Glad I'll Be Frank" (Stoppard)   4:524; 29:394, 397

The Ignoramus and the Madman (Bernhard)
   See *Der Ignorant und der Wahnsinnige*

"Ignorance" (Middleton)   13:389

Der Ignorant und der Wahnsinnige (*The Fool and the Madman*; *The Ignoramus and the Madman*) (Bernhard)   32:24; 61:12, 20

"Igor Stravinsky: The Selected Phone Calls" (Frazier)   46:164-65

Igor-The Paris Years Chez Pleyel (The Brothers Quay)   95:330-31, 336, 344, 353

Igre (*Games*) (Popa)   19:373

L'iguana (*The Iguana*) (Ortese)   89:191-97, 199

The Iguana (Ortese)
   See *L'iguana*

Ikarian Dreamers (Nakos)   29:323

"Ike" (Dove)   81:137

"Ike and Nina" (Boyle)   36:63

"Ikey" (Brown)   100:82-3

Ikiru (*Doomed*) (Kurosawa)   16:396, 400, 402

"Ikons" (Mahapatra)   33:279

The Ikons and Other Poems (Durrell)   4:145

Ikuisen rauhau aika (*Age of Eternal Peace*) (Haavikko)   34:180-81

Il cardillo addolorato (Ortese)   89:199

IIll castello dei destini incrociati (*The Castle of Crossed Destinies*) (Calvino)   8:126-28, 130-32; 22:89; 33:98, 100; 39:306-07, 310, 313-14, 316-17; 73:48, 51, 58

"Il cinema di poesia" (Pasolini)   106:237

"Il continente sommerso" ("The Submerged Continent") (Ortese)   89:198-99

"Il diaul cu la mari" (Pasolini)   106:230

Il Duetto (The Brothers Quay)   95:329

"Il est des nuits" ("There Are Nights") (Damas)   84:173-74, 177

Il est par là, le soleil (*Is It the Sun, Philibert?*; *It's Over There, the Sun*; *There Is the Sun, Philibert*) (Carrier)   13:141-44; 78:39-40, 44, 46, 49, 51, 57, 61-2, 67-70, 79, 81, 83

Il était une fois dans l'est (Tremblay)   102:361, 369

Il Fanfani rapito (Fo)   109:104

Il mare non bagna Napoli (*The Bay Is Not Naples*; *The Sea Does Not Wash Naples*) (Ortese)   89:191-92

"Il medioevo è già cominciato" (Eco)   28:131

"Il neo-sperimentalismo" (Pasolini)   106:212

"Il n'est pas de midi qui tienne" (Damas)   84:158

"Il nini muart" (Pasolini)   106:227-28, 233, 260-61

"Il n'y a pas d'amour heureux" ("There Is No Such Thing as a Happy Love") (Aragon)   22:38

Il n'y a pas de pays sans grand-père (*No Country without a Grandfather*; *No Country without Grandfathers*) (Carrier)   13:144; 78:61, 63, 65-7, 70, 72, 80

Il porto di Toledo (Ortese)   89:195, 198

"Il sangue, il mare" ("Blood, Sea") (Calvino)   8:127

"Il se pourrait bien que les arbres voyagent" (Carrier)   78:63

"Il se sauve" (Davison)   28:104

Il sesso inutile (*The Useless Sex*) (Fallaci)   11:190; 110:189

"Il signor Lin" ("L'inquilino"; "The Tenant") (Ortese)   89:198

Il sogno di una cosa (Pasolini)   106:231, 254

L'ile de la demoiselle (Hebert)   29:240-41

L'ile introuvable (Theriault)   79:408

The Ilex Tree (Murray)   40:333-34

Ílios o prótos (*Sun the First*) (Elytis)   15:220; 49:106, 115; 100:155, 175, 190

"I'll Be Home for Christmas" (Anderson)   23:31

"I'll Be Waiting for You When the Swimming Pool Is Empty" (Tiptree)   48:385-86

"I'll Be Your Baby Tonight" (Dylan)   12:185

"I'll Bet He's Nice" (Wilson)   12:651-52

"I'll Bring You Back Something Nice" (Levine)   54:295

"I'll Cover You"   99:161, 164, 184

"I'll Do Anything" (Lightfoot)   26:283

"I'll Fly Away" (Bottoms)   53:32

"I'll Follow My Secret Heart" (Coward)   1:65

I'll Get There; It Better Be Worth the Trip (Donovan)   35:139-41, 143

I'll Leave It to You (Coward)   29:139

I'll Love You When You're More Like Me (Kerr)   12:300

I'll Never Be Young Again (du Maurier)   59:284-86

"I'll Never See Johanna" (Sondheim)   30:398

"I'll See You Again" (Coward)   1:65; 29:138

Ill Seen Ill Said (Beckett)
   See *Mal vu mal dit*

"I'll Start Out by Talking" (Moure)   88:220

"I'll Take My Stand" (Tate)   4:535; 11:527

"I'll Take My Stand" (Warren)   8:538

Illa (Cixous)   92:63

The Illearth War (Donaldson)   46:140-43

The Ill-Fated Peregrinations of Fray Servando (Arenas)
   See *El mundo alucinante: Una novela de aventuras*

Illiberal Education: The Politics of Race and Sex On Campus (D'Souza)   70:400, 403-04

Illicit Interlude (Bergman)
   See *Sommarlek*

"Illimitable Kingdom" (Parini)   54:360

"The Illinois Enema Bandit" (Zappa)   17:592

"The Illiterate" (Meredith)   13:374; 55:192

The Ill-Made Knight (White)   30:440-41, 444-46

"Illness as Metaphor" (Muske)   90:314

Illness as Metaphor (Sontag)   10:487; 13:519; 31:411-13, 417; 105:206, 214-15, 227

The Ill-Tempered Clavichord (Perelman)   49:261, 272

"The Illuminated Man" (Ballard)   36:34

Illumination Night (Hoffman)   51:206-08

"Illuminations" (Gluck)   22:176

Illuminatus! (Wilson)   9:576

"The Illumined Graves" (Lamming)   66:220, 225

"Illusion" (Rhys)   51:356

The Illusion (Caute)   29:114-15, 118, 122

The Illusion (Kushner)   81:197, 204

The Illusion of Technique (Barrett)   27:20-1

"The Illusionists" (Friel)   42:166

The Illusionists: A Tale (Fuller)   62:198, 201, 203-05

"Illusions" (Blunden)   56:38, 52

Illusions (Bach)   14:36

"The (Illustrated) Body Politic" (Leyner)   92:293-94

The Illustrated Man (Bradbury)   10:70

"The Illustrated Woman" (Bradbury)   42:33

"Illustration" (Ashbery)   77:58

Illustrations (Butor)   15:114, 119

The Illustrations (Dubie)   36:131-33, 137-39

Illywhacker (Carey)   40:130-35; 55:112-18; 96:26-9, 31-7, 43-7, 50, 53, 55, 58-9, 61, 63, 65, 70, 72, 74, 76, 81

"Ils ont" ("Their Thing") (Damas)   84:167, 174

"Ils sont venus ce soir" ("They Came That Night") (Damas)   84:169, 171, 182, 185

Ilsa (L'Engle)   12:344

"Ilu, the Talking Drum" (Knight)   40:283-84, 287

La ilusion viaja en tranvia (Bunuel)   80:24

Ilya Ehrenburg; Revolutionary, Novelist, Poet, War Correspondent, Propagandist: The Extraordinary Epic of a Russian Survivor (Goldberg)
   See *Ilya Ehrenburg: Writing, Politics, and the Art of Survival*

Ilya Ehrenburg: Writing, Politics, and the Art of Survival (*Ilya Ehrenburg; Revolutionary, Novelist, Poet, War Correspondent,*

Propagandist: The Extraordinary Epic of a Russian Survivor) (Goldberg)　**34**:433-34, 436, 438

Ilyitch Slept Here (Carlisle)　**33**:103

"I'm a Boy" (Townshend)　**17**:529-31, 539

"I'm a Loser" (Lennon and McCartney)　**35**:274

I'm a Lucky Guy (Gilbreth and Carey)　**17**:153-54

I'm a Stranger Here Myself (Nash)　**23**:318, 320

"I'm Carrying" (McCartney)　**35**:285

"I'm Crazy" (Salinger)　**56**:336

"I'm Dreaming of Rocket Richard" (Blaise)　**29**:70

I'm Dying Laughing (Stead)　**80**:341

"Im Ei" ("In the Egg") (Grass)　**32**:198, 201; **88**:179

I'm Everyone I Ever Loved (Mull)　**17**:300

I'm Expecting to Live Quite Soon (West)　**7**:523

"I'm Free" (Townshend)　**17**:526

I'm Getting My Act Together and Taking It on the Road (Cryer)　**21**:81-2

"I'm Going to Cut You into Little Pieces" (Pink Floyd)
　See "One of These Days"

"I'm Herbert" (Anderson)　**23**:31

"I'm Here" (Roethke)　**19**:397

"I'm Here" (Sondheim)　**30**:389

"Im Lande der Rujuks" ("In the Land of the Rujuks") (Boell)　**27**:66; **72**:72

"I'm Losing You" (Lennon)　**35**:272-73

"I'm Not Angry" (Costello)　**21**:67

"I'm Not Down" (Clash)　**30**:46-7

"I'm Not in Love" (Byrne)　**25**:96

"I'm Not like Everybody Else" (Davies)　**21**:95

I'm Not Rappaport (Gardner)　**44**:208-12

I'm Not Stiller (Frisch)
　See *Stiller*

"I'm Over Twenty-Nine" (Musgrave)　**54**:341

I'm Really Dragged but Nothing Gets Me Down (Hentoff)　**26**:182-84

"I'm Set Free" (Reed)　**21**:303, 322

"I'm So Bored with the U.S.A." (Clash)　**30**:43-5, 51-2

"I'm So Cute" (Zappa)　**17**:592

"I'm Stepping Out" (Lennon)　**35**:275-76

"I'm Still Here" (Sondheim)　**30**:387, 396, 400

"I'm Sure" (Ignatow)　**40**:259

I'm Talking about Jerusalem (Wesker)　**3**:517-19

"I'm the Face" (Townshend)　**17**:534, 538

I'm the King of the Castle (Hill)　**113**:281-82, 290, 293, 297, 300, 303, 305, 309-10, 312-14, 318, 321, 325, 330

"I'm Too Big but I Love to Play" (Tiptree)　**48**:385

Im Wechsel der Zeit: Autobiographische Skizzen und Essays (Hochwalder)　**36**:239

Im Westen nichts Neues (*All Quiet on the Western Front*) (Remarque)　**21**:324-27, 329-31, 334-37

"I'm Wide" (Lish)　**45**:230

"Image" (Guillevic)　**33**:193

"The Image" (Hass)　**18**:212-13; **39**:147-48

"The Image" (Singer)　**69**:306

Image and Idea (Rahv)　**24**:351-52, 360

The Image, and Other Stories (Singer)　**69**:305, 308-09

The Image and the Law (Nemerov)　**6**:361; **36**:301, 304, 307

"The Image as Guide to Meaning in the Historical Novel" (Lytle)　**22**:294

"An Image from Beckett" (Mahon)　**27**:286, 288

"An Image from Propertius" (Longley)　**29**:294

Image in the Snow (Deren)　**16**:252

The Image Men (Priestley)　**34**:361

"An Image of Leda" (O'Hara)　**13**:427; **78**:354

"Image of Man as a Gardener after Two World Wars" (Ciardi)　**44**:382

"Image of Man is Australian Poetry" (Buckley)　**57**:129

The Image of Misfortune (Onetti)
　See *La cara de la desgracia*

"An Image of Success" (Gordimer)　**18**:185; **33**:180

The Image of the Beast (Farmer)　**19**:164, 167

"The Image of the Shark Confronts the Image of the Little Match Girl" (Ashbery)　**25**:54, 56

"The Image System of Grotesque Realism" (Oe)　**86**:229, 242

Image—Music—Text (Barthes)　**83**:80-1

"Imagens em Castela" ("Images in Castille") (Cabral de Melo Neto)　**76**:167

"Images" (Aldington)　**49**:2, 9, 12, 17

"Images" (Gluck)　**81**:170

"Images" (Hass)　**99**:129-30, 135, 145, 148

"Images" (Munro)　**19**:344; **95**:287, 292, 298

Images (Altman)　**16**:23-4, 28, 35, 38, 41, 43; **116**:3-7, 21, 23, 67, 69, 73-4

Images (1910-1915) (Aldington)
　See *Images Old and New*

"Images à Crusoe" ("Pictures for Crusoe") (Perse)　**46**:301

"Images and Images" (Simic)　**68**:369

Images de Marque (Leiris)　**61**:362

"Images for Godard" (Rich)　**11**:476; **36**:373

"Images for Piano" (Corn)　**33**:114

"Images in Castille" (Cabral de Melo Neto)
　See "Imagens em Castela"

"Images of Angels" (Page)　**7**:291

Images of Desire (Aldington)　**49**:2-3, 7, 9-10, 17-18

"Images of Elspeth" (Berryman)　**62**:64

Images of Kin (Harper)　**22**:209

Images of Truth (Wescott)　**13**:592

Images of War (Aldington)　**49**:2-3, 5, 7-10, 17

Images Old and New (*Images (1910-1915)*) (Aldington)　**49**:2, 17

"A imaginação do pouco" ("Imagination on a Small Scale") (Cabral de Melo Neto)　**76**:160, 165

Imaginación y violencia en América (Dorfman)　**77**:155

L'imaginaire: Psychologie phénoénologique de l'imagination (Sartre)　**24**:413; **44**:498

"The Imaginary Assassin" (Mukherjee)　**53**:269

"The Imaginary Dead Baby Sea Gull" (Shields)　**97**:431, 433

Imaginary Friends (Lurie)　**4**:306-07; **5**:260

The Imaginary Girlfriend (Irving)　**112**:174-76

"Imaginary Homelands" (Rushdie)　**55**:241

"The Imaginary Iceberg" (Bishop)　**32**:43

"The Imaginary Jew" (Berryman)　**3**:71; **10**:45

An Imaginary Life (Malouf)　**28**:266, 268; **86**:196, 203, 208-09, 211

Imaginary Magnitude (Lem)　**40**:292, 298-99

Imaginary Paintings, and Other Poems (Baxter)　**78**:24-25, 28

Imaginary Timber (Galvin)　**38**:197-98

"The Imagination" (Richards)　**24**:396-97

Imagination Dead Imagine (Beckett)
　See *Imagination morte imaginez*

Imagination morte imaginez (*Imagination Dead Imagine*) (Beckett)　**16**:76-82, 85, 95-8, 102, 105, 107, 122, 123

"Imagination on a Small Scale" (Cabral de Melo Neto)
　See "A imaginação do pouco"

Imaginations (Williams)　**2**:468-69; **5**:510

Imaginative Qualities of Actual Things (Sorrentino)　**3**:461-62; **7**:449-52; **14**:499; **22**:391-93; **40**:385-86

"Imagine" (Lennon)　**35**:263-65, 267, 270, 272-73, 275

Imagine (Lennon)　**12**:366, 381; **35**:263-66, 269-70, 273

"Imagine a Man" (Townshend)　**17**:535-37

Imagine a Woman, and Other Tales (Selzer)　**74**:285, 287

Imagine Kissing Pete (O'Hara)　**42**:319, 326-27

"Imagined Scenes" (Beattie)　**8**:56

Imaging American Women: Ideas and Ideals in Cultural History (Banta)　**65**:327

"Imagining a Unicorn" (Spacks)　**14**:511

Imagining a Unicorn (Spacks)　**14**:511

"Imagining How It Would Be to Be Dead" (Eberhart)　**56**:87

"Imagining Jews" (Roth)　**9**:459

"Imagining the Reservation" (Alexie)　**96**:4, 7

Imaginings of Sand (Brink)　**106**:134-38

Imago Bird (Mosley)　**43**:318-20, 322; **70**:202, 205

Iman (*Pro patria*) (Sender)　**8**:479-80

"Imelda" (Colwin)　**84**:146, 149, 151

"Imefda" (Selzer)　**74**:274-76

Imerológhio enós athéatou Aprilíou (Elytis)　**100**:175

Imitation of Christ (Warhol)　**20**:420

"The Imitation of the Rose" (Lispector)　**43**:268-70

Imitations (Lowell)　**1**:180, 182; **2**:246, 249; **3**:300; **4**:297-28, 301; **5**:257; **8**:354

L'immaculée conception (Breton)　**54**:32

Immanuel Kant (Bernhard)　**32**:25; **61**:13, 26-7

"Immanuel Kant and the Hopi" (Stern)　**40**:408

Immanuel Kant in England, 1793-1838 (Wellek)　**28**:446, 452

The Immaterial Murder Case (Symons)　**14**:523

"The Immigrant" (Rothenberg)　**57**:374

The Immigrant Experience: The Long, Long Journey (Silver)　**20**:341, 345

The Immigrant Jews of New York, 1881 to the Present (Howe)
　See *World of Our Fathers: The Journey of the Eastern European Jews to America and the Life They Found and Made*

"Immigrant Song" (Page and Plant)　**12**:474-75

"Immigrant Voyage" (Murray)　**40**:338, 340

The Immigrants (Fast)　**23**:159-60

"Immigration Blues" (Santos)　**22**:365

The Immobile Wind (Winters)　**32**:469

"An Immodest Proposal" (Brodsky)　**100**:63, 72

"Immolatus" (Komunyakaa)　**94**:241

"Immoral Allure" (Leyner)　**92**:293

"The Immoral Proposition" (Creeley)　**78**:124, 126

"The Immortal" (Borges)
　See "El inmortal"

"An Immortal" (Murray)　**40**:344

"The Immortal" (Simic)　**68**:376

"Immortal" (Van Doren)　**10**:496

"Immortal Autumn" (MacLeish)　**68**:273-74,

285, 288
"Immortal Element" (Jacobsen) 48:190
"Immortal Longings" (Pinsky) 94:
The Immortal One (Robbe-Grillet)
  See *L'immortelle*
"The Immortal Story" (Dinesen) 10:145;
  95:53-4
The Immortal Story (Welles) 20:442, 445-47;
  80:391-93, 395-97
L'immortalité (*Immortality*) (Kundera) 68:250-
  66; 115:347-48, 357, 359
Immortality (Kundera)
  See *L'immortalité*
"Immortality over the Dakotas" (Warren)
  39:270
"The Immortals" (Amis) 62:7, 10
"The Immortals" (Bioy Casares) 88:78
"The Immortals" (Tate) 2:432
L'immortelle (*The Immortal One*) (Robbe-
  Grillet) 1:287; 2:376; 6:466
"Immortelles" (Merwin) 88:210, 212
The Immovable Pilgrims (Lopez y Fuentes)
  See *Los peregrinos inmóviles*
"Immram" (Muldoon) 32:320-21; 72:267-68,
  270, 273-74, 278, 280
"Imogene Knode" (Broumas) 73:3-4
"The Impalpabilities" (Tomlinson) 6:534;
  13:549
"Impasse" (Stegner) 49:351
Impatience (Trifonov)
  See *Neterpenie*
"Impeccable Conception" (Angelou) 35:32
"An Imperfect Copy of Antichrist" (Ayrton)
  7:18
"Imperfect Critics" (Eliot) 24:169, 180
"The Imperfect Eye" (L'Heureux) 52:272
"L'imperfection est la cime" (Bonnefoy)
  58:49, 59
"Imperial Adam" (Hope) 51:210-12, 214, 216,
  219-20
Imperial Caesar (Warner) 45:436
Imperial City (Rice) 7:359, 363
Imperial Earth (Clarke) 13:150-51, 153, 155;
  18:106-07
The Imperial German Dinner Service (Hughes)
  48:184-85
The Imperial Presidency (Schlesinger) 84:364-
  65, 367-68, 376, 381, 386
"The Imperial Theme" (Simmons) 43:414
Imperial Woman (Buck) 7:32
"Imperialism" (Graham) 48:155
"Impersonal Narration" (Booth) 24:86
Implements in Their Places (Graham) 29:196-
  98
"The Implements of Augury" (Simic) 49:343
"Implosions" (Rich) 6:457-58
"The Importance of Artists' Biographies"
  (Goldbarth) 38:205-06
"The Importance of Being Earnest" (Ewart)
  46:153
"The Importance of Elsewhere" (Larkin)
  13:339; 64:262
"The Importance of Green" (Galvin) 38:199
"The Importance of Mozart's Operas" (Brophy)
  105:13
"The Important Thing" (Williams) 45:447
Important to Me (Johnson) 7:184; 27:222
"Impossible" (Sondheim) 30:378
Impossible Buildings (Sherwin) 7:414
"Impossible Iambics" (Sandburg) 35:356
"The Impossible Indispensibility of the Ars
  Poetica" (Carruth) 84:136
The Impossible Loves (Arrabal) 9:39

Impossible Object (Mosley) 43:314-16, 318-
  19, 321-22
The Impossible Proof (Nossack)
  See *Un moegliche Bewiesaufrahme*
The Impossible Railway (Berton) 104:39
"An Impossible Song" (Townshend) 42:378,
  380
Impossible Vacation (Gray) 112:114-17, 119,
  126-27, 129-130
The Imposter (Brady) 86:130, 133-34
"El impostor inverosímil Tom Castro" ("Tom
  Castro,   the   Implausible
  Imposter")(Borges) 48:36
"Impotence" (Williams) 42:443
"Imprecated upon a Postal Clerk" (Nemerov)
  36:309
"Impresario on the Lam" (Perelman) 23:336
"Impressions II" (Cummings) 68:51
"The Imprisonment of Obatala" (Clark)
  38:126, 128
L'improbable (Bonnefoy) 58:57
*L'impromptu de l'alma; ou, Le cameleon du
  berger* (*Improvisation; or, The Shepherd's
  Chameleon*) (Ionesco) 4:251; 6:248-49;
  15:298
L'impromptu du Palais-Royal (Cocteau)
  8:148-50; 43:112
"Impromptu for Francis Webb" (Buckley)
  57:130
Impromptu in Moribundia (Hamilton) 51:186,
  195
The Impromptu of Outremont (Tremblay)
  29:424
"The Improved Binoculars" (Layton) 15:322
"Improvisation" (Gunn) 81:176, 187
"Improvisation" (L'Heureux) 52:272
"An Improvisation for the Stately Dwelling"
  (Ammons) 108:56
Improvisation; or, The Shepherd's Chameleon
  (Ionesco)
  See *L'impromptu de l'alma; ou, Le cameleon
    du berger*
"Improvisations on Themes from Guillevic"
  (Justice) 102:263
"The Improvisors" (Morgan) 2:294
"Imprudent Lover" (Coles) 46:113
"The Impstone" (Musgrave) 13:401
The Impstone (Musgrave) 13:401; 54:341
Les impudents (Duras) 6:149; 11:165; 40:179;
  68:92, 99; 100:145-47, 149
"Impuissance" (Livesay) 79:340
"Impulse" (Aiken) 10:1-2
"The Impulse" (Smith) 64:391
The Impuritans (Clarke) 6:111
"In 1929" (Spender) 91:266
"In 1940" (Akhmatova) 25:29
"In a Bad Light" (Boland) 113:100, 115, 126
"In a Boat" (Ashbery) 15:34
"In a Buggy at Dusk" (Milosz) 82:306
"In a Café" (Rhys) 19:390-91
In a Café (Lavin) 18:307
"In a Caledonian Forest" (MacDiarmid) 4:309;
  11:333
"In a Churchyard" (Wilbur) 53:402
"In a Cold Season" (Hamburger) 14:234
"In a Country Church" (Thomas) 13:543;
  48:381
"In a Country Churchyard" (Blunden) 56:39
In a Dark Garden (Slaughter) 29:373-75
"In a Dark Square" (Merwin) 2:277
"In a Dark Time" (Roethke) 3:433-34; 8:456,
  460; 11:485; 46:361, 364; 101:267, 289,
  309

In a Dark Wood (Warner) 59:216
"In a Darkness" (Bowers) 9:122
"In a Deserted Rest Home" (Akhmadulina)
  See "V opustevshem dome otdykha"
In a Dusty Light (Haines) 58:217, 219, 221
In a Farther Country (Goyen) 5:148-49;
  14:210, 214; 40:218
"In a Father's Place" (Tilghman) 65:105, 108,
  111-12
In a Father's Place (Tilghman) 65:105-06,
  108-09, 111-12
"In a Flemish Garden" ("Tlactocatzine del jardin
  de Flandes"; "Tlactocatzine in the Garden
  of Flanders"; "Tlactocatzine, of the Flem-
  ish Garden") (Fuentes) 22:171
In a Free State (Naipaul) 4:373-75; 7:253-54;
  9:391-92; 13:402, 404-05, 407; 18:359;
  37:320, 329; 105:142-43, 146, 157-58,
  161, 164, 170, 176, 181
"In a Garden" (Clarke) 61:73
"In a Great Man's House" (Jhabvala) 8:312-
  13
"In a Green Night" (Walcott) 42:421; 76:273,
  277-80, 282
In a Green Night: Poems, 1948-1960 (Walcott)
  14:549, 551; 25:448-50; 42:421; 67:344
"In a Hand or a Face" (Townshend) 17:535
In a Harbour Green (Kiely) 23:259, 261-62;
  43:245
"In a Hard Intellectual Light" (Eberhart) 56:75,
  80
"In a Jon-Boat during a Florida Dawn" (Bot-
  toms) 53:32-3
"In a Manner That Must Shame God Himself"
  (Vonnegut) 5:469
In a Marine Light (Carver)
  See *Ultramarine*
"In a Mexican City" (Hughes) 108:323
In a Mirror (Stolz) 12:547-49
In a Moscow Street (Ehrenburg)
  See *In Protochny Lane*
In a Narrow Grave (McMurtry) 7:214-15;
  27:324, 328; 44:260-62
"In a Notebook" (Fenton) 32:165-67, 169
"In a Polish Home for the Aged" (Hirsch)
  50:197
In a Province (van der Post) 5:463
"In a Railway Compartment" (Fuller) 62:200-
  02
"In a Right Angle: A Cycle of Quatrains"
  (Amichai) 57:44
"In a Room and a Half" (Brodsky) 50:132-33,
  137
In a Shallow Grave (Purdy) 10:424-25; 52:348
"In a Simple Way I Love You" (Cryer) 21:81
"In a Small Moment" (Simon) 26:411-12
"In a Space" (Davies) 21:105
"In a Station of the Metro" (Pound) 18:428;
  48:283; 50:436
"In a Strange Country" (Ellison) 114:126
In a Strange Land (Middleton) 38:332-33
In a Summer Season (Taylor) 29:408, 411-12
In a Time of Violence (Boland) 113:87, 90, 92-
  5, 99, 101, 108, 110, 112, 115, 119-21,
  125-27
"In a Troubled Key" (Hughes) 15:291
"In a U-Haul North of Damascus" (Bottoms)
  53:32
In a U-Haul North of Damascus (Bottoms)
  53:31-3
In a Vast Dominion (Aleixandre)
  See *En un vasto dominio*
"In a Warm Bath" (Rakosi) 47:344

In a Year of Thirteen Moons (Fassbinder) 20:119

In a Yellow Wood (Vidal) 4:558; 22:431-33

In Abraham's Bosom (Green) 25:192-93, 195-96, 198-99

In Adversity Be Ye Steadfast (Boyle) 19:68

In Africa Even the Flies Are Happy (Breytenbach) 23:84

In Agony (Krleza)
  See *U agoniji*

"In Alien Flesh" (Benford) 52:75-6

In Alien Flesh (Benford) 52:75-6

In America's Shoes (Codrescu) 46:104-05

"In Amicitia" (Ransom) 5:365

In and Out (Hine) 15:282

"In Another Country" (Hemingway) 3:241; 10:269; 30:182, 184-85, 196, 200; 61:194, 203; 80:136

"In Another Country" (Laughlin) 49:221-23

In Another Country: Poems, 1935-1975 (Laughlin) 49:220-22

In Any Case (Stern) 4:523; 39:236

"In April, In Princeton" (Kumin) 13:327

"In Apulia" (Bachmann) 69:61

"In Arden" (Tomlinson) 13:549-50; 45:394

"In Argos" (Davis) 49:93

"In at the Birth" (Trevor) 71:326

"In Atrim" (Paulin) 37:352

"In August" (Soto) 80:289

In Aunt Mahaly's Cabin (Green) 25:193

"In Balthazar's Village" (Middleton) 13:388

In Battle for Peace (Du Bois) 96:148

"In Bed" (Koch) 44:248

"In Bed One Night" (Coover) 32:127

In Bed One Night and Other Brief Encounters (Coover) 32:126-27

"In between the Sheets" (McEwan) 66:281

In between the Sheets (McEwan) 13:371; 66:275, 279-80, 282, 294

"In Blackwater Woods" (Oliver) 34:249; 98:273

In Bluebeard's Castle: Some Notes toward the Redefinition of Culture (Steiner) 24:431-33

In Broken Country (Wagoner) 15:559-60

"In Broken Images" (Graves) 45:174

In Camera (Sartre) 44:495

In Celebration (Anderson) 20:17

In Celebration (Storey) 2:424-25; 4:529-30; 5:414-15

"In Celebration of My Uterus" (Sexton) 53:316

"In Challenge, Not Defence" (MacLeish) 68:288

In Character (Mortimer) 43:304-05

"In Childhood" (Blunden) 56:31

"In Church" (Thomas) 48:383

"In City Hall Square" (Farrell) 66:130

"In Clown Clothes" (Phillips) 28:363

In Cold Blood: A True Account of a Multiple Murder and Its Consequences (Capote) 3:99-100; 8:132-33; 13:133, 135-39; 19:82-5, 87; 34:320, 322-25, 327; 38:78, 80, 82-5, 87; 58:85-136

In Cold Hell, in Thicket (Olson) 5:328; 29:334

"In Cold Storm Light" (Silko) 74:347

In Constant Flight (Tallent) 45:386-90

"In Corner B" (Mphahlele) 25:340, 342

In Corner B (Mphahlele) 25:339, 341

In Country (Mason) 43:286-90; 82:236-39, 244, 251, 254, 256-58, 260

In Cuba (Cardenal) 31:71-2

In Custody (Desai) 37:71-2; 97:

"In Cytherea" (Hoffman) 6:243

"In Danger from the Outer World" (Bly) 10:57

In Darkest America (Oates) 108:376

"In Darkness" (Durban) 39:44, 47

In Darkness and Confusion (Petry) 18:403

"In Deep Waters" (Arghezi)
  See "Apa mare"

In Defence of a Friend (Leonov) 92:277

In Defence of Fantasy: A Study of the Genre in English and American Literature since 1945 (Swinfen) 34:576-77

"In Defense of a Passionate and Incorruptible Heart" (Lytle) 22:294

"In Defense of Ellis Hollow Creek" (Crase) 58:164

In Defense of Ignorance (Shapiro) 4:484, 487; 53:328, 330

"In Defense of Metaphysics" (Tomlinson) 45:400

"In Defense of Milton" (Leavis) 24:296

"In Defense of Purple Prose" (West) 96:393

In Defense of Reason (Winters) 4:589-90; 8:552; 32:459-60, 470

In Defense of Sensuality (Powys) 46:319

In Defense of the Earth (Rexroth) 1:283; 6:450; 22:346; 49:277, 283; 112:370

"In Defense of the Word" (Galeano) 72:130

In den Wohnungen des Todes (*In the Dwellings of Death; In the Habitation of Death; In the Houses of Death*) (Sachs) 14:476; 98:321-22, 324-25, 327-28, 332, 344-45, 348, 352-54, 356, 365

"In der Finsternis" (Boell) 72:69

"In Distrust of Merits" (Moore) 8:400; 10:352

"In Dream: The Privacy of Sequence" (Young Bear) 94:362, 366

"In Dreams Begin Responsibilities" (Schwartz) 4:479; 10:462-63, 466; 45:353-55, 359; 87:334-36, 339-43, 346-47

In Dreams Begin Responsibilities, and Other Stories (Schwartz) 45:355; 87:333

In Dubious Battle (Steinbeck) 1:325; 5:405; 9:512, 514-18, 520; 13:529-34; 21:366, 371, 373, 381-83, 389-91; 34:405, 412, 414; 45:370, 374, 376; 59:317, 333, 335-37, 344, 347, 354; 75:341, 343-44, 348-49, 352-55, 357, 360

"In Due Form" (Riding) 7:374

"In Due Season" (Auden) 43:15

"In Durance" (Pound) 7:337; 13:456; 48:288

"In Ego with Us All" (Ciardi) 40:155-56

In England's Green And (Williams) 13:600-01

"In Eporphyrial Harness" (Avison) 97:77, 82

"In Evening Air" (Roethke) 101:309

"In Evening Air" (Roethke) 3:433

"In Every World" (Lane) 25:288

In Evil Hour (Garcia Marquez)
  See *La mala hora*

"In Exchange for Haiku" (Niedecker) 10:360

"In Exile" (Boland) 113:93

In Fact (Ciardi) 10:105; 40:161

In Famine's Shadow (Jones) 52:245

In Favor of the Sensitive Man (Nin) 14:385-86

"In Fear of Harvests" (Wright) 3:540; 10:545

"In Festubert" (Blunden) 56:41

In Fires of No Return (Baxter) 14:62

"In Florida" (Swenson) 61:402, 404

"In Fog, Taeit, Outside Cherbourg" (Hollander) 5:186

"In Football Season" (Updike) 23:473

In Form: Digressions on the Act of Fiction (Sukenick) 48:368-69

"In France" (Dabrowska)
  See "We Francji"

"In Gallarus Oratory" (Heaney) 5:171; 7:148; 91:121

"In Genesis" (Lowell) 11:329

"In Green Solariums" (Livesay) 79:342, 352

"In Greenwich There Are Many Gravelled Walks" (Calisher) 8:125; 38:67

"In Guinea" (Cabral de Melo Neto)
  See "Na Guiné"

"In Hardwood Groves" (Frost) 26:118

"In Hefnerland" (Amis) 62:5

In Her Day (Brown) 18:73, 75; 79:153, 155-56, 158-59, 169

"In Her Own Image" (Boland) 40:99; 67:44; 113:58-60, 62

In Her Own Image (Boland) 40:97-8, 100; 67:41, 43-6; 113:57-8, 60, 63, 74, 80-1, 87-8, 94, 96-7, 108-09, 117, 122-23

"In High Waters" (Graham) 48:147

In His Country (Willard) 37:462

In His Own Country (Callaghan) 41:89

"In His Own Image" (Boland) 40:100; 67:44; 113:58-60, 123

In His Own Write (Lennon) 12:354-55; 35:267

"In His Sixty-Fifth Year" (Fuller) 28:157

"In Honour of Chris. Brennan" (McAuley) 45:246

"In Illo Tempore" (Heaney) 74:169

"In India" (Ezekiel) 61:102-03, 105

"In Isfahan" (Trevor) 7:478; 71:340; 116:333, 374

"In It" (Johnston) 51:239, 244, 249, 251

In Iwa's Country (Le Clezio) 31:249

"In Jack-O'-Lantern's Weather" (Williams) 45:443

"In January" (Clarke) 61:83

In Joy Still Felt: The Autobiography of Isaac Asimov, 1954-1978 (Asimov) 19:29; 26:52

"In Just Spring" (Cummings) 12:159

"In Khandesh" (Rao) 56:291-92

"In Kildare Street" (Clarke) 9:168

"In Lieu of the Lyre" (Moore) 13:396

"In Lilliput" (O'Faolain) 70:314

"In Limbo" (Wilbur) 9:570; 53:412; 110:357

"In Llandough Hospital" (Abse) 29:18

In London (Creeley) 36:118; 78:140, 159

"In Love" (Prince) 35:323

In Love and Anger (Acorn) 15:10

In Love and Trouble: Stories of Black Women (Walker) 5:476-77; 6:553-54; 27:449; 46:428; 103:356-57, 363, 366, 372, 396, 398-99, 402, 406-13, 422

"In Love Made Visible" (Swenson) 106:337, 347-48

"In Love with Ariadne" (Trevor) 71:341, 348-49; 116:363-64

"In Love's Place" (Padilla) 38:351

"In Loving Memory of the Late Author of Dream Songs" (Meredith) 55:193

"In Lower Town" (Levine) 54:297, 300-01

"In Luss Churchyard" (Smith) 64:388, 397

In Mad Love and War (*Mad Love*) (Harjo) 83:272, 274-77, 280-86

"In March" (Stevenson) 33:380

În marea trecere (*The Great Passage; In the Great Passage; In the Great Passing*) 75:62, 67, 69-70, 77

"In May, 1916: Near Richebourg St. Vaast" (Blunden) 56:44

"In Me Two Worlds" (Day Lewis) 10:128
"In Memoriam" (Longley) 29:292
"In Memoriam" (Schnackenberg) 40:379
"In Memoriam" (Senghor) 54:407
In Memoriam (Reznikoff) 9:450
"In Memoriam Francis Ledwidge" (Heaney) 25:247
In Memoriam James Joyce (MacDiarmid) 4:309, 312; 11:333, 337-38; 19:289-90; 63:242, 250, 255
"In Memoriam Mae Noblitt" (Ammons) 108:56
"In Memoriam Miss B." (Stevenson) 33:379
"In Memoriam: Robert Fitzgerald" (Heaney) 74:174
"In Memoriam Stratton Christensen" (Meredith) 13:374
In Memoriam to Identity (Acker) 111:34-6
"In Memoriam: Wallace Stevens" (Duncan) 41:129
"In Memory: After a Friend's Sudden Death" (Levertov) 66:250
"In Memory of an Aristocrat" (Williams) 45:453
"In Memory of Anton Webern" (Mueller) 51:279
"In Memory of Arthur Winslow" (Lowell) 1:182; 4:297; 8:358
"In Memory of Boris Pasternak" (Levertov) 15:336
In Memory of David Archer (Barker) 8:45; 48:21, 24
"In Memory of Elena" (Forche)
  See "The Memory of Elena"
"In Memory of Francis Webb" (Shapcott) 38:402
"In Memory of H. F." (Klappert) 57:256-57, 259-60
"In Memory of Leopardi" (Wright) 3:543
"In Memory of My Cat Domino" (Fuller) 28:151
"In Memory of My Country" (Crase) 58:163
"In Memory of My Feelings" (O'Hara) 78:339, 350-51, 355-60, 365-66
In Memory of My Feelings (O'Hara) 2:323; 13:427, 430
"In Memory of Robert Macbryde" (Barker) 48:19
"In Memory of Segun Awolowo" (Soyinka) 44:277
"In Memory of Sigmund Freud" (Auden) 14:31; 43:27
"In Memory of the Horse David, Who Ate One of My Poems" (Wright) 3:543; 5:520
"In Memory of the Master Poet Robert Browning" (Nemerov) 36:309
"In Memory of W. B. Yeats" (Auden) 43:16, 27-8
"In Memory of W. H. Auden" (Matthews) 40:320-21
"In Memory of W. H. Auden" (Stern) 100:328
In Memory Yet Green (Asimov) 19:27-9; 26:51-2; 76:312; 92:5
"In Midas' Country" (Plath) 111:200
"In Milan" (Milosz) 56:248
"In Mind" (Levertov) 66:238
"In Modern Dress" (Raine) 103:186
"In Montgomery" (Brooks) 49:28
"In My Day We Used to Call It Pussy-Whipped" (Bukowski) 82:14
"In My Dream I Always Hear a Step on the Stairs" (Moravia) 46:286-87
In My Father's Court (Singer)

  See *Mayn Tatn's bes-din shtub*
In My Father's House (Gaines) 11:217-18; 86:173
"In My Father's House There Are a Few Mansions, More Hovels, and Probably Even More Ranch Houses" (Ciardi) 40:161
"In My Life" (Dubus) 97:195, 204-05, 208
"In My Mind" (MacCaig) 36:284
"In My Room" (Wilson) 12:644, 649, 651
"In My Time" (Blunden) 56:44
"In My Time, In My Place" (Amichai) 57:36
"In My Time of Dying" (Page and Plant) 12:477, 479
"In Mysie's Bed" (MacDiarmid) 4:310; 11:334
"In Nature" (Haines) 58:216
"In Nature There Is Neither Right Nor Left Nor Wrong" (Jarrell) 9:298
In New England Winter (Bullins) 5:83
"In Nine Sleep Valley" (Merrill) 34:233
In Nueva York (Mohr) 12:447
"In Ohnmacht gefallen" ("Powerless, with a Guitar") (Grass) 32:199
In, on, or about the Premises: Being a Small Book of Poems (Blackburn) 43:62
In Orbit (Morris) 1:233; 3:343; 7:246; 37:310-13
In Other Words (Katz)
  See *Creamy and Delicious: Eat My Words*
In Other Words (Swenson) 61:402-04; 106:323, 333, 336, 340, 342-43, 346
In Our Lifetime (Gaye) 26:134
In Our Terribleness (Some Elements and Meaning in Black Style) (Baraka) 2:35; 5:48; 33:56
In Our Time (Hemingway) 1:142; 3:241-43; 6:226, 233-34; 8:285, 288-89, 292; 10:263; 13:273; 19:210; 30:178, 180-82, 184-86, 188-92, 195, 198-201; 34:478; 39:398, 401; 41:197; 61:191-92, 214; 80:148, 150
In Our Time (Montale)
  See *Nel nostro tempo*
"In Pain" (Simon) 26:413
In Parenthesis (Jones) 2:216-19; 4:259-62; 7:186-89, 191; 13:307-12; 42:238-43, 246-48
"In parte ove non e che" (Chappell) 40:145
In Patagonia (Chatwin) 28:70-5; 57:141-43, 147-48, 150; 59:274-78
In Peace as in War (Cabrera Infante)
  See *Así en la paz como en la guerra*
In Place (Hollander) 14:265
In Plain Russian (Voinovich) 49:375-77
"In Plaster" (Plath) 17:353; 51:346; 111:166, 180-81, 211
"In Plaster, with a Bronze Wash" (Meredith)
  See "Thoughts on One's Head"
"In Praise of Ancestors" (Kunene) 85:176-77
"In Praise of Cities" (Gunn) 32:208
"In Praise of Darkness" (Borges)
  See *Elogio de la sombra*
In Praise of Darkness
  See *Elogio de la sombra*
In Praise of Darkness (Borges)
  See *Elogio de la sombra*
"In Praise of Diversity" (McGinley) 14:367
"In Praise of Feeling Bad about Yourself" (Szymborska) 99:205
"In Praise of Grief" (Bly) 15:68
"In Praise of Limestone" (Auden) 3:26; 6:16, 20, 24; 9:57; 14:29
In Praise of Love (Rattigan) 7:355
"In Praise of Marriages" (Wright) 53:428

"In Praise of Ms Navratilova" (Brophy) 105:21
In Praise of Older Women: The Amorous Recollections of András Vajda (Vizinczey) 40:432-34, 436-39
"In Praise of Shadows" (Tanizaki) 14:526; 28:416, 420
In Praise of Sleep
  See *Lauda somnului*
In Praise of the Dangerous Life (Cendrars) 106:191
"In Praise of the Earth" (Kunene) 85:165
In Praise of the Stepmother (Vargas Llosa)
  See "Elogio de la madrastra"
"In Praise of the Sword" (Wittlin) 25:469
"In Praise of Unwashed Feet" (Willard) 7:539
"In Praise of Vespasian" (Chester) 49:54-6
"In Praise of Women's Bodies" (Steinem) 63:383
"In Preparation" (Macdonald) 13:356
"In Prison" (Bishop) 32:40, 44
In Protochny Lane (*In a Moscow Street*; *Protochny Lane*) (Ehrenburg) 18:131; 62:175, 178-79
In Public, In Private (Denby) 48:81, 83
"In Pursuit of the Angel" (Lieberman) 36:261
In Pursuit of the English (Lessing) 22:277-78
"In Quebec City" (Levine) 54:296
In quel preciso momento (Buzzati) 36:88, 96
In Radical Pursuit: Critical Essays and Lectures (Snodgrass) 10:477-78
"In Railroad Yards" (Lane) 25:288
In Re: Sherlock Holmes (Derleth) 31:137
"In Re Solomon Warshawer" (Klein) 19:261
"In Response to a Question" (Stafford) 29:380
"In Retrospect" (Ezekiel) 61:93, 103
"In Ruth's Country" (Bass) 79:5
"In Salem" (Clifton) 19:110
"In Santa Maria del Popolo" (Gunn) 18:203; 81:177
In Search (Levin) 7:204-06
In Search of a Character (Greene) 9:250
In Search of a Genre (Aksyonov) 101:22
"In Search of a Language" (Boland) 113:125
"In Search of a Majority" (Baldwin) 13:53
In Search of Ancient Gods (von Daniken) 30:425-26
In Search of Bisco (Caldwell) 50:300
In Search of Columbus (Davies) 70:339
In Search of Columbus: The Sources of the First Voyage (Henige) 70:351, 353, 355
In Search of J. D. Salinger (Hamilton) 55:334-37, 341
In Search of Love and Beauty (Jhabvala) 29:261-63; 94:171-72, 174, 183, 185-87, 194-96, 203-5
In Search of Melancholy Baby (*V poiskakh grustnogo bebi: Kniga ob Amerike*) (Aksyonov) 101:36-7, 39, 41-2, 52
"In Search of Our Mother's Gardens" (Walker) 103:357
In Search of Our Mother's Gardens: Womanist Prose (*Mother's Garden*) (Walker) 46:428; 58:408-09, 415; 103:364, 367-70, 396-97, 400, 402, 414, 418
In Search of Owen Roblin (Purdy) 14:432
In Search of Theatre (Bentley) 24:47, 50
"In Season" (Davison) 28:100
In Sepia (Anderson) 9:31
In Sicily (Vittorini)
  See *Conversazione in Sicilia*
"In Sickness and Health" (Humphrey) 45:193
"In Sickness and in Health" (Auden) 2:23

"In Sickness and in Health" (Gellhorn) **14**:195; **60**:184-85
"In Small Townlands" (Heaney) **14**:243
"In Snow, a Possible Life" (Smith) **42**:348
"In So Many Words" (Abish) **22**:19
"In So Sustained a Remarkable Amount of Motion" (Everson) **27**:134
"In Society" (Ginsberg) **36**:182
In soffitta (Buzzati) **36**:84
"In Some Doubt but Willingly" (Ciardi) **44**:382
In sonno e in veglia (Ortese) **89**:194-95, 197
"In Spring" (Squires) **51**:383
In Such a Night (Deutsch) **18**:118
In Suspect Terrain (McPhee) **36**:299
"In Sydney by the Bridge" (Cassity) **42**:98
"In Sylvia Plath Country" (Jong) **6**:267
"In Sympathy with Another Motherless Child (One View of the Profession of Writing" (Giovanni) **117**:189
"In Terror of Hospital Bills" (Wright) **5**:520
In That Dawn (Paustovsky)
See *The Beginning of an Unknown Century*
"In That Month of May" (Akhmadulina)
See "V tot mesiats Mai"
In That Time (Lagerkvist)
See *I den tiden*
In the Absence of Angels (Calisher) **38**:67-8
"In the Absence of Horses" (Hearne) **56**:127
In the Absence of Horses (Hearne) **56**:126-27
"In the Alien Corn" (McNickle) **89**:184
"In the Alley" (Elkin) **51**:98
In the American Grain (*Ars Poetica: In the American Grain*) (Williams) **2**:467-68; **5**:508; **13**:602, 605; **22**:466; **42**:449, 451-53, 455; **67**:416, 427
"In the Aran Islands" (Mahon) **27**:287
"In the Attic" (Justice) **19**:233-34; **102**:256
"In the Attic" (Motion) **47**:286
"In the Back of My Car" (Zappa)
See "Cheap Thrills"
"In the Baggage Room at Greyhound" (Ginsberg) **36**:188
"In the Bahamas" (Hass) **99**:141
In the Bar of a Tokyo Hotel (Williams) **2**:465; **8**:549; **11**:571; **19**:472; **45**:449-52
"In the Basement" (Dybek) **114**:66
"In the Beach House" (Sexton) **10**:468
"In the Beauty of the Lillies" (Auchincloss) **9**:54
"In the Beech" (Heaney) **74**:169
"In the Beginning" (Lamming) **66**:227
"In the Beginning" (Sanchez) **116**:299, 300
In the Beginning (Potok) **7**:321-22; **26**:372-73; **112**:284
In the Beginning, Love: Dialogues on the Bible (Van Doren) **6**:541
"In the Beginning of the War" (Smith) **25**:421
In the Beginning Was Love: Psychoanalysis and Faith (Kristeva)
See *Au commencement était l'amour: Psychanalyse et foi*
"In the Beginning Was the Word: Logos or Mythos" (Fiedler) **4**:163; **13**:211
"In the Bleak Mid-Winter" (Thomas) **37**:419, 422; **107**:327
"In the Bodies of Words" (Swenson) **61**:402
In the Boom Boom Room (Rabe) **4**:425-27; **8**:450
"In the Bosom of the Country" (O'Faolain) **14**:405
"In the Briar Patch" (Garrett) **51**:144, 152
In the Briar Patch (Garrett) **51**:143-45
In the Burning Darkness (Buero Vallejo)

See *En la ardiente oscuridad*
"In the Café" (Kadare)
See "Në kafe"
In the Cage (Abse) **29**:21
In the Castle of My Skin (Lamming) **2**:235; **4**:280; **66**:217, 219-21, 223-24, 227-30
"In the Cell" (Olds) **85**:292, 298
"In the Cemetery Where Al Jolson Is Buried" (Hempel) **39**:68-70
"In the Children's Wing" (Johnson) **58**:291, 293
"In the City" (Weller) **26**:442-43, 448
In the City (Weller) **26**:442-43, 445
In the City of Fear (Just) **27**:229-30
"In the City of Red Dust" (Okri) **87**:319, 321
"In the Clear" (Transtroemer) **65**:223
"In the Clearing" (Butler) **81**:124
In the Clearing (Frost) **4**:176; **9**:220, 223; **13**:230
In the Cold Country (Howes) **15**:288-89
"In the Cold Kingdom" (Van Duyn) **116**:401
"In the Compartment" (Voinovich) **10**:505
"In the Corridor" (Fuller) **62**:196-97
In the Country of Last Things (Auster) **47**:16
"In the Country of Modern Art" (Asturias) **8**:25
In the Country of Ourselves (Hentoff) **26**:183-84
"In the Country of the Black Pig" (Hope) **52**:209
In the Country of the Black Pig (Hope) **52**:208-09
In the Country of the Skin (Redgrove) **6**:445; **41**:349, 352, 355-56
In the Court of Yearning
See *La curtile dorului*
"In the Courtyard" (Montale) **9**:388
"In the Courtyard of the Isleta Mission" (Bly) **38**:59
In the Courtyard of Yearning
See *La curtile dorului*
"In the Crevice of Time" (Jacobsen) **48**:198
In the Crevice of Time (Jacobsen) **102**:242
"In the Crowd" (Weller) **26**:444
"In the Crypt at Bourges" (Grigson) **7**:136
"In the Dark" (Raine) **32**:352 ; **103**:184-85, 193
"In the Dark" (Smith) **64**:399
"In the Darkness" (Ding Ling)
See "Zai heianzhong"
"In the Darkness of Cities" (Purdy) **50**:246
"In the Days of Prismatic Color" (Moore) **47**:260, 262-63
In the Days of Simon Stern (Cohen) **7**:50-1; **31**:93
In the Dead of the Night (Dubie) **36**:129-30, 140
"In the Deep Museum" (Sexton) **53**:316
In the Deepest Part of Sleep (Fuller) **25**:180
"In the Department" (Sargeson) **31**:365
"In the Desert" (Coupland) **85**:35, 37, 41
"In the Desert War" (Simmons) **43**:407
In the Ditch (Emecheta) **14**:160; **48**:97-8, 101
"In the Dream of My Grandmother's Tree" (Coles) **46**:113
"In the Dreaming" (Dickey) **28**:119
"In the Dry" (Pancake) **29**:346-48
In the Dwellings of Death (Sachs)
See *In den Wohnungen des Todes*
"In the Early Cretaceous" (Purdy) **50**:247
In the Early Morning Rain (Berrigan) **37**:44
"In the Egg" (Grass)

See "Im Ei"
"In the Egyptian Museum" (Lewis) **41**:254, 262
"In the Elegy Season" (Wilbur) **6**:570
"In the Evening" (Rich) **7**:365
"In the Eye of the Storm" (Spinrad) **46**:384
"In the Eyes of God" (Cheever) **15**:127
"In the Fall" (MacLeod) **56**:193, 200
In the Fictive Wish (Everson) **5**:122
"In the Field" (O'Brien) **103**:174
"In the Fifties" (Michaels) **6**:325
"In the Finland Woods" (Nowlan) **15**:398
"In the Flesh" (Barker) **52**:52, 55
In the Flesh (Barker) **52**:55-6
In the Flesh (Bowering) **15**:83; **47**:22
In the Flesh (Wolitzer) **17**:563-64
In the Fog of the Season's End (La Guma) **19**:272-76
"In the Foothills" (Purdy) **14**:432
In the Footsteps of the Prophet
See *Pasii profetului*
In the Frame (Francis) **42**:150, 156-57; **102**:127, 131, 139
In the Freest State in the World (Traven) **11**:535
In the Future Perfect (Abish) **22**:17-18
"In the Gallery" (Abse) **29**:20
"In the Gallery" (Squires) **51**:382
"In the Garden" (Dylan) **77**:185-86, 190
"In the Garden" (Paley) **37**:333
"In the Garden of the North American Martyrs" (Wolff) **64**:448, 455
In the Garden of the North American Martyrs (*Hunters in the Snow*) (Wolff) **64**:446-49, 450-51, 456-57
"In the Garret" (Van Vechten) **33**:385
"In the Giving Vein" (Porter) **5**:347; **33**:322
In the Great Passage
See *În marea trecere*
In the Great Passing
See *În marea trecere*
"In the Greyness of Isolated Time" (Brutus) **43**:92
"In the Groove" (Thomas) **107**:337-40
In the Habitation of Death (Sachs)
See *In den Wohnungen des Todes*
"In the Hands of the Senecas" (Edmonds) **35**:153, 156
"In the Heart of the Beast" (Williams) **33**:443-44
In the Heart of the Country (*From the Heart of the Country*) (Coetzee) **23**:121-23, 125; **33**:106, 111; **117**:33, 44, 47-8, 65, 67-9, 72-3, 81, 83-4
"In the Heart of the Heart of the Country" (Gass) **8**:244-45; **15**:257-58
In the Heart of the Heart of the Country, and Other Stories (Gass) **2**:154-55; **8**:244, 246-47; **11**:224-25; **39**:478, 482
In the Heart of the Seas (Agnon)
See *Bilvav yamim*
In the Heart or Our City (Rudnik) **7**:384
"In the Heat of the Summer" (Ochs) **17**:331
"In the Highlands" (Gellhorn) **60**:189, 192
"In the Hill at New Grange" (Jeffers) **54**:246
"In the Hills South of Capernaum, Port" (Olson) **29**:330
"In the Hills, the Cities" (Barker) **52**:53
"In the Hole" (Ciardi) **44**:383
In the Hollow of His Hand (Purdy) **52**:348-50
"In the Hospital" (Ding Ling) **68**:65
"In the Hospital" (Jensen) **37**:187-88
"In the Hospital for Tests" (Van Duyn) **63**:437
"In the Hotel of Lost Night" (Kinnell) **13**:322

In the Hours Waiting for the Blood to Come (MacBeth)   9:340

In the House of the Judge (Smith)   42:349, 351, 353, 357

In the Houses of Death (Sachs)
See *In den Wohnungen des Todes*

"In the Icebound Hothouse" (Goyen)   40:217

In the Illusion of the Threshhold (Bonnefoy)
See *Dans le leurre du seuil*

"in the inner city" (Clifton)   66:68

"In the Jungle" (Dillard)   60:74

"In the Kalahari Desert" (Raine)   32:350; 103:185, 188

"In the King's Rooms" (Steele)   45:365

In the Labyrinth (Robbe-Grillet)
See *Dans le labyrinthe*

In the Lake of the Woods (O'Brien)   103:163-68, 176

"In the Land of Dreamy Dreams" (Gilchrist)   48:114, 116

In the Land of Dreamy Dreams (Gilchrist)   34:165-66; 48:114-18, 120

In the Land of Israel (Oz)   54:348-49, 351; 33:300-04

In the Land of Morning (Petrakis)   3:383

"In the Land of the Great Aunts" (Cassity)   42:97

"In the Land of the Rujuks" (Boell)
See "Im Lande der Rujuks"

In the Last Analysis (Heilbrun)   25:255

"In the Light" (Page and Plant)   12:477, 479, 481

In the Lure of the Threshold (Bonnefoy)
See *Dans le leurre du seuil*

"In the Margin" (Blunden)   56:40

"In the Matter of Miracles" (Feinstein)   36:168

In the Meantime (Smart)   54:425

"In the Mecca" (Brooks)   49:28

In the Mecca (Brooks)   2:82; 4:78; 5:75-6; 15:92-3; 49:22, 27-31, 34-7

"In the Memory of Andrée Rexroth" (Rexroth)   49:279; 112:375

"In the Men's Room" ("s") (Piercy)   27:373

"In the Middle" (Smith)   64:392, 400

In the Middle (Smith)   64:394

In the Middle Distance (Delbanco)   6:130

In the Middle of a Life (Wright)   6:581-82

"In the Middle of America" (Haines)   58:222

In the Middle of Nowhere (Howe)   47:176-77

"In the Middle of the Fields" (Lavin)   99:322

In the Middle of the Fields (Lavin)   4:281; 18:306-07; 99:312, 322

"In the Middle of the Night" (Pearce)   21:289

In the Middle of the Wood (Smith)   64:401

"In the Middle of This Century" (Amichai)   116:138

"In the Midst of Life" (Rozewicz)   9:463, 465; 23:363

"In the Midst of Life" (Sargeson)   31:370, 373

In the Midst of My Fever (Layton)   15:318

"In the Miro District" (Taylor)   18:527-29; 37:409; 50:253; 71:304, 306-07

In the Miro District, and Other Stories (Taylor)   18:527-28

"In the Missouri Ozarks" (Van Duyn)   63:442

"In the Mist" (MacCaig)   36:285

"In the Mood" (Dowell)   60:107

In the Mood (Waterhouse)   47:422

"In the Morning" (Koch)   44:246, 249

"In the Mortuary" (Raine)   32:350, 352-53; 103:200

"In the Mountains"   75:77

"In the Mountains" (Strand)   18:516

"In the Mountains" (Warren)   10:521

"In the Mountains of Jerusalem" (Amichai)   116:97

"In the Movies" (O'Hara)   78:354

"In the Naked Bed, in Plato's Cave" (Schwartz)   10:462; 45:356; 87:341, 347

In the Native State (Stoppard)   91:192

"In the New Sun" (Levine)   14:320

"In the Night" (Himes)   7:159

"In the Night" (Kincaid)   43:247-48

In the Night Café (Johnson)   58:291-93

"In the Night the Night Sound Woke Us" (Rukeyser)   27:411

"In the Nile Delta" (Transtroemer)   65:226, 233

In the Ocean of Night (Benford)   52:59-61, 63-5, 70-2, 76-7

"In the Old People's Home, 1914" (Ewart)   46:148, 153

"In the Old Sun" (Hesse)   17:218

In the Outer Dark: Poems (Plumly)   33:310-13

In the Penal Colony (Berkoff)   56:14

"In the Penile Colony" (Jong)   8:314

"In the Penny Arcade" (Millhauser)   54:325-26

In the Penny Arcade (Millhauser)   109:157-58, 169-70, 174

In the Pink (Blackwood)   100:16, 18

"In the Pond" (Johnston)   51:239, 251

In the Presence of the Sun: Stories and Poems, 1961-1991 (Momaday)   85:279-81

"In the Privacy of the Home" (Strand)   18:516

"In the Protestant Cemetery, Rome" (Watkins)   43:452

"In the Public Garden" (Moore)   47:263

"In the Public Gardens" (Betjeman)   43:41

"In the Reading Room of the British Museum" (Faludy)   42:137

"In the Realm of the Herons" (Kaplan)   50:55-7

In the Realm of the Senses (Oshima)
See *L'empire de sens*

"In the Red Light: A History of the Republican Convention in 1964" (Mailer)   111:105-07

"In the Red Mountains" (Merwin)   45:278

"In the Red Room" (Bowles)   53:45

"In the Region of Ice" (Oates)   3:360; 19:348-49; 52:338

"In the Reign of Peace" (Nissenson)   4:381

In the Reign of Peace (Nissenson)   4:380-81; 9:399-400

"In the Ruins of New York City" (Merton)   83:395

In the Scarlet Star (Williamson)   29:454

In the Shade of the Old Apple Tree (Barker)   8:44

"In the Shadow of War" (Okri)   87:319

"In the Shetland Islands" (MacDiarmid)   4:309; 11:334

In the Skin of a Lion (Ondaatje)   51:318-21; 76:198, 202, 204, 206

"In the Small Hotel" (Dunn)   6:149

"In the Smoking Car" (Wilbur)   53:405

In the Soop (Mull)   17:300

In the Spirit of Crazy Horse (Matthiessen)   32:292-95; 64:315, 325

"In the Spring" (Fante)   60:133

In the Stoneworks (Ciardi)   40:158

"In the Stopping Train" (Davie)   8:165-66; 31:112, 118

In the Stopping Train, and Other Poems (Davie)   31:111-12, 116-19

"In the Street" (Tanizaki)   28:414

"In the Street Today" (Weller)   26:443

"In the Suburbs" (Simpson)   4:498

"In the Suburbs" (Urdang)   47:399

In the Summer House (Bowles)   68:4-7, 9-15, 18, 21

"In the Tank" (Gunn)   32:211

In the Terrified Radiance (Burnshaw)   3:91

"In the Theatre: A True Incident" (Abse)   7:2; 29:18-19

"In the Thick of Darkness" (Salinas)   90:332

"In the Thriving Season: In Memory of My Mother" (Mueller)   51:279-80

"In the Time of the Blossoms" (Merwin)   45:276-77

In the Time of the Butterflies (Alvarez)   93:13-19

"In the Tradition" (Baraka)   33:62

In the Tradition (Baraka)   115:11, 18, 39

"In the Train" (O'Connor)   14:398; 23:326

"In the True Light of Morning" (Swan)   69:361-64

"In the Tunnel" (Gallant)   38:194

In the Twelfth Year of the War (Appleman)   51:13

"In the Underworld" (Rukeyser)   27:412

"In the Vacuum" (Williams)   42:441

In the Valley of the Statues (Holdstock)   39:152

"In the Village" (Bishop)   9:90, 92; 13:93; 32:34, 40-1, 44

"In the Waiting Room" (Bishop)   9:91, 97; 13:89-90, 94; 15:61; 32:30-1, 33, 37, 39, 42-3

"In the Wake of Home" (Rich)   36:378

"In the Wall" (Fisher)   25:159

"In the Ward" (Lowell)   37:238

"In the Ward: The Sacred Wood" (Jarrell)   13:300

"In the Waxworks" (Shapiro)   53:332

"In the Wee, Wee Hours" (Berry)   17:51

"In the Wheatfield"   75:69

"In the White Night" (Beattie)   63:14, 16-17, 19

"In the Wilderness" (Graves)   45:169-70

"In the Wilderness" (Smith)   15:515

"In the Wilderness" (Swan)   69:363, 365

In the Wilderness, and Other Poems (Simmons)   43:407, 411

"In the Wind My Rescue Is" (Ammons)   9:28

In the Wine Time (Bullins)   1:47; 5:83

In the Winter of Cities (Williams)   45:443

"In the Wood" (Pasternak)   63:278

"In the Woods" (Rich)   3:428; 11:478

"In the Woods" (Robison)   98:308, 317

In the World (Elliott)   2:131

"In the X-Ray Room" (Moss)   50:353

"In the Year of the Longest Cadillac" (Ciardi)   40:155

"In the Zone" (Pynchon)   18:440

"In the Zoo" (Stafford)   7:459; 19:431; 68:422-23, 431-32

In Their Wisdom (Snow)   6:517-18; 9:498; 19:427

"In This Age of Hard Trying, Nonchalance Is Good and ..." (Moore)   8:400; 13:397; 47:261

"In This Country" (Brutus)   43:89

In This House of Brede (Godden)   53:160-62

In This Our Life (Huston)   20:158, 164

In This Sign (Greenberg)   7:135; 30:162, 166

"In Thy Sleep/Little Sorrows Sit and Weep" (Rakosi)   47:344

"In Time Like Air" (Sarton)   91:253

In Time Like Air (Sarton) 4:470
"In Time of Cloudburst" (Frost) 34:475
"In Time of Plague" (Gunn) 81:177, 181, 187-88
"In Time of the Hungarian Martyrdom" (Buckley) 57:125
"In Times When My Head" (Simon) 26:410-11, 413
"In Touch" (Fisher) 25:160
In Tragic Life (Fisher) 7:103
"In Transit" (Auden) 43:27
In Transit: An Heroi-Cyclic Novel (Brophy) 6:100; 29:97; 105:7, 10-11, 13-14, 22-30, 33
"In Trust" (Gilliatt) 53:145
"In Tuscany" (Garrett) 3:192
"In Two Degrees Cold" (Appleman) 51:15
"In Umbria" (Moss) 45:290
"In Verdi Square" (Tomlinson) 45:403
"in viewpoint: poem for 14 catfish and the town of tama, iowa" (Young Bear) 94:363, 366
"In Warsaw" (Milosz) 56:248
In Watermelon Sugar (Brautigan) 1:45; 3:86-7, 90; 5:67-8, 70-1; 9:123; 12:58-62, 66, 68, 70; 34:314-15, 317-18; 42:50, 57, 60, 62, 66
"In Weather" (Hass) 18:209
"In West Flanders" (Blunden) 56:44
"In Westminster Abbey" (Betjeman) 6:68-9; 43:33, 44
In What Hour (Rexroth) 1:284; 22:344-45; 49:275, 277, 279-80, 284, 286; 112:365, 374, 387, 390, 396-97, 400
"In Which the Ancient History I Learn is Not My Own" (Boland) 113:93
In Which We Serve (Coward) 29:136, 140
"In White" (Frost) 10:199
In White America (Duberman) 8:185
"In Whose Garden I Am Sleeping / In Whose Garden I Am Sleeping Perfectly" (Moure) 88:223
"In Willesden Churchyard" (Betjeman) 43:45-6
"In Winter" (MacBeth) 5:264
"In Winter" (Stevenson) 33:379
In Winter (Ryan) 65:211, 213
"In with the Doctor" (Kelman) 58:298-99
In Words and the Poet (Thomas) 6:530
"In Your Movements I See Drownings" (Lerman) 9:329
"In Youth Is Pleasure" (Gallant) 38:192
"In Zeno's World" (Nemerov) 36:306
"The Inability" (Bronk) 10:75
"Inaction" (Fuller) 28:159
Inadmissible Evidence (Osborne) 1:263; 2:328; 5:332-33; 11:421-22; 45:313-16, 319-21
The Inadvertent Epic (Fiedler) 24:204-05
"Inaugural Lecture, Collège de France" (Barthes) See *Leçon inaugurale faite le vendredi 7 janvier 1977*
"Inaugural Rose" (Jordan) 114:146
"Inca" (Raine) 103:186, 189
Incandescence (Nova) 31:297-99
"Incantation" (Akhmadulina) See "Zaklinanie"
"incantation" (Clifton) 66:84
"Incantation" (Milosz) 56:233, 251; 82:303
"Incantation" (Swenson) 106:351
The Incarnate (Campbell) 42:90-1, 93
"Incarnation" (Rexroth) 49:281; 112:399
"The Incarnation of Sirius" (McAuley) 45:248, 253

Incarnations of Immortality (Anthony) 35:40
Incarnations: Poems, 1966-1968 (Warren) 4:578; 6:557-58; 8:539; 10:520; 13:577; 18:534, 536; 39:265-66
"The Incendiary" (Scannell) 49:326, 331
"L'incendio in via Keplero" (Gadda) 11:209
"Incense to Idols" (Ashton-Warner) 19:21
"The Inception of the Poem" (McAuley) 45:248
"Incertus" (Heaney) 74:193
"Incespicare" ("Stumbling") (Montale) 7:225
"Incident" (Adcock) 41:18
"Incident" (Fuller) 62:206
"The Incident" (Smith) 64:391
"Incident" (Stafford) 29:387
Incident at Hawk's Hill (Eckert) 17:107-08
"An Incident at Krechetovka Station" (Solzhenitsyn) 7:435; 10:479
"Incident at Twilight" (Durrenmatt) 15:195
Incident at Vichy (Miller) 1:218; 2:278-80; 6:329-30; 10:342-44; 15:373-75; 47:256
"Incident at Yalentay" (Castellanos) 66:60
"An Incident at Yanagiyu" (Tanizaki) 28:417
"Incident in a Saloon Bar" (Scannell) 49:326
"Incident in Azania" (Waugh) 27:477
"Incident in Hyde Park, 1803" (Blunden) 56:33
"Incident in San Domingo" (Booth) 23:75
"An Incident in the Early Life of Ebenezer Jones, Poet, 1928" (Betjeman) 43:41
"An Incident in the 'Metropole': A True Story Resembling a Thriller" (Voinovich) 10:507
"Incident on a Picnic" (Steele) 45:362
"Incident on Fifty-Seventh Street" (Springsteen) 17:477, 480, 488, 490
"An Incident with Jacob Pichunk" (Leonov) 92:
Incidental Music (Sagan) 36:382-83
Incidents at the Shrine (Okri) 87:314, 322, 325
"Incipit" (Robbe-Grillet) 8:454; 14:462
Incitación al Nixonicidio y alabanza de la revolución Chilena (A Call for Nixonicide and Glory to the Chilean Revolution) (Neruda) 28:314
The Incline (Mayne) 12:399
"Including Myself" (Moure) 88:219
Inclus (Guillevic) 33:192, 194
"The Incognito Lounge" (Johnson) 52:232-34
The Incognito Lounge, and Other Poems (Johnson) 52:231-34
"The Incoherent Radio" (Ratushinskaya) 54:385
The Incomparable Atuk (Richler) 5:373, 376; 13:481, 484, 486; 46:347, 349; 70:225, 230
"Incompatibilities" (Hughes) 9:284
L'inconnu sur la terre (Le Clezio) 31:250
The Increased Difficulty of Concentration (Havel) 25:223, 225-26; 58:240, 242
The Incredible Brazilian (Ghose) See *The Native*
The Incredible Feeling Show (Swados) 12:560
Incredible Floridas (Weir) 20:424
The Incredible Planet (Campbell) 32:74
"Incunabula #3" (Daitch) 103:78
Indecent Dreams (Lustig) 56:188-90
Indecent Exposure (Sharpe) 36:399, 402
An Indecent Obsession (McCullough) 27:321-22; 107:135-36, 154
"Indecision" (Swados) 12:557

"Indelible, Inedible" (Ashbery) 25:54
"Independence" (Bennett) 28:27-8
Independence (Motion) 47:287-94
"Independence Day" (Bukowski) 82:14
"Independence Day" (Morrison) 21:233
Independence Day 99:104, 107-15, 118-27
Independent People (Laxness) See *Sjálfstaett fólk*
"The Independent Woman" (Govier) 51:166-67
Les Indes (Glissant) 10:231; 68:171, 173, 179-80, 188
"A indesjada das gentes" ("The Undesireables") (Cabral de Melo Neto) 76:168
"Indeterminacy" (Cage) 41:80
"India" (Mahapatra) 33:277
India: A Million Mutinies Now (Naipaul) 105:174
India: A Wounded Civilization (Naipaul) 9:393; 13:407; 18:363-64; 37:321, 324, 328; 105:155, 176
"India Again" (Forster) 77:242
India Song (Duras) 100:125, 127, 145, 148
India Song (Duras) 6:150; 20:100-04; 34:162; 40:178-80; 68:77, 81, 89, 91, 95-6
Indian (Ryga) 14:472-73
The Indian Affair (Deloria) 21:113
"Indian Boarding School: The Runaways" (Erdrich) 54:165
"Indian Bread" (Kinnell) 5:217; 13:321
"Indian Camp" (Hemingway) 6:231; 8:289, 291; 10:269; 13:273; 19:211; 30:180, 186-87, 190, 192, 194, 196, 198-99; 50:429; 80:138
"Indian Country" (Simpson) 7:428-29
Indian Country (Matthiessen) 32:295-97; 64:315-16, 325
"Indian Dances" (Sarton) 49:320
"Indian Education" (Alexie) 96:7, 11
Indian Foe, Indian Friend (Archer) 12:17
Indian Ink (Stoppard) 91:192
Indian Journals, March 1962-May 1963 (Ginsberg) 2:163; 3:195; 6:200; 36:181, 186; 109:351
Indian Man: A Life of Oliver La Farge (McNickle) 89:181
"Indian Pipe" (Piercy) 27:376
"The Indian Renaissance" (Waters) 88:365
Indian Short Stories (Anand) 93:42
"Indian Summer" (Barnes) 29:27
"Indian Summer" (Hirsch) 50:197
"Indian Summer" (Howes) 15:290
"Indian Summer" (Pasternak) 63:313
Indian Summer (Knowles) 1:169; 4:271-72; 26:254-56, 258
"Indian Summer Poem" (Mahapatra) 33:277, 282
Indian Tales and Others (Neihardt) 32:331
the Indian Theatre (Anand) 93:23
"The Indian Tribes of the United States: Ethnic and Cultural Survival" (McNickle) 89:160-61
"The Indian Uprising" (Barthelme) 5:53; 8:50; 23:44-5; 46:36, 43; 115:56-8, 65
The Indian Wants the Bronx (Horovitz) 56:147-48, 150, 154
Indiana (Eshleman) 7:97, 99
"Indianapolis/Summer/1969/Poem" (Sanchez) 116:272, 278
"The Indians" (Wild) 14:581
Indians (Coles) 108:194
Indians (Kopit) 1:170-71; 18:290; 33:247, 249-52

Indians and Other Americans: Two Ways of Life Meet (McNickle)   **89**:168, 173, 175, 180-81

"Indians at the Guthrie" (Vizenor)   **103**:281, 296

The Indians in the Woods, 1918-1928 (Lewis)   **41**:252, 260-61

Indians of the Pacific Northwest (Deloria)   **21**:114

"The Indians on Alcatraz" (Muldoon)   **32**:315

Indicateur des chemins de coeur (*Heartway Guide*) (Tzara)   **47**:390

The Indifferent Children (Auchincloss)   **45**:23-4

Gli indifferenti (*The Time of Indifference*) (Moravia)   **2**:293; **7**:240-41, 244; **11**:382-83; **18**:343-49; **27**:354

"The Indigo Engineers" (Vollmann)   **89**:277

El indio (*They That Reap*) (Lopez y Fuentes)   **32**:278-80, 282-83

Indira Gandhi's Emergence and Style (Sahgal)   **41**:372-73

"Indirect Method" (King)   **53**:209, 212

Indirect Method, and Other Stories (King)   **53**:209

Das indische Grabmal (Lang)   **103**:86, 89

"Indischer Lebenslauf" (Hesse)   **11**:272

Indiscretion (De Sica)
   See *Stazione termini*

Indiscretions (Pound)   **13**:461

"Indisposed" (Banks)   **37**:24

The Individual and His Times (Fuller)   **28**:157-59

"Individual and Mass Behavior in Extreme Situations" (Bettelheim)   **79**:123, 125

"The Individualist" (Ritsos)   **31**:324

"Individuals" (Simpson)   **7**:428

"The Indivisible Incompatibles" (Swenson)   **106**:348

"Indonesia" (Oliver)   **98**:280, 290

"Indoor Games near Newbury" (Betjeman)   **2**:60

"Indoor Perennials" (Hall)   **51**:170

"Indosincrasia" (Ulibarri)   **83**:412

"Indulgences" (Godwin)   **8**:248

"Industrija" (Bagryana)   **10**:12

Inées Perée et Inat Tendu (Ducharme)   **74**:61, 63-5

"The Ineffectual Marriage" (Loy)   **28**:251

Inessential Woman: Problems of Exclusion in Feminist Thought   **65**:314

"The Inexhaustible Beginning" (Trifonov)   **45**:411

"The Infallible Executors of Roman Law" (Haavikko)   **34**:175

"Infant" (Smith)   **44**:442

Infante's Inferno (Cabrera Infante)
   See *La Habana para un infante difunto*

"Infantiev" (Bitov)   **57**:114-15

Les infants du sabat (*Children of the Black Sabbath*) (Hebert)   **13**:267-68; **29**:232, 238-41

Infants of the Spring: The Memoirs of Anthony Powell (Powell)   **10**:417; **31**:313-16, 319-20, 322

"Infare" (Still)   **49**:363

"The Infection" (King)   **8**:321

The Infernal Desire Machines of Doctor Hoffman (Carter)   **41**:114-15; **76**:323, 329

The Infernal Machine (Cocteau)
   See *La machine infernale*

The Infernal World of Branwell Brontë (du Maurier)   **59**:286

"Inferno, I, 32" (Borges)   **44**:354

The Inferno of Dante (Pinsky)   **94**:

Infidels (Dylan)   **77**:179, 184

"El infierno tan temido" ("Dreaded Hell") (Onetti)   **10**:376

L'infini turbulent (*The Infinite Storm*) (Michaux)   **8**:392; **19**:312

The Infinite Atom (Campbell)   **32**:74

Infinite Dreams (Haldeman)   **61**:174-76, 178, 181

Infinite Jest (Wallace)   **114**:366-68, 370, 372-76, 383-93, 395

"The Infinite Passion of Expectation" (Berriault)   **109**:94

The Infinite Passion of Expectation (Berriault)   **54**:4-5, 7; **109**:90, 92, 98

The Infinite Plan (Allende)
   See *The Infinite Plan*

The Infinite Storm (Michaux)
   See *L'infini turbulent*

"The Infinity Box" (Wilhelm)   **7**:538

The Infinity Box (Wilhelm)   **7**:538

An Infinity of Mirrors (Condon)   **4**:107; **45**:93-6, 104; **100**:102, 111-12

"Infirmity" (Roethke)   **3**:433; **46**:357

Inflation (Forman)   **21**:121

"Influences" (Alexie)   **96**:9

"Influences" (Carruth)   **84**:127

The Influences (Watkins)   **43**:455

"Influenza" (Adcock)   **41**:18

"An Influx of Poets" (Stafford)   **68**:443, 449

The Information (Amis)   **101**:84-86, 88-99

"Information Density" (Ammons)   **57**:53

El informe de Brodie (*Doctor Brodie's Report*) (Borges)   **2**:71-2, 77; **3**:81; **4**:75; **6**:88, 91; **10**:66-8; **13**:104; **44**:356-58, 364, 368; **48**:38, 40; **83**:182, 189

"Informe sobre ciegos" (Sabato)   **10**:444-46

The Informed Heart: Autonomy in a Mass Age (Bettelheim)   **79**:110, 134-35

Informer (Ford)   **16**:303, 315

The Informer (O'Flaherty)   **5**:321; **34**:355-57

The Informers (Ellis)   **117**:147-50

"The Ingoldsby Legends" (Wilson)   **3**:540

Ingrid Babendererde: Reifeprüfung, 1953 (Johnson)   **40**:270-71

The Inhabitant (Turco)   **11**:550-51

"The Inhabitant of the Lake" (Campbell)   **42**:92

The Inhabitant of the Lake and Less Welcome Tenants (Campbell)   **42**:83, 89-91

The Inhabitants (Morris)   **1**:232; **37**:313, 316

The Inhabited Island (Strugatskii and Strugatskii)   **27**:434

Inhale and Exhale (Saroyan)   **29**:363

"Inheritance" (Barnard)   **48**:26

"Inheritance" (Ingalls)   **42**:234

"Inheritance" (Louie)   **70**:81

"Inheritance" (Merwin)   **88**:213

"Inheritances" (Hacker)   **72**:184

"Inheritor" (Wright)
   See "Eroded Hills"

"The Inheritors" (Waters)   **88**:333

The Inheritors (Golding)   **1**:121-22; **2**:166, 168-69; **3**:197-98, 200; **8**:249; **10**:233-36, 239; **17**:158-62, 165-66, 171-72, 174, 177, 179; **27**:159-64, 167-68; **58**:185, 202; **81**:317-21, 323, 326

The Inheritors (Robbins)   **5**:378

"The Inhuman Condition" (Barker)   **52**:55

The Inhuman Condition (Barker)   **52**:53-6

"The Inhumanist" (Jeffers)   **54**:241; **3**:260; **11**:311

"Inicial" (Neruda)   **28**:310-11

Inishfallen, Fare Thee Well (O'Casey)   **88**:238-39, 262

"The Initiate" (Simic)   **68**:375

"Initiation" (McIlvanney)   **42**:282

"Initiations" (Okigbo)   **25**:349; **84**:299, 307-09, 313, 325, 327

"Initram" (Thomas)   **13**:538, 540; **37**:416; **107**:319, 347

"Injun or Indian?" (Fiedler)   **24**:198

Injury Time (Bainbridge)   **10**:15-17; **14**:37; **62**:25, 30, 33, 36

The Injustice Collectors (Auchincloss)   **4**:31; **45**:24-5

"Ink Drawings" (Levertov)   **28**:242

"The Ink Feather" (Swan)   **69**:360-61

The Ink Truck (Kennedy)   **6**:275; **28**:203-04; **53**:194, 197

The Inkling (Chappell)   **40**:137-38, 140; **78**:97, 109

Inklings (Wolff)   **41**:458-59

Inklings: Selected Stories (Jacobson)   **14**:290

"Inland" (Motion)   **47**:285-86, 289

"The Inlet" (Gluck)   **7**:119

"Inmarypraise" (Grass)   **6**:209

The Inmates (Powys)   **7**:349; **46**:321-22

"El inmortal" ("The Immortal") (Borges)   **1**:39; **2**:69, 72, 76; **8**:98; **10**:66; **19**:47; **83**:156-57, 166

The Inmost Leaf (Kazin)   **38**:272-74

Innansveitark-Skáldatími (Laxness)   **25**:300

"Innard Life" (Macdonald)   **13**:355

"Inner City Blues" ("Make Me Wanna Holler") (Gaye)   **26**:130, 132

The Inner Experience (Bataille)
   See *L'expérience intérieure*

"The Inner Harbour" (Adcock)   **41**:15-16

The Inner Harbour (Adcock)   **41**:15-17

Inner Landscape (Sarton)   **49**:308-09, 320; **91**:245, 254

The Inner Live of the Middle Class (Ehrenreich)   **110**:180

"The Inner Room" (Aickman)   **57**:6

"Inner Voice" (Herbert)   **9**:273

Inner Weather (Phillips)   **28**:361, 363

The Inner Wheel (Roberts)   **14**:463

Innervisions (Wonder)   **12**:656-57

The Innerworld of the Outerworld of the Innerworld (Handke)   **5**:165; **15**:266; **38**:219

The Innkeeper's Song (Beagle)   **104**:33-4

"Innocence" (Bates)   **46**:52, 54

"Innocence" (Brodkey)   **56**:58-60, 62, 65, 67

"Innocence" (Broumas)   **10**:77; **73**:3, 16

"The Innocence" (Creeley)   **8**:153

"Innocence" (Gunn)   **18**:203; **32**:208

"Innocence" (Kavanagh)   **22**:239

Innocence (Fitzgerald)   **51**:125-27; **61**:118-20, 122

Innocence and Memory (Ungaretti)   **7**:485

Innocence in Extremis (Hawkes)   **49**:158-60

The Innocent (McEwan)   **66**:290-95

The Innocent (Visconti)
   See *L'innocente*

"The Innocent and Infinite Windows of Childhood" (Schwartz)   **45**:361

The Innocent and the Guilty (Warner)   **7**:512

The Innocent Assassins (Eiseley)   **7**:92

Innocent Blood (James)   **18**:274-76; **46**:205-06

Innocent Bystander (Sissman) 9:492
An Innocent Millionaire (Vizinczey) 40:436-39
The Innocent Party (Hawkes) 4:213, 215; 7:140
Innocent Sorcerers (Wajda) 16:577-78
The Innocent Traveller (Wilson) 13:607-09, 611
L'innocente (*The Innocent*) (Visconti) 16:573-74
The Innocents (Capote) 34:322
Les innocents (Chabrol) 16:182
The Innocents (Slaughter) 56:412
"The Innocents Abroad" (Stafford) 4:517
"Innoculated City" (Clash) 30:52
L'innommable (*The Unnameable*) (Beckett) 2:44-5; 3:45; 4:52; 6:36-7, 42-3; 9:78-9, 83-4, 87; 10:28, 32; 11:32-4, 37; 14:71, 73, 76-7; 18:41, 47, 50-1; 29:53, 55-9, 61-2, 65-7; 59:253, 257
"L'inoffensif" (Char) 14:128
"Inquest" (Snodgrass) 18:491
The Inquest (Lem) 40:295, 297
"L'inquilino" (Ortese)
   See "Il signor Lin"
"The Inquisition" (Elytis) 49:110
Inquisition (Arrabal) 58:28-9
L'inquisitoire (*The Inquisitory*) (Pinget) 7:305-06; 37:359-61, 363-64
The Inquisitory (Pinget)
   See *L'inquisitoire*
"L'insaisissable Breyon!" (Theriault) 79:407
"Insane Decisions" (Ashbery) 77:66
"Inscribed in War-Books" (Blunden) 56:30
"Inscription Facing Western Sea" (Merwin) 13:386
"Inscription for the Tank" (Wright) 5:520
The Insect Colony (Larson) 31:239
"The Insect World" (Rhys) 14:447
"Inselhin" ("Toward the Island") (Celan) 19:90
L'inserzione (Ginzburg) 54:207; 70:283
Inshallah (Fallaci) 110:215-17
"Inside and Out" (Motion) 47:293-94
"Inside Barbara Walters" (Grayson) 38:211
Inside Big League Baseball (Kahn) 30:230
"Inside from the Outside" (Jiles) 58:280
Inside Mr. Enderby (Burgess) 4:81, 84; 5:88-9, 91; 8:112; 10:88; 22:69; 40:114, 122-23; 62:130; 81:301
"Inside Norman Mailer" (Apple) 9:32; 33:18, 21
The Inside of His Head (Miller)
   See *Death of a Salesman*
"Inside Out" (Creeley) 78:131
Inside, Outside (Wouk) 38:452-53
"An Inside Outside Complex" (O'Faolain) 7:274
"The Inside Rooms" (Giovanni) 4:189
"Inside the Apple" (Amichai) 57:47
Inside the Blood Factory (Wakoski) 4:571; 7:507; 9:554
"Inside the Drop of Rain" (Plumly) 33:311
Inside the Easter Egg (Engel) 36:160-62
"Inside the Onion" (Nemerov) 36:309
Inside the Onion (Nemerov) 36:309
"Inside the Story" (Strand) 6:521
"Inside the Tulip" (Bowering) 47:28
"Inside-Out" (Knight) 40:283-84, 286
"Insight at Flame Lake" (Amis) 62:7-10
"Insignificant Elephants" (Auden) 4:33
"Insomnia" (Bishop) 32:39
"Insomnia" (Bowers) 9:122
Insomnia; or, The Devil at Large (Miller) 9:380
"Insomniac" (Plath) 111:171, 180, 214

L'insoumise (Blais) 6:82; 13:96
L'insourenable l'égrèté de l'être (*The Unbearable Lightness of Being*) (Kundera) 33:262-64, 267-68, 271; 68:232-36, 238, 244-47, 249-50, 252-54, 256, 259-62, 264-66; 115:309, 311, 315, 317, 321, 326, 329-30, 333, 344-45, 347-48, 351, 353-54, 359
"Inspeak: Your Streetwise Guide to Linguistics and Structuralism" (Bradbury) 61:48
"The Inspector" (Reid) 33:350
The Inspector (de Hartog) 19:131
An Inspector Calls (Priestley) 5:350; 34:361-63, 365-66
Inspector Maigret and the Dead Girl (Simenon)
   See *Maigret and the Young Girl*
Inspector Maigret and the Killers (*Maigret and the Gangsters*) (Simenon) 47:373, 377
Inspector Maigret and the Strangled Stripper (Simenon)
   See *Maigret au "Picratt"*
Inspector Queen's Own Case (Queen) 11:464
Inspector Saito's Small Satori (van de Wetering) 47:411
"The Inspired Chicken Motel" (Bradbury) 42:34
Instamatic Poems (Morgan) 31:275-76
"L'instance de la lettre" ("The Agency of the Letter in the Unconscious; or, Reason Since Freud") (Lacan) 75:286, 295
"Instances of Communication" (Jacobsen) 102:241
"Instancing" (Ammons) 57:50
"The Instant" (Levertov) 66:241
The Instant Enemy (Macdonald) 1:185; 2:256; 14:335
"L'instant II" (Chedid) 47:87
An Instant in the Wind (Brink)
   See *File on a Diplomat*
"Instant Karma!" (Lennon) 35:265, 270-71, 273-74
"Instant of the Hour After" (McCullers) 12:433
"Instead of an Essay" (Tomlinson) 45:397-98
"Instead of an Interview" (Adcock) 41:16
"Instead of Camargue" (Swenson) 106:320
"Instead of You" (Dunn) 36:155
Instinct and Intelligence (Cousteau) 30:107
The Institute (Cain) 11:87; 28:54
Institute Benjamenta, or This Dream Which People Call Human Life (The Brothers Quay) 95:348, 351, 354, 356-58
"Instrucciones para John Howell" (Cortazar) 5:109
"The Instruction Manual" (Ashbery) 9:42; 41:40; 77:58, 70
"Instructions for Bombing with Napalm" (Frame) 96:200
"Instructions for Exiting the Building in Case of Fire" (Zoline) 62:463
"Instructions for John Howell" (Cortazar) 5:109
Instructions for Undressing the Human Race (Alegria) 57:11
"Instructions from the Dean of Menopause" (Klappert) 57:257-58
"Instructions to the Double" (Gallagher) 18:170; 63:122, 124
Instructions to the Double (Gallagher) 18:168, 170; 63:116, 118-20, 122
"Instructions to the Orphic Adept" (Graves) 45:162, 166
"Instructions to the Player" (Rakosi) 47:346

"Instructions to Vampires" (Adcock) 41:13
"Instructions toward a Nude" (Dacey) 51:79
The Instrument (O'Hara) 42:319
"Instrument and Agent" (MacCaig) 36:279
"Instrument of Destruction" (Spencer) 22:406
Instrument of Thy Peace (Paton) 25:364
"Instruments of Seduction" (Rush) 44:91, 94-5
Insufficient Poppy (Enright) 31:152
An Insular Possession (Mo) 46:261-62
The Insurance Man (Bennett) 45:59; 77:91
"Una insurrección permanente" ("A Permanent Insurrection") (Vargas Llosa) 85:354
Insurrection (O'Flaherty) 5:321; 34:355-56
"Intacta" (Davison) 28:100
"The Integers" (Leithauser) 27:242
"Integraciones" (Neruda) 28:309
"Integrity" (Rich) 36:369, 377
"The Intellectual" (Ritsos) 31:324
"The Intellectual Physiognomy of Literacy Characters" (Lukacs) 24:316
Intellectual Things (Kunitz) 11:319; 14:313
"The Intellectuals" (Shapiro) 53:326
The Intellectuals on the Road to Class Power: A Sociological Study of the Role the Intelligentsia in Socialism (Konrad)
   See *Az értlemiség utja az oszatályhatalomhoz*
Intelligent Life in the Universe (Sagan) 112:416, 438
Intense Pleasure (McFadden) 48:244-46, 250
"Intensive Care" (Smith) 73:353, 356-57, 359
Intensive Care (Bennett) 77:93
Intensive Care (Frame) 6:190; 96:173, 179-82, 191-92, 197, 199, 200, 217
L'intention poétique (Glissant) 68:173, 179, 181-82, 185, 189
Inter Ice Age 4 (Abe)
   See *Daiyon kampyoki*
"Intercession" (Avison) 97:115
"The Intercessors" (Derleth) 31:133
The Intercom Conspiracy (Ambler) 9:18, 20
"An Interest in Life" (Paley) 6:393; 37:338
"Interference" (Ammons) 108:21
"Interferences" (Morgan) 31:275-76
"Intérieur" (Bagryana) 10:14
"L'intérieur" (Butor) 15:117
"Interim" ("Prologue: An Interim") (Levertov) 5:247-49
"Interim" (Wilson) 49:416
"Interim in a Waiting Room" (Corn) 33:114
Interim Report (Shapcott) 38:401
"Interims" (Amichai) 116:122
"The Interior Castle" (Stafford) 7:457; 19:431; 68:422-23, 434, 449
"Interior Decorating" (Simmons) 43:412
"Interior Decorator" (Betjeman) 43:51
"The Interior Dialogue" (Mauriac) 9:363
The Interior Landscape: The Literary Criticism of Marshall McLuhan, 1943-1962 (McLuhan) 83:360
Interior Landscapes: Autobiographical Myths and Metaphors (Vizenor) 103:311, 340
The Interior Life (Moravia)
   See *La vita interiore*
"Interior Space" (Irving) 172, 175
"Interiors" (Fisher) 25:158
Interiors (Allen) 16:9-11, 13-16; 52:40, 46-8
"Interiors with Various Figures" (Fisher) 25:161
"Interjection Number Four: Bad Year, Bad War: A New Year's Card, 1969" (Warren) 8:538
"Interjection Number Three: I Know a Place Where All Is Real" (Warren) 8:537
"Interjection Number Two: Caveat" (Warren)

8:537

"Interlopers" (Wilding)   73:399

"An Interlude of Winter Light" (Duncan)
    41:128-29

Interlunar (Atwood)   84:68, 98, 102, 104

"An Intermediate Stop" (Godwin)   8:249;
    69:232

"Intermission" (Coover)   46:121

The Intermittent Quest (Ionesco)
    See *La quête intermittent*

Internal Colloquies: Poetries (Richards)
    14:453; 24:401

Internal Foreigner (Klappert)   57:266

"The International Crime of Genital Mutila-
    tion" (Steinem)   63:384

"International Lover" (Prince)   35:326, 328

The International Stud (Fierstein)   33:152-53

"Interoffice Memorandum to James Seay"
    (Harmon)   38:244

*Interpersonal Perception: A Theory and a
    Method of Research* (Laing)   95:134, 141,
    145, 174, 176

"Interplay" (Wright)   53:424, 429

Interpretation in Teaching (Richards)   24:400-
    01

"The Interpretation of Dreams" (Koch)   44:249

"The Interpretation of Dreams" (Matthews)
    40:323-24

"The Interpretation of Dreams" (Smith)
    73:353, 356-58

The Interpretation of Dreams (Breton)   15:88,
    90

"Interpretations" (Urdang)   47:400

"The Interpreter" (Aldiss)   14:11

The Interpreters (Soyinka)   3:462; 5:397;
    14:508, 509; 36:410-11; 44:291, 294-96

Interpreter's House (Dickey)   28:118

"Interpreting the Past" (Lively)   32:273

The Interrogation (Le Clezio)   31:242-43, 246,
    249

"The Interrogation of the Prisoner Bung by
    Mister Hawkins and Sergeant Tree"
    (Huddle)   49:181-82

The Interrupted Act (Rozewicz)   9:464-65

"The Interrupted Class" (Hesse)   3:248-49

Interrupted Praise: New and Selected Poems
    (Honig)   33:216

"An Interruption" (Ciardi)   44:383

Intersect (Shields)   113:412, 441

"I-80 Nebraska, m.490—m.205" (Sayles)
    14:483

"Interstellar Overdrive" (Pink Floyd)   35:307

The Interstellar Search (Campbell)   32:74

"Interstitial Office" (Berryman)   3:69

Intertidal Life (Thomas)   37:422-24; 107:328,
    330, 336-37, 340, 347, 349

"The Interval" (Motion)   47:288, 291

"Interval in Sunlight" (Bradbury)   42:35

Intervalle (Butor)   15:119-20

"The Interview" (Blackwood)   6:80

"The Interview" (Bruce)   21:44

"The Interview" (Creeley)   78:136

"Interview" (Havel)
    See "Audience"

"The Interview" (Ignatow)   40:259

"The Interview" (Jhabvala)   94:184

"The Interview" (Singer)   69:306

Interview (van Itallie)   3:493

"An Interview Unlike Any Other" (Wiesel)
    37:451

"Interview with a Spirit Healer" (Abse)   29:16

"Interview with Doctor Drink" (Cunningham)
    31:98

Interview with History (Fallaci)
    See *Intervista con la storia*

Interview with the Vampire (Rice)   41:361-67

"The Interviewer" (Hinde)   6:239

*Interviewing Matisse, or, The Woman Who Died
    Standing Up* (Tuck)   70:117-21

Interviewing the Audience (Gray)   112:103,
    111

Intervista (Fellini)   85:
    See *Federico Fellini's intervista*

Intervista con la storia (*Interview with History*)
    (Fallaci)   110:194-95, 207

"Intifada" (Jordan)   114:147

"Intimacy" (Carver)   53:62, 64-6; 55:275, 277

"Intimacy" (Collins)   44:37-8

"Intimacy" (Colwin)   84:150

"Intimacy" (Montague)   46:277

Intimacy, and Other Stories (Sartre)
    See *Le mur*

"Intimate Exchanges" (Ayckbourn)   33:47, 50;
    74:20

"Intimate Parnassus" (Kavanagh)   22:238

Intimate Relations (Cocteau)
    See *Les parents terribles*

Intimate Strangers (Prichard)   46:337-38, 340-
    42

"Intimations" (Michaels)   25:314

"Intimations of Mortality" (McGinley)   14:366

"Intimidations of an Autobiography" (Tate)
    6:528

"Into Each Rain Some Life Must Fall"
    (Robinson)   21:348-50

*Into Eternity: The Life of James Jones, Ameri-
    can Writer* (MacShane)   39:404-14

"Into Hades" (Young)   5:523-25

"Into Mexico" (Van Duyn)   116:400, 402

"Into My Own" (Frost)   26:117-18

"Into My Own" (Levine)   33:274

"Into the American Maw" (Frazier)   46:164

"Into the Black" (Young)
    See "Hey Hey, My My"

"Into the Dark Chamber" (Coetzee)   117:74,
    90, 98

"Into the Dusk-Charged Air" (Ashbery)   77:57,
    69

"Into the Green Night" (Faust)   8:215

Into the Music (Morrison)   21:238

"Into the Night" (Carroll)
    See "When the City Drops"

Into the Night (Woolrich)   77:405

"Into the Night Life" (Miller)   84:250

"Into the Salient" (Blunden)   56:30

Into the Slave Nebula (Brunner)   8:111

"Into the Stone" (Dickey)   7:79, 83; 109:236,
    244, 265

"Into the Tree" (Milosz)   82:300

Into the Valley: A Skirmish of the Marines
    (Hersey)   40:226; 81:332, 334-35;
    97:297, 301, 303-04, 310

"Into the Wood" (Aickman)   57:6-7

Into Their Labours (Berger)   19:41

Into Your Tent I'll Creep (De Vries)   2:114;
    3:125; 7:76; 28:107

"Intoxication" (Pasternak)   63:313

"Intracom" (Le Guin)   45:213, 216-17

"Intra-Political: An Exercise in Political As-
    tronomy" (Avison)   97:76, 79, 91, 109,
    127

"Între doua nopti" ("Between Two Nights")
    (Arghezi)   80:6

"The Intrinsic Study of Literature" (Wellek)
    28:442

Introducción a los vasos órficos (Lezama Lima)
    4:288

*Introducing David Jones: A Selection of His
    Writings* (Jones)   42:238, 241

Introducing Eavan Boland (Boland)   40:97-9;
    113:69, 81

Introducing Shirley Braverman (Wolitzer)
    17:562

"Introduction (Queens of the Universe)"
    (Sanchez)   116:299

An Introduction to English Literature (Borges)
    9:117

"Introduction to History" (Galeano)   72:130

Introduction to Metaphysics (Heidegger)
    24:270

Introduction to Objectivist Epistemology (Rand)
    30:304

"Introduction to Poe and Performance"
    (Berkoff)   56:15

"Introduction to the 'Collected Plays'" (Miller)
    47:250-51

An Introduction to the Metaphysical Poets
    (Beer)   58:33

Introduction to the New Existentialism (Wil-
    son)   14:586

"Introduction to the Structural Analysis of
    Narrative" (Barthes)   83:80

"Introduction to the Twentieth Century"
    (Dunn)   36:155

"The Intruder" (Borges)
    See "La intrusa"

"The Intruder" (Dixon)   52:98

"The Intruder" (Dubus)   97:234, 237

"The Intruder" (Fisher)   25:157

"The Intruder" (Kizer)   80:172, 182

Intruder in the Dust (Faulkner)   3:149, 156-
    57; 14:179-80; 28:143; 52:139

"Intruders" (Abe)   81:294, 296-97

The Intruders (Garner)   13:236

"L'intrus" (Theriault)   79:408

"La intrusa" ("The Intruder") (Borges)   1:39;
    2:77; 6:88; 44:364; 48:34; 83:186, 188

Intrusion (Maugham)   93:244

Intrusions (Aickman)   57:3

"Intuition" (Lennon)   35:266

The Intuitive Journey and Other Works (Edson)
    13:190

"The Inundation" (Dickey)   7:79

"The Invaders" (Campbell)   32:76, 78, 80

"The Invaders" (Winters)   32:469

The Invaders (Plomer)   4:406

"Invaders from the Infinite" (Campbell)
    32:72-3

The Invaders Plan (Hubbard)   43:206-07

The Invading Asteroid (Wellman)   49:391

"The Invalid" (Merwin)   8:390

"Invalid, Convalescing" (Raine)   103:179

The Invasion (Adamov)
    See *L'invasion*

L'invasion (*The Invasion*) (Adamov)   4:5;
    25:12-15, 18-20

The Invasion (Leonov)
    See *Nashestvie*

*The Invasion: A Narrative of Events concern-
    ing the Johnston Family of St. Mary's*
    (Lewis)   41:251-52, 259, 261-62

Invasion Earth (Harrison)   42:207

"Invasion Exercise on the Poultry Farm"
    (Betjeman)   43:34

"Invasion Footnote" (Ellison)   42:131

Invasion from Aldebaran (Lem)   40:290

The Invasion of Canada, 1812-1813 (Berton)
    104:41-4, 59

"The Invasion of the Airline Stewardesses"

(Ritter)　**52**:355

Invasion of the Space Invaders: An Addict's Guide (Amis)　**38**:16

"Invective against Denise, a Witch" (Hecht)　**19**:208

La invención de Morel (The Invention of Morel, and Other Stories (from "La trama celeste")) (Bioy Casares)　**4**:63; **8**:94; **13**:84-5, 87; **88**:59-62, 64-5, 73, 75-7, 82, 84-7, 89, 91-3

Inventing the Flat Earth: Columbus and Modern Historians　**70**:341, 344

"L'invention" (Carrier)　**78**:58

The Invention (Soyinka)　**14**:505

"Invention for Shelagh" (Rule)　**27**:420

"The Invention of Comics" (Baraka)　**3**:35

The Invention of Morel, and Other Stories (from "La trama celeste") (Bioy Casares)
See *La invención de Morel*

The Invention of Poetry (Quarrington)　**65**:203

"The Invention of Robert Herendeen" (Millhauser)　**109**:158-59, 161

The Invention of Solitude (Auster)　**47**:10-12

"The Invention of the Telephone" (Klappert)　**57**:258

The Invention of the World (Hodgins)　**23**:228-36

The Inventor (Lind)　**82**:143-44

"The Inventor of Franglais?" (Ewart)　**46**:153

"Inventory" (Eich)
See "Inventur"

The Inventory (Josipovici)　**43**:213-14, 218, 227-28

"The Inventory of Fontana Bella" (Williams)　**5**:502

"Inventur" ("Inventory") (Eich)　**15**:204

"The Inverted Forest" (Salinger)　**12**:498, 514

Investigating Psychics: Five Life Histories (Kettelkamp)　**12**:307-08

Investigating UFO's (Kettelkamp)　**12**:306

The Investigation (Lem)　**8**:344; **15**:327; **40**:290

The Investigation (Weiss)
See *Die Ermittlung: Oratorium in Elf Gesëngen*

Investigative Poetry (Sanders)　**53**:309

"The Investigator" (Hinde)　**6**:239

"Investigator" (Waddington)　**28**:437

"The Investor" (Friedman)　**56**:97

"Invictus" (Lattimore)　**3**:277

"The Invincible" (Livesay)　**79**:342

The Invincible (Lem)　**8**:343-44; **15**:328; **40**:296

An Invincible Memory (Ribeiro)
See *Vivo o povo brasileiro*

"The Invincible Slave-Owners" (Dinesen)　**29**:159; **95**:35, 42

"Invischiato" (Moravia)　**11**:382

"Invisibility in Academe" (Rich)　**73**:322

"The Invisible Arch of Viñales" (Lezama Lima)
See "Arco invisible de Viñales"

Invisible Cities (Calvino)
See *Le città invisibili*

The Invisible Knight (Calvino)
See *Il cavaliere inesistente*

"The Invisible Man" (Phillips)　**28**:362-63

Invisible Man (Ellison)　**1**:93-5; **3**:141-46; **11**:179-81, 184; **54**:106-48; **86**:318-26, 328-29; **114**:85, 88-9, 91-3, 95, 98-9, 101-05, 107-08, 111-12, 114-15, 117, 124-27, 131-38

"Invisible Mending" (Morrissy)　**99**:78

Invisible Mending (Busch)　**47**:59-61

The Invisible Musician (Young Bear)　**94**:371-

73, 376

The Invisible One (Lagerkvist)
See *Den osynlige*

Invisible presencia (Alonso)　**14**:23

The Invisible Pyramid (Eiseley)　**7**:91

The Invisible River (Neruda)
See *El rio invisible*

"Invisible Sun" (Police, The)　**26**:365

Invisible Threads (Yevtushenko)　**26**:468

"The Invisible Woman" (Morgan)　**2**:295

Invisible Woman: New and Selected Poems, 1970-1982 (Oates)　**33**:292, 294; **108**:348

The Invisible Writing (Koestler)　**15**:312; **33**:235

"An Invitation" (Gunn)　**81**:178, 182, 187

Invitation à un concert officiel et autres récits (Kadare)　**52**:261

L'invitation au château (Ring round the Moon: A Charade with Music) (Anouilh)　**1**:7-8; **3**:11; **13**:17, 22; **40**:51, 54, 60; **50**:278-80

"L'invitation au voyage" (Wilbur)　**14**:577

Invitation to a Beheading (Nabokov)　**1**:239, 242-43; **2**:302; **3**:353; **8**:415, 418; **15**:393, 395-97; **46**:292; **64**:350-51

"Invitation to Juno" (Empson)　**19**:155

"Invitation to the Dance" (Hughes)　**9**:285

Invitation to the Waltz (Lehmann)　**5**:235, 239

"Invitations" (Shields)　**113**:425

"Invite" (O'Hara)　**42**:320-21

L'invitée (She Came to Stay) (Beauvoir)　**1**:19; **2**:43; **8**:58; **31**:34, 40-2; **44**:343, 350; **71**:48-9, 51-6, 72, 85

Invocaciones (Invocations) (Cernuda)　**54**:41-2, 47, 58, 60

"The Invocation" (Campbell)　**42**:89

"The Invocation" ("Pygmalion") (Hope)　**51**:213, 215-16

"Invocation" (Jeffers)　**54**:235

"Invocation" (Levertov)　**66**:236

"Invocation" (McAuley)　**45**:249-50

"Invocation" (Musgrave)　**13**:401

"Invocation" (Raine)　**45**:330, 341

"Invocation" (Sarton)　**91**:244

"Invocation" (Sitwell)　**67**:320

"Invocation and Ritual Dance of the Young Pumpkin" (Zappa)　**17**:585

"Invocation to Kali" (Sarton)　**91**:254

"Invocation to the Guardian" (Montague)　**46**:277

"Invocation to the Social Muse" (MacLeish)　**8**:363; **68**:282, 290-92

Invocations (Cernuda)
See *Invocaciones*

"Invulnerable" (Ellison)　**42**:131

"Inward Bound" (MacCaig)　**36**:284-85

The Inward Eye (MacCaig)　**36**:284

"The Inward Generation" (de Man)　**55**:414

Inwards to the Sun (Shapcott)　**38**:399

"Io" (Broumas)　**73**:6

Io e lui (Two: A Phallic Novel; The Two of Us) (Moravia)　**2**:293-94; **7**:242; **18**:347; **46**:284-85

"Ion Ion" (Arghezi)　**80**:7

"Iona: The Graves of the Kings" (Jeffers)　**54**:246

Ionesco the Great (Jacobsen)　**102**:227

"Iork" (Brodsky)
See "York: In Memoriam W. H. Auden"

"Iota" (Tolson)　**105**:255

IOU's (Sebestyen)　**30**:349-51

"Iowa" (Klappert)　**57**:258

The Iowa Baseball Confederacy (Kinsella)　**43**:257-60

The Ipcress File (Deighton)　**4**:119; **7**:75-6; **22**:113-14; **46**:125, 128-29

"Iphigenia" (Dodson)　**79**:194

Iphigenia at Aulis (Rexroth)　**11**:472; **22**:345

"Ipomoea" (Gluck)　**81**:164

"Irani Restaurant Instructions" (Ezekiel)　**61**:95

"Ireland" (Muldoon)　**32**:320; **72**:266, 268

"Ireland, 1972" (Durcan)　**43**:116

Ireland and the English Crisis (Paulin)　**37**:355-56

Irene; o, El tesoro (Irene; or, The Treasure) (Buero Vallejo)　**15**:102

Irene; or, The Treasure (Buero Vallejo)
See *Irene; o, El tesoro*

Irisches Tagebuch (Irish Journal) (Boell)　**2**:68; **3**:75; **9**:109; **15**:70-2; **27**:60

The Irish (O'Faolain)　**2**:275; **70**:317-18

"An Irish Childhood in England: 1951" (Boland)　**67**:46; **113**:86, 92-93, 106, 108, 125

Irish Elegies (Colum)　**28**:91

An Irish Faustus (Durrell)　**4**:145; **13**:184

"The Irish Genius" (Allen)　**52**:35

"Irish Hierarchy Bans Colour Photography" (Durcan)　**43**:114-16

Irish Journal (Boell)
See *Irisches Tagebuch*

Irish Miles (O'Connor)　**14**:397

The Irish Novelists, 1800-1850 (Flanagan)　**25**:163

"Irish Revel" (O'Brien)　**5**:313; **36**:338; **116**:207-11, 222

The Irish Signorina (O'Faolain)　**47**:328-29, 331; **108**:407

Irish Sketch Book (Behan)　**79**:30-1

"The Irish Unionist's Farewell to Greta Hellstrom in 1922" (Betjeman)　**43**:34, 44, 52

Irma La Douce (Wilder)　**20**:460-61

"Iron" (Levi)　**37**:226-27

"The Iron Age"　**75**:79

Iron and Man (Lagerkvist)
See *Järn och människor*

The Iron Breadboard (Baxter)　**14**:60

Iron Cage (Norton)　**12**:465, 470

The Iron Cross (Rice)　**7**:364

"The Iron Door" (Pratt)　**19**:378, 385-86

The Iron Dream (Spinrad)　**46**:386-87

The Iron Duke (Tunis)　**12**:593

Iron Earth, Copper Sky (Kemal)
See *Yer demir gök bakir*

The Iron Giant (Hughes)　**4**:236

"Iron Horse" (Ginsberg)　**36**:187, 193, 196

The Iron Horse (Ford)　**16**:302

Iron John: A Book About Men (Bly)　**70**:420-21, 424-26, 428-30, 435-61

"The Iron Lady" (Ochs)　**17**:331

"Iron Landscapes" (Gunn)　**18**:199

"Iron Larks" (Gilliatt)　**13**:237

"The Iron Lung" (Plumly)　**33**:313

Iron Mountain (Clark)　**12**:130

"Iron Palace" (Graves)　**45**:166

"Iron Staircase" (Yevtushenko)　**26**:467

"The Iron Thread" (Olsen)　**114**:237

"The Iron Throat" (Olsen)　**114**:221

"Iron Woman" (Rooke)　**25**:391

Ironweed (Kennedy)　**28**:205-06; **34**:206-11; **53**:191-97, 199-201

"Irony and Ironic Poetry" (Brooks)　**24**:104

"Irracionalismo y eficacia" (Cortazar)　**92**:154

Irrational Man: A Study in Existential Philosophy (Barrett)　**27**:16-17, 20

Irrefuhrung der Behörden (Becker)　**7**:27

"The Irrelevant" (Campbell)　**32**:74

"An Irrelevant Death" (Abe)   81:297-98
"The Irresponsibles" (MacLeish)   68:292
"Irtnog" (White)   10:527
is 5 (Cummings)   12:154, 158, 161; 15:159-62; 68:26-7, 34-6, 45-7
"Is Fiction the Art of Lying?" (Vargas Llosa)   42:412
"Is It Far to Go?" (Day Lewis)   10:131
"Is It in My Head?" (Townshend)   17:532
"Is It Me?" (Townshend)   17:532
"Is It Really Important to Think?" (Foucault)   69:191-92
Is It Safe to Drink the Water? (Buchwald)   33:90
Is It Something I Said? (Pryor)   26:378
Is It the Sun, Philibert? (Carrier)
   See *Il est par là, le soleil*
"Is It True?" (Sexton)   6:494
"Is Literary Criticism Possible?" (Tate)   24:443
"Is/Not" (Atwood)   13:44; 84:65
"Is Paris Burning?" (hooks)   94:152
"Is Phoenix Jackson's Grandson Really Dead?" (Welty)   105:333
"Is Poetry an American Art?" (Shapiro)   8:486; 53:328
Is Summer This Bear (Kenny)   87:245-47
"Is That What You Are" (Merwin)   88:192
Is That You, Miss Blue? (Kerr)   12:298-99, 301; 35:250-51
"Is the Pope Capitalized?" (Blount)   38:46
Is There a Case for Foreign Missions? (Buck)   7:32
"Is There No Love Can Link Us?" (Peake)   54:373, 375
"Is There No Way Out?" (Paz)
   See "¿No hay salida?"
"Is There Nowhere Else Where We Can Meet?" (Gordimer)   18:185
"Is This Love" (Marley)   17:270, 272
"Is This Useful? Is This Boring?" (Grayson)   38:211
"Is Verse a Dying Technique?" (Wilson)   24:472
"Is Wisdom a Lot of Language?" (Sandburg)   35:356
"Is You or Is You Ain't, Goober Man?" (Perelman)   23:336
"Isaac" (Michaels)   25:316
Isaac Asimov, The Complete Stories: Volume 2 (Asimov)   76:319
Isaac Asimov's Book of Facts (Asimov)   26:51
"Isaac Starbuck" (Sillitoe)   57:388-89
"Isaak Babel" (Dubie)   36:130
Isabel si apele diavolului (Eliade)   19:145
Isabella, tre caravelle e un cacciaballe (Fo)   109:113, 115
"Isba Song" (McGuckian)   48:278
"Ishmael, the Archer" (Colum)   28:91
"Ishmael's Dream" (Stern)   100:328
"Ishtar" (Wright)   53:419
"Isidor" (Simpson)   7:429
"Isis in Darkness" (Atwood)   84:96-7
"Isis Wanderer" (Raine)   45:332, 338
La isla (Goytisolo)   23:183
"La isla a mediodía" ("The Island at Noon") (Cortazar)   5:109; 34:333
"Isla en Manhattan" (Marques)   96:240-41
"La Isla III" ("The Island III") (Neruda)   62:334
Isla Negra: A Notebook (Neruda)
   See *Memorial de Isla Negra*
"Island" (Ezekiel)   61:105, 107
"The Island" (Forche)   83:211, 214
"The Island" (Honig)   33:211-12

"The Island" (Jarrell)   9:298
"The Island" (Longley)   29:296
"Island" (MacLeod)   56:200
"The Island" (Rukeyser)   27:408
"The Island" (Thomas)   6:530
The Island (Creeley)   2:105; 8:151-52; 36:122; 78:125, 128, 144
The Island (Fugard)   9:229-34; 14:191; 25:175; 40:197-98; 80:62-3, 65-6, 69, 70,74-5, 80, 82
Island (Huxley)   1:152; 3:255; 4:237-41, 243; 5:193-94; 8:303-04; 11:282, 284-88; 18:266-67; 35:238-40, 242-44; 79:309-10
"The Island at Noon" (Cortazar)
   See "La isla a mediodía"
An Island Called Moreau (Aldiss)   40:16
An Island Death (Yurick)   6:583-84
"The Island Dream" (Hesse)   3:248-49
Island Fling (Coward)
   See *South Sea Bubble*
"Island Funeral" (MacDiarmid)   4:309, 313; 11:333
"The Island III" (Neruda)
   See "La Isla III"
Island in the City: The World of Spanish Harlem (Wakefield)   7:502-03
Island in the Sky (Gann)   23:162
The Island of Crimea (Aksyonov)
   See *Ostrov Krym*
The Island of Horses (Dillon)   17:93, 95
"Island of Summer" (Warren)   10:520
Island of the Blue Dolphins (O'Dell)   30:267-71, 273-74, 276-77
The Island of the Mighty (Arden)   6:10
Island People (Dowell)   60:96-101, 105-06, 109
The Island Stallion (Farley)   17:116
"Island Storm" (Honig)   33:211, 215
"The Island Ven" (Berriault)   109:97
"The Islanders" (Booth)   23:74
"The Islands" (Atwood)   4:27
"The Islands" (H. D.)   73:121
"The Islands" (Hayden)   37:156
"Islands" (Merwin)   88:203
"Islands" (Walcott)   67:362
Islands (Brathwaite)   11:67
Islands in the Net (Sterling)   72:370-71, 373
Islands in the Sky (Clarke)   13:153
Islands in the Stream (Hemingway)   1:144; 3:237, 243; 6:229-30, 232; 8:285, 288; 10:269; 30:199; 39:430; 41:204, 206; 50:423; 80:148, 151
Islands in the Stream (White)   7:529
The Islands of Scotland (MacDiarmid)   4:309; 11:334
Islands of Space (Campbell)   32:73
The Islands of Unwisdom (Graves)   45:172
Íslandsklukkan (Laxness)   25:297
"The Isle of Aves" (Hope)   51:226
"Isle of Man Christmas 1967" (Kunene)   85:165
Isle of the Dead (Zelazny)   21:464, 470
Isle of the Sea Horse (Brinsmead)   21:28
Isma (Sarraute)   8:471; 31:381
"Ismael" (Chester)   49:55-6
"Ismene" (Ritsos)   13:488
Ismos (Gomez de la Serna)   9:238
Isn't It Romantic (Wasserstein)   32:440-43; 59:219-21, 223-24; 90:407-9, 412-15, 418-21, 425, 429-30, 431-33, 436
"Isn't She Lovely" (Wonder)   12:659, 662
L'isola di Arturo (*Arturo's Island*) (Morante)   47:275, 280-81, 283

"Isolated Incidents" (Mukherjee)   53:266, 268, 270
"Isolation" (Lennon)   35:262
"Isolationist" (Page)   7:291
"Isolt of Brittany" (*Exposition of the Orthodox Faith*) (Christie)   110:126
"Isomorphism" (L'Heureux)   52:273
"Ispoved" (Voznesensky)   15:554
"The Israeli Navy" (Bell)   8:66
The Issa Valley (Konwicki)
   See *Dolina Issy*
The Issa Valley (Milosz)
   See *Dolina Issy*
"L'issue" (Char)   14:128
"The Issue" (Grass)   49:139
"The Issues" (Olds)   39:187; 85:290
"Iswaran" (Narayan)   28:303
"It" (Olds)   85:295
"It" (Sturgeon)   39:361, 365-66
IT (King)   61:318-25, 329-37; 113:388-89, 391, 393
It (Mayne)   12:405-06
It Ain't All for Nothin' (Myers)   35:296-97
"It Ain't Me, Babe" (Dylan)   77:167, 173
It Ain't Me Babe (Robbins)   21:338
It All Adds Up (Amis)   101:83
"It Always Breaks Out" (Ellison)   114:100
It Catches My Heart in Its Hands: New and Selected Poems, 1955-1963 (Bukowski)   5:80-1; 41:64, 66-7; 108:110, 114
It Changed My Life: Writings on the Women's Movement (Friedan)   74:93-8
"It Fills You Up" (Morrison)   21:237
"It Had Wings" (Gurganus)   70:192, 194, 196
"It Happened in Broad Daylight" (Duerrenmatt)   102:60
It Happened One Night (Capra)   16:153-54, 157-60, 163
It Happens Tomorrow (Fo)   32:176
It Has No Choice (Bullins)   5:83
"It Is 12.20 in New York a Friday" (O'Hara)   13:423
"It Is a Living Coral" (Williams)   42:462
"It Is Dangerous to Read Newspapers" (Atwood)   15:38
"It is my own bones, Creeping" (Moure)   88:229
"It Is Only Me" (Moure)   88:217
It Is the Law (Rice)   7:364; 49:302
"It Is the Season" (Jacobsen)   48:193
"It Is This Way with Men" (Williams)   33:442
It Is Time, Lord (Chappell)   40:137; 78:97
"It Is Very Distinct at the Ballpark" (Loewinsohn)   52:284
"It Is Wonderful" (Ignatow)   40:261
It Is Written (Duerrenmatt)   102:56, 58, 60
It Is Written (Durrenmatt)
   See *Es steht geschrieben*
"It Isn't the Heat, It's the Cupidity" (Perelman)   49:265
It Looked Like for Ever (Harris)   19:205
"It May Not Always Be So: And I Say" (Cummings)   68:30, 43-4
"It Must Be Sophisticated" (Ashbery)   77:79
"It Spoke of Exactly the Things" (Hannah)   38:233-34; 90:138
"It Sure Is Cold Here at Night" (Freeman)   55:57
"It Sure Was" ("Love") (Kristofferson)   26:268
It Takes a Long Time to Become Young (Kanin)   22:232
"It Takes a Lot to Laugh, It Takes a Train to Cry" (Dylan)   77:175

"It Takes a Thief" (Miller)   30:262
"It Takes Two to Tango, but Only One to Squirm" (Perelman)   15:418
"It Used to Be Green Once" (Grace)   56:117
It Was (Zukofsky)   4:599
"It Was a Funky Deal" (Knight)   40:279, 287
"It Was Beginning Winter" (Roethke)   46:362
"It Was Nothing—Really!" (Sturgeon)   22:411
"It Was the Grape Autumn" (Neruda)   1:247
"It Wasn't Me" (Berry)   46:74
"It Will Be Darkness Soon" (Salinas)   90:332
"It Won't Be Long" (Lennon and McCartney)   35:274
Italian American Reconciliation (Shanley)   75:323-25, 332
The Italian Element in Milton's Verse (Prince)   22:339
"Italian Extravaganza" (Corso)   11:123
Italian Folktales (Calvino)
   See *Fiabe Italiene*
The Italian Girl (Murdoch)   1:236; 3:347; 6:348-49; 8:406; 31:288-89
The Italian Lesson (Elliott)   47:115
"Italian Morning" (Bogan)   46:79-80, 85, 90
"Italian Postcards" (Urquhart)   90:386
The Italian Straw Hat (Clair)   20:59, 63, 70
An Italian Straw Hat (Cooney)   62:145
An Italian Visit (Day Lewis)   6:127; 10:128
The Italian Wife (Humphreys)   47:179-80, 188
Italianamerican (Scorsese)   20:326, 329, 333-34; 89:254
Itan no passporto (*Pagan Passport*) (Abe)   81:289
"Itansha no kanashimi" ("The Sorrow of the Pagan Outcast") (Tanizaki)   28:415
"The Itching Bear" (Edmonds)   35:156
An Item from the Late News (Astley)   41:48-9
"Items of a Night" (Grigson)   7:136
"Ithaka" (Borges)   6:93
"Ithaka" (Davenport)   14:142
It's a Battlefield (Greene)   6:219; 18:194; 72:148-49, 152-53, 158, 160-61
"It's a Dirty World" (Bukowski)   41:73
"It's a Good Night" (Robinson)   21:348
"It's a New Day" (Sanchez)   116:301-02
It's a New Day: Poems for Young Brothas and Sistuhs (Sanchez)   116:301, 309
"It's a Pity You Weren't With Us" (Aksyonov)   101:18
It's a Slippery Slope (Gray)   112:135-36
"It's a Woman's World" (Boland)   40:100; 113:79, 90, 109, 124
It's a Wonderful Life (Capra)   16:156, 159-60, 162, 164-65
"It's All Over Now, Baby Blue" (Dylan)   77:168, 173-74, 178
It's All True (Welles)   80:413-16
It's Beautiful (Sarraute)
   See *C'est beau*
It's Called the Sugar Plum (Horovitz)   56:147-48, 150
"Its Great Emptiness" (Pinsky)   38:361
"It's Great to Be Back" (Heinlein)   26:165
"It's Growing" (Robinson)   21:346
"It's Half an Hour Later Before" (Ammons)   108:12
"It's Hard to Be a Saint in the City" (Springsteen)   7:487-88
"It's Hard to Dislike Ewart" (Ewart)   46:147
Its Image on the Mirror (Gallant)   18:172
"It's Just Another Day in Big Bear City, California" (Beattie)   63:3, 9, 11-12
It's Like This, Cat (Neville)   12:449-53

"Its Many Fragments" (Pinsky)   38:361
It's Me, Eddie (Coles)
   See *Eto ja—Edichka*
It's My Way! (Sainte-Marie)   17:431
It's Never Over (Callaghan)   14:100, 102; 41:89
"It's Nice to Think of Tears" (Stern)   40:413, 415
"It's Not for Me to Understand" (Nelson)   17:305
It's Not the End of the World (Blume)   12:44; 30:20, 22
"It's Not True" (Townshend)   17:530
It's Not What You Expect (Klein)   30:237
"It's O.K." (Wilson)   12:648
It's OK If You Don't Love Me (Klein)   30:240
"It's Only Culture" (Epstein)   39:468
It's Only a Play (McNally)   41:292-93; 91:159
"It's Only Rock 'n Roll" (Jagger and Richard)   17:232-34, 236, 238
It's Over There, the Sun (Carrier)
   See *Il est par là, le soleil*
"It's So Hard" (Lennon)   35:263-64
"It's Still Rock 'n' Roll to Me" (Joel)   26:220-21
It's Time, My Friend, It's Time (*Pora, moi drug, pora*) (Aksyonov)   22:26; 101:3-4, 6, 10-11, 17, 29
"It's Too Dark in Here" (Berry)   17:51
It's Too Late to Stop Now (Morrison)   21:235
It's Trad Dad! (Lester)   20:220
"It's Warm under Your Thumb" (Laughlin)   49:222
"It's Worth Believin'" (Lightfoot)   26:279
Itsuka (Kogawa)   78:194-95
"Iva" ("The Willow") (Akhmatova)   25:24
"Ivan Meets G.I. Joe" (Clash)   30:48
Ivan the Terrible and Ivan the Fool (Yevtushenko)   26:468
Ivanca (*There Are Facts*)   75:65-6
The Ivankiad; or, The Tale of the Writer Voinovich's Installation in His New Apartment (Voinovich)
   See *Ivan'kiada: Ili rasskaz o vselenii pisatelia Voinovicha v novuiu kvartiru*
Ivan'kiada: Ili rasskaz o vselenii pisatelia Voinovicha v novuiu kvartiru (*The Ivankiad; or, The Tale of the Writer Voinovich's Installation in His New Apartment*) (Voinovich)   10:507-08; 49:373-75, 377, 383-84
"Ivanovo Calicoes" (Yevtushenko)   26:468
Ivanovo Detstvo (*The Childhod of Ivan; Ivan's Childhood; My Name Is Ivan*) (Tarkovsky)   75:369-72, 374, 382, 385, 388, 397-98, 402, 407
Ivan's Childhood (Tarkovsky)
   See *Ivanovo Detstvo*
"Ivbie" (Clark)   38:116, 125, 127-28
I've Always Been Crazy (Jennings)   21:204-05
I've Been a Woman (Sanchez)   116:272, 274-75, 281-82, 293, 298, 300, 302, 309-10, 315, 319
"I've Been Dead 400 Years" (Cliff)   21:63
I've Got the Blues (Odets)   28:332
"I've Got the Drimoleague Blues" (Durcan)   43:114
"I've Got Time" (Seger)   35:379-80
"I've Got to Tell You" (O'Hara)
   See "Poem"
"I've Had Enough" (McCartney)   35:285-86
"I've Had Her" (Ochs)   17:331, 334
"I've Lost My Pal" (Sargeson)   31:363-64
"I've Loved These Days" (Joel)   26:215, 219-

20
I've Tasted My Blood: Poems, 1956-1968 (Acorn)   15:10
Ivona, Princess of Burgundia (Gombrowicz)
   See *Iwona; Ksiezniczka Burgunda*
"Ivory, Apes, and People" (Thurber)   5:434
The Ivory Grin (Macdonald)   14:334; 41:265, 269, 271
The Ivory Swing (Hospital)   42:218-21
"The Ivory Tower" (Ashbery)   25:54; 77:61
"Ivy Gripped the Steps" (Bowen)   15:77
Ivy Gripped the Steps (Bowen)
   See *The Demon Lover and Other Stories*
Ivy: The Life of I. Compton-Burnett (Spurling)   34:494, 499, 501
The Ivy Tree (Stewart)   7:467; 35:390, 392
Iwona; Ksiezniczka Burgunda (*Ivona, Princess of Burgundia; Yvonne, Princess of Burgundy*) (Gombrowicz)   11:239; 49:121-26, 128
Ixion's Wheel (Gustafson)   36:213, 216, 218
"Iz okna samoloyta" (Voznesensky)   15:555
Iz shesti knig (Akhmatova)   25:24
Izlet u Rusiju (*A Trip to Russia*) (Krleza)   114:168, 177
"The Izu Dancer" (Kawabata)
   See "Izu no Odoriko"
"Izu no Odoriko" ("The Izu Dancer") (Kawabata)   107:100, 104, 106, 109
Izu no Odoriko (Kawabata)   107:104-05, 108, 119
"J" (Merrill)   8:384, 387
J. B. (Kazan)   63:234
J. B. (MacLeish)   3:310; 8:362; 14:336
"The J Car" (Gunn)   81:179
"J. P. Donleavy's Dublin" (Mahon)   27:286
J. P. Donleavy's Ireland: In All Her Sins and Some of Her Graces (Donleavy)   45:127-29
J. P. Morgan Saves the Nation   99:160, 168, 171, 180, 186
J R (Gaddis)   6:194-95; 8:226-30; 10:210-14; 19:186-87; 43:156-62; 86:147-49, 151, 153, 155-58, 162-64, 166
J. S. Manifold: An Introduction to the Man and His Work (Hall)   51:174
J'abats mon jeu (*I Lay My Cards on the Table*) (Aragon)   3:14; 22:38
Jablko z klína (*An Apple from One's Lap; An Apple From the Lap; An Apple from Your Lap*) (Seifert)   34:256; 44:425; 93:306, 318, 341
The Jacaranda Tree (Bates)   46:64-5
J'accuse; the Dark Side of Nice (Greene)   27:177; 70:294
Jack (Sinclair)   14:488
"Jack and Jill" (Thesen)   56:414, 418-19
Jack and Jill (De Marinis)   54:98-9
Jack and the Beanstalk (Hunter)   31:228
The Jack and the Joker (Ringwood)   48:330, 333, 335-39
"Jack Frost" (Jacobsen)   102:241
Jack Gelber's New Play: Rehearsal (Gelber)   14:193-94
Jack Holborn (Garfield)   12:215-17, 220, 224-28, 231, 235-36, 239
Jack in the Box (Kotzwinkle)   35:255-56
Jack London, Hemingway, and the Constitution (Doctorow)   113:174, 176
"The Jack of Diamonds" (Leonov)   92:237
"The Jack of Hearts" (Ferlinghetti)   111:65
Jack of Shadows (Zelazny)   21:466, 473
Jack; or, The Submission (Ionesco)

See *Jacques; ou, La soumission*
"The Jack Randa Hotel" (Munro) **95**:319, 325
"Jack Schmidt, Arts Administrator" (Keillor) **40**:273
Jack Straw (Maugham) **11**:367-68; **15**:366
"Jack Stringer" (Nowlan) **15**:398
"Jack the Idiot Dunce" (Davies) **21**:101
Jack the Ripper (West)
   See *Jack the Ripper*
"Jack U Off" (Prince) **35**:324-26
Jack Winter's Dream (Baxter) **14**:64
"The Jackal-Headed Cowboy from Ra" (Reed) **13**:478
"The Jackdaw" (Hamburger) **5**:159
"The Jackdaw" (Hesse) **25**:259, 261-62
"A Jackeen Cries at the Loss of the Blaskets" (Behan) **79**:37, 51
"Jackhammer" (Dumas) **62**:155
Jacklight (Erdrich) **54**:164-65
Jacko the Great Intruder (Keneally) **117**:241-44
Jackpot: The Short Stories of Erskine Caldwell (Caldwell) **14**:96
"Jack's Straw Castle" (Gunn) **18**:201; **32**:209, 211
Jack's Straw Castle, and Other Poems (Gunn) **18**:199, 201-02; **32**:209, 211-12; **81**:178
Jackson Browne (Browne) **21**:34-5, 38
Jackson Pollock (Friedman) **7**:108
Jackson Pollock (O'Hara) **78**:375
"The Jackstraws" (Fisher) **87**:131
"Jacob and the Angel" (Auden) **4**:35
Jacob Have I Loved (Paterson) **30**:283-85, 287-90
"Jacob: The Faith-Healing Priest" (Head) **67**:98
Jacob the Liar (Becker)
   See *Jakob der Lügner*
Jacob Two-Two Meets the Hooded Fang (Richler) **5**:378
"Jacob y el otro" (Onetti) **10**:376
Jacobowsky and the Colonel (Behrman) **40**:88
The Jacob's Ladder (Levertov) **2**:242; **5**:246; **8**:345; **15**:336-37; **66**:235, 237-39, 253
"Jacob's Voice" (Celan)
   See "Jakobs Stimme"
Jacob's Wake (Cook) **58**:154-55, 157-58
"Jacqueline Ess: Her Will and Testament" (Barker) **52**:51
"Jacquemard et Julia" (Char) **9**:165
Jacques and His Master (Kundera)
   See *Jacques et son maitre: Hommage à Denis Diderot*
Jacques et son maitre: Hommage à Denis Diderot (Jacques and His Master)(Kundera) **68**:235, 240
Jacques; ou, La soumission (Jack; or, The Submission) (Ionesco) **4**:250-51; **6**:247-48, 253; **11**:290; **41**:222-23, 225, 230; **86**:332, 334, 340
"Jael's Part" (Avison) **97**:91
Die Jagdgesellschaft (The Hunting Party) (Bernhard) **32**:24-5; **61**:27-8
"Jäger des Spotts" (Lenz) **27**:245
"Jäger, mein Sternbild" (Sachs) **98**:330
The Jagged Orbit (Brunner) **8**:105-07, 110; **10**:78
Jagua Nana (Ekwensi) **4**:151-52
"The Jaguar" (Hughes) **14**:270
The Jaguar Smile (Rushdie) **59**:438
"Jah Live" (Marley) **17**:268
Jahrestage: Aus dem Leben von Gesine

Cresspahl (Days of the Year) (Johnson) **40**:263
Jahrestage: Aus dem Leben von Gesine Cresspahl III (Anniversaries: From the Life of Gesine Cresspahl) (Johnson) **40**:269-70
Jahrestage: Aus dem Leben von Gesine Cresspahl IV (Anniversaries: From the Life of Gesine Cresspahl) (Johnson) **5**:201-02; **10**:284; **15**:307; **40**:263, 266-70
The Jail Diary of Albie Sachs (Edgar) **42**:114, 116, 120
"Jail Guitar Doors" (Clash) **30**:44-5
"Jail Poems" (Kaufman) **49**:204
Jailbird (Vonnegut) **22**:446-47, 449-51; **40**:441, 444-46; **111**:354-55, 358, 360-61
"The Jailer" (Plath) **9**:426; **14**:424; **51**:340, 345; **111**:166
"Jailer's Son" (Ferron) **94**:126
"Jailhouse Blues" (Guthrie) **35**:186
"The Jain Bird Hospital in Delhi" (Meredith) **55**:192
Jak daleko stad, jak blisko (How Far It Is From Here, How Near; So Far and Yet So Near) (Konwicki) **117**:257, 282-83
Jake and the Kid (Mitchell) **25**:322-23, 327-28
"Jake Bluffstein and Adolf Hitler" (Faust) **8**:215
Jake's Thing (Amis) **13**:14-15; **44**:135, 140, 144
Jake's Women (Simon) **70**:238-40
Jakob der Lügner (Jacob the Liar) (Becker) **7**:27
Jakobowsky and the Colonel (Kazan) **63**:225
"Jakobs Stimme" ("Jacob's Voice") (Celan) **53**:77
"À Jakobson" (Lacan) **75**:304
Jalna (de la Roche) **14**:148-49
La jalousie (Jealousy) (Robbe-Grillet) **1**:286-90; **2**:374-75; **4**:446-50; **6**:464-66, 468; **10**:437; **14**:455-62; **43**:360, 364-66
Jalsaghar (The Music Room) (Ray) **16**:476-77, 479-80, 482-83, 487, 491-93; **76**:360, 362, 367
Jamaica (Abrahams) **4**:2
"Jamaica Elevate" (Bennett) **28**:28
Jamaica Inn (du Maurier) **11**:162; **59**:280, 282-87
Jamaica Labrish (Bennett) **28**:27, 29-30
"Jamaica, Say You Will" (Browne) **21**:34-5
"Jambalaya" (Berry) **17**:52
"James" (Joel) **26**:215
"James" (Simon) **26**:413
James and the Giant Peach (Dahl) **79**:177, 182
The James Bond Dossier (Amis) **2**:7, 10
"James Dean" (Ai) **69**:18
The James Dean Story (Altman) **16**:19, 41; **116**:11-12
James Joyce (Ellmann) **50**:305-06
"James Joyce, Marcel Duchamp, Erik Satie: An Alphabet" (Cage) **41**:85-6
The James Joyce Murder (Heilbrun) **25**:252
"Jamesie" (Powers) **1**:282
Jamie Is My Heart's Desire (Chester) **49**:53-4, 56, 58
Jamie on a Flying Visit (Frayn) **7**:107
"Jamini Roy" (Ezekiel) **61**:91, 100
Jammin' the Greek Scene (Williams) **13**:600
"Jamming" (Marley) **17**:272
"Jamming with the Band at the VFW" (Bot-

toms) **53**:29-30
Jamming with the Band at the VFW (Bottoms) **53**:31
"Jamrag" (Lennon) **35**:265
"Jan. 6th" (Musgrave) **13**:400
Jan. 31 (Goldbarth) **5**:145; **38**:203
"Jan Godfrey" (Frame) **96**:185
Jana Aranya (The Middleman) (Ray) **16**:495; **76**:358, 362, 367
Jane (Behrman) **40**:87-8
Jane and Prudence (Pym) **37**:368, 372-73, 379; **111**:229, 234, 243-48, 263-66, 269, 274, 279-81, 283-85
"Jane at Two" (Nowlan) **15**:399
Jane Eyre (Welles) **80**:379
Jane Franklin's Obsession (Berton) **104**:61
The Jane Poems (Spivack) **6**:520-21
"Jane, Steve, and Sarah" (Willingham) **51**:403
"Jane Witnesses the Destruction of the World" (Spivack) **6**:520
"Janek" ("The Little John") (Dabrowska) **15**:165
"Janet Waking" (Ransom) **4**:431
"Janice" (Cohen) **19**:113
"Janie Crawford" (Walker) **103**:371
"Janie Jones" (Clash) **30**:44-5
Janis Ian (Ian) **21**:184, 188
"Januaries" (Bishop) **13**:89
"January" (Barthelme) **59**:250
"January" (Chappell) **40**:142
"January" (Hass) **99**:140
"January 1918" (Pasternak) **63**:280
"January First" (Paz) **65**:187
"January Fugue" (Shapcott) **38**:404
The January Man (Shanley) **75**:325-27, 330
"January Oranges" (Brosman) **9**:135
"Janus" (Beattie) **63**:14, 16, 18
Janus (Barker) **48**:10
Janus: A Summing Up (Koestler) **33**:242
"Japan" (Hecht) **8**:266-67; **19**:207
Japan and Her Ghosts (Gironella) **11**:237
Japan, the Beautiful, and Myself (Kawabata) **107**:108
Japan, the Beautiful, and Myself (Kawabata) **107**:108
The Japanese Corpse (van de Wetering) **47**:406-07, 410
"Japanese in Warsaw" (Endo) **99**:301
"Japanese Jottings" (Aksyonov) **101**:17
"Japanese Movies" (Thesen) **56**:417
The Japanese of the Menam River (Endo) **99**:285
"Japanese Papers" (Sarton) **49**:307
"Japanese Print" (Clarke) **6**:112; **9**:168
"Japanese River Tales" (Hughes) **37**:179
"Japanese Tea Garden Golden Gate Park in Spring" (Whalen) **6**:566
El jardin de al lado (The Garden Next Door) (Donoso) **32**:161; **99**:218, 220, 222-28, 233-38, 242-43, 245-49, 252-54, 274-77
"Jardín de invierno" ("Winter Garden") (Neruda) **7**:261; **28**:310; **62**:333-35
"El jardín de senderos que se bifurcan" ("The Garden of Forking Paths") (Borges) **1**:39; **3**:80; **6**:93; **8**:102; **19**:54; **44**:362-63, 370; **48**:45-6; **83**:167
El jardin de senderos que se bifurcan (The Garden of Forking Paths) (Borges) **48**:43; **83**:163-64
Le jardin des délices (The Garden of Earthly Delights) (Arrabal) **18**:21-2; **58**:17
Le jardin des délices (The Garden of Delights)

(Carrier) **78**:65, 67-72, 79, 82
"Jardin du Palais Royal" (Gascoyne) **45**:159
Les jardins et les fleuves (Audiberti) **38**:33
The Jargoon Pard (Norton) **12**:469
Järn och människor (Iron and Man) (Lagerkvist) **54**:286
Jaro sbohem (Farewell, Spring!; Goodbye Spring) (Seifert) **93**:306, 332, 341
"Jasmine" (Mukherjee) **53**:270-71; **115**:364-65, 367-69
Jasmine (Mukherjee) **115**:365, 370, 373-75, 377-79, 386, 390-91
"Jason" (MacLeish) **8**:359
Jason and Medeia (Gardner) **3**:184-87; **5**:131, 133-35; **7**:115; **8**:236-238; **10**:219; **28**:167
Jason and the Money Tree (Levitin) **17**:265
Jason's Quest (Laurence) **3**:281; **50**:321
Jaune le soleil (Duras) **68**:94
"Jauregg" (Bernhard) **32**:27
"Javelina" (Harjo) **83**:274
"Javni" (Rao) **56**:312
Jawbreakers (Acorn) **15**:10
"Jaws" (Barthelme) **59**:251
Jaws (Benchley) **4**:53-4; **8**:82
Jaws (Spielberg) **20**:359-61, 363-66
Jazz (Morrison) **81**:241-48, 250, 252-62, 268, 270, 272
"A Jazz Age Clerk" (Farrell) **66**:131
Jazz Country (Hentoff) **26**:182, 184
"Jazz Fantazia" (Sandburg) **35**:358
Jazz Is (Hentoff) **26**:185
The Jazz Singer (Diamond) **30**:113-14
"Jazzonia" (Hughes) **108**:296
Jazz-set (Milner) **56**:225
Je l'entends encore (Cayrol) **11**:108
Je me souviens (I Remember) (Perec) **116**:241
"Je suis perdu" (Taylor) **18**:526
Je t'aime! (Simenon) **47**:374
Je t'aime, Je t'aime (Resnais) **16**:510-12
The Jealous God (Braine) **1**:43; **41**:57, 60
"Jealous Guy" (Lennon) **35**:263-65, 267, 274
"Jealous Twin" (Carroll) **35**:80-1
Jealousy (Robbe-Grillet)
　　See *La jalousie*
Jean Baudrillard: Selected Writings (Baudrillard) **60**:29, 33, 38-9
"Jean Beicke" (Williams) **42**:458
"Jean Harlow's Wedding Night" (Wasserstein) **90**:429
Jean le bleu (Giono) **4**:184; **11**:233
Jean Rhys: The Collected Short Stories (Rhys) **51**:375
Jean Rhys: The Complete Novels (Rhys) **51**:367
"Jeanne d'Arc" (Smith) **12**:535, 541
"La Jeannette" (Theriault) **79**:410
"Jean's TV" (Carver) **55**:276
Jeeves and the Tie That Binds (Much Obliged, Jeeves) (Wodehouse) **2**:480-81; **5**:515
Los jefes (Vargas Llosa) **15**:550
Jefferson and/or Mussolini (Pound) **112**:315, 338
The Jeffersons (Lear) **12**:331-32, 336
"Jeffrey, Believe Me" (Smiley) **53**:348
"Jeffty Is Five" (Ellison) **42**:129-30
J-E-L-L-O (Baraka) **5**:46
"A Jellyfish" (Moore) **8**:401
JEM: The Making of Utopia (Pohl) **18**:412-13
Jemima Shore's First Case (Fraser) **107**:50
"Jen jedno jsem spatril..." ("Only Once I Caught a Glimpse...") (Seifert) **93**:343
Jennifer (Sherburne) **30**:361

"Jenny" (Davison) **28**:100
Jenny Kimura (Cavanna) **12**:100-02
Jenseits der Liebe (Walser) **27**:463, 466
"Jeopardy" (Dorris) **109**:308
"The Jerboa" (Moore) **2**:291; **4**:362; **8**:399; **10**:351; **47**:260, 265
Jeremy's Version (Purdy) **2**:350; **10**:421, 424; **28**:381; **52**:342-43, 347-48
"Jericho" (Ai) **69**:7
"Jericho" (Dickey) **7**:86
Jericho Road (Kogawa) **78**:181
Jericho Sleep Alone (Bermant) **40**:89-90
"Jericho's Brick Battlements" (Laurence) **62**:282
The Jerk (Martin) **30**:249, 251-52
The Jero Plays (Soyinka) **5**:398; **44**:286
"Jerome" (Fair) **18**:139, 141
"Jerome" (Jarrell) **13**:302-03
"Jeronimo" (Bishop) **9**:97
Jero's Metamorphosis (Soyinka) **44**:287-88
The Jersey Shore (Mayne) **12**:401-02
"Jerusalem" (Silkin) **43**:401
"Jerusalem 1967" (Amichai) **57**:39, 44
"Jerusalem Address" (Kundera) **115**:321, 324
Jerusalem Daybook (Baxter) **14**:66
"Jerusalem Prize Acceptance Speech" (Coetzee) **117**:89-90, 92
Jerusalem Sonnets (Baxter) **14**:66
Jerusalem Syndrome (Sobol) **60**:385-86
Jerusalem the Golden (Drabble) **2**:118; **3**:128; **5**:117; **10**:165; **22**:121; **53**:121
"Jerusalem's Lot" (King) **26**:237
Jeruzalemski dijalog (Krleza) **114**:169
"Jesse" (Douglas) **73**:66-7, 73, 81
"Jesse" (Simon) **26**:413
"Jesse and Meribeth" (Munro) **50**:208-09, 211, 217-18, 221
The Jesse James Poems (Jiles) **58**:281-82
"Jesse Younger" (Kristofferson) **26**:268
Jessica (Campbell) **85**:4, 19-23, 26-7
Jessica Fayer (L'Heureux) **52**:278
"Jessica Kelley" (Hersey) **81**:329
A Jest of God (Laurence) **3**:278-81; **13**:341; **50**:311-17, 319, 321; **62**:269-71, 273, 279-81, 284-85, 289-91, 294-95, 306
Jestina's Calypso (Lovelace) **51**:271
Jesting Pilate (Huxley) **3**:255
"Jesus and Isolt" (Pinsky) **94**:306, 308, 310
"The Jesus Apparition" (Redgrove) **41**:352
Jesus, Break His Fall (Durcan) **43**:113
"Jesus Children of America" (Wonder) **12**:657
"Jesus Christ's Half-Brother Is Alive and Well on the Spokane Indian Reservation" (Alexie) **96**:5
Jesus Christ—Superstar (Rice and Webber) **21**:422-33
The Jesus Incident (Herbert) **23**:219; **35**:204-05, 209-10; **44**:393-94
"Jesus Is Easy" (Mull) **17**:299
The Jesus Myth (Greeley) **28**:170
Jesus on Mars (Farmer) **19**:168
"The Jesus Papers" (Sexton) **6**:491; **53**:321-23
"Jesus Suckles" (Sexton) **53**:322
Jesus Tales (Linney) **51**:260
Jesus Was a Capricorn (Kristofferson) **26**:268
"Jet" (McCartney) **35**:282, 284, 289
"Jet Plane/Dhla-nuwa" (Allen) **84**:5
"Jet Plane/Dhla-nuwa" (Allen) **84**:5
"Jet Stream: Betsy, 1980" (McNally) **82**:262
"Jets from Orange" (Ghose) **42**:178
Jets from Orange (Ghose) **42**:178-79
Le jeu du souterrain (The Underground Game)

(Mallet-Joris) **11**:356
"La jeune fille" (Carrier) **78**:60
"La jeune fille et la mort" (Tournier) **23**:452
Le Jeune née (Cixous)
　　See *Le Jeune née*
Les jeunes filles (Montherlant) **8**:393; **19**:322-23, 325, 328
Jeunesse (Green) **77**:273-74, 277-78, 281
Jeux de massacre (The Killing Game) (Ionesco) **86**:341
Les jeux incompris (Misunderstood Games) (Carrier) **78**:65
"Jew" (Abse) **29**:15
The Jew as Pariah (Arendt) **98**:27
"The Jew from Babylon" (Singer) **69**:310-11
A Jew in Love (Hecht) **8**:270
"A Jew of Persia" (Helprin) **7**:152; **10**:260
A Jew Today (Wiesel) **37**:450-51
"The Jewbird" (Malamud) **18**:317-19; **27**:298, 300; **44**:413, 417, 420; **85**:217
"The Jewel" (Moure) **88**:231
"A Jewel Box" (McFadden) **48**:251
The Jewel in the Crown (Scott)
　　See *The Raj Quartet*
The Jewel in the Skull (Moorcock) **58**:349
"Jewel Lotus Harp" (Broumas) **73**:9
"The Jewel of Amitaba" (Kotzwinkle) **35**:254
"The Jewel Stair's Grievance" (Pound) **10**:400
The Jewel-Hinged Jaw: Notes on the Language of Science Fiction (Delany) **14**:147; **38**:159
"The Jewels" (Clarke) **9**:168
"The Jewels of the Cabots" (Cheever) **7**:49; **11**:122
The Jewish Americans: A History in Their Own Words (Meltzer) **26**:308
"The Jewish Blues" (Roth) **66**:386, 389
"The Jewish Cemetery" (Kaufman) **8**:317
"A Jewish Cemetery by Leningrad" (Brodsky) **50**:120
"The Jewish Hunter" (Moore) **68**:298, 300
"A Jewish Patient Begins His Analysis" (Roth) **66**:386, 407
"Jewish Princess" (Zappa) **17**:592-93
"The Jewish Refugee" (Malamud)
　　See "The German Refugee"
"The Jews and Contemporary Literature" (de Man)
　　See "Les Juifs dans la littérature actuelle"
"Jews at Haifa" (Jarrell) **6**:261
"Jews in Contemporary Literature" (de Man)
　　See "Les Juifs dans la littérature actuelle"
"Jews in Present-Day Literature" (de Man)
　　See "Les Juifs dans la littérature actuelle"
"Jews in Today's Literature" (de Man)
　　See "Les Juifs dans la littérature actuelle"
The Jews of Silence: A Personal Report on Soviet Jewry (Wiesel)
　　See *Les Juifs du silence*
Jézabel (Anouilh) **13**:19; **40**:51, 55
JFK (Stone) **73**:384-86
JFK and LBJ (Wicker) **7**:533
A Jig for the Gypsy (Davies) **42**:104
The Jig of Forslin: A Symphony (Aiken) **52**:20-1, 27-8
Jiggery-Pokery (Hollander) **2**:197
Jig-Saw (Powell) **66**:368-69
"Jigsaw Puzzle" (Jagger and Richard) **17**:223, 241
Jill (Larkin) **5**:223-24, 229; **8**:333, 337-39; **9**:323-24; **13**:335, 337-38; **33**:262-66; **39**:334, 336, 340, 346-48; **64**:260, 280
Jill the Reckless (Wodehouse) **10**:538

"The Jilting of Granny Weatherall" (Porter) 7:315; **101**:209, 212, 224, 244, 248, 253
"Jim Crow's Funeral" (Hughes) **108**:284
Jim Crow's Last Stand (Hughes) **108**:283
Jim Dandy: Fat Man in a Famine (Saroyan) 8:467; **56**:376
"Jim Dean of Indiana" (Ochs) 17:332
"Jim O'Neill" (Farrell) **66**:129-30
"Jimble" (Prichard) 46:345
Jimmie Higgins (Sinclair) 15:502; **63**:346, 349
"Jimmy Jazz" (Clash) 30:46-7
Jimmy the Kid (Westlake) 33:437, 440
"Jimmy's Chicky-Run" (Phillips) 28:363
"Jingle" (Cohen) 38:131
"Jinx" (Dickinson) 49:102-03
Jitney (Wilson) **63**:454
Jitterbug Perfume (Robbins) 32:373-74; **64**:377, 381-82, 384
"Jiving" (Dove) 81:144
Jo Stern (Slavitt) 14:491
"Joal" (Senghor) **54**:401, 409
Joan Armatrading (Armatrading) 17:7-8, 10
Joan Makes History (Grenville) **61**:156, 159-60, 167
Joan Miró (Cabral de Melo Neto) **76**:168
Joanna's Husband and David's Wife (Hailey) 40:223-24
Joanna's Luck (Jones) **52**:254-55
"The Job" (Stafford) 7:460
The Job (Burroughs) **75**:107-08, 111-13, 115
Job: A Comedy of Justice (Heinlein) **55**:303
Jobber Skald (Powys)
  See *Weymouth Sands*
Job's Comforting (Richards) 14:453
"Job's Discount" (Porter) 33:319
Jobs in Fine Arts and Humanities (Berger) 12:40
"Job's New Children" (Stanton) 9:508
Job's Year (Hansen) 38:239-40
"The Jockey" (McCullers) 12:433; **100**:246
"Jody and the Kid" (Kristofferson) 26:267, 270
"Jody Girl" (Seger) 35:380-81, 383
Joe (Brown) **73**:24-8
"Joe and Pete" (Gellhorn) **60**:178
Joe Gould's Secret (Mitchell) **98**:168-70, 172-73, 175, 177, 180-81, 183, 187
Joe Hill: A Biographical Novel (Stegner)
  See *The Preacher and the Slave*
Joe Louis Uncovers Dynamite (Wright) 14:596
"Joe the Lion" (Bowie) 17:66
"Joe the Painter and the Deer Island Massacre" (King) **89**:76-78
Joe Turner's Come and Gone (Wilson) **50**:268; **63**:447-48, 450-54, 456, 458
Joe Versus the Volcano (Shanley) **75**:329-32
Joe's Ark (Potter) **86**:353
Joe's Bed-Stuy Barbershop: We Cut Heads (Lee) **105**:85, 102
Joe's Garage, Act I (Zappa) 17:593-95
Joe's Garage, Act II (Zappa) 17:594-95
Joe's Garage, Act III (Zappa) 17:594-95
"Joey the Midget" (Soto) **32**:403
"Johann Joachim Quantz's Five Lessons" (Graham) **29**:196
"Johanna" (Sondheim) 30:394, 398
John A.—Himself! (Findley) **102**:105
John and Mary (Jones) **52**:243, 245, 253
John Aubrey and His Friends (Powell) 7:343; 31:317
"John Aubrey's Antique Shop" (Szirtes) 46:394
John Barry (Fearing) **51**:113

"John Billy" (Wallace) **114**:347, 349
"John Brown" (Hayden) 37:158
John Brown (Du Bois) **64**:103
"John Cat" (Kinsella) 27:236
"John Chapman" (Oliver) **98**:256, 258, 260
"John Chrysostom" (Wilbur) **110**:386
John Deth: A Metaphysical Legend and Other Poems (Aiken) **52**:20, 22, 26
John Dollar (Wiggins) **57**:436-41
"John Dos Passos and the Whole Truth" (Schwartz) 10:462-63
"John Dryden" (Carruth) **84**:135
"John Duffy's Brother" (O'Brien) 7:270
John Ford (Sinclair) 14:489
"John John" (Arghezi) 80:9
"John Keats, Surgeon" (Belitt) 22:52
"John Knox" (Smith) **64**:397
John Lennon/Plastic Ono Band (Lennon) 12:366, 380; **35**:261-62, 264-68, 271, 273-74
"John Marin" (Jones) 10:285
"John Marston Advises Anger" (Porter) 33:318, 322, 325
"John Maydew; or, The Allotment" (Tomlinson) 13:549-50
"John Milton and My Father" (Beer) 58:36
"John Napper Sailing through the Universe" (Gardner) 5:133; 7:111, 116
"The John O'Groats Theory" (Reading) 47:350
John, Paul, George, Ringo, and Bert (Russell) **60**:319-20
"John Quixote" (MacCaig) 36:282
"John Redding Goes to Sea" (Hurston) 7:172; 30:218
"John Sinclair" (Lennon) 35:264
"John the Baptist" (Simpson) 7:427
John Wesley Harding (Dylan) 4:148; 6:155, 158; 12:185, 190, 199; 77:169
"Johnnie Brewer" (Warner) 7:512
Johnnie Cross (White) 49:409-10
Johnno (Malouf) 28:265, 267
"Johnny B. Goode" (Berry) 17:54
"Johnny Bear" (Steinbeck)
  See "The Ears of Johnny Bear"
"Johnny Carson" (Wilson) 12:651-52
Johnny Crackle Sings (Cohen) 19:111
Johnny Got His Gun (Trumbo) 19:444-48
Johnny, I Hardly Knew You (*I Hardly Knew You*) (O'Brien) 13:415; **36**:337-38; 116:185, 189, 191-92, 194
Johnny Johnson (Green) **25**:195, 198
Johnny Mangano and His Astonishing Dogs (Tremblay) **102**:365-66
"Johnny Mnemonic" (Gibson) **39**:139, 143; **63**:129, 134, 139
"Johnny on the Spot" (Woolrich) 77:402
"Johnny Panic and the Bible of Dreams" (Plath) 11:450-51; 17:364; **111**:184, 212-13
Johnny Panic and the Bible of Dreams (Plath) 3:390; 11:450-51; 17:364; **111**:179
"Johnny Spain's White Heifer" (Carruth) **84**:135
"Johnny Thomas" (Brown) **59**:262
Johnny Tremain (Forbes) 12:207, 210-11
"Johnny Was" (Marley) 17:269, 272
"John's Mysteries" (Stern) **100**:341-43
"Johnson as Critic and Poet" (Eliot) 24:172, 178
"The Johnson Girls" (Bambara) 19:33; **88**:21, 49
Johnson over Jordan (Priestley) 2:347
"Johnson's Cabinet Watched by Ants" (Bly) 5:64

Joie de vivre (Rattigan) 7:355
"Join Together with the Band" (Townshend) 17:531
"Joke" (Dixon) 52:100
"The Joke" (Singer) 3:454
The Joke (Kundera)
  See *Zert*
The Joker of Seville (Walcott) **25**:455; **67**:347, 350, 352; **76**:275
"Jokerman" (Dylan) 77:179
"The Joker's Greatest Triumph" (Barthelme) **115**:65, 76
Jokes to Mislead the Police (Parra) **102**:347, 356
Joking Apart (Ayckbourn) 18:30; **33**:44, 47-9
"Jokund ile Si-Ya-U" ("Gioconda and Si-Ya-U") (Hikmet) **40**:245, 249-51
Jolis deuils, petites tragédies pour adultes (*Pretty Mournings, Small Tragedies*) (Carrier) **78**:46, 51, 59-60, 63, 65, 67
"Jonah" (Phillips) 28:363
Jonah (Porter) 5:347
Jonah: Christmas 1917 (Huxley) 11:282-83
The Jonah Man (Carlisle) **33**:104-05
Jonah's Gourd Vine (Hurston) 7:170-71; **30**:208-11, 215, 226-27; **61**:270
"Jonas ou l'artiste au travail" ("The Artist at Work") (Camus) 9:144; 14:114
Jonathan (Chedid) 47:84-5
"Jonathan Edwards in Western Massachusettes" (Lowell) 8:351
"Jonathan Livingston Seagull" (Diamond) 30:113
Jonathan Livingston Seagull (Bach) 14:35-6
Jonathan Livingston Seagull (Diamond) 30:114
"Jonathan Sitting in Mud" (Giovanni) **117**:205
Jonathan Troy (Abbey) 36:14
"Jonathan's Song" (Dodson) **79**:194
Jones (Humphreys) 47:189
Jonica 66:176
"Jonna" (Haines) 58:218
Jonoah and the Green Stone (Dumas) **62**:156-57, 159, 164
"Jools and Jim" (Townshend) 17:541-42
Jordan County: A Landscape in Narrative (Foote) **75**:230-32, 239, 254, 257
The Jordans (Millin) 49:239, 246
"Jorinda and Jorindel" (Gallant) 38:190-91, 193-94
"Jornada de la soltera" (Castellanos) 66:52
"José Ortega y Gasset" (Paz) **51**:332
"Joseph" (Forche) **25**:172; **83**:210
"Joseph" (Soyinka) **36**:415-17; **44**:285
Joseph (Jones) **52**:244-46
Joseph (Rathbone) 41:340-42
"Joseph and His Brother" (Thomas) 37:416; **107**:316, 318
Joseph and the Amazing Technicolor Dreamcoat (Rice and Webber) 21:423, 427-28, 430
"Joseph Haydn and Captain Bligh" (MacLennan) **92**:342-43
Joseph Pasquier's Passion (Duhamel)
  See *La passion de Joseph Pasquier*
"Joseph Pockets" (Stern) **40**:411
Josephine Herbst: The Story She Could Never Tell (Langer) **34**:448, 450-51, 453-54
"Jose's Country" (Winters) 32:469
Joshua Then and Now (Richler) 18:452-56; 70:219, 231
"Joshua Tree" (Ammons) **108**:21
"Josie" (Becker and Fagen) 26:84

"Jottings of a Writer" (Olesha) **8**:430
Un joualonais, sa joualonie (*St. Lawrence Blues*) (Blais) **6**:80-2
"Un jouf" (Michaux) **8**:390
Le jour (*The Accident*) (Wiesel) **3**:529; **5**:491
Le jour est noir (*The Day Is Dark*) (Blais) **6**:82; **13**:96; **22**:57-8
"Le jour où je devins un apostat" (Carrier) **78**:71
"Le jour qui fut" (Hebert) **29**:237
"Journal" (Pinget) **37**:364-65
"The Journal" (Shields) **113**:425
Journal (Green) **77**:273, 275, 283-84
Journal (Mauriac) **56**:210, 212
Journal, 1928-1958 (Green) **3**:204-05
Journal, 1936-1937 (Gascoyne) **45**:157-58
"Journal, August, 1968" (Blackburn) **9**:100
Journal du voleur (*The Thief's Journal*) (Genet) **5**:138; **14**:202; **44**:386-88, 390; **46**:175-76, 178, 182
Journal du voyageur (Green) **77**:284-85
Journal d'un contre-révolutionnaire (Kohout) **13**:323
Journal d'un curé de campagne (*Diary of a Country Priest*) (Bresson) **16**:103-04, 107-18
Le journal d'une femme de chambre (*Diary of a Chambermaid*) (Bunuel) **16**:141, 148; **80**:47, 57
Journal en miettes (Ionesco) **41**:227-28; **86**:335, 340
Journal from Ellipsia (Calisher) **38**:71
"A Journal from France" (Clarke) **61**:78
Journal intime (Brossard) **115**:121
"Journal, June, 1971" (Blackburn) **9**:100
"Journal Night Thoughts" (Ginsberg) **36**:184; **109**:345
Journal/Nocturnal (Broner) **19**:70-1
Journal of a Living Experiment (Lopate) **29**:300
"Journal of a Poet" (Bogan) **93**:74
Journal of a Solitude (Sarton) **4**:471; **49**:317-18; **91**:247-48, 250-52
The Journal of Albion Moonlight (Patchen) **2**:332; **18**:391-94
"Journal of an Airman" (Auden) **11**:18; **14**:32
The Journal of Arthur Stirling (Sinclair) **63**:345, 347-48
The Journal of John Cardan (Cunningham) **31**:103
Journal of the Fictive Life (Nemerov) **2**:307-08; **36**:304
Journal sans date (Jouve) **47**:209
"The Journalist" (Ai) **69**:9-10, 17
The Journalists (Wesker) **3**:519-20; **42**:426-30
The Journals (Blackburn) **9**:99-100; **43**:65-6, 68
Journals, 1939-1983 (Spender) **91**:264
Journals and Dreams (Waldman) **7**:509
Journals: Early Fifties, Early Sixties (Ginsberg) **13**:241; **36**:185-86; **69**:219; **109**:348, 351
Journals Mid-Fifties (1954-1958) (Ginsberg) **109**:350-51
The Journals of Susanna Moodie (Atwood) **3**:20; **8**:29-30, 32; **13**:42; **15**:37; **25**:63-4, 67-8; **84**:51, 62, 68, 97
The Journals of Sylvia Plath (Plath) **50**:448; **51**:347, 349-53; **111**:200
The Journals of Thornton Wilder, 1939-1961 (Wilder) **82**:377, 379, 380
"The Journey" (Abse) **29**:12
"The Journey" (Boland) **67**:36, 40, 42, 45-6; **113**:82, 84-5, 92, 94, 98, 110, 124

"Journey" (Clarke) **61**:73
"Journey" (Cook-Lynn) **93**:123
"A Journey" (Gordimer) **70**:177-78, 180
"Journey" (Grace) **56**:117, 119, 120, 123
"A Journey" (O'Brien) **5**:311; **8**:429
"The Journey" (Oliver) **98**:260
"The Journey" (Porter) **13**:451; **15**:429
"Journey" (Scott) **22**:373
"The Journey" (Thomas) **13**:544
"The Journey" (Thomas) **13**:542
"Journey" (Transtroemer) **65**:223
"The Journey" (Wright) **53**:428
Journey (Michener) **60**:261-62; **109**:376, 381
The Journey (Winters) **32**:469
The Journey, and Other Poems (Boland) **67**:36, 39, 45; **113**:69, 72-4, 77, 82, 84, 86-7, 94, 98, 108-09, 124
"Journey around My Room" (Bogan) **46**:88; **93**:103
Journey around My Room: The Autobiography of Louise Bogan, A Mosaic (Bogan) **39**:388-89, 391, 393-94; **46**:88; **93**:61, 73, 75-7, 88, 99
"Journey Back to the Source" (Carpentier)
   See "Viaje a la semilla"
"Journey beyond the Hills" (Still) **49**:363
"Journey by Air" (White) **49**:407
"A Journey by Night" (Warner) **19**:460
Journey Continued (Paton) **55**:311, 314; **106**:305-06
"The Journey East" (Livesay) **79**:338
The Journey Home (Abbey) **36**:14, 19; **59**:238, 241-42, 245
"A Journey in Love" (Shapcott) **38**:398, 400
Journey into Autumn (Bergman)
   See *Kvinnodröm*
Journey into Dustlessness (Sachs) **98**:326
Journey into Fear (Ambler) **6**:4; **9**:19, 21
Journey into Fear (Welles) **20**:444, 449
Journey into the Beyond (Sachs)
   See *Fahrt ins Staublose*
"A Journey into the Mind of Watts" (Pynchon) **33**:334-35; **72**:332, 335
"Journey into the Night" (Lind) **82**:130
Journey into the Whirlwind **59**:384
Journey Inward (George) **35**:179
"The Journey of a Lifetime" (Carey) **96**:25, 38
"The Journey of a Poem Compared to All the Sad Variety of Travel" (Schwartz) **45**:355
The Journey of August King (Ehle) **27**:104-05
The Journey of Tai-me (Momaday) **85**:276
The Journey of the Fifth Horse (Ribman) **7**:357-58
"Journey of the Magi" (Eliot) **10**:168; **15**:217; **41**:151-52; **55**:374
Journey through Dark Night (Shiga) **33**:363-68
"Journey through the Past" (Young) **17**:582
Journey through the Past (Young) **17**:571, 574
Journey to a Known Place (Carruth) **4**:93
Journey to a War (Auden) **3**:25; **14**:26; **43**:18, 28
Journey to a War (Isherwood) **14**:278-79, 282; **44**:397-98
Journey to America (Levitin) **17**:263-64
Journey to Chaos: Samuel Beckett's Early Fiction (Federman) **47**:118-19, 129
Journey to Ithaca (Desai) **97**:189-90, 192
Journey to Ixtlan (Castaneda) **12**:88-9, 92, 95
"Journey to Love" (McFadden) **48**:256
Journey to Love (Williams) **22**:465; **42**:451,

463
"Journey to Nine Miles" (Walker) **58**:409
Journey to Nowhere: A New World Tragedy (Naipaul)
   See *Black and White*
"Journey to Nuremburg" (Hesse) **2**:191
Journey to the Alcarria (Cela)
   See *Viaje a la Alcarria*
Journey to the East (Hesse)
   See *Die Morgenlandfahrt*
Journey to the End of the Night (Celine)
   See *Voyage au bout de la nuit*
"Journey to the Forks" (Still) **49**:364
"The Journey to the Interior" (Atwood) **8**:33
"Journey to the Interior" (Roethke) **8**:458; **19**:396; **101**:289, 306-07, 314-16, 319, 330
A Journey to the Interior (Newby) **2**:310; **13**:411
"Journey to the Sacred Mountains" (Kunene) **85**:176-77
"Journey to the Sahel" (Cabral de Melo Neto)
   See "Viagem ao Sahel"
"A Journey to the Seven Streams" (Kiely) **23**:266; **43**:241
A Journey to the Seven Streams: Seventeen Stories (Kiely) **43**:239, 244
"Journey with Anita" (Fellini) **85**:64
The Journey with Jonah (L'Engle) **12**:347-48
Journey with My Selves: A Memoir, 1909-1963 (Livesay) **79**:354-55
Journey without Maps (Greene) **1**:134; **70**:293; **72**:149-50, 152, 161
Journeying and the Returns (Nichol) **18**:366, 368-69
Journeyman (Caldwell) **8**:122; **50**:299-300, 303; **60**:46-7, 49, 54, 64
"Journeys" (Prokosch) **48**:306
Journeys among the Dead (Ionesco)
   See *Voyages chez les morts: Thèmes et variations*
"Journeys and Faces" (Abse) **29**:14
Journeys between Wars (Dos Passos) **25**:137
Journey's End (Neruda)
   See *El fin del viaje*
Journey's End (O'Casey) **11**:407
Journeys to the Other Side (Le Clezio) **31**:249
Jours effeuillés: Poémes, essais, souvenirs, 1920-1965 (Arp) **5**:33
"Jóvenes" ("Youngsters") (Parra) **102**:343
"Joy" (Enzensberger) **43**:144-45
"Joy" (Gaye) **26**:135
"Joy" (Hughes) **108**:332
"Joy" (Moore) **68**:299-301
"Joy" (Rosenthal) **28**:395
"Joy" (Singer) **6**:508; **11**:502
"Joy" (Warren) **13**:577
Joy (Hunt) **70**:65-8
"Joy and Margaret" (Blunden) **56**:46-7
Joy in the Morning (Smith) **19**:424
"Joy inside My Tears" (Wonder) **12**:662
The Joy Luck Club (Tan) **59**:89-99
The Joy of Gay Sex (White) **27**:480; **110**:321, 323, 329
The Joy of Sex (Comfort) **7**:54
"The Joy of the Job" (Ferber) **93**:140, 142
"The Joy of the Just" (Gardner) **28**:162-63
Joy of the Worm (Sargeson) **31**:366-67, 374
"Joyce and the Modern Novel" (Wilder) **82**:356, 359
"The Joycelin Schranger Story" (Disch) **7**:87
"Jóyenes alemanes" (Neruda) **62**:326
"The Joyful Black Demon of Sister Clara Flies

through the Midnight Woods on Her Snow-mobile" (Wakoski)   4:573
"Joyful Mystery" (Castellanos)   66:60
"Joyous Sound" (Morrison)   21:237
Joyride (Cavanna)   12:101
"The Joys of Being a Business Man" (Fearing)   51:111
"The Joys of Gay Life" (White)   110:335
The Joys of Motherhood (Emecheta)   14:160; 48:97, 99-101; 65:329-33
Joysprick: An Introduction to the Language of James Joyce (Burgess)   4:83
"József" (Murray)   40:337
"J's Marriage" (Coover)   15:145
"J's Wife" (Coover)   7:58
"Juan" (Graves)   45:166
Juan Bobo and the Lady of the Occident (Marques)
   See *Juan Bobo y la dama de occidente*
Juan Bobo y la dama de occidente (*Juan Bobo and the Lady of the Occident*) (Marques)   96:225
"Juan in Limbo" (Scannell)   49:332
"Juan Muraña" (Borges)   2:77; 10:67
Juan sin tierra (*Juan the Landless*) (Goytisolo)   10:245; 23:185, 187-88
Juan the Landless (Goytisolo)
   See *Juan sin tierra*
"Juan's Song" (Bogan)   4:68; 46:81
Jubal Sackett (L'Amour)   55:306-08
Jubb (Waterhouse)   47:418, 421
Jubiabá (Amado)   13:11; 40:25-7, 34, 36; 106:57-8, 62-3, 71
"Jubilare" (Moure)   88:227, 229
"Jubilate Matteo" (Ewart)   46:151
Jubilee (Hart)   66:176, 182
Jubilee Blues (Davies)   23:145
"Jubilee Hymn" (Betjeman)   34:308
Judah the Pious (Prose)   45:322-24
"Judaism and Harold Bloom" (Ozick)   62:349-51
"Judas" (Brunner)   8:107
"Judas" (Chappell)   40:141-42
"Judas" (O'Connor)   14:399; 23:332
The Judas Boy (Raven)   14:441
The Judas Cloth (O'Faolain)   108:423-24
"The Judas Goat" (Musgrave)   54:334
The Judas Goat (Parker)   27:364, 366-67
"Judas Iscariot" (Spender)   10:487
Judas, My Brother (Yerby)   22:489
The Judas Tree (Cronin)   32:139
The Judas Window (Carr)   3:101
The Judge (Mortimer)   28:285-86
The Judge (West)   7:525; 31:451, 457; 50:395, 398, 408
The Judge and His Hangman (Duerrenmatt)   102:83
The Judge and His Hangman (Durrenmatt)
   See *Der Richter und sein Henker*
"The Judge and Other Snakes" (Dubus)   97:234
"The Judge Is Fury" (Cunningham)   31:97, 100, 102
"Judge Not" (Roethke)   46:356
"The Judgement" (Lind)   82:128, 130
"Judgement Day" (O'Connor)   1:257; 3:366; 6:382; 21:268, 277, 279; 104:103, 108, 115, 135, 160, 178, 187-88, 190, 198
Judgement Day (Lively)   32:274-75
A Judgement in Stone (Rendell)   28:385; 48:320-21
The Judgement of Deke Hunter (Higgins)   10:273-74
"The Judgement of Paris" (Merwin)   88:205

"The Judge's Wife" (Allende)   97:3, 33, 35
"The Judgment" (Akhmatova)   64:12
"Judgment Day" (Hughes)   108:297
Judgment Day (Farrell)   1:98; 4:157; 66:112, 120, 127
Judgment Day (Rice)   7:360-61; 49:299-300, 302-03, 305
The Judgment of Paris (Vidal)   2:448-49; 6:549; 22:434
Judgment on Deltchev (Ambler)   6:3; 9:18
Judgment on Janus (Norton)   12:457, 461, 469
"Judith" (Smith)   12:535, 540
Judith (Abell)   15:1, 5
Judith (Mosley)   43:322; 70:202-04
Judith, and Other Stories (Farrell)   4:157-58; 8:205
Judith Hearne (Moore)
   See *The Lonely Passion of Judith Hearne*
"Judith Kane" (Spencer)   22:402
Judith Madrier (Troyat)   23:457
Judy Garland and the Cold War (Simmons)   43:409, 412
Juegos de manos (*The Young Assassins*) (Goytisolo)   10:243; 23:186
"El juez, mi rehén" (Ulibarri)   83:416
"Jug and Bottle" (Ross)   13:496
"Jug Band Blues" (Pink Floyd)   35:307
"Jug of Silver" (Capote)   1:55
"Juggernaut" (Bass)   79:3, 12
Juggernaut (Lester)   20:229-30
"Juggernaut's Little Scrapbook" (Murray)   40:335-36
"Juggler" (Wilbur)   53:399, 407
Jugglers Three (Williamson)   56:433-34
Juhannustanssit (*A Midsummer Dance*) (Salama)   18:460-61
Juhlat (*The Festivity*) (Haavikko)   34:170
Juicios sumarios (Castellanos)   66:54
"Les Juifs dans la littérature actuelle" ("The Jews and Contemporary Literature"; "Jews in Contemporary Literature"; "Jews in Present-Day Literature"; "Jews in Today's Literature") (de Man)   55:383-84, 386, 398, 403-04, 408, 412, 419-20, 422
Les Juifs du silence (*The Jews of Silence: A Personal Report on Soviet Jewry*) (Wiesel)   3:529; 37:455
"Juilliard Lecture" (Cage)   41:78, 80
"Juke Box Music" (Davies)   21:102
Jules and Jim (Truffaut)
   See *Jules et Jim*
Jules et Jim (*Jules and Jim*) (Truffaut)   20:382, 387, 391-92, 394-97, 402-03; 101:371, 373-75, 377-81, 383-85, 387-88, 391-94, 396, 406-408, 410, 412, 414-17
"Julia" (Hellman)   8:282; 44:530, 532; 52:190-92, 194-95, 197-98, 200, 202-05
"Julia" (Lennon and McCartney)   35:264, 266
Julia (Straub)   28:409; 107:264-66, 268, 274, 276-78, 281-83, 292, 304-10
Julia and the Bazooka, and Other Stories (Kavan)   5:206; 82:119-20, 122
Julia Paradise (Jones)   50:51-4
Julian (*Julian the Apostate*) (Vidal)   2:449; 4:553-55, 557; 6:549-50; 8:528; 10:502; 22:433-35; 33:407; 72:386-87, 389, 399, 406
Julian the Apostate (Vidal)
   See *Julian*
Julian the Magician (MacEwen)   13:357
"Julie: A Memory" (Brown)   73:20
Julie of the Wolves (George)   35:177-80

"Julie's on the Drug Squad" (Clash)   30:43
Juliet of the Spirits (Fellini)
   See *Giulietta degli spiriti*
"Julieta" (Guillen)   79:241
Julio Jurenito (Ehrenburg)
   See *The Extraordinary Adventures of Julio Jurenito and His Disciples*
Julius Caesar (Welles)   80:379
"July" (Lane)   25:284
"July" (Swan)   69:358-60, 363-64
July 7th (McCorkle)   51:273-76, 278
July's People (Gordimer)   33:181-85; 51:156-59, 161-62; 70:163, 165-67, 170-71, 182, 187
"Jumbo's Wife" (O'Connor)   23:329
La jument verte (*The Green Mare*) (Ayme)   11:21-3
Jump, and Other Stories (Gordimer)   70:166, 168, 176-77, 180
Jump Ship to Freedom (Collier and Collier)   30:73-5
Jumpers (Stoppard)   3:470; 4:525-27; 5:411-14; 8:501-04; 15:518-20, 524; 29:394,397, 399-400, 402, 406; 34:273-74, 280-81; 63:404; 91:184, 189-90
"Jumpin' Jack Flash" (Jagger and Richard)   17:224, 229, 231
"Jumping Beans" (Lopate)   29:302
Jumping Jupiter (Gilbreth and Carey)   17:154
Jumping the Train Tracks with Angela (Durcan)   43:116-17
"June" (Gunn)   32:213
"June 30, 1974" (Schuyler)   23:391
June 30th, June 30th (Brautigan)   12:73-4
"June Cherries" (Asturias)   8:25
"June: Dutch Harbor" (Meredith)   22:302
"June Fugue" (Shapcott)   38:402
"June Light" (Wilbur)   110:351
June Moon (Kaufman)   38:265
"June Rain" (Aldington)   49:17
"June Rain" (Merwin)   18:336-37
"June Recital" (Welty)   14:564; 22:456-58; 33:420; 105:299
The Juneberry Tree (Ferron)
   See *L'amélanchier*
"Juneteenth" (Ellison)   114:99, 102
Jung and Feminism: Liberating the Archetypes   65:325
"Jung and the Theatre" (Davies)   13:174
Jungfrukällen (*The Virgin Spring*) (Bergman)   16:50, 61, 64-7, 74
"The Jungle" (Kavanagh)   22:242
The Jungle (Samarakis)
   See *I zoungla*
The Jungle (Sinclair)   1:310; 11:497-98; 15:498-501; 63:345-51, 354, 359-61, 366-70, 373-74, 376
"The Jungle and the Sea" (Aleixandre)   36:29
"Jungle Fever" (Komunyakaa)   86:192
Jungle Fever (Lee)   105:95-97, 99-103, 111, 113, 127-30
"Jungle Knot" (Ammons)   25:42
"The Jungle Line" (Mitchell)   12:439
Jungle Lovers (Theroux)   5:427; 8:512; 28:424-25
"The Jungle of Lord Lion" (Jacobsen)   102:241
"Jungle Surrender" (Komunyakaa)   94:230, 245
"Jungleland" (Springsteen)   17:480-81, 489-90
"Jungletime" (Diamond)   30:112
"The Juniata Diary: With Timely Repartees" (Codrescu)   46:106
"Juninachmittag" (Wolf)   29:464

"Junior Addict" (Hughes) **15**:295

The Junior Bachelor Society (Williams) **13**:599

Junior Bonner (Peckinpah) **20**:276, 278

Junior Miss Series (Benson) **17**:48, 50

The Juniper Tree (Straub) **107**:304-05, 307-09

"Junk" (Wilbur) **6**:570; **53**:405; **110**:351

The Junkers (Read) **4**:444; **25**:375-76, 379

"Junkie Slip" (Clash) **30**:48

Junkie: The Confessions of an Unredeemed Drug Addict (Junky) (Burroughs) **15**:111-12; **22**:83, 86; **42**:74-5, 77-8; **75**:97, 103-04

Junkies Are Full of Shhh. . . (Baraka) **115**:36

Junky (Burroughs)
    See *Junkie: The Confessions of an Unredeemed Drug Addict*

Juno and Avos (Voznesensky) **57**:424

Juno and the Paycock (O'Casey) **5**:317-20; **9**:407-08; **11**:409-10; **15**:404-05; **88**:234-37, 242, 244, 247, 252, 254-58, 261-63, 265

Junta, the Body Snatcher (Onetti)
    See *Juntacadaveres*

Juntacadaveres (Junta, the Body Snatcher) (Onetti) **7**:279-80; **10**:376

"Junto al Río de Cenizas de Rosa" (Sarduy) **97**:382, 384-86

The Jupiter Legacy (Harrison) **42**:207

The Jupiter Plague (Harrison) **42**:207

Jupiter Project (Benford) **52**:63

Jupiter: The Largest Planet (Asimov) **26**:50

"El juramento" (Marques) **96**:241, 245

Jurassic Park (Crichton) **90**:70, 72, 84-5, 87, 89, 91, 93, 96-7

Jürg Reinhart (Frisch) **3**:167; **9**:218; **44**:183, 185-86, 193, 204

The Jury (Klima) **56**:162-63, 165-67, 170

"Juryrigged" (Haldeman) **61**:174, 177

"Just a Little One" (Parker) **68**:335

Just a Little Simple (Childress) **86**:309, 311, 314

"Just a Smack at Auden" (Empson) **33**:142

"Just a Song at Twilight" (Aickman) **57**:4

"Just About Asleep Together" (Peacock) **60**:292

Just above My Head (Baldwin) **15**:41-4; **17**:41-5; **42**:17; **50**:297; **90**:31, 33

Just Add Water and Stir (Berton) **104**:47

The Just and the Unjust (Cozzens) **1**:67; **4**:112-13, 115; **11**:124, 128, 131-32; **92**:178-81, 184-86, 189, 196, 211-12

"A Just Anger" (Piercy) **6**:404; **18**:406; **27**:375

Just Another Band from L.A. (Zappa) **17**:588, 593

"Just as It Was" (Amichai) **57**:36

The Just Assassins (Camus)
    See *Les justes*

Just before Nightfall (Chabrol)
    See *Juste avant la nuit*

Just between Ourselves (Ayckbourn) **18**:30; **33**:41, 48-9; **74**:8, 18, 21, 23

"Just Boys" (Farrell) **66**:131

"Just Don't Never Give Up on Love" (Sanchez) **116**:287, 302, 310, 317

"Just Enough for the City" (McPherson) **77**:359, 378, 381-82

"Just for a Time" (Angelou) **77**:30

"Just Friends" (Davies) **21**:92

Just Give me a Cool Drink of Water 'fore I Diiie (Angelou) **12**:13; **64**:32; **77**:15, 22, 28-9

Just, Human Time (Padilla)
    See *El justo tiempo humano*

"Just like a Tree" (Gaines) **3**:179; **18**:167

"Just Like a Woman" (Dylan) **12**:182; **77**:177

"Just like Her Mother" (Callaghan) **41**:98

"(Just like) Starting Over" (Lennon) **35**:271-72, 274

Just Like the Resurrection (Beer) **58**:31, 36, 38

"Just like This Train" (Mitchell) **12**:443

"Just like Tom Thumb's Blues" (Dylan) **4**:149

"Just Living" (Lane) **25**:289

"Just Not True" (Simon) **26**:409

Just Relations (Hall) **51**:176-79

Just Representations: A James Gould Cozzens Reader (Cozzens) **92**:194, 203, 208

"Just Say Yes Calypso" (Ginsberg) **109**:318

"Just Tell Me Who It Was" (Cheever) **15**:131

"Just the Way You Are" (Joel) **26**:217, 221

"Just to Keep You Satisfied" (Gaye) **26**:133

"Just Us" (Pryor) **26**:378

"Just Us Kids" (Crumb) **17**:83

"Just Walking Around" (Ashbery) **41**:35, 38

Juste avant la nuit (Just before Nightfall) (Chabrol) **16**:179, 183

"Juste présent" (Tzara) **47**:388

Les justes (The Assassins; The Just Assassins) (Camus) **1**:54; **9**:146; **14**:108, 114-15; **32**:84-8, 90-2, 94, 96-101; **63**:63, 86

"A Justice" (Faulkner) **68**:128

"Justice" (Hughes) **15**:295

"Justice" (O'Hara) **42**:319

Justice and Her Brothers (Hamilton) **26**:152-53, 155-56

"Justice at Midnight" (Barker) **48**:15

"Justice Is Reason Enough" (Wakoski) **9**:554

Justification and Application: Remarks on Discourse Ethics (Habermas) **104**:91

Justine (Durrell) **1**:87; **4**:144, 146; **8**:190-92; **13**:185, 187-88; **27**:97-8; **41**:133, 136-37

El justo tiempo humano (Just, Human Time; The Right Moment for Humanity) (Padilla) **38**:350, 352

Juvenile Court (Wiseman) **20**:474, 476

Juvenile Justice and Injustice (Hyde) **21**:178

"Juvenilia" (Smart) **54**:425

Juvenilia I (Nye) **42**:302, 304-05

Juvenilia II (Nye) **42**:302, 304-05

"Juventad" (Paz) **10**:392

Juxtaposition (Anthony) **35**:37

Jyotaro (Tanizaki) **28**:418

"K" (Merrill) **8**:385, 387

"The K" (Olson) **29**:330

"K, der Käfer" ("K, the Beetle") (Grass) **32**:201

"K filosofii postupka" ("Towards a Philosophy of the Act") (Bakhtin) **83**:36, 38

"K Likomedu, na Skiros" ("On the Way to Lycomedes of Scyrus"; "To Lycomedes on Scyros") (Brodsky) **50**:122-23

"K, the Beetle" (Grass)
    See "K, der Käfer"

K Uranii (Brodsky)
    See *To Urania: Selected Poems 1965-1985*

"The Kabbalah" (Borges) **48**:47-8

Kabbalah and Criticism (Bloom) **24**:79; **103**:2, 6-8, 12-13, 25, 27-8, 41, 48

"Kabnis" (Toomer) **4**:549; **13**:550-52, 554, 556; **22**:429

"Lo kabrosh" ("Not Like a Cypress") (Amichai) **116**:119-21, 124

"Kaddish" (Ginsberg) **2**:164; **3**:194-95; **4**:181; **6**:199; **13**:241; **36**:181, 183-85, 187-89, 192, 195, 197; **69**:217, 223, 225; **109**:324-26, 330, 332-33, 336, 338, 351, 358-62, 364, 371-72

"Kaddish" (Ignatow) **40**:259

Kaddish, and Other Poems (Ginsberg) **1**:119; **2**:162-64; **6**:198-99; **13**:239-40; **36**:183, 186, 193, 196, 199; **109**:328, 338-43, 348, 352, 359, 362-63

Kafatasi (The Skull) (Hikmet) **40**:245

Kaff auch Mare Crisium (Schmidt) **56**:391-92, 401, 405

"Kafka and His Executors" (Grass) **49**:138

"Kafka and His Precursors" (Borges) **8**:100; **44**:359; **48**:44; **83**:192, 194

"Kafkas" (Wiggins) **57**:434-36, 439

Kafka's Dick (Bennett) **45**:58-60; **77**:90-1

Kafka's Other Trial: The Letters to Felice (Canetti)
    See *Der andere Prozeß: Kafkas Briefe an Felice*

Kagemusha (Kurosawa) **16**:406

Kagi (The Key) (Ichikawa) **20**:177, 181

Kagi (The Key) (Tanizaki) **8**:510-11; **14**:525, 527; **28**:417

Kahawa (Westlake) **33**:439

"Kaiser and the War" (Ortiz) **45**:309, 311

Kak nam obustroit' Rossiiu?: Posil'nye soobrazheniia (Rebuilding Russia: Reflections and Tentative Proposals) (Solzhenitsyn) **78**:427, 429-30, 432-33

Kakemono hôtel (Cayrol) **11**:110

"Kalaloch" (Forche) **25**:168-70; **83**:209, 211

Kalendarz i klepsydra (A Calander and an Hourglass) (Konwicki) **117**:257-58, 272, 279, 284, 286

"Kali" (Clifton) **66**:80

"Kali's Galaxy" (Reed) **5**:368

Kalki (Vidal) **10**:501-04; **22**:435-36; **33**:407; **72**:386-87

Das Kalkwerk (The Lime Works) (Bernhard) **3**:64-5; **32**:17-21, 26; **61**:14-15, 19-21, 23-4, 28-9

Die Kälte: Eine Isolation (Bernhard) **32**:26; **61**:11

Kameliadamen (The Lady of the Camelias) (Abell) **15**:2, 7

Kamen no kokuhaku (Confessions of a Mask) (Mishima) **2**:286-87, 289; **4**:355; **6**:338; **9**:381-82, 385; **27**:337-41, 345-46

Kammený most (The Stone Bridge) (Seifert) **44**:425; **93**:306, 328, 343

Kamouraska (Hebert) **4**:220; **29**:231-33, 235-38, 240-41

Kämpande ande (Struggling Spirit) (Lagerkvist) **54**:286

Kanal (Wajda) **16**:577-79, 581-82

Kanchenjunga (Ray) **16**:481, 492, 494

"The Kandy-Kolored Tangerine-Flake Streamline Baby" (Wolfe) **51**:418, 420

The Kandy-Kolored Tangerine-Flake Streamline Baby (Wolfe) **35**:449-50, 452, 456, 458, 460, 465-66; **51**:418-20

Kane and Abel (Archer) **28**:12-14

Kangaroo (Aleshkovsky) **44**:29-32

Kansakunnan linja (The National Line) (Haavikko) **34**:181

"Kansas City" (Harjo) **83**:271

Kansas City (Altman) **116**:71-4

Kanthapura (Rao) **25**:366-67, 369-72; **56**:284, 286-87, 289, 292-93, 295-96, 298-99, 301-04, 306-07, 315

Kaos (Chaos) (Lagerkvist) **54**:274, 277

"Kapetan Michalis" (Levi) **41**:245

"Das kapital" (Baraka) **33**:62

Kara-Bugaz (Paustovsky) **40**:363, 368
Karaoke (Potter) **86**:343-46, 348
"Karate" (Plumly) **33**:312
Karate Is a Thing of the Spirit (Crews) **6**:117-18; **23**:138; **49**:71-2, 76
"The Karate Kid" (Soto) **80**:298
"Karintha" (Toomer) **4**:549; **22**:425
The Karl Marx Play (Owens) **8**:434
"Kärleken och döden" ("Love and Death") (Lagerkvist) **54**:276, 286
"Karma" (Hughes) **37**:173
"Karma" (Raine) **103**:182
alKarnak (Mahfuz) **52**:297, 302-03
Karoton (*City of Splintered Gods*) (Faludy) **42**:136
"Kartofel'nyy el'f" (Nabokov)
    See "The Potato Elf"
Kartoteka (*Personal File*) (Rozewicz) **23**:359
Die Kaschuben (Grass) **88**:144
"Kashmir" (Page and Plant) **12**:477-82
"A Kashmir Idyll" (Anand) **23**:18
"Kas-Kas" (Bennett) **28**:29
Kaspar (Handke) **5**:163, 165; **8**:262-63; **10**:254-56; **15**:267-68, 270; **38**:215, 217, 219
Kaspar and Other Plays (Handke) **38**:215, 219
Kassandra and the Wolf (Karapanou) **13**:314-15
"Kata Ucle" ("One Arm") (Kawabata) **107**:73, 77, 86
Kate Vaiden (Price) **50**:229-33; **63**:323, 325-27, 329-30, 332-33, 335-36, 339, 341
"Kate Whiskey" (Muldoon) **32**:315
"Kategorier" ("Categories") (Ekelof) **27**:111
"Käthe Kollwitz" (Rukeyser) **15**:457; **27**:413
"Katherine Anne Porter: The Eye of the Story" (Welty) **105**:322
Kathie and the Hippopotamus (Vargas Llosa)
    See *Kathie y el hipopótamo*
Kathie y el hipopótamo (*Kathie and the Hippopotamus*) (Vargas Llosa) **42**:407; **85**:380
Kathleen and Frank (Isherwood) **9**:292; **11**:298; **14**:281, 286; **44**:397-98
Kathleen Listens In (O'Casey) **88**:270
Kathleen, Please Come Home (O'Dell) **30**:275
"Kathleen's Field" (Trevor) **71**:332, 341, 348; **116**:363-64, 379-80, 395
Kathy and the Mysterious Statue (Kingman) **17**:244
Kathy Goes to Haiti (Acker) **45**:14; **111**:8-9, 11, 25
Katia (Almedingen)
    See *Little Katia*
"Katia Reading" (Dobyns) **37**:79, 81
"Katmandu" (Seger) **35**:380-81, 383
"Kato slunce" ("Like the Sunshine") (Bagryana) **10**:14
Katy Lied (Becker and Fagen) **26**:79-80, 83-4
Katz und Maus (*Cat and Mouse*) (Grass) **2**:171-72; **4**:202-03, 206; **32**:198; **49**:143; **88**:137, 143-45, 159
Katzelmacher (Fassbinder) **20**:106, 113
"Kava" (Marley) **17**:270
Kawa no Aru Shitamachi o Hanashi (Kawabata) **107**:121
Kaya (Marley) **17**:270-73
"Kayenta, Arizona, May, 1977" (Lewis) **41**:260-61
Kean (Sartre) **7**:391; **13**:500
"Keats and the Embarrassments of Poetic Tradition" (Bloom) **24**:70
"Keats at Highgate" (Gunn) **32**:215

"Keel and Kool" (Frame)
    See "Keel, Kool"
"Keel, Kool" ("Keel and Kool") (Frame) **96**:184-85
"Keel, Ram, Stauros" (Jones) **7**:190
"Keela, the Outcast Indian Maiden" (Welty) **33**:414; **105**:329, 349
"Keen" (Muldoon) **32**:318
Keep It Crisp (Perelman) **49**:259-60, 270
"Keep it Holy" (Ferber) **93**:162
"Keep Talking" (Levine) **33**:275
"Keep the Customer Satisfied" (Simon) **17**:460, 465
Keep the Faith, Baby! (Powell) **89**:206-07, 209
Keep Tightly Closed in a Cool Dry Place (Terry) **19**:440
"Keep under Cover" (McCartney) **35**:292
Keep Your Eyes Down (Russell) **60**:319
"Keep Your Eyes on the Sparrow" (Cliff) **21**:64
"Keep Your Pity" (Boyle) **58**:66
"The Keeper of the Key" (Guthrie) **23**:199
The Keepers of the House (Grau) **4**:207-08
Keepers of the House (Teran) **36**:419-22
"Keeping Close to Home" (hooks) **94**:144
"Keeping Fit" (Gordimer) **70**:177-78
"Keeping Informed in D.C." (Nemerov) **6**:361
"Keeping Things Whole" (Strand) **18**:518; **41**:436-38; **71**:278, 282, 284-85, 290
"Keeping Track" (Levertov) **66**:239
Keeping Watch (Pack) **13**:439
"Keeping Watch by Night" (O'Brien) **103**:145
"Keepsake" (Montale) **7**:232
Kein Ort. Nirgends (*No Place on Earth*) (Wolf) **29**:463-64, 466-67; **58**:428, 431, 433-35, 437
"Keine Delikatessen" ("No Delicacies") (Bachmann) **69**:57
Der Keller (*The Cellar*) (Bernhard) **32**:25; **61**:11-13
Der Keller (Bernhard) **32**:25
The Kelpie's Pearls (Hunter) **21**:155
Kemet, Afrocentricity and Knowledge (Asante) **70**:389
"Ken Kesey at Stanford" (Cowley) **39**:461
Kennedy for the Defense (Higgins) **18**:234-35
Kennedy or Nixon: Does It Make Any Difference? (Schlesinger) **84**:375
Kennedy without Tears (Wicker) **7**:533
"Kennedy's Inauguration" (Bly) **38**:57
Kennis van die Aand (*Darkness; Looking on Darkness*) (Brink) **18**:66-7; **36**:68; **106**:95-7, 99, 101, 122-25, 137
"The Kensington Mass" (Jones) **42**:242
Kent Family Chronicles (Jakes) **29**:249-50
Kent State: What Happened and Why (Michener) **1**:214; **5**:290; **29**:311; **109**:375, 378-79, 382
"Kentucky Derby Day, Belfast, Maine" (Dobyns) **37**:82
Kentucky Fried Movie (Landis) **26**:271-73
Kentucky Is My Land (Stuart) **11**:509-10; **34**:373
"Kentucky Mountain Farm" (Warren) **6**:557
The Kentucky Trace: A Novel of the American Revolution (Arnow) **7**:15-16
"Kentucky Woman" (Diamond) **30**:110-11, 113
Kenyatta's Escape (Goines) **80**:94
Kenyatta's Last Hit (Goines) **80**:94
"*Kenyon Review*, After the Sandstorm" (Bukowski) **82**:14
"Keokuk" (Hugo) **32**:242

"Kepa" (Grace) **56**:116
Kepler (Banville) **46**:29, 31
"Kept" (Bogan) **46**:80-1, 86, 89; **93**:65
"The Kerner Report on Camp Creek Road" (Allen) **84**:5, 38
Kerrisdale Elegies (Bowering) **47**:30-3
Kersti (Friis-Baastad) **12**:213
"Kerzen für Maria" (Boell) **72**:70
Kesey's Garage Sale (Kesey) **3**:267-68; **64**:231
Kesten and Cul-de-sac (Theriault)
    See *Cul-de-sac*
The Kestrel (Alexander) **35**:27-8
"Kettle of Fire" (Davis) **49**:92, 94
Kettle of Fire (Davis) **49**:92-3
"Kew" (Sarton) **49**:307
"The Kew Stakes" (Hope) **51**:226
"The Key" (Asimov) **19**:25; **26**:45
"The Key" (Muldoon) **72**:282
"The Key" (Singer) **6**:509; **23**:419
The Key (Ichikawa)
    See *Kagi*
The Key (Tanizaki)
    See *Kagi*
Key Largo (Huston) **20**:159, 165
Key out of Time (Norton) **12**:468
"The Key to Everything" (Swenson) **106**:314, 345
A Key to Modern British Poetry (Durrell) **1**:84, 87
The Key to Rebecca (Follett) **18**:157
Key To the Door (Sillitoe) **1**:307; **3**:448; **6**:500; **57**:387, 392-93, 402-03
A Key to the Suite (MacDonald) **3**:307; **44**:408
"Keys and Watercress" (Metcalf) **37**:306
"The Keys of Death" (Green)
    See "Les clefs de la mort"
The Keys of the Kingdom (Cronin) **32**:135-36, 140
"The Keystone" (Powers) **57**:349
Keystone Kids (Tunis) **12**:594-95, 598
The K-Factor (Caute) **29**:124
"al-Khala" ("The Wilderness") (Mahfuz) **55**:188
"Khalil'" (Leonov) **92**:237, 263-64
Khammarat al-qitt al-aswad (*The Black Cat Tavern; The Tavern of the Black Cat*) (Mahfuz) **52**:297-98; **55**:174, 176, 188
Khan al-Khalili (Mahfuz) **52**:292-93, 300
"Khironomíes" (Ritsos) **6**:463
"Khudozhnik" (Brodsky) **13**:115
"Kichli" (*Thrush*) (Seferis) **11**:493, 495
Kicking against the Pricks (Metcalf) **37**:307
Kicking the Leaves (Hall) **13**:259-60; **37**:146-48; **59**:152, 154
"Kicks" (Reed) **21**:311
"Kiczowaty" (Szymborska)
    See "Kitschy"
"The Kid" (Ai) **69**:7, 13
"Kid" (Creeley) **11**:138
The Kid **7**:406
The Kid (Aiken) **10**:4; **52**:20, 24, 26, 32
Le kid (Beckett) **6**:39
The Kid (Chaplin) **16**:203, 207
The Kid (Coover) **32**:120; **46**:116; **87**:35
"Kid Charlemagne" (Becker and Fagen) **26**:81, 83
The Kid Comes Back (Tunis) **12**:595
"The Kid from Hell" (Strugatskii and Strugatskii) **27**:438
The Kid from Tomkinsville (Tunis) **12**:593, 598
"Kid MacArthur" (Vaughn) **62**:456, 459
"Kid Punch" (Beecher) **6**:48

Kid Stakes (Lawler)   58:333, 336-37, 340-44
"Kidnap Poem" (Giovanni)   19:192
The Kidnapped Saint (Traven)   11:535
"Kidnapper" (Gallagher)   63:123, 126
"The Kids Are All Right" (Townshend)   17:525, 529
The Kids Are All Right (Townshend)   17:539
"The Kids Downstairs" (Ihimaera)   46:200
"The Kid's Guide to Divorce" (Moore)   39:84; 45:279-80
"Kierkegaard" (Smith)   64:397
"Kierkegaard en la Zonz Rosa" (Fuentes)   113:250-51
"Kierkegaard: The Singular Universal" (Sartre)   7:472
"Kierkegaard Unfair to Schlegel" (Barthelme)   8:50; 13:56; 46:40-1; 115:60, 65, 70
"Kiev" (Ehrenburg)   62:170
Kifah Tiba (*Thebes' Struggle*) (Mahfuz)   52:299
Kiiroi hito (*Yellow Man*) (Endo)   54:154, 159; 99:285-86
Kika (Almodovar)   114:34-7
"Kiku on the Tenth" (Mishima)   27:341
"Kilbinnen Men" (Dunn)   40:171
"The Kilfenora Teaboy" (Durcan)   43:114, 118
Kilgaren (Holland)   21:149
"Kilka dni wojny o ktorej nie wiadomo, czy byla" ("A Few Day's War Which One is Not Certain Happened") (Konwicki)   117:284
Kill Cure (Rathbone)   41:338
"Kill Day on the Government Wharf" (Thomas)   13:540; 37:416; 107:326
"Kill Your Sons" (Reed)   21:309
Kill Zone (Estleman)   48:105-06
The Killdeer (Reaney)   13:472, 474-75
Killdeer Mountain (Brown)   47:39-40
"Killdozer" (Sturgeon)   39:361, 365, 368
"Killer" (Kesey)   46:227
The Killer (Ionesco)
    See *Tueur sans gages*
The Killer Angels (Shaara)   15:474
Killer at Large (Thompson)   69:378
"Killer Barracuda" (Kristofferson)   26:270
Killer Dolphin (Marsh)   53:248, 260
The Killer Elite (Peckinpah)   20:281-83
The Killer Inside Me (Thompson)   69:375-78, 380-81, 383-86, 388
"The Killer Poet" (Strand)   41:439-41
"The Killers" (Bukowski)   41:74; 108:85
"The Killers" (Hemingway)   13:273; 30:179, 182, 184, 195-96; 41:200; 80:104
Killer's Head (Shepard)   6:496-97
Killer's Kiss (Kubrick)   16:376, 379-80, 385-86
"Killhope Wheel" (Silkin)   6:498-99; 43:403-04
The Killing (Kubrick)   16:377, 379-80, 383-84, 386-87, 389
The Killing Doll (Rendell)   48:323-24
Killing Everybody (Harris)   19:204
"Killing Floor" (Ai)   69:4
Killing Floor (Ai)   14:8-9; 69:3-8, 11-14, 16
A Killing for Christ (Hamill)   10:251
The Killing Game (Ionesco)
    See *Jeux de massacre*
The Killing Ground (Settle)   61:369-74, 376, 383-87
Killing in Verse and Prose, and Other Essays (Fussell)   74:139
Killing Mr. Griffin (Duncan)   26:104-06
Killing Mr. Watson (Matthiessen)   64:325-29

The Killing of a Chinese Bookie (Cassavetes)   20:51-2
"The Killing of Hastings Banda" (Theroux)   46:401
Killing Rage: Ending Racism (hooks)   94:159-61
The Killing Room (Bowering)   32:47
"Killing the Calves" (Hayden)   37:156
"Killing the Pig" (Montague)   46:271
"Killing the Whale" (Plumly)   33:310
Killing Time (Berger)   3:63; 5:60; 8:83; 18:57; 38:41
Killing Time (Warner)   14:553
The Killing Tree (Bennett)   35:43
"Killings" (Dubus)   36:145-46; 97:201-02, 221, 223-24, 229-30
"The Killings in Atlanta" (Amis)   62:2, 5
The Killings in Trinidad (Naipaul)   18:363
The Kill-Off (Thompson)   69:382, 386
Killshot (Leonard)   71:218-19, 223
"Kilmainham Jail" (Day Lewis)   10:131
"Kilpeck" (Adcock)   41:15
"Kilroy Was Here" (Farrell)   66:129
"Kilroy's Carnival" (Schwartz)   45:355, 360
The Kilterman Legacy (McCaffrey)   17:281
"Kim" (Spivack)   6:520
"Kimberley Solzhenitsyn's Calendar" (Frazier)   46:164-65
"Kimberly" (Smith)   12:539
Kimen (*The Seed*) (Vesaas)   48:404-07, 409
"Kimono" (Merrill)   13:380
"Kimyona shigoto" ("A Queer Job") (Oe)   36:349
"Kin" (Angelou)   77:30
"Kin" (Szirtes)   46:393
"Kin" (Welty)   105:299, 323
"Kin" (Williams)   56:426
"Kind" (Ammons)   108:24
"Kind" (Miles)   14:369
Ein Kind (Bernhard)   61:11
Kind Are Her Answers (Renault)   17:390
Kind Hearts and Gentle Monsters (Yep)   35:472-73
A Kind of Alaska (Pinter)
    See *Other Places*
A Kind of Anger (Ambler)   9:18
"A Kind of Happiness" (Mahapatra)   33:284
A Kind of Magic (Ferber)   18:152; 93:186
"A Kind of Nature" (Silkin)   43:400
A Kind of Order, a Kind of Folly: Essays and Conversations (Kunitz)   6:287; 11:319
"A Kind of Parlance" (Peacock)   60:297
"The Kind of Poetry I Want" (MacDiarmid)   63:256
A Kind of Religion (MacInnes)   23:286
"A Kind of Scar" (Boland)   113:66, 90
A Kind of Scar (Boland)   113:74
"A Kind of Survivor" (Steiner)   24:428
A Kind of Testament (Gombrowicz)   49:126-27, 134
"A Kind of Weakness" (Strand)   18:516
"Kind Offices" (Johnston)   51:250
Kinda Kinks (Davies)   21:89
Kinder Brauchen Märchen (Bettelheim)
    See *The Uses of Enchantment: The Meaning and Importance of Fairy Tales*
Kinder Capers (Snodgrass)   68:388, 398-99
Kindergarten (Rushforth)   19:405-07
"Kinderlied" (Grass)   2:173; 32:198
Ein Kinderspiel (*Child's Play*) (Walser)   27:462
"Kindertotenlieder" (Dubie)   36:130
"Kindertotenlieder" (Longley)   29:293
Kindheitsmuster (*A Model Childhood*; *Patterns*

of Childhood) (Wolf)   14:594-95; 29:464-68; 58:422, 428, 430-36
The Kindling (Elliott)   47:106-07
Kindling (Shute)   30:365
Kindly Light (Wilson)   33:451
The Kindly Ones (Powell)   3:400-02; 7:340; 9:435, 439
"Kindness" (Plath)   1:271; 3:392; 9:426; 14:424; 17:360; 50:446; 111:203
A Kindness Cup (Astley)   41:46-8
"The Kindness of Mrs. Radcliffe" (Coward)   51:74
The Kindness of Strangers: Poems, 1969-1974 (Whalen)   29:445
The Kindness of Strangers: The Life of Tennessee Williams (Spoto)   39:444-47, 449-53
Kindred (Butler)   38:62, 65-6
Kindred (Carroll)   10:96-7
Kinds of Affection (Miles)   2:278; 14:369; 39:353
Kinds of Love (Sarton)   4:471; 49:313-14; 91:241
Kindui nogaku shu (Mishima)   4:353; 27:339
Kinflicks (Alther)   7:11-14; 41:19-24
Kinfolk (Buck)   11:77
The King (Lagerkvist)
    See *Konungen*
King and Joker (Dickinson)   12:175-76; 35:133-34, 138
The King and Me (Kureishi)   64:246
"King and Shepard" (Brown)   48:60
The King and the Queen (Sender)
    See *El rey y la reina*
"King Bee" (Boyle)   90:45, 48
King Blood (Thompson)   69:384
"King Borborigmi" (Aiken)   52:28
"King Caliban" (Wain)   46:415
King Coal (Sinclair)   15:498-99, 502; 63:346, 348, 361-62, 371-73
"King Cobra" (Young Bear)   94:370
"The King Cobra as Political Assassin" (Young Bear)   94:370
King Coffin (Aiken)   52:26
King Cole (Masefield)   11:358; 47:229
"King David Dances" (Berryman)   3:66; 6:64; 25:92
The King David Report (Heym)   41:215-16
"King Death" (Gallagher)   63:122, 124
The King Dies (Ionesco)
    See *Le roi se meurt*
King Fisher Lives (Rathbone)   41:338-39, 341
The King Goes Forth to France (Haavikko)   34:175, 177-78
A King in New York (Chaplin)   16:197-98, 203-04
"The King Is Dead" (Vanderhaeghe)   41:450, 452
The King Is Dead (Queen)   11:463
King James VI of Scotland, I of England (Fraser)   32:183-84; 107:32
King Jesus (Graves)   1:128; 39:322-23, 325; 45:172-73
King John (Duerrenmatt)
    See *König Johann*
King John (Durrenmatt)   43:126
"King Kong" (Ondaatje)   51:310
"King Kong Meets Wallace Stevens" (Ondaatje)   51:310-12
King Lazarus (Beti)
    See *Le roi miraculé*
"King Lear" (Simmons)   43:410-12
King Leary (Quarrington)   65:203-04
"A King Listens" (Calvino)   73:50, 53, 60

King Log (Hill)   8:293-96; **45**:178-79, 181-82, 184-87

"King Lord/Queen Freak" (Sanders)   **53**:304

King Lord/Queen Freak (Sanders)   **53**:304

King Midas: A Romance (Sinclair)
    See *Springtime and Harvest: A Romance*

The King Must Die (Renault)   3:426; **11**:472; 17:393-97, 400-01

The King of a Rainy Country (Brophy)   **11**:68; 29:91; **105**:2, 7-10, 12, 30, 34-5

"The King of Asine" (Seferis)   5:385

"King of Beasts" (MacCaig)   **36**:283

The King of Comedy (Scorsese)   **89**:237-42, 252, 261-68

"King of Death" (Honig)   **33**:213

King of Egypt, King of Dreams (MacEwen)   13:357

"The King of Harlem" (Kaufman)   **49**:205

King of Hearts (Kerr)   **22**:254

King of Hearts (Slavitt)   14:491

King of Kazoo (Peck)   17:341

"King of Pain, The" (Police, The)   **26**:366

King of the Beggars (O'Faolain)   **14**:402; 70:317, 321

"King of the Bingo Game" (Ellison)   **86**:324; **114**:113, 125, 131

King of the Castle (Russell)   **60**:320

The King of the Fields (Singer)   **69**:313-16

"King of the Gypsies" (Mitchell)   **98**:153, 180

King of the Gypsies (Maas)   **29**:305-07

"The King of the Hill" (Mailer)   74:205

King of the Hill (Fleming)   **37**:121-22

King of the Hill: On the Fight of the Century (Mailer)   2:262; 3:315; **8**:370

King of the Jews (Epstein)   **27**:128-32

"King of the Mountain" (Garrett)   **51**:140

King of the Mountain (Garrett)   **51**:140, 142-43, 145

The King of the Rainy Country (Freeling)   **38**:184

"King of the River" (Kunitz)   6:286; 14:313

"King of the World" (Becker and Fagen)   **26**:80

King Phoenix (Davies)   7:73

King, Queen, Knave (Nabokov)   1:243; 2:299; 6:352; **8**:417-18; 15:396; 23:312-13; 44:465; 46:294; **64**:348

King, Queen, Knave (Skolimowski)   **20**:353-54

King Rat (Clavell)   **25**:124-26, 128; **87**:2-3, 7, 9, 11-12, 17-19

"King Richard's Prison Song" (Blackmur)   24:66

"King Saul and I" (Amichai)   9:22; **116**:85, 87, 96

The King Snake (Eckert)   17:106

"King Solomon's Ring" (Zelazny)   **21**:466

"King Tut" (Martin)   **30**:248

King Warrior Magician Lover: Rediscovering the Archetypes of the Mature Masculine 70:426, 431, 458

"The King Who Lived on Air" (Bates)   **46**:50

"King Yu" (Hesse)   **25**:259

"The Kingdom" (MacNeice)   1:186

A Kingdom (Hanley)   13:261-62

"The Kingdom and the Glory" (McGinley)   14:365

The Kingdom and the Power (Talese)   **37**:391-93, 403-04

The Kingdom by the Sea: A Journey around Great Britain (Theroux)   **28**:428; **46**:404

"Kingdom County Come" (Mosher)   **62**:313

A Kingdom in a Horse (Wojciechowska)   26:451

The Kingdom of Death (*Sweet Danger*) (Allingham)   19:14, 16

"The Kingdom of Earth" (Williams)   **15**:580; **45**:452, 455

Kingdom of Earth: The Seven Descents of Myrtle (*The Seven Descents of Myrtle*) (Williams) 1:369; 2:464-66; 5:503; **11**:571, 573, 577; **45**:455

"Kingdom of Heaven" (Levertov)   **66**:244

"The Kingdom of Poetry" (Schwartz)   10:464

The Kingdom of the Wicked (Burgess)   **40**:124-26

The Kingdom of This World (Carpentier)
    See *El reino de este mundo*

The Kingdoms of Elfin (Warner)   19:459-60

Kingdoms of Gold, Kingdoms of Jade: The Americas Before Columbus   **70**:331, 342

"The Kingfisher" (Clampitt)   **32**:115

"Kingfisher" (Oliver)   **98**:292

The Kingfisher (Clampitt)   **32**:115-18

"The Kingfishers" (Olson)   2:326; 5:328-29; 6:388; **9**:412; **11**:417-20; **29**:329-30, 334

"Kingfishers at Condat" (Clarke)   **61**:78, 82

"The Kingfisher's Boxing Gloves" (Fenton)   **32**:165

Kingfishers Catch Fire (Godden)   **53**:156-57

"Kinglidoma" (Ritsos)   6:463

"The Kings" (Hope)   **51**:215

The King's Fifth (O'Dell)   **30**:268-70, 273

"The King's Indian" (Gardner)   **5**:133-34; 7:112-13, 115; 8:238; **28**:167-68

The King's Indian (Gardner)   **5**:132-35; 7:111-14, 116; 8:238; **18**:183; **28**:167

The King's Iron (Peck)   17:341

The King's Persons (Greenberg)   7:134; **30**:160-61

King's Ransom (Hunter)   **31**:220

"Kingsbury Mill" (Fisher)   **25**:161

"Kingsmeat" (Card)   **47**:67

Kingstree Island (Ehle)   **27**:102-03

"Kinju" ("Of Birds and Beasts") (Kawabata)   **107**:73, 77, 86

Kink Kontroversy (Davies)   **21**:88-9

The Kink Kronikles (Davies)   **21**:93

Kinkakuji (*The Temple of the Golden Pavillion*) (Mishima)   2:286; **4**:353-54, 357; 6:338; 9:383-84; **27**:335-36, 338-41

"Kinkies" (Trevor)   116:371

The Kink's Greatest Celluloid Heroes (Davies)   21:101

The Kinks Greatest Hits! (Davies)   **21**:89

Kinks Kinkdom (Davies)   **21**:89

Kinks Size (Davies)   **21**:89

"Kinky Reggae" (Marley)   **17**:267, 269

"The Kinnehorah" (Weidman)   7:517

"Kinosaki nite" ("At Kinosaki") (Shiga)   33:370

"Kinot al hametim bamilkhama" ("Lamentations on the War Dead") (Amichai)   **116**:110-11

"The Kinsey Report" (Trilling)   24:452

"Kinship" (Bottoms)   **53**:31, 33

"Kinship" (Heaney)   14:242, 244; **25**:243, 246, 251; **91**:117

Kinsman (Bova)   **45**:71-3

Kiowa Trail (L'Amour)   **25**:280

"Kip" (Grace)   **56**:116-17, 120

Kipper's Game (Ehrenreich)   **110**:175-79, 181-84

"Kirchbachstrasse 121, 2800 Bremen" (Grayson)   **38**:209

"Die Kirche im Dorf" (Boell)   72:77

"The Kirk" (MacCaig)   **36**:287

Kirlian Quest (Anthony)   35:37

"Kirsten" (Shapcott)   **38**:400

"Kiskatinaw Songs" (Musgrave)   **13**:401

"The Kiss" (Blunden)   **56**:39

"The Kiss" (Landolfi)   **49**:216

"The Kiss" (Sassoon)   **36**:385

Kiss (Warhol)   **20**:421

A Kiss before Dying (Levin)   3:294

"A Kiss in Galloway" (Fuller)   **62**:197

Kiss, Kiss (Dahl)   **79**:175-77, 183

Kiss Me Again, Stranger: A Collection of Eight Stories, Long and Short (du Maurier)
    See *The Apple Tree: A Short Novel and Some Stories*

"Kiss Me Baby" (Wilson)   12:644

Kiss Me, Deadly (Spillane)   **13**:526-27

Kiss Me Stupid (Wilder)   **20**:461

The Kiss of Kin (Settle)   **61**:374, 385

"The Kiss of Life" (Gardam)   **43**:171

Kiss of the Spider Woman (McNally)   **91**:159, 163

Kiss of the Spider Woman (Puig)
    See *El beso de la mujer araña*

"Kiss on the Lips" (Prichard)   **46**:332-33

Kiss on the Lips, and Other Stories (Prichard)   **46**:332, 337, 343, 345

Kiss, Orchestra, Fish, Sausage (Aksyonov)
    See *Potseluj, orkestr, ryba, kolbasa*

The Kiss to the Leper (Mauriac)
    See *Le baiser au lépreux*

"The Kissing Place" (Szirtes)   **46**:394-95

"The Kissing Seat" (Muldoon)   **32**:317

"Kissing Stieglitz Goodbye" (Stern)   **100**:333

Kissing the Rod: An Anthology of Seventeenth-Century Women's Verse (Greer)   **65**:316-17

"Kissing the Toad" (Kinnell)   **29**:284

"Kitchen" (Jensen)   **37**:191

"The Kitchen" (Lee)   **90**:201

"The Kitchen" (O'Faolain)   **32**:342

The Kitchen (Wesker)   3:518; 5:481-83; **42**:425-28, 430

Kitchen (Yoshimoto)
    See *Kitchin*

"A Kitchen Allegory" (Fisher)   **87**:128, 130

"The Kitchen Side of the Door" (Ferber)   93:140-41

"The Kitchen Stairs" (Gombrowicz)   **49**:127

"Kitchenette Building" (Brooks)   **49**:31

Kitchin (*Kitchen*) (Yoshimoto)   **84**:421-31

"The Kite" (Eberhart)   **11**:178; **56**:88

"The Kite" (Elytis)   **100**:172

"Kite" (Jensen)   **37**:191

"The Kite" (Strand)   **71**:283

Kite (Minus)   **39**:79-81

The Kite (Mitchell)   **35**:322, 325-27

"Kite and Paint" (Robison)   **42**:339

"A Kite for Michael and Christopher" (Heaney)   37:165, 169

"Kite Man" (Wild)   14:580

"Kites" (Merwin)   **88**:210

"Kites" (Urdang)   **47**:400

"Kitschy" ("Kiczowaty") (Szymborska)   **99**:208

"Kitsilano Beach on a May Evening" (McFadden)   **48**:258

"The Kitten" (Oliver)   **34**:246, 249; **98**:256, 267

"Kittiwake" (Hall)   **51**:170

"Kitty" (Appelfeld)   **47**:5

Kitty Foyle (Trumbo)   19:445

"Kitty Hawk" (Frost)   **13**:230-31; **26**:120

"Kitty Partners" (Apple)   **33**:22

"Kitty's Back" (Springsteen) 17:488

Ki-Yu: A Story of Panthers (*Panther*) (Haig-Brown) 21:134, 139-40, 143-46

Kjeldene (*The Springs*) (Vesaas) 48:404

"KKK" (Guillen) 48:159

"Kladenec" (Bagryana) 10:14

"Klagemauer Nacht" (Sachs) 98:327

Klanger och spår (*Eagles and Traces; Echoes and Traces; Resonance and Foot-Tracks*) (Transtroemer) 52:410, 412; 65:222-23, 229, 233

Klara and Two Men (Klima) 56:166, 168

"Klare gerührt" (Jandl) 34:196

"Klassik Komix #1" (Millhauser) 109:160

"Klasyk" (Herbert) 43:187

"Kleckerburg" (Grass) 32:198

"Klee Dead" (Coover) 15:145

Klein und Wagner (Hesse) 69:289, 297

"Kleine Aufforderung zum grossen Mundaufmachen" (Grass) 15:263

"Eine Kleine mathmusik" (Perelman) 23:336

Kleinzeit (Hoban) 7:161; 25:264, 266

Klingsor's Last Summer (Hesse)
See *Klingsors letzter Sommer*

Klingsors letzter Sommer (*Klingsor's Last Summer*) (Hesse) 17:206

The Klondike Stampede (Berton) 104:61

Klondike: The Life and Death of the Last Great Gold Rush (Berton) 104:39, 44-5, 47, 57

"Klounut govori" (Bagryana) 10:14

The Knack (Jellicoe) 27:206-10

The Knack (Lester) 20:219, 223, 228-29

"The Knave of Diamonds" (Leonov)
See "Bubnovy valet"

Knave of Dreams (Norton) 12:469-70

Kneading the Blood (Kenny) 87:241

"Kneel to the Rising Sun" (Caldwell) 1:51; 14:96; 60:61

Kneel to the Rising Sun, and Other Stories (Caldwell) 60:47, 50, 60-1

"Kneeling before You in a Gesture" (Brutus) 43:91-2

"Kneeling Down to Look into a Culvert" (Bly) 38:53

"Kneeshaw Goes to War" (Read) 4:439

Der Knekht (*The Slave*) (Singer) 1:313; 3:453, 455, 457; 15:504, 507; 23:413-15, 418; 69:316; 111:294, 304-05, 307, 321-23, 328

"Knife" (Oates) 108:382

"The Knife" (Samarakis) 5:381

"The Knife" (Selzer) 74:277-78

"Knife" (Simic) 9:479; 22:383; 49:337, 339, 342; 68:370, 379

"The Knife" (Tillinghast) 29:416-17

A Knife All Blade (Cabral de Melo Neto)
See *Uma faca só lâmina*

The Knife and Other Poems (Tillinghast) 29:415-17

"The Knife and the Bread" (Broumas) 73:9

"Knife Blows" (Mauriac)
See "Coups de couteaux"

Knife in the Water (Polanski) 16:463-65, 467, 471-72

"The Knife Sharpener's Daughter" (Dybek) 114:61

"The Knife Thrower" (Boell)
See "Der Mann mit den Messern"

"The Knight" (Rich) 6:457; 11:475-76; 36:366

"The Knight, Death, and the Devil" (Jarrell) 13:298

A Knight in Dried Plums (McFadden) 48:245-46, 251

The Knight of the Swords (Moorcock) 27:350

The Knightly Quest (Williams) 39:449; 45:447, 453

The Knightly Quest: A Novella and Four Short Stories (Williams) 1:369; 45:447

Knights and Dragons (Spencer) 22:401, 405-06

Knight's Fee (Sutcliff) 26:427-28, 431-36, 439, 441

Knight's Gambit (Faulkner) 3:149, 156; 14:179; 18:148-49; 52:128

The Knights of the Golden Table (Almedingen) 12:1

"Knights of the Paper Spaceship" (Aldiss) 40:17

The Knights of the Round Table (Cocteau)
See *Les chevaliers de la table ronde*

"Knights of the White Camellia & Deacons of Defense" (Komunyakaa) 94:249

"Knives" (Welch) 52:428

"Knives of Pernambuco" (Cabral de Melo Neto)
See "As facas Pernambucanas"

Knjiga lirike (*A Book of Lyrics*) (Krleza) 114:166

"Knock, Knock" (Wilding) 73:401, 403

Knock Knock (Feiffer) 8:216; 64:149-50, 159, 161

Knock on Any Door (Motley) 18:355-57

"Knock on the Door" (Ochs) 17:332

Knock upon Silence: Poems (Kizer) 15:308; 39:171; 80:173-74, 177-79, 181

Knockdown (Francis) 22:151-52; 42:148-50, 155-58; 102:140

"A Knocker" (Herbert) 9:273

"Knockin' On Heaven's Door" (Dylan) 77:187

"Knocking Around" (Ashbery) 15:33

"Knocking Donkey Fleas off a Poet from the Southside of Chi" (Madhubuti) 73:193, 214

Knocking on the Door (Paton) 10:388; 25:364

"Knocks Me off My Feet" (Wonder) 12:660, 664

"Knole" (Fuller) 28:152

Knots (Laing) 95:132, 137

The Knotting Sequence (Booth) 13:103-04

Know about Alcohol (Hyde) 21:179

Know about Drugs (Hyde) 21:180

Know Nothing (Settle) 19:409; 61:372-73, 375-76, 381-87

Know Your Feelings (Hyde) 21:177

"Know Your Rights" (Clash) 30:51-2

"Knowing He Was Not my Kind Yet I Followed" (Hannah) 90:148-49

"Knowing the Human Condition" (Childress) 86:314; 96:104, 115

"Knowing Where to Stop" (Booth) 24:91

"Knowledge" (Bogan) 46:89; 93:67

Knowledge and Experience in the Philosophy of F. H. Bradley (Eliot)
See "Experience and the Objects of Knowledge in the Philosophy of F. H. Bradley"

Knowledge and Human Interests (Habermas)
See *Erkenntnis und Interesse*

"Knowledge and the Image of Man" (Warren) 13:576

Knowledge from the Abyss (Michaux)
See *Connaissance par les gouffres*

"Knowledge of Age" (Avison) 97:76

"Knox" (Ellison) 13:206

"Knoxville, Tennessee" (Giovanni) 117:194-96

Knuckle (Hare) 29:213-14, 216-17; 58:233

Knulp (Hesse) 6:237; 17:218

Den knutna näven (*The Clenched Fist*) (Lagerkvist) 54:274-75

Ko; or, A Season on Earth (Koch) 5:219; 44:248

"The Kobzar" (Gustafson) 36:221

Kochu byt' chestnym (*I Want to Be Honest*) (Voinovich) 10:505, 507-08; 49:373

"Kodachrome" (Simon) 17:466

Kodak (*Documentaires; Kodak Documentaires*) (Cendrars) 18:95; 106:153, 158-59, 175, 185-86, 190-91, 198

Kodak Documentaires (Cendrars)
See *Kodak*

Kogda razglyaetsya (*When the Skies Clear*) (Pasternak) 18:383

"Kogda v mrachneyshey iz stolits" ("When in the Gloomiest of Capitals") (Akhmatova) 64:9

"Koi" (Merrill) 91:233

"Koisimi Buddhist of Altitudes" (Kinnell) 13:320

Kojinteki na taiken (*A Personal Matter*) (Oe) 10:327, 374; 36:343-48; 86:215-16, 230, 236, 241, 244

"Koka Kola" (Clash) 30:46

Koko (Straub) 107:282-86, 288-91, 293-96, 298-302, 304, 306-07, 309-10

"Kolbel'naya treskovogo mysa" (Brodsky)
See "A Cape Cod Lullaby"

"Kolelo" (Bagryana)
See "Surce coveško"

Kolkhida (Paustovsky) 40:363, 368

Kollegi (Aksyonov)
See *Colleagues*

The Kolokol Papers (Bograd) 35:62-3

Kolyma Tales (Shalamov) 18:478-80

The Komagata Maru Incident (Pollock) 50:224, 226

Kommentar till ett stjärnfall (Johnson)
See *Commentary on a Falling Star*

Die Komödie der Eitelkeit (*Comedy of Vanity*) (Canetti) 14:121; 75:127-28, 143, 145-47; 86:298, 301, 303

Komödie der Politik (Durrenmatt) 15:199

Kompleks polski (*The Polish Complex*) (Konwicki) 28:207-10; 54:256-60, 262, 264; 117:256-60, 262, 264, 271, 279-80, 284, 286, 290-91

"Kompromise Kompromisovich" (Yevtushenko) 26:468

"Konarka" (Mahapatra) 33:284

Koncert na ostrove (*Concert on the Island*) (Seifert) 93:336-37, 343

Konec prekrasnoj èpox (Brodsky)
See *Konets prekrasnoy epokhi*

Konek Landing (Figes) 31:162

Konets melkogo cheloveka (*The End of a Little Man; The End of a Petty Man; The End of a Trivial Man; The End of an Insignificant Man*) (Leonov) 92:237-38, 242, 256, 265, 275, 278

Konets prekrasnoy epokhi (*The End of a Fine Epoch; Konec prekrasnoj èpox*) (Brodsky) 13:116-17

Konfessions of an Elizabethan Fan Dancer (Nichol) 18:369

Kongi's Harvest (Soyinka) 5:396; 36:417-18; 44:281-83, 286-88, 290

König Johann (*King John*) (Duerrenmatt) 102:53, 55, 57, 62, 64

König Johann (Durrenmatt) 15:199

Kontakion for You Departed (*For You De-*

parted) (Paton)   25:363-64
Kon-Tiki: Across the Pacific by Raft (Heyerdahl)
   26:189-93
The Kon-Tiki Expedition (Heyerdahl)   26:191,
   193
"Kontrapunkti" ("Parola") (Bagryana)   10:11,
   13
Kontynenty (Milosz)   56:236
Konungen (*The King*) (Lagerkvist)   54:269-
   70, 275
"Kooks" (Bowie)   17:58
Köp den blindes sång (Ekelof)   27:110
Kopfgeburten (Grass)   32:201
Kora (Popa)   19:373
Kora in Hell: Improvisations (Williams)   2:468-
   70; 5:507-09; 22:466; 42:449, 452, 460,
   462-64; 67:410
"Korab ot Ispanja" (Bagryana)   10:12
"Kore" (Creeley)   8:153; 36:118
"Kore" (Merwin)   8:389; 13:384; 18:335-36;
   88:203-04
"Korea" (McGahern)   48:262
"Korea" (Selzer)   74:269, 273, 285
Korrektur (*Correction; Revisions*) (Bernhard)
   32:21-3, 26; 61:10, 14-15, 19, 21; 32:21-
   2
Korsoniloff (Cohen)   19:111
Koshikei (*Death by Hanging*) (Oshima)
   20:246-49, 251-52
Kosmos (*Cosmos*) (Gombrowicz)   7:123, 127;
   49:121, 123, 127, 129, 133-34
Koto (Kawabata)   107:98-9, 102, 104, 107-12
Koviakin's Notes (Leonov)
   See *Zapisi nekotorykh epizodov, sdelannye v
      gorode Goguleve Andreem Petrovichem
      Koviakinym*
Kovyakin's Diary (Leonov)
   See *Zapisi nekotorykh epizodov, sdelannye v
      gorode Goguleve Andreem Petrovichem
      Koviakinym*
Kovyakin's Journal (Leonov)
   See *Zapisi nekotorykh epizodov, sdelannye v
      gorode Goguleve Andreem Petrovichem
      Koviakinym*
The Kozlotur Constellation (Iskander)
   See *Sozvezdie Kozlotura*
Kozui wa waga tamashii ni oyobi (*The Flood
   unto my Soul; The Waters Are Come in
   unto My Soul*) (Oe)   36:350; 86:215-17,
   228, 230-32, 234, 238-39, 241
"Kral Majales" (Ginsberg)   36:184; 109:346-
   47, 355-56
"Kranich and Bach" (Hollander)   8:299
"Krankheit und Liebesentzug" (Wolf)   58:430
Krapp's Last Tape (Beckett)   1:20; 2:45-6;
   6:39, 45-7; 9:77, 83-6; 10:32; 11:37-9;
   14:74; 18:42-3, 47; 29:58, 63; 57:79, 89;
   59:252, 255, 257-58; 83:114
*Krasnoe koleso: Povestvovanie v otmerennykh
   srokakh. Uzel I, Avgust chetyrnadsatogo*
   (Solzhenitsyn)
   See *Avgust chetyrnadtsatogo*
Krazy Kat: The Unveiling and Other Stories
   (Dawson)   6:125-26
The Kremlin Letter (Huston)   20:171
"Kremlin of Smoke" (Schnackenberg)   40:380-
   81
"Krestova Solitaire" (Lane)   25:285
"Kretschmer's Types" (Durrell)   27:97
Krik? Krak! (Danticat)   94:93-100
Krilon: A Novel about the Probable (Johnson)
   14:295
Krippendorf's Tribe (Parkin)   43:336-39

Kris (*Crisis*) (Bergman)   72:51
"Krishnamurti and His Hallucinating Devotees"
   (Asturias)   8:25
Krisis: Ein Stuck Tagebuch (*Crisis: Pages from
   a Diary*) (Hesse)   69:275, 293, 297
"Kristallnacht" (Ai)   69:9, 17
Kristlein Trilogy (Walser)   27:463
Kristnihald undir jökli (Laxness)   25:300
Kristofferson (Kristofferson)   26:266
Kristofor Kolombo (*Cristoval Colon*) (Krleza)
   114:166, 174-76
"Kristu Du" (Carey)   96:25, 28, 36-7, 39
Kristy's Courage (Friis-Baastad)   12:213
Kroliki i udavy (*Rabbits and Boa Constrictors*)
   (Iskander)   47:195, 200-01
Kronika wypadków milosnych (*A Chronicle of
   Love Affairs; A Chronicle of Love Events*)
   (Konwicki)   117:257, 283, 285, 287
Kroniki (Milosz)   82:297
Kroxotnye rasskazy (*Poems in Prose; Short
   Sketches*) (Solzhenitsyn)   2:412
Kruger's Alp (Hope)   52:211-14, 217
Kruglie sutki non-stop (Aksyonov)
   See *'Round the Clock Non-Stop*
Krumnagel (Ustinov)   1:346
"Kto my,—fishki ili velikiye?" (Voznesensky)
   57:416
"Kto ty?" (Voznesensky)   15:555
"Kublaikansky" (Raine)   32:351
Kucá nasred druma (*A House in the Middle of
   the Highway*) (Popa)   19:375
"Kudo" (Endo)   99:293
"Kudzu" (Dickey)   15:173
"The Kugelmass Episode" (Allen)   52:41, 48
Kühe in Halbtrauer (Schmidt)   56:391-92
Kujira no shimetsu suru hi (*The Day the Whales
   Shall be Annihilated*) (Oe)   86:214
"Kukuvitsa" (Bagryana)   10:12
Kullus (Pinter)   27:388
"Kuma" (Shiga)   33:368
"Kumpel mit dem langen Haar" (Boell)   72:69
"A Kumquat for John Keats" (Harrison)   43:179,
   181
"Kuniko" (Shiga)   33:367
"Kunst und Religion" (Boell)   27:67
Der Künstliche Baum (Jandl)   34:197
Kunstmakher fun Lublin (*The Magician of
   Lublin*) (Singer)   1:313; 3:455, 457; 6:508;
   9:488; 11:500, 503; 15:504-05, 508;
   23:414-15, 418, 422; 69:307, 317;
   111:294, 300, 305, 307, 319, 321-22, 324-
   25, 328, 345
"Kurodiasu no nikki" ("Claudius' Diary";
   "Claudius' Journal") (Shiga)   33:366-67,
   371
Kuroi ame (*Black Rain*) (Ibuse)   22:224-27
Kuroi junin no ohna (*Ten Dark Women*)
   (Ichikawa)   20:186
Kurt Gerstein ou l'ambiguité du bien (*Coun-
   terfeit Nazi: The Ambiguity of Good; Kurt
   Gerstein: The Ambiguity of Good*) (Fried-
   lander)   90:105-7, 112, 118
Kurt Gerstein: The Ambiguity of Good (Fried-
   lander)
   See *Kurt Gerstein ou l'ambiguité du bien*
"Kurt Vonnegut and His Critics: The Aesthet-
   ics of Accessibility" (Irving)   38:250
"Kurzgefasster Lebenslauf" (Hesse)   17:204
Kuslar da gitti (*The Birds Too Are Gone*)
   (Kemal)   14:301
Kvaedakver (*Poems*) (Laxness)   25:295
"Kväll Morgon" (Transtroemer)   65:235

Kvetch (Berkoff)   56:17-19
Kvinnodröm (*Dreams; Journey into Autumn*)
   (Bergman)   72:41, 62
Kvinnor ropar heim (*Women Calling Home*)
   (Vesaas)   48:404, 406
Kvinnors väntan (*Secrets of Women; Waiting
   Women*) (Bergman)   16:66; 72:40, 62
"Kwa Mamu Zetu Waliotuzaa (for our mothers
   who gave us birth)" (Sanchez)   116:273,
   274, 281, 298, 301, 316
"Kyofu" ("The Fear") (Tanizaki)   28:417
Kyoko no ie (*Kyoko's House*) (Mishima)   9:383,
   385; 27:341
Kyoko's House (Mishima)
   See *Kyoko no ie*
"A Kyoto Garden" (Enright)   31:149
"Kyoto: Her Nature, Food...and Women"
   (Tanizaki)   28:416
"Kyrie" (Gascoyne)   45:149
Kyrie (Jouve)   47:212
"L" (Merrill)   8:383-84, 387
"L" (Walcott)   67:358
"La" (Tolson)   105:262
"L.A." (Young)   17:572
LA (Cixous)   92:74, 93
L.A. (*Light Album*) (Wilson)   12:653-54
"A la créole" (Audiberti)   38:21
De la grammatologie (*Of Grammatology; On
   Grammatology*) (Derrida)   24:137-40,
   145, 147, 156; 87:72-74, 77-80, 89-91,
   100, 102, 104
"De la littérature considérée comme une
   tauromachie" (Leiris)   61:341, 343, 352,
   357-58
De la séduction (*On Seduction*) (Baudrillard)
   60:24, 26, 33
De la vigilia estéril (Castellanos)   66:45, 50
L.A. Woman (Morrison)   17:290-91, 295-96
Labels: A Mediterranean Journal (Waugh)
   19:462; 107:394
El laberinto (Arrabal)
   See *La Labyrinthe*
El laberinto de la soledad (*The Labyrinth of
   Solitude*) (Paz)   3:375-76; 6:397; 10:393;
   19:364, 366-67; 51:331; 65:176, 179,
   181, 185-86, 188, 195
Laberinto de Pasiones (*Labyrinth of Passions*)
   (Almodovar)   114:3, 14, 16-7, 30-2, 45,
   46-9, 55
Labor in Vain (Garfield)   12:234
Laboratories of the Spirit (Thomas)   13:544-
   45; 48:379-81
Labors of Love (Cassill)   23:109
"Labour Day Dinner" (Munro)   95:302
"The Labours of Hercules" (Fuller)   62:186-
   87, 193-94, 201
LaBrava (Leonard)   28:236-37; 34:213-16;
   71:208-13, 216, 220, 222-23
"The Labrenas" (Landolfi)
   See "La labrene"
"La labrene" ("The Labrenas") (Landolfi)
   49:216-17
Laburnum Grove (Priestley)   2:346; 34:361
Labyrinth of Passions (Almodovar)
   See *Laberinto de Pasiones*
The Labyrinth of Solitude (Paz)
   See *El laberinto de la soledad*
La Labyrinthe (*El laberinto*) (Arrabal)   58:5-8,
   12, 17-18
Le labyrinthe du monde (Yourcenar)   19:484;
   38:461; 87:382, 396, 432
Labyrinths of Voice (Kroetsch)   57:287, 293
Labyrinths: Selected Stories, and Other Writ-

ings (Borges) 2:72; 3:80; 8:99; 44:356; 48:44, 46; 83:171, 185, 188

Labyrinths, with Path of Thunder (Path of Thunder) (Okigbo) 25:349, 352, 355-56; 84:305-06, 310, 312, 314, 316-19, 322-23, 328-34, 339-43

"Lac en coeur" (Dudek) 11:161; 19:137

"Laca" (Guillen) 79:238

"Lace" (Boland) 67:39; 113:84

"The Lace Maker" (Watkins) 43:446

"Der Lacher" ("The Laughter") (Boell) 2:55; 15:69; 27:66

"Lachesis lapponica" (Enzensberger) 43:145-46

"Lachrimae; or, Seven Tears Figured in Seven Passionate Pavans" (Hill) 8:296; 18:238, 242; 45:178, 180-85, 187, 189

"The Lackawanna at Dusk" (Parini) 54:361

Laços de familia (Family Ties) (Lispector) 43:267-72

"'Lacrimae rerum'" (Corn) 33:116

"The Ladder" (Prince) 35:331-32

"The Ladder" (Pritchett) 41:334

"The Ladder and the Tree" (Golding) 58:197

Ladder of Years (Tyler) 103:274-77

Ladders to the Fire (Nin) 4:376; 60:279

Ladera este (East Slope; Eastern Slope) (Paz) 51:324, 333; 65:177, 181-83, 189, 198, 200

The Ladies (Grumbach) 64:198-201

"Ladies Advice" (Thesen) 56:421

Ladies Almanack (Barnes) 29:27-9

Ladies and Escorts (Thomas) 37:416-17; 107:316, 318, 326, 348

"Ladies and Gentlemen" (Oates) 108:385

"Ladies' and Gentlemen's Guide to Modern English Usage" (Thurber) 5:435

"Ladies and Red Nights" (Vollmann) 89:276, 304

"Ladies Auxiliary" (Guthrie) 35:185

"Ladies by Their Windows" (Justice) 19:232, 236; 102:256

"Ladies from Lapland" (Chappell) 78:114

"The Ladies in the Library" (Vidal) 33:407

"Ladies, Listen to Me" (Wakoski) 7:504

"Ladies Looking for Lice" (Kennedy) 42:258

Ladies Love Outlaws (Jennings) 21:201

Ladies' Man (Price) 12:491-92

"Ladies Need Only Apply" (Astley) 41:47

The Ladies of Missalonghi (McCullough) 107:152, 154, 162

The Ladies of St. Hedwig's (Almedingen) 12:1, 3

Ladies of the Canyon (Mitchell) 12:436-37

Ladies of the Corridor (Parker) 68:331, 333, 337

"Ladies Pay" (Reed) 21:312-13

"The Ladies Who Lunch" (Sondheim) 30:385-86, 391, 395, 400

The Ladies-in-Waiting (Buero Vallejo)
   See *Las meninas*

"El lado de la sombra" (Bioy Casares) 88:94

El lado de la sombra (Bioy Casares) 88:94

Ladri di biciclette (The Bicycle Thief) (De Sica) 20:85-9, 91-7

"Lady" (Carruth) 84:135

"A Lady" (Donoso)
   See "Una señora"

The Lady (Richter) 30:316, 319, 324, 330

Lady (Tryon) 11:548

"The Lady and the Pedlar" (Anand) 23:18

"The Lady and the Unicorn" (Porter) 33:322

"Lady Bates" (Jarrell) 2:209; 6:260

"Lady Cab Driver" (Prince) 35:326-28

"Lady Day" (Reed) 21:307

Lady Frederick (Coward) 29:134

Lady Frederick (Maugham) 15:366; 67:215, 223, 228

The Lady from Dubuque (Albee) 25:36-40; 53:21-3, 25; 86:120; 113:28, 31-3, 40

"The Lady from Ferme-Neuve" (Ferron) 94:120

"The Lady from Guatemala" (Pritchett) 5:353-54; 41:333

"The Lady from Lucknow" (Mukherjee) 53:267

The Lady from Nowhere-At-All (Carroll) 10:98

The Lady from Shanghai (Welles) 20:434, 441, 443-44; 80:382-84, 386, 388-91, 393, 395

"The Lady from the Land" (Thurber) 5:433

"Lady Godiva" (Moravia) 7:244

Lady Godiva and Other Stories (Moravia)
   See *Un'altra vita*

"Lady Godiva's Horse" (Rooke) 25:394

"Lady Godiva's Operation" (Reed) 21:307

"Lady Immoraline" (Sitwell) 67:325

"Lady in a Green Dress" (Callaghan) 41:98

The Lady in Kicking Horse Reservoir (Hugo) 6:244-45; 18:260; 32:239, 241-44, 246, 250

The Lady in the Car with Glasses and a Gun (Japrisot)
   See *La dame dans l'auto avec des lunettes et un fusil*

Lady in the Dark (Hart) 66:176, 178, 180, 182-83, 188-90

Lady into Fox (Garnett) 3:188-89

The Lady Is Cold (White) 10:528-29

Lady L (Gary) 25:184

"Lady Lazarus" (Plath) 2:335-36; 3:390; 5:342-44; 9:427; 11:445-48, 450; 14:423, 425-26, 428; 17:348, 354, 359, 361, 363, 365-66; 50:440, 449; 51:342-44, 346, 351, 353; 62:390, 405; 111:159, 173-74, 176-78, 180-81, 185, 199, 208-11, 216, 221

"Lady Lucifer" (O'Faolain) 70:312

"Lady Luncheon Club" (Angelou) 35:30

"A Lady of Fashion" (Phillips) 28:362

The Lady of Larkspur Lotion (Williams) 45:448

Lady of Luzon (Connelly) 7:55

The Lady of the Camelias (Abell)
   See *Kameliadamen*

"The Lady of the House of Love" (Carter) 41:117

"The Lady of the Lake" (Malamud) 9:349; 11:353; 27:297; 44:419; 85:199

"Lady Olga" (Mitchell) 98:168, 180

Lady Oracle (Atwood) 8:30-31, 33-34; 13:44-6; 15:39; 25:62-5, 67-8; 44:147; 84:70, 72, 77-9, 86, 90-5, 105-07

"Lady Stardust" (Bowie) 17:65

The Lady Vanishes (Hitchcock) 16:337-38, 340, 345, 347

The Lady Who Sold Furniture (Metcalf) 37:299

"Lady with a Lamp" (Parker) 68:326, 334, 339

Lady with Chains (Carrier)
   See *La dame qui avait des chaines aux chevilles*

"The Lady with No One at All" (Williams) 45:444

The Lady with the Compass (Haviaras) 33:202

"The Lady with the Dog" (Baxter) 78:28

"The Lady with the Pet Dog" (Oates) 52:338;

108:354, 368, 371

The Lady with the Unicorn (Watkins) 43:441, 446, 451, 456

Lady Yesterday (Estleman) 48:107

"Lady-Oh" (Diamond) 30:112

"Lady's Boogie" (Hughes) 108:299-304

The Lady's Not for Burning (Fry) 2:143, 145; 10:200

"La'em" ("To the Mother") (Amichai) 116:132

"El lago de los cisnes" ("Swan Lake") (Neruda) 62:332

"Lagoon" (Brodsky) 36:78

"The Lagoon" (Frame) 96:183-85, 188

The Lagoon and Other Stories (Frame) 66:143-45; 96:183-85, 188-89, 194, 209, 216

"Laguna Ladies Luncheon" (Allen) 84:8

Le lai de Barabbas (Arrabal) 18:21

Laid Back in Washington (Buchwald) 33:95

Laidlaw (McIlvanney) 42:282-85

The Laird of Abbotsford: A View of Sir Walter Scott (Wilson) 33:452-53

"The Laird's Son" (Brown) 100:82

"Le lait de la mort" ("Milk of Death ") (Yourcenar) 38:463; 87:390

"Lajwanti" (Anand) 23:21

Lak tar miyo kinyero wi lobo (Are Your Teeth White? Then Laugh!) (p'Bitek) 96:300

"The Lake" (Fuller) 28:153

"The Lake" (Hall) 51:171

"The Lake" (Jeffers) 54:234

"The Lake" (Merwin) 13:386

"The Lake" (Wright) 53:424

The Lake (Kawabata) 5:207-08; 9:316; 107:106, 108

"Lake Chelan" (Stafford) 4:520

Lake Effect Country (Ammons) 57:49-51, 59; 108:16, 57

"Lake in Spring" (Wright) 11:578

"The Lake in the Sky" (Haines) 58:218

"The Lake in Winter" (Shapcott) 38:397

"Lake Michigan Morning" (Sandburg) 35:356

The Lake of Darkness (Rendell) 28:386-87; 48:320-21

"The Lake of Loneliness" (Sagan) 17:428

Lake of the Woods (Tesich) 40:417, 422; 69:373

"The Lake of Tuonela" (Roberts) 14:464

"A Lake Scene" (Swenson) 61:400; 106:326

"Lake Stephen" (Baxter) 78:26

"Lake Superior" (Niedecker) 42:297, 300

Lake Wobegon Days (Keillor) 40:275-77; 115:261, 263-64, 269, 274-75, 277, 296

Lakeboat (Mamet) 46:252

"Lakeshore" (Scott) 22:372-74, 377-78

"Lakeside Incident" (Skelton) 13:507

The Lakestown Rebellion (Hunter) 35:229

Lakota Woman (Crow Dog) 93:109-112

"Lamarck Elaborated" (Wilbur) 3:533

"The Lamb" (Oliver) 19:362

Lamb (Mac Laverty) 31:253, 255-56

The Lamb (Mauriac) 56:219

"Lamb to the Slaughter" (Dahl) 79:180

"Lambda" (Tolson) 105:284

The Lambert Mile (The Lambert Revels) (White) 49:401-04

The Lambert Revels (White)
   See *The Lambert Mile*

"Lambkin: A Fable" (Hope) 51:217

The Lamb's War (de Hartog) 19:133

"The Lame" (Bottoms) 53:29

"Lame de fond" (Montague) 46:269

"The Lame Duck" (Wright) 53:425

"A Lame Idyll" (MacNeice) 53:233

"The Lame Shall Enter First" (O'Connor) 3:366; 13:418; 15:410; 21:261, 263, 272, 276; 104:103, 106, 108, 100, 113, 123, 135, 138, 141, 156, 173, 178-79, 184-85, 194, 196

"Lament" (Dodson) 79:191

"Lament" (Gunn) 81:179, 181, 184, 186-87

"Lament" (Livesay) 79:345

"Lament" (Morrison) 17:295-96

"Lament" (Plath) 17:360

"Lament" (Sexton) 53:318

Lament and Triumph (Barker) 48:10-11, 16, 20

"Lament: Fishing with Richard Hugo" (Wright) 28:469

"Lament for a Dead Policeman" (Simmons) 43:414

"Lament for a Proprietor" (Porter) 33:318

"Lament for Barney Flanagan" (Baxter) 14:62

"Lament for Doormen" (Tomlinson) 45:403

"The Lament for Galadriel" (Tolkien) 38:440

Lament for Harmonica (Ringwood) 48:330, 334-35, 339

"Lament for Moths" (Williams) 71:360

"Lament for Pasiphaé" (Graves) 2:175

"Lament for the Duke of Medina Sidonia" (Beer) 58:38

"Lament for the Great Music" (MacDiarmid) 4:309-10, 313; 11:333

"Lament For The Lakes" (Frame) 96:200

"Lament for the Makers" (Buckley) 57:131

"Lament for the O'Neills" (Montague) 46:275-76

"Lament for the Poles of Buffalo" (Hass) 18:209, 211

"Lament fot the Makers" (Pinsky) 94:308

"The Lament of Edward Blastock" (Sitwell) 67:325

"Lament of the Drums" (Okigbo) 84:310-11, 315, 321, 326-27, 336, 341

"Lament of the Flutes" (Okigbo) 25:351; 84:328-30, 332

"Lament of the Frontier Guard" (Pound) 112:344

"Lament of the Lavender Mist" (Okigbo) 25:351, 354; 84:310, 328-29, 331, 336

"The Lament of the Masks: For W. B. Yeats: 1865-1939" (Okigbo) 25:353; 84:311, 321

"Lament of the Normal Child" (McGinley) 14:366

"Lament of the Sacred Python" (Achebe) 7:6; 11:4

"Lament of the Silent Sisters" (Okigbo) See "Silences: Lament of the Silent Sisters"

"The Lament of the Tortured Lover" (Christie) 110:126

"The Lament on the Death of a Master of Arts" (Anand) 23:16; 93:34

"Lament over Love" (Hughes) 35:221

"The Lament upon the Waters" (Ashbery) 77:45

"Lamentación de Dido" ("Dido's Lament") (Castellanos) 66:45-6, 50-1, 53

"Lamentations" (Gluck) 22:175-77

"Lamentations on the War Dead" (Amichai) See "Kinot al hametim bamilkhama"

"Lamento" (Transtroemer) 52:410; 65:235

Laments (Heaney) 91:124

Laments for the Living (Parker) 15:414; 68:325

"Lamium" (Gluck) 81:173

De l'amour dans la ferraille (Heartbreaks along the Road) (Carrier) 78:79-82

"Lamp" (Rakosi) 47:344

The Lamp and the Veil (Watkins) 43:441-42

"The Lamp at Noon" (Ross) 13:493

The Lamp at Noon, and Other Stories (Ross) 13:492

A Lamp for Nightfall (Caldwell) 50:302; 60:64

"A Lamp in the Window" (Capote) 19:85

"The Lamp of God" (Queen) 11:461

A Lamp on the Plains (Horgan) 53:172-75

"La lámpara en la tierra" (Neruda) 7:259

Lampes à arc (Morand) 41:303, 307

"Lampfall" (Walcott) 76:279

The Lamplighter's Funeral (Garfield) 12:234-35, 237

The Lamplit Answer (Schnackenberg) 40:380-81

"Lamp-Posts" (Dunn) 40:169

"Lampshades" (Yevtushenko) 26:467

Lamy of Santa Fe (Horgan) 9:279

Lanark: A Life in Four Books (Gray) 41:176-84

Lancelot (Percy) 8:442-46; 14:411, 414-15, 419; 18:399, 402; 47:341; 65:257

Lancelot (Vansittart) 42:396-98

Lancelot du Lac (Bresson) 16:119

"Land" (Heaney) 5:172

The Land (Colum) 28:86-7, 90

Land (Lopez y Fuentes) See Tierra

The Land and People of Ghana (Sale) 68:349

The Land and the Promise (Slaughter) 29:376

"The Land around Us" (Carson) 71:104

"The Land Below" (Dorn) 10:158-59

The Land beyond the River (Stuart) 11:510; 34:374

The Land Breakers (Ehle) 27:103

The Land Is Bright (Kaufman) 38:264, 266

"Land Israel" (Sachs) 98:357

Land Israel (Sachs) 98:357

"The Land Itself" (O'Brien) 8:430

The Land Leviathan (Moorcock) 27:348-49

Land of Carnival (Amado) See O pais do carnaval

"The Land of Cockaigne, 1568" (Dubie) 36:135

"Land of Cotton" (Sorrentino) 7:448

The Land of Lost Content (Hill) 113:287

The Land of Lost Content (Phillips) 28:362

Land of Muscovy (Almedingen) See Rus into Muscovy

"Land of Promise" (Swan) 69:363-64

The Land of Promise (Maugham) 11:368; 93:254

Land of Silence and of Darkness (Herzog) 16:328

The Land of Silence and Other Poems (Sarton) 49:312

The Land of the Blessed Virgin (Maugham) 93:268

Land of the Free—U.S.A. (MacLeish) 8:361; 14:338; 68:286, 292

"The Land of the Freeze" (Ekelof) 27:115

The Land of the Living (Connelly) 7:57

The Land of Ulro (Milosz) See Ziemia Ulro

Land of Unlikeness (Lowell) 1:183; 4:295, 297-98, 302; 5:257; 8:348, 356; 37:235, 239, 241

"The Land of Veils" (Peacock) 60:293

"The Land They Gave Us" (Rulfo) See "Nos han dado la tierra"

The Land Unknown (Raine) 7:353

"Land Where My Fathers Died" (Dubus) 97:208, 213-16

Land Where My Fathers Died (Dubus) 97:209

Land without Bread (Bunuel) See Las Hurdes—Tierra sin pan

Land without Stars (Kiely) 23:259, 261-62; 43:239, 245

"Land Workers" (Masefield) 11:358

"Landed Fish" (Piercy) 27:374

Landed Gentry (Maugham) 11:368

Landessprache (Enzensberger) 43:146

"Landfall" (Mosley) 43:317

Landfill Meditations (Vizenor) 103:288

"Landing on the Moon" (Swenson) 61:391

"Landing Zone Bravo" (O'Brien) 103:145

"The Landlady" (Dahl) 79:181

The Landlady (Behan) 79:36, 53

Landlocked (Lessing) 3:290, 292; 6:291; 94:281-82

"The Landlord" (Pritchett) 41:334

The Landlord (Hunter) 35:224-25, 227

Landlord (Vansittart) 42:395

"The Landlord's Flower Beds" (Thesen) 56:420

"The Landlord's Tiger Lilies" (Thesen) 56:422

Lando (L'Amour) 25:278

Landor's Poetry (Pinsky) 38:360; 94:302

Landru (Chabrol) 16:169, 181

"Land's End" (MacLeish) 68:273, 284, 287

Land's End (Stolz) 12:555

"Landscape" (Ashbery) 41:37

"Landscape" (Hooker) 43:196-97

"Landscape" (Oliver) 98:261, 267

Landscape (Pinter) 3:386-87; 6:416-17, 420; 9:420; 11:442-43; 15:423-24; 27:385, 394-96; 73:268

Landscape after the Battle (Wajda) 16:582

"Landscape as Poetic Focus" (Davie) 10:125

"Landscape at Champrovent" (Dobyns) 37:81

"Landscape, Figure, Cavern" (Le Guin) 45:213

"Landscape for the Disappeared" (Komunyakaa) 94:240

"Landscape, History and the Pueblo Imagination" (Silko) 114:305-06

Landscape in Concrete (Lind) See Landschaft in Beton

"Landscape in Spring" (Soto) 80:290

"Landscape Near an Aerodrome" (Spender) 41:427; 91:260

Landscape of a Nightmare (Baumbach) 6:32; 23:52-3

"A Landscape of Cries" (Sachs) See "Landschaft aus Schreien"

"Landscape of Fire" (Hooker) 43:201

"Landscape of Love" (Page) 18:376

"Landscape of My Young World" (Brutus) 43:93

"The Landscape of Return" (Mahapatra) 33:277

"Landscape of Screams" (Sachs) See "Landschaft aus Schreien"

Landscape of the Body (Guare) 14:221; 29:204-06, 208; 67:81-2, 85

Landscape of the Daylight Moon (Hooker) 43:197, 199-200

"Landscape of the Star" (Rich) 7:368

Landscape Painted with Tea (Pavic) See Predeo slikan cajem

"Landscape Poetry Is a Dead Letter" (Bernard) 59:45

Landscape West of Eden (Aiken) 52:26

"Landscape with a Wish" (Levi) 41:244

Landscape with Figures (Hildesheimer) See Landschaft mit Figuren

"Landscape with Little Figures" (Justice)

19:234
"Landscape with Orphans" (Porter)　33:320
"Landscape with Poet" (Levi)　41:244
Landscape with Rain (Gustafson)　36:220-22
"Landscape with Tractor" (Taylor)　44:302-03
"Landscape without Figures" (McGinley)　14:366
"Landscapeople" (Ashbery)　25:53
"Landscapes" (Eliot)　13:201; 15:213
"Landscapes" (Oates)　3:359; 6:367
Landscapes of Living and Dying (Ferlinghetti)　27:139; 111:59
Landscapes of Watt (Beckett)　29:59
Landscapes with Figures (Cabral de Melo Neto)
　See *Paisagens com figuras*
"Landscapes with Termites" (Cabral de Melo Neto)
　See "Paisagens com cupim"
The Landscapes Within (Okri)　87:314, 316-19, 322, 325
"Landschaft aus Schreien" ("A Landscape of Cries"; "Landscape of Screams") (Sachs)　98:331, 335, 338-41, 343-44
Landschaft in Beton (*Landscape in Concrete*) (Lind)　1:177-78; 2:245; 4:292-93; 27:271; 82:128, 131-40, 142, 145
Landschaft mit Figuren (*Landscape with Figures*) (Hildesheimer)　49:167
"Landslides" (Coles)　46:112
Landslides: Selected Poems, 1975-1985 (Coles)　46:113
"Lane" (Ali)　69:31
Le langage et son double/The Language and Its Shadow (Green)　77:285
"A l'ange avantgardien" (Scott)　22:374, 377
"Der Lange Marsch" (Hofmann)　54:225
"Der Längere Arm" (Lenz)　27:245
The Langoliers (King)　113:366-67, 385-87
Langston Hughes: A Biography (Meltzer)　26:299
The Langston Hughes Reader (Hughes)　108:285
"Langston, McKay, and Dubois: The Contradicitions of Art and Politics during the Harlem Renaissance" (Baraka)　115:11
"Language" (Ciardi)　40:156
"The Language" (Creeley)　78:162
"Language" (hooks)　94:157
Language (Spicer)　8:499; 72:346, 348, 351
"Language and Gnosis" (Steiner)　24:435
"Language and Literature from a Pueblo Perspective" (Silko)　114:294-95, 303, 305-06, 311
"Language (and Other) Problems" (Richler)　46:352
"Language and Politics" (McCarthy)　39:488-89
Language and Silence (Steiner)　24:427-30, 432
"Language as an Escape from the Discrete" (Jacobsen)　48:192, 194-95
"Language as an Instrument of Domination" (Castellanos)　66:56
Language as Gesture (Blackmur)　24:57, 59-60, 63, 66
Language as Symbolic Action (Burke)　24:132
"Language Barrier" (Warren)　39:273
"The Language in the Present Day" (Brooks)　86:282
"Language Is a Tool of Production" (Solzhenitsyn)　10:480
Language Lattice (Celan)

　See *Sprachgitter*
Language Made Plain (*English Made Plain*) (Burgess)　81:301
The Language of Clothes (Lurie)　39:180
The Language of Fiction (Lodge)　36:267-70
The Language of Goldfish (Oneal)　30:279-80
"The Language of Love" (Hearne)　56:127
"A Language of New York" (Oppen)　7:281
"The Language of Shadows" (Koch)　44:246
The Language of the American South (Brooks)　86:278, 283
"The Language of the Brag" (Olds)　32:346; 39:189
"The Language of the Gentry and the Folk" (Brooks)　86:281
The Language of the Night: Essays on Fantasy and Science Fiction (Le Guin)　22:269, 274
"The Language of the Self" (Lacan)
　See "Fonction et champ de la parole et du langage en psychanalyse"
"The Language of Weather" (Young Bear)　94:369
"Language, Power, Force" (Eco)　60:113
"Language-Mesh" (Celan)
　See "Sprachgitter"
"Languages and Culture" (Brink)　106:120
The Languages of Criticism and the Structure of Poetry (Crane)　27:70-1
The Languages of Love (Brooke-Rose)　40:102
The Languages of Love (Maitland)
　See *Daughter of Jerusalem*
The Languages of Pao (Vance)　35:422-23, 425
Langue (Jouve)　47:206-08
"Langue de pierres" (Breton)　15:91
"L'anguilla" ("The Eel") (Montale)　9:387
"Lantana" (Wakoski)　40:456
The Lantern Bearers (Sutcliff)　26:427, 429, 430, 432-37, 439
"Lantern Slides" (O'Brien)　65:168, 171; 116:210-11
Lantern Slides (O'Brien)　65:167-71, 173; 116:203-04, 222
Lanterna Magica (*The Magic Lantern*) (Bergman)　72:60-2
"La lanterne magique de Picasso" (Prevert)　15:439
"The Lanterns" (Koch)　44:241
Lanterns across the Snow (Hill)　113:309
Lanterns and Lances (Thurber)　5:433; 11:534
"Laocoon" (Piercy)　62:367
"Lap Dissolves" (Coover)　46:122
A Lap of Honour (MacDiarmid)　4:310
"Lapis Lazuli" (Durcan)　70:152
"L'Lapse" (Barthelme)　115:65
"Lares" (Longley)　29:293
"Large Bad Picture" (Bishop)　9:94; 13:95; 32:29
"The Large Cool Store" (Larkin)　64:269, 276
"A Large Number" (Szymborska)　99:200
A Large Number (Szymborska)　99:199
The Large Scale Structure of Space-Time (Hawking)　63:149; 105:44-5
"Largely an Oral History of My Mother" (Brodkey)　56:60-1, 67
Larger than Life (Buzzati)
　See *Il grande ritratto*
"The Largess" (Eberhart)　56:86
"Largess" (Muldoon)　32:319; 72:265
"Largo" (Celan)　53:74
Largo Desolato (Havel)　58:243, 245; 65:420, 429, 435, 439, 441

"Lark"　75:77
"The Lark" (Merwin)　1:213
The Lark (Anouilh)
　See *L'alouette*
Lark Ascending (de la Roche)　14:149
"Lark Descending" (Blunden)　56:30
"The Lark in the Clear Air Still Sings" (O'Casey)　88:261
"The Larkin Automatic Car Wash" (Ewart)　46:149
"Larkinesque" (Ryan)　65:215
"Larmes de soleil" (Soupault)　68:406-07
"Larry" (Gallant)　38:195
Larry and the Undersea Raider (Farley)　17:115
Larry's Party (Shields)　113:444-46
"Las Vegas Tilt" (Ferlinghetti)　6:183-84
"Lascelles Abercrombie" (Blunden)　56:40
Lasi Claudius Civiliksen salaliittolaisten pöydällä (*The Glass on the Table of Claudius Civilis's Conspirers*) (Haavikko)　34:170
"A Lass in Wonderland" (Scott)　22:377
"The Lass of Aughrim" (Muldoon)　72:277
"Lasser" (Ammons)　5:29
"Last Acts" (Olds)　85:302
"The Last Adam" (Cozzens)　4:112, 115; 11:124, 128, 131-32
The Last Adam (Cozzens)　92:179-81, 186, 192-93, 199
The Last Analysis (Bellow)　3:49; 6:49, 51; 8:69, 76; 13:70-1; 33:71
Last and Lost Poems of Delmore Schwartz (Schwartz)　45:354-57; 87:344
The Last and the First (Compton-Burnett)　1:63
"The Last Battle" (Parra)　102:353-54
The Last Battle (Lewis)　6:308; 27:264
The Last Battle (Ryan)　7:385-86
The Last Beautiful Days of Autumn (Nichols)　38:344-45
The Last Billionaire (Clair)
　See *Le dernier milliardaire*
"The Last Bus" (Strand)　18:516, 518
The Last Carousel (Algren)　4:17-18; 33:14-15
The Last Castle (Vance)　35:417, 423, 426-27
The Last Catholic in America: A Fictionalized Memoir (Powers)　66:379-80, 382-83
"The Last Charge" (Davidson)　13:170
"Last Child" (Kennedy)　42:255
"Last Class" (Roethke)　101:266
The Last Command (Sternberg)　20:377-78
"The Last Commander" (Yehoshua)　13:617; 31:468
The Last Cop Out (Spillane)　3:469
"The Last Cottage" (Leavitt)　34:77
Last Courtesies and Other Stories (Leffland)　19:279-80
"The Last Covenant" (Riding)　7:374
"The Last Crop" (Jolley)　46:221
"Last Dance" (Young)　17:572
"The Last Dance" (Zamora)
　See "El último baile"
"The Last Dane" (Mahon)　27:290
"The Last Day" (Dinesen)　10:148
"Last Day" (Kogawa)　78:167
"The Last Day" (Matheson)　37:246
"The Last Day" (Stafford)　29:379
The Last Day and the First (Weiss)　14:557
"Last Day at the Job" (Cryer)　21:81
"The Last Day in the Field" (Gordon)　29:188; 83:231, 247
The Last Day of Summer (Konwicki)
　See *Ostatni dzien lata*

The Last Day the Dogbushes Bloomed (Smith) **25**:406, 408, 410; **73**:355

"Last Days" (Oates) **33**:296

Last Days (Oates) **33**:296

"Last Days at Teddington" (Gunn) **18**:199

"Last Days of a Charming Lady" (Tate) **9**:523

"The Last Days of a Famous Mime" (Carey) **40**:129; **96**:53

"Last Days of a Squaw Man" (Cook-Lynn) **93**:127

"The Last Days of Alice" (Tate) **4**:535, 539; **6**:525; **9**:522

The Last Days of America (Erdman) **25**:155-56

The Last Days of British Honduras (Tavel) **6**:529

The Last Days of Louisiana Red (Reed) **5**:370-71; **6**:447-50; **13**:477, 480; **32**:357-59, 364; **60**:302, 305, 313

"Last Days of Prospero" (Justice) **19**:233; **102**:277

"The Last Decision" (Bova) **45**:73

The Last Defender of Camelot: A Collection by Roger Zelazny (Zelazny) **21**:478-79

Last Delivery before Christmas (Buckler) **13**:120

"The Last Demon" (Singer) **38**:407; **111**:296, 329-32

The Last Detail (Towne) **87**:350-53, 360, 369, 374-77

"Last Diary" (Arguedas) **18**:8

"The Last Diet" (Gilchrist) **48**:120, 122

The Last Ditch (MacNeice) **4**:315; **53**:237

Last Ditch (Marsh) **53**:247-51, 253

The Last Don (Puzo) **107**:210-214

"The Last Dream" (Young Bear) **94**:362

The Last Enchantment (Stewart) **35**:395-96; **117**:369, 372, 374-76, 379

The Last Epiphany (Aleixandre)
   See *Nacimiento último*

"Last Evening" (Justice) **102**:267

"The Last Evolution" (Campbell) **32**:73-4

Last Exit to Brooklyn (Selby) **1**:306-07; **2**:390; **4**:481-82; **8**:474-77

"The Last Experiment of Dr. Brugge" (Gustafson) **36**:220

"The Last Fantasy" (Allen) **84**:5

"The Last Flight of Doctor Ain" (Tiptree) **48**:389, 394, 396; **50**:357

The Last Flower, a Parable of Pictures (Thurber) **5**:431-33, 435, 442; **25**:437

Last Fragments (Pound) **48**:286

The Last Frontier (Fast) **23**:153-54

The Last Frontier (MacLean) **50**:349-50

"The Last Galway Hooker" (Murphy) **41**:312, 314, 316

The Last Galway Hooker (Murphy) **41**:311

The Last Gamble (Graham) **23**:192

"Last Gang in Town" (Clash) **30**:44, 46

"Last Gangster" (Corso) **11**:123

"The Last Gas Station" (Grau) **4**:210; **9**:240

The Last Gentleman (Percy) **2**:332-34; **3**:379-81; **6**:399-400; **8**:440, 442, 444-45; **14**:413, 417; **18**:396-99, 401-02; **47**:338; **65**:254, 257-58, 260

"The Last Good Country" (Hemingway) **10**:269; **30**:194, 198-99

The Last Good Time (Bausch) **51**:54-5

The Last Guru (Pinkwater) **35**:317-18

"The Last Head" (Gascoyne) **45**:157

"Last Hill in a Vista" (Bogan) **46**:89

Last Holiday (Priestley) **34**:362

The Last Hours of Sandra Lee (Sansom) **6**:484

The Last Houseparty (Dickinson) **35**:136, 138

The Last Human Being (Lagerkvist)
   See *Sista mänskan*

The Last Hurrah (Ford) **16**:313, 315

The Last Hurrah (O'Connor) **14**:389-90, 392-94

"The Last Husband" (Humphrey) **45**:193, 203-04

The Last Husband, and Other Stories (Humphrey) **45**:193, 195

"The Last Incantation" (Smith) **43**:423, 425

The Last Jew in America (Fiedler) **4**:161; **13**:213

"Last Journey" (Montague) **46**:269

"The Last Kiss" (Gordimer) **33**:179-80

"The Last Laugh" (Betjeman) **43**:49

The Last Laugh (Perelman) **23**:338-40; **44**:502; **49**:269

"The Last Leaf" (Porter) **7**:310; **15**:429

"Last Letter" (Livesay) **79**:344

The Last Love (Costain) **30**:100

The Last Lunar Baedeker (Loy) **28**:251, 253

The Last Magi (Conde)
   See *Les derniers rois mages*

The Last Man (Lagerkvist)
   See *Sista mänskan*

The Last Man and Other Verses (Daryush) **19**:118, 120

The Last Man's Head (Anderson) **37**:19

"Last May" (Dixon) **52**:94-5

The Last Metro (Truffaut) **20**:407-08; **101**:387, 396, 410

"The Last Mohican" (Malamud) **9**:346-48; **18**:317; **27**:297, 306; **44**:412

"The Last Moon" (Dubus) **97**:236-37

"The Last Morning" (Smith) **22**:385

Last Mornings in Brooklyn (Kenny) **87**:249

"The Last Mowing" (Frost) **4**:175; **10**:195

"The Last Mummer" (Heaney) **5**:170, 172

"Last Names and Empty Pockets" (Kinsella) **27**:237

Last Night at the Brain Thieves Ball (Spencer) **30**:404, 406

"Last Night I Drove a Car" (Corso) **11**:123

"Last Night in Darkness" (Lane) **25**:287

The Last Night of the Earth Poems (Bukowski) **82**:28

Last Nights of Paris (Soupault)
   See *Les dernières nuits de Paris*

Last Notes from Home (Exley) **6**:172

"The Last of Autumn" (Blunden) **56**:28

The Last of England (Porter) **5**:346; **33**:319, 322

The Last of Mankind (Lagerkvist)
   See *Sista mänskan*

The Last of Mr. Norris (*Mr. Norris Changes Trains*) (Isherwood) **1**:156; **9**:293; **11**:298-300; **14**:283-84, 286; **44**:396-97, 399-400, 402

"The Last of Saturdays" (Elytis) **100**:190

Last of the Breed (L'Amour) **55**:306-07

"The Last of the Caddoes" (Humphrey) **45**:203

The Last of the Country House Murders (Tennant) **13**:536-37; **52**:397

The Last of the Crazy People (Findley) **27**:140-41; **102**:97, 105, 108, 111-16

The Last of the Duchess (Blackwood) **100**:18-21, 25, 27-8, 31

"The Last of the Fire Kings" (Mahon) **27**:288-90

The Last of the Just (Schwarz-Bart) **2**:388-89; **4**:479-80

The Last of the Lowries (Green) **25**:198

"The Last of the Masters" (Dick) **72**:113

The Last of the Pleasure Gardens (King) **53**:206-07

Last of the Red Hot Lovers (Simon) **11**:495; **31**:395-96, 403-04

The Last of the Savages (McInerney) **112**:211, 213, 215-19

"The Last of the Spanish Blood" (Garrett) **51**:152

The Last of the Wine (Renault) **3**:425-26; **17**:392-401

"The Last One" (Merwin) **13**:385; **88**:205-06

Last One Home Sleeps in the Yellow Bed (Rooke) **25**:390-91

Last Orders, and Other Stories (Aldiss) **40**:14-15, 20

The Last Outing (Leonov) **92**:278

The Last Pad (Inge)
   See *Don't Go Gentle*

"The Last Painting or the Portrait of God" (*Le dernier tableau ou le portrait de Dieu*) (Cixous) **92**:81, 94, 96

"The Last Pennant before Armageddon" (Kinsella) **43**:253, 255-57

"The Last People" (Merwin) **13**:383

"The Last Picasso" (Diamond) **30**:113

"The Last Picture Show" (Brown) **79**:154

The Last Picture Show (McMurtry) **2**:272; **3**:333; **7**:213-15; **11**:371; **27**:324-25, 328-31; **44**:254, 256-57

The Last Plantagenets (Costain) **30**:100

"The Last Poem in the Series" (Jiles) **58**:277

Last Poems (Celan) **53**:82-3; **82**:34-6

Last Poems (Sexton) **53**:313

"The Last Post" (Graves) **39**:327

"Last Post" (O'Connor) **23**:331

"Last Quarter" (Hollander) **5**:186

"The Last Quatrain of the Ballad of Emmett Till" (Brooks) **49**:36

"The Last Question" (Asimov) **9**:50, 52; **26**:55

"The Last Quixote" (Coover) **3**:114; **46**:115

"The Last Remarkable Man" (Cook-Lynn) **93**:115

The Last Resort (Johnson) **27**:217-18

Last Resort (Sommer) **25**:426

A Last Resort—For These Times (Rathbone) **41**:342

"Last Respects" (Kis) **57**:251, 253

"Last Respects" (Roth) **104**:284

Last Respects (Weidman) **7**:517

The Last Ride of Wild Bill (Brown) **59**:265, 266, 268

"Last Rites" (Scott) **22**:372, 376

"The Last River" (Kinnell) **5**:216; **29**:283

Last Round (Cortazar)
   See *Ultimo round*

"Last Rung on the Ladder" (King) **113**:338

"Last Scene in the First Act" (Piercy) **18**:405; **27**:374

"Last Seen" (Ai) **69**:18

The Last September (Bowen) **11**:59-64; **15**:79

The Last Seven Wounds (Duhamel)
   See *Les sept dernières plaies*

"Last Sheet" (Fuller) **28**:151

"The Last Song" (Harjo) **83**:270

The Last Song (Harjo) **83**:272, 278

The Last Song of Manuel Sendero (Dorfman)
   See *La última canción de Manuel Sendero*

The Last Spike (Berton) **104**:44-5, 57

"Last Spring They Came Over" (Callaghan) **65**:250

Last Stand at Saber River (Leonard) **71**:224

Last Stands: Notes from Memory (Masters) **48**:220-24

"The Last Stop" (Seferis)   **11**:492
"The Last Straw" (Brown)   **79**:154
"The Last Struggle" (Davies)   **23**:142
"The Last Summer" (Pasternak)
   See "Provest'"
Last Summer (Hunter)   **11**:279; **31**:222, 225
The Last Summer (Pasternak)
   See *Povest*
Last Sunday (Peck)   **17**:341-42
"Last Supper" (Endo)   **99**:288, 296-97, 301, 307
"The Last Supper" (Nye)   **42**:302
The Last Supper (Bermant)   **40**:93
"The Last Supplement" (Kesey)   **3**:267
The Last Sweet Days of Isaac (Cryer)   **21**:78-9
Last Tales (Dinesen)   **10**:145, 150; **29**:156; **95**:37, 47-50, 52, 55, 68
"Last Tango" (Steele)   **45**:365
Last Tango in Paris (Bertolucci)   **16**:89-94, 97-8, 100
"The Last Tea" (Parker)   **68**:326, 339
The Last Temptation of Christ (Scorsese)   **89**:249-54, 258, 260-63, 265, 267-68
The Last Testament of Oscar Wilde (Ackroyd)   **52**:4-7, 10-12, 14-15
"Last Things" (Nemerov)   **36**:309
"Last Things" (Plath)   **5**:341
Last Things (Snow)   **4**:505; **6**:517; **9**:497-98; **19**:427
"The Last Thoughts of Sir Walter Raleigh in the Tower of London" (Padilla)   **38**:352
"The Last Throw" (Pritchett)   **41**:334
"The Last Time" (Jagger and Richard)   **17**:231
"The Last Time" (Kristofferson)   **26**:270
"The Last Time I Saw Her" (Lightfoot)   **26**:278
"The Last Time I Saw Richard" (Mitchell)   **12**:440
"The Last Time I Saw Trout Fishing in America" (Brautigan)   **3**:88
"Last Time the Angels Came Up" (Kesey)   **46**:228
"The Last to See Them Alive" (Capote)   **13**:137
The Last Train Robbery (Theroux)   **15**:533
"The Last Train to Malakhovka" (Voznesensky)   **57**:415
"Last Trams" (Slessor)   **14**:496-97
Last Treatments (Yehoshua)   **13**:616; **31**:470
The Last Tresilians (Stewart)   **7**:465
"Last Trip to Tulsa" (Young)   **17**:572
The Last Trolley Ride (Calisher)   **38**:72-3
The Last Trump (Gardner)   **30**:156
The Last Tycoon (Kazan)   **16**:373-74; **63**:225, 229
The Last Unicorn (Beagle)   **7**:25-6; **104**:3-10, 15, 18-21, 23-34
The Last Valley (Guthrie)   **23**:200-01
"The Last Veil" (L'Heureux)   **52**:274
"The Last Virgin" (Howe)   **47**:172
"The Last Voyage of the Ghost Ship" (Garcia Marquez)
   See "El último viaje del buque fantasma"
"Last Walk" (Lowell)   **37**:238
The Last Waltz (Scorsese)   **20**:332-34; **89**:260, 265
Last Waltz in Santiago, and Other Poems of Exile and Disappearance (Dorfman)
   See *Pastel de choclo*
"The Last Wasp in the World" (Fiedler)   **13**:213
The Last Wave (Weir)   **20**:427-30
"The Last Will and Testament" (Auden)   **43**:16
"Last Will and Testament" (Larkin)   **64**:261
"The Last Will and Testament of Art Evergreen" (Pack)   **13**:438

The Last Will of Dr. Mabuse (Lang)   **20**:204
"Last Wishes" (Trevor)   **9**:529
The Last Woman in His Life (Queen)   **11**:464-65
The Last Word and Other Stories (Greene)   **70**:289
"Last Words" (Abse)   **29**:20
"Last Words" (Plath)   **3**:389; **14**:425; **51**:340, 346; **111**:214
"Last Words" (Roethke)   **46**:356
The Last Words of Dutch Schultz (Burroughs)   **5**:93
"Last Words to James Wright" (Hugo)   **32**:250
"A Last World" (Ashbery)   **41**:40; **77**:52
The Last Worthless Evening (Dubus)   **97**:208-09, 213-16, 224
Last Year at Marienbad (Resnais)
   See *L'annee derniére a Marienbad*
Last Year at Marienbad (Robbe-Grillet)
   See *L'année dernière à Marienbad*
"Lastness" (Kinnell)   **13**:322
Latakia (Thomas)   **37**:417-18, 423; **107**:330, 333-36, 340-41, 347-48
"Late" (Bogan)   **93**:65, 92
"Late Afternoon of a Faun" (Brophy)   **29**:91; **105**:9, 15, 30
"A Late Answer" (Levine)   **14**:318
"Late at Night" (Rosenthal)   **28**:395
"Late at Night" (Stafford)   **29**:380
"A Late Aubade" (Wilbur)   **53**:413; **110**:385
"Late August" (Atwood)   **13**:44
"Late August" (Hacker)   **72**:192
Late Autumn (Ozu)   **16**:448-49, 451, 453-56
"Late Autumn in Venice" ("After Rilke") (Schwartz)   **45**:355
The Late Bourgeois World (Gordimer)   **5**:145, 147; **7**:132; **10**:239; **18**:186; **33**:182; **51**:161; **70**:162-65, 170, 172, 180
The Late Breakfasters (Aickman)   **57**:2
Late But in Earnest (Simmons)   **43**:407, 411
Late Call (Wilson)   **2**:472, 474; **3**:534-36; **5**:513-14; **25**:459, 461
A Late Divorce (Yehoshua)   **31**:474-76
"Late Echo" (Ashbery)   **15**:33-4; **41**:38
"A Late Encounter with the Enemy" (O'Connor)   **21**:256, 268-69; **104**:175
"Late Fall" (Jacobsen)   **48**:192; **102**:242
Late for the Sky (Browne)   **21**:35-6, 38
The Late George Apley (Kaufman)   **38**:264
The Late George Apley (Marquand)   **10**:329-31
"Late Gothic" (Gotlieb)   **18**:191
The Late Great Human Road Show (Jiles)   **58**:273-74, 278-79
The Late Great Me (Scoppettone)   **26**:401-02
The Late Hour (Strand)   **18**:517-18, 520-21; **41**:432, 434, 436; **71**:279, 287
"Late in the Evening" (Simon)   **17**:467-68
"Late in the Season" (Matthiessen)   **64**:321, 324
Late Innings (Angell)   **26**:32-3
"Late, Late" (Starbuck)   **53**:354
"Late Love" (Oz)   **8**:436-37
Late Love (Oz)
   See *Ad m'avet*
"Late Loving" (Van Duyn)   **116**:411, 413, 415, 429
"Late Moon" (Bly)   **38**:57
"The Late Mother" (Macdonald)   **13**:356
"Late Naps" (Bell)   **31**:51
"Late Night in Autumn" (Merwin)   **88**:193
"Late Night, San Francisco" (Codrescu)   **46**:103
"Late Night Telephone" (Jiles)   **58**:271

Late Night Thoughts on Listening to Mahler's Ninth Symphony (Thomas)   **35**:415-16
"Late Night with Fog and Horses" (Carver)   **55**:273
A Late Picking: Poems, 1965-1974 (Hope)   **51**:222
"Late Poem to My Father" (Olds)   **85**:295, 299, 304
"The Late Public Figure" (Bates)   **46**:55-6
"Late Requests" (Longley)   **29**:295
"The Late Show" (Browne)   **21**:36
"Late Sonnet" (Carruth)   **84**:130
"Late Spring" (Hass)   **99**:140-41
Late Spring (Ozu)   **16**:448, 450-51, 453-56
"Late Summer" (Dunn)   **36**:155
"A Late Sunday Afternoon by the Huron" (Baxter)   **45**:52-3; **78**:17-18
"Late Tutorial" (Buckley)   **57**:130
"Late Winter" (Dudek)   **11**:159
"Late-Flowering Lust" (Betjeman)   **43**:34
The Latent Heterosexual (Chayefsky)   **23**:116
"Latent Rapists" (Shange)   **25**:402
"Later" (Creeley)   **78**:162
"Later" (Sondheim)   **30**:391, 402
Later (Creeley)   **15**:153; **36**:121; **78**:141, 148, 150-52
"Later: Four Fragments" (Barnard)   **48**:27
Later Poems (Thomas)   **48**:381
"The Later Poetry of W. B. Yeats" (Blackmur)   **24**:63
"Later Sonnets" (Denby)   **48**:84
"Later Testament" (Belitt)   **22**:49
Later than You Think (Kaye)   **28**:198
Later the Same Day (Paley)   **37**:333-35, 337, 339
"Later Today" (Stern)   **100**:338-39
"Latest Face" (Larkin)   **64**:262
"The Latest Injury" (Olds)   **85**:293
Late-Winter Child (Buckley)   **57**:133-36
The Lathe of Heaven (Le Guin)   **13**:345, 350; **22**:273; **45**:213, 221
"The Latin Lesson" (Boland)   **113**:92, 111
"Latitude" (Gotlieb)   **18**:191
A látogáto (*The Case Worker*) (Konrad)   **4**:273; **10**:304; **73**:174, 176-81, 184, 187
"Latorre, Prado, and My Own Shadow" (Neruda)   **62**:325
"Latrine" (Eich)   **15**:204
A Lattice for Momos (Everson)   **27**:133-34
"Lauda" (Milosz)   **56**:250; **82**:298, 303
Lauda somnului (*In Praise of Sleep*)   **75**:67, 70, 77-8
Laudatur (Faludy)   **42**:139
"Das Läufer" (Lenz)   **27**:245
"Laugh and Learn" (Royko)   **109**:408
"Laugh? I Thought I'd Die" (Royko)   **109**:408
"The Laugh of the Medusa" (Cixous)
   See "The Laugh of the Medusa"
Laughable Loves (Kundera)
   See *Smesné lásky*
"The Laughing Man" (Salinger)   **12**:520; **56**:329
The Laughing Matter (Saroyan)   **1**:301-02; **8**:467; **29**:361-62
The Laughing Policeman (Wahloo)
   See *Den skrattande polisen*
Laughing Stalks (Dudek)   **11**:159; **19**:137-38
Laughing Stock (Linney)   **51**:262
Laughing to Keep from Crying (Hughes)   **10**:281; **108**:285
"Laughing with One Eye" (Schnackenberg)   **40**:378-79
"Laughs in the Open Tombs" (Shapcott)   **38**:403
"The Laughter" (Boell)

See "Der Lacher"
"Laughter" (Dybek)   114:72, 81-2
"Laughter" (O'Connor)   23:329
Laughter! (Auschwitz; Tsar) (Barnes)   56:4, 6, 8-9
"Laughter Beneath the Bridge" (Okri)   87:314-15
Laughter in the Dark (Nabokov)   1:239; 2:302; 3:353-55; 6:359; 8:417; 15:396; 44:465; 46:291, 294; 64:348
A Laughter in the Mind (Layton)   15:319
"Laughter in the Peroration" (Klappert)   57:268
The Laughter of Carthage (Moorcock)   58:355-59
"The Laughter of Leen" (Richter)   30:320
"The Laughter of the Wapishanas" (Harris)   25:217
"Launcelot in Hell" (Ciardi)   40:158
Laundromats (Altman)   116:68
"Laura" (Aickman)   57:4
"Laura" (Joel)   26:223
"Laura's Funeral" (Johnston)   51:249
"The Laureate" (Graves)   45:173
"Laurel" (Walker)   27:449; 103:407, 409-10
"The Laurel Axe" (Hill)   45:190
"Laurel Hole in the Day" (Vizenor)   103:297
"Laurentian Shield" (Scott)   22:372, 377
"Laurie" (Merwin)   45:272
Laut und Luise (Jandl)   34:196, 198
Lautaro (Alegria)   57:9
Lautgedichte (Jandl)   34:195
Lava (Konwicki)
   See Lawa
"Lava Cameo: A brooch carved on volcanic rock" (Boland)   113:91-2, 94, 115, 125
Lavender-Green Magic (Norton)   12:466
"Laventille" (Walcott)   25:452; 67:353-54; 76:274
Laverne and Shirley (Marshall)   17:276-78
"Lavin" (McGahern)   48:262, 266, 268
"Lavinia: An Old Story" (Paley)   37:339
Law and Disorder (Forman)   21:119
Law and Order (Wiseman)   20:471-72
"The Law and the Grace" (Smith)   64:398
The Law and the Grace (Smith)   64:394, 398
The Law at Randado (Leonard)   71:224
"Law Clerk, 1979" (Leithauser)   27:240-41
A Law for the Lion (Auchincloss)   45:25, 29
"Law like Love" (Auden)   43:18
Law of Desire (Almodovar)
   See La Ley del Deseo
The Law of Karma (Hall)   51:170-72
"Law Song" (Sissman)   9:491
Lawa (Lava) (Konwicki)   117:283, 290
Lawd Today (Wright)   1:379; 4:594-95; 14:596; 21:440, 448, 452, 460
The Lawless (Jakes)   29:249
The Lawless Roads (Greene)   27:173; 37:137; 72:150-51, 155, 160
Lawley Road, and Other Stories (Narayan)   28:293, 296, 301, 303; 47:306
"Lawn" (Ezekiel)   61:109
"The Lawn Party" (Beattie)   13:65
"The Lawnmower" (Bowering)   47:24
Lawrence and the Arabs (Graves)   39:322
The Laws of Ice (Price)   63:325, 333
The Laws of Practical Morality (Arghezi)
   See Pravila de morala practica
Laws That Changed America (Archer)   12:15-16
The Lawyers Know Too Much (Sandburg)   35:341

"Lax though the Longing May Wear" (Barker)   48:12
Lay By (Hare)   29:216
"Lay Down Your Weary Tune" (Dylan)   6:154
"Lay, Lady, Lay" (Dylan)   77:162, 186-87
The Lay of Barrabas (Arrabal)   58:15
"Lay of Errantry" (Cesaire)   32:112
"The Lay of Ike" (Berryman)
   See "Dream Song 23"
"Lay of Maid Marion" (Hoffman)   6:243
"The Lay of the Romance of the Associations" (O'Hara)   13:424
"Lay Your Sleeping Head, My Love" (Auden)   11:19; 43:22
"Layaways" (Dixon)   52:98, 100
"Laying a Lawn" (Raine)   103:195-96
"Laying on Our Backs Looking at the Stars" (Keillor)   115:283
"Laying the Dust" (Levertov)   66:237
A Layman Looks at Cancer (MacLean)   50:349
"A Layman Looks at Medical Men" (MacLennan)   92:342
Lazare (Malraux)   57:307-08; 9:358-59; 15:354-55
Lazaretti; oder, Der Säbeltiger (Lazaretti; or, The Saber-Toothed Tiger) (Hochwalder)   36:237, 239-40
Lazaretti; or, The Saber-Toothed Tiger (Hochwalder)
   See Lazaretti; oder, Der Säbeltiger
"Lázaro" (Cernuda)   54:48
"Lazarus" (Achebe)   11:4
"Lazarus" (Dybek)   114:61, 63
"Lazarus" (Vanderhaeghe)   41:452
"Lazarus and the Sea" (Redgrove)   41:351
The Lazarus Effect (Herbert)   35:204-06; 44:393-94
A Lazy Eye (Morrissy)   99:76-8
"Lazy Mornin'" (Lightfoot)   26:279
"Lazy Sons" (Calvino)   33:101
L.C. (Daitch)   103:58-66, 70-8
Leadbelly (Parks)   16:460-61
"The Leader" (Clark)   38:118, 125
"The Leader" (Clash)   30:48
Leader (Horovitz)   56:149
"Leader from a Quality Newspaper" (Kelman)   58:300
"The Leader of the People" (Steinbeck)   9:515; 13:530; 21:376-78; 34:409
"The Leaders" (Vargas Llosa)   31:444
"The Leading Lady" (Ferber)   93:140
"Lead's the Best" (Auden)   9:60
"The Leaf" (Warren)   8:539; 18:536; 39:266-67
"Leaf by Niggle" (Tolkien)   12:566, 570, 573-74, 586
"A Leaf of Sage" (McAuley)   45:250
Leaf Storm (Garcia Marquez)
   See La hojarasca
The Leafless American (Dahlberg)   7:67
"Leaflets" (Rich)   6:458
Leaflets: Poems, 1965-1968 (Rich)   3:427; 6:457-59; 7:365-66, 371-72; 11:476; 18:445-46; 36:372-73, 375; 73:326, 328, 334; 76:219
Leafy Rivers (West)   7:520; 17:549-51
The League of Frightened Men (Stout)   3:471
League of Frightened Philistines (Farrell)   66:132
"Léah" (Migueis)   10:341
Léah e outras histórias (Migueis)   10:341
"Leah Goldberg Died" (Amichai)
   See "Yehuda Halevi, Ibn Gabirol, Leah Goldberg meta"

"Lean Times in Lankhmar" (Leiber)   25:310
"Leander of the Diving Board" (Cassity)   42:97
"The Leaning Tower" (Porter)   7:309, 311, 314-17; 10:398
The Leaning Tower, and Other Stories (Porter)   7:309, 314; 101:210, 215, 217, 224, 249, 255
"The Leap" (Barthelme)   13:60-1; 46:38, 41; 115:66
Leap Before You Look (Oe)   86:225, 227
Leap Before You Look (Stolz)   12:554
Leap Year (Erickson)   64:142-43, 145
"Leaping Falls" (Kinnell)   13:322
"The Leaping Fire" (Montague)   46:270
Lear (Bond)   6:87; 13:99, 102; 23:64, 68
Learn This Poem of Mine By Heart (Faludy)   42:141-42
"The Learners" (Van Duyn)   63:443
"Learning" (Scannell)   49:332
"Learning a Dead Language" (Merwin)   5:285; 45:269; 88:206
"Learning About the Indians" (Oliver)   98:291
"Learning from the 60s" (Lorde)   71:244
"Learning from the Tyrants" (Cioran)   64:98
Learning Laughter (Spender)   91:261
"Learning the Trees" (Nemerov)   9:394
"Learning to Fall" (Beattie)   40:64, 66; 63:11-12, 17, 19
"Learning to Fly" (Hope)   52:210
"Learning to Let Water Heal" (Bottoms)   53:29-31
"Learning to See" (Welty)   105:320-21, 378, 380-81
"Learning to Swim" (Swift)   41:446
Learning to Swim, and Other Stories (Swift)   41:443, 445-46; 88:290, 318
"Learning to Write" (Lorde)   71:256
The Learning Tree (Parks)   1:265; 16:457-59
"Learning Where to Stop" (Booth)   24:91
"The Leather Man" (Doctorow)   37:91, 93-4; 113:135-36, 153-54
"Leave for Cape Wrath Tonight" (Auden)   3:24; 11:15
Leave It to Beany (Weber)   12:632
Leave It to Me (Mukherjee)   115:391-93
Leave It to Psmith (Wodehouse)   2:479; 22:482-83
Leave Well Enough Alone (Wells)   12:638-39
Leaven of Malice (Davies)   13:171, 173; 25:130-31; 42:101-04, 106; 75:184, 191, 213-14; 91:203, 204
"Leaves" (Updike)   15:543-44
Leaves and Flowers (Davenport)   6:124
"Leaves Compared with Flowers" (Frost)   26:117
Leaves from Satan's Book (Dreyer)   16:259-60, 266
Leaves, News (Haavikko)   34:169
Leaves of Hypnos (Char)
   See Feuillets d'Hypnos
"Leaves that Talk" (Sexton)   15:473
Leaves the Leaves (Haavikko)
   See Lehdet lehtiä
"Leaves Without Trees" (Amichai)   116:95
The Leavetaking (McGahern)   5:280-81; 9:369-70, 372-74; 48:263-64, 269-73
The Leavetaking (Weiss)
   See Abschied von den Eltern: Erzählung
"Leaving" (Harjo)   83:271
"Leaving" (Suknaski)   19:432
"Leaving" (Wilbur)   53:409; 110:361
"Leaving an Island" (Muldoon)   32:316

"Leaving Barra" (MacNeice)   **53**:231
"Leaving Belfast" (Motion)   **47**:291
Leaving Cheyenne (McMurtry)   **2**:272; **7**:213-15; **27**:325, 328-31, 333; **44**:255, 257
"Leaving Church Early" (Updike)   **43**:430
"Leaving Early" (Plath)   **3**:389; **5**:345; **51**:344
"Leaving Home" (Suknaski)   **19**:432
Leaving Home (Keillor)   **115**:267, 269, 274, 277, 288-92
"Leaving Inishmore" (Longley)   **29**:292
"Leaving Ithaca" (Snodgrass)   **68**:397
"Leaving School" (Walcott)   **67**:342
"Leaving the Atocha Station" (Ashbery)   **9**:43
"Leaving the Cherries" (Smith)   **64**:391
Leaving the Door Open (Ignatow)   **40**:260-61
Leaving the Land (Unger)   **34**:114-17
"Leaving the Yellow House" (Bellow)   **25**:84
"Leaving This Island Place" (Clarke)   **53**:89
"Leaving Town" (Brown)   **73**:20
"Leaving Waterloo" (Wakoski)   **40**:456
"Leavings" (Heaney)   **91**:115
Lebensläufe (Hesse)   **17**:197-98˙
Lebenszeichen (*Signs of Life*) (Herzog)   **16**:321-23, 331
"Lección de cocina" (Castellanos)   **66**:58-9
Lecherous Limericks (Asimov)   **76**:315
"Lechery" (Phillips)   **15**:420
La leçon (*The Lesson*) (Ionesco)   **1**:154; **4**:251-52; **6**:248, 253-54, 257; **9**:286; **11**:290; **15**:297-98; **41**:224-25, 230; **86**:332-33, 340
Leçon de choses (*The World about Us*) (Simon)   **9**:485; **15**:495-97; **39**:212, 214-15
Leçon inaugurale faite le vendredi 7 janvier 1977 ("Inaugural Lecture, Collège de France") (Barthes)   **24**:37; **83**:96
"Lectura de domingo" ("Sunday Reading") (Guillen)   **79**:229
"A Lecture by My Books" (Porter)   **33**:320
"Lecture Noir" (Thesen)   **56**:421
"Lecture on Nothing" (Cage)   **41**:82
"Lecture Overheard" (Redgrove)   **41**:358
Lectures and Essays (Heidegger)
    See *Vorträge und Aufsätze*
Lectures on Literature (Nabokov)   **23**:310-11, 314
"Led" (Voznesensky)   **15**:554
Led Zeppelin (Page and Plant)   **12**:473, 476-78
Led Zeppelin II (Page and Plant)   **12**:473-74, 482
Led Zeppelin III (Page and Plant)   **12**:474-75, 479
Led Zeppelin IV (Page and Plant)   **12**:475-76, 478, 482
"Leda" (Huxley)   **11**:284
"Leda" (Smith)   **15**:517
"Leda" (Van Duyn)   **63**:439; **116**:420
Leda (Chabrol)   **16**:168
Leda (Krleza)   **8**:329; **114**:168
"Leda and the Swan" (Van Duyn)   **116**:401
"Leda Reconsidered" (Van Duyn)   **63**:437, 440; **116**:400, 414, 419-20
"The Ledge" (Mathews)   **52**:308
The Ledge between the Streams (Mehta)   **37**:296-97
"The Ledger" (Kroetsch)   **23**:273-75
Lee in the Mountains and Other Poems (Davidson)   **2**:111-12; **13**:166, 170; **19**:128
"Leela's Friend" (Narayan)   **28**:302
"Left" (Ammons)   **57**:58
The Left Bank (Rice)   **7**:360-61, 363; **49**:295-

96, 298, 300, 302
The Left Bank, and Other Stories (Rhys)   **6**:452, 454-55; **14**:446; **19**:390; **51**:355-56, 359, 376
"The Left Eyelid" (Sagan)   **17**:428
The Left Hand of Darkness (Le Guin)   **8**:343; **13**:346-51; **22**:266-68, 272; **45**:214, 216-18, 221-23; **71**:187
The Left in Europe since 1789 (Caute)   **29**:110
"left with the day" (Bukowski)   **108**:75
"The Left-Behind" (MacNeice)   **53**:238
Left-Handed Liberty (Arden)   **13**:26, 29; **15**:21
The Left-Handed Woman (Handke)   **15**:268; **38**:221-23, 227
The Left-Hander's World (Silverstein and Silverstein)   **17**:456
"The Leg" (Bitov)   **57**:115
"The Leg" (Shapiro)   **53**:331
A Leg to Stand On (Sacks)   **67**:289-90, 292-96
"Legacies" (Giovanni)   **64**:187
"Legacies" (Mahon)   **27**:290-91
"Legacies" (Padilla)   **38**:353
Legacies, after Villon (Mahon)   **27**:286
Legacies: Selected Poems (Padilla)   **38**:349-54
"Legacy" (Harjo)   **83**:275, 281
"Legacy" (Kenny)   **87**:241, 256
"The Legacy" (Motion)   **47**:286, 293
"Legacy" (Ritsos)   **13**:488
"Legacy" (Vinge)   **30**:413-14
Legacy (Fast)   **23**:161
Legacy (Michener)   **60**:258; **109**:382, 386
The Legacy (*A Town like Alice*) (Shute)   **30**:368-69
The Legacy of the Civil War (Warren)   **59**:296
Legacy of the Desert: Understanding the Arabs (Archer)   **12**:22
"Legal Fiction" (Empson)   **19**:155; **34**:336
"The Legal System" (Hogan)   **73**:158-59
"Legend" (Auden)   **14**:33; **43**:17
"Legend" (Gluck)   **44**:218
"Legend for a Painting" (O'Faolain)   **47**:327-28
"Legend in Bronze" (Davidson)   **13**:169
"A Legend in Its Own Time" (Robinson)   **21**:343
"Legend in Your Own Time" (Simon)   **26**:407-08, 410
"Legend of Kalafaat" ("The Tale of the Furious Kalafat") (Leonov)   **92**:257
"The Legend of Success, the Salesman's Story" (Simpson)   **7**:426
The Legend of Tarik (Myers)   **35**:297-98
"Legend of the Last Jew on Earth" (Cohen)   **7**:51
"The Legend of the Sleepers" (Kis)   **57**:251, 253
The Legend of the Thousand Bulls (Kemal)   **29**:266
"A Legend of Viable Women" (Eberhart)   **56**:91
Legenda (Krleza)   **114**:166-67, 171-72, 174
Legenda emöke (*The Bass Saxophone*) (Skvorecky)   **15**:511-121; **39**:221, 224, 229, 231-32; **69**:330-32, 334, 337, 341, 343-44, 346-48
"Legende" (Celan)   **82**:54
Legenden und Erzühlungen (Sachs)   **98**:324
Légendes africanes (Tchicaya)   **101**:355
"Legends" (Boland)   **113**:94, 100, 126
Legends of Our Times (Wiesel)   **3**:529
"Legends of the Fall" (Harrison)   **66**:155-56, 159-60
Legends of the Fall (Harrison)   **14**:235-37;

33:196-97, 199-200; **66**:154, 156, 158, 167-71
"Leggende" (Ungaretti)   **7**:483
Legion: Civic Choruses (Harmon)   **38**:242-43
The Legion of Space (Williamson)   **29**:455-56, 461
The Legion of Time (Williamson)   **29**:450-53, 456, 459-60
Legitimationsprobleme im Spätkapitalismus (Habermas)   **104**:66, 69, 72
"The Legs" (Graves)   **45**:169
Legs (Kennedy)   **6**:274-75; **28**:204-06; **34**:206-10; **53**:192-94, 199
"The Legs of the Lame" (Garner)   **13**:237
The Legs of the Lame (Garner)   **13**:237
Lehdet lehtiä (*Leaves the Leaves*) (Haavikko)   **34**:170; **34**:170
"Leicestershire" (Davie)   **31**:120
Leila (Donleavy)   **45**:125-26
"Leila Lee" (Oates)   **108**:384
Leiret og hjulet (*The Clay and the Wheel*) (Vesaas)   **48**:406
Leisure Garden (Pa Chin)
    See *Ch'i-yüan*
"Lejana" ("The Distances"; "Faraway Image") (Cortazar)   **10**:114; **33**:128; **34**:332; **92**:155
"Leli" (Hrabal)   **67**:121
"Lembrando Manolete" ("Recalling Manolete") (Cabral de Melo Neto)   **76**:161
"The Lemmings" (Masefield)   **47**:233
"The Lemon" (Lustig)   **56**:185
"Lemon Ode" ("For Neruda") (Galvin)   **38**:198
Lemon Sky (Wilson)   **7**:547
"The Lemon Song" (Page and Plant)   **12**:474-76
"Lemonade" (Findley)   **102**:108, 111-14
"Lemonade" (Lavin)   **99**:322
Lemprière's Dictionary (Norfolk)   **76**:86-92
"Lemuel's Blessing" (Merwin)   **88**:194, 199, 201
"Léna ou le secret" (Yourcenar)   **87**:385, 387
Lend Me a Tenor (Ludwig)   **60**:251-53
"Lend Me Your Light" (Mistry)   **71**:266
"The Lengthening Silence of a Poet" (Yehoshua)   **31**:472-73
Lengua poética (Alonso)   **14**:20
"Lenin" (Hughes)   **108**:321
Lenin in Zurich (Solzhenitsyn)   **7**:444-45; **18**:499; **34**:484, 489
"Lenin na tribune 18-ogo goda" (Voznesensky)   **15**:555
"Lenny" (Asimov)   **26**:47
Lenny (Fosse)   **20**:123-25
"Lenny Bruce, American" (Bruce)   **21**:44
Lenny Bruce at Carnegie Hall (Bruce)   **21**:51
Lenny Bruce: I Am Not a Nut, Elect Me (Bruce)   **21**:44
Lenny Bruce Live at the Curran Theater (Bruce)   **21**:49, 51
"Lenny Bruce's Interviews of Our Times" (Bruce)   **21**:44
"Lenore" (Moure)   **88**:217, 229
"The Lens" (Williams)   **56**:427
"Lenten Flowers" (Raine)   **45**:340
"Lenten Thoughts of a High Anglican" (Betjeman)   **10**:52; **43**:47
Lenuska (Leonov)
    See *Lyonushka*
Leo and Theodore (*The Drunks*) (Newlove)   **6**:363-64
Léocadia (*Time Remembered*) (Anouilh)   **8**:23-4; **13**:16, 20; **40**:51, 54; **50**:279

"Un león en el bosque de Palermo" (Bioy Casares) 88:94
Leon Gaspard (Waters) 88:363
Leon Trotsky (Trotsky) (Howe) 85:128
"Leonard Commits Redeeming Adulteries with All the Women in Town" (Erdrich) 54:165
Leonardo's Last Supper (Barnes) 56:5, 7-8
"Leontes, Solus" (Fuller) 62:184
"The Leopard" (Nabokov) 3:355
The Leopard (Bodker) 21:11-12
The Leopard (Visconti) 16:565-67, 574-75
The Leopard Hunts in Darkness (Smith) 33:378
"Leopardi" (Strand) 41:432-33
"The Leopard-Nurser" (Jacobsen) 48:193
Leos Janacek: Intimate Excursions (The Brothers Quay) 95:330, 332, 341-42, 344, 350, 353
The Leper Prince (Mishima) 2:289
"The Leper's Helix" (Coover) 87:52
"Lerici" (Gunn) 18:199
"LeRoi Jones Talking" (Baraka) 115:49
"Lesbia" (Aldington) 49:6
The Lesbian Body (Wittig) 22:476
Lesbian Images (Rule) 27:417-20, 422
"Lesbos" (Plath) 14:424; 17:347-48; 51:342; 62:415; 111:161, 169, 203
Leslie (Sherburne) 30:363
"Leslie in California" (Dubus) 36:147; 97:228
De l'espirt: Heidegger et la question (Of Spirit: Heidegger and the Question) (Derrida) 87:108
"The Less Deceived" (Larkin) 8:339; 18:294
The Less Deceived (Larkin) 3:275; 5:223, 225-28, 230-31; 8:332-33, 336, 338, 340; 13:335-38, 340; 18:293-94, 297-99, 301; 33:256, 261-63; 39:334, 339, 341-42; 64:259, 267-68, 270-71, 278-80
"Less Delicate than the Locust" (Bukowski) 41:73
"Less Is Less: The Dwindling American Short Story" (Bell) 102:16
Less than Angels (Pym) 37:367-68, 373-74, 376-77; 111:227, 234-36, 243-47, 249, 254-58, 263-67, 269, 271, 281-84
"Less Than One" (Brodsky) 50:133; 100:43
Less Than One (Brodsky) 50:126, 130-33, 135-36; 100:37, 49-50, 55, 58, 60-4
"Less than Zero" (Costello) 21:66-7
Less than Zero (Ellis) 39:55-9; 71:147, 149-51, 157, 159, 162-64, 166, 168, 170, 172; 117:105-09, 112-16, 118-24, 128-29, 131-32, 135, 138, 143, 146-48, 150
Lesser Evils: Ten Quartets (Soto) 80:291, 300
Lesser Lives: The True History of the First Mrs. Meredith (Johnson) 48:201-02
"Lesser Magellan" (Young) 82:411
Lessico famigliare (Family Sayings) (Ginzburg) 11:228-30; 54:195-96, 200-07, 211, 214; 70:280, 282-83
Lessness (Beckett)
   See Sans
"The Lesson" (Bambara) 19:33; 88:12-13, 15, 21, 27
"The Lesson" (Lowell) 4:303
"The Lesson" (Purdy) 28:378
"The Lesson" (Simic) 49:340
"The Lesson" (Tomlinson) 45:396
The Lesson (Ionesco)
   See La leçon
A Lesson before Dying (Gaines) 86:170-79
"Lesson for the Day" (Stern) 39:243-44
"A Lesson for This Sunday" (Walcott) 25:451

"The Lesson for Today" (Frost) 10:195
A Lesson from Aloes (Aloes) (Fugard) 25:174-76; 40:201, 203; 80:62, 68, 70-2, 80-1
A Lesson from the Cyclops and Other Poems (Rudnik) 7:384
A Lesson in Dead Language (Kennedy) 66:214
"A Lesson in Geography" (Rexroth) 22:346; 49:285; 112:397
"A Lesson in History" (Farrell) 66:129
A Lesson in Love (Bergman)
   See En lektion i kärlek
"A Lesson in Ourselves" (Brosman) 9:135
"Lesson Number Eight" (Sondheim) 39:174
"The Lesson of Mont Sainte-Victoire" (Handke)
   See "The Lesson of Sainte-Victoire"
"The Lesson of Poetry" (Cabral de Melo Neto)
   See "A licão de poesia"
"The Lesson of Sainte-Victoire" ("The Lesson of Mont Sainte-Victoire") (Handke) 38:224-25, 228
"The Lesson of the Falling Leaves" (Clifton) 66:81
"Lesson of the Master" (Dickey) 28:117
"The Lesson of the Master" (Howard) 7:169
"The Lesson of the Master" (Ozick) 28:354
"Lesson One" (Johnston) 51:255
Lesson Park and Belsize Square (Straub) 107:304
"Lessons" (Amis) 40:44
"Lessons: From Attica to Soledad" (Davis) 77:108
"Lessons from the Art" (Selzer) 74:264
The Lessons of Modernism, and Other Essays (Josipovici) 43:220-21, 223, 226
"The Lessons of Stendhal" (Ehrenburg) 62:178
"Lester Leaps In" (Kerouac) 14:306
"Let America Be America Again" (Hughes) 108:283
"Let Be" (Avison) 97:117
Let Each Man Remember (Jacobsen) 48:189, 196; 102:235
"Let 'Em In" (McCartney) 35:284-85
"Let Go" (Johnston) 51:255
"Let Him Run Wild" (Wilson) 12:644, 649
"Let History Be My Judge" (Auden) 6:22
"Let It Be" (Lennon and McCartney) 12:380; 35:278-79, 292, 294
Let It Be (Lennon and McCartney) 12:380
"Let It Begin" (Levine) 14:318
Let It Bleed (Jagger and Richard) 17:227, 229-32, 235, 236-37
Let It Come Down (Bowles) 1:41; 2:78; 19:57; 53:40-1, 43, 46
"Let It Go" (Empson) 8:202
"Let It Go" (Nye) 13:412
"Let It Last" (Armatrading) 17:10
"Let It Loose" (Jagger and Richard) 17:224
"Let It Rock" (Jagger and Richard) 17:229
"Let It Rock" (Seger) 35:381
"Let It Shine" (Young) 17:576
"Let Koras and Balafong Accompany Me" (Senghor)
   See "Que m'accompagnent Kôras et Balafong"
Let Live (Mphahlele) 25:341
Let Love Come Last (Caldwell) 39:302
Let Man Live (Lagerkvist) 54:272
"Let Me Alone (Kavan) 5:205-06; 82:121
"Let Me Be Your Clock" (Robinson) 21:348-50
"Let Me Begin Again" (Levine) 33:271
Let Me Breathe Thunder (Attaway) 92:25, 27-8, 32, 34-5, 37-8

Let Me Count the Ways (De Vries) 28:106
"Let Me Die in My Footsteps" (Dylan) 77:166
Let Me Fall before I Fly (Wersba) 30:431-32
Let Me Hear You Whisper (Zindel) 26:472
"Let Me Make This Perfectly Clear" (MacEwen) 55:166-67
"Let Me Roll It" (McCartney) 35:282
"Let My Love Open the Door" (Townshend) 17:541-42
"Let My People Go" (Miller) 30:264
Let No Man Write My Epitaph (Motley) 18:357
Let Noon Be Fair (Motley) 18:357
"Let Not This Plunder Be Misconstrued" (Brutus) 43:92
Let the Buyer Beware (Bruce) 21:54
"Let the Old Dead Make Room for the Young Dead" (Kundera) 32:260; 115:308
"Let the Rockets Roar" (Heinlein) 14:249
"Let Them Call It Jazz" (Rhys) 14:447; 51:375
"Let Them Remember Samangan" (Bunting) 39:299; 47:45
Let There Be Light (Huston) 20:165, 175
"Let Us Be Content with Three Little Newborn Elephants" (Miller) 43:298
"let us begin again the / circle of Blackness" (Sanchez) 116:300
"let us begin the real work" (Sanchez) 116:327
Let Us Compare Mythologies (Cohen) 38:130-32
"Let Us Go On This Way" (Wilson) 12:652
"Let Us Save the Universe" (Lem) 40:295
Let X Be Excitement (Harris) 12:263
"Let Your Hand Play First" (Livesay) 79:347
Let Your Mind Alone! and Other More or Less Inspirational Pieces (Thurber) 5:434, 437, 442; 25:435
"Let Your Yeah Be Yeah" (Cliff) 21:64
"Lethargy" (Justice) 6:271
"Lethe" (Barnard) 48:25, 27
"Lethe" (H. D.) 73:109
"Letishta" (Bagryana) 10:13
"Letizia" (Espriu) 9:192
"Let's All Help the Cowboys Sing the Blues" (Jennings) 21:203
Let's Do It Again (Poitier) 26:360
"Let's Do the Time Warp Again" (O'Brien) 17:322
Let's Get It On (Gaye) 26:131-33, 135
Let's Get Small (Martin) 30:246-47
"Let's Go Crazy" (Clash) 30:49
"Let's Go Crazy" (Prince) 35:329
"Let's Go, Daddy" (Bell) 31:47
"Let's Hear It for a Beautiful Guy" (Friedman) 56:106-07
Let's Hear It for a Beautiful Guy (Friedman) 56:107
Let's Hear It for the Queen (Childress) 86:309
Let's Hear It from the Deaf Man (Hunter) 11:279
Let's Kill Uncle Lionel (Creasey) 11:135
"Let's Pretend We're Married" (Prince) 35:326-27
"Let's Put Our Hearts Together" (Wilson) 12:652
"Let's Say" (Dunn) 36:154
"Let's See Action" (Townshend) 17:531
"Let's See If I Have It Right" (Dunn) 36:154-55
"Let's Seize the Time" (Cliff) 21:62
"Let's Spend the Night Together" (Jagger and Richard) 17:226, 238
Let's Talk about Men (Wertmueller) 16:595-97
"Let's Work" (Prince) 35:324-25

"The Letter" (Auden) 6:24; 11:15, 17
"The Letter" (Blackburn) 43:62
"A Letter" (Bogan) 93:92-3
"Letter" (Cohen) 38:131
"The Letter" (Creeley) 78:135
"Letter" (Fuller) 62:204
"A Letter" (Hecht) 13:269
"Letter" (Hughes) 108:291
"A Letter" (Justice) 6:271; 102:265
"The Letter" (MacEwen) 55:168
"The Letter" (Malamud) 8:375; 44:416
"A Letter" (Mathias) 45:238
"The Letter" (Maugham) 67:206, 210
"The Letter" (Motion) 47:288, 291, 293-94
"A Letter" (O'Faolain) 70:314
"A Letter" (Simic) 68:377
"Letter" (Strand) 18:517; 71:285-86
"Letter I" (Empson) 19:157-58
"Letter II" (Empson) 8:202; 19:158
"Letter III" (Empson) 19:157-58
"Letter IV" (Empson) 19:159; 34:335
"Letter V" (Empson) 19:159
"A Letter about Unequivocal and Ambigious Meaning, Definiteness and Indefiniteness, about Ancient Conditions and New View Scopes, and about Objectivity" (Wolf) 58:421
"Letter concerning the Yellow Fever" (Epstein) 7:97
"Letter for Jan" (Lorde) 71:240
"A Letter for Marian" (McGrath) 59:181
"Letter for Those Who Grew Up Together" (Ciardi) 40:153
"Letter from a City Dweller" (Davison) 28:100
"Letter from a Distant Land" (Booth) 23:73-4, 77
"Letter from a Far Country" (Clarke) 61:74-6, 78-80
Letter from a Far Country (Clarke) 61:74-7, 79, 82-3
"Letter from a Metaphysical Countryside" (Ciardi) 40:157
"Letter from a Pander" (Ciardi) 40:161
"Letter from a Region in My Mind" (Baldwin) See "The Fire Next Time"
Letter from Birmingham Jail (King) 83:330, 332-34, 336-37, 346-48
"A Letter from Brooklyn" (Walcott) 25:449; 67:353
"Letter from Campus" (Turco) 63:429
"Letter from Chicago" (Sarton) 91:254
"A Letter from Copenhagen" (Keillor) 115:267, 288
"A Letter from Gwyther Street" (Mathias) 45:238
"Letter from Highgate Wood" (Adcock) 41:16
"Letter from Johannesburg, 1976" (Gordimer) 70:170
A Letter from Li Po, and Other Poems (Aiken) 52:24, 26
"A Letter from Little Tobago" (Howes) 15:289
"Letter from New Paltz" (Eshleman) 7:99
"Letter from Our Man in Blossomtime" (Gluck) 22:173
"Letter from Paris" (Ciardi) 40:155
"A Letter from Phillis Wheatley" (Hayden) 14:240; 37:153, 155, 158
"A Letter from Rome" (Hope) 51:227
"Letter from the Alpes-Maritimes" (Hacker) 72:189
"Letter from the House of Questions" (Atwood) 84:98
"Letter from the North" (Bukowski) 41:64

"A Letter from the Old Guard" (Walcott) 67:360
"A Letter from the Pigmies" (Weiss) 14:555
"Letter I" (Eberhart) 56:82
"Letter I" (Olson) 29:334
"The Letter I" (Simpson) 7:429
"A Letter in a Bottle" (Brodsky) 6:96
"Letter in November" (Plath) 9:427; 111:204
"The Letter in the Cedarchest" (Goyen) 40:217
"A Letter More Likely to Myself" (Graham) 29:193
"Letter Number Forty-One" (Olson) 29:329
"Letter of Recommendation" (Amichai) 9:25
"A Letter of the Times, or Should This Sado-Masochism Be Saved?" (Walker) 103:407-08, 412
"Letter on August 15" (Hacker) 72:188, 190
"Letter on Humanism" (Heidegger) 24:265
"A Letter That Never Reached Russia" (Nabokov) 8:418; 15:393
"Letter to a Bourgeois Friend Whom Once I Loved (and Maybe Still Do If Love Is Valid)" (Giovanni) 64:194
Letter to a Child Never Born (Fallaci) See *Lettera a un bambino mai nato*
"Letter to a Conceivable Great-Grandson" (Birney) 6:74
"Letter to a Faraway Friend" (Cioran) 64:99
"Letter to a Friend About Girls" (Larkin) 64:280
"Letter to a Poet" (Scannell) 49:325
"Letter to a Poet" (Senghor) 54:406
"Letter to a Psychiatrist" (Sarton) 14:481
"Letter to a Sailor" (Walcott) 76:288
"Letter to a Sister Underground" (Morgan) 2:294
"Letter to a Wrong Child" (Ciardi) 10:105
"Letter to a Young Lady in Paris" (Cortazar) See "Carta a un senorita en París"
"Letter to a Young Poet" (Barker) 48:17
"Letter to a Young Writer" (Price) 63:326-27
"A Letter to Alex Comfort" (Abse) 29:19
"Letter to an Exile" (Motion) 47:292-93
"Letter to an Imaginary Friend" (McGrath) 59:176, 183
Letter to an Imaginary Friend (McGrath) 59:174-75, 177, 180-81
Letter to an Imaginary Friend: Parts One and Two (McGrath) 28:276-79
"A Letter to Any Friend" (Riding) 7:374
"A Letter to Basil" (Brutus) 43:94
"Letter to Ben, 1972" (Durcan) 43:113
"Letter to Bob Kaufman" (Komunyakaa) 94:239
"Letter to California" (Mueller) 51:284
"Letter to Dante" (Ciardi) 40:152
"Letter to Dr. Gustáv Husák" (Havel) 65:438
"A Letter to Dr. Martin Luther King" (Sanchez) 116:317
"Letter to Elaine Feinstein" (Olson) 11:415
"A Letter to Elizabeth Mayer" (Auden) 3:29
"Letter to Goldbarth from Big Fork" (Hugo) 32:241, 250
"Letter to Hans Bender" (Celan) 53:83
"Letter to Hanson" (Hugo) 32:242
"Letter to Hitler" (Laughlin) 49:220-21
"Letter to Horace" (Brodsky) 100:61
"A Letter to Ismael in the Grave" (Brown) 32:64
"A Letter [to J] from Unwritten 'Greed, Part 10'" (Wakoski) 40:456
"Letter to J. R. R., the Last Transcendentalist" (Ciardi) 40:157

"A Letter to James Stephens" (Sarton) 49:319
Letter to Jane (Godard) 20:150
"Letter to Joe Brainard" (Waldman) 7:509
"A Letter to John Dryden" (McAuley) 45:246, 252
"Letter to John Fuller" (Fenton) 32:166
"A Letter to John Steinbeck" (Yevtushenko) 26:464
"Letter to Julie in a New Decade" (Hacker) 91:110
"Letter to Levertov from Butte" (Hugo) 32:247
Letter to Lord Byron (Auden) 14:29; 43:18-19, 27
"Letter to Man's Reasonable Soul" (Riding) 7:374
"Letter to Marcel Proust" (Walker) 13:566
"Letter to Mother" (Ciardi) 40:152; 44:379
"Letter to My Father" (McFadden) 48:257-58
"A Letter to My Grandad on the Occasion of a Letter from Cousin Wanda Lee Saying Grandad is Too Infirm to Feed the Cows and Is Not Long for This World" (Jiles) 58:281
Letter to My Judge (Simenon) See *Lettre à mon juge*
Letter to My Mother (Simenon) See *Lettre à ma mère*
"Letter to My Sisters at Home" (Ciardi) 40:151
"Letter to N.Y." (Bishop) 32:39
"A Letter to Pausanias" (Squires) 51:377
A Letter to Queen Victoria (Wilson) 7:550
"Letter to Reed" (Hugo) 32:242
"Letter to Seferis the Greek" (Durrell) 27:97
Letter to Sister Benedicta (Tremain) 42:383-84
Letter to Soviet Leaders (Solzhenitsyn) See *Pis' mo vozhdiam Sovetskogo Soiuza*
"Letter to the Academy" (Hughes) 108:294
Letter to the Alumni (Hersey) 81:335
"Letter to the Finalists of the Walt Whitman First-Book Poetry Contest" (Wakoski) 40:452-53
"Letter to the Fourth Congress of Soviet Writers" (Solzhenitsyn) 7:445
Letter to Three Students (Solzhenitsyn) 78:408
"Letter to Time" ("Time") (Alegria) 75:34, 37, 39, 42
"Letter to Tony: Suitable for Presentation as a Gift" (Goldbarth) 38:201
"Letter to Virginia Johnson" (Ciardi) 40:152
"A Letter to William Carlos Williams" (Rexroth) 112:378, 394
"Letter to William Kinter of Muhlenberg" (Levertov) 66:243
"Letter, Towards and Away" (Atwood) 4:27
"The Letter Writer" (Singer) 38:410
"Letter Written on a Ferry Crossing Long Island Sound" (Sexton) 6:493; 53:319
Lettera a un bambino mai nato (*Letter to a Child Never Born*) (Fallaci) 11:189-91; 110:194-95, 207, 208
Lettera amorosa (Char) 9:162
Lettere d'amore a Maria Cumani (Quasimodo) 10:429
"The Letters" (Mott) 15:380
"The Letters" (White) 69:393
LETTERS (Barth) 14:55-9; 27:26-8; 51:20-2, 26-8; 89:47, 49
Letters (Duncan) 15:188
"The Letters II" (Mott) 15:381
"Letters and Other Worlds" (Ondaatje) 51:314,

316

"Letters and Poems to Nazim Hikmet" (Otero)
11:425

Letters for Origin (Olson)   6:387; 11:417

"Letters for the Dead" (Levine)   4:288; 14:318

"Letters for the Next Time" (Ciardi)   40:157

"Letters from a Father" (Van Duyn)   116:408-
10, 421, 425, 430

Letters from a Father (Van Duyn)   63:441-44;
116:408, 410, 412, 420, 426

Letters from a Lost Uncle from Polar Regions
(Peake)   54:369, 373

"Letters from a Man in Solitary" (Hikmet)
40:248

Letters from Africa, 1914-1931 (Dinesen)
29:163-64; 95:54-6, 58-60, 68-9, 77

"Letters from France" (Ousmane)   66:350

Letters from Iceland (Auden)   3:25; 43:16, 18,
27

Letters from Iceland (MacNeice)   53:234

"Letters from Jack" (Keillor)   115:283

Letters from Maine (Sarton)   49:321

"Letters from My Father" (Butler)   81:129

"Letters from Rome" (Ciardi)   40:155

Letters from the Earth to the Earth (McFadden)
48:242-44, 246, 249, 251

Letters from the Field, 1925-1975 (Mead)
37:281

"Letters from the Life-Watch" (Cixous)   92:81

"Letters from the Ming Dynasty" (Brodsky)
36:78

"Letters from the Poet Who Sleeps in a Chair"
(Parra)   102:351-53

"Letters from the Samantha" (Helprin)   22:222

Letters from the Savage Mind (Lane)   25:283,
285

"Letters from Tula" (Pasternak)
See "Pis'ma iz Tuly"

"Letters from Whetu" (Grace)   56:116-17,
120

Letters Home (Nichol)   18:366

Letters Home: Correspondence, 1950-1963
(Plath)   14:427; 17:367-68; 50:441, 447-
48; 51:349; 62:415; 111:179

"Letters I Did or Did Not Get" (Ashbery)   77:68

"Letters in a Time of Crisis" (Merton)   83:383

"Letters in the Family" (Rich)   73:332

Letters of Delmore Schwartz (Schwartz)   45:357-
59; 87:344

Letters of E.B. White (White)   34:431; 39:377

The Letters of Evelyn Waugh (Waugh)   19:465;
27:474-76; 44:520, 524; 107:387, 392

Letters of Ezra Pound, 1907-1941 (Pound)
4:410; 7:335

The Letters of Great Ape (Orlovitz)   22:337

The Letters of J. R. R. Tolkien (Tolkien)   38:432-
34

The Letters of Jean Rhys (Rhys)   51:365-67

Letters of Katherine Anne Porter (Porter)
101:243, 250

Letters of Marshall McLuhan (McLuhan)
83:372-74

The Letters of Robert Frost to Louis Untermeyer
(Frost)   44:459

*The Letters of Sean O'Casey, Volume I, 1940-
1941* (O'Casey)   9:411; 88:258

*The Letters of T. S. Eliot: Volume One, 1898-
1922* (Eliot)   55:352-55, 359, 362, 369

The Letters of William S. Burroughs (Burroughs)
109:227

Letters on Art and Literature (Mauriac)   56:219

Letters on Literature and Politics (Wilson)
24:486, 490

Letters to a German Friend (Camus)
See *Lettres à un ami allemand*

"Letters to a Roman Friend" (Brodsky)   36:76

"Letters to a White Liberal" (Merton)   83:382,
384

Letters to a Young Doctor (Selzer)   74:272,
281

Letters to Alice on First Reading Jane Austen
(Weldon)   36:447-48

Letters to Allen Ginsberg, 1953-1957
(Burroughs)   42:72

*Letters to Christopher: Stephen Spender's Let-
ters to Christopher Isherwood, 1929-1939*
(Spender)   41:424-25

Letters to Five Artists (Wain)   11:561-63; 15:561

Letters to Friends (Hugo)   6:244

"Letters to Irish Poets" (Longley)   29:293,
296

"Letters to Josef in Jerusalem" (MacEwen)
55:163-65, 167-69

Letters to Malcolm: Chiefly on Prayers (Lewis)
3:297; 6:308

*Letters to Martha and Other Poems from a South
African Prison* (Brutus)   43:87-9, 92-4,
96

Letters to Mrs. Z (Brandys)   62:119

Letters to Olga: June 1979 to September 1982
(Havel)   65:414-15, 419, 435, 438, 442

Letters to Olga: June 1979-September 1985
(Havel)   58:240-44, 247

"Letters to Salonika" (Kroetsch)   57:292

"Letters to Taranta-Babu" (Hikmet)
See "Taranta-Babuya mektuplar"

Letters to Tomasito (McGrath)   59:176, 178

Letters to Yesenin (Harrison)   14:235; 33:197;
66:158

"Letting Down the Side" (Garnett)   3:189

"Letting Go" (McCartney)   35:283

Letting Go (Roth)   31:334-35, 343-44, 346;
66:386, 401, 405, 415

"Letting in Cold" (Bell)   31:50

Letting in the Rumour (Clarke)   61:83

Lettre à ma mère (*Letter to My Mother*)
(Simenon)   8:487-88

"Lettre à Maurice Thorez" (Cesaire)   112:20,
25

Lettre à mon juge (*Letter to My Judge*)
(Simenon)   2:399; 18:482; 47:379

La lettre aérienne (*The Aerial Letter*) (Brossard)
115:117, 127-28, 135, 137-39, 156

"Lettre d'amour" ("A Love Letter") (Ferron)
94:106-7, 126

"Lettre d'Angleterre" (Eliot)   24:176

Lettres à un ami allemand (*Letters to a German Friend*) (Camus)   11:95; 69:105

Lettres au Castor (Sartre)   52:380

Letty Fox: Her Luck (Stead)   5:404; 32:412,
414-15; 80:326-28, 331-33, 341-43, 345-
46, 348-49

"Leuké" (H. D.)   31:207

"leukemia as white rabbit" (Clifton)   66:84

The Levant Trilogy (Manning)   19:303-04

The Levanter (Ambler)   6:2-3

"The Level at Which Sky Began" (Soto)   80:287

"Levelling with Death" (Roberts)   48:342

"Levels" (Mahapatra)   33:277, 283

"Levels of Reality in Literature" (Calvino)
73:39, 48

Levels of the Game (McPhee)   36:294

"Leviathan" (Merwin)   13:384; 45:276

"Leviathan" (Wolff)   64:451-52

Leviathan (Schmidt)   56:392-93, 405

Leviathan (Wilson)   9:576

"Lèviathan: La traversée inutile" (Green)
77:265

Levine (Westlake)   33:440

"Lévi-Strauss at the Lie-Detector" (Morgan)
31:276

"Levitation" (Dacey)   51:81

"Levitation" (Ozick)   62:351, 353-54

Levitation: Five Fictions (Ozick)   28:349-50,
355; 62:350

Lew Archer, Private Investigator (Macdonald)
14:336

Lewis and Irene (Morand)
See *Lewis et Irène*

"Lewis Carroll au pays des petites Filles"
(Tournier)   95:378

Lewis et Irène (*Lewis and Irene*) (Morand)
41:297, 303

"Lexicon Rhetoricae" (Burke)   24:118

"La ley" (Azorin)   11:24

La Ley del Deseo (*Law of Desire*) (Almodovar)
114:2-5, 7-16, 19-23, 30-32, 38, 53

"Leyenda" (Borges)   6:90

La Lézarde (*The Ripening*) (Glissant)   10:231;
68:170, 172-79, 181-82, 184, 187-89,
191

"Lezhat velosipedy" (Voznesensky)   57:416

"Li letanis dal biel fi" (Pasolini)   106:261

"Liaisons" (Sondheim)   30:384-85

"Liaisons" (Tate)   25:428

Liana (Gellhorn)   14:194; 60:182, 190, 194

"Liar!" (Asimov)   19:27; 26:55, 64; 92:4, 6,
11

"The Liar" (Baraka)   5:45; 115:30-1

"The Liar" (Ihimaera)   46:199

"The Liar" (Wolff)   64:449-51, 454

The Liar (Savage)   40:371-72

Liar, Liar (Yep)   35:473-74

"The Liars" (Pritchett)   41:334

Liars in Love (Yates)   23:482-83

"Libbard's Last Case" (Turner)   48:398-99

"Libby" (Simon)   26:410

Le libera (*The Libera Me Domine*) (Pinget)
13:441-43; 37:359-64

The Libera Me Domine (Pinget)
See *Le libera*

The Liberal Imagination (Trilling)   9:530;
11:539-42, 545-46; 24:449, 450-54, 458-
59, 461-62

"Liberality and Order: The Criticism of John
Bayley" (Eagleton)   63:106

"Liberation" (Gluck)   44:218; 81:173

"The Liberation" (Stafford)   68:423, 431-32,
449

"La libertà stilistica" (Pasolini)   106:246

"Libertad" (Aleixandre)   9:14

Libertad bajo palabra (*Freedom under Parole*;
Liberty behind the Words) (Paz)   65:176,
189

Liberté d'action (*Freedom of Action*) (Michaux)
8:392

"La liberté des mers" (Reverdy)   53:286

Liberté I: Négritude et humanisme (Senghor)
54:399

The Liberties (Howe)   72:208

Le libertinage (Aragon)   22:40

"The Libertine" (MacNeice)   4:315

Liberty Bar (Simenon)   47:373, 376

Liberty behind the Words (Paz)
See *Libertad bajo palabra*

Liberty Tavern (Fleming)   37:126

Liberty Tree (Paulin)   37:354-55

Liberty Two (Lipsyte)   21:210-11

Libra (DeLillo)   54:86-94; 76:171-72, 174-

77, 179-83, 186
"The Librarian" (Olson)　5:328
"The Library" (Calisher)　38:75
"The Library Horror" (Gardner)　28:162-63
"The Library Is on Fire" (Char)　55:289
"The Library of Babel" (Borges)
　See "La biblioteca de Babel"
The Library Policeman (King)　113:367
"The Library Revisited" (Weiss)　8:546
"Libretto" (Thesen)　56:414
Libretto for the Republic of Liberia (Tolson)
　36:425-27; 105:231-35, 240, 254, 258,
　261, 263, 271, 277, 281, 283-84, 286-
　88, 290-94
El libro de arena (Borges)　9:117; 44:364
Libro de las preguntas (*Book of Questions*)
　(Neruda)　7:261; 28:310; 62:333, 336-37
The Libro de las profecias of Christopher Co-
　lumbus: An en Face Edition　70:340-41,
　355
El libro de levante (*Superrealismo*) (Azorin)
　11:27
El libro de los libros de Chilam Balam (Asturias)
　13:37
Libro de Manuel (*A Manual for Manuel*)
　(Cortazar)　5:109; 10:115-16, 118;
　13:164; 15:147-48; 33:123, 125; 34:329-
　30, 333-34
Libro que no muerde (*Book That Doesn't Bite*)
　(Valenzuela)　31:438; 104:363, 377-78
"A licão de poesia" ("The Lesson of Poetry")
　(Cabral de Melo Neto)　76:152, 157
"Lice" (Merwin)　18:334; 88:187
Lice (Cendrars)
　See *La Main Coupée*
The Lice (Merwin)　1:212-13; 2:277; 3:339;
　5:286, 288; 8:389; 13:383-86; 18:335;
　45:274, 278; 88:187, 191, 195, 197, 199,
　202, 204-06, 211
"A License" (Tuohy)　37:430
License Renewed (Gardner)　30:156-57
License to Carry a Gun (Codrescu)　46:101-03
"License to Kill" (Dylan)　77:184
"Lichen" (Munro)　50:209, 211-12, 216-17,
　220
Lichtzwang (*Force of Light; Light Compulsion*)
　(Celan)　53:73, 82; 19:91; 53:73, 78, 82;
　82:34
Licking Hitler (Hare)　29:215; 58:225, 232
"Licorice" (Theriault)　79:408
"Liddy's Orange" (Olds)　85:295, 300
"The Lie" (Angelou)　77:31
"The Lie" (Banks)　37:23
"The Lie" (Carver)　36:106
The Lie (Moravia)
　See *L'attenzione*
Lie Down in Darkness (Styron)　1:329-30;
　3:472-74; 5:418; 11:515-16, 520-21;
　15:525; 60:392
The Lie of the Land (Beer)　58:37-8
A Lie of the Mind (Shepard)　44:263-72
Eine Liebe in Deutschland (*A German Love*
　Story) (Hochhuth)　18:255-56
Lieber Fritz (Kroetz)　41:234
"Liebesgedicht" (Voigt)　54:430-31
"(Liebeslied.)" ("(Lovesong.)") (Celan)　82:50-
　2
"Lieblingsspeise der Hyänen" (Lenz)　27:245
Lieblose Legenden (Hildesheimer)　49:173-74
"Ein Lied in der Wüste" ("A Song in the Wil-
　derness") (Celan)　53:69
"Liedholz" (Read)　4:439
"Liejyklos" (Brodsky)　36:77

"Lies" (Canin)　55:39
"Lies" (Endo)　99:296
"Lies" (Shields)　97:433
Lies (Newlove)　14:377-78
Lies (Williams)　33:441-42, 444-45
Lies and Secrets (Fuller)　62:196-98, 201, 204
Lies of Silence (Moore)　90:289-96, 298, 301
Lies of the Night (Bufalino)
　See *Le menzogne della notte*
Lies of the Night (Bufalino)
　See *Le menzogne della notte*
"Lieu de la salamandre" ("Place of the Sala-
　mander") (Bonnefoy)　15:76
The Lieutenant (Dubus)　13:183; 97:203, 209,
　224, 230
"Lieutenant Bligh and Two Midshipmen"
　(Brown)　100:82-3
Lieutenant Hornblower (Forester)　35:169-70
Lieutenant Lookeast, and Other Stories (Ibuse)
　22:226-27
Lieutenant Schmidt (Pasternak)　18:382;
　63:288, 292-93, 308, 313
"Life" ("Vida") (Aleixandre)　36:29
"Life" (Head)　67:96
"A Life" (Plath)　111:181, 185
A Life (Leonard)　19:282
A Life (Morris)　3:343-44; 7:246
A Life (Tesich)　40:421
Life: A User's Manual (Perec)
　See *La vie, mode d'emploi*
"The Life Adventurous" (Farrell)　66:129
Life after God (Coupland)　85:35-41
"The Life Ahead" (Levine)　14:321
Life among Others (Halpern)　14:231-32
"Life among the Constipated" (Crumb)　17:83
The Life and Adventures of Nicholas Nickleby
　(Edgar)　42:117-21, 123
Life and Death in a Coral Sea (Cousteau)
　30:104-05
Life and Death in the Charity Ward (*Erections,*
　Ejaculations, Exhibitions, and General
　Tales of Ordinary Madness) (Bukowski)
　2:84; 5:80; 41:68; 82:3-4, 8; 108:83
"Life and Death in the South Side Pavilion"
　(Carey)　96:37, 67
Life and Death of an Oilman: The Career of E.
　W. Marland (Mathews)　84:205, 211
The Life and Death of Nikolay Kurbov
　(Ehrenburg)　62:174-75
The Life and Death of Yellow Bird (Forman)
　21:120
The Life and Extraordinary Adventures of Pri-
　vate Ivan Chonkin (Voinovich)
　See *Zhizn i neobychainye prikliucheniia*
　soldata Ivana Chonkina
Life and Fate (Grossman)
　See *Zhizn' i sud'ba*
Life and Limb (Reddin)　67:265, 267, 270-71
The Life and Loves of a She-Devil (Weldon)
　36:448-49
Life and Sun (Sillanpaa)
　See *Elämä ja aurinko*
The Life and Times of an Involuntary Genius
　(Codrescu)　46:103-04
The Life and Times of Chaucer (Gardner)
　10:220; 28:164
The Life and Times of Joseph Stalin (Wilson)
　7:549-51; 9:576
Life and Times of Michael K (Coetzee)　33:106-
　12; 66:91-2, 95-7, 99, 105-06; 117:30-3,
　39, 45-9, 59-60, 62-3, 66, 69, 71, 73, 75,
　79, 81-7, 92, 102-03
"The Life and Times of Multivac" (Asimov)

26:56; 92:9
The Life and Times of Sigmund Freud (Wilson)
　7:549, 551
The Life and Work of Semmelweiss (Celine)
　3:104; 4:99, 103; 7:43; 9:154
Life at the Top (Braine)　1:43-4; 41:57
"Life at War" (Levertov)　5:248-49; 66:239
Life before Man (Atwood)　15:38-40; 25:70;
　84:97
"Life before Science" (Carlson)　54:37-9
"Life Being the Best" (Boyle)　58:77
Life Being the Best, and Other Stories (Boyle)
　58:77
"Life between Meals" (De Marinis)　54:99-
　100
"Life Class" (Montague)　13:391; 46:273
Life Class (Storey)　4:530; 5:415-17; 8:505
Life Collection (Ivask)　14:287
"Life Comparison" (Dugan)　6:143
"Life Cycle of Common Man" (Nemerov)
　6:361
"Life Drawing" (Mac Laverty)　31:255
"Life during Wartime" (Byrne)　26:97
Life during Wartime (Reddin)　67:270-72
"Life for a Life" (Paton)　25:359
A Life for the Stars (Blish)　14:85
"Life from a Goldfish Bowl" (Johnston)
　51:239, 243
"Life from a Window" (Weller)　26:443-44
"Life Goes On" (Davies)　21:102
Life Goes On (Sillitoe)　57:399-400
"The Life Guard" (Wain)　46:417
The Life Guard (Wain)　46:417
"The Life I Led" (Giovanni)　64:191
The Life I Really Lived (West)　17:554
Life in a Quiet House (Kohout)　13:325
"Life in a Small Neighborhood" (Crase)　58:165
"Life in an Explosive Forming Press" (Brunner)
　8:109
Life in an Explosive Forming Press (Brunner)
　8:109
Life in Folds (Michaux)
　See *La vie dans les plis*
Life in Schools: An Introduction to Critical
　Pedagogy in the Foundations of Educa-
　tion　70:366
Life in the Forest (Levertov)　15:338-39;
　28:242; 66:236, 253
A Life in the Theatre (Mamet)　9:360; 15:355-
　56, 358; 46:250-51
Life in the Universe (Silverstein and Silverstein)
　17:450
"Life in the Valley" (Strand)　71:289
Life in the West (Aldiss)　40:15, 19, 21
"Life in Windy Weather" (Bitov)　57:114-15
Life in Windy Weather (Bitov)　57:113-15, 117,
　119
Life Is a Platform (Levi)　41:245
Life Is Elsewhere (Kundera)
　See *La vie est ailleurs*
"Life Is No Abyss" (Stafford)　7:457; 68:423
"Life Is Trying to Be Life" (Hughes)　37:172
Life, Law, and Letters (Auchincloss)　18:25
Life Lessons (Scorsese)　89:265, 267-68
"Life Line" (Heinlein)　14:248
Life/Lines: Theorizing Women's Autobiography
　65:315
"A Life Membership" (Tuohy)　37:430
Life Notes (Waldman)　7:508
The Life of a Poet (Cocteau)
　See *La vie d'un poète*
The Life of a Woman (Endo)
　See *Onna no Issho*

"The life of Borodin" (Bukowski) 108:111
The Life of Henry James (Edel) 34:537
A Life of Jesus (Endo) 19:161; 54:160; 99:285, 287, 301, 308
The Life of Jesus (Olson) 28:342-44
The Life of John Milton (Wilson) 33:455
"The Life of John Voe" (Brown) 48:62
The Life of Juanita Castro (Warhol) 20:415, 417
The Life of Langston Hughes, Volume I, 1902-1941: I, Too, Sing America (Rampersad) 44:507-09, 511-13
"The Life of Lincoln West" (Brooks) 49:23, 28, 36-7
The Life of Mahalia Jackson, Queen of the Gospel Singers (Jackson) 12:291
"The Life of Poetry" (Tate) 25:429
The Life of Poetry (Rukeyser) 15:459-60; 27:407, 412-13
A Life of Poetry: 1948-1994 (Amichai) 116:137
The Life of Raymond Chandler (MacShane) 39:411
The Life of Riot (Sherwin) 15:479
"The Life of Tadeo Isidoro Cruz" (Borges)
   See "Biografía de Tadeo Isidoro Cruz"
The Life of the Automobile (Ehrenburg) 18:137-38
The Life of the Drama (Bentley) 24:47-50
The Life of the Mind (Arendt) 98:14-15, 38, 48, 52
The Life of the Self: Toward a New Psychology (Lifton) 67:149, 151
"A Life of Wonder" (Ignatow) 40:259
"Life on Mars" (Bowie) 17:58, 64
"Life on the Moon" (Smith) 73:356, 358
"Life on the Road" (Davies) 21:101
"Life on the Rocks: The Galápagos" (Dillard) 60:75
"Life Portrait" (Steele) 45:365
Life Quest (Aldington) 49:17
Life Sentences (Hailey) 40:222-23
Life/Situations (Sartre) 18:472
Life Sketches (Hersey) 81:329, 332
"Life Story" (Barth) 3:41; 7:24; 9:68-9; 14:53-4, 56; 51:23; 89:5-6, 9-10, 16, 19, 24, 28-30, 32, 34-6, 44-5, 47-8, 56, 61-2
Life Studies (Lowell) 1:180-84; 2:246-48; 3:299-302, 304-06; 4:295-96, 298-304; 5:257-58; 8:348, 350-51, 353, 355-58; 9:333-35, 339; 11:325-27, 331; 15:342-48; 37:232-33, 235-36, 238, 241-43
Life, the Universe, and Everything (Adams) 27:13-15; 60:2
"The Life to Come" (Forster) 3:161; 13:220; 22:135; 45:136
The Life to Come, and Other Stories (Forster) 2:136; 3:161-62; 15:229, 231; 22:135; 45:131, 143
Life under Water (Greenberg) 57:227-29
Life Vanquished (Lagerkvist)
   See Det besegrade livet
"The Life with a Hole in It" (Larkin) 64:272
"Life with Atlas" (West) 96:363, 384
"Life with the Blob" (Macdonald) 41:270
Life with the Lions: Unfinished Music Number Two (Lennon) 35:267, 270
"The Life You Live (May Not Be Your Own)" (Cooper) 56:71-2
"The Life You Save May Be Your Own" (O'Connor) 1:257; 21:256, 264, 276; 104:104, 120, 123, 135
Lifeboat (Harrison) 42:204
Lifeboat (Hitchcock) 16:339, 345

"The Lifeguard" (Dickey) 4:120
"Lifeguard" (Updike) 7:486; 13:558
"Lifeline" (Heinlein) 55:300, 302
Life's Long Days (Johnson)
   See Livsdagen läng
"A Life's Unity" (Blunden) 56:50
"Life's Work" (Kumin) 13:327
The Lifestyle of Robie Tuckerman (Corcoran) 17:71-2
Life-Terms (Canetti)
   See Die Befristeten
Lifetime (Sommer) 25:424
A Lifetime Burning (Douglas) 73:76-8, 84-8, 90, 97-9
"The Lift Man" (Betjeman) 43:51
"The Lift That Went Down into Hell" (Lagerkvist)
   See "Hissen som gick ner i helvete"
"Lifting" (Heaney) 14:243
"The Lifting" (Olds) 85:308
"The Light" 75:74
"light" (Clifton) 66:87
"Light" (Jacobsen) 48:190
"The Light" (Sarton) 91:244
Light (Figes) 31:168-70
Light Album (Wilson)
   See L.A.
"Light and Dark" (Howes) 15:289-90
Light and Dark (Bronk) 10:75
Light and Darkness (Kawabata) 9:314
The Light and the Dark (Snow) 1:317; 4:501, 504; 6:516; 13:509-10; 19:425
The Light and the Grief (Bufalino)
   See La luce e il lutto
The Light around the Body (Bly) 1:37; 2:65-6; 5:61-5; 10:54-7; 15:62, 65-8; 38:55, 57
"The Light at Birth" (Berriault) 54:7; 109:98
The Light Beyond the Forest: The Quest for the Holy Grail (Sutcliff) 26:440
"A Light Breather" (Roethke) 8:455; 101:304
Light Can Be Both Wave and Particle (Gilchrist) 65:349
Light Compulsion (Celan)
   See Lichtzwang
"Light Fiction" (Johnston) 51:251
A Light for Fools (Ginzburg)
   See Tutti i nostri ieri
"The Light from Beyond" (Smith) 43:424
Light in August (Faulkner) 1:100, 102; 3:149-50, 152-53, 156-58; 6:174, 176, 178, 180-81; 8:207-09, 211; 9:200-01; 11:200, 202, 206; 14:169, 172, 179-80; 18:149; 28:135-38, 140-45; 68:116
The Light in the Forest (Richter) 30:319-23
The Light in the Piazza (Spencer) 22:399-400, 403
"The Light in the Window" (Woolrich) 77:402
"A Light in Winter" (MacBeth) 2:252
"A Light Left On" (Sarton) 91:254
"Light Listened" (Roethke) 8:456; 101:332
"Light Music" (Mahon) 27:292
"Light My Candle" 99:169
"Light My Fire" (Morrison) 17:288, 290, 295
The Light of Day (Ambler) 4:19; 6:4; 9:18
"The Light of Paradise" 75:74
"The Light of the World" (Hemingway) 3:241; 30:185, 192
"The Light of the World" (Walcott) 67:342, 359, 361-63; 76:275
"Light on the Subject" (Komunyakaa) 94:246
"The Light Put Out" (Moss) 45:290
Light Shining in Buckinghamshire (Churchill)

31:83-4
"The Light Symbolism in 'L'Allegro-Il Peneroso'" (Brooks) 110:36-7
"the light that came to lucille clifton" (Clifton) 66:85
Light Thickens (Marsh) 53:260
"The Light Tree" (Elytis) 49:111
The Light Tree and the Fourteenth Beauty (Elytis) 49:108, 117; 100:168, 170, 175, 180, 183, 185-86, 190
The Light under Islands (Squires) 51:378
Light Up the Cave (Levertov) 28:242-43; 66:239
Light Up the Sky (Hart) 66:176-79, 182-86, 188, 190
"Light Verse" (Asimov) 19:28
Light Years (Gee) 57:221-22
Light Years (Salter) 7:387-38; 52:360-61, 363, 365-67; 59:195-98
"The Light-blue Sea Cannons" (Aksyonov) 101:20
"Lightenings" (Heaney) 74:188
Lightfall (Monette) 82:316
"The Lighthouse" (Walcott) 67:360; 76:299
"Lighting Fires in Snow" (Richards) 14:455
"Lightly Bound" (Smith) 25:420
"Lightness" (Wilbur) 53:397
"Lightnin' Blues" (Dove) 50:157; 81:144
"Lightning" (Barthelme) 46:39-40, 43
"Lightning" (Oliver) 34:247-48
"The Lightning" (Swenson) 106:349
Lightning (Pa Chin)
   See Tien
"The Lightning Rod Man" (Belitt) 22:53, 52
"The Lightning Speed of the Past" (Carver) 55:275
"Lightning Storm" (Schaeffer) 6:489; 11:491
"Lights" (Cardenal)
   See "Luces"
"Lights among Redwood" (Gunn) 18:200
"The Lights Are Always Near" (Kenny) 87:256
"The Lights in the Sky are Stars" (Rexroth) 112:377
The Lights of Earth (Berriault) 54:5-7; 109:90, 94
Lights On in the House of the Dead (Berrigan) 4:58
"Lights Out" (Cassity) 42:97
"The Lightship" (Lenz)
   See "Das Feverschiff"
"The Light-Years" (Calvino) 8:127
"Like a Banner" (Greenberg) 30:166
Like a Bulwark (Moore) 8:400; 47:262
Like a Conquered Province (Goodman) 2:171
"Like a Hurricane" (Young) 17:577
"Like a Leaf" (McGuane) 45:265-66
"Like a Message on Sunday" (Dorn) 10:157
Like a Ripple in the Pond (Giovanni) 117:185
"Like a Ripple on a Pond" (Giovanni) 117:191
"Like a Rolling Stone" (Dylan) 6:155; 12:182, 193; 77:165, 168, 171, 174-75, 179, 182, 186
"Like a Winding Sheet" (Petry) 1:266
"Like an Old Proud King in a Parable" (Smith) 15:516-17
Like Any Other Man (Boyle) 19:67
Like Birds, Like Fishes (Jhabvala) 4:257; 29:256
"Like Dolmens round My Childhood, the Old People" (Montague) 13:390; 46:266, 275, 278
"Like Father, Like Sun" (Kaufman) 49:207
Like Ghosts of Eagles (Francis) 15:236

"Like Glass" (Beattie) 63:18
Like I Say (Whalen) 29:446
"Like Life" (Moore) 68:297, 300-01
Like Life (Moore) 68:297-302
Like Men Betrayed (Mortimer) 28:282
"Like Mexicans" (Soto) 80:284
"Like Morning Light" (Rosenthal) 28:394
"Like Myself" (Ortiz) 45:306
"Like O. M." (Cabral de Melo Neto)
    See "A maneria de Olegário Mariano"
"Like Olegário Mariano" (Cabral de Melo Neto)
    See "A maneria de Olegário Mariano"
Like One of the Family: Conversations from a Domestic's Life (Childress) 86:309, 311; 96:94-5
"Like Son" (Van Doren) 10:495
"Like That" (McCullers) 12:433
"Like the Inner Wall of a House" (Amichai) 116:89, 93
Like the Lion's Tooth (Kellogg) 2:224-25
"Like the Night" (Carpentier) 38:94
"Like the Sad Heart of Ruth" (Taylor) 37:407
"Like the Sun" (Narayan) 47:304
"Like the Sunshine" (Bagryana)
    See "Kato slunce"
"Like Things Made of Clay" (Kunze) 10:310
"Like This One" (Moure) 88:221
"Like This Together" (Rich) 6:458; 7:368
"Like This...So This" (Oates) 6:367
"Like Three Fair Branches from One Root Deriv'd" (Hass) 18:213
"Like Whipporwills" (Simic) 22:381, 383
"Likenesses" (MacCaig) 36:282
"Lila" (Brodkey) 56:57, 59
Lila: An Inquiry into Morals (Pirsig) 73:309-10
Lila the Werewolf (Beagle) 104:5, 8, 19-23, 25
"Lilacs" (Lavin) 99:322
"The Lilacs" (Wilbur) 6:570
Lilacs out of the Dead Land (Billington) 43:54
"Liliana llorando" ("Liliana Weeping") (Cortazar) 33:123-24
"Liliana Weeping" (Cortazar)
    See "Liliana llorando"
Lilian's Story (Grenville) 61:152-67
"Lilies" (Oliver) 98:279, 281, 283
"The Lilies Break Open Over the Dark Water" (Oliver) 98:283, 290
"The Lilies of the Field Know Which Side Their Bread Is Buttered On" (Harmon) 38:243-44
Liliom (Lang) 20:217; 103:122
Lilít e altri racconti ("Lilith, and Other Stories"; *Moments of Reprieve*) (Levi) 37:224; 50:323, 325, 334, 336
"Lilith" (Kennedy) 42:255
Lilith (Salamanca) 4:461-62; 15:464-65
"Lilith, and Other Stories" (Levi)
    See *Lilít e altri racconti*
"Det lilla fälttåget" ("The Children's Campaign") (Lagerkvist) 54:276, 287
Lillian Hellman: The Image, the Woman (Wright) 44:526-32
"Lilly's Story" (Wilson) 13:607
Lilo's Diary (Elman) 19:149
"The Lily" (Bates) 46:52, 54, 63
"Lily" (Smiley) 53:348
"Lily Coe" (White) 49:409
Lily Dale (Foote) 51:135-37
"Lily Daw and the Three Ladies" (Welty) 2:462; 22:458; 105:298, 385
"The Lily of the Valley Lay-By" (Tournier) 36:439

"The Lily Pond" (Johnston) 51:241, 243
Lily Tomlin on the Way to Broadway (Tomlin) 17:517
"Lily's Party" (Purdy) 52:350
The Lilywhite Boys (Poole) 17:371
"Limbé" ("Blues"; "Love Sickness") (Damas) 84:168-69, 171-72, 176, 178, 182
"Limbo" (Carpenter) 41:103
"Limbo" (Cernuda) 54:58
"Limbo" (Heaney) 5:170; 7:148
Limbo (Huxley) 11:284
"Limbo River" (Hillis) 66:195
Limbo River (Hillis) 66:194, 196-99
The Lime Twig (Hawkes) 1:138; 2:183, 185; 3:221-23; 4:214-18; 7:141, 144, 146; 9:263-64, 266, 268-69; 15:271; 27:191-92, 196, 199; 49:161-62, 164
The Lime Works (Bernhard)
    See *Das Kalkwerk*
Limelight (Chaplin) 16:194-97, 201-02, 204
Limericks: Too Gross (Asimov) 76:315
Limit of Darkness (Hunt) 3:251
"Limited" (Sandburg) 10:450
"Limites" ("Limits") (Borges) 6:87; 10:65
"Limits" (Ammons) 57:50
"Limits" (Borges)
    See "Limites"
"Limits" (Okigbo) 25:349-50, 352, 355; 84:317, 319
Limits (Okigbo) 25:348-54; 84:302, 306-10, 314-15, 319, 322, 325-28, 331, 336-37
The Limits of Interpretation (Eco) 60:123
The Limits of Love (Raphael) 2:366-67
"The Limits of the Novel" (Cowley) 39:458
Lina (Arghezi) 80:6
Lincoln: A Novel (Vidal) 33:409-11; 72:386-87, 389-93, 395-400, 402-04, 406
"The Lincoln-Pruitt Anti-Rape Device: Memoirs of the Woman's Combat Army in Vietnam" (Prager) 56:276-78
Lincoln's Doctor's Dog, and Other Stories (Grayson) 38:210-11
"A Lincolnshire Church" (Betjeman) 43:40, 42
"Linda" (Fuller) 62:199
"Linda" (Smith) 12:535
"Linda Paloma" (Browne) 21:38
"The Linden Branch" (MacLeish) 8:359
Linden Hills (Naylor) 52:321-26
Linden Hills (Leffland) 19:280
The Linden Tree (Priestley) 2:347
"Lindenbloom" (Clampitt) 32:118
Lindmann (Raphael) 2:366-67
"Lindow Man" (Selzer) 74:287
"Lindsay and the Red City Blues" (Haldeman) 61:181
"The Line" (Carruth) 84:129
"The Line" (Hoffman) 6:243
Line (Horovitz) 56:149-50, 153
"Line and Form" (Dudek) 11:160
"The Line of Apelles" (Pasternak)
    See "Il tratto di Apelle"
The Line of Least Existence (Drexler) 2:119
"The Lineman" (Miller) 30:262, 264
"The Linen Industry" (Longley) 29:296
"Linen Town" (Heaney) 7:148
"The Linen Workers" (Longley) 29:296
"Lines" (Dacey) 51:82
"The Lines" (Motion) 47:288
"Lines about the Recent Past" (Galvin) 38:198
Lines at Intersection (Miles) 39:353
"Lines for a 21st Birthday" ("Birthday") (Fuller) 62:206

"Lines for a Bamboo Stick" (Dudek) 11:159
"Lines for an Internment" (MacLeish) 68:285
"Lines for Mr. Stevenson" (Turco) 63:430
"Lines for My Grandmother's Grave" (Urdang) 47:397
"Lines for Roy Fuller" (Spender) 91:269
"Lines for the English" (Squires) 51:383
"Lines for the Twice-Drowned" (Logan) 5:255
"Lines for Translation into Any Language" (Fenton) 32:169
"Lines for Winter" (Strand) 18:517, 520
"Lines from My Grandfather's Journal" (Cohen) 38:131
"Lines in Stasis in the Form of Sonnet That Didn't Get Written" (Montgomery) 7:233
Lines of Life (Mauriac)
    See *Destins*
"Lines on a Young Lady's Photograph Album" (Larkin) 5:231; 18:301; 33:263; 64:267, 279
Lines Scibbled on an Envelope and Other Poems (L'Engle) 12:348
"Lines to Be Recited While Burning at the Stake" (L'Heureux) 52:275
"Lines to Myself" (Heaney) 74:152
"Lines to Robert Lowell" (Voznesensky) 57:421
"Lines with a Gift of Herbs" (Lewis) 41:262
"Lines Written for Allen Tate on His Sixtieth Anniversary" (Davidson) 2:113
"Lines Written in a Guest Book" (Van Duyn) 116:425
"Lines Written in the Euganean Hills" (Tomlinson) 45:393-94
"Lines Written in the Library of Congress after the Cleanth Brooks Lecture" (Kumin) 28:222
"Lines Written on Dry Grape Leaves" 75:76
"The Linesman" (Frame) 96:182
Lingard (Wilson) 14:589
"The Lingham and the Yoni" (Hope) 51:214, 216
"La lingua seritta della realtà" (Pasolini) 106:235
"Lining Up" (Howard) 47:170-71
Lining Up (Howard) 47:170
"Links on the Chain" (Ochs) 17:330-31
"Linoleum" (Gallagher) 63:118
"Linoleum Roses" (Cisneros) 69:146, 147
Linotte: The Early Diary of Anaïs Nin, 1914-1920, Vol. I (Nin) 11:398-99
"Lint" (Brautigan) 12:65
"Liompa" (Olesha) 8:432
"Lion" (Garrett) 51:145
"The Lion" (Merton) 83:388
"Lion" (Swenson) 61:395, 400; 106:326
The Lion and the Archer (Hayden) 37:156, 160
The Lion and the Honeycomb: Essays in Solicitude and Critique (Blackmur) 24:58-60, 65-6, 68
The Lion and the Jewel (Soyinka) 3:463; 14:506-07; 44:280-83, 287, 290
The Lion and the Rose (Sarton) 49:310, 320
Lion Country (Buechner) 2:82-4; 4:80; 6:102-03; 9:137
"The Lion for Real" (Ginsberg) 36:181, 199; 109:356
"Lion Grove, Suzhou" (Seth) 90:351
"Lion Hunt" (Beer) 58:36
The Lion in Love (Delaney) 29:144-47
The Lion in the Gateway (Renault) 17:397
The Lion of Boaz-Jachin and Jachin-Boaz

(Hoban)   7:161; 25:263
The Lion of Comarre (Clarke)   35:121
"A Lion on the Freeway" (Gordimer)   18:189
Lion on the Hearth (Ehle)   27:103
The Lion Skin (Baxter)   14:63
The Lion, the Witch, and the Wardrobe (Lewis)   1:177; 27:262-63, 265
"A Lion upon the Floor" (Olson)   29:329
Lions and Shadows: An Education in the Twenties (Isherwood)   1:157; 9:290-93; 14:279-80, 283; 44:397-402
"Lions, Harts, Leaping Does" (Powers)   57:356, 358
"Lions' Jaws" (Loy)   28:251, 253
Lions Love (Varda)   16:558
The Lion's Mouth: Concluding Chapters of Autobiography (Raine)   45:340-41
Lionushka (Leonov)
    See *Lyonushka*
"Lip Service" (Costello)   21:68
"The Lippia Lawn" (Stafford)   4:517; 19:430
"Lips of My Love" (Prichard)   46:337
Lips Together, Teeth Apart (McNally)   91:159, 161, 164
"Lips Twisted with Thirst" (Ammons)   57:49-50
Lipstick on Your Collar (Potter)   86:347
"Lipstick Vogue" (Costello)   21:68
The Liquidator (Gardner)   30:151-52
Lire "Le Capital" (Reading Capital) (Althusser)   106:12, 17-19, 21, 29, 31, 38, 42-3
Lirika (Krleza)   114:167
"Lisa" (Beauvoir)   31:42
Lisa, Bright and Dark (Neufeld)   17:308, 310
"Lisa Says" (Reed)   21:304-05, 311
The Lisbon Traviata (McNally)   41:291-92; 91:159
al-Liss wa-al-kilab (Mahfuz)
    See *al-Liss wa-'l-kilab*
al-Liss wa-'l-kilab (*al-Liss wa-al-kilab*; *The Thief and the Dogs*) (Mahfuz)   52:295-96, 300-01, 303-05; 55:174, 181, 183
The List of Adrian Messenger (Huston)   20:168
"A List of Assets" (Olesha)
    See "Spisok blagodeyany"
"A List of Benefits" (Olesha)
    See "Spisok blagodeyany"
"listen children" (Clifton)   66:69
Listen for the Whisperer (Whitney)   42:434
"Listen Put On Morning" (Graham)   29:198
Listen! The Wind (Lindbergh)   82:148, 150, 153, 158, 166-67
"Listen. This Is the Noise of Myth" (Boland)   67:40, 46; 113:86, 88, 98
Listen to the Mockingbird (Perelman)   49:260, 272
Listen to the Warm (McKuen)   1:211
Listen to the Wind (Brinsmead)   21:29-30
Listen to the Wind (Reaney)   13:475
"Listen to What the Man Said" (McCartney)   35:282-83
"Listen with Mother" (Raine)   103:186, 189
"Listenen to Big Black at S.F. State" (Sanchez)   116:295
The Listener (Caldwell)   28:62-3
"The Listener in the Corner" (Thomas)   13:545
"Listening" (Paley)   37:336-37, 339
"Listening" (Welty)   105:320-21, 378-80, 382
Listening: A Chamber Play (Albee)   9:10; 11:13; 53:21, 26; 113:15, 17, 22, 24, 30-1, 33-5
The Listening Landscape (Zaturenska)   11:579
Listening to America: A Traveler Rediscovers His Country (Moyers)   74:249-51, 255

Listening to Billie (Adams)   13:2; 46:13-16, 21
"Listening to Distant Guns" (Levertov)   28:242
"Listening to Marianne Moore on a Record" (Cabral de Melo Neto)
    See "Ouvindo Marianne Moore em disco"
"Listening to the Mourners" (Wright)   10:544
"Listening to the Orchestra" (Hill)   113:330
Listening to the Orchestra (Hill)   113:330-31
"Listening Wind" (Byrne)   26:98
The Listening Woman (Hillerman)   62:251, 253, 256
"Liston Cows Patterson and Knocks Him Silly" (Rosenthal)   28:394
Lisztomania (Russell)   16:549
"The Litanies of the Beautiful Bay" (Pasolini)   106:261
"Litany" (Ashbery)   15:33-6; 25:52-3, 58-9; 41:33, 38; 77:43
"A Litany for Mad Masters" (Zamora)   89:387
"The Litany for Survival" (Lorde)   71:241, 247, 257
"A Litany of Atlanta" (Du Bois)   64:114, 116; 96:130
A Literary Affair (Blais)   22:60
Literary Biography (Edel)   34:534-35, 537
"The Literary Consequences of the Crash" (Wilson)   24:481
Literary Criticism: A Short History (Brooks)   110:9, 31
"Literary Criticism and Philosophy" (Leavis)   24:298
"A Literary Discovery" (Betjeman)   43:33
The Literary Essays of Ezra Pound (Pound)   4:416
The Literary Essays of Thomas Merton (Merton)   83:396
"The Literary Gathering" (Ewart)
    See "Sestina: The Literary Gathering"
"A Literary History" (Brophy)   6:100
"Literary History and Literary Modernity" (de Man)   55:384, 386, 396
"A Literary History of Anton" (Cohen)   19:113
"The Literary Life Today" (Epstein)   39:467-68
Literary Lifelines (Durrell)   27:96
"Literary Observations" (Fuller)   62:196
"The Literary Process in Russia" (Sinyavsky)   8:490
Literary Reflections (Michener)   109:383
Literary Theory: An Introduction (Eagleton)   63:95-100, 104-05, 113
"Literary Theory and the Black Tradition" (Gates)   65:386
"Literary Unions" (Ewart)   46:150
"The Literate Farmer and the Planet Venus" (Frost)   26:118
Literatur und Lustprinzip (Wellershoff)   46:436-37
Literatur und Veränderung: Versuche zu einer Metakritik der Literatur (Wellershoff)   46:434, 437
"A literatura como turismo" ("Literature as Tourism") (Cabral de Melo Neto)   76:169
"La literatura es fuego" ("Literature Is Fire") (Vargas Llosa)   85:354, 370-71
Literature and Existentialism (Sartre)
    See *Qu'est-ce que la littérature?*
Literature and Morality (Farrell)   66:132, 136
"Literature and Offence" (Brink)   36:68
"Literature and Revolution; or, The Idylist's Snorting Hobby-Horse" (Grass)   49:140
Literature and Science (Huxley)   4:241; 5:192; 35:242

"Literature and Society" (Leavis)   24:298
"Literature and Technology" (MacLennan)   14:343
Literature and the Press (Dudek)   19:138
Literature and the Sixth Sense (Rahv)   24:354-55
Literature and Western Man (Priestley)   34:362-63
"Literature as Knowledge" (Tate)   11:522; 24:444
"Literature as Tourism" (Cabral de Melo Neto)
    See "A literatura como turismo"
"Literature as Utopia" (Bachmann)   69:57
"Literature Is Fire" (Vargas Llosa)
    See "La literatura es fuego"
The Literature Machine (Calvino)
    See *Una pietra sopra: Discorsi di letteratura e societa*
"The Literature of Exhaustion" ("Exhaustion") (Barth)   3:41; 7:22; 14:55; 51:20-2, 24-5; 89:17, 21, 25, 35, 38-9, 44-7, 57
"The Literature of Replenishment" (Barth)   51:20-2, 24-5; 89:57
"The Literature of the Holocaust" (Alvarez)   5:17
"Literature versus the Universities" (Hope)   51:218
Literatuur in die strydperk (Brink)   106:109
Lithium for Medea (Braverman)   67:49, 53
"Lithuanian Divertissement" (Brodsky)
    See "Litoviskij divertisment"
"Lithuanian Nocturne" ("Litovskii noktyurn") (Brodsky)   100:45, 53
"The Litigants" (Singer)   69:306
"Litoviskij divertisment" ("Lithuanian Divertissement") (Brodsky)   36:77; 50:125, 131
"Litovskii noktyurn" (Brodsky)
    See "Lithuanian Nocturne"
Litsom k litsu (Face to face) (Aitmatov)   71:13-14, 16
La littérature et le mal (Bataille)   29:46-7
"Littérature et metaphysique" (Beauvoir)   44:345
"Littérature littérale" (Barthes)   24:27
"Littérature objective" (Barthes)   24:27
Little (Zukofsky)   2:487
Little Badger and Fire Spirit (Campbell)   85:15
"Little Ballad of Ploudiv" (Guillen)   79:229
"A Little Beaded Bag" (Callaghan)   41:98
Little Big Man (Berger)   3:63-4; 5:60; 8:83-4; 11:46; 18:54-8; 38:36-9, 41
Little, Big; Or the Fairies' Parliament (Crowley)   57:158-60, 162-64
"Little Billy" (Townshend)   17:534
"Little Bird" (Wilson)   12:641
Little Birds: Erotica (Nin)   14:387; 60:269, 275
"Little Bit of Emotion" (Davies)   21:105
"The Little Black Box" (Dick)   72:113
"Little Black Heart of the Telephone" (Warren)   18:537
"The Little Blond Fellow" (Farrell)   66:113
"Little Bombadier" (Bowie)   17:65
Little Book of Evening (Arghezi)
    See *Carticica de seara*
"Little Boy and Lost Shoe" (Warren)   8:538
"Little Boy Impelling a Scooter" (Murray)   40:343
A Little Boy in Search of God: Mysticism in a Personal Light (Singer)   11:499; 23:422; 38:412; 69:303
"Little Boy Sick" (Smith)   25:418; 44:442

"Little Boy Soldiers" (Weller) **26**:446

"The Little Boys" (Hughes) **4**:236

"Little Brother" (Wideman) **67**:379, 382-83, 385

"The Little Coat" (Spender) **41**:427

"The Little Cousins" (Taylor) **18**:523; **37**:411; **44**:305-06, 309

"Little Creatures" (Coupland) **85**:35-6, 39

"Little Curtis" (Parker) **68**:326-27, 334-36

The Little Dark Thorn (Arthur) **12**:26, 28

A Little Decorum, for Once (Spackman) **46**:380-81

"Little Deuce Coupe" (Wilson) **12**:651

Little Deuce Coupe (Wilson) **12**:642

The Little Disturbances of Man (Paley) **4**:391-92, 394; **6**:391-93; **37**:330-32, 334-35, 337

"Little Dreams of Mr. Morgan" (Willingham) **51**:403

The Little Drummer Girl (le Carre) **28**:226-32

"The Little Duffer" (Stewart) **32**:421

Little Eden: A Child at War (Figes) **31**:166

"The Little Elderly Lady Visits" (Gustafson) **36**:212

"Little Elegy" (Kennedy) **42**:255, 257

"Little Elegy for Cello and Piano" (Justice) **102**:271

"Little Exercise" (Bishop) **9**:94-5

"Little Expressionless Animals" (Wallace) **114**:347-48, 350, 352, 359, 361

"Little Extras" (McGuane) **45**:265

"The Little Farm" (Bates) **46**:59

"Little Fishes" (Bates) **46**:63

"Little Flower" (Anand) **23**:18

The Little Flowers of Madame de Montespan (Urquhart) **90**:374-5, 381, 398

Little Footsteps (Tally) **42**:368

The Little Foxes (Hellman) **2**:187; **8**:281; **14**:256, 258-59; **18**:221; **34**:348-49, 351; **44**:527-28, 531-32; **52**:189, 191, 202

Little Friend, Little Friend (Jarrell) **2**:209-10; **6**:260; **13**:298, 300

"Little Fugue" (Plath) **5**:345; **111**:204, 214

A Little Geste (Hoffman) **6**:243; **13**:287; **23**:238

The Little Ghost (Preussler) **17**:375

"Little Gidding" (Eliot) **1**:89, 92; **2**:126; **3**:138; **6**:164-65; **9**:185, 187-88; **10**:171; **13**:196, 202; **15**:215-16; **34**:400, 524, 526, 530-32; **41**:147; **55**:346, 353, 360, 366, 374; **113**:183, 193, 219

"Little Gidding" (H. D.) **8**:257

"The Little Girl" (Paley) **6**:392; **37**:338

"The Little Girl Continues" (Barnes)
See "The Grande Malade"

"Little Girl Lost" (Kristofferson) **26**:267

"Little Girl, My String Bean, My Lovely Woman" (Sexton) **53**:316, 324

"The Little Girl Sold with the Pears" (Calvino) **22**:94

"A Little Girl Tells a Story to a Lady" (Barnes)
See "Cassation"

The Little Girls (Bowen) **3**:82; **6**:94-5; **11**:63-4; **15**:79; **22**:62

"The Little Girl's Room" (Bowen) **22**:62

"The Little Gram Shop" (Rao) **56**:312

Little Ham (Hughes) **35**:217

"A Little Holiday" (O'Brien) **65**:173

The Little Horses of Tarquinia (Duras)
See *Les petits chevaux de Tarquinia*

The Little Hotel (Stead) **5**:403-05; **8**:499-500; **80**:336, 339

"The Little Hours" (Parker) **68**:326, 335

"Little Imber" (Forster) **22**:137; **45**:131, 133

"A Little Is Enough" (Townshend) **17**:541-42

"The Little John" (Dabrowska)
See "Janek"

Little Katia (*Katia*) (Almedingen) **12**:2, 5-7

The Little Kingdom (Humphreys) **47**:184, 186-87

Little Kingdoms (Millhauser) **109**:165, 167, 170, 174

"Little Lamb" (Sondheim) **30**:377

"Little Lamb Dragonfly" (McCartney) **35**:281

"Little League Try-Outs" (Soto) **80**:279

A Little Learning (Waugh) **27**:477; **44**:520, 522, 524; **107**:370, 392-93

"A Little Light" (Johnston) **51**:240, 245

"Little Lion Face" (Swenson) **106**:343

Little Little (Kerr) **35**:247-50

"Little Lobeila's Song" (Bogan) **4**:69; **39**:388; **93**:81

"Little Lost Robot" (Asimov) **9**:50; **92**:6, 11, 14

"The Little Man at Chehaw Station" (Ellison) **114**:108-12

"The Little Mariner" ("The Little Sailor"; "The Little Seafarer") (Elytis) **100**:170-71, 175-76, 182, 184, 187, 189

The Little Mariner (*The Little Sailor*; *The Little Seafarer*) (Elytis) **100**:186-88

"Little Miracles, Kept Promises" (Cisneros) **69**:148

"Little Miss Queen of Darkness" (Davies) **21**:88

Little Murders (Feiffer) **2**:133; **8**:216; **64**:148-50, 159-64

"A Little Night Music" (Seth) **43**:388

A Little Night Music (Sondheim) **30**:383-85, 387, 389, 391-92, 395-97, 399, 401-02

The Little Nugget (Wodehouse) **5**:515

Little Ocean (Shepard) **6**:495; **17**:447

"A Little Old Funky Homeric Blues for Herm" (Carruth) **84**:129

"Little Old Lady Passing By" (King) **53**:209

"Little Old Miss Macbeth" (Leiber) **25**:304

"Little Old Spy" (Hughes) **108**:324

"The Little Old Woman" (Carroll) **10**:98

"The Little Ones" (Soto) **32**:402

A Little Order (Waugh) **27**:476

"Little Oscar" (Dybek) **114**:66

"Little Pad" (Wilson) **12**:645

Little People, Little Things (Pa Chin)
See *H siao-jen, h siao shih*

A Little Portable Cosmogony (Queneau)
See *Petite cosmogonie portative*

Little Portia (Gray) **36**:200

Little Prayers and Finite Experience (Goodman) **2**:170

"The Little Prince" (Lavin) **99**:320

"The Little Puppy That Could" (Amis) **62**:7-9, 10

A Little Raw on Monday Mornings (Cormier) **12**:133-34

"Little Red Corvette" (Prince) **35**:326-31

"Little Red Riding Hood" (Ferron) **94**:103, 123

"Little Red Rooster" (Jagger and Richard) **17**:227

"The Little Robber Girl Considers Some Options" (Hacker) **72**:190

"Little Rock" (Guillen) **48**:164; **79**:229-30

A Little Romance (Hill) **26**:207-08, 211-12

"The Little Room" (Carver) **53**:61

"The Little Sailor" (Elytis)
See "The Little Mariner"

The Little Sailor (Elytis)
See *The Little Mariner*

The Little Saint (Simenon)
See *Le petit saint*

"The Little Seafarer" (Elytis)
See "The Little Mariner"

The Little Seafarer (Elytis)
See *The Little Mariner*

"The Little Shoemakers" (Singer) **3**:453; **38**:407, 410; **69**:311; **111**:297

"Little Sister Pond" (Oliver) **98**:257

Little Sisters (Weldon) **11**:566; **19**:469

"The Little Soldier" (Aitmatov) **71**:16

Little Songs of the Chief Officer of Hunar Louse, or This Unnameable Little Broom (*The Epic of Gilgamesh*) (The Brothers Quay) **95**:334, 337, 341-42, 344-45, 347, 351, 353-54

Little Tales of Misogyny (Highsmith) **14**:261; **42**:214; **102**:173, 186, 190, 197

A Little Tea, a Little Chat (Stead) **32**:413-16; **80**:327, 329, 341

"Little Tembi" (Lessing) **22**:279

The Little That Is All (Ciardi) **40**:161; **44**:379, 381

The Little Theater of Jean Renoir (Renoir)
See *Le petit théâtre de Jean Renoir*

"Little Things" (Olds) **85**:296

"The Little Things You Do Together" (Sondheim) **30**:380, 391, 395, 402

"The Little Time-Keeper" (Silkin) **43**:401

The Little Time-Keeper (Silkin) **43**:400, 404

"Little Triggers" (Costello) **21**:69

"Little Victories" (Seger) **35**:387

"The Little Virtues" (Ginzburg) **54**:209

The Little Virtues (Ginzburg) **70**:280

"The Little Ways that Encourage Good Fortune" (Stafford) **29**:384

"Little Whale, Varnisher of Reality" (Aksyonov) **101**:10, 18

Little Wheel, Spin and Spin (Sainte-Marie) **17**:431

"Little Willie" (Gordimer) **33**:179-80

Little Wilson and Big God (Burgess) **62**:126-28; **81**:300, 302, 305-06, 310; **94**:87

The Little Witch (Preussler) **17**:374

"The Little Wrens and Roses" (Kiely) **43**:239

"A Liturgy of Rofes" (Williams) **45**:444

Liubov'k elektrichestvu (Aksyonov)
See *Love of Electricity*

"Live" (Sexton) **10**:468; **53**:319

Live (Marley) **17**:269, 272

Live and Let Die (Fleming) **30**:132-33, 136, 138, 143, 148-49

Live Another Day (Ciardi) **40**:152-54, 156-57; **44**:375

Live at Leeds (Townshend) **17**:527-29

"Live Bait" (Tuohy) **37**:433

Live Bait, and Other Stories (Tuohy) **37**:430-32

Live Bullet: Bob Seger and the Silver Bullet Band (Seger) **35**:380-83, 385

Live Flesh (Rendell) **48**:326-27

Live Flesh (Vine) **50**:263-64

Live Like Pigs (Arden) **6**:4-5, 7-10; **13**:23-5, 28; **15**:18-19

Live Not by Lies! (Solzhenitsyn) **34**:482

Live or Die (Sexton) **2**:390-91; **4**:482; **6**:492-93; **8**:484; **10**:468; **15**:471-72; **53**:312, 316-17, 319-21, 324

Live Peace in Toronto (Lennon) **35**:267, 271

Live Rust (Young) **17**:583

The Live Wire (Kanin) **22**:230

"Live with Me" (Jagger and Richard) **17**:226,

238

The Lively Dead (Dickinson) 35:131, 133-34

"Lives" (Rukeyser) 15:458; 27:409, 413

Lives (Mahon) 27:286-90

The Lives and Times of Bernardo Brown (Household) 11:277

The Lives and Times of Jerry Cornelius (Moorcock) 27:349

The Lives of a Cell: Notes of a Biology Watcher (Thomas) 35:408-12, 414-15

"Lives of Girls and Women" (Munro) 95:300

Lives of Girls and Women (Munro) 6:341-42; 10:357; 19:345-46; 50:210, 215; 95:284-87, 289, 291, 293, 297, 299-303, 306, 311, 314-15, 317-18, 320, 323, 325

"The Lives of Gulls and Children" (Nemerov) 36:304

"The Lives of Mrs. Gale" (Belitt) 22:52

Lives of Short Duration (Richards) 59:187, 189, 192

"Lives of the Artists" (Merwin) 88:213

"The Lives of the Chosen" (Dobyns) 37:76

"The Lives of the Dead" (O'Brien) 103:136, 162, 175

"Lives of the Poest" (Van Duyn) 116:410

"Lives of the Poets" (Atwood) 13:45-6

"Lives of the Poets" (Doctorow) 37:93; 113:135, 149-50, 152-55

Lives of the Poets: Six Stories and a Novella (Doctorow) 37:91-4; 44:166-68, 172, 175; 113:135-36, 151-53, 155-56, 163, 171-72, 174, 176-77, 179

"Lives of the Saints" (Berriault) 109:95

"Lives of the Saints" (Muldoon) 32:315

Lives of the Saints (Lemann) 39:75-8

Lives of the Saints (The Book of Saints) (Ricci) 70:207-17

Lives of the Twins (Oates) 52:335, 339-40

Lives of X (Ciardi) 10:106; 40:163; 44:375, 379, 381

Livia; or, Buried Alive (Durrell) 13:189; 27:95, 98-100; 41:134-35, 137-38

Livid Light (Castellanos)
  See Lívida luz

Lívida luz (Livid Light) (Castellanos) 66:47, 52

"Livin' above My Station" (Mull) 17:298

"Living" (Cooper) 56:71

"Living" (Paley) 4:392; 37:332, 337

"The Living" (Pinsky) 38:358; 94:299

The Living (Dillard) 115:194-96, 198, 201

Living (Green) 2:178-79; 13:251, 153-54; 97:242, 245, 247-48, 254, 257-58, 267-68, 279-81, 284, 286-89, 292-93

"Living Alone in Iota" (Abbott) 48:6

"Living among the Dead" (Matthews) 40:320-21

"The Living and Dead" (Mphahlele) 25:338, 342, 344

The Living and Dead, and Other Short Stories (Mphahlele) 25:338, 341, 344

Living and Dying (Lifton) 67:148

The Living and the Dead (White) 4:586; 5:486; 7:531-32; 65:275, 277, 279; 69:394, 396, 401, 403, 407

"Living at Random" (Landolfi) 49:214

Living at the Movies (Carroll) 35:78

The Living Bread (Merton) 83:403

The Living Buddha (Morand)
  See Bouddha vivant

Living by Fiction (Dillard) 60:70-4; 115:169-71, 175, 177, 179, 182-88, 198-201

Living by the Word: Selected Writings, 1973-

1987 (Walker) 58:408-10, 412

The Living End (Elkin) 14:157-59; 27:124-25; 51:89, 91, 98, 100; 91:213, 216, 224

"The Living Flag" (Keillor) 115:272

"Living for Now" (Stevenson) 7:464

"Living for the City" (Wonder) 12:657

Living Free (Adamson) 17:2-4

Living in a Calm Country (Porter) 13:451-52; 33:320, 325

Living in America (Stevenson) 33:379-80

Living in Imperial Rome (Dillon) 17:99

"Living in Paradise" (Costello) 21:68

"Living in Sin" (Rich) 7:370; 18:446; 36:372

"Living in the Cave" (Rich) 3:428

"Living in the Country" (Kavanagh) 22:237

Living in the Maniototo (Frame) 22:148-49; 66:145-46; 96:186, 191, 193-94, 197-98, 202-05, 211, 217

"Living in the New Middle Ages" (Eco) 60:113

Living in the Open (Piercy) 14:420, 422; 27:373

"Living in the Present" (Wain) 2:457; 46:408-10

Living in Time (Raine) 7:352; 45:330-32, 334

Living in Truth (Havel) 65:442

Living Lights: The Mystery of Bioluminescence (Silverstein and Silverstein) 17:451

"Living Like Weasels" (Dillard) 60:74-5; 115:202

"Living Loving Maid" (Page and Plant) 12:473

"Living Memory" (Rich) 73:328, 330, 332

The Living Novel and Later Appreications (Pritchett) 15:440; 41:328, 331

Living off the Country (Haines) 58:221-22

"Living On: Border Lines" (Derrida) 87:92

Living on the Dead (Megged) 9:374-75

"A Living Pearl" (Rexroth) 49:280; 112:376, 399-400

The Living Principle (Leavis) 24:307-08, 310, 314

Living Quarters (Canby) 13:131

Living Quarters (Friel) 42:173-74; 115:224-25, 227-29, 233, 235, 237, 241-43

"The Living Reality of the Medicine World" (Allen) 84:46

The Living Reed (Buck) 7:32

"The Living Room" (Dobyns) 37:81

"Living Room" (Jordan) 114:147

The Living Room (Greene) 1:135; 6:212-13; 70:292, 294

Living Room (Jordan) 114:146-47

The Living Sea (Cousteau) 30:102-03

"Living Together" (Bowers) 9:121-22

"Living Together" (Merwin) 88:195

Living Together (Ayckbourn) 5:36-7; 74:4-6

Living Together (Wilding) 73:395, 397-98

"Living under a Threat" (Sachs) 98:361

Living up the Street: Narrative Recollections (Soto) 80:283-84, 298, 300

"Living with Beautiful Things" (McCarthy) 39:485, 488, 490-91

"Living With Other Women" (Brown) 79:154

Living with Your First Motorcycle (Felsen) 17:124

Livingdying (Corman) 9:169

"The Livingroom" (Turco) 11:551

"Livings" (Larkin) 5:230-31; 8:337; 33:259; 64:261, 268

"Livings II" (Larkin) 5:230; 33:261

"Livings III" (Larkin) 18:301; 33:261

Livingstone's Companions (Gordimer) 3:202; 5:147; 10:241; 18:184; 33:183

Un Livre (A Book) (Brossard) 115:106-07,

110-11, 117, 154-55

Le livre de mon bord: Notes, 1930-1936 (Reverdy) 53:283-84, 286, 291-92

Le livre de mon pierrot (The Deflowered One) (Nakos) 29:322-23

Le livre du rire et de l'oubli (The Book of Laughter and Forgetting) (Kundera) 19:268-71; 32:260-71; 68:232-36, 244-47, 252-54, 256-60; 115:310-11, 317, 335-45, 347, 351, 354, 359

"Le livre est sur la table" (Ashbery) 77:50-1

"Le livre, pour vieillir" (Bonnefoy) 15:74

"Livres" (Butor) 15:114

Livret de famille (Modiano) 18:338

Livro de histórias (Ribeiro) 67:276

Livsdagen läng (Life's Long Days) (Johnson) 14:296

"Livvie" (Welty) 105:302-03, 385

Liza of Lambeth (Maugham) 15:370; 67:215, 227; 93:227, 234, 244, 247, 271

The Lizard in the Cup (Dickinson) 12:169-71; 35:133-34

Lizard in the Grass (Hill) 113:284-85, 295

Lizard Music (Pinkwater) 35:319

The Lizard Woman (Waters) 88:359

The Lizards (Wertmueller) 16:586-87

The Lizard's Tail (Valenzuela)
  See Cola de lagartija

"Lizbeth: The Caterpillar Story" (Wideman) 36:455

Lizzie (Hunter) 31:228-29

"Ljubov" (Bagryana) 10:12

Ljubov (Love) (Brodsky) 13:116

"Llama el océano" ("The Call of the Sea") (Neruda) 62:335

"El llano en llamas" ("The Plain in Flames") (Rulfo) 80:216, 224

El llano en llamas, y otros cuentos (The Burning Flames, and Other Stories; The Burning Plain, and Other Stories; The Plain in Flames; Plain of Fire) (Rulfo) 8:462; 80:199-200, 210, 213, 221, 223

"Llegada" (Guillen) 48:166; 79:240

Llegada de los dioes (Arrival of the Gods) (Buero Vallejo) 46:93-94, 96, 98

"Llyr" (Clarke) 61:77

"De lo real-maravilloso americano" (Carpentier) 38:98

"Lo, the Dear, Daft Dinosaur!" (Bradbury) 42:42

Loaded (Reed) 21:303, 308

"Loading Boxcars" (Lane) 25:287

"The Load-Out" (Browne) 21:39-40

"A Loaf of Bread" (McPherson) 19:310; 77:366

The Loafers (Fellini)
  See I vitelloni

"The Loan" (Malamud) 44:418-19

Loaves and Fishes (Brown) 5:78; 48:51, 57; 100:84

Loaves and Fishes (Maugham) 93:249

Loblolly (Gilbreth and Carey) 17:155

"Lobster" (Rakosi) 47:343

"Lobsters in the Brain Coral" (Lieberman) 4:292

Local Anaesthetic (Grass) 2:172-73; 4:202, 206; 6:209; 11:248; 15:261; 32:204; 49:139, 143

Local Assays: On Contemporary American Poetry (Smith) 42:355-56

Local Color (Capote) 3:100; 8:133; 19:87; 34:320; 38:84; 58:87

"Local Customs" (Thomas) 107:333

"Local Family Keeps Son Happy" (Keillor) 40:274
Local Lives (Brand) 7:29-31
Local Measures (Miles) 1:215; 39:353
"Local Quarrels" (Bottoms) 53:33
"Local Troublemaker Abramashvili" (Aksyonov) 101:18
"Locale" (Crase) 58:165
"Localizing" (Ammons) 57:50, 52
Locations (Harrison) 6:223
"Loch na Bearraig" (MacCaig) 36:281
"The Loch Ness Monster's Song" (Morgan) 31:276
The Lock at Charenton (Simenon) 47:371
A Locked House (Snodgrass) 68:388, 399
The Locked Room (Auster) 47:14-16
The Locked Room (Wahloo)
  See *Det slutna rummet*
Locked Rooms and Open Doors: Diaries and Letters of Anne Morrow Lindbergh, 1933-1935 (Lindbergh) 82:152-53
"The Locket" (Montague) 46:277
"Locking Yourself Out, Then Trying to Get Back In" (Carver) 36:107
"Locks" (Bukowski) 82:14
"Locks" (Koch) 5:219
The Lockwood Concern (O'Hara) 42:316-17, 323-24
Locos: A Comedy of Gestures (Alfau) 66:2-12
"Locus" (Allen) 84:38
"Locus" (Hayden) 37:157
"Locus Solus" (Bowering) 47:19
"Locust Songs" (Hill) 8:295
"The Locust Trees" (Klappert) 57:257
The Locusts Have No King (Powell) 66:359-60, 362, 364, 372, 374-76
The Lodge (Ringwood) 48:335-39
Lodger (Bowie) 17:66
The Lodger (Hitchcock) 16:343-44, 352
"Lofty" (Beattie) 63:18
"Lofty" (O'Connor) 23:327
"Lofty in the Palais de Danse" (Gunn) 18:200; 32:207
"Log" (Merrill) 13:380
The Log from the Sea of Cortez (Steinbeck) 34:412
The Log of Christopher Columbus 70:331, 351
"Logan Airport, Boston" (Lowell) 11:331
Logan in Overtime (Quarrington) 65:203
Logan Stone (Thomas) 13:542
"Logarithms" (Singer) 69:311
La logeuse (*The Boardinghouse Keeper*) (Audiberti) 38:23, 26, 29
"Logging and Pimping and 'Your Pal, Jim'" (Maclean) 78:221-22, 231-32
"Logic" (Moore) 13:396
"Logic of Empire" (Heinlein) 26:163; 55:302
"Logopandocy" (Gray) 41:179
"Logos" (Durrell) 27:96
"Logos" (Hughes) 37:173, 175
"Logos" (Warren) 10:521
"Lohengrin's Tod" (Boell) 27:59; 72:70
Loin de rueil (*The Skin of Dreams*) (Queneau) 5:358; 42:333
The Loiners (Harrison) 43:174-78, 180
Loitering with Intent (Spark) 40:393-96, 398-400
Lola vs. Powerman and the Moneygoround, Part One (Davies) 21:91, 97
"Lolita" (Parker) 68:337
Lolita (Albee) 25:38-9; 86:120, 123; 113:49
Lolita (Kubrick) 16:377-80, 382, 384-87, 389, 392
Lolita (Nabokov) 1:239-45; 2:299-304; 3:352-55; 6:352, 355, 357-59; 8:407-13, 417-18; 11:391, 393, 395; 15:390, 393, 395-96; 23:304-05, 307; 44:464-68; 46:290-96; 64:332-69
Lollingdon Downs, and Other Poems (Masefield) 11:357; 47:227, 229, 234
Lollipop (Southern)
  See *Candy*
"Lollipops of the Pomeranian Baroque" (Fenton) 32:165
"Lollocks" (Graves) 39:323; 45:170
Lolly Willowes (Warner) 19:460
The Loman Family Picnic (Margulies) 76:190, 193-94
A l'ombre des majorits silencieuses ou la fin du social (Baudrillard) 60:14-15
Lona Hanson (Savage) 40:370
"London" (Ezekiel) 61:105
"London" (Morgan) 31:275
"London" (Naipaul) 105:160
London (Morand)
  See *Londres*
"London Ballads" (Plomer) 4:406
"The London Boys" (Bowie) 17:65
"London Bridge" (Ashbery) 77:67
"London Calling" (Clash) 30:48
London Calling (Clash) 30:45-7, 49-51
The London Embassy (Theroux) 28:428; 46:398-99
"London Fantasy" (Peake) 54:375
London Fields (Amis) 62:12-20; 101:63-67, 69-70, 77-79, 84-86, 88-90, 92, 95, 99
"London Girl" (Weller) 26:443-44
"London Letters" (Eliot) 9:190
London Lickpenny (Ackroyd) 52:2
London Match (Deighton) 46:131-32
The London Novels of Colin MacInnes (MacInnes) 23:283
"London, Ontario" (Bowering) 47:31
"London Rain" (MacNeice) 53:237
"London, Rainy Day" (Ferlinghetti) 111:65
"London Revisited" (Livesay) 79:332
"London Songs" (Fuller) 62:186
"London Town" (McCartney) 35:285-87
London Town (McCartney) 35:285
"London Traffic" (Weller) 26:443
"London Welshman" (Mathias) 45:235
Londoners (Duffy) 37:116-17
Londoners (Ewart) 46:147-50
"London's Burning" (Clash) 30:43-4
Londres (*London*) (Morand) 41:304, 306
"The Lone Pilgrim" (Colwin) 84:140, 150-51
The Lone Pilgrim (Colwin) 23:129-30; 84:142, 146, 149-51
"The Lone Ranger" (Hall) 37:142
The Lone Ranger (Baraka) 115:29
The Lone Ranger and Tonto Fistfight in Heaven (Alexie) 96:4-9, 11-13, 15-17
"A Lone Striker" (Frost) 34:475
The Lone Woman and Others (Urdang) 47:399-400
"The Lone Woman of San Nicolas Island" (Urdang) 47:399
Loneliest Girl in the World (Fearing) 51:115-16, 121
"Loneliness" (Betjeman) 10:52; 43:48
"Loneliness" (Bukowski) 108:86
"Loneliness" (Transtroemer) 52:410; 65:227
Loneliness (Paz)
  See *Soledad*
"Loneliness: An Outburst of Hexasyllables" (Carruth) 84:129
The Loneliness of Mia (*That Early Spring*) (Beckman) 26:88-9
"The Loneliness of the Long-Distance Runner" (Sillitoe) 1:307-08; 6:500; 19:421; 57:386, 391-92, 394-95
The Loneliness of the Long-Distance Runner (Sillitoe) 1:308; 3:448-49; 6:501; 57:388-89, 392, 396, 401
"Lonely Ache" (Ellison) 42:126
Lonely Crusade (Himes) 2:195; 4:229; 7:159; 58:251, 255; 108:220-21, 224, 228, 231-32, 236, 253-61, 271, 274
Lonely for the Future (Farrell) 66:129, 132
The Lonely Girl (O'Brien) 3:365; 5:313; 116:193
"The Lonely Guy's Apartment" (Friedman) 56:105
The Lonely Guy's Book of Life (Friedman) 56:105, 108
"The Lonely Guy's Cookbook" (Friedman) 56:105-06
"Lonely Hearts Column" (Dorfman) 77:141-43
"The Lonely Land" (Smith) 15:515-17
"Lonely Looking Sky" (Diamond) 30:111
"Lonely Love" (Blunden) 56:40, 48, 52
"The Lonely Love of Middle Age" (Waddington) 28:438
The Lonely Men (L'Amour) 25:280
The Lonely Passion of Judith Hearne (*Judith Hearne*) (Moore) 1:225; 3:340-41; 5:294-95; 297; 7:235-37; 8:394-95; 19:330-31, 333-35; 32:309, 312-13; 90:238-40, 242, 249-52, 254, 256-7, 261-3, 267, 269, 273, 278, 288-90, 292, 301, 304
"The Lonely Psalmist" (Arghezi)
  See "Psalmistul singuratic"
"Lonely School Days" (Berry) 17:52
The Lonely Sea (MacLean) 50:348; 63:268-70
The Lonely Silver Rain (MacDonald) 44:409
The Lonely Suppers of V.W. Balloon (Middleton) 13:388-89
Lonely Vigils (Wellman) 49:393-94
The Lonely Voice (O'Connor) 14:397
"Lonely, White Fields" (Oliver) 98:288
The Lonely Wife (Ray) 76:357, 359
"Lonely Women" (Nyro) 17:315
"A Loner" (Arghezi)
  See "Un singuratic"
"The Loner" (Young) 17:572, 582
The Loner: A Story of the Wolverine (Corcoran) 17:77-8
Lonesome Cowboys (Warhol) 20:420, 423
"The Lonesome Death of Hattie Carroll" (Dylan) 12:180-81; 77:166
"The Lonesome Death of Jordy Verrill" (King) 26:243
Lonesome Dove (McMurtry) 44:253-62
"The Lonesome Dream" (Mueller) 51:280
The Lonesome Gods (L'Amour) 55:308
Lonesome, On'ry, and Mean (Jennings) 21:201
"Lonesome Road" (Berriault) 54:4
Lonesome Road (Green) 25:193
"Lonesome Shorty" (Keillor) 115:294
Lonesome Traveler (Kerouac) 14:305
Long after Midnight (Bradbury) 42:35
The Long Afternoon of Earth (*Hothouse*) (Aldiss) 14:10-12; 40:18
"Long Ago" (Durrell)
  See "Far Away"

The Long Ago (Lavin)   99:312

Long Ago in France: The Years in Dijon (Fisher)   76:333-36, 339

"The Long Alley" (Roethke)   11:480; 46:362; 101:274, 280, 283, 335, 337-38

A Long and Happy Life (Price)   3:404-06; 6:425; 43:342-44, 346-47, 349, 353; 50:230-32; 63:323-32, 334-36, 338, 341

"The Long and Winding Road" (Lennon and McCartney)   35:281

Long before Forty (Forester)   35:172

The Long Black Coat (Bennett)   33:43-5

"Long Black Song" (Wright)   4:595; 14:596; 21:445, 453-54

The Long Christmas Dinner (Wilder)   82:363-66, 386-87, 390

The Long Christmas Dinner, and Other Plays in One Act (Wilder)   5:495; 10:532-33; 15:569, 574; 82:345, 362, 386

"The Long Coyote Line" (Lane)   25:289

The Long Dark Tea-Time of the Soul (Adams)   60:4-7

"The Long Day" (Gordon)   13:247; 29:187; 83:232

"The Long Day Called Thursday" (Neruda)   62:326

A Long Day in November (Gaines)   11:217; 86:173

The Long Day Wanes: The Malayan Trilogy (Burgess)
   See *The Malayan Trilogy*

A Long Day's Dying (Buechner)   2:83; 4:79-80

Un long demanche de fiancailles (A Very Long Engagement) (Japrisot)   90:170-73

A Long Desire (Connell)   45:112-14

"Long Distance" (Ferber)   93:139

"Long Distance" (O'Brien)   65:168

"Long Distance" (Smiley)   53:348-49

Long Distance (Mortimer)   5:298-99

"Long Distance: An Octave" (Thesen)   56:415

"Long Distance, II" (Harrison)   43:180

"The Long Distance Runner" (Paley)   6:392; 37:336, 338

"Long Division" (Rose)   85:311

Long Division (Roiphe)   3:435

Long Division: A Tribal History (Rose)   85:311-12

The Long Divorce (Crispin)   22:109

The Long Dream (Wright)   4:595-96; 9:584; 14:598; 21:436-37, 446, 449; 74:380

Long Drums and Cannons (Laurence)   50:314-15, 321; 62:278

The Long Farewell (Stewart)   14:512

The Long Farewell (Trifonov)
   See *Dolgoe proshchanie*

"The Long Flight" (Scannell)   49:334

"A Long Fourth" (Taylor)   18:524, 528; 37:407, 409-11, 413; 44:305; 50:259-60; 71:296-98, 308

A Long Fourth, and Other Stories (Taylor)   1:334; 18:523-24, 526

The Long Good-Bye (Altman)   16:27-9, 31-2, 35-6, 43; 116:3-7, 11, 13-14, 23, 44-6, 48, 59, 68

The Long Goodbye: Three Novellas (Trifonov)   45:411-12, 417, 420

"Long Haired Lady" (McCartney)   12:366, 372

"The Long Home" (Berryman)   13:78

"Long House Valley Poem" (Ortiz)   45:308

Long is the Cypress' Shadow (Delibes)
   See *La sombra del ciprés es alrgada*

Long Island Light: Poems and a Memoir (Heyen)   18:231-33

"The Long Island Night" (Moss)   45:287

"Long Island Springs" (Moss)   45:289

"Long Journey" (Fearing)   51:114

The Long Journey (Corcoran)   17:70

Long Lankin (Banville)   46:24-7

The Long Lavender Look (MacDonald)   27:274; 44:408

"A Long Line of Doctors" (Kizer)   80:180

"Long Lines" (Goodman)   4:196

Long Live Death (Arrabal)
   See *Viva la muerte*

"Long Live Lord Kor!" (Norton)   12:468

"Long Live the Bride" (Tchicaya)   101:349

The Long Love (Buck)   11:76

The Long March (Beauvoir)
   See *La longue marche*

The Long March (Styron)   1:329-30; 5:418; 11:514, 516-17; 15:525; 60:392

"Long May You Run" (Young)   17:576, 582

Long May You Run (Young)   17:575-76

The Long Naked Descent into Boston (Eastlake)   8:201

"The Long Naked Walk of the Dead" (Williams)   33:442

"The Long Night" (Bambara)   88:22, 28, 54, 55

The Long Night (Lytle)   22:292, 296

The Long Night of Francisco Sanctis (Costantini)   49:63-5

The Long Night of White Chickens (Goldman)   76:46-55

"Long Nook" (Wieners)   7:537

"Long Nose" (Stern)   40:408

"Long Nose Tragedy, Short Nose Comedy" (Szirtes)   46:394

"A Long Novel" (Ashbery)   77:58

Long Remember (Kantor)   7:194

"The Long River" (Hall)   37:142-43; 59:156

The Long River (Smith)   64:397

The Long Road to Paradise (Settle)   19:410

"The Long Road to Ummera" (O'Connor)   14:399; 23:331-32

"The Long Shadow of Lincoln: A Litany" (Sandburg)   35:354

The Long Shot (Monette)   82:318

"Long Story Short" (Boyd)   28:39

The Long Street (Davidson)   2:112; 13:167, 169; 19:127

The Long Summer Still to Come (Simmons)   43:408-09

"The Long Thoughts" (Dybek)   114:64-5, 76

Long Time between Kisses (Scoppettone)   26:404-05

Long Time Coming and a Long Time Gone (Farina)   9:195

"Long Track Blues" (Brown)   59:266

"Long Trip" (Hughes)   108:333

The Long Valley (Steinbeck)   9:516; 13:531, 534; 21:381, 385; 34:405; 45:372, 374; 59:348, 351

The Long View (Howard)   29:242, 245

The Long Voyage Home (Ford)   16:306-07

The Long Voyage: The Life Cycle of a Green Turtle (Silverstein and Silverstein)   17:453

The Long Wait (Spillane)   13:526-28

The Long Walk (King)   37:201, 207; 61:331, 333; 113:388, 391

"The Long War" (Lee)   90:177

"The Long Waters" (Roethke)   8:456-57;

19:399; 101:285, 289, 299, 307, 316-19

"The Long Way Around" (Handke)   38:228

A Long Way from Verona (Gardam)   43:164-66

The Long Way Home (Benary-Isbert)   12:33

The Long Way Home (Teran)   36:419, 421

"The Long Years" (Bradbury)   42:38

"The Longe Nightes When Every Creature..." (Winters)   32:468

The Longest Day (Ryan)   7:385-86

The Longest Journey (Forster)   77:226, 236

"The Longest Night" (Piercy)   27:379

The Longest Weekend (Arundel)   17:13-15, 17-18

"Longfellow Serenade" (Diamond)   30:112

"Longfellow, Virgil, and Me" (Selzer)   74:278, 283

"Longing" (Brutus)   43:92

"Longing" (Oz)   11:428-29

"The Longing" (Roethke)   8:455; 19:396, 398; 101:305-06, 308, 312, 314, 316

"Longing for Lermontov" (Akhmadulina)   53:9-10

"Longing for Mother" (Tanizaki)
   See "Haha no kouru ki"

A Longing for the Light: Selected Poems of Vicente Aleixandre (Aleixandre)   36:27, 29-30, 32

"Longjumeau" (Voznesensky)   57:415

Longleaf (Hansen)   38:237

The Long-Legged House (Berry)   27:32, 38

"Long-Line Poems" (Laughlin)   49:224

"The Longobards" (Herbert)   9:274

The Longships in Harbour (McIlvanney)   42:281, 285

Longshot (Francis)   102:137-39, 141, 152, 158

Longshot O'Leary's Garland of Practical Poesie (McGrath)   59:175-76

Longshot Peoms for Broke Players (Bukowski)   41:64

"The Longstop" (Bainbridge)   62:37

Longtime Companion (Lucas)   64:296

Longtime Passing (Brinsmead)   21:32

La longue marche (The Long March) (Beauvoir)   8:62; 44:342-43

"Lonzhyumo" (Voznesensky)   57:418

The Loo Sanction (Trevanian)   29:430-32

"The Look" (Olds)   85:306

"The Look" (Sartre)   13:501

"Look" (Swenson)   61:397

"Look" (Thomas)   48:374

The Look (Marques)
   See *La Mirada*

"Look a Little on the Sunny Side" (Davies)   21:94

Look after Lulu (Coward)   29:140

"A Look at Alfred Metraux" (Leiris)   61:362

Look at All Those Roses (Bowen)   11:66; 22:67

"Look at Me" (Lennon)   35:262

Look at Me (Brookner)   32:60-1; 34:137, 139, 142; 51:62-3, 65

"Look at Me Go" (Robison)   42:342

Look at the Harlequins! (Nabokov)   6:354-56, 358-60; 8:412-14; 15:393; 44:464, 466, 472-73; 46:292

"Look at Us Play with Our Meat" (Stern)   40:408

Look Back in Anger (Osborne)   1:263; 2:327-28; 5:330-33; 11:421, 423-24; 45:313-21

Look Behind You, Neighbor (Ringwood)   48:330, 334-36

Look for Your Words, Look for Your Steps (Carrier)

See *Cherche tes mots, cherche tes pas*
"Look Homeward, Jack" (Ferlinghetti) 27:139
"Look How the Fish Live" (Powers) 1:282; 8:447
Look How the Fish Live (Powers) 8:447-48; 57:349, 356-58
"Look Me in the Eyes" (Simon) 26:409-10
"Look Out" (Redgrove) 6:445
"Look Out for My Love" (Young) 17:580
A Look round the Estate: Poems, 1957-1967 (Amis) 2:6; 40:41
"Look, Stranger, on This Island Now" (*On This Island*) (Auden) 3:22, 24; 6:20, 22-3; 11:15; 14:26-7, 32-4; 43:15, 17-18
Look to the Lady (Allingham)
   See *The Gyrth Chalice Mystery*
"Look to the Market" (Neruda) 62:326
Look Who's Talking! (Perelman) 49:257
"Lookalikes" (Beer) 58:37
Looker (Crichton) 90:69-71
"Lookin' Back" (Seger) 35:380-82
"Lookin' for a Love" (Young) 17:575
"Looking" (Snodgrass) 68:397
"Looking at a Dry Tumbleweed Brought in from the Snow" (Bly) 15:63
"Looking at Each Other" (Rukeyser) 27:411
"Looking at My Father" (Olds) 85:292
"Looking at Native Prose" (Callaghan) 65:246
Looking at the Dance (Denby) 48:81
"Looking at the Rain" (Lightfoot) 26:278-79
"Looking at Them Asleep" (Olds) 85:295-96
"Looking Back" (Beer) 58:31
"Looking Back" (Heaney) 74:167
Looking Back (Maugham)
   See *Looking Backward*
Looking Back (Maynard) 23:288-90
"Looking Back at the First Story" (Welty) 105:306
"Looking Back at the Tin Drum" (Grass) 22:195
"Looking Back from the Mud" (Rose) 85:314
Looking Backward (*Looking Back*) (Maugham) 11:370; 67:228
"Looking Down from Above" (Hood) 28:193
"Looking 'Em Over" (Farrell) 66:112
"Looking for a Rain God" (Head) 67:98
"Looking for Buckhead Boys" (Dickey) 2:117
"Looking for Chekov's House" (Simpson) 7:428
"Looking for Climatic Asylum" (Aksyonov) 101:41
Looking for Holes in the Ceiling (Dunn) 36:151-52, 155
"Looking for Love" (Reed) 21:317
Looking for Mr. Goodbar (Rossner) 6:469-70; 9:457; 29:352-56
"Looking for Mr. Green" (Bellow) 6:52; 10:44
"Looking for Mushrooms" (Oliver) 98:265
"Looking for Mushrooms at Sunrise" (Merwin) 88:203
"Looking for Rilke" (Hass) 39:150
"Looking for Snakes" (Oliver) 98:282
"Looking for Something?" (Herbert) 35:208; 44:393
"Looking for Women" (Wieners) 7:537
Looking for Work (Cheever) 18:100-02; 48:64-5
"Looking for Zora" (Walker) 58:409
The Looking Glass War (le Carre) 3:282; 5:232-33; 9:327
"Looking in a Mirror" (Atwood) 8:32; 25:67
"Looking in the Mirror" (Sherwin) 15:480
"Looking into a Tide Pool" (Bly) 15:63

"Looking into Chaos" (Hesse) 69:275
"Looking into You" (Browne) 21:40
Looking on Darkness (Brink)
   See *Kennis van die Aand*
Looking over Hills (Kherdian) 6:281; 9:317-18
"Looking Over the Acreage" (Ammons) 5:27
"Looking Sideways" (Beer) 58:38
"Looking Up" (Merwin) 88:212
Looking Up at Leaves (Howes) 15:289-90
"Looking Uptown" (Swenson) 14:521
"Looking-Glass" (Levertov) 66:239
"The Look-Out" (H. D.) 73:104, 108, 120
Lookout Cartridge (McElroy) 5:279-80; 47:238-44, 246
"Lookout Joe" (Young) 17:574
"Lookout's Journal" (Snyder) 32:389
"Looks" (Gunn) 81:183
The Loom of Light (Brown) 48:61
"Loon and Bebert" (Connell) 45:109
Loon Lake (Doctorow) 18:124-27; 37:86-8, 90, 92-4; 44:168, 170, 172, 175, 177, 179; 65:137; 113:144, 146-47, 150, 152, 156, 158, 160-61, 175-76, 180
"The Loon on Forrester's Pond" (Carruth) 84:120, 132, 135
"The Loons" (Laurence) 50:320; 62:277
"The Loon's Cry" (Nemerov) 36:304
The Loony-Bin Trip (Millett) 67:258-62
"Loop" (Ondaatje) 51:310
Der Loop Der Loop (The Brothers Quay) 95:329
"Loose" (Ortiz) 45:310
"The Loose and Baggy Monsters of Henry James" (Blackmur) 24:59, 64
Loose Change (Davidson) 9:174-75
"Loose Ends" (Mukherjee) 53:271; 115:364
Loose Ends (Weller) 53:386-93
"A Loose Mountain" ("Telescopic") (Frost) 26:118
"Loose Reins" (Tilghman) 65:106-08, 112
Loosely Tied Hands (Rosenblatt) 15:448
"Loot" (Gunn) 6:221
Loot (Orton) 4:387-88; 13:435-37; 43:326-27, 329-30, 332-34
"Lopey" (Johnston) 51:241, 243
"Loppy Phelan's Double Shoot" (Callaghan) 41:98
Loquitur (Bunting) 39:297; 47:45-6, 49-50
The Lorca Story: Scenes from a Life (Albee) 113:51-2
Lord Byron's Doctor (West) 96:366, 373-74, 379-80, 387, 390, 392, 395
Lord Edgware Dies (Christie)
   See *Thirteen at Dinner*
Lord Emsworth and Others (Wodehouse) 10:537
Lord Foul's Bane (Donaldson) 46:140-42
"The Lord Giveth" (Yezierska) 46:449
Lord Hornblower (Forester) 35:167-68, 170
Lord Malquist and Mr. Moon (Stoppard) 91:184
Lord Malquist and Mr. Moon (Stoppard) 1:328; 29:394; 34:278
"Lord Mountdrago" (Maugham) 67:219
Lord Mullion's Secret (Stewart) 32:421
"Lord Myth" (Dubie) 36:137
Lord of Dark Places (Bennett) 5:57-9
Lord of Light (Zelazny) 21:463-65, 467
"Lord of the Chalices" (Amis) 8:11
Lord of the Far Island (Hibbert) 7:157
Lord of the Flies (Golding) 1:119-22; 2:165-68; 3:196-98, 200; 10:233-36, 239; 17:157-58, 160-64, 166, 168-70, 172-77,

179; 27:159-67, 169-70; 58:169-212; 81:315-19, 323, 325
The Lord of the Rings (Bakshi) 26:72-4
The Lord of the Rings (Tolkien) 1:335-41; 2:433-36; 3:477, 479-83; 8:515-16; 12:565-74, 576-84, 586; 38:431-35, 437-43
Lord of the Shadow (Espriu) 9:192
Lord of Thunder (Norton) 12:457, 461
Lord Pengo (Behrman) 40:85, 87-8
Lord Richard's Passion (Jones) 52:248-49, 254
Lord Rochester's Monkey: Being the Life of John Wilmot, Second Earl of Rochester (Greene) 6:220; 70:293
"Lord Short Shoe Wants the Monkey" (Shacochis) 39:199-201
Lord Weary's Castle (Lowell) 1:178-79, 182; 2:246-47; 3:302, 304-05; 4:295, 298, 300, 302-03; 5:257; 8:348, 350-51, 353, 355-56; 9:337-39; 11:325-26, 328; 15:343-44; 37:235, 242
"The Lordly and Isolate Satyrs" (Olson) 29:335
The Lords and the New Creatures (Morrison) 17:289
"The Lord's Chameleons" (Klappert) 57:260
The Lords of Akchasaz: Murder in the Ironsmiths Market (Kemal) 29:266, 268
The Lords of Discipline (Conroy) 30:79-80; 74:44-7, 49-52
The Lords of Limit: Essays on Literature and Ideas (Hill) 45:186-89
The Lord's Pink Ocean (Walker) 14:552
The Lord's Will (Green) 25:193
"Lore" (Longley) 29:295
"Lorelei" (Plath) 51:343-44; 111:178, 210
"Lorenzo de Medici, about 1480" (Faludy) 42:137
"Lorgneau le grand" (Theriault) 79:410
Los Alamos Light (Bograd) 35:63-4
"Los Angelenos" (Joel) 26:214
"Los Angeles 1980" (Allen) 84:8, 10
"The Loser" (Carroll) 10:98
"The Loser" (Rich) 18:445
The Loser (Konrad)
   See *A cinkos*
Loser and Still Champion: Muhammad Ali (Schulberg) 48:350
"Losers" (Friel)
   See *Lovers*
"Losers" (Sandburg) 4:463
Losers (Friel) 42:166-67
"Losers, Finders: Strangers at the Door" (Findley) 102:104, 106-08
"Losing Battles" (Welty) 2:462-63; 5:478, 479; 14:564; 22:462; 33:415-16, 419, 421-24
Losing Battles (Welty) 105:300, 303-06, 310, 312, 314, 329, 335, 349, 353-59, 363, 370-77, 390
"A Losing Game" (Powers) 1:280; 57:358
"Losing Game" (Swan) 69:362
"Losing Merrygorounds" (Waddington) 28:437
"Losing My Mind" (Sondheim) 30:381
"The Losing Side" (Monette) 82:332
"Loss" (King) 53:212
"Loss" (Montague) 46:270, 274
"Loss" (Williams) 33:441
The Loss of El Dorado (Naipaul) 7:252-53; 9:393; 18:361; 105:137, 139, 154, 156, 160
The Loss of India (Ghose) 42:177, 179

"Loss, of Perhaps Love, in Our World of Contingency" (Warren) 59:295

A Loss of Roses (Inge) 8:307-08; 19:226-29

"The Loss of Strength" (Clarke) 9:168

"The Loss of the Creature" (Percy) 3:378

"The Loss of the Magyar" (Beer) 58:36

Loss of the Magyar (Beer) 58:36, 38

"The Loss of The Nabara" (Day Lewis)
  See "The Nabara"

Losses (Jarrell) 2:207, 209-10; 6:260; 13:298, 300

"The Lost" (Boyle) 58:81-2

"Lost" (Bukowski) 108:113

"The Lost" (Campbell) 42:84-5

"Lost" (Haines) 58:220

"Lost" (Singer) 9:486

The Lost (Nakos) 29:322-23

Lost and Found (Gloag) 40:211-12

The Lost and Found Man (Guild) 33:186

The Lost and Found Stories of Morley Callaghan (Callaghan) 41:98

The Lost and the Lurking (Wellman) 49:390-91, 396

"The Lost Angel" (Levine) 4:287

"The Lost Baby Poem" (Clifton) 19:109; 66:64, 73

"The Lost 'Beautifulness'" (Yezierska) 46:441

"The Lost Camelia of the Bartrams" (Merwin) 88:213

"Lost Child" (Anand) 23:21

"The Lost Child" (Lavin) 99:322

"The Lost Child" (Phillips) 28:362

The Lost Childhood, and Other Essays (Greene) 3:211; 6:217; 9:250-51

"The Lost Children" (Jarrell) 2:210

"The Lost Children" (Oliver) 34:249; 98:258

"Lost City of Mars" (Bradbury) 42:34

The Lost Colony (Green) 25:195-96, 199

"Lost Commagene" (Elytis) 100:189

"The Lost Continent" (Spinrad) 46:384

Lost Copper (Rose) 85:312-13, 315, 317

"The Lost Cottage" (Leavitt) 34:77-8

The Lost Country (Raine) 7:353

The Lost Country (Salamanca) 4:461-62; 15:464

"Lost Cove and the Rose of San Antone" (Tillinghast) 29:416

"The Lost Displays" (Wright) 6:581

Lost Empires (Priestley) 5:351; 34:361

"The Lost Explorer" (McGrath) 55:73

The Lost Father (Warner) 59:211-17

"The Lost Federation" (Walcott) 14:549; 76:281

The Lost Flying Boat (Sillitoe) 57:397-98

"Lost Garden" (Lewis) 41:254-55

"The Lost Girls" (Hogan) 73:158-59

"Lost Ground" (Trevor) 116:383, 396

The Lost Honor of Katharina Blum: How Violence Develops and Where It Can Lead (Boell)
  See *Die verlorene Ehre der Katharina Blum: oder, Wie Gewalt entstehen und wohin sie führen kann*

Lost Horizon (Capra) 16:154-55, 160-62

"Lost in a Roman" (Morrison) 17:286

Lost in America (Singer) 23:422-23; 38:408; 69:303; 111:320

"Lost in Calcutta" (Ginsberg) 36:184

"Lost in Heaven" (Frost) 26:118

"Lost in the Badlands" (Purdy) 50:247

Lost in the Barrens (Mowat) 26:336-37, 339, 341-43

Lost in the Bonewheel Factory (Komunyakaa)
94:218-19, 246

Lost in the City (Jones) 76:64-70

Lost in the Cosmos: The Last Self-Help Book (Percy) 47:333-35, 339-40; 65:257

"Lost in the Flood" (Springsteen) 17:488

"Lost in the Funhouse" ("Funhouse") (Barth) 9:66-7, 69; 14:52-3; 51:23; 89:3-4, 6, 8-10, 13-17, 19-22, 33, 42-3, 45, 49-50, 54-5, 57, 59-60

Lost in the Funhouse: Fiction for Print, Tape, Live Voice (*Funhouse*) (Barth) 1:18; 2:36-8; 3:39, 41-2; 5:51-2; 7:22-5; 9:65-6, 69, 71-2, 74; 10:24; 14:51, 53-4, 56; 51:20-4, 26, 29; 89:3-64

"Lost in the Supermarket" (Clash) 30:46

"Lost in Translation" (Merrill) 8:381; 13:376; 18:328; 34:241

Lost in Yonkers (Simon) 70:235-36, 239-45

The Lost Island (Dillon) 17:93

Lost Island (Whitney) 42:434

The Lost Lands (Vansittart) 42:393

"The Lost Language" (Feldman) 7:101

"The Lost Leader" (Blunden) 56:47

"Lost Luggage" (Adams) 46:17

"The Lost Man" (Wright) 53:419

The Lost Ones (Beckett)
  See *Le dépeupleur*

Lost Originals (Feldman) 7:102-03

"Lost Paradise" (Seifert) 34:362; 93:331

The Lost Pilot (Tate) 2:431; 25:427-29

Lost Profile (Sagan) 9:468; 17:427

"The Lost Romans" (Rukeyser) 15:458

"The Lost Salt Gift of Blood" (MacLeod) 56:196

A Lost Season (Fuller) 4:177; 28:152, 158

"The Lost Son" (Roethke) 11:480-81; 19:397; 46:357, 362-64; 101:263-64, 274, 277, 282-91, 301, 312, 325, 334-41

The Lost Son, and Other Poems (Roethke) 1:291; 3:433-34; 8:455, 459-60; 11:484-85; 19:396-97; 46:355-56, 358, 360-63; 101:263, 265-66, 273, 285-89, 291-92, 298, 300-01, 303, 305, 312, 322-26, 334-35, 337-38

"Lost Sons" (Salter) 52:369; 59:196

"The Lost Speakers" (MacLeish) 68:287-88

The Lost Steps (Carpentier)
  See *Los pasos perdidos*

"A Lost Tradition" (Montague) 46:276

"The Lost Tribe" (Muldoon) 32:317

"Lost Unfound" (Gotlieb) 18:191

The Lost Weekend (Wilder) 20:456

"The Lost World" (Jarrell) 2:210; 9:296

The Lost World (Crichton) 90:96-7

The Lost World (Jarrell) 2:207-08, 210-11; 6:260-62; 13:301; 49:200

Lost Worlds (Smith) 43:419

The Lost Worlds of 2001 (Clarke) 13:151; 35:122

"The Lost Young Intellectual" (Howe) 85:147-48

"Lot and His Daughters" (Hope) 51:216

"Lot Ninety-Six" (Day Lewis) 10:131

"La lotería en Babilonia" ("The Babylon Lottery"; "The Lottery in Babylon"; "The Lottery of Babylon") (Borges) 1:39; 2:69, 77; 6:90; 9:116-17; 19:51; 83:156-57, 164

The Lothian Run (Hunter) 21:157-58

Le lotissement du ciel (Cendrars) 18:96; 106:167, 172, 190

Lotna (Wajda) 16:578, 582

"Lots" (Gunnars) 69:260

"Lots of Ghastlies" (O'Faolain) 6:383

"Lots of Lakes" (Loewinsohn) 52:285

"Lot's Wife" (Akhmatova) 64:16

"Lot's Wife" (Nemerov) 6:361

"Lot's Wife" (Simmons) 43:411

"Lot's Wife" (Szymborska) 99:201

"Lotta Love" (Young) 17:580

"The Lottery" (Jackson) 11:302; 60:211-16, 218, 221, 224-30, 232, 235-38; 87:222-35

"The Lottery in Babylon" (Borges)
  See "La lotería en Babilonia"

"The Lottery of Babylon" (Borges)
  See "La lotería en Babilonia"

The Lotus Flowers (Voigt) 54:432-34

Lou in the Limelight (Hunter) 35:229-30

"Lou Marsh" (Ochs) 17:330-32

Lou Reed (Reed) 21:304

The Loud Boy's Life (Barker) 37:37

The Loud, Resounding Sea (Bonham) 12:51

"The Loudest Voice" (Paley) 37:337

Lough derg (Kavanagh) 22:244

"A Lough Neagh Sequence" (Heaney) 5:170-71; 7:147; 14:243; 74:157

Louie and Ophelia (Edwards) 43:141-42

Louis 'David' Riel: Prophet of the New World (Flanagan) 25:164

"Louisa, Please Come Home" (Jackson) 60:235

Louise Bogan: A Portrait (Frank) 39:383-84, 386-88, 390-91, 393

"Loulou; or, The Domestic Life of the Language" (Atwood) 84:67

Le loup (*The Wolf*) (Blais) 6:81; 13:97-8

"Loup Garoup Means Change Into" (Reed) 5:368

"The Louse and the Mosquito" (Seth) 90:353

"Lovborg's Women" (Allen) 52:36

"Love" (Boland) 113:92

"Love" (Butler) 81:122, 129

"Love" (Char)
  See "L'amour"

"Love" (Creeley) 36:118

"Love" (Graham) 48:149

"Love" (Kristofferson)
  See "It Sure Was"

"Love" (Lennon) 35:262

"Love" (Lispector) 43:268-69

"Love" (MacDiarmid) 2:253

"Love" (Milosz) 56:233

"Love" (O'Hara) 13:424

"Love" (Olesha) 8:430, 432, 433-34

"Love" (Paley) 37:333, 336

"Love" (Stevenson) 33:379-80

"Love" (Wilson) 49:413-16

Love (Brodsky)
  See *Ljubov*

Love (Carter) 5:103; 41:113-14; 76:328-30

Love (Dabrowska)
  See *Milos*

Love (Duras)
  See *L'amour*

Love (Martin) 89:116, 118

Love (Schaeffer) 22:369

"Love, 20 the First Quarter Mile" (Fearing) 51:117

"Love, 1944" (Rozewicz) 9:463

Love: A Building on Fire (Byrne) 26:98

Love: A Trilogy (Pa Chin)
  See *Ai-ch'ing ti san-pu ch u*

A Love Affair (Buzzati)
  See *Un amore*

Love Affair (Towne) 87:378, 379

"Love after Love" (Walcott) 42:422

"Love Again" (Larkin) 64:263, 277, 281

Love Ain't Nothing but Sex Misspelled (Ellison) **13**:206; **42**:126-27

Love Alone: Eighteen Elegies for Rog (Monette) **82**:317, 321-23, 328, 331-34

Love Always (Beattie) **40**:66-9; **63**:15

Love among the Cannibals (Morris) **1**:232; **37**:311-13

Love among the Ruins (Rice) **7**:363

"Love and Affection" (Armatrading) **17**:8-9

Love and Anarchy (Wertmueller) **16**:587-90, 595-96

"Love and Death" (Lagerkvist)
See "Kärleken och döden"

Love and Death (Allen) **16**:7, 10, 17; **52**:37, 39, 44, 48

Love and Death in a Hot Country (Naipaul)
See *A Hot Country*

Love and Death in the American Novel (Fiedler) **4**:159, 161; **13**:213; **24**:189-92, 197-99, 203-05

Love and Exile (Singer) **69**:304, 306

Love and Fame (Berryman) **2**:56-60; **3**:65-8, 70; **4**:60, 62-3; **6**:63-5; **8**:92-3; **10**:51; **13**:81-2; **25**:91-2, 95; **62**:43-4, 46, 54, 56-8, 66, 74-6

Love and Friendship (Lurie) **4**:305-06; **5**:259-60; **39**:180, 182

"Love and How to Cure It" (Wilder) **82**:362

"Love and Its Derangements" (Oates) **6**:367

Love and Its Derangements (Oates) **1**:251; **3**:359; **6**:367; **15**:401

"Love and Like" (Gold) **42**:195, 197-98

Love and Like (Gold) **42**:189, 197

"Love and Maple Syrup" (Lightfoot) **26**:280

"Love and Marilyn Monroe" (Schwartz) **45**:360

"Love and Marriage" (Johnston) **51**:249

Love and Napalm: Export USA (Ballard)
See *The Atrocity Exhibition*

Love and Other Deaths (Thomas) **13**:541-42

Love and Other Euphemisms (Klein) **30**:235-36

Love, and Other Stories (Olesha) **8**:432

Love and Salt Water (Wilson) **13**:608, 612

"Love and Separation" (Spender) **41**:427

Love and Separation (Spender) **41**:420

"The Love and the Hate" (Jeffers) **11**:311

Love and War, Art and God (Shapiro) **53**:330-31

Love and Work (Price) **3**:405-06; **43**:344-46, 353; **50**:229, 232; **63**:335, 341

"Love at First Sight" (Szymborska) **99**:202

"Love at Night" (Williams) **42**:443

"Love at Roblin Lake" (Purdy) **50**:239-41

Love at the Greek (Diamond) **30**:113

Love at Twenty (Truffaut) **101**:382, 386, 413

"Love Awake" (McCartney) **35**:286

"Love beyond Keeping" (Sandburg) **35**:356

Love Breeze (Robinson) **21**:347

"Love by Ambition" (Auden) **14**:32; **43**:15

"Love Calls Us to the Things of This World" (Wilbur) **6**:570; **53**:399, 401, 412; **110**:357, 359, 374, 385-87

Love Child (Duffy) **37**:115

Love Comes to Eunice K. O'Herlihy (Corcoran) **17**:76

Love, Dad (Hunter) **31**:224-26

"The Love Day" (Dunn) **40**:165

Love, Death, and the Changing of the Seasons (Hacker) **72**:185, 187-88, 191-92

"Love, Death, and the Ladies' Drill Team" (West) **7**:519; **17**:546, 548

Love, Death, and the Ladies' Drill Team (West) **7**:519, 521; **17**:546

The Love Department (Trevor) **7**:475; **71**:326, 345

The Love Eaters (Settle) **19**:408-09; **61**:374, 385

Love Feast (Buechner) **6**:102-03; **9**:136-37

"The Love for October" (Merwin) **88**:204

The Love for Three Oranges (The Brothers Quay) **95**:347, 350

"Love Fossil" (Olds) **32**:345-46; **39**:190

"The Love Gift" (Masefield) **11**:357

The Love Girl and the Innocent (Solzhenitsyn)
See *Olen'i shalashovka*

Love Goes to Press (Gellhorn) **60**:181-82

"Love Has Its Own Action" (Dixon) **52**:95, 97-8

"Love Having You Around" (Wonder) **12**:656

"Love I Hear" (Sondheim) **30**:378

Love in a Burning Building (Purdy) **14**:430-31

"Love in a Bus" (McGrath) **59**:181

Love in a Cold Climate (Mitford) **44**:485, 491-92

Love in a Dry Season (Foote) **75**:231, 236, 238, 243, 252

"Love in a Song" (McCartney) **35**:282

"Love in a Valley" (Betjeman) **43**:35

"Love in a Valley" (Ewart) **46**:153

"Love in America?" (Moore) **47**:265

Love in Amsterdam (Freeling) **38**:185-86

"Love in Blood Time" (Olds) **85**:298

"Love in High Places" (Johnston) **51**:240-43, 247, 252

"Love in Idleness (O Mistress Mine)" (Rattigan) **7**:354

"Love in Moonlight" (Gluck) **81**:167-69, 172

"Love in Reverse" (Amichai) **116**:107

Love in the Afternoon (Wilder) **20**:459

"Love in the Air" (Jin) **109**:54

Love in the Backrooms: The Sequel to City of Night (Rechy) **107**:259

Love in the Days of Rage (Ferlinghetti) **111**:59

"Love in the Depression" (McGinley) **14**:365

Love in the Environs of Voronezh (Sillitoe) **1**:308

"Love in the Luncheonette" (Rosenthal) **28**:391, 394

"Love in the Marble Foot" (O'Faolain) **47**:325

"Love in the Museum" (Rich) **7**:370

Love in the Ruins: The Adventures of a Bad Catholic at a Time Near the End of the World (Percy) **2**:334-35; **3**:378-79, 381; **6**:399-400; **8**:440, 442, 444-45; **14**:412-13, 418; **18**:397-98, 401-02; **47**:334, 336, 338-41; **65**:257-58

Love in the Time of Cholera (Garcia Marquez) **55**:134-40, 142-48

"Love Is" (Swenson) **106**:347

Love Is a Fervent Fire (Jenkins) **52**:221, 225, 227-28

"Love: Is a Human Condition" (Giovanni) **64**:192; **117**:203

Love Is a Missing Person (Kerr) **12**:298, 301; **35**:251

"Love Is a Piece of Paper Torn to Bits" (Bukowski) **41**:65-6

"Love Is a Rose" (Young) **17**:577

Love Is a Summer Word (Daly) **17**:90

"Love Is a Woman" (Wilson) **12**:652

"Love is an Art of Time" (Rexroth) **112**:395

Love Is Colder than Death (Fassbinder) **20**:105

Love Is Eternal (Stone) **7**:469

"Love Is Not Concerned" (Walker) **58**:407

Love Is Not Enough: The Treatment of Emotionally Disturbed Children (Bettelheim) **79**:108, 111

"Love Is Not Relief" (Aleixandre) **36**:29

Love Is Not What You Think (West) **17**:547

Love Is One of the Choices (Klein) **30**:240-41

"Love Is So Short, Forgetting Is So Long" (Neruda)
See "Es tan corto el amor, y es tan largo el olvido"

Love Is the Crooked Thing (Abbott) **48**:4-7

"Love Is the Plan, the Plan Is Death" (Tiptree) **48**:386, 389, 392, 395-96; **50**:357-58

Love, Laurie (Cavanna) **12**:99

"Love Letta" (Bennett) **28**:29

"A Love Letter" (Ferron)
See "Lettre d'amour"

"Love Letter" (Plath) **111**:210

"Love Letter" (Schnackenberg) **40**:380-81

Love Letter from an Impossible Land (Meredith) **4**:348; **13**:373-74; **55**:193

Love Letters from Asia (Hochman) **3**:250; **8**:297

"Love Letters on Blue Paper" (Wesker) **5**:483-84

Love Letters on Blue Paper (Wesker) **5**:483-84; **42**:427

"Love Lies Sleeping" (Bishop) **1**:34; **32**:37

Love Life (Mason) **82**:244-45, 251-52, 254-56, 258-59

Love, Love at the End (Berrigan) **4**:56

The Love Machine (Susann) **3**:475

"Love Me, I'm a Liberal" (Ochs) **17**:334

"Love Me Now or Love Me Later" (Gaye) **26**:135

"Love Me till the Sun Shines" (Davies) **21**:90

Love Me Tonight (Mamoulian) **16**:419-20, 423-26, 428

"Love Me Two Times" (Morrison) **17**:292, 295

Love Medicine (Erdrich) **54**:165-73; **39**:128-34

"Love Minus Zero/No Limit" (Dylan) **6**:156; **77**:176-77

"Love Needs a Heart" (Browne) **21**:40

"The Love Object" (O'Brien) **8**:429; **36**:340; **116**:186, 208

The Love Object (O'Brien) **36**:337-38, 340; **116**:207-09, 222

The Love of a Good Man (Barker) **37**:34-7, 41

The Love of a Good Man. All Bleeding (Barker) **37**:37

Love of Electricity (*Liubov'k elektrichestvu*) (Aksyonov) **101**:12, 22

A Love of Innocence (Jenkins) **52**:222-23, 225-27

The Love of Jenny Ney (Ehrenburg) **62**:174

The Love of Marcel Faber-Fabriczy for Miss Laura Warronigg (Krleza) **8**:330

"Love of Solitude" (Yevtushenko) **26**:467

"Love of the City" (Johnston) **51**:243-44, 247

"Love of the Scorching Wind" (Nagy) **7**:251

Love of the Scorching Wind (Nagy) **7**:251

A Love, on a Season (Stolz)
See *Two by Two*

"Love on My Mind" (Young) **17**:571

"Love on the Rocks" (Diamond) **30**:113

"Love on the Rocks" (Louie) **70**:79-80

Love on the Run (Truffaut) **20**:406; **101**:388, 396, 398, 400, 411-13

"Love on Toast" (Willingham) **51**:403

Love One Another (Dreyer) **16**:259-61

Love or Nothing (Dunn) **6**:148; **40**:167

"Love Out in the Street" (Simon)   26:409
Love out of Season (Leffland)   19:278-79
The Love Parlour (Rooke)   25:391-92
"Love Passes" (Christie)   110:126
"Love: Petulance" (Williams)   56:429
"Love Philtre" (Prichard)   46:337
"Love Poem" (Appleman)   51:15
"Love Poem" (Ezekiel)   61:101
"A Love Poem" (Knight)   40:279, 283
"A Love Poem" (Kumin)   28:224
"Love Poem" (Purdy)   14:431
"Love Poem" (Raine)   7:352; 45:338
"Love Poem" (Rich)   73:331
"Love Poem" (Steele)   45:365
"Love Poem For Real" (Giovanni)   117:186
"Love Poem on a Theme by Whitman" (Ginsberg)   6:198; 109:354, 358
"Love Poems" (Roethke)   8:455; 101:304
Love Poems (Amichai)   22:33; 57:36; 116:96
Love Poems (Barker)   48:14
Love Poems (Sanchez)   272, 274, 278-79, 281, 289, 298, 301-02, 309, 315, 323
Love Poems (Sexton)   2:391; 4:482-84, 6:492, 494; 15:471-72, 474; 53:319, 321
Love Poems (Wild)   14:580
Love Poems (Yevtushenko)   13:620
Love Poems and Elegies (Smith)   64:393, 399
"The Love Poems of Marichiko" (Rexroth)   112:370, 383, 393, 398
The Love Poems of Marichiko (Rexroth)   49:276, 286-88; 112:387
The Love Poems of May Swenson (Swenson)   106:336-37, 343-44, 347-48
The Love Poems of Myrrhine and Konallis (Aldington)   49:2-3, 10
"Love Reign O'er Me" (Townshend)   17:532
Love Respelt (Graves)   45:166
Love, Roger (Webb)   7:515
The Love Run (Parini)   54:359
Love Scene (Coover)   15:145; 32:120
"Love Sickness" (Damas)
   See "Limbé"
"Love So Fine" (Robinson)   21:348
"Love Song" (Achebe)   11:4; 26:22
"Love Song" (Amichai)   116:93
"Love Song" (Dabydeen)   34:149
"A Love Song" (Dubus)   97:235
"Love Song in Absence" (Wright)   53:432
Love Song of a Puritan (Smith)   64:388
"The Love Song of J. Alfred Prufrock" (Eliot)   1:89, 91; 2:127; 3:136, 138-41; 6:163, 167; 9:183, 187; 10:169-70; 13:196-99, 201; 15:210-211, 213; 24:176; 34:390, 397-98, 402, 525-26; 41:146, 149-5; 55:351-52, 371, 374; 57:168, 175, 179, 181, 190, 207-08, 210;113:182-86, 188-97, 199-200, 202-11, 214-18, 220-23, 226
"Love Song to Idi Amin" (Knight)   40:282
Love Songs (Loy)   28:247, 251-52
Love Songs (Sanders)   41:377
"Love Songs in Age" (Larkin)   3:276; 33:258
Love Songs to Joannes (Loy)   28:247
"Love Sonnet" (Ezekiel)   61:92, 100
"Love Story" (Abse)   29:14
"A Love Story" (Bates)   46:51
"A Love Story" (Bowen)   22:62
"A Love Story" (Graves)   2:175; 45:162, 173
Love Story (Segal)   3:446-47; 10:466-67
Love Story Black (Demby)   53:114
"Love Street" (Morrison)   17:288, 295
"Love Suffered" (Aleixandre)   36:29
The Love Suicide at Schofield Barracks

(Linney)   51:259, 265
"Love Suicides" (Kawabata)   107:113
"Love That I Bear" (H. D.)   73:118
"Love the Butcher Bird Lurks Everywhere" (Stafford)   29:381
"Love the Wild Swan" (Jeffers)   54:249; 11:306
"Love Thoughts" (Giovanni)   117:177
"Love to Patsy" (Tuohy)   37:431
"Love Too Long" (Hannah)   90:141, 144-45
Love! Valour! Compassion! (McNally)   91:164-65
"Love Wrapped Me in Darkness" (Rosenthal)   28:394
"Love You by Heart" (Simon)   26:413
Love You till Tuesday (Bowie)
   See *David Bowie*
"Love, Your Only Mother" (Kaplan)   50:55-7
"Love-Child" (O'Brien)   5:311
The Loved and Envied (Bagnold)   25:74-5
The Loved and the Lost (Callaghan)   14:101-02; 41:90, 92, 95; 65:248-50
The Loved One (Isherwood)   44:397
The Loved One: An Anglo-American Tragedy (Waugh)   1:358-59; 3:509; 19:461; 27:470, 477; 107:360, 368-69, 374-76, 380, 382, 384, 400-02, 404-05
"Loved to Death" (Cooper)   56:70
Love-Hate Relations: English and American Sensibilities (Spender)   5:401-02; 91:278, 280
"Loveland" (Sondheim)   30:391
Loveland (Swarthout)   35:401
The Loveliest Afternoon of the Year (Guare)   29:204; 67:79
Love-Life (Williams)   42:443-45
"Lovelight" (Blunden)   56:48
"The Loveliness of the Long Distance Runner" (Maitland)   49:235
"Lovely" (Amis)   40:40
"Lovely" (Sondheim)   30:378
The Lovely Ambition (Chase)   2:101
"The Lovely April" (Grau)   4:210; 9:240
"A Lovely Bit of Wood" (Gilliatt)   13:237
The Lovely Ladies (Freeling)   38:184
"The Lovely Leave" (Parker)   68:328, 335, 339-40
"The Lovely Linda" (McCartney)   35:278
"A Lovely Love" (Brooks)   49:27
A Lovely Monster: The Adventures of Claude Rains and Dr. Tellenbeck (De Marinis)   54:96-8
A Lovely Morning (Yourcenar)   87:405
A Lovely Summer for Crève Coeur (Williams)   19:471
"Loveman's Comeback" (Campbell)   42:88
"The Lover" (Aldington)   49:5-6
"The Lover" (Creeley)   78:134
"The Lover" (Walker)   103:407-10, 412
"The Lover" (Yehoshua)
   See "Facing the Forests"
The Lover (Duras)
   See *L'amant*
The Lover (Pinter)   1:267; 3:385-86; 6:408; 15:423-24; 27:385-86, 394; 58:373, 384; 73:257
"Lover in a Mad World" (Salinas)   90:332
"The Lover of Horses" (Gallagher)   63:121, 124
The Lover of Horses (Gallagher)   63:120-22, 124
Loveroot (Jong)   6:270; 8:314-15; 18:277; 83:290, 299, 301
"The Lovers" (Berryman)   10:45

"Lovers" (Cohen)   38:131
"The Lovers" (Head)   67:111
"Lovers" (MacBeth)   5:265
"Lovers" (Oates)   9:403
"The Lovers" (Souster)   14:502
The Lovers (Farmer)   19:165, 167
Lovers ("Losers"; "Winners") (Friel)   42:166-67, 169; 59:148; 115:241
"Lovers Again" (MacBeth)   5:265
Lovers and Cohorts: Twenty-Seven Stories (Gold)   42:197
Lovers and Tyrants (Gray)   22:200
A Lover's Discourse: Fragments (Barthes)
   See *Fragments d'un discours amoureux*
"The Lovers Go Fly a Kite" (Snodgrass)   68:397
"Lovers in Middle Age" (Hall)   37:142
"The Lovers Leave by Separate Planes" (Kumin)   28:224
"Lovers of the Lake" (O'Faolain)   7:274; 14:405; 32:341, 344; 70:319
"Lovers of the Poor" (Brooks)   5:75
"Lovers of Their Time" (Trevor)   14:537; 25:443; 71:349; 116:377, 385
Lovers of Their Time, and Other Stories (Trevor)   14:535-37; 25:444-45; 71:325, 346; 116:374, 376
The Lovers of Viorne (Duras)
   See *L'amante anglaise*
"Lovers on Aran" (Heaney)   25:240; 74:182
"The Lover's Quarter" (Mahfuz)   52:292
"Lover's Rock" (Clash)   30:46-7
"A Lover's Woods" (Watkins)   43:441
"Love's in Need of Love Today" (Wonder)   12:659-60, 664
Love's Labor: An Eclogue (O'Hara)   78:364
Loves Lies Bleeding (Crispin)   22:108-09
Love's Lovely Counterfeit (Cain)   3:97; 28:45, 47, 53
Love's Mansion (West)   96:391-94, 396, 400
The Loves of Cass McGuire (Friel)   5:128; 42:164-65; 115:216, 241-42, 244
The Loves of Harry Dancer (Sanders)   41:382
The Loves of Ondine (Warhol)   20:422
"Loves of the Puppets" (Wilbur)   53:398, 405
Love's Old Sweet Song (Saroyan)   34:458; 56:376
Love's Pilgrimage (Sinclair)   63:348-49
"Love's Progress" (Roethke)   3:433; 8:458; 101:328
"Love's Young Dream" (O'Faolain)   70:312, 319
Lovesick (Stern)   100:327
"(Lovesong.)" (Celan)
   See "(Liebeslied.)"
"Lovesong" (Hughes)   37:177
Lovey Childs: A Philadelphian's Story (O'Hara)   2:324; 42:323-24
Lovhers (Brossard)
   See *Amantes*
Loving (Green)   2:178; 13:253, 255; 97:243, 245, 247-49, 251-57, 263, 269-70, 280-82, 288-91, 293
"Loving Blackness as Political Resistance" (hooks)   94:153
A Loving Eye (Elliott)   47:109-10
The Loving Game (Scannell)   49:330
Loving Hands at Home (Johnson)   5:198; 48:201
"Loving, Losing, Loving a Man" (Oates)   6:370
"Loving Mad Tom" (Ashbery)   13:30
"The Loving Shepherdess" (Jeffers)   11:305
The Loving Spirit (du Maurier)   59:284-87
"Loving the Crone" (Piercy)   62:378

Low (Bowie) 17:65-8
"Low Budget" (Davies) 21:104
Low Budget (Davies) 21:104-06
Low Company (Fuchs) 8:220-21; 22:158
Low Flying Aircraft (McNally) 82:262-64, 267, 269-70
"Low Sunday" (Klappert) 57:269
"Low Tide" (Szirtes) 46:393
Low Tide (Eberstadt) 39:48-51
"Low to High" (Hughes) 35:222
The Lower Depths (Kurosawa) 16:396, 401
"Lower Field—Enniscorthy" (Olson) 29:329
"The Lowering" (Swenson) 106:320-21
The Lowest Trees Have Tops (Gellhorn) 60:193
Low-Flying Aircraft, and Other Stories (Ballard) 14:39, 41; 36:37-8
"Lowland" (Gascoyne) 45:153
"Low-Lands" (Pynchon) 33:333-34, 338-40; 62:432
"The Lowliest Bush a Purple Sage Would Be" (Keillor) 40:274
"Loyal" (Matthews) 40:323, 325
"LSD" (Ginsberg) 109:325
The LSD Leacock (Rosenblatt) 15:446-47
"The L-Shaped Room" (Banks) 23:40-1
Lu Ann Hampton Laverty Oberlander (Jones) 10:297
"Luau" (Wilson) 12:647
"Luc and His Father" (Gallant) 38:195
Luca (Moravia)
    See *Luca*
Luca (Moravia) 27:354
La lucarne ovale (Reverdy) 53:285, 288
"Lucas, His Partisan Arguments" (Cortazar)
    See "Lucas, sus discusiones partidarias"
"Lucas, sus discusiones partidarias" ("Lucas, His Partisan Arguments") (Cortazar) 34:334
La luce e il lutto (*The Light and the Grief*) (Bufalino) 74:40
"Luces" ("Lights") (Cardenal) 31:77
"The Luceys" (O'Connor) 14:399
Lucha (Urdang) 47:401
Luci del varieta (*Variety Lights*) (Fellini) 16:274, 298; 85:55, 59, 67, 69, 71, 75, 78, 81
"Lucifer" (Seger) 35:378
Lucifer (Powys) 7:347
Lucifer and the Lord (Sartre)
    See *Le diable et le bon Dieu*
"Lucifer Ashore" (Davison) 28:100
Lucifer Falling (White) 49:400-01
"Lucifer in the Train" (Rich) 7:368
"Lucifer Praying" (Klappert) 57:259-60
Lucifer Wilkins (Garfield) 12:235
"Lucinda" (Swan) 69:359-61
"Luck" (Prichard) 46:345
Luck and Pluck (Swarthout) 35:403
The Luck of Ginger Coffey (*Ginger Coffey*) (Moore) 1:225; 5:295, 297; 19:331;32:307, 309; 90:238-9, 242-44, 251-2, 263, 277, 278, 280
"The Luck of the Irish" (Lennon) 35:264-65
"Luckenbach, Texas" ("Back to the Basics of Love") (Jennings) 21:204
"Luckily the Account Representative Knew CPR" (Wallace) 114:347, 349
"Lucky" (Nyro) 17:315
"Lucky Boy" (Pearce) 21:289
"The Lucky Coin" (Clarke) 9:168
Lucky Jim (Amis) 1:5-6; 2:4-10; 3:9-10; 5:20-3; 8:11-12; 13:12; 40:41, 47-8; 44:138, 140, 142
Lucky Life (Stern) 40:405-08, 410-12; 100:329

"The Lucky Pair" (Lavin) 99:321
Lucky Poet (MacDiarmid) 4:312-13; 19:288
Lucky Starr and the Big Sun of Mercury (Asimov) 26:36, 41, 64
Lucky Starr and the Moons of Jupiter (Asimov) 26:41, 64
Lucky Starr and the Oceans of Venus (Asimov) 26:35-6, 41, 64
Lucky Starr and the Pirates of the Asteroids (Asimov) 26:41, 64
Lucky Starr and the Rings of Saturn (Asimov) 26:36, 41, 64
"Lucky You" (Gerstler) 70:156, 159
"Lucretius versus the Lake Poets" (Frost) 15:243
"Luctus in Morte Infantis" (Barker) 48:9, 12
Lucy (Kincaid) 68:215-21
"lucy and her girls" (Clifton) 66:69
Lucy Crown (Shaw) 7:411
"Lucy in the Sky with Diamonds" (Lennon and McCartney) 12:357, 373; 35:368
"Lucy's Daffodil" (Fuller) 62:207
"Lud and Marie Meet Dracula's Daughter" (Tomlin) 17:522-23
Lud Heat (Sinclair) 76:227
Ludwig (Visconti) 16:570, 575
"Ludwig Wittgenstein: Zu einem Kapital der jüngsten Philosophiegeschichte" (Bachmann) 69:57
Ludzie stamtad (*The People from Yonder*) (Dabrowska) 15:166-68
"Lugar llamado Kindberg" (Cortazar) 33:124, 34:333
El lugar sin límites (*Hell Has No Limits*; *A Place without Boundaries*) (Donoso) 4:126-29; 8:178-79; 11:145-46; 32:153-54, 159, 161; 99:216, 218, 221, 223, 236, 240
Lugging Vegetables to Nantucket (Klappert) 57:256-60, 263, 265-66
"Luigi's House" (Gellhorn) 60:180-81
"Luis" (Selzer) 74:287
Luisa en el páis de la realidad (*Luisa in Realityland*) (Alegria) 75:43-6, 48, 50-1
Luisa in Realityland (Alegria)
    See *Luisa en el páis de la realidad*
Lukács and Heidegger: Towards a New Philosophy (Goldmann) 24:251, 254
"Lukas, Sanftmütiger Kneeht" (Lenz) 27:245
"The Lull" (Green) 97:276-77
"Lull" (Muldoon) 72:266
"The Lull" (Peacock) 60:294
"Lullabies" (Greenberg) 7:134
Lullabies Twisters Gibbers Drags (Williams) 13:600
"Lullaby" (Auden) 9:56
"Lullaby" (Boland) 40:100
"Lullaby" (Fearing) 51:107
"Lullaby" (Gluck) 81:172-73
"The Lullaby" (Riding) 7:374
"Lullaby" (Sexton) 10:468
"Lullaby" (Silko) 23:409; 74:344; 114:314, 340
"Lullaby" (Sitwell) 67:318-19, 325, 333, 336
"Lullaby" (Waddington) 28:438
"Lullaby for Rachel" (Simmons) 43:411
Lullaby for Sinners: Poems, 1970-1979 (Braverman) 67:49
"Lullaby through the Side of the Mouth" (Wagoner) 3:508
"Lullabye" (Broumas) 73:9, 11
"Lulu" (Hesse) 25:259
"Lumber" (Barthelme) 36:52; 117:2
"The Lumens" (Olds) 85:306

Lumeton aika (*The Snowless Time*) (Haavikko) 34:170
"La lumière, changée" (Bonnefoy) 15:74
"Luminism" (Strand) 71:288-89
"The Luminosity of Life" (Smith) 22:386
"Lump" (Phillips) 28:365
Lumpy Gravy (Zappa) 17:588, 591
"Lumumba Lives" (Matthiessen) 64:322, 325
Luna (Bertolucci) 16:100
Luna de enfrente (*Moon Across The Way*; *Moon across the Way*) (Borges) 19:44-5; 44:367
"Luna e G N A C" ("The Moon and GNAC") (Calvino) 33:100; 73:33
Luna silvestre (Paz) 65:176, 196
"La luna sul muro" ("Moonlight on the Wall") (Ortese) 89:198
Lunar Attractions (Blaise) 29:72
"Lunar Baedecker" (Loy) 28:246, 248-49
"Lunar Changes" (Wright) 28:470
"The Lunar Cycle" (Piercy) 27:379
Lunar Landscapes (Hawkes) 4:212
Lunatic Villas (Engel) 36:164-65
Lunatics and Lovers (Kingsley) 44:236, 238
"The Lunatic's Tale" (Allen) 52:42
"The Lunch" (Cortazar)
    See "El almuerzo"
"Lunch" (Koch) 5:219; 44:243, 248
"Lunch and Afterwards" (Abse) 29:20
Lunch and Counter Lunch (Murray) 40:336-38
"Lunch Hour" (O'Hara) 13:431
Lunch Hour (Kerr) 22:258-59
Lunch Hour (Mortimer) 28:283-84
"Lunch in Winter" (Trevor) 71:333
Lunch Poems (O'Hara) 2:323; 13:428; 78:333
"Lunch with Pancho Villa" (Muldoon) 32:318-19, 321; 72:265-66, 268
"The Luncheon" (Archer) 28:14
"Lunches of 1943" (Aksyonov) 101:11, 15, 18, 20
Lunes en papier (Malraux) 4:332; 15:354-55
"Les lunettes" (Carrier) 78:68
Lupercal (Hughes) 2:197-98, 201-02; 4:236; 9:280-83; 14:270, 273; 37:171, 175, 180
"Lupercalia" (Hall) 51:172
"The Lure of the Open Window" (Jong) 6:268
"Lush Triumphant" (McGrath) 55:75
Das Lusitania Songspiel (Durang) 27:88
"Luss Village" (Smith) 64:397
"Lust" (Urquhart) 90:386
Lust for Life (Stone) 7:468-71
"Lust in Action" (Glassco) 9:237
"Lustig" (Jandl) 34:195
"Lustra" (Okigbo) 25:349, 355; 84:299-300, 309, 313, 326
"Lustra" (Pound) 4:408
Lustra (Pound) 1:276; 10:400; 13:460; 48:283-84
O lustre (Lispector) 43:261, 265
Lusts (Blaise) 29:76-7
O lutador (*The Wrestler*) (Andrade) 18:3
"Luther" (Huddle) 49:182
Luther (Osborne) 2:328; 5:331, 333; 11:421-22; 45:313-16
Lutheran Letters (Pasolini) 37:351; 106:259
Luv (Schisgal) 6:489
"Luvina" (Rulfo) 80:200, 213, 217
"Luxury" (Amichai) 116:95
"Luzina Takes a Holiday" (Roy) 14:467
Lvíce (*Miss Silver's Past*) (Skvorecky) 15:510; 69:339, 341
"Lychees for Tone" (Gardam) 43:169
Den lyckliges väg (*The Path of the Happy Man*)

(Lagerkvist)   54:274

Lydie Breeze (Guare)   29:205-08; 67:78-81

"Lyell's Hypothesis Again" (Rexroth)   49:280, 285, 289; 112:376, 383-84, 398, 400

"Lying" (Wilbur)   53:405, 412; 110:357, 360, 372

"The Lying Art" (Porter)   13:452-53; 33:320

"Lying Awake in a Desert" (Wagoner)   15:560

The Lying Days (Gordimer)   10:239; 18:186; 33:177-79; 70:162-65, 170

"The Lying Dear" (Graham)   29:196

"Lying Doggo" (Mason)   82:234, 236

Lying Figures (Warner)   14:552

"Lying In" (Broumas)   73:16

"Lying in a Hammock at William Duffy's Farm in Pine Island, Minnesota" (Wright)   3:540, 543; 10:546; 28:468

"Lying in Politics: Reflections on the Pentagon Papers" (Arendt)   98:11

Lying in State (Rathbone)   41:345

Lying Low (Johnson)   13:305-06; 48:208

"Lying Together..." (Loewinsohn)   52:285

"Lynch" (Guillen)   48:159

The Lynchers (Wideman)   5:489-90; 36:452-54

"The Lynching" (Scannell)   49:325, 331

"The Lynchings of Jesus" (Rukeyser)   27:405

"Lyndon" (Wallace)   14:348

"Lynn" (Dybek)   114:62

"Lynz" (Orlovitz)   22:337

Lyonesse (Vance)   35:427-28

Lyonushka (*Lenuska; Lionushka*) (Leonov)   92:260, 270, 277

The Lyre of Orpheus (Davies)   75:196-202, 206-08, 210-14, 216-17; 91:203-4

"Lyric" (Raine)   7:352

"The Lyric Physiognomy and Lyric Daring of Andreas Kalvos" (Elytis)   100:177

"Lyric Sarcastic" (Gustafson)   36:214

Lyrical and Critical Essays (Camus)   9:146; 14:108

Lyrical Ballads (Sandburg)   10:448

The Lyrics of Noël Coward (Coward)   29:134

Lyrics Unromantic (Gustafson)   36:216

Lysistrata and NATO (Hochhuth)   18:255

"M" (Merrill)   8:383

M (Lang)   20:202, 204, 213; 103:90-5, 115

M. Butterfly (Hwang)   55:150-55

"M. François Mauriac et la liberté" (Sartre)   24:417

M. le modéré (Adamov)   25:18, 21

"M. M. and the Rivers" (Cabral de Melo Neto)   See "Murilo Mendes e os rios"

"M., Singing" (Bogan)   93:78

M/T (Oe)   86:241

M: Writings, '67-'72 (Cage)   41:81-3, 86

"Ma" (Muldoon)   32:318

"Ma grand-mère toute-puissante" (Roy)   10:440

"Ma lamadti bamilhamot" ("What I have Learned in the Wars") (Amichai)   116:121

"Ma Lord" (Hughes)   108:298

Ma mère (*My Mother*) (Bataille)   29:44-5

A ma mère (Conde)   92:

Ma nuit chez Maud (*My Night at Maud's*) (Rohmer)   16:529-31, 533, 536, 540

"Ma Provence" (Koch)   44:243, 251

"Ma Rainey" (Brown)   59:266, 270

Ma Rainey's Black Bottom (Wilson)   39:276-82; 50:267-68, 270-71; 63:447-54, 457

"Má vlast" ("My Country"; "My Homeland") (Klima)   56:172-73

Mabel: A Story and Other Prose (Creeley)   78:128

"Mabinog's Liturgy" (Jones)   42:241

"Mabuti" (Highsmith)   102:201

"Mac in Love" (Dixon)   52:94, 96-7

A maçã no escuro (*The Apple in the Dark*) (Lispector)   43:261-66, 269-71

"Macabre" (Colter)   58:146

"Macao" (Auden)   14:26

"Macario" (Rulfo)   80:200, 213, 216

Macario (Traven)   8:520

"Macaroon" (Cunningham)   12:164

"Macaw" (Bogan)   46:77

"Macbech" (Updike)   43:431

Macbeth (Polanski)   16:469, 472

Macbeth (Welles)   20:433-35, 438-39, 441-43, 447-49, 451, 453-54; 80:382, 391, 397, 401, 410

Macbett (Ionesco)   6:252-53; 11:292; 86:341

"Macchu Picchu" (Lane)   25:284, 286

Macchu Picchu (Neruda)   See *Alturas de Macchu Picchu*

The MacGuffin (Elkin)   91:213-14, 223

"Macherey and Marxist Literary Theory" (Eagleton)   63:107

"The Machine" (Campbell)   32:76, 78, 80

"La machine à detecter tout ce qui est américain" (Carrier)   78:63

La machine àecrire (Cocteau)   43:105-06, 108

Machine Dreams (Phillips)   33:305-08

La machine infernale (*The Infernal Machine*) (Cocteau)   8:144, 147, 149; 15:134; 16:220; 43:99-102, 105-06, 110-11

"The Machine Stops" (Forster)   77:230

The Machine Stops (Forster)   10:183; 22:129-30

"The Machine-Gun Corps in Action" (O'Connor)   23:329

The Machine-Gunners (Westall)   17:555-58

The Machineries of Joy (Bradbury)   42:33

"Machinery" (Kauffman)   65:348

Machines and Men (Roberts)   14:463

Macho Comancho's Beat (Sanchez)   23:383-86

Die Macht der Gewohnheit (*The Force of Habit*) (Bernhard)   32:20, 23-4; 61:12, 20, 26-8

"Macht und Überleben" ("Power and Survival") (Canetti)   75:129, 132

"Machu Picchu" (Birney)   6:75

"Mackenzie River North" (Musgrave)   13:400

"Mackerel" (Hoffman)   6:244

The Mackerel Plaza (De Vries)   7:76; 10:136-38; 28:106-07; 46:135

"Mackinnon's Boat" (Tomlinson)   4:548

"Mackintosh" (Maugham)   67:206

The Mackintosh Man (Huston)   20:173

Macquarie (Buzo)   61:53-9, 64, 68

"Macquarie as Father" (Shapcott)   38:398

Mad Dog Blues (Shepard)   4:490-91; 17:438, 443-44, 448; 41:409, 412

Mad Dog Blues and Other Plays (Smith)   12:534

"Mad Dogs and Englishmen" (Coward)   51:76

Mad Ducks and Bears: Football Revisited (Plimpton)   36:354-56

"The Mad Farmer in the City" (Berry)   27:33

"The Mad Farmer Manifesto: The First Amendment" (Berry)   6:61

"A Mad Fight Song for William S. Carpenter" (Wright)   5:520; 28:465

"Mad Housewife" (Nemerov)   36:309

Mad in Pursuit (Leduc)   See *La folie en tête*

"The Mad Kitchen and Dong, the Cave Adolescent" (Jiles)   58:273, 275

"The Mad Lomasneys" (O'Connor)   14:399; 23:332

Mad Love (Harjo)   See *In Mad Love and War*

"Mad Marga" (O'Faolain)   47:328

"A Mad One" (Gordimer)   18:189

"The Mad One" (Mahfuz)   See "al- Majnuna"

The Mad Pomegranate and the Praying Mantis: An Andalusian Adventure (Luke)   38:318

"The Mad Pomegranate Tree" (Elytis)   49:106, 114

Mad Puppetstown (Keane)   31:231-32

Mad Shadows (Blais)   See *La belle bête*

"The Mad Tea-Party" (Queen)   11:462

"Mad Yak" (Corso)   11:123

"Madam" (Hughes)   108:326

"Madam and Her Madam" (Hughes)   108:326

"Madam and the Number Writer" (Hughes)   108:297

Madam, Will You Talk? (Stewart)   7:467; 35:388-89, 391

Madame Bovary (Renoir)   20:286, 293-94, 310

Madame de Pompadour (Mitford)   44:485, 488-89

Madame de Sade (Mishima)   2:286; 27:337-38

"Madame Dodin" (Duras)   40:184-85

Madame Edwarda (*The Naked Beast at Heaven's Gate*) (Bataille)   29:45

Madame Maigret's Friend (Simenon)   18:484-85

"Madame Moth" (Reaney)   13:473

"Madame Rosette" (Dahl)   79:174

Madame Sousatzka (Rubens)   31:350-51

"Madame Zelena" (Carlson)   54:38

"Madame Zilensky" (McCullers)   12:433

"Madame Zilensky and the King of Finland" (McCullers)   100:246

"Madam's Music" (Hall)   51:170

Die Mädchen aus Viterbo (Eich)   15:203

Madder Music (De Vries)   10:137-38; 28:107, 110, 112

Made in America (Maas)   29:306-07

Made in Canada (Souster)   5:395

"Made in Goatswood" (Campbell)   42:85

Made in U.S.A. (Godard)   20:137, 149

"Made to Last" (Durban)   39:46

"Mademoiselle Claude" (Miller)   84:262

Mademoiselle Colombe (Anouilh)   See *Colombe*

Mademoiselle Jaïre (Ghelderode)   11:226

"Mademoiselle O" (Nabokov)   8:414

"Mademoiselle Veronique" (Brodsky)   36:81

The Maderati (Greenberg)   57:227-30

Madigan (Polonsky)   92:387-88, 405, 415

"Madimba: Gwendolyn Brooks" (Harper)   7:139

"The Madison Experience" (Jordan)   114:146

"The Madman" (Achebe)   26:23; 75:14

"The Madman" (Urdang)   47:397

"The Madman and the Book" (Wiesel)   5:490

The Madman and the Medusa (Tchicaya)   101:356

"Madman of the Uncharmed Debris of the South Side" (Major)   19:293

Madmen and Specialists (Soyinka)   3:463; 5:397; 14:509; 36:411, 417; 44:286-88

"Madness" (Arghezi)   See "Streche"

"Madness" (Dickey)   2:117; 109:272

"Madness" (Schaeffer) 6:489

Madness and Civilization: A History of Insanity in the Age of Reason (Foucault)
  See *Folie et déraison: Histoire de la folie à l'âge classique*

The Madness of George III (Bennett) 77:103

"The Madness of Saul" (Sitwell) 67:324

"Madoc" (Mathias) 45:236

"Madoc: A Mystery" (Muldoon) 72:279-82

Madoc: A Mystery (Muldoon) 72:279, 281-83

"The Madonna" (Barker) 52:52, 55

La madonna dei filosofi (Gadda) 11:210

Madonna Red (Carroll) 38:104, 107

"Madonnas Touched Up with a Goatee" (Simic) 49:336; 68:372

"The Madras Rumble" (Faust) 8:215

"La madre" (Ginzburg) 54:206

Una madre (Fo) 109:109

"Madrid, 1974" (Van Duyn) 63:442

"Madrid, May, 1977" (Van Duyn) 63:442

"Madrigal" (Guillen) 48:157; 79:232, 238-40

Madrigal (Gardner) 30:152

A Madrigal (H. D.)
  See *Bid Me to Live (A Madrigal)*

"Madrigal trirrimo" (Guillen) 79:238

"Madrigals" (Shapcott) 38:400

Madrugada (*Dawn*) (Buero Vallejo) 15:99, 101

"The Madwoman" (Nakos) 29:321

"Maenad" (Plath) 11:446, 448; 111:159, 164-65

"Maestranzas de noche" ("Arsenal by Night"; "Dockyards at Night") (Neruda) 62:322

"Maeterlinck in Ontario" (Cassity) 42:99

Mafia Vendetta (Sciascia)
  See *Il giorno della civetta*

"Magdalena" (Zappa) 17:588

"Magdalene" (Kristofferson) 26:270

Magdalene (Slaughter) 56:408-09

The Magellan Nebula (Lem) 40:289-90

The Magellanic Clouds (Wakoski) 2:459; 9:555

"Maggid" (Piercy) 62:379

Maggie Cassidy (Kerouac) 1:167; 5:215; 29:270, 272; 61:309

"Maggie Meriwether's Rich Experience" (Stafford) 68:422, 449

Maggie Muggins (Waterhouse) 47:421-22

"Maggie of the Green Bottles" (Bambara) 88:16-17, 21, 23, 27, 47

Maggie-Now (Smith) 19:424

"Maggie's Farm" (Dylan) 77:176

"Maggie's Gift" (Paterson) 30:283

A Maggot (Fowles) 87:147, 149, 159, 161-62, 173-78, 181, 183

"Magi" (Brown) 48:59

"The Magi" (Gluck) 7:118, 120

"Magi" (Plath) 5:345; 51:340; 111:159

"Magias parciales del Quijote" ("Partial Enchantments of the *Quixote*"; "Partial Magic in the *Quixote*") (Borges) 13:112; 83:161

"Magic" (Kaplan) 50:55, 57

"Magic" (Klein) 30:236

"Magic" (Porter) 7:320; 15:432; 101:209-210, 224

Magic (Elliott) 47:114-15

Magic (Goldman) 48:127-28

"Magic Affinities" (Moss) 7:250

The Magic Animal (Wylie) 43:472

Magic Animals: Selected Poems Old and New (MacEwen) 13:358

The Magic Apple Tree (Feinstein) 36:168

The Magic Apple Tree (Hill) 113:326

"The Magic Apples" (O'Brien) 116:187

"Magic at Ruth Lake" (Bass) 79:17

"The Magic Barrel" (Malamud) 2:266, 269; 3:323; 8:376; 18:317; 27:297, 306; 44:412, 419-20; 78:249, 264, 271; 85:190-224

The Magic Barrel (Malamud) 1:195-96, 200; 3:320-24; 5:269; 8:376; 9:346, 348; 11:345-46; 18:321; 27:298, 301-02; 44:411, 413, 415-16, 420; 78:252, 281; 85:191. 195, 200, 209

"The Magic Box" (Sillitoe) 57:388

"The Magic Bus" (Townshend) 17:527, 530, 536

The Magic Carpet, and Other Tales (Douglas) 73:99

The Magic Carpets of Antonio Angelini (Ringwood) 48:334

"Magic Castle" (Barthelme) 117:5

The Magic Change: Metamorphosis (Silverstein and Silverstein) 17:453-54

The Magic Christian (Southern) 7:453

Magic City (Komunyakaa) 86:191; 94:218-220, 234, 237, 239, 240-41, 246, 248-49

The Magic Finger (Dahl) 79:177

"The Magic Flute" (Moore) 13:396

The Magic Flute (Bergman)
  See *Trollflöjten*

"Magic Fox" (Welch) 52:428

"Magic, Inc." (Heinlein) 55:302

The Magic Journey (Nichols) 38:342, 344

The Magic Kingdom (Elkin) 91:214, 220, 223-24

The Magic Lantern (Bergman)
  See *Lanterna Magica*

The Magic Lantern of Marcel Proust (Moss) 50:352

Magic Man, Magic Man (Wagman) 7:500

"A Magic Mountain" (Milosz)
  See "Duzo spiè"

"Magic Mountains" (Stafford) 4:517

The Magic of Shirley Jackson (Jackson) 60:211-13

The Magic of the Guts (Adler) 35:13

Magic Papers (Feldman) 7:101

"The Magic Poker" (Coover) 7:58

"The Magic Strength of Need" (Cooper) 56:70

"The Magic Striptease" (Garrett) 51:149

The Magic Striptease (Garrett) 51:149

The Magic Summer (*The Growing Summer*) (Streatfeild) 21:409-10

The Magic Toyshop (Carter) 5:102; 41:111-12, 114; 76:323, 329

The Magic Will: Stories and Essays of a Decade (Gold) 42:192-93

"The Magical" (Eberhart) 56:85

"Magical Lady" (Thurber) 11:533

"Magical Mystery Pool" (McFadden) 48:243

"The Magician" (Kotzwinkle) 35:253

"Magician" (Rooke) 25:391

"The Magician" (Tanizaki) 14:527

The Magician (Abse) 29:15, 17

The Magician (Bergman)
  See *Ansiktet*

The Magician (Nabokov)
  See *Volshebnik*

The Magician in Love (Rooke) 25:393

The Magician of Lublin (Singer)
  See *Kunstmakher fun Lublin*

The Magician's Feastletters (Wakoski) 40:456-57

The Magician's Girl (Grumbach) 64:201-05

The Magician's Nephew (Lewis) 27:262-64

The Magicians of Caprona (Jones) 26:230

The Magician's Wife (Cain) 28:49, 52-3

Magie noire (*Black Magic*) (Morand) 41:300-01, 303-04, 306

Magie rouge (Ghelderode) 11:226

"Magiel" (Herbert) 43:186

"Der magische Tänzer" (Sachs) 98:364, 367

Magister Ludi (Hesse)
  See *Das Glasperlenspiel*

"Magna Mater" (Oates) 6:373

"Magna Takes the Calls" (Dixon) 52:100

The Magnanimous Cuckold (Crommelynck)
  See *Le cocu magnifique*

"The Magnet" (Sarton) 49:310

Magnet Fragments (Lezama Lima)
  See *Fragmentos a su imán*

Magnetic Field (s) (Loewinsohn) 52:285-90

The Magnetic Fields (Breton and Soupault)
  See *Les champs magnétiques*

The Magnetic Mountain (Day Lewis) 6:128; 10:132

"Magneto and Titanium Man" (McCartney) 35:282-83

"Magnificat" (Guillevic) 33:193

"Magnificat in Transit from the Toledo Airport" (Starbuck) 53:354

Magnificence (Brenton) 31:57, 60, 62, 64-7

The Magnificent Ambersons (Welles) 20:435-36, 440, 444, 446-50, 452-54; 80:368-69, 372-75, 377, 382, 386, 388-91, 393, 395-97, 409, 414-16

The Magnificent Century (Costain) 30:96-7, 99

The Magnificent Cuckold (Crommelynck)
  See *Le cocu magnifique*

The Magnificent Seven (*The Seven Samurai*) (Kurosawa) 16:395-99, 403

The Magnificent Showboats of the Lower Vissel River, Lune XXIII South, Big Planet (Vance)
  See *Showboat World*

The Magnificent Spinster (Sarton) 49:321-23; 91:240, 246-47, 249-50

"Magnolia Flower" (Hurston) 7:172

"Magnum Opus" (Reid) 33:350

Magnus (Brown) 48:58-9, 61; 100:78, 86

Magog (Sinclair) 2:402; 14:488

"Magpies" (King) 89:97-8

"Magpies" (Wright) 53:423

"Magpiety" (Milosz)
  See "Sroczosc"

"Magrette's Secret Agent" (Lee) 46:234

"Magritte Dancing" (Stern) 100:333, 343

"Mags" (Trevor) 116:377

The Magus (Fowles) 1:109; 2:137-39; 3:162-63; 4:170-73; 6:185, 187-89; 9:210-17; 10:184-87, 189; 15:233-34; 33:163, 166, 169, 171-75; 87:136, 139-40, 147, 150-52, 154, 157-62, 176, 178-82

The Mahabharata: A Shortened Modern Prose Version of the Indian Epic (Narayan) 28:301

Mahagony (Glissant) 68:178-80, 182-84, 187

Mahanagar (*The Big City*) (Ray) 16:480-84, 492; 76:357

"The Maharajah" (White) 30:451

The Maharajah, and Other Stories (White) 30:451

Mahatma Gandhi and His Apostles (Mehta) 37:292

"Mahavaton Ki Ek Raat" ("One Rainy Night of Winter") (Ali) 69:25

Mahler (Russell) 16:548, 551

Mahler Grooves (Williams)   13:600-01

"Mahoney the Bad Traveler" (Klappert)   57:267

"Mahpiyato" (Cook-Lynn)   93:124, 126, 130

Mai devi domandarmi (Ginzburg)   11:228; 54:196-97, 212

Mai Mai Peñi (Parra)   102:356

The Maid (Audiberti)
   See *La pucelle*

The Maid Silja (Sillanpaa)
   See *Fallen Asleep While Young*

"The Maiden" (Stafford)   7:457

Maiden Castle (Powys)   7:348-50; 9:441; 15:433; 46:320-21, 324

"Maiden Name" (Larkin)   39:339

"Maiden Voyage" (Wolff)   64:450

The Maids (Genet)
   See *Les bonnes*

Maidstone: A Mystery (Mailer)   1:193; 4:323; 14:351; 28:256-57, 259; 74:217-18

"Maighdean Mara" (Heaney)   7:148; 74:157

Maigret à New York (*Maigret in New York's Underworld*) (Simenon)   2:399; 47:381

Maigret Abroad (Simenon)   47:370

Maigret Afraid (Simenon)   47:382

Maigret and His Corpse (Simenon)
   See *Maigret et son mort*

Maigret and M. Labbé (Simenon)   47:372

Maigret and Monsieur Charles (Simenon)   47:376

Maigret and the Apparition (Simenon)   8:487; 18:481

Maigret and the Black Sheep (Simenon)   8:486

Maigret and the Bum (Simenon)   47:377

Maigret and the Calame Report (Simenon)
   See *Maigret and the Minister*

Maigret and the Coroner (Simenon)
   See *Maigret chez le coroner*

Maigret and the Enigmatic Lett (Simenon)
   See *Pietr-le-Letton*

Maigret and the Flea (Simenon)   47:376

Maigret and the Gangsters (Simenon)
   See *Inspector Maigret and the Killers*

Maigret and the Hotel Majestic (Simenon)   18:486

Maigret and the Hundred Gibbets (Simenon)
   See *Le pendu de Saint-Pholien*

Maigret and the Killer (Simenon)   47:376

Maigret and the Loner (Simenon)   47:377

Maigret and the Man on the Bench (Simenon)
   See *Maigret et l'homme du banc*

Maigret and the Millionaires (Simenon)   47:377

Maigret and the Minister (*Maigret and the Calame Report*) (Simenon)   47:375

Maigret and the Nahour Case (Simenon)   47:378

Maigret and the Old Lady (Simenon)
   See *Maigret et la vieille dame*

Maigret and the Wine Merchant (Simenon)
   See *Maigret et le marchand de vin*

Maigret and the Young Girl (*Inspector Maigret and the Dead Girl*) (Simenon)   47:373, 375

Maigret at the Coroner's (Simenon)
   See *Maigret chez le coroner*

Maigret at the Crossroads (Simenon)
   See *The Crossroad Murders*

Maigret au "Picratt" (*Inspector Maigret and the Strangled Stripper*) (Simenon)   47:373

Maigret Bides His Time (Simenon)   47:382

Maigret chez le coroner (*Maigret and the Coroner*; *Maigret at the Coroner's*) (Simenon)   47:378; 47:378, 381

Maigret cinq (Simenon)   47:375

Maigret et la grande perche (Simenon)   3:451

Maigret et la vieille dame (*Maigret and the Old Lady*) (Simenon)   8:487; 47:375

Maigret et le client du samedi (Simenon)   47:381

Maigret et le marchand de vin (*Maigret and the Wine Merchant*) (Simenon)   47:376, 381

Maigret et les vieillards (Simenon)   3:450

Maigret et l'homme du banc (*Maigret and the Man on the Bench*; *La main*) (Simenon)   2:398; 47:377

Maigret et son mort (*Maigret and His Corpse*) (Simenon)   47:380-81

Maigret Has Doubts (Simenon)   47:378

Maigret Hesitates (Simenon)   2:398

Maigret in Exile (Simenon)   18:486; 47:378

Maigret in New York's Underworld (Simenon)
   See *Maigret à New York*

Maigret in Vichy (Simenon)   18:481

Maigret Keeps a Rendez-Vous (Simenon)   47:370

Maigret Loses His Temper (Simenon)   47:375

Maigret Mystified (Simenon)
   See *The Shadow in the Courtyard*

Maigret on the Defensive (Simenon)   47:378

Maigret Rents a Room (Simenon)
   See *Maigret Takes a Room*

Maigret Returns (Simenon)   47:372

Maigret se trompe (Simenon)   47:381

Maigret Sets a Trap (Simenon)   47:376

Maigret Sits It Out (Simenon)   47:371-72

Maigret Stonewalled (Simenon)
   See *Monsieur Gallet, décédé*

Maigret Takes a Room (*Maigret Rents a Room*) (Simenon)   47:374-75

Maigret to the Rescue (Simenon)   47:371

Maigret Travels South (Simenon)   47:369-70

A Maigret Trio (Simenon)   2:399

Maigret's Boyhood Friend (Simenon)   47:376

Maigret's Little Joke (*None of Maigret's Business*) (Simenon)   47:374-75

Maigret's Memoirs (Simenon)   8:487; 47:374, 383

Maigret's Pickpocket (Simenon)   47:375

Maigret's Revolver (Simenon)   47:382

Maigret's Rival (Simenon)   47:378

Maigret's War of Nerves (Simenon)
   See *A Battle of Nerves*

Maihime (*The Dancer*) (Kawabata)   107:121

"Mail at Your New Address" (Klappert)   57:258

"Mail Call" (Jarrell)   9:298

Mailer: His Life and Times (Manso)   39:416-25

"The Mailman" (Strand)   18:514, 516; 41:437; 71:283

"The Maimed Man" (Tate)   2:429, 431; 11:525, 527; 14:529

"Maimutoii judecatori" ("The Ape Judges") (Arghezi)   80:3

"La main" (Carrier)   78:60, 68

La main (Simenon)
   See *Maigret et l'homme du banc*

The Main (Trevanian)   29:431-32

La Main Coupée (*Lice*) (Cendrars)   106:167, 183, 187-88, 190

"Main Currents of American Thought" (Shaw)   34:369

Main Line West (Horgan)   53:172, 175

"The Main of Light" (Heaney)   74:188

La main passe (Tzara)   47:387

La main sèche (*Dried Hand*) (Tchicaya)   101:354-55, 363, 366

"Main Theme" (Gaye)   26:131

The Maine Massacre (van de Wetering)   47:407-10

"Les mains" (Hebert)   29:238

Les mains négatives (Duras)   68:92, 96

Les mains sales (*Crime Passionel*; *Dirty Hands*) (Sartre)   4:476; 9:471; 13:499-500; 18:472; 50:382; 52:375, 381, 388

"Mainstreet" (Seger)   35:381

"Maintaining a Home" (Dorris)   109:311

Maíra (Ribeiro)   34:102-04

Maisie (Taylor)   4:543

Maison basse (Ayme)   11:22

La maison de rendez-vous (*The House of Assignation*) (Robbe-Grillet)   1:287, 290; 2:376; 4:446, 448, 450; 6:465-66; 8:452-54; 10:437; 14:457, 462; 43:361

La maison du canal (Simenon)   47:379

"Maison flake" (Tzara)   47:393

La maison sans racines (Chedid)   47:87-8

Le maître de la parole: Kouma lafôlô kouma (*The Guardian of the Word*) (Laye)   38:286-87, 290, 292

Le maitre de Milan (Audiberti)   38:33

Le maître de Santiago (Montherlant)   19:326-27, 329-30

"La maîtresse servante" (Damas)   84:179

Maitreya (Sarduy)   97:390, 393-96, 399-400, 402-03, 405-07, 409-10

Maitreyi (Eliade)   19:145

"The Maja" (Nin)   60:276

"Majestic" (Johnston)   51:249

"The Majesty of the Law" (O'Connor)   14:398, 400; 23:331-33

"al- Majnuna" ("The Mad One") (Mahfuz)   55:176

The Major (Hughes)   48:182, 184

The Major and the Minor (Wilder)   20:455

Major André, Brave Enemy (Duncan)   26:102

Major Dundee (Peckinpah)   20:273, 279, 283-84

"Major Hoople" (Coles)   46:112

"The Major of Hussars" (Bates)   46:60

"Major Pugachov's Last Battle" (Shalamov)   18:479-80

Makassar Reef (Buzo)   61:63-7

Makbara (Goytisolo)   23:188-89

Make and Break (Frayn)   31:191-93

"Make Believe Ballroom Time" (Strand)   71:282

Make Death Love Me (Rendell)   28:386

"Make It New" (Pound)   7:327

"Make Me Wanna Holler" (Gaye)
   See "Inner City Blues"

Make No Sounds (Corcoran)   17:77

"Make Room for Me" (Sturgeon)   39:363

Make Room! Make Room! (Harrison)   42:205-06

"Make the Old Man Sing" (Shapcott)   38:404

"Make Up" (Reed)   21:305

"Make Way" (Lightfoot)   26:282

"The Make-Believe Dance Hall" (Purdy)   10:424

"The Maker" (Borges)
   See "El hacedor"

"The Maker" (Wright)   53:428

The Maker (Borges)
   See *El hacedor*

"The Makers" (Nemerov)   36:307-08

Makers and Finders (Brooks)   29:85, 87-9

Makes Me Wanna Holler: A Young Black Man in America (McCall)   86:73-81

"Makin' Thunderbirds" (Seger)   35:386-87

"Making a Break" (Thesen) **56**:423
"Making a Movie" (Richler) **46**:351-52
"Making a Sacher Torte" (Wakoski) **40**:456
Making a TV Play (Taylor) **27**:441
"Making Amends" (Packer) **65**:350
Making Certain It Goes On (Hugo) **32**:250-51
"Making Change" (Busch) **47**:63
"Making Changes" (Michaels) **25**:317
Making Do (Goodman) **4**:197
"Making Good with Mother" (Ferber) **93**:136
Making History (Friel) **115**:237, 239, 243-46, 248-50
"Making, Knowing, and Judging" (Auden) **4**:34; **6**:16
"Making Much of Orioles" (Davison) **28**:103
The Making of a Martyr (Warren) **59**:296
"The Making of a New Zealander" (Sargeson) **31**:363-64, 370
The Making of Ashenden (Elkin) **6**:169; **27**:122, 125
"The Making of *The Black Book*" (Morrison) **87**:278
"The Making of the Book" (Fisher) **25**:160
The Making of the Popes, 1978 (Greeley) **28**:173-74
The Making of the Representative for Planet Eight (Lessing) **40**:302-06
"Making Peace" (Levertov) **66**:251
"Making Room" (Ammons) **57**:50
"Making Strange" (Heaney) **37**:169; **74**:168
"Making Tracks" (Grenville) **61**:152
Making Tracks (Ayckbourn) **33**:46, 50
"Making Tracks to Chittagong" (Theroux) **46**:402
"Making Up" (Boland) **67**:44; **113**:60, 63
"Making Up the Past" (Alvarez) **93**:17
"The Makings of a Music" (Heaney) **74**:178
The Makioka Sisters: A Tale of Disarrayed Chrysanthemums (Tanizaki)
   See *Sasame yuki*
Makom aher (*Elsewhere, Perhaps*) (Oz) **8**:436
Mal aimées (Kavan)
   See *Neige suivi de mal aimées*
Les mal aimés (Mauriac) **56**:215
Le mal court (*Evil Is Abroad*; *The Evil Runs*) (Audiberti) **38**:22-4, 26, 28-31
Mal vu mal dit (*Ill Seen Ill Said*) (Beckett) **29**:61-3, 65, 67; **59**:256
Mala apokalipsa (*A Minor Apocalypse*) (Konwicki) **28**:207-08, 211; **54**:254-63; **117**:264-65, 268, 271, 279-80, 283-84, 287-8, 292
La mala hora (*The Evil Hour*; *In Evil Hour*) (Garcia Marquez) **2**:148; **15**:253-54; **27**:147, 151, 155; **47**:153; **68**:153, 156
The Malacia Tapestry (Aldiss) **14**:14; **40**:14, 21
"Malacoda" (Beckett) **9**:80
Le maladie de la mort (*Malady*; *The Malady of Death*) (Duras) **68**:73-4, 79-80, 87, 90-1, 99
Malady (Duras)
   See *Le maladie de la mort*
The Malady of Death (Duras)
   See *Le maladie de la mort*
The Malady of the Ideal (Brooks) **29**:86
Malafrena (Le Guin) **22**:270, 274-75; **45**:214, 216, 221
Malatesta (Montherlant) **19**:327, 329
"Malatesta Cantos" (Pound) **10**:402; **13**:461
The Malayan Trilogy (*The Long Day Wanes: The Malayan Trilogy*) (Burgess) **2**:85; **4**:81-2; **5**:89; **13**:124; **22**:69, 73-4, 77-8;

40:113-14; **81**:301; **94**:56
Malcauchon; or, The Six in the Rain (Walcott) **9**:556; **25**:451
"Malcolm" (Sanchez) **116**:272, 274, 294
Malcolm (Albee) **5**:13; **9**:6; **13**:5; **25**:38; **113**:40
Malcolm (Purdy) **2**:347-50; **4**:422-24; **10**:422-24; **28**:376-78, 380-81; **52**:344, 347, 350-51
Malcolm Lowry's 'Volcano': Myth, Symbol, Meaning (Markson) **67**:190, 195
Malcolm Mooney's Land (Graham) **29**:196-98
"Malcolm Spoke/Who listened? (This Poem Is for My Consciousness Too)" (Madhubuti) **73**:199, 210
Malcolm X (Lee) **105**:104, 106, 109-10, 112-14, 127-29
Malcolm X Speaks: Selected Speeches and Statements (Malcolm X) **82**:173, 176, 188, 226; **117**:319
Malcolm X: The Last Speeches (Malcolm X) **82**:226-27
"Malcolm X: the Longed-for-Feminist-Manhood" (hooks) **94**:158
The Malcontents (Snow) **4**:503
"Maldrove" (Jeffers) **54**:235
Male and Female (Mead) **37**:273
The Male Animal (Thurber) **5**:432, 434-35, 442
Male Armor (Duberman) **8**:185
A Male Child (Scott) **60**:320
"The Male Prison" (Baldwin) **42**:21
El male rahamim (Amichai) **116**:100-05, 118
"A *Malebolge* of Fourteen Hundred Books" (Shapiro) **53**:329-30
"Malediction" (Spacks) **14**:511
"The Malediction" (Williams) **15**:580; **45**:447
The Malefactors (Gordon) **6**:203-04, 206; **29**:190; **83**:236, 241-42, 244, 246, 251, 258-60
"Malefic Things" (Seth) **90**:350
Malemort (Glissant) **10**:231; **68**:174-82, 187, 189
Malempin (Simenon) **47**:371
"Malenkii gigant bol'shogo seksa" ("A Sexy Little Giant") (Iskander) **47**:201
Le malentendu (*Cross Purpose*; *The Misunderstanding*) (Camus) **1**:52; **9**:141-42, 146; **11**:93; **14**:108, 115; **32**:84-8, 92-6, 99-101; **69**:136
"Malest Cornifici Tuo Catullo" (Ginsberg) **109**:358
Malgudi Days (Narayan) **28**:301-03; **47**:302
"Malheur County" (Le Guin) **45**:216-17
"The Malice of Objects" (Gerstler) **70**:157
Malina (Bachmann) **69**:35-6, 51-2, 54, 59-62
"Malinche" (Castellanos) **66**:45, 53
"La Malnou" (Theriault) **79**:410
Malone Dies (Beckett)
   See *Malone meurt*
Malone meurt (*Malone Dies*) (Beckett) **1**:23; **2**:44; **3**:45; **4**:52; **6**:37, 42-3; **9**:78, 80; **11**:33-4; **14**:71-3, 76; **18**:47, 50, 52; **29**:53, 55-7, 59, 65-7; **59**:253-54, 257
Malraux (Hartman) **27**:182
The Maltese Falcon (Hammett) **3**:219; **5**:162; **19**:193, 195-99; **47**:156-57, 161-64
The Maltese Falcon (Huston) **20**:157, 162, 165, 169, 172
Mama (McMillan) **50**:67-9; **61**:363-65; **112**:223, 226-27, 230, 234, 236-37, 239-40, 243, 247-49, 252
"Mama Come Home" (Tiptree) **48**:385

Mama Day (Naylor) **52**:324-27
Mama Grande's Funeral (Garcia Marquez)
   See *Los funerales de la Mamá Grande*
"Mamá guantes" (Ulibarri) **83**:416
"Mama Mercy" (Armatrading) **17**:8
The Mama Poems (Kenny) **87**:242, 245, 253-54, 258-59
"Mama Tuddi Done Over" (Rooke) **25**:394
Mama Turns 100 (Saura) **20**:322
Mamaji (Mehta) **37**:294
The Mambo Kings Play Songs of Love (Hijuelos) **65**:146-50
Maminka (*Mother*) (Seifert) **44**:427; **93**:307, 317, 335, 343, 345
Mamma Roma (Pasolini) **20**:259-60, 265; **37**:347; **106**:206-08, 221-22, 226, 253, 273
Mammonart: A Study in Economic Interpretation (Sinclair) **63**:346
"Mammorial Stunzas for Aimee Simple McFarcin" (Birney) **6**:71, 75
The Mammoth Hunters (Auel) **107**:4-5, 8-10, 14-15, 19-20, 24-25
"A Mammy Encomium" (Nolan) **58**:366
"The Man" (Bradbury) **10**:71; **42**:34
"A Man" (Bukowski) **108**:86
"The Man" (Clarke) **53**:91
"Man!" (MacLeish) **68**:270, 291
"The Man" (McCartney) **35**:291-92
"Man" (Roberts) **14**:463
"The Man" (Rulfo)
   See "El hombre"
"The Man" (White) **30**:451
A Man (Fallaci)
   See *Un uoma*
The Man (Wallace) **7**:509-10; **13**:567-69
"The Man Accursed" (Ali) **69**:31
"Man Alone" (Bogan) **46**:80, 83-4, 87; **93**:64
A Man and a Woman (Mull) **17**:299
"Man and Boy" (Heaney) **74**:188, 194
Man and Boy (Morris) **1**:232; **37**:310-11
Man and Boy (Rattigan) **7**:355
Man and God (Alonso)
   See *Hombre y Dios*
"A Man and His Little Sister" (Wiesel) **37**:450
The Man and His Times (Malcolm X) **117**:317
"A Man and His Wife" (Sargeson) **31**:364
"Man and Socialism in Cuba" (Guevara) **87**:201, 216
Man and Time (Priestley) **34**:365
"A Man and Two Women" (Lessing) **2**:239; **22**:278
A Man and Two Women (Lessing) **94**:261
"Man and Wife" (Lowell) **4**:297; **15**:343
"Man and Wife" (Sorrentino) **7**:449
Man as an End: A Defense of Humanism; Literary, Social, and Political Essays (Moravia) **46**:283
A Man Asleep (Perec)
   See *Un homme qui dort*
"The Man beneath the Tree" (Wright) **53**:420
"The Man Born to Farming" (Berry) **46**:73
"Man Bring This Up Road" (Williams) **45**:446, 453, 455
"Man Can Face the Truth" (Bachmann) **69**:42
"Man Coming of Age" (Warren) **13**:573
"Man Descending" (Vanderhaeghe) **41**:448-49, 451-52
Man Descending (Vanderhaeghe) **41**:448-53
The Man Died: Prison Notes of Wole Soyinka (Soyinka) **3**:463; **5**:397; **44**:284-85
"Man Does, Woman Is" (Graves) **45**:172
Man Does, Woman Is (Graves) **11**:256

"The Man Doors Said Hello To" (Tiptree) 48:385-86

"Man Dying on a Cross" (Scott) 43:370

A Man Escaped (Bresson) 16:115, 117

The Man Everybody Was Afraid Of (Hansen) 38:237-38

A Man for All Seasons (Bolt) 14:88-90

"Man Friday" (Hope) 51:217, 221, 224, 226

"A Man from Benin" (Transtroemer) 52:410; 65:222, 227

The Man from Everywhere (Simenon) 47:372

"The Man from Mars" (Atwood) 13:46; 84:70

The Man from Monticello: An Intimate Life of Thomas Jefferson (Fleming) 37:123

"The Man from P.I.G." (Harrison) 42:203

"The Man from R.O.B.O.T." (Harrison) 42:203

The Man from the Broken Hills (L'Amour) 25:281

"Man from the South" (Dahl) 79:189

"Man Gave Names to All the Animals" (Dylan) 77:184, 186

"Man, God Ain't Like That" (Wright) 21:438-39

Man Hunt (Lang) 20:207; 103:88

"The Man I Killed" (O'Brien) 103:139, 142-43

"A Man I Knew" (Klappert) 57:256, 259-60

A Man in a Mirror (Llewellyn) 80:196

"A Man in Assynt" (MacCaig) 36:284, 286

"Man in Black" (Plath) 9:425; 14:423

"The Man in Bogotá" (Hempel) 39:68

A Man in Charge (Philipson) 53:275

"A Man in Louisiana" (McGuane) 45:266

A Man in My Position (MacCaig) 36:284, 286

Man in Space to the Moon (Branley) 21:19

The Man in the Black Coat Turns (Bly) 38:53-60

"The Man in the Brooks Brothers Shirt" (McCarthy) 3:329

The Man in the Brooks Brothers Shirt (McCarthy) 59:290

The Man in the Brown Suit (Christie) 12:113-14

The Man in the Cage (Vance) 35:427

"Man in the Cellar" (O'Faolain) 108:407, 413

Man in the Cellar (O'Faolain) 6:382-83; 47:330

A Man in the Divided Sea (Merton) 83:390

"Man in the Drawer" (Malamud) 3:323

The Man in the Glass Booth (Shaw) 5:390-91

The Man in the Gray Flannel Suit (Wilson) 32:444-49

The Man in the Gray Flannel Suit II (Wilson) 32:449

The Man in the Gray Flannel Suit Twenty Years Before and After (Wilson) 32:448

The Man in the High Castle (Dick) 30:117, 121-22, 125, 127; 72:105, 107, 117-22

Man in the Holocene (Frisch)
See *Der Mensch erscheint im Holozän*

"A Man in the House" (Colter) 58:140, 146-47

"The Man in the Manmade Moon" (Kennedy) 42:254

The Man in the Middle (Wagoner) 3:507; 5:473-74; 15:558

"The Man in the Mirror" (Strand) 18:516, 518; 41:437; 71:283-84

"A Man in the Moon" (MacDiarmid) 19:286-87

"The Man in the Overstuffed Chair" (Williams) 45:455-56

"The Man in the Toolhouse" (Swados) 5:420

"The Man in the Tree" (Strand) 18:515; 71:284

"The Man in the Wind" (Stevenson) 33:382

The Man in the Yellow Boots (Bowering) 15:82

The Man in the Yellow Raft (Forester) 35:172, 174

A Man in the Zoo (Garnett) 3:188

Man Is an Onion (Enright) 4:156

"Man Is—Nothing Is—No One" (Haavikko)
See "Mies ei—Mitään, ei—Kukaan"

A Man Lay Dead (Marsh) 7:210; 53:247-48, 252

Man Lying on a Wall (Longley) 29:294, 296

A Man Made of Smoke (Middleton) 38:331

"The Man Made of Words" (Momaday) 85:274; 95:260, 262

"Man Must Live" (Mphahlele) 25:336, 341

Man Must Live (Mphahlele) 25:336, 338, 342

Man Must Speak: The Story of Language and How We Use It (Gallant) 17:128

The Man Named East, and Other New Poems (Redgrove) 41:358-59

"A Man Needs a Maid" (Young) 17:570, 578

"Man of All Work" (Wright) 21:438-39

"A Man of Destiny" (Castellanos) 66:56

Man of England Now (Sargeson) 31:366-67

A Man of Honour (Maugham) 1:204; 11:368

"Man of Letters" (Dixon) 52:97

A Man of Letters (Pritchett) 41:335-36

"The Man of Letters in the Modern World" (Tate) 24:443, 445

A Man of Little Evils (Dobyns) 37:75

Man of Marble (Wajda) 16:583-84

"Man of My Time" (Quasimodo) 10:428

Man of Nazareth (Burgess) 13:126; 22:78; 40:125

A Man of Power (Colegate) 36:308, 113-14

"The Man of Sentiment" (Slessor) 14:495

The Man of Slow Feeling: Selected Short Stories (Wilding) 73:396

Man of Steel: Joseph Stalin (Archer) 12:15

Man of the Moment (Ayckbourn) 74:18-20, 27-9, 34-5

Man of the Monitor: The Story of John Ericsson (Latham) 12:323

A Man of the People (Achebe) 1:1-2; 3:1-3; 5:1, 3; 7:3, 5-6; 11:1, 3; 26:13, 15- 20, 25, 27; 51:3, 6-7, 9; 75:3-4, 6-8, 12, 14, 16, 18-26

"A Man of the Thirties" (Grigson) 7:135

Man of Two Worlds (Herbert) 44:392

Man of Words/Man of Music (Bowie) 17:58, 64, 67

Man Off Beat (Hughes) 48:181

Man on a Tightrope (Kazan) 16:361

The Man on All Fours (Derleth) 31:127

"The Man on His Death Bed" (Aleixandre) 36:28

The Man on the Balcony (Wahloo)
See *Mannen på balkongen*

The Man on the Horse (Baxter) 14:63

"Man on the Moon" (Ortiz) 45:304, 309

"Man on the Pink Corner" (Borges)
See "Hombre de la esquina rosada"

The Man on the Rock (King) 53:205

"The Man on the Train: Three Existential Modes" (Percy) 14:416; 65:260

Man Plus (Pohl) 18:410, 412

"The Man Seeking Experience Enquires His Way of a Drop of Water" (Hughes) 14:270

"The Man She Loved" (Simpson) 32:377

Man Should Rejoice (MacLennan) 92:306,

308

Man Shy (Davison) 15:170

The Man Sitting in the Corridor (Duras) 100:130-31

"Man Smoking a Cigarette in the Barcelona Métro" (Durcan) 43:118

"Man Spricht Deutsch" (Enzensberger) 43:145-46

"Man the Master" (Merton) 83:397

Man the Measurer: Our Units of Measure and How They Grew (Gallant) 17:129

"Man Thinks, God Laughs" (Kundera) 115:350

A Man to Conjure With (Baumbach) 6:32; 23:53-4

A Man to Marry, A Man to Bury (Musgrave) 54:333-34, 340

"The Man to Send Rainclouds" (Silko) 23:408; 74:347; 114:316

"A Man Told Me the Story of His Life" (Paley) 37:339

"Man Track Here" (Derleth) 31:131, 133

"The Man under the Bed" (Jong) 6:268; 83:291

"A Man Walks beneath the Moon" (Neruda)
See "Un hombre anda bajo la luna"

"Man We Was Lonely" (McCartney) 35:278-79

"A Man Whistling" (Simmons) 43:411

"The Man Who Became Afraid" (Wesker) 3:519; 5:483-84

"The Man Who Blew Away" (Bainbridge) 62:34, 37

"The Man Who Brought Happiness" (Federspiel) 42:146

"The Man Who Came Back" (Singer) 111:314

The Man Who Came to Dinner (Hart and Kaufman) 38:262,265; 66:174-76, 178, 182-87, 190-91

The Man Who Cried I Am (Williams) 5:496-98; 13:598-99

The Man Who Dared the Lightning: A New Look at Benjamin Franklin (Fleming) 37:125

"The Man Who Didn't Eat Food" (Ulibarri) 83:418

The Man Who Died at Twelve O'Clock (Green) 25:193

The Man Who Fell to Earth (Bowie) 17:68

The Man Who Fell to Earth (Tevis) 42:370-72, 374

"The Man Who Gave Up His Name" (Harrison) 14:236-37; 66:154-55, 159, 161

The Man Who Got Away (Elliott) 38:179-80

"The Man Who Grew Younger" (Charyn) 5:104

The Man Who Grew Younger, and Other Stories (Charyn) 5:103

The Man Who Had All the Luck (Miller) 1:216, 218

The Man Who Had No Idea (Disch) 36:127

The Man Who Had Three Arms (Albee) 25:40; 53:18-21, 24-6; 86:118, 120-21, 124-25; 113:40-1

"The Man Who Invented Pain" (Raine) 32:353; 103:186, 189-90

"The Man Who Invented Sin" (O'Faolain) 1:259; 32:343-44; 70:313, 318

The Man Who Invented Sin (O'Faolain)
See *Teresa, and Other Stories*

The Man Who Invented Tomorrow (Hughes) 48:182, 184, 186

"The Man Who Killed a Shadow" (Wright) 9:585; 21:439

The Man Who Killed Himself (Symons) 2:426; 14:523; 32:424

The Man Who Killed His Brother (Donaldson)

46:140

The Man Who Killed the Deer (Waters) **88**:330, 334-37, 342-43, 345, 347, 349-52, 354-56, 358, 361-63

"The Man Who Knew Belle Starr" (Bausch) **51**:56-7

The Man Who Knew Kennedy (Bourjaily) **62**:96-9

The Man Who Knew Too Much (Hitchcock) **16**:342, 345

The Man Who Left His Will on Film (Oshima) **20**:249, 254

The Man Who Lived Alone (Hall) **37**:148-49

The Man Who Lived His Life Over Again (Lagerkvist)
   See *Han som fik leva om sitt liv*

"The Man Who Lived Underground" (Wright) **9**:585; **14**:597; **21**:438-40, 443, 445-46, 449; **74**:380

"The Man Who Lost His Memory Twice" (Mahfuz) **52**:292

The Man Who Lost His Wife (Symons) **14**:524

The Man Who Loved Children (Stead) **2**:420-23; **5**:403-05; **8**:499-500; **32**:408-09, 411-12, 414-18; **80**:305, 307, 309-10, 319, 322, 324-26, 331-34, 336, 339-42, 348-51, 353

"The Man Who Loved the Nereids" (Yourcenar) **38**:463

The Man Who Loved Women (Truffaut) **20**:404-05, 407; **101**:407, 411-13

"The Man Who Loves Hegel" (Dunn) **36**:154

"The Man Who Married Magdalene" (Hecht) **8**:268

The Man Who Mistook His Wife for a Hat, and Other Clinical Tales (Sacks) **67**:298-302, 304

"The Man Who Never Loses His Balance" (Dunn) **36**:153

The Man Who Risked His Partner (Donaldson) **46**:143

"The Man Who Saw the Flood" (Wright) **9**:585; **14**:598

The Man Who Shook Hands (Wakoski) **11**:564; **40**:455

The Man Who Shot Liberty Valance (Ford) **16**:308-11, 315, 319-20

The Man Who Shot the Albatross (Lawler) **58**:333

"The Man Who Sold the Moon" (Heinlein) **3**:224

The Man Who Sold the World (Bowie) **17**:57-9, 61-2, 64, 67

"The Man Who Studied Yoga" (Mailer) **3**:315; **4**:319; **74**:224; **111**:135-36

"The Man Who Turned into a Statue" (Oates) **6**:370

The Man Who Turned into a Stick (Abe)
   See *Bo ni natta otako*

"The Man Who Walked Home" (Tiptree) **48**:386; **50**:357

"The Man Who Was Almos' a Man" (Wright) **9**:585; **21**:438

The Man Who Was Given His Life to Live Again (Lagerkvist)
   See *Han som fik leva om sitt liv*

"The Man Who Was Heavily into Revenge" (Ellison) **42**:129

"The Man Who Was Left Behind" (Ingalls) **42**:230

The Man Who Was Left Behind, and Other Stories (Ingalls) **42**:230-31

The Man Who Was Not with It (Gold) **4**:189,
191; **42**:191, 195

The Man Who Was There (Morris) **1**:232; **37**:311

The Man Who Wasn't There (Barker) **94**:3

The Man Who Watched the Trains Go By (Simenon) **1**:309

"The Man Who Went to Chicago" (Wright) **3**:545

The Man Who Went Up in Smoke (Wahloo)
   See *Mannen som gick upp i rök*

The Man Who Won the Pools (Stewart) **7**:464

The Man Who Would Be King (Huston) **20**:173

"The Man Who Would Never Write Like Balzac" (Wesker) **42**:426

The Man Who Would Not Come Back **59**:395

"The Man Who Would Not Die" (Davidson) **13**:169

"The Man Who Wrote Books in His Head" (Highsmith) **14**:261; **102**:192

The Man Whose Dreams Come True (Symons) **2**:426; **14**:523

Man with a Bull-Tongue Plow (Stuart) **8**:507; **11**:509; **14**:513; **34**:373-74, 376

"Man with a Family" (Humphrey) **45**:193

"A Man with a Field" (Watkins) **43**:452

Man with a Sling (Neruda)
   See *El hondero entusiasta, 1923-1924*

Man with Bags (Ionesco)
   See *L'homme aux valises*

"The Man with Clam Eyes" (Thomas) **107**:333

"The Man with Night Sweats" (Gunn) **81**:178, 186

The Man with Night Sweats (Gunn) **81**:176-89

"Man with One Small Hand" (Page) **7**:291

The Man with Red Suspenders (Dacey) **51**:82-3

The Man with Seven Toes (Ondaatje) **14**:408; **29**:341; **51**:310-11, 316

The Man with the Coat (Callaghan) **65**:246-47

"The Man with the Dog" (Jhabvala) **4**:259; **94**:184

The Man with the Golden Arm (Algren) **4**:16; **10**:6; **33**:12-17

The Man with the Golden Gun (Fleming) **30**:137-39, 143-44, 148, 150

"The Man with the Knives" (Boell)
   See "Der Mann mit den Messern"

"The Man with Three Violins" (MacEwen) **55**:164

The Man with Two Brains (Martin) **30**:251-52

The Man Within (Greene) **3**:211; **18**:193-94; **27**:175; **70**:291, 293; **72**:148-50, 177

The Man without a Face (Holland) **21**:148, 150-53

"Man without a Fig Leaf" (Garrett) **51**:147

Man without a Shadow (Wilson)
   See *The Sex Diary of Gerard Sorme*

The Man without a Soul (Lagerkvist)
   See *Mannen utan själ*

"A Man Writes to a Part of Himself" (Bly) **10**:57; **38**:58, 60

"The Management of Grief" (Mukherjee) **53**:272; **115**:366

El manana efímero (Goytisolo) **23**:186

Mañana los guerreros (*Tomorrow the Warriors*) (Alegria) **57**:10-11

"Las Mañanitas" (Fuentes) **113**:257-58

Manassas: A Novel of the War (Sinclair) **63**:345-46, 348, 350, 366

Manchild in the Promised Land (Brown) **30**:33-41

"Manchouli" (Empson) **33**:142

The Manchurian Candidate (Condon) **4**:105-
07; **6**:115; **8**:150; **45**:92, 96, 99, 101-02, 104; **100**:91, 94, 97-100, 102-07, 110-12

Mandabi (*Le Mandat*; *The Money Order*) (Ousmane) **66**:334-36, 338, 340-42

"Mandala" (Merrill) **2**:275

Mandala (Buck) **7**:33

Les mandarins (*The Mandarins*) (Beauvoir) **2**:43; **4**:47-8; **8**:60-1; **14**:68; **31**:34, 38-9, 41-2; **44**:342-43, 345-46, 350; **50**:390; **71**:48-52, 54-6, 67-8, 70, 72, 74-5

The Mandarins (Beauvoir)
   See *Les mandarins*

Le Mandat (Ousmane)
   See *Mandabi*

The Mandelbaum Gate (Spark) **2**:416-18; **3**:463-67; **5**:400; **8**:495; **18**:502-03, 505; **40**:393, 400; **94**:333, 339

"Mandolin" (Dove) **50**:153, 155

"Mandorla" (Celan) **53**:70

The Man-Eater of Malgudi (Narayan) **28**:296-99; **47**:304, 308

Le manège espagnol (*Through the Hoop*) (del Castillo) **38**:166-67

Man'en gan'nen no futtoboru (*The Football Game of the First Year of Manen*; *A Game of Football*; *The Silent Cry*) (Oe) **10**:374; **36**:346; **86**:219, 225-26, 230, 232, 234, 241-42, 244

"A maneria de Olegário Mariano" ("Like O. M."; "Like Olegário Mariano") (Cabral de Melo Neto) **76**:163

The Maneuver (Adamov)
   See *La grande et la petite manoeuvre*

"Man-Fate" (Everson) **5**:123; **14**:166

Man-Fate: The Swan Song of Brother Antoninus (Everson) **5**:122

The Mangan Inheritance (Moore) **19**:332-35; **32**:310, 312-13; **90**:243, 247, 249-51, 254-5, 257, 260-61, 272-3, 277, 281, 289, 296, 305

"The Mangler" (King) **12**:311

"The Mango Community" (Jacobsen) **48**:196, 198; **102**:242

"Mango Says Goodbye Sometimes" (Cisneros) **69**:148

"Mango Seedling" (Achebe) **11**:4; **26**:21

Mango Street (Cisneros)
   See *The House On Mango Street*

Manhattan (Allen) **16**:11-14, 18; **52**:39-41, 46-9

"Manhattan Island" (Stafford) **4**:517

Manhattan Made Me (Edwards) **43**:141

"Manhattan May Day Midnight" (Ginsberg) **109**:364

Manhattan Pastures (Hochman) **3**:250

Manhattan Transfer (Dos Passos) **1**:77-9; **4**:131-32, 137-38; **11**:152, 154; **15**:183-85; **25**:137-38, 141-42, 145-47; **34**:419-24; **82**:61-2, 65-6, 68, 70, 73-4, 76, 86, 88, 102, 104-06

"Manhole Covers" (Shapiro) **15**:478

"Manhole Sixty-Nine" (Ballard) **36**:41

"Manhood" (Wain) **46**:415

Manhood: A Journey from Childhood into the Fierce Order of Virility (Leiris)
   See *L'age d'homme*

Manhood in the Making: Cultural Concepts of Masculinity (Gilmore) **70**:425, 431

"Manhunt" (Carpentier) **11**:104

A Mania for Sentences (Enright) **31**:155-56

"Manic and Depressive" (Matthews) **40**:325

"Manichean Geography" (Paulin) **37**:354

"The Manicheans" (Burgess)   94:
Manifest Manners (Vizenor)   103:337-40
"The Manifestation" (Roethke)   3:433
Manifeste dada (Tzara)   47:393
Manifeste du surréalisme. Poisson soluble (*Manifesto of Surrealism; Soluble Fish; Surrealist Manifesto*) (Breton)   54:16, 19-21, 33
"Manifesto" (Ewart)   13:208
"Manifesto" (Monette)   82:322-23, 332-33
"Manifesto" (Otero)   11:427
"Manifesto" (Parra)   102:348-49, 352-53
Manifesto of Surrealism (Breton)
    See *Manifeste du surréalisme. Poisson soluble*
"Manifesto: The Mad Farmer Liberation Front" (Berry)   6:61
Manifestoes of Surrealism (Breton)   54:15-16
"The Manipulator" (Bell)   31:46
La manivelle (Pinget)   13:442
"Mankiewitz Won't Be Bowling Tuesday Nights Anymore" (Kinsella)   27:237-38
"Mankind Journeys Through Forests of Symbols" (Chappell)   78:117
The Mankind Thing (Shapcott)   38:398, 400
"Manley Buckminster" (Avison)   97:128
"The Man-Moth" (Bishop)   1:34; 9:98; 32:33, 37-8, 43
"Der Mann mit den Messern" ("The Knife Thrower"; "The Man with the Knives") (Boell)   11:58; 27:66-7; 72:69, 76
Mannen på balkongen (*The Man on the Balcony*) (Wahloo)   7:501
Mannen som gick upp i rök (*The Man Who Went Up in Smoke*) (Wahloo)   7:501-02
Mannen utan själ (*The Man without a Soul*) (Lagerkvist)   54:269-70, 272, 275, 278
"Le mannequin" (Robbe-Grillet)   4:449
Männer Sache (*Men's Business; Through the Leaves*) (Kroetz)   41:234, 238, 240
"Manners" (Bishop)   32:39
"Manners" (Peterkin)   31:308
"Manners, Morals, and the Novel" (Trilling)   9:531; 24:450, 461
Människor (*People*) (Lagerkvist)   54:273, 286
Manny and Rose (Peters)   39:91-3
"La mano" (Aleixandre)   36:26
"Mano entregada" (Aleixandre)   9:12
"Mano rubato" (Landolfi)   49:214
The Manor (Singer)   1:313; 3:455-56; 9:488; 11:501; 15:505; 23:415-16
"The Manor Garden" (Plath)   14:425; 111:164, 179, 203
Las manos del día (*The Hands of Day*) (Neruda)   7:261; 7:261; 28:315
"Manos Karastefanís" (Merrill)   13:376
A Man's Blessing (Sciascia)
    See *A ciascuno il suo*
A Man's Blessing (Sciascia)
    See *A ciascuno il suo*
A Man's Estate (Humphreys)   47:179-80, 185-88
"Man's Fate" (Dubus)   97:201
Man's Fate (Malraux)
    See *La condition humaine*
"Man's Fulfillment in Order and Strife" (Duncan)   41:130
Man's Hope (Malraux)
    See *L'espoir*
Man's Life Is This Meat (Gascoyne)   45:148, 153, 157
A Man's Place (Ernaux)
    See *La place*

A Man's Place (Sender)   8:481
"Man's Power over Things" (Kunene)   85:165, 178
Man's Reach for the Stars (Gallant)   17:128-29
Man's Reach into Space (Gallant)   17:127-28
A Man's Road (Sillanpaa)
    See *Miehen tie*
Man's Search for Meaning: An Introduction to Logotherapy (Frankl)
    See *Ein psycholog erlebt das konzentrationslager*
"Manscape" (Tomlinson)   6:534-35
Manseed (Williamson)   29:461
Manservant and Maidservant (*Bullivant and the Lambs*) (Compton-Burnett)   1:60; 15:137, 139, 141-42; 34:496, 500, 502
"Mansion" (Ammons)   108:21
The Mansion (Faulkner)   3:151, 156; 14:178-79; 18:149; 28:145; 68:121
The Manticore (Davies)   2:113; 7:72-4; 13:173-74; 25:129, 131, 133, 136; 42:102, 105-07, 109; 75:180, 184, 190, 192, 199, 215-16, 224; 91:198, 201, 203, 204
Mantissa (Fowles)   33:171-73, 175; 87:149, 159, 162-67, 179-80
"The Mantle of Whistler" (Parker)   68:336
Manual de morala practica (*A Handbook of Practical Morality*) (Arghezi)   80:12
A Manual for Manuel (Cortazar)
    See *Libro de Manuel*
"Manual for Sons" (Barthelme)   8:51-52; 23:47, 49; 115:64
Manual Labor (Busch)   7:38-9; 10:91-3
A Manual of Instruction in Military Maps and Aerial Photographs (Maclean)   78:244
"Manual System" (Sandburg)   35:340
Manuale minimo dell'Attore (Fo)   109:113, 119, 131, 135
Manuel de déification (Romains)   7:381
"Manuela em dia de chuva" (Dourado)   23:151
"Manuelzinho" (Bishop)   13:89; 32:37-8, 42
"Manuscript Found in a Pocket" (Cortazar)
    See "Manuscrito hallado en un bolsillo"
"Manuscript Found under a Mattress in a Hotel Room" (Rudnik)   7:384
The Manuscripts of Pauline Archange (Blais)   2:63; 4:67; 6:80-2; 22:58
"Manuscrito hallado en un bolsillo" ("Manuscript Found in a Pocket") (Cortazar)   33:124
"Many Are Disappointed" (Pritchett)   41:332
"Many as Two" (Avison)   4:37; 97:92
The Many Colored Coat (Callaghan)   14:102-03; 41:89-90; 65:247-49, 252
"Many famous feet have trod" (Larkin)   64:259
"Many Happy Returns" (Paterson)   30:283
Many Happy Returns (Berrigan)   37:43-4
Many Long Years Ago (Nash)   23:320
"Many Loves" (Ginsberg)   36:198; 109:357
"The Many Mansions" (Levertov)   66:245
"Many Mansions" (Roth)   104:284
Many Moons (Thurber)   5:430, 438, 442; 25:437
"Many of Our Waters: Variations on a Poem by a Black Child" (Wright)   10:544
"Many Problems" (Tate)   25:428
"Many Rivers to Cross" (Cliff)   21:61, 63-4
"Many Rivers to Cross" (Jordan)   114:153
"Many Senses: Mexico City" (Moss)   45:287
Many Smokes, Many Moons: A Chronology of American Indian History through Indian Art (Highwater)   12:288
"Many Things of Death" (Salinas)   90:326,

330, 331
Many Thousand Gone: An American Fable (Fair)   18:140, 142
"Many Thousands Gone" (Baldwin)   42:16; 67:5
"Many Wagons Ago" (Ashbery)   15:36
"Many without Elegy" (Graham)   29:193
The Many Worlds of Magnus Ridolph (Vance)   35:422
"Manyone Flying" (Swenson)   106:344, 346
A Many-Windowed House (Cowley)   39:461
The Manzoni Family (Ginzburg)
    See *La famiglia Manzoni*
Mao II (DeLillo)   76:170-87
Mao Tse-Tung (Archer)   12:18-21
Maori Girl (Hilliard)   15:279
Maori Woman (Hilliard)   15:279
"The Map" (Bishop)   9:89, 93, 97; 32:29, 32, 37, 43, 45
"Map" (Enright)   31:150
"The Map" (Strand)   18:516
"The Map of Harlem" (Dumas)   62:159
A Map of Misreading (Bloom)   24:74-5, 79, 81; 103:2-4, 6, 12, 14, 20, 23-4, 26-7, 32-3, 41, 44, 46, 53-4
"A Map of Skye" (Hugo)   32:244
"Map of the Antilles" (Walcott)   76:279-80
"A Map of the City" (Gunn)   18:203
A Map of the New Country: Women and Christianity (Maitland)   49:231-32
"A Map of the Small Town" (Cassity)   42:95
"A Map of the Western Part of the County of Essex in England" (Levertov)   5:246
A Map of the World (Hare)   29:219-22; 58:230, 233
"Map to the Treasure" (Nyro)   17:313, 316, 318
"Maple" (Frost)   9:219
Mapmakers (Brink)   36:68-9; 106:109, 119-20
"Mappemonde" (Levertov)   66:241
"Mappemounde" (Birney)   6:72, 76, 78
"The Mapping of the Currents" (Olson)   28:343
"Maps" (Reaney)   13:473
Maps (Farah)   53:140
Maps (Olson)   28:342-43
Maps of Another Town: A Memoir of Provence (Fisher)   76:335
Maquettes (Warner)   14:552
"Mar del paraíso" (Aleixandre)   9:16
"El mar del tiempo perdido" ("The Sea of Lost Time") (Garcia Marquez)   15:254; 27:148
"O mar e o canavial" ("The Sea and the Canefield") (Cabral de Melo Neto)   76:168
"Mar en la tierra" (Aleixandre)   9:14
Mar morto (*Sea of Death; Sea of the Dead*) (Amado)   13:11; 40:26-7, 36; 106:58-60, 63
"Mar y aurora" (Aleixandre)   9:12, 15
El mar y las campanas (*The Sea and the Bells*) (Neruda)   7:261; 28:310-11; 62:333, 335-36
"Mar y noche" ("Sea and Night") (Aleixandre)   9:15
El mar y sus pescaditos (Castellanos)   66:54
"Mara" (Jeffers)   11:307
"Marat Dead" (Tomlinson)   13:550; 45:401
Marat/Sade (Weiss)   3:513-15; 15:563, 565-69; 51:386, 388, 391, 393-97
"Maratea Porto: The Dear Postmistress There" (Hugo)   32:235
"Marathon" (Gluck)   44:216-17, 219-21, 223-24

Marathon Man (Goldman) **48**:126-28, 131
"The Marauder" (Johnston) **51**:254
al- Maraya (*Mirrors*) (Mahfuz) **52**:299, 302
The Marble Faun (Faulkner) **9**:201; **68**:127
Marbles (Brodsky) **100**:58
Marbot: A Biography (Hildesheimer)
    See *Marbot: Eine Biographie*
Marbot: Eine Biographie (*Marbot: A Biography*) (Hildesheimer) **49**:173, 175-79
Marbre (Mandiargues) **41**:278-79
"Marburg" (Pasternak) **18**:382
Marcel Duchamp: Appearance Stripped Bare (Paz)
    See *Marcel Duchamp o el castillo de la castillo de la pureza*
Marcel Duchamp o el castillo de la castillo de la pureza (*Marcel Duchamp: Appearance Stripped Bare*; *Marcel Duchamp, or The Castle of Purity*) (Paz) **3**:375; **19**:365; **65**:176
Marcel Duchamp, or The Castle of Purity (Paz)
    See *Marcel Duchamp o el castillo de la castillo de la pureza*
"Marcella" (Wilson) **12**:650
"The March" (Blaise) **29**:70-1
"The March" (Lowell) **3**:302
"March" (MacLeish) **68**:286
"March" (Pasternak) **63**:305, 313
"March 1, 1847. By the First Post" (Boland) **113**:110
"March 21" (Daryush) **19**:120
"A March Calf" (Hughes) **37**:180
"march eight/1979" (Young Bear) **94**:363
"March Evening" (Martinson) **14**:357
The March Hare (White) **49**:403
"March Moon" (Hughes) **108**:330
"March Morning" (Ciardi) **40**:157
"March Morning Unlike Others" (Hughes) **37**:175
"A March on Washington" (Squires) **51**:381
"The March Past" (Larkin) **64**:262
"March Snow" (Berry) **4**:59
"March Snow" **108**:20
March to the Monteria (Traven) **8**:522
Le marchand de regrets (*The Merchant of Regrets*) (Crommelynck) **75**:152, 168
Marchbanks' Almanack (Davies)
    See *Samuel Marchbanks' Almanack*
"Marche" (Soupault) **68**:405
"Marche" ("Walk") (Tchicaya) **101**:350
"Marche Funèbre" (Seifert) **93**:337
Les marches de sable (Chedid) **47**:82
"Les marchés du temple" (Mandiargues) **41**:279
"Marching" (Simic) **22**:380
Marching Blacks: An Interpretive History of the Rise of the Black Common Man (Powell) **89**:202, 204-06
The Marchington Inheritance (Holland) **21**:153
The Marchioness of Loria (Donoso)
    See *La misteriosa desaparición de la Marquesita de Loria*
"Marco Polo" (Slessor) **14**:492
Marco Polo, If You Can (Buckley) **37**:60-1
Marco Polo Sings a Solo (Guare) **8**:253; **29**:204-05; **67**:79
"Marcovaldo at the Supermarket" (Calvino) **33**:100; **73**:34
Marcovaldo: or, The Seasons in the City (Calvino)
    See *Marcovaldo ouvero le stagioni in citta*
Marcovaldo ouvero le stagioni in citta (*Marcovaldo: or, The Seasons in the City*) (Calvino) **8**:127; **11**:91-2; **33**:99-100;

39:306-07, 310-11; **73**:33-4, 42, 46
"The Mare" (Watkins) **43**:451-52, 454
Il mare colore del vino (Sciascia) **9**:475
La marea (*The Tide*) (Gironella) **11**:234, 238
La marée du soir (Montherlant) **8**:394
"Mares escarlatas" (Cernuda) **54**:52
"Margaret Are You Grieving" (Durcan) **70**:152
Margaret Mead: Some Personal Views (Mead) **37**:282-83
"Margaret Thatcher Joins the IRA" (Durcan) **43**:115
"Marge" (Carruth) **84**:135
La marge (*The Margin*) (Mandiargues) **41**:275-77, 279
Marges de la philosophie (Derrida) **87**:72, 84, 89
The Margin (Mandiargues)
    See *La marge*
A Margin of Hope: An Intellectual Autobiography (Howe) **85**:132-35, 137, 139, 143-47, 155
The Marginal Farm (Buzo) **61**:70
"Marginal Notes in a Theology Text" (L'Heureux) **52**:273
"Marginalia" (Avison) **97**:93
"Marginalia" (Wilbur) **53**:412; **110**:357
"Margins" (Buckley) **57**:126
Margins (Booth) **23**:75-6
"Margrave" (Jeffers) **54**:248; **2**:212
"Marguerite" (Beauvoir) **31**:42
"Marguerite Landmine" (Kauffman) **65**:348
"Maria" (Sondheim) **30**:386
"María Concepción" (Porter) **7**:314; **13**:449; **101**:209-11
"Maria Giuseppa" (Landolfi) **49**:216
Maria Irene Fornes: Plays (*The Conduct of Life; The Danube; Mud; Sarita*) (Fornes) **39**:136-38; **61**:134-41
"Maria Minor" (Avison) **97**:71
Maria Neféli (*Maria Nephele*) (Elytis) **49**:108-15, 117-18; **100**:170, 172-73, 175, 192
Maria Nephele (Elytis)
    See *Maria Neféli*
"Maria Nephele's Song" (Elytis) **100**:173
"Maria Reiche: The Riddle of the Pampa" (Chatwin) **57**:153
Mariaagélas (*Mariaagelas: Maria, Daughter of Gelas*) (Maillet) **54**:303-04, 307, 310-11, 314, 318
Mariaagelas: Maria, Daughter of Gelas (Maillet)
    See *Mariaagélas*
Le mariage (Gombrowicz)
    See *Slub*
Mariamne (*Herod and Mariamne*) (Lagerkvist) **7**:200; **10**:312; **13**:333; **54**:288
Mariana o el alba (*Mariana, or the Dawn*) (Marques) **96**:241-43
Mariana, or the Dawn (Marques)
    See *Mariana o el alba*
"Marianne" (Celan) **10**:104
Marianne (Davies) **23**:146
A Marianne Moore Reader (Moore) **2**:291; **47**:267
Marianne Thornton, 1797-1887: A Domestic Biography (Forster) **4**:167; **77**:221
"Marie" (Jones) **76**:65
"Marie" (Kotzwinkle) **35**:253-54
"La Marie" (Theriault) **79**:410
Marie: A True Story (Maas) **29**:307-08
Marie and Bruce (Shawn) **41**:397-400, 402
Marie Blythe (Mosher) **62**:314-15
Marie Laveau (Prose) **45**:324, 326

"Marie, Marie, Hold On Tight" (Barthelme) **46**:40-1
La mariée etait en noir (*The Bride Wore Black*) (Truffaut) **20**:383-84, 387, 390; **101**:375, 377-81, 383, 386, 390
Les mariés de la Tour Eiffel (*The Wedding on the Eiffel Tower*) (Cocteau) **8**:146, 148; **15**:134; **43**:102, 105-06, 108-09
Marigolds (Zindel)
    See *The Effect of Gamma Rays on Man-in-the-Moon Marigolds*
Marigolds in August (Fugard) **25**:173
"Marihuana" (Woolrich) **77**:389-90, 396, 399
"Marijuana Notation" (Ginsberg) **109**:325
Marilyn (Steinem) **63**:385-88
Marilyn: A Biography (Mailer) **3**:315-20; **8**:372-73; **11**:344; **14**:351; **28**:259; **74**:205-06, 225, 227-28, 245; **111**:103, 114-15, 148
"Marilyn Miller" (Smith) **12**:535
Marilyn the Wild (Charyn) **8**:135-36
Marilyn's Daughter (Rechy) **107**:256, 258
"Marin" (Merwin) **88**:211
Le marin de Gibraltar (*The Sailor from Gibraltar*) (Duras) **6**:149-50; **11**:165; **40**:180-83; **68**:74, 79-80, 88, 98
"Marina" (Eliot) **9**:186-87, 189; **15**:210, 213, 217; **34**:529; **41**:148, 151; **55**:346, 374; **57**:206
"Marin-an" (Snyder) **32**:387
Marine (Clancy) **112**:86-7
"Marine Surface, Law Overcast" (Clampitt) **32**:114
Mariner Dances (Newby) **2**:311
Marinero en tierra (Alberti) **7**:8-9
"Mariner's Carol" (Merwin) **5**:285
Mariners, Renegades, and Castaways (James) **33**:222
"Mariposa" (Guillen) **79**:238
"Mariposa de obsidiana" ("Obsidian Butterfly") (Paz) **19**:366; **51**:327
"Marita" (Mason) **82**:255
"Marital Sonnets" (Simmons) **43**:408
Marjorie Morningstar (Wouk) **1**:376; **38**:444-47
"The Mark" (Bogan) **46**:77, 90; **93**:61, 90-1, 98
"The Mark" (Pancake) **29**:348, 350
Mark Coffin, U.S.S. (Drury) **37**:110
"Mark Ingestre: The Customer's Tale" (Aickman) **57**:4
Mark Lambert's Supper (Stewart) **7**:464
"The Mark of Apelles" (Pasternak)
    See "Il tratto di Apelle"
"The Mark of Cain" (Yevtushenko) **26**:462
The Mark of Conte (Levitin) **17**:265
The Mark of the Horse Lord (Sutcliff) **26**:433-36, 439-40
Mark of the Vampire (Browning) **16**:125-26
The Mark of the Warrior (Scott) **60**:340
"The Mark of Vishnu" (Singh) **11**:505
The Mark of Zorro (Mamoulian) **16**:425, 428
Mark Twain and Southwestern Humor (Lynn) **50**:426
The Mark Twain Murders (Yep) **35**:472-73
"Mark Van Doren and the Brook" (MacLeish) **8**:363
Marked by Fire (Thomas) **35**:405-07
"The Market" (Snyder) **32**:387, 399
"Market Day" (Buckley) **57**:131
"Market Day" (Hacker) **72**:192
"The Market Where the Rivers Go" (Cabral de Melo Neto)

See "O mercado a que os rios"
"Markings" (Heaney)   74:188
Marks of Identity (Goytisolo)
   See *Señas de identidad*
Marksizm i filosofija jazyka (*Marxism and the Philosophy of Language*) (Bakhtin)   83:3-7, 14, 16, 21, 25-6, 28-30, 33, 38, 45
Det märkvärdiga landet (*The Strange Country*) (Lagerkvist)   54:287
"The Marl Pits" (Tomlinson)   13:548
"The Marlboro Man" (Cisneros)   69:155
Marle (Chambers)   35:98
"Marlene American Horse" (Vizenor)   103:281
Marlenes Schwester: Zwei Erzählungen (Strauss)   22:407
"Marlin off the Moro" (Hemingway)   34:478
"The Marlon Brando Memorial Swimming Pool" (Alexie)   96:3, 12
"Marlon Brando, Pocahontas, and Me" (Young)
   See "Pocahontas"
The Marlow Chronicles (Sanders)   41:378
The Marmalade Bird (Sansom)   6:483
"Marmilion" (McGrath)   55:74, 76
The Marmot Drive (Hersey)   7:153; 40:227-28, 231, 239-40; 81:334; 97:302
Marnie (Graham)   23:193
Marnie (Hitchcock)   16:349-50, 353
"Maroon" (Dybek)   114:61, 67
"Marooned" (Keillor)   115:286
Marooned (Campbell)   32:80
"Marooned off Vesta" (Asimov)   76:313
The Marquis de Sade (Beauvoir)   14:66
Le marquis qui perdit (Ducharme)   74:63, 65-6
The Marquise Goes Out at Five (Mauriac)
   See *La Marquise sortit à cinq heures*
The Marquise of O (Rohmer)
   See *Die Marquise von O*
La Marquise sortit à cinq heures (*The Marquise Goes Out at Five*) (Mauriac)   9:363-66
"Die Marquise von O" (Pasternak)   18:385
Die Marquise von O (*The Marquise of O*) (Rohmer)   16:537-39
"Marrakesh" (Munro)   6:342; 10:357; 95:302, 304
"Marriage" (Aickman)   57:3
"Marriage" (Clarke)   9:168
"Marriage" (Corso)   11:124
"A Marriage" (Creeley)   36:118
"Marriage" (Ezekiel)   61:92, 94
"A Marriage" (Hoffman)   23:237
"A Marriage" (Lavin)   99:320
"Marriage" (Lowell)   11:331
"Marriage" (Moore)   4:362; 10:351; 13:393; 19:336, 340, 342-43; 47:260, 262
"Marriage" (Oates)   6:367
"The Marriage" (Strand)   18:518; 41:438; 71:283-84
"The Marriage" (Summers)   10:494
"Marriage" (Wilson)   49:413-15
Marriage (Feinstein)   36:170
The Marriage (Gombrowicz)
   See *Slub*
The Marriage Ceremony (Gombrowicz)
   See *Slub*
"The Marriage Feast" (Lagerkvist)   54:276-77
Marriage in Philippsburg (Walser)
   See *Die Ehen in Philippsburg*
"Marriage Is a Private Affair" (Achebe)   26:22; 75:13
"Marriage Is Belonging" (Porter)   101:241
Marriage Italian Style (De Sica)   20:97

"Marriage No Field of Daisies" (Royko)   109:407
The Marriage of Bette and Boo (Durang)   38:173-74
The Marriage of Cadmus and Harmony (Calasso)
   See *Le nozze di Cadmo e Armonia*
"A Marriage of Convenience" (Morrissy)   99:78
The Marriage of Maria Braun (Fassbinder)   20:118-19
The Marriage of Mr. Mississippi (Duerrenmatt)
   See *Die Ehe des Herrn Mississippi*
The Marriage of Mr. Mississippi (Durrenmatt)
   See *Die Ehe des Herrn Mississippi*
"The Marriage of Pocohantas" (Simpson)   7:427
"The Marriage of Strongbow and Aoife" (Muldoon)   72:279
"The Marriage of Theseus and Hippolyta" (Nemerov)   6:360
"Marriage of Two" (Day Lewis)   10:131
Marriage Play (Albee)   53:26; 86:119, 124
"A Marriage Poem" (Voigt)   54:430-31
Marriage Poem (Ezekiel)   61:105, 107
"A Marriage Poem for Peg and John" (Johnston)   51:248
"A Marriage Portion" (Foote)   75:230-31
"The Marriage Sculptor" (Van Duyn)   116:422
"Marriage with Beasts" (Van Duyn)   3:491; 63:436, 439; 116:401-01, 419, 429
"Marriages" (Larkin)   64:262, 283
Marriages (Straub)   28:408-09; 107:266, 268, 274, 282-83, 291-92, 304-05
Marriages and Infidelities (Oates)   2:315-16; 6:370-71; 9:402; 15:400; 19:351; 52:338; 108:354, 369, 370
The Marriages between Zones Three, Four, and Five (Lessing)   15:334-36; 22:285-86; 40:303, 306; 94:274-75
"Marriages, Births, Deaths" (Johnston)   51:248-49, 254
"Married Dialogue" (Day Lewis)   10:131
The Married Lovers (Horwitz)   14:266
"The Married Man" (Phillips)   28:362-63
A Married Man (Read)   25:377-80
The Married Woman: Fragments of a Film Made in 1964 (Godard)
   See *Une femme mariée*
"Married Woman's Complaint" (Bowering)   32:47
"Le marronier" (Mandiargues)   41:279
"The Marrow" (Le Guin)   45:213
"The Marrow" (Roethke)   3:433; 19:396; 46:364
"Marry Me a Little" (Sondheim)   30:398
Marry Me: A Romance (Updike)   9:536-40; 13:559, 563; 23:472; 43:431-32, 434
"Marrying Damian" (Trevor)   116:394-95
"Marrying the Hangman" (Atwood)   15:36; 25:69
La Marseillaise (Renoir)   20:293, 295-98, 302, 311-12
"Marsh, Hawk" (Atwood)   84:69
"Marshall Washer" (Carruth)   84:135
"Marshallene at Work" (Engel)   36:162
"Marshall's Dog" (Beattie)   63:10-12
"Marshe O Pyus" (Voznesensky)   57:416
Marshes (Konwicki)
   See *Rojsty*
Le marteau sans maître (Char)   9:164; 11:114, 117; 55:287-88
"Martello" (Paulin)   37:354

Martello Towers (Buzo)   61:58-67, 70
Martereau (Sarraute)   2:384; 4:464, 467, 469; 8:471; 31:377, 380; 80:230, 236, 239-40, 252, 254
"Martha" (Lorde)   71:235-36, 260
Martha (Fassbinder)   20:108
"Martha Blake" (Clarke)   6:113; 9:168
"Martha Blake at Fifty-One" (Clarke)   6:112-13; 9:168
"Martha Graham" (Dodson)   79:194
Martha Quest (Lessing)   3:287, 290-91; 15:334; 22:283; 94:255-57, 288
"Marthe" (Rexroth)   112:388
"Marthe Away" (Rexroth)   49:284
"The Martian" (Bradbury)   42:38
The Martian Chronicles (Bradbury)   1:42; 10:68, 70; 15:86; 42:32, 35, 37-40, 43; 98:111-12, 121, 141, 144
"A Martian Sends a Postcard Home" (Raine)   103:191-94
A Martian Sends a Postcard Home (Raine)   32:350-52, 354; 103:181, 183, 186, 188, 190-91, 197-201, 211
Martian Time-Slip (Dick)   10:138; 30:116-17, 123, 125, 127; 72:108, 114, 119, 121-22
The Martian Way, and Other Stories (Asimov)   3:16
The Martians' Second Invasion (Strugatskii and Strugatskii)   27:432, 434, 437
Martin and John (*Fucking Martin*) (Peck)   81:89-100
Martin Dressler: The Tale of an American Dreamer (Millhauser)   109:165-69, 171-74
Martin Heidegger (Steiner)   24:435-36
Martin Heidegger and the Question of Literature: Toward a Postmodern Literary Hermeneutics (Heidegger)   24:277
Martin Mull (Mull)   17:298-99
Martin Mull and His Fabulous Furniture (Mull)   17:299
"Martin the Fisherman" (Knowles)   26:258
"Martine" (Ferron)   94:127-28
"The Martinique" (Ondaatje)   51:310
Martiries (Ritsos)   13:487
The Martlet's Tale (Delbanco)   6:130
Marty (Chayefsky)   23:111, 115
"The Martyr" (Ngugi wa Thiong'o)   36:317
"The Martyr" (Porter)   101:235, 237, 239-40
The Martyr (O'Flaherty)   5:321
"The Martyrdom of Bishop Farrar" (Hughes)   9:284
"The Martyrdom of Saint Sebastian" (Durcan)   70:153
"The Martyrdom of St. Magnus" (Brown)   100:84, 86
The Martyrology, Books I-II (Nichol)   18:368-70
"The Martyr's Corner" (Narayan)   28:293
"The Martyr's Crown" (O'Brien)   10:362
Maru (Head)   25:233-38; 67:92-7, 108-09
Marune (Vance)   35:421
"The Marvelous Children" (Williams)   45:443
"The Marvelous Girl" (Pritchett)   13:468
The Marvelous Misadventures of Sebastian (Alexander)   35:25
Marvelous Possessions: The Wonder of the New World   70:356-57
"Marvelous Truth" (Levertov)   66:236
"The Marvels of the City" (Simic)   49:343
"Marvin McCabe" (Carruth)   84:131, 135
Marx: The Man and His Work (Prichard)   46:337
Marxism and Literary Criticism (Eagleton)

63:94, 102-03
"Marxism and Literature" (Wilson)　24:467, 470, 474
Marxism and the Philosophy of Language (Bakhtin)
　See *Marksizm i filosofija jazyka*
Marxisme et le sciences humaines (Goldmann)　24:242
Mary (Nabokov)
　See *Mashen'ka*
"Mary and the Seasons" (Rexroth)　22:346; 49:283; 112:377
Mary Anne (du Maurier)　59:286
Mary Barnes (Edgar)　42:113, 116
"The Mary Celeste Move" (Herbert)　44:394
Mary Christmas (Chase)　2:101
Mary Glenn (Millin)　49:242-43, 246, 248
Mary Hartman, Mary Hartman (Lear)　12:333-36, 338
Mary Hartman, Mary Hartman (Mull)　17:300
"Mary in the Mountains" (Tilghman)　65:106, 109, 111
"Mary Jane" (Smith)　12:535
"Mary Jordan" (Kerrigan)　6:276
"Mary Lou" (Seger)　35:381
"Mary Magdalene at Easter" (Davison)　28:100
Mary, Mary (Kerr)　22:256
"Mary Moody Emerson, R.I.P." (Turco)　11:549, 551
Mary of Scotland (Ford)　16:312-13
Mary O'Grady (Lavin)　18:304; 99:312, 319
"Mary O'Reilley" (Farrell)　66:129-30
"Mary, Queen of Arkansas" (Springsteen)　17:487
Mary, Queen of Scots (Fraser)　32:178-80, 183, 185; 107:29,35,37,43,60-61,67
Mary Queen of Scots: The Fair Devil of Scotland (Hibbert)　7:157
Mary Reilly (Martin)　89:120-35, 137
"Mary Shelley" (Bowering)　32:48
"Mary Stuart to James Bothwell" (Sitwell)　9:493
"Mary Ure" (Murphy)　41:319
"Mary Winosky" (Hughes)　108:292
Marya: A Life (Oates)　52:329-32, 334, 336-38; 108:386, 390, 393
"Mary's Piece" (Dixon)　52:97
"Mary's Song" (Plath)　111:178, 199, 217, 219
"El más bello amor" (Aleixandre)　9:14
Masante (Hildesheimer)　49:170, 175, 179
Mascara (Dorfman)　77:134-36, 139-42, 149-50, 152
Mascarets (Mandiargues)　41:279
Die Maschine (Perec)　56:256-57
Masculine Feminine (Godard)　20:136, 139
M<indexhang>A<indexhang>S<indexhang>H (Altman)　16:20-1, 24-5, 28-9, 33, 40-1; 116:3-6, 11, 14, 16-17, 21-3, 31, 36, 46, 48, 51, 54, 59, 66-7, 72
M<indexhang>A<indexhang>S<indexhang>H (Gelbart)　21:126-27, 129, 132
"Mash Flat" (Bennett)　28:29
Mashen'ka (*Mary*) (Nabokov)　1:243, 245; 2:300-01; 8:418; 11:395; 15:396; 44:469; 46:295; 64:348
The Mask (Koontz)　78:203
A Mask for Janus (*A Masque for Janus*) (Merwin)　1:212; 2:277; 5:284, 287; 8:388; 18:335; 45:268-70; 88:194, 205, 207
The Mask of Apollo (Renault)　3:425; 17:398-99, 402

The Mask of Dimitrios (*A Coffin for Dimitrios*) (Ambler)　4:18-19; 6:3-4; 9:19-20
"The Mask of the Bear" (Laurence)　62:271
The Masked Days (Fuentes)
　See *Los dís enmascarados*
Masked Gods: Navaho and Pueblo Ceremonialism (Waters)　88:341-43, 345-47, 352, 356, 362-64, 369
"The Masked Marvel's Last Toehold" (Selzer)　74:279
"Masked Woman's Song" (Bogan)　4:69; 39:396
"The Mask-Maker" (Abse)　29:14-15
"The Masks" (Prokosch)　48:309
Masks (Brathwaite)　11:67
Masks (Enchi)　31:141
Masks: A Love Story (Bennett)　35:43
The Masks of God (Campbell)　69:72, 74, 76-7, 81-4, 88-9, 94-5, 99
The Masks of God: Creative Mythology (*Creative Mythology*) (Campbell)　69:74, 76
The Masks of God: Occidental Mythology (*Occidental Mythology*) (Campbell)　69:73
The Masks of God: Oriental Mythology (*Oriental Mythology*) (Campbell)　69:72-3
The Masks of God: Primitive Mythology (*Primitive Mythology*) (Campbell)　69:70-1, 73
"The Masks of Love" (Scannell)　49:325
The Masks of Love (Scannell)　49:325, 331-32
"Masks of Satan" (Davies)　13:174
"Mas'ot Binyamin ha'aharon mitudela" ("Travels of a Latter-Day Benjamin of Tudela"; "Travels of the Last Benjamin Tudela") (Amichai)　22:31, 57:38, 40-2, 44, 46; 116:119, 123, 138
A Masque for Janus (Merwin)
　See *A Mask for Janus*
"A Masque of Italy" (Christie)　110:125, 128
A Masque of Mercy (Frost)　3:170-71, 173; 9:222; 10:196-97; 13:225-26; 15:242-43
"The Masque of Princes" (Brown)　48:57
A Masque of Reason (Frost)　3:170, 173; 9:222; 10:193, 196; 13:225-26; 15:241-42
Masquerade (Berton)　104:43-4, 47-8
The Masquerade (Clark)　38:113, 115-16, 119, 122
The Masquerade of Souls (Lagerkvist)
　See *Själarnas maskerad*
"Masquerades" (Okri)　87:314
"Mass" (Jiles)　58:271, 279
"Mass for the Day of St. Thomas Didymus" (Levertov)　28:243; 66:244
"Mass Man" (Walcott)　76:274
Massachusetts Trust (Terry)　19:440
"The Massacre" (Broumas)　73:15
The Massacre at Fall Creek (West)　7:522; 17:553
"Massacre of the Boys" (Rozewicz)　9:465
"The Massacre of the Innocents" (Davison)　28:100
"Massacre of the Innocents" (Hope)　51:212, 216
Masse und Macht (*Crowds and Power*) (Canetti)　14:119-21, 124; 25:106-07, 109-14; 75:124, 128-32, 134, 137, 139-42, 144-45; 86:293-97, 299, 301-03
"Masses of Men" (Caldwell)　60:60
"The Masses The Implosion of the Social in the Media" (Baudrillard)　60:35
"The Masseuse" (Broumas)　73:15-16
"Massive Retaliation" (Ciardi)　40:155
"Mastectomy" (Boland)　40:100; 67:44, 46; 113:58, 60, 90, 109, 117
"Master" (Carter)　5:103

"The Master" (Merwin)　45:268
The Master (Klima)　56:164-65
The Master (White)　30:444
The Master, and Other Stories (Kaufman)　8:317
"The Master and the Victim" (Kunene)　85:175
"Master Halcrow, Priest" (Brown)　48:55
"Master Harold" ... and the Boys (Fugard)　25:176-78; 40:203; 80:61, 63, 65, 68-70, 72, 77, 80-1
"Master Misery" (Capote)　3:99; 13:133-36, 138; 19:79; 58:86, 98
"Master of Days" (Kunene)　85:165
"The Master of Doornvlei" (Mphahlele)　25:344
The Master of Go (Kawabata)　5:208; 18:281; 107:73-8, 81, 91, 101, 108
The Master of Petersburg (Coetzee)　117:74-6, 79, 81, 87-93
"Master of the Asteroid" (Smith)　43:420, 422
Master of the House (Dreyer)　16:259-63
Master of the Moor (Rendell)　28:388; 48:321
The Master Puppeteer (Paterson)　12:484; 30:283-86, 288
"Master Richard" (Wain)　46:411
"The Master Speech" (Frost)　34:475
"Mastera" (Voznesensky)　15:555-56; 57:414-15, 417, 423
Master-Builder Manole
　See *Mesterul Manole*
"Masterful" (Matthews)　40:325
Mastergate: A Play on Words (Gelbart)　61:145-50
"Mastering the Craft" (Scannell)　49:332
"MAsterMANANiMAL" (Swenson)　61:397
"Masters" (Amis)　40:44
"The Masters" (Heaney)　74:169
The Masters (Duhamel)　8:189
The Masters (Snow)　1:315-17; 4:502-03; 6:517; 9:496; 13:509-11; 19:425, 427
Masters in Israel (Buckley)　57:125-26, 129-31, 133
"Master's in the Garden Again" (Ransom)　2:363; 11:466
The Masters of Bow Street (Creasey)　11:135
Masters of Modern Music (Berger)　12:38-9
"The Master's Tools Will Never Dismantle the Master's House" (Lorde)　71:244
"The Mastodon Palace of Westminster" (Aickman)　57:2
"Masts" (Merwin)　88:194
"Masts at Dawn" (Warren)　13:577; 39:267, 271
"A Mat to Weave" (Tchicaya)　101:346
Matador (Almodovar)　114:3-4, 6, 8-9, 11, 13-4, 19-20, 22-3, 29-34, 57-8
The Matador (Montherlant)
　See *Le bestiaires*
"Matador: A Soliloquy" (Hall)　51:170
The Matarese Circle (Ludlum)　22:290-91
Matatabi (*The Wanderers*) (Ichikawa)　20:183-84
"The Match" (Sillitoe)　6:501
"Match Boxes" (Bowering)　47:29
The Matchmaker (Wilder)　82:368, 376, 379
"Materia" (Aleixandre)　9:12
Materia memorable (Castellanos)　66:52-3
"Material" (Munro)　6:341; 19:344
Matérialisme et révolution (Sartre)　24:406
Materials (Oppen)　7:285; 34:358-59
Materinskoe pole (*Mother Earth*; *Mother Field*; *Mother's Field*) (Aitmatov)　71:6, 13-14, 16, 22, 33
"The Maternal Feminine" (Ferber)　93:139,

146

"Maternal Grief" (Raine) **45**:341

"Maternity Ward" (Selzer) **74**:272-73

"The Mathematicians of Grizzly Drive" (Skvorecky) **69**:339

"Mathematics of Love" (Hamburger) **5**:159

"Mathew VIII, 28ff" (Wilbur) **110**:385

Matière céleste (Jouve) **47**:208-09

Matière de Bretagne (Celan) **53**:71

Matière de rêves (Butor) **8**:120; **15**:115

Matière de rêves III (Butor) **15**:120

Matilda (Gallico) **2**:147

"Matilda's England" (Trevor) **116**:371, 374

Matilda's England (Trevor) **14**:536-37; **71**:325-27, 348; **116**:362, 367-68, 371, 374, 385

Les matinaux (Char) **11**:114; **55**:288

"Matinée" (Reverdy) **53**:289

"Matinees" (Merrill) **91**:229

Mating Birds (Nkosi) **45**:295-99

"Mating Calls" (Beer) **58**:38

"Matins" (Levertov) **66**:235, 243

"Matisse" (Hirsch) **31**:216

The Matlock Paper (Ludlum) **22**:289; **43**:274

The Matriarch (Ihimaera) **46**:202-03

"Matrix" (Fisher) **25**:160-61

Matrix (Fisher) **25**:159

"Matrix of Morning" (Watkins) **43**:454

The Matrix Trilogy (Johnson) **9**:301-03

The Matrons (Auchincloss) **18**:24

"Matryona's Home" (Solzhenitsyn)
    See "Matryonin Dvor"

"Matryona's House" (Solzhenitsyn)
    See "Matryonin Dvor"

Matryona's House (Solzhenitsyn) **34**:489; **78**:408, 418

"Matryonin Dvor" ("Matryona's Home"; "Matryona's House") (Solzhenitsyn) **2**:412; **4**:507; **7**:432, 436, 446; **10**:480; **18**:495; **26**:419, 423

Matsushima: Pine Islands (Vizenor) **103**:308

"Matter and Energy" (Oates) **3**:360

"A Matter of Chance" (Nabokov) **6**:358

A Matter of Conviction (Hunter) **31**:219-21

A Matter of Gravity (Bagnold) **25**:78-9

"A Matter of Origin" (Zamora)
    See "Asunto de prinicpio"

"A Matter of Principle" (Archer) **28**:14

"A Matter of Taste" (La Guma) **19**:272

The Matter of This World: New & Selected Poems (Olds) **85**:302

A Matter of Time (West) **7**:520; **17**:549, 551, 553

"A Matter of Vocabulary" (McPherson) **19**:309; **77**:358-61, 364, 366

Matters of Fact and Fiction: Essays, 1973-1976 (Vidal) **8**:528-29; **10**:501; **22**:436; **33**:404-405

Matthew Arnold (Trilling) **24**:458

"Matthew in the Marshes I" (Klappert) **57**:261

"Matthew in the Marshes II" (Klappert) **57**:261

"Matthew V. 29-30" (Mahon) **27**:290, 292

"The Mattress in the Tomato Patch" (Williams) **45**:447; **71**:364

"Mature Art" (MacDiarmid) **63**:242

Maud Martha (Brooks) **2**:82; **4**:79; **5**:75; **49**:23-5, 28

"Maude" (Auchincloss) **45**:24

Maude (Lear) **12**:331

Maudits soupirs pour une autre fois: Une version primitive de Féerie pour une autre fois (Celine) **47**:76-7

Maui the Demigod: An Epic Novel of Mythical Hawaii (Goldsberry) **34**:54-6

Maule's Curse (Winters) **8**:552; **32**:454, 457, 463-65, 471

"Mau-Mauing the Flak Catchers" (Wolfe) **9**:578; **35**:454

"Mau-Maus" (Guillen) **79**:229-30, 236-37

"Maumee Ruth" (Brown) **59**:262-63, 265

Maundy (Gloag) **40**:208-10

A Mauriac Reader (Mauriac) **56**:216

Maurice (Forster) **1**:109; **2**:135; **3**:161-62; **4**:165-66, 168; **9**:206-09; **10**:181-83; **13**:220-21; **15**:229-30; **22**:136; **45**:134, 137, 140-41, 143

"Maurits Escher's Impossible/Buildings" (Sherwin) **7**:415

Maus: A Survivor's Tale II: And Here My Troubles Began (Spiegelman) **76**:239-50

Maus: A Survivor's Tale: My Father Bleeds History (Spiegelman) **76**:240-42, 244-45, 247-48

Mausoleum (Enzensberger) **43**:149, 151

Le mauvais démiurge (*The New Gods*) (Cioran) **64**:88-9, 93-4

Le mauvais lieu (Green) **77**:278, 280-82

Le Mauvais Sang (*Bad Blood*) (Tchicaya) **101**:348-49, 353, 357, 359

Mauve Desert (Brossard)
    See   *Le de‹indexing›‹indexing›‹indexing›‹indexing›sert mauve*

Mauve Gloves and Madmen, Clutter and Vine (Wolfe) **9**:578-79; **15**:583, 585; **35**:457, 459

Mawrdew Czgowchwz (McCourt) **5**:277-79

"Mawu" (Lorde) **71**:262

Max: A Play (Grass)
    See *Davor*

Max and the White Phagocytes (Miller) **1**:224; **2**:281; **9**:380; **84**:236

Max Jamison (Sheed) **2**:394-95; **4**:487-88; **10**:473

"Max Perkins in 1944" (Cowley) **39**:461

"Maxie Allen" (Brooks) **49**:31

"Maxims in Limbo" (Pack) **13**:439

Maximum Bob (Leonard) **71**:215, 227-28

"Maximum Consumption" (Davies) **21**:94

Maximum Ned (Hannah) **90**:126

"Maximus, from Dogtown I" (Olson) **29**:334

The Maximus Letters (Olson) **5**:329

"Maximus of Gloucester" (Olson) **2**:326

The Maximus Poems (Olson) **1**:263; **2**:326-27; **5**:326, 328; **6**:386-88; **9**:412-13; **11**:417, 420; **29**:328-29, 335-36

"Maximus, to Himself" (Olson) **29**:334

Maximus, Vol. I (Olson) **29**:334

Maximus, Vol. III (Olson) **9**:413

Maximus, Vol. IV (Olson) **5**:327; **9**:413

Maximus, Vol. V (Olson) **5**:327

Maximus, Vol. VI (Olson) **5**:327

Max's Dream (Mayne) **12**:405

"Maxwell's Silver Hammer" (Lennon and McCartney) **12**:364, 380

"May" (Oliver) **34**:246; **98**:256-57

"May 15, 1982" (Kenny) **87**:242

"May 24, 1980" (Brodsky) **100**:55

"May, 1945" (Warner) **45**:433

"May and June" (Rendell) **48**:320

"May Be Left Untitled" (Szymborska) **99**:193

"The May Day Garland" (Blunden) **56**:47

"May Day Sermon" (Dickey) **7**:84; **10**:141; **109**:266-68, 273

"May Days" (Ginsberg) **109**:329

"May I Ask You a Question, Mr. Youngstown Sheet and Tube?" (Patchen) **18**:395

May I Cross Your Golden River? (Corcoran) **17**:74-5

"May I Feel Said He (I'll Squeal Said She)" (Cummings) **68**:29

"May It Be" (Pasternak) **63**:281

"May Night" (O'Connor) **23**:331, 331

May Out West (Swenson) **106**:351

"May the Ridge Rise" (Anand) **93**:57

May We Borrow Your Husband? and Other Comedies of the Sexual Life (Greene) **3**:211, 213, 215; **70**:293

"May We Entertain You?" (Sondheim) **30**:377

"May Wind" (Szirtes) **46**:393

Mayan Letters (Olson) **29**:326

Maybe: A Story (Hellman) **18**:227-29; **34**:349, 352; **52**:190, 192-94, 198, 200, 204-05

"Maybe All This" (Szymborska) **99**:203

"Maybe I'm Amazed" (McCartney) **35**:278, 284, 289

Maybe the Moon (Maupin) **95**:204-10

"Maybe Your Baby" (Wonder) **12**:663

"Maybellene" (Berry) **17**:51, 53-5

Mayday (Faulkner) **28**:141-42

Maydays (Edgar) **42**:122-24

"Mayflower" (Aiken) **10**:3; **52**:24

"Maymeys from Cuba" (Ferber) **93**:141

Mayn Tatn's bes-din shtub (*In My Father's Court*) (Singer) **3**:453; **11**:500; **15**:505; **23**:417, 419; **38**:412; **69**:310, 317; **111**:305

"The Mayo Accent" (Durcan) **70**:153

"Mayo Monologues" (Longley) **29**:295-96

"The Mayonnaise Chapter" (Brautigan) **12**:71

"Mayoo Sto Hoon" (Sainte-Marie) **17**:431

The Mayor of Castro Street: The Life and Times of Harvey Milk (Shilts) **85**:319, 321, 340-43

"The Mayors" (Asimov) **19**:26; **26**:63

"May-Ry" (Calisher) **38**:69

Mayta (Vargas Llosa)
    See *La historia de Mayta*

"Mazatlán Sea" (Creeley) **78**:162

"Maze" (Eberhart) **56**:77

The Maze Maker (Ayrton) **7**:16-18, 20

A Maze of Death (Dick) **30**:124-25; **72**:121-22

"The Mazel Tov Revolution" (Haldeman) **61**:174, 176

Mazeppa (The Brothers Quay) **95**:347, 350

"Mazes" (Le Guin) **45**:213

"Mazie" (Mitchell)
    See "Except That She Smokes, Drinks Booze and Talks Rough, Miss Mazie Is a Nun"

"M.B." (Brodsky) **36**:81

M.C. Higgins, the Great (Hamilton) **26**:149-52, 154, 157

McAuslan in the Rough (Fraser) **7**:106

The McBain Brief (Hunter) **31**:228

McCabe and Mrs. Miller (Altman) **16**:21-2, 25-6, 28-31, 35, 39, 41; **116**:3, 6-9, 11, 13-14, 17, 20, 22-3, 31, 37, 39-42, 44, 46, 48, 59, 65, 67, 72, 74

McCarthy and His Enemies: The Record and Its Meaning (Buckley) **37**:57

"McCarthy and the Intellectuals" (Fiedler) **4**:163

McCartney (McCartney) **12**:371; **35**:278-80, 285, 287

McCartney II (McCartney) **35**:287-89

"McCrimmon and the Blue Moonstones" (MacLean) **63**:269

"McDuff on the Mound" (Coover) **87**:25

"McKane's Falls" (Merrill)　13:376

The McPhee Reader (McPhee)　36:297

"McSorley's Wonderful Saloon" (Mitchell)　98:165

McSorley's Wonderful Saloon (Mitchell)　98:153-60, 164-65, 168-69, 171-73, 175, 177, 180-81, 183, 185

"M.D." (Fearing)　51:114

"Me Again" (Rexroth)　112:386, 400

Me Again: Uncollected Writings of Stevie Smith (Smith)　25:420-22; 44:435-36, 441, 444

"Me and Bobby McGee" (Kristofferson)　26:267-70

"Me and Julio Down by the Schoolyard" (Simon)　17:461, 465-66

"Me and Miss Mandible" (Barthelme)　46:35, 40; 59:247; 115:65-7, 79

"Me and My Baby View the Eclipse" (Smith)　73:357

Me and My Baby View the Eclipse (Smith)　73:353, 356-59

Me and My Bones (Gallant)　17:129-30

"Me and My Town" (Sondheim)　30:387

"Me and Paul" (Nelson)　17:303

"Me and the Girls" (Coward)　29:141; 51:74

"Me and the Runner" (MacEwen)　55:164

"Me and the World" (Simmons)　43:410

"Me and You and a Dog Named Blue" (Corcoran)　17:78

"Me Bredda" (Bennett)　28:29, 31

"Me Cago en la Leche (Robert Jordan in Nicaragua)" (Boyle)　90:45

"Me, Hood!" (Spillane)　13:528

Me, I'm Afraid of Virginia Woolf (Bennett)　77:85-6, 88-9

Me Me Me Me Me: Not a Novel (Kerr)　35:249-50, 252

Me, Myself, and I (Ayckbourn)　33:50

Me Myself I (Armatrading)　17:10-11

"Mea culpa" (Sondheim)　30:398

Mea culpa (Celine)　47:79

"The Meadow" (Carver)　55:275

"Mead's Theory of Subjectivity" (Habermas)　104:88

"A Meal" (Atwood)　4:27

"The Meal" (Olds)　85:294

"Mean Drunk Poem" (Thesen)　56:418-19

"Mean Mother Mary" (Carroll)　35:77

Mean Rufus (Smith)　22:389

Mean Spirit (Hogan)　73:160-64

Mean Streets (Scorsese)　20:324-26, 337-38, 340; 89:219-23, 231-32, 235-36, 239-40, 243-45, 247-49, 252-56, 260-61, 266-67

"The Meaning of a Literary Idea" (Trilling)　24:456, 460-61

The Meaning of Contemporary Realism (Lukacs)　24:320

The Meaning of Culture (Powys)　7:349

"The Meaning of Life" (Keillor)　115:283

The Meaning of Meaning (Richards)　24:370, 375, 385, 389, 400-01

"A Meaning of Robert Lowell" (Carruth)　84:121, 124

"The Meaning of Simplicity" (Ritsos)　31:331

Meaning of the Stars (Ivask)
　See *Tähtede tähendus*

The Meaning of Treason (West)　9:561, 563; 31:455, 458; 50:394-95, 398, 401, 404-06, 408, 410

"The Meaning of Western Defense" (Mailer)　111:104

"A Meaningless Institution" (Ginsberg)　36:182

"Meaningless Midnight Musings" (McFadden)　48:244, 250

"Meaningless Story" (Valenzuela)　31:437-38

Meanings (Walcott)　25:454; 76:282

Means of Evil (Rendell)　28:386-87

"Means of Protection" (Watkins)　43:450

"Meant for You" (Wilson)　12:641

"Measles" (Ashbery)　77:42

"The Measure" (Lane)　25:289

"The Measure" (Silkin)　6:498

"Measure" (Williams)　13:604

The Measure (Lane)　25:288-89

The Measure of Man (Krutch)　24:280

"The Measure of Poetry" (Nemerov)　9:396

Measure of the Year (Haig-Brown)　21:142

Measure with Metric (Branley)　21:21

Measures (MacCaig)　36:282, 288

"Measures for G.C." (Hoffman)　6:243

"Measuring Death" (Mahapatra)　33:281

"Meat" (Gunn)　81:178

Meat (Wiseman)　20:476-77

Meat Air: Poems, 1957-1969 (Loewinsohn)　52:284-85

Meat Science Essays (McClure)　6:318, 320; 10:332

Mécanique jongleuse (Daydream Mechanics) (Brossard)　115:104-05

La meccanica (Gadda)　11:215

The Mechanical Bride: Folklore of Industrial Man (McLuhan)　37:252, 254, 256, 259-61, 263; 83:354, 359, 361, 363, 366, 369, 373

"A Mechanic's Life" (Masters)　48:224

"The Mechanics of Good Times" (Kauffman)　42:252

"Mechanism" (Ammons)　108:3, 4

"Les méchins" (Ferron)　94:103

"Médaille d'or" (Soupault)　68:406

"Les medailles flottent-elles sur la mer?" (Carrier)　78:71

"Medal from Jerusalem" (Shaw)　7:411; 23:396; 34:370

"Medallion" (Plath)　11:446; 111:199, 203

"Medallion" (Pound)　112:313-14

"Medallions" (Davie)　8:166

Meddle (Pink Floyd)　35:311, 313

"Medea" (Raine)　45:339

Medea (Anouilh)
　See *Médée*

Medea (Fo)　32:174-76

Medea (Jeffers)　54:247; 11:306, 310

Medea (Pasolini)　20:265-68; 106:226, 256

Medea at Kolchis (Duncan)　55:293

Médée (Medea) (Anouilh)　8:22; 13:16-17, 20; 40:51, 57; 50:278

"Media Event" (Baxter)　45:51, 53; 78:17

"Media Man" (Vinge)
　See "Mediaman"

"Media Vitae" (Duncan)　1:82

"Mediaman" ("Media Man") (Vinge)　30:410

Le Médianoche amoureux (The Midnight Love Feast) (Tournier)　95:377, 382, 390

"Mediation at Spring Hill" (Raine)　32:349

Medical Center Lab (Berger)　12:41

"A Medical Unit and a Half" (Aksyonov)　101:9

A Medicine for Melancholy (Bradbury)　3:86; 15:85; 42:32

Medicine in Action (Hyde)　21:172

"The Medicine Man" (Caldwell)　14:96

"Medicine Man" (De Marinis)　54:98, 102

Medicine River (King)　89:79-82, 84, 86-91, 93-4, 97, 101

"Medicine Song" (Allen)　84:39

"The Medieval" (Hall)　51:175

Medieval Scenes (Duncan)　15:187

"Medievalism" (Pound)　4:410

Medina (McCarthy)　14:358-59

Una meditación (A Meditation) (Benet)　28:18-20, 22-3

"The Meditated Death" (Ungaretti)　7:485

"Meditation" (Aldington)　49:6

A Meditation (Benet)
　See *Una meditación*

"Meditation Addressed to Hugh MacDiarmid" (Smith)　64:397

"Meditation at Lagunitas" (Hass)　18:210, 213; 39:148; 99:130, 144-46

"Meditation at Oyster River" (Roethke)　1:291; 19:399; 46:364; 101:289, 299, 306, 313-14, 319

"Meditation in Sunlight" (Sarton)　49:310

"Meditation on a Bone" (Hope)　51:213

"Meditation on a Constable Picture" (Betjeman)　6:67

"A Meditation on John Constable" (Tomlinson)　13:547; 45:392

"Meditation on Play, Thoughts on Death" (Collins)　44:36-7

"Meditation on Saviors" (Jeffers)　54:237

Meditation on Statistical Method (Cunningham)　31:97, 99, 102

"Meditation on the BMT" (Blackburn)　43:63

"Meditation on the Threshold" (Castellanos)　66:60

Meditation on Violence (Deren)　16:252-54; 102:28, 31, 38, 40, 42-3, 48-9

"Meditation Two" (Eberhart)　11:179

"Meditations" (Eberhart)　11:178

"Meditations for a Savage Child" (Rich)　7:373; 11:477

"Meditations in an Emergency" (O'Hara)　5:324; 78:355

Meditations in an Emergency (O'Hara)　13:424; 78:347

Meditations in Green (Wright)　33:467-70

"Meditations in Time of Divorce" (Simmons)　43:412

"Meditations of an Old Woman" (Roethke)　3:433; 8:455, 459-60; 11:486; 19:398-99; 101:288-89, 291, 304, 310, 312-13, 318-19, 327, 329-31, 333-34

"Meditations on History" (Williams)　89:327, 343

"Meditations on Romans" (Garrett)　3:192

"Meditations on the Problem of the Nation" (Herbert)　43:189

"Meditations upon Survival" (Klein)　19:262

"Mediterranean" (Senghor)　54:392

"The Mediterranean" (Tate)　2:429; 4:535, 539; 6:525; 9:522; 11:522, 525, 527

Mediterranean Cities (Denby)　48:82-5

"Mediterraneo" (Montale)　7:222, 227; 18:339

"The Medium" (Voigt)　54:431

The Medium (Weiss)　3:516; 14:557

The Medium Is the Massage: An Inventory of Effects (McLuhan)　37:262-64; 83:362, 366

"Medium Loser and Small Winner" (Brooke-Rose)　40:106

"Medley" (Bambara)　88:22-23, 28

"Medley" (McCartney)　35:281

"Medusa" (Bogan)　46:81-3, 86, 90; 93:64, 67-9, 81, 85-7, 90, 93, 96

"Medusa" (Dove)　81:152

"Medusa" (Plath)　5:345; 9:427; 11:449; 17:369; 51:340; 111:207

"Medusa" (Smith)   43:422

The Medusa and the Snail: More Notes of a Biology Watcher (Thomas)   35:410-12, 415

Les Méduses, ou les orties de mer (Tchicaya)   101:355

"Mee Too Buggi" (Cendrars)   106:190

Meek Heritage (Sillanpaa)   19:417

Meet John Doe (Capra)   16:156, 160-62, 166

Meet Marlon Brando (Maysles and Maysles)   16:443-44

Meet Me at Tamerlane's Tomb (Corcoran)   17:74-5

Meet Me at the Morgue (Macdonald)   41:271-72

Meet Me in St. Louis (Benson)   17:48

Meet Me in the Green Glen (Warren)   1:356; 4:579, 581; 8:540

Meet My Father (Ayckbourn)   33:44

Meet the Austins (L'Engle)   12:346-47, 350

Meet the Beatles (Lennon and McCartney)   12:382

Meet the Maitlands (Streatfeild)   21:417

Meet the Malones (Weber)   12:631

Meet Whiplash Willie (Wilder)
   See *The Fortune Cookie*

"The Meeting" (Abse)   29:15

"The Meeting" (Bogan)   93:81

"The Meeting" (Borges)   1:39; 2:77; 10:67; 48:33

"The Meeting" (Cortazar)
   See "Reunión"

"The Meeting" (Dixon)   52:97

"The Meeting" (Ewart)   46:152-53

"Meeting" (Hughes)   9:281

"Meeting" (Merwin)   88:192

"A Meeting" (Montague)   13:391

"A Meeting" (Nabokov)   1:243

"A Meeting" (O'Faolain)   32:341

"Meeting" (Pasternak)   63:313

"Meeting" (Peterkin)   31:308

"The Meeting" (Sillitoe)   57:391, 396

"Meeting, 1944" (Szirtes)   46:395

"Meeting a Person" (Enright)   8:204

The Meeting at Telgte (Grass)   22:195-97

A Meeting by the River (Isherwood)   1:157; 9:294; 11:300; 14:280, 282, 285-86; 44:397-98, 402

"Meeting Cheever" (Ryan)   65:209, 214-15

Meeting Ends: A Play (Warner)   14:553

"A Meeting in Rauch" (Bioy Casares)   88:92, 94-5

"A Meeting in the Dark" (Ngugi wa Thiong'o)   36:311-12, 317

"The Meeting in the Kitchen, 1740" (Schnackenberg)   40:379

"A Meeting in Valladolid" (Burgess)   62:139

"Meeting Mrs. Milllar" (Aickman)   57:5

"A Meeting of Eyes in Mexico" (Ferlinghetti)   111:60

"A Meeting of Minds" (Lorde)   71:256

"Meeting of Strangers" (Birney)   6:74-5

"Meeting Place" (Ammons)   57:50-1

Meeting Place (Mosley)   43:312, 321

"Meeting Point" (MacNeice)   53:231

The Meeting Point (Clarke)   8:142; 53:85, 87-9, 93-5

"Meeting the British" (Muldoon)   72:276

Meeting the British (Muldoon)   72:273-74, 277-79

"Meeting the Folks" (Grenville)   61:152

"Meeting the Man Who Warns Me" (Bly)   10:60

"Meeting the Mountains" (Snyder)   5:393

"Meeting Together of Poles and Latitudes: in Prospect" (Avison)   97:70, 76, 80, 90

"A Meeting with Medusa" (Clarke)   13:148; 18:107; 35:123

Mefisto (Banville)   46:31-3

Meg (Gee)   29:178-79

La meglio gioventù (Pasolini)   37:348; 106:227, 231, 243

Meier Helmbrecht (Hochwalder)   36:235-38

Le meilleur de la vie (Gascar)   11:222

"Mein Judentum" (Hildesheimer)   49:179

"Mein Karren knarrt nicht mehr" (Celan)   82:52

Mein Name sei Gantenbein (*A Wilderness of Mirrors*) (Frisch)   3:167; 9:218; 18:163; 32:188-90, 192; 44:183-85, 188-90, 193, 197, 199

"Mein Onkel Fred" (Boell)   72:72

"Mein teures Bein" ("My Expensive Leg") (Boell)   27:65

"Mein trauriges Gesicht" (Boell)   27:59; 72:70-1

"Mein verdrossenes Gesicht" (Lenz)   27:245

"Mein Vogel" (Bachmann)   69:41

"Meiosis" (Auden)   43:21, 27

"Mejdoub" (Bowles)   19:59

"Los mejor calzados" (Valenzuela)
   See "The Best Shod"

"Meksikanskij romansero" ("Mexican Romancero") (Brodsky)   50:131; 100:53

"Melancholia" (Bly)   10:56

Melancholia (Sartre)
   See *La nausée*

Melancholy Baby (O'Faolain)   47:330

"Melancholy Breakfast" (O'Hara)   13:424

Mélancolie nord (Rio)   43:354-55

"Melancthon" (Moore)   47:266

"Mélange adultère de tout" (Eliot)   3:140

Meles Vulgaris (Boyle)   19:68

"Mélie and the Bull" (Ferron)   94:123

Melissa (Caldwell)   28:59

The Melodeon (Swarthout)   35:403-04

"Melodic Trains" (Ashbery)   13:30, 35-6; 15:30

Melodien, der blev vaek (Abell)   15:1

Melodrama Play (Shepard)   4:489; 6:497; 17:436, 438, 441, 443; 41:412

Mélodrame (Jouve)   47:209-10

"The Melongene" (Wilbur)   110:383

Melville Goodwin, U.S.A. (Marquand)   10:329

"Melville's Withdrawal" (Updike)   34:290, 293

The Member for the Marsh (Mayne)   12:386

"Member of the European Parliament" (Durcan)   70:152

"A Member of the Family" (Spark)   40:402

The Member of the Wedding (McCullers)   1:208, 210; 4:344-45; 10:338; 12:410-18, 420-24, 426, 430, 432; 48:230-31, 234-36, 240; 100:242-46, 249, 251-56, 260, 263, 270

"Membrane of Air" (Buckley)   57:136

Memed, My Hawk (Kemal)   14:299-300

"Memento" (Gotlieb)   18:191

"Memento" (Spender)   41:420

Memento mori (Spark)   2:414-17; 3:464-66; 5:399; 13:520-21, 525; 18:501, 505-06; 40:395-96, 400, 402; 94:326-328, 332, 336, 353

Memleketimden insan manzaralari (*Human Landscapes; Human Landscapes from My Land; Humanscapes from My Land*) (Hikmet)   40:244-45, 247, 251

"Memo" (Fearing)   51:106

"Memo" (Jordan)   114:146, 152

"Memo from Turner" (Jagger and Richard)   17:226

"Memo: Preliminary Draft of a Prayer to God the Father" (Ciardi)   40:161; 44:382

"Memo to the 21st Century" (Appleman)   51:15

"Memoir" (Pinsky)   94:308

"Memoir" (Van Duyn)   63:444-45; 116:412

Memoir of a Russian Punk (Coles)
   See *Podrostak Savenko*

Mémoires d'Hadrien (*Hadrian's Memoirs*; *The Memoirs of Hadrian*) (Yourcenar)   19:480-82; 38:455-61, 463-64; 50:361-65; 87:383, 385-86, 390, 394-97, 401, 403-06, 409, 411-12, 417-19, 421, 423-24, 427-28, 431-32

Mémoires d'une jeune fille rangée (*Memoirs of a Dutiful Daughter*) (Beauvoir)   1:19; 4:48; 8:58; 31:42; 44:343, 345, 349-50; 50:389; 71:59, 76, 80-1

Mémoires intérieurs (Mauriac)   56:218

Memoirs (Neruda)
   See *Confieso que he vivido: memorias*

Memoirs (Williams)   7:545-46; 8:547-48; 11:573-75; 15:581, 583; 19:470, 472; 39:445, 449-51, 453; 45:443-44, 446, 452-53, 455; 111:390-91

Memoirs, 1921-1941 (Ehrenburg)   18:135, 137

Memoirs and Opinions (Tate)   9:521; 11:526

Memoirs Found in a Bathtub (Lem)   8:344; 15:327; 40:291, 300

Memoirs from a Young Republic (Keneally)   117:240-41

Memoirs from the Time of Immaturity (Gombrowicz)
   See *Pamietnik okresu dojrzewania*

"Memoirs in Oxford" (Prince)   22:339-40

Memoirs of a Dutiful Daughter (Beauvoir)
   See *Mémoires d'une jeune fille rangée*

Memoirs of a Fox-Hunting Man (Sassoon)   36:387, 390, 394, 396-97

Memoirs of a Peon (Sargeson)   31:365-67, 371, 373-74

"Memoirs of a Private Detective" (Hammett)   19:195

The Memoirs of a Shy Pornographer (Patchen)   18:392-93

Memoirs of a Space Traveler: Further Reminiscences of Ijon Tichy (Lem)   40:294, 296

Memoirs of a Survivor (Lessing)   6:299-305; 10:315-16; 15:333; 40:312; 94:253, 258, 261, 264, 282-83, 286

Memoirs of an Anti-Semite (Rezzori)   25:382-85

Memoirs of an Ex-Prom Queen (Shulman)   2:395

"Memoirs of an Infantry Officer" (Sassoon)   36:387, 392, 394-97

Memoirs of an Invisible Man (Saint)   50:73-6

The Memoirs of Christopher Columbus   70:352

The Memoirs of George Sherston (Sassoon)   36:388, 394, 396

The Memoirs of Hadrian (Yourcenar)
   See *Mémoires d'Hadrien*

Memoirs of Hecate County (Wilson)   1:373; 2:474-75, 478; 8:551

Memoirs of Many in One, by Alex Xenophon Demirjian Gray (White)   65:275, 278, 282; 69:410-13

Memoirs of Montparnasse (Glassco)   9:236

The Memoirs of Solar Pons (Derleth)   31:137-38

"The Memoirs of Stefan Czarniecki" (Gombrowicz) **49**:127
"Memoranda" (Dickey) **28**:117
The Memorandum (Havel) **25**:219-24, 226, 229; **58**:237, 239-40, 242, 244-45; **65**:419, 421, 429, 432, 435, 439-40
"Memorial" (Munro) **10**:357
"Memorial" (Sanchez) **294**, 325-26
"Memorial II" (Lorde) **71**:260
"The Memorial, 1914-1918" (Blunden) **56**:30, 39, 44-5
"Memorial Address" (Heidegger) **24**:266
"Memorial Day" (Berrigan) **37**:46
"Memorial Day" (Cameron) **44**:33, 35
"Memorial Day" (Lowell) **4**:304
"Memorial Day" (Simon) **26**:412-13
"Memorial Day" (Voigt) **54**:433
"Memorial Day, 1950" (O'Hara) **13**:423, 426-27; **78**:344, 348, 373-74
Memorial Day, 1950 (O'Hara) **13**:423
Memorial de Isla Negra (*Black Island Memorial; Isla Negra: A Notebook; Memorial to Isla Negra; Notes from Isla Negra*) (Neruda) **5**:303-04; **7**:261; **9**:399; **28**:312, 314-16; **62**:323, 325-26
"Memorial de Tlatelolco" (Castellanos) **66**:46, 53
"Memorial for the City" (Auden) **2**:23; **14**:27, 29
"The Memorial Fountain" (Fisher) **25**:158, 160
The Memorial: Portrait of a Family (Isherwood) **1**:155-56; **9**:293; **11**:295, 297-300; **14**:280-82; **44**:396-97, 400-03
"Memorial Rain" (MacLeish) **68**:284-85, 293
"Memorial to Ed Bland" (Brooks) **49**:32
Memorial to Isla Negra (Neruda)
　　See *Memorial de Isla Negra*
"Memorial to Luthuli" (Paton) **10**:388
Memorials of a Tour in Yorkshire (Simmons) **43**:408
Memorias: Infancia, adolescencia y còmo sehace un escritor (Bioy Casares) **88**:95
Memorias inmemoriales (Azorin) **11**:27
"memories for no one" (Young Bear) **94**:363
Memories of a Catholic Girlhood (McCarthy) **14**:363; **59**:290-93
"Memories of a Cross-Country Man" (Rooke) **25**:391
Memories of an Auctioneer (Auchincloss) **18**:24
Memories of Dying (Hughes) **48**:183-84
"Memories of Earth" (Morgan) **31**:274, 276
Memories of Happy Days (Green) **77**:276
"Memories of the Depression Years" (Justice) **102**:255
Memories of the Future (Horgan) **53**:181-82
"Memories of the Linen Room" (Raine) **103**:188
"Memories of West Street and Lepke" (Lowell) **11**:326-27; **15**:343
"Memories of Youghal" (Trevor) **116**:338
"Memory" (Bogan) **46**:83; **93**:64
"A Memory" (Hughes) **37**:176
"A Memory" (Lavin) **4**:282; **18**:305; **99**:312
"Memory" (Merwin) **18**:333-34
"Memory?" (Plath) **11**:449
"Memory" (Queneau) **42**:337
"Memory" (Raine) **32**:349
"Memory" (Roethke) **101**:329
"A Memory" (Welty) **14**:563; **33**:414; **105**:297, 334, 378-79
Memory (Jensen) **37**:191-92

"Memory, 1930" (Creeley) **36**:122; **78**:152
"Memory Albums" (Stuart) **8**:507
A Memory, and Other Stories (Lavin) **4**:282
Memory Gardens (Creeley) **78**:153-54, 158, 160, 162
"Memory Green" (MacLeish) **68**:273, 286
"Memory Hotel" (Jagger and Richard) **17**:236, 242
"Memory of a Porch" (Justice) **102**:252
"A Memory of Asia" (Ghose) **42**:185
A Memory of Asia: New and Selected Poems (Ghose) **42**:185
"The Memory of Elena" ("In Memory of Elena") (Forche) **83**:211, 214, 216, 218-19
Memory of Fire (Galeano) **72**:131, 133-37, 139-41, 143-44
Memory of Fire: Century of the Wind (Galeano) **72**:135-38, 140
Memory of Fire: Faces and Masks (Galeano) **72**:132-37
Memory of Fire: Genesis (Galeano) **72**:131-38
A Memory of Murder (Bradbury) **42**:42
The Memory of Old Jack (Berry) **4**:59; **6**:62; **8**:85-6; **46**:73
"A Memory of Ottawa" (Levine) **54**:300
A Memory of Two Mondays (Miller) **1**:216, 219; **6**:329; **15**:373
A Memory of War (Fenton) **32**:166-67
"Memory of Wilmington" (Kinnell) **29**:285
"Memory pieces for Baby Jane" (Broumas) **73**:10-11
"Memory Unsettled" (Gunn) **81**:180, 188
Memos from Purgatory (Ellison) **13**:205
"Memphis" (Gilchrist) **48**:120-22
"Memphis" (Mason) **82**:251, 258
"Memphis Blues" (Brown) **23**:96; **59**:262,265
Me-mushiri Kouchi (*Pluck the Flowers, Gun the Kids*) (Oe) **86**:226-27, 240-41
"Men" (Jong) **6**:267
"Men" (MacLeish) **68**:273, 283, 287-88, 293
"Men and Brethren" (Cozzens) **4**:113, 115; **11**:128, 131, 133
Men and Brethren (Cozzens) **92**:179-80, 182, 184, 198, 201
Men and Gods (Vittorini)
　　See *Uomini e no*
Men and Gods (Warner) **45**:439
Men and Wives (Compton-Burnett) **15**:138; **34**:500
"Men and Women" (Dabydeen) **34**:149
"Men and Women" (Seidel) **18**:475
Men at Arms (Waugh) **8**:543; **19**:461-62; **27**:471-72; **107**:371, 406
"Men at Forty" (Justice) **102**:261
Men at War (Waugh) **107**:406
Men Call It Dawn (Bunuel)
　　See *Cela s'appelle l'aurore*
The Men from P.I.G. and R.O.B.O.T. (Harrison) **42**:202-03
"Men Have Forgotten God" (Solzhenitsyn) **78**:402
Men in Battle (Bessie) **23**:59-60
Men in Dark Times (Arendt) **98**:9, 11, 45, 52-3
The Men in the Jungle (Spinrad) **46**:383
Men in White (Kingsley) **44**:230-32, 234, 237-38
Men Inside (Bogosian) **45**:62
"Men Loved Wholly beyond Wisdom" (Bogan) **39**:387; **46**:83, 86; **93**:64, 66, 69, 93
"Men Marry What They Need; I Marry You"

(Ciardi) **44**:380
"Men Must Die" (Woolrich) **77**:403
Men of Distinction (Condon) **100**:93
"Men of Good Fortune" (Reed) **21**:306
"Men of Good Will" (MacNeice) **53**:231
Men of Good Will (Romains)
　　See *Les hommes de bonne volonté*
Men of Maize (Asturias)
　　See *Hombres de maíz*
"Men of Maize: Myth as Time and Language" (Dorfman) **77**:155
Men of Men (Smith) **33**:377-78
"Men of My Century Loved Mozart" (MacLeish) **68**:286
"Men of Our People" (Laurence) **50**:320, 322
Men of Stones (Warner) **45**:434-35, 437-40
"Men of the Great Man" (Cassity) **42**:98
Men of the Mountains (Stuart) **14**:513; **34**:373, 376
The Men of Tohoku (Ichikawa) **20**:181
Men on Bataan (Hersey) **40**:226; **81**:329, 332, 334-35; **97**:301, 303, 305, 310
"Men Running" (Cozzens) **92**:189
"Men Sign the Sea" (Graham) **29**:194, 198
"Men Suspected of Faggotry" (Donnell) **34**:159
"Men: The Man Who Ended His Story" (Wilson) **49**:413-16
"The Men with Long Faces" (Dobyns) **37**:78
Men Without Shadows (Sartre)
　　See *Morts sans sépulture*
Men without Women (Hemingway) **1**:143; **19**:211; **30**:180, 185, 192, 198-99; **39**:430; **44**:519
Men, Women, and Children (Sillitoe) **3**:449; **6**:500; **57**:392
Men, Women, and Dogs (Thurber) **25**:436-37
"The Men XIX" (Neruda)
　　See "Los hombres XIX"
"Las ménades" (Cortazar) **33**:126-29
"Menage" (Luzi) **13**:353
"Ménage à trois" (Moss) **45**:292
"Menagerie" (Salinas) **90**:329
"Menagerie, a Child's Fable" (Johnson) **51**:234
Mencius on the Mind (Richards) **24**:390, 395
"A Mendicant Order" (Williams) **45**:444
"Mending Wall" (Frost) **3**:170, 174; **10**:197-98; **15**:240, 245-48; **26**:111-12, 116, 118, 123, 125-28
The Mendiola Trilogy (Goytisolo) **23**:185
"Mene, Mene, Tekel, Upharsin" (Cheever) **64**:65
"Menelaiad" (Barth) **2**:39; **3**:39, 41; **5**:50-1; **9**:70; **51**:23; **89**:6, 9-10, 15-17, 19, 21, 26-7, 45, 48, 54, 59, 61-3
Menéndez Pelayo, crítico literario (Alonso) **14**:20
"Meneseteung" (Munro) **95**:306, 311, 314, 320
"Los Menestrales" ("The Minstrels") (Valenzuela) **104**:382, 387
Menfreya in the Morning (Hibbert) **7**:155
"Mengke" (Ding Ling) **68**:55, 64-5
Las meninas (*The Ladies-in-Waiting*) (Buero Vallejo) **15**:97-9, 101; **46**:95-6
"Menino de engenho" ("Plantation Boy") (Cabral de Melo Neto) **76**:160
"Meniscus" (Longley) **29**:295
Menneskebonn (*Children of Men*) (Vesaas) **48**:404-05, 411
The Menorah (Skvorecky)
　　See *Sedmiramenný svícen*
Men's Business (Kroetz)
　　See *Männer Sache*

The Men's Club (Michaels) 25:317-20

Men's Lives: The Surfmen and Baymen of the South Fork (Matthiessen) 64:317-19, 325, 327

"The Men's Room in the College Chapel" (Snodgrass) 68:397

"Men's Studies: 'Roman de la rose'" (Fulton) 52:161

Der Mensch erscheint im Holozän (*Man in the Holocene*) (Frisch) 18:162-63; 32:192-94; 44:192, 204, 206-07

Mensch Meier (Kroetz) 41:240-41

Das Menschenbild der Seelenheilkunde (Frankl) 93:194

"Menses" (Boland) 40:98; 67:44, 46; 113:60-1, 109

Le mensonge (Sarraute) 10:457; 31:381-82; 80:241

Mensonge: Structuralism's Hidden Hero (Bradbury) 61:43-4, 47

Les mensonges (Mallet-Joris) 11:355

"Menstruation at Forty" (Sexton) 4:482

"Menthol Sweets" (Amichai) 116:93

Mention My Name in Mombosa (Daly) 17:89-90

"Menuchat kayits u-milam" ("Summer Rest and Words") (Amichai) 116:133-35

"Menudo" (Carver) 53:62; 55:278

"Menus" (Cendrars) 106:191

Menzogna e sortilegio (*House of Liars*) (Morante) 47:274-75, 279-80, 282-83

Le menzogne della notte (*Lies of the Night*; *Lies of the Night*; *Night's Lies*; *Night's Lies*) (Bufalino) 74:41

Mephisto (O'Hara) 78:368-69

Le mépris (*Contempt*) (Godard) 20:133, 143

"La mer" (Loewinsohn) 52:283

Le meraviglie d'Italia (Gadda) 11:215

Los mercaderes (Matute)
  See *La trampa*

"O mercado a que os rios" ("The Market Where the Rivers Go") (Cabral de Melo Neto) 76:165

"The Mercedes" (Kavan) 82:120

"A Mercedes Funeral" (Ngugi wa Thiong'o) 7:267; 36:318

"Mercedes Hospital" (Bishop) 32:44

"The Mercenaries" (Hemingway) 39:399

"A Mercenary" (Ozick) 7:288; 62:353-54

Mercenary (Anthony) 35:40-1

The Merchant (Wesker) 42:425-26, 428-30

"The Merchant of Bristol" (Foote) 75:230

"The Merchant of Heaven" (Laurence) 13:341

The Merchant of Regrets (Crommelynck)
  See *Le marchand de regrets*

The Merchant of the Four Seasons (Fassbinder) 20:105-08, 119

The Merchant of Yonkers: A Farce in Four Acts (Wilder) 82:359, 376, 379

"The Merchant Princes" (Asimov) 26:63

Merchanter's Luck (Cherryh) 35:109

Mercian Hymns (Hill) 5:184; 8:293-94, 296-97; 18:238-43; 45:178-83, 185-88, 191

Mercier and Camier (Beckett) 6:42-5; 9:84; 14:70; 18:52; 29:55-6; 59:254

Merciful Disguises: Published and Unpublished Poems (Van Duyn) 3:491-92; 7:499; 63:438-39, 443; 116:402, 406, 408

"Mercy" (Broumas) 73:15-16

"Mercy" (Dickey) 47:96; 109:267-69, 272

"Mercy" (Kunene) 85:175

"Mercy, Mercy Me" (Gaye) 26:130-31, 133

Mercy of a Rude Stream (Roth) 104:284-86,
289, 317-21, 323-24, 326-29

Mercy Street (Sexton) 53:321-22

"Mercy, the Cat's Got into the Budget" (Perelman) 49:258

Mere Christianity (Lewis) 6:311; 14:323; 27:263, 265-66

"La Mère Noel" (Tournier) 95:368

Meredithian Sonnets (Fuller) 28:150-51

"Merging Traffic" (Greenberg) 30:166

"Mericans" (Cisneros) 69:155

"Der Meridian" ("The Meridian") (Celan) 53:74, 83; 82:51, 57

"The Meridian" (Celan)
  See "Der Meridian"

Meridian (Walker) 9:557-58; 19:452; 27:449-51; 46:424, 428, 431; 58:404, 406, 410; 103:357, 366-67, 373, 383, 385-90, 392, 394-95, 405, 412

"La meridiana" ("The Sundial") (Piccolo) 13:440

Merlin (Nye) 13:414; 42:305-06, 308

Merlin and the Snake's Egg (Norris) 14:388

Merlin Trilogy (Stewart) 35:397

"The Mermaid" (Mueller) 51:279-80

Mermaids and Ikons (MacEwen) 13:358

Mermaids in the Basement: Poems for Women (Kizer) 39:170; 80:181-83, 185

"Mermaids on the Golf Course" (Highsmith) 42:216

Mermaids on the Golf Course (Highsmith) 42:215

"The Merman" (Hesse) 25:260

"The Merman" (Muldoon) 32:318-19; 72:264

"The Merman's Children" (Anderson) 15:14

"Merriggi e ombre" (Montale) 7:228

Merrily We Go to Hell (Arzner) 98:69-70, 76, 78-9, 91

"Merrily We Pentagon" (Baker) 31:31

Merrily We Roll Along (Hart and Kaufman) 33:259-60, 263, 266; 66:175, 182, 188-89

Merrily We Roll Along (Sondheim) 30:399-403; 39:174

The Merry Month of May (Jones) 3:261-62; 10:292; 39:406-07, 412

The Merry Vineyard (Zuckmayer)
  See *Der Fröliche Weinberg*

"Merry-Go-Round" (Crispin) 22:112

"Merry-Go-Round" (Day Lewis) 10:130-31

"Merry-Go-Round" (Hughes) 35:218

The Merry-Go-Round (Maugham) 15:365, 370; 93:229-30

The Merry-Go-Round (Van Vechten) 33:385

The Merry-Go-Round in the Sea (Stow) 23:433; 48:357-58, 360

"Merry-go-round with White Swan" (Seifert) 93:330

Mert and Phil (Burr) 6:104-05

Merton of the Movies (Connelly) 7:56

Merton of the Movies (Kaufman) 38:257

Mes débuts (Morand) 41:304

Mes propriétés (*My Properties*) (Michaux) 8:392; 19:313

"A mesa" ("The Table") (Cabral de Melo Neto) 76:151

"Mescaline" (Ginsberg) 109:325

"Mesh Cast for Mackerel" (Bunting) 39:299

Meshes of the Afternoon (Deren) 16:251-53; 102:28-31, 35-47

Meshugah (Singer) 111:346-47

"Mesmerism" (Pound) 48:288

"Mesopotamia" (Carver) 53:61

"Mesquakie Love Song" (Young Bear) 94:373

"Mess" (King) 53:212

"A Mess of Clams" (Mitchell) 98:174

"Message" (Berryman) 3:66; 25:95

"The Message" (Boell)
  See "Die Botschaft"

"Message" (Forche) 25:171; 83:214

"Message" (Whalen) 29:445

"A Message All Blackpeople Can Dig (& A Few Negroes Too)" ("And a Few Negroes Too") (Madhubuti) 6:313; 73:199, 210

"Message Clear" (Morgan) 31:275

"Message for the Sinecurist" (Gallagher) 63:125

Message from Malaga (MacInnes) 39:351

"Message from Mars" (McGinley) 14:365

"Message in a Bottle" (Gordimer) 33:180

"Message in a Bottle" (Police, The) 26:364

"The Message in the Bottle" (Percy) 65:257, 260

The Message in the Bottle: How Queer Man Is, How Queer Language Is, and What One Has to Do with the Other (Percy) 6:400-01; 8:438-41; 14:416; 18:396, 402; 47:333-35, 338-39

"the message of crazy horse" (Clifton) 66:82

"Message to a Black Soldier" (Madhubuti) 73:208

"Messages" (Dickey) 47:96

"Messages" (Senghor) 54:410

"The Messenger" (Gunn) 18:201

"The Messenger" (Merton) 83:390

"Messenger" (Smith) 22:389; 42:353

"The Messenger" (Steele) 45:362

The Messenger (Wright) 49:425-27, 430-31, 434

Messenger Huskuld (Vesaas)
  See *Sendemann Huskuld*

"Messengers" (Gluck) 7:120

"Messengers" (Martin) 89:118

Messengers of Day: The Memoirs of Anthony Powell (Powell) 10:417; 31:316, 319, 322

Messengers of God: Biblical Portraits and Legends (Wiesel) 11:570; 37:459

The Messengers Will Come No More (Fiedler) 13:212

Messiah (Vidal) 6:549; 10:502, 504; 22:435; 33:406-07; 72:387

The Messiah of Stockholm (Ozick) 62:345-49, 353-54, 356-57

Mesterul Manole (*Master-Builder Manole*) 75:64, 66

Mesto v slzách (*The City in Tears; Town in Tears*) (Seifert) 34:256; 44:424; 93:305, 308, 316, 318, 331, 338-39

"A Meta Physic in Things" (Bowering) 47:19

"Metafantasia: The Possibilities of Science Fiction" (Lem) 40:300

The Metal Horde (Campbell) 32:73

The Metal Man (Williamson) 29:454, 456

"Metamorfosis de la hechicera" ("Metamorphosis of a Witch") (Castellanos) 66:46, 53

"Metamorphic Journal" (Levertov) 15:338

"Metamorphoses" (Cheever) 64:65

"Metamorphoses" (Fisher) 25:161

"Metamorphoses, I / Moon" (Walcott) 76:270

"Metamorphosis" (Gluck) 44:215

"Metamorphosis" (Longley) 29:295

"Metamorphosis" (Moravia) 46:282

"The Metamorphosis" (Oates) 108:354

"Metamorphosis" (Porter) 33:322

"Metamorphosis" (Sachs) 98:322

"Metamorphosis" (Sandburg) 35:356
"Metamorphosis" (Sitwell) 9:494, 496; 67:324-25, 335
"The Metamorphosis" (Tomlinson) 45:393
Metamorphosis (Berkoff) 56:14, 16, 23
"Metamorphosis of a Witch" (Castellanos)
    See "Metamorfosis de la hechicera"
"Metaphor and Reality" (Zamora) 89:393
"Metaphor as Mistake" (Percy) 8:439
"Metaphors" (Plath) 111:167
"The Metaphysical Amorist" (Cunningham) 31:102
"The Metaphysical Horse" (Hearne) 56:125, 127
"Metaphysical Pictures of the Thistle" (MacDiarmid) 63:244
"Metaphysical Poems" (Gascoyne) 45:153
"The Metaphysical Poets" (Eliot) 10:172; 24:167, 171-72, 178; 55:346; 113:218, 220
Metapolitics (Viereck) 4:560
"Meta-Rhetoric" (Jordan) 114:146
Metel (*The Blizzard*; *The Snowstorm*) (Leonov) 92:250, 252, 260, 268-70, 277
"Metempsychosis" (Slessor) 14:492
Meteor (Behrman) 40:73-4, 76, 78, 82, 87-8
The Meteor (Duerrenmatt)
    See *Der Meteor*
Der Meteor (*The Meteor*) (Duerrenmatt) 102:54, 56, 62
Der Meteor (*The Meteor*) (Durrenmatt) 8:194; 15:199, 201
The Meteor (Durrenmatt)
    See *Der Meteor*
Les Météores (Tournier) 95:361-63, 368-69, 373, 376-77, 381-82
"The Meterological Lighthouse at O" (Raine) 103:182, 193-94
"Meters and Memory" (Justice) 102:263, 284
"Metho Drinker" (Wright) 53:418
"Method for Calling up Ghosts" (Purdy) 50:238
Méthode de méditation (Bataille) 29:38-9
The Methods of Maigret (Simenon)
    See *Mon ami Maigret*
Methods of the Novel (Oe)
    See *Shosetsu no hoho*
Methuselah's Children (Heinlein) 3:225; 8:275; 14:249; 26:169; 55:302, 304
"Métier: Why I Don't Write Like Franz Kafka" (Wilson) 49:414, 416
"Metric Blues" (Scott) 22:376
"Metrical Exercises" (Aldington) 49:10
"Le métro" (Carrier) 78:58-9, 68
Metro: A Novel of the Moscow Underground (Kaletski) 39:72-4
"Metro-Goldwyn-Mayer" (Schwartz) 45:356
Metroland (Barnes) 42:24-7
"Metropolis" (Shapcott) 38:398
Metropolis (Lang) 20:201-03, 210, 213, 215; 103:82-5, 95, 108-10, 112, 114, 117-20, 122-28
The Metropolis (Sinclair) 63:346, 348
Metropolitan Life (Lebowitz) 11:322; 36:248-49
"The Metropolitan Railway" (Betjeman) 43:44
"Mews Flat Mona" (Plomer) 4:407
"The Mexican Connection" (Joel) 26:214
"Mexican Divertimento" ("Mexican Divertissement") (Brodsky) 36:81; 50:125
"Mexican Divertissement" (Brodsky)
    See "Mexican Divertimento"
"Mexican Games" (Hughes) 108:323
"Mexican Movies" (Cisneros) 69:153

"Mexican Romancero" (Brodsky)
    See "Meksikanskij romansero"
The Mexican Stove (Condon) 100:91, 102, 110
"A Mexican Tale" (Kaplan) 50:55, 57
"The Mexican Trinity" (Porter) 101:241
"The Mexican Woman" (Simpson) 32:379-80
"Mexicans Begin Jogging" (Soto) 32:403; 80:278, 297
"Mexico" (Bass) 79:5, 11
"Mexico" (Gilchrist) 65:349
Mexico (Michener) 109:383, 386
"Mexico Age Four" (Salinas) 90:322, 329
Mexico and the United States (Archer) 12:19
Mexico Bay: A Novel of the Mid-Century (Horgan) 53:186-88
Mexico City Blues (Kerouac) 29:270-71
"Mexico Is a Foreign Country" (Warren) 13:574
Mexico Mystique: The Coming Sixth World of Consciousness (Waters) 88:349-51, 361, 364-65
Mexico Set (Deighton) 46:130-31
The Mezzanine (Baker) 61:2-5
Mezzotints (Miller) 14:372-74
MF (Burgess) 2:86-7; 4:80-1, 83; 5:85; 10:87-8; 22:75; 40:115-18, 120; 62:125; 81:303, 307; 94:40, 51
"Mi" (Tolson) 105:262
Mi abuela fumaba puros y otros cuentos de Tierra Amarilla/My Grandma Smoked Cigars, and Other Tales of Tierra Amarilla (*My Grandma Smoked Cigars, and Other Tales of Tierra Amarilla*) (Ulibarri) 83:409, 414, 418
"Mi caballo blanco" (Ulibarri) 83:413
"Mi chiquita" ("My Honey") (Guillen) 79:245
Mi general! (Lopez y Fuentes) 32:279-81
Mi idolatrado hijo sisi (Delibes) 18:110
"Mi vida entere" ("My Entire Life") (Borges) 44:367
Mia (*Mia Alone*) (Beckman) 26:87-9
Mia Alone (Beckman)
    See *Mia*
Miami (Wasserstein) 90:417
"Miami 2017" ("Seen the Lights Go Out on Broadway") (Joel) 26:215, 220, 222
Miami and the Siege of Chicago: An Informal History of the Republican and Democratic Conventions of 1968 (Mailer) 1:192; 2:263; 3:314; 4:323; 8:370-72; 11:344; 14:351; 28:256-57; 74:225; 111:103, 107
"Miami Beach" (Moss) 45:291
"MIA's (Missing in Action and Other Atlantas)" (Sanchez) 116:302, 305, 317-18
Mica Mountain Poems (Wild) 14:580
"Michael" (Brown) 5:79
Michael (Dreyer) 16:260-62
"Michael Angelo Looks Up Not Sleeping" (Gustafson) 36:216
Michael Collins (Jordan) 110:309-10
Michael Scarlett (Cozzens) 11:124, 128, 131; 92:196-97
"Michael X and the Black Power Killings in Trinidad" (Naipaul) 18:363; 105:155, 157, 163-64
"Michael's Wife" (O'Connor) 14:398
"Micheaux's Films" (hooks) 94:153
Michelangelo (Krleza)
    See *Michelangelo Buonarroti*
Michelangelo Buonarroti (*Michelangelo*; *Mikelandjelo*) (Krleza) 114:166, 174

Michelet (*Michelet par lui-même*) (Barthes) 24:25-6, 33; 83:67
Michelet par lui-même (Barthes)
    See *Michelet*
"Michelle" (Lennon and McCartney) 12:358-59; 35:278
Michigan: A Bicentennial History (Catton) 35:94
Mick and Mick (*All the Nice People*) (Leonard) 19:281
Mick Jagger (Highwater) 12:285
Mickelsson's Ghosts (Gardner) 28:163-66; 34:548
The Microcosm (Duffy) 37:113-14
"Microcosmic God" (Sturgeon) 22:410, 412; 39:361, 364-65
"The Microscopic Army Ants of Corsica" (Acorn) 15:10
Microworlds: Writings on Science Fiction and Fantasy (Lem) 40:299-300
"MidAmerica" (Urdang) 47:399
Midaq Alley (Mahfuz)
    See *Zuqaq al-Midaqq*
"Midas" (Winters) 4:593
The Midas Consequence (Ayrton) 7:19-20
Midas oder Die schwarze Leinwand (Duerrenmatt) 102:91
Midas of the Rockies: The Story of Stratton and Cripple Creek (Waters) 88:351, 360, 362
"Mid-August at Sourdough Mountain Lookout" (Snyder) 5:393; 9:501
"Mid-Autumn" (Butler) 81:124-26
Midcentury (Dos Passos) 1:79; 4:132, 137; 15:187; 25:141, 143, 145-46; 34:420, 422-23
"Mid-Day" (H. D.) 73:119
"The Middle against Both Ends" (Fiedler) 4:160
"Middle Age" (Beer) 58:33
"Middle Age" (Lowell) 8:351
The Middle Age of Mrs. Eliot (Wilson) 2:471-73; 3:536; 5:514-15; 25:461, 463-64
"The Middle Ages" (Haines) 58:216
The Middle Ages (Gurney) 54:216-17; 32:220-21; 50:178-79, 183-84
Middle Class (Millin) 49:239
Middle Class Radicalism: The Social Bases of the British Campaign for Nuclear Disarmament (Parkin) 43:338
The Middle Ground (Drabble) 22:125-28; 53:122, 124, 126, 128-29
The Middle Mist (Renault) 3:425
The Middle of a War (Fuller) 28:152-53, 158
The Middle of My Tether (Epstein) 39:465
"The Middle of Nowhere" (Wagoner) 3:508
The Middle of the Journey (Trilling) 9:530-31; 11:540-42, 544
Middle of the Night (Chayefsky) 23:112
The Middle of the Night (Mahfuz)
    See *Qalb al-layl*
"The Middle of the Night: The Hands" (Kallman) 2:222
"Middle Passage" (Hayden) 5:168-69; 14:240-41; 37:153, 155, 157-58, 160
Middle Passage (Johnson) 65:152-59
The Middle Passage; Impressions of Five Societies: British, French, and Dutch—in the West Indies and South America (Naipaul) 4:371-72, 374; 13:406; 18:363; 37:323; 105:138, 147-51, 154, 159, 180
The Middle Sister (Duncan) 26:100
"The Middle-Aged" (Rich) 7:368; 36:372
"The Middle-Aged Man and the Gulf" (Hannah) 90:137

The Middle-Aged Man on the Flying Trapeze: A Collection of Short Pieces (Thurber) 5:438, 442

"The Middle-American Prose Style" (Cowley) 39:460

A Middle-Class Education (Sheed) 4:487; 10:473; 53:339

"The Middle-Class Housewife" (Highsmith) 102:197

"Middle-Class Poem" (Dunn) 36:156

The Middleman (Ray)
    See *Jana Aranya*

The Middleman, and Other Stories (Mukherjee) 53:269-72; 115:363-64, 366-67, 386-87, 389

"Middle-Sea and Lear-Sea" (Jones) 42:241

"Middlesex" (Davie) 8:164

"The Midget" (Levine) 5:251; 14:317

Midis gagnés (Noontimes Gained) (Tzara) 47:387, 390

Midland in Stilfs (Bernhard) 32:17; 61:9

"The Mid-Life Crisis of Dionysus" (Keillor) 115:286

"Midnight" (Wright) 53:428

Midnight (Green)
    See *Minuit*

"Midnight and I'm Not Famous Yet" (Hannah) 38:232; 90:126, 148, 151, 163

The Midnight Bell: A Love Story (Twenty Thousand Streets under the Sky: A London Trilogy) (Hamilton) 51:184-86, 190, 194-95, 197-98

"Midnight Chippie's Lament" (Hughes) 35:221

A Midnight Clear (Wharton) 37:439-43

"The Midnight Club" (Strand) 71:288

"Midnight Cowboy" (Herlihy) 6:234-35

Midnight Express (Stone) 73:362-65, 367, 369-70, 382

The Midnight Folk (Masefield) 11:356

The Midnight Fox (Byars) 35:73

Midnight in the Desert (Priestley) 34:365

Midnight in the Garden of Good and Evil: A Savannah Story (Berendt) 86:33-40

"Midnight in the Mirror World" (Leiber) 25:303

Midnight Is a Place (Aiken) 35:18

"Midnight Lady" (Gaye) 26:135

Midnight Line (Savage) 40:374

"Midnight Log" (Clash) 30:48

Midnight Love (Gaye) 26:135

The Midnight Love Feast (Tournier)
    See *Le Médianoche amoureux*

"Midnight Magic" (Mason) 82:245, 256

The Midnight Man (Estleman) 48:104, 107

Midnight Mass (Bowles) 53:39-40, 45

"Midnight Meat Train" (Barker) 52:51, 53

A Midnight Moon at the Greasy Spoon (Pinero) 55:317-18

Midnight Oil (Pritchett) 5:352-53; 13:466; 41:335

"Midnight on the Bay" (Young) 17:576

"Midnight Rambler" (Jagger and Richard) 17:224, 227, 230, 235-36

"The Midnight Reader" (Gardner) 5:133

"The Midnight Skaters" (Blunden) 56:30, 33, 45-7, 52

"Midnight Turning Gray" (Matthiessen) 64:321, 324-25

Midnight Turning Gray (Matthiessen) 64:321

"Midnight Verses" (Akhmatova) 64:13

Midnight Was My Cry: New and Selected Poems (Kizer) 15:309; 80:179-80

Midnight's Children (Rushdie) 23:364, 366-69; 31:353-60; 55:216-19, 223-25, 253-54, 263; 59:406, 410, 412, 415, 417, 432, 434, 445, 447-48, 450; 100:287-88, 290, 292, 295-96, 304, 310, 312, 315-18, 322-24

"Midnite Blue" (Nyro) 17:318

"Midpoint" (Updike) 7:486; 23:465, 474-75; 43:430

Midpoint, and Other Poems (Updike) 2:441; 3:485, 487; 13:558; 23:474-75; 43:431

Midquest: A Poem (Chappell) 40:143-48; 78:91-7, 102, 111-12, 114-15

Midsommardalen (Martinson) 14:355

"Midsummer" (Gluck) 81:167

Midsummer (Walcott) 42:415-18, 421, 423; 67:344, 348-49, 358-60; 76:275, 300

Midsummer Century (Blish) 14:83, 86

"Midsummer Christmas" (Avison) 97:117

A Midsummer Dance (Salama)
    See *Juhannustanssit*

"Midsummer, England" (Walcott) 14:550

"Midsummer in Town" (Beer) 58:37

"Midsummer Meditations" (McGinley) 14:366

Midsummer Night and Other Tales in Verse (Masefield) 11:358

"Midsummer Night Madness" (O'Faolain) 7:273-74

Midsummer Night Madness, and Other Stories (O'Faolain) 1:259; 7:275; 14:402;32:340, 343; 70:313, 315-16, 321

Midsummer Night's Dream in the Workhouse (Lagerkvist) 54:278

A Midsummer Night's Sex Comedy (Allen) 52:48

A Midsummer-Night's Dream (Brenton) 31:67

"The Midway Song" (Mitchell) 12:435

The Midwich Cuckoos (Wyndham) 19:474-76

The Midwife (Hochhuth) 18:254-55

"The Midwives" (Enzensberger) 43:144, 146

"El miedo" (Marques) 96:244

Miehen tie (A Man's Road) (Sillanpaa) 19:417-18, 420

"Mientras dura vida, sobra el tiempo" (Forche) 25:169

Miernes (Breytenbach) 23:86

"Mies ei—Mitään, ei—Kukaan" ("Man Is—Nothing Is—No One") (Haavikko) 34:175

The Mightiest Machine (Campbell) 32:72, 74, 76

"A Mighty Trauma Is Our Beginning" (Spielberg) 6:519

Mignon (Cain) 28:49, 52-3

"Mignotta" (Pasolini) 37:347

Migraine: Evolution of a Common Disorder (Migraine: Understanding a Common Disorder) (Sacks) 67:296-97

Migraine: Understanding a Common Disorder (Sacks)
    See *Migraine: Evolution of a Common Disorder*

"Migrant Swift" (Wright) 53:423

Migrants (Coles) 108:194, 210-12

"Migration" (Boland) 40:100; 113:109

"Migration" (Carver) 55:275

"A Migration" (Heaney) 74:168

"Migration" (Neruda) 62:332

Migrations (Josipovici) 43:220-21

Migrations: An Arabesque in Histories (Scott) 43:374, 385

Miguel Street (Naipaul) 4:372, 375; 13:403, 406; 37:323-25, 327-28; 105:142, 147-48, 150, 154-56, 165, 179

"Miisa" (Diamond) 30:110

"Mike" (Acorn) 15:8

Mikelandjelo (Krleza)
    See *Michelangelo Buonarroti*

"Mike's View" (Royko) 109:395

Mikey and Nicky (May) 16:435-37

Mikkai (Secret Rendezvous) (Abe) 22:14-15; 53:5-6; 81:297

Mila Eighteen (Uris) 7:491; 32:433, 435

O milagre secundo Salomé (Migueis) 10:340-41

The Milagro Beanfield War (Nichols) 38:341-42, 344-47

"El milagro de Anaquillé" (Carpentier) 11:102-03

"El milagro secreto" ("The Secret Miracle") (Borges) 2:76; 8:98-9, 102; 44:363; 83:183

De milagros y de melancolías (Of Miracles and Melancholies) (Mujica Lainez) 31:280, 282

Mildred Pierce (Cain) 3:97; 11:84; 28:45, 47, 49-53

Mile High (Condon) 45:97-8, 101-03

"The Mile Runner" (Waddington) 28:438

"Mile Zero" (Kroetsch) 57:292-93

"Miles City, Montana" (Munro) 50:209-12, 216, 218-20; 95:309-10, 314

Miles of Aisles (Mitchell) 12:438

"Milford Junction, 1939: A Brief Encounter" (Coover) 46:122

"Milgate" (Lowell) 11:331

The Military Half: An Account of Destruction in Quang Ngai and Quang Tin (Schell) 35:362-63

Military Men (Just) 4:266; 27:227

The Military Philosophers (Powell) 3:400, 402; 7:345; 9:435; 10:415; 31:317

"Milk" (Carlson) 54:37-8

Milk and Honey (Jolley) 46:217-21

Milk and Honey (Lennon) 35:275-76

"Milk Bread Beer Ice" (Shields) 113:405

"Milk Is Very Good for You" (Dixon) 52:95

"Milk of Death " (Yourcenar)
    See "Le lait de la mort"

"The Milk of Paradise" (Tiptree) 48:388, 392, 396

"Milk the Mouse" (Ryan) 65:215

The Milk Train Doesn't Stop Here Anymore (Williams) 2:465; 5:499, 503; 11:573; 19:472; 45:446, 450, 453, 455; 71:387; 111:379-80, 383, 391

Milkbottle H (Orlovitz) 22:333-35

The Milk-Cheese (Pasolini)
    See *La Ricotta*

"Milkman 2" (King)
    See "Big Wheels: A Tale of the Laundry Game"

"Milkweed" (Levine) 14:321

"Milkweed" (Wright) 3:540; 5:518

The Milky Way (Bunuel)
    See *La voie lactée*

The Milky Way: Galaxy Number One (Branley) 21:18

"Milky Way Vegetation I" (Gunnars) 69:262

"Milky Way Vegetation II" (Gunnars) 69:262

"The Mill" (Bates) 46:66-7

"The Mill" (Morgan) 31:275

"The Mill" (Wilbur) 53:410; 110:353

"Mill Cry" (Lane) 25:288

"Mill Mountain" (Brown) 59:265

"The Mill on the Po" (Bacchelli) 19:31-2

Mille chemins ouverts (Green) 3:204

"Millenium" (McGinley)   14:366

Millennium: A Novel about People and Politics in the Year 1999 (Bova)   45:69-70, 72-3

"Millennium Also Ran" (Bates)   46:52

"The Millennium, and What They Can Do With It" (Perelman)   9:416

Millennium Approaches (Kushner)   81:196-213

Miller's Crossing (The Coen Brothers)   108:145-47, 149-51, 153, 156-58, 161-63, 166-67, 169

"The Miller's Tale" (Bates)   46:66

Millie's Boy (Peck)   17:337-39

Le million (Clair)   20:58-61, 67-8, 70

"Million Miles" (McCartney)   35:286

"The Millionaire" (McGuane)   45:265-66

"Millionaire" (Scannell)   49:327

"Millions in His Firing Squad" (Royko)   109:408

Millions of Strange Shadows (Hecht)   8:269-70; 13:269; 19:207

"The Million-Year Picnic" (Bradbury)   42:38

Un millón de muertos (One Million Dead) (Gironella)   11:235, 238

"The Millpond" (Komunyakaa)   94:238

"Millpond Lost" (Warren)   39:265

"The Mills of the Kavanaughs" (Lowell)   1:179, 182; 2:246; 4:295-96, 298, 300, 303; 8:348, 351, 353, 356; 15:344; 37:232, 242

The Mills of the Kavanaughs (Lowell)   1:179, 182; 2:246; 4:295-96, 303; 8:348, 351, 353, 356; 15:344; 37:232, 242

The Millstone (Thank You All Very Much) (Drabble)   2:118-19; 5:118-19; 10:162, 165; 22:122-24; 53:117-18, 121

"Millstream Memories" (Blunden)   56:48

"Milne's Bar" (MacCaig)   36:285

Milos (Love) (Dabrowska)   15:167

"A Miltonic Sonnet for Mr. Johnson on His Refusal of Mr. Peter Hurd's Official Portrait" (Wilbur)   110:371, 381

Milton's God (Empson)   8:202; 33:146, 148, 151; 34:336-38

Milton's "Paradise Lost" (Wilding)   73:390, 396

"Mimesis and the Motive for Fiction" (Alter)   34:515

"Mimi the Fish" (Mazer)   26:291

The Mimic Men (Naipaul)   4:373, 375; 7:253; 9:391-92; 13:403-05; 18:360-61; 37:325; 105:154, 156, 161, 170, 180-81

Minä, Olli ja Orvokki (I, Olli, and Orvokki) (Salama)   18:460-62

"Mind" (Wilbur)   9:569-70; 110:351

Mind Breaths: Poems, 1972-1977 (Ginsberg)   13:241; 36:185-86, 188, 191, 196; 109:331

Mind Drugs (Hyde)   21:174

The Mind Game (Spinrad)   46:385

"Mind Games" (Lennon)   35:265-66, 270-71

Mind Games (Lennon)   35:265-67

The Mind Has Mountains (Hocking)   13:285

Mind in the Modern World (Trilling)   11:539; 24:458

"The Mind Is Still" (Le Guin)   45:212

The Mind Murders (van de Wetering)   47:408-09, 411-12

"A Mind of His Own" (Haldeman)   61:174, 177

Mind of My Mind (Butler)   38:61-2, 64, 66

"Mind on My Man" (Simon)   26:409

Mind over Murder (Kienzle)   25:275

The Mind Parasites (Wilson)   3:537

"Mind to Body" (Fuller)   4:178

A Mind to Murder (James)   18:273; 46:205, 208

Mindbridge (Haldeman)   61:171-73, 176, 185

"The Mind-Reader" (Wilbur)   9:568, 570; 53:402-03

The Mind-Reader: New Poems (Wilbur)   9:568-70; 14:578-79; 53:398-99, 401-02, 405, 409-11; 110:352, 355, 361, 380

"The Mind's Games" (Williams)   42:450

"Mind's Heart" (Creeley)   78:156

Minds Meet (Abish)   22:17, 22

The Minds of Billy Milligan (Keyes)   80:166-67, 169

Mine Boy (Abrahams)   4:1-2

"Mine Field" (Calvino)   33:101

"The Mine Is Also of Nature" (Acorn)   15:10

"Mined Country" (Wilbur)   53:397

"Mineral" (Page)   7:291

"Minerals of Cornwall, Stones of Cornwall" (Redgrove)   41:351

"Miners" (Wright)   10:543

The Miner's Pale Children (Merwin)   1:214; 2:277-78; 5:288; 8:390; 18:332-33; 88:198-200

"The Miner's Wake" (Parini)   54:360

Minetoza (Paustovsky)   40:362

Minetti (Bernhard)   32:25; 61:12-13

Minick (Kaufman)   38:258

"The Minimal" (Roethke)   8:456; 19:397; 101:263

"Minimal Mahoney, in His Cups" (Klappert)   57:265

The Minimal Self (Lasch)   102:289-90, 295-96, 301-02

"Minims" (Leithauser)   27:242

The Minister (Thomas)   13:542; 48:383

The Minister for Justice (Mr. Stephen) (White)   49:404

"Minister Opens New Home for Battered Husbands" (Durcan)   43:115-16

The Ministry of Fear (Greene)   1:130-31; 9:250; 18:194; 37:140; 70:289; 72:148-50, 169-72

The Ministry of Fear (Lang)   20:207, 213

"Mink" (Muldoon)   32:321

The Min-Min (Clark)   12:129-30

"The Minneapolis Poem" (Wright)   3:541, 543; 5:520; 28:465

"Minneapolis Story" (Warren)   39:259

Minnie and Moskowitz (Cassavetes)   20:47-8, 55

"Minnie and Mrs. Hoyne" (Fearing)   51:108

The Minnow Leads to Treasure (Pearce)   See *Minnow on the Say*

Minnow on the Say (The Minnow Leads to Treasure) (Pearce)   21:280-81, 283-89

"Minnows and a Monster" (Young)   82:411

A Minor Apocalypse (Konwicki)   See *Mala apokalipsa*

Minor Characters (Johnson)   58:286-92

"Minor Heroism: Something About My Father" (Gurganus)   70:190, 193, 195-96

Minor Monuments: Selected Essays (Moss)   45:292; 50:353

"A Minor Mood" (Dybek)   114:74-5

"The Minor Novelist" (Sheed)   53:341

Minor Poems (Eliot)   15:213

"Minority Poem" (Ezekiel)   61:97-9

"Minority Report" (Blunden)   56:31

Minority Report (Rice)   7:363

"Minotaur" (Dickey)   28:117

"Minotaur" (Shapcott)   38:399

"Le minotaure ou la halte d'oran" (Camus)   69:112

Der Minotaurus (Wellershoff)   46:435

The Minstrel Boy (Cronin)   32:140

"The Minstrels" (Valenzuela)   See "Los Menestrales"

"The Mint Quality" (Blackburn)   43:63

Minty Alley (James)   33:220

Minuit (Midnight) (Green)   11:259; 77:270, 276, 279-81

Minus Sign (Williamson)   29:455

Minute by Glass Minute (Stevenson)   33:381-82

"Minutes of the Last Meeting" (Updike)   15:544, 546

Minutes to Go (Burroughs)   109:183, 194-95

"La minutieuse" ("Thoroughgo") (Char)   9:163

"Mio marito" (Ginzburg)   11:229

Mirabell: Books of Numbers (Merrill)   13:382; 18:329-31; 34:226-31, 235-38; 91:228

"A Miracle" (Mahfuz)   52:297

"The Miracle" (Pasternak)   63:312

The Miracle (Jordan)   110:304

Miracle (Skvorecky)   See *Mirákl*

Miracle at Indian River (Nowlan)   15:398-99

Miracle de la rose (Miracle of the Rose) (Genet)   1:115-17; 5:135, 137-39; 10:225; 44:386-90; 46:173, 176-82

Miracle en Bohàme (Skvorecky)   See *Mirákl*

"A Miracle for Breakfast" (Bishop)   1:36

The Miracle Game: A Political Whodunit (Skvorecky)   See *Mirákl*

Miracle in Saville (Michener)   109:383

"Miracle Man" (Costello)   21:67

"The Miracle of the Birds" (Amado)   106:73

Miracle of the Rose (Genet)   See *Miracle de la rose*

"Miracle on St. David's Day" (Clarke)   61:79, 81-3

Miracle Play (Oates)   3:364; 33:289

Miracle Play (Shreve)   23:404-05

Miracle Row (Ian)   21:187

The Miracle Woman (Capra)   16:153, 165-66

The Miracle Worker (Gibson)   23:174-78

"Miracles" (Abse)   29:18

Miracles (Lewis)   3:296; 6:311; 14:323; 27:262

Miracles of the Gods (von Daniken)   30:426

Miracolo a Milano (De Sica)   20:85, 93

The Miraculous Day of Amalia Gómez (Rechy)   107:254, 256, 257

"Miraculous Weapons" (Cesaire)   See "Les armes miraculeuses"

La Mirada (The Gaze; The Look) (Marques)   96:233, 235, 237-40, 244

Mirage (Ringwood)   48:334-36, 338-39

"Mirages" (Boland)   113:76

Mirages (Burnshaw)   13:129

Mirákl (Miracle; Miracle en Bohàme; The Miracle Game: A Political Whodunit) (Skvorecky)   39:229; 69:330, 339, 341-43, 348-53

Miramar (Mahfuz)   52:299, 301, 304-05; 55:177-79, 181, 183, 185

"Miranda" (Barker)   8:47

"Miranda Grows Up" (Van Duyn)   116:427

"Miranda over the Valley" (Dubus)   13:183; 97:196, 201, 212

"Mirando aquellos desde los campos" (Zamora)   89:368

"Miriam" (Capote)   3:99; 13:133; 19:79; 34:321

"Miriam" (Kerrigan)   6:276

"Miriam" (Klima)
   See "Myriam"

Miriam at Thirty-Four (Lelchuk)   5:244-45

"Miriam Tazewell" (Ransom)   11:470

"Miró in the Third Person: Eight Statements" (Cage)   41:78

En miroir (Jouve)   47:206

Le miroir de la production: ou, l'illusion critique du matérialism historique (The Mirror of Production) (Baudrillard)   60:11-14

"Miroir de la tauromachie" (Leiris)   61:341

Le miroir des limbes (The Mirror of Limbo) (Malraux)   9:359; 15:354; 57:306-09, 319

Le miroir qui revient (Robbe-Grillet)   43:366

"The Mirror" (Bowers)   9:122

"The Mirror" (Haines)   58:222

"Mirror" (Plath)   5:340; 111:206-12

"Mirror" (Robison)   98:306, 308

"The Mirror" (Singer)   15:505; 38:413-16; 111:329-31

The Mirror (Singer)   38:413-16

The Mirror and the Lamp (Abrams)   24:11-12, 14, 18

"The Mirror and the Mask" (Borges)   13:111; 48:41

The Mirror Crack'd from Side to Side (Christie)   110:121

A Mirror for Artists (Davidson)   19:123-24

A Mirror for the Sky (West)   7:520; 17:544

A Mirror for Witches (Forbes)   12:203

"Mirror Image" (Asimov)   26:43-4

Mirror in My House: The Autobiographies of Sean O'Casey (O'Casey)   5:318

The Mirror in the Roadway (O'Connor)   14:397

"The Mirror in Which Two Are Seen as One" (Rich)   18:447

"Mirror, Mirror" (Tillinghast)   29:414

Mirror, Mirror (Garfield)   12:234-35

Mirror, Mirror (Waugh)   6:559-60

The Mirror of Criticism: Selected Reviews, 1977-1982 (Josipovici)   43:224-26

The Mirror of Her Dreams (Donaldson)   46:143-45

Mirror of Her Own (Guy)   26:145-46

The Mirror of Limbo (Malraux)
   See *Le miroir des limbes*

The Mirror of Production (Baudrillard)
   See *Le miroir de la production: ou, l'illusion critique du matérialism historique*

"The Mirror of the Enigmas" (Borges)   44:355; 83:162

The Mirror of the Mother: Selected Poems, 1975-1985 (Roberts)   48:342-44

"The Mirror of the Unknown" (Kis)   57:251

Mirror on the Floor (Bowering)   47:19-20

"Mirror Sermon" (Brutus)   43:92

"The Mirror Stage as Formative of the Function of the I as Revealed in Psychoanalytic Experience" (Lacan)
   See "Le stade du miroir"

"The Mirrored Man" (Avison)   97:75, 80, 86, 90

"Mirrors" (Borges)
   See "Los espejos"

"Mirrors" (Giovanni)   64:192

"Mirrors" (Grace)   56:116, 118-19

"Mirrors" (Graham)   48:145

Mirrors (Creeley)   36:120-22; 78:141-42, 151-53, 158

Mirrors (Mahfuz)
   See *al- Maraya*

Mirrors and Windows (Nemerov)   2:308; 36:302-03, 305

Mirrorshades: The Cyberpunk Anthology (Sterling)   72:370

A Misalliance (Brookner)   51:61-4

The Misanthrope (Wilbur)   14:576

"Misanthropos" (Gunn)   18:203; 32:208, 211

"Miscellaneous" (MacInnes)   23:286

"A Miscellany of Characters That Will Not Appear" (Cheever)   7:49

"The Mischief Done" (Crispin)   22:112

The Mischief Makers (Truffaut)   20:380, 397

"Misdeal" (Landolfi)   11:321

La mise à mort (Aragon)   22:38

"Mise Eire" (Boland)   67:40, 45-6; 113:70, 82, 86, 98, 103, 105-08

Miserable Miracle (Michaux)
   See *Misérable miracle*

Misérable miracle (Miserable Miracle) (Michaux)   8:392; 19:312-13

"Misère noire" (Damas)   84:181

"Miserere" (Gascoyne)   45:147, 153, 157

"Misericords" (Raine)   103:186

"Misericords" (Szirtes)   46:392

"Misery" (Ian)   21:183

Misery (King)   61:325-29, 337; 113:350, 369-70, 388, 392

"Misery and Splendor" (Hass)   99:140

"Misfit" (Heinlein)   3:225; 14:248; 55:302

"Misfit" (Simon)   26:408-09

Misfits (Davies)   21:103-04

The Misfits (Huston)   20:168

The Misfits (Miller)   1:216, 218; 6:332; 15:374

"Misgiving" (Frost)   26:117

Misgivings (Howard)   47:169

Mishima: A Vision of the Void (Yourcenar)
   See *Mishima; ou, La vision du vide*

Mishima; ou, La vision du vide (Mishima: A Vision of the Void) (Yourcenar)   50:363; 87:401

"Mismatched Shoes" (Komunyakaa)   94:238

"Miss Amao" (Ding Ling)
   See "Amao guniang"

"Miss Book World" (Abse)   29:18

"Miss Briggs" (Sargeson)   31:370

"'Miss Buttle' and 'Mr. Eliot'" (Wilson)   2:477

"Miss Coynte of Green" (Williams)   5:502-03; 45:454

"Miss Drake Proceeds to Supper" (Plath)   111:170-71

The Miss Firecracker Contest (Henley)   23:217

"Miss Foote" (Thomas)   107:333

"Miss Gada-Nigi" (Seifert)   93:341

"Miss Gee" (Auden)   11:16

"Miss God" (Ewart)   46:153

Miss Gomez and the Brethren (Trevor)   7:476; 9:529; 71:345; 116:334-35

"Miss Gradenko" (Police, The)   26:366

"Miss Hamilton in London" (Adcock)   41:17

Miss Herbert (The Suburban Wife) (Stead)   8:500-01; 32:411-12, 414; 80:326-27, 329, 342-44, 347-48

"Miss Holland" (Lavin)   18:303

Miss Jane Pittman (Gaines)
   See *The Autobiography of Miss Jane Pittman*

"Miss Jee" (Jin)   109:52

"Miss Leonora When Last Seen" (Taylor)   37:412

Miss MacIntosh, My Darling (Young)   82:400-21

"Miss Marnell" (Clarke)   6:112

Miss Morissa, Doctor of the Gold Trail (Sandoz)   28:404

"Miss Muriel" (Petry)   1:266; 7:305

Miss Muriel, and Other Stories (Petry)   1:266; 7:305

"Miss Nora Kerrin Writes to Her Betrothed" (Shapcott)   38:403

Miss Peabody's Inheritance (Jolley)   46:215-19, 221

"Miss Peskova Regrets" (Skvorecky)   69:345

"Miss Pulkinhorn" (Golding)   81:319

"Miss Quirke" (Trevor)   116:378

"Miss Rosie" (Clifton)   66:73, 86

"Miss Scarlett, Mr. Rhett and Other Latter Day Saints" (Angelou)   77:28

Miss Silver's Past (Skvorecky)
   See *Lvíce*

Miss Smilla's Feeling for Snow (Hoeg)
   See *Smilla's Sense of Snow*

"Miss Smith" (Trevor)   71:347; 116:338

"Miss Twye" (Ewart)   46:148

Miss Universal Happiness (Foreman)   50:168, 171

"Miss Winczewska" (Dabrowska)   15:169

"A Miss X" (Alberti)   7:7

"Miss You" (Jagger and Richard)   17:239-40, 242

"Miss Zilphia Gant" (Faulkner)   18:149

"Missile Base 612" (Yehoshua)   13:617; 31:471-72, 474

"The Missing" (Gunn)   81:180

Missing Continents (Dorfman)   77:150-52

"Missing Dates" (Empson)   19:156

"The Missing Girl" (Jackson)   60:230

"The Missing Line" (Singer)   69:312

"The Missing Peace" (Danticat)   94:98

"A Missing Person" (Mahapatra)   33:282

"The Missing Person" (Wolff)   64:450-51, 454

The Missing Person (Grumbach)   22:205-06; 64:198

Missing Persons, and Other Essays (Boell)   9:112

The Missing Persons League (Bonham)   12:55

"Missing the Sea" (Kallman)   2:221

"The Mission" (Friedman)   56:97

"The Mission" (Warren)   18:537

Mission Earth (Hubbard)   43:206-08

Mission terminée. (Mission to Kala) (Beti)   27:41-4, 46-9, 51-2

"Mission Tire Factory, 1969" (Soto)   80:278, 293

Mission to Kala (Beti)
   See *Mission terminée*

Mission to the Heart Stars (Blish)   14:86

"The Missionaries" (Duncan)   41:129

The Missionaries (Jenkins)   52:221, 223, 227-28

"The Missionary" (Smith)   64:392

"The Missionary Visits Our Church in Scranton" (Parini)   54:362

"Mississippi" (Bass)   79:4-5, 7

"Mississippi" (Dove)   81:140, 150

"Mississippi, Ham Rider" (Bambara)   88:27

"Mississippi Levee" (Hughes)   15:292

Mississippi Mermaid (Truffaut)   20:386, 389-92; 101:375, 379, 380-81, 383, 390, 407

"Missives to Max" (Hildesheimer)   49:180

The Missolonghi Manuscript (Prokosch)   48:316

"Missoula Softball Tournament" (Hugo)   32:241

"Missouri" (Urdang)   47:399-400

Missouri Bittersweet (Kantor)   7:195-96

The Missouri Breaks (McGuane)   45:261-62

"Missy" (Hill) **113**:281, 294, 297
"Missy's Twins" (Peterkin) **31**:306, 308
The Mist (King) **37**:207; **113**:341, 344-45, 359, 379-80
The Mist in the Mirror (Hill) **113**:315-16, 318
"The Mist Net" (Muldoon) **72**:277
"The Mistake" (Singer) **69**:306
Mistaken Ambitions (Moravia)
  See *Le ambizioni sbagliate*
"Mr. Andrews" (Forster) **77**:213
Mister Corbett's Ghost, and Other Stories (Garfield) **12**:217-18, 225, 237
Mister McGregor (Lytle) **22**:295, 298
Mister, Mister (Grass) **4**:201
Mr. (Calvino)
  See *Palomar*
"Mr. Parker" (Colwin) **5**:108
"Mister Rock of Ages" (Lightfoot) **26**:282
"Mister Sparks: A Self-Portrait" (Tolson) **105**:249
"Mr. Tambourine Man" (Dylan) **6**:155; **12**:188-89; **77**:187
"Mister Toussan" (Ellison) **11**:183; **114**:93-4, 131
Mister White Eyes (Gold) **42**:196-97
Mr. Wilson's War (Dos Passos) **25**:145; **34**:424; **82**:96
El misterio del ramo de rosas (*The Mystery of the Boquet of Roses*) (Puig) **65**:273
"Misterios gozosos" (Castellanos) **66**:45, 50
La misteriosa desaparición de la Marquesita de Loria (*The Marchioness of Loria; The Mysterious Disappearance of the Young Marchioness of Loria*) (Donoso) **32**:160-61; **99**:242
Mistero Buffo (Fo) **109**:101, 104-06, 108-09, 113-18, 124-25, 127, 131, 142, 146
Il mistero di oberwald (Antonioni) **20**:42
Les mistons (Truffaut) **20**:380, 397; **101**:379, 382, 388, 405, 410
"Mistral" (Faulkner) **18**:147-48; **28**:136
"The Mistress" (Berriault) **54**:3; **109**:96
The Mistress and Other Stories (Berriault) **54**:3-4; **109**:90
"Mistress Mary" (Macdonald) **13**:356
Mistress Masham's Repose (White) **30**:441, 449
The Mists of Avalon (Bradley) **30**:31-2
"Misty Morning" (Marley) **17**:271
"Misty Mountain Hop" (Page and Plant) **12**:475
The Misunderstanding (Camus)
  See *Le malentendu*
A Misunderstanding (Farrell) **66**:129
"Misunderstood" (Townshend) **17**:537
Misunderstood Games (Carrier)
  See *Les jeux incompris*
"Mit Wechselndem Schlüssel" ("With Changing Key") (Celan) **19**:90
"The Mitchells" (Murray) **40**:339, 341
"Der Mitmacher" (Duerrenmatt) **102**:61
Der Mitmacher (*The Accomplice*) (Duerrenmatt) **102**:61-2, 64, 69
Der Mitmacher: Ein Komplex (Duerrenmatt) **102**:61
Mito (*Myth*) (Buero Vallejo) **15**:101-02
"Mittags um zwei" (Eich) **15**:202
Mitteilungen an Max: Über der Stand der Dinge und anderes (Hildesheimer) **49**:179
"Mittelbergheim" (Milosz) **31**:265
Mixed Company (Shaw) **7**:411
"Mixed Doubles" (Shaw) **34**:370
"Mixed Feelings" (Ashbery) **15**:28, 32

"The Mixed Marriage" (Muldoon) **32**:319
"Mixed Sequence" (Roethke) **46**:364; **101**:304
"The Mixer" (MacNeice) **4**:318; **53**:243
A Mixture of Frailties (Davies) **13**:171; **25**:130-33; **42**:101-05; **75**:184, 192, 199, 204-05, 211-15; **91**:203-4
"Mizu kara waga namida o nuguitamo hi" ("The Day He Himself Shall Wipe My Tears Away"; "My Tears"; "Waga namida o nuguitamo, hi") (Oe) **36**:347-48; **86**:218, 225, 228, 239-40, 244
"M=L/T" (Goldbarth) **38**:205
"Mnemoka" (Smith) **43**:425
"A Mnemonic Wallpaper Pattern for Southern Two Seaters" (Williams) **13**:600
Mnemosyne Lay in Dust (Clarke) **6**:110, 112; **9**:168
Mo' Better Blues (Lee) **105**:89-91, 93, 95, 98, 102-03, 111, 127-28
"The Mob" (Brutus) **43**:92, 94
Mobile (Butor) **3**:93; **8**:117-18, 120; **15**:115, 118, 120
"The Mobile Bed-Object" (Highsmith) **102**:197
Mobius the Stripper (Josipovici) **6**:270
Moby Dick (Huston) **20**:163, 165-67
"Mocassin" (Kenny) **87**:240
"The Moccasin Telegraph" (Kinsella) **43**:254
The Moccasin Telegraph, and Other Stories (Kinsella) **43**:253, 257-58, 260
"The Mock Auction" (Lavin) **99**:319, 322
"Mock Orange" (Gluck) **44**:216, 218, 221
Mockingbird (Tevis) **42**:371-73, 376-77
Mockingbird, Wish Me Luck (Bukowski) **5**:80; **82**:4
Mockinpott (Weiss) **51**:391, 395-96
"Mode of Existence of a Literary Work" (Wellek) **28**:452
"The Model" (Auden) **9**:59
"The Model" (Baxter) **78**:17
"The Model" (Malamud) **27**:307
"The Model" (Nin) **60**:277
The Model (Aickman) **57**:4-5
Model (Wiseman) **20**:477-78
The Model Apartment (Margulies) **76**:188
A Model Childhood (Wolf)
  See *Kindheitsmuster*
A Model for Death (Bioy Casares)
  See *Un modelo para la muerte*
Un modelo para la muerte (*A Model for Death*) (Bioy Casares) **88**:78
Moderate Fable (Young) **82**:396, 400, 405-06, 409, 411-12, 414
Moderato cantabile (Duras) **3**:129; **6**:149-50; **11**:165, 167-68; **34**:162; **40**:180-81, 184; **68**:74, 91; **100**:123-24, 130
The Modern American Novel (Bradbury) **32**:57
"Modern Dance Class" (Dunn) **36**:153
A Modern Day Yankee in a Connecticut Court, and Other Essays on Science (Lightman) **81**:76
Modern Dogma and the Rhetoric of Assent (Booth) **24**:92, 99
"The Modern Element in Modern Literature" (Trilling) **9**:532
The Modern Hebrew Poem Itself (Burnshaw) **3**:91
"Modern Literature and Sex" (Oe) **86**:229
"Modern Literature: Between the Whirlpool and the Rock" (Wilson) **24**:466
"Modern Love" (Boyle) **90**:47-8, 61
"Modern Love" (Morgan) **2**:295
Modern Poetry: A Personal Essay (MacNeice) **10**:324, 326; **53**:234-35, 244

"Modern Poetry and the Imagists" (Aldington) **49**:16
Modern Poetry and the Tradition (Brooks) **24**:101, 103-04; **86**:278-79, 286; **110**:3-4, 9, 11, 13-14, 26, 28-9, 32
"Modern Poetry Is Prose (But It Is Saying Plenty)" (Ferlinghetti) **27**:139
The Modern Poets (Rosenthal) **28**:389-90
Modern Rhetoric (Brooks) **86**:278
"Modern Saint #271" (Janowitz) **43**:211
Modern Scream (Tomlin) **17**:516-17
The Modern Short Story: A Critical Survey (Bates) **46**:67
The Modern Temper (Krutch) **24**:281, 286-87, 289
"Modern Theatre" (Lagerkvist) **54**:271
"Modern Times" (Parra) **102**:355
Modern Times (Chaplin) **16**:190-92, 194-95, 197, 201-04, 207
"The Modern Writer and His Community" (Brooks) **24**:111; **110**:8
"Moderne AE gteskab og andre Betragtninger" (Dinesen) **95**:61
Modernism and the Harlem Renaissance (Baker) **65**:381
"Modernism" in Modern Drama: A Definition and Estima tion (Krutch) **24**:286
Modernities and Other Writings (Cendrars) **106**:190-91
The Modes of Modern Writing: Metaphor, Metonymy, and the Typology of Modern Literature (Lodge) **36**:271-72, 274
"Modes of Pleasure" (Gunn) **18**:199
"A Modest Proposal" (Hughes) **14**:270
"A Modest Proposal" (Stafford) **7**:457; **68**:449
"A Modest Self-Tribute" (Wilson) **24**:480
"The Modesty of History" (Borges) **10**:65
La modification (*A Change of Heart*) (Butor) **3**:92; **8**:113, 116-17, 119-21; **11**:78-9; **15**:112-13, 115-17, 119
"Modified Sonnets" (Moss) **14**:376
"Modulations for a Solo Voice" (Levertov) **15**:338-39
Modus Vivendi (Levinson) **49**:227-29
"Moe, Nat, and Yrd" (Pesetsky) **28**:358
Un moegliche Bewiesaufrahme (*The Impossible Proof*) (Nossack) **6**:365-66
A Moelna Elegy (Ekelof)
  See *En Mölna-elegi*
Moetsukita chizu (*The Ruined Map*) (Abe) **8**:1; **22**:12, 14; **53**:2-3, 5-6; **81**:285, 287, 289, 294, 297
"Moeurs contemporaines" (Pound) **10**:405
"Mogollon Morning" (Momaday) **85**:281
Mogu, the Wanderer (Colum) **28**:86
"Mohaq" (Shamlu) **10**:469
"The Mohawks in High Steel" (Mitchell) **98**:180, 184, 187
Mohn und Gedächtnes (*Poppy and Memory*) (Celan) **10**:101-02; **19**:89; **53**:69, 71, 74, 76-7, 80
M.O.I. American Pageant (Zappa) **17**:584-85
Moi, Laminaire (*I, Laminarian*) (Cesaire) **32**:112-13; **112**:12, 22-3, 26, 30
Moi, Pierre Huneau (Theriault) **79**:414
"Moi, Pierre Rivière, ayant égurgé ma mer, ma soeur, et mon frère" ("I, Pierre Rivière, Having Slaughtered My Mother, My Sister, and My Brother") (Foucault) **31**:185
Moi, Tituba, sorciére, noire de Salem (*I, Tituba, Sorceress, Black Woman of Salem*) (Conde) **52**:84-5; **92**:101-02, 108, 113-14, 124-31, 133-35

Moïra (Green)   77:270-71, 274, 276-78, 290

Moires (Jouve)   47:209

Moise and the World of Reason (Williams)   5:505-06; 7:544; 11:574-75; 15:581; 19:472; 45:453

Moj obracun s njima (*My Squaring of Accounts with Them*) (Krleza)   114:169, 175

"Moja ratna lirika" ("My War Poetry") (Krleza)   114:170

Moje první lásky (*My First Loves*) (Klima)   56:172-74

Mojo: A Black Love Story (Childress)   86:309, 316; 96:91, 103-04, 111

Mojo and the Russians (Myers)   35:296

"The Mole" (Kawabata)
   See "The Mole"

Mole Notes (Benedikt)   4:55

"The Mole-Catcher" (Blunden)   56:37

"The Molecule as Mosaic" (Hall)   51:175

Molecules Today and Tomorrow (Hyde)   21:174

"Moles" (Oliver)   34:247; 98:274

"The Molesters" (Oates)   11:402

"Molitva rezanova" (Voznesensky)   15:554

Molloy (Beckett)   2:44; 3:45; 4:52; 6:34, 37, 42-3, 45; 9:78-80, 84, 86; 11:32-5; 14:71-2, 76-7; 18:47; 29:53, 55-7, 59, 65-7; 57:65, 92; 59:253-54, 257, 260

"Molly" (Dubus)   97:208, 213, 215-16, 218

Molly (Gray)   14:214; 36:203

"Molly Brant, Iroquois Matron, Speaks" (Allen)   84:24

Molly Brant: Poems of War (Kenny)
   See *Tekonwatoni/Molly Brant (1735-1795): Poems of War*

Molly Cottontail (Caldwell)   50:302

"Molly: Passions" (Kenny)   87:257

"Molly's Dog" (Adams)   46:21

Molly's Dream (Fornes)   39:138; 61:129-31

En Mölna-elegi ("Elegy"; *A Moelna Elegy*) (Ekeloef)   27:114-15

Molnen över Metaponthion (*The Clouds over Metaponthion*) (Johnson)   14:296

"Moly" (Gunn)   32:208; 81:179

Moly (Gunn)   3:215-16; 6:221-22; 18:200, 203; 32:208, 211

"Mom" (Smith)   73:356, 358

"Mom in Your Boots" (Carroll)   38:103

"Mom Luby and the Social Worker" (Hunter)   35:226

Mom, the Wolf Man, and Me (Klein)   30:236-37, 239, 241

Momatkom (Livesay)   79:345

"Moment" (Nemerov)   36:303

"The Moment" (Raine)   45:332, 338

"The Moment" (Roethke)   3:433; 8:456

"The Moment before the Gun Went Off" (Gordimer)   70:177

The Moment Is All (Gustafson)   36:222

"Moment of Eternity" (MacDiarmid)   4:309; 11:334

"The Moment of Green" (Merwin)   88:213

"A Moment of Green Laurel" (Vidal)   33:406-07

"The Moment of My Father's Death" (Olds)   85:302

A Moment of True Feeling (Handke)   8:264; 10:255-56, 259-60; 38:218-21, 223, 227

"The Moment of Truth" (Castellanos)   66:56

"The Moment of Vision" (Eberhart)   56:80

A Moment of War: A Memoir of the Spanish Civil War (Lee)   90:200, 204-7, 209-10

"Moment of Wisdom" (Fisher)   87:124

"The Moment the Two Worlds Meet" (Olds)   85:293, 296

"Momentary Bafflement with Return Home at Dawn" (Codrescu)   46:106

A Momentary Taste of Being (Tiptree)   48:388-89, 392

Moments (Hine)   15:282

"Moments of Light" (Chappell)   40:141

Moments of Light (Chappell)   40:141-43; 78:95, 113

Moments of Reprieve (Levi)
   See *Lilít e altri racconti*

Moments of the Italian Summer (Wright)   28:469, 472

"Momma" (Barthelme)   46:37

"Momma" (Seger)   35:380

"Momma and the Neutron Bomb" (Yevtushenko)   51:432

"Momma Welfare Roll" (Angelou)   35:30

Momo (Gary)
   See *La vie devant soi*

"Momoku monogatari" ("A Blind Man's Tale"; "The Story of a Blind Man") (Tanizaki)   28:414

Moms: A Praise Play for a Black Comedienne (Childress)   86:309; 96:110

Mon ami Maigret (*The Methods of Maigret*) (Simenon)   8:487; 47:373

Mon oncle d'Amerique (Resnais)   16:518

Mon temps n'est pas le vôtre (Marcel)   15:361

"Mona" (Wilson)   12:651-52

"Mona Lisa" (Herbert)   43:189, 192

Mona Lisa (Jordan)   110:274-76, 278, 282, 304, 306-09

Mona Lisa Overdrive (Gibson)   63:134-38

Mona Minim and the Smell of the Sun (Frame)   96:189

The Monarch (Vassilikos)   8:524

The Monarch of the Glen (Mackenzie)   18:316

"Monarchs" (Olds)   32:345

"The Monastery of Hosios Louikas" (Bowering)   32:46

Moncrieff (Holland)   21:149-50

Monday Begins on Saturday (Strugatskii and Strugatskii)   27:434-35

"A Monday Dream at Alameda Park" (Thomas)   13:538-39

Monday Morning (Hamilton)   51:183, 194

Monday Night (Boyle)   5:65; 58:64, 66, 70, 73-4

Monday the Rabbi Took Off (Kemelman)   2:225

The Monday Voices (Greenberg)   7:134

Le monde cassé (Marcel)   15:361, 364

Le Monde extérieur (Duras)   100:134-35

"Le monde objet" (Barthes)   24:27

Mondo et autres histoiries (Le Clezio)   31:249-50

Il mondo salvato dai ragazzini (Morante)   47:281, 283

"Monet" (Nemerov)   36:307

"MONET: Les Nymphéas" (Snodgrass)   68:393

"Monet's 'Waterlilies'" (Hayden)   37:152

"Money" (Larkin)   8:332; 9:323; 64:282

"Money" (Lennon)   35:267

"Money" (Nemerov)   2:308

"Money" (Nowlan)   15:399

"Money" (Nyro)   17:318-19

"Money" (Pink Floyd)   35:306, 311, 313

Money: A Jazz Opera (Baraka)   115:10, 29

Money: A Suicide Note (Amis)   38:16, 18-19; 62:5-7, 9, 11, 13-17, 19; 101:65-70, 77, 79-84, 86-91, 95

"Money and How It Gets That Way" (Miller)   43:298

Money Is Love (Condon)   6:115; 8:150; 100:113

Money Is Love (Glanville)   6:202

The Money Juggler (Auchincloss)   18:24

Money, Money, Money (Wagoner)   3:507; 5:473

The Money Order (Ousmane)
   See *Mandabi*

Money Pamphlets by £ (Pound)   7:328

"Money Talks" (Davies)   21:98

Money with Menaces (Hamilton)   51:193

"Money Won't Save You" (Cliff)   21:63

Money Writes! (Sinclair)   11:498

The Moneychangers (Hailey)   5:157-58

The Moneychangers (Sinclair)   63:346, 348

"The Moneygoround" (Davies)   21:91, 105

The Moneyman (Costain)   30:93-5, 97

The Money-Order; with White Genesis (Ousmane)
   See *Véhi-Ciosane; ou, Blanche-Genèse, suivi du Mandat*

"Mongolian Whiskey" (Katz)   47:220, 222-23

The Mongrel (Rice)   7:360

Mongrel (Seger)   35:378, 381

Mongrel Mettel (Stuart)   34:376

"Mónico" (Ulibarri)   83:411, 415

"Monique" (Gardam)   43:167

"Monk" (Faulkner)   52:128

Monk Dawson (Read)   4:444-45; 10:434, 436; 25:376, 379

"Monkberry Moon Delight" (McCartney)   35:279

"The Monkey" (Dinesen)   10:152; 29:154-55; 95:59

"The Monkey" (King)   37:207

Monkey Bridge (Cao)   109:44-5

Monkey Business (Perelman)   9:414-15; 44:501-02, 504-05; 49:270

The Monkey Grammarian (Paz)
   See *El mono gramático*

The Monkey King (Mo)   46:257-59

"Monkey Man" (Jagger and Richard)   17:227, 228, 234

"The Monkey Puzzle" (Moore)   13:394

The Monkey Wrench Gang (Abbey)   36:13, 17, 19; 59:238-39, 241-45

"The Monkeys" (Moore)   8:399; 47:260

Monkeys (Minot)   44:77-81

The Monkey's Wrench (Levi)
   See *La chiave a stella*

Monkfish Moon (Gunesekera)   91:33, 37, 41

"Monk's House, Rodmell" (Muske)   90:316

"Monkshood" (Gunnars)   69:260-61

El mono gramático (*The Monkey Grammarian*) (Paz)   10:393; 51:323-25

Monodromos (*One Way Street*) (Engel)   36:159, 162

"Monody on the Death of Aldersgate Street Station" (Betjeman)   34:306; 43:40

"The Monogram" (Elytis)   49:109; 100:173

The Monogram (Elytis)   100:175, 188

"Monolog bitnika" (Voznesensky)   57:417

"Monolog Merlin Monro" (Voznesensky)   57:416

"Monolog rybaka" (Voznesensky)   57:416

"Monólogo de la extranjera" ("Monologue of a Foreign Woman") (Castellanos)   66:45-6

Monologue (Beauvoir)   14:70

Monologue (Pinter)   15:423; 27:395-96; 58:381

"Monologue of a Broadway Actress" (Yevtushenko)   26:462

"Monologue of a Foreign Woman" (Castellanos)

See "Monólogo de la extranjera"
"Monologue of a Fox on an Alaskan Fur Farm"
   (Yevtushenko)   26:464
"Monologue of a Shell" (Hooker)   43:197
Monologue of a Whore in a Lunatic Asylum
   (Fo)   32:176
"Monologue of an American Poet"
   (Yevtushenko)   26:462
"Monologue of Dr. Spock" (Yevtushenko)
   26:462
"Monologue of Isabel Watching It Rain in
   Macondo" (Garcia Marquez)   3:180
"Monologue of the Beatniks" (Yevtushenko)
   26:463
"Monologue on Life and Death" (Faludy)
   42:138
Monologues (Kundera)   19:267
Monorail (Audiberti)   38:32-3
"The Monosyllable" (Jacobsen)   48:193;
   102:240
Monotones (Nichol)   18:367
"Monotonies" (Boland)   113:72
Monsieur (Durrell)   6:151-54; 13:187, 189;
   27:95, 98-100
"Monsieur Colin's Paint-Box Garden" (Grigson)
   7:136
Monsieur Gallet, décédé (*Maigret Stonewalled;
   Mr. Gallet, Deceased*) (Simenon)   47:371,
   374, 380
"Monsieur les deux chapeaux" (Munro)
   50:208-09, 211-12, 220
Monsieur Levert (Pinget)
   See *Le fiston*
"Monsieur Maurice" (Pinget)   37:364
Monsieur Monde Vanishes (Simenon)   8:488
Monsieur; or, The Prince of Darkness (Durrell)
   41:134-35, 137-38
Monsieur Toussaint (Glissant)   68:173, 180-81
Monsieur Verdoux (Chaplin)   16:193-97, 199-
   202, 204-06
Monsieur Vincent (Anouilh)   50:279
"Monsieur X., Here Called Pierre Rabier"
   (Duras)   40:188; 68:75-6, 78, 83, 99
"Monsignor Missalwait's Interstate" (Vizenor)
   103:309
Monsignor Quixote (Greene)   27:174, 176-77;
   70:287, 294; 72:163-64
"The Monster" (Buzzati)   36:94
Monster (Morgan)   2:294-95
"The Monster and the Maiden" (Zelazny)
   21:466
"Monster Deal" (Barthelme)   36:50; 117:18
Monster in a Box (Gray)   112:116-19, 126-27,
   129-33, 135
Monster Lecture about Justice and Law
   (Duerrenmatt)
   See *Monstervortrag über Gerechtigkeit und
   Recht*
The Monsters and the Critics, and Other Essays
   (Tolkien)   38:439, 442
Monstervortrag über Gerechtigkeit und Recht
   (*Monster Lecture about Justice and Law*)
   (Duerrenmatt)   102:58-9, 82
Les monstres sacrés (*Sacred Monsters*)
   (Cocteau)   43:105, 112
Mont de piété (*Pawnshop*) (Breton)   9:126;
   54:29-30
Montage of a Dream Deferred (Hughes)   10:280;
   35:214, 218, 220-22; 108:283, 291, 299,
   328, 334-35
"La montagne du dieu vivant" (Le Clezio)
   31:250
La montagne secrète (*The Hidden Mountain*)

(Roy)   10:441; 14:467
"Montana" (Zappa)   17:589
"Montana Ecologue" (Stafford)   4:521
"Montana Ranch Abandoned" (Hugo)   32:237
Montauk (Frisch)   9:217; 14:183-85; 18:163;
   32:193; 44:190-93, 204-07
Mont-Cinère (*Avarice House*) (Green)   3:205;
   77:264, 266, 269, 271, 273, 288, 290
"Monte Niko" (Ulibarri)   83:416
"Monte Sant' Angelo" (Miller)   10:345-46;
   47:249-50
"Montego Bay—Travelogue II" (Walcott)
   25:452
Montezuma's Revenge (Harrison)   42:201
A Month and a Day (Saro-Wiwa)   114:260,
   262, 274-76
"A Month in Summer" (Kizer)   15:308
A Month in the Country (Friel)   115:250
A Month of Sundays (Updike)   5:457-61; 7:488-
   90; 9:537-38; 13:557, 559, 562; 43:432
"The Month Was April" (Auden)   43:16-17
The Months (Brandys)   62:117, 119
"Montjuich" (Levine)   14:321
"Montmarte" (Hughes)   1:149
"Montraldo" (Cheever)   7:49; 15:131
"La montre de Pâcome" (Theriault)   79:408
Le montreur (Chedid)   47:82, 87
Montserrat (Hellman)   2:187; 18:222
Monty Python and the Holy Grail (Monty Py-
   thon)   21:224-25, 228
Monty Python: Live! At City Center (Monty
   Python)   21:227
Monty Python's Big Red Book (Monty Python)
   21:223
Monty Python's Contractual Obligation Album
   (Monty Python)   21:230
Monty Python's Flying Circus (Monty Python)
   21:224-25
Monty Python's Life of Brian (Monty Python)
   21:228-29
*Monty Python's Matching Tie and Handker-
   chief* (Monty Python)   21:225-26
Monty Python's Previous Album (Monty Py-
   thon)   21:224, 226
"Montypythonscrapbook" (Monty Python)
   21:229
"The Monument" (Bishop)   1:34; 9:92, 98;
   32:32-8, 41, 43
"A Monument" (Hughes)   37:176
"Monument" (Jeffers)   54:248
The Monument (Johnson)   27:213-14
The Monument (Strand)   18:517, 520; 41:434-
   35
The Monument Rose (Garrigue)   2:153
*Monuments and Maidens: The Allegory of Fe-
   male Form* (Warner)   59:217
"A Mood of Quiet Beauty" (Ashbery)   77:63,
   67
"Moods of Love" (Day Lewis)   10:129
Moon Across The Way
   See *Luna de enfrente*
Moon across the Way (Borges)
   See *Luna de enfrente*
"Moon and Flowering Plum" (Pollitt)   28:366-
   68
"The Moon and GNAC" (Calvino)
   See "Luna e G N A C"
The Moon and Sixpence (Maugham)   15:368-
   70; 67:219, 226; 93:229-30, 233, 243-
   44, 250, 262-63, 267
"The Moon and the Yew Tree" (Plath)   1:270;
   5:345; 9:427, 433; 14:425; 51:353;
   111:203, 214

The Moon by Night (L'Engle)   12:346
The Moon Children (Williamson)   29:455
"The Moon Dance Skunk" (Guthrie)   23:199
"Moon Deluxe" (Barthelme)   36:52; 117:17-
   18
Moon Deluxe (Barthelme)   36:50-2, 54; 117:2,
   5, 9, 11, 13-18, 21
The Moon: Earth's Natural Satellite (Branley)
   21:17, 20
The Moon Era (Williamson)   29:454
Moon Eyes (Poole)   17:370-72
"The Moon, Falling" (Shields)   97:429-30
"Moon Fishing" (Mueller)   51:279
"The Moon in Its Flight" (Sorrentino)   22:393
"Moon in My Window" (Sondheim)   30:379
"The Moon in the Orange Street Skating Rink"
   (Munro)   50:209, 211, 215-17, 219-20
"The Moon in Your Hands" (H. D.)   14:223
The Moon Is a Gong (*The Garbage Man*) (Dos
   Passos)   4:133; 15:84; 25:144
The Moon Is a Harsh Mistress (Heinlein)   3:226;
   14:254-55; 26:174, 176; 55:300, 303
The Moon Is Always Female (Piercy)   27:375-
   77, 379; 62:373
The Moon Is Down (Steinbeck)   1:325; 9:514;
   13:531-33; 21:382; 34:405, 411; 59:335,
   353
"The Moon Is Hell" (Campbell)   32:75, 80
"The Moon Is the Number Eighteen" (Olson)
   29:334
"Moon Lake" (Welty)   105:339
"Moon Landing" (Auden)   6:19; 9:59; 14:28
Moon Marigolds (Zindel)
   See *The Effect of Gamma Rays on Man-in-
   the-Moon Marigolds*
"The Moon Momens" (Mahapatra)   33:281,
   284
"The Moon Moth" (Vance)   35:419, 426
"Moon Object" (Abse)   7:2
Moon of Desire (Prichard)   46:337
Moon of Gomrath (Garner)   17:135-43, 149
Moon of the Three Rings (Norton)   12:458,
   460, 462, 468
Moon on the Nile (Christie)   39:437
"The Moon on the Water" (Derleth)   31:138
"Moon on the Water" (Kawabata)
   See "Moon on the Water"
"Moon over the Gasworks" (Seifert)   93:333
The Moon Shines on Kylenamoe (O'Casey)
   88:269
"The Moon, The Owl, My Sister" (Dowell)
   60:108-09
Moon Tiger (Lively)   50:200-05
Moon-Bells and Other Poems (*Moon-Whales
   and Other Moon Poems*) (Hughes)   14:271
Moonchildren (Weller)
   See *Cancer*
Mooncranker's Gift (Unsworth)   76:252
Moondance (Morrison)   21:232
Moonfleet (Lang)   20:209, 216; 103:89
"Moon-Freaks" (Hughes)   14:271
"Moonlight" (Harjo)   83:271
"Moonlight Alert" (Winters)   4:591
"Moonlight Among the Pines" (MacDiarmid)
   63:252
"Moonlight Drive" (Morrison)   17:290-91
"Moonlight Mile" (Jagger and Richard)   17:224,
   228
"Moonlight on the Wall" (Ortese)
   See "La luna sul muro"
"Moonlight Shadow" (Yoshimoto)   84:421-
   24, 427-29
Moonlight Sonata (Ritsos)   13:488; 31:325,

328
"Moonlighters" (Lieberman)   **36**:262
Moonraker (Fleming)   **30**:139, 149
"Moonrise" (Plath)   **111**:164, 178
Moonrise Moonset (Konwicki)   **117**:266, 275, 279, 284, 288-89
"Moon's Farm" (Read)   **4**:440
Moon's Farm (Read)   **4**:439
The Moons of Jupiter (Munro)   **95**:297, 301-02, 305-06, 308, 315-16, 320, 325
Moon's Ottery (Beer)   **58**:34-5
"The Moon's Skull in the Lake" (Ivask)   **14**:288
"Moonshine" (Marsh)   **53**:255
Moonshine Light, Moonshine Bright (Fox)   **22**:139-40
The Moonshine War (Leonard)   **71**:224
"Moonshine Whiskey" (Morrison)   **21**:232-33
"Moonshot" (Sainte-Marie)   **17**:431
Moonshot (Sainte-Marie)   **17**:431
"Moonshot: 1969" (Allen)   **84**:4, 8
The Moon-Spinners (Stewart)   **7**:467; **35**:390, 392
Moonstruck (Shanley)   **75**:321-31
"Moontan" (Strand)   **71**:284-85
"Moon-Watcher" (Clarke)   **35**:122
Moon-Whales and Other Moon Poems (Hughes)
  See *Moon-Bells and Other Poems*
"Moonwriter" (Bullins)   **7**:37
"Moony-Art" (Hughes)   **14**:271
Moorcock's Book of Martyrs (Moorcock)   **58**:352
"Moorings" (MacCaig)   **36**:282
The Moor's Last Sigh (Rushdie)   **100**:285-324
"Moortown" (Hughes)   **37**:175, 177
Moortown (Hughes)   **37**:172, 174-76, 178-80
Moortown Elegies (Hughes)   **37**:175
"The Moose" (Bishop)   **9**:91-2, 96; **13**:89-91, 94-5; **32**:32, 37-8, 42
"Moose in the Morning, Northern Maine" (Van Duyn)   **63**:442; **116**:410
"Moose Island" (H. D.)   **31**:208
"Moot" (Colter)   **58**:140, 147
"Moral Censorship" (Farrell)   **66**:134
The Moral Circus (Honig)   **33**:210
Moral Consciousness and Communicative Action (Habermas)
  See *Moralbewusstsein und Kommunikatives Handeln*
"Moral Education" (Lustig)   **56**:182
"Moral Fibre" (Amis)   **40**:43, 45
The Moral Intelligence of Children (Coles)   **108**:216
The Moral Life of Children (Coles)   **108**:184, 186-88, 208, 211-12, 216
"Moral Problem" (Scannell)   **49**:327, 331
Moralbewusstsein und Kommunikatives Handeln (*Moral Consciousness and Communicative Action*) (Habermas)   **104**:79-80, 82
"Moraldo in the City" (Fellini)   **85**:64
Morale élémentaire (Queneau)   **10**:430
"Morales élémentaires" (Perec)   **56**:258
"The Moralists" (Winters)   **4**:591
"A Morality" (Forster)
  See "What Does It Matter? A Morality"
"The Morality of Impersonal Narration" (Booth)   **24**:88
"The Morality of Indian Hating" (Momaday)   **85**:264-65; **95**:244, 275
Moravagine (Cendrars)   **18**:91, 95, 97; **106**:166, 183-85, 187-90, 192
Mord paas 31: A vaangin (*Murder on the*

Thirty-First Floor) (Wahloo)   **7**:501
"Mordent for a Melody" (Avison)   **97**:76, 90
Mordre en sa chair (*To Bite the Flesh*) (Brossard)   **115**:102
"More" (Ai)   **69**:9
More (Pink Floyd)   **35**:311
"The More a Man Has, the More a Man Wants" (Muldoon)   **32**:321; **72**:270, 274, 279, 282
"More Benadryl, Whined the Journalist" (Vollmann)   **89**:305, 307, 314
More Caviar (Buchwald)   **33**:88-9
More Classics Revisited (Rexroth)   **112**:387
"More Clues" (Rukeyser)   **27**:410
More Collected Poems (MacDiarmid)   **4**:313; **63**:246
More Collected Stories (Pritchett)   **41**:334
"More de A.D." (Beckett)   **14**:74
More Die of Heartbreak (Bellow)   **63**:27-35, 40
"More Enterprise" (Merrill)   **2**:274
"More Essay Poems" (Davie)   **31**:117
More Experiments in Science (Branley)   **21**:16
More Hardcore (Thompson)   **69**:383
More Issues at Hand (Blish)   **14**:83
More Joy (Comfort)   **7**:54
More Joy in Heaven (Callaghan)   **14**:100-01, 103; **41**:88, 90, 95; **65**:250, 252
"More Life" (Strand)   **41**:439-41
"More Light! More Light!" (Hecht)   **8**:268; **19**:207
"The More Little Mummy in the World" (Thomas)   **37**:417; **107**:326,348
More Lives than One (Krutch)   **24**:289
"More of a Corpse than a Woman" (Rukeyser)   **27**:404, 412
"More of the Insane" (Rosenblatt)   **15**:448
"More Pleasant Adventures" (Ashbery)   **41**:34, 39
More Poems, 1961 (Graves)   **1**:127
More Poems for People (Acorn)   **15**:10
More Poems to Solve (Swenson)   **61**:402; **106**:340
More Pricks than Kicks (Beckett)   **6**:38, 43; **10**:34; **11**:32, 36; **14**:79; **18**:41, 43; **29**:59, 62; **83**:135
More Shapes Than One (Chappell)   **78**:116-17
More Songs about Buildings and Food (Byrne)   **26**:95-8
"More Sonnets at Christmas" (Tate)   **14**:531
More Tales of Pirx the Pilot (Lem)   **40**:295, 297
More Tales of the City (Maupin)   **95**:191-94, 197, 199-201, 202
More Than a New Discovery (Nyro)
  See *The First Songs*
More than Enough (Sargeson)   **31**:369
More than Human (Sturgeon)   **22**:410-11; **39**:361-62, 364-68
"More Than the Sum of His Parts" (Haldeman)   **61**:181
More Than You Deserve (Weller)   **53**:390
The More the Merrier (Weber)   **12**:633
More under Saturn (Dickey)   **3**:126-27
More Women than Men (Compton-Burnett)   **15**:138, 140; **34**:494
More Words of Science (Asimov)   **26**:38
More Work for the Undertaker (Allingham)   **19**:13, 18
Morgan's Passing (Tyler)   **18**:529-31; **28**:432; **44**:315; **59**:205; **103**:217, 222-24, 228, 235, 241-42, 244-45, 254, 259-60, 263
"Morgengabe" (Jeffers)   **54**:234

Die Morgenlandfahrt (*Journey to the East*) (Hesse)   **1**:146; **17**:204, 211; **25**:261; **69**:279
"Morgenlied" (Williams)   **45**:443
"Moritat" (Jandl)   **34**:197
Mork and Mindy (Marshall)   **17**:277-78
Mörkerseende (*Dark Adaptation*; *Night Vision*; *Seeing in the Dark*) (Transtroemer)   **52**:410; **65**:220, 222-23, 225, 229
Morley Callaghan's Stories (Callaghan)   **65**:248
"Morn Advancing" (Keates)   **34**:202-03
"Morning" (Arghezi)   **80**:9
"A Morning" (Atwood)   **84**:68
"Morning" (Barthelme)   **13**:59-60, 62; **46**:37-8
"Morning" (Creeley)   **78**:143
"Morning" (Davie)   **31**:116, 118
"Morning" (Fuller)   **62**:197
"Morning" (Gluck)   **44**:216, 218
"Morning" (MacCaig)   **36**:279
"Morning" (Oliver)   **98**:293
"A Morning" (Strand)   **41**:432, 438
"Morning" (Williams)   **42**:459
"The Morning" (Winters)   **32**:469
Morning (Horovitz)
  See *Chiaroscuro*
"Morning After" (Zamora)   **89**:368
The Morning After (Sheed)   **10**:473
The Morning after Optimism (Murphy)   **51**:301-02, 304
"Morning and Evening" (Transtroemer)   **65**:222
"Morning at Great Pond" (Oliver)   **34**:246
Morning at Jalna (de la Roche)   **14**:149
"Morning at the Window" (Eliot)   **41**:151-52; **113**:187
"Morning Bedroom" (Dunn)   **40**:165-66
"Morning Birds" (Transtroemer)   **65**:227
"Morning Coffee" (Hope)   **3**:250
"Morning Express" (Sassoon)   **36**:386
Morning Face (Anand)   **93**:29-30, 32-3, 36-7, 41, 55, 57
Morning Girl (Dorris)   **109**:306-07, 309
"Morning Glory" (Moss)   **45**:290
"Morning Glory" (Nemerov)   **36**:308
The Morning Glory, Another Thing That Will Never Be My Friend (Bly)   **15**:63, 65-6; **38**:50, 57-9
"Morning Glory Blue" (Sandburg)   **35**:356
"The Morning Half-Life Blues" (Piercy)   **27**:373
"Morning in a New Land" (Oliver)   **98**:294
Morning in Antibes (Knowles)   **1**:169; **4**:272; **26**:247-48, 255-56, 258, 262
"Morning in Massachusetts" (Oliver)   **19**:362
"Morning in Norfolk" (Barker)   **48**:24
"A Morning in the Life of Intelligent People" (Mosley)   **43**:314
"Morning in the Park" (Ciardi)   **40**:157
Morning Is a Long Time Coming (Greene)   **30**:170
"Morning Jitters" (Ashbery)   **77**:66
"morning mirror" (Clifton)   **66**:83
"The Morning Moon" (Walcott)   **67**:351
Morning, Noon, and Night (Cozzens)   **1**:67; **4**:116; **11**:132; **92**:189-94
"The Morning of the Day They Did It" (White)   **10**:528
"The Morning of the Dead" (Wright)   **53**:423-24
The Morning of the Poem (Schuyler)   **23**:390-92
"Morning On This Street" (Soto)   **80**:282

"Morning Poem" (Oliver) **98**:267
"Morning Prayer" (Berryman) **10**:46
"Morning Prayer" (Ezekiel) **61**:92
"The Morning Prayers of the Hasid, Rabbi Levi Yitzhak" (Gotlieb) **18**:193
"Morning Scene" (Huxley) **11**:284
"Morning Song" (Plath) **9**:428; **14**:422; **111**:207
The Morning Song of Lord Zero: Poems Old and New (Aiken) **52**:26
Morning Star (Dabrowska)
    See *Gwiazda zaranna*
Morning Star (Williams) **15**:577
The Morning Star: Poems and Translations (Rexroth) **22**:349; **49**:275; **112**:370-71, 393
"Morning Sun" (MacNeice) **1**:186; **53**:234
"Morning Thinking of Empire" (Carver) **36**:100
"Morning Train" (Cliff) **21**:65
"The Morning Train" (Merwin) **88**:211
"A Morning Walk" (Ezekiel) **61**:92, 100, 104
"Morning with Broken Window" (Hogan) **73**:158
Morning Yet on Creation Day (Achebe) **75**:5
"Mornings After" (Adcock) **41**:14, 17-18
"Mornings in a New House" (Merrill) **13**:381
"Mornings in Mexico" (West) **9**:562
Mornings Like This (Dillard) **115**:209
"morning-water train woman" (Young Bear) **94**:363
"Morocco" (Faludy) **42**:139
Morocco (Sternberg) **20**:369, 372
The Moronic Inferno and Other Visits to America (Amis) **62**:2-6; **101**:68, 77, 80, 82
Moros en la costa (*Hard Rain*) (Dorfman) **77**:145-46
Morový sloup (Seifert)
    See *The Plague Column*
Morreion: A Tale of the Dying Earth (Vance) **35**:422
"Morris Smith: The Man and the Myth" (Frazier) **46**:164-65
Morrison Hotel (Morrison) **17**:289, 291-92, 295-96
"Morse Moose and Grey Goose" (McCartney) **35**:286
Morskiye nabroski (Paustovsky) **40**:362
"Un Morso Doo Pang" (Ferber) **93**:139
"La mort" (Lee)
    See "Elle est trois,"
Mort à crédit (*Death on the Installment Plan*) (Celine) **1**:56; **3**:102, 104-05; **4**:98, 100-02; **7**:43, 46-7; **9**:152, 158; **15**:125; **47**:71-5, 77, 79
La mort conduit l'attelage (Yourcenar) **50**:364; **87**:383
La mort dans l'âme (*Troubled Sleep*) (Sartre) **1**:305; **50**:383
Le mort de demain (Marcel) **15**:363
"La mort de l'auteur" ("The Death of the Author") (Barthes) **83**:81, 97
La Mort de Siegfried (Lang) **103**:88-9
Mort d'Oluwémi d'Ajumako (Conde) **52**:79, 81; **92**:99-100
La mort en ce jardin (*Death in This Garden*) (Bunuel) **16**:147-48; **80**:25, 28, 30-1, 38-40
La mort heureuse (*A Happy Death*) (Camus) **2**:98-9; **9**:149-50
"La mort rose" (Breton) **54**:33
Mortal Acts, Mortal Words (Kinnell) **29**:284-

86, 288-89
Mortal Coils (Huxley) **1**:151
Mortal Consequences: A History from the Detective Story to the Crime Novel (Symons) **14**:524; **32**:424-25
"The Mortal Danger" (Solzhenitsyn) **78**:403-06
"A Mortal Day of No Surprises" (Kumin) **13**:328; **28**:225
Mortal Engines (Lem) **8**:345; **40**:296
Mortal Friends (Carroll) **38**:104-08
Mortal Lessons: Notes on the Art of Surgery (Selzer) **74**:263-64, 268, 270, 276, 278-79, 281
"Mortal Limit" (Warren) **39**:265, 268, 270
"The Mortal Mountain" (Zelazny) **21**:465-66
A Mortal Pitch (Scannell) **49**:324, 330, 332
"Mortal Pride" (Clarke) **9**:168
Mortal Stakes (Parker) **27**:363-64, 366
"Mortality" (Betjeman) **6**:66
"Mortality and Mercy in Vienna" (Pynchon) **6**:430; **33**:333, 339
Morte accidentale di un anarchico (*Accidental Death of an Anarchist*) (Fo) **32**:172-74, 176-77; **109**:104, 106, 117-18, 120-21, 136, 142, 144-45
La morte dell'inquisitore (*Death of the Inquisitor*) (Sciascia) **41**:388, 395
Morte d'urban (Powers) **1**:279-82; **4**:419; **57**:349-50, 352-54, 356-58
"A Morte e a morte de Quincas Berro Dágua" (*Berro Dágua*; *Two Deaths*; *The Two Deaths of Quincas Wateryell*) (Amado) **40**:30-1, 34; **106**:65-6, 70-1, 73, 77
Morte e vida severina e outraos poemas em voz alta (*Death and Life of a Severino*) (Cabral de Melo Neto) **76**:153, 155-56, 158, 160, 168-69
Une morte très douce (*A Very Easy Death*) (Beauvoir) **4**:47; **8**:62; **14**:67; **31**:35, 43; **44**:344-45, 349-51; **71**:58, 78-9
The Mortgaged Heart (McCullers) **1**:210; **4**:344-45; **12**:427, 432
"The Mortician's Twelve-Year-Old Son" (Ai) **69**:7
"Mortmain" (Warren) **13**:573; **39**:260, 266
"Morts pour la France" (Damas) **84**:176
Morts sans sépulture (*The Dead Without Burial*; *Men Without Shadows*; *The Victors*) (Sartre) **9**:470-71; **13**:499; **52**:381
"Morvin" (Fuller) **62**:184-85
Morwyn; or, The Vengeance of God (Powys) **7**:350; **46**:322
"Mosaic" (Cage) **41**:78
"Mosaic Harlem" (Dumas) **62**:155
"The Mosaic Hunchback" (Macdonald) **19**:290
Mosby's Memoirs, and Other Stories (Bellow) **25**:85; **33**:67, 69, 71; **63**:43
"Moschus Moschiferus" (Hope) **51**:223
"Moscow" (Stern) **40**:414
Moscow 2042 (Voinovich) **49**:383-85
Moscow Does Not Believe in Tears (Ehrenburg) **18**:131; **62**:176
"Moscow in the Wilderness, Segovia in the Snow" (Ferlinghetti) **27**:139; **111**:65
Moscow Saga (*Moskovskaia saga*) (Aksyonov) **101**:55-6
"The Moscow Symphony" (Hikmet) **40**:248
The Moscow Symphony and Other Poems (Hikmet) **40**:248
Mosén Milán (*Requiem for a Spanish Peasant*; *Requiem por un campesino espanol*)

(Sender) **8**:479, 481
Moses (Burgess) **8**:113; **22**:71, 78
"Moses at Darwin Station" (Purdy) **50**:247
Moses, Man of the Mountain (Hurston) **7**:171; **30**:212-13, 216, 219, 228
The Moses Of Beale Street (Tolson) **105**:281
Moses, Prince of Egypt (Fast) **23**:158
Moshauer Novelle (*Moskaver Novelle*) (Wolf) **14**:593; **58**:432
Moskaver Novelle (Wolf)
    See *Moshauer Novelle*
Moskovskaia saga (Aksyonov)
    See *Moscow Saga*
"Mosler Safe" (Lowell) **15**:343
The Mosquito Coast (Theroux) **28**:426-28; **46**:399-400, 403
"Mosquito Kingdom" (Cardenal)
    See "Reino mosco"
"Mosquitoes" (Jones) **81**:63, 65, 67
Mosquitoes (Faulkner) **9**:199; **11**:200-01; **28**:140-41; **68**:127-28, 130-31
Moss and Blister (Garfield) **12**:234
"The Moss of His Skin" (Sexton) **53**:316-17
"Mossbawn: Sunlight" (Heaney) **25**:249; **74**:166, 193
"Moss-Gathering" (Roethke) **3**:432; **46**:362; **101**:294
Most (Bagryana) **10**:11
The Most Beautiful (Kurosawa) **16**:399
"The Most Beautiful Legs in the World" (Kelley) **22**:247
"The Most Beautiful Protestant Girls in Muggalnagrow" (Durcan) **43**:118
The Most Beautiful World (Hall) **51**:176
"The Most Costly Passion of All" (Mayle) **89**:150
"The Most Difficult Position" (Fuller) **62**:196-97, 201, 203-04
"Most Exclusive Residence for Sale" (Davies) **21**:88
"The Most Humble Poem" (Seifert)
    See "Básezn nejpokornejší"
"The Most Incredible Meal" (Kotzwinkle) **35**:253
"Most like an Arch This Marriage" (Ciardi) **40**:156-58
Most Likely to Succeed (Dos Passos) **4**:135; **15**:186; **25**:141, 146; **34**:422
"Most Lovely Shade" (Sitwell) **67**:324
"The Most of It" (Frost) **4**:175; **9**:219, 222, 228-29; **10**:194-95; **26**:128; **34**:471
"Most of My Life" (Stern) **100**:336
The Most of S. J. Perelman (Perelman) **15**:417-18; **44**:505
"A Most Peculiar Man" (Simon) **17**:458
"Mostly about Myself" (Yezierska) **46**:442
Mostly Baseball (Hall)
    See *Fathers Playing Catch with Sons: Essays on Sport*
Mostly Canallers (Edmonds) **35**:146, 150-51
Il mostro (Buzzati) **36**:84
"Mostru o pavea" (Pasolini) **106**:229
"Mota Shel Assia G." ("The Death of Assia G.") (Amichai) **116**:118
The Mote in God's Eye (Niven) **8**:426
Motel (van Itallie) **3**:493
"A Motel in Troy, New York" (Jacobsen) **48**:193, 197
"A Motet for Tomas Luis de Victoria" (Shapcott) **38**:404
"The Moth" (Dobyns) **37**:81
"The Moth" (Scannell) **49**:328
"The Moth" (Wakoski) **40**:456

The Moth (Cain)   28:48

"Moth Sonata" (Rosenblatt)   15:448

"The Mother" (Brooks)   5:75

"Mother" (Carruth)   84:133

"Mother" (Hacker)   72:182

"Mother" (Lennon)   35:261-62, 266, 270

"The Mother" (Olds)   85:286

"The Mother" (Ousmane)   66:349

"Mother" (Police, The)   26:366

"The Mother" (Snodgrass)   68:381-82, 397

"The Mother" (Stevenson)   33:382

The Mother (Buck)   11:70, 74, 77; 18:79

Mother (Seifert)
   See *Maminka*

Mother and Child (Vinge)   30:409-10, 413-14

"Mother and Child Reunion" (Simon)   17:461, 465-66

"A Mother and Her Daughter" (Wiesel)   37:450

"Mother and 'Miss E.'" (Fisher)   87:131

"Mother and Son" (Tate)   9:523; 14:529, 531

Mother and Son (Compton-Burnett)   15:140; 34:495, 500

A Mother and Two Daughters (Godwin)   31:194-96, 198; 69:232, 234-35, 237-39, 241, 246, 252-53

"Mother Coming" (Bly)   15:62

Mother Courage & Her Children (Shange)   25:399-400

"Mother Dressmaking" (Raine)   103:182, 186, 189

"Mother Earth" (Asimov)   26:42

"Mother Earth" (Gunn)   18:200

Mother Earth (Aitmatov)
   See *Materinskoe pole*

"Mother Earth, or the Folly of National Boundaries" (Kunene)   85:178

Mother Field (Aitmatov)
   See *Materinskoe pole*

Mother Figure (Ayckbourn)   18:28; 33:40

"Mother Geese" (Niedecker)   42:298-300

"Mother Goose" (Rexroth)   112:400

"Mother in the Sky with Diamonds" (Tiptree)   48:385

Mother Ireland (O'Brien)   8:429-30; 116:181-82, 185, 193-95, 197, 199

"Mother Knows Best" (Ferber)   93:153, 162, 180

Mother Knows Best (Ferber)   93:153

Mother Küsters Goes to Heaven (Fassbinder)   20:112

Mother London (Moorcock)   58:358-60

"Mother Marie Therese" (Lowell)   8:353, 356; 15:344

Mother Night (Vonnegut)   1:348; 2:453, 455; 3:495-97, 499, 501-03, 505-06; 4:561-65, 567; 5:467-69; 8:531, 533; 12:601, 604, 606-07, 609-12, 614, 618-23; 40:441, 443, 448-49; 60:424, 431-32, 440; 111:351, 354-55, 359, 361, 366

The Mother of Captain Shigemoto (Tanizaki)
   See *Shosho Shigemoto no haha*

Mother of Pearl (Morrissy)   99:73-8

"The Mother of the Child in Question" (Lessing)   94:265

"The Mother of Toads" (Smith)   43:422

Mother Russia (Littell)   42:276

"Mother to Son" (Hughes)   35:216; 108:296, 309

"Mother Tongue" (Simic)   9:479

Mother World (Campbell)   32:74

"Motherhood" (Swenson)   106:335

"Motherhood according to Bellini" (Kristeva)   77:312

Mothering Sunday (Streatfeild)   21:400

"The Mother-in-Law" (Betts)   3:73

Motherlode (Ferlinghetti)   111:63

"Mothers" (Endo)   54:158, 161

"Mothers" (Giovanni)   117:196

Mothers and Daughters (Hunter)   31:220

"Mother's Boy" (Durcan)   70:152

"The Mother's Curses" (Schaeffer)   11:491

"The Mother's Dance" (Kinsella)   43:254

Mother's Field (Aitmatov)
   See *Materinskoe pole*

Mother's Garden (Walker)
   See *In Search of Our Mother's Gardens: Womanist Prose*

A Mother's Kisses (Friedman)   3:165; 5:127; 56:95-6, 99, 102-3, 107-08

"Mother's Little Helper" (Jagger and Richard)   17:226, 234-35

"The Mother's Tale" (Ai)   69:9

"Mother's Voice" (Creeley)   36:120; 78:153

Mothersill and the Foxes (Williams)   13:599

"Mothlady" (Rosenblatt)   15:446

"Moths" (Boland)   113:92

"The Motion" (Jacobsen)   48:195

"The Motion" (Roethke)   3:433; 19:396

"Motion for Motion" (Ammons)   5:28; 108:23

The Motion of History and Other Plays (Baraka)   14:48; 33:57; 115:10, 28-9

"Motion's Holdings" (Ammons)   57:51, 56-7

Motives for Fiction (Alter)   34:515-17

"Los motivos de son" (Guillen)   79:238

Motivos de son (*Son Motifs*) (Guillen)   48:157, 159, 161, 163, 165-69; 79:228-29, 240-41, 244-46, 248

"Moto Shel Celan" ("The Death of Celan") (Amichai)   116:118

La motocyclette (*The Motorcycle*) (Mandiargues)   41:275-77

"The Motor Car" (Clarke)   53:89

Motor City (*Biography of a Buick*) (Morris)   76:77-85

Motor City Blue (Estleman)   48:103-04, 107

"A Motorbike" (Hughes)   37:172

"Motorbike" (Williams)   42:441

The Motorcycle (Mandiargues)
   See *La motocyclette*

The Motorcycle Betrayal Poems (Wakoski)   2:459; 4:571-72; 7:507; 9:555

"Motorcycle Mama" (Young)   17:580

"Motorcycle Stunts on the Vertical Wall" (Voznesensky)   57:419

"O motorneiro de Caxangá" ("The Caxangá Driver") (Cabral de Melo Neto)   76:168

Les mots (*The Words*) (Sartre)   1:305; 4:474, 476; 7:389, 397; 13:501; 18:472-73; 24:411; 44:493, 496;50:370-72, 374, 376, 378, 381-82, 384; 52:379, 385, 387

Les mots dans la peinture (Butor)   15:114

Les mots et les choses: Une archéologie des sciences humaines (*The Order of Things: An Archaeology of the Human Sciences*) (Foucault)   31:174-78, 181, 185-86; 34:339, 341; 69:159, 168, 170

Mots sans memoire (Leiris)   61:346

"Les mots sans rides" (Breton)   9:125

"Motteti" (Montale)   7:223-24; 18:340

"The Motto on the Sundial" (Rexroth)   112:396

Les mouches (*The Flies*) (Sartre)   4:473; 7:389; 9:470-71; 13:498-99; 18:470; 44:493; 50:371, 373, 375, 381, 383; 52:373, 388

Mouchette (Bresson)   16:112-13, 115, 119

Mouchoir de nuages (*Cloud Handkerchief; Handkerchief of Clouds*) (Tzara)   47:388, 390; 47:388

"Mougins Provence, September, 1971" (Morgan)   31:275

Le moulin de la sourdine (Ayme)   11:22

Moulin premier (Char)   55:288

Moulin Rouge (Huston)   20:162

The Mound Builders (Wilson)   7:548-49; 14:590; 36:463

"Mount Blank" (Hollander)   8:299

"Mount Eagle" (Montague)   46:279

"The Mount of Olives" (Arghezi)
   See "Muntele Maslinilor"

"Mount Royal" (Scott)   22:374

"Mt. Zion" (Amichai)   116:85, 88

Mount Zion; or, In Touch with the Infinite (Betjeman)   34:306

"The Mountain" (Frost)   9:219; 15:247; 26:112

"The Mountain" (Gluck)   44:216, 222

"The Mountain" (Mathias)   45:238

"The Mountain" (Merwin)   1:213; 88:205

The Mountain (Troyat)
   See *La neige en deuil*

"The Mountain and Maryann" (Lightfoot)   26:278

"The Mountain and the Man Who Was Not God" (Jordan)   114:151-52

The Mountain and the Valley (Buckler)   13:118, 120

"Mountain and Tidewater Songs" (Epstein)   7:97

"The Mountain Ash Tree" (Pack)   13:438-39

Mountain City (Sinclair)   15:498

"The Mountain Day" (Stafford)   68:433

Mountain Dialogues (Waters)   88:365

The Mountain in the Sea (Fuller)   62:190-92, 195-97, 201-02, 204

Mountain Interval (Frost)   10:193; 15:248; 26:117-19, 124, 128; 34:468

Mountain Language (Pinter)   58:385

"Mountain Liar" (Ammons)   108:20

The Mountain Lion (Stafford)   4:517; 7:455, 456-59; 19:430; 68:421, 424-28, 430, 434-36, 439, 444, 447-49

"Mountain Meddler" (Guthrie)   23:199

"Mountain Medicine" (Guthrie)   23:203

"Mountain Mystery" (Warren)   39:258

"Mountain Oysters" (Lane)   25:285, 287

Mountain Paths (Arnow)   7:15-16; 18:10

"Mountain Pines" (Jeffers)   54:234

"Mountain Plateau" (Warren)   18:535

"Mountain Talk" (Ammons)   25:44

Mountain Wolf Woman, Sister of Crashing Thunder: The Autobiography of a Winnebago Indian (Mountain Wolf Woman)   92:356-372

"The Mountaineers" (Abse)   29:16

Mountaineers and Eskimos (Coles)   108:194, 210

"Mountains" (Gascoyne)   45:153

Mountains and Rivers without End (Snyder)   32:387-89, 399

"The Mountains of Dawn" (McIntyre)   18:327

"The Mountains of Guatemala" (Connell)   45:112

"The Mountains of Sunset" (McIntyre)   18:327

"The Mountains of the Moon" (Powys)   7:349

"Mountains, Polecats, Pheasants" (Norris)   14:387

Mountains, Polecats, Pheasants and Other Elegies (Norris)   14:387-88

Mounted Police Patrol (Haig-Brown)   21:139

Mountolive (Durrell)   1:87; 4:144-45, 147; 8:191; 13:185-86

"The Mourner" (Friedman)　56:107
"The Mourners" (Malamud)　9:348; 27:306; 85:190
Mourners Below (Purdy)　28:381-82; 52:342-43, 346-48
The Mournful Demeanor of Lieutenant Boruvka (Skvorecky)　69:333-34, 338, 346-47
"Mourning" (Strand)　6:522
"Mourning Letter" (Dorn)　10:159
"Mourning Poem for the Queen of Sunday" (Hayden)　37:160
Mouroir (Breytenbach)　37:47-50
"The Mouse" (Ashbery)　77:67
"The Mouse" (Nin)　60:267
"The Mouse" (Snodgrass)　68:382, 388
The Mouse and His Child (Hoban)　7:161; 25:263, 265
"Mouse Elegy" (Olds)　85:295-96
Mouse on the Moon (Lester)　20:220
Mouse Woman and the Mischief-Makers (Harris)　12:268
Mouse Woman and the Vanished Princesses (Harris)　12:266, 268
The Mousetrap (Christie)　6:110; 12:118, 125; 39:437, 440-41; 48:78; 110:122-23, 146-48
La moustache (*The Mustache*) (Carrere)　89:67-71
"The Mouth of the Hudson" (Lowell)　5:258
"Mouths" (Dudek)　11:158
Le mouvement perpétual (Aragon)　22:40
Mouvements (*Movements*) (Michaux)　8:392; 19:316
"Movable Feast" (Weidman)　7:517
"The Move" (Roy)　14:467
Move! (Lieber)　6:311
"Move On" (Sondheim)　30:403
"Move On Up" (Bell)　102:5-6, 8
Move Over, Mountain (Ehle)　27:101-03
Move Over, Mrs. Markham (Cooney)　62:144, 146
"Move Still, Still So" (Howard)　47:171
"Move Un-noticed to be Noticed: A Nationhood Poem" (Madhubuti)　73:215
A Moveable Feast (Hemingway)　3:243; 6:228; 8:283; 13:275; 19:215, 224; 39:402, 430, 432-33; 41:198, 203-04, 207; 44:519; 50:427, 430; 80:146
"The Move-In" (Bowen)　6:96; 15:78
"The Movement" (Bambara)　88:54
Movement (Miner)　40:327-31
"Movement of Autumn" (Watkins)　43:450
"The Movement of Fish" (Dickey)　7:83
"Movements" (Tomlinson)　4:545; 13:549
Movements (Michaux)
　See *Mouvements*
"Movements IV" (Tomlinson)　13:549
"The Movers" (Louie)　70:79-80
The Movie at the End of the World (McGrath)　28:277-78; 59:175, 178, 181
"Movie House" (Updike)　23:474
Movie Movie (Gelbart)　21:130; 61:149
"The Movie Run Backward" (Creeley)　78:142
Movie Shoes (*The Painted Garden*) (Streatfeild)　21:399, 414-15
The Moviegoer (Percy)　2:333-34; 3:378-81; 6:399-401; 8:439-40, 442, 444-45; 14:413, 416-18; 18:396-400, 402; 47:333, 336, 338, 340-41; 65:255-60
"Moviegoing" (Hollander)　8:299
Moviegoing and Other Poems (Hollander)　8:298
"Movies" (Dixon)　52:98

"Movies" (Hughes)　35:222
Movies (Dixon)　52:98-101
"Movin' Out" ("Anthony's Song") (Joel)　26:215-17, 221
"Moving" (Jarrell)　2:209
"The Moving" (Still)　49:364, 366
"Moving Day" (Coles)　46:107, 113
"The Moving Finger" (Masters)　48:223
The Moving Finger (Christie)　39:438; 48:73
"The Moving Floor" (Szirtes)　46:394
"Moving from Cheer to Joy, from Joy to All" (Jarrell)　9:296
"Moving From Pain to Power: Black Self-Determination" (hooks)　94:159
"The Moving Image" (Wright)　11:578; 53:416, 418-19, 423-24, 426-27, 431
The Moving Image (Wright)　11:578; 53:416, 418-19, 423, 426-28, 430-31
Moving in Winter (Rich)　36:378
"Moving Inward at Last" (Bly)　10:57
"Moving: New York—New Haven Line" (Corn)　33:117
Moving On (McMurtry)　2:271-72; 3:333; 7:214-15; 27:326, 328-30, 333; 44:254
Moving Parts (Katz)　47:217-19, 223
"Moving Pictures" (Johnson)　51:234, 236
Moving Pictures: Memories of a Hollywood Prince (Schulberg)　48:350-51
"A Moving Target" (Golding)　81:321
A Moving Target (Golding)　27:164-65, 168-69
The Moving Target (Macdonald)　1:185; 14:328, 334; 34:417; 41:265, 267-68, 270-71
The Moving Target (Merwin)　1:212-13; 2:276-77; 3:340; 5:285-86, 288; 88:191-93, 197, 199, 201, 203-05
"Moving the Walls" (Simpson)　7:428
"Moving through Spain" (Dobyns)　37:77
"Moving to a New House" (Hesse)　17:216
"The Moving to Griffin" (Ondaatje)　14:407
Moving Towards Home (Jordan)　114:152, 156
The Moving Toyshop (Crispin)　22:108
Moviola (Kanin)　22:232
"The Mower" (Bates)　46:67
"The Mower" (Garrett)　51:144
"Mowing" (Frost)　4:177; 13:227; 15:246, 248; 26:112, 115-16, 118
Mozaika (Voznesensky)　15:555
Mozart (Hildesheimer)　49:171, 175-76, 178-79
Mozart and the Wolf Gang (*On Mozart: A Paean for Wolfgang*) (Burgess)　81:304, 307-10
Mozart the Dramatist (Brophy)　29:93-4, 98; 105:3-4, 30, 37
"Mozart's Clarinet Concerto" (Dunn)　40:171
Mr. Aa the Antiphilosopher (Tzara)　47:390
Mr. Ames against Time (Child)　19:101, 103
"Mr. and Mrs. Baby" (Strand)　41:438-39, 441
Mr. and Mrs. Baby, and Other Stories (Strand)　41:438-41; 71:280
"Mr. and Mrs. Edgehill" (Coward)　29:141
"Mr. and Mrs. Elliot" (Hemingway)　30:191
"Mr. and Mrs. Jack Sprat in the Kitchen" (Van Duyn)　116:421-22, 427
"Mr. & Mrs. Van Winkle" (Dybek)　114:67
"Mr. Appollinax" (Eliot)　41:160
"Mr. Arcularis" (Aiken)　5:9; 52:26
Mr. Arcularis (Aiken)　5:9
Mr. Arkadin (*Confidential Report*) (Welles)　20:434-35, 437, 440-41, 449; 80:395, 413
Mr. Armitage Isn't Back Yet (Jones)　52:246, 253

"Mr. Austin" (Farrell)　4:158
"Mr. Bedford" (Godwin)　31:197-99
Mr. Bedford and the Muses (Godwin)　31:197-98; 69:247
Mr. Beluncle (Pritchett)　41:332
"Mr. Big" (Allen)　52:35
"Mr. Bleaney" (Larkin)　8:339; 39:341, 343; 64:263, 272
"Mr. Blue" (Creeley)　4:118; 8:152; 36:122; 78:126, 132
Mr. Bridge (Connell)　4:108; 6:116; 45:111-12, 116
Mr. Campion's Lady (Allingham)　19:17
"Mr. Churchill Says" (Davies)　21:91
"Mr. Clean" (Weller)　26:444
Mr. Cogito (Herbert)
　See *Pan Cogito*
"Mr. Cogito and Pure Thought" (Herbert)　9:275
"Mr. Cogito and the Imagination" (Herbert)　43:191, 193
"Mr. Cogito and the Soul" (Herbert)　43:191
"Mr. Cogito Laments the Pettiness of Dreams" (Herbert)　9:275
"Mr. Cogito on the Need for Precision" (Herbert)　43:195
"Mr. Cogito on Virtue" (Herbert)　9:276
"Mr. Cogito Reads the Newspaper" (Herbert)　9:275
"Mr. Cogito Tells about the Temptation of Spinoza" (Herbert)
　See "Pan Cogito opowiada o kuszeniu Spinozy"
"Mr. Costyve Duditch" (Toomer)　22:429
Mr. Deeds Goes to Town (Capra)　16:154-55, 158, 160-62, 164
"Mr. Durant" (Parker)　68:326
"Mr. Eliot's Sunday Morning Service" (Eliot)　1:92; 15:210, 216
"Mr. Extinction, Meet Ms. Survival" (Appleman)　51:17
Mr. Fairlie's Final Journey (Derleth)　31:138
Mr. Gallet, Deceased (Simenon)
　See *Monsieur Gallet, décédé*
Mr. Gourd (Endo)
　See *Hechima kun*
"Mr. Green Genes" (Zappa)　17:585
Mr. Happiness (Mamet)　15:358; 46:254
"Mr. Harrington's Washing" (Maugham)　67:219
"Mr. Heine" (Smith)　64:392
"Mr. Hunter's Grave" (Mitchell)　98:161, 173, 182-84
"Mr. Jonas" (Green)　97:274-77
"Mr. Jones" (Capote)　19:85
"Mr. Krösing's Top Hat" (Seifert)　34:261; 93:310
"Mr. Levi" (Oz)　11:429
"Mr. Lincoln and His Gloves" (Sandburg)　35:358
Mr. Lincoln's Army (Catton)　35:83-7
Mr. Love and Justice (MacInnes)　4:314; 23:282-87
"Mr. Loveday's Little Outing" (Waugh)　27:477
Mr. MacKinley's Flight (Leonov)
　See *Begstvo Mistera Mak-Kinli*
"Mr. Mahoney" (Jacobsen)　48:195
Mr. Majestyk (Leonard)　71:223
"Mr. McGregor's Garden" (McGuckian)　48:276-77
Mr. McKinley Runs Away (Leonov)
　See *Begstvo Mistera Mak-Kinli*
"Mr. McMirty" (Jacobsen)　102:237
"Mr. McNamara" (Trevor)　71:324, 335;

116:361, 377
"Mr. Mendelsohn" (Mohr)   12:446
Mr. Midshipman Hornblower (Forester)
    35:169
"Mr. Moore" (Dourado)   23:151
"Mr. More and the Mithraic Bull" (Wilson)
    2:477
"Mr. Morgan" (Michener)   109:378
Mr. Nicholas (Hinde)   6:238, 241
Mr. Norris Changes Trains (Isherwood)
    See *The Last of Mr. Norris*
Mr. Parker Pyne, Detective (Christie)   110:112
Mr. Pope and Other Poems (Tate)   11:527
"Mr. Powers" (Gordon)   13:248; 83:231
Mr. Pu (Ichikawa)
    See *Poo-san*
Mr. Pye (Peake)   54:366, 369-70, 375, 378
"Mr. Quintillian" (Hersey)   81:330
"Mr. S. Karuma's Crime" (Abe)
    See "S. Karuma-shi no hanzai"
Mr. Sammler's Planet (Bellow)   1:33; 2:52-3;
    3:51, 54-8; 6:52-4, 56, 58-9, 61; 8:71,
    74-5, 78-80; 10:39-42, 44; 13:70-4;
    15:47, 49-50, 52, 54-5, 57; 25:81-2;
    33:66-7, 69, 71; 34:545; 63:27, 33, 37-9
Mr. Sampath (Narayan)   28:292, 298, 300
Mr. Scobie's Riddle (Jolley)   46:213-15, 217-
    18, 221
"Mr. Seurat's Sunday Afternoon" (Schwartz)
    See "Seurat's Sunday Afternoon along the
    Seine"
"Mr. Slaughterboard" (Peake)   54:372
Mr. Smith Goes to Washington (Capra)   16:155-
    58, 160-62
"Mr. Soul" (Young)
    See "Hello Mr. Soul"
Mr. Stephen (White)
    See *The Minister for Justice*
Mr. Stimpson and Mr. Gorse (Hamilton)
    51:192-95, 197
Mr. Stone and the Knights Companion (Naipaul)
    4:374-75; 7:253; 13:403-06; 105:136,
    147, 154, 156, 180
"Mr. Trill in Hades" (Smith)   64:401
"Mr. Vidal: Unpatriotic Gore" (Amis)   62:3
"Mr. Waterman" (Redgrove)   41:348, 359
Mr. Welk and Jersey Jim (Sackler)   14:479
Mr. Whatnot (Ayckbourn)   33:40, 42; 74:29
"Mr. Whitney" (Kinsella)   27:237
"Mr. Wilson, the World" (Jones)   10:286
Mr. Witt among the Rebels (Sender)   8:480
Mr. Wrong (Howard)   7:164-65
"Mrs. Acland's Ghosts" (Trevor)   7:477-78
Mrs. Beer's House (Beer)   58:34-5
"Mrs. Benson" (Purdy)   28:379
"Mrs. Bixby and the Colonel's Coat" (Dahl)
    79:176, 182
Mrs. Blood (Thomas)   7:472; 37:417, 423;
    107:316-21, 333-35, 340, 344-45, 348,
    351
Mrs. Bridge (Connell)   4:108; 6:116; 45:107-
    09, 111-12, 116
Mrs. Caldwell habla con su hijo (*Mrs. Caldwell
    Speaks to Her Son*) (Cela)   4:96, 98
Mrs. Caldwell Speaks to Her Son (Cela)
    See *Mrs. Caldwell habla con su hijo*
Mrs. Caliban (Ingalls)   42:230-31, 233-35
Mrs. Craddock (Maugham)   15:370; 93:244,
    247, 257
"Mrs. Cross and Mrs. Kidd" (Munro)   95:315
"Mrs. Darcy Meets the Blue-Eyed Stranger at
    the Beach"   25:409
Mrs. deWinter (Hill)   113:316-19, 328-29

Mrs. Doremi (Nakos)   29:323
Mrs. Dot (Maugham)   15:366
Mrs. Eckdorf in O'Neill's Hotel (Trevor)   7:476;
    71:345; 116:334-35, 338, 367, 374, 377,
    382-83
"Mrs. Evan Nr. Six" (Davies)   23:144
"Mrs. Fanchier at the Movies" (Fearing)
    51:114
Mrs. Fay Dines on Zebra (Calisher)   38:69
Mrs. Fish, Ape, and Me, the Dump Queen (Ma-
    zer)   26:293
"Mrs. Fornheim, Refugee" (Layton)   15:322
"Mrs. Frankenstein" (Piercy)   62:367
"Mrs. Franklin Ascends" (Chappell)   40:141
"Mrs. Frost" (Clarke)   61:78
Mrs. God (Straub)   107:304-07
"Mrs. Golightly and the First Convention"
    (Wilson)   13:609
"Mrs. Grobnik a Checker-Upper" (Royko)
    109:407
"Mrs. Hackett" (Dowell)   60:107-08
"Mrs. Hofstadter on Josephine Street" (Parker)
    68:336
"Mrs. Jinny's Shroud" (Prichard)   46:333
"Mrs. Macintosh" (Hall)   51:172
"Mrs. Mandford's Drawing Room" (Brophy)
    29:91
"Mrs. Mandrill" (Nemerov)   6:361; 9:394;
    36:300
"Mrs. Martino the Candy Store Lady" (Turco)
    11:552
Mrs. McGinty's Dead (Christie)   12:117;
    110:133
"Mrs. McGonigle on Decorum" (Johnston)
    51:244
"Mrs. Mean" (Gass)   2:154; 8:244
Mrs. Munck (Leffland)   19:277-79
Mrs. October was Here (Dowell)   60:96, 99-
    100, 108
Mrs. Palfrey at the Claremont (Taylor)   29:408-
    09, 412
"Mrs. Plum" (Mphahlele)   25:339, 342
Mrs. Pooter's Diary (Waterhouse)   47:423-24
"Mrs. Razor" (Still)   49:366
"Mrs. Reinhardt" (O'Brien)   116:186
"Mrs. Robinson" (Simon)   17:460, 463, 465
"Mrs. Silly" (Trevor)   71:336
Mrs. Silly (Bennett)   77:97
"Mrs. Small" (Brooks)   15:92
"Mrs. Snow" (Justice)   102:285
Mrs. Stevens Hears the Mermaids Singing
    (Sarton)   4:471-72; 14:481; 49:322-23;
    91:246-47, 249-50
Mrs. Ted Bliss (Elkin)   91:114-15, 221-25
"Mrs. Todd's Shortcut" (King)   37:206
"Mrs. Turner Cutting the Grass" (Shields)
    113:427, 429-30
"Mrs. Vandebilt" (McCartney)   35:282
Mrs. Wallop (De Vries)   2:113-14; 3:126; 28:107
"Mrs. Wentworth" (Reaney)   13:473
"Mrs. Wienckus" (White)   10:527
"Ms. Found in an Anthill" (Le Guin)   45:217
"Mt. Vernon and Fairway" (Wilson)   12:647
"MTX" (Moure)   88:229
"Mu" (Tolson)   105:250-51, 255
Much Obliged, Jeeves (Wodehouse)
    See *Jeeves and the Tie That Binds*
"Mud Toe the Cannibal" (Purdy)   52:350
"The Mud Vision" (Heaney)   74:161
"Mudbone" (Pryor)   26:378
"A Muddy Cup" (Montague)   46:277
Muder Ahoy! (Christie)   110:124
"The Mudtower" (Stevenson)   33:381

Las muertas (*The Dead Girls*) (Ibarguengoitia)
    37:182-84
"La muerte" (Aleixandre)   9:14, 16
"La muerte" (Marques)   96:227
"Muerte constante más allá der amor" ("Death
    Constant beyond Love") (Garcia Marquez)
    3:182; 15:254; 47:146, 151
La muerte de Artemio Cruz (*The Death of
    Artemio Cruz*) (Fuentes)   8:224; 13:232;
    22:165; 41:167, 171-72, 174; 60:156-58,
    160, 163, 172; 113:230, 238, 253, 256-
    57, 262-63
"Muerte de Narciso" ("Death of Narcissus")
    (Lezama Lima)   101:121, 125
La muerte no entrará en palacio (*Death Shall
    Not Enter the Palace*) (Marques)   96:224,
    226-30, 232, 240-42, 250-52, 257-58,
    260-61
"La muerte y la brújula" ("Death and the Com-
    pass") (Borges)   1:39; 2:72; 6:87, 89, 91;
    8:97, 99; 10:66; 19:54; 44:358, 362-63;
    48:33, 45; 83:155, 177
"El muerto" ("The Dead Man") (Borges)   19:46;
    48:34, 38
"Les muets" ("The Silent Men") (Camus)   9:144;
    14:114
La muette (Chabrol)   16:170, 174-75
"Mugging" (Ginsberg)   109:365
A Mug's Game (Hamburger)   5:159
"Mugumo" (Ngugi wa Thiong'o)   36:317
"Mujer" ("Woman") (Neruda)   62:336
Mujer del río (Alegria)   75:49
"Mujer imagen" (Ulibarri)   83:407
Mujer, levántate y anda (*Woman, Arise and
    Walk*) (Gironella)   11:234, 236
"Mujer nueva" ("The New Woman") (Guillen)
    48:157, 164, 166; 79:233, 238-40
Mujer que sabe latín (*Woman Who Knows Latin*)
    (Castellanos)   66:43, 46-7, 54, 57, 61
Una mujer sin amor (Bunuel)   80:23
"La mujer y su imagen" ("Woman and Her Im-
    age") (Castellanos)   66:46, 54
"Mujeres" (Parra)   102:341
Mujeres al borde de un ataque de nervios
    (*Women on the Verge of a Nervous Break-
    down*) (Almodovar)   11-14, 19, 21-3,
    37-45, 49, 52-5, 57
Mul Hayaarot (Yehoshua)   31:470
"Mulata" (Guillen)   48:161; 79:240, 245, 248
Mulata de tal (Asturias)   13:37
"Mulatto" (Hughes)   10:280; 35:212, 217;
    108:327
Mulatto (Hughes)   108:284, 291
"The Mulch" (Kunitz)   6:286
"The Mule" (Asimov)   9:52; 26:46, 62-5
Mule Bone (Hurston)   61:273
"Mule Song" (Ammons)   5:29
"Mule Team and Poster" (Justice)   102:255,
    270
"Mules" (Muldoon)   32:318-19
Mules (Muldoon)   32:317-21; 72:264-65, 273-
    74, 276
Mules and Men (Hurston)   7:171; 30:209-12,
    215, 217, 220-21, 223-27; 61:263, 267,
    270, 275
"Mulleins Are My Arms" (Kenny)   87:256
Mulligan Stew (Sorrentino)   14:499-501;
    22:394-97; 40:384-85, 389, 391
"Multiple Choice" (Brunner)   8:109
The Multiple Man (Bova)   45:69
"Multitude" (Johnston)   51:243
"Multiversity" (Duncan)   41:128, 130
"Mulvihill's Memorial" (Trevor)   25:445-46;

71:348; 116:377, 384
"Mum and Mr. Armitage" (Bainbridge) **62**:34, 37
Mum and Mr. Armitage: Selected Stories (Bainbridge) **62**:34-8
"Mumbo" (McCartney) **35**:280
Mumbo Jumbo (Reed) **2**:367-69; **3**:424; **5**:368-70; **6**:447-50; **13**:479-80; **32**:357, 359-60, 364; **60**:300, 302-05, 307-10, 312
Mummy Slept Late and Daddy Fixed Breakfast (Ciardi) **44**:378
Münchhausen (Haavikko) **18**:208; **34**:169-70, 173
Munchmeyer (Thomas) **37**:415-16; **107**:314-15
Munchmeyer. Prospero on the Island (Thomas) **37**:415-16, 423; **107**:333, 348-49
Mundo a solas (*World Alone*) (Aleixandre) **9**:15; **36**:24, 28, 30
El mundo alucinante: Una novela de aventuras (*Hallucinations; The Ill-Fated Peregrinations of Fray Servando*) (Arenas) **41**:26-7
"El mundo está bien hecho" (Aleixandre) **9**:13
Mundo grande (*Big World*) (Andrade) **18**:3
Mundome (Mojtabai) **5**:293; **9**:385-86; **15**:377-79
The Mundy Scheme (Friel) **42**:167; **115**:246
"La muñeca reina" ("The Doll Queen"; "The Queen Doll") (Fuentes) **113**:237
Una muñeca rusa (*A Russian Doll, and Other Stories*) (Bioy Casares) **88**:92-5
"Munich" (MacNeice) **4**:315
"The Munich Mannequins" (Plath) **5**:345; **9**:427; **111**:168, 182, 185-86, 206
"The Municipal Park" (L'Heureux) **52**:275
"Muntele Maslinilor" ("The Mount of Olives") (Arghezi) **80**:2
Le mur (*Intimacy, and Other Stories; The Wall, and Other Stories*) (Sartre) **1**:305-06; **4**:473; **24**:406; **44**:495; **50**:371, 374, 382; **52**:379, 381
"Mural" (Scott) **22**:375
"The Murder" (Steinbeck) **21**:387-88
Murder à la mod (De Palma) **20**:72, 78
Murder After Hours (Christie)
   See *The Hollow*
"Murder at Cobbler's Hulk" (O'Faolain) **7**:274
Murder at McQueen (Ritter) **52**:356-57
Murder at the ABA: A Puzzle in Four Days and Sixty Scenes (Asimov) **9**:49; **76**:313
Murder at the Gallop (Christie) **110**:124
Murder at the Savoy (Wahloo)
   See *Polis, polis potatismos*
The Murder at the Vicarage (Christie) **12**:122; **39**:438; **48**:74, 76; **110**:111-12, 116
Murder Being Once Done (Rendell) **28**:383, 385, 387
"Murder By Capitol" (Pound) **112**:315
Murder in Mesopotamia (Christie) **48**:74
Murder in Retrospect (*Five Little Pigs*) (Christie) **12**:123; **48**:72, 74; **110**:120
Murder in the Calais Coach (*Murder on the Orient Express*) (Christie) **1**:58; **6**:108; **8**:142; **12**:112-13, 117, 120, 122, 124; **48**:73, 77; **110**:112, 121-22, 132
Murder in the Cathedral (Eliot) **1**:89, 91; **2**:129; **6**:166-68; **13**:193, 195; **15**:206-08, 215; **34**:401; **41**:144, 152, 155; **55**:372; **57**:186, 208
Murder in the Dark (Atwood) **84**:70
Murder in the English Department (Miner) **40**:328, 330-31

"The Murder, Inc. Sutra" (Rothenberg) **57**:374
A Murder Is Announced (Christie) **12**:124; **39**:438; **48**:71-5; **110**:112, 116
Murder Most Foul (Christie) **110**:124
"Murder Mystery" (Reed) **21**:303, 307
"Murder Mystery" (Rooke) **25**:394
"Murder Mystery" (Wagoner) **3**:508
The Murder of Aziz Khan (Ghose) **42**:178-79
"A Murder of Crows" (Lane) **25**:287
"The Murder of Harry Keyes" (Durcan) **70**:147
The Murder of Otsuya (Tanizaki)
   See *Otsuya Koroshi*
A Murder of Quality (le Carre) **3**:281; **5**:232-33
The Murder of Roger Ackroyd (Christie) **1**:58; **6**:108-09; **8**:140, 142; **12**:111-12, 114, 117-18, 120, 122-23; **39**:437, 440-41; **48**:71-3, 77; **110**:116, 122
"The Murder of the Frogs" (Carpenter) **41**:103
The Murder of the Frogs, and Other Stories (Carpenter) **41**:103, 105, 108
Murder on the Links (Christie) **12**:110, 122; **48**:74
Murder on the Orient Express (Christie)
   See *Murder in the Calais Coach*
Murder on the Thirty-First Floor (Wahloo)
   See *Mord paas 31: A vaangin*
Murder, She Said (Christie) **110**:124
Murder Stalks the Wakely Family (Derleth) **31**:127
Murder with Mirrors (Christie) **48**:75
"The Murderer" (Smith) **44**:438
Murderer (Shaffer) **19**:415
The Murderer (Simenon) **1**:309
The Murderer Is a Fox (Queen) **11**:462
"The Murderers of Kings" (Herbert) **43**:191, 193
Murders in Volume 2 (Daly) **52**:87
Murdo and Other Stories (Smith) **64**:391
"Mureau" (Cage) **41**:82
Muriel (Elliott) **2**:131
Muriel (Resnais) **16**:501-02, 504, 506, 509-11, 515
"Murilo Mendes e os rios" ("M. M. and the Rivers") (Cabral de Melo Neto) **76**:163
Murke's Collected Silences (Boell)
   See *Doktor Murkes gesammeltes Schweigen, und andere Satiren*
"The Murmurers" (Jacobsen) **48**:190-91
Murmurs of Earth (Sagan) **30**:337; **112**:417
Murphy (Beckett) **2**:44, 48; **6**:34, 38-9, 43; **9**:78, 81; **10**:27-9, 34; **11**:34, 36-7; **14**:71, 75-6, 79-80; **18**:43, 50; **29**:53, 56, 65; **57**:92; **59**:253, 256, 258, 260
"Murphy in Manchester" (Montague) **46**:273
Murther & Walking Spirits (Davies) **75**:224-25; **91**:200-1, 204, 206, 209
The Muscular System: How Living Creatures Move (Silverstein and Silverstein) **17**:454
"The Muse" (Akhmatova) **64**:16
"The Muse" (Dunn) **36**:153
"The Muse" (Ewart) **46**:150
"The Muse" (Heaney) **37**:165
"The Muse" (Hope) **51**:215
"The Muse" (Kizer) **39**:169-70
"The Muse" (Sarton) **49**:314
"A Muse" (Simmons) **43**:410
"The Muse in Armor" (Benedikt) **14**:81
"The Muse Mother" (Boland) **67**:43, 45
"The Muse of History: An Essay" (Walcott) **67**:353
"A Muse of Water" (Kizer) **80**:172-73, 181, 185

"Muse, Poet, and Fountain" (Watkins) **43**:453
"Musée des Beaux Arts" (Auden) **3**:23-4; **9**:59; **11**:17; **43**:22
"Musée imaginaire" (Montague) **46**:266
Le musée imaginaire de la sculpture mondiale (Malraux) **15**:352
Le musée noir (Mandiargues) **41**:278
"Musées" (Butor) **15**:114
Museo d'ombre (Bufalino) **74**:39
The Muses Are Heard: An Account of the Porgy and Bess Tour to Leningrad (Capote) **3**:100; **8**:132-33; **34**:320, 322; **58**:87, 94
Museu de tudo (*Museum of Everything*) (Cabral de Melo Neto) **76**:155-56, 160, 162, 169
"The Museum" (Duncan) **41**:129
"Museum" (Fearing) **51**:114
"Museum" (Hass) **99**:152
"Museum" (Niedecker) **10**:360
Museum (Dove) **50**:152; **81**:132-34, 136-38, 142-43, 145, 149
Museum (Friedman) **7**:108-09
Museum (Howe) **48**:171-75
The Museum of Cheats (Warner) **7**:511
Museum of Everything (Cabral de Melo Neto)
   See *Museu de tudo*
"Museum of the Year 1937" **59**:387
"Museum Piece" (Wilbur) **110**:385
"A Museum Piece" (Zelazny) **21**:465-66
Museum Pieces (Plomer) **4**:406
Museum Pieces (Tallent) **45**:388-90
"Museums and Women" (Updike) **9**:537; **23**:475
Museums and Women, and Other Stories (Updike) **2**:444-45; **3**:487-88; **7**:488; **13**:562; **23**:473, 475
Mushroom Book (Cage) **41**:82
"The Mushroom Gatherers" (Davie) **8**:162; **31**:109
"Mushroom Gathering" (Muldoon)
   See "Gathering Mushrooms"
"Mushrooms" (Atwood) **84**:69
"Mushrooms" (Bradbury) **15**:85-6
"Mushrooms" (Derleth) **31**:138
"Mushrooms" (Fuller) **62**:195
"Mushrooms" (Oliver) **34**:246-47, 249; **98**:256
"Mushrooms" (Plath) **11**:447; **17**:350; **51**:344
"Mushrooms in the City" (Calvino) **33**:100; **73**:33
"The Music" (Baraka) **115**:12
"Music" (Nabokov) **6**:357
"Music" (O'Hara) **13**:428-29
"Music" (Oliver) **34**:247; **98**:298
"Music" (Trevor) **71**:329, 333
Music (Slessor) **14**:497
The Music and Life of Carl Michael Bellman (Zuckmayer)
   See *Ulla Winblad*
Music and Silence (Redmon) **22**:342
Music at Night (Huxley) **5**:192; **79**:310
A Music behind the Wall: Selected Stories, Volume One (Ortese) **89**:197-99
"The Music Box" (Montague) **46**:277
The Music Box Bird (Sarton) **91**:241
"The Music Critic's Tale" (Stead) **80**:326
Music for Chameleons: New Writing (Capote) **19**:84-5; **34**:320-21, 323, 326
"Music for Four Doors" (Graver) **70**:52
"Music from Spain" (Welty) **22**:461; **105**:339
Music from the Body (Pink Floyd) **35**:311
"Music in the Air" (Johnston) **51**:247
Music Late at Night (McAuley) **45**:253-54
"Music Lessons" (Oliver) **98**:267

Music Lessons (Akhmadulina)   **53**:13
"The Music Lover" (Gardner)   **28**:162-63
The Music Lovers (Russell)   **16**:542, 544-46, 548
Music Maker (Cliff)   **21**:62-3
"Music Must Change" (Townshend)   **17**:538-39, 542
"Music of Colonis" (Watkins)   **43**:454
"Music of Colours" (Watkins)   **43**:451, 453, 457
"Music of Colours—Dragonfoil and the Furnace of Colours" (Watkins)   **43**:444
"Music of Colours—White Blossom" (Watkins)   **43**:447, 451
Music of My Mind (Wonder)   **12**:656, 661, 663
"The Music of Poetry" (Eliot)   **15**:215; **113**:194
The Music of This Sphere (Thomas)   **35**:409
Music of Time (Newby)   **2**:310
"Music on the Water" (Johnston)   **51**:240, 242
The Music: Reflections on Jazz and Blues (Baraka)   **115**:12, 37
The Music Room (McFarland)   **65**:67-74
The Music Room (Ray)
See *Jalsaghar*
The Music School (Updike)   **3**:488; **7**:487; **15**:543; **23**:473
"Music Swims Back to Me" (Sexton)   **53**:318
"The Music Teacher" (Cheever)   **7**:49
"The Music That Hurts" (Komunyakaa)   **94**:235
Music Walk (Cage)   **41**:79
La musica (Duras)   **20**:99
La música en Cuba (Carpentier)   **11**:103; **110**:59, 78
"Musical Chairs" (Fuller)   **62**:196-97, 201
"Musical Moment in Assynt" (MacCaig)   **36**:285
"Musical Offering" (Fuller)   **28**:157
"Musician" (Bogan)   **93**:78
"Musk" (Johnston)   **51**:241, 243
Mussarniks (Grade)   **10**:246, 248
"Mussel Hunter at Rock Harbour" (Plath)   **11**:447
Mussolini's Italy (Gallo)   **95**:93, 95-6
"Must the Novelist Crusade" (Welty)   **14**:565
The Mustache (Carrere)
See *La moustache*
Mustain (Price)   **63**:330
Muswell Hillbillies (Davies)   **21**:92-3, 95-7
"Mutability" (Snodgrass)   **68**:388
"Mutable Hearts" (Avison)   **97**:111
"Les mutations radieuses" (*Radiant Mutations*) (Tzara)   **47**:387, 390
"The Mute" (Landolfi)   **11**:321; **49**:211-12
Mute (Anthony)   **35**:36
"Muted Music" (Warren)   **39**:270
"Muteness" (Akhmadulina)
See "Nemota"
"The Mutes" (Levertov)   **66**:238
The Mutilated (Williams)
See *The Gnädiges Fräulein*
"Mutilated Prayer" (Cocteau)
See "Prière mutilée"
Mutmassungen über Jakob (*Speculations about Jacob*) (Johnson)   **5**:200-02; **10**:283-84; **15**:302-04, 307; **40**:263, 267-68, 270
"Mutra" (Paz)   **65**:182
Mutterschaft   **65**:445-48
The Mutual Friend (Busch)   **10**:93-4; **18**:84, 86; **47**:64
Mutuwhenua: The Moon Sleeps (Grace)   **56**:114-17, 119-21, 123
Muzeeka (Guare)   **8**:253; **14**:220; **29**:204-05

M.V. Sexton Speaking (Newton)   **35**:301-02
"Mwilu/or Poem for the Living" (Madhubuti)   **73**:215
"My '48 Pontiac" (Purdy)   **50**:238
My Achilles Heart (Voznesensky)
See *Akillesovo serdtse*
"My Adolescent Days" (Tanizaki)
See "Sheishun monogatari"
My Aim Is True (Costello)   **21**:66-70
My Amputations: A Novel (Major)   **48**:215-18
"My Ancestors" (Cliff)   **21**:65
"My Appearance" (Wallace)   **114**:348, 350, 352
My Argument with the Gestapo: A Macaronic Journal (Merton)   **11**:373-74
My Aunt Christina (Stewart)   **32**:422
"My Baby Gives It Away" (Townshend)   **17**:537
"My Back Pages" (Dylan)   **6**:154; **77**:167
My Beautiful Laundrette (Kureishi)   **64**:246-52, 254
"My Beginnings as a Writer" (Farrell)   **66**:135
"My Belief" (Hesse)   **17**:218
"My Belongings" (Endo)   **54**:158, 161
"My Best Friend" (Reed)   **21**:311
"My Best Soldier" (Jin)   **109**:54
"My Big-Assed Mother" (Bukowski)   **41**:68
My Body Was Eaten by Dogs: Selected Poems of David McFadden (McFadden)   **48**:254-55
"My Bones Flew Apart" (Eberhart)   **56**:76
My Brother Fine with Me (Clifton)   **66**:67
My Brother Michael (Stewart)   **7**:467; **35**:389, 391-92; **117**:367
My Brother Sam Is Dead (Collier and Collier)   **30**:71-5
"My Butterfly" (Frost)   **10**:199
"My Cherie Amour" (Wonder)   **12**:655, 661
"My Children at the Dump" (Updike)   **3**:485
My Children! My Africa (Fugard)   **80**:76-8
"My Children's Book" (Ewart)   **46**:152
"My Company" (Read)   **4**:437, 439
My Confession (Solzhenitsyn)   **4**:508
"My Conversion" (Spark)   **94**:344
"My Country" (Klima)
See "Má vlast"
"My Country" (Wright)   **53**:423
"My Country Wrong" (Rule)   **27**:419
My Cousin, My Gastroenterologist (Leyner)   **92**:282, 284-85, 290-94
My Cousin Rachel (du Maurier)   **11**:163; **59**:280, 284-85, 287
"My Cousins who could eat cooked turnips" (Frame)   **96**:188
"'My Craft and Sullen Art': The Writers Speak—Is There a Feminine Voice in Literature?" (Thomas)   **107**:348
"My Credo" (Fiedler)   **4**:163; **13**:212
"My Crow" (Carver)   **53**:61
"My Crow, Pluto—A Fantasy" (Moore)   **47**:266
My Crowd (Addams)   **30**:16
"My Dad's Wallet" (Carver)   **36**:107
"My Daily Horse" (Valenzuela)   **104**:377
My Darling Clementine (Ford)   **16**:305, 308, 310-11, 317
My Darling, My Hamburger (Zindel)   **6**:586; **26**:471-73, 475, 479-80
"My Daughter" (Pack)   **13**:438
My Daughter, Nicola (Arthur)   **12**:24, 28-9
"My Daughter the Junkie on a Train" (Lorde)
See "To My Daughter the Junkie on a Train"
My Days: A Memoir (Narayan)   **7**:254-55; **28**:296, 303

My Days of Anger (Farrell)   **66**:129
"My Dear Palestrina" (Mac Laverty)   **31**:254
"My Death" (Smith)   **15**:514
"My Death" (Strand)   **18**:517; **41**:432
"My Ding-a-Ling" (Berry)   **17**:54-5
My Dinner with André (Shawn)   **41**:400-02
"My Dream" (Bennett)   **28**:31
"My Dream" (Berry)   **17**:52
"my dream about the cows" (Clifton)   **66**:83
"My Dream by Henry James" (Ryan)   **65**:209
"My Dungeon Shook" (Baldwin)   **13**:53; **42**:19
"My Early Poems" (Justice)   **19**:233
My Ears Are Bent (Mitchell)   **98**:152-54, 163-64, 172, 177, 181, 183-84
My Education: A Book of Dreams (Burroughs)   **109**:182, 230-31
My Emily Dickinson (Howe)   **72**:195-201, 203, 209
My Enemy, My Brother (Forman)   **21**:117
"My Enemy's Enemy" (Amis)   **40**:43-5
My Enemy's Enemy (Amis)   **40**:45
"My Entire Life" (Borges)
See "Mi vida entere"
"My Erotic Double" (Ashbery)   **15**:33
"My Evolving Program" (Du Bois)   **96**:158
"My Expensive Leg" (Boell)
See "Mein teures Bein"
My Faith in Women's Suffrage (Masefield)   **47**:233
"My Faithful Mother Tongue" (Milosz)   **56**:246; **82**:290
"My Father" (Berrigan)   **4**:58
"My Father" (Hillis)   **66**:194
"My Father Burns Washington" (Chappell)   **78**:91
"My Father Died Imperfect as a Man" (Ciardi)   **44**:379, 381
"My Father in the Dark" (Simpson)   **7**:427
"My Father in the Night Commanding No" (Simpson)   **7**:427-28
"My Father Leaves Home" (Gordimer)   **70**:177
"My Father Moved through Dooms of Feel" (Cummings)
See "My Father Moved through Dooms of Love"
"My Father Moved through Dooms of Love" ("My Father Moved through Dooms of Feel") (Cummings)   **15**:162; **68**:50, 52
"My Father Paints the Summer" (Wilbur)   **53**:397
My Father Photographed with Friends (Bronk)   **10**:75
My Father Sits in the Dark (Weidman)   **7**:516
"My Father Speaks to Me from the Dead" (Olds)   **85**:306, 308
"My Father Was a River" (Dowell)   **60**:104, 107-09
"My Father's Breasts" (Olds)   **39**:187; **85**:302
"My Father's Country Is the Poor" (Walker)   **103**:369
"My Father's Deaths" (Amichai)
See "The Times My Father Died"
"My Father's Face" (Carruth)   **84**:
"My Father's Fights" (Dybek)   **114**:61
"My Father's God" (Fante)   **60**:133
"My Father's House" (Rule)   **27**:420
My Father's House (Troyat)   **23**:458
My Father's House: A Memoir of Incest and Healing (Fraser)   **64**:179-80
"My Father's Knee" (Scannell)   **49**:326
"My Father's Life" (Richler)   **46**:351-53
"My Father's Love Letters" (Komunyakaa)   **94**:238, 241

"My Father's Red Indian" (Abse)   29:21
My Father's Son (O'Connor)   23:326
"My Father's Telescope" (Dove)   81:135, 138
"My Father's Watch" (Ciardi)   40:154
"My Father's Wedding" (Bly)   38:58
My Fellow Devils (Hartley)   22:214-15
"My Final Hour" (Laurence)   50:316
"My First and Only House" (Adams)   46:21
"My First Ball" (Ihimaera)   46:199
"My First Hard Springtime" (Welch)   52:429
My First Loves (Klima)
    See *Moje první lásky*
"My First Marriage" (Jhabvala)   8:312; 29:256
My First Sorrow (Sarraute)   80:243
"My First Two Women" ("The Pretender")
    (Gordimer)   33:179
"My Flower Garden" (Christie)   110:126
My Foot My Tutor (Handke)   5:166; 8:262;
    10:256-57; 15:267; 38:217
"My Forefathers" (Kunene)   85:176
My Friend Hitler (Mishima)
    See *Wagatomo Hitler*
My Friend Judas (Sinclair)   2:401
My Friend Says It's Bullet-Proof (Mortimer)
    5:298-99
"My Friend the Instrument" (Simmons)   43:414
My Friend Wants to Run Away (Hyde)   21:180
"My Genealogy" (Akhmadulina)   53:14
"My Generation" (Townshend)   17:525, 528-
    33, 536, 539-40
"My Generation Was Lost" (Milosz)   56:233-
    34
"My Girl" (Robinson)   21:347
"My God" (Amichai)   22:33
"My Good Father" (Kizer)   80:182-83
"My Good-Byes" ("My Goodbyes") (Alegria)
    75:38-40
"My Goodbyes" (Alegria)
    See "My Good-Byes"
My Granddad the Monument (Aksyonov)
    101:22
"My Grandfather Gets Doused" (Chappell)
    40:145
"My Grandfather's Church Goes Up" (Chappell)
    40:145
"My Grandfather's Country" (Purdy)   50:240-
    41
"My Grandfather's Wake" (Muldoon)   72:273
*My Grandma Smoked Cigars, and Other Tales
    of Tierra Amarilla* (Ulibarri)
    See *Mi abuela fumaba puros y otros cuentos
    de Tierra Amarilla/My Grandma Smoked
    Cigars, and Other Tales of Tierra Amarilla*
"My Grandmother's Dream of Plowing"
    (Chappell)   78:92, 115
My Happy Days in Hell (Faludy)   42:135-36,
    141
"My Hate" (Bell)   8:65
"My Heart" (O'Hara)   78:364
"My Heart Is Broken" (Gallant)   7:110;
    18:171-72
My Heart's in the Highlands (Saroyan)   10:452-
    53; 29:362; 56:367-71, 373, 375-80
"My Heavenly Shiner" (Lowell)   3:306
My Holy Satan (Fisher)   7:103
My Home Is Far Away (Powell)   66:358-59,
    371
"My Homeland" (Klima)
    See "Má vlast"
"My Honey" (Guillen)
    See "Mi chiquita"
My Horse Gonzalez (Alegria)
    See *Caballo de copas*

"My Hotel Year" (Coupland)   85:35, 39
"My House" (Giovanni)   64:187, 194; 117:198-
    99
My House (Giovanni)   4:189; 19:192; 64:186-
    87, 191, 194; 117:181-86, 191-92, 196-
    97, 199
"My House in Umbria" (Trevor)   116:372-73
My House in Umbria (Trevor)
    See *Two Lives: Reading Turgenev; My House
    in Umbria*
My House Is on Fire (Dorfman)
    See *Cría ojos*
My Hustler (Warhol)   20:420, 422
My Kinsman, Major Molineux (Lowell)   8:350,
    352; 11:324-25
"My Lady the Lake" (Davison)   28:104
"My Land Has a Voice" (Stuart)   34:373, 376
"My Last Afternoon with Uncle Devereux
    Winslow" (Lowell)   11:327; 15:342;
    37:243
"My Last Name" (Guillen)   48:158; 79:229-
    30
"My Last Story" (Frame)   96:
My Last Two Thousand Years (Gold)   4:193;
    7:121-22
My Left Foot (Brown)   63:47-8, 55-6
"My Life" (Howe)   72:198, 200
"My Life" (Joel)   26:217
"My Life" (Ochs)   17:332
My Life and Hard Times (Thurber)   5:431-37,
    439-40, 442; 11:533; 25:437, 439
My Life and Times (Miller)   2:283
My Life as a Man (Roth)   4:454-59; 6:475-76;
    9:459, 461; 15:451-52, 455; 22:353-54;
    47:357, 361-64, 366; 66:416-17; 86:250,
    258
"My Life as An Echo" (Miller)   84:293
"My Life by Somebody Else" (Strand)   18:517-
    19; 71:279, 285
"My Life by Water: Collected Poems, 1936-
    1968" (Niedecker)   10:360-61; 42:297,
    299
My Life in the Bush of Ghosts (Byrne)   26:99
My Life in the Bush of Ghosts (Tutuola)   5:443;
    14:538-39, 541; 29:438, 440, 442
My Life, My Death by Pier Paolo Pasolini
    (Acker)   45:17; 111:8-10, 17, 21, 25-6,
    32-3
My Life of Absurdity (Himes)   18:250; 58:263,
    269-70; 108:228-29, 234, 241, 256
"My Life on the Road with Bread and Water"
    (Willard)   37:464
My Life to Live (Godard)
    See *Vivre sa vie*
"My Life with R. H. Macy" (Jackson)   60:211,
    235
"My Life with the Wave" (Paz)   3:375
My Little Poplar in the Red Kerchief (Aitmatov)
    See *Topolek moi v krasnoi kosynke*
"My Little Town" (Simon)   17:466
"My Little Utopia" (Simic)   22:383
"My Little Woman" (Guillen)   79:229
"My Livelihood" (Dickinson)   49:103
"My Love" (McCartney)   35:281, 283
"My Love Affair with James I" (Tremain)
    42:385
"My Love, My Umbrella" (McGahern)
    48:262, 268
"My Love Shooting the Buddha" (Lieberman)
    36:264
"My Lover John" (Smart)   54:425
"My Lucy Friend Who Smells Like Corn"
    (Cisneros)   69:153

My Madness (Kavan)   82:125-26
"My Man Bovanne" (Bambara)   88:19-20, 27,
    47
My Man-Coated Man (Lee)   90:181-2, 185
"My Meadow" (Carruth)   84:129, 132
"My Memory's Hyperbole" (Kristeva)   77:320
My Merry Mornings: Stories from Prague
    (Klima)   56:170-72, 174
My Michael (Oz)   54:351-53, 355; 5:334-35;
    8:436; 11:427-28; 27:359-60; 33:302
"My Mind Reads ..." (Levi)   41:243
"My Mistress" (Colwin)   84:142
"My Moby Dick" (Humphrey)   45:201
"My Mother" (Brophy)   105:8
"My Mother" (Kincaid)   43:248; 68:207-08
My Mother (Bataille)
    See *Ma mère*
"My Mother Breathing Light" (Vaughn)   62:458
My Mother: Demonology (Acker)   111:41
"My Mother Has Me Surrounded" (Kauffman)
    42:252-53
My Mother, My Father, and Me (Hellman)
    18:222, 224; 34:348
"My Mother on an Evening in Late Summer"
    (Strand)   41:432-33, 438
"My Mother Once Told Me" (Amichai)   116:95
"My Mother Remembers She Was Beautiful"
    (Gallagher)   18:170
"My Mother Remembers That She Was Beauti-
    ful" (Gallagher)   63:118, 126
"My Mother Would Be a Falconress" (Duncan)
    41:128; 55:298
My Mother's Body (Piercy)   62:370-71, 373
"My Mother's Hard Row to Hoe" (Chappell)
    40:143
"My Mother's Lips" (Williams)   33:448
My Mother's Music (West)   96:399, 400
"My Mother's Nipples" (Hass)   99:155
"My Mother's Novel" (Piercy)   27:376
"My Mummy's Dead" (Lennon)   35:262, 266
"My Muse" (Smith)   25:420
"My My, Hey Hey" ("Out of the Blue")
    (Young)   17:581-82
"My nacional'nyj geroj" ("We Are the Na-
    tional Hero") (Coles)   67:173, 175, 179
"My Name" (Brautigan)   34:318
"My Name" (Cisneros)   69:146
"My Name" (Levine)   33:275
"My Name and I" (Graves)   45:169
"My Name Blew Like a Horn Among The
    Payira" (p'Bitek)   96:309
My Name is Aram (Saroyan)   1:301; 8:468
My Name Is Asher Lev (Potok)   2:338-39;
    7:321; 26:371-72; 263, 266, 269, 290-92
    295
My Name Is Ivan (Tarkovsky)
    See *Ivanovo Detstvo*
My Name Is Legion (Zelazny)   21:472
"My Name Is Red Hot. Yo Name Ain Doodley
    Squat" (Brooks)
    See "Five Men against the Theme, 'My
    Name is Red Hot. Yo Name ain Doodley
    Squat'"
My Name Is Saroyan (Saroyan)   29:362-63
"My Native Land" (Ignatow)   7:177
"My Neighbor" (Ignatow)   7:180
"My Neighborhood" (Dybek)   114:62, 65, 67
My Next Bride (Boyle)   58:64, 66, 77-80
My Night at Maud's (Rohmer)
    See *Ma nuit chez Maud*
"My North Dakota Railroad Days" (Keillor)
    40:273-74
"My Nose Is Growing Old" (Brautigan)   3:87

"My Oakland, There is a There There" (Reed) 60:310

"My Oedipus Complex" (O'Connor) 14:399; 23:332

"My Old Man" (Hemingway) 6:233; 8:283; 19:211; 30:179, 191

"My Old Man" (Mitchell) 12:436

"My Old Man" (Reed) 21:320

"My Olson Elegy" (Feldman) 7:102

My Organic Uncle (Pownall) 10:419

My Own Ground (Nissenson) 9:399-400

"My Own Native Land" (Singh) 11:504

"My Papa's Waltz" (Roethke) 101:262, 264

"My Perfect Soul Shall Manifest Me Rightly: An Essay on Blackfolks and the Constitution" (Jordan) 114:151

My Petition for More Space (Hersey) 7:154-55; 40:240

"My Philosophy" (Allen) 52:35

"My Poem" (Giovanni) 19:191; 64:182, 186

"My Pony Won't Go" (Lightfoot) 26:279

My Present Age (Vanderhaeghe) 41:450-53

My Properties (Michaux)
See *Mes propriétés*

"My Quarrel with Hersh Rasseyner" (Grade) 10:247

"My Real Estate" (Apple) 9:32

My Red Kerchiefed Young Poplar (Aitmatov)
See *Topolek moi v krasnoi kosynke*

"My Rival" (Becker and Fagen) 26:85

"My Room" (Ali) 69:31

"My Routine" (Matthews) 40:319

"My Sad Captains" (Gunn) 18:199; 32:208, 211; 81:180

My Sad Captains, and Other Poems (Gunn) 3:215; 6:221; 18:200, 202; 32:208, 211

My Saint Petersburg (*I Remember Petersburg*) (Almedingen) 12:1, 5-6

"My Second Marriage to My First Husband" (Fulton) 52:162

"My Secret Identity Is" (Simic) 68:378

"My Shoes" (Simic) 9:479; 49:337, 339, 341; 68:370

"My Side of the Matter" (Capote) 1:55; 19:79-80

My Side of the Mountain (George) 35:175-79

My Sister, Life (Pasternak)
See *Sestra moia zhizn*

My Sister's Hand in Mine: An Expanded Edition of The Collected Works of Jane Bowles (Bowles) 68:10-11, 13

"My Sisters, O My Sisters" (Sarton) 4:472; 14:481; 49:310; 91:253

"My Son and I" (Levine) 14:316, 318

"My Son Austin" (O'Faolain) 14:402

"My Son the Murderer" (Malamud) 8:375; 27:306; 44:415

"My Son the Rastafarian" (Vargas Llosa) 42:412

"My Songs Induce Prophetic Dreams" (Whalen) 6:566

My Son's Story (Gordimer) 70:167, 171-76, 180, 184, 187

"My Soul and I" (Tolson) 105:282

My Soul in China (Kavan) 5:206

"My Speech to the Graduates" (Allen) 52:42

My Squaring of Accounts with Them (Krleza)
See *Moj obracun s njima*

"My Strange Quest for Mensonge" (Bradbury) 61:48

"My Swazi Boy or Song of the Frog" (Kunene) 85:176

"My Sweet Old Etcetera" (Cummings) 3:119; 68:46

"My Tears" (Oe)
See "Mizu kara waga namida o nuguitamo hi"

"My Three Hoboes" (Scannell) 49:327

My Times (Berton) 104:62

"My Trip Abroad" (Wilson) 24:483

My True Love Waits (Weber) 12:632-33

"My True Story" (Roth) 4:454, 458-59; 9:459

"My Uncle Daniel" (Cummings) 12:159

My Uncle Dudley (Morris) 1:232; 37:310-12

My Uncle Oswald (Dahl) 18:108-09; 79:176, 179

My Uncle Silas (Bates) 46:62-3, 66

"My Universities" (Yevtushenko) 51:432

"My Vocation" (Ginzburg) 54:201, 205

"My Voice Not Being Proud" (Bogan) 46:83; 93:64

"My War" (Fussell) 74:125, 127, 134

"My War Poetry" (Krleza)
See "Moja ratna lirika"

My War with the Twentieth Century (Berton) 104:47

"My Warszawa: 1980" (Oates) 33:296

"My Weariness of Epic Proportions" (Simic) 68:378

"My Wicked Uncle" (Mahon) 27:290

My Wicked Wicked Ways (Cisneros) 69:144, 150-51

"My Wife, My Car, My Color, and Myself" (Olson) 29:328

My Wife's the Least of It (Gerhardie) 5:139

My World (Stuart) 34:375

My World—And Welcome to It (Thurber) 5:438

My Younger Brother (Aksyonov) 101:15

"My Youngest Child" (Shiga) 33:368

My zdes' zhivem (*We Live Here*) (Voinovich) 10:504-05, 507

"Mycenae" (Denby) 48:83

"Myeza and His Musical Instrument" (Kunene) 85:176

Myko (Boyle) 19:68

"Mymosh the Self-Begotten" (Lem) 8:344

"My-ness" (Milosz) 56:239

"Myopia: A Night" (Lowell) 11:327-28

"Myra" (Berriault) 54:3

Myra Breckinridge (Vidal) 2:449; 4:553-55, 557-58; 6:548-50; 8:525, 528; 10:502, 504; 22:438; 33:408-09; 72:386-87, 389

"Myriam" ("Miriam") (Klima) 56:172-73

"Myrisai to áriston" (Elytis)
See "Smelling the Best"

Myron (Vidal) 6:548-50; 10:502; 33:409; 72:387

"Le myrte" (Bonnefoy) 15:74

"Myself" (Ashton-Warner) 19:22

"Myself" (Creeley) 78:152

Myself in India (Jhabvala) 4:259; 94:172, 177-79, 183, 185, 188

Myself When Young (du Maurier) 11:164

Myself with Others: Selected Essays (Fuentes) 60:162-64, 170; 113:251, 256

Le mystère d'Alceste, Suivi de Qui n'a pas son minotaure? (Yourcenar) 87:420

Mystère de la parole (Hebert) 29:230, 236-38

"The Mysteries" (H. D.) 73:121

Mysteries (Wilson) 14:584-85

"The Mysteries of Life in an Orderly Manner" (West) 7:519

Mysteries of Motion (Calisher) 38:73-5

The Mysteries of Pittsburgh (Chabon) 55:41-5

"The Mysteries of the Joy Rio" (Williams) 45:453-54

Mysteries of the Mind (Hyde) 21:176

Mysteries of Winterthurn (Oates) 33:294-96; 52:329, 331, 339; 108:348-49, 351, 354, 385, 391

Les mystérieuses noces (Jouve) 47:209

The Mysterious Affair at Styles (Christie) 1:58; 6:107-09; 12:111, 114, 120, 122, 124, 127; 39:438, 441; 48:77; 110:110, 116, 118, 122, 129

The Mysterious Disappearance of the Young Marchioness of Loria (Donoso)
See *La misteriosa desaparición de la Marquesita de Loria*

"Mysterious Doings in the Metropolitan Museum" (Leiber) 25:311

The Mysterious History of Columbus: An Exploration of the Man, the Myth, the Legacy (Wilford) 70:331, 340, 342, 345, 354

"Mysterious Kôr" (Bowen) 22:64-7

The Mysterious North (Berton) 104:37-8, 47, 51-2

Mystery (Straub) 107:283-86, 289-90, 302, 304, 306-07, 309-10

Mystery and Manners (O'Connor) 3:365; 6:380; 13:417-18, 420-21

"Mystery at Euston" (Scannell) 49:331

Mystery at Love's Creek (Cavanna) 12:101

Mystery at the Edge of Two Worlds (Harris) 12:269

"Mystery Dance" (Costello) 21:67

Mystery in Little Tokyo (Bonham) 12:50, 54

"Mystery in São Cristovão" (Lispector) 43:267-68

"Mystery Mile" (Allingham) 19:11, 14

The Mystery of Being (Marcel) 15:359, 364

"The Mystery of Emily Dickinson" (Bell) 31:49

"The Mystery of Hunter's Lodge" (Christie) 110:111

The Mystery of Irma Vep: A Penny Dreadful (Ludlam) 46:243-44; 50:342-44

"The Mystery of Job's Suffering" (Spark) 40:399

The Mystery of Kaspar Hauser (Herzog)
See *Every Man for Himself and God against All*

"The Mystery of Personality in the Novel" (Gold) 42:189

The Mystery of Phillis Wheatley (Bullins) 7:37

The Mystery of Stonehenge (Branley) 21:18

The Mystery of the Boquet of Roses (Puig)
See *El misterio del ramo de rosas*

The Mystery of the Buddha (Cavanna) 12:102

The Mystery of the Charity of Charles Péguy (Hill) 45:182-87, 189-91

Mystery of the Fat Cat (Bonham) 12:50-2

"The Mystery of the Initiate" 75:62

Mystery of the Verb (Hebert) 13:268; 29:232

Mystery of the Witch Who Wouldn't (Platt) 26:350

"Mystic" (Plath) 5:342; 11:449; 14:425; 17:360; 51:345; 111:205

The Mystic Adventures of Roxie Stoner (Morgan) 6:340

The Mystic Masseur (Naipaul) 4:372, 375; 7:252; 13:402-04, 406; 18:360; 37:324-25; 105:147-48, 155, 170, 179

"A Mystic of the Air Age" (Johnston) 51:239, 251

Mysticism and Witchcraft (Waters) 88:343

Mystics and Zen Masters (Merton) 1:211

"Myten om människorna" ("The Myth of Mankind") (Lagerkvist) 54:286-87

"The Myth" (Levine) **33**:274
"Myth" (Mahapatra) **33**:278, 282
"The Myth" (Oates) **108**:355, 357
"Myth" (Ritsos) **31**:325
Myth (Buero Vallejo)
  See *Mito*
Myth and Metaphor: Selected Essays, 1974-1980 (Frye) **70**:274
The Myth and the Powerhouse (Rahv) **24**:353, 361
"Myth, Dream, and Poem" (Read) **4**:444
"Myth in Education" (Hughes) **37**:171
Myth, Literature, and the African World (Soyinka) **14**:509; **36**:412
"The Myth Makers" (Lane) **25**:285
The Myth Makers (Pritchett) **15**:441-42; **41**:331
"The Myth of Arthur" (Jones) **7**:189-90; **13**:309
The Myth of Deliverance (Frye) **70**:277
"The Myth of Mankind" (Lagerkvist)
  See "Myten om människorna"·
"Myth of Mountain Sunrise" (Warren) **39**:266
"The Myth of Sisyphus" **75**:69
The Myth of Sisyphus (Camus)
  See *Le mythe de Sisyphe*
"Myth on Mediterranean Beach: Aphrodite as Logos" (Warren) **10**:520
"Myth Today" (Barthes) **83**:93-4
Mythago Wood (Holdstock) **39**:151-54
Le mythe de Sisyphe (*The Myth of Sisyphus*) (Camus) **1**:54; **2**:97; **4**:89, 91; **9**:141, 152; **11**:93, 95-6; **14**:104-05, 108-12, 117; **32**:88, 100; **63**:60-2, 83-4; **69**:105-06, 113-18, 121, 126, 128-29, 133-34, 136
"Mythic Fragment" (Gluck) **44**:219, 222
The Mythic Image (Campbell) **69**:77-9, 81-2, 87
Mythistorema (Seferis) **5**:384; **11**:492-94
The Mythmakers (Barnard) **48**:27, 29
"The Mythmaker's Office" (Frame) **96**:192
"Mythological Beast" (Donaldson) **46**:143
"Mythological Introduction" (Larkin) **64**:262, 282
"The Mythological Poet" (Ashbery) **41**:40
Mythological Sonnets (Fuller) **28**:149, 151
"A Mythological Subject" (Colwin) **84**:149-50
Mythologies (Barthes) **24**:25-6, 30-1, 37; **83**:67, 69-71, 73-8, 80, 83, 85-7, 90, 93, 94-6, 98, 104
Mythologies: An Introduction to a Science of Mythology (Levi-Strauss)
  See *Mythologiques*
Mythologiques (*Mythologies: An Introduction to a Science of Mythology*) (Levi-Strauss) **38**:303, 305, 308
"Mythos" (Gustafson) **36**:211
"Myths I" (Mott) **15**:381
"Myths VII" (Mott) **15**:381
Myths and Texts (Snyder) **5**:395; **9**:499, 503; **32**:387-89, 391, 396, 398-99
Myths of Power: A Marxist Study of the Brontës (Eagleton) **63**:101-02, 104
Myths of the Near Future (Ballard) **36**:44, 47
Myths to Live By (Campbell) **69**:77, 94
"Myxomatosis" (Larkin) **5**:225; **8**:340
"N" (Cummings) **15**:160
N or M? (Christie) **110**:111, 113
La ná (Audiberti) **38**:22, 32-3
"Na audiart" (Pound) **48**:288
"Na cidade po porto" (Cabral de Melo Neto) **76**:161

"Na Guiné" ("In Guinea") (Cabral de Melo Neto) **76**:167
Na rannikh poezdakh (*On Early Trains*) (Pasternak) **18**:383; **63**:288, 290, 312
Na reke Baidamtal (*On the River Baidamtal*) (Aitmatov) **71**:15
Na rubu pameti (*On the Brink of Reason*; *On the Edge of Reason*; *On the Edge of Reason*) (Krleza) **8**:329, 331; **114**:168, 174, 176-77, 186
Na vlnách T. S. F. (*On Radio Waves*; *On the Radio Waves*; *On the Waves of Wireless Telegraphy*) (Seifert) **34**:256; **44**:424; **93**:305, 318, 333, 340
"Na vystavke Karla Veilinka" (Brodsky)
  See "At Karl Weilink's Exhibition"
Nabakov's Garden: A Guide to "Ada" (Mason) **82**:255
"The Nabara" ("The Loss of The Nabara") (Day Lewis) **10**:131
"Nabo: The Black Man Who Made the Angels Wait" (Garcia Marquez) **2**:150; **3**:181; **47**:148, 150
Nabokov: His Life in Art; A Critical Narrative (Field) **44**:465, 467-69
Nabokov: His Life in Part (Field) **44**:464-68, 470
Nachdenken über Christa T. (*The Quest for Christa T.*) (Wolf) **14**:593-94; **29**:464-67; **58**:422-23, 431-36
Die nachholende Revolution (Habermas) **104**:87
Nachmetaphysisches Denken (*Postmetaphysical Thinking*) (Habermas) **104**:87, 89
"Nachtflug" ("Night Flight") (Bachmann) **69**:38, 54
Nachtstück (*Night Play*) (Hildesheimer) **49**:169-71
Nacimiento último (*The Last Epiphany*) (Aleixandre) **9**:17
Nada (Chabrol) **16**:179, 183-84
"Nadie" (Aleixandre) **9**:15
"Nadir" (Le Guin) **45**:216
Nadja (Breton) **54**:22-6, 28, 32-4; **2**:80-1; **15**:87
Nafsika (Nakos) **29**:323
"La nageur" (Soupault) **68**:406-07
Några steg mot tystnaden (Johnson) **14**:296-97
"Nähe der gräber" ("Nearness of Graves") (Celan) **19**:89
"Naiad" (Davidson) **13**:168; **19**:129
"A Nail" (Guillevic) **33**:191
"The Nail in the Middle of the Hand" (Brunner) **8**:108
Nail Polish (Layton) **2**:236
"The Nailhead" (Ignatow) **40**:258
"The Nails" (Merwin) **88**:199
"Le nain rouge" (Tournier) **23**:452
"Nairobi" (Oates) **52**:331
Naissance de la clinique: Une archélologie du regard médical (*The Birth of the Clinic: An Archaeology of Medical Perception*) (Foucault) **31**:178-80; **34**:339; **69**:170
Naissance de l'Odyssée (Giono) **4**:188; **11**:232
The Naive and Sentimental Lover (le Carre) **3**:281; **5**:232-33; **15**:325
"A Naive Poem" (Milosz)
  See "The World"
"The Naive Reader" (Reid) **33**:350
"Naked" (Oates) **108**:382
The Naked and the Dead (Mailer) **1**:187-93;

2:258, 262-63, 265; **3**:311-15, 318; **4**:318-19, 321, 323; **5**:266; **8**:364, 368-73; **11**:339-40, 342-43; **14**:352; **28**:256-57; **39**:417-18, 420, 425; **74**:202-03, 205-06, 208-09, 211, 217, 219-21, 233, 238; **111**:94, 97, 108, 113, 126, 135-36, 139-42, 144-46, 148, 151
"The Naked and the Nude" (Graves) **45**:169
The Naked Beast at Heaven's Gate (Bataille)
  See *Madame Edwarda*
"Naked Body" (Ritsos) **31**:332
"The Naked Eye" (Santos) **22**:363-64
"Naked Eye" (Townshend) **17**:534
"Naked Girl and Mirror" (Wright) **53**:425-26, 429
The Naked God (Fast) **23**:157-58
Naked in Garden Hills (Crews) **6**:117; **23**:132, 138; **49**:68, 70, 72
"The Naked Lady" (Bell) **41**:54
Naked Lunch (Burroughs) **1**:48-9; **2**:90-3; **5**:91-2; **15**:108, 110-11; **22**:80-6; **42**:68-9, 71-7, 80; **75**:83-117; **109**:180-91, 194-95, 197, 207, 210-16, 220-22, 224, 226, 227-31
"Naked Moon" (Rosenblatt) **15**:448
A Naked Needle (Farah) **53**:132, 134-35, 137-38
The Naked Night (Bergman)
  See *Gycklarnas afton*
Naked Poems (Webb) **18**:540-42
The Naked Sun (Asimov) **9**:50-1; **19**:28; **26**:40, 42, 46-8, 50, 53, 58; **76**:314; **92**:13
Naked Youth (Oshima) **20**:247
"Nakedness" (Ezekiel) **61**:105
Nalini (Ezekiel) **61**:97-9
"Namaste" (Broumas) **73**:14
"The Name" (Transtroemer) **52**:412; **65**:222-23
"Name and Address" (McCartney) **35**:286
"Name Changes" ("Changes of Name") (Parra) **102**:348, 350
A Name for Evil (Lytle) **22**:293, 300
The Name of Action (Greene) **18**:194; **70**:291; **72**:158-59, 161
The Name of Annabel Lee (Symons) **32**:429
The Name of the Rose (Eco)
  See *Il nome della rosa*
"The Name, the Nose" (Calvino) **73**:51, 53, 60
"Named for Victoria, Queen of England" (Achebe) **75**:13
"Name-Day Night" (Olson) **29**:330
The Nameless (Campbell) **42**:90, 93
"Nameless Flower" (Wright) **53**:424, 428, 431
"A Nameless One" (Avison) **97**:128
"The Nameless One" (Nakos) **29**:322
"The Nameless Stream" (Blunden) **56**:29
"Names" (Carruth) **84**:135
"Names" (Dixon) **52**:95
"Names" (Walcott) **76**:281-86
The Names (DeLillo) **27**:83-6; **39**:116-17, 119, 122, 125; **54**:79-83; **76**:171-72, 177, 179-80, 182, 185
The Names: A Memoir (Momaday) **19**:318, 320; **85**:235, 250, 256-57, 262, 267-68, 273, 279; **95**:267
"The Names and Faces of Heroes" (Price) **43**:341
The Names and Faces of Heroes (Price) **3**:404, 406; **43**:341-42, 344; **50**:229-30; **63**:325, 341
The Names of the Lost (Levine) **9**:332; **14**:315-16, 318-20; **33**:270-72, 274

"The Name's the Same" (Findley) **102:**110-11

"Naming a Poem Called Tucker Drugs" (Moure) **88:**230

"The Naming of Beasts and Other Poems" (Stern) **40:**414

"The Naming of Names" (Bradbury)
See "Dark They Were, and Golden-Eyed"

Naming Our Destiny: New and Selected Poems (Jordan) **114:**143, 146, 149, 153, 157, 162

"Naming the Losses" (Parini) **54:**360

Nana (Arzner) **98:**66, 69, 71, 75, 87, 90, 92-7, 99

Nana (Renoir) **20:**301

"The Nana-Hex" (Sexton) **53:**321

"Nancy and Sluggo" (Katz) **47:**216

"Nancy Culpepper" (Mason) **28:**274; **43:**288-89; **82:**235, 240

Nancy Mitford: A Biography (Hastings) **44:**483-84, 486-88, 491-92

"Nancy Reagan Wears a Hat: Feminism and Its Cultural Consensus" (Stimpson) **65:**339

"Nanji mo mata" (Endo) **99:**289, 290-95

Nanji mo mata (*And You, Too*) (Endo) **54:**159; **99:**285-86

Nanna-ya (Conde) **52:**84

"Nanny" (Dick) **72:**118

"Naoise at Four" (Boland) **40:**96; **67:**43

Naomi's Road (Kogawa) **78:**183, 194

"The Nap" (Banks) **37:**23

"The Nap" (Hine) **15:**282

"Napier Court" (Campbell) **42:**84, 92

Napis (Herbert) **43:**186

Napoleon Symphony (Burgess) **4:**83-5; **5:**85-7, 90; **22:**78; **40:**118, 126; **62:**132; **81:**303, 307, 310; **94:**51, 61, 69, 75

Nappy Edges (Shange) **25:**397-99; **38:**393

"Naptha" (O'Hara) **78:**334

Nära livet (*Brink of Life; So Close to Life*) (Bergman) **16:**47, 50, 80

"Narcissa" (Auchincloss) **45:**33

Narcissa, and Other Fables (Auchincloss) **45:**33

"Narcissus" (Disch) **36:**127

Narcissus (Scott) **43:**371-73

Narcissus and Goldmund (Hesse)
See *Narziss und Goldmund*

"Narcissus as Narcissus" (Tate) .**6:**526; **14:**528

"Narcissus Explains" (Howard) **47:**171

"Narcissus Moving" (Berryman) **13:**78

Narracions (Espriu) **9:**192

The Narrative (Pasternak)
See *Povest*

"Narrative Art and Magic" (Borges)
See "El arte narrativo y la magia"

"Narrative Authority" (Sukenick) **48:**369

"The Narrative of Jacobus Coetzee" (Coetzee) **23:**121, 124; **117:**34-6, 38, 44, 52, 79, 83

"Narrative Poetry" (Strand) **71:**288

"A Narrative with Scattered Nouns" (Dorn) **10:**160

"The Narrator" (Graham) **29:**193

The Narrow Corner (Maugham) **15:**367; **67:**206, 229-30

"A Narrow Heart: The Portrait of a Woman" (Gordon) **13:**244

The Narrow House (Scott) **43:**370-73, 380

The Narrow Land (Vance) **35:**427

Narrow Road to the Deep (Bond) **4:**69; **6:**85; **13:**98, 102

"The Narrow Road to the North" (Muldoon) **32:**318

Narrow Rooms (Purdy) **10:**425-26; **52:**343, 347-48

"The Narrow Way" (Pink Floyd) **35:**305

The Narrowing Circle (Symons) **14:**524

"Narrows" (Ammons) **8:**14

"The Narrows" (Jones) **42:**242-43

The Narrows (Petry) **7:**305; **18:**403-04

"Narsiga" (Rao) **56:**291, 306

"Narthex" (H. D.) **31:**208

Narziss und Goldmund (*Narcissus and Goldmund*) (Hesse) **2:**189-92; **3:**243, 245-47; **11:**270-72; **17:**195, 204-06, 217-18; **69:**287, 289

Nascita d'aurora (Ungaretti) **15:**536

Nashestvie (*The Invasion*) (Leonov) **92:**246, 260, 270-72, 277

Nashville (Altman) **16:**33-44; **116:**13-20, 22-6, 28-30, 36-7, 48, 50-1, 60-2, 64, 66,68, 70, 72, 74

"Nashville Gone to Ashes" (Hempel) **39:**68-9

Nashville Skyline (Dylan) **3:**131; **4:**150; **6:**155; **12:**186-87, 189, 199; **77:**169

Nasty, Very: A Mock Epic in Six Parts (Rathbone) **41:**344

"Nat Bacon's Bones" (MacLeish) **68:**290

"Nat Koffman" (Ignatow) **40:**258

Natalie Mann (Toomer) **22:**425, 428, 430

Natalie Natalia (Mosley) **43:**316, 319, 321

"Natalya Nikolayevna Goncharov" (Coles) **46:**113

"Natasha" (Olesha) **8:**431

Nathalie Granger (Duras) **20:**99, 101

Nathan Coulter (Berry) **46:**73

"Nathan La Freneer" (Mitchell) **12:**436-37

Nathaniel (Saul) **46:**368-69

"Nathaniel Hawthorne" (Borges) **83:**164

Nathan's Run (Gilstrap) **99:**43-5

Natica Jackson (O'Hara) **42:**319, 327

"A Nation" (Milosz) **82:**297

Nation et voie africaine du socialisme (*The Concept of Nation and the African View of Socialism*) (Senghor) **54:**399, 401

"A Nation of Sheep" (Ferlinghetti) **111:**60

"A Nation of Wheels" (Barthelme) **46:**36

"National Day of Mourning for Twelve Protestants" (Durcan) **43:**114

"The National Debt" (Apple) **33:**21

National Dream (Berton) **104:**44-5

The National Dream (Findley) **102:**104, 106

The National Health (Nichols) **5:**305-07, 309; **36:**329, 331-32

National Health (Nichols) **65:**162

The National Interest (Edgar) **42:**116, 123

National Lampoon's Animal House (Landis) **26:**272-77

"National Liberation Movements" (Baraka) **14:**49

The National Line (Haavikko)
See *Kansakunnan linja*

"The National Pastime" (Cheever) **3:**107

"The National Pastime" (Spinrad) **46:**384

National Reality from the Bed (Valenzuela)
See *Realidad nacional desde la cama*

The National Theatre (Edgar) **42:**114-15

"National Thoughts" (Amichai) **57:**41

"National Trust" (Harrison) **43:**177

National Velvet (Bagnold) **25:**72-4

The National Weather Service (Berger) **12:**38

National Winner (Humphreys) **47:**181, 184

"La nationalisation de la littérature" (Sartre) **24:**419

The Native (*The Incredible Brazilian*) (Ghose) **42:**180, 183-84

"The Native American Broadcasting System" (Alexie) **96:**12

Native American Tribalism: Indian Survivals and Renewals (McNickle) **89:**160-61, 181

Native Americans: 500 Years After, A Guide to Research in Native American Studies (Dorris) **109:**296

A Native Argosy (Callaghan) **41:**89

The Native Country (Haavikko)
See *Synnyinmaa*

"A Native Hill" (Berry) **27:**38, 40

The Native in Literature: Canadian and Comparative Perspectives (King) **89:**75

Native Intelligence (Sokolov) **7:**430-31

Native Land (Rich)
See *Your Native Land, Your Life*

Native Realm: A Search for Self-Definition (Milosz)
See *Rodzinna Europa*

"Native Resistances" (Dickey) **3:**127

Native Son (Welles) **80:**382

Native Son (Wright) **1:**377-80; **3:**545-46; **4:**594-96; **9:**584-86; **14:**595-99; **21:**435, 441-42, 446-47, 458-59, 462; **48:**416, 418-21, 423-30; **74:**356, 359, 361, 363, 370, 378, 380-81, 383, 385, 390-91

Native Speaker (Lee) **91:**53-58

"Native Village" **75:**78

"Natives Don't Cry" (Boyle) **58:**66-7

Natives of My Person (Lamming) **2:**235; **4:**279; **66:**220, 223-25, 227-28, 230

"The Nativity" (Archer) **28:**14

"Nativity" (Livesay) **79:**334-36

"Nativity" (Raine) **45:**331, 335

"Nativity, Caucasian" (Gurganus) **70:**191, 193, 195

"Nativity Poem" (Gluck) **7:**118

"Nativity Scene" (Bottoms) **53:**32

"A Nativity Tale" (Brown) **100:**83

"Natrabach i na cytrze" ("With Trumpets and Zithers") (Milosz) **56:**235, 244, 249; **82:**295

Natsukashii toshi e no tegami (Oe) **86:**244

Natten är här (*The Night Is Here*) (Johnson) **14:**295

Nattvardsgästerna (*The Communicants; Winter Light*) (Bergman) **16:**52-5, 58, 61-2, 64, 74, 78, 80; **72:**33, 38-41, 46-7, 49, 52, 54-5, 59

Natty Dread (Marley) **17:**267-68, 270, 272-73

The Natural (Malamud) **1:**196-98, 201; **2:**266, 269; **3:**321, 324; **8:**375-76; **9:**341, 346, 348-50, 352; **11:**345-46, 349-53; **18:**321; **27:**295-96, 298-99, 301; **44:**411-17; **78:**248-49, 251-52, 264, 271-72, 282-83; **85:**200

Natural Affection (Inge) **8:**309; **19:**227-28

Natural Child (Willingham) **5:**511; **51:**404-05, 411

Natural Enemies (Horwitz) **14:**267

"Natural Freaks" (Maitland) **49:**233

"A Natural Girl" (Yates) **23:**483

"Natural History" (Thomas) **37:**418-19, 421; **107:**325-26, 328, 349

"Natural History" (Warren) **8:**537

Natural History (Urdang) **47:**397-98, 401

"Natural History II" (Walcott) **76:**285

"A Natural History of the Dead" (Hemingway) **30:**188

"A Natural Man" (Dumas) **62:**155

"Natural Mystic" (Marley) **17:**269-70

Natural Numbers: New and Selected Poems (Rexroth) **1**:284; **22**:346; **49**:274, 283, 285

A Natural Perspective: The Development of Shakespearean Comedy and Romance (Frye) **24**:213; **70**:271, 277

"Natural Resources" (Rich) **36**:374, 379

Natural Selection (Barthelme) **117**:9, 11, 13-14, 18, 21-3

Natural Shocks (Stern) **39**:241-43

Natural Stories (Levi)
　See *Storie naturali*

Natural Supernaturalism (Abrams) **24**:12, 14, 16, 18

"Natural Theology" (Hass) **99**:142-43, 145-47

"Natural Tilts" (Vizenor) **103**:293

"Natural/Unnatural" (Avison) **97**:80-1

"Naturally" (Gallagher) **63**:116

"Naturally the Foundation Will Bear Your Expenses" (Larkin) **3**:275; **8**:340; **33**:258; **64**:272-74

"Nature" (McFadden) **48**:246

"Nature" (Oliver) **98**:292

"Nature and New Painting" (O'Hara) **78**:358

The Nature and Purpose of the Universe (Durang) **27**:88

"Nature Displayed" (Blunden) **56**:37

"Nature, Humanism, Tragedy" (Robbe-Grillet) **43**:360

"Nature in Literature" (Gerstler) **70**:158

"Nature morte" (Brodsky) **4**:78; **13**:116; **36**:81

"La nature morte de Samuel Beckett" (Sherwin) **7**:415

"The Nature of a Mirror" (Warren) **8**:537

The Nature of Alexander (Renault) **11**:472; **17**:401

"The Nature of Almost Everything" (Robison) **42**:342-43

The Nature of Catastrophe (Moorcock) **58**:347-48

"The Nature of Cold Weather" (Redgrove) **41**:347, 351, 354

The Nature of Cold Weather and Other Poems (Redgrove) **41**:347, 349

"The Nature of Evidence" (Graham) **48**:144

"The Nature of Literature" (Wellek) **28**:442

The Nature of Love (Bates) **46**:65

The Nature of Love (Wright) **53**:425

The Nature of Passion (Jhabvala) **29**:253-54, 260; **94**:166-68, 170, 180

The Nature of Space and Time (Hawking) **105**:73-7

The Nature of the Universe (Gallant) **17**:126

"The Nature of Tragedy" (Miller) **10**:346

Nature: Poems Old and New (Swenson) **106**:346, 351

"Nature with Man" (Silkin) **6**:498; **43**:397, 400

Nature with Man (Silkin) **6**:498; **43**:397, 399, 404

Les naturels du Bordelais (*The Bordelais Natives*) (Audiberti) **38**:22-4, 26

"Nature's Beauty" (Blunden) **56**:39

"Naufragi" (Ungaretti) **11**:559

"Naughty Boy" (Creeley) **36**:118

Nausea (Sartre)
　See *La nausée*

La nausée (*Melancholia*; *Nausea*) (Sartre) **1**:305; **4**:473, 477; **7**:396, 398-99; **9**:472; **13**:503-06; **18**:463-66; **24**:406, 410, 421; **44**:493, 495; **50**:370-74, 377-80, 382-84; **52**:378-79, 384, 387-89

"A Navajo Blanket" (Swenson) **61**:398

Navegação de Cabotagem (Amado) **106**:91

"Navigator" (Sarton) **49**:310

The Navigator (Keaton) **20**:195

The Navigator (West) **33**:430-31

"The Navigator Returns to His Country" (Bioy Casares) **88**:92

Le navire night (Duras) **40**:178 .

Nayak (*Nayak—The Hero*) (Ray) **16**:487, 494

Nayak—The Hero (Ray)
　See *Nayak*

Näyelmät (Haavikko) **18**:208

The Nazarene Gospel Restored (Graves) **6**:211; **39**:325; **45**:173

Nazarin (Bunuel) **16**:130-31, 135, 148, 151; **80**:20, 25-6, 28, 30, 34, 38-41, 44, 47-50, 53

The Nazi Doctors: Medical Killing and the Psychology of Genocide (Lifton) **67**:155-61

Nazism (Forman) **21**:121

"Ndbele's People" (Hope) **52**:210

"The *ndioso* Driver" (Cabral de Melo Neto)
　See *O automobilista Infundioso*

"Në kafe" ("In the Café") (Kadare) **52**:259

"Ne pisat' o groze" ("Don't Write about the Storm") (Akhmadulina) **53**:13

Ne réveillez pas madame (Anouilh) **40**:59-60

Ne vahvimmat miehet ei ehjiksi jää (*The Strongest Men Don't Stay Unscathed; or, Mother Always Knows Best*) (Haavikko) **34**:173, 178

"Neal vs. Jimmy the Fag" (Gelber) **79**:223

"Near Alexandria" (Brodsky) **100**:36

Near and Far (Blunden) **56**:49

"The Near and the Far" (Tomlinson) **45**:397

"Near Changes" (Van Duyn) **116**:414

Near Changes (Van Duyn) **63**:443-45; **116**:411-15, 418, 420, 423, 425, 427

The Near East (Asimov) **76**:312

Near False Creek Mouth (Birney) **6**:73-4

"Near Keokuk" (Sandburg) **35**:355

"Near Olympic" (Steele) **45**:364-66

"Near Pala" (Rush) **44**:91-2, 94-5

"Near Perigord" (Pound) **112**:352-53

"Near Périgord" (Stern) **40**:414

"Near the Haunted Castle" (Williams) **33**:445-46

"Near the Heart Place of Grue" (Abbott) **48**:3

"Near the Ocean" (Lowell) **8**:354; **9**:338; **11**:326; **15**:345; **37**:236

Near the Ocean (Lowell) **1**:181-82, 184; **2**:247, 249; **4**:302; **8**:351, 357; **11**:325, 331; **15**:342-43; **37**:234

"Nearing La Guarira" (Walcott) **76**:279-80

"Nearing the Ancre Battlefield" (Blunden) **56**:30

"Nearing the Lights" (Moss) **14**:375

Nearing's Grace (Sommer) **25**:424-25

The Nearly Complete Collection of Woody Guthrie Folk Songs (Guthrie) **35**:184-85

"Nearly True Stories" (Riding) **7**:375

"Nearness of Graves" (Celan)
　See "Nähe der gräber"

The Nearness of You (Kizer) **80**:182, 185-86

The Nearness of You (Kizer) **80**:182, 185-86

"Neato Keeno Time" (Crumb) **17**:83

Neb (Thomas) **48**:382-83

Nebanuitele trepte (*The Unsuspected Stair*) **75**:67, 71-2

Nebraska (Reddin) **67**:270

"Necessary Clarifications" (Aitmatov)
　See "Neobkhodimye utochneniia"

Necessary Doubt (Wilson) **3**:537; **14**:589

Necessary Secrets: The Journals of Elizabeth Smart (Smart) **54**:425-26

"Necessities" (Mueller) **51**:283-84

Necessities of Life: Poems, 1962-1965 (Rich) **3**:427; **6**:457; **7**:365-66, 368, 371-72; **11**:476; **18**:446; **36**:366, 372, 375; **73**:325-26

"Necessity" (Eberhart) **56**:77

"Necessity" (Hughes) **35**:222

"The Necklace" (Pritchett) **41**:334

The Necklace (Tomlinson) **2**:437; **4**:543-44, 546; **13**:545-46; **45**:393, 398-400, 402, 404

"Necrobes" (Lem) **40**:298

"Necrological" (Ransom) **2**:362; **4**:431, 435; **5**:365

"Necropsy of Love" (Purdy) **14**:432

Nectar in a Sieve (Markandaya) **8**:377; **38**:319-21, 323, 325

"The Nectarine Tree" (Sitwell) **9**:493

Ned Kelly (Buzo) **61**:58

"Ned Skinner" (Muldoon) **32**:317-18; **72**:276

"Need: A Chorale for Black Women's Voices" (Lorde) **71**:246

"The Need for Sleep" (Dybek) **114**:62

"A Need for Something Sweet" (Gordimer) **18**:190

"The Need of Being Versed in Country Things" (Frost) **3**:174; **15**:250

"The Need to Hold Still" (Mueller) **51**:280

The Need to Hold Still (Mueller) **51**:280, 282

"Need Ya" (Seger) **35**:380

Needful Things (King) **113**:388, 390, 392-93

"Needle" (Simic) **9**:480

The Needle (King) **8**:321-22

"The Needle and the Damage Done" (Young) **17**:570

"A Needle for the Devil" (Rendell) **48**:320

"The Needlecase" (Bowen) **22**:66

"Needles" (Cabral de Melo Neto)
　See "Agulhas"

The Needle's Eye (Drabble) **2**:117-19; **3**:128; **5**:117-19; **10**:162-63; **53**:118-19, 121-23

"Nefarious Times We Live In" (Allen) **52**:41-2

"Nefelegeretes" (Elytis) **100**:173

Nefertiti et le rêve d'Akhnaton (Chedid) **47**:86

"The Negative" (Williams) **39**:449

"Negative Capability and Its Children" (Simic) **49**:339

"Negative Pluses" (Ammons) **57**:50

"Negative Symbiosis" (Ammons) **57**:53

"Negative: The Little Engine That Could" (Smith) **42**:350

"Negatives" (Walcott) **14**:551

"The Neglect of Ford Madox Ford's *Fifth Queen*" (Gass) **39**:482

"Negotations" (Rich) **73**:330

Les nègres: Clownerie (*The Blacks: A Clown Show*) (Genet) **2**:157-58; **5**:136-37; **10**:225; **14**:199, 207; **44**:385-89, 391; **46**:173, 178

"The Negress: Her Monologue of Dark Crepe with Edges of Light" (Dubie) **36**:132

"Negro" (Hughes) **108**:309

The Negro (Du Bois) **64**:116, 131; **96**:146

"The Negro Artist and the Racial Mountain" (Hughes) **35**:220; **108**:290, 294, 307, 320, 323, 325, 333

"Negro bembón" ("Fat Lip"; "Thick-Lipped Nigger") (Guillen) **48**:161, 168; **79**:245

The Negro Caravan (Brown) **59**:267

"The Negro Hero" (Brooks) **15**:93

The Negro in American Fiction (Brown) 1:47; 59:271

"The Negro in Art" (Du Bois) 64:124

The Negro in Virginia (Brown) 59:272

"El negro mar" (Guillen) 79:240

"The Negro Mother" (Hughes) 108:297

"A Negro Playwright Speaks Her Mind" (Childress) 86:309

Negro Poetry and Drama (Brown) 1:47; 59:271

"A Negro Saw the Jewish Pageant, 'We Will Never Die'" (Dodson) 79:194

"Negro Servant" (Hughes) 35:214

"A Negro Speaks of Rivers" (Hughes) 5:191; 10:280; 44:507, 511; 108:296, 309, 311-12, 323, 334

"The Negro Writer and His World" (Lamming) 66:226

"Negroes are anti-Semitic because they are anti-White" (Baldwin) 42:22

"Nehotarîre" (Arghezi) 80:2

"Neige" (Kavan) 13:317

La neige en deuil (*The Mountain*) (Troyat) 23:458, 461

La neige était sale (*The Snow Was Black*) (Simenon) 1:309; 2:399; 18:484, 486

Neige noir (*Black Snow; Hamlet's Twin*) (Aquin) 15:17

Neige suivi de mal aimées (*Mal aimées*) (Kavan) 13:317

"Neige sur Paris" (Senghor) 54:395-96

"Neiges" ("Snows") (Perse) 4:399-400; 46:303-05, 307, 309

"Neighbor" (Hugo) 32:247-49

"Neighbor" (Silverberg) 7:425

"Neighbor" (Simak) 55:320

"Neighborhood Drunk" (Dybek) 114:64, 74

"Neighborhood House" (Guillen) 79:230

Neighboring Lives (Disch) 36:125-26

"Neighbors" (Carver) 22:97-8; 55:277, 279-81

"The Neighbors" (Friedman) 56:97

"Neighbors" (Hogan) 73:160

"Neighbors" (Singer) 111:333

Neighbors (Berger) 18:56-8; 38:37-40

"Neighbours" (Clarke) 61:83

Neil Young (Young) 17:569, 572, 579

Neither Fish nor Fowl (Kroetz) 41:240

"Neither in God nor in Marx" (Montale) 9:387

"Neither Out Far nor in Deep" (Frost) 1:110; 9:219, 221; 13:228; 15:250; 26:125

"Neither the Most Terrifying nor the Least Memorable" (Valenzuela) 31:437; 104:378

"Neither Wanting More" (Swenson) 106:347

"Nekkid: Homage to Edgar Allan Poe" (Smith) 42:353, 357

Nekrassov (Sartre) 13:500-01

Nekrofánia (Haviaras) 33:202

"Nel Bagno" (Jacobsen) 48:192; 102:241-42

Nel magma (Luzi) 13:352-53

Nel nostro tempo (*In Our Time*) (Montale) 18:340

NELLIGAN (Tremblay) 102:380

"Nelly Meyers" (Ammons) 5:29; 108:4

Nelly Sachs zu Ehren (Sachs) 98:323

Nelly's Version (Figes) 31:164-65

Nelson (Rattigan) 7:355

Nemesis (Christie) 6:108

"Nemota" ("Muteness") (Akhmadulina) 53:12

"Nemureru bijo" ("House of the Sleeping Beauties") (Kawabata) 5:208; 107:77-8, 86, 114

Nemureru bijo (*House of the Sleeping Beau-*

ties, and Other Stories) (Kawabata) 9:309; 18:280, 286; 107:77-78, 86, 106-09, 114

"Neobkhodimye utochneniia" ("Necessary Clarifications") (Aitmatov) 71:14

Neobyknovennie rasskazy o muzhikakh (*Stories about Unusual Muzhiks; Unusual Stories about the Peasants*) (Leonov) 92:258

"The Neo-Classic Drama" (Merwin) 45:268-69

"The Neo-Classical Urn" (Lowell) 8:351, 353; 11:328

"Le néo-Français en déroute" (Queneau) 42:333

"Neo-HooDoo Manifesto" (Reed) 3:424; 13:478; 60:315

The Neon Bible (Toole) 64:412, 415-17, 421-24

"Neon Sky" (Seger) 35:379

Neon Vernacular: New and Selected Poems (Komunyakaa) 86:190-94; 94:239, 242, 246-49

The Neon Wilderness (Algren) 4:16; 10:5; 33:13-15

The Nephew (Purdy) 2:348, 350; 10:423-24; 28:376-78, 380; 52:343-44

The Nerd (Shue) 52:392-93

"Nertheless" (Bernard) 59:44

"Nerthus" (Heaney) 25:245

Neruda and Vallejo: Selected Poems (Neruda) 1:247

The Nerve (Bragg) 10:72

Nerve (Francis) 2:143; 22:150; 42:147, 149-50, 153, 155, 158; 102:131-32, 144

Nerves (Wieners) 7:536-37

"The Nervous Father" (Martin) 30:248

Nervous Horses (Hearne) 56:124-28

"Nervous Songs" (Berryman) 3:67, 70; 8:91; 13:78; 62:71

The Nervous System: The Inner Networks (Silverstein and Silverstein) 17:452

"Nesselrode to Jeopardy" (Perelman) 49:261, 272

"The Nest" (Nyro) 17:320

The Nest (Kroetz) 41:235-36, 239-40

"Nest Egg" (Stuart) 34:374

"A Nest Egg for Paradise" (Singer) 69:306-07

A Nest of Ninnies (Ashbery) 2:17-18; 25:50

A Nest of Ninnies (Schuyler) 23:389

A Nest of Simple Folk (O'Faolain) 2:275; 13:402, 404-05; 70:312-13, 315-16, 320-21

"Nest of Vampires" (Fenton) 32:166

"Nested" (Nyro) 17:320-21

The Nesting Ground (Wagoner) 3:508; 5:473

"The Nestling" (Williams) 42:442

"Nestor's Bathtub" (Dove) 81:137

"Nests" (Kinsella) 43:253-54

"Nests in a Stone Image" (Goyen) 8:251; 14:212-13

"Net of Law" (Ding Ling) 68:67

"The Net of Place" (Blackburn) 9:100

Neterpenie (*Impatience*) (Trifonov) 45:417, 422

Netherwood (White) 69:410

The Nets (Blackburn) 43:63

The Nets (Ghiselin) 23:169

"Netting" (Graham) 48:145

"Nettles" (Pollitt) 28:366

"The Network" (Mathews) 52:308

Network (Chayefsky) 23:117-18

Netzahualcóyotl (Cardenal) 31:73

"Neues Hörspiel" (Jandl) 34:200

Neuromancer (Gibson) 39:139-44; 63:129-39

"Neurotics" (MacNeice) 53:233

"The Neutral Love Object" (Kumin) 28:223

"Nevada" (Cernuda) 54:55

"Nevada" (Updike) 15:545, 547

"Neve Forschungen über logik" (Heidegger) 24:276

"Neve Lebansansichten eines Katers" (Wolf) 29:465

"Never Again Would Birds' Song Be the Same" (Frost) 3:174; 9:228-29; 15:250; 26:114; 34:471

"Never Any Dying" (Silkin) 6:498

"Never Before" (Levine) 33:274-75

Never Call Retreat (Catton) 35:92-4

Never Come Morning (Algren) 4:16; 10:5; 33:11, 13-14, 16

Never Cry Wolf (Mowat) 26:335-36, 343, 346

Never Die (Hannah) 90:140-41

Never Die Alone (Goines) 80:96

"The Never Ending Wrong" (Porter) 15:432

Never Enough! (Sargeson) 31:371

"Never Give a Bum an Even Break" (Welch) 14:559; 52:429-30

"Never Had a Dream Come True" (Wonder) 12:656

"Never Is Too Late" (Armatrading) 17:8-9

"Never Marry a Mexican" (Cisneros) 69:153-54

"Never More Will the Wind" (H. D.) 73:119

Never Put Off to Gomorrah (Frayn) 31:189

"Never Stronger" (Fuller) 62:193

"Never to Dream of Spiders" (Lorde) 71:262

Never to Forget: The Jews of the Holocaust (Meltzer) 26:303-04

"Never Too Close" (Lightfoot) 26:281

Never Victorious, Never Defeated (Caldwell) 28:60-1; 39:302-03

"Never Visit Venice" (Aickman) 57:6-7

Never You Must Ask Me (Ginzburg) 70:283

The Neverending Story (Ende) 31:142-44

"Neverness; or The One Ship Beached on One Far Distant Shore" (Avison) 97:70-2, 94, 111, 120

"Nevertheless" (Moore) 47:264

Nevertheless (Moore) 8:400

Neveryona (Delany) 38:159-60

Névralgies (Damas) 84:156, 158-60, 167, 170, 176, 179-80, 185

"New" (Matthews) 40:322, 324

The New Adventures of Ellery Queen (Queen) 3:422; 11:461

"The New Aestheticism" (Davie) 8:163

"New Age" (Reed) 21:303, 323

The New Age/Le nouveau siècle (Hood) 15:287; 28:191, 193, 195-96

The New Air Book (Berger) 12:40

The New American Arts (Kostelanetz) 28:213

New and Collected Poems (Wilbur) 53:409-10, 413; 110:352, 357, 359-61, 372, 377, 380

New and Collected Poems, 1917-1976 (MacLeish) 8:363; 14:337

New and Collected Poems, 1950-1980 (Scannell) 49:330-32

A New and Different Summer (Weber) 12:633-34

New and Old Selected Writings (Clifton) 66:78

New and Selected Poems (Davie) 31:108-09

New and Selected Poems (Fearing) 51:116-18

New and Selected Poems (Garrigue) 2:154

New and Selected Poems (McGrath) 28:276

New and Selected Poems (Meredith) 13:374

New and Selected Poems (Nemerov) 2:306;

9:393

New and Selected Poems (Oliver) 98:285-88, 290, 293-94, 302

New and Selected Poems (Richards) 14:454-55

New and Selected Poems (Smith) 6:512

New and Selected Poems (Wagoner) 3:508

New and Selected Poems (Wild) 14:580

New and Selected Poems: 1923-1985 (Warren) 39:264-70

New and Selected Poems, 1932-1967 (Viereck) 4:559

New and Selected Poems, 1940-1986 (Shapiro) 53:334

New and Selected Poetry (Warren) 59:298

New and Selected Things Taking Place (*Things Taking Place*) (Swenson) 14:520-21; 61:394-96, 398-99, 401; 106:321-22, 324, 328-29, 331, 336, 338, 343-45

"New Approach Needed" (Amis) 2:6

New Arrivals, Old Encounters (Aldiss) 14:15

A New Athens (Hood) 28:192-95

The New Atlantis (Le Guin) 45:214, 216-17

New Axis (Newman) 2:311

"New Babylons" (Abse) 29:17

"The New Baseball" (Keillor) 40:274

New Bats in Old Belfries (Betjeman) 34:309; 43:34

New Bearings in English Poetry (Leavis) 24:292, 294, 298, 300, 306, 308

"New Best Friends" (Adams) 46:22

"New Birds" (Davis) 49:83

"A New Birth" (Hoffman) 6:243; 23:239

New Bodies for Old (Vance) 35:419

The New Book of Forms: A Handbook of Poetics (Turco) 63:431

"New Boots and Contracts" (Clash)
  See "All the Young Punks"

"The New Boy" (Dubus) 36:147

"New Brunswick" (Nowlan) 15:399

New Cairo (Mahfuz)
  See al- *Qahira al-jadida*

"The New Cathedral in Galway" (Clarke) 9:168

The New Centurions (Wambaugh) 3:509; 18:532-33

The New City: A Prejudiced View of Toronto (Berton) 104:47

New Collected Poems (Graves) 39:325; 45:168-69, 173-74

The New Confessions (Boyd) 53:54-8; 70:132-33, 135

The New Conservatism: Cultural Criticism and the Historians' Debate (Habermas) 104:77-80

"The New Cosmogony" (Lem) 15:329

New Country (Spender) 10:491

The New Criticism (Ransom) 2:364; 4:433-34, 436-37; 24:363, 367

"New Dawn" (Warren) 39:264-65

"A New Day for Willa Mae" (Sapphire) 99:80-1

New Days: Poems of Exile and Return (Jordan) 5:203

A New Decade: Poems, 1958-1967 (Neruda) 5:301

"A New Diary" (Abse) 7:2

"The New Divan" (Morgan) 31:276-77

The New Divan (Morgan) 31:274, 276

A New Dominion (*Travelers*) (Jhabvala) 4:256-59; 8:311; 29:256-61; 94:171-74, 178-79, 181-86, 188, 192-94, 199, 201, 204

"New England" (Wright) 53:430

"New England, 1868" (Dubie) 36:130

"A New England Bachelor" (Eberhart) 56:91

"A New England Farm, August, 1914" (Murray) 40:333

New England: Indian Summer (Brooks) 29:81-2, 84-5, 88-9

"New England Theocritus" (MacCaig) 36:283

"A New England View: My Report" (Eberhart) 11:178

The New Equality (Hentoff) 26:180-81

"The New Evangelical Right" (Amis) 62:5

"New Every Morning" (Simmons) 43:414

The New Ewart: Poems, 1980-1982 (Ewart) 46:151-53

The New Food Book: Nutrition Diet, Consumer Tips, and Foods of the Future (Berger) 12:41-2

"New Forest Ponies" (Walker) 13:566

New Found Land: Fourteen Poems (MacLeish) 8:361; 14:337; 68:272-75, 292

"New Friends" (Rukeyser) 10:443

"The New Frontier" (Gary) 25:186

"The New Frontier" (Seidel) 18:475

"The New Gardener" (Lavin) 99:322

The New Genetics (Hyde) 21:176

"The New Girl Friend" (Rendell) 48:326

The New Girl Friend and Other Stories of Suspense (Rendell) 48:326

"The New Gods" (Cioran) 64:89, 94

The New Gods (Cioran)
  See *Le mauvais démiurge*

New Green World (Herbst) 34:452

"New Guinea Legend: The Finding of the Moon" (Wright) 53:425

New Hampshire (Frost) 3:170, 174; 9:220, 228; 10:195:15:240, 243-44, 249; 26:110, 113, 119, 124; 34:468, 471

"New Hampshire, February" (Eberhart) 11:179; 56:80, 85

"New Heaven and Earth" (Oates) 108:356

A New Herball: Poems (Willard) 37:462

A New History of Torments (Ghose) 42:183-84

"New Home" (Richter) 30:307

"The New Honesty" (Busch) 47:63

"The New Hospital" (Raine) 103:181

The New India (Mehta) 37:293-94

New Jersey: A Bicentennial History (Fleming) 37:127

"New Jerusalem" (McAuley) 45:251

"New Journalism" (Wolfe) 51:417-18

The New Journalism, with an Anthology (Wolfe) 35:457, 459, 463

"The New Kid" (Callaghan) 41:98

"A New King for the Congo: Mobutu and the Nihilism of Africa" (Naipaul) 105:155, 158

"New Lace Sleeves" (Costello) 21:76

A New Leaf (May) 16:431-37

A New Lease of Death (Vine) 50:264

"The New Leda" (Howes) 15:290

The New Left Church (Eagleton) 63:101

"New Liberal Coalition" (Schlesinger) 84:374

"New Liberty Hall" (Clarke) 9:168

"A New Life" (Heaney) 5:172

A New Life (Malamud) 1:196-98; 2:265-66, 268-69; 3:321, 323-24; 9:343, 346, 348-53; 11:345-46, 349-53; 18:321-22; 27:295-96, 298, 302; 44:413-14, 417; 85:191

New Life (Pa Chin) 18:373

A New Life (Rice) 7:360; 49:300, 304

"A New Look at the Language Question" (Paulin) 37:355-57

"New Lots" (Simpson) 32:378

"New Mama" (Young) 17:574

"The New Man" (Jones) 76:65

The New Meaning of Treason (West) 7:525-26; 9:562

The New Men (Snow) 1:316; 4:501-02; 6:516; 9:498; 13:508-11; 19:427

The New Modern Poetry (Rosenthal) 28:390-91

"The New Mood in Politics" (Schlesinger) 84:355

"The New Moon Party" (Boyle) 36:63

"The New Moreton Bay" (Murray) 40:343

"New Morning" (Dylan) 77:162

New Morning (Dylan) 77:162

"The New Moses" (Stern) 100:340

"New Mother" (Olds) 39:187, 192; 85:289

"The New Mothers" (Shields) 113:441

"New Murders in the Rue Morgue" (Barker) 52:51

"The New Music" (Barthelme) 13:59-60

New Music (Price) 63:325

"New Names" (Scott) 22:373

The New Net Goes Fishing (Ihimaera) 46:195, 198, 200

The New Nobility (Broner) 19:70

"A New Notebook" (Hoffman) 13:289

"New Objectives, New Cadres" (Rexroth) 112:397

The New Order (Prichard) 46:337

"New Orleans Nuptials" (Shange) 74:311

"The New Owner" (Barthelme) 59:251

"A New Pair" (Swenson) 61:404

"The New Pastoral" (Boland) 40:99; 113:71

A New Path to the Waterfall (Carver) 55:279-80

"A New Place" (McPherson) 77:359

"New Poems" (Simpson) 7:429

"New Poems" (Wright) 28:471

New Poems (Fuller) 4:178; 28:151, 153, 157, 159

New Poems (Hope) 3:251

New Poems (Montale) 7:231; 9:386-88

New Poems (Rexroth) 112:386, 393

New Poems (Roethke)
  See *Shorter Poems, 1951-53*

New Poems (Slavitt) 14:490

New Poems (Transtroemer) 65:223

New Poems, 1973 (Kinsella) 4:271; 19:252

"The New Poetries" (Kostelanetz) 28:219

The New Poetry (Alvarez) 5:16-18

"The New Poetry Handbook" (Strand) 71:286, 290

The New Poets (Rosenthal) 28:390-91

"A New Proletarian Art" (Seifert) 34:263; 93:340

New Provinces (Scott) 22:371

The New Radicalism in America (Lasch) 102:293, 297, 316-24

"The New Realism" (Ashbery) 2:19

The New Realism (Spender) 10:492

"A New Refutation of Time" (Borges) 19:55-6; 83:160, 161-62, 178

"The New Ring" (Shapiro) 53:332

A New Romance (McFadden) 48:248, 251-53, 255, 257

"New Rose Hotel" (Gibson) 39:144; 63:129-31, 134, 139

"The New Saddhus" (Pinsky) 38:356

"The New Sculpture" (Pound) 112:315

"New Season" (Levine) 9:332; 14:316, 318-19

"The New Season" (Merwin) 45:276

"New Secondhand Clothes" (Raine) 103:204

New Seeds of Contemplation (Merton) 83:403
New Selected Poems (Hughes) 37:177-78, 181
New Selected Poems (Moss) 45:290-91;
  50:352-53
New Selected Poems (Rothenberg) 57:380,
  382-83
New Shoes (Streatfeild)
  See *New Town*
"A New Siege" (Montague) 13:390; 46:270-
  71, 275-76
"A New Song" (Heaney) 7:148; 14:242-43;
  25:249; 37:162; 74:157
"New Song" (Townshend) 17:538
A New Song (Hughes) 10:279; 108:295, 297
New Songs (Arghezi)
  See *Cintece noi*
"The New Spirit" (Ashbery) 77:49, 59
The New Spirit (Ashbery) 2:19; 25:50
"New Stanzas to Augusta" (Brodsky)
  See "Novye stansy k Avguste"
"New Styles in Leftism" (Howe) 85:156
"New Tables" (MacCaig) 36:285
The New Tenant (Ionesco)
  See *Le nouveau locataire*
"The New Tendency of the Avant-Garde Writ-
  ers" (Kawabata) 9:311
"New Territory" (Boland) 113:96, 109
New Territory (Boland) 40:100; 67:46; 113:69,
  72, 74, 76, 81, 93, 96, 108-10, 114, 121-
  22
The New Testament (Asimov)
  See *Asimov's Guide to the Bible, Volume II:*
  The New Testament
The New Theologian (Mehta) 37:290
A New Time for Mexico (Fuentes) 113:270-73
"The New Tourist" (Sarton) 49:312
New Town (*New Shoes*) (Streatfeild) 21:402,
  406
"The New Tradition" (Sukenick) 48:369
"The New U" (Klappert) 57:268
New Wanderings and Misfortunes of Lazarillo
  de Tormes (Cela)
  See *Nuevas andanzas y desventuras de*
  Lazarillo de Tormes
The New Water Book (Berger) 12:40
New Weather (Muldoon) 32:315-17, 319-21;
  72:264-65, 276, 279
New Wind in a Dry Land (Laurence)
  See *The Prophet's Camel Bell*
"A New Window Display" (Mohr) 12:446
"The New Woman" (Guillen)
  See "Mujer nueva"
"New World" (Momaday) 85:268
"New World" (Walcott) 76:285
The New World (Banks) 37:24; 72:4, 12, 14
The New World (Bronk) 10:73, 76
The New World (Turner) 48:399-402
New World Avenue and Vincinity (Konwicki)
  See *Nowy swiat i okolice*
New World Writing (Roethke) 8:456
"New Year" (Clark) 38:126
"A New Year Greeting" (Auden) 43:27
New Year Letter (Auden) 1:9-10; 2:23; 3:24;
  4:33, 14:29; 35; 9:55; 11:19; 43:16, 26-7
"New Year on Dartmoor" (Plath) 111:202
"New Year Poem" (Larkin) 64:282, 285
"New Year Verses" 59:383
"New Year's at Lawrence's Grave" (Monette)
  82:332
"New Year's Day at Lepe" (Hooker) 43:199
"New Year's Day at the End of a Decade"
  (Squires) 51:379, 381-82
"New Year's Eve" (Ciardi) 40:157

"New Year's Eve" (Eberhart) 56:76
"New Year's Eve" (Prokosch) 48:306-07
"New Year's Eve" (Schwartz) 4:479; 45:354;
  87:334
"A New Year's Garland for My Students"
  (Levertov) 3:292
"New Year's Poem" (Avison) 97:69, 74-5
"New Year's Resolution" (Appleman) 51:15
"New Year's Song" (Seifert) 93:334
"New York" (Gunn) 32:213
"New York" (Hollander) 5:187
"New York" (Moore) 8:398; 19:340
"New York" (Senghor) 54:407
New York (Morand) 41:301, 304, 306
New York: A Serendipiter's Journey (Talese)
  37:390-91
"New York Airport at Night" (Voznesensky)
  57:414, 419
"New York City" (Lennon) 35:264
"New York City Serenade" (Springsteen)
  17:482-83
"New York Day Women" (Danticat) 94:96-8
The New York Head Shop and Museum (Lorde)
  71:240, 248-49, 251
"The New York Intellectuals" (Howe) 85:121-
  22, 149, 151, 153-54
New York Jew (Kazin) 34:561; 38:280-83
"New York Lady" (Parker)
  See "From the Diary of a New York Lady"
New York, New York (Scorsese) 20:330-32,
  336, 339; 89:231-32, 235-36, 241, 243,
  245-46, 260, 263, 265, 267-68
"New York Power Crisis" (Matthias) 9:361
"New York State of Mind" (Joel) 26:219-20
New York Stories (Scorsese) 89:265
New York Tendaberry (Nyro) 17:312-15, 317
"New York to Detroit" (Parker) 68:325, 334,
  339
The New York Trilogy (Auster) 47:13-16
"The New York Woman" (Sissman) 9:491
"The New Yorkers" (Giovanni) 117:198
The New Yorkers (Calisher) 2:96; 4:87; 38:74
The New Youth (Pasolini)
  See *La nuova gioventù*
New Zealand (Marsh) 53:255
"Newark, before Black Men Conquered"
  (Baraka) 14:48
"Newcastle Is Peru" (Harrison) 43:175
"Newcomer" (Okigbo) 25:347, 351; 84:300,
  306, 308-10, 314
"The Newest Bath Guide" (Betjeman) 43:47
New-Found-Land (Stoppard) 8:503-04
"Newhouse" (Major) 19:297
Newly Born Woman (Cixous) 65:328; 92:51,
  55, 64, 69-70, 72-3, 78-80, 83
The Newly Fallen (Dorn) 18:128
"Newness" (Paulin) 37:352
"Newport Jazz Festival" (Jordan) 114:145
"The News" (Busch) 47:63
"The News" (Cliff) 21:63
News (Delbanco) 6:130
"News Flash" (Cendrars) 106:197
"News for the Mineshaft" (Price) 3:406
"News from Avignon" (Weiss) 8:546
News from Cold Point (Bowles) 2:79
"The News from Ireland" (Trevor) 71:329-
  33, 340, 346; 116:367, 372, 382, 396
The News from Ireland, and Other Stories
  (Trevor) 71:329, 332; 116:367
News from Lake Wobegon (Keillor) 115:296
"News from the Cabin" (Oliver) 98:289
"News from the Cabin" (Swenson) 61:399;
  106:325

News from the City of the Sun (Colegate) 36:111
"News from the Glacier" (Haines) 58:219
News from the Glacier: Selected Poems, 1960-
  1980 (Haines) 58:220-22
"News from the Old Country" (Rakosi) 47:343
"News of the Death of the World's Biggest Man"
  (Macdonald) 13:356
"News of the Human Universe" (Tillinghast)
  29:415
"News of the Phoenix" (Smith) 15:516
News of the Phoenix (Smith) 15:512-13
News of the Universe (Bly) 38:51, 53-5
News of the World (Barker) 48:17, 21, 23
The News of the World (Carlson) 54:37-9
"News Photo" (Warren) 8:537
"News Report at Ameliasburg" (Purdy) 50:242
"News Wires of April 15, 1912" (Enzensberger)
  43:152
"New-Sense" (Baraka) 33:56
"The Newspaper" (Gustafson) 36:222
The Newspaper of Claremont Street (Jolley)
  46:213, 217
"Newspapers" (Lopate) 29:302
"Newsreel" (Daryush) 19:121
"Newsreel" (Day Lewis) 6:127; 10:133
"Newsreel: Man and Firing Squad" (Atwood)
  25:68
The Newton Letter (Banville) 46:29-30, 32
"A New-Wave Format" (Mason) 28:272-73;
  82:235
"Next" (Sondheim) 30:388, 391
Next (McNally) 4:347; 7:217; 41:292
"Next Day" (Jarrell) 13:302
"Next Door" (Wolff) 64:446, 448
"The Next Glade" (Aickman) 57:3, 7
"The Next Logical Step" (Bova) 45:69
"Next My Spade's Going" (Graham) 29:193
Next: New Poems (Clifton) 66:81-5
Next of Kin (Hopkins) 4:234
"Next, Please" (Larkin) 5:223; 8:332; 13:336;
  18:294-301; 33:256
The Next Room of the Dream (Nemerov)
  36:302
"Next to Last Things" (Kunitz) 6:288
Next to Nature, Art (Lively) 32:275-76
"Next to the Cafe Chaos" (Broumas) 73:15
"Next to You" (Police, The) 26:363
"Next Turn" (Slessor) 14:492
"Next Year" (Carver) 36:107
Nexus (Miller) 84:251
Le nez qui voque (Ducharme) 74:57, 59-61,
  68
Ngaahika Ndeenda (*I Will Marry When I Want*)
  (Ngugi wa Thiong'o) 36:319, 322
"Ngiculela/Es una historia/I Am Singing" (Won-
  der) 12:661
"Ngoma" (Dumas) 6:146
N'Goola and Other Stories (Prichard) 46:343,
  345
"Niagara" (Jandl) 34:195
"Niagara Daredevil, 37, Buried near the Falls"
  (MacEwen) 55:168
"Niagara Falls" (Barth) 9:67
Niaye (Ousmane) 66:335
Die Nibelungen (*The Niebelungs*) (Lang)
  20:200-01, 203; 103:110, 121, 123-24
The Nibelungenlied (Almedingen) 12:1
Nic albo nic (*Nothing or Nothing*) (Konwicki)
  8:327; 117:258, 277, 284-87
Nic w plaszczu Prospera (*Nothing in Prospero's*
  Cloak) (Rozewicz) 23:359-60
"Nicaraguan canto" (Cardenal)
  See "Canto nacional"

The Nice and the Good (Murdoch) 2:297-98;
3:347; 6:344, 348; 11:385
"A nice day" (Bukowski) 108:112
"Nice Day at School" (Trevor) 71:336
Nice Feeling Tonight (Ayckbourn) 33:44
A Nice Pair (Pink Floyd) 35:307
A Nice Place to Visit (Garner) 13:235
"Nice to Be Nice" (Kelman) 58:295
"A Nice Way to Go" (King) 8:322
"Nice Weather, Aren't We?" (Grayson) 38:211
Nichijoseikatsu no boken (*Adventures in Ev-
eryday Life*) (Oe) 86:230, 241
The Nicholas Factor (Myers) 35:299
Nicholson at Large (Just) 27:227-28
"Nicht nur zur Weihnachtzeit" ("Christmas
Every Day") (Boell) 15:70; 27:56-7;
72:72, 90-4
Nichts in den Windbruch getragen (Celan)
10:101
The Nick Adams Stories (Hemingway) 3:239,
241-42; 10:269-70; 30:193-94, 197-98
"Nick and the Candlestick" (Plath) 9:426,
428; 111:181-82, 199
"A Nickel Bet" (Knight) 40:279
Nickel Mountain: A Pastoral Novel (Gardner)
3:187-88; 5:131-35; 7:112, 114-15;
8:237-38; 10:218; 18:177-78; 28:167;
34:550
"Ha nidah" ("The Banished One") (Agnon)
14:3
The Niebelungs (Lang)
See *Die Nibelungen*
Die Niemandsrose (*The No One's Rose*; *The
Nobody's Rose*; *No-man's Rose*) (Celan)
10:101; 19:88, 90, 93; 53:70, 72-7, 82;
82:33, 37, 45
Niente e cosi (*Nothing, and So Be It*) (Fallaci)
110:192, 197, 203, 210, 214-15
Niepokój (*Anxiety*) (Rozewicz) 23:358, 362-
63
"Nietzsche, Genealogy, History" (Foucault)
69:194
Nigel Mole's Diary 61:411
"Nigerian Unity/or Little Niggers Killing Little
Niggers" (Madhubuti) 73:199, 210-11
"A Nigger" (Himes) 108:235
"Nigger" (Sanchez) 116:276-77, 293
"Nigger" (Shapiro) 15:475; 53:330
"Nigger Can You Kill?" (Giovanni) 117:177
Nigger Heaven (Van Vechten) 33:390-400
"Nigger Song: An Odyssey" (Dove) 81:134
The Niggerlovers (Tabori) 19:437
"Nigger's Leap: New England" (Wright)
53:418, 427, 432
"Night" (Akhmadulina)
See "Noch'"
"Night" (Bly) 5:63; 10:57
"Night" (Bogan) 4:68; 39:393; 93:69, 78, 81-
3
"The Night" (Bradbury) 42:36-7
"Night" (Campbell) 32:74-5
"Night" (Celan) 82:37
"Night" (Giovanni) 117:197
"Night" (Jeffers) 54:236, 244
"The Night" (Kunene) 85:165
"Night" (O'Brien) 116:195
"Night" (Springsteen) 17:489
Night (O'Brien) 3:365; 5:312-13; 36:337;
116:180, 184-85, 192, 194, 211, 227
Night (Pinter) 6:417; 15:423-24; 27:394-95;
58:373
Night (Wiesel)
See *La nuit*

"The Night / 1" (Galeano) 72:139
"Night after Bushfire" (Wright) 53:419
"A Night among the Horses" (Barnes) 3:37;
29:27
A Night among the Horses, and Other Stories
(Barnes) 3:36; 29:26-7
Night and Day (Stoppard) 15:521, 524; 29:397,
401; 91:187
Night and Fog (Resnais)
See *Nuit et brouillard*
Night and Hope (Lustig) 56:182, 184
"Night and Morning" (Clarke) 9:168
Night and Morning (Clarke) 6:112; 9:167-68
"The Night Apple" (Ginsberg) 36:197
"Night Arrival at Seatrout" (Hughes) 37:180
A Night at Green River (Hilliard) 15:279
*A Night at the Movies, or You Must Remember
This* (Coover) 46:121-23
"A Night at the Opera" (Tomlinson) 13:550
Night at the Vulcan (Marsh)
See *Opening Night*
Night Bathers (Walker) 13:565
The Night before Christmas (Perelman) 49:258
"The Night before Great Babylon" (Sitwell)
67:318, 325
"The Night before Morning" (Bowering) 47:19
"The Night before the Night before Christmas"
(Jarrell) 2:210
"Night Blooming Flowers" (Pollitt) 28:367
"Night Call, Collect" (Bradbury) 42:34
Night Chills (Koontz) 78:203, 212, 216-17
"The Night City" (Graham) 29:198
"The Night Club in the Woods" (Calisher)
38:69
The Night Comers (Ambler)
See *A State of Siege*
*Night Comes Softly: An Anthology of Black
Female Voices* (Giovanni) 117:190
The Night Country (Eiseley) 7:91
Night Cries (Benedikt) 14:81-2
Night Crossing (Mahon) 27:286-87, 289-90
"Night Crow" (Roethke) 19:397; 101:263,
324
"The Night Dances" (Plath) 5:345; 9:427-28;
111:167, 204
Night Desk (Ryga) 14:472-73
"The Night Dream" (MacLeish) 68:290
Night Dreams (Hoeg)
See *Fortællinger om Natten*
"The Night Driver" (Calvino) 73:31-2
"Night Duty" (Transtroemer) 52:415-16;
65:220, 236
"The Night Express" (Moss) 45:286, 289
"The Night Face Up" (Cortazar)
See "La noche boca arriba"
"Night Falls on Shiva's Hills" (Anand) 93:57
"Night Feed" (Boland) 67:42, 46; 113:79, 92,
98, 124
Night Feed (Boland) 67:41-4, 46; 40:99-101;
113:57, 72, 74, 79, 81, 87, 94, 97-99,
101, 108-09, 123-24
"Night Flight" (Bachmann)
See "Nachtflug"
"Night Flight" (Page and Plant) 12:477
"Night Flight" (Updike) 23:476
"Night Flight to Attiwapiskat" (Jiles) 58:273
Night Flight to Hanoi (Berrigan) 4:56
Night Flights (Cohen) 19:112-13
"Night for Voyeurs" (Dybek) 114:62
"The Night Game" (Pinsky) 94:306-308
Night Has a Thousand Eyes (Woolrich)
77:389-91, 393-97, 400, 402, 404-05
"The Night He Cried" (Leiber) 25:304

"The Night He Was Left Alone" (Rulfo)
See "La noche que lo dejaron solo"
"A Night in June" (Williams) 42:458
The Night in Lisbon (Remarque) 21:332-33
"Night in Martindale" (Raine) 45:340
A Night in May (Yehoshua) 13:616; 31:470,
472
The Night in Motion (Michaux)
See *La nuit remue*
"Night in the City" (Mitchell) 12:440
"Night in the Forest" (Kinnell) 29:284
"A Night in the Garden" (Dickinson) 49:102-
03
"Night in the Province" (Krleza)
See *Noc u provinci*
Night in Tunisia (Jordan) 110:275, 278
The Night Is Dark and I Am Far from Home
(Kozol) 17:252-54
The Night Is Here (Johnson)
See *Natten är här*
*The Night Is Long: The Autobiography of a
Person Who Can't Sleep* (Millin) 49:254
"Night Journey in the Cooking Pot" (Bly)
10:60-1
"Night Letter" (Kunitz) 6:286
"Night Letter" (Wright) 6:580
"Night Letters" (Jordan) 114:143
"The Night Lies" (Ciardi) 40:157
"The Night Life" (Ignatow) 7:177
Night Life (Kingsley) 44:237-38
"Night Light" (Willard) 37:463
Night Light (Justice) 19:232-33; 102:263-64,
270, 277, 283
"The Night Manny Mota Tied the Record"
(Kinsella) 43:255
Night Marc (Anthony) 35:38-9
Night March (Lancaster) 36:245
"Night Meeting" (Bradbury) 42:38
The Night Mirror (Hollander) 2:197; 5:186-
87; 8:299; 14:264
Night Monsters (Leiber) 25:303
'*night, Mother* (Norman) 28:319-21
"Night Movement" (Sandburg) 35:341
"Night Moves" (Seger) 35:383-86
Night Moves (Seger) 35:381-86
"Night Muse & Mortar Round" (Komunyakaa)
94:229
Night Music (Odets) 28:328-29, 332-33, 341;
98:198-200, 210, 229, 235, 237, 241, 244
"Night Must Fall" (Landolfi) 11:321; 49:212
Night Must Fall (Williams) 15:577
"Night Notes" (Booth) 23:78
Night of Camp David (Knebel) 14:308
"Night of Endless Radiance" (McFadden)
48:257-58
"The Night of Frost" (Harper) 7:138
Night of January 16 (*Penthouse Legend*;
Woman on Trial) (Rand) 44:451; 79:369-
70, 373-77
Night of Light (Farmer) 19:168
The Night of Long Knives (Gallo) 95:87-90,
92-4
Night of Masks (Norton) 12:468
The Night of One Hundred Heads (Sender)
See *La noche de las cien cabezas*
"Night of Six Days" (Morand)
See "La nuit de seis jours"
"The Night of St. Bartholomew" (Akhmadulina)
53:11
The Night of Stones (MacBeth) 2:251
Night of the Aurochs (Trumbo) 19:447-48
"Night of the Cabala and Passion" (Dourado)
See "Noite de cala e paixão"

"Night of the Chickens, North of Joplin" (Smith) 42:346
"The Night of the Curlews" (Garcia Marquez) See "La noche de los alcaravanes"
"The Night of the Gifts" (Borges) 48:47
"The Night of the Iguana" (Williams) 15:579; 45:446-47, 453, 455; 111:380, 382-83, 388, 391-92
The Night of the Iguana (Huston) 20:169
The Night of the Iguana (Williams) 1:368; 2:465; 5:499-501; 7:543; 8:548-49; 11:571, 573; 15:580; 19:472; 30:466; 39:444-46, 448, 451, 453; 45:445-46, 449-50, 453-55; 71:368-69, 371, 387
The Night of the Man on Stilts (Haviaras) 33:202
"Night of the Meek" (Serling) 30:358
Night of the Poor (Prokosch) 48:307, 312
"Night of the Scorpion" (Ezekiel) 61:102, 105-06
"Night of the Weeping Children" (Sachs) 98:335
A Night of Their Own (Abrahams) 4:1
Night on Bald Mountain (White) 7:532
"A Night Out" (Abse) 7:1; 29:18-19
A Night Out (Pinter) 11:438-39; 15:423; 27:385-86, 394; 58:372-74, 383
"Night Out, 1925" (Rhys) 14:446
Night over Day over Night (Watkins) 55:92-5
"The Night Parade" (Hirsch) 50:196-97
"Night Passage" (Leiber) 25:307
"Night Piece" (Belitt) 22:49
"Night Pieces" (Strand) 18:517, 520-21; 41:432
"Night Pieces, II" (Strand) 18:518
Night Play (Hildesheimer) See *Nachtstück*
"The Night Raider" (Edmonds) 35:155
"Night Rain" (Clark) 38:117, 120-21, 125-29
"Night Rally" (Costello) 21:68-9
"The Night Rhonda Ferguson Was Killed" (Jones) 76:64
"Night Ride" (Saro-Wiwa) 114:253
Night Rider (Warren) 1:352-54; 4:577-80, 582; 10:518-19; 13:570-71; 53:359, 366, 376; 59:298
"Night Scenes" (Duncan) 41:128
"Night School" (Carver) 36:106
Night School (Pinter) 11:441; 27:394; 58:372, 383
Night Seasons (Foote) 91:99
The Night Shapes (Blish) 14:86
"Night Shift" (Marley) 17:269
The Night Shift (Baxter) 14:61
Night Shift (King) 12:310; 26:237; 37:202, 207; 113:335
"Night Song" (Clark) 38:129
"Night Song" (Gluck) 44:217, 220
"Night Song for a Woman" (Purdy) 50:238, 241
Night Studies (Colter) 58:142-45
"Night Stuff" (Sandburg) 35:341
"Night Sung Sailor's Prayer" (Kaufman) 49:205
"Night Sweat" (Lowell) 11:328; 15:347
The Night Swimmers (Byars) 35:73
"Night Taxi" (Gunn) 32:212
"The Night the Bed Fell" (Thurber) 25:440
"The Night the Ghost Got In" (Thurber) 11:534
"The Night the Playoffs Were Rained Out" (Jacobsen) 102:241
"The Night They Left Him Alone" (Rulfo) See "La noche que lo dejaron solo"
"The Night They Murdered Boyle Somerville"

(Durcan) 43:114
"The Night They Put John Lennon Down" (Durcan) 43:117
Night Thoughts (Gascoyne) 45:148-53, 155, 157
"Night Thoughts in Greenwich Village" (O'Hara) 13:426
"Night Thoughts of a Media Watcher" (Steinem) 63:381
"Night Time" (Creeley) 78:141
"Night Train" (Reaney) 13:473
The Night Traveler (Oliver) 19:362; 98:259
Night unto Night (Wylie) 43:463-64, 470
Night Vision (Transtroemer) See *Mörkerseende*
"The Night Visitor" (Traven) 11:536
"Night Visits with the Family" (Swenson) 106:344
Night Voices: Strange Stories (Aickman) 57:3-4
Night Walk (Daly) 52:90
"The Night Was Young" (Wilson) 12:651-52
"The Night Watchman" (Jacobsen) 48:193; 102:240
"The Night We Rode with Sarsfield" (Kiely) 23:266; 43:245
A Night with Cindy (Hugo) 18:261
Night without End (MacLean) 13:361-63; 50:348-49; 63:263
Night without Stars (Graham) 23:192
"Night Women" (Danticat) 94:94
"Night Words" (Steiner) 24:429
"The Night Workers of Ragnarök" (Gunnars) 69:263
The Night Workers of Ragnarök (Gunnars) 69:262-63
Nightbirds on Nantucket (Aiken) 35:20
The Night-Blooming Cereus (Hayden) 37:151, 154, 160
Night-Blooming Cereus (Reaney) 13:473, 475
Nightbook (Kotzwinkle) 5:220; 35:257
Nightclub Cantata (Swados) 12:556-58, 560-61
"Nightfall" (Asimov) 19:28; 26:50; 76:313-14; 92:22
"Nightfall" (Mahapatra) 33:283
"Nightfall" (Urdang) 47:398
"The Nightfishing" (Graham) 29:197, 199
The Nightfishing (Graham) 29:195-98
"Nightgame" (Cherryh) 35:107
"The Nightgown" (Dacey) 51:83
"Nightgown" (Davies) 23:145, 148
"Nightgown" (Merrill) 13:380
"Nighthawks" (Dybek) 114:68, 70-1, 81-2
"The Nightingale and the Frog" (Seth) 90:354
The Nightingale of the Catholic Church (Pasolini) See *L'usignuolo della Chiesa Cattolica*
The Nightingale Sings Badly (Seifert) See *Slavík zpívášpatne*
The Nightingale Sings out of Tune (Seifert) See *Slavík zpívášpatne*
The Nightingale Sings Poorly (Seifert) See *Slavík zpívášpatne*
Nightlines (McGahern) 48:262-63, 267-69, 271
"Nightmare" (Longley) 29:293
The Nightmare (Forester) 35:174
"Nightmare and Flight" (Arendt) 98:51
Nightmare Begins Responsibility (Harper) 7:138-39
"Nightmare Boogie" (Hughes) 108:299, 301, 303-04

The Nightmare Factory (Kumin) 28:221, 224-25
"Nightmare Island" (Sturgeon) 39:361
"Nightmares" (Borges) 48:47, 49
"Nightmusic" (Oates) 6:370
"Night-Music" (Rukeyser) 27:404, 410
"A Night-Piece to Mrs. Treed" (Johnston) 51:243
"Nightride" (Clarke) 61:73
"The Night-Ride" (Slessor) 14:492
"Nights and Days" (Salinas) 90:323, 326, 328
Nights and Days (Dabrowska) See *Noce i dnie*
Nights and Days (Merrill) 2:273-75; 13:376, 380; 91:228, 230-31
Nights as Day, Days as Night (Leiris) See *Nuits sans nuit et quelques jours sans jour*
Nights at Serampore (Eliade) 19:146-47
Nights at the Alexandra (Trevor) 71:348,350; 116:367, 383
Nights at the Circus (Carter) 41:119-21; 76:329
"Nights before Battle" (Blunden) 56:30
Nights below Station Street (Richards) 59:186-92
Night's Black Agents (Leiber) 25:307
"Night's Fall Unlocks the Dirge of the Sea" (Graham) 29:194
"The Night's for Cryin'" (Himes) 58:265
Nights in Aruba (Holleran) 38:246-47
"Nights in Hackett's Cove" (Strand) 41:432, 434
Nights in the Gardens of Brooklyn (Swados) 5:420, 422
"Nights in the Gardens of Clare" (Durcan) 70:149, 152
"Nights in the Gardens of Spain" (Berriault) 109:97
Nights in the Underground: An Exploration of Love (Blais) See *Les nuits de l'underground*
Night's Lies (Bufalino) See *Le menzogne della notte*
Night's Lies (Bufalino) See *Le menzogne della notte*
Night's Master (Lee) 46:231, 234
"Night's Negation" (Read) 4:439
"Night's Nothings Again" (Sandburg) 35:341
"Nights of 1964-1966: The Old Reliable" (Hacker) 72:191
The Nights of Cabiria (Fellini) See *Le notti di Cabiria*
"The Nights of Goliadkin" (Bioy Casares) See "Las noches de Goliadkin"
"The Nights of Goliadkin" (Borges) 48:42
The Night's Orbit (FitzGerald) 19:175
"Night-Sea Journey" (Barth) 2:39; 9:66; 14:51; 27:26; 51:20, 23, 26; 89:4, 6-10, 15-23, 27-8, 30, 32-3, 36, 39-45, 47-9, 52, 55, 59, 61, 64
"Nightshade" (Voigt) 54:434
Night-Side (Oates) 9:406; 11:404; 52:339
Nightsong (Williams) 5:497
"Nightsong: City" (Brutus) 43:91, 95-6
"Nightsong: Country" (Brutus) 43:90
Nightspawn (Banville) 46:25-7
"The Night-Tender" (Govier) 51:166-67
"Night-Time in the Cemetery" (Smith) 25:419
Nighttime Talk with a Despised Man (Duerrenmatt) 102:53
"Nightwalker" (Kinsella) 4:271; 19:251, 255
Nightwalker (Kinsella) 4:271; 19:251, 253
Nightwatch (Sachs) 98:322

Nightwatchmen (Hannah)　23:208-09; 38:232; 128, 152, 155, 156-59

Nightwebs (Woolrich)　77:400

"Nightwind" (Banville)　46:25

"Nightwind" (Swenson)　106:318

Nightwing (Smith)　25:412

Nightwood (Barnes)　3:36-8; 4:43-4; 8:47-8; 11:29-31; 29:23-32

Nightwork (Hansen)　38:240

Nightwork (Shaw)　7:414

Night-World (Bloch)　33:83-4

Der Nihilist (*Die Falle; The Traps*) (Duerrenmatt)　1:81; 4:140; 8:195; 11:170; 15:195; 43:120, 128

"The Nihilist as Hero" (Lowell)　8:355

Niin katosi voitto maailmasta (*So Profit Disappeared from the World*) (Haavikko)　34:170

"Nike Who Hesitates" (Herbert)　43:184

"Nikki-Rosa" (Giovanni)　19:191; 64:191; 117:167, 194, 201

Nilda (Mohr)　12:445-46, 448

"The Nile" (Christie)　110:127

"Nimram" (Gardner)　28:161-63

"Nina" (Bates)　46:49

"La niña que murió de amor" (Ulibarri)　83:416

"Nine" (Creeley)　78:139

"IX" (Dunn)　40:170

Nine (Kopit)　33:251-52

"Nine Bean-Rows on the Moon" (Purdy)　14:433

"Nine Beatitudes to Denver" (Barker)　48:18

"Nine Below" (Harjo)　83:272

Nine Coaches Waiting (Stewart)　7:467; 35:389, 392

Nine Days to Mukalla (Prokosch)　4:421; 48:312, 314-15

The Nine Guardians (Castellanos)
　See *Balún-Canán*

"Nine Lives" (Le Guin)　8:343

"Nine Lives" (Merrill)　91:238

Nine Men Who Laughed (Clarke)　53:96-7

The Nine Mile Walk (Kemelman)　2:225

Nine Months in the Life of an Old Maid (Rossner)　9:456

"Nine Months Making" (Mueller)　51:280

"Nine Nectarines and Other Porcelain" (Moore)　2:291; 13:394, 397; 19:340

The Nine O'Clock Mail (Sackler)　14:479

The Nine Planets (Branley)　21:16, 19, 23

Nine Poems (Goyen)　40:218

"Nine Points of the Law" (Porter)　33:318

"Nine Shaman Songs Resung" (Ferlinghetti)　6:184

Nine Stories (Salinger)　1:298; 8:463; 12:519

Nine Tonight (Seger)　35:385-86

Nine-Headed Dragon River: Zen Journals, 1969-1982 (Matthiessen)　64:316-21, 326

The Ninemile Wolves (Bass)　79:20

"MCMXIV" (Larkin)　8:340; 33:261; 39:336

1918 (Foote)　51:132-36

1985 (Burgess)　13:124-28; 22:78; 40:120; 62:130-32; 94:60-1

"1984" (Bowie)　17:61

1984, Spring: A Choice of Futures (Clarke)　35:128-29

"1989 cont./Gorilla in the Midst #6" (Sapphire)　99:80

"1982" (Kenny)　87:242

1982 Janine (Gray)　41:179-84

Nineteen Elastic Poems (Cendrars)
　See *Dix-neuf poèmes élastiques*

"1911" (Kenny)　87:242

"1915:The Queen's Own Oxfordshire Hussars" (Raine)　103:211

"1958" (MacEwen)　55:167

"Nineteen Fifty-Five" (Walker)　103:407, 412-13

"1959" (Tillinghast)　29:415

"1959 Valentine" (Zukofsky)　18:558

"1957, a Romance" (Gilchrist)　48:115-16

"1956—Ein Pilzjahr" (Hildesheimer)　49:173-74

"1953" (MacNeice)　4:316

"Nineteen Forty" (Dubie)　36:131

"1940" (McFadden)　48:251-52

"1948: Jews" (Rich)　76:210

"1945-1985: Poem for the Anniversary" (Oliver)　98:261

1941 (Spielberg)　20:366

"1947 Blue Buick Convertible" (Sorrentino)　7:448

"1942" (Brautigan)　12:59, 61

"Nineteen Hadley Street" (Schnackenberg)　40:378-79

1900 (Bertolucci)　16:100

1900 (Morand)　41:304

1900 (West)　31:459-60

"1901: In All Latin America" (Galeano)　72:138

"1905" (Graves)　39:323

Nineteen Masks for the Naked Poet (Willard)　7:540; 37:462

1919 (Dos Passos)　1:77; 11:152-53; 15:186; 34:419, 424; 82:62, 64-8, 71, 73, 80, 83-4, 86, 89, 91-2, 95, 98-103, 105, 108-10

"1919: Back from the Front" (Raine)　103:211

1999 (Prince)　35:326-28, 330-32

"1978 Reunion of Palmakh Veterans at Ma'ayan Harod" (Amichai)　57:44

"1971" (Justice)　102:277

"1977: Poem for Mrs. Fannie Lou Hamer" (Jordan)　114:147

"1972" (Brodsky)　36:76, 78; 100:54

"1906" (Raine)　103:208

"1916 Seen from 1921" (Blunden)　56:30, 38, 51

"1968" (Rakosi)　47:345

1968 (Stern)　4:523; 39:239-40

1968, Year of Crisis (Archer)　12:18

"1965 cont./Gorilla in the Midst #3" (Sapphire)　99:80

1969 Velvet Underground Live (Reed)　21:308

"1966" (Achebe)　26:21, 24

"1966 and All That" (Montague)　46:271

"1963" (Dove)　81:134

Nineteen Stories (Greene)　37:140

"Nineteen Thirty-seven" ("1937") (Danticat)　94:94, 96-7, 99

"1937" (Danticat)
　See "Nineteen Thirty-seven"

"1933" (MacLeish)　68:281, 287

"Nineteenth Century as a Song" (Hass)　18:213

"Nineteenth Nervous Breakdown" (Jagger and Richard)　17:234-35

"The Nineteenth New York" (Doctorow)　113:167

"The Nineteenth-Century Mexican Woman" (Castellanos)　66:55

"The 1913 Massacre" (Guthrie)　35:191, 193

"The Nineteen-Thirties Are Over" (Waddington)　28:439

"1938" (Dacey)
　See "A Surrealistic Photograph by Manuel Alvarez Bravo"

"1934" (Phillips)　15:421; 33:305

1934 (Moravia)　27:355-57; 46:285

"1939" (Taylor)　18:526

1936... Peace? (Huxley)　35:241

1933 (Levine)　4:288; 5:250-52; 9:332; 14:319-20; 33:271

1933 Was a Bad Year (Fante)　60:133-34

"1928" (Sadoff)　9:467

"1924: Lenin Takes a Long Bath" (Raine)　103:212

"1921" (Townshend)　17:538

"Ninetieth Birthday" (Thomas)　6:534

"Ninety Miles from Nowhere" (Phillips)　28:364-65

"Ninety North" (Jarrell)　6:260

"91, Revere Street" (Raine)　103:189

98 (Sukenick)　6:523-24; 48:365-70

95 Poems (Cummings)　1:68; 8:160; 12:154; 15:163; 68:40-2, 48

Ninety-Nine Novels: The Best in English Since 1939 (Burgess)　81:301

"91 Revere Street" (Kizer)　80:183

"Ninety-One Revere Street: An Autobiographical Fragment" (Lowell)　4:303; 5:258; 8:350; 9:334-35

"A Ninety-Six-Year-Old Big Sister" (Gold)　42:198

"92" (Brown)　73:24

Ninety-Two Days (Waugh)　27:477

Ninety-Two in the Shade (McGuane)　3:330-31; 7:212-13; 18:323-26; 45:258, 260, 262-63

Un niño azul para esa sombra (*A Blue Child for that Shadow*) (Marques)　96:224, 226-28, 241-43, 245, 250-52

"El nino en el arbol" (Marques)　96:245

"Ninth Elegy: The Antagonists" (Rukeyser)　27:407

"Ninth Fytte: *La Donna*" (Barnard)　48:29

"The Ninth Part of Speech" (Davidson)　2:113

"The Ninth Symphony of Beethoven Understood at Last as a Sexual Message" (Rich)　7:367, 373

The Ninth Wave (Ehrenburg)　34:440; 62:177-78

"Niobe" (Watkins)　43:446

Niobjeta ziemia (*Unattainable Earth*) (Milosz)　56:238-40, 243, 246; 82:290, 297

A Nip in the Air (Betjeman)　6:66; 10:53; 34:306; 43:46

"Nipples Rise to Spirit" (Dacey)　51:80

"The Nipplewhip" (Benedikt)　14:81

The Nirvana Blues (Nichols)　38:344, 346

"Nirvana Small by a Waterfall" (Perelman)　49:261

"Nirvana Stair" (Broumas)　73:17

"A Nite with Beau Willie Brown" (Shange)　25:404

"Nitrous Oxide" (Ginsberg)　109:325

The Nitty Gritty (Bonham)　12:50-1, 53

"Nitya" (Narayan)　47:304

Nkrumah and the Ghana Revolution (James)　33:221

"nNight Before the Journey" (Swenson)　106:337

"No" (Berryman)　13:83

"The No" (Dacey)　51:83

"No" (Milosz)　82:280

No (Ionesco)
　See *Non*

NO (Major)　3:320; 19:293-94; 48:212, 215

"No Answer" (Ignatow)　7:175

"No Answer" (Thomas)　6:530

"No Assistance" (Shange)   25:402
"No Bells to Believe" (Hugo)   32:247
"No Bird Does Call" (Warren)   39:265
No Bugles Tonight (Lancaster)   36:243-44
"No Bull Shit" (Smith)   12:541
No Cause for Panic (Baker)   31:26
No Chinese Stranger (Wong)   17:567
"No Chocolates for Breakfast" (Jordan)   114:152
No Clouds of Glory (Engel)   36:157-58, 162
No Comebacks (Forsyth)   36:176
"No Compassion" (Byrne)   26:95
"No Connection" (Asimov)   26:41
No Continuing City (Longley)   29:291, 293-96
The No 'Count Boy (Green)   25:193
No Country for Young Men (O'Faolain)   19:360-61; 47:326, 328, 330-31; 108:406, 409-10, 414-15, 417-18, 422
No Country without a Grandfather (Carrier)
   See *Il n'y a pas de pays sans grand-père*
No Country without Grandfathers (Carrier)
   See *Il n'y a pas de pays sans grand-père*
"No Dancing" (Costello)   21:67
No Deadly Drug (MacDonald)   44:408
No Decency Left (Graves)   45:171
"No Delicacies" (Bachmann)
   See "Keine Delikatessen"
"No Direction Home" (Spinrad)   46:384
No Direction Home (Spinrad)   46:383-84
No Directions (Hanley)   13:261
"No Dogs Bark" (Rulfo)   80:200
"No Dove, No Covenant" (Vonnegut)   12:607
No End of Blame (Barker)   37:37-8
"No End of Fun" (Szymborska)   99:201
No End of Fun (Szymborska)   99:199
"No existe el hombre" (Aleixandre)   9:15
No Exit (Sartre)
   See *Huis clos*
No Fond Return of Love (Pym)   37:373-74, 376-77, 379; 111:227, 234, 238, 243-48, 263, 265-66, 269, 282-85
No Hassles (Waldman)   7:508
"¿No hay salida?" ("Is There No Way Out?") (Paz)   19:366; 65:180-81
No Highway (Shute)   30:367-68
"No I Don't" (Ashbery)   77:64, 68
No, I'm Not Afraid (Ratushinskaya)   54:380-82
No! in Thunder: Essays on Myth and Literature (Fiedler)   4:163; 13:211; 24:189-91, 203
"No Joke" (Mac Laverty)   31:255
"No Kaddish for Weinstein" (Allen)   52:36-7
"No Land Is Waste" (Simmons)   43:410, 412
No Land Is Waste, Dr. Eliot (Simmons)   43:408
No Laughing Matter (Wilson)   2:472-74; 3:534-36; 5:513-14; 25:459, 463-64; 34:581, 584
No Longer at Ease (Achebe)   1:1; 3:1-3; 5:1, 3-4; 7:3-6; 11:1-3; 26:12, 15-16, 18, 25-7; 51:3-5; 75:3, 6-7, 11, 13, 26
No Longer Two People (Lane)   25:286, 288
"No Man Could Bind Him" (Vanderhaeghe)   41:450, 452
No Man Is an Island (Merton)   83:380, 382
"No Man, No Woman" (Rosa)   23:353
"No Man's Land" (Heaney)   14:244
"No Man's Land" (Seger)   35:384-85
No Man's Land (Pinter)   6:418-19; 9:418-21; 11:444; 15:423-25; 27:387, 395-96; 58:370, 374-76, 379, 383; 73:277
No Man's Land (Shammas)   55:86
No Man's Land: The Place of the Woman Writer in the Twentieth Century (Gilbert and Gubar)   65:344-45, 347
No Man's Meat (Callaghan)   41:89-92
No Man's Meat. The Enchanted Pimp (Callaghan)   41:89, 91; 65:248
No Man's Time (Yanovsky)   2:485; 18:550-51
"No Matter for History" (Brutus)   43:89
No me agarran viva: La mujer salvadoreñña en lucha (*They Won't Take Me Alive*) (Alegria)   75:42-3
"No Money Down" (Berry)   17:52-3
"No Moon Floods the Memory of That Night" (Knight)   40:283
"No Moon for Me" (Miller)   30:263
No More Dying Then (Rendell)   28:383, 385; 48:321
"No More Ghosts" (Graves)   45:173
"No More Lonely Nights" (McCartney)   35:293
"No More Looking Back" (Davies)   21:101
"no more love poems" (Shange)   25:402, 404
No More Love Poems, Number Two (Shange)   25:404
"No More Marching" (Madhubuti)   73:209
"No More Sacrifices" (Ortiz)   45:309
"No More Songs" (Ochs)   17:332, 334
"No More Than Is" (Riding)   7:374
"No Name" (Atwood)   84:102
"No Name for It" (Martinson)   14:357
"No Name in the Street" (Baldwin)   13:52; 42:17, 19
"No Name in the Street" (Sillitoe)   19:422; 57:395
No Name in the Street (Baldwin)   2:32-4; 4:41; 13:53; 15:42; 17:38; 42:15, 17-19, 22
"No Neck and Bad as Hell" (Bukowski)   108:86
"No News from the Old Country" (Motion)   47:292
No Night without Stars (Norton)   12:470
"No No No No" (Angelou)   77:28
No, Not Bloomsbury (Bradbury)   61:42
No Nudes Is Good Nudes (*A Pelican of Blondings*) (Wodehouse)   2:479
"No One" (Merwin)   45:270
"No One Remembers" (Levine)   14:318-19
"No One Talks about This" (Rakosi)   47:344
"No One Will Laugh" ("Nobody Will Laugh") (Kundera)   32:260; 68:241; 115:332
No One Writes to the Colonel (Garcia Marquez)
   See *El colonel no tiene quien le escribe*
The No One's Rose (Celan)
   See *Die Niemandsrose*
"No Orpheus, No Eurydice" (Spender)   41:428; 91:269
No Other Life (Moore)   90:297-300, 302-3
"No oyes ladrar los perros" ("Don't You Hear the Dogs Barking?"; "Hear the Dogs Barking") (Rulfo)   80:224
No Parasan! (They Shall Not Pass): A Story of the Battle of Madrid (Sinclair)   15:499; 63:363
No Part in Your Death (Freeling)   38:188
"No Particular Place to Go" (Morrison)   17:291
No Particular Place to Go (Williams)   42:444
"No Place" (O'Brien)   116:210-11
No Place for an Angel (Spencer)   22:401, 403, 405
No Place for Hiding (L'Heureux)   52:275
"No Place for You, My Love" (Welty)   22:459, 462; 105:299
No Place on Earth (Wolf)
   See *Kein Ort. Nirgends*
No Place to Be Somebody (Gordone)   1:124-25; 4:198-99
"No Pleasure" (Newlove)   14:378
"No Quarter" (Page and Plant)   12:476
No Quarter Given (Horgan)   53:170-71, 175
No Regrets for Our Youth (Kurosawa)   16:399-400
No Relief (Dixon)   52:93-7, 101
No Retreat (Hart)   66:176, 182
"No Road" (Larkin)   13:336, 340; 18:294; 33:258; 64:258, 260, 262, 266
"No Room at the Inn" (Ferber)   93:180
No saco nada de la escuela (Valdez)   84:395
"No Sale" (Wagoner)   3:508
"No Sanctuary" (Heaney)   14:244
"No se culpa a nadie" (Cortazar)   10:118
"No sé por qué piensas tú" ("I Don't Know Why You Think") (Guillen)   79:251
No Secrets (Simon)   26:408
"No Smiles"   59:378
"No Solution" (Gascoyne)   45:157
No Souvenirs: Journal, 1957-1969 (Eliade)   19:148
No Star is Lost (Farrell)   66:114, 116-17, 119-20
"No Starch in the Dhoti, s'il vous plaît" (Perelman)   49:265
"No Succour!" (Stern)   100:329
No Such Liberty (Comfort)   7:52
"No Such Thing As a Free Lunch" (Grenville)   61:152
"No Swan So Fine" (Moore)   10:353
"No Swan so Fine" (Swenson)   106:340
No Thanks (Cummings)   12:145, 154; 15:157, 161-62; 68:35, 49
"No Theory" (Ignatow)   7:179
No Third Path (Kosinski)   2:232; 70:300, 305
"No Ties" (Simmons)   43:408
No Time (Avison)   97:121-22
"No Time Ago" (Cummings)   8:160
No Time for Comedy (Behrman)   40:80-3
No Time for Sergeants (Levin)   6:306
"No Time Is Passing" (Aickman)   57:3
No Time like Tomorrow (Aldiss)   14:11
No Time to Be Young (Jones)   52:253
"No Title Required" (Szymborska)   99:203
"No Turtles" (Klappert)   57:258
"No Understand" (Sondheim)   30:380
"No Use to Talk to Me" (Le Guin)   45:213
No Vacancies in Hell (Epstein)   7:97
No Vacation for Maigret (Simenon)   47:373, 375
No Villain Need Be (Fisher)   7:103, 105
"No Voyage" (Oliver)   19:361; 98:266
No Voyage (Oliver)   19:361; 98:256, 276-77, 288, 293
No Way (Ginzburg)
   See *Caro Michele*
"No Way Out" (Johnston)   51:241, 243, 252
"No Way Out but Through" (Maitland)   49:235
No Way to Treat a Lady (Goldman)   48:128
"No Whistle Slow" (Rooke)   25:391
"No Woman, No Cry" (Marley)   17:271-72
Noah (Seger)   35:378, 381
Noah and the Waters (Day Lewis)   10:131, 133
"Noah's Ark" (Abe)   81:298
Noah's Ark   75:65
Noaptea (Arghezi)   80:6, 8
Nobel Lecture by Aleksandr Solzhenitsyn (Solzhenitsyn)
   See *Nobelevskaia lektsii politerature 1970 goda*
The Nobel Prize (Krotkov)   19:264-66
Nobelevskaia lektsii politerature 1970 goda

(*Nobel Lecture by Aleksandr Solzhenitsyn*) (Solzhenitsyn) 4:508, 512

Nobi (*Fires on the Plain*) (Ichikawa) 20:177-78

Noble House: A Novel of Contemporary Hong Kong (Clavell) 25:126-27; 87:2, 8, 17-19

The Noble Tale of Sir Lancelot of the Lake (Steinbeck) 21:387

"Noblesse oblige" (O'Hara) 6:385

Noblesse Oblige: An Enquiry into the Identifiable Characteristics of the English Aristocracy (Mitford) 44:486, 491

Nobodaddy (MacLeish) 8:360-61; 14:336; 68:271

Nobodaddy's Kinder: Trilogie (Schmidt) 56:390, 393, 405

Nobody Answered the Bell (Davies) 23:147

"Nobody Answers the Door" (Tyler) 103:258

"Nobody Better, Better than Nobody" (Frazier) 46:166

Nobody Better, Better than Nobody (Frazier) 46:165

"Nobody Gives" (Davies) 21:98

Nobody Hears a Broken Drum (Miller) 2:284

Nobody Knew They Were There (Hunter) 31:222

"Nobody Knows" (McCartney) 35:287-88

"Nobody Knows Anything about Art Anymore" (Donnell) 34:158

"Nobody Knows My Name" (Baldwin) 42:16

Nobody Knows My Name (Baldwin) 90:28, 31, 34

Nobody Knows My Name: More Notes of a Native Son (Baldwin) 2:31-2; 5:42; 13:52-3; 17:21-3, 32, 38; 42:14, 16, 18-19; 50:282, 289, 292, 296

"Nobody Loses All the Time" (Cummings) 3:119

"Nobody Loves Anybody Anymore" (Kristofferson) 26:270

"Nobody Loves You" ("When You're Down and Out") (Lennon) 35:268-69

Nobody Owns th Earth (Bissett) 18:58

"Nobody Said Anything" (Carver) 22:96; 53:65

Nobody to Blame (Greene) 37:140

"Nobody Told Me" (Lennon) 35:275-76

"Nobody Wanted to Sit behind a Desk" (Gray) 49:152

"Nobody Will Laugh" (Kundera) See "No One Will Laugh"

Nobody's Angel (McGuane) 45:258-62, 265

"Nobody's Business" (Gilliatt) 10:229

Nobody's Business (Gilliatt) 2:160-61; 10:229

Nobody's Fault (Jones) 52:250

"Nobody's Fault but Mine" (Page and Plant) 12:480

"Nobody's In Town" (Ferber) 93:169

Nobody's In Town (Ferber) 93:169

The Nobody's Rose (Celan) See *Die Niemandsrose*

Noc u provinci ("Night in the Province") (Krleza) 114:167

Noce i dnie (*Nights and Days*) (Dabrowska) 15:165-68

Noces (*Nuptials*) (Camus) 1:53; 14:106-07, 111; 32:86, 96; 63:74, 84; 69:112, 117, 127, 133

Les noces (Jouve) 47:207-09, 212

Les noces rouges (Chabrol) 16:178

"Noch'" ("Night") (Akhmadulina) 53:12

Noch feiert der Tod das Leben (Sachs) 98:324

"La noche boca arriba" ("The Night Face Up"; "On His Back under the Night") (Cortazar) 10:113; 34:332

"La noche cíclica" (Borges) 4:71

La noche de las cien cabezas (*The Night of One Hundred Heads*) (Sender) 8:480-81

"La noche de los alcaravanes" ("The Night of the Curlews") (Garcia Marquez) 3:181; 47:148-49

"Noche de negros junto a la catedral" (Guillen) 48:165

"Noche del hombre y su demonio" (Cernuda) 54:49

"Noche en claro" ("Clear Night") (Paz) 51:337

"Noche final" (Aleixandre) 9:12

"Noche incial" (Aleixandre) 9:12

"La noche que lo dejaron solo" ("The Night He Was Left Alone"; "The Night They Left Him Alone") (Rulfo) 80:200

"Nochebuena cincuenta y una" (Cernuda) 54:46

"Las noches de Goliadkin" ("The Nights of Goliadkin") (Bioy Casares) 88:68, 71, 77

"Noctamble" (Johnston) 51:238, 240, 245

"Noctambule" (Smith) 15:517

"Noctambules" (Gascoyne) 45:152, 155, 159

Nocturna Artificialia: Those Who Desire Without End (The Brothers Quay) 95:329-30, 333-34, 339, 347, 350-51, 353

"Nocturnal Games" (Hesse) 25:260-61

"Nocturne" (Faulkner) 9:201

"Nocturne" (Livesay) 79:350

"Nocturne" (MacLeish) 68:286

"Nocturne" (O'Hara) 78:341

"Nocturne" (Prokosch) 48:309

"Nocturne" (Transtroemer) 52:410; 65:222-23, 235

"Nocturne" (Voigt) 54:434

Nocturne (Swinnerton) 31:420-23, 425

"Nocturne among Grotesqueries" (Cernuda) See "Nocturno entre las musarañas"

"Nocturne at Bethesda" (Bontemps) 1:38; 18:64

Nocturne of Remembered Spring and Other Poems (Aiken) 52:22

"Nocturne with Neon Lights" (Tuohy) 37:431

Nocturnes (Senghor) 54:390, 402, 408-09

Nocturnes for the King of Naples (White) 27:479-80, 482; 110:316, 326-27, 330, 336-38

"Nocturno" (Castellanos) 66:52-3

"Nocturno de San Ildefonso" ("San Ildefonso Nocturne") (Paz) 51:337; 65:188, 190, 197, 200

"Nocturno entre las musarañas" ("Nocturne among Grotesqueries") (Cernuda) 54:55, 58

Noé (Giono) 4:188

The Noël Coward Diaries (Coward) 29:139-41

Le noeud de vipères (Mauriac) 4:339-40; 56:206, 216, 219

Nog (*The Octopus*) (Wurlitzer) 2:482-84; 4:597-98; 15:587-89

No-Good Friday (Fugard) 14:189; 80:61, 63, 67-9, 80

"Noh Lickle Twang" (Bennett) 28:29-30

Noh; or, Accomplishment (Pound) 48:289

La noia (*The Empty Canvas*) (Moravia) 7:240-42, 244; 11:382-83; 18:344, 349; 46:283-85

La Noire de... (*The Black Girl*) (Ousmane) 66:335

"noire et lippue, bien sûr" (Tchicaya) 101:354

Noise in the Trees: A Memoir (Heyen) 13:282, 284; 18:230

"The Noise of a Match" (Char) 55:288

"Noise of Strangers" (Garrett) 51:149, 152

Noises Off (Frayn) 31:192-93; 47:137-40

"Noite de cala e paixão" ("Night of the Cabala and Passion") (Dourado) 60:85

Le Nom d'Oedipe (Cixous) 92:88

"Nomad and Viper" (Oz) 27:359-62

"Nomad Invasions" (Chatwin) 57:153; 59:277

"Nomad Songs" (Merwin) 88:194

No-man's Rose (Celan) See *Die Niemandsrose*

Les nombres (Chedid) 47:82, 87

Il nome della rosa (*The Name of the Rose*) (Eco) 28:130-33; 60:111-14, 117-22, 124

Non (*No*) (Ionesco) 41:225; 86:334-35

"Non Linear" (Webb) 18:541

"Non piangere, liù" (Porter) 13:453

Non Sequitur O'Connor (Klappert) 57:260-61

"Non serviam" (Lem) 15:330

Non Serviam (Ekeloef) 27:114

"Nona" (King) 37:207; 61:333

"Nonaspettavano altro" (Buzzati) 36:86

"Non-Commitment" (Achebe) 11:4; 26:22

None but the Lonely Heart (Llewellyn) 80:192, 194-96

None but the Lonely Heart (Odets) 98:197, 199, 244-47

None Genuine without This Signature (Hood) 28:194-95

None of Maigret's Business (Simenon) See *Maigret's Little Joke*

"None of the Above" (Wells) 12:637-38

"None of the Other Birds" (Smith) 25:421

None Shall Look Back (Gordon) 6:202-03, 207; 13:242; 29:186; 83:227-29, 233, 240, 242, 247, 252-54, 258-59

The Nonexistent Knight (Calvino) See *Il cavaliere inesistente*

The Nonexistent Knight and the Cloven Viscount (Calvino) See *Il visconte dimezzato*

Nongogo (Fugard) 14:189, 191-92; 80:61, 63, 67-8

"Non-Hymns" (Wittlin) 25:468

The Nonny Poems (Kherdian) 6:281; 9:317-18

Nonsense and Happiness (Handke) 38:218-19

Nonsequences: Selfpoems (Middleton) 13:387

Non-Stop (*Starship*) (Aldiss) 14:10; 40:20-1

"Non-Stop Dancing" (Weller) 26:442

"Nonstop Jetflight to Halifax" (Johnston) 51:245

"Non-Stop to Mars" (Williamson) 29:455, 458

"Noon" (Apple) 9:32

"Noon" (Dudek) 19:136

"Noon" (Levine) 33:271

Noon (McNally) 4:347; 7:217; 41:292

Noon: Twenty-Second Century (Strugatskii and Strugatskii) 27:436

"Noon Wine" (Porter) 101:224, 229, 242, 253

Noon Wine (Porter) 1:273; 7:311-14, 316-17, 319; 10:394-96, 398-99; 13:446, 448-50; 15:429; 27:398-99, 401; 101:219

"Noon Wine: The Sources" (Porter) 101:224

"Nooncoming" (Benford) 52:75

"Noonday Axeman" (Murray) 40:333-34, 340

Noonday Demons (Barnes) 56:5-8

No-One Was Saved (Barker) 37:32

Noontimes Gained (Tzara) See *Midis gagnés*

Nopalgarth (Vance) 35:427

Nor All Thy Tears (Swinnerton) 31:428

Nor Shall My Sword (Leavis) 24:306, 308, 310, 314

"Nora and Hilda" (Durcan) 43:114

"Nora's Journal" (Klappert) 57:259-60

Nord (*North*) (Celine) 1:57; 3:104-05; 4:98, 102; 7:43, 45; 9:152, 158; 47:74-5, 79

Nordic Twilight (Forster) 1:107

The No-Return Trail (Levitin) 17:266

"Norfolk, 1969" (Tilghman) 65:107-08, 110-11

The Norfolk Poems (Carruth) 4:94

"Noria" (Cesaire) 32:113

Norm and Ahmed (Buzo) 61:52-4, 56, 59-61, 64

"Norma" (Sanchez) 116:302-03, 306

The Normal Heart (Kramer) 42:270-73

The Norman Conquests (Ayckbourn) 5:35, 37; 8:34; 18:27-9; 33:42-3, 45, 49; 74:6-7, 34

"Norman Mailer: The Avenger and the Bitch" (Amis) 62:4-5

"North" (Heaney) 7:151; 14:244-45; 25:245

"North" (Hoffman) 6:244

"North" (Justice) 102:258

"North" (Walcott) 76:275

North (Celine)
See *Nord*

North (Heaney) 7:148-52; 14:242-45; 25:243-51; 37:163, 165, 168; 74:156-60, 162-63, 165, 167, 171, 173-75, 180, 183, 190-91, 193; 91:118, 121, 123, 128

"North America" (Newlove) 14:377

A North American Education (Blaise) 29:69-71, 73-5

"North American Sequence" (Roethke) 3:433; 8:457, 460; 11:484-85; 19:398-400; 46:356, 361, 364; 101:288-92, 299, 304-06, 308-13, 315-16, 318, 321, 327, 334

"North American Time" (Rich) 36:378

The North American Turbine (Dorn) 10:158; 18:128

"North and South" (Walcott) 25:457; 42:422; 67:348, 356

North and South (Bishop) 4:65; 9:89, 91, 93-4, 97; 13:89, 91, 93, 95; 32:28-9, 37-9, 41-2

North and South (Jakes) 29:250

"North Beach Birth" (Musgrave) 54:335

North by Northwest (Hitchcock) 16:346-47, 349, 353, 359

"North by the Creek" (Davison) 28:102

North Central (Niedecker) 10:360

"North Country" (Slessor) 14:497

North Dallas Forty (Gent) 29:180-83

"North Dublin" (Davie) 8:167

North Face (Renault) 3:425; 17:392; 94:353

"North in Winter" (Kenny) 87:241

"North Light" (Helprin) 22:221

North of Boston (Frost) 3:172; 4:176; 13:222-23; 15:239-40, 246-51; 26:111, 118-19, 121, 124, 127; 34:468, 470

North of Jamaica (Simpson) 4:500; 7:429

"North of Sixty" (Richler) 46:352

North of South: An African Journey (Naipaul) 32:325-27; 39:355-58

North of Summer (Purdy) 50:246

North of the Danube (Caldwell) 50:299

"The North Rim" (Swenson) 61:401; 106:329

"North Sea Off Carnoustie" (Stevenson) 33:380-81

"North Sea Poem" (Musgrave) 13:400

"The North Sea Undertaker's Complaint" (Lowell) 4:299

"The North Ship" (Larkin) 13:338

The North Ship (Larkin) 5:223, 225-27, 230; 8:338-40; 13:335, 337; 18:293, 298-300; 33:261-62; 39:334, 341-42, 344-45; 64:257-61, 266-68, 270, 278

"North Shore" (Davison) 28:100

North Shore Fish (Horovitz) 56:157

The North Star (Hellman) 52:191

"North Stream" (Scott) 22:373

North to the Orient (Lindbergh) 82:153, 158, 166-67

"North Winter" (Carruth) 4:94; 84:119

"Northern Elegies" (Akhmatova) 25:26; 64:5

"Northern Exposure" (Simic) 68:373

"Northern Express" (Montague) 46:277

"The Northern Gate" (Montague) 46:269

"A Northern Hoard" (Heaney) 5:170; 7:148; 14:243-44; 25:241

"A Northern Legion" (Read) 4:439

The Northern Light (Cronin) 32:138-39

Northern Lights (O'Brien) 7:272; 19:357; 103:134-35, 143, 166

"Northern Pass" (Rulfo)
See "El pasa del norte"

"Northern Philosopher" (Van Doren) 6:541

"Northern Pike" (Wright) 5:520

"Northern River" (Wright) 11:578

The Northern Story (Paustovsky) 40:367

"Northern Summer" (Faludy) 42:141

Northfield Poems (Ammons) 2:12; 5:26; 57:59; 108:5

"Northhanger Ridge" (Wright) 6:581

Northrop Frye on Shakespeare (Frye) 70:271, 274-75

"Northumbrian Sequence" (Raine) 45:332, 335, 337

"N.W.5 and N.6" (Betjeman) 43:36, 40

Northwest Ecolog (Ferlinghetti) 27:139

The Norton Book of Modern War (Fussell) 74:133

"Norwegian Wood" (Lennon and McCartney) 12:360-61

"Nos han dado la tierra" ("The Land They Gave Us"; "They've Given Us the Land"; "La tierra que nos han dado") (Rulfo) 80:200, 210, 216, 221, 223

No's Knife (Beckett) 4:51

"Nos mains au jardin" ("Our Hands in the Garden") (Hebert) 29:228, 232

De nos oiseaux (Tzara) 47:392-93

"Nos vemos" (Allen) 84:6

"The Nose" (Jong) 6:269

The Nose of Sisyphus (Ferlinghetti) 111:63

"Noses Run in My Family" (Mull) 17:300

Nosferatu—The Vampyre (Herzog) 16:330, 333-36

Nostalghia (Tarkovsky) 75:385, 388-89, 392-94, 396, 398-99, 402, 411-13

"Nostalgia" (Mukherjee) 53:267-68

"Nostalgia" (Strand) 71:285

Nostalgia and Sexual Difference: Resistance to Contemporary Feminism (Doane and Hodges) 65:324

Nostalgia for the Present (Voznesensky) 15:557; 57:420-22, 426

"Nostalgia of the Lakefronts" (Justice) 102:272

"Nostalgic Suffering" (Voinovich) 49:382

"Nostalgie de bonheur" (Coles) 46:113

"Nostasia in Asia" (Perelman) 5:338

The Nostradamus Traitor (Gardner) 30:155

I nostri antenati (*Our Ancestors*) (Calvino) 5:97-8; 8:127; 11:88-9, 91; 22:88, 90; 33:97; 39:307, 310, 314-15; 73:34, 58

"A Nosty Fright" (Swenson) 61:405; 106:323

"Not" (Orlovitz) 22:336

"Not a Day Goes By" (Sondheim) 30:399-400

Not a Penny More, Not a Penny Less (Archer) 28:11

Not a Word about Nightingales (Howard) 5:188

Not after Midnight (*Don't Look Now*) (du Maurier) 6:146; 59:285-87

"Not All There" (Frost) 13:228

Not at These Hands (Wellman) 49:388

"Not by Rain Alone" (Ross) 13:492

"Not Charles" (Dixon) 52:98, 100

"Not Correcting His Name Misspelled on the Mailing Label" (Dacey) 51:82

Not Dancing (Dunn) 36:156

"La not di maj" (Pasolini) 106:229

"Not Dying" (Strand) 18:515, 517; 71:285-86

"Not Fade Away" (Jagger and Richard) 17:227

"Not for an Age" (Aldiss) 5:15

Not for Children (Rice) 7:363; 49:301-03

"Not for Publication" (Gordimer) 33:180, 182

Not for Publication, and Other Stories (Gordimer) 33:180; 70:162

"Not for the Sabbath" (Singer) 23:421

"Not Forgotten" (Davison) 28:99-100, 102

Not George Washington (Wodehouse) 22:485

"Not Going to New York: A Letter" (Hass) 18:210

"Not Going to See a Movie about a Nuclear Holocaust's Aftermath" (Dacey) 51:83

"Not Honey" (H. D.) 73:105

Not I (Beckett) 3:47; 4:51; 6:36-7, 39, 43; 9:81-4, 86; 11:37, 39; 14:74; 18:46-7; 29:57, 65; 59:253, 255

"Not in Baedeker" (Auden) 9:60

Not in God's Image (O'Faolain) 108:414

Not Just to Remember (Amichai) 22:30

"Not Leaving the House" (Snyder) 32:399

"Not Like a Cypress" (Amichai)
See "Lo kabrosh"

"Not Looking at Pictures" (Forster) 4:169

"Not Marble in the Gilded Monuments" (MacLeish) 68:286

"Not Not While the Giro" (Kelman) 58:295

Not Not While the Giro, and Other Stories (Kelman) 58:295; 86:181

Not Now But Now (Fisher) 76:337, 342; 87:119, 122, 126

Not Now, Darling (Cooney) 62:141-44, 146, 148

"Not Now John" (Pink Floyd) 35:315

Not of This Time, Not of This Place (Amichai) 9:22-4; 57:40, 46; 116:78, 84, 128

"Not One of Us" (Highsmith) 42:215; 102:199

"Not Only Here" (Clash)
See "Up in Heaven"

"Not Palaces" (Spender) 41:428

"Not Quite Bernadette" (Bukowski) 41:73

Not Responsible for Personal Articles (Gould) 10:243

Not So Deep as a Well (Parker) 68:326

"Not Somewhere Else, but Here" (Rich) 18:449

Not That He Brought Flowers (Thomas) 48:374, 380

"Not the End of the World" (Ryan) 65:213

"Not the Sweet Cicely of Gerardes Herball" (Adams) 97:89

Not This Pig (Levine) 2:244; 4:285-87; 5:251; 9:332; 14:317; 33:271, 273-74

"Not to be Printed, Not to be Said, Not to be Thought" (Rukeyser) 10:443

Not to Disturb (Spark) 2:417-19; 3:464; 5:400; 8:495; 13:524; 40:400

"Not Waiting for Godot" (O'Casey) 88:260

"Not Waving but Drowning" (Smith) 25:420, 422-23; 44:438, 440, 443, 445

"Not While I'm Around" (Sondheim) 30:394

Not With My Wife, You Don't! (Gelbart) 21:125-26

Not without Laughter (Hughes) 1:147, 149; 5:190; 10:280, 282; 35:213; 108:285, 293-94, 326

"Not Worth the Record" (Mathias) 45:238

"Not Yet" (Alegria) 75:45, 49

The Notary from Le Havre (Duhamel) 8:188

"Notas de viaje" (Parra) 102:338-39

Notations (Cage) 41:81

"The Notations of Love" (Livesay) 79:337, 343

"Notations of Love" (Rosenthal) 28:394-95

"The Note" (Arghezi)
See "Biletul"

"A Note" (Turco) 63:428

"Note eternelle du présent" (Reverdy) 53:293

A Note in Music (Lehmann) 5:235, 238

"A Note on a Poem by Thomas Hardy" (Hooker) 43:199

"A Note on Balance at the Trot" (Hearne) 56:126

"Note on Blues" (Hughes) 15:291

"A Note on Eugenics" (Huxley) 79:316

A Note on Literary Criticism (Farrell) 66:111, 113, 131-32, 137

"Note on Local Flora" (Empson) 8:202; 19:155; 33:142

"A Note on Metrics" (Dudek) 11:160

"A Note on Poetry" (Barnard) 48:27

"A Note on Puritans" (Smith) 64:396

"A Note on Sherwood Anderson" (Farrell) 66:138

"A Note on the Esthetic Significance of Photography" (Scott) 43:385

"A Note on the Literary Life" (Schulberg) 48:350

"A Note on the Truth of the Tales" (Vollmann) 89:279

"Note on the Way" (Forster) 15:227

"A Note on the Work of the Imagination" (Levertov) 66:241

"A Note on War Poetry" (Eliot) 41:150

"A Note on Wittgenstein and Literary Criticism" (Abrams) 24:13

"A Note on Wyatt" (Amis) 40:44

"Note Slipped under a Door" (Simic) 22:383

"Note sur la poésie" (Tzara) 47:393

"A Note to Donald Davie in Tennessee" (Abse) 29:20

"A Note to Olga" (Levertov) 66:240, 246

"Note to Wang Wei" (Berryman) 62:76

"Notebook" (Durrell) 27:96

"Notebook" (Levertov)
See "From a Notebook, October '68—May '69"

Notebook, 1970 (Lowell) 1:184; 3:301-04; 4:300, 302, 304; 5:256-58; 8:349, 356-58; 9:334, 336, 338-39; 11:328-31; 15:342, 344, 347; 37:232, 234, 236-37, 240

Notebook 1967-68 (Lowell) 1:181-84; 2:248; 3:301-04; 4:300, 302, 304; 5:256-58; 8:349, 356-58; 9:334, 336, 338-39; 11:328-31; 15:342, 344, 347-48; 37:232,
234, 236-37, 240

"Notebook of a Return to the Native Land" (Cesaire)
See *Cahier d'un retour au pays natal*

A Notebook on William Shakespeare (Sitwell) 67:332

Notebooks (Camus)
See *Carnets*

Notebooks, 1960-1977 (Fugard) 40:198-201, 203

The Notebooks of Captain Georges (Renoir) 20:305

The Notebooks of David Ignatow (Ignatow) 4:249; 7:175, 177-79

The Notebooks of Lazarus Long (Heinlein) 55:303

"The Notebooks of Robinson Crusoe" (Smith) 64:389-90

The Notebooks of Robinson Crusoe (Smith) 64:389-90, 400

The Notebooks of Susan Berry (Mott) 15:379

"Notes" (Ciardi) 40:161

"Notes" (Frost) 15:243

"Notes" (Moore)
See "How to Talk to Your Mother"

"Notes" (O'Brien) 103:139, 174

"Notes" (Saroyan) 29:362

Notes (Canetti)
See *Aufzeichnungen, 1942-48*

Notes and Counter-notes (Ionesco)
See *Notes et contre-notes*

"Notes d'un retour au pays natal" (Conde) 92:130

Notes et contre-notes (*Notes and Counter-notes*) (Ionesco) 4:251; 41:222, 224; 86:332

"Notes et variantes" (Camus) 63:75

"Notes for a Case History" (Lessing) 22:278

"Notes for a Hypothetical Novel" (Baldwin) 13:53

Notes for a New Culture: An Essay on Modernism (Ackroyd) 52:3, 13

"Notes for a Novel about the End of the World" (Percy) 47:338

"Notes for a Preface" (Merwin) 88:191, 208

"Notes for a Speech" (Baraka) 14:42

"Notes for a Story" (Godwin) 8:248-49

Notes for an African Orestes (Pasolini) 20:270

"Notes for an Elegy" (Meredith) 13:374; 22:302

Notes for Another Life (Bridgers) 26:92

"Notes for Oscar Wilde" (Wright) 6:580

"Notes for the First Line of a Spanish Poem" (Galvin) 38:198

"Notes for the Legend of Salad Woman" (Ondaatje) 51:317

Notes from a Bottle Found on the Beach at Carmel (Connell) 4:108-10; 6:116; 45:109-11

Notes from a Child of Paradise (Corn) 33:119-21

"Notes from a Confession" (Birkerts) 150

Notes from a Lady at a Dinner Party (Malamud) 8:375

"Notes from a Nonexistent Himalayan Expedition" (Szymborska) 99:199

"Notes From a Sububan Heart" (Van Duyn) 116:424

"Notes from an Unfinished Novel" (Fowles) 87:182

Notes from Isla Negra (Neruda)
See *Memorial de Isla Negra*

Notes from New York, and Other Poems (Tomlinson) 45:403-04

"Notes from the Castle" (Moss) 45:286, 289

Notes from the Castle (Moss) 45:285-89, 292

Notes from the Century Before (Hoagland) 28:180-81

"Notes from the Corner" (Bitov) 57:114-15, 119

"Notes from the Delivery Room" (Pastan) 27:368

"Notes from the Land of the Dead" (Kinsella) 4:271; 19:255-56

Notes from the Land of the Dead, and Other Poems (Kinsella) 4:271; 19:252-54, 257

"Notes Inspired by *The Sleepwalkers*" (Kundera) 115:321

"Notes Made in the Piazzo San Marco" (Swenson) 61:395

"Notes Mainly at the Clinic" (Abse) 29:21

Notes of a Baden Patient (Hesse) 2:190

"Notes of a Dirty Old Man" (Bukowski) 9:138; 41:74; 108:80, 83

"Notes of a Native Son" (Baldwin) 1:13, 15; 2:31-3; 3:32; 4:41-2; 5:42; 8:41; 13:52; 15:43; 17:21-4, 26, 28, 31, 38, 43; 42:14, 16, 18; 50:282, 291, 296

Notes of a Native Son (Baldwin) 90:5, 10, 13

Notes of a Night Watchman (Zinoviev) 19:488

"Notes of a Potential Suicide" (Bukowski) 41:68

"Notes of a Submariner" (Szirtes) 46:396

Notes of an Alchemist (Eiseley) 7:91

Notes of the Author (Kosinski) 53:221

Notes of Woe (Tate) 25:427

"Notes on a Native Son" (Cleaver) 30:54

Notes on a Poetry of Release (Graham) 29:192

Notes on an Endangered Species and Others (Richler) 5:378

"Notes on Camp" (Sontag) 105:215-19, 226

"Notes on Class" (Fussell) 74:125

"Notes on Dangerous Game" (Hemingway) 34:478

"Notes on Poetics regarding Olson's 'Maximus'" (Duncan) 15:189

"Notes on the Decline of Outrage" (Dickey) 7:86; 109:239

"Notes on the English" (Forster) 77:227

"Notes on the Language of Aeschylus" (Warner) 45:434, 439

"Notes on the Responsibility and the Teaching of Creative Writing" (Smith) 42:356

"Notes on the Road: The SS. Formosa" (Cendrars) 106:158

"Notes on the Wasteland" (Eliot) 113:210-11

"Notes on the Writing of Horror: A Story" (Ligotti) 44:54-5

"Notes on Thought and Vision" (H. D.) 73:139

Notes on Translating Shakespearean Tragedies (Pasternak) 63:291

"Notes on Writing a Novel" (Bowen) 15:78

"Notes toward a Nature Poem" (Ghose) 42:185

"Notes toward a Poem That Can Never Be Written" (Atwood) 25:65, 68; 84:69

"Notes toward an Understanding of My Father's Novel" (Durban) 39:44, 46

"Notes Toward Home" (Jordan) 114:146

Notes towards an Aesthetic (Baxter) 14:62

Notes towards the Definition of Culture (Eliot) 2:126, 128; 6:165; 24:177, 184; 41:157-59, 162

Nothing (Green) 2:178; 13:252-54; 97:245, 248, 250, 254, 257, 266, 276, 279, 283, 290-91, 293

"Nothing: A Preliminary Account" (Barthelme) 46:36; 115:71, 76, 98

Nothing, and So Be It (Fallaci)
  See *Niente e cosi*
"Nothing Began as It Is" (Merwin)   **18**:334
"Nothing but Color" (Ai)   **14**:8; **69**:5-6, 11
Nothing but Light (Pack)   **13**:438-39
Nothing but Love (Seifert)
  See *Samá láska*
"Nothing but Poking" (Redgrove)   **41**:348
Nothing Can Go Wrong (MacDonald)   **44**:408
Nothing Can Rescue Me (Daly)   **52**:88
"Nothing Down" (Dove)   **50**:153, 157; **81**:139
"Nothing Ever Breaks Except the Heart"
  (Boyle)   **58**:70-1
Nothing Ever Breaks Except the Heart (Boyle)
  5:67; **58**:70-1
"Nothing Ever Happens on the Moon"
  (Heinlein)   **26**:175
Nothing for Anyone (Reading)   **47**:350
Nothing Happens in Carmincross (Kiely)
  43:240-46
"Nothing in Heaven Functions As It Ought"
  (Kennedy)   **42**:255-56
Nothing in Prospero's Cloak (Rozewicz)
  See *Nic w plaszczu Prospera*
"Nothing Is Everything" (Townshend)   **17**:528
*Nothing Like the Sun: A Story of Shakespeare's
  Love-Life* (Burgess)   **2**:86; **4**:80, 84; **5**:86;
  8:112; **10**:89-90; **22**:70-1, 78; **40**:114,
  116, 122, 126; **81**:313; **94**:41
"Nothing Makes Sense" (Giovanni)   **117**:201
The Nothing Man (Thompson)   **69**:379, 382,
  385-86, 389
Nothing Missing but the Samovar (Lively)
  32:273
Nothing More than Murder (Thompson)
  69:379, 383, 387
Nothing More to Declare (Holmes)   **56**:138-41
Nothing New under the Sun (Bacchelli)   **19**:31-
  2
"Nothing Now Astonishes" (Graves)   **45**:173
Nothing or Nothing (Konwicki)
  See *Nic albo nic*
Nothing Personal (Baldwin)   **17**:28; **42**:18
Nothing Sacred (Carter)   **41**:119; **76**:327, 329
Nothing Sacred (Walker)   **61**:430-31, 433
"Nothing to Be Said" (Larkin)   **64**:271
"Nothing to Fear" (Amis)   **2**:6
"Nothing to Say" (Davies)   **21**:91
"Nothing Twice" (Szymborska)   **99**:204, 207
"Notice" (Lowell)   **11**:330
"Notice of Loss" (Enzensberger)   **43**:151
"Notice the Convulsed Orange Inch of Moon"
  (Cummings)   **68**:30
"Notiunile" ("Some Notions") (Arghezi)   **80**:11
*Not-Knowing: The Essays and Interviews of
  Donald Barthelme* (Barthelme)   **115**:99
Notorious (Hitchcock)   **16**:342, 345-46, 348,
  359
"Notre Dame de Chartres" (Meredith)   **4**:348
Notre dame des fleurs (*Our Lady of the Flow-
  ers*) (Genet)   **1**:115-17; **2**:157; **5**:137-38;
  10:225; **44**:386-90; **46**:168-76, 180, 182
"Notre hublot" (Chedid)   **47**:87
Notre pain quotidien (Cendrars)   **18**:96; **106**:173
"Notre petit continent" (Arp)   **5**:34
La notte (Antonioni)   **20**:19, 22, 26, 31
"La notte brava" (Pasolini)   **37**:347
Le notti bianche (Visconti)   **16**:563, 565
Le notti di Cabiria (*Cabiria; The Nights of
  Cabiria*) (Fellini)   **16**:271, 273, 274, 292;
  85:59-60, 62, 74-6, 78-9
Le notti difficili (Buzzati)   **36**:90
Nottingham Lace (Forster)   **22**:136-37; **45**:131

"Nouns" (Wright)   **6**:580
Nourish the Beast (Tesich)
  See *Baba Goya*
"Nourishments of Love" (Kunene)   **85**:175
A nous la liberté (Clair)   **20**:59-62, 70
Nous n'irons plus au bois (Crommelynck)
  75:152
"Nous tombons" (Char)   **14**:128
Le nouveau locataire (*The New Tenant*)
  (Ionesco)   **4**:251; **6**:248; **9**:286, 288;
  41:231; **86**:332, 340
Un Nouveau Patron pour l'Aviation (Cendrars)
  106:172
Nouveau recueil (Ponge)   **18**:414
"nouvelle bonte" (Cesaire)   **112**:31
La nouvelle origine (Audiberti)   **38**:21
La nouvelle somme de poèsie du monde noir
  (Damas)   **84**:175, 180
Les nouvelles noces (Jouve)   **47**:210
Nouvelles orientales (*Oriental Tales*)
  (Yourcenar)   **38**:462-64; **50**:363-64;
  87:401-02
Nouvelles pièces noires (Anouilh)   **13**:19-20
"Nova" (Sherwin)   **7**:415
Nova (Delany)   **8**:168; **14**:146-47; **38**:150-51,
  153-57, 160-62
Nova Express (Burroughs)   **2**:91-3; **5**:92; **15**:108,
  110; **22**:83; **42**:71, 73, 77, 79; **75**:93, 96-
  8, 102, 106, 108, 111; **109**:183, 186, 195-
  96, 207, 209, 212, 229
"Nova Scotia Chronolog Number Three and
  Number Five" (Dunn)   **36**:153
"The Novel" (Rich)   **73**:332
The Novel (Michener)   **109**:383
"The Novel and Europe" (Kundera)
  See "The Depreciated Legacy of Cervantes"
The Novel and Our Time (Comfort)   **7**:53
"The Novel and the Nation in South Africa"
  (Gordimer)   **70**:163
"The Novel as Form" (Faulkner)   **3**:156
"The Novel as History" (Mathews)   **52**:312-
  13, 315
The Novel as Research (Butor)   **8**:120
"The Novel as Spectacle" (Calvino)   **73**:48
The Novel in the Third World (Larson)   **31**:240-
  41
*The Novel Now: A Guide to Contemporary Fic-
  tion* (Burgess)   **4**:82; **8**:112; **62**:131; **94**:33,
  76
"The Novel of Manners Today" (Auchincloss)
  45:28
The Novel of the Future (Nin)   **1**:248; **4**:379;
  14:384, 386; **60**:271
*Novel on Yellow Paper; or, Work It Out for Your-
  self* (Smith)   **25**:416, 422-23; **44**:432-35,
  437-39, 443-45
"Novel, Tale, and Romance" (McCarthy)
  39:485, 490
"The Novel Today" (Coetzee)   **117**:65, 90, 93
Novela negra con arentinos (*Black Novel (with
  Argentines)*) (Valenzuela)   **104**:379-82,
  384-85, 389, 392-98
Novelario de donga novais (Dourado)   **23**:151
A Novelette, and Other Prose (Williams)   **2**:468-
  69
"The Novelist and His Characters" (Mauriac)
  56:211
The Novelist and the Narrator (Wilson)   **34**:580
The Novelist at the Crossroads (Lodge)   **36**:270
Novelist before the World (Gironella)
  See *El novelista ante del mundo*
"The Novelist, Diagnostician of the Contem-
  porary Malaise" (Percy)   **65**:261

"A Novelist to His Readers" (Green)   **97**:293
El novelista ante del mundo (*Novelist before
  the World*) (Gironella)   **11**:234-35
"Novella" (Hass)   **99**:143
Novelle del ducato in fiamme (Gadda)   **11**:215
Novellen (Boell)   **11**:55
"Novels and Children" (Barthes)   **83**:95
The Novels of Dashiell Hammett (Hammett)
  5:161
"Novelty Booth" (Nowlan)   **15**:399
"November" (Frost)   **26**:128
"November" (Merwin)   **18**:335
"November" (Smith)   **25**:419
"November, 1889" (Howard)   **7**:168
"November, 1961" (Smith)   **64**:388
November and May (Szirtes)   **46**:391-93, 395
"November Graveyard" (Plath)   **111**:202
"November, 1968" (Rich)   **36**:366
"November: San Joaquin Valley" (Rose)   **85**:314
"November through a Giant Copper Beech"
  (Honig)   **33**:213
"November Walk near False Creek Mouth"
  (Birney)   **6**:74, 76-7; **11**:51
"Novembers" (Peacock)   **60**:293
Novembre (Simenon)   **2**:398
"Novices" (Moore)   **10**:350; **47**:260
"Noviembre" (Rodriguez)   **10**:440
"Novilladas democráticas" (Murray)   **40**:335
"Novotny's Pain" (Roth)   **31**:335
"Novye stansy k Avguste" ("New Stanzas to
  Augusta") (Brodsky)   **50**:125
"Now" (Barnard)   **48**:26
"Now" (Jacobsen)   **48**:198
"Now" (Sondheim)   **30**:391, 402
Now about These Women (Bergman)
  See *For att ente tala om alla dessa kvinnor*
Now and Another Time (Hearon)   **63**:159-60
Now and at the Hour (Cormier)   **12**:133
Now and In Other Days (Amichai)
  See *Akhshav Uveyamim*
Now and on Earth (Thompson)   **69**:380, 383
"Now and Then" (Fuller)   **62**:185
Now and Then: Poems, 1976-1978 (Warren)
  13:581; **18**:534-38; **39**:257-58, 260, 265,
  270; **59**:296
Now Don't Try to Reason with Me (Booth)
  23:89, 99
Now Dowager (Bermant)   **40**:92-3
"Now Full of Silences" (Pack)   **13**:438
"Now I Become Myself" (Sarton)   **91**:253
"Now I Come before You" (Cohen)   **38**:137
"Now I Lay Me" (Hemingway)   **8**:283; **10**:269;
  13:270; **30**:183, 187, 192, 196-97, 200
"now I love somebody more than" (Shange)
  25:402
"Now I'm a Farmer" (Townshend)   **17**:534
Now Is Not Too Late (Holland)   **21**:154
"Now Is the Air Made of Chiming Bells"
  (Eberhart)   **19**:143; **56**:86
"Now Is the Time" (Himes)   **7**:159
Now Is the Time for All Good Men (Cryer)
  21:77-9
"Now Let Us Praise Stupid Women" (Atwood)
  84:105
Now Playing at Canterbury (Bourjaily)   **8**:103-
  04; **62**:101-04
Now Sheba Sings the Song (Angelou)   **64**:38;
  77:22, 32
"Now That April's Here" (Callaghan)   **65**:250
Now That April's Here, and Other Stories
  (Callaghan)   **14**:100
"Now That I Am Forever a Child" (Lorde)
  71:251

"Now That Men Can Cry..." (Sheed)　**53**:336
"Now That My Father Lies Down beside Me"
　(Plumly)　**33**:313
Now That the Buffalo's Gone (Sainte-Marie)
　17:431-32
"Now the Sidewise Easing into Night" (Plumly)
　33:310
"Now the Sky" (Van Doren)　**10**:496
"Now the Sturdy Wind" (Graham)　**48**:145
Now They Sing Again (Frisch)
　See *Nun singen sie wieder*
Now They've Started Singing Again (Frisch)
　See *Nun singen sie wieder*
"Now This Cold Man" ("This Cold Man")
　(Page)　**7**:291; **18**:378
Now Wait for Last Year (Dick)　**30**:115-16;
　72:121
Now We Are Enemies (Fleming)　**37**:118, 120
"Now We Know How Many Holes It Takes to
　Fill the Albert Hall" (Kesey)　**46**:228
"Now When We Think of Compromise"
　(Mahapatra)　**33**:276, 282
"Nowadays Clancy Can't Even Sing" (Young)
　See "Clancy"
The Nowaks (Isherwood)　**11**:300; **14**:278
Nowhere (Berger)　**38**:41-2
"Nowhere but Here" (Fisher)　**87**:128
Nowhere but Light (Belitt)　**22**:50, 52-3
The Nowhere City (Lurie)　**4**:305-07; **5**:259-
　60; **18**:310; **39**:182-83
The Nowhere Man (Markandaya)　**8**:377;
　38:324
"No-Winter Country" (Lewis)　**41**:255
Nowy swiat i okolice (*New World Avenue and
　Vincinity*) (Konwicki)　**117**:276-77, 279,
　281, 286, 289-90
Les noyers de l'Altenburg (*The Walnut Trees of
　Altenburg*) (Malraux)　**1**:202; **4**:325-26,
　328-29, 333, 336; **9**:355, 358-59; **13**:366-
　67, 369; **15**:352-54; **57**:302, 306, 308-
　09, 321
Le nozze di Cadmo e Armonia (*The Marriage
　of Cadmus and Harmony*) (Calasso)
　81:39-52
NP (Yoshimoto)　**84**:430-31
N'Tsuk (Theriault)　**79**:416
N.U.: Nettezza urbana (Antonioni)　**20**:28
"Le nu parmi les cercueils" (Mandiargues)
　41:274
Le nu perdu, 1964-1970 (Char)　**55**:288
"Le nu provençal" (Middleton)　**13**:388
Le nuage rouge (Bonnefoy)　**58**:56-7, 60
"Nube feliz" (Aleixandre)　**9**:14
"Las nubes" (Azorin)　**11**:25
Las nubes (*The Clouds*) (Cernuda)　**54**:42, 46,
　53, 58, 60-1
The Nuclear Age (O'Brien)　**40**:345-48;
　103:132, 134-37, 143, 166
"Nuclear Umbrella" (Padilla)　**38**:352
Nude Descending a Staircase (Kennedy)
　42:254-55
"Nude Pictures" (Komunyakaa)　**94**:231
The Nude Restaurant (Warhol)　**20**:419, 422-
　23
"Nude Resting" (Dobyns)　**37**:81
Nude with Violin (Coward)　**29**:136, 139
"Nude Women" (Asturias)　**8**:25
Nuestra Natacha (Casona)　**49**:40-5
La nueva narrativa hispanoamericana
　(Fuentes)
　See *La nueva novela hispanoamericana*
La nueva novela hispanoamericana (*La nueva
　narrativa hispanoamericana*)(Fuentes)

　10:208
*Nuevas andanzas y desventuras de Lazarillo de
　Tormes* (*New Wanderings and Misfortunes
　of Lazarillo de Tormes*) (Cela)　**4**:96;
　59:126, 135, 142
Nuevos sermones (Parra)　**102**:356
La nuit (*Les confitures de coings*; *Quince Jam*)
　(Ferron)　**94**:106, 108, 110, 117-18, 124-
　26
La nuit (*Night*) (Wiesel)　**3**:526-30; **5**:491;
　11:570; **37**:452
La nuit américaine (*Day for Night*) (Truffaut)
　20:393, 396-97, 400, 406; **101**:379-80,
　382-86, 396, 400, 407, 409-13
"Nuit blanche" ("Sleepless Night") (Damas)
　84:177-78, 183
"La nuit Catalane" ("The Catalan Night"; "the
　Catalonian Night") (Morand)　**41**:297, 308
Une nuit dans la fôret (Cendrars)　**18**:96;
　106:166
La nuit de la Saint-Jean (*Saint John's Eve*)
　(Duhamel)　**8**:189
"La nuit de seis jours" ("Night of Six Days";
　"The Six-Day Night") (Morand)　**41**:297,
　308
"Nuit de Sine" (Senghor)　**54**:390
La nuit d'orage (*The Stormy Night*) (Duhamel)
　8:187-88
La nuit du carrefour (Renoir)　**20**:309-10
La nuit du décret (del Castillo)　**38**:168-69
Nuit et brouilland (*Night and Fog*) (Resnais)
　16:502-03, 506, 512
"La nuit Hongroise" ("The Hungarian Night")
　(Morand)　**41**:296-97, 308
La nuit remue (*The Night in Motion*) (Michaux)
　8:392; **19**:315
"La nuit Romaine" ("The Roman Night")
　(Morand)　**41**:297, 308
La nuit talismanique (Char)　**14**:128; **55**:287-
　88
"La nuit Turque" ("The Turkish Night")
　(Morand)　**41**:296-97, 307-08
"La nuit viennoise" (Lang)　**103**:87
Les nuits de l'underground (*Nights in the Un-
　derground: An Exploration of Love*)
　(Blais)　**22**:59-60
Nuits sans nuit et quelques jours sans jour
　(*Nights as Day, Days as Night*) (Leiris)
　61:347, 360-61
Nuket (*The Dolls*; *The Puppets*) (Haavikko)
　34:169-170, 173
"Nul ne se rappelle avoir vu" (Damas)　**84**:180
"Null Class" (Young)　**82**:396, 412
"Nullipara" (Olds)　**85**:308
"Num bar da Calle Sierpes, Sevilha" (Cabral de
　Melo Neto)　**76**:169
"Numa" (Benet)　**28**:23
"# 5" (Alegria)　**57**:10
"No. 80" (Amichai)　**116**:98-9
"No. 52 (Amichai)　**116**:97
"Number Four" (Major)　**19**:297
"No. 14 (Amichai)　**116**:95
"Number Man" (Sandburg)　**15**:466
"Number Nine Dream" (Lennon)　**35**:268, 270-
　71
The Number of the Beast (Heinlein)　**26**:174-
　75; **55**:303
The Number of the Beast (Wilson)　**33**:465
"No. 1" (Amichai)　**116**:97
Number One (Dos Passos)　**11**:156; **15**:183,
　187; **34**:420
"Number One Rip-Off Man" (Cliff)　**21**:63
"No. 74" (Amichai)　**116**:97

"No. 21" (Amichai)　**116**:96
"No. 23" (Amichai)　**116**:95
"No. 2" (Amichai)　**116**:98
The Numbered (Canetti)
　See *Die Befristeten*
"Numbered Apartment" (Merwin)　**45**:274
"Numbers" (Creeley)　**36**:121
"Numbers" (Hughes)　**35**:222
"Numbers" (Sachs)
　See "Zahlen"
"Numbers" (Weller)　**26**:444
Numbers (Creeley)　**2**:106; **78**:144
Numbers (Rechy)　**7**:357; **18**:442; **107**:223-
　26, 228, 230, 238, 243, 254, 256, 258
"Numbers: 63" (Orlovitz)　**22**:334-35
Numbers: A Further Autobiography (Lind)
　2:245; **4**:293
"Le numéro barbette" (Cocteau)　**8**:148-49
Numero deux (Godard)　**20**:153, 155
"The Nun at Court" (Blunden)　**56**:48
"Nun, Geometry, Grief" (Lerman)　**9**:330
"A Nun No More" (Fante)　**60**:133
Nun singen sie wieder (*Now They Sing Again*;
　Now They've Started Singing Again;
　They're Singing Again Now) (Frisch)
　9:217; **14**:181-82; **32**:190; **44**:185, 194-
　96, 199, 204
"The Nun Who Returned to Ireland" (Carrier)
　See "La religieuse qui retourna en Irlande"
"Nunc dimittis" (Brodsky)　**4**:78; **36**:76, 79
"Nunc Dimittis" (Dahl)　**79**:175, 178, 180
"Nunc Dimittis" (Lee)　**46**:234
Nunca llegarás a nada (*See You Will Never Get
　Anywhere*) (Benet)　**28**:23-4
"Nuncle" (Wain)　**46**:411
Nuncle and Other Stories (Wain)　**46**:411
Nuni (Griffin)　**68**:196-201
Nunquam (Durrell)　**6**:153; **8**:193; **13**:185;
　41:136-37
Nuns and Soldiers (Murdoch)　**22**:328-31;
　31:289, 291, 294
"A Nun's Mother" (Lavin)　**99**:316
Nuorena nukkunit (Sillanpaa)　**19**:420
La nuova gioventù (*The New Youth*) (Pasolini)
　106:265, 267
Nuovi strani amici (Buzzati)　**36**:84
Il nuovo questore (Buzzati)　**36**:84
"Nuptial Hymn" (McAuley)　**45**:254
Nuptials (Camus)
　See *Noces*
"Nur auf Sardinien" (Lenz)　**27**:245
"Nuremburg" (Slessor)　**14**:492
"Nurse Cora" (Cortazar)　**3**:115
"Nurse Sharks" (Matthews)　**40**:320
"The Nurselog" (Purdy)　**50**:247
"A Nursery Tale" (Nabokov)　**6**:357
"Nursie" (Kinsella)　**43**:253, 255
The Nursing-Home Murder (Marsh)　**53**:250
La nuvola di smog (*Smog*) (Calvino)　**5**:98,
　100; **11**:91, 92; **33**:100; **39**:315; **73**:42
"N.Y. Telephone Conversation" (Reed)　**21**:305
"Nyassa" (Jeffers)　**54**:234
Nyatt School (Gray)　**49**:146-47; **112**:108
The Nylon Curtain (Joel)　**26**:222-23
"N'yu-yorkskaya ptitsa" (Voznesensky)
　57:416
"O" (Merrill)　**8**:386-87
"O" (Nowlan)　**15**:398
"O" (Voznesensky)　**57**:426-29
O Albany!: An Urban Tapestry (Kennedy)
　53:190-92, 194
O Babylon (Walcott)　**25**:454; **76**:275
O Beulah Land (Settle)　**19**:408-09; **61**:372-

74, 376, 381-87
"O Canada" (Richler) 46:352
O Canada (Wilson) 2:475
"O Cities, through Which the Armies Marched" (Haavikko) 34:175
"O City of Broken Dreams" (Cheever) 64:65
"The O. D. and Hepatitis Railroad or Bust" (Boyle) 90:49
"O Daedalus, Fly Away Home" (Hayden) 5:168
"O die Schornsteine" ("O the Chimneys") (Sachs) 98:334, 348, 352, 355, 362
O Dreamland (Anderson) 20:11, 17
"O Dreams, O Destinations" (Day Lewis) 10:131
"O Earth, Turn!" (Johnston) 51:251
"O Fat White Woman" (Trevor) 71:337; 116:363
O Gato Malhado e a Andorinha Sinhá (The Swallow and the Tom Cat: A Love Story) (Amado) 106:73
O Genteel Lady! (Forbes) 12:202
"O Gentle Queen of the Afternoon" (Graham) 29:193
"O Happy Melodist" (Hood) 15:284; 28:188
"The O in Jose" (Aldiss) 40:21
"O întîlnire de necrezut" ("Unbelievable Encounter") (Arghezi) 80:13
"O Love, Sweet Animal" (Schwartz) 45:356
O Lucky Man! (Anderson) 20:16-18
"O Lull Me, Lull Me" (Roethke) 101:274, 282, 335, 340
"O Lung Flowering Like a Tree" (Frame) 96:200
"O ma martelée" (Char) 9:162
"O Marcel...Otherwise/I Also Have Been to Louise's" (Loy) 28:253
O Master Caliban (Gotlieb) 18:193
"O me donzel" (Pasolini) 106:228
O Mikrós naftilos (Elytis) 100:175, 187
O Mistress Mine (Rattigan)
    See *Love in Idleness*
"O My God" (Police, The) 26:366
O Pays, mon beau peuple (Ousmane) 66:334
O risco do bordado (Pattern for a Tapestry) (Dourado) 60:85, 93-4
O saisons, o chateaux (Varda) 16:556
O Shepherd, Speak (Sinclair) 63:365
O sorriso do lagarto (Ribeiro) 67:282
"O Taste and See" (Levertov) 66:250
O Taste and See (Levertov) 2:242; 5:246, 249; 15:336; 66:235-39
"O the Chimneys" (Sachs)
    See "O die Schornsteine"
O the Chimneys (Sachs) 14:475-76; 98:362
"O, Thou Opening, O" (Roethke) 101:273-74, 281, 284
O to Be a Dragon (Moore) 8:400; 13:396
"O Ugly Bird!" (Wellman) 49:395
O Westport in the Light of Asia Minor (Durcan) 43:113
"O Wha's the Bride" (MacDiarmid) 11:334
"O What Is That Sound Which So Thrills the Ear" (Auden) 11:15-16
"O Who Will Speak from a Womb or a Cloud" (Barker) 48:10
"O Ye Tongues" (Sexton) 53:320, 322-23
"O Yes" (Olsen) 114:192, 194, 213, 220-21, 223
"O Youth and Beauty!" (Cheever) 7:49-50; 64:46, 48
The Oak and the Calf (Solzhenitsyn)
    See *Bodalsia telenok s dubom*
The Oak and the Ram (Moorcock) 5:294

Oak Leaves and Lavender; or, A World on Wallpaper (O'Casey) 5:318; 11:408-09; 88:239
"Oak Tree at the Entrance to Blackwater Pond" (Oliver) 98:280
"Oasis" (p'Bitek) 96:286
The Oasis (A Source of Embarrassment) (McCarthy) 3:326-27; 14:363; 39:488; 59:289, 291-92
Oasis in Space (Cousteau) 30:105
The Oath (Wiesel)
    See *Le serment de Kolvillàg*
"Oaxaca" (Shields) 97:431
Obakasan (Wonderful Fool) (Endo) 7:96; 54:152, 156, 157, 159; 99:284-85, 287, 302
"Obalaji as drummer, Ras as Poet" (Baraka) 115:12
Obasan (Kogawa) 78:165-69, 177, 179, 181, 183, 185-87, 192, 194-95
"Obatala" (Clark) 38:126
"Obeah Win de War" (Bennett) 28:29
The Obedient Wife (O'Faolain) 47:326-29, 331; 108:413
"The Obelisk" (Forster) 45:143
"Oberfeldwebel Beckstadt" (Raine) 32:350, 352
Oberflächenübersetzungen (Jandl) 34:195
"Obit Page" (Blackburn) 43:68
"Obits" (Busch) 47:65
Obituaries (Saroyan) 29:360-61
"Obituary" (Asimov) 76:320
"Obituary" (McGrath) 28:277
"Obituary for a Living Lady" (Brooks) 49:22
"Obituary of a Democracy" (Gellhorn) 60:196
"Obituary of a Gin Mill" (Mitchell) 98:165, 178, 180, 184
"Obituary of R. Fuller" (Fuller) 28:151, 158
"Object Lessons" (Boland) 113:94
Object Lessons: The Life of the Woman and the Poet in Our Time (Boland) 113:108-09, 112-16, 120-21, 125-27
The Object of My Affection (McCauley) 50:62-5
"Object Trouvé: Piazza San Marco" (Fuller) 62:203
Objections to Sex and Violence (Churchill) 31:82-3
"The Objectivist Ethics" (Rand) 79:387
An "Objectivists" Anthology (Zukofsky) 1:385
"Objects at Brampton Ash" (Middleton) 13:387
Objects of Affection (Bennett) 77:93
"Oblique Prayers" (Levertov) 66:245
Oblique Prayers (Levertov) 66:237, 239-41, 250
The Oblivion Ha-Ha (Tate) 2:431; 25:430
Obmen (The Exchange) (Trifonov) 45:408-10, 413, 415-17, 419-21, 423
"La obra" (Bioy Casares) 88:94
Obra gruesa (Parra) 102:353
Obra poética (Guillen) 48:162
Obras completas (Complete Works) (Aleixandre) 9:12, 17
Obras completas (Borges) 2:73; 9:117; 44:361
Obras completas (Neruda) 2:309; 28:310
The Obscene Bird of Night (Donoso)
    See *El obsceno pájaro de la noche*
Obscene Gestures for Women (Kauffman) 65:347
Obscenities (Casey) 2:100
El obsceno pájaro de la noche (The Obscene Bird of Night) (Donoso) 4:126-30; 8:178-80; 11:146-47, 149-52; 32:153-55, 159-

61; 99:216, 218-20, 222-23, 231-32, 240-41, 249-51, 254-56, 258, 267, 269, 274
"The Obscure" (Dubie) 36:130
An Obscure Man (Yourcenar) 87:404
Obscured by Clouds (Pink Floyd) 35:311
"Obscurity and Clarity in Poetry" (Neruda) 5:302
"The Obscurity of the Poet" (Jarrell) 9:298
"Obsequies" (Longley) 29:296-97
"Observance" (Berry) 46:69
"Observation Car" (Hope) 51:213, 216-17
Observations (Moore) 1:228; 4:363; 13:393; 19:337, 342
"Observations on the Uses of Autobiography in Fiction" (Stafford) 68:441
"The Observer" (Rich) 36:372
"Obsession" (Damas) 84:173
"Obsession" (Montague) 46:267-68
"Obsession" (Phillips) 28:362
Obsession (Campbell) 42:91-2
The Obsession (Levin) 7:204-06
Obsession (De Palma) 20:76-8
"Obsidian Butterfly" (Paz)
    See "Mariposa de obsidiana"
Obsluhoval jsem anglického krále (I Served the King of England; I Waited on the King of England) (Hrabal) 67:114, 116, 120-26, 128-52
"Obsolescence" (Ciardi) 44:383
"Obsolete Youth" (Bettelheim) 79:126
"Obstacles" (Frame) 96:189
"An Obstinate Exile" (Lee) 90:203
"The Obvious" (Laing) 95:141, 146
Obyknovenny chelovek (An Ordinary Man; An Ordinary Person) (Leonov) 92:246, 250-51, 260, 270, 277
Ocalenie (Rescue) (Milosz) 11:377; 56:236-37, 245; 82:289
Occasion for Loving (Gordimer) 7:132; 18:186; 33:183; 70:161-62, 164
Occasion of Sin (Billington) 43:57-8
Occasional Prose (McCarthy) 39:484-91
"The Occasional Room" (Loewinsohn) 52:283
Le occasioni (The Occasions) (Montale) 7:222-24, 228, 230-32; 18:340
"The Occasions" (Thesen) 56:423
The Occasions (Montale)
    See *Le occasioni*
The Occasions of Poetry (Gunn) 32:210, 212-14
Occidental Mythology (Campbell)
    See *The Masks of God: Occidental Mythology*
The Occult: A History (Wilson) 3:538; 14:583
"Occupant" (Summers) 10:494
Occupant Please Forward (Summers) 10:494
"The Occupation" (Abse) 29:14
The Occupation (Caute) 29:114-16, 122
Occupations (Griffiths) 13:256; 52:171-72, 174, 178, 180-82, 185
"The Ocean" (Cheever) 3:107; 7:49
"The Ocean" (Grace) 56:112
"The Ocean" (Mason) 82:240, 254
"Ocean 1212-W" (Plath) 62:410; 111:159, 209
"Ocean Girl" (Young) 17:576
Ocean of Night (Ali) 69:23
Ocean of Story (Stead) 80:341-42
"Ocean of Words" (Jin) 109:54
Ocean of Words (Jin) 109:53-4
"Ocean Poem" (Moure) 88:224
The Ocean World of Jacques Cousteau

(Cousteau) **30**:105-07, 109
Oceanography Lab (Berger) **12**:39
"Ocean's Love to Ireland" (Heaney) **25**:245; **74**:157, 162
The Ocean's Musical March (Ritsos) **31**:324
L'océantume (Ducharme) **74**:57, 59-61, 68
Ochii Maicii Domnului (The Eyes of the Madonna) (Arghezi) **80**:6
Ocnos (Cernuda) **54**:42, 53
Octaedro (Cortazar) **13**:164; **34**:333
Octagon Magic (Norton) **12**:458, 471
Octavian Shooting Targets (Gregor) **9**:253, 256
"October" (Johnston) **51**:248
"October" (Lane) **25**:284
"October" (Swenson) **61**:395, 397-98, 402; **106**:322
October 1916 (Solzhenitsyn)
  See *Oktyabr' shestnadtsatogo*
"October, 1940" (Fuller) **28**:158
"October 1950" (Muldoon) **32**:319-20; **72**:265
"October Arriving" (Simic) **49**:343
"October at the Window" (Ashbery) **77**:66
The October Circle (Littell) **42**:275-76
"October Comes" (Blunden) **56**:30, 45
The October Country (Bradbury) **42**:46
"October Dawn" (Hughes) **9**:280-81
"October Fugue" (Shapcott) **38**:402
"The October Game" (Bradbury) **42**:35
"October Ghosts" (Wright) **28**:466
"October in the Railroad Earth" (Kerouac) **61**:296, 309, 313
October Light (Gardner) **8**:233-38; **10**:220; **18**:183; **28**:162-63, 165, 167; **34**:550
"October Picnic Long Ago" (Warren) **39**:272
"October Prayer" (Pack) **13**:340
"An October Salmon" (Hughes) **37**:177, 179-81
"October Snow" (Johnston) **51**:253
"October Spring" (Appleman) **51**:14
October Wind: A Novel of Christopher Columbus **70**:332, 349
"Octogenarians Die in Crash" (Leyner) **92**:281
"An Octopus" (Moore) **10**:348; **47**:260
The Octopus (Wurlitzer)
  See *Nog*
"Oda a la pobreza" (Neruda) **9**:397
"Oda a las Américas" (Neruda) **9**:396-97
"Oda al átomo" (Neruda) **9**:397
"Oda al caldillo de congrio" (Neruda) **9**:397
"Odalisque" (Padilla) **38**:351
Odas elementales (The Elemental Odes; Elementary Odes; Odes to Simple Things) (Neruda) **5**:301, 303; **7**:259; **9**:396; **28**:307, 310-11, 313; **62**:333
"Odd" (Abse) **7**:1; **29**:16-17
The Odd Couple (Simon) **6**:503, 506; **31**:393, 396-98, 400, 403; **70**:235, 237-38, 240-41
Odd Girl Out (Howard) **7**:164
"An Odd Job" ("A Strange Job") (Oe) **36**:346; **86**:226-27, 236
"Odd Jobs" (Cameron) **44**:33
Odd Man Out (Pinter)
  See *Old Times*
Odd Number (Sorrentino) **40**:390-91
Odd Obsession (Ichikawa) **20**:177
The Odd Woman (Godwin) **5**:142-43; **8**:247-48; **22**:180-83; **31**:195-96, 198; **69**:232, 237-39, 243-46
"Oddball" (Aksyonov) **101**:11, 17
"Oddjob, a Bull Terrier" (Walcott) **14**:549
"The Odds" (Salinas) **90**:332

Odds Against (Francis) **2**:143; **22**:151; **42**:148-50, 153-54, 156; **102**:127, 146, 156-57, 162
Odds and Ends (Enzensberger)
  See *Einzelheiten*
Odds and Sods (Townshend) **17**:534
"Odds: Roughs for Theatre and Radio" (Beckett) **9**:84; **14**:74
"Ode" (Kennedy) **42**:255
"Ode" (MacNeice) **10**:325
"Ode" (Prokosch) **48**:306, 309-10
Ode (Jouve) **47**:206
"Ode 32" (Bunting) **47**:45
"Ode 34" (Bunting) **47**:45
Ode à Charles Fourier (Breton) **9**:128
"Ode at the Spring Equinox" (Watkins) **43**:443
"Ode auf N" (Jandl) **34**:198
"Ode for James Downey" (Johnston) **51**:249
"Ode for the American Dead in Asia" (McGrath) **59**:181
"Ode on a Common Fountain" (Wieners) **7**:535
"Ode on Causality" (O'Hara) **13**:430
"Ode, on Contemplating Clapham Junction" (Middleton) **13**:387
"Ode on Human Destinies" (Jeffers) **54**:235
"An Ode on Nativity" (Olson) **29**:334
"Ode: On the Death of William Butler Yeats" (Smith) **15**:517
"Ode pour l'élection de son sépulchre" (Pound) **10**:405
"Ode: The Eumenides" (Smith) **15**:516
"The Ode to a Chinese Paper Snake" (Eberhart) **56**:82-3
"Ode to a Koala Bear" (McCartney) **35**:292
"Ode to a Model" (Nabokov) **8**:407
"Ode to a Paperclip" (Dunn) **40**:169
"Ode to Afternoon" (Porter) **33**:324
"Ode to an Absconding Bookie" (Algren) **33**:15
"Ode to Bill" (Ashbery) **15**:28
"Ode to Bread" (Neruda) **28**:307
"Ode to Duplicitous Men" (Holmes) **56**:145
"Ode to Ennui" (Dos Passos) **25**:143
"Ode to Failure" (Ginsberg) **36**:198
"Ode to Healing" (Updike) **43**:436
"Ode to Joy" (O'Hara) **13**:430
"Ode to Lenin" (Neruda) **2**:309
"Ode to Man" (Arghezi)
  See "Cîntare omului"
"Ode to Michael Goldberg's Birth and Other Births" (O'Hara) **5**:324
"Ode to Our Young Pro-Consuls of the Air" (Tate) **14**:533
"Ode to Picasso" (Elytis) **100**:173
"Ode to Rot" (Updike) **43**:436
"Ode to Stalin on His Seventieth Birthday" (Faludy) **42**:138
"Ode to Suburbia" (Boland) **67**:43; **113**:96, 122
"Ode to Terminus" (Auden) **43**:28
"Ode to the Bath" (McGinley) **14**:366
"Ode to the Brown Paper Bag" (Galvin) **38**:198
"Ode to the Confederate Dead" (Tate) **2**:427, 429-30; **4**:535, 539; **6**:527; **9**:523; **11**:522, 524, 527; **14**:528, 530
"Ode to the Runaway Caves" (Lieberman) **36**:262, 264-65
"Ode to the Spectral Thief, Alpha" (Dubie) **36**:139
"Ode to Willem de Kooning" (O'Hara) **5**:324
"Odes" (Senghor) **54**:391
Odes to Simple Things (Neruda)
  See *Odas elementales*
The Odessa File (Forsyth) **2**:136-37; **36**:175

Odin den' Ivana Denisovicha (One Day in the Life of Ivan Denisovich) (Solzhenitsyn) **1**:319-20; **2**:407-08, 410, 412; **4**:506-07, 511, 513-15; **7**:432, 436, 440, 444-45, 447; **10**:481; **18**:496; **24**:414-16, 418-23; **34**:481-82, 484-85, 489, 491; **78**:381, 389, 394, 408-09, 411, 416, 418
Odlévání zvonu (The Casting of Bells; The Casting of the Bells; Casting the Bells) (Seifert) **34**:257; **44**:422; **93**:310, 317, 324, 329, 332, 343
"Odnazhdy, pokanuvshis' na kraiu" ("Once, Rocking on the Edge") (Akhmadulina) **53**:13
Ododo (Walker) **19**:454
"An Odor of Verbena" (Faulkner) **52**:132
"Odour of Eucalyptus" (Wilding) **73**:398
An Odour of Sanctity (Yerby) **22**:488
ODTAA (Masefield) **11**:358
"Odysseus" (Merwin) **13**:384; **18**:333
"Odysseus at Rush Hour" (Dunn) **36**:155
Odysseus Elytis: Selected Poems (Elytis) **100**:192
"Odysseus on Hermes" (Gunn) **81**:182, 186
"Odysseus Speaking" (Barnard) **48**:27
"Odysseus to Telemachus" (Brodsky) **36**:76
"Odyssey" (Elytis) **100**:175, 187-88
"Odyssey" (Honig) **33**:211
The Odyssey (Walcott) **76**:297
"The Odyssey of a Manuscript" (Tolson) **105**:239
"The Odyssey of a Wop" (Fante) **60**:133
"Odyssey of Big Boy" (Brown) **23**:96; **59**:266
Odyssey of Courage: The Story of Alvar Nuñez Cabeza de Vaca (Wojciechowska) **26**:450-52
"Odyssey of Rancor" (Cioran) **64**:98
Oe Kenzaburo dojidai ronshu (Essays on Contemporary Issues) (Oe) **86**:228-29
"Oeconomic divina" (Milosz) **11**:381
"Oedipus at Colonus" (Forster) **3**:162
"Oedipus Complex" (Durrell) **27**:97
Oedipus Rex (Oedipus the King) (Cocteau) **8**:147; **43**:109, 111
Oedipus Rex (Pasolini)
  See *Edipo Re*
Oedipus the King (Cocteau)
  See *Oedipus Rex*
L'oeil du malin (The Third Lover) (Chabrol) **16**:169
L'oeuvre au noir (The Abyss) (Yourcenar) **19**:482-84; **38**:454-60, 464-65; **50**:361, 363-65; **87**:386, 395-97, 399, 412, 433
Oeuvre de chair (Theriault) **79**:412-13
Oeuvres complètes (Bataille) **29**:41-2
Oeuvres complètes (Breton) **54**:32
Oeuvres complètes (Char) **55**:288
Oeuvres complètes (Genet) **44**:387
Oeuvres complètes (Green) **77**:279-81, 284-85
Oeuvres complètes, Volume I: 1912-1924 (Tzara) **47**:391, 393
Oeuvres complètes, Volume II: 1925-1933 (Tzara) **47**:391, 393
Of a Fire on the Moon (Mailer) **1**:192-93; **2**:262-63; **3**:318; **4**:323; **8**:369-71, 373; **11**:344; **14**:350; **74**:205, 225; **111**:103, 133
"Of a Jar You Are" (Nye) **13**:412
Of Age and Innocence (Lamming) **2**:235; **4**:279; **66**:218-19, 222-24, 227, 229-30
"Of Alexander Crummell" (Du Bois) **64**:130
"Of an Etching" (Bowers) **9**:122

"Of Answers and Her Asleep" (Gustafson) 36:217

Of Art and the Future (Miller) 84:242

"Of Being Numerous" (Oppen) 7:282-84, 286

Of Being Numerous (Oppen) 7:282-84; 13:434; 34:358-59

"Of Birds and Beasts" (Kawabata)
See "Kinju"

"Of Cabbages and Kings" (McPherson) 19:309;77:359-61, 365-66

"Of Commerce and Society" (Hill) 8:294

"Of Daumiers a Portfolio" (Klein) 19:259

"Of Eastern Newfoundland, Its Inns and Outs" (Dorn) 10:160

"Of Faith" (Clark) 38:127

"Of Forced Sightes and Trusty Ferefulness" (Graham) 48:152

"Of Friendship" (Steele) 45:364

"Of Goats and Monkeys" (Walcott)
See "Goats and Monkeys"

"Of God and of the Gods" (Levertov) 66:245

"Of Gods" (Levertov) 66:241

Of Good and Evil (Gann) 23:166

Of Grammatology (Derrida)
See De la grammatologie

"Of History Fiction" (Ciardi) 40:156

"Of How the Lizards Live" (Brosman) 9:135

Of Human Bondage (Maugham) 1:204; 11:370; 15:366, 370; 67:203-07, 211-14, 217-22, 228; 93:225-73

Of Human Bondage, with a Digression on the Art of Fiction (Maugham) 93:242

Of Human Freedom (Barzun) 51:33-5

"Of Itzig and His Dog" (Abse) 29:20

"Of John Davidson" (MacDiarmid) 255

"Of Land and Love" (Ghose) 42:177

"Of Liberation" (Giovanni) 64:182-83

Of Light and Sounding Brass (Yanovsky) 2:485; 18:551-52

"Of Love: A Testimony" (Cheever) 64:65

Of Love and Death and Other Journeys (Holland) 21:149

Of Love and Dust (Gaines) 11:218; 18:165-66; 86:173

Of Love and Shadows (Allende)
See De amor y de sombra

"Of Memory and Desire" (Swan) 69:358-360

Of Memory and Desire (Swan) 69:359-60, 363

"Of Men and Cities" (Tolson) 105:260

Of Mice and Men (Steinbeck) 1:324-25; 5:406, 408-09; 9:512, 514, 517-18, 520; 13:529, 531-32; 21:366, 372, 378-86, 389-92; 34:405, 410-11, 414; 45:370-71, 382; 59:322, 332-34, 351; 75:335-65

Of Miracles and Melancholies (Mujica Lainez)
See De milagros y de melancolías

"Of Missing Persons" (Browne) 21:41-2

Of Mist and Grass and Sand (McIntyre) 18:326

Of Mortal Love (Gerhardie) 5:140-41

"Of Mourners" (Livesay) 79:332

"Of Natural Reticence" (Garrett) 51:141

"Of Necessity" (Levertov) 66:241

Of Nightingales That Weep (Paterson) 12:484-85; 30:284-86, 288

"Of Rabbi Yose" (Abse) 29:20

Of Rats and Diplomats (Ali) 69:31-2

"Of Rivers" (Levertov) 66:241

"Of Robin Hood and Womanhood" (Dubus) 97:233

"Of Rounds" (Swenson) 106:339

Of Sanctity and Whiskey (O'Faolain) 14:406

Of Smiling Peace (Heym) 41:211-12

Of Snails and Skylarks (Brown) 63:56

"Of Space/Time and the River" (Benford) 52:76

Of Spirit: Heidegger and the Question (Derrida)
See De l'esprit: Heidegger et la question

"Of Suicide" (Berryman) 25:95; 62:74

Of Surrealism in Its Living Works (Breton)
See Du surréalisme en ses oeuvres vives et d'ephemerides surréalistes

"Of That Fire" (Ignatow) 40:260

"Of the Coming of John" (Du Bois) 64:117-18, 130, 133

"Of the Dead of a Forsaken Country" (Davis) 49:93

"Of the Faith of the Fathers" (Du Bois) 64:134

Of the Farm (Updike) 1:344-45; 3:487; 5:451; 9:538, 540; 15:540, 543; 23:469; 43:430-31, 433; 70:249

Of the Festivity (Dickey) 28:117-18

"Of the Passing of the First-Born" (Du Bois) 64:130, 133

"Of the Quest of the Golden Fleece" (Du Bois) 64:110

"Of the Scythians" (Pollitt) 28:368

"Of the Sorrow Songs" (Du Bois) 64:130

"Of the Training of Black Men" (Du Bois) 96:129

Of the War: Passages (Duncan) 55:293

Of the Well and Numa: An Essay and a Legend (Benet)
See Del pozo y del Numa: Un ensayo y una leyenda

"Of the Wings of Atlanta" (Du Bois) 64:110, 130; 96:129

Of Thee I Sing (Kaufman) 38:258, 265

"Of This Time, of That Place" (Trilling) 9:532; 11:540

"Of Three or Four in a Room" (Amichai) 57:41; 116:89

"Of Tuor and His Coming to Gondolin" (Tolkien) 38:431

"Of Tyranny, in One Breath: (translated from a Hungarian poem by Gyula Illyes, 1956)" (Avison) 97:78

Of Whales and Women (Gilbreth and Carey) 17:155

Of Women and Their Elegance (Mailer) 74:225, 227

Of Women and Thomas Harrow (Marquand) 2:271; 10:328, 331

Of Women Born: Motherhood as Experience and Institution (Rich) 11:474-76,479; 18:444; 36:365, 375-76; 73:323-24; 76:219

Off into Space! Science for Young Travelers (Hyde) 21:172

Off Limits (Adamov) 25:16, 20-2

"Off Reservation Blues" (Allen) 84:3

"Off The Campus: Wits" (Brutus) 43:92

Off the Mainland (Shaw) 5:390

"Off the Track" (Adcock) 41:16

"Off to the Cemetery" (Ignatow) 7:182

Offending the Audience (Handke) 5:166; 8:262-63; 10:256; 15:265-68; 38:215, 217, 228

Der Öffentliche Ankläger (The Public Prosecutor, and Other Plays) (Hochwalder) 36:235, 237-40

"Öffentlichkeit als Partner" (Frisch) 44:191

"An Offering" (Apple) 33:21-2

"An Offering" (Stafford) 29:386

The Offering (Edwards) 43:137-39, 141-42

"An Offering for Mr. Bluehart" (Wright) 3:543

"Offerings" (Mason) 82:235, 242

"The Office" (Munro) 10:358; 95:294, 297

The Office (Fornes) 39:138

Office Life (Waterhouse) 47:421

Office Politics (Sheed) 2:392-94; 4:488; 10:473; 53:336

"Office Primitive" (Ewart) 46:150

"Office Romances" (Trevor) 116:333, 377

"Officers" (Miles) 34:245

Officers and Gentlemen (Waugh) 8:544; 19:461; 27:471-72; 107:371, 406

"Officers' Mess" (Ewart) 46:148, 150

The Officers' Wives (Fleming) 37:128-29

"Offices" (Page) 18:377

"Official Americans" (Rush) 44:91-3, 95-6

Officina (Pasolini) 106:232

Offret (Tarkovsky) 75:385, 391-94, 396-99, 401, 411-13

Offshore (Fitzgerald) 19:173-74; 51:124-25; 61:115-18, 120, 122

"Offshore Breeze" (Ashbery) 77:67

"Offspring of the First Generation" (Pesetsky) 28:357

Oficia de tinieblas cinquo (Cela) 13:147

Oficio de tinieblas (Rite of Darkness) (Castellanos) 66:60

"Oficio de tiniebles" (Carpentier) 110:76-7

Un oficio del siglo XX (Cabrera Infante) 25:105

"Oft in a Stilly Night" (O'Brien) 65:167, 169-71, 173; 116:203

"Often I Am Permitted to Return to a Meadow" (Duncan) 41:124

Ogon no kuni (Endo) 7:95

The Ogoni Nationality Today and Tomorrow (Saro-Wiwa) 114:275

The Ogre (Tournier)
See Le roi des Aulnes

The Ogre Downstairs (Jones) 26:224-26

Ogre, Ogre (Anthony) 35:38

"Oh" (Sexton) 4:483

Oh! (Robison) 42:340-43; 98:306, 308, 317-18

Oh, Boy! (Wodehouse) 22:478

"Oh, Brother" (Leyner) 92:293

Oh Dad, Poor Dad, Mamma's Hung You in the Closet and I'm Feelin' So Sad (Kopit) 18:286-87; 33:247-50, 252

"Oh! Darling" (Lennon and McCartney) 12:364, 380

Oh, God! (Gelbart) 21:128

"Oh Jamaica" (Cliff) 21:60-1

"Oh, Joseph, I'm So Tired" (Yates) 23:483

"Oh Khrushchev, My Khrushchev" (Grayson) 38:212

Oh, Lady! Lady!! (Wodehouse) 22:478

"Oh Louisiana" (Berry) 17:52

"Oh Max" (Creeley) 36:122

Oh Mercy (Dylan) 77:181-85

"Oh, Moon of Mahagonny!" (Harrison) 43:180

"Oh, My Love" (Lennon) 35:263-64, 267

"Oh No" (Creeley) 36:118

Oh Pray My Wings Are Gonna Fit Me Well (Angelou) 12:13; 64:32; 77:15, 22, 29-30

"Oh, Sister" (Dylan) 77:187

Oh, to Be a Swinger (Buchwald) 33:93

Oh! What a Lovely War (Deighton) 46:127

Oh What a Paradise It Seems (Cheever) 25:119-22; 64:49-52, 57, 59

"Oh What a Thrill" (Berry) 17:56

"Oh, What Avails" (Munro) 95:309, 314

"Oh Yoko!" (Lennon) 35:263

"Oh! You Pretty Things" (Bowie) 17:58

Ohayo (Good Morning) (Ozu) 16:447-48, 452-

55
"Ohio" (Young)　17:572
"Ohio Impromptu" (Beckett)　29:59, 65-6
"Ohio River Blues" (Patchen)　18:395
Ohio Town (Santmyer)　33:357-58, 360
Ohitika Woman (Crow Dog)　93:109. 111-12
Der Ohrenzeuge: Fünfzig Charaktere (Earwitness: Fifty Characters) (Canetti)　25:108; 75:145; 86:294, 300-01
Oi for England (Griffiths)　52:184
"Oil" (Hogan)　73:154
Oil! (Sinclair)　11:498; 15:498-99; 63:346, 349, 351, 361, 371, 373
"Oil at St. A. Barbara" (Eigner)　9:181
Oil Notes (Bass)　79:7-16, 18, 20
"L'oiseau des ruines" (Bonnefoy)　58:53
"L'oiseau migrateur" (Breton)　9:134
"L'oiseau spirituel" (Char)　14:128
Oiseaux (Birds) (Perse)　4:398-400
"Les oiseaux du souci" (Prevert)　15:437
Los ojos vendados (Blindfolded) (Saura)　20:320, 322
"Okay, Mr. Pappendass, Okay" (Fuchs)　22:157
"O'Keefe Retrospective" (Swenson)　61:397
"Oklahoma" (Transtroemer)　52:409
"Oklahoma Hills" (Guthrie)　35:183
Oktyabr' shestnadtsatogo (October 1916) (Solzhenitsyn)　2:411; 7:444; 78:413
Okurete kita seinen (The Young Man Who Arrived Late; The Youth Who Came in Late) (Oe)　86:228, 230
Ol' Waylon (Jennings)　21:204
"Olber's Paradox (Ferlinghetti)　111:65-6
"Old" (Coles)　46:108-09
Old Acquaintance (Guild)　33:187
"Old Adam" (Avison)　97:71
The Old Adam (Enright)　31:147
"The Old Address" (Kavan)　82:120
Old Age (Beauvoir)
　See *La vieillesse*
"Old Age of an Eagle" (Ransom)　11:466; 24:366
"The Old Age of Michelangelo" (Prince)　22:340
"The Old and the New Masters" (Jarrell)　9:296
"The Old Army Game" (Garrett)　51:147
"The Old Artist: Notes on Mr. Sweet" (Walker)　58:409
"The Old Asylum of the Narragansetts" (Dubie)　36:133
"Old Bapu" (Anand)　23:21
"The Old Bird, a Love Story" (Powers)　1:282
"Old Bones" (Narayan)　28:293
"The Old Books" (Scannell)　49:327, 331
"Old Bottles" (Bowering)　47:29
The Old Boys (Trevor)　7:475-76; 25:444-45; 71:321, 333, 340, 342, 345; 116:331, 334, 348, 366, 374-75, 381
"The Old Bucket" (Solzhenitsyn)
　See "Staroe vedro"
"Old Bull" (Trevor)　116:378
The Old Bunch (Levin)　7:204, 206
The Old Capital (Kawabata)
　See *The Old Capital*
An Old Captivity (Shute)　30:365-66
"The Old Century" (Sassoon)　36:387
The Old Century and Seven More Years (Sassoon)　36:394
"The Old Chevalier" (Dinesen)　29:162; 95:36, 42, 45
"The Old Chief Mshlanga" (Lessing)　22:279
"Old Complaints Revisited" (Sontag)　13:517-18

The Old Country (Bennett)　45:58; 77:83-5, 87, 100
"The Old Country Waltz" (Young)　17:576
"Old Countryside" (Bogan)　46:78, 83; 93:64, 68-69, 78, 80-81, 96-97
"Old Coyote in the Adirondacks" (Kenny)　87:253
"An Old Cracked Tune" (Kunitz)　6:287
The Old Crowd (Bennett)　45:58; 77:86, 88-9, 90-1,98
Old Dan's Records (Lightfoot)　26:279, 282
The Old Dark House (Priestley)
　See *Benighted*
"Old Desire" (Ammons)　57:49
The Old Devils (Amis)　44:134-44
"Old Dirt Road" (Lennon)　35:268
"Old Doc Rivers" ("Doc Rivers") (Williams)　9:572; 42:458
The Old Dog Barks Backwards (Nash)　23:323
"Old Dominion" (Hass)　18:213
"Old Dwarf Heart" (Sexton)　53:318
The Old English "Exodus": Text, Translation, and Commentary (Tolkien)　38:438, 440, 442
The Old English Peep-Show (A Pride of Heroes) (Dickinson)　12:168; 35:133
"The Old Faith" (O'Connor)　23:333
"The Old Fascist in Retirement" (Baxter)　78:27, 30
Old Fashioned Pilgrimage (Clarke)　6:112-13
"Old Fashioned Wedding" (Porter)　33:325
"Old Favorites" (Santos)　22:364
"An Old Field Mowed for Appearances' Sake" (Meredith)　4:347
"Old Flame" (Lowell)　4:303
"Old Flame" (Warren)　18:535-36
"Old Florist" (Roethke)　101:295
"Old Folks at Home" (Highsmith)　102:199
"Old Folk's Home, Jerusalem" (Dove)　81:152
The Old Foolishness (Carroll)　10:98
"The Old Fools" (Larkin)　5:230; 8:332, 337; 9:323; 18:298-301; 33:260, 262, 269; 39:339, 341, 344; 64:266, 270, 285
"The Old Forest" (Taylor)　37:411-13; 44:305-06, 309; 50:251, 253, 255, 260; 71:295-96, 298
The Old Forest, and Other Stories (Taylor)　37:410-13; 44:304-07, 309-10; 50:251
"Old Francis" (Kelman)　58:297, 300-01
"An Old Friend" (Abse)　29:21
"Old Friends" (Bromell)　5:74
"Old Friends" (Endo)　54:161
"Old Friends" (Moure)　88:218
"Old Gardener" (Simmons)　43:410
The Old Glory (Lowell)　4:299; 5:256; 8:350-53, 357; 11:324-25
"The Old Gods" (Kizer)　80:172
The Old Gods Waken (Wellman)　49:389, 396
"An Old Gourd" (Turco)　63:429
"The Old Gray Couple" (MacLeish)　8:363-64
The Old Gringo (Fuentes)
　See *El gringo viejo*
"Old Harp" (Davidson)　13:168; 19:126
"Old Homes" (Blunden)　56:37
"The Old Horns" (Campbell)　42:84-5
"The Old Hotel" (Swan)　69:365
"Old House" (Redgrove)　6:445
"The Old House at Home" (Mitchell)　98:156, 184
"Old Houses" (Hall)　37:142
"The Old Huntsman" (Sassoon)　36:388-90
The Old Huntsman and Other Poems (Sassoon)　36:385, 389-90, 392, 394

"The Old Icons" (Heaney)　74:169
"The Old Italians Dying" (Ferlinghetti)　27:139
"Old Jewelry" (Snodgrass)　68:388, 399
"Old John's Place" (Lessing)　22:279
Old Jules (Sandoz)　28:400-02, 404-05, 407
"The Old Lady" (Jhabvala)　8:312
"Old Lady Mandel" (Ferber)　93:139, 142
"An Old Lady's Winter Words" (Roethke)　8:455; 46:363; 101:304, 329
"An Old Lament Renewed" (Scannell)　49:326, 329
"The Old Land Dog" (Betjeman)　43:51
"Old Larkinian" (Ewart)　46:151
"Old Leaves" (Squires)　51:381
"Old Letters" (Schwartz)　45:361
"Old Letters" (Steele)　45:365
"The Old Liberals" (Betjeman)　43:35, 37, 40
Old Lights for New Chancels: Verses Topographical and Amatory (Betjeman)　43:34
"Old Lone Wolf" (Guthrie)　35:185
"Old Love" (Archer)　28:13-14
"Old Love" (Singer)　6:511; 9:487; 15:507
Old Love (Singer)　15:507-09; 23:420-21; 111:332-33
"The Old Lovers" (Aleixandre)
　See "Los amantes viejos"
"Old Lovers at a Ballet" (Sarton)　91:254
An Old Magic (Arthur)　12:27-9
"The Old Man" (Coover)　32:127
"Old Man" (Faulkner)　6:174; 8:211
"Old Man" (Hillis)　66:194
"The Old Man" (Johnston)　51:243
"Old Man" (MacCaig)　36:288
"The Old Man" (Singer)　111:294, 296-7
"Old Man" (Young)　17:571
The Old Man (Trifonov)
　See *Starik*
"The Old Man and the Child" (Roy)
　See "Le veillard et l'enfant"
"The Old Man and the Child" (Wiesel)　5:490
The Old Man and the Sea (The Sea in Being) (Hemingway)　1:143; 3:231-34, 237, 241, 243; 6:227-28, 230-32; 8:283-85; 10:264, 267; 13:273, 275, 278-81; 19:212, 224; 34:478; 39:428, 430; 41:198, 202, 204; 50:424, 427, 429; 61:201, 225; 80:146
"The Old Man and the Sun" (Aleixandre)　36:28, 30
"Old Man at the Bridge" (Hemingway)　80:135-36
The Old Man at the Railroad Crossing (Maxwell)　19:307
"An Old Man Awake in His Own Death" (Strand)　41:432
"Old Man Buzzard" (Brown)　59:265, 268
"Old Man in the Crystal Morning" (Schwartz)
　See "Poem"
"Old Man Isbell's Wife" (Davis)　49:91
Old Man Joseph and His Family (Linney)　51:260
"Old Man Minick" (Ferber)　93:145, 179-80
"Old Man of the Temple" (Narayan)　28:293
"Old Man Playing with Children" (Ransom)　4:435
Old Man Rubbing His Eyes (Bly)　15:63
"Old Man's Fugue" (Shapcott)　38:404
"An Old Man's Winter Night" (Frost)　1:110; 9:226; 15:250; 26:123-24
"Old Marrieds" (Brooks)　49:21-2, 26
"The Old Master" (O'Faolain)　14:402; 32:342; 70:317-18
"Old Master" (Shapcott)　38:402
Old Masters (Bernhard)

See *Alte Meister*
Old Mazurka to the Rhythm of Rain (Ritsos) 31:324
"The Old McGrath Place" (McGrath) 59:175
"Old Meg" (Gunn) 81:178
The Old Men at the Zoo (Wilson) 2:471-474; 3:535-36; 5:513-14; 25:463
"Old Men at Union Street Corner" (McIlvanney) 42:282
"Old Men Go Mad at Night" (Williams) 45:445
"Old Men Pitching Horseshoes" (Kennedy) 42:256-57
"The Old Mill" (Tillinghast) 29:415
"The Old Morality" (Fuentes)
See "Vieja moralidad"
"The Old Morality" (Fuentes) 22:170-71
"Old Mortality" (Porter) 101:224, 232, 251-52
Old Mortality (Porter) 1:272; 3:393; 7:310, 312, 317, 319; 10:396-99; 13:448-51; 15:428; 27:401
Old Mother (Lane) 25:289
"Old Mother Hubbard" (Guthrie) 23:199
"Old Mr. Busybody" (Capote) 34:322
Old Mr. Flood (Mitchell) 98:158-59, 165-66, 169, 172-73, 175, 177, 180-84
"Old Mr. Marblehall" (Welty) 14:561; 33:415; 105:385-86
"Old Music for Quiet Hearts" (Sandburg) 35:356
"Old Mythologies" (Montague) 46:278
"Old Names Taste Like Ashes" (Haavikko) 34:172
"Old New England" (Walcott) 25:455, 457; 42:421
"Old, Old Woodstock" (Morrison) 21:232
The Old Ones (Wesker) 3:518-20; 42:426-28, 430
"The Old Order" (Porter) 3:393; 7:310; 13:450
Old Order: Stories of the South (Porter) 10:396; 13:451
"Old Palaces" (Mahapatra) 33:277-78
The Old Patagonian Express: By Train through the Americas (Theroux) 15:533-35; 28:425; 46:402
"Old Peasant Woman Walks along the Beach" (Rozewicz) 9:465
"Old People on the Nursing Home Porch" (Strand) 71:282, 285
"Old Pewter" (Heaney) 37:165; 91:119
Old Phantoms (Edwards) 43:139, 142
"An Old Photo in an Old Life" (Hoffman) 13:287
"Old Photograph of the Future" (Warren) 39:270
"The Old Play" (Slessor) 14:496
"Old Pleasures Deserted" (Blunden) 56:44
"Old poet" (Bukowski) 108:111
The Old Poetries and the New (Kostelanetz) 28:218
"The Old Poet's Tale" (Rakosi) 47:348
Old Possum's Book of Practical Cats (Eliot) 55:354
"The Old Prison" (Wright) 53:418, 431
"Old Property" (Acorn) 15:9
"An Old Pub near the Angel" (Kelman) 86:185
"The Old Quarry, Part One" (Jones) 42:242-43
"The Old Quarry, Part Two" (Jones) 42:242
"Old Red" (Gordon) 29:187-88; 83:233, 239, 247-48
Old Red, and Other Stories (Gordon) 13:245; 29:189
"Old Sailor's Choice" (Davidson) 2:112

"The Old Saybrook House" (Holmes) 56:145
Old School Ties (Trevor) 71:345
Old Shirts and New Skins (Alexie) 96:2, 4, 8, 11
"Old Siam" (McCartney) 35:286-87
Old Snow Just Melting (Bell) 31:51
"Old Soldier" (Simpson) 7:426
"Old Soldiers" (Brown) 73:24
Old Soldiers (Bailey) 45:45-7
"Old Song" (Livesay) 79:340, 351
"Old Song" (Scott) 22:373-74
"Old Song" (Voznesensky) 57:427
"The Old Song and Dance" (Rexroth) 49:289
"Old Souls" (Giles) 39:64-6
"An Old Story" (Kelman) 58:298-99
An Old Story about Travellers (Costantini)
See *Una vieja historia de caminantes*
"The Old System" (Bellow) 6:53; 33:71
"Old Tale" (Sorrentino) 40:386
Old Tales of Old Castile (Delibes)
See *Viejas historias de castilla la vieja*
The Old Testament (Asimov)
See *Asimov's Guide to the Bible, Volume I: The Old Testament*
"Old Things" (Dunn) 40:168
"Old Things" (Mason) 28:273-74; 82:242
"An Old Time Indian Attack" (Silko) 74:328
"Old Time Rock and Roll" (Seger) 35:384
Old Times (*Odd Man Out*) (Pinter) 3:387-88; 6:415-19; 9:420-21; 11:444; 15:423-24; 27:394-95; 58:374, 376, 384; 73:276
"Old Town" 75:70
"Old Voices" (Norris) 14:387
"Old Walt" (Hughes) 108:333
The Old Ways (Snyder) 32:394, 399
"The Old White Man" (Redgrove) 41:348
"Old Whitey" (Van Doren) 10:495
"An Old Whorehouse" (Oliver) 98:256
"Old Wildwood" (Goyen) 40:217
The Old Wives' Fairy Tale Book (Carter) 76:329
"An Old Woman" (Sitwell) 67:320, 335
"Old Woman" (Smith) 64:388-89, 393-94, 398
"An Old Woman and Her Cat" (Lessing) 94:261
The Old Woman and the Cow (Anand) 23:13, 17
"The Old Woman and the Mayflowers" (Purdy) 50:245
"An Old Woman Asked Me..." (Lopate) 29:302
The Old Woman Broods (Rozewicz) 9:463
"The Old Woman of Portrush" (Simmons) 43:414
"An Old Woman of the Roads" (Colum) 28:90
"Old Woman on Yonge Street" (Souster) 14:504
"Old Woman with Flowers" (Smith) 64:393
"Old Words" (Sanchez) 116:272, 279-80
The Olden Days Coat (Laurence) 50:314
"Older Sister" (Simon) 26:408-09
The Oldest Confession (Condon) 4:105-07; 6:115; 45:95-6; 100:91, 93, 110-11, 113
The Oldest Killed Lake in North America (Carruth) 84:136
Oldest Living Confederate Widow Tells All (Gurganus) 70:190, 195-96
"The Oldest Man" (Fisher) 87:124
The Oldest Man, and Other Timeless Stories (Kotzwinkle) 35:254
"Oldfashioned" (McGahern) 48:273
"Old-Fashioned Chords" (Johnston) 51:240
An Old-Fashioned Darling (Simmons) 57:405
"An Old-Fashioned Story" (Colwin) 84:146
"Old-Time Childhood in Kentucky" (Warren) 39:265

"Olduvai and All That" (Connell) 45:114
Ole Doc Methuselah (Hubbard) 43:204
Oleanna (Mamet) 91:147-50
Olen'i shalashovka (*The Love Girl and the Innocent*) (Solzhenitsyn) 10:479
"Oleo: Demon Briefs and Dopey Ditties" (Kesey) 46:227-28
Olinger Stories: A Selection (Updike) 15:543; 23:473
"The Olive Garden" (Gordon) 13:246; 29:188-90
The Olive of Minerva; or, The Comedy of a Cuckold (Dahlberg) 7:71
The Olive Tree, and Other Essays (Huxley) 11:286
"Oliver Plunkett" (Longley) 29:296
"Oliver's Army" (Costello) 21:71
Oliver's Story (Segal) 10:466-67
"Olivia" (Rich) 76:213
"Olivia" (Salinas)
See "Poem for Olivia"
Ölmez otu (*The Undying Grass*) (Kemal) 14:300-301
Los olvidados (*The Young and the Damned*) (Bunuel) 16:131-33, 143, 146-47, 149; 80:19-22, 27, 30-1, 38, 47, 51
Olympiad (*Olympic Games*) (Riefenstahl) 16:521-22, 525-26
"The Olympian" (Dickey) 109:246
The Olympian (Glanville) 6:202
The Olympians (Priestley) 34:362, 364
Olympic Games (Riefenstahl)
See *Olympiad*
"The Olympic Girl" (Betjeman) 43:41
"Om pseudonumerog Gengaedelsens veje" (Dinesen) 95:68
Omaenimo tsumi ga aru (*You, Too Are Guilty*) (Abe) 81:294
"Omagh Hospital" (Montague) 46:269
"Gli Ombra" ("The Ombras") (Ortese) 89:198
"The Ombras" (Ortese)
See "Gli Ombra"
"Omega" (Tolson) 105:247, 253, 274, 284-85
"Omegaman" (Police, The) 26:365
"Omen" (Avison) 97:111
"Omen" (Hirsch) 50:195-96, 198-99
Omensetter's Luck (Gass) 1:114; 2:154-55; 8:240-42, 245-46; 11:224-25; 15:255, 257; 39:478, 482
Omeros (Walcott) 67:361-68; 76:288, 296-98
"Omicron" (Tolson) 105:242, 274
Ommateum with Doxology (Ammons) 2:12-13; 5:25-6, 28; 8:17; 25:41; 57:53-4; 108:5, 12, 14, 26, 46, 60
The Omni-Americans: New Perspectives on Black Experience and American Culture (Murray) 73:218-21, 230, 235-41
"Omnibus" ("Busride") (Cortazar) 34:332
Omnivore (Anthony) 35:40
"Omo" (Thomas) 107:316-18
"On?" (Avison) 97:112
"On a Beach in Southern Connecticut" (Klappert) 57:257
"On a Bicycle" (Yevtushenko) 1:382
"On a Book Entitled *Lolita*" (Nabokov) 64:344, 365
"On a Bust of an Army Corporal Killed ... in the Boer War" (Coles) 46:108
"On a Certain Engagement South of Seoul" (Carruth) 4:93
"On a Child Who Lived One Minute"

(Kennedy) 42:257

On a Dark Night (The Vintage) (West) 50:360

On a Darkling Plain (Saro-Wiwa) 114:258, 267, 275

On a Darkling Plain (Stegner) 49:346-47; 81:352

On a Deserted Shore (Raine) 7:353; 45:341

"On a Field Trip at Fredericksburg" (Smith) 42:353

"On a Line from Julian" (Kizer) 80:179

"On a Line from Sophocles" (Kizer) 80:179

On a mangé la dune (Maillet) 54:305-06

"On a Morning Full of Sun" (Appleman) 51:15

"On a Painting by Patient B of the Independence State Hospital for the Insane" (Justice) 102:261

On a Pale Horse (Anthony) 35:39-41

"On a Photo of Sgt. Ciardi a Year Later" (Ciardi) 40:157, 161; 44:381

"On a Picture by Dürer" (Blunden) 56:30

"On a Picture of Ezra Pound" (Carruth) 84:127

"On a Pig's Head" (Tomlinson) - 45:401

"On a Portrait of a Scholar" (Winters) 32:470

"On a Question Preliminary to Any Possible Treatment of Psychosis" (Lacan) 75:288, 293

"On a Raised Beach" (MacDiarmid) 4:312; 11:338; 19:287; 63:242, 244-46, 249

"On a Small Steamboat" (Ding Ling)
  See "Xiaohuolun shang"

"On a Son Returned to New Zealand" (Adcock) 41:14

"On a Streetcar Named Success" (Williams) 45:445

"On a Train to Rome" (Farrell) 8:205; 66:129

"On A Wagon" (Singer) 6:509

"On a Winded Civilization" (Cioran) 64:76, 78, 82, 96

"On Angels" (Barthelme) 115:71

"On Angels" (Milosz) 82:296, 302

"On Balance" (Brunner) 8:109

On Bear's Head (Whalen) 6:565-66; 29:445-46

"On Beauty" (Koch) 44:249

On Becoming a Novelist (Gardner) 34:548-49

"On Becoming a Writer" (Ellison) 86:328; 114:109-10

"On Being an Intellectual" (McAuley) 45:253

"On Being Asked to Write a Poem Against the War in Vietnam" (Carruth) 7:41

"On Being Asked What It's Like to Be Black" (Giovanni) 64:183

"On Being Blue" (Gass) 39:477

On Being Blue: A Philosophical Inquiry (Gass) 8:246-47; 11:224; 15:256, 258; 39:478

"On Being Busted at Fifty" (Fiedler) 13:212

"On Being Shot Again" (Hemingway) 34:478

"On Being Twenty-Six" (Larkin) 64:258, 260

"On Being Wrong: Convicted Minimalist Spills Beans" (Barthelme) 117:9

On Boxing (Oates) 52:333-35; 108:362-63, 365-67, 374

"On Breaking the Forms" (Wain) 11:563

On Call: New Political Essays (Jordan) 114:152-53, 162

"On Charon's Warf" (Dubus) 97:233

"On Chesterton" (Borges) 48:46

"On Circe's Island" (Simmons) 43:410

"On Credo ut Intelligam" (Bronk) 10:74

On Crime Writing (Macdonald) 41:269

"On Criticism in General" (Pound) 10:402

On Darkening Green (Charyn) 5:104

"On Deck" (Plath) 111:166

On Difficulty, and Other Essays (Steiner) 24:435, 437

"On Discovering Who We Are" (MacLennan) 92:306, 341

On Distant Ground (Butler) 81:121, 127

On Drink (Amis) 3:9; 5:22

"On Dry Land" (Motion) 47:294

"On Each Journey" (Merwin) 88:193

"On Each Other's Time" (Gilliatt) 53:146

On Early Trains (Pasternak)
  See *Na rannikh poezdakh*

"On Earth" (Broumas) 73:17

"On Edge of Time Future" (Okri) 87:324

On est toujours trop bon avec les femmes (We Always Treat Women Too Well) (Queneau) 42:332-33, 335

"On Fairy Stories" (Tolkien) 3:481; 12:573, 581; 38:440, 442-43

"On Falling Asleep by Firelight" (Meredith) 13:375; 22:301

"On Falling Asleep to Bird Song" (Meredith) 13:375

"On Finding a Bird's Bones in the Woods" (Mueller) 51:279

On First Looking Down from Lions Gate Bridge (Suknaski) 19:432

"On Flower Wreath Hill" (Rexroth) 49:276, 286; 112:402-04

"On Flying to a Political Convention" (Ciardi) 40:157

"On for the Long Haul" (Boyle) 90:46

"On F.R. Leavis and D.H. Lawrence" (Rahv) 24:355

"On Freedom" (Ignatow) 40:259

"On Freedom of Expression" (Warner) 45:433

"On Freedom's Ground" (Wilbur) 53:409, 411; 110:356, 361, 384

"On Gay Wallpaper" (Williams) 42:462

On Glory's Course (Purdy) 52:345-48

On Going to Bed (Burgess) 40:119

"On Goodbye" (Avison) 97:116

On Grammatology (Derrida)
  See *De la grammatologie*

On Grief and Reason (Brodsky) 100:61-5, 68-70, 73

"On Guard" (Waugh) 27:477

On Guerrilla Warfare (Guevara)
  See *La guerra de guerrillas*

"On Handling Some Small Shells from the Windward Islands" (Swenson) 4:532-34

"On Hearing a Recording of Marianne Moore" (Cabral de Melo Neto)
  See "Ouvindo Marianne Moore em disco"

"On Hearing Russian Spoken" (Davie) 10:125; 31:109

"On Hearing the Airlines Will Use a Psychological Profile to Catch Potential Skyjackers" (Dunn) 36:152

On Her Majesty's Secret Service (Fleming) 30:143, 149

On Heroes and Tombs (Sabato)
  See *Sobre héroes y tumbas*

"On Heroic Leadership and the Dilemma of Strong Men and Weak People" (Schlesinger) 84:356

"On Highgate Hill" (Hope) 52:209

"On His Back under the Night" (Cortazar)
  See "La noche boca arriba"

"On His Own Face in a Glass" (Pound) 112:330

"On His Sixty-Fifth Birthday" (Fuller) 28:157

"On Hypotheses in 'Historical Criticism'" (Crane) 27:74

"On Ibrahim Balaban's 'Spring Picture'"

(Hikmet) 40:249

On Ice (Gelber) 79:217, 223-24

On Ice (Ingalls) 42:233-35

"On 'Identity'" (Roethke) 101:291, 328-29, 331

"On Inhabiting an Orange" (Miles) 14:368

"On Initiation Rites and Power: Ralph Ellison Speaks at West Point" (Ellison) 114:109

"On Its Way" (Swenson) 61:396

"On John Donne" (Merwin) 45:268

On Keeping Women (Calisher) 38:73

"On Knowing Nothing" (Smith) 15:514

On Learning to Read: The Child's Fascination with Meaning (Bettelheim) 79:132-33

"On Leaving Norway, from a Mission, without a Penny" (Kunene) 85:176

"On Leaving Wantage, 1972" (Betjeman) 10:53; 43:48

On Lies, Secrets, and Silence: Selected Prose, 1966-1978 (Rich) 18:447-48; 73:319, 321-22; 76:215, 219

"On Listening: A Good Way to Hear" (Jordan) 23:256

"On Living in Aztlán" (Zamora) 89:361, 386

"On Looking Into Henry Moore" (Livesay) 79:342, 346

"On Looking Up by Chance at the Constellations" (Frost) 3:175; 26:118

"On Magical Thinking" 75:63

"On Making Certain Anything Has Happened" (Frost) 26:118

"On Medicine and Literature" (Coles) 108:192

"On Minding One's Own Business" (Wright) 28:463

On Modern Marriage, and Other Observations (Dinesen) 95:60

On Moral Fiction (Gardner) 10:222-23; 18:176-77, 179, 180-81, 183-84; 28:161-66; 34:548-49

"On Moral Leadership as a Political Dilemma" (Jordan) 114:146

On Mozart: A Paean for Wolfgang (Burgess)
  See *Mozart and the Wolf Gang*

"On My Birthday" (Amichai) 116:95, 99

"On My Father" (Faludy) 42:138

"On My Life" (Cliff) 21:60

On My Master Döblin (Grass)
  See *Über Mein Lehrer Döblin*

"On My Own Work" (Wilbur) 14:577

"On My Way Out I Passed over You and the Verrazano Bridge" (Lorde) 71:258-59

On Native Grounds (Kazin) 34:556-57, 561; 38:269-75, 279-80

"On Not Being a Jew" (Updike) 43:431

"On Not Being Banned by the Nazis" (Acorn) 15:10

"On Not Being Milton" (Harrison) 43:177, 180

"On Not Saying Everything" (Day Lewis) 10:131

"On Open Form" (Merwin) 88:193

"On Pasternak Soberly" (Milosz) 82:292

On Photography (Sontag) 10:484-87; 13:515, 518; 31:411-13, 417-18; 105:206, 208, 215, 226

"On Poetry" (Dudek) 11:160

On Poetry and Poets (Eliot) 24:171-72, 177-78; 113:194

On Poets and Others (Paz) 51:331-32

"On Poets and Poetry" (Olson) 11:415

"On Prayer" (Milosz) 56:248

On purge bébé (Renoir) 20:309

"On Quicksand Creek" (Still) 49:366

"On Quitting a Little College" (Stafford) 29:379

On Racine (Barthes)
See *Sur Racine*

On Radio Waves (Seifert)
See *Na vlnách T. S. F.*

"On Raglan Road" (Kavanagh) 22:243

"On Reading Dickens" (Warner) 45:434

"On Reading John Cage" (Paz) 51:333

"On Reading That the Rebuilding of Ypres Approached Completion" (Blunden) 56:43

"On Reading 'The Country of the Pointed Firs'" (Garrigue) 8:239

"On Reading to Oneself" (Gass) 39:478, 481

"On Realising He Has Written Some Bad Poems" (Purdy) 50:246

"On Receiving a Postcard from Japan" (Van Duyn) 63:445

"On Renoir's 'The Grape Pickers'" (Boland) 40:100-01; 113:108

"On Returning to Teach" (Bell) 8:66

On Revolution (Arendt) 98:11, 22-5, 39, 48, 51

"On Saturday Afternoon" (Sillitoe) 57:388

On Seduction (Baudrillard)
See *De la séduction*

"On Seeing Diana go Maddddddddd" (Madhubuti) 73:213

"On Seeing Larry River's *Washington Crossing the Delaware* at the Museum of Modern Art" (O'Hara) 78:352

"On Seeing 'The Day of the Dolphin'" (Livesay) 79:332, 348

"On Self-Respect" (Didion) 8:177; 14:155

"On Sickness" (Cioran) 64:88

"On Social Plays" (Miller) 47:251

On Socialist Realism (Sinyavsky) 8:488

"On Some Lines of Virgil" (Davenport) 38:145, 148

"On Squaw Peak" (Hass) 99:139, 142

On Stage (Tomlin) 17:522-23

"On Style" (Sontag) 105:201, 226

"On Sunday Walks" (Fuller) 62:193

"On Talking to Oneself" (Gass) 39:478, 481

"On Tearing up a Cynical Poem" (Blunden) 56:51

"On That Century" (Milosz) 56:232

"On the Air" (Jong) 6:269

"On the Air" (Roth) 2:379

"On the Appian Way" (Farrell) 8:205

"On the Beach" (Abse) 7:1

"On the Beach" (Young) 17:576

On the Beach (Shute) 30:369-74

On the Beach (Young) 17:573-74, 576, 582

"On the Beach at Forte Dei Marmi" (Barker) 8:47

On the Bearpaw Sea (Purdy) 14:432

"On the Bestial Floor" (Merwin) 45:269

"On the Birth of a Black/Baby/Boy" (Knight) 40:286

"On the Birth of Bomani" (Clifton) 66:77

"On the Birth of Good and Evil during the Long Winter of '28" (Levine) 14:319

On the Black Hill (Chatwin) 28:73-5; 57:139, 141-42, 146, 148, 150; 59:274-75,278

"On the Blue Water" (Hemingway) 34:478

"On the Body Politic" (Boyle) 58:75

On the Brink of Reason (Krleza)
See *Na rubu pameti*

"On the Calculus" (Cunningham) 31:97-8

"On the Cobb at Lyme Regis" (Beer) 58:36

On the Contrary (Brink) 106:130, 132-33, 137

On the Contrary (McCarthy) 14:357; 24:343; 39:489; 59:292

On the Contrary (McGinley) 14:365

"On the Death of a Child" (Enright) 31:155

"On the Death of a Murderer" (Wain) 11:563

"On the Death of Friends in Childhood" (Justice) 102:261, 268

"On the Death of Ghandi" (Scott) 22:377

"On the Death of May Street" (MacBeth) 5:265

"On the Death of My Father" (Kherdian) 6:280

On the Death of My Father, and Other Poems (Kherdian) 6:280; 9:317

"On the Death of Senator James Walsh" (Winters) 32:468

"On the Death of Shukskin" (Voznesensky) 57:421

"On the Death of W. B. Yeats" (Hope) 51:217

On the Decay of Humanism (Spackman) 46:380

"On the Decipherment of Linear B" (Purdy) 6:428

"On the Deck" (Barthelme) 59:251

"On the Decline of Oracles" (Plath) 9:422

"On the Demo, London, 1968" (McCarthy) 39:485

"On the Disposal of My Body" (Disch) 36:127

"On the Dressing Gown Lent Me by My Hostess the Brazilian Counsul in Milan, 1958" (Smith) 25:422

"On the Edge" (Levine) 5:251

"On the Edge" (Lorde) 71:257

On the Edge (Koch) 44:250

On the Edge (Levine) 4:287; 5:251; 14:316; 33:275

"On the Edge of Darkness: What Is Political Poetry?" (Levertov) 66:239

On the Edge of Reason (Krleza)
See *Na rubu pameti*

On the Edge of Reason (Krleza)
See *Na rubu pameti*

"On the Edge of the Cliff" (Pritchett) 15:442, 444; 41:334

On the Edge of the Cliff, and Other Stories (Pritchett) 15:443-44; 41:330

"On the Edge of the Desert" (Swan) 69:355-56, 359, 362

On the Edge of the Desert (Swan) 69:359, 363-64

"On the Edge of the Woods" (Gardner) 18:178

"On the Eve of a Birthday" (Steele) 45:365-66

"On the Eve of the Next Revolution" (Swan) 69:358, 360-63

"On the Eyes of an SS Officer" (Wilbur) 110:362, 381

"On the Far Edge of Kilmer" (Stern) 40:413

"On the Ferry across Chesapeake Bay" (Bly) 5:61

"On the Ferry from Suduroy to Torshavn" (Johnston) 51:253

"On the Fragility of the Mind" (Eberhart) 56:83

On the Frontier (Auden) 1:9; 11:17

On the Frontier ... (Isherwood) 44:396, 399

"On the Function of the Novel" (Farrell) 66:137

"On the Ganges greenest isle" (Seth) 90:353

"On the Geneology of Ethics: An Overview of Work in Progress" (Foucault) 34:343-44

On the Golden Porch (Tolstaya) 59:370-01, 385

On the Great Water Divide
See *La cumpana apelor*

"On the Hall at Stowey" (Tomlinson) 45:393

"On the Heart's Beginning to Cloud the Mind" (Frost) 9:228; 34:475

On the High Wire (Arrabal)
See *En la cuerda floja*

On the Highest Hill (Haig-Brown) 21:136, 141

"On the Home Front—1942" (Denby) 48:85

"On the Human Condition" (Boyle) 58:75

On the Inside (Murphy) 51:303, 305

"On the Island" (Jacobsen) 48:192

On the Island (Jacobsen) 102:241-42

"On the Lake" (Douglas) 73:94

"On the Last Afternoon" (Tiptree) 48:389, 396; 50:357

On the Ledge (Simpson) 32:380

"On the Life That Waits" (Lieberman) 36:262, 264

On the Limits of Poetry: Selected Essays, 1928-1948 (Tate) 24:441

On the Line (Swados) 5:420, 423

"On the Magellanic Clouds" (Wakoski)
See "George Washington Meets the King of Spain"

"On the Margin" (Burgess) 4:82

On the Margin (Huxley) 3:256; 5:192

"On the Materialist Dialectic" (Althusser) 106:23

On the Motion and Immobility of Douve (Bonnefoy)
See *Du mouvement et de l'immobilité de Douve*

"On the Mountain" (Gellhorn) 60:188-89, 192

"On the Move" (Gunn) 32:207; 81:185

"On the Murder of Lieutenant José Del Castillo by the Falangist Bravo Martinez, July 12, 1936" (Levine) 9:333; 14:318

"On the Nature and Use of This Book" (Davies) 75:182

On the Night of the Seventh Moon (Hibbert) 7:155

"On the Ocean Floor" (MacDiarmid) 63:255

"On the Old Way" (Merwin) 88:210-11

"On the Open Side" (Fisher) 25:159

"On the Orthodoxy and Creed of My Power Mower" (Ciardi) 44:383

"On the Other Side" (Milosz) 56:237

On the Outside (Murphy) 51:303, 305

On the Outskirts (Frayn) 31:189; 47:135

On the Perimeter (Blackwood) 100:4-9, 11-12, 27

"On the Perpetuum Mobile" (Raine) 32:351; 103:180

"On the Persistence of Pastoral" (Fussell) 74:129

"On the Philosophical Bases of the Humanities" (Bakhtin) 83:13

"On the Photographs of Ansel Adams" (Salinas) 90:332

"On the Platform" (Nemerov) 2:308

"On the Pleasures of Formal Poetry" (Bogan) 93:78

On the Poet and His Craft: Selected Prose (Roethke) 1:292

"On the Poet as a Marionette" (Ciardi) 10:107

"On the Porch" (Johnston) 51:245

On the Prejudices, Predilections, and Firm Beliefs of William Faulkner (Firm Beliefs of William Faulkner) (Brooks) 86:278, 284-85, 287

"On the Quai at Smyrna" (Hemingway)　**30**:189

On the Radio Waves (Seifert)
　See *Na vlnách T. S. F.*

"On the Railway Platform" (Fuller)　**4**:178

"On the Rainy River" (O'Brien)　**103**:139

On the Razzle (Stoppard)　**29**:398, 402

"On the Rebound" (Purdy)　**52**:350

"On the Republic" (Elytis)　**49**:108

On the Rim of the Curve (Cook)　**58**:154

On the River Baidamtal (Aitmatov)
　See *Na reke Baidamtal*

"On the River Styx" (Matthiessen)　**64**:322-23, 325

On the River Styx, and Other Stories (Matthiessen)　**64**:321-22, 324-25, 327

"On the Rivershore" (Tilghman)　**65**:107-08, 110-12

"On the Road" (Adams)　**65**:348

"On the Road" (Didion)　**14**:153

"On the Road" (Heaney)　**74**:169, 197

"On the Road" (Richler)　**46**:352

On the Road (Kerouac)　**1**:165-67; **2**:226-29; **3**:265-66; **5**:212-15; **14**:303-07; **29**:271-74, 276-78; **61**:278-315

On the Road: A Search for American Character (Smith)　**86**:266

On the Road Again (McFadden)　**48**:247-48, 251, 255

"On the Screaming of the Gulls" (Redgrove)　**41**:353

"On the Self-Evident" (Grass)　**49**:139

On the Shore of the Dead Sea (Endo)　**99**:285, 287

"On the Skeleton of a Hound" (Wright)　**28**:462

"On the Square and Across the River" (Aksyonov)　**101**:11, 19-20

On the Staircase (Swinnerton)　**31**:423

"On the Staten Island Ferry" (Kenny)　**87**:259

"On the Steps of the Conservatory" (Barthelme)　**13**:61

"On the Subway" (Olds)　**85**:293, 298

"On the Teaching of Modern Literature" (Trilling)　**11**:546; **24**:460

"On the Tennis Court at Night" (Kinnell)　**29**:284-85

"On the Threshold of His Greatness, the Poet Comes Down with a Sore Throat" (Nemerov)　**36**:301

"On the Time When the Surrealists Were Right" (Breton)　**54**:16

"On the Turmoil of Many Religions" (Milosz)　**56**:232

"On the Via Margritta" (Connell)　**45**:110

"On the Wagon" (Mitchell)　**98**:157

On the Wasteland (Arthur)　**12**:27-9

On the Waterfront (Kazan)　**16**:362-74; **63**:222, 224, 226-29, 232-35

On the Waterfront (Schulberg)　**7**:403; **48**:346-47, 351

"On the Waves" (Brodkey)　**56**:64

On the Waves of Wireless Telegraphy (Seifert)
　See *Na vlnách T. S. F.*

"On the Way" (McCartney)　**35**:287-88

"On the Way" (Wiebe)　**11**:568

"On the Way to Lycomedes of Scyrus" (Brodsky)
　See "K Likomedu, na Skiros"

"On the Way to School" (Aleixandre)　**36**:29

On the Way to the Sky (Diamond)　**30**:114

"On the Wild Side" (Coles)　**67**:177-78

On the Wire (Arrabal)
　See *En la cuerda floja*

"On the Yankee Station" (Boyd)　**28**:38

On the Yankee Station (Boyd)　**28**:38-9; **53**:52

"On the Year of Many Conversions Etc." (Ciardi)　**40**:157

"On the Zattere" (Trevor)　**71**:329, 333

On This Island (Auden)
　See "Look, Stranger, on This Island Now"

"On This Short Day of Frost and Sun" (Kumin)　**28**:224

On This Side Nothing (Comfort)　**7**:53

"On Those Islands (A Poem for Hector MacIver)" (MacNeice)　**53**:231, 235

On Tour (Streatfeild)　**21**:408

"On Trains" (McPherson)　**77**:361, 364, 366

"On Translating 'Eugene Onegin'" (Nabokov)　**6**:359

On Trial (Rice)　**7**:358, 363; **49**:291-92, 294, 300-02, 304

On Troublesome Creek (Still)　**49**:364, 366-67, 369

"On Tyranny" (Brodsky)　**50**:132

"On Understanding" (Rao)　**56**:306

"On Universalism" (Knight)　**40**:279, 284

"On Utilitarianism" (Bell)　**8**:66

"On Vacation" (Creeley)　**78**:140

On Valentine's Day (Foote)　**51**:134-36

On Violence (Arendt)　**98**:12

"On Watching a World Series Game" (Sanchez)　**116**:295

"On Which Side of the Curtain?" (Alegria)
　See "A què lado de la cortina?"

On Wings of Song (Disch)　**36**:124-25

"On Writers and Writing" (Boyle)　**58**:75

"On Writing" (Carver)　**36**:99; **53**:66-7

"On Writing" (Hemingway)　**10**:269; **30**:194, 198

"On Writing" (Welty)　**14**:565, 567

On Writing and Politics, 1967-1983 (Grass)　**49**:136-38

"On Your Feet" (Tchicaya)
　See "Debout"

"On Your Own" (Gallagher)　**18**:170

"Once" (Celan)　**82**:46

"Once" (Thomas)　**6**:530

Once (Walker)　**6**:553; **9**:558; **58**:405, 408-09; **103**:356, 364-65, 405

"Once a Great Love" (Amichai)　**22**:33; **57**:37

Once a Greek... (Durrenmatt)
　See *Grieche sucht Griechin*

Once and for All: Poems for William Bronk (Corman)　**9**:170

The Once and Future King (White)　**30**:445-52

Once Bitten, Twice Bitten: Poems (Porter)　**33**:317-18, 322, 324

"Once by the Pacific" (Frost)　**15**:241, 250; **26**:121, 124

"Once High upon a Hill" (Birney)　**11**:51

"Once in a Lifetime" (Byrne)　**26**:98-9

Once in a Lifetime (Hart and Kaufman)　**38**:258, 265; **66**:175-78, 180-86, 188, 190-91

"Once in a Lifetime, Snow" (Murray)　**40**:334

"Once in May" (Levine)　**14**:318

Once Is Enough (Sargeson)　**31**:368-69

Once Is Not Enough (Susann)　**3**:476

"Once More" (Carruth)　**84**:132

Once More the Sea (Arenas)
　See *Otra vez el mar*

"Once More to the Lake" (White)　**10**:529; **34**:431; **39**:380

Once More upon a Totem (Harris)　**12**:263, 266-67

"Once More with Feeling" (Kristofferson)　**26**:270

"Once More with Feeling" (Williams)　**42**:443-44

"Once on a Hill" (Blunden)　**56**:47

"Once, Rocking on the Edge" (Akhmadulina)
　See "Odnazhdy, pokanuvshis' na kraiu"

Once There Was a War (Steinbeck)　**45**:382

Once upon a Droshky (Charyn)　**5**:104

"Once upon a Picnic Ground" (Wagoner)　**3**:508

"Once Upon a Time" (Gordimer)　**70**:178

Once upon a Time (Dreyer)　**16**:260-62

Once upon a Totem (Harris)　**12**:261, 265, 267

"Den onda ängeln" ("The Evil Angel") (Lagerkvist)　**54**:286

Onda sagor (*Evil Sagas*; *Evil Tales*) (Lagerkvist)　**54**:274, 286

"Ondine" (Barnard)　**48**:25-6

"1" (Cummings)　**15**:161-62

"1" (Donnell)
　See "Positions"

"one" (Shange)　**25**:402

One (Kinsella)　**19**:253-54

"The One About Coyote Going West" (King)　**89**:101

One Across, Two Down (Rendell)　**28**:383; **48**:322

"One Afternoon in 1939" (Brautigan)　**12**:70

One against Another (Adamov)
　See *Tous contre tous*

One against the Legion (Williamson)　**29**:455, 460

"One against Thebes" ("The Dragon's Teeth") (Gordon)　**29**:188-90; **83**:258

One A.M. (Chaplin)　**16**:204

"One A.M. with Voices" (Kennedy)　**42**:257

One and Last Love (Braine)　**41**:60-2

"The One and the Universe" (Sabato)
　See *Uno y el universo*

"One Arab Flute" (MacEwen)　**55**:163

"One Arm" (Kawabata)
　See "Kata Ucle"

"One Arm" (Williams)　**15**:579-80; **45**:447, 453, 456

One Arm (Wilson)　**7**:547

One Arm, and Other Stories (Williams)　**15**:579; **45**:447; **71**:366, 373

"One Art" (Bishop)　**9**:98; **15**:60; **32**:36, 39, 44

"One Blink of the Moon" (Aldiss)　**14**:15

"One Body: Some Notes on Form" (Hass)　**39**:149; **99**:145

One by One (Gilliatt)　**2**:160; **53**:142-43

"One Child of One's Own" (Walker)　**103**:357

"One Chooses a Language" (Ghose)　**42**:178

One Christmas (Capote)　**38**:87

"One Christmas Knitting" (Jolley)　**46**:220

One Clear Call (Sinclair)　**63**:356-57

"One Crowded Hour of Glorious Strife" (McGinley)　**14**:367

One Damn Thing after Another (Garner)　**13**:235-36

"One Day" (Goldemberg)　**52**:165

"One Day" (Lennon)　**35**:266

"One Day" (Sapphire)　**99**:82

One Day (Morris)　**1**:233; **37**:311-12

The One Day: A Poem in Three Parts (Hall)　**59**:151-57

"One Day After Saturday" (Garcia Marquez)　**27**:147, 154; **47**:146, 150-51

One Day at a Time (Lear)　**12**:334

"One Day in Spring" (Sitwell)　**67**:319

One Day in the Afternoon of the World (Saroyan)　**1**:301

One Day in the Life of Ivan Denisovich

(Solzhenitsyn)
  See *Odin den' Ivana Denisovicha*
"One Day in Wall Street" (Ferber) **93**:162
"One Day of Happiness" (Singer) **69**:309
One Day of the Life (Argueta)
  See *Un dia en la vida*
One Day When I Was Lost (Baldwin) **3**:32;
  17:38-9
One Deadly Summer (Japrisot)
  See *L'ete meurtrier*
"The One Desire" (Muldoon) **72**:267
One Dozen Roses (Robinson) **21**:343
*One Earth, Four or Five Worlds: Reflections on
  Contemporary History* (Paz) **51**:327-28,
  330
"One Evening" (Lavin) **99**:322
One Eye and a Measuring Rod (L'Heureux)
  52:274
"One Fair Daughter and No More" (O'Faolain)
  32:341
One Fat Englishman (Amis) **1**:6; **2**:8-10; **3**:9;
  5:21-2
One Fat Summer (Lipsyte) **21**:212
*One Fell Soup; or, I'm Just a Bug on the Wind-
  shield of Life* (Blount) **38**:46-8
One Fine Day (Bennett) **77**:86-7
One Flew over the Cuckoo's Nest (Kesey) **1**:167;
  3:266-68; **6**:277-79; **11**:314, 316-18;
  46:224, 226, 228-29; **64**:206-44
One Foot in the Grave (Dickinson) **35**:132
One for My Baby (Bessie) **23**:61-2
One for the Pot (Cooney) **62**:144
One for the Road (Davics) **21**:106
One for the Road (Pinter)
  See *Other Places*
One for the Road (Russell) **60**:319, 322
One for the Rose (Levine) **33**:272-75
"One Friday Morning" (Hughes) **35**:215;
  108:285
One Generation After (Wiesel) **37**:450
"The One Girl at the Boys' Party" (Olds)
  39:189; **85**:289
"One Good Story, That One" (King) **89**:77-8,
  98, 101
One Good Story, That One (King) **89**:98-9,
  101
*One Half of Robertson Davies: Provocative
  Pronouncements on a Wide Range of Top-
  ics* (Davies) **13**:174; **25**:131-32; **75**:184;
  91:204
One Hand Clapping (Burgess) **4**:81; **22**:74;
  40:115-16; **81**:301; **94**:41
"One Hard Look" (Graves) **45**:166-67
One Hell of an Actor (Kanin) **22**:232
"One Holy Night" (Cisneros) **69**:153
One Hundred and One Poems (Arghezi) **80**:10
"100 Dollars and Nothing!" (Cooper) **56**:70
"The 184th Demonstration" (Piercy) **27**:374
The 158-Pound Marriage (Irving) **13**:293;
  23:244-45; **38**:250; **112**:155-57, 159, 165
One Hundred Love Sonnets (Neruda)
  See *Cien sonetos de amor*
One Hundred More Poems from the Japanese
  (Rexroth) **112**:393
One Hundred More Poems from the Japanese
  (Rexroth) **11**:474
"One Hundred Per Cent" (Ferber) **93**:139
100%: The Story of a Patriot (Sinclair) **15**:502;
  63:346, 348
One Hundred Poems (Slessor) **14**:495
One Hundred Poems from the Chinese
  (Rexroth) **112**:370, 386, 392
One Hundred Poems from the Japanese

  (Rexroth) **11**:474; **112**:392
"107 Poems" (Fisher) **25**:159
"$106,000 Blood Money" (Hammett) **47**:161
110 Coca-Cola Bottles (Warhol) **20**:418
"110 West Sixty-First Street" (Barthelme)
  46:35
The 120 Days of Sodoma (Pasolini)
  See *Salo: 120 Days of Sodom*
"125th Street and Abomey" (Lorde) **71**:232-
  33, 236
"One Hundred Years Ago" (Jagger and Richard)
  17:228, 232
"One Hundred Years of Proust" (Moss) **45**:287
One Hundred Years of Solitude (Garcia Marquez)
  See *Cien años de soledad*
One/ Interior/ Day (Harwood) **32**:225-26
One Is a Wanderer and Other Stories (King)
  53:212
"One Is One and All Alone" (Thomas) **13**:539;
  107:316-18
"One Life" (Motion) **47**:293-94
"One Life" (Rich) **73**:330
One Life (Rukeyser) **15**:457-58; **27**:411
One Life at a Time Please (Abbey) **59**:238,
  242
"One Life Furnished in Early Poverty" (Ellison)
  13:207
One Life to Live (Nixon) **21**:242-47
One Lonely Night (Spillane) **13**:526-28
One Long Poem (Harmon) **38**:243-44
"One Love" (Marley) **17**:269-70
"One Love/People Get Ready" (Marley)
  17:269
A One Man Protest (Ayckbourn) **74**:21
"One Man's Goose" (Starbuck) **53**:352
One Man's House (Ringwood) **48**:330, 335-
  36
"One Man's Hysteria—Real and Imagined—in
  the Twentieth Century" (Louie) **70**:80
One Man's Initiation—1917 (First Encounter)
  (Dos Passos) **15**:184; **25**:137-38, 143-
  44, 146; **82**:78, 83, 86, 107
One Man's Meat (White) **10**:527-29; **34**:430;
  39:370, 372-73, 377, 379
"One: Many" (Ammons) **25**:42; **57**:59
One Million Dead (Gironella)
  See *Un millón de muertos*
"One More Brevity" (Frost) **9**:228
"One More Day" (Milosz) **56**:250
One More July (Plimpton) **36**:355-56
"One More Kiss" (McCartney) **35**:281
One More Manhattan (McGinley) **14**:365
"One More Round" (Angelou) **35**:30
One More Sunday (MacDonald) **44**:407, 409
"One More Thing" (Carver) **22**:103
"One More Time" (Gordon) **29**:187-89;
  83:247
"One More Time" (Simon) **26**:407
"One More Way to Die" (Himes) **7**:159
"One Morning" (Steele) **45**:364
"One Morning in New Hampshire" (Swenson)
  106:321, 338
"One Must Have Willpower" (Guillen)
  See "Hay que tené boluntá"
One Nation (Stegner) **81**:349
"One Night" (Merwin) **88**:194
"One Night in Turin" (O'Faolain) **1**:259
One Night Stand (Gardner) **44**:210
One Night Stand, and Other Poems (Spicer)
  72:352, 363
One Night Stood: A Minimal Fiction
  (Kostelanetz) **28**:218
"One Night's Standing" (Kogawa) **78**:167

"One of Many Epilogs" (Pasolini)
  See "Uno dei tanti epiloghi"
"One of My Turns" (Pink Floyd) **35**:312
"One of Ours" (Boyle) **58**:66
"One of the Boys" (Dacey) **51**:80
One of the Children Is Crying (*The Grass Dies*)
  (Dowell) **60**:96, 98-9, 109
One of the Founders (Newby) **13**:408
"One of the Muses" (Davison) **28**:100
"One of the Muses" (Williams) **33**:447-48
"One of the Three Is Still Alive" (Calvino)
  33:99
"One of These Days" (Garcia Marquez) **27**:147;
  47:146
"One of These Days" (McCartney) **35**:287
"One of These Days" ("I'm Going to Cut You
  into Little Pieces") (Pink Floyd) **35**:306,
  311, 313
"One of Those Big-City Girls" (Carpenter)
  41:103
"One of Those Springs" (Seifert) **93**:337
"One of Us" (Fante) **60**:130
"One of Us Must Know (Sooner or Later)"
  (Dylan) **77**:174
"One Off the Short List" (Lessing) **22**:278
"1, 1/3, 1/3" (Brautigan) **12**:71
One or Another (Drexler) **2**:119-20
"One or Two" (Frost) **13**:230
"One or Two Things" (Oliver) **98**:259
"One Ordinary Day, with Peanuts" (Jackson)
  60:235
"One out of Many" (Naipaul) **4**:373; **13**:407;
  37:320; **105**:157
"One Owner, Low Mileage" (Hood) **28**:189
One Plus One (*Sympathy for the Devil*) (Godard)
  20:140-41, 150
"One Pocket" (Carpenter) **41**:107-08
One Police Plaza (Caunitz) **34**:35-7
"A One Pound Stein" (Williams) **5**:510
"One Quiet Afternoon" (Buckler) **13**:120
"One Rainy Night of Winter" (Ali)
  See "Mahavaton Ki Ek Raat"
"One Ran Before" (Winters) **32**:467
"1 September 1939" (Berryman) **62**:56, 71
"One Sided Shoot-Out" (Madhubuti) **73**:191,
  214
One Sings, the Other Doesn't (Varda)
  See *Une chant et l'autre pas*
"One Sister" (Jiles) **58**:278
"One XVI" (Cummings) **68**:26
One Size Fits All (Zappa) **17**:591
"One Slip-Slouch Twi" (Cummings) **15**:162
*One Small Candle: The Pilgrims' First Year in
  America* (Fleming) **37**:121
"The One Song" (Strand) **71**:285
"One Song Glory" ("Glory") **99**:162, 169,
  180, 187
"One Sort of Poet" (Smith) **15**:516
"One Spring Day" (Abse) **29**:15
One Step from Earth (Harrison) **42**:200
"One Step Towards Gomorrah" (Bachmann)
  See "Ein Schritt nach Gomorrah"
"One Summer" (Lavin) **4**:281; **99**:319, 322
"One Summer Morning" (Ihimaera) **46**:199
"One Sunday" (Mistry) **71**:270, 272
"One Sunday Afternoon" (Abse) **29**:20
"1. the supremes—cuz they dead" (Sanchez)
  116:294
One Thing and Another (Forbes) **12**:211
"One Thousand Cranes" (Purdy) **3**:408
"$1,000 a Week" (Farrell) **66**:129
$1,000 a Week, and Other Stories (Farrell)
  66:130

"One Thousand Fearful Words for Fidel Castro" (Ferlinghetti) 6:182
1001 Afternoons in Chicago (Hecht) 8:270
1003 (Hochwalder) 36:236-38
"1,000 Years (Life after God)" (Coupland) 85:36-7, 39
The 1,000-Year Plan (Asimov) 92:21
One Tiger to a Hill (Pollock) 50:226
One Time, One Place (Welty) 14:565; 22:459; 105:300, 324, 334
1x1 (Cummings) 8:158; 12:156; 15:162-63, 68:35, 48
"One Too Many Mornings" (Dylan) 77:172-73
One Touch of Venus (Kazan) 63:225
One Touch of Venus (Perelman) 44:500-01, 503
The One Tree (Donaldson) 46:141
One, Two, Buckle My Shoe (*The Patriotic Murders*) (Christie) 12:124; 48:71-2
One, Two, Three (Endo) 99:285
One, Two, Three (Wilder) 20:459-60
"One Volume Missing" (Dove) 50:157-58
"One Way Conversation" (Livesay) 79:349
"One Way Journey" (MacCaig) 36:285
One Way or Another (Cameron) 44:33-5
One Way or Another (Sciascia) 9:476
One Way Pendulum (Simpson) 29:366-70
One Way Street (Engel)
  See *Monodromos*
One Way Ticket (Hughes) 10:279; 35:214; 108:291
One Way Ticket (Levine) 54:292-93, 295, 297, 300
"One Way Ticket Home" (Ochs) 17:333
"One Way to Spell Man" (Stegner) 49:358-59
One Way to Spell Man (Stegner) 49:358-59
One Who Became Lost (Bowering) 32:46-7
"The One Who Thinks Alone" (Arghezi)
  See "Cel ce gîndeste singur"
"One Winter Morning by the Footbridge" (L'Heureux) 52:272
"The One with the Dog" (Kelman) 58:298, 300
One Wonderful Sunday (Kurosawa)
  See *Subarashiki nichiyobi*
"One World (Not Three)" (Police, The) 26:365-66
One Writer's Beginnings (Welty) 33:423-26; 105:316, 319, 321-23, 326, 334, 349, 359-62, 367, 369, 377-80, 382-84, 387-88
"One Year" (Olds) 85:306
"One Year Later" (Sagan) 36:382
One-Act Plays for Stage and Study (Rice) 7:358
"The One-Armed Crucifixion" (Durcan) 70:153
"One-Eye" (Merwin) 1:212
"One-Eye, Two-Eyes, Three-Eyes" (Sexton) 53:314
"The One-Eyed King" (Levine) 4:287
One-Eyed Moon Maps (Gunnars) 69:257-61
"The One-Horned Mountain Goat" (Harris) 12:265
"One-Legged Man" (Sassoon) 36:392
"The One-Legged Man" (Sexton) 4:483
One-Man Masque (Reaney) 13:475
"One-Night Homecoming" (Kennedy) 42:256
"One-Play Oscar" (Fante) 60:133
"One's a Heifer" (Ross) 13:492
"Onesided Dialog" (Jordan) 114:155
One-Trick Pony (Simon) 17:467-68
One-Woman Plays (Fo) 32:174

Oni srazhalis' za rodinu (*They Fought for Their Country*) (Sholokhov) 15:482-83
The Onion Eaters (Donleavy) 4:124-25; 6:139, 141; 10:154
The Onion Field (Wambaugh) 3:509
Onion John (Krumgold) 12:317-20
The Onion, Memory (Raine) 32:348-52; 103:179, 182, 186, 188-90, 197, 200
Onkel, Onkel (Grass) 15:260
Onliness (Smith) 42:346-47, 351
"Only a Few Left" (Madhubuti) 73:209
"Only a Hobo" (Dylan) 77:166
"Only among Walkers" (Padilla) 38:349
Only as Far as Brooklyn (Kenny) 87:241
"The Only Child" (Browne) 21:39
"Only Child" (Page) 7:291; 18:377
"An Only Child" (Welty) 105:363
An Only Child (O'Connor) 14:395-96; 23:326
Only Children (Lurie) 18:310-11; 39:180
"The only cool day of summer" (Broumas) 73:12
The Only Daughter (Anderson) 37:21
"The Only Death in the City" (Cherryh) 35:107
Only Love (Seifert) 34:256
Only Love (Seifert)
  See *Samá láska*
"Only Love Can Break Your Heart" (Young) 17:569-70
Only Make Believe (Potter) 58:389, 391
"The Only Man on Liberty Street" (Kelley) 22:246
The Only Neat Thing to Do (Tiptree) 48:394-95
"Only Once I Caught a Glimpse..." (Seifert)
  See "Jen jedno jsem spatril..."
The Only Ones Left (Char)
  See *Seuls demeurants*
"Only People" (Lennon) 35:266
"The Only Poem" (Warren) 39:272
The Only Problem (Spark) 40:396-400
The Only Sense Is Nonsense (Simpson) 29:367
The Only Sun (Ozu) 16:453
Only Ten Minutes to Buffalo (Grass) 4:202; 15:260; 88:147
"Only the Dreamer Can Change the Dream" (Logan) 5:255
"Only the Good Die Young" (Joel) 26:216
Only the Heart (Foote) 51:129
"Only the Little Bone" (Huddle) 49:183-84
Only the Little Bone (Huddle) 49:183-84
"Only the Red Fox, Only the Crow" (Olson) 29:329-30
"Only the World" (Urdang) 47:401
Only the World (Urdang) 47:400
"The Only Traffic Signal on the Reservation Doesn't Flash Red Anymore" (Alexie) 96:4
"The Only Way Around Is Through" (Ammons) 57:49
"The Only Way to Make It in New York" (Brown) 32:63
Only When I Larf (Deighton) 46:126
Only When I Laugh (Simon) 70:238
"Only Woman Blues" (Hughes) 15:292
Onna no Issho (*The Life of a Woman*) (Endo) 99:283, 285, 287
"Onnagata" (Mishima) 6:339
Onnazaka (*The Waiting Years*) (Enchi) 31:140-41
"The Onset" (Frost) 13:228; 26:123
"Onset" (Johnston) 51:248
De ontaarde slapers (*The Depraved Sleepers*)

(Ruyslinck) 14:472
"Ontario" (Muldoon) 72:273
Ontological Proof of My Experience (Oates) 33:289
"The Ontology of the Sentence; or, How to Make a World of Words" (Gass) 11:224
"Oo You" (McCartney) 35:278
"Oo-Ee Baby" (Reed) 21:311
"Oona, The Jolly Cave Woman" (Highsmith) 102:186
O.P.: Orden público (*Public Order*) (Sender) 8:477, 480-81
Open Air (Straub) 28:408; 107:304
Open All Night (Morand)
  See *Ouvert la nuit*
"Open Arms" (Butler) 81:125, 129
"The Open Boat" (Steinbeck) 9:519
"Open Book" (Elytis) 100:168
Open Book (Elytis)
  See *Anihtá hártia*
The Open Cage: An Anzia Yezierska Collection (Yezierska) 46:449
Open Couple (Fo) 109:119
The Open Door (Sillitoe) 57:401-03
Open Door (Valenzuela) 104:376, 380, 382, 388
Open Doorways (Appleman) 51:14-15
"Open Eye, Open Heart" (Ferlinghetti) 27:139
Open Eye, Open Heart (Ferlinghetti) 6:183-84; 27:139; 111:65
Open Heart (Buechner) 2:83-4; 4:80; 6:102-03; 9:137
"Open House" (Gordimer) 18:189
"Open House" (Roethke) 19:396-97
Open House (Roethke) 1:291; 8:455, 459-60; 19:396-97; 46:356-57, 360-62; 101:265-66, 287, 298, 301, 312
"Open It, Write" (Ekeloef) 27:114
"Open Letter" (Dodson) 79:194
"Open Letter" (Munro) 95:291
"Open Letter" (Roethke) 19:396-97; 101:262-63, 334-36, 339, 341
"Open Letter from a Constant Reader" (Van Duyn) 116:430
"Open Letter, Personal" (Van Duyn) 63:440; 116:408, 429
"An Open Letter to My Sister, Miss Angela Davis" (Baldwin) 50:296
"Open Letter to President Husák" (Havel) 65:419
"Open Letter to Richard Crossman" (Fenton) 32:165
"An Open Letter to the South" (Hughes) 108:294
"The Open Mind" (White) 49:408
Open Papers (Elytis) 100:190-91
The Open Poem (Rozewicz)
  See *Poemat otwarty*
An Open Prison (Stewart) 32:423
"The Open Road" (Farrell) 66:129
Open Road (Dawson) 6:126
The Open Sea (Meredith) 13:374-75; 22:301-02; 55:193
Open Season: Sporting Adventures (Humphrey) 45:205
"Open Secrets" (Motion) 47:288, 290
Open Secrets (Munro) 95:301, 319-25
Open Songs (McGrath) 59:178
Open Songs: Sixty Short Poems (McGrath) 28:278
"Open the Gates" (Kunitz) 6:287
The Open Veins of Latin America: Five Centuries of the Pillage of a Continent (Galeano)

72:127-29, 131, 136, 143

"The Open Window" (Transtroemer)   65:223

"Open Windows" (Hacker)   72:182

"Open Winter" (Davis)   49:91, 94, 97

The Open Work (Eco)   60:118, 123

The Opener of the Way (Bloch)   33:82

"The Opening" (Olds)   32:346

Opening Day (Gascoyne)   45:152, 158

"Opening Her Jewel Box" (Matthews)   40:320

Opening Night (Cassavetes)   20:52-3

Opening Night (*Night at the Vulcan*) (Marsh)   53:253

The Opening of the Field (Duncan)   1:82; 2:122-23; 41:126, 128-29; 55:292-93, 295, 299

"The Opening of the Road" (Buzzati)   36:92, 94

"Opening the Door of a Barn I Thought Was Empty on New Year's Eve" (Bly)   15:63

Opening the Hand (Merwin)   45:273-76; 88:191, 194-95, 205-06

"Opening Up the Canon" (Fiedler)   24:205

Openings (Berry)   4:59; 27:32, 34; 46:70

Opéra (Cocteau)   8:146; 15:133

"L'opéra des falaises" (Mandiargues)   41:278

Ópera dos mortos (*Opera of the Dead; Voices of the Dead*) (Dourado)   23:149-52; 60:83-4

L'opera mouffe (Varda)   16:554, 556-57

Opera of the Dead (Dourado)
   See *Ópera dos mortos*

Opéra parlé (*Spoken Opera*) (Audiberti)   38:23, 25-6, 29-30

Opera Wonyosi (Soyinka)   36:412-13

"The Operation" (Livesay)   15:341; 79:338, 340, 343-44

"The Operation" (Sexton)   8:483; 15:472; 53:312

"The Operation" (Snodgrass)   18:491

Operation ARES (Wolfe)   25:472

Operation Chaos (Anderson)   15:11-12

Operation Harvest Moon (Harper)   22:208

Operation Iskra (Edgar)   42:115, 121

Operation Shylock: A Confession (Roth)   86:247-64

Operation Sidewinder (Shepard)   4:489-90; 6:497; 17:436-37, 440, 447; 41:409, 412

Operation Time Search (Norton)   12:458, 468

Operation Wandering Souls (Powers)   93:291-95, 299-301

Operetta (Gombrowicz)   4:195; 49:128-29

"Ophelia" (Hughes)   37:179

"Ophelia" (Watkins)   43:447

Ophelia (Chabrol)   16:169-70, 177

"An Opinion on the Question of Pornography" (Szymborska)   99:201

The Opinions of Oliver Allston (Brooks)   29:82-4

"Opinions of the Press" (Reading)   47:354

"Opium" (Ellison)   42:130

The Opoponax (Wittig)   22:471-74

Oppiano Licario (Lezama Lima)   101:121, 129

"Opportunity" (Armatrading)   17:8

The Opposing Self (Trilling)   9:530; 11:542-43, 546; 24:452-53, 456, 458, 461-62

The Opposing Shore (Gracq)
   See *Le rivage des Syrtes*

Opposite the Forests (Yehoshua)
   See *Facing the Forests*

"Opposite the House of the Caryatids" (Pasternak)   7:294

"Opposites" (Wilbur)   110:364

Opposites (Wilbur)   6:571; 110:382, 387

Opposites—React (Williamson)   29:455

"The Oppositional Gaze: Black Female Spectators" (hooks)   94:153

"Oppressed Hair Puts a Ceiling on the Brain" (Walker)   58:409

"Oppression" (Hughes)   15:295

Opticks: A Poem in Seven Sections (Goldbarth)   5:143-44; 38:203

"Optimism" (Hikmet)   40:252

The Optimist (Gold)   4:190-92; 42:191

"Optimists"   99:115

"The Optimist's Daughter" (Welty)   105:364

The Optimist's Daughter (Welty)   2:463-64; 5:479; 14:564; 22:462; 33:415-16, 424; 105:300, 308, 312, 322, 325, 335, 349-51, 353, 359-64, 367-70, 382-83, 390

"Optional" (Avison)   97:71, 75

Opus 21 (Wylie)   43:465, 467, 470, 472

Opus 100 (Asimov)   26:48

Opus 200 (Asimov)   19:27-8

"Opus Dei" (Berryman)   3:66, 68, 70; 13:82; 25:92

Opus Pistorum (Miller)   43:301-02

"Op. posth. Nos. 1-14" (Berryman)   13:80; 25:93, 96, 98

L'or (*Gold; Sutter's Gold*) (Cendrars)   18:95, 97; 106:149, 153-54, 167, 182-83, 185, 190, 194

Or Else: Poem/Poems, 1968-1974 (Warren)   6:555-59; 8:536-37, 539, 542; 10:520-22; 13:577; 39:260, 270-71

"Or, Solitude" (Davie)   5:114

"...Or Traveller's Joy" (Tomlinson)   45:394

"Or When Your Sister Sleeps Around for Money" (Knight)
   See "The Violent Space (or when your sister sleeps around for money)"

"Una oracion" (Borges)   6:90

Oración (Arrabal)
   See *Oraison*

Oración (*Oraison; Orison*) (Arrabal)   9:33, 38; 18:18, 20; 58:3, 7, 9, 11, 16, 18

"Oracle"
   See "Oraculoe"

"The Oracle" (Merton)   83:391

"An Oracle" (White)   110:340

The Oracle (O'Connor)   14:392-93

The Oracle in the Heart, and Other Poems, 1975-1978 (Raine)   45:339

"Oracle over Managua" (Cardenal)
   See "Oráculo sobre Managua"

"Oracles" (Jiles)   58:277-78

"Oráculo sobre Managua" ("Oracle over Managua") (Cardenal)   31:77

"Oraculoe" ("Oracle") (Cardenal)   31:77

"Orage" (Reverdy)   53:289

Oraison (*Oración; Orison*) (Arrabal)   58:3, 7, 9, 11, 16, 18

Oraison (Arrabal)
   See *Oración*

"Oral History" (Gordimer)   18:190

Oral History (Smith)   73:340-45, 347, 350, 352, 355, 357

"Oral Messages" (Ferlinghetti)   27:138

"The Oral Tradition" (Boland)   67:36; 113:73, 82-3, 98, 119

"Orange County Plague" (Lieberman)   36:263

"The Orange Fish" (Shields)   113:408, 432

The Orange Fish (Shields)   113:404-05, 407-08, 410-11, 413-14

"An Orange from Portugal" (MacLennan)   92:340

"Orange Roses" (Stern)   40:413

"The Orange Tree" (Belitt)   22:53

The Orange Tree (Fuentes)   113:262-65

The Orangery (Sorrentino)   14:498-500; 40:384, 386

"Oranges" (O'Hara)   78:352, 355

Oranges (McPhee)   36:293

Oranges (O'Hara)   2:323; 13:423, 426

"Oranges and Apples" (Munro)   95:310

Oranges Are Not the Only Fruit (Winterson)   64:426-27, 429-32, 434-35, 439-40, 442, 444

"Oranges from Morocco" (Aksyonov)   22:27

Oranges from Morocco (*Apel'siny iz Marokko*) (Aksyonov)   101:6-7, 10, 12, 16, 29-30

"Oranges on Her Windowsill" (Federspiel)   42:145

"Orange-throats" (Zamora)   89:392

"Orange-Tree" (Wright)   53:419

"The Oranging of America" (Apple)   9:32-3; 33:19

The Oranging of America, and Other Stories (Apple)   9:33; 33:18-22

L'orare du discours (*The Discourse on Language*) (Foucault)   34:341

"Oration at a Bonfire, Fourteen Years Late" (Dinesen)   95:56

The Orators: An English Study (Auden)   2:22; 6:24; 9:60; 11:15, 18-19; 14:31-2; 43:15-16, 18, 21, 25

The Orb Weaver (Francis)   15:235-36, 238

Orbita de Lezama Lima (Lezama Lima)   101:109-10

"Orbital Radio Relays" (Clarke)   35:128

"Orbiter 5 Shows How Earth Looks from the Moon" (Swenson)   61:397

"Orbiting" (Mukherjee)   53:271; 115:385-87, 389

"Orchard" (Eberhart)   56:77, 89

"Orchard" (H. D.)
   See "Priapus"

The Orchard Keeper (Leonov)
   See *Polovchanskie sady*

The Orchard Keeper (McCarthy)   4:342-43; 57:327-28, 330-32; 101:133, 135, 147-48, 150, 154, 166-67, 175-78, 182, 185, 195, 197, 202-04

"Orchard Love" (Carlson)   54:37

The Orchards of Polovchansk (Leonov)
   See *Polovchanskie sady*

"Orchestra" (Purdy)   50:247

"The Orchestra" (Turco)   11:552

Orchestra and Beginners (Raphael)   14:436

The Orchestra Rehearsal (Fellini)
   See *Provo d'orchestra*

Orchéstration Théâtrale (Arrabal)   58:4, 13-14

L'orchestre (Anouilh)   40:58-9

"Orchids" (Roethke)   8:461; 11:484; 101:294

Orchids in the Moonlight (Fuentes)
   See *Orquideas a la luz de la luna*

"L'ordalie" (Bonnefoy)   58:53

Ordeal (*What Happened to the Corbetts?*) (Shute)   30:364-65, 369

Ordeal by Ice (Mowat)   26:334

Ordeal by Innocence (Christie)   12:116, 124; 48:75

The Ordeal of Gilbert Pinfold (Harwood)   32:225

The Ordeal of Gilbert Pinfold: A Conversation Piece (Waugh)   1:357; 3:510, 513; 8:544; 27:474, 477; 44:522-23; 107:373, 385, 393, 398

The Ordeal of Mark Twain (Brooks)   29:79-81,

86-7
The Order of Assassins (Wilson)   14:589
"Order of Insects" (Gass)   8:245; 15:258
"The Order of Saying" (Tomlinson)   45:398
"Order of the Black Cross" (p'Bitek)   96:299
The Order of Things: An Archaeology of the Human Sciences (Foucault)
   See *Les mots et les choses: Une archéologie des sciences humaines*
"Order to View" (MacNeice)   10:323
"Orders" (Duncan)   55:297
Orders of Chivalry (Vansittart)   42:390-91
Orders of the Retina (Disch)   36:127
Ordet (*The Word*) (Dreyer)   16:258, 260-61, 263-65, 267-69
L'Ordinaire (Brossard)   115:106, 110
"An Ordinary Evening in Cleveland" (Turco)   63:429
An Ordinary Evening in New Haven (Aiken)   3:3
"Ordinary Homecoming" (MacCaig)   36:282
Ordinary Love and Goodwill (Smiley)   76:230, 233
An Ordinary Lunacy (Anderson)   37:18
"Ordinary Man" (Lightfoot)   26:279
An Ordinary Man (Leonov)
   See *Obyknovenny chelovek*
Ordinary Money (Jones)   65:56-62
Ordinary, Moving (Gotlieb)   18:192-93
"Ordinary Pain" (Wonder)   12:660
"Ordinary People" (Davies)   21:100
"Ordinary People" (Musgrave)   54:341
Ordinary People (Guest)   8:253-54; 30:172-76
An Ordinary Person (Leonov)
   See *Obyknovenny chelovek*
An Ordinary Woman (Clifton)   19:109-10, 66:66-7, 75-6, 80-1, 84-5
Ordkonst och bildkonst (*Verbal and Pictorial Art*; *Word Art and Picture Art*) (Lagerkvist)   54:271, 273, 286, 289
"Ordo" (Westlake)   33:438
The Ordways (Humphrey)   45:195-200, 202
"Oread" (H. D.)   14:223; 31:205, 207; 73:118, 121
Ore'ah natah lalun (*A Guest for the Night*) (Agnon)   4:12; 8:8-9; 14:5
"Oregano" (Neruda)   28:309
"Oregon" (Davis)   49:92
L'oreille de l'autre (*The Ear of the Other*) (Derrida)   87:92
Oreste (Anouilh)   40:58; 50:279
The Oresteia of Aeschylus (Lowell)   15:344, 348-49
"Orestes" (Davies)   23:142, 145
"Orestes" (Ritsos)   31:325
Orestes (Fugard)   14:189; 40:197; 80:62, 64
Orestes (Ritsos)   13:488
Orestes A. Brownson: A Pilgrim's Progress (Schlesinger)   84:346
"Orestes at Tauris" (Jarrell)   2:209; 13:300
"Orf" (Hughes)   37:174
The Organdy Cupcakes (Stolz)   12:545-46, 549
"Organelle" (Swenson)   106:314
"Organized Guilt and Universal Responsibility" (Arendt)   98:52
"The Organizer's Wife" (Bambara)   88:7, 28, 37, 48, 52-54
"Organs" (Swenson)   106:339
"The Orgasm: A Reappraisal" (Blount)   38:46
Orgasmo Adulto Escapes from the Zoo (Fo)   32:175-76; 109:119

La orgía perpetua: Flaubert y "Madame Bovary" (*Flaubert y "Madame Bovary"*; *The Perpetual Orgy: Flaubert and "Madame Bovary"*) (Vargas Llosa)   10:500-01; 85:355, 363, 385
Orgie (Brink)   106:101
"The Orgy" (Amichai)   116:107
The Orgy (Rukeyser)   27:409
"O'Riada's Farewell" (Montague)   46:272
"Orielton Empty" (Mathias)   45:235-36
"Orient and Immortal Wheat" (Walcott)   67:353
"The Orient Express" (Jarrell)   13:298
Orient Express (Greene)
   See *Stamboul Train*
"The Oriental Ballerina" (Dove)   50:155, 158
Oriental Mythology (Campbell)
   See *The Masks of God: Oriental Mythology*
Oriental Tales (Yourcenar)
   See *Nouvelles orientales*
"Orientation Day in Hades" (Fulton)   52:161
Orientations (Elytis)
   See *Prosanatolizmi*
Orientations (Maugham)   67:220
"Oriflamme" (Williams)   5:502-03
An Origin Like Water: Collected Poems 1967-1987 (Boland)   113:108, 112, 114, 120-21, 124, 127
"The Origin of Centaurs" (Hecht)   8:268
The Origin of Evil (Queen)   11:459, 463
"The Origin of Extermination in the Imagination" (Gass)   39:481-82
"The Origin of Man" (Bowering)   32:47
Origin of Satan (Pagels)   104:222-28, 230, 233, 234
The Origin of the Brunists (Coover)   3:114; 7:57; 32:124-26; 46:116, 119, 121; 87:23-6, 28-9, 32-3, 37-8, 43-6
"The Origin of the Scarecrow" (Farrell)   66:131
"Original Child Bomb" (Merton)   83:384
Original Child Bomb: Points for Meditation to Be Scratched on the Walls of a Cave (Merton)   11:373
Original Light: New and Selected Poems, 1973-1983 (Goldbarth)   38:204-07
"Original Memory" (Harjo)   83:282
The Original Michael Frayn: Satirical Essays (Frayn)   47:135
"Original Sin" (Jeffers)   15:301
Original Sin (Tabori)   19:435-36
"Original Sin: A Short Story" (Warren)   8:539; 13:582; 39:264
"Original Sin on the Sussex Coast" (Betjeman)   43:38, 41
Original Sins (Alther)   41:19-23
"The Original Sins of Edward Tripp" (Trevor)   71:322, 335
"The Originators" (Merton)   83:385, 397
"Origins" (Bowen)   6:95
"Origins" (Walcott)   42:418, 421
"Origins and History of Consciousness" (Rich)   36:374, 376
"Origins of a Poem" (Levertov)   66:241-43
Origins of Marvel Comics (Lee)   17:258
"Origins of the Beat Generation" (Kerouac)   61:310
Origins of the Sexual Impulse (Wilson)   14:589
The Origins of Totalitarianism (*The Burden of Our Time*; *Totalitarianism*) (Arendt)   66:15-18, 22, 26, 31-2, 40; 98:3, 9, 11, 17-18, 20-2, 31, 36, 45, 48, 50-2
Origins: The Lives and Worlds of Modern Cosmologists (Lightman)   81:78

"O'Riley's Late-Bloomed Little Son" (Kennedy)   42:256-57
"Orion" (Oliver)   98:261
"Orion" (Rich)   18:447; 36:369
Orion (Bova)   45:73-4
Orion aveugle (Simon)   39:206
"Orion Iroquois" (Char)   55:285
Orison (Arrabal)
   See *Oración*
Orison (Arrabal)
   See *Oraison*
"Orissa" (Mahapatra)   33:283
"Orizont si stil" ("Horizon and Style")   75:72
Orkney: Pictures and Poems (Brown)   100:84
An Orkney Tapestry (Brown)   48:52; 100:84
Orlando at the Brazen Threshold (Colegate)   36:110, 113
Orlando King (Colegate)   36:110, 113
Ormen's ägg (*The Serpent's Egg*) (Bergman)   16:80-2; 72:55, 57, 59
Orn (Anthony)   35:35, 40
"The Ornamental Water" (Blunden)   56:45
Ornifle; ou, Le courant d'air (Anouilh)   13:17, 20
El oro de los tigres (*The Gold of the Tigers: Selected Later Poems*) (Borges)   6:90; 13:109-10; 48:37; 83:190
L'oro di Napoli (De Sica)   20:90
"Orphan" (Jong)   6:268
The Orphan (Rabe)   4:425; 8:450
The Orphan Genius (Dabrowska)
   See *Geniusz sierocy*
"The Orphanage" (McCullers)   4:345; 12:432
"The Orphanage" (Reaney)   13:473
"Orphanage Boy" (Warren)   18:536
"The Orphaning" (Belitt)   22:50, 52-3
"The Orphans" (Dubie)   36:130
The Orphans (Murphy)   51:300
Orphans and Other Children (Webb)   7:515-16
The Orphan's Home (Foote)   51:132-33, 136-37
Orphans of the Sky (Heinlein)   3:225
Orphée (*Orpheus*) (Cocteau)   8:145, 147-49; 15:134; 16:223-29; 43:102, 104-07, 109-10
"Orpheus" (Dybek)   114:63
"Orpheus" (Rukeyser)   15:457; 27:407-08, 410-14
"Orpheus" (Smith)   64:399-400
Orpheus (Cocteau)
   See *Orphée*
"Orpheus Alone" (Strand)   71:287-88, 290
"Orpheus and Eurydice" (Graham)   48:154
"Orpheus and His Lute" (O'Connor)   14:398
Orpheus and Other Poems (Smith)   64:399
"Orpheus Below" (Honig)   33:214
"Orpheus' Brother" (Brunner)   8:108
Orpheus Descending (Williams)   5:499, 502; 11:571-72, 577; 15:578-79; 30:466; 71:369, 386, 405; 111:393
"Orpheus in the Underworld" (Gascoyne)   45:148
"Orpheus in the Underworld" (Simpson)   7:426
Orpheus in the Underworld of the Twentieth Century (Wittlin)   25:467
"Orpheus to Eurydice" (Morgan)   23:301-02
Orquideas a la luz de la luna (*Orchids in the Moonlight*) (Fuentes)   41:168-72
Orsinian Tales (Le Guin)   8:343; 45:214, 216
Ortadirek (*The Wind from the Plain*) (Kemal)   14:299-300
"The Orthodoxy of Enlightenment" (Leavis)

24:305
Örtlich betäubt (Grass) **15**:263
O'Ryan (Olson) **5**:328
The Osages: Children of the Middle Waters
   (Mathews) **84**:206, 209, 211, 221, 226
"Osai to minosuke" (Tanizaki) **8**:509
Oscar and Lucinda (Carey) **55**:112-19; **96**:36,
   47, 49-50, 59, 61, 63, 70, 72, 76-82
Oscar Wilde (Ellmann) **50**:306, 309
"Oscar Wilde and San Miniato" (Wright) **6**:580
Osceola (Dinesen) **95**:67, 70
Oscura noticia ("Copla") (Alonso) **14**:16, 23,
   26
"Osen'" (Voznesensky) **15**:555
Osm dnu (*Eight Days*) (Seifert) **44**:425;
   93:306, 317, 334, 342
"Un oso y un amor" ("A Bear and a Love")
   (Ulibarri) **83**:415
"Osobny zeszyt" ("The Separate Notebooks")
   (Milosz) **56**:231-32, 234, 239, 244, 251
"The Osprey" (Longley) **29**:292
The Osprey Suicides (Lieberman) **4**:291;
   36:261, 263
Ossessione (Visconti) **16**:563-64, 572, 575
Ossi di seppia (*Bones of the Cuttlefish*; *Cuttle-
   fish Bones*) (Montale) **7**:222, 224, 226-
   29, 231; **9**:387-88; **18**:339-40
"Ostanovka v pustyne" ("A Halt in the Desert")
   (Brodsky) **6**:96; **50**:123-24; **6**:96; **13**:114,
   116; **50**:121-24, 131
Ostatni dzien lata (*The Last Day of Summer*)
   (Konwicki) **117**:282
"Ostensibly" (Ashbery) **77**:63
Österjöar (*Baltics*) (Transtroemer) **52**:413-
   18; **65**:219, 226, 229, 233, 235
The Osterman Weekend (Ludlum) **22**:289;
   43:273
"Ostia Antica" (Hecht) **8**:268
Ostre sledované vlaky (*Closely Observed Trains*;
   Closely Watched Trains) (Hrabal) **13**:290-
   91; **67**:121-22, 124-27, 129-31
Ostrov Krym (*The Island of Crimea*) (Aksyonov)
   37:12-13, 16; **101**:23-5, 29, 35, 47, 50
Den osynlige (*The Invisible One*) (Lagerkvist)
   54:268, 270-71, 274, 277
Othello (Welles) **20**:433-35, 438-41, 448-50;
   80:367, 410
"The Other" (Borges)
   See "El otro"
"The Other" (Dickey) **109**:235
"The Other" (Greene) **27**:174
"The Other" (Plath) **9**:426; **17**:361; **51**:340;
   111:203
"The Other" (Roethke) **101**:328
The Other (Tryon) **3**:483; **11**:548
"The Other Boat" (Forster) **2**:136; **4**:168;
   15:231; **22**:135-36; **45**:136, 140
"The Other Celia" (Sturgeon) **39**:366
Other Days (Haines) **58**:220
Other Dimensions (Smith) **43**:418-19
"The Other Eye of Polyphemus" (Ellison)
   42:130
"The Other Face" (Mahfuz)
   See "al-Wahj al-akhar"
"Other Factors" (Gaitskill) **69**:199-200
The Other Father (Hobson) **25**:271
Other Gods (Buck) **11**:75
"The Other Half" (Wright) **53**:425-26, 429
The Other Half (Wright) **53**:426, 429, 431
Other Inquisitions, 1937-1952 (Borges)
   See *Otras inquisiciónes, 1937-1952*
"The Other K" (Fuentes) **60**:162
"Other Kingdom" (Forster) **9**:207; **45**:140

"The Other Labrynth" (Bioy Casares)
   See "El otro labertino"
"Other Manifestations of the American Scene"
   (Stafford) **4**:517
"The Other Margaret" (Trilling) **11**:544
"The Other Me" (McCartney) **35**:292
Other Men's Daughters (Stern) **4**:522-23;
   39:240-41
"Other Modes" (Updike) **2**:444; **3**:488
"Other Nations" (Kumin) **28**:223
"The Other One" (Borges)
   See "El otro"
The Other One (Green)
   See *L'autre*
The Other Paris (Gallant) **18**:170
Other People: A Mystery Story (Amis) **38**:14-
   15; **62**:5, 17; **101**:65, 89
Other People's Children (Findley) **102**:106
"Other People's Legs" (Oe) **86**:226-27
Other People's Money (Weidman) **7**:517
"Other People's Stories" (Ozick)
   See "Usurpation (Other People's Stories)"
Other People's Worlds (Trevor) **25**:442-44,
   446; **71**:323, 326, 346, 348; **116**:338, 364,
   377
Other Places (*A Kind of Alaska*; *One for the
   Road*; *Victoria Station*) (Pinter) **27**:392-
   93, 396-97; **58**:371, 375-78, 385
Other Poems (Kinsella) **19**:252-53
"The Other Rib of Death" (Garcia Marquez)
   See "La otra costilla de la muerte"
"The Other Shore" (Paz) **10**:392
"The Other Side" (Heaney) **25**:241
The Other Side (Alvarez)
   See *El Otro Lado*
The Other Side (Middleton) **38**:333
"The Other Side of Death" (Garcia Marquez)
   See "La otra costilla de la muerte"
The Other Side of Hugh MacLennan
   (MacLennan) **14**:343
"The Other Side of Lethe" (Howe) **47**:173-74
"The Other Side of the Border" (Greene) **72**:149
"The Other Side of the Fence" (Ihimaera)
   46:196, 199
The Other Side of the Fence (Tunis) **12**:596
The Other Side of the Fire (Ellis) **40**:192-93
The Other Side of the Hill (Luke) **38**:318
"The Other Side of the Lake" (Aldiss) **40**:21
The Other Side of the Sky (Clarke) **13**:148
The Other Side of the Sun (L'Engle) **12**:349
Other Skies (Ciardi) **40**:152-54; **44**:378
"The Other Tiger" (Borges)
   See "El otro tigre"
"Other Times" (Nye) **13**:412
Other Times (Lawler) **58**:333, 336-37, 340-44
"The Other Tradition" (Ashbery) **77**:45, 54
The Other Trial (Canetti)
   See *Der andere Prozeß: Kafkas Briefe an
   Felice*
"The Other Voice" (Paulin) **37**:353
"The Other Voices" (Hogan) **73**:159
Other Voices, Other Rooms (Capote) **1**:55;
   3:99; **8**:132-33; **13**:132-35, 138-40;
   19:79-80, 85-7; **34**:320-25; **38**:78-9, 82-
   3, 85-7; **58**:86, 94, 102, 122, 133
"The Other Way" (Grau) **4**:210; **9**:240
"Other Weapons" (Valenzuela) **104**:372, 374
Other Weapons (Valenzuela)
   See *Cambio de armas*
"The Other Whitman" (Borges) **83**:163
"The Other Woman" (Boland) **113**:78
"The Other Woman" (Dacey) **51**:83
"The Other Woman" (Lessing) **6**:292; **10**:316

"Other Women" (Vaughn) **62**:458-59
Other Women (Alther) **41**:22-4
Others (Shields) **113**:407, 412, 441
"Otherwise" (Ashbery) **15**:36
"Otherwise" (Niedecker) **42**:299
Otherwise Engaged (Gray) **9**:241-42; **36**:201-
   07, 210
Otherwise Known as Sheila the Great (Blume)
   30:22
"Otis and Marlena" (Mitchell) **12**:443
"Otkazom" (Brodsky) **13**:115
"L'otobiographie de Nietzsche" (Derrida) **87**:
"Otoño" ("Autumn"; "Fall") (Neruda) **62**:335
La otra casa de Mazón (Benet) **28**:20-1
"La otra costilla de la muerte" ("The Other Rib
   of Death"; "The Other Side of Death")
   (Garcia Marquez) **3**:181; **47**:147
"Otra no amo" (Aleixandre) **9**:12
Otra vez el diablo (Casona) **49**:40, 42-5, 47
Otra vez el mar (*Farewell to the Sea: A Novel of
   Cuba*; *Once More the Sea*)(Arenas) **41**:29-
   30
"Otras aires" (Cernuda) **54**:60
Otras inquisiciónes, 1937-1952 (*Other Inqui-
   sitions, 1937-1952*) (Borges) **2**:72; **3**:80;
   8:100; **10**:63; **44**:363, 366; **48**:39, 46-7;
   83:160-64, 166, 169, 171, 184
"El otro" ("The Other"; "The Other One")
   (Borges) **13**:111; **44**:360, 365; **48**:38, 41
"El otro cielo" (Cortazar) **10**:113; **33**:126,
   129
"Otro día nuestro" (Marques) **96**:228, 243
"El otro labertino" ("The Other Labrynth")
   (Bioy Casares) **88**:59
El Otro Lado (*The Other Side*) (Alvarez) **93**:17
"Otro rio: O Ebro" ("Another River: The Ebro")
   (Cabral de Melo Neto) **76**:168
El otro rostro del peronismo (Sabato) **23**:378
"El otro tigre" ("The Other Tiger") (Borges)
   3:81; **13**:107
Otros poemas (Parra) **102**:334, 341, 343, 356
"Otros tulipanes amarillos" (Cernuda) **54**:60
Otsu junkichi (Shiga) **33**:371
Otsuya Koroshi (*The Murder of Otsuya*)
   (Tanizaki) **8**:509
"The Ottawa Valley" (Munro) **19**:345; **95**:291
"The Otter" (Heaney) **14**:246; **25**:244; **37**:162
"An Otter" (Hughes) ·**2**:203; **4**:235
"Otto" (Roethke) **8**:457
"Otto and the Magi" (Connell) **45**:109
Otto e Mezzo (*8 1/2*) (Fellini) **16**:274, 277,
   282-84, 286-89, 291-92, 297-98; **85**:47-
   9, 55, 57-62, 64-6, 68-70, 73-6, 78-81
"Otto tis erate" (Elytis) **100**:178
Où boivent les loups (Tzara) **47**:387
Où: Le génie de lieu, Volume II (Butor) **11**:80;
   15:118, 120
L'oubli (Mauriac) **9**:366
Oublier Foucault (*Forget Foucault*)
   (Baudrillard) **60**:13, 15
"Oughtiness Ousted" (Avison) **97**:121
"Oui" (Dorris) **109**:309
"Ouija" (Plath) **11**:447; **51**:344; **111**:178
"Ould Biddy—The Newsmonger" (Carroll)
   10:98
"Our Actors and the Critics" (McCarthy)
   24:344
"Our Aims Our Dreams Our Destinations"
   (Brutus) **43**:92-3
Our Ancestors (Calvino)
   See *I nostri antenati*
Our Betters (Maugham) **1**:204; **11**:369; **15**:366;
   67:207, 223, 225; **93**:257

Our Blood: Prophecies and Discourses on Sexual Politics (Dworkin)　43:132-33
"Our Bog Is Dood" (Smith)　25:419
"Our Bourgeois Literature" (Sinclair)　63:348
Our Conquest (Hofmann)　54:226, 229
Our Country and Our Children: Improving America's Schools and Affirming the Common Culture　70:362
"Our Cousin, Mr. Poe" (Tate)　24:445
Our Day Out (Russell)　60:320
Our Dead Behind Us (Lorde)　71:254-55, 257-59, 261-63
"Our Dead Poets" (Lowell)　11:329
"Our Death" (Strand)　18:516-17
Our England Is a Garden (Stewart)　14:513
"Our Exagimation Round His Factification for Incamination of Work in Progress" (Beckett)　59:254
"Our Father" (Durcan)　70:153
Our Father (King)　8:322
Our Father's Failing (Horovitz)　56:155
"Our Fear" (Herbert)　43:193
"Our Fearful Innocence" (O'Faolain)　32:342
"Our First Day Together" (Simon)　26:407
"Our Forward Shadows" (Swenson)　106:339
Our Friends from Frolix-8 (Dick)　72:121-22
Our Gang (Roth)　2:378-80; 3:437, 439; 4:452-53, 456-57, 459; 6:476; 15:452; 22:352; 47:363
Our Golden Ironburg (Aksyonov)　101:25
"Our Grandmothers" (Angelou)　64:41
Our Ground Time Here Will Be Brief (Kumin)　28:222-25
"Our Hands in the Garden" (Hebert)
　See "Nos mains au jardin"
Our Hospitality (Keaton)　20:188
Our House in the Last World (Hijuelos)　65:150
"Our Hunting Fathers" (Auden)　43:17
"Our Hunting Fathers" (Simmons)　43:411
"Our Impossibilities" (Borges)
　See "Our Inadequacies"
"Our Inadequacies" ("Our Impossibilities") (Borges)　48:45, 47; 83:162
"Our King is Dead" (Dumas)　62:160
"Our Lady of Ardboe" (Muldoon)　72:266
Our Lady of Babylon (Rechy)　107:259-60
Our Lady of Darkness (Leiber)　25:306, 308
Our Lady of the Flowers (Genet)
　See *Notre dame des fleurs*
Our Lady of the Snows (Callaghan)　41:97-8
"Our Lady of the Well" (Browne)　21:37
"Our Land" (Ritsos)　13:488
"Our Lane" (Ali)
　See "Hamari Gali"
Our Late Night (Shawn)　41:396-97, 399-400
Our Little Trip (Ferlinghetti)　111:63
"Our Love Is So Natural" (Wright)　53:431
"Our Love Was" (Townshend)　17:531
"Our Love Was Is" (Townshend)　17:539
Our Man in Havana (Greene)　3:212-13; 9:250; 14:219; 18:197; 27:176; 37:140; 70:289-90, 294; 72:163-65, 169, 171-72
"Our Many Different Businesses with Art" (Booth)　24:98
Our Mother's House (Gloag)　40:205-07, 210-11
Our Mrs. McChesney (Ferber)　93:141
Our New Front Yard (Simak)　55:320
Our Next President (Baker)　31:27
"Our Northern Kind" (Carruth)　84:129
"Our Old Aunt Who Is Now in a Retirement Home" (Shields)　113:442

"Our Own or Other Nations" (Brand)　7:30
"Our Padre" (Betjeman)　43:42
"Our Place in Winter" (Dobyns)　37:77
Our Republic (Keneally)　117:243
"Our Room" (Peacock)　60:292
"Our Secret" (Allende)　97:4, 10
"Our Story Begins" (Wolff)　64:451-52, 454
"Our Strange and Loveable Weather" (Matthews)　40:322
"Our Text for Today" (Pryor)　26:378
Our Town (Wilder)　1:364, 366; 5:494-96; 6:572-78; 10:532; 15:569-73, 575; 35:346-47; 82:345-48, 352, 355, 357-66, 368, 373, 376, 379-80, 385-87, 389-90
"Our Trip (A Diary)" (Bioy Casares)　88:92-3
"Our Turn" (Reed)　5:368
"Our Vera Ivanovna" (Aksyonov)　101:13
"Our Very Best People" (Ferber)　93:153
"Our Visit to Niagara" (Goodman)　4:196
"Our Western Furniture" (Fenton)　32:164-65, 169
"Our Whole Life" (Rich)　7:366
"Our Work and Why We Do It" (Barthelme)　23:46
"Our Working Day May Be Menaced" (Avison)　97:72, 91, 110
"Ourselves or Nothing" (Forche)　83:212, 219
Ourselves to Know (O'Hara)　2:324; 42:312, 318, 321-24
"Ousia and Grammé" (Derrida)　87:85
"Out" (Hughes)　37:180
Out (Brooke-Rose)　40:104, 111
Out (Sukenick)　3:475; 4:531; 6:523; 48:363-70
"Out at Sea" (Martinson)　14:356
Out Cry (Williams)
　See *The Two-Character Play*
"Out Here" (Leavitt)　34:77
"Out in the Midday Sun" (Thomas)　37:419-21; 107:316, 320, 328, 330
"Out in the Open" (Transtroemer)　65:229
"Out in the Stream" (Hemingway)　34:478
"Out Like a Lamb" (Dubus)　97:233
Out of Africa (Dinesen)　10:148-50, 152-53; 29:153, 155-56, 158-60, 163-64; 95:32-3, 37-8, 40-5, 47-9, 54, 56, 68, 72, 75, 77, 80-2
Out of Chaos (Ehrenburg)　18:136; 62:168
"Out of Darkness" (La Guma)　19:274
"Out of Depth" (Waugh)　44:520
"Out of His Window" (Van Doren)　6:542
Out of India (Jhabvala)　94:187-88
Out of Love (Wolitzer)　17:563
"Out of Luck" (Tevis)　42:372
"Out of Mind, Out of Sight" (Kristofferson)　26:268
"Out of My Head" (Swenson)　106:345
Out of My House (Foote)　51:129
Out of My League (Plimpton)　36:351-52, 356
"Out of My Mind" (Young)　17:578
"Out of Night" (Campbell)　32:75
"Out of Our Heads" (Jagger and Richard)　17:232, 237
"Out of Season" (Aksyonov)　101:22
"Out of Season" (Hemingway)　30:181, 191; 61:219
"Out of Sleep Awakened" (MacLeish)　68:290
"Out of Superstition" (Pasternak)
　See "From Superstition"
"Out of the Blue" (Young)
　See "My My, Hey Hey"
"Out of the Closet, onto the Bookself" (White)　110:333, 342

"Out of the Dead City" (Delany)　14:144
Out of the Everywhere and Other Extraordinary Visions (Tiptree)　48:389-90
"Out of the Garden" (Hall)　37:148
Out of the Garden (MacInnes)　4:314-15
"Out of the Hospital and Under the Bar" (Ellison)　54:131-32; 114:99
Out of the Picture (MacNeice)　10:326; 53:233, 237
"Out of the Pulver and the Polished Lens" (Klein)　19:262
"Out of the Rubbish" (Piercy)　62:371
"Out of the Sea, Early" (Swenson)　4:533
Out of the Shelter (Lodge)　36:270
"Out of the Silence" (Findley)　102:108
Out of the Silent Planet (Lewis)　1:177; 3:297-99; 6:309-10; 14:323-326; 27:259-60
"Out of the Snow" (Dubus)　97:234, 237-38
"Out of the Sun" (Clarke)　13:148
Out of the Sun (Bova)　45:66
"Out of the Wardrobe" (Davies)　21:103-04
Out of the Way: Later Essays (MacInnes)　23:286
"Out of the Whirlpool" (Sillitoe)　57:400-01
"Out of the Wood" (Fuller)　62:185
Out of This World (Swift)　88:284-90, 307, 310, 313, 315, 317-18, 322
"Out of Tune" (Davison)　28:100
"Out of War" (Willard)　37:464
"Out of Work Blues" (Hughes)　35:221
"Out on the Week-End" (Young)　17:571
"Out, Out—" (Frost)　9:222
"Out to the Hard Road" (Lorde)　71:258
"Out Tonight"　99:
Out Went the Candle (Swados)　5:420, 422
Outback (Keneally)　43:232-33; 117:240
"Outbound" (Sissman)　18:488
Outcast (Sutcliff)　26:426, 429-30, 439
The Outcasts of Heaven Belt (Vinge)　30:414, 416
The Outcry (Antonioni)
　See *Il grido*
"The Outdoor Amphitheatre" (Corn)　33:117-19
"The Outdoor Concert" (Gunn)　18:202
"Outdoors" (Johnston)　51:248, 252-53
"The Outer Banks" (Rukeyser)　15:459
Outer Dark (McCarthy)　4:341-43; 57:326-32, 334-36; 101:135, 147-50, 154, 176-77, 183, 185, 195, 197, 201-04
"Outer Drive" (Honig)　33:211
"The Outer Island" (Cassill)　4:95
"The Outing" (Baldwin)　13:52; 17:33
"An Outing" (O'Brien)　5:313
An Outland Piper (Davidson)　13:166, 168; 19:124, 126, 129
"Outlander" (Rule)　27:423
Outlander (Rule)　27:422-23
Outlanders (Weiss)　3:515; 14:555
"Outlandish Agon" (Van Duyn)　63:440; 116:402, 420
Outlandos d'amour (Police, The)　26:363-64
"The Outlaw" (Heaney)　7:148; 25:244
"The Outlaw" (Ross)　13:492
Outlaw Culture: Resisting Representations (hooks)　94:156-59, 161-62
"Outlaws" (Graves)　45:166-67
"Outlaws of Callisto" (Wellman)　49:391
Outline for the Study of the Poetry of American Negroes (Brown)　59:267
Outline of a Jungian Aesthetics (Philipson)　53:273
"Outlines" (Lorde)　71:257

"The Outlook for American Culture, Some Reflections in a Machine Age" (Huxley) 18:266

Outlyer and Ghazals (Harrison) 6:224; 33:197

Out-of-the-Body Travel (Plumly) 33:312-16

The Out-of-Towners (Simon) 31:395

"The Outpost" (Transtroemer) 65:221, 226, 234, 236

Outrageous Acts and Everyday Rebellions (Steinem) 63:378-79, 381-83

"The Outrider" (Livesay) 79:342

Outrider (Stow) 23:436

Outside (Duras) 68:90

Outside (Norton) 12:470-71

An Outside Chance: Essays on Sport (McGuane) 45:257-58

"Outside History" (Boland) 113:65-6, 73-4, 89, 92, 94, 104, 106, 125-26

Outside History 1980-1990 (Boland) 113:68-9, 72-5, 80-1, 83, 87, 92-94, 99, 108, 111-12, 116, 118-19

"Outside of a Small Circle of Friends" (Ochs) 17:333-34

"Outside the Diner" (Gunn) 81:188

Outside the House of Baal (Humphreys) 47:180-81, 184, 187-89

Outside the Law (Browning) 16:124

"Outside the Machine" (Rhys) 6:453, 456

"Outside the Ministry" (Lessing) 22:278

"Outside the Operating Room of the Sex-Change Doctor" (Olds) 85:294

"Outside the Wall" (Pink Floyd) 35:313

"Outside-In" (Knight) 40:283-84, 286

The Outsider (Camus)
　See *L'étranger*

The Outsider (Sabato)
　See *El túnel*

The Outsider (Wilson) 3:537; 14:583-85

The Outsider (Wright) 1:379; 4:596-97; 9:584, 586; 14:596-97; 21:436, 443, 446, 448, 450-51, 462

Outsider in Amsterdam (van de Wetering) 47:404-08

The Outsiders (Hinton) 30:203-04, 206; 111:75-83, 85-90

Outskirts (Kureishi) 64:246

"The Outstation" (Maugham) 67:206; 93:257

The Outward Room (Brand) 7:29-30

"Outwork, Prefacing" (Derrida) 87:92

Ouvert la nuit (*Open All Night*) (Morand) 41:296-98, 303, 306-08

"Ouvindo Marianne Moore em disco" ("Listening to Marianne Moore on a Record"; "On Hearing a Recording of Marianne Moore") (Cabral de Melo Neto) 76:160

"L'ouvrier modèle" (Carrier) 78:58

The Oval Portrait, and Other Poems (Raine) 45:339

"La oveja negra" (Matute) 11:364

"The Oven Bird" (Frost) 4:174; 26:123

"Ovenstone" (Guillen) 79:229

"Over" (O'Brien) 5:311; 8:429; 36:340-41

"Over 2,000 Illustrations and a Complete Concordance" (Bishop) 9:97; 13:94; 15:59; 32:37, 41

Over and Above (Hobson) 25:272

"Over Back" (Frost) 13:230

"Over Cities" (Milosz) 31:262; 82:294

Over on the Dry Side (L'Amour) 25:281

"Over Russia's Wheatfields Once" (Ratushinskaya) 54:386

Over the Border (Kesey) 3:267-68; 46:225

Over the Brazier (Graves) 1:127; 39:323;

45:166

"Over the Edge" (Adcock) 41:15

Over the Frontier (Smith) 25:422; 44:439

Over the High Side (Freeling) 38:184

"Over the Hills and Far Away" (Page and Plant) 12:476

Over the Hills and Far Away (Mayne) 12:392, 398, 401

"Over the Hills in the Rain, My Dear" (Purdy) 50:248

"Over the Moon" 99:167, 183-84

"Over the Ozarks, Because I Saw Them, Stars Came" (Smith) 22:390

"Over the Red Line" (Wiebe) 14:574

"Over the River" (Peterkin) 31:306, 308

"Over the River and through the Wood" (O'Hara) 42:326-27

"Over the Roof ..." (Levi) 41:243

"Over the Valley" (Blunden) 56:45

Over to You (Dahl) 79:174, 177, 183

"The Overcoat" (Berriault) 109:96

"The Overcoat II" (Boyle) 36:63; 90:

"Overcome" (Gerstler) 70:158

"Overcoming White Supremacy" (hooks) 94:159

The Overcrowded Barracoon (Naipaul) 7:252-53; 13:407; 105:135-37, 155

An Overdose of Death (Christie) 110:135

Overdrive (Buckley) 37:61

"Overdue Pilgrimage to Nova Scotia" (Merrill) 91:238

Overhead in a Balloon: Stories of Paris (Gallant) 38:195

"Overheard" (Levertov) 66:236

"Overheard in County Sligo" (Clarke) 61:79, 82

Overlaid (Davies) 42:104

Overland to the Islands (Levertov) 28:242; 66:235, 237, 241

"The Overload" (Byrne) 26:98

"The Overloaded Packing Barrels" (Aksyonov) 101:21

"Overlooking the Pile of Bodies at One's Feet" (Leet) 11:323

Overnight (Inge) 8:308

"The Over-Night Bag" (Greene) 3:213

"Overnight to Many Distant Cities" (Barthelme) 46:39, 43

Overnight to Many Distant Cities (Barthelme) 46:38-9, 41-3; 59:247, 249; 115:80

Over-Nite Sensation (Zappa) 17:589, 591

"Overpowered by Funk" (Clash) 30:50-2

The Overreachers (Talese) 37:391

"Overs" (Simon) 17:459, 466

Overture (Scott) 22:371

"Overture and Incidental Music for *A Midsummer Night's Dream*" (Carter) 41:122

Overture to Death (Marsh) 53:247, 250

Overtures to Death and Other Poems (Day Lewis) 10:131, 133

"Ovid in the Third Reich" (Hill) 8:293, 295; 45:179-80, 183-84, 187, 189

"Ovid, Old Buddy, I Would Discourse with You a While" (Carruth) 84:136

"O ovo da galinha" ("The Chicken's Egg") (Cabral de Melo Neto) 76:167

"O ovo e a galinha" ("The Egg and the Hen") (Lispector) 43:262

Owarishi michino shirubeni (*The Road Sign at the End of the Street*) (Abe) 81:292

Owen Glendower (Powys) 7:348-50; 46:320-22

"Owl" (Plath) 111:200

The Owl (Hawkes) 2:183, 185; 3:223; 4:212-13; 7:141, 145; 15:270, 273; 27:199; 49:161, 164

The Owl Answers (Kennedy) 66:202-07, 209

"The Owl Flower" (Hughes) 37:173

The Owl in the Attic (Thurber) 5:435-36

"The Owl King" (Dickey) 47:93

The Owl Service (Garner) 17:136-49

"The Owls Are Leaving" (Ewart) 46:152

Owls Do Cry (Frame) 6:190; 22:143, 145-47; 66:144; 96:166-67, 172-76, 178-83, 188-91, 195-96, 203, 206-09. 218

Owls in the Family (Mowat) 26:335-36, 338-39, 343-44

The Owl's Insomnia (Alberti) 7:10

The Owls of North America (Eckert) 17:108

"The Owner of My Face" (Hall) 51:175

Ownerless Earth (Hamburger) 5:158-59

Owners (Churchill) 31:81-3; 55:126

"Owning a Wife" (Dacey) 51:83

Owning Jolene (Hearon) 63:168-70

"Owning Up" (Bowering) 47:25

"The Ox" (Bates) 46:55-6, 67

Ox (Anthony) 35:35

Ox Bells and Fireflies (Buckler) 13:122

The Ox-Bow Incident (Clark) 28:76-83

Ox-Cart Man (Hall) 37:145, 148

"Oxen: Ploughing at Fiesole" (Tomlinson) 13:547

"Oxenhope" (Warner) 7:513

"Oxford" (Auden) 14:26; 43:16

"Oxford" (Dorn) 10:159

Oxford Addresses on Poetry (Graves) 11:254

Oxford Blood (Fraser) 107:52

Oxford Book of Canadian Verse (Smith) 15:514

"Oxford Leave" (Ewart) 46:150

"Oxford Town" (Dylan) 77:166

"The Oxford Volunteers" (Huxley) 11:283

Oxherding Tale (Johnson) 51:229, 231-33, 235; 65:156-57

Oye, patria, mi aflicción (*Hear, My Country, My Affliction*) (Arrabal) 58:27-8

"Oysters" (Heaney) 14:244; 25:247-48; 74:159, 164-66; 91:118

"Oysters" (McGahern) 48:264

"Oysters" (Sexton) 53:324

"Oysters" (Snyder) 32:387

The Oysters of Locmariaquer (Clark) 19:105

"Oza" (Voznesensky) 57:413, 415, 426

Ozhog (*The Burn*) (Aksyonov) 22:28; 37:14-16; 101:24-6, 28-38, 41-2, 44, 47-8, 50, 52

Ozidi (Clark) 38:118, 124

"Oznob" ("Fever") (Akhmadulina) 53:10, 13-14

"Ozone" (Dove) 81:149, 151

O-Zone (Theroux) 46:403-05

"P" (Merrill) 8:385-88

"P. & O." (Maugham) 67:206

P. D. Kimerakov (Epstein) 27:127-28, 131

"P. S." (Reading) 47:352

Pabellón de reposo (*Rest Home; Rest Pavillion; Rest Ward*) (Cela) 4:96, 98; 59:126, 129, 142

Pábitelé (*The Palaverers*) (Hrabal) 67:121

"Pacelli and the Ethiop" (Cassity) 42:97

"Pacific Door" (Birney) 11:50

Pacific Highway (Wilding) 73:394-96, 398-99

Pacific Interlude (Wilson) 32:449

"Pacific Lament" (Olson) 29:330

"Pacific Letter" (Ondaatje) 51:314

Pacific Overtures (Sondheim) 30:387-88, 390-

82, 395-97, 399-402
"Pacing..." (Creeley)   78:141
Pack My Bag (Green)   13:253-54; 97:249-50, 257, 278, 280, 286-88, 291-92
Pack of Lies (Whitemore)   37:445-48
"The Package Store" (Dixon)   52:100
"Packages" (Stern)   39:243-44
Packages (Stern)   39:243-44
"A Packet for Ezra Pound" (Pound)   48:290
Paco's Story (Heinemann)   50:186-93
"The Pact" (Musgrave)   54:338
"The Paddiad" (Kavanagh)   22:235, 240, 243
Paddy Clarke Ha Ha Ha (Doyle)   81:156-61
"Paean to Place" (Niedecker)   10:360; 42:297-98, 300
Pagan Passport (Abe)
   See *Itan no passporto*
A Pagan Place (O'Brien)   5:313; 116:179, 183-84, 192, 227
"The Pagan Rabbi" (Ozick)   7:287, 288-89; 62:341-44, 350-51, 353-54
The Pagan Rabbi, and Other Stories (Ozick)   3:372; 7:287-88; 28:349-50, 355
Pagan Spain (Wright)   4:596; 21:443
"The Paganini Break" (West)   96:375
The Pageant of England (Costain)   30:95-6, 98-100
Pages from a Cold Island (Exley)   6:170-72; 11:186-87
"Pages from a Velvet Photograph Album" (Kis)   57:246
"Pages from a Voyage" (Corn)   33:114
"Pages from a Western Journal" (Richler)   46:352
"Pages from a Young Girl's Diary" ("A Young Girl's Journal") (Aickman)   57:3
"Pages from an Abandoned Journal" (Vidal)   33:406-07
"Pages from Cold Point" (Bowles)   19:61; 53:46
Pages from Parra (Parra)
   See *Hojas de Parra*
"Pages of a Wound Dresser's Diary" (Selzer)   74:281-82
Pagoda of Long Life (Pa Chin)   18:374
"Paho at Walpi" (Lewis)   41:260
Paid on Both Sides (Auden)   2:22; 6:24; 11:17; 14:30-1, 33-4; 43:17, 21, 24, 29
"The Pail" (Bly)   10:62
"Pain" (Mahapatra)   33:284
"Pain" (Simic)   9:479
"Pain" (Webb)   18:540
"The Pain Continuum" (Brodkey)   56:61
"Pain for a Daughter" (Sexton)   10:468
"A Pain I Dwell In" (Char)   9:166
"The Pain Is Not Excessive" (Lenz)
   See "Die Schmerzen sin zumutbar"
"Paingod" (Ellison)   13:203, 206
Paingod and Other Delusions (Ellison)   13:202; 42:126
"Pains" (Enright)   31:155
Paintbox Summer (Cavanna)   12:98
The Painted Bird (Kosinski)   1:171-72; 2:231-32; 3:272-73; 6:282-85; 10:306-09; 15:313-17; 53:218-22, 224-28; 70:297-98, 300-09
"Painted Desert" (Barthelme)   117:25-7
A Painted Devil (Billington)   43:55
Painted Devils (Aickman)   57:3
"The Painted Door" (Ross)   13:492-93
Painted Dresses (Hearon)   63:161-63
"Painted Finches" (Prichard)   46:345
The Painted Garden (Streatfeild)

   See *Movie Shoes*
"Painted Head" (Ransom)   4:431; 5:365
The Painted King (Davies)   23:147
The Painted Lady (Sagan)   36:380-82
Painted Rain   59:400-02
"Painted Steps" (Gallagher)   63:118
The Painted Veil (Maugham)   15:367, 370
"The Painted Window: Notes on Post-Realist Fiction" (Bowering)   47:29
The Painted Word (Wolfe)   15:585; 35:455-56, 460, 464; 51:416, 420
"The Painter" (Ashbery)   9:42; 13:35
"The Painter" (Hesse)   25:261
"A Painter" (Matthias)   9:361
"The Painter Dreaming in the Scholar's House" (Nemerov)   36:301
The Painter Gabriel (Newlove)   6:363
"Painter in Xyochtl" (Jacobsen)   48:190
The Painter of Signs (Narayan)   7:256; 28:299, 302
The Painter Went Poor into the World (Seifert)
   See *Šel malir chude do sveta*
"Painters" (Rukeyser)   10:443
Painting Churches (Howe)   48:174-78
Painting the Roses Red (Malone)   43:280
"Painwise" (Tiptree)   48:385
"Le pair" (Carrier)   78:58
A Pair of Baby Lambs (McFadden)   48:257
"A Pair of Glasses" (Gallagher)   63:122
"A Pair of Socks" (Sargeson)   31:363
"Pairing" (Ammons)   57:50
O país do carnaval (*Carnival Country*; *Carnival Land*; *Land of Carnival*) (Amado)   40:24-7; 106:55, 57, 89-90
"Paisagens com cupim" ("Landscapes with Termites") (Cabral de Melo Neto)   76:167
Paisagens com figuras (*Landscapes with Figures*) (Cabral de Melo Neto)   76:153, 158, 168
"Paisley Park" (Prince)   35:331-32
Paix dans les brisements (Michaux)   19:312-14
A paixão segundo G. H. (Lispector)   43:261-62, 266
"Pajaros sin descenso" (Aleixandre)   9:16
Pal Joey (O'Hara)   1:261; 6:384; 11:413; 42:312
"La palabra" (Aleixandre)   9:13
"Palabras antes de una lectura" (Cernuda)   54:50
"Palabras en el trópico" (Guillen)   48:166
"The Palace" (Transtroemer)   65:226
The Palace (Simon)
   See *Le palace*
Le palace (*The Palace*) (Simon)   4:495-96; 9:484; 15:487, 489-90, 492-93; 39:203-05, 207, 209-11
"The Palace at 4 A.M." (Barthelme)   46:38-9, 43; 59:251
"Palace Days" (White)   110:340
Palace of Ice (Vesaas)
   See *The Ice Palace*
Palace of Strangers (Masters)   48:220
Palace of the Peacock (Harris)   25:202-05, 210, 213, 218
Palace without Chairs (Brophy)   11:68-9; 105:16-18, 31, 33
"Palais de justice" (Helprin)   22:220-21, 223
Le palais de sable (Marcel)   15:360, 363
"Palais des Arts" (Gluck)   22:177; 81:173
Palaver: Political   Considerations (Enzensberger)
   See *Palaver: Politische Überlegungen*

Palaver: Politische Überlegungen (*Palaver: Political Considerations*) (Enzensberger)   43:154
The Palaverers (Hrabal)
   See *Pábitelé*
"A Pale and Perfectly Oval Moon" (Adams)   46:16
Pale Blue Dot (Sagan)   112:431, 433-34
"Pale Blue Eyes" (Reed)   21:305, 308, 311, 318, 322
Pale Fire (Nabokov)   1:240-41, 243-46; 2:299-303; 3:352-56; 6:351-53, 355-59; 8:407-15, 418; 11:392-93, 396; 15:392-93, 396-98; 23:311; 44:464-68; 46:291-92; 64:348, 366
"Pale Hands I Loathe" (Perelman)   49:265
The Pale Horse (Christie)   12:116; 110:113, 122
"Pale Horse, Pale Rider" (Porter)   101:228, 234, 252, 256
Pale Horse, Pale Rider (Porter)   3:393; 7:311, 315, 317; 10:398; 13:449-51; 15:429; 27:400-01
Pale Horse, Pale Rider: Three Short Novels (Porter)   7:309, 312, 314, 317; 10:398; 13:446; 101:212, 219, 229, 243, 249, 255
"Pale Light" (Montague)   46:269
"The Pale Ones" (Spacks)   14:511
"The Pale Panther" (MacNeice)   10:324
"The Pale Pink Roast" (Paley)   37:337
"Pale Tepid Ode" (Justice)   102:258
A Pale View of Hills (Ishiguro)   27:202-04; 56:158-61; 59:159, 163, 166-67; 110:220-25, 227-28, 231, 234, 236, 240, 246-47, 249-50, 257, 259, 261-62
The Paleface (Keaton)   20:188
"Paleface and Redskin" (Rahv)   24:352, 359
"A Paleolithic Fertility Fetish" (Szymborska)   99:200
"Paleontology" (Cioran)   64:89, 94
Palimpsest (H. D.)   31:204, 208, 210; 73:110-12, 123, 128-33, 135, 140
"Palindrome" (Perec)   56:254
"Palinode" (Hamburger)   5:159
"Palinodie" (Audiberti)   38:21
Il palio dei buffi (Palazzeschi)   11:432
"A Palladian Bridge" (Tuohy)   37:429
Palladium (Fulton)   52:160-62
"Pallinode" (H. D.)   31:207
"Palm Beach: Don't You Love It?" (Amis)   62:5
Palm Latitudes (Braverman)   67:50-3, 55
"Palm Sunday" (Bowers)   9:121-22
"Palm Sunday" (Clampitt)   32:114
"Palm Sunday" (Clifton)   19:109
"Palm Sunday" (Muldoon)   72:267-68
Palm Sunday (Marques)   96:224, 243
Palm Sunday: An Autobiographical Collage (Vonnegut)   22:449-52; 40:445-46; 111:368
"A Palm Tree in the Desert" (Christie)   110:125
Palm-of-the-Hand Stories (Kawabata)
   See *Palm-of-the-Hand Stories*
"The Palms" (Merwin)   88:213
The Palm-Sized Stories (Kawabata)
   See "Tanagokoro no Shosetsu"
The Palm-Wine Drinkard (Tutuola)   5:443, 445; 14:537-42; 29:434-37, 439, 441-43
"A palo seco" (Cabral de Melo Neto)   76:154, 161, 163
La paloma de vuelo popular: Elegiás (*The Dove of Popular Flight—Elegies*) (Guillen)   48:158, 161, 164; 79:229-30, 241

Paloma por dentro (*Dove Inside*) (Neruda) 62:336

Palomar (*Mr.; The Silent Mr. Palomar*) (Calvino) 39:306, 311, 314-17; 73:40-1, 43-7, 51, 57-9

"Palomas negras" (Ulibarri) 83:416

Palomino (Jolley) 46:213, 217

A Palpable God (Price) 13:464-65

Pals (Margulies) 76:193

"Palymyra" (Plomer) 4:407

Pamietnik okresu dojrzewania (*Memoirs from the Time of Immaturity*) (Gombrowicz) 49:121, 127

"Pamjati T. B." (Brodsky) 50:131

The Pamperers (Loy) 28:251

A Pamphlet against Anthologies (Riding) 7:373

"Pan" 75:76

"Pan and Syrinx" (Rodgers) 7:378

"Pan at Lane Cove" (Slessor) 14:492

Pan Cogito (*Mr. Cogito*) (Herbert) 9:274-76; 43:188

"Pan Cogito opowiada o kuszeniu Spinozy" ("Mr. Cogito Tells about the Temptation of Spinoza") (Herbert) 9:275; 43:187

"Pan with Us" (Frost) 26:117

Panama (McGuane) 18:323-26; 45:259-60, 262

"Panama, etc." (Cendrars) 106:158

"Le Panama ou les aventures de mes sept oncles" ("The Adventures of My Seven Uncles") (Cendrars) 18:92, 94; 106:152, 154, 158-59, 163, 167, 177, 181, 184, 186, 190-92, 196-97

"Pancakes for the Queen of Babylon" (Levi) 41:246

Pancakes for the Queen of Babylon: Ten Poems for Nikos Gatsos (Levi) 41:244-45, 248

Pandora (Fraser) 64:166-68, 171, 175-77

"Panel Game" (Coover) 87:40

Panels for the Walls of Heaven (Patchen) 18:392

"The Pangolin" (Moore) 8:401; 10:353; 19:340; 47:265

"The Pangs of Love" (Gardam) 43:171

"Pangs of Love" (Louie) 70:78

Pangs of Love (Louie) 70:78-81

The Pangs of Love, and Other Stories (Gardam) 43:170-71

Panic: A Play in Verse (MacLeish) 68:286, 293

Panic Encyclopedia: The Definitive Guide to the Postmodern Scene (Kroker) 77:344

Panic in the Streets (Kazan) 16:362, 367; 63:225

Pankraz Awakens (Zuckmayer) 18:554

Die Panne (*The Breakdown*) (Duerrenmatt) 102:61-2, 64

"Panorama" (Guillen) 11:262

Pantagleize (Ghelderode) 6:198; 11:227

Pantaleón y las visitadoras (*Captain Pantoja and the Special Service*) (Vargas Llosa) 6:543; 10:498, 501; 15:552; 31:443-45, 449; 42:404; 85:352, 355, 362, 380, 389, 395

"Pantaloon in Black" (Faulkner) 3:152; 8:213-14

Panther (Haig-Brown)
See *Ki-Yu: A Story of Panthers*

The Panther and the Lash: Poems of Our Times (Hughes) 10:279; 15:294; 35:218-20; 108:286, 290, 334

"The Panther Waits" (Ortiz) 45:309, 311

"A Panting" (Enzensberger) 43:145

"Pantomime" (Fearing) 51:106

Pantomime (Walcott) 25:454-55; 67:342, 346, 351-52; 76:275

"Pantoum" (Ashbery) 13:34; 25:50

"Panus Angelicus" (Muske) 90:313

Paolo Paoli (Adamov) 4:5; 25:12, 15, 20-1

Les Paons (Tremblay) 29:426

"Papa!" (Aksyonov) 101:11

Papa Boss (Ferron) 94:106, 110, 113

"Papa Montero's Wake" (Guillen)
See "Velorio de Papá Montero"

"Papa, What Does It Spell?" (Aksyonov) 101:10, 15, 20

Paper Boy (Huddle) 49:182-83

"Paper Children" (Jolley) 46:213

"Paper Cities" (Schnackenberg) 40:382

"Paper Cuts" (Jong) 6:268

Paper Dragon (Hunter) 31:221

The Paper Landscape (Aksyonov)
See *Bumazhnyi peizazh*

Paper Lion (Plimpton) 36:352-56

"Paper Matches" (Jiles) 58:271, 279, 281

The Paper Men (Golding) 81:315, 319-20, 322-23

"The Paper on the Floor" (Bukowski) 41:63

The Paper People (Findley) 102:98-9, 104

Paper Trail (Dorris) 109:298, 310

"Paperback Writer" (Lennon and McCartney) 35:288

"Papers" (Popa) 19:373

Papers from Lilliput (Priestley) 34:361

"The Papers of Professor Bold" (Orlovitz) 22:332

The Papers of Samuel Marchbanks (Davies) 42:105; 75:182-83, 187-89; 91:204, 207

The Papers of Tony Veitch (McIlvanney) 42:283-85

"The Paper-Spike" (Gustafson) 36:220

"The Paperweight" (Schnackenberg) 40:378

Papiers d'identité (Morand) 41:304

"Paprika Plains" (Mitchell) 12:443

"Papyrus" (Pound) 13:460; 48:292

Les pâques (*Easter in New York*) (Cendrars) 18:93; 106:159, 163, 177-78, 180, 184, 189-90, 195

"Par la fenêtre ouverte à demi" (Damas) 84:180

Para esta noche (Onetti) 7:277

Para leer al Pato Donald (*How to Read Donald Duck: Imperialist Ideology in the Disney Comic*) (Dorfman) 48:87-8, 94; 77:134-36, 153

"Para llegar a Montego Bay" ("The Approach to Montego Bay") (Lezama Lima) 101:121

"Para quién escribo" (Aleixandre)
See "Whom I Write For"

"Para una poética" (Cortazar) 92:158

Para una tumba sin nombre (*For a Nameless Tomb; Una tumba sin nombre*) (Onetti) 10:376

"A Parable" (Gluck) 44:222

"Parable" (Wilbur) 110:385

"Parable Island" (Heaney) 74:161

Parable of a Drowning Man (Delibes)
See *Parábola del náufrago*

The Parable of the Blind (Hofmann)
See *Der Blindensturz*

"The Parable of the Palace" (Borges) 13:112

Parabola (Voznesensky) 15:555

Parábola del náufrago (*Parable of a Drowning Man*) (Delibes) 8:169; 18:114-15

"Parabolas" (Voznesensky) 57:425

"Parabolicheskaya ballada" (Voznesensky) 57:416

Paracelsus (Ryga) 14:473

"Parachute" (Jagger and Richard) 17:223

Parachutes & Kisses (Jong) 83:310-2

"Parade" (Grace) 56:111-13, 120

Parade (Cocteau) 8:148; 15:134; 43:106, 108-09

The Parade Ends (Arenas)
See *Termina el desfile*

"A Parade in Town" (Sondheim) 30:379, 387

The Parade is Over (Arenas)
See *Termina el desfile*

"Parade of Painters" (Swenson) 61:390

"Parades Parades" (Walcott) 14:549; 76:274, 281

"Paradigm" (Allen) 84:4

Le paradis perdu (Jouve) 47:207

Paradísarheimt (*Paradise Reclaimed*) (Laxness) 25:292, 299

"Paradise" (O'Brien) 36:340-41; 116:186, 189, 191

Paradise (Barthelme) 46:43-5; 59:247, 249; 115:80-5

Paradise (Castedo) 65:31-41

Paradise (Forbes) 12:203-04

Paradise, and Other Stories (Moravia)
See *Il paradiso*

"Paradise Flycatcher" (Ezekiel) 61:101-02, 105, 107

"Paradise Found" (White) 110:333

Paradise Illustrated (Enright) 31:152-53, 155

Paradise Lost (Odets) 2:318-19; 28:324-25, 328, 332-33, 336, 340; 98:198, 200, 204-05, 207, 212, 217-24, 229-31, 233, 236, 238, 241-42

"The Paradise Lounge" (Trevor) 25:446; 116:363

"Paradise of Children" (Mahfuz) 52:298

"The Paradise of the Theologians" (Herbert) 9:275

"Paradise Park" (Millhauser) 109:170

Paradise Poems (Stern) 40:411-14; 100:333, 342

Paradise Postponed (Mortimer) 43:305-09

Paradise Reclaimed (Laxness)
See *Paradísarheimt*

Paradiso (Lezama Lima) 4:288-91; 10:317, 319-22; 101:102-03, 106-15, 118-22, 124, 128

Il paradiso (*Paradise, and Other Stories*) (Moravia) 2:293; 7:239, 242

"Paradox of Time" (Warren) 39:262

The Paradox Players (Duffy) 37:114

"Paradoxes and Oxymorons" (Ashbery) 25:54

"The Paraffin Lamp" (Brown) 100:82-3

"Paráfrase de reverdy" ("Free Translation Of Reverdy") (Cabral de Melo Neto) 76:163

Parages (Derrida) 87:92

The Paragon (Knowles) 1:169; 4:271-72; 10:303; 26:261-62

"Paragraphs" (Carruth) 18:88-9; 84:119, 136

The Paraguayan Experiment (Wilding) 73:396-97, 399, 405

"The Parallax Monograph for Rodin" (Dubie) 36:135

"The Parallel World" ("Parallel Worlds") (Martin) 89:111-12, 118

"Parallel Worlds" (Martin)
See "The Parallel World"

"Paralytic" (Plath) 9:427-28; 17:360; 51:341; 111:160, 163

"Paraphrases" (Fisher) 25:160

"Parapsyche" (Vance)   35:425
Paras pathar (*The Philosopher's Stone*) (Ray)
   16:477, 482, 491-93
"Parashut" (Bagryana)
   See "Vurni me"
The Parasite (*To Wake the Dead*) (Campbell)
   42:86-7, 90, 93
"A Parasite of Rui Barbosa" (Cabral de Melo
   Neto)
   See "Um piolho de Rui Barbosa"
Parasites of Heaven (Cohen)   38:135-36
Les paravents (*The Folding Screens*) (Genet)
   1:117; 2:158; 14:200; 44:385-89, 391;
   46:173, 183
"Parce que la comédie" (Damas)   84:159
"The Parcel" (Boland)   113:93, 100, 127
A Parcel of Patterns (Walsh)   35:434
A Parcel of Trees (Mayne)   12:389-90, 404,
   407
"Pardon" (Shields)   113:426
"The Pardon" (Wilbur)   6:570
Pardon Me, You're Stepping on My Eyeball!
   (Zindel)   26:474, 479-80
The Pardoner's Tale (Wain)   11:564; 15:561-
   62; 46:418
"Pareille à la légende" (Damas)   84:177
"Parentheses" (Ritsos)   31:328, 330
Parentheses, 1946-47 (Ritsos)   31:328-29
Parentheses, 1950-61 (Ritsos)   31:328-29
"Parents" (Barthelme)   117:5
"Parents" (Buckley)   57:126, 131
"Parents" (Smith)   3:460
Parents and Children (Compton-Burnett)
   34:500
"The parents left the child" (Amichai)   116:98
"The Parents: People Like Our Marriage, Maxie
   and Andrew" (Brooks)   49:26
Les parents terribles (*Intimate Relations*)
   (Cocteau)   8:148-49; 15:132, 134; 16:226,
   228; 43:104-06, 108-11
"Parergon" (Ashbery)   2:19
"Parergon" (Derrida)   87:92
"Paring the Apple" (Tomlinson)   13:546;
   45:392, 399
"Paris" (Muldoon)   32:319; 72:266
"Paris" (Ondaatje)   29:341
Paris (Green)   77:288, 294
"Paris, 1968" (Rosenthal)   28:394
"Paris and Helen" (Schwartz)   45:355
Paris Journal, 1937-1939 (Gascoyne)   45:155,
   157-58
Paris, New York: 1982-1984 (Brandys)   62:116-
   17, 119-20
Paris! Paris! (Shaw)   34:370
Paris qui dort (*The Crazy Ray*) (Clair)   20:57,
   66, 69
Paris, Texas (Shepard)   41:413-14
"Paris: The May Revolution" (Fuentes)   60:164
"Paris: This April Sunset Completely Utters;
   Post Impressions" (Cummings)   15:155
Paris Trout (Dexter)   55:129-32
"Paris Without Rhyme" (Voznesensky)   57:420
Parish Churches (Betjeman)   43:49
Paris—Tombouctou (Morand)   41:304
"The Park" (Fisher)   25:157
"The Park" (Levertov)   1:176
"The Park" (Williams)   56:427
"Park-Bench Vacation" (Calvino)   33:100
"Parker's Back" (O'Connor)   21:268, 271,
   276-77, 279; 104:112, 115, 124, 138,
   158-59, 166-67, 178, 187-88, 197
"Parker's Band" (Becker and Fagen)   26:79
"Parker's Dog" (Vanderhaeghe)   41:450, 452

"The Parking Lot" (Beattie)   63:10
Parktilden Village (Elliott)   2:130-31
Les parleuses (*Woman to Woman*) (Duras)
   6:151; 68:86-9; 100:129
"Parliament Hill Fields" (Betjeman)   43:32
"Parliament Hill Fields" (Plath)   51:345;
   111:167, 201
Parlor, Bedlam, and Bath (Perelman)   23:334;
   44:503
La parodie (*The Parody*) (Adamov)   4:5; 25:11-
   12, 17-20
The Parody (Adamov)
   See *La parodie*
"Parody for the Poem 'Paterson'" (Williams)
   42:455
"Paroi" (Guillevic)   33:194
"Parola" (Bagryana)
   See "Kontrapunkti"
La parole des femmes (Conde)   92:100-01,
   112
La parole en archipel (Char)   14:127; 55:288
"Parole in agitazione" (Landolfi)   49:215
Paroles (Prevert)   15:437
"Parousia" (Gluck)   81:166
La parrocchie di Regalpetra (*Salt in the Wound*)
   (Sciascia)   8:473; 9:475; 41:392-93
"The Parrot" (Ferron)   94:126
"The Parrot Who Met Papa" (Bradbury)   42:35
"The Parrotfish" (Szirtes)   46:393
Parrot's Perch (Rio)
   See *Le perchoir du perroquet*
Parry of the Arctic (Berton)   104:61
The Parsifal Mosaic (Ludlum)   43:276
"Parsley" (Dove)   81:134, 138
"The Parsley Garden" (Saroyan)   8:468
Parsley, Sage, Rosemary, and Thyme (Simon)
   17:459-60, 464, 466
"Parsnips" (Tomlinson)   45:397
Parson's Nine (Streatfeild)   21:394-95
"Parson's Pleasure" (Dahl)   79:176, 178, 183
The Parson's Progress (Mackenzie)   18:314
Parson's Widow (Dreyer)   16:259-61, 265
A Part (Berry)   27:37; 46:69-70
La part maudite (Bataille)   29:42, 49-50
"Part of a Letter" (Wilbur)   53:404, 407
"Part of a Novel, Part of a Poem, Part of a
   Play" (Moore)   13:395
"Part of Mandevil's Travels" (Empson)   19:154
"A Part of Speech" (Brodsky)
   See "Cast reci"
A Part of Speech (Brodsky)
   See *Cast reci*
"Part of the Doctrine" (Baraka)   5:48
"Part of What Might Have Been a Short Story,
   Almost Forgotten" (Warren)   39:272
"Part Song, with Concert of Recorders"
   (Dickey)   28:117
Partage formel (Char)   9:161
"Parthenope" (West)   50:405
Le parti pris de choses (Ponge)   18:419
"Partial Accounts" (Meredith)   55:191
Partial Accounts: New and Selected Poems
   (Meredith)   55:190-93
"Partial Eclipse" (Snodgrass)   18:491
"Partial Enchantments of the *Quixote*" (Borges)
   See "Magias parciales del Quijote"
"Partial Magic in the *Quixote*" (Borges)
   See "Magias parciales del Quijote"
"A Partial State" (Paulin)   37:353
"A Partial View" (Scannell)   49:331
"La participación de la mujer mexicana en la
   educación formal" (Castellanos)   66:46
Parti-Colored Blocks for a Quilt (Piercy)

62:373
The Particularity of the Aesthetic (Lukacs)
   24:330
Particularly Cats...and Rufus (Lessing)   94:271-
   72
Une partie de campagne (Renoir)   20:310-11
La Partie pour le tout (Brossard)   115:103-05
Parties (Van Vechten)   33:394-95, 397-99
"Parting" (Ammons)   25:45; 108:56
"Parting" (Bennett)   28:26
"Parting" (Layton)   15:319
"Parting" (Lorde)   71:252
"Parting" (Pasternak)   63:313
"Parting Is Such Sweet Sorrow" (Adcock)   41:13
"Parti-pris" (Damas)   84:179
Partir avant le jour (*To Leave before Dawn*)
   (Green)   3:204; 77:271-73, 276-77, 289
Partisans (MacLean)   63:266-67
Partisans (Matthiessen)   32:285, 290; 64:327
Partner (Bertolucci)   16:87, 91, 94, 100
"Partners" (McGuane)   45:265
The Partners (Auchincloss)   4:30-1; 6:15
Partners in Crime (Christie)   12:112; 110:111
A Partnership of Mind and Body (Kettelkamp)
   12:307
"The Partridge Festival" (O'Connor)   104:178,
   187-88
"Parts of Speech" (Thesen)   56:415
"Parts of the Eagle" (Kinsella)   43:254
"Part-Time" (p'Bitek)   96:287
"Partway round the Course" (Sagan)   36:382
"The Party" (Avison)   97:68-9, 71
"The Party" (Barthelme)   115:65
"The Party" (Creeley)   78:126
"The Party" (Elkin)   51:96
"Party" (Lively)   32:273
"The Party" (Ochs)   17:331-32
The Party (Griffiths)   13:255-56; 52:171-72,
   174, 178, 185
"Party at Bannon Brook" (Nowlan)   15:399
"A Party Down at the Square" (Ellison)
   114:125-26, 131, 138
"A Party for the Girls" (Bates)   46:67
Party Frock (Streatfeild)   21:415
"Party Game" (Urquhart)   90:375
Party Going (Green)   2:178; 13:251, 253-55;
   97:242-43, 245-49, 254-55, 257, 268,
   270-72, 277-82, 287-88, 290, 292
"Party Piece" (Muldoon)   72:265
Party Shoes (Streatfeild)   21:399
"Party Up" (Prince)   35:324-25
"The Party-Givers" (Adams)   46:16
The Party's Over (*Fin de fiesta*) (Goytisolo)
   23:189
"Parvardigar" (Townshend)   17:528
"Les pas" (Carrier)   78:60
"Le pas de Gamelin" (Ferron)   94:129
Les pas perdus (Breton)   54:32
"El pasa del norte" ("Northern Pass") (Rulfo)
   80:200
"El pasado" (Borges)   6:90
Pasado en claro (*A Draft of Shadows*) (Paz)
   10:393; 19:368; 51:326-27, 333, 337;
   65:197, 200
Pasajes de la guerra revolucionaria (*Episodes
   of the Revolutionary War; Passages from
   the Revolutionary War; Reminiscences of
   the Cuban Revolutionary War*) (Guevara)
   87:199-200, 203-04, 206, 210
"Pasar" (Otero)   11:427
"Pascal" (Huxley)   35:241
"Pascal" (Muldoon)   72:280
Pascal (Ringwood)   48:330

Pascali's Island (*The Idol Hunter*) (Unsworth)
76:252, 256, 259
"Pascal's Sphere" ("The Sphere of Pascal")
(Borges) 8:100; 83:160, 163
Páscoa feliz (Migueis) 10:341
"Pascoli e Montale" (Pasolini) 106:232
Pascual Duarte's Family (Cela)
See *La familia de Pascual Duarte*
"Paseo" (Donoso) 11:146-48; 32:156-58
Pasii profetului (*The Footprints of the Prophet*;
In the Footsteps of the Prophet; *The
Prophet's Steps*) 75:65, 67-9, 74, 76-7
Pasión de la tierra (*Passion of the Earth*)
(Aleixandre) 9:10-11, 15; 36:23, 25-6,
28-31
"Pasiphae" (Hope) 51:220
Pasmore (Storey) 2:425-26; 4:529-30; 8:505
"El Paso" (Phillips) 15:420
El Paso de los Gansos (*The Chilean Spring*;
The Goosesteppers) (Alegria) 57:12, 13-
14
Los pasos perdidos (*The Lost Steps*)
(Carpentier) 8:134; 11:100, 102, 104-
07; 38:89-90, 92-6, 98-9; 110:53, 56, 60,
64-7, 84, 90, 96-7, 103, 105
Pasqualino settebellezze (*Seven Beauties*)
(Wertmueller) 16:590-93, 595-99
Pasque Flower (Ringwood) 48:330, 334-39
The Pass (Savage) 40:369-70
"Pass Away" (Berry) 17:56
"Pass fe White" (Bennett) 28:29
"Pass on by" (Guillen)
See "Sigue"
Pass th Food Release th Spirit Book (Bissett)
18:60
Passacaille (*Recurrent Melody: Passcaglia*)
(Pinget) 7:306; 13:442-44; 37:359-361
"Passage" (Levertov) 66:245
"Passage" (Okigbo) 25:347-48, 351, 355;
84:300, 307-10, 312-13, 324, 326-27,
329, 331-32, 337, 342
"Passage" (Vliet) 22:443
"Le passage de l'oiseau divin" (Breton) 9:134
Passage de Milan (Butor) 3:92; 8:114-19,
121; 11:79-80; 15:115-17
Passage du malin (Mauriac) 56:215
Passage of Arms (Ambler) 9:19
"Le passage Pommeraye" (Mandiargues)
41:277-79
"Passage to Godhead" (Rukeyser) 27:405
A Passage to India (Forster) 1:103-04, 106-
08; 2:135; 3:159-61; 4:165, 167-69;
9:206-09; 10:179-81; 13:215, 218-22;
15:223, 227-28; 22:130-35, 137; 45:132-
33, 135-39, 141-44; 77:194- 257
"Passages" (Duncan) 41:124, 128-30
Passages (Duncan) 2:122; 4:141; 15:190-92
Passages (Michaux) 8:392
Passages 24 (Duncan) 55:297-98
Passages from the Revolutionary War (Guevara)
See *Pasajes de la guerra revolucionaria*
The Passages of Joy (Gunn) 32:212-15; 81:184
"Passages toward a Long Poem" (Aldington)
49:11
"Passato prossimo" (Levi) 37:224
"La passeggiata" (Landolfi) 49:215
"The Passenger" (Calisher) 38:76
"The Passenger" (Nabokov) 15:394
The Passenger (Antonioni) 20:39-42
Passenger (Keneally) 14:301-03; 19:248;
43:236-37; 117:224, 226-27
"Passenger Pigeons" (Jeffers) 54:247
Passenger to Frankfurt (Christie) 12:117-18;

39:438
"Passengers" (Johnson) 52:234
"Passengers" (Silverberg) 7:425
"Passengers" (Wolff) 64:446, 449
Passengers of Destiny (Aragon)
See *Les voyageurs de l'impériale*
"Passers-By on a Snowy Night" (Warren)
18:539; 39:265, 272
"A Passing" (Christie) 110:127
Passing (Larsen) 37:211-19
Passing Game (Tesich) 40:420-21
"Passing It On" (Saner) 9:469
The Passing of the Dragons (Roberts) 14:464
The Passing of the Third-Floor Buck
(Waterhouse) 47:420
"Passing over Your Virtues" (Hearne) 56:128
The Passing Scene (Ritter) 52:354, 357
"Passing the Word" (Dobyns) 37:75
"Passing Time" (Angelou) 77:29
"Passing Time" (Ihimaera) 46:200
Passing Time (Butor)
See *L'emploi du temps*
"Passion" (Elytis) 100:156, 159, 161, 163,
165, 183
"Passion" (Oates) 108:382
"Passion" (O'Faolain) 32:341
A Passion (Bergman)
See *En Passion*
Passion (Bond) 23:66
Passion (Nichols)
See *Passion Play*
The Passion (Winterson) 64:428-30, 432-35,
440-42, 444
Passion and Affect (*Dangerous French Mistress,
and Other Stories*) (Colwin) 5:107-08;
23:128; 84:146, 149-51
The Passion Artist (Hawkes) 15:276-79;
27:194-96, 198-99; 49:163-65
La passion de Jeanne d'Arc (*The Passion of
Joan of Arc*) (Dreyer) 16:255-57, 259-
66
La passion de Joseph Pasquier (*Joseph
Pasquier's Passion*) (Duhamel) 8:189
La passion des femmes (*The Passion of Women;
Women in Evidence*) (Japrisot) 90:169
"A Passion in Eden" (Greenberg) 7:134
A Passion in Rome (Callaghan) 14:102; 41:90,
96; 65:246, 248, 250
Passion: New Poems, 1977-1980 (Jordan)
23:255-56, 258; 114:142, 146, 155, 158,
161
The Passion of Anna (Bergman)
See *En Passion*
The Passion of Ayn Rand (Branden) 44:448,
450, 452-54
The Passion of Joan of Arc (Dreyer)
See *La passion de Jeanne d'Arc*
The Passion of Joseph D (Chayefsky) 23:114
The Passion of Molly T. (Sanders) 41:382
The Passion of New Eve (Carter) 41:115-16;
76:324, 329
Passion of the Earth (Aleixandre)
See *Pasión de la tierra*
The Passion of Women (Japrisot)
See *La passion des femmes*
Passion Play (Kosinski) 15:315-17; 53:216,
220-22, 227; 70:298, 306
Passion Play (*Passion*) (Nichols) 36:329-31
Passion simple (*Simple Passion*) (Ernaux)
88:113-19
The Passionate Past of Gloria Gaye (Kops)
4:274
"The Passionate Shopping Mall" (Baxter)

78:29
"La passione" (Pasolini) 106:268
Passione (Innaurato) 21:197-99; 60:200-01,
205-06
Passione e ideologia (Pasolini) 106:245
Passionless Moments (Campion) 95:2, 6
"Passions" (Singer) 9:487, 489
Passions and Impressions (Neruda) 62:324-
27
Passions, and Other Stories (Singer) 6:510-
11; 9:487, 489; 11:499; 15:509; 23:420
The Passions of the Mind (Stone) 7:470-71
The Passions of Uxport (Kumin) 28:221-22
Passions Spin the Plot (Fisher) 7:103
The Passport (Samarakis)
See *To diav*
"The Passport Officer" (Bunting) 47:53
Passport to Fame (Ford) 16:307-08
Passport to the War (Kunitz) 14:312
"Past" (Sanchez) 116:274, 280
The Past (Jordan) 110:269-70, 272, 275
Past All Dishonor (Cain) 28:51-3
"Past and Present" (Jones) 42:245
The Past as Future (Habermas) 104:98-99
The Past Is the Past (Wesley) 7:518-19
"The Past Is the Present" (Moore) 8:399
"Past Midnight" (Motion) 47:293
The Past Now: New Poems (Gregor) 9:255-56
"Past Paradise" (Wonder)
See "Pastime Paradise"
"The Past, Present and Future" (Tolson)
105:280
"The Past Reordered" (Ignatow) 7:176
The Past through Tomorrow (Heinlein) 8:275
Le Pastaga des loufs ou Ouverture orang-outan
(Arrabal) 58:18
Pastel de choclo (*Last Waltz in Santiago, and
Other Poems of Exile and Disappearance*)
(Dorfman) 77:133
"Pastime Paradise" ("Past Paradise") (Won-
der) 12:659, 662
Pastimes of a Red Summer (Vansittart) 42:394
"Pastor Dowe at Tacaté" (Bowles) 19:60;
53:36-7
Pastor Prayers (Ezekiel) 61:107
"Pastor Prayers—8" (Ezekiel) 61:109
"Pastor Prayers—9" (Ezekiel) 61:108
"A Pastoral" (Ashbery) 13:35
"Pastoral" (Carver) 55:279
"Pastoral" (Dove) 81:150
"Pastoral" (Dubie) 36:130
"Pastoral" (Hall) 59:151, 154-56
"Pastoral" (Landolfi) 49:209
"Pastoral" (Mathias) 45:235
"Pastoral" (Simic) 68:368-69
Pastoral (Shute) 30:372
"Pastoral Care" (Gardner) 5:133-34; 7:112-
13, 116; 8:238
Pastoral Jazz (Broumas) 73:8-9, 13-14
Pastoral; or, Time for Cocoa (Hildesheimer)
See *Pastorale; oder, Die Zeit für Kakao*
"Pastorale" (Cain) 28:47
Pastorale; oder, Die Zeit für Kakao (*Pastoral;
or, Time for Cocoa*) (Hildesheimer)
49:167, 171
"A Pastorale of Sorts" (Turco) 63:429
Pastorals: A Book of Verses (Blunden) 56:40,
49
"Pastorela di Narcis" (Pasolini) 106:230
Os pastores da noite (*Shepherds of the Night*)
(Amado) 40:31-2; 106:64, 73, 77
Pastors and Masters (Compton-Burnett) 1:61;
3:112; 10:109-10; 15:135, 138; 34:495,

498, 500
"Pastrami Brothers" (Swados)   12:558
"The Pasture" (Frost)   3:170; 15:247-48
"The Pasture Pond" (Blunden)   56:29, 39, 51
The Pastures of Heaven (Steinbeck)   1:325; 9:513, 518; 13:531; 21:366, 380-81, 385; 34:415; 45:373-74, 382:59:317, 333-334; 75:360
"Pastures of Plenty" (Guthrie)   35:187, 194
Pastures of the Blue Crane (Brinsmead)   21:25-6, 30
"Pat Collins" (O'Hara)   42:319
Pat Garrett and Billy the Kid (Peckinpah)   20:278-79, 282, 284-85
Pat Hobby and Orson Welles (Welles)   80:413
"Pat McGee" (Farrell)   66:129
Pataphysical Poems (Queneau)
   See *Pounding the Pavements, Beating the Bushes, and Other Pataphysical Poems*
"Pataxanadu" (Middleton)   13:389
Pataxanadu and Other Prose (Middleton)   13:389
The Patch Boys (Parini)   54:363
"Patchwork" (Boland)   113:124
"Patchwork" (Longley)   29:296
"Patent Leather" (Brooks)   49:26
"Paterson" (Ginsberg)   4:183; 36:182; 109:354
Paterson (Williams)   1:369-72; 2:466-70; 5:506-10; 9:571-73; 13:602-05; 22:465-69; 42:449-52, 455-57, 459-61, 464; 67:395-427
Paterson I (Williams)   9:572-73; 13:603; 22:465, 467-68; 42:455-56
Paterson II (Williams)   9:572-73; 22:465, 467; 42:452-54, 456
Paterson III (Williams)   5:508; 9:572-73; 22:465, 467
Paterson IV (Williams)   9:571-73; 22:465, 467
Paterson V (Williams)   5:508; 9:571-73; 13:603; 22:465-68; 42:451, 460
"Path" (Hoffman)   6:244
"Path" (Merwin)   8:390
The Path (Delibes)
   See *El camino*
Path of Dalliance (Waugh)   7:513-14
Path of Hunters: Animal Struggle in a Meadow (Peck)   17:337-38
The Path of the Happy Man (Lagerkvist)
   See *Den lyckliges väg*
"The Path of the Moon's Dark Fortnight" (Gordimer)   33:180
"Path of Thunder" (Okigbo)   84:336, 342
The Path of Thunder (Abrahams)   4:3
Path of Thunder (Okigbo)
   See *Labyrinths, with Path of Thunder*
The Path to the Nest of the Spiders (Calvino)
   See *Il sentiero dei nidi di ragno*
A Path Where No Man Thought (Sagan)   112:429-30
Pather panchali (*The Song of the Little Road*; *The Song of the Road*) (Ray)   16:474-80, 482, 484-85, 489-91; 76:356-58, 360-64, 366
"Pathology of Colours" (Abse)   29:18
"Paths" (Miles)   14:369
Paths (Transtroemer)
   See *Stigar*
Paths of Glory (Kubrick)   16:377-80, 382-87
Pathways to the Gods (von Daniken)   30:428
"Patience" (Reid)   33:348
"Patience" (Reverdy)   53:290
"Patience Is a Leveling Thing" (Jensen)   37:189

The Patience of Maigret (Simenon)   47:370
Les patients (Audiberti)   38:31
"Patisserie" (Willard)   37:463
"Patmos" (Elytis)   49:110
Patooie (Peck)   17:342
"Patria de retorno" (Ulibarri)   83:412
Patria mia (Pound)   13:457; 112:315-18, 320, 338
Patria o muerte! The Great Zoo, and Other Poems by Nicolás Guillén (Guillen)
   See *El gran zoo*
"The Patriarch" (Grau)   9:240
The Patriarch (Bermant)   40:94-5
Patriarchal Attitudes (Figes)   31:162-63, 167
"Patricia's Poem" (Jordan)   114:145
Patrick Kentigern Keenan (Hunter)
   See *The Smartest Man in Ireland*
Patrimony: A True Story (Roth)   86:249, 254, 257, 263
"The Patriot" (O'Faolain)   70:314
The Patriot (Buck)   11:75, 77
The Patriot (Connell)   45:108-09
A Patriot For Me (Osborne)   5:332; 11:421; 45:313-16, 321
Patriot Games (Clancy)   112:50-1, 55-6, 63, 66-7, 72, 74-5, 77, 84, 90, 93
"Patriotic" (Kauffman)   42:251-52
Patriotic Gore (Wilson)   1:372-73; 2:476; 3:538; 8:550; 24:478, 481, 487-89
The Patriotic Murders (Christie)
   See *One, Two, Buckle My Shoe*
"Patriotic Poem" (Wain)   11:562
Patriotic Suite (Montague)   46:264, 270-71
"Patriotism" (Mishima)   6:339; 27:341-42
The Patriots (Kingsley)   44:234
"The Patriot's Dream" (Lightfoot)   26:278
"The Patrol" (Lem)   40:291
"A Pattern" (Jennings)   14:292
The Pattern (Buckley)   57:133-36
Pattern for a Tapestry (Dourado)
   See *O risco do bordado*
Pattern for a Tapestry (Dourado)
   See *Risco do bordado*
"Pattern for Death" (Still)   49:363
"Pattern for Survival" (Matheson)   37:246
The Pattern of the Future (Comfort)   7:52
Patternmaster (Butler)   38:61-2, 64, 66
"Patterns" (Janowitz)   43:212
Patterns (Serling)   30:353, 358
Patterns and Coincidences (Neihardt)   32:336
Patterns in Comparative Religion (Eliade)   19:147
Patterns of Childhood (Wolf)
   See *Kindheitsmuster*
"The Patterns of Dorne" (Sturgeon)   22:411
"Patty Hearst" (Coupland)   85:36
Paul Celan: Poems (*Poems of Paul Celan*) (Celan)   19:95; 82:34, 38-39, 41
"Paul Eluard" (Guillen)   79:229
"Paul Klee" (Haines)   58; 220
"Paul Laurence Dunbar" (Hayden)   37:153
"Paul Revere" (Jiles)   58:273
Paul Revere and the World He Lived In (Forbes)   12:205-07
"Paul Revere's Ride" (Whittemore)   4:588
"Paul Robeson" (Brooks)   49:30
Paul Robeson: The Life and Times of a Free Black Man (Hamilton)   26:150
Paul Simon (Simon)   17:461-66
Paula (Allende)   97:56-64
Paulina, 1880 (Jouve)   47:203, 210
"Paulo Freire" (hooks)   94:156
"Paul's Wife" (Frost)   9:218; 26:119

"The Pauper Witch of Grafton" (Frost)   1:110; 9:224-25; 15:244
"Paura alla scala" ("The Scala Scare") (Buzzati)   36:83-4, 86, 94, 96
Pauvre Bitos; ou, Le dîner de têtes (*Poor Bitos*) (Anouilh)   1:7; 13:17, 20-2; 40:56-8; 50:279-81
Le pauvre Christ de Bomba (*The Poor Christ of Bomba*) (Beti)   27:42-5, 49, 52
"Pavan for a Dead Prince" (Delaney)   29:146
"Pavana dolorosa" (Hill)   45:180
Pavane (Roberts)   14:464
Pavannes (Pound)   7:326
Pavarotti: My Own Story (Wright)   44:527
"Paved Roads" (Aksyonov)   101:13-14
Pavilion of Women (Buck)   11:76-7
Pawley's Peepholes (Wyndham)   19:474
"Pawn to Bishop's Five" (Masefield)   47:233
The Pawnbroker (Wallant)   5:478; 10:511-15
"The Pawnbroker's Wife" (Spark)   13:519-20
Pawnshop (Breton)
   See *Mont de piété*
"Pax magna"   75:68
Pay Day (Chaplin)   16:191
"Pay It Back" (Costello)   21:67
Payday (Carpenter)   41:107
"The Paying Guests" (Mistry)   71:272
Payment Deferred (Forester)   35:165-66, 170
"Payne Whitney" (Schuyler)   23:390
Les pays lointains (*The Distant Lands*) (Green)   77:283-90, 292-94
Pays mêlé (Conde)   52:83-4; 92:101
"Pays Natal" (Walcott)   76:278
"Pays Perdu" (Garrigue)   8:239
"Paysage de répons" (Butor)   3:93
"Paysage de répons illustré par dialogues des règnes" (Butor)   3:93
"Paysage Moralisé" (Auden)   11:17; 14:27
Le paysan de Paris (*The Peasant from Paris*) (Aragon)   3:14; 22:36, 40
Le paysan de Paris (Breton)   15:90
"Les paysans" (Malraux)
   See "*L'espoir*"
Pe o palma de tarîna (*A Strip of Land*) (Arghezi)   80:13
"Pea Soup" (Reid)   33:349
Pea Soup (Reid)   33:349-51
"Peace" (Levine)   33:271
"Peace" (Simon)   17:461
Peace Breaks Out (Knowles)   26:263-65
Peace Eye (Sanders)   53:304
"Peace Frog" (Morrison)   17:295-96
"Peace in Mind" (Armatrading)   17:9
Peace in Our Time (Coward)   29:136
"Peace in the Welsh Hills" (Watkins)   43:453-54
"Peace Is a Stratified Concept" (Allen)   84:40
Peace like a River (Fisher)   7:103
"The Peace of Cities" (Wilbur)   53:397
"Peace of Mind" (Boyle)   90:45, 48
"Peace of Mind" (Young)   17:580
"The Peace of Utrecht" (Munro)   10:358; 95:305
Peace Shall Destroy Many (Wiebe)   6:567; 14:572-74
"The Peaceable Kingdom" (Piercy)   6:401; 18:406; 27:374
The Peaceable Kingdom (de Hartog)   19:132-33
The Peaceable Kingdom (Silkin)   6:498; 43:397-401
"The Peaceable Kingdom of Emerald Windows" (Chappell)   40:144

"The Peacefulness of Vivyan" (Tiptree) 48:385
"The Peacelike Mongoose" (Thurber) 5:434
The Peacemaker (Forester) 35:165-66
"The Peach Tree" (Sitwell) 67:324
"The Peach Tree" (Swan) 69:364
"Peaches" (McGahern) 48:263, 266, 268
"The Peach-Tree" (Bates) 46:50
"The Peacock" (Mosher) 62:313
The Peacock Feather Murders (The Ten Tea-cups) (Carr) 3:101
The Peacock Poems (Williams) 89:320, 324-25, 332, 358
"Peacock's Superette" (Peacock) 60:292
The Peacock's Tail (Hoagland) 28:180
"Peak" (Ammons) 8:16; 9:30; 57:59
Peake's Progress: Selected Writings and Draw-ings of Mervyn Peake (Peake) 54:372, 378
"The Pealing" (Broumas) 73:17
"Peals of Crying" (p'Bitek) 96:287
"Peanuts" (Police, The) 26:363
Peanuts (Schulz) 12:522, 524-25, 527-31, 533
Peanuts Jubilee (Schulz) 12:531-33
Peanuts Treasury (Schulz) 12:525
"Pear Tree" (H. D.) 14:223; 73:118
"Pear Tree" (Livesay) 79:338, 342, 350, 352
"Pear Tree Dance" (Jolley) 46:220-21
"Pear-Brown Rome" (Denby) 48:83
The Pearl (Steinbeck) 1:325; 5:407; 13:533-34; 21:368, 370-71, 382; 45:374, 383; 75:343
Pearl at the Bottom (Hrabal)
    See Perlicka na dne
Pearl of the Deep (Hrabal)
    See Perlicka na dne
The Pearlkillers (Ingalls) 42:234
"The Pearls" (Dinesen) 29:159; 95:35
Pearls before Swine (Allingham)
    See Coroner's Pidgin
Pearl's Progress (Kaplan) 59:70-73
"Pears" (Kis) 57:246
"Peasant" (Merwin) 88:206
"A Peasant" (Thomas) 6:534
The Peasant from Paris (Aragon)
    See Le paysan de Paris
The Peasant Mandarin (Murray) 40:338-39
"Peasants" (O'Connor) 14:398; 23:332-33
La peau douce (The Soft Skin; The Tender Skin) (Truffaut) 20:383, 389, 405; 101:375, 377, 379, 385
Peau noire, masques blancs (Black Skins and White Masks; Black Skins, White Masks) (Fanon) 74:71-2, 74-81, 83
"Pebble" (Herbert) 9:272
Pebble in the Sky (Asimov) 26:48, 64; 76:315
Peckham's Marbles (De Vries) 46:137-38
A Peculiar Treasure (Ferber) 93:171, 177, 179, 186-87, 190
The Peddler and Other Domestic Matter (Sum-mers) 10:493
"A Peddler's Memories" (Goldemberg) 52:165
"The Pedersen Kid" (Gass) 2:154; 11:224; 15:255-56; 39:478
"The Pedestrian" (Bradbury) 42:32, 34
The Pedestrian (Bradbury) 42:33
"A Pedestrian Accident" (Coover) 46:116
"Pedestrian Crossin'" (Bennett) 28:27, 29
"Pedestrian Pastoral" (Ryan) 65:213
Pedigree (Simenon) 1:309
The Pedlar's Revenge, and Other Stories (O'Flaherty) 34:356
Pedra do sono (Stone of Sleep) (Cabral de Melo

Neto) 76:150, 152, 156
"Pedro imaginário" ("Pedro the Image Carver") (Dourado) 60:85
Pedro Páramo (Rulfo) 8:462; 80:199-208, 210-14, 216-19, 221-24
"Pedro the Image Carver" (Dourado)
    See "Pedro imaginário"
Peel: An Exercise in Discipline (Campion) 95:6, 11
"Peeling" (Carey) 40:128-29; 96:24, 27, 35, 37, 67
"Peeling Fence Posts" (Kumin) 28:223
"The Peeper" (Davison) 28:100
"The Peeping Tom" (Knowles) 26:258
"Peerless Jim Driscoll" (Scannell) 49:331
"Peg" (Becker and Fagen) 26:84
"Pegasus" (Kavanagh) 22:235, 237
Pegasus and Other Poems (Day Lewis) 6:126; 10:128-29, 131
"Peggety's Parcel of Shortcomings" (Hersey) 81:329
Peggy (Duncan) 26:102
"Peggy Day" (Dylan) 12:186
Pegil pes, begushchij kraem moria (Piebald Dog Running along the Shore; The Skew-bald Dog Running along the Seashore; The Skewbald Dog Running at the Edge of the Sea; A Spotted Dog) (Aitmatov) 71:7-8, 11-12, 15, 21, 32-3
The Pegnitz Junction (Gallant) 7:110-11; 38:194
"Peirce and Communication" (Habermas) 104:87
"Pel Tvardovsky v nochnoy Florentsii, B'yut zhenschinu" (Voznesensky) 57:417
Die Pelerine (The Cape) (Eliade) 19:147
"Pelican" (Wright) 53:423
The Pelican Brief (Grisham) 84:193-95, 198-99
A Pelican of Blondings (Wodehouse)
    See No Nudes Is Good Nudes
"The Pen" (Carver) 55:276
"Pen in the Mouth" (Hope) 52:209
Pen, Sword, Camisole: A Fable to Kindle a Hope (Amado) 40:36-7
"Penal Rock/Altamuskin" (Montague) 46:270
"Penalty of Godhead" (Achebe) 11:4
"Penance" (Dybek) 114:62
"Penance" (Kinsella) 27:237
"Penance" (Williams) 33:443
"The Pencil" (Crispin) 22:111-12
Pencil Letter (Ratushinskaya) 54:382
"Penda's Fen" (Rudkin) 14:471
Le pendu de Saint-Pholien (Maigret and the Hundred Gibbets) (Simenon) 3:451; 8:487; 47:371, 374
"The Pendulum's Swing" (Brodsky) 100:40
"Penelope" (Bitov) 57:115
Penelope (Maugham) 15:366; 67:223
Penelope (Happy Birthday, Wanda June) (Vonnegut) 2:452; 3:500; 8:530; 12:605, 610, 619, 626; 40:443
"Penelope at Her Loom" (Graham)
    See "Self-Portrait as Hurry and Delay"
"Penelope's Despair" (Ritsos) 6:464
"Penelope's Hall" (Bowering) 32:48
"Penguin in Bondage" (Zappa) 17:591
Penguin Touquet (Foreman) 50:163
Penhally (Gordon) 6:203-05, 207; 13:242; 29:185; 83:226-27, 229, 232-33, 240-42, 247, 251, 253-54, 257, 259
"Penis Poem" (Phillips) 28:363
The Penitent (Singer)

    See Der Bal-tshuve
"Penitentes" ("Penitents") (Zamora) 89:363, 368, 382, 384, 387, 394
"Penitents" (Zamora)
    See "Penitentes"
"The Pennacesse Leper Colony for Women, Cape Cod, 1922" (Dubie) 36:130
"Pennants Must Have Breezes" (Weidman) 7:517
Pennies from Heaven (Potter) 58:389, 391-92, 395, 399-400; 86:345-46, 348, 350-53
Penniless Painter Goes Out into the World (Seifert)
    See Šel malír chude do sveta
"A Penniless Painter Went Out into the World" (Seifert)
    See Šel malír chude do sveta
The Penniless Redeemer (Ferron)
    See Le Ciel de Québec
Penniless till Doomsday (Hall) 51:170
"Pennstuwehniyaahtsi: Quuti's Story" (Ortiz) 45:309
"Pennsylvania" (Sandburg) 10:450
Pennsylvania Gothic (Sheed) 2:392-94; 53:339
"Penny Dreadful" (Coward) 51:74
"Penny in the Dust" (Buckler) 13:119-20
"Penny Parker's Mistake" (Ashbery) 25:54
A Penny Saved Is Impossible (Nash) 23:324
The Penny Wars (Baker) 8:39
Penny Wheep (MacDiarmid) 11:334, 338; 19:286, 290; 63:239
"El pensamiento en blanco" ("Blank Thought") (Paz) 65:182, 184
Pensamiento serpentino (Valdez) 84:414
La Pensée (Brossard) 115:106
La pensée sauvage (Levi-Strauss) 38:294, 296-97, 299, 304
Penser/Classer (Perec) 56:264
"Penshurst Place" (Mahon) 27:292
"Il pensiero fluttuante ddella felicità" (Luzi) 13:353
"The Pension Grillparzer" (Irving) 112:172, 175
"Pentagon: A Memory" (Carroll) 38:103
"Pentecost" (Ai) 14:8; 69:4, 8
"The Pentecost Castle" (Hill) 18:238; 45:178, 180, 182, 185, 190
Penthesilea (Riefenstahl) 16:526
Penthesilia (Nye) 13:413
"The Penthouse Apartment" (Trevor) 71:322, 326, 339; 116:371
Penthouse Legend (Rand)
    See Night of January 16
Pentimento: A Book of Portraits (Three) (Hellman) 4:220-22; 8:280-82; 14:259; 34:348-50, 352-53; 44:527-28, 530; 52:190, 192-203
The Penultimate Truth (Dick) 30:127; 72:108, 123-24
"Peonies" (Oliver) 98:287
"Peony Stalks" (Van Duyn) 116:417, 424
"People" (Armatrading) 17:10
"The People" (Silkin) 6:499; 43:404-05
People (Lagerkvist)
    See Människor
People and Life, 1891-1921 (Ehrenburg) 18:134
"People Are Fascinating" (Benson) 17:46-7
People Are Living There (Fugard) 9:232; 14:189-90; 40:197, 201; 80:62, 69, 74
"People Are Strange" (Morrison) 17:295
"The People at the Party" (Mueller) 51:279

"The People behind This Peculiar Nation" (MacLennan)　14:341
"People Don't Want Us" (Lewis)　41:254
"People for Lunch" (Bainbridge)　62:36-8
The People from Yonder (Dabrowska)
　See *Ludzie stamtad*
"People Getting Divorced" (Ferlinghetti)　111:65
The People Immortal (Grossman)　41:188
People in a Diary: A Memoir (Behrman)　40:86-7
"People in Dreams" (O Hehir)　41:322
People in Glass Houses (Hazzard)　18:214-17
People in Summer Night (Sillanpaa)　19:417-18
People Live Here: Selected Poems, 1949-1983 (Simpson)　32:378, 380-84
The People Machines (Williamson)　29:458
The People Named Chippewa: Narrative Histories (Vizenor)　103:289, 291, 299, 311, 317, 348
People of Darkness (Hillerman)　62:251-52, 256, 259
The People of Japan (Buck)　7:33
The People of Kau (Riefenstahl)　16:524-25
The People of Peoples and Their Gifts to Men (Du Bois)　96:144-45
"A People of Solitaries" (Cioran)
　See "Un peuple de solitaires"
People of the Buffalo (Campbell)　85:4, 22
People of the City (Ekwensi)　4:151
People of the Deer (Mowat)　26:329-34, 341, 347
People of the Dream (Forman)　21:119
"The People of the Night" (Duras)　100:120
"People of the Shell" (Piercy)　14:420
People of the Valley (Waters)　88:329, 334-37, 345, 351, 361, 366-70
People on a Bridge (Szymborska)　99:192-93, 199, 203
"The People on the Bridge" (Szymborska)　99:200
"People to People" (Ingalls)　42:234
"The People v. Abe Lathan, Colored" (Caldwell)　1:51
The People vs Ranchman (Terry)　19:440
"People Who Died" (Carroll)　35:79-81
People Who Knock on the Door (Highsmith)　42:215-16; 102:184, 209
People Who Led to My Plays (Kennedy)　66:209-10
People Will Always Be Kind (Sheed)　4:488-89
The People with the Dogs (Stead)　32:413, 416; 80:341
People, Years, Life (Ehrenburg)　34:434, 436; 62:180-81
The People, Yes (Sandburg)　4:463; 10:448, 450-51; 15:466, 468-70; 35:347-48, 351-53, 357-58
A Peopled Landscape (Tomlinson)　2:436-37; 4:544, 546; 13:545, 547; 45:405
The Peoples of Kenya (Adamson)　17:4
The People's Otherworld (Murray)　40:342, 344
"People's Parties" (Mitchell)　12:442
"People's Surroundings" (Moore)　13:396
Pepi, Lucy, Bom and a Whole Lot of Other Girls (Almodovar)
　See *Pepi, Lucy, Mom y Otros Chicas del Monton*
Pepi, Lucy, Mom y Otros Chicas del Monton (*Pepi, Lucy, Bom and a Whole Lot of Other Girls*) (Almodovar)　114:3, 16-17, 22,

25-6, 30-1, 35, 45
"The Pepper Plant" (Wakoski)　9:555
Peppercanister Poems, 1972-1978 (Kinsella)　19:254-56
"Peppergrass" (Plumly)　33:316
Peppermint frappé (Saura)　20:320
Pequeña crónica de grandes días (*Small Chronicle of Great Days*) (Paz)　65:190
"Pequeña oda a un negro boxeador cubano" ("Small Ode to a Black Cuban Boxer") (Guillen)　48:163; 79:229-30
"Pequnea ode mineral" ("Short Mineral Ode") (Cabral de Melo Neto)　76:159, 165
Perceval (Rohmer)　16:538-40
Le perchoir du perroquet (*Parrot's Perch*) (Rio)　43:355-57
"Percy" (Cheever)　11:122
Percy (Davies)　21:92
"Percy Lawson" (Purdy)　14:434
"Percy's Song" (Dylan)　77:166
Perdido (Robinson)　10:438-39
"Perdón si por mis ojos..." (Neruda)　7:261
"El peregrino" (Parra)　102:338-39
Los peregrinos inmóviles (*The Immovable Pilgrims*) (Lopez y Fuentes)　32:282-83
"A Pereira da Costa" ("For P. da C.") (Cabral de Melo Neto)　76:163
Perelandra (Lewis)　1:177; 3:297-99; 6:309, 311; 14:323-26; 27:260-61, 266
Perelman's Home Companion: A Collector's Item (The Collector Being S. J. Perelman) of Thirty-Six Otherwise Unavailable Pieces by Himself (Perelman)　49:262
"The Perennial Answer" (Rich)　6:459; 73:330
The Perennial Philosophy (Huxley)　1:152; 4:239-41; 5:193; 8:303; 11:286; 18:269-70; 35:241, 243-44; 79:317
"The Perennial Poetry" (McAuley)　45:249
Perestroika (Kushner)　81:197-98, 200-02, 207-08, 212
"The Perfect Body" (Kumin)　28:223
A Perfect Circle of Sun (Pastan)　27:368-69
A Perfect Couple (Altman)　16:43-4; 116:37
"The Perfect Critic" (Eliot)　24:169, 180; 55:356
"A Perfect Day for Bananafish" ("A Great Day for a Bananafish") (Salinger)　3:444; 12:499, 503, 514, 520; 56:324, 352
The Perfect Fiction (Sorrentino)　7:449, 451-52; 22:391; 40:384
A Perfect Ganesh (McNally)　91:159
Perfect Happiness (Lively)　32:275-77
"The Perfect Life" (Katz)　47:222
"Perfect Morning" (MacCaig)　36:282
"The Perfect Nazi Family Is Alive and Living in Modern Ireland" (Durcan)　43:117
The Perfect Party (Fuller)
　See *The Village: A Party*
The Perfect Party (Gurney)　54:216-18, 220, 222; 50:180-81, 183
A Perfect Peace (Oz)　54:345-53, 355
"The Perfect Sky" (Gallagher)　63:119
The Perfect Storm (Junger)　109:56-62
"Perfect Things" (Barthelme)　117:6
A Perfect Vacuum (Lem)　15:329-30; 40:292, 296, 298
"The Perfect Warrior" (Bova)　45:69, 75
"Perfect Weather" (Piercy)　62:379
A Perfect Woman (Slaughter)　56:411-12
"Perfect Women Who Are Bearable" (Wasserstein)　90:430, 432
"Perfection" (Nabokov)　6:357
"The Perfection of Dentistry" (Bell)　8:65-6;

31:47
"Perfection of Orchard View" (Edmonds)　35:155
The Perfectionist (Williamson)　56:439-41
The Perfectionists (Godwin)　5:142; 8:248; 22:179-80; 31:198; 69:246-47
"Perfections" (Tomlinson)　45:392-93
"A Perfectly, Clear View of Basketball" (Royko)　109:408
"Perfectly Independent" (Ferber)　93:153
"Perfectly Lovely Couple" (Sondheim)　30:380
Perfil del aire (Cernuda)　54:57-8
"The Performance" (Dickey)　15:177; 109:238, 287
"Performance" (Mahapatra)　33:277, 283
"The Performance of a Lifetime" (King)　53:208
The Perfume Sea (Laurence)　62:278
Perfume: The Story of a Murderer (Suskind)　44:111-17
"Perhaps Hand" (Cummings)　68:37
Perhaps Never (Derleth)　31:131
"Perhaps No Poem But All I Can Say and I Cannot Be Silent" (Levertov)　66:239
"Perhaps We Shall Meet Again" (Bates)　46:55-6
"Perhaps You Should Talk to Someone" (Bainbridge)　62:37
"Pericalypsis" (Lem)　15:330
"Perichoresis and the Single Seminarian" (L'Heureux)　52:274
"Peril" (Giles)　39:64-5
Peril at End House (Christie)　6:108; 12:113, 122; 48:71-2, 77; 110:116, 137
"Perils of the Nile" (Gilchrist)　48:115
"Period" (Thomas)　6:530
Period of Adjustment (HiH)　26:196, 201
Period of Adjustment: High Point over a Cavern (Williams)　1:368; 5:500, 504; 11:577; 15:580; 19:472; 71:368-69
A Period of Transition (Morrison)　21:237
The Periodic Table (Levi)
　See *Il sistema periodico*
"Periphery" (Ammons)　5:27; 57:59
The Perishable Quality (Davies)　23:147
"El perjurio de la nieve" ("The Perjury of the Snow") (Bioy Casares)　88:60
"The Perjury of the Snow" (Bioy Casares)
　See "El perjurio de la nieve"
Perlicka na dne (*Pearl at the Bottom; Pearl of the Deep*) (Hrabal)　67:121-22
"Perlmutter at the East Pole" (Elkin)　51:99
Permanence and Change (Burke)　24:119-21, 127-28
Permanent Errors (Price)　3:406; 6:423; 43:344-45, 353; 63:331, 341
"The Permanent Hell" (Ignatow)　7:176
"A Permanent Insurrection" (Vargas Llosa)
　See "Una insurrección permanente"
Permitted Fruit (Tzara)
　See *Le fruit permis*
"Permutations" (Donnell)　34:156
"The Pernambucan M. B." (Cabral de Melo Neto)
　See "O pernambucano Manual Bandeira"
"O pernambucano Manual Bandeira" ("The Pernambucan M. B.") (Cabral de Melo Neto)　76:163
"Perpetua" (Broumas)　73:13-17
"The Perpetual Light" (Fulton)　52:159
The Perpetual Orgy: Flaubert and "Madame Bovary" (Vargas Llosa)
　See *La orgía perpetua: Flaubert y "Madame*

Bovary"
"The Perpetual Present" (Paz)   4:398
Perpétue (Beti)   27:46-7, 53
"Perplex" (Bennett)   28:29
Persécuté persécuteur (Aragon)   3:14
"Persecution Smith" (Seger)   35:378, 381
"El perseguidor" (Cortazar)   10:113, 116; 13:164; 33:125-26, 128; 34:332
"El Perseguidor" ("The Pursuer") (Cortazar)   34:332; 92:149, 155-56
"Perseid" (Barth)   5:52; 14:54-5; 89:38
"Persephone" (Barnard)   48:26-7
"Persephone" (Ritsos)   13:488
"Persephone Pauses" (Kizer)   80:172-73
Persephone's Flowers (Grigson)   39:332
"Pershore Station; or, A Liverish Journey First Class" (Betjeman)   43:34, 36, 41
The Persian Boy (Renault)   3:426; 17:401
Persian Nights (Johnson)   48:206-09
Persian Paintings (Anand)   93:24
"Persistences" (Ammons)   25:45
"Persistent Explorer" (Ransom)   4:431
"The Person" (Laughlin)   49:225
"...Person, or A Hymn on and to the Holy Ghost" (Avison)   97:79, 93, 99, 104, 116
Person, Place, and Thing (Shapiro)   4:485; 15:475-76; 53:331
"Person to Person" (Williams)   71:368
Person to Person (Ciardi)   40:159
"The Person Who Held the Job Before You" (Pesetsky)   28:358
"Persona" (Banville)   46:25
Persona (Bergman)   16:56-9, 62, 67-9, 74, 78, 80; 72:40, 46, 48-52, 55, 57, 59
Personae (Pound)   1:276; 2:343; 7:323, 325; 13:456; 48:288, 299; 112:340
"Personal and Sexual Freedom" (Major)   19:293
Personal Anthology (Borges)
   See *Antologia personal*
Personal Best (Towne)   87:365-71, 373-78
Personal File (Rozewicz)
   See *Kartoteka*
"Personal Helicon" (Heaney)   25:244
A Personal History of the American Theater (Gray)   49:148
A Personal History of the "Boom" (Donoso)
   See *Historia personal del 'boom'*
"The Personal is Political" (White)   110:336, 341, 343
"Personal Letter No. 2" (Sanchez)   116:272, 278, 295
"Personal Letter No. 3" (Sanchez)   116:274, 278, 295
A Personal Matter (Oe)
   See *Kojinteki na taiken*
"Personal Poem" (O'Hara)   78:350-51, 376
"Personal Remarks" (McGinley)   14:366
"A Personal Statement" (Longley)   29:291, 293, 295-96
"Personal Tour" (Hall)   51:172
Personality Plus (Ferber)   93:136, 141, 147
Personality Quotient (Daly)
   See *What's Your P.Q.*
"Personals" (Ginsberg)   109:364
Personals (Bontemps)   18:64
"Personism: A Manifesto" (O'Hara)   2:322; 13:423-24; 78:350-51, 354, 362
"Persons" (MacNeice)   53:234
"Persons from Porlock" (Hope)   51:217, 221, 223, 225
Persons, Ideas, and Seas (Gironella)   11:237
Persons of Consequence: Queen Victoria and Her Circle (Auchincloss)   18:25

"Persons Unknown" (Capote)   13:137
"Perspective" (Avison)   97:67-71, 100, 102-04, 111
"Perspectives" (Ezekiel)   61:93, 101
"The Perspectives and Limits of Snapshots" (Smith)   42:353
Perto do coração selvagem (Lispector)   43:261, 266
"Peru" (McNally)   82:263
Peru (Lish)   45:230-33
Pervigilium veneris (Tate)   4:536
Pervyi uchitel' (*Duishen; The First Teacher*) (Aitmatov)   71:3, 6, 14, 16, 22
"A pesar de proponérselo" (Castellanos)   66:56
Pešcanik (*Hourglass*) (Kis)   57:243-44, 246-50, 252
La peste (*The Plague*) (Camus)   1:52-4; 2:97-8; 4:89-93; 9:139-41, 144-46, 148, 150; 11:93-4, 96-7; 14:107, 110, 113, 115-17; 32:86-8, 90; 63:62, 64-8, 71, 73-7, 82-4, 86; 69:109, 122, 128, 135-36
"Pet Milk" (Dybek)   114:77
Pet Sematary (King)   37:203-07; 61:319, 321, 328, 331, 333, 335; 113:335-36, 338, 346, 363-64, 367-68, 371-72, 374, 388-89, 391
Pet Sounds (Wilson)   12:640-46, 649-52
Pet zvezdi (Bagryana)   10:11
Petals of Blood (Ngugi wa Thiong'o)   13:583-84; 36:313-17, 319, 322-24
"Peter" (Moore)   47:261
"Peter" (Ondaatje)   14:407; 29:341
"Peter and Rosa" (Dinesen)   29:159
Peter Breaks Through   59:399-402
Peter Camenzind (Hesse)   2:190; 17:195, 207-09, 216-17; 69:287
"Peter in the Park" (Mazer)   26:291
"Peter Kürten to the Witness" (Thomas)   31:434
The Peter Pan Bag (Kingman)   17:245-46
Peter Smart's Confessions (Bailey)   45:42-4, 46-7
Peter Whiffle (Van Vechten)   33:385, 388-89, 393-95, 398-99
"Peters" (Tolstaya)   59:371
"The Peters Family" (Stafford)   29:379
"Petersburg Tale" (Akhmatova)   11:8
Petersen (Williamson)   56:434
"Petey and Yotsee and Mario" (Roth)   104:249
"Petit Cachou" (Bell)   102:5, 7
"Petit désespoir" (Hebert)   29:228
Le petit saint (*The Little Saint*) (Simenon)   2:397; 18:482-83
"Le petit salvié" (Williams)   2:397; 56:426, 428
Le petit soldat (Godard)   20:130, 132
Le petit théâtre de Jean Renoir (*The Little Theater of Jean Renoir*) (Renoir)   20:300, 302
Petite cosmogonie portative (*A Little Portable Cosmogony*) (Queneau)   5:360-61
La petite marchande d'allumettes (Renoir)   20:300, 309
La petite poule d'eau (*Where Nests the Water Hen*) (Roy)   10:442; 14:465-66
"Petition" (Barth)   7:24; 9:67; 51:23, 29; 89:4-6, 8-10, 13, 15-16, 20, 26, 33, 43, 48, 53-5, 59-60
Les petits chevaux de Tarquinia (*The Little Horses of Tarquinia*) (Duras)   6:149; 11:164; 40:180; 68:78, 80, 96; 100:145
"Petit-Thouars" (Davie)   31:124
"Pétres" (Ritsos)   6:463

"The Petrified Man" (Welty)   5:479; 14:564; 33:414-15; 105:298, 310, 313, 323, 385-86
"The Petrified Woman" (Gordon)   29:187; 83:257
Pétrinos hrónos (*Rocky Time*) (Ritsos)   13:487
Petrolio (Pasolini)   106:272, 274
The Pets (Shaw)   5:390
"Petting and Being a Pet" (Peacock)   60:295, 297
Petulia (Lester)   20:225, 227, 229
"Petunias" (Walker)   58:405; 103:412
Petushikha's Breakthrough (Leonov)
   See *Petushikhinsky Prolom*
Petushikhin Notch (Leonov)
   See *Petushikhinsky Prolom*
The Petushikhino Breakthrough (Leonov)
   See *Petushikhinsky Prolom*
Petushikhinsky Prolom (*The Breakthrough of Petushikhino; Petushikha's Breakthrough; Petushikhin Notch; The Petushikhino Breakthrough*) (Leonov)   92:237, 242, 257, 264-65
"Un peuple de solitaires" ("A People of Solitaries") (Cioran)   64:74, 82, 84, 98
"Phaedo; or, The Dance" (Yourcenar)   38:456
"Phaedra" (H. D.)   73:105
Phaedra (Rexroth)   11:472; 22:345
"Phakeni's Farewell" (Kunene)   85:176
Les phalènes (Tchicaya)   101:357
"The Phallic Forest" (Wilding)   73:395, 398
The Phallic Forest (Wilding)   73:398
"Phallus in Wonderland" (Ewart)   46:147, 150
"Phantasia for Elvira Shatayev" (Rich)   73:332
"Die Phantasie" (Lenz)   27:251
"Phantasmagoria" (Gascoyne)   45:152
Phantom Africa (Leiris)   61:361
Phantom City: A Ghost Town Gallery (Beecher)   6:49
Phantom Dwelling (Wright)   53:432
"Phantom Eclipse" (Zamora)   89:393
Phantom Fortress (Lancaster)   36:244
Phantom Lady (Woolrich)   77:389-97, 400, 403-04
Phantom of Liberty (Bunuel)
   See *Le fantôme de la liberté*
"The Phantom of the Movie Palace" (Coover)   46:121-22
"The Phantom of the Opera's Friend" (Barthelme)   115:65, 70
Phantom of the Paradise (De Palma)   20:75-6, 78
"Phantom Palace" (Allende)   97:4
Phantoms (Koontz)   78:197, 203, 206-12
Phantoms of My Brain (Gironella)
   See *Los fantasmos de mi cerebo*
"Phar Lap in the Melbourne Museum" (Porter)   33:318
La pharisienne (Mauriac)   9:369; 56:212, 219
Pharos and Pharillon (Forster)   13:215, 221; 15:228
Phases and Stages (Nelson)   17:303-04, 306
The Phases of Love (Livesay)   79:348
"Pheasant" (Plath)   51:349; 111:204, 214
"A Pheasant" (Szirtes)   46:394
"Phenomena" (Carlson)   54:38
"Phenomenal Woman" (Angelou)   35:30; 77:30
"The Phenomenology of Anger" (Rich)   6:459; 7:373; 11:477
"The Phenomenon" (Shapiro)   53:332
"A Phenomenon of Nature" (Howard)   10:277
"Phi" (Tolson)   105:271, 274
Phil Ochs' Greatest Hits (Ochs)   17:332-34

Phil Ochs in Concert (Ochs)　17:331
Philadelphia Fire (Wideman)　67:380, 385-91
Philadelphia, Here I Come! (Friel)　5:128-29;
　42:163-66, 169, 173-74; 59:147, 149;
　115:213-14, 216, 224-25, 227-29, 231,
　233-35, 237, 240-42, 251, 254-57
"Philadelphia Lawyer" (Guthrie)　35:183, 191
The Philadelphia Negro (Du Bois)　64:115,
　128, 131; 96:142, 146
The Philanthropist (Hampton)　4:212
"Philemon and Baucis" (Gunn)　81:178
Philip Larkin: A Writer's Life (Motion)　81:417-
　64
Philip the King and Other Poems (Masefield)
　47:229
The Philippines' Fight for Freedom (Archer)
　12:18
"Phillida" (Fowles)　9:214
"Phillis Goldberg" (Durcan)　70:151
"Philoclea in the Forest" (Huxley)　11:282
"Philoctetes" (McAuley)　45:250-51
"Philoctetes" (Ritsos)　31:325
Philoctetes (Ritsos)　13:488
Philoctetes: The Wound and the Bow (Wilson)
　See *The Wound and the Bow*
"Philology Recapitulates Ontology, Poetry Is
　Ontology" (Schwartz)　45:356
"The Philosopher" (Farrell)　66:131
"The Philosopher and the Birds" (Murphy)
　41:317
"The Philosophers" (Merton)　83:384
The Philosopher's Pupil (Murdoch)　31:290-
　95; 51:287
"Philosopher's Songs" (Huxley)　11:284
The Philosopher's Stone (Lagerkvist)　54:278
The Philosopher's Stone (Ray)
　See *Paras pathar*
Philosophical Problems of Many Valued Logic
　(Zinoviev)　19:485
"A Philosophico-Political Profile" (Habermas)
　104:87
"Philosophy" (Ezekiel)　61:101
"Philosophy and Postwar American Criticism"
　(Wellek)　28:446
"Philosophy as Stand-In and Interpreter"
　(Habermas)　104:99
"The Philosophy Lesson" (Stafford)　68:431,
　433, 441-45
The Philosophy of Jean-Paul Sartre (Sartre)
　1:304
The Philosophy of Literary Form (Burke)
　24:121-22, 125-28
The Philosophy of Rhetoric (Richards)　24:387-
　88, 394, 396, 399, 401
"Philosophy of Solitude" (Merton)　83:403
A Philosophy of Solitude (Powys)　46:319
"The Philosophy of Style"　75:71
"The Philosophy of the Beat Generation"
　(Holmes)　56:140
Phineas, and Other Stories (Knowles)　26:257-
　58, 262
"Phobias" (Appleman)　51:17
"The Phoenix" (Cunningham)　31:98-9, 102,
　104
"Phoenix" (Ellison)　42:127
"The Phoenix" (Le Guin)　45:216
"Phoenix" (Nemerov)　36:304
"The Phoenix" (Sarton)　91:243
"The Phoenix and the Tortoise" (Rexroth)
　49:276-77; 112:386, 394
The Phoenix and the Tortoise (Rexroth)　1:284;
　22:345, 348; 49:277; 112:365-70, 373,
　377, 387, 392, 400

"Phoenix in the Ashes" (Vinge)　30:413
"Phoenix Park Vespers" (Durcan)　43:114
A Phoenix Too Frequent (Fry)　2:144; 10:200;
　14:187-88
Phoenix under the Rain (Shamlu)　10:470
*Phogey! How to Have Class in a Classless Soci-
　ety* (Bradbury)　32:55
"Phone" (Creeley)　36:118
"Phone for the Fishknives, Norman"
　(Betjeman)　43:33
"A Phone of Her Own" (Wasserstein)　90:429
"Phone-In" (Gilliatt)　13:237
"Phonenix Park" (Kinsella)　19:251-52, 255
"Phools" (Lem)　40:294
"Phosphorus" (Levi)　37:227
"Photini" (Nakos)　29:322
"Photo of the Timbó Plantation" (Cabral de
　Melo Neto)
　See "Fotografia do engenho Timbó"
Photo-Finish (Marsh)　53:250, 255-56, 260
"Photograph" (Coles)　46:107-08, 113
"Photograph" (Halpern)　14:233
"The Photograph" (Oliver)　98:256
"Photograph" (Page)　18:376
*A Photograph: A Still Life with Shadows/A
　Photograph: A Study of Cruelty* (Shange)
　See *A Photograph: Lovers in Motion*
Photograph: Cruelty (Shange)
　See *A Photograph: Lovers in Motion*
A Photograph: Lovers in Motion (*A Photo-
　graph: A Still Life with Shadows/A Photo-
　graph: A Study of Cruelty; Photograph:
　Cruelty; Photograph: Still Life*) (Shange)
　25:397-98; 74:294, 307
"Photograph of the Girl" (Olds)　85:291
"The Photograph of the Unmade Bed" (Rich)
　6:458
Photograph: Still Life (Shange)
　See *A Photograph: Lovers in Motion*
"The Photographer" (Munro)　95:291
"The Photographer in Winter" (Szirtes)
　46:395-96
The Photographer in Winter (Szirtes)　46:395-
　96
"Photographer of Snow" (Hillis)　66:194
"The Photographic Image" (Barthes)　83:80,
　85
"The Photographs" (Dobyns)　37:78
"Photographs" (Van Duyn)　63:441-42;
　116:408, 430
"Photographs" (Wright)　6:581
The Photographs (Fuller)　28:157
The Photographs (Vassilikos)　4:551; 8:524
"Photographs Courtesy of the Fall River His-
　torical Society" (Olds)　85:285
The Photographs of Chachaji (Mehta)　37:294-
　95
"Photographs of Stanley's Grandfather" (Dunn)
　40:171
"photon scanner blue spruce" (Moure)　88:232
"Photos of a Salt Mine" (Page)　7:291-92
Phrases from Orpheus (Jones)　10:285, 288
"Phrases in Common Use" (Jacobsen)　102:240
"Phrenfy" (Reading)　47:351
"The Phylactery" (Szirtes)　46:391
Phyllis (Fast)　23:158
Physical Graffiti (Page and Plant)　12:477-80,
　482
"Physical Universe" (Simpson)　32:381-82
The Physicists (Duerrenmatt)
　See *Die Physiker*
The Physicists (Durrenmatt)
　See *Die Physiker*

"Physics" (Janowitz)　43:212
Die Physiker (*The Physicists*) (Duerrenmatt)
　102:55-6, 59-60, 65, 69, 74, 77, 83
Die Physiker (*The Physicists*) (Durrenmatt)
　8:194, 197; 11:171, 173; 15:195-96, 198-
　99; 43:128-30
The Physiology of Taste (Fisher)　87:122, 129,
　131
"Pi" (Tolson)　105:242, 274
"Pi shnayim" ("Twice as Much") (Agnon)　8:9
"La pia" (Merwin)　45:272; 88:200
"Pian dei Giullari" (Ewart)　46:152
"Piano" (Neruda)　7:260
The Piano (Campion)　95:9, 11-30
"Piano after War" (Brooks)　15:95
The Piano Lesson (Wilson)　63:452-58
"Piano Man" (Joel)　26:213, 218-19, 222
Piano Man (Joel)　26:213-15, 217-18, 223
The Piano Man's Daughter (Findley)　102:120-
　21
"A Piano Piece for the Left and Right Hand"
　(Jandl)　34:196
"Piano Pieces" (Shapcott)　38:404
"The Piano Player" (Barthelme)　46:40
"Piano Practice" (Moss)　45:290
"The Piano Tuner's Wives" (Trevor)　116:394-
　95
The Pianoplayers (Burgess)　62:124-26
"Piazza di Spagna, Early Morning" (Wilbur)
　53:413; 110:348-49, 382
"Piazza Piece" (Ransom)　4:431
Picasso (Reverdy)　53:280
Picasso and Poetry (Tzara)　47:389
"The Picasso Poem" (Stern)　100:333
"The Picasso Summer" (Bradbury)　42:35
Picasso's Mask (Malraux)
　See *La tête d'obsidienne*
Piccadilly (Seifert)
　See *Deštník z Piccadilly*
The Piccadilly Bushman (Lawler)　58:331-33,
　337
"Piccola commedia" (Wilbur)　14:578
"Pick and Poke" (Stern)　40:409
Picked-Up Pieces (Updike)　9:540; 34:284-
　87, 290, 292; 43:427-29
"Picking and Choosing" (Moore)　13:393
"Picking Cloudberries by Moonlight"
　(Musgrave)　54:334
"Picking Gooseberries" (Kenny)　87:254
"Picking the Roses" (Stern)　40:412
"Picking Up the Beer Cans" (Carruth)　84:129
"Pickle Belt" (Roethke)　19:397
Pickpocket (Bresson)　16:104-05, 114-15, 117
"The Picnic" (Creeley)　78:134
"Picnic" (Scott)　22:372
Picnic (*Summer Brave*) (Inge)　1:153; 8:308;
　19:226-28, 230
"Picnic 1960" (Christie)　110:125
Picnic at Hanging Rock (Weir)　20:425-29
The Picnic at Sakkara (Newby)　2:311; 13:408
"A Picnic Contata" (Schuyler)　23:388
Pic-nic en campaña (*Picnic on the Battlefield;
　Pique-nique en Campagne*) (Arrabal)
　9:38; 18:19; 53:3, 8
*Picnic in Babylon: A Jesuit Priest's Journal,
　1963-1967* (L'Heureux)　52:273, 275,
　277, 279
The Picnic in the Cemetery (Urdang)　47:398-
　99
Picnic on Paradise (Russ)　15:461-62
Picnic on the Battlefield (Arrabal)
　See *Pic-nic en campaña*
Picnic on the Grass (Renoir)

See *Le déjeuner sur l'herbe*

"Picnic on the Lawn" (Scannell)   **49**:330

"Picnic with Moonlight and Mangoes" (Jhabvala)   **8**:313

"Pico Blanco" (Zamora)   **89**:392-93

A Pictorial History of English Architecture (Betjeman)   **34**:308

"Pictor's Metamorphoses" (Hesse)   **25**:259, 261

Pictor's Metamorphoses, and Other Fantasies (Hesse)   **25**:259-61

"A Picture History of the War" (Barthelme)   **115**:67

"Picture Layout in 'Life' Magazine" (Purdy)   **50**:246

"Picture of a Black Child with a White Doll" (Merton)   **83**:393, 397

"Picture of a Nativity" (Hill)   **8**:294

"The Picture of J. T. in a Prospect of Stone" (Tomlinson)   **13**:547, 549

"A Picture of Lee Ying" (Merton)   **83**:393

"The Picture of Little J. A. in a Prospect of Flowers" (Ashbery)

  See "The Portrait of Little J. A. in a Prospect of Flowers"

"A Picture of Soldiers" (Bell)   **8**:66

"A Picture of the Virgin" (Kinsella)   **27**:237-38

Picture Palace (Theroux)   **11**:529-32; **15**:533; **28**:425; **46**:398, 400, 405

Picture Show (Sassoon)   **36**:385

The Picture Story of Britain (Streatfeild)   **21**:401

Picture Theory (Brossard)   **115**:106, 108-09, 111, 121, 132, 134-36, 140-45

"The Picture: Wolves in the Tree" (Schaeffer)   **11**:491

The Picturegoers (Lodge)   **36**:266-67

"The Pictures" (Frame)   **96**:188

"The Pictures" (Grace)   **56**:116, 119

Pictures and Conversations (Bowen)   **6**:94-6; **11**:64; **15**:78

Pictures at a Prosecution (Feiffer)   **64**:153

"Pictures for Crusoe" (Perse)

  See "Images à Crusoe"

"Pictures from a Japanese Printmaker" (Redgrove)   **41**:355

Pictures from an Institution (Jarrell)   **2**:208; **6**:261; **9**:297; **13**:300; **49**:186-96, 201

"Pictures from Breughel" (Williams)   **9**:575

Pictures from Brueghel, and Other Poems (Williams)   **5**:507-08; **42**:455; **67**:407

Pictures in the Hallway (O'Casey)   **5**:320; **88**:280

"Pictures of a Long-Lost World" (Souster)   **14**:504

Pictures of Fidelman: An Exhibition (Malamud)   **1**:200; **2**:266, 268; **3**:322, 324; **5**:269-70; **8**:375; **9**:346, 350; **11**:349, 351; **18**:321; **27**:296-97; **44**:413, 415, 417, 420; **85**:200

"Pictures of Lily" (Townshend)   **17**:529-31, 535, 539

"Pictures of People in the War" (Gluck)   **22**:173

"Pictures of the Dead" (Price)   **43**:351

Pictures of the Gone World (Ferlinghetti)   **10**:174; **27**:137-38; **111**:50-4, 64, 71-2

"Pictures of the Ice" (Munro)   **95**:315

"The Picturesque, the Sublime, and the South African Landscape" (Coetzee)   **66**:99

Picturing Will (Beattie)   **63**:20-3

Pido la paz la palabra (Otero)   **11**:425

"Pie Country" (Barthelme)   **117**:17

"Pie Dance" (Giles)   **39**:64

"Pie Song" (Sondheim)   **30**:398

Pie XII et le IIIe Reich; documents (*Pius XII and the Third Reich: A Documentation*) (Friedlander)   **90**:100-4, 106-7, 112, 118

Piebald Dog Running along the Shore (Aitmatov)

  See *Pegil pes, begushchij kraem moria*

"A Piece" (Creeley)   **78**:161

"A Piece of Advice" (Singer)   **6**:508

A Piece of Mine (Cooper)   **56**:69-72

"A Piece of Monologue" (Beckett)   **29**:59, 65

A Piece of My Heart   **99**:105, 110, 116, 120-21

A Piece of My Heart (Ford)   **46**:156-59

A Piece of My Mind (Greeley)   **28**:178

A Piece of My Mind (Wilson)   **8**:550; **24**:478

"A Piece of News" (Welty)   **14**:561; **105**:325, 349, 368

A Piece of the Action (Poitier)   **26**:361-62

A Piece of the Night (Roberts)   **48**:340-42

"Pieces" (Rich)   **7**:372

Pieces (Creeley)   **1**:67; **2**:106-07; **4**:117; **8**:151, 153; **11**:138; **15**:151; **36**:117-21; **78**:124, 127-28, 130, 138-41, 147

Pieces and Pontifications (Mailer)   **74**:207

Pièces brillantes (Anouilh)   **1**:7; **13**:17, 19-20

Pièces costumées (Anouilh)   **13**:19, 21

Pièces grinçantes (Anouilh)   **13**:17, 19-20

Pièces noires (Anouilh)   **1**:7; **8**:22; **13**:16, 19-21; **50**:278

Pieces of Another World: The Story of Moon Rocks (Branley)   **21**:19

Pieces of Life (Schorer)   **9**:473-74

Pieces of Soap (Elkin)   **91**:213-14

Pieces of the Frame (McPhee)   **36**:296

"Pieces of the One and a Half Legged Man" (Klappert)   **57**:256, 258

Pièces roses (Anouilh)   **1**:7; **13**:16, 19-21; **50**:278

"Pied à terre" (Johnston)   **51**:240, 243, 247

Pied Piper (Shute)   **30**:366-67

"Piedra" ("The Stone") (Soto)   **80**:287, 291-92

Piedra de sol (*Sun Stone*; *Sunstone*) (Paz)   **6**:395; **10**:389, 391; **51**:333, 336-37; **65**:181, 185-87, 195, 199-200

Las piedras de Chile (*The Stones of Chile*) (Neruda)   **28**:313-14

Piege pour Cendrillon (*Trap for Cinderella*) (Japrisot)   **90**:167-68

"Piere Vidal Old" (Pound)   **10**:408; **48**:288

"The Pier-Glass" (Graves)   **2**:176; **45**:167, 169

The Pier-Glass (Graves)   **6**:210

Pierre écrite (*Words in Stone*; *Written Stone*) (Bonnefoy)   **9**:115; **58**:43-6, 49-54

"Pierre Menard, Author of the *Quixote*" (Borges)

  See "Pierre Menard, autor del *Quixote*"

"Pierre Menard, autor del *Quixote*" ("Pierre Menard, Author of the *Quixote*") (Borges)   **3**:77; **4**:74; **6**:87, 93; **8**:96; **9**:118; **13**:108; **19**:49; **44**:362, 369; **48**:37, 44-5; **83**:156-157, 161, 171-72, 181-82, 192

"La pierre qui pousse" ("The Growing Stone") (Camus)   **9**:144, 150-51; **14**:114; **63**:71

"Pierre Ronsard and His Rose" (Lattimore)   **3**:278

Pierrot le fou (Godard)   **20**:139, 145, 149

Pierrot mon ami (Queneau)   **5**:359-62; **42**:333

Pierrot ou les secrets de la nuit (Tournier)   **95**:368, 372, 378-82

"Pieta" (Gascoyne)   **45**:147

"Pietà" (Gluck)   **22**:178

"Pieta" (Krleza)   **114**:170

"Pietà" (McAuley)   **45**:252

"Pieta" (Thomas)   **13**:543; **48**:374, 379

"La pietà" (Ungaretti)   **7**:485; **11**:556; **15**:536

"The Pieta" (Van Duyn)   **7**:498; **116**:425

Le piéton de l'air (*A Stroll in the Air*; *The Stroller in the Air*) (Ionesco)   **4**:252; **6**:252, 254-55; **9**:286-87; **11**:292; **41**:227, 229, 231; **86**:332, 340

La pietra lunare (Landolfi)   **49**:216

Una pietra sopra: Discorsi di letteratura e societa (*The Literature Machine*; *The Uses of Literature*) (Calvino)   **73**:39, 48

Pietr-le-Letton (*Maigret and the Enigmatic Lett*) (Simenon)   **18**:481; **47**:379

"Piety" (Simic)   **49**:337

"Pig" (Hecht)   **8**:269

"The Pig" (Lessing)   **3**:288

"The Pig Boy" (Gardam)   **43**:171

Pig Earth (Berger)   **19**:39-41

"Pig Glass, 1973-1978" (Ondaatje)   **51**:316-17

Pig in the Middle (Mayne)   **12**:390, 392, 397

Pig in the Poke (Gray)   **36**:201

Pig Island Letters (Baxter)   **14**:62

The Pig Pen (Bullins)   **5**:83

"Pig Pig" (Walker)   **13**:566

Pig/s Book (Olson)   **28**:343

"Pig Song" (Atwood)   **13**:44

"The Pigeon" (Oe)   **86**:227

The Pigeon (Bennett)   **35**:45

"Pigeon Eggs" (Van Duyn)   **63**:445

Pigeon Feathers, and Other Stories (Updike)   **3**:488; **5**:455; **13**:557, 562; **23**:473

Pigeon Pie (Mitford)   **44**:492

"Pigeons" (Larkin)   **64**:271, 280

"The Pigeons" (Shapiro)   **53**:334

"Pigeons at Daybreak" (Desai)   **97**:152, 176

The Pigman (Zindel)   **6**:586-87; **26**:470-76, 478-80

The Pigman's Legacy (Zindel)   **26**:478, 480

Pigments (Damas)   **84**:156-57, 159-61, 163-65, 169-71, 173-80, 182-83, 185-86

Pignight (Wilson)   **33**:459, 464

Pigpen (*Pigsty*) (Pasolini)   **20**:264, 267

"Pigs" (Levi)   **41**:246

Pigs (Fugard)

  See *A Place with the Pigs*

Pigs in Heaven (Kingsolver)   **81**:190-95

Pigsty (Pasolini)

  See *Pigpen*

"The Pike" (Blunden)   **56**:29, 32, 37, 45

"Pike" (Hughes)   **4**:235-36; **9**:280-81; **37**:179

Pike's Peak: A Family Saga (Waters)   **88**:349-51, 359, 364, 369

"Pilatus" (Durrenmatt)   **15**:194

"Pile of Feathers" (Stern)   **40**:408

A Pile of Stone (Nissenson)   **4**:380; **9**:399

"A Pilgramage" (Ewart)   **46**:154

The Pilgrim (Chaplin)   **16**:188, 191, 201

Pilgrim at Sea (Lagerkvist)   **54**:281-85

Pilgrim at Tinker Creek (Dillard)   **9**:175, 177-78; **60**:70, 74, 76-7, 79, 80-1; **115**:160-61, 164-71, 175-82, 194, 197, 202-09

The Pilgrim Hawk, Love Story (Wescott)   **13**:591-92

Pilgrim of the Sea (Lagerkvist)

  See *Pilgrim på havet*

The Pilgrim on the Earth (Green)   **77**:264

Pilgrim på havet (*Pilgrim of the Sea*) (Lagerkvist)   **7**:200; **10**:312; **13**:332

"Pilgrimage" (Olds)   **32**:346; **85**:286

"Pilgrimage" (Pinsky)   **94**:308

Pilgrimage (Clarke)   **9**:167

The Pilgrimage of Festus (Aiken)   **52**:20, 22,

28

The Pilgrimage of Henry James (Brooks) 29:81, 86-7

"Pilgrimage to Non-Violence" (King) 83:347

"Pilgrimages" (Thomas) 48:383

"The Pilgrim—Chapter Thirty-Three" (Kristofferson) 26:267, 269

The Pilgrim's Regress (Lewis) 3:299, 6:310; 14:322-24; 27:265-66

Piling Blood (Purdy) 50:246, 248

Pili's Wall (Levine) 2:244; 4:286; 14:317

"The Pill Box" (Lively) 32:277

The Pill versus the Springhill Mine Disaster (Brautigan) 3:86-90; 12:58-60, 69; 34:315; 42:61

"Pillar of Fire" (Bradbury) 42:34; 98:111

"Pillar of Fire" (Foote) 75:230-31, 253, 257

A Pillar of Iron (Caldwell) 28:65; 39:303

"Pillar of Salt" (Jackson) 60:211-12

Pillars of the Nation (Laurence) 50:319

"Pillbox" (Blunden) 56:43

"Pillow" (Hogan) 73:158

"The Pilot" (Turco) 11:549, 551

"A Pilot from the Carrier" (Jarrell) 9:298; 13:300

"A Pilot Is Speaking" (Faludy) 42:140

"Pilots, Man Your Planes" (Jarrell) 13:300

Pimm's Cup for Everybody (Corcoran) 17:76

Pinball (Kosinski) 53:223-28; 70:298, 307

"Pinball Wizard" (Townshend) 17:527, 535

The Pinballs (Byars) 35:72, 75

Pincher Martin (*The Two Deaths of Christopher Martin*) (Golding) 1:121-22; 2:166-69; 3:196, 198-99; 8:249; 10:233, 237; 17:159-66, 172, 174, 179; 27:159, 162-64, 167-68; 81:317-18, 320, 323

Pinchirannaa chosho (*The Pinchrunner Memorandum*) (Oe) 36:350; 86:215-18, 220-24, 228, 230-31, 238-40

The Pinchrunner Memorandum (Oe)
  See *Pinchirannaa chosho*

Pindare (Yourcenar) 87:383

"Pine" (Dickey) 4:120; 109:266-67, 270-72

The Pine Barrens (McPhee) 36:295

"Pine Tree Tops" (Snyder) 5:395; 32:389

The Pineapple Bay Hotel (Gardam)
  See *Black Faces, White Faces*

"Pineapple Cake" (Desai) 97:150

"The Pinewoods, Crows, and Owl" (Oliver) 34:249

"Piney Wood Hills" (Sainte-Marie) 17:432

"The Pineys" (Stern) 100:329

Ping (Beckett)
  See *Bing*

Le ping-pong (*Ping-Pong*) (Adamov) 4:5-6; 25:16, 20-1

Ping-Pong (Adamov)
  See *Le ping-pong*

"The Pink Corner Man" (Borges)
  See "Hombre de la esquina rosada"

"Pink Dog" (Bishop) 32:37-8

Pink Floyd: The Wall (Pink Floyd) 35:313-14

"Pink Hands" (Soto) 80:302

"Pink Moon the Pond" (Oliver) 98:266, 272

"Pink Tights and Ginghams" (Ferber) 93:141

Pink Triangle and Yellow Star (Vidal)
  See *The Second American Revolution and Other Essays, 1976-1982*

Pinktoes (Himes) 2:195; 7:159; 58:253, 257, 261; 108:228, 234

Pinky (Kazan) 16:360-61; 63:225, 229, 234

"Pinnacle Range" (Crase) 58:163

"Pinnochio" (McFadden) 48:258

Pinocchio in Venice (Coover) 87:64-66, 68

"The Pinprick Speech" (Grass) 49:139

Pin-Ups (Bowie) 17:61-2, 64

"Um piolho de Rui Barbosa" ("A Parasite of Rui Barbosa") (Cabral de Melo Neto) 76:164

The Pioneers (Prichard) 46:327, 332, 335-36, 338

The Pious Agent (Braine) 41:59

"The Pious Brother" (Lind) 82:128

Pipali Sahab: Story of a Childhood under the Rag (Anand) 93:49

"Pipefish" (Oliver) 98:283

The Piper at the Gates of Dawn (Pink Floyd) 35:307

"Pipes of Peace" (McCartney) 35:291

Pipes of Peace (McCartney) 35:291-93

"Pipistrel" (Selzer) 74:287

"A Pippa Lilted" (Stafford) 29:382

Pippa's Challenge (Adamson) 17:5

Piracy Preferred (Campbell) 32:73

Pirandello e la Sicilia (Sciascia) 41:395

"The Piranha Brothers" (Monty Python) 21:223

"Le pirate" (Soupault) 68:406

The Pirate (Mamoulian) 16:427

The Pirate (Robbins) 5:380

"The Pirate of Penance" (Mitchell) 12:437

"Pirates" (Skvorecky) 69:333, 346

Les pirates du Texas (Simenon) 47:374

"The Pirate's Ghost" (Brown) 48:55

"Pis ma rimskomu drugu" (Brodsky) 50:131

"Pis mo generalu Z." (Brodsky) 50:131

Pis' mo vozhdiam Sovetskogo Soiuza (*Letter to Soviet Leaders*) (Solzhenitsyn) 4:514; 7:435, 439; 34:488, 493; 78:400, 403, 405, 424, 428-30

The Pisan Cantos (Pound) 3:395, 399; 4:417; 7:326, 328-29; 13:460-61, 463; 34:505; 48:282, 284-85, 287, 290, 293, 295, 299; 50:434-38; 112:301, 303-08, 332, 337, 339-40, 354-55, 357

"Písen o lásce" ("Song About Love") (Seifert) 93:342

Písen o Viktorce (Seifert)
  See *The Song of Viktorka*

"Pis'ma iz Tuly" ("Letters from Tula") (Pasternak) 7:293; 10:387; 18:385

"Piss Factory" (Smith) 12:539

"Pissaro's Tomb" (Lane) 25:287

"Pissing in a River" (Smith) 12:539-40

The Pistachio Prescription (Danziger) 21:84

The Pistol (Jones) 3:261; 10:290; 39:406

A Pistol in Greenyards (Hunter) 21:156-57, 161, 165

"The Pit" (Lessing) 94:265

"The Pit" (Roethke) 11:481

The Pit (Onetti)
  See *El pozo*

"Pit Viper" (Momaday) 85:262-63

Pitch Dark (Adler) 31:14-18

"Pitch Memory" (Canin) 55:37-8

"The Pitcher" (Dubus) 36:146; 97:210-11, 229

"Pitcher" (Francis) 15:237, 239

"The Pitcher" (Hood) 28:192

"The Pitchfork" (Heaney) 74:194

"Pitching and Rolling" (Yevtushenko) 3:547

"The Pitll Pawob Division" (Ellison) 42:127

"The Pitt-Rivers Museum, Oxford" (Fenton) 32:165-66

Pity in History (Barker) 37:41

Pity Is Not Enough (Herbst) 34:449, 451, 455

"A Pity. We Were Such a Good Invention" (Amichai) 57:41; 116:84, 90, 114-15

La più belle pagine di Tommaso Landolfi (Landolfi) 49:216

Pius XII and the Third Reich: A Documentation (Friedlander)
  See *Pie XII et le IIIe Reich; documents*

"A pizca" (Alonso) 14:25

Pjesme u tmini (*Poems in the Darkness*) (Krleza) 114:167

Placard pour un chemin des écoliers (Char) 14:127

"Placating the Gods" (Dacey) 51:83

"Place" (Creeley) 78:152

"The Place" (Warren) 39:270

La place (*A Man's Place; Positions*) (Ernaux) 88:98-99, 106-09, 111-13, 116-17, 120

Place (Forbes) 12:211

A Place among People (Hall) 51:173

"A Place as Good as Any" (Brodsky) 100:69

The Place at Whitton (Keneally) 5:210; 117:209-11, 227, 245

Place Called Estherville (Caldwell) 60:53

La Place de la Concorde Suisse (McPhee) 36:299

A Place for Lovers (De Sica) 20:95

A Place in England (Bragg) 10:72

"Place in Fiction" (Welty) 14:565-67; 105:321-22

The Place in Flowers Where Pollen Rests (West) 96:363, 365-67, 371, 373, 375-76, 378, 381, 385-86

"A Place in the Country" (Simic) 49:341

"A Place in the Sun" (Wonder) 12:656

The Place of Dead Roads (Burroughs) 42:73-6; 109:197-99, 201

"The Place of Death" (Jarrell) 2:207

"Place of Fire" (Purdy) 50:246

Place of Hawks (Derleth) 31:128-31

"Place of Learning" (Sarton) 49:310

"The Place of O" (Young Bear) 94:362

"The Place of Pain in the Universe" (Hecht) 8:266

"Place of the Salamander" (Bonnefoy)
  See "Lieu de la salamandre"

The Place of the Skull (Aitmatov)
  See *Plakha*

A Place on Earth (Berry) 8:85; 46:71, 73-4

"Place Pigalle" (Wilbur) 110:381

"The Place the Musician Became a Bear on the Streets of a City Meant to Kill Him" (Harjo) 83:286

A Place to Come to (Warren) 8:540-42; 10:523; 59:302

A Place to Die (Bowering) 47:29-30

A Place to Stand (Wagoner) 5:473

"A Place to Stand On" (Laurence) 50:320; 62:280

The Place Whrere Souls are Born (Keneally) 117:237

"The Place with No Name" (Ellison) 42:127-29

A Place with the Pigs (*Pigs*) (Fugard) 80:76, 78-80, 81, 83

A Place without Boundaries (Donoso)
  See *El lugar sin límites*

Place Your Bets (Tzara)
  See *Faites vos jeux*

"Placed by the Gideons" (Reading) 47:350

Los placeres prohibidos (*Forbidden Pleasures*) (Cernuda) 54:41, 43, 52-4, 58

"Place-Rituals" (Rukeyser) **15**:457

"Places" (Buckley) **57**:128, 131, 133

"Places in the World a Woman Could Walk" (Kauffman) **42**:250-51

Places in the World a Woman Could Walk (Kauffman) **42**:250-53

"Places I've Never Been" (Hood) **28**:189

"Places, Loved Ones" (Larkin) **64**:272

"Places to Look for Your Mind" (Moore) **68**:298-301

Places Where They Sing (Raven) **14**:442

"Plague" (Hubbard) **43**:204

The Plague (Camus)
  See *La peste*

"The Plague Children" (Hodgins) **23**:236

The Plague Column (*Morový sloup*; *The Plague Monument*) (Seifert) **34**:256-57, 259-61; **44**:422-23; **93**:304-05, 316-17, 320-22, 324, 329, 337-38, 341, 344, 346

The Plague Dogs (Adams) **18**:1

The Plague from Space (Harrison) **42**:207

The Plague Monument (Seifert)
  See *The Plague Column*

Plague Ship (Norton) **12**:467

Plague Ship (Slaughter) **29**:378

Plagued by the Nightingale (Boyle) **5**:65; **19**:61; **58**:64-5, 70, 75

The Plague-Sower (Bufalino)
  See *Diceria dell'untore*

The Plague-Sower (Bufalino)
  See *Diceria dell'untore*

The Plain (Rozewicz)
  See *Równina*

A Plain Brown Rapper (Brown) **79**:153-54, 168

"Plain Fare" (Hine) **15**:282

"The Plain in Flames" (Rulfo)
  See "El llano en llamas"

The Plain in Flames (Rulfo)
  See *El llano en llamas, y otros cuentos*

The Plain Man (Symons) **14**:523

Plain Murder (Forester) **35**:165-66

Plain of Fire (Rulfo)
  See *El llano en llamas, y otros cuentos*

"Plain Pleasures" (Bowles) **68**:3, 6, 11, 16

Plain Pleasures (Bowles) **68**:3, 9, 16

"Plain Song" (Raine) **103**:186

Plain Song (Harrison) **33**:197

"A Plain Song for Comadre" (Wilbur) **53**:397, 405, 407, 410, 413; **110**:353

"A Plain Sonnet" (Mueller) **51**:280

"The Plain, the Endless Plain" (Aldiss) **40**:21

"Plain-chant" (Cocteau) **8**:145

The Plains of Cement (*Twenty Thousand Streets under the Sky: A London Trilogy*) (Hamilton) **51**:185-86, 190, 193-95, 197-98

The Plains of Passage (Auel) **107**:19-22, 24-25

Plains Song: For Female Voices (Morris) **18**:353-55; **37**:313

Plainsongs (Livesay) **15**:341; **79**:332, 337-38, 340

"Plaint" (Roethke) **3**:433

"Plainview: 1" (Momaday) **85**:256, 264-65

"Plainview: 2" (Momaday) **85**:247-48, 264-65, 269

"Plainview: 3" (Momaday) **85**:265

"Plainview: 4" (Momaday) **85**:265

Le plaisir du texte (*The Pleasure of the Text*) (Barthes) **24**:28-30, 37, 39; **83**:80, 96, 99-100, 102-04

Plakha (*The Executioner's Block*; *The Place of the Skull*) (Aitmatov) **71**:21-33

Plameni vjetar (*The Burning Wind*) (Krleza) **114**:167

"The Plan" (Cohen) **38**:137

"The Plan" (O'Brien) **36**:340

"Plan B" (Himes) **108**:234, 241-42, 251-53

Plan de evasión (*A Plan for Escape*) (Bioy Casares) **13**:84-7; **88**:62-3, 65-6, 73, 75-6, 79-81, 85-7, 91-2

Le plan de l'aiguille (*Antarctic Fugue*) (Cendrars) **18**:97; **106**:169, 185-86

A Plan for Escape (Bioy Casares)
  See *Plan de evasión*

"Plan for the Young English King" (Pound) **10**:407

El plan infinito (Allende) **97**:21-2, 24-6, 41-3, 57

"Plan Now to Attend" (Purdy) **28**:380

"Plan of Future Works" (Pasolini) **106**:241, 250

"The Planctus" (Hope) **3**:251

"Plane Landing in Tokyo" (Scott) **22**:373

A Planet Called Treason (Card) **47**:67; **50**:143

Planet News: 1961-1967 (Ginsberg) **2**:163; **4**:181-82; **6**:198; **13**:240; **36**:183-85, 190-91, 194, 196

Planet of Adventure (Vance) **35**:423

Planet of Exile (Le Guin) **13**:345, 348; **22**:265, 273; **45**:213, 215, 218, 222

The Planet of Junior Brown (Hamilton) **26**:148-49, 154, 156

The Planet of Lost Things (Strand) **41**:435-36

Planet of the Apes (Serling) **30**:357

"Planet of the Damned" (Vance) **35**:420

The Planet Savers (Bradley) **30**:26

Planet Waves (Dylan) **4**:150; **12**:199; **77**:190

"Planetarium" (Rich) **11**:478; **18**:447; **36**:372

Le planétarium (*The Planetarium*) (Sarraute) **1**:302; **2**:386; **4**:464, 466-67, 469; **8**:472; **31**:377-78, 380, 386; **80**:229-30, 236, 240, 252

The Planetarium (Sarraute)
  See *Le planétarium*

Planets and Dimensions: Collected Essays of Clark Ashton Smith (Smith) **43**:420-21

"Planks" (Barnard) **48**:26

"The Planner's Dream Goes Wrong" (Weller) **26**:447

"Planning" (Ezekiel) **61**:104-05

"Planning the Perfect Evening" (Dove) **81**:134

Plans for Departure (Sahgal) **41**:374-75

"The Planster's Vision" (Betjeman) **6**:68; **43**:36-7, 40

Plant and Phantom (MacNeice) **4**:315; **53**:232

Plant Dreaming Deep (Sarton) **49**:316-17; **91**:251

The Plant, the Well, the Angel (Vassilikos) **4**:551

Plantain (Akhmatova) **25**:27; **64**:10

Plantain (Akhmatova)
  See *Podorozhnik*

"Plantation Boy" (Cabral de Melo Neto)
  See "Menino de engenho"

"Plantation Mistress or Soul Sister?" (hooks) **94**:150, 152

"Planting a Magnolia" (Snodgrass) **68**:393

"Planting Strawberries" (Stern) **40**:408

"Planting Trees" (Updike) **43**:436

Plants Today and Tomorrow (Hyde) **21**:173

Planus (Cendrars)
  See *Bourlinguer*

"The Plaster Mask" (Oe) **86**:226-27

"The Plastic Abyss" (Wilhelm) **7**:537-38

"Plastic Man" (Katz) **47**:216

"Plastic People" (Zappa) **17**:585

Un plat de porc aux bananes vertes (Schwarz-Bart) **2**:389

"A Plate" (Popa) **19**:373

"The Platform Man" (Snodgrass) **68**:397

Platinum Blonde (Capra) **16**:159

Platitudes (Ellis) **55**:50-4

"Platko" (Alberti) **7**:7

"Platonic" (Ezekiel) **61**:93, 101, 105

"Platonic Drowse" (Warren) **39**:256

"Platonic Love" (Reaney) **13**:473

Platonic Scripts (Justice) **102**:268, 281, 283

Platoon (Stone) **73**:367-79, 381-83, 385

"Plato's Pharmacy" (Derrida) **24**:155; **87**:92

"Plato's Year" (Sherwin) **7**:414

"Platsch" (Jandl) **34**:196

"Platypus" (Murray) **40**:334

Plausible Prejudices: Essays on American Writing (Epstein) **39**:464-69

"A Play" (Alta) **19**:19

Play (Beckett) **6**:39, 43, 47; **9**:84, 86; **11**:37-9, 42-3; **18**:43, 46-8; **29**:54

The Play about the Baby (Albee) **113**:54

A Play by Aleksandr Solzhenitsyn (Solzhenitsyn) **1**:321

Play by Play (Goldemberg)
  See *Tiempo al Tiempo*

"Play Ebony Play Ivory" (Dumas) **62**:155

Play Ebony Play Ivory (Dumas)
  See *Poetry for My People*

"Play in Four Acts" (Dobyns) **37**:76

Play It Again, Sam (Allen) **16**:3-5; **52**:39, 44, 48

"Play It as It Lays" (Braverman) **67**:52

Play It as It Lays (Didion) **1**:74-5; **3**:127-28; **8**:173-77; **14**:151, 153; **32**:143, 149

A Play of Giants (Soyinka) **36**:417-18

"A Play of Memory" (Updike) **23**:475

The Play of the Eyes (Canetti)
  See *Das Augenspiel: Lebensgeschichte 1931-1937*

Play Parade: Collected Plays of Noël Coward (Coward) **29**:134

Play Strindberg (Duerrenmatt) **102**:60-1

Play Strindberg (Durrenmatt) **8**:195; **15**:195; **43**:126-27

Play with a Tiger (Lessing) **94**:272

La playa (Sarduy) **97**:370

"De playa a playa" (Otero) **11**:427

"Playa ignorante" (Aleixandre) **9**:15

"Playback" (Beattie) **63**:2, 9, 12, 19

"Playbox" (Reaney) **13**:473

"Playboy" (Wilbur) **110**:384

The Player (Altman) **116**:50-2, 55, 58-9, 62, 66-7, 71, 73

The Player King (Rovit) **7**:383

The Player on the Other Side (Queen) **3**:421; **11**:461, 464-65

"The Player Piano" (Jarrell) **13**:302

Player Piano (*Utopia Fourteen*) (Vonnegut) **1**:348; **2**:453; **3**:495-96, 498, 500-01; **4**:562-63, 565-67; **5**:466-67, 469; **12**:600-03, 606, 609-12, 614, 616-18, 620-21, 623; **22**:445; **40**:441, 444; **60**:429, 431; **111**:351, 355, 363

Players (DeLillo) **8**:172; **10**:134-35; **13**:175, 178; **27**:80, 85-6; **39**:117, 123, 125; **54**:80, 82; **76**:171-72, 174, 182

Players (Williamson)
  See *The Club*

The Players and the Game (Symons) **2**:426; **14**:523

Playground (Buell) **10**:81-2

The Playground (Levine)   54:293, 299
"The Playhouse Called Remarkable" (Spark)
    13:523
"Playing an Obsolete Instrument" (Hollander)
    5:186
"Playing Cards" (Atwood)   4:27
Playing for Time (Miller)   26:326-28
Playing House (Wagman)   7:500
*Playing in the Dark: Whiteness and the Literary
    Imagination* (Morrison)   81:239-40, 245-
    46, 248, 250-51, 255, 258, 260
"Playing in the Mines" (Parini)   54:361
Playing Possum (Simon)   26:409-10
"Playing with Fire" (Simmons)   43:414
"Playing with My Kinsman" (Kunene)   85:176
Playland (Fugard)   80:83
The Playmaker (Keneally)   117:240, 243
"The Playroom" (Barnard)   48:25-6
"The Playroom" (Turco)   11:550
Plays for England (Osborne)   2:328; 5:332;
    45:314
Plays for the Poor Theatre (Brenton)   31:69
Plays in Which Darkness Falls (Hildesheimer)
    See *Spiele in denen es dunkel wird*
The Plays of J. P. Donleavy (Donleavy)   4:125
"Plays: Self" (Foreman)
    See "How I Write My"
The Playwright as Thinker (Bentley)   24:45-7
"Plaza Real with Palm Trees" (Blackburn)
    9:100
"Plaza Real with Palm Trees: Second Take"
    (Blackburn)   9:100
Plaza Suite (Simon)   6:504; 31:395-96, 403-
    04; 70:240, 243
"Plea" (Kaufman)   49:205
"A Plea to the Protestant Churches" (Brooks)
    110:28, 30
"Plea to Those Who Matter" (Welch)   52:429-
    30
"A Pleasant Thought from Whitehead"
    (O'Hara)   13:427
"A Pleasant Walk" (Enright)   31:154
"Please" (Komunyakaa)   94:242
Please Don't Eat the Daisies (Kerr)   22:255
"Please Forward" (Summers)   10:494
"Please Hello" (Sondheim)   30:388
"Please Let Me Wonder" (Wilson)   12:643
"Please, Master" (Ginsberg)   109:333, 357,
    364, 366
Please Pass the Guilt (Stout)   3:472
"Please Please Me" (Lennon and McCartney)
    35:274
"Please Stay in the Family Clovis" (Durcan)
    43:114, 116
"Please Turn Off the Moonlight" (Wheelock)
    14:571
"Pleasure" (Schwartz)   10:465
"Pleasure" (Wiggins)   57:434-36
Pleasure City (Markandaya)
    See *Shalimar*
The Pleasure Garden (Garfield)   12:232-33,
    236
"The Pleasure Ground" (Murphy)   41:315-16
"The Pleasure of Her Company" (Smiley)
    53:348
The Pleasure of the Text (Barthes)
    See *Le plaisir du texte*
The Pleasure Principle (Wilson)   33:460-61,
    464
Pleasure Seeker's Guide (Leet)   11:323
"The Pleasure Steamers" (Motion)   47:289,
    291, 293-94
The Pleasure Steamers (Motion)   47:285-86,

288-89, 292-94
Pleasure-Dome (Madden)   15:350
*The Pleasure-Dome: The Collected Film Criti-
    cism, 1935-40 (Graham Greene on Film:
    Collected Film Criticism, 1935-1940)*
    (Greene)   70:294
The Pleasures of Exile (Lamming)   2:235;
    66:221-22, 224-27, 231
The Pleasures of Helen (Sanders)   41:377
"The Pleasures of Peace" (Koch)   44:243
The Pleasures of Peace and Other Poems
    (Koch)   44:241, 243, 248-49
Pleasures of the Flesh (Ewart)   13:208; 46:148,
    150
The Pleasures of the Harbour (Ochs)   17:330-
    34
"Pleasuring Sunday" (Nagy)   7:251
*The Plebeians Rehearse the Uprising: A Ger-
    man Tragedy* (Grass)   4:201, 203; 6:207;
    15:261; 49:139
The Pledge (Duerrenmatt)   102:59
The Pledge (Durrenmatt)
    See *Das Versprechen: Requiem auf den
    Kriminalroman*
"The Pleiades" (Barnard)   48:26
"The Plentitude" (Thesen)   56:415
Plenty (Hare)   29:213-20; 58:225, 230, 233-
    35
"*Plessy vs. Ferguson*: Theme and Variations"
    (Merton)   83:397
Plexus (Miller)   2:281
"Plitsch" (Jandl)   34:196
"Ploaie" ("Rain") (Arghezi)   80:8
"Ploja fòur di dut" (Pasolini)   106:267
"Ploja tai cunfins" (Pasolini)   106:226-28,
    267
"Pløjeren" (Dinesen)   95:70-1
"Plot" (Oates)   6:370-71
The Plot (Wallace)   13:568
"The Plot against Proteus" (Smith)   15:513,
    516
The Plot Against Roger Rider (Symons)   32:425
The Plot to Seize the White House (Archer)
    12:19-20
Plotting and Writing Suspense Fiction
    (Highsmith)   102:185, 196, 209, 213
"Plotting with the Dead" (Szymborska)   99:201
The Plough and the Stars (O'Casey)   5:317-
    20; 11:406-11; 15:404-06; 88:239, 242,
    244-45, 247, 250, 254, 256-59, 262, 276-
    77
"The Plougher" (Colum)   28:90
"Ploughman" (Kavanagh)   22:238
Ploughman and Other Poems (Kavanagh)
    22:236
The Ploughman's Lunch (McEwan)   66:286
Ploughmen of the Glacier (Ryga)   14:474
"Plow Cemetery" (Updike)   43:436
Plowshare in Heaven (Stuart)   34:373, 376
Pluck the Flowers, Gun the Kids (Oe)
    See *Me-mushiri Kouchi*
"Plug Body" (Howe)   47:172-73
"Pluie" (Hebert)   29:237
La Pluie d'Eté (Duras)   100:120, 131
La pluie et le beau temps (Prevert)   15:438
*Pluie et vent sur Télumée Miracle (The Bridge
    of Beyond)* (Schwarz-Bart)   7:404-05
"Pluies" ("Rains") (Perse)   11:433; 46:303-
    05, 307, 309
"Plum Blossoms" (Peterkin)   31:308
Plum Bun (Fauset)   19:169, 171; 54:176-77,
    180-82, 187, 189-90
"The Plum Trees" (Oliver)   34:247; 98:257,

260, 296-97
"Plumb" (Zamora)   89:369, 394
Plumb (Gee)   29:177-79
The Plumber (Weir)   20:429-30
"The Plumber as the Missing Letter"
    (Wheelock)   14:571
"The Plumbing" (Merwin)   45:277
Plume à Casablanca (Michaux)   19:311
Plume au restaurant (Michaux)   19:311
Plumelia (Piccolo)   13:441
"The Plumet Basilisk" (Moore)   4:362; 10:353;
    13:396
"The Plum's Heart" (Soto)   80:289
"Plunder" (Ammons)   25:48
Plunder Squad (Westlake)   33:437
"Plunge" (Gunn)   18:199, 202
"A Plunge into Real Estate" (Calvino)
    See "La speculazione edilizia"
"plunging into the improbable" (Broumas)   73:5
"Plunking the Skagit" (Hugo)   32:237
"Plurality" (MacNeice)   4:317
Plus (McElroy)   47:240-41, 243-44, 246
"Plutonian Ode" (Ginsberg)   36:192, 196
Plutonian Ode: Poems, 1977-1980 (Ginsberg)
    36:188, 191-91, 194, 196
"Plutonium-186" (Asimov)   19:26
PM/AM: New and Selected Poems (Pastan)
    27:371
Pnin (Nabokov)   1:239, 243-45; 2:299, 303;
    3:352-53, 355-56; 6:351, 356; 8:412, 418;
    15:393; 44:467-68; 46:291; 64:351
The Poume (Vance)   35:422, 424
"Po' Boy Blues" (Hughes)   35:221
"Po jagody" (Yevtushenko)   13:620
"Po' Sammy" (Bennett)   28:29
"Po' Ting" (Bennett)   28:27
The Poacher (Bates)   46:53-6
"Poachers Early Morning" (MacCaig)   36:282
"Poaching" (Wolff)   64:446, 449
Poarta neagra (The Black Gate) (Arghezi)
    80:6-7, 11
"Pobeda" (Aksyonov)
    See "The Victory"
"Pocahontas" ("Marlon Brando, Pocahontas,
    and Me") (Young)   17:581
La poche parmentier (Perec)   56:257-58
"Pochti elegiia" ("Almost an Elegy") (Brodsky)
    13:116; 50:121
"The Pocket Elephants" (Middleton)   13:389
A Pocket Full of Miracles (Robinson)   21:343
A Pocket Full of Rye (Christie)   12:115-16,
    124; 48:75
The Pocket Mirror (Frame)   22:145; 96:189,
    198, 201
"The Pocket Remembered" (Singer)   69:306-
    07
"The Pocket Song" (Goldbarth)   38:201
"The Pocket Wars of Peanuts Joe" (Harrison)
    43:175
Pocketful of Miracles (Capra)   16:157, 160,
    163
Pocketful of Rye (Cronin)   32:140
Pocoangelini: A Fantography (Turco)   11:552
Pocock and Pitt (Baker)   8:39-40
"Pocock Passes" (Pritchett)   41:334
"Pocomania" (Walcott)   42:421; 76:279
"Pocta Vladimíru Holanovi" ("Eulogy on
    Vladimír Holan") (Seifert)   93:343
"Pod of the Milkweed" (Frost)   9:223; 10:199
"Poderío de la noche" (Aleixandre)   9:16
Podkayne of Mars (Heinlein)   55:303
*Podniataia tselina (The Seeds of Tomorrow;
    Virgin Soil Upturned)* (Sholokhov)   7:416-

17, 420-21; 15:481-84
Podorozhnik (*Buckthorn*; *Plantain*) (Akhmatova) 25:24
Podrostak Savenko (*Memoir of a Russian Punk*) (Coles) 67:177, 182-83
Poe Poe Poe Poe Poe Poe Poe (Hoffman) 6:242; 13:286-87; 23:240-41
"Poem" (Ashbery) 13:35
"Poem" (Bishop) 9:94-5, 97-8; 13:95
"Poem" (Gluck) 22:174
"The Poem" (Hall) 37:142
"The Poem" (Hoffman) 13:289
"Poem" (Jensen) 37:192
"Poem" (Justice) 6:272; 19:235; 102:285
"The Poem" (Kinnell) 3:269; 29:284
"Poem" (McGrath) 59:183
"Poem" ("I've Got to Tell You") (O'Hara) 13:423-25, 427, 430; 78:333, 346
"Poem" (Oliver) 98:260
"The Poem" (Paz) 4:397
"Poem" (Purdy) 14:431
"Poem" (Rukeyser) 27:409
"Poem" ("Old Man in the Crystal Morning") (Schwartz) 45:355; 45:355
"Poem" (Simic) 9:478, 481
"Poem" (Smith) 64:395
"Poem" (Strand) 71:281
"Poem" (Tomlinson) 13:546
"Poem" (Turner) 48:398-99
"The Poem" (Williams) 13:605
"Poem" (Zweig) 34:379
"Poem 1" (Ferlinghetti) 111:50-1
"Poem I" (Larkin) 18:293
"Poem II" (Larkin) 18:298
"Poem 5" (Ferlinghetti) 111:51
"Poem 6" (Ferlinghetti) 111:53
"Poem 13" (Ferlinghetti) 111:54
"Poem 14" (Ferlinghetti) 111:54, 56
"Poem 15" (Ferlinghetti) 111:57
"Poem 17" (Ferlinghetti) 111:52
"Poem XX" (Larkin) 8:340; 18:293, 299
"Poem 22" (Ferlinghetti) 111:55
"Poem 24" (Ferlinghetti) 111:54, 58
"Poem 25" (Ferlinghetti) 111:54
"Poem XXIX" (Larkin) 18:298
"Poem XXXII" (Larkin) 8:339-40
"Poem 177: The Law School Riots, Athens, 1973" (Levi) 41:246
"Poem about a Ball in the Nineteenth Century" (Empson) 8:201
"A Poem about George Doty in the Death House" (Wright) 5:519
"A Poem about Intelligence for My Brothers and Sisters" (Jordan) 23:255
"Poem about Morning" (Meredith) 13:375
"Poem About My Rights" (Jordan) 114:143-47, 158, 161, 163
"Poem about People" (Pinsky) 38:359; 94:305
"A Poem about Poland" (Donnell) 34:158
"Poem About Police Violence" (Jordan) 114:142
"Poem about the Future" (Enzensberger) 43:144
"Poem (All the Mirrors in the World)" (O'Hara) 78:339
"The Poem and the Spear" (Laurence) 62:280
"The Poem and the Water" (Cabral de Melo Neto)
  See "O poema e a água"
"The Poem as a Field of Action" (Williams) 42:450
"The Poem as Mask: Orpheus" (Rukeyser) 15:459; 27:413-14

"Poem at Thirty" (Sanchez) 116:272, 275, 278, 280, 313
"Poem Beginning 'The'" ("The") (Zukofsky) 18:558
"A Poem Beginning with a Line by Pindar" (Duncan) 2:122; 15:190, 192; 41:124
"Poem Dedicatory" (MacLeish) 68:273
"Poem Ended by a Death" (Adcock) 41:16-17
"A Poem for 3rd World Brothers" (Knight) 40:282, 285
"Poem for a Birthday" (Plath) 17:368; 111:164, 177-81, 203, 212
"A Poem for a Certain Lady on Her Thirty-Third Birthday" (Knight) 40:283
"Poem for a Fatherless Son" (Plath) 111:167
"Poem for a Gone Woman" (Lane) 25:287
"Poem for a Painter" (O'Hara) 13:425
"Poem for a Poet" (Lorde) 71:247
"A Poem for a Poet" (Madhubuti) 73:213
"Poem for a Time of Change" (MacLeish) 68:287
"Poem for a Tremendous Drunk" (Salinas) 90:331
"Poem for Angela Elston" (Mahapatra) 33:284
"Poem for Aretha" (Giovanni) 64:186
"A Poem for Atheists" (Dunn) 36:151
"Poem for Benn's Graduation from High School" (Ciardi) 40:161
"A Poem for Black Hearts" (Baraka) 5:48
"A Poem for Black Relocation Centers" (Knight) 40:284
"Poem (For BMC No. 2)" (Giovanni) 117:194
"Poem for Conrad" (Watkins) 43:450, 453
"Poem for Etheridge" (Sanchez) 116:295, 315
"Poem for Half-White College Students" (Baraka) 5:48
"poem for jennifer, marla, tawana and me" (Sapphire) 99:81
"Poem for Joy" (Jordan) 114:154
"A Poem for Julia" (Hecht) 8:266
"Poem for L. C." (Klappert) 57:259
"Poem for Marie" (Heaney) 14:243-44
"Poem for Mark" (Jordan) 114:154
"A Poem for My Father" (Sanchez) 116:281, 295, 313
"Poem for My Thirty-Second Birthday" (Ciardi) 40:157
"A Poem for My Wife" (Sorrentino) 40:386
"A Poem for Myself" (Knight) 40:284
"Poem for Nana" (Jordan) 114:143
"A Poem for Negro Intellectuals (If There Bes Such a Thing)" (Madhubuti) 73:199
"Poem for Olivia" ("Olivia") (Salinas) 90:325
"Poem for One of the Annettes" (Purdy) 50:245
"Poem for Personnel Managers" (Bukowski) 41:64-5
"Poem for South African Women" (Jordan) 114:158
"A Poem for Sterling Brown" (Sanchez) 116:301
"A Poem for the Blue Heron" (Oliver) 98:273
"A Poem for the Students of Greece" (Boyle) 58:76
"A Poem for the Teesto Diné of Arizona" (Boyle) 58:76
"A Poem for Willie Best" (Baraka) 10:20; 115:33
"Poem XLII" (Cummings) 68:47
"Poem From Taped Testimony in the Tradition of Bernhard Goetz" (Jordan) 114:144
"Poem in April" (Gustafson) 36:218
"Poem in March" (Levi) 41:244

"Poem in Memory of an Earlier Poem" (Thesen) 56:422-23
"Poem in Praise of the British" (Dunn) 40:166
"Poem in Prose" (Bogan) 46:90; 93:65
A Poem in Time Frozen (*A Poem on Frozen Time*) (Milosz) 22:312; 82:298
"A Poem in Translation" (Gallagher) 18:170
"Poem Instead of a Columbus Day Parade" (Jordan) 114:146
"A Poem Is a Walk" (Ammons) 5:26
"Poem Issued by Me..." (Starbuck) 53:353
"The Poem Itself" (Jacobsen) 48:195
The Poem Itself (Burnshaw) 3:91; 13:129
"Poem (Khrushchev Is Coming on the Right Day!)" (O'Hara) 78:360
"A Poem Looking for a Reader" (Madhubuti) 73:193
"A Poem Nearly Anonymous" (Ransom) 24:366
"Poem No. 4" (Sanchez) 116:279
"Poem No. 7" (Sanchez) 116:272, 274
"Poem No. 8" (Sanchez) 116:315
"Poem (No Name No. 3)" (Giovanni) 64:182
"Poem #5" (L'Heureux) 52:273
"A Poem of Ecstasy" (Aksyonov) 101:21
"The Poem of Flight" (Levine) 33:274
"Poem of Lewis" (Smith) 64:396-97
"Poem of Liberation" (Stern) 40:410-11
"A Poem of Praise" (Sanchez) 116:315
"Poem of the Wintry Fisherman" (Haines) 58:215
"Poem of These States" (Ginsberg) 36:191
"Poem on an Underground Wall" (Simon) 17:459, 461
A Poem on Frozen Time (Milosz)
  See *A Poem in Time Frozen*
"Poem on My Birthday" (Amichai) 9:22
"A Poem on the First Battles" (Amichai)
  See "Shir al hakravot harishonim"
"A Poem on the Nuclear War, from Pompeii" (Tillinghast) 29:415
"Poem on the Road" (Jordan) 114:146
"Poem, or Beauty Hurts Mr. Vinal" (Cummings) 8:159; 68:46
"Poem out of Childhood" (Rukeyser) 15:457
"Poem Read at Joan Mitchell's" (O'Hara) 78:372
"Poem LXVII" (Cummings) 68:47
"Poem to a Foreign Lady" (Perse)
  See "Poème à l'étrangère"
"Poem to Camus" (Kaufman) 49:204
"A Poem to Complement Other Poems" (Madhubuti) 73:199, 212
"Poem to My Daughter" (Stevenson) 33:382
"Poem to My Husband from My Father's Daughter" (Olds) 32:346; 85:287
"Poem Two" (Snyder) 32:387
"Poem V (F) W" (O'Hara) 78:358
"A Poem with Children" (Guillen)
  See "Poema con niños"
"Poem with One Fact" (Hall) 37:146
Poem without a Hero (Akhmatova)
  See *Poema bez geroia*
"Poem without Theme" (Squires) 51:377
"Poem Written After Reading Wright's 'American Hunger'" (Sanchez) 116:303
Poema a fumetti (Buzzati) 36:97
Poema bez geroia (*Poem without a Hero*) (Akhmatova) 11:8-9; 25:28-30; 64:11, 13-15, 18-19
"Poema con niños" ("A Poem with Children") (Guillen) 79:241
"Poema de los dones" (Borges) 6:89

"O poema e a água" ("The Poem and the Water"; "Water and the Poem") (Cabral de Melo Neto) 76:150, 165

Poemas, 1923-1959 (Borges) 44:363

Poemas (1953-1955) (Castellanos) 66:50

"Poema(s) da cabra" ("Poems of the Goat") (Cabral de Melo Neto) 76:167

Poemas de amor (Guillen) 79:241

Poemas de la consumación (*Poems of Consummation*) (Aleixandre) 9:12, 17; 36:25-7, 30-1

Poemas de un novelista (Donoso) 32:161; 99:270-72

Poemas para combatir la calvicie (Parra) 102:356

Poemas puros (Alonso) 14:16

Poemas y antipoemas (*Poems and Antipoems*) (Parra) 2:331; 102:334, 337-38, 340, 342, 344-45, 348, 356

Poemat otwarty (*The Open Poem*) (Rozewicz) 23:362

"Poème" (Char) 14:127

"Poème à l'étrangère" ("Poem to a Foreign Lady") (Perse) 4:399; 46:305, 307, 309

Poeme noi (Arghezi) 80:8

Le poème pulverisé (Char) 9:161, 164

Poemele luminii (*Poems of Light*) 75:67-70, 74-7

Poèmes (Genet) 44:391

Poemes des deux années, 1953-1954 (Char) 9:159

Poèmes en prose (Reverdy) 53:286

Poèmes et poésies (1917-1973) (Soupault) 68:408

Poèmes militants (Char) 14:127

Poèmes nègres sur des airs africains (*African Songs of Love, War, Grief and Abuse*) (Damas) 84:177, 179, 181, 184

Poèmes: Un champ d'iles, La terre inquiète, Les Indes (Glissant) 68:182

Poem-Paintings (O'Hara) 13:427

Poems (Amichai) 116:84, 89-90, 95-6

Poems (Auden) 2:22; 3:24; 6:19-24; 14:26, 33; 43:17

Poems (Barker) 48:9, 11, 20

Poems (Beer) 58:38

Poems (Berryman) 13:77; 62:71

Poems (Bishop) 4:65

Poems (Celan) 53:71, 74

Poems (Christie) 110:125-26, 128

Poems (Clark) 38:120, 125, 127

Poems (Eliot) 13:193; 41:151; 55:350; 57:167

Poems (Fearing) 51:104-08, 110-11, 114-15

Poems (Finch) 18:153

Poems (Fowles) 9:216

Poems (Fuller) 28:151-52

Poems (Golding) 27:164; 81:318

Poems (Hebert) 13:268; 29:231-32

Poems (Hope) 51:213, 216-21

Poems (Ignatow) 7:175, 177; 14:274, 276; 40:258

Poems (Klein) 19:260

Poems (Koch) 44:240, 244

Poems (Laxness)
  See *Kvaedakver*

Poems (MacNeice) 4:315; 53:233-34

Poems (Nabokov) 3:351

Poems (Pasolini)
  See *Poesi*

Poems (Ratushinskaya)
  See *Stikhi/Poems/Poèmes*

Poems (Reaney) 13:472

Poems (Slessor) 14:492

Poems (Smith) 6:512

Poems (Spender) 10:488, 492; 41:418, 424; 91:263, 266, 269

Poems (Walcott) 25:452; 76:273

Poems (Warner) 45:428-29

Poems, 1930 (Auden) 3:25; 4:34; 11:15, 17; 14:32; 43:15-16, 18, 23-4, 26, 29

Poems, 1934 (Auden) 6:19; 11:18

Poems, 1934 (Empson) 34:335

Poems, 1935 (Empson) 19:152, 157, 159; 34:335

Poems, 1950 (Bunting) 39:297; 47:44-5, 49

Poems, 1953 (Graves) 1:127

Poems 1960 to 1967 (Levertov) 66:251

"Poems 1946-56" (Spicer) 72:362

Poems 1968-72 (Levertov) 66:251-52

Poems, 1914-1926 (Graves) 1:127; 45:162-63

Poems, 1914-1930 (Blunden) 56:30, 38, 40-1

Poems, 1918-1936 (Reznikoff) 9:450

Poems, 1920-1945: A Selection (Tate) 14:532

Poems, 1922-1947 (Tate) 4:539; 14:532

Poems, 1922-1961 (Davidson) 2:112

Poems, 1923-1954 (Cummings) 15:154; 68:35, 40, 42

Poems, 1924-1933 (MacLeish) 8:360; 68:286

Poems, 1924-1944 (Lewis) 41:255

Poems, 1925-1940 (MacNeice) 53:231, 235

Poems, 1926-1930 (Graves) 45:162

Poems, 1930-1940 (Blunden) 56:30, 44

Poems, 1934-1969 (Ignatow) 4:247-49; 7:177, 180-82

Poems, 1937-1942 (Gascoyne) 45:146-51, 153, 156, 158

Poems, 1938-1945 (Graves) 1:126-27

Poems, 1938-1949 (Lowell) 9:335

Poems, 1940-1953 (Shapiro) 8:486; 15:478

Poems, 1943-1947 (Day Lewis) 10:130-31

Poems, 1943-1956 (Wilbur) 53:396

Poems, 1955-1980 (Fisher) 25:160-62

Poems, 1956-1973 (Kinsella) 19:254-55

Poems, 1957-1967 (Dickey) 1:73; 2:115; 4:120; 7:79; 15:174; 47:92; 109:264

Poems, 1962-1978 (Mahon) 27:291-92

Poems, 1964-1967 (Rothenberg) 6:477

Poems, 1964-1980 (Rosenthal) 28:398

Poems (1965-1973) (Van Duyn) 116:426

Poems, 1965-1975 (Heaney) 25:249-51; 37:162

Poems, 1968-1970 (Graves) 2:177; 6:212

Poems, 1970-1972 (Graves) 1:127; 2:177; 6:212; 45:168-69

"Poems about Birch Trees" (Haines) 58:218

Poems about God (Ransom) 2:365; 4:431, 436; 5:366

"Poems about Paintings" (Snodgrass) 10:477; 68:393

"Poems about St. Petersburg, II" (Akhmatova) 64:9

"Poems about War" (Achebe) 26:21

Poems against Economics (Murray) 40:335, 338

Poems All Over the Place, Mostly '70s (Ginsberg) 36:196

Poems Ancient and Modern (Porter) 33:318

Poems and Antipoems (Parra)
  See *Poemas y antipoemas*

Poems and Epistles (Fuller) 62:192, 194

Poems and Essays (Ransom) 2:364; 5:364

Poems and New Poems (Bogan) 39:390; 46:80-1, 83, 90

Poems and Poets (Grigson) 7:135

Poems and Problems (Nabokov) 2:304; 8:407

Poems and Prose, 1949-1977 (Pinter) 27:387

Poems and Satires (Graves) 1:127

Poems and Songs (Ewart) 13:208; 46:147-49

"Poems Are a Complex" (Creeley) 78:120

Poems by an Unknown (Abe)
  See *Poems of an Unknown Poet*

"Poems by Women" (Levertov) 66:244

"Poems for a Woman" (Amichai) 57:43

Poems for All the Annettes (Purdy) 6:428-29; 14:433; 50:236, 246

"Poems for Haruko" (Jordan) 114:155

Poems for People Who Don't Read Poems (Enzensberger) 43:144-46

Poems for the Game of Silence (Rothenberg) 6:477

"Poems for the Living" (Olds) 85:346

Poems Four (Dugan) 6:144

"Poems from a Cycle Called 'Patriotic Songs'" (Amichai) 116:91-2

"Poems from a Small Island" (Brown) 48:57

Poems from a Voyage across the Sound (Haavikko) 34:177

Poems from Prison (Knight) 40:278-80, 282-84

Poems from the House of Novgorod Merchant (Haavikko) 34:177

"Poems from the Margins of Thom Gunn's 'Moly'" (Duncan) 41:130; 55:298

Poems from Three Decades (Lattimore) 3:277-78

Poems, Golders Green (Abse) 29:15-16

"The Poems I Have Lost" (Ortiz) 45:307

Poems in Prose (Solzhenitsyn)
  See *Kroxotnye rasskazy*

Poems in the Darkness (Krleza)
  See *Pjesme u tmini*

Poems in the Porch (Betjeman) 43:34, 49

Poems in the Shape of a Rose (Pasolini)
  See *Poems in the Shape of a Rose*

"Poems in Transit" (Ferlinghetti) 6:184; 27:139

"Poems Looking In" (Ciardi) 40:154

Poems New and Collected (Smith) 15:517

Poems New and Selected (Brown) 48:53, 57

Poems, New and Selected (Eberhart) 56:79

Poems New and Selected (Lane) 25:286-88

Poems New and Selected (Silkin) 43:397-400

Poems New and Selected (Whittemore) 4:588

"Poems Not about War" (Achebe) 26:20, 22, 24

Poems of 9-10 P.M. (Hikmet)
  See *Saat 21-22 siirleri*

Poems of a Jew (Shapiro) 4:484; 53:330-31, 333

"Poems of Air" (Strand) 18:520

Poems of Akhmatova (Akhmatova) 25:26; 64:13-14

Poems of an Unknown Poet (*Poems by an Unknown*) (Abe) 81:292-93

Poems of André Breton: A Bilingual Anthology (Breton) 54:30

Poems of Consummation (Aleixandre)
  See *Poemas de la consumación*

Poems of Dedication (Spender) 91:261, 263

"Poems of Exile" (Jordan) 5:203

Poems of Jerusalem (Amichai) 116:127-28

Poems of Light
  See *Poemele luminii*

"Poems of Many Places" (Hall) 51:171

Poems of Many Years (Blunden) 2:65; 56:29, 36, 40

Poems of Night (Kinnell) 29:281

Poems of Paul Celan (Celan)

See *Paul Celan: Poems*

Poems of Places and People (Barker) **8**:46; **48**:19, 24

Poems of R. S. Thomas (Thomas) **48**:383

Poems of René Char (Char) **55**:287

The Poems of Richard Aldington (Aldington) **49**:11-13

The Poems of Richard Wilbur (Wilbur) **53**:405, 410; **110**:350, 352

The Poems of Stanley Kunitz, 1928-1978 (Kunitz) **14**:313

"Poems of the Forgotten" (Haines) **58**:220

"Poems of the Goat" (Cabral de Melo Neto) See "Poema(s) da cabra"

Poems of the War and After (Brittain) **23**:89

Poems of Thirty Years (Morgan) **31**:276

Poems of Two Worlds (Morgan) **23**:298, 301

Poems of Various Years (Yevtushenko) See *Stikhi raznykh let*

Poems Old and New, 1918-1978 (Lewis) **41**:261-62

Poems Retrieved (O'Hara) **13**:423

Poems Selected and New (Page) **7**:292; **18**:379

Poems: Selected and New, 1950-1974 (Rich) **6**:459; **7**:369, 372-73; **36**:371, 375; **73**:323, 328

"Poems to a Brown Cricket" (Wright) **3**:541; **10**:544

Poems to Solve (Swenson) **61**:402; **106**:320, 339

Poems Unpleasant (Baxter) **14**:61

"Poems without Legs" (Hall) **37**:148

Poems Worth Knowing (McFadden) **48**:245

"Poems Written to Accompany Photographs by Rudy Burckhardt" (Denby) **48**:83

Poesi (Poems) (Pasolini) **37**:348; **106**:250, 253

Poesi española: Ensayo de métodos y límites estilísticos (Alonso) **14**:20

Poesía, 1953-1966 (Rodriguez) **10**:439

"Poesía de comunión y poesía de soledad" ("Poetry of Solitude and Poetry of Communion") (Paz) **65**:176, 180

La poesía de San Juan de la Cruz (Alonso) **14**:23

La poesia dialettale del Novecento (Pasolini) **37**:345; **106**:226, 231,

"Poesia e compoiçao—A inspiração e o trabalho de arte" (Cabral de Melo Neto) **76**:152, 157

Poesía en movimiento (Paz) **65**:177

Poesia in forma di rosa (Pasolini) **37**:346, 350; **106**:220, 253, 263

Poesía no eres tú: Obra poética, 1948-1971 (You Are Not Poetry) (Castellanos) **66**:44, 53

"La poesia popolaine italiana" (Pasolini) **106**:231, 245

La poesia populace Italiana (Pasolini) **37**:343

Poesía y literatura (Cernuda) **54**:48

Poesias completas (Alberti) **7**:9

Poesias completas (Cabral de Melo Neto) **76**:156

Poesie a Casarsa (Pasolini) **37**:343, 348; **106**:228-29, 231, 234, 243, 271

La poésie antillaise (Conde) **92**:100

Poésie et connaissance (Cesaire) **112**:13-14

Poesie IV (Jouve) **47**:208-09

Poésie pour pouvoir (Poetry to Enable) (Michaux) **8**:392

Poesie und Politik (Poetry and Politics) (Enzensberger) **43**:154

Poésies complètes: 1917-1937 (Soupault) **68**:404, 408

"The Poet" (Aleixandre) See "El poeta"

"Poèt" (Bagryana) **10**:14

"The Poet" (Dinesen) **10**:145; **95**:42, 48, 53-4, 73

"A Poet" (Feldman) **7**:102

"The Poet" (Frost) **13**:227

"The Poet" (Kaufman) **49**:205

"The Poet" (Lowell) **37**:237

"The Poet" (Oates) **33**:294

"Poet" (Shapiro) **53**:334

"The Poet" (Williams) **15**:579

"Poet: A Lying Word" (Riding) **7**:374

"Poet and Critic" (Livesay) **79**:351

Poet and Dancer (Jhabvala) **94**:202-5

"Poet and Goldsmith" (Watkins) **43**:452

A Poet and His Camera (Parks) **1**:265

"The Poet and Revolution" (Day Lewis) **10**:132

"The Poet as a Creator of Social Values" (Sanchez) **116**:316

"The Poet as Hero: Keats in His Letters" (Trilling) **11**:543

"The Poet as Painter" (Tomlinson) **45**:404

"The Poet as Refugee" (Dobyns) **37**:76

"The Poet as Troublemaker" (Meredith) **4**:348

"Poet at Seventy" (Milosz) **56**:246; **82**:290

"Poet at the Market" (Yevtushenko) **26**:467

"The Poet Contemplates His Inaction" (Ezekiel) **61**:106

"Poet for Time" (Lerman) **9**:331

Poet in Our Time (Montale) **9**:390

"The Poet in Residence in Spite of Himself" (Montgomery) **7**:233

A Poet in the Family (Abse) **29**:20

The Poet in the Imaginary Museum: Essays of Two Decades (Davie) **10**:124-25; **31**:112

"The Poet in the World" (Levertov) **8**:346

The Poet in the World (Levertov) **3**:293; **5**:246-47, 250; **8**:346-47

"The Poet Is Dead" (Everson) **14**:163

"The Poet Is Not a Rolling Stone" (Neruda) **62**:324

"Poet, Lover, Birdwatcher" (Ezekiel) **61**:93-4, 101, 105, 110

"A Poet of the Thirteenth Century" (Borges) See "Un poeta del siglo XIII"

"The Poet on the Island" (Murphy) **41**:311, 317

"The Poet Ridiculed by Hysterical Academics" (Snodgrass) **68**:388

"The Poet Says Good-Bye to the Birds" (Neruda) **62**:332

"Poet to Tiger" (Swenson) **61**:402; **61**:397; **106**:329, 343

"The Poet Turns on Himself" (Dickey) **47**:97

"Poet, When You Rhyme" (Jacobsen) **48**:190

The Poet Who Became a Worm (Alegria) See *El poeta que se Volvío Gusano*

"El poeta" ("The Poet") (Aleixandre) **9**:16

"Un poeta del siglo XIII" ("A Poet of the Thirteenth Century") (Borges) **44**:367

El poeta que se Volvio Gusano (The Poet Who Became a Worm) (Alegria) **57**:11

"El poeta recuerda su via" (Aleixandre) **9**:12

"O poeta Thomas Hardy fala" ("So Speaks the Poet T. H.") (Cabral de Melo Neto) **76**:163

Les poetès (Poets) (Aragon) **22**:38

Poètes d'expression française (Damas) **84**:179

"Poet—For Irina Ratushinskaya" (Seth) **90**:351

"The Poetic Diction of John M. Synge" (Davie) **10**:124

A Poetic Equation: Conversations between Nikki Giovanni and Margaret Walker (Giovanni) **117**:192, 201, 204

"The Poetic Faculty" (MacDiarmid) **63**:248

The Poetic Image (Day Lewis) **10**:128

The Poetic Image in Six Genres (Madden) **5**:265

Poetic Justice (Heilbrun) **25**:255, 257

Poetic Meter and Poetic Form (Fussell) **74**:117

"The Poetic Process" (Burke) **24**:118

"The Poetic Revelation" (Paz) **4**:397

"A Poetic State" (Milosz) **82**:307

"Poetic Structure in the Language of Aristotle" (Crane) **27**:71

Poetic Values (Neihardt) **32**:333

"Poetics" (Nemerov) **36**:309

"A Poetics for Bullies" (Elkin) **4**:154

"The Poetics of the Physical World" (Kinnell) **29**:282-83

Poetries and the Sciences (Richards) **24**:400

"Poetry" (Borges) **48**:47, 49

"Poetry" (Moore) **1**:227, **8**:397; **10**:349, **19**:342; **47**:271

"Poetry" (O'Hara) **78**:352, 364, 375-76

"Poetry" (Pasternak) **63**:281

"Poetry" (White) **10**:528

Poetry (Cocteau) **8**:145

"Poetry: A Note on Ontology" (Ransom) **5**:364-65, 367; **24**:365-68

"Poetry and Ambition" (Hall) **59**:153

Poetry and Drama (Eliot) **6**:167; **24**:184

"Poetry and Experience" (Rich) **7**:371

Poetry and Fiction (Nemerov) **6**:360

"Poetry and History" (Paz) **4**:397

"Poetry and Landscape" (Wilbur) **53**:400

"Poetry and Marriage" (Berry) **46**:75

Poetry and Metamorphosis (Tomlinson) **45**:405

Poetry and Morality (Buckley) **57**:132

"Poetry and Other Modern Arts" (Davie) **10**:125

"Poetry and Personality" (Carruth) See "The Act of Love: Poetry and Personality"

"Poetry and Pleasure" (Pinsky) **94**:301, 303

"Poetry and Politics" (Enzensberger) **43**:148

Poetry and Politics (Enzensberger) See *Poesie und Politik*

Poetry and Repression (Bloom) **24**:80; **103**:2-4, 6, 8-9, 11-14, 24, 45, 47

"Poetry and Revolution" (Spender) **10**:489

"Poetry and Social Criticism" (Wain) **11**:563

"Poetry and the Absolute" (Tate) **24**:441, 445, 447

Poetry and the Age (Jarrell) **6**:261; **9**:296; **13**:299

Poetry and the Common Life (Rosenthal) **28**:392-94

"Poetry and the New Christians" (Buckley) **57**:130

"Poetry and the Primitive" (Snyder) **9**:499

"Poetry and the Public World" (MacLeish) **68**:288

Poetry and the Sacred (Buckley) **57**:132

Poetry and the World (Pinsky) **94**:300-5, 311-12, 316

"Poetry as Imitation" (Schwartz) **4**:479

Poetry by Canadian Women (Sullivan) **65**:356

Poetry for My People (Play Ebony Play Ivory) (Dumas) **6**:145-46; **62**:151, 155, 158, 160

Poetry for Supper (Thomas) **13**:542; **48**:374, 376, 380

"Poetry for the Advanced" (Baraka) **14**:49

Poetry, Gongorism, and a Thousand Years (Jeffers) 54:244
A Poetry Handbook (Oliver) 98:293, 302
"Poetry in English" (Dudek) 11:160
Poetry in the Making (Hughes) 2:203; 37:171
"Poetry Is an Occupation" (Neruda) 9:399
"Poetry is Not a Luxury" (Lorde) 71:243, 263
"Poetry is the Smallest" (Ammons) 57:58
"Poetry Manual" (Brooks) 110:33
"Poetry Modern and Unmodern" (Tate) 11:522
"Poetry of Departures" (Larkin) 33:257, 268; 39:345; 64:272
The Poetry of Maya Angelou (Angelou) 77:28
The Poetry of Place: Essays and Reviews, 1970-1980 (Hooker) 43:200-02
"Poetry of Solitude and Poetry of Commun-ion" (Paz)
    See "Poesía de comunión y poesía de soledad"
The Poetry of Stephen Crane (Hoffman) 23:240
"The Poetry of Tradition" (Pasolini) 106:265
The Poetry of W. B. Yeats (MacNeice) 53:244
The Poetry of Yevgeny Yevtushenko, 1953-1965 (Yevtushenko) 26:461-62
"Poetry, or Poems?" (Davie) 10:124
"Poetry, Personality, and Death" (Kinnell) 29:282
"Poetry Reading" (Ezekiel) 61:94, 97, 101, 103
"Poetry Reading" (Szymborska) 99:206
"Poetry, Regeneration, and D.H. Lawrence" (Rexroth) 49:278; 112:371
"Poetry Review" (Jiles) 58:279
"Poetry Shall Not Have Sung in Vain" (Neruda) 62:324
"Poetry That Is Life" (Shamlu) 10:470-71
Poetry to Enable (Michaux)
    See *Poésie pour pouvoir*
The Poetry Wreck: Selected Essays, 1950-1970 (Shapiro) 8:486
"The Poets" 75:63, 79
"The Poets" (Boland) 113:114
"Poets" (Boyle) 58:76
"Poets" (Brown) 48:59
"Poets" (Frame) 96:200
"Poets" (Kennedy) 8:320; 42:257
Poets (Aragon)
    See *Les poetès*
A Poet's Alphabet: Reflections on the Literary Art and Vocation (Bogan) 4:68; 39:388, 391; 46:87; 93:69-71, 105
Poets and Presidents (Doctorow) 113:165
"Poets Are Still Writing Poems about Spring and Here Is Mine: Spring" (Waddington) 28:440
"Poets, Children, Soldiers" (Hirsch) 31:214
Poet's Circuits (Colum) 28:91-2
"Poets in Canada" (Avison) 97:105-11
"Poets in Late Winter" (Van Duyn) 116:427
"A Poet's Lament: Concerning the Massacre of American Indians at Wounded Knee" (Cook-Lynn) 93:122
"A Poet's Life" (MacBeth) 9:340
"The Poet's Mother" (Kroetsch) 57:292-93
A Poet's Notebook (Sitwell) 67:332
"The Poets Observe the Absence of God from the St. Louis Zoo" (Kumin) 28:224
Poets of the 1950's (Enright) 31:148
The Poet's Progress (McFadden) 48:247, 251
"Poet's Pub" (MacDiarmid) 11:334
"Poets Return" (Faludy) 42:138
"Poets Survive in Fame" (Cunningham) 31:102
The Poet's Town (Neihardt) 32:331

"The Poet's Voice" (Moss) 45:292
"Poets without Laurels" (Ransom) 5:365; 24:367
"The Poet's Words" (Ciardi) 10:107
"Poet's Work" (Niedecker) 10:360
A Poet's Year (MacBeth) 5:264
Poezii: texte comentate 75:76
"Poezijata" (Bagryana) 10:14
Poezje zebrane (Rozewicz) 23:363
"Poggio" (Durrell) 27:97
"The Point" (Heaney) 74:197
"The Point" (Montague) 46:275
"The Point" (Soto) 32:402
Point Counter Point (Huxley) 1:150-51; 3:252, 254-55; 4:237-40, 243-44; 5:192-94; 8:304; 11:281, 283-88; 18:265, 268, 270-71; 35:232, 235, 240-41, 243-44; 79:304, 310, 312, 315, 326-27
"Point of Departure" (Calisher) 8:125
"A Point of Identity" (Mphahlele) 25:339, 342
Point of No Return (Marquand) 10:329, 331
"Point Pelee in March" (Snodgrass) 68:397
"Point Pinos and Point Lobos" (Jeffers) 11:312
Point Reyes Poems (Bly) 15:65
"Point Shirley" (Plath) 11:446; 17:367-68; 111:177
La pointe courte (Varda) 16:553, 556-57
Pointe-aux-coques (Maillet) 54:303, 306
Points for a Compass Rose (Connell) 4:108-10; 6:116
Points in Time (Bowles) 53:38-40
The Points of My Compass (White) 10:528, 530
Points of View (Maugham) 15:368; 67:219
Points on the Grid (Bowering) 15:82; 47:19
Point-to-Point (Keane)
    See *Conversation Piece*
Poirot Investigates (Christie) 12:110; 48:71
"Poison Oak" (Huddle) 49:183-84
The Poison Oracle (Dickinson) 12:171-72; 35:131, 133-34
Poison Pen (Garrett) 51:152-54
The Poison Tree (Ribman) 7:358
The Poisoned Kiss and Other Stories from the Portuguese (Oates) 6:373-74; 9:402
"Poisoned Lands" (Montague) 46:266, 275-76
Poisoned Lands and Other Poems (Montague) 13:391; 46:266, 273, 278-79
"The Poisonous Rabbit" (Calvino) 33:100
Poisson soluble (Breton) 9:132, 134; 54:15, 17, 29, 33
Les poissons rouges; ou, Mon père, ce héros (The Goldfish) (Anouilh) 13:21-2; 40:57-60
"Poker Face" (Sturgeon) 22:410
"The Poker Party" (Kelley) 22:252
The Poker Session (Leonard) 19:281
Pokolenie zimy (Aksyonov)
    See *Generations of Winter*
Poland (Michener) 29:316-17; 60:258; 109:375, 377, 379, 382, 386, 388
"Poland/1931" (Rothenberg) 57:380-81
Poland/1931 (Rothenberg) 6:477-78; 57:373-74, 382-83
"Poland: Legends" (Agnon)
    See "Polin: Sipure agadot"
Polar Bear Hunt (Bissett) 18:61
"Polar Bears and Others" (Boyle) 19:62
"Polaris, or Gulag Nightscapes" (MacEwen) 55:164-65

"Polarities" (Atwood) 4:26; 13:46; 25:62
"The Polatski Man" (Dybek) 114:62, 64, 67, 71, 73, 75-6, 78
"Polder" (Heaney) 37:162; 74:162
"Poldi" (McCullers) 12:433
"Pole Star" (MacLeish) 8:361
"Pole Star for this Year" (MacLeish) 68:286
Police (Baraka) 115:36
Police at the Funeral (Allingham) 19:14
"The Police Band" (Barthelme) 8:50
"Police Dreams" (Bausch) 51:55-7
Police Lab (Berger) 12:40
"The Police: Seven Voices" (Murray) 40:340
Police State: Could It Happen Here (Archer) 12:23
"The Policeman and the Rose" (Rao) 56:312-14
"Polin: Sipure agadot" ("Poland: Legends") (Agnon) 4:11; 14:3
Polis, polis potatismos (Murder at the Savoy) (Wahloo) 7:502
"A Polish Anecdote" (Rothenberg) 57:374
The Polish Complex (Konwicki)
    See *Kompleks polski*
"Polish Displaced Persons" (Spender) 41:421
"The Polish Question" (Weiss) 14:554
Polismördaren (Cop Killer) (Wahloo) 7:502
"Polite Conversation" (Stafford) 7:457; 68:434, 450
"Politic" (Rose) 85:314
"Political Code and Literary Code: The Testimonial Genre in Chile Today" (Dorfman) 77:156
A Political Fable (Coover) 32:122
Political Fictions (Wilding) 73:393, 399, 405
The Political Life of Children (Coles) 108:184, 186-88, 210, 214
"Political Meeting" (Klein) 19:262-63
Political Position of Art Today (Breton) 15:90
"The Political Prisoner" (Kunene) 85:166
"Political Relations" (Lorde) 71:260
"Politician" (Garrett) 51:144
"Politics" (Bukowski) 108:87
"Politics" (Meredith) 13:375
"Politics" (Paley) 4:392; 37:337
Politics (Acker) 111:20
Politics and Crime (Enzensberger)
    See *Politik und Verbrechen*
"Politics and the Novel" (McCarthy) 39:485
Politics and the Novel (Howe) 85:117-19, 135, 147
Politics of Experience (Castaneda) 12:86
The Politics of Experience (Laing) 95:124, 128, 131-34, 136, 138, 140-41, 144-47, 153, 167, 177-79, 182-83
The Politics of Hope (Schlesinger) 84:355
"The Politics of Language" (Sukenick) 48:370
"The Politics of Rich Painters" (Baraka) 5:45
The Politics of the Family and Other Essays (Laing) 95:132, 137, 149, 183-84
The Politics of Upheaval (Schlesinger) 84:382, 384
The Politics of Waste (Adamov)
    See *La politique des restes*
Politik und Verbrechen (Politics and Crime) (Enzensberger) 43:147-48, 150, 154
La politique des restes (The Politics of Waste) (Adamov) 25:14-15, 17, 20-1
"Polka" (Sitwell) 67:324
"Polling Day" (Scannell) 49:330-31
"Pollock and Canvas" (Graham) 48:150-51
Pollution Lab (Berger) 12:39
Polonaise (Read) 10:434-36; 25:379

"Polonaise: A Variation" (Brodsky) 100:41-2
Polovchansk Gardens (Leonov)
  See *Polovchanskie sady*
Polovchanskie sady (*The Orchard Keeper; The Orchards of Polovchansk; Polovchansk Gardens*) (Leonov) 92:246, 260, 268-71, 277
"Polycarp" (Durcan) 43:114, 116
The Polyglots (Gerhardie) 5:140
"Polynesian" (Scott) 22:373
"Pomade" (Dove) 81:139
"The Pomegranate" (Boland) 113:91, 120, 126
Pomes for Yoshi (Bissett) 18:59, 61
Pomme, pomme, pomme (Audiberti) 38:31
"Les pommes" (Carrier) 78:59
"Pompeii" (Updike) 23:475
Pompes funèbres (*Funeral Rites*) (Genet) 1:115; 2:158; 5:138-39; 44:386-88, 390; 46:173, 180-83
"The Pond" (Nemerov) 36:303, 305
"Pond" (Smith) 42:353
The Ponder Heart (Welty) 1:361; 2:462-64; 5:478; 14:564; 33:415-16, 419, 424; 105:300, 318, 325, 335, 349
"Pondicherry Blues" (Jacobsen) 48:195; 102:240
"The Ponds" (Oliver) 98:294
"Pondy Woods" (Warren) 18:535
The Ponsonby Post (Rubens) 19:403-04
Le pont aux trois arches (Kadare)
  See *Ura me tri harqe*
Le pont de Londres: Guignol's band II (Celine) 47:71, 77
"Pont Neuf at Nightfall" (Kinnell) 29:284
Pony from Tarella (Clark) 12:132
"Pony Rock" (MacLeish) 68:286, 290
"Poodles. . .Great Eating!" (Martin) 30:248
"The Pool" (Creeley) 78:136-37
"The Pool" (H. D.) 73:119
"The Pool" (Johnston) 51:249-51
"The Pool" (Maugham) 15:368; 67:219
Pool and Rapid: The Story of a River (Haig-Brown) 21:133, 141
"Pool Lights" (Barthelme) 117:17
"Pool of Bethesda" (Sandburg) 35:356
"The Pool Player" (Williams) 42:440
"Pool Room in the Lion's Club" (Merwin) 45:270
"The Pool Table Caper" (Hunter) 35:226
"Pools" (Wesker) 5:484
"The Poor" (Wild) 14:581
Poor and Simple (Ortese)
  See *Poveri e semplici*
"The Poor Are Always with Us" (Wolff) 64:451-52
"Poor Baby" (Sondheim) 30:401
Poor Bitos (Anouilh)
  See *Pauvre Bitos; ou, Le dîner de têtes*
"Poor Charley's Dream" (Hope) 51:222
The Poor Christ of Bomba (Beti)
  See *Le pauvre Christ de Bomba*
"A Poor Christian Looks at the Ghetto" (Milosz) 56:234
Poor Clare (Hartley) 2:181-82
"Poor Edward" (Johnston) 51:239, 245
Poor Fool (Caldwell) 50:300
Poor George (Fox) 2:139-40
"Poor Gum" (Bennett) 28:29
"Poor Innocent" (Smith) 15:515, 517
"A Poor Jew" (Bell) 8:65
"Poor Koko" (Fowles) 6:184, 187-88; 10:188; 33:174; 87:154, 158

"The Poor Man's Pig" (Blunden) 56:26-7
The Poor Mouth: A Bad Story about the Hard Life (O'Brien)
  See *An Béal Bocht*
Poor Murderer (Kohout) 13:323, 326
"Poor North" (Strand) 18:520; 41:432
"The Poor Poet" (Milosz) 56:242
Poor Richard (Kerr) 22:256-57
Poor Russell's Almanac (Baker) 31:28
"A Poor Scholar of the 'Forties" (Colum) 28:90
"Poor Slave" (Cliff) 21:60
"Poor Superman" (Leiber) 25:303-04
"The Poor Thing" (Powers) 1:280, 282
The Poorhouse Fair (Updike) 1:343-44; 2:439, 442; 3:485, 489; 5:450, 453, 459-60; 9:539; 13:557-58, 562; 23:463; 43:431, 433; 70:253
Poo-san (*Mr. Pu*) (Ichikawa) 20:181-82, 186
Pop. 1280 (Thompson) 69:378-81, 383, 385-86, 389
"Pop Life" (Prince) 35:332
The Pope and the Witch (Fo) 109:142, 144
"The Pope's Penis" (Olds) 85:294, 296, 303
The Pope's Wedding (Bond) 4:69; 13:99; 23:64
Popeye (Altman) 116:47, 59, 65
"Popham of the New Song" (Dubie) 36:130
"Poplar Garden" (Bogan) 93:93
"Poplar, Sycamore" (Wilbur) 6:570
"The Poplars" (Fisher) 25:159
Popo and Fifina (Hughes) 108:294
Popol vuh (Asturias) 13:37
"Popper's Disease" (Johnson) 51:234-35
"Poppies" (Oliver) 98:287, 291
"Poppies" (Smith) 12:540
"Poppies" (Smith) 64:388
"Poppies in July" (Plath) 5:345; 17:365-66; 51:345; 111:203-04
"Poppies in October" (Plath) 2:336; 17:359; 111:203-04
Poppy (Nichols) 36:329, 331-32; 65:161
Poppy and Memory (Celan)
  See *Mohn und Gedächtnes*
"Poppycock" (Francis) 15:237
Pops (Linney) 51:263
"Popular Songs" (Ashbery) 77:58
"Populist Manifesto" (Ferlinghetti) 27:137; 111:66
Popytka k begstvu (*An Attempted Escape; Escape Attempt*) (Strugatskii and Strugatskii) 27:433, 438
Pora, moi drug, pora (Aksyonov)
  See *It's Time, My Friend, It's Time*
"The Porcelain Salamander" (Card) 47:67
"Porcellina di terra" (Landolfi) 49:214
"Porch" (Szirtes) 46:393
"Porch Song" (Carroll) 35:77
Porcilè (Pasolini) 106:241, 256
"Porciúncula" (Amado)
  See "De como o Mulato Porciúncula Descarregou seu Defunto"
"The Porcupine" (Kinnell) 2:230; 3:268-69; 29:282, 284, 288
"The Porcupine Puffer Fish" (Lieberman) 36:263
"Porcupines at the University" (Barthelme) 23:46; 115:81
"Pore Perrie" (Goyen) 14:211
Porgy (Mamoulian) 16:424
Porius: A Romance of the Dark Ages (Powys) 7:348; 15:435; 46:321-22
The Pork Butcher (Hughes) 48:185-88
"Pork Chop Paradise" (Himes) 58:265

"Porn" (MacBeth) 5:265
"Porn" (Walker) 27:448, 450; 103:407-08, 410-12
"Porno Flick" (Valenzuela) 31:438
"Porno Love" (Dacey) 51:79
Pornografia (Gombrowicz) 4:194-95; 7:122-25; 11:242; 49:123, 126-29, 133-34
The Pornographer (McGahern) 48:264-67, 269, 271-73
"A Pornographer Woos" (Mac Laverty) 31:253
"The Pornographic But Serious History" (Bell) 8:67
"The Pornographic Imagination" (Sontag) 13:516; 105:225
"Pornography" (McEwan) 66:279-80
"Pornography" (Raine) 103:190
"The Pornography Box" (Smith) 42:346, 350, 353-54
Pornography: Men Possessing Women (Dworkin) 43:132-33, 135
"Port" (Reverdy) 53:281
Port Eternity (Cherryh) 35:113-15
"Port of Call" (Abse) 29:15
Port of Call (Bergman)
  See *Hamnstad*
Port of Saints (Burroughs) 22:83-5; 42:80; 109:195
The Portable Nabokov (Nabokov) 6:357
Portable People (West) 96:375, 392
"The Portable Phonograph" (Clark) 28:78
Portable Steinbeck (Steinbeck) 59:343, 345
"Porte cochère" (Taylor) 37:409, 412-13; 44:305-06; 50:253, 258; 71:299, 307
Porte des lilas (Clair) 20:64-5
Porte dévergondée (Mandiargues) 41:278
A Porter Folio: New Poems (Porter) 5:346; 33:318, 323
"The Porter Song Book" (Porter) 33:318
Porterhouse Blue (Sharpe) 36:399-400
"Porter's Metamorphoses" (Porter) 33:318
Les portes de la forêt (*The Gates of the Forest*) (Wiesel) 3:529; 5:492-93; 37:452
"Porth Cwyfan" (Mathias) 45:237
"Portland, 1968" (Gluck) 22:176
"The 'Portland' Going Out" (Merwin) 13:383
Portnoy's Complaint (Roth) 1:293; 2:378-80; 3:435-38, 440; 4:451, 453-57, 459; 6:475-76; 9:459, 460-62; 15:449, 451-52, 455; 22:350-52; 47:357-65; 66:386-422; 86:250-51, 255-57
"Il porto sepolto" (Ungaretti) 7:484; 11:559
"The Portobello Road" (Spark) 40:403
"Portrait" (Ammons) 108:24
"Portrait" (Bogan) 46:77
"Portrait" (Boyle) 19:62
"Portrait" (Fearing) 51:106, 108
"Portrait" (Gluck) 22:177
"The Portrait" (Graves) 45:169, 173
"Portrait" (Guillevic) 33:191
"Portrait" (Thomas) 6:534
"Portrait" (Urdang) 47:399-400
The Portrait (Silkin) 43:399
Portrait de l'artiste en jeune singe (Butor) 11:81-2; 15:114-15, 117-18
Portrait du soleil (Cixous) 92:56
"Portrait d'un élu" (Camus) 14:107
Portrait d'un inconnu (*Portrait of a Man Unknown*) (Sarraute) 1:302; 2:384-85; 4:464, 466-67; 8:469, 471-72; 10:458-59; 31:377, 380, 383; 80:229, 236-37, 239, 241, 252, 254
"Portrait d'une femme" (Pound) 2:343; 4:408;

10:401, 404
Portrait eines Planeten (Durrenmatt)   15:196
"The Portrait: Emmanuel Romano" (Williams)
    22:464
Portrait in Brownstone (Auchincloss)   4:28,
    30-1
"The Portrait of a Clown" (Turco)   11:550
"Portrait of a Cog" (Fearing)   51:108
"Portrait of a Deaf Man" (Betjeman)   43:34
"Portrait of a Germanophile" (Borges)   48:45
"Portrait of a Girl in Glass" (Williams)   5:502;
    15:580; 45:446-47, 452-54; 71:365, 373
"Portrait of a Jew Old Country Style"
    (Rothenberg)   57:374
"Portrait of a Lady" (Eliot)   1:89-90; 3:139;
    9:186-87, 189; 13:201-02; 15:213;
    34:397; 41:146, 150; 55:346, 362, 374;
    57:168, 207; 113:183, 187, 190, 205, 209,
    223
"Portrait of a Lady" (Gellhorn)   60:179-181,
    191
"Portrait of a Lady" (Ryan)   65:215
"Portrait of a Lady" (Wakoski)   2:459
"Portrait of a Lady" (White)   49:409
Portrait of a Man Unknown (Sarraute)
    See *Portrait d'un inconnu*
Portrait of a Planet (Duerrenmatt)
    See *Porträt eines Planeten*
Portrait of a Romantic (Millhauser)   54:324,
    326-27; 21:218-21; 109:170, 174
"Portrait of a Short Story Writer" (Konwicki)
    117:281
"Portrait of an Artist" (Kavanagh)   22:243
Portrait of an Artist with Twenty-Six Horses
    (Eastlake)   8:199-200
"Portrait of Captain Logan" (Shapcott)
    38:399
*Portrait of Delmore: Journals and Notes of
    Delmore Schwartz, 1939-1959* (Schwartz)
    45:360-61; 87:344-46
"The Portrait of Diana Prochink" (Baker)
    8:40
"A Portrait of Elmer" (Faulkner)   18:149
"Portrait of Georgia" (Toomer)   13:551
Portrait of India (Mehta)   37:290-92
Portrait of Ivan (Fox)   2:139
Portrait of Jason (Clarke)   16:218-19
Portrait of Joanna (McGuckian)   48:274
"Portrait of Lady" (Smith)   42:353
"The Portrait of Little J. A. in a Prospect of
    Flowers" ("The Picture of Little J. A. in a
    Prospect of Flowers") (Ashbery)   25:57;
    41:40
"Portrait of Malcolm X" (Knight)   40:279
Portrait of Margarita (Arthur)   12:25, 28-9
"Portrait of Marina" (Page)   18:377
*Portrait of Max: An Intimate Memoir of Sir
    Max Beerbohm* (Behrman)   40:85
Portrait of Orkney (Brown)   48:59; 100:86
"A Portrait of Shunkin" (Tanizaki)
    See "Shunkin sho"
"Portrait of the Artist" (Davie)   10:121
"Portrait of the Artist" (Harrison)   42:203
"Portrait of the Artist as a Middle-aged Man"
    (Abse)   7:2
"Portrait of the Artist as a New World Driver"
    (Murray)   40:337
"Portrait of the Artist as a Young Woman"
    (Bogan)   39:392
Portrait of the Poet as Landscape (Klein)
    19:260
"Portrait with Flashlight" (Justice)   102:265
"Portraits" (Cummings)   15:160, 162

Portraits and Elegies (Schnackenberg)   40:378-
    81
Porträt eines Planeten (*Portrait of a Planet*)
    (Duerrenmatt)   102:61, 81
"Portret epizodzisty" (Konwicki)   117:281
The Poseidon Adventure (Gallico)   2:147
"Poseshchenie muzeia" (Nabokov)
    See "The Visit to the Museum"
"Posesión" (Aleixandre)   9:13
"Position" (Damas)   84:177
Position de l'inconscient (Lacan)   75:295
"The Position of the Afrikaans Writer" (Brink)
    36:68
"Positional" (Sherwin)   7:415
"Positions" ("1") (Donnell)   34:158
Positions (Derrida)   87:72, 87, 105
Positions (Ernaux)
    See *La place*
"Positive Edges" (Ammons)   57:50
"Positive Vibration" (Marley)   17:268, 272
"Positively 4th Street" (Dylan)   77:174-75
Positives (Gunn)   32:211
"Positives: For Sterling Plumpp" (Madhubuti)
    73:215
"Posjaščaetsja Jalte" (Brodsky)   50:131
"Poslanie k stikham" ("Epistle to His Verses")
    (Brodsky)   13:116
Posle skazki (Belyj parokhod) (Aitmatov)
    See *Belyj parokhod*
"Poslushnitsa" (Bagryana)   10:12
Les possédés (*The Possessed*) (Camus)   32:88,
    99-100; 63:64
"The Possessed" (Barnes)   11:31
"Possessed" (Olds)   39:186
"The Possessed" (Sacks)   67:299
The Possessed (Camus)
    See *Les possédés*
Possessed (Gombrowicz)   49:131-32
Possessing the Secret of Joy (Walker)   103:419,
    421, 424
Possession (Delbanco)   13:174
Possession (de la Roche)   14:150
Possession (Markandaya)   38:322-23
Possession: A Romance (Byatt)   65:122-29,
    131-33
"Possibilities" (Morrissy)   99:78
Possibilities (Bradbury)   32:51; 61:40
"The Possibility of a Poetic Drama" (Eliot)
    24:175, 181
"The Possibility of Evil" (Jackson)   60:215
"Possible" (Avison)   97:79
"A Possible Fake" (Hollander)   5:186
"Post aetatem nostram" (Brodsky)   50:122-
    23, 131
"The Post Card" (Boell)
    See "Die Postkarte"
*The Post Card: From Socrates to Freud and
    Beyond* (Derrida)
    See *La carte postale: De Socrate à Freud et
    au-delà*
"Post Modernism" (Apple)   33:21
"Post mortem" (Jeffers)   15:300
Post Mortem (Coward)   1:64; 29:131-32, 135,
    138
Post Office (Bukowski)   41:68, 70; 82:4, 10-
    13, 15-17, 24, 28; 108:66, 70, 72, 81-3,
    90, 96-7, 100, 106
"Post scriptum" (Bataille)   29:38
Postal Variations (Brandys)   62:119
"Postcard" (Garrett)   3:192
"Postcard" (McGrath)   59:178
"The Postcard Collection" (Koch)   5:219
"The Postcard from Chinatown" (Brautigan)

12:59
"Postcard from Cornwall" (Abse)   29:15
"Postcard from Florida" (Oliver)   34:247
"A Postcard from Iceland" (Heaney)   74:162
"A Postcard from John Ashbery" (O'Hara)
    13:427
"A Postcard from North Antrim" (Heaney)
    74:163
"Postcard to the Social Muse" (Winters)
    32:468
Postcards   81:274-77, 279
"Postcards from Cape Split" (Van Duyn)
    63:442; 116:400, 403, 406, 428
"Postcards from China" (Kroetsch)   57:292
"Postcards to Columbus" (Alexie)   96:11
Postcripts (Priestley)   34:361, 364
"Poste restante" (Thomas)   48:379
The Poster in History (Gallo)   95:97
"Posterity" (Larkin)   5:229; 9:323; 33:261;
    39:336
Postern of Fate (Christie)   12:120; 110:116,
    125
"Posthumous Autobiography" (Scannell)
    49:332
"Posthumous Fiction" (Bowering)   47:31
"A Posthumous Sketch" (Oates)   9:403
*The Posthumous Writings and Poems of
    Hermann Lauscher* (Hesse)
    See *Hinterlassene Schriften und Gedichte von
    Hermann Lauscher*
"Postigo" ("Back Gate") (Cabral de Melo Neto)
    76:161
A Postillion Struck by Lightning (Bogarde)
    19:41-2
"A Post-Impressionist Susurration for the First
    of November, 1983" (Carruth)   84:136
"Post-Impressions" (Cummings)   15:160-162
"Die Postkarte" ("The Post Card") (Boell)
    11:54; 72:71
The Postman Always Rings Twice (Cain)   3:96-
    7; 11:85-6; 28:43-5, 47-54
The Postman Always Rings Twice (Mamet)
    46:246
"Postman Cheval" (Breton)
    See "Facteur Cheval"
"Postmark" (Abse)   29:15
Postmarked the Stars (Norton)   12:458-60,
    467
Postmetaphysical Thinking (Habermas)
    See *Nachmetaphysisches Denken*
"Postmodern Blackness" (hooks)   94:145
*The Postmodern Scene: Excremental Culture
    and Hyper-Aesthetics* (Kroker)   77:343,
    345
Poštovní holub (*The Carrier Pigeon*) (Seifert)
    93:306, 333-34, 340
Post-Prison Writings and Speeches (Cleaver)
    30:62-3, 65-6
Postriziny (*The Haircutting*) (Hrabal)   67:114-
    15, 120-21, 123
"Postscript" (Hooker)   43:197
"Postscript" (Livesay)   79:336
"Postscript" (Thomas)   6:530
"Postscript" (Wright)   6:580
"Postscript: A Reply to the Angel at Blythburg"
    (Szirtes)   46:394
"Postscript to an Erotic Novel" (Vizinczey)
    40:435
"Postscript to Duncan McNaughton" (Thesen)
    56:421
"A Postscript with Ntozake Shange" (Shange)
    74:307, 309
"Postulation" (Ammons)   57:51

"The Postulation of Reality" (Borges) **83**:163, 165

Postures (*Quartet*) (Rhys) **2**:371-73; **6**:453-54, 457; **14**:446, 450; **51**:356-57, 359, 365, 368-70

"Postures of Unease" (Ashbery) **77**:68

"The Pot of Earth" (MacLeish) **8**:360-62; **68**:270-72, 275, 284, 286, 290, 293

"The Pot of Gold" (Cheever) **64**:65

"A Pot of Soothing Herbs" (O'Faolain) **47**:325; **108**:408-09

"Pot Pourri from a Surrey Garden" (Betjeman) **43**:41

"Pot Roast" (Strand) **18**:518, 520; **41**:435

"Potato" (Wilbur) **110**:383

"The Potato Dealer" (Trevor) **116**:395

"The Potato Elf" ("Kartofel'nyy el'f") (Nabokov) **3**:354

"Potato Flower" (Yevtushenko) **26**:467

Potch and Colour (Prichard) **46**:337, 343, 345

"Potential" (Campbell) **42**:92

The Pothunters (Wodehouse) **2**:478

Potiki (Grace) **56**:121-22

"The Potlatch of Esmerelda" (Tuohy) **37**:434

"Potomka" (Bagryana) **10**:12

"Pots and Pans" (Ammons) **57**:56

Potseluj, orkestr, ryba, kolbasa (*Kiss, Orchestra, Fish, Sausage*) (Aksyonov) **37**:12

Potter's Field (Green) **25**:199

The Potting Shed (Greene) **6**:213; **70**:292, 294

Pounamu, Pounamu (Ihimaera) **46**:192, 195-96, 198-201

"The Pound Is Sinking" (McCartney) **35**:289-91

Pounding the Pavements, Beating the Bushes, and Other Pataphysical Poems (*Pataphysical Poems*) (Queneau) **42**:336-37

Pour Dante: Discours (Perse) **4**:399-400; **11**:433

"Pour faire le portrait d'un oiseaux" (Prevert) **15**:437

"Pour fêter une enfance" (Perse) **46**:300

Pour finir encour et Autres Foirades (Beckett)
See *Foirades*

"Pour Khalam" (Senghor) **54**:408

Pour la révolution africaine: Ecrits politiques (*Toward the African Revolution: Political Essays*) (Fanon) **74**:72, 74

"Pour le sport" (Sondheim) **30**:398

Pour Marx (*For Marx*) (Althusser) **106**:3, 17, 19, 29, 31, 39, 42

"Pour que tout soit en tout" ("That All Be in All") (Damas) **84**:160

Pour saluer Melville (Giono) **4**:184

"Pour sûr" (Damas) **84**:175, 177

"Pour toi et moi" (Damas) **84**:167

Pour un malherbe (Ponge) **18**:413, 418

"Pour un oui ou pour un non" (Sarraute) **80**:241-42

"Pour un prométhée saxifrage" (Char) **9**:162

Pour une critique de l'économie politique du signe (*For a Critique of the Political Economy of the Sign; Towards a Critique of a Political Economy of Signs*) (Baudrillard) **60**:11-13, 15-16

Pour une morale de l'ambiguité (Beauvoir) **44**:344

Pour une sociologie du roman (Goldmann) **24**:235-36, 241, 243, 246

"Pouring the Milk Away" (Rukeyser) **27**:411

"Pourquoi la négritude? Négritude ou révolution?" (Conde) **52**:79, 82

'Pourquoi Pas?'—A Letter from Ottawa (Richler) **46**:352

Pouvoirs de l'horreur (*Powers of Horror*) (Kristeva) **77**:306, 308-09, 324-25

Povatek Filipa Latinovicza (*The Return of Philip Latinovicz*) (Krleza) **8**:329-30; **114**:168, 176-81, 185

Poveri e semplici (*Poor and Simple*) (Ortese) **89**:191

Poverkh barierov (*Above the Barriers*) (Pasternak) **18**:381-82; **63**:289

"Poverty" (Ammons) **57**:49, 52

"Poverty" (Merwin) **8**:390

"Poverty in Athens, Ohio" (Bell) **8**:65

"The Poverty of Poverty" (Bernard) **59**:46

"Poverty Train" (Nyro) **17**:315, 318

Povest (*The Last Summer; The Narrative; The Story; A Tale*) (Pasternak) **7**:298; **10**:384

Povest' o lesakh (Paustovsky) **40**:363

Povest' o zhizni (*The Story of a Life; The Tale of Life*) (Paustovsky) **40**:358-61, 364-66

Povestri gor i stepei (*Tales of the Mountains and Steppes*) (Aitmatov) **71**:3, 21

Povestri i rasskazy (*Cingiz Ajtmatov: Povesti i rasskazy*) (Aitmatov) **71**:7

"Pow Wow" (Alexie) **96**:4

"Powder Monkey" (Carver) **55**:275

"Powderday's Red Hen" (Stuart) **11**:511

Powdered Eggs (Simmons) **57**:404-05, 407-08

"Powder-White Faces" (Hughes) **108**:324

"Power" (Lorde) **71**:233, 236, 241, 246

"Power" (Redgrove) **41**:351

"Power" (Rich) **36**:376

Power (Konwicki)
See *Wladza*

"Power and Light" (Dickey) **2**:115; **15**:174

"Power and Light (An Idea for Film)" ("An Idea for Film") (Hannah) **38**:234-35; **90**:126, 138-39

"Power and Love" (MacLennan) **92**:342

"Power and Survival" (Canetti)
See "Macht und Überleben"

The Power and the Glory (Greene) **1**:130-33, 135; **3**:207-10, 213-14; **6**:215-19; **9**:251; **14**:216-18; **18**:195, 197; **27**:173, 175-76; **37**:136-37, 140; **70**:287, 289-91, 293, 295; **72**:148, 151-55, 157, 178-79

The Power House (Comfort) **7**:54

Power/Knowledge: Selected Interviews and Other Writings (Foucault) **34**:343

"The Power of Creativity" (Kunene) **85**:166

"The Power of Darkness" (Anand) **23**:21

"The Power of Division" (Culler) **65**:339

The Power of Horses, and Other Stories (Cook-Lynn) **93**:124-27, 129-30

The Power of Light (Singer) **69**:306

"Power of Love" (Dorris) **109**:311

"The Power of Maples" (Stern) **40**:406

"The Power of Music to Disturb" (Mueller) **51**:279

The Power of Myth (Campbell and Moyers) **69**:87, 90-1, 93, 96, 98

The Power of Myth (Moyers) **74**:254

The Power of One (Courtenay) **59**:52-8

"The Power of Taste" (Herbert) **43**:193

The Power of the Dog (Barker) **37**:41

The Power of the Dog (Savage) **40**:371, 373, 376

"The Power of the Powerless" (Havel) **58**:243

Power of Three (Jones) **26**:226-28

"Power Plays" (Ammons) **57**:51, 53

The Power Plays (*The Art of War; Filthy Rich; Gossip*) (Walker) **61**:424, 426-30, 432-33

Power Politics (Atwood) **2**:20; **3**:19-20; **4**:25; **8**:28-30; **13**:42-3; **15**:37; **25**:62-3, 67; **84**:68, 106

Power Shift: The Rise of the Southern Rim and Its Challenge to the Eastern Establishment (Sale) **68**:345-50, 353, 359

"A Power Struggle" (Head) **67**:98

The Power That Preserves (Donaldson) **46**:140

The Power to Change Geography (O Hehir) **41**:323-24

"Power to the People" (Lennon) **35**:264, 270-71

"Power to the Pussy" (hooks) **94**:157

"Power-Cut" (McGuckian) **48**:276

"Powerfinger" (Young) **17**:581, 583

Powerful Long Ladder (Dodson) **79**:187-88, 190-91, 194, 198

"Powerhouse" (Welty) **14**:561; **33**:415, 424; **105**:314-15, 327, 329, 331, 336, 349

"Powerless, with a Guitar" (Grass)
See "In Ohnmacht gefallen"

"The Powerline Incarnation" (Murray) **40**:337

"Powers" (Milosz) **82**:303

Powers of Attorney (Auchincloss) **4**:30; **9**:52; **45**:29

Powers of Darkness (Aickman) **57**:2

Powers of Horror (Kristeva)
See *Pouvoirs de l'horreur*

"Powrót prokonsula" ("The Return of the Pronconsul") (Herbert) **9**:274; **43**:184, 186, 189

"A Pox on You, Mine Goodly Host" (Perelman) **49**:259

El pozo (*The Pit; The Well*) (Onetti) **7**:276, 280; **10**:376-80

Practical Criticism (Richards) **24**:376, 386, 389, 392-93, 395-96, 398-400

"A Practical Joke" (Farrell) **66**:127

"Practical Recommendations in the Event of a Catastrophe" (Herbert) **43**:184

Practicalities (Duras)
See *La vie materielle*

The Practice Effect (Brin) **34**:135

"The Practice of the Craft" (Metcalf) **37**:299-300

A Praed Street Dossier (Derleth) **31**:138

Prague (Krizanc) **57**:274-76, 278-80

Prague (Seifert)
See *Praha*

"The Prague Orgy" (Roth) **47**:357-59, 362

Praha (*Prague*) (Seifert) **93**:343

"Prairie" (Sandburg) **10**:448, 450; **35**:339-41, 343, 352

"Prairie" (Waddington) **28**:440

Prairie du chien (Mamet) **46**:254

"A Prairie Home Companion" (Keillor) **40**:272-75; **115**:261, 266, 268-69, 274, 276-77, 281, 284, 288, 293-94, 296

A Prairie Home Companion Anniversary Album (Keillor) **40**:274

The Prairie Home Companion Folk Song Book (Keillor) **115**:277

A Prairie Nightmare (Berton) **104**:61

"Prairie Poems" (Lane) **25**:289

Prairie-Town Boy (Sandburg) **35**:354, 357

"Praise" (Ciardi) **44**:381

"Praise" (Jensen) **37**:189

"Praise" (Oliver) **98**:283

Praise (Hass) **18**:209-13; **99**:139-42, 144,

148-50, 154, 157
"Praise/Complaint" (Goldbarth) 38:205
"Praise for Sick Women" (Snyder) 5:394;
32:387
"Praise in Summer" (Wilbur) 9:569-70; 53:399,
406
"Praise of Margins" (Gustafson) 36:222
The Praise Singer (Renault) 11:472; 17:402
"Praise to the End!" (Roethke) 101:274, 277-
78, 281, 283, 334, 337-41
Praise to the End! (Roethke) 1:291; 8:455,
458; 11:482; 19:396-97; 46:355, 360-61,
363; 101:264, 266-67, 273, 286-88, 290-
91, 303-05, 326-27, 334-35, 340-41
"Praised Be" (Elytis) 100:155
"The Praises" (Olson) 5:329; 11:419
"Praises IV" (McGrath) 59:181
Praisesong for the Widow (Marshall) 27:314-
15; 72:231-32, 236-37, 242-46, 248-50,
252-54
"Praising Dark Places" (Komunyakaa) 86:192
"Praiso" (Hass) 18:212
Prancing Novelist (Brophy) 6:98; 29:98; 105:8,
14, 18, 29-30, 33
Der Präsident (*The President*) (Bernhard)
61:27
Prater Violet (Isherwood) 1:157; 9:293; 11:297,
299; 14:278, 280, 282-85; 44:397-98,
401-04
"Pratfalls" (Klein) 30:235-36
Pratidwandi (*The Adversary*; *The Anniversary*)
(Ray) 16:487, 489, 492-93; 76:358, 360
"Pravaya kist" ("The Right Hand")
(Solzhenitsyn) 4:507; 7:432; 18:495
Pravda (Godard) 20:141, 150
Pravda: A Fleet Street Comedy (Hare) 58:225-
30
Pravila de morala practica (*The Laws of Prac-
tical Morality*) (Arghezi) 80:11
Praxis (Weldon) 11:566; 19:468-69; 36:447
"Pray Eros" (Honig) 33:211
Pray Love, Remember (Stolz) 12:548-49
"Pray without Ceasing" (Ammons) 8:14, 17;
9:30; 57:59
"Prayer" (Akhmatova) 64:4
"Prayer" (Ezekiel) 61:97
"Prayer" (Levertov) 15:337
"Prayer" (Olds) 85:297, 305
"Prayer" (Sanders) 53:304
"Prayer Against Too Much" (Zweig) 34:379
"Prayer before Birth" (MacNeice) 4:315-16;
53:239, 243
"Prayer for Aroniateka/Hendrick" (Kenny)
87:254
A Prayer for Katerina Horovitzova (Lustig)
56:183-84, 186-88
"Prayer for My Daughter" (Durcan) 70:152
"A Prayer for My Daughter" (Van Duyn)
116:426
A Prayer for Owen Meany (Irving) 112:152-
54, 156-58, 165, 173
"Prayer for Peace" (Lindbergh) 82:155-56
"A Prayer for Rain" (Mueller) 51:280
"Prayer for Russia" (Ehrenburg) 62:174
"Prayer in the Pacific" (Silko) 74:347; 114:316
"Prayer Meeting" (Hughes) 108:297
The Prayer Meeting (Green) 25:192
"Prayer of Mr. Cogito—Traveler" (Herbert)
43:191
"Prayer of the Middle Class at Ease in Zion"
(Nemerov) 36:309
"The Prayer of the Middle-Aged Man"
(Berryman) 13:82

"Prayer Service in an English Church" (Bly)
38:56
"A Prayer to Go to Paradise with the Don-
keys" (Wilbur) 14:577
"Prayer to Hermes" (Creeley) 78:152
"Prayer to the Good Poet" (Wright) 28:466
"Prayer to the Lady, Queen Freak" (Sanders)
53:304
"A Prayer to the Mountain" (Ciardi) 40:161
"Prayers" (Ciardi) 40:154
"Prayers" (Sondheim) 30:388
Prayers (MacBeth) 5:264
"Prayers and Sayings of the Mad Farmer"
(Berry) 27:33
Prayers of a Very Wise Child (Carrier)
See *Prières d'un enfant très très sage*
"Praying for Rain" (Bass) 79:15
The Praying Man (Santos) 22:365
"Prayrs for th One Habitation" (Bissett) 18:58
"Praze" (Seifert) 93:319
"Le pré" (Ponge) 18:418-19
"Preach on Dusty Roads" (Shaw) 23:396
"The Preacher" (Townshend) 17:542
The Preacher and the Slave (*Joe Hill: A Bio-
graphical Novel*) (Stegner) 49:350-51
"The Preacher at the Corner" (Stafford)
29:381
"Preaching to the Converted" (Porter) 5:347;
13:451
"Pre-Amphibian" (Atwood) 25:66
"The Precedent" (Dodson) 79:194
"Precession of the Equinoxes" (Rexroth)
112:395
"Precious Angel" (Dylan) 77:186-87
"Precious Five" (Auden) 14:28
"Preciousness" (Lispector) 43:267-68
"The Precipice" (Wright) 53:420
The Precipice (MacLennan) 2:257; 14:339-
40, 342; 92:306-07, 313-18, 322, 326,
328-31, 341, 344, 347
"Precipice—Encurled" (Byatt) 65:125
Precipitations (Scott) 43:370, 384
Précis de décomposition (*A Short History of
Decay*) (Cioran) 64:73, 91-2
"Precision" (Wakoski) 40:455
A Precocious Autobiography (Yevtushenko)
26:460; 51:430
"The Predators" (Allen) 52:35
Predatory Things of Our Age (Strugatskii and
Strugatskii) 27:433
Predeo slikan cajem (*Landscape Painted with
Tea*) (Pavic) 60:288
"A Predicament" (Callaghan) 65:250
"Prediction" (Himes) 7:159; 58:268
"Prediction" (Himes) 108:234, 251, 278
"The Prediction" (Strand) 18:515, 518-20;
71:284
Predilections (Moore) 47:267
Predvaritel'nye itogi (*Taking Stock*) (Trifonov)
45:408, 411, 413, 416-17, 420
Prefabrications (Miles) 39:353
"La préface" (Olson) 29:330
"Préface" (Tchicaya) 101:351-52
Préface à la Gita-Govinda (Yourcenar) 38:457
"Preface: Deciding to Live" 78:2
Preface to a Twenty Volume Suicide Note
(Baraka) 2:34; 5:44-46; 10:21; 14:42;
115:3, 10, 38, 40
"Preface to an Adaptation of Ibsen's *An En-
emy of the People*" (Miller) 10:346
"Preface to Blackness: Text and Pretext"
(Gates) 65:383
"Preface to My Poems—Frivolous Version"

(Williams) 45:443
"Preface to 'The Galton Case'" (Macdonald)
14:333
"Preface to the Reader" (Rukeyser) 15:456
"Preface to *The Unending Rose*" (Borges)
13:110
"Prefigurations: Prato" (Landolfi) 49:217
"Pregão turístico do Recife" ("Tourist Pitch
for Recife"; "Tourist Proclamation For
Recife") (Cabral de Melo Neto) 76:153-
54, 167-68
"The Pregnant Dream" (Swenson) 106:337
The Pregnant Man (Phillips) 28:362-64
"Preguntas" (Neruda) 28:309
"Pre-History" (Akhmatova) 11:8
"Preliminary Investigation of an Angel"
(Herbert) 9:272; 43:188
"Prelude" (Avison) 97:74-7, 80-1, 106, 128
"The Prelude" (Frost) 9:227
"Prelude" (Kavanagh) 22:237
"Prelude" (Walcott) 25:449; 67:352; 76:278,
280, 286
A Prelude (Wilson) 2:475, 478; 24:483
"Prelude for Spring" (Livesay) 79:332, 334-
36, 38
"Prelude to a Fairy Tale" (Sitwell) 67:313
Prelude to a Kiss (Lucas) 64:294-99
"Prelude to a Parting" (Angelou) 77:31
"Prelude to an Evening" (Ransom) 2:363;
5:365
"Prelude to Darkness" (Salinas) 90:332
*Prelude to Downfall: Hitler and the United
States 1939-1941* (Friedlander)
See *Hitler et les États-Unis (1939-1941)*
Prelude to Foundation (Asimov) 76:313
*Prelude to Space: A Compellingly Realistic
Novel of Interplanetary Flight* (Clarke)
35:118, 120-21, 124
Prelude to Terror (MacInnes) 27:283-84
"Preludes" (Eliot) 13:199, 201; 15:213;
41:152, 156; 57:174; 113:187
"Preludes" (Transtroemer) 52:410; 65:222-
23
Preludes for Memnon; or, Preludes to Attitude
(Aiken) 3:3; 5:9; 10:3; 52:22-4, 26, 29
Premier amour (*First Love*) (Beckett) 6:38;
10:34-6
Le premier homme (Camus) 32:99
Le Premier quartier de la lune (Tremblay)
102:379
La première enquête de Maigret, 1913
(Simenon) 3:451
Les premiers poèmes (Tzara) 47:389
Los premios (*The Winners*) (Cortazar) 15:146;
33:135-36; 34:329; 92:138-39, 141, 155
"Premonition" (Montague) 13:390; 46:268
"The Premonition" (Roethke) 8:460; 46:361
"Pre-Mortem" (Purdy) 50:247
Prenez Garde (White) 49:399-400
Prenn Drifting (Lengyel) 7:202
Prénom de Dieu (Cixous) 92:56
Prénoms de personne (Cixous) 92:52-3, 70,
90, 94
Preoccupations in Australian Poetry (Wright)
11:578; 53:432
Preoccupations: Selected Prose, 1968-1978
(Heaney) 25:248-51; 74:162, 165, 169,
173, 177-78, 181, 183, 193; 91:115, 118,
121, 124, 128
"Preparation" (Butler) 81:127
"Preparation" (Milosz) 56:246, 251; 82:290
"Preparation" (Silko) 74:347
Preparation for the Ascent (Rogin) 18:458-59

"Preparations for Victory" (Blunden) **56**:43

"Preparatory Exercise (Dyptych with Votive Tablet)" ("Diptych with VotiveTablet") (Paz) **65**:198

Prepositions (Zukofsky) **4**:599

"The Pre-Presidential T.R." (Wilson) **24**:481

"A Pre-Raphaelite Ending, London" (Howard) **7**:168

"A Pre-Raphaelite Notebook" (Hill) **45**:180

"Pres Spoke in a Language" (Baraka) **115**:39

"Pre-School" (Purdy) **50**:246

"Prescience" (Angelou) **35**:32

"The Prescriptive Stalls As" (Ammons) **108**:13

Préséances (Mauriac) **4**:340; **56**:204, 206

"The Presence" (Elytis) **49**:109

"The Presence" (Gordon) **29**:188; **83**:247

"Presence" (Kunene) **85**:166

"Presence" (Levertov) **66**:241

Presence (Page and Plant) **12**:480

"The Presence of Grace" (Powers) **1**:280

The Presence of Grace (Powers) **4**:419; **8**:447; **57**:356

"The Presence of Presence" (Dacey) **51**:80-1

A Presence with Secrets (Spackman) **46**:377-78

"The Presences" (Jacobsen) **48**:198

"Presences" (Justice) **19**:233-34; **102**:263

Presences (Creeley) **78**:128, 130-33, 144, 147, 159

Présences (Jouve) **47**:203

Presences: Seven Dramatic Pieces (Taylor) **4**:542-43; **18**:524-27

"The Present" (Bell) **8**:67

"Present" (Sanchez) **116**:280

"The Present" (Stafford) **7**:457

The Present (Josipovici) **6**:270-71

The Present and the Past (Compton-Burnett) **34**:500

"Present Discontents" (Blunden) **56**:30

"A Present for Miss Merriam" (Buckler) **13**:120

Present Laughter (Coward) **29**:134-35, 138; **51**:68-70

Présent passé, passé présent (*Present Past, Past Present*) (Ionesco) **41**:227-28; **86**:332, 335, 341

"The Present Past" (Nemerov) **36**:309

Present Past, Past Present (Ionesco)
   See *Présent passé, passé présent*

The Present Takers (Chambers) **35**:101

"The Present Tense" (Oates) **33**:294

Present Tense (Gilroy) **2**:161

"Présentation des temps modernes" (Sartre) **24**:419-20

Presentation Piece (Hacker) **91**:94

"Presenting a Watch" (Howard) **47**:168

"Presents" (Wideman) **67**:379, 385

"Preservation" (Carver) **36**:100, 104

Preservation, Act 1 (Davies) **21**:96-8

Preservation, Act 2 (Davies) **21**:98, 100

Preservation Hall (Spencer) **30**:404-07

Preserve and Protect (Drury) **37**:105, 107

"The President" (Barthelme) **8**:50; **23**:46

The President (Asturias)
   See *El Señor presidente*

The President (Bernhard)
   See *Der Präsident*

The President (Cassill) **23**:104-05

The President (Dreyer) **16**:259-61

The President (Hersey) **81**:332

"The President of the Louisiana Live Oak Society" (Gilchrist) **48**:116, 121

Presidential Agent (Sinclair) **63**:355

Presidential Lottery (Michener) **109**:383, 386

Presidential Mission (Sinclair) **63**:355, 357

The Presidential Papers (Mailer) **1**:190, 192; **8**:370; **28**:256, 263; **74**:219; **111**:95-96, 100, 116

The President's Child (Weldon) **36**:445-47

The President's Man (Guild) **33**:188

"Presque Isle" (Gluck) **81**:167

"La presqu'île" (Gracq) **48**:141

La presqu'île (Gracq) **48**:141

"Press Clippings" (Cortazar)
   See "Recortes de prensa"

"Pressed Duck" (Seidel) **18**:475

"Pressing On" (Dylan) **77**:186, 190

"Pressure" (Davies) **21**:105-06

"Pressure" (Joel) **26**:223

"Pressure" (Waldman) **7**:508

Prêt-à-Porter (*Ready to Wear*) (Altman) **116**:59, 61, 68, 70-1

"Pretend I'm Not Here" (Theroux) **11**:528

"Pretend We're French" (Freeman) **55**:57

"Pretended Homes" (Dunn) **40**:171

"The Pretender" (Browne) **21**:39-40

"The Pretender" (Gordimer)
   See "My First Two Women"

The Pretender (Browne) **21**:38-41

Pretender to the Throne: The Further Adventures of Private Ivan Chonkin (Voinovich) **49**:376, 379-82

Pretending to Be Asleep (Davison) **28**:100-01

"Preternaturally Early Snowfall in Mating Season" (Warren) **39**:272

Prétexte: Roland Barthes (Barthes) **83**:89-90

"The Prettiest Star" (Bowie) **17**:60

Pretty Boy (Poliakoff) **38**:379-80, 385

"Pretty Boy Floyd" (Guthrie) **35**:183, 185, 190-91

"The Pretty Girl" (Dubus) **36**:147-48; **97**:199-202, 217, 221, 223, 228-30

"Pretty Ice" (Robison) **42**:339

"Pretty Lady" (Sondheim) **30**:397

Pretty Leslie (Cassill) **23**:104

"Pretty Maggie Moneyeyes" (Ellison) **13**:203, 206; **42**:126

Pretty Mournings, Small Tragedies (Carrier)
   See *Jolis deuils, petites tragédies pour adultes*

The Pretty Pictures (Beauvoir)
   See *Les belles images*

"Pretty Polly Barlow" (Coward) **51**:74

Pretty Poplar in a Red Kerchief (Aitmatov)
   See *Topolek moi v krasnoi kosynke*

Pretty Tales for Tired People (Gellhorn) **60**:185, 187-88

"Pretty Woman" (Sondheim) **30**:393, 398

Pretzel Logic (Becker and Fagen) **26**:79, 83

"Preview of Death" (Woolrich) **77**:401

"The Previous Tenant" (Simpson) **32**:381

"Las previsiones de Sangiácomo" (Bioy Casares) **88**:67, 69

"Priapus" ("Orchard") (H. D.) **14**:223; **31**:205

Priapus and the Pool and Other Poems (Aiken) **52**:20, 22

Príbeh inzenýra lidských duší (*The Engineer of Human Souls: An Entertainment of the Old Themes of Life, Women, Fate, Dreams, the Working Class, Secret Agents, Love, and Death*) (Skvorecky) **39**:221-22; **69**:327-30, 332, 335-37, 339, 342-44, 346-52

The Price (Miller) **2**:279-80; **6**:330-33; **10**:342-43; **15**:373-74; **47**:251, 254-55

The Price of Diamonds (Jacobson) **4**:256; **14**:289

The Price of Gold (Waddington) **28**:439

"The Price of Peace" (Cliff) **21**:60-1

The Price of Salt (Highsmith) **42**:211; **102**:210, 212, 219-21

"The Price of Stone" (Murphy) **41**:319

The Price of Stone: New and Selected Poems (Murphy) **41**:319-20

The Price of the Ticket: Collected Nonfiction, 1948-1985 (Baldwin) **42**:15-21

"Pricing" (Ignatow) **7**:177

The Prick of Noon (De Vries) **46**:134-36

Prick Up Your Ears (Bennett) **77**:85, 89-90, 98, 100, 102

"Prickli" (Tournier)
   See "Prickli"

"Prickly" (Tournier) **36**:438; **95**:383-84, 387-89

Pricksongs and Descants (Coover) **3**:113-14; **7**:58; **32**:121-24, 126; **46**:119, 121-22; **87**:25, 32, 43

"The Pride" (Newlove) **14**:377

"Pride" (Urquhart) **90**:385

The Pride of Chanur (Cherryh) **35**:108-09

A Pride of Heroes (Dickinson)
   See *The Old English Peep-Show*

Pride of the Bimbos (Sayles) **7**:399; **10**:460; **14**:484

"Pride of the Village" (Blunden) **56**:37

"Prière" (Damas) **84**:179

"Prière mutilée" ("Mutilated Prayer") (Cocteau) **8**:146

Prières d'un enfant très très sage (*Prayers of a Very Wise Child*) (Carrier) **78**:83

"The Priest" (Thomas) **48**:375

"The Priest and the Matador" (Bukowski) **41**:64

"The Priest Says Goodbye" (Cohen) **38**:131-32

"A Priest to His People" (Thomas) **13**:542

"Priestly Fellowship" (Powers) **8**:447; **57**:349, 357-58

"The Priest's Confession" (Ai) **69**:9, 10

"The Priest's Wife" (L'Heureux) **52**:279

"Prikliuchenie v antikvarnom magazine" ("Adventure in an Antique Shop") (Akhmadulina) **53**:12-13

Prilba hlíny (Seifert)
   See *Helmet of Clay*

Prilli i thyer (*Avril brisé*) (Kadare) **52**:260

La prima Angélica (*Cousin Angélica*) (Saura) **20**:315-18, 321-22

The Primal Urge (Aldiss) **14**:10-11

The Primary English Class (Horovitz) **56**:153-54

The Primary Language of Poetry in the 1640's (Miles) **39**:354

The Primary Language of Poetry in the 1740's and 1840's (Miles) **39**:354

The Primary Language of Poetry in the 1940's (Miles) **39**:354

Primate (Wiseman) **20**:475, 477

"La primavera Hitleriana" ("The Hitlerian Spring") (Montale) **9**:390

"Prime" (Ungaretti) **11**:559

"Prime Colours" (Watkins) **43**:451

"Prime Minister" (Enright) **31**:155

The Prime Minister (Clarke) **53**:89-90, 92, 95

"The Prime of Life" (Asimov) **26**:50

The Prime of Life (Beauvoir)
   See *La force de l'âge*

The Prime of Miss Jean Brodie (Spark) **2**:415-17; **3**:465-67; **8**:493-94; **13**:520, 522-23; **18**:501-06; **40**:393-96, 399-400; **94**:327-

28, 331-344, 350, 353-356, 358-359
Primeiras estorias (*The Third Bank of the River, and Other Stories*) (Rosa) **23**:352-54
Primer for Blacks (Brooks) **49**:29
Primer for Combat (Boyle) **58**:70
A Primer for Poets (Shapiro) **4**:487
A Primer of Ignorance (Blackmur) **2**:62
Primera història d'Esther (Espriu) **9**:192
Primera memoria (Matute) **11**:362-63, 365
"Primero sueño" ("First Dream") (Guillen) **79**:246
Primeros encuentros/First Encounters (*First Encounters*) (Ulibarri) **83**:410-11, 415
"The Primitive" (Madhubuti) **73**:192
"The Primitive" (Swenson) **4**:533; **61**:391
The Primitive (Himes) **2**:195; **4**:229; **18**:248; **58**:252, 256-57, 263; **108**:229, 232, 254, 259
Primitive (Oppen) **13**:434; **34**:358
Primitive Mythology (Campbell)
  See *The Masks of God: Primitive Mythology*
"Primitive Sources" (Atwood) **25**:66
Primitivism and Decadence (Winters) **32**:451-52, 455, 460, 463, 466, 469
The Primrose Path (Nash) **23**:317-18
"The Prince" (Winters) **32**:468
Prince (Prince) **35**:323-24
The Prince and Betty (Wodehouse) **10**:538
"The Prince and the Pauper" (Auchincloss) **45**:30
The Prince and the Showgirl (Olivier) **20**:238-39, 244
The Prince and the Wild Geese (Brophy) **29**:98-9
Le Prince de Jaffar (*The Prince of Jaffar*) (Duhamel) **8**:187
"Prince Ferrix and Princess Crystal" (Lem) **15**:328
A Prince of a Fellow (Hearon) **63**:160-62
"Prince of Darkness" (Powers) **57**:355-56
Prince of Darkness (Mortimer) **43**:307
Prince of Darkness and Other Stories (Powers) **1**:279; **4**:419; **57**:356-7
The Prince of Jaffar (Duhamel)
  See *Le Prince de Jaffar*
Prince of Naples (Walker) **61**:424, 428
Prince of Peace (Carroll) **38**:108-11
Prince of Players (Hart) **66**:182
"Prince of the Punks" (Davies) **21**:103
The Prince of Tides (Conroy) **74**:44-6, 50-3
"The Prince of Wales" (Pesetsky) **65**:349
The Prince of West End Avenue (Isler) **91**:45-52
"Princes and Powers" (Baldwin) **50**:292
"The Princes and the Feathers" (Harris) **12**:268
"The Prince's Land" (Murray) **40**:334
"Princess" (Mohr) **12**:446
"The Princess and the Bears" (Harris) **12**:268
"The Princess and the Pea" (Muldoon) **72**:278
The Princess Bride: S. Morgenstern's Classic Tale of True Love and Adventure; The "Good Parts" Version, Abridged (Goldman) **48**:126, 128
Princess in Denim (Sherburne) **30**:361
"The Princess with the Golden Hair" (Wilson) **8**:551
"Princesse, ton épître" (Senghor) **54**:396
"The Princessess" **75**:62
"Princeton Speech" (Weiss) **51**:386
"Principal in a Prairie Town" (Suknaski) **19**:432
Principato (McHale) **3**:331; **5**:281-82
"Le principe d'utilité" (Cendrars) **18**:92

The Principle of Water (Silkin) **6**:499; **43**:400, 404
The Principles of Literary Criticism (Richards) **24**:370-76, 379-81, 384-85, 387-89, 393-400
Print of a Hare's Foot (Davies) **23**:146
Le printemps 71 (*Spring 71*) (Adamov) **25**:13-21
Printer's Devil (Moorcock) **58**:351
"Printer's Pie" (Hope) **51**:226
"The Prinzhorn Collection" (Coles) **46**:111-13
The Prinzhorn Collection (Coles) **46**:111-13
The Pripet Marshes (Feldman) **7**:103
"Priscilla" (Calvino) **11**:92
Prismatic Ground (Young) **82**:395-97, 405-06, 409, 411-12, 414
Prison (Bergman)
  See *Fängelse*
The Prison (Simenon) **2**:398
Prison and Chocolate Cake (Sahgal) **41**:369
Prison and Peace (*Tiur'ma i mir*) (Aksyonov) **101**:55
The Prison Cell and Barrel Mystery (Reading) **47**:350
"The Prison House" (Ali) **69**:31
The Prison House (Ali) **69**:31
"Prison Island" (Fenton) **32**:165-66
"Prison Mass" (Himes) **108**:235
Prison Poems (Berrigan) **4**:57-8
The Prison Tree and the Women (Ritsos) **6**:463
"The Prisoner" (Ai) **69**:9, 15
"The Prisoner" (Jong) **6**:268
"The Prisoner" (Klappert) **57**:260
"The Prisoner" (Malamud) **3**:321
"The Prisoner" (Nkosi) **45**:295
"The Prisoner" (Paz)
  See "El prisonero"
"The Prisoner" (Roa Bastos)
  See "El prisonero"
"The Prisoner" (Simic) **22**:380
"Prisoner at a Desk" (Sarton) **91**:253
"The Prisoner of Las Lomas" (Fuentes) **113**:242
The Prisoner of Second Avenue (Simon) **6**:504, 506; **31**:394-96; **70**:241
The Prisoner of Sex (Mailer) **2**:262; **3**:315; **4**:321-23; **8**:370, 373; **11**:341, 344; **39**:417, 420; **74**:205, 225-27; **111**:103
"The Prisoner of Zenda" (Wilbur) **110**:385
"Prisoner Who Wore Glasses" (Head) **67**:111
"El prisonero" ("The Prisoner") (Paz) **19**:366
"El prisonero" ("The Prisoner") (Roa Bastos) **45**:345
"Prisoners" (Boland) **40**:98; **67**:43
"Prisoners" (Komunyakaa) **94**:226
Prisoner's Dilema (Powers) **93**:277, 279-86, 301
"A Prisoner's Ode to a Fine Lady from the Past" (Faludy) **42**:142
Prisoners of Jebs (Saro-Wiwa) **114**:254
Prisoners of Power (Strugatskii and Strugatskii) **27**:437
The Prisoners of September (Garfield) **12**:231-32, 236, 238-39
Prisoners of Silence: Breaking the Bonds of Adult Illiteracy in the United States (Kozol) **17**:255
Prisons (Settle) **61**:372-74, 379-86
"Privacy" (Rexroth) **112**:404
The Private Art (Grigson) **39**:332
"Private Audience" (Roa Bastos)
  See "Audiencia privada"

Private Contentment (Price) **63**:325
"A Private Correspondence on Reality" (Graves) **45**:165
The Private Dining Room (Nash) **23**:322
"Private Domain" (McPherson) **19**:309; **77**:360, 366
"Private Drive" (Howard) **7**:165
The Private Ear (Shaffer) **5**:387
"Private Eye Lettuce" (Brautigan) **12**:59
Private Eyes: Adventures with the Saturday Gang (Kingman) **17**:245
A Private Function (Bennett) **77**:98, 101
"Private Ground" (Plath) **111**:203-04
Private Ground (Levi) **41**:247-48
"Private Hell" (Weller) **26**:445-46
"Private John Daniel Ramey" (Hersey) **81**:329
"Private Joy" (Prince) **35**:324-26
"The Private Life" (Mueller) **51**:281
Private Life (Elliott) **47**:108, 110
The Private Life (Mueller) **13**:399-400; **51**:281
A Private Life (Seton) **27**:429-30
Private Life of an Indian Prince (Anand) **23**:13, 17; **93**:24-5, 29, 43, 50-2
"The Private Life of Mr. Bidwell" (Thurber) **5**:431
The Private Life of Sherlock Holmes (Wilder) **20**:463-64
Private Lives: An Intimate Comedy (Coward) **1**:64; **9**:173; **29**:133, 135-39; **51**:69-73, 75, 77
"A Private Lot" (Ghose) **42**:179
A Private Mythology (Sarton) **4**:471; **49**:314, 320
"Private Parts" (Hope) **52**:211
Private Parts: A Memoir (Metcalf) **37**:301-03, 305-06
Private Parts, and Other Tales (Hope) **52**:210-11, 217
Private Potter (Harwood) **32**:222
"Private Sadness" (Kaufman) **49**:206
A Private Signal (Howes) **15**:289-90
"Private Tuition by Mr. Bose" (Desai) **97**:150, 152-53, 171
A Private View (Havel) **58**:237-41, 243, 245
"The Private War of Private Jacob" (Haldeman) **61**:177
"Private Worship" (Van Doren) **10**:495
The Private Wound (Day Lewis) **6**:128
Privateers (Bova) **45**:74
Privates on Parade (Nichols) **36**:327-28, 332; **65**:160-65
"Privilege" (Smith) **12**:543
The Privilege (Kumin) **28**:220
"Privilege of Being" (Hass) **99**:140, 142
"A Privileged Moment" (Day Lewis) **10**:131
Privileged Ones (Coles) **108**:194
"Privilegio del suicida" (Castellanos) **66**:53
The Prize (Wallace) **7**:509; **13**:567-68, 570
Prize Stock (Oe)
  See *Shiiku*
"Prize-Winning Blank Verse" (Wilson) **24**:481
Prizzi's Family (Condon) **45**:104; **100**:92-5, 100, 109-11, 113
Prizzi's Glory (Condon) **100**:93-5, 100, 109-11, 113
Prizzi's Honor (Condon) **45**:99, 104-05; **100**:91-5, 97-8, 100, 102, 104-07, 109-13
Prizzi's Money (Condon) **100**:108-13
"The Pro" (Updike) **23**:473
"Pro femina" (Kizer) **39**:171; **80**:174-75, 178-79, 181-82, 184
Pro patria (Sender)

See *Iman*
"Próba rozwiazania mitologii" (Herbert) 43:187

A Probable Volume of Dreams (Bell) 8:64-6; 31:46-7, 49

Probing the Limits of Representation: Nazism and the Final Solution (Friedlander) 90:120-1

"A Problem from Milton" (Wilbur) 3:533

"A Problem in Spatial Composition" (Warren) 10:522; 39:270, 274

"The Problem of Anxiety" (Koch) 44:246

"The Problem of Belief and the Problems of Cognition" (Brooks) 110:15, 34-5

"The Problem of Fornication in the Blarney Chronicle" (Durcan) 43:116

The Problem of Pain (Lewis) 3:296; 6:308; 14:322-23

The Problem of the Green Capsule (*The Black Spectacles*) (Carr) 3:101

"The Problem of the Text" (Bakhtin) 83:9, 40

"The Problem Shop" (Rooke) 25:394

"Problemas del subdesarrollo" (Guillen) 48:159

"Problematica de la actual novela Latinoamericano" (Carpentier) 38:94

"Problems" (Updike) 15:544

Problems, and Other Stories (Updike) 15:544-48

"The Problems of a Catholic Writer" (Endo) 99:285

"Problems of Adjustment in Survivors of Natural/Unnatural Disasters" (Oates) 6:370

Problems of Dostoevsky's Poetics (Bakhtin)
See *Problemy tvorcestva Dostoevskogo*

"Problems of Knowledge" (Warren) 13:573

Problems of the Theatre (Durrenmatt) 8:194, 197; 11:170, 173; 15:199; 43:123

"Problems of Underdevelopment" (Guillen)
See "Problems of Underdevelopment"

"Problems Problems" (Bachmann) 69:46-7

Problemy tvorcestva Dostoevskogo (*Dostoevsky; Problems of Dostoevsky's Poetics*) (Bakhtin) 83:3-4, 6, 9, 13, 16, 18, 24-5, 30, 33, 40

"Procedures for Underground" (Atwood) 25:67

Procedures for Underground (Atwood) 3:20; 4:24; 8:30-1; 13:44; 25:63, 67; 84:68

Proceed, Sergeant Lamb (Graves) 39:322

Le procès (*The Trial*) (Welles) 20:438-42, 444-45, 448, 450; 80:389, 391, 396

Procès de Jeanne d'Arc (*The Trial of Joan of Arc*) (Bresson) 16:105, 109, 113-15

Le procès de Shamgorod (Wiesel) 37:452

"Process" (Livesay) 79:338

"Processes" (Tomlinson) 13:549

"The Procession" (Brodsky) 50:120

"Procession" (Soyinka) 44:285

"A Procession at Candlemas" (Clampitt) 32:115-17

"The Procession of Life" (O'Connor) 23:329

"Procession with the Madonna" (Yevtushenko) 3:547

"Processional" (Enright) 31:150

Le procès-verbal (Le Clezio) 31:243-44, 251

Prochain Episode (Aquin) 15:15, 17

"Prochorus Thompson" (Beer) 58:36

"The Prodigal" (Vanderhaeghe) 41:452

The Prodigal Daughter (Archer) 28:13-14

"The Prodigal Parent" (Gallant) 38:190

"The Prodigal Son" (Bishop) 4:66

"The Prodigal Son" (Bly) 38:57-8

"Prodigal Son" (Montague) 46:265

"The Prodigal Son" (White) 69:403

The Prodigal Son (Hughes) 35:218

"La prodigiosa tarde de Baltazar" ("Balthazar's Marvelous Afternoon") (Garcia Marquez) 27:147-48; 47:146, 151

"Prodigy" (Simic) 22:382; 49:337-38, 341

"The Produce District" (Gunn) 32:211

The Producers (Brooks) 12:75-6, 78-82

"Proem" (McAuley) 45:250

"Proem" (Paz) 65:190

Proêmes (Ponge) 18:417

The Profane Art (Oates) 33:293

"La profesora" ("The Professor") (Valenzuela) 104:357

Le Professeur Taranne (*Professor Taranne*) (Adamov) 25:12, 14, 19-20

Professing Poetry (Wain) 11:563-64

"Profession" (Asimov) 26:53

Professional Foul (Stoppard) 29:395, 397, 404; 34:272; 91:190

"A Professional of Rememberances" (Cabral de Melo Neto)
See "O profissional da memória"

Professional Secrets (Cocteau) 8:145-46

"The Professor" (Farrell) 66:129

"Professor" (Hughes) 35:215

"The Professor" (Valenzuela)
See "La profesora"

The Professor (Warner) 45:429-32, 435, 437-41

"Professor Cheeta" (Anand) 23:18

"Professor Heller and the Boots" (Davie) 10:124

"Professor Klaeber's Nasty Dream" (Raine) 32:349

"Professor Nobody's Little Lectures on Supernatural Horror" (Ligotti) 44:53-4

The Professor of Desire (Roth) 9:460-62; 15:449, 451-52, 455; 22:354; 47:359, 364; 66:417, 420; 86:255, 258

"Professor Sea Gull" (Mitchell) 98:168, 181, 187

Professor Taranne (Adamov)
See *Le Professeur Taranne*

Professors and Gods: Last Oxford Lectures on Poetry (Fuller) 4:178

The Professor's Daughter (Read) 4:444; 25:376, 379

"The Professor's Morning Ride" (Simmons) 43:414

"Profile" (Auden) 14:27; 43:15

Profiles of the Future: An Enquiry into the Limits of the Possible (Clarke) 35:117, 128-29

"O profissional da memória" ("A Professional of Rememberances") (Cabral de Melo Neto) 76:169

The Profits of Religion: An Essay in Economic Interpretation (Sinclair) 63:346-47

Profound Today (Cendrars) 106:191-92

"Profumo" (Muldoon) 72:277

"De profundis" (Gascoyne) 45:157

"Progenitor" (Zamora) 89:384, 387

"Pro-Girl" (Ian) 21:183

"Prognosis" (MacNeice) 53:237

"Prognosis" (Roethke) 19:397

"Prognostic" (Laughlin) 49:220

"Program" (Burke) 24:119

"The Program" (Fearing) 51:106

A Program for Survival (Ruark) 3:441

"Programme Note" (Tomlinson) 45:397-98

"Progress" (MacCaig) 36:285

The Progress of a Crime (Symons) 14:522

"The Progress of Faust" (Shapiro) 53:334

The Progress of Julius (du Maurier) 59:284, 286

"The Progress of Love" (Munro) 50:208-09, 211-12, 215, 217-18; 95:306, 309

The Progress of Love (Munro) 50:208-13, 215-19; 95:318, 320

Progress of Stories (Riding) 7:375

"Progression" (Christie) 110:126

"Progulka" (Akhmadulina) 53:15

Prohibido suicidarse en primavera (*Suicide Prohibited in Springtime*) (Casona) 49:42-5, 48, 50

"Project" (Ammons) 25:43

Project for a Revolution in New York (Robbe-Grillet)
See *Projet pour une révolution à New York*

"Project for a Trip to China" (Sontag) 13:516, 518

Projective Verse (Olson) 6:386; 11:415-17; 29:326, 335-37

Projet pour une révolution à New York (*Project for a Revolution in New York*) (Robbe-Grillet) 2:376-77; 4:448, 450; 6:464-65; 8:454; 10:437; 14:462; 43:366

"Prolegomena to a Third Surrealist Manifesto or Not" (Breton) 54:16

A Prolegomenon to a Theodicy (Rexroth) 22:344; 49:279, 285; 112:375

"Proletarian Literature: A Political Autopsy" (Rahv) 24:355

The Prolific and the Devourer (Auden) 14:31; 43:14-15, 26

"Prolog" (Dixon) 52:97

"Prolog" (Herbert) 43:186

"Prólogo" (Guillen) 48:160

"Prologue" (MacLeish) 8:361

"Prologue" (Seifert) 93:329-30

"Prologue" (Silkin) 43:401

"Prologue" (Yevtushenko) 26:461

Prologue (Brady)
See *The Unmaking of a Dancer*

"Prologue: An Interim" (Levertov)
See "Interim"

"Prologue at Sixty" (Auden) 14:27; 43:18

"Prologue for a Play" (Ciardi) 40:157

"Prologue in Heaven" (Butor) 8:118

"Prologue in the Theater" (Butor) 8:118

"Prologue to an Autobiography" (Naipaul) 37:325-29

A Prologue to Love (Caldwell) 28:63

"Prologue to 'The Invention of Morel'" (Borges) 48:47

"La prolongada busca de Tai An" (Bioy Casares) 88:69

Proluky (*Vacant Sites*) (Hrabal) 67:122

"Promenade" (Ignatow) 40:258

Promenade (Fornes) 39:138; 61:130-33, 140

"Promeny" ("Transformations") (Seifert) 93:342

La promesse de l'aube (*Promise at Dawn*) (Gary) 25:185-86

"Prometheus" (Gray) 41:179, 181

"Prometheus" (McAuley) 45:246

"Prometheus" (Tomlinson) 4:544; 13:546, 548-49; 45:392-93, 401

Prometheus Bound (Lowell) 3:301; 8:357; 11:324; 15:349

"Prometheus in Straits" (Ransom) 2:363

"Prometheus Loved Us" (Barnard) 48:25, 27

"Prometheus on His Crag" (Hughes) 37:174-75, 177

"The Promise" (Steinbeck) 9:515

The Promise (Buck) 11:76-7
The Promise (Potok) 2:338-39; 7:321; 26:369-70, 372-73, 376; 112:260-61, 267, 276, 282, 290
Promise and Fulfillment: Palestine 1917-1949 (Koestler) 3:271
Promise at Dawn (Gary)
  See *La promesse de l'aube*
The Promise of Joy (Drury) 37:107
Promise of Love (*Purposes of Love*) (Renault) 17:389-90
"Promise of Rain" (Taylor) 37:411; 44:305-06; 50:260; 71:299, 304
The Promise of Space (Clarke) 35:117-18
The Promise: Requiem to the Detective Novel (Durrenmatt) 8:196
The Promised Land (Berton) 104:44-6
Promised Land (Parker) 27:363, 366-67
Promised Lands (Sontag) 31:411
"The Promised One" (Wright) 53:419
The Promisekeeper (Newman) 2:311
Promises: Poems, 1954-1956 (Warren) 4:578; 6:557; 8:539, 542; 10:520, 522; 13:572, 575, 577-78, 581; 39:265-66, 270; 59:297
"Promises, Promises" (Cassity) 42:99
"Promises, Promises" (Muldoon) 32:321; 72:268
Promises, Promises (Simon) 31:394, 403-04; 70:235
Promises to Keep (Corcoran) 17:73-4
Promises to Keep (Fleming) 37:127-28
"A Promising Career" (Gellhorn) 60:187-88
A Promising Career (Brown) 63:56-7
"Proof" (Milosz) 22:308
"The Proof" (Wilbur) 110:386
"The Proof" (Winters) 32:467-68
Proof (Francis) 42:153, 159-60; 102:131, 139, 148
"The Proofreader" (Huddle) 49:182
A Proper Gentleman (Scannell) 49:332
"A Proper Halo" (Redgrove) 41:359
A Proper Marriage (Lessing) 2:238; 3:291; 94:256-57, 281, 286
"The Proper Respect" (Allende) 97:29, 32
Proper Studies: The Proper Study of Mankind Is Man (Huxley) 18:269; 35:242; 79:309
"Property" (Gilliatt) 10:229
Property Of (Hoffman) 51:199-202
"The Property of Colette Nervi" (Trevor) 71:329; 116:358
"The Prophecy" (Miller) 47:249
Prophecy (Handke) 8:262; 15:266
"The Prophet" (Blunden) 56:29
"The Prophet" (Pasternak) 63:
"The Prophet of the New World" (Livesay) 79:345
The Prophets (Mrozek) 3:345
Prophets (Walker) 1:351
The Prophet's Camel Bell (*New Wind in a Dry Land*) (Laurence) 50:314, 319; 62:274, 278-81
The Prophet's Steps
  See *Pasii profetului*
"Proposal for a Survey" (Adcock) 41:16
"Propositions on the Death of Ana" (Guillen) 48:159
The Proprietor (Schlee) 35:374-76
"Propriety" (Moore) 2:291
Proprioception (Olson) 5:326
"Prosa aus der flüstergalerie" (Jandl) 34:196
Prosanatolizmí (*Orientations*) (Elytis) 15:220; 49:106, 108, 115; 100:155, 187, 189
"Prosas da maré na Jaqueira" ("Chatting with

the Tide at Jaqueira"; "Conversations of the Tide at Jaqueira") (Cabral de Melo Neto) 76:169
Proschai, Gul'sary! (Farewell, Gul'sary!) (Aitmatov) 71:3, 7, 13-15, 17-19, 21-2
"Prose" 59:370-71, 378-79
"Prose and Poetry of It All; Or, Dippy Verses" (Barth) 51:26
"Prose and Verse" (Eliot) 113:220
"Prose du transsibérien et de la petite Jeanne de France" ("Prose of the Trans-Siberian"; "Prosody of the Transsiberian"; "Transsiberian") (Cendrars) 18:90, 92, 94, 97; 106:151, 158-59, 163, 167, 177, 180-81, 184, 186, 189-90, 192, 196-97
"Prose of the Trans-Siberian" (Cendrars)
  See "Prose du transsibérien et de la petite Jeanne de France"
"Prose Poem" (Tomlinson) 45:393, 401
"Prose Rhythms" (Voznesensky) 57:425
"Proseball: Sports, Stories, and Style" (Hall) 37:149
The Proselytizer (Mano) 2:270
"Proserpina" (Lewis) 41:253
Proserpina and the Devil (Wilder) 82:384
"Prosody of the Transsiberian" (Cendrars)
  See "Prose du transsibérien et de la petite Jeanne de France"
"Prospect" (Creeley) 78:153
"Prospect" (Plath) 111:201
The Prospect before Us (Dos Passos) 25:145
The Prospect before Us (Gold) 4:189; 42:188
"A Prospect of Swans" (Blunden) 56:45
"Prospecting" (Ammons) 108:20
"Prospective Immigrants Please Note" (Rich) 18:446
"Prospects for an Expedition" (Federspiel) 42:146
"Prospero and the Sycorax" (Hughes) 37:177
Prospero on the Island (Thomas) 37:416; 107:315, 330, 349
Prospero's Cell: A Guide to the Landscape and Manners of the Island of Corcyra (Durrell) 8:193; 13:188
"Prospero's Soliloquy" (Zaturenska) 6:586
Prostho Plus (Anthony) 35:36
"Protean Man" (Lifton) 67:142
"Protection" (Jacobsen) 48:196, 198
"Protective Footwear" (Bowering) 47:24-5
Protective Footwear: Stories and Fables (Bowering) 47:24-5
"Protest" (Havel) 25:227-28, 230; 58:237-40, 243; 65:413, 439
"A Protest against the Sun" (Millhauser) 54:324-27
Protestant and Roman Catholic Ethics: Prospects for Rapprochement (Gustafson) 100:197
"Protestant Drums, Tyrone, 1966" (Heaney) 74:167
"Protestant Old Folks' Coach Tour" (Durcan) 43:114
"Proteus" (Borges) 13:110
Proteus (West) 33:431-32
"Prothalamium" (Smith) 15:514
"Protivosloyaniye ochery" (Voznesensky) 15:556
Protochny Lane (Ehrenburg)
  See *In Protochny Lane*
"Protocol" (Lightfoot) 26:281
"Proud Are the Dead" (Oe) 86:226-27
Proud Are the Dead (Oe) 86:227
Proud Flesh (Humphrey) 45:198-99

Proud Flesh (Warren) 8:536; 53:369
The Proud Highway: Saga of a Desperate Southern Gentleman (Thompson) 104:348, 350
"The Proud Lady" (Dinesen) 10:149
Proud Riders and Other Poems (Davis) 49:83
"The Proud Walkers" (Still) 49:364
"Proust" (Beckett) 1:22; 10:33, 35; 11:36, 40; 18:46; 57:79, 95
The Proust Screenplay: À la recherche du temps perdu (Pinter) 15:421-23; 73:277
"Provazolezci" ("The Tightrope Walkers") (Klima) 56:172
"Prove It All Night" (Springsteen) 17:483, 490
"Prove It to You One More Time" (Kristofferson) 26:270
Provence (Mayle) 89:152
The Proverb, and Other Stories (Ayme) 11:21
"Proverbs" (Bennett) 28:29
"Proverbs" (Gotlieb) 18:193
"Provest'" ("The Last Summer") (Pasternak) 18:386
"Provide, Provide" (Frost) 1:110; 9:228; 15:250; 44:457
"Provided For" (Reznikoff) 9:450
Providence (Brookner) 32:59-61; 34:139, 142; 51:61-2, 65
Providence (Resnais) 16:515-18
Providence (Wolff) 41:461-62
Providence Island (Willingham) 5:511-12; 51:408-09, 411
The 'Province of the Heart (McGinley) 14:367
The Province of the Human (Canetti)
  See *Die Provinz des Menschen: Aufzeichnungen, 1942-1972*
"Provincetown" (Dudek) 11:159
Provincetown (Oliver) 98:276
"Provincetown: Short-Suite" (Olson) 28:343
"Provincial" (Barnard) 48:25
"Provincial I" (Barnard) 48:26
"Provincial II" (Barnard) 48:26
"The Provincial Consciousness" (Stegner) 49:359; 81:339
"Provincial Narratives" (Paulin) 37:352
"The Provincial Night" (Landolfi) 49:217
A Provincial Story (Leonov)
  See *Provintsialnaya istoriya*
"Provincialism the Enemy" (Pound) 7:332; 112:315
The Proving Trail (L'Amour) 25:282
Provintsialnaya istoriya (*A Provincial Story*) (Leonov) 92:270
Die Provinz des Menschen: Aufzeichnungen, 1942-1972 (*The Human Province; The Province of the Human*) (Canetti) 75:144; 86:295, 301
"Provisional Conclusions" (Montale) 7:224
Provo d'orchestra (*The Orchestra Rehearsal*) (Fellini) 16:300; 85:60, 69, 81
Provocations (Padilla) 38:351
"The Prowler" (Malouf) 28:269
The Prowler (Gunnars) 69:264-66, 268
"Prowlers" (Baxter) 78:27, 30
Proxopera (Kiely) 23:264-66; 43:240, 242-43, 245
Der Proze um des Esels Schatten (Duerrenmatt) 102:62
The Prudent Heart (Steele) 45:364
Prufrock and Other Observations (Eliot) 41:150, 161; 55:350, 352, 354-55, 374
"Prufrock's Dilemma" (Berryman) 8:91; 10:45
"The Pruned Tree" (Moss) 50:353

"Pruning Fruit Trees" (Pack)   13:439
"Prurient" (Matthews)   40:325
Prussian Nights: A Poem (Solzhenitsyn)
   See *Prusskie nochi: pozma napisappaja vlagere v 1950*
Prusskie nochi: pozma napisappaja vlagere v 1950 (*Prussian Nights: A Poem*) (Solzhenitsyn)   9:506-07; 10:479, 483; 18:499
Prywatne obowiazki (Milosz)   56:237
"Przesluchanie aniola" (Herbert)   43:187
Przy budowie (*At the Building Site*) (Konwicki)   117:284
"Ps. 19" (Avison)   4:37; 97:78, 81, 88, 93
P.S Wilkinson (Bryan)   29:100-01
P.S. Your Cat Is Dead (Kirkwood)   9:319
"Psalm"   75:74, 77
"A Psalm" (Blunden)   56:39
"Psalm" (Celan)   19:94; 53:70, 73, 75-6; 82:42, 46, 48
"Psalm" (Rosenthal)   28:394
"Psalm I" (Ginsberg)   36:182, 195
"Psalm 72: Man Declared a Treasure" (Enright)   31:149
"Psalm Concerning the Castle" (Levertov)   66:236
Psalmi (*Psalms*) (Arghezi)   80:5-8
"Psalmistul singuratic" ("The Lonely Psalmist") (Arghezi)   80:2, 4-5
"Psalms" (Stern)   40:408
Psalms (Arghezi)
   See *Psalmi*
Psalms of Struggle (Cardenal)   31:70, 80
The Psalms with Their Spoils (Silkin)   43:401-03
"Psi" (Tolson)   105:257, 277, 285
"Psi i knjige" ("Dogs and Books") (Kis)   57:240, 243
A psicologia da composicão com a fábula de Anfion e antiode (*Psychology of Composition*) (Cabral de Melo Neto)   76:152-53, 157
Psion (Vinge)   30:412
"P-s-s-t, Partner, Your Peristalsis Is Showing" (Perelman)   49:259
Psuedo (Gary)   25:188
"The Psychedelic Children" (Koontz)   78:201
"Psycho" (Ian)   21:183
Psycho (Bloch)   33:83-5
Psycho (Hitchcock)   16:342-43, 347-49, 352, 356, 359
Psycho II (Bloch)   33:84-6
"Psycho Killer" (Byrne)   26:94-5
"Psychoanalysis" (Durrell)   27:97
"Psychoanalysis: An Elegy" (Spicer)   18:508
"Psychoanalysis and History" (Lifton)   67:142
"The Psychohistorians" (Asimov)   26:60
Ein psycholog erlebt das konzentrationslager (*From Death-Camp to Existentialism: A Psychiatrist's Path to a New Therapy; Man's Search for Meaning: An Introduction to Logotherapy*) (Frankl)   93:193-95, 202, 206, 208-10, 216, 222-23
The Psychological Novel, 1900-1950 (Edel)   29:168
La psychologie de l'art (*The Psychology of Art*) (Malraux)   4:324-25; 9:353, 358; 15:351; 57:301
"Psychology and Art" (Auden)   4:34
"Psychology and Form" (Burke)   24:118
"Psychology and the Troubadours" (Pound)   48:285; 112:310
Psychology in Action (Hyde)   21:174

The Psychology of Art (Malraux)
   See *La psychologie de l'art*
Psychology of Composition (Cabral de Melo Neto)
   See *A psicologia da composicão com a fábula de Anfion e antiode*
Psychoneurotic Phantasies   65:444-48
"The Psychopathology of Everyday Life" (Matthews)   40:323-24
"Psychopolis" (McEwan)   66:278-82
Psychotherapy and Existentialism: Selected Papers on Logotherapy (Frankl)   93:208, 218
"Ptitsata s motornoto surtse" (Bagryana)   10:12
Pubis angelical (Puig)   28:372; 65:266, 269-70
"Public and Political Poems" (Ferlinghetti)   6:184; 27:139
"Public Bar" (Enright)   31:150
"Public Bart" (Hughes)   14:271
The Public Burning (Coover)   15:142-43, 145; 32:122, 124-25; 46:116-17, 119-22; 87:24-5, 28-32, 35-9, 41-3, 46-7, 50, 56
"Public House Drunk" (Betjeman)   2:61
The Public Image (Spark)   2:416, 418; 3:464; 5:400; 13:524; 40:399-400
"Public Life" (Fearing)   51:110
Public Order (Sender)
   See *O.P.: Orden público*
"Public Outcry" (Oates)   15:402
"A Public Pool" (Adams)   46:21
The Public Prosecutor, and Other Plays (Hochwalder)
   See *Der Öffentliche Ankläger*
"The Public Son of a Public Man" (Spender)   41:428-29
"Public Speech and Private Speech in Poetry" (MacLeish)   68:288, 290
Public Speech: Poems (MacLeish)   8:361
"The Public Ward" (Johnston)   51:250
"The Public-House" (Davies)   23:142
"The Publisher to the Poet" (Laughlin)   49:220
La pucelle (*The Maid*) (Audiberti)   38:23
"Pueblo, 1950" (Zamora)   89:384, 386, 394
Los pueblos (Azorin)   11:24
Puella (Dickey)   47:93-4; 109:245, 264-65
"Puella Mea" (Cummings)   12:146
The Puerile Lovers (Crommelynck)
   See *Les amants puérils*
"La puerta cerrada" ("The Closed Door") (Donoso)   4:127; 32:157
"Las puertas del cielo" (Cortazar)   33:128
"Puerto Rican Song" (Guillen)   48:158
Puffball (Weldon)   19:468-70; 36:446
"Puget Sound Country" (Davis)   49:92
"The Pugilist at Rest" (Jones)   81:63, 65, 67, 69
The Pugilist at Rest (Jones)   81:61-70
I pugnalatori (Sciascia)   8:474
Puhua, vastata, opettaa (*Speak, Answer, Teach*) (Haavikko)   34:179
"Pukeko" (Frame)   96:201
"The Pull" (Olds)   85:306, 308
Pull Down Vanity and Other Stories (Fiedler)   4:160
"Pull My Daisy" (Ginsberg)   109:365
"Pull of the Earth" (Plumly)   33:312
"Pulled Up" (Byrne)   26:94-5
"The Pulling" (Olds)   85:307-08
Pullman Car Hiawatha (Wilder)   82:345, 359, 364, 386-87, 390
Pulp (Bukowski)   108:93-95, 115, 116

"Pulse" (Dickey)   3:127
"The Pulse" (Levertov)   5:249
The Pump House Gang (Wolfe)   35:451-54, 459, 464
"Pump It Up" (Costello)   21:69
"Pumping" (Smith)   12:539
The Pumpkin Eater (Mortimer)   5:298-99
Pumpkin Seed Point (Waters)   88:347, 356, 363-65
"The Pumpkins" (Pinget)   37:364
"The Punch" (Friedman)   56:97
Punch and Judy (The Brothers Quay)   95:330-31
Punch: The Immortal Liar, Documents in His History (Aiken)   52:20, 22, 24
Punch's Secret (Sarton)   4:472
"Punctuation as Score" (Metcalf)   37:307
"Puncture" (Ransom)   2:363; 4:431
The Puncture (Duerrenmatt)   102:54
Punish the Sinners (Saul)   46:366
"Punishable Innocence" (Breytenbach)   23:87
"Punishment" (Heaney)   7:149; 25:243; 74:158, 193
"Punishment" (Ritsos)   31:325
Punishment Room (Ichikawa)   20:181-82
Punk et Punk et Colégram (Arrabal)   58:18
"Punky Reggae Party" (Marley)   17:271-72
"Punky's Dilemma" (Simon)   17:459
"The Pupils of the Eyes of Hungry People" (Hikmet)   40:244
The Puppet Masters (Heinlein)   1:139; 3:225; 14:247, 249, 254; 26:178; 55:303
Puppet on a Chain (MacLean)   50:348; 63:270
"The Puppet Show" (Rule)   27:423
The Puppets (Haavikko)
   See *Nuket*
The Puppy Sister (Hinton)   111:90
Pupurupú (Ulibarri)   83:415-16
"Purdah" (Plath)   5:345; 17:363, 366; 51:340-41, 343, 345; 111:178, 210
"A Pure Accident" (Lavin)   4:281; 99:322
"Pure and Easy" (Townshend)   17:528, 534
"Pure and Impure Poetry" (Warren)   8:541
"The Pure and the Good" (Maclean)   78:234-35
The Pure Clear Word: Essays on the Poetry of James Wright (Smith)   42:346
"The Pure Food Act" (Murray)   40:336
"The Pure Fury" (Roethke)   11:486; 46:363; 101:265, 328, 331, 333
"Pure Memory" (Ondaatje)   51:317
"Pure Sin" (Simon)   26:413
Pure Smokey (Robinson)   21:345-46, 349
"The Pure Suit of Happiness" (Swenson)   61:395; 106:322
"Purgation" (Dickey)   47:93
"Purgatory" (Berryman)   62:74
"Purgatory, Formerly Paradise" (Howard)   7:170; 10:276
Purification (Williams)   71:363, 369
"Puritan Poet Reel" (Buckley)   57:126
Purity of Diction in English Verse (Davie)   5:115; 8:162, 167; 10:123; 31:113, 122
Purl and Plain, and Other Stories (Garnett)   3:189
"Purple Blooms" (Shields)   113:426
The Purple Decades (Wolfe)   35:464-66
Purple Dust (O'Casey)   5:318, 320; 9:407; 11:408-10; 15:405; 88:270
Purple Gold Mountain (Ali)   69:32
"The Purple Hat" (Welty)   1:362; 14:563
"Purple Loosestrife" (Ferron)   94:120-21, 126
The Purple Plain (Bates)   46:59-61, 64-5

Purple Rain (Prince)   35:328-32
"The Purpose of the Moon" (Robbins)   32:370
"The Purpose of This Creature Man" (Abbott)   48:4-7
Purposes of Love (Renault)
    See *Promise of Love*
"Les Pur-Sang" (Cesaire)   19:98
"Purse" (Gilliatt)   53:145-46
A Purse of Coppers (O'Faolain)   1:259; 14:402; 32:340, 343; 70:317
"The Purse-Seine" (Blackburn)   9:100; 43:63
"The Pursuer" (Cortazar)
    See "El Perseguidor"
"Pursuit" (Plath)   111:165
"Pursuit" (Warren)   10:525
Pursuit (Morgan)   6:339-40
"The Pursuit of Gloom" (Willingham)   51:403
Pursuit of Happiness (Jones)   52:249
The Pursuit of Happiness (Rogers)   57:360-64, 366-67
Pursuit of Honor (Sissman)   9:491; 18:488
The Pursuit of Love (Mitford)   44:483, 485-87, 489-92
Pursuit of the Prodigal (Auchincloss)   9:54; 45:27
"A Pursuit Race" (Hemingway)   30:179
"La Push" (Hugo)   32:236
Push (Sapphire)   99:82-8
A Pushcart at the Curb (Dos Passos)   15:184; 25:142-43
Pushkin (Troyat)   23:457
Pushkin House (Bitov)
    See *Pushkinskii dom*
"Pushkin's Photograph (1799-2099)" (Bitov)   59:378
Pushkinskii dom (*Pushkin House*) (Bitov)   57:114-24
The Pussy (McClure)   6:317
"Pussywillows" (Lightfoot)   26:278
Put On by Cunning (Rendell)   28:387
Put Out More Flags (Waugh)   1:359; 3:513; 13:585; 44:522; 107:359, 362, 370-71, 385, 393
Put Out the Lights (Seifert)
    See *Zhasnete svetla*
"Put the Money Down" (Townshend)   17:534
"Put Your Head on My Shoulder" (Wilson)
    See "Don't Talk"
"Put Yourself in My Shoes" (Carver)   55:280
"Putamadre" (Dorfman)   77:141-42, 144
"Putney Garage" (Durcan)   70:151-52
"Puttermesser and Xanthippe" (Ozick)   28:349, 351; 62:350-51
"Puttermesser: Her Work History, Her Ancestry, Her Afterlife" (Ozick)   28:349
"Putting in the Person: Character and Abstraction in Current Writing and Painting" (Bradbury)   61:34
"Putting in the Seed" (Frost)   26:112
"Putting It All Away" (Dobyns)   37:76
"Putting It Together" (Sondheim)   39:174
"Putting to Sea" (Bogan)   46:84
"Putting Your Body to Sleep" (Dacey)   51:81
Puut, kaikki heidän vihreytensä (*The Trees, All Their Greenness*) (Haavikko)   18:205; 34:170
"Puzzle" (Parra)   102:350
"The Puzzle Factory" (Cassill)   4:95
The Puzzle of Hind Foot (Strugatskii and Strugatskii)   27:433
"The Puzzleheaded Girl" (Stead)   32:408; 80:305
The Puzzleheaded Girl (Stead)   2:422-23;

5:404; 32:408-09; 80:305, 323
"The Puzzling Nature of Blue" (Carey)   40:133; 96:25
"Pygmalion" (H. D.)   73:104
"Pygmalion" (Hope)
    See "The Invocation"
"Pygmy Twylyte" (Zappa)   17:591
Pylon (Faulkner)   3:153; 18:143; 28:140; 52:112
"The Pylons" (Spender)   41:418, 428
"pyramid" (Shange)   25:402
The Pyramid (Golding)   1:121-22; 2:168; 3:196, 198-200; 10:237; 17:172, 174, 176, 180; 27:161, 163; 81:315, 317-18, 322-23
"Pyramis; or, The House of Ascent" (Hope)   51:213, 215, 217, 221
"Pyrography" (Ashbery)   13:36; 15:30; 25:57; 77:46
"Pyrography" (White)   110:339, 343
"Pyrrhus et Cinéas" (Beauvoir)   31:40-1
Pythagoras (Abse)   29:17, 21-2
"Pythagoras in America" (Muldoon)   72:281
Pythagorean Silence (Howe)   72:195, 202, 207-08
"The Pythoness" (Raine)   45:333-34
The Pythoness and Other Poems (Raine)   45:331-32, 334, 340
The Pyx (Buell)   10:82
"Q" (Merrill)   8:385-86; 13:381
"Q & A" (Fearing)   51:106
al- Qahira al-jadida (*New Cairo*) (Mahfuz)   52:292-93, 300; 55:176
Qalb al-layl (*The Middle of the Night*) (Mahfuz)   55:175
Qasr al-Shawq (Mahfuz)   52:293, 300; 55:171, 174
QB VII (Uris)   32:432-34
"Qiana" (Dorris)   109:307
Quaderna (*Four Spot*) (Cabral de Melo Neto)   76:154, 158-59, 161, 168-69
Quaderno de quattro anni (*Depends: A Poet's Notebook*; *The Four Years' Notebook*) (Montale)   18:340
Quadrille (Coward)   29:136
Quadrille (Swinnerton)   31:427
Quadrophenia (Townshend)   17:532-40; 42:379
Quag Keep (Norton)   12:471
"The Quagga" (Enright)   31:154
"Quai d'Orléans" (Bishop)   32:42
Quail and Autumn (Mahfuz)
    See *al-Summan wa-al-kharif*
"Quail for Mr. Forester" (Humphrey)   45:193, 204
"A Quaint Disorder" (Scannell)   49:328
Quake (Wurlitzer)   2:484; 4:597-98; 15:588-89
"Quake Theory" (Olds)   32:346; 85:286
"The Quaker Graveyard at Nantucket (for Warren Winslow, Dead at Sea)" (Lowell)   1:183; 2:248; 4:302; 8:348, 350, 355, 358; 9:335-37; 37:234, 236
"Qualcosa era successo" ("Catastrophe") (Buzzati)   36:88, 92, 94, 96
The Quality of Hurt (Himes)   2:195-96; 4:229; 7:159; 18:248, 250; 58:263-65; 108:223, 228-29, 234, 241, 259-60
A Quality of Mercy (West)   96:368
Quand prime le spirituel (*When Things of the Spirit Come First: Five Early Tales*) (Beauvoir)   31:38-9, 42; 44:344-45; 71:84
Quand vient le souvenir (*When Memory Comes*) (Friedlander)   90:111, 114-16,118, 121

Quantities (Howard)   7:168; 10:276; 47:167-68
"Il quarantotto" (Sciascia)   8:474
The Quare Fellow (Behan)   1:26; 8:63-4; 11:44; 15:45; 79:24-7, 34-6, 40-3, 47-9, 52-5, 58
"The Quarrel" (Brodkey)   56:55-6, 63
"The Quarrel" (Buckler)   13:119
"Quarrel" (Voigt)   54:430
"A Quarreling Pair" (Bowles)   68:6-7
"The Quarry" (Clampitt)   32:115
"Quarry" (Honig)   33:212
"The Quarry" (Nemerov)   36:305
The Quarry (Durrenmatt)
    See *Der Verdacht*
The Quarry (Eberhart)   11:176
The Quarry Adventure (Kingman)   17:243-44
Quartermaine's Terms (Gray)   36:205-10
Quartet (Rhys)
    See *Postures*
Quartet in Autumn (Pym)   13:469-71; 19:389; 37:369, 372-73, 376-77; 111:225-29, 231-32, 234-36, 242-44, 248-53, 258, 263, 266-71, 273, 275, 278, 280-85, 287
"Quartet: Uncollected Stories, 1979-1981" (O'Brien)   36:340
"The Quartz-Stone" (Popa)   19:373
"Quasi una fantasia" (Montale)   18:339
Quatorze juillet (Clair)   20:61-2, 70
Quatrains (Rubailer) (Hikmet)   40:245
Les quatre cents coups (*The 400 Blows*) (Truffaut)   20:380, 382, 395, 399-400, 402-05, 407; 101:370, 373, 375, 379, 381-82, 384-91, 396, 398-400, 403, 405-08, 410-11, 413
Les quatre vérités (Ayme)   11:23
"89 et nous les noirs" (Damas)   84:181
Le quatrième siècle (Glissant)   10:231; 68:172-78, 180-81, 183, 187-89
"Que así invade" (Aleixandre)   9:12
"Que cante quetzal" (Allen)   84:10
"Qué color" (Guillen)   48:163-64
"Lo que el difunto dijo de sí mismo" (Parra)   102:340
Qué He Hecho Yo para Merecer Ésto? (What Have I Done to Deserve This?) (Almodovar)   114:4, 6-7, 9, 11-13, 18-9, 23-8, 35, 39, 45-6, 49-53, 55
"A què lado de la cortina?" ("On Which Side of the Curtain?") (Alegria)   57:11-12
Que ma joie demeure (Giono)   4:184; 11:234
"Que m'accompagnent Kôras et Balafong" ("Let Koras and Balafong Accompany Me") (Senghor)   54:390, 395-98, 407, 409
"Lo que no se marchita" (Rodriguez)   10:440
"Que siga el son" (Guillen)   79:244
Que trate de España (Otero)   11:425
"Quebec Night" (Gustafson)   36:212
"The Queen" (Chappell)   40:146
"Queen" (De Marinis)   54:101
The Queen (Maysles and Maysles)   16:440
Queen After Death (Montherlant)
    See *Le reine morte*
The Queen against Defoe, and Other Stories (Heym)   41:216-17
"Queen Bee" (Ihimaera)   46:199-200
"Queen Bitch" (Bowie)   17:58, 64
Queen Christina (Mamoulian)   16:420-21, 423-24, 428
"The Queen Doll" (Fuentes)
    See "La muñeca reina"
The Queen Elizabeth Story (Sutcliff)   26:427-

28, 432-33, 435, 439
"Queen for a Day" (Banks)   72:5
"Queen Jane Approximately" (Dylan)   77:174
The Queen of a Distant Country (Braine)   3:86; 41:58
"The Queen of Air and Darkness" (Anderson)   15:12
The Queen of Air and Darkness (White)   30:445-46
The Queen of Drum (Lewis)   27:265
"The Queen of Egypt" (Schaeffer)   22:369
The Queen of Egypt (Schaeffer)   22:368-70
Queen of Greece (Tavel)   6:529
"The Queen of Lop" (Johnston)   51:239, 244
"Queen of Scots" (MacCaig)   36:288
Queen of Stones (Tennant)   52:399-401
Queen of Swords (Kotzwinkle)   35:258
The Queen of the Legion (Williamson)   29:461
"Queen of the Night" (Oates)   33:289
The Queen of What Ifs (Klein)   30:242-43
The Queen on Tour (Abell)   15:5
Queen Victoria (Streatfeild)   21:402
Queen Victoria's Revenge (Harrison)   42:202, 205
Queenie (Calisher)   2:96
"Queenie Fat and Thin" (Brooke-Rose)   40:106
"Queenie White" (Bates)   46:63
"Queens and Duchesses" (Johnston)   51:244
The Queen's Gambit (Tevis)   42:374-76
The Queens of France (Wilder)   15:574; 82:345, 362
The Queens of the Hive (Sitwell)   67:325-28
"Queens of the Universe" (Sanchez)   116:300
"The Queen's Red Race" (Asimov)   76:320
Queer (Burroughs)   42:77-8, 80-1; 109:221, 229
"A Queer Heart" (Bowen)   22:63
"A Queer Job" (Oe)
   See "Kimyona shigoto"
"A Queer Streak" (Munro)   50:210, 214-16, 218-19
"Quel histoire" (Grigson)   7:137
Quel petit vélo à guidon chromé au fond de la cour? (Perec)   56:257-58; 116:232
Quelqu'un (Pinget)   13:442
Quer pasticciacco brutto de via Merulana (Gadda)   11:209, 216
Querelle de Brest (Querelle of Brest) (Genet)   5:137-39; 44:386, 388, 390; 46:173,176-77
Querelle of Brest (Genet)
   See Querelle de Brest
Queremos tanto a Glenda (Glenda; We Love Glenda So Much, and Other Tales) (Cortazar)   33:125-39; 34:329, 334
"Queridinha da familia" ("The Family Sweetheart") (Dourado)   60:85
"The Query" (Allen)   52:42
"Query, Not to Be Answered" (Oates)   33:294
"The Quest" (Auden)   9:59
"The Quest" (Olds)   85:295-97
"The Quest" (Wright)   10:544
Quest Crosstime (Norton)   12:457, 471
Quest for an Island (Aksyonov)   101:41-2
"The Quest for Blank Claveringi" (Highsmith)   102:205
The Quest for Christa T. (Wolf)
   See Nachdenken über Christa T.
Quest for Food (Cousteau)   30:105-06
"The Quest for the South Land" (McAuley)   45:251
"The Quest of Erebor" (Tolkien)   38:431
The Quest of the Gole (Hollander)   5:185

"The Quest of the Opal" (Cunningham)   31:99-102, 106
The Quest of the Silver Fleece (Du Bois)   1:80; 13:182; 64:110, 114, 117-18; 96:133, 137
"Qu'est-ce que la critique?" ("What Is Criticism?") (Barthes)   24:26; 83:88, 100
Qu'est-ce que la littérature? (Literature and Existentialism; What Is Literature?) (Sartre)   13:502; 18:467; 24:407, 410-12, 415, 417-21; 44:494-96; 50:380; 52:373
"Question" (Creeley)   78:142
"The Question" (Rukeyser)   27:410
"Question" (Swenson)   106:346, 350
"Question at Cliff-Thrust" (Warren)   39:270
"A Question for the Frankfurt School" (Padilla)   38:352
A Question of Attribution (Bennett)   77:95, 97-8, 100, 103-04
"A Question of Climate" (Lorde)   71:256
"A Question of Essence" (Lorde)   71:260
Question of Loyalty (Freeling)
   See Gun before Butter
"A Question of Manners" (Hall)   51:172
The Question of Max (Heilbrun)   25:254, 257
"The Question of Poetic Form" (Carruth)   84:117
A Question of Power (Head)   25:233, 235-38; 67:92-7, 99-100, 102-04, 109, 111
A Question of Proof (Day Lewis)   6:129
A Question of Reality (Unreality) (Brandys)   62:111-12, 119-20
"A Question of Re-Entry" (Ballard)   36:37
A Question of Upbringing (Powell)   3:400, 402-03; 7:338, 340, 342; 9:435; 10:409, 412-14, 416, 418; 31:317, 319-20
"The Question Party" (Barthelme)   115:65
Questioned (Grass)   15:259
The Questioning of Nick (Kopit)   33:248-49
"The Questionnaire" (Snodgrass)   6:514
"The Questions" (Pinsky)   38:363; 94:298
The Questions (Hawkes)   4:213, 215
"Questions about a Spaniel of Eleven" (Dickey)   28:117
Questions de méthode (Search for a Method) (Sartre)   18:473; 24:407; 52:380-81, 386
"Questions for the Heart of Darkness" (Sapphire)   99:81
Questions of Literature and Aesthetics (Bakhtin)   83:2
"Questions of Method" (Foucault)   69:190
"Questions of Travel" (Bishop)   13:93-4; 15:59; 32:32, 36, 41
Questions of Travel (Bishop)   9:90; 13:89, 91-3; 32:38-42
Questions Put to Myself (Szymborska)   99:194, 199, 207, 211
"Questions to Tourists Stopped by a Pineapple Field" (Merwin)   45:274
"Questions You Might Ask" (Oliver)   98:294
La quête de l'ourse (Theriault)   79:410-11, 414, 416
La quête intermittent (The Intermittent Quest) (Ionesco)   86:332, 337-38
"Quetzalcóatl" (Cernuda)   54:48
Quetzalcoatl (Lopez Portillo)   46:235-37
The Queue   59:369
"Quevedo" (Borges)   83:162
Qui a ramené Doruntine? (Kadare)   52:261
Qui je fus (What I Was) (Michaux)   19:311-12, 315
Quia pawper amavi (Pound)   4:408
Quick as Dandelions (L'Heureux)   52:271-74
A Quick Graph: Collected Notes and Essays

(Creeley)   78:119-20, 145
"A Quick One While He's Away" (Townshend)   17:524-25, 529-31
The Quick Red Fox (MacDonald)   27:275; 44:409
"The Quickening of St. John Baptist" (Merton)   83:391
"Quicker with Arrows" (Santos)   22:365
"The Quickest Way Out of Manchester" (Wain)   46:411
"Quicksand" (Wiggins)   57:435-36
Quicksand (Larsen)   37:209-11, 213-16, 218
The Quicksilver Pool (Whitney)   42:431
Quién matú a Palomino Molero? (Who Killed Palomino Molero) (Vargas Llosa)   85:362, 365-66, 368-69, 391, 395
"The Quiet" (Berry)   4:59
Quiet Adventures (Lezama Lima)
   See Aventuras sigilosas
"A Quiet Afternoon at Home" (Van Duyn)   63:437
The Quiet American (Greene)   1:131-33; 3:208, 210, 212-14; 6:219; 18:194-95; 27:173-74, 176; 37:136-38; 70:289-92, 294, 296; 72:155-56, 173, 177
Quiet as a Nun (Fraser)   32:184-85; 107:34,51-52
Quiet Days in Clichy (Miller)   9:379; 84:255
"Quiet Desperation" (Simpson)   32:379
The Quiet Don (Sholokhov)
   See Tikhii Don
The Quiet Duel (Kurosawa)   16:403
"Quiet Girl" (Hughes)   35:214
Quiet in the Land (Chislett)   34:144-46
"Quiet Lies the Locust Tells" (Ellison)   42:131
A Quiet Life (Bainbridge)   8:37-8; 10:15-17; 62:30, 36
The Quiet Man (Ford)   16:307, 315, 317
"Quiet Places" (Sainte-Marie)   17:431
Quiet Places (Sainte-Marie)   17:431
A Quiet Storm (Robinson)   21:346
"Quiet Town" (Stafford)   29:381
"The Quiet Woman of Chancery Lane" (Redgrove)   41:359
"Quietness among Old Things"   75:61
Quiller (Cook)   58:151, 154, 157
"The Quince" (L'Heureux)   52:273
"The Quince Bush" (Ammons)   25:43
Quince Jam (Ferron)
   See La nuit
"De Quincey's Status in the History of Ideas, 1944" (Wellek)   28:446
"De Quincey's Three Opium Dream Sonnets on the Wordsworth Family" (Ewart)   46:154
The Quincunx (Palliser)   65:81-8
Quinn's Book (Kennedy)   53:197-201
"La quinque rue" (Blunden)   56:43
Quintana and Friends (Dunne)   28:128
Quintet (Altman)   16:43; 116:30, 59
Quintet (Vansittart)   42:395-96
"Quintets for Robert Morley" (Murray)   40:341
Quinx; or, The Ripper's Tale (Durrell)   41:135-39
"Quisiera estar solo en el sur" (Cernuda)   54:55
Quite Contrary: The Mary and Newt Story (Dixon)   52:97-8, 101
"A Quite Incredible Dance" (Kinsella)   27:238
"Quitting Time" (Lane)   25:285, 288
A Quiver Full of Arrows (Archer)   28:13-14
"Quixotic Expectation" (Salinas)   90:328
A Quizaine for the Yule (Pound)   112:331
Quo vadimus? or, The Case for the Bicycle

(White)   10:527, 529; 39:377
Quoat-Quoat (Audiberti)   38:22-5, 27-30
"Quod tegit omnia" (Winters)   32:468
Quodlibet (Handke)   8:262; 15:267-68
Quoi? L'éternité (What? Eternity) (Yourcenar)   87:382, 396, 405, 411-12, 417, 433
Quoof (Muldoon)   32:321-22; 72:270, 272-74, 276, 282
"Quotations" (Sandburg)   35:356
Quotations from Chairman Mao Tse-Tung (Albee)   113:8-9, 15, 22-3
Quotations from Other Lives (Gilliatt)   53:144-45
Qyteti i jugut (The Southern City) (Kadare)   52:258-59
"R" (Merrill)   8:383, 385-86
R. Crumb and His Cheap Suit Serenaders (Crumb)   17:85
R. Crumb's Big Yum Yum Book (Crumb)   17:83, 86
The R Document (Wallace)   7:510
R Is for Rocket (Bradbury)   42:46
"R. S. I." (Lacan)   75:287
The Ra Expeditions (Heyerdahl)   26:192-93
"The Rabbi" (Hayden)   37:160
The Rabbi of Lud (Elkin)   51:96-8; 91:213, 224
"La rabbia" (Pasolini)   106:265
"The Rabbi's Daughter" (Calisher)   38:71
"The Rabbit" (Barnes)   3:37; 29:27
Rabbit at Rest (Updike)   70:248-65
"The Rabbit Catcher" (Plath)   51:340; 111:204
"The Rabbit Fights for His Life the Leopard Eats Lunch" (Williams)   33:443
"Rabbit in the Moon" (Swan)   69:363-64
Rabbit Is Rich (Updike)   23:467-72, 477; 43:432-34; 70:248-53, 255, 260
"Rabbit Man" (Sapphire)   99:81
The Rabbit Race (Walser)
   See *Eiche und Angora*
Rabbit Redux (Updike)   1:345-46; 2:442-45; 3:486; 5:451, 453-54, 456, 458, 460; 7:485, 487-89; 9:538-39, 541; 13:558-59, 563; 15:540-43; 23:466-71, 477; 43:430-31; 70:248-53, 257, 259-60, 263
Rabbit, Run (Updike)   1:344-46; 2:439-44; 3:485-86, 488; 5:450-51, 453, 457-58; 7:485-86, 488-89; 9:537, 539, 541; 13:562; 15:540-42; 23:463, 456-70, 473, 477; 34:284, 291; 70:248-49, 252-53, 257, 260-61
"The Rabbit-Hunter" (Frost)   26:128
Rabbits and Boa Constrictors (Iskander)
   See *Kroliki i udavy*
Rabbits and Redcoats (Peck)   17:340
"The Rabbits Who Caused All the Trouble" (Thurber)   11:533
Rabelais and His World (Bakhtin)
   See *Tvorcestva Fransua Rable i narodnaja kul'tura srednevekov'ja i Renessansa*
Rabindranath Tagore (Ray)   16:491
"Raby Head" (Everson)   27:135
I racconti (Calvino)   5:97; 11:90; 39:314
I racconti di Canterbury (The Canterbury Tales) (Pasolini)   20:266; 106:226, 266
I racconti Romani (Roman Tales) (Moravia)   2:293; 7:240; 18:343
Racconto d'autunno (Landolfi)   2:293; 49:216
"Raccoon" (Selzer)   74:260
"The Race" (Bates)   46:62
"The Race" (Bukowski)   41:66
"The Race" (Olds)   85:306
"The Race" (Tomlinson)   45:394

Race: A Study in Modern Superstition (Barzun)   51:32-3
Race and Class   70:370
"Race at Morning" (Faulkner)   18:149
Race des hommes (Audiberti)   38:21
Race et histoire (Levi-Strauss)   38:294
"The Race of the Flood" (Williams)   33:445
"Race Problems and Modern Society" (Toomer)   22:424
Race Rock (Matthiessen)   7:212; 32:285; 64:309, 327
'Race,' Writing and Difference   65:380
The Rachel Papers (Amis)   4:19-21; 9:25; 38:11-12; 62:5, 9, 11-12, 17; 101:59, 61-63, 65-67, 69, 84, 86, 89, 92
"Racial Musings" (Christie)   110:127
Les racines du ciel (The Roots of Heaven) (Gary)   25:183-84, 186, 189
"Racing in the Street" (Springsteen)   17:483-86, 490
"Racing with Utopias" (Grass)   49:137
Racism 101 (Giovanni)   117:200
"Racism: The Continuing Saga of the American Dream" (Giovanni)   117:192
The Rack (Serling)   30:353
Racketeers in the Sky (Williamson)   29:455
"Rada" (Arghezi)   80:9
"Radar" (Bagryana)   10:13
"Radar" (Spicer)   72:361-63
Radcliffe (Storey)   2:425; 4:528; 8:505
"The Radiance" (Rosenthal)   28:394
The Radiant Future (Zinoviev)   19:488-90
Radiant Mutations (Tzara)
   See "Les mutations radieuses"
The Radiant Way (Drabble)   53:123-29
"Radiare" (Moure)   88:229
"Radical Chic" (Wolfe)   15:584; 35:454-57, 463-64
Radical Chic and Mau-Mauing the Flak Catchers (Wolfe)   2:481; 15:586; 35:454, 465; 51:422
"A Radical Departure" (Tate)   25:428
"Radical Departures" (Moss)   50:353
Radical Poems, 1932-1938 (Klein)   19:260
"Radio" (Bagryana)   10:13
"The Radio" (Levine)   33:275
"Radio I" (Beckett)   9:84
"Radio II" (Beckett)   9:84
Radio Days (Keillor)   115:294
Radio Ethiopia (Smith)   12:538, 540
Radio Ethiopia (Smith)   12:538-39, 543
"The Radio in the Ivory Tower" (Pratt)   19:385
"Radio Jazz" (Bowering)   15:82
"Radio New France Radio" (Thesen)   56:415, 421
"Radio, Radio" (Costello)   21:71
"Radio Rick in Heaven and Radio Richard in Hell" (Foreman)   50:165, 167
"Radio Waves" (Carver)   53:61
"Radioactive Red Caps" (Hughes)   108:284
The Radish Memoirs (White)   49:406-07
Raditzer (Matthiessen)   32:286, 290; 64:309, 327
Radubis (Mahfuz)   52:292, 299
"Radwick: A Child's Scrapbook" (Brown)   100:81
"Rael" (Townshend)   17:525, 530
The Raffle (De Sica)   20:90
"The Raft" (King)   37:206-07; 61:331
The Raft (Clark)   38:113-15, 119-20, 122-23
"The Raft of the Medusa" (Dickey)   28:119
"Raftsman, Lumberjack" (Derleth)   31:136

Rag and Bone Shop (Birney)   4:64; 6:77-8
The Ragazzi (Pasolini)
   See *Ragazzi di vita*
Ragazzi di vita (The Ragazzi) (Pasolini)   37:341-43, 346-47; 106:211, 216-18, 231, 242, 251, 253-54, 271
"Rage" (Oliver)   98:259-60, 272, 293
Rage (King)   37:207; 61:331; 113:375-77, 388, 391
"The Rage for the Lost Penny" (Jarrell)   6:261
A Rage in Harlem (Himes)
   See *For Love of Imabelle*
Rage in Heaven (Isherwood)   44:397
The Rage of the Vulture (Unsworth)   76:252, 259
A Rage to Live (O'Hara)   2:324-25; 6:386; 42:313, 315, 317, 319
Raging Bull (Schrader)   26:396-98
Raging Bull (Scorsese)   20:334-36; 89:233-36, 240-43, 247-49, 252, 254, 260-66, 268
"Raging Canal" (Edmonds)   35:155
Ragioni d'una poesia (Ungaretti)   11:555
"The Ragman's Daughter" (Sillitoe)   57:393
The Ragman's Daughter, and Other Stories (Sillitoe)   57:388-89, 392
"Ragnarök" (Borges)   8:101
"Ragtime" (Nin)   60:267
Ragtime (Doctorow)   6:131-38; 11:140-45; 15:178; 18:120-27; 37:83-9, 91-4; 44:166-68, 170-72, 174-77, 179; 65:137, 145; 113:135-36, 144-48, 150, 152, 156, 158-60, 162, 166, 168-71, 176, 178, 180
Ragtime (Weller)   53:393
Rahel Varnhagen: The Life of a Jewish Woman (Arendt)   98:12, 53
"The Raid" (Steinbeck)   21:381
Raiders of the Lost Ark (Spielberg)   20:367
Raids and Reconstructions: Essays on Politics, Crime, and Culture (Enzensberger)   43:149-50
"The Rail" (Roth)   2:378
"Railroad Bill, a Conjure Man" (Reed)   5:368
"Railroad Bridge" (Ashbery)   77:63, 67
Railroad Earth (Kerouac)   3:265
"Railroad Sketches" (Dubus)   97:233
The Railroad Track Triangle (Grass)   15:259
"The Railway Children" (Heaney)   37:165; 74:190
The Railway Police and The Last Trolley Ride (Calisher)   38:71-2
"Rain" (Arghezi)
   See "Ploaie"
"The Rain" (Creeley)   8:151
"Rain" (Hogan)   73:158
"Rain" (Hughes)   37:175
"Rain" (Johnston)   51:250
"Rain" (Kenny)   87:246-47, 249
"Rain" (Lennon and McCartney)   35:274
"A Rain" (Mahapatra)   33:277
"Rain" (Maugham)   1:204; 15:369; 67:206; 93:249
"Rain" (Millhauser)   109:160
"Rain" (Oliver)   98:288
"Rain" (Soto)   80:287
Rain (Brink)
   See *Rumours of Rain*
Rain (Pa Chin)
   See *Yü*
Rain, and Other Fictions (Kenny)   87:247-49, 253
"Rain at Bellagio" (Clampitt)   32:116
"Rain Check" (Barthelme)   117:3, 18

"The Rain Child" (Laurence) 62:278
"Rain Dance" (Carroll) 38:103
"Rain Down Home" (Foote) 75:230-31, 253-57
"Rain Eyes" (Berry) 17:53
"The Rain Falling" (Mahapatra) 33:284
The Rain Forest (Manning) 5:273; 19:301
Rain from Heaven (Behrman) 40:77-80, 82, 88
"The Rain Glass" (Haines) 58:222
"The Rain Guitar" (Dickey) 15:177-78; 47:91, 93, 98
"Rain in Ohio" (Oliver) 34:247
"Rain in the Heart" (Taylor) 18:526; 44:305-06
The Rain in the Trees (Merwin) 88:197, 205-06, 208, 212
"Rain Moving In" (Ashbery) 41:35-6, 39
"A Rain of Rites" (Mahapatra) 33:282
A Rain of Rites (Mahapatra) 33:276-80, 282-83
"A Rain of Women" (Bukowski) 82:8
"Rain on Tanyard Hollow" (Stuart) 14:517
"Rain on the Battlefield" (Amichai)
See "Geshem bisdeh hakrav"
The Rain People (Coppola) 16:232-33, 235, 239, 244-45, 249
"The Rain Song" (Page and Plant) 12:476, 481
The Rain Stopped (Abell)
See Regnen holdt op
Rain upon Godshill (Priestley) 34:365
"Rain Your Love on Me" (Cryer) 21:79
The Rainbearers (Mosley) 43:311
The Rainbirds (Frame) 2:141; 6:189; 22:146; 96:170-72, 179-80, 182, 189-91, 196, 200, 203, 216-17
"The Rainbow" (Kinnell) 29:289
"Rainbow" (Plumly) 33:313
Rainbow (Ragni and Rado) 17:387-88
The Rainbow Grocery (Dickey) 28:119
Rainbow Jordan (Childress) 86:309; 96:108, 114-18
Rainbow on the Road (Forbes) 12:209-10
"The Rainbow Sign" (Kureishi) 64:247-48
The Rainbow Stories (Vollmann) 89:276, 278-83, 285-86, 291, 296-304, 306-07, 311, 313
"Rainbow Trout" (Lightfoot) 26:280-81
"Rainbow-Bird" (Wright) 53:423
Rainbow's End (Cain) 28:53-4
The Raining Tree War (Pownall) 10:418-19
"The Rainmaker" (Humphrey) 45:204
The Rainmaker (Ringwood)
See Hatfield, the Rainmaker
"Rains" (Perse)
See "Pluies"
"The Rainshore: Field, Rain, Heat" (Moure) 88:230
Rainsong (Whitney) 42:437
"Rainy" (Ritsos) 31:330
"Rainy Day in June" (Davies) 21:88
"Rainy Day People" (Lightfoot) 26:281
"Rainy Day Women #12 8 35" (Dylan) 77:168
Rainy Mountain (Momaday)
See The Way to Rainy Mountain
"Rainy Mountain Cemetery" (Momaday) 85:248, 266, 278
"Rainy Season: Sub-Tropics" (Bishop) 32:31, 35-6, 42
"Raise High the Roofbeam, Carpenters" ("Carpenters"; "Hoist High the Roof Beam, Carpenters"; "Roof Beam") (Salinger)

1:299; 3:444, 446; 8:463; 12:499, 503, 513, 518, 521
Raise High the Roofbeam, Carpenters and Seymour: An Introduction (Seymour: An Introduction) (Salinger) 1:299; 12:518
Raise, Race, Rays, Raze: Essays since 1965 (Baraka) 14:48; 33:56
"Raised on Robbery" (Mitchell) 12:442
A Raisin in the Sun (Hansberry) 17:182-85, 187-92; 62:211-12, 214-21, 223-30, 232, 236-43, 247
Raising Arizona (The Coen Brothers) 108:129-33, 135-44, 146-47, 149, 151, 156-57, 159-62, 165-66, 168-72, 175
Raising Demons (Jackson) 60:211-12, 216, 228-29, 233-34
"The Raising of Elvira Tremlett" (Trevor) 71:336, 350; 116:377, 385
"Raising the Demon" (Kaplan)
See "Elisabetta, Carlotta, Catherine"
"Raising the Flag" (Vizenor) 103:281
Raising the Moon Vines (Vizenor) 103:296, 308
The Raj Quartet (The Day of the Scorpion; A Division of the Spoils; The Jewel in the Crown; The Towers of Silence) (Scott) 9:477-78; 60:329-51
"Raj teologów" (Herbert) 43:186-87
The Rake's Progress (Auden) 43:26
Rakovyi korpus (The Cancer Ward) (Solzhenitsyn) 1:319-21; 2:407-08; 4:507-10, 512, 515; 7:432, 434, 436, 442-45; 10:480; 18:495, 497-98; 26:419; 34:485, 492; 78:381-83, 393-94, 396, 398, 409, 411, 420, 424
"Raleigh Was Right" (Williams) 67:408
Ralentir travaux (Breton) 54:32
Ralentir travaux (Char) 9:165; 55:286
Ralph and Tony (Forster) 22:136-37; 45:131-32
"Ram" (Clarke) 61:79-80
Ram (McCartney) 12:366, 371-72; 35:279-80, 283, 289
"The Ram beneath the Barn" (Davison) 28:104
"The Ram in the Thicket" (Morris) 37:310
"Ramblin' Gamblin' Man" (Seger) 35:380, 384, 386
Ramblin' Gamblin' Man (Seger) 35:378
Rambling Rose (Willingham) 5:511-12; 51:409-10
"Rambling Round" (Guthrie) 35:190
"Ramifications" (Squires) 51:379, 382
Ramona and the White Slaves (Walker) 61:424, 426-27, 432
Rancho Deluxe (McGuane) 45:261-62
Rancho Notorious (Lang) 20:216; 103:89
"Randal" (Nye) 42:309
Randall and the River of Time (Forester) 35:172
"Randall Jarrell" (Lowell) 3:302
Randall Jarrell's Letters: An Autobiographical and Literary Selection (Jarrell) 49:197-201
"Randall, My Son" (Davidson) 13:170
"Randevu" (Aksyonov)
See "Rendezvous"
Random Descent (Govier) 51:163-64, 166
"R-and-R" (Enright) 8:204
Raney (Edgerton) 39:52-4
"Range" (Ammons) 25:45
"The Range in the Desert" (Jarrell) 9:299
Rangoon (Barthelme) 36:49
Rani jadi (Chagrins précoces) (Kis) 57:245-

47
Rannie zhuravli (The Cranes Fly Early; The Early Cranes) (Aitmatov) 71:5, 7, 10-15, 32-3
Ransom (Duncan) 26:101
Ransom (McInerney) 112:180-82, 184, 203-04, 207-08, 212
"A Rant" (O'Hara) 78:351
A Rap on Race (Baldwin) 90:30
A Rap on Race (Mead) 37:277-79
"Rape" (Andrade)
See "Rapta"
"Rape" (Rich) 3:427, 429; 7:367, 370, 373
Rape (Lennon) 35:267
"Rape Fantasies" (Atwood) 25:61
"Rape is Not a Poem" (Jordan) 114:146, 148
The Rape of Clarissa: Writing, Sexuality and Class Struggle in Samuel Richardson (Eagleton) 63:97, 104
"The Rape of Persephone" (Dybek) 114:61, 63, 66
"The Rape of Philomel" (Shapiro) 8:486
The Rape of Shavi (Emecheta) 48:99-100
The Rape of Tamar (Jacobson) 4:254-56
"The Rape of the Drape" (Perelman) 49:272
"Rape Poem" (Piercy) 62:379
"Rape, Racism and the Myth of the Black Rapist" (Davis) 77:124
"Rapids" (Ammons) 25:45; 108:56
"The Rapids" (Barnard) 48:25
"Rappel" (Damas) 84:173, 176
"Rapport" (Colter) 58:147
"Rapta" ("Rape") (Andrade) 18:4
"Rapture" (Johnston) 51:239
"Rapunzel" (Sexton) 53:321
"Rapunzel" (Thomas) 13:540; 37:417; 107:316, 318, 320, 335
"Rapunzel, Rapunzel" (Chester) 49:56
Rare Angel (McClure) 6:319-21; 10:333
"Rascacielos" (Guillen) 11:262
The Rascals from Haskell's Gym (Bonham) 12:55
"Rascasse" (Van Duyn) 116:417, 422
Rashomon (Kurosawa) 16:394-402, 404
"Raspberry Beret" (Prince) 35:332
The Raspberry Picker (Hochwalder)
See Der Himbeerpflücker
"Rassvet" (Pasternak) 18:389
Rastaman Vibration (Marley) 17:268-72
"the rat" (Bukowski) 108:75
"The Rat" (McFadden) 48:258
The Rat (Grass)
See Die Rättin
"A Rat and Some Renovations" (Mac Laverty) 31:254
Rat Jelly (Ondaatje) 29:341; 51:310-12, 315-17
Rat Man of Paris (West) 96:362, 365, 368-69, 377, 382, 385, 390, 393, 399-400
"Rat Race" (Marley) 17:268-69, 272
Rat Race (Francis) 2:142; 22:151-52; 42:148-50; 102:131
Las ratas (Delibes) 18:110
"Ratatouille" (Dunn) 40:169
Rates of Exchange (Bradbury) 32:56-8; 61:39-41, 43, 45
"Rat-Faced Auntie" (Hannah) 90:159
"A Rather Dull Introduction" (Pound) 48:288
"Rather Like a Dream" (Warren) 18:536
"Rational Man" (Rukeyser) 27:411
Ratner's Star (DeLillo) 8:171-72; 10:134-35; 13:175-76, 178; 27:78-80, 82-3, 85; 39:116-17, 119; 54:81-2; 76:171, 180,

182
"Rats" (Hoffman)   6:243-44
"The Rats" (Levine)   4:287
The Rats (Sillitoe)   1:307
"The Rats and Cats in the House of Culture" (Singh)   11:504
Rats and Mice: Friends and Foes of Man (Silverstein and Silverstein)   17:452
"Rat's Eye" (Hall)   51:170
A Rat's Mass (Kennedy)   66:208-09
"The Rats on the Waterfront" (Mitchell)   98:161, 167, 182
Die Rättin (*The Rat*) (Grass)   49:140-44
"Rattlesnake" (Wild)   14:580
"Rattlesnake Country" (Warren)   8:537; 10:524; 39:264-65
"Rattling Hail's Ceremonial" (Vizenor)   103:281
Ravages (Leduc)   22:262
"The Ravages of Spring" (Gardner)   5:132; 7:111, 113, 116
"Raven" (Hoffman)   6:244
"The Raven" (Rich)   3:428
"Raven II" (Bowering)   32:47
"Ravenna" (Denby)   48:82
"Ravens" (Hughes)   37:175-76
"Ravens" (Jiles)   58:279, 281
Raven's Cry (Harris)   12:262, 264, 267
"Raven's Wing" (Oates)   52:331-32
Raven's Wing (Oates)   52:331-32
Ravensgill (Mayne)   12:394-95, 397-98, 402-03
Ravenswood (McNally)   4:347; 7:218
"Le ravin" (Bonnefoy)   58:53
"The Ravine" (Ai)   14:8
"The Ravine" (Carruth)   84:132, 135
"Raving and Drooling" (Pink Floyd)   35:311
A Raving Monarchist (Rathbone)   41:340
The Ravishing of Lol V. Stein (Duras)
    See *Le ravissement de Lol V. Stein*
Le ravissement de Lol V. Stein (*The Ravishing of Lol V. Stein*) (Duras)   40:178, 180; 68:73-4, 79, 81, 85, 87-9, 91, 93, 95, 99; 100:122, 130, 143
The Raw and the Cooked (Levi-Strauss)
    See *Le cru et le cuit*
Raw Heaven (Peacock)   60:292-94, 296-98
Raw Material (Sillitoe)   3:448; 6:500
"Rawhead Rex" (Barker)   52:53
The Rawhide Knot, and Other Stories (Richter)   30:328-29
Ray (Hannah)   23:210-13; 38:232-35; 90:127-30, 132, 134-37, 139-40, 144, 151, 160
"Raymond Bamber and Mrs. Fitch" (Trevor)   7:475; 71:334; 116:364
"Raymond of the Rooftops" (Durcan)   43:118
"Raymond's Run" (Bambara)   88:16, 18-19, 21, 39-40, 47, 49, 51
Rayuela (*Hopscotch*) (Cortazar)   2:102-05; 3:114-15; 5:110; 10:114, 118; 13:157, 164; 15:146-47; 33:123, 125-26, 128, 130, 136; 34:329-33; 136-74
"The Razor" (Shiga)   33:367
"The Razor Shell" (Watkins)   43:450
The Razor's Edge (Maugham)   1:204; 11:370; 15:367; 67:217, 219, 227, 229; 93:245
"Re" (Duncan)   7:88
"Re" (Tolson)   105:262
Re: Colonised Planet 5 (Lessing)   94:253
Re:Creation (Giovanni)   64:186, 188, 195; 117:183, 191-92, 195-97
Re Joyce (Burgess)
    See *Here Comes Everybody: An Introduc-

tion to James Joyce for the Ordinary Reader*
"The Reach" ("Do the Dead Sing?") (King)   37:207; 61:332-33
Reach for Tomorrow (Clarke)   18:106
Reach to the Stars (Willingham)   5:510; 51:403-04
"Re-Act for Action" (Madhubuti)   73:207
"The Reacting of Richard" (Updike)   9:539
Reactionary Essays on Poetry and Ideas (Tate)   11:527; 14:530; 24:439-40, 446
"Reactive Agent Tape Cut by Lee the Agent in Interzone" (Burroughs)   109:195
"Reader" (Dorfman)   77:141-43
Reader (Dorfman)   77:136, 139, 152
"The Reader over My Shoulder" (Graves)   45:167
Reader's nuestro que estás en la tierra: Ensayos sobre el imperialismo cultural(*The Empire's Old Clothes: What the Lone Ranger, Babar, and Other Innocent Heroes Do to Our Minds*) (Dorfman)   48:88-91, 93; 77:134-35, 143, 150-51
"Readiness" (Monette)   82:323
"Reading a View" (Malouf)   28:268
"Reading Aloud" (Gallagher)   63:124
"The Reading and Writing of Short Stories" (Welty)   105:327, 333
"Reading Apollinaire by the Rouge River" (Ferlinghetti)   111:59
Reading Capital (Althusser)
    See *Lire "Le Capital"*
"Reading Early Sorrow" (Williams)   56:428
Reading for the Plot: Design and Intention in Narrative (Brooks)   34:519-22
"A Reading Glass" (Sherwin)   7:415
Reading Henry James (Auchincloss)   9:53
"Reading Her Old Letter about a Wedding" (Raine)   103:179
"Reading Holderlin on the Patio with the Aid of a Dictionary" (Dove)   81:137
"Reading: I Dream My Schooling" (Acker)   111:14
"A Reading in Trollope" (Stewart)   32:421
"Reading Late at Night, Thermometer Falling" (Warren)   6:556-58; 39:260
"Reading Late in Winter" (Tillinghast)   29:414
"The Reading Lesson" (Murphy)   41:318
"Reading Miss Turgenev" (Trevor)   116:372
"Reading Myself" (Lowell)   8:355
Reading Myself and Others (Roth)   6:476; 22:357; 66:417, 420-21; 86:263
"Reading Nietzsche" (Moure)   88:218
"A Reading of Rex Stout" (Van Duyn)   63:442; 116:411
"The Reading of the Will" (Knowles)   26:258
"Reading Pascal in the Lowlands" (Dunn)   40:171
"Reading 'Pericles' in New London" (Corn)   33:117-18
"Reading Plato" (Graham)   48:149
"Reading Pornography in Old Age" (Nemerov)   36:309
"A Reading Problem" (Stafford)   68:423, 431
"Reading Robert Southey to My Daughter" (Nye)   42:305
"Reading the Books Our Children Have Written" (Smith)   42:346, 353
"Reading 'The Bostonians' in Algeciras Bay" (Fuller)   28:153
"Reading the River" (McPhee)   36:296
Reading the Signs (Wilding)   73:396-97, 399, 401, 403

"Reading the South African Landscape" (Coetzee)   66:99
Reading the Spirit (Eberhart)   11:178; 19:143; 56:425, 429
"Reading: The Subway" (Williams)   56:425, 429
"Reading to My Sick Daughter" (Buckley)   57:126, 130
Reading to You (Hustvedt)   76:58
"Reading Trip" (Kennedy)   8:320; 42:256
Reading Turgenev (Trevor)
    See *Two Lives: Reading Turgenev; My House in Umbria*
"The Reading Wars" (Birkerts)   116:166-67
"Reading, Writing, and the Rackets" (Fearing)   51:117-18
"Reading Your Poems in Your House While You Are Away (for Richard Shelton)" (Kizer)   80:183
"Readings" (Milosz)   56:237
Readings (Cixous)   92:95
"Readings, Forecasts, Personal Guidance" (Fearing)   51:109
"Readings of History" (Rich)   18:447
Reads (Brophy)   105:31
Ready or Not (Stolz)   12:546-47, 549
Ready to Wear (Altman)
    See *Prêt-à-Porter*
"Reaffirmation" (Lindbergh)   82:155-58
"Reagan, Begin, and God" (Blount)   38:47
"Reaganism: The Spirit of the Times" (Howe)   85:153
The Real Cool Killers (Himes)   58:265, 267, 269; 108:237-38, 242, 244, 246-47, 250, 267, 275
The Real David Copperfield (Graves)   6:211
Real Dreams (Griffiths)   52:185
"Real Estate" (Muske)   90:308
"Real Estate" (Waddington)   28:440
Real Estate (Hamburger)   14:234-35
Real Estate (Page)   40:352-55
"A Real Fright" (Betjeman)   34:309
"The Real Hero" (Amichai)   116:130
"The Real Hero of the Agedah" (Amichai)
    See "Hagibor ha'amiti shel ha'agedah"
"Real Impudence" (Calisher)   38:75
"The Real Inspector Hound" (Stoppard)   1:328; 3:470; 4:524-25, 527; 5:412; 8:504; 15:518-19, 522-24; 29:394, 397, 399-401; 34:275; 63:404, 91:187, 190
"A Real Life" (Munro)   95:320-21, 324
The Real Life of Alejandro Mayta (Vargas Llosa)
    See *La historia de Mayta*
The Real Life of Sebastian Knight (Nabokov)   1:240; 2:302, 304; 3:352; 6:352, 354; 8:412, 418; 11:393; 15:391; 46:292; 64:348, 366
"Real Life Writes Real Bad" (Findley)   102:110-11
Real Losses, Imaginary Gains (Morris)   7:247; 18:351
"The Real Magic Opera Begins" (Ferlinghetti)   111:65
"The Real Me" (Townshend)   17:532-33
"Real Mothers" (Thomas)   37:419-20, 422; 107:328
Real Mothers (Thomas)   37:418-20; 107:316, 326-28, 330, 332, 349
"Real People" (Grayson)   38:209
Real People (Lurie)   4:306; 5:259-60; 39:179
"Real People in a Real Place" (Smith)   64:400
Real Presence (Bausch)   51:51-4, 57
"The Real Revolution Is Love" (Harjo)   83:273,

282

The Real Russia (Prichard) **46**:337
"Real Situation" (Marley) **17**:273
The Real Story of Alejandro Mayta
  See *La historia de Mayta*
The Real Story of Alejandro Mayta (Vargas
  Llosa)
  See *La historia de Mayta*
"The Real Thing" (Stewart) **32**:421
The Real Thing (Lessing) **94**:265, 272-73,
  287
The Real Thing (Stoppard) **29**:402-06; **34**:273-
  82; **91**:187, 190
The Real Work: Interview and Talks, 1964-1979
  (Snyder) **32**:389-90, 393-94, 396, 399
The Real World (Aragon) **3**:13
"The Real World of Manuel Córdova" (Merwin)
  88:211
Realidad nacional desde la cama (*National
  Reality from the Bed*) (Valenzuela)
  104:389, 391
La realidad y el deseo (Cernuda) **54**:41-3, 46-
  52, 58-61
Realignment (Eshleman) **7**:99
Realism in Our Time (Lukacs) **24**:330
The Realists (Snow) **13**:514
"Réalité" ("Reality") (Damas) **84**:173, 176
"Realities" (MacLeish) **8**:359
"Realities" (Slessor) **14**:492
"Realities" (Williams) **42**:440
"Reality" (Damas)
  See "Réalité"
"Reality" (Dudek) **19**:137
"A Reality" (Ekelof) **27**:119
"Reality" (Pasolini) **106**:241, 250
"Reality Demands" (Szymborska) **99**:202
"Reality in America" (Trilling) **11**:541; **24**:460
Reality Sandwiches (Ginsberg) **6**:198; **13**:239;
  36:183, 185, 189, 195-96
"Realization" (Kunene) **85**:165
"Really, *Doesn't* Crime Pay?" (Walker)
  58:404; **103**:358-61, 372, 398-99, 406-
  07, 410
"Really Gone" (Redgrove) **41**:352
"The Really Practical People" (Snodgrass)
  6:514
The Really Short Poems of A.R. Ammons
  (Ammons) **108**:47, 61
"Realm" (Eberhart) **56**:77
The Realms of Gold (Drabble) **8**:183-85;
  10:162-65; **22**:127; **53**:118-20, 122
"The Reaper and the Flowers" (Stuart) **11**:512
The Rear Column (Gray) **14**:215; **36**:205-06
"Rear Window" (Woolrich) **77**:400-01
Rear Window (Hitchcock) **16**:340-41, 346,
  355, 358-59
"The Reardon Poems" (Blackburn) **43**:64
"Rearmament" (Jeffers) **3**:259
"Reason" (Asimov) **9**:51; **92**:4, 7, 9, 11, 21
"Reason" (McClure) **6**:318-19
"Reason" (Miles) **14**:369
Reason and Energy (Hamburger) **14**:233-34
*Reason and Violence: A Decade of Sartre's
  Philosophy* (Laing) **95**:123-25, 134, 140-
  42, 144, 171
"A Reason for Moving" (Strand) **18**:516
The Reason for the Pelican (Ciardi) **44**:378
Reason in Madness (Tate) **6**:527; **24**:440, 446
The Reason Why the Closet Man Is Never Sad
  (Edson) **13**:191
"A Reasonable Man" (Beattie) **13**:65; **63**:3, 9
"Reasonable People" (Fuentes) **113**:242-43
"Reasons for Attendance" (Larkin) **13**:336;

33:256; **64**:258, 277
Reasons for Moving (Strand) **18**:514-16, 518;
  41:436; **71**:278, 282-86
Reasons of State (Carpentier)
  See *El recurso del método*
Reasons of the Heart (Dahlberg) **7**:62
Reasons to Live (Hempel) **39**:67-70
"Reasons Why" (Hughes) **15**:295
"The Reassurance" (Gunn) **81**:179
"Reassurance" (Gurganus) **70**:190, 192, 195
The Reawakening (Levi)
  See *La tregua*
Rebecca (du Maurier) **6**:147; **11**:162-63;
  59:280-81, 283-87
Rebecca (Hitchcock) **16**:338, 343, 345, 357
The Rebecca Notebook and Other Memories
  (du Maurier) **59**:286
Rebecca West: A Celebration (West) **31**:458
Rebecca West: A Life (Glendinning) **50**:394-
  97, 399-401, 403, 405-10
The Rebel (Camus)
  See *L'homme révolté*
The Rebel Angels (Davies) **25**:132-35; **42**:106-
  07, 109; **75**:184-85, 187, 190-202, 204,
  206, 208, 211, 213, 215-16, 218, 223;
  91:201, 203-4
A Rebel in Time (Harrison) **42**:207
"Rebel Music" (Marley) **17**:267, 272
"Rebel, Rebel" (Bowie) **17**:62
"Rebel Waltz" (Clash) **30**:48
"Rebellion" (Campbell) **32**:74, 78, 80
"Rebellion" (Lowell) **8**:350; **11**:326
*The Rebellion of Young David, and Other Sto-
  ries* (Buckler) **13**:119
The Rebels (Jakes) **29**:248-49
Rebels of the Heavenly Kingdom (Paterson)
  30:287-88
"Rebirth" (Sanchez) **116**:280
Re-Birth (Wyndham) **19**:475
"Rebours" (Tchicaya) **101**:354
"Rebreaking Outlaw Horses in the Desert"
  (Hearne) **56**:127
Rebuilding Coventry **61**:417
*Rebuilding Russia: Reflections and Tentative
  Proposals* (Solzhenitsyn)
  See *Kak nam obustroit' Rossiiu?: Posil'nye
    soobrazheniia*
"Recalling Manolete" (Cabral de Melo Neto)
  See "Lembrando Manolete"
"Recalling War" (Graves) **39**:328; **45**:169
Recapitulation (Stegner) **49**:356-58, 361;
  81:350, 352
"Recapturing the Past in Fiction" (Settle)
  61:385-88
"Receipt" (Reading) **47**:352
A Recent Martyr (Martin) **89**:109, 111, 113,
  116-19, 123, 125-27, 129
"Recent Negro Fiction" (Ellison) **114**:107
Recent Trends in New Zealand Poetry (Baxter)
  14:60
"The Reception" (Jordan) **114**:145, 154
"Reception" (McCartney) **35**:286
Recessional (Michener) **109**:383, 386, 388-
  89
Recherche de la base et du sommet (*Search for
  the Base and the Summit*) (Char) **55**:289
Recherches dialectiques (Goldmann) **24**:239
Recherches pour une sémanalyse (Kristeva)
  See *Semeiotke: Recherches pour une
    sémanalyse*
"The Recital" (Ashbery) **2**:19; **15**:28; **25**:50;
  77:54
"A Recital for the Pope" (Stern) **39**:244

"Recitatif" (Morrison) **81**:266
"Recitative of Palinurus" (Ungaretti) **7**:481,
  485
Reckless (Lucas) **64**:290-96
Reckless Eyeballing (Reed) **60**:300-02, 304-
  06, 313
The Reckoning (Elman) **19**:149-50
The Reckoning (Jellicoe) **27**:210-11
A Reckoning (Sarton) **14**:482; **49**:315, 322;
  91:245-46, 251
The Reckoning (Ward) **19**:457
"The Recluse" (L'Heureux) **52**:274
"Recluse" (O Hehir) **41**:324
"The Recluse" (Singer) **69**:312
"Recognition" (Blunden) **56**:43
The Recognitions (Gaddis) **1**:113-14; **3**:177;
  6:193-95; **8**:227-30; **10**:209-14; **19**:185-
  90; **43**:156-63; **86**:147-49, 151-53, 156-
  57, 161-62, 164, 166, 168
Recoil (Thompson) **69**:386
Recollected Essays, 1965-1980 (Berry) **27**:37-
  9; **46**:75
"Recollection in Upper Ontario, from Long
  Before" (Warren) **39**:256, 272
"Recollection of Childhood" (Eberhart) **56**:86
Recollections of a Golden Triangle (Robbe-
  Grillet)
  See *Souvenirs du triangle d'or*
Recollections of Gran Apacheria (Dorn)
  10:159
"Recollections of the Works Department"
  (Hood) **28**:187
"The Recompense" (Tomlinson) **45**:400, 403
"Reconaissance" (Bontemps) **1**:38
Reconciliation (Shiga)
  See *Wakai*
"Reconsidering the Madman" (Hugo) **32**:241
"Reconstruction and Its Benefits" (Du Bois)
  64:107
Record of a Living Being (Kurosawa) **16**:399,
  401
"The Record of a Man" (Willingham) **51**:403
The Record of a Tenement Gentleman (Ozu)
  16:451
*A Record of Certain Episodes Made in the Town
  of Gogulev by Andrey Petrovich Kovyakin*
  (Leonov)
  See *Zapisi nekotorykh epizodov, sdelannye v
    gorode Goguleve Andreem Petrovichem
    Koviakinym*
"A Record of Longing for Mother" (Tanizaki)
  See "Haha no kouru ki"
"Records" (Giovanni) **19**:191; **64**:191
"Records" (Tate) **11**:525
"Recortes de prensa" ("Press Clippings")
  (Cortazar) **33**:126
"Recourse" (Gallagher) **63**:121, 124
"Recoveries" (Ammons) **57**:53
The Recoveries (Adamov)
  See *Les retrouvailles*
Recoveries (Jennings) **14**:291
Recovering: A Journal, 1978-1979 (Sarton)
  49:315, 317-18; **91**:251
"The Recovery" (Blunden) **56**:30
"The Recovery" (Dacey) **51**:79
"Recovery" (Milosz) **31**:268
"Recovery" (Scott) **22**:372
Recovery (Berryman) **3**:69, 71-2; **4**:63-4; **6**:63;
  13:83; **25**:95-7; **62**:45
"Recovery of Sexual Desire after a Bad Cold"
  (Chappell) **40**:147
"The Recruiting Officer" (McGahern) **48**:268
"Rectitude" (Ammons) **25**:42-3

The Rector of Justin (Auchincloss)   4:29-31; 9:52, 54; **18**:27; **45**:36-7

"Recuerdo" (Allen)   84:6-8, 40

"Recuerdos de juventud" (Parra)   102:338, 341

Recurrent Melody: Passcaglia (Pinget)
    See *Passacaille*

El recurso del método (Reasons of State) (Carpentier)   8:134-35; **11**:99-101, 107; **38**:101; **110**:57-9, 69, 91, 94-6

Recyclings (Kostelanetz)   28:216

"Red" (Maugham)   1:204; **15**:368

Red (Van Vechten)   33:387

"The Red and Green Beads" (Hill)   113:282, 312

The Red and the Green (Murdoch)   1:236; **3**:346-47; **4**:368; **6**:348; **22**:326-27; **51**:291

The Red and the White (Troyat)   23:459

"Red Angel Dragnet" (Clash)   30:50-2

Red Anger (Household)   11:277

Red Azalea (Min)   86:82-97

The Red Badge of Courage (Huston)   20:161, 163, 165

"The Red Balloon" (Abse)   29:16

Red Beard (Kurosawa)   16:402-03

The Red Book and the Great Wall (Moravia)   7:243

The Red Box (Stout)   3:471

Red Burning Light; or, Mission XQ3 (Fornes)   61:129, 131-32

"Red Buses" (Dunn)   40:168

The Red Cabbage Café (Treitel)   70:114-16

The Red Carnation (Vittorini)   6:551

A Red Carpet for the Sun (Layton)   15:320

"Red Chair" (De Marinis)   54:102

Red Chameleon (Kaminsky)   59:171

"The Red Coal" (Stern)   40:410

The Red Coal (Stern)   40:409-12; **100**:329, 333

"The Red Cockatoos" (Kelman)   58:298, 302

"The Red Cocoon" (Abe)
    See "Akai mayu"

Red Cross (Shepard)   4:489-90; **17**:434-36, 439, 448; **41**:409, 411

A Red Death (Mosley)   97:331-39, 344-45, 348, 352-53, 355

The Red Desert (Antonioni)
    See *Il deserto rosso*

The Red Devil Battery Sign (Williams)   11:576; **45**:455

"The Red Dog" (Jensen)   37:189

Red Dust (Levine)   4:286-87; **14**:317; **33**:270-71

"The Red Dwarf" (Tournier)   36:438-39

"The Red Flower Poems" (Zweig)   42:465

The Red Fox (Hyde)   42:225-28

"The Red Front" (Aragon)   22:34

The Red Gang of Asakusa (Kawabata)   9:311
    See *The Red Gang of Asakusa*

"The Red Girl" (Kincaid)   43:249

The Red Glove (Rozewicz)
    See *Czerwona rekawiczka*

Red Hart Magic (Norton)   12:471

Red Harvest (Amado)
    See *Seára vermelha*

Red Harvest (Hammett)   3:218-19; **19**:193, 195-97; **47**:156-58, 160-63

The Red Heart (Reaney)   13:473

"Red Hills" (Davies)   23:144

Red Is for Murder (Whitney)   42:431

The Red Kimono (Arzner)   98:87

"Red Leaves" (Faulkner)   8:212-13; **18**:147; **28**:143

"Red Maple Leaves" (Rexroth)   112:404

The Red Monarch (Krotkov)   19:264

"Red Money" (Bowie)   17:66

"The Red Mullet" (Warren)   39:267; **59**:295

"Red Music" (Skvorecky)   15:511; **69**:343

"Red Neck Friend" (Browne)   21:35

Red Noses (Red Noses, Black Death) (Barnes)   56:6-10

Red Noses, Black Death (Barnes)
    See *Red Noses*

"Red Pawn" (Rand)   79:374-75, 377-78

Red Planet: A Colonial Boy on Mars (Heinlein)   3:225; **14**:249; **26**:160, 163, 168, 171, 175-76; **55**:302

The Red Pony (Steinbeck)   1:324-25; **9**:515-18; **13**:529, 533; **21**:378, 386, 389; **34**:405, 409, 415; **45**:374; **59**:317

"The Red Poppy" (Gluck)   81:165, 169-70

Red Rebel: Tito of Yugloslavia (Archer)   12:16

Red Ribbon on a White Horse (Yezierska)   46:445, 447

Red River (Ford)   16:318

"Red Rose and a Beggar" (H. D.)   14:224

Red Rose Speedway (McCartney)   35:280-83

Red Roses for Bronze (H. D.)   31:208; **73**:113, 121, 139

Red Roses for Me (O'Casey)   5:318; **11**:407-10; **15**:404-05; **88**:257, 260, 262-70, 275-76, 280

"Red Runner" (Guthrie)   35:185

"Red Sails" (Bowie)   17:66

Red Sand (Stribling)   23:445

"Red Shift" (Ammons)   57:53

Red Shift (Garner)   17:145-47, 149-50

"The Red Shoes" (Sexton)   4:483

"Red Stamps with Lenin's Picture" (Kis)   57:251, 253-54

"Red Star, Winter Orbit" (Gibson)   63:130

Red Storm Rising (Clancy)   45:87-90; **112**:49-50, 52, 55-6, 62-3, 69, 74-7, 88, 90

"Red Termites" (Perelman)   49:257

"Red Trousseau" (Muske)   90:318

Red Trousseau (Muske)   90:318

Red Wagon (Berrigan)   37:44

The Red Wheel, Knot I: August 1914 (Solzhenitsyn)
    See *Avgust chetyrnadtsatogo*

"The Red Wheelbarrow" (Williams)   42:450, 457, 460

Red Wolves and Black Bears (Hoagland)   28:182

"Rede und Nachrede" (Bachmann)   69:56

"Rededication" (Cohen)   38:130

"Redeeming the Time" (Hill)   45:183, 186, 189

"Redemption" (Gardner)   28:162

"Redemption Song" (Marley)   17:273

"Redemption Songs" (Shacochis)   39:199-200

"Redeployment" (Nemerov)   36:304

"Redfish" (Bass)   79:5, 12

"The Red-Haired Miss Daintreys" (Lehmann)   5:240

Red-Headed Stranger (Nelson)   17:303-06

Redimiculum Matellarum (Bunting)   39:297; **47**:43

"Rediscovering Lost Values" (King)   83:340

"Rediscovery" (McGrath)   59:181

The Rediscovery of North America   70:344

"Redondo Beach" (Smith)   12:536, 539

"The Redress of Poetry" (Heaney)   74:189

The Redress of Poetry (Heaney)   91:124, 127-9

"Red-Tail Hawk and Pyre of Youth" (Warren)   13:581-82; **18**:534-36; **39**:266

"Redwing" (Gallagher)   63:125

"Redwing Blackbirds" (Warren)   39:262

"Red-Winged Blackbirds" (Cooper)   56:72

"Redwood Hill" (Lightfoot)   26:280

The Reed Cutter (Tanizaki)   8:510; **28**:414, 416, 418

A Reed in the Tide (Clark)   38:116-17, 125, 127-29

Reef (Gunesekera)   91:33-39

"Reeling Back the Saffron" (Fulton)   52:158

The Reeling Earth (Millin)   49:251

"Reeling in the Years" (Becker and Fagen)   26:79-80

"Reena" (Marshall)   27:312; **72**:222

"Reencounter" (Kawabata)
    See "Reencounter"

"Reference Back" (Larkin)   39:334; **64**:282

Refiner's Fire (Helprin)   10:260-62; **22**:223; **32**:229, 233

"The Refinery" (Pinsky)   94:305, 308-309

"The Reflecting Trees of Being and Not Being" (Rexroth)   112:373

"Reflection from Anita Loos" (Empson)   8:201

"Reflection in an Ironworks" (MacDiarmid)   63:255

"Reflections" (Carter)   5:101-03

"Reflections after a Poem" (McClure)   6:319

Reflections at Fifty (Farrell)   4:157; **66**:132

"Reflections before a Glass Cage" (Enzensberger)   43:149

Reflections from a Village (Swinnerton)   31:427-28

"Reflections from Glass Breaking" (Sapphire)   99:80

Reflections in a Golden Eye (Huston)   20:170

Reflections in a Golden Eye (McCullers)   1:208; **10**:338; **12**:409, 412-15, 417-18, 421-26; **48**:227-30, 240-41; **100**:246, 249, 251-52, 254, 256, 259, 261, 263

"Reflections in a Mirror" (Frye)   24:225

Reflections of a Jacobite (Auchincloss)   9:52; **45**:33

"Reflections of a Kept Ape" (McEwan)   66:280

"Reflections of a Middle-Aged Novelist" (Raven)   14:440

"Reflections of India" (Forster)   77:237, 239

Reflections of Nazism: An Essay of Kitsch and Death (Friedlander)
    See *Reflets du nazisme*

Reflections on a Marine Venus (Durrell)   8:193; **13**:188

"Reflections on Deafness" (Davie)   31:108-09

Reflections on Espionage: The Question of Cupcake (Hollander)   8:301-02; **14**:261, 264-65

"Reflections on Foreign Literature" (Enright)   8:203

"Reflections on History in Missouri" (Urdang)   47:400

"Reflections on My Life" (Lem)   40:300

"Reflections on My Own Name" (Porter)   33:318

"Reflections on My Profession" (Giovanni)   64:196

"Reflections on the Black Woman's Role in the Community of Slaves" (Davis)   77:122-23

Reflections on the Civil War (Catton)   35:95

"Reflections on the Composition of *Memoirs of Hadrian*" (Yourcenar)   87:394, 406-07, 411

Reflections on the Guillotine: An Essay on Capital Punishment (Camus)

See *Réflexions sur la peine capitale*
"Reflections on the Novel" (Anand)   93:52
Reflections on the Psalms (Lewis)   3:296
"Reflections on Two Decades" (MacLennan)   92:347
"Reflections outside a Gymnasium" (McGinley)   14:366
Reflections upon a Sinking Ship (Vidal)   8:528
"Reflective" (Ammons)   57:59
Reflets du nazisme (*Reflections of Nazism: An Essay of Kitsch and Death*) (Friedlander)   90:118-19
Reflex (Francis)   22:153-54; 42:150, 154-58; 102:144
Reflex and Bone Structure (Major)   19:294-96; 48:212-15
Réflexions sur la peine capitale (*Reflections on the Guillotine: An Essay on Capital Punishment*) (Camus)   4:89; 14:112, 117
"Reformers, Saints, and Preachers" (McGinley)   14:368
"Refrain" (Dove)   81:144
"The Refrigerator" (Moss)   14:376
"The Refuge of the Roads" (Mitchell)   12:442
Refugee (Anthony)   35:39-41
"Refugee in America" (Hughes)   1:149
"Refugee Mother and Child" (Achebe)   11:3; 26:21, 24
"The Refugees" (Read)   4:437, 439
"Refugees" (Tallent)   45:387
"A Refusal to Mourn" (Mahon)   27:290
"Refusal to Mourn the Death by Fire of a Child in London (Ammons)   108:21
"Refusing the Necessary" (Dobyns)   37:77
"O regaço urbanizado" ("The Urbanization of a Shelter") (Cabral de Melo Neto)   76:167
Regain (Giono)   4:186
Le Regard des femmes (Gallo)   95:100
Le regard du roi (Laye)   4:282-85; 38:285-86, 288-91
"Regarding Chainsaws" (Carruth)   84:132, 134-35
"Regarding Places" (Wilbur)   53:406
"Regarding Wave" (Snyder)   32:399
Regarding Wave (Snyder)   1:318; 2:406-07; 5:393, 395; 32:387-88, 391-92, 399
"The Regatta" (Wilbur)   53:400-01
"Regency Houses" (Day Lewis)   10:131
Regeneration (Barker)   94:4, 9-16, 18-19
"Regent's Park Sonnets" (Hacker)   72:182
"Regents' Professor Berryman's Crack on Race" (Berryman)   4:62
Reggatta de blanc (Police, The)   26:364
Un régicide (Robbe-Grillet)   43:361, 364-67
Regiment of Women (Berger)   3:63-4; 5:60; 18:57; 38:39
Regina (Epstein)   27:131-32
Regina V. Rumpole (Mortimer)   28:287
La región más transparente (*Where the Air Is Clear*) (Fuentes)   8:223-24; 13:232; 22:163-65; 41:166-67, 171-72; 60:153-54, 156-57, 163, 171-73; 113:230, 235, 238, 244-45, 248-51, 253
"Regionalism; or, Portrait of the Artist as a Model Farmer" (Montague)   46:266
La règle du jeu (*The Rules of the Game*) (Leiris)   61:341, 343-44, 347-60
La regle du jeu (*The Rules of the Game*) (Renoir)   20:287, 294-95, 297, 299, 302-12
Regnen holdt op (*The Rain Stopped*) (Abell)   15:5
"Regraduating the Lute" (Snodgrass)   68:397

"Regreso" ("Return") (Neruda)   62:335
"The Rehabilitation of Ginevra Leake" (Calisher)   38:69
Rehabilitations and Other Essays (Lewis)   27:265
The Rehearsal; or, The Punished Lover (Anouilh)
See *La répétition; ou, L'amoureux puni*
Rehearsals for Extinct Anatomies (The Brothers Quay)   95:345-48, 351, 353, 355
Rehearsals for Retirement (Ochs)   17:332
"Rehumanize Yourself" (Police, The)   26:365-66
"Reichs-Kommissar, 1915-1944" (Hall)   51:170
The Reign of Sparrows (Fuller)   28:156-57, 159
Reilly's Luck (L'Amour)   25:282
"Reincarnation I" (Dickey)   109:273
"Reincarnation II" (Dickey)   109:247, 273
La Reine des Pommes (Himes)   108:232, 241
Le reine morte (*Queen After Death*) (Montherlant)   8:393; 19:324, 327-28, 330
Reinhart in Love (Berger)   3:63; 5:60; 8:83; 18:53-4, 57; 38:36-8
Reinhart's Women (Berger)   38:36-8
El reino de este mundo (*The Kingdom of This World*) (Carpentier)   11:100-05, 107; 38:90-6, 98-9; 110:61, 63, 69, 75-80, 82
"Reino mosco" ("Mosquito Kingdom") (Cardenal)   31:77
"Re-Interments: Recollections of a Grandfather" (Warren)   39:265
Reinventing a Continent: Essays on South African Writing and Politics (Brink)   106:138
"Reinventing America" (Urdang)   47:399
Reinventing Womanhood (Heilbrun)   25:254-55
"Die Reisebergegnung" (Seghers)   7:409
The Reivers (Faulkner)   14:178; 28:140
La reivindicación del Conde Don Julián (*Count Julian; Don Julián*) (Goytisolo)   5:150-51; 10:245; 23:184, 186-87
"Rejoicing with Henry" (Kumin)   28:223
Rejoicings: Selected Poems, 1966-1972 (Stern)   40:408, 412-14; 100:329, 333
"Rejoinder to a Critic" (Davie)   10:125
"Relación del peregrino" (Castellanos)   66:50
"Related Histories" (Adams)   46:16-17
"The Relation of Environment & Anti-Environment" (McLuhan)   83:370
The Relation Of My Imprisonment (Banks)   37:27; 72:8
The Relation of the Alabama-Georgia Dialect to the Provincial Dialects of Great Britain (Brooks)   86:279
"Relations" (Allen)   84:3
"Relations" (Robison)   42:339
Relations (Slaughter)
See *The Story of the Weasel*
Relations and Contraries (Tomlinson)   4:543, 546; 13:546; 45:396, 404
Relationship (Mahapatra)   33:284
Relationships (Jennings)   14:292
"A Relative and an Abosolute" (Van Duyn)   116:406, 416
"A Relative Stranger" (Baxter)   78:25, 27
A Relative Stranger, and Other Stories (Baxter)   78:25-28, 30, 32
Relative Values (Coward)   29:136
Relatively Speaking (Ayckbourn)   5:35-6; 18:27-8; 33:40, 45, 47; 74:19, 30-4

Relatives (Plante)   7:307; 23:344
"Relativistic Effects" (Benford)   52:75-6
"Relativity" (Amichai)   57:38
"Relato con un fondo de agua" (Cortazar)   10:114
Relatos completos (Arguedas)   10:10
"Relearning the Alphabet" (Levertov)   5:249; 66:242, 244-45
Relearning the Alphabet (Levertov)   3:293; 5:248-49; 28:239, 241; 66:235-37, 239, 245, 251
"The Release" (Gregor)   9:254
"The Release" (MacLeish)   8:361
Release (Schevill)   7:400
"Release the Cranes" (Voznesensky)   57:429
"Releases" (Fisher)   25:161
Relentless as the Tarantula (Bukowski)   82:22
"Relevance of African Cosmological Systems to African Literature Today" (Kunene)   85:180
La relève du matin (Montherlant)   8:394
"Relic" (Butler)   81:122, 127, 129
"Relics" (Thomas)   107:333
"Relief" (Blaise)   29:70
"Relief" (Hughes)   35:222
"Relief" (Padilla)   38:349
"La religieuse qui retourna en Irlande" ("The Nun Who Returned to Ireland") (Carrier)   78:73, 78
"Religio Medici, 1643" (Borges)   6:90
Religion and Career (Greeley)   28:169
"Religion and Literature" (Brooks)   110:9
Religion and Literature (Endo)   99:285
"Religion and the Old South" (Tate)   4:537; 11:522; 24:440
Religion and the Rebel (Wilson)   14:587
"Religion and the Romantics" (Blunden)   56:49
Religion in the Year 2000 (Greeley)   28:171
"The Religion of My Time" (Pasolini)   106:239, 241, 253
La religione del mio tempo (Pasolini)   106:220, 263, 265
La religione del nostro tempo (Pasolini)   37:346
Religions East and West (Kettelkamp)   12:306
"Religions, Inc." (Bruce)   21:48, 53
"The Religious Button" (Brooke-Rose)   40:106
"The Religious Poet" (Merwin)   88:191
"The Reliquary" (Skelton)   13:507
"Relocation" (Ortiz)   45:303
"The Reluctant Poetess: Alicia Medina" (Kunene)   85:166
"The Reluctant Voyage" (Bullins)   7:37
Remain in Light (Byrne)   26:98-9
The Remainderman (White)   49:400
"The Remains" (Strand)   18:515, 518; 41:432; 71:285
Remains (Snodgrass)   6:514; 18:491, 494; 68:381-84, 388-90, 397
Remains of Elmet (Hughes)   14:273; 37:172-73, 175, 178
The Remains of the Day (Ishiguro)   59:158-64, 166-69; 110:227, 229-34, 238-40, 243-46, 252-54, 256-65
"Remake the World" (Cliff)   21:63
Re-Making Love (Ehrenreich)   110:159-64, 178
"A Remark on Dedication" (Ekelof)   27:119
The Remarkable Andrew (Trumbo)   19:445, 447
"The Remarkable Case of Mr. Bruhl" (Thurber)   5:438
"Remarks of Soul to Body" (Warren)   6:557;

10:522
"Remarks of the Scholar Graduate" (Mathews)
    52:313-14
"Remarks on Discourse Ethics" (Habermas)
    104:91
"Rembrandt" (Lowell)   5:256
"Rembrandt's Hat" (Malamud)   27:306
Rembrandt's Hat (Malamud)   3:323-25; 5:269;
    9:349; 18:318; 44:411, 413, 415
"Remedies, Maladies, and Reasons" (Van Duyn)
    63:438, 441; 116:408, 416, 424, 430
Remedy Is None (McIlvanney)   42:279-81
"Remember" (Lennon)   35:262
"Remember" (Rulfo)
    See "Acuérdate"
"Remember" (Stafford)   29:379
Remember Me (Tremblay)
    See *Les anciennes odeurs*
Remember Me (Weldon)   9:559-60; 11:565;
    19:467, 469; 36:446
Remember Ruben (Beti)   27:53
"Remember Thy Creator" (Simmons)   43:407
"Remember Young Cecil" (Kelman)   58:295
"A Remembered Beat" (Kaufman)   49:203
"Remembered Morning" (Lewis)   41:254
Remembering Babylon (Malouf)   86:195-211
"Remembering Christopher Smart" (Newlove)
    14:378
"Remembering Eliot" (Spender)   41:421
"Remembering Esquimalt" (Skelton)   13:507
"Remembering Hiroshima" (Purdy)   3:408;
    14:432; 50:246-47
Remembering Laughter (Stegner)   9:510;
    49:345-47; 81:344, 348-49
"Remembering Lunch" (Dunn)   40:169
"Remembering Malibu" (Heaney)   74:167
"Remembering Mykinai" (Corn)   33:117
"Remembering Needleman" (Allen)   52:40-2,
    49
"Remembering Poets" (Hall)   13:260
*Remembering Poets: Reminiscences and Opin-
    ions* (Hall)   37:143-45, 148; 59:157
"Remembering the Children of Auschwitz"
    (McGrath)   59:184
"Remembering the Movement" (Davie)
    10:124
"Remembering the Old Family Farmhouse"
    (Faludy)   42:142
"Remembering the Thirties" (Davie)   8:162;
    10:125; 31:109
"Remembering Williams" (Tomlinson)   4:548
"Remembrance" (Christie)   110:126
"Remembrance" (Enzensberger)   43:153
Remembrance (Walcott)   14:550-51; 25:454-
    55; 67:352; 76:275, 298
"Remembrance Day" (Achebe)   26:21
"Remembrance Day" (Johnston)   51:252
"Remembrance Day : 2010" (MacLennan)
    92:344
A Remembrance of Miracles (Ringwood)
    48:335, 338-39
"Remembrance of Things Past" (Ali)   69:31
Remembrance Rock (Sandburg)   10:448;
    15:467-68; 35:351, 354
"Reminders of Bouselham" (Bowles)   19:59
"Reminiscence of Carousels and Civil War"
    (Hirsch)   31:216
"Reminiscence of My Beloved Mother"
    (Tanizaki)
    See "Haha no kouru ki"
Reminiscences of the Cuban Revolutionary War
    (Guevara)
    See *Pasajes de la guerra revolucionaria*

"Reminiscences: Places and People" (Allen)
    52:42
"The Remission" (Gallant)   18:172
"Remittance Man" (Wright)   53.427
"Remnant Water" (Dickey)   47:92
"Remorse" (Betjeman)   43:34
"Remorse" (Merwin)   8:390
Remote (Shields)   97:430, 433-36
"Remote Control" (Clash)   30:44
Remote People (Waugh)   107:381
"Remous" (Montague)   46:269
"The Removal" (Merwin)   13:386
The Removalists (Williamson)   56:431-35,
    439-40, 442
"The Remove" (Ghose)   42:179
Remove Protective Coating a Little at a Time
    (Donovan)   35:141
Le rempart des béguines (Mallet-Joris)   11:355
"The Renaissance" (Pound)   112:316-17
Renaldo and Clara (Dylan)   12:197-98
Renaud et Armide (Cocteau)   8:149; 43:112
"Rendevous-Vous with my Son" (Aitmatov)
    71:16
"Rendezvous" ("Randevu") (Aksyonov)
    101:11, 22, 28, 30
"Rendezvous" (MacLean)   63:270
Le rendez-vous (Robbe-Grillet)
    See *Djinn*
The Rendez-Vous (Strugatskii and Strugatskii)
    27:433
The Rendezvous and Other Stories (du Maurier)
    59:286
Le rendez-vous de Senlis (Anouilh)   8:24; 13:16-
    17; 40:51, 54-5
Rendezvous in a Landscape (Derleth)   31:137
Rendezvous in Black (Woolrich)   77:400, 403
"Rendezvous with America" (Tolson)   36:424-
    25; 105:259-60, 288, 291-92
Rendezvous with America (Tolson)   424-25,
    427; 105:231, 236, 239, 258-61, 263,
    281-83, 285-86
Rendezvous with Rama (Clarke)   4:105; 13:150-
    51, 153-55; 18:106-07; 35:120, 123-24,
    127
"Renee" (Kelman)   58:300-01
"The Renegade" (Camus)
    See "Le renégat"
"Renegade" (Jackson)   60:211-12
The Renegade (Graham)   23:191
"Le renégat" ("The Renegade") (Camus)   4:92;
    9:146; 14:114
"The Renewal" (Roethke)   3:433; 19:396;
    101:265, 329
"Renewed Homage to Marianne Moore" (Cabral
    de Melo Neto)
    See "Homenagem renovada a Marianne
    Moore"
Renga (Paz)   10:390
Renga (Tomlinson)   4:547; 45:398
Renifleur's Daughter (Fraze)   50:43-4
"Renner" (Powers)   1:282
Renoir, My Father (Renoir)   20:305
"Renouncing Sexual 'Equality'" (Dworkin)
    43:132
Rent   99:160-90
"Rent Control" (Tevis)   42:372
Rent; or, Caught in the Act (Edgar)   42:116,
    123
"Rent-a-Womb" (Highsmith)   102:201
"The Renunciatory Beauty" (Gascoyne)   45:157
The Re-Ordering of the Stones (Silkin)   6:498;
    43:396-98, 400, 404
"Repeat" (Kunene)   85:178

"'Repent, Harlequin!' Said the Ticktockman"
    (Ellison)   42:131-32
"Repentance" (Behan)   79:36-8
"Repentance" (Clarke)   9:168
"Repentance" (Herbert)   24:253, 268, 276
"Repentance and Self-Limitation in the Life of
    Nations" (Solzhenitsyn)   78:385, 405-06
"Reperdiation of the *Trilogy of Life*" (Pasolini)
    106:268
Répertoire (Butor)   11:78; 15:119
Répertoire II (Butor)   11:78; 15:119
Répertoire III (Butor)   15:114, 119
Répertoire IV (Butor)   15:114, 119
La répétition; ou, L'amoureux puni (*The Re-
    hearsal; or, The Punished Lover*) (Anouilh)
    1:7; 13:17; 40:54-5; 50:279
"The Replica" (Watkins)   43:454
"The Reply" (Ginsberg)   36:182
"The Reply" (Ignatow)   40:259
"The Reply" (L'Heureux)   52:275
"Reply to Mr. Wordsworth" (MacLeish)   8:362
"Report" (Barthelme)   6:29; 8:50; 115:59
"A Report" (Jin)   109:54
"Report Cards" (Humphrey)   45:193
"Report for Northrop Frye" (Everson)   27:135
"Report from Normalia" (Hesse)   25:261
"Report from Paradise" (Herbert)   9:275;
    43:184
Report from Part One (Brooks)   2:81-2; 4:78-
    9
"Report from Starship 26" (Fowles)   87:
Report from the Aleutians (Huston)   20:164
"Report from the Besieged City" (Herbert)
    43:191-93, 195
*Report from the Besieged City and Other Po-
    ems* (Herbert)   43:191-92, 194-95
"Report from the Skull's Diorama"
    (Komunyakaa)   94:245
Report of the Country Chairman (Michener)
    109:375, 378-79, 383, 386
"Report on Experience" (Blunden)   56:30, 33,
    39, 49
*Report on Planet Three and Other Specula-
    tions* (Clarke)   35:119, 122
Report on Probability A (Aldiss)   14:10, 13;
    40:19-20
"Report on the Shadow Industry" (Carey)
    40:127; 96:28, 37, 53
"Report on the Threatened City" (Lessing)
    2:242; 10:316; 94:261
"A Report to an Academy" (Oates)   33:294
"Reportazh s otkrytiya GES" (Voznesensky)
    57:417
"Reports from the Global Village" (Eco)   60:112
*Reports on the Ideological Situation of the
    Nation* (Boell)
    See *Berichte zur Gesinnungslage der Nation*
"Representation and the War for Reality" (Gass)
    39:477, 479-81
The Representative (Hochhuth)   18:252
Representing Super Doll (Peck)   21:296
"Representing T. A. Buck" (Ferber)   93:139
"Repression" (Williams)   56:429
The Reprieve (Sartre)
    See *Le sursis*
"The Reproach" (Gluck)   44:218, 221
"Reproach" (Graves)   45:167
"Reproach to Dead Poets" (MacLeish)   68:273,
    287
*The Reproductive System: How Living Crea-
    tures Multiply* (Silverstein and Silverstein)
    17:453
"The Republic" (Ondaatje)   51:310

A Republic of Insects and Grass (Schell) **35**:366-67

The Republic of Love (Shields) **91**:168, 171; **113**:433, 441, 445

Repulsion (Polanski) **16**:463-65, 467, 471

"Requa" (Olsen) **114**:206-09, 223, 232

Request Concert (Kroetz)
See *Wunschkonzert*

"Request for Offering" (Eberhart) **56**:77

"Request to a Year" (Wright) **53**:420, 428

"Requiem" (Fearing) **51**:107

"Requiem" (Heinlein) **55**:302

"Requiem" (Ignatow) **40**:259

"Requiem" (Miller) **6**:334-35; **15**:372

Requiem (Akhmatova) **11**:8; **25**:25-8; **59**:384, 388, 391; **64**:6, 11-20

Requiem (Bagryana)
See *Vechnata i svjatata*

Requiem (Guillevic) **33**:194

Requiem (Warner) **14**:553

Requiem for a Futurologist (Soyinka) **44**:298

Requiem for a Heavyweight (Serling) **30**:354-55, 358

Requiem for a Nun (Camus)
See *Requiem pour une nonne*

Requiem for a Nun (Faulkner) **3**:151, 156; **6**:175-76, 180; **28**:140

Requiem for a Princess (Arthur) **12**:25-6, 28-9

Requiem for a Spanish Peasant (Sender)
See *Mosén Milán*

"Requiem for Aberfam" (Thomas) **13**:541

"The Requiem for Christine Latrobe" (Epstein) **7**:97

Requiem for Fanny Goldmann (Bachmann)
See *Requiem für Fanny Goldmann*

"Requiem for the Champ" (Jordan) **114**:151

"Requiem for the Croppies" (Heaney) **74**:155; **91**:117

"Requiem for the Spanish Dead" (Rexroth) **49**:284-85

Requiem für Fanny Goldmann (*Requiem for Fanny Goldmann*) (Bachmann) **69**:36, 59

Requiem por un campesino espanol (Sender)
See *Mosén Milán*

Requiem pour une nonne (*Requiem for a Nun*) (Camus) **9**:145; **14**:114; **32**:86, 88, 91, 96, 100

"Requiescat" (Hersey) **81**:329

"Requiescat" (Parker) **68**:325

Required Writing (Larkin) **33**:266-68; **39**:337, 341, 343; **64**:282, 284

"Reredos Showing the Assumption into Heaven of Frank O'Hara" (Feldman) **7**:102

"De rerum natura" **75**:62

"De rerum natura" (Boyle) **36**:58

"De rerum virtute" (Jeffers) **54**:244

Reruns (Baumbach) **6**:31-2

"Resaca" (Aleixandre) **9**:14

La resaca (Goytisolo) **23**:186

El rescate del mundo (Castellanos) **66**:45, 50

"The Rescue" (Goyen) **14**:211

"A Rescue" (Green) **97**:274-76

"The Rescue" (McGuane) **45**:266

Rescue (Milosz)
See *Ocalenie*

"Rescue Mission" (Kristofferson) **26**:268-69

The Rescue of Miss Yaskell and Other Pipe Dreams (Baker) **31**:31-2

"Rescue Party" (Clarke) **35**:127

"Rescue, Rescue" (Bell) **8**:66

"Rescue the Dead" (Ignatow) **4**:247; **7**:180;

14:274; **40**:258

Rescue the Dead (Ignatow) **4**:247-48; **7**:175, 180-81; **14**:276; **40**:258

"Rescue with Yul Brynner" (Moore) **47**:261, 263

The Rescued Year (Stafford) **4**:519-20; **7**:461-62; **29**:385

"Research in Jiangsu Province" (Seth) **43**:388

"The Research of Dancers" (Moss) **45**:286-87

Réseau aérien (Butor) **8**:118, 120

"The Resemblance between a Violin Case and a Coffin" (Williams) **5**:502; **39**:450; **45**:447, 452-53; **111**:423

"Resentment" (Aldington) **49**:7

The Reservation (Ruyslinck) **14**:471

Reservation Blues (Alexie) **96**:13, 15-17

"Reservation Drive-In" (Alexie) **96**:8

"The Reservoir" (Frame) **96**:184-85, 191

Reservoir Ravine (Hood) **28**:195-96

The Reservoir: Stories and Sketches (Frame) **22**:143; **96**:188-89, 192, 216

Residence on Earth (Neruda)
See *Residencia en la tierra*

Residence on Earth and Other Poems (Neruda)
See *Residencia en la tierra*

Residencia en la tierra (*Residence on Earth*; *Residence on Earth and Other Poems*; *Residencia en la tierra, Vol. 1, 1925-31*; *Residencia en la tierra, Vol. 2, 1931-35*; *Residencia I*; *Residencia II*; *Residencia III*) (Neruda) **1**:246; **2**:309; **5**:301, 303-05; **7**:257-60, 262; **9**:398; **28**:309, 311-13

Residencia en la tierra, Vol. 1, 1925-31 (Neruda)
See *Residencia en la tierra*

Residencia en la tierra, Vol. 2, 1931-35 (Neruda)
See *Residencia en la tierra*

Residencia I (Neruda)
See *Residencia en la tierra*

Residencia II (Neruda)
See *Residencia en la tierra*

Residencia III (Neruda)
See *Residencia en la tierra*

"Resident at the Club" (Motion) **47**:291, 294

Residential Quarter (Aragon)
See *Les beaux quartiers*

"Residents and Transients" (Mason) **82**:243

Residua (Beckett) **6**:36; **14**:80

The Residual Years: Poems, 1934-1948 (Everson) **1**:96; **14**:163

"Residue of Song" (Bell) **31**:48

Residue of Song (Bell) **8**:67; **31**:47-50

"Resign! Resign!" (Richards) **14**:455

Resignation; or, The Story of a Marriage (Hochhuth) **18**:253

"The Resistance" (Olson) **29**:329

Resistance (Archer) **12**:20

"The Resistance Cabaret" (Simmons) **43**:409

Resistance, Rebellion, and Death (Camus) **2**:97

The Resistance to Theory (de Man) **55**:403-05, 409-10

"Resisting Amnesia" (Rich) **73**:322

"Resolution of Dependence" (Barker) **48**:16, 20

Resonance and Foot-Tracks (Transtroemer)
See *Klanger och spår*

A Resounding Tinkle (Simpson) **29**:364-70

"Respectabilities" (Silkin) **43**:398, 400, 404

"Respected Graves" (Ignatow) **40**:259

Respected Sir (Mahfuz) **52**:305

The Respiratory System: How Creatures Breathe (Silverstein and Silverstein) **17**:451

"El resplandor del ser" ("The Splendor of Be-

ing") (Castellanos) **66**:45, 51, 60

"The Resplendent Quetzal" (Atwood) **13**:46; **25**:62

"Responding to Pain" (Govier) **51**:166

Résponses (Sagan) **17**:428-29

Responses (Wilbur) **14**:578

"Responsibilities of the Poet" (Pinsky) **94**:300-304, 312

"The Responsibility of Parentage" (Young) **82**:396

"Resposta a vinicius de moraes" (Cabral de Melo Neto) **76**:162

"The Rest" (Carver) **53**:61

Rest and Be Thankful (MacInnes) **27**:280

Rest beyond the Peaks (Bernhard)
See *Über allen Gipfeln ist Ruh: ein deutscher Dichtertag um 1980*

Rest Home (Cela)
See *Pabellón de reposo*

"Rest Hour" (Johnston) **51**:250

"The Rest House" (MacNeice) **10**:323

Rest in Pieces (Brown) **79**:171

The Rest of the Robots (Asimov) **26**:37, 42, 46-7, 53; **92**:5, 9, 13

Rest Pavillion (Cela)
See *Pabellón de reposo*

"Rest Stop" (Swan) **69**:362-64

Rest Ward (Cela)
See *Pabellón de reposo*

The Restaurant at the End of the Universe (Adams) **27**:12-15; **60**:2

"The Restaurant Window" (Moss) **45**:290

"Resting Places" (Watkins) **43**:450

"Restless" (Matthews) **40**:325

Restless Is the River (Derleth) **31**:131-33

Restless Nights: Selected Stories of Dino Buzzati (Buzzati) **36**:94-5

"Restless Serpents" (Zamora) **89**:380, 384, 386-87, 392

Restless Serpents (Zamora) **89**:361-63, 368-71, 373, 378, 381-82, 385, 388-91, 395

The Restless Years (*The Restless Youth*) (Paustovsky) **40**:366-68

The Restless Youth (Paustovsky)
See *The Restless Years*

"Restlessness and Experience" (Kunene) **85**:166

The Restoration of Arnold Middleton (Storey) **2**:425; **5**:415

Restoree (McCaffrey) **17**:280

"Restraint" (Barthelme) **117**:6

"The Resurrection of Lazarus" (Fo) **109**:125

"Resurgam" (Tate) **14**:532

"The Resurgence of Miss Ankle-Strap Wedgie" (Ellison) **42**:126

"Resurrection" (Atwood) **15**:37

"Resurrection" (Davies) **23**:145

"Resurrection" (Harjo) **83**:273

"Resurrection" (Konwicki) **117**:281

"Resurrection" (Lind) **82**:129-30

"Resurrection" (Major) **19**:298

Resurrection **75**:64

The Resurrection (Gardner) **7**:112, 115; **8**:234, 237-38; **10**:218; **28**:167

Resurrection (Gerhardie) **5**:140

"La résurrection des morts" (Jouve) **47**:213

"Resurrection: Easter Sunday" (Allen) **84**:8

"Resurrection of Arp" (Smith) **15**:516

The Resurrection of Joseph Bourne (Hodgins) **23**:231-33, 235-36

"The Resurrection of the Dead" (Oates) **15**:402

"The Retarded Children Find a World Built Just for Them" (O Hehir) **41**:324

"Reticent" (Thomas) 13:541
"The Retired Life of the Demons" (Enright) 31:154
"The Retired Postal Clerk" (Betjeman) 43:51
"Retirement" (Shapiro) 53:334
"Retort" (Richards) 14:453
Retour amont (Char) 55:288
Retour de Guyane (Damas) 84:160, 164, 176, 179, 181
"Le retour de l'enfant prodigue" ("The Return of the Prodigal Son") (Senghor) 54:400, 406
"Retratos anónimos" (Aleixandre) 9:12
"The Retreat" (Mason) 82:241, 246, 248-49
"Retreat" (Shaw) 23:396
The Retreat (Appelfeld) 47:5-7
Retreat (Blunden) 56:46
The Retreat (Newby) 2:310; 13:408, 410
The Retreat from Moscow (Almedingen) 12:4
Retreat to Glory: The Story of Sam Houston (Latham) 12:323-24
Retreat to Innocence (Lessing) 22:280
"Retreating Wind" (Gluck) 81:164, 167, 169, 174
"Retribution" (Allen) 52:40-1
"The Retrieval System" (Kumin) 28:222
The Retrieval System (Kumin) 13:327; 28:222
"Retroduction to American History" (Tate) 11:522; 14:528, 532
"Retrospect" (Huxley) 11:283
"Retrospective Forelook" (Eberhart) 56:79
Les retrouvailles (*The Recoveries*; *The Reunions*) (Adamov) 25:12
Retrouver la foi (Romains) 7:381
"Return" 75:78
"The Return" (Allen) 84:3
"Return" (Bontemps) 18:64
"A Return" (Faulkner) 18:148
"Return" (Forche) 25:172; 83:198-99, 211, 214, 216; 86:144
"The Return" (Gluck) 22:177
"Return" (Heaney) 14:243
"A Return" (Johnston) 51:249
"Return" (Lerman) 9:331
"The Return" (Lustig) 56:182, 184
"Return" (MacLeish) 68:273
"The Return" (MacLeod) 56:192, 194
"The Return" (McGrath) 28:279-80
"Return" (Montague) 46:267
"Return" (Neruda)
  See "Regreso"
"The Return" (O'Brien) 36:340
"Return" (Paz)
  See "Vuelta"
"The Return" (Pound) 2:343; 10:405, 408; 18:429; 48:283
"The Return" (Roethke) 11:481; 46:362; 101:263
"The Return" (Silkin) 43:400
"Return" (Tillinghast) 29:416-17
"The Return" (Watkins) 43:452
"Return" (Wright) 53:424
Return (Paz)
  See *Vuelta*
The Return (Turner) 48:399-400
"Return from Ein Gedi" (Amichai) 116:96
"The Return from the Freudian Islands" (Hope) 51:211, 216, 221
Return from the Stars (Lem) 40:289, 292-94, 296
"The Return from Unlikeness" (Hine) 15:280
"Return in Hinton" (Tomlinson) 13:549
The Return of A. J. Raffles (Greene) 9:250;

70:292
"Return of a Popular Statesman" (Buckley) 57:126
The Return of Ansel Gibbs (Buechner) 4:79
"The Return of Chorb" (Nabokov) 15:394
"The Return of Eva Perón" (Naipaul) 105:155
The Return of Eva Perón (Naipaul) 18:361-65; 37:321, 323-24, 328-29; 105:155, 171, 176
The Return of Frank James (Lang) 20:206
"The Return of Inspiration" (Kunene) 85:176
The Return of Iphigenia (Ritsos) 13:488
The Return of Lanny Budd (Sinclair) 15:500; 63:357-59, 365
The Return of Lieutenant Boruvka (Skvorecky) 69:346
"The Return of McCaughey" (Behan) 79:36
The Return of Moriarty (Gardner) 30:153-54
"Return of Peace" (Kunene) 85:175
"The Return of Persephone" (Hope) 51:216
The Return of Philip Latinovicz (Krleza)
  See *Povatek Filipa Latinovicza*
"The Return of Robinson Jeffers" (Hass) 18:211
The Return of Service (Baumbach) 23:55
The Return of Solar Pons (Derleth) 31:138
The Return of the Brute (O'Flaherty) 5:321
"The Return of the Fisherman" (Clark) 38:127
"The Return of the Goddess" (Graves) 2:174
"Return of the Golden Age" (Kunene) 85:175
"Return of the Hood" (Spillane) 13:528
Return of the Jedi: The Storybook Based on the Movie (Vinge) 30:415
"The Return of the Middle Ages" (Eco) 60:112
"Return of the Native" (Blunden) 56:43
"The Return of the Native" (Cabral de Melo Neto) 76:163
"The Return of the Prodigal Son" (Senghor)
  See "Le retour de l'enfant prodigue"
"The Return of the Pronconsul" (Herbert)
  See "Powrót prokonsula"
The Return of the Rivers (Brautigan) 34:315
The Return of the Soldier (West) 7:526-27; 9:561; 31:451, 454, 457, 459; 50:395, 398, 401-02, 405-06
"The Return of the Son of Monster Magnet" (Zappa) 17:589
"Return of the Sphinx" (MacLennan) 14:342, 344; 92:307, 344, 347
Return of the Sphinx (MacLennan) 92:326, 343, 349-50
Return of the Traveller (Warner)
  See *Why Was I Killed?*
The Return of the Vanishing American (Fiedler) 4:161; 13:211; 24:197-99
"Return the Bridewealth" (p'Bitek) 96:299
"The Return to a Cabin" (Leithauser) 27:242
Return to a Place Lit by a Glass of Milk (Simic) 6:502; 9:478-79, 481; 49:340
"Return to Air" (Pearce) 21:289
"Return to Cardiff" (Abse) 29:15, 17
"Return to Chartres" (Sarton) 49:310
"Return to D'Ennery, Rain" (Walcott) 67:353; 76:279
"Return to Frisco, 1946" (Snodgrass) 18:490
Return to Goli (Abrahams) 4:1
Return to Ithaca: The "Odyssey" Retold as a Modern Novel (Johnson)
  See *Strändernas svall*
"Return to Kraków in 1880" (Milosz) 82:305
"Return to Lewis" (Smith) 64:396
"A Return to Me" (Neruda)
  See "Se vuelve a yo"

Return to My Native Land (Cesaire)
  See *Cahier d'un retour au pays natal*
"The Return to Mysticism" (Sadoff) 9:467
Return to Night (Renault) 17:391
"Return to Oneself" (Neruda)
  See "Se vuelve a yo"
Return to Paradise (Michener) 29:310-11; 109:378, 382
"Return to Pernambuco" (Cabral de Melo Neto)
  See "Volta a Pernambuco"
"Return to Return" (Hannah) 38:232
Return to Sender or, When the Fish in the Water Was Thirsty (Mungo) 72:290
"Return to Solitude" (Bly) 5:63; 10:57; 38:56
Return to the River (Haig-Brown) 21:134-36, 141, 144-46
"The Return to the Trees" (Walcott) 76:284
Return to Thebes (Drury) 37:108-09
Return to Tomorrow (*To the Stars*) (Hubbard) 43:204
"Return to Varyinko" (Pasternak) 18:388
"Return Trip Tango" (Cortazar) 33:129-30
"Return Trips" (Adams) 46:21
Return Trips (Adams) 46:21-3
"Return Your Call" (Pinsky) 9:417
"Returned to Say" (Stafford) 29:381, 385
"Returning" (Pastan) 27:371
"Returning" (Rosenthal) 28:394
Returning (O'Brien) 36:336, 338, 341
"Returning a Lost Child" (Gluck) 22:173
"Returning North of Vortex" (Ginsberg) 36:184
Returning to Earth (Harrison) 14:235; 33:197
"Returning to the Continent" (Brutus) 43:89
Reubella and the Old Focus Home (Newton) 35:301
Reuben (Wideman) 67:374-78, 384
"Reuben James" (Guthrie) 35:193-94
Reuben, Reuben (De Vries) 2:114; 3:125; 10:137; 28:106, 112; 46:137
"A Reunion" (Amis) 40:40, 45
"ReUnion" (Bowering) 47:24-5
"Reunion" (Cheever) 3:106
"Reunión" ("The Meeting") (Cortazar) 5:109; 92:149
"The Reunion" (Dodson) 79:193
"Reunion" (Swan) 69:358, 361-64
"A Reunion" (Szirtes) 46:392
"Reunion" (Vanderhaeghe) 41:449
Reunion (Mamet) 15:358; 46:250-51
"Reunion in Brooklyn" (Miller) 1:224; 84:243
"Reunion in the Avenue" (Boell)
  See "Wiedersehen in der Allee"
"Reunioning Dialogue" (Dickey) 15:177
"Reunions" (Simon) 26:406
The Reunions (Adamov)
  See *Les retrouvailles*
"rev pinps" (Sanchez) 116:294
Revaluation, Tradition, and Development in English Poetry (Leavis) 24:293-94, 298, 300, 308
Un rêve fait à Mantoue (Bonnefoy) 58:57
"Revealed at Last! What Killed the Dinosaurs! And You Don't Look So Terrific Yourself" (Ellison) 13:208
"Le réveille-matin" (Carrier) 78:58
"The Revelation" (Bates) 46:63
"The Revelation" (Elytis) 49:110
"Revelation" (O'Connor) 3:366; 13:419; 15:410; 21:262-63, 271-72, 275-77, 279; 104:103, 107, 110, 112, 115, 123-24, 138, 157, 159, 179-80, 185-89, 196-97
Revelation (Welty) 105:359
"Revelations" (Barker) 52:53, 55

"Revelations" (Dubie)   36:142
"Revelations" (Macpherson)   14:347
"Revenant" (McAuley)   45:249
Les revenentes (The Ghosts) (Perec)   56:256-57; 116:233, 245, 267
"Revenge" (Allende)   97:33, 36
"Revenge" (Barth)   51:26
"Revenge" (Gilchrist)   48:115
"Revenge" (Harrison)   14:236-37; 66:155-56, 159
"Revenge" (Sillitoe)   57:388-89
"Revenge" (Smith)   12:544
Revenge (Brenton)   31:56-7, 59-62, 65
"The Revenge of Hannah Kemhuff" (Walker)   58:407; 103:363, 365, 371, 406, 410, 412, 423
The Revenge of Moriarty (Gardner)   30:154
Revenge of the Lawn: Stories, 1962-1970 (Brautigan)   1:45; 3:88-90; 12:64-6, 70; 34:315
Revenge of the Tribes (Berton)   104:58-9
"Revenge of Truth" (Dinesen)   95:49
The Revenge of Truth (Sandhedens Haevn) (Dinesen)   10:145; 95:41-2, 49, 61-2, 64, 67-8
The Revenger's Comedies (Ayckbourn)   74:18, 28-9, 34-6
Reverberation Machines (Foreman)   50:166
"Reverdure" (Berry)   27:36
"Reverend Father Gilhooley" (Farrell)   66:113, 131
The Reverend Ghost (Garrett)   3:192; 51:141, 145
Reverie (Aldington)   49:2
"A Reverie of Bone" (Peake)   54:369, 373
"Reveries on a pillow, Recife" (Cabral de Melo Neto)
    See "Coisas de cabeceira, Recife"
"Reveries on a Pillow, Seville" (Cabral de Melo Neto)
    See "Coisas de cabeceira, Sevilha"
"Reversal" (Ammons)   2:14; 9:28
"Reversal" (Dixon)   52:100-01
Reversals (Stevenson)   7:462
Reverse Psychology (Ludlum)   46:242; 50:342
"Reverse Pygmalion" (Avison)   97:123
"Reverting Still Again" (Carruth)   7:41
Les rêves et la jambe (Dream and the Leg) (Michaux)   19:315
"Reviewers in Flat Heels: Being a Postface to Several Novels" (Markson)   67:191
"Reviewing" (Wakoski)   9:555
"Reviewing and Being Reviewed" (Epstein)   39:467
"The Revisionist" (Crase)   58:159-61, 165
The Revisionist (Crase)   58:159-66
Revisions (Bernhard)
    See Korrektur
"Revisited Waters" (Watkins)   43:447
"The Revival of Poetry" (Scott)   22:371
"The Revival of Vaudeville" (Dickey)   28:119
"Revolt against the Crepuscular Spirit in Modern Poetry" (Pound)   48:288
Revolt in 2100: The Prophets and the Triumph of Reason over Superstition (Heinlein)   3:225
Revolt in the South (Wakefield)   7:503
The Revolt of the Fisherman of St. Barbara (Seghers)   7:408-09
Révolte dans les Asturies (Camus)   32:88, 100-01
"Revolucinations" (Morgan)   2:295
"Revolution" (Fuller)   62:185

"Revolution" (Lennon and McCartney)   12:363; 35:264, 266, 270
"Revolution" (Marley)   17:267
"Revolution" (Montague)   46:270
Revolution (Taylor)   27:441
Revolution and Roses (Newby)   2:311; 13:408
"Revolution Blues" (Young)   17:573
La révolution du langage poétique: L'avant-garde à la fin du XIXe siècle, Lautréamont et Mallarmé (Revolution in Poetic Language) (Kristeva)   77:299-302, 310, 313, 319-21, 323
"Revolution I" (Lennon and McCartney)   12:365
Revolution in Our Time (Archer)   12:18
Revolution in Poetic Language (Kristeva)
    See La révolution du langage poétique: L'avant-garde à la fin du XIXe siècle, Lautréamont et Mallarmé
A Revolution in Taste (Simpson)   32:380
Revolution in Writing (Day Lewis)   10:133
"Revolution Number Nine" (Lennon and McCartney)   35:261, 270
"The Revolution of 1905" (Sadoff)   9:467
"Revolution Rock" (Clash)   30:47
The Revolution Script (Moore)   3:341; 5:296-97; 7:236; 90:255, 259, 269, 289
"Revolutionaries" (Ritsos)   31:324
"Revolutionary Dreams" (Giovanni)   64:186; 117:201
Revolutionary Immortality: Mao Tse-Tung and the Chinese Cultural Revolution (Lifton)   67:140-41
"Revolutionary Music" (Giovanni)   19:191; 64:186
"Revolutionary Petunias" (Walker)   9:558
Revolutionary Petunias (Walker)   103:357, 364-66, 375, 395, 405
Revolutionary Road (Yates)   7:553-56; 8:556; 23:482
"Revolutionary Situations" (Buckley)   57:131
"A Revolutionary Tale" (Giovanni)   19:192; 64:183
"The Revolutionary Tradition in Afro-American Literature" (Baraka)   14:49
A Revolutionary Woman (Fugard)   48:110-12
"The Revolutionist" (Hemingway)   30:189, 191; 80:143
"Revolutions Revalued: The Attack on Credit Monopoly from a Cultural Viewpoint" (Williams)   22:464
Revolver (Lennon and McCartney)   12:357, 361, 376, 379, 384
Le revolver á cheveux blancs (The White-Haired Revolver) (Breton)   9:127-28; 54:18, 27, 30
"The Revolver in the Corner Cupboard" (Greene)   6:216; 72:151-52
The Revolving Door (Jones)   52:247
"Rewards of the Fountain" (Watkins)   43:453
El rey y la reina (The King and the Queen) (Sender)   8:478-79
Los reyes (Cortazar)   2:101; 10:113-14
Reynard the Fox; or, The Ghost Heath Run (Masefield)   11:356-58; 47:229-31, 233-34
"Reynolds & Chevrolet" (Kenny)   87:241
The Rez Sisters (Highway)   92:215-17, 219-21, 223-24, 227
"Rhapsody of Naked Light" (Ritsos)   31:324
"Rhapsody on a Windy Night" (Eliot)   41:156, 161; 55:350, 374; 57:169
"Rhenish Fourteenth C." (Van Duyn)   7:498

"'Rhetoric' and Poetic Drama" (Eliot)   24:185
"Rhetoric of a Journey" (Fuller)   28:159
"The Rhetoric of Blindness" (de Man)   55:401
The Rhetoric of Fiction (Booth)   24:84-6, 89-92, 94-6
"The Rhetoric of Hitler's 'Battle'" (Burke)   24:128
A Rhetoric of Irony (Booth)   23:90-3
The Rhetoric of Romanticism (de Man)   55:400, 404
"The Rhetoric of Temporality" (de Man)   55:410
"The Rhetoric of the Image" (Barthes)   83:85
A Rhetoric of the Unreal (Brooke-Rose)   40:109, 111
"Rhetorical Meditations in Times of Peace" (Montague)   46:265
The Rhetorical World of Augustan Humanism: Ethics and Imagery from Swift toBurke (Fussell)   74:115, 137, 144
Rhine Journey (Schlee)   35:372-76
The Rhinemann Exchange (Ludlum)   22:288-89
"Rhinestone in the Rough" (Sorrentino)   40:389
"The Rhino" (Soto)   80:299
Rhinoceros (Ionesco)
    See Rhinocéros
Rhinocéros (Rhinoceros) (Ionesco)   1:154; 4:250-52; 6:250-53, 257; 9:286, 289; 11:289-90, 294; 15:298-99; 41:226, 229-31; 86:331-34, 340
"Rho" (Tolson)   105:255
"Rhobert" (Toomer)   13:556
Rhoda in Potatoland (Foreman)   50:168, 172
"Rhode Island" (Meredith)   13:373; 22:303
"Rhododendron" (Stern)   40:414
"Rhododendron Estranged in Twilight" (Middleton)   13:387
"Rhododendrons" (Gallagher)   63:124
"Rhody's Path" (Goyen)   14:211
"Rhossili" (Watkins)   43:454
"The Rhubarbarians" (Harrison)   43:180
"Rhyme of the Flying Bomb" (Peake)   54:373
Rhymed Ruminations (Sassoon)   36:389
"The Rhymer"   75:63
"Rhymes" (Tomlinson)   13:548
"Rhymes on Béthune, 1916" (Blunden)   56:44
Rhymes without Reason (Peake)   54:369
"Rhyming Max" (Updike)   23:474
"The Rhythm" (Creeley)   8:153; 78:144, 156, 162
"Rhythm and Blues" (Baraka)   5:45
The Rhythm of Violence (Nkosi)   45:294-95
"Rhythms of Love" (Riding)   7:374
"The Ribbon" (Williams)   42:443
"Ribs, Roast, Chops, Bacon" (Johnston)   51:254
"Ricardo and the Flower" (Bowering)   47:22
"La ricchezza" (Pasolini)   37:346
I ricci crescenti (Buzzati)   36:84
"Rice" (Harris)   25:212
"Rich" (Gilchrist)   48:115-16, 120
"Rich" (Raine)   103:186
"The Rich" (Tomlinson)   6:535
Rich (Raine)   103:185-90, 197-98, 206, 210
Rich and Famous (Guare)   8:252-53; 14:220; 29:204-05
"Rich and Rare Were the Gems She Wore" (Kiely)   23:261
Rich and Strange (Hitchcock)   16:345
"Rich Boy's Birthday Through a Window" (Avison)   97:69

"The Rich Brother" (Wolff) 64:451-52, 454
Rich in Love (Humphreys) 57:233-38
Rich Like Us (Sahgal) 41:373, 375
Rich Man, Poor Man (Shaw) 7:413; 23:398-400; 34:368
The Rich Pay Late (Raven) 14:441, 443
Rich Rewards (Adams) 46:14-16, 21
"Richard Cory" (Simon) 17:461
Richard III (Olivier) 20:237, 239-40, 243
Richard Pryor Live in Concert (Pryor) 26:379, 381-84
Richard Pryor Live on Sunset Strip (Pryor) 26:380-84
Richard Wright Reader (Wright) 14:596
"Richard Wright's Blues" (Ellison) 11:185
Richard's Cork Leg (Behan) 79:27, 40, 47
Richard's Things (Raphael) 14:437
Der Richter und sein Henker (Duerrenmatt) 102:66, 69
Der Richter und sein Henker (*The Judge and His Hangman*) (Durrenmatt) 4:140-41; 11:171, 174; 43:122-23, 128
"The Rick of Green Wood" (Dorn) 10:156, 159
"La ricotta" (Pasolini) 20:271; 37:347
La Ricotta (*The Milk-Cheese*) (Pasolini) 106:206-208, 221
"The Riddle" (Heaney) 74:161
"Riddle" (Snodgrass) 18:491; 68:388
"Riddle in the Garden" (Warren) 39:266
"Riddle Me" (Ashbery) 77:63, 65, 68-9
"The Riddle of the Ordinary" (Ozick) 62:349, 352
"The Riddle of the Sphinx" (Du Bois) 64:109, 112, 116
"Riddles" (Guillen) 48:157
"Riddles" (Parra)
   See "Rompecabezas"
Riddley Walker (Hoban) 25:264-67
"Ride" (Miles) 14:370
"The Ride" (Wilbur) 53:412; 110:357, 360, 372
Ride a Pale Horse (MacInnes) 39:349-50
The Ride across Lake Constance (Handke) 5:163; 8:262; 10:257; 15:268-70
"Ride, Fly, Penetrate, Loiter" (Hannah) 38:233; 90:138
"Ride My Llama" (Young) 17:581
"Ride Natty Ride" (Marley) 17:273
"Ride Off Any Horizon" (Newlove) 14:377
"A Ride on the Short Dog" (Still) 49:366-67
Ride Out (Foote) 75:230-31, 236, 239
Ride Out the Wilderness: Geography and Identity in Afro-American Literature (Dixon) 65:381
Ride Proud, Rebel! (Norton) 12:457
Ride the Dark Trail (L'Amour) 25:279
Ride the High Country (*Guns in the Afternoon*) (Peckinpah) 20:272-75, 277, 279, 282-84
Ride with Me (Costain) 30:93
"Rideau rideau" (Breton) 9:127
"Riderless Horses" (Bly) 10:57
"Riders" (Frost) 15:241
"The Riders" (Voigt) 54:433
"The Riders Held Back" (Simpson) 7:427
Riders in the Chariot (White) 3:521-22, 524; 4:583-84; 5:484-88; 7:530, 532; 18:545; 65:275-79, 281-82; 69:392-97, 400-01, 405-06, 408
Riders on the Earth: Essays and Recollections (MacLeish) 14:338
"Riders on the Storm" (Morrison) 17:294-95

"Riders to the Blood-Red Wrath" (Brooks) 5:75; 15:93; 49:36
"The Ridge Farm" (Ammons) 57:51-2, 54-6
Ridiculous Loves (Kundera)
   See *Smesné lásky*
Ridin' the Moon in Texas: Word Paintings (Shange) 74:311, 313
"Ridin' up Front with Carl and Marl" (Wiggins) 57:433-34, 439
"Riding a Jumper" (Hearne) 56:124
"Riding a Nervous Horse" (Hearne) 56:127
Riding High (Weber) 12:632
Riding Lights (MacCaig) 36:279-80, 284
"Riding the 'A'" (Swenson) 61:401; 106:328
Riding the Earthboy 40 (Welch) 14:559; 52:425-26, 428, 430, 433
Rien que la terre (Morand) 41:304
Rien va (Landolfi) 49:215-16
"RIF" (Barthelme) 59:251
The Rifle and the Cross (Endo) 99:287
Rifleman Dodd (*Death to the French*) (Forester) 35:165, 168, 170
The Rifles (Vollmann) 89:286, 297, 304, 306, 309-13
Rigadoon (Celine)
   See *Rigodon*
"Right" (Matthews) 40:324
"Right across the Great Plains" (Muldoon) 32:317
"Right and Wrong Political Uses of Literature" (Calvino) 73:48
"The Right Arm" (Muldoon) 72:272
"Right Dress" (Scannell) 49:330
"The Right Hand" (Solzhenitsyn)
   See "Pravaya kist"
Right Hand Left Hand (Livesay) 15:342; 79:354
The Right Madness on Skye (Hugo) 32:242-43, 250-51
The Right Moment for Humanity (Padilla)
   See *El justo tiempo humano*
"The Right of Eminent Domain versus the Rightful Domain of the Eminent" (Lebowitz) 36:249
"Right of Sanctuary" (Carpentier) 38:94
"Right On" (Ammons) 25:43
"Right On" (Gaye) 26:130
"The Right Profile" (Clash) 30:47
Right Royal (Masefield) 11:357
The Right Stuff (Wolfe) 15:584-87; 35:458-60, 464-66; 51:415, 418-21
The Right to an Answer (Burgess) 2:85; 4:81; 22:70, 77; 40:115-16; 62:129; 94:23-24, 26, 40-41
"The Right to Life" (Piercy) 27:379
"Right to Loathsome Ideas" (Schlesinger) 84:372
The Right to Remain Silent (Meltzer) 26:300-01
"The Rightangled Creek: A Sort of Ghost Story" (Stead) 2:423; 32:408; 80:306, 323
"The Rightful One" (Ignatow) 7:175, 179
Rights of Passage (Brathwaite) 11:66-7
Right-Wing Women (Dworkin) 43:133-34
Rigodon (*Rigadoon*) (Celine) 4:101-04; 7:45; 9:153, 158; 47:74-5, 79
"Rigor Viris" (Avison) 97:69, 71, 106
"Rihaku" (Pound) 112:343
"Rikki Don't Lose That Number" (Becker and Fagen) 26:79
Rima in the Weeds (McNamer) 70:83-90
"Rimbaud and Verlaine" (Aiken) 52:23
"Rimbaud and Verlaine" (O'Hara) 13:424

"Rimbaud Fire Letter to Jim Applewhite" (Chappell) 78:93, 96
"Rimbaud's Piano" (Merwin) 88:213
"Rime of the Palmers" (Merwin) 45:269
"Rimrock, Where It Is" (Carruth) 7:41
"Rind of Earth" (Derleth) 31:136
The Ring (Hitchcock) 16:343
Ring around the Sun (Simak) 55:320
Der Ring Gott Farblonjet (Ludlam) 50:342, 344-45
"The Ring Of" (Olson) 5:328
Ring of Truth (Scannell) 49:333
Ring Roads (Modiano)
   See *Le boulevards de ceinture*
Ring round the Moon: A Charade with Music (Anouilh)
   See *L'invitation au château*
Ring the Judas Bell (Forman) 21:116, 118
"Ringa Ringa Rosie" (Levine) 54:293, 295
The Ringers on the Tower (Bloom) 24:70, 73; 103:3-4, 41
"Ringing the Bells" (Sexton) 53:313
"Ringing the Changes" (Aickman) 57:2, 5
Ringing the Changes: An Autobiography (de la Roche) 14:150
"Ringling Brothers, Barnum and Bailey" (Van Duyn) 63:443; 116:410
Rings around Us (Gilbreth and Carey) 17:155
Rings on a Tree (MacCaig) 36:283, 286
The Rink (Chaplin) 16:207
The Rink (McNally) 41:290-91
"Río" (Aleixandre) 9:12
El río (Matute) 11:364
"Rio e/ou poço" ("River and/or Well") (Cabral de Melo Neto) 76:169
El rio invisible (*The Invisible River*) (Neruda) 62:336
O rio ou relaçãode viagem que faz o Capibaribe sua nascente à cidade do Recife (*The River*) (Cabral de Melo Neto) 76:153, 158, 162, 167-68
Un río, un amor (*A River, A Love*) (Cernuda) 54:41, 51, 53-60
El rio y la muerta (Bunuel) 80:24
"Riordan's Fiftieth" (Stern) 39:244
Los ríos profundos (*Deep Rivers*) (Arguedas) 10:8; 18:6-7, 9-10
"Riot" (Brooks) 49:28
Riot (Brooks) 4:78; 15:92-3; 49:23, 28, 31, 35, 37-8
Riot: A History of Mob Action in the United States (Archer) 12:20
Riotous Assembly (Sharpe) 36:398-99, 402
"R.I.P." (Avison) 97:76
Rip Awake (Coover) 32:120
"Rip Off" (Cliff) 21:60
Rip van Winkle (Frisch) 44:194
The Ripening (Glissant)
   See *La Lézarde*
Ripley Bogle (Wilson) 59:105-08
Ripley under Ground (Highsmith) 4:225; 42:212; 102:179, 193-95, 197, 207-09, 212
Ripley under Water (Highsmith) 102:212
Ripley's End (Highsmith) 4:226
Ripley's Game (Highsmith) 4:226; 42:214; 102:174, 179-80, 183, 185, 193, 195, 208-09
The Rip-Off (Thompson) 69:382-83, 387
"Riposte" (Hacker) 72:191
Ripostes (Pound) 4:408; 10:405; 48:288
A Ripple from the Storm (Lessing) 2:238; 3:290-92; 6:298; 94:256, 281-82

Riprap (Snyder)   5:393-94; 9:500-03; 32:387-90, 396-98

"Le Rire de la Méduse" (Cixous)   92:54, 57, 69-70, 72, 75, 78-80, 87-9, 95-6

Risco do bordado (*Pattern for a Tapestry; The Texture of the Embroidery*) (Dourado)   23:150-51; 60:85, 93-4

"The Rise" (Berry)   27:38

"Rise and Fall" (Busch)   47:62

"Rise and Fall" (Dacey)   51:78

The Rise and Fall of Ziggy Stardust and the Spiders from Mars (Bowie)   17:58-9, 61-3, 67-8

Rise of English Literary History (Wellek)   28:443, 452

The Rise of Life on Earth (Oates)   108:379, 381, 385

"The Rise of the Angry Generation" (Kunene)   85:175

"The Rise of the Middle Class" (Banks)   37:24

Risibles Amours (Kundera)
   See *Smesné lásky*

"Risiko für Weihnachtsmänner" (Lenz)   27:245

Rising and Falling (Matthews)   40:320-22

The Rising Fire (MacEwen)   13:357

The Rising Generation (Jellicoe)   27:208-10

The Rising Gorge (Perelman)   5:338; 9:415; 23:336

The Rising of the Moon (Ford)   16:315

"The Rising of the Sun" (Milosz)
   See "From Where the Sun Rises"

"The Rising Out" (McGuckian)   48:278

Rising Sun (Crichton)   90:76-83, 88, 90-1, 93, 96

"The Rising Tide" (Yehoshua)   31:472

The Rising Tide (Keane)   31:233

"Rising Up" (Gerstler)   70:156

"Risk" (Asimov)   26:55; 92:13

"Risk" (Dickinson)   49:102-03

Risk (Francis)   22:151; 42:150, 155, 157

"The Risk and the Clock" (Char)
   See "Le risque et le pendule"

"Risky Bizness" (Kristofferson)   26:269

"Le risque et le pendule" ("The Risk and the Clock") (Char)   11:117

Risques et périls (Reverdy)   53:286

"Risvegli" (Ungaretti)   11:555

Rita Hayworth and Shawshank Redemption (King)   26:240-42; 113:351-52

"Rital and Raton" (Pasolini)   106:270

The Rite (Bergman)
   See *Riten*

"Rite and Fore-Time" (Jones)   7:190; 42:241

Rite of Darkness (Castellanos)
   See *Oficio de tinieblas*

"Rite of Passage" (Olds)   39:187, 192; 85:290

Rite of Passage (Fugard)   48:110

Riten (*The Rite; The Ritual*) (Bergman)   16:75; 72:46-7, 56, 61

"Rites" (Cohen)   38:130

"The Rites" (Creeley)   78:133

"The Rites for Cousin Vit" (Brooks)   49:27

"Rites for the Extrusion of a Leper" (Merton)   83:397

"The Rites of Hysteria" (Gascoyne)   45:148, 151

"Rites of Passage" (Gunn)   18:200

"Rites of Passage" (Rexroth)   22:345

Rites of Passage (Golding)   27:160-63, 165-69; 81:315, 317-25

Rites of Passage (Greenberg)   30:162-63, 166

The Rites of Spring (Abbey)   36:21

Ritmuri (Arghezi)   80:6, 8

"Il ritorno di Lorenzo" (Levi)   37:224

Ritsos in Parentheses (Ritsos)   31:328-31

"Ritual" (Gregor)   9:254

"Ritual" (Ignatow)   4:248; 7:180; 40:258

"A Ritual" (Mahapatra)   33:282

"Ritual" (Purdy)   50:246

The Ritual (Bergman)
   See *Riten*

"Ritual One" (Ignatow)   7:180

"Ritual Two" (Ignatow)   7:180

"Ritual Three" (Ignatow)   7:180

"Ritual Drama as the Hub" (Burke)   24:126

"Ritual for Eating the World" (Ammons)   108:20

Ritual in the Dark (Wilson)   3:537; 14:588

Ritual in Transfigured Time (Deren)   16:252; 102:28, 31, 35, 38-9, 43-47

"The Ritual of Memories" (Gallagher)   18:170; 63:123

Ritual of the Wind: North American Indian Ceremonies, Music, and Dances (Highwater)   12:287

"Ritual XVII" (Blackburn)   9:100

"Rituals" (Giovanni)   4:189

"Rituals of Rejection" (Valenzuela)
   See "Ceremonias de rechazo"

Rituals of Surgery (Selzer)   74:263, 281, 285, 287

The Ritz (Lester)   20:231

The Ritz (McNally)   7:219; 41:293; 91:163

Le rivage des Syrtes (*The Opposing Shore*) (Gracq)   11:245; 48:136, 138-43

"A Rival" (Hughes)   37:179

"The Rival" (Plath)   9:427; 51:344; 111:214

"The Rivals" (Garrett)   51:140

"The Rivals" (Scannell)   49:331

The Rivals (Aitmatov)
   See *Soperniki*

"Riven Doggeries" (Tate)   25:429-30

Riven Doggeries (Tate)   25:429

"River" (Ammons)   108:22

"The River" (Carver)   55:276

"The River" (Dybek)   114:72-3

"The River" (Merwin)   88:213

"The River" (O'Connor)   1:257; 6:381; 10:368; 15:412; 21:256-57, 261, 271; 66:309; 104:120, 173

"The River" (Oliver)   98:258

"The River" (Salinas)   90:322, 324

"The River" (Soto)   80:301

The River (Cabral de Melo Neto)
   See *O rio ou relaçãode viagem que faz o Capibaribe sua nascente à cidade doRecife*

The River (Godden)   53:154-58, 161

The River (Hughes)   37:178-81

The River (Renoir)   20:287, 304

A River, A Love (Cernuda)
   See *Un rio, un amor*

River: A Poem (Chappell)   40:143-45, 147; 78:91

The River and I (Neihardt)   32:335

"River and/or Well" (Cabral de Melo Neto)
   See "Rio e/ou poço"

River at Her Feet (Sherburne)   30:361

"The River Awakening to the Sea" (Chappell)   78:111

"River Barrow" (Hughes)   37:179

The River Between (Ngugi wa Thiong'o)   3:358; 7:262, 264-66; 13:583; 36:312-13, 315-17, 319

"The River Bridged and Forgot" (Berry)   46:72

"The River Flows Slowly along the Valley" (Akhmatova)   25:27

River George (Lee)   52:267-69

"River Going By" (Derleth)   31:136

"The River House" (Blunden)   56:29

"River Incident" (Roethke)   19:397

River Lady (Waters)   88:362

"The River Merchant's Wife: A Letter" (Pound)   1:275; 112:343, 346-47

A River Never Sleeps (Haig-Brown)   21:135-36, 142

The River Niger (Walker)   19:455

River of Death (MacLean)   63:266

River of Earth (Still)   49:363-69

"River of Names"   78:2

"River People" (Bass)   79:17

River Rats, Inc. (George)   35:178

"River Roads" (Sandburg)   10:450

River Root: A Syzygy for the Bicentennial of These States (Everson)   14:164, 167

A River Runs Through It (Maclean)   78:221-27, 229, 232, 235-37, 239-41

A River Runs Through It, and Other Stories (Maclean)   78:221-22, 232, 235, 242, 244

"The River Song" (Pound)   112:347

The River Sot' (Leonov)
   See *Sot'*

The River Styx, Ohio (Oliver)   98:276-77, 291

"The River That Is East" (Kinnell)   29:281, 283-84, 287

The River to Pickle Beach (Betts)   3:73; 28:34

A River Town (Keneally)   117:246-47, 249

Riverbed (Wagoner)   3:508

"The Riverman" (Bishop)   9:97; 13:89; 32:33-4, 42

"The Rivermen" (Mitchell)   98:173, 182

"Riverroad" (Tilghman)   65:107

"Rivers" (Milosz)   82:298

Rivers among Rocks (Gustafson)   36:212, 214, 216-18, 222

"Rivers and Mountains" (Ashbery)   77:59-60

Rivers and Mountains (Ashbery)   2:16, 19; 4:22-3; 9:43-4; 15:26-7, 30; 25:49, 58; 41:40

Rivers of Canada (*Seven Rivers of Canada*) (MacLennan)   92:306, 319, 343-44

The Rivers of Eros (Colter)   58:138-41, 143-44, 146

"The Rivers of Roa Bastos" (Dorfman)   77:156

"River's Story" (Tate)   25:430

Rivers West (L'Amour)   25:280-81

Riverside (Hamilton)
   See *The Slaves of Solitude*

Riverside Drive (Simpson)   4:499; 32:379

The Riverside Villas Murder (Amis)   3:7-10; 5:22; 40:41-3

La rivière sans repos (Roy)   10:442; 14:468

"Rivkala's Ring" (Gray)   112:111

R.L.'s Dream (Mosley)   97:348, 354-61

The Roaches (Tchicaya)
   See *Les cancrelats*

"The Road" (Avison)   97:111

"The Road" (Hillis)   66:194

"The Road" (Simpson)   7:428

The Road (Anand)   23:12, 17; 93:48, 50, 55

The Road (Ehle)   27:104

The Road (Fellini)
   See *La strada*

The Road (Martinson)
   See *Vägen till Klockrike*

The Road (Soyinka)   3:463; 14:508; 36:410; 44:277, 279-81, 283, 286-88, 290

The Road (Tesich)   40:421

The Road Allowance People (Campbell)   85:13-

4

"The Road and the Sky" (Browne)   21:36, 41
"The Road Atlas" (McGuane)   45:265
The Road Back (Remarque)   21:326-27, 330
"Road Ends at Tahola" (Hugo)   32:238
"The Road from Colonus" (Forster)   45:136, 140-42
"Road from the Isles" (Laurence)   50:320, 322; 62:280-81
"A Road in Indiana" (Colwin)   84:151
"The Road Not Taken" (Frost)   10:193; 13:230; 15:248; 26:116-17, 121, 123, 128; 34:470, 474
"The Road of Dreams" (Christie)   110:125
The Road of Dreams (Christie)   39:437; 110:125
"The Road of El Sueno by the Sea" (Salinas)   90:332
The Road Past Altamont (Roy)
See *La route d'Altamont*
"Road Show" (Carpenter)   41:103
The Road Sign at the End of the Street (Abe)
See *Owarishi michino shirubeni*
The Road through the Wall (Jackson)   60:216-18, 232-34, 236
The Road to a Kingdom (Endo)   99:287
The Road to Bithynia (Slaughter)   29:374-75
The Road to Camlann: The Death of King Arthur (Sutcliff)   26:440-41
"The Road to Emmaus" (Brown)   100:82-3
The Road to Gandolfo (Ludlum)   43:275
The Road to Joy (Merton)   83:404
The Road to Klockrike (Martinson)
See *Vägen till Klockrike*
The Road to Lichfield (Lively)   32:273
The Road to Los Angeles (Fante)   60:133-35
Road to Mandalay (Browning)   16:124
The Road to Many a Wonder (Wagoner)   5:474-75
The Road to Mecca (Fugard)   40:200-02; 80:72, 74, 78-81, 84, 87
The Road to Miltown; or, Under the Spreading Atrophy (Perelman)   23:335
"The Road to Rankin's Point" (MacLeod)   56:193, 196-97
The Road to Ruin (Sassoon)   36:389
"The Road to Santiago" (Carpentier)   38:94
The Road to Stratford (O'Connor)   14:397
The Road to the City (Ginzburg)
See *La strada che va in città*
The Road to the Graveyard (Foote)   51:133
Road to the Ocean (Leonov)
See *Doroga na okean*
"The Road to the Sea" (Clarke)   35:122
Road to the Stilt House (Richards)   59:187-89
The Road to Wellville (Boyle)   90:56-9, 61, 64
"The Road to Yesterday" (Davison)   15:170
"The Road You Didn't Take" (Sondheim)   30:386, 391
Roadmarks (Zelazny)   21:472, 474
"The Road's End" (Montague)   46:267
"The Roads Must Roll" (Heinlein)   26:171; 55:302, 304
The Roads of Earth (Drury)   37:111-12
The Roads of Freedom (Sartre)
See *Les chemins de la liberté*
"The Roads Round Pisa" (Dinesen)   10:145, 152; 95:35, 41, 49, 52, 64-5
The Roads That Lead Far Away (Haavikko)
See *Tiet eäisyyksiin*
Roadside Picnic (Strugatskii and Strugatskii)   27:435-36
Roadside Valentine (Adler)   35:14-15

"Roadways" (Masefield)   11:358
Roadwork (King)   37:207-08
"Roan Stallion" (Jeffers)   54:236, 238, 241, 243-44, 246; 3:258
Roan Stallion, Tamar, and Other Poems (Jeffers)   11:305; 54:233, 235-37, 244
Roanoke: A Novel of the Lost Colony (Levitin)   17:264
"Roar Lion Roar" (Faust)   8:215
Roar Lion Roar (Faust)   8:215
The Roar of Thunder (Smith)
See *The Sound of Thunder*
A Roaring in the Wind (Taylor)   14:534-35
The Roaring Nineties: A Story of the Goldfields of Western Australia (Prichard)   46:334, 337-38, 340, 342-43
"Roas Turkey" (Bennett)   28:28
The Roast (Marshall)   17:278
Roast Beef, Medium: The Business Adventures of Emma McChesney and Her Son, Jock (Ferber)   93:135, 140-41, 147
"Roast Opossum" (Dove)   50:153-54; 81:139
Robbed in Light (Seifert)   44:423
The Robber Bride (Atwood)   84:108
The Robber Bridegroom (Uhry)   55:265-66
The Robber Bridegroom (Welty)   1:361; 2:462-63; 14:562; 22:460; 33:417-21; 105:325, 341-46, 349, 384-85
The Robber Hotzenplotz (Preussler)   17:374, 376
"The Robbery" (Mohr)   12:447
"Robbie" (Asimov)   9:50; 26:54, 58; 92:4, 10
"La robe de laine" (Theriault)   79:407-08
"La robe déchirée" (Theriault)   79:407
La robe mauve de Valentine (Sagan)   17:424
La robe prétexte (Mauriac)   56:206
"Robert Frost at Bread Loaf His Hand against a Tree" (Swenson)   61:394
Robert Frost Himself (Burnshaw)   44:457-61
Robert Graves: The Assault Heroic, 1895-1926 (Graves)   44:475-76, 479-80
Robert Hayden: Collected Poems (Collected Poems) (Hayden)   37:159-60
"Robert Kennedy" (Seidel)   18:475
Robert Kennedy and His Times (Schlesinger)   84:368, 385
"Robert Kennedy Saved from Drowning" (Barthelme)   5:53; 6:30; 8:50; 23:46, 48; 46:35, 43; 115:57, 87, 92
"Robert Schumann" (Oliver)   98:290
"Robert Schumann, Or: Musical Genius Begins with Affliction" (Dove)   81:137
"Roberta" (Joel)   26:214, 219
Robeson Street (Howe)   47:177
Robespierre the Incorruptible: A Psychobiography (Gallo)   95:87
"Robin" (Merwin)   18:334
"The Robin" (Stolz)   12:552
"The Robin" (Vidal)   33:406-07
Robin and Marian (Lester)   20:230-31
"Robin Redbreast" (Kunitz)   6:287
"The Robin's House" (Barnes)   29:27
Robinson (Spark)   2:414-15, 417; 13:520-21; 18:505; 40:393; 94:326, 328, 331-333, 336, 353
Robinson Crusoe (Bunuel)
See *Las aventuras de Robinson Crusoe*
"Roblin's Mills" (Purdy)   50:237
"Robot" (Davenport)   6:124-25; 14:140; 38:144
"Robul'a ("The Thrall") (Arghezi)   80:2
"Robust Meteors" (Char)   9:167
Rocannon's World (Le Guin)   13:345, 348,

351; 22:265, 272; 45:218, 222
Rocco and His Brothers (Visconti)   16:570
"The Rock" (Jackson)   60:214
Rock (Wagoner)   3:507
The Rock: A Pageant Play (Eliot)   55:348
"Rock and Fern" (Hooker)   43:197
Rock and Other Four-Letter Words (Highwater)   12:285
"Rock and Roll" (Page and Plant)   12:475, 477-78
"Rock and Roll" (Reed)   21:305, 307, 322-23
Rock and Roll Heart (Reed)   21:312-13
"Rock and Roll Music" (Berry)   17:53
"Rock and Roll Suicide" (Bowie)   17:58, 61
"Rock and Roll Time" (Kristofferson)   26:268-69
"Rock Bottom" (Ondaatje)   51:313-14
"Rock Climbing" (Jiles)   58:273
The Rock Cried Out (Douglas)   73:70-6, 83, 85-6, 88, 90, 95-7, 99
The Rock Garden (Shepard)   17:441; 41:410
Rock It (Berry)   17:55
"Rock Me on the Water" (Browne)   21:35
Rock 'n' Roll (Lennon)   35:269-71, 275
Rock 'n Roll Animal (Reed)   21:307-09
"A Rock 'n' Roll Fantasy" (Davies)   21:103-05
"Rock 'n' Roll Never Forgets" (Seger)   35:385-86
"Rock 'n' Roll Nigger" (Smith)   12:543
"Rock River" (Wideman)   67:379, 385
"Rock Show" (McCartney)   35:282-83
"Rock Springs" (Ford)   46:161
Rock Springs   99:105-06, 110, 115-16, 120
"Rock Study with Wanderer" (Berryman)   62:71
"Rock the Casbah" (Clash)   30:50-2
"A Rock Thrown into the Water Does Not Fear the Cold" (Lorde)   71:247
Rock Wagram (Saroyan)   29:361-62
The Rock Woman (Baxter)   14:63
"Rockaby" (Beckett)   29:65
Rockaby, and Other Short Pieces (Beckett)   29:59, 63-5; 59:253, 255
"The Rocket and the Future of Warfare" (Clarke)   35:128
"The Rocket Man" (Bradbury)   42:44
"Rocket Man" (Jones)   81:64-5, 67
Rocket Ship Galileo (Heinlein)   55:302
"Rocket Show" (Baxter)   14:62
"Rocket Summer" (Bradbury)   42:38
Rocket to the Moon (Odets)   2:320; 28:327-28, 332-33, 335; 98:195, 198-200, 209, 215, 229-32, 237, 244, 252
Rocketship Galileo (Heinlein)   14:247, 249; 26:165, 171, 175
"Rockin' after Midnight" (Gaye)   26:135
Rocking Back and Forth (Grass)   15:260
The Rocking Chair (Klein)   19:259-62
"A Rocking Horse on Mars" (West)   96:362
Rockinghorse (Kaniuk)   19:239-40
"The Rockpile" (Baldwin)   17:33
"The Rocks" (Creeley)   78:144
"The Rocks" (Guillevic)   33:191
"Rocks" (Mahon)   27:288
"Rocks in Our Beds" (Holmes)   56:143-44
"Rocks Off" (Jagger and Richard)   17:224-25, 229, 236
Rockspring (Vliet)   22:441-42
Rockway (Shanley)   75:319
"Rocky Acres" (Graves)   45:166-67, 169, 173
"Rocky Flats" (Levertov)   66:239
The Rocky Horror Picture Show (O'Brien)   17:322, 327

Rocky Mountain Foot (Bowering) 15:82; 47:20
Rocky Mountain Poems (Gustafson) 36:212-13, 216-17
The Rocky Summer (Kingman) 17:243
Rocky Time (Ritsos)
  See *Pétrinos hrónos*
"The Rococo Seducer" (Brophy) 105:8
Rod (Buzo) 61:58
Rod Serling's Night Gallery (Serling) 30:357
Rodmoor (Powys) 7:348, 350; 46:313-14, 324
"Rodrigo Poems" (Cisneros) 69:144
Rodzinna Europa (*Native Realm: A Search for Self-Definition*) (Milosz) 22:309, 311-12; 31:263-64, 267-68, 270; 56:232, 242, 244, 250; 82:277, 279, 281, 289, 291, 297
Roger's Version (Updike) 43:437-39; 70:249, 262-63
RoGoPaG (Pasolini) 106:226
Rogue Male (Household) 11:277
"La roi Cophetua" (Gracq) 48:141
Le roi des Aulnes (*The Erlking*; *The Ogre*) (Tournier) 6:536-38; 23:452; 36:433-44; 95:361, 364, 366-67, 371-73, 375-78, 381, 390, 395
Le roi d'Yvetat (Renoir) 20:300
Le roi miraculé (*King Lazarus*) (Beti) 27:41-6, 49, 52
Le roi pêcheur (Gracq) 11:246; 48:134, 141
"Le roi s'amuse" (Urquhart) 90:374
Un roi sans divertissement (Giono) 4:184
Le roi se meurt (*Exit the King*; *The King Dies*) (Ionesco) 4:252; 6:253; 9:286; 11:290-94; 15:298; 41:224, 227, 229, 231; 86:332, 340
Rojsty (*Marshes*) (Konwicki) 8:325; 117:256, 260, 274, 283-84
Rok mysliwego (*The Hunter's Year*) (Milosz) 82:307-08
Roland Barthes by Roland Barthes (Barthes)
  See *Roland Barthes par Roland Barthes*
Roland Barthes par lui-même (Barthes)
  See *Roland Barthes par Roland Barthes*
Roland Barthes par Roland Barthes (*Roland Barthes by Roland Barthes*; *Roland Barthes par lui-même*) (Barthes) 24:31, 36; 83:79, 83-4, 88-9, 102-04
"Roland Hayes Beaten" (Hughes) 108:319
"The Role of the Writer in a New Nation" (Achebe) 51:2
"Roll Another Number" (Young) 17:574
"The Roll Call" (Johnston) 51:238
Roll, Jordan, Roll (Peterkin) 31:305, 307, 309, 311
"Roll Me Away" (Seger) 35:386-87
Roll of Thunder, Hear My Cry (Taylor) 21:419-21
"Roll On Bloomin' Death" (Luke) 38:313
"Roll On, Columbia" (Guthrie) 35:188, 194
"Roll Over, Beethoven" (Berry) 17:51-5
Roll Shenandoah (Lancaster) 36:245
Roll Sweet Chariot (Green) 25:195, 198-200
"Roller Coaster" (Parra) 102:348-49, 351
"Roller Skating Child" (Wilson) 12:651-52
"Rolling Back" (Haines) 58:222
"The Rolling Machine" (Kelman) 58:301
"rolling motion" (Moure) 88:224
The Rolling Season (Mayne) 12:392
The Rolling Stones (*Space Family Stone*) (Heinlein) 26:162, 165, 171-72, 176; 55:302
Rolling Stones Now (Jagger and Richard) 17:225, 232, 237
"Rolling Thunder" (Abbott) 48:6
Rolling Thunder (Schrader) 26:388-89, 399
Rolling Thunder Logbook (Shepard) 17:445-46
Roma (*Fellini Roma*; *Fellini's Roma*) (Fellini) 16:282-84, 298-300; 85:53, 55, 59, 65-6, 69, 71, 74, 76, 78-9, 81
Roma (Palazzeschi) 11:432
"Romaiosyni" ("Romiosini") (Ritsos) 31:325-26, 328
Le roman antillais (Conde) 92:100, 112-13
Roman Balcony and Other Poems (Gascoyne) 45:148, 150-51, 154
"Le roman comme recherche" (Butor) 3:92
"Roman Diary, 1951" (Ciardi) 40:162
The Roman Empire (Asimov) 76:312
"Roman Fountain" (Bogan) 39:387, 393; 46:79-80, 86-7; 93:76
Roman Hat (Queen) 11:458
"A Roman Holiday" (Hecht) 8:267
Roman Holiday (Sinclair) 15:498
Le roman inachevé (*The Unfinished Novel*) (Aragon) 22:38
"Roman Incident" (Porter) 33:322
"The Roman Night" (Morand)
  See "La nuit Romaine"
"Roman Poem III" (Barker) 48:18
"Roman Poem Number Five" (Jordan) 5:203
"Roman Poems" (Garrett) 51:144
"Roman Portrait Busts" (Updike) 23:475
"The Roman Quarry" (Jones) 42:242
The Roman Quarry and Other Sequences (Jones) 42:242-43, 246-48
"Roman Reasons" (Enright) 31:150
The Roman Republic (Asimov) 76:312
"A Roman Sarcophagus" (Lowell) 1:182
The Roman Spring of Mrs. Stone (Williams) 15:580-81; 45:453
Roman Tales (Moravia)
  See *I racconti Romani*
La Romana (*The Woman of Rome*) (Moravia) 7:240-41; 11:382; 18:344, 349; 46:283, 285
"Romance" (Amis) 40:40
"A Romance" (Dunn) 36:153
"Romance" (Fuller) 28:151
"Romance: A Prose Villanelle" (De Marinis) 54:101
"Romance I Think, Must Remain" (Lerman) 9:330
"Romance in the Twilight" (Salinas) 90:332
Romance of a Horse Thief (Polonsky) 92:402, 415-17
The Romance of Atlantis (Caldwell) 39:302-03
"A Romance of the Equator" (Aldiss) 40:19
"Romance of the Thin Man and the Fat Lady" (Coover) 15:145; 46:115
Romancero (Pasolini) 106:230-31
Le romancier et ses personnages (Mauriac) 56:205
"Romania, Romania" (Stern) 40:413
The Romanovs (Almedingen) 12:2
Romans, Countrymen, Lovers (Fleming) 37:123-24
The Romans in Britain (Brenton) 31:64, 66-9
"The Romantic" (Bogan) 46:77-8, 83-4; 93:64-5
Romantic Comedy (Slade) 46:371-72
The Romantic Egoists (Auchincloss) 45:26
"The Romantic Entanglement" (Ashbery) 77:69
The Romantic Manifesto (Rand) 79:369
Romantic Times (Nabokov)
  See *Glory*
"A Romantic Weekend" (Gaitskill) 69:199-203
Romanticism and Consciousness (Bloom) 103:47
Romanticism and the Modern Ego (*Classic, Romantic, and Modern*) (Barzun) 51:39-40
Romantics (Paustovsky) 40:367
"Rome" (Williams) 13:605
Rome 1630 (Bonnefoy) 58:60
Rome and a Villa (Clark) 5:106; 19:105
"Rome, Anno Santo" (Montague) 46:265-66
"The Rome Discourse" (Lacan)
  See "Fonction et champ de la parole et du langage en psychanalyse"
Rome Haul (Edmonds) 35:144-46, 148-49, 151, 153-54, 156-57
Rome n'est plus dans Rome (Marcel) 15:360
"Rome: The Night Before" (Moss) 50:353
Romeo and Jeannette (Anouilh)
  See *Roméo et Jeannette*
Romeo and Juliet (Cocteau)
  See *Roméo et Juliette*
Roméo et Jeannette (*Romeo and Jeannette*) (Anouilh) 13:16-17, 20; 40:51, 55-6
Roméo et Juliette (*Romeo and Juliet*) (Cocteau) 8:144; 43:109
"Romiosini" (Ritsos)
  See "Romaiosyni"
Rommel Drives On Deep into Egypt (Brautigan) 3:87-8; 12:59-60; 42:61
"Rompecabezas" ("Riddles") (Parra) 102:346
Romulus (Vidal) 4:553
"Romulus and Remus" (Hall) 51:172
Romulus der Grosse (*Romulus the Great*) (Duerrenmatt) 102:53, 55, 58, 60, 74, 77, 79, 83
Romulus der Grosse (*Romulus the Great: An Unhistorical Comedy*) (Durrenmatt) 8:194; 11:168-69, 171; 15:194
Romulus the Great (Duerrenmatt)
  See *Romulus der Grosse*
Romulus the Great: An Unhistorical Comedy (Durrenmatt)
  See *Romulus der Grosse*
"Rondeau Redoublé" (Avison) 97:76
Rondo (Brandys) 62:118-21
Rond-Point des Champs Elysées (Morand) 41:304
"Ronnie, Talk to Russia" (Prince) 35:324-26
The Roof (De Sica)
  See *Il tetto*
"Roof Beam" (Salinger)
  See "Raise High the Roofbeam, Carpenters"
"The Roof Tableau of Kashikojima" (Lieberman) 36:262
"The Roof, the Steeple and the People" (Ellison) 114:99
"Roof Tree" (Murphy) 41:320
"Roofs" (Levine) 33:274
"Rooftop" (Moss) 45:289
"The Roofwalker" (Rich) 7:371; 11:477-78; 18:446; 36:366
"Roog" (Dick) 72:113
"The Rookers" (Mason) 28:271
Rookie of the Year (Tunis) 12:595
"The Room" (Aiken) 52:22
"The Room" (Ignatow) 7:180; 40:258
"A Room" (Lessing) 94:261, 263-64
"The Room" (Sartre)

See "La chambre"
"The Room" (Strand)   6:521; 18:519
The Room (Altman)   116:59
The Room (Day Lewis)   10:128
The Room (Pinter)   1:268; 6:408, 410, 416-17; 9:419; 11:436-38, 440-41, 444; 15:422; 27:385, 388, 393-94; 58:371-75, 377-78, 381, 384; 73:252
The Room (Selby)   1:307; 2:390; 4:481-82
"The Room and the Cloud" (Seidel)   18:475
Room at the Top (Braine)   1:43-4; 41:55-60, 62
Room Enough to Caper (Brammer)   31:53-4
"A Room Forever" (Pancake)   29:346-47, 349
"Room Number Five" (Carey)   40:129
"A Room of Frail Dancers" (Helprin)   22:222
"Room of God and Door to Heaven" (Cook-Lynn)   93:116
A Room of His Own (Beckman)   26:87
Room Temperature (Baker)   61:5-6
A Room with a View (Forster)   4:169; 9:207; 13:215-16, 218-20; 22:131; 45:136, 138, 142; 77:241
A Room with a View (Jhabvala)   94:185, 187-88
"The Room with the Tapestry Rug" (Giovanni)   117:199
"A Roomful of Hovings and Other Profiles" (McPhee)   36:294, 297
The Roominghouse Madrigals: Early Selected Poems, 1946-1966 (Bukowski)   82:26-7
Rooms in the House of Stone (Dorris)   109:310
"The Roosevelt and the Antinoe" (Pratt)   19:379, 383
"The Rooster" (Orlovitz)   22:333, 336
"Roosters" (Bishop)   1:34-5; 4:66; 9:92; 32:29, 37-8, 42-3
"Root Cellar" (Roethke)   3:432; 11:484; 19:397; 101:293
"Root Hog or Die" (Guthrie)   35:183
The Root of It (MacCaig)   36:284
Rootabaga Stories (Sandburg)   10:448; 15:468; 35:347, 357
Rooted (Buzo)   61:51-6, 58-62, 64, 67-8
"Root-Light; or, The Lawyer's Daughter" (Dickey)   47:91-2, 98
"Roots" (Clifton)   66:70, 87
"Roots" (Haines)   58:217
"Roots" (Heaney)   14:244
"Roots" (Livesay)   79:336, 350, 352
"Roots" (Meredith)   4:349; 22:302
"Roots" (Thomas)   107:337, 340-41, 346
"Roots" (Walcott)   76:277-78
Roots (Haley)   76:343-45, 347-52
Roots (Wesker)   3:517-19; 5:481-82; 42:425, 427
Roots and Branches (Duncan)   2:122-23; 4:141; 7:87; 15:192; 41:129-30; 55:293, 295
The Roots of Heaven (Gary)
   See *Les racines du ciel*
The Roots of Heaven (Huston)   20:163, 165
The Roots of Treason: Ezra Pound and the Secret of St. Elizabeths (Torrey)   34:503-07, 509-12
"Roots, Rock, Reggae" (Marley)   17:268
Roots: The Next Generations (Haley)   12:253-55; 76:344-45, 348
Roots: The Saga of an American Family (Haley)   8:259-61; 12:246-53; 76:343-52, 346, 348
"Rope" (Porter)   15:429; 101:209-10
Rope (*Rope's End*) (Hamilton)   51:187, 189-90, 192, 194, 198
Rope (Hitchcock)   16:340, 345, 355
Rope of Gold (Herbst)   34:449, 451, 455
"Rope of Wind" (Dumas)   62:162
Rope of Wind (Dumas)   62:159, 164
"The Rope Trick" (Sillitoe)   57:388
"The Rope-Makers" (Longley)   29:293
"Ropes" (Townshend)   42:379
Rope's End (Hamilton)
   See *Rope*
"Rosa" (Morrissy)   99:78-9
"Rosa" (Ozick)   62:353, 357-58
La rosa separada: obra póstuma (*The Separate Rose*) (Neruda)   28:310, 313; 62:332-35
Rosaire (Ferron)   94:126
"Rosalie" (Seger)   35:379
"Rosalie's Folly" (Grenville)   61:162
Rosalind Passes (Swinnerton)   31:428
"Rosalinda's Eyes" (Joel)   26:217
"Rosalita" (Springsteen)   17:477, 482-85, 491
"Rosamund's Bower" (Aickman)   57:4
A Rosario Castellanos Reader: An Anthology of Her Poetry, Short Fiction, Essays, and Journals (Castellanos)   66:60-1
The Rosary Murders (Kienzle)   25:274-75
Rosas (Masefield)   11:357
"The Rose" (Carey)   96:25
"The Rose" (Cohen)   38:137
"Rose" (Dixon)   52:95
"Rose" (Dubus)   97:203, 208, 214-16, 218, 222-24, 227-28, 230
"Rose" (Guillevic)   33:193
"The Rose" (Roethke)   11:485; 101:289, 305, 308-09, 319-21
"The Rose and the Mignonette" (Aragon)
   See "La rose et la reseda"
The Rose and the Puritan (Nowlan)   15:398
The Rose and the Yew Tree (Christie)   12:115
"The Rose Beetle" (Merwin)   88:206
"The Rose Bush" (Giovanni)   64:191
Rose Cottage (Stewart)   117:394
La rose de sable (*Desert Love*) (Montherlant)   8:393; 19:325
"La rose des vents" (Wilbur)   53:405
Rose des vents (Soupault)   68:404-05
"La rose et la reseda" ("The Rose and the Mignonette") (Aragon)   22:37-8
"A Rose for Ecclesiastes" (Zelazny)   21:466-68, 474
"A Rose for Emily" (Faulkner)   8:213; 18:149; 28:143, 145; 52:142
A Rose for Winter: Travels in Andalusia (Lee)   90:179-80, 184-5, 187
"Rose Harbours Whaling Station" (Bowering)   32:47
A Rose in the Heart (O'Brien)   13:415-16
"A Rose in the Heart of New York" (O'Brien)   13:416; 36:339-41; 116:186, 189, 194
Rose Madder (King)   113:383, 386-87
The Rose of Solitude (Everson)   5:121; 14:166
"Rose Petals" (Jhabvala)   94:
"Rose Street" (Lustig)   56:182, 184
The Rose Tattoo (Williams)   1:368; 2:465; 5:498, 500; 30:470; 39:446; 45:446; 71:382
"The Rose Warehouse" (Stern)   40:410
Rose, Where Did You Get That Red? Teaching Great Poetry to Children (Koch)   44:245
Roseanna (Wahloo)   7:501-02
"Rosedale Afternoon" (Phillips)   28:361
Roseland (Jhabvala)   94:184
"Roselily" (Walker)   58:406; 103:358-61, 363, 406, 410, 412
Rosemary (Stolz)   12:548-49
Rosemary's Baby (Levin)   3:294-95; 6:305-07
Rosemary's Baby (Polanski)   16:464-67, 471-73
A Rosen by Any Other Name (Horovitz)   56:156
Rosencrantz and Guildenstern Are Dead (Stoppard)   1:327-28; 3:470; 4:524-25, 527; 5:412, 414; 8:501-02, 504; 15:518-19, 522-24; 29:393-94, 397, 399-401, 406; 34:273, 280-81; 63:391-426; 91:184, 187, 188-89
"Rosendo's Tale" (Borges)   10:67; 13:104; 48:35
"Rosenschimmer" (Celan)   82:49
"Roses" (Dove)   81:138
"The Roses" (Oliver)   98:256
Roses Are Blooming in Picardy (Bermant)   40:93
Roses Are Dead (Estleman)   48:105-06
"Roses, Late Summer" (Oliver)   98:281, 287
The Roses of Tretower (Mathias)   45:235
"Roses, Rhododendron" (Adams)   46:20
Les roses sauvages (*Wild Roses*) (Ferron)   94:104-8, 112, 118, 124-27
"Rose's Turn" (Sondheim)   30:389-90
The Rosewater Revolution: Notes on a Change of Attitude (Hughes)   48:182
"Rosewood, Ohio" (Matthews)   40:322
"Rosie" (Browne)   21:39
"Rosie Baby" (Huddle)   49:182
"Rosie Won't You Please Come Home?" (Davies)   21:88
Rosinante to the Road Again (Dos Passos)   1:77; 25:146; 82:105
"Rosita, the Future Waits with Hands of Swans" (Salinas)   90:332
Ross Macdonald (Bruccoli)   34:416-17
Rosshalde (Hesse)   2:190; 17:195, 202, 217
"Rostered Duty" (Murray)   40:337
"The rosy aureole of your affection" (Brutus)   43:90
"Rosy Cheeks" (Howe)   47:172
The Rosy Crucifixion (Miller)   2:282; 9:379; 14:373; 43:294, 297-98; 84:277
Rosy Starling (Garfield)   12:235
"Rotation of Crops" (Hollander)   8:300
The Rotten Book (Rodgers)   12:493
"Rotten Lake" (Rukeyser)   27:406, 408
The Rotten Years (Wojciechowska)   26:455-57
"Rouge High" (Hughes)   35:215
"Rough Boys" (Townshend)   17:541
The Rough Field (Montague)   13:390-92; 46:269-77, 279
Rough Mix (Townshend)   17:537-38, 540
"Rough Outline" (Simic)   49:336; 68:373
"Rough Sketch" (Simmons)   43:407
Rough Strife (Schwartz)   31:387-90
"Rough Translations" (Giles)   39:65-6
Rough Translations (Giles)   39:64-6
Rough Treatment (Wajda)   16:584-85
Roughneck (Thompson)   69:383-84
Rougon-Macquart (Ehrenburg)   62:179
Round about America (Caldwell)   50:302
"Round and Round" (Seth)   90:351
Round and Round the Garden (Ayckbourn)   5:36-7; 74:4-6
"The Round Dozen" (Maugham)   67:209
A Round of Applause (MacCaig)   36:281-82
"Round Song" (McGrath)   28:280
'Round the Clock Non-Stop (*Kruglie sutki non-stop*) (Aksyonov)   101:22, 29

"The Roundhouse Voices" (Smith)   **22**:389;
   42:346, 352-53
*The Roundhouse Voices: Selected and New
   Poems* (Smith)   **42**:352, 354, 356-57
"Rounds" (Selzer)   **74**:272
Rounds (Arghezi)
   See *Hore*
Rounds (Busch)   **18**:85-6; **47**:59, 64
"Rouse Him Not" (Wellman)   **49**:396
"La route" (Gracq)   **48**:141
"Route" (Oppen)   **7**:283
La route d'Altamont (The Road Past Altamont)
   (Roy)   **10**:440; **14**:467
La route des Flandres (The Flanders Road)
   (Simon)   **4**:495-96; **9**:482, 484; **15**:487,
   491-94; **39**:203-07, 209-11
Route Two and Back (Dorris)   **109**:298
Routines (Ferlinghetti)   **111**:63
"The Rover" (Page and Plant)   **12**:477-78
A Row of Tigers (Corcoran)   **17**:70
Row with Your Hair (Tate)   **6**:528
Rowan Farm (Benary-Isbert)   **12**:31-2
"Rowayton at 4 P. M." (Klappert)   **57**:256
"Rowing" (Sexton)   **6**:492, 494; **53**:322
"The Rowing Endeth" (Sexton)   **6**:492, 494;
   53:322
"Równina" (Milosz)   **56**:236
Równina (The Plain) (Rozewicz)   **23**:362
"Rows of Cold Trees" (Winters)   **32**:468
"Roxanne" (Police, The)   **26**:363-64
Roxy and Elsewhere (Zappa)   **17**:590-91
"Roy Bradley, Boy Broodcaster" (Keillor)
   115:286, 295
The Roy Murphy Show (Buzo)   **61**:52-3, 56, 60
"Royal Beatings" (Munro)   **95**:290
"Royal Blue" (Loewinsohn)   **52**:285
Royal Charles: Charles II and the Restoration
   (Fraser)   **32**:184-85; **107**:35,42,67
Royal Chronicles (Mujica Lainez)
   See *Crónicas reales*
"The Royal Commission" (Johnston)   **51**:242,
   252
"Royal Ebony" (Guillen)
   See "Ebano real"
The Royal Family (Ferber)   **93**:159, 165, 171
The Royal Family (Kaufman)   **38**:258, 262
Royal Harry (Mayne)   **12**:395, 399, 407
The Royal Hunt of the Sun (Shaffer)   **5**:386-
   89; **14**:485-87; **18**:475-77; **37**:383-84;
   60:359, 361, 363, 373
"Royal Jelly" (Dahl)   **79**:176, 180, 183
"Royal Orleans" (Page and Plant)   **12**:480
"The Royal Palms" (Walcott)   **76**:278
The Royal Pardon (Arden)   **15**:21
"The Royal Scam" (Becker and Fagen)   **26**:80
The Royal Scam (Becker and Fagen)   **26**:80-1,
   83, 85
"A Royal Visit" (Montague)   **46**:266
The Royal Way (Malraux)
   See *La voie royale*
Royaume farfelu (Malraux)   **57**:301
"Rozmowa na Wielkanoc 1620 r." (Milosz)
   56:237
"R.T.S.L." (Walcott)   **42**:421
Le ru d'Ikoué (Theriault)   **79**:418
Rubailer (Hikmet)
   See *Quatrains*
"Rubaiyat" (Borges)   **4**:75
Rubber Band (Bowie)   **17**:65
Rubber Soul (Lennon and McCartney)   **12**:357,
   360, 366, 371-72, 375; **35**:274, 278
Rubbers (Reynolds)   **38**:390
"Rubbing the Faces of Angels" (Bottoms)

   53:31
"Rubble" (Thomas)   **13**:542
Rubble (Solzhenitsyn)
   See *From under the Rubble*
"Rubens' Innocents" (Slessor)   **14**:495
Rubicon Beach (Erickson)   **64**:138-40, 142,
   144
"Rublyovskoye shosse" (Voznesensky)   **57**:416-
   17
Rubrics for a Revolution (L'Heureux)   **52**:272-
   73
Ruby (Guy)   **26**:142-43, 145
"Ruby and Amethyst" (Graves)   **45**:166
"Ruby Brown" (Hughes)   **108**:326
Ruby Red (Fox)   **22**:139-40
Rubyfruit Jungle (Brown)   **18**:72-5; **43**:80-5;
   79:153, 155-57, 159-61, 163-69, 172
Ruce Venušiny (Seifert)
   See *The Arms of Venus*
A Rude Awakening (Aldiss)   **40**:15
Un rude hiver (A Hard Winter) (Queneau)   **5**:362
"Rudie Can't Fail" (Clash)   **30**:46-7
Rudyard Kipling (Stewart)   **7**:466
Rudyard Kipling and His World (Amis)   **8**:11
Rue des boutiques obscures (Modiano)   **18**:338
Rue deschambault (Street of Riches) (Roy)
   14:465-66, 468
Rue traversière (Bonnefoy)   **9**:114; **58**:60
*La rueda dentada (The Serrated Wheel; The
   Serrated Wheel)* (Guillen)   **48**:159-60,
   164; **79**:229
The Ruffian on the Stair (Orton)   **4**:388; **43**:328-
   29, 331-34
Ruffles and Drums (Cavanna)   **12**:101-02
Rufus (Fair)   **18**:142
"The Rug" (O'Brien)   **5**:313
"Rugaroo" (Erdrich)   **54**:166
"Rugby Football Excursion" (MacNeice)
   53:231
"Rugby Road" (Garrett)   **51**:147
"Ruidoso" (McPhee)   **36**:296
"The Ruin" (Tomlinson)   **13**:549
Ruin the Sacred Truths (Bloom)   **103**:36-9
"Las ruinas circulares" ("The Circular Ruins")
   (Borges)   **1**:38; **2**:76; **3**:80; **6**:87; **8**:97,
   99, 102; **9**:121; **10**:65; **19**:46; **48**:33-5,
   46; **83**:156-57, 175, 177, 181
Le ruine presque cocasse d'un polichinelle
   (Beti)   **27**:53
The Ruined Boys (That Distant Afternoon)
   (Fuller)   **28**:149
The Ruined Map (Abe)
   See *Moetsukita chizu*
Ruining the New Road: Poems (Matthews)
   40:318-19
"Ruins" (Thomas)   **6**:530
Ruins and Visions: Poems, 1934-1942
   (Spender)   **41**:428; **91**:263
"Ruins of a Great House" ("Great House")
   (Walcott)   **25**:450-51, 455; **42**:421;
   76:273, 278, 281
The Ruins of Isis (Bradley)   **30**:32
Ruka a plamen (The Arm and the Flame)
   (Seifert)   **93**:343
"Rule 18" (Simak)   **55**:321
Rule Britannia (du Maurier)   **6**:147; **59**:284,
   287
"The Rule of Names" (Le Guin)   **71**:186
"Rule of Three" (Sturgeon)   **39**:366
Rulers of the City (Fleming)   **37**:127
The Rules of Attraction (Ellis)   **71**:147, 149-
   51, 157, 162, 164, 166; **117**:105-07, 113,
   123, 132-33, 135-38, 141, 143, 147, 150

*The Rules of Chaos; or, Why Tomorrow Doesn't
   Work* (Vizinczey)   **40**:434-36
"Rules of Sleep" (Moss)   **45**:290
Rules of Sleep (Moss)   **45**:289-90; **50**:353
The Rules of the Game (Leiris)
   See *La règle du jeu*
The Rules of the Game (Renoir)
   See *La regle du jeu*
The Ruling Class (Barnes)   **5**:49-50; **56**:2-5, 7-
   8
Rum and Coke (Reddin)   **67**:265-68, 270-71
"Rumba" (Guillen)   **48**:163; **79**:234, 239-40
Rumble Fish (Hinton)   **30**:205; **111**:77-83, 85,
   90
"Rumble in Bavaria" (Royko)   **109**:406
"Ruminant" (Scannell)   **49**:327
"Rumination" (Eberhart)   **56**:81, 87
"Ruminations of Luke Johnson" (Brown)
   59:263
Rumming Park (Mortimer)   **28**:281
A Rumor of War (Caputo)   **32**:102-06
"Rumor Verified" (Warren)   **39**:258
Rumor Verified: Poems, 1979-1980 (Warren)
   39:257-61, 265
Rumors (Simon)   **70**:240-41
Rumors of Peace (Leffland)   **19**:278-80
Rumour at Nightfall (Greene)   **18**:194; **72**:148,
   158-59, 161
"Rumours of Foot" (Hillis)   **66**:199
Rumours of Our Death (Walker)   **61**:428
Rumours of Rain (Rain) (Brink)   **18**:68-9;
   36:65, 68; **106**:96-7, 99, 123-24, 130, 146
"Rumpelstiltskin" (Broumas)   **73**:4, 7, 13
"Rumpelstiltskin" (Sexton)   **53**:314
Rumplestiltskin (Hunter)   **31**:226-27
"Rumpole for the Defence" (Mortimer)   **28**:287
Rumpole of the Bailey (Mortimer)   **43**:308
Rumpole's Return (Mortimer)   **28**:287; **43**:305
Rumstick Road (Gray)   **49**:146-47; **112**:97, 107,
   114
"The Run for the Elbertas" (Still)   **49**:366-68
The Run for the Elbertas (Still)   **49**:369-70
"Run for the Stars" (Ellison)   **42**:127
Run for Your Wife! (Cooney)   **62**:143-48
Run Man Run (Himes)   **18**:245; **58**:254, 257,
   263; **108**:234
A Run of Jacks (Hugo)   **6**:244; **32**:234-38,
   244, 247, 249
Run River (Didion)   **3**:128; **8**:174, 177; **32**:143,
   147, 150
Run Softly, Go East (Wersba)   **30**:430-31
Run with the Hunted (Bukowski)   **41**:64;
   108:94-5
"Runagate, Runagate" (Hayden)   **5**:168; **37**:155,
   157, 160
"Runaround" (Asimov)   **26**:54; **76**:319; **92**:4,
   11, 20
"The Runaway" (Frost)   **26**:112
"The Runaway" (Ross)   **13**:492
Runaway Horse (Walser)   **27**:466-67
Runaway Horses (Mishima)   **4**:355-58; **6**:337-
   38; **27**:341-42
Runaway Voyage (Cavanna)   **12**:102-03
Runaways (Swados)   **12**:558-61
"Runaways Café I" (Hacker)   **72**:187
"Runaways Café II" (Hacker)   **72**:187
"Runes" (Brown)   **5**:77
"Runes" (Nemerov)   **6**:361-62; **9**:394; **36**:304-
   05
Runes (Baxter)   **14**:60
"Runes from the Island of Horses" (Brown)
   48:57
"Rungstedlund: A Radio Address" (Dinesen)

95:58
"The Runner" (Dacey)   51:81
"The Runner" (Simpson)   4:499; 7:426-28
Runner in the Sun: A Story of Indian Maize
    (McNickle)   89:160, 165, 168-69, 171-
    73, 175-79, 181
The Runner Stumbles (Stitt)   29:389-91
"The Runners" (Purdy)   50:242
"Runners" (Waddington)   28:439
Runners (Poliakoff)   38:385-86
"Running" (Dobyns)   37:76-7
"Running" (Dubus)   97:231
"Running" (Wilbur)   53:413; 110:384
"Running Away" (Marley)   17:271
"Running Away from Home" (Kizer)   39:169-
    71
"Running Child" (Coles)   46:113
Running Dog (DeLillo)   13:178-79; 27:85-6;
    39:117, 123, 125-26; 54:82, 90; 76:177-
    78, 180, 182
"Running Dreams" (Beattie)   40:64; 63:12, 19
"Running Dry" (Young)   17:569
"Running Gun Blues" (Bowie)   17:57
Running in the Family (Ondaatje)   29:342-43;
    51:313-14, 318, 320; 76:202, 206
The Running, Jumping, and Standing Still Film
    (Lester)   20:219, 228
The Running Man (King)   37:201, 207; 113:388
"Running of Streight" (Davidson)   13:166
"The Running of the Grunion" (Rukeyser)
    10:442
The Running of the Tide (Forbes)   12:208-09
"Running on Empty" (White)   110:330, 340,
    344
Running on Empty (Browne)   21:39-41
Running on Empty (Phillips)   28:364-65
"Running on the Spot" (Weller)   26:447
"Running Stream" (Blunden)   56:49
"Rupee" (Willingham)   51:403
"Rupert Beersley and the Beggar Master of
    Sivani-Hotta" (Boyle)   36:63
"Rupture" (Pasternak)   63:280, 291
La rupture (Chabrol)   16:175, 182
"Rural Colloquy with a Painter" (Steele)   45:363
"Rural Hazards" (Queneau)   42:337
"Rural Objects" (Ashbery)   2:17
Rus into Muscovy (Land of Muscovy)
    (Almedingen)   12:6-7
Rush/What Fuckan Theory (Bissett)   18:59
Rushes (Rechy)   18:442-43; 107:254-56, 258
"Rushing" (Young Bear)   94:362
Ruski (Burroughs)   109:182
"Russia and the Virus of Liberty" (Cioran)   64:98
"A Russian Beauty" (Nabokov)   6:351-53
A Russian Beauty, and Other Stories (Nabokov)
    3:354-55; 6:351-52
"The Russian Dancer" (Bates)   46:51
Russian Dictionary of Linguistic Expression
    (Solzhenitsyn)   78:434
"A Russian Doll" (Bioy Casares)   88:92-3, 95
A Russian Doll, and Other Stories (Bioy
    Casares)
    See *Una muñeca rusa*
The Russian Forest (Leonov)
    See *Russkii les*
Russian Hide-and-Seek (Amis)   40:42
The Russian Interpreter (Frayn)   31:189-90
Russian Journal (Lee)   36:252-55, 257
The Russian People (Odets)   98:196
"Russian Winter Journal" (Ferlinghetti)   27:139
The Russians and the Americans (Archer)
    12:21-2
Russkii les (The Russian Forest) (Leonov)

92:240, 247-48, 250-52, 254-55, 260,
    266, 274, 277-78
Russkoe (Coles)   67:175
Rust Never Sleeps (Young)   17:580-81, 583
Rustic Elegies (Sitwell)   67:312-13
"The Rustle of History's Wings, As They Said
    Then" (Amichai)   57:37
The Rustle of Language (Barthes)
    See *Le bruissement de la langue*
"Rustling Taffetas" (Milosz)   56:239
"Ruth" (Engel)   36:162
"Ruth" (Oates)   19:353
"Ruth" (Plumly)   33:313
"Ruthanna Elder" (Purdy)   52:350
"Ruthie and Edie" (Paley)   37:334, 336, 338
"Ruth's Song (Because She Could Not Sing It)"
    (Steinem)   63:379, 382-83
Rvach (The Grabber) (Ehrenburg)   62:175-76,
    178
"Ryder" (Haines)   58:220
"Ryder" (Rukeyser)   15:457
Ryder (Barnes)   3:36-7; 8:47; 29:27-9
Rysopis (Identification Marks: None)
    (Skolimowski)   20:348-50, 353
*Rzeka podziemna, podziemne ptaki (Under-
    ground River, Underground Birds)*
    (Konwicki)   117:275, 279, 284, 288, 290-
    91
"s" (Piercy)
    See "In the Men's Room"
s (Loewinsohn)
    See *Magnetic Field*
S. (Updike)   70:248-49
"S. Dead" (Piercy)   27:374
"S/He" (Paulin)   37:354
S Is for Space (Bradbury)   42:34, 39
S. J. Perelman: A Life (Herrmann)   44:500-04
"S. Karuma-shi no hanzai" ("The Crime of S.
    Karma"; "Mr. S. Karuma's Crime") (Abe)
    81:293, 297
*S. Karuma-shi no hanzai (The Crime of S.
    Karma)* (Abe)   81:285, 288
"S. L." (Brodkey)   56:60, 68
S/Z (Barthes)   24:28-31, 35-7; 83:74, 77-8,
    83, 85-7, 89-91, 95-6, 99, 103
S-1 (Baraka)   10:19-20; 14:48; 33:57
Saat 21-22 siirleri (Poems of 9-10 P.M.)
    (Hikmet)   40:245, 247
"Sabás" (Guillen)   48:157, 162
"Sabbath Park" (McGuckian)   48:277-78
"Sabbatha and Solitude" (Williams)   5:502;
    15:580
Sabbatical: A Romance (Barth)   27:25-31;
    51:22, 24, 26-9
Sabella; or, The Blood Stone (Lee)   46:231
"Sabélo" (Ulibarrí)   83:414
"Sabeth" (Eich)   15:202
Sabine (Freeling)   38:186
"The Sabine Farm" (Parini)   54:360, 362
"Les sabines" (Ayme)   11:23
Sabotage (Hitchcock)   16:345, 358
The Sabre Squadron (Raven)   14:441-42
"Sabrina" (Turco)   63:429
Sabrina (Wilder)   20:457
Sac Prairie People (Derleth)   31:131
Sackett's Land (L'Amour)   25:280-81
Sacktown Rag (Walker)   61:425
"Le sacré dans la vie quotidienne" (Leiris)
    61:357
"Le Sacre du Printemps" (Piercy)   62:377
Le sacre du printemps (Simon)   4:495; 9:485;
    15:487, 490-92; 39:203-04, 209-11
"Sacred" (Silkin)   43:398

The Sacred and Profane Love Machine
    (Murdoch)   4:367-70; 6:342-47; 8:404;
    15:388-89; 31:294
Sacred and Profane Memories (Van Vechten)
    33:395
Sacred and Secular Elegies (Barker)   48:14,
    17, 21
"The Sacred and the Suburban" (Phillips)
    28:363
"Sacred Chant for the Return of Black Spirit
    and Power" (Baraka)   5:48
Sacred Cows and Other Edibles (Giovanni)
    64:195-96; 117:189
"Sacred Elegies" (Barker)   8:46
"The Sacred Factory" (Toomer)   22:428, 430
Sacred Families (Donoso)   8:179-80; 32:154,
    159-60; 99:220
Sacred Families; Three Novellas (Donoso)
    See *Tres novelitas burguesas*
The Sacred Flame (Maugham)   67:225
"The Sacred Hearth" (Gascoyne)   45:147, 154,
    157
"The Sacred Hoop: A Contemporary Indian
    Perspective on Native American Litera-
    ture" (Allen)   84:13, 29-30, 35
*The Sacred Hoop: Recovering the Feminine in
    American Indian Traditions* (Allen)
    84:14-15, 19-19, 22-4, 26-9, 31-3, 35-6,
    39, 45
Sacred Hunger (Unsworth)   76:252-60
"The Sacred Marriage" (Oates)   19:351;
    108:354-58, 368-69
Sacred Monsters (Cocteau)
    See *Les monstres sacrés*
"The Sacred Mound" (Foote)   75:230, 232,
    257
"The Sacred Rhino of Uganda" (Amis)   40:43
*The Sacred Wood: Essays on Poetry and Criti-
    cism* (Eliot)   6:166; 9:190; 24:158, 160-
    61, 163, 169, 171, 173, 178-84, 186;
    34:398 55:352; 57:211-13
"The Sacred Wood Revisited" (McIlvanney)
    42:285
The Sacred Zone (Fuentes)
    See *Zona sagrada*
"The Sacrifice" (Auchincloss)   45:30
"The Sacrifice" (Hamburger)   5:159
The Sacrifice (Bidart)   33:77, 79-81
The Sacrifice (Slavitt)   14:491
Sacrifice (Vachss)   106:362
The Sacrifice Consenting (Dickey)   28:119
"A Sacrifice in the Orchard" (Bly)   38:54-5,
    57
"Sacrifice in the Temple" (Robbins)   21:340
"Sacrifice of a Virgin in the Mayan Bull Court"
    (Dubie)   36:134
"The Sacrificial Egg" (Achebe)   26:22-3; 75:13-
    14
Sacrificio en el Monte Moriah (Marques)
    96:242-45, 250, 252
The Sacrilege of Alan Kent (Caldwell)   60:46-
    8, 67
Sad as She (Onetti)
    See *Tan triste como ella*
"The Sad Ballad of the Fifteen Consecutive
    Rhymes" (Starbuck)   53:354
"The Sad Boy" (Riding)   7:374
Sad Cypress (Christie)   39:438; 48:72-3, 76
*Sad Dust Glories: Poems during Work Summer
    in Woods* (Ginsberg)   36:188
A Sad Heart at the Supermarket (Jarrell)   2:208;
    6:260; 9:297
Sad Ires (Enright)   8:203

"The Sad Phoenician" (Kroetsch)   23:273-76
"Sad Steps" (Larkin)   5:229; 8:341; 13:335;
   33:261; 39:344; 64:272, 276, 282
"Sadako" (Soto)   80:294
"Sadastor" (Smith)   43:424
The Saddest Summer of Samuel S (Donleavy)
   1:76; 4:125; 6:139, 141; 10:154; 45:126
"Saddle Up the Palomino" (Young)   17:576
Sade, Fourier, Loyola (Barthes)   24:31-2; 83:83
*The Sadeian Woman: An Exercise in Cultural
   History* (Carter)   41:117, 119; 76:324,
   327, 329
"Sad-Eyed Lady of the Lowlands" (Dylan)
   12:183; 77:177-78
"Sadie" (Matthiessen)   64:321-22, 324
"Sadie and Maude" (Brooks)   49:22
Sadler's Birthday (Tremain)   42:382-84
"Sadness" (Galvin)   38:198
Sadness (Barthelme)   2:41-2; 3:43-4; 5:53;
   6:30-1; 8:50; 13:55; 23:44, 47; 46:35-6,
   41; 59:247, 250; 115:60, 68
"Sadness and Happiness" (Pinsky)   9:416;
   38:355
Sadness and Happiness: Poems (Pinsky)
   9:416-17; 38:359, 362; 94:299, 308
"Sadness and Joy" (Amichai)
   See "Atsvut vesimha"
The Sadness of Days: New and Selected Poems
   (Salinas)   90:332-33
"Sadness on a Deserted Evening" (Kunene)
   85:162
"Sado Machismo" (White)   110:332
"Safe and Sound" (Simon)   26:408
Safe Conduct (Pasternak)   7:295-96; 10:384;
   18:381; 63:290-93
"Safe European Home" (Clash)   30:43, 46
"Safe Houses" (Gordimer)   70:177
"Safe Lives" (Beer)   58:32
"Safe Places" (Urdang)   47:399
"Safe Subjects" (Komunyakaa)   94:239
The Safety Net (Boell)
   See *Fürsorgliche Belagerung*
"The Safety-Valve" (Fuller)   62:185
"Safeway" (Barthelme)   36:50
"Saga" (Voznesensky)   57:426
The Saga of a Seagull (Kemal)
   See *Seagull*
The Saga of Anathan (Sternberg)   20:373, 376
Saga of the Patient Footsoldier (Wittlin)
   25:466
Sagan om Fatumeh (*The Tale of Fatumeh*)
   (Ekeloef)   27:116-17
Sagarana (Rosa)   23:348-51, 354-55
"Sagesse" (H. D.)   14:223; 31:208; 73:143
"Sagg Beach" (Crase)   58:162, 165
Sagittario (Ginzburg)   11:228; 54:209, 210,
   213-14
La Sagouine (Maillet)   54:303-06, 308, 310-
   11, 313-16, 318
Said the Don (FitzGerald)   19:178
"Said the Old Man to the Young Man" (Wesker)
   42:426
Said the Old Man to the Young Man (Wesker)
   42:426
Saigon Rose (Edgar)   42:120-21
"Saikai" (Kawabata)   107:104
"Sail Away" (Young)   17:580
Sail Away (Coward)   1:65
"Sail On, Sailor" (Wilson)   12:646
"A Sailboat of Occasions" (Mahapatra)   33:284
"Sailfish off Mombasa" (Hemingway)   34:478
"Sailing" (Dacey)   51:83
"Sailing Home from Rapallo" (Lowell)   8:353;

37:243
*Sailing into the Unknown: Yeats, Pound, and
   Eliot* (Rosenthal)   28:395-96
"Sailing Nights" (Seger)   35:380
"Sailing the Back Water" (Smith)   22:386
Sailing through China (Theroux)   46:398
"Sailing to an Island" (Murphy)   41:311, 314,
   316, 318
Sailing to an Island (Murphy)   41:311-12,
   314-16, 318-19
"Sailor Ashore" (Merwin)   5:288
"Sailor Boy of the Garden" (Elytis)   100:175
"The Sailor Boy's Tale" (Dinesen)   29:159;
   95:61
The Sailor from Gibraltar (Duras)
   See *Le marin de Gibraltar*
The Sailor from Gibralter (Isherwood)   44:397
"A Sailor in Africa" (Dove)   81:138
"Sailor off the Bremen" (Shaw)   7:411; 23:395;
   34:370
Sailor off the Bremen (Shaw)   23:395
The Sailor Who Fell from Grace with the Sea
   (Mishima)
   See *Gogo no eiko*
"Sailors" (Nowlan)   15:398
"Sailors" (Wild)   14:581
The Sailor's Return (Garnett)   3:188
"A Saint" (Johnston)   51:239, 245
"Saint" (Rosenthal)   28:395
The Saint and Mary Kate (O'Connor)   14:395,
   397, 400; 23:328-30
"St. Anthony of the Desert" (Colwin)   84:151
Saint Carmen de la main (*Saint Carmen of the
   Main*) (Tremblay)   29:419, 422, 424-25;
   102:362, 372, 374-75, 381
Saint Carmen of the Main (Tremblay)
   See *Saint Carmen de la main*
"Saint Daniel the Paranoiac" (Klappert)
   57:269
The Saint Elias (Ferron)
   See *Le Saint-Elias*
Saint Genet, Actor and Martyr (Sartre)
   See *Saint Genet, comédien et martyr*
Saint Genet, comédien et martyr (*Saint Genet,
   Actor and Martyr*) (Sartre)   4:475-76;
   7:393; 13:498; 18:473; 24:404, 407-10;
   44:497; 50:370; 52:380
"Saint George and the Dragon: An Elizabethan
   Pageant" (Beer)   58:38
Saint Glinglin (Queneau)   5:361
Saint Jack (Theroux)   5:427-28; 8:512; 46:405
"Saint Joey" (Demby)   53:101
Saint John's Eve (Duhamel)
   See *La nuit de la Saint-Jean*
"Saint Judas" (Wright)   10:542
Saint Judas (Wright)   3:540-43; 5:520; 10:542,
   544-45; 28:463, 468, 470-71
Saint Maybe (Tyler)   103:247-48, 255-56, 261,
   263, 267-70
"Saint Valentine" (Moore)   10:348
"Sainte Lucie" (Walcott)   9:557; 14:549-51;
   42:421-22
Sainte-Europe (*Holy Europe*) (Adamov)   25:14-
   15, 17-18, 20-1
Le Saint-Elias (*The Saint Elias*) (Ferron)
   94:106, 120, 124, 127
"The Saintly Men of Safed" (Michener)   5:289
"Saints" (Gerstler)   70:158
"Saints" (Mukherjee)   53:266, 268, 270
"Saints" (Trevor)   116:338-40, 345
Saints and Scholars (Eagleton)   63:107-10
Saints and Strangers (Carter)
   See *Black Venus*

"The Saints in Caesar's Household" (Tyler)
   103:258
"Saints Lose Back" (Willard)   7:539
"The Saint's Path" (Seger)   75:77
Saint-Watching (McGinley)   14:365, 368
Une saison à Rihata (*A Season in Rihata*)
   (Conde)   52:81-2, 85; 92:99-100, 109,
   111, 130-31
Une saison au Congo (*A Season in the Congo*)
   (Cesaire)   112:3-4, 7, 21, 24, 28
Une saison dans la vie d'Emmanuel (*A Season
   in the Life of Emmanuel*) (Blais)   2:63;
   4:66-7; 6:80-1; 13:96; 22:60
"The Sake of Words for Their Own Sake"
   (Simpson)   32:381
Sakhar-the-Pouch (Solzhenitsyn)   4:507
Sakonnet Point (Gray)   49:146; 112:106-07
"Sakyamuni Coming Out from the Mountain"
   (Ginsberg)   3:194; 4:182
*Sal Si Puedes: Cesar Chavez and the New
   American Revolution* (Matthiessen)
   7:212; 32:289-90, 292; 64:303-04
"La sala" (Marques)   96:245
"Salad" (Nichol)   18:369
"Salad Days" (Musgrave)   54:335
Salad Days (Sagan)
   See *Le chien couchant*
"The Saladmaker" (McFadden)   48:246
The Saladmaker (McFadden)   48:246-48
"Salamander" (McCartney)   35:286
"Salamander" (Rukeyser)   27:408
The Salamander (Paz)
   See *Salamandra*
The Salamander (West)   6:563-64
Salamandra (*The Salamander*) (Paz)   51:324;
   65:181
"Salami" (Levine)   4:286; 9:332
Salammbô (Ludlam)   50:342
"Sale" (Desai)   97:149, 171
"Sale Day" (Sargeson)   31:370
"Salem" (Lowell)   8:356
Salem's Lot (King)   12:309; 26:237, 239, 242;
   37:199, 201, 204-05; 61:319, 323, 327,
   331, 333; 113:341, 344-47, 349, 354-55,
   362, 365, 384, 387-91, 393
Salesman (Maysles and Maysles)   16:438-39,
   443
Salesman in Beijing (Miller)   47:253-54
"A Salesman Is an It That Stinks, Excuse"
   (Cummings)   68:41
"The Salesman's Son Grows Older" (Blaise)
   29:75
"Saliences" (Ammons)   5:26-7; 8:13, 16; 9:26-
   8, 30; 57:59; 108:11, 23
"Salinas Sees Romance Coming His Way" (Sali-
   nas)   90:332
The Saliva Milkshake (Brenton)   31:65-7
Salka valka (Laxness)   25:290, 295
"Sally" (Durcan)   70:152
Sally Bowles (Isherwood)   11:300; 14:284, 286;
   44:397, 399-400
Sally Can't Dance (Reed)   21:308-09
Salmos (Cardenal)   31:75
Salo: 120 Days of Sodom (*The 120 Days of
   Sodoma*) (Pasolini)   20:268-70; 106:238-
   39, 241, 248-50, 257, 268, 273
Saloma (Krleza)   114:172-73
"Salome" (Ai)   69:9
"Salome" (Garrett)   51:147-48
"Salome" (Komunyakaa)   94:241
Salome of the Tenements (Yezierska)   46:441-
   42, 444-45
"Salon des indépendents" (Szirtes)   46:392

"Salon des refusés" (Thomas) 13:539

Salonika (Page) 40:351, 353-55

"Salsa" (Walcott) 67:361

"Salt" (Levine) 33:274

Salt (Gold) 4:191-92; 42:190-92, 198

Salt (Szymborska) 99:199, 203

The Salt Eaters (Bambara) 19:33-35; 88:9-11, 20-21, 23-24, 26-29, 31, 33-41, 43-44

"The Salt Garden" (Nemerov) 36:304-05

The Salt Garden (Nemerov) 2:305, 308; 6:361; 36:303, 305

Salt in the Wound (Sciascia)
   See *La parrocchie di Regalpetra*

The Salt Lands (Shaffer) 14:484

"Salt of the Earth" (Jagger and Richard) 17:222, 238, 241

"The Salt of the Earth" (West) 31:454; 50:399

Salt of the Earth (Humphreys) 47:190

Salt of the Earth (Wittlin) 25:467-69, 471

"Salt Water" (Pinsky) 94:302-3

"Salt Water Story" (Hugo) 32:250

"Saltcod Red" (Lieberman) 36:262

The Salterton Trilogy (Davies) 42:102, 104; 75:184, 191, 199; 91:201, 204

Salto (Konwicki) 8:326

Salto (*Somersault*) (Konwicki) 117:282

Salt-Water Ballads (Masefield) 11:357; 47:229, 233

Saltwater Summer (Haig-Brown) 21:139-40

"Salud decimos cada día" ("We Say 'Cheers' Every Day") (Neruda) 62:335

"Salut à l'oiseau" (Prevert) 15:437

Le salut de l'Irlande (*The Salvation of Ireland*) (Ferron) 94:112, 115

"A Salute to My Friend Zo Nozizwe" (Kunene) 85:176

"Salute to the Orient" (Forster) 15:229

"Salute to the Passing" (Himes) 108:235

Salvador (Didion) 32:144-46

Salvador (Stone) 73:365-67, 369-70, 375-77, 381-82

"El Salvador: An Aide Memoire" ("Aide-Memoire") (Forche) 83:197, 213-15

The Salvation Hunters (Sternberg) 20:371

Salvation Now (Wilson) 33:464

The Salvation of Ireland (Ferron)
   See *Le salut de l'Irlande*

"The Salvation of Me" (Pancake) 29:347, 350

Salwàre (Zuckmayer) 18:556

The Salzburg Connection (MacInnes) 27:282; 39:349-50

The Salzburg Tales (Stead) 2:422-23; 32:407, 415; 80:305, 307, 321-24, 326, 334, 340

Sam (Corcoran) 17:69-70

Sam Ego's House (Saroyan) 8:467

Sam O'Shanker (Russell) 60:320

"Sam Palka and David Vishkover" (Singer) 6:510

"Sam Sam the Candy Man" (Lane) 25:284-85

"Sam Smiley" (Brown) 59:262, 265-66

"Sam, Soren, and Ed" (Vanderhaeghe) 41:448-49, 451-52

Sam the Sudden (Wodehouse) 5:515

Sam Tucker (Green) 25:192

Samá láska (*All Love; Nothing but Love; Only Love*) (Seifert) 34:259; 44:425-26; 93:318, 339-41

Samapti (Ray) 16:494

"Samaritans" (Kelman) 58:301

The Same Door (Updike) 1:343; 3:488

"The Same Gesture" (Montague) 46:278

"Same in Blues" (Hughes) 108:328

"The Same Moon Above Us" (Stern) 100:334

"Same Old Song" (Kristofferson) 26:268

The Same Old Story (Fo) 32:175

"The Same Poem Over and Over" (Rexroth) 112:395

The Same River Twice (Walker) 103:428

"Same Situation" (Mitchell) 12:438, 440

Same Time, Next Year (Slade) 11:507-08; 46:370-73

"Same Time, Same Place" (Peake) 54:372

Sammy and Rosie Get Laid (Kureishi) 64:248-51, 254-55

Sammy and Rosie Get Laid: The Script and the Diary (Kureishi) 64:249, 254

"Sammy Chester" (Brooks) 15:94

"Samos" (Merrill) 18:331; 34:235

Les samouraïs (*The Samurai*) (Kristeva) 77:325-26, 328, 334-37

Sam's Cross (Durcan) 43:113

Samson (Wajda) 16:578, 582

"Samson and Delilah" (Abse) 29:14

"Samson and Samsonella" (Aksyonov) 101:9

"Samuel" (Paley) 37:338

A Samuel Beckett Reader (Beckett) 29:67

"Samuel Beckett's Dublin" (Davie) 31:109

Samuel Johnson (Krutch) 24:286

Samuel Johnson: A Biography (Wain) 15:561

Samuel Johnson and the Life of Writing (Fussell) 74:117, 119

Samuel Marchbanks' Almanack (*Marchbanks' Almanack*) (Davies) 13:173; 25:129; 42:103, 105; 75:182-83

The Samurai (Endo) 54:153-57, 160, 162; 99:284-85, 287, 293

The Samurai (Kristeva)
   See *Les samouraïs*

The Samurai (MacBeth) 9:340

San Andreas (MacLean) 50:348; 63:267, 269

San Camilo, 1936 (Cela) 59:141-43

"San Fernando Road" (Soto) 80:286, 293-94

"San Francisco" (Olds) 85:298

"San Francisco Dues" (Berry) 17:52

"San Fruttuoso: The Divers" (Tomlinson) 45:398

San Giorgio in casa Brocchi (Gadda) 11:209

"San Ildefonso Nocturne" (Paz)
   See "Nocturno de San Ildefonso"

San Martín Copybook (Borges)
   See *Cuaderno San Martín*

"San Onofre, California" (Forche) 83:214-16

The San Sebastian (Dillon) 17:92-3

"Sanatorium" (Maugham) 67:218

Sancho Panza en la ínsula Barataria (Casona) 49:40

The Sanctity of Marriage (Mamet) 15:358

"Sanctuary" (Larsen) 37:218

"Sanctuary" (Wright) 53:420

Sanctuary (Faulkner) 1:100; 3:149, 156; 6:179-81; 8:207-09, 211; 9:201; 11:198; 14:179-80; 18:143-44, 148-49; 28:135-36, 140-42; 52:107, 109, 112-13, 139

Sanctuary (*Donde esta la casa de Dios*) (Shange) 74:314

Sanctuary V (Schulberg) 7:403

"Sanctuary and the Southern Myth" (Tate) 4:537

The Sanctuary Lamp (Murphy) 51:303, 305, 307

"Sanctus" (Gascoyne) 45:147

"Sanctus" (Moure) 88:227

Sand (Mayne) 12:390, 392-93, 397

Der Sand aus den Urnen (*Sand from the Urns*) (Celan) 10:104; 19:89; 53:73, 81; 82:48

"Sand Creek Survivors" (Vizenor) 103:297

Sand from the Urns (Celan)
   See *Der Sand aus den Urnen*

"Sand Pail" (Ashbery) 15:28

Sand Rivers (Matthiessen) 32:290-92; 64:310-11, 326

The Sandalwood Tree (Vesaas)
   See *Sandeltreet*

The Sandbox (Albee) 5:10, 14; 9:2-3, 9; 13:7; 25:33; 53:22, 27; 86:119-21; 113:3, 17-8, 26, 47

The Sandbox Tree (Fleming) 37:124

The Sandboy (Frayn) 31:191

The Sandburg Range (Sandburg) 35:354

The Sandburg Treasury: Prose and Poetry for Young People (Sandburg) 35:357

"Sandcastle" (Coles) 46:113

The Sandcastle (Murdoch) 1:236; 2:295; 3:347; 6:345, 349; 8:406; 15:384-85; 22:327

Sandeltreet (*The Sandalwood Tree*) (Vesaas) 48:405

"Sanders Theater" (Eberhart) 11:179

Sandhedens Haevn (Dinesen)
   See *The Revenge of Truth*

"Sandia Man" (Suknaski) 19:432

Sandinista (Clash) 30:47-51

"The Sandman" (Barthelme) 13:57

"Sandpiper" (Bishop) 13:93; 32:42

"The Sandpit" (Heaney) 74:167

"Sandra's Mobile" (Dunn) 40:172

Sandro from Chegem (Iskander)
   See *Sandro iz Chegema*

Sandro iz Chegema (*The Gospel according to Chegem; Sandro from Chegem; Sandro of Chegem*) (Iskander) 47:193-200; 59:394

Sandro of Chegem (Iskander)
   See *Sandro iz Chegema*

The Sands of Mars (Clarke) 13:153; 35:121

"Sandstone Keepsake" (Heaney) 37:165, 169; 91:117

"Sandstone Mountain" (MacCaig) 36:283

"Sandwiched Between Proust and the Mummy: Seven Notes and an Epilogue on Carpentier's Reasons of State" (Dorfman) 77:156

"Sandy" (Springsteen) 17:488, 490-91

Sanford and Son (Lear) 12:329, 330

"San-Fran-York on the Lake" (Royko) 109:405

"Sång" (Transtroemer) 65:235

Le sang des autres (*The Blood of Others*) (Beauvoir) 1:19-20; 8:59; 31:40-1; 44:343, 345, 350; 50:389; 71:48-9, 55, 67-9, 72, 84

Le sang des gitanes (Simenon) 47:374

Le sang d'un poète (*The Blood of a Poet*) (Cocteau) 8:145, 148; 15:133-34; 16:220-23, 225-30

Sång och strid (*Song and Strife*) (Lagerkvist) 54:275

Le sang rive (Glissant) 68:179, 181

"Sang satisfait du sens ancien du dit" (Damas) 84:167

Sangre de amor correspondido (*Blood of Requited Love*) (Puig) 65:268, 271

Sangschaw (MacDiarmid) 11:334, 338; 19:285-86, 290; 63:239

"A Sanguinary" (Goldbarth) 38:205-06

Sanitized Sonnets (Porter) 33:319, 324

"Sanity" (Leiber) 25:304

Sanity, Madness and the Family (*The Families of Schizophrenics*) (Laing) 95:125, 127,

130, 135-36, 138, 141, 160, 168, 171, 174-76

Sanjuro (Kurosawa)   16:399, 403-04

Sanningbarriären (The Truth Barrier; Truth Barriers) (Transtroemer)   52:410, 414-16, 418; 65:226, 229-30

Sans (Lessness) (Beckett)   4:52; 6:36-8, 45; 11:40; 14:80; 18:43; 29:57, 59, 61

Sans coup férir (Tzara)   47:395

"Sans remède" (Montherlant)   19:325

"Sanskrit" (Mahapatra)   33:282

"Santa Ana in the Dark" (Alegria)   75:36, 38-9

"Santa Barbara Road" (Hass)   99:140, 142

Santa Claus (Cummings)   15:157-58

Santa Cruz (Frisch)   14:181, 183; 18:160; 44:193-98, 200

"Santa Cruz Propositions" (Duncan)   41:129-30

"Santa Fe"   99:167

"Santa Lucia" (Hass)   18:211-13

"Santarém" (Bishop)   32:37

Santaroga Barrier (Herbert)   12:276, 279; 23:226; 35:196; 44:393-94

"Santelices" (Donoso)   11:147-48; 32:158

Santorini (MacLean)   50:347; 63:270-71

"Santos: New Mexico" (Sarton)   49:320

São Jorge dos Ilhéus (St. George of Ilhéus) (Amado)   40:25, 27; 106:60-1, 89

Sapetchatlionnoye vremya (Sculpting in Time: Reflections on the Cinema) (Tarkovsky)   75:389-91, 396, 401, 408-09, 412-13

"The Sapper" (Federspiel)   42:145-46

"Sapphics against Anger" (Steele)   45:366

Sapphics against Anger and Other Poems (Steele)   45:365-66

A Sapphire for September (Brinsmead)   21:27-8

Sappho (Delbanco)   6:130

Sappho (Durrell)   13:184

Sappho (Elytis)   100:170

Sappho: A New Translation (Barnard)   48:25, 27

"Sara" (Dylan)   77:178

al-Sarab (Mahfuz)   52:292

The Saracen Lamp (Arthur)   12:26, 28

Sarafina! (Ngema)   57:344-47

"Sarah" (Lavin)   99:316-18

Sarah (Sackler)   14:479

Sarah and Son (Arzner)   98:69-71, 86-7, 90

Sarah Bastard's Notebooks (Engel)   36:157, 163

Sarah Bishop (O'Dell)   30:276-77

"Sarah Cole: A Type of Love Story" (Banks)   72:3-5

Sarah Phillips (Lee)   36:255-58

"Sarandapikhou Street" (Vassilikos)   4:552

"Saratoga" (Moss)   7:249

Saratoga Headhunter (Dobyns)   37:82

"Saratoga, Hot" (Calisher)   38:75-6

Saratoga, Hot (Calisher)   38:75-6

Saratoga Longshot (Dobyns)   37:76, 78-9

Saratoga Swimmer (Dobyns)   37:78-9

Saratoga Trunk (Ferber)   93:173-75, 181, 186-87, 189-90

"Sarcophagi I" (Montale)   9:388

"Sarcophagi II" (Montale)   9:388

"Sarcophagus" (Selzer)   74:262

"The Sarcophagus of the Esophagus" (Benedikt)   14:81

Sard Harker (Masefield)   11:357

Sardana Dancers (Jenkins)   52:227-28

Sardines (Farah)   53:132-40

Sargasso of Space (Norton)   12:467

Sargento Getúlio (Sergeant Getúlio) (Ribeiro)   10:436; 67:273-79, 282

"Sarnesfield" (Mathias)   45:238

Saroyan: A Biography (Gifford)   34:457-59

Saroyan: A Biography (Lee)   34:457-59

Sarton Selected (Sarton)   91:240

"The Sartorial Revolution (I)" (Bioy Casares)   88:78

Sartoris (Flags in the Dust) (Faulkner)   3:153, 155, 158; 6:180; 8:210-11, 214; 9:197, 199; 11:197, 200, 202, 206; 14:179-80; 28:135, 140, 142-43; 52:109, 112-13; 68:127-30, 132

Sartre: A Life (Cohen-Solal)   50:370-72, 374-76, 378, 381-82

Sartre on Theater (Sartre)   18:473; 52:372, 375

Sartre: Romantic Rationalist (Murdoch)   3:348; 15:386; 51:288

Sasame yuki (The Makioka Sisters: A Tale of Disarrayed Chrysanthemums) (Tanizaki)   8:510; 14:525; 28:414-15, 420-21

Sasha, My Friend (Corcoran)   17:70

"Saskatchewan" (Lane)   25:284

Såsom i en spegel (Through A Glass Darkly) (Bergman)   16:50, 52, 54-5, 57, 59, 61-2, 64, 74, 79; 72:33, 37-41, 47, 50, 52, 57, 59, 62

Sassafrass (Shange)   8:485

Sassafrass, Cypress Indigo (Shange)   38:392-94, 396; 74:303, 307

Sassinak (McCaffrey)   17:280-81

"Satan" (Tanizaki)
   See "Akuma"

The Satan Bug (MacLean)   50:348-49

"Satan Comes to Georgia" (Pritchett)   41:331

Satan in Goray (Singer)
   See *Shoten an Goray*

Satan Says (Olds)   32:345-46; 39:190-93; 85:285, 288-90, 292, 297, 305-06

"Satan Speaks" (Smith)   25:420

"Satanic Form" (Swenson)   106:337

The Satanic Mill (Preussler)   17:376-77

The Satanic Verses (Rushdie)   55:215-28, 230-51, 253-56, 258-59, 261-63; 59:406-29, 431-55; 100:287, 293-96, 299, 301-03, 305, 307-09, 311-12, 315-19, 321-23

Satan's Brew (Fassbinder)   20:115

"Satellite" (Morgan)   2:294

"Satellite of Love" (Reed)   21:305, 314

"Sati Sapni" (Anand)   93:57

"Satin Bower-Birds" (Wright)   53:423

Satin-Legs Smith (Brooks)
   See "The Sundays of Satin-Legs Smith"

"Satires" (Loy)   28:253

"Satires and Occasions" (Garrett)   51:144

The Satires of Persius (Merwin)   45:269

Satirical Poems (Sassoon)   36:387

"The Satirist" (MacNeice)   4:318

"Satis Passio" (Murray)   40:343

"Satisfaction" (Jagger and Richard)   17:222, 225-27, 231, 234-35, 237, 239-40

"Satisfaction Guaranteed" (Asimov)   92:13

"The Satisfactions of the Mad Farmer" (Berry)   8:85

"The Satisfactory" (Pritchett)   41:334

"Satisfied" (Morrison)   21:239-40

"Satisfy My Soul" (Marley)   17:270

Satori in Paris (Kerouac)   2:227-28; 61:296

Satura (Montale)   7:224-25, 226, 230-01; 9:386-87, 389; 18:340

"Saturday" (Gallant)   38:191, 194

"Saturday" (Salinas)   90:324, 328

"Saturday Afternoon" (Caldwell)   8:123

The Saturday Gang (Kingman)   17:244-45

"Saturday Kids" (Weller)   26:445-46

"Saturday Night" (Gunn)   81:180

"Saturday Night" (Hughes)   108:297

"Saturday Night" (Kenny)   87:241

"Saturday Night" (Sondheim)   30:398

"Saturday Night" (Wakoski)   40:456

Saturday Night (Sondheim)   30:387, 400

Saturday Night and Sunday Morning (Sillitoe)   1:307-08; 3:448-49; 6:501; 19:421; 57:387, 389, 392, 396, 400-03

"A Saturday of Sun, Sand, and Sleep" (Calvino)   33:100

"Saturday People" (Packer)   65:350

"Saturday Sundae" (Scott)   22:375

"Saturday Sweeping" (Levine)   4:286

Saturday the Rabbi Went Hungry (Kemelman)   2:225

Saturday, the Twelfth of October (Mazer)   26:290-91

"Saturday under the Sky" (Soto)   80:283

"Saturn" (Grass)   32:198, 200

"Saturn" (Olds)   85:292, 294, 298, 304

"Saturn" (Wonder)   12:660

Saturn and Beyond (Asimov)   26:50-1

"Saturn, November 11th" (Ellison)   42:131

"Saturn Rising" (Clarke)   13:148

"Saturnalia" (Gluck)   22:173

Saturne (Malraux)   4:335

"The Satyr" (Lewis)   27:258

"The Satyr in the Periwig" (Sitwell)   67:312

"The Satyr Shall Cry" (Garrett)   51:149

Satyricon (Fellini's Satyricon) (Fellini)   16:280-81, 283, 286-90, 292-93, 299; 85:51, 53, 63-6, 68-70, 74, 76, 78, 82

Der Satz vom Grund (Heidegger)   24:271

Sauce for the Goose (De Vries)   28:108-10

"The Saucer Has Landed" (Buzzati)   36:94

"The Saucer of Larks" (Friel)   115:253

The Saucer of Larks (Friel)   42:163; 115:216

"Saucer of Loneliness" (Sturgeon)   39:366

"A Saucerful of Secrets" (Pink Floyd)   35:305

A Saucerful of Secrets (Pink Floyd)   35:307, 310

Sauerkraut Soup (Dybek)   114:64-4, 67-8, 76

"Saul Alone" (Gardam)   43:167

"Saul and Patsy Are Getting Comfortable in Michigan" (Baxter)   45:53; 78:30

"Saul and Patsy Are Pregnant" (Baxter)   78:26, 30

Saúl ante Samuel (Benet)   28:21

Saul Bellow: Drumlin Woodchuck (Harris)   19:206

"Saul Bellow in Chicago" (Amis)   62:4

Saul Bellow: Vision and Revision (Fuchs)   34:545-46

Das Sauspiel (Walser)   27:463

La sauvage (The Savage) (Anouilh)   13:17, 19, 21; 40:50, 52, 55-6

Sauve qui peut (Durrell)   41:139

Sauve qui peut (La vie) (Every Man for Himself; La vie) (Godard)   20:153-55

The Savage (Anouilh)
   See *La sauvage*

The Savage Gentleman (Wylie)   43:461

The Savage God (Alvarez)   5:18-19

Savage Holiday (Wright)   1:379; 4:596; 21:443, 446

Savage in Limbo (Shanley)   75:320

Savage Journey (Eckert)   17:109

Savage/Love (Shepard) **41**:407
"Savage Memories" (Amichai) **116**:96
"Savage Menace" (Ashbery) **77**:62
Savage Messiah (Russell) **16**:543-44, 546, 548
Savage Night (Thompson) **69**:386, 389
Savage Sleep (Brand) **7**:29-30
"Savages" (O'Brien) **36**:339; **116**:186
Savages (Hampton) **4**:212
Savannah Bay (Duras) **34**:162
"Savata, My Fair Sister" (Goyen) **14**:211
"Save a Kitty from Extinction" (Royko) **109**:407
Save Every Lamb (Stuart) **34**:373, 376
Save Me, Joe Louis (Bell) **102**:17-19
"Save One for Mainz" (Huddle) **49**:183
"Save the Children" (Gaye) **26**:131
"Save the Country" (Nyro) **17**:316, 318
"Saved" (Dylan) **77**:186, 190-91
Saved (Bond) **4**:69; **6**:84, 86; **13**:98; **23**:63
Saved (Dylan) **77**:185, 188, 190
Saville (Storey) **8**:505-06
"Saving Grace" (Dylan) **77**:185-86, 189
Saving St. Germ (Muske) **90**:317
"Saving the Life That Is Your Own" (Walker) **103**:368, 414
Saving the Queen (Buckley) **7**:35-6; **37**:61
Saving the Text: Literature/Derrida/Philosophy (Hartman) **27**:187, 189
"Savings" (Hogan) **73**:158-59
Savings (Hogan) **73**:158-60
"Savior Machine" (Bowie) **17**:57
Savior, Savior, Hold My Hand (Thomas) **17**:498-501
"The Saviour" (Bullins) **7**:37
"Savitri" (Anand) **93**:57
Le savon (Ponge) **18**:413
Saw (Katz) **47**:216
"Sawdust" (Moss) **7**:250; **14**:376
Sawdust and Tinsel (Bergman)
     See *Gycklarnas afton*
"Sawmill, Limekiln" (Montague) **46**:274
Say Cheese! (*Skazhi izjum!*) (Aksyonov) **101**:29, 42-7, 50
"Say Goodbye to Hollywood" (Joel) **26**:214
Say Hello to the Hit Man (Bennett) **35**:44
"Say It with Music" (Soupault) **68**:406
"Say Never" (Wallace) **114**:347
Say Nothing (Hanley) **5**:167
"Say Pardon" (Ignatow) **7**:177
Say Pardon (Ignatow) **7**:173-76, 179; **14**:275-76; **40**:258
"Say Say Say" (McCartney) **35**:291-93
Say Something Happened (Bennett) **77**:98
Say Who You Are (*Help Stamp Out Marriage*) (Waterhouse) **47**:418
"Say Yes" (Wolff) **64**:454
"Say You Love Me" (Peacock) **60**:297-98
"Saying Good-Bye to Hannah, 1907-1975" (McCarthy) **39**:487
"Saying Goodbye to Sally" (Yates) **23**:483
"Saying It to Keep It from Happening" (Ashbery) **77**:45-6
"A Saying of Anaximander" (Heidegger) **24**:270
Sayings and Doings (Berry) **27**:35
Sayonara (Michener) **11**:375; **29**:311; **109**:376, 378-79, 382
"The Scala Scare" (Buzzati)
     See "Paura alla scala"
"A Scale in May" (Merwin) **88**:199-200
"The Scales" (Koch) **44**:242, 249
"The Scales of the Eyes" (Nemerov) **6**:361-62; **36**:302, 304-05

"Scaling Desire" (Ammons) **57**:53
Scandal (Endo) **54**:162-63; **99**:284-85, 289-91, 294, 299-300
Scandal (Kurosawa) **16**:399
Scandal (Wilson) **33**:456-57
"Scandal d'Estime" (Hannah) **90**:162
"The Scandal on Via Sesotri" (Buzzati) **36**:93
The Scandalmonger (White) **30**:449
"A Scandalous Woman" (O'Brien) **36**:339-41; **116**:187, 194, 196, 198-99, 212, 216, 219-21
A Scandalous Woman, and Other Stories (O'Brien) **5**:311-12
"Scandinavian Skies" (Joel) **26**:223
A Scanner Darkly (Dick) **10**:138; **72**:110
The Scapegoat (du Maurier) **59**:280-81, 284
The Scapegoat (Settle) **19**:410-12; **61**:371-76, 382-87
"Scape-Goats" (Barker) **52**:55
"The Scar" (Campbell) **42**:84
"Scar" (Lorde) **71**:259
"Scar" (McPherson)
     See "The Story of a Scar"
"Scarborough Fair/Canticle" (Simon) **17**:462
A Scarcity of Love (Kavan) **5**:205; **82**:121
"The Scarecrow" (Farrell) **66**:131
"Scarecrow" (Pink Floyd) **35**:307
The Scarf (Bloch) **33**:83
"The Scarf of June" (Eberhart) **56**:77
Scarface (Hecht) **8**:274
Scarface (Norton) **12**:455
Scarface (Stone) **73**:364-65, 367, 369-70, 382
The Scarlatti Inheritance (Ludlum) **22**:288-89, 291
"The Scarlatti Tilt" (Brautigan) **12**:65
The Scarlet Cord (Slaughter) **29**:375
The Scarlet Empress (Sternberg) **20**:370, 372, 374
The Scarlet Goose (Almedingen) **12**:5-6
"Scarlet Ibis" (Atwood) **84**:67
The Scarlet Letters (Queen) **11**:464
"The Scarlet Moving Van" (Cheever) **7**:49
The Scarlet Patch (Lancaster) **36**:243
Scarlet Pilgrim (Robbins) **21**:338
The Scarlet Ruse (MacDonald) **3**:307; **27**:275
The Scarlet Sail (Cavanna) **12**:100
Scarlet Sister Mary (Peterkin) **31**:303-07, 309-10
Scarlet Song (Ba)
     See *Un chant ecarlate*
Scarlet Street (Lang) **20**:207, 216; **103**:88, 102, 104-08
The Scarlet Sword (Bates) **46**:64-5
The Scarlet Thread (Betts) **28**:33-4
The Scarperer (Behan) **79**:25, 27
"Scars" (Williams) **42**:440
Scars (Kinsella) **27**:236-37; **43**:260
Scars on the Soul (Sagan)
     See *Des bleus à l'âame*
Scattered Images of Childhood (Ionesco) **11**:290
Scattered Poems (Kerouac) **3**:264
Scattered Returns (Sissman) **9**:490; **18**:488
A Scattering of Salts (Merrill) **91**:227-28, 232, 237-38
"Scavengers at the Palm Beach County Landfill" (Bottoms) **53**:31
"Scenario" (Dunn) **36**:154
"Scenario" (Perelman) **44**:502; **49**:265
"Scenario for a Walk-On Part" (Fuller) **62**:186
"Scene" (Robbe-Grillet) **43**:361
Scène blanche (Brossard) **115**:110-11

La scène capitale (Jouve) **47**:203-06
"A Scene of the Memorial Service for the War Dead" (Kawabata) **2**:222
"The Scene of War" (Read) **4**:439
"Scene Twelve: Take Seven" (Ciardi) **40**:162
"La sceneggiatura come 'struttura che vuol essene altia struttura'" (Pasolini) **106**:237
Scener ur ett äktenskap (*Scenes from a Marriage*) (Bergman) **16**:75, 77, 80-2; **72**:57, 59-61
Scenes from a Marriage (Bergman)
     See *Scener ur ett äktenskap*
Scenes from American Life (Gurney) **54**:217; **32**:216-17, 219; **50**:175, 177-78
Scenes from American Life (Oates) **19**:350; **108**:389
Scenes from an Album (Trevor) **116**:338, 346
"Scenes from an Italian Restaurant" (Joel) **26**:215-16, 222
Scenes from Bourgeois Life (Jones) **52**:250
Scenes from the Life of a Faun (Schmidt)
     See *Aus dem Leben eines Fauns: Kurzroman*
"Scenes from the Life of Behemoth" (Howard) **7**:168
Scenes from the Life of the Future (Duhamel) **8**:188
"Scenes from the Lives of the Saints" (Nichol) **18**:368
"Scenes of J. C.'s Life" (Cabral de Melo Neto)
     See "Cenas da vida de Joaquim Cardozo"
"Scenes of Passion and Desire" (Oates) **19**:352
Scenic Drive (Wilding) **73**:395, 398
The Scenic Route (Adcock) **41**:14-15, 17
Scent of Apples (Santos) **22**:365-66
"Scent of Camomile" (Derleth) **31**:138
Scented Gardens for the Blind (Frame) **2**:141; **6**:190; **96**:173-74, 176, 178-79, 182, 185-86, 189-91, 194, 196, 199, 203, 216-17
Die Schatten (Wellershoff) **46**:435
Der Schatten des Körpers des Kutschers (*The Shadow of the Coachman's Body*) (Weiss) **15**:563; **51**:389, 395
Der Schatten eines Traumes (Wolf) **58**:431, 433
Die Schattengrenze (Wellershoff) **46**:433-34, 436
"Scheherazade" (Baxter) **78**:26
"Scheherazade in South Dakota" (Cassity) **42**:99
Der Schein trügt (*Appearances Are Deceiving*) (Bernhard) **61**:11, 26
"Scherzo" (Berryman) **10**:51
Scherzo (Wheelock) **14**:571
Scherzo capriccioso (*Dvořák in Love*) (Skvorecky) **69**:327-32, 336, 344, 347
"Schicksal einer henkellosen Tasse" (Boell) **15**:69
"Schiffman's Ape" (Sayles) **14**:483
Schinderhannes (Zuckmayer) **18**:555
Schindler's Ark (Keneally)
     See *Schindler's List*
Schindler's List (*Schindler's Ark*) (Keneally) **27**:231-34; **43**:230-37; **117**:226-27, 229, 231, 233-35, 237, 239, 241, 243, 245, 250-51
"Schinz" (Frisch) **44**:194, 199
The Schirmer Inheritance (Ambler) **9**:19
Schismatrix (Sterling) **72**:368, 370
"Schizophrenic Girl" (Kennedy) **42**:256-57
"Schläferung" (Hildesheimer) **49**:173
Schlaflose Tage (*Sleepless Days*) (Becker) **19**:36
"Schmährede des alten B. auf seinen Sohn"

(Hofmann) **54**:225

"Schmerz durch reibung" (Jandl) **34**:196

"Die Schmerzen sin zumutbar" ("The Pain Is Not Excessive") (Lenz) **27**:252

Schmoedipus (Potter) **58**:400

"Schneebett" ("Snowbed") (Celan) **53**:72; **82**:39-40

Schneeglöckchenfeste (Hrabal)
See *Slavnosti snezenek*

Schneepart (Celan) **82**:34

"The Scholar" (Clarke) **6**:113

"Scholar and Gypsy" (Desai) **97**:150, 152

"Scholars at the Orchid Pavillion" (Berryman) **25**:96

"Scholar's Wife" (Kennedy) **8**:320

Ein schöner Tag (*A Beautiful Day*) (Wellershoff) **46**:434-35

Die Schönheit des Schimpansen (Wellershoff) **46**:436-37

"Das Schönste Fest der welt" (Lenz) **27**:246

"The School Children" (Gluck) **7**:119; **22**:174

"School Days" (Berry) **17**:53-5

School Daze (Lee) **105**:81-86, 95, 102, 109, 111, 128

"School Drawing" (Turco) **11**:550

"School Figures" (Matthews) **40**:323

A School for Fools **59**:369, 388

"The School for Love" (Porter) **5**:347

"The School for Tenors" (Grass)
See "Die Schule der Tenöre"

"The School Friend" (Aickman) **57**:2

"The School Globe" (Reaney) **13**:473

The School of Darkness (Wellman) **49**:396-97

"The School of Desire" (Swenson) **106**:339, 347

The School of Donne (Alvarez) **5**:19

"The School of Eloquence" (Harrison) **43**:176-78, 181

"The School of Gordon Lish" (Birkerts) **116**:148, 151

"School of Knives" (Cabral de Melo Neto)
See "A escola das facas"

The School of Knives (Cabral de Melo Neto)
See *A escola das facas*

"A School Story" (Trevor) **71**:336; **116**:375

"School Teacher" (Smith) **64**:389

School Ties: Good and Bad at Games, and Dutch Girls (*Good and Bad at Games*) (Boyd) **53**:53-4

Schoolboys in Disgrace (Davies) **21**:100-01

"Schooling" (Ammons) **2**:14

"Schoolmaster" (Larkin) **64**:261

"Schoolmaster" (Yevtushenko) **1**:382

The Schoolmaster (Lovelace) **51**:267, 271

"The Schoolmaster in Spring" (Winters) **32**:470

"Schoolroom on a Wet Afternoon" (Scannell) **49**:324

"The Schooner Blue Goose" (Acorn) **15**:10

Schooner Cove (Jiles) **13**:304

"The Schooner *Flight*" (Walcott) **14**:551; **42**:420-22; **76**:272, 274-75, 296

"Schopenhauer und Marbot" (Hildesheimer) **49**:179

Das Schreien der Katze im Sack (Wellershoff) **46**:435

"The Schreuderspitze" (Helprin) **22**:221-22

"Ein Schritt nach Gomorrah" ("One Step Towards Gomorrah") (Bachmann) **69**:35, 37

"Schrödinger's Cat" (Le Guin) **45**:213, 216

"Schtzngrmm" (Jandl) **34**:196, 198, 200

Schubertiana (Transtroemer) **52**:418

Die Schule der Atheisten: Novellen-Comödie in 6 Aufzügen (Schmidt) **56**:393-94

"Die Schule der Tenöre" ("The School for Tenors") (Grass) **32**:198

Schultz (Donleavy) **45**:123-26

The Schva (Broner) **19**:70

Das Schwanenhaus (*The Swan Villa*) (Walser) **27**:466-67

"Schwarze Flocken" ("Black Flakes") (Celan) **19**:89; **19**:89

Der schwarze Schwan (*The Black Swan*) (Walser) **27**:462, 465

Schwarze Spiegel (Schmidt) **56**:390, 393, 405

"Die schwarzen schafe" ("The Black Sheep") (Boell) **2**:68

Schwarzenberg (Heym) **41**:219-20

"Schwierige Traver" (Lenz) **27**:245-46

Die Schwierigen; oder, J'adore ce qui me brûle (*The Difficult Ones*) (Frisch) **9**:218; **44**:183-86, 188-89, 193, 203

Lo scialle andaluso (Morante) **47**:280

Lo sciecco bianco (*The White Sheik*) (Fellini) **16**:270, 272-74; **85**:52, 59, 66-7, 69, 71-2, 74, 76

"Science" (Jeffers) **11**:304

Science (Asimov)
See *Words of Science*

Science and Poetry (Richards) **24**:373, 378, 382, 387-89, 395, 400

"Science Fiction" (Bova) **45**:75

"Science Fiction" (Heinlein) **14**:252

"Science Fiction" (Levi) **41**:244

"Science Fiction: A Hopeless Case—With Exceptions" (Lem) **40**:299

The Science Fiction Source Book (Wingrove) **68**:456

The Science Fiction Stories of Walter M. Miller, Jr. (Miller) **30**:262

"Science, Liberty and Peace" (Huxley) **4**:239; **18**:270

The Science of Hatred (Sholokhov) **15**:482

"The Scientific Method" (Skvorecky) **69**:333

"Scilla" (Gluck) **81**:164-65, 171

Scimitar (De Marinis) **54**:97-9

"Scintillant Orange" (Vollmann) **89**:277-78, 304

Scion (Dickey) **109**:245

"Lo sciopero dei telefoni" (Buzzati) **36**:86

"Scissors" (Baxter) **78**:26

Sciuscia (De Sica) **20**:84, 92

La scomparsa di Majorana (Sciascia) **9**:476; **41**:389

Scoop (Waugh) **1**:359; **3**:512; **13**:585, 589; **27**:470; **44**:522; **107**:362, 370-71, 381, 383, 398, 400-01

The Scorched-Wood People (Wiebe) **11**:569; **14**:573

"The Score" (Bernard) **59**:46

"Score" (Rose) **85**:315

"A Score Settled" (Dourado)
See "Um ajuste de contas"

"The Scorpion" (Bowles) **19**:56-7

Scorpion and Other Poems (Smith) **25**:417

"The 'Scorpion' Departs but never Returns" (Ochs) **17**:332

The Scorpion God (Golding) **1**:122; **2**:168-69; **3**:200-01; **17**:177; **27**:163-64, 167; **81**:318, 323, 325-26

Scotchman's Return and Other Essays (MacLennan) **92**:298, 300, 306, 320

"Scotland's Fate: Canada's Lesson" (MacLennan) **14**:343

Scots Unbound (MacDiarmid) **63**:249, 255

Scotsman's Return and Other Essays (MacLennan)
See *Scotsman's Return and Other Essays*

Scott of the Antarctic (Brenton) **31**:59, 65

"Scottish Bards and an English Reviewer" (Barker) **48**:18

Scott-King's Modern Europe (Waugh) **27**:470; **107**:368-69

"Scottsboro" (Hughes) **108**:330

"Scoundrel" (Fante) **60**:133

The Scoundrel (Hecht) **8**:274

Scoundrel Time (Hellman) **8**:281-82; **14**:257, 260; **18**:225, 228-29; **34**:348, 350, 352; **44**:526, 528; **52**:189-90, 192-94, 198-205

"The Scour" (Ammons) **57**:49

"The Scoutmaster" (Taylor) **1**:334; **37**:412; **44**:305, 308; **50**:253; **71**:304-05

"Scram You Made the Pants Too Short" (Perelman) **23**:339-40

"The Scrap Merchant" (Mahfuz) **52**:292

"Scrapbook" (Appleman) **51**:15

"The Scrape" (Still) **49**:364

"Scrapeaway" (Weller) **26**:446

"Scrapers and Bluey" (Frame) **96**:

"The Scrapper" (Pancake) **29**:346-47, 350

"Scraps" (Graver) **70**:52

"Scratch" (Pesetsky) **28**:358

"Scratch Your Head" (Carroll) **35**:77

"Scratching the Surface: Some Notes on Barriers to Women and Loving" (Lorde) **71**:231, 244-46

"The Scream" (Smith) **64**:392

"The Scream" (Tomlinson) **45**:394

The Scream (Abell) **15**:3, 7

"A Scream of Toys" (Sillitoe) **19**:422; **57**:391, 396

"The Scream on Fifty-Seventh Street" (Calisher) **8**:125; **38**:69

"The Screamers" (Baraka) **33**:55-6, 62-3

"Screech Owl" (Davie) **31**:124

"A Screen Depicting the Fifty-Four Episodes of the Tale of Genji on a Background of Gold Leaf" (Pollitt) **28**:366

Screen Test (Warhol) **20**:415

"SCREENO" (Schwartz) **87**:342

The Screens and Other Poems (Richards) **14**:452, 455

"Screw: A Technical Love Poem" (Wakoski) **4**:573

"The Screwfly Solution" (Tiptree) **48**:389, 396

The Screwtape Letters (Lewis) **1**:177; **3**:295, 297, 299; **6**:308; **14**:322-23; **27**:260, 263, 266

"Screwtop" (McIntyre) **18**:327

Scribble, Scribble (Ephron) **17**:113-14; **31**:159

"Scribbles" (Ammons) **57**:50

"Scribe" (H. D.) **73**:118

Scrieri (*Writings*) (Arghezi) **80**:13

"Script" (Adcock) **41**:18

The Script (Anouilh) **50**:279

"Scripts for the Pageant" (Merrill) **18**:330-32; **34**:226, 228-31, 235-36; **91**:228

Scripture of the Blind (Ritsos) **31**:329, 331

Scritti corsair (Pasolini) **106**:245

"The Scriveners" (Buzzati) **36**:94

"Scroppo's Dog" (Swenson) **61**:398

Scuba Duba (Friedman) **5**:125, 127; **56**:98-9, 109

Le sculpteur de masques (*The Sculptor of Masks*) (Crommelynck) **75**:152, 155, 162-63, 166, 168

Sculpting in Time: Reflections on the Cinema

(Tarkovsky)
See *Sapetchatlionnoye vremya*
"The Sculptor" (Christie) **110**:127
"The Sculptor" (Plath) **9**:423; **11**:447; **111**:201
The Sculptor of Masks (Crommelynck)
See *Le sculpteur de masques*
"Sculptors" (Purdy) **14**:433
Scum (Singer) **69**:316-21; **111**:341
"Scum Grief" (Bukowski) **41**:73
Scum of the Earth (Koestler) **15**:309; **33**:228-29
"Scumbag" (Lennon) **35**:265
Scumbler (Wharton) **37**:441-43
"Scyros" (Shapiro) **15**:478
"The Scythes" (Dubie) **36**:130
"Scything" (Clarke) **61**:80
SDS (Sale) **68**:343-44, 348, 353, 359
Se il sole muore (*If the Sun Dies*) (Fallaci) **110**:180, 191-92
"Se la vita e sventura...?" (Strand) **71**:288
"Se me ocurren ideas luminosas" (Parra) **102**:342
Se non ora, quando? (*If Not Now, When?*) (Levi) **37**:225, 228-30; **50**:327-28, 330, 332, 337, 339-40
"Se querían" (Aleixandre) **9**:12
Se questo è un uomo (*Survival in Auschwitz: The Nazi Assault on Humanity*) (Levi) **37**:220, 223, 225, 227; **50**:323-26, 332, 334, 336-37, 340
Se tavallinen tarina (Salama) **18**:461
Se una notte d'inverno un viaggiatore (*If on a Winter's Night a Traveler*) (Calvino) **22**:90-1; **73**:31, 34, 41, 48, 53-4, 56, 58, 60
"Se vuelve a yo" ("A Return to Me"; "Return to Oneself") (Neruda) **62**:336
"The Sea" (Dudek) **11**:160
"Sea" (Ghiselin) **23**:170
"The Sea" (Oliver) **98**:271, 296-97, 299
The Sea (Bond) **4**:70; **13**:102; **23**:65
The Sea Anchor (Whitehead) **5**:488-89
"The Sea and Its Shore" (Bishop) **9**:90; **32**:40, 43
"Sea and Night" (Aleixandre)
See "Mar y noche"
The Sea and Poison (Endo)
See *Umi to dokuyaku*
"Sea and Sardinia" (West) **9**:562
The Sea and the Bells (Neruda)
See *El mar y las campanas*
"The Sea and the Canefield" (Cabral de Melo Neto)
See "O mar e o canavial"
"The Sea and the Mirror: A Commentary on Shakespeare's *Tempest*" (Auden) **1**:9-10; **2**:24; **3**:24, 27; **4**:33; **6**:20; **9**:59; **11**:17, 19; **14**:31; **43**:15
"The Sea and the Shore" (Amichai) **116**:122
"The Sea and the Shore" (Thurber) **5**:431
The Sea and the Wedding (Johnson) **27**:217
"The Sea and Tricks" (Aksyonov) **101**:22
"The Sea, around Us" (Loewinsohn) **52**:285
The Sea around Us (Carson) **71**:92-4, 99-111
The Sea at Dauphin (Walcott) **2**:460; **9**:556; **25**:451, 453-54; **67**:351
"Sea Bells" (Waddington) **28**:438
"The Sea Birds Are Still Alive" (Bambara) **88**:7-9, 20-23, 53-54
The Sea Birds Are Still Alive: Collected Stories (Bambara) **19**:33; 7, 27-28, 40, 42-3, 52, 54-5
"Sea Burial from the Cruiser 'Reve'" (Eberhart)

11:178
"Sea Canes" (Walcott) **76**:285
"The Sea Caves of Dogashima" (Lieberman) **36**:261
"Sea Change" (Broumas) **73**:9
"The Sea Change" (Hemingway) **19**:219
"Sea Change" (Moss) **45**:291
The Sea Change (Howard) **29**:243
A Sea Change (Salamanca) **4**:462; **15**:463-65
The Sea Change of Angela Lewes (Seton) **27**:424, 426
"Sea Changes" (Bowering) **32**:48
"Sea Changes" (Montague) **46**:268-69
"Sea Charm" (Hughes) **35**:214
"The Sea Cliffs at Kailua in December" (Merwin) **45**:276
"The Sea Creature" (O Hehir) **41**:324
The Sea Does Not Wash Naples (Ortese)
See *Il mare non bagna Napoli*
"Sea Fever" (Masefield) **11**:358; **47**:233
Sea Garden (H. D.) **31**:205, 207-08, 211; **73**:106, 109
Sea Glass (Yep) **35**:470-71
"Sea Gods" (H. D.) **73**:121, 139
"Sea Graces" (Pollitt) **28**:367
"Sea Grapes" (Walcott) **42**:422; **76**:279, 285-86
Sea Grapes (Walcott) **9**:556-57; **14**:548-51; **25**:452, 457; **42**:421-22 **76**:274
The Sea Gulls Woke Me (Stolz) **12**:546, 549
"Sea Heroes" (H. D.) **73**:105, 121
"The Sea Horse" (Graves) **39**:328
"Sea Horse" (Szirtes) **46**:393
The Sea in Being (Hemingway)
See *The Old Man and the Sea*
The Sea in Danger (Cousteau) **30**:107
"The Sea in Winter" (Mahon) **27**:292
"The Sea Is History" (Walcott) **42**:421
Sea Island Song (*Gullah*) (Childress) **86**:308-09, 314
Sea Lanes Out (Hugo) **32**:251-52
"Sea Lovers" (Martin) **89**:111-12, 118
"Sea Monster" (Merwin) **5**:288
"The Sea Mouse" (Oliver) **98**:303
Sea of Cortez: A Leisurely Journal of Travel and Research (Steinbeck) **9**:515-16; **21**:382-83, 389, 392; **34**:405, 412; **45**:383; **75**:344
Sea of Death (Amado)
See *Mar morto*
The Sea of Fertility: A Cycle of Novels (Mishima)
See *Hojo no umi*
Sea of Grass (Kazan) **63**:225, 229
The Sea of Grass (Richter) **30**:307-09, 311-14, 316, 318-19, 324, 329
"The Sea of Hesitation" (Barthelme) **46**:38-9, 42-3
A Sea of Legends (Cousteau) **30**:107
Sea of Lentils (Benitez-Rojo) **70**:348, 359
"The Sea of Lost Time" (Garcia Marquez)
See "El mar del tiempo perdido"
"The Sea of Sinbad" (Clarke) **35**:123
Sea of the Dead (Amado)
See *Mar morto*
"Sea of Tranquility" (Lightfoot) **26**:282
"Sea Poppies" (H. D.) **73**:119
Sea Routes to Polynesia (Heyerdahl) **26**:191-92
"Sea Sea Rider" (Brautigan) **12**:64
"The Sea Shell" (Bradbury) **98**:135
Sea Siege (Norton) **12**:467
The Sea, the Sea (Murdoch) **11**:388-89; **22**:328; **31**:287-89; **51**:287, 296

"The Sea to Hart Crane" (Moss) **45**:291
Sea Trilogy (Golding) **81**:320, 325-26
"Sea Violet" (H. D.) **73**:119
"Sea Voyage" (Empson) **3**:147
The Sea Wall (Dillon) **17**:96
The Sea Wall (Duras)
See *Un barrage contre le Pacifique*
"The Sea When Absent" (Hemingway) **8**:285
"The Sea When Young" (Hemingway) **8**:285
"Sea Wolves" (Moorcock) **58**:347-48
"Sea Worms" (Ryan) **65**:215-16
"Sea-Beach" (Wright) **53**:428
A Sea-Change (Gould) **10**:241-42
"A Sea-Chantey" (Walcott) **76**:273, 279-80
"The Seacoast of Bohemia" (Garrett) **51**:140
Seademons (Yep) **35**:470
"The Seafarer" (Pound) **4**:408; **7**:336; **10**:408; **13**:454; **112**:305, 340, 343, 345-46
"The Sea-Gull" (Loewinsohn) **52**:283
Seagull (*The Saga of a Seagull*) (Kemal) **29**:267
The Seagull on the Step (Boyle) **58**:67
"The Seahorse and the Reef" (Ihimaera) **46**:200
"Seahorses" (Porter) **33**:323
"Seal" (Clarke) **61**:83
Seal Island Anthology (Brown) **48**:60
Seal Secret (Chambers) **35**:100
Sealed with a Loving Kiss (Hughes) **48**:181
The Seals (Dickinson)
See *The Sinful Stones*
The Seals (Dillon) **17**:97-8, 101
"Seals at High Island" (Murphy) **41**:313-14, 317
"Seals, Terns, Time" (Eberhart) **19**:144; **56**:86
Seamarks (Perse)
See *Amers*
"The Seamless Garment" (MacDiarmid) **11**:335; **63**:253
The Seamless Web (Burnshaw) **3**:90-1; **13**:128-30
The Seamless Web (Dickey) **10**:141
"Seamstress at St. Leon" (Clarke) **61**:83
"Seamus" (Pink Floyd) **35**:306
Seamus Heaney and Tom Paulin (Paulin) **37**:354
"Seamus Heaney's Fiftieth Birthday" (Durcan) **70**:151
"Sea-Music for My Sister Travelling" (Watkins) **43**:441
"The Sean Bhean Bhoct" (Montague) **46**:265-66, 275, 278
"Sean Flynn" (Clash) **30**:50-2
The Sean O'Casey Reader: Plays, Autobiographies, Opinions (O'Casey) **88**:253
"The Seance" (Creeley) **8**:152
The Séance, and Other Stories (Singer) **6**:508
"Seanchas" (Muldoon) **32**:315
Seára vermelha (*Red Harvest*) (Amado) **40**:27-8; **106**:57-59
"The Search" (Berryman) **25**:95
"The Search" (Blackburn) **43**:63
The Search (Snow) **4**:500, 505
"Search by the Foundation" (Asimov) **26**:46, 60-3, 65
"Search by the Mule" (Asimov) **26**:63, 64
"A Search for a Future" (Miller) **47**:250
Search for a Method (Sartre) **52**:380-81, 386
Search for a Method (Sartre)
See *Questions de méthode*
The Search for Charlie (Corcoran) **17**:75
The Search for Harry Allway (Buzo) **61**:70-1
"The Search for J. Kruper" (Berriault) **54**:5; **109**:94

"The Search for Life—Is Anybody There?" (Branley) 21:22

"The Search for Marvin Gardens" (McPhee) 36:296

Search for Poetry (Andrade) 18:4

Search for the Base and the Summit (Char)
    See Recherche de la base et du sommet

A Search for the King (Vidal) 22:433; 33:406-07

"The Search for Tom and Lucy" (Turner) 48:398

Search for Tomorrow (Nixon) 21:241, 245

"The Search for Wholes" (Livesay) 79:348

"Search Party" (Merwin) 88:210

"Search under Every Veil" (Bunting) 47:54

The Searchers (Ford) 16:310, 314, 316-17, 319

Searches and Seizures (Eligible Men) (Elkin) 4:153-54; 6:168-69; 9:191; 14:158; 27:121-23; 91:213

"Searching and Sounding" (Avison) 97:80, 84-5

Searching for Caleb (Tyler) 7:479; 11:552; 28:434; 44:315, 320; 59:202, 205; 103:226, 235, 239-40, 243-44, 247-48, 259, 263, 265, 268-69, 273

Searching for Survivors (Banks) 37:22-3; 72:4-5, 12, 14

"Searching for Survivors II" (Banks) 37:23

Searching for the Ox (Simpson) 7:429-30; 9:485-86

The Searching Image (Dudek) 19:136

"Searching, Not Searching" (Rukeyser) 6:480; 27:413

The Searching Spirit (Adamson) 17:5-6

The Searching Wind (Hellman) 2:187; 8:282; 18:222; 52:191

"Searchlight" (Heinlein) 26:165

"Searchlight Practice" (Wright) 53:428

"Sea-Rose" (H. D.) 73:105, 117, 121

Seascape (Albee) 5:12-14; 9:6; 11:13; 25:38; 53:24; 86:120, 124; 113:15-6, 24, 28-31, 33, 40

Seascape: Needle's Eye (Oppen) 7:284-85

"Seascape with Sun & Eagle" (Ferlinghetti) 111:59

"A Seashell" (Snodgrass) 68:388

Seashells and Sandalwood" (Stow) 23:436

"A Seaside Garden" (Gardam) 43:171

"Seaside Resort" (Porter) 5:347

"Season" (Soyinka) 44:277

The Season at Sarsaparilla (White) 7:531; 69:407

A Season in England (Newby) 2:311

A Season in Paradise (Breytenbach) 23:85-6

Season in Purgatory (Keneally) 8:319; 10:298; 14:303; 19:247; 117:225, 235, 242

A Season in Rihata (Conde)
    See Une saison à Rihata

"The Season in Scarborough, 1923" (Raine) 32:353; 103:186, 189-90

A Season in the Congo (Cesaire)
    See Une saison au Congo

A Season in the Life of Emmanuel (Blais)
    See Une saison dans la vie d'Emmanuel

A Season in the Sun (Kahn) 30:232

Season of Adventure (Lamming) 2:235; 4:279; 66:219, 223-24, 227-32

Season of Anomy (Soyinka) 5:398; 14:509; 44:294

The Season of Comfort (Vidal) 22:432-33; 33:405

A Season of Delight (Greenberg) 30:167

A Season of Fear (Polonsky) 92:378, 381, 402, 415, 417

"Season of Hard Wind" (Piercy) 27:376

Season of Lights (Nyro) 17:319

"Season of Lovers and Assassins" (Kizer) 80:182

"The Season of Phantasmal Peace" (Walcott) 25:456; 67:355-56

Season of Ponies (Snyder) 17:469

Season of the Briar (Brinsmead) 21:26-7

"The Season of the Small, Small Spider" (Souster) 14:505

Season of the Two-Heart (Duncan) 26:100-01

"The Season of the Witch" (Herlihy) 6:235-36

Season Songs (Hughes) 9:282; 14:271; 37:175, 180

"Seasonal Greeting" (Simmons) 43:412

"The Seasonless" (Wright) 28:462

"The Seasons" (Fugard) 48:109

"Seasons" (Haldeman) 61:181

"Seasons" (Tomlinson) 13:549; 45:393

"Seasons and Meters" (Johnston) 51:254

The Season's Difference (Buechner) 4:79

Season's Greetings (Ayckbourn) 33:43; 74:7

Seasons in Flight (Aldiss) 40:21

The Season's Lovers (Waddington) 28:436

"Seasons of Love" 99:161, 173, 177, 180, 185, 187, 190

"The Seasons of the Soul" (Tate) 2:428-30; 4:540; 11:522, 525, 527; 14:529-31

Season's Reasons (Milner) 56:225

The Sea-Thing Child (Hoban) 7:161

"Seattle Art Society" (Acker) 111:33

Seaview (Olson) 28:344-45

Seawitch (MacLean) 13:364

Sebastian; or, Ruling Passions (Durrell) 41:133-35, 137-38

"La seca españa" (Azorin) 11:24

"sechita" (Shange) 25:402

"Der Sechste Geburtstag" (Lenz) 27:246

"Un secolo di studi sulla poesia popolare" (Pasolini) 106:245

The Second American Revolution and Other Essays, 1976-1982 (Pink Triangle and Yellow Star) (Vidal) 33:403-05, 409; 72:386

"The Second Angel" (Levine) 4:287

"Second Avenue" (O'Hara) 78:344, 355, 359-60

Second Avenue (O'Hara) 2:323; 13:423, 426-27

"The Second Best Bed" (Nye) 42:309

The Second Birth (Pasternak) 7:292; 10:383-84; 18:382; 63:289, 306

"The Second Birth of the Great Shaka of the Zulus" (Kunene) 85:176

"Second Chance" (Auchincloss) 45:30

"The Second Chance" (Sillitoe) 57:391, 395

The Second Chance, and Other Stories (Sillitoe) 19:422; 57:391, 395

Second Chance: Tales of Two Generations (Auchincloss) 45:30-1

"Second Chances" (Hugo) 32:239

The Second Chronicles of Thomas Covenant, the Unbeliever (Donaldson) 46:140-41

"The Second Coming" (Abse) 7:1

"Second Coming" (Livesay) 15:340; 79:339

The Second Coming (Percy) 18:398-403; 47:334, 337-38; 65:257

The Second Confession (Stout) 3:472

"Second Cup of Coffee" (Lightfoot) 26:278-79

The Second Curtain (Fuller) 4:178; 28:148

The Second Day (Ehrenburg) 34:439; 62:176, 178-79

The Second Deadly Sin (Sanders) 41:379

The Second Death (Schell) 35:366-67

The Second Dune (Hearon) 63:160, 166

Second Ending (Hunter) 31:218-20

"The Second Essay on Interest" (Murray) 40:343

The Second Face (Ayme) 11:21

Second Fall (O'Casey) 11:406

A Second Flowering (Cowley) 39:458-59

Second Foundation (Asimov) 3:17; 26:46, 58, 61, 64; 76:313-14

Second Generation (Fast) 23:160

Second Growth (Stegner) 49:349-50

Second Heaven (Guest) 30:174-76

"Second Hymn to Lenin" (MacDiarmid) 4:311; 63:253-55

Second Hymn to Lenin, and Other Poems (MacDiarmid) 63:245, 250, 255

"The Second Interment" (Smith) 43:420

"Second Language" (Gallagher) 63:120

Second Language (Mueller) 51:283-85

The Second Life (Morgan) 31:272-73, 275-76

"A Second Look" (MacLennan) 92:346

The Second Man (Behrman) 40:72-3, 75-6, 78, 81, 87

Second Manifeste du surréalisme (Second Manifesto of Surrealism) (Breton) 54:20, 31

Second Manifesto of Surrealism (Breton)
    See Second Manifeste du surréalisme

Second Marriage (Barthelme) 36:52-5; 117:4, 7, 11, 21, 26

"Second Meeting" (Dinesen) 10:149, 152

"A Second Meeting with my Father" (Amichai) 116:126

The Second Mrs. Whitberg (Bermant) 40:94

Second Nature (Stolz) 12:551

Second Poems (Graham) 29:193

"Second Populist Manifesto" (Ferlinghetti)
    See "Adieu á Charlot"

The Second Ring of Power (Castaneda) 12:95

"Second Sally" (Lem) 40:296

The Second Scroll (Klein) 19:258

"The Second Sermon on the Warpland" (Brooks) 15:93

The Second Sex (Beauvoir)
    See Le deuxième sexe

The Second Shell (Williamson) 29:454

"A Second Siege" (Montague) 13:392

Second Skin (Hawkes) 1:138; 2:185-86; 3:221-22; 4:215, 218; 7:141, 144-45; 9:266-69; 15:274-77; 27:190-92, 199; 49:161-64

"Second Son" (Pastan) 27:368

"Second Son Day" (Honig) 33:213, 215

"Second Song" (Bogan) 46:81; 93:67, 69

Second sous-sol (Butor) 15:115

"Second Spring" (MacLeod) 56:198-200

The Second Stage (Friedan) 74:99-111

The Second Stone (Fiedler) 4:160

"The Second Swimming" (Boyle) 36:58

"Second Thoughts about Humanism" (Eliot) 6:160

"Second Time Around" (Cortazar)
    See "Segunda vez"

"The Second Time Around" (Fisher) 87:124

The Second Tree from the Corner (White) 10:527-28; 39:370, 373, 375

"Second Wind" (Chappell) 78:92

The Secondary Sky (Popa) 19:373-74

Secondary Worlds (Auden) 6:16; 43:25

Second-Class Citizen (Emecheta) 14:159;

48:97-8, 101
"Second-Class Matter" (Perelman)   **49**:264
"The Second-Fated" (Graves)   **45**:169
"Secrecý" (Watkins)   **43**:454, 456
"The Secret" (Cohen)   **19**:113
"The Secret" (Frame)   **96**:184
"The Secret" (Mahapatra)   **33**:284
"A Secret" (Plath)   **51**:340
A Secret (Akhmadulina)   **53**:15
Secret (Andrade)
   See *Segrafedo*
The Secret Adversary (Christie)   **48**:73-4;
   110:111, 113, 123
Secret Agent (Hitchcock)   **16**:345
The Secret beyond the Door (*Le Secret derrière
   la Porte*) (Lang)   **20**:207, 216; **103**:87
"Le secret de Justine" (Theriault)   **79**:408
Le Secret derrière la Porte (Lang)
   See *The Secret beyond the Door*
The Secret Diary of Adrian Mole, Aged 13 3/4
   (*The Adrian Mole Diaries*)   **61**:407-16,
   418-420
*The Secret Diary of Margaret Hilda Roberts,
   Aged 14 1/2*   **61**:420
Secret Friends (Potter)   **86**:346, 353
The Secret Glass (Bainbridge)
   See *The Dressmaker*
*The Secret Government: The Constitution in
   Crisis* (Moyers)   **74**:252
"A Secret Gratitude" (Wright)   **10**:544
*The Secret Heart of the Clock: Notes, Apho-
   risms, Fragments, 1973-1985* (Canetti)
   See *Das Geheimherz der Uhr:
   Aufzeichnungen 1973-1985*
The Secret History (Tartt)   **76**:119-37
The Secret History of the Lord of Musashi
   (Tanizaki)
   See *Bushuko hiwa*
Secret Honor (Altman)   **116**:59, 68
"Le secret humain" (MacLeish)   **68**:270, 285
"The Secret in the Cat" (Swenson)   **14**:518
Secret in the Stlalakum Wild (Harris)   **12**:263-
   67
"The Secret Integration" (Pynchon)   **33**:334,
   338-40; **62**:431, 434
Secret Isaac (Charyn)   **18**:99
"Secret Journal" (Willingham)   **51**:403
The Secret Journey of the Silver Reindeer
   (Kingman)   **17**:245-46
The Secret Ladder (Harris)   **25**:203, 205, 214
The Secret Life of Cartoons (Barker)   **52**:54
"The Secret Life of Henry K" (Bova)   **45**:75
The Secret Life of the Lord of Musashi (Tanizaki)
   See *Bushuko hiwa*
"The Secret Life of Walter Mitty" (Thurber)
   5:432, 440; **11**:533-34; **25**:440
Secret Lives, and Other Stories (Ngugi wa
   Thiong'o)   **36**:313, 317, 322
Secret Marriages (Longley)   **29**:295
The Secret Meaning of Things (Ferlinghetti)
   10:174-75; **27**:139; **111**:65
"The Secret Miracle" (Borges)
   See "El milagro secreto"
Secret Narratives (Motion)   **47**:288-94
The Secret of Chimneys (Christie)   **110**:111,
   113
The Secret of Dr. Honigberger (Eliade)
   See *Secretul Doctorului Honigberger*
The Secret of Heaven (Lagerkvist)
   See *Himlens hemlighet*
The Secret of J. Eddy Fink (Ian)   **21**:183
The Secret of Luca (Silone)   **4**:493
The Secret of the Lodge (*The House in Cornwall*;

The House of Cornwall) (Streatfeild)
   21:398, 406
Secret of the Lost Race (Norton)   **12**:468
Secret Passage (Cavanna)   **12**:98
The Secret Passion (Huston)
   See *Freud*
The Secret People (Wyndham)   **19**:476
"Le secret perdu dans l'eau" (Carrier)   **78**:63,
   72, 77-8
Secret Places (Elliott)   **47**:112-14
The Secret Rapture (Hare)   **58**:231-35
Secret Rendezvous (Abe)
   See *Mikkai*
The Secret Road (Lancaster)   **36**:244
"The Secret Room" (Robbe-Grillet)   **14**:462;
   43:361
"The Secret Sits" (Frost)   **13**:228
Secret Stories of the Lord of Musashi (Tanizaki)
   See *Bushuko hiwa*
The Secret Tales of the Lord of Musashi
   (Tanizaki)
   See *Bushuko hiwa*
"The Secret Town" (Nash)   **23**:317
Secret Training (Codrescu)   **46**:104
Secret Understandings (Philipson)   **53**:276
"A Secret Vice" (Tolkien)   **38**:439-40, 442
Secret Villages (Dunn)   **40**:170-71
The Secret Ways (MacLean)   **13**:361; **63**:262-
   63
"Secret Weapons" (Cortazar)
   See "Las armas secretas"
Secret Window, Secret Garden (King)   **113**:367
"Secretary" (Gaitskill)   **69**:199, 201
"Secretary" (Hughes)   **2**:198; **9**:284
"The Secretary Chant" (Piercy)   **6**:403
"Secrets" (Fuller)   **62**:201
"Secrets" (Mac Laverty)   **31**:253-54
Secrets, and Other Stories (Mac Laverty)
   31:252-54
Secrets and Surprises (Beattie)   **13**:64-6; **18**:37;
   40:63, 66; **63**:3, 11, 15, 17
Secrets from the Center of the World (Harjo)
   83:272-73, 275-77, 279
*Secrets of a Woman's Heart: The Later Life of I.
   Compton-Burnett, 1920-1969* (Spurling)
   34:495-98
"Secrets of Hans's Harem" (Sansom)   **2**:383
"Secrets of Lord Bushu" (Tanizaki)
   See *Bushuko hiwa*
Secrets of the Shopping Mall (Peck)   **21**:300
"Secrets of the Universe" (McFadden)   **48**:257
Secrets of Women (Bergman)
   See *Kvinnors väntan*
"Secrets of Wonder Women" (Hochman)   **8**:297
Secrets on the Road (Transtroemer)
   See *Hemligheter på vägen*
"Secrets on the Way" (Transtroemer)   **65**:222-
   23
Secrets on the Way (Transtroemer)
   See *Hemligheter på vägen*
Secretul Doctorului Honigberger (*The Secret
   of Dr. Honigberger*) (Eliade)   **19**:145-47
"The Sect of the Phoenix" (Borges)
   See "La secta del Fénix"
"The Sect of Thirty" (Borges)
   See "La secta de los treintas"
"La secta de los treintas" ("The Sect of
   Thirty") (Borges)   **9**:117; **19**:51; **48**:38-9
"La secta del Fénix" ("The Sect of the Phoe-
   nix") (Borges)   **83**:156-57
Section: Rock-Drill, 85-95 de los cantares
   (Pound)   **4**:412, 414; **7**:331; **13**:463;
   48:282-83, 285-86, 293

"Secuestro de la mujer de Antonio" (Guillen)
   48:163
"Secular Conversions" (Burke)   **24**:127
Secular Love (Ondaatje)   **51**:313-15, 317, 320
The Secular Scripture (Frye)   **24**:226, 229
"The Security Guard" (Dixon)   **52**:95, 98
"Security Precedes Credibility" (Carr)   **86**:47
"Sedan Chair" (Young)   **17**:581
"Sediment" (Ignatow)   **40**:258
Sedmiramenný svícen (*The Menorah*)
   (Skvorecky)   **39**:221; **69**:343
Seduced (Shepard)   **17**:447-49; **41**:408-09
"Seduction" (Giovanni)   **19**:190; **64**:186-87,
   194-95
"Seduction and Betrayal" (hooks)   **94**:158
Seduction and Betrayal (Hardwick)   **13**:264-
   66
The Seduction, and Other Stories (Oates)
   6:373; **9**:403
The Seduction of Mimi (Wertmueller)   **16**:587-
   89, 595, 597-98
The Seduction of Peter S. (Sanders)   **41**:381-82
Seduction of the Minotaur (Nin)   **4**:376, 378-
   79; **14**:385; **60**:275, 279-81
"See Everything New" (Cryer)   **21**:79
"See My Friends" (Davies)   **21**:89
See Naples and Die (Rice)   **7**:360; **49**:300
*See No Evil: Prefaces, Essays, and Accounts,
   1976-1983* (Shange)   **38**:395
"See the Moon?" (Barthelme)   **115**:62, 86
See the Old Lady Decently (Johnson)   **6**:264-
   65; **9**:301
"See the Sky about to Rain" (Young)   **17**:573
See Them Die (Hunter)   **31**:220
See Under: Love (Grossman)   **67**:65-72, 74
See You at Mao (Godard)   **20**:141
See You Later Alligator (Buckley)   **37**:62-3
See You Will Never Get Anywhere (Benet)
   See *Nunca llegarás a nada*
The Seed (Vesaas)
   See *Kimen*
The Seed beneath the Snow (Silone)   **4**:493
"Seed Catalogue" (Kroetsch)   **23**:273
Seed Catalogue: Poems (Kroetsch)   **23**:273
"The Seed Cutters" (Heaney)   **7**:152; **25**:245
"A Seed in the Sky" (Honig)   **33**:216
"Seed Leaves" (Wilbur)   **3**:533; **6**:568; **9**:568;
   53:404-05
"The Seed of My Father" (Swenson)   **106**:351
"The Seed Picture" (McGuckian)   **48**:275-77
"The Seed Thrower" (Scott)   **22**:373
Seeds and Bran (Tzara)
   See *Grains et issues*
Seeds for a Hymn (Paz)
   See *Semillas para un himno*
*Seeds of Change: A Quincentennial Com-
   memoration*   **70**:332, 344
Seeds of Contemplation (Merton)   **1**:211;
   83:403
Seeds of Destruction (Merton)   **1**:211; **83**:382-
   83
Seeds of Man (Guthrie)   **35**:194
The Seeds of Tomorrow (Sholokhov)
   See *Podniataia tselina*
Seedtime on the Cumberland (Arnow)   **7**:15-
   16; **18**:12
"Seeing Death in the Murderous Look of an
   Unknown Black Man Whom I Admire and
   Deducing from This Certain Proprietorial
   Privileges" (Hall)   **51**:175
"Seeing Gender" (Acker)   **111**:46
"Seeing Her Leave" (Davie)   **31**:117
"Seeing in the Dark" (Komunyakaa)   **94**:230

Seeing in the Dark (Transtroemer)
See *Mörkerseende*
Seeing Is Believing (Tomlinson) **2**:436-37;
4:543-44, 546-47; **13**:545, 547; **45**:392-
93, 396, 398-400, 402, 404
"Seeing Pablo Neruda" (Spacks) **14**:511
"Seeing Things" (Heaney) **74**:188, 194-95
"Seeing Things" (Peterkin) **31**:307
Seeing Things (Heaney) **74**:188-95, 197,
91:124-25
Seeing through the Sun (Hogan) **73**:150-52,
154, 157, 159
*Seeing Voices: A Journey into the World of the
Deaf* (Sacks) **67**:303-05
"Seeing You Have" (Snodgrass) **18**:491
Seek the House of Relatives (Cook-Lynn)
93:121
"The Seeker" (Townshend) **17**:529, 531
"The Seekers" (McGrath) **59**:177, 181
The Seekers (Jakes) **29**:248
The Seekers and Other Poems (Sachs) **14**:476;
98:362
"Seeking a Job" (Bennett) **28**:29
Eine Seele aus Holz (*Soul of Wood, and Other
Stories*) (Lind) **1**:178; **2**:245; **4**:292-93;
27:271, 273; **82**:128-30, 132-38, 140,
142, 145
"Seele im Raum" (Jarrell) **6**:260; **13**:298
Die Seele und die Formen (*Soul and Form*)
(Lukacs) **24**:324-25, 330
"Der Seelische Ratgeber" (Lenz) **27**:245
Seembadha (Ray)
See *Simabaddha*
"Seen and Not Seen" (Byrne) **26**:98-9
"Seen the Lights Go Out on Broadway" (Joel)
See "Miami 2017"
"Seesaw" (Gerstler) **70**:156
"See-Saw" (Pink Floyd) **35**:307
The Seesaw Log (Gibson) **23**:175-76
Seetee Ship (Williamson) **29**:450
Seetee Shock (Williamson) **29**:450
Sefer ha-Maasim (*The Book of Deeds*; *Book of
Fables*) (Agnon) **8**:8; **14**:4
Seger i mörker (*Victory in the Dark*) (Lagerkvist)
54:269-70, 272, 275, 278
Ségou: La terre en miettes (*Children of Segu*)
(Conde) **52**:83-5; **92**:108, 130
Ségou: Les murailles de terre (*Segu*) (Conde)
52:81-5; **92**:100, 102-03, 108-11, 113,
126, 130-31, 133-34
Segrafedo (*Secret*) (Andrade) **18**:3
Segrêdo (Andrade) **18**:3
Segregation: The Inner Conflict in the South
(Warren) **8**:538; **59**:298
La segretaria (Ginzburg) **54**:207
Il segreto del bosco vecchio (Buzzati) **36**:83,
97
Segu (Conde)
See *Ségou: Les murailles de terre*
Segues (Bell) **31**:51-2
"Seguir siguiendo" (Otero) **11**:427
"Segunda vez" ("Second Time Around")
(Cortazar) **33**:125
"Le sei della sera" ("Donat"; "6 della sera")
(Ortese) **89**:198
Sein und Zeit (*Being and Time*) (Heidegger)
24:257, 260, 262, 264-65, 267, 269-71,
273, 275, 277, 279
"Las seis" (Aleixandre) **9**:12
Seis calas (Alonso) **14**:20
Seis problemas para Don Isidro Parodi (*Six
Problems for Don Isidro Parodi*) (Bioy
Casares) **13**:84, 106; **48**:36, 41-4; **88**:66,

69-73, 77-8, 85
"Seismograf" (Bagryana) **10**:13
"Seismograf na surtseto" (Bagryana) **10**:12,
14
Seize the Day (Bellow) **1**:27-8, 30-1; **2**:49, 51,
53; **3**:49-50, 52, 55-7, 60-1; **6**:56, 61;
8:70, 72, 74, 77; **10**:37-9, 44; **13**:70, 72-
3; **15**:47-8, 50, 52-3, 55, 57; **25**:80, 84-5;
33:64, 67, 71; **63**:28, 36, 42-3; **79**:60-
104
"Seizing Control" (Robison) **98**:306-08, 317
"The Seizure" (Blaise) **29**:70-1
Seizure (Stone) **73**:364
A Seizure of Limericks (Aiken) **52**:26
The Seizure of Power (Milosz)
See *Zdobycie wladzy*
Sekrya (*The Guinea Pigs*) (Vaculik) **7**:494-97
Šel malir chude do sveta (*The Painter Went
Poor into the World*; *Penniless Painter
Goes Out into the World*; "A Penniless
Painter Went Out into the World")
(Seifert) **93**:306, 332, 335, 343
Le sel noir (Glissant) **68**:187
"Selahl" (Hughes) **108**:308
"Selbdritt, Selbviert" ("The Three of Us, the
Four of Us") (Celan) **53**:77
"The Select Party" (Ewart) **46**:150
Selected and New Poems (Dubie) **36**:139-41
Selected and New Poems, 1961-1981
(Harrison) **33**:197-98
Selected Cantos (Pound) **4**:416; **48**:295
Selected Criticism: Prose, Poetry (Bogan)
46:84; **93**:65
Selected Declarations of Dependence (Mathews)
52:307, 314, 316
Selected Essays (Eliot) **24**:173, 177, 183;
113:218
Selected Essays (Farrell) **66**:132
Selected Essays (Montale) **18**:342-43
Selected Essays (Montherlant) **19**:324
Selected Essays (Williams) **5**:510; **67**:411
Selected Essays and Criticism (Dudek) **19**:139
Selected Essays of Delmore Schwartz (Schwartz)
45:359
Selected Essays of Hugh MacDiarmid
(MacDiarmid) **2**:254
Selected Failings (Neruda)
See *Defectos escogidos: 2000*
The Selected James Simmons (Simmons)
43:411-12
Selected Letters (Frost) **44**:459, 462
Selected Letters, 1917-1961 (Hemingway)
See *Ernest Hemingway: Selected Letters,
1917-1961*
Selected Letters of Conrad Aiken (Aiken)
52:30-2
*Selected Letters of E. M. Forster, Volume I: 1879-
1920* (Forster) **45**:137-38, 143
*Selected Letters of E. M. Forster, Volume II:
1921-1970* (Forster) **45**:138-40, 143
Selected Letters of James Thurber (Thurber)
25:438-40
Selected Letters of John O'Hara (O'Hara)
11:414; **42**:318
*The Selected Letters of Philip Larkin, 1940-
1985* (Thwaite) **81**:417-64
Selected Letters of Theodore Roethke (Roethke)
46:356
Selected Letters of William Faulkner (Faulkner)
9:203
A Selected Life (Kinsella) **19**:253
Selected Literary Criticism of Louis MacNeice
(MacNeice) **53**:244

Selected Longer Poems (Ammons) **25**:44;
57:59
Selected Notebooks: 1960-1967 (Cozzens)
92:211
The Selected Paul Durcan (Durcan) **43**:115-
18
Selected Plays (Friel) **115**:224
*Selected Plays and Prose of Amiri Baraka/LeRoi
Jones* (Baraka) **14**:48
Selected Poems (Abse) **7**:1
Selected Poems (Adcock) **41**:17-18
Selected Poems (Aiken) **1**:4
Selected Poems (Akhmatova) **25**:25
Selected Poems (Ali) **69**:32
Selected Poems (Ammons) **2**:11-12; **5**:26;
9:26; **25**:48; **57**:59; **108**:5, 17, 21-2, 24
Selected Poems (Ashbery) **41**:40-1; **77**:56,
60, 62
Selected Poems (Avison) **97**:120-22
Selected Poems (Baraka) **115**:38-9
Selected Poems (Barker) **48**:13-14
Selected Poems (Beer) **58**:36
Selected Poems (Betjeman) **6**:67
Selected Poems (Boland) **67**:45-6; **113**:108,
110
Selected Poems (Breton) **54**:17
Selected Poems (Brooks) **49**:23, 27, 32, 35
Selected Poems (Ciardi) **40**:162; **44**:375, 379-
82
Selected Poems (Clarke) **61**:78-9, 82
Selected Poems (Clarke) **9**:169
Selected Poems (Creeley) **8**:153; **78**:161
Selected Poems (Daryush) **6**:122; **19**:119
Selected Poems (Day Lewis) **6**:127-28
Selected Poems (Dorn) **18**:129
Selected Poems (Eberhart) **3**:135; **56**:80-4
Selected Poems (Eigner) **9**:181
Selected Poems (Ekelof) **27**:113, 116
Selected Poems (Elytis) **49**:113-14
Selected Poems (Frost) **9**:219
Selected Poems (Glassco) **9**:236
Selected Poems (Graham) **29**:198-99
Selected Poems (Grass) **32**:197
Selected Poems (Gregor) **9**:253, 255
Selected Poems (Guillevic) **33**:191
Selected Poems (Gustafson) **36**:214, 216
Selected Poems (H. D.) **31**:203
Selected Poems (Hacker) **91**:110
Selected Poems (Hall) **51**:173-75
Selected Poems (Harrison) **43**:179-81
Selected Poems (Hayden) **5**:168; **14**:240;
37:160
Selected Poems (Hikmet) **40**:244, 247
Selected Poems (Hope) **51**:226-27
Selected Poems (Hugo) **18**:263-64; **32**:244-
46
The Selected Poems (Ignatow) **7**:178-79, 181-
82
Selected Poems (Jarrell) **9**:297; **13**:300
Selected Poems (Justice) **19**:232-34, 236-37;
102:248-51, 253, 256, 261, 267-68, 270,
275, 277, 283
Selected Poems (Kinnell) **29**:288-89
Selected Poems (Kinsella) **19**:252
Selected Poems (Laughlin) **49**:220
Selected Poems (Levertov) **66**:249-50
Selected Poems (Levine) **33**:275
Selected Poems (Lowell) **8**:353, 355-57
Selected Poems (MacCaig) **36**:284, 288
Selected Poems (Masefield) **47**:233
Selected Poems (Merrill) **91**:235
Selected Poems (Merton) **83**:393-94
Selected Poems (Merwin) **88**:204-06

Selected Poems (Milosz)　5:292; 22:308, 312; 31:259, 262, 267; 56:239-40, 244; 82:297-98

Selected Poems (Montague)　46:275-77, 279

Selected Poems (Moore)　1:228-30; 2:291; 13:393; 19:339; 47:260

Selected Poems (Moss)　7:247-49; 14:375-76; 45:289; 50:352

Selected Poems (Murphy)　41:319

Selected Poems (Neruda)　5:301-02; 62:333

Selected Poems (O'Hara)　13:424

Selected Poems (Orlovitz)　22:333, 336-37

Selected Poems (Pastan)　27:370

Selected Poems (Patchen)　18:394

Selected Poems (Paz)　51:326-27, 334

Selected Poems (Pound)　4:415

Selected Poems (Purdy)　3:408

Selected Poems (Rakosi)　47:342-43

Selected Poems (Ransom)　2:365; 11:467

Selected Poems (Rexroth)　49:283-86

Selected Poems (Rich)　18:446 ·

Selected Poems (Riding)　7:374-75

Selected Poems (Ritsos)　31:325

Selected Poems (Sachs)
　See *Ausgewählte Gedichte*

Selected Poems (Sandburg)　35:345

Selected Poems (Scannell)　49:328-29

Selected Poems (Scott)　22:373, 375, 377

Selected Poems (Shapcott)　38:403-04

Selected Poems (Shapiro)　8:486; 15:478; 53:331

Selected Poems (Silkin)　43:403-04

Selected Poems (Simpson)　4:497-99; 7:428-29

Selected Poems (Sitwell)　67:324

Selected Poems (Skelton)　13:506-07

Selected Poems (Smith)　43:417, 422

Selected Poems (Strand)　41:431-37; 71:278, 286-88, 290

Selected Poems (Thomas)　31:431, 434

Selected Poems (Transtroemer)　52:415-16

Selected Poems (Voznesensky)　15:552-53

Selected Poems (Walcott)　67:353

Selected Poems (Warren)　59:295-96

Selected Poems (Watkins)　43:441

Selected Poems (Webb)　18:542

Selected Poems (Wieners)　7:536-37

Selected Poems, 1949 (Williams)　42:462

Selected Poems, 1968 (Herbert)　43:183, 188, 194

Selected Poems, 1977 (Herbert)　43:188

Selected Poems, 1984 (Williams)　42:461-62

Selected Poems 1954-82 (Fuller)　62:203-04

Selected Poems: 1968-86 (Muldoon)　72:275-76

Selected Poems, 1920-1970 (Everson)　27:135

Selected Poems, 1923-1943 (Warren)　8:539-40, 542; 10:523, 525; 13:578, 573-74; 18:535

Selected Poems, 1923-1967 (Borges)　2:71-2; 48:46

Selected Poems, 1923-1975 (Warren)　8:539-40, 542; 10:523, 525; 13:573, 578; 39:265, 267

Selected Poems, 1928-1958 (Kunitz)　6:285-86; 14:312

Selected Poems, 1930-1960 (Watkins)　43:447, 455

Selected Poems, 1933-1980 (Faludy)　42:142

Selected Poems, 1935-1985 (Laughlin)　49:223-24

Selected Poems (1938-1958): Summer Knowl-edge (Schwartz)

See *Summer Knowledge: New and Selected Poems, 1938-1958*

Selected Poems: 1938-1988 (McGrath)　59:180-84

Selected Poems, 1940-1966 (Birney)　6:74-5, 78

Selected Poems, 1946-1968 (Thomas)　6:531; 48:380

Selected Poems 1947-1995 (Ginsberg)　109:362-63, 365

Selected Poems, 1950-1975 (Gunn)　18:202-04; 81:184

Selected Poems, 1950-1982 (Koch)　44:248, 250

Selected Poems, 1951-1974 (Tomlinson)　13:546, 548-49; 45:392, 394-96, 401

Selected Poems, 1951-1977 (Ammons)　25:41-4

The Selected Poems, 1951-1986 (Ammons)　57:51-2

Selected Poems, 1953-1976 (Alvarez)　13:9

Selected Poems, 1954-1986 (Transtroemer)　52:418

Selected Poems, 1954-1992 (Brown)　100:88

Selected Poems, 1955-1976 (Honig)　33:215

Selected Poems, 1955-1980 (Smith)　64:393-96

Selected Poems, 1957-1967 (Hughes)　4:235-36; 9:281

Selected Poems, 1957-1987 (Snodgrass)　68:387, 389, 395, 397-99

Selected Poems, 1958-1980 (Sorrentino)　40:384, 386

Selected Poems, 1963-1980 (Longley)　29:296

Selected Poems, 1963-1983 (Simic)　49:337-43

Selected Poems 1965-1975 (Atwood)　8:29-30; 15:36-8; 25:64, 67; 84:68

Selected Poems 1966-1987 (Heaney)　74:192-93, 195; 91:124

Selected Poems, 1970-1980 (Codrescu)　46:104-05

The Selected Poems: Expanded Editions (Ammons)　108:24

Selected Poems, Joseph Brodsky (Brodsky)　4:77-8; 6:97-8; 36:74, 76-9, 81; 100:49, 51-2, 58

Selected Poems: Loki Is Buried at Smoky Creek (Wah)　44:328

Selected Poems: New and Old, 1923-1966 (Warren)　8:539; 18:534; 39:266

Selected Poems of Dorothy Livesay 1926-1956 (Livesay)　15:339

The Selected Poems of Langston Hughes (Hughes)　10:279; 35:216; 108:292, 295, 315, 319, 334-35

Selected Poems of Luis Cernuda (Cernuda)　54:58

Selected Poems of May Sarton (Sarton)　14:482

The Selected Poems of Rosario Castellanos (Castellanos)　66:60

Selected Poems: Poems Selected and New 1976-1986 (Atwood)　84:68-9

Selected Poems: The Self-Completing Tree (The Self-Completing Tree) (Livesay)　79:332-33, 336, 338, 353

Selected Poetry (Walcott)　14:548; 25:452; 42:421

Selected Poetry of Amiri Baraka/LeRoi Jones (Baraka)　14:48

The Selected Poetry of Hayden Carruth (Carruth)　84:131, 133-34

The Selected Poetry of Jaroslav Seifert (Seifert)

44:423; 93:329, 331, 345

The Selected Poetry of Robinson Jeffers (Jeffers)　54:238, 244, 246, 249; 11:304

Selected Poetry of W. H. Auden (Auden)　2:24

The Selected Poetry of Yehuda Amichai (Amichai)　57:40-4; 116:114, 130

Selected Prose (Celan)　82:37

Selected Prose, 1909-1965 (Pound)　3:397-99; 5:349; 7:333

Selected Short Stories of Mulk Raj Anand (Anand)　23:21

Selected Shorter Poems (Reaney)　13:476

Selected Stories (Gordimer)　7:132-33; 10:240; 33:182; 70:163

Selected Stories (Hood)　28:193

Selected Stories (Levine)　54:295-97

Selected Stories (Pritchett)　13:467; 15:443; 41:330

Selected Stories of Andre Dubus (Dubus)　97:221-22, 227, 229-30, 235

Selected Stories of Roald Dahl (Dahl)　1:71

Selected Stories of Seán O'Faoláin (O'Faolain)　14:405-07

"Selected Strawberries" (Musgrave)　54:340

Selected Tales of Jacques Ferron (Ferron)　94:124

Selected Translations, 1968-1978 (Merwin)　45:276

Selected Verse Translations (Watkins)　43:455

Selected Writings (Barnes)　29:25

Selected Writings (Capote)　3:99; 13:139; 58:93

Selected Writings (Cendrars)　106:177

Selected Writings (Olson)　5:326

Selected Writings 1950-1990 (Howe)　85:151-52

Selected Writings of William Goyen: Eight Fa-vorites by a Master American Story-Teller (Goyen)　8:250

Selecteda Poems of Tudor Arghezi (Arghezi)　80:9

"Selene Afterwards" (MacLeish)　68:271, 286

"Self" (Hacker)　72:191

"Self" (de Man)　55:410

The Self and Others: Further Studies in Sanity and Madness (Laing)　95:124, 129, 131, 133-35, 138, 141, 156, 170-71, 173-74, 182

"The Self and the Mulberry" (Bell)　31:49

"Self as an Eye" (Squires)　51:380

Self defence: Critique esthétique (Reverdy)　53:280, 283, 285-86

"Self Defense" (Giles)　39:65

"The Self in Fiction" (Barth)　51:24

"Self Is a Very Iffy Word for Me" (Bell)　31:51

"Self Portrait" (Castellanos)
　See "Autorretrato"

Self Portrait (Dylan)　4:150; 6:157; 12:190, 199; 77:164, 175, 178

Self Portrait (Kavanagh)　22:236

"Self Portrait at Fourty-Four" (Pastan)　27:369

Self-Accusation (Handke)　5:166; 8:262-63; 15:266-67; 38:215

The Self-Completing Tree (Livesay)
　See *Selected Poems: The Self-Completing Tree*

Self-Consciousness (Updike)　70:253, 263

"Self-Counsel in Old Age" (Wheelock)　14:571

"The Self-Hatred of Don L. Lee" (Madhubuti)　73:206

"Self-Help" (Beer)　58:32

Self-Help (Moore)　39:82-5; 45:279-83; 68:296-301

"Self-Interview" (Reed)　60:313

Self-Interviews (Dickey) 1:73; 2:116; 109:249-50

"The Selfish One" (Neruda)
See "El egoísta"

"Self-Portrait" 75:61, 77

"Self-Portrait" (Creeley) 36:120

"Self-Portrait" (Dixon) 52:100

"Self-Portrait" (Graham) 48:145

"Self-Portrait" (Stern) 40:407

"Self-Portrait, 1969" (Bidart) 33:74, 76

"Self-Portrait as a Bear" (Hall) 37:142

"Self-Portrait as Apollo and Daphne" (Graham) 48:154

"Self-Portrait as Hurry and Delay" ("Penelope at Her Loom") (Graham) 48:155

"Self-Portrait as the Gesture between Them" (Graham) 48:150

Self-Portrait: Ceaselessly into the Past (Macdonald) 34:416; 41:269-70

"Self-Portrait in a Convex Mirror" (Ashbery) 9:44, 48; 13:31, 33-4; 15:28, 32, 35; 25:52, 56; 41:33, 37-8, 40-1; 77:44, 46, 48-9, 55-6, 60, 62, 77-9

Self-Portrait in a Convex Mirror (Ashbery) 6:11-14; 9:41-2, 44, 47-9; 13:30-1, 33; 15:28-9, 31, 35; 25:58; 41:38, 40

"Self-Portrait, Nude with Steering Wheel" (Durcan) 70:147

"Self-Portrait on a Summer Evening" (Boland) 113:73, 82-3, 89, 94, 98

"Self-Portraits" (Wright) 28:460

"Self's the Man" (Larkin) 18:299; 33:258, 268; 39:343; 64:267-68, 282

"The Self-Seeker" (Frost) 15:240

"Sell Me?" (Guillen) 79:229

"Sell Me a Coat" (Bowie) 17:65

"Sell Out" (Damas)
See "Solde"

"Selling Hot Pussy" (hooks) 94:150

The Selling of the President, 1968 (McGinniss) 32:299-302

The Sell-Outs (Valdez)
See *Los vendidos*

Selvä johdatus myöhempään historiaan (*A Clear Introduction to Later History*) (Haavikko) 34:170; 34:170

"La selva y el mar" (Aleixandre) 9:14, 16

Sem' puteshestvii (*Seven Journeys*) (Bitov) 57:115

La semaine sainte (*Holy Week*) (Aragon) 3:14; 22:35-6, 38

"The Semantic Waltz" (L'Heureux) 52:273

Semeiotke: Recherches pour une sémanalyse (*Recherches pour une sémanalyse*) (Kristeva) 77:299, 303

"Semejante a la noche" (Carpentier) 110:48

"Semele Recycled" (Kizer) 39:169-71

"Semicolon; for Philip Whalen" (Loewinsohn) 52:284

"Semi-Fraudulent Direct from Hollywood Overture" (Zappa) 17:587

Semillas para un himno (*Seeds for a Hymn*) (Paz) 19:368

Semi-Monde (Coward) 51:70

Séminaire XX (*Encore*) (Lacan) 75:304-05, 310

Séminaire, 1974-75 (Lacan) 75:287

The Seminarian (del Castillo) 38:167-68

Semiotics and Structuralism (Bakhtin) 83:24

Semiotics and the Philosophy of Language (Eco) 60:116, 125

"Semiprivate, Female" (Selzer) 74:272

"The Semi-Sapphics" (Ewart) 46:152-53

Semmel Weiss (Sackler) 14:480

Il sempione strizza l'occhio al frejus (*The Twilight of the Elephants*) (Vittorini) 9:546; 14:544

La señal que se espera (*The Awaited Sign*) (Buero Vallejo) 15:101-02

Señas de identidad (*Marks of Identity*; *Signs of Identity*) (Goytisolo) 5:151; 10:244-45; 23:181, 186, 189

"Send in the Clowns" (Sondheim) 30:384-85, 387, 396, 401

"Send No Money" (Larkin) 5:227; 18:299; 33:256

Send No More Roses (Ambler)
See *The Siege of the Villa Lipp*

Send Somebody Nice (Hilliard) 15:280

Sendemann Huskuld (*Huskuld the Herald*; *Messenger Huskuld*) (Vesaas) 48:404-05, 410

"Send-Off" (Adcock) 41:16

"The Send-Off" (Jong) 6:268; 83:300

"Séneca en las orillas" (Borges) 48:47

A Seneca Journal (Rothenberg) 57:374, 382

"Seneca Journal I" (Rothenberg) 57:382

Senior Citizens (Jones) 52:250

"Senior Service" (Costello) 21:71

Seniority (Ziegenhagen) 55:377-80

Senlin: A Biography (Aiken) 52:20, 22, 24

Sennik wspólczesny (*A Dreambook for Our Time*) (Konwicki) 8:326; 117:255, 257-58, 272, 282, 284-85, 287

"Señor Ong and Señor Ha" (Bowles) 53:37

El Señor presidente (*The President*) (Asturias) 3:17-8; 8:28; 13:37

"Señor (Tales of Yankee Power)" (Dylan) 77:182

"Una señora" ("A Lady") (Donoso) 11:145; 32:157

"La señora mayor" (Borges) 44:365

Le Sens apparent (*Surface of Meaning*; *Surface of Sense*) (Brossard) 115:107, 111, 114-15, 121, 136

Le sens de la marche (*The Direction of the March*) (Adamov) 25:12-13

"Sensation Time at the Home" (Merton)
See "A Song: Sensation Time at the Home"

A Sense of Danger (Scannell) 49:326, 328, 331

A Sense of Detachment (Osborne) 45:316, 320

"A Sense of Direction" (Gellhorn) 60:180-81

The Sense of Glory (Read) 4:441

A Sense of Honor (Webb) 22:453-54

"Sense of Identity" (Herbert) 9:275

"A Sense of Measure" (Creeley) 78:147

A Sense of Measure (Creeley) 4:118

The Sense of Movement (Gunn) 3:215; 18:200; 32:207, 210; 81:183-85

The Sense of Occasion (Kallman) 2:221

"A Sense of Pilgrimage" (Levertov) 66:242

"A Sense of Porpoise" (Grayson) 38:211

"A Sense of Proportion" (Frame) 96:189

A Sense of Reality (Greene) 3:211; 70:293

"A Sense of Shelter" (Updike) 23:473

"A Sense of Story" (McPherson) 77:365

"The Sense of the Past" (Trilling) 24:450

A Sense of Values (Wilson) 32:447

A Sense of Where You Are (McPhee) 36:296

"The Sense of Wonder" (Carson) 71:112

The Sense of Wonder (Carson) 71:101, 103-08, 112-13

The Sense Organs: Our Link with the World (Silverstein and Silverstein) 17:452

"Sensemayá" (Guillen) 79:248

"Sensibility! O La!" (Roethke) 101:274, 282, 335, 340

"The Sensitive Goldfish" (Stead) 80:334

"The Sensitive Knife" (Stern) 40:408

Senso (Visconti) 16:564-66, 568-69, 572

"Il senso recondito" (Buzzati) 36:96

"The Sensualists" (Roethke) 46:363

"Sensuality" (Slessor) 14:496

"The Sensuality of Truth" (Ezekiel) 61:109

The Sensuous Dirty Old Man (Asimov) 76:315

Sent for You Yesterday (Wideman) 34:298-300; 67:374, 378-79, 381-82, 384, 388

Sent off the Field (Padilla)
See *Fuera del juego*

"The Sentence" (Barthelme) 23:45; 115:61

"The Sentence" (Graves) 45:168

A Sentence of Life (Gloag) 40:206-07

"Sentences" (Scannell) 49:334

Sentences (Nemerov) 36:305-08

"The Sententious Man" (Roethke) 101:328

Il sentiero dei nidi di ragno (*The Path to the Nest of the Spiders*) (Calvino) 5:97-8; 8:127, 129; 11:87-90, 92; 22:89; 33:97; 39:306-07, 309, 314, 317; 73:52, 58

"Sentiment" (Parker) 68:326, 334, 339

Sentiment of Time (Ungaretti)
See *Sentimento del tempo*

"Sentimental Education" (Brodkey) 56:55-6

A Sentimental Education (Oates) 19:356; 33:289

"Sentimental Memory" (Colwin) 23:129; 84:149-50

"Sentimental Summer" (Huxley) 11:282

Sentimento del tempo (*Sentiment of Time*) (Ungaretti) 7:481-82, 485; 11:555-57, 559-60; 15:536-39

Sentimento do mundo (Andrade) 18:5

"Sentiments fanés" (Reverdy) 53:283

"Sentiments for a Dedication" (MacLeish) 68:287

"The Sentinel" (Clarke) 35:122

"Sentry Duty" (Transtroemer) 65:230

Separate but Unequal (Harlan) 34:186

Separate Checks (Wiggins) 57:431-33, 435, 439-40

A Separate Development (Hope) 52:209-12, 217

"Separate Flights" (Dubus) 97:197, 199, 201, 204, 206-07, 209, 215, 218

Separate Flights (Dubus) 13:182-83; 36:144, 146-48; 97:195, 197, 199, 204, 209, 215, 218, 231, 235

"The Separate Notebooks" (Milosz)
See "Osobny zeszyt"

The Separate Notebooks (Milosz) 31:267, 269; 56:231-32, 234, 239, 244; 82:283, 297-98, 301, 305, 310

A Separate Peace (Knowles) 1:169; 4:271-72; 10:303; 26:245-50, 252-53, 255-65

"Separate Planes" (Adams) 46:21

A Separate Reality (Castaneda) 12:86-90, 95

The Separate Rose (Neruda)
See *La rosa separada: obra póstuma*

Separate Tables (Rattigan) 7:355-56

"Separating" (Coles) 46:108

"Separating" (Updike) 7:489; 15:545-47

"The Separation" (Broumas) 73:16

"A Separation" (Spender) 41:427

La séparation (Simon) 39:208

Separations (Hacker) 9:257-58; 23:205; 72:188

"The Sepia Postcard" (Millhauser) 109:157-58

Les sept dernières plaies (*The Last Seven Wounds*) (Duhamel) 8:187-88
"September" (Hughes) 14:270
September (Swinnerton) 31:423
"September 1, 1939" (Auden) 4:35; 6:20; 9:56-7; 43:16
"September 1, 1939" (Rexroth) 112:396
"September 17" (Herbert) 43:194
September, 1939 (Spender) 41:427
September Blackberries (McClure) 6:320
"September Dawn" (O'Connor) 23:329
"September Eclogue" (Reaney) 13:474
"September Elegy" (Moss) 45:292; 50:353
"September Fires" (Read) 4:439
"September in Great Yarmouth" (Mahon) 27:290
"September in the Park" (Snodgrass) 18:491
"September Journal" (Spender) 41:422-23
"September Moon" (Harjo) 83:271
"September on Jessore Road" (Ginsberg) 36:181
September September (Foote) 75:262-63
"September Song" (Heaney) 74:160, 165
"September Song" (Hill) 8:293; 18:236
"September Street" (Avison) 97:76
"September Sun, 1947" (Gascoyne) 45:147
"September, the First Day of School" (Nemerov) 6:363
September Tide (du Maurier) 59:286
"September Twilight" (Gluck) 81:167, 172
Septième (Audiberti) 38:22
Septuagenarian Stew (Bukowski) 82:25-8
"Septuagesima" (Betjeman) 34:309-10
"Sepulture South: Gaslight" (Faulkner) 18:149
"The Sequel" (Roethke) 3:433; 8:456
"Sequelae" (Lorde) 71:241
"Sequence" (Ciardi) 40:159
A Sequence for Francis Parkman (Davie) 5:114-15; 10:123
"Sequence, Sometimes Metaphysical" (Roethke) 11:485; 46:361, 364; 101:288, 304, 326-27
"Sequences" (Sanchez) 116:274, 279-80
Sequences (Sassoon) 36:390, 392
Les séquestrés d'Altona (*The Condemned of Altona*) (Sartre) 4:476; 7:392-93; 9:470; 13:502; 18:471; 44:493; 50:381-82; 52:381
Les séquestrés d'Altona (*The Condemned of Altona*) (De Sica) 20:90-1
"Ser de Sansueña" (Cernuda) 54:61
Ser Visal's Tale (Donaldson) 46:143
The Seraglio (Merrill) 13:376-77, 381; 91:228-29
"The Seraph and the Zambesi" (Spark) 13:519; 40:401, 403
Seraph on the Suwanee (Hurston) 30:214, 216-17, 219, 228-29
The Seraphim (Barker) 48:24
"Seraphion" (Baxter) 14:62
"La serata a Colono" (Morante) 47:281
"Serena" (Blunden) 56:34
"Serena I" (Beckett) 9:81
"Serena III" (Beckett) 9:81
Serena Blandish (Bagnold) 25:74, 76
Serena Blandish; or, The Difficulty of Getting Married (Behrman) 40:73, 76, 78
Serena Cruz or True Justice (Ginzburg) 70:282
"Sérénade" (Damas) 84:179
Serenade (Cain) 3:97; 11:85-7; 28:44-5, 47-8, 51-3
Serenade (Diamond) 30:112-13
"Serenade: Any Man to Any Woman" (Sitwell) 67:318-19, 322

"Serenade for Strings" (Livesay) 79:354
Serenading Louie (Wilson) 7:549; 36:464-65
"Serengeti" (Oliver) 98:282
Serenissima: A Novel of Venice (Jong) 83:321
"The Sergeant" (Barthelme) 8:52
Sergeant Getúlio (Ribeiro)
  See *Sargento Getúlio*
Sergeant Lamb of the Ninth (Graves) 39:322, 325
Sergeant Pepper's Lonely Hearts Club Band (Lennon and McCartney) 12:357-58, 361, 365, 373, 376, 379; 35:267, 273, 275, 289-90
Sergeant Rutledge (Ford) 16:308, 319
Sergio (Mujica Lainez) 31:283
"The Serial" (Nemerov) 36:308
Serial (Cabral de Melo Neto) 76:154, 158-59
"Series and Nexus in the Family" (Laing) 95:171-72
"A Series of Popes Had Been Devils" (Silko) 114:333
"The Serious Artist" (Pound) 10:405; 112:318, 321
"A Serious Case" (Van Duyn) 63:440-41
"Serious Comedy in Afro-American Literature" (Reed) 60:310
Serious Money (Churchill) 55:121-27
"A Serious Step Lightly Taken" (Frost) 10:193
"A Serious Talk" (Carver) 22:101; 36:101
"Seriousness and the Inner Poem" (Carruth) 84:117
Serjeant Musgrave's Dance (Arden) 6:4-10; 13:23-6, 28; 15:18, 20, 23, 25
Le serment de Kolvillàg (*The Oath*) (Wiesel) 3:528-30; 5:490; 37:453-54
"Sermon" (Purdy) 28:378
"The Sermon" (Redgrove) 41:348, 351
A Sermon (Mamet) 46:246
"A Sermon Beginning with the Portrait of a Man" (Ciardi) 40:157
"A Sermon by Doctor Pep" (Bellow) 33:71
A Sermon on Swift (Clarke) 6:112
Sermones y moradas (Alberti) 7:10
Sermones y prédicas del Cristo de Elqui (*Sermons and Homilies of the Christ of Elqui*) (Parra) 102:347, 356
Sermons and Homilies of the Christ of Elqui (Parra)
  See *Sermones y prédicas del Cristo de Elqui*
Sermons and Soda Water (O'Hara) 6:384; 42:319, 325-26
Serowe: Village of the Rain Wind (Head) 25:238-39; 67:97-8
"The Serpent" (Rothenberg) 57:383
Serpent (Mosley) 43:319-20; 70:202
The Serpent (van Itallie) 3:493
The Serpent and the Rope (Rao) 25:365-68, 370-73; 56:284-87, 289, 292-99, 301, 306-09, 312-15
Le serpent d'etoiles (Giono) 4:184
"Serpent Knowledge" (Pinsky) 19:372
The Serpent's Children (Yep) 35:474
The Serpent's Egg (Bergman)
  See *Ormen's ägg*
The Serpent's Gift (Lee) 86:68-72
Serpent's Reach (Cherryh) 35:106, 110-11
Serpico (Maas) 29:304-05
The Serrated Wheel (Guillen)
  See *La rueda dentada*
The Serrated Wheel (Guillen)
  See *La rueda dentada*
"O sertanejo falando" ("The Speech of a Man from the Backlands"; "The Way a

Sertanejo Speaks") (Cabral de Melo Neto) 76:164
"Servant" (Thomas) 48:380
The Servant (Pinter) 11:443; 27:391
"Servant Boy" (Heaney) 25:245
"Servant Boy" (Heaney) 74:157
"The Servant Problem" (Kelley) 22:246
"Servant Problem—Oriental Style" (Clarke) 35:123
"A Servant to Servants" (Frost) 1:110; 10:198; 15:240; 26:119, 123
The Servants and the Snow (Murdoch) 4:367-68
Servants of the Wankh (Vance) 35:422, 424
Serve It Forth (Fisher) 76:334, 336, 340-42; 87:118, 120, 128-29, 132
"Service" (Thomas) 48:374
Service inutile (Montherlant) 19:326
Sesame, and Other Stories (Lem) 40:289
62: Modelo para armar (*Sixty-Two: A Model Kit*) (Cortazar) 2:104-05; 3:115; 10:113, 116, 118; 15:147; 33:126-27; 34:329, 333; 92:149
"Seskilgreen" (Montague) 46:271
"Sestina" (Bishop) 9:90; 15:60; 32:38
"Sestina" (Eberhart) 56:85
"Sestina: Altaforte" (Pound) 2:343; 10:408; 13:461; 48:288
"Sestina of Sandbars and Shelters" (Lattimore) 3:278
"Sestina on Six Words by Weldon Kees" (Justice) 102:277, 283
"Sestina: The Literary Gathering" ("The Literary Gathering") (Ewart) 46:151-53
Sestra moia zhizn (*My Sister, Life*) (Pasternak) 7:293; 10:382-83; 18:383; 63:275, 280, 289
Set in Motion (Martin) 89:104-09, 116, 125, 129-30
A Set of Variations (O'Connor) 14:396
A Set of Wives (Jones) 52:242-43
Set on Edge (Rubens) 31:350
Set the Bird Free! (Voznesensky) 15:554
"Set the Controls for the Heart of the Sun" (Pink Floyd) 35:305, 307
Set This House on Fire (Styron) 1:329-30; 3:472, 474; 5:418; 11:514-17; 15:525, 527; 60:397-98, 400-01
"Sette figli" (Moravia) 11:383
I sette messaggeri (*The Seven Messengers*) (Buzzati) 36:87, 93-4, 96-7
"Sette piani" (Buzzati) 36:97
Setting Free the Bears (Irving) 13:292; 23:244-45; 38:250-51; 112:155-57, 159, 166
Setting Sons (Weller) 26:444-46
The Setting Sun (Pa Chin) 18:373
Setting the World on Fire (Wilson) 25:461-64
"Settings" (Heaney) 14:243; 74:188-89
"The Settle Bed" (Heaney) 91:125
Settle Down Simon Katz (Kops) 4:275
"The Settlement of Mars" (Busch) 47:62
Settlement Poems I (Gunnars) 69:257-61
Settlement Poems II (Gunnars) 69:257-61
Settlements (Donnell) 34:155-59
"The Settlers" (Bradbury) 42:38
The Settlers (Levin) 7:204-06
"Settling Down" (Sadoff) 9:466
Settling Down (Sadoff) 9:466
Seuls demeurants (*The Only Ones Left*) (Char) 55:287-88
"Seurat" (Dubie) 36:130
"Seurat" (Sadoff) 9:466
"Seurat's Sunday Afternoon along the Seine"

("Mr. Seurat's Sunday Afternoon") (Schwartz) 45:361; 87:346-47
Seven (Seger) 35:380
The Seven Ages of Man (Wilder) 82:363
"Seven and the Stars" (Haldeman) 61:181
Seven Arrows (Storm) 3:470
"Seven Attempted Moves" (Fisher) 25:158
Seven Beauties (Wertmueller)
    See *Pasqualino settebellezze*
Seven Chances (Keaton) 20:190, 193, 196
Seven Dada Manifestos and Lampisteries (Tzara) 47:392
"The Seven Days" (Whittemore) 4:588
Seven Days in May (Knebel) 14:307-08
Seven Days in May (Serling) 30:354-55
"The Seven Deadly Sins" (Smith) 73:357
The Seven Deadly Sins (Nye) 13:413
The Seven Deadly Sins (Shapcott) 38:401
The Seven Descents of Myrtle (Williams)
    See *Kingdom of Earth: The Seven Descents of Myrtle*
The Seven Dials Mystery (Christie) 12:115; 110:111, 113
"Seven Floors" (Buzzati) 36:94
Seven Gothic Tales (Dinesen) 10:147, 149-50, 152-53; 29:154, 156-59, 161, 163-64; 95:32, 35-7, 41, 43-7, 49-50, 53-4, 59, 61, 64, 68-9, 72-4
The Seven Hells of Jigokv Zoshi (Rothenberg) 6:477
"Seven Island Suite" (Lightfoot) 26:280
Seven Japanese Tales (Tanizaki) 28:421
Seven Journeys (Bitov)
    See *Sem' puteshestvii*
The Seven Journeys (Graham) 29:193-94
Seven Long Times (Thomas) 17:500-02
"Seven Love Songs Which Include the Collective History of the United States of America" (Alexie) 96:8, 10
The Seven Messengers (Buzzati)
    See *I sette messaggeri*
"7, Middagh Street" (Muldoon) 72:274, 277, 280, 282
The Seven Minutes (Wallace) 7:510; 13:568
"Seven Moments of Love" (Hughes) 15:292
The Seven Mountains of Thomas Merton (Mott) 34:460-67
Seven Nights (Borges) 44:361; 48:47-8
Seven Occasions (Summers) 10:493
"Seven O'Clock News/Silent Night" (Simon) 17:462, 466
"Seven O'Clock of a Strange Millennium" (Gilliatt) 53:145
"Seven Odes to Seven Natural Processes" (Updike) 43:436
"Seven Poems" (Strand) 18:519; 71:285
"Seven Points for an Imperilled Star" (Murray) 40:335
Seven Poor Men of Sydney (Stead) 2:422; 5:403; 32:406-09, 411-12, 414; 80:307, 315, 319, 326, 331, 335-37
"Seven Rail Poems" (Moure) 88:218
Seven Red Sundays (Sender)
    See *Siete domingos rojos*
Seven Rivers of Canada (MacLennan)
    See *Rivers of Canada*
"Seven Roses Later" (Celan)
    See "Sieben Rosen später"
The Seven Samurai (Kurosawa)
    See *The Magnificent Seven*
"Seven Say You Can Hear Corn Grow" (Boyle) 58:71
Seven Scenes from a Family Album (Gray)

49:147
The Seven Sisters (Prokosch) 4:421
"Seven Stanzas at Easter" (Updike) 23:474
"Seven Steps to Love" (Day Lewis) 10:131
The Seven Storey Mountain (Merton) 1:211; 3:337; 11:372; 34:461-65, 467; 83:379, 382, 398-400, 403-04
Seven Summers (Anand) 23:17; 93:23-4, 29, 32, 37, 41-2, 55-6
Seven Suspects (*Death at the President's Lodging*) (Stewart) 14:511; 32:419
Seven Tales and Alexander (Bates) 46:49-50
Seven Types of Ambiguity (Empson) 3:147; 8:201-02; 19:153-55; 33:137-38, 140-41, 145-50; 34:336-38, 543
"Seven Ways of Going" (Smith) 12:544
The Seven Who Fled (Prokosch) 4:421; 48:304-06, 309, 312-15
Seven Winters (Bowen) 11:61
Seven Women (Ford) 16:312, 317, 319-20
The Seven Year Itch (Wilder) 20:457, 464
"Seven Years from Somewhere" (Levine) 33:271
Seven Years from Somewhere (Levine) 14:320-21; 33:270-72, 274
The Seven-League Crutches (Jarrell) 2:207-08, 210; 13:298
"Seventeen" (Farrell) 66:128
Seventeen (Benson) 17:49-50
Seventeen (Welles) 80:380
Seventeen Chirps (Vizenor) 103:296
17 Poems (Transtroemer)
    See *17 dikter*
"The Seventeen Virgins" (Vance) 35:428
"Seventeen Warnings in Search of a Feminist Poem" (Jong) 4:263; 6:267; 83:289
1776, Year of Illusions (Fleming) 37:126
"A Seventeenth Century Suite" (Duncan) 55:298
The Seventeenth Degree (McCarthy) 5:276-77
Seventeenth Summer (Daly) 17:87-9, 91
"A Seventeenth-Century Suite in Homage to the Metaphysical Genius in English Poetry, 1590-1690" (Duncan) 41:128-30
The Seventeenth-Street Gang (Neville) 12:450
Seventh Avenue Poems (Shapcott) 38:402
The Seventh Babe (Charyn) 18:99
The Seventh Book (Akhmatova) 11:8; 64:21
The Seventh Cross (Seghers) 7:407-08
"Seventh Day" (Raine) 45:333
The Seventh Game (Kahn) 30:234
"Seventh Heaven" (Smith) 12:535
Seventh Heaven (Smith) 12:535, 540, 542
A Seventh Man (Berger) 19:38-9
The Seventh Raven (Dickinson) 35:135-36
"Seventh Seal" (Gotlieb) 18:191
The Seventh Seal (Bergman)
    See *Det sjunde inseglet*
"Seventh Street" (Toomer) 4:549
"The Seventh Trunk" (Boell)
    See "Warum ich kurze Prosa wie Jakob Maria Hermes and Heinrich Knecht schreibe"
"Seventh Voyage" (Lem) 40:296
"Seventy Thousand Assyrians" (Saroyan) 29:361
The 75th (Horovitz) 56:155
"Seventy-five Dollars" (Hughes) 108:292
Seventy-One Poems for People (Bowering) 47:31, 33
Seventy-Seven Dream Songs (Berryman) 2:56-7; 3:65, 67-8, 70; 10:48-9; 13:75, 80; 25:88-91, 93, 98; 62:60, 71, 76

73 Poems (Cummings) 3:118; 8:160; 12:154; 15:163; 68:40-2, 50
Several Observations (Grigson) 7:135
Several Perceptions (Carter) 5:102; 41:112; 76:323
"Several Species of Small Furry Animals Gathered Together in a Cave and Grooving with a Pict" (Pink Floyd) 35:305, 311
"Several Voices Out of a Cloud" (Bogan) 39:388; 46:86, 90
"Several Voices out of a Cloud" (Gunn) 18:202
Severance Pay (Whalen) 29:447
"The Severed Head" (Lowell) 4:299
"The Severed Head" (Montague) 46:270
A Severed Head (Murdoch) 1:234-37; 2:296, 298; 3:345, 347; 4:367; 6:343-45, 348; 15:381-33, 385, 387; 31:287-89, 295
"Severence Pay" (Macdonald) 13:356
"Severnside" (Tomlinson) 45:403
"Severo's Phases" (Cortazar)
    See "Las fases de Severo"
Sevilha andando (*Walking Through Seville*) (Cabral de Melo Neto) 76:161, 163
"A sevilhana que não se sabiae" ("The Seville Woman Unknown to Herself") (Cabral de Melo Neto) 76:161
"The Seville Woman Unknown to Herself" (Cabral de Melo Neto)
    See "A sevilhana que não se sabiae"
"The Sewing Harems" (Ozick) 62:351
"Sex" (Carruth) 84:136
Sex (Allen) 52:43
Sex and Death (Purdy) 6:428-29; 14:432; 50:246-47
"Sex and Death to the Age 14" (Gray) 49:148-49, 152; 112:97-8, 111, 114
Sex and Death to the Age 14 (Gray) 49:148, 151
"Sex and Love" (MacInnes) 23:286
Sex and Power: The Rise of Women in America, Russia, Sweden, and Italy (Meyer) 65:325
Sex and Subterfuge: Women Novelists to 1850 (Figes) 31:168
Sex and Temperament in Three Primitive Societies (Mead) 37:271-72
The Sex Diary of Gerard Sorme (*Man without a Shadow*) (Wilson) 3:537; 14:588
"The Sex of Poetry" (Smith) 22:385
"The Sex Opposite" (Sturgeon) 39:361
The Sex War and Others: A Survey of Recent Murder Principally in France (Heppenstall) 10:272
"Sex without Love" (Olds) 39:188
"Le Sexe ou la tête?" (Cixous)
    See "Castration or Decapitation?"
"The Sexes" (Parker) 68:335-36
Sexing the Cherry (Winterson) 64:434-44
"Sexism: An American Disease in Blackface" (Lorde) 71:245
"Sex-'n'-Violence" (Brophy) 105:9
"Sexplosion" (Lem) 15:329
"Sext" (Berryman) 3:69
Sextet in A Minor (Klein) 30:242-43
El sexto (Arguedas) 10:8; 18:10
"Sexual Healing" (Gaye) 26:135
The Sexual Liberals and the Attack on Feminism (Leidholdt and Raymond) 65:317-19
The Sexual Outlaw (Rechy) 14:445; 107:236, 243-45, 247-51, 254, 256
Sexual Personae: Art and Decadence from Nefertiti to Emily Dickinson (Paglia) 65:346; 68:303-20

Sexual Perversity in Chicago (Mamet) 9:360;
    15:356-57; **34**:223; **46**:247-48, 251-52,
    255
Sexual Politics (Millett) 67:234-43, 245, 247-
    48, 252-53, 256, 258, 260, 262
"Sexual Water" (Neruda)
    See "Agua sexual"
"Sexuality" (Prince) 35:325-26, 331
*Sexuality Today—And Tomorrow: Contempo-
    rary Issues in Human Sexuality* (Gordon)
    26:138
Sexus (Miller) 2:282-83; 14:371
"Sexy Dancer" (Prince) 35:323
"A Sexy Little Giant" (Iskander)
    See "Malenkii gigant bol'shogo seksa"
"Seyh Bedreddin destani" ("The Epic of Sheik
    Bedreddin") (Hikmet) 40:244-47, 249-
    51
"Seymour: An Introduction" (Salinger) 1:295;
    3:444; 8:463; 12:503, 514, 518
Seymour: An Introduction (Salinger)
    See *Raise High the Roofbeam, Carpenters
    and Seymour: An Introduction*
"Sezoni dimëror i Kafe Rivierës" (Kadare)
    52:259
Shabbytown Calendar (Shapcott) 38:402-03
"The Shack" (Laurence) 62:280
Shackles (Cesaire)
    See *Ferrements*
"The Shad-Blow Tree" (Gluck) 7:120
A Shade of Difference (Drury) 37:100-03, 105
"Shades of Caesar" (Weiss) 14:556
"Shades of Scarlet Conquering" (Mitchell)
    12:439
"Shades of the Prison House" (O'Faolain)
    32:341
The Shade-Seller: New and Selected Poems
    (Jacobsen) 48:191-92, 195; **102**:233
"Shadow" (Oliver) 98:276
Shadow (Green) 77:271
"Shadow: 1970" (Wright) 53:426, 428-29,
    432
Shadow and Act (Ellison) 54:129; **86**:319,
    323, 326; **114**:91-2, 104, 108-10, 112,
    115-17, 123, 128
Shadow and Substance (Carroll) 10:95-100
The Shadow Box (Cristofer) 28:94-6, 98
Shadow Box (Plimpton) 36:356-57
*The Shadow Cage and Other Tales of the Su-
    pernatural* (Pearce) 21:290, 292
"Shadow Country" (Allen) 84:10
Shadow Country (Allen) 84:2, 10-11, 28, 39-
    40
Shadow Dance (*Honeybuzzard*) (Carter) 5:102;
    41:109-12; 76:323, 328
Shadow Distance (Vizenor) 103:340-41
"The Shadow Goes Away" (Bly) 10:59
Shadow Hawk (Norton) 12:460
The Shadow in the Courtyard (*Maigret Mysti-
    fied*) (Simenon) 47:369, 379
The Shadow Knows (Johnson) 5:199-200;
    13:304-05; 48:207-08
Shadow Land (Straub) 28:411; **107**:265, 274-
    77, 279-82, 305-10
The Shadow Land (Vansittart) 42:394
"The Shadow Life of Reading" (Birkerts)
    116:167
The Shadow Master (Feinstein) 36:170
Shadow of a Bull (Wojciechowska) 26:449-
    53, 455-56, 458
"The Shadow of a Crib" (Singer) 111:304-05
Shadow of a Doubt (Hitchcock) 16:338, 340-
    41, 343, 345-46, 349-50, 355, 359

The Shadow of a Gunman (Carroll) 10:97
The Shadow of a Gunman (*The Gunman*)
    (O'Casey) 5:317, 320; 11:409-13, 15:403,
    405; **88**:234-37, 239, 242-43, 245-46,
    254-55, 257-58, 262, 269
Shadow of a Man (Sarton) 49:310-11
Shadow of a Sun (Byatt) 19:75; 65:127
The Shadow of Cain (Sitwell) 67:336-37
The Shadow of Captain Bligh (MacLennan)
    See *The Shadow of Captain Bligh*
"Shadow of Night" (Derleth) 31:136
Shadow of Paradise (Aleixandre)
    See *Sombra del paraiso*
"The Shadow of Sound" (Voznesensky) 57:425
The Shadow of the Coachman's Body (Weiss)
    See *Der Schatten des Körpers des Kutschers*
"The Shadow of the Gods" (Miller) 10:344
The Shadow of the Hawk (Forester) 35:165-
    66
The Shadow of the Hawk (Scott) 43:383
The Shadow of the Lynx (Hibbert) 7:155
Shadow of the Moon (Kaye) 28:197-201
The Shadow of the Torturer (Wolfe) 25:473-
    79
The Shadow of Vesuvius (Dillon) 17:100
A Shadow on Summer (Brown) 63:51-3, 55-6
The Shadow on the Hills (Thiele) 17:496
"Shadow Path (the encounter group)" (Allen)
    84:38
Shadow Play (Baxter) 78:30-33
Shadow Play (Coward) 51:70
Shadow Train: Fifty Lyrics (Ashbery) 25:54,
    56-60; 41:38; 77:44
Shadowfires (Koontz) 78:200, 203
The Shadow-Maker (MacEwen) 13:358;
    55:163, 165
"Shadows" (Allen) 84:37-8
"Shadows" (Endo) 99:296-97, 301, 307
"Shadows" (Norris) 14:388
"Shadows" (Williams) 22:465
Shadows (Cassavetes) 20:44, 55
Shadows (Clarke) 16:216
Shadows (Lightfoot) 26:283
"Shadows and Light" (Mitchell) 12:439
Shadows in Paradise (Remarque) 21:333-34
Shadows Offstage (Bennett) 35:43-4
Shadows on Little Reef Bay (Adler) 35:14-15
Shadows on the Grass (Dinesen) 10:146;
    29:156; **95**:35, 37, 43, 45-6, 48, 56, 81
"Shadows There Are" (Smith) 15:516
"Shadow-Shamans" (Musgrave) 13:401
"Shad-Time" (Wilbur) 110:361
"Shafei nüshi de riji" ("The Diary of Miss
    Sophie") (Ding Ling) 68:57, 59-60, 64-
    5, 67, 69
"The Shaft" (Tomlinson) 13:548
Shaft (Parks) 16:458-59
The Shaft (Tomlinson) 13:548, 550; 45:392-
    95, 401
Shaft's Big Score (Parks) 16:459-61
Shagbark (Peck) 3:377-78
al- Shahhadh (Mahfuz) 52:296, 300
Shake a Spear with Me, John Berryman (Honig)
    33:214
Shake Hands for Ever (Rendell) 28:384, 387;
    48:320
Shake Hands with a Murderer (Rendell) 48:324
"Shake Hands with the Devil" (Kristofferson)
    26:270
"Shakedown" (Waddington) 28:437
"Shaker, Why Don't You Sing?" (Angelou)
    77:31
Shaker, Why Don't You Sing? (Angelou) 35:32;

77:22, 31
Shakespeare and Society (Eagleton) 63:101,
    112
Shakespeare and the Nature of Time (Turner)
    48:398
Shakespeare and the Students (Enright) 31:150
"Shakespeare at Sonnets" (Ransom) 24:362
"Shakespeare at Thirty" (Berryman) 10:45-6
"Shakespeare in Harlem" (Hughes) 35:220-21
"Shakespeare Say" (Dove) 81:137
Shakespeare Wallah (Jhabvala) 29:259;
    94:174, 185, 192
"A Shakespearean Sonnet: To a Woman
    Liberationist" (Knight) 40:287
Shakespeare's Boy Actors (Davies) 13:173;
    25:136
Shakespeare's Dog (Rooke) 34:250-54
"Shakespeare's Grave" (Jeffers) 54:246
"A Shakespearian Cycle" (Zaturenska) 11:580
Shakha Proshakha (*Branches of the Trees*)
    (Ray) 76:358-60, 364-65
*Shaking the Pumpkin: Traditional Poetry of
    the Indian North Americans* (Rothenberg)
    57:373, 375-77, 382
Shalako (L'Amour) 55:308
Shalimar (*Pleasure City*) (Markandaya)
    38:326-27
"Shall Gaelic Die?" (Smith) 64:395-96
"Shall I Compare Thee to a Summer's Day?"
    (Simmons) 43:411
Shall We Gather at the River (Wright) 3:540-
    43; 5:518-20; 10:543-45; 25:463, 465-
    66, 469
Shall We Tell the President? (Archer) 28:11-
    12
"Shallots" (Raine) 32:350; **103**:184, 191
"The Shallowest Man" (Allen) 52:40
"Shallowly Quicker" (Rozewicz) 9:465
"Shaman's Blues" (Morrison) 17:288
"Shame" (Oates) 6:370; 19:348
"Shame" (Wilbur) 53:405; **110**:384-85
Shame (Bergman)
    See *Skammen*
Shame (Rushdie) 31:353-60; **55**:216-19, 224,
    253, 263; 59:415-16, 431, 434, 444, 447,
    450; **100**:287, 318-19, 322
Shame and Glory (Viereck) 4:560
Shame the Devil (Appleman) 51:15-16
Shame the Devil (O'Flaherty) 34:357
"Shammu Khan" (Ali) 69:31
"The Shampoo" (Bishop) 9:93; 32:37
Shampoo (Towne) 87:354-55, 359-60, 366,
    369, 372, 375-76
Shampoo Planet (Coupland) 85:31-6, 39-41
"Shancoduff" (Kavanagh) 22:238
"Shandy" (Kristofferson) 26:269
Shanghai Express (Sternberg) 20:370, 372,
    379
The Shanghai Gesture (Sternberg) 20:372,
    378
"Shanghai, June 1989" (Durcan) 70:147
"Shangri-La" (Davies) 21:91, 93
"Shanley" (Farrell) 66:129
Shannon's Way (Cronin) 32:136
"The Shape of Death" (Swenson) 106:328,
    350
"The Shape of Flesh and Bone" (MacLeish)
    8:362
*The Shape of Further Things: Speculations on
    Change* (Aldiss) 14:14
"A Shape of Light" (Goyen) 8:251
"The Shape of the Fire" (Roethke) 11:480,
    482; 19:397; 46:363; **101**:262-63, 274,

281, 335, 337-40
"The Shape of the Sword" (Borges)
  See "La forma de la espada"
"The Shape of Things" (Hogan) 73:151
"The Shape of Things to Come" (Brown)
  79:153
Shapes and Sounds (Peake) 54:366, 369, 373-74
"Shapes of Winter" (Sorrentino) 40:386
A Shaping Joy: Studies in the Writer's Craft
  (Brooks) 24:111, 113-14, 116; 86:286-87; 110:8, 15, 20
The Shaping of England (Asimov) 76:312
The Shaping Spirit (Alvarez) 5:16
"Shaping the World of My Art" (Marshall)
  72:249
Shardik (Adams) 5:5-7
Shards of God: A Novel of the Yippies (Sanders)
  53:304
Shards of Memory (Jhabvala) 94:212-13
Sharecroppers (Coles) 108:194, 210
"The Shared Mystery" (Everson) 27:134
"The Shark" (Pratt) 19:380
"Shark Hunter" (Ciardi) 40:155
"Shark in the Window" (Dickey) 109:244
"The Shark: Parents and Children" (Wakoski)
  40:457
The Shark: Splendid Savage of the Sea
  (Cousteau) 30:104
"Sharks" (Oliver) 98:267
"The Shark's Parlor" (Dickey) 47:97; 109:266
"A Sharp Attack of Something or Other"
  (White) 30:451
Sharra's Exile (Bradley) 30:29
Shatranj Ke Khilari (*The Chess Players*) (Ray)
  16:495; 76:357-59, 362-63, 365
"Shatterday" (Ellison) 42:129-30
Shatterday (Ellison) 42:129-30
"Shattered" (Jagger and Richard) 17:240
The Shattered Chain (Bradley) 30:26, 30-2
"Shattered Image" (Betjeman) 10:53-4
"Shattered Like a Glass Goblin" (Ellison)
  42:127
Shaved Fish (Lennon) 35:270-71
Shaved Splits (Shepard) 17:443; 41:407
"The Shawl" (Ozick) 62:357-58
The Shawl (Mamet) 46:254-55
The Shawl (Ozick) 62:357-58
"She" (Konwicki) 117:281
"She" (Nemerov) 36:309
She (Rosenthal) 28:394-95
"She and the Muse" (Levertov) 66:238, 250
"She Being Brand-New" (Cummings) 68:43, 46, 51
"She Belongs to Me" (Dylan) 77:176-77
She Came to Stay (Beauvoir)
  See *L'invitée*
"She Carries a 'Fat Gold Watch'" (Ondaatje)
  14:407
"She Contrasts with Herself Hippolyta" (H. D.)
  73:128
"She Didn't Even Wave" (Ai) 69:7, 13
She Had Some Horses (*Horses*) (Harjo) 83:266, 268, 272, 276, 279, 285
She Had to Do Something (O'Faolain) 70:315
"She Hid in the Trees from the Nurses" (Wright)
  10:545
"She in Summer" (Dickey) 28:118
"She Knows Me Too Well" (Wilson) 12:643, 651
"She Lays" (Peacock) 60:292
"She Loves" (Broumas) 73:15-16
"She Loves You" (Lennon and McCartney)

12:374
"She Rebukes Hippolyta" (H. D.) 73:105
"She Seemed to Know" (Laughlin) 49:224
"She Shall Be Called Woman" (Sarton) 14:481; 49:307
"She Shook Me Cold" (Bowie) 17:57
"She Touches Him" (Elliott) 2:131
She Used to Wanna Be a Ballerina (Sainte-Marie) 17:431
"She Waits for All Men Born" (Tiptree) 48:388, 391, 397
She Walks in Beauty (Powell) 66:366
"She Was Afraid of Upstairs" (Aiken) 35:20
"She Went to Stay" (Creeley) 78:144
"she won't ever forgive me" (Clifton) 66:82
She Wore a Yellow Ribbon (Ford) 16:305, 308
"Shearing" (Clarke) 61:78
"The Shearwaters" (Levi) 41:247
"Sheeba the Outcast Drag Queen" (Dickey)
  28:119
"Sheep" (Bates) 46:51
"Sheep" (Oe) 10:373
"Sheep" (Pink Floyd) 35:311, 313
"Sheep" (Zoline) 62:461-65
"The Sheep Child" (Dickey) 15:173, 177; 47:97; 109:273
"Sheep Herding" (Davis) 49:92
"Sheep in a Fog" (Plath) 51:341; 111:205, 215
The Sheep Look Up (Brunner) 8:105-07, 110-11; 10:78, 80-1
"Sheep Shearing at Ayot St. Lawrence" (Szirtes)
  46:391
"Sheep Trails Are Fateful to Strangers" (Spicer)
  72:349
"The Sheep Went On Being Dead" (Hughes)
  14:273
Sheepfold Hill: Fifteen Poems (Aiken) 52:26
"Sheep-Fuck Poem" (Sanders) 53:304
Sheepish Beauty, Civilian Love (Moure)
  88:231-32
Sheer Fiction (West) 96:362, 394
Sheer Fiction II (West) 96:394-95
"The Sheer Joy of Amoral Creation" (Shields)
  97:429, 431
"Sheet Lightning" (Blunden) 56:52
Sheik Yerbouti (Zappa) 17:592-93
Sheiks and Adders (Stewart) 32:421-22
"Sheishun monogatari" ("My Adolescent
  Days") (Tanizaki) 28:417
The Shelbourne Hotel (Bowen) 11:61
"Shelf Life" (Heaney) 37:165
"Shell" (Hoffman) 6:244
"The Shell" (Humphrey) 45:193
"Shell Game" (Dick) 72:109
The Shell Lady's Daughter (Adler) 35:13-14
"Shell Story" (Brown) 100:83
Shella (Vachss) 106:363-64
Shelley (Jellicoe) 27:209
Shelley's Mythmaking (Bloom) 103:11-12, 19, 22, 24
"Shells" (Redgrove) 41:359
"Shells by a Stream" (Blunden) 56:29
"Shelter" (Baxter) 78:25-26, 29, 30
"The Shelter" (Narayan) 47:304
Shelter (Cryer) 21:80
The Shelter (Phillips) 96:342, 354-55
"The Shelter of Your Arms" (Nelson) 17:305
"Sheltered Garden" (H. D.) 31:201; 73:118
"A Sheltered Life" (Reed) 21:312-13
"The Sheltered Sex: 'Lotus Eating' on Seven-and-Six a Week" (West) 31:460
The Sheltering Sky (Bowles) 1:41; 2:78-9;

19:56, 58-9; 53:37-40, 42-4, 46
"Shema" (Levi) 37:223
Shema: Collected Poems of Primo Levi (Levi)
  37:223
Shenandoah, or the Naming of the Child
  (Schwartz) 4:479; 87:334-36, 339, 341-42
"The Shepards" (O'Connor) 23:332
"The Shepherd" (Blunden) 56:27, 32, 37
"The Shepherd" (Soto) 32:401, 403; 80:277, 282
"The Shepherd" (Williams) 31:464
*The Shepherd and Other Poems of Peace and
  War* (Blunden) 56:25, 28-9, 32, 36-8, 40-3, 51
"The Shepherd Corydon" (Howard) 10:277
"The Shepherd Makhaz" (Iskander) 47:196
Shepherd of the Streets (Ehle) 27:102
Shepherdess of Sheep (Streatfeild) 21:395-97
"Shepherds of the Nation" (Davies) 21:98
Shepherds of the Night (Amado)
  See *Os pastores da noite*
"Shepherd's Song" (Milosz) 11:380
Sheppey (Maugham) 1:204; 15:366-67; 67:225-26
"Sheraton Gibson" (Townshend) 17:528
Sherbrookes (Delbanco) 13:174
"Sheridan" (Lowell) 11:330
"Sheridan" (Merwin) 45:274-76
"The Sheriff of McTooth County Kansas"
  (Dorn) 10:161
*Sherlock Holmes vs. Dracula; or, The Adven-
  ture of the Sanguinary Count by John H.
  Watson* (Estleman) 48:102
Sherlock Jr. (Keaton) 20:195, 197-99
"Sherlock Spends a Day in the Country" (Fear-
  ing) 51:119
"Sherston's Progress" (Sassoon) 36:387, 395-97
Sherwood Anderson (Howe) 85:115
"She's a Woman" (Lennon and McCartney)
  35:285
"She's Always a Woman" (Joel) 26:216-17
"She's Goin' Bald" (Wilson) 12:643
"She's Gone" (Marley) 17:271
"She's Got a Way" (Joel) 26:217
"She's Got Medals" (Bowie) 17:65
She's Gotta Have It (Lee) 105:80-85, 95, 98, 100, 110, 119, 122-23, 128
"She's Leaving Home" (Lennon and
  McCartney) 12:357; 35:280
"She's My Baby" (McCartney) 35:284-85
"She's Right on Time" (Joel) 26:223
"She's the One" (Springsteen) 17:489
Shibumi (Trevanian) 29:431-32
"The Shield of Achilles" (Auden) 11:20; 43:26
The Shield of Achilles (Forman) 21:116
The Shield of the Valiant (Derleth) 31:136-37
"The Shield of Two Dreams" (Momaday)
  85:281
"The Shield of Which Less Said the Better"
  (Momaday) 85:280
The Shield Ring (Sutcliff) 26:426, 430-32, 434-35, 439
"The Shield That Died" (Momaday) 85:280
"The Shield That Was Touched by Pretty
  Mouth" (Momaday) 85:280
"Shift of Scene at Grandstand" (Swenson)
  61:405
"Shifting Colors" (Lowell) 37:238
Shifting Landscape (Roth) 104:282-85, 311, 317, 324
Shiiku (*The Catch*; *Prize Stock*) (Oe) 10:374;

36:348; **86**:216, 226-27, 244
Shikasta (Lessing) **15**:331-36; **22**:285; **40**:303-04, 306, 309; **94**:253, 260-61
"Shiloh" (Mason) **28**:272, 274; **82**:235, 241, 246, 248, 250, 254-58, 260
"Shiloh" (Mott) **15**:381
Shiloh (Foote) **75**:230, 238-40, 243, 251, 258
Shiloh, and Other Stories (Mason) **28**:271-74; **43**:286-88; **82**:233, 238-40, 244, 246, 249-50, 258-59
"Shine" (Damas) **84**:172, 176
"Shine a Light" (Jagger and Richard) **17**:225, 236
Shine On, Bright and Dangerous Object (Colwin) **23**:128-29; **84**:146, 150
"Shine on You Crazy Diamond" (Pink Floyd) **35**:308, 313
"Shine, Perishing Republic" (Jeffers) **54**:233, 245; **3**:259
"Shingles for the Lord" (Faulkner) **6**:179
"Shingling the New Roof" (Bottoms) **53**:33
The Shining (King) **12**:309-11; **26**:234, 237, 239-42; **37**:198-99, 201, 203, 205, 207-08; **61**:319, 321, 323, 328, 331, 335; **113**:335-36, 344, 347, 351, 353, 355, 362, 369, 378-79, 381-82, 388, 391-92
The Shining (Kubrick) **16**:393
"Shining Agate" (Dorris) **109**:309
"Shining Earth: A Summer Without Evil" (Buckley) **57**:126
"The Shining Houses" (Munro) **95**:285, 297
"The Shining One" (Bova) **45**:73
"The Shining Ones" (Brown) **5**:79
"The Shining Ones" (Clarke) **13**:148
"The Ship" (Bates) **46**:55-6
The Ship (Forester) **35**:164-68, 170, 174
Ship Island, and Other Stories (Spencer) **22**:402
"Ship Master" (Graves) **45**:165
A Ship Named Hope (Klima) **56**:162-63, 174
Ship of Fools (Porter) **1**:271-74; **3**:393-94; **7**:311-21; **10**:398; **15**:426-27, 429-30, 432; **27**:401-02; **101**:215, 218-22, 224, 242-43, 249-50, 253, 255-56
The Ship of Men (Dourado)
  See *A barca dos homens*
Ship of the Line (Forester) **35**:162-63, 166, 170
"The Ship Sails at Midnight" (Leiber) **25**:304
The Ship Sails On (Fellini)
  See *E la nave va*
"Shipapu iyetico" (Allen) **84**:38
"Shipbuilding Office" (O'Connor) **18**:377
"Shipbuilding Office" (Page) **18**:377
"A Ship-Load of Crabs" (Calvino) **39**:314
The Shipping News **81**:274-80
"Ships" (Masefield) **47**:233
"The Ships" (Redgrove) **41**:359
Ships and Other Figures (Meredith) **13**:374; **22**:302; **55**:193
"Ships of Ashes" **75**:79
The Ship's Orchestra (Fisher) **25**:157-58, 160-61
Shipwrecked (Maugham) **15**:365
The Shipyard (Onetti) **7**:277, 280
"Shir al hakravot harishonim" ("A Poem on the First Battles") (Amichai) **116**:109
Shira (Agnon) **4**:14
"The Shires" (Betjeman) **43**:51
The Shires (Davie) **5**:115-16; **8**:163-67; **31**:112-13, 117-20, 123
Shirley Valentine (Russell) **60**:321-25
Shiroi hito (Endo) **54**:154; **99**:283, 285, 307

"Shirt" (Pinsky) **94**:306, 308, 312
"Shirt" (Simic) **49**:337
"The Shirt" (Soto) **80**:298
"The Shirt Poem" (Stern) **40**:410-11
"A Shirtsleeve Wedding" (Redgrove) **41**:358
"Shisei" ("Tattooer") (Tanizaki) **8**:509-10; **29**:415, 418
"Shisha no ogori" ("The Extravagance of the Dead") (Oe) **36**:349
"Shiva and Parvati Hiding in the Rain" (Pinsky) **94**:306, 308-9
Shiva Descending (Benford) **52**:66-7, 74
Shlemiel the First (Singer) **38**:415-16
"Shloimele" (Singer) **6**:509; **9**:488
"Shneynu beyahad vekhol ehad lehud" ("The Two of Us Together and Each of Us Alone") (Amichai) **116**:122
"The Shoals Returning" (Kinsella) **4**:271
Shock III (Matheson) **37**:245
"The Shock of Recognition" (Anderson) **23**:32
The Shock of Recognition (Wilson) **24**:472, 481, 488-89
The Shockwave Rider (Brunner) **10**:81
The Shoe Bird (Welty) **105**:335
Shoe Shine (De Sica) **20**:86-7, 94-5
"Shoe Soul" (Robinson) **21**:348
"Shoe Store" (Souster) **5**:396
"the shoelace" (Bukowski) **108**:75
Shoeless Joe (Kinsella) **27**:238-39; **43**:253, 255-60
"Shoeless Joe Jackson Comes to Iowa" (Kinsella) **27**:237-38
Shoeless Joe Jackson Comes to Iowa (Kinsella) **27**:237-38
"Shoes in the Rain Jungle" (Warren) **13**:573
The Shoes of the Fisherman (West) **6**:564; **33**:432-33
"Shoeshine Boys on the Avenida Juarez" (Purdy) **50**:241
Shogun: A Novel of Japan (Clavell) **6**:113-14; **25**:126-28; **87**:2, 4-12, 16-19
Sholay (The Flames) (Ali) **69**:25
"Shonen" ("Children") (Tanizaki) **28**:415
Shoot the Piano Player (Truffaut)
  See *Tirez sur le pianiste*
"The Shooting" (Dubus) **36**:143; **97**:201
"Shooting Ducks in South Louisiana" (Tillinghast) **29**:417
Shooting in the Dark (Hougan) **34**:60-2
"The Shooting Party" (Bates) **46**:63
The Shooting Party (Colegate) **36**:112-14
"The Shooting Range" (Brodkey) **56**:60, 62, 64-5
"Shooting Rats at the Bibb County Dump" (*The Tunnel*) (Bottoms) **53**:29-30
Shooting Rats at the Bibb County Dump (Bottoms) **53**:28-33
"A Shooting Script" (Heaney) **74**:161
"Shooting Script" (Rich) **18**:446
"A Shooting Season" (Tremain) **42**:386
"Shooting Star" (Reed) **21**:314, 316
The Shooting Star (Benary-Isbert) **12**:31
A Shooting Star (Stegner) **9**:510; **49**:352-53
"Shooting Whales" (Strand) **41**:432-33
"Shootism versus Sport" (Hemingway) **34**:478
The Shootist (Swarthout) **35**:403
"Shoot-Out" (Moure) **88**:229
Shootout at Carnegie Hall (Ochs) **17**:333
"Shootout at Gentry's Junction" (Coover) **46**:121-22
"Shopgirls" (Barthelme) **36**:51-2; **117**:14, 17
"Shoppe Keeper" (Ellison) **42**:129
"Shopping" (Oates) **108**:381-82

"Shopping in Oxford" (Masefield) **47**:233
"The Shopping List" (Dacey) **51**:83
Shops and Houses (Swinnerton) **31**:421, 423
The Shopworn Tare of Barrels (Aksyonov)
  See *The Tare of Barrels*
"The Shore" (Hearne) **56**:128
"Shore Leave" (Sturgeon) **39**:364
"Shore Life" (Brosman) **9**:135
"Shore Line" (Rakosi) **47**:346
"Shore Woman" (Heaney) **7**:148
The Shorebirds of North America (Matthiessen) **32**:288-89
"Shorelines" (Moss) **7**:249-50
"Shorelines" (Murray) **40**:335
The Shores of Light (Wilson) **3**:538; **8**:550; **24**:474-75, 479, 481
The Shores of Space (Matheson) **37**:246
"The Shorn Lamb" (Stafford) **7**:457
"The Short Biography of A. A. Darmolatov" (Kis) **57**:252
The Short Cases of Inspector Maigret (Simenon) **47**:374
"A Short Course in Nietzschean Ethics" (Baxter) **45**:51; **78**:16
"Short Easterly Squall, With Low Visibility and Rising Gorge" (Perelman) **49**:265
"The Short End" (Hecht) **19**:207, 209-10
Short Eyes (Pinero) **4**:401-02; **55**:316-18
"Short Friday" (Singer) **38**:407, 409-10; **111**:295, 305, 311
Short Friday, and Other Stories (Singer) **3**:456; **15**:504; **23**:415-16, 418; **69**:313; **111**:299
"Short Glossary of Words Used by Poorer People" (Lebowitz) **36**:250
"Short Grotesque Litany on the Death of Senator McCarthy" (Guillen) **79**:229
"The Short Happy Life of Francis Macomber" (Hemingway) **3**:233-34; **8**:283; **10**:264; **13**:277-78; **19**:212; **30**:184; **39**:430-31; **41**:203, 205; **50**:424, 427, 429-31; **80**:141
"Short Histories of the Sea" (Muske) **90**:309
A Short History of a Small Place (Pearson) **39**:86-90
A Short History of Decay (Cioran)
  See *Précis de décomposition*
"A Short History of Judaic Thought in the Twentieth Century" (Pastan) **27**:369
"A Short History of Oregon" (Brautigan) **3**:88
"A Short History of Sex" (Soto) **80**:291
Short Letter, Long Farewell (Handke) **5**:164-65, 167; **10**:255-56, 258; **38**:218-20, 222-23, 227
"The Short Life of Kazno Yamomoto" (Enright) **31**:155
"Short Mineral Ode" (Cabral de Melo Neto)
  See "Pequnea ode mineral"
"Short Papa" (Purdy) **52**:350
"Short Poem" (Sanchez) **116**:277, 294
"Short Poem for Armistice Day" (Read) **4**:439
"A Short Poem in Color" (Boyle) **1**:42
Short Poems (Berryman) **6**:63; **8**:91; **25**:93
"A Short Recess" (Milosz) **31**:262
The Short Reign of Pippin IV: A Fabrication (Steinbeck) **21**:369, 382; **34**:405; **45**:382; **59**:353
A Short Sad Book (Bowering) **15**:81, 84; **47**:25
A Short Sharp Shock (Brenton) **31**:63-4
Short Sketches (Solzhenitsyn)
  See *Kroxotnye rasskazy*
"Short Stories" (Moss) **14**:376
Short Stories from Berlin (Grass) **32**:200
"A Short Story" (Bowering) **47**:29
"Short Story" (Voigt) **54**:433

The Short Story Embassy: A Novel (Wilding) 73:391, 393, 395-96, 398

"Short Story on a Painting of Gustav Klimt" (Ferlinghetti) 111:65

"Short Summary" (Bogan) 46:87

A Short Survey of Surrealism (Gascoyne) 45:156-57

The Short Throat, the Tender Mouth (Grumbach) 22:204

"Short Time" (Ewart) 13:209

A Short Time to Live (Jones) 52:251-52, 254

"Short Views in Africa" (Jacobsen) 48:192, 197

A Short Walk (Childress) 15:131-32; 86:309, 312; 96:91, 93, 108

"Short Wave" (Szirtes) 46:393-94

Short Wave (Szirtes) 46:393-95

Short Work of It: Selected Writing by Mark Harris (Harris) 19:205-06

Shortcuts (Altman) 116:51-3, 58-62, 64-9, 71, 73-4

Shorter Poems, 1951-53 (*New Poems*) (Roethke) 6:451; 8:455; 22:346; 49:274, 283, 286

"The Shorter View" (Kennedy) 42:257

"The Shortest Way Home" (Kiely) 43:244

"The Short-Story in England 1700-1753" (Jhabvala) 94:207

"Shorty" (Gellhorn) 60:183

"Shorty Leach" (Farrell) 66:127

Shosetsu no hoho (*Methods of the Novel; The Technique of Fiction*) (Oe) 86:227, 229, 240, 242

Shosetsu no Kenkyu (Kawabata) 107:97

Shosha (Singer) 11:499-503; 23:416, 419-20; 69:312; 111:307, 310, 312, 321-24, 327-28, 333, 344-46

Shosho Shigemoto no haha (*Captain Shigemoto's Mother; The Mother of Captain Shigemoto*) (Tanizaki) 28:414, 419

The Shoshoneans (Dorn) 10:159

"Shot Actress—Full Story" (Bates) 46:55

"A Shot from Nowhere" (Highsmith) 42:215

"Shot of Redeye" (Bukowski) 41:67

Shoten an Goray (*Satan in Goray*) (Singer) 1:313; 3:452, 455; 9:488; 11:500; 15:503-04, 506, 508; 23:413-20; 38:408; 69:306; 111:293-94, 306, 311, 314-15, 318-22, 342-43

"Shotgun Days" (Lerman) 9:329

Shotgun Willie (Nelson) 17:302, 306

"Shots" (Ozick) 62:350, 353-54

"Shottle Bop" (Sturgeon) 22:410; 39:361

"Should I Stay or Should I Go?" (Clash) 30:51-2

"Should, Should Not" (Milosz) 82:308

"Should Wizard Hit Mommy?" (Updike) 5:455

The Shout (Graves) 45:171, 173

The Shout (Skolimowski) 20:354-56

Shout across the River (Poliakoff) 38:382-83, 386

Shout at the Devil (Smith) 33:377

"The Shovel Man" (Sandburg) 10:448; 15:468; 35:355

Shovelling Trouble (Richler) 3:431

The Show (Browning) 16:123, 124, 126

"Show Biz" (Dickey) 28:119

"Show Biz Connections" (Friedman) 56:97

Show Boat (Ferber) 18:151; 93:149-52, 154, 156, 160, 164-65, 171-77, 179, 181, 185-87, 189-90

The Show Must Go On (Rice) 7:363

"Show Saturday" (Larkin) 5:230; 8:332-33, 336, 339; 13:340; 18:301; 33:259-60, 263; 64:265, 282, 284-85

Show Some Emotion (Armatrading) 17:8-9

Showboat World (*The Magnificent Showboats of the Lower Vissel River, Lune XXIII South, Big Planet*) (Vance) 35:427

Showdown (Amado)
See *Tocaia grande*

Showdown at Yellow Butte (L'Amour) 25:279

"A Shower of Gold" (Barthelme) 46:40; 115:59, 65, 68, 69, 78, 79

"Shower of Gold" (Gustafson) 36:220

"Shower of Gold" (Welty) 22:459; 33:419; 105:338-39, 386-87

A Shower of Summer Days (Sarton) 49:311

"The Showings; Lady Julian of Norwich, 1342-1416" (Levertov) 66:251

Showman (Maysles and Maysles) 16:442-43

Shrapnel (MacBeth) 5:264

Shrapnel. Poet's Year (MacBeth) 5:265

The Shrewsdale Exit (Buell) 10:81-2

The Shrimp and the Anemone (Hartley) 22:211, 214

"Shrine" (Gerstler) 70:156-57

"The Shrine" (H. D.) 73:109

The Shrine, and Other Stories (Lavin) 99:312, 319

"Shrines" (Mahapatra) 33:284

The Shrinking Man (Matheson) 37:246-50

"The Shrink's Wife" (Olds) 85:294

Shrivings (Shaffer)
See *The Battle of Shrivings*

Shroud for a Nightingale (James) 18:272; 46:205

Shroud My Body Down (Green) 25:197, 199

"The Shrouding" (Livesay) 79:341

"Shrovetide" (Reed) 13:480

Shrovetide in Old New Orleans (Reed) 13:480; 32:358-60; 60:313

"Shrubs Burnt Away" (Hall) 59:152-56

"The Shrunken Head of Pancho Villa" (Valdez) 84:403, 405, 407, 413, 417

"Shucking Corn" (Steele) 45:365

"Shujia zhong" (Ding Ling) 68:58

"Shunkin sho" ("A Portrait of Shunkin") (Tanizaki) 8:510; 14:527; 28:414, 418

"Shut a Final Door" (Capote) 13:133, 136, 140

Shut Down, Vol. 2 (Wilson) 12:643-44

"Shutter Door" (Moure) 88:231

A Shuttle in the Crypt (Soyinka) 36:415; 44:284-85

Shuttlecock (Swift) 41:442-44; 88:284-85, 287-90, 293-96, 307, 309, 311, 321-22

"Shuttles" (Swenson) 61:403, 405; 106:333

"The Shy Man" (Roethke) 101:332-33

"Shy Rights: Why Not Pretty Soon?" (Keillor) 40:273

Si j'étais vous (Green) 77:275

Si l'été revenait (Adamov) 25:16, 21-2

Une si longue lettre (*So Long a Letter*) (Ba)

"Si souvent" ("So Often") (Damas) 84:173, 176

"Si tú supiera" (Guillen)
See "Ay negra, si tu supiera"

Si usted no puedo, yo sí (Bunuel) 80:22

The Siamese Twin Mystery (Queen) 11:460

"Siamo spiacenti di..." (Buzzati) 36:86

Siberian Lady Mac Beth (Wajda) 16:579, 582

"The Siberian Olive Tree" (Johnston) 51:243, 252

"Sibirskiye bani" (Voznesensky) 57:417

"Sibling Mysteries" (Rich) 36:374

"Siblings" (Gordimer) 18:189; 70:183

"The Sibling's Woodcut" (Dubie) 36:134

"A Sibyl" (Atwood) 25:66

"Sibyl" (Heaney) 74:159

"The Sibyl" (Watkins) 43:450

The Sibyl (Lagerkvist) 54:278-79, 281-83, 285; 13:331

"Sicilia est insula" (Haavikko) 34:175

The Sicilian (Puzo) 36:361-63; 107:196-99, 207, 213, 216

Sicilian Carousel (Durrell) 8:193

Sicilian Uncles (Sciascia)
See *Gli zii di Sicilia*

"Sicilian Vespers" (White) 5:487; 7:532

"Sick Again" (Page and Plant) 12:477

"A Sick Call" (Nowlan) 15:398

"The Sick Child" (Gluck) 22:177

"The Sick Humor of Lenny Bruce" (Bruce) 21:44

"Sick Love" (Graves) 39:328; 45:173

"Sick Visits" (Thomas) 48:379

The Sickest Don't Always Die the Quickest (Jackson) 12:290

"Sickness" (Akhmadulina)
See "Bolezn'"

"Sickness" (Sommer) 25:425

"The Sickness unto Death" (Sexton) 6:492

Siddhartha (Hesse) 1:145; 2:191-92; 3:245-48; 11:271; 17:195, 199, 206, 210-11, 214-17, 219; 69:279, 289, 293

Side by Side by Sondheim (Sondheim) 30:389

Side Effects (Allen) 52:40-2

"Side Street" (Farrell) 66:131

Side Street, and Other Stories (Farrell) 66:129

"Sidere Mens Eadem Mutato" (Murray) 40:337

"A Sidewalk Cafe: Budapest, Autumn" (Padilla) 38:351

"The Sidmouth Letters" (Gardam) 43:169-70

The Sidmouth Letters (Gardam) 43:169, 171

"The Sidney Greenstreet Blues" (Brautigan) 12:59

The Sidney Poet Heroical, in Twenty-Nine Scenes (Baraka) 10:19; 115:10, 20, 28

"Sieben Rosen später" ("Seven Roses Later") (Celan) 19:90

17 dikter (*17 Poems*) (Transtroemer) 52:408-10, 412, 415, 418; 65:222, 226, 229, 231, 233-37

"Siefried's Journey" (Sassoon) 36:387-88, 394, 396-97

Sieg des Glaubens (*Victory of Faith*) (Riefenstahl) 16:520

"The Siege" (Mueller) 51:280

The Siege (*The Friends of God*) (Vansittart) 42:391, 393

Le siége de l'air (Arp) 5:33

The Siege of Krishnapur (Farrell) 6:173-74

"The Siege of Mullingar" (Montague) 46:268

The Siege of Pleasure (*Twenty Thousand Streets under the Sky: A London Trilogy*) (Hamilton) 51:185-86, 190-91, 193-94, 197-98

The Siege of the Villa Lipp (*Send No More Roses*) (Ambler) 9:21-2

Der Sieger nimmt alles (*Winner Takes All*) (Wellershoff) 46:438-39

Siegfried (Lang) 20:201, 204, 210; 103:85

Siegfried Sassoon Diaries, 1915-1918 (Sassoon) 36:396-97

Siegfried Sassoon Diaries, 1920-1922 (Sassoon) 36:396-97

Siegfried's Journey, 1916-1920 (Sassoon) 36:388-89, 396

"Siegmund Freud" (Parra) 102:343
"Siena" (Milosz) 56:237
"Sierpes Street" (Cabral de Melo Neto)
See "Calle Sierpes"
"Sierra Leone" (McGahern) 48:264
"Siesta" (Transtroemer) 65:222
"Siesta in Xbalba and Return to the States"
(Ginsberg) 36:189-90
"Siesta: Mexico/Vermont" (Belitt) 22:52
"Siestas" (Cortazar) 10:113; 33:129
Siete domingos rojos (Seven Red Sundays)
(Sender) 8:477-78, 480
Sift in an Hourglass (Gustafson) 36:212-13,
216-18
"The Sighing Time" (Blunden) 56:37
Sight Unseen (Margulies) 76:188-95
Sightings (Rothenberg) 6:477; 57:372
Sights and Spectacles, 1937-1956 (McCarthy)
24:341-42
The Sightseer (Wolff) 41:456-57
*El siglo de las luces (Explosion in the Cathe-
dral)* (Carpentier) 11:99-100, 102, 105-
07; 38:91-2, 94, 96-101; 110:58, 60, 74,
78
"Sigma" (Tolson) 105:255
The Sign (Harrison) 6:223
"Sign for My Father, Who Stressed the Bunt"
(Bottoms) 53:33
"A Sign in Space" (Calvino)
See "Sign of Space"
"Sign In Stranger" (Becker and Fagen) 26:81
The Sign in Sydney Brustein's Window
(Brustein's Window) (Hansberry) 17:184-
89, 191-92; 62:216-18, 220
"The Sign of Apelles" (Pasternak)
See "Il tratto di Apelle"
The Sign of Jonas (Merton) 83:379, 397-403
"Sign of Space" ("A Sign in Space") (Calvino)
8:128
The Sign of the Chrysanthemum (Paterson)
12:484; 30:286
Sign of the Unicorn (Zelazny) 21:468, 470,
473
The Signal (Vesaas)
See *Signalet*
Signalet (The Signal) (Vesaas) 48:407
Signature (Scott) 22:373
"Signature Event Context" (Derrida) 87:84
"Signature for Tempo II" (MacLeish) 68:270
"The Signature of All Things" (Rexroth)
112:385, 399
*The Signature of All Things: Poems, Songs,
Elegies, Translations, and Epigrams*
(Rexroth) 6:450; 22:345, 348-49;
49:279; 112:387, 405
"Signatures" (Dixon) 52:99
"Signe ascendant" (Breton) 15:91
Le signe de la croix (Marcel) 15:364
Le signe de vie (Tzara) 47:396
Le signe du lion (Rohmer) 16:528, 530
"Le Signe du Mauvais Sang" (Tchicaya)
101:349
"Signed, Sealed, Delivered" (Wonder) 12:656,
663
Signed, Sealed, Delivered (Wonder) 12:655-
56
"Significant Moments in the Life of My
Mother" (Atwood) 84:67
Significant Others (Maupin) 95:192-99, 201,
203-04, 208
"The Signifying Darkness" (Dodson) 79:191
*The Signifying Monkey: A Theory of Afro-
American Literary Criticism* (Gates)

65:380, 387-91, 393-94, 404-05
Signifying Rappers (Wallace) 114:360, 363
La Signora Senza Camelie (Antonioni) 20:20-
1
Signpost (Livesay) 15:340; 79:339
"Signs" 75:70
"Signs" (Diamond) 30:112
"Signs" (Merwin) 45:273
"The Signs" (Olds) 85:296
"Signs" (Redgrove) 41:348
"Signs and Portents" (Kunitz) 14:313
"Signs and Symbols" (Nabokov) 15:393
Signs of Identity (Goytisolo)
See *Señas de identidad*
Signs of Life (Dabrowska)
See *Znaki zycia*
Signs of Life (Elliott) 38:181-82
Signs of Life (Herzog)
See *Lebenszeichen*
Signs of the Gods (von Daniken) 30:427
"Sigue" ("Pass on by") (Guillen) 79:245-46
Siinä näkijä missä tekiyä (Salama) 18:460-62
S'il vous plait (If You Please) (Breton and
Soupault) 68:408-13
Silabe (Arghezi) 80:6-8
Silas and Ben-Godik (Bodker) 21:13-14
"Silas and Goliath" (Bates) 46:62
Silas and the Black Mare (Bodker) 21:11-13
Silas and the Runaway Coach (Bodker) 21:13-
14
Silas Crockett (Chase) 2:101
"The Silence" (Berry) 46:75
"Silence" (Bly) 5:61
"Silence" (Ginzburg) 54:201, 203-04; 70:280
"Silence" (Moore) 47:264
The Silence (Bergman)
See *Tystnaden*
Silence (Endo)
See *Chinmoku*
Silence (Pinter) 3:386-87; 6:416-17, 420;
9:420; 11:442-43; 15:423; 27:394-95;
58:372, 374, 377; 73:268
The Silence (Sarraute)
See *Le silence*
Le silence (The Silence) (Sarraute) 8:470;
10:457-58; 31:381-82; 80:241
"Silence and the Poet" (Steiner) 24:429
Le silence des pierres (del Castillo) 38:168
Le silence est d'or (Clair) 20:64, 71
The Silence in the Garden (Trevor) 71:339-
42, 346, 349; 116:348, 352, 354, 365,
376-77, 382-83, 396
Silence in the Snowy Fields (Bly) 2:66; 5:61,
63-5; 10:54-7; 15:62-3, 65-8; 38:54-7
Silence: Lectures and Writings (Cage) 41:76-
83
The Silence Now (Sarton) 91:244
A Silence of Desire (Markandaya) 38:322-23
The Silence of History (Farrell) 11:193; 66:129,
139
"The Silence of Oswald" (Holmes) 56:140
"The Silence of the Valley" (O'Faolain) 1:259;
14:402, 406; 32:343-44; 70:313, 318
Silence over Dunkerque (Tunis) 12:598
"The Silences" (Dunn) 40:169
Silences (Okigbo) 25:349, 354
Silences (Olsen) 13:432-33; 114:199-202,
210, 215, 219, 221-24, 231, 237, 239
The Silences Between: Moeraki Conversations
(Hulme) 39:160
"Silences: Lament of the Silent Sisters" ("La-
ment of the Silent Sisters"; "Silent Sis-
ters") (Okigbo) 25:354; 84:302, 312,

315, 321-23, 325-26, 328, 332, 336
"Silences, When Writers Don't Write" (Olsen)
114:193, 195-96
"The Silent Areas" (Feinstein) 36:171
The Silent Areas (Feinstein) 36:171
The Silent Cry (Oe)
See *Man'en gan'nen no futtoboru*
"The Silent Generation" (Simpson) 4:498
"Silent in America" (Levine) 5:252; 9:332
"Silent in Gehenna" (Ellison) 13:206
"The Silent Man" (Phillips) 28:364
"The Silent Marriage" (Simmons) 43:410-11
"The Silent Men" (Camus)
See "Les muets"
Silent Movie (Brooks) 12:80-2
The Silent Mr. Palomar (Calvino)
See *Palomar*
"Silent Night, Lonely Night" (Anderson)
23:30-2
"The Silent Poet Sequence" (Kroetsch) 23:273-
75
The Silent Rooms (Hebert)
See *Les chambres de bois*
"Silent Service" (Sassoon) 36:389
"Silent Sisters" (Okigbo)
See "Silences: Lament of the Silent Sisters"
The Silent Sky (Eckert) 17:104-05
"The Silent Slain" (MacLeish) 68:290
"Silent Snow, Secret Snow" (Aiken) 52:26
The Silent Speaker (Stout) 3:472
Silent Spring (Carson) 71:97-9, 101-08, 110-
13
"The Silent Towns" (Bradbury) 42:38
The Silent World (Cousteau) 30:101-04, 109
"Silhouette" (Ashbery) 15:33
"Silhouette" (Hughes) 108:328
Silhouette du scandale (Ayme) 11:23
"Silhouettes" (Jones) 81:65
"Sililoquy on the Rocks" (Bowering) 47:19
"Silk of a Soul" (Herbert) 9:271
Silk Stockings (Kaufman) 38:268
Silk Stockings (Mamoulian) 16:425, 428-30
Silkeborg (Abell) 15:1, 5
Silken Eyes (Sagan) 9:468; 17:427-28
The Silken Net (Bragg) 10:72
"The Silken Swift" (Sturgeon) 39:361
"The Silken Tent" (Frost) 13:228
"The Silken Tent" (Loewinsohn) 52:285
Silkwood (Ephron) 31:160
"The Silky Veils of Ardor" (Mitchell) 12:443-
44
"Sillat" (*Bridges*) (Haavikko) 34:174
"Silly Boy Blue" (Bowie) 17:65
"Silly Love Songs" (McCartney) 35:284-85,
287-88, 290, 293-94
"Silly Talk about Suicide" (Valenzuela) 31:437
The Silmarillion (Tolkien) 1:338; 3:481;
8:515-16; 12:585-87; 38:431-32, 434-38,
441-43
"Siloam" (Davie) 31:124
"Silvae" (Montale) 7:222
"Silver" (Ammons) 5:29; 108:4
"The Silver Bangles" (Anand) 23:21
The Silver Bears (Erdman) 25:154
"The Silver Bird of Herndyke Mill" (Blunden)
56:27, 31, 37
The Silver Branch (O'Faolain) 70:315, 317
The Silver Branch (Sutcliff) 26:426-28, 430,
433-35
"The Silver Bullet" (McPherson) 19:310;
77:365
The Silver Chair (Lewis) 27:263
The Silver Chalice (Costain) 30:97-8

"The Silver Crown" (Malamud) 3:325; 8:375; 18:317-18; 27:306
"A Silver Dish" (Bellow) 25:84-5; 33:68; 63:29
The Silver Eggheads (Leiber) 25:303
"Silver Gift Poem" (Elytis) 49:114; 100:175
"Silver Lamé" (Carpenter) 41:103
"The Silver Lily" (Gluck) 81:172
"The Silver Locket" (McNickle) 89:180
The Silver Metal Lover (Lee) 46:232
Silver out of Shanghai: A Scenario for Josef von Sternberg, Featuring Wicked Nobles, a Depraved Religious Wayfoong, Princess Ida, the China Clipper, and Resurrection Lily (Cassity) 42:96-7
"A Silver Plate" (Raine) 103:210
"The Silver Porcupine" (Kinsella) 43:258
"The Silver Stag" (Raine) 45:332
The Silver Swan: Poems Written in Kyoto, 1974-1975 (Rexroth) 49:283, 286; 112:372, 404
"The Silver Swanne" (Dowell) 60:108-09
The Silver Tassie (The Tassie) (O'Casey) 5:320; 11:407-09; 15:405-06, 408; 88:242, 248, 251-54, 257, 259-61, 263-65, 267-70, 273, 275-77, 281
Silver: The Life of an Atlantic Salmon (Haig-Brown) 21:139-40, 142-44
The Silver Tongued Devil and I (Kristofferson) 26:267, 269-70
"Silver Wedding" (Scannell) 49:329
Silver Wedding 59:364
The Silver Wire (Bowering) 15:82
Silverhill (Whitney) 42:434
"Silvester-Unfall" (Lenz) 27:245
"Silvia" (Cortazar) 10:113
Sima kindynou (Danger Signal) (Samarakis) 5:381
Simabaddha (Company Limited; Seembadha) (Ray) 16:487, 493, 495; 76:357-58, 360, 362
"Simaetha" (H. D.) 73:105
Simbi and the Satyr of the Dark Jungle (Tutuola) 5:443; 14:539; 29:441-42
"Similar Triangles" (Raphael) 14:438
"Simile" (Meredith) 55:192
"Simile" (Momaday) 85:247
"Similkameen Deer" (Lane) 25:284
Simon (Sutcliff) 26:425, 428-29, 432-35, 439
Simon and Garfunkel's Greatest Hits (Simon) 17:463
"Simon Buckminster (SR)" (Avison) 97:128
Simon del desierto (Simon of the Desert) (Bunuel) 16:134-35, 139, 141, 151; 80:41, 46
"Simon Frailman" (Scannell) 49:331-32
"Simon le Mage" ("Simon Magus") (Kis) 57:249, 251-52
"Simon Magus" (Kis)
  See "Simon le Mage"
Simon of the Desert (Bunuel)
  See Simon del desierto
Simon Plunges Through Thousands of Years: A Dramatic Happening in Fourteen Scenes (Sachs) 98:322
Simone de Beauvoir: A Life... a Love Story (Francis and Gontier) 50:387-92
Simonetta Perkins (Hartley) 22:211, 213
"Simple Autumnal" (Bogan) 46:77-8, 89; 93:92-3, 95-6
A Simple Honorable Man (Richter) 30:317, 321-22, 326
"A Simple Language" (Clifton) 66:86
"Simple Language, Simple People: Smith, Paton,

Mikro" (Coetzee) 66:99
"The Simple Life" (Bates) 46:59-60
"The Simple Life" (Beer) 58:38
"The Simple Life" (Richter) 30:328
A Simple Lust: Selected Poems Including Sirens, Knuckles, Boots; Letters to Martha; Poems from Algiers, Thoughts Abroad (Brutus) 43:88-9, 94, 96-7
"Simple Maria" (Allende) 97:30, 32
Simple Passion (Ernaux)
  See Passion simple
Simple People (Gray) 9:241
Simple Speaks His Mind (Hughes) 10:281
Simple Stakes a Claim (Hughes) 10:281; 35:215-16; 108:284
Simple Takes a Wife (Hughes) 10:281
The Simple Truth (Hardwick) 13:264
"Simple Twist of Fate" (Dylan) 77:178
Simple's Uncle Sam (Hughes) 35:219; 108:286
"The Simpleton" (Garfield) 12:218
"Simplicity" (Rakosi) 47:345
"The Simplification" (Piercy) 27:374
Simply Heavenly (Hughes) 35:217-18
"Simply Passing Through" (Walcott) 25:448
"Simply the Human Form" (Forster) 45:131, 133
La simulación (Sarduy) 97:404-06
The Simulacra (Dick) 30:127; 72:104, 121
Simulacra and Simulations (Baudrillard)
  See Simulacres et simulations
"Le simulacre" (Pinget) 13:443
Simulacres et simulations (Simulacra and Simulations) (Baudrillard) 60:19
"Simultan" ("Three Paths to the Lake") (Bachmann) 69:47-8
Simultan (Three Paths to the Lake) (Bachmann) 69:36, 46, 48, 59
Sin (Ai) 69:8-10, 15-17
The Sin (Ichikawa)
  See Hakai
The Sin Eater (Ellis) 40:189-91
"Sin título" ("Untitled") (Zamora) 89:387
"Sinaï, bis" (Tchicaya) 101:353
The Sinai Sort (MacCaig) 36:279-80
"Sinaloa" (Birney) 6:75
"Sinbad" (Barthelme) 59:251
"Since" (Auden) 4:33; 6:19-20
"Since 1939" (Lowell) 11:330; 37:238
"Since Donovan Died" (Scannell) 49:327
"Since I Had You" (Gaye) 26:132
"Since I've Been Loving You" (Page and Plant) 12:480
"Since then" (Amichai) 116:97
Sincerely, Willis Wayde (Marquand) 10:329-30
"Sincerity and Art" (Huxley) 11:283
Sincerity and Authenticity (Trilling) 9:530; 11:539, 543, 545; 24:457-59
Sindbad and Me (Platt) 26:348-50
"Sinew" (Carver) 55:276
"Sinful City" (Seifert)
  See "Hříšné mesto"
Sinful Davy (Huston) 20:171
"The Sinful Life and Death of Tinkori" (Anand) 93:57
Sinful Minds (Dourado)
  See As imaginações pecaminosas
The Sinful Stones (The Seals) (Dickinson) 12:169; 35:133
Sinful Woman (Cain) 3:97; 28:53
Sing Down the Moon (O'Dell) 30:269-70
Sing for Your Supper (Weber) 12:632
"Sing My Songs to Me" (Browne) 21:35
"Sing Shaindele, Sing" (Charyn) 5:104

"Sing This All Together" (Jagger and Richard) 17:221
Sing to Me Through Open Windows (Kopit) 18:287; 33:249
"Singalong Junk" (McCartney) 35:278-79
"Singapore" (Oliver) 98:278, 280-81, 284
"The Singapore Hotel" (Hood) 28:189
Singer of Sad Songs (Jennings) 21:201
"The Singers" (Ai) 69:5
"The Singers" (Boland) 113:110, 119
"The Singer's House" (Heaney) 25:247
"The Singer's Song" (Ekelof) 27:110
Singin' and Swingin' and Gettin' Merry Like Christmas (Angelou) 12:13-14; 35:31; 64:24, 27, 29-31, 36, 39; 77:3-4, 6-8, 10-13, 15, 22, 24-5
"Singing" (Shapcott) 38:401
"Singing" (Stern) 40:413-14
"Singing Aloud" (Kizer) 80:174, 179, 181
"The Singing Bell" (Asimov) 26:44-5
The Singing Cave (Dillon) 17:94-5
The Singing Detective (Potter) 58:393-401; 86:345-53
Singing from the Well (Arenas)
  See Celestino antes del alba
The Singing Head (Elliott) 47:104
"Singing in the Clump" (Dowell) 60:107-09
Singing in the Shrouds (Marsh) 53:250
"The Singing Lesson" (West) 7:519
"Singing Nigger" (Sandburg) 35:352
"Singing School" (Heaney) 25:245-46; 74:163
Singing Strings (Kettelkamp) 12:304
"Singing the Monthly Blues" (Jong) 83:300
"Singing the Tree" (Goldbarth) 5:144
Single Handed (Forester) 35:159, 163
The Single Hound (Sarton) 49:307-08; 91:240, 245
A Single Lady, and Other Stories (Lavin) 99:312
A Single Light (Wojciechowska) 26:454, 458-59
A Single Man (Isherwood) 1:156-57; 9:294; 11:300; 14:280, 285; 44:398-99, 402
A Single Pebble (Hersey) 1:144; 7:153; 40:228-29, 231, 239-42; 81:334-35; 97:302
"Single Pigeon" (McCartney) 35:281
"Single Sonnet" (Bogan) 46:81, 90
Single Spies (Bennett) 77:94-5, 97-8, 100-02
"Singleminded" (Brunner) 8:107
"Singling & Doubling Together" (Ammons) 57:49-51, 59-60; 108:16, 38, 57, 58
A Singular Man (Donleavy) 1:76; 4:123, 125; 6:139, 141-42; 10:153-54
Singularities (Howe) 72:209
"The Singularly Ugly Princess" (Brophy) 6:99
"Un singuratic" ("A Loner") (Arghezi) 80:12
Sinister Street (Mackenzie) 18:313-17
"Sink" (Celan) 53:78
Sink the Belgrano! (Berkoff) 56:17
"The Sinking House" (Boyle) 90:48
"The Sinking of the Bismarck" (MacLean) 63:270
The Sinking of the Odradek Stadium (Mathews) 6:315-16; 52:307, 309-10, 315-16, 318
The Sinking of the Odradek Stadium and Other Novels (Mathews) 52:307
The Sinking of the Titanic (Enzensberger)
  See Der Untergang der Titanic
Sinking Ship Blues (Breytenbach) 23:84
"Sinn Fein: 1957" (Buckley) 57:126
"Sinner" (Hughes) 10:279; 108:297
Sinning with Annie, and Other Stories

(Theroux) 5:427
Sins For Father Knox (Skvorecky) 69:337-38, 344, 346-47
"Sins Leave Scars" (Cooper) 56:70
The Sins of Philip Fleming (Wallace) 13:567-68
"The Sins of the Fathers" (Porter) 33:318
"Sins of the Third Age" (Gordimer) 33:185; 70:182
"Sintra" (Adams) 46:21
"The Sipapu" (Loewinsohn) 52:285
Sippi (Killens) 10:300-02
Sippur pashut (Agnon) 4:15
"Sipsy in the Rain" (Bass) 79:17
"Sir" (McCartney) 35:287
Sir Donald Wolfit (Harwood) 32:224
"Sir Duke" (Wonder) 12:660, 662
"Sir Francis Bacon" (Moore) 47:268
"Sir Gawain and the Green Knight" (Winters) 4:591; 32:467
"Sir John Piers" (Betjeman) 43:34
Sir Slob and the Princess: A Play for Children (Garrett) 51:145
"Sir William Herschel's Long Year" (Hope) 51:226
"Sir William Johnson: His Daily Journal" (Kenny) 87:257
Sire Halewyn (Ghelderode) 11:226
The Siren (Buzzati) 36:95
"Siren Limits" (Okigbo) 25:350, 352; 84:301, 306-07, 314, 317-22, 326, 333
"The Siren of Sandy Gap" (Prichard) 46:345
"Siren Song" (Atwood) 8:29
La sirena varada (Casona) 49:40, 42-6
Die Sirene (Wellershoff) 46:437
"The Sirens" (Ferron) 94:103, 125
"Sirens" (Gerstler) 70:157-58
The Sirens (Wesley) 7:519
"Sirens and Voices" (Swan) 69:363-64
The Sirens of Titan (Vonnegut) 2:453, 455; 3:495-501, 503; 4:561-63, 565-67, 569; 5:466-67, 469; 8:530-31; 12:603-04, 606, 609, 612-14, 618, 620-21, 623, 628; 40:448-49; 60:424, 430-31, 438, 440; 111:351, 358, 359, 366
"The Sirens' Welcome to Cronos" (Graves) 2:174
The Sirian Experiments: The Report by Ambien II, of the Five (Lessing) 15:336; 22:285-87; 40:303-06, 309
"Sirius: Midnight" (Derleth) 31:138
"Sirmione Peninsula" (Spender) 41:426
"Sirocco" (Piccolo) 13:441
Sirocco (Coward) 29:131
"Sirriamnis" (Lee) 46:231-32
"Sirventes" (Blackburn) 43:61
Sissie (Williams) 5:498; 13:598
Sista mänskan (*The Last Human Being*; *The Last Man*; *The Last of Mankind*) (Lagerkvist) 54:268, 274, 277
Il sistema periodico (*The Periodic Table*) (Levi) 37:223, 226-27; 50:323-24, 327-28, 332-34, 336, 338-40
"Sister" (Dunn) 36:153
"Sister" (Farrell) 4:158; 8:205
"Sister" (Herbert) 9:274
"Sister" (Hughes) 108:328
"Sister" (Prince) 35:324
"Sister" (Taylor) 5:425
"Sister" (Voigt) 54:429
"Sister" (Wolff) 64:454
Sister Age (Fisher) 76:341; 87:124-25, 127-28, 130, 133

"Sister and Brother" (Welty) 105:341
"Sister Ann of the Cornfields" (Kinsella) 27:238
"Sister Imelda" (O'Brien) 36:336, 339, 341; 116:186, 195, 216-18
"Sister Lou" (Brown) 1:47
"Sister Madeleine Pleads for Our Mary" (Fulton) 52:161
Sister Mary Ignatius Explains It All for You (Durang) 27:90-3; 38:172-74
"Sister Morphine" (Jagger and Richard) 17:223-24, 229, 234
"Sister Outsider" (Lorde) 71:243
Sister Outsider: Essays and Speeches (Lorde) 71:243-45, 260
"Sister Ray" (Reed) 21:303, 314
Sister Son/ji (Sanchez) 116:283, 301, 308, 316
"Sister Water" (Warren) 13:582
"Sisterhood" (Steinem) 63:379
Sisterhood Is Powerful (Morgan) 2:294
Sisterly Feelings (Ayckbourn) 18:29-30; 33:42-3; 74:31, 34
"The Sisters" (Jacobsen) 48:198-99
"The Sisters" (Wright) 53:418
The Sisters (Angelou) 77:21
The Sisters (Littell) 42:277-78
Sisters (*Blood Sisters*) (De Palma) 20:74-8
"Sisters in Arms" (Lorde) 71:260
The Sisters Materassi (Palazzeschi)
   See *Sorelle Materassi*
The Sisters: New and Selected Poems (Jacobsen) 48:197-99; 102:240
Sisters of Darkness (Almodovar)
   See *Entre Tinieblas*
"The Sisters of Mercy" (Cohen) 3:109
"Sisters of the Princess" (Boyle) 58:74
"Sisters of the Rain" (Cooper) 56:71-2
Sisters of the Yam: Black Women and Self-Recovery (hooks) 94:154-55, 159
The Sisters Rosenweig (Wasserstein) 90:435-40
"Sisters Under Their Skin" (Ferber) 93:140
Sisyphus and Reilly: An Autobiography (Luke) 38:317-18
"Sit Down Young Stranger" (Lightfoot) 26:281
Sit Opposite Each Other (Summers) 10:493
Sita (Millett) 67:252-53, 258
"Sitalkas" (H. D.) 73:104-05, 119
"Sites" (Butor) 15:114
The Sittaford Mystery (Christie) 48:72-3
"The Sitting" (McGuckian) 48:278
"Sitting in Limbo" (Cliff) 21:65
Sitting in Mexico (Bowering) 15:83
"Sitting in My Hotel" (Davies) 21:95
Sitting In: Selected Writings on Jazz, Blues, and Related Topics (Carruth) 84:132
Sitting in the Club Car Drinking Rum and Karma Cola: A Manual for Ladies Crossing Canada by Train (Jiles) 58:273-75
"Sitting in the Waters of Grasse River" (Kenny) 87:255
Sitting Pretty (Young) 19:479-80
"La situación insostenible" (Neruda) 28:309
"The Situation at the End of the War" (Leavis) 24:293
"Situation Comedy" (Jiles) 58:272, 279
A Situation in New Delhi (Sahgal) 41:372
"Situation in the West" (Ferlinghetti) 27:139
Situation Normal (Miller) 1:216
The Situation of Poetry: Contemporary Poetry and Its Traditions (Pinsky) 19:369-70; 38:355-56, 359-60; 94:299-300, 302,

308
Situations (Sartre) 1:304; 7:397; 18:473; 24:416, 418, 421; 50:370
Situations 2 (Sartre) 24:419, 421
Situations 10 (Sartre) 9:473
"VI" (Dunn) 40:170
Six and One Remorses for the Sky (Elytis) 15:220-21; 49:107-09, 111, 117; 100:175, 180, 192
"Six Beautiful in Paris" (McNickle) 89:183-84
"Six Cemetery Poems" (Silkin) 43:404
Six Darn Cows (Laurence) 50:314
"Six Days before Christmas" (Kherdian) 6:280
Six Days in Marapore (Scott) 60:320
Six Degrees of Separation (Guare) 67:86-90
"The Six Deliberate Acts" (Fisher) 25:161
"6 della sera" (Ortese)
   See "Le sei della sera"
Six Epistles to Eva Hesse (Davie) 5:114-15; 8:163, 165
Six Feet of the Country (Gordimer) 18:185; 33:178-79; 70:162
"603 West Liberty Street" (Fulton) 52:160
"Six Inches" (Bukowski) 41:75; 108:85
"Six Lectures in Verse" (Milosz) 56:248; 82:297-98, 301, 304
6 litres d'eau par seconde (Butor) 15:115, 118
"Six Meditations after the Event" (Coles) 46:108
Six Memos for the Next Millenium (Calvino) 73:42, 49, 57, 59-60
"Six Nuns Die in Convent Inferno" (Durcan) 70:151
Six of One (Brown) 18:73-5; 43:81; 79:153, 155, 157-59, 169
"Six Places in New York State" (Crase) 58:159-60
Six Plays of Clifford Odets (Odets) 98:209, 211, 217
Six Problems for Don Isidro Parodi (Bioy Casares)
   See *Seis problemas para Don Isidro Parodi*
"Six Sailors" (Feldman) 7:103
Six San Francisco Poets (Kherdian) 6:281
Six Sections from Mountains and Rivers without End (Snyder) 1:318; 32:388, 398
"Six Sentences" (Clarke) 9:167
"Six Songs for Clöe" (Hope) 3:251
"Six Songs for Tamar" (Amichai) 116:96
Six Stories (Bates) 46:63
"Six Sundays in January" (Wesker) 3:519; 5:484
"The 6000" (Pratt) 19:379-80
Six Troubadour Songs (Snodgrass) 18:492
"Six Underrated Pleasures" (Piercy) 62:370-71
"Six Varieties of Religious Experience" (L'Heureux) 52:275
"Six Winter Privacy Poems" (Bly) 10:55, 61; 15:63
The Six Wives of Henry VIII (Fraser) 107:60-2, 64-5, 67
"Six Years" (Snyder) 32:387, 391
"Six Years Later" (Brodsky) 36:78
"The Six-Day Night" (Morand)
   See "La nuit de seis jours"
Le sixième jour (Chedid) 47:84-6
Sixpence in Her Shoe (McGinley) 14:368
Sixteen, and Other Stories (Daly) 17:90
"1614 Boren" (Hugo) 32:244-47
"1692 Cotton Mather Newsreel" (Brautigan) 12:69

"Sixteen-Year-Old Susan March Confesses to the Innocent Murder of All the Devious Strangers Who Would Drag Her Down" (Rooke) 25:394

Sixth Column (Heinlein) 14:247

The Sixth Commandment (Sanders) 41:380

"The Sixth Fleet Still Out There in the Mediterranean" (Starbuck) 53:354

The Sixth Heaven (Hartley) 22:211

Sixth Sense (Kettelkamp) 12:305-06

"The Sixties" (Shields) 97:430-31, 433

"Sixty Answers to Thirty-Three Questions from Daniel Charles" (Cage) 41:83

Sixty Poems (Ezekiel) 61:96

Sixty Stories (Barthelme) 23:47-9; 46:42; 59:246-47; 115:78, 81

"A Sixty Year Old Man" (Endo) 99:296, 301, 307

"'65'" (Reading) 47:351

63: Dream Palace (Purdy) 2:348-50; 4:424; 10:421-24; 28:379; 52:343-44

"Sixty-three Words" (Kundera) 115:321

Sixty-Two: A Model Kit (Cortazar)
    See *62: Modelo para armar*

"Sixty-Two Mesostics re Merce Cunningham" (Cage) 41:82

"The Size of a Universe" (Ciardi) 40:154

"The Size of Song" (Ciardi) 10:107; 40:159

"Sizwe Bansi Is Dead" (Purdy) 6:429

Sizwe Bansi Is Dead (Fugard) 9:229-34; 14:191; 25:175; 40:197-98, 203; 80:61-3, 65-6, 69-70, 74-5, 77, 79

Själarnas maskerad (*The Masquerade of Souls*) (Lagerkvist) 54:276, 288-90

Sjálfstaett fólk (*Independent People*) (Laxness) 25:291, 296

En Självbiografi: EfterKauamnade brev och anteckningar (Ekelof) 27:116

Det sjunde inseglet (*The Seventh Seal*) (Bergman) 16:45-50, 52-5, 59-62, 64-7, 69, 71, 73-4, 77, 82; 72:27-40, 52, 54-6, 59-60

Skammen (*Shame*) (Bergman) 16:60, 62, 74-5, 80-1; 72:40, 49-50, 52, 54, 57, 59

Skapelsemorgon (Lagerkvist) 13:331

"Skater in Blue" (Parini) 54:360-61

"The Skaters" (Ashbery) 2:19; 4:23; 9:43; 15:27; 25:50-1, 56; 41:33, 40-1; 77:52, 62

"The Skaters" (Jarrell) 13:299

"Skating" (Motion) 47:292

The Skating Party (Warner) 59:212, 216

Skating Shoes (*White Boots*) (Streatfeild) 21:400, 406-07, 410, 415

"Skaza harmonii" (Milosz) 56:237

Skazhi izjum! (Aksyonov)
    See *Say Cheese!*

"Skazka" ("A Fairy Tale") (Pasternak) 18:387-89; 63:313, 318

"The Skein" (Kizer) 80:174, 180

The Skeletal System (Silverstein and Silverstein) 17:456

"The Skeleton" (Aldiss) 40:19

"The Skeleton" (Pritchett) 13:467

Skeleton Crew (King) 37:207

"Skeleton Crow" (Szirtes) 46:393

"Skeleton Key: Opening and Starting Key for a 1954 Dodge Junked Last Year" (Hollander) 2:197

A Skeleton Key to "Finnegans Wake" (Campbell and Robinson) 69:65-7, 90

"The Skeleton of Dreams" (Appleman) 51:17

"The Skeleton of the Future" (MacDiarmid) 19:287; 63:253, 255

"The Skeletonizers" (Lieberman) 36:261

"Skeletons" (Beattie) 63:18

Skeletons (Swarthout) 35:404

"Skepparhistoria" (Transtroemer) 65:235

"Skeptic" (Frost) 13:231; 26:118

"Skeptic and Barbarian" (Cioran) 64:88

"Skepticism and the Depth of Life" (Bellow) 10:40

Skerrett (O'Flaherty) 5:321; 34:355-56

"SKETCH: CNR London to Toronto (II)" (Avison) 97:113, 117

"SKETCH: End of a Day: OR, I as a blurry" (Avison) 97:117

"Sketch for a Landscape" (Swenson) 106:313

"Sketch from Life" ("A Good Boy") (Sargeson) 31:364

"Sketch in October" (Transtroemer) 65:223

"Sketch of a Long Poem" (Voznesensky) 57:418

"A Sketch of the Great Dejection" (Gunn) 81:178, 182

"Sketch of the Old Graveyard at Col de Castillon" (Middleton) 13:388

Sketchbook, 1946-1949 (Frisch)
    See *Tagebuch, 1946-1949*

Sketchbook, 1966-1971 (Frisch)
    See *Tagebuch, 1966-1971*

The Sketches (Turco) 11:550, 552

Sketches from the Land of Kuty (Arghezi)
    See *Tablete din tara ke Kuty*

Sketches in Criticism (Brooks) 29:83

The Skewbald Dog Running along the Seashore (Aitmatov)
    See *Pegil pes, begushchij kraem moria*

The Skewbald Dog Running at the Edge of the Sea (Aitmatov)
    See *Pegil pes, begushchij kraem moria*

"The Skewer" (McGrath) 55:73, 75-6

"Skiddah and Kuziba" (Singer) 111:305

The Skies of Crete (Forman) 21:115

The Skies of Europe (Prokosch) 48:311-12

"The Skills of Xanadu" (Sturgeon) 39:364

"The Skimming Stone" (Steele) 45:365

"Skin" (Selzer) 74:278

The Skin (Silverstein and Silverstein) 17:456

"Skin Boat" (Ondaatje) 51:314

Skin Deep (Dickinson)
    See *The Glass-Sided Ants' Nest*

"The Skin Game" (Phillips) 28:362-63

The Skin of Dreams (Queneau)
    See *Loin de rueil*

Skin of Grace (Willard) 37:462-63

The Skin of Our Teeth (Kazan) 63:225, 230, 234

The Skin of Our Teeth (Wilder) 1:364-66; 5:495-96; 6:572-73, 575-78; 10:531-32, 535; 15:570-71, 573-75; 35:442, 444; 82:346-48, 352-53, 357-61, 363-64, 368, 376-77, 379-82, 384, 390-91

Skin Screen Utopia (Brossard) 115:109-11

Skinflick (Hansen) 38:238

"Skinned Alive" (White) 110:340

Skinned Alive (White) 110:339-40, 342-43

"Skinning a Deer" (Holmes) 56:145

Skinny Legs and All (Robbins) 64:380-84

"Skins" (Wright) 13:612; 28:457, 460

Skins and Bones (Allen) 84:24

Skinwalkers (Hillerman) 62:260

"The Skip" (Fenton) 32:166

Skipper (Corcoran) 17:78

Skippy (Sackler) 14:479

Skipton (Johnson) 1:161

"A Skirmish" (McGuane) 45:265

Skirmish: The Great Short Fiction of Clifford D. Simak (Simak) 55:319

"The Skokie Theatre" (Hirsch) 50:198

"Skookumchuk" (Musgrave) 54:336, 341

Den skrattande polisen (*The Laughing Policeman*) (Wahloo) 7:501-02

The Skull (Hikmet)
    See *Kafatasi*

"The Skull Ballad" (Voznesensky) 57:414

The Skull beneath the Skin (James) 46:205-07

A Skull in Salop and Other Poems (Grigson) 7:135

"A Skull Picked Clean" (Day Lewis) 10:131

"Skull Valley, Utah" (Squires) 51:379

"The Skunk" (Heaney) 14:245-46; 25:242-44, 247; 74:167

"Skunk Cabbage" (Oliver) 34:246-47; 98:257

"Skunk Hour" (Lowell) 3:302; 4:301; 5:258; 8:351, 354; 9:336; 11:326-27; 15:344, 346-47; 37:241, 243

Skutarevsky (Leonov)
    See *Skutarevsky*

Skutarevsky (*Skutarevski*) (Leonov) 92:232, 240, 246, 250, 253, 259, 270, 274, 276-78

"The Sky" (Findley) 102:111

"Sky" (Szymborska) 99:198

Sky (Benedikt) 4:54

"Sky and Earth" (Nagy) 7:251

"The Sky and I" (McFadden) 48:246

The Sky and the Forest (Forester) 35:169

Sky Blue (Bataille)
    See *Le bleu du ciel*

The Sky Changes (Sorrentino) 7:451-52; 22:392; 40:387

The Sky Is Free (Clark) 12:131-32

"The Sky is Gray" (Gaines) 86:178

"Sky Line" (Taylor) 37:407

Sky Man on the Totem Pole? (Harris) 12:263-67

"Sky of Grasses" (Young) 82:411

Sky Stones (Neruda) 28:313-14

"Sky Valley Rider" (Wright) 6:581

"Skybird" (Diamond) 30:111

Skye Cameron (Whitney) 42:432

Skyfall (Harrison) 42:203-06

"Skylarks" (Hughes) 14:271

"Skylight" (Mosley) 43:317

"Skylight" (Muske) 90:312

"Skylight" (Pastan) 27:368

Skylight (Muske) 90:309, 312-13

"Skylight One" (Aiken) 52:26

Skylight One: Fifteen Poems (Aiken) 52:26

"Skylights" (Gallagher) 63:118

"Skyscape" (Oates) 33:294

Skyscraper (Clarke) 16:215

"The Skyscraper Loves Night" (Sandburg) 35:341

"Skywriting" (Harrison) 43:179

"Slabs of the Sunburnt West" (Sandburg) 35:343

Slabs of the Sunburnt West (Sandburg) 15:466; 35:342-43, 352

"Slack" (Hooker) 43:197

Slag (Hare) 29:211, 213; 58:233

"Slam, Dunk, & Hook" (Komunyakaa) 94:237

The Slant Door (Szirtes) 46:390-92, 394

Slap Shot (Hill) 26:205-07

Slapstick; or, Lonesome No More! (Vonnegut) 8:532-34; 12:614, 618-20, 625-26, 628-29; 22:446; 40:441-42, 444-46; 111:360, 368

Slapstick Tragedy (Williams)

See *The Gnädiges Fräulein*
"Slash Burning on Silver Star" (Lane) 25:285
"Slate Mine" (Clarke) 61:84
Slats Grobnik and Some Other Friends (Royko) 109:404
"Slattery's Sago Saga; or, From Under the Ground to the Top of the Trees" (O'Brien) 7:270; 10:362
"The Slaughterer" (Singer) 3:458
"The Slaughterer's Testimony" (Rothenberg) 57:374
Slaughterhouse (Mrozek) 13:399
Slaughterhouse-Five (Hill) 26:198-201, 208, 211
Slaughterhouse-Five; or, The Children's Crusade: A Duty-Dance with Death (Vonnegut) 1:347; 2:451-53, 455-56; 3:495-506; 4:560, 562-64, 566-67, 569; 5:465-70; 8:529-32, 534-35; 12:602-05, 607-11, 613-15, 617, 619, 623-24, 626-27, 629; 60:416-41; 111:351, 355, 358-59, 362-64, 366, 368-72
"Slave" (Phillips) 15:419, 421
"Slave" (Simon) 26:409-10
The Slave (Baraka) 1:163; 2:35; 3:35-6; 5:44-5; 14:43-4; 33:54, 57, 59-60; 115:10-1, 33, 35
The Slave (Singer)
    See *Der Knekht*
The Slave Girl (Emecheta) 14:159; 48:97, 99, 101
"Slave Quarters" (Dickey) 2:115; 15:174
Slave Ship: A Historical Pageant (Baraka) 14:48-9; 33:60; 115:28, 34-5
Slave Song (Dabydeen) 34:147-50
Slave Trade (Gold) 14:208-09
Slavery: From the Rise of Western Civilization to the Renaissance (Meltzer) 26:300-01
Slavery, Volume II: From the Renaissance to Today (Meltzer) 26:301
"Slaves and Masters" (Brink) 36:68
"The Slaves in New York" (Janowitz) 43:211-12
Slaves of New York (Janowitz) 43:210-12
Slaves of Sleep (Hubbard) 43:207
The Slaves of Solitude (Riverside) (Hamilton) 51:189-91, 193-95, 197-98
Slaves of Spiegel: A Magic Moscow Story (Pinkwater) 35:319
"Slaves on the Block" (Hughes) 108:328
"Slave-Woman's Song" (Dabydeen) 34:149
Slavík zpívášpatne (*The Nightingale Sings Badly; The Nightingale Sings out of Tune; The Nightingale Sings Poorly*) (Seifert) 34:256, 260; 44:424; 93:305, 318, 333, 340-41
Slavnosti snezenek (*Schneeglöckchenfeste; Snowdrop Festivities*) (Hrabal) 67:121
"Slavnostní den" ("A Festive Day") (Seifert) 44:424
Slayground (Westlake) 33:437
"Slaying the Dream: The Black Family and the Crisis of Capitalism" (Davis) 77:128
Slayride (Francis) 42:148, 154, 156-57
"The Sledding Party" (Millhauser) 54:324-27
Sleek for the Long Flight: New Poems (Matthews) 40:319
"Sleep" (Slessor) 14:492-93
"The Sleep" (Strand) 71:285
Sleep (Gelber) 14:193
Sleep (Warhol) 20:414-15, 417, 421
Sleep and Dreams (Silverstein and Silverstein) 17:454

Sleep and His Brother (Dickinson) 12:170-71; 35:131, 133
Sleep Has His House (Kavan)
    See *The House of Sleep*
"Sleep in the Majave Desert" (Plath) 111:200-01
"Sleep Is the Silence Darkness Takes" (Lane) 25:288
Sleep It Off, Lady (Rhys) 14:446-47; 19:390
"Sleep like a Hammer" (Ai) 14:8; 69:7
A Sleep of Prisoners (Fry) 2:143-44; 10:200, 202
The Sleep of Reason (Buero Vallejo)
    See *El sueño de la razón*
The Sleep of Reason (Snow) 4:501-02; 19:427-28
The Sleep of the Great Hypnotist: The Life and Death and Life after Death of a Modern Magician (Redgrove) 41:356
"Sleep of the Valiant" (Elytis) 49:107; 100:175
"Sleep Tight" (Purdy) 52:350
Sleep Two, Three, Four! A Political Thriller (Neufeld) 17:309
Sleep Watch (Tillinghast) 29:414-15, 417
"The Sleeper" (Hope) 51:214
"The Sleeper" (Moss) 45:287
Sleeper (Allen) 16:4-6, 9, 15; 52:38-9
"The Sleeper Wakes" (Fauset) 54:183-84, 186-87
"Sleepers" (Honig) 33:211
The Sleepers (Tate) 25:427
Sleepers Awake (Patchen) 18:392
Sleepers in Moon-Crowned Valleys (Purdy) 2:350; 10:424
"Sleepers Joining Hands" (Bly) 38:52, 57
Sleepers Joining Hands (Bly) 2:66; 10:55-9, 61-2; 15:63, 65-6
The Sleepers of Roraima (Harris) 25:217
"Sleeping Beauty" (Broumas) 73:3, 13
"The Sleeping Beauty" (Sitwell) 9:494-95
The Sleeping Beauty (Carruth) 84:118-21, 123, 128-31, 136
Sleeping Beauty (Macdonald) 3:308-09; 14:328, 332, 335-36; 41:270
The Sleeping Beauty (Sitwell) 67:312, 317-18, 324, 334
The Sleeping Beauty (Taylor) 29:407, 411-12
"The Sleeping Beauty Syndrome: The New Agony of Single Men" (Wasserstein) 90:432
The Sleeping Car Murders (Japrisot)
    See *Compartiment tueurs*
"Sleeping Compartment" (MacCaig) 36:283
Sleeping Dog (Gray) 36:200
Sleeping Dogs Lie (Gloag) 40:210
"The Sleeping Fury" (Bogan) 39:388, 390, 393, 395-96; 46:80-1, 84; 93:60-1, 67-8, 81, 85, 87-90
The Sleeping Fury (Bogan) 46:79-81, 83, 89-90; 93:105
The Sleeping Gypsy and Other Poems (Garrett) 3:192; 51:141-42, 145
"Sleeping in a Jar" (Zappa) 17:586
"Sleeping in the Forest" (Oliver) 98:267, 269, 271
"Sleeping in the Jon-Boat" (Bottoms) 53:32
Sleeping in the Sun (Bioy Casares)
    See *Dormir al sol*
Sleeping in the Woods (Wagoner) 5:475; 15:558
A Sleeping Life (Rendell) 28:386-87; 48:320
"Sleeping like Dogs" (Calvino) 33:102
"The Sleeping Lord" (Jones) 7:191; 42:240
The Sleeping Lord and Other Fragments (Jones)

4:260, 262; 7:187-89, 191; 13:311; 42:238, 242, 246-49
Sleeping Murder (Christie) 8:142; 12:121
"Sleeping on the Ceiling" (Bishop) 9:97
"Sleeping on the Wing" (O'Hara) 78:346
"Sleeping Out at Easter" (Dickey) 109:265
"Sleeping Overnight on the Shore" (Swenson) 14:518
The Sleeping Partner (Graham) 23:192
"Sleeping Standing Up" (Bishop) 32:34
"The Sleeping Trees" (Shapcott) 38:400, 403
"Sleeping with One Eye Open" (Strand) 71:282-83
Sleeping With One Eye Open (Strand) 18:514-16; 41:436; 71:278, 281-82, 284, 518
"Sleeping with the Television On" (Joel) 26:220-22
"Sleeping with Women" (Koch) 44:243, 251
"Sleeping with You" (Updike) 43:435
"Sleepless at Crown Point" (Wilbur) 14:580; 110:383
"Sleepless Atlantic Boy" (Schwartz) 10:465
Sleepless Days (Becker)
    See *Schlaflose Tage*
"Sleepless Night" (Damas)
    See "Nuit blanche"
"Sleepless Night" (Davies) 21:102
Sleepless Nights (Hardwick) 13:265-66
"Sleep's Dark and Silent Gate" (Browne) 21:39
Sleeps Six (Raphael) 14:439
Sleeps Six, and Other Stories (Raphael) 14:438
"A Sleepwalker" (Moravia) 7:244
Sleepwalker (Davies) 21:101, 104
The Sleepwalkers (Ezekiel) 61:97-9
The Sleepwalkers: A History of Man's Changing Vision of the Universe (Koestler) 33:235
"Sleepwalking Solo" (Dybek) 114:62
"Sleepy-Heads" (Sandburg) 35:352
"Sleet" (MacCaig) 36:283
Sleuth (Shaffer) 19:413-15
"A Slice of Wedding Cake" (Graves) 45:173
Slick But Not Streamlined: Poems and Short Pieces (Betjeman) 6:68; 34:305; 43:32
"Slick Gonna Learn" (Ellison) 114:93
Slide Rule (Shute) 30:372
"The Slides" (Rich) 73:330
Slides (Plante) 23:342-44
"Slides from Our Recent European Trip" (Piercy) 62:377
"Slides of Verona" (Wright) 6:580
Sliding (Norris) 14:388
Slight Abrasions (Vizenor) 103:296
A Slight Ache (Pinter) 6:408, 413, 420; 11:437-38, 440-41; 15:422; 27:385-86, 393; 58:373-74, 384; 73:247, 251, 279
"A Slight Disorder" (Keates) 34:201-03
"A slight relax of air where cold was" (Larkin) 64:258
The Slightest Distance (Bromell) 5:74
"Slightly Higher in Canada" (Grayson) 38:212
The Slightly Irregular Fire Engine: Or; The Hithering Thithering Djinn (Barthelme) 59:246
"Sligo and Mayo" (MacNeice) 53:237
"Slim Greer" (Brown) 59:262, 265-66
"Slim Hears 'The Call'" (Brown) 59:262
"Slim in Atlanta" (Brown) 59:266
"Slim in Hell" (Brown) 59:266
"Slim Slow Slider" (Morrison) 21:236
Slinger (Dorn) 10:156-57, 161
"Slip Kid" (Townshend) 17:536
"Slip, Slidin' Away" (Simon) 17:467

"Slipfoot and How He Nearly Always Never Gets What He Goes After" (Sandburg) 15:468

"Slippery Ice in New York" (Yevtushenko) 26:464

A Slipping-Down Life (Tyler) 59:202-04, 206; 103:236-39, 241, 244, 259, 263-64, 267

"A Slip-Up" (McGahern) 48:271

"Sliverlick" (Avison) 97:114

"Sloe Gin" (Heaney) 37:165

"Sloe Whisky" (Johnston) 51:243

Slogum House (Sandoz) 28:400-02, 405-07

"Sloop John B." (Wilson) 12:643, 653

"The Slope" (Wright) 53:429

"Sloth" (Dobyns) 37:76

"Sloth Moth" (Fuller) 28:157

Slouching towards Bethlehem (Didion) 3:127-28; 8:174-77; 14:151, 153; 32:149

Slouching towards Kalamazoo (De Vries) 28:111-12; 46:137

"Slough" (Betjeman) 6:69; 43:33, 37, 44-5, 50

"Slovenski vecheri" (Bagryana) 10:12

"Slovo" ("The Word") (Akhmadulina) 53:12

Slow Approach of Thunder (Paustovsky) 40:360-61

"Slow Black Dog" (McFadden) 48:248

"A Slow Burn" (Weiss) 8:546

"The Slow Classroom" (Baxter) 78:29

A Slow Dance (Montague) 13:392; 46:271-74, 279

"Slow Death" (Caldwell) 60:60

"Slow Dissolve" (Grenville) 61:155

Slow Homecoming (Handke)
See *Slow Journey Home*

Slow Journey Home (*Slow Homecoming*) (Handke) 38:224-25, 228-29

Slow Learner: Early Stories (Pynchon) 33:338-40; 62:431, 433, 451

"Slow Music" (Tiptree) 48:389; 50:357

The Slow Natives (Astley) 41:45-6, 48

"The Slow of Despond" (Thomas) 107:338-42

"Slow Pace of the Future" (Char) 55:288

"The Slow Pacific Swell" (Winters) 4:593

"Slow Sculpture" (Sturgeon) 22:412; 39:361, 364, 366, 368

"Slow Tango for Six Horses" (Szirtes) 46:394-95

"Slow Train" (Dylan) 77:186-87, 189

Slow Train Coming (Dylan) 77:176, 186-87, 189

The Slow Train to Milan (Teran) 36:420-22

"Slow Walker" (Gunn) 32:214

Slowly by Thy Hand Unfurled (Linney) 51:257-58

Slowly, Slowly I Raise the Gun (Bennett) 35:46

Slowly, Slowly in the Wind (Highsmith) 14:261

"Slowly./Town" (Cummings) 68:37

Slowness (Kundera) 115:357, 359-60

Slub (*Le mariage; The Marriage; The Marriage Ceremony*) (Gombrowicz) 11:239; 49:122-26, 128-29

Sluchai na stantsii Krechetovka [i] *Matrenin dvor* (*We Never Make Mistakes*) (Solzhenitsyn) 7:435

"Slug in Woods" (Birney) 6:78

"Sluggishness" (Akhmadulina) 53:15

Slumber Party Massacre (Brown) 79:169

Slumgullion Stew (Abbey) 36:21

"The Slump" (Updike) 23:473

Det slutna rummet (*The Locked Room*) (Wahloo) 7:502

Sly Fox (Gelbart) 21:127-28

"The Small" (Roethke) 3:433

"Small Action Poem" (Tomlinson) 13:548

"Small Animals at Night" (Hogan) 73:149

"The Small Assassin" (Bradbury) 42:35, 42

"Small Bear" (Dixon) 52:98

"The Small Blue Heron" (Wright) 3:541

A Small Book of Poems (Laughlin) 49:221

A Small Boy and Others (Baldwin) 13:48

"Small Brother of the Sea Gulls" (Ritsos) 31:324

Small Ceremonies (Shields) 91:169, 176; 113:395-401, 404-08, 410, 412-13, 424, 429, 437-38, 440, 442-45

Small Change (Truffaut)
See *L'argent de la poche*

Small Changes (Piercy) 3:384-85; 6:402-03; 27:373, 378, 380; 62:362-65, 373, 376, 381

Small Chronicle of Great Days (Paz)
See *Pequeña crónica de grandes días*

"Small Comment" (Sanchez) 116:277

Small Craft Warnings (Williams) 2:465-66; 5:502, 504; 7:544, 546; 8:549; 11:573, 575; 15:581-82; 19:472; 45:450; 111:392

A Small Desperation (Abse) 29:16

"Small Dirge" (Redgrove) 41:348

"Small Elegy" (Ciardi) 44:382

Small Faces (Soto) 80:284-85

"The Small Family" (Kelman) 58:298

A Small Family Business (Ayckbourn) 74:16-17, 19-20, 22, 24, 27-9, 31, 34-5

"Small Frogs Killed on a Highway" (Wright) 5:520

Small g: A Summer Idyll (Highsmith) 102:217-19, 221

"Small Game" (Levine) 14:317

"Small Garden near a Field" (Gallagher) 63:125-26

"A Small Girl Swinging" (Szirtes) 46:395

"A Small, Good Thing" (Carver) 36:101-04; 53:63, 65

"Small Green Sea" (Elytis) 100:173

Small Heroics (Richards) 59:187

The Small Hours (Kaufman) 38:266

Small Is Beautiful: Economics As If People Mattered (Schumacher) 80:261-66, 268, 272-74

"Small Is My Cinema, Deep Is My Doze" (Perelman) 23:336

"Small Island Republics" (Apple) 33:21

"The Small Lady" (O'Faolain) 70:315

"Small Memoriam for Myself" (Kaufman) 49:205

"Small Ode to a Black Cuban Boxer" (Guillen)
See "Pequeña oda a un negro boxeador cubano"

"A Small Personal Voice" (Lessing) 94:252, 256, 287, 293

A Small Personal Voice: Essays, Reviews, Interviews (Lessing) 1:175; 6:296; 22:280

"Small Philosophical Poem" (Stevenson) 33:382

"A Small Piece of Blue" (Levine) 54:300

A Small Place (Kincaid) 68:206-07, 209, 217

"The Small Rain" (Pynchon) 33:332-33, 338-40; 62:431

Small Rain (Delbanco) 6:130

The Small Rain (L'Engle) 12:344

"The Small Room" (Fisher) 25:158

The Small Room (Sarton) 4:471; 49:322; 91:245

"A Small Room in Qingyün Lane" (Ding Ling)

68:57

"Small Suite in Red Major" (Ritsos) 31:332

"A Small Summit" (Ezekiel) 61:107

"Small Tactics" (Atwood) 25:67

A Small Town (Hearon) 63:165-67

Small Town (Wilson) 32:448-49

A Small Town in Germany (le Carre) 5:232-34

"A Small Variation" (Paz) 65:201

The Small War of Sergeant Donkey (Daly) 17:91

"Small White House" (Warren) 8:538

"Small World" (Gotlieb) 18:191

"Small World" (Sondheim) 30:377

Small World (Lodge) 36:277-78

The Smaller Sky (Wain) 46:416-19

"The Smallest Part" (Gold) 42:197

"The Smallest Woman in the World" (Lispector) 43:269

"Smart" (Robison) 42:342-43

Smarter and Smoother (Daly) 17:88

The Smartest Man in Ireland (*Patrick Kentigern Keenan*) (Hunter) 21:155-56

"The Smartest Woman in America" (Colwin) 5:108

Smash (Kanin) 22:233

"The Smatterers" (Solzhenitsyn) 78:403

"The Smell" (Clarke) 53:96

"Smell" (Peacock) 60:294

"The Smell of Death and Flowers" (Gordimer) 33:178-79

"The Smell of Gasoline Ascends in My Nose" (Amichai) 57:44

The Smell of Hay (Bassani) 9:77

"Smelling the Best" ("Myrisai to áriston") (Elytis) 100:171, 176

"Smerdyakov with a Guitar" (Belitt) 22:52

Smesné lásky (*Laughable Loves; Ridiculous Loves; Risibles Amours*) (Kundera) 4:276-78; 9:320; 19:267, 269-70; 32:259-60, 266; 68:232, 234, 239-42, 244,250, 254, 266; 115:307-08, 322, 346, 350

"The Smile" (Bradbury) 98:109

"The Smile" (Finch) 18:154

"The Smile" (Hughes) 2:203

"The Smile" (Morgan) 23:297

Smile (Nyro) 17:317-19

"Smile a Beast-Smile" (Dacey) 51:79

"Smile Away" (McCartney) 35:279-80, 283

"The Smile beneath the Smile" (Colwin) 84:146, 149-50

A Smile in His Lifetime (Hansen) 38:238, 240

A Smile in the Mind's Eye (Durrell) 27:94-5

"The Smile of a Turtle" (De Marinis) 54:99

The Smile of the Lamb (Grossman) 67:73-6

"The Smile of Winter" (Carter) 5:101-03

"Smile Please" (Abse) 29:20

Smile Please: An Unfinished Autobiography (Rhys) 19:391-95; 51:366-67, 370-71

"The Smile Was" (Abse) 29:18

"Smilers" (Johnston) 51:240

Smiles of a Summer Night (Bergman)
See *Sommarnattens leende*

Smiles on Washington Square (Federman) 47:130, 132

Smiley Smile (Wilson) 12:641-43, 645, 649-50, 652

Smiley's People (le Carre) 15:324-26; 28:228-29, 231

Smilla's Sense of Snow (*Miss Smilla's Feeling for Snow*) (Hoeg) 95:103-19

Smith (Garfield) 12:217-18, 224-25, 227-32, 234-36, 239

Smith (Maugham) 15:366
Smith of Wooton Major (Tolkien) 2:434; 12:570, 574
"Smithy" (Duerrenmatt) 102:61-2
"SMLE" (Murray) 40:336
Smog (Calvino)
   See *La nuvola di smog*
"Smoke" (Faulkner) 3:157
"Smoke" (Robison) 42:339
"Smoke" (Ryan) 65:209
Smoke, and Other Early Stories (Barnes) 29:32
"Smoke and Steel" (Sandburg) 10:450
Smoke and Steel (Sandburg) 10:448-51; 15:466; 35:340-41, 343, 352
Smoke Ghost (Leiber) 25:303
Smoke on the Ground (Delibes) 8:169
"Smoke over the Prairie" (Richter) 30:307
"The Smoke Shop Owner's Daughter" (Garrigue) 8:240
"Smokers" (Wolff) 64:448-49
Smokescreen (Francis) 2:142-43; 42:148, 154, 156-57; 102:156, 158
"Smokey" (Kristofferson) 26:267
Smokey (Robinson) 21:344
Smokey Robinson and the Miracles, 1957-1972 (Robinson) 21:344
Smokey's Family Robinson (Robinson) 21:347
Smokin' (Robinson) 21:348
"Smokin' O.P.'s" (Seger) 35:378-79
The Smoking Mountain: Stories of Postwar Germany (Boyle) 19:64; 58:64, 66, 74
"Smoky the Bear Bodhisattva" (Rexroth) 112:364
"Smooth Gnarled Crape Myrtle" (Moore) 13:396
"Smothered by the World" (Bly) 10:57
"Smudging" (Wakoski) 7:505
Smudging (Wakoski) 2:459; 4:572-73
Smug Minority (Berton) 104:44, 47
"The Smuggler" (Singer) 69:314
A Smuggler's Bible (McElroy) 47:236-39, 241-42, 244
"The Smugglers of Lost Souls' Rock" (Gardner) 8:234-36
Smultronstället (*Wild Strawberries*) (Bergman) 16:47-50, 52-5, 59-62, 64-5, 69, 73-4, 79; 72:31-7, 39-41, 52
"Smut-Hunting in Pretoria" (Fussell) 74:124
"The Snail on the Slope" (Strugatskii and Strugatskii) 27:432, 434, 437
"Snail Pie" (Still) 49:366
"The Snail Watcher" (Highsmith) 102:185, 205
"Snails" (Oliver) 98:303
The Snail-Watcher, and Other Stories (Highsmith) 2:194
"The Snake" (Abse) 29:20
"The Snake" (Berry) 4:59
"The Snake" (Steinbeck) 13:529
"Snake Eyes" (Baraka) 5:45
The Snake Has All the Lines (Kerr) 22:256
The Snake Pit (Brand) 7:29
"Snakecharmer" (Plath) 9:432-33; 111:201
"Snakes" (Mahapatra) 33:281
"The Snakes" (Oliver) 34:249
Snakes (Young) 19:477-79
Snakes and Ladders (Bogarde) 19:42
"Snakes in the Winter" (Oliver) 19:362
"Snake's Shoes" (Beattie) 8:57
"The Snake-Song" (Narayan) 28:303
"Snap Snap" (Barthelme) 6:29
The Snapper (Doyle) 81:156, 158-61
"Snapshot" (Fuller) 62:185

"A Snapshot of the Auxiliary" (Hugo) 6:245
"Snapshots" (Elytis) 100:171, 179, 189
Snapshots (Robbe-Grillet) 43:360
"Snapshots of a Daughter-in-Law" (Rich) 7:366, 371; 11:477-78; 18:445, 447; 36:366, 372-73, 375, 379; 76:210
Snapshots of a Daughter-in-Law: Poems, 1954-1962 (Rich) 6:457-58; 7:365, 368-69, 371-72; 11:476-77; 18:446; 36:366, 371-73, 375; 73:314, 324-25, 332; 76:209
The Snare (Spencer) 22:402-03, 405
The Snare of the Hunter (MacInnes) 27:282; 39:351
"A Snark in the Night" (Benford) 52:61
The Snarkout Boys and the Avocado of Death (Pinkwater) 35:318-20
The Snarkout Boys and the Baconburg Horror (Pinkwater) 35:320-21
The Snarling Citizen (Ehrenreich) 110:184-85
Sneaky People (Berger) 5:60-1; 8:83; 11:47; 18:58; 38:39-41
"The Sneering" (Campbell) 42:89
"The Sniper" (Sillitoe) 57:391, 395
Snipe's Castle (Mathias) 45:236-37
Snoopy and the Red Baron (Schulz) 12:527
"*Snoopy Come Home*" *Movie Book* (Schulz) 12:529
The Snoopy Festival (Schulz) 12:531
"Snoring in New York—An Elegy" (Denby) 48:84
"The Snow" (Amichai) 116:105
"Snow" (Avison) 97:99-100, 102-04, 116, 121-22, 124, 126, 128-36
"Snow" (Baxter) 78:25
"Snow" (Beattie) 63:14, 16-18
"Snow" (Butler) 81:127
"Snow" (Dobyns) 37:78
"Snow" (Frost) 26:112
"The Snow" (Hall) 37:143
"Snow" (Kawabata) 107:108
"Snow" (MacNeice) 4:316
"Snow" (Mowat) 26:347
"Snow" (Phillips) 15:421
"The Snow" (Quasimodo) 10:428
Snow (Pa Chin) 18:373
"Snow Angel" (Vaughn) 62:456
"Snow at Roblin Lake" (Purdy) 14:434
The Snow Ball (Brophy) 6:99-100; 29:92-4, 97-8; 105:8, 10, 14, 29-30, 38
The Snow Ball (Gurney) 50:180
"The Snow Child" (Carter) 41:118
Snow Country (Kawabata)
   See *Yukiguni*
"Snow Country Weavers" (Welch) 14:558
"The Snow Curlew" (Watkins) 43:450, 454
"Snow Door" (Moure) 88:223-24
"Snow Drops" (Gluck) 81:173
Snow Falling on Cedars (Guterson) 91:103-08
"Snow in New York" (Swenson) 14:522
"Snow in San Anselmo" (Morrison) 21:234-35
"The Snow King" (Dove) 81:137
"The Snow Lamp" (Hayden) 37:157-59
The Snow Leopard (Matthiessen) 11:358-61; 32:290-91; 64:308-11, 316-17, 320, 325-27
The Snow Leopard (West) 14:568; 96:383
"Snow Leopards at the Denver Zoo" (Matthews) 40:320
"Snow Line" (Berryman) 25:96
"Snow Log" (Ammons) 25:42

"Snow Moon—Black Bear Gives Birth" (Oliver) 98:265
Snow on Snow (Stanton) 9:507-08
Snow on the Mountain (Clarke) 61:73-4
"Snow out of Season" (Warren) 39:262
"The Snow Party" (Mahon) 27:288-89, 292
The Snow Party (Mahon) 27:287-91
The Snow Pasture (Newby) 2:311
"Snow People" (Blaise) 29:73, 75
The Snow Poems (Ammons) 9:30-1; 25:41-3, 45; 57:58-9; 108:10-3, 24, 27-8, 35, 37, 55, 58
The Snow Queen (Vinge) 30:410-16
"Snow Signs" (Tomlinson) 45:400-01, 403
The Snow Walker (Mowat) 26:340-41, 344-45, 347
The Snow Was Black (Simenon)
   See *La neige était sale*
"Snow White" (Broumas) 73:5
"Snow White" (Sexton) 53:314
Snow White (Barthelme) 1:18; 2:39-42; 5:53-7; 6:29-31; 8:49-50; 13:54-5, 58, 62; 23:44-6, 48, 50; 46:38-9, 43, 45; 59:247-49; 115:53, 55, 57-9, 64-5, 68-9, 71-4, 76-9, 81, 86, 94, 99
"Snowball" (Janowitz) 43:212
"A Snowball in Hell" (Ashbery) 77:65
"Snowbed" (Celan)
   See "Schneebett"
"Snowdrift" (Scott) 22:373
Snowdrop Festivities (Hrabal)
   See *Slavnosti snezenek*
"Snowfall" (Gunn) 32:211
"The Snowfall" (Justice) 102:269
"Snowfall" (Merwin) 18:332
"Snowfall" (Oates) 33:294
"Snowfall" (Strand) 41:432
"Snowgoose" (Allen) 84:4
"Snowing in Greenwich Village" (Updike) 13:563
The Snowless Time (Haavikko)
   See *Lumeton aika*
"The Snowman on the Moor" (Plath) 111:165, 202
"Snowman, Snowman" (Frame) 66:144; 96:185-86, 192
Snowman, Snowman: Fables and Fantasies (Frame) 22:143; 96:188-89, 191
"Snowmen" (Millhauser) 54:326-27
"Snows" (Perse)
   See "Neiges"
"The Snows Are Melted, the Snows Are Gone" (Tiptree) 48:385
"The Snows of Kilimanjaro" (Hemingway) 3:234; 6:226, 229-31; 8:283; 10:266; 13:271, 277; 19:212-13, 219; 30:179, 183; 34:478; 39:430; 41:197, 203, 206; 50:427, 431; 61:203; 80:121, 150
"Snowshoeing Back to Camp in Gloaming" (Warren) 18:539
The Snowstorm (Leonov)
   See *Metel*
"A Snowy Day" (Shiga) 33:367
"Snowy Heron" (Ciardi) 40:157-58; 44:382
"A Snowy Night on West Forty-Ninth Street" (Brennan) 5:73
So All Their Praises (MacLennan) 92:306, 308
"So Bad" (McCartney) 35:292
So Big (Ferber) 18:150; 93:149, 156, 164, 171, 176-77, 179, 186-87
So Close to Life (Bergman)
   See *Nära livet*

"So ein Rummel" (Boell) 72:69

"So Far" (Merwin) 88:209, 213

So Far and Yet So Near (Konwicki)
See *Jak daleko stad, jak blisko*

So Far, So Good (Souster) 5:395

"So, for the Moment, Sweet, Is Peace" (Brutus)
43:91

"So Frost Astounds" (Warren) 13:573

"So Glad to See You Here" (McCartney) 35:286

*So Going Around Cities: New and Selected
Poems, 1958-1979* (Berrigan) 37:45

"So I Said I Am Ezra" (Ammons) 57:49; 108:14

"So I Went Down to the Ancient Harbor"
(Amichai) 57:44

"So I Wrote You a Song" (Seger) 35:379

"So Little He Is" (Cummings) 15:156

So Little Time (Marquand) 10:329, 331

"So Lonely" (Police, The) 26:364

So Long a Letter (Ba)
See *Une si longue lettre*

So Long, and Thanks for All the Fish (Adams)
60:2-4, 6-7

"So Long, Frank Lloyd Wright" (Simon)
17:460-61, 465

So Long, It's Been Good to Know You (Guthrie)
35:183-85, 189, 194

So Long on Lonely Street (Deer) 45:119-21

So Long, See You Tomorrow (Maxwell) 19:308-
09

"So Long? Stevens" (Berryman)
See "Dream Song 219"

"'So Long' to the Moon from the Men of
Apollo" (Swenson) 61:400; 106:327

"So Many Summers" (MacCaig) 36:284

"So Many Things Terrify, So Many" (Cisneros)
See "Tantas Cosas Asustan, Tantas"

"So Much Things to Say" (Marley) 17:270

"So Much Water So Close to Home" (Carver)
36:100; 53:64

"So Not to be Mottled" (Zamora) 89:369,
388, 390-91, 395

"So Often" (Damas)
See "Si souvent"

So Profit Disappeared from the World
(Haavikko)
See *Niin katosi voitto maailmasta*

"So Speaks the Poet T. H." (Cabral de Melo
Neto)
See "O poeta Thomas Hardy fala"

So the Wind Won't Blow It All Away (Brautigan)
34:315; 42:59-60

So This Is Depravity (Baker) 31:28-9

"So This Is Male Sexuality" (Blount) 38:46

"So Tired of Waiting for You" (Davies) 21:89,
97

So ward Abend und Morgen (Boell) 27:57;
72:71, 74

"So Why Not a Visit..." (Thesen) 56:419

"So You Say" (Strand) 41:432

*So, You're Getting Braces: A Guide to Orth-
odontics* (Silverstein and Silverstein)
17:456

"Soap" (Farrell) 66:112, 129

"Soap" (Stern) 40:413-14

Soap Opera (Davies) 21:99-100

"The Soap-Pig" (Muldoon) 72:273

Sobranie sochnenii (Voznesensky) 57:425

Sobre cultura femenina (*I On Feminine Culture*) (Castellanos) 66:54, 57

Sobre héroes y tumbas (*On Heroes and Tombs*)
(Sabato) 10:444-46; 23:378-82

Sobre los ángeles (Alberti) 7:7, 9

Sobrevivo (Alegria) 75:33-4

"So-Called Sonnets" (Ewart) 46:151

*The Social Context of Modern English Litera-
ture* (Bradbury) 32:51

Social Organization of Manua (Mead) 37:285

"Social Revolution in England" (Abse) 29:16

"Social Science" (Louie) 70:79-80

"Social Science Fiction" (Asimov) 92:20

Social Studies (Lebowitz) 36:248-50

Socialism and America (Howe) 85:138-39,
145, 150

La société de consommation (*Consumer Society*) (Baudrillard) 60:14-15, 25, 33

"Society, Morality, and the Novel" (Ellison)
114:112-13

"Society's Child" (Ian) 21:184

Society's Child (Ian) 21:182-84, 188

"Sociodowser" (Vizenor) 103:293, 297-98

Sociologie d'une révolution (Fanon)
See *L'an V de la révolution algérienne*

"Sock It to Me Santa" (Seger) 35:381

"Socks" (Hood) 28:193

Les socles (Tremblay) 29:426

"The Sod of Battlefields" (Davidson) 13:169

"Sodomy" (Ragni and Rado) 17:385

"Sofa Art" (Dickinson) 49:102-04

"Soft and Hard" (Phillips) 28:363

"Soft Come the Dragons" (Koontz) 78:198

The Soft Machine (Burroughs) 2:93; 5:92;
15:110-11; 22:82-3; 42:71, 73, 77, 79;
75:93, 97, 102, 106; 109:183, 185-86,
191, 194-96, 199, 207, 212, 229

The Soft Parade (Morrison) 17:288-89, 291-
92, 295

"The Soft Psyche of Joshua Logan" (Talese)
37:393, 403

The Soft Skin (Truffaut)
See *La peau douce*

Soft Targets (Poliakoff) 38:386

"The Soft Voice of the Serpent" (Gordimer)
70:178

The Soft Voice of the Serpent (Gordimer)
33:176-79; 70:162

"Soft Voices at Passenham" (White) 30:451

Softcops (Churchill) 31:90

"Soho" (Morgan) 31:273

"Soho Cinema" (Lorde) 71:260

"The Soho Hospital for Women" (Adcock)
41:16-17

"Soho: Saturday" (Abse) 29:14

Soie sauvage (Broumas) 73:8, 13-14

La soif et la faim (*Hunger and Thirst*) (Ionesco)
6:251, 253-54; 11:292, 294; 41:225, 227;
86:340

"The Soil-Map" (McGuckian) 48:277

"The Soirée of Velvel Kleinburger" (Klein)
19:258

"Sojourn in X" (Boell)
See "Aufenthalt in X"

"Sojourner" (Dillard) 60:75; 115:205

"The Sojourner" (McCullers) 10:335; 12:413,
433

"Sol" (Tolson) 105:262

"Sol de lluria" (Guillen) 79:240

El sol y los MacDonald (Marques) 96:224-25,
228, 240

"Sola la muerte" ("Death Alone") (Neruda)
7:257

"Solar" (Larkin) 5:229-31; 8:333; 18:295-
96; 33:259-61; 64:265, 268-69, 285

"The Solar Corona" (Swenson) 61:397

Solar Lottery (Dick) 72:120

"Solar System" (Wilson) 12:652

"Solar Throat Slashed" (Cesaire) 32:113

Solaris (Lem) 8:343-45; 15:327-28; 40:290,
293, 295-98, 300

Solaris (Tarkovsky) 75:370-72, 375-80, 382-
85, 387, 389-90, 398, 402-03, 406-12

Soldado razo (*Buck Private; The Chicano Soldier*) (Valdez) 84:396, 406, 413, 415

"Soldados en Abisinia" ("Soldiers in Abyssinia")
(Guillen) 48:158; 79:235-37

Le soldat Dioclès (Audiberti) 38:30

"Solde" ("Sell Out") (Damas) 84:171-72, 176-
77

"The Soldier" (Bitov) 57:114

"A Soldier" (Frost) 13:227

"Soldier" (Ignatow) 40:258

The Soldier (Aiken) 52:26

"Soldier Asleep" (McGinley) 14:367

A Soldier Erect (Aldiss) 5:14; 14:14

"Soldier from the Wars Returning" (Brown)
48:55

"Soldier in the Blanket" (Kotzwinkle) 35:254

Soldier in the Rain (Goldman) 48:124, 128

Soldier of Fortune (Gann) 23:164

A Soldier of the Revolution (Just) 27:226

Soldier, Soldier (Arden) 13:28; 15:19

The Soldiers (Hochhuth) 4:231-32; 18:251,
253

The Soldier's Art (Powell) 3:400; 7:345

"Soldiers Bathing" (Prince) 22:338-39

"A Soldier's Declaration" (Sassoon) 36:394

"The Soldier's Dream" (Scannell) 49:329-30,
332

A Soldier's Embrace (Gordimer) 18:188-91

"Soldier's Home" (Hemingway) 3:242; 19:211;
30:181, 189-90, 192, 201-02; 50:428

"Soldiers in Abyssinia" (Guillen)
See "Soldados en Abisinia"

Soldiers in Hiding (Wiley) 44:118-20

"Soldier's Joy" (Wolff) 64:450, 453-54

Soldier's Joy (Bell) 102:4-5, 8, 11, 17, 22

The Soldiers of No Country (Ferlinghetti)
111:63

"Soldiers of the Republic" (Parker) 68:328,
336

Soldiers' Pay (Faulkner) 8:214; 9:199-201;
11:201; 28:140-41, 145; 52:108, 112;
68:127

A Soldier's Play (Fuller) 25:181-82

"A Soldier's Son" (Boland) 40:96, 98; 113:122

"Soldiers Surround" (Ignatow) 40:261

"The Soldier's Wish" (Smith) 64:388

Sold-Out (*Turn of a Pang*) (Brossard) 115:105-
06, 110-11, 155

Sole Survivor (Gee) 29:178-79

Soledad (*Loneliness*) (Paz) 19:367

"Soledad. =f. Solitude, Loneliness, Homesickness; Lonely Retreat" (Rich) 76:219

"Soledades of the Sun and Moon" (Hope)
51:215, 217-18, 226

"Soleil" (Reverdy) 53:289

Soleil Cou-Coupé (Cesaire) 112:7, 15, 29

Soleil de la conscience (Glissant) 68:180-81,
187

Le soleil des eaux (Char) 11:115

Soleil des loups (Mandiargues) 41:278

Soleil noir: Dépression et melancholie (*Black
Sun: Depression and Melancholia*)
(Kristeva) 77:314, 317-19, 324-25, 327,
333

"Le soleil placé en abîme" (Ponge) 18:418

Soleils (Gascar) 11:222

"Les soleils chanteurs" (Char) 14:127

The Solemn Communion (Arrabal)
See *La communion solonelle*

Solemn Tightrope Walking (Oe)
See *Genshuku natsunawatari*
"A Solemne Musick" (L'Heureux) **52**:272, 274
Solemnly Walking the Tightrope (Oe)
See *Genshuku natsunawatari*
Solent Shore (Hooker) **43**:197-201
"Solent Winter" (Hooker) **43**:197
"Soles occidere et redire poussunt" (Huxley) **5**:192; **11**:284
Los soles truncos (Marques) **96**:224, 226-28, 240-41, 249-50, 252
"Solfeggietto" (Rich) **73**:330
"Solid Geometry" (McEwan) **13**:370
The Solid Gold Cadillac (Kaufman) **38**:267
The Solid Gold Kid (Mazer) **26**:291-92
The Solid Mandala (White) **3**:521-23; **4**:583-86; **5**:485-88; **7**:529, 532; **65**:275-77, 279-82; **69**:401, 403-06, 408, 410, 412
"Solid Rock" (Dylan) **77**:185-89, 191
Solidão solitude (Dourado) **23**:150
Soliloquies of a Chalk Giant (Hooker) **43**:197-99, 201
"Soliloquio del individuo" (Parra) **102**:344
"Soliloquy" (Jeffers) **54**:237, 242
"Soliloquy" (Prokosch) **48**:310
"Soliloquy of the Spanish Cloister" (Howard) **7**:168
"Soliloquy on a Southern Strand" (Montague) **46**:265-66
"Solipsism and Theology" (Warren) **6**:558
"The Solipsist" (Cunningham) **31**:100
"Solitaire" (Garrett) **3**:192; **51**:144
Solitaire (Anderson) **23**:33
Le solitaire (*The Hermit*) (Ionesco) **6**:252, 256-57; **11**:290, 292-94; **86**:332
Solitaire/Double Solitaire (Anderson) **23**:33
The Solitaries (Walker) **13**:565
"El solitario" (Aleixandre) **9**:13
"Solitary" (Boland) **113**:60-1
"Solitary" (Wideman) **36**:455
A Solitary Blue (Voigt) **30**:420
"Solitary Confinement" (Kennedy) **42**:255
"The Solitary Daffodil" (Richards) **14**:455
"A Solitary Ewe" (Hood) **28**:189
"Solitary Man" (Diamond) **30**:111
"Solitary Swedish Houses" (Transtroemer)
See "Svenska hus ensligt belägna"
"Solitary Travel" (MacNeice) **4**:316
"A Solitude" (Levertov) **15**:338
"Solitude" (Transtroemer) **52**:412
"Solitude Late at Night in the Woods" (Bly) **10**:57
Solitudes (Vliet) **22**:441-43
Solitudes Crowded with Loneliness (Kaufman) **49**:202-03, 205
"Solja Work" (Bennett) **28**:29
Solo: An American Dreamer in Europe, 1933-34 (Morris) **37**:314-16
"Solo Dance" (Phillips) **15**:419
Solo Faces (Salter) **52**:361-63, 366-68
Solo for Two Voices (Paz) **3**:377
"A Solo Song: For Doc" ("Doc For Doc") (McPherson) **19**:309; **77**:351-52, 364, 366-67, 369
Solomon Gursky Was Here (Richler) **70**:219-33
"Solomon's Mines" (Hill) **45**:182
Solomon's Temple (Hoffman) **5**:184-85
"Solstice" (Lorde) **71**:236
Solstice (Oates) **33**:297-98; **52**:329, 336; **108**:386, 389-90
Solstice and Other Poems (Jeffers) **54**:237
Solstices (MacNeice) **4**:318; **53**:241

Solteria (Castellanos) **66**:48
Soluble Fish (Breton)
See *Manifeste du surréalisme. Poisson soluble*
"Solus Rex" (Nabokov) **3**:354
"Solution Unsatisfactory" (Heinlein) **55**:302-03
"Solving the Riddle" (Simic) **9**:478
Solzhenitsyn: A Biography (Scammell) **34**:480-82, 484, 487, 489-92
"Somali Legend" (Jensen) **37**:192
"Somber Prayer" (Berryman) **13**:82
La sombra del ciprés es alrgada (*Long is the Cypress' Shadow*) (Delibes) **18**:109, 111, 117
Sombra del paraiso (*Shadow of Paradise*) (Aleixandre) **9**:11, 16; **36**:24, 26, 28, 30
Sombra e exílio (Dourado) **23**:150-51
"Sombre" (Reverdy) **53**:290
Sombrero Fallout: A Japanese Novel (Brautigan) **9**:124; **12**:73; **42**:49, 56
Some Achieve Greatness (Swinnerton) **31**:428
"Some Against Natural Selection" (Hirsch) **31**:214
Some American Feminists (Brossard) **115**:117
Some American People (Caldwell) **60**:53, 60-1, 66
Some Americans: A Personal Record (Tomlinson) **45**:395-96, 402-03, 405
Some Angry Angel: A Mid-Century Faerie Tale (Condon) **4**:107; **45**:92, 96; **100**:111-12
"Some Any" (Ammons) **57**:53
"Some Approaches to the Problem of the Shortage of Time" (Le Guin) **45**:216
"Some Are Born to Sweet Delight" (Gordimer) **70**:177, 180
"Some Autumn Characters" (Stafford) **29**:379
"Some Beasts" (Neruda) **1**:247
"Some Blind Alleys: A Letter" (Cioran) **64**:78, 99
Some Business Recently Transacted in the White World (Dorn) **10**:160
Some Came Running (Jones) **1**:162; **3**:261; **10**:292; **39**:405-07, 412, 415
Some Changes (Jordan) **5**:203
"Some Children of the Goddess" (Mailer) **8**:371
Some Corner of an English Field (Abse) **29**:12
"Some Correspondence with Theodore Dreiser" (Farrell) **66**:138
"Some Dangers to American Writing" (Cowley) **39**:460
"Some Day I'll Find You" (Coward) **1**:65
"Some Day You'll Be Sorry" (Cozzens) **92**:201
Some Deaths in the Delta (Brown) **32**:62-3
"Some Different Meanings of the Concept of 'Difference'" **65**:339
Some Doves and Pythons (Elliott) **38**:178
"Some Dreamers of the Golden Dream" (Didion) **14**:153
"Some Dreams They Forgot" (Bishop) **32**:34
"Some Echo" (Creeley) **36**:121
"Some Final Questions" (Webb) **18**:540
Some Follow the Sea (Felsen) **17**:120
"Some Foreign Letters" (Sexton) **15**:472; **53**:312, 321
"Some General Instructions" (Koch) **8**:323; **44**:244, 249, 251
"Some Get Wasted" (Marshall) **72**:248
Some Girls (Jagger and Richard) **17**:239-40, 242
"Some Impediments to Christian Commitment" (Smith) **25**:421
Some Inner Fury (Markandaya) **38**:320-23

"Some Kind of a Love Story" (Miller) **47**:253
Some Kind of Grace (Jenkins) **52**:219, 225-26, 228
Some Kind of Hero (Kirkwood) **9**:320
"Some Kinda Love" (Reed) **21**:309, 311, 322
"Some Last Questions" (Merwin) **13**:385
Some Lie and Some Die (Rendell) **28**:384-85; **48**:320
Some Like It Hot (Wilder) **20**:459, 463, 465-66
"Some Like Poetry" (Szymborska)
See "Some People Like Poetry"
"Some Limitations of English" (Bunting) **47**:52
"Some Lines on the State of the Universe" (Faludy) **42**:141
"Some Love" (Ginsberg) **36**:197
"Some Marvelous Quarry" (Squires) **51**:383
"Some Memories of the Glorious Bird and an Earlier Self" (Vidal) **8**:527-28; **10**:501
Some Men Are Brothers (Enright) **31**:146, 148
Some Merry-Go-Round Music (Stolz) **12**:551
"Some Monday for Sure" (Gordimer) **10**:239; **33**:182-83
"Some Money" (Ashbery) **77**:68
"Some Mother" (Bukowski) **41**:73
"Some Mother's Son" (Davies) **21**:91
"Some Musicians Play Chamber Music for Us" (Bronk) **10**:75
"Some Natural Things" (Laughlin) **49**:224
"Some New Ruins" (Corn) **33**:116
"Some Notes on Organic Form" (Levertov) **66**:242
"Some Notes on Recent American Fiction" (Bellow) **6**:58; **13**:73
"Some Notes on Silence" (Graham) **48**:151
"Some Notes on Time in Fiction" (Welty) **14**:567; **105**:378-80, 382
"Some Notions" (Arghezi)
See "Notiunile"
"Some Novelists I Have Known" (Maugham) **67**:216
"Some Observations on Naturalism, So-Called, in Fiction" (Farrell) **66**:134-35, 137
"Some of These Days" (Purdy) **52**:350
"Some of Us Are Exiles from No Land" (O Hehir) **41**:322
Some of Your Blood (Sturgeon) **39**:361, 364-67
"Some Old Tires" (Ashbery) **25**:56
Some One Sweet Angel Chile (Williams) **89**:321, 324, 330, 332
Some Other Summer (Adler) **35**:13
"Some Passages of Isaiah" (Pinsky) **94**:303
"Some People" (Jordan) **114**:146, 149
"Some People Like Poetry" ("Some Like Poetry") (Szymborska) **99**:208-10
"Some People Never Know" (McCartney) **35**:280
Some People, Places, and Things That Will Not Appear in My Next Novel (Cheever) **15**:127
"Some Poems for Max Ernst" (Bly) **15**:62
Some Prefer Nettles (Tanizaki)
See *Tade ku mushi*
"Some Quadrangles" (Swenson) **61**:403; **106**:335
"Some Reasons Why I Tell the Stories I Tell the Way I Tell Them rather than Some Other Sort of Stories Some Other Way" (Barth) **51**:24-5
Some Recent Attacks: Essays Cultural and Po-

litical (Kelman)   **86**:185

"Some Remarks on Humor" (White)   **10**:531

"Some Secrets" (Stern)   **40**:412

Some Soul to Keep (Cooper)   **56**:71-2

"Some South American Poets" (Koch)   **44**:243

"Some Sunny Day" (Beer)   **58**:38

Some Sweet Day (Williams)   **42**:442, 445

"Some Talk of Peace" (Blunden)   **56**:30

Some Tame Gazelle (Pym)   **37**:375-79; **111**:233-38, 240, 243-48, 254, 263-64, 267, 269-71, 273, 278, 283-87

"Some There Are Fearless" (Page)   **18**:379

"Some Thoughts about the Line" (Simic)   **68**:366

"Some Thoughts on Juvenile Delinquency" (Steinbeck)   **21**:380

"Some Thoughts on Playwriting" (Wilder)   **82**:356, 385

"Some Trees" (Ashbery)   **41**:40

Some Trees (Ashbery)   **2**:16-17; **4**:22-4; **9**:42-4; **13**:31, 34-5; **15**:26; **25**:49, 55, 57-8; **41**:40; **77**:42, 44, 50, 52, 58, 70

Some Unease and Angels (Feinstein)   **36**:170

Some Versions of Pastoral (*English Pastoral Poetry*) (Empson)   **8**:202; **19**:153-54; **33**:145, 147-48, 150; **34**:336-38, 340

"Some Women" (Garrett)   **3**:192

"Some Words" (Ashbery)   **4**:21

Some Write to the Future: Essays on Contemporary Latin American Fiction (Dorfman)   **77**:153, 155

"Somebody Always Grabs the Purple" (Roth)   **104**:249, 267

Somebody Else's Life (Philipson)   **53**:276-77

Somebody in Boots (Algren)   **4**:16; **10**:5; **33**:13

Somebody Owes Me Money (Westlake)   **33**:436

"Somebody Who Cares" (McCartney)   **35**:290-91

Somebody's Darling (McMurtry)   **11**:371; **27**:331-33; **44**:254

"Somebody's Life" (Urdang)   **47**:400

Someday (Seger)   **35**:378

Someday, Maybe (Stafford)   **4**:521; **7**:460-61

"Someday We're Gonna Tear Them Pillars Down" (Dodson)   **79**:192

"Somehow we survive" (Brutus)   **43**:90

Someone (Pinget)   **37**:361

Someone Else (Tindall)   **7**:473-74

Someone Else Is Still Someone (Pomerance)   **13**:444

"Someone Has Disturbed the Roses" (Garcia Marquez)
See "Alguien desordena estas rosas"

"Someone in a Tree" (Sondheim)   **30**:388, 390, 397, 400, 402

"Someone in the Review Board" (Carroll)   **38**:103

"Someone Is Beating a Woman" (Voznesensky)   **57**:414

"Someone Is Probably Dead" (Bell)   **31**:51

Someone Just Like You (Yurick)   **6**:583-84

Someone Like You (Dahl)   **79**:175, 177

Someone to Love (Mazer)   **26**:296

"Someone Walking Around" (Cortazar)
See "Alguien que anda por ahí"

"Someone Writes to the Future: Meditations on Hope and Violence in García Márquez" (Dorfman)   **77**:156

"Someone You Have Seen Before" (Ashbery)   **77**:63-4

"Somersault" (MacDiarmid)   **19**:286

Somersault (Konwicki)
See *Salto*

"Somerville" (Hill)   **113**:281, 291, 312

"Something" (Oliver)   **34**:247, 249; **98**:257

Something about a Death, Something about a Fire (Straub)   **107**:305

Something about a Soldier (Harris)   **19**:200, 203

"Something about a Viet Cong Flag" (Bukowski)   **108**:87

"Something about England" (Clash)   **30**:48

"Something about Him" (Williams)   **45**:454

"Something about It" (Hollander)   **8**:300

"Something Else" (Akhmadulina)
See "Drugoe"

Something Else (Davies)   **21**:90, 105

"Something, Everything, Anything, Nothing" (O'Faolain)   **14**:406

Something Going (Lipsyte)   **21**:210

Something Happened (Heller)   **5**:173-83; **8**:278-80; **11**:268; **36**:225-28, 230; **63**:203-04

"Something Happened to Me Yesterday" (Jagger and Richard)   **17**:231, 238

Something I'll Tell You Tuesday (Guare)   **29**:204

Something in Common, and Other Stories (Hughes)   **10**:281

Something in Disguise (Howard)   **29**:245-46

"Something in the Night" (Springsteen)   **17**:483

"Something in the Water" (Prince)   **35**:328

Something in the Wind (Smith)   **25**:406-07, 410; **73**:342, 355

"Something Is in the Air" (Strand)   **18**:516

"Something I've Been Meaning to Tell You" (Munro)   **95**:286

Something I've Been Meaning to Tell You (Munro)   **6**:341-42; **10**:356-57; **19**:344; **50**:210; **95**:284, 293, 297, 301, 304, 313, 320, 322, 325

Something Left to Lose (Brancato)   **35**:66, 68

"Something Like a Sonnet for Phillis Miracle Wheatley" (Jordan)   **114**:145

"Something Missing" (L'Heureux)   **52**:278

"Something Must Happen" (Boell)   **39**:292

"Something Nice" (Gaitskill)   **69**:199

"Something Other than Our Own" (Lane)   **25**:289

Something Out There (Gordimer)   **33**:183-85; **51**:157; **70**:163-66, 182

Something Said (Sorrentino)   **40**:389-90

"Something So Right" (Simon)   **17**:466

"Something Strange" (Amis)   **40**:43

"Something the Cat Dragged In" (Highsmith)   **42**:215

"Something There Is about You" (Dylan)   **4**:150

Something to Answer For (Newby)   **13**:409

Something to Be Desired (McGuane)   **45**:263-65

"Something to Be Said for Silence" (Giovanni)   **64**:191

"Something to Look Forward To" (Piercy)   **62**:378

"Something to Nibble on in My Igloo" (Breytenbach)   **23**:84

Something to Say: William Carlos Williams on Younger Poets (Williams)   **42**:462

"Something to Tell Mother" (Orlovitz)   **22**:333

"Something to Tell the Girls" (Gardam)   **43**:167

"Something to Write Home About" (Ingalls)   **42**:230

Something Unspoken (Williams)   **11**:576

Something Wicked This Way Comes (Bradbury)   **3**:85; **10**:68-9; **42**:36, 42, 46; **98**:111, 144

"Something's Coming" (Sondheim)   **30**:389, 395, 400

"Something's Going On" (Ortiz)   **45**:301

Sometime in New York City/Live Jam (Lennon)   **12**:372-73; **35**:264-66, 271, 273

"Sometime—Later—Not Now" (Findley)   **102**:107-08

"Sometimes" (Nowlan)   **15**:399

"Sometimes a Fantasy" (Joel)   **26**:221

Sometimes a Great Notion (Kesey)   **6**:277-78; **11**:318; **46**:224, 226; **64**:216

Sometimes a Stranger (Weber)   **12**:635

"Sometimes All Over" (Coles)   **46**:111

Sometimes All Over (Coles)   **46**:107-11

"Sometimes, as a Child" (Broumas)   **73**:2, 8

"Sometimes I Am Very Happy and Desperate" (Amichai)   **116**:93

"Sometimes I Don't Mind" (Lightfoot)   **26**:282

Sometimes I Live in the Country (Busch)   **47**:63-5

"Sometimes . . . Injustice" (Kenny)   **87**:259

"Sometimes They Come Back" (King)   **113**:336

"Sometown" (Hoffman)   **6**:243

"A Somewhat Static Barcarolle" (Cassity)   **42**:98

Somewhere a Master: Further Hasidic Portraits and Legends (Wiesel)   **37**:456-57

"Somewhere a Roscoe ..." (Perelman)   **49**:258

"Somewhere above the Victim" (Yevtushenko)   **26**:468

"Somewhere along the Line" (Joel)   **26**:213

Somewhere among Us a Stone Is Taking Notes (Simic)   **9**:480; **68**:376

"Somewhere Behind" (Kundera)   **115**:321

"Somewhere, Belgium" (Kincaid)   **43**:249

"The Somewhere Doors" (Chappell)   **78**:116-17

"Somewhere Else" (Paley)   **37**:339

Somewhere Else (Kotlowitz)   **4**:275

"Somewhere Far from This Comfort" (Coles)   **46**:113

"Somewhere I Have Never Travelled, Gladly Beyond" (Cummings)   **3**:117; **15**:154; **68**:44

"Somewhere in Argentina" (Rosenblatt)   **15**:447

Somewhere in the House (Daly)   **52**:90

Somewhere in the Night (*The Chinese Agent*) (Moorcock)   **58**:347-49, 351

"Somewhere Is Such a Kingdom" (Ransom)   **2**:363; **4**:431

Somewhere Is Such a Kingdom: Poems, 1952-1971 (Hill)   **8**:293-94, 296

"Somewhere, My Man" (Mahapatra)   **33**:276

"Somewhere Near Phu Bai" (Komunyakaa)   **94**:226, 228

"Somewhere U.S.A." (Lightfoot)   **26**:280

Sommaren med Monika (*Summer with Monika*) (Bergman)   **16**:46, 60, 66

Sommarlek (*Illicit Interlude*; *Summer Interlude*; *Summerplay*) (Bergman)   **16**:46-7, 51-2, 60, 66, 72; **72**:40-1, 62

Sommarnattens leende (*Smiles of a Summer Night*) (Bergman)   **16**:46-7, 49, 51-3, 61, 64, 66, 69, 73, 79, 82; **72**:30-1, 40, 52, 54-5, 60-2

Somme athéologique (*Atheological Summa*) (Bataille)   **29**:44

Somme athéologique (Bataille)
See *Summa Atheologica*

Le sommeil délivré (*From Sleep Unbound*) (Chedid)   **47**:83-5, 88

"Sommerbericht" ("Summer Report") (Celan)   **53**:77

The Somnambulists (Elliott)   **47**:103

"Son" (Ian)   **21**:183

"The Son" (Levertov)   66:235, 237
"The Son" (MacBeth)   5:263
"Son" (Olds)   39:187
"The Son" (Swift)   41:443, 446
The Son (Berriault)   54:4; 109:90, 92
"Son and Heir" (Cozzens)   92:202
"Son and Heir" (Smith)   15:517
"Son de cloche" (Reverdy)   53:290
El son entero (*The Entire Son*) (Guillen)
   48:158, 162, 164, 168; 79:229, 240, 250
"A *son* for Antillian Children" (Guillen)   79:230
"The Son From America" (Singer)   6:509;
   111:337
Son Motifs (Guillen)
   See *Motivos de son*
Son nom de Venise dans Calcutta désert (Duras)
   40:178; 68:89, 96; 100:145
"Son number 6" (Guillen)
   See "Son numero 6"
Son number 6 (Guillen)
   See *Son número 6*
"Son numero 6" ("Son number 6") (Guillen)
   48:162; 79:250
Son número 6 (*Son number 6*) (Guillen)   79:231
Son of a Hundred Kings (Costain)   30:96
Son of a Smaller Hero (Richler)   5:371-75;
   13:485-86; 18:455; 46:347
"The Son of Andrés Aparicio" ("El hijo de
   Andrés Aparicio") (Fuentes)   22:171;
   60:165
"Son of Celluloid" (Barker)   52:53-4
"The Son of Karmaria" (Valenzuela)
   See "El hijo de Karmaria"
"The Son of Man" (Ginzburg)   70:280
The Son of Man (Mauriac)   56:219
Son of Man (Potter)   86:346
Son of Man (Roa Bastos)
   See *Hijo de hombre*
"Son of Msippi" (Dumas)   6:145; 62:155
"The Son of My Skin" (Redgrove)   41:351-52
"Son of Orange County" (Zappa)   17:591
"The Son of Perdition" (Cozzens)   11:125,
   131; 92:196, 198-99, 201
"Son of Satan" (Bukowski)   82:25
The Son of Someone Famous (Kerr)   12:297-
   99
Son of the Black Stallion (Farley)   17:115
A Son of the Circus (Irving)   112:173-74
Son of the Great Society (Buchwald)   33:91
Son of the Morning (Oates)   11:404; 15:401-
   02; 19:350, 354; 33:289
*Son of the Morning Star: Custer and the Little
   Bighorn* (Connell)   45:117-18
"Son of the Tree" (Vance)   35:420
Son of the Valley (Tunis)   12:596, 598
"Son the Beatiful Ones" (Kunene)   85:175
"Son venezolano" (Guillen)   48:161, 164
"A Son with a Future" (Reznikoff)   9:450
Un soñador para un pueblo (*A Dreamer for a
   People*) (Buero Vallejo)   15:97, 99, 101;
   46:96
Sonar Kella (*The Golden Fortress*) (Ray)
   76:356
"Sonata" (Schnackenberg)   40:380-81
"Sonatina in Blue" (Justice)   102:253
"Sonatina in Green" (Justice)   102:262-63,
   265
"Sonatina in Yellow" (Justice)   102:251-53,
   255, 258, 264-65
Sonderbare Begegnungen (Seghers)   7:409
Sondheim: A Musical Tribute (Sondheim)
   30:385, 387
"Sondra" (Van Duyn)   116:422, 429

"Song" (Abse)   29:16
"Song" (Bogan)   46:81, 86, 89
"Song" (Boland)   40:98, 100
"Song" (Creeley)   78:152
"Song" (Durrell)   27:97
"Song" (Fenton)   32:165-66
"Song" (Gluck)   81:167, 173
"Song" (H. D.)   73:118
"Song" (Heaney)   74:159, 163
"The Song" (Johnson)   52:232
"Song" (Justice)   102:269
"The Song" (Milosz)   56:233, 247
"The Song" (Roethke)   3:433; 19:399;
   101:263, 332
"Song" (Sitwell)   67:320
"Song" (Snodgrass)   18:491; 68:395
"Song" (Thomas)   6:530
"Song" (Winters)   32:467
"Song III" (Bishop)   15:59
"Song IV" (Bishop)   15:59
A Song, a Twilight (Coward)   29:139-40
Song about Death (Seifert)   34:260
"Song About Love" (Seifert)
   See "Písen o lásce"
"A Song about Major Eatherly" (Wain)   11:562
"Song against Broccoli" (Blount)   38:47
"Song and Dance" (Livesay)   79:349, 351
Song and Idea (Eberhart)   11:178; 19:143;
   56:76-8
Song and Strife (Lagerkvist)
   See *Sång och strid*
Song at the Year's Turning: Poems, 1942-1954
   (Thomas)   6:532; 13:542; 48:377, 380
"Song But Oblique to '47" (Avison)   97:68, 71
"Song by the Sea" (Lee)   90:182
"Song for a Dark Girl" (Hughes)   108:299
Song for a Dark Queen (Sutcliff)   26:437
"Song for a Lyre" (Bogan)   4:68; 46:81; 93:78,
   81-3
"Song for a Slight Voice" (Bogan)   4:68; 46:81,
   83; 93:64, 96
"Song for Adam" (Browne)   21:34
"Song for an Engraved Invitation" (McGinley)
   14:366
Song for an Equinox (Perse)   11:436
"Song for Bob Dylan" (Bowie)   17:58
"Song for Disheartened Lute" (Dickey)   28:118
"Song for Easter" (Wright)   53:419
"Song for Marian" (Lamming)   66:220
"Song for My Name" (Hogan)   73:157
"Song for Myself" (Tolson)   105:260, 282
"A Song for New-Ark" (Giovanni)   117:198-
   99
"Song for Puerto Rico" (Guillen)   79:230
"Song for Resurrection Day" (Buckley)   57:125
"A Song for Rising" (Bowers)   9:121
"Song for Sharon" (Mitchell)   12:440
"A Song for Simeon" (Eliot)   15:217; 41:149,
   151
"A Song for Soweto" (Jordan)   114:161
"Song for Tamar" (Amichai)   57:36
"A Song for the Asking" (Simon)   17:460
"Song for the Death of Averroës" (Merton)
   83:394
"Song for the Deer and Myself to Return On"
   (Harjo)   83:282
"A Song for the Degrees" (Pound)   13:461
"Song for the Last Act" (Bogan)   39:385;
   46:87; 93:68-9, 76, 96
"Song for the Mothers of Dead Militiamen"
   (Neruda)
   See "Canto a las madres de los milicianos
   muertos"

"Song for the Rainy Season" (Bishop)   13:89
"Song for Thomas Nashe" (Buckley)   57:128
"Song for War" (Rodgers)   7:378
"A Song from Armenia" (Hill)   8:296
"Song (from Goodbye, Spring)" (Seifert)
   93:334
*Song from the Earth: American Indian Paint-
   ing* (Highwater)   12:285-86
"Song from the Multitude" (Livesay)   79:353
Song: I Want a Witness (Harper)   7:138-39
"A Song in Passing" (Winters)   32:468
"Song in Praise of Willy" (Grass)   49:139
"Song in Sligo" (Garrigue)   8:240
"A Song in the Wilderness" (Celan)
   See "Ein Lied in der Wüste"
"Song of a Child" (Morgan)   31:275
"Song of a Citizen" (Milosz)   56:238
Song of a Goat (Clark)   38:113, 115-16, 118-
   22, 124
"Song of a Hebrew" (Abse)   29:16
"The Song of a Shift" (O'Casey)   88:239
Song of a Soldier (p'Bitek)   96:299
"The Song of Abraham in the Fire" (Shamlu)
   10:472
"Song of Advent" (Winters)   32:468
"A Song of Degrees" (Nemerov)   36:304
Song of Deprivation (Ezekiel)   61:97-9
"A Song of Experience" (Amis)   40:40, 44
"The Song of Fire" (75:79
The Song of Hendele (Seifert)   93:328
"The Song of Hugh Glass" (Neihardt)   32:329-
   31, 334, 338
"A Song of Innocence" (Ellison)   114:108,
   112
"The Song of Jed Smith" (Neihardt)   32:334,
   338
Song of Jubilee (Forman)   21:119
Song of Kali (Simmons)   44:273-75
Song of Lawino (p'Bitek)   96:264-72, 277-
   79, 281-82, 290-91, 293-96, 299-312
The Song of Lazarus (Comfort)   7:54
Song of Malaya (p'Bitek)   96:274, 281-82,
   286, 298-99, 301, 305
"The Song of Maria Neféli" (Elytis)   49:109
The Song of My Sister (Ritsos)   31:324
Song of Ocol (p'Bitek)   96:268, 270, 280-81,
   290-91, 294-99, 301, 305
"Song of Patience" (Cohen)   38:131
"A Song of Praise" (Sanchez)   116:316
Song of Prisoner (p'Bitek)   96:265-67, 270-
   73, 278, 280-81, 284-86, 288-89, 296-
   99, 301, 303-05
"Song of Reasons" (Pinsky)   38:361
A Song of Sixpence (Cronin)   32:139-40
"A Song of Sojourner Truth" (Jordan)   114:145
Song of Solomon (Morrison)   10:355-56;
   22:316-17, 319-20; 55:195-96, 200, 205,
   207-08, 210; 81:217-18, 221, 223-25,
   227-28, 230-38, 250, 256-57, 259-60,
   262, 265, 268-69, 272; 87:263-65, 292-
   94
"The Song of Songs" (Davies)   23:144
Song of Songs (Mamoulian)   16:421
"Song of the Blackbird" (Turco)   63:429
"The Song of the Bongo" (Guillen)
   See "La canción del bongo"
"Song of the Books" (Clarke)   6:112
Song of the City (Abrahams)   4:3
"The Song of the Cold" (Sitwell)   67:336
The Song of the Cold (Sitwell)   2:403
"Song of the Deportees" (Guthrie)   35:193
"A Song of the Dust" (Sitwell)   67:337
"The Song of the Final Meeting" (Akhmatova)

64:8

"Song of the First and Last Beatnik" (Gold)
42:192

"Song of the Flaming Sword" (Avison)   97:111

"Song of the Forest" (Okigbo)   25:350, 354;
84:330, 332

"Song of the German Mercenaries" (Faludy)
42:138-39

"Song of the GI's and MG's" (Laughlin)   49:221

"Song of the Immediacy of Death" (Bell)   8:67

"The Song of the Indian Wars" (Neihardt)
32:330-32, 334, 337-38

The Song of the Little Road (Ray)
See Pather panchali

"Song of the Lonely Bachelor" (Montague)
46:265

Song of the Lusitanian Bogey (Weiss)
See Gesang vom lusitanischen Popanz

Song of the Lusitanian Bogeyman (Weiss)
See Gesang vom lusitanischen Popanz

"The Song of the Man of Light Who Passed
into Gloom" (Shamlu)   10:472

"The Song of the Messiah" (Neihardt)   32:332-
34, 338

"Song of the Native Land" (Seifert)   93:335

"The Song of the Necromancer" (Smith)
43:422-25

"Song of the Past" (Mahapatra)   33:283

"The Song of the Poet" (Elytis)   49:109

"Song of the River Sweep" (Lieberman)   36:262

The Song of the Road (Ray)
See Pather panchali

"Song of the Shirt, 1941" (Parker)   68:328,
334-35, 339-40

"The Song of the Shrouded Stranger of the
Night" (Ginsberg)   36:196

"Song of the Smoke" (Du Bois)   64:114; 96:130

"Song of the Son" (Toomer)   13:551; 22:425-
26

"A Song of the Soul of Central" (Hughes)
108:309

"Song of the Spasskaya Tower" (Padilla)
38:351

"Song of the Sweepings" (Seifert)   93:331

"Song of the Taste" (Snyder)   32:387

Song of the Trees (Taylor)   21:418-20

"Song of the Whales" (Seifert)   34:261-62

The Song of Three Friends (Neihardt)   32:329-
31, 334, 337

The Song of Viktorka (Písen o Viktorce; Viktorka)
(Seifert)   34:262-63; 44:422; 93:307, 309,
323, 326-28, 332, 335-36, 343

"A Song of Wrinkles" (Whittemore)   4:588

"Song Off-Key" (Wagoner)   3:508

"Song on Porcelain" (Milosz)   82:297-98

"A Song on the End of the World" (Milosz)
11:381; 31:259, 262; 56:234

"The Song Remains the Same" (Page and Plant)
12:481

The Song Remains the Same (Page and Plant)
12:480, 482

"A Song: Sensation Time at the Home" ("Sensation Time at the Home") (Merton)
83:397

Song, Speech, and Ventriloquism (Kettelkamp)
12:304

"The Song the Body Dreamed in the Spirit's
Mad Behest" (Everson)   5:122

"Song, the Brian Coral" (Rukeyser)   15:457

"Song: The Organic Years" (Bell)   8:66

"Song to Alfred Hitchcock and Wilkinson"
(Ondaatje)   14:407

Song to Grow On (Guthrie)   35:187

"Song to Ishtar" (Levertov)   66:235, 238

"A Song to No Music" ("Song without Music")
(Brodsky)   36:78, 81; 100:52

"Song to Pie" (Blount)   38:47

"A Song to Sing You" (Wright)   53:419

"Song to Woody" (Dylan)   77:166

"Song without Music" (Brodsky)
See "A Song to No Music"

"The Songbook of Sebastian Arrurruz" (Hill)
8:293-95; 45:178-79, 183, 190

Le songe (The Dream) (Montherlant)   8:393;
19:322-23

Le songe du critique (Anouilh)   40:57

Les songes en equilibre (Hebert)   29:227, 230,
236-37

The Songlines (Chatwin)   57:139-48, 150, 153

Songlines (Chatwin)   59:275-77

Songmaster (Card)   47:67-9; 50:143

Sóngoro cosongo: Poemas mulatos (Guillen)
48:157, 159, 161-63, 166-68; 79:229,
231, 238-40, 246-48, 250

"Songs" (Prokosch)   48:309

Songs and Other Musical Pieces (Auden)   6:17

"Songs and Recitations" (Simmons)   43:414

"Songs for a Colored Singer" (Bishop)   1:34;
9:97; 15:59; 32:38

Songs for a Son (Peters)   7:303

Songs for a Summer Day (MacLeish)   68:285

"Songs for a Woman" (Amichai)   116:96

Songs for an Autumn Rifle (Caute)   29:109,
115

Songs for Eve (MacLeish)   8:362

"Songs for Five Companionable Singers" (Corn)
33:116, 118

"Songs for Masters" (Hope)   52:209

"Songs for My Father" (Komunyakaa)   86:192-
93; 94:239

Songs for Naëtt (Senghor)
See Chants pour naëtt

"Songs/for Sanna" (Broumas)   73:9

Songs for Soldiers and Tunes for Tourists
(Guillen)
See Cantos para soldados y sones para
turistas

"Songs for the Air" (Hecht)   8:266

"Songs from Libretti" (Denby)   48:83

Songs from the Stars (Spinrad)   46:384-86

Songs in a Time of War (Saro-Wiwa)   114:253

Songs in the Attic (Joel)   26:222

Songs in the Key of Life (Wonder)   12:659-62,
664

Songs My Mother Taught Me (Thomas)   7:472;
13:538; 37:424; 107:348

Songs of a Dead Dreamer (Ligotti)   44:53-5

Songs of a Mountain Plowman (Stuart)   11:509

"The Songs of Adrien Zielinsky" (Milosz)
11:378

Songs of Enchantment (Okri)   87:329-31

"Songs of Jerusalem and Myself" (Amichai)
116:89, 114

"Songs of Life" (Diamond)   30:113

"The Songs of Maximus" (Olson)   5:329

"The Songs of Reba Love Jackson" (Wideman)
36:455

Songs of Something Else (Ekeloef)   27:119

"Songs of the Desert" (Baxter)   14:61

Songs of the Doomed (Thompson)   104:338-
44, 347

Songs of the Heart (Lagerkvist)
See Hjärtats sånger

"Songs of the Land of Zion Jerusalem"
(Amichai)   22:30

"Songs of the Old Sod" (Simmons)   43:412

"Songs of the Sea-Witch" (Musgrave)   13:400

Songs of the Sea-Witch (Musgrave)   13:400;
54:341;

"Songs of the Shade" (Senghor)
See Chants d'ombre

"Songs of the Transformed" (Atwood)   8:29;
13:44; 15:37-8; 25:67; 84:65

Songs of Woody Guthrie (Guthrie)   35:191

"Songs of Zion the Beautiful" (Amichai)
57:41, 44

"Songs the Minstrel Sang" (Lightfoot)   26:282

Songs to a Handsome Woman (Brown)   79:153

"Songs to Survive the Summer" (Hass)   18:212;
99:140

Songs to the Seagull (Mitchell)   12:435, 437,
440

"The Songs We Know Best" (Ashbery)   41:34,
38

Sonim, di Geschichte fun a Liebe (Enemies: A
Love Story) (Singer)   3:456, 459; 11:499,
501, 503; 23:416, 419, 422; 111:307, 309-
12, 321-24, 327-28, 333, 341, 346

"Sonnet" (Bishop)   32:37

"Sonnet" (Bogan)   46:78; 93:90, 96

"Sonnet" (Carruth)   84:136

"Sonnet" (Hass)   99:155

"Sonnet" (Justice)   102:269, 278

"Sonnet" (Plumly)   33:314

"Sonnet" (Reading)   47:350

"Sonnet" (Watkins)   43:450

"Sonnet" (Winters)   32:468

"Sonnet" (Wright)   53:427

"Sonnet VIII" ("How Do I Love You?")
(Shapiro)   4:486

"Sonnet 14" (Berryman)   62:51

"Sonnet 15" (Berryman)   62:53

"Sonnet 16" (Berryman)   62:51

"Sonnet 20" (Berryman)   62:51

"Sonnet 23" (Berryman)   62:52

"Sonnet 25" (Berryman)   62:53

"Sonnet 40" (Berryman)   62:50

"Sonnet 47" (Berryman)   62:72

"Sonnet 52" (Berryman)   62:51

"Sonnet 58" (Berryman)   62:52

"Sonnet 75" (Berryman)   62:51

"Sonnet 97" (Berryman)   62:52

"Sonnet 100" (Berryman)   62:50

"Sonnet 101" (Berryman)   62:52

"Sonnet 103" (Berryman)   62:52

"Sonnet 105" (Berryman)   62:51

"Sonnet for Minimalists" (Van Duyn)   116:412,
415

"Sonnet, Freely Adapted" (Zamora)   89:361,
370, 372, 375, 394

"A Sonnet from the Stony Brook" (Jordan)
114:145

"The Sonnet Hobby" (Pasolini)   106:265-66

"Sonnet Number Eight" (Orlovitz)   22:336

"Sonnet Number Ninety" (Orlovitz)   22:336

"Sonnet on Rare Animals" (Meredith)   55:192

"A Sonnet Sequence: Dishonor" (Denby)
48:81, 84

"Sonnet: The Greedy Man Considers Nuclear
War" (Ewart)   46:151

"Sonnet III" (Cummings)   68:44

"Sonnet to My Father" (Justice)   102:268,
285

The Sonnets (Berrigan)   37:42-5

Sonnets (Carruth)   84:136

"Sonnets for Five Seasons" (Stevenson)   33:383

"Sonnets for Roseblush" (Hollander)   5:187

Sonnets of Love and Opposition (Brenton)
31:63

"Sonnets of the Blood" (Tate)   **11**:525, 527

Sonnets to Chris (Berryman)
   See *Berryman's Sonnets*

"Sonnets—Actualities" (Cummings)   **15**:159, 160

"Sonnets—Realities" (Cummings)   **15**:159, 160, 162

"Sonnets—Unrealities" (Cummings)   **15**:159

"Sonnet—To the Ocean" (Masefield)   **11**:358

"Sonny Jim" (Williams)   **42**:446

"Sonny's Blues" (Baldwin)   **13**:53-4; **17**:33; **90**:2-41

Sons (Buck)   **7**:32; **11**:73, 77

Sons (Hunter)   **31**:222

"Sons and Lovers" (Roth)   **104**:283

Sons Come and Go, Mothers Hang in Forever (Saroyan)   **8**:468

Sons of Cain (Williamson)   **56**:439-42

Sons of Darkness, Sons of Light (Williams)   **5**:497

"The Sons of Medea" (Squires)   **51**:381

The Sons of Mrs. Aab (Millin)   **49**:247-48

Sons of My Skin: Selected Poems, 1954-1974 (Redgrove)   **6**:447; **41**:350-54

Sons of the Conquistador (Fuentes)   **113**:262

The Sons of the Falcon (Garnett)   **3**:189

"Sons of the Silent Age" (Bowie)   **17**:66

"Sons of Unless and Children of Almost" (Cummings)   **68**:52

"Sons of Vulindlela" (Kunene)   **85**:162

"Soolaimon" (Diamond)   **30**:110

"Soon" (Sondheim)   **30**:391, 402

"Soon I'll Be Loving You Again" (Gaye)   **26**:132

Soon One Morning (Dodson)   **79**:189

"Soonest Mended" (Ashbery)   **13**:30, 33-4; **15**:33; **41**:40-1; **77**:51, 57-8

Soperniki (*The Rivals*) (Aitmatov)   **71**:5

Sophie's Choice (Styron)   **15**:525, 528-31; **60**:392, 394-402

Sor Juana Inés de la Cruz, o, Las trampas de la fe (*Sor Juana; Or, The Traps of Faith*) (Paz)   **65**:176, 186, 189, 197

Sor Juana; Or, The Traps of Faith (Paz)
   See *Sor Juana Inés de la Cruz, o, Las trampas de la fe*

"Sora no kaibutsu Aguwee" ("Aghwee the Sky Monster") (Oe)   **36**:348; **86**:215-16, 244

"The Sorcerer Postponed" (Borges)
   See "El brujo postergado"

"The Sorcerer's Apprentice" (Johnson)   **51**:234-36

The Sorcerer's Apprentice (Johnson)   **51**:234, 236

"The Sorcerer's Daughter" (Bogan)   **4**:69

"Sorcery" (Livesay)   **79**:338, 348, 353

"Sorcery or Foolishness" (Ulibarri)
   See "Brujerías o tonterías"

Sore Throats (Brenton)   **31**:63, 67

Sorelle Materassi (*The Sisters Materassi*) (Palazzeschi)   **11**:431-32

"La sorgue: Chanson pour Yvonne" (Char)   **11**:117

"Sorôco, His Mother, His Daughter" (Rosa)   **23**:352-53

"Sorrel" (Fuller)   **62**:199, 202

"Sorrow" (Alegria)   **75**:34, 36-7, 39, 41, 53-5

The Sorrow and the Terror (Mukherjee)   **115**:366, 386

A Sorrow beyond Dreams: A Life Story (Handke)
   See *Wunscholses Unglück*

The Sorrow Dance (Levertov)   **2**:242; **5**:248-49; **28**:238; **66**:236-39, 245-46

"Sorrow Is the Only Faithful One" (Dodson)   **79**:191-92

"The Sorrow of the Pagan Outcast" (Tanizaki)
   See "Itansha no kanashimi"

"Sorrow-Acre" (Dinesen)   **10**:144, 146-47, 149-52; **29**:154; **95**:35, 38-42, 46, 48, 50, 52

"Sorrowful Mysteries" (Dubus)   **97**:

"The Sorrows of Captain Carpenter" (Berryman)   **10**:45

The Sorrows of Frederick (Linney)   **51**:260, 262

"The Sorrows of Gin" (Cheever)   **15**:131; **64**:47, 65

The Sorrows of Priapus (Dahlberg)   **7**:64-5, 67, 71

"Sorry..." (Havel)
   See "Sorry..."

"Sorry Fugu" (Boyle)   **90**:45-7

"A Sort of a Song" (Williams)   **42**:457

"A Sort of Ecstasy" (Smith)   **15**:516

A Sort of Forgetting (Vansittart)   **42**:391

A Sort of Life (Greene)   **3**:213; **6**:219-20; **27**:171-72, 174; **37**:138; **70**:289, 293; **72**:160, 179

"Sorties" (Cixous)   **92**:52-3, 69, 78-9, 84-90, 92, 95

Sorties (Dickey)   **2**:117; **7**:84; **10**:141; **47**:93

"Sorties: Out and Out: Attacks/Ways Out/Forays" (Cixous)   **92**:77

"S.O.S" (Bagryana)   **10**:14

"S.O.S." (Damas)   **84**:169, 172, 177

Sos the Rope (Anthony)   **35**:34-5

Sot' (*The River Sot'; Soviet River*) (Leonov)   **92**:236-37, 245, 248, 256, 258-59, 276, 278

Sotto il sole giaguro (*Under the Jaguar Sun*) (Calvino)   **73**:50, 53, 59-60

The Sot-Weed Factor (Barth)   **1**:17-18; **2**:35-9; **3**:38-9, 42; **5**:52; **7**:22-5; **9**:61, 68, 72-4; **10**:24; **14**:49-51, 56; **27**:28; **51**:20-1; **89**:8, 11, 14, 17

Le souci de soi (Foucault)
   See *Histoire de la sexualité, Vol. 3: Le souci de soi*

Soudce z Milosti (Klima)   **56**:173

"Souffrance" (Soupault)   **68**:404

La soufriere (Herzog)   **16**:328

"The Soul" (Amichai)   **22**:33

"The Soul" (Amichai)
   See "Hanefesh"

The Soul and Body of John Brown (Rukeyser)   **27**:404

Soul and Form (Lukacs)
   See *Die Seele und die Formen*

"Soul and Money" (Berriault)   **109**:95

The Soul Brothers and Sister Lou (Hunter)   **35**:225-29

Soul Catcher (Herbert)   **12**:273; **35**:196; **44**:394

Soul Clap Hands and Sing (Marshall)   **27**:309, 311-13, 315; **72**:212, 227, 231, 248, 254

A Soul for Sale (Kavanagh)   **22**:234

Soul Gone Home (Hughes)   **1**:148; **35**:217

"The Soul inside the Sentence" (Gass)   **39**:479-80, 482

"Soul Kitchen" (Morrison)   **17**:286, 290, 292

"The Soul Longs to Return Whence It Came" (Eberhart)   **56**:77, 80, 87

Soul/Mate (Oates)   **108**:386-88

The Soul of a Jew (Sobol)   **60**:385

"The Soul of a Woman's College" (Rich)   **73**:322

The Soul of Kindness (Taylor)   **29**:408, 412

"The Soul of the Village"   **75**:70, 78

Soul of the White Ant (Wilson)   **33**:461, 464-65

Soul of Wood, and Other Stories (Lind)
   See *Eine Seele aus Holz*

Soul on Fire (Cleaver)   **30**:68-9

"Soul on Ice" (Cleaver)   **30**:59

Soul on Ice (Cleaver)   **30**:54-9, 61-2, 65, 67-9

"Soul Survivor" (Jagger and Richard)   **17**:224, 236

"Soul under Water" (Aleixandre)   **36**:29

Souls and Bodies (Lodge)   **36**:274-76

The Souls of Black Folk (Du Bois)   **1**:80; **2**:120-21; **13**:180, 182; **64**:103-05, 110, 116-17, 127-34; **96**:127-32, 137, 142, 146-48, 153-61

"The Souls of White Folk" (Du Bois)   **64**:104

Souls on Fire: Portraits and Legends of Hasidic Masters (Wiesel)
   See *Célébration hasidique: Portraits et legendes*

The Sound and the Fury (Faulkner)   **1**:98, 100, 102; **3**:149-55, 157; **6**:176, 180; **8**:207-08, 211; **9**:197-203; **11**:197-202, 206; **14**:168-69, 171, 173, 175, 178-80; **18**:144, 148; **28**:140-42, 145; **68**:106-36

The Sound in Your Mind (Nelson)   **17**:304

A Sound Investment (Sanchez)   **116**:301

"The Sound Machine" (Dahl)   **79**:181

Sound of a City (Farrell)   **66**:127, 129

"Sound of a Wound" (Montague)   **46**:276

The Sound of Bow Bells (Weidman)   **7**:517

A Sound of Chariots (Hunter)   **21**:159-60, 163, 165, 167-68

The Sound of Coaches (Garfield)   **12**:230-31, 235, 237, 241

The Sound of Mountain Water: The Changing American West (Stegner)   **49**:359

"The Sound of Pines" (Masters)   **48**:224

"The Sound of Poets" (Sondheim)   **30**:389

The Sound of the Mountain (Kawabata)   **2**:223; **5**:207; **9**:309, 314-17; **18**:285; **107**:73, 87-89, 91, 101-02, 106, 111-12, 114, 117, 119-22

"Sound of the Sinners" (Clash)   **30**:48

"The Sound of the Trees" (Frost)   **10**:193; **26**:117

"A Sound of Thunder" (Bradbury)   **42**:42

The Sound of Thunder (Caldwell)   **28**:61

The Sound of Thunder (*The Roar of Thunder*) (Smith)   **33**:376

The Sound of Waves (Mishima)   **2**:286; **4**:354; **6**:337; **9**:382, 385; **27**:340

"Sound Track" (Calisher)   **38**:75-6

"Sounding Harvey Creek" (Bottoms)   **53**:32

"Sounding My Name" (Kroetsch)   **57**:292-93

"Soundings" (Baraka)   **115**:12

"Soundings" (Muske)   **90**:314

"Soundings: Block Island" (Belitt)   **22**:52-4

"The sounds begin again" (Brutus)   **43**:91, 96

Sounds, Feelings, Thoughts (Szymborska)   **99**:192-93

"Sounds in the Night" (Lowell)   **11**:329

"The Sounds of Silence" (Simon)   **17**:459, 461, 463-64, 466

"Soup" (Creeley)   **78**:141

"Soup" (Simic)   **6**:502

Soup (Peck)   **17**:338, 340

Soup and Me (Peck)   **17**:339-40

"Soup du jour" (Shields)   **113**:406-08

Soup for President (Peck)   **17**:342

"Sour Milk" (Wakoski)   **4**:573

Sour Sweet (Mo)   **46**:259-61

"The Source" (Porter)   7:310
"Source" (Walker)   103:407, 410-13, 423
Source (Chappell)   40:147, 149; 78:97
The Source (Michener)   5:288-90; 11:375; 29:311-14; 109:375, 377, 379, 380, 382, 386
A Source of Embarrassment (McCarthy)
   See The Oasis
"A Source of Innocent Merriment" (Tiptree)   48:389
The Source of Light (Price)   43:347-50, 353; 50:229, 232
The Source of Magic (Anthony)   35:35
"Sources" (Rich)   73:316
Sources (Rich)   36:371-72, 374, 377; 73:327; 76:210
Sources of Unrest (Vansittart)   42:392
Le sourd dans la ville (Blais)   22:60
"Sourdough Mountain Lookout" (Whalen)   29:446
Sous bénéfice d'inventaire (The Dark Brain of Piranesi, and Other Essays) (Yourcenar)   19:484; 87:412
Sous les toits de Paris (Under the Roofs of Paris) (Clair)   20:57-62, 69-70
"Sousa" (Dorn)   10:159
"The South" (Borges)   8:97; 9:116; 44:362; 48:36, 46
"South" (Hoffman)   6:244
"South" (Justice)   102:258
"South" (Walcott)   76:275
South (Green)
   See Sud
"South Africa, 1986" (Levertov)   66:251
The South African Quirt (Edmonds)   35:157
The South Africans (Millin)   49:246
"South America" (Dunn)   40:170-71
South by Java Head (MacLean)   13:361; 63:262-64
"South Country" (Slessor)   14:493
The South Goes North (Coles)   108:210-11, 214
South of Heaven (Thompson)   69:384
"South of My Days" (Wright)   53:423, 427, 430
South of No North (Bukowski)   108:77, 86-87
South of the Angels (West)   7:519, 521; 17:548, 551, 553
"South Parade Pedler" (Bennett)   28:26
"South Parks Road" (Fenton)   32:165
South Pole Station (Berger)   12:38
South Sea Bubble (Island Fling) (Coward)   29:136, 139
South Street (Bradley)   23:79-80
"South: The Name of Home" (Walker)   58:405
South to a Very Old Place (Murray)   73:222-24, 235-41
The South Wind of Love (Mackenzie)   18:313
"Southbound on the Freeway" (Swenson)   106:319
"Southeast Arkansia" (Angelou)   77:29
"Southeast Corner" (Brooks)   49:26
Southern Adventure (Paustovsky)
   See Brosok na yug
The Southern City (Kadare)
   See Qyteti i jugut
"Southern Cop" (Brown)   59:265-66
"The Southern Cross" (Konwicki)   117:281
"The Southern Cross" (Wright)   28:458
The Southern Cross (Wright)   28:458-60
Southern Discomfort (Brown)   43:81-3; 79:153, 155, 158-59, 167-71
A Southern Family (Godwin)   69:239, 241-49,

251-52
Southern Fried (Fox)   22:140
Southern Fried Plus Six (Fox)   22:140
"Southern Gentlemen, White Prostitutes, Mill-Owners, and Negroes" (Hughes)   108:318
"A Southern Landscape" (Spencer)   22:406
"Southern Mammy Sings" (Hughes)   35:221; 108:325-26
"Southern Man" (Young)   17:570, 572-73, 582
"Southern Mansion" (Bontemps)   1:38; 18:64
"A Southern Mode of Imagination" (Tate)   4:537; 11:522
"The Southern Quality" (McLuhan)   83:360
Southern Road (Brown)   1:47; 23:95-8; 59:262, 264-65, 267-68, 270-71, 273
"The Southern Thruway" (Cortazar)
   See "La autopista del sur"
"The Southerner" (Shapiro)   15:476, 478
The Southerner (Renoir)   20:287-88, 304
Southmost Twelve (FitzGerald)   19:175
"Southpaw" (Mueller)   51:284
The Southpaw (Harris)   19:200, 203
Southways (Caldwell)   14:96
"Souvenir" (Joel)   26:214, 219
"Souvenir de temps perdu" (Smith)   15:516
A Souvenir from Qam (Connelly)   7:57
"A Souvenir of Japan" (Carter)   5:102
Souvenirs (Fuller)   28:156-58
Souvenirs du triangle d'or (Recollections of a Golden Triangle) (Robbe-Grillet)   43:361-62, 365-68
Souvenirs pieux (Dear Departed) (Yourcenar)   19:484; 87:389, 396, 412, 417-18, 432-34
"Sovereign" (Voinovich)
   See "Vladychitsa"
The Sovereign Sun: Selected Poems (Elytis)   15:219-20; 49:109; 100:158, 174
The Sovereignty of Good over Other Concepts (Murdoch)   15:387, 389; 51:291
Soviet Poems (Gustafson)   36:217-18, 221
Soviet River (Leonov)
   See Sot'
"Sow" (Plath)   5:345; 9:432; 17:344, 348, 350; 51:343; 111:164
"The Sow and Silas" (Bates)   46:63
"The Soy Cowboy" (Vollmann)   89:314
Sozaboy (Saro-Wiwa)   114:258, 267, 275
Sozvezdie Kozlotura (The Goatibex Constellation; The Kozlotur Constellation) (Iskander)   47:193, 196, 199-200
"The Space" (Soto)   80:277
Space (Aleixandre)
   See Ambito
Space (Michener)   29:314-16; 60:258; 109:378-79, 381, 386
Space Ache (Wilson)   33:463-66
The Space Beyond (Campbell)   32:80
Space Cadet (Heinlein)   14:250; 26:161, 171, 175; 55:302
Space Family Stone (Heinlein)
   See The Rolling Stones
"A Space in the Air" (Silkin)   6:498; 43:397, 399-400
The Space Merchants (Pohl)   18:412
"Space Monkey" (Smith)   12:543
"Space Mowgli" (Strugatskii and Strugatskii)   27:438
"Space Oddity" (Bowie)   17:57, 59
The Space Pirate (Vance)   35:420
"Space Rats of the C.C.C." (Harrison)   42:203
"Space Sonnet and Pollyfilla" (Morgan)   31:276
"The Space Spiders" (Hall)   37:146

Space, Time, and Nathaniel (Aldiss)   14:10
The Space Vampires (Wilson)   14:589
"Spaced In" (Baker)   31:29
Spaces of the Dark (Mosley)   43:321
"The space-ship" (Smith)   64:393
"Spaceships Have Landed" (Munro)   95:320, 325
Spacious Earth (Pasternak)
   See Zemnoy prostor
"Spadanie czyli; o, Elementach wertykalnych i horyzontalnych w zyciu czlowieka wspolczesnego" ("Falling; or, On the Vertical and Horizontal Elements in the Life of Contemporary Man") (Rozewicz)   23:359
"Spain" (Cocteau)
   See "Espagne"
Spain (Auden)   3:25; 14:33; 43:18, 21
"Spain, 1937" (Auden)   6:20, 23; 11:14, 19; 14:27; 43:16
"Spain, 1934-1936" (Leiris)   61:361
Spain: A Poem in Four Anguishes and a Hope (Guillen)
   See España: Poema en cuatro angustias y una esperanza
Spain Again (Bessie)   23:60
Spain at Heart (Neruda)
   See España en el corazón: himno a las glorias del pueblo en la guerra (1936-1937)
Spain in My Heart (Neruda)
   See España en el corazón: himno a las glorias del pueblo en la guerra (1936-1937)
Spain in the Heart (Neruda)
   See España en el corazón: himno a las glorias del pueblo en la guerra (1936-1937)
Spain under Franco (Gallo)   95:90, 92, 94, 96
"Span" (Avison)   97:91
A Spaniard in the Works (Lennon)   12:355; 35:267
"The Spaniards Arrive in Shanghai" (Middleton)   13:389
The Spanish Armadas (Graham)   23:194
"Spanish Artifacts" (Dacey)   51:80-1
"Spanish Balcony" (Beer)   58:37
"The Spanish Bed" (Pritchett)   15:442, 444
"Spanish Bombs" (Clash)   30:46-7
The Spanish Cape Mystery (Queen)   11:460
"The Spanish Civil War" (Carruth)   7:41
"The Spanish Earl" (White)   30:451
The Spanish Earth (Hemingway)   6:226; 50:412; 80:107
The Spanish Gardener (Cronin)   32:137
"The Spanish Lady" (Munro)   95:293
The Spanish Letters (Hunter)   21:155-56, 161, 166
"The Spanish Lie" (MacLeish)   68:289
"Spanish Point" (Buckley)   57:136
Spanish Roundabout (Daly)   17:90
The Spanish Smile (O'Dell)   30:277
The Spanish Temper (Pritchett)   41:335
Spanish Testament (Koestler)   15:309; 33:243
The Spanish Virgin, and Other Stories (Pritchett)   41:332
The Spanish World   70:341
Spanking the Maid (Coover)   32:125; 46:117
Spare Ass Annie (Burroughs)   109:185
"Spare Us from Loveliness" (H. D.)   73:115
Spared (Horovitz)   56:155
"A Spark in the Tinder of Knowing" (Rexroth)   112:404

Spark of Life (Remarque) 21:330-31
Spark of Opal (Clark) 12:130-32
Sparkling Cyanide (Christie) 12:124
"Sparks Street Echo" (Creeley) 78:161
"Sparrow" (Gaye) 26:133-34
"Sparrow" (Gunn) 18:202
"Sparrow Come in My Window" (Nowlan) 15:398
A Sparrow Falls (Smith) 33:376
"A Sparrow Hawk in the Suburbs" (Boland) 113:111
"Sparrow Hills" (Pasternak) 63:278
"Sparrows" (Lessing) 94:265
"Sparrows in March" (Raine) 45:330
Spartacus (Fast) 23:156
Spartacus (Kubrick) 16:379-80, 382, 385-86, 389
Spartina (Casey) 59:119-23
"Spasskoye" (Pasternak) 63:279
"Spat" (Schaeffer) 11:491
"Spät und tief" (Celan) 10:102
"Spatiul mioritic" 75:72
"Spats" (Martin) 89:111-12
The Spawning Run (Humphrey) 45:198
"Speak" (Wright) 10:544
Speak 59:364
Speak, Answer, Teach (Haavikko)
    See *Puhua, vastata, opettaa*
Speak for England (Bragg) 10:72
Speak, Memory: An Autobiography Revisited (Conclusive Evidence: A Memoir) (Nabokov) 1:242, 245; 2:299, 301, 304; 3:354-55; 6:357, 359; 8:409, 412-15, 417-18; 11:391-92, 395; 15:390, 394; 46:292
Speak Now (Yerby) 7:557; 22:491
Speak Out on Rape! (Hyde) 21:177-78
"Speak to Me" (Pink Floyd) 35:306
"Speak, You Also" (Celan) 19:94; 53:74-5; 82:47
Speaker for the Dead (Card) 47:69; 50:143-51
Speaker of Mandarin (Rendell) 48:323
Speaking and Language: Defense of Poetry (Goodman) 2:169, 171; 4:198
"Speaking in Tongues" (Moure) 88:227
Speaking in Tongues (Byrne) 26:99
"Speaking into Darkness" (Bottoms) 53:29-31
"Speaking of Courage" (O'Brien) 103:136, 139, 147, 163, 168, 174
"Speaking of *LETTERS*" (Barth) 51:26
"Speaking of Which" (Moure) 88:224
Spearpoint (Ashton-Warner) 19:23
"Special Lovers" (Ransom) 4:431
Special Occasions (Slade) 46:372-73
A Special Providence (Yates) 7:554; 23:480
"A Special Sense of Place" (Momaday) 85:237
"A Special Train" (Hoffman) 6:243
The Special View of History (Olson) 11:418-20
"Special-Constable" (Sassoon) 36:385
Species of Spaces (Perec)
    See *Espèces d'espaces*
"Speck's Idea" (Gallant) 38:195
Spectacle (Prevert) 15:438
The Spectacle at the Tower (Hofmann)
    See *Auf dem Turm*
"The Spectacle of Youth" (Kunene) 85:166
"Spectacles" (Butor) 15:114
The Spectator Bird (Stegner) 9:509; 49:356; 81:344, 348, 350
A Specter Is Haunting Texas (Leiber) 25:304-05, 310
Spectral Emanations: New and Selected Po-

ems (Hollander) 8:302; 14:263-64
"Spectral Lovers" (Ransom) 5:365
"Spectre de la rose" (Davies) 23:142
"The Spectrum Dream" (Shapcott) 38:402
"The Speculation of the Building Constructors" (Calvino)
    See "La speculazione edilizia"
Speculations about Jacob (Johnson)
    See *Mutmassungen über Jakob*
"Speculations on the Present through the Prism of the Past" (Jordan) 114:155
Speculative Instruments (Richards) 24:390, 394-96
"La speculazione edilizia" ("A Plunge into Real Estate"; "The Speculation of the Building Constructors") (Calvino) 11:89-91; 33:100; 39:315-16
"The Speech" (Pritchett) 41:333
"Speech" (Sandburg) 35:356
Speech and Phenomena, and Other Essays on Husserl's Theory of Signs (Derrida)
    See *La voix et le phénomène: Introduction au problème su signe dans le phénoménologie de Husserl*
"Speech and Silence" (Ezekiel) 61:105
"Speech for an Ideal Irish Election" (Montague) 46:278
"Speech for the Repeal of the McCarran Act" (Wilbur) 14:577; 53:404; 110:382
"Speech, Near Hope in Providence" (Honig) 33:211
"Speech #38" (Baraka) 115:39
"The Speech of a Man from the Backlands" (Cabral de Melo Neto)
    See "O sertanejo falando"
"The Speech of Birds" (Raine) 7:352
Speech on the Occasion of Receiving the Literature Prize of the Free Hanseatic City of Bremen (Bremen Speech) (Celan) 53:83; 82:54
"Speech Rhythm" (Williams) 13:604; 42:460-61
"Speech to a Crowd" (MacLeish) 68:287
"Speech to the Detractors" (MacLeish) 68:287
"Speeches at the Barriers" (Howe) 72:195
The Speeches of Malcolm X at Harvard (Malcolm X) 117:317, 340
"Speech-Grille" (Celan)
    See "Sprachgitter"
Speech-Grille, and Selected Poems (Celan)
    See *Sprachgitter*
The Speed of Darkness (Rukeyser) 27:409, 411
The Speed of Darkness (Tesich) 69:368, 370-74
"Speed Queen among the Freudians" (Robbins) 21:339-40
Speedboat (Adler) 8:4-7; 31:14, 16-17
Spektorsky (Pasternak) 10:384; 18:382-83; 63:289, 311, 315
"Speleology" (Warren) 18:539; 39:265, 274
"The Spell" (Allen) 52:35
"The Spell" (Kumin) 28:220
"The Spell" (Lowell) 37:238
"The Spell against Spelling" (Starbuck) 53:354
A Spell before Winter (Nemerov) 36:304
"Spell for a Traveller" (Mueller) 13:400
A Spell for Chameleon (Anthony) 35:35
A Spell for Green Corn (Brown) 48:53-4
Spell #7: Geechee Jibara Quik Magic Trance Manual for Technologically Stressed Third World People (Shange) 25:397-98; 74:300-02, 307-10

The Spell of Time (Levin) 7:205
The Spell Sword (Bradley) 30:27-8
Spella Ho (Bates) 46:54-5
"Spellbound" (Zaturenska) 6:586
Spellbound (Hitchcock) 16:339, 345, 357
The Spellcoats (Jones) 26:229-30
"Spelling" (Atwood) 25:65
"Spelling" (Munro) 95:293, 304
"Spells" (Raine) 45:336
Spence + Lila (Mason) 82:238-40, 245, 255, 257-58, 260
Spencer's Mountain (Hamner) 12:257-58
"Spending the New Year with the Man from Receiving at Sears" (Wakoski) 40:455-56
La speranza (Hope) (Moravia) 46:282
"Sphere" (Ammons) 57:59; 108:27
Sphere (Crichton) 54:74-5
The Sphere (Sender)
    See *La esfera*
"The Sphere of Pascal" (Borges)
    See "Pascal's Sphere"
Sphere: The Form of a Motion (Ammons) 5:30-1; 8:13-16, 18; 9:27-9; 25:42; 57:49, 57, 59; 108:11, 13, 15, 24, 27-8, 35-8, 54-5, 60
Sphinx (Cook) 14:131
The Spice-Box of Earth (Cohen) 38:131-35, 137
"The Spider" (Cortazar)
    See "La araña"
"The Spider" (Leiber) 25:307
"Spider Blues" (Ondaatje) 51:311-12
Spider Boy (Van Vechten) 33:393-94, 397-98
"The Spider Mathematician" (Ratushinskaya) 54:385
"Spider on the Clothesline" (Hall) 51:170
"The Spider Outside Our Window" (Souster) 5:396
"Spider Rose" (Sterling) 72:368
Spider Web (Dourado)
    See *Teia*
Spider Woman's Granddaughters: Traditional Tales and Contemporary Writing by Native American Women (Allen) 84:22, 24-7, 37, 45
"Spiders" (Schwartz) 45:354
The Spiders (Lang)
    See *Die Spinnen*
The Spider's House (Bowles) 1:41; 19:58; 53:41-2, 46-9
The Spider's Strategy (Bertolucci) 16:86-90, 92-5, 100
Spider's Web (Christie) 12:125
Spiele in denen es dunkel wird (Plays in Which Darkness Falls) (Hildesheimer) 49:167, 171
"Spillway" ("Beyond the End") (Barnes) 3:37; 29:27, 31
Spillway, and Other Stories (Barnes) 29:30, 32
Spin a Soft Black Song: Poems for Children (Giovanni) 117:168, 191
"A Spin around the House" (Pack) 13:340
"Spin It On" (McCartney) 35:286
"Spindrift" (Kinnell) 29:289
Die Spinnen (The Spiders) (Lang) 20:206, 209-10
"Spinnin' and Spinnin'" (Wonder) 12:663
"Spinning" (Purdy) 50:238
The Spinning Ladies (Wagoner) 3:507
"The Spinning Wheel in the Attic" (Smith) 42:356

"The Spinoza of Market Street" (Singer) 15:505; 69:306, 309

The Spinoza of Market Street, and Other Stories (Singer) 3:456; 11:502; 15:504; 23:413, 415, 418

"Spinster" (Ashton-Warner) 19:20

"Spinster" (Plath) 111:165

"The Spinsters and the Knitters in the Sun" (Beer) 58:37

Spinsters in Jeopardy (Marsh) 53:249-51, 254

"A Spinster's Tale" (Taylor) 18:523; 37:409

"Spinster's Wake" (Dunn) 40:168

Spione (The Spy) (Lang) 20:203, 209, 211; 103:88

"The Spiral" (Calvino)
See "La spirale"

"Spiral" (Oates) 6:370

Spiral (Leonov) 92:274

"The Spiral of Perspectives" (Laing) 95:145

"The Spiral Rag" (Ammons) 57:49

The Spiral Road (de Hartog) 19:130-31

"La spirale" ("The Spiral") (Calvino) 8:127; 11:91

"Spirals" (Fuller) 62:196-97

"The Spire" (Voigt) 54:430-31

The Spire (Golding) 1:121-22; 2:166-68; 3:196-98, 200; 10:237; 17:166-68, 171-72, 174, 179; 27:161, 163-64; 81:315-18, 320-21, 323, 326

Spirit Lake (Kantor) 7:196

The Spirit Level (Heaney) 91:124, 129

"Spirit of America" (Wilson) 12:643

"The Spirit of Place" (Rich) 36:367, 370, 379; 73:315

The Spirit of Romance (Pound) 7:332, 335; 13:457; 48:288; 112:331

The Spirit of St. Louis (Wilder) 20:458

"Spirit of Transgression" (Doctorow) 113:162

Spirit Reach (Baraka) 115:10

"The Spirit the Triumph" (Williams) 33:443

"Spirits" (Bausch) 51:55-7

Spirits, and Other Stories (Bausch) 51:55-6

Spirits in Bondage: A Cycle of Lyrics (Lewis) 27:265

"Spirits in the Night" (Springsteen) 17:487-88

Spirits of the Dead (Fellini) 16:279

"Spirit's Song" (Bogan) 4:68; 46:81, 83; 93:64-5, 81

"Spiritual" (Arghezi)
See "Sufleteasca"

"Spiritual" (Thesen) 56:414

Spiritual (Pasolini) 106:230

"The Spiritual Alchemy of Thomas Vaughn" (Rexroth) 112:364

"A Spiritual Call" (Jhabvala) 94:181, 184

The Spiritual Life of Children (Coles) 108:203, 206-07, 209, 216

"The Spiritual Plan of Aztlán" (Zamora) 89:378

"Spiritual View of Lena Horne" (Giovanni) 64:183

"Spiritus" (Beattie) 63:14, 18

Spiritus, I (Rakosi) 47:345

Spiritus Mundi (Frye) 70:275

"The Spirokeet" (Ewart) 46:150

"A Spism and a Spasm" (Mitchell) 98:169

"Spisok blagodeyany" ("A List of Assets"; "A List of Benefits") (Olesha) 8:430-32

"Spit" (Williams) 33:445

Spit Delaney's Island (Hodgins) 23:230, 232

Spite Marriage (Keaton) 20:189

Splash! (Friedman) 56:108

"Spleen" (O'Hara) 78:351

Splender in the Grass (Inge) 8:308

Splendid Lives (Gilliatt) 10:229-30; 13:237

The Splendid Wayfaring (Neihardt) 32:331

Splendide-Hôtel (Sorrentino) 3:462; 7:448-50, 452; 14:498; 22:392-93; 40:385-86, 389

Splendor and Death of Joaquin Murieta (Neruda)
See Fulgor y muerte de Joaquin Murieta

Splendor in the Grass (Kazan) 16:367-71; 63:226, 233, 235

"The Splendor of Being" (Castellanos)
See "El resplandor del ser"

"A Splinter" (Ryan) 65:209

Split (Abroad; At Home) (Weller) 53:387, 391-92

"Split, 1962" (Dunn) 36:154

"Split at the Root" (Rich) 73:321, 324

Split Images (Leonard) 28:234-35

Split Infinity (Anthony) 35:36, 38

The Splits (Ritter) 52:352, 357

"Splitting Wood at Six Above" (Kumin) 13:327

"Splittings" (Rich) 18:450

Spock Must Die! (Blish) 14:86

The Spoil of the Flowers (Grumbach) 22:204

Spoiled (Gray) 9:241; 36:201-03, 206-07

"The Spoiled Brat" (McFadden) 48:250

"The Spoiler's Return" (Walcott) 42:422; 67:357; 76:275

"The Spoiler's Revenge" (Walcott) 67:356

"Spoils" (Gordimer) 70:176, 178

The Spoils (Bunting) 10:83-4; 47:46, 48-50, 52-5

"Spoils of War" (Brodsky) 100:61, 68

The Spoils of War (Fleming) 37:129

Spoils of War (Weller) 53:392-94

The Spoilt City (Manning) 19:300-01

"Spokane Tribal Celebration, September, 1987" (Alexie) 96:2

Spoken Opera (Audiberti)
See Opéra parlé

"The Spoken Word" (Davie) 10:124

The Sponge Room (Waterhouse) 47:417-18

"Sponono" (Paton) 25:359-60

Sponono (Paton) 25:361

Spookhouse (Fierstein) 33:157

"Spooks" (Cooper) 56:71

Spooky Lady's Sideshow (Kristofferson) 26:268-69

Spooky Magic (Kettelkamp) 12:304

"The Spool" (Belitt) 22:49

"The Spoon" (Simic) 9:479; 49:337, 339, 342

"Spoons with Realistic Dead Flies on Them" (Simic) 49:336

A Sport and a Pastime (Salter) 7:387; 52:359-60, 363-69; 59:195-97

The Sport of My Mad Mother (Jellicoe) 27:205-08

A Sport of Nature (Gordimer) 51:156-61; 70:172, 175, 187

The Sport of Queens (Francis) 22:150; 42:148, 153-54; 102:126, 140, 143-44, 153

The Sporting Club (McGuane) 3:329-30; 7:213; 18:323, 325; 45:258, 260, 262

"A Sporting Life" (Moure) 88:227

"A Sporting Man" (Mitchell) 98:180

"Sports" (Guillen) 48:164; 79:230

Sport$ (Tunis) 12:592

"Sports Day in the Park" (Raine) 103:186

Sports in America (Michener) 109:382

"Sportsfield" (Hope) 51:216

"The Sportsmen" (Dunn) 40:167

"Sportsmen" (McGuane) 45:265

Sportsworld (Lipsyte) 21:211

The Sportswriter 99:105-08, 110-14, 116-25

The Sportswriter (Ford) 46:159-62

"A Spot of Konfrontation" (Aldiss) 14:15

A Spotted Dog (Aitmatov)
See Pegli pes, begushchij kraem moria

The Spotted Sphinx (Adamson) 17:5

Die Sprache (Heidegger) 24:276

"Sprachgitter" ("Language-Mesh"; "Speech-Grille") (Celan) 53:70; 82:33, 37, 40, 57

Sprachgitter (The Grid of Language; Language Lattice; Speech-Grille, and Selected Poems; The Straightening) (Celan) 10:101-02; 19:90, 94-5; 53:69-70, 72, 75-7

"Sprawozdanie z raju" (Herbert) 43:186

"Spraying Sheep" (MacCaig) 36:282

"Spread of Mrs. Mobey's Lawn" (Jacobsen) 48:195

Spreading Fires (Knowles) 4:272; 26:262

Sprechblasen (Jandl) 34:197-98

"The Spree" (Pritchett) 5:353; 13:467

"A Sprig of Dill" (Nemerov) 36:309

Sprightly Running: Part of an Autobiography (Wain) 46:411, 413, 420

"Spring" (Christie) 110:127

"Spring" (Larkin) 64:262, 266

"Spring" (Oliver) 98:

"Spring" (Oliver) 98:256, 280, 287

"The Spring" (Pound) 2:343

"Spring" (Rexroth) 49:283;

"Spring" (Sitwell) 67:319

"Spring" (Squires) 51:382

The Spring (Ehrenburg) 62:178; 18:132-34, 136; 34:434, 440

The Spring (Ehrenburg)
See The Thaw

Spring (Pa Chin)
See Ch'un

Spring 71 (Adamov)
See Le printemps 71

"Spring, 1941" (Scott) 22:372

"Spring, A Violin in the Void" (MacDiarmid) 63:244

Spring and All (Williams) 2:468-70; 5:508-09; 9:572-73; 22:470; 42:454-55, 457, 460, 462; 67:407

"Spring and Summer" (Corn) 33:116

"Spring Azures" (Oliver) 98:294

"Spring Bulletin" (Allen) 52:35

"Spring Chorus" (Johnston) 51:248, 255

"Spring Cleaning" (MacNeice) 10:325

"Spring, Coast Range" (Rexroth) 112:390

Spring Comes Riding (Cavanna) 12:98-9

"Spring Day" (Ashbery) 2:17-18

"Spring Drawing" (Hass) 99:141, 143

"Spring Drawing 2" (Hass) 99:141, 143

"Spring Evening" (Farrell) 66:129, 131

"Spring Flood" (Pasternak) 63:313

"Spring in the Academy" (Cassity) 42:95

"Spring in the Classroom" (Oliver) 98:288, 291

"Spring in the Igloo" (Atwood) 25:66

"Spring in the New World" (Parini) 54:360-61

"Spring Journal" (Honig) 33:212

Spring Journal: Poems (Honig) 33:212-13, 216

"Spring Light" (Ashbery) 15:30

"Spring MCMXL" (Gascoyne) 45:154

"Spring Moon" (Johnston) 51:243, 248

Spring Moon: A Novel of China (Lord) 23:278-80

"Spring Night" (Gustafson) **36**:215
Spring Night (Vesaas)
   See *Vårnatt*
"Spring Northbound" (Honig) **33**:214, 216
"Spring Oak" (Kinnell) **5**:217
Spring of the Thief (Logan) **5**:252
"Spring on Troublesome Creek" (Still) **49**:363
"Spring Poem" (Atwood) **13**:44
"The Spring Poem" (Smith) **42**:353
"Spring Pools" (Frost) **10**:195; **15**:241
"Spring Pools" (Nemerov) **9**:394
"A Spring Serpent" (Winters) **4**:593
Spring Shade (Fitzgerald) **39**:319, 473
"Spring Snow" (Matthews) **40**:321
Spring Snow (Mishima) **2**:287-88; **4**:355-56, 358; **6**:338; **9**:384; **27**:341-43
Spring Sonata (Rubens) **19**:405; **31**:350-51
"Spring Song" (Ciardi) **40**:151, 153, 157
"Spring Song" (Clifton) **66**:85
"A Spring Song" (Davie) **31**:116, 118
"Spring Song" (Purdy) **50**:244
Spring Sowing (O'Flaherty) **34**:356-57
"Spring Strains" (Williams) **42**:459
Spring Symphony (Ritsos) **31**:324
"Spring Thing" (Blackburn) **43**:63
"Spring Tide" (MacCaig) **36**:284
"Spring Victory" (Stuart) **34**:374
"Spring Voices" (MacNeice) **53**:234
Springboard (MacNeice) **4**:315
"Spring-Dance" (Rodgers) **7**:377
Springer's Progress (Markson) **67**:186-88, 191, 193, 195-97
The Springing of the Blade (Everson) **5**:122
The Springs (Vesaas)
   See *Kjeldene*
"The Springs of Poetry" (Bogan) **93**:104
Springtime and Harvest: A Romance (*King Midas: A Romance*) (Sinclair) **63**:345, 348
"The Sprinter's Mother" (Dickey) **47**:92
"Sprouts the Bitter Grain" (Webb) **18**:540
"Spunk" (Hurston) **7**:172; **30**:211, 215
Spurs: Nietzsche's Styles (Derrida)
   See *Eperons: Les styles de Nietzsche*
"Spurwing Plover" (Murray) **40**:338
"Sputnik 57" (Guillen) **79**:229
"Spy" (Amichai) **116**:114
The Spy (Lang)
   See *Spione*
Spy (Simon) **26**:412-13
A Spy in the House of Love (Nin) **60**;269, 273-74, 279; **4**:376; **8**:422; **14**:383
The Spy in the Ointment (Westlake) **7**:528; **33**:439
A Spy of the Old School (Rathbone) **41**:343
Spy Story (Deighton) **4**:119; **7**:74-6
The Spy Who Came in from the Cold (le Carre) **3**:281-82; **5**:233-34; **9**:327; **15**:324;**28**:227-28
The Spy Who Loved Me (Fleming) **30**:135-36, 139-40, 148
The Spyglass Tree (Murray) **73**:241-43
"SQ" (Le Guin) **45**:213
"Squandering the Blue" (Braverman) **67**:54
Squandering the Blue (Braverman) **67**:52-5
Le square (*The Square*) (Duras) **3**:129; **6**:149; **11**:165; **40**:174, 180; **68**:76; **100**:129
The Square (Duras)
   See *Le square*
the Square Cat (Ayckbourn) **74**:30-1
Square Dance (Boyle) **19**:68
Square in the Eye (Gelber) **79**:217, 222-24
Square One (Tesich) **69**:367-69

The Square Root of Wonderful (McCullers) **10**:334; **12**:425-26, 430
The Squares of the City (Brunner) **8**:105; **10**:78-9
Square's Progress (Sheed) **2**:393; **4**:487
Squaring the Circle (Stoppard) **91**:190
"Squarings" (Heaney) **74**:188-91, 193-95, 197
Squat Betty (Waterhouse) **47**:417-18
"Squatter" (Mistry) **71**:266, 272
"Squatter's Children" (Bishop) **9**:93; **13**:89; **32**:31, 34
"Squeeze Box" (Townshend) **17**:535, 537
The Squire of Bor Shachor (Bermant) **40**:94
"Squirrel Disappears" (Peacock) **60**:292
The Squirrel Wife (Pearce) **21**:287-89
"The Squirrels of Summer" (Jacobsen) **48**:196
"S.R.O." (Ellison) **42**:127
"Sroczosc" ("Magpiety") (Milosz) **56**:244
"An S.S. Officer" (Spicer) **18**:513
S.S. San Pedro (Cozzens) **4**:111; **11**:125, 128, 131; **92**:178, 186, 199-200
SS-GB: Nazi-Occupied Britain, 1941 (Deighton) **22**:116-17; **46**:128
"S.S.R., Lost at Sea" (Gustafson) **36**:214
"S-sss-ss-sh!" (Hughes) **108**:330
"St. Andrew's" (MacBeth) **2**:252; **5**:263
"St. Anne's Reel" (Ai) **69**:9
St. Augustine (West) **7**:525, 527; **31**:453
"St. Augustine and the Bullfight" (Porter) **101**:223
"St. Augustine's Pigeon" (Connell) **45**:109, 112, 115
St. Augustine's Pigeon: The Selected Stories of Evan S. Connell (Connell) **45**:114-15
"St. Barnabas, Oxford" (Betjeman) **34**:313
St. Burl's Obituary (Akst) **109**:39-42
"St Cecilia's Day" (Porter) **33**:323
"St. Christopher" (Brown) **100**:83
"St. Christopher" (Clarke) **9**:168
St. Dominic's Preview (Morrison) **21**:233-34
"St. Ebba of Coldingham" (Slavitt) **14**:491
"St. Francis and the Birds" (Heaney) **14**:243
"St. Francis of Assisi" (Elytis) **49**:110
St. Francis of Assisi (Almedingen) **12**:3
"St. George and the Dragon: Piecing It All Together" (Hearne) **56**:125-26
St. George and the Godfather (Mailer) **3**:315; **74**:225; **111**:103, 115
St. George of Ilhéus (Amado)
   See *São Jorge dos Ilhéus*
"St. George's Basilica" (Seifert) **93**:345
"St. John" (Godwin) **31**:197
"St. Kilda's Parliament" (Dunn) **40**:170
St. Kilda's Parliament (Dunn) **40**:168-69, 171
St. Lawrence Blues (Blais)
   See *Un joualonais, sa joualonie*
"St. Lawrence of the Cross" (McFadden) **48**:251
"St. Lawrence River" (Kenny) **87**:241
"St. Lemuel's Travels" (Amis) **8**:11
"St. Mark's" (Stern) **100**:344
St. Martin's (Creeley) **2**:108; **4**:117
"St. Paul Could Hit the Nail on the Head" (Mac Laverty) **31**:254
"St. Paul's Cathedral" (Hall) **51**:170
"St. Paul's Revisited" (Davie) **31**:112, 117
"St. Roach" (Rukeyser) **10**:443
"St. Saviour's, Aberdeen Park" (Betjeman) **43**:351
"St. Thomas's Day" (Clarke) **61**:83
"St. Urbain Street Then and Now" (Richler) **46**:351-53
St. Urbain's Horseman (Richler) **3**:429-30;

5:378; **18**:453, 455-56; **46**:347-51; **70**:220, 231-32
"St. Vincent's" (Merwin) **18**:334; **45**:274
Staalspanget (*The Steel Spring*) (Wahloo) **7**:501
"Stabat Mater" (Kristeva) **77**:317, 334
"Stabat mater" (Wittlin) **25**:467
Stad i ljus (*Town in Light*) (Johnson) **14**:294
Stad i möerker (*Town in Darkness*) (Johnson) **14**:294
"Le stade du mirior" ("The Mirror Stage as Formative of the Function of the I as Revealed in Psychoanalytic Experience") (Lacan) **75**:282, 287, 292
Die Stadt (Durrenmatt) **4**:140; **15**:193-96
Stadtgespräch (*The Survivor*) (Lenz) **27**:244, 246, 249, 252-54
"The Staech Affair" (Boell)
   See "Veränderungen in Staech"
"The Staff of Aesculapius" (Moore) **2**:291; **47**:263
"Staffordshire" (Davie) **8**:166
Stage Blood (Ludlam) **46**:241; **50**:343
Stage Door (Ferber) **93**:165
Stage Door (Kaufman) **38**:260
Stage Fright (Hitchcock) **16**:346
"The Stage Is Unlit" (Williams) **42**:440
Stage Struck (Gray) **36**:205, 207
Stagecoach (Ford) **16**:304, 310, 314-15, 317
"Stages" (Gold) **42**:197
"Stages of a Journey Westward" (Wright) **3**:542
Stags and Hens (Russell) **60**:319-20
"Stained Glass" (Baxter) **45**:51, 53
Stained Glass (Buckley) **18**:81-3; **37**:60-1
Stained Glass Elegies (Endo) **54**:157, 160-61; **99**:301
"The Stained Glass Man" (Macdonald) **13**:356
"The Stained Glass Woman" (Macdonald) **19**:290
The Stainless Steel Rat (Harrison) **42**:200, 204-05
The Stainless Steel Rat for President (Harrison) **42**:207
The Stainless Steel Rat Saves the World (Harrison) **42**:204
The Stainless Steel Rat Wants You (Harrison) **42**:204
The Stainless Steel Rat's Revenge (Harrison) **42**:200-01, 204
"The Stains" (Aickman) **57**:4-5, 7
A Staircase in Surrey (Stewart) **14**:512
"The Stairs" (Moss) **14**:376
Stairs to the Roof (Williams) **71**:363, 367
"Stairway to Heaven" (Page and Plant) **12**:478-79, 481-82
"Staking Claim" (Ammons) **57**:58
"The Stalactite" **75**:61
Stalag 17 (Wilder) **20**:457, 460
"Stalin" (Elytis) **49**:110
The Stalingrad Elegies (Schevill) **7**:400
"Stalin's Heirs" ("The Heirs of Stalin") (Yevtushenko) **3**:547; **26**:461, 464; **51**:431
"The Stalker" (Momaday) **85**:256
Stalker (Tarkovsky) **75**:382-85, 388-89, 394, 396-98, 401-02, 406-07, 412
Stalking the Nightmare (Ellison) **42**:131
"Stalkings" (Oates) **108**:371, 374
Stallerhof (*Farmyard*) (Kroetz) **41**:234, 236-37
Stal'naja ptica (Aksyonov)
   See *The Steel Bird, and Other Stories*
Stamboul Train (*Orient Express*) (Greene)

3:209, 213; 27:173, 175; 37:139; 70:289-91, 293; 72:159, 169, 171, 176
Stampe dell' ottocento (Palazzeschi) 11:432
"The Stampede" (Williams) 42:443
Stampede (Ringwood) 48:329-30, 333, 335-38
The Stand (King) 12:311; 26:238, 240; 37:200-01, 203, 205; 61:327, 331-33, 335; 113:343-47, 362, 364-66, 379, 388-93
"Stand, and Be Recognized" (Busch) 47:61, 63
Stand Fast Beloved City (Almedingen) 12:6
"Stand in a Row and Learn" (Abbott) 48:4
A Stand in the Mountains (Taylor) 71:295-96
Stand on Zanzibar (Brunner) 8:105-07; 10:78, 80
Stand Still like the Hummingbird (Miller) 43:298
"Stand Up" (Marley) 17:269
"Stand Up" (Salinas) 90:324, 327
Stand Up, Nigel Barton (Potter) 86:346, 349
Stand We at Last (Fairbairns) 32:163
Stand with Me Here (Francis) 15:234-35, 239
"Stand with Your Lover on the Ending Earth" (Cummings) 68:41
Standard Dreaming (Calisher) 2:96-7; 4:87
A Standard of Behavior (Trevor) 71:339, 345; 116:331, 334, 381
"The Standard of Living" (Parker) 68:329, 335, 337
"Standardisation" (Hope) 51:216
"Standards" (Doctorow) 113:175
"Standards" (Moss) 45:286
"Standards" (Weller) 26:443
Standing by Words (Berry) 46:71, 75
Standing Fast (Swados) 5:422-23
"Standing Fast: Fox into Hedgehog" (Davison) 28:103
"Standing In for Nita" (Rooke) 25:394
"Standing in My Ideas" (MacCaig) 36:288
"Standing on the Streetcorner" (Denby) 48:81
Standing Room Only (Ayckbourn) 74:3
Standing Still and Walking in New York (O'Hara) 78:358, 371, 375
"Standing under a Cherry Tree at Night" (Bly) 15:63
"The Stand-To" (Day Lewis) 10:131
Stanley and the Women (Amis) 40:45-8; 44:135-36, 139, 141-42, 144
Stanley Elkin's The Magic Kingdom (Elkin) 51:92-6; 91:213, 217
"Stanley Kunitz" (Oliver) 98:290
"Stanza" (Bogan) 93:92
"Stanzas" (Brodsky) 100:51
"Stanzas Written at Night in Radio City" (Ginsberg) 6:199
"The Star" (Clarke) 18:107; 35:122
"The Star" (Neruda)
   See "La estrella"
Star (McClure)
   See *The Surge*
The Star Beast (Heinlein) 26:160-61, 172, 176-77
Star Born (Norton) 12:464
Star Bridge (Williamson) 29:461
"Star Bright" (Williamson) 29:455, 458
The Star Conquerors (Bova) 45:65-6, 70
The Star Diaries (Lem) 8:344-45; 15:327; 40:290, 296
The Star Dwellers (Blish) 14:86
"Star Food" (Canin) 55:36-8
A Star for the Latecomer (Zindel) 27:477-78
Star Gate (Norton) 12:456, 461, 467

Star Guard (Norton) 12:461, 463, 467
Star Hunter (Norton) 12:467
"A Star in a Stone-Boat" (Frost) 13:223
A Star in the Family (Faust) 8:215
A Star in the Sea (Silverstein and Silverstein) 17:450, 453
A Star Is Born (Hart) 66:182
The Star King (Vance) 35:421, 423
"Star Lummox" (Heinlein) 55:303
Star Man's Son: 2250 A.D. (Norton) 12:456, 461, 467
"Star of Bethlehem" (Young) 17:577, 582
"Star of Day" (H. D.) 14:224
The Star of Ethiopia (Du Bois) 64:111, 121; 96:145-46
"The Star of the Axletree" (Gray) 41:183
Star Quality (Coward) 29:140
Star Rangers (Norton) 12:456, 461, 467
A Star Shines Over Mt. Morris Park (Roth) 104:317, 319, 324-25, 327
Star Smashers of the Galaxy Rangers (Harrison) 42:202-03, 205, 207
Star Songs of an Old Primate (Tiptree) 48:388-89
"Star Spangled Banner" ("Whores Die Hard") (Kristofferson) 26:269
"Star Star" ("Starfucker") (Jagger and Richard) 17:228, 234, 236, 238
A Star to the North (Corcoran) 17:70, 72
"Star Trek" (Roddenberry) 17:403-15
The Star Turns Red (O'Casey) 5:320; 11:406-09; 15:406; 88:257-58, 270
Star Wars (Lucas) 16:411-17
Star Watchman (Bova) 45:66, 70
"The Star-Apple Kingdom" (Walcott) 42:421-22; 67:355
The Star-Apple Kingdom (Walcott) 14:550-51; 25:457; 42:418, 421-22; 67:358, 360; 76:274
Starbuck Valley Winter (Haig-Brown) 21:138-41
The Starched Blue Sky of Spain (Herbst) 34:452
The Starcrossed (Bova) 45:68-9
"Stardust" (Simon) 26:413
Stardust Memories (Allen) 52:46, 48-9
"Star-Fall" (Warren) 13:582; 18:535
"Starfish" (Oliver) 98:
"Starfucker" (Jagger and Richard)
   See "Star Star"
"Stargazer" (Diamond) 30:112-13
"Star-Gazer" (MacNeice) 53:239
"Stargazing at Barten" (Steele) 45:362
Starik (*The Old Man*) (Trifonov) 45:413-14, 417, 419-25
"Staring at the Sea on the Day of the Death of Another" (Swenson) 106:328
"Stark Boughs on the Family Tree" (Oliver) 98:266
"Stark County Holidays" (Oliver) 19:362; 98:265
"The Starlight Express" (Gilchrist) 65:349
"Starlight Scope Myopia" (Komunyakaa) 94:228, 240, 243-244, 247
"Starlight Scope Myopia" (Komunyakaa) 94:228, 240, 243-44, 247
"Starman" (Bowie) 17:59, 65
Starman Jones (Heinlein) 8:275; 14:250; 26:162-63, 170-72, 176
"Staroe vedro" ("The Old Bucket") (Solzhenitsyn) 10:479
Starring Sally J. Freedman as Herself (Blume) 12:46
"Starry Night" (Sexton) 10:468; 53:316, 320

"The Starry Night" (Snodgrass) 68:388
The Starry Rift (Tiptree) 48:394-95
A Starry Ticket (*A Ticket to the Stars*; *Zvezdnyi bilet*) (Aksyonov) 22:25, 27-8; 101:3-4, 6, 9, 14-15, 28-9, 47
Starryveldt (Morgan) 31:272
"Stars" (Hayden) 9:270; 37:153
"Stars" (Moss) 45:287, 289
"Stars" (Slessor) 14:494
"Stars" (Wright) 53:418, 431
Stars and Bars (Boyd) 53:50-3, 55-6; 70:132, 134-35
The Stars Are Ours! (Norton) 12:456, 467
"The Stars are the Styx" (Sturgeon) 39:366
The Stars at Noon (Johnson) 52:239-41
"The Stars Below" (Saro-Wiwa) 114:253
Stars in Her Eyes (Cavanna) 12:100
Stars in My Pocket Like Grains of Sand (Delany) 38:162
The Stars in Shroud (*Deeper than the Darkness*) (Benford) 52:60, 65
The Stars in Shroud (Benford)
   See *Deeper than the Darkness*
"Stars in Your Name" (Broumas) 73:15
The Stars, like Dust (Asimov) 26:48
The Stars Look Down (Cronin) 32:132-34
"Stars of the New Curfew" (Okri) 87:319, 321
Stars of the New Curfew (Okri) 87:315, 319-22
The Stars of the South (Green)
   See *Les étoiles du sud*
Stars over Paradise Garden (Seifert)
   See *Hvezdy nad rajskou zahradou*
"Stars Over the Dordogne" (Plath) 111:200, 214
"Stars Wheel in Purple" (H. D.) 73:118
Stars Which See, Stars Which Do Not See (Bell) 31:49-51
"Stars Won't You Hide Me" (Bova) 45:73
Starship (Aldiss)
   See *Non-Stop*
Starship Troopers (Heinlein) 14:246-47, 250-254; 26:162-63, 165-66, 170-71, 173, 177-78; 55:303
The Star-Spangled Crunch (Condon) 100:104
The Star-Spangled Future (Spinrad) 46:384
The Star-Spangled Girl (Simon) 31:393-94, 396
"The Star-Splitter" (Frost) 10:195
Starswarm (Aldiss) 14:11
"Start Again Somewhere" (Gallagher) 63:118
Start from Home (Summers) 10:493
A Start in Life (*The Debut*) (Brookner) 32:59-61; 34:139, 142
A Start in Life (Sillitoe) 1:308; 57:397, 399-400
"Start of a Late Autumn Novel" (Transtroemer) 52:416; 65:230
Startide Rising (Brin) 34:133-35
"Starting" (O'Brien) 13:415
"Starting a New Life" (Morrison) 21:232
"Starting Back" (Hugo) 32:242
Starting: Early, Anew, Over, and Late (Yglesias) 22:492
Starting from San Francisco (Ferlinghetti) 10:175; 27:139; 111:64
Starting from Scratch (Castellanos)
   See *Al pie de la letra*
Starting from Scratch: A Different Kind of Writer's Manual (Brown) 79:166, 168, 171
Starting Out (Berton) 104:62
Starting Out in the Thirties (Kazin) 38:275-

77, 280, 283

Starting Over (Wakefield) 7:503

"Starving" (Faludy) 42:141

"Starving Again" (Moore) 68:300

Starworld (Harrison) 42:206-07

"The State" (Pound) 112:319-20

"State Champions" (Mason) 82:244, 252

"State of Affairs" (Gustafson) 36:222

"The State of Art" (Elkin) 14:158

A State of Change (Gilliatt) 2:160; 53:143-44

"The State of Grace" (Brodkey) 56:55-6, 63-4

State of Grace (Williams) 31:461-63

A State of Independence (Phillips) 96:317-18, 325, 333, 340, 343, 352, 354

The State of Ireland: A Novella and Seventeen Stories (Kiely) 23:265-67; 43:241-43, 245

A State of Justice (Paulin) 37:352-53

A State of Peace (Elliott) 47:107-08, 110

A State of Siege (*The Night Comers*) (Ambler) 4:19; 9:19

The State of Siege (Camus)
See *L'état de siège*

A State of Siege (Frame) 22:144, 146; 96:169, 179-80, 189-90, 192, 196, 203, 217, 219

State of the Nation (Dos Passos) 15:183

State of the Union (Capra) 16:159-61

"The Stately Roller Coaster" (Tremain) 42:386

"Statement" (Francis) 15:238

"Statement By a Responsible Spinster" (Smith) 64:394

"Statement of Conservation" (Giovanni) 117:203

Statements after an Arrest under the Immorality Act (Fugard) 9:229, 232-35; 40:197-98; 80:65-6, 68, 70, 74

Statements: Two Workshop Productions (Fugard) 40:197-98

States of Desire: Travels in Gay America (White) 27:480-81; 110:313-14, 316, 322-23, 327, 332

States of Emergency (Brink) 106:107-08, 119-20, 123-25, 137

"Static" (Barnard) 48:27

"Station Island" (Heaney) 37:164-66, 168-69; 74:162-63, 165, 168, 175, 181, 184, 186-87, 193; 91:115-17, 120, 122

Station Island (Heaney) 37:164-69; 74:162, 164-67, 169, 172, 174, 186, 189-90, 193, 197; 91:119, 124

Station to Station (Bowie) 17:63-4, 66, 68

Station Zima (Yevtushenko)
See "Zima Station"

"Stations" (Lorde) 71:260

"Stations" (Stow) 23:436

Stations (Heaney) 74:193; 91:122

"The Statue" (Creeley) 78:137

"The Statue" (Finch) 18:155

"The Statue" (Fuller) 62:184

"The Statue" (Gregor) 9:254

"Statue and Birds" (Bogan) 46:86; 93:93

"Statue at Tsarskoye Selo" (Akhmatova) 64:9

"The Statue in the Café" (Ritsos) 31:331

"The Statue in the Hills" (Brown) 48:57

"The Statue of Liberty" (Wideman) 67:379, 382, 385

"The Statues" (Durcan) 70:152

"The Statues" (Schwartz) 10:462, 465

"Statues" (Wilbur) 53:399

Statues and Lovers (Hall) 51:170

Statues in a Garden (Colegate) 36:109-11

Les statues meurent aussi (Resnais) 16:505

"The Statues of Athens" (Squires) 51:381

"The Status of Art" (Burke) 24:119

"A Statute of Wine" (Neruda)
See "Estatura del vino"

Stavisky (Resnais) 16:511, 513-15

"Stay" (Sondheim) 30:379

"Stay Free" (Clash) 30:43, 46

Stay with Me till Morning (*The View from Tower Hill*) (Braine) 41:58, 61

"Staying Alive" (Levertov) 8:347; 66:245-48

"Staying Alive" (Wagoner) 15:558-59

Staying Alive (Wagoner) 5:474

"Staying Alive by Going to Pieces" (Wagoner) 5:474

"Staying at Ed's Place" (Swenson) 61:397, 401

Staying On (Scott) 9:478; 60:336, 339, 341

"Staying Thin" (Dacey) 51:82

Stazione termini (*Indiscretion*) (De Sica) 20:94

"Steady, Steady, Six Already" (Cortazar) 34:334

Steady Work: Essays in the Politics of Democratic Radicalism, 1953-1966 (Howe) 85:150

The Steagle (Faust) 8:215

"Steak Worship" (Priestley) 34:362

The Stealer of Souls, and Other Stories (Moorcock) 58:350

"Stealing Trout on a May Morning" (Hughes) 37:181

"Steam" (Wain) 46:415

"The Steam Boiler Effect" (Grass)
See "Der Dampfkessel-Effekt"

"Steam Song" (Brooks) 49:36, 38

Steambath (Friedman) 5:127; 56:98-100

Steamboat Bill Junior (Keaton) 20:190, 193-96

"Steamed Carp's Cheeks" (Fuller) 62:199

"The Steel" (Murray) 40:343

Steel Across the Plains (Berton) 104:61

"Steel and Glass" (Lennon) 35:268, 271

The Steel Bird, and Other Stories (*Stal'naja ptica*) (Aksyonov) 22:26; 101:19, 28-29

"Steel Gang" (Davis) 49:93

Steel Magic (Norton) 12:457

Steel Magnolias (Harling) 53:165-67

The Steel Spring (Wahloo)
See *Staalspanget*

Steelwork (Sorrentino) 3:462; 7:447-48, 450-52; 22:392-93; 40:386-87

"Steely Silence" (Wakoski) 4:573

The Steep Ascent (Lindbergh) 82:166-67

Steeple Bush (Frost) 3:169-70; 9:220; 15:241-42, 245; 26:119

"A Steeple on the House" (Frost) 15:242

"The Steeple-Jack" (Moore) 8:397; 10:348; 19:338, 340; 47:260-61, 264, 266, 270

Steeplejacks in Babel (Cassity) 6:107; 42:95, 97-8

"Steersman, My Brother" (Walcott) 25:450

"Stefano's Two Sons" (Landolfi) 11:321; 49:210, 212

Steffie Can't Come Out to Play (Arrick) 30:17

"Steh auf, steh doch auf" (Boell) 72:69

A Steinbook and More (Rothenberg) 6:477

Das steinerne Herz: Historischer Roman aus dem Jahre 1954 (Schmidt) 56:391-93, 405

The Steinway Quartet (Epstein) 27:128

"Stele" (Aldington) 49:3, 6

"Stèle aux mots" (Audiberti) 38:21

"Stellar Manipulator" (Durcan) 70:153

Der Stellvertreter (*The Deputy*) (Hochhuth) 4:230; 11:276

"The Stenographer" (Nowlan) 15:399

"The Stenographers" (Page) 18:379

The Step (Loewinsohn) 52:285

"A Step Away from Them" (O'Hara) 13:425; 78:348-51, 353, 364, 376

"The Step Beyond" (Livesay) 79:348

"Step on His Head" (Laughlin) 49:220

A Step to Silence (Newby) 2:310; 13:408, 410-12

"Step-and-a-Half Waleski" (Erdrich) 54:165

"Stepanida Ivanovna's Funeral" (Soloukhin) 59:378

"The Stepchildren" (Elytis) 49:111

The Stepdaughter (Blackwood) 9:101; 100:2-3, 9, 14-15, 19, 27, 31

Stepen' doveriia (*Degree of Trust*) (Voinovich) 10:506

The Stepford Wives (Levin) 3:294; 6:305-06

"Stephano Remembers" (Simmons) 43:411

"Stephanotis" (Day Lewis) 10:131

Stephen Crane: A Critical Biography (Berryman) 3:71; 13:76

Stephen D (Leonard) 19:280

Stephen Hawking's A Brief History of Time: A Reader's Companion (Hawking) 105:67-8

Stephen King's Danse Macabre (King) 26:243; 37:197-99, 202; 61:326-27

A Stephen Sondheim Evening (Sondheim) 30:400

Stephen Spender: Journals, 1939-1983 (Spender) 41:426-27, 429

Stephen's Light (Almedingen) 12:4-5

Steppenwolf (Hesse)
See *Der Steppenwolf*

Der Steppenwolf (*Steppenwolf*) (Hesse) 1:145-47; 2:191; 3:243-49; 6:236; 11:270-72; 17:196-97, 201-02, 204, 206, 208, 211-16, 219; 25:261; 69:272, 274-79, 284, 286-87, 289, 292-98

"Steppin' Out" (Armatrading) 17:10

"Stepping Outside" (Gallagher) 18:168; 63:120

"Stepping Westward" (Levertov) 66:235

Stepping Westward (Bradbury) 32:51, 53-6, 58; 61:34, 39-40

"Steps" (O'Hara) 78:334

Steps (Kosinski) 1:171-72; 2:231-33; 3:272-73; 6:282-85; 10:306-08; 15:313-14, 316-17; 53:216-17, 219-20, 222, 226, 228; 70:287-98, 300-01, 303, 306

The Steps of the Sun (Tevis) 42:376-77

"Das Sterben der Pythia" ("The Death of the Pythia") (Duerrenmatt) 102:61-2, 64, 69

The Sterile Cuckoo (Nichols) 38:336-41, 343

"Sterling" (Hope) 52:209

"The Sterling Letters" (Harper) 7:140

Stern (Friedman) 3:165; 5:126-27; 56:93-7, 99, 101-05, 107-09

Sternverdunkelung (*Eclipse of Stars*) (Sachs) 98:321-22, 324, 343-45, 352, 356-57, 364

Stet (Reading) 47:354-55

"The Stethoscope" (Abse) 29:18

"Steven Spielberg Plays Howard Beach" (Reed) 60:310

"Stevens" (Harmon) 38:243

Stevie (Whitemore) 37:444-45

Stevie: A Biography of Stevie Smith (Barbera and McBrien) 44:432-35, 437, 440-41, 443-45

Stevie Smith: A Selection (Smith)   44:433, 441
Stevie Wonder Presents Syreeta (Wonder)   12:663
Stewards of Excellence (Alvarez)   5:16
"Stick" (Abe)   81:293
Stick (Leonard)   28:235-36; 71:207-08, 210-11, 213, 216-17, 219, 221-22, 224, 226
"A Stick of Green Candy" (Bowles)   68:4-6, 9
"A Stick-Nest in Ygdrasil" (MacDiarmid)   63:244
Sticks and Bones (Rabe)   4:425-27; 8:449-51; 33:341-44
"Sticks and Stones" (Michaels)   25:315-16
Sticks and Stones (Bowering)   15:81
Sticks and Stones (Reaney)   13:475-76
Sticky Fingers (Jagger and Richard)   17:224-26, 228-30, 232-33, 236, 238, 242
Stiff Upper Lip: Life among the Diplomats (Durrell)   41:139
Stigar (*Paths*) (Transtroemer)   65:221, 233
"Stikhi pod epigrafom" (Brodsky)   13:115
Stikhi/Poems/Poèmes (*Poems*) (Ratushinskaya)   54:379-80, 384, 386
Stikhi raznykh let (*Poems of Various Years*) (Yevtushenko)   13:620
"Stikhii" (Bagryana)   10:12
"Stiletto" (Joel)   26:216-17, 220-21
"Still" (Ammons)   25:48; 57:58; 108:23
"Still" (Beckett)   14:74
"Still Afternoon Light" (Merwin)   1:213
Still Another Day (Neruda)   62:333
The Still Centre (Spender)   5:401; 10:492; 41:424, 429
"Still, Citizen Sparrow" (Wilbur)   53:410-11; 110:354-55
"Still Crazy after All These Years" (Simon)   17:465-66
"Still Hot from Filing" (Williams)   42:439
"Still Hunting" (Lane)   25:286
Still Is the Summer Night (Derleth)   31:129
Still It Is the Day (Delibes)
   See *Aún es de día*
"Still Jim and Silent Jim" (Pearce)   21:288
"Still Just Writing" (Tyler)   103:225, 257, 266
"Still Life" (Gluck)   22:174
"Still Life" (Hughes)   14:271
"Still Life" (MacCaig)   36:282
"Still Life" (Olds)   85:295
"Still Life" (Tchicaya)   101:347
"Still Life" (Thomas)   31:430
Still Life (Byatt)   65:125, 131
Still Life (Coward)   51:69
Still Life (Daryush)   19:119, 122
"Still Life with Flowers" (Thomas)   13:539
"Still Life with Fruit" (Betts)   6:70
Still Life with Pipe (Donoso)   99:222, 255, 273-75
"Still Life with Watermelon" (Mason)   28:274
Still Life with Woodpecker (Robbins)   32:367-69, 371, 373-74; 64:377, 381-83
"Still Lives" (Goldbarth)   38:205
"A Still Moment" (Welty)   14:563; 33:424; 105:299, 307, 385
"Still on Water" (Rexroth)   49:281; 112:398
Still Stands the House (Ringwood)   48:329-39
"Still the Same" (Seger)   35:383
"Still They Call It Marriage" (Musgrave)   54:333
"The Still Time" (Kinnell)   29:285
"Still Turning" (Swenson)   106:351
Still Water (Nichol)   18:369
Still Waters (Middleton)   38:331
"Stillborn" (Plath)   5:341; 14:424; 111:181, 212

Stille Nacht I (The Brothers Quay)   95:351-52, 354
Stille Nacht II (The Brothers Quay)   95:346-47, 351-52, 354
Stille Nacht III (The Brothers Quay)   95:351-32, 355
Stille Nacht IIIA (The Brothers Quay)   95:354
Stille Nacht IV (The Brothers Quay)   95:354
Stiller (*I'm Not Stiller*) (Frisch)   3:167; 9:217-18; 18:163; 32:188-94; 44:183-90, 193-94, 200, 203
"Stillness" (Gardner)   28:162
A Stillness at Appomattox (Catton)   35:85-6, 88, 90
"The Stillness of the Poem" (Loewinsohn)   52:282-83
"Stillpoint Hill at Midnight" (Chappell)   40:145
"Stillpoint Hill That Other Shore" (Chappell)   40:145; 78:92
"Stills" (Montague)   46:266
"Stimme des Heilegen Landes" ("The Voice of the Holy Land") (Sachs)   98:349
"Stimmen" ("Voices") (Celan)   53:69, 77
Stimmen (*Voices*) (Eich)   15:204
Die Stimmen von Marrakesch: Aufzeichnungen nach einer Reise (*The Travels of Marrakesh*; *The Voices of Marrakesh: A Record of a Visit*) (Canetti)   14:124; 25:107-09, 111-12; 75:130, 139; 86:301, 303
Der Stimmenimitator (Bernhard)   61:9
Stimmungen der See (Lenz)   27:244-45
The Sting (Hill)   26:201-05, 207-08, 211-12
"Stings" (Plath)   9:424, 426, 431, 433; 17:361, 366; 111:169, 177
Stir Crazy (Friedman)   56:108
Stir Crazy (Poitier)   26:361-62
"Stir It Up" (Marley)   17:268, 272
"The Stir-Off" (Still)   49:364
Stirrings Still (Beckett)   59:253, 255, 259
Stitch (Stern)   4:523; 39:237-39
"Stixi na smert T. S. Èliota" ("Verses on the Death of T. S. Eliot") (Brodsky)   4:77; 6:97; 13:114; 50:131
"Stoat" (McGahern)   48:264
"Stobhill" (Morgan)   31:275-76
The Stochastic Man (Silverberg)   7:425
"The Stocking" (Campbell)   42:92
Stolen Apples (Yevtushenko)   1:383; 3:547
Stolen Hours (West)   17:548
Stolen Kisses (Truffaut)
   See *Baisers volés*
The Stolen Lake (Aiken)   35:19-20
The Stolen Melody (Nossack)
   See *Die gestohlene Melodie*
"Stolen Pleasures" (Berriault)   109:97
"Stolen Poems" (Laughlin)   49:224
"The Stolen Stories" (Katz)   47:222
Stolen Stories (Katz)   47:220, 222-23
"Stolen Trees" (Hogan)   73:156
Stomping the Blues (Murray)   73:231-36, 242
"The Stone" (Ezekiel)   61:104
"The Stone" (Herbert)   43:193
"Stone" (Hoffman)   6:244
"Stone" (Simic)   9:479; 49:338-40, 342; 68:370, 378
"The Stone" (Soto)
   See "Piedra"
"The Stone" (Thesen)   56:420
"Stone" (Thomas)   13:542
"Stone and Fern" (Norris)   14:388

Stone and Flower Poems, 1935-1943 (Raine)   45:330-32, 334, 341
The Stone Angel (Laurence)   3:280; 13:342-43; 50:312-20; 62:267, 269-71, 273, 278-84, 288-89, 306-07
"The Stone Bear" (Haines)   58:218
The Stone Bird (Purdy)   50:246, 248
The Stone Book (Garner)   17:147-50
"The Stone Boy" (Berriault)   54:3-4; 109:95
The Stone Bridal Bed (Mulisch)   42:287-88
The Stone Bridge (Seifert)
   See *Kamenný most*
The Stone Bull (Whitney)   42:435
"A Stone Church Damaged by a Bomb" (Larkin)   64:261, 282
"Stone City" (81:275
A Stone Country (La Guma)   19:274-76
"The Stone Crab: A Love Poem" (Phillips)   28:362-63
The Stone Diaries (Shields)   91:167-80; 113:437-41, 444-45
A Stone for Danny Fisher (Robbins)   5:379
The Stone from the Green Star (Williamson)   29:454
"The Stone from the Sea" (Celan)   82:36
The Stone Hammer Poems (Kroetsch)   23:272, 276
The Stone Harp (Haines)   58:215-17, 219, 221
"Stone Idols" (Silko)   114:341
"The Stone in the Field" (Munro)   95:305-06, 314
"Stone inside a Stone" (Simic)   9:480
"Stone Keep" (Ammons)   57:51
"The Stone Man" (Hill)   45:179
"Stone Mania" (Murphy)   41:319-20
Stone of Sleep (Cabral de Melo Neto)
   See *Pedra do sono*
"The Stone on the Island" (Campbell)   42:83
"Stone or Flame" (Swenson)   106:337
Stone, Paper, Knife (Piercy)   27:381; 62:366-68, 373
"Stone Reality Meditation" (Ferlinghetti)   111:65
"Stone Serpents" (Zamora)   89:386, 391, 393-94
Stone Telling (Le Guin)   45:219
"Stone Trees" (Gardam)   43:171
"The Stone Verdict" (Heaney)   74:160
Stone Virgin (Unsworth)   76:252-54
"The Stone without Edges" (Ciardi)   40:156
"Stonebreaking" (Forster)   45:134
"The Stonecarver's Poem" (Levertov)   66:249
"Stoned Immaculate" (Morrison)   17:293
"Stoned Soul Picnic" (Nyro)   17:313
Stonehenge (Harrison)   42:201
The Stonemason (McCarthy)   101:168, 191-92, 194, 202-03
"The Stones" (Plath)   1:270; 11:446; 14:425; 17:365-68; 51:340, 344, 346, 348-49; 111:165, 178-79
"Stones" (Transtroemer)   65:222
Stones (Findley)   102:110, 117
The Stones (Hall)   1:137
Stones (O'Hara)   13:424, 427
"Stones and Angels" (MacEwen)   55:165
Stones for Ibarra (Doerr)   34:151-54
"Stones for My Temple"   75:71
Stones from the Rubble (Montgomery)   7:233
"Stones in My Passway, Hellhound on My Trail" (Boyle)   36:64
The Stones of Chile (Neruda)
   See *Las piedras de Chile*

The Stones of Florence (McCarthy)   **14:**357; **59:**290

The Stones of the Field (Thomas)   **6:**532; **13:**542; **48:**380

Stones Speak (Endo)   **99:**285

The Stonewall Brigade (Slaughter)   **29:**378

Stonewall Jackson: The Good Soldier (Tate)   **11:**526-27

"Stonewall Jackson's Wife" (Wiggins)   **57:**433-35

"Stoney End" (Nyro)   **17:**315

"Stony Grey Soil" (Kavanagh)   **22:**239

Stony Limits (MacDiarmid)   **4:**309; **11:**333; **19:**290; **63:**249, 255

"Stop" (Dixon)   **52:**99

"Stop" (Wilbur)   **6:**570; **53:**413

A Stop in the Desert (Brodsky)   **100:**59

Stop Press (Stewart)   **14:**512

"Stop Staring at My Tits, Mister" (Bukowski)   **41:**74; **108:**85

"Stopped Dead" (Plath)   **5:**345; **17:**366; **51:**340, 345

"Stopped Frames and Set-Pieces" (Fisher)   **25:**161

"Stopping by Woods on a Snowy Evening" (Frost)   **3:**170, 174; **9:**220; **10:**198; **13:**223-24, 228, 230; **15:**240, 244, 246, 249; **26:**114-17, 119, 121-23; **34:**475

A Stopping Place (Mojtabai)   **15:**378-79

"The Store" (Jones)   **76:**65-6

The Store (Stribling)   **23:**440, 442, 448-49

Det store spelet (*The Great Game*) (Vesaas)   **48:**404, 406, 409

"The Storeroom" (Weiss)   **8:**546; **14:**554, 557

La storia (*History: A Novel*) (Morante)   **8:**402-03; **47:**276-77, 281-83

Storia della Tigre (Fo)   **109:**101, 108, 115

"La storia di Regalpetra" (Sciascia)   **41:**392

Storie naturali (*Natural Stories*) (Levi)   **50:**331

"Stories" (Anderson)   **9:**31

"The Stories" (Dunn)   **40:**171

"Stories" (Jarrell)   **13:**301; **49:**196

"Stories" (Oliver)   **98:**303

Stories (Lessing)   **10:**316; **15:**331

Stories (Pasternak)   **63:**290

Stories about Unusual Muzhiks (Leonov)   See *Neobyknovennie rasskazy o muzhikakh*

Stories and Plays (O'Brien)   **4:**385; **7:**269-70; **10:**362

Stories and Prose Poems: by Aleksandr Solzhenitsyn (Solzhenitsyn)   **4:**507; **78:**427

Stories, Fables, and Other Diversions (Nemerov)   **6:**360, 363

Stories for Children (Singer)   **69:**306

"Stories from behind the Stove" (Singer)   **3:**454

Stories from El Barrio (Thomas)   **17:**502

Stories from Western Canada (Wiebe)   **6:**567

"Stories I Tell Myself" (Cortazar)   **33:**126, 130

Stories in an Almost Classical Mode (Brodkey)   **56:**59-63, 65-7

The Stories of Bernard Malamud (*Collected Stories*) (Malamud)   **27:**305-07; **44:**413

The Stories of Breece D'J Pancake (Pancake)   **29:**346-51

The Stories of Elizabeth Spencer (Spencer)   **22:**405

The Stories of Eva Luna (Allende)   **97:**2-4, 9-11, 25-6, 28, 56, 63

Stories of Five Decades (Hesse)   **2:**192; **3:**249

The Stories of Heinrich Böll (Boell)   **72:**99

"Stories of Ideas" (Riding)   **7:**375

The Stories of John Cheever (Cheever)   **11:**120-21; **15:**129-31; **64:**66

"Stories of Lives" (Riding)   **7:**375

Stories of Love (Agnon)   **4:**11

"The Stories of Love and Sickness" (Calvino)   **39:**314

The Stories of Mary Lavin (Lavin)   **99:**322

Stories of Misbegotten Love (Gold)   **42:**197

The Stories of Muriel Spark (Spark)   **40:**400-03

"The Stories of Our Daughters" (Smith)   **42:**350

The Stories of Ray Bradbury (Bradbury)   **42:**35-7

The Stories of Raymond Carver (Carver)   **36:**106; **53:**66

The Stories of Seán O'Faoláin (O'Faolain)   See *Finest Short Stories of Seán O'Faoláin*

"Stories of Snow" (Page)   **7:**291-92; **18:**379

Stories of the Gods and Heroes (Benson)   **17:**47

The Stories of William Trevor (Trevor)   **71:**321, 324-5, 334; **116:**367

Stories that Could Be True: New and Collected Poems (Stafford)   **29:**383, 385

Stories up to a Point (Pesetsky)   **28:**357-59

Stories We Listened To (Haines)   **58:**223

"The Storm" (Brown)   **48:**57

"Storm" (H. D.)   **73:**118

"The Storm" (L'Heureux)   **52:**274

"Storm" (O'Brien)   **65:**167-71

"Storm" (Oliver)   **98:**266

The Storm (Ehrenburg)   **18:**132; **62:**177-80

Storm and Echo (Prokosch)   **48:**312-15

The Storm and Other Poems (Brown)   **100:**84

The Storm and Other Things (Montale)   See *La bufera e altro*

The Storm and Other Things (Montale)   See *La bufera e altro*

The Storm and the Silence (Walker)   **14:**552

Storm at Castelfranco (Kallman)   **2:**221

"Storm Awst" (Clarke)   **61:**73

Storm Below (Garner)   **13:**234

Storm Boy (Thiele)   **17:**493, 496

"The Storm Cleared Rapidly" (Jacobsen)   **48:**190

"Storm Coming in Wales" (Grigson)   **7:**136

"Storm Ending" (Toomer)   **1:**341

"Storm Fear" (Frost)   **26:**113

"Storm Glass" (Urquhart)   **90:**384-5

Storm Glass (Urquhart)   **90:**383-5

Storm Haven (Slaughter)   **29:**375

Storm in Chandigarh (Sahgal)   **41:**371

"Storm in the Desert" (Squires)   **51:**380, 382

Storm of Fortune (Clarke)   **8:**142; **53:**93-4

"Storm on Fifth Avenue" (Sassoon)   **36:**387

Storm over Warlock (Norton)   **12:**467

"Storm Warnings" (Rich)   **36:**365

"Storm Weather" (Shapcott)   **38:**402

"Storm Windows" (Nemerov)   **36:**305

The Storm Within (Cocteau)   **16:**223

"The Storm-Cock's Song" (MacDiarmid)   **63:**255

The Storming of Velikoshumsk (Leonov)   See *Vziatie Velikoshumska*

"Stormpetrel" (Murphy)   **41:**314

Stormqueen (Bradley)   **30:**27-8, 30

The Stormy Life of Lasik Roitschwantz (Ehrenburg)   **18:**134; **34:**437, 439; **62:**173

"Stormy Night" (Blunden)   **56:**49

The Stormy Night (Duhamel)   See *La nuit d'orage*

The Stormy Petrel (Stewart)   **117:**384

"Stormy Sky" (Davies)   **21:**102

"A Story" (Avison)   **97:**115

"Story" (Cohen)   **38:**131

"A Story" (Rich)   **73:**330

"Story" (Sanchez)   **116:**328

The Story (Pasternak)   See *Povest*

"A Story about Greenery" (Valenzuela)   **104:**388

"The Story Behind 'Foundation'" (Asimov)   **92:**21

"Story Books on a Kitchen Table" (Lorde)   **71:**247, 250

A Story for Teddy—And Others (Swados)   **5:**422

"Story from Bear Country" (Silko)   **114:**316

"The Story Hearer" (Paley)   **37:**336

"A Story in an Almost Classical Mode" (Brodkey)   **56:**60, 66-7

"Story in Harlem Slang" (Hurston)   **30:**219

A Story like the Wind (van der Post)   **5:**464

"The Story of a Blind Man" (Tanizaki)   See "Momoku monogatari"

"The Story of a Citizen" (Gallagher)   **63:**123, 125

"Story of a Coin" (Levi)   **50:**335

The Story of a Country Boy (Powell)   **66:**367

"The Story of a Dead Man" ("Dead Man") (McPherson)   **77:**367-68, 373, 378-79, 382

The Story of a Humble Christian (Silone)   **4:**494

The Story of a Life (Paustovsky)   See *Povest' o zhizni*

The Story of a Little Girl (Almedingen)   **12:**1-2, 7

"Story of a Marriage" (Foote)   **51:**137-38

"The Story of a Novel" (MacLennan)   **92:**347

"The Story of a Panic" (Forster)   **9:**207; **45:**140

The Story of a Round-House and Other Poems (Masefield)   **47:**225

"The Story of a Scar" ("Scar") (McPherson)   **77:**361, 365-69, 378, 380-82

The Story of a Shipwrecked Sailor (Garcia Marquez)   **47:**152-54

Story of a Staircase (Buero Vallejo)   See *Historia de una escalera*

Story of a Stairway (Buero Vallejo)   See *Historia de una escalera*

"The Story of a Story" (Smith)   **25:**421

The Story of a Three-Day Pass (Van Peebles)   **20:**409-10

A Story of a Town with a River (Kawabata)   See *A Story of a Town with a River*

"The Story of a Well-Made Shield" (Momaday)   **85:**247

The Story of Adele H. (Truffaut)   See *L'histoire d'Adele H.*

"The Story of Africa" (Du Bois)   **64:**112

The Story of an African Farm (Paton)   **4:**395

"The Story of an Olson" (Olson)   **29:**329

The Story of Aunt Shlomzion the Great (Kaniuk)   **19:**240

"The Story of Counter-Octave" ("The History of a Contraoctave") (Pasternak)   **10:**387

A Story of Floating Weeds (Ozu)   **16:**451

The Story of Folk Music (Berger)   **12:**41

The Story of Gudrun (Almedingen)   **12:**3

The Story of Henri Tod (Buckley)   **37:**61-2

"A Story of How a Wall Stands" (Ortiz)   **45:**303

The Story of Israel (Levin)   **7:**206

"The Story of Lowry Maen" (Colum)   **28:**91

The Story of Marie Powell: Wife to Mr. Milton (*Wife to Mr. Milton: The Story of Marie Powell*) (Graves)   **39:**322, 325; **45:**173

The Story of Mist (Dybek)   **114:**74

"The Story of My Experiment with a White Lie" (Anand)   **93:**41-2

Story of My Life (McInerney) 112:181-86, 190-91, 196, 202-04, 208-09, 212, 215, 218

"The Story of Our Lives" (Strand) 6:521; 18:519; 41:433, 437; 71:279, 289

The Story of Our Lives (Strand) 6:521-23; 18:519, 521; 41:434, 436; 71:279

"The Story of Richard Maxfield" (Wakoski) 7:504

"The Story of Studs Lonigan" (Farrell) 66:134

"Story of Sun House" (Silko) 74:334-35, 338

"The Story of the Arrowmaker" (Momaday) 95:238

Story of the Eye (Bataille)
    See *Histoire de l'oeil*

The Story of the Heart (Aleixandre)
    See *Historia del corazón*

"The Story of the Master and the Disciple" (Kis) 57:251

The Story of the Siren (Forster) 9:207

"Story of the Warrior and the Captive" (Borges)
    See "Historia del guerrero y de la cautiva"

The Story of the Weasel (*Relations*) (Slaughter) 56:407-08, 410

"A Story of Tomoda and Matsunaga" (Tanizaki)
    See "Tomoda to Matsunaga no hanashi"

"The Story of Tsoai" (Momaday) 85:256

"The Story of Two Dogs" (Lessing) 22:279

"Story of Two Gardens" (Paz)
    See "Cuento de dos jardines"

The Story on Page One (Odets) 28:336-37; 98:211, 246

"The Story Teller" (Brown) 48:52

"The Story Teller" (O'Connor) 23:331

Story Teller (Kantor) 7:195

The Story Teller (Vansittart) 42:394, 400

"Story under Full Sail" (Voznesensky) 57:422

"A Story Wet as Tears" (Piercy) 62:366

"Story Which Should Have Happened" (Porter) 5:347

"A Story with a Pattern" (Lavin) 18:306

"The Storyteller" (Hillis) 66:196, 199

"Storyteller" (Silko) 23:411; 74:322, 333, 338, 344; 114:314

The Story-Teller (Highsmith)
    See *A Suspension of Mercy*

Storyteller (Silko) 23:411; 74:326-27, 329, 331-32, 335-38, 341-44, 346-51; 114:304, 310-12, 314-15, 317-19, 337-40, 343

The Storyteller (Sillitoe) 19:420-21; 57:403

The Storyteller (Vargas Llosa)
    See *El hablador*

"Storyteller's Escape" (Silko) 74:349

"Storytelling" (Silko) 74:337; 114:315

"Storytown" (Daitch) 103:78

Storytown (Daitch) 103:77-8

Stowaway to Mars (Wyndham) 19:476

La strada (*The Road*) (Fellini) 16:270-73, 275-76, 278-79, 284, 286-87, 290, 292, 294, 297; 85:46-8, 58-9, 66-7, 74, 76, 78, 80

La strada (Pasolini) 106:230

La strada che va in città (*The Road to the City*) (Ginzburg) 11:227; 54:193, 196, 205; 70:281-83

Straight (Francis) 102:135-37, 139, 158

Straight Cut (Bell) 102:15-16

Straight from the Ghetto (Pinero) 55:317

Straight Through the Night (Allen) 59:337

"Straight to Hell" (Clash) 30:50-2

"Straight-Creek—Great Burn" (Snyder) 5:395

The Straightening (Celan)
    See *Sprachgitter*

Strains (Brutus) 43:88-9

The Strait of Anian (Birney) 6:74; 11:51

"The Straitening" (Celan)
    See "Engführung"

The Straitjacket (Parra) 102:355

"The Strand at Lough Beg" (Heaney) 25:248; 37:164; 74:159-60, 163, 168, 171; 91:115, 117

Strändernas svall (*Return to Ithaca: The "Odyssey" Retold as a Modern Novel*) (Johnson) 14:295

"Strandhill, the Sea" (McGahern) 48:268

"The Strange Aberration of Mr. Ken Smythe" (Metcalf) 37:300

The Strange Adventures of David Gray (*Vampyr*) (Dreyer) 16:258-61, 263-65, 269

The Strange Affair of Adelaide Harris (Garfield) 12:223, 226, 230, 232, 235, 237

"A Strange and Sometimes Sadness" (Ishiguro) 27:202

"The Strange and True Story of My Life with Billy the Kid" (Momaday) 85:280

"Strange Archaeology" (Skvorecky) 69:333, 346

The Strange Case of Mademoiselle P. (Norfolk) 76:93-7

The Strange Children (Gordon) 6:203, 207; 29:190; 83:232, 234-36, 244, 246-48, 258, 260-61

The Strange Country (Lagerkvist)
    See *Det märkvärdiga landet*

Strange Days (Morrison) 17:289, 291-92, 295

The Strange Death of Mistress Coffin (Begiebing) 70:35-42

"Strange Encounters" (Chatwin) 57:153

Strange Eons (Bloch) 33:84

"Strange Fire" (Oz) 27:359-60, 362

"Strange Fruit" (Harjo) 83:272, 274

"Strange Fruit" (Heaney) 25:243; 74:158

Strange Fruit (Phillips) 96:332, 334

Strange Fugitive (Callaghan) 14:100, 102-03; 41:89, 98; 65:251-52

A Strange God (Savage) 40:373-74

"Strange Hurt" (Hughes) 108:330

The Strange Islands (Merton) 83:394

"A Strange Job" (Oe)
    See "An Odd Job"

"Strange Juice (or the murder of Latasha Harlins)" (Sapphire) 99:81

"Strange Legacies" (Brown) 59:265

Strange Meeting (Hill) 4:226-28; 113:280, 287, 291-92, 296-97, 300, 303-05, 312, 322-24, 330

Strange Moon (Stribling) 23:445

"The Strange Museum" (Paulin) 37:354

The Strange Museum (Paulin) 37:353

The Strange Necessity (West) 7:526; 31:452, 459; 50:394

Strange News from Another Star, and Other Tales (Hesse) 3:249

"Strange People" (Erdrich) 54:165

The Strange River (Green)
    See *Epaves*

"Strange Things Happen Here" (Valenzuela) 104:382

Strange Things Happen Here (Valenzuela) 31:436-37; 104:364, 376-78

"Strange Town" (Weller) 26:446

Strange Wine (Ellison) 13:208

"The Stranger" (Brown) 48:57

"The Stranger" (Joel) 26:221

The Stranger (Camus)
    See *L'étranger*

The Stranger (Joel) 26:215-17, 221-22

The Stranger (Ray)
    See *Agantuk*

The Stranger (Ringwood) 48:330, 334-35, 338-39

The Stranger (Visconti) 16:567-68, 575

The Stranger (Welles) 20:433, 441; 80:382, 387, 391, 393-96

"Stranger at Coney Island" (Fearing) 51:114-15

Stranger at Coney Island and Other Poems (Fearing) 51:113-14

The Stranger at the Gate (Neihardt) 32:331

"Stranger at the Table" (Apple) 33:21

"Stranger, Bear Words to the Spartans We..." (Boell)
    See "Wanderer, kommst du nach Spa..."

A Stranger Came Ashore (Hunter) 21:163-64

Stranger in a Strange Land (Heinlein) 3:225-27; 8:274-75; 14:247, 250-252, 254-55; 26:161-63, 166-70, 174; 55:300-04

"Stranger in My Own Land" (Allen) 84:18

"A Stranger in My Own Life: Alienation in American Indian Prose and Poetry" (Allen) 84:3, 36

The Stranger in Shakespeare (Fiedler) 24:200, 202

"Stranger in the House" (Costello) 21:71

"Stranger in the House" (Wilhelm) 7:537-38

Stranger in the House (Sherburne) 30:363

A Stranger in the Kingdom (Mosher) 62:315-18

"Stranger in the Village" (Baldwin) 2:32; 42:18; 50:291; 90:12

Stranger in Town (Hunt) 3:252

Stranger in Town (Seger) 35:382-86

"Stranger on a Train" (Theroux) 46:402

Stranger on Horseback (L'Amour) 55:308

"A Stranger with a Bag" (Warner) 7:512

Stranger with My Face (Duncan) 26:107-08

"Strangers" (Graham) 48:144-45

"Strangers" (Singer) 69:309

Strangers (Jones) 52:247-48, 253

Strangers (Koontz) 78:197-98, 200, 203

The Strangers (Schlee) 35:371-72

The Strangers All Are Gone (Powell) 31:321-22

Strangers and Brothers (Snow) 1:314-17; 4:500-05; 6:515-18; 9:496-97; 13:508-10, 511; 19:425-28

Strangers in Paradise (Abbott) 48:6-7

"The Stranger's Kingdom" (Carroll) 10:98

Strangers on a Train (Highsmith) 2:193; 4:225-26; 42:211; 102:169-170, 172-73, 185-88, 190, 192-93, 199-201, 206, 210-13, 219-20

Strangers on a Train (Hitchcock) 16:340, 344, 346, 349, 355, 358-59

Strangers on Earth (Troyat) 23:459-60

Strangers to Ourselves (Kristeva)
    See *Etrangers à nous-mêmes*

Strangers When We Meet (Hunter) 31:219-21, 226

The Strangest Kind of Romance (Williams) 15:580

"Strangled Thoughts" (Cioran) 64:89, 94

Strapless (Hare) 58:233

"Strata" (FitzGerald) 19:180

Les stratégies fatales (*Fatal Strategies*) (Baudrillard) 60:25-5, 33

"Strategy" (Gallagher) 63:119

"Straus Park" (Stern) **40**:406, 408
Straw Dogs (Peckinpah) **20**:278, 282
"Straw Hat" (Dove) **50**:156; **81**:139
"Strawberries under the Snow" (Duncan) **15**:187
Strawberry Fields (Poliakoff) **38**:378-81, 386
"Strawberry Fields Forever" (Lennon and McCartney) **35**:268
"Strawberry Hill" (Ewart) **46**:150
"Strawberry Hill" (Hughes) **14**:270
"Strawberry Moon" (Oliver) **98**:265
"The Strawberry Window" (Bradbury) **42**:32
"Strawberrying" (Swenson) **61**:405; **106**:333
"Straw-Blond" (Hikmet) **40**:247, 251
Strawhead (Mailer) **74**:227
"Stray Cat Blues" (Jagger and Richard) **17**:222-23, 230, 235, 240
"Stray Children" (Oates) **52**:338
Stray Dog (Kurosawa) **16**:402-03
"The Stray Dog by the Summerhouse" (Justice) **19**:233
"Stray Dog Near Ecully" (Avison) **97**:70-1
"Strayed Crab" (Bishop) **32**:42
"The Straying Student" (Clarke) **9**:168
"The Stream" (Simic) **22**:381
"The Stream" (Van Duyn) **63**:441-42, 444; **116**:409-10, 421, 425, 430
Streamers (Altman) **116**:47
Streamers (Rabe) **8**:450-51; **33**:341-45
"Streams" (Auden) **14**:29; **43**:27
"Streamside Exchange" (Clark) **38**:120-21, 128-29
"Streche" ("Madness") (Arghezi) **80**:7
"The Street" (Dobyns) **37**:81
"The Street" (Pinsky) **38**:361-62; **94**:299
"The Street" (Soto) **80**:276-77, 281, 287, 292, 295-96
The Street (Petry) **1**:266; **7**:304; **18**:403-04
The Street (Richler) **9**:450
"Street Boy" (Bennett) **28**:26, 29
"Street Crossing" (Transtroemer) **65**:229-30
"Street Fighting Man" (Jagger and Richard) **17**:222-24, 226, 229, 236-37, 241
Street Games (Brown) **32**:63-5
The Street Has Changed (Daly) **52**:88
Street Hassle (Reed) **21**:314-17, 319-21
"A Street in an Autumn Morning" (Krleza)
   See "Ulica u jesenje jutro"
A Street in Bronzeville (Brooks) **1**:46; **2**:82; **5**:75-6; **15**:92-4; **49**:21-2, 25-6, 30-2, 35
A Street in Moscow (Ehrenburg) **62**:168
"Street in the City" (Townshend) **17**:537
Street Legal (Dylan) **12**:197; **77**:189-90
"Street Life" (Diamond) **30**:112
Street of Crocodiles (The Brothers Quay) **95**:333-35, 338-45, 347-48, 350-57
"The Street of Furthest Memory" (Pinsky) **94**:307
Street of Riches (Roy)
   See *Rue deschambault*
The Street of Today (Masefield) **11**:357
Street Players (Goines) **80**:91-2
Street Rod (Felsen) **17**:122
Street Scene (Rice) **7**:358-64; **49**:294-97, 299-302, 304-05
Street Scenes, 1970 (Scorsese) **20**:324
"Street Scenes II" (Hacker) **91**:110
Streetbird (van de Wetering) **47**:410, 412
"Streetcar" (Avison) **97**:106
A Streetcar Named Desire (Kazan) **16**:361, 367-69, 374; **63**:222, 225, 231, 234
A Streetcar Named Desire (Williams) **1**:367-69; **2**:465-66; **5**:498, 500-01, 503-06;

7:541, 543, 545; **8**:547-48; **11**:572, 574-77; **15**:581; **19**:472; **30**:454-73; **39**:445-46, 449-50, 452-53; **45**:446-48; **71**:265-66, 382, 387, 399, 405; **111**:377, 380, 387-91, 398-404, 408-09, 411-19, 421-25
"Streetcorner Man" (Borges)
   See "Hombre de la esquina rosada"
Streetlife Serenade (Joel) **26**:214, 217, 219
"Streetlife Serenader" (Joel) **26**:214, 217
"The Streets" (Winters) **32**:468
Streets in the Moon (MacLeish) **8**:362; **68**:270-71, 273, 291
"The Streets of Ashkelon" (Harrison) **42**:203
"Streets of Fire" (Springsteen) **17**:483-85
Streets of Gold (Hunter) **11**:280; **31**:223
"The Streets of Laredo" (MacNeice) **1**:187
Streets of Night (Dos Passos) **15**:184; **25**:137, 144
"Streets of Pearl and Gold" (Kizer) **80**:180, 182, 185
Strega (Vachss) **106**:355-59, 361, 365
"The Strength of Fields" (Dickey) **15**:177-78; **47**:92, 98; **109**:243
The Strength of Fields (Dickey) **15**:177-78; **47**:90-3, 95-6, 98; **109**:245
Strength of Steel (Serling) **30**:353
"Strength through Joy" (Rexroth) **112**:389
The Strength to Dream: Literature and the Imagination (Wilson) **14**:588
Strength to Love (King) **83**:328-30, 341
"The Stricken Child" (Dacey) **51**:79
A Stricken Field (Gellhorn) **60**:178-79, 190-91, 196
"Strictly Business" (Himes) **108**:235
Strictly from Hunger (Perelman) **49**:257
"Strictly Genteel" (Zappa) **17**:587
Strictly Personal (Maugham) **15**:367
Stride toward Freedom: The Montgomery Story (King) **83**:327, 331, 337-38, 347
"Striders" (Nemerov) **36**:309
"Strike" (Selby) **4**:481; **8**:475, 477, 475-76
"Strike and Fade" (Dumas) **6**:145; **62**:154-55
Strike the Father Dead (Wain) **46**:412, 418
Strike Three, You're Dead (Rosen) **39**:194-97
The Strikers (Valdez)
   See *Huelgistas*
Strikes, Bombs, and Bullets: Big Bill Haywood and the IWW (Archer) **12**:19
"Striking at the Heart of the System" (Eco) **60**:113
Striking the Stones (Hoffman) **6**:243; **13**:287; **23**:237
Strindberg (Wilson) **14**:589
The String (Akhmadulina)
   See *Struna*
String (Childress) **12**:104; **86**:309
String Horses (Holden) **18**:257, 259
String Too Short to Be Saved (Hall) **37**:146-47, 149; **59**:152
Stringer (Just) **4**:266-67
"Strings" (Kinsella) **43**:253
The Strings Are False (MacNeice) **53**:244
The Strings, My Lord, Are False (Carroll) **10**:95-6, 98
"S-Trinity of Parnassus" (Tolson) **105**:256
Strip Jack Naked (Hill) **113**:296
"Strip/La Baleine" (Moure) **88**:219, 229
A Strip of Land (Arghezi)
   See *Pe o palma de tarina*
"Stripper" (Phillips) **15**:419
Striptease (Mrozek) **3**:345
Striptease of Jealousy (Arrabal) **9**:39

"Striptiz" (Voznesensky) **57**:417
Stripwell (Barker) **37**:32, 35-7
"Strivings of the Negro People" (Du Bois) **96**:154
"Strof och motstrof" (Transtroemer) **52**:410; **65**:235
"Strofy" (Brodsky)
   See "Strophes"
"Stroke" (Buckley) **57**:126, 128, 131, 133
"The Stroke" (Dove) **50**:153; **81**:139
"The Stroke" (Smith) **25**:419
"The Stroke of Apelles" (Pasternak)
   See "Il tratto di Apelle"
A Stroke of Genius (West) **96**:397
"A Stroke of Good Fortune" (O'Connor) **3**:366; **6**:381; **21**:268
"A Stroke of Luck" (Kotzwinkle) **35**:253-54
A Stroll in the Air (Ionesco)
   See *Le piéton de l'air*
A Stroll with William James (Barzun) **51**:48, 50
The Stroller in the Air (Ionesco)
   See *Le piéton de l'air*
The Strong Are Lonely (Hochwalder)
   See *Das Heilige Experiment*
"The Strong Are Saying Nothing" (Frost) **10**:196
The Strong Breed (Soyinka) **14**:506-07; **36**:410-11; **44**:283, 287-90
The Strong City (Caldwell) **28**:57; **39**:302
A Strong Dose of Myself (Abse) **29**:20
"Strong Horse Tea" (Walker) **5**:476; **103**:407, 412, 423
Strong Medicine (Foreman) **50**:168
"Strong Men" (Brown) **23**:96
"Strong Men Riding Horses: Lester after the Western" (Brooks) **15**:92; **49**:32
"A Strong New Voice Pointing the Way" (Madhubuti) **73**:215
Strong Opinions (Nabokov) **3**:355; **8**:413-14; **23**:304
"A Strong Wind" (Clarke) **6**:112
Strong Wind (Asturias)
   See *The Cyclone*
Stronger Climate (Jhabvala) **4**:257-58
The Strongest Men Don't Stay Unscathed; or, Mother Always Knows Best (Haavikko)
   See *Ne vahvimmat miehet ei ehjiksi jää*
The Stronghold (Hunter) **21**:160, 165
The Stronghold (Levin) **7**:205
"Strophes" ("Strofy") (Brodsky) **13**:115; **36**:77; **100**:55
"Strophes elegiaque: A la memoire d'Alban Berg" ("Elegiac Stanzas for Alban Berg") (Gascoyne) **45**:150, 158
Stroszek (Herzog) **16**:326-29, 331, 333
Strountes (Ekeloef) **27**:115
Structural Anthropology (Levi-Strauss)
   See *Anthropologie structurale*
"The Structural Study of Myth" (Rothenberg) **57**:383
The Structural Transformation of the Public Sphere (Habermas)
   See *Strukturwandel der Offenlichkeit*
"La structure, le signe, et le jeu dans le discours des sciences humaines" (Derrida) **24**:153
"The Structure of Bad Taste" (Eco) **60**:118
"The Structure of Orlando Furioso" (Calvino) **73**:48
"The Structure of Rime" (Duncan) **41**:124, 128-29
The Structure of Rime (Duncan) **4**:141; **15**:190; **55**:297-98

"The Structure of the Plane" (Rukeyser) 15:459; 27:404

"Structures" (MacCaig) 36:284

Les structures élémentaires de la parenté (Levi-Strauss) 38:294, 297, 300

Structures mentales (Goldmann) 24:242

The Structures of Complex Words (Empson) 8:201-02; 33:145, 147-51; 34:336-38

"The Struggle After Justice" (Neruda) 62:328

The Struggle against Shadows (Duhamel) 8:189

Struggle Is Our Brother (Felsen) 17:119-20

"Struggle of Wings" (Williams) 42:450

"The Struggle Staggers Us" (Walker) 6:554

Struggling Man (Cliff) 21:62

"The Struggling Masseur" (Naipaul) 13:402

Struggling Spirit (Lagerkvist)
    See *Kämpande ande*

Strukturwandel der Offenlichkeit (*The Structural Transformation of the Public Sphere*) (Habermas) 104:85-6

Struna (*The String*) (Akhmadulina) 53:9-11, 13, 15

Struna swiatla (Herbert) 43:192

Stuart Little (White) 34:425-26, 430; 39:369-70, 375-77, 380

The Stubborn Heart (Slaughter) 29:374

"Stubborn Hope" (Brutus) 43:89

Stubborn Hope: New Poems and Selections from "China Poems" and "Strains" (Brutus) 43:89-90, 97

"The Stubborn Spearmen" (Davis) 49:91, 97

The Stubborn Structure (Frye) 70:275

"Stuck-Up" (Cryer) 21:79

"The Student Aulach" (Spender) 41:421

"The Students" (Bell) 8:65

Students (Trifonov)
    See *Studenty*

"The Students Take Over" (Rexroth) 49:275

Studenty (*Students*) (Trifonov) 45:407-11, 413, 417, 420-22

The Studhorse Man (Kroetsch) 5:220-21; 23:270-72; 57:283-84, 288

Studies (Ritsos) 13:487

"Studies for an Actress" (Garrigue) 8:239

Studies for an Actress and Other Poems (Garrigue) 8:239

"Studies for an Andalusian Dancer" (Cabral de Melo Neto)
    See "Estudos para uma bailadora andaluza"

Studies in a Dying Colonialism (Fanon)
    See *L'an V de la révolution algérienne*

Studies in American Indian Literature: Critical Essays and Course Designs (Allen) 84:13-14, 23, 28, 31, 34-6

Studies in Black American Literature: Black American Prose Theory, Volume I 65:365

Studies in European Realism (Lukacs) 24:315, 317, 321, 323

"Studies in Power" (Smith) 64:398

"Studies in the Park" (Desai) 97:149, 151-53, 171

"The Studies of Narcissus" (Schwartz) 45:356

Studies of the Novel (Kawabata)
    See *Studies of the Novel*

"Studies on the Life of Testaccio (Pasolini) 106:270

The Studio (Dunne) 28:121, 125

"Studio Tan" (Zappa) 17:592

Studium przedmiotu (*Study of the Object*) (Herbert) 9:274; 43:184, 192

Studs Lonigan: A Trilogy (Farrell) 1:198; 4:158; 8:205; 11:193, 195-96; 66:112-14, 120-

26, 128-29, 132, 134-36

"Study" (Harrison) 43:180

A Study in Choreography for Camera (Deren) 16:252, 254

A Study in Choreography for Camera (Deren) 102:28, 31, 37-8, 40-3

A Study in French Poets (Pound) 10:400

"Study in Kore" (Plumly) 33:311

A Study of Courage and Fear (Coles) 108:193

"The Study of History" (Rich) 7:368

"A Study of Reading Habits" (Larkin) 5:223, 227; 39:336, 343; 64:266

"The Study of the Classics" (Warner) 45:433

"Study of the Object" (Herbert) 43:184-85, 188, 193

Study of the Object (Herbert)
    See *Studium przedmiotu*

"Study War" (Styron) 11:519

"The Stuff of Madness" (Highsmith) 42:216

The Stuff of Sleep and Dreams: Experiments in Literary Psychology (Edel) 29:174-75; 34:534

"Stumbling" (Montale)
    See "Incespicare"

"Stumbling" (Soupault) 68:406

"The Stump" (Hall) 37:142-43

"Stump" (Heaney) 14:244

"Stumps" (Davison) 28:101

Eine Stunde hinter Mitternacht (*An Hour Beyond Midnight*) (Hesse) 3:248; 17:198; 69:287

"Stupid Girl" (Jagger and Richard) 17:230, 233, 235

"Stupid Girl" (Young) 17:579

"Stupid Man" (Reed) 21:317

Sturgeon Is Alive and Well (Sturgeon) 22:411, 413

Sturgeon's West (Sturgeon) 39:366

Der Sturz (Durrenmatt) 15:196

Der Sturz (Walser) 27:461

"Stuttgart: In a Nightclub" (Laughlin) 49:221

"The Stygian Banks" (MacNeice) 10:325

"Style" (Durrell) 27:97

"Style" (Moore) 10:349; 47:263, 270

Le style Apollinaire (Zukofsky) 4:600

"Style as Risk" (Cioran) 64:75, 78-9

"The Style of Byron's 'Don Juan' in Relation to the Newspapers of His Day" (Avison) 97:112

Styles of Radical Will (Sontag) 31:407-10; 105:225

"Stylistics, Poetics, and Criticism" (Wellek) 28:452

"Styx" (Duncan) 55:295-96

Su fondamenti invisibili (Luzi) 13:352, 354

"The Sub" (Dixon) 52:99

"Sub Contra" (Bogan) 93:64, 67, 79-81

Sub Rosa (Benet) 28:23, 25

"A Subaltern's Love Song" (Betjeman) 2:60

Subarashiki nichiyobi (*One Wonderful Sunday*) (Kurosawa) 16:398

Subida al cielo (Bunuel) 80:23, 29-30, 36

"Subiectul" ("The Topic") (Arghezi) 80:11

"The Subject and Power" (Foucault) 69:190

A Subject of Scandal and Concern (Osborne) 2:328; 45:313

The Subject Was Roses (Gilroy) 2:161

The Subjection of Women (Mill) 65:323

"Subject-Matter of Poetry" (Huxley) 5:192

"The Subjects of Discontent" (Klappert) 57:268

"The Sublime and the Beautiful" (Murdoch) 8:406

"The Sublime and the Beautiful Revisited" (Murdoch) 6:347

"The Sublime and the Good" (Murdoch) 6:346, 349

"The Sublime Art" (Hamburger) 14:234

"The Sublime Child" (Berriault) 109:96

"Subliminal Code" (Moure) 88:218

"The Subliminal Man" (Ballard) 3:32-3; 14:41; 36:33, 36

Submarine (Clancy) 112:77

Submarine Sailor (Felsen) 17:120

"The Submerged Continent" (Ortese)
    See "Il continente sommerso"

"Subpoena" (Barthelme) 5:53

"Substitute" (Townshend) 17:529-30, 532

"Subterranean Homesick Blues" (Dylan) 77:161, 165, 188

The Subterraneans (Kerouac) 1:165; 2:226-27; 3:265; 5:214; 14:303-04, 307; 29:271-72; 61:296, 298, 309

Os subterrâneos da liberdade (Amado) 106:57, 59

"The Subtitle of This Book" (Barth) 51:25

"The Subtle Calm" (Blunden) 56:46

Subtle Flame (Prichard) 46:344-45

Subtraction (Robison) 98:314-18

Suburb (Dos Passos) 25:144

Suburban Strains (Ayckbourn) 33:42-4

The Suburban Wife (Stead)
    See *Miss Herbert*

"Suburban Woman: A Detail" (Boland) 40:98; 67:39; 113:89, 92, 96

"Suburbanite" (Moravia) 7:244

"The Suburbans" (Kizer) 80:172-73

"Suburbia" (Ciardi) 40:162

The Suburbs of Hell (Stow) 48:356-61

"The Subverted Flower" (Frost) 9:229; 34:471

"Subverting the Standards" (Fiedler) 24:205

"Subway" (Woolrich) 77:401

The Subway (Rice) 7:360, 362; 49:300-02, 305

"Success" (Masters) 48:223-24

Success (Amis) 38:12-16; 62:5, 11-12, 16-17; 101:59, 61-63, 84, 86, 89-90

The Success and Failure of Picasso (Berger) 2:54-5

Success Stories (Banks) 72:2-5, 9, 11

"Success Story" (Townshend) 17:535-36

The Successful Life of 3 (Fornes) 39:138; 61:129-33, 140

Successful Love, and Other Stories (Schwartz) 10:462

The Succession: A Novel of Elizabeth and James (Garrett) 51:149-51, 153

"Succotash" (Harmon) 38:244

Such (Brooke-Rose) 40:104-05, 111

Such a Gorgeous Kid Like Me (Truffaut)
    See *A Gorgeous Bird like Me*

Such a Long Journey (Mistry) 71:273-76

Such a Love (Kohout) 13:323

"Such a Lovely Girl" (Jones) 52:250

"Such Counsels" (Plumly) 33:313

"Such Counsels You Gave to Me" (Jeffers) 54:238, 245-46

Such Counsels You Gave to Me and Other Poems (Jeffers) 11:307; 54:238

Such Darling Dodos (Wilson) 2:470; 3:534; 25:464

Such Good Friends (Gould) 4:199; 10:241

Such Is My Beloved (Callaghan) 14:101-03; 41:90-1, 93, 95; 65:246, 248-52

Such Nice People (Scoppettone) 26:403-04

"Such Silences" (Livesay) 79:333-34

Such Stuff as Screams Are Made Of (Bloch) 33:84

"Such Things Only Happen in Books" (Wilder) 82:362

Such Was the Season (Major) 48:218

"Suchen wissen" (Jandl) 34:199

"Sucker" (McCullers) 4:345; 12:432-33

Sud (*South*) (Green) 11:258, 260; 77:271, 276-77, 288-91, 294

Sudden Death (Brown) 43:82-3, 85; 79:153, 155, 169

"Sudden Illness at the Bus-Stop" (Betjeman) 43:32, 34

"The Sudden Sixties" (Ferber) 93:145

"Sudden Things" (Hall) 37:146

"A Sudden Trip Home in the Spring" (Walker) 103:366, 407, 409-10, 412

"Suddenly" (Thomas) 48:383

Suddenly Last Summer (Williams) 1:368; 2:465-66; 5:499, 501; 7:543; 11:571-72, 576; 39:446; 45:448; 71:368, 386; 111:380-83, 388, 391, 393, 424

"Suddenly, Walking along the Open Road" (Peake) 54:375

Suder (Everett) 57:214-17

"Sudor y látigo" ("Sweat and the Lash"; "Sweat and the Whip") (Guillen) 48:158, 162, 164

"Sueño" (Soto) 80:278

El sueño de la razón (*The Sleep of Reason*) (Buero Vallejo) 15:100-02; 46:93-5

"Sueño de las dos ciervas" (Alonso) 14:25

El sueño de los héroes (*The Dream of Heroes*) (Bioy Casares) 13:85; 88:88-93

"Sueño Real" (Ferlinghetti) 111:65

Un sueño realizado y otros cuentos (*A Dream Fulfilled, and Other Stories*) (Onetti) 7:276

"Sueños" (Soto) 80:278

Sueur de sang (Jouve) 47:207-08, 212

"Suffer the Children" (Lorde) 71:260

Suffer the Children (Saul) 46:365, 369

Sufficient Carbohydrate (Potter) 58:390-91

The Suffrage of Elvira (Naipaul) 4:372, 375; 13:402, 406; 37:324-25; 105:140,147, 155, 179-80

"Suffragette City" (Bowie) 17:61

"Sufleteasca" ("Spiritual") (Arghezi) 80:8

Sugar (Byatt) 65:125

Sugar and Rum (Unsworth) 76:254

"The Sugar Crock" (Gass) 8:242

Sugar Daddy (Williams) 42:441-42

"Sugar for the Horse" (Bates) 46:62-3

Sugar for the Horse (Bates) 46:62-3

"Sugar Loaf" (Hughes) 14:271

"Sugar Mountain" (Young) 17:572, 583

"Sugar Rises" (Goldbarth) 38:201

"Sugarcane" (Guillen) 48:157

The Sugarland Express (Spielberg) 20:357-58, 365

Sugartown (Estleman) 48:105, 107

"The Sugawn Chair" (O'Faolain) 32:343; 70:319

"The Suggestiveness of One Stray Hair in an Otherwise Perfect Coiffure" (Leyner) 92:283

"The Suicide" (Davison) 28:100

"The Suicide" (Ignatow) 14:277

"Suicide" (Schaeffer) 6:489

"Suicide" (Sturgeon) 22:411

Suicide in B-Flat (Shepard) 41:406, 412

"Suicide in the Trenches" (Sassoon) 36:393

"Suicide Notes" (Suknaski) 19:432

"The Suicide of Hedda Gabler" (Dubie) 36:130

"Suicide off Egg Rock" (Plath) 14:424

"Suicide on Pentwyn Bridge" (Clarke) 61:78

Suicide Prohibited in Springtime (Casona) See *Prohibido suicidarse en primavera*

Suicide: The Hidden Epidemic (Hyde) 21:179

"Suicides" (Gilchrist) 48:115-16, 121

"The Suicides" (Justice) 102:264

"Suicides" (Voigt) 54:429

"Suicidio" (Aleixandre) 9:14

"Suigetsu" (Kawabata) 107:104

"Suisho Genso" ("The Crystal Fantasy") (Kawabata) 107:114

A Suit of Nettles (Reaney) 13:474, 476

A Suitable Boy (Seth) 90:351-60, 365-9

"The Suitcase" (Mphahlele) 25:338, 342, 344

"The Suitcase" (Ozick) 28:353; 62:352

Suitcase (Abe) 81:291

"A Suite for Augustus" (Dove) 81:134

"Suite for Marriage" (Ignatow) 40:258

Suite furlana (Pasolini) 106:229, 233

"Suite in Prison" (Eberhart) 19:143

Suite in Three Keys (Coward) 29:135-36, 139

Suite logique (Brossard) 115:106

"A Suite of Lies" (Webb) 18:540

Suite to Appleness (Harrison) 6:223

"Suites I and II" (Webb) 18:540

The Suitors of Spring (Jordan) 37:194

"Sujam o suicído" ("They Dirty the Suicide") (Cabral de Melo Neto) 76:164

"Le sujet en procès" (Kristeva) 77:302

al-Sukkariyya (Mahfuz) 52:293, 300; 55:171-72, 175-76

"Sul credere o non credere in Dio" (Ginzburg) 54:207

Sula (Morrison) 4:365-66; 10:355; 22:315-16, 318-19; 55:196, 205, 207-08; 81:217-19, 225-26, 228, 230, 232, 235-37, 254, 256, 260, 270; 87:263-65, 291-94, 304, 306

Sulla poesia (Montale) 18:341

Sullivan and Gilbert (Ludwig) 60:251

"Sultry Rain" (Pasternak) 63:277

"The Sum of All" (Blunden) 56:34, 39

The Sum of All Fears (Clancy) 112:56-9, 61-2, 77, 90

The Sum of Things (Manning) 19:303-04

Suma y sigue (Alegria) 75:38

Sumerian Vistas (Ammons) 57:51-3, 55-6, 59; 108:24

Summa Atheologica (*Somme athéologique*) (Bataille) 29:38

al-Summan wa-al-kharif (*Quail and Autumn*) (Mahfuz) 52:295-96; 301

"Summary" (Sanchez) 116:276, 280, 282, 294

"Summary" (Sarton) 49:320

"Summer" 75:69

"Summer" (Ashbery) 2:17

"Summer" (Cortazar) See "Verano"

"Summer" (Crase) 58:162

"Summer" (Gluck) 44:216, 218, 221

"Summer" (Soto) 80:287

Summer (Camus) See *L'été*

Summer (Grunwald) 44:49-51

Summer (Leonard) 19:282, 284

"Summer '68" (Pink Floyd) 35:305

Summer: A European Play (Bond) 23:72

A Summer Affair (Klima) 56:173

The Summer after the Funeral (Gardam) 43:165-66, 173

Summer and Smoke (Williams) 1:367; 2:465; 5:498, 500; 7:541, 543-44; 8:548-49; 11:572, 576; 30:466; 39:446, 448; 45:446, 451, 453; 71:405; 111:380, 388, 392-93

"The Summer Anniversaries" (Justice) 102:261, 270

The Summer Anniversaries (Justice) 19:232-33; 102:261, 263-64, 268, 270, 277, 283

The Summer before the Dark (Lessing) 3:285-88, 291; 6:300-01, 304; 15:334; 22:281; 40:303; 94:258, 261-62, 283-84, 286

"The Summer Belvedere" (Williams) 45:443

A Summer Bird Cage (Drabble) 2:118; 22:120; 53:121, 126

Summer Brave (Inge) See *Picnic*

"A Summer by the Sea" (Jhabvala) 94:171-73

"Summer Camp" (Scott) 22:376

"Summer Canyon" (Merwin) 45:273

Summer Celestial (Plumly) 33:315-16

Summer Crossing (Tesich) 40:423-24

"The Summer Day" (Oliver) 98:281, 294

"A Summer Day" (Stafford) 7:457; 19:430; 68:422, 433

Summer Days (And Summer Nights) (Wilson) 12:649-50

"Summer Doorway" (Merwin) 18:334

"Summer Dust" (Gordon) 29:189; 83:231-32, 241, 258

"The Summer Farmer" (Cheever) 15:127

"The Summer Fire" (Dodson) 79:199

The Summer Game (Angell) 26:28-32

"Summer Garden" (Harrison) 43:176

Summer Girls, Love Boys, and Other Short Stories (Mazer) 26:295

"A Summer Gone" (Moss) 50:353

"Summer Haiku" (Cohen) 38:132

Summer Holiday (Mamoulian) 16:427-28

"Summer Home" (Heaney) 25:241; 74:158

"Summer House" (Heaney) 7:148

A Summer in Italy (O'Faolain) 70:318

"A Summer in Rouen" (Endo) 99:289, 293-95

Summer in Salandar (Bates) 46:65

Summer in the City (Stevens) 34:111-13

Summer in the Spring: Ashinaabe Lyric Poems and Stories (Vizenor) 103:341-47

Summer in the Spring: Ojibwe Lyric Poems and Tribal Songs (Anishinabe Adisokan) (Vizenor) 103:296, 298, 335-36, 342-48

A Summer in the Twenties (Dickinson) 35:135

"Summer in Town" (Pasternak) 63:313

Summer in Williamsburg (Fuchs) 8:220-21

Summer Interlude (Bergman) See *Sommarlek*

Summer Knowledge: New and Selected Poems, 1938-1958 (Selected Poems (1938-1958): Summer Knowledge) (Schwartz) 2:387; 10:465; 45:354, 356

"Summer Landscape" (Eberhart) 56:86

"Summer Landscape" (Sarton) 49:309

A Summer Life (Soto) 80:298, 300-01

"Summer Lightning" (Clarke) 9:168

"Summer Lightning" (Simmons) 43:410-11

Summer Love and Surf (Appleman) 51:13

"Summer Moon" (Winters) 32:469

Summer Moonshine (Wodehouse) 22:479

"Summer Morning" (Simic) 9:480-81; 22:380

"A Summer Morning" (Wilbur) 53:405, 413

"Summer near the River" (Kizer) 80:174, 180

"A Summer Night" (Auden) 43:17

"Summer Night" (Bowen) 22:65-6

"The Summer Night" (Bradbury) 42:38

"Summer Night" (Ekelof) 27:110

"Summer Night" (Harjo) 83:276, 280

"A Summer Night" (Mahapatra) 33:283-84
The Summer of 1925 (Ehrenburg) 18:131; 62:178
"A Summer of Discovery" (Williams) 45:445
Summer of Fear (Duncan) 26:104
The Summer of My German Soldier (Greene) 30:169-71
The Summer of the Falcon (George) 35:176
Summer of the Red Wolf (West) 6:563
Summer of the Seventeenth Doll (Lawler) 58:329-44
The Summer of the Swans (Byars) 35:71-3, 75
Summer of the White Goat (Corcoran) 17:76-7
The Summer Party (Poliakoff) 38:383, 386
"Summer People" (Beattie) 63:14, 18
"Summer People" (Hemingway) 10:269; 30:194; 39:403
"Summer People" (Kaplan) 50:55-7
"The Summer People" (Merrill) 6:323
Summer People (Elliott) 47:111-12
Summer People (Piercy) 62:379-81
"A Summer Pilgrim" (Tuohy) 37:431
"Summer Place" (Ammons) 11, 36, 37
"A Summer Place" (Stevenson) 33:381
A Summer Place (Wilson) 32:445-46
"Summer Plain" (Transtroemer) 65:223
"Summer Poem" (Enzensberger) 43:144-45
"Summer Rain" (Read) 4:439
Summer Rain (Duras)
  See *Summer Rain*
"Summer Report" (Celan)
  See "Sommerbericht"
"Summer Resort" (Gellhorn) 60:181
"Summer Rest and Words" (Amichai)
  See "Menuchat kayits u-milam"
"Summer School" (Davison) 28:100
"Summer Session" (Ammons) 5:29; 8:15, 18; 25:43-5
"Summer Session 1968" (Ammons) 57:23, 59
Summer Side of Life (Lightfoot) 26:278, 282
"Summer Soft" (Wonder) 12:659-60
The Summer Soldier (Guild) 33:186-87
"Summer Solstice, New York City" (Olds) 85:299
"Summer Song I" (Barker) 48:24
"Summer Storm" (Montague) 46:268
Summer Storm (Swinnerton) 31:423
"Summer Storm in Japanese Hills" (Blunden) 56:50
"The Summer Thunder" (Moss) 45:290
"Summer time T. V. (is witer than ever)" (Sanchez) 116:295
A Summer to Decide (Johnson) 1:161; 7:184
"A Summer Tragedy" (Bontemps) 1:37
"Summer Tragedy Report" (Hillis) 66:195-99
"Summer Vertigo" (Corn) 33:116
"Summer Waterfall, Glendale" (MacCaig) 36:283
"Summer Wish" (Bogan) 46:78-9, 84, 90; 93:65, 81, 90, 97
Summer with Monika (Bergman)
  See *Sommaren med Monika*
"Summer Words of a Sistuh Addict" (Sanchez) 116:280
Summering (Greenberg) 7:134
Summerplay (Bergman)
  See *Sommarlek*
"A Summer's Day" (Collins) 44:36, 38
"Summer's Day Song" (McCartney) 35:287-89
"A Summer's Dream" (Bishop) 32:34
"A Summer's Fancy" (Blunden) 56:29

"Summer's Lease" (Haldeman) 61:177-78
A Summer's Lease (Sachs) 35:333
Summertime and Other Stories (Donoso)
  See *Veraneo y otros cuentos*
"Summertime and the Living..." (Hayden) 37:160
"Summertime Blues" (Townshend) 17:525
Summertime Dream (Lightfoot) 26:281
"Summertime in England" (Morrison) 21:239
Summertime Island (Caldwell) 14:95
The Summing Up (Maugham) 15:367; 67:211, 215-16, 219, 223, 226, 228; 93:238-39, 246-47, 250, 253, 267, 270
"Summing Up by the Defendant" (Dodson) 79:198
"Summit Beach, 1921" (Dove) 81:147-48, 150
Summoned (O Hehir) 41:322, 324
Summoned by Bells (Betjeman) 6:69; 34:306; 43:37-9, 41-2
A Summoning of Stones (Hecht) 8:266, 268-69; 13:269; 19:207
"Summons" (Dickey) 47:94
A Summons to Memphis (Taylor) 50:251-61; 71:298
"The Sumo Revisions" (Hodgins) 23:236
"Sumptuous Destitution" (Wilbur) 3:532
"The Sun" (Ashbery) 15:33-4; 41:40
"The Sun" (Bottoms) 53:30-1
"Sun" (Dickey) 7:82
"Sun" (Kenny)
  See "I Am the Sun"
"Sun" (Livesay) 79:339
"Sun" (Moore) 4:362; 10:353
Sun: A Poem for Malcolm X Inspired by His Murder (Kennedy) 66:205
The Sun Also Rises (*Fiesta*) (Hemingway) 1:141-44; 3:231, 234-38, 240-41; 6:226-27, 229-31, 233; 8:283, 287, 289-90; 10:263-64, 267; 13:271-72, 274, 276, 278-79; 19:211, 216-19, 221; 30:179; 61:190-232; 80:111, 113, 117-18, 137, 141, 145-46, 151
The Sun Always Shines for the Cool (Pinero) 55:316-18
"Sun and Fun" (Betjeman) 43:35-6
Sun and Moon (Page) 18:376-78
"Sun and Moon Flowers: Paul Klee, 1879-1940" (Dubie) 36:131
Sun and Steel (Mishima) 2:286-87, 289; 4:354; 9:381-83; 27:342-43
The Sun and the Moon (Reaney) 13:474
The Sun at Midnight: Notes on the Story of Civilization Seen as the History of the Great Experimental Work of the Supreme Scientist (Gascoyne) 45:154
"The Sun between Their Feet" (Lessing) 94:288-89, 295-96
"The Sun Came" (Knight) 40:279
"The Sun Dance Shield" (Momaday) 85:280
The Sun Dog (King) 113:367
"Sun Dried" (Ferber) 93:142
"The Sun Going Down upon Our Wrath" (Levertov) 66:250
The Sun Has Begun to Eat the Mountain (Lane) 25:284
Sun Horse, Moon Horse (Sutcliff) 26:437
The Sun Is Axeman (Jones) 10:285, 288
"Sun Is Shining" (Marley) 17:270
"Sun King" (Lennon and McCartney) 12:365, 380
The Sun King (Mitford) 44:485, 488-89
The Sun My Monument (Lee) 90:176-7, 181,

194
"Sun Poem" (Wakoski) 2:459
"The Sun Rises Twice" (Bates) 46:56
Sun Rock Man (Corman) 9:170
"The Sun Room" (O'Hara) 6:385
The Sun Shines Bright (Ford) 16:316, 319
The Sun Shines on the Sanggan River (Ding Ling) 68:62, 64, 66
The Sun: Star Number One (Branley) 21:18
Sun Stone (Paz)
  See *Piedra de sol*
"Sun the First" (Elytis) 100:171-72
Sun the First (Elytis)
  See *Ílios o prótos*
"Sun Threnody" (Komunyakaa) 94:226-27
Sun Under Wood (Hass) 99:155, 157-58
Suna no onna (*The Woman in the Dunes*) (Abe) 8:1-2; 22:11, 13; 53:2-6; 81:285, 287, 290-97
"Sunbathing on a Rooftop in Berkeley" (Kumin) 28:225
The Sunbird (Smith) 33:374-75
sunblue (Avison) 97:111-18, 121
"Sunburst" (Mahapatra) 33:280, 283
"Sunburst" (Seger) 35:381
"Sundance" (Silverberg) 7:425
Sunday after the War (Miller) 43:298; 84:242-43
"Sunday Afternoon" (Munro) 95:287, 297
"Sunday Afternoon" (Steele) 45:362
"Sunday Afternoon at Home" (McFadden) 48:256
"Sunday Afternoon at Two O'Clock" (Frame) 96:201
"Sunday Afternoon in Buffalo, Texas" (Justice) 102:259
"Sunday Afternoon near the Naval Air Base" (Ciardi) 40:153
"Sunday Afternoon Service in St. Enodoc Church, Cornwall" (Betjeman) 43:34
"Sunday at Home" (Smith) 25:420-21
"Sunday at the Zoo" (Dybek) 114:67
"Sunday before Noon" (Bukowski) 108:113
Sunday Best (Rubens) 19:403, 405; 31:351
"Sunday Bloody Sunday" (Lennon) 35:264
Sunday Bloody Sunday (Gilliatt) 2:160-61; 53:146
"Sunday Brunch in the Boston Restoration" (Starbuck) 53:354
"Sunday by the Combination" (Hughes) 108:297
"Sunday... Dig the Empty Sounds" (Salinas) 90:324, 328
Sunday Dinner (Oates) 11:400
"Sunday Drinks" (Trevor) 25:445
"A Sunday Drive" (Atwood) 84:69
"A Sunday Evening" (Kelman) 58:298, 300
Sunday Father (Neufeld) 17:310
"The Sunday Following Mother's Day" (Jones) 76:65-6
Sunday in the Park with George (Sondheim) 30:400, 402-03; 39:172-74
"Sunday Lemons" (Walcott) 76:285
Sunday, Monday and Always (Powell) 66:372
"Sunday Mornin' Comin' Down" (Kristofferson) 26:266, 270
"Sunday Morning" (Ammons) 5:26
"Sunday Morning" (Avison) 97:71
"Sunday Morning" (Ciardi) 40:157
"Sunday Morning" (Dubus) 97:237
"Sunday Morning" (Hass) 18:212
"Sunday Morning" (Jacobsen) 48:196
"Sunday Morning" (MacNeice) 1:186; 53:231,

238
"Sunday Morning, June 4, 1989" (Thomas)
    107:340, 346
"Sunday Morning Walk" (Smith)   64:388, 394
The Sunday of Life (Queneau)
    See *Le dimanche de la vie*
"The Sunday Poem" (Bowering)   15:82
Sunday Punch (Newman)   14:378-79
"Sunday Reading" (Guillen)
    See "Lectura de domingo"
Sunday Runners in the Rain (Horovitz)   56:154
"Sunday Siesta" (Garcia Marquez)   47:146
Sunday the Rabbi Stayed Home (Kemelman)
    2:225
"Sundays" (King)   53:209, 212
"Sundays before noon" (Bukowski)   108:112
"Sunday's Best" (Costello)   21:71
"Sundays in Summer" (Oates)   108:384
"Sundays Kill More Men than Bombs"
    (Bukowski)   41:64
"The Sundays of Satin-Legs Smith" (*Satin-Legs
    Smith*) (Brooks)   5:76; 15:92; 49:26, 32-
    3, 35
The Sundered Worlds (*The Blood Red Game*)
    (Moorcock)   58:350
"The Sundial" (Clarke)   61:73
"The Sundial" (Piccolo)
    See "La meridiana"
The Sundial (Clarke)   61:73-4, 79, 82
The Sundial (Jackson)   11:303; 60:211, 217,
    219-20, 234
Sundiver (Brin)   34:133-35
Sundog (Harrison)   33:199-201; 66:157, 160-
    61, 169
"Sundown" (Lightfoot)   26:280-81
Sundown (Lightfoot)   26:280
Sundown (Mathews)   84:203-04, 207, 209-
    11, 216, 225-26, 229-30
Sunfall (Cherryh)   35:107
"Sunfast" (Livesay)   15:340; 79:337-38, 351
"Sunflower" (Breton)
    See "Tournesol"
Sunflower (De Sica)   20:95
Sunflower (West)   50:394, 399
"Sunflower Sonnet Number Two" (Jordan)
    11:312
"Sunflower Sutra" (Ginsberg)   3:194; 13:239;
    36:181, 187; 109:333, 365
"The Sunflowers" (Oliver)   98:261
"Sunken Evening" (Lee)   90:182
"Sunlight" (Gunn)   3:216
"Sunlight" (Heaney)   7:151; 25:245
Sunlight (Van Peebles)   20:410
The Sunlight Dialogues (Gardner)   2:151-52;
    3:184-88; 5:131-35; 7:112, 114; 8:234,
    237-38; 10:218-20; 28:166-67; 34:550
Sunlight on Cold Water (Sagan)
    See *A Few Hours of Sunlight*
"The Sunlit Vale" (Blunden)   56:44
"Sunny Afternoon" (Davies)   21:88-90, 97
"A Sunny Place" (Kawabata)   107:104, 107
"Sunny Prestatyn" (Larkin)   39:340; 64:262,
    269-70
"Sunrise" (Hass)   18:212-13
"Sunrise" (Seidel)   18:475
"Sunrise" (Townshend)   17:531
Sunrise (Seidel)   18:474-75
Sunrise on Sarah (Ryga)   14:473
"A Sunrise on the Veld" (Lessing)   22:279
*Sunrise with Seamonsters: Travels and Discov-
    eries, 1964-1984* (Theroux)   46:401-03
The Sun's Burial (Oshima)   20:247, 251
The Sun's Net (Brown)   48:55-6

"Sunset" (Ginsberg)   36:182
"Sunset" (Gluck)   81:165, 172
Sunset and Evening Star (O'Casey)   88:240-
    41
Sunset at Blandings (Wodehouse)   22:484
Sunset Boulevard (Wilder)   20:456-57, 462
Sunset Gun (Parker)   68:324
"Sunset Limited" (Harrison)   66:167-71
"The Sunset Maker" (Justice)   102:271
The Sunset Maker (Justice)   102:269-72, 277,
    283
The Sunset of a Clown (Bergman)
    See *Gycklarnas afton*
"The Sunset Perspective" (Moorcock)   58:348
"The Sunset Piece" (MacLeish)   68:287-88
Sunset Village (Sargeson)   31:369-70
"Sunshine" (Klein)   30:239
"Sunshine and Shadow" (Beattie)   40:64, 66;
    63:19
The Sunshine Boys (Simon)   6:506-07; 11:496;
    31:399-401, 403; 39:218; 70:236, 238
The Sunshine Years (Klein)   30:239
"Sunspot Baby" (Seger)   35:381
Sunstone (Paz)
    See *Piedra de sol*
"Sunstroke" (Landolfi)   11:321
Suomalainen sarja (*A Finnish Suite*)
    (Haavikko)   34:170
Suor (*Sweat*) (Amado)   40:25-7
Superbia   99:160-61, 168, 171, 180, 186
*Superboy—The Adventures of Superman When
    He Was a Boy* (Siegel and Shuster)   21:359
The Supercops (Parks)   16:461
The Superhero Women (Lee)   17:261-62
The Superintendent (Haavikko)
    See *Ylilääkäri*
Superior Women (Adams)   46:17-22
"Superiorities" (Wilbur)   110:385
"Superman" (Davies)   21:105
"Superman" (Updike)   23:473
Superman (Puzo)   107:213
Superman (Siegel and Shuster)   21:354, 356,
    359-60
"The Superman Comes to the Supermarket"
    (Mailer)   28:257; 111:96, 103-05, 107,
    113
Superman II (Lester)   20:232
Superman III (Kotzwinkle)   35:257
"A Supermarket in California" (Ginsberg)
    13:239; 36:192-93; 69:211, 214; 109:355
Supernation at Peace and War (Wakefield)
    7:502
The Supernatural: From ESP to UFOs (Berger)
    12:41-2
Superrealismo (Azorin)
    See *El libro de levante*
"Supersonic Rocket Ship" (Davies)   21:94
Superspies: The Secret Side of Government
    (Archer)   12:23
"Superstition" (Wonder)   12:657, 660, 663-
    64
Superstizione (Antonioni)   20:28
"Superwoman" (Wonder)   12:657
"Superwoman Drawn and Quartered, The Early
    Forms of *She*" (Atwood)   84:89
"The Supper after the Last" (Kinnell)   29:281
"The Supper at Elsinore" (Dinesen)   29:157,
    162
"Supper on the Blackbird's Field" (Popa)
    19:375
"Supplizio" ("Torture") (Ortese)   89:198

"Suppose" (Mahapatra)   33:284
A Supposedly Funny Thing I'll Never Do Again
    (Wallace)   114:388-89
"Supposing You Have Nowhere to Go"
    (Musgrave)   54:341
*The Suppression of the African Slave-Trade to
    the United States of America, 1638-1870*
    (Du Bois)   64:128; 96:127, 146, 151, 160
"Supreme Fictions" (Squires)   51:382
"Sur" (Le Guin)   45:216
Sur la route de San Romano (Breton)   9:128
"Sur le sein" (Damas)   84:180
Sur les femmes (Montherlant)   19:322
Sur Nietzsche (Bataille)   29:38-9, 47
Sur Racine (*On Racine*) (Barthes)   24:23, 25-
    6, 36, 41-2; 83:67, 78, 98-9
"Sur une carte postale" (Damas)   84:174
"Surce coveško" ("Kolelo") (Bagryana)   10:14
"Surcease" (Lane)   25:287
The Sure Hand of God (Caldwell)   60:53
Sure of You (Maupin)   95:197-204, 208
"'Sure,' Said Benny Goodman" (Carruth)
    84:136
"Surf" (Hansen)   38:240
"The Surface" (Swenson)   106:346
"Surface Calm" (Martin)   89:116
The Surface of Earth (Price)   6:423-26; 13:463-
    64; 43:348-50, 353; 50:229, 232; 63:332,
    341
Surface of Meaning (Brossard)
    See *Le Sens apparent*
Surface of Sense (Brossard)
    See *Le Sens apparent*
Surface Tension (Blish)   14:85
"Surface Textures" (Desai)   97:149, 152-53,
    171
Surfacing (Atwood)   2:20; 3:19-20; 4:24-7,
    28; 8:28-31, 33-4; 13:42-4; 15:37, 39;
    25:61-4, 66, 68-9; 44:146-48, 152-53,
    160; 84:49-53, 56, 59-60, 66, 69, 79, 90,
    105, 107
"Surfacing in Private Spaces" (Allen)   84:5
Surfeit of Lampreys (Marsh)
    See *Death of a Peer*
"Surfer Girl" (Wilson)   12:642-43, 648
"Surfer in Winter" (Kessler)   4:270
"Surfiction" (Wideman)   67:379, 381-82, 384
Surfiction: Fiction Now and Tomorrow
    (Federman)   47:121-23, 126
"Surfiction—Four Propositions in Form of an
    Introduction" (Federman)   47:121, 126
"Surfin'" (Wilson)   12:644, 647
"Surfin' Safari" (Wilson)   12:647, 650
Surfin' Safari (Wilson)   12:642, 644
"Surfin' U.S.A." (Wilson)   12:647-48
Surfin' U.S.A. (Wilson)   12:651
Surf's Up (Wilson)   12:645, 648, 650
The Surge (*Star*) (McClure)   6:317, 320
"The Surgeon as Priest" (Selzer)   74:264, 276
"Surgeon at Two A.M." (Plath)   5:345; 9:433;
    111:203, 214
"The Surname" (Guillen)
    See "El apellido"
Surplussed Barrelware (Aksyonov)
    See *The Tare of Barrels*
"A Surprise in the Peninsula" (Adcock)   41:14,
    17
"Surprise, Surprise!" (Abse)   29:15, 17
"Surprise Surprise" (Lennon)   35:268
Surprise! Surprise! (Tremblay)   29:419;
    102:367-68
"'Surprise, Surprise!' from Matron" (Jolley)
    46:214

"Surprised by Evening" (Bly) 38:56
"Surprised by Joy" (Baxter) 45:53; 78:17-18
Surprised by Joy: The Shape of My Early Life (Lewis) 3:296; 6:310
"Surprises" (Aksyonov) 101:9
Surprises of the Sun (McAuley) 45:249, 252
Surreal Thing (Kristofferson) 26:269
Surrealism (Read) 4:443
Le surréalisme et l'après-guerre (Tzara) 47:385
Surrealist Manifesto (Breton)
  See *Manifeste du surréalisme. Poisson soluble*
"Surrealist Situation of the Object" (Breton) 54:16
"A Surrealistic Photograph by Manuel Alvarez Bravo" ("1938") (Dacey) 51:79-80
"The Surrogate" (Blackburn) 43:65
The Surrounded (McNickle) 89:157-59, 161, 164-73, 175-88
"Surrounded by Children" (Smith) 25:420
Surroundings (MacCaig) 36:283
Le sursis (*The Reprieve*) (Sartre) 1:305; 50:383
"Surveillance" (Berryman) 62:45
Surveiller et punir: Naissance de la prison (*Discipline and Punish: The Birth of the Prison*) (Foucault) 31:180-81, 184-85; 34:339-42; 69:168-69, 174, 185, 190
A Survey of Modernist Poetry (Graves) 11:254; 45:173
A Survey of Modernist Poetry (Riding) 7:375
"The Surveyor" (Roth) 104:311
"A Survival" (Gold) 42:193
"Survival" (Marley) 17:272-73
Survival: A Thematic Guide to Canadian Literature (Atwood) 3:20; 4:25; 8:31; 13:42-3; 15:37; 25:62, 64; 84:50-1, 55-6, 64, 68, 70, 89, 94
"Survival Course" (Bowering) 47:31
Survival in Auschwitz: The Nazi Assault on Humanity (Levi)
  See *Se questo è un uomo*
"The Survival of the Bark Canoe" (McPhee) 36:296
"The Survival of the Fittest" (Thomas) 107:340-42
The Survival of the Fittest (Johnson) 27:221, 224
Survival Techniques (Calisher) 38:76
Survival Zero (Spillane) 13:527-28
Survivals (Honig) 33:213, 216
Le survivant (Chedid) 47:84-5
"Surviving" (Bettelheim) 79:123, 136, 143
Surviving (Green) 97:291-93
Surviving, and Other Essays (*Surviving the Holocaust*) (Bettelheim) 79:122, 124, 125-26
Surviving the Holocaust (Bettelheim)
  See *Surviving, and Other Essays*
"Surviving the Life" (Diamond) 30:112
"The Survivor" (Bambara) 88:21, 27
"Survivor" (Cheever) 15:127
"Survivor" (MacLeish) 8:363
"Survivor" (O Hehir) 41:324
"The Survivor" (Rozewicz) 23:363
Survivor (Butler) 38:62-4
The Survivor (Forman) 21:121
A Survivor (Jones) 52:244-45, 254
The Survivor (Keneally) 5:210-11; 10:299; 117:215-16, 224, 248
The Survivor (Lenz)
  See *Stadtgespräch*
The Survivor (MacBeth) 9:340
The Survivor and Other Poems (Rozewicz) 23:361, 363

"A Survivor in Salvador" (Tuohy) 37:427
The Survivor: The Story of Eddy Hukov (Ehle) 27:102
"Survivor Type" (King) 37:206-07
"The Survivors" (Snodgrass) 68:382, 388
The Survivors (Beer) 58:36, 38
The Survivors (Feinstein) 36:171
The Survivors (Hunter) 35:228-29
The Survivors (Raven) 14:442-43
The Survivors (Shaw) 23:397
The Survivors of the Crossing (Clarke) 8:143; 53:84-7, 91-2
"Susan and the Serpent—A Colonial Fiction" (Murray) 40:334
A Susan Sontag Reader (Sontag) 31:416-18; 105:216-19
Susana, carne y demonio (Bunuel) 80:29, 34
Susanna Moodie: Voice and Vision (Shields) 113:396, 400, 413, 442
"Sushi" (Muldoon) 72:273-74, 277
The Suspect (Wright) 44:334-35
The Suspect in Poetry (Dickey) 109:244
"The Suspended Life" (Ashbery) 2:19
"A Suspense Story" (Macdonald) 13:356
A Suspension of Mercy (*The Story-Teller*) (Highsmith) 2:192; 42:212; 102:170, 173-74, 177, 192
The Suspicion (Duerrenmatt) 102:56, 59
Suspicion (Durrenmatt) 4:140
Suspicion (Hitchcock) 16:338, 355
"Sussex" (Davie) 8:165-66
"Suterareru made" ("Until Forsaken") (Tanizaki) 28:418
"Suttee" (Auchincloss) 45:30
Sutter's Gold (Cendrars)
  See *L'or*
Suttree (McCarthy) 57:329-31, 333-35; 101:135-37, 147, 152-57, 167-69, 175-76, 178, 180-82, 186, 195, 198, 202-04
"Suvetski khora" (Bagryana) 10:11
"Suzanne" (Cohen) 3:109
Suzanne and the Young Men (Duhamel) 8:189
"Suzerain" (Char) 9:166
Den svåra stunden (*The Trying Hour*) (Lagerkvist) 54:268, 274
Svärmare och harkrank (Martinson) 14:355
Svatby v dome (*Weddings in the House*) (Hrabal) 67:128
Svayamvara and Other Poems (Mahapatra) 33:282
Svecha na vetru (*Candle in the Wind*) (Solzhenitsyn) 4:510-11; 7:432, 443; 10:479
"Svengali" (Dybek) 114:61
"Svenska hus ensligt belägna" ("Solitary Swedish Houses") (Transtroemer) 65:233
Svetlem odená (*Clad in Light*; *Clothed in Light*; *Dressed in Light*) (Seifert) 44:425; 93:306, 309, 319, 328, 343
"Svijazhsk" (Aksyonov) 101:29
Swag (Leonard) 28:233; 71:207, 213, 219, 224
Swallow (Thomas) 31:434
The Swallow and the Tom Cat: A Love Story (Amado)
  See *O Gato Malhado e a Andorinha Sinhá*
Swallow the Lake (Major) 19:292
The Swallower Swallowed (Ducharme)
  See *L'avalée des avalés*
"Swallowing" (Barthelme) 115:85
"Swallowing Darkness Is Swallowing Dead Elm Trees" (Waddington) 28:437
"Swallows" (McGahern) 48:264

Swami and Friends: A Novel of Malgudi (Narayan) 7:255; 28:299-300, 302; 47:303, 307
"The Swamp" (Walcott) 42:418
Swamp Angel (Wilson) 13:607-08, 610-11
The Swamp Dwellers (Soyinka) 14:506; 44:281, 287
Swamp Man (Goines) 80:91, 93, 97
"Swamp Pheasant" (Wright) 53:423
Swamp Water (Renoir) 20:304
"Swamps" (Oates) 6:370; 108:371
"The Swan" (Dacey) 51:83
"Swan" (Hall) 37:143
"The Swan" (L'Heureux) 52:273
"The Swan" (Oliver) 98:289
"The Swan" (Roethke) 19:402
"Swan and Fox" (L'Heureux) 52:278
"Swan and Shadow: The Last Shape" (Hollander) 2:197; 5:186
"The Swan Café" (Pinget) 37:364
The Swan in the Evening (Lehmann) 5:239
"Swan Lake" (Neruda)
  See "El lago de los cisnes"
Swan Song (Binyon) 34:32-4
The Swan Villa (Walser)
  See *Das Schwanenhaus*
"Swanny Lake" (Aksyonov) 101:22
"Swans" (Frame) 96:184, 188
Swans on an Autumn River (Warner) 7:512
"A Swan's Song Came from the Sky" 75:69
"Swansong" (Muske) 90:308, 311
The Swap (Klein) 30:243
"The Swarm" (Murray) 40:338
"The Swarm" (Plath) 9:431; 14:423
"Swarm" (Sterling) 72:368, 372
A Swarm in May (Mayne) 12:387-90, 397, 401-02
"The Swarming Bees" (Laughlin) 49:220
The Swastika Poems (Heyen) 8:231; 13:282-84
"Sway" (Johnson) 52:234
"Sway" (Simpson) 32:377-78, 380
"Swaziland" (Giovanni) 117:197
"Sweat" (Hurston) 7:172
"Sweat" (Redgrove) 41:352
Sweat (Amado)
  See *Suor*
"Sweat and the Lash" (Guillen)
  See "Sudor y látigo"
"Sweat and the Whip" (Guillen)
  See "Sudor y látigo"
"A Sweating Proust of the Pantry Shelves" (Van Duyn) 7:498; 116:402
Sweeney Agonistes: Fragments of an Aristophanic Melodrama (Eliot) 6:166-68; 9:190; 15:206, 208; 41:161; 55:346-47, 350-51, 369, 371, 55:346-47, 350-51, 369, 371
"Sweeney among the Nightingales" (Eliot) 1:92; 10:168; 34:394; 55:364-65
Sweeney Astray (Heaney) 37:163-65, 167, 169; 74:165-68, 193, 195, 197; 91:122, 124
"Sweeney Erect" (Eliot) 1:92; 57:206
Sweeney in the Trees (Saroyan) 56:376
"Sweeney Redivivus" (Heaney) 37:169; 74:162, 169, 174, 193, 197
Sweeney Todd: The Demon Barber of Fleet Street (Sondheim) 30:392-402
"Sweeney's Return" (Heaney) 74:169
Sweet Adelaide (Symons) 32:428
Sweet and Sour Animal Book (Hughes) 108:335-36

Sweet and Sour Milk (Farah)   **53**:132, 134-40

Sweet Bells Jangled out of Tune (Brancato)   **35**:69

Sweet Bird of Youth (Williams)   **1**:368; **2**:466; **5**:499; **7**:545; **11**:572; **15**:581; **19**:472; **30**:466-67; **39**:446; **45**:444-47; **71**:368; **111**:380, 391, 424

"Sweet Blindness" (Nyro)   **17**:319

"Sweet Boy, Give me Yr Ass" (Ginsberg)   **109**:358

"Sweet Burning" (Bogan)   **93**:96

"Sweet Caroline" (Diamond)   **30**:110-11, 113-14

Sweet Charity (Fosse)   **20**:121

Sweet Charity (Simon)   **70**:240

Sweet Danger (Allingham)
    See *The Kingdom of Death*

Sweet Desserts (Ellmann)   **61**:85-9

The Sweet Dove Died (Pym)   **13**:470; **19**:386-87; **37**:377-78; **111**:227, 230, 232, 234-37, 242-48, 258, 262-63, 266, 269-71, 273, 281-82, 285

Sweet Dreams (Frayn)   **3**:164-65

"Sweet Dreams, Son" (Tolstaya)   **59**:372

"Sweet Everlasting" (Voigt)   **54**:430

The Sweet Flypaper of Life (Hughes)   **5**:190; **35**:215; **108**:289-90

Sweet Genevieve (Derleth)   **31**:135

"Sweet Guinevere" (Lightfoot)   **26**:282

"Sweet Harmony" (Robinson)   **21**:344

The Sweet Hereafter (Banks)   **72**:19-24

"Sweet Jane" (Reed)   **21**:303, 306-07, 311, 315, 322

"Sweet Jesus" (Oliver)   **98**:289

"Sweet like a Crow" (Ondaatje)   **51**:317

"Sweet Little Girl" (Wonder)   **12**:656

"Sweet Little Sixteen" (Berry)   **17**:52, 54-5

Sweet Memories (Nelson)   **17**:305

Sweet Reason (Littell)   **42**:275

The Sweet Second Summer of Kitty Malone (Cohen)   **19**:113-16

The Sweet Smell of Success (Odets)   **98**:197, 245-48

Sweet Sue (Gurney)   **54**:217-20, 223; **50**:180, 182-83

Sweet Sweetback's Baadassss Song (Van Peebles)   **2**:448; **20**:411-13

"Sweet Talk" (Vaughn)   **62**:459

Sweet Talk (Vaughn)   **62**:456-59

"Sweet Thing/Candidate" (Bowie)   **17**:61

Sweet Thursday (Steinbeck)   **1**:325; **5**:407; **9**:514, 517; **21**:382; **34**:405

"Sweet Time" (Peacock)   **60**:292

"Sweet Town" (Bambara)   **88**:12, 15, 27

"The Sweet Voice" (Kunene)   **85**:166

Sweet Whispers, Brother Rush (Hamilton)   **26**:157-59

Sweet William (Bainbridge)   **8**:37; **10**:16; **18**:34; **62**:30

"Sweetened Change" (Ammons)   **25**:45; **108**:56

"Sweetest Little Show" (McCartney)   **35**:291-92

"Sweetgrass" (Kenny)   **87**:239

"The Sweetheart of the Song Tra Bong" (O'Brien)   **103**:174

"Sweethearts"   **99**:115

"Sweethearts in a Mulberry Tree" (Knight)   **40**:279

Sweetie (Campion)   **95**:2-6, 8-9, 11-12, 18, 20, 23, 26

"Sweetly Sings the Donkey" (Delaney)   **29**:146

Sweetly Sings the Donkey (Delaney)   **29**:145-46

"The Sweetness of Life" (Stern)   **40**:408

The Sweets of Pimlico (Wilson)   **33**:450-51

The Sweet-Shop Owner (Swift)   **41**:442-44, 446-47; **88**:288, 290-91, 294, 296, 307, 309, 311-12, 321

The Sweetshoppe Myriam (Klima)
    See *Café Myriam*

Sweetsir (Yglesias)   **22**:493-94

Sweetwater (Yep)   **35**:469, 471

The Swell Season: A Text on the Most Important Things in Life (Skvorecky)   **39**:229; **69**:329, 332, 341, 343, 348, 352

A Swell-Looking Babe (Thompson)   **69**:382, 386, 389

"Swells" (Ammons)   **25**:45; **108**:56

Swept Away by an Unusual Destiny in the Blue Sea of August (Wertmueller)   **16**:589-90, 592-96

"Swept for You Baby" (Robinson)   **21**:343, 348

"Swept Sky" (Johnston)   **51**:248

"Swiadomosc" ("Consciousness") (Milosz)   **56**:243

Swiatlo dzienne (Milosz)   **56**:238

"Swift Current" (Smith)   **15**:515, 517

Swiftie the Magician (Gold)   **7**:120-22; **14**:208; **42**:195

A Swiftly Tilting Planet (L'Engle)   **12**:352

"Swifts" (Stevenson)   **33**:382

"The Swim" (Longley)   **29**:296

A Swim Off the Rocks (Moss)   **14**:375-76

"The Swimmer" (Cheever)   **3**:107; **7**:49-50; **11**:120; **64**:46, 48, 53, 63, 66

"The Swimmer" (Ransom)   **11**:469

"The Swimmer at Lake Edward" (Hugo)   **32**:241

"The Swimmer in Hard Light" (De Marinis)   **54**:103

"A Swimmer in the Air" (Moss)   **7**:248

Swimmer in the Secret Sea (Kotzwinkle)   **35**:254-55

"Swimmers" (Swenson)   **106**:339

"The Swimmers" (Szirtes)   **46**:395-96

"The Swimmers" (Tate)   **2**:429; **4**:541; **11**:525-26; **14**:529

The Swimmers and Other Selected Poems (Tate)   **2**:430; **11**:526

"The Swimmer's Moment" (Avison)   **97**:76, 80-1, 84, 121-22, 131, 135

"Swimming Chenango Lake" (Tomlinson)   **13**:548; **45**:401

Swimming Lessons, and Other Stories from Firozsha Baag (Mistry)
    See *Tales from Firozsha Baag*

"The Swimming Pool" (Moss)   **45**:291

The Swimming Pool Season (Tremain)   **42**:387-88

"Swimming to Cambodia" (Gray)   **49**:149

Swimming to Cambodia (Gray)   **49**:148-52; **112**:97-8, 101-04, 111-20, 122-25, 127-31, 134

Swimming to Cambodia: The Collected Works of Spalding Gray (Gray)   **49**:149, 152

The Swimming-Pool Library (Hollinghurst)   **55**:55-63; **91**:132-34, 136-39, 141

The Swindle (Fellini)
    See *Il bidone*

Swing, Brother, Swing (Marsh)
    See *A Wreath for Rivera*

The Swing in the Garden (Hood)   **15**:286; **28**:190-92, 195-96

"Swing Out, Sweet Chariot" (Perelman)   **49**:259

Swinger (Ferlinghetti)   **111**:64

"Swinging" (Clarke)   **61**:73

"The Swinging Bridge" (Davidson)   **13**:169; **19**:126

Swinging in the Rain (Bermant)   **40**:92

Swinnerton (Swinnerton)   **31**:425

The Swiss Family Perelman (Perelman)   **49**:260-61, 266

The Switch (Leonard)   **71**:221

Switch Bitch (Dahl)   **6**:121-22; **79**:177, 181-82

"Switchblade" (Ryan)   **65**:209, 211, 215

"Sword" (Hacker)   **72**:184

"The Sword" (Landolfi)   **11**:321; **49**:210-12

The Sword and the Circle: King Arthur and the Knights of the Round Table (Sutcliff)   **26**:437, 440

The Sword and the Sickle (Anand)   **23**:14, 20; **93**:24, 30-2, 41, 43, 48, 50

The Sword and the Stallion (Moorcock)   **5**:294

Sword at Sunset (Sutcliff)   **26**:432-33, 435, 438, 440

"Sword Eulogising Itself after a Massacre" (Kunene)   **85**:175

The Sword in the Stone (White)   **30**:436-41, 444-47, 449-50

The Sword of Aldones (Bradley)   **30**:27, 29, 31

Sword of Honor (Waugh)   **1**:358-59; **3**:510, 512; **19**:461; **27**:475; **107**:370, 372, 393, 401

Sword of the Lictor (Wolfe)   **25**:476-77

"The Swords" (Aickman)   **57**:3

Swords Like Lips (Aleixandre)
    See *Espadas como labios*

"The Sybarites" (Wilding)   **73**:398

Sybil (Auchincloss)   **45**:25

"Sycamore" (Watkins)   **43**:450

The Sycamore Tree (Brooke-Rose)   **40**:102-03

"The Sylko Bandit" (Raine)   **103**:190

Syllogismes de l'amiertume (Cioran)   **64**:73

"Sylvester's Dying Bed" (Hughes)   **108**:297

Sylvia (Sinclair)   **63**:348

Sylvia Plath: A Biography (Wagner-Martin)   **50**:439-41, 443-50

Sylvia Scarlett (Mackenzie)   **18**:314

Sylvia's Marriage (Sinclair)   **63**:348

The Symbol (Bessie)   **23**:62

"Symbol as Hermeneutic in Existentialism" (Percy)   **65**:260

"Symbol as Need" (Percy)   **14**:415

"The Symbol of the Archaic" (Davenport)   **38**:143

"Symbolic Action in an Ode by Keats" (Burke)   **24**:125

The Symbolic City in Modern Literature (Ferlinghetti)   **10**:174

Symbolic Exchange and Death (Baudrillard)
    See *L'échange symbolique et la mort*

"The Symbolic Imagination: The Mirrors of Dante" (Tate)   **2**:429; **6**:527; **14**:528

Symbolic Wounds: Puberty Rites and the Envious Male (Bettelheim)   **79**:106-09

"Symbolism and Immortality" (Pasternak)   **7**:296

"Symmetrical Companion" (Swenson)   **106**:336, 348

"A Symmetry of Thought" (Ammons)   **9**:27

"A Sympathy, a Welcome" (Berryman)   **62**:76

"Sympathy for the Devil" (Jagger and Richard)   **17**:222-24, 226, 236, 241

Sympathy for the Devil (Godard)
    See *One Plus One*

"Sympathy in White Major" (Larkin)   **64**:283

"Symphonic Night" (Aleixandre)   **36**:29

"Symphony No. Three in D Minor, II" (Williams) 13:600-01

"The Symposium" (Cunningham) 31:102

"A Symposium" (Kundera) 9:321; 32:260

"The Symposium of the Gorgon" (Smith) 43:422

Symposium of the Whole (Rothenberg) 57:382

"Symptoms of Loss" (Williams) 42:443

Symptoms of Loss (Williams) 42:439-42

Synchronicity (Police, The) 26:366

"Synchronicity I" (Police, The) 26:366

"Synchronicity II" (Police, The) 26:366

The Syncopated Cake Walk (Major) 19:294, 299

"Syncrétisme et alternance" (Montherlant) 19:325

"Syndrome" (Dunn) 40:167

"The Syndrome" (Jones) 52:250

"Synecdoche" (Corn) 33:116

Synnyinmaa (*Birthplace; The Native Country*) (Haavikko) 18:205-07; 34:168-69

"Synopsis" (Williams) 42:442

"Synthetic World" (Cliff) 21:64

"Sypaichi" (Aitmatov) 71:15

"The Syphilis Oozes" (Smith) 12:541

"Syphoning the Spring" (Clarke) 61:79

"Syracuse" (Denby) 48:84

"Syracuse; or, The Panther Man" (Morand) 41:300-01

"Syringa" (Ashbery) 13:30, 36; 15:30; 41:41; 77:42, 45, 55

"Syros" (Transtroemer) 52:409; 65:226

"Syrup of Figs Will Cast Our Fear" (Porter) 33:322

"The System" (Ashbery) 2:19; 15:28; 25:50; 77:61

"The System" (Galeano) 72:130

The System of Dante's Hell (*The System of Dante's Inferno*) (Baraka) 3:35; 5:44; 14:46; 33:52, 55, 57, 59, 63; 115:3, 10, 15, 17, 49

The System of Dante's Inferno (Baraka)
　See *The System of Dante's Hell*

The System of Objects (Baudrillard)
　See *Le systéme des objets*

Système de la mode (*The Fashion System*) (Barthes) 24:31, 36; 83:94

Le systéme des objets (*The System of Objects*) (Baudrillard) 60:9-11, 15, 25, 33

"*Szyrk v. Village of Tantamount et al.*" (Gaddis) 86:163

The T. E. Lawrence Poems (MacEwen) 55:163

"'T' Plays It Cool" (Gaye) 26:131

"T. S. Eliot" (McFadden) 48:244

T. S. Eliot (Spender) 91:263

T. S. Eliot: A Life (Ackroyd) 34:387-89, 392-96, 398-99, 402; 52:7, 9-11, 14-15

T. V. Baby Poems (Ginsberg) 109:338

T. Zee (O'Brien) 17:324

"'t zero" (Calvino) 5:99-101; 8:127; 73:31-2

t zero (Calvino)
　See *Ti con zero*

"Ta" (Cummings) 15:160

"Ta eleyía tis Oxó petras" (Elytis) 100:189

"Ta zou hou" ("After He Left") (Ding Ling) 68:59

"Las tablas" (Parra) 102:339-40

"The Table" (Cabral de Melo Neto)
　See "A mesa"

"Table" (Simic) 22:383

"The Table" (Trevor) 7:475; 71:339, 348

Table Manners (Ayckbourn) 5:35, 37; 8:35; 74:4-6

Table Money (Breslin) 43:76-8

"Table of Delectable Contents" (Simic) 22:381

Table Talk (Ayckbourn) 33:44

The Table Talk of Samuel Marchbanks (Davies) 13:173; 25:129; 42:103, 105; 75:182-83

Le tableau (Ionesco) 41:229

"Tablet" (Shamlu) 10:471

"Tableta de cronicar" ("Chronicler's Notice") (Arghezi) 80:11

"Tablete. Despre cîteva lucruri stiute" (Arghezi) 80:13

Tablete din tara ke Kuty (*Sketches from the Land of Kuty; Tablets from the Land of Kuty*) (Arghezi) 80:6, 11

Tablets from the Land of Kuty (Arghezi)
　See *Tablete din tara ke Kuty*

"Tabula rasa" (Carruth) 7:41

Il taccuino del vecchio (Ungaretti) 11:556

Tacey Cromwell (Richter) 30:308, 310-11, 316, 319-20, 322, 324, 329

"Tacitus" (Trilling) 24:450

Tacones lejanos (*High Heels*) (Almodovar) 114:37, 55

"Tact and the Poet's Force" (Snodgrass) 10:478

"The Tactful Saboteur" (Herbert) 44:394

"The Tactics of Motivation" (Burke) 24:127

Tade ku mushi (*Some Prefer Nettles*) (Tanizaki) 8:509-10; 14:525; 28:417, 419, 421

"Tadeo Limardo's Victim" (Bioy Casares)
　See "La victima de Tadeo Limardo"

"Tadeo Limardo's Victim" (Borges) 48:42

"Tag och skriv" (Ekeloef) 27:112

"Tage mit Hähern" (Eich) 15:202

Tagebuch, 1946-1949 (*Sketchbook, 1946-1949*) (Frisch) 14:183-84; 44:185-86, 190, 192, 194-96, 199-203, 207

Tagebuch, 1966-1971 (*Sketchbook, 1966-1971*) (Frisch) 14:184; 44:192-93, 199, 204

Taht al-mizalla (Mahfuz) 55:172

Tähtede tähendus (*Meaning of the Stars*) (Ivask) 14:287

"Tai An's Long Search" (Borges) 48:41-2

"Taiko Dojo Messages from Haruko" (Jordan) 114:154

"The Tailor's Wedding" (Simpson) 7:428

"Tailpiece" (Barth) 9:68

Tai-pan: A Novel of Hong Kong (Clavell) 6:113; 25:125-27; 87:2-3, 8, 10, 17-19

Tajinko Village (Ibuse) 22:227

"Tak durno zhit', kak ia vchera zhila" ("To Live as Foolishly as I Lived Yesterday") (Akhmadulina) 53:12

Tak fordi du kom, Nick (*Thanks for Coming Home, Nick*) (Abell) 15:5

Tak pobedim! (shest' p'es o Lenine) (*That's How We'll Win! (Six Plays about Lenin)*) 59:359, 362

Take a Call, Topsy (*Ballet Fever*) (Cavanna) 12:98, 103

Take a Girl like You (Amis) 1:6; 2:4, 7-10; 5:20; 8:11; 13:13; 44:135, 143-44

"Take a Lesbian to Lunch" (Brown) 79:153

"Take a Look at the Horizon" (Salinas) 90:324

Take Heart (Peacock) 60:296-98

"Take It Away" (McCartney) 35:289-90

"Take It Easy" (Browne) 21:35, 38

Take It or Leave It (Federman) 6:181; 47:122-24, 127, 129-30

Take Me Back (Bausch) 51:53-4

"Take Me or Leave Me" 99:164, 169

"Take Me to the Mardi Gras" (Simon) 17:466

Take Me Where the Good Times Are (Cormier)

12:134

"Take Me with You" (Prince) 35:331

"Take My Saddle from the Wall: A Valediction" (McMurtry) 27:328

"Take Off Your Socks!!" (Laughlin) 49:224

"Take Pity" (Malamud) 27:306; 44:418

"Take the Moment" (Sondheim) 30:379

Take the Money and Run (Allen) 16:2-3, 5, 12, 15-16; 52:39

"Take Them Out!" (Jordan) 114:146

Take This Man (Busch) 47:57-9

Take Three Tenses (*A Fugue in Time*) (Godden) 53:153-56, 159, 161

"Take Your Clothes Off When You Dance" (Zappa) 17:591

"Taken at the Flood" (Matthews) 40:322

Taken at the Flood (Christie)
　See *There Is a Tide*

"Takeoff" (Snodgrass) 68:397

The Takeover (Spark) 8:493-96; 40:394-95, 398

The Taker/Tulsa (Jennings) 21:201

"The Takers" (Olds) 39:187

"Taking" (Ondaatje) 51:311

Taking a Grip (Johnston) 51:248, 253-54

"Taking a Visitor to See the Ruins" (Allen) 84:24

"Taking a Walk with You" (Koch) 44:243

"Taking a Walk with You" (Strand) 41:436; 71:281-82

"Taking Care" (Williams) 31:464-65

Taking Care (Williams) 31:464-65

Taking Care of Mrs. Carroll (Monette) 82:315, 318, 328

Taking Chances (Keane) 31:231

"Taking In Wash" (Dove) 50:153; 81:139

"Taking It All Off in the Balkans" (Fussell) 74:139

Taking Liberties (Costello) 21:75

"Taking My Baby Up Town" (Armatrading) 17:9-10

Taking Notice (Hacker) 23:204-05; 72:182-83

The Taking of Miss Janie (Bullins) 5:83-4; 7:37

The Taking of Velikoshumsk (Leonov)
　See *Vziatie Velikoshumska*

Taking Sides (Klein) 30:238

Taking Steps (Ayckbourn) 33:42-4, 50

Taking Stock (Trifonov)
　See *Predvaritel'nye itogi*

Taking Terri Mueller (Mazer) 26:294

"Taking the World in for Repairs" (Selzer) 74:273, 275

Taking the World in for Repairs (Selzer) 74:274-75, 281

Un tal Lucas (*A Certain Lucas*) (Cortazar) 33:135-36; 34:333-34

"Talbingo" (Slessor) 14:492

"Talbot Road" (Gunn) 32:213, 215

"A Tale" (Bogan) 46:78; 93:81, 85, 87, 92

A Tale (Pasternak)
　See *Povest*

"A Tale about Rain in Several Episodes" (Akhmadulina)
　See "A Fairytale about the Rain"

The Tale Bearers: Literary Essays (Pritchett) 41:328-29, 331

A Tale for Midnight (Prokosch) 48:315

Tale for the Mirror: A Novella and Other Stories (Calisher) 2:96; 38:69

The Tale of Fatumeh (Ekeloef)
　See *Sagan om Fatumeh*

The Tale of Life (Paustovsky)
   See *Povest' o zhizni*
"The Tale of Macrocosmic Horror" (Smith)
   43:420
A Tale of Satisfied Desire (Bataille)   **29**:45
The Tale of Sunlight (Soto)   **32**:401-03; **80**:276-
   77, 281-83, 293, 295
"The Tale of the Beautiful Princess Kalito"
   (Maitland)   **49**:233, 235
"The Tale of the Black Ring" (Akhmatova)
   64:16, 20
"The Tale of the Children of Hurin" (Tolkien)
   38:431
"The Tale of the Furious Kalafat" (Leonov)
   See "Legend of Kalafaat"
The Tale of the Triumvirate (Strugatskii and
   Strugatskii)
   See *The Tale of the Troika*
The Tale of the Troika (*The Tale of the Triumvi-
   rate*) (Strugatskii and Strugatskii)   **27**:434,
   436
"Tale of the Wicker Chair" (Hesse)   **25**:260-
   61
"The Tale of Three Story Telling Machines"
   (Lem)   **8**:344; **15**:327
"Tale of Time" (Warren)   **13**:578; **39**:264
A Tale of Time: New Poems, 1960-1966 (War-
   ren)   **8**:539; **13**:573-74
"A Tale of Two Gardens" (Paz)
   See "Cuento de dos jardines"
"A Tale of Two Liars" (Singer)   **111**:297, 305
A Tale Told (Wilson)   **36**:459-61, 463
"A Tale without Beginning or End" (Mahfuz)
   52:292
Talent and Work (Leonov)   **92**:277
A Talent for Loving; or, The Great Cowboy Race
   (Condon)   **4**:107; **45**:92, 96; **100**:94, 111,
   113
Talent Is Not Enough (Hunter)   **21**:164
The Talented Mr. Ripley (Highsmith)   **2**:193;
   4:226; **42**:211; **102**:177, 179-80, 182-84,
   193-94, 207-08, 211-12, 220
Tales (Baraka)   **5**:45, 48; **14**:56; **33**:55, 57, 63;
   115:10, 15
Tales and Stories for Black Folks (Bambara)
   88:6
Tales and Texts for Nothing (Beckett)   **2**:44
*Tales for the Telling: Irish Folk and Fairy Sto-
   ries* (O'Brien)   **116**:187
"Tales from a Family Album" (Justice)   **102**:268
Tales from a Troubled Land (Paton)   **4**:395;
   25:359
Tales from Bective Bridge (Lavin)   **99**:312
Tales from Firozsha Baag (*Firozsha Baag*; *Swim-
   ming Lessons, and Other Stories from
   Firozsha Baag*) (Mistry)   **71**:266-67, 269-
   74, 276
Tales from the Plum Grove Hills (Stuart)   **34**:374
Tales from the Uncertain Country (Ferron)
   See *Contes du pays incertain*
Tales from the White Hart (Clarke)   **13**:148-49;
   18:106
Tales I Told My Mother (Nye)   **42**:304-05, 308
Tales of a Fourth Grade Nothing (Blume)   **12**:47;
   30:20
"Tales of Afrikaners" (Coetzee)   **117**:48
Tales of Beatnik Glory (Sanders)   **53**:307
Tales of Known Space (Niven)   **8**:426
Tales of Love (Kristeva)
   See *Histoires d'amour*
Tales of Love and Death (Aickman)   **57**:3
Tales of Manhattan (Auchincloss)   **4**:29; **18**:24;
   45:36

Tales of Natural and Unnatural Catastrophes
   (Highsmith)   **102**:201
Tales of Nevèryön (Delany)   **14**:148; **38**:159
Tales of Pirx the Pilot (Lem)   **15**:330; **40**:291,
   293, 295-96
Tales of Power (Castaneda)   **12**:91-2, 95
"Tales of Queen Louisa" (Gardner)   **5**:133;
   8:238
Tales of Tenderness and Power (Head)   **67**:111
"Tales of the Art World" (Chatwin)   **57**:153
Tales of the City (Maupin)   **95**:192-97, 199,
   201-07, 211
"Tales of the Islands" (Walcott)   **25**:448;
   42:421; **67**:353-54; **76**:273, 275, 279
"Tales of the Marvellous and the Ridiculous"
   (Wilson)   **24**:481
Tales of the Mountains and Steppes (Aitmatov)
   See *Povestri gor i stepei*
Tales of the Quintana Roo (Tiptree)   **48**:393-
   95; **50**:357
Tales of the South Pacific (Michener)   **1**:214;
   5:289; **11**:375; **29**:309-12; **60**:258, 262;
   109:375-80, 382, 384, 385, 387, 388
"Tales of the Swedish Army" (Barthelme)
   13:59
Tales of the Unexpected (Dahl)   **18**:108
"Tales of Two Old Gentlemen" (Dinesen)
   95:56
"Tales Told of the Fathers" (Hollander)   **8**:301
Tales Told of the Fathers (Hollander)   **8**:299-
   302
"Taliesin, 1952" (Thomas)   **48**:377
"Taliesin and the Spring of Vision" (Watkins)
   43:447, 451, 453-54
"Taliesin in Gower" (Watkins)   **43**:442, 451,
   454
"A Taliessin Answer" (Redgrove)   **41**:349
"A Talisman" (Moore)   **13**:392; **19**:336
The Talisman (Alegria)   **75**:51-2
The Talisman (King)   **37**:205-06; **61**:328, 331;
   113:388-89, 391, 393
The Talisman (Straub)   **107**:267-73, 275-77,
   279-80, 282, 289, 291, 304-08, 310
"Talk I" (Cage)   **41**:80
A Talk in the Park (Ayckbourn)   **33**:41
Talk Radio (Stone)   **73**:374-77, 382
"Talk Show" (Baxter)   **45**:53; **78**:17, 21
"Talk to Me" (Mitchell)   **12**:444
Talk to Me about Funes (Costantini)
   See *Háblenme de Funes*
"A Talk with Doris Lessing" (Lessing)   **94**:293
Talkative Man (Narayan)   **47**:306-09
"Talkin 'Bout Sonny" (Bambara)   **88**:21
"Talkin, John Birch Paranoid Blues" (Dylan)
   77:166, 168
*Talkin' Moscow Blues: Essays about Literature,
   Politics, Movies, and Jazz* (Skvorecky)
   69:334-36
"Talkin' World War III Blues" (Dylan)   **77**:161
Talking All Morning (Bly)   **38**:50-4
"The Talking Back of Miss Valentine Jones"
   (Jordan)   **114**:145-46
*Talking Back: Thinking Feminist, Thinking
   Black* (hooks)   **94**:143-45, 159
"Talking Back (to W. H. Auden)" (Meredith)
   55:192
"Talking Birmingham Jam" (Ochs)   **17**:331
Talking Book (Wonder)   **12**:657, 659-60, 663
"Talking Cuba" (Ochs)   **17**:330-31
"Talking Dust Bowl" (Kennedy)   **42**:256
"Talking Dustbowl" (Guthrie)   **35**:188
The Talking Earth (George)   **35**:180
Talking God (Hillerman)   **62**:262

Talking Heads (Bennett)   **77**:92, 95, 98, 101-
   03
Talking Heads: Seventy-Seven (Byrne)   **26**:94-
   5
"Talking Horse" (Malamud)   **3**:323, 325;
   27:298, 300; **44**:417
"Talking in Bed" (Larkin)   **33**:258
"Talking in the Train" (White)   **49**:409
"Talking in the Woods with Karl Amorelli"
   (Knight)   **40**:286
"Talking Myself to Sleep at One More Hilton"
   (Ciardi)   **40**:160
Talking Pictures (Foote)   **91**:99
"Talking Shop Tanka" (Porter)   **33**:323
"The Talking Stone" (Asimov)   **26**:44
"Talking to a Stranger" (Grayson)   **38**:209
"Talking to My Grandmother Who Died Poor
   (While Hearing Richard Nixon Declare 'I
   Am Not a Crook')" (Walker)   **58**:405
"Talking to Myself" (Auden)   **2**:28; **6**:18-19
Talking to Myself: A Memoir of My Times
   (Terkel)   **38**:424-25
Talking to Strange Men (Rendell)   **48**:327
"Talking to the Moon" (Matthews)   **40**:321
Talking to the Moon (Mathews)   **84**:209-11,
   216-18, 220-22, 224-26
"Talking to You Afterwards" (Porter)   **33**:321
The Talking Trees (O'Faolain)   **7**:273; **32**:342-
   43; **70**:319
"Talking United States" (Wilson)   **24**:481
"Talking Vietnam Blues" (Ochs)   **17**:330
"The Tall Grass" (Daly)   **17**:90
Tall Houses in Winter (Betts)   **28**:33
Tall in the Saddle (Armatrading)   **17**:9
"The Tall Men" (Davidson)   **2**:111; **13**:166-
   67, 169; **19**:124-26
"The Tall Men" (Faulkner)   **3**:149
"The Tall Sailing Ship" (Quasimodo)
   See "L'alto veliero"
"Tall Windows" (Hass)   **99**:143
"Taller Today" (Auden)   **14**:32; **43**:15
The Talley Method (Behrman)   **40**:80, 83, 87
Talley's Folly (Wilson)   **14**:591-93; **36**:459-
   61, 465
"A Tally" (Creeley)   **78**:137
"Talpa" (Rulfo)   **80**:200-01, 216
Talvipalatsi (*The Winter Palace*) (Haavikko)
   18:205-06; **34**:170-71, 177
Tam o' the Wilds and the Many-Faced Mystery
   (MacDiarmid)   **63**:249
"Tamar" (Helprin)   **22**:221, 223; **32**:230-31
"Tamar" (Jeffers)   **54**:233, 235-37, 244-46,
   248-49; **2**:215; **3**:258; **11**:304-07; **15**:300
Tamar and Other Poems (Jeffers)   **54**:235, 240,
   250; **11**:304-05
Tamara (Krizanc)   **57**:271-79
"The Tamarind Tree" (Anand)   **23**:21
"Tambourine" (Prince)   **35**:332
"The Tambourine Lady" (Wideman)   **67**:379,
   385
"Tambourine Life" (Berrigan)   **37**:43, 46
"Tambourines" (Hughes)   **108**:297
Tambourines to Glory (Hughes)   **35**:216-18
Les tambours de la pluie (Kadare)   **52**:261
"Tamer and Hawk" (Gunn)   **18**:204; **32**:210
"The Taming" (Livesay)   **15**:340-41; **79**:337,
   339
The Taming of Badadoshkin (Leonov)
   See *Usmirenie Badadoshkina*
"The Taming of the Shrew" (Peacock)   **60**:295
Taming the Star Runner (Hinton)   **111**:84-86
"Tamurlane" (Mukherjee)   **53**:265-66, 268
An tan revolisyon (Conde)   **92**:132

Tan triste como ella (*As Sad as She Is*; *Sad as She*) (Onetti)   10:377-80

"Tanagokoro no Shosetsu" (*The Palm-Sized Stories*) (Kawabata)   107:103, 108, 112

"Tancredi Continues" (Cixous)   92:81-2, 93-4

Tanecni hodiny pro starši a pokrocilé (*Dance Lessons for Adult and Advanced Pupils*) (Hrabal)   67:121

"Tang" (Himes)   108:234-35

The Tangent Factor (Sanders)   41:379-80

The Tangent Objective (Sanders)   41:378-80

"Tangerine" (Page and Plant)   12:475

"Tangi" (Ihimaera)   46:196

Tangi (Ihimaera)   46:193-97, 199, 202

Tangier Buzzless Flies (Hopkins)   4:233

"Tangled Up in Blue" (Dylan)   6:157; 12:191; 77:178

"A Tangled Web" (Haldeman)   61:181

"Tango" (Gluck)   22:177

Tango (Mrozek)   3:344-45; 13:398

"The Tango Bear" (Hansen)   38:240

"Tango: Maureen"   99:167, 169

Tango Palace (Fornes)   39:138; 61:129-30, 137, 139

"Tanhum" (Singer)   15:507

Tanin no kao (*The Face of Another*) (Abe)   22:12-13; 53:2, 4, 6; 81:285, 287-88, 293-94, 297

The Tank Corps (Skvorecky)
   See *L'Escadron blindé*

"The Tank Trapeze" (Moorcock)   58:347

"Tankas" (Borges)   13:110

Tankový prapor (Skvorecky)
   See *L'Escadron blindé*

Tanner '88: The Dark Horse (Altman)   116:50, 59

"Tantas Cosas Asustan, Tantas" ("So Many Things Terrify, So Many") (Cisneros)   69:151

La tante (Simenon)   47:379

"Tantric Ballad2dq2" (Ferlinghetti)   111:65

"Tantrum" (Jensen)   37:189

Tantrum (Feiffer)   64:153

"Die Tänzerin (D.H.)" (Sachs)   98:354

"Tao in the Yankee Stadium Bleachers" (Updike)   23:473

Tap Root Manuscript (Diamond)   30:110-11

Tape for the Turn of the Year (Ammons)   2:12-13; 5:29, 31; 8:14-15, 17-18; 9:27; 25:47; 57:55, 58-9; 108:5, 11-2, 48, 52-5, 58-9, 61

"Tape from California" (Ochs)   17:332

Tape from California (Ochs)   17:332

"Tapestries of Time" (Tolson)   105:260, 282

"Tapestry" (Ashbery)   15:33-4; 41:40

"A Tapestry for Bayeaux" (Starbuck)   53:353, 355

"Tapestry Makers" (Willard)   37:463

"Tapiama" (Bowles)   2:79

"Tapioca Surprise" (Goyen)   14:211

Tapping the Source (Nunn)   34:94-6

"The Taps" (Soto)   80:298

Taps for Private Tussie (Stuart)   11:511; 14:517; 34:373, 376

"Tapwater" (Jensen)   37:191

Tar (Williams)   33:447-49; 56:426, 428-29

The Tar Baby (Charyn)   5:104

Tar Baby (Morrison)   22:320-23; 55:195-96, 207-08; 81:225, 228, 231-33, 236, 238, 256-57, 260; 87:263, 288, 290-92, 294

Tara (White)   49:401

Taran Wanderer (Alexander)   35:24-6

"Taranta-Babuya mektuplar" ("Letters to

Taranta-Babu") (Hikmet)   40:245, 247

Tarantula (Dylan)   4:148; 12:184, 187; 77:176

Taratuta (Donoso)   99:222, 255, 273-75, 277

"Tardy" (Matthews)   40:325

"Tardy Autumn" (Arghezi)
   See "Tîrzui de toamna"

The Tare of Barrels (*Bochkotara*; *The Shopworn Tare of Barrels*; *SurplussedBarrelware*; *Zatovarennaia bochkotara*) (Aksyonov)   101:11-12, 28, 30

Tares (Thomas)   48:374, 380

al-Tariq (Mahfuz)   52:295-96; 55:174, 181-82

"The Tarn and the Rosary" (Brown)   48:55, 60

Tårnet (*The Tower*) (Vesaas)   48:407

The Tarot of Cornelius Agrippa (Morgan)   23:299

"Tarquin" (O'Hara)   13:426

"Tarry, Delight" (Belitt)   22:48

"Tarsisius" (Buckley)   57:129

"Tartan" (Brown)   48:52

The Tartar Steppe (Buzzati)
   See *Il deserto dei tartari*

Tarts and Muggers (Musgrave)   54:338, 340

Tarzan and the City of Gold (Leiber)   25:303

"Tarzan Is an Expatriate" (Theroux)   46:402

"Tashlich" (Piercy)   62:370

"A Task" (Milosz)   56:238; 82:307

Tasks and Masks: Themes and Styles of African Literature (Nkosi)   45:295

The Tassie (O'Casey)
   See *The Silver Tassie*

"The Taste" (Bitov)   57:114-15

"Taste" (Dahl)   79:180

"Taste" (Thomas)   13:544

A Taste for Death (James)   46:209-11

"A Taste for Perfection" (Vanderhaeghe)   41:449-50

A Taste of Honey (Delaney)   29:143-48

A Taste of Salt Water (Shapcott)   38:398, 400

"The Taste of the Age" (Jarrell)   6:260

"Tasting the Wild Grapes" (Oliver)   98:267, 297

"Tatlin!" (Davenport)   6:123

Tatlin! (Davenport)   6:123-25; 14:139-142; 38:139-40, 144, 146, 148

"Tatoos Twelve" (Wright)   13:613

"Tattered Kaddish" (Rich)   76:210, 212-14

"Tattoo" (Moss)   7:249

"Tattoo" (Townshend)   17:531, 533, 539

The Tattooed Countess (Van Vechten)   33:387-88, 392, 398

"The Tattooed Man" (Hayden)   37:155

"The Tattooed Man" (Raine)   103:179

"Tattooer" (Tanizaki)
   See "Shisei"

"Tattoos" (Wright)   13:612; 28:456, 460

"Tau" (Tolson)   105:255

Tau Zero (Anderson)   15:11, 13

"Tauben" (Eich)   15:202

Die tausend Augen des Dr. Mabuse (Lang)
   See *The Thousand Eyes of Dr. Mabuse*

Tauw (Ousmane)   66:336

Se tavallinen tarina (*The Usual Story*) (Salama)   18:461

"The Tavern of Crossed Destinies" (Calvino)   8:131

"The Tavern of the Black Cat" (Mahfuz)   52:298

The Tavern of the Black Cat (Mahfuz)
   See *Khammarat al-qitt al-aswad*

"Tavistock Square" (Williams)   42:442

"Tawny Owl" (Clarke)   61:82-3

The Tax Inspector (Carey)   96:69-74, 76-8, 80-1, 83

The Taxi (Leduc)   22:263

Taxi Driver (Schrader)   26:385-89, 393-95

Taxi Driver (Scorsese)   20:327-30, 334, 336-38, 340; 89:223-26, 228-30, 232-33, 235-36, 239-41, 243-45, 248-49, 252, 254, 260-64, 266-67

"The Taxpayer" (Bradbury)   42:38

Tayaout, fils d'Agaguk (Theriault)   79:407, 418, 420

"Tayga" (Voznesensky)   57:417

"T.B. Sheets" (Morrison)   21:235

T.B. Sheets (Morrison)   21:235

"TCB" (Sanchez)   116:295

"Te lucis ante terminum" (Hill)   45:180

"Tea and Sympathy" (Anderson)   23:28-9, 31, 33

Tea and Sympathy (Kazan)   63:234

"Tea for One" (Page and Plant)   12:480

"Tea in the Rain" (Cryer)   21:79

"Tea in the Sahara" (Police, The)   26:366

Tea Party (Pinter)   15:423; 27:385, 394; 58:373

"The Tea Time of Stouthearted Ladies" (Stafford)   68:430

"Tea with an Artist" (Rhys)   51:356

Tea with Dr. Borsig (Boell)
   See *Zum Tee bei Dr. Borsig*

"Tea with Mrs. Bittell" (Pritchett)   15:442; 41:330

"Tea with the Devil" (Hope)   51:226

"Teach the Gifted Children" (Reed)   21:320-21

Teach Us to Outgrow Our Madness (Oe)
   See *Warera no kyoki o ikinobiru michi o oshieyo*

"Teacher" (Ashton-Warner)   19:21

"The Teacher's Mission" (Pound)   4:416; 112:322

"Teacher's Pet" (Thurber)   5:432

"Teaching a Stone to Talk" (Dillard)   60:74

Teaching a Stone to Talk: Expeditions and Encounters (Dillard)   60:74-5; 115:170, 197-99, 202-03, 205-06, 208-09

"Teaching and Story Telling" (Maclean)   78:239

"The Teaching of Literature" (O'Connor)   104:167

"The Teaching Poet" (Roethke)   101:266

"Teaching Poetry at Votech High, Santa Fe, the Week John Lennon Was Shot" (Allen)   84:24

"Teaching the Ape to Write Poems" (Tate)   2:432

Teaching the Penguins to Fly (Spacks)   14:510

Teaching to Transgress: Educating as the Practice of Freedom (hooks)   94:155-59

"The Teachings of Don B.: A Yankee Way of Knowledge" (Barthelme)   115:85-6

The Teachings of Don Juan (Castaneda)   12:84-6, 88, 95

"Team Bells" (Davis)   49:91

Team Bells Woke Me (Davis)   49:90-1

"Tear" (Kinsella)   19:252, 254

"A Tear" (Yevtushenko)   26:467

"Tear Gas" (Rich)   6:459

"Tears, Idle Tears" (Bowen)   22:65

"Tears in Sleep" (Bogan)   46:78; 93:90, 95-6

"The Tears of a Clown" (Robinson)   21:342, 344, 347

"Tears of an Excavator" (Pasolini)   106:241-

249
"Tears of Rage" (Dylan) 6:155
"Tears, Spray, and Steam" (Logan) 5:255
"The Teasers" (Empson) 19:156
Teater (Theater) (Lagerkvist) 54:273-74
El teatro en soledad (Gomez de la Serna) 9:238
"Tecendo a manhã" ("Weaving the Morning") (Cabral de Melo Neto) 76:155
Technical Difficulties: African-American Notes on the State of the Union (Jordan) 114:150-51, 153, 156
"Technical Notes" (Laughlin) 49:220-21
"Technical Notes on My House-Arrest" (Havel) 65:421
Technicians of the Sacred: A Range of Poetries from Africa, America, Asia, and Oceania (Rothenberg) 57:373, 375, 379, 382
The Technicolor Time Machine (Harrison) 42:200, 205
Technik und Wissenschaft als "Ideologie" (Habermas) 104:68
"Technique as Discovery" (Schorer) 9:473
Technique du roman (Queneau) 5:360
The Technique of Fiction (Oe)
See *Shosetsu no hoho*
"Technologies" (Oppen) 7:281
Technology and Culture (Dudek) 19:139
Technology and the Canadian Mind: Innis/ McLuhan/Grant (Kroker) 77:341-42, 344
"Technology and the Soul" (Martinson)
See "Tekniken och själen"
"Tecumseh" (Oliver) 34:246; 98:257-58, 272, 278
Tecumseh (Eckert) 17:108
Ted Hughes and Paul Muldoon (Hughes) 37:179
Tedderella (Edgar) 42:116
"Teddungal" (Senghor) 54:410
"Teddy" (Salinger) 12:520
"Teddy Bears" (Swenson) 106:333
"Teddy Boy" (McCartney) 35:278
"The Teddy-Bears' Picnic" (Trevor) 116:364
"Ted's Wife" (Thomas) 37:421
Teeftallow (Stribling) 23:439, 441, 445
Teen Kanya (Two Daughters) (Ray) 16:479-80, 483-84, 490-491, 493; 76:360
Teenage Survival Book (Gordon) 26:139
A Teen-Ager's First Car (Felsen) 17:124
Teendreams (Edgar) 42:113
"Teeth" (Stern) 39:237
Teeth, Dying, and Other Matters (Stern) 39:237
Teeth 'n' Smiles (Hare) 29:211-14, 216; 58:233
"The Teeth of My Father" (Metcalf) 37:301, 306
The Teeth of My Father (Metcalf) 37:299-300
"The Teeth-Mother Naked at Last" (Bly) 2:66; 5:64; 10:55, 58-9; 15:62-3; 38:55
Tehanu: The Last Book of Earthsea (Le Guin) 71:181-82, 184, 188-89, 191, 196, 198, 200-01
Teia (Spider Web) (Dourado) 23:149-51
"Teibele and Her Demon" (Singer) 15:509; 38:414-16
Teile dich Nacht (Sachs) 14:477; 98:347, 358-59
Teitlebaum's Window (Markfield) 8:379-80
La tejedora de sueños (Buero Vallejo) 15:99; 46:96
"Tekniken och själen" ("Technology and the Soul") (Martinson) 14:355
Tekonwatoni/Molly Brant (1735-1795): Poems of War (Molly Brant: Poems of War)

(Kenny) 87:250-53, 258-59
"Telecommunication" (Reading) 47:352
"Telegram" (Berrigan) 37:44
"Telemachus" (Dickey) 28:119
"Le téléphone" (Carrier) 78:68
"Telephone Call" (Kenny) 87:242
"A Telephone Call" (Parker) 68:325, 329, 334, 339
"A Telephone Call on Yom Kippur" (Singer) 69:305
"Telephone Conversation" (Soyinka) 14:506; 44:279
"The Telephone Number" (Scannell) 49:326
"The Telephone Number of the Muse" (Justice) 19:234, 236; 102:265, 269
"Telephone Poles" (Updike) 23:474
Telephone Poles, and Other Poems (Updike) 1:344; 23:474-75
Telepinus (Olson) 11:420
"The Telescope" (Derleth) 31:138
"Telescopic" (Frost)
See "A Loose Mountain"
"Television" (Bennett) 28:26
La télévision (Lacan) 75:301
"Television Is a Baby Crawling Toward That Death Chamber" (Ginsberg) 36:184; 109:344
Television Plays (Chayefsky) 23:111
"The Television Poems" (Dobyns) 37:76-7
"Television's Junkyard Dog" (Crews) 49:73
"Tell All the People" (Morrison) 17:289
Tell Freedom (Abrahams) 4:2
Tell It Me Again (Fuller) 62:205
"Tell Me a Riddle" (Olsen) 114:192-94, 197-99, 201-02, 207, 212-13, 215, 218-20, 222-24, 236-38, 240-42, 244
Tell Me a Riddle (Olsen) 4:386-87; 13:433; 114:193, 195, 197-99, 201, 206, 232, 236, 239
"Tell Me a Story" (Warren) 13:582
Tell Me Again How the White Heron Rises and Flies Across the Nacreous River at Twilight Toward the Distant Islands (Carruth) 84:133, 136
"Tell Me, Doctor" (Redgrove) 41:352
Tell Me How Long the Train's Been Gone (Baldwin) 1:16; 2:32; 4:41-2; 5:43; 13:52; 15:42-3; 17:34-7, 45; 50:283, 293, 296; 90:31, 33
Tell Me If the Lovers Are Losers (Voigt) 30:418
Tell Me, Tell Me: Granite, Steel, and Other Topics (Moore) 8:401; 47:263
Tell Me that You Love Me, Junie Moon (Kellogg) 2:223-24
"Tell Me Who to Kill" (Naipaul) 13:407; 105:157
"Tell Me Why" (Young) 17:570
"Tell Me Yes or No" (Munro) 6:342; 10:358; 19:344
"Tell Miss Sweeny Good-Bye" (Tomlin) 17:522-23
Tell My Horse (Voodoo Gods: An Inquiry into Native Myths and Magic in Jamaica and Haiti) (Hurston) 30:212, 217
"Tell the Women We're Going" (Carver) 22:102, 104
"Tell Them Good-by" (Foote) 75:231
"Tell Them Not to Kill Me" (Rulfo)
See "Díles que no me maten!"
Tell Them Willie Boy Is Here (Polonsky) 92:382-83, 387, 391-92, 396-97, 402-03, 405, 415-16
The Telling (Riding) 7:375-77

"Telling about Coyote" (Ortiz) 45:304, 306
"Telling Fortunes" (Brown) 59:265
"Telling Moves" (Ammons) 57:53
The Telling of Lies (Findley) 102:112, 118
Telling Tales (Maitland) 49:233-34
"Telling Them" (Beer) 58:36
The Tell-Tale Heart (Symons) 32:426-27
"Tema del traidor y del héroe" ("The Theme of the Traitor and the Hero") (Borges) 6:91; 19:47; 48:45; 83:156
"Tema para San Jorge" (Cortazar) 10:118
"Temenos" (Lane) 25:288
Le témoignage de l'enfant de choeur (Simenon) 3:450
Temol shilshom (Agnon) 14:6
"Tempered Copper" (Richter) 30:323
The Tempers (Williams) 42:458
A Tempest: After "The Tempest" by Shakespeare, Adaptation for the Negro Theatre (Cesaire)
See *Une tempête: d'après "La tempête" de Shakespeare, Adaptation pour un théâtre nègre*
Tempest-Tost (Davies) 13:171, 173; 25:129-31; 42:101-02, 104; 75:184, 191-93, 198, 213-14; 91:201, 203-4
Une tempête: d'après "La tempête" de Shakespeare, Adaptation pour un théâtre nègre (A Tempest: After "The Tempest" by Shakespeare, Adaptation for the Negro Theatre) (Cesaire) 19:99; 112:21, 26, 28, 39, 44
The Temple (Spender) 91:264-68
The Temple (Weidman) 7:518
The Temple of Dawn (Mishima) 4:356, 358; 6:338; 27:341-42
The Temple of Gold (Goldman) 48:123-24, 128
The Temple of My Familiar (Walker) 58:410-17
The Temple of the Golden Pavillion (Mishima)
See *Kinkakuji*
"A Temple of the Holy Ghost" (*Woman of the River*) (O'Connor) 6:376, 378; 13:417; 15:412; 21:261, 263, 267-68
Tempo de amar (Time to Love) (Dourado) 23:150
The Temporary Kings (Powell) 3:401-04; 7:338-39, 343; 9:436-37; 10:415-16
A Temporary Life (Storey) 4:529-30; 5:416-17; 8:505
"Temporary Secretary" (McCartney) 35:287-89
"Temporary Thing" (Reed) 21:312
Le temps, ce grand sculpteur (That Mighty Sculptor, Time) (Yourcenar) 50:363-64; 87:412, 433
Le temps d'Anaïs (Simenon) 18:483
Le temps des assassins (Age of Assassins: The Story of Prisoner No. 1234) (Soupault) 68:402-04
Le temps des morts (Gascar) 11:220
Les temps du Carcajou (Theriault) 79:417
Le temps du mépris (Days of Wrath) (Malraux) 4:324-26, 331, 336; 9:354; 13:366; 57:301-02, 305-06, 312
Le temps immobile (Mauriac) 9:367
Le temps sauvage (Hebert) 29:237-38
"Temptation" (Milosz) 82:295, 298
"Temptation" (Prince) 35:331-32
"The Temptation of Jack Orkney" (Lessing) 94:261, 264
The Temptation of Jack Orkney, and Other Stories (Lessing) 2:241-42; 3:286; 6:300;

94:261

"The Temptation of Modernity" (Powell) 89:206

"The Temptation of St. Anthony" (Barthelme) 13:57; 46:35

"The Temptation of St. Ivo" (Gardner) 8:238

The Temptation to Exist (Cioran)
See *La tentation d'exister*

The Temptations of Big Bear (Wiebe) 6:566-67; 14:574

"The Temptations of Doctor Antonio" (Fellini)
See "Le tentazioni del Dottor Antonio"

The Temptations of Eileen Hughes (Moore) 32:307-11, 313; 90:260, 265, 268, 274, 304

The Temptations of Oedipus (Baxter) 14:65

"Tempul Firing" (Bissett) 18:58

Temy i variatsi (*Temy i var'iatsii*; *Themes and Variations*) (Pasternak) 7:293, 300; 18:381-82; 63:275, 280, 289

Temy i var'iatsii (Pasternak)
See *Temy i variatsi*

"10" (Reading) 47:350

"Ten Accounts of a Monogamous Man" (Meredith) 4:349

Ten Blocks on the Camino Real (Williams)
See *Camino Real*

"Ten Burnt Offerings" (MacNeice) 4:317

"Ten Cents a Coup" (Ochs) 17:333

Ten Dark Women (Ichikawa)
See *Kuroi junin no ohna*

"Ten Days Leave" (Snodgrass) 68:387

Ten Days of Wonder (Queen) 11:461-64

"Ten Degrees and Getting Colder" (Lightfoot) 26:278

Ten Green Bottles (Thomas) 7:472; 13:539; 37:417; 107:314, 316-17, 326, 334, 347, 348, 350

Ten Horsepower (Ehrenburg) 62:176

"Ten Indians" (Hemingway) 10:269; 30:181

"Ten Jack-Offs" (Bukowski) 41:68

Ten Little Indians (Christie)
See *And Then There Were None*

Ten Little Niggers (Christie)
See *And Then There Were None*

Ten Million Ghosts (Kingsley) 44:232

Ten North Frederick (O'Hara) 2:324; 6:385-86; 42:313, 315, 319, 323-24

Ten Novelists and Their Novels (Maugham) 15:368

10 Pastoral Poems (Alegria) 57:10

"Ten Pecan Pies" (Major) 19:298

"Ten Shots of Mr. Simpson" (Graham) 29:198-99

The Ten Teacups (Carr)
See *The Peacock Feather Murders*

Ten Theatre Poems (Morgan) 31:274

The 10:30 from Marseilles (Japrisot)
See *Compartiment tueurs*

Ten Thousand Light-Years from Home (Tiptree) 48:385-86, 389, 393

"10,000 Men" (Dylan) 77:182, 185

"Ten Thousand Words a Minute" (Mailer) 111:106-07

Ten Times Table (Ayckbourn) 33:41, 45

Ten Tiny Fingers, Nine Tiny Toes (Foreman) 61:419

Ten Working Theses of the Writer in a Divided World (Weiss) 15:567

"Ten Years Ago When I Played at Being Brave" (Ciardi) 44:381

Ten Years Beyond Baker Street (Van Ash) 34:118-19

"Ten Years Gone" (Page and Plant) 12:479

"Ten Years' Sentences" (Laurence) 3:280; 50:321; 62:269-70

Ten' zvuka (Voznesensky) 15:554, 557

"Tenancies" (Thomas) 48:375

"A Tenancy" (Merrill) 13:379

"The Tenant" (Mukherjee) 53:272; 115:364, 366-67, 369

"The Tenant" (Ortese)
See "Il signor Lin"

"The Tenant" (Phillips) 28:363

The Tenant (Polanski) 16:472-73

The Tenants (Malamud) 1:201; 2:266-69; 3:322, 325; 8:375; 9:343-46, 348-50; 11:346-48, 351-54; 18:319-21; 27:295-96, 298, 300-04; 44:413, 415, 419; 85:200

The Tenants of Moonbloom (Wallant) 5:478; 10:512, 514-17

Tenants of the House (Abse) 29:12-18

"Tenants of the Last Tree-House" (Gordimer) 33:180

The Tenants of Time (Flanagan) 52:153-56

Tenda dos milagres (*Tent of Miracles*) (Amado) 13:11; 40:33-4; 106:56, 60, 62, 65

"Ten-Day Leave" (Meredith) 4:348

"A Tender Man" (Bambara) 22, 28, 42

Tender Mercies (Brown) 32:67-70

Tender Mercies (Foote) 51:131-36, 138; 91:101

"The Tender Offer" (Auchincloss) 45:33

Tender Offer (Wasserstein) 32:441

The Tender Skin (Truffaut)
See *La peau douce*

"The Tenderfoot and the Tramp" (Solzhenitsyn) 7:432

"Tenderfoot in Space" (Heinlein) 26:177

"Tenderloin" (Gunn) 81:176, 178

Tenderness and Gristle: The Collected Poems (Niedecker) 42:295

Tending to Virginia (McCorkle) 51:275-78

Tendres stocks (*Fancy Goods*; *Green Shoots*) (Morand) 41:295-98, 303, 306-08

"Tendril in the Mesh" (Everson) 5:123; 14:166

"Tenebrae" (Celan) 10:104; 19:88; 53:75; 82:45

"Tenebrae" (Clarke) 9:168

"Tenebrae" (Gascoyne) 45:148

"Tenebrae" (Hill) 45:180

Tenebrae (Hill) 18:238-40, 242-43; 45:178-82, 185-87

Tenement of Clay (West) 96:367-68, 384

"Tengo" ("All Is Mine"; "I Have") (Guillen) 48:161

Tengo (*All Is Mine*; *I Have*) (Guillen) 48:158-59, 164, 167; 79:229

Tennessee (Linney) 51:260, 262

Tennessee Day in St. Louis (Taylor) 18:522; 71:293

"Tennessee June" (Graham) 48:145

Tennessee Williams's Letters to Donald Windham, 1940-1965 (Williams) 19:470; 45:444-45

"Tennis" (Avison) 97:69, 76, 81, 111, 129, 130-36

"Tennis: A Portrait" (Moss) 14:376

"The Tennis Court" (Dunn) 40:171

"The Tennis Court" (Trevor) 9:529

"The Tennis Court Oath" (Ashbery) 9:43

The Tennis Court Oath (Ashbery) 2:16, 18-19; 4:22-3; 9:42-43, 45; 15:26-8, 34, 36; 25:52, 55, 58; 41:40-1; 42, 48, 52, 73

The Tennis Handsome (Hannah) 38:231-35; 90:137, 148, 151

"Tennis Instructor, 1971" (Leithauser) 27:240

Tennis Shoes (Streatfeild) 21:397, 414

"Te-non-an-at-che" (Kenny) 87:252

"Tenor" (Jensen) 37:191

"Tense Night" (Faludy) 42:140

"Tension in Poetry" (Tate) 4:536; 6:526; 11:525

Tent of Miracles (Amado)
See *Tenda dos milagres*

The Tent of Orange Mist (West) 96:397-99

"Tent on the Home Ground" (Ihimaera) 46:200

"Tentation de la permanence" (de Man) 55:404

La tentation d'exister (*The Temptation to Exist*) (Cioran) 64:73-5, 77-84, 87, 90, 92-3, 96-9

Tentativa del hombre infinito ("Assay of the Infinite Man"; *Endeavors of Infinite Man*; *Venture of the Infinite Man*) (Neruda) 28:313

"Tentative Conclusion" (Frye) 24:209

"Tentative Decisions" (Byrne) 26:94

"Tentative Hour" (Avison) 97:123

"A Tentative Welcome to Readers" (Stafford) 29:387

"Le tentazioni del Dottor Antonio" ("The Temptations of Doctor Antonio") (Fellini) 16:277; 85:71

"Tenth Avenue Freeze-Out" (Springsteen) 17:489

"The Tenth Child" (Calisher) 38:76

"The Tenth Clew" (Hammett) 47:164

The Tenth Commandment (Sanders) 41:380-82

The Tenth Man (Chayefsky) 23:113, 117

The Tenth Man (Greene) 37:139-40; 70:289

The Tenth Man (Maugham) 11:368

The Tenth Month (Hobson) 7:163

The Tenth Moon (Powell) 66:367

"Tenth Symphony" (Ashbery) 15:32

Ten-Thirty on a Summer Night (Duras)
See *Dix heures et demie du soir en été*

"Tents for the Gandy Dancers" (Engel) 36:162

The Tents of Wickedness (De Vries) 2:113; 3:126; 28:106, 110

"Tenzone" (Ciardi) 10:105; 44:381

Teorema (*Theorem*) (Pasolini) 20:261-65, 267; 37:346-47, 349-51; 106:226, 248, 256, 265, 273

"Teoria delle giunte" (Pasolini) 106:236

"Teo's Bakery" (Suknaski) 19:434

Tequila Sunrise (Towne) 87:369-72, 374-78

"Ter le milicien" ("Ter of the Militia") (Duras) 40:188; 68:75-6, 78, 83, 90, 94

"Ter of the Militia" (Duras)
See "Ter le milicien"

"Teraloyna" (Gordimer) 70:177-78

"Teran" (Salinas) 90:324

"The Tercentenary Incident" (Asimov) 26:50, 56; 76:320

Tercera residencia, 1935-1945 (*Third Residence*; *The Third Residence*) (Neruda) 7:258; 62:328-29, 333, 336

"La tercera resignación" ("The Third Resignation") (Garcia Marquez) 3:181; 47:147

"Teresa" (Adams) 46:17

"Teresa" (Wilbur) 9:570

Teresa, and Other Stories (*The Man Who Invented Sin*) (O'Faolain) 14:402; 32:340, 343-44; 70:318

Teresa of Jesus (Sender) 8:480

"Teresa's Bar" (Durcan) 43:113-14

Teresa's Bar (Durcan) 43:113

"Teresa's Wedding" (Trevor) 71:326; 116:385,

395

"Tereseta-que-baixava-les-escales" (Espriu) 9:192

Tereza Batista cansada de guerra (*Tereza Batista Home from the Wars*) (Amado) 13:11; 40:34-6; 106:55, 59, 62, 73, 76, 86

Tereza Batista Home from the Wars (Amado) See *Tereza Batista cansada de guerra*

"The Term" (Blackburn) 43:61

Termina el desfile (*The Parade Ends*; *The Parade is Over*) (Arenas) 41:28

"The Terminal Beach" (Ballard) 3:34; 14:40; 36:34, 46

The Terminal Beach (Ballard) 3:33

"Terminal Day at Beverly Farms" (Lowell) 37:243

Terminal Hip (Wellman) 65:239, 242

The Terminal Man (Crichton) 2:109; 6:119; 54:67-71, 76

Terminal Moraine (Fenton) 32:164-66

"Terminal Note" (Forster) 3:161; 9:207; 15:230

"Terminal Thoughts" (Brown) 63:57

Terminos del presagio (*Terms of the Presage*) (Sender) 8:480-81

"Terminus" (Ammons) 25:43

"Terminus" (Barthelme) 59:251

"The Termitary" (Gordimer) 18:189

"The Terms in Which I Think of Reality" (Ginsberg) 4:182

Terms of Endearment (McMurtry) 7:214-15; 11:371; 44:255-57

Terms of Reference (Middleton) 38:329-30

Terms of the Presage (Sender) See *Terminos del presagio*

"The Terns" (Oliver) 98:283

Terra amata (Le Clezio) 31:245-47, 249

"Terra Australis" (McAuley) 45:248

"Terra incognita" (Nabokov) 3:354

Terra nostra (Fuentes) 8:223-25; 10:205-08; 41:167-68, 171; 60:152-53, 156, 162, 164-68, 171-72; 113:243, 262-64

Terra nova (Tally) 42:365-68

La terra promessa (Ungaretti) 7:481-82; 11:556, 558; 15:537-39

La terra trema (Visconti) 16:561-62, 564, 570

"Terrain" (Ammons) 108:22

"The Terrapin" (Highsmith) 102:172, 204, 220

Terraqué (Guillevic) 33:192, 194

Terras do sem fim (*The Violent Land*) (Amado) 13:11; 40:24-5, 27, 29; 106:58, 61-2

"La terre des hommes" (Durcan) 43:113, 116

La terre inquiète (Glissant) 68:171, 179

Terre lointaine (Green) 3:204; 77:276-80, 289

Terre sur terre (*Earth upon Earth*) (Tzara) 47:388, 390, 396

"Les terres impossibles" (Theriault) 79:408

"Terrestrial Magnetism" (Fulton) 52:160

"Terribilis est locus iste: Gauguin and the Pont-Aven School" (Hill) 45:181, 190

"Terrible" (Roethke) 11:486

"Terrible Man, Barney" (Carroll) 10:98

"The Terrible Redeemer Lazarus Morell" (Borges) See "El espantoso redentor Lazarus Morell"

The Terrible Shears (Enright) 4:155-56; 8:203; 31:154-56

Terrible Swift Sword (Catton) 35:91-4

The Terrible Temptation (Arundel) 17:15-18

The Terrible Threes (Reed) 60:310-11, 313

The Terrible Threshold (Kunitz) 6:287

The Terrible Twos (Reed) 32:359-62; 60:310-11, 313

Territorial Rights (Spark) 13:525; 18:505-06; 40:395, 397, 400

"Territory" (Leavitt) 34:77, 79

The Territory Ahead (Morris) 7:245; 18:353; 37:311-13

"The Territory Is Not the Map" (Spicer) 72:349

"Terror" (Aldington) 49:7

Terror and Decorum (Viereck) 4:559

"Terror and Erebus" (MacEwen) 55:163-64, 166, 169

"The Terrorist, He Watches" ("The Terrorist, He's Watching") (Szymborska) 99:192, 196

"The Terrorist, He's Watching" (Szymborska) See "The Terrorist, He Watches"

"Le terroriste" (Theriault) 79:408

Terrorists and Novelists (Johnson) 48:202-03

The Terrors of Dr. Treviles (Shuttle) 6:446; 7:423

The Terrors of Dr. Treviles: A Romance (Redgrove) 6:446; 41:355

Terrors of Pleasure (Gray) 49:148; 112:97-8, 119, 124, 130

"Terrors of Pleasure: The House" (Gray) 49:152

"Terry Street" (Raine) 103:189

Terry Street (Dunn) 6:148; 40:164-68, 172

"Tertiaries" (Ammons) 57:57

Tess (Polanski) 16:473

Tessie (Jackson) 12:289-90

"The Test" (Lem) 40:291, 296

"The Test" (Matheson) 37:246

"Test" (Parra) 102:350, 353

"The Test Is, If They Drown" (Grenville) 61:156

"Test of Atlanta 1979" (Jordan) 114:148

Test of Fire (Bova) 45:72-3

"A Test of Poetry" (Zukofsky) 18:561

"A Testament" (Creeley) 78:140

"Testament" (Hoffman) 23:238

The Testament (Wiesel) 37:453-55

"Testament Coran" (Pasolini) 37:348; 106:243

Le testament d'Orphée (*The Testament of Orpheus*) (Cocteau) 16:226-30

Le Testament du docteur Mabuse (Lang) See *The Testament of Dr. Mabuse*

Le testament du Dr. Cordelies (*The Testament of Dr. Cordelies*) (Renoir) 20:291, 298

"Testament for My Students" (Boyle) 58:71-2

Testament for My Students (Boyle) 1:42

Testament for My Students, 1968-1969, and Other Stories (Boyle) 1:42; 58:71-2

"The Testament of Athammaus" (Smith) 43:420, 424

The Testament of Daedalus (Ayrton) 7:20

The Testament of Dr. Cordelies (Renoir) See *Le testament du Dr. Cordelies*

The Testament of Dr. Mabuse (*Le Testament du docteur Mabuse*) (Lang) 20:206, 211; 103:88, 121-22

Testament of Experience (Brittain) 23:92-3

The Testament of Man (Fisher) 7:103-04

The Testament of Orpheus (Cocteau) See *Le testament d'Orphée*

"Testament of the Royal Nirvana" (Kallman) 2:221

"Testament of the Thief" (Kinnell) 29:283

"Testament of Youth" (Brittain) 23:88-93

"Testamento de Hécuba" (Castellanos) 66:53

Testaments Betrayed (Kundera)

See *Les testaments trahis*

Les testaments trahis (*Testaments Betrayed*) (Kundera) 115:355-56, 358, 360

Un testigo fugaz y disfrazado (Sarduy) 97:404

Testimonies (Ritsos) 31:327

Testimony (Reznikoff) 9:449

"The Testimony of J. Robert Oppenheimer" (Ai) 69:9-10

"The Testimony of Light" (Forche) 86:139, 141, 145

"Testimony of Pilot" (Hannah) 90:132, 143, 164

Testimony of the Invisible Man: William Carlos Williams, Francis Ponge, Rainer Maria Rilke, Pablo Neruda (Willard) 37:461-63

Testimony of Two Men (Caldwell) 2:95; 39:302-03

"The Testimony of Wine" (Smith) 22:384-86

"Testimony on the War in France" (de Man) 55:384

Testing the Current (McPherson) 34:85-9

The Testing-Tree (Kunitz) 6:285-87; 14:313

"Tête" (Reverdy) 53:290

Tête blanche (Blais) 4:67; 6:82; 13:96

La tête d'obsidienne (*Picasso's Mask*) (Malraux) 9:358; 57:307

La tête du roi (Ferron) 94:108, 112, 125

"Tetélestai" (Aiken) 52:24, 27

Il tetto (*The Roof*) (De Sica) 20:88, 94

Tex (Hinton) 30:205-06; 111:77-85

"Texarcana Was a Crazy Town" (Garrett) 51:147, 152

Texas (Michener) 60:255-57, 260-61; 109:376-77, 379-81, 383, 386

Texas by the Tail (Thompson) 69:386-87

Texas Celebrity Turkey Trot (Gent) 29:181-82

"The Texas Girls" (Lerman) 9:331

"The Texas Principessa" (Goyen) 40:217-18

Texas Town (Foote) 51:129

A Texas Trilogy (Jones) 10:296-97

"Text in a Notebook" (Cortazar) 33:130, 132

"A Textbook of Poetry" (Spicer) 18:511-12

La texte du roman: Approache semiologique d'une structure discursive transformationelle (Kristeva) 77:299-300

Textes pour rien (*Texts for Nothing*) (Beckett) 4:52-3; 6:45; 9:80; 10:29; 11:40; 29:56, 59

Texts for Nothing (Beckett) See *Textes pour rien*

Text-Sound Art in North America (Kostelanetz) 28:219

The Texture of the Embroidery (Dourado) See *Risco do bordado*

Textures of Life (Calisher) 38:70

The Textures of Silence (Vorster) 34:121-23

Thaddeus Stevens and the Fight for Negro Rights (Meltzer) 26:298

"Thalassa" (MacNeice) 10:325; 53:238

"Thalidomide" (Plath) 5:345; 51:340; 111:163

"The Thames at Chelsea" (Brodsky) 36:80

"Thames Forest" (Watkins) 43:441

"Thammuz" (Mahon) 27:288, 290

The Thanatos Syndrome (Percy) 47:336-41; 65:256-58

"Thank God for the Atom Bomb" (Fussell) 74:129, 134, 140

Thank God for the Atom Bomb, and Other Essays (Fussell) 74:129, 137

"Thank the Lord for the Nightime" (Diamond)

30:111

Thank U Very Much for the Family Circle (Taylor) **27**:441

"Thank You" (Koch) **44**:243, 249

"Thank You" (Page and Plant) **12**:473

Thank You All Very Much (Drabble)
See *The Millstone*

Thank You and Other Poems (Koch) **44**:241, 248, 251

"Thank You, Christine" (Berryman) **2**:59

Thank You, Fog: Last Poems (Auden) **6**:18-20, 24-5; **9**:56; **43**:26, 29

"Thank You for the Lovely Tea" (Gallant) **38**:190, 194

Thank You, Masked Man (Bruce) **21**:58

Thank You, Miss Victoria (Hoffman) **40**:253

"Thank You Very Much" (Sondheim) **30**:379

"Thankfulness" (Milosz) **56**:239

"Thanking My Mother for Piano Lessons" (Wakoski) **4**:572

Thanks for Coming Home, Nick (Abell)
See *Tak fordi du kom, Nick*

"Thanks for the Ride" (Munro) **19**:344; **95**:285, 297

"Thanks to Joyce" (Behan) **79**:37-8

"Thanks to Miss Morrissey" (Ferber) **93**:141

Thanks to Murder (Krumgold) **12**:316

"A Thanksgiving" (Auden) **6**:25; **9**:55

"Thanksgiving" (Gluck) **22**:173, 75

"Thanksgiving" (Nemerov) **36**:306

"Thanksgiving for a Habitat" (Auden) **11**:20; **43**:29

"Thanksgiving Spirit" (Farrell) **66**:131

The Thanksgiving Visitor (Capote) **34**:322; **38**:84, 87

"A Thank-You Letter" (Swenson) **61**:405; **106**:323

Tharthara fawq al-Nil (*Chatter on the Nile*; *Chatting on the Nile*; *Chit-Chat on the Nile*) (Mahfuz) **52**:296, 300-01; **55**:183

"Thasos" (Squires) **51**:381

"That" (Thomas) **48**:375

"That Abomination in the By-Now Twentieth Century Aesthetic Tradition: Meditation on a Wet Snowy Afternoon" (Wakoski) **4**:572

"That All Be in All" (Damas)
See "Pour que tout soit en tout"

"That Apple Was Mental" (Young) **82**:397, 412

That Championship Season (Miller) **2**:284-85

"That Chance" (Young) **82**:396-97, 412

"That Cloud" (Young) **82**:412

That Cold Day in the Park (Altman) **116**:47, 74

That Cold Day in the Park (Altman) **16**:20, 24-5, 31; **116**:11

"That Dirty Old Man" (Sondheim) **30**:378

That Distant Afternoon (Fuller)
See *The Ruined Boys*

"That Distant Winter" (Levine) **5**:251

That Early Spring (Beckman)
See *The Loneliness of Mia*

"That Evening Sun" (Faulkner) **3**:156; **8**:213-14; **18**:147; **68**:128

"That Falling We Fall" (Galvin) **38**:198

"That Girl Could Sing" (Browne) **21**:42

That Good between Us (Barker) **37**:33-5, 37

That Good between Us. Credentials of a Sympathiser (Barker) **37**:37

That Hideous Strength: A Modern Fairy Tale for Grown-Ups (Lewis) **1**:177; **3**:297-99;

6:309-11; **14**:323-26; **27**:264, 266, 268

That Horse (Hogan) **73**:153-54

"That I Had the Wings" (Ellison) **11**:183; **114**:93-4, 126, 131

"That Kind of Thing" (Gallagher) **63**:124, 126

"That Lovely April" (Grau) **9**:240

That Mighty Sculptor, Time (Yourcenar)
See *Le temps, ce grand sculpteur*

"That Mortal Knot" (L'Heureux) **52**:273

That Most Distressful Nation: The Taming of the American Irish (Greeley) **28**:170-71

"That Mouth" (Rich) **76**:214

"That New Man, the American" (Stegner) **49**:359

That Night (McDonald) **90**:217-22, 224-26, 230-33
See *A Bigamist's Daughter*

That None Should Die (Slaughter) **29**:372

That Obscure Object of Desire (Bunuel)
See *Cet obscure objet du désir*

That Old Gang O' Mine: The Early and Essential S. J. Perelman (Perelman) **49**:268-69

"That Old Picayune-Moon" (Keillor) **115**:294

"That Quick and Instant Flight" (Lane) **25**:285

That Red Wheelbarrow (Coles) **108**:195

"That Room" (Montague) **46**:267

"That Same Old Obsession" (Lightfoot) **26**:279

"That Seed" (Wright) **53**:429

"That Star" (Dodson) **79**:193-94

"That Straightlaced Christian Thing between Your Legs" (Simic) **9**:479, 481

"That Summer" (Sargeson) **31**:366, 368, 371

That Summer in Paris: Memories of Tangled Friendships with Hemingway, Fitzgerald, and Some Others (Callaghan) **3**:97; **14**:102-03; **41**:94; **65**:245-48, 250-53

"That Summer Shore" (Ciardi) **40**:156

That Summer—That Fall (Gilroy) **2**:161

That Tantalus (Bronk) **10**:74

"That the Science of Cartography Is Limited" (Boland) **113**:91, 100, 110, 113, 115

"That the Soul May Wax Plump" (Swenson) **61**:398, 402; **106**:329, 344

"That Thou Art Mindful of Him" (Asimov) **26**:50, 56; **92**:6-9

That Time (Beckett) **9**:84; **14**:74; **18**:46, 49; **29**:63-4; **59**:255

"That Time in Odessa" (Boell)
See "Damals in Odessa"

That Uncertain Feeling (Amis) **1**:5-6; **2**:4-5, 10; **5**:20-1, 23

That Voice (Pinget) **37**:361, 363-66

"That Was Close, Ma" (Hannah) **90**:160

"That Was the President" (Ochs) **17**:331

That Was Then, This Is Now (Hinton) **30**:204; **111**:77-78, 80-85

"That Which Convinces" (Elytis) **49**:114

"That Would Be Something" (McCartney) **35**:278-79

"That Year" (McGuckian) **48**:275-76

"That Year" (Olds) **32**:346; **85**:285

"Thatch Retaliates" (Chappell) **40**:141

"The Thatcher" (Heaney) **25**:244

"That'll Show Him" (Sondheim) **30**:378

That's All (Duras) **100**:150

That's How We'll Win! (Six Plays about Lenin)
See *Tak pobedim! (shest' p'es o Lenine)*

"That's Marriage" (Ferber) **93**:138

"That's No Way to Spend Your Youth" (Clash) **30**:43-4

"That's Saul, Folks" (Grayson) **38**:211-12

"That's the Way" (Page and Plant) **12**:474-75

"That's the Way I've Always Heard It Should Be" (Simon) **26**:406-08, 410-11

That's What We Live For (*That's Why We Are Alive*) (Szymborska) **99**:194, 199, 203, 206, 211

That's Why We Are Alive (Szymborska)
See *That's What We Live For*

"Thaw" (Avison) **97**:77

"Thaw" (Longley) **29**:295

The Thaw (*A Change of Season*; *The Spring*) (Ehrenburg) **18**:132-34, 136; **34**:434, 440; **62**:171-73, 178

"Thaw on a Building Site" (MacCaig) **36**:282

"Thawing Out" (Boyle) **90**:46-8, 50

"The" (Zukofsky)
See "Poem Beginning 'The'"

"'The Black Swan' Revisted" (Selzer) **74**:273

"'The Monk' and Its Author" (Berryman) **10**:45

"Theater" (Toomer) **4**:549; **22**:425

Theater (Lagerkvist)
See *Teater*

The Theater Essays of Arthur Miller (Miller) **10**:346; **47**:250

Theater Piece (Cage) **41**:79

"Theater Problems" (Duerrenmatt) **102**:74

"Theaterprobleme" (Durrenmatt) **15**:197

"Theatre" (Hellman) **52**:192

Theatre (Maugham) **67**:211

Théâtre (Sarraute) **31**:380-81

"Theatre I" (Beckett) **9**:84

Théâtre I (Arrabal) **58**:3, 11

"Theatre II" (Beckett) **9**:84

Théâtre III (Arrabal) **58**:10

Théâtre IV (Arrabal) **58**:9

Théâtre bouffe (Arrabal) **58**:16, 18

Théâtre cérémonie 'panique' (Arrabal) **58**:9, 19

Théâtre complet (Ionesco) **86**:340

Théâtre de Poche (Cocteau) **43**:107

Théâtre Eight (Arrabal) **9**:35

Théâtre et religion (Marcel) **15**:359

The Theatre of Commitment (Bentley) **24**:49, 51-2

"The Theatre of Hope and Despair" (Friel) **115**:251

The Theatre of Mixed Means (Kostelanetz) **28**:213

Theatre of War (Bentley) **24**:52

"Theatre Party" (Coward) **51**:74

Theatre Shoes (Streatfeild) **21**:399

"Thebais" (Howard) **47**:169-70

The Theban Mysteries (Heilbrun) **25**:252

Thebes' Struggle (Mahfuz)
See *Kifah Tiba*

"Thee" (Aiken) **10**:4

"Theft" (Porter) **7**:314, 319-20; **10**:396; **27**:399; **101**:227, 253

Theft (Ingalls) **42**:229

"The Theft of Melko" (Tolkien) **38**:441

"The Theft Partial" (Simmons) **43**:407

"Their Behaviour" (Brutus) **43**:96

Their Blood is Strong (Steinbeck) **59**:340-41, 347

"Their Cities, Their Universities" (Murray) **40**:337, 340

Their Days Are Numbered (Canetti)
See *Die Befristeten*

Their Eyes Were Watching God (Hurston) **7**:171; **30**:210-12, 215-16, 218-19, 222-25, 227-28; **61**:237-75

Their Heads Are Green and Their Hands Are Blue (Bowles) 19:58; 53:43

"Their Oxford" (Amis) 40:45

"Their Quiet Lives" (Warner) 7:512

Their Satanic Majesties Request (Jagger and Richard) 17:220-21, 224, 229, 235, 237

"Their Son" (Green) 97:292

"Their Thing" (Damas)
  See "Ils ont"

"Their Very Memory" (Blunden) 56:29, 43

Their Very Own and Golden City (Wesker) 3:519; 5:483; 42:426, 428, 430

"Them" (Simon) 26:413

them (Oates) 1:251-52; 2:314; 3:359, 361-62, 364; 6:368-69, 371-72; 9:403-06; 15:400-01; 19:349-50, 353; 33:288-89, 293; 52:329, 334-36, 338-39; 108:374, 377-78, 391-92

"Them and Us" (Bukowski) 82:28

"Them Belly Full" ("But We Hungry") (Marley) 17:267, 269, 271-72

Them, Featuring Van Morrison (Morrison) 21:234-35

Them That Glitter and Them That Don't (Greene) 30:171

"Theme for Diverse Instruments" (Rule) 27:420

Theme for Diverse Instruments (Rule) 27:419-20

A Theme for Hyacinth (Symons) 32:429

The Theme Is Freedom (Dos Passos) 25:145

"The Theme of the Traitor and the Hero" (Borges)
  See "Tema del traidor y del héroe"

Themes and Variations (Cage) 41:84

Themes and Variations (Huxley) 4:240

Themes and Variations (Pasternak)
  See *Temy i variatsi*

Themes and Variations for Sounding Brass (Gustafson) 36:213-14, 216-18, 221

Themes in My Poems (Jeffers) 54:250

"Then" (Hacker) 72:191

Then Again, Maybe I Won't (Blume) 30:22

Then and Now (Maugham) 1:204; 15:368; 67:207-09, 217

Then Badger Said This (Cook-Lynn) 93:115, 118-120

"Then I Shall Be Able to Find Peace and Slumber" (Le Clezio) 31:244

"Then Oblique Stroke Now" (Johnston) 51:245

Then Shall the Dust Return (Green) 77:271

"Then We Were Three" (Shaw) 34:370

Thendara House (Bradley) 30:32

"Theodicy" (Milosz) 56:239

"Theodore Dreiser" (Farrell) 66:139

"Theodore Dreiser: In Memoriam" (Farrell) 66:139

Theodore Roethke: An American Romantic (Parini) 54:358-59, 361

"The Theologians" (Borges) 13:105; 44:353; 83:164

"Theological" (Ezekiel) 61:108

A Theological Position (Coover) 3:114; 15:145; 32:120, 124; 87:24-5

Theology and Christian Ethics (Gustafson) 100:196

Theophilus North (Wilder) 6:577-78; 10:536; 82:367, 376, 378

Theorem (Pasolini)
  See *Teorema*

Theorie des kommunikativen Handelns I-II (*The Theory of Communicative Action*) (Habermas) 104:85-6

Die Theorie des Romans (*The Theory of the Novel*) (Lukacs) 24:320, 323, 326-28

Theorie und Praxis (Habermas) 104:66

"Theory" (Simic) 22:381

"The Theory and Practice of Rivers" (Harrison) 66:162

The Theory and Practice of Rivers and New Poems (Harrison) 66:162-63

The Theory and Practice of Rivers and Other Poems (Harrison) 66:157, 161

"Theory as Liberatory Practice" (hooks) 94:157

The Theory of Communicative Action (Habermas)
  See *Theorie des kommunikativen Handelns I-II*

A Theory of Fiction (Gass) 15:257

Theory of Flight (Rukeyser) 10:442; 15:456, 458-59; 27:403-05, 408, 410-11, 414

"A Theory of Language" (Percy) 6:400; 8:441

Theory of Literature (Wellek) 28:441-44, 446, 452

Theory of Prosody in Eighteenth-Century England (Fussell) 74:144

"The Theory of Sets" (Pesetsky) 28:358

The Theory of the Novel (Lukacs)
  See *Die Theorie des Romans*

"Theory of Truth" (Jeffers) 54:250

Theory of War (Brady) 86:130-36

"A Theory of Wind" (Goldbarth) 38:205

"Therapy 2000" (Roberts) 14:463

"there" (Clifton) 66:83

"There" (Creeley) 36:121

"There" (Hooker) 43:196

"There" (Taylor) 18:526; 37:412

"There Are Delicacies" (Birney) 4:64

There Are Facts
  See *Ivanca*

"There Are More Things" (Borges) 48:38, 40-1

"There Are Nights" (Damas)
  See "Il est des nuits"

"There Are No Honest Poems About Dead Women" (Lorde) 71:254

"There Are No Such Trees in Alpine, California" (Haines) 58:218

"There Are No Thieves in This Town" (Garcia Marquez) 27:148, 154; 47:146, 150-51

"There Are Roughly Zones" (Frost) 10:196; 26:125

"There Are So Many Houses and Dark Streets without Help" (Bukowski) 82:14

"There Are the Steps" (Ekeloef) 27:119

"There Are Things I Tell to No One" (Kinnell) 29:285

"There But for Fortune" (Ochs) 17:329, 331-32

"There But Where, How" (Cortazar) 33:125

There Goes Rhymin' Simon (Simon) 17:464-65

"There Has to Be a Jail for Ladies" (Merton) 83:393

"There Is a Dream Dreaming Us" (Dubie) 36:134, 136

"There Is a Happy Land" (Bowie) 17:65

"There Is a Legend about a Piano That Somehow Got Flushed into the Sewers of Chicago" (Goldbarth) 38:205

"There Is a Lone House" (O'Connor) 23:331

"There Is a Right Way" (Welch) 52:426

There Is a Tide (*Taken at the Flood*) (Christie) 12:124; 48:73

There Is a Tree More Ancient Than Eden

(Forrest) 4:163-64

There is Confusion (Fauset) 54:175-76, 178, 180-81, 185, 187, 189; 19:169-71

"There Is No Conversation" (West) 31:453-54

"There Is No Such Thing as a Happy Love" (Aragon)
  See "Il n'y a pas d'amour heureux"

"There Is Only One of Everything" (Atwood) 13:44; 15:37

There Is the Sun, Philibert (Carrier)
  See *Il est par là, le soleil*

There Must Be More to Love Than Death (Newman) 8:419

There Shall Be No Darkness (Blish) 14:84

"There She Breaches" (Hemingway) 34:478

"There Was a Child Went Forth" (Levine) 14:317

There Was a Father (Ozu) 16:451, 453, 456

There Was a Time (Caldwell) 28:59

"There Was a Woman Bending" (Lane) 25:284, 287

There Was an Ancient House (Kiely) 23:263; 43:245

"There Was an Old Woman" (Queen) 11:462-63

"There Was Earth inside Them" (Celan) 53:75

"There Was Once" (Atwood) 84:105

"There Was When Morning Fell" (Graham) 29:193

"There Will Be Harvest" (Everson) 5:122

"There Will Come Soft Rains" (Bradbury) 42:38

Therefore (Grass)
  See *Davor*

Therefore Be Bold (Gold) 4:190-91; 42:188-89

"The Therefore Hag" (Guthrie) 23:199

There'll Be No Teardrops Tonight (Nelson) 17:305

There's a Bat in Bunk Five (Danziger) 21:85-6

"There's a Better Shine" (Niedecker) 42:298

"There's a Change in the Weather" (Davies) 21:98

"There's a Garden of Eden" (Gilchrist) 48:115, 120

"There's a Grandfather's Clock in the Hall" (Warren) 8:538

"There's a Maniac Loose Out There" (Vonnegut) 12:610

"There's a Place" (Lennon and McCartney) 12:375

There's a Trick with a Knife I'm Learning to Do: Poems, 1963-1978 (Ondaatje) 14:410; 29:341; 51:316-17

"There's a Window" (Sapphire) 99:80-1

"There's a World" (Young) 17:570, 578

"There's No Difference" (Ashbery) 15:36

"There's No Place like London" (Sondheim) 30:398

"There's Not That Much to Say" (Neruda) 28:311

"There's Nothing like a Good Foundation" (Asimov) 26:63

There's Something in the Air (Bates) 46:56-7

"There's the Sound of Rain" (Akhmadulina)
  See "Vot zvuk dozhdia"

There's Wisdom in Women (Kesselring) 45:206-07

Thérèse Desqueyrous (Mauriac) 4:339, 341; 9:368; 56:204, 206

Thérèse et Pierrette à l'école des Saints-Agnes (Tremblay) 29:424, 427; 102:370-74,

376-77, 379

Thérèse's Creed (Cook) **58**:154

"The Thermal Stair" (Graham) **29**:196-97

"Theroux Metaphrastes" (Theroux) **25**:432

"These". (Williams) **42**:452

"These Are My People" (Hayden) **37**:156

"These Beautiful Girls" (Sondheim) **30**:382

"These Days" (Browne) **21**:41

These Golden Days (Braine) **41**:62

These Green-Going-to-Yellow (Bell) **31**:50-1

"These Lacustrine Cities" (Ashbery) **9**:44; 77:56

These Our Mothers, or The Disintegrating Chapter (Brossard)
See *L'Amer*

"These Streets" (Milner) **56**:225

These the Companions (Davie) **31**:121-22, 124

These Thirteen (Faulkner) **3**:156; **8**:213; 28:141

These Thousand Hills (Guthrie) **23**:197-98, 201

These Three (Hellman) **34**:348; **52**:191

"These Trees Stand" (Snodgrass) **18**:491

These Words: Weddings and After (McIlvanney) **42**:285

"These Yet to Be United States" (Angelou) **64**:40

"Theseus and Ariadne" (Graves) **2**:174; **45**:166, 173

"Thesis" (Dorn) **10**:159

"Theta" (Tolson) **105**:234

"Thetis" (Broumas) **73**:13

"They" (Creeley) **78**:140, 154, 157

"They" (Heinlein) **26**:165

"They" (Sassoon) **36**:385

"They" (Thomas) **48**:374, 381

"They Ain't the Men They Used to Be" (Farrell) **66**:131

"They All Go to the Mountains Now" (Brooke-Rose) **40**:106

"They All Made Peace—What Is Peace?" (Hemingway) **19**:218

"They Are All in Love" (Townshend) **17**:535-36

They Are Dying Out (Handke)
See *Die Unvernünftigen Sterben aus*

"They Are Not Ready" (Madhubuti) **73**:207

"They Arrive This Morning" (O Hehir) **41**:324

They Both Were Naked (Wylie) **43**:469

They Brought Their Women (Ferber) **93**:161-62

"They Called for More Structure..." (Barthelme) **46**:38, 42

They Came Here First: The Epic of the American Indian (McNickle) **89**:169, 172, 175, 181

They Came Like Swallows (Maxwell) **19**:305-06

"They Came That Night" (Damas)
See "Ils sont venus ce soir"

They Came to Baghdad (Christie) **12**:115; **39**:438; **48**:71, 74; **110**:113, 129

They Came to Cordura (Swarthout) **35**:399-400, 403

They Caught the Ferry (Dreyer) **16**:268

"They Clapped" (Giovanni) **117**:197

"They Dirty the Suicide" (Cabral de Melo Neto)
See "Sujam o suicído"

They Do It with Mirrors (Christie) **110**:121

"They Dream Only of America" (Ashbery) 77:42, 56

"They Feed They Lion" (Levine) **2**:244; **4**:286,

288; **9**:332; **14**:317-19

They Feed They Lion (Levine) **2**:244; **4**:286-87; **5**:250-52; **9**:332; **14**:317, 320-21; 33:271, 273

"They Flee from Me" (Ewart) **46**:152

They Fought for Their Country (Sholokhov)
See *Oni srazhalis' za rodinu*

They Hanged My Saintly Billy: The Life and Death of Dr. William Palmer (Graves) 39:322-23

"They Have Not Survived" (Mathias) **45**:237

"They Like" (Ashbery) **41**:37

They Never Came Home (Duncan) **26**:101-02

"They Never Were Found" (Jacobsen) **102**:237

"They Only Move" (Amis) **40**:44

"They Reach the Gulf of Mexico, 1493" (Neruda) **5**:302

"They Say Etna" (Bunting) **47**:45

They Shall Have Stars (Blish) **14**:85

They Shall Inherit the Earth (Callaghan) **14**:101-03; **41**:95; **65**:246, 248-50

"They Shall Not Grow Old" (Dahl) **79**:183

"They Shall Not Pass" (Ai) **69**:10

"They Sleep without Dreaming" (Gilliatt) **53**:145-46

They Sleep without Dreaming (Gilliatt) **53**:145-46

They That Reap (Lopez y Fuentes)
See *El indio*

They Went Thataway (Brown) **47**:36

They Were Expendable (Ford) **16**:306-07, 313, 315

"They Were Showing a Film of Bermuda in Hammond II" (Jacobsen) **48**:190

They Winter Abroad (White) **30**:449

They Won't Demolish Me! (Carrier)
See *Le deux-millième étage*

They Won't Take Me Alive (Alegria)
See *No me agarran viva: La mujer salvadoreña en lucha*

"They're Not Your Husband" (Carver) **36**:101

They're Playing Our Song (Simon) **31**:398, 400

They're Singing Again Now ("The Auld Farmer's New Year Morning Salutation"; "The Auld Farmer's New Year Morning Salutation") (Frisch)
See *Nun singen sie wieder*

"They've Given Us the Land" (Rulfo)
See "Nos han dado la tierra"

"Thick As Thieves" (Weller) **26**:446

"Thickening the Plot" (Delany) **38**:153

"Thicker than Liquor" (Berry) **46**:74

Thicker Than Water (Harrison) **70**:55-8

The Thicket of Spring (Bowles) **19**:60

"Thick-Lipped Nigger" (Guillen)
See "Negro bembón"

"The Thief" (Anand) **23**:21

"The Thief" (Govier) **51**:166

"The Thief" (Tanizaki) **28**:414

"The Thief" (Tillinghast) **29**:416

The Thief (Leonov)
See *Vor*

The Thief and the Dogs (Mahfuz)
See *al-Liss wa'l-kilab*

"The Thief Coyote" (Goyen) **14**:211

"The Thief of Poetry" (Ashbery) 77:47

A Thief of Time (Hillerman) **62**:260-63

The Thief's Journal (Genet)
See *Journal du voleur*

"A Thief's Tale" (Klima) **56**:171

Thieves (Gardner) **44**:210

Thieves' Carnival (Anouilh)

See *Le bal des voleurs*

Thieves in the Night: Chronicle of an Experiment (Koestler) **1**:170; **3**:270; **15**:310-11; **33**:231-33, 242

"Thieves' Kitchen" (Slessor) **14**:497

Thieves Like Us (Altman) **16**:28-31, 39; **116**:3-4, 7, 11-12, 14, 16, 21, 23, 31, 36-7

Thieves of the Kings and Queens of England (Fraser) **107**:33-34

"Thieving" (Rush) **44**:92-3, 95-6

"Thin Air" (Hass) **99**:139, 142

"The Thin Edge of Your Pride" (Rexroth) **49**:280; **112**:376

"Thin Ice" (Levine) **54**:298, 301

The Thin Man (Hammett) **3**:218-20; **5**:162; **19**:193-96; **47**:157, 163

The Thin Mountain Air (Horgan) **9**:279; 53:185-86

"The Thin People" (Plath) **51**:340, 344; 111:218

The Thin Red Line (Jones) **1**:162; **3**:261; **10**:290-94; **39**:406-08, 414

The Thin Snow (Tanizaki) **8**:509

"The Thing" (Moravia) **46**:286-87

The Thing about Joe Sullivan (Fisher) **25**:159

"Thing from Inner Space" (Fuller) **62**:197

The Thing He Loves (Glanville) **6**:202

"The Thing Made Real" (Loewinsohn) **52**:283

A Thing of Beauty (Cronin) **32**:138

The Thing of It Is... (Goldman) **1**:123; **48**:125, 128

"A Thing of the Past" (Gordimer) **33**:180

"The Thing That Happened to Uncle Adolphe" (Callaghan) **41**:98

"A Thing They Wear" (Metcalf) **37**:299

"The Things" (Jacobsen) **48**:194

Things (Ponge) **18**:415

"Things as They Are" (Pritchett) **41**:332

Things as They Are (Horgan) **9**:278; **53**:180-82, 185

Things Fall Apart (Achebe) **1**:1-2; **3**:1-2; **5**:1-3; **7**:3-7; **11**:1-4; **26**:11-16, 18-19, 21-2, 25-7; **51**:2-9; **75**:2-6, 8-13, 20, 23

Things Gone and Things Still Here (Bowles) 19:59

"Things I Can Do in My Situation" (Swenson) 61:394

"Things I Didn't Know I Loved" (Hikmet) 40:251

Things I Didn't Know I Loved (Hikmet) **40**:246, 248

Things Invisible to See (Willard) **37**:464-66

"Things Not Solved Though Tomorrow Came" (Taylor) **44**:301

"Things of the World" (Waddington) **28**:440

"Things of This World" (Parini) **54**:363

Things of This World (Wilbur) **3**:530; **6**:568; **9**:569; **14**:576-77; **53**:396, 398-99, 404, 407-08, 410; **110**:348-49, 353

"Things Past" (Baker) **31**:31

"Things Past" (Skelton) **13**:508

Things Taking Place (Swenson)
See *New and Selected Things Taking Place*

Things That Are Caesar's (Carroll) **10**:95-9

"Things That Are Worse Than Death" (Olds) **39**:189; **85**:290

"Things That Fly" (Coupland) **85**:36, 39

Things that Happen Where There Aren't Any People (Stafford) **29**:386-87

"Things that have been lost" (Amichai) **116**:98

Things That I Do in the Dark: Selected Poetry (Jordan) **11**:312-13; **114**:146

The Things That I Know (Hemingway)

See *Across the River and into the Trees*
Things Themselves: Essays and Scenes (Price)
　43:346-47
"The Things They Carried" (O'Brien)　103:143
The Things They Carried (O'Brien)　103:133-
　34, 136-38, 140-43, 159-66, 168-69,
　174-75
Things to Come (Norton)　12:458
"Things to Do in Providence" (Berrigan)　37:46
Things We Dreamt We Died For (Bell)　31:46-7
The Things Which Are (Nowlan)　15:398-99
Think Back on Us .?.?. (Cowley)　39:461
"Think before You Shoot" (Adcock)　41:13
Think Black! (Madhubuti)　2:238; 6:313;
　73:199-200, 202, 204-11, 214-15
"Think It Over" (Reed)　21:320
"Think It Over America" (Beecher)　6:49
"Think of It" (Celan)　53:75
"Thinkability" (Amis)　62:6-7, 9-10
"Thinking about El Salvador" (Levertov)
　66:239, 250
"Thinking about Shelley" (Stern)　40:410;
　100:333
"Thinking about the Past" (Justice)　102:257,
　285
"Thinking against Oneself" (Cioran)　64:96-7,
　99
"The Thinking Man's Wasteland" (Bellow)
　8:74
"Thinking of Death and Dogfood" (Kumin)
　28:228
"Thinking of That Contest" (Lane)　25:287
"Thinking of the Goldfish" (Muldoon)　32:315
"Thinking of the Lost World" (Jarrell)　2:210;
　9:298
"Thinking of the World as Idea" (Pollitt)
　28:367
The Thinking Reed (West)　31:454, 457, 459;
　50:405-07
Thinks (Waterhouse)　47:423
Thinner (King)　37:206-08; 113:369
The Third (Ezekiel)　61:97
"The Third Autumn" (Dabrowska)
　See "Trzecia jesién"
The Third Bank of the River, and Other Stories
　(Rosa)
　See *Primeiras estorias*
The Third Book about Achim (Johnson)
　See *Das Dritte Buch über Achim*
The Third Book of Criticism (Jarrell)　9:296
The Third Deadly Sin (Sanders)　41:381-82
"Third Degree" (Hughes)　35:216
"The Third Dimension" (Levertov)　28:242
"The Third Expedition" (Bradbury)　42:37-8
The Third Eye (Hunter)　21:169-70
The Third Face (Rozewicz)
　See *Twarz trzecia*
"The Third Floor" (Rooke)　25:391
The Third Generation (Fassbinder)　20:118,
　120
The Third Generation (Himes)　2:195; 4:229;
　7:159; 18:247; 58:250, 256, 263-65;
　108:224, 228-31, 259
Third Girl (Christie)　12:117; 110:121, 138
"Third Hymn to Lenin" (MacDiarmid)　63:254-
　56
The Third Life of Grange Copeland (Walker)
　5:476-77; 6:553; 9:558; 19:451-52;
　27:451, 453-54; 46:423, 428, 431;
　58:404, 406, 408; 103:356-57, 364-65,
　368, 383, 385-89, 392, 395-96, 398, 405,
　414, 418
"The Third Light" (Longley)　29:296

The Third Lover (Chabrol)
　See *L'oeil du malin*
The Third Man (Greene)　1:134; 3:207-210;
　37:139-40; 70:288-89, 294; 72:165-66,
　168, 173-76
The Third Mind (Burroughs)　15:112; 42:71-2;
　109:182
"Third Monday" (Mason)　28:271; 82:245-
　46, 249-50
"Third or Fourth Day of Spring" (Miller)
　14:375
"The Third Party" (Trevor)　71:343, 348,
　349; 116:347, 375
The Third Policeman (O'Brien)　1:252; 4:383,
　385; 5:314, 317; 7:270; 10:362, 364;
　47:312-22
"A Third Presence" (Gordimer)　18:185
Third Residence (Neruda)
　See *Tercera residencia, 1935-1945*
The Third Residence (Neruda)
　See *Tercera residencia, 1935-1945*
"The Third Resignation" (Garcia Marquez)
　See "La tercera resignación"
"The Third Story" (Bitov)　57:114-15
"Third Time Lucky" (Ingalls)　42:234
"Third Voice: The Widower" (Davison)　28:101
"Third Ypres" (Blunden)　56:29-30, 38, 42-3,
　51
"Thirst" (Avison)　97:117
"Thirst" (O'Brien)　7:270; 10:362
Thirst (Bergman)
　See *Törst*
Thirst (Trifonov)　45:420
Thirst for Love (Mishima)　9:382
*Thirsting for Peace in a Raging Century: Se-
　lected Poems, 1961-1985* (Sanders)
　53:310
A Thirsty Evil (Vidal)　33:406-07
"13" (Jones)　10:287
"Thirteen" (Townshend)　42:380-81
Thirteen (Morrison)　17:290
Thirteen at Dinner (*Lord Edgware Dies*)
　(Christie)　6:108; 12:113-14
The Thirteen Clocks (Thurber)　5:430, 432,
　438, 440, 442; 25:437-38
Thirteen Hands (Shields)　91:178; 113:440
"Thirteen O'Clock" (Fearing)　51:116
"Thirteen Phantasms" (Smith)　43:422
Thirteen Pipes (Ehrenburg)　62:176, 179
The Thirteen Problems (Christie)　110:139-46
Thirteen Stories and Thirteen Epitaphas
　(Vollmann)　89:286, 291, 296-97, 302,
　313
"Thirteen to Centaurus" (Ballard)　36:37
The Thirteenth Labor of Herucles (Iskander)
　See *Trinadtsaty podvig Gerakla*
The Thirteenth Member (Hunter)　21:158, 165
Thirteenth Night (Brenton)　31:69
*The Thirteenth Tribe: The Khazar Empire and
　Its Heritage* (Koestler)　8:324-25
The Thirteenth Valley (Del Vecchio)　29:149-
　51
"The Thirties" (Sadoff)　9:467
*The Thirties and After: Poetry, Politics, People,
　1933-1970* (Spender)　41:420-23, 427;
　91:242
Thirtieth Anniversary Report to the Class of '41
　(Nemerov)　36:302
"The Thirtieth Year" (Bachmann)
　See "Das dreissigste Jahr"
The Thirtieth Year (Bachmann)
　See *Das dreissigste Jahr*
"Thirty Days" (Berry)　17:53

"XXXI" (Auden)　14:26
Thirty Poems (Merton)　83:389-91
Thirty Preliminary Poems (Barker)　48:9, 11,
　21
Thirty Seconds over Tokyo (Trumbo)　19:445
Thirty Stories (Boyle)　5:65; 19:62; 58:64, 70,
　76
Thirty Things (Creeley)　11:139
"Thirty Ways of Drowning in the Sea" (Levi)
　41:244
The Thirty-First of February (Symons)　14:523
Thirty-Nine Poems (Ciardi)　40:155, 158
The Thirty-Nine Steps (Hitchcock)　16:337-
　38, 340, 345, 354, 357
Thirty-One Letters and Thirteen Dreams (Hugo)
　18:260, 262-63; 32:241, 244, 250-51
Thirty-One Sonnets (Eberhart)　3:134
Thirty-One Sonnets (Guillevic)
　See *Trente et un sonnets*
"Thirty-Seven Haiku" (Ashbery)　41:37
"XXXVI" (Walcott)　67:358
Thirty-Six Poems (Warren)　1:353; 13:573,
　575
Thirty-Two Votes before Breakfast (Stuart)
　34:376
"This" (Olds)　85:295, 297
"This" (Rich)　73:332
"This Age of Conformity" (Howe)　85:134
"This Be the Verse" (Larkin)　9:323; 33:261,
　268; 39:336, 343; 64:282
This Bed Thy Centre (Johnson)　1:160; 27:213
"This Black Rich Country" (Ammons)　57:59
*This Blessed Earth: New and Selected Poems,
　1927-1977* (Wheelock)　14:571
*This Body Is Made of Camphor and
　Gopherwood* (Bly)　10:62; 15:66-7; 38:50
This Body the Earth (Green)　25:195, 197
This Boy's Life (Wolff)　64:456-61
"This Bright Day" (Ammons)　2:14; 57:59
"This City!" (Stevenson)　33:380
"This Cold Man" (Page)
　See "Now This Cold Man"
This Crooked Way (Spencer)　22:398-99, 403
This Crowded Planet (Hyde)　21:173
"This Day" (Creeley)　15:153
"This Day" (Fearing)　51:114
"This Day" (Hoffman)　23:238
"This Day" (Levertov)　66:241
This Day's Death (Rechy)　1:283; 107:222-23,
　225-26, 228, 230, 238, 254, 258
This Dear-Bought Land (Latham)　12:323
"This Destination Not to Be Found in a Star"
　(Barker)　48:9
"This Farm for Sale" (Stuart)　11:513
"This Fevers Me, This Sun on Green" (Eberhart)
　19:143; 56:80
"This Form of Life Needs Sex" (Ginsberg)
　36:183; 109:358
"This Golden Summer" (Lowell)　11:331
"This Ground So Bare" (Van Doren)　10:496
This Gun for Hire (Greene)
　See *A Gun for Sale*
*This Hallowed Ground: The Story of the Union
　Side in the Civil War* (Catton)　35:87-90
"This Hand, These Talons" (Cassill)　4:94
This Happy Breed (Coward)　29:135-36, 138;
　51:69
"This Heat" (Durban)　39:44-6
This Hidden God (Goldmann)
　See *Le Dieu caché*
"this house" (Young Bear)　94:363
This Hunger... (Nin)　60:267-68
"This I Believe" (Stegner)　49:359

This Immortal (Zelazny) **21**:469
This in Which (Oppen) **7**:281; **34**:359
"This Is" (Ammons) **25**:42; **108**:28
"This Is" (Steele) **45**:362-64
This Is (An Entertainment) (Williams) **11**:575
"This Is a Photograph of Me" (Atwood) **4**:27; **25**:66
"This Is a Poem I Wrote at Night, before the Dawn" (Schwartz) **45**:355
This Is a Recording (Corcoran) **17**:71
"This Is a Story about My Friend George, the Toy Inventor" (Paley) **37**:333
This is a Test (Waters) **81**:
"This Is It" (Stern) **40**:406, 408
This Is My Country Too (Williams) **5**:498
This Is My God (Wouk) **9**:580; **38**:444, 448, 452-53
"This Is Not a Film, This Is a Precise Act of Disbelief" (Abish) **22**:17
This Is Not a Letter and Other Poems (Boyle) **58**:75-6
This is Not a Pipe (Foucault) **31**:186-87
"This Is Not For John Lennon (And This Is Not a Poem)" (Giovanni) **117**:198
This Is Not for You (Rule) **27**:417
"This Is the Beat Generation" (Holmes) **56**:139-40
This Is the Castle (Freeling) **38**:184
"This Is the Garden: Colors Come and Go" (Cummings) **68**:44
This Is the Modern World (Weller) **26**:443, 445
This Is the Rill Speaking (Wilson) **7**:547
"this is the tale" (Clifton) **66**:82
"This Is Their Fault" (Forche) **83**:209
"This Is Tibet!" (Boell)
  See "Hier ist Tibten"
"This Is What It Means to Say Phoenix, Arizona" (Alexie) **96**:5
"This Is What Killed Dylan Thomas" (Bukowski) **108**:86
"This Island Formed You" (Smith) **64**:393
This Island Now (Abrahams) **4**:1-2
This Journey (Wright) **28**:467-69, 473
"This Land Is Your Land" (Guthrie) **35**:185, 188-91, 194
"This Last Pain" (Empson) **19**:155, 158; **33**:142; **34**:336
"This Life" (Dove) **81**:137
"This Life of Mine" (Van Doren) **6**:542
"This Loved One" (Fuller) **62**:193
This Man and Music (Burgess) **40**:119
This Man and This Woman (Farrell) **66**:128
"This Man for Fuck Sake" (Kelman) **58**:297
This Man Must Die (Chabrol) **16**:175-76
"This Man, My Father" (Callaghan) **41**:98
"This Morning Again It Was in the Dusty Pines" (Oliver) **98**:285
This Music Crept by Me on the Water (Eberhart) **11**:176
"This Must Be Wrong" (Ian) **21**:186
"This My Modest Art" (Nemerov) **36**:309
"This Neutral Realm" (Montague) **46**:277
"This Night Only" (Rexroth) **22**:346
This Noble Land (Michener) **109**:383
"This One's on Me" (Gotlieb) **18**:191
"This Page My Book" (Livesay) **79**:348
This Perfect Day (Levin) **6**:305-07
"This Poem May Not Be Just What You Wrote to Santa for, But" (Sherwin) **7**:415
"This Praying Fool" (Kumin) **28**:220
This Proud Heart (Buck) **11**:74-5
This Quiet Dust and Other Writings (Styron)

60:392-94, 396
This Real Night (West) **9**:562
This Rock within the Sea (Mowat) **26**:338, 346-47
This Rough Magic (Stewart) **35**:390, 392; **117**:367
"This Sandwich Has No Mayonnaise" (Salinger) **12**:498
This School Is Driving Me Crazy (Hentoff) **26**:184-85, 187
"This Seems True" (Simmons) **43**:407
This Side Jordan (Laurence) **13**:342; **50**:314, 319, 322; **60**:278-79, 290, 306; **62**:278-79, 290, 306
This Side of Innocence (Caldwell) **28**:59; **39**:302-03
This Sporting Life (Anderson) **20**:12-13, 16-18
This Sporting Life (Storey) **2**:423-25; **4**:528; **5**:417; **8**:505
This Strange Passion (Bunuel)
  See *El*
This Strangest Everything (Ciardi) **40**:160
"This Stupid Bitch" (p'Bitek) **96**:271-72
"This Summer" (Scannell) **49**:327
This Sunday (Donoso)
  See *Este Domingo*
This Sweet Sickness (Highsmith) **2**:193; **42**:211; **102**:170, 173, 193
"This, That, and the Other" (Nemerov) **2**:307
This Thing Don't Lead to Heaven (Crews) **6**:117; **23**:132, 138; **49**:68
This Time (Jennings) **21**:202
"This Time Alone" (Wright) **53**:432
This Time of Morning (Sahgal) **41**:370
"This Time Tomorrow" (Davies) **21**:92
This Time Tomorrow (Ngugi wa Thiong'o) **7**:266; **36**:320-21
"This Tokyo" (Snyder) **32**:399
"This Tournament" (MacNeice) **53**:233
This Tree Will Be Here for a Thousand Years (Bly) **15**:64, 68; **38**:50, 53, 56-7, 59
"This Urn Contains Earth from German Concentration Camps" (Lorde) **71**:256
"This Was a Man" (Coward) **29**:131
This Was the Old Chief's Country (Lessing) **22**:279; **94**:261, 266
"This Way Down" (Johnston) **51**:244
"This Wilderness in My Blood: The Spiritual Foundations of the Poetry of Five American Indian Women" (Allen) **84**:11, 15, 36
"This World" (Creeley) **78**:148-49
This World and Nearer Ones: Essays Exploring the Familiar (Aldiss) **14**:15
This World, Then the Fireworks (Thompson) **69**:385, 387-88
"This Year's Girl" (Costello) **21**:68
This Year's Model (Costello) **21**:68, 70
"This You May Keep" (Zweig) **34**:379
The Thistle and the Grail (Jenkins) **52**:220, 225, 227-28
"The Thistle, The Nettle" (Milosz) **82**:311
"Thistles" (Hughes) **9**:284; **14**:271; **37**:179
"Thistles" (Levine) **4**:286
Thistles and Roses (Smith) **64**:393-94, 397-98
Thomas and Beulah (Dove) **50**:152-58; **81**:132, 136, 138, 140-47, 151-52, 154
Thomas and the Warlock (Hunter) **21**:157
"Thomas at the Wheel" (Dove) **50**:153; **81**:139
"Thomas Bewick" (Gunn) **18**:199, 202
Thomas Hardy and British Poetry (Davie)

5:114; **8**:162
"Thomas Jefferson" (Niedecker) **42**:296, 300
Thomas l'imposteur (Thomas the Imposter) (Cocteau) **8**:146; **15**:132; **16**:220; **43**:103
"Thomas Mann" (Szymborska) **99**:202
The Thomas Merton Reader (Merton) **83**:404
Thomas Muskerry (Colum) **28**:86-7, 90
"Thomas Nashe and 'The Unfortunate Traveler'" (Berryman) **10**:45
Thomas the Imposter (Cocteau)
  See *Thomas l'imposteur*
"Thomas Traherne's Meditation for Love, 1672" (Dubie) **36**:130
"Thomasine" (Blunden) **56**:34, 38
Thor, with Angels (Fry) **10**:200
"Thoreau Z" (Lowell) **37**:237
The Thorn Birds (McCullough) **27**:318-22; **107**:127-45, 147-63, 166-68, 170-71
Thorn in Our Flesh: Castro's Cuba (Archer) **12**:17-18
"Thornapple" (Rendell) **48**:320
"Thornbills" (Wright) **53**:423
Thornyhold (Stewart) **117**:384
The Thoroughbreds (Cesaire) **112**:12
"Thoroughgo" (Char)
  See "La minutieuse"
Thoroughly Modern Millie (Hill) **26**:196, 200-01, 204
"Thorow" (Howe) **72**:205, 209
"Those Awful Dawns" (Highsmith) **14**:261
Those Barren Leaves (Huxley) **1**:151; **4**:238-40, 244; **11**:281-82, 284-85; **18**:265, 267-69; **79**:304, 326
"Those before Us" (Lowell) **8**:351
"Those Being Eaten by America" (Bly) **15**:62
"Those Gods Are Children" (Achebe) **26**:24
Those Other People (Childress) **86**:309
"Those Paperweights with Snow Inside" (Peacock) **60**:295
"Those Times" (Sexton) **53**:322
"Those Various Scalpels" (Moore) **13**:392; **19**:335
"Those Who Have Burned" (Dickey) **28**:118
"Those Who Have No Turkey" (Hughes) **108**:292
Those Who Love (Stone) **7**:469-70
Those Who Perish (Dahlberg) **7**:66
Those Who Ride the Night Winds (Giovanni) **64**:192; **117**:170, 177, 187-88, 193, 198-99, 205
Those Who Walk Away (Highsmith) **2**:193; **4**:225; **102**:173, 185, 205-06
"Those Winter Sundays" (Hayden) **37**:153, 160
Those without Shadows (Sagan) **17**:419-20
"The Thou" (Montale)
  See "Il tu"
"Thou Art Lovelier Than the Sky and Sea" (Cendrars) **106**:159
"Thou Didst Say Me" (Waddington) **28**:438
"Thou Good and Faithful" (Brunner) **8**:111
"Thou Shalt Not Kill" (Rexroth) **22**:346, 348; **49**:276-77, 280, 284; **112**:376, 400, 403
"Thought" (Dumas) **62**:151-52
"Thought by Rembrandt's Wife and Model during the Painting of 'Flora'" (Rudnik) **7**:384
"The Thought Machine" (Stafford) **7**:460
"The Thought of Something Else" (Berry) **46**:70
"Thought of the Future" (Mahapatra) **33**:284
"Thought on June 26" (Kunene) **85**:166
Thought Reform and the Psychology of

Totalism: A Study of 'Brainwashing' in China (Lifton) 67:135-36, 140, 145, 154

"The Thought-Fox" (Hughes) 9:281; 37:172, 178-79

"Thoughts about Lessing" (Arendt) 98:50

"Thoughts about the Christian Doctrine of Eternal Hell" (Smith) 25:417

"Thoughts about the Person from Porlock" (Smith) 25:423

Thoughts after Lambeth (Eliot) 2:126; 24:177, 182-83

"Thoughts/Images" (Dumas) 62:155

Thoughts in Solitude (Merton) 83:389

"Thoughts on a Narrow Night" (Gustafson) 36:222

"Thoughts on Being Bibliographed" (Wilson) 24:474, 476

"Thoughts on Looking into a Thicket" (Ciardi) 44:375, 382

"Thoughts on March 8" (Ding Ling) 68:62, 68-9

"Thoughts on One's Head" ("In Plaster, with a Bronze Wash") (Meredith) 13:375

"Thoughts on Politics and Revolution" (Arendt) 98:11

"Thoughts on the *Diary of a Nobody*" (Betjeman) 43:36

"Thoughts on the Poetic Discontent" (Ransom) 4:436

"Thoughts on Women's Day" (Ding Ling) 68:65

Thoughts, Words, and Creativity (Leavis) 24:308-09, 314

A Thousand Acres (Smiley) 76:229-38

"The Thousand and One Nights" (Borges) 48:47

"The Thousand and One Nights" (Fuller) 62:185

"The Thousand and Second Night" (Merrill) 2:273-74; 13:380-81

A Thousand Clowns (Gardner) 44:209-10

Thousand Cranes (Kawabata) 2:223; 5:206-08; 9:309, 316; 18:285; 107:73-4, 76, 98-101, 103-04, 106, 108-12, 114, 121

A Thousand Days: John F. Kennedy in the White House (Schlesinger) 84:357, 359-60, 368, 375-76, 379-80, 384-85

The Thousand Eyes of Dr. Mabuse (*Die tausend Augen des Dr. Mabuse*) (Lang) 20:208, 211; 103:86

"The Thousand Islands" (Cendrars) 106:190

A Thousand Summers (Kanin) 22:231

"The Thousand Things" (Middleton) 13:387

"The Thousand Ways" (Chappell) 40:142; 78:95

Thousandstar (Anthony) 35:36-7

"The Thrall" (Arghezi) See "Robul''a

"Thrall" (Kizer) 80:181-83, 185

"Thrasher" (Young) 17:581

The Thread That Runs So True (Stuart) 14:516; 34:373, 375

Thread-Suns (Celan) See *Fadensonnen*

"Threatened" (O Hehir) 41:323-24

"The Threatened One" (Borges) 83:190

Threats Instead of Trees (Ryan) 65:209, 211, 213

"Three" (Cummings) 15:161

"Three" (Grau) 9:240

"Three" (Gunn) 18:199; 32:208

"III" (Kinnell) 13:322

"Three" (Lish) 45:230

Three (Ashton-Warner) 19:23

Three (Hellman) See *Pentimento: A Book of Portraits*

Three (Quin) 6:441-42

Three Act Tragedy (Christie) 48:71-2

Three Acts of Recognition (Strauss) See *Trilogie des Wiedersehens*

Three Adventures: Galápagos, Titicaca, The Blue Holes (Cousteau) 30:106

The Three Ages (Keaton) 20:191

"3 AM" (Harjo) 83:278-79

"3 A.M. Kitchen: My Father Talking" (Gallagher) 63:126

The Three Arrows (Murdoch) 4:367-68

"The Three Avilas" (Jeffers) 11:306

"Three Awful Picnics" (L'Heureux) 52:274

Three Bad Men (Ford) 16:317

"Three Beyond" (Davie) 31:124

"Three Blind Mice" (Christie) 48:71

Three Blind Mice, and Other Stories (Christie) 12:119

"The Three Boxes" (Chappell) 40:141

Three by Ferlinghetti (Ferlinghetti) 2:134

Three by Peter Handke (Handke) 38:218

Three Cheers for the Paraclete (Keneally) 5:210-11; 19:245; 43:236; 117:215-17, 221, 224, 227

The Three Coffins (Carr) 3:101

Three Comrades (Remarque) 21:327-28, 330-31

"Three Conservations" (Rosenthal) 28:394

Three Continents (Jhabvala) 94:186-87, 194-96, 204, 207-10, 213

"Three Critics" (Silkin) 43:400

"Three Darknesses" (Warren) 39:265, 270

"Three Days" (Simon) 26:407

"Three Days and a Child" (Yehoshua) 31:472

Three Days and a Child (Yehoshua) 13:618; 31:468-71

"Three Derivative Poems" (Sissman) 9:490

Three Desks (Reaney) 13:474

Three Dialogues (Beckett) 6:36

Three Dozen Poems (Everson) 27:133

"Three Drawings" (Heaney) 74:188

The Three Edwards (Costain) 30:98-100

Three Essays on America (Brooks) 29:83-4

Three Fantasies (Powys) 46:324

"Three Fantasies in Minor Key" (Bioy Casares) 88:92-3

Three Farmers on Their Way to a Dance (Powers) 93:275-79, 281, 283-86, 289, 293, 296, 299, 301

The Three Fat Men (Olesha) See *Tri tolstiaku*

"Three Fat Women of Antibes" (Maugham) 67:211

"Three Fate Tales" (Creeley) 11:135

"Three for Water-Music" (Davie) 31:119

Three for Water-Music (Davie) 31:119, 123

"Three Freuds" (Lowell) 37:238

"Three from Tu Fu" (Kizer) 39:171

The Three Generations of Superman (Siegel and Shuster) 21:358

"3 Geniuses" (Wiggins) 57:433, 435, 439

Three Godfathers (Ford) 16:317

The Three Graces (Eliade) See *Die drei Grazien*

"Three Halves of a House" (Hood) 28:187, 193

Three Hundred and Sixty Degrees of Blackness Comin at You (Sanchez) 116:293

"Three Hundred Men Made Redundant"

(Durcan) 43:116

365 Days (Glasser) 37:131-34

334 (Disch) 36:124

Three Hundred Years of Gravitation (Hawking) 105:55

The Three Ill-Loved Ones (Cabral de Melo Neto) See *Os três mal-amados*

"Three Illuminations in the Life of an American Author" (Updike) 43:430

"Three Journeys" (Hirsch) 50:196, 198

Three Journeys: An Automythology (Zweig) 34:378-79; 42:467

"Three Kills for One" (Woolrich) 77:403

"Three Kinds of Pleasures" (Bly) 10:56

"Three Knots in the Net" (Castellanos) 66:60-1

"Three Laws of Robotics" (Asimov) 3:17

Three Legions (Sutcliff) 26:441

"Three Legs" (McCartney) 35:279

"Three Lindens" (Hesse) 25:259-60

"Three Little Birds" (Marley) 17:269

"Three Long Songs" (Coles) 67:171-72, 174

Three Lovers (O'Faolain) 19:359; 108:399, 424-25, 428

The Three Lovers (Swinnerton) 31:423

Three Loves (Cronin) 32:130-31

"Three Meditations" (Levertov) 15:337

"Three Men" (Sargeson) 31:365

Three Men Die (Millin) 49:248

"Three Miles Up" (Howard) 7:164

"Three Modes of History and Culture" (Baraka) 115:38

"Three Moods of Princeton" (Clark) 38:118, 128

"The Three Musicians" (Walcott) 67:360

The Three Musketeers (Lester) 20:227-28

"Three Notes toward Definitions" (Steele) 45:363

Three Novels (Naipaul) 37:324

Three Novels: The Blackmailer, A Man of Power, and The Geat Occasion (Colegate) 36:113

"Three O'Clock" (Woolrich) 77:403

Three of a Kind (Cain) 11:85; 28:45-7, 50

Three of a Kind (Ingalls) See *I See a Long Journey*

"The Three of Us in the Dark" (Simon) 26:413

"The Three of Us, the Four of Us" (Celan) See "Selbdritt, Selbviert"

Three Old Brothers (O'Connor) 14:401

Three on the Tower: The Lives and Works of Ezra Pound (Simpson) 9:486

"Three Parabolic Tales" (Baxter) 78:28

"Three Paths to the Lake" (Bachmann) See "Simultan"

Three Paths to the Lake (Bachmann) See *Simultan*

Three Pick-Up Men for Herrick (Van Peebles) 20:410

"Three Pieces for Voices" (Redgrove) 41:352

Three Places in Rhode Island (Gray) 49:146; 112:105, 118

Three Players of a Summer Game, and Other Stories (Williams) 5:502; 45:446-47, 452-53, 455

Three Plays (Brown) 48:61

Three Plays (Buzo) 61:67

Three Plays (Clark) 38:113-15

Three Plays (Mrozek) 3:345

Three Plays (Walker) 61:424, 432

Three Plays (Wilder) 15:572; 35:442; 82:361, 383, 385

Three Plus Three (Felsen) 17:124

"Three Poems" (Elytis)   100:175

"Three Poems" (Parra)
   See "Tres Poesías"

Three Poems (Ashbery)   2:18-19; 3:15-16; 4:22-4; 9:43; 13:33; 15:26-8, 32, 35; 25:58; 41:35, 40-1; 77:41-2, 52, 54, 60-1

Three Poems (Wild)   14:580

"Three Poems for James Wright" (Oliver)   98:294

"Three Poems for Music" (Porter)   33:318

"Three Poems in Memory of My Mother, Miriam Murray nee Arnall" (Murray)   40:344

"Three Poems of Drowning" (Graham)   29:194

"Three Poems of Sicily" (Davie)   31:119

"Three Poems on Aaron Siskind's Photographs" (Logan)   5:255

"Three Poems under a Flag of Convenience" (Elytis)   100:179

"Three Poems with Yevtushenko" (Dickey)   47:93

"III Poems Written in Surrey" (Barker)   48:24

"Three Poets" (Rosenthal)   28:394

Three Port Elizabeth Plays (Fugard)   9:233

"Three Poses" (Sherwin)   15:480

Three Postcards (Lucas)   64:289-90, 292

"Three Princes Carouse" (Iskander)   47:200

"Three Prompters from the Wings" (Hecht)   8:269

"Three Quatrains" (Sorrentino)   7:449

"The Three Readings of the Law" (Handke)   5:165

"three reasons for transgression" (Young Bear)   94:363

"Three Rings" (Monette)   82:323, 331-33

The Three Roads (Macdonald)   14:332-33; 41:268

Three Rooms in Manhattan (Simenon)   2:399

Three Secret Poems (Seferis)   11:493

"Three Sentences for a Dead Swan" (Wright)   3:541

"Three Sermons to the Dead" (Riding)   7:374

"Three Sheets in the Wind" (Chappell)   40:145

Three Short Novels (Boyle)   5:65; 58:73

"Three Shots" (Hemingway)   10:269; 30:194

"Three Shrines" (Sandburg)   35:356

The Three Sirens (Wallace)   7:509; 13:567-68

"Three Sisters" (Carroll)   35:80

"The Three Sisters" (Cisneros)   69:147

Three Sisters (Olivier)   20:241, 244

Three Six Seven: Memoirs of a Very Important Man (Vansittart)   42:397-98

"Three Skethces from *House Made of Dawn*" (Momaday)   85:228

"Three Skies" (Stern)   100:342

Three Soldiers (Dos Passos)   4:137-38; 11:154; 15:184; 25:140, 143, 147; 34:419-20, 422-23; 82:62-3, 78, 86

"Three Songs for a Cadaver" (Ciardi)   40:154

"Three Sonnets" (Smith)   64:398

The Three Stigmata of Palmer Eldritch (Dick)   30:115-17, 121-22, 127; 72:113, 117-19, 121-22

"Three Stories" (Sexton)   4:482

Three Stories and Ten Poems (Hemingway)   6:225

Three Stories and Ten Poems (McFadden)   48:257

"Three Stratagems" (Vidal)   33:406

"Three Subjects on the Study of Realism" (Herbert)   43:188

"Three Swiss Inns" (Fisher)   87:122

Three Tall Women (Albee)   86:117-27; 113:48-

51, 53-4

"Three Tears" (Stern)   40:408

Three Thousand Red Ants (Ferlinghetti)   2:134; 111:63

"Three Translations of Villon" (Gotlieb)   18:193

"Three Transportations" (Porter)   33:323

Three Trapped Tigers (Cabrera Infante)
   See *Tres tristes tigres*

Three Travellers (Blais)
   See *Les voyageurs sacrés*

"Three Travelogues" (Ammons)   8:17; 9:30

"Three Types of Poetry" (Tate)   11:522; 24:439

Three Uneasy Pieces (White)   69:413-14

"Three Valentines to the Wide World" (Van Duyn)   63:444; 116:406, 421, 424

"Three Versions of Judas" (Borges)
   See "Tres versiones de Judas"

"Three Views of Mount Rainier" (Deutsch)   18:119

"Three Voices" (Abse)   29:15

The Three Voices of Poetry (Eliot)   6:167; 24:184

"Three White Vases" (Swenson)   106:333

Three Who Died (Derleth)   31:128

Three Winters (Milosz)   11:377; 22:312

"Three Witches Go for Lunch in Elora" (Musgrave)   54:341

Three Wogs (Theroux)   2:433; 25:431-34

"Three Women" (Ortiz)   45:310

"Three Women" (Sargeson)   31:364

Three Women (Altman)   16:38-9, 41, 43; 116:20-2, 28-30, 37-8, 59, 66-7, 69, 73-4

Three Women (Plath)   2:338; 3:391; 5:342; 9:428; 17:361; 51:342, 345, 349

"Three Women: A Poem for Three Voices" (Plath)   111:159-60, 168, 177, 185, 203

"Three Women of the Country" (Hodgins)   23:230

"Three Worlds" (Kunene)   85:166

Three Years to Play (MacInnes)   23:284

The Three-Arched Bridge (Kadare)
   See *Ura me tri harqe*

"The Three-Cornered Pear" (Voznesensky)
   See "The Triangular Pear"

"The Three-Day Blow" (Hemingway)   3:242; 10:267; 30:180, 187, 189-90, 195-98

"The Three-Penny Opera" (O'Hara)   78:349, 354-55

A Three-Pipe Problem (Symons)   14:523

"The Thresher" (Ochs)   17:331

Threshold (Fugard)   48:109-10

Threshold (Le Guin)
   See *The Beginning Place*

Threshold of Eternity (Brunner)   8:105, 110

"The Thrice-Thrown Tranny Man; or, Orgy at Palo Alto High School" (Kesey)   46:225

"Thrift" (Faulkner)   18:149

"The Thrill of the Grass" (Kinsella)   43:256

The Thrill of the Grass (Kinsella)   43:253-57

Thrilling Cities (Fleming)   30:135

The Throat (Straub)   107:284-86, 288-92, 302, 304-10

Throne of Blood (Kurosawa)   16:396, 401, 404

"The Throne of Good" (Nissenson)   4:381

The Throne of Saturn: A Novel of Space and Politics (Drury)   37:105-06

Thrones, 96-109 de los cantares (Pound)   4:412, 414; 7:331; 13:463; 34:505; 48:282-83, 285-86, 293

Through a Brief Darkness (Peck)   21:296, 298

"Through a Crack" (Ryan)   65:211

"Through a Glass Brightly" (Bainbridge)   62:35, 37

Through A Glass Darkly (Bergman)
   See *Sásom i en spegel*

"Through Corralitos under Rolls of Cloud" (Rich)   73:336; 76:210

"Through Lifetime" (Young Bear)   94:361

"Through My Sails" (Young)   17:582

"Through Our Love" (McCartney)   35:292

"Through Streets Where Smiling Children" (Rosenthal)   28:395

Through the Broken Mirror with Alice (Wojciechowska)   26:457

Through the Fields of Clover (De Vries)   1:73

"Through the Hills of Spain" (Salinas)   90:324-5, 329

Through the Hoop (del Castillo)
   See *Le manège espagnol*

"Through the Inner City to the Suburbs" (Angelou)   35:30

Through the Ivory Gate (Dove)   81:140-41, 148, 152-55

Through the Leaves (Kroetz)
   See *Männer Sache*

"Through the Long Night" (Joel)   26:220

"Through the Mirror" (Elytis)   49:110

Through the Night (Griffiths)   52:173-74, 183

Through the Purple Cloud (Williamson)   29:454

Through the Safety Net (Baxter)   45:51-3; 78:16-19, 21-22, 24-26, 32

Through the Vanishing Point: Space in Poetry and Painting (McLuhan)   83:366, 368

Through the Villages (Handke)   38:225-26

"Through *Tristes Tropiques*" (Leiris)   61:361

"Through with Buzz" (Becker and Fagen)   26:79

"Throughout Our Lands" (Milosz)   31:259; 56:240-41, 251

"Throw Back the Little Ones" (Becker and Fagen)   26:80

A Throw to the South (Paustovsky)
   See *Brosok na yug*

The Throwback (Sharpe)   36:401

"The Thrower-Away" (Boell)
   See "Der Wegwerfer"

Thru (Brooke-Rose)   40:107-09, 111

Thrump-o-moto (Clavell)   87:10, 13, 19

Thrush (Seferis)
   See "Kichli"

"Thrush Song at Dawn" (Eberhart)   56:87

"Thrushes" (Hughes)   9:281; 37:176, 179

"Thrushes" (Moure)   88:226-28, 230

"Thrust and Riposte" (Montale)
   See "Botta e riposta"

al-Thulatthiyya (*The Cairo Trilogy*; *The Trilogy*) (Mahfuz)   55:171, 174, 181-85, 187-88

"Thumb" (Dacey)   51:80

"The Thumb Mark of Saint Peter" (Christie)   110:142, 146

The Thumbstick (Mayne)   12:388, 392

"Thunder among the Leaves" (Roa Bastos)   45:346-47

Thunder among the Leaves (Roa Bastos)
   See *El trueno entre las hojas*

"Thunder and Lightning" (Moravia)   11:384

Thunder and Lightning (Klima)   56:168

"Thunder and Roses" (Sturgeon)   39:361

"Thunder Can Break" (Okigbo)
   See "Come Thunder"

Thunder Heights (Whitney) **42**:433

Thunder on the Right (Stewart) **7**:467; **35**:389, 392

"Thunder Road" (Springsteen) **17**:479-81, 485, 489

"The Thunder Steers" (Elytis) **49**:110

Thunderball (Fleming) **30**:149-50

"Thunderbolt" (Tuohy) **37**:430

Thunderbolt (Sternberg) **20**:377

Thunderbolt and Lightfoot (Cimino) **16**:208

The Thurber Album (Thurber) **5**:430-31, 436, 442; **25**:437

A Thurber Carnival (Thurber) **11**:534

"Thurber: The Comic Prufrock" (De Vries) **7**:76

"Thursday Out" (Berryman) **10**:45

Thursday's Child (Streatfeild) **21**:410-11, 416

Thursday's Children (Anderson) **20**:15, 17

"Thurso's Landing" (Jeffers) **11**:306

Thurso's Landing, and Other Poems (Jeffers) **11**:306; **54**:237

"Thus" (Justice) **102**:250

"Thus" (Simic) **49**:336

"Thus Sings a Mockingbird in El Turquino" (Guillen) **79**:229-30

THX 1138 (Lucas) **16**:407-08, 411, 415-16

Thy Brother's Wife (Greeley) **28**:175-77

Thy Neighbor's Wife (O'Flaherty) **34**:355-57

Thy Neighbor's Wife (Talese) **37**:394-402

Thymus Vulgaris (Wilson) **36**:461

Ti con zero (*t zero*; *Time and the Hunter*) (Calvino) **5**:99; **8**:127; **11**:89, 91-2; **22**:89; **73**:44, 47

Ti Jean l'horizon (*Between Two Worlds*) (Schwarz-Bart)

"Ti ssu ping shih" ("Ward Number Four") (Pa Chin) **18**:374

"Ti2dq2" (Tolson) **105**:262

La tiá Julia y el escribidor (*Aunt Julia and the Scriptwriter*) (Vargas Llosa) **10**:500; **85**:352, 355, 365, 368, 379, 383-84, 386, 389, 392, 394, 396

Tick, Tick . . . Boom! **99**:160, 168, 180, 186

A Ticket for a Seamstitch (Harris) **19**:200, 203

The Ticket That Exploded (Burroughs) **1**:48; **2**:90, 93; **5**:92; **15**:108, 110; **22**:82; **42**:71, 73-4, 79; **75**:93, 102, 106, 109-10; **109**:183, 186, 195, 207, 212, 229

Ticket to Ride (Potter) **58**:391-92, 401; **86**:346, 350, 352

A Ticket to the Stars (Aksyonov)
   See *A Starry Ticket*

Tickets for a Prayer Wheel (Dillard) **115**:170, 201

The Tide (Gironella)
   See *La marea*

"The Tide at Long Point" (Swenson) **106**:315

"Tide Pools" (Smith) **42**:354

"Tide Wash" (Clark) **38**:121, 126

"Tide-Reach" (Mathias) **45**:236

Tides (Montague) **13**:390-91; **46**:268-69, 271, 273-74, 278

The Tides of Lust (Delany) **14**:144; **38**:157-59

The Tidewater Tales (Barth) **51**:27-9

"Tidings" (Milosz) **82**:291, 294-96

Tie Me Up, Tie Me Down (Almodovar)
   See *Atame!*

The Tie That Binds (Haruf) **34**:57-9

Tied Up in Tinsel (Marsh) **7**:209

Tiefland (Riefenstahl) **16**:521, 523, 525-26

El tiempo (Matute) **11**:365

Tiempo al Tiempo (*Play by Play*) (Goldemberg) **52**:167-69

Tiempo mexicano (Fuentes) **60**:152-53

Tien (*Lightning*) (Pa Chin) **18**:372-73

Tientos y diferencias (Carpentier) **11**:105; **38**:94; **110**:59

"Tieresias" (Harris) **25**:212

Tierra (*Land*) (Lopez y Fuentes) **32**:279-81

Tierra Amarilla: Cuentos du Nuevo México (*Tierra Amarilla: Stories of New Mexico/ Cuentos de Nuevo México*) (Ulibarri) **83**:408-09, 413

Tierra Amarilla: Stories of New Mexico/Cuentos de Nuevo México (Ulibarri)
   See *Tierra Amarilla: Cuentos du Nuevo México*

Tierra de nadie (Onetti) **7**:276

"La tierra que nos han dado" (Rulfo)
   See "Nos han dado la tierra"

Tierra sin pan (Bunuel)
   See *Las Hurdes—Tierra sin pan*

"The Ties That Bind" (Miller) **30**:263-64

Tiet eäisyyksiin (*The Roads That Lead Far Away*) (Haavikko) **34**:170

Tieta do Agreste, pastora de cabras; ou, A volta da filha pródiga (*Tieta, the Goat Girl; or, The Return of the Prodigal Daughter*) (Amado) **13**:11-12; **40**:34-5; **106**:86

Tieta, the Goat Girl; or, The Return of the Prodigal Daughter (Amado)
   See *Tieta do Agreste, pastora de cabras; ou, A volta da filha pródiga*

"Tiffany Alexander" (L'Heureux) **52**:275

Tiffany Street (Weidman) **7**:518

La tiganci (Eliade) **19**:146

"Tiger" (Hughes) **108**:307

The Tiger (Schisgal) **6**:489-90

The Tiger (Teran) **36**:422-23

The Tiger and the Horse (Bolt) **14**:90

The Tiger and the Rose (Scannell) **49**:328-29, 332-34

"Tiger Dream" (Raine) **45**:341

Tiger Eyes (Blume) **30**:22-4

A Tiger for Malgudi (Narayan) **47**:302-04

The Tiger in the Smoke (Allingham) **19**:13

The Tiger in the Tiger Pit (Hospital) **42**:220-21, 224

The Tiger of Gold (Jenkins) **52**:222-23, 226

"Tiger Thoughts" (Hope) **51**:222

Der Tiger von Eschnapur (Lang)
   See *Tigress of Bengal*

"Tigers" (Adcock) **41**:13

Tigers (Adcock) **41**:13

Tigers Are Better-Looking (Rhys) **6**:452-56; **14**:446; **19**:390

"The Tiger's Bride" (Carter) **41**:117

The Tiger's Daughter (Mukherjee) **53**:262-64, 268-70; **115**:386

The Tigers of Subutopia, and Other Stories (Symons) **32**:428-29

The Tiger's Revenge (Robbins) **21**:341

Tigers Wild (Rechy) **107**:256

Tight White Collar (L'Heureux) **52**:275-77, 279

"Tightrope Walker" (Scannell) **49**:327

The Tightrope Walker (Levine) **54**:292

"The Tightrope Walkers" (Klima)
   See "Provazolezci"

Le Tigre du Bengale (Lang)
   See *Tigress of Bengal*

A Tigress in Prothero (Swinnerton) **31**:427

Tigress of Bengal (*Der Tiger von Eschnapur*; *Le Tigre du Bengale*) (Lang) **20**:209; **103**:86-9

The Tigris Expedition (Heyerdahl) **26**:194

Ti-Jean and His Brothers (Walcott) **2**:460; **4**:574; **9**:556; **25**:451, 454-55; **67**:351-52; **76**:273

Tikhii Don (*The Quiet Don*) (Sholokhov) **7**:415-16, 418-21; **15**:480-85

Til Death (Hunter) **31**:219

"The Tilemaker's Hill Fresco" (Lieberman) **36**:262, 264

"Till Death Do Us Part" (Gellhorn) **14**:195; **60**:184

Till glädje (*To Joy*) (Bergman) **16**:72; **72**:62

"Till I Die" (Wilson) **12**:650

"Till It Shines" (Seger) **35**:384

"Till September Petronella" (Rhys) **19**:390-91; **51**:375

Till the Break of Day: Memories, 1939-1942 (Wojciechowska) **26**:457-58

"Till the Day I Die" (Odets) **28**:323-24, 332

Till the Day I Die (Odets) **98**:198, 201, 207, 213-15, 218, 224, 229, 231, 233-34, 241

"Till Victory" (Smith) **12**:543

Till We Have Faces: A Myth Retold (Lewis) **6**:310-11; **14**:324; **27**:266

"The Tillotson Banquet" (Huxley) **3**:256

Tillträde till festen (*Admission to the Feast*) (Beckman) **26**:86-7, 89

Tiln (Cook) **58**:157

"Tilth" (Graves) **45**:170, 175

Tim (McCullough) **27**:317; **107**:127-33, 137, 152, 154, 159

Tim, Tim: Anthologie de la littérature antillaise en néerlandais (Conde) **92**:100

Tim tim? Bois sec! (Conde) **92**:100

Timans and Justice (Johnson)
   See *Timas och rä-ttfärdigheten*

Timas och rä-ttfärdigheten (*Timans and Justice*) (Johnson) **14**:294

Timber (Haig-Brown) **21**:135, 141

"Timbuktu" (Thomas) **37**:421-22; **107**:316, 320-21, 327

"Time" (Alegria)
   See "Letter to Time"

"Time" (Creeley) **36**:121

"Time" (Merrill) **2**:273-74

"Time" (Pink Floyd) **35**:306-07

"Time" (Stafford) **29**:382

Time (Amichai) **22**:31-2; **116**:95, 97-9

Time (Burroughs) **109**:184

Time after Time (Keane) **31**:234-35

A Time and a Place (Humphrey) **45**:197-98

"Time and Again" (Bowering) **47**:22

"Time and Again" (Pancake) **29**:347-48

Time and Again (Simak) **55**:320

"Time and Description in Fiction Today" (Robbe-Grillet) **8**:453; **43**:360

"Time and Love" (Nyro) **17**:318

"Time and Music" (Lewis) **41**:261

"Time and Place" (Howe) **47**:174

Time and Place (Trifonov)
   See *Vremia i mesto*

"Time and the City" (Le Guin) **45**:220

Time and the Conways (Priestley) **2**:346; **5**:350; **34**:361, 365

"Time and the Garden" (Winters) **32**:469

Time and the Hunter (Calvino)
   See *Ti con zero*

Time and the White Tigress (Barnard) **48**:28-9

Time and Tide (O'Brien) **116**:204-07, 212

Time and Time Again (Ayckbourn) **5**:35; **33**:40, 44; **74**:31, 33-6

"Time and Times" (Montale) **9**:387

"Time and Violence" (Boland) **113**:100

"The Time around Scars" (Ondaatje) **51**:310,

312
"Time as Hypnosis" (Warren)   6:558; 10:522;
    39:270
"Time as Now" (Scott)   22:373
"The Time Bomb" (Stewart)   32:421
"The Time Capsule" (Gilchrist)   65:349
Time Cat (Alexander)   35:22
"Time Considered as a Helix of Semi-Precious
    Stones" (Delany)   38:149, 154
"Time Did" (Gordimer)   18:190
"The Time Disease" (Amis)   62:7-8
*Time Enough for Love: The Lives of Lazarus
    Long* (Heinlein)   3:227; 14:251-53, 255;
    26:169; 55:303
"Time Fades Away" (Young)   17:571
Time Fades Away (Young)   17:571-75
Time for a Tiger (Burgess)   15:103; 22:73; 81:301
A Time for Judas (Callaghan)   41:92-8; 65:252
"Time for Perjury" (Oe)   86:226-27
"A Time for the Eating of Grasses" (Kumin)
    13:326
Time for the Stars (Heinlein)   26:161, 171,
    173, 177; 55:302
"Time for Truth" (Weller)   26:443
"Time Future" (White)   10:527
"Time, Gentlemen!" (Calisher)   38:69
Time Given (McAuley)   45:253-54
"The Time Has Come" (Van Doren)   10:496
Time in a Red Coat (Brown)   48:60-1
Time in Ezra Pound's Work (Harmon)   38:243
Time in Its Flight (Schaeffer)   11:491-92
Time in the Rock: Preludes to Definition (Aiken)
    3:3; 5:8-9; 10:3; 52:21, 23-4, 26-7, 30
"Time Is Money" (Busch)   47:62
The Time Is Noon (Buck)   7:33
The Time Is Ripe (Odets)   98:247
"Time Is the Artery of Space" (Ivask)   14:287
"Time Is the Mercy of Eternity" (Rexroth)
    49:282-83; 112:391, 399-400
Time Is the Simplest Thing (Simak)   55:320
"Time Lapse with Tulips" (Gallagher)   63:125
Time Must Have a Stop (Huxley)   1:151-52;
    4:239-41, 243; 8:303
Time No Longer (Caldwell)   39:302-03
"A Time of Bees" (Van Duyn)   63:435, 440;
    116:401, 403, 420, 426
A Time of Bees (Van Duyn)   3:491; 7:498;
    63:435-36, 440
"The Time of Death" (Munro)   95:296
A Time of Death (Cosic)
    See *Vreme smrti*
Time of Desecration (Moravia)
    See *La vita interiore*
Time of Drums (Ehle)   27:104-05
"A Time of Dying" (Wesker)   5:483-84
"The Time of Friendship" (Bowles)   53:44
The Time of Friendship (Bowles)   2:79; 19:60;
    53:40
The Time of Great Expectations (*Years of Hope*)
    (Paustovsky)   40:364-65, 368
"The Time of Her Time" (Mailer)   3:315;
    28:256, 261; 74:207-08; 111:135-37
Time of Hope (Snow)   13:509-11; 19:426-27
The Time of Illusion (Schell)   35:363-64
The Time of Indifference (Moravia)
    See *Gli indifferenti*
"A Time of Learning" (West)   7:519
*Time of Need: Forms of Imagination in the
    Twentieth Century* (Barrett)   27:18-20
"Time of Passage" (Ballard)   3:33
A Time of Terror (Eckert)   17:104
The Time of the Angels (Murdoch)   1:236; 2:296;
    3:347; 6:348-49; 11:386-87; 22:327

The Time of the Assassins: A Study of Rimbaud
    (Miller)   9:380; 84:251
Time of the Butcherbird (La Guma)   19:277
The Time of the Crack (Tennant)   13:536-37;
    52:396, 398
The Time of the Ghost (Jones)   26:231-32
The Time of the Hero (Vargas Llosa)
    See *La ciudad y los perros*
"The Time of Their Lives" (O'Faolain)   32:342
*Time of Trial, Time of Hope: The Negro in
    America, 1919-1941* (Meltzer)   26:297-
    98
"The Time of Year" (Trevor)   71:348
The Time of Your Life (Saroyan)   8:468; 10:453,
    455; 29:359-60; 34:459; 56:367-85, 387-
    88
Time on Fire (Shapcott)   38:397, 400
Time Out for Happiness (Gilbreth and Carey)
    17:156
Time Out of Joint (Dick)   30:116, 125; 72:110
"Time out of Mind" (Becker and Fagen)   26:85
"Time Passing" (Townshend)   17:528
"Time Passing, Beloved" (Davie)   5:114;
    31:109, 118
"Time Past" (White)   10:527
"Time Present" (White)   10:527
Time Present (Osborne)   5:333; 11:421, 423;
    45:313-16, 320
"Time Quarry" (Simak)   55:319
Time Remembered (Anouilh)
    See *Léocadia*
"Time Shards" (Benford)   52:76
"Time Sharing Angel" (Tiptree)   48:389
"Time Spirals" (Rexroth)   112:399-400
Time Thieves (Koontz)   78:203
A Time to Be Born (Powell)   66:357-59, 361,
    363, 370-71
A Time to Be Happy (Sahgal)   41:369
"A Time to Break Silence" (King)   83:345-46,
    349
A Time to Change (Ezekiel)   61:104-05
"A Time to Dance" (Mac Laverty)   31:255
A Time to Dance and Other Poems (Day Lewis)
    6:128; 10:128, 131
A Time to Dance and Other Stories (Mac
    Laverty)   31:254-55
A Time to Dance, No Time to Weep (Godden)
    53:163-64
A Time to Die (Wicker)   7:534-35
"Time to Go" (Dixon)   52:99-100
Time to Go (Dixon)   52:99-101
Time to Go (O'Casey)   15:405
"A Time to Keep" (Brown)   48:52
"A Time to Keep" (Sillitoe)   57:391, 396
A Time to Keep and Other Stories (Brown)
    48:52-5; 100:83
A Time to Kill (Grisham)   84:190, 195, 198-99
A Time to Laugh (Davies)   23:141
Time to Love (Benary-Isbert)   12:34
Time to Love (Dourado)
    See *Tempo de amar*
A Time to Love and a Time to Die (Remarque)
    21:331-32
"A Time to Talk" (Frost)   15:248
"The Time Tombs" (Ballard)   36:37
The Time Traders (Norton)   12:467
"Time Waits for No One" (Jagger and Richard)
    17:233, 236, 238
"Time Was Away" (MacNeice)   4:315
"The Time We Climbed Snake Mountain"
    (Silko)   74:335, 345
"Time We Took to Travel" (Bell)   8:65
Time Will Darken It (Maxwell)   19:306

"Time Will Tell" (Cliff)   21:60
*Time within Time: The Diaries of Andrey
    Tarkovsky* (Tarkovsky)   75:412
Time without Number (Berrigan)   4:58
Time-Jump (Brunner)   8:108
Timeless Meeting (Graves)   6:212
"Timeless, Twinned" (Warren)   39:256
"The Timeless World of a Play" (Williams)
    111:394
"Timelight" (Skelton)   13:507
Timelight (Skelton)   13:507
Timequake (Vonnegut)   111:371-73
"Timer" (Harrison)   43:178
"Times" (Beattie)   63:18
"Times" (Cummings)   15:162
*The Times Are Never So Bad: A Novella and
    Eight Short Stories* (Dubus)   36:146, 148;
    97:199, 201, 208-10, 224, 233
Time's Arrow (Amis)   101:69-71, 77-78, 86-
    87, 89, 95
"The Times My Father Died" ("My Father's
    Deaths") (Amichai)   116:106-07
The Times of Melville and Whitman (Brooks)
    29:88-9
"Times of Sickness and Health" (Shields)
    113:405
Times of Surrender (Coles)   108:192, 196
Time's Power: Poems, 1985-1988 (Rich)
    73:328, 330-32; 76:211
"Time's Rub" (Benford)   52:76
"Times Square" (Clark)   38:118, 128
"The Times They Are A-Changin'" (Dylan)
    77:164
The Times They Are A-Changin' (Dylan)   4:149;
    12:182, 198-99
Times Three (McGinley)   14:366, 368
Timescape (Benford)   52:65-9, 72-4, 76-7
"Times-Square-Shoeshine   Composition"
    (Angelou)   77:28
"Timesweep" (Sandburg)   10:449; 35:356
Timmerlis (Bodker)   21:12
"Timor dei" (Cunningham)   31:102
"Timor Mortis" (Porter)   5:347
Timothy Archer (Dick)
    See *The Transmigration of Timothy Archer*
"Ti-Moune" (Gold)   42:197-98
"The Tin Can" (Smith)   6:513
The Tin Can and Other Poems (Smith)   6:512
The Tin Can Tree (Tyler)   28:430-31; 59:203,
    205, 207; 103:236-37, 241, 244, 258,
    264, 271, 273
The Tin Drum (Grass)
    See *Die Blechtrommel*
The Tin Flute (Roy)
    See *Bonheur d'occasion*
The Tin Lizzie Troop (Swarthout)   35:402-03
The Tin Men (Frayn)   31:189-90
"Tin Roof" (Ondaatje)   51:313, 315
"Tin Roof Blues" (Brown)   23:96
"Tin Soldier" (Vinge)   30:410
"Tinder" (Heaney)   14:244
"Tinieblas y consolación" (Castellanos)   66:50
Tinker, Tailor, Soldier, Spy (le Carre)   5:232-
    35; 9:327; 15:324-26
"Tinkers" (Powers)   8:447
Tinsel (Goldman)   48:127-28
Tiny Alice (Albee)   1:5; 2:1-4; 3:7; 5:10, 12-13;
    9:1, 5-7, 9; 11:11; 13:3-5; 25:34, 37-8,
    40; 53:21, 23, 26; 86:118, 123; 113:15-
    17, 19-21, 25-6, 28, 30, 32, 34-6
"The Tiny Baby" (Strand)   41:438-40
"Tiny Tears" (Fuller)   28:157
"Tiny Treaties" (Alexie)   96:8

"Tio e sobrinho" ("Uncle and Nephew") (Cabral de Melo Neto)   76:163
"Tip on a Dead Jockey" (Shaw)   34:370
Tip on a Dead Jockey (Shaw)   7:412
Tips for Teens (Lebowitz)   36:248
"Tirade for the Mimic Muse" (Boland)   67:43; 113:58-9, 87, 97-8, 122-23
"A Tirade Turning" (Roethke)   46:361; 101:266
"The Tire Hangs in the Woods" (Smith)   42:346, 349
"Tired" (Hughes)   108:320
"Tired and Unhappy, You Think of Houses" (Schwartz)   10:462
"Tired Eyes" (Young)   17:574
"Tires on Wet Asphalt at Night" (Warren)   39:273
"Tiresias" (Clarke)   6:112
"Tiresome Company" (Ferron)   94:103
Tirez sur le pianiste (*Shoot the Piano Player*) (Truffaut)   20:381-83, 397, 402-03; 101:369, 373, 377, 380, 382·85, 387-91, 396, 406, 409-10
Les tiroirs de l'inconnu (Ayme)   11:23
Tirra Lirra by the River (Anderson)   37:20-1
"Tîrzui de toamna" ("Tardy Autumn") (Arghezi)   80:7
Tis Pity She's a Whore (Ayckbourn)   74:19
"Tis the Season to Be Jolly" (Matheson)   37:245
Tissue (Page)   40:355
"Titan" (Dorfman)   77:141
Titania's Lodestone (Corcoran)   17:75
"The Titanic" (Feldman)   7:103
"The Titanic" (Milosz)   82:299
Titanic (Durang)   27:88
The Titanic (Pratt)   19:378, 381-84
Titans (Pratt)   19:378, 382
"Tithonus" (Brown)   48:55
Titicut Follies (Wiseman)   20:467-69, 471-72, 476
"Title" (Barth)   3:41; 9:67, 69; 14:53-4; 51:23; 89:5-6, 8-10, 12-16, 18-19, 23-24, 27, 30, 32, 34-5, 37, 44-6, 48, 50, 56, 59, 61-2
"The Title of This Book" (Barth)   51:25
"Titre à Préciser" (Derrida)   87:92
"Titties and Beer" (Zappa)   17:592
"Titties Prayer" (Carrier)   78:83
Titus Alone (Peake)   54:367-68, 370-72, 376-78; 7:302
Titus Andronicus (Duerrenmatt)   102:54-6, 59, 61
Titus Groan (Peake)   54:366-75, 377-78
Tiur'ma i mir (Aksyonov)
   See *Prison and Peace*
"Tlactocatzine del jardin de Flandes" (Fuentes)
   See "In a Flemish Garden"
"Tlactocatzine in the Garden of Flanders" (Fuentes)
   See "In a Flemish Garden"
"Tlactocatzine, of the Flemish Garden" (Fuentes)
   See "In a Flemish Garden"
"Tlön, Uqbar, Orbis Tertius" (Borges)   2:69, 72; 3:77; 6:87, 92; 8:94, 96, 98, 100; 9:116-118; 10:66; 44:362, 369; 48:33, 42-3, 45-6; 83:155-57, 161, 164, 176, 183
Tlooth (Mathews)   6:314-16; 52:307, 309-10, 315-16, 318
"To a Beautiful Old Lady" (Christie)   110:125
"To a Blackbird" (Kavanagh)   22:236
To a Blossoming Pear Tree (Wright)   10:546-

47; 28:466, 468, 472-73
"To A British Jar Containing Stephen's Ink" (Blunden)   56:37
"To a Brother in the Mystery" (Davie)   31:109
"To a Cedar Tree" (Christie)   110:127
"To a Chameleon" (Moore)   8:401
"To a Child" (Snodgrass)   68:382
"To a Child" (Wright)   53:419
"To a Communist" (MacNeice)   53:234
"To a Conscript of 1940" (Read)   4:439
"To a Contemporary Bunk-Shooter" (Sandburg)   35:347
"To a Dead Lover" (Bogan)   93:104
"To a Distant Statue of King George V" (Hall)   51:170
"To a Friend Going Blind" (Graham)   48:154
"To a Friend in Time of Trouble" (Gunn)   81:184
"To a Friend in Trouble" (Wain)   11:562
"To a Friend Parting" (Warren)   8:539
"To a Friend Who Cannot Accept My Judgment of Him" (Wakoski)   4:572
"To a Friend Who Has Moved to the East Side" (Ignatow)   14:274
"To a Friend Who Threw Away Hair Dyes" (Van Duyn)   116:415
"To a Friend Who Wished Always to Be Alone" (Wright)   13:614
"To a Friend Whose Family Was Killed or Ngenimpi (A Late Recruit)" (Kunene)   85:176
"To a Friend Whose Work Has Come to Triumph" (Sexton)   53:316
To a God Unknown (Steinbeck)   1:325; 5:406-07; 9:512-13; 13:530, 533; 21:366, 381, 390; 34:412; 59:333; 75:343
"To a Greek Marble" (Aldington)   49:2-3, 6, 16
"To A. H., New Year, 1943" (Wright)   53:427
"To a Happy Day" (Neruda)   7:259
"To a Hostess Saying Goodnight" (Wright)   28:462
"To a Husband" (Angelou)   77:28
"To a Jealous Cat" (Sanchez)   116:277, 294
"To a Lady in a Phone Booth" (McGinley)   14:366
"To a Little Girl, One Year Old in a Ruined Fortress" (Warren)   39:266
"To A. M., a Flamenco Singer" (Cabral de Melo Neto)
   See *A Antonio Mairena, cantador*
"To a Mad Friend" (Davison)   28:99-100
"To a Man" (Angelou)   64:33-4
"To a Man on His Horse" (Prince)   22:340
"To a Military Rifle" (Winters)   32:468, 470
"To a Moth Seen in Winter" (Frost)   9:226
"To a Muse" (Corn)   33:116
"To a Navaho Boy Playing the Flute" (Kunene)   85:176
"To a New Mother" (Levine)   33:274
"To a Now-Type Poet" (Kennedy)   42:257
"To a Painter in England" (Walcott)   76:277
"To a Plum-Coloured Bra Displayed in Marks and Spencer" (Ewart)   46:153
"To a Poet Who Has Had a Heart Attack" (Eberhart)   11:177
"To a Red Hell" (Himes)   58:264
"To a Sad Daughter" (Ondaatje)   51:314, 317
"To a Snail" (Moore)   8:400; 47:272
"To a South African Policeman" (Kunene)   85:175
"To a Steam Roller" (Moore)   47:268
"To a Stranger" ("At the End of a Caboose")

(Jensen)   37:192
"To a Teacher of French" (Davie)   31:116, 118
"To a Ten-Months' Child" (Justice)   102:269
To a Tensed Serenity (Char)
   See *À une sérénité crispée*
"To a Thinker" (Frost)   10:193
"To a Wandering Albatross" (Neruda)   62:331
"To a Waterfowl" (Hall)   37:146
"To a Watertower" (Crase)   58:160, 163
"To a Western Bard Still a Whoop and a Holler Away from English Poetry" (Meredith)   22:302
"To a Winter Squirrel" (Brooks)   49:28
"To a Woman on Her Defense of Her Brother" (Winters)   32:468
"To a Young American the Day after the Fall of Barcelona" (Ciardi)   40:157
"To a Young Girl Leaving the Hill Country" (Bontemps)   18:64
"To a Young Writer" (Winters)   32:470
"To Abolish Children" (Shapiro)   53:329
To Abolish Children, and Other Essays (Shapiro)   53:328-30
"To Acquire a Beautiful Body" (Dybek)   114:62
"To Aegidius Cantor" (Howard)   10:277
"To Alexander Graham" (Graham)   29:199
To All Appearances: Poems New and Selected (Miles)   14:369, 370
"To All Black Women, from All Black Men" (Cleaver)   30:56, 59
"To All Sisters" (Sanchez)   116:282
"To All Telephone Subscribers" (Enzensberger)   43:145
"To an Adolescent Weeping Willow" (Bell)   31:51
"To an American Poet Just Dead" (Wilbur)   110:383
"To an Artist, to Take Heart" (Bogan)   46:83; 93:64
To an Early Grave (Markfield)   8:378-79
"To an Honest Friend" (Sarton)   91:254
"To an Old Lady" (Empson)   3:147; 8:202; 19:155; 33:142; 34:540
"To an Unknown American Friend" (Leonov)   92:277
"To an Unknown Poet" (Kizer)   80:183, 185
"To and Fro" (McEwan)   66:275, 279, 281
"To Any Dead Officer" (Graves)   45:166
"To Any Dead Officer Who Left School for the Army in 1914" (Sassoon)   36:385
"To Any Poet" (McAuley)   45:249
"To Apollo" (Herbert)   43:189
"To Artemis" (Carruth)   10:100
"To Artina" (Hughes)   108:333
"To Auden on His Fiftieth" (Eberhart)   11:177
"To Aunt Rose" (Ginsberg)   2:17
"To Autumn" (Gluck)   7:118
"To Autumn" (Logan)   5:254
"To Autumn" (Smith)   64:399
"To Be a Man" (Soto)   80:284
"To Be a Poet" (Stevenson)   33:381
To Be a Poet (Seifert)
   See *Býti básnikem*
"To Be Collected" (Sillitoe)   57:391
"To Be in Love" (Brooks)   49:27-8
To Be of Use (Piercy)   6:402-04; 18:406; 27:375; 62:376
"To Be Quicker for Black Political Prisoners" (Madhubuti)   73:215
"To Be Sung on the Water" (Bogan)   93:65, 78
"To Be Sung on the Water" (Bogan)   39:387; 46:81; 93:77

To Be Young, Gifted, and Black (Hansberry) 17:187-88

To Bedlam and Part Way Back (Sexton) 2:390-91; 4:482-84; 6:491; 8:483; 15:471-72; 53:312, 316-18, 320-21

"To Begin" (Strand) 6:521

To Begin Again: Stories and Memoirs, 1908-1929 (Fisher) 87:128, 130, 132-33

"To Belkis, When She Paints" (Padilla) 38:349

"To Bev" (Behan) 79:38

"To Bill Williams" (Eberhart) 11:177

"To Bird-watching" (Neruda) 62:331

To Bite the Flesh (Brossard)
  See *Mordre en sa chair*

"'To Bodies Gone': Pygmalion Remembering" (Rosenthal) 28:395

"To Build a House" (Hall) 59:154-56

"To C. E. B." (Blunden) 56:40

"To Canidia" (Jeffers) 54:234

"To Carry the Child" (Smith) 44:437

To Catch a Thief (Hitchcock) 16:341, 346, 359

"To Cease" (Montague) 46:269

"To Certain Friends" (Scott) 22:377

"To Certain Negro Leaders" (Hughes) 108:319

"To Change in a Good Way" (Ortiz) 45:310-11

"To Christ" (Ritsos) 31:324

"To Chuck" (Sanchez) 116:278, 294

"To Cipriano, in the Wind" (Levine) 33:273

To Circumjack Cencrastus (MacDiarmid) 11:336; 19:289-90; 63:239

"To Cleave" (Bowering) 15:82

"To Confirm a Thing" (Swenson) 106:314, 341

"To Criticize the Critic" (Eliot) 24:178

To Criticize the Critic (Eliot) 113:193

"To Da-duh, In Memoriam" (Marshall) 27:313-14

"To Delmore Schwartz" (Lowell) 3:300

To Demosia ké ta Idiotika (Elytis) 100:187

To diav (*The Passport*) (Samarakis) 5:381-82

To diavatírio (Samarakis) 5:381

"To Die for One's Country Is Glorious" (Kis) 57:251

To Die in Italbar (Zelazny) 21:466, 468-69

"To Die in Milltown" (Hugo) 32:240

"To Dinah Washington" (Knight) 40:279

To Disembark (Brooks) 49:23, 29

"To Don at Salaam" (Brooks) 49:29

"To Dorothy" (Bell) 31:50

"To Draw the Warmth of Flesh from Subtle Graphite" (Broumas) 73:17

"To Dwell in Time" (Cabral de Melo Neto)
  See "Habitar o tempo"

"To Earthward" (Frost) 9:218; 26:112

To Eat a Peach (Willingham) 51:407

"To Elizabeth Ann Fraser" (McFadden) 48:251

"To Elsie" (Williams) 67:408

"To Eugene" (Brodsky) 50:125

"To Eve in Bitterness" (Jones) 10:286

"To Every Thing There Is a Season" (MacLeod) 56:197-99

"To F." (Swenson) 106:343

"To Fill" (Moore) 39:82-3

"To Free Nelson Mandela" (Jordan) 114:162

"To Gerhardt" (Olson) 11:420

"To Girls at the Turn of Night Love Goes On Knocking" (Graham) 29:193

"to gloria, who is she: on using a pseudonym" (hooks) 94:143

"To Happiness" (Neruda) 7:259

To Have and Have Not (Hemingway) 1:141;

3:232, 235-36, 240; 6:226-27, 229; 8:283; 13:271, 274, 278; 30:179; 39:430, 435; 41:197-98; 80:101, 103-04, 106, 108, 118, 135, 137, 143, 150-51

To Have and to Lose (Aitmatov)
  See *Topolek moi v krasnoi kosynke*

"To Have Done Nothing" (Williams) 42:460

To Heaven One Climbs on Foot (Ulibarri)
  See *Al cielo se sube a pie*

"To Helen" (Simic) 49:341

"To Helen Whose Remembrance Leaves No Peace" (Jeffers) 54:234

"To Hell with Dying" (Walker) 6:553-54; 58:409; 103:399, 402, 409, 412, 423

"To Here and the Easel" (Sturgeon) 22:411; 39:365

"To His Other Spirit" (Rosenthal) 28:394-95

"To His Skeleton" (Wilbur) 110:385

"To Hold a Poem" (Smith) 15:515-16

"To Howard Hughes: A Modest Proposal" (Haldeman) 61:174, 176-77

"To Hummingbirds" (Neruda) 62:331

"To Isherwood Dying" (Gunn) 81:186

To Jerusalem and Back: A Personal Account (Bellow) 8:79-82; 15:58; 25:82, 86

"To Joy" (Blunden) 56:39

To Joy (Bergman)
  See *Till glädje*

"To Juan at the Winter Solstice" (Graves) 1:126; 2:174; 39:321; 45:169, 173, 176

"To Judith Asleep" (Ciardi) 40:153-54, 156-58; 44:380

To Keep Moving: Essays, 1959-1969 (Hall) 37:148

To Keep the Ball Rolling: The Memoirs of Anthony Powell (Powell) 31:314, 317, 319-20, 322

"To Keorapetse Kgositsile (Willie)" ("Willie") (Brooks) 49:29

To Kill a Mockingbird (Foote) 51:131, 133; 91:101

To Kill a Mockingbird (Lee) 12:340-42; 60:240-50

To Leave before Dawn (Green)
  See *Partir avant le jour*

"To Life" (Neruda) 7:259

To Live and Die in Dixie (Beecher) 6:48-9

"To Live as Foolishly as I Lived Yesterday" (Akhmadulina)
  See "Tak durno zhit', kak ia vchera zhila"

To Live Forever (Vance) 35:420, 423, 426

"To Lose the Earth" (Sexton) 6:493

"To Love" (Neruda) 7:259

"To Lucasta on Going to the Wars" (Graves) 45:166

"To Lycomedes on Scyros" (Brodsky)
  See "K Likomedu, na Skiros"

"To Maeve" (Peake) 54:369, 372

"To Make a Play" (Swenson) 106:339

"To Make a Poem in Prison" (Knight) 40:279, 283

"To Marina" (Koch) 44:246, 250

"To Marx" (Ritsos) 31:324

"To Mary Gilmore" (Wright) 53:429

To Meet the Sun (FitzGerald) 19:176

"To M.E.L.M. in Absence" (Christie) 110:126

"To Military Progress" (Moore) 8:398

To Mix with Time: New and Selected Poems (Swenson) 4:533; 61:390-92, 395, 400; 106:316, 319-20, 327, 336, 341, 345, 349

"To Ms. Ann" (Clifton) 66:67

"To My Brother" (Bogan) 46:80, 83, 87; 93:64, 76

"To My Brother Hanson" (Merwin) 88:192, 201

"To My Brother on the Death of a Young Poet" (Levine) 33:270

"To My Daughter the Junkie on a Train" ("My Daughter the Junkie on a Train") (Lorde) 71:232, 236

"To My Dog" (Aleixandre) 36:30

"To My Elder Kinsman (Polycarp Dlamini)" (Kunene) 85:176

"To My Father" (Bidart) 33:76

"To My Father" (Olds) 85:306

"To My First White Hairs" (Soyinka) 36:409

"To My Friend, Behind Walls" (Kizer) 80:12

"To My Friends" (Silkin) 43:400

"To My God in His Sickness" (Levine) 14:319

"To My Godson, on His Christening" (Van Duyn) 63:439; 116:399, 425

"To My Mother" (Barker) 48:22

"To My Mother" (Smith)
  See "For My Mother"

"To My Mountain" (Raine) 45:330

"To My Sister" (Roethke) 8:455

To My Son in Uniform (Felsen) 17:124

"To My Wife" (Cunningham) 3:122; 31:98

"To My Wife" (Larkin) 64:262

"To My Wife at Midnight" (Graham) 29:197-98

"To No End Ever" (Ciardi) 40:159

"To Nomazwi—Reluctant Poetess" (Kunene) 85:175-76

"To Old Asclepius—Lyric at Epidaurus" (Gustafson) 36:218

"To One 'Investigated' by the Last Senate Committee, or the Next" (Ciardi) 40:153, 157

To Our Father Creator Tupac (Arguedas)
  See *Tupac amaru kampa Taytanchisman*

To Painting: A Poem of Color and Line (Alberti) 7:10

"To Please a Shadow" (Brodsky) 50:132; 100:61

"To Poets' Worksheets in the Air-Conditioned Vault of a Library" (Van Duyn) 116:403

To Possess the Land: A Biography of Arthur Rochford Manby (Waters) 88:364

To Praise the Music (Bronk) 10:74

"To Professor X, Year Y" (Avison) 97:133-34

"To Raja Rao" (Milosz) 56:240; 82:301

"To Ramona" (Dylan) 77:174

"To Remember is a Kind of Hope" (Amichai) 116:90

"To Revive Anarchism" (Shapiro) 53:328

To Ride Pegasus (McCaffrey) 17:281

"To Robinson Jeffers" (Milosz) 56:241, 244; 82:295-96, 300

"To Room Nineteen" (Lessing) 40:310

To Room Nineteen (Lessing) 94:261

To Sail beyond the Sunset (Heinlein) 55:303

"To Say It" (Creeley) 78:141

To See the Dream (West) 17:546-47

"To See the Sun" (Amis) 40:43, 45

To See, To Take (Van Duyn) 3:491; 7:498-99; 63:436-38, 440, 442, 444; 116:400-03, 406, 414, 419, 426

"To See You Again" (Adams) 46:17

To See You Again (Adams) 46:15-17, 21-2

"To September Wings" (Neruda) 62:331

"To Sing a Song of Palestine" (Jordan) 114:146

To Sir with Love (Clavell) 87:18

To Skin a Cat (McGuane) 45:265-66

"To Sleep, Perchance to Steam" (Perelman)

49:265
To Smithereens (Drexler) 6:142
"To Speak of My Influences" (Garrigue) 8:240
"To Speak of Woe That Is in Marriage" (Lowell) 15:343
"To Start, to Hesitate; to Stop" (Cummings) 8:160
"To Statecraft Embalmed" (Moore) 8:401; 47:260
To Stay Alive (Levertov) 2:243; 3:293; 5:248-250; 66:245-46, 249, 251
"To Suzanne, from Prison" (Faludy) 42:137-38
"To Take Objects Outs" (Herbert) 9:275
To Teach, to Love (Stuart) 34:375
To Tell Your Love (Stolz) 12:545-46, 549, 552
"To the Adversary" (Wittlin) 25:469
To the Air (Gunn) 18:200
"To the August Fallen" (Wright) 5:520
"To the Birds of Chile" (Neruda) 62:331
"To the Blessed Virgin" (Buckley) 57:125
To the Bone (Kristofferson) 26:270
"To the Botequim and Back" (Bishop) 32:43
"To the Butterflies" (Dickey) 109:246
"To the Chicago Abyss" (Bradbury) 98:112
To the Chicago Abyss (Bradbury) 42:33-4
"To the Dark Star" (Silverberg) 7:425
To the Dark Tower (King) 53:204
"To the Diaspora" (Brooks) 49:23, 29
"To the End of the Pier" (Corn) 33:115
To the End of the World (Cendrars)
  See *Emmène-moi au bout du monde!*
To the Ends of the Earth (Golding) 81:320
"To the Film Industry in Crisis" (O'Hara) 78:354
To the Finland Station (Wilson) 1:372-73; 2:476; 3:539-40; 24:467, 473, 482-83, 486-87
"To the Foot from Its Child" (Neruda) 7:260
"To the Governor and Legislature of Massachusetts" (Nemerov) 2:308
"To the Gull" (Neruda) 62:331
"To the Gulls of Antofagasta" (Neruda) 62:331
"To the Hawk" (Justice) 19:235
"To the Holy Spirit" (Winters) 4:591; 32:468-69
"To the Immaculate Virgin, on a Winter Night" (Merton) 83:391
To the Indies (Forester) 35:163-64
"To the Insects" (Merwin) 88:206
To the Is-Land (Frame) 66:143, 145, 150; 96:187-88, 193-94, 201, 203, 206, 209-10, 217-18, 220
To the Islands (Stow) 23:432-34; 48:355-56, 358
"To the Lacedemonians" (Tate) 4:539; 9:522
To the Ladies! (Connelly) 7:56
To the Ladies! (Kaufman) 38:257, 264
To the Land of the Cattails (*To the Land of the Reeds*) (Appelfeld) 47:7-9
To the Land of the Reeds (Appelfeld)
  See *To the Land of the Cattails*
To the Limit (Armatrading) 17:9-10
"To the Little Fort, San Lázaro, on the Ocean Front Havana" (Hughes) 108:324
"To the Living" (Sarton) 49:310
"To the Man Who Sidled Up to Me and Asked: 'How Long You In fer, Buddy?'" (Knight) 40:279
"To the Members of the D.A.R." (Greenberg) 30:163
"To the Migration of Birds" (Neruda) 62:331
"To the Mother" (Amichai)

  See "La'em"
"To the Mothers of the Dead Militia" (Neruda)
  See "Canto a las madres de los milicianos muertos"
"To the Muse" (Levertov) 66:238-39, 242
"To the Muse" (Wright) 3:541, 543; 28:466
"To the New Tenant" (Brodsky) 13:114
"To the Nightingale" (McGuckian) 48:278
To the North (Bowen) 3:84; 11:62, 65-6; 15:79; 22:61, 63
"To the Oriole" (Neruda) 62:331
"To the Painters: On the United States, Considered as a Landscape" (Howard) 47:169
"To the Poet Who Happens to Be Black and the Black Poet Who Happens to Be a Woman" (Lorde) 71:254, 256
"To the Poetry of Hugh McRae" (Slessor) 14:496-97
"To the Poets in New York" (Wright) 3:543
"To the Poets of Chile" (Levine) 14:315, 318-19
To the Precipice (Rossner) 9:456
To the Public Danger (Hamilton) 51:190, 193
"To the Reader" (Cunningham) 31:101-02
"To the Reader" (Jong) 6:268
"To the Readers" 75:62
"To the Sea" (Larkin) 5:226, 230-31; 8:332, 337, 339; 9:323; 13:340; 18:301; 33:259; 64:277, 280, 282, 284
"To the Sea Serpent" (Fuentes)
  See "A la Víbora de la mar"
"To the Sky" (Bell) 8:67
"To the Snake" (Levertov) 66:252
"To the Snake of the Sea" (Fuentes)
  See "A la Víbora de la mar"
"To the Southdowns" (Blunden) 56:45
"To the Soviet Union" (Ritsos) 31:324
To the Stars (Hubbard)
  See *Return to Tomorrow*
"To the Statues of the Gods" (Cernuda) 54:58
"To the Stone-Cutters" (Jeffers) 54:243, 248
"To the Storming Gulf" (Benford) 52:71-2, 75-6
"To the Sun" (Bachmann)
  See "An die Sonne"
"To the Unknown God" (Moravia) 46:286
To the Unknown Hero (Nossack)
  See *Dem unbekannten Sieger*
"To the Unknown Lady Who Wrote the Letters Found in the Hatbox" (Justice) 102:279
To the Victors the Spoils (MacInnes) 23:283
"To the Virgin as She Now Stands" (Codrescu) 46:103
"To the Watcher of the Gates" (Kunene) 85:166
"To the Western World" (Simpson) 7:426; 9:486
To the White Sea (Dickey) 109:236, 257-60, 262-63, 273, 275, 287
"To the Wilderness" (Kinnell) 13:320
"To the World Beyond I'm Posting" (Ratushinskaya) 54:384, 386
"To Thom Gunn in Los Altos, California" (Davie) 31:111
"To Thy Chamber Window, Sweet" (Gordon) 83:247
To Transfigure, To Organize (Pasolini)
  See *Trasumanar e organizzar*
"To Tu Fu, Beethoven, Va Dong, Magolwane and All the Great Poets of Humankind" (Kunene) 85:176
"To Urania" (Brodsky) 100:45-6

To Urania: Selected Poems 1965-1985 (*K Uranii*) (Brodsky) 100:41-2, 49-50, 53-5, 58, 61
"To Victor Hugo of My Crow Pluto" (Moore) 8:401; 47:263
"To Violet Lang" (O'Hara) 13:424
To Wake the Dead (Campbell)
  See *The Parasite*
To Walk a Crooked Mile (McGrath) 28:275-76; 59:177-78
"To Westward" (Ciardi) 40:151-52
To What End: Report from Vietnam (Just) 4:266; 27:227-28
"To What Red Hell" (Himes) 108:227
To What Strangers, What Welcome (Cunningham) 3:120-21
To Whom She Will (Jhabvala)
  See *Amrita*
"To Wine" (Bogan) 93:67
"To Wine" (Neruda) 7:259
To X (Fuller) 28:151
"To You" (Koch) 44:251
To Your Scattered Bodies Go (Farmer) 19:165
"To Yvor Winters, 1955" (Gunn) 18:200
"Toad" (Oliver) 98:304
"Toads" (Larkin) 3:275; 13:336; 33:257, 263, 268; 39:336, 342, 345; 64:266, 272, 282
"Toad's Mouth" (Allende) 97:9, 28-9, 32
"Toads Revisited" (Larkin) 5:226; 33:257, 268; 39:341; 64:282
"The Toad's Watch" (Castellanos)
  See "La velada del sapo"
"A Toast" (MacNeice) 53:231
A Toast to the Lord (Jenkins) 52:225-26
Tobacco Road (Caldwell) 1:51; 8:123-24; 14:94-5, 97-9; 50:298-303; 60:44-50, 53, 55-9, 61-7
Tobogán de hambrientos (Cela) 4:97
"Toby Dammit" (Fellini) 16:279-81, 299; 85:63-6, 81-2
Toby Lived Here (Wolitzer) 17:564
Tocaia grande (*Showdown*) (Amado) 106:84-5, 91
"Toccata and Fugue for the Foreigner" (Kristeva) 77:336
"Der Tod der Elsa Baskoleit" ("The Death of Elsa Baskoleit") (Boell) 72:68, 71
Todas las sangres (Arguedas) 10:9; 18:6-7
"Today" (Mahapatra) 33:284
"Today" (O'Hara) 78:345-46, 375-76
"Today a Leaf" (Stern) 40:413
"Today I Was So Happy I Made This Poem" (Wright) 5:518
"Today in the Cafe Trieste" (Tillinghast) 29:416-17
"Today Is Friday" (Hemingway) 13:280
"Today Is the Day" (Shields) 113:408, 432
Today the Struggle (Jones) 10:295; 52:252-53
"Today Will Be a Quiet Day" (Hempel) 39:68-70
Today's a Holiday (Buero Vallejo)
  See *Hoy es fiesta*
"Today's Wish" (Kunene) 85:175
Today's Young Barbarians (Arrabal) 58:17
Todesarten (*Ways of Death*) (Bachmann) 69:36, 59-60, 62
"Todesfuge" ("Death Fugue") (Celan) 82:33, 40, 44-5, 49
"Todo esto por amor" (Cernuda) 54:54
Todo modo (Sciascia) 41:387-88, 393-94
Todos los fuegos el fuego (*All Fires the Fire, and Other Stories*) (Cortazar) 3:115;

5:109; **10**:115; **33**:123; **34**:329

Todos los gatos son pardos (Fuentes) **22**:168-70; **41**:168, 171; **113**:232

"Todos mis pecados" ("All My Sins") (Fuentes) **10**:206

Todos somos fugitivos (*We Are All Fugitives*) (Gironella) **11**:236

"Todtnauberg" (Celan) **53**:74

"To-Em-Mei's 'The Unmoving Cloud'" (Pound) **112**:341, 348

"Toe'Osh: A Laguna Coyote Story" (Silko) **23**:412

"The Toe-Tag" (Muldoon) **72**:273

A toi, pour toujours, ta Marie-Lou (Tremblay) **29**:419, 421-22, 425-26; **102**:360, 362, 370-71, 374-75, 381

The Toilet (Baraka) **5**:44; **14**:43, 46; **33**:54, 59; **115**:29, 47

"Toilet of a Dandy" (Slessor) **14**:492

Toinen taivas ja maa (*Another Heaven and Earth*) (Haavikko) **34**:170

"Token Drunk" (Bukowski) **82**:14

"Toki" (Grace) **56**:111, 118

Tokyo Boshoku (*Tokyo Twilight*) (Ozu) **16**:449, 453

Tokyo Monogatari (*The Tokyo Story*) (Ozu) **16**:446-48, 450, 454, 456

Tokyo Olympiad (Ichikawa) **20**:179-80

The Tokyo Story (Ozu) **16**:446-48, 450, 454, 456

The Tokyo Story (Ozu)
   See *Tokyo Monogatari*

Tokyo Twilight (Ozu)
   See *Tokyo Boshoku*

Tokyo Woes (Friedman) **56**:108-09

The Tokyo-Montana Express (Brautigan) **34**:315; **42**:49-50, 55-6, 60

"Told in the Desert" (Smith) **43**:423, 425

The Toll (Mewshaw) **9**:376

"The Tollund Man" (Heaney) **5**:170; **14**:243; **25**:243, 245, 248; **74**:155; **91**:116

Tolstoy (Troyat) **23**:460-61

Tolstoy and Dostoevsky (Steiner) **24**:423-24, 427

Tolstoy's Dictaphone: Technology and the Muse (Birkerts) **116**:174

"Tom" (Lavin) **99**:319

Tom (Buzo) **61**:53, 59-62, 64-5

Tom (Cummings) **12**:146; **68**:35

"Tom Carroll" (Farrell) **4**:158

"Tom Castro, the Implausible Imposter" (Borges)
   See "El impostor inverosímil Tom Castro"

Tom Fobble's Day (Garner) **17**:147-50

Tom Horn (McGuane) **45**:261-62

"Tom Joad" (Guthrie) **35**:183-84, 189-91

"Tom Mooney" (Hughes) **108**:294

Tom o'Bedlam's Beauties (Reading) **47**:351-52

"Tom Pringle" (Simpson) **7**:426

"Tom Riley" (Delaney) **29**:146

"Tom Rivers" (Gordon) **13**:247; **29**:187; **83**:231

"Tom Thumb Runs Away" (Tournier)
   See "Tom Thumb Runs Away"

"Tom Whipple" (Edmonds) **35**:155

"Toma de conciencia" (Castellanos) **66**:52

Tomas Tranströmer: Selected Poems, 1954-1986 (Transtroemer) **65**:224-27, 235

"Tomato" (Pollitt) **28**:367

"Tomatoes" (Merwin) **45**:272

A Tomb (Benet)
   See *Una tumba*

"The Tomb at Akr Çaar" (Pound) **4**:408

"A Tomb for Boris Davidovich" (Kis) **57**:241

A Tomb for Boris Davidovich (Kis) **57**:240-44, 249-53

"The Tomb of Heracles" (McAuley) **45**:249

The Tomb of Ligeia (Towne) **87**:355-56

"The Tomb of Penthesilia" (Hope) **51**:220

"The Tomb of Pletone" (Forster) **45**:131-32

The Tomb of the Kings (Hebert)
   See *Le tombeau des rois*

Tomb Tapper (Blish) **14**:86

Tombe (Cixous) **92**:90

"Le tombeau des rois" (Hebert) **4**:219; **29**:228-30, 236-38

Le tombeau des rois (*The Tomb of the Kings*) (Hebert) **13**:268; **29**:227-30, 232, 236-38

Le tombeau des secrets (Char) **11**:114

Le Tombeau hindou (Lang) **103**:86-9

"Les tombeaux de Ravenne" (Bonnefoy) **58**:58

The Tombs of Atuan (Le Guin) **13**:347; **22**:266, 271; **71**:180-82, 184, 188-89, 191, 196, 198, 200-01

"Tombstone Blues" (Dylan) **4**:149; **77**:161, 180

"Tombstones" (Ammons) **57**:53, 55-6

"Tom-Dobbin" (Gunn) **32**:208

Tommy (Russell) **16**:547-59

Tommy (Townshend) **17**:525-27, 529-31, 533-38, 540; **42**:379

"The Tommy Crans" (Bowen) **22**:65, 67

Tommy Gallagher's Crusade (Farrell) **66**:130

The Tommyknockers (King) **61**:328-30; **113**:369, 388-93

"Tomoda to Matsunaga no hanashi" ("A Story of Tomoda and Matsunaga") (Tanizaki) **14**:527

Tomodachi, enemoto takekai (*Friends*) (Abe) **8**:1; **81**:295, 297

"Tomorrow" (Fearing) **51**:106

"Tomorrow" (McCartney) **35**:280

"Tomorrow" (Strand) **71**:286

Tomorrow! (Foote) **51**:131

Tomorrow! (Wylie) **43**:467-68

"Tomorrow and Tomorrow" (Farrell) **4**:158

Tomorrow and Yesterday (Boell)
   See *Haus ohne Hüter*

The Tomorrow Boy (Chislett) **34**:146

The Tomorrow File (Sanders) **41**:378

"Tomorrow Is a Long Time" (Dylan) **77**:172

Tomorrow Morning, Faustus! (Richards) **14**:453

Tomorrow the Warriors (Alegria)
   See *Mañana los guerreros*

Tomorrow to Fresh Woods (Davies) **23**:143, 145

"Tomorrow, Tomorrow" (Walcott) **67**:361

Tomorrow Will Be Better (Smith) **19**:423

Tomorrow Will Come (Almedingen) **12**:1, 3-4

"Tomorrow You Shall Reap" (Mphahlele) **25**:336

"Tomorrow's Arrangement" (Gardam) **43**:170

The Tomorrow-Tamer, and Other Stories (Laurence) **13**:341; **50**:314-15, 319; **62**:278-79

Tomorrow-Today (Kureishi) **64**:246

Tom's Midnight Garden (Pearce) **21**:281, 283-87, 289

The Tom-Walker (Sandoz) **28**:407

"Ton père. Ta soeur" (Sarraute) **31**:383

Tone Clusters (Oates) **108**:376

"Tong Raa" (p'Bitek) **96**:307

"Tongue" (Herbert) **9**:271

Tongue of Flame: The Life of Lydia Maria Child (Meltzer) **26**:297

The Tongue Set Free: Remembrance of a European Childhood (Canetti)
   See *Die gerettete Zunge: Geschichte einer Jugend*

"Tongues" (Govier) **51**:166

"Tongues" (Wright) **6**:580

Tongues (Shepard) **41**:407

The Tongues of Angels (Price) **63**:339-41

"Tongues of Fire" (Smith) **73**:353, 357-59

"Tongues of Men" (Steiner) **24**:433

"Tongues of Men and of Angels" (Goyen) **40**:217

"Tongues of Stone" (Plath) **11**:451

Toni (Renoir) **20**:304, 309-10

To-Night at 8:30 (Coward) **51**:69

"Tonight at Noon" (Weller) **26**:443

"Tonight I Hear the Water Flowing" (Mahapatra) **33**:281

"Tonight Is a Favor to Holly" (Hempel) **39**:68-9

"Tonight My Body" (Moure) **88**:218

"Tonight the Famous Psychiatrist" (Simpson) **7**:428

Tonight We Love (Linney) **51**:263

Tonight's the Night (Young) **17**:573-76, 580, 582-83

The Tontine (Costain) **30**:97-8

"Tonton-Macoute" (Guillen) **48**:159

"Tony's Story" (Silko) **23**:408; **74**:322, 346, 349; **114**:315-16

"Too Bad" (Parker) **68**:326, 335, 338

Too Bad about the Haines Girl (Sherburne) **30**:362

Too Bad Galahad (Cohen) **19**:115

"Too Dear" (Fuller) **62**:193

Too Dear for My Possessing (Johnson) **1**:161; **27**:214-15

Too Early Lilac (Almedingen) **12**:8

Too Far to Go: The Maples Stories (*Your Lover Just Called: Stories of Joan and Richard Maple*) (Updike) **13**:563; **43**:433

Too Far to Walk (Hersey) **40**:236-37, 240

Too Great a Vine (Clarke) **9**:167

"Too Happy, Happy Tree" (Ashbery) **77**:62, 69

"Too High" (Wonder) **12**:657

"Too Late" (Jin) **109**:54

"Too Late" (Thomas) **48**:376

Too Late (Dixon) **52**:96-7, 101

Too Late American Boyhood Blues (Busch) **47**:61-4

Too Late Blues (Cassavetes) **20**:45

"The Too Late Born" (MacLeish) **68**:272

"Too Late for Prayin'" (Lightfoot) **26**:280, 282-83

Too Late for the Mashed Potato (Mortimer) **28**:285

Too Late the Phalarope (Paton) **4**:395; **25**:357-63; **106**:288-89, 292-94, 296-97, 300, 304-06

Too Loud a Solitude (Hrabal)
   See *Une trop bruyante solitude*

"Too Many Mornings" (Sondheim) **30**:387

"Too Many People" (McCartney) **12**:371

"Too Much" (Moore) **47**:265

Too Much Flesh and Jabez (Dowell) **60**:97-9, 101

"Too Much Information" (Police, The) **26**:365

Too Much Is Too Much (Cendrars) **106**:177-78

"Too Much Monkey Business" (Berry) **17**:53,

55

Too Much of Everything (Wylie)　43:463
"Too Much of Nothing" (Dylan)　77:178
"Too Much on My Mind" (Davies)　21:88-9
"Too Much Trouble" (Amis)　40:43, 45
"Too Nice a Day to Die" (Woolrich)　77:390, 392, 396
"Too Sensitive" (Bukowski)　41:74; 108:85
"Too Vague" (Fuller)　62:193
Tool of the Trade (Haldeman)　61:181-84
Tools of Modern Biology (Berger)　12:38
"Toome" (Heaney)　7:148; 14:242-43; 25:245
"The Toome Road" (Heaney)　74:163; 91:101, 117
"The Tooth" (Jackson)　60:212, 235
"Tooth" (Swan)　69:363
Tooth Imprints on a Corn Dog (Leyner)　92:292-94
The Tooth of Crime (Shepard)　4:490-91; 6:496-97; 17:441-44, 448; 41:406, 410, 412; 44:270
"Toothache" (Sargeson)　31:365, 374
Tootsie (Gelbart)　61:146-47
Top Girls (Churchill)　31:87-9; 55:122, 126-27
The Top of the Hill (Shaw)　23:399
"Top of the Pops" (Davies)　21:91
"Top Rock" (Stern)　40:408
Top Soil (Rosenblatt)　15:448
"The Top Ten Best Sellers" (Vidal)　8:528
Topaz (Hitchcock)　16:348, 353
Topaz (Uris)　7:492; 32:432-33
"The Topic" (Arghezi)
　See "Subiectul"
Topoemas (Paz)　65:199
"The Topography of History" (McGrath)　59:180
Topolek moi v krasnoi kosynke (*My Little Poplar in the Red Kerchief; My RedKerchiefed Young Poplar; Pretty Poplar in a Red Kerchief; To Have and to Lose*) (Aitmatov)　71:3, 13-14, 16, 33
Topologie d'une cité fantôme (*Topology of a Phantom City*) (Robbe-Grillet)　8:453-54; 10:438; 14:462; 43:361-62, 367-68
Topology of a Phantom City (Robbe-Grillet)
　See *Topologie d'une cité fantôme*
Tops and Bottoms (Streatfeild)　21:395
"Topsy Turvy" (Powys)　46:325
Tor Ha-pela'ot (*The Age of Amazement; The Age of Wonders*) (Appelfeld)　23:35, 38; 47:2-5
The Torch in My Ear (Canetti)
　See *Die Fackel im Ohr: Lebensgeschichte 1921-1931*
"Torch Procession" (Celan)
　See "Fackelzug"
"Torch Song" (Cheever)　15:127, 130; 64:65
Torch Song (Roiphe)　9:455-56
Torch Song Trilogy (Fierstein)　33:152-57
Torches (Tate)　25:427
"Torguyut arbuzami" (Voznesensky)　15:555
Torment (Bergman)
　See *Hets*
"Tormento del amor" (Aleixandre)　9:12
"The Torments of Conscience" (Yevtushenko)　3:547
"Tormer's Lay" (Le Guin)　22:265
"The Torn Cloth" (Duncan)　41:129
Torn Curtain (Hitchcock)　16:347-48, 353
Torn Curtain (Moore)　90:262
"The Torn Sky" (Jordan)　114:146
"Torna Zeffiro" (Ekelof)　27:119

"Tornado" (Stafford)　29:380
"Tornado Blues" (Brown)　23:96; 59:266
"Tornant al pais" (Pasolini)　106:229
"Toronto Means the Meeting Place" (Crase)　58:162
"Toronto the Ugly" (Lane)　25:284
"Torpid Smoke" (Nabokov)　3:354
"The Torque" (Forster)　3:161
Torquemada (Fast)　23:158
"La torre" (Olson)　29:334
Le torrent (*The Torrent*) (Hebert)　4:219-20; 13:266-67; 29:229-31, 237-38, 240
The Torrent (Hebert)
　See *Le torrent*
A Torrent of Faces (Blish)　14:85
The Torrents of Spring: A Romantic Novel in Honor of the Passing of a Great Race (Hemingway)　6:227; 8:283; 30:191; 39:401, 403; 41:200; 61:192
"Torridge" (Trevor)　14:536-37; 71:323; 116:374-75
Torse Three (Middleton)　13:387
"Torso" (Brodsky)　36:76
Törst (*Thirst*) (Bergman)　16:51, 66, 72; 72:40, 52
The Tortilla Curtain (Boyle)　90:64-5
Tortilla Flat (Steinbeck)　1:325; 5:406-07; 9:513-14, 517-18, 520; 13:530-31; 21:366, 368, 381-82, 386, 389-91; 34:405, 409-10, 413-14; 45:370, 373-74; 59:317, 322, 334, 351; 75:353, 357
Tortuga (Anaya)　23:26
"Tortuous Road" (Arghezi)
　See "Cale frînta"
"Torture" (Atwood)　25:65
"Torture" (Ortese)
　See "Supplizio"
"The Torturer" (Durrenmatt)
　See "Der Folterknecht"
"Tortures" (Szymborska)　99:195, 206
"Tosca" (Allende)　97:12
Tossing and Turning (Updike)　23:475-76; 43:429-30
Total Eclipse (Hampton)　4:211
"The Total Library" (Borges)　48:44
Total Loss Farm: A Year in the Life (Mungo)　72:288-92
"Total Love" (Aleixandre)　36:29
"Total Stranger" (Cozzens)　92:202
Totalitarianism (Arendt)
　See *The Origins of Totalitarianism*
"The Totally Rich" (Brunner)　8:108; 10:77
"Totem" (King)　89:98
"Totem" (Plath)　9:426-27, 433; 17:365; 111:182, 205
Le totémisme aujourd'hui (Levi-Strauss)　38:294, 305
Das Totenschiff (*The Death Ship*) (Traven)　8:517-23; 11:535-39
"Totentanz: The Coquette" (Hope)　3:250; 51:220
"Ein totes Kind spricht" (Sachs)　98:364
"Tou Wan Speaks to Her Husband, Liu Sheng" (Dove)　81:135, 137
"The Touch" (Blackburn)　9:100
The Touch (Bergman)
　See *Beröringen*
Touch (Gunn)　3:215; 6:221; 32:208, 211; 81:180
The Touch (*The Contaminated Man*) (Keyes)　80:164
Touch (Leonard)　71:217, 221
Touch and Go (Fisher)　76:342

Touch and Go (Kerr)　22:254
Touch and Go (Poole)　17:373
"Touch Me" (Morrison)　17:289
Touch Not the Cat (Stewart)　7:468; 35:394
"A Touch of Autumn in the Air" (O'Faolain)　32:343; 70:312
A Touch of Chill (Aiken)　35:18-19
A Touch of Danger (Jones)　3:262
Touch of Evil (Welles)　20:435, 442, 449, 452; 80:386, 388-89, 391, 393, 395-96, 414
"A Touch of Gothic" (Gardam)　43:169
A Touch of Infinity: Thirteen New Stories of Fantasy and Science Fiction (Fast)　23:159
A Touch of Magic (Cavanna)　12:100
"A Touch of Snow" (Davidson)　13:168
Touch: Selected Poems, 1960-1970 (Bowering)　47:21-2
Touch the Water, Touch the Wind (Oz)　5:334-35; 8:435
"Touched" (Broumas)　73:15
"The Touching" (Livesay)　79:337, 343, 350-51
Touching (Neufeld)　17:308-09
Touching Bottom (Tesich)　40:421
"Touch-up Man" (Komunyakaa)　94:240
"The Tough Guy" (Ferber)　93:138
Tough Guys Don't Dance (Mailer)　39:422, 424; 74:207-10, 218-19, 224, 336
Toujours (Audiberti)　38:21
Toujours Provence (Mayle)　89:145-47, 149-51, 153-54
"The Tour" (Plath)　14:427; 51:343; 111:172-74
"La tour" (Theriault)　79:407
"Tour 5" (Hayden)　37:157-58
Tour of Duty (Dos Passos)　25:145
"Touris" (Bennett)　28:27
"The Tourist and the Geisha" (Enright)　4:154
"The Tourist and the Town" (Rich)　7:368; 73:330
"The Tourist from Syracuse" (Justice)　102:279-80
"Tourist Pitch for Recife" (Cabral de Melo Neto)
　See "Pregão turístico do Recife"
"Tourist Proclamation For Recife" (Cabral de Melo Neto)
　See "Pregão turístico do Recife"
"Tourist Promotion" (Enright)　31:150
"Tourists" (Amichai)　116:127
"The Tourists" (McGrath)　59:178
A Tourist's Guide to Ireland (O'Flaherty)　34:356
"Tourists of the Revolution" (Enzensberger)　43:148
"Tourists on Paros" (Ryan)　65:209, 216
Tourmaline (Stow)　23:433-35; 48:356, 360
Tournament (Foote)　75:230-31, 236-37, 240
The Tournament (Vansittart)　42:392
"Tournesol" ("Sunflower") (Breton)　54:27
Tours of the Black Clock (Erickson)　64:139-42, 144-45
Tous contre tous (*All against All; One against Another*) (Adamov)　4:5; 25:12-13, 17-18, 20
Tous les hommes sont mortels (*All Men Are Mortal*) (Beauvoir)　1:19; 8:60; 31:40-1; 44:343, 345, 350; 71:48-9, 56, 67-8, 85
"toussaint" (Shange)　25:402
Toussaint l'Ouveture: La Révolution Française et la problème colonial (Cesaire)　19:96
Tout compte fait (*All Said and Done*) (Beauvoir)　4:47-9; 8:58, 63; 44:343, 349-50; 71:79-

80, 82-3

Tout l'or du monde (Clair) 20:65-6

Tout va bien (Godard) 20:146-47, 150

"Toute à ce besoin d'évasion" (Damas) 84:180

Toute la mémoire du monde (Resnais) 16:496, 503, 506, 510

"Toutes Directions" (Howard) 7:164

Toutes les femmes sont fatales (*All Women Are Fatal*) (Mauriac) 9:363

"Toward" (Loewinsohn) 52:284

"Toward a Definition of Marriage" (Van Duyn) 63:435, 440; 116:413, 426, 429

"Toward a More Feminist Criticism" (Rich) 73:322

Toward a New Life (Nakos) 29:322-23

"Toward a New Yiddish" (Ozick) 28:352; 62:349

"Toward a Poetic Art" (Queneau) 42:337

Toward a Radical Middle: Fourteen Pieces of Reporting and Criticism (Adler) 31:12-13

Toward a Recognition of Androgyny (Heilbrun) 25:253-54

"Toward a Successful Marriage" (Gordon) 26:139

"Toward a Woman-Centered University" (Rich) 18:448

"Toward an Organic Philosophy" (Rexroth) 22:345; 49:280, 284-85; 112:376, 390, 397, 404

"Toward Certain Divorce" (Bell) 8:65; 31:47

"Toward Clairvoyance" (Fulton) 52:158

"Toward Nightfall" (Simic) 49:341

Toward the African Revolution: Political Essays (Fanon)
 See *Pour la révolution africaine: Ecrits politiques*

"Toward the Imagination of Buffoonery and Regeneration" (Oe)
 See "Doke to saisei e no sozoryku"

"Toward the Island" (Celan)
 See "Inselhin"

"Toward the Jurassic Age" (Alegria) 75:36, 38-9

"Toward the Piraeus" (H. D.) 73:121

Toward Yoknapatawpha and Beyond (Brooks)
 See *William Faulkner: Toward Yoknapatawpha and Beyond*

Towards a Better Life (Burke) 2:87-8

Towards a Critique of a Political Economy of Signs (Baudrillard)
 See *Pour une critique de l'économie politique du signe*

Towards a New Novel (Robbe-Grillet) 4:449

Towards a New Poetry (Wakoski) 40:452-53, 458

"Towards a Philosophy of the Act" (Bakhtin)
 See "K filosofii postupka"

"Towards a Theory of Treason" (Enzensberger) 43:149

"Towards Autumn" (Hacker) 72:182

Towards the Human (Smith) 64:400

"Towards the Imminent Days" (Murray) 40:335-36, 340

Towards the Last Spike (Pratt) 19:376, 380, 383-84

Towards the Mountain (Paton) 25:361, 364; 55:311, 313-14; 106:299, 305

Towards Zero (Christie) 8:142; 12:114, 125; 48:72; 110:133

"The Tower" (Neruda) 7:261

The Tower (Vesaas)
 See *Tårnet*

The Tower (Weiss) 15:563; 51:387

"The Tower beyond Tragedy" (Jeffers) 54:233, 235, 237-38, 246, 248; 11:304-06, 310

The Tower Beyond Tragedy (Jeffers) 54:251

The Tower of Babel (Arrabal) 58:17

The Tower of Babel (Canetti)
 See *Die Blendung*

The Tower of Babel (Merton) 83:396

Tower of Ivory (MacLeish) 68:285

The Tower Struck by Lightning (Arrabal) 58:23-4

Towers of Healing (Oe)
 See *Chiryo-to*

The Towers of Silence (Scott)
 See *The Raj Quartet*

"The Towers of Toron" (Delany) 14:144

"Town" (Soto) 80:287, 294

The Town (Faulkner) 6:176; 14:178-79

The Town (Richter) 30:312-15, 318-19, 324-25, 328

"Town and Country Lovers" (Gordimer) 18:190-91

Town and Country Matters (Hollander) 5:187; 8:302

The Town and the City (Kerouac) 2:226; 3:264; 5:214-15; 14:304; 29:270, 272; 61:310

The Town beyond the Wall (Wiesel)
 See *La ville de la chance*

Town Burning (Williams) 14:581, 583

"A Town Called Malice" (Weller) 26:447

The Town Cats, and Other Tales (Alexander) 35:28

"Town Center in December" (Corn) 33:118

"The Town Clerk's Views" (Betjeman) 6:68; 43:37, 40, 42

"Town Crier Exclusive, Confessions of a Princess Manque: How Royals Found Me Unsuitable to Marry Their Larry" (Elkin) 91:218-19

"The Town Dump" (Nemerov) 2:308

"Town Edge" (Shapcott) 38:402

Town in Darkness (Johnson)
 See *Stad i mörker*

"A Town in Eastern Oregon" (Davis) 49:91

Town in Light (Johnson)
 See *Stad i ljus*

Town in Tears (Seifert)
 See *Mesto v slzách*

Town Life (Parini) 54:363-64

A Town like Alice (Shute)
 See *The Legacy*

"The Town of Hill" (Hall) 37:147

The Town of Hill (Hall) 37:146-47

"Town Report, 1942" (Cowley) 39:460

The Town Scold (Sherwin) 15:480

"Townend, 1976" (Davie) 31:112, 118

"Townies" (Dubus) 36:145; 97:201, 204, 206, 208, 223

The Townsman (Buck) 11:76

Toxique (Sagan) 17:424

A Toy Epic (Humphreys) 47:180, 186-87

The Toy Fair (Moss) 7:247; 45:292

"The Toy Pilgrim" (Cohen) 19:113

"Toyland" (Fisher) 25:158-59

Toys in a Field (Komunyakaa) 94:236

Toys in the Attic (Hellman) 2:187; 4:220; 18:224; 34:349, 351-52; 44:529; 52:191, 202

Toys in the Attic (Hill) 26:204

"Toys of Tamison" (Norton) 12:467

"Tra notte e giorno" (Luzi) 13:353

"The Trace" (Fisher) 25:159

"The Trace of Being" (Lane) 25:286

"Traceleen at Dawn" (Gilchrist) 48:120, 122

Tracer (Barthelme) 3-4, 7, 11-12, 20

"Traces of Living Things" (Niedecker) 42:296-97

The Traces of Thomas Hariot (Rukeyser) 6:479; 15:459-60

Tracey and Hepburn (Kanin) 22:231

Track 29 (Potter) 58:400; 86:346

"The Track Meet" (Schwartz) 45:355-56; 87:334

The Track of the Cat (Clark) 28:77-84

"Tracking Level" (Ellison) 42:131

"Tracks" (Montague) 13:390

"Tracks" (Transtroemer) 65:223, 226, 228

Tracks (Erdrich) 54:170-73

"The Tracks of My Tears" (Robinson) 21:344, 347-48, 351

"Tractor" (Hughes) 37:174

Tractor (Ritsos) 31:324

"The Tractor in Spring" (Levi) 41:244, 248

Trade Wind (Kaye) 28:199, 202

"Trade Winds" (Cortazar) 33:124

"A Traded Car" (Updike) 15:540-41

Trader to the Stars (Anderson) 15:11

"The Traders" (Asimov) 26:63

Il tradimento (Landolfi) 49:216

Tradition and Poetic Structure (Cunningham) 31:101, 103

"Tradition and the Individual Talent" (Eliot) 6:160, 164; 13:195-96; 15:213; 24:159, 163, 165, 170-72, 174-75, 178, 180-83, 187; 34:528; 41:155, 157; 55:347, 356; 57:206; 113:218

"Tradition and the Individual Talent: The Bratislava Spiccato" (Mathews) 52:308, 312-13

"Tradition and the West Indian Novel" (Harris) 25:204-05

"Tradition, Society, and the Arts" (McAuley) 45:251

Tradition, the Writer, and Society: Critical Essays (Harris) 25:204

Traditional Hungarian Songs (Snodgrass) 18:494

"Traditional Songs" (Shapcott) 38:404

"Traditions" (Heaney) 7:148; 14:242; 74:157

"Traducción do James Jogeo, la ultima hojo de Ulises" (Borges) 4:71

Traduction et introduction à l'origine de la géométrie d'Edmund Husserl (*Edmund Husserl's "Origin of Geometry": An Introduction*) (Derrida) 87:72

Traed mewn cyffion (*Feet in Chains*) (Roberts) 15:445

"Traffic" (Transtroemer) 65:223

El tragaluz (*The Basement Window*) (Buero Vallejo) 15:98, 101-02; 46:95-6

"The Tragedians" (Prokosch) 48:309

"La tragédie du langage" (Ionesco) 41:225

La tragédie du Roi Christophe (*The Tragedy of King Christophe*) (Cesaire) 19:96, 99; 32:112; 112:3-4, 7, 21, 28-9

"Tragedy" (Graham) 48:149

"A Tragedy" (Lavin) 4:281

Tragedy and Social Evolution (Figes) 31:164-65

"Tragedy and the Common Man" (Miller) 6:333; 10:346; 15:375; 26:315-16; 47:251

"Tragedy and the Whole Truth" (Huxley) 79:310

"The Tragedy at Maradon Manor" (Christie) 110:111

The Tragedy of King Christophe (Cesaire)
See *La tragédie du Roi Christophe*
The Tragedy of Nan, and Other Plays (Masefield) 47:225, 229
The Tragedy of Pompey the Great (Masefield) 11:358
"The Tragedy of Taliped Decanus" (Barth) 9:64, 69
"The Tragedy of the Leaves" (Bukowski) 41:65; 108:110
The Tragedy of X (Queen) 3:421; 11:459
The Tragedy of Y (Queen) 3:421; 11:459
The Tragedy of Z (Queen) 11:459
"The Tragic Fallacy" (Krutch) 24:282
Tragic Ground (Caldwell) 14:97; 50:300; 60:54-5, 66
"The Tragic Tryst" (MacDiarmid) 11:334
Tragic Ways of Killing a Woman 65:327
La traicion de Rita Hayworth (*Betrayed by Rita Hayworth*) (Puig) 3:407; 5:354-56; 10:420; 28:369-72; 65:268, 271-73
Trail Blazer of the Seas (Latham) 12:322
"Trail Crew Camp at Bear Valley, 9000 Feet. Northern Sierra—White Bone and Threads of Snowmelt Water" (Snyder) 5:394
Trail Driving Days (Brown) 47:36-7
"The Trail into Kansas" (Merwin) 13:386
Trailerpark (Banks) 37:26-7; 72:4, 9, 11, 14, 17
"The Train" (Le Guin) 45:219
"The Train" (Salinas) 90:326
"The Train" (Walcott) 25:452
The Train (Simenon)
See *Le train*
Le train (*The Train*) (Simenon) 1:397; 47:379
Le train bleu (Cocteau) 15:134
"Train for Dublin" (MacNeice) 53:231, 234
"The Train from Bordeaux" (Duras) 100:120
"Train from Rhodesia" (Gordimer) 18:184
"Train in Vain" (Clash) 30:46-7, 52
"Train Journey" (Wright) 53:419, 431
A Train of Powder (West) 7:525-26; 9:561, 563; 50:404
"Train Ride" (Berrigan) 37:46
"Train Rising out of the Sea" (Ashbery) 15:34; 41:38
The Train Robbers (Read) 25:376-77
"Train Song" (Bogan) 93:77
"Train Time" (Bogan) 46:90
Train to Pakistan (Singh) 11:505-07
"Train Tune" (Bogan) 93:65, 78
"The Train Was on Time" (Boell)
See "Der Zug war pünktlich"
Train Whistle Guitar (Murray) 73:226-29, 231, 235-36, 238-42, 244
"The Trainee 1914" (Murray) 40:333
"The Trains" (Aickman) 57:4, 6-7
"The Trains" (Wright) 53:427
Traité du pianiste (Bonnefoy) 58:57
Traité du style (*Treatise on Style*) (Aragon) 22:37, 41
"The Traitor" (Maugham) 67:216
The Traitor (Wouk) 38:446-47
"Traitors" (Stern) 40:408
The Traitors (Forman) 21:117, 123
Traitor's Purse (Allingham) 19:16, 17
"Traits and Stories" (Montague) 46:270
"Trakat poetycki" ("Treatise on Poetry") (Milosz) 56:235; 82:297-300, 306
"Tralala" (Selby) 8:475-76
"La trama" (Borges) 6:90
La trama celeste (*The Celestial Plot*) (Bioy Casares) 88:60

"Tramp" (Thomas) 48:376
"The Tramp at Piraeus" (Naipaul) 105:157
"A Tramp at the Door" (Roy) 14:469
"La trampa" (Parra) 102:337-38
La trampa (*Los mercaderes*) (Matute) 11:364-68
"Trampled under Foot" (Page and Plant) 12:477, 480, 482
"The Tranced" (Roethke) 3:433
"Tranquil River" (Milosz) 11:378
"Transaction" (Updike) 15:547
Trans-Atlantic (Gombrowicz)
See *Trans-Atlantyk*
Transatlantic Blues (Sheed) 10:472-74; 53:336, 339
A Transatlantic Tunnel, Hurrah! (Harrison)
See *Tunnel through the Deeps*
Trans-Atlantyk (*Trans-Atlantic*) (Gombrowicz) 7:124; 49:122, 129-31
Transbluency (Baraka) 115:38
"Transcedental Etude" (Rich) 18:450; 36:376
Transcendent Censorship
See *Cenzura transcendenta*
"Transcendental Experience in Relation to Religion and Psychosis" (Laing) 95:178
"Transcendental Meditation" (Wilson) 12:641
Transcendental Style in Film (Schrader) 26:385, 387
"Transcendental View" 75:78
"Transcending Destiny" (Ellison) 42:131
"Transcontinental" (Derleth) 31:136
Trans-Europ-Express (Robbe-Grillet) 6:466; 14:457
"Transfer of Title" (Phillips) 28:363-64
The Transfiguration of Benno Blimpie (Innaurato) 21:190, 192; 60:199-202, 204, 206-07
The Transformation (MacBeth) 5:265
Transformation: Understanding the Three Levels of Masculine Consciousness 70:426
"Transformations" (Engel) 36:160
"Transformations" (Harjo) 83:269
"Transformations" (Oates) 108:354
"Transformations" (Seifert)
See "Promeny"
"Transformations" (Waddington) 28:438
Transformations (Sexton) 2:392; 4:482-83; 6:494; 8:483; 10:468-69; 15:470-72; 53:314, 319, 321, 323
"Transformed Nonconformist" (King) 83:347
Transformer (Reed) 21:304-06, 312
"Trans-Global Express" (Weller) 26:447
The Transgressors (Thompson) 69:384
"Transient Barracks" (Jarrell) 9:299
"Transit" (Wilbur) 53:413
Transit (Seghers) 7:408
"Transit Bed" (Calvino) 33:102
"Transit of the Gods" (Raine) 45:337
The Transit of Venus (Hazzard) 18:218-20
"Transit Passengers" (Gardam) 43:169
A Transit to Narcissus (Mailer) 111:135
"The Transition" (Grace) 56:111
"Transition" (Okigbo) 84:306-07, 309
Transitional Poem (Day Lewis) 6:128; 10:126-27, 131, 133
"The Translatability of Poetry" (Davie) 10:124
"Translation" (Fuller) 28:150, 159
"Translation" (Strand) 71:280, 287-88
"Translation" (Wheelock) 14:570
"Translations" (Rich) 7:372
Translations (Friel) 42:171-74; 59:146-49; 115:221-24, 227-31, 233, 235, 237, 239-

48, 250, 257
Translations (Tomlinson) 45:405
"Translations from the English" (Starbuck) 53:355
"The Translators of the 1001 Nights" (Borges) 83:163
The Transmigration of Timothy Archer (*Timothy Archer*) (Dick) 72:114, 119-20
"The Transmutation into English" (Rakosi) 47:347
"Transparencies" (L'Heureux) 52:273
"Transparencies" (Stevenson) 33:382-83
Transparencies (Sherwin) 15:480
"Transparent Garments" (Hass) 18:213
The Transparent Sea (Dudek) 11:159
Transparent Things (Nabokov) 2:302-03, 305; 3:353-54; 6:351, 355; 8:410, 412, 416, 418; 15:393-95
"Transparently" (Ezekiel) 61:105, 108
"Les transparents" (Char) 9:161
"Transplanting" (Roethke) 101:295
Transplants (Macdonald) 13:355-56; 19:290-91
"Transport" (Meredith) 55:192
Transport from Paradise (Lustig) 56:184
"The Transport of Slaves from Maryland to Mississippi" (Dove) 81:137
"Transportation" (Oe) 86:227
Transsiberian (Cendrars)
See "Prose du transsibérien et de la petite Jeanne de France"
"The Trap" (Tuohy) 37:429
The Trap (Jacobson) 14:289
Trap for Cinderella (Japrisot)
See *Piege pour Cendrillon*
"Trap Lines" (King) 89:97
"Trapped Dingo" (Wright) 53:418, 427
Trapped in the Arctic (Berton) 104:61
"The Trapper" (Klappert) 57:259
Trappers (Williams) 33:442
"The Trappist Cemetery, Gethsemani" (Merton) 83:393
Traps (Churchill) 31:84
The Traps (Duerrenmatt)
See *Der Nihilist*
"Tras os montes" (Sissman) 18:488, 490
"Trash" (Thomas) 107:338, 340, 342
"Trash" (Williams) 33:441
Trash 78:2-3, 5-7, 9, 11
"Trashabet" (Redgrove) 41:354
"Trastevere" (Denby) 48:82
Trasumanar e organizzar (*To Transfigure, To Organize*) (Pasolini) 106:253, 265-66
Tratados en la habana (*Havana Treatises*) (Lezama Lima) 4:288; 101:121
"Il tratto di Apelle" ("Apellesova cherta"; "The Line of Apelles"; "The Mark of Apelles"; "The Sign of Apelles"; "The Stroke of Apelles") (Pasternak) 7:293; 10:387; 18:385
Träume (*Dreams*) (Eich) 15:203-05
Travaux d'approche (Butor) 3:93
"Travel" (Avison) 97:123
"Travel" (Colwin) 23:129
"Travel from Home" (Bullins) 7:37
Travel Notes (Cendrars) 106:190-91, 194, 198
"A Travel Piece" (Atwood) 25:62
"Travel Report" (Wolf) 58:421
"The Travel Sack" (Elytis)
See "Traveling Bag"
"The Traveler" (Stegner) 49:351; 81:346
The Traveler (Connelly) 7:57
"Traveler, Conjuror, Journeyman" (Page)

18:379
Traveler from a Small Kingdom (Neville) 12:450-51
The Traveler in Black (Brunner) 8:106
Travelers (Jhabvala)
    See *A New Dominion*
"Traveler's Song" (White) 39:376
Traveler's Tree (Tzara)
    See *L'arbre des voyageurs*
"Travelin Man" (Matthiessen) 64:321, 323-24
"Travelin' Man" (Seger) 35:381, 383
"Traveling Bag" ("The Travel Sack") (Elytis) 100:171, 178, 187
"The Traveling Companion" (Padilla) 38:349, 352
"Traveling Home: High School Reunion" (Theroux) 46:401
"Traveling IV" (Hamburger) 5:159
The Traveling Lady (Foote) 51:130
"Traveling Light" (Fulton) 52:160
Traveling on Credit (Halpern) 14:231-32
"The Traveling Photographer: Circa 1880" (Smith) 42:349
"Traveling Salesman" (Dybek) 114:62-3, 67
"Traveling through the Dark" (Stafford) 29:382
Traveling through the Dark (Stafford) 4:520; 7:460, 462; 29:384
"Traveling with You" (Oates) 3:359
Travelingue (Ayme) 11:22-3
"The Traveller" (Berryman) 13:76
"The Traveller" (Livesay) 79:332
"A Traveller" (Paulin) 37:352
"The Traveller" (Reid) 33:350
"The Traveller" (Stevenson) 33:379
The Traveller and His Child (Tindall) 7:474
"Traveller, If You Come to the Spa" (Boell)
    See "Wanderer, kommst du nach Spa..."
"Traveller, If You Go to Spa" (Boell)
    See "Wanderer, kommst du nach Spa..."
"A Traveller in Time" (Young) 5:524
Traveller without Luggage (Anouilh)
    See *Le voyageur sans bagage*
"The Travellers" (Aldiss) 14:13
"Traveller's Curse after Misdirection" (Graves) 45:169
Traveller's Litany (Baxter) 14:61
"Travellin' Man" (McFadden) 48:255
"Travelling" (Merwin) 88:194
"Travelling" (Simic) 9:481
Travelling (Hamburger) 5:158; 14:234
Travelling behind Glass (Stevenson) 7:462-63; 33:382
The Travelling Entertainer (Jolley) 46:213
"Travelling Even Farther North" (Astley) 41:49
Travelling North (Williamson) 56:435-36
Travelling People (Johnson) 6:262; 9:301
"Travelling to My Second Marriage on the Day of the First Moonshot" (Nye) 42:305
A Travelling Woman (Wain) 2:457; 46:409-10
"Travelogue" (Reading) 47:350
"Travelogue in a Shooting Gallery" (Fearing) 51:110
Travels (Amichai) 57:41-2
Travels (Crichton) 54:75-6
Travels (Merwin) 88:209-13
"Travels in Georgia" (McPhee) 36:296
"Travels in Hyperreality" (Eco) 60:111
Travels in Hyperreality (Eco) 60:111-13, 124
Travels in Nihilon (Sillitoe) 3:448; 57:397
"Travels of a Latter-Day Benjamin of Tudela"

(Amichai)
    See "Mas'ot Binyamin ha'aharon mitudela"
The Travels of Jaimie McPheeters (Taylor) 14:533-35
The Travels of Marrakesh (Canetti)
    See *Die Stimmen von Marrakesch: Aufzeichnungen nach einer Reise*
"Travels of the Last Benjamin Tudela" (Amichai)
    See "Mas'ot Binyamin ha'aharon mitudela"
Travels through New England (Gray) 49:147
Travels to the Enu: Stories of a Shipwreck (Lind) 27:270-72; 82:143-44
Travels with Charley in Search of America (Steinbeck) 5:405; 21:370, 392-93; 34:409; 45:382; 59:353
Travels with My Aunt (Greene) 3:208, 211, 214; 14:219; 27:173; 72:164; 70:292-93, 295
Travels with Myself and Another (Gellhorn) 14:196; 60:193, 195
Traversée de la mangrove (*Crossing the Mangrove*) (Conde) 92:115-26, 132
Travesties (Stoppard) 4:527; 5:412-13; 8:501-04; 15:519-21, 524; 29:394, 397, 399-401, 403, 406; 34:280-81; 63:404; 91:187, 189
Travesty (Hawkes) 7:143-45; 9:269; 15:278; 27:190-91, 194-95; 49:162-63
A Travesty (Westlake) 33:438
Travnik Chronicle (Andric) 8:20
Trawl (Johnson) 6:262-63; 9:300-01, 303
Trayectoria del polvo (Castellanos) 66:44, 50-1
Tread the Dark (Ignatow) 14:275-77; 40:259
Tread the Green Grass (Green) 25:197, 199
Treasure Hunt (Buechner) 9:136-37
Treasure in Earthen Vessels (Gustafson) 100:229
The Treasure Is the Rose (Cunningham) 12:166
"The Treasure of Gold" (Carroll) 10:98
The Treasure of Siegfried (Almedingen) 12:1
The Treasure of the Sierra Madre (Huston) 20:158, 162, 165
The Treasure of the Sierra Madre (Traven) 8:518-20, 522
Treasures of Time (Lively) 32:273-74
Treasury Holiday: Thirty-Four Fits for the Opening of Fiscal Year 1968 (Harmon) 38:241-42
A Treasury of Yiddish Poetry (Howe) 85:147
A Treasury of Yiddish Stories (Howe) 85:126, 147
"Treat Her Gently—Lonely Old People" (McCartney) 35:282
"Treatise on Poetry" (Milosz)
    See "Trakat poetycki"
Treatise on Poetry (Milosz) 11:377
Treatise on Style (Aragon)
    See *Traité du style*
"The Treble Recorder" (Seifert) 93:336
Trece fábulas y media (Benet) 28:21
"Tree" (Abse) 29:14
"Tree" (Hoffman) 6:244
"The Tree" (Pound) 48:283
The Tree (Ehrenburg) 62:170
"A Tree. A Rock. A Cloud." (McCullers) 12:413, 416, 425, 433
Tree and Leaf (Tolkien) 12:566, 581
"Tree and Sky" (Transtroemer) 65:223
"Tree at My Window" (Frost) 13:229; 15:242; 26:121
"Tree Change" (Fisher) 87:130-31

"Tree Children" (Hall) 51:173
"Tree Ferns" (Plumly) 33:316
A Tree for Poverty: Somali Poetry and Prose (Laurence) 50:312, 314; 62:278, 280
"The Tree Fort" (Gilchrist) 65:349
A Tree Grows in Brooklyn (Kazan) 16:360, 362; 63:225, 229, 231, 234
A Tree Grows in Brooklyn (Smith) 19:422-23
"Tree in a Snowstorm" (Dudek) 11:159
The Tree of Childhood (Iskander)
    See *Dereva detstva*
The Tree of Hands (Rendell) 48:323-24
Tree of Life (Conde)
    See *La vie scélérate*
The Tree of Man (White) 3:521-23; 4:585-86; 5:487; 7:531; 18:545, 548; 65:275-77, 279, 282; 69:392-97, 399-403, 405-06, 412
"A Tree of Night" (Capote) 1:56; 3:99; 13:133; 19:79; 58:86
A Tree of Night, and Other Stories (Capote) 1:55; 19:79-80, 85-6; 34:321; 38:84, 87; 58:94
"Tree of Rivers" (Rukeyser) 15:457
The Tree of Swords and Jewels (Cherryh) 35:113-14
The Tree of the Sun (Harris) 25:211
A Tree on Fire (Sillitoe) 3:448; 6:500
"Tree Surgeons" (Graham) 48:154
"A Tree Telling of Orpheus" (Levertov) 66:250
"The Tree that Became a House" (Haines) 58:218
The Tree That Walked (Fuller) 62:185-86, 201
"The Tree, the Bird" (Roethke) 3:433; 19:396
The Tree Where Man Was Born (Matthiessen) 5:273; 7:210; 11:358, 360; 32:290, 294; 64:306-07, 309
"A Treeful of Cleavage Flared Branching" (Ammons) 108:19
"The Trees" (Larkin) 5:229; 8:333, 339, 341; 13:335; 39:347; 64:258, 266
"Trees" (Merwin) 13:384
"Trees" (Nemerov) 36:305
"The Trees" (Sarton) 49:307
"Trees" (Williams) 42:459
The Trees (Richter) 30:308-15, 318-19, 324, 327
"Trees Abandon Something inside a Circle of Fog" (Ponge) 18:419
The Trees, All Their Greenness (Haavikko)
    See *Puut, kaikki heidän vihreytensä*
"Trees at the Arctic Circle" (Purdy) 50:245
"Trees Die at the Top" (Ferber) 93:170, 180
"Trees in the Open Country" (Simic) 49:341, 343
Trees of Heaven (Stuart) 14:514, 516; 34:373, 376
Trees of Strings (MacCaig) 36:286
"Treetops" (Bell) 8:65; 31:47, 49
"Der Treffpunkt" (Seghers) 7:409
"Trefoil" (Ashbery) 41:40
"Tregardock" (Betjeman) 10:52; 43:46
La tregua (*The Reawakening*; *The Truce: A Survivor's Journey Home from Auschwitz*) (Levi) 37:222-23, 226-27, 229; 50:323, 326-32, 334, 336-37
"Le 13 l'echelle a frôlé le firmament" (Breton) 9:134
Le treizième César (Montherlant) 8:394
Trelawny (Holland) 21:149
"The Trellis" (Connell) 45:107
"A Trellis for R." (Swenson) 4:534; 106:321,

344

"Tremayne" (Justice) **102**:270

"The Trembler" (Merwin) **88**:200

The Trembling Hills (Whitney) **42**:432

The Trembling of a Leaf (Maugham) **15**:369

A Trembling upon Rome (Condon) **45**:100-01; **100**:91, 110

The Tremor of Forgery (Highsmith) **2**:193-94; **102**:171, 173-78, 209

Tremor of Intent (Burgess) **10**:87, 90; **22**:70-1; **40**:114, 117; **62**:132; **94**:40, 51, 58-59

"Tren Fortynbrasa" ("Elegy of Fortinbras") (Herbert) **9**:274; **43**:183-84, 188, 193-94

"Trenchtown Rock" (Marley) **17**:267

The Trend is Up (West) **50**:360

"Trends" (Asimov) **26**:39

Trente et un sonnets (*Thirty-One Sonnets*) (Guillevic) **33**:191, 194

Trepleff (Harris) **9**:258-59

Os três mal-amados (*The Three Ill-Loved Ones*) (Cabral de Melo Neto) **76**:156, 165, 169

Tres novelitas burguesas (*Sacred Families; Three Novellas*) (Donoso) **8**:179-80; **32**:154, 159-60; **99**:241-42

Las tres perfectas casadas (Casona) **49**:46

"Tres poemas" (Castellanos) **66**:52

"Tres Poesías" ("Three Poems") (Parra) **102**:344, 350

"Tres sorores" (Espriu) **9**:192

Tres tristes tigres (*Three Trapped Tigers*) (Cabrera Infante) **5**:95-7; **25**:100-04; **45**:78-81, 83

"Tres versiones de Judas" ("Three Versions of Judas") (Borges) **19**:51; **48**:38; **83**:156, 164

Tres y un sueño (Matute) **11**:364

"Trespass" (Matheson) **37**:246

Trespass (Knebel) **14**:308

The Trespassers (Hobson) **25**:268-69

Trespasses (Bailey) **45**:39-44

Treugol'naya grusa (*Trevgol'naya grusa; Triangular Pear*) (Voznesensky) **15**:553-54, 556

Trevayne (Ludlum) **43**:274-75

"Trêve" (Damas) **84**:173-74, 177

"Trevenen" (Davie) **8**:167

Trevgol'naya grusa (Voznesensky)
    See *Treugol'naya grusa*

Tri Simfonije (Krleza) **114**:173

Tri tolstiaku (*The Three Fat Men*) (Olesha) **8**:430, 432

Tría piímata me siméa efkerías (Elytis) **100**:175

"Triad" (Watkins) **43**:450

"The Trial" (Abse) **29**:16

"The Trial" (Lem) **40**:291

The Trial (Berkoff) **56**:14

The Trial (Welles) **80**:389, 391, 396
    See *Le procès*

Trial Balances (Miles) **34**:244

"The Trial by Existence" (Frost) **10**:196; **13**:223; **15**:244; **26**:125-26

"Trial by Fury" (Bochco and Kozoll) **35**:60

Trial Impressions (Mathews) **52**:308, 314

Trial of a City (Birney) **6**:71-2, 78

Trial of a Judge (Spender) **10**:491; **41**:423-24; **91**:257, 261, 263

Trial of a Poet (Shapiro) **4**:485-86; **15**:476, 478

The Trial of Dedan Kimathi (Ngugi wa Thiong'o) **36**:315, 321-22, 324

The Trial of God (Wiesel) **37**:452, 455, 459

"The Trial of Jean Rhys" (Rhys) **19**:394

The Trial of Joan of Arc (Bresson)
    See *Procès de Jeanne d'Arc*

"The Trial of Plucking Buds and Shooting Lambs" (Oe) **86**:241

The Trial of Sören Qvist (Lewis) **41**:254-58, 263

The Trial of the Catonsville Nine (Berrigan) **4**:57-8

"The Trial of the Old Watchdog" (Thurber) **5**:434

"The Trial of Thomas Builds-the-Fire" (Alexie) **96**:5

"Trial Run" (Jacobsen) **48**:194

Trial Run (Francis) **22**:152; **42**:156-57

"Trial Translation" ("From 'Twelfth Night'") (Burke) **24**:128

The Trials of Brother Jero (Soyinka) **3**:462; **14**:505, 507; **44**:281-82, 287-88

"Triangle" (Lightfoot) **26**:283

"Le triangle ambigu" (Mandiargues) **41**:279

"Triangle at Rhodes" (Christie) **48**:72

Triangle Junction (Grass)
    See *Gleisdreieck*

Le triangle noir (Malraux) **4**:333

"The Triangular Pear" ("The Three-Cornered Pear") (Voznesensky) **57**:425-26

Triangular Pear (Voznesensky)
    See *Treugol'naya grusa*

"Tribal Dance" (Montague) **46**:270

Tribal Justice (Blaise) **29**:70-1, 74-6

"Tribal Poems" (Ciardi) **40**:156

Tribal Scars (Ousmane)
    See *Voltaïque*

Tribal Scenes and Ceremonies (Vizenor) **103**:296-97

"Tribal Stumps" (Vizenor) **103**:296

Tribunals Passages (Duncan) **41**:128-30

Tribunals: Passages 31-35 (Duncan) **2**:123; **4**:141

"Tribune or Bureaucrat" (Lukacs) **24**:339

The Tribune's Visitation (Jones) **4**:259; **7**:186-87; **13**:311

"The Tribute" (H. D.) **73**:104-05, 120

Tribute (Slade) **46**:370-72

"Tribute of a Legs Lover" (Dunn) **40**:167

"Tribute to a Reporter in Belfast, 1974" (Durcan) **43**:116

Tribute to Freud (H. D.) **8**:258; **14**:228; **31**:204, 208-10; **73**:122-27, 129-30, 137, 140

"Tribute to Mshongweni" (Kunene) **85**:176

Tribute to the Angels (H. D.) **8**:255, 257-58; **14**:223, 225-27; **31**:202-03, 208; **34**:445

"Tribute to Upanishads" (Ezekiel) **61**:109

"Tricentennial" (Haldeman) **61**:174, 176, 178

A Triche-coeur (*By Cheating the Heart*) (Tchicaya) **101**:348, 350-51

Le tricheur (*The Trickster*) (Simon) **4**:494-95; **9**:484; **15**:485-86, 489-92; **39**:203-04, 206, 209, 211

El triciclo (Arrabal)
    See *Le tricycle*

"The Trick" (Campbell) **42**:88-9

"The Trick Is Consciousness" (Allen) **84**:3

A Trick of Light (Corcoran) **17**:71

The Trick of the Ga Bolga (McGinley) **41**:286-87

"Trick Scenery" (Barthelme) **117**:5-6

"Tricks" (Moure) **88**:217-19

"Tricks out of Time Long Gone" (Algren) **33**:15

"Tricks with Mirrors" (Atwood) **8**:29; **13**:44; **84**:50

The Trickster (Simon)
    See *Le tricheur*

"Trickster 1977" (Rose) **85**:311

"Trickster Discourse" (Vizenor) **103**:325

The Trickster of Liberty (Vizenor) **103**:332-34

The Tricycle (Arrabal)
    See *Le tricycle*

Le tricycle (*El triciclo; The Tricycle*) (Arrabal) **9**:38; **18**:17, 21; **58**:4-5, 8, 17, 21

Trifles for a Massacre (Celine)
    See *Bagatelles pour un massacre*

"The Triflin' Man" (Miller)
    See "You Triflin' Skunk"

Trig (Peck) **17**:341

Trig Sees Red (Peck) **17**:342

The Triggering Town: Lectures and Essays on Poetry and Writing (Hugo) **18**:263; **32**:243, 245-47, 250

Trillion Year Spree: The History of Science Fiction (Wingrove) **68**:452, 456

"Trillium" (Gluck) **81**:170

Trilobite, Dinosaur and Man (Simak) **55**:320

"Trilobites" (Pancake) **29**:346-50

Trilogia culturii **75**:58-61, 67

Trilogia cunoasterii (*The Trilogy of Knowledge*) **75**:58, 67, 79-80

Trilogia della vita (Pasolini) **106**:248, 266, 268

Trilogia valorilor (*The Trilogy of Values*) **75**:58, 67

Trilogie des Wiedersehens (*Three Acts of Recognition*) (Strauss) **22**:407

The Trilogy (Beckett) **6**:40; **29**:59

Trilogy (*War Trilogy*) (H. D.) **8**:255-57; **14**:225-28, 230; **31**:201, 206, 208-09, 211; **34**:442, 445; **73**:139-40, 142

The Trilogy (Mahfuz)
    See *al-Thulatthiyya*

The Trilogy of Knowledge
    See *Trilogia cunoasterii*

Trilogy of Life (Pasolini)
    See *Trilogy of Life*

The Trilogy of Values
    See *Trilogia valorilor*

Trinadtsaty podvig Gerakla (*Forbidden Fruit, and Other Stories; The Thirteenth Labor of Herucles; Zapretnyi plod*) (Iskander) **47**:192-93, 198-99

"A Trinity" (Trevor) **71**:342-43, 348

Trinity (Uris) **7**:492; **32**:433, 437

"Trinity Peace" (Sandburg) **35**:340

"Trinity Place" (McGinley) **14**:365-66

"Trinket" (Bell) **31**:49-50

"The Trinket Box" (Lessing) **3**:288

"Trionfo della morte" (Ekeloef) **27**:111

Trios (White) **110**:331

"Trip" (Barthelme) **117**:15

"A Trip" (Hoffman) **6**:243

"The Trip" (Seidel) **18**:475

A Trip around Lake Erie (McFadden) **48**:253-56

A Trip around Lake Huron (McFadden) **48**:253-56

"The Trip Back" (Butler) **81**:128-29

The Trip Back Down (Bishop) **10**:54

The Trip to Bountiful (Foote) **51**:130-31, 134-36, 138; **91**:99

Trip to Hanoi (Sontag) **105**:197, 227

A Trip to Italy and France (Ferlinghetti) **27**:139

The Trip to Jerusalem (Lind) **4**:294

The Trip to London (Davies) **23**:142

"Trip to New York" (Cardenal)
    See "Viaje a Nueva York"

A Trip to Russia (Krleza)

See *Izlet u Rusiju*
A Trip to the North (Yevtushenko) 26:466
Trip to the Village of Crime (Sender)
    See *Viaje a la aldea del crimen*
"A Trip to Vigia" (Bishop) 32:43
Trip Trap (Rathbone) 41:338
Tripes d'or (*Golden Tripe*) (Crommelynck)
    75:153, 156, 160, 162-63, 168-69
Triple (Follett) 18:156
The Triple Echo (Bates) 46:59, 61, 65-6
The Triple Thinkers (Wilson) 8:550; 24:470,
    472-74, 481, 487
"Triple Time" (Larkin) 33:256
"Triplicate" (Fuchs) 22:156, 160
Tripmaster Monkey: His Fake Book (Kingston)
    58:318, 324-27
"Tripping" (Williams) 31:462
Tripticks (Quin) 6:442
"Triptych" (Eberhart) 56:79
"Triptych" (Heaney) 25:248
Triptych (Simon)
    See *Triptyque*
"Triptych I, After a Killing" (Heaney) 74:159
Triptych: Three Scenic Panels (Frisch)
    See *Triptychon*
Triptychon (*Triptych: Three Scenic Panels*)
    (Frisch) 14:184; 44:192, 199, 204, 206-
    07
Triptyque (*Triptych*) (Simon) 4:497; 15:490,
    493-96; 39:208, 210-12, 214
"The Triskelion" (Stead) 80:324
Tristan and Iseult (Sutcliff) 26:435
"Tristan Vox" (Tournier) 36:439; 95:361
Tristana (Bunuel) 16:135, 140, 147; 80:40,
    50, 57
"Tristan's Singing" (Masefield) 11:357
"Triste conción para aburrir a cualquiera"
    (Neruda) 28:309
Tristes tropiques (Levi-Strauss) 38:294, 296-
    99, 303, 311-12
Tristessa (Kerouac) 3:265; 5:214; 29:271-72;
    61:296, 309
Triton (Delany) 8:169; 14:143-44, 146-47;
    38:151, 161-62
"Triumf" (Arghezi) 80:2
"Triumph" (James) 33:221
Triumph (Wylie) 43:468-69
"The Triumph of Achilles" (Gluck) 44:214,
    217-18, 222
The Triumph of Achilles (Gluck) 44:214-24;
    81:164, 173
The Triumph of Inspector Maigret (Simenon)
    47:379
"The Triumph of Life: Mary Shelley" (Mueller)
    51:280-81
"Triumph of Man" (Kunene) 85:165
"The Triumph of Poetry" (Frame) 96:189
"The Triumph of Principles" (Boyle) 58:74
The Triumph of the Spider Monkey (Oates)
    33:289; 108:386
Triumph of the Will (Riefenstahl) 16:519-26
"Triumph of Thought" (Kunene) 85:165
The Triumph of Time (Blish) 14:85
Triumphal March (Eliot) 1:89
Triumphs of Modern Science (Berger) 12:37
"Triunfo del amor" (Aleixandre) 9:14
Trivial, Vulgar, and Exalted (Cunningham)
    31:99
Troe (Coles) 67:175
"The Troika Fairy Tale" (Strugatskii and
    Strugatskii) 27:432
"Troilus" (Olson) 29:329
Trois acteurs: Un drame (Ghelderode) 11:227

"Les trois frères" (Damas) 84:179
Les trois Lumières (Lang) 103:85, 88
Trois petits tours (Tremblay) 29:419, 425
"Trois poèmes spontanés" (Ferlinghetti)
    27:139
"Les trois soeurs" (Char) 9:164
Trois villes saintes (Le Clezio) 31:251
Troisième bélvèdere (Mandiargues) 41:277-79
The Trojan Brothers (Johnson) 27:215-16
The Trojan Ditch (Sisson) 8:490
The Trojan Horse: A Play (MacLeish) 68:289-
    90
"The Trojan War" (Elytis) 49:110
"The Troll" (White) 30:452
Trollflöjten (*The Magic Flute*) (Bergman)
    16:77; 72:61
"Trolling for Blues" (Wilbur) 53:412; 110:357,
    361
Trollope: His Life and Art (Snow) 9:498
"Trompe l'oeil" (Perec) 56:254
"Troop Train Returning" (Murray) 40:335⁰
Une trop bruyante solitude (*Too Loud a Soli-
    tude*) (Hrabal) 67:128-33
"Tropes of the Text" (Gass) 39:480-81
"The Trophy" (Hope) 51:219
Tropic of Cancer (Miller) 1:219-224; 2:281-
    83; 4:350; 9:378-80; 14:370, 372-75;
    43:293, 295-301; 84:232-94
Tropic of Capricorn (Miller) 1:220-22, 224;
    9:379-81; 14:372-73; 43:297-300;
    84:239, 241-42, 244-47, 250-51, 254,
    258, 266, 269, 273, 287, 290
"Tropic Zone" (Walcott) 42:416
Tropical Night Falling (Puig)
    See *Cae la noche tropical*
A Tropical Nightfall (Puig)
    See *Cae la noche tropical*
"Tropics" (Voigt) 54:429
Tropismes (*Tropisms*) (Sarraute) 2:384; 4:464,
    466-67, 470; 8:472; 10:460; 31:377, 380,
    382-83, 386; 80:233, 236, 238-40, 242,
    250-52, 254-55, 257
Tropisms (Sarraute)
    See *Tropismes*
"The Tropville Evening Express" (Yehoshua)
    See "The Evening Journey of Yatir"
Trotsky (Howe)
    See *Leon Trotsky*
Trotsky in Exile (Weiss)
    See *Trotzki im Exil*
Trotsky: World Revolutionary (Archer) 12:19-
    21
The Trotter-Nama (Sealy) 55:78-83
Trotzki im Exil (*Trotsky in Exile*) (Weiss) 15:568;
    51:386-87, 391, 393-94
Trou de mémoire (Aquin) 15:17
"The Trouble" (Powers) 1:280, 282
"Trouble Child" (Mitchell) 12:438
"Trouble Coming Everyday" (Zappa) 17:585,
    588
Trouble Follows Me (Macdonald) 14:332-33
Trouble in July (Caldwell) 1:51; 50:300; 60:54-
    5
"Trouble in Mind" (Dylan) 77:189
Trouble in Mind (Childress) 12:104-05, 108;
    86:309-10, 314-15; 96:88, 103-04, 109-
    10
The Trouble I've Seen (Gellhorn) 60:177-79,
    190-91, 195-96
"Trouble Man" (Gaye) 26:131, 133
The Trouble with Being Born (Cioran) 64:90,
    98
"The Trouble with Being Food" (Busch) 10:93

The Trouble with England (Raphael) 2:367
The Trouble with Francis (Francis) 15:236
The Trouble with Harry (Hitchcock) 16:341,
    346
"The Trouble with Heroes" (Vanderhaeghe)
    41:450
The Trouble with Heroes, and Other Stories
    (Vanderhaeghe) 41:450, 452
The Trouble with Lazy Ethel (Gann) 23:165
Trouble with Lichen (Wyndham) 19:475
The Trouble with Nigeria (Achebe) 75:6, 17,
    24
Troubled Air (Shaw) 7:411; 23:397
"The Troubled Genius of Oliver Cromwell"
    (Carr) 86:47
Troubled Sleep (Sartre)
    See *La mort dans l'âme*
Troublemaker (Hansen) 38:237
"Troubles" (Stern) 39:244
Troubles (Farrell) 6:173
"The Troubles of a Book" (Riding) 7:374
"The Troubles of Dr. Thoss" (Ligotti) 44:53-
The Troubling of the Waters 75:64-6
Trouées (Guillevic) 33:194-95
"Trout" (Heaney) 5:173; 14:243
"The Trout" (Montague) 46:267, 275
"The Trout Farm2dq2 (Raine) 103:201
Trout Fishing in America (Brautigan) 1:44-5;
    3:86-90; 5:68-71; 12:57-66, 69-73;
    34:314-17; 42:49-53, 56-8, 60, 62-6
"Troy Town" (Ondaatje) 14:408
"The Truant" (Pratt) 19:377, 379, 385
The Truants (Barrett) 27:22-4
Truants (Carlson) 54:36
*Truants from Life: The Rehabilitation of Emo-
    tionally Disturbed Children* (Bettelheim)
    79:111
"Truce" (Muldoon) 72:266
*The Truce: A Survivor's Journey Home from
    Auschwitz* (Levi)
    See *La tregua*
"The Truce and Peace" (Jeffers) 11:305
Truck (Dunn) 71:133-35
The Truck (Duras)
    See *Le camion: Suivi de entretien avec
    Michelle Porte*
"A Trucker" (Gunn) 3:215
"A Trucker Breaks Down" (Bottoms) 53:29
"A Trucker Drives through His Lost Youth"
    (Bottoms) 53:29
The True Adventures of Huckleberry Finn
    7:405-06
The True Adventures of John Steinbeck, Writer
    (Benson) 34:404-08, 410, 412-15
The True and Only Heaven (Lasch) 102:290-
    92, 295, 297-99, 301-03, 305, 311-12,
    322, 324-25
"True Colors" (Adams) 46:16
The True Confession of George Barker (Barker)
    8:46; 48:16-18, 21-4
"True Confessional" (Ferlinghetti) 6:184;
    111:65
True Confessions (Dunne) 28:123-26
*True Confessions of Adrian Albert Mole, Mar-
    garet Hilda Roberts and Susan Lilian
    Townsend* 61:419-21
The True Confessions of an Albino Terrorist
    (Breytenbach) 37:50-2
"The True Discovery of Australia" (McAuley)
    45:248
*The True History of Squire Jonathan and His
    Unfortunate Treasure* (Arden) 15:21

"The True Import of Present Dialogue, Black vs. Negro" (Giovanni) **64**:182, 185, 188, 191, 193

The True Life Story of Jody McKeegan (Carpenter) **41**:103-08

True Love (Gold) **42**:195-96

"True Love Isn't Hard to Find" (Donnell) **34**:158

"True Loves" (Strand) **41**:438-41

"The True Nature of Time" (Warren) **6**:557; **13**:577

"The True Person" (Rexroth) **112**:372

"A True Picture Restored" (Watkins) **43**:452

True Repose (Oz) **33**:299

"The True Song" (Montague) **46**:268

True Stories (Atwood) **25**:65, 68-9; **84**:69

"True Stories of Bitches" (Mamet) **46**:255

"The True Story of Lavinia Todd" (Auchincloss) **9**:52

"True Tenderness" (Akhmatova) **64**:11

"True Thomas" (Nye) **42**:309

"True Trash" (Atwood) **84**:95, 97

"The True Tyrant" (Smith) **25**:419

True West (Shepard) **34**:266, 269-70; **41**:407-08, 411-12; **44**:264-65, 268-70

El trueno entre las hojas (*Thunder among the Leaves*) (Roa Bastos) **45**:344-47

Trullion (Vance) **35**:421

"The Truly Great" (Spender) **41**:428

"Truman Capote: Knowing Everybody" (Amis) **62**:5

Trumpet in Arms (Lancaster) **36**:243

The Trumpet of the Swan (White) **34**:426-27, 430; **39**:369, 375-78, 380

"The Trumpet Part" (Celan) **53**:75-6

Trumpet to the World (Harris) **19**:199, 203

"Trumpeter" (Gardner) **28**:162-63

Trumpets and Rasperrries (Fo)
  See *Clascon trombette e penacchi*

"Trunk in Petöcki" (Boell) **72**:69

Trust (Costello) **21**:75

Trust (Ozick) **3**:372; **7**:287; **28**:349, 355; **62**:355

Trust in Chariots (Savage) **40**:370-71

The Truth about Stone Hollow (Snyder) **17**:472

"The Truth About the Floods" (Ezekiel) **61**:104, 107

The Truth about the Ku Klux Klan (Meltzer) **26**:309

Truth and Consequence (Stolz) **12**:547-48

"The Truth and Life of Myth" (Duncan) **2**:123; **4**:142; **7**:88

"Truth and Power" (Foucault) **69**:194

"Truth and the Novelist" (Stafford) **68**:441

The Truth Barrier (Transtroemer)
  See *Sanningbarriären*

Truth Barriers (Transtroemer)
  See *Sanningbarriären*

"The Truth Game" (Klima)
  See "Hra na pravdu"

"Truth in Fiction" (Stafford) **68**:441

"Truth in Melodrama" (Davies) **75**:197

The Truth in Painting (Derrida)
  See *La verité en peinture*

"The Truth Is" (Hogan) **73**:151, 157

Truth Is More Sacred (Dahlberg) **7**:69; **14**:138

"Truth Is Never" (Miles) **14**:369

"Truth is on its Way" (Giovanni) **117**:191

"The Truth of Departure" (Merwin) **88**:195

The Truth of Poetry (Hamburger) **5**:158

"The Truth of the Matter" (Ihimaera) **46**:200

"Truth or Consequences" (Adams) **46**:17

"The Truth the Dead Know" (Sexton) **10**:469;

53:318

"Try a Dull Knife" (Ellison) **42**:127

"Try a Little Priest" (Sondheim) **30**:398

"Try to Remember" (Herbert) **44**:394

"Try to See My Sister" (Walker) **58**:408

Try! Try! (O'Hara) **13**:431; **78**:332-33, 365-68

"Trying" (Robison) **98**:306-08

Trying Hard to Hear You (Scoppettone) **26**:400-03

The Trying Hour (Lagerkvist)
  See *Den svåra stunden*

"Trying Out for the Race" (Yates) **23**:483

"Trying to Be" (Gaitskill) **69**:199, 201

Trying to Explain (Davie) **31**:115, 119

"Trying to Hold It All Together" (Eberhart) **19**:144

"Trying to Pray" (Wagoner) **15**:559

Trying to Save Piggy Sneed (Irving) **112**:174

"Trying to Talk with a Man" (Rich) **3**:428; **7**:369; **11**:478

"Trying to Write" (Smart) **54**:426

"Tryst" (Broumas) **73**:15

"Trzecia jesién" ("The Third Autumn") (Dabrowska) **15**:166

T.S. Eliot: A Study in Character and Style (Bush) **34**:524, 526-27, 530-32

"T.S. Eliot's Later Poetry" (Leavis) **24**:310

Tsar (Barnes)
  See *Laughter!*

"Le tsar noir" ("The Black Tsar") (Morand) **41**:301

Tschai (Vance) **35**:422-24

Tsemakh Atlas (*The Yeshira*) (Grade) **10**:248

Tsing-Boum! (Freeling) **38**:184

Tsotsi (Fugard) **25**:173, 175-76; **40**:201; **80**:65, 67, 69

Tsuga's Children (Williams) **14**:582

"Tsvety" ("Flowers") (Akhmadulina) **53**:11

"T.T. Jackson Sings" (Baraka) **5**:48

"Il tu" ("The Thou") (Montale) **7**:224

"Tu Do Street" (Komunyakaa) **94**:236-37

"Tu entendras..." (Bonnefoy) **58**:53

Tu étais si gentil quand tu étais petit (Anouilh) **40**:57-8

Tu ne t'aimes pas (*You Don't Love Yourself*) (Sarraute) **80**:253, 256-57

"Tú no sabe inglé" ("You Speak No English") (Guillen) **79**:245

"Tu ti spezzasti" ("You Shattered") (Ungaretti) **7**:485; **11**:556

"Tuatamur" (Leonov) **92**:237, 256, 263-64

"The Tub, 1934, Halifax, Mississippi" (Dubie) **36**:131-32

"Tubal-Cain Forges A Star" (Garcia Marquez)
  See "Tubal-Caín forja una estrella"

"Tubal-Caín forja una estrella" ("Tubal-Cain Forges A Star") (Garcia Marquez) **3**:181

The Tubs (McNally) **4**:346; **7**:219

"Tucker Drugs" (Moure) **88**:230

"Tucson: First Night" (Allen) **84**:2

El tuerto es rey (Fuentes) **113**:233

"The Tuesday Afternoon Siesta" (Garcia Marquez)
  See "Tuesday Siesta"

"Tuesday and Wednesday" (Wilson) **13**:606

"The Tuesday Night Club" (Christie) **110**:141, 144

"Tuesday Night with Cody, Jimbo, and a Fish of Some Proportion" (Crews) **49**:73

"Tuesday Siesta" ("The Tuesday Afternoon Siesta") (Garcia Marquez) **27**:147-48; **47**:148, 150-51; **55**:148; **68**:151, 166

"Tuesday's As Good As Any" (O'Hara) **6**:385

Tueur sans gages (*The Killer*; *The Unrewarded Killer*) (Ionesco) **4**:251-52; **6**:248-49, 253-54; **9**:286; **11**:290-92, 294; **15**:296; **41**:224, 229; **86**:332, 340

"The Tuft of Flowers" (Frost) **3**:174-75; **15**:246, 248; **26**:118, 121-22

Tug of War (McCartney) **35**:289-93

"Tugela River" (Plomer) **4**:407

The Tugman's Passage (Hoagland) **28**:186

"Tulane" (Berry) **17**:55

"Tulips" (Cummings) **15**:159

"Tulips" (McGuckian) **48**:274, 276

"Tulips" (Plath) **5**:341, 345; **9**:426, 428, 433; **11**:448-49; **14**:423, 425, 429; **17**:347, 355, 365, 368-69; **50**:446; **51**:340, 343-46; **111**:161-62, 168, 171-74, 210

"Tulips, Again" (Schaeffer) **11**:491

Tulips and Chimneys (Cummings) **3**:118-19; **8**:156, 158; **12**:139-40, 144-45, 160-61; **15**:159-60, 162, 164; **68**:27, 31, 35, 41, 44-6, 50

Tulku (Dickinson) **12**:177; **35**:131-32

"Tulpen" (Celan) **82**:49

"Tumannaya ulitsa" (Voznesensky) **15**:555

Tumatumari (Harris) **25**:207, 210, 213

Una tumba (*A Tomb*) (Benet) **28**:19-20, 23

Una tumba sin nombre (Onetti)
  See *Para una tumba sin nombre*

"La tumba viva" (Roa Bastos) **45**:345

Tumbleweed (van de Wetering) **47**:405-07, 410

"Tumbling Dice" (Jagger and Richard) **17**:229, 236

Tunc (Durrell) **1**:87; **6**:153; **8**:193; **13**:185; **41**:136-37

"A Tune for Festive Dances in the Nineteen Sixties" (Merton) **83**:397

"Tune, in American Type" (Updike) **23**:473

"Tuned In Late One Night" (Stafford) **29**:387

Tuned Out (Wojciechowska) **26**:454-55

"El túnel" (Parra) **102**:338

El túnel (*The Outsider*) (Sabato) **23**:375-77, 379

Tunes for a Small Harmonica (Wersba) **30**:432-34

"Tuning of Perfection" (MacLeod) **56**:197-200

"Der Tunnel" (Durrenmatt) **11**:172

"The Tunnel" (Rukeyser) **27**:404

"The Tunnel" (Strand) **18**:516, 518; **41**:437; **71**:281

"Tunnel" (Summers) **10**:494

The Tunnel (Gass) **15**:256-57; **39**:478

The Tunnel (Sabato)
  See "Shooting Rats at the Bibb County Dump"

Tunnel in the Sky (Heinlein) **26**:161, 172, 176-77; **55**:302

The Tunnel of Love (De Vries) **1**:73; **3**:126; **28**:106, 112-13; **46**:137

Tunnel through the Deeps (*A Transatlantic Tunnel, Hurrah!*) (Harrison) **42**:201-02, 205

Tunnel Vision (Arrick) **30**:18

"Tunstall Forest" (Davie) **8**:164

"Tuolomne" (Starbuck) **53**:353

"Tupac amaru kampa Taytanchisman" (Arguedas) **18**:7

Tupac amaru kampa Taytanchisman (*To Our Father Creator Tupac*) (Arguedas) **18**:7-8

"Tupelo Honey" (Morrison) **21**:233

Tupelo Honey (Morrison) **21**:232-33

Tupelo Nights (Bradley) **55**:31-4

"Tupic" (Tournier)   95:361

Turbott Wolfe (Plomer)   4:406

Un turbulent silence (Brink)   36:68

Turbulent Stream (Pa Chin)
  See *Chi-liu*

"Turds" (Martin)   30:248

La turista (Shepard)   4:490; 17:433-34; 41:412

Turkey Hash (Nova)   7:267; 31:297, 299

"The Turkey Season" (Munro)   95:302, 306

"Turkeyneck Morning" (Bukowski)   41:73

"Turkish Delight" (O'Faolain)   108:415

"The Turkish March" (Swan)   69:363

"The Turkish Night" (Morand)
  See "La nuit Turque"

"A Turkish Story" (Pollitt)   28:366

"The Turmoil" (Pasternak)   10:386

"Turn" (Saner)   9:469

Turn, Magic Wheel (Powell)   66:353-54, 356, 368

Turn of a Pang (Brossard)
  See *Sold-Out*

"The Turn of the Moon" (Graves)   45:166

"The Turn of the Screw" (Oates)   108:354

The Turn of the Years (Pritchett)   41:332

Turn Off the Lights (Seifert)
  See *Zhasnete svetla*

Turn Out the Lights (Seifert)
  See *Zhasnete svetla*

"Turn the Page" (Seger)   35:379, 381, 384

"Turn, Turn Your Face Away" (Barker)   48:14

"A Turn with the Sun" (Knowles)   26:258

Turnaround (Carpenter)   41:106-08

"The Turncoat" (Baraka)   5:45; 14:42

"turning" (Clifton)   66:75

"The Turning" (Levine)   14:317

"Turning" (Rich)   73:330

"Turning Away" (Dickey)   4:120

"Turning Fifty" (Wright)   53:431

"Turning Forty" (Jiles)   58:272-73, 275, 278

"Turning Out the Bedside Lamp" (Williams)   45:444

"The Turning Point" (Allen)   84:5

"The Turning Point" (Stolz)   12:552

Turning Point (Seferis)   5:384

"Turning Thirty" (Pollitt)   28:367

"Turning to You" (Merwin)   45:273

A Turning Wind (Rukeyser)   15:456, 458; 27:404, 406, 408, 410-11

Turns (Matthias)   9:361-62

Turns and Movies and Other Tales in Verse (Aiken)   52:20-2, 27

"Turns: Toward a Provisional Aesthetic and a Discipline" (Matthias)   9:361

Turnstiles (Holden)   18:257-59

Turnstiles (Joel)   26:214-15, 219-20

"Turpentine" (Gallagher)   63:121

"Turquoise Carnations" (Thesen)   56:421

The Turquoise Lament (MacDonald)   3:307

The Turquoise Mask (Whitney)   42:435

"Turtle" (Hellman)   52:193

"Turtle" (Lowell)   15:238

"The Turtle" (Oliver)   98:261, 274, 294

Turtle Diary (Hoban)   7:160-62; 25:266

Turtle Diary (Pinter)   58:381

"The Turtle Dove" (Hill)   8:294

Turtle Island (Snyder)   5:395; 9:498; 32:387-88, 394, 396, 399-400

"The Turtle Who Conquered Time" (Thurber)   5:430

Turvey (Birney)   6:70-1; 11:49

"Tusten" (Vesaas)   48:407

"The Tutelar of the Place" (Jones)   7:188-89; 13:311

Tutti i nostri ieri (*All Our Yesterdays*; *Dead Yesterdays*; *A Light for Fools*) (Ginzburg)   5:142; 11:228-29; 54:193-94, 196, 201-05, 211; 70:280, 283

Tutti unitil tutti insiemel ma scusa quello non e'il padrone? (Fo)   109:104, 112

TV (van Itallie)   3:493

"TV in Black and White" (Soto)   80:278

"TV Off" (Hughes)   37:180

"TV Room at the Children's Hospice" (Ryan)   65:212-14

"T.V. Talkin' Song" (Dylan)   77:184

Två sagor om livit (*Two Tales About Life*) (Lagerkvist)   54:286

"TVC One Five" (Bowie)   17:67

"Tvoi dom" ("Your House") (Akhmadulina)   53:11

Tvoj ubijca (Aksyonov)
  See *Vash ubiytsa*

Tvorcestva Fransua Rable i narodnaja kul'tura srednevekov'ja i Renessansa (*Rabelais and His World*) (Bakhtin)   83:13, 15, 17, 26, 28, 32, 57

Twarz trzecia (*The Third Face*) (Rozewicz)   23:362

"Twelfth Morning; or, What You Will" (Bishop)   9:92; 32:34, 43

Twelve around the World (Daly)   17:89

"Twelve Bagatelles" (Shapcott)   38:400

Twelve Chairs (Brooks)   12:78-9, 82

The Twelve Dancers (Mayne)   12:398, 406

"Twelve Études for Voice and Kazoo" (Sorrentino)   40:386

"The Twelve Figures of the World" (Borges)   48:41-2

"Twelve Flying Monkeys Who Won't Copulate Properly" (Bukowski)   41:75; 108:85

$1,200 a Year (Ferber)   93:147

Twelve Million Black Voices: A Folk History of the Negro in the United States (Wright)   1:377; 4:595; 14:598; 74:390

Twelve Moons (Oliver)   19:362-63; 98:265, 269, 276-77, 290

"The Twelve Mortal Men" (McCullers)   12:429; 48:241

"Twelve O'Clock News" (Bishop)   9:97-8; 13:90; 32:35, 39

Twelve Poems (Warner)
  See *Azrael*

Twelve Poems for Cavafy (Ritsos)   31:328

"Twelve Propositions" (Burke)   24:127

The Twelve Seasons (Krutch)   24:289

"12527th Birthday of the Buddha" (Komunyakaa)   94:230, 232

"Twelve Versions of God" (Broumas)   10:77

The Twelve-Spoked Wheel Flashing (Piercy)   14:421-22

The Twenties (Wilson)   24:483

Twenties in the Sixties (Kostelanetz)   28:218

"Twentieth Century Fiction and the Black Mask of Humanity" (Ellison)   114:108, 117

"Twentieth Century Fox" (Morrison)   17:294

20th Century Pleasures (Hass)
  See *Twentieth Century Pleasures: Prose on Poetry*

Twentieth Century Pleasures: Prose on Poetry (*20th Century Pleasures*) (Hass)   39:146-49; 99:129-40, 144-50, 156-57

The Twentieth Century Revue (Arrabal)   58:17

"Twentieth-Century Blues" (Fearing)   51:116

Twentieth-Century Caesar: Benito Mussolini (Archer)   12:15

Twentieth-Century Faith: Hope and Survival

(Mead)   37:280

"Twentieth-Century Pharisee" (Thomas)   48:379

20 (Wilson)   12:645

"Twenty and One" (Haavikko)   34:178

Twenty Forty (Jong)   83:319

Twenty Love Poems and a Despairing Song (Neruda)
  See *Veinte poemas de amor y una canción desesperada*

Twenty Love Poems and a Desperate Song (Neruda)
  See *Veinte poemas de amor y una canción desesperada*

Twenty Love Poems and a Song of Despair (Neruda)
  See *Veinte poemas de amor y una canción desesperada*

Twenty Love Poems and One Song of Despair (Neruda)
  See *Veinte poemas de amor y una canción desesperada*

"Twenty Minutes" (Salter)   52:368-69; 59:196-97

"Twenty or So" (Gregor)   9:254

Twenty Poems (Aleixandre)   36:25, 28, 32

Twenty Poems (Haines)   58:217, 221

XX Poems (Larkin)   5:230; 64:257

Twenty Poems (Neruda)
  See *Veinte poemas de amor y una canción desesperada*

Twenty Poems (Spender)   91:260

Twenty Thousand Streets under the Sky: A London Trilogy (Hamilton)
  See *The Siege of Pleasure*

Twenty Thousand Streets under the Sky: A London Trilogy (Hamilton)
  See *The Plains of Cement*

Twenty Thousand Streets under the Sky: A London Trilogy (Hamilton)
  See *The Midnight Bell: A Love Story*

"XXII" (Auden)   14:26

"Twenty Years Gone, She Returns to the Nunnery" (Dickey)   28:117

The Twenty-Eighth Day of Elul (Elman)   19:148

"The Twentyfifth Anniversary of a Republic, 1975" (Mahapatra)   33:277, 281, 283

"Twenty-Fifth Floor" (Smith)   12:543

Twenty-First Century Sub (*The Dragon in the Sea*; *Under Pressure*) (Herbert)   12:270, 273; 23:224-26; 35:196-98; 44:392-95

"25 Norfolk Crescent" (Ewart)   46:153

Twenty-Five Poems (Tzara)
  See *Vingt-cinq poèmes*

25 Poems (Walcott)   42:421; 67:344; 76:273, 288

Twenty-Four Poems (Dudek)   19:136

"Twenty-Nine Inventions" (Oates)   6:369; 15:400

Twenty-One Love Poems (Rich)   11:478; 18:450; 76:209

"Twenty-One Points about The *Physicists*" (Durrenmatt)
  See "Einundzwanzig Punkte du zen *Physikern*"

Twenty-One Stories (Greene)   3:211

Twentyone Twice (Harris)   19:201

"Twenty-Seven Wagons Full of Cotton" (Williams)   45:454

The Twenty-Seventh Kingdom (Ellis)   40:191-92

"Twenty-Six" (Ferlinghetti)   27:138

"26 Days, On Earth" (Haldeman)   61:176-77

Twenty-Six Starlings Will Fly through Your Mind (Wersba) **30**:433
"Twenty-Third Flight" (Birney) **6**:75
22 Stories (Gilliatt) **53**:146-47
"Twice as Much" (Agnon)
   See "Pi shnayim"
"Twice Born" (Warren) **39**:259
Twice in Time (Wellman) **49**:387
Twice Shy **59**:399-402
Twice Shy (Francis) **42**:150-57; **102**:162
Twiddledum Twaddledum (Spielberg) **6**:519-20
"Twilight" (Campbell) **32**:74-5, 78-80
"Twilight" (Faludy) **42**:139-40
"Twilight" (Faulkner) **68**:128
The Twilight Book (Neruda)
   See *Crepúsculario*
"Twilight Excursion" (Davidson) **19**:129
Twilight for the Gods (Gann) **23**:165
Twilight in Delhi (Ali) **69**:20, 23-7, 29-32
"Twilight in Southern California" (Fuchs) **22**:157, 161
Twilight: Los Angeles, 1992 (Smith) **86**:265-73
Twilight of the Day (Jones) **10**:295
The Twilight of the Elephants (Vittorini)
   See *Il sempione strizza l'occhio al frejus*
"Twilight of the Gods" (MacNeice) **53**:233
The Twilight of the Gods of the Steppe (*The Twilight of the Steppe Gods*) (Kadare) **52**:259, 262
The Twilight of the Steppe Gods (Kadare)
   See *The Twilight of the Gods of the Steppe*
The Twilight Zone (Serling) **30**:354, 358-59
The Twin In the Clouds (Pasternak)
   See *Bliznets v tuchakh*
"Twin Peaks" (Whalen) **6**:566
Twin Peaks (Lynch) **66**:265-70
Twinkle, Twinkle, Little Spy (*Catch a Falling Spy*) (Deighton) **7**:76; **46**:127-29
"The Twins" (Bukowski) **41**:64; **108**:111
"Twins" (Kelley) **22**:247
"The Twins" (Livesay) **79**:348
"Twins" (Oates) **108**:384
"The Twins" (Spark) **13**:519; **40**:401
"The Twins" (Van Duyn) **116**:402
"Twin-Sets and Pickle Forks" (Dunn) **40**:170-72
"The Twist" (Olson) **29**:334
The Twisted Thing (Spillane) **13**:528
"The Twisted Trinity" (McCullers) **100**:260
"The Twitching Colonel" (White) **69**:406-07
"Two" (Allen) **84**:41
"Two" (Creeley) **78**:139
"Two" (Cummings) **15**:161
"2" (Seger) **35**:380
"Two" (Singer) **23**:421
The Two (Wallace) **13**:570
Two: A Phallic Novel (Moravia)
   See *Io e lui*
Two Against One (Barthelme) **117**:7-8, 11, 14, 19, 21-2
"Two American Haikus" (Stern) **100**:329
The Two Americas (Fuentes) **113**:263
"Two and a Half Acres" (Shapcott) **38**:400
Two and the Town (Felsen) **17**:121-22
"Two Annas" (Greenberg) **7**:134
"Two Appearances" (Scannell) **49**:331
"Two Armies" (Spender) **41**:425
"Two Arts" (Rich) **76**:218
"The Two Audens" (Schwartz) **87**:346
"Two Bodies" (Paz) **51**:327
Two Books (Pasternak) **63**:289

"Two Boys" (Moore) **68**:297, 300
"Two Brothers" (Ai) **69**:9-10, 15, 17
"The Two Brothers" (Hesse) **25**:260
"The Two Brothers" (Pritchett) **4T**:334
Two Brothers (Middleton) **38**:331-32
Two Bucks without Hair, and Other Stories (Millin) **49**:252
Two by Two (Gellhorn) **14**:195; **60**:184-85
Two by Two (*A Love, on a Season*) (Stolz) **12**:548, 553
"Two Campers in Cloud Country" (Plath) **11**:448; **111**:200-01, 210
"Two Castilians in Seville" (Cabral de Melo Neto)
   See "Dois castelhanos em Sevilha"
"Two Centuries of Canadian Cities" (Avison) **97**:72
Two Cheers for Democracy (Forster) **1**:104; **2**:135; **45**:144; **77**:242
"Two Children" (Guillen)
   See "Dos niños"
"Two Circuses Equal One Cricket Match" (Raine) **103**:180
Two Citizens (Wright) **3**:544; **5**:519-21; **10**:547; **28**:463, 465-66, 471-73
"Two Colonials" (Calisher) **38**:70
"Two Comrades" (Voinovich)
   See "Dva tovarishcha"
"Two Conceits" (Tate) **14**:532
"Two Corpses Go Dancing" (Singer) **9**:487; **11**:499; **111**:314
Two Crimes (Ibarguengoitia)
   See *Dos crímenes*
The Two Cultures and the Scientific Revolution (Snow) **1**:315-16; **13**:512-13
Two Daughters (Ray)
   See *Teen Kanya*
"Two Deaths" (Ashbery) **13**:36
Two Deaths (Amado)
   See "A Morte e a morte de Quincas Berro Dágua"
The Two Deaths of Christopher Martin (Golding)
   See *Pincher Martin*
The Two Deaths of Quincas Wateryell (Amado)
   See "A Morte e a morte de Quincas Berro Dágua"
"Two Dreamers" (Soto) **80**:298, 300
"Two Dreamtimes" (Wright) **53**:432
"Two Egrets" (Ciardi) **40**:154; **44**:382
"The Two Elenas" (Fuentes)
   See "Las dos Elenas"
Two English Girls (Truffaut)
   See *Deux Anglaises et le continent*
"The Two Environments" (Trilling) **24**:460
The Two Executioners (Arrabal)
   See *Les deux bourreaux*
The Two Faces of January (Highsmith) **2**:192; **4**:225; **42**:212; **102**:173, 189, 193, 196
The Two Faces of the Boss (Valdez)
   See *Las dos caras del patroncito*
"Two Families" (Lish) **45**:230
The Two Fiddlers: Tales from Orkney (Brown) **48**:55
Two Figures (Momaday) **85**:270
"The Two Fires" (Wright) **53**:420, 431
The Two Fires (Wright) **53**:419-20, 423, 428-29, 431
"Two for Heinrich Bleucher" (Weiss) **14**:557
Two for the Seesaw (Gibson) **23**:173-78
"Two Fragments: March 199-" (McEwan) **66**:280-81
"The Two Fraternities" (Peake) **54**:373
"The Two Freedoms" (Silkin) **43**:399-400

The Two Freedoms (Silkin) **6**:498; **43**:395-96
"Two Friends" (Voinovich)
   See "Dva tovarishcha"
"Two from Ireland" (Davie) **31**:124
"Two Funerals" (Buckley) **57**:126
Two Gentlemen in Bonds (Ransom) **4**:436
"Two Ghosts" (Dubus) **97**:233
Two Giants (O'Brien) **116**:187
Two Girls, Fat and Thin (Gaitskill) **69**:203-08
"Two Hangovers" (Wright) **5**:519
"Two History Professors Found Guilty of Murder" (Durcan) **43**:114, 116
"Two Horses" (Merwin) **45**:276-77
"Two Horses" (Oliver) **98**:265
"Two Horses Playing in the Orchard" (Wright) **3**:540
"Two Hours in an Empty Tank" (Brodsky) **4**:77; **6**:97
"Two Hours to a Kill" (McGuane) **45**:266
"Two Houses" (Merwin) **45**:275
"252 or at the End of a Volume" (Kunene) **85**:176
"201 Upper Terrace, San Francisco" (Olds) **85**:297
200 Motels (Zappa) **17**:587-88
The 290 (O'Dell) **30**:274-75
"Two Images" (Ezekiel) **61**:93, 103
"Two Images of Continuing Trouble" (Silkin) **43**:404
Two in One (Smith) **3**:460
"Two in the Bush" (Thomas) **107**:316, 318, 320
"Two in the Bush, and Other Stories" (Thomas) **107**:316, 332
"Two Insomniacs" (Oates) **9**:403
Two Into One (Cooney) **62**:144
Two Is Lonely (Banks) **23**:42
The Two Jakes (Towne) **87**:369-70, 373, 377-78
"Two Kinds of Angel" (Edgar) **42**:123
"Two Kitchens in Provence" (Fisher) **87**:128
"Two Ladies in Retirement" (Taylor) **18**:522-23; **37**:409, 411; **44**:305
"Two Leading Lights" (Frost) **26**:118
Two Leaves and a Bud (Anand) **23**:15-16; **93**:33, 36, 42
"Two Letters" (Strand) **71**:288
"Two Little Hitlers" (Costello) **21**:71-2
Two Lives and a Dream (Yourcenar)
   See *Comme l'eau qui coule*
Two Lives: Reading Turgenev; My House in Umbria (*My House in Umbria; Reading Turgenev*) (Trevor) **71**:350-52; **116**:365, 367, 372, 377
"Two Look at Two" (Frost) **26**:111
Two Lovely Beasts, and Other Stories (O'Flaherty) **34**:356-57
"Two Loves" (Eberhart) **56**:77
"Two Mayday Selves" (Avison) **4**:37; **97**:92
"Two Meditations" (Barth) **9**:67; **89**:5-6, 16, 21, 26, 44, 61-2
"Two Men" (Prichard) **46**:333
Two Men and a Wardrobe (Polanski) **16**:462, 464, 471
Two Moons (Heppenstall) **10**:272-73
"Two More Gallants" (Trevor) **71**:333
"Two More under the Indian Sun" (Jhabvala) **8**:312
"Two Morning Monologues" (Bellow) **1**:31
"Two Motions" (Ammons) **8**:18
Two Much (Westlake) **7**:529
"The Two Numantias" (Fuentes) **113**:262, 264
"Two of a Kind" (O'Faolain) **14**:405

"Two of Hearts" (Hogan) **73**:158

The Two of Them (Russ) **15**:462

The Two of Us (Braine) **41**:61-2

The Two of Us (Moravia)
    See *Io e lui*

"Two of Us Staring into Another Dimension" (Oates) **3**:359

"The Two of Us Together and Each of Us Alone" (Amichai)
    See "Shneynu beyahad vekhol ehad lehud"

"The Two Old Maids" (Landolfi) **49**:209-10

"Two on a Party" (Williams) **45**:452, 454

Two on an Island (Rice) **7**:361, 363; **49**:298, 300

"Two or Three Graces" (Huxley) **11**:281

Two or Three Things I Know about Her (Godard)
    See *Deux ou trois choses que je sais d'elle*

"Two Organs" (Berryman) **62**:58

"Two Pair" (Nemerov) **9**:395

"Two Peas in a Pod" (Skvorecky) **69**:337

Two People (Dreyer) **16**:263, 269

"II Peter, ii, 22" (Blunden) **56**:43

"Two Pilgrims" (Taylor) **18**:524, 526

Two Plays (O'Casey) **88**:234, 236

Two Plays (Rice) **7**:361

"Two Poems" (Madhubuti) **73**:191

"Two Poems" (Plumly) **33**:313-14

Two Poems (Merrill) **3**:334

"Two Poems about President Harding" (Wright) **3**:541

"2 Poems from the Ohara Monogatari" (O'Hara) **78**:336

Two Poems in the Air (Dickey) **109**:244

"Two Poems of Flight-Sleep" (Dickey) **15**:178

"Two Poems of the Military" (Dickey) **15**:177

"Two Poems on the Catholic Bavarians" (Bowers) **9**:121

"Two Poems on the Passing of an Empire" (Walcott) **42**:421

"Two Portraits" (Abse) **29**:14

"Two Portraits of Sex" (Larkin) **64**:262, 282

"The Two Presences" (Bly) **15**:64

"Two Private Lives" (Tuohy) **37**:433

"Two Quatrains" (Amichai) **116**:95

"Two Rides on a Bike" (Ryan) **65**:215

Two Rode Together (Ford) **16**:319

"The Two Roots of Judaism" (Wesker) **42**:430

"Two Scenes" (Ashbery) **4**:23; **77**:57-8

"Two Seaside Yarns" (Katz) **47**:223

"Two Seedings" (Clark) **38**:126

"The Two Selves" (Avison) **4**:36; **97**:92

Two Serious Ladies (Bowles) **3**:84; **68**:2-13, 16, 18, 20-21

"Two Ships" (Boyle) **90**:46

The Two Shorts (Fuentes) **113**:262

"The Two Sides of a Drum" (Smith) **15**:514

"Two Sides of a Story" (Wright) **53**:432

"Two Sisters" (Farrell) **66**:131

"The Two Sisters" (Fuller) **62**:186, 192, 203

The Two Sisters (Arundel) **17**:12-13, 17

The Two Sisters (Bates) **46**:47-9, 54, 56

Two Sisters (Vidal) **2**:449; **4**:554; **6**:549-50; **8**:525; **33**:407; **72**:387

"Two Sisters of Persephone" (Plath) **17**:354

"Two Sketches from *House Made of Dawn*" (Momaday) **85**:228

"Two Soldiers" (Faulkner) **3**:149

Two Solitudes (MacLennan) **2**:257; **14**:339, 340, 342-43; **92**:298, 300-05, 307-10, 312-18, 321-23, 325-26, 341-43, 346, 350

"Two Songs for the Round of the Year" (Smith) **42**:350

"Two Songs from 'The Hunted Revolutionaries'" (McGrath) **59**:182

"Two Songs of Advent" (Winters) **32**:469

Two Sought Adventure (Leiber) **25**:302

Two Stars for Comfort (Mortimer) **28**:283-86

"Two Statements on Ives" (Cage) **41**:78

"Two Stories" (Gallagher) **18**:169

"Two Summer Jobs" (Leithauser) **27**:240-42

"Two Suns in the Sunset" (Pink Floyd) **35**:315

Two Tales About Life (Lagerkvist)
    See *Två sagor om livit*

Two Tales and Eight Tomorrows (Harrison) **42**:199

Two Tales of the Occult (Eliade) **19**:146-47

"Two Things, Dimly, Were Going At Each Other" (Hannah) **90**:160

2001: A Space Odyssey (Clarke) **1**:59; **4**:104-05; **13**:150-51, 153-55; **18**:105-06; **35**:118, 122-27

2001: A Space Odyssey (Kubrick) **16**:382-89, 391

Two Thousand Seasons (Armah) **33**:28-9, 32-6

2010: Odyssey Two (Clarke) **35**:125-29

"The 2003 Claret" (Amis) **40**:43

"2x2" (Dylan) **77**:183-84

Two to Conquer (Bradley) **30**:29-30

The Two Towers (Tolkien) **12**:565; **38**:434

Two Trains Running (Wilson) **63**:458

"Two Tramps in Mud Time" (Frost) **10**:195, 198; **26**:122; **34**:475

"221-1424 (San/francisco/suicide/number)" (Sanchez) **116**:295

Two Valleys (Fast) **23**:153

"Two Variations" (Levertov) **5**:248

"Two Venetian Pieces" (Montale) **9**:388

Two Views (Johnson)
    See *Zwei Ansichten*

"Two Views of a Cadaver Room" (Plath) **11**:446; **14**:426

"Two Views of Marilyn Monroe" (Clark) **38**:128

"Two Views of Nature: White and Indian" (Waters) **88**:343, 347

"Two Views of Withens" (Plath) **111**:202, 206

Two Virgins (Markandaya) **8**:376-77; **38**:325-26

Two Virgins: Unfinished Music Number One (Lennon) **35**:261, 267, 270

"Two Visits" (Barnard) **48**:27

"Two Voices" (Abse) **29**:17

"Two Voices" (Blunden) **56**:43

Two Voices (Cabral de Melo Neto)
    See *Dois palamentos*

Two Voices (Thomas) **13**:541

"Two Voices in a Meadow" (Wilbur) **14**:577; **110**:374

Two Waters (Cabral de Melo Neto)
    See *Duas aguas*

"Two Weddings and One Divorce" (Singer) **15**:509

Two Weeks in Another Town (Shaw) **7**:414; **23**:398, 400; **34**:368

"Two Went to Sleep" (Cohen) **38**:136

Two Wings the Butterfly (Vizenor) **103**:308

Two Wise Children (Graves) **39**:325

"Two Wise Generals" (Hughes) **9**:284

"Two Wise Men" (Kunene) **85**:166

Two Witches (Frost) **9**:224

Two Women (Lee) **90**:201

Two Women (Moravia)
    See *La ciociara*

Two Women (Mulisch) **42**:288-89

Two Women (De Sica)
    See *La ciociara*

Two Women and Their Man (Jones) **52**:252

"Two Words" (Allende) **97**:

"Two Working" (Clarke) **61**:73

"Two Worlds" (Maclean) **78**:239

Two Worlds and Their Ways (Compton-Burnett) **15**:140

"The Two Worlds of Ernst" (Wain) **46**:411

Two Years (O'Flaherty) **34**:357

Two-and-Twenty (Forester) **35**:165-66

The Two-Character Play (*Out Cry*) (Williams) **5**:501-02, 504; **15**:582-83; **19**:472; **45**:444, 447-52, 455

The Twofold Vibration (Federman) **47**:127-29

"The Two-Headed Eagle" (Haavikko) **34**:175

Two-Headed Poems (Atwood) **15**:36-7; **18**:37; **25**:65, 69; **84**:66, 68

Two-Headed Woman (Clifton) **66**:68, 80-1, 84-6

Two-Lane Blacktop (Wurlitzer) **15**:589

Two-Part Inventions (Howard) **7**:167-68; **10**:274-76; **47**:168-69, 171

"Two-Part Pear Able" (Swenson) **61**:399; **106**:325

Twopence Coloured (Hamilton) **51**:183, 194

Two's Company (Middleton) **38**:329

"Two's Enough of a Crowd" (Hunter) **35**:226

2000 (Neruda) **28**:310

The Two-Thousand-Pound Goldfish (Byars) **35**:74-5

Two-Way Traffic (Lieber) **6**:312

The Twyborn Affair (White) **18**:546-49; **65**:275-76, 278, 281-82; **69**:410

"Tying One On in Vienna" (Kizer) **80**:172, 185

Tynset (Hildesheimer) **49**:167-68, 170, 175, 179

Types of Shape (Hollander) **2**:197; **5**:186; **8**:302

The Typewriter (Cocteau) **43**:110, 112

Typewriter in the Sky (Hubbard) **43**:205, 207

The Typewriter Revolution and Other Poems (Enright) **4**:155

"Typhoid Epidemic" (Faludy) **42**:140

"Typhus" (Simpson) **32**:377-78, 380

Typical American (Jen) **70**:69-77

"A Typical Canadian Family Visits Disney World" (McFadden) **48**:250

"A Typical Day in Winnipeg" (Purdy) **50**:247

The Typists (Schisgal) **6**:489

"The Typographer's Ornate Symbol at the End of a Chapter or Story" (Avison) **97**:111

Tyrannus Nix? (Ferlinghetti) **111**:68

"The Tyranny of Trivia" (Thurber) **5**:433

"Tyrant of the Syracuse" (MacLeish) **8**:362

"Tyrants Destroyed" (Nabokov) **6**:357-60

Tyrants Destroyed, and Other Stories (Nabokov) **11**:391

Tystnaden (*The Silence*) (Bergman) **16**:56, 58, 62, 64, 67-8, 70-1, 74, 79-80; **72**:39-41, 52, 54-5, 59, 62

Tzili: The Story of a Life (Appelfeld) **47**:2-3, 5-6

"U" (Merrill) **8**:383-84, 387

U agoniji (*In Agony*) (Krleza) **8**:329; **114**:167, 177

U predvecerje (Krleza) **114**:173

The U.A.W. and Walter Reuther (Howe) **85**:115

Über allen Gipfeln ist Ruh: ein deutscher Dichtertag um 1980 (*Rest beyond the Peaks*) (Bernhard) **61**:26

Über das selbstverständliche: Politische Schriften (Grass) **49**:139; **88**:168

"Über die Brücke" (Boell)　11:53; 27:56-7; 72:69

Über Mein Lehrer Döblin (*On My Master Döblin*) (Grass)　88:147

Über mein Theater (Hochwalder)　36:237

"Die Überflutung" (Hofmann)　54:225

Die Überflutung: Vier Hörspiele (Hofmann)　54:225

"Überlebende" (Sachs)　98:328

Ubik (Dick)　30:115-17, 119; 72:104, 108, 110-12, 117, 119, 121-22

"Ubiquity" (Pinget)　37:365

Uccellacci e uccellini (*The Hawks and the Sparrows*) (Pasolini)　20:260, 271; 106:220, 226, 273

"The UFO Menace" (Allen)　52:42

"The Ugliest Woman" (Souster)　5:396

"Ugly Corner" (MacCaig)　36:285

"Ugly Honkies; or, The Election Game and How to Win It" (Giovanni)　19:191; 64:183

"The Ugly Little Boy" (Asimov)　76:321

An Ugly Little Secret: Anti-Catholicism in North America (Greeley)　28:173

"The Ugly Poem That Reluctantly Accepts 'Itself' As Its Only Title" (Dubie)　36:132

Ugly Swans (Strugatskii and Strugatskii)　27:434, 436

"Ugolino" (Heaney)　25:248; 74:190; 91:115

Uh Huh; But How Do It Free Us? (Sanchez)　116:284-85, 301

"Uh, Philosophy" (Ammons)　57:52

"Uh-Oh, Love Comes to Town" (Byrne)　26:94

Die Uhren (*The Clocks*) (Hildesheimer)　49:167

"Ukhod Khama" ("Ham's Departure") (Leonov)　92:237, 264

Ukulele Music (Reading)　47:353-54

"Ulan Dhor Ends a Dream" (Vance)　35:420

"Ulcer" (Pesetsky)　28:358

"Ulica u jesenje jutro" ("A Street in an Autumn Morning") (Krleza)　114:166

"El *Ulises* de Joyce" (Borges)　4:71

Ulla Winblad (*The Music and Life of Carl Michael Bellman*) (Zuckmayer)　18:556

"Ullswater" (Gunesekera)　91:37

"Ulrich and the Doctor" (Vollmann)　89:305

"Ulrike" (Borges)　13:110; 48:39-41; 83:189

"Ulster Today" (Simmons)　43:408

"An Ulster Twilight" (Heaney)　74:167

La última canción de Manuel Sendero (*The Last Song of Manuel Sendero*) (Dorfman)　48:92-5; 77:133, 135, 137-43, 146-49, 152-53

"Ultima Thule" (Nabokov)　3:354

The Ultimate Adventure (Hubbard)　43:203

"The Ultimate City" (Ballard)　14:39, 41-2; 36:38

The Ultimate Good Luck　99:105, 110, 116-17, 120-21

The Ultimate Good Luck (Ford)　46:158-59, 161

"Ultimate Professor" (Redgrove)　41:354

"The Ultimate Safari" (Gordimer)　70:177-78, 180

Ultimate Values (Sassoon)　36:392

"Ultimatum" (Gustafson)　36:214

Ultimatum (Vesaas)　48:406

"Ultime" (Ungaretti)　11:559

"Ultimi cori" (Ungaretti)　7:483

"El último amor" (Aleixandre)　9:12

"El último baile" ("The Last Dance") (Zamora)　89:384, 386

Ultimo round (*Last Round*) (Cortazar)　5:110; 92:158

"El último viaje del buque fantasma" ("The Last Voyage of the Ghost Ship") (Garcia Marquez)　2:149; 27:147; 47:151

Ultimo viene il corvo (Calvino)　39:314

Ultramarine (*In a Marine Light*) (Carver)　53:60-1; 55:275

"Uluru Wild Fig Song" (Snyder)　32:396

"Ulysses" (Ciardi)　40:156

"Ulysses" (Ferron)　94:103, 123, 125

"Ulysses" (Graves)　45:161, 173

"Ulysses" (Soyinka)　36:417; 44:285

"Ulysses and Circe" (Lowell)　11:325, 330; 37:238

Ulysses in Traction (Innaurato)　21:194-96; 60:200-01, 205

"Ulysses, Order, and Myth" (Eliot)　10:172

"De um avião" ("From an Airplane") (Cabral de Melo Neto)　76:167

Umberto D (De Sica)　20:86-94, 96

Der umbewusste Gott: Psychotherapie und religion (*The Unconscious God: Psychotherapy and Theology*) (Frankl)　93:209-10, 216, 222

"The Umbilical Cord" (Gordimer)　18:185

"The Umbrella" (Plomer)　4:407; 8:446

An Umbrella from Piccadilly (Seifert)　34:257, 261-62; 44:423

Umbrella from Piccadilly (Seifert)
　See *Deštník z Piccadilly*

The Umbrella from Piccadilly (Seifert)
　See *Deštník z Piccadilly*

An Umbrella from Piccadilly (Seifert)
　See *Deštník z Piccadilly*

"U.M.C." (Seger)　35:380

Umi to dokuyaku (*The Sea and Poison*) (Endo)　19:161; 54:151-53, 159; 99:283, 285, 299

"L'umile Itallia" (Pasolini)　106:265

Ummagumma (Pink Floyd)　35:305-08, 311

"Die Umsiedler" (Schmidt)　56:391, 405

"Umykanie, ili Zagadka Endurtsev" ("Abduction of the Endursky Enigma"; "The Abduction; or, The Mystery of the Endurtsies") (Iskander)　47:196, 198

"U.N. Hymn" (Auden)　2:28

U.N. Journal (Buckley)　7:35

"Unaccompanied Sonata" (Card)　47:68

Unaccompanied Sonata, and Other Stories (Card)　47:67-8

"Unacknowledged Legislators and Art pour Art" (Rexroth)　49:278; 112:373

Un'altra vita (*Lady Godiva and Other Stories*) (Moravia)　7:242, 244

The Un-Americans (Bessie)　23:60, 62

"The Un-Angry Young Men" (Fiedler)　24:191

Unassigned Frequencies: American Poetry in Review, 1964-77 (Lieberman)　36:259-60, 264

Unattainable Earth (Milosz)
　See *Niobjeta ziemia*

"The Unattained" (Gascoyne)　45:157

The Unbearable Lightness of Being (Kundera)
　See *L'insoutenable l'égrèté de l'être*

"Unbelievable" (Dylan)　77:182, 184-85

"Unbelievable Encounter" (Arghezi)
　See "O întîlnire de necrezut"

"The Unbeliever" (Bishop)　9:96; 32:37

Unberechenbare Gäste (Boell)　72:71

The Unblinding (Lieberman)　36:261, 263

"Unborn" (Muldoon)　32:316

"The Unborn" (Wright)　53:419, 428

"Unborn Child" (Oates)　6:367

"Unborn Song" (Rukeyser)　27:411

"Unborn Things" (Lane)　25:286

Unborn Things: South American Poems (Lane)　25:284-85

"Unbroken Lineage" (Avison)　97:76, 129-30, 133-34

"The Uncanny" (Hemingway)　8:289

The Uncertain Certainty (Simic)　49:339; 68:370-71

Uncertain Friend (Heym)　41:216

Uncertainties and Rest (Steele)　45:362-65

"Unchain My Heart" (Jones)　81:61, 63-5, 67

"The Unchangeable" (Blunden)　56:41

Uncharted Stars (Norton)　12:466-67

Uncivil Seasons (Malone)　43:282

"Unclaimed" (Seth)　43:388; 90:338

"Uncle" (Tate)　6:528

"Uncle Albert/Admiral Halsey" (McCartney)　35:279, 290-91

"Uncle and Nephew" (Cabral de Melo Neto)
　See "Tio e sobrinho"

"Uncle Anne" (Boyle)　19:62

"Uncle Arthur" (Bowie)　17:65

"Uncle Ben's Choice" (Achebe)　26:23; 75:14

"Uncle Bernie's Farm" (Zappa)　17:585

"Uncle Bullboy" (Jordan)　114:146

"Uncle Casper" (Stuart)　14:518

"Uncle Dockery and the Independent Bull" (Mitchell)　98:187

"Uncle Fremmis" (Sturgeon)　22:411

"Uncle Grant" (Price)　43:341

"Uncle Jack" (Simmons)　43:408, 410

"Uncle Jeff" (Stuart)　14:514

Uncle Louis (Bowering)　47:28-9

Uncle Meat (Zappa)　17:585-87, 589, 591

"Uncle Meat Variations" (Zappa)　17:585

"Uncle Roger" (Van Doren)　10:495

Uncle Sandro and the End of the Goatibex (Iskander)
　See *Diadia Sandro i konets kozlotura*

"Uncle Sandro and the Slave Khazarat" (Iskander)　47:197

"Uncle Spencer" (Huxley)　11:281

"Uncle T" (Moore)　90:277

"Uncle Theodore" (Dinesen)　10:148-49; 95:67

Uncle Tom's Children (Wright)　1:379-80; 4:594-95; 9:585; 14:596-98; 21:435, 444, 452; 74:363, 370, 378, 383, 385, 390, 393

"Uncle Tony's Goat" (Silko)　23:412; 74:347

"Uncle Wiggily in Connecticut" (Salinger)　12:498

"Uncles" (Atwood)　84:96

"Uncles" (Taylor)　37:409

"Uncle's Letters" (Narayan)　47:305

Uncollected Poems (Betjeman)　34:306; 43:50-1

Uncollected Poems (Plath)　9:425

The Uncollected Stories of William Faulkner (Faulkner)　18:148-49

The Uncollected Wodehouse (Wodehouse)　22:483-84

"Uncommon Visage" (Brodsky)　100:69

Uncommon Women and Others: A Play about Five Women Graduates of a Seven Sisters College Six Years Later (Wasserstein)　32:439-40; 59:219-21, 223; 90:405, 407-8, 410-413, 416, 418-23, 429-31, 433

Unconditional Surrender (Waugh)　1:358-59; 8:543; 19:461; 27:472

The Unconquered (Ray)
　See *Aparajito*

"Unconscious" (Breton)　54:30

The Unconscious God: Psychotherapy and The-

ology (Frankl)
   See *Der umbewusste Gott: Psychotherapie und religion*
Unconscious Motives of the Motion Picture Industry (Foreman)   50:168
"The Unconsidered Life" (Musgrave)   54:341
The Unconsoled (Ishiguro)   110:257-58, 260-63, 265
"Uncontrollable Feeling of Ecstasy" (Kunene)   85:176
The Uncorrected World (Hanson)   13:263
"The Uncreating Chaos" (Spender)   41:427, 429
"The Uncreation" (Pinsky)   94:309
"Unctuous Platitudes" (Ashbery)   77:59
Und Niemand weiss weiter (*And No One Knows Where to Go*) (Sachs)   98:321-22, 324
Und Sagte kein einziges Wort (*Acquainted with the Night; And Never Said a Word*) (Boell)   6:83; 9:102-04, 106-07, 109; 11:57-9; 27:54-9
"Und wir die Ziehlen" (Sachs)   98:341
"The Undead" (Graves)   11:256
"The Undead" (Wilbur)   53:405; 110:384
"The Undecided" (Ritsos)   31:324
"The Undefeated" (Hemingway)   13:280; 19:212; 30:179, 182; 61:190; 80:137
"The Undelivered" (Cioran)   64:89, 94
Under a Changing Moon (Benary-Isbert)   12:34
"Under a Glass Bell" (Nin)   60:267
Under a Glass Bell (Nin)   14:381-82; 60:267, 269
Under a Soprano Sky (Sanchez)   116:302, 307-08, 310-11, 318, 324-25
"Under a White Shawl of Pine" (Smith)   42:350
Under Aldebaran (McAuley)   45:245-47, 249, 252-54
"Under Arcturus" (Jones)   42:242-43
"Under Black Leaves" (Merwin)   13:383
"Under Capricorn" (Hollander)   2:197
Under Capricorn (Hitchcock)   16:345
"Under Cows" (Plumly)   33:312
"Under Glass" (Atwood)   13:46; 25:62
"Under House Arrest" (Brutus)   43:93
"Under Icebergs" (Hall)   51:170
Under My Skin (Lessing)   94:276-81, 283-84, 286-87
"Under My Thumb" (Jagger and Richard)   17:226, 230, 234-35, 239
"Under One Small Star" (Szymborska)   99:201
Under Plain Cover (Osborne)   45:313-14, 316
"Under Pressure" (Transtroemer)   52:411; 65:223
Under Pressure (Herbert)
   See *Twenty-First Century Sub*
"Under Sedation" (Hope)   51:222
Under Sentence of Death (Genet)   44:386
"Under St. Paul's" (Davie)   31:109
"Under Stars" (Gallagher)   63:122
Under Stars (Gallagher)   18:169-70; 63:119-20, 122
Under the Banyan Tree and Other Stories (Narayan)   47:304-06
"Under the Bell Jar" (Nemerov)   6:361
"Under the Boathouse" (Bottoms)   53:32-3
"Under the Dog Star" (Ekelof)   27:110
Under the Eye of the Clock (Nolan)   58:362-67
Under the Eye of the Storm (Hersey)   40:237-39
"Under the Falling Sky" (Browne)   21:38
"Under the Garden" (Greene)   3:213, 215
Under the Ice (Nowlan)   15:398

"Under the Influence" (Bowering)   32:48
Under the Jaguar Sun (Calvino)
   See *Sotto il sole giaguro*
"Under the Knife" (Singer)   15:504
"Under the Lights" (Dubus)   97:231-33
"Under the Maud Moon" (Kinnell)   5:216-17
"Under the Moon's Reign" (Tomlinson)   45:394
Under the Mountain Wall: A Chronicle of Two Seasons of the Stone Age (Matthiessen)   7:210; 11:360; 32:287, 290; 64:309
Under the Net (Murdoch)   1:234, 236; 2:295, 297; 4:367-69; 6:342, 345; 8:404; 11:386; 15:384-86; 22:328; 31:293; 51:289
Under the Red Flag (Jin)   109:54
Under the Red Sky (Dylan)   77:181-85
Under the Roofs of Paris (Clair)
   See *Sous les toits de Paris*
"Under the Rose" (Pynchon)   33:338, 340; 62:433
Under the Rose (Davies)   23:145
Under The Sea Wind: A Naturalist's Picture of Ocean Life (Carson)   71:100, 102-09
Under the Sign of Saturn (Sontag)   31:411-13, 415-16
Under the Skin of the Statue of Liberty (Yevtushenko)   13:619
Under the Skin: The Death of White Rhodesia (Caute)   29:122-24
"Under the Sky" (Bowles)   19:60
Under the Sweetwater Rim (L'Amour)   25:280
"Under the Tree" (Johnston)   51:240-43, 245, 252
"Under the Tree" (Levertov)   28:239
"Under the Trees" (Kaufman)   8:317
"Under the Viaduct" (Dove)   50:153; 81:139
"Under the Vulture-Tree" (Bottoms)   53:33
Under the Vulture-Tree (Bottoms)   53:33-4
Under the Weather (Bellow)   6:49-50
"Under the Wheat" (De Marinis)   54:99-101
Under the Wheel (Hesse)
   See *Unterm Rad*
Under Venus (Straub)   107:274, 283, 292, 304-05, 307, 310
"Under Water" (Strand)   41:440
"Under Which Lyre" (Auden)   14:28
Undercliff: Poems, 1940-1953 (Eberhart)   3:133; 11:178; 19:144; 56:81-3
"The Underdog" (Tolson)   105:260
"The Underground" (Heaney)   74:167, 190
Underground Alley (Mayne)   12:389, 395, 405
The Underground Game (Mallet-Joris)
   See *Le jeu du souterrain*
"The Underground Garage" (Beer)   58:31
The Underground Man (Macdonald)   1:185; 2:255-56; 14:332, 335-36; 41:267, 269-70
Underground Man (Meltzer)   26:301-02
The Underground River (Sarton)   91:241
Underground River, Underground Birds (Konwicki)
   See *Rzeka podziemna, podziemne ptaki*
"Underground the Darkness Is the Light" (Carruth)   84:134, 136
The Underground Woman (Boyle)   5:66-7
"Undergrowth" (p'Bitek)   96:286
"The Undersea Farmer" (Howes)   15:290
"Understanding Alvarado" (Apple)   33:18-19
"Understanding and Politics" (Arendt)   98:50, 52
"Understanding but not Forgetting" (Madhubuti)   73:206-07, 209
Understanding Drama (Brooks)   110:20, 29, 33

Understanding Fiction (Brooks)   110:14, 20, 29, 33
Understanding Fiction (Warren)   59:297, 299
Understanding Media: The Extensions of Man (McLuhan)   37:255-63, 265-66; 83:359-64, 367, 369, 373
Understanding Poetry (Brooks)   24:111, 116; 86:278-79; 110:3, 14-15, 20, 29, 31, 33, 38, 40
Understanding Poetry (Warren)   39:257; 59:297, 299-300
Understrike (Gardner)   30:151-52
The Understudy (Kazan)   6:274; 63:219
The Undertaker (Hawkes)   4:213, 215
The Undertaker's Gone Bananas (Zindel)   26:475-77, 479-80
"The Undertaking" (Gluck)   22:174
Undertones of War (Blunden)   2:65; 56:28, 31, 33, 38, 42-4, 51
"Underture" (Townshend)   17:526
"Underwater" (Bioy Casares)   88:92-3, 95
Underworld (Hecht)   8:274
Underworld (Sternberg)   20:368
"The Undesirables" (Huddle)   49:184
Undesirables (Gunn)   81:178
"The Undesireables" (Cabral de Melo Neto)
   See "A indesjada das gentes"
"Undine" (Heaney)   37:162; 74:154
"Undine geht" ("Undine Goes") (Bachmann)   69:35, 37, 45
"Undine Goes" (Bachmann)
   See "Undine geht"
The Undoing (Mastrosimone)   36:291
"Undress the Bureaucrat" (Alegria)   57:11
The Undying Grass (Kemal)
   See *Ölmez otu*
"Uneasy Love" (Kunene)   85:166
Unemi románu: Cesta Vladislava Vancuryza velkou epikou (*The Art of the Novel: Vladislav Vancura's Search for the Great Epic*) (Kundera)   68:242-46, 248-50, 253-54, 263; 115:320-21, 324-25, 355-56, 358, 360
"Unemployment Monologue" (Jordan)   114:145
Unending Blues (Simic)   49:339, 341-43
"The Unending Rose" (Borges)   13:110
The Unending Rose (Borges)   13:110
"Unes" (Bagryana)   10:14
"An Unexpected Adventure" (Gerstler)   70:158
"Unexpected Freedom" (Peacock)   60:298
The Unexpected Guest (Christie)   12:125
Unexpected Night (Daly)   52:86-7
The Unexpected Universe (Eiseley)   7:90
"Unexpected Visit" (Adcock)   41:18
Unexplained Laughter (Ellis)   40:193-94
The Unexpurgated Code: A Complete Manual of Survival and Manners (Donleavy)   6:142; 10:153-55; 45:125
Unfair Arguments with Existence (Ferlinghetti)   2:134; 111:63
"Unfinished After-Portrait (or: Stages of Mourning)" (Avison)   4:36; 97:76, 90
"Unfinished America" (Mott)   15:380-81
"The Unfinished Business of Childhood" (Abbott)   48:7
Unfinished Cathedral (Stribling)   23:443-45, 447
The Unfinished Man (Ezekiel)   61:91-2, 95-7, 100-01
The Unfinished Novel (Aragon)
   See *Le roman inachevé*
Unfinished Ode to Mud (Ponge)   6:422

"Unfinished Poem" (Larkin) **64**:276-77
Unfinished Portrait (Christie) **48**:78
"Unfinished Short Story" (Forster) **45**:133
Unfinished Tales of Númenor and Middle-Earth (Tolkien) **38**:431-32, 442
An Unfinished Woman: A Memoir (Hellman) **4**:221-22; **8**:280-82; **14**:259; **18**:224, 226, 228; **34**:349, 352; **44**:527-28, 530; **52**:189-204
"Unflushed Urinals" (Justice) **102**:259, 261, 269
"Unfold! Unfold!" (Roethke) **101**:274, 281, 284, 335, 339-40
Unfolding in Fog (Shamlu) **10**:469-70
"The Unforeseen" (Gerstler) **70**:158
The Unforgiven (Huston) **20**:168
The Unfortunates (Johnson) **9**:300-03
"Unframed Originals" (Merwin) **88**:189
Unframed Originals: Recollections (Merwin) **45**:271-74, 276-77; **88**:198, 200, 202
"Unfriendly Witness" (Starbuck) **53**:353, 355
Ungenach (Bernhard) **32**:17-18; **61**:9
"El ungido" (Castellanos) **66**:50
"The Unglamorous but Worthwhile Duties of the Black Revolutionary Artist" (Walker) **103**:365
The Ungrateful Garden (Kizer) **15**:308; **39**:171; **80**:171-75, 177, 179
The Ungrateful Land (Carrier) **78**:66
Unguarded Hours (Wilson) **33**:450-51
The Unguarded House (Boell)
  See *Haus ohne Hüter*
"Unguided Tour" (Sontag) **13**:516, 518; **105**:206
"The Unhappy Composer" (Kunene) **85**:175
The Unheard Cry for Meaning: Psychotherapy and Humanism (Frankl) **93**:219-20
"Unholy Living and Half Dying" (O'Faolain) **32**:341
Unholy Loves (Oates) **15**:402-03; **33**:292; **52**:338; **108**:386, 390
The Unholy Three (Browning) **16**:122, 124
The Unicorn (Murdoch) **1**:236; **3**:345, 347; **6**:345; **8**:406; **11**:386-87; **15**:381-83; **22**:324-26
The Unicorn (Walser)
  See *Das Einhorn*
The Unicorn and Other Poems, 1935-1955 (Lindbergh) **82**:158
"The Unicorn in the Garden" (Thurber) **5**:442; **11**:533
El unicornio (Mujica Lainez) **31**:282-83
"Uninvited Guests" **75**:77
Union Dues (Sayles) **10**:460-62; **14**:483-84
L'union libre (Breton) **54**:17, 30; **9**:133
"Union Maid" (Guthrie) **35**:191, 194
Union Street (Barker) **32**:11; **94**:2-3, 9, 11, 14
"The Unique/Universal" (Oates) **108**:356
Unit of Five (Dudek) **19**:136
"The United Church Observer" (McFadden) **48**:246, 248
"United Rapes Unlimited, Argentina" (Valenzuela) **31**:438
United States (Gelbart) **21**:131
"U.S. 1946 King's X" (Frost) **9**:223
U.S. Grant and the American Military Tradition (Catton) **35**:87-8
U.S.A. (Dos Passos) **1**:77-80; **4**:131-38; **8**:181-82; **11**:154-58; **15**:180-83, 185-87; **25**:137-38, 140-48; **34**:419-24; **82**:59-114
"U.S. One" (Rukeyser) **27**:406
U.S. One (Rukeyser) **15**:457-59; **27**:404-05,

408, 410
"The Unity" (Stern) **40**:414
The Unity of Marlowe's Doctor Faustus (Brooks) **24**:111
Unity of the Stream (Watkins) **43**:456-57
The Universal Baseball Association, Inc., J. Henry Waugh, Prop. (Coover) **3**:114; **7**:59-60; **15**:143; **32**:124-25; **46**:116-17, 119, 121; **87**:24-5, 27, 29, 35-8, 41, 43, 48, 50-1, 53, 58
A Universal History of Infamy (Borges)
  See *Historia universal de la infamia*
"Universal Love" (Cliff) **21**:65
"Universe" (Heinlein) **26**:163; **55**:304
"The Universe" (Swenson) **61**:390; **106**:316, 345
The Universe, and Other Fictions (West) **96**:363, 373, 384
"The Universe as Seen Through a Keyhole" (Galeano) **72**:130
"Universe into Stone" (Smith) **15**:516
"The Universe Is Closed and Has REMs" (Starbuck) **53**:354
"The Universe Is Not Really Expanding" (Willingham) **51**:403
"The Universe of Death" (Miller) **84**:252
A Universe of Time (Farrell) **11**:192
"The Universe Responds" (Walker) **58**:410
"University" (Shapiro) **15**:476; **53**:331
"University Examinations in Egypt" (Enright) **4**:154
"University Hospital, Boston" (Oliver) **34**:247; **98**:257, 267
"The University Is Something Else You Do" (Bell) **31**:51
"The University Toilet" (Simmons) **43**:408
An Unkindness of Ravens (Rendell) **48**:325
The Unknown (Browning) **16**:121, 123-25
The Unknown (Maugham) **11**:368
Unknown Assailant (Hamilton) **51**:192-93, 195
"An Unknown Child" (Gardam) **43**:171
"Unknown Citizen" (Auden) **3**:23
"Unknown Girl in the Maternity Ward" (Sexton) **53**:317
Unknown Man, No. 89 (Leonard) **28**:233; **71**:219
The Unknown Men (Vesaas)
  See *Dei ukjende mennene*
"The Unknown Soldier" (Morrison) **17**:287, 291-92, 295-96
Unlawful Assembly (Enright) **31**:150, 154
Unleaving (Walsh) **35**:431-34
"Unless" (Warren) **18**:537
"The Unlikely" (MacCaig) **36**:284
Unlikely Stories, Mostly (Gray) **41**:178-79, 181-83
Unlimited (Cliff) **21**:60-1
The Unlimited Dream Company (Ballard) **14**:40
"The Unlived Life" (Boland) **113**:77, 84
The Unloved: From the Diary of Perla S. (Lustig) **56**:186-87
The Unlovely Child (Williams) **39**:100-01
The Unmade Bed (Sagan) **17**:428
"Unmailed Letter" (Harjo) **83**:273
"Unmailed, Unwritten Letters" (Oates) **19**:348, 351; **52**:338; **108**:369
The Unmaking of a Dancer (*Prologue*) (Brady) **86**:130, 133-34, 136
The Unmediated Vision (Hartman) **27**:179, 182
"The Unmentionable Subject" (Brophy)

105:11
"The Unmirroring Peak" (Ammons) **8**:14
The Unnameable (Beckett)
  See *L'innommable*
Unnatural Causes (James) **46**:205
Unnatural Scenery (Canby) **13**:132
"Unnatural State of the Unicorn" (Komunyakaa) **86**:191; **94**:240
"Uno dei tanti epiloghi" ("One of Many Epilogs") (Pasolini) **106**:266
Uno y el universo ("The One and the Universe") (Sabato) **23**:378
An Unofficial Rose (Murdoch) **1**:236-37; **3**:347; **8**:406; **22**:327
The Unoriginal Sinner and the Ice-Cream God (Powers) **66**:381-83
Unpaniere di chiocciole (Landolfi) **49**:215
"The Unpeaceable Kingdom" (Mott) **15**:380
The Unpopular Ones (Archer) **12**:16
The Unquiet Bed (Livesay) **15**:340-41; **79**:332, 335-41, 349-52
"Unraveling" (Swan) **69**:355
"Unready to Wear" (Vonnegut) **12**:617
"Unreal City" (Eliot) **13**:198-99
Unreality (Brandys)
  See *A Question of Reality*
"The Unregenerate" (Belitt) **22**:49
"Unregierbarkeit" (Enzensberger) **43**:152
"Unreleased Movie" (Ashbery) **77**:65, 67
Unrequited Loves (Baker) **8**:40
"Unrest" (Bly) **10**:56
"Unresting Death" (Larkin) **64**:258
"The Unreturning Footsteps" (Carroll) **10**:98
The Unrewarded Killer (Ionesco)
  See *Tueur sans gages*
"Unrhymed Sonnet" (Ekelof) **27**:117
"An Un-Romantic American" (Boland) **113**:103, 106, 108
"Unsaid" (Ammons) **25**:43; **108**:9
"An Unscheduled Stop" (Adams) **46**:17
Der Unschuldige (Hochwalder) **36**:237
"Unscientific Postscript" (Nemerov) **6**:361
Unsecular Man: The Persistence of Religion (Greeley) **28**:171-72
"The Unseen" (Pinsky) **38**:359, 361-63; **94**:298-99
"The Unseen" (Singer) **38**:407; **111**:314
The Unseen Hand (Shepard) **4**:490; **6**:496-97; **17**:437-38, 442, 448; **41**:409
Unsent Letters: Irreverent Notes from a Literary Life (Bradbury) **61**:48
"Unsere Gier nach Geschdichten" (Frisch) **44**:188
"Unsere gute, alte Renée" (Boell) **72**:70
The Unsettling of America (Berry) **27**:36, 38
The Unshaven Cheek (Lawler) **58**:332
Unshorn Locks and Bogus Bagels (Perelman) **9**:415
Unsilent Night (Lee) **46**:231
"The Unspeakable" (Avison) **97**:81-4
The Unspeakable Gentleman (Marquand) **10**:330
Unspeakable Practices, Unnatural Acts (Barthelme) **2**:39; **6**:30; **8**:49, 50, 52; **13**:55; **23**:44; **46**:35-6, 39; **59**:247; **115**:57, 76
The Unspeakable Skipton (Johnson) **27**:217-18, 220, 224
"Unspoken" (Gascoyne) **45**:157
"An Unstamped Letter in Our Rural Letter Box" (Frost) **26**:118
"The Unsuccessful Husband" (Creeley) **4**:118
An Unsuitable Attachment (Pym) **37**:369-72;

111:229-30, 232, 234, 236, 239, 242-44, 248, 258, 263, 265-66, 269-70, 279, 281-83, 285, 287

An Unsuitable Job for a Woman (James) 18:272; 46:205-06

The Unsuspected Stair
See *Nebanuitele trepte*

The Unteleported Man (Dick) 72:110, 121

"The Untelling" (Strand) 6:521-22; 18:520; 41:433, 438; 71:279, 289

Unter den Linden (Wolf) 29:464, 467

"Unter Mördern und Irren" ("Among Murderers and Madmen") (Bachmann) 69:35-6, 45, 56

Der Untergang der Titanic (*The Sinking of the Titanic*) (Enzensberger) 43:150-53

Der Untergeher (Bernhard) 61:22

Unterm Rad (*Beneath the Wheel*; *Under the Wheel*) (Hesse) 2:189; 3:245; 17:195-96, 201-02, 211, 215-17

"Das Unternehmen der Wega" (Durrenmatt) 15:196

Unterweggs zur Sprache (Heidegger) 24:265, 277

"Until" (Tillinghast) 29:415

"Until Forsaken" (Tanizaki)
See "Suterareru made"

"Until It's Time for You to Go" (Sainte-Marie) 17:432

Until the Celebration (Snyder) 17:474

"Until the Night" (Joel) 26:216-17, 220-21

"Until They Sail" (Michener) 109:378

Until Your Heart Stops (McNally) 82:264-70

Untilovsk (Leonov) 92:255, 260, 270, 277

Untinears and Antennae for Maurice Ravel (Williams) 13:601

"Untitled" (Ashbery) 25:54

"Untitled" (Giovanni) 19:192

"Untitled" (Swenson) 106:336, 349

"Untitled" (Zamora)
See "Sin título"

"Untitled Piece" (McCullers) 12:433

"Untitled Poem" (Silkin) 43:400

Untitled Subjects (Howard) 7:166-69; 10:276; 47:168-69

Unto Deatht (Oz)
See *Ad m'avet*

Untold Millions (Hobson) 25:272-73

"An Untold Story" (Colter) 58:146-47

Untouchable (Anand) 23:11, 13, 15, 17, 20-1; 93:22, 24, 29-30, 36-8, 40-2, 45-6, 48-50

The Untouchables (Mamet) 46:255-56

The Untuning of the Sky (Hollander) 8:298

The Unusual Adventures of Julio Jurenito and His Disciples (Ehrenburg)
See *The Extraordinary Adventures of Julio Jurenito and His Disciples*

The Unusual Life of Tristan Smith (Carey) 96:75-80, 82, 84

Unusual Stories about the Peasants (Leonov)
See *Neobyknovennie rasskazy o muzhikakh*

Unutulan adam (*The Forgotten Man*) (Hikmet) 40:245

The Unvanquished (Fast) 23:154

The Unvanquished (Faulkner) 3:149; 14:179; 18:148-49; 28:138; 52:137

"The Unveiling" (Milosz) 31:262-63

Unveiling Claudia: A True Story of a Serial Murder (Keyes) 80:169

Die Unvernünftigen Sterben aus (*They Are Dying Out*) (Handke) 8:261; 10:257; 15:268-69

"The Unwanted" (Day Lewis) 10:131

"Unwanted" (Lowell) 37:238

"The Unworldliness That He Creates" (Gregor) 9:253

"The Unworthy Friend" (Borges) 10:67; 13:104

"Unworthy of the Angel" (Donaldson) 46:143

"Unwritten Episodes" (Mphahlele) 25:336

"The Unwritten Poem" (Simpson) 32:380

"Unwritten Poem Review" ("Evaluation of an Unwritten Poem") (Szymborska) 99:193, 202-03

Un uoma (*A Man*) (Fallaci) 110:195-97

Uomini e no (*Men and Gods*) (Vittorini) 9:546, 548

L'uomo che guarda (*The Voyeur*) (Moravia) 46:287-88

Up (Sukenick) 3:475; 4:530-31; 48:363, 366-67, 370

Up above the World (Bowles) 2:78; 53:38, 40-1, 43-5, 49

Up Against It (Royko) 109:404

Up against It: A Screenplay for the Beatles (Orton) 43:327-28, 331

"Up, Aloft in the Air" (Barthelme) 115:65

"Up Among the Eagles" ("Where the Eagles Dwell") (Valenzuela) 104:377, 388

Up Among the Eagles (Valenzuela)
See *Donde viven las águilas*

"Up and Down" (Fuller) 62:191-92, 197

"Up and Down" (Merrill) 3:335; 13:378, 381; 18:331

Up and Out (Powys) 46:322

"Up at La Serra" (Tomlinson) 13:547, 549

Up at the Villa (Maugham) 67:217

"Up Country" (Kumin) 28:224

Up Country: Poems of New England (Kumin) 5:222

Up from Liberalism (Buckley) 37:58, 60

"Up from the Earth" (Kumin) 13:327

Up From the Kitchen Floor (Friedan) 74:92

"Up in Heaven" ("Not Only Here") (Clash) 30:48

"Up in Michigan" (Hemingway) 30:180, 198; 44:518; 50:415, 418-19, 426, 428

Up in Seth's Room (Mazer) 26:292-93, 295

"Up in the Old Hotel" (Mitchell) 98:161, 166, 173, 179, 182, 184

Up in the Old Hotel (Mitchell) 98:169, 171-72, 174-78, 180, 183, 185, 187

"Up on Fong Mountain" (Mazer) 26:291

Up the Agency: The Funny Business of Advertising (Mayle) 89:150, 152

"Up the Bare Stairs" (O'Faolain) 1:259

"Up the Dark Valley" (McGrath) 59:183

Up the Sandbox! (Roiphe) 3:434-35; 9:455

"Up the Shore" (Heaney) 14:243

Up the Walls of the World (Tiptree) 48:386-88, 391, 393, 397; 50:355, 357-58

"Up to the Crater of an Old Volcano" (Hughes) 108:323

Up to Thursday (Shepard) 17:433; 41:411

"An Upland Field" (Day Lewis) 10:131

"Uplands" (Ammons) 5:27; 57:59

Uplands (Ammons) 2:12; 5:26-7; 9:26-7; 25:45; 57:59; 108:55

"Upon Apthorp House" (Hollander) 8:299

"Upon Finding Dying: An Introduction, by L.E. Sissman, Remaindered at Is" (Sissman) 9:490

"Upon Meeting Don L. Lee, in a Dream" (Dove) 81:133, 137

Upon the Sweeping Flood, and Other Stories (Oates) 3:360; 6:370; 108:341

"Upon This Evil Earth" (Oz) 27:359, 361

Upon This Rock (Slaughter) 29:377

Upper Austria (Kroetz) 41:239-40

"Upper Berth" (Spielberg) 6:519

"The Upper Class Twit of the Year Race" (Monty Python) 20:223

"Upprätt" (Transtroemer) 52:410

"Upprörd meditation" (Transtroemer) 65:235

"Up-Rising" (Duncan) 7:88; 41:130

"Uprising" (Marley) 17:273

"Upriver Incident" (Muldoon) 32:315, 317

"Ups and Downs" (Kinsella) 27:236

"Upsilon" (Tolson) 105:249-50, 252, 255-56

"Upstairs by a Chinese Lamp" (Nyro) 17:313, 316, 318

"Upstairs, Downstairs" (Raphael) 14:438

"Upstairs, Mona Bayed for Dong" (Hannah) 90:160

The Upstart (Read) 4:444-45; 10:434-35; 25:379

Upstate (Wilson) 2:475-77; 8:550

"Uptight" ("Everything's Alright") (Wonder) 12:655, 661

Uptight (Grass)
See *Davor*

"Uptown" (Prince) 35:324

Uptown Saturday Night (Poitier) 26:359-60

"Ur en afrikansk dagbok" ("From the African Diary") (Transtroemer) 52:409-10

Ura me tri harqe (*Le pont aux trois arches*; *The Three-Arched Bridge*) (Kadare) 52:259-60, 262

"L'uranium" (Theriault) 79:408

Uranium Poems (Sherwin) 7:414; 15:479

Uranus (Ayme) 11:22-3

"Urban" (Ezekiel) 61:91, 100

"An Urban Convalescence" (Merrill) 6:323; 13:379

Urban Scrawl (Ritter) 52:355-56

"The Urbanization of a Shelter" (Cabral de Melo Neto)
See "O regaço urbanizado"

"Ur-Cantos" (Pound) 10:401; 48:285

Urfaust (Duerrenmatt) 102:61

"The Urge to Self-Destruction" (Koestler) 6:282

Urgent Copy (Burgess) 94:56-7

"Uriah Preach" (Bennett) 28:29

Urlicht (Innaurato) 60:205, 207

"The Urn" (Olds) 85:306

Die Ursache (*The Cause*) (Bernhard) 32:25-6; 61:11

"Der Ursprung des Kunstwerkes" (Heidegger) 24:259

Urujac (Audiberti) 38:32-3

"Úryvek z dopisu" ("Excerpt from a Letter") (Seifert) 93:344

"US" (O'Hara) 13:424

"Us" (Sexton) 53:324

"Us and Them" (Pink Floyd) 35:309, 313

Us Number One (Crumb) 17:83

"Us Together" (Johnston) 51:243

L'usage de la parole (*The Use of Speech*) (Sarraute) 31:381-83, 386

L'usage des plaisirs (Foucault)
See *Histoire de la sexualité, Vol. 2: L'usage des plaisirs*

The Use and Abuse of Art (Barzun) 51:42-4

"The Use of Books" (McGrath) 59:180

"The Use of Force" (Williams) 13:606; 42:458

"The Use of History" (Simmons) 43:412

The Use of Pleasure: The History of Sexuality, Vol. 2 (Foucault)

See *Histoire de la sexualité, Vol. 2: L'usage des plaisirs*
The Use of Poetry and the Use of Criticism: Studies in the Relation of Criticism to Poetry in England (Eliot)   6:167; 24:161, 182-83; 41:156; 113:205
A Use of Riches (Stewart)   7:464
The Use of Speech (Sarraute)
   See *L'usage de la parole*
The Use of Words (Castellanos)
   See *El uso de la palabra: Una mirada a la realidad*
"A Used Car Lot at Night" (Dacey)   51:83
"Useful Fictions" (Roth)   4:457; 9:459
The Useless Mouths (Beauvoir)
   See *Les bouches inutiles*
The Useless Sex (Fallaci)
   See *Il sesso inutile*
"The Uses of Anger" (Lorde)   71:243
The Uses of Enchantment: The Meaning and Importance of Fairy Tales (*Kinder Brauchen Märchen*) (Bettelheim)   79:113-14, 123, 126, 135, 143-44, 146-47, 149-50,
"The Uses of Literature" (Brooks)   24:111; 110:8
The Uses of Literature (Calvino)
   See *Una pietra sopra: Discorsi di letteratura e societa*
"The Uses of the Erotic, The Erotic as Power" (Lorde)   71:241, 243
"The Uses of Williamson Wood" (Carey)   96:28, 38
USFS 1919: The Ranger, The Cook and a Hole in the Sky (Maclean)   78:221, 231-33, 235-36
Ushant: An Essay (Aiken)   3:3-5; 5:8-9; 10:3; 52:19, 23-5, 31
"Usher II" (Bradbury)   98:114
L'usignuolo della Chiesa Cattolica (*The Nightingale of the Catholic Church*) (Pasolini)   37:347-48; 106:228, 242, 250, 263, 265, 267-68
Using Biography (Empson)   34:338, 538-43
Usmirenie Badadoshkina (*The Taming of Badadoshkin*) (Leonov)   92:270, 277
El uso de la palabra: Una mirada a la realidad (*The Use of Words*) (Castellanos)   66:49, 54, 56
Uspravna zemlja (*Earth Erect*) (Popa)   19:374-75
"Ustica" (Paz)   4:396
"A Usual Prayer" (Berryman)   13:82
The Usual Story (Salama)
   See *Se tavallinen tarina*
"Usufruct" (Clarke)   6:112
"The Usurers" (Guillen)   48:159
"Usurpation (Other People's Stories)" ("Other People's Stories") (Ozick)   7:288-90; 28:348; 62:341, 343, 353-54
The Usurpers (Milosz)
   See *Zdobycie wladzy*
Utah Blaine (L'Amour)   25:279
"Utah Stars" (Matthews)   40:322
Uterine Hunger (Miller)   84:253
Utolenie zhazhdy (Trifonov)   45:407-08, 410
"Utopia" (MacNeice)   10:325
"Utopia" (Szymborska)   99:192, 195
"Utopia de un hombre que está cansada" ("Utopia of a Tired Man") (Borges)   9:117; 48:39
Utopia Fourteen (Vonnegut)
   See *Player Piano*

Utopia, Inc. (Ludlam)   46:241
"Utopia of a Tired Man" (Borges)
   See "Utopia de un hombre que está cansada"
Utsikt från en grästuva (*View from a Tussock*) (Martinson)   14:355
Utsukushisa to kanashimi (Kawabata)   2:222; 5:208-09; 9:316
Utwory poetyckie (Milosz)   11:381; 22:307
Utz (Chatwin)   57:146-51; 59:275-77
Las uvas y el viento (*The Grapes and the Wind*) (Neruda)   5:301; 5:301; 28:312, 314
"V" (Merrill)   8:383, 387
V. (Harrison)   43:181
V. (Pynchon)   2:353-57; 3:408-12, 414-15, 417, 419-20; 6:430, 432-38; 9:444-46; 11:452-55; 18:430, 433-35; 33:327-30, 333-34, 338-40; 62:431-33, 439, 443, 451, 453; 72:296-99, 301-02, 308-09, 311, 325, 339
"V Amerika, propakhshey mrakom" (Voznesensky)   57:416
"V, der Vogel" ("V, the Bird") (Grass)   32:201
"V dni neslykhanno bolevyye" (Voznesensky)   15:556
"V gribnuiu osen" (Trifonov)   45:408
V kruge pervom (*The First Circle*) (Solzhenitsyn)   1:319-21; 2:407-10, 412; 4:511, 515; 7:432-36, 439, 440-42, 445; 9:504; 10:481; 18:497-98; 26:419; 34:481, 485, 487, 491-92; 78:382-85, 406-12, 418, 420, 424
"V opustevshem dome otdykha" ("In a Deserted Rest Home") (Akhmadulina)   53:12
V poiskakh grustnogo bebi: Kniga ob Amerike (Aksyonov)
   See *In Search of Melancholy Baby*
"V, the Bird" (Grass)
   See "V, der Vogel"
"V tot mesiats Mai" ("In That Month of May") (Akhmadulina)   53:11
"Vaarlem and Tripp" (Garfield)   12:218
"The Vacant Lot" (O'Connor)   15:409; 104:123
"A Vacant Possession" (Fenton)   32:165-66
A Vacant Possession (Fenton)   32:165
Vacant Sites (Hrabal)
   See *Proluky*
"The Vacation" (Bradbury)   42:33
Vacation Time: Poems for Children (Giovanni)   117:178, 193
"The Vacuum" (Nemerov)   36:305
"Vacuum Genesis" (MacEwen)   55:163
Vaegen till Klockrike (Martinson)
   See *Vägen till Klockrike*
"The Vagabond King" (Arzner)   98:69
Vagabundos (Bonham)   12:51
Vagadu (Jouve)   47:203
"El vagamundo" (Otero)   11:427
Vägen till Klockrike (*The Road; The Road to Klockrike; Vaegen till Klockrike*) (Martinson)   14:356
Vaghe stelle dell Orsa (Visconti)   16:569
"A Vagrant" (Gascoyne)   45:150, 157
A Vagrant and Other Poems (Gascoyne)   45:147-51, 153
The Vagrant Mood (Maugham)   15:368; 67:219
"A Vague Word" (Mahfuz)   52:297
Vägvisare till underjorden (Ekeloef)   27:117
The Vaiden Trilogy (Stribling)   23:446, 448
"Vain and Careless" (Graves)   45:166-67
"The Vain Life of Voltaire" (Riding)   7:373
Ein vakker dag (*A Fine Day*) (Vesaas)   48:407
The Valachi Papers (Maas)   29:303-05, 307

"Valaida" (Wideman)   67:379, 382-84
"Valarie" (Zappa)   17:586
Valdez Is Coming (Leonard)   71:224
The Vale of Laughter (De Vries)   3:125
"A Vale of Soulmaking" (Levertov)   66:243
"Valediction" (Ciardi)   40:151, 156
"Valediction" (Heaney)   25:244
"Valediction" (MacNeice)   53:231
"Valediction" (Thomas)   48:380
"A Valediction Forbidding Mourning" (Rich)   36:373
"Valentine" (Ashbery)   13:36; 77:45-7
"A Valentine" (Fuller)   62:199, 204
"The Valentine" (Jones)   39:410
The Valentine (Garfield)   12:234
"Valentine Day" (McCartney)   35:279
"Valentine for Ophelia" (L'Heureux)   52:273
Valentines to the Wide World (Van Duyn)   3:491; 63:443; 116:398, 406, 413, 426
Valentino (Ginzburg)   11:228-29; 54:210, 213-14
Valentino (Russell)   16:551
"Valère et le grand canot" (Theriault)   79:407
Valère et le grand canot (Theriault)   79:407
"The Valiant Vacationist" (Avison)   97:70-1, 76, 94, 100, 103-04, 131
"The Valiant Woman" (Powers)   1:282
Validity in Interpretation (Hirsch)   79:254-55, 257-58, 260-61
"Valina kukla" ("Valya's Doll") (Leonov)   92:237, 262
VALIS (Dick)   72:109, 116-20
El valle de las hamacas (Argueta)   31:19
"La vallée" (Audiberti)   38:21
"Valley" (Grace)   56:112-13, 118-19, 121
"The Valley Between" (Marshall)   72:254
The Valley of Bones (Powell)   3:400; 7:340, 345; 10:418; 31:317
Valley of Decision (Middleton)   38:335
The Valley of Horses (Auel)   31:23-4; 107:3-5, 8-11, 13-14, 24
The Valley of Issa (Milosz)
   See *Dolina Issy*
"The Valley of Rest" (Kunene)   85:165
Valley of the Dolls (Susann)   3:475
"Valley of the Dragon" (Davidson)   13:168; 19:129
"Valo do Capibaribe" ("The Capibaribe Valley") (Cabral de Melo Neto)   76:168-69
La valse aux adieux (*The Farewell Party*) (Kundera)   9:321-22; 19:268, 270; 32:261-62, 266; 68:232, 239-43, 245, 260-61; 115:351
La valse des toréadors (*The Waltz of the Toreadors*) (Anouilh)   3:11-12; 8:24; 13:17, 20-1; 40:54-5, 59-60; 50:278-80
La Valse mauve (Dinesen)   95:69
"Valuable" (Smith)   3:460
"The Value of Money" (Berger)   19:39
"Values" (Blunden)   56:33, 39
"Valya's Doll" (Leonov)
   See "Valina kukla"
Vamp till Ready (Fuller)   28:157-58
"Vampire" (Hughes)   2:198; 9:280
"Vampire" (Muldoon)   72:265
Vampire (Wilson)   33:460-64
"Vampire Blues" (Young)   17:573
The Vampire Lestat (Rice)   41:365-66
The Vampires (Rechy)   107:223, 225-26, 228, 239, 256
Vampyr (Dreyer)
   See *The Strange Adventures of David Gray*
The Van (Doyle)   81:157-59, 161

"Van Gogh" (L'Heureux) 52:272

Van Gogh (Resnais) 16:502, 505, 508

Van Gogh's Room at Arles (Elkin) 91:213-14, 217, 219-20

"Van Wyck Brooks on the Civil War Period" (Wilson) 24:481

"Vanadium" (Levi) 37:227

"Vancouver Lights" (Birney) 6:74

The Vandal (Schlee) 35:373

"Vandals" (Munro) 95:320

Vandals of the Void (Vance) 35:420

"Vandergast and the Girl" (Simpson) 7:429

"The Vane Sisters" (Nabokov) 6:360; 11:391

The Vanek Plays: Four Authors, One Character (Havel) 65:440

"Vanessa's Bower" (McGuckian) 48:277

Il vangelo secondo Matteo (*The Gospel according to St. Matthew*) (Pasolini) 20:260, 263, 265-66, 271; 106:202-05, 207-09, 221, 226, 248-49, 265, 272-73

Vanguard from Alpha (Aldiss) 14:10

The Vanished Jet (Blish) 14:86

"Vanished Mansard" (Hollander) 5:186

Vanishing Act (Greenberg) 57:227-28

Vanishing Cornwall (du Maurier) 59:286

The Vanishing Hero (O'Faolain) 14:404

Vanishing Point (Mitchell) 25:323, 327

"Vanishing Point: Urban Indian" (Rose) 85:311

"The Vanishing Red" (Frost) 26:111

Vanities (Heifner) 11:264

"Vanity" (Dobyns) 37:76

"Vanity" (Merwin) 8:390

"Vanity" (Oates) 6:367

Vanity of Duluoz: An Adventurous Education, 1935-1946 (Kerouac) 2:227, 229; 5:214; 29:270; 61:296, 298, 309-10

"The Vanity of Human Wishes" (Ammons) 108:22

"The Vanity of Human Wishes" (Gunn) 32:213

The Vanquished (Antonioni)
   See *I vinti*

"The Vantage Point" (Frost) 3:174; 26:117

"Vanvild Kava" (Singer) 38:407

"Vanzetti—A Tribute and an Appeal" (Sinclair) 63:371

"Vapor Trail Reflected in the Frog Pond" (Kinnell) 29:290

"Vaquero" (Muldoon) 32:318; 72:264

Var the Stick (Anthony) 35:35

Vargtimmen (*The Hour of the Wolf*) (Bergman) 16:58-60, 68, 74, 81; 72:40-1, 50, 52, 55, 62

"Variant" (Ashbery) 13:35

"Variation and Reflection on a Poem by Rilke" (Levertov) 66:253

"Variation for Two Pianos" (Justice) 102:258, 262

"Variation on a Noel" (Ashbery) 41:36

Variation on a Theme (Rattigan) 7:355

"Variation on a Theme of A. Huxley" (Ewart) 46:150

"Variation on Gaining a Son" (Dove) 50:156

"Variations" (Gregor) 9:254

"Variations on a Text by Vallejo" (Justice) 19:235; 102:261, 263, 277, 283

"Variations on a Theme by William Carlos Williams" (Koch) 44:250

"Variations on a Theme from James" (Justice) 102:263, 283

"Variations on a Theme of the Seventeenth Century" (Hope)
   See "The Elegy"

"Variations on Hopkins on the Theme of Child Wonder" (Clark) 38:116, 127

Variations on the Theme of an African Dictatorship (Farah) 53:134, 138-39

Varicose Moon (Leyner) 92:285

"Varieties of Dramatic Criticism" (Crane) 27:75

"Varieties of Exile" (Gallant) 38:193

Varieties of Parable (MacNeice) 10:323-24; 53:240, 244

Variety Lights (Fellini)
   See *Luci del varieta*

"Variety of Literary Utopias" (Frye) 24:221

"A Variety of Religious Experience" (Brady) 86:136

"Varioni Brothers" (Salinger) 12:498

"The Various Arts of Poverty and Cruelty" (Bly) 15:68

The Various Light (Corn) 33:116-20

"Various Miracles" (Shields) 113:429

Various Miracles (Shields) 113:403, 405-08, 410, 414, 419, 421, 424-25, 429

Various Persons Named Kevin O'Brien (Nowlan) 15:399

Vårnatt (*Spring Night*) (Vesaas) 48:407-08, 412

The Varnishing Day (Havel)
   See *Vernissage*

A várósalapító (*The City Builder*) (Konrad) 10:304-05; 73:173, 175-77, 179-82, 187

"Varsell Pleas" (Hersey) 81:329

The Varsity Story (Callaghan) 65:253

"The 'Varsity Students' Rag" (Betjeman) 43:35

"The Vase and the Rose" (Major) 19:298

"The Vase of Tears" (Spender) 41:420

"The Vasectomy Bureau in Lisdoonvarna" (Durcan) 43:117

Les vases communicants (Breton) 54:21, 25-6; 9:126-27; 15:88

Vash ubiytsa (*Tvoj ubijca*; *Your Murderer*) (Aksyonov) 22:26-7; 37:12

"A Vast Common Room" (Price) 63:333, 335

"A Vast Confusion" (Ferlinghetti) 111:65

The Vast Earth (Pasternak) 63:290

"Vaster than Empires and More Slow" (Le Guin) 45:221

"The Vastness of the Dark" (MacLeod) 56:193

"Vaucanson" (Ashbery) 77:64, 67

"Vaucanson's Duck" (Bernard) 59:45

Vaudeville for a Princess, and Other Poems (Schwartz) 10:462; 45:359; 87:348

The Vaudeville Marriage (Hochman) 3:250

"Vault Centre" (Soyinka) 44:285

"The Vaults of Yoh-Vombis" (Smith) 43:418-19, 422

"Vaunting Oak" (Ransom) 5:365

VD: The Silent Epidemic (Hyde) 21:176

"V-Day" (McGinley) 14:366

Vecher (*Evening*) (Akhmatova) 25:23-4; 64:3, 8, 21

"Vecher na stroyke" (Voznesensky) 15:556

Vechnata i svjatata (*Requiem*) (Bagryana) 10:11, 13

Den vedervaerdige mannen fraan saeffle (*The Abominable Man*) (Wahloo) 7:502

Vedi (Mehta) 37:295

Veedon Fleece (Morrison) 21:236-37

Vefarinn mikli frá Kasmír (Laxness) 25:291, 293

Vega and Other Poems (Durrell) 4:147

Vegas (Dunne) 28:121-23, 126

"Las Vegas (What?) Las Vegas (Can't Hear You! Too Noisy) Las Vegas!!!" (Wolfe) 51:418

"The Vegetable King" (Dickey) 109:272

The Vegetable Kingdom (Colum) 28:91

Vegetable Poems (Pollitt) 28:367

"Vegetables" (Wilson) 12:643

"Veglia" ("Watch") (Ungaretti) 7:485; 11:556

"Vegnerà el vero Cristo" (Pasolini) 106:230

"Vehaya he'akov lemishor" ("And the Crooked Shall Become Straight"; "The Crooked Made Straight") (Agnon) 14:3

Véhi-Ciosane; ou, Blanche-Genèse, suivi du Mandat (*The Money-Order; with White Genesis*) (Ousmane) 66:334-35, 338-44

"Vehicle" (Ammons) 57:59

"Vehicles" (Honig) 33:212

"Vehicles" (Williams) 56:429

The Veil (Johnson) 52:241

Veilchenfeld (Hofmann) 54:228

"Le veillard et l'enfant" ("The Old Man and the Child") (Roy) 14:469

Veillées noires (Damas) 84:176, 178-81

"The Vein in the Pulse" (Cabral de Melo Neto) 76:163

A Vein of Riches (Knowles) 10:303-04; 26:263

Veinte poemas de amor y una canción desesperada (*Twenty Love Poems and a Despairing Song; Twenty Love Poems and a Desperate Song; Twenty Love Poems and a Song of Despair; Twenty Love Poems and One Song of Despair; Twenty Poems*) (Neruda) 2:309; 7:257, 259, 262; 9:398; 28:308, 311-13; 62:333

Vejir Bozeny Nemcové (*Bozena Nemcová's Fan*) (Seifert) 93:342

"La velada del sapo" ("The Toad's Watch") (Castellanos) 66:45, 47

The Veldt (Bradbury) 42:33-4

Os velhos marinheiros (*Home Is the Sailor*) (Amado) 13:11; 40:29-30, 32; 106:57, 63-4

"Velocity Meadows" (Strand) 71:288-89

"Velorio de Papá Montero" ("Papa Montero's Wake"; "Wake for Papa Montero"; *White Genesis*) (Guillen) 48:161-63; 79:248

"The Velvet Hand" (McGinley) 14:367

The Velvet Horn (Lytle) 22:293-97, 300

The Velvet Room (Snyder) 17:469, 472

The Velvet Underground and Nico (Reed) 21:303, 307, 314

"Ven al jardín" (Guillen) 79:238

Venceremos! The Speeches and Writings of Ernesto Che Guevara (Guevara) 87:200-02

Le vendeur d'étoiles, et autres contes (Theriault) 79:401, 408

Les vendeurs du temple (Theriault) 79:400, 412, 416-17

Los vendidos (*The Sell-Outs*) (Valdez) 84:395, 404, 416

The Vendor of Sweets (Narayan) 7:254-55; 28:295

Vendredi; ou, La vie sauvage (*Friday; or, The Other Island*) (Tournier) 6:536, 538; 23:454; 36:433, 435-37, 441; 95:366-67, 369, 371-73, 375, 378, 380

Vendredi ou les limbes du Pacifique (Tournier) 95:361, 377-78, 382, 390

The Venerable Bead (Condon) 100:105-08

The Venetian Affair (MacInnes) 27:281; 39:349-51

"Venetian Interior, 1889" (Howard) 10:275

"Venetian Stanzas" (Brodsky) 100:38, 44-5

"Venetian Stanzas II" ("Venetsianskie strofy 2") (Brodsky) 100:38, 44, 50

"The Venetian Vespers" (Hecht) 19:207-09

The Venetian Vespers (Hecht)   19:208-10
"Venetsianskie strofy 2" (Brodsky)
    See "Venetian Stanzas II"
"Una venganza" (Allende)
    See "Una venganza"
"Vengeance" (Iskander)
    See "Vozmezdie"
"Vengeance" (Simon)   26:412-13
La Vengeance de Krimhilde (Lang)   103:88
"Vengeance for Nikolai" (Miller)   30:265
Vengeance Is Mine (Spillane)   13:526, 528
"Vengeance Is Mine, Inc." (Dahl)   79:181
"The Vengeance of Nitocris" (Williams)
    45:452-55
"The Vengeful Creditor" (Achebe)   7:6; 26:23;
    75:15-16
"Veni creator" (Milosz)   56:248
Veni, Vedi...Wendt (Stern)   4:523; 39:239
"Venice" (Denby)   48:82
"Venice" (Moss)   7:247; 50:353
"Venice" (Tomlinson)   45:399
"Venice 182-" (Berryman)   3:70
"Venice Now and Then" (Lively)   32:277
Venice Observed (McCarthy)   59:292
"The Venice Poem" (Duncan)   15:187; 55:292
The Venom Business (Crichton)   54:65-6
Le vent (*The Wind*) (Simon)   4:494-96; 9:484;
    15:485-87, 490-92, 494; 39:203-04, 206-
    07, 209-11
Le vent de la memoire (Cayrol)   11:108
Le vent d'est (*Wind from the East*) (Godard)
    20:142, 144, 150
Le vent paraclet (Tournier)   23:451-52; 36:437;
    95:361-62, 364-65, 372, 376-80, 383-84,
    387
"Vento a Tindare" (Quasimodo)   10:428
Le Ventre (*The Belly*) (Tchicaya)   101:348,
    352, 358-59, 363
"le ventre reste" (Tchicaya)   101:358
"Ventriloquist's Dummy" (Garrett)   51:148
The Ventriloquist's Wife (Ludlam)   46:241;
    50:342-44
Vents (*Winds*) (Perse)   4:399-400; 46:303-05,
    307-09
Venture of the Infinite Man (Neruda)   28:313
Venture of the Infinite Man (Neruda)
    See *Tentativa del hombre infinito*
Venture Once More (Graham)   23:192
"Venture to the Moon" (Clarke)   13:148
"La Venue à l'écriture" (Cixous)   92:90-1
La Venue à l'écriture (Cixous)   92:52, 54-6,
    69, 74-5, 82, 90-1
Venus and Mars Are Alright Tonight
    (McCartney)   12:379; 35:282-85
Venus and the Rain (McGuckian)   48:277-79
"Venus and the Sun" (McGuckian)   48:277-78
"Venus Androgyne" (Gascoyne)   45:157
"Venus Ascendant" (Gellhorn)   60:184
"Venus, Cupid, Folly, and Time" (Taylor)
    18:524; 37:409, 413; 71:299, 301, 303
Venus Envy (Brown)   79:171
"The Venus Hunters" (Ballard)   36:37
Venus in Sparta (Auchincloss)   4:28, 30
Venus, Near Neighbor of the Sun (Asimov)
    26:57-8
Venus Observed (Fry)   2:143; 10:200
"The Venus of Azombeii" (Smith)   43:423
Venus on the Half-Shell (Farmer)   19:166
Venus Plus X (Sturgeon)   22:411; 39:361, 363-
    64, 367
"Venus Rising" (Swan)   69:365
"Venus Will Now Say a Few Words" (Auden)
    14:32; 43:17

"Venusberg" (Barker)   8:47
Venusberg (Powell)   10:410-11
"Venus's-flytraps" (Komunyakaa)   94:234, 241
"Venus—The Lark ..." (Blackburn)   43:63
Vera Baxter (Duras)   68:89-90
"Vera i Zoika" (Trifonov)   45:408
"A Veranda on the Cane Field" (Cabral de Melo
    Neto)
    See "O alpendre no canavial"
"Verandah" (Walcott)   76:273, 281-82
"Veränderungen in Staech" ("The Staech Af-
    fair") (Boell)   72:77, 101
"Veraneo" (Donoso)   8:178; 32:156
Veraneo y otros cuentos (*Summertime and
    Other Stories*) (Donoso)   11:145; 99:239
"Verano" ("Summer") (Cortazar)   13:164;
    33:123
"The Verb to Kill" (Valenzuela)   31:438;
    104:382
Verbal and Pictorial Art (Lagerkvist)
    See *Ordkonst och bildkonst*
"The Verbalist of Summer" (Eberhart)   56:82-
    3
Verbliuzhii glaz (*The Camel's Eye*; *The Eye of
    the Camel*) (Aitmatov)   71:3-4, 16, 18
Der Verdacht (Duerrenmatt)   102:66-7, 69
Der Verdacht (*The Quarry*) (Durrenmatt)
    4:140-41; 11:171, 174; 15:195; 43:122-
    23, 128
"The Verdict" (Dodson)   79:193
Verdict (Christie)   12:125
The Verdict (Mamet)   46:253
"Vereda del cuco" (Cernuda)   54:59
"Vergüenza" (Zamora)   89:363
Das Verhör von Habana (*The Havana Inquiry*)
    (Enzensberger)   43:146-47
Verikivi (*Bloodstone*) (Ivask)   14:287
"The Veritable Years, 1949-1966" (Everson)
    14:167
La verité en peinture (*The Truth in Painting*)
    (Derrida)   87:90, 92-3, 96, 104, 106-08
Verklighet till döds (Martinson)   14:355
"Verlie I Say unto You" (Adams)   13:2
*Die verlorene Ehre der Katharina Blum: oder,
    Wie Gewalt entstehen und wohin sie führen
    kann* (*The Lost Honor of Katharina Blum:
    How Violence Develops and Where It Can
    Lead*) (Boell)   6:84; 11:58-9; 27:67;
    39:292, 295-96; 72:85-86, 88, 90
Der Verlust (Lenz)   27:256
Vermilion Sands (Ballard)   3:35; 6:27-8; 36:35
"Vermont" (Beattie)   63:22
"Vermont" (Carruth)   18:88-9; 84:123
"Vermont Ballad: Change of Season" (Warren)
    39:258
The Vermont Notebook (Ashbery)   6:11-12;
    25:55
"A Vermont Tale" (Helprin)   22:221
"Vermont Thaw" (Warren)   39:265
Verna, U.S.O. Girl (Innaurato)   21:195
The Vernacular Republic: Poems, 1961-1981
    (Murray)   40:340-41
Vernissage (*The Varnishing Day*) (Havel)
    25:224, 227, 230
Veronica's Room (Levin)   3:294-95; 6:306
"Vers de Société" (Larkin)   5:227, 230; 8:332,
    337; 9:323; 18:299; 33:256, 258, 268;
    39:345-46; 64:258, 263, 270, 282
"Versben bujdosó" ("Hiding in Poems") (Nagy)
    7:251
Versben bujdosó (*Hiding in Poems*) (Nagy)
    7:251
Das Verschwinden im Bild: Essays (Wellershoff)

46:437
"Verse for Urania" (Merrill)   8:384
Verses and Poems (Brodsky)   100:59
"Verses for a Centennial" (MacLeish)   68:286
Verses: Fourth Book (Daryush)   19:118, 120
"Verses in April" (Brodsky)   13:114, 116
"Verses on the Death of T. S. Eliot" (Brodsky)
    See "Stixi na smert T. S. Èliota"
"Verses versus Verses" (Bell)   8:65
Versos de salón (Parra)   102:340-42, 356
Versos del capitán (*The Captain's Verses*; *Los
    versos del capitán*) (Neruda)   5:305; 28:312
Los versos del capitán (Neruda)
    See *Versos del capitán*
Die Verspätung (*The Delay*) (Hildesheimer)
    49:171
Das Versprechen (Duerrenmatt)   102:65, 68
*Das Versprechen: Requiem auf den
    Kriminalroman* (*The Pledge*)
    (Durrenmatt)   4:140-41; 11:171; 15:195-
    96; 43:120, 122-23, 128
Verstörung (*Disturbances*; *Gargoyles*)
    (Bernhard)   3:65; 32:16-22, 26-7; 61:14,
    18-19, 23-4, 29
Versus (Nash)   23:321
Verteidigung der Wölfe (Enzensberger)   43:146
The Vertical Smile (Condon)   4:106; 6:115
"Vertigo" (Graham)   48:153
"Vértigo" (Ulibarri)   83:407
Vertigo (Hitchcock)   16:343, 350, 354, 356
"A Very Continental Weekend" (Stolz)   12:552
A Very Easy Death (Beauvoir)
    See *Une morte très douce*
The Very Eye of Night (Deren)   16:254; 102:28,
    31, 36, 38, 40-1, 48-9
Very Far Away from Anywhere Else (*Far Away
    from Anywhere Else*; *A Very Long Way from
    Anywhere Else*) (Le Guin)   45:212, 214
"A Very Good Second Man" (Heym)   41:217
"A Very Indian Poem in Indian English"
    (Ezekiel)   61:95
"Very Like a Whale" (White)   49:408
A Very Long Engagement (Japrisot)
    See *Un long demanche de fiancailles*
A Very Long Way from Anywhere Else (Le Guin)
    See *Very Far Away from Anywhere Else*
"A Very Private Eye" (Pym)   37:377-78; 111:236-
    37, 263, 269, 272, 275
A Very Private Life (Frayn)   31:190
The Very Rich Hours of Count von Stauffenberg
    (West)   96:362, 367, 370, 372-73, 377,
    380, 382, 387, 392, 399
"The Very Sad Story of Salah Bourguine"
    (Chatwin)   57:154; 59:277
A Very Scotch Affair (Jenkins)   52:223-24, 227-
    28
"A Very Short Story" (Hemingway)   30:181,
    189-90, 192, 196
"A Very Stern Discipline" (Ellison)   114:91
The Very Thing That Happens (Edson)   13:190
"Vespers" (Berryman)   62:46
"Vespers" (Johnson)   52:234
"Vespers" (Muldoon)   32:315-17
"The Vessel of Wrath" (Maugham)   1:204
Vessels (Bloom)
    See *The Breaking of the Vessels*
Vestal Fire (Mackenzie)   18:314
"La vestibule" (Butor)   15:117
"Vestiges" (Brown)   23:99
"Vestiges" (Bunting)   47:45
"Vestigia" (Purdy)   6:428
"Vesuvius" (Tolson)   105:259

"Vesuvius at Home: The Power of Emily Dickinson" (Rich) 18:447-48; 76:218

"The Veteran" (Blunden) 56:37, 42

"Veterans" (Coles) 46:109

"Veterans" (Johnston) 51:241, 243

"Veteran's Dream" (Heaney) 7:148

"Vetiver" (Ashbery) 77:63-5, 67-8

Vetsera blomstrer ikke for enhver (Abell) 15:2

"La veuve Aphrodissia" ("Aphrodissia, the Widow") (Yourcenar) 38:463; 87:390

La veuve couderc (Simenon) 2:398

La veuve enragée (Maillet) 54:304, 313-17

"Via Appia" (Denby) 48:84

"Via negativa" (Salter) 52:368; 59:196

"Via negativa" (Thomas) 6:530; 48:382

"VIA: Tourism" (Moure) 88:218

Les viaducs de la Seine-et-Oise (Duras) 11:164-66; 40:182

"Viagem ao Sahel" ("Journey to the Sahel") (Cabral de Melo Neto) 76:169

I viaggi la morte (Gadda) 11:211

"Viaggio agli inferni del secolo" (Buzzati) 36:97

"Viaggio d'inverno" ("Winter Voyage") (Ortese) 89:199

Viaggio in Sardegna (Vittorini) 9:548

Viaje a la Alcarria (*Journey to the Alcarria*) (Cela) 13:145, 147; 59:128-30, 143

Viaje a la aldea del crimen (*Trip to the Village of Crime*) (Sender) 8:481

"Viaje a la semilla" ("Journey Back to the Source") (Carpentier) 38:94-5, 99; 110:48, 52, 76, 88

"Viaje a Nueva York" ("Trip to New York") (Cardenal) 31:76-7, 79

Un viaje de invierno (Benet) 28:20

"La víbora" (Parra) 102:334, 337-39, 342

A Vicarage Family (Streatfeild) 21:404, 416

The Vicar's Wife (Bennett) 77:89

"Vice" (Baraka) 14:46

"The Vice President of Insurance" (Kunitz) 6:287

"The Vice-Consul" (Pritchett) 15:443; 41:334

The Vice-Consul (Duras)
   See *Le vice-consul*

Le vice-consul (*The Vice-Consul*) (Duras) 6:149; 20:101; 40:178, 180; 68:73, 89, 91; 100:143, 148-49

The Viceroy of Ouidah (Chatwin) 28:72-3; 57:141-42, 148, 150, 153; 59:274-75, 279

"Los vicios del mundo moderno" (Parra) 102:342-43

"Vicious Circle" (Reed) 21:312-13

Vicissitude eforma (Luzi) 13:354

"Vicissitudes of Presidential Reputations" (Schlesinger) 84:380

"The Victim" (Garrett) 51:143

"Victim" (O Hehir) 41:323-24

The Victim (Bellow) 1:27-31; 2:49, 51, 53; 3:48, 50-2, 56-7, 59, 61; 6:50-3, 56, 61; 8:74, 78; 13:71-2; 15:47-8, 50, 53-5; 25:80-1, 85; 33:66, 69, 71; 63:31, 41; 79:62, 76, 80, 83,88

"The Victim of Aulis" (Abse) 7:1; 29:14

A Victim of the Aurora (Keneally) 10:298-99; 19:243, 246-47; 117:227

"La victima de Tadeo Limardo" ("Tadeo Limardo's Victim") (Bioy Casares) 88:69

"La victime" (Jouve) 47:203-05

Victimes du devoir (*Victims of Duty*) (Ionesco) 4:251; 6:247-51, 253-54; 41:225-27; 86:332-33

"The Victims" (Olds) 39:190; 85:290

"The Victims" (Raine) 45:334, 338

The Victims of Amnesia (Ferlinghetti) 2:134; 111:63

Victims of Duty (Ionesco)
   See *Victimes du devoir*

"Victor" (Auden) 11:16

"A Victor" (Hoffman) 6:243

"Victor Blue" (Beattie) 63:11

"Victoria" (Davies) 21:91

"Victoria" (Haines) 58:218

Victoria Station (Pinter)
   See *Other Places*

Victorian House, and Other Poems (Child) 19:101

"The Victorians" (Blunden) 56:51

The Victors (Sartre)
   See *Morts sans sépulture*

"The Victory" ("Pobeda") (Aksyonov) 101:11-12, 18, 28, 30-1

"Victory" (Dickey) 2:117; 47:95; 109:267, 273-75

"Victory" (Taylor) 5:426

Victory: Choices in Revolution (Barker) 37:38-41

Victory in the Dark (Lagerkvist)
   See *Seger i mörker*

Victory of Faith (Riefenstahl)
   See *Sieg des Glaubens*

Victory on Janus (Norton) 12:461, 469

Victory over Japan (Gilchrist) 34:164-66; 48:119, 121

"Vida" (Aleixandre)
   See "Life"

Vida (Piercy) 18:406-09; 27:376, 378, 380; 62:373, 376

La vida breve (*A Brief Life*) (Onetti) 7:276-81; 10:376, 380-81

"Vida de perros" (Parra) 102:340-41

Uma vida em segredo (*A Hidden Life*) (Dourado) 23:149-51; 60:83, 85

"Vidal vs. Falwell" (Amis) 62:5

La vie (Godard)
   See *Sauve qui peut (La vie)*

"La Vie Bohème" 99:162, 168-69, 178, 182, 185-86, 190

La vie dans les plis (*Life in Folds*) (Michaux) 19:314, 316

La vie devant soi (*Momo*) (Gary) 25:187-89

La vie d'un poète (*The Life of a Poet*) (Cocteau) 8:147

"La vie écarlate" (Gascar) 11:222

La vie est ailleurs (*Life Is Elsewhere*) (Kundera) 4:276-78; 9:320; 19:270; 32:260-61, 263; 68:237-42, 244, 247, 257, 260-61, 264; 115:307-08, 337-38, 342, 347, 350

Vie et aventures de Salavin (Duhamel) 8:186

Vie et mort dÉmile Ajar (Gary) 25:191

La vie materielle (*Practicalities*) (Duras) 68:99-102; 100:118-120, 124

La vie, mode d'emploi (*Life: A User's Manual*) (Perec) 56:255, 257-58, 260, 262-65, 267-74; 116:232, 235-38, 242-43, 246, 248-53, 262, 264-65, 267, 270

"La vie parisienne" (Gallant) 38:195

La vie passionnée de Rodney Buckthorne (Cassill) 23:107

La vie scélérate (*Tree of Life*) (Conde) 92:102, 104, 107, 112-14, 125, 130-31, 133-34

La vie tranquille (Duras) 6:149; 11:165; 40:179; 100:145, 147

La vie unanime (Romains) 7:379

"Le vieillard et l'enfant" (Roy) 10:440

La vieillesse (*The Coming of Age*; *Old Age*) (Beauvoir) 2:43-4; 4:47, 49; 44:343-44, 350; 71:60-1, 75, 77-80, 82

Una vieja historia de caminantes (*An Old Story about Travellers*) (Costantini) 49:61

"Vieja moralidad" ("The Old Morality") (Fuentes) 22:170-71; 113:237

"La vieja rosa" (Arenas) 41:28

Viejas historias de castilla la vieja (*Old Tales of Old Castile*) (Delibes) 18:113

"Vienna" (Spender) 10:489-90

Vienna (Spender) 91:260

"Vienna Blood" (Rothenberg) 57:381

"Vienne" (Rhys) 51:356

"Vientos aliseos" (Cortazar) 34:333

La vierge de Paris (Jouve) 47:207-08, 212-13

Viet Journal (Jones) 39:405, 410

Viet Nam Diskurs (*Discourse on Vietnam*; *Vietnam Discourse*) (Weiss) 15:566, 568; 51:387, 391-92, 395

Viet Rock (Terry) 19:438-40

"Vietnam" (Cliff) 21:60-1, 64

Vietnam (McCarthy) 14:358-59

"The Vietnam Call of Samuel V. Reimer" (Wiebe) 14:575

Vietnam Discourse (Weiss)
   See *Viet Nam Diskurs*

"Vietnam Memorial" (Shapiro) 53:334

"The Vietnam Project" (Coetzee) 23:121, 124; 117:34, 38, 44

"The Vietnam War" (Bly) 15:68

A Vietnamese Wedding (Fornes) 61:129, 131

The Vietnamization of New Jersey (Durang) 27:88-9, 93

Vieux carré (Williams) 8:549; 39:452; 45:443, 447-49, 455

"The View" (Milosz) 82:299

"View" (Pastan) 27:368

"A View" (Van Duyn) 63:438, 440; 116:404

The View from a Blind I (Barker) 48:18

"View from a Height" (Vinge) 30:410, 416

View from a Tussock (Martinson)
   See *Utsikt från en grästuva*

"View from a Wheelchair" (Scannell) 49:328

A View from Calvary (Boyle) 19:68

"View from Charles Bridge" (Seifert) 93:336

"The View from Here" (Stafford) 29:380

"The View from Misfortune's Back" (Porter) 33:323

The View from Serendip (Clarke) 35:123

"The View from the Balcony" (Stegner) 49:350

A View from the Bridge (Miller) 1:216-17, 219; 2:278, 280; 6:326, 329-30; 15:372-73; 26:315, 318; 47:252, 254; 78:306, 318-19, 323

The View from the Ground (Gellhorn) 60:190-191, 193-96

The View from the Peacock's Tail (Rosenthal) 28:392, 394

"View from the screen" (Bukowski) 108:111

A View from the Source: Selected Poems (Hooker) 43:200-01

"The View from the Stars" (Miller) 30:260

The View from Tower Hill (Braine)
   See *Stay with Me till Morning*

"The View Minus One" (Moss) 7:247

A View of Dawn in the Tropics (Cabrera Infante)
   See *Vista del amanecer en el trópico*

A View of the Harbour (Taylor) 2:432; 29:410

A View of the Promised Land (Duhamel) 8:189

"A View of the Woods" (O'Connor) 10:367; 21:276; 104:103, 108, 114, 135, 138, 154, 166-68, 173, 179, 183-84, 188, 192

"A View on Contemporary German Fiction"

(de Man) **55**:420-21

"View with a Grain of Sand" (Szymborska) **99**:203

View with a Grain of Sand (Szymborska) **99**:194, 199, 203-04, 206

"Viewing a Leopard" (Honig) **33**:216

"Viewing the Body" (Snodgrass) **68**:382, 388, 397

"Viewpoint" (Hall) **51**:170

Views (Milosz) **56**:232

Views and Spectacles (Weiss) **14**:555

Views from a Window (Vidal) **22**:435

"Views of My Father Weeping" (Barthelme) **1**:18; **23**:46-8; **46**:36, 40, 43; **115**:67, 87, 89-93, 95

"Vigil" (Carver) **53**:61

"The Vigil" (Livesay) **79**:340

"The Vigil" (Winters) **32**:467

"Vigilance" (Breton) **54**:30; **9**:127

"Vik" ("Cry") (Bagryana) **10**:14

"Viking Dublin: Trial Piece" (Heaney) **14**:244; **74**:193

The Viking Portable Library Dorothy Parker (Parker) **68**:328-30

Viktorka (Seifert)

See *The Song of Viktorka*

Det vilda torget (*The Wild Marketplace*; *The Wild Market-Square*) (Transtroemer) **65**:226, 229, 233

Vile Bodies (Waugh) **1**:357-59; **3**:509-12; **8**:544; **13**:584, 586-89; **19**:461, 466; **44**:521-22, 524; **107**:356-57, 359-60, 362, 364, 366, 370-71, 376, 378-79, 383, 393, 394-97, 400-01

"Villa Adriana" (Rich) **7**:368

The Villa Golitsyn (Read) **25**:379-80

A Villa in France (Stewart) **32**:421-22

Villa Magdalena (Santos) **22**:362-63

Villa Stellar (Barker) **48**:19-20, 22, 24

"The Village" (Corn) **33**:117

"The Village" (Smith) **64**:402

"The Village" (Walcott) **76**:285-86

"The Village" (Wilhelm) **7**:538

The Village (Anand) **23**:12, 19; **93**:22, 24, 32, 43

The Village (Hinde) **6**:240

The Village (Smith) **64**:402

The Village: A Party (*The Perfect Party*) (Fuller) **25**:179

The Village Band Mystery (Kingman) **17**:244

The Village by the Sea (Desai) **37**:68; **97**:175-76, 180, 190

Village Daybook (Derleth) **31**:137

"Village Ghetto Land" (Wonder) **12**:659, 662-63

The Village Green Preservation Society (Davies) **21**:90, 97

"The Village Idiot" (Hirsch) **50**:198

"The Village Inn" (Betjeman) **43**:37

"The Village Inside" (Hood) **28**:193

"A Village Life" (Walcott) **42**:419; **76**:286

The Village of Ben Sue (Schell) **35**:361-63

Village of God and the Devil (Alegria) **75**:51-2

"The Village of Miracles" **75**:78

The Village of Souls (Child) **19**:100, 103

"Village of the Sun" (Zappa) **17**:591

"Village of Winter Carols" (Lee) **90**:200

"A Village Priest" (Dubie) **36**:136

"The Village Priest" (Ngugi wa Thiong'o) **36**:313

"The Village Saint" (Head) **67**:98

"Village Snow" (Levi) **41**:247-48

"Village Song" (Blunden) **56**:48

"The Village That Lost Its Children" (Lee) **90**:199

Village Year (Derleth) **31**:134

"Villages démolis" (Read) **4**:439

"Villa-Lobos" (Stern) **100**:333

"Villanelle: The Psychological Hour" (Pound) **13**:460

"Ville" (Guillevic) **33**:194

Ville cruelle (Beti) **27**:45-6

La ville de la chance (*The Town beyond the Wall*) (Wiesel) **3**:529; **5**:490, 492

La ville dont le prince est un enfant (Montherlant) **19**:327, 329

"Villon" (Bunting) **10**:83; **39**:298; **47**:44-5, 49, 52-5

"Vilota" (Pasolini) **106**:228

Vimy (Berton) **104**:49

Vincent and Theo (Altman) **116**:46-8, 50, 65

Vindane (*The Winds*) (Vesaas) **48**:407

Vindication (Sherwood) **81**:101-10

Vindication of the Rights of Women (Wollstonecraft) **65**:323

"The Vindictives" (Frost) **10**:194-95

"The Vine" (Williams) **15**:580; **45**:447

"The Vinegar Mother" (Rendell) **28**:385

Vinegar Puss (Perelman) **5**:337-38

Vinegar Tom (Churchill) **31**:84

Vineland (Pynchon) **62**:439-54

"The Vine—The Willow ..." (Blackburn) **43**:63

"The Vineyard Woman" (Wright) **53**:425

Vingt-cinq poèmes (*Twenty-Five Poems*) (Tzara) **47**:390-95

Vinland (Brown) **100**:77-81

Vinland the Good (Shute) **36**:367

"Vinland, Vinland" (Connell) **45**:113

"Víno a cas" ("Wine and Time") (Seifert) **93**:341

"Vintage" (Hass) **99**:140

The Vintage (West)

See *On a Dark Night*

Vintage London (Betjeman) **6**:67

Vintage Murder (Marsh) **7**:210; **53**:247, 249-50, 255-60

"The Vintage of River Is Unending" (Hughes) **37**:181

Vintage Stuff (Sharpe) **36**:403

"A Vintage Thunderbird" (Beattie) **13**:64; **63**:17

Vintage Thurber (Thurber) **5**:433

Vinter-Eventyr (Dinesen)

See *Winter's Tales*

"Vinterns formler" ("Winter's Formulae") (Transtroemer) **52**:409, 411

Vinterns formler (*Winter's Formulae*) (Transtroemer) **65**:222

I vinti (*The Vanquished*) (Antonioni) **20**:19

Vinyl (Warhol) **20**:417, 422

Viola di morte (Landolfi) **49**:216

The Violated (Bourjaily) **62**:87-93, 101, 105-06

Violence and Glory: Poems, 1962-1968 (Schevill) **7**:401

The Violent Bear It Away (O'Connor) **1**:253-54, 257-58; **3**:365-67; **6**:375, 379; **10**:364, 367-70; **13**:418, 420, 422; **15**:408, 410-11, 413; **21**:257-63, 266, 271-73; **66**:309-10; **104**:103-06, 108, 120, 123, 135, 141, 178-79

The Violent Land (Amado)

See *Terras do sem fim*

"The Violent Noon" (Ballard) **14**:40

"The Violent Space (or when your sister sleeps around for money)" ("Or When Your Sister Sleeps Around for Money") (Knight) **40**:279-81, 284, 286

"Violent Storm" (Strand) **41**:436; **71**:279, 282

The Violent West (Ghose) **42**:179

The Violent World of Hugh Greene (*The World of Violence*) (Wilson) **3**:537; **14**:588

Violet Clay (Godwin) **22**:180-83; **31**:195; **69**:232-33, 235, 238, 246

"Violet Hair" (Vollmann) **89**:278

"The Violet Rock" (Stafford) **7**:457

"Violets" (Gluck) **81**:164, 170

"Violets" (O'Brien) **36**:340

Violette noziere (Chabrol) **16**:184

"A Violin" (Popa) **19**:373

The Violin Book (Berger) **12**:39-40

Violins and Shovels: The WPA Art Projects, a New Deal for America's Hungry Artists of the 1930's (Meltzer) **26**:304-05

Viollet (Cunningham) **12**:163-64

Viper Jazz (Tate) **25**:427-29

"Vipers" (Walker) **13**:567

La virgen del tepeyac (Valdez) **84**:397

The Virgin and the Nightingale: Medieval Latin Poems (Adcock) **41**:18

"The Virgin and the Petri Dish" (Selzer) **74**:272-73

"Virgin Forest, Southern New South Wales" (Shapcott) **38**:400

The Virgin in the Garden (Byatt) **19**:76-7; **65**:125, 131

"The Virgin in the Rose-Bower; or, The Tragedy of Glen Mawr Manor" (Oates) **108**:349, 351, 353

"The Virgin of Guadalupe" (Hughes) **108**:323

Virgin Planet (Anderson) **15**:15

Virgin Soil Upturned (Sholokhov)

See *Podniataia tselina*

The Virgin Spring (Bergman)

See *Jungfrukällen*

The Virgin Suicides (Eugenides) **81**:53-60

Virgin Territory (Maitland) **49**:233-35

"Virgin Violeta" (Porter) **101**:235, 237-38

"Virginal" (Ezekiel) **61**:96, 101

Virginia (O'Brien) **36**:335-36, 341-42

"Virginia Britannia" (Moore) **2**:291; **8**:399

"Virginia Woolf: A Capsule Biography" (Borges) **48**:45

Virginie: Her Two Lives (Hawkes) **27**:196-98, 200-01; **49**:163-65

"Virgins" (Trevor) **71**:329, 332-33

Virgins and Vampires (Rosenblatt) **15**:447-48

"Virgo Descending" (Wright) **13**:614

"Virgo Hibernica" (Montague) **46**:267, 278

Viridiana (Bunuel) **16**:130-31, 134-35, 139; **80**:27-9, 31-2, 34-5, 37, 41, 45, 47, 49-51

"Virility" (Ozick) **7**:288; **28**:347; **62**:353-54

"Virtu" (Ammons) **2**:14; **9**:28

The Virtue of Selfishness: A New Concept of Egoism (Rand) **30**:304; **79**:369

"Virtuoso" (Greenberg) **7**:134

Virtuoso Literature for Two and Four Hands (Wakoski) **7**:504-05, 507

"Virtuoso of the X" (Bell) **8**:66

A Virtuous Woman (Gibbons) **88**:123-28, 130-32

"Le visage nuptial" (Char) **9**:161-62; **11**:114; **55**:287

"Visakha" (Nye) **42**:309

Il visconte dimezzato (*The Cloven Viscount*; *The Nonexistent Knight and the Cloven Viscount*) (Calvino) **5**:97-8; **8**:129-30;

11:88; **22**:87-8, 90; **33**:97; **39**:314, 317; **73**:58

Viscous Circle (Anthony)   **35**:37-8

Vishnevaya kostochka (*The Cherry Stone*) (Olesha)   **8**:432

"The Visible Moments" (Squires)   **51**:377

"Vision" (MacLeod)   **56**:197-200

"Vision" (Scott)   **22**:374

"The Vision" (Wright)   **53**:432

The Vision (Koontz)   **78**:203, 212, 214-17

"Vision and Late Supper" (Willard)   **37**:464

Vision and Resonance (Hollander)   **8**:298-99, 301-02; **14**:262

"A Vision beyond Time and Space" (Momaday)   **95**:241

"Vision by Sweetwater" (Ransom)   **4**:431

"La vision capitale" (Mandiargues)   **41**:279

"Vision: Fire Underground" (O Hehir)   **41**:324

"Vision of a Woman Hit by a Bird" (Moure)   **88**:229

A Vision of a World Language (MacDiarmid)   **63**:255

"The Vision of Adam" (Ghiselin)   **23**:169

A Vision of Battlements (Burgess)   **4**:81; **5**:85; **10**:89-90; **13**:124; **22**:70, 72-4; **40**:113-14; **62**:132; **94**:49, 51, 56, 75

A Vision of Beasts and Gods (Barker)   **48**:15-16, 18

"Vision of Cathkin Braes" (Morgan)   **31**:276

A Vision of Ceremony (McAuley)   **45**:249, 252, 254

"A Vision of Democracy in the County of Meath" (Durcan)   **70**:152

"Vision of England, '38" (Barker)   **48**:10-11

"A Vision of the World" (Cheever)   **15**:131; **64**:53, 58, 60-3

"A Vision of World Language" (MacDiarmid)   **19**:289

"A Vision of Zosukuma" (Kunene)   **85**:176

"Vision out of the Corner of the Eye" (Valenzuela)   **31**:438; **104**:382

"The Vision Test" (Van Duyn)   **63**:443

"Vision through Timothy" (Eberhart)   **19**:144

"Vision under the October Mountain: A Love Poem" (Warren)   **8**:537

"Visionary" (Ellison)   **42**:131

The Visionary (Le Guin)   **45**:219

The Visionary Company (Bloom)   **24**:70, 75; **103**:11, 19, 30, 36-7, 41-3, 45, 47-8

The Visionary Farms (Eberhart)   **11**:175, 178; **56**:81,88

"A Visionary Gleam" (Warner)   **7**:513

"The Visionary Picnic" (Matthews)   **40**:320

Le visionnaire (*The Dreamer*) (Green)   **11**:259; **77**:267, 269, 276-77, 290

"Visions" (Heaney)   **14**:243

"Visions" (Mukherjee)   **53**:268

"Visions" (Wonder)   **12**:657-58

Visions and Revisions of American Poetry (Turco)   **63**:431-33

Visions from San Francisco Bay (Milosz)   See *Widzenia nad Zatoka San Francisco*

Visions from the Ramble (Hollander)   **5**:186; **8**:299

Visions of America (Lynn)   **50**:426

"Visions of Budhardin" (Dybek)   **114**:62, 64-65, 71, 74, 76

Visions of Cody (Kerouac)   **2**:228-29; **3**:264, 266; **5**:212-13; **29**:270, 272-74; **61**:297, 308-09

"Visions of Daniel" (Pinsky)   **94**:309, 311-12

Visions of Eight (Ichikawa)   **20**:185

Visions of Gerard (Kerouac)   **1**:167; **14**:307;

29:270; 61:309

"Visions of Jesus" (Rothenberg)   **57**:381, 383-84

Visions of Kerouac (Duberman)   **8**:185-86

"Visit" (Ammons)   **25**:45; **108**:28

"The Visit" (Ciardi)   **40**:151

"A Visit" (Kavan)   **82**:120

"A Visit" (Levertov)   **15**:339

"A Visit" (Levine)   **54**:297, 301

"The Visit" (Smith)   **64**:392

"The Visit" (Spencer)   **22**:406

"The Visit" (Wesker)   **42**:426

"The Visit" (Young)   **82**:411

The Visit (Duerrenmatt)   **102**:53-4, 83

A Visit (Fornes)   **61**:129, 140

The Visit: A Tragi-Comedy (Durrenmatt)   See *Der Besuch der alten Dame*

"A Visit at Tea-Time" (Wain)   **46**:415

"A Visit from Mother" (Tevis)   **42**:372, 377

"A Visit from Reverend Tileston" (Cook-Lynn)   **93**:124, 127

"A Visit from the Footbinder" (Prager)   **56**:276-77

A Visit from the Footbinder, and Other Stories (Prager)   **56**:276-80

"A Visit in Bad Taste" (Wilson)   **34**:581

"A Visit of Charity" (Welty)   **105**:333

"The Visit of the Queen of Sheba" (Amichai)   **9**:22; **57**:40, 44

Visit to a Small Planet (Vidal)   **4**:558

"A Visit to Eggeswick Castle" (Davies)   **23**:148

"A Visit to Grandmother" (Kelley)   **22**:246

"The Visit to the Museum" ("Poseshchenie muzeia") (Nabokov)   **3**:354

"A Visit to the Painter Vladimir Komarek" (Seifert)   **34**:362

"A Visit to the Ruins" (Hope)   **3**:251

"Visit with the Artist in Her Own Studio" (Robbins)   **21**:341

"The Visitant" (Roethke)   **11**:483; **101**:263

Visitants (Stow)   **23**:437-38; **48**:358, 360-61

"Visitation" (Cesaire)   **32**:111

"Visitation" (Merwin)   **88**:194

"A Visitation" (Snodgrass)   **18**:491, 493; **68**:397

The Visitation (Roberts)   **48**:341-42

Visitations (MacNeice)   **4**:318; **53**:242

"Visite" (Reverdy)   **53**:290

"Visiting a Dead Man on a Summer Day" (Piercy)   **18**:405-06; **27**:374

A Visiting Card (Pound)   **112**:356-57

Visiting Mrs. Nabokov (Amis)   **101**:77-78, 83

"Visiting Thomas Hart Benton and His Wife in Kansas City" (Bly)   **15**:63

"The Visitor" (Dahl)   **6**:122; **79**:180-81, 183

"The Visitor" (Forche)   **25**:172; **83**:216

"The Visitor" (Voigt)   **54**:433

The Visitor (Poole)   See *Billy Buck*

The Visitor (Ray)   See *Agantuk*

"Visitor from Forest Hills" (Simon)   **31**:396-97

"Visitor from Hollywood" (Simon)   **31**:396

"Visitor: Jack Kerouac in Old Saybrook" (Holmes)   **56**:143

"Visitors" (Barthelme)   **46**:40, 43; **59**:249; **115**:80

"Visitors" (Lowell)   **37**:238

"Visitors" (Mukherjee)   **53**:267, 269

"Visitors" (Munro)   **95**:305-06, 316, 318

The Visitors (Kazan)   **16**:369

The Visitors (Simak)   **55**:319

"Visitors from Mlok" (Smith)   **43**:422

The Visitors Have All Returned (Bowering)   **32**:48

"Visitors to the Black Belt" (Hughes)   **35**:214

"Visits to St. Elizabeths" (Bishop)   **15**:60; **32**:37, 42

Viskningar och rop (*Cries and Whispers*) (Bergman)   **16**:70-2, 75-6, 79, 82; **72**:52, 54-5, 57, 59, 62

La víspera del hombre (*The Eve of Manhood*) (Marques)   **96**:233, 241, 244

"Vissi d'arte" (Moore)   **68**:300

Vista del amanecer en el trópico (*A View of Dawn in the Tropics*) (Cabrera Infante)   **25**:100, 103-05; **45**:78

The Vistants (Waddington)   **28**:440

Visual Language (Kostelanetz)   **28**:218

"Vita amicae" (Le Guin)   **45**:213

Vita d'un uoma (Ungaretti)   **7**:483; **11**:556

Vita immaginaria (Ginzburg)   **54**:197

La vita interiore (*The Interior Life*; *Time of Desecration*) (Moravia)   **18**:346-49; **27**:356; **46**:284-85

Una vita violenta (Pasolini)   **37**:341-43, 347; **106**:209, 216, 218-19, 242, 253, 254, 269-70

The Vital Center: The Pollitics of Freedom (Schlesinger)   **84**:348, 350, 355, 370-71, 374, 380-81

"Vital Message" (Phillips)   **28**:363

Vital Parts (Berger)   **3**:63; **5**:60; **38**:36-8

Vital Provisions (Price)   **43**:350-51, 353; **63**:333

Vital Signs (Slavitt)   **14**:490-91

"Vitamins" (Carver)   **36**:104

I vitelloni (*The Loafers*; *The Young and the Passionate*) (Fellini)   **16**:271-77, 281, 283, 290-91, 293, 297, 299; **85**:55, 59, 64, 74-6, 78

"Vitrail" (Guillevic)   **33**:195

Viudas (*Widows*) (Dorfman)   **48**:89-90, 92, 94; **77**:138, 141-42, 146, 148-49, 152-54

ViVa (*VV*) (Cummings)   **15**:161-62, **68**:35, 47-8

Viva and Louis (Warhol)   See *Blue Movie*

Viva la muerte (*Long Live Death*) (Arrabal)   **58**:14, 26, 28

"Viva Mi Fama" (Fuentes)   **113**:242-43

"Viva Stalin" (Parra)   **102**:354

Viva Zapata! (Kazan)   **16**:368-69, 371-72; **63**:225, 235

Viva Zapata! (Steinbeck)   **34**:415

"Vivaldi" (Dybek)   **114**:66

"Vivaldi" (Schwartz)   **45**:361

"Vivaldi, Bird and Angel" (Hope)   **3**:251; **51**:227

"Vivaldi Years" (Stern)   **40**:413

"Vivat! Vivat Regina!" (Bolt)   **14**:91

Vive en poésie (Guillevic)   **33**:194-95

Vive guitare (Audiberti)   **38**:21

Vive Moi! (O'Faolain)   **7**:272-73, 275; **70**:315, 319, 321

The Vivid Air (Gustafson)   **36**:221-22

"Vivir para ver" (Otero)   **11**:426

Vivir sin estar viviendo (Cernuda)   **54**:60

The Vivisector (White)   **3**:522-23; **4**:583-84; **5**:484-85, 487-88; **7**:529, 532; **65**:275-76, 278-79; **69**:400-02, 405

Vivo o povo brasileiro (*An Invincible Memory*) (Ribeiro)   **67**:280-82

Vivre l'orange (Cixous)   **92**:58, 62

Vivre sa vie (*My Life to Live*) (Godard)   **20**:129, 148-49

Vivre! Vivre!: La suite des manuscrits de Pauline Archange (Blais)　4:67

The Vixens (Yerby)　22:487

Vizio di forma (Levi)　50:331

Vladimir and Rosa (Godard)　20:151

"Vladychitsa" ("Sovereign") (Voinovich)　10:506

Vlaminck (Duhamel)　8:188

"Vlemk the Box-Painter" (Gardner)　28:161-63

"V-Letter" (Shapiro)　15:475, 478; 53:330, 334

V-Letter and Other Poems (Shapiro)　15:475-76, 478; 53:326, 331, 334

VN: The Life and Art of Vladimir Nabokov (Field)　44:463-72

Vocabulaire (Cocteau)　15:133

"Vocation" (Stafford)　7:462; 29:388

"The Vocation of the Poet in the Modern World" (Schwartz)　87:335

"Vocational Guidance" (Howard)　10:276

La voce della luna (*The Voice ˙of the Moon; Voices of the Moon*) (Fellini)　85:75, 77-8, 80

Le voci della sera (*Voices in the Evening*) (Ginzburg)　11:228-29; 54:194-96, 198, 200-01, 206, 211-12; 70:279-80, 282-83

The Vodi (Braine)　41:56

"Vodka" (Ciardi)　10:105, 107

"Vodka and Small Pieces of Gold" (Delaney)　29:146

Voetskrif (Breytenbach)　23:83

"Vogel" (Cohen)　19:113

Vogue la galère (Ayme)　11:22

"The Vogue of the Marquis de Sade" (Wilson)　24:481

"The Voice" (Levine)　33:275

"The Voice" (Nin)　14:383-84; 60:265-66

"The Voice" (Pritchett)　41:333

The Voice at the Back Door (Spencer)　22:399-400, 403

"A Voice from Croisset" (Rozewicz)　23:360-61

Voice from the Attic (Davies)
See *A Voice in the Attic*

A Voice from the Chorus (Sinyavsky)　8:488-90

"A Voice from under the Table" (Wilbur)　3:533; 110:349

A Voice in the Attic (*Voice from the Attic*) (Davies)　13:172-74; 75:184, 197, 205, 212; 91:204

The Voice in the Closet/La voix dans le cabinet de débarras (Federman)　47:123-25, 127-28, 132

A Voice in the Mountain (Davison)　28:103-04

"Voice of a Dove" (p'Bitek)　96:271, 286

The Voice of a Stranger (Humphreys)　47:186

The Voice of Asia (Michener)　29:310-11; 109:376, 379, 382

The Voice of Experience (Laing)　95:165

"The Voice of Night" (Arghezi)
See "Graiul noptii"

"The Voice of Rock" (Ginsberg)　6:199

The Voice of Scotland (MacDiarmid)　63:254

"The Voice of St. Lucia" (Walcott)　67:344

"The Voice of the Beach" (Campbell)　42:92

"The Voice of the Canefield" (Cabral de Melo Neto)
See "A voz do canavial"

"The Voice of the Holy Land" (Sachs)
See "Stimme des Heilegen Landes"

The Voice of the Moon (Fellini)
See *La voce della luna*

The Voice of the Mountain (Wellman)　49:394-95

The Voice of the Sea, and Other Stories (Moravia)　11:384

"The Voice of the Soul" (Pasternak)　7:295

The Voice of the Victims　70:339

The Voice of the Void (Campbell)　32:73

The Voice of Things (Ponge)　6:422-23; 18:415

The Voice That Is Great Within Us: American Poetry of the Twentieth Century (Carruth)　84:118, 124

"A Voice through the Door" (Taylor)　18:526

"Voices" (Celan)
See "Stimmen"

"Voices" (Josipovici)　6:270

"Voices" (Plumly)　33:310

"Voices" (Szymborska)　99:198

Voices (Eich)
See *Stimmen*

Voices: A Memoir (Prokosch)　48:317-18

Voices at Play (Spark)　13:519

"Voices by a River" (Blunden)　56:29

"Voices from the Forest" (Mueller)　51:282-83

Voices from the Forest (Mueller)　51:280, 282

"Voices from the Moon" (Dubus)　36:148-49; 97:221, 223, 227, 229-30

Voices From the Moon (Dubus)　97:203, 209-11, 213, 216, 224-25

"Voices from the Other World" (Merrill)　8:387; 34:235

Voices from the Sky: Previews of the Coming Space Age (Clarke)　35:123

Voices from the Yiddish (Howe)　85:147

Voices in an Empty Room (King)　53:210-11

Voices in the City (Desai)　19:133; 37:64, 66, 69; 97:142, 149, 152, 156, 161-62

Voices in the Evening (Ginzburg)
See *Le voci della sera*

Voices in the Whirlwind (Mphahlele)　25:334-35, 341

Voices in Time (MacLennan)　92:340, 343-45, 350

Voices of a Summer Day (Shaw)　7:412

Voices of America (Bogosian)　45:62

The Voices of Marrakesh: A Record of a Visit (Canetti)
See *Die Stimmen von Marrakesch: Aufzeichnungen nach einer Reise*

"Voices of Poor People" (Milosz)　11:377-78; 56:237-38

The Voices of Silence (Malraux)
See *Les voix du silence*

Voices of the Dead (Dourado)
See *Ópera dos mortos*

The Voices of the Heroic Dead (Mishima)　27:341

Voices of the Moon (Fellini)
See *La voce della luna*

"The Voices of Time" (Ballard)　14:40; 36:37, 39-41, 44

"Voices under the Ground" (Ekeloef)　27:117

A Void (Perec)
See *La disparition*

The Void Captain's Tale (Spinrad)　46:387-89

"Void Only" (Rexroth)　112:404

La voie lactée (*The Milky Way*) (Bunuel)　16:134-35, 139; 80:41, 47, 51

La voie royale (*The Royal Way*) (Malraux)　4:324-25, 330-31, 333, 336; 13:367-68; 57:300-01, 304, 308-09, 321

Voies de pères, voix de filles (Conde)　92:104

Voina i tiur'ma (Aksyonov)
See *War and Prison*

"Voir la figure," de Jacques Chardonne (de Man)　55:420

Les voisinages de Van Gogh (Char)　55:288

Les voix du silence (*The Voices of Silence*) (Malraux)　4:324; 13:366; 57:301, 307, 314, 324

La voix et le phénomène: Introduction au problème su signe dans le phénoménologie de Husserl (*Speech and Phenomena, and Other Essays on Husserl's Theory of Signs*) (Derrida)　24:136, 140; 87:72, 103-04

Vol à voile (Cendrars)　18:96

Le vol d'Icare (*The Flight of Icarus*) (Queneau)　5:362; 10:430; 42:331-32

Le Vol du Vampire (Tournier)　95:370-71

"The Volcano" (Stegner)　81:345

"Volcano" (Walcott)　76:285-86

Volcano (Endo)　19:161; 54:152, 155; 99:285

The Volcano (Santos)　22:362-63

The Volcano Lover (Sontag)　105:185-86, 188, 190-213, 224-25

Vole-moi un petit millard (Arrabal)　58:18

"Les voleurs" (Burroughs)　42:76

"Volhynia Province" (Simpson)　7:428

Volk (*Begstvo Sandukova; The Flight of Sandukov; The Wolf*) (Leonov)　92:246, 260, 268, 270, 277

La volonté de savoir (Foucault)
See *Histoire de la sexualité, Vol. 1: La volonté de savoir*

Volshebnik (*The Enchanter; The Magician*) (Nabokov)　44:469; 46:290-96; 64:366

"Volta a Pernambuco" ("Return to Pernambuco") (Cabral de Melo Neto)　76:167

"De volta ao Cabro de Santo Agostinho" ("Going Back to Cape de Santo Agostinho") (Cabral de Melo Neto)　76:160

Voltaïque (*Tribal Scars*) (Ousmane)　66:334-35, 347

Voltaire in Love (Mitford)　44:485, 488

The Voluntad (Azorin)　11:26

"The Volunteer" (Stegner)　49:351

Volunteers (Friel)　42:169, 173-74; 115:242-43, 246, 248

"Voluptuaries and Others" (Avison)　4:36; 97:72, 91, 94, 103-04, 107

Volverás a región (Benet)　28:15-20

Volverás a región (Delibes)　8:170

"Vom einem Land, einem Fluss und den Seen" (Bachmann)　69:56

"Vom Sinn der Dichtung in Unserer Zeit" (Durrenmatt)　15:197

"Vom Steppenwolf" (Hesse)　6:237

The Von Bülow Affair (Wright)　44:527

"Von diesen Stauden" (Celan)　82:49

Von Schwelle zu Schwelle (*From Threshold to Threshold*) (Celan)　10:101-02; 19:90; 53:69, 71, 74, 77

"Von Wesen der Wahrheit" (Heidegger)　24:259

The Voodoo Gods (Deren)
See *Divine Horsemen: The Living Gods of Haiti*

Voodoo Gods: An Inquiry into Native Myths and Magic in Jamaica and Haiti (Hurston)
See *Tell My Horse*

"The Voodoo of Hell's Half-Acre" (Wright)　74:387

Voprosy literatury i estetiki (*The Dialogic Imagination*) (Bakhtin)　83:2, 14, 19, 32-4, 37, 44, 57, 59-60

Vor (*The Thief*) (Leonov)　92:236-39, 243-50, 252, 254-55, 257-60, 266, 268, 274-79

Vor dem Ruhestand (*Before Retirement*; *Eve of Retirement*) (Bernhard) **61**:11, 13, 26

Voraussetzungen einer Erzählung: Kassandra (*Cassandra: A Novel and Four Essays*) (Wolf) **58**:419-28, 431-34, 436-37

Das Vorbild (*An Exemplary Life*) (Lenz) **27**:250-51

The Vortex (Coward) **29**:132-35, 137-39; **51**:69

"Vorticism" (Pound) **10**:400

Vorträge und Aufsätze (*Lectures and Essays*) (Heidegger) **24**:264, 277

Die Vorzüge der Windhühner (Grass) **6**:207; **32**:197-98, 200-01; **6**:207; **32**:197-98, 200-01

Voskhozhdenie na Fudzhiamu (*The Ascent of Mount Fuji*) (Aitmatov) **71**:23

Voss (White) **3**:521-23; **4**:584-85; **5**:485-87; **9**:563, 565; **18**:545-46; **65**:275-76, 279-82; **69**:392-94, 396-97, 403, 405, 411

"Vot zvuk dozhdia" ("There's the Sound of Rain") (Akhmadulina) **53**:11

Vote, Vote, Vote for Nigel Barton (Potter) **86**:346, 348-50

"The Voter" (Achebe) **26**:20; **75**:14

"Votes and Boys" (Forster) **45**:133

"Votin' Ink" (Bennett) **28**:30

Votive Tablets: Studies Chiefly Appreciative of English Authors and Books (Blunden) **56**:46

"De votre bonheur etc." (MacLeish) **68**:286

Votre Faust: Fantaisie variable genre opéra (Butor) **3**:92; **8**:118-19

La vouivre (Ayme) **11**:22

Vous les entendez? (*Do You Hear Them?*) (Sarraute) **2**:385-86; **4**:468-70; **31**:380; **80**:238, 241

Vous m'oublierez (*You Will Forget Me*) (Breton and Soupault) **68**:411-15

"A Vow" (Ginsberg) **36**:184, 191

"A Vow" (Hecht) **8**:269; **19**:207

The Vow of Conversation (Merton) **83**:403

"Voyage" (Levertov) **66**:243

"The Voyage" (Prokosch) **48**:309

"Voyage" (Rukeyser) **27**:406

Le voyage (Morand) **41**:304

The Voyage (De Sica) **20**:97

Voyage au bout de la nuit (*Journey to the End of the Night*) (Celine) **1**:56-7; **3**:101, 103, 105; **4**:98, 100-03; **7**:42, 44-7; **9**:152-53, 155, 158; **15**:124; **47**:71-4, 77-9

Le voyage de Patrice Périot (Duhamel) **8**:186

Voyage en Grande Garabagne (*Voyage to Great Garabagne*) (Michaux) **8**:392

Voyage en Italie (Giono) **4**:184

"A Voyage from Stockholm" (Tate) **25**:428

"The Voyage Home" (Appleman) **51**:17

Voyage Home (Hochman) **3**:250

Le voyage imaginaire (Clair) **20**:63, 69

"Voyage in the Blue" (Ashbery) **3**:16; **15**:28

Voyage in the Dark (Rhys) **2**:371-73; **6**:453-55; **14**:446-49, 451; **19**:393; **51**:359, 361, 364, 368-71

The Voyage of Saint Brandon (Brown) **48**:61

The Voyage of the Destiny (Nye) **42**:307-08

"The Voyage of the Needle" (Dickey) **47**:92

A Voyage round My Father (Mortimer) **28**:286

Voyage to a Beginning: A Preliminary Autobiography (Wilson) **14**:584, 589

Voyage to Great Garabagne (Michaux)
    See *Voyage en Grande Garabagne*

A Voyage to Pagany (Williams) **13**:602

Voyage to Somewhere (Wilson) **32**:444

"Voyage to Spring" (Aiken) **52**:24

Voyage to the First of December (Carlisle) **33**:103-04

"Voyage to the Moon" (Pinsky) **94**:309

"Voyager" (Mueller) **51**:284

Voyager in Night (Cherryh) **35**:114

Voyagers (Bova) **45**:71-2, 75

Voyagers II: The Alien Within (Bova) **45**:75-6

"Les voyagerurs traques" (Montherlant) **19**:325

Voyages (Brown) **48**:60; **100**:80

Voyages and Homecomings (Neruda) **28**:314

Voyages chez les morts: Thèmes et variations (*Journeys among the Dead*) (Ionesco) **41**:227-28; **86**:332, 341

Voyages de l'autre côte (Le Clezio) **31**:251

Le voyageur sans bagage (*Traveller without Luggage*) (Anouilh) **8**:24; **13**:19, 21; **40**:52-3, 60; **50**:279

"Le voyageur sur la terre" (Green) **77**:266

Le voyageur sur la terre (*Christine, and Other Stories*) (Green) **11**:260; **77**:265, 274-76

Les voyageurs de l'impériale (*Passengers of Destiny*) (Aragon) **22**:37

Les voyageurs sacrés (*Three Travellers*) (Blais) **2**:62; **4**:67; **6**:82; **13**:96; **22**:57

"The Voyeur" (Van Duyn) **63**:440; **116**:403, 426

The Voyeur (Moravia)
    See *L'uomo che guarda*

Le voyeur (*The Voyeur*) (Robbe-Grillet) **1**:286-87, 289; **2**:373, 375; **4**:446, 449; **6**:464-66, 468; **8**:453; **10**:437; **14**:455-59, 461; **43**:361-62, 364, 366

The Voyeur (Robbe-Grillet)
    See *Le voyeur*

Voyou Paul. Brave Virginie. (Celine) **47**:72

"A voz do canavial" ("The Voice of the Canefield") (Cabral de Melo Neto) **76**:155, 165

Una voz en la montana (Marques) **96**:225

"Vozdushnye puti" (Pasternak)
    See "Aerial Ways"

"Vozmezdie" ("Vengeance") (Iskander) **47**:201

Voznesensky: Selected Poems (Voznesensky) **57**:413-15

"Vozvrashcheniye v Siguldu" (Voznesensky) **57**:417

Vreme smrti (*A Time of Death*) (Cosic) **14**:132

Vremia i mesto (*Time and Place*) (Trifonov) **45**:418, 420, 423

"V.R.T." (Wolfe) **25**:472

Všecky krásy sveta (Seifert) **44**:426; **93**:322, 326

Vsegda v prodaze (*Always on Sale*) (Aksyonov) **22**:26-7; **37**:12

Vstrechniye korabli (Paustovsky) **40**:362

Vucja so (*Wolf's Salt*) (Popa) **19**:375

El vuelo de la celebración (Rodriguez) **10**:440

"Vuelta" ("Return") (Paz) **51**:333, 335

Vuelta (*Return*) (Paz) **65**:198

La vuelta al dia en ochenta mundos (*Around the Day in Eighty Worlds*) (Cortazar) **10**:118; **92**:155, 158

Vulcan's Hammer (Dick) **30**:127

"Vulthoon" (Smith) **43**:419

"The Vulture" (Beckett) **9**:81

"Vulture" (Wakoski) **2**:459

"Vultures" (Achebe) **11**:4

"Vultures" (Oliver) **34**:246; **98**:274

Vuodet (*The Years*) (Haavikko) **34**:170

"Vurni me" ("Parashut") (Bagryana) **10**:12

Vurt (Noon) **91**:59-66

VV (Cummings)
    See *ViVa*

"Vying" (Davie) **8**:164

"Vysokaya bolesn" ("The High Malady") (Pasternak) **7**:293-94; **18**:382

Vzgljad: Stix i poèmy (Voznesensky) **15**:553-54, 557

Vziatie Velikoshumska (*Chariot of Wrath*; *The Storming of Velikoshumsk*; *The Taking of Velikoshumsk*) (Leonov) **92**:240, 242, 247, 260, 277

"W" (Merrill) **8**:387-88

"W. D. Assists in the Protection of Cock Robin's Roost" (Snodgrass) **68**:394

"W. D., Don't Fear That Animal" (Snodgrass) **68**:398

"W. D. Picks a Bouquet for Cock Robin but Cannot Separate the Thorns from the Flowers" (Snodgrass) **68**:394

"W. D. Tries to Warn Cock Robin" (Snodgrass) **68**:394, 398

"W drodze do Delf" (Herbert) **43**:187

W; or, The Memory of Childhood (Perec)
    See *W; ou, Le souvenir d'enfance*

W; ou, Le souvenir d'enfance (*W; or, The Memory of Childhood*) (Perec) **56**:258-62, 268, 271-73; **116**:233-35, 238, 246-47, 256-59, 267, 269

"W. S. Landor" (Moore) **47**:263

W. S. Merwin: The First Four Books of Poems (Merwin) **8**:388; **13**:384

"Wa ta se Na ka mo ni, Viet Nam Memorial" (Young Bear) **94**:373

"Die Waage der Baleks" ("The Balek Scales") (Boell) **11**:55; **27**:57; **72**:71, 74-6

"Wading at Wellfleet" (Bishop) **32**:37-8, 43

"Waga namida o nuguitamo, hi" (Oe)
    See "Mizu kara waga namida o nuguitamo hi"

Wagatomo Hitler (*My Friend Hitler*) (Mishima) **2**:289

The Wager (Medoff) **6**:322-23

"The Wages of Fun" (Blount) **38**:47

Wages of Virtue (Middleton) **38**:330

"The Waggoner" (Blunden) **2**:65

The Waggoner and Other Poems (Blunden) **56**:25, 28-9, 32-3, 36-7, 40-2, 48

"Wagon Wheel" (Reed) **21**:305

Wagonmaster (Ford) **16**:306-07, 311, 316

"al-Wahj al-akhar" ("The Other Face") (Mahfuz) **55**:172-74

Wah'Kon-tah: The Osage and the White Man's Land (Mathews) **84**:203, 205, 207, 209, 211, 218-19, 226

Die Wahrheit der Literatur: Sieben Gespräche (Wellershoff) **46**:437

"Waiariki" (Grace) **56**:112

"Waif" (Leiber) **25**:307

Wailing Monkey Embracing a Tree (Shuttle) **7**:422

"The Wait" (Clancy) **112**:63

"Wait" (Kinnell) **29**:285

"Wait" (Reed) **21**:315

"Wait" (Steele) **45**:362

"Wait for Me" (Creeley) **8**:153

Wait for Me, Michael (Stolz) **12**:552

"Wait till the Sun Shines" (Wain) **46**:417

Wait Until Spring, Bandini (Fante) **60**:128-29, 133-34

Wait until the Evening (Bennett) **5**:59

"Waiting" (Beattie) **40**:66; **63**:12, 18

"Waiting" (Creeley) **78**:151

"Waiting" (Dubus) **36**:145; **97**:202, 228

"Waiting" (Levine) **14**:316

"Waiting" (Mahapatra) **33**:279, 284

"Waiting" (Montague)　46:267-68
"The Waiting" (Olds)　85:308
"Waiting" (Thomas)　48:382
"Waiting" (Warren)　13:582
"Waiting" (Wright)　53:427, 432
Waiting (Mahapatra)　33:278-80, 282-83
"Waiting at Dachau" (Price)　3:406; 6:423
"Waiting for a Taxi" (Jordan)　114:151
"Waiting for Ada" (Howard)　10:277
Waiting for Cordelia (Gold)　14:208; 42:197
"Waiting for Evening" (Sadoff)　9:466
Waiting for Godot (Beckett)
　See *En attendant Godot*
"Waiting for It" (Swenson)　61:399; 106:326
"Waiting for Lefty" (Odets)　2:318-20; 28:323-25, 329, 332, 338-40
Waiting for Lefty (Odets)　98:194-95, 199-201, 205-07, 210, 212, 215, 218, 220-21, 224, 229, 231, 233-34, 236, 239, 243, 250, 252
"Waiting for Merna" (Sommer)　25:425
Waiting for My Life (Pastan)　27:370-71
"Waiting for Santy" (Perelman)　49:259, 263
Waiting for Saskatchewan (Wah)　44:323, 326-28
Waiting for Sheila (Braine)　41:59
"Waiting for Stella" (Adams)　46:22
Waiting for the Angel (McGrath)　28:278-79
Waiting for the Barbarians (Coetzee)　23:124-26; 33:106-11; 66:90-2, 95-7, 99, 102, 105-06; 117:30-1, 33, 39-41, 43-5, 47, 59-60, 67, 74, 80-3, 86, 97-8, 100-03
Waiting for the Boat: Dennis Potter on Television (Potter)　86:349
"Waiting for the Call" (Kinsella)　27:237
Waiting for the End (Fiedler)　4:161; 24:193, 195-98
"Waiting for the End of the World" (Costello)　21:70
Waiting for the End of the World (Bell)　41:52-4; 102:4, 6, 11, 16, 22
"Waiting for the Fire" (Appleman)　51:15
"Waiting for the Girls Upstairs" (Sondheim)　30:385, 397
Waiting for the King of Spain (Wakoski)　9:554-55
Waiting for the Mahatma (Narayan)　7:255; 28:291, 300-01; 47:307
Waiting for the Music (Fuller)　62:204
"Waiting for the Poem to Come Through" (Souster)　14:505
"Waiting for the Story to Start" (Martin)　89:131
Waiting for the Sun (Morrison)　17:289, 295
"The Waiting Grounds" (Ballard)　36:37
"Waiting in the Bone" (Squires)　51:378, 382-83
Waiting in the Bone and Other Poems (Squires)　51:378, 380-81
Waiting in the Wings (Coward)　29:139
"Waiting in Vain" (Marley)　17:269-70
"Waiting Room" (Justice)　102:258
The Waiting Room (Harris)　25:208, 215
"Waiting to Be Fed" (Young Bear)　94:362, 366
Waiting to Exhale (McMillan)　112:226-34, 236-42, 244-45, 247, 49, 251-52
"Waiting Ward" (Wright)　53:419
Waiting Women (Bergman)
　See *Kvinnors väntan*
The Waiting Years (Enchi)
　See *Onnazaka*
"Waiting—Afield at Dusk" (Frost)　26:127

Waka Jawaka (Zappa)　17:590
Wakai (Reconciliation) (Shiga)　33:366-67, 371
"The Wake" (Dybek)　114:64, 71, 73-4
"Wake for Papa Montero" (Guillen)
　See "Velorio de Papá Montero"
A Wake for the Living (Lytle)　22:298
Wake of the Great Sealers (Mowat)　26:338
"Wake the World" (Wilson)　12:641
Wake Up, Jonathan (Rice)　7:360; 49:301, 305
Wake Up, Stupid (Harris)　19:200-01, 204
Wakefield Express (Anderson)　20:17
"Wake-Pick" (Gunnars)　69:260-61
Wake-Pick Poems (Gunnars)　69:259-61
"Wake-Up Niggers" (Madhubuti)　6:313; 73:199, 207
"The Waking" (Roethke)　101:271, 326
Waking (Figes)　31:167-70
"Waking an Angel" (Levine)　4:287
"Waking Early Sunday Morning" (Lowell)　8:351; 15:343; 37:237
"Waking in a Newly-Built House" (Gunn)　6:221
"Waking in the Blue" (Lowell)　11:327; 15:343
"Waking in the Dark" (Rich)　3:428; 7:369, 373
"Waking in the Endless Mountains" (Smith)　42:357
"Waking Jed" (Williams)　33:449
The Waking: Poems, 1933-1953 (Roethke)　1:291; 8:455; 19:397; 46:360, 363; 101:266, 273, 287, 295, 302, 304
Waking Slow (Mewshaw)　9:376-77
"Waking This Morning" (Swados)　12:557
Waking Up (Fo)　32:174, 176
"Waking Up in the Middle of Some American Dreams" (Jordan)　114:152
"Wakulla: Chasing the Gator's Eye" (Bottoms)　53:33
"Waldo" (Heinlein)　14:250; 55:302-03
Waldo (Theroux)　28:422-23
"Wales and the Crown" (Jones)　7:191
"Wales Visitation" (Ginsberg)　36:184, 189-91; 109:347
"Walimai" (Allende)　97:9, 31
"A Walk" (Snyder)　32:391
"Walk" (Tchicaya)
　See "Marche"
Walk Gently This Good Earth (Craven)　17:80-1
"A Walk in Kyoto" (Birney)　6:78
"A Walk in Late Summer" (Roethke)　3:433
"A Walk in the Country" (Raine)　103:184, 190
A Walk in the Night, and Other Stories (La Guma)　19:272-73, 275-76
"A Walk in the Woods" (Davis)　49:92
A Walk in the Woods (Blessing)　54:8-13
A Walk in Wolf Wood (Stewart)　117:369
Walk like a Dragon (Clavell)　87:18
Walk Me to the Distance (Everett)　57:216-17
Walk My Way (Corcoran)　17:78
"A Walk on Moss" (Viereck)　4:559
"A Walk on Snow" (Viereck)　4:559
"A Walk on the Cliff" (Lavin)　99:321-23
"Walk on the Moon" (Momaday)　85:231
"Walk on the Water" (Broumas)　73:15
A Walk on the Water (Leonard)　19:280
A Walk on the Water (Stoppard)　15:518; 29:398
A Walk on the West Side: California on the Brink (Gold)　42:194
"Walk on the Wild Side" (Reed)　21:304-05, 314
A Walk on the Wild Side (Algren)　4:17; 10:6-7; 33:12, 15-16

Walk on the Wild Side: The Best of Lou Reed (Reed)　21:314
"Walk with Eros" (O'Casey)　11:406
A Walk with Love and Death (Huston)　20:171-72
"A Walk with Raschid" (Jacobsen)　48:192, 196
"A Walk with Raschid" (Jacobsen)　102:241
A Walk with Raschid, and Other Stories (Jacobsen)　48:192, 196; 102:225
"A Walk with the Accuser" (Gordon)　29:188
"The Walker" (Hope)　51:213
"Walker Brothers Cowboy" (Munro)　50:210; 95:287, 298
"Walker in Darkness" (Wright)　53:419
A Walker in the City (Kazin)　34:561; 38:272-73, 275, 280, 282
Walker Percy: An American Search (Coles)　108:179
"Walkers Passing Each Other in the Park" (Rakosi)　47:345
"Walkers with the Dawn" (Hughes)　35:214
"Walking" (Creeley)　15:151
"Walking at Whitsun" (Gascoyne)　45:154, 158
Walking Dead (Dickinson)　12:176-77; 35:133-34
"Walking Down Park" (Giovanni)　117:195-98
Walking down the Stairs (Kinnell)　29:281-82
The Walking Drum (L'Amour)　55:308
"Walking Home at Night" (Ginsberg)　36:182
Walking in Dead Diamond River (Hoagland)　28:181
"Walking in the rain in Guyana" (Sanchez)　116:318-19
"Walking in Your Footsteps" (Police, The)　26:366
"Walking into Love" (Piercy)　18:406; 27:375
"Walking Lessons" (Price)　3:406; 6:423; 43:345
"The Walking Man of Rodin" (Sandburg)　10:448
"Walking on Sunday" (Murphy)　41:317
"Walking on the Prayerstick" (Rose)　85:312
"Walking on Water" (Munro)　10:357; 19:345; 95:302, 304
"Walking Our Boundaries" (Lorde)　71:232, 240, 247
"Walking Out" (Plumly)　33:312
"Walking out Alone in Dead of Winter" (Kinnell)　13:321
Walking Papers (Hochman)　8:297-98
"Walking Parker Home" (Kaufman)　49:203-04
The Walking Stones (Hunter)
　See *The Bodach*
"Walking the Boundaries" (Davison)　28:103
Walking the Boundaries: Poems, 1957-1974 (Davison)　28:102-03
"Walking the Dog: a Diatribe" (Van Duyn)　63:439
Walking the Indian Streets (Mehta)　37:288-89
"Walking the Trestle" (Parini)　54:361
Walking Through Seville (Cabral de Melo Neto)
　See *Sevilha andando*
"Walking to Sleep" (Wilbur)　14:577; 53:412; 110:357, 360
Walking to Sleep: New Poems and Translations (Wilbur)　3:532-33; 6:568; 14:577; 53:396, 402, 406-07, 410-11; 110:352, 355, 360, 372, 384-85
"Walking to the Cattle-Place" (Murray)

40:335-36

Walking under Water (Abse)   29:13-17

"Walking with Jackie, Sitting with Dog" (Soto)
32:403

"Walking Wounded" (Scannell)   49:327, 329,
332

"Walking Wounded" (Shaw)   7:411; 23:396

Walking Wounded: Poems, 1962-1965
(Scannell)   49:327-29, 331-32

"Walk-On" (Young)   17:573

Walkover (Skolimowski)   20:348, 350-51, 353

"The Wall" (Brooks)   49:28, 38

"Wall" (Creeley)   2:108; 78:154

"The Wall" (Jones)   4:259

"A Wall" (Simic)   49:337

The Wall (Hersey)   1:144; 7:153; 40:227, 230-
31, 234, 241; 81:332-34, 337; 97:302-
03, 305-06

The Wall (Pink Floyd)   35:309-15

The Wall (Ringwood)   48:330, 335-36, 338

The Wall, and Other Stories (Sartre)
See *Le mur*

"The Wall and the Books" (Borges)   13:105;
83:160, 162, 176

Wall around a Star (Williamson)   29:462

"The Wall of All Earth" (Akhmatova)   25:28

"Wall of Death" (Voznesensky)   57:428

"A Wall of Fire Rising" (Danticat)   94:93, 98-
9

The Wall of the Plague (Brink)   36:70-2;
106:119-22, 124

"Wall Songs" (Hogan)   73:150-51, 153

Wall Street (Stone)   73:367-68, 376-77, 381-
82

The Wall: The Crime of Mr. S. Karuma (Abe)
22:13

Wallace Stevens: Musing the Obscure
(Sukenick)   3:475

Wallace Stevens: The Poems of Our Climate
(Bloom)   103:12, 14, 16, 24

"A Walled Garden" (Taylor)   44:305

Wallflower at the Orgy (Ephron)   17:110-11,
113

"The Wallpaper Flower" (Snodgrass)   6:514

The Wallpaper Fox (Philipson)   53:274-75,
277

Walls and Bridges (Lennon)   12:377; 35:268-
71, 274

The Walls Do Not Fall (H. D.)   8:255, 257-58;
14:223, 225-27; 31:202-04, 208; 34:445-
46; 73:117

"The Walls of Anagoor" (Buzzati)   36:93-4

"The Walls of Shimpundu" (Pownall)   10:419

"Walls That Hear You" (Woolrich)   77:401

"Wally Whistles Dixie" (Beattie)   63:12

The Walnut Door (Hersey)   9:277

The Walnut Trees of Altenburg (Malraux)
See *Les noyers de l'Altenburg*

Walsh (Pollock)   50:224, 226

"Walt and Will" (Apple)   33:21

"Walt Whitman" (Dahlberg)   7:63

"Walt Whitman" (Honig)   33:211

"Walt Whitman at Bear Mountain" (Simpson)
4:499; 7:427, 429; 9:486; 32:380

Walt Whitman: The Making of the Poet (Zweig)
34:378-79; 42:468-69

Walter (Taylor)   27:443

*Walter Benjamin; or, Towards Revolutionary
Criticism* (Eagleton)   63:97, 104, 110

"Walter Clark's Frontier" (Stegner)   81:347

"Walter Llywarch" (Thomas)   6:534

The Walter Mosley Omnibus (Mosley)   97:360

"The Waltons" (Hamner)   12:258-59

"The Waltz" (Parker)   15:417; 68:326, 335-
36, 338

Waltz in Marathon (Dickinson)   49:99-103

Waltz Into Darkness (Woolrich)   77:389, 391,
393, 395-98

The Waltz of the Toreadors (Anouilh)
See *La valse des toréadors*

Wampeters, Foma, and Granfalloons: Opinions
(Vonnegut)   4:568-69; 5:466, 469-70;
12:610, 620, 626-27; 22:449, 451; 60:434

"The Wanderer" (Auden)   11:15

"The Wanderer" (Christie)   110:126

"The Wanderer" (Masefield)   47:229

"The Wanderer" (Williams)   67:405-06

The Wanderer (Leiber)   25:302-03, 311

"The Wanderer Awaiting Preferment" (Stafford)
7:462

A Wanderer in Japan (Blunden)   56:50

"Wanderer, kommst du nach Spa..." ("Stranger,
Bear Words to the Spartans We..."; "Traveller, If You Come to the Spa"; "Traveller, If You Go to Spa") (Boell)   6:83;
27:56, 58-9, 65-7; 39:293-95; 72:69, 70,
73, 76, 78, 79-84, 94, 98, 100

"Wanderers" (Stern)   39:237

"The Wanderers" (Welty)   33:420; 105:340,
386

The Wanderers (Ichikawa)
See *Matatabi*

The Wanderers (Mphahlele)   25:332-34, 340-
42, 345

The Wanderers (Price)   6:426-27; 12:488-91

Wanderers and Travellers (Strugatskii and
Strugatskii)   27:433

"A Wanderer's Song" (Masefield)   11:358

"The Wandering Islands" (Hope)   51:216, 219-
20, 224

"The Wandering Islands" (Walcott)   76:279

The Wandering Islands (Hope)   51:210, 213,
215-17, 219-20

The Wandering Jew (Heym)   41:218-19

The Wandering of Desire (Montgomery)   7:232

The Wandering Prince (Hibbert)   7:156

"The Wandering Scholar's Prayer to St.
Catherine of Egypt" (Cunningham)
31:99, 101

The Wandering Unicorn (Mujica Lainez)
31:283-85

Wanderings: Chaim Potok's History of the Jews
(Potok)   14:429-30; 26:373-74; 112:261-
62, 269, 295

"Wanderlust" (McCartney)   35:290-91

"Wanderung" (Jandl)   34:195

"A Waning Moon" (Sansom)   6:484

"The Want" (Olds)   85:305

The Want Bone (Pinsky)   94:305-12, 322

"Want More" (Marley)   17:268-69, 271

"Wantage Bells" (Betjeman)   43:35

Wanted (Pryor)   26:379

Wanted! A Horse! (Friis-Baastad)   12:214

Wanted Alive (Moure)   88:216-19, 227-29

"Wanted: An Ontological Critic" (Ransom)
4:437; 5:365; 24:365

Wanted: Hope (Samarakis)
See *Zititai elpis*

"Wanted—An Enemy" (Leiber)   25:304

The Wanting Seed (Burgess)   2:85-6; 4:84;
8:112; 10:87-8; 13:123, 126; 22:69-70,
74; 40:116-17, 121; 62:130-31; 94:25-
29, 31, 34, 39, 41, 43, 49, 51, 55, 57, 59,
65, 74, 77

"Wanting to Die" (Sexton)   6:492; 53:313,
316, 319-20

"Wanting to Experience All Things" (Bly)
38:57

"Wanting to Help" (Bell)   8:65

"Wanting to Live in Harlem" (Seidel)   18:474

"The Wanton Song" (Page and Plant)   12:477

"Wants" (Larkin)   5:227; 18:296, 301; 64:260,
266

"Wants" (Paley)   37:337

The Wapshot Chronicle (Cheever)   3:107, 109;
7:50; 15:127; 25:118, 120; 64:44, 48, 57,
65-7

The Wapshot Scandal (Cheever)   3:106-07,
109; 7:50; 25:118; 64:44, 48-9, 57-9, 66

"The War" (Duras)
See "La douleur"

"War" (Findley)   102:108, 111-12, 116

"A War" (Jarrell)   49:201

"War" (Scott)   22:372

"War" (Williams)   56:427

War (Le Clezio)   31:247, 249

The War (Ehrenburg)   62:177

The War: A Memoir (Duras)
See *La douleur*

War All the Time: Poems, 1981-1984 (Bukowski)
41:73; 82:13

"War and Memory" (Jordan)   114:146, 148,
157

War and Prison (*Voina i tiur'ma*) (Aksyonov)
101:55

War and Remembrance (Wouk)   38:449-52

War and War (Barthelme)   36:49

"War Autobiography" (Blunden)   56:41

"The War between Desire and Dailiness"
(Pastan)   27:371

"The War between Men and Women" (Thurber)
11:533; 25:437

The War between the Tates (Lurie)   4:305-07;
5:259-61; 18:310; 39:178-80

"War Cemetary" (Blunden)   56:30, 45

"War Cemetery, Ranville" (Scannell)   49:330

War Comes to Willy Freeman (Collier and
Collier)   30:74-5

"War Crimes" (Carey)   96:28, 36, 38-9, 68, 71

"War Crimes" (Muske)   90:309-10, 312

War Crimes (Carey)   96:22, 24-5, 36, 38-9, 53,
55, 62-3, 68, 72

*The War Diaries of Jean-Paul Sartre, Novem-
ber 1939-March 1940* (Sartre)   52:377-
80

"War Games" (Morgan)   2:295

War Games (Morris)   7:245

"The War Horse" (Boland)   40:96, 98; 113:96,
122

The War Horse (Boland)   40:96-8, 100; 67:43-
6; 113:74, 78, 81, 87, 94, 96, 99, 108-09,
114, 122

The War Hound and the World's Pain
(Moorcock)   58:354

"War: Impacts and Delayed Actions" (Blunden)
56:38

"The War in the Bathroom" (Atwood)   13:46;
25:62

War Is Heaven! (Mano)   2:270

"War Is Over" (Lennon)
See "Happy Xmas"

"The War Is Over" (Ochs)   17:332, 335

The War Lords of Washington (Catton)   35:82-
3

The War Lover (Hersey)   40:230-32, 234, 238-
40; 81:332, 334; 97:302, 304

"War Memoir" (Kaufman)   49:203

"War Movie Veteran" (Scannell)   49:332

The War of Dreams (Carter)   5:101

The War of the End of the World (Vargas Llosa)
    See *La guerra del fin del mundo*
The War of the Saints (Amado) 106:86-91
"War of the Two Directions" (Wingrove)
    68:456
The War of the Worlds (Welles) 80:378-81,
    414-16
The War of Time (Carpentier)
    See *Guerra del tiempo*
"The War of Vaslav Nijinsky" (Bidart) 33:77-
    81
"The War on Poverty" (Shields) 97:429-31
War on the Fourth Floor (Kohout) 13:325
"War on the Periphery" (Johnston) 51:240,
    243, 250, 253
"The War Piece" (Bell) 8:66
"War Poems" (Ciardi) 40:154
"War Poems" (MacBeth) 5:265
"War Profit Litany" (Ginsberg) 36:184
"A War Requiem" (Sissman) 9:491
"War Sonnet" (Meredith) 13:374
War Suite (Harrison) 6:223
War Trilogy (H. D.)
    See *Trilogy*
"War Winters" (Birney) 6:74
War with the Newts (Kohout) 13:324
*War Within and Without: Diaries and Letters of
    Anne Morrow Lindbergh,1939-1944*
    (Lindbergh) 82:156-57, 159
"War Wounds" (Shields) 97:430, 433
War Year (Haldeman) 61:169
Ward 402 (Glasser) 37:132-33
"Ward Number Four" (Pa Chin)
    See "Ti ssu ping shih"
"The Warden" (Gardner) 7:111, 116; 8:238
"The Warden Said to Me the Other Day"
    (Knight) 40:283
"The Warden's Wife" (Trevor) 116:389
"Wardrobe Trunk" (Woolrich) 77:399
"Warehouse Three" (Aldiss) 5:15
Warera no jidai (Oe) 36:350; 86:214, 230,
    239, 241
Warera no kyoki o ikinobiru michi o oshieyo
    (*Teach Us to Outgrow Our Madness*) (Oe)
    86:215-17, 225, 228, 243-44
Warlock (Harrison) 33:196-201; 66:155-56,
    161, 169
Warlock of the Witch World (Norton) 12:468
The Warlord of the Air (Moorcock) 27:348;
    58:349
"Warm and Beautiful" (McCartney) 35:284-
    85
A Warm December (Poitier) 26:358-60
"Warm Flesh-Colored Ode" (Justice) 102:258
"Warm Love" (Morrison) 21:234
The Warm Nights of January (Tuohy) 37:428,
    431
"A Warm Room" (Tillinghast) 29:414-15
"Warm Thoughts" (Robinson) 21:348-50
Warm Worlds and Otherwise (Tiptree) 48:386,
    388-89, 393
"Warming Trends" (Louie) 70:81
"The Warmth of the Sun" (Wilson) 12:651
"Warning" (Cohen) 38:131
"The Warning" (Creeley) 36:120; 78:134
"A Warning" (Ezekiel) 61:96
"Warning" (Frost) 15:246
"Warning" (Hughes) 35:218
Warning (Fassbinder) 20:106
"Warning Sign" (Byrne) 26:96
"Warning to Children" (Graves) 2:176; 39:328;
    45:170
"Warnings" (Parra) 102:353

Warnings from the Grave (Plath) 9:429
"Warnings to the Reader" (Parra) 102:348-51
"A Warrant for Pablo Neruda" (McGrath)
    28:277
"Warren Pryor" (Nowlan) 15:398
Warrendale (Maysles and Maysles) 16:440
"Warrior" (Kenny) 87:241
Warrior Marks (Walker) 103:419-22
"The Warrior Princess Ozimbu" (Price) 43:341
The Warrior Queens (Fraser)
    See *The Warrior Queens*
Warrior Scarlet (Sutcliff) 26:426, 428, 430-
    36, 441
The Warriors (Jakes) 29:248-49
The Warriors of Day (Blish) 14:84
"The Wars" (Moss) 45:291
The Wars (Findley) 27:141-45; 102:97, 99-
    101, 104-06, 109, 111-14, 116-17, 121
"The Wars in New Jersey" (Merwin) 88:208
The Wars of the Jews (Sobol) 60:385-86
A Warsaw Diary, 1978-1981 (Brandys) 62:112-
    17, 119-20
"Warszawa" (Bowie) 17:65
"A Wartime Dawn" (Gascoyne) 45:154, 158-
    59
Wartime Journalism, 1939-1943 (de Man)
    55:411, 413
*Wartime: Understanding and Behavior in the
    Second World War* (Fussell) 74:130-32,
    135-39, 143
"The Wartons" (Blunden) 56:37
"Warum ich kurze Prosa wie Jakob Maria
    Hermes and Heinrich Knecht schreibe"
    ("The Seventh Trunk") (Boell) 27:67
"Was" (Faulkner) 6:174-75
"Was" (Scott) 22:374
Was Europe a Success? (Krutch) 24:284, 289
Was Heisst Denken? (*What Is Called Thinking?*)
    (Heidegger) 24:264, 267
"Was ich Rom sah und hörte" ("What I Saw
    and Heard in Rome") (Bachmann) 69:42-
    3
*Was soll aus dem Jungen bloss werden?: oder,
    Irgendwas mit Büchern* (*What's to Become
    of the Boy? or, Something to Do with
    Books*) (Boell) 27:294; 72:101
"Wash" (Faulkner) 52:138-39
"Wash Far Away" (Berryman) 10:45
"Wash of Cold River" (H. D.) 73:108, 120
"The Washing Machine Tragedy" (Lem)
    40:294
"Washington Bullets" (Clash) 30:48-9
Washington, D.C. (Vidal) 2:449; 4:559; 6:549-
    50; 8:525; 22:435; 33:407, 409; 72:377-
    79, 382-84, 389, 391-93, 395-97, 400-03
"Washington in Love" (Berryman) 8:93; 25:96
Washington Is Leaking (Buchwald) 33:94
Washington Jitters (Trumbo) 19:446
Washington Square (Auchincloss) 9:55
The Washington Square Ensemble (Bell) 41:51-
    4; 102:3-4, 16-17
*Washington vs. Main Street: The Struggle be-
    tween Federal and Local Power* (Archer)
    12:21
"The Washroom Ballet" (Lieberman) 36:261
"The Wasp" (Morrison) 17:295
"Wasp" (Nowlan) 15:399
The Wasp Factory (Banks) 34:29-31
"Wasp Nest" (Fuller) 62:199
"A WASP Woman Visits a Black Junkie in
    Prison" (Knight) 40:285
"Wassermann Test" (Pasternak) 7:297
"Die Wasserstrasse" (Schmidt) 56:392

The Waste Land (Eliot) 1:89-92; 2:125-30;
    3:136-41; 6:160-61, 164-66; 9:182-88,
    190; 10:168-72; 13:198, 201-02; 15:210,
    212, 214-17; 24:163, 167, 172, 176, 185;
    34:388, 390,; 55:346-48, 351-56, 358-
    60, 362, 366-70, 372, 374; 57:167-213;
    113:182, 186, 189-91, 197, 209, 217, 219,
    223
*The Waste Land: A Facsimile and Transcript of
    the Original Drafts, Including the Anno-
    tations of Ezra Pound* (Eliot) 57:201-09
"Waste Sonata" (Olds) 85:306
"Wasted on the Young" (Brunner) 8:111
"Wasteland" (Weller) 26:446
"The Watch" (Bass) 79:4-6, 9
"The Watch" (Dixon) 52:98
"The Watch" (Swenson) 14:518; 61:392
"The Watch" (Swift) 41:443, 446; 88:320
"Watch" (Ungaretti)
    See "Veglia"
"The Watch" (Wagoner) 3:508
The Watch (Bass) 79:3-7, 10-11, 14-17, 19-20
"Watch Any Day His Nonchalant Pauses"
    (Auden) 14:32; 43:15
"Watch for Flag Man" (Loewinsohn) 52:284
The Watch House (Westall) 17:557-59
Watch It Come Down (Osborne) 45:319-20
Watch on the Rhine (Hellman) 2:187; 8:281;
    14:258-59; 18:222, 225, 227; 34:348-49,
    353; 44:530; 52:191, 202
"Watch Repair" (Simic) 49:340
The Watch That Ends the Night (MacLennan)
    2:257; 14:339-42, 344; 92:305, 307-08,
    321, 324-28, 331-40, 342-50
"Watch That Man" (Bowie) 17:60
Watch the North Wind Rise (Graves) 11:256;
    45:171-73
"Watch Your Step" (Costello) 21:76
Watchboy, What of the Night? (Cassity) 42:94-
    5
"The Watcher" (Cooper) 56:71
"The Watcher" (Vanderhaeghe) 41:449-50,
    453
The Watcher, and Other Stories (Calvino)
    See *La giornato d'uno scruttatore*
Watcher in the Shadows (Household) 11:277
"A Watcher of the Dead" (Gordimer) 33:177
"The Watchers" (Blackburn) 43:62
"The Watchers" (Bradbury) 42:38
Watchers (Koontz) 78:198, 200-01, 203, 219
"Watches of Grandfathers" (Dunn) 40:168
Watchfires (Auchincloss) 45:32
"The Watchful Gods" (Clark) 28:79-80
The Watchful Gods, and Other Stories (Clark)
    28:78-9
"The Watching" (Dodson) 79:194
"Watching" (O Hehir) 41:324
"Watching 'Dark Circle'" (Levertov) 66:239
"Watching Football on TV" (Nemerov) 36:305
"Watching Him" (McFadden) 48:243
Watching Me, Watching You (Weldon) 36:443-
    45
"Watching Post" (Day Lewis) 10:131
"Watching Running Water" (Blunden) 56:29
"Watching the Detectives" (Costello) 21:68,
    74
Watching the Detectives (Rathbone) 41:344
"Watching the Jets Lose to Buffalo at Shea"
    (Swenson) 61:402; 106:330
"Watching the River Flow" (Dylan) 6:158
"Watching the Wheels" (Lennon) 35:272-75
The Watchmaker of Everton (Simenon) 2:396,
    399

"Watchman, What of the Night?" (Barnes) 29:24

"Water" (Creeley) 78:137

"Water" (Larkin) 33:259; 39:344; 64:268, 282-84

"Water" (Lowell) 4:299

"Water" (Snyder) 32:386

Water and Stone (Vliet) 22:443

"Water and the Poem" (Cabral de Melo Neto)
See "O poema e a água"

"Water and the Wine" (Armatrading) 17:8

"The Water Bearer" (Williams) 42:442

The Water Beetle (Mitford) 44:489

"The Water Carrier" (Montague) 46:275

"The Water Clock" (Boland) 113:120

"The Water Diviner" (Abse) 29:15

"The Water Drop" (Elytis) 49:110-11

"Water Element Song for Sylvia" (Wakoski) 7:504

The Water Engine: An American Fable (Mamet) 15:355, 358; 46:246, 249, 252-54

The Water Is Wide (Conroy) 30:76-7; 74:47-51

The Water Is Wide (Le Guin) 45:213-14

"Water Island" (Moss) 45:291-92

"Water Liars" (Hannah) 90:143-45, 147, 160

"Water Maid" (Clark) 38:121

Water Music (Boyle) 36:58-60, 62-3; 90:43, 49, 58-9, 61

"Water Music for the Progress of Love in a Life-Raft down the Sammamish Slough" (Wagoner) 5:474

"The Water of Izli" (Bowles) 53:36

"Water of Life" (MacDiarmid) 63:244

"The Water of the Flowery Mill" (Rothenberg) 57:374

Water on the Brain (Mackenzie) 18:316

The Water Pourer (Coover) 87:45

"The Water Rats" (Colwin) 5:108; 84:149

Water, Rock, and Sand (Levi) 41:243-44

"Water Song" (Kogawa) 78:167

Water Street (Merrill) 2:273, 275; 13:378-80; 91:228, 230

Water under the Bridge (Elliott) 38:181

"Water Widow" (Jensen) 37:186

Water with Berries (Lamming) 2:235; 4:279; 66:220, 225, 227-30

Water with the Wines (Armatrading) 17:9

"The Water Works" (Doctorow) 37:91, 93; 113:151-52

"Water Writes Always in Plural" (Paz) 19:365

"Waterbird" (Swenson) 61:402-03

"Waterclap" (Asimov) 19:26

"Watercolor of Grantchester Meadows" (Plath) 51:344; 111:200, 203

"The Watercress Girl" (Bates) 46:67

"The Water-Diviner" (Clarke) 61:79-80, 83

"Waterfall" (Clarke) 61:73

"The Waterfall" (Daryush) 19:121

"Waterfall" (Heaney) 25:242

"Waterfall" (O Hehir) 41:323-24

"The Waterfall" (Oliver) 98:288

"Waterfall" (Simon) 26:409

The Waterfall (Drabble) 2:117-19; 3:128-29; 5:118; 10:165; 22:122, 124-25; 53:118-19, 121-22

"Waterfalls" (McCartney) 35:287

"Waterfalls" (Watkins) 43:444, 453

Waterfront (Schulberg) 48:346-47

Watergate: America in Crisis (Archer) 12:21-2

"The Watergaw" (MacDiarmid) 11:336;

19:286-87; 63:252

Watering (Brosman) 9:135-36

Waterland (Swift) 41:443-47; 88:284-92, 294-303, 307-10, 313, 315-18, 320-22

"Waterlily Fire" (Rukeyser) 27:408

Waterlily Fire: Poems, 1935-1962 (Rukeyser) 15:456; 27:408

"Waterloo Bridge" (Middleton) 13:387

"Waterloo Express" (Jiles) 13:304; 58:271-73

"Waterloo Sunset" (Davies) 21:90, 97

"Watermaid" (Okigbo) 25:347-48, 351, 354; 84:301, 305, 308-10, 313, 329-31

Watermark (Brodsky) 100:38, 47, 56, 58

"Watermarked" (White) 110:339-40

Watermelon Man (Van Peebles) 20:410-12

Watermelons (Loewinsohn) 52:283

"Water-Message" (Barth) 9:66, 69; 89:3, 6, 8-10, 14-16, 19, 22, 36, 41, 48-50, 54, 56, 59, 64

The Water-Method Man (Irving) 13:292-93; 23:244; 38:250-51; 155-157, 159, 165

"A Waterpiece" (Blunden) 56:29

"The Waters" (Matthews) 40:322, 324

"The Waters" (Merwin) 45:275

The Waters Are Come in unto My Soul (Oe)
See *Kozui wa waga tamashii ni oyobi*

"The Water's Edge" (Hooker) 43:197

The Waters of Babylon (Arden) 6:4, 9; 13:26, 28; 15:19

The Waters of Kronos (Richter) 30:316-17, 321-22, 326

"Waters of Melis" (Kerrigan) 6:276

The Waters of Siloe (Merton) 83:398, 403

"The Watershed" (Auden) 6:24

"Watershed" (Avison) 97:128

Watership Down (Adams) 4:6-10; 5:4-7; 18:2

The Waterworks (Doctorow) 113:166-80

Watson's Apology (Bainbridge) 62:32, 34

Watt (Beckett) 3:45; 6:34, 41-4; 9:80, 84; 10:27-8, 34-6; 11:33-4, 36, 39, 40, 43; 14:70-3, 75-6, 80; 18:41, 50, 52; 29:53, 56, 63, 65; 57:65; 59:253-54, 260; 83:121

Watten: Ein Nachlass (Bernhard) 61:9

Watusi (Clavell) 87:18

"A Wave" (Ashbery) 41:33-4, 36-41; 77:62

"The Wave" (MacLeish) 8:362

"Wave" (Smith) 12:543

A Wave (Ashbery) 41:33-40

The Wave (Scott) 43:376-78, 383, 385

The Wave of the Future (Lindbergh) 82:155-158, 164, 166-67

Wave the High Banner (Brown) 18:70

Wave without a Shore (Cherryh) 35:107-09, 112

Wavelength (Morrison) 21:238

"The Waves" (Oliver) 98:267

Waves (Pasternak) 63:288

The Waves behind the Boat (King) 53:207

The Waves of Night (Petrakis) 3:382

"Waving" (Smith) 42:348

The Wax Museum (Hawkes) 4:213, 215

"The Way" (Creeley) 78:127, 133

"The Way a Ghost Dissolves" (Hugo) 32:247-48

"The Way a *Sertanejo* Speaks" (Cabral de Melo Neto)
See "O sertanejo falando"

"The Way Back" (Grau) 9:240

The Way Home (Singer) 69:306

"The Way I Feel" (Giovanni) 117:192

"The Way In" (Tomlinson) 13:549

The Way In and Other Poems (Tomlinson) 6:534-36; 13:548-49; 45:396, 398, 401

A Way in the World (Naipaul) 105:175-77, 179, 181-82

"The Way Is Not a Way" (Snyder) 32:392

"The Way It Is" (Strand) 18:516, 519; 41:436; 71:285

"The Way It Mostly Was" (O'Brien) 103:144-45

"The Way It Sometimes Is" (Taylor) 44:300

"the Way it Was" (Clifton) 66:69

"The Way Love Used to Be" (Davies) 21:92

The Way of a World (Tomlinson) 2:437; 4:544, 546-47; 13:545-46, 548; 45:393-94, 396, 398, 402

The Way of All Flesh (Compton-Burnett) 10:109

Way of All the Earth (Akhmatova) 64:13

The Way of It (Thomas) 13:545; 48:380-81

"The Way of Keys" (Dobyns) 37:75

A Way of Life, like Any Other (O'Brien) 11:405

A Way of Seeing (Mead) 37:277-78

"A Way of Talking" (Grace) 56:111-12

The Way of the Animal Powers (Campbell)
See *The Historical Atlas of World Mythology*

The Way of the Seeded Earth (Campbell)
See *The Historical Atlas of World Mythology*

"The Way of the Wind" (Oz) 27:359

"The Way of the Wind" (Riding) 7:374

"The Way of the World" (Martin) 89:110, 112, 118

The Way of the World (Connelly) 7:57

"A Way Out" (Adcock) 41:16

A Way Out (Frost) 15:249

Way Out in the Centre (Abse) 29:20

The Way Some People Die (Macdonald) 14:334; 41:265, 267, 269, 271

The Way Some People Live (Cheever) 15:127; 64:66

"The Way the Bird Sat" (Young Bear) 94:361, 366

The Way the Future Was (Pohl) 18:412

"The Way Things Work" (Graham) 48:145

The Way to Dusty Death (MacLean) 13:359; 50:348

"The Way to Eden" (Roddenberry) 17:412

"The Way to Hump a Cow Is Not" (Cummings) 15:162

"A Way to Love God" (Warren) 13:578; 39:267-69

The Way to Rainy Mountain (*Rainy Mountain*) (Momaday) 2:290; 19:317-20; 85:227-28, 231-33, 235, 238, 246, 250-51, 253, 255-56, 258, 262, 266-67, 269, 273-79; 95:218, 222, 234, 237-38, 274, 276-77

Way to the Ocean (Leonov)
See *Doroga na okean*

"The Way up to Heaven" (Dahl) 79:176

Way Upstream (Ayckbourn) 33:45-6, 48; 74:19-20, 24, 27, 29, 31

"The Way We Live" (Haines) 58:216

"The Way We Live Now" (Bernard) 59:46

"The Way We Live Now" (Sontag) 105:197

The Way We Live Now (Sontag) 105:206

The Way West (Guthrie) 23:197-98, 201

A Way with Words (Bowering) 47:28

"The Way You Do the Things You Do" (Robinson) 21:343, 346-47

"A Way You'll Never Be" (Hemingway) 10:267; 30:179, 183, 187-88, 196-97

"The Wayfarer" (Colum) 28:85

"The Wayfarer" (Coover) 46:116

"Ways" (O'Brien) 13:416; 36:341; 116:209-10

"Ways and Means" (Eberhart) 11:178

Ways of a Sleeping Man, Ways of a Waking Man (Michaux)
  See *Façons d'endormi, façons d'éveillé*
Ways of Death (Bachmann)
  See *Todesarten*
Ways of Escape (Greene) 27:171-74; 37:138; 70:289-90, 292; 72:179
"Ways of Feeling" (Cassity) 42:94
The Ways of White Folks (Hughes) 1:149; 10:281; 108:313, 315
The Waystation (Simak) 55:319-20, 322
The Wayward and the Seeking: A Collection of Writing by Jean Toomer (Toomer) 22:428-29
The Wayward Bus (Steinbeck) 1:325; 5:406; 9:517-18; 21:366, 371, 382-83, 391; 34:405; 45:370, 372, 378; 75:343, 350
"The Wayward Path" (Swan) 69:362
The Wayward Saint (Carroll) 10:97-100
"We" (McClure) 10:333
We a BadddDDD People (Sanchez) 116:272, 274-75, 278, 281, 295-96, 298, 301-02, 309, 313, 326
"We a BadddDDD People (for gwendolyn brooks/a fo real bad one)" (Sanchez) 116:295, 309, 315
"We All Begin in a Little Magazine" (Levine) 54:298, 301
We All Die Naked (Blish) 14:86
We All Have the Same Story (Fo) 32:176
"We All Wore a Green Carnation" (Coward) 29:138
"We Also Walk Dogs" (Heinlein) 14:249
We Always Treat Women Too Well (Queneau)
  See *On est toujours trop bon avec les femmes*
"We and Europe" (Ehrenburg) 62:177
"We and Them" (Marley) 17:273
We Are All Fugitives (Gironella)
  See *Todos somos fugitivos*
"We Are Always Too Late" (Boland) 113:92
We Are Betrayed (Fisher) 7:103
"We Are for the Dark" (Aickman) 57:4
"We Are in Your Area" (Van Duyn) 116:427
We Are Many (Neruda) 5:303
"We Are Muslim Women" (Sanchez) 116:299
"We Are Norsemen" (Boyle) 36:57
We Are Still Married (Keillor) 115:283, 286
"We Are the Dead" (Bowie) 17:61
We Are the Living (Caldwell) 14:96; 60:48
"We Are the National Hero" (Coles)
  See "My nacional'nyj geroj"
"We Are the Nighttime Travelers" (Canin) 55:35-6, 38-9
"We Are the Only Animals Who Do This" (Boland) 113:92
"We Are Very Poor" (Rulfo)
  See "Es que somos muy pobres"
We Bombed in New Haven (Heller) 11:265
We Can Build You (Dick) 30:123, 127-28; 72:104
"We Can Remember It for You Wholesale" (Dick) 72:123-24
"We Can Work It Out" (Lennon and McCartney) 12:361
We Can't Breathe (Fair) 18:140-41
"We Come Back" (Rexroth) 112:400
We Come to the River (Bond) 23:66
"We Don't Live Here Anymore" (Dubus) 36:144, 146, 148-49; 97:195-96, 199-200, 210, 218, 226
We Don't Live Here Anymore (Dubus) 97:209, 218-20
"We Don't Want No Education" (Pink Floyd)

35:313
"We Drink the Wine in France" (Walker) 103:407
"We Encounter Nat King Cole as We Invent the Future" (Harjo) 83:275, 282
"We Feed on Shadow" (Aleixandre) 36:30
We Fished All Night (Motley) 18:356-57
"We Francji" ("In France") (Dabrowska) 15:165
"We Free Singers Be" (Knight) 40:285, 287
"We Get Smashed and Our Endings Are Swift" (Abbott) 48:4-5
We Have Always Lived in the Castle (Jackson) 11:301; 60:211, 213-14, 217, 221-25, 234-35
"We Have Been Believers" (Walker) 6:554
"We Have Known" (Bell) 31:49
"We Have No Secrets" (Simon) 26:408, 410, 413
"We in Some Strange Power's Employ, Move on a Rigorous Line" (Delany) 38:154
We Killed Christ (Bruce) 21:54
"We Know You're Busy Writing, but We Thought You Wouldn't Mind If We Dropped In for a Minute" (Crispin) 22:112
"We Laughed at Him" (Achebe) 11:4
"We Learned" (Jong) 8:314
We Live Again (Mamoulian) 16:423
We Live Here (Voinovich)
  See *My zdes' zhivem*
We Love Glenda So Much, and Other Tales (Cortazar)
  See *Queremos tanto a Glenda*
"We Loved Here" (Amichai)
  See "Ahavnu Kan"
We Might See Sights! and Other Stories (O'Faolain) 47:325, 329
"We Must Call a Meeting" (Harjo) 83:269, 280, 285
"We Never Know" (Komunyakaa) 94:228, 243
We Never Make Mistakes (Solzhenitsyn)
  See *Sluchai na stantsii Krechetovka [i] Matrenin dvor*
"We Real Cool" (Brooks) 15:93
"We Say 'Cheers' Every Day" (Neruda)
  See "Salud decimos cada día"
We Talk, You Listen: New Tribes, New Turf (Deloria) 21:109-10, 113
"We Teach" (Howard) 7:168
We the Living (Rand) 30:291-92, 296-98, 300; 44:451; 79:362, 371, 373-75, 377-81, 389
We, the People (Rice) 7:360-61, 363; 49:296-97, 300-05
"We Two" (H. D.) 73:109
"We Walk the Way of the New World" (Madhubuti) 6:313
We Walk the Way of the New World (Madhubuti) 2:238; 73:205, 212, 214-15
"We, We Ourselves" (Ammons) 57:49-50
"We Went" (Montale) 9:388
We Were Strangers (Huston) 20:160-62
"We Were Three" (Alegria) 75:36-7, 39
We Who Are About To (Russ) 15:461-62
"We Who Stole the 'Dream'" (Tiptree) 48:389
We Won't Pay! We Won't Pay! (Fo) 32:173-76; 109:100-01, 119-20, 122, 144, 146
"The Weaker Sex" (Kawabata)
  See "Yowaki Utsuwa"
The Weaker Vessel (Fraser) 32:186-87; 107:35-36, 38, 40, 41-43, 45, 47, 51, 57, 59, 61, 67

The Weaker Vessel (Kawabata)
  See *The Weaker Vessel*
"The Weald of Youth" (Sassoon) 36:387, 394
"The Wean and That" (Kelman) 58:298
Weapons of Happiness (Brenton) 31:60-7
"The Weary Blues" (Hughes) 44:507-09, 511
The Weary Blues (Hughes) 1:147; 10:279; 15:292; 35:212, 214; 108:282, 290, 293-94, 296, 310, 312, 319, 323
"Weary Kingdom" (Irving) 112:173, 175
"Weasels and Ermines" (Kinsella) 27:239
Weasels Ripped My Flesh (Zappa) 17:586, 590, 593
"The Weather" (Chappell) 40:142; 78:95
"The Weather" (Soto) 80:299
Weather and Season (Hamburger) 14:234
"The Weather as Cultural Determinator" (Giovanni) 19:191
"Weather Bestiary" (Brown) 5:76
Weather Forecast for Utopia and Vicinity: Poems, 1967-1982 (Simic) 49:336-37, 339
"The Weather Gifts" (Szirtes) 46:391
The Weather in Africa (Gellhorn) 14:195; 60:188-89, 192
The Weather in the Streets (Lehmann) 5:235, 238
"The Weather Is Hot on the Back of My Watch" (Bukowski) 41:67
The Weatherboard Cathedral (Murray) 40:334, 336, 338
"Weathering by a Fire" (Brosman) 9:135
"Weathering Out" (Dove) 50:154; 81:139
The Weathermakers (Bova) 45:66-7
"Weatherman" (Dunn) 36:153-54
The Weathermonger (Dickinson) 12:167-68, 170, 172
Weathers and Edges (Booth) 23:74-5
A Weave of Women (Broner) 19:71-2
"The Weaver in the Vault" (Smith) 43:420
Weaveworld (Barker) 52:56-7
"Weaving the Morning" (Cabral de Melo Neto)
  See "Tecendo a manhã"
"The Web" (Glassco) 9:237
"Web" (Oliver) 34:248
Web (Wyndham) 19:476
"The Wedding" (Bates) 46:52, 63
"The Wedding" (Carrier) 78:38
"Wedding" (Dobyns) 37:82
"Wedding" (Nagy) 7:251
"The Wedding" (Pritchett) 15:443; 41:330, 334
"The Wedding" (Rothenberg) 57:374
A Wedding (Altman) 16:39-40, 42-44
The Wedding (Altman) 116:30, 37-8, 51, 61, 66, 70
The Wedding (Canetti)
  See *Die Hochzeit*
The Wedding (Kadare)
  See *Dasma*
The Wedding (Wajda) 16:580, 583
Wedding Album (Lennon) 35:267
Wedding Band: A Love/Hate Story in Black and White (Childress) 12:104-06; 86:305-06, 309-10, 312, 314-16; 96:88-93, 103-04, 109, 118-20, 123-24
"Wedding Bells Will Ring So Merrily" (Farrell) 66:129
"Wedding Day" (Boyle) 58:66-7, 71
"Wedding Day" (Hall) 51:170
"Wedding Day" (Hemingway) 3:240
Wedding Day, and Other Stories (Boyle) 5:65; 19:61
The Wedding Feast (Canetti)

See *Die Hochzeit*

The Wedding Feast (Wesker)   3:519; 42:426-27

The Wedding Group (Taylor)   2:432-33; 29:412

Wedding in Blood (Chabrol)   16:179

"The Wedding in the Garden" (Trevor)   71:329, 348

"Wedding Night" (Landolfi)   11:321; 49:209

"The Wedding Night" (Sexton)   53:316

"Wedding Night" (Tremain)   42:386

"The Wedding of Galia" (Yehoshua)   31:474

The Wedding on the Eiffel Tower (Cocteau)
   See *Les mariés de la Tour Eiffel*

"The Wedding Party" (Dubie)   36:132

The Wedding Party (De Palma)   20:73, 78

"Wedding Pictures" (Phillips)   15:420

"Wedding Song" (Dylan)   4:150

"Wedding Song" (Robinson)   21:346

"Wedding Song" (Smith)   42:353

Wedding Song (Mahfuz)   52:304-05

"A Wedding Toast" (Wilbur)   110:385

"Wedding Wind" (Clarke)   61:75

"Wedding Wind" (Larkin)   5:227; 8:332, 339; 18:298; 33:259; 39:336, 345; 64:259, 282

"The Wedding-Party" (Pasternak)   63:313

Weddings (Yevtushenko)   26:461

The Weddings at Nether Powers and Other New Poems (Redgrove)   41:356

Weddings in the House (Hrabal)
   See *Svatby v dome*

The Wedge (Williams)   42:455

"The Wedge-Tailed Eagle" (Buckley)   57:126

"Wednesday" (Fuller)   62:206

"Wednesday" (Levine)   14:318

"Wednesday at the Waldorf" (Swenson)   4:534; 106:339

Wednesday Morning Three A.M. (Simon)   17:459

"Wednesday Night at Our House" (Grayson)   38:210

"The Wee Boy Who Got Killed" (Kelman)   58:300. 302

"Wee Horrors" (Kelman)   58:295

"The Weed" (Bishop)   1:34; 9:92; 32:34, 36-7, 42

"Weed" (Hass)   99:140

The Weed Garden (Turco)   11:551-52

"The Weed of Time" (Spinrad)   46:383

"Weed Puller" (Roethke)   11:484; 19:397; 101:293-94, 334

The Weedkiller's Daughter (Arnow)   7:15-16; 18:12, 16

"Weeds" (De Marinis)   54:100

"The Weeds" (Stern)   40:408, 413

"Week of Sun" (Landolfi)   11:321; 49:212

"The Week of the Small Leaves" (Souster)   14:505

"Weekend" (Beattie)   63:17

"Weekend" (Weldon)   36:444

Weekend (Godard)   20:137, 140, 151

"Weekend Glory" (Angelou)   35:32

Weekend in Dinlock (Sigal)   7:423-24

"Weekend in the Country" (Sondheim)   30:397

"Weekend in the Neighborhood of Summer" (Ritsos)   31:324

The Weekend Man (Wright)   6:581-82

"Weekend Song" (Joel)   26:214

A Weekend with Claude (Bainbridge)   4:39, 22:44; 62:23-5, 30

"A Weekend with the Angels" (White)   10:527

Weep before God (Wain)   11:563

Weep Not, Child (Ngugi wa Thiong'o)   3:358; 7:263-66; 13:583; 36:311, 313, 315-17, 319, 324

Weep Not for Me (Edwards)   43:139-42

"Weeping and Wailing" (Stern)   40:413

"The Weeping Headstones of the Isaac Becketts" (Durcan)   43:114

"Weeping Willow" (Hikmet)   40:244

"Weg zum Bahnhof" (Eich)   15:204

"Weggebeizt" (Celan)   53:79

"Der Wegwerfer" ("The Thrower-Away") (Boell)   27:66-7; 72:67, 72-3, 107

Wei hu (Ding Ling)   68:64-5

"Weiß sind die Tulpen" (Celan)   82:50

"The Weight" (Lane)   25:289

The Weight of the Evidence (Stewart)   14:512

The Weight of the World (Handke)   38:223-27

"Weights" (Baxter)   45:50-2; 78:17

Weihnacht (*Christmas*) (Durrenmatt)   8:195; 15:193-94

"The Weird of Avoosl Wuthoqquan" (Smith)   43:420

Weird Scenes inside the Gold Mines (Morrison)   17:290

"Weird Sister" (Phillips)   28:361

"Weird Tales" (Chappell)   78:116

Weird Tales (Hamilton)   1:137

The Weirdstone of Brisingamen: A Tale of Alderly (Garner)   17:134-38, 142-44, 149

Weitere Aussichten (Kroetz)   41:235

"The Welcome" (Blunden)   56:43

Welcome! (Shapcott)   38:404

"Welcome Back, Mr. Knight: Love of My Life" (Knight)   40:287

Welcome Eumenides (Taylor)   5:425-26

"Welcome Morning" (Sexton)   6:493

"The Welcome Table" (Walker)   6:554; 103:361-63, 407

Welcome to Hard Times (Doctorow)   6:136; 11:143-45; 37:84, 88-91, 93-4; 44:168, 170, 176; 113:131, 150-52, 156-58, 160-61, 166, 173, 176, 180

Welcome to Mars (Blish)   14:86

"Welcome to the Machine" (Pink Floyd)   35:308, 311

Welcome to the Monkey House: A Collection of Short Works (Vonnegut)   1:348; 3:495; 5:467; 12:602, 619; 40:441

Welcome to the Moon (Shanley)   75:319

"Welcome to the Working Week" (Costello)   21:67

Welcome to Thebes (Swarthout)   35:400

Welcoming Disaster (Macpherson)   14:346-47

Welfare (Wiseman)   20:475-77

"Welfare Mothers" (Young)   17:581

"Well" (Lennon)   35:265

"The Well" (Levertov)   66:238, 242-43, 253

"The Well" (Wiebe)   14:575

The Well (Brown)   48:61

The Well (Jolley)   46:220-22

The Well (Onetti)
   See *El pozo*

The Well (Ross)   13:495-96

"Well Dennis O'Grady" (Gunn)   81:176

"The Well Dreams" (Montague)   46:277

"We'll Have Dinner at Eight" (Mphahlele)   25:338, 342

"Well Moused, Lion" (Moore)   47:272

"The Well of Baln" (Le Guin)   45:213

"The Well of Bethlehem" (Goodman)   4:197

"The Well of Lycopolis" (Bunting)   10:83; 47:45, 52, 54

Well of Shiuan (Cherryh)   35:104-05, 112

"A Well Respected Man" (Davies)   21:89, 95, 97

"We'll Run Away" (Wilson)   12:651

We'll Shift Our Ground; Or, Two on a Tour (Blunden)   56:47

We'll Take It from Here, Sarge (Trudeau)   12:590

"Well Then" (Parra)   102:355

"Well Water" (Jarrell)   2:210; 13:302

"Well Water" (Jensen)   37:189

"Well We All Had Our Willie and Wade Records..." (Barthelme)   46:42

"Well, Well, Well" (Lennon)   35:262

"Well, What Are You Going to Do?" (Wright)   28:466

The Well Wrought Urn (Brooks)   24:102-08, 116; 86:278-79, 286, 289; 110:9, 14-17, 31-4, 36-7

The Well-Dressed Explorer (Astley)   41:44, 46

Welle und Granit (Sachs)   98:321

"Die Wellen des Balaton" (Lenz)   27:252

"Wellesley Free" (Lowell)   11:331; 37:238

"Well-Found Poem" (Davie)   31:123

"The Well-Intentioned Question" (Rose)   85:313

The Well-Tempered Critic (Davies)   75:191

The Well-Tempered Critic (Frye)   24:214; 70:275

"Welsh Blacks" (Clarke)   61:80

"The Welsh Hill Country" (Thomas)   13:543

"Welsh Incident" (Graves)   39:328

The Welsh Sonata (Hanley)   13:261-62

Welt im Kopf (Canetti)   75:127

Weltanschauung (Ionesco)   9:288

Der Weltverbesserer (*The World Reformer*) (Bernhard)   61:13, 26

Wembly Arena (Zappa)   17:595

Wenceslas Square (Shue)   52:393-94

"Wendy" (Wilson)   12:644, 650

"Wenishet-Jusmene" (Kunene)   85:165

"Wenn ich nur wusste" ("If I only knew") (Sachs)   98:348

Went South (Wiggins)   57:431, 435, 438

Wer pa Lawino (p'Bitek)
   See *Wer pa Lawino*

"We're at the Graveyard" (Ondaatje)   51:310

We're Friends Again (O'Hara)   42:319, 325

"We're Gonna Be All Right" (Sondheim)   30:379

We're No Angels (Jordan)   110:275-76, 278

"We're Not Gonna Take It" (Townshend)   17:530

"We're Not Learnen to Be Paper Boys (for the young brothas who sell Muhammad Speaks)" (Sanchez)   116:301

We're Not Pregnant: An Illustrated Guide to Birth Control (*Congratulations! You're Not Pregnant: An Illustrated Guide to Birth Control*) (Mayle)   89:142

"We're on TV in the Universe" (Vaughn)   62:456-57

We're Only in It for the Money (Zappa)   17:588-91

"We're Open Tonight" (McCartney)   35:286-87

We're Right behind You, Charlie Brown (Schulz)   12:532

"We're So Close" (Simon)   26:412-13

"We're Very Poor" (Rulfo)
   See "Es que somos muy pobres"

"The Wereman" (Atwood)   25:67

"The Werewolf" (Carter)   41:117

The Werewolf Trace (Gardner)   30:154-55

Werke: Essayistiche Schriften und Reden I, 1952-1956 (Boell)   72:97

"Werner Herzog in Ghana" (Chatwin)   59:277,

279

"The Werther Level" (Porter)   33:321

Wesley (Brenton)   31:59, 65

"West" (Hoffman)   6:244

"The West" (Longley)   29:293

"West" (Moure)   88:219-20

West (Berkoff)   56:21

"West Branch Ponds, Kokadjo, Maine" (Van Duyn)   63:441

"West by the Road" (Davison)   28:102

"West Central Pub" (Suknaski)   19:432

"The West Coast" (Disch)   36:127

"West Coast" (Livesay)   79:346

West Country Churches (Betjeman)   34:308

"West Indian Dutch Party" (Lamming)   66:220

"The West Indian People" (Lamming)   66:226

West Indies, Ltd.: Poemas (Guillen)   48:157-59, 162-63, 166-69; 79:229, 240, 244, 248-50

"West Marginal Way" (Hugo)   32:236

"The West Midland Underground" (Wilding)   73:398

The West Midland Underground (Wilding)   73:397-98

West of Eden (Harrison)   42:208-09

West of Suez (Osborne)   2:328; 45:316, 320

West of the Rockies (Fuchs)   8:221; 22:155-56, 159

West of Your City (Stafford)   7:460, 462

West of Zanzibar (Browning)   16:124

The West Pier (Hamilton)   51:191-93, 195, 197

"West Point" (Vidal)   8:529

West Side Story (Sondheim)   30:376-78, 380, 385-87, 389-90, 395, 400, 402

West Strand Visions (Simmons)   43:409

"West Twenty-Third" (Motion)   47:291-92

"West Wind" (Wright)   53:420

"West Window" (Jensen)   37:192

West Window: The Selected Poetry of George Bowering (Bowering)   47:28

West with the White Chiefs (Harris)   12:262

"Westcottes Glanz und Ende" (Hildesheimer)   49:174

"Westering" (Heaney)   74:167

The Western Angler (Haig-Brown)   21:136

The Western Approaches: Poems, 1973-1975 (Nemerov)   9:394-96; 36:301-02

"Western Australia" (Faludy)   42:138

The Western Borders (Howe)   72:202

The Western Canon (Bloom)   103:50-6

The Western Coast (Fox)   2:140-41; 8:217-18

"Western Country" (Merwin)   13:386

The Western Lands (Burroughs)   109:197-99, 201, 230

"The Western Novel: A Symposium" (Waters)   88:337, 364

"Western Star" (Wright)   53:428

Western Union (Lang)   20:206

"Western Wind" (Oppen)   7:285

"Westland" (Baxter)   78:25-27

Westmark (Alexander)   35:27-8

Westmark Trilogy (Alexander)   35:28

"West-Running Brook" (Frost)   13:230; 15:245, 250; 26:125

West-Running Brook (Frost)   13:223, 230; 15:241, 249; 26:117, 119, 124

Westviking (Mowat)   26:342

Westward Ha!; or, Around the World in Eighty Clichés (Perelman)   5:338; 9:416; 23:335; 44:502; 49:263, 266

"Westward the Course of Empire Takes Its Way

(Wallace)   114:347, 349-50, 352, 354, 357-58, 361, 364

Westwego (Soupault)   68:404-05

Westworld (Crichton)   54:70-1, 76; 90:69, 72-6

"Wet" (Colwin)   5:108

"Wet" (Johnston)   51:239

"Wet Are the Boards" (Ashbery)   77:66, 69

"Wet Casements" (Ashbery)   13:30; 15:30, 33; 41:40

"Wet Moccasins" (Kenny)   87:249

"A Wet Night" (Beckett)   11:32

The Wet Parade (Sinclair)   11:497; 63:349

"A Wet Sunday in Spring" (Fuller)   28:159

"Der Wetterfleck" (Bernhard)   32:20

"We've Got Tonight" (Seger)   35:383

Weymouth Sands (*Jobber Skald*) (Powys)   9:440; 46:318-19, 324

"Wezwanie" (Milosz)   56:238

"W.H. Auden as a Literary Critic" (Brooks)   24:114

"Whacking Off" (Roth)   4:451; 66:386, 389

"The Whale" (Ihimaera)   46:196, 199

"Whale Constellations" (Gunnars)   69:261

A Whale for the Killing (Mowat)   26:337, 343, 346-47

"The Whale, His Bulwark" (Walcott)   76:281

Whale Music (Quarrington)   65:203-04

The Whale People (Haig-Brown)   21:138-39

"The Whaleboat Struck" (Ammons)   108:19

"The Whaler's Return" (Brown)   48:52, 54

"Whales" (Olson)   28:344

"The Whales" (Young)   82:396

"The Whales' Graveyard" ("Cemetery of Whales") (Yevtushenko)   3:547; 26:462, 464

"Whales Off Sasketeewan" (Booth)   13:103

Whanau (Ihimaera)   46:194-95, 197, 202

"Wharf" (Merwin)   88:192

"What" (Creeley)   78:160

What? (Polanski)   16:469-70

What a Kingdom It Was (Kinnell)   13:321; 29:279-80, 284

What a Nighmare, Charlie Brown (Schulz)   12:533

"What a Sky" (O'Brien)   65:168

"What a View" (Montague)   46:277

What a Way to Go (Morris)   1:232-33; 37:311-13

What Am I Doing Here (Chatwin)   57:152-54; 59:276-79

"What America Would Be without Blacks" (Ellison)   114:101

What Are the Bugles Blowing For? (*The Bugles Blowing*) (Freeling)   38:186-87

"What Are the Leftists Saying?" (Thurber)   25:435

"What Are the Odds?" (Acorn)   15:10

"What Are Years" (Moore)   19:339

What Are Years (Moore)   2:292; 8:399; 10:346

What Are You Going to Do about It (Huxley)   35:241

What Are You Up to, William Thomas (Newton)   35:301

What Became of Jane Austen? And Other Questions (Amis)   3:10; 5:22

"What Became of What-Was-His-Name?" (Enright)   31:150

What Came Ashore at Lirios (Tiptree)   48:395

"What Can I Do for You?" (Dylan)   77:185-86, 189-90

"What Can You Do to Me Now?" (Nelson)   17:306

What Century? (O'Hara)   78:368-69

"What Comes Next" (Baumbach)   23:54

"What Dante Means to Me" (Eliot)   113:193

"What Destiny Wanted" (Fuentes)
    See "Fortuna lo que ha querido"

"What Do the Scalds Tell Us?" (Johnston)   51:248

What Do We Believe? (Greeley)   28:172

"What Do You Say?" (Giles)   39:64-5

"What Does a Woman Need to Know?" (Rich)   73:322

"What Does It Matter? A Morality" ("A Morality") (Forster)   22:135

"What Does Not Change" (Lane)   25:284

"What Does Poetry Communicate" (Brooks)   110:36

What Dreams May Come (Matheson)   37:248

What Dreams May Come (Wellman)   49:394, 396

What? Eternity (Yourcenar)
    See *Quoi? L'éternité*

"What Feels like the World" (Bausch)   51:55-6

"What Frightens Me..." (Ezekiel)   61:105

"What Furies" (Hass)   39:150; 99:146

"What Gets In" (Hogan)   73:160

"What Gives" (Eberhart)   56:87

"What Goes On" (Reed)   21:307

What Happened to the Corbetts? (Shute)
    See *Ordeal*

What Happened When the Hopi Hit New York (Rose)   85:315

What Happens Next? (Rogin)   18:457-59

"What Has Happpened to These Working Hands?" (Hogan)   73:158

What Hath a Man? (Millin)   49:249-50

What Have I Done to Deserve This? (Almodovar)
    See *Qué He Hecho Yo para Merecer Ésto?*

What Have You Been Eating? (Hyde)   21:177

"What Holds Them Apart" (Galvin)   38:199

What I Believe (Forster)   1:108; 9:204, 206; 15:227, 229; 45:132; 77:218

What I Did Last Summer (Gurney)   54:219; 32:219; 50:178

"What I Expected" (Spender)   41:419

"What I Fear ..." (Oates)   6:367

"What I Have Been Doing Lately" (Kincaid)   43:248

"What I have Learned in the Wars" (Amichai)
    See "Ma lamadti bamilhamot"

What I Know So Far (Lish)   45:228-30

"What I Learned from Caesar" (Vanderhaeghe)   41:449, 453

What I Lived For (Oates)   108:394-95

What I Love (Elytis)   100:172-74, 186-87

"What I Might Have Been" (Voinovich)   49:375-76

What I Really Think of You (Kerr)   35:248-51

"What I Saw and Heard in Rome" (Bachmann)
    See "Was ich Rom sah und hörte"

"What I Want to Say" (Van Duyn)   63:437-38; 116:403

What I Was (Michaux)
    See *Qui je fus*

"What if God" (Olds)   85:297, 299, 304

"What If I Said the Dinosaur's Not Dead" (Bradbury)   42:42

What If You Died Tomorrow (Williamson)   56:433-35, 442

What I'm Going to Do, I Think (Woiwode)   10:542

"What Indians Do" (Ortiz)   45:309-10

"What Is a Classic?" (Eliot) 24:178; **41**:155
"What Is a Protestant, Daddy?" (Durcan) 43:114, 116
What Is a Welshman? (Thomas) 48:381
"What Is and Is Not" (Williams) 33:441
What Is Called Thinking? (Heidegger)
  See *Was Heisst Denken?*
What Is Contemplation? (Merton) 34:465
"What Is Criticism?" (Barthes)
  See "Qu'est-ce que la critique?"
What Is Existentialism? (Barrett) 27:18
"What Is Fixed to Happen" (Paulin) 37:354
"What is it?" (Oliver) 98:279, 292
"What Is Left to Link Us" (Lish) 45:230
"What Is Left to Say" (Mueller) 51:285
"What is Literature?" (p'Bitek) 96:300
What Is Literature? (Sartre)
  See *Qu'est-ce que la littérature?*
"What Is Minor Poetry?" (Eliot) 24:178
What Is Money For (Pound) 7:333
"What is Poetry" (Ashbery) 77:47, 59
"What Is Possible" (Rich) 36:367, 370
"What Is Poverty" (Salinas) 90:331
"What Is Rape?" (Willingham) 51:403
"What Is Seized" (Moore) 39:82-3; 45:280
"What Is the Basis of My Faith?" (Solzhenitsyn) 4:508
"What Is the Connection between Men and Women" (Oates) 15:401; 19:348-49
"What Is the Language Using Us For?" (Graham) 29:196, 198
"What Is the Voice That Speaks" (Warren) 39:273
What Is Theatre? (Bentley) 24:50-2
"What Is This Movie?" (Freeman) 55:57
What Is to Be Done? (Gallant) 38:190-93
What Is to Be Given? (Schwartz) 10:463; 87:346
"What is Winter?" (Blunden) 56:46
"What It Cost" (Forche) 83:208-09
"What It Costs" (Piercy) 27:377
"What It Is I Think I'm Doing Anyhow" (Bambara) 88:32-35
"What It Minns to Be a Minnow" (Perelman) 49:264
"What Kind of Day Did You Have?" (Bellow) 33:67-70
"What Kind of Formation Are B Specials?" (Paulin) 37:354
"What Kind of Man" (Amichai)
  See "Eyze min adam"
"What Lies Under" (Olson) 29:327
What Love Has Joined Together (Robinson) 21:342
"What Love Intended" (Boland) 113:119
What Mad Pursuit (Gellhorn) 60:177-78
What Makes Sammy Run? (Schulberg) 7:401-03; 48:346-47, 350, 352
What Men Don't Tell Women (Blount) 38:47-8
"What Men Have Instead of Skirts" (Donnell) 34:159
What Moon Drove Me to This? (Harjo) 83:268, 270, 272
"What Mrs. Felton Knew" (Findley) 102:108
What Mrs. McGillicuddy Saw! (Christie) 48:75; 110:112
"What My House Would Be Like If It Were a Person" (Levertov) 66:236
"What Not to Say to Poorer People" (Lebowitz) 36:248
"What Remains" (Piercy) 62:370-71
"What Remains" (Silone) 4:493
"What Shall I Wear, Darling, to 'The Great Hunger'?" (Durcan) 70:152

What Shall We Tell Caroline? (Mortimer) 28:282-86
"What Shall We Tell Our Children?" (Grass) 49:137
What Shall We Wear to This Party? (Wilson) 32:447-48
"What Should I Have Done?" (Adams) 46:19
"What Songs the Soldiers Sang" (Bell) 8:65; 31:46
"What the Bones Know" (Kizer) 80:172
What the Butler Saw (Orton) 4:388; 13:435-36; 43:326-30, 334-35
What the Chairman Told Tom (Bunting) 39:298
"What the Chroniclers Did Not Record" (Kenny) 87:254
What the Crow Said (Kroetsch) 57:283-84, 287
"What the Deceased Had to Say About Himself" (Parra) 102:350-51, 354
"What the Doctor Said" (Carver) 55:282
"What the End Is For" (Graham) 48:151, 153
"What the Fox Agreed to Do" (Bly) 38:55, 57
"What the Frog's Eye Tells the Frog's Brain" (Fenton) 32:166
What the Grass Says (Simic) 9:480; 22:379; 68:376
"What the Heart Wants" (Moss) 45:287
"what the mirror said" (Clifton) 66:85, 88
"What the Motorcycle Said, A Small Excursion" (Van Duyn) 63:439
What the Neighbors Did, and Other Stories (Pearce) 21:288-90
"What the Pencil Writes" (Laughlin) 49:220, 222
"What the Tapster Saw" (Okri) 87:315, 320, 322
"What the Thunder Said" (Eliot) 10:169; 41:156
"What the White Had to Say" (Simic) 49:340
What the Wine-Sellers Buy (Milner) 56:222-28
What the Woman Lived: Selected Letters of Louise Bogan, 1920-1970 (Bogan) 4:69; 39:390, 394; 46:87-8; 93:71, 77, 84-5, 88
"What the Women Said" (Bogan) 93:73
"What They Ate" (Le Guin) 45:219
"What They Carried" (O'Brien) 103:140
"What They Say about C. L." (Cabral de Melo Neto)
  See "Contam de Clarice Lispector"
"What They Wore" (Le Guin) 45:219
What Thou Lovest Well, Remains American (Hugo) 6:245; 32:241-42, 244, 250
"What to Do? A Problem Play" ("After Feydeau") (Schuyler) 23:388
"What to Do Next" (Barthelme) 115:70-1
"What to Think Of" (Strand) 71:284-86
What Use Are Flowers? (Hansberry) 17:192-93
"What Use Have I Got for a Carnival" (Moravia) 46:287
What Vedanta Means to Me (Isherwood) 14:282
What Was Literature? Class Culture and Mass Society (Fiedler) 24:205-06
What Was the Relationship of the Lone Ranger to the Means of Production?: A Play in One Act (Baraka) 115:31
"What We Lost" (Boland) 113:73, 99
"What We Talk about When We Talk about Love" (Carver) 55:276-77
What We Talk about When We Talk about Love (Carver) 22:101-04; 36:103-06; 53:60
What Where (Beckett) 29:65-6
"What Whilwind Man Told Kochinanako, Yel-

low Woman" (Silko) 74:333
"What Why When How Who" (Pinsky) 94:308, 322
"What Will Happen to the Land?" (Momaday) 85:229
"What Will Remain" (Mahon) 27:288, 290
"What Would I Do White" (Jordan) 114:146
"What You Hear from 'Em?" (Taylor) 18:526, 528; 37:409, 413
"Whatever Gets You Through the Night" (Lennon) 35:269-70
Whatever Is Moving (Moss) 45:287-88; 50:353
Whatever Love Declares (Kessler) 4:270
"Whatever Time Is Past Was Worse" (Guillen) 79:229
"Whatever You Say Say Nothing" (Heaney) 7:149; 14:245; 25:246, 248
"Whatever's for Us" (Armatrading) 17:7-8
What's Become of Waring (Powell) 10:411-12; 31:317, 319
What's Bred in the Bone (Davies) 42:106-09; 75:180-81, 184-87, 192, 196-202, 204-08, 211, 216-20, 222-24; 91:201, 203-4
What's for Dinner? (Schuyler) 23:389, 391
"What's Going On" (Gaye) 26:130
What's Going On (Gaye) 26:130-35
"What's Happening Brother" (Gaye) 26:130
What's Happening! The Beatles in the U.S.A. (Maysles and Maysles) 16:442-43
What's Happening to Me? (Mayle) 89:141-42
"What's in Alaska?" (Carver) 22:99; 53:65
"What's in Your Life for Me" (Robinson) 21:348-49, 351
"What's My Name" (Clash) 30:44
What's So Big about Green? (Birney) 4:64
"What's That Smell in the Kitchen?" (Piercy) 27:382
"What's That You're Doing" (McCartney) 35:290-91
"What's the Purpose of the Bayonet?" (Garrett) 51:145, 152
"What's the Trouble: Social Crisis, Crisis of Civilization, or Both" (Howe) 85:131
"What's the Use of Theorizing about the Arts?" (Abrams) 24:13
What's to Become of the Boy? or, Something to Do with Books (Boell)
  See *Was soll aus dem Jungen bloss werden?: oder, Irgendwas mit Büchern*
What's Up, Tiger Lily? (Allen) 16:1, 3, 5, 15-16
"What's Wrong with Being a Slob?" (Naipaul) 105:157
What's Wrong with This Picture? (Margulies) 76:188, 193
What's Your P.Q. (Personality Quotient) (Daly) 17:89
Wheat that Springeth Green (Powers) 57:349-54, 356-58
"The Wheel" (Ghiselin) 23:170
The Wheel (Berry) 27:40; 46:71-2
The Wheel (Cendrars) 106:185
The Wheel in Midsummer (Lewis) 41:252
"The Wheel of Love" (Oates) 19:348
The Wheel of Love, and Other Stories (Oates) 2:313, 315; 6:370; 19:348, 351; 52:338
"The Wheelbarrow" (Pritchett) 13:467; 41:334
"Wheels" (Dixon) 52:99-100
"Wheels" (McGahern) 48:267-68
Wheels (Hailey) 5:156
Wheels (Huxley) 11:283-84
Wheels of Justice (Duerrenmatt) 102:83

"Wheels Slowly Turning" (Montague) **46**:274
"Wheels within Wheels" (Heaney) **74**:188, 194
Wheelworld (Harrison) **42**:206
"Whelks" (Oliver) **98**:291
"When" (Lane) **25**:286
"When" (Olds) **39**:193; **85**:295
"When a Man Needs a Woman" (Wilson) **12**:641, 643
"When Aliens Come" (Clarke) **35**:122
"When and Where and Whose Country is This, Anyway" (Jordan) **114**:152
When Angels Fall (Polanski) **16**:471
"When Are You Going Back?" (Gilliatt) **53**:145
"When Boyhood Dreams Come True" (Farrell) **66**:129
"When Death Came April Twelve 1945" (Sandburg) **10**:448
"When Death Comes" (Oliver) **98**:291, 294
"When Did You Stop Loving Me, When Did I Stop Loving You" (Gaye) **26**:133-34
When Dinah Shore Ruled the Earth (Durang) **27**:88
When Dinah Shore Ruled the Earth (Wasserstein) **90**:418
"When Doves Cry" (Prince) **35**:329-30
When Eight Bells Toll (MacLean) **13**:362; **50**:348
"When Everyone Was Pregnant" (Updike) **9**:537
"When first we faced" (Larkin) **64**:258
"when god decided to invent" (Cummings) **15**:162
"When Golden Flies upon My Carcass Come" (Eberhart) **56**:87
"When Half the Time They Don't Know Themselves" (Ashbery) **77**:65, 68
"When He Returns" (Dylan) **77**:185-87
When He Was Free and Young and He Used to Wear Silks (Clarke) **53**:89, 95-6
"When Heart Is Open" (Morrison) **21**:239-40
"When I Am Dead" (Dodson) **79**:193
"When I Am Dead" (MacBeth) **5**:263
"When I Banged My Head on the Door" (Amichai) **116**:136
"When I Die" (Giovanni) **19**:192; **64**:191
"When I Die" (Nyro) **17**:315, 319
"When I Grow Up to Be a Man" (Wilson) **12**:644, 649
"When I have a stomachache" (Amichai) **116**:97, 116
"When I Loved Her" (Kristofferson) **26**:267
"When I Nap" (Giovanni) **64**:187
"When I Sat Down to Play the Piano" (Purdy) **50**:247
"When I Set Fire to the Reed Patch" (Ammons) **108**:19
"When I Was a Freeport and You Were the Main Drag" (Nyro) **17**:313, 316, 319
"When I Was in Xia Village" (Ding Ling) **68**:67
"When I Was Young, the Whole Country Was Young" (Amichai) **57**:44
When I Whistle (Endo) **14**:161; **19**:160; **54**:152; **99**:285
"When I Wrote a Little" (Carruth) **84**:133
"When I'm among a Blaze of Lights" (Sassoon) **36**:388
"When I'm Gone" (Ochs) **17**:331
"When I'm Sixty-Four" (Lennon and McCartney) **12**:357, 360; **35**:279
When in Rome (Marsh) **7**:209; **53**:248
"When in Rome-Apologia" (Komunyakaa) **94**:235

"When in the Gloomiest of Capitals" (Akhmatova)
See "Kogda v mrachneyshey iz stolits"
"When It Comes" (Wain) **11**:562
"When It Happens" (Atwood) **13**:46; **44**:146
"When It's Human instead of When It's Dog" (Hempel) **39**:67-8
"When Its Shoesies That I Need" (Perelman)
See "Don't Bring Me Oscars"
"When It's Time to Go" (Wideman) **67**:379, 381, 385
"When Johnny ...." (Kelley) **22**:248
"When last I ranged and revelled" (Brutus) **43**:91
"When Life Begins" (Warren) **39**:272
"When Love Becomes Words" (Riding) **7**:374
"When Love Is Gone" (Hughes) **5**:191
"When Man Enters Woman" (Sexton) **6**:493
When Memory Comes (Friedlander)
See *Quand vient le souvenir*
"When My Girl Comes Home" (Pritchett) **13**:468; **41**:332, 334
"When My Ship Comes Home" (Coward) **29**:139
"When My Sorrow Came Home" (Honig) **33**:211, 215
"When Our Dream World Finds Us, and These Hard Times Are Gone" (Abbott) **48**:5, 7
"When Poisoned Socrates" (Levi) **41**:242
When Queens Collide (Ludlam)
See *Conquest of the Universe*
When Rain Clouds Gather (Head) **25**:232-34, 236-38; **67**:92-3, 95, 110
When She Was Good (Roth) **1**:292-93; **2**:378-79; **3**:436-38, 440; **4**:451, 457, 459; **6**:475-76; **9**:459, 461; **15**:449, 451-52; **22**:351-52; **31**:334-35, 343-44; **66**:386, 388, 391, 405
"When She Wears Red" (Hughes) **108**:293, 309
When the Atoms Failed (Campbell) **32**:72-3
When the Bough Breaks (Kellerman) **44**:225-28
When the Bridges Go Up (Aksyonov) **101**:17
"When the City Drops" ("Into the Night") (Carroll) **35**:79
"When the Clover Field Stirs" (Yevtushenko) **51**:432
"When the Dumb Speak" (Bly) **15**:68
"When the Fleet Was in in Mobile" (Highsmith) **102**:205-06
"When the Levee Breaks" (Page and Plant) **12**:475
"When the Light Falls" (Kunitz) **6**:287
"When the Lights Return" (Okri) **87**:315, 321-22
When the Lion Feeds (Smith) **33**:376
"When the Moment Is Over" (Pastan) **27**:371
"When the Music's Over" (Morrison) **17**:290-91
"When the Night" (McCartney) **35**:281
"When the Pipes Froze" (Collins) **44**:36-8
When the Rattlesnake Sounds (Childress) **12**:107; **86**:309, 316; **96**:103
When the Reds ... (Russell) **60**:319
"When the Saints Go Ma'chin Home" (Brown) **59**:263
"When the Shoe Is on the Other Foot for a Change" (Waddington) **28**:440
When the Siren Wailed (Streatfeild) **21**:412, 415
When the Skies Clear (Pasternak)
See *Kogda razglyaetsya*

When the Sky Burned (Bova) **45**:67, 73
"When the Stars Get Angry and Coo above Our Heads" (Salinas) **90**:332
"When the Statue Fell" (Blunden) **56**:34
When the Sun Tries to Go On (Koch) **44**:242-43
"When the Sun Went Down" (Ashbery) **41**:33
"When the Swimmers on the Beach Have All Gone Home" (Rooke) **25**:390-91
When the Tree Flowered (Neihardt) **32**:335
When the Tree Sings (Haviaras) **33**:203-07
"When the Vacation Is Over for Good" (Strand) **18**:516; **71**:281-82, 285
When the War Began (Boell)
See "Als der Krieg ausbrach"
When the War Ended (Boell)
See *Als der Krieg zu Ende war*
When the War Started (Boell)
See "Als der Krieg ausbrach"
When the War Was Over (Boell)
See *Als der Krieg zu Ende war*
When the War Was Over (Frisch)
See *Als der Krieg zu Ende war*
"When the Whip Comes Down" (Jagger and Richard) **17**:240
When the Wind Blows (Sargeson) **31**:362-63
When the Wind Blows (Saul) **46**:366-67
"When the World Is Running Down, You Make the Best of What's Still Around" (Police, The) **26**:365
"When the World Stands Still" (Herbert) **9**:274
When Things of the Spirit Come First: Five Early Tales (Beauvoir)
See *Quand prime le spirituel*
"When Thou Hast Taken Thy Last Applause, and When" (Cummings) **68**:44
"When We are Able" (Zamora) **89**:384
When We Are Married (Priestley) **2**:347; **34**:361, 365-66
"When We Dead Awaken: Writing as Re-Vision" (Rich) **11**:477; **18**:445; **73**:321-23; **76**:215
When We First Met (Mazer) **26**:295-96
"When We Were Children" (MacNeice) **53**:237
"When We with Sappho" (Rexroth) **49**:289; **112**:383, 392, 398
When Women Rule (Clarke) **53**:91, 95
"When You and I Were All" (Jarrell) **2**:209
"When You Are Silent, Shining Host by Guest" (Cummings) **8**:160
When You Comin' Back, Red Ryder? (Medoff) **6**:321-23
"When You Dance I Can Really Love" (Young) **17**:569, 582
"When You Gonna Wake Up?" (Dylan) **77**:186-87
"When You Kisses Me" (Armatrading) **17**:10
"When You Speak to Me" (Gallagher) **18**:169
"When You Were Mine" (Prince) **35**:324, 327
"When You're Down and Out" (Lennon)
See "Nobody Loves You"
"When You've Forgotten Sunday" (Brooks) **49**:38
"Where" (Berry) **27**:36
Where All the Ladders Start (Loewinsohn) **52**:288-90
"Where Am I Kenneth?" (Koch) **44**:241
Where Angels Fear to Tread (Forster) **1**:103, 107; **2**:134; **4**:169; **9**:207; **13**:215-16, 219; **15**:222; **45**:136, 138, 142; **77**:241
"Where Are the Waters of Childhood?" (Strand) **18**:521; **41**:432, 434, 438; **71**:280

Where Are They Now? (Stoppard) 29:394, 397

"Where Are Those People Who Did Hair" (Swados) 12:558

"Where Are We Going? And What Are We Doing?" (Cage) 41:77

"Where Are We Now" (Canin) 55:38-9

"Where Are You Going, Where Have You Been?" (Oates) 3:360; 9:405; 11:402-03; 19:349-51; 52:338; 108:375, 386

"Where but What" (Kelman) 58:298

Where Did I Come From? The Facts of Life without Any Nonsense and with Illustrations (Mayle) 89:141-42, 151

"Where Did the Spring Go?" (Davies) 21:95

"Where Did They Go?" (Berry) 46:74

"Where Do People Go?" (Swados) 12:559

Where Do We Go from Here: Chaos or Community? (King) 83:324, 328-31

Where Eagles Dare (MacLean) 13:362; 50:348-49; 63:265, 268, 270

Where East Is East (Browning) 16:123-24

Where Elephants Go to Die (Donoso) 99:223

Where Has Tommy Flowers Gone? (McNally) 4:347; 7:217-18

"Where Have All the Good Times Gone" (Davies) 21:89

"Where Have You Gone, Charming Billy?" (O'Brien) 103:144, 148-49

"Where I Come from God Is a Grandmother" (Allen) 84:29, 31, 34

"Where I Live in This Honorable House of the Laurel Tree" (Sexton) 53:317

Where I Live: Selected Essays (Williams) 19:471; 45:445-46

"Where I Lived, and What I Lived For" (Oates) 6:370

"Where I Read What I Read" (Elkin) 51:96

"Where I'd Quit" (Kauffman) 65:348

"Where I'm Calling From" (Carver) 36:101, 103-04; 53:62-3, 65; 55:275

Where I'm Calling From (Carver) 53:62-3, 65

Where I'm Coming From (Wonder) 12:656, 662

"Where Is Everybody?" (Serling) 30:354

"Where Is Everyone?" (Carver) 36:100

"Where Is Garland Steeples Now?" (Abbott) 48:6

"Where is Home?" (Peacock) 60:295

Where Is My Wandering Boy Tonight? (Wagoner) 5:474

"Where Is the Love" (hooks) 94:159

"Where is the Voice Coming From" (Welty) 33:425; 105:298, 311, 314-15, 319

Where Is the Voice Coming From? (Wiebe) 6:567

"Where It Came From" (Brooks) 86:280

"Where I've Been All My Life" (Kizer) 80:181

"Where Knock Is Open Wide" (Roethke) 19:396; 101:273-74, 277-79, 290, 335, 339-40

Where Late the Sweet Birds Sang (Wilhelm) 7:538

"Where Moth and Dust Doth Corrupt" (Wright) 13:614

"Where Mountain Lion Lay Down with Deer" (Silko) 114:316

Where Nests the Water Hen (Roy)
  See *La petite poule d'eau*

"Where Scars Come From" (Harmon) 38:244

Where Shall We Go This Summer? (Desai) 37:65, 67, 69-71; 97:141, 144, 152, 158, 161-63, 172-73

"Where Solomon Was Wanting" (McAuley)

45:251

Where Sparrows Work Hard (Soto) 32:403; 80:277, 282, 291, 293, 296

Where Speed Is King (Hyde) 21:172

"Where, Tall Girl, Is Your Gypsy Babe" (Akhmatova)
  See "Gde, vysokaya, tvoy tsyganyonok"

"Where the Action Is" (Highsmith) 42:216

Where the Air Is Clear (Fuentes)
  See *La región más transparente*

Where the Bluebird Sings to the Lemonade Springs: Living and Writing in the West (Stegner) 81:341, 347-48, 353

Where the Boys Are (Swarthout) 35:399-400

"Where the Car Turns at Eighteenth" (Ferber) 93:140

Where the Compass Spins (Squires) 51:381

Where the Dreams Cross (Douglas) 73:73-5, 83, 89

"Where the Eagles Dwell" (Valenzuela)
  See "Up Among the Eagles"

"Where the Girls Were Different" (Caldwell) 14:96

Where the Going Was Good (Waugh) 107:359-60

"Where the Hayfields Were" (MacLeish) 68:289

"Where the Heart Is" (Shange) 74:311

"Where the Hell Would Chopin Be?" (Bukowski) 41:64

Where the Jackals Howl and Other Stories (Oz)
  See *Artsot hatan*

Where the Long Grass Blows (L'Amour) 25:278, 281

"Where the Rainbow Ends" (Lowell) 8:348, 355; 11:326

"Where the Rhododendrons Grow" (Aksyonov) 101:10

Where the Rivers Flow North (Mosher) 62:311-15

"Where the Sidewalk Ends" (Dumas) 62:155

"Where the Slow Fig's Purple Sloth" (Warren) 39:266

Where the Soul Was Shallow (Gironella)
  See *Un hombre*

"Where the Tides Meet" (Mac Laverty) 31:253

"Where the Track Vanishes" (Kinnell) 13:320

"Where the World Began" (Laurence) 62:280

"Where the World Begins" (Laurence) 50:321

"Where There Is a Song" 75:63

Where There's Smoke (Hunter) 11:280

Where There's Smoke (Robinson) 21:348

"Where They Disembarked" (Jiles) 58:272

Where Water Comes Together with Other Water (Carver) 36:107; 53:60

"Where We Are Today, You Will Notice Is" (Smith) 22:386

"Where We Must Look for Help" (Bly) 38:60

"Where We Were" (Dacey) 51:81

"Where Will You Go, Sam Lee Wong" (Roy) 14:469

"Where You'll Find Me" (Beattie) 63:18, 22

Where You'll Find Me, and Other Stories (Beattie) 63:14-18

Where's Daddy? (Inge) 8:309

"Where's Esther?" (Goyen) 40:217-18

"Wherever Home Is" (Wright) 28:469

"Which New Era Would That Be?" (Gordimer) 7:133; 33:178-79

Which Ones Are the Enemy? (Garrett) 3:190; 11:220; 51:143, 145

Which Tribe Do You Belong To? (Moravia) 7:243

The Whicharts (Streatfeild) 21:394

While Gods Are Falling (Lovelace) 51:266-68, 271-72

"While Home" (Robison) 98:306-07

"While Love Is Unfashionable" (Walker) 103:364

"While Reading Hamlet" (Akhmatova) 64:15

While Reagan Slept (Buchwald) 33:95

"While Seated on a Plane" (Swenson) 106:335

"While Shepherds Watched" (Bunting) 47:44

"While Sitting in the Tuileries and Facing the Slanting Sun" (Swenson) 106:349

While Still We Live (MacInnes) 27:279

While the City Sleeps (Lang) 20:208; 103:87, 89, 95-7

While the Sun Shines (Rattigan) 7:354

"Whim" (Muldoon) 32:320

The Whip (Creeley) 2:106; 78:130, 134

Whip Hand (Francis) 22:152-53; 42:150, 154, 156-57; 102:128, 157, 162

"Whip Lady" (Davies) 21:92

"A Whipbird Straps the Light Awake" (Shapcott) 38:401

"Whiplash" (Matthews) 40:325

Whipperginny (Graves) 45:162-63

"The Whipping" (Hayden) 37:160

Whipping Star (Herbert) 12:279; 23:221; 35:196; 44:393-94

Whipple's Castle (Williams) 14:583

"The Whip-Poor-Will" (Thurber) 5:432

The Whir of Gold (Ross) 13:494, 496

The Whirlpool (Tanizaki) 28:414-15

The Whirlpool (Urquhart) 90:382-84, 386-93, 398, 401

Whirlwind (Clavell) 87:10-15, 17-19

Whiskey (McNally) 4:347

"Whiskey and Blood" (Blount) 38:46

The Whiskey Vigil (Moure) 88:229

"Whiskey, Whiskey" (Kristofferson) 26:270

A Whisper in the Night: Stories of Horror, Suspense, and Fantasy (Aiken) 35:20

"Whisper My Name" (Lightfoot) 26:282

The Whisper of Madness (Mahfuz)
  See *Hams al-junun*

The Whisper of the Axe (Condon) 6:115; 8:150; 45:101, 103; 100:91

Whisper to the Earth (Ignatow) 40:259-60

The Whispering Roots and Other Poems (Day Lewis) 6:128-29; 10:130-31

"Whispers" (Oliver) 98:260, 267

Whispers (Koontz) 78:197, 203-12, 215-17

Whispers in Bedlam (Shaw) 7:413

"Whispers of Immortality" (Eliot) 1:92

"Whistle" (Galvin) 38:199

"The Whistle" (Komunyakaa) 94:241

Whistle (Jones) 10:290-94; 39:406-09, 412, 415

A Whistle in the Dark (Murphy) 51:300-01, 303-06, 308

"The Whistler" (Justice) 102:254

The Whistling Boy (Arthur) 12:25-6, 28

"Whit Monday" (MacNeice) 53:239

"White" (Johnston) 51:249

"White" (Simic) 49:338-40

"White" (Strand) 18:517

"White" (Wright) 6:580

White (Simic) 9:478, 481; 49:339-40, 342

The White Album (Didion) 14:151-54

The White Album (Lennon and McCartney) 12:376, 379; 35:266, 272

"White Apples" (Hall) 37:146-47

"White as Snow" (Boyle) 58:71

"The White Azalea" (Spencer) 22:402

"The White Bird" (MacCaig) 36:284-85
White Biting Dog (Thompson) 39:250-53
"The White Boat" (Roberts) 14:464
White Book (Kohout) 13:325
White Boots (Streatfeild)
　See *Skating Shoes*
"White Boots Marching in a Yellow Land"
　(Ochs) 17:332, 334
White Boy Running (Hope) 52:216-17
"White Boys" (Ragni and Rado) 17:385
The White Bus (Anderson) 20:18
"The White Butterfly" (Longley) 29:296
White Butterfly (Mosley) 97:333-38, 344-46,
　348, 352-53, 357
"The White Canoe" (Mowat) 26:347
"White Center" (Hugo) 32:243
White Center (Hugo) 32:239, 250-51, 243
White Chappell, Scarlet Tracings (Sinclair)
　76:225, 227-28
White Coal or the Tears of Werther (Ehrenburg)
　62:176
White Coats (*White Robes*) 59:388-89
"The White Coffin" (Bowering) 47:24
The White Crow (Forman) 21:121
The White Deer (Thurber) 5:430, 433, 436,
　442; 25:437-38
"The White Devil" (Tate) 2:428
White Dog (Gary) 25:187
"The White Donkey" (Le Guin) 45:216
The White Dragon (McCaffrey) 17:283-84
White Dresses (Green) 25:192
"White Dump" (Munro) 50:209-12, 215-17,
　220
"White Dwarfs" (Ondaatje) 29:341-42;
　51:311-14
White Eagles over Serbia (Durrell) 1:85
White Figure, White Ground (Hood) 15:283,
　285-86; 28:188, 190
White Flock (Akhmatova)
　See *Belaya staya*
"White Flowers" (Oliver) 98:289
The White Gate (Chase) 2:101
White Genesis (Ousmane)
　See "Velorio de Papá Montero"
The White German Shepherd (Hearne) 132-
　34
"White Goat, White Ram" (Merwin) 13:384;
　45:270
*The White Goddess: A Historical Grammar of
　Poetic Myth* (Graves) 1:128; 2:177; 6:210;
　11:255, 257; 39:321-26, 328; 45:165-66,
　173
White Gold Wielder (Donaldson) 46:141-44
"The White Holster" (Smith) 22:390
"The White Horse" (Dumas) 62:163
"The White Horse" (Jones) 81:64-5
"The White Horse" (MacEwen) 55:167
White Horses (Hoffman) 51:203-04, 208
"The White Horses of Vienna" (Boyle) 58:64,
　66-7, 71, 75
The White Hotel (Thomas) 22:418-22; 31:430-
　35
"The White House" (Hughes) 108:307
The White House (*Conversations on a Home-
　coming*) (Murphy) 51:302, 307-08
The White House Murder Case (Feiffer) 64:150,
　160
"The White Isle of Leuce" (Read) 4:439
"White Key" (Muske) 90:312
"White Kid Gloves" (Prichard) 46:333
"The White Knights" (Vollmann) 89:277-78
"The White Lantern" (Connell) 45:113
The White Lantern (Connell) 45:113-14

White Liars (Shaffer) 14:487
"White Lies" (Theroux) 28:425
White Light/White Heat (Reed) 21:303-04, 307,
　314, 319
"The White Lilies" (Gluck) 81:166, 172
White Lotus (Hersey) 40:235, 239; 81:332,
　335; 97:302-03
"White Magic" (Walcott) 67:361
"White Man in Hammersmith Palais" (Clash)
　30:44-6
White Man, Listen! (Wright) 1:377; 4:596;
　9:585; 74:383
White Man's Justice, Black Man's Grief (Goines)
　80:91-3
White Marriage (Rozewicz) 23:361-62
"White Moon" (Swenson) 106:351
White Mule (Williams) 2:468; 5:509-10
"White Mythology" (Derrida) 87:85-6
"The White Negro" (Mailer) 1:189; 3:312;
　8:364, 366; 11:341; 14:349; 28:256;
　74:211-12, 219, 223-24; 111:94, 101,
　104, 117, 121-22, 125, 133, 137, 148
"White Night" (Oliver) 98:271, 296
"White Night" (Pasternak) 63:313
"White Night" (Rich) 6:459
"White Nocturne" (Aiken) 52:22
White Noise (DeLillo) 39:115-27; 54:81-6;
　76:171-72, 174-75, 177, 179-82, 185-86
"White Noises" (Hollander) 2:197
The White Noon (Smith) 64:397
"White Notes" (Justice) 102:262
"White Oak" (Lewis) 41:255
The White Oaks of Jalna (Findley) 102:104,
　106
White on Black on White (Dowell) 60:99, 101-
　03, 106-07
"White on White" (Ferlinghetti) 27:139
"White Owl Flies Into and Out of the Field"
　(Oliver) 98:283, 289-90
White Palace 50:77-81
White Paper (Starbuck) 53:353
White People (Gurganus) 70:189-96
"White Petal Nanitch" (Davis) 49:93
"White Pickney" (Bennett) 28:29
White Pine (Oliver) 98:302-04
The White Plague (Herbert) 35:200-01, 205;
　44:394
"The White Pony" (Bates) 46:56, 67
"The White Quail" (Steinbeck) 9:516
"The White Rabbit" (Lustig) 56:185
"The White Rabbit Caper" (Thurber) 5:440;
　11:533
White Rain (Aitmatov)
　See *Belyi dozhd*
"White Riot" (Clash) 30:44-5, 51
White Robes
　See *White Coats*
"The White Rooster" (Goyen) 8:250-51;
　40:217-18
The White Rose (Traven) 11:535
White Sail (Sorrentino) 40:386
The White Sheik (Fellini)
　See *Lo sciecco bianco*
The White Ship (After the Fairy Tale) (Aitmatov)
　See *Belyj parokhod*
"White Shroud" (Ginsberg) 36:193
White Shroud (Ginsberg) 109:324, 338, 356,
　358
"White Shrouds" (Bottoms) 53:34
White Stag of Exile (Shapcott) 38:404-05
The White Steamer (Aitmatov)
　See *Belyj parokhod*
The White Steamship (Aitmatov)

　See *Belyj parokhod*
The White Steed (Carroll) 10:95-100
"The White Stick" (Tuohy) 37:431
White Sun, Black Sun (Rothenberg) 6:477;
　57:371
"The White Sybil" (Smith) 43:424
The White Thorntree (Davison) 15:171
The White Threshold (Graham) 29:194-95,
　198
"The White Tiger" (Thomas) 48:380
White Tiger (Browning) 16:125
"The White Tower: A Novel in the Form of a
　Poem" (Leet) 11:323
"White Trash" (Oates) 108:383
"White, White Collars" (Johnson) 52:234
"The White Wild Bronco" (Kiely) 43:244
"White World" (H. D.)
　See "The Whole White World"
*White Writing: On the Culture of Letters in South
　Africa* (Coetzee) 66:98-101, 105; 117:50-
　1, 70-5, 79=80
"Whitebait" (Grace) 56:116
White-Haired Lover (Shapiro) 4:486-87;
　15:479; 53:333
The White-Haired Revolver (Breton)
　See *Le revolver á cheveux blancs*
Whites (Rush) 44:91-6
"Whites Only" (Hope) 52:211
"Whitewash" (Damas)
　See "Blanchi"
Whitewater (Horgan) 9:278; 53:183-84
Whither (Powell) 66:366
"Whither Thou Goest" (Selzer) 74:287
"Whitman: The Invisible World" (Hall) 37:148
"Whitsun" (Plath) 5:345
"The Whitsun Weddings" (Larkin) 3:276;
　5:227, 230-31; 8:332, 334-37, 339-40;
　9:325; 13:335, 337, 340; 18:297; 33:259-
　60; 39:342, 345; 64:265-66, 269-71, 275,
　282-84
The Whitsun Weddings (Larkin) 3:275-76;
　5:223, 225-28, 230-31; 8:332, 336-
　38,340; 13:337-38; 18:293, 296-97, 299-
　301; 33:256, 261-62; 39:334, 338,
　341-45; 64:259-60, 269-72, 278-80, 283
"The Whittrick" (Morgan) 31:275
Whity (Fassbinder) 20:106
"Who" (Plath) 11:448; 111:159, 164
"Who Actually Creates Gaps?" (Royko)
　109:405
"Who Are the Brain Police" (Zappa) 17:588
Who Are the Violets Now (Waugh) 7:514
Who Are We Now? (Ferlinghetti) 27:139; 59,
　65
Who Are You (Townshend) 17:538-41
"Who Be Kind To" (Ginsberg) 6:198; 36:184,
　188; 109:347
"Who Began It and What For" (Gustafson)
　36:221
Who Brought Back Doruntine? (*Who Brought
　Doruntine Back?*) (Kadare) 52:261-62
Who Brought Doruntine Back? (Kadare)
　See *Who Brought Back Doruntine?*
The Who by Numbers (Townshend) 17:535-
　39, 542
Who Calls from Afar? (Brinsmead) 21:30
Who Came First (Townshend) 17:527, 531,
　534
Who Can Replace a Man? (Aldiss) 14:11
"Who Cares, Long as It's B-Flat" (Carruth)
　84:129
"Who Cares Who Killed Roger Ackroyd?"
　(Wilson) 24:481

Who Do You Think You Are? (Bradbury) **32**:53; **61**:39, 43

Who Do You Think You Are? (*The Beggar Maid: Stories of Flo and Rose*) (Munro) **19**:345-47; **50**:208, 210-12; **95**:283, 285-89, 291-95, 297, 301, 304-05, 310-11, 313, 321

Who Fears the Devil? (Wellman) **49**:389, 391, 393-94, 396

Who Gathered and Whispered behind Me (Goldbarth) **38**:203-04

"Who Goes There?" (Campbell) **32**:75-7, 80-2

"Who Has Lived from a Child with Chickens" (Kauffman) **42**:251

"Who Has Seen The Wind?" (Dodson) **79**:192

"Who Has Seen the Wind" (McCullers) **12**:432

Who Has Seen the Wind (Mitchell) **25**:321-22, 325-26

"Who Is Alienated from What?" (Rexroth) **49**:287

"Who is an SF Writer?" (Dick) **72**:106

Who Is Angelina? (Young) **19**:479

"Who Is Cherubino, What Is He?" (Brophy) **105**:37

Who Is Harry Kellerman and Why Is He Saying Those Terrible Things about Me? (Gardner) **44**:210

"Who Is It?" (Byrne) **26**:94-5

"Who Is It Can Tell Me Who I Am?" (Berriault) **109**:94-7

Who Is Teddy Villanova? (Berger) **8**:83-4; **11**:46; **18**:58; **38**:39, 41-2

"Who Is Your Mother? Red Roots of White Feminism" (Allen) **84**:29, 34

Who Killed Palomino Molero (Vargas Llosa)
See *Quién matú a Palomino Molero?*

Who Killed Richard Cory? (Gurney) **32**:220

"Who Knows One?" (Gotlieb) **18**:191

Who Look at Me (Jordan) **114**:141, 153

Who Lost an American? (Algren) **33**:12

"Who Needs a Heart" (Shange) **74**:311

"Who Needs the Peace Corps" (Zappa) **17**:591

"Who Needs Theater Anymore" (Ionesco) **86**:332

"Who or What Was It" (Amis) **40**:43

Who Really Cares? (Ian) **21**:184

"Who Said It Was Simple" (Lorde) **71**:246

The Who Sell Out (Townshend) **17**:530-31, 533, 535, 537, 541

Who Shall Be the Sun? (Wagoner) **15**:559

Who Shall Die? (Beauvoir)
See *Les bouches inutiles*

The Who Sings My Generation (Townshend) **17**:524; **42**:379

Who Speaks for the Negro? (Warren) **8**:538; **59**:298

"Who Stands, the Crux Left of the Watershed" (Auden) **43**:17

"Who the Cap Fit" (Marley) **17**:268-69

"Who Then Is Crazy" (Spacks) **14**:511

Who Wants Music on Monday? (Stolz) **12**:552-53

Who Wants War? (Prichard) **46**:337

"Who Was Leslie A. Fiedler?" (Fiedler) **24**:205

Who Was Oswald Fish? (Wilson) **33**:453-54, 457

"Who Will Know Us?" (Soto) **80**:302

Who Will Know Us?: New Poems (Soto) **80**:300-01, 303

"Whoever Was Using This Bed" (Carver) **53**:64-5; **55**:277

"Whoever You Are" (Purdy) **6**:428

The Whole Armour (Harris) **25**:203-05, 209, 214

Whole Days in the Trees (Duras)
See *Des journées entières dans les arbres*

"Whole Lotta Love" (Page and Plant) **12**:474-75, 478-79, 482

"Whole Love" (Graves) **45**:166

The Whole Man (Brunner) **8**:105; **10**:77

"A Whole School of Bourgeois Primitives" (Reid) **33**:348

"The Whole Story" (Nye) **42**:309

"The Whole Story" (Strand) **18**:515; **71**:281, 284

The Whole Voyald, and Other Stories (Saroyan) **1**:301

"The Whole White World" ("White World") (H. D.) **73**:105, 118

"The Wholeness" (Silkin) **43**:399-400

(W)holes (Macdonald) **19**:290-91

"Who'll Be the Next in Line?" (Davies) **21**:89

Who'll Save the Plowboy? (Gilroy) **2**:161

"Wholly Numbers; or, The Meditations of St. Stitch" (Ciardi) **40**:159

Whom Do We Write For? (Calvino) **73**:48

"Whom I Write For" ("Para quién escribo") (Aleixandre) **36**:30

"Whooping Cranes" (Erdrich) **54**:165

Whoops-a-Daisy (Waterhouse) **47**:419

"The Whore of Mensa" (Allen) **52**:36-7, 40

"The Whorehouse in a Calcutta Street" (Mahapatra) **33**:279, 283

"Whores Die Hard" (Kristofferson)
See "Star Spangled Banner"

Whores for Gloria: Or, Everything Was Beautiful until the Girls Got Anxious (Vollmann) **89**:284-86, 290-91, 296, 304, 311, 313

Whoreson: The Story of a Ghetto Pimp (Goines) **80**:92, 95-6

"Whorl" (Young) **82**:411

"Whoroscope" (Beckett) **9**:82, 87; **14**:78

Who's Afraid of Virginia Woolf? (Albee) **1**:5; **2**:1-4; **3**:6-7; **5**:10-14; **9**:1-3, 5-7, 9-10; **11**:10-11, 13; **13**:3-7; **25**:34-8, 40; **53**:20-1, 24, 26; **86**:119-20, 122-25; **113**:5-7, 13, 15, 19-21, 26, 28, 30-3, 36, 40-1, 44, 49, 52, 54

Who's Got His Own (Milner) **56**:221-22

"Who's Most Afraid of Death? Thou Art of Him" (Cummings) **1**:68; **3**:117; **68**:44

Who's Next (Townshend) **17**:527-28, 535, 539-41

"Who's on First?" (Janowitz) **43**:212

Who's on First (Buckley) **18**:83; **37**:60-1

"Who's Paying for This Call?" (Hood) **28**:189

Who's Pinkus, Where's Chelm? (Taylor) **27**:440-41

Who's That Knocking at My Door? (Scorsese) **20**:323, 325, 329-30; **89**:219-20, 249, 254-56, 260, 266-67

"Who's That Woman?" (Sondheim) **30**:382

"Who's to Bless and Who's to Blame" (Kristofferson) **26**:269

"Who's Who" (Auden) **9**:60

"Whose Deduction?" (Skvorecky) **69**:333

"Whose Dream Is This Anyway? Remythologizing and Self-Definition in Contemporary Indian Fiction" (Allen) **84**:36, 43

"Whose Goat?" (Stevenson) **33**:383

Whose Life Is It Anyway? (Clark) **29**:126-29

"Whose Timeless Reach" (Ammons) **108**:19

"Whose Who" (Blount) **38**:46

"The Whosis Kid" (Hammett) **47**:164

Why are Cross With Me, oh, Wind? (Arghezi)
See *Ce-ai cu mine, vîntule?*

Why Are We in Vietnam? (Mailer) **1**:191-92; **2**:262-63, 265; **3**:313-14; **4**:319, 323; **5**:267; **8**:370, 372-73; **11**:340, 342-43; **14**:352; **28**:256-57, 263; **74**:204, 206-07, 209, 224; **111**:95, 101-02, 108, 113, 117-18, 120-21, 141, 148

Why Are We So Blest? (Armah) **5**:32; **33**:27-32, 36-8

"Why Be a Poet?" (Heidegger) **24**:269

"Why Brownlee Left" (Muldoon) **72**:267, 272

Why Brownlee Left (Muldoon) **32**:319-21; **72**:365-66, 268-69, 273-74, 276-78

Why Call Them Back from Heaven (Simak) **55**:320

Why Can't They Be Like Us? America's White Ethnic Groups (Greeley) **28**:170

"Why Can't They Tell You Why?" (Purdy) **2**:349

Why Can't We Live Together Like Civilized Human Beings? (Kumin) **28**:222-25

"Why Clowns" (Fellini) **85**:82

"Why Crime is Good for America" (Puzo) **107**:189

"Why Did Benerjee Kill Himself?" (Hikmet)
See "Benerci kendini nicin öldürdü"

Why Didn't They Ask Evans? (*The Boomerang Clue*) (Christie) **6**:108; **110**:113

"Why Do Human Beings Produce Literature?" (Oe) **86**:228, 241

Why Do You Live So Far Away? (Levine) **54**:299

"Why Do You Sing My Bird" (Ekeloef) **27**:119

"Why Do You Write about Russia" (Simpson) **32**:377

Why Does Herr R. Run Amok? (Fassbinder) **20**:109, 115

"Why Does It Hurt When I Pee" (Zappa) **17**:593

"Why Dolphins Don't Bite" (Sturgeon) **39**:361

"Why Don't You Come Live with Me It's Time" (Oates) **108**:384

"Why Don't You Dance" (Carver) **22**:101; **36**:107; **55**:273, 277

"Why Don't You Look Where You're Going?" (Clark) **28**:78

"Why Don't You Write for Me?" (Ciardi) **10**:107

"Why Fortune Is Empress of the World" (Cassity) **42**:99

"Why Has Socialism Failed in America?" (Howe) **85**:151

"Why Have I Wandered the Asphalt of Midnight?" (Warren) **18**:539; **39**:273

Why Have the Birds Stopped Singing? (Sherburne) **30**:363

"Why Heisherik Was Born" (Singer) **69**:306

"Why Honey?" (Carver) **22**:96; **53**:65

"Why I Am Not a Painter" (O'Hara) **78**:354

"Why I Died" (Jong) **83**:290

Why I Don't Write Like Franz Kafka (Wilson) **49**:414-16

"Why I like Country Music" (McPherson) **77**:366-67

"Why I Like England" **61**:420

"Why I Live at the P. O." (Welty) **14**:563; **22**:456; **33**:414-15; **105**:298, 309, 318, 385

"Why I Love Country Music" (Tallent) **45**:387

"Why I Love Sleep" (Lebowitz) **36**:249

"Why I Quit the Gowanus Liberation Front" (Brown) **32**:63

"Why I Write" (Paton) **10**:388

"Why I'm Jewish" (Ginsberg) 109:328
"Why Irish Heroines Don't Have to be Good Anymore" (O'Brien) 116:188, 197
"Why Is Your Writing So Violent?" (Oates) 52:337
"Why Marry at All?" (Piercy) 62:371
Why Me? (Westlake) 33:440
Why Men Are The Way They Are 70:422
"Why My Mother Made Me" (Olds) 85:294
Why Should I Have All the Grief? (Gotlieb) 18:192
"Why So Many Shamuses?" (Skvorecky) 69:339
"Why, Soldier, Does It Seem to You . . ." (Guillen) 48:158
"why some people be mad at me sometimes" (Clifton) 66:82
"Why Study Power: The Question of the Subject" (Foucault) 34:343
"Why Suffering" (Paton) 25:364
"Why the Castle" (Schaeffer) 22:369
"Why the Classics" (Herbert) 9:273; 43:188
"Why There Will Never Be a Great Bowling Novel" (Blount) 38:46
"Why Van Johnson Believes in ESP" (Grayson) 38:211
Why Was I Killed? (Return of the Traveller) (Warner) 45:430-31, 434, 438-40
Why We Act Like Canadians: A Personal Exploration of Our National Character (Berton) 104:46-8, 60
Why We Can't Wait (King) 83:328, 330, 347
"Why We Die" (Swenson) 106:314
"Why We Do It" (Bass) 79:2
Why We Fight (Capra) 16:160
"Why We Tell Stories" (Mueller) 51:283
"Why We're Here" (McGahern) 48:262
"Why, You Reckon?" (Hughes) 35:215
"Whys/Wise" (Baraka) 115:12
"Wichita Vortex Sutra" (Ginsberg) 2:163; 4:181, 183; 36:183-84, 190, 192-93, 196-97; 109:347, 372
Wichita Vortex Sutra (Ginsberg) 109:338
The Wicked Cooks (Grass) 4:202; 15:260
The Wicked Day (Stewart) 35:396-97
The Wicked Enchantment (Benary-Isbert) 12:32, 34
"Wicked Girl" (Allende) 97:9
The Wicked One (Hunter) 21:167
The Wicked Pavilion (Powell) 66:361, 372, 374-76
"A Wicked Story" (Shaw) 7:412
"The Wickedness of Peter Shannon" (Nowlan) 15:398
"A Wicker Basket" (Creeley) 78:161
"Wicket Maiden" (Scannell) 49:330-31
Wickford Point (Marquand) 2:271; 10:329-31
"The Widder" (Bates) 46:62
Wide Fields (Green) 25:194
The Wide House (Caldwell) 28:58; 39:303
Wide Is the Gate (Sinclair) 15:500; 63:364
"The Wide Land" (Ammons) 25:43-4; 108:20
"The Wide Net" (Welty) 2:462; 14:562-63; 22:459; 33:419; 105:307, 327-28, 368
The Wide Net, and Other Stories (Welty) 1:362; 14:562-63; 22:460; 105:384
"The Wide Prospect" (Jarrell) 13:300
Wide Sargasso Sea (Rhys) 2:371-73; 4:445; 6:452-55, 457; 14:446-448, 451; 19:392-93, 395; 51:360-61, 364-72, 374-76
The Wide Sleeve of Kwannon (Lancaster) 36:241
"Widgeon" (Heaney) 37:165

Widger's Way (Ringwood) 48:329, 333, 335-36, 338
Die Widmung (Devotion) (Strauss) 22:407-08
"The Widow" (Honig) 33:211
"Widow" (Mueller) 51:284
"The Widow" (O'Brien) 65:169; 116:203
"Widow" (Plath) 11:448; 111:214
"Widow" (Reading) 47:350
"The Widow" (Smith) 64:389, 394
The Widow (Fornes) 39:138
The Widow (Freeling) 38:187
The Widow Claire (Foote) 51:136-37
The Widow in the Bye Street (Masefield) 47:225-28, 230
"A Widow in Wintertime" (Kizer) 80:172-73
"The Widow Interviewed" (Day Lewis) 6:128
"The Widow Perez" (Soto) 32:403
"Widower" (Raine) 103:190
"The Widower" (Redgrove) 6:445; 41:351
"Widower" (Robison) 42:339
"Widowers" (Davie) 31:116
The Widower's Son (Sillitoe) 10:477; 19:421; 57:395-96
"The Widows" (White) 49:408
Widows (Dorfman)
　　See *Viudas*
Widows and Children First! (Fierstein) 33:153, 155
"Widows and Orphans" (McPherson) 19:310; 77:359
The Widow's Children (Fox) 8:218-19
"Widow's Lament" (Brautigan) 12:69
The Widows of Thornton (Taylor) 71:293
"The Width of a Circle" (Bowie) 17:57, 59
Widzenia nad Zatoka San Francisco (Visions from San Francisco Bay) (Milosz) 31:263-64; 56:232, 242-44, 250
"Wie bei Gogol" (Lenz) 27:252
"Wie das Gesetz es befahl" (Boell) 72:98
"Wie sagen wir es den Kindern?" ("How Shall We Tell the Children") (Grass) 22:195
Wieczne zmartwienie (Eternal Worry) (Dabrowska) 15:167, 169
"Wieder Mitte geworden" (Sachs) 98:359
"Wiedersehen in der Allee" ("Reunion in the Avenue") (Boell) 72:69, 101
"Wiedersehen mit Drüng" (Boell) 72:69
Die Wiedertäufer (The Anabaptists) (Durrenmatt) 4:140; 15:194, 197-98
Wier & Pouce (Katz) 47:220-23
"Wife" (Faludy) 42:139
"The Wife" (Highsmith) 102:186, 197
Wife (Mukherjee) 53:263-65, 268-69; 115:386
The Wife of Martin Guerre (Lewis) 41:253, 255-59, 262
"A Wife of Nashville" (Taylor) 18:524; 50:251
"The Wife of the Autumn Wind" (Kawabata) 107:77
Wife to Mr. Milton: The Story of Marie Powell (Graves)
　　See *The Story of Marie Powell: Wife to Mr. Milton*
"The Wifebeater" (Sexton) 4:483
"The Wife's Story" (Le Guin) 45:216-17
"A Wife's Story" (Mukherjee) 115:364, 367-69
"The Wife's Tale" (Bausch) 51:55
"The Wife's Tale" (Heaney) 7:148; 25:244
"Wife-Wooing" (Updike) 9:537; 13:561
The Wig: A Mirror Image (Wright) 49:426-31, 433-34
"Wiggle Wiggle" (Dylan) 77:182, 184
Wigs on the Green (Mitford) 44:483, 486, 492

"Wigtime" (Munro) 95:307, 324
De wijn in drinkbaar dank zij het glas (Mulisch) 42:288
Wild 90 (Mailer) 74:217
"A Wild and Crazy Guy" (Martin) 30:248
A Wild and Crazy Guy (Martin) 30:247-48
Wild Angels (Le Guin) 45:214
Wild at Heart (Lynch) 66:266-73
Wild Berries (Yevtushenko) 51:425-30
"Wild Billy's Circus Song" (Springsteen) 17:481
"Wild Bird in a Living Room" (Walker) 13:567
"The Wild Birds" (Berry) 46:74
The Wild Birds: Six Stories of the Port William Membership (Berry) 46:73-4
"The Wild Blue Yonder" (Thomas) 107:342
The Wild Blue Yonder (Thomas) 107:336-37, 339-41, 346
"Wild Boar Clough" (Davie) 31:119, 124
The Wild Boys: A Book of the Dead (Burroughs) 2:94; 5:91-2; 15:110-11; 22:86; 42:75, 78-80; 75:102; 109:184, 195
The Wild Bunch (Peckinpah) 20:273-76, 279, 281, 284
Wild Cat (Peck) 17:339-40
"The Wild Cherry Tree" (Bates) 46:60
"Wild Child" (Reed) 21:304-05
The Wild Child (Truffaut)
　　See *L'enfant sauvage*
"Wild Children" (Morrison) 21:234
The Wild Colonial Boy (Hynes) 65:51-5
Wild Conquest (Abrahams) 4:1, 3
"The Wild Dog Rose" (Montague) 13:390; 46:268-70, 276
Wild Dreams of a New Beginning (Ferlinghetti) 111:59-60
"The Wild Duck" (Faludy) 42:142
Wild Earth and Other Poems (Colum) 28:85, 87
The Wild Earth's Nobility (Waters) 88:327-28, 337, 339, 345, 349, 359
"Wild Escapes" (Pollitt) 28:366
The Wild Flag: Editorials from The New Yorker on Federal World Government and Other Matters (White) 10:529; 39:377, 379
The Wild Frontier (Berton) 104:47
Wild Frontier (Berton) 104:47
The Wild Garden; or, Speaking of Writing (Wilson) 3:534; 5:512; 34:581
"Wild Geese" (Oliver) 98:260
The Wild Girl (Roberts) 48:341-43
"The Wild Goose" (Buckler) 13:123
The Wild Goose Chase (Warner) 45:427-31, 433, 435, 437-38, 440-41
Wild Grape Wine (Purdy) 50:246
"Wild Grapes" (Frost) 15:244; 26:111-12
"Wild Gratitude" (Hirsch) 50:195-96, 198-99
Wild Gratitude (Hirsch) 50:195-98
Wild Grow the Lilies: An Antic Novel (Brown) 63:53-4
Wild Honey (Frayn) 47:136-37, 139-41
Wild Honey (Wilson) 12:641-43, 645, 649, 651-54
"Wild Horses" (Bass) 79:5-7, 12
"Wild Horses" (Jagger and Richard) 17:224, 229-30
"Wild Horses" (Lane) 25:287
Wild Horses (Francis) 102:158, 160-62
"The Wild Hunter in the Bush of the Ghosts" (Tutuola) 29:439
Wild in the Country (Odets) 98:247
Wild in the World (Donovan) 35:140-42
"The Wild Iris" (Gluck) 81:165-66

The Wild Iris (Gluck) 81:163-74
The Wild Island (Fraser) 32:185; 107:37
Wild Justice (Smith) 33:376
"Wild Life" (McCartney) 35:280
Wild Life (McCartney) 12:372; 35:280, 293
"Wild Love" (Zappa) 17:592
Wild Man Fragment (Olson) 11:421
The Wild Man of Borneo (Connelly) 7:56
The Wild Marketplace (Transtroemer)
   See *Det vilda torget*
The Wild Market-Square (Transtroemer)
   See *Det vilda torget*
Wild Nights (Tennant) 52:398-99, 406
"Wild Oats" (Larkin) 18:299; 33:258; 64:272
Wild Oats (Epstein) 19:162-63
The Wild Oats of Han (Prichard) 46:332, 335
A Wild Old Man on the Road (Callaghan)
   65:245-47, 250, 252
The Wild Old Wicked Man (MacLeish) 8:362
The Wild One (Anouilh) 50:279
The Wild Palms (Faulkner) 3:152, 156; 8:207,
   211; 18:149; 28:138, 140, 145
"The Wild Parrots of Bloody Bay" (Jacobsen)
   48:191
The Wild Party (Arzner) 98:63, 69, 74
A Wild Patience Has Taken Me This Far: Po-
   ems, 1978-1981 (Rich) 36:366-68,370,
   376; 73:315, 317, 326, 330
"Wild Raspberries" (Fuller) 62:191, 202
Wild River (Kazan) 16:367-69; 63:226, 233,
   235
"Wild Roses" (Christie) 110:125
"Wild Roses" (Christie) 110:126
Wild Roses (Ferron)
   See *Les roses sauvages*
Wild Season (Eckert) 17:105-06
Wild Seed (Butler) 38:62, 66
The Wild Shore (Robinson) 34:105-07
"The Wild Sky" (Rich) 7:368
"Wild Sports of the West" (Montague) 46:266
Wild Strawberries (Bergman)
   See *Smultronstället*
"Wild Strawberry" (Kenny) 87:239, 241, 248
A Wild Surmise (Raphael) 2:366-67
Wild Swans: Three Daughters of China (Chang)
   71:114-29
The Wild, the Innocent, and the E Street Shuffle
   (Springsteen) 17:477, 481, 484, 488,
   490-91
"Wild Thing" (Sapphire) 99:81-4
Wild to the Heart (Bass) 79:3, 10, 15, 17-19
Wild Town (Thompson) 69:382, 385
"Wild Water" (Swenson) 106:337, 347
"Wild, Wild Night" (Morrison) 21:232-33
"Ein Wildermuth" ("A Wildermuth";
   "Wildermuth's Passion") (Bachmann)
   69:35, 37, 44
"A Wildermuth" (Bachmann)
   See "Ein Wildermuth"
"Wildermuth's Passion" (Bachmann)
   See "Ein Wildermuth"
"The Wilderness" (Fuller) 62:197
"The Wilderness" (Mahfuz)
   See "al- Khala"
"Wilderness" (Sandburg) 35:339
Wilderness (Danvers) 70:43-7
Wilderness (Parker) 27:364
Wilderness: A Tale of the Civil War (Warren)
   1:356; 4:578; 8:540
Wilderness Empire (Eckert) 17:106
"Wilderness Gothic" (Purdy) 14:431; 50:248
Wilderness of Ladies (Taylor) 5:425-26
A Wilderness of Mirrors (Frisch)

   See *Mein Name sei Gantenbein*
A Wilderness of Vines (Bennett) 5:57-9
Wilderness Road (Green) 25:198
Wilderness Stair: Poems, 1938-1954 (Belitt)
   22:49, 52
"A Wilderness Station" (Munro) 95:319-22
"Wilderness Tips" (Atwood) 84:97
Wilderness Tips (Atwood) 84:95-7
The Wilderness War (Eckert) 17:109
Wildest Dreams (Ayckbourn) 74:30
Wildfire (Clark) 12:131
Wildfire at Midnight (Stewart) 35:388-90, 392
"Wildflowers" (Howard) 7:169; 10:274
Wildlife 99:104, 110, 116-17, 123
Wildlife in America (Matthiessen) 32:285;
   64:309
"Wildness Makes a Form" (Silkin) 43:402
Wild's Magical Book of Cranial Effusions (Wild)
   14:580
Wildtrack (Wain) 2:458; 11:562
"Wilf McKenzie" (Purdy) 50:248
Wilkin's Tooth (*Witch's Business*) (Jones)
   26:224-25
"The Will" (Lavin) 99:319
"The Will" (Merrill) 8:386; 13:377; 34:235
"The Will" (Miller) 30:262
The Will (Swados) 5:420, 422
"Will I?" 99:184, 188
"Will I Go to Heaven?" (Mayle) 89:141
"Will Not Come Back" (Lowell) 8:354
"The Will of Stanley Brooke" (Campbell)
   42:83
"Will Scarlet" (Hoffman) 6:243
Will Shakespeare: The Untold Story (Mortimer)
   28:286
"Will Someone Who Is Not Guilty" (Lerman)
   9:329
"Will the Circle Be Unbroken" (Dumas) 6:145;
   62:154, 160-61, 163
The Will to Change: Poems, 1968-1970 (Rich)
   3:427-28; 6:457-58; 7:364, 366, 368,
   371-72; 11:476; 18:446-47; 36:366, 372-
   73, 375; 73:323, 325-26, 334; 76:217
"Will to Love" (Young) 17:577, 579
The Will to Meaning: Foundations and Appli-
   cations to Logotherapy (Frankl) 93:210
The Will to Power (Foucault)
   See *Histoire de la sexualité, Vol. 1: La volonté*
   de savoir
"Will to Win" (Scott) 22:372
"Will You Please Be Quiet, Please?" (Carver)
   22:100; 55:280
Will You Please Be Quiet, Please? (Carver)
   22:96-9, 101, 103; 36:101, 103; 53:60
"Will You Please Go Now" (O'Faolain) 47:328
"Will You Tell Me" (Barthelme) 115:56
"Will You Turn a Deaf Ear" (Auden) 14:32;
   43:15
Willard and His Bowling Trophies: A Perverse
   Mystery (Brautigan) 9:124; 12:70-2;
   42:50, 56-7, 60
Willard Gibbs (Rukeyser) 6:479; 15:459-60
"The Willets" (Swenson) 61:397-99; 106:324-
   25, 337
"Willi" (Doctorow) 37:91, 93; 113:152, 163-
   65
"William" (Oliver) 98:303
"William and Mareon Clark" (Brown) 48:60
"William and Mary" (Dahl) 79:181, 183
"William Butler Yeats" (Hope) 51:217
"William Butler Yeats Visits Lincoln Park and
   Escapes Unscathed" (Ochs) 17:332
"William Carlos Williams: By Day and by

Night" (Soupault) 68:416
William Carlos Williams on Art and Artists (Wil-
   liams) 22:464
William Dean Howells: An American Life (Lynn)
   50:426
William Faulkner: A Critical Study (Howe)
   85:116
William Faulkner: First Encounters (Brooks)
   86:278, 285, 287
William Faulkner: The Yoknapatawpha Coun-
   try (*The Yoknapatawpha Country*)
   (Brooks) 24:107-08, 114, 116; 86:278,
   285, 287; 110:5, 15, 24-5
William Faulkner: Toward Yoknapatawpha and
   Beyond (*Toward Yoknapatawpha and Be-*
   yond) (Brooks) 86:285, 287; 110:15, 24-
   5
"William Faulkner: Vision of Good and Evil"
   (Brooks) 86:287
"William Street" (Slessor) 14:497
"Williams Creek" (Oliver) 98:303
"Willie" (Angelou) 35:30; 77:30
"Willie" (Brooks)
   See "To Keorapetse Kgositsile (Willie)"
"Willie" (Tryon) 11:549
Willie and Family Live (Nelson) 17:305
Willie Masters' Lonesome Wife (Gass) 1:114;
   2:155; 8:242-43, 245-46; 15:255; 39:478
"Willie the Wandering Gypsy and Me"
   (Jennings) 21:202
The Willie Way (Nelson) 17:302
"The Willing" (Bell) 8:67
"A Willing Slave" (Narayan) 28:302
"Willingly" (Gallagher) 63:123
Willingly (Gallagher) 63:116-18, 120, 122,
   124-25
Williwaw (Vidal) 2:448; 4:556-58; 22:431, 433;
   72:387
"The Willow" (Akhmatova)
   See "Iva"
"Willow" (Armatrading) 17:8
"Willow and Fig and Stone" (Buckley) 57:131
"Willow He Walk" (Wellman) 49:396
Willow Run (Swarthout) 35:398
"Willow's Money" (Hansen) 38:240
"Willowware Cup" (Merrill) 34:235
Will's Boy: A Memoir (Morris) 37:313-16
Willy Remembers (Faust) 8:215
Wilt (Sharpe) 36:400
The Wilt Alternative (Sharpe) 36:401-02
Wilt on High (Sharpe) 36:403-04
"The Wimp" (Gallagher) 63:122, 124-25
"Winchester" (Squires) 51:381, 383
"Wind" (Carver) 55:275
"Wind" (Fenton) 32:169
"Wind" (Hughes) 4:235; 9:281; 14:270
"The Wind" (Pasternak) 63:313
"The Wind" (Simic) 22:382
"Wind" (Soto) 32:405; 80:286-87, 293
The Wind (Simon)
   See *Le vent*
"The Wind and the Boy" (Head) 67:98
"The Wind and the Snow of Winter" (Clark)
   28:78-9
"Wind and Trees" (Muldoon) 32:317, 321
"Wind and Water and Stone" (Paz) 51:336
"The Wind at Your Door" (FitzGerald) 19:176-
   77
The Wind Changes (Manning) 19:299-300
"Wind Chimes" (Wilson) 12:650
"Wind Chimes in a Temple Ruin" (Birney) 6:75
"The Wind Coming Down From" (Ammons)
   108:21

The Wind Eye (Westall)   17:556, 558-59

Wind from an Enemy Sky (McNickle)   89:165-74, 181, 187

The Wind from Nowhere (Ballard)   3:32; 14:41; 36:33

Wind from the East (Godard)
See *Le vent d'est*

The Wind from the Plain (Kemal)
See *Ortadirek*

"The Wind in the Cloisters" (Amis)   8:11

A Wind in the Door (L'Engle)   12:350

"The Wind in the Dooryard" (Walcott)   14:550

Wind in the Eyes (Dabrowska)   15:169

"Wind in the Street" (Gunn)   18:203

The Wind in the Willows (Bennett)   77:102

Wind Mountain: A Poem (Chappell)   40:144-45; 78:91

The Wind off the Small Isles (Stewart)   35:391

Wind over All (Day Lewis)   1:72

Wind over Wisconsin (Derleth)   31:130, 133

"Wind Saves Woman in Leap from Building" (Jensen)   37:192

The Wind Shifting West (Grau)   4:210; 9:240

"The Wind Sleepers" (H. D.)   73:118

Wind Song (Sandburg)   10:450; 35:357

Wind, What Do You Want of Me? (Arghezi)
See *Ce-ai cu mine, vintule?*

Windfalls (O'Casey)   11:405

"Windigo" (Erdrich)   54:165

"Winding Down the War" (Appleman)   51:15

The Winding Stair: Francis Bacon, His Rise and Fall (du Maurier)   11:163

"Winding Up" (Walcott)   42:422

"Windingo" (Bowering)   15:82

Windlestraws (Prichard)   46:332, 335

"A Windmill in the West" (Carey)   40:129, 133; 96:27-8, 37

"Windmills of Dwinelle Hall" (Vizenor)   103:288

"Windmühlen" (Schmidt)   56:391

"The Window" (Carver)   53:61

"The Window" (Creeley)   78:137

"The Window" (Garrett)   51:144

"Window" (Hoffman)   6:244

"The Window" (Levine)   33:275

"The Window" (Mahon)   27:290

"A Window" (Merton)
See "The Blessed Virgin Mary Compared to a Window"

"Window" (Pinsky)   94:305

"The Window" (Ritsos)   13:488

"The Window" (Samarakis)   5:381

"The Window" (Sarton)   49:310

The Window (Dorris)   109:298

"A Window Affair" (Dunn)   40:166

"The Window Is an Almanach" (Goldbarth)   38:203

"The Window of His Room" (Carroll)   38:103

A Window on Russia (Wilson)   24:482

"Window Seat" (Birney)   11:51

"Windows" (Livesay)   79:353

"The Windows" (Merwin)   8:389

"Windows" (Tuohy)   37:434

Windows (Creeley)   78:160-62

Windows and Stones (Transtroemer)   65:221-22

"Windröschen" (Celan)   82:49

Windrose: Poems, 1929-1979 (Ghiselin)   23:171-72

"Winds" (Auden)   43:27

Winds (Perse)
See *Vents*

The Winds (Vesaas)

See *Vindane*

"Winds in the Western Suburbs" (Ritsos)   31:324

The Winds of Altair (Bova)   45:73

The Winds of Darkover (Bradley)   30:27

The Winds of March (Weber)   12:633

Winds of Morning (Davis)   49:86-8, 90-1, 97-8

"The Winds of Orisha" (Lorde)   71:231

"Winds of Passage" (Martinson)   14:357

The Winds of Time (Corcoran)   17:72

The Winds of War (Wouk)   1:377; 9:580-81; 38:444, 449-52

The Wind's Twelve Quarters (Le Guin)   8:342

Windswept (Chase)   2:101

"The Windy City" (Sandburg)   35:342-43

"Windy Evening" (Simic)   68:377

"Windy Streets" (Johnston)   51:243

"Wine and Milk" (Barthes)   83:94

"Wine and Time" (Seifert)
See "Víno a cas"

"The Wine Breath" (McGahern)   48:263

Wine in the Wilderness: A Comedy Drama (Childress)   12:106; 86:310, 314, 316; 96:91, 103-04, 107, 112-13

The Wine of Absurdity (West)   7:522; 96:383, 386

The Wine of Astonishment (Gellhorn)   60:182, 192

The Wine of Astonishment (Lovelace)   51:270-71

Wine of Choice (Behrman)   40:79, 82

The Wine of the Puritans (Brooks)   29:86

"Wine of Wyoming" (Hemingway)   30:185

The Wine of Youth: Selected Stories (Fante)   60:133

Wine, Writing (Haavikko)   18:208; 34:175

"The Wine-Dark Sea" (Aickman)   57:6-7

The Wine-Dark Sea (Aickman)   57:7

"The Winemaker's Beat-Étude" (Purdy)   50:244

"Winesaps" (Smith)   42:356-57

"Winged Flight" (Gustafson)   36:221

Winged Seeds (Prichard)   46:334, 338, 342-43

Winged Victory (Hart)   66:178, 189

"Wingfoot Lake" (Dove)   50:157

"Wings" (Goldbarth)   38:207

"Wings" (Hughes)   2:202

"The Wings" (Levertov)   66:243

"Wings" (Voznesensky)   57:419

Wings (Kopit)   18:291; 33:246-52

Wings of the Morning (Cunningham)   12:165-66

"Wings over Africa" (Hemingway)   34:478

Winkelberg (Hecht)   8:271-72

The Winner (Rice)   49:304

Winner Take All (Federman)   6:182

Winner Take Nothing (Hemingway)   10:271; 30:180, 185, 192; 39:430

"Winner Takes All" (Wasserstein)   90:432

"Winner Takes All" (Waugh)   27:477

Winner Takes All (Wellershoff)
See *Der Sieger nimmt alles*

"Winners" (Friel)
See *Lovers*

The Winners (Cortazar)
See *Los premios*

Winners (Finders) (Friel)   42:166-67

"winnie song" (Clifton)   66:83

Winning (Brancato)   35:66, 68-9

"The Winning of Etain" (Boland)   113:96

A Winnipeg Childhood (Livesay)   4:295; 79:354

"The Winnower to the Winds" (Carruth)

84:129

"The Winnowing" (Asimov)   26:50

The Winslow Boy (Rattigan)   7:354-56

"Winston" (Townshend)   42:379-80

"Winter" (Celan)   82:57

"Winter" (Dubus)   97:223

"Winter" (Giovanni)   64:194

Winter (Callaghan)   65:249

Winter, 1671 (Ritter)   52:354

"Winter: 1978" (Beattie)   40:64, 66; 63:12-13

The Winter Alone (Scott)   43:377

"Winter at Roblin Lake" (Purdy)   14:434

"Winter at the Track" (Voznesensky)   15:557; 57:420

"Winter Bouquet" (Snodgrass)   18:491

"Winter Castle" (Jacobsen)   102:235, 240

"A Winter Come" (Moss)   7:248

"A Winter Convalescence" (Abse)   29:18

"Winter Dog" (MacLeod)   56:197-99

"Winter Drought" (Ryan)   65:209, 212, 214

"A Winter Eden" (Frost)   15:241

"Winter Evening" (Winters)   32:469

"Winter Evening Poem" (Jensen)   37:186

"A Winter Fable" (Boyle)   58:69

"The Winter Father" (Dubus)   36:146; 97:209, 227

"Winter Fire" (Raine)   45:331

"Winter Garden" (Neruda)
See "Jardín de invierno"

Winter Garden (Bainbridge)   22:45-7; 62:30-1

"Winter Harbour" (Bowering)   32:47

The Winter Hero (Collier and Collier)   30:72-3

"Winter Honey" (Jordan)   114:148

"The Winter House" (Crase)   58:161, 165

"Winter in Castile" (Dos Passos)   25:143

"Winter in July" (Lessing)   6:292; 22:279

"Winter in the Abruzzi" (Ginzburg)   54:201, 204, 208

Winter in the Blood (Welch)   6:560-62; 14:558-61; 52:426, 428-36, 438

"Winter in the Country" (Oliver)   19:362; 98:266

A Winter in the Hills (Wain)   46:416-18

"Winter Is Lovely, Isn't Summer Hell" (Rooke)   25:394

"Winter Journey" (Baxter)   45:53; 78:17-18

Winter Journey (Broughton)   19:73-4

Winter Journey (Figes)   31:162-63

"Winter Kestrel" (Wright)   53:417

Winter Kills (Condon)   4:107; 6:115; 8:150; 45:101-03; 100:91, 94, 97, 100, 104, 110-11, 113

"Winter Landscape" (Berryman)   13:77

"A Winter Landscape near Ely" (Davie)   5:114

"Winter Landscape, with Rooks" (Plath)   111:201-02, 205

"A Winter Legend" (Brown)   48:59

"A Winter Light" (Haines)   58:217

Winter Light (Bergman)
See *Nattvardsgästerna*

"Winter Lightning" (Nemerov)   36:305

The Winter Lightning (Nemerov)   2:306

"Winter Love" (H. D.)   73:143

Winter Love (H. D.)   31:208

"The Winter Man" (Scannell)   49:329

The Winter Man (Scannell)   49:329-30

"Winter Market" (Gibson)   39:144

"The Winter Market" (Gibson)   63:129

"Winter Mask" (Tate)   2:429; 14:529

Winter Morning in Charlottesville (Hass)   18:213

The Winter Name of God (Carroll)   38:103

"Winter Nelis" (Jolley)   46:213

"Winter News" (Haines) **58**:214
Winter News (Haines) **58**:214-21
"A Winter Night" (Aldington) **49**:10
"Winter Night" (Boyle) **58**:80
"Winter Night" (Pasternak) **63**:313, 315, 317
Winter: Notes from Montana (Bass) **79**:12-20
Winter Numbers (Hacker) **91**:109-11
"Winter of '73" (Gold) **42**:197
"The Winter of Artifice" (Nin) **60**:265-66
The Winter of Artifice (Nin) **4**:379; **8**:421; **14**:381-83; **60**:265, 279
Winter of Madness (Walker) **14**:552
The Winter of Our Discontent (Steinbeck) **1**:326-27; **5**:405-06; **9**:520; **21**:371, 382, 391; **34**:405, 407, 410-11; **45**:382; **59**:350-51
Winter of the Luna Moth (Rosenblatt) **15**:446
Winter of the Salamander: The Keeper of Importance (Young Bear) **94**:363-64, 369-73, 376
The Winter of the World (Anderson) **15**:15
"Winter on Earth" (Toomer) **22**:429
The Winter Palace (Haavikko)
  See *Talvipalatsi*
The Winter Palace (Haavikko) **18**:205-06; **34**:168-69, 177
The Winter People (Ehle) **27**:106-07
The Winter People (Whitney) **42**:434
"Winter Piece" (Tomlinson) **45**:393
"Winter Rain" (Adams) **13**:2
"The Winter Rain" (Berry) **4**:59
"Winter Remembered" (Ransom) **5**:365
"Winter Scene" (Ammons) **5**:30; **25**:43; **108**:24
"Winter Sleep" (Oliver) **98**:270
"Winter Sleepers" (Atwood) **25**:66
"Winter Solace" (Squires) **51**:379
Winter Soldiers (Santiago) **33**:354
"Winter Solstice" (Blackburn) **43**:69
"Winter Solstice" (Livesay) **79**:353
"Winter Song" (Kizer) **80**:180
"Winter Stars" (Blunden) **56**:47
Winter Station (Yevtushenko)
  See "Zima Station"
Winter Sun (Avison) **4**:36; **97**:73-7, 79-86, 88-92, 105, 110-14, 117, 122, 128-30, 137
Winter Sun/The Dumbfounding: Poems 1940-1966 (Avison) **97**:110, 121, 128
"Winter Swan" (Bogan) **4**:68; **46**:90; **93**:65, 80, 90-1
A Winter Talent and Other Poems (Davie) **5**:114; **8**:162-63; **10**:125
Winter Tales (Brown) **100**:82-3
Winter Tales from Poland (Wojciechowska) **26**:457-58
Winter Thunder (Sandoz) **28**:407
"Winter Trees" (Oliver) **98**:271
Winter Trees (Plath) **2**:337-38; **3**:389-91; **5**:340-41, 343, 345; **9**:434; **14**:424-26; **17**:355, 361-64, 366, 368; **51**:340, 353; **111**:158, 167-69, 181, 204
"Winter Tryst" (Van Doren) **6**:541
"Winter Verse for His Sister" (Meredith) **4**:349
"Winter Vineyard Workers" (Saroyan) **8**:468
"A Winter Visit" (Abse) **29**:20
"Winter Voyage" (Ortese)
  See "Viaggio d'inverno"
"Winter Walk" (Blunden) **56**:46
"Winter Walking" (Purdy) **14**:433; **50**:238
"Winter Wind" (Munro) **95**:304
"Winterfold" (Brown) **48**:57
Winterfold (Brown) **48**:57-8; **100**:84
"Wintergreen Ridge" (Niedecker) **10**:360-62;

42:297-98
"Wintering" (Plath) **9**:427, 431; **111**:177, 185
"Wintering in Victoria" (Rooke) **25**:391
Wintering Out (Heaney) **5**:170-72; **7**:147-48, 150-51; **14**:241-45; **25**:243, 245-46, 248; **37**:165; **74**:156-58, 167, 171, 193; **91**:121, 128
"Winterkill" (Ford) **46**:161
"Winterlong" (Young) **17**:577
Winterlude (Scannell) **49**:332
"A Winter-Piece" (Berryman) **13**:78
Winter's Edge (Miner) **40**:331
"Winter's Formulae" (Transtroemer)
  See "Vinterns formler"
Winter's Formulae (Transtroemer)
  See *Vinterns formler*
"Winter's Morning" (Deighton) **46**:127
"A Winter's Tale" (Brown) **48**:57
"A Winter's Tale" (Heaney) **7**:148
"The Winter's Tale" (Jarrell) **2**:209
"A Winter's Tale" (Plath) **51**:340
"A Winter's Tale" (Thomas) **13**:539; **107**:326, 343, 350
Winter's Tale (Helprin) **32**:229-33
"A Winter's Tale, by a Wife" (Van Duyn) **116**:410
Winter's Tales (Vinter-Eventyr) (Dinesen) **10**:146, 150; **29**:156, 158-59, 161; **95**:37-8, 46, 50-1, 68
The Winthrop Covenant (Auchincloss) **9**:54; **45**:32
"Winthrop Mackworth *Redivivus*" (Betjeman) **43**:37
"Winthrop Thorpe Tortuga" (Keillor) **115**:294
Wintle's Wonders (Dancing Shoes) (Streatfeild) **21**:402-03
"Wipeout" (Jones) **81**:63-5, 67
"The Wiper" (MacNeice) **53**:241-42
"Wir Besenbinder" (Boell) **11**:55; **72**:69
"Wire" (Goldbarth) **38**:200
"Wired into Now" (Blount) **38**:46
"Wires" (Larkin) **64**:262
"Wisconsin in Their Bones" (Derleth) **31**:138
Wisdom, Madness and Folly: The Making of a Psychiatrist (Laing) **95**:155, 184, 187
The Wisdom of the Heart (Miller) **43**:298; **84**:260
The Wisdom Tooth (Connelly) **7**:56
Wise Blood (Huston) **20**:174
Wise Blood (O'Connor) **1**:254-57; **3**:366; **6**:376, 379-81; **10**:364, 367-70; **13**:420-21; **15**:408-09, 411, 413; **21**:255-59, 261-62, 266, 271; **66**:299-330; **104**:104-06, 108, 119-20, 122, 124, 164, 179
Wise Child (Gray) **36**:201-04, 207
Wise Children (Carter) **76**:324-31
The Wise Have Not Spoken (Carroll) **10**:95, 97
"The Wise Men" (Carpentier) **38**:94
"Wise Men at Their End" (Bausch) **51**:55-7
Wise Virgin (Wilson) **33**:454, 457
Wise, Why's, Y'z (Baraka) **115**:39
The Wise Wound (Carter) **76**:330
The Wise Wound: Everywoman and Eve's Curse (Redgrove) **41**:355-56, 359
"Wish" (Mason) **82**:258
"Wish" (Merwin) **5**:286
"Wish for a Young Wife" (Roethke) **46**:364; **101**:266, 333
"Wish Fulfilment" (Simmons) **43**:408
Wish in the Dark (Weber) **12**:631
"Wish to Be a Red Indian" (Plumly) **33**:312
"Wish You Were Here" ("Zhal', chto vas ne bylo s nami") (Aksyonov) **101**:28-9, 35

"Wish You Were Here" (Pink Floyd) **35**:313
Wish You Were Here (Brown) **79**:171
Wish You Were Here (Pink Floyd) **35**:307-13, 315
"The Wishbone" (Muldoon) **72**:277, 279
"Wishes" (Wright) **13**:614
Wishes, Lies, and Dreams: Teaching Children to Write Poetry (Koch) **8**:323; **44**:245
Wishful Thinking (Buechner) **4**:80
"The Wishing Box" (Plath) **3**:390
"Wishing More Dear" (Riding) **7**:374
"Wisteria" (Spencer) **22**:402
"A Wistful Poem Called 'Readers'" (Davie) **31**:112, 118
The Wit to Woo (Peake) **54**:366, 372-73, 375
"The Witch" (Beer) **58**:36
"The Witch" (Singer) **9**:487
"Witch Burning" (Plath) **17**:361; **111**:159, 163
The Witch Diggers (West) **7**:520; **17**:544-46, 552-53
"Witch Doctor" (Hayden) **37**:152, 158
The Witch from the Sea (Hibbert) **7**:156
The Witch in the Wood (White) **30**:438-41, 444-46
"The Witch of Coös" (Frost) **1**:110; **9**:218, 224-25; **15**:250
Witch Week (Jones) **26**:232-33
"Witchbird" (Bambara) **19**:33; **88**:28
"Witchcraft" (Head) **67**:93-5
The Witchcraft of Salem Village (Jackson) **60**:217, 223, 237
"The Witches' Brew" (Pratt) **19**:377-78, 383, 385
The Witches of Eastwick (Updike) **43**:432-35, 437; **70**:248-49, 253
The Witches of Worm (Snyder) **17**:471-72
"Witch-Girl" (Dunn) **40**:168
"Witchgrass" (Gluck) **81**:170
The Witch-Herbalist of the Remote Town (Tutuola) **29**:441-43
"Witching" (Boland) **40**:99-100; **67**:44; **113**:60, 62-3
"The Witchmark" (McGuckian) **48**:276-77
Witch's Business (Jones)
  See *Wilkin's Tooth*
Witch's Cradle (Deren) **102**:37-9
"With a Gun" (Becker and Fagen) **26**:79-80
"With a Little Help from My Friends" (Lennon and McCartney) **12**:358
"With a Little Luck" (McCartney) **35**:285-86, 289
"With a Potpourri from Down Under" (Howard) **47**:169
"With All Deliberate Speed" (Madhubuti) **73**:215
"With All Due Respect" (Aleixandre) **36**:30
With All My Might (Caldwell) **50**:299
"With an Axe and an Auger" (Haines) **58**; 220
With Bold Knife and Fork (Fisher) **76**:342; **87**:122
"With Burney and Dudek on Mount Royal" (Everson) **27**:133
"With Changing Key" (Celan)
  See "Mit Wechselndem Schlüssel"
With Closed Eyes (Arenas)
  See "Con los ojos cerrados"
"With Delicate Mad Hands" (Tiptree) **48**:389
With Eye and Ear (Rexroth) **112**:371
With Eyes at the Back of Our Heads (Eyes at the Back of Our Heads) (Levertov) **2**:242-43; **15**:336; **28**:242; **66**:238, 241, 252

"With Eyes Closed" (Paz) 65:188
"With Folded Hands..." (Williamson) 29:455-59
"With God on Our Side" (Dylan) 12:183; 77:161
"With Hands Like Leaves" (Still) 49:363
With Hitler in New York, and Other Stories (Grayson) 38:210
"With Hopes of Hemp" (Ammons) 108:19
"With Horace" (Ignatow) 40:259
"With Ignorance" (Williams) 33:445
With Ignorance (Williams) 33:444-48; 56:426, 428-29
"With Janice" (Koch) 44:248-49
"With Life and With Death" (Elytis) 100:171, 177, 187
With Love to Lesbia: A Sheaf of Poems (Kenny) 87:245
With Malice Toward All (Herrmann) 44:503-04
"With Meaning" (Wieners) 7:537
"With Mercy for the Greedy" (Sexton) 53:319
With My Knives I Know I'm Good (Rathbone) 41:338
With My Little Eye (Fuller) 4:178
"With My Sons at Boarhills" (Stevenson) 33:381
"With One Launched Look" (Stafford) 29:381
With Open Eyes: Conversations with Matthieu Galey (Yourcenar)
  See *Les yeux ouverts; entretiens avec Matthieu Galey*
"With or Without" (Dickinson) 49:102-03
With or Without (Dickinson) 49:102-03
With ou l'art de l'innocence (Cixous) 92:62, 69, 94
"With Our Youth and with Our Aged" (Agnon)
  See "Bin'arenu uvizkenenu"
"With Quevedo during Spring" (Neruda)
  See "Con Quevedo en primavera"
With Shuddering Fall (Oates) 2:314; 33:293; 52:335; 108:341, 362, 386
"With So Little to Be Sure Of" (Sondheim) 30:379, 400
With the Beatles (Lennon and McCartney) 12:384
"With the Deep Voice of a Prophet" (Akhmadulina)
  See "Glubokim golosom proroka"
"With the Grain" (Davie) 8:165; 31:109
"With the Old Ones" 75:78
"With the Remover to Remove" (Howard) 47:169
With the Victors (Gallo)
  See *Le cortège des vainqueurs*
"With the World in My Bloodstream" (Merton) 83:397
"With Trumpets and Zithers" (Milosz)
  See "Natrabach i na cytrze"
"With Warm Regards to Miss Moore and Mr. Ransom" (Van Duyn) 63:441
With Your Body upon My Hands (Grade) 10:247
"Withdrawal" (Carey) 40:127-28
"The Withdrawal" (Lowell) 37:238-39
"Withdrawal" (Williams) 42:441
Withered Murder (Shaffer) 19:413
The Withered Root (Davies) 23:140, 143
"Withered Skin of Berries" (Toomer) 22:428-29
"Within That Context, One Style: Eclectic, Reminiscent, Amused, Fickle, Perverse" (Trow)
  See "Ahmet Ertegun"

"Within the Context of No Context" (Trow) 52:420, 422
Within the Context of No Context (Trow) 52:420, 422, 424
Within the Gates (O'Casey) 5:320; 9:407, 409-11; 11:406-09; 15:404, 406; 88:239, 258, 270
Within the Zodiac (Gotlieb) 18:191
"Without a Counterpart" (Gunn) 18:200
"Without a Hero" (Boyle) 90:62-3
Without a Hero, and Other Stories (Boyle) 90:62-3
"Without a Sough of Wind" (Simic) 49:341
Without a Stitch in Time (De Vries) 2:114
Without Anesthesia (Wajda) 16:584
"Without Bark" (Zamora) 89:393
"Without Benefit of Tape" (Livesay) 79:336, 350
"Without Desolation" (Wakoski) 2:459
Without Feathers (Allen) 52:35-7, 40
"Without Love" (Cooper) 56:70
Without Me You're Nothing (Herbert) 44:393
Without Pausing for a Breath (Ehrenburg) 62:176-78
Without Remorse (Clancy) 112:67, 77, 90
Without Sorcery (Sturgeon) 39:361, 364, 366
Without Stopping (Bowles) 53:43-5
"Without You" 99:164
"The Witness" (Garrett) 51:140
"Witness" (L'Heureux) 52:279
"The Witness" (Oates) 33:296
"The Witness" (Porter) 7:310; 15:429
Witness (McNally) 7:217
"Witness for the Prosecution" (Christie) 110:112
Witness for the Prosecution (Christie) 12:125; 48:78; 110:122-23
Witness for the Prosecution (Wilder) 20:463
The Witness of Poetry (Milosz) 31:264-66, 269; 56:233, 250; 82:284, 296, 299
"Witness, Secret and Not" (Alexie) 96:5
A Witness Tree (Frost) 9:220; 10:194; 13:230; 15:241-42; 26:118; 34:468, 470, 475
"The Witnesses" (Auden) 43:16
"The Witnesses" (Hooker) 43:197
The Witnesses (Simenon) 2:397
"Wittgenstein on Egdon Heath" (Morgan) 31:276
Wittgenstein's Mistress (Markson) 67:187-90, 193-94, 198-200
Wittgensteins Neffe: eine Freundschaft (Wittgenstein's Nephew) (Bernhard) 61:22, 24
Wittgenstein's Nephew (Bernhard)
  See *Wittgensteins Neffe: eine Freundschaft*
Wives and Other Women (Klein) 30:242
The Wives of Henry VIII (Fraser)
  See *The Wives of Henry VIII*
The Wizard Bird (Millin) 49:251
A Wizard of Earthsea (Le Guin) 8:343; 13:347; 22:266, 270, 273; 71:178-84, 187-92, 194-98, 200-01, 203-04
The Wizard of Loneliness (Nichols) 38:338-39, 341
Wizards (Bakshi) 26:72, 74
"Wizard's World" (Norton) 12:468
Wladza (Power) (Konwicki) 8:325; 54:256; 117:256, 284
"W.L.M.K." (Scott) 22:371, 376
"WLT" ("The Edgar Era") (Keillor) 40:274
WLT: A Radio Romance (Keillor) 115:284-85
Wniebowstapienie (Ascension) (Konwicki) 8:326; 117:257-58, 284

Wo warst du, Adam? (Adam, Where Art Thou?; And Where Were You, Adam?) (Boell) 2:68; 6:83; 9:102-03, 105, 107-08; 11:53, 57-8; 27:55-6, 58; 39:293-94; 72:78-80, 100
Der Wobbly (Die Baumwollpflücker) (Traven) 11:535
"Woden's Day" (Stafford) 68:443
Wodwo (Hughes) 2:197-98, 201-03; 4:235-36; 9:280, 283; 14:271; 37:172-75, 181
"Woe or Wonder" (Cunningham) 31:101, 103
Woe or Wonder (Cunningham) 31:101-02
"Wohin" (Sachs) 98:328
"The Wolf" (Davidson) 13:168-69
The Wolf (Blais)
  See *Le loup*
The Wolf (Leonov)
  See *Volk*
Wolf: A False Memoir (Harrison) 6:224-25; 33:199; 66:153, 155, 157-58, 160, 166
"Wolf Alice" (Carter) 41:117
"Wolf Dreams" (Beattie) 63:3, 10
"Wolf Knife" (Hall) 13:259
"Wolf Moon" (Oliver) 98:288
"Wolf Net" (McClure) 6:317
Wolf Solent (Powys) 7:347-48; 9:440-41; 15:433-35; 46:315-18, 320-21, 324
Wolf Willow: A History, a Story, and a Memory of the Last Plains Frontier (Stegner) 9:510; 81:339-40, 345, 349-50, 352
"Wolfbane" (Thomas) 13:541
Wolfnight (Freeling) 38:187
The Wolfpen Poems (Still) 49:370-71
Wolf's Salt (Popa)
  See *Vucja so*
"The Wolves" (Kinnell) 13:320
"The Wolves" (MacNeice) 53:234
"Wolves Defended against the Lambs" (Enzensberger) 43:145
"The Wolves of Aguila" (Matthiessen) 64:321, 323-24
The Wolves of Willonghby Chase (Aiken) 35:17, 19
"The Woman" (Creeley) 78:134
"Woman" (Jarrell) 9:297-98
"The Woman" (Jensen) 37:192
"The Woman" (Lennon) 35:272, 274-75
"The Woman" (Levertov) 66:238
"The Woman" (Livesay) 79:343, 353
"Woman" (Lorde) 18:309; 71:252
"The Woman" (Mphahlele) 25:337
"Woman" (Neruda)
  See "Mujer"
"Woman" (Salinas) 90:328
The Woman (Bond) 23:67
"The Woman Alone" (Day Lewis) 10:131
A Woman Alone (Fo) 32:175-76
A Woman Alone (Head) 67:111
"A Woman and a Man" (Ding Ling)
  See "Yige nüren he yige nanren"
"Woman and Her Image" (Castellanos)
  See "La mujer y su imagen"
"Woman and the Sea" (Mott) 15:381
"Woman and Tree" (Graves) 39:325
Woman, Arise and Walk (Gironella)
  See *Mujer, levántate y anda*
"The Woman as a Mummy's Head" (Boland) 40:99-100
"Woman as Artist" (Taylor) 5:425
"Woman as Knower" (Lifton) 67:142
"Woman as Market" (Rukeyser) 15:458
"Woman as Operator" (Williams) 22:464
The Woman at Otowi Crossing (Waters)

88:337, 342, 347-49, 358, 363-64

"The Woman at the Washington Zoo" (Jarrell) **2**:210; **9**:298

The Woman at the Washington Zoo (Jarrell) **2**:208, 210; **9**:296; **13**:302

Woman Beware Woman (*The Half-Mother*) (Tennant) **52**:401-02

"The Woman Changes Her Skin" (Boland) **40**:99-100

"Woman Chopping Wood" (Hogan) **73**:157

The Woman Destroyed (Beauvoir)
See *La femme rompue*

"The Woman Follows Me Home as I Walk" (Salinas) **90**:332

The Woman from Sicily (Swinnerton) **31**:427

"The Woman Hanging from the Thirteenth Floor" (Harjo) **83**:267

Woman Hating: A Radical Look at Sexuality (Dworkin) **43**:131-32

Woman Hollering Creek and Other Stories (Cisneros) **69**:153-56

The Woman I Abandoned (Endo)
See *The Girl I Left Behind*

"Woman in a Lampshade" (Jolley) **46**:221

Woman in a Lampshade (Jolley) **46**:213, 220-21

"The Woman in Black" (Moravia) **46**:286

The Woman in Black (Hill) **113**:316, 326-27

"A Woman in Heat Wiping Herself" (Olds) **85**:295

"Woman in Kitchen" (Boland) **113**:109, 124

Woman in Mind (Ayckbourn) **74**:9, 11, 13-15, 17-20, 23-4

A Woman in Sunshine (Swinnerton) **31**:426

"Woman in the Bar" (Shapcott) **38**:400

"the woman in the camp" (Clifton) **66**:81

The Woman in the Dunes (Abe)
See *Suna no onna*

"Woman in the House" (Stuart) **34**:376

The Woman in the Moon (Lang)
See *Die Frau im Mond*

"The Woman in the Ordinary" (Piercy) **27**:373

"Woman In the Rose Colored Dress" (Berriault) **109**:96

A Woman in the Sky (Hanley) **5**:167-68

Woman in the Window (Lang) **20**:207, 211, 216

Woman in the Woods (Kogawa) **78**:166

"Woman Is the Death of the Soul" (Oates) **6**:367

"Woman Is the Nigger of the World" (Lennon) **12**:273; **35**:264, 270-71

A Woman like That (Shreve) **23**:402-03

"The Woman Lit by Fireflies" (Harrison) **66**:168-71

The Woman Lit by Fireflies (Harrison) **66**:167-71

A Woman Named Solitude (Schwarz-Bart) **2**:388-89; **4**:480

"A Woman Observed" (Ezekiel) **61**:96

The Woman of Andros (Wilder) **1**:364, 366; **5**:495; **6**:575, 577; **10**:536; **15**:572-74; **35**:442; **82**:339-40; 342-44, 364-65, 368, 372-73, 376, 379, 382

A Woman of Character (Gloag) **40**:209-10

A Woman of Destiny (Card) **47**:69

A Woman of Independent Means (Hailey) **40**:220-24

A Woman of Means (Taylor) **37**:408; **44**:305; **50**:252-53, 258; **71**:297

A Woman of No Importance (Bennett) **77**:98

The Woman of Paris (Chaplin) **16**:187-88, 198, 201

The Woman of Rome (Moravia)
See *La Romana*

A Woman of Singular Occupation (Gilliatt) **53**:147

Woman of the Ganges (Duras)
See *La femme du Gange*

"The Woman of the House" (Murphy) **41**:311-12, 316, 320

Woman of the Inner Sea (Keneally) **117**:238-40, 243, 245

Woman of the River (Alegria)
See "A Temple of the Holy Ghost"

"The Woman of the Sumpul River" (Alegria) **75**:49

Woman on the Edge of Time (Piercy) **14**:419-20; **18**:406; **27**:376; **62**:362-67, 371-74, 376

"The Woman on the Stair" (MacLeish) **8**:361; **68**:286-87

Woman on Trial (Rand)
See *Night of January 16*

"A Woman Pacing Her Room" (Levertov) **15**:339

"A Woman Painted on a Leaf" (Boland) **113**:92, 94-5, 111

"A Woman Playwright Speaks Her Mind" (Childress) **86**:316

"Woman Posing" (Boland) **40**:99, 101; **113**:108

A Woman Run Mad (L'Heureux) **52**:280-81

The Woman Said Yes: Encounters with Life and Death (West) **7**:522; **17**:553

"Woman Singing" (Ortiz) **45**:309

A Woman Speaks (Nin) **14**:385

"The Woman Takes Her Revenge on the Moon" (Boland) **113**:87

"The Woman, the Place, the Poet" (Boland) **113**:84, 105-06, 126

"The Woman Thing" (Lorde) **71**:232

"Woman to Child" (Wright) **53**:419, 427, 431

"Woman to Man" (Wright) **53**:418-19, 427, 431

Woman to Man (Wright) **53**:417, 419-20, 423-24, 427-28, 431

Woman to Woman (Duras)
See *Les parleuses*

"The Woman Turns Herself into a Fish" (Boland) **40**:99-100; **113**:124

"A Woman Unconscious" (Hughes) **9**:280, 285

A Woman under the Influence (Cassavetes) **20**:48-51, 55

The Woman Warrior: Memoirs of a Girlhood among Ghosts (Kingston) **12**:312-14; **19**:249-50; **58**:308-18, 324, 327

"The Woman Who Came at Six O'Clock" (Garcia Marquez) **15**:254; **47**:148, 150

"The Woman Who Died Too Soon" (Steinem) **63**:380

"The Woman Who Fainted" (Dybek) **114**:74-6

"The Woman Who Had Imagination" (Bates) **46**:52, 54, 66

The Woman Who Had Imagination, and Other Stories (Bates) **46**:51-2

"The Woman Who Kept Her Poet" (Godwin) **8**:248

"The Woman Who Knew Too Much" (Ai) **69**:4

Woman Who Knows Latin (Castellanos)
See *Mujer que sabe latin*

"The Woman Who Loved to Cook" (Jong) **6**:267

The Woman Who Owned the Shadows (Allen)

84:13, 17-20, 24, 28-33, 37-8, 41, 44

"The Woman Who Raised Goats" (Gallagher) **18**:169; **63**:119

"The Woman Who Tried to Be Good" (Ferber) **93**:138, 180

"The Woman Who Was a Tree" (Huxley) **11**:282

The Woman Who Was Changed (Buck) **18**:80

The Woman Who Was God (King) **53**:213-14

"The Woman Who Was Never Satisfied" (Martin) **89**:111-12, 116, 118

"The Woman Who Was Not Allowed to Keep Cats" (White) **69**:398

A Woman Whose Heart Is Too Small (Crommelynck)
See *Une femme qu'a le coeur trop petit*

"Woman with Chrysanthemums" (Mueller) **51**:279

"Woman with Girdle" (Sexton) **8**:483

The Woman without a Face (Bergman) **72**:51

"Woman Work" (Angelou) **77**:30

"A Woman, Young and Old" (Paley) **37**:337

"Woman-Enough" (Gallagher) **18**:170; **63**:120

"The Womanhood" (Brooks) **5**:75; **49**:31

A Woman's Age (Billington) **43**:55-7

"A Woman's Breast" (Landolfi) **49**:214, 217

A Woman's Hand (White) **5**:486-87

"A Woman's Illness" (Ghose) **42**:179

"A Woman's Issue" (Atwood) **25**:65; **84**:68

"Woman's Song" (Wright) **53**:418-19, 427, 431

A Woman's Story (Ernaux)
See *Une femme*

"the woman's vision" (Young Bear) **94**:363

"Womanwork" (Allen) **84**:6

Womberang **61**:408-11

"Women" (Bogan) **39**:388, 390, 392; **46**:87

"The Women" (Boland) **113**:70, 92, 124

"The Women" (Kenny) **87**:240

"Women" (Rich) **36**:372

"Women" (Scott) **43**:370

"Women" (Swenson) **61**:394, 397; **106**:342

"The Women" (Walker) **58**:405

Women (Bukowski) **41**:70-1, 73; **82**:10-11, 13, 28; **108**:96, 100-03, 105-09

Women and Angels (Brodkey) **56**:57-9

Women and Children First (Benson) **17**:49

"Women and Honor: Some Notes on Lying" (Rich) **18**:448; **73**:324

Women and Men (McElroy) **47**:244-46

The Women and the Men (Giovanni) **19**:192; **64**:188-89, 191; **117**:184, 192, 197

Women and Wallace (Sherman) **55**:377-80

"The Women Are Grieving" (Hogan) **73**:148

The Women at Point Sur (Jeffers)
See *The Women of Point Sur*

Women Calling Home (Vesaas)
See *Kvinnor ropar heim*

Women, Class, and the Feminist Imagination: A Socialist-Feminist Reader **65**:342

Women, Culture, & Politics (Davis) **77**:127-29

"Women in Egypt: A Personal View" (Davis) **77**:129

Women in Evidence (Japrisot)
See *La passion des femmes*

"Women in Love" (Mahapatra) **33**:284

Women in Love (Russell) **16**:541-42, 548

"Women in Marriage" (Stevenson) **7**:463

"Women in the Locker Room!" (Blount) **38**:47

Women in the Wall (O'Faolain) **6**:383; **19**:360; **47**:330-31; **108**:400-01

Women in Their Beds: New and Selected Stories

(Berriault) 109:95, 98

"Women Like Taverns I've Dreamt" (Salinas) 90:332

"Women like You" (Ondaatje) 51:313

"The Women Men Don't See" (Tiptree) 48:389-90, 392; 50:356-57

"Women, Men, Theories, and Literature" (Heilbrun) 65:344

The Women of Brewster Place (Naylor) 28:304-05; 52:320-24

Women of Crisis (Coles) 108:188

"The Women of Dan Dance With Swords in Their Hands to Mark the Time When They Were Warriors" (Lorde) 71:236

Women of Messina (Vittorini)
   See *Le donne di Messina*

The Women of Point Sur (*The Women at Point Sur*) (Jeffers) 11:305, 311; 54:233, 236-37, 243, 245

The Women of Whitechapel and Jack the Ripper (West) 96:369, 376, 386-90, 392-93, 396

The Women on the Porch (Gordon) 6:203, 206; 29:186, 190; 83:234, 239, 243-44, 247-48, 250-51, 257, 260

Women on the Verge of a Nervous Breakdown (Almodovar)
   See *Mujeres al borde de un ataque de nervios*

"The Women on the Wall" (Stegner) 49:350; 81:346

The Women on the Wall (Stegner) 49:350; 81:346

Women, Race, & Class (Davis) 77:120-23, 128

"The Women Speaking" (Hogan) 73:150

"Women Who Are Writers in Our Century: One Out of Twelve" (Olsen) 114:197

The Women Who Hate Me 78:2-3, 7

The Women Who Walk (Packer) 65:350

Women Whose Lives Are Food, Men Whose Lives Are Money (Oates) 15:402

"Women without Gardens" (Dunn) 40:171

Women Writers of the Seventeenth Century 65:343

"Women-Identified" (Brown) 79:159

"Women's House" (Muske) 90:308

"A Women's Restaurant" (Boyle) 36:56-8

The Women's Room (French) 10:191; 18:158-59; 60:138, 141, 144, 147-50

"Women's Time" (Kristeva) 77:306-09

"Woncha Come on Home" (Armatrading) 17:8-9

"The Wonder Woman" (Giovanni) 64:185-87

"Wonderful" (Wilson) 12:645

The Wonderful Clouds (Sagan) 17:422-23

Wonderful Fool (Endo)
   See *Obakasan*

"Wonderful Future" (Nelson) 17:302

"Wonderful Holidays" (Lehmann) 5:240

The Wonderful O (Thurber) 5:432, 438; 25:437

"The Wonderful Old Gentleman" (Parker) 68:326-27, 335, 337

"Wonderful Plant" (Goyen) 40:218

The Wonderful Story of Henry Sugar and Six More (Dahl) 79:177, 181

Wonderful Tennessee (Friel) 115:237-38

Wonderful Words, Silent Truth (Simic) 68:376

"Wonderful World, Beautiful People" (Cliff) 21:60

Wonderful World, Beautiful People (Cliff) 21:60-1

"The Wonderful World of Winnebagos" (Crews)

49:73

The Wonderful Years (Kunze) 10:310

Wonderland (Oates) 1:252; 2:314-15, 3:360-62; 6:368-69; 9:406; 15:400-02; 19:353; 52:335, 338; 108:374-75, 378, 385, 386, 391

"Wonderment" (Sassoon) 36:385

"Wonders of Obligation" (Fisher) 25:160-62

The Wonder-Worker (Jacobson) 4:253-56

"Wonga Vine" (Wright) 53:431

"Won't Get Fooled Again" (Townshend) 17:527, 531, 535

Won't Know Till I Get There (Myers) 35:298-99

Woo Havoc (Bell) 8:67

"The Wood" (Green) 97:292

"A Wood" (Merwin) 88:192

"Wood" (Munro) 95:311-12

"A Wood" (Wilbur) 53:410-11; 110:354-55

Wood and Stone (Powys) 7:348; 46:313

"The Wood Dove at Sandy Spring" (MacLeish) 8:362

"Wood Has No Mouth" (Lorde) 71:255

Wood Mountain Poems (Suknaski) 19:432-33

"The Woodcarver" (Brown) 100:83

"Woodchucks" (Kumin) 28:225

The Woodcock (Tournier)
   See *Le coq de bruyère*

Woodcutters (Bernhard)
   See *Holzfällen: Eine Erregung*

"Woodcutting on Lost Mountain" (Gallagher) 63:124

"The Wooden Dove of Archytas" (Davenport) 14:142

A Wooden Horse (Brandys) 62:119

The Wooden Horse (Hine) 15:282

Wooden Hunters (Cohen) 19:115

Wooden Icons (Arghezi)
   See *Icoane de lemn*

"The Wooden Madonna" (Coward) 51:74

"The Wooden Queen" (Leonov)
   See "Dereviannaia koroleva"

The Wooden Shepherdess (Hughes) 11:278

"The Wooden Umbrella" (Porter) 7:310; 101:223

"Wooding" (Motion) 47:288-90

"The Woodlot" (Clampitt) 32:114

"Woodpigeons at Rahenny" (Davie) 10:122

"The Wood-Pile" (Frost) 9:227; 15:248; 26:112, 122

"Woodrow Wilson (February, 1924)" (Jeffers) 54:246

"The Woods" (Erdrich) 54:165

The Woods (Mamet) 15:356; 46:251-52, 254

The Woods (Plante) 23:347; 38:365-67, 370-71

Woods and River Tales (Haig-Brown) 21:146

"The Woods, New York" (Bronk) 10:75

"Woodstock" (Mitchell) 12:441

"The Wood-Weasel" (Moore) 8:400

Woody Guthrie: Library of Congress Recordings (Guthrie) 35:185

Woody Sez (Guthrie) 35:193

Woody's Story (Guthrie) 35:193

"Wool Tea" (Dowell) 60:107-08

"The Wool Trade" (Heaney) 5:170; 7:151; 14:242

The Woolgatherer (Mastrosimone) 36:289-91

"Woolworth's" (Hall) 37:142

The Worcester Account (Behrman) 40:84

"Worcestershire" (Davie) 8:165

"The Word" (Akhmadulina)
   See "Slovo"

"The Word" (Smith) 25:418

Word (Booth) 23:77

The Word (Dreyer)
   See *Ordet*

The Word (Wallace) 7:510; 13:567

A Word about Tolstoy (Leonov) 92:277

Word Art and Picture Art (Lagerkvist)
   See *Ordkonst och bildkonst*

The Word Became Sex (Sender) 8:480

A Word Carved on a Sill (Wain) 11:562

A Word Child (Murdoch) 6:347-48; 8:404-06; 11:384, 389; 31:288, 290, 294; 51:288

"The Word Crys Out" (Ammons) 108:12

"Word, Dialogue, and Novel" (Kristeva) 77:310

"A Word for Me...Also" (Giovanni) 64:192; 117:177

"A Word for the Wind" (Ezekiel) 61:104

"Word for Word" (Bachmann) 69:46

The Word for World Is Forest (Le Guin) 8:343; 13:348, 350-51; 22:266; 45:222-23

"Word from the Right Wing" (Baraka) 5:48

"A Word in Your Ear on Behalf of Indifference" (Davison) 28:101

"The Word of Unbinding" (Le Guin) 71:186, 199

Word over All (Day Lewis) 6:127; 10:131

"A Word with You" (Bishop) 32:38

Wordarrows (Vizenor) 103:281, 284, 296-98

"Wordless Winter" (Davison) 28:104

"Wordlists" (Harrison) 43:176

"Wordlists II" (Harrison) 43:177

"Words" (Creeley) 15:152

"Words" (Enright) 31:154

"Words" (Levine) 33:271

"Words" (Plath) 5:346; 9:428, 433; 14:422, 424-25, 429; 17:366; 62:406

"Words" (Shields) 113:426

Words (Creeley) 1:67; 2:106-07; 8:151, 153; 11:138; 15:151-52; 36:117-20; 78:125, 127, 137, 143-44, 149

Words (Josipovici) 43:214, 218-19, 227

The Words (Sartre)
   See *Les mots*

Words and Experience (Hughes) 9:282

Words and Music (Beckett) 6:45, 47; 9:83-4

Words and Music (Mayne) 12:389-90, 403

Words and Things (Foucault) 34:340

"Words Asleep" (Lee) 90:194

Words by Heart (Sebestyen) 30:345-51

"The Words Continue Their Journey" (Atwood) 84:68

"Words for a Bike-Riding, Osprey-Chasing, Wine-Drunk Squaw Man" (Allen) 84:10

Words for a Deaf Daughter (West) 7:523; 14:568-69; 96:385, 393, 400

"Words for a Nursery" (Plath) 111:167

"Words for a Song" (Lewis) 41:261

Words for Dr. Y (Sexton) 53:313

"Words for Love" (Berrigan) 37:43

"Words for Music" (Aldington) 49:9-10, 17

"Words for the Dumb" (Van Duyn) 116:427

"Words for the Wind" (Roethke) 46:363; 101:266, 328

Words for the Wind: The Collected Verse of Theodore Roethke (Roethke) 3:432-33; 8:455, 460; 46:360, 363; 101:265-67, 269, 285, 287, 290, 295, 302, 304, 311, 327-33

"Words for Winter" (Blaise) 29:70

Words from History (Asimov) 76:312

Words from the Exodus (Asimov) 76:312

"The Words He Said" (Lessing) 22:279

"Words heard, by accident, over the phone" (Plath) **111**:203

"Words in Commotion" (Landolfi) **49**:216-17

Words in Commotion, and Other Stories (Landolfi) **49**:215-17

Words in Genesis (Asimov) **76**:312

Words in Stone (Bonnefoy)
See *Pierre écrite*

Words in th Fire (Bissett) **18**:59

Words in the Mourning Time (Hayden) **5**:168; **37**:151-52, 160

The Words in the Sand (Buero Vallejo) **15**:100, 102

"Words in the Tropics" (Guillen) **79**:229-30

"Words into Fiction" (Welty) **105**:333

Words Made to Measure (Arghezi)
See *Cuvinte potrivite*

"Words of a Pilgrim" (Gregor) **9**:254

Words of Advice (Weldon) **11**:565

"Words of Comfort" (Ammons) **108**:12

The Words of My Roaring (Kroetsch) **5**:220-21; **23**:269-70; **57**:282-83, 288

Words of Science (Science) (Asimov) **26**:36, 38; **76**:312

"Words on a Page" (Raine) **103**:186

"The Words on Magnet" (Seifert) **93**:341

Words on the Map (Asimov) **76**:312

"Words Rising" (Bly) **38**:55, 59-60

Words That Must Somehow Be Said: Selected Essays, 1927-1984 (Boyle) **58**:74-5

"Words to a Young Revolutionist" (Carruth) **84**:129

"Words to Frank O'Hara's Angel" (O'Hara) **78**:339

"Words with Marigold" (Tremain) **42**:386

Words with Power: Being a Second Study of 'The Bible and Literature' (Frye) **70**:272-73, 275, 278

"Wordsharp" (Brunner) **8**:109

"Wordsworth and the Paradox of the Imagination" (Brooks) **110**:35

"A Wordsworthian Sonnet for Arnold Feinstein, Who Mended My Spectacles in Yugoslavia" (Ewart) **46**:154

Wordsworth's Poetry, 1787-1814 (Hartman) **27**:178, 182

"Work" (Arghezi) **80**:10

"Work" (Oliver) **98**:304

"Work" (Shields) **113**:442

Work (Dixon) **52**:94-7, 101

Work and Love (Dunn) **36**:155

"Work Diary" (Wolf) **58**:421

Work in Progress (Redgrove) **41**:348-49

"The Work of Art" (Oliver) **98**:302

"A Work of Artifice" (Piercy) **18**:405; **62**:379

"Work Problem" (Hollander) **5**:186

"Work Song" (Berry) **27**:35-6

Work Suspended (Waugh) **13**:588-60; **19**:461

"Workday" (Hogan) **73**:159

"The Worker" **75**:70

The Workhouse Donkey (Arden) **6**:8; **13**:23-4, 29; **15**:20

"Working" (Harrison) **43**:176

Working Bullocks (Prichard) **46**:328, 330-32, 334, 336-38, 340-41, 343-44

"Working Class Hero" (Lennon) **35**:261-62, 267

Working Cotton (Williams) **89**:358

The Working Days: The Journals of 'The Grapes of Wrath,' 1938-1941 (Steinbeck) **59**:340-41, 346-49, 351, 353-54

Working Girls (Arzner) **98**:62, 71, 81, 87-90, 94

"Working Late" (Simpson) **32**:378

Working Men (Dorris) **109**:298, 307-10

"The Working Novelist and the Myth-Making Process" (Lytle) **22**:293, 297

The Working of Water (Redgrove) **41**:359-60

"Working on Wall Street" (Swenson) **14**:521

"Working Out" (Ammons) **57**:53

Working Papers: Selected Essays and Reviews (Carruth) **84**:115, 118, 121, 123-24, 127

Working: People Talk about What They Do All Day and How They Feel about What They Do (Terkel) **38**:422-25, 428

"Working the Face" (Parini) **54**:361

Working with Structuralism (Lodge) **36**:274, 276

"Workingman with Hand So Hairy-Sturdy" (Cummings) **68**:46

"The Workman" (Smith) **64**:390

The Works of Love (Morris) **1**:230-33; **3**:343; **7**:246; **18**:354; **37**:310, 312-13

"The World" (Bowen) **11**:60

"The World" ("A Naive Poem") (Milosz) **11**:381; **31**:265-66, 268; **55**:232, 237,245, 248, 251; **82**:285, 289, 298

The World about Us (Simon)
See *Leçon de choses*

The World Above (Polonsky) **92**:375-76, 402

The World according to Garp (Hill) **26**:208-10

The World according to Garp (Irving) **13**:293-97; **23**:244-47, 253; **38**:250, 252; **112**:139-40, 142-56, 158-60, 164-72, 174-75

"The World according to Hsü" (Mukherjee) **53**:265-67, 270

World Alone (Aleixandre)
See *Mundo a solas*

The World and Africa (Du Bois) **64**:118

The World and the Book: A Study of Modern Fiction (Josipovici) **43**:214-20, 223

"The World and the Jug" (Ellison) **86**:320

"The World as a Vision of the Unity in Flesh, Homage to Henry James" (Spacks) **14**:510

The World as I Found It (Duffy) **50**:33-6

"A World Awash with Fascism and Fear" (Ferlinghetti) **6**:183-84

The World before Us: Poems, 1950-70 (Weiss) **3**:517; **8**:545; **14**:557

"The World Began in Eden but Ended in Los Angeles" (Ochs) **17**:332

"The World behind Watergate" (Sale) **68**:346

A World Between (Spinrad) **46**:384

"The World Book, 1927" (Rich) **36**:366

"World Breaking Apart" (Gluck) **22**:175

The World by Itself (Aleixandre) **36**:30

World Citizen: Woodrow Wilson (Archer) **12**:16

"The World Contracted to a Recognizable Image" (Williams) **9**:575

"The World Dance" (Le Guin) **45**:219

The World Doesn't End (Simic) **68**:370, 376, 378-79

World Enough and Time (Warren) **1**:355; **4**:577-81; **8**:539, 541; **10**:518-19; **39**:266; **53**:376; **59**:298

World Enough: Rethinking the Future (Mead) **37**:280-81

"World Hymn 1914" (Christie) **110**:125, 127

A World I Never Made (Farrell) **66**:112, 114, 116, 120, 132, 136

A World in a Drop of Water (Silverstein and Silverstein) **17**:450

The World in the Attic (Morris) **1**:232; **7**:247

The World in the Evening (Isherwood) **1**:155, 157; **9**:293-94; **11**:294, 296-300; **14**:278, 280-81, 285; **44**:397-99, 402

"The World Is a Beautiful Place" (Ferlinghetti) **27**:137

The World Is a Room, and Other Stories (Amichai) **57**:38, 46; **116**:105, 107, 128

"The World Is a Wedding" (Schwartz) **45**:353-54

The World Is a Wedding (Schwartz) **4**:478; **10**:462-63; **45**:354; **87**:333-36

"The World Is Alive" (Le Clezio) **31**:243

"The World Is Almost Rotten" (Abbott) **48**:6

"The World Is Full of Poets" (Urdang) **47**:400

The World Is Made of Glass (West) **33**:433-34

The World Is My Home: A Memoir (Michener) **109**:375, 381, 385, 387-89

"The World Is Round Like an Orange" (Grenville) **61**:156

The World Jones Made (Dick) **30**:116

"The World Keeps Going Round" (Davies) **21**:89

World Light (Laxness)
See *Heimsljós*

A World More Attractive: A View of Modern Literature and Politics (Howe) **85**:121

"The World of 2001" (Clarke) **35**:123-24

World of Adventure (Vance) **35**:427

"The World of Apples" (Cheever) **3**:107; **7**:48, 50; **64**:50, 53

The World of Apples (Cheever) **3**:107-08; **7**:48-9; **25**:120

The World of Apu (Ray)
See *Apur sansar*

The World of Dance (Berger) **12**:42

The World of Dew (Enright) **8**:203; **31**:148

A World of Difference (MacCaig) **36**:287-88

The World of Doonesbury (Trudeau) **12**:590

The World of Farley Mowat (Mowat) **26**:346-47

The World of Gwendolyn Brooks (Brooks) **1**:46; **4**:79; **49**:23

The World of Henry Orient (Hill) **26**:197, 204, 207-08

"World of Heroes" (Kavan) **82**:122

A World of Ideas: Conversations with Thoughful Men and Women about American Life Today and the Ideas Shaping Our Future (Moyers) **74**:253-54

"The World of J. Edgar Hoover" (MacBeth) **5**:264

The World of J.B. Priestley (Priestley) **34**:362

The World of Jesse Stuart (Stuart) **8**:507; **34**:373

The World of Lenny Bruce (Bruce) **21**:53

A World of Love (Bowen) **3**:82, 84; **11**:63-4

The World of Mr. Mulliner (Wodehouse) **5**:517

"World of Nothing" (Fair) **18**:139, 141

World of Nothing (Fair) **18**:139

World of Og (Berton) **104**:47

World of Our Fathers: The Jews of Eastern Europe (Meltzer) **26**:302-03

World of Our Fathers: The Journey of the Eastern European Jews to America and the Life They Found and Made (*The Immigrant Jews of New York, 1881 to the Present*) (Howe) **85**:123, 126-28, 133, 137, 147-49

The World of Paul Slickey (Osborne) **2**:328; **5**:331; **45**:313-14, 320

"World of Peace" (Cliff) **21**:61

A World of Profit (Auchincloss) **4**:29-30

World of Ptavv's (Niven)　8:427

The World of Ray Bradbury (Bradbury)　42:33

The World of Sex (Miller)　84:242, 249-50, 252, 266, 287, 292

"The World of Simon Raven" (Porter)　33:325

A World Of Strangers (Gordimer)　10:239-40; 18:186; 70:162-63, 165-66, 169-70

The World of the Lie (Loewinsohn)　52:283-85

"World of the Myth" (Ellison)　42:126

"World of the Red Sun" (Simak)　55:320-21

The World of Violence (Wilson)
See *The Violent World of Hugh Greene*

The World of Washington Irving (Brooks)　29:88

"World of Women" (Durban)　39:44-6

World of Wonders (Davies)　7:73-4; 13:173-74; 25:133, 136; 42:102, 105, 107, 109; 75:180, 184, 192, 199, 204, 216; 91:208

"World on a String" (Young)　17:574

World Outside the Window: The Selected Essays of Kenneth Rexroth (Rexroth)　49:286-87

The World Reformer (Bernhard)
See *Der Weltverbesserer*

World Revolution, 1917-1936: The Rise and Fall of the Communist International (James)　33:218

World Series (Tunis)　12:593

"The World Still Needs" (Avison)　97:89

"World Telegram" (Berryman)　62:56, 71

"The World That Couldn't Be" (Simak)　55:320

The World, the Worldless (Bronk)　10:73, 75

"The World (This One), the Flesh (Mrs. Oedipa Maas), and the Testament of Pierce Inverarity" (Pynchon)　72:309, 323, 333

The World Upside Down (Mayne)　12:386, 388-89

WWII (Jones)　39:405

World War I (Smith)　64:388

"The World War I Los Angeles Airplane" (Brautigan)　3:89; 12:65, 70

"World War III" (Bell)　8:65

The World We Make (Kingsley)　44:232-33

"The World Well Lost" (Sturgeon)　39:361, 363, 366

"World Wisdom" (Kunene)　85:175

"A World within a War" (Read)　4:440

The World within the Word (Gass)　11:224-25; 15:258; 39:477, 479-80, 482

World within Walls (Keene)　34:567, 569

World within World (Spender)　5:401; 41:420-27; 91:256-57, 261-65, 267-69

"World without End" (Gascoyne)　45:153

World without End (Gray)　22:201-02

World without End, Amen (Breslin)　4:76-7; 43:72, 74, 76, 78

"A World without Objects Is a Sensible Emptiness" (Wilbur)　6:570; 53:399, 406; 110:387

World without Stars (Anderson)　15:13

"Worldliness" (Gregor)　9:254

"Worldly Goods" (Wolff)　64:448-49

Worldly Hopes (Ammons)　25:46; 57:49-50, 59

"Worlds" (Goldbarth)　38:205

"Worlds" (Wilbur)　53:413

The Worlds (Bond)　23:71

Worlds: A Novel of the Near Future (Haldeman)　61:178-80, 182-83

Worlds Apart: A Novel of the Near Future (Haldeman)　61:179-80, 182, 186

The World's Body (Ransom)　2:362, 364; 4:433, 436-37; 5:364; 24:362, 365-66

World's End (Boyle)　55:106-11; 90:43-5, 47, 49, 51-2, 54, 57-60, 65

World's End (Johnson)　27:212-14, 216

World's End (Neruda)　28:315

World's End (Sinclair)　63:354, 358

World's, End and Other Stories (Theroux)　28:425; 46:399

"World's Fair" (Berryman)　62:71

World's Fair (Doctorow)　37:94-6; 44:166-79; 65:137, 141; 113:137, 150-51, 168, 170, 175-76, 178

"The World's Fastest Human" (Faust)　8:215

The World's Flesh (Buckley)　57:126, 129, 131, 133

The Worlds of Fritz Leiber (Leiber)　25:307

The Worlds of Robert A. Heinlein (Heinlein)　55:303

The World's Room (MacCaig)　36:285

"Worlds that Flourish" (Okri)　87:315

"Worlds to Kill" (Ellison)　42:127

"The World's Worst Boyfriends" (Wasserstein)　90:432

The World-Thinker (Vance)　35:419

The World-Wreckers (Bradley)　30:31

"The Worm" (Ezekiel)　61:104

The Worm and the Ring (Burgess)　2:86; 5:85; 40:113-15, 117; 81:301; 94:49

"Worm Moon" (Oliver)　98:265

"The Worms" (Kizer)　80:172

Worms into Nails (Olson)　28:343

The Worms of Kukumlima (Pinkwater)　35:319-20

"Wormwood" (Kinsella)　19:251, 254

"The Wormwood Star" (Milosz)　82:302, 305

"A Worn Path" (Welty)　33:414, 419, 424; 105:298, 301, 307, 319, 326, 349

"Worry" (Muske)　90:309-10

Worse Things Waiting (Wellman)　49:389, 392, 394, 396

"Worsewick" (Brautigan)　12:64

"Worship" (Starbuck)　53:353

"The Worshippers" (Pritchett)　15:442-43; 41:330, 334

"The Worst of All Loves" (Dunn)　40:167

"The Worst Pies in London" (Sondheim)　30:398

"The Worst Policy" (Bainbridge)　62:35, 37-8

"The Worst Thing in His Life" (Paton)　25:360

"The Worst Thing of All" (Gordimer)　33:181

The Worst Years of Our Lives (Ehrenreich)　110:178, 180, 187

Worstward Ho (Beckett)　29:66-8; 59:253

The Worthing Chronicle (Card)　47:68; 50:143

"Worthy It Is" (Elytis)　100:155

Worthy It Is (Elytis)
See *The Axion Esti*

Woton's Wake (De Palma)　20:75

"Would You Do It for a Penny?" (Ellison)　42:130

"Would You Like to Try for Infinity Years" (Montgomery)　7:233

"Would You Suggest Writing as a Career?" (Bukowski)　41:74-5; 108:85

"The Would-Be Father" (Baxter)　45:51-2

A Would-Be Saint (Jenkins)　52:226, 229

"Wouldn't It Be Nice" (Wilson)　12:647, 649

"The Wound" (Barthelme)　59:251

"The Wound" (Gluck)　22:173

"The Wound" (Gunn)　18:203

The Wound and the Bow (Philoctetes: The Wound and the Bow) (Wilson)　8:550; 24:468-70, 473, 476, 480-81, 487

The Wound and the Weather (Moss)　45:290-91; 50:352-53

"Wounded Knee" (Eiseley)　7:92

The Wounded Land (Donaldson)　46:140-41

"The Wounded Soldier" (Garrett)　51:147, 152

The Wounded Stag (Santos)　22:361

"Wounds" (Longley)　29:292-93, 295-96

Wounds (Duffy)　37:114-15, 117

"Wounds in the Rain" (McGrath)　28:275

Woyzeck (Duerrenmatt)　102:61

Woyzeck (Herzog)　16:333-34

Woza Albert! (Mtwa)　47:295-97

Woza Albert! (Ngema)　57:340, 342, 344

"WPLJ" (Zappa)　17:586

"Wrack" (Barthelme)　46:43

"Das Wrack" (Lenz)　27:245

Wraiths of Time (Norton)　12:470-71

"Wrapped around Your Finger" (Police, The)　26:366

"Wrapped in Black" (Bowering)　15:82

"Wrapping the Wind" (Shange)　74:311

"The Wrath of God" (Fante)　60:131

"The Wreath" (Bates)　46:56

"The Wreath" (Jacobsen)　102:241

"Wreath for a Bridal" (Plath)　51:344

"A Wreath for Alun Lewis" (Watkins)　43:452

A Wreath for Rivera (Swing, Brother, Swing) (Marsh)　53:250, 254

"Wreath for the Dead" (Akhmatova)　64:6

"A Wreath for the Gamekeeper" (Porter)　101:223

A Wreath for Udomo (Abrahams)　4:1

A Wreath of Christmas Legends (McGinley)　14:368

A Wreath of Roses (Taylor)　29:410

A Wreath of Sonnets (Seifert)　93:346

A Wreath to Gorky (Leonov)　92:277

"Wreaths" (Longley)　29:296

"The Wreck" (Fuller)　62:193

"The Wreck" (Haines)　58:216

The Wreck of the 5:25 (Wilder)　6:576

The Wreck of the Archangel (Brown)　100:77, 80

The Wreck of the Cassandra (Prokosch)　4:421

"The Wreck of the Edmund Fitzgerald" (Lightfoot)　26:281

"The Wreck of the Thresher" (Meredith)　22:303; 55:191

The Wreck of the Thresher (Meredith)　4:349; 13:373, 375; 22:302

"The Wreck of the *Titanic*" (Tolson)　105:279

"Wreckage" (Momaday)　85:281

The Wreckage of Agathon (Gardner)　2:150-52; 3:187; 5:131, 135; 8:237; 10:218-19; 28:167

Wrecked Eggs (Hare)　58:230-31

Wreckers (Edgar)　42:116

The Wrench (Levi)
See *La chiave a stella*

Wrestle with an Angel (Everson)　27:133-34

The Wrestler (Andrade)
See *O lutador*

The Wretched of the Earth (Fanon)
See *Les damnés de la terre*

Wright Morris: A Reader (Morris)　3:343; 37:310

"The Wrights' Biplane" (Frost)　13:230

A Wrinkle in Time (L'Engle)　12:346-52

"Wrinkled Linen" (Prager)　56:276-77

"Wrinkles" (Jong)　6:270

Wrinkles (Simmons)　57:406-08

"Write, Then" (Ekeloef)　27:111

"The Writer" (Wilbur)　9:569; 53:413; 110:361-63, 377, 385

"Writer and Critic" (Bradbury)　61:42

"Writer and Critic" (Lukacs) 24:316
"The Writer and the Concept of Adulthood" (Stegner) 49:359
"The Writer as Detective Hero" (Macdonald) 41:270
"The Writer as Exile" (Moore) 90:277
"The Writer as Independent Witness" (Doctorow) 113:162
"The Writer as Moralist" (Bellow) 8:78
"Writer Devoured by Children" (Tournier) 95:389
"The Writer in a State of Siege" (Brink) 106:103
The Writer in America (Brooks) 29:87-8
The Writer in Disguise (Bennett) 45:58; 77:93
"The Writer in the Family" (Doctorow) 37:91-3; 44:175, 177; 113:136, 150-51, 153-55
"Writers and Writing" (McCullers) 12:427
A Writer's Capital (Auchincloss) 18:25
"The Writer's Commitment" (Alegria) 75:53
Writers from the Other Europe (Roth) 15:451
Writers in Politics (Ngugi wa Thiong'o) 36:318-19
A Writer's Ireland: Landscape in Literature (Trevor) 71:327-29, 331; 116:377
A Writer's Notebook (Maugham) 15:368; 67:218, 228-29
"The Writers of the American Revolution" (Williams) 13:604
"Writers on Strike" (Lebowitz) 11:322
The Writer's Point of View (Maugham) 15:368
"The Writer's Situation" (Carruth) 84:117
"A Writer's Story" (Levine) 54:297-98, 300
Writin' is Fightin': 37 Years of Boxing on Paper (Reed) 60:310
"Writing" (Motion) 47:288, 293
"Writing" (Nemerov) 36:305
"Writing a Book" (Hill) 113:326
"Writing a First Novel" (Jong) 6:270
Writing a Novel (Braine) 41:59-61
"Writing a Résumé" (Szymborska) 99:205
"Writing a Sketch of a Forgotten Poet" (Blunden) 56:40
Writing a Woman's Life (Heilbrun) 65:313
"Writing about Jews" (Roth) 15:453
"Writing Again" (Bly) 38:56
Writing Against: A Biography of Sartre (Hayman) 44:493-94, 496-98
Writing against Time (Moss) 50:353
"Writing American Fiction" (Roth) 4:459
Writing and Difference (Derrida)
   See L'écriture et la différence
Writing and the Body (Josipovici) 43:223-26
"Writing and the Holocaust" (Howe) 85:151-52
"writing autobiography" (hooks) 94:143
"Writing Autobiography" (Lee) 90:199, 201
"The Writing Condition" (Sheed) 53:341
Writing Degree Zero (Barthes)
   See Le degré zéro de l'écriture
"Writing for Children Is No Child's Play" (Tournier) 95:378-80
"Writing for Television" 61:420
"Writing for the Fourth Time through 'Finnegans Wake'" (Cage) 41:86
Writing Home (Williams) 42:445
Writing in a State of Siege (Brink) 36:68-70, 72; 106:101, 103
"Writing in a Time of Violence" (Boland) 113:93-4, 100, 111, 115-17, 127
"Writing in Latin America" (Allende) 57:20
Writing in Restaurants (Mamet) 46:255
"Writing in Wartime: The Uses of Innocence" (Fussell) 74:140
The Writing Life (Dillard) 60:79-81; 115:193-94, 201
"Writing Lives" (Merwin) 88:209-10, 213
Writing Lives: Principia Biographica (Edel) 34:534-37
Writing on a Body (Sarduy)
   See Escrito sobre un cuerpo
"Writing on Napkins at the Sunshine Club" (Bottoms) 53:29-30
The Writing on the Wall and Other Literary Essays (McCarthy) 24:344-46; 39:487
"Writing Poetry in a Hotel Room" (Enright) 31:150
Writing the Australian Crawl (Stafford) 29:386
"Writing 'The Galton Case'" (Macdonald) 14:333; 41:270
"Writing through 'Finnegans Wake'" (Cage) 41:84
Writing through 'Finnegans Wake' (Cage) 41:84
"Writing through the Cantos" (Cage) 41:85
"Writing to Aaron" (Levertov) 15:339
"Writing Your Love Down" (Jensen) 37:188
Writings (Arghezi)
   See Scrieri
Writings and Drawings (Dylan) 3:130; 12:189
"Writings on a Cave Wall" (Dowell) 60:107-08
"Writings to an Unfinished Accompaniment" (Merwin) 88:187
Writings to an Unfinished Accompaniment (Merwin) 3:339-40; 5:286-87; 8:389; 13:383; 45:276; 88:192-94, 200, 202, 205
"Written, Directed By, and Starring..." (Simmons) 43:410
"Written in 1938" (Ewart) 46:148
"Written in Dejection near Rome" (Bly) 10:56
"Written in My Dream by W.C. Williams" (Ginsberg) 109:324
"Written Off" (Enright) 31:146
Written on Water (Tomlinson) 4:544, 547-48; 13:548-49; 45:398
Written Stone (Bonnefoy)
   See Pierre écrite
"Written Water" (Ammons) 57:50
"Written While Riding the Long Island Rail Road" (Swenson) 61:397
"Wrong" (Matthews) 40:324
"Wrong Beauty" (Grass)
   See "Falsche Schönheit"
The Wrong Box (Gelbart) 21:125
"Wrong 'Em Boyo" (Clash) 30:46-7
"The Wrong Folks" (Powers) 4:419
"Wrong Formula" (McGinley) 14:366
"The Wrong Lunch Line" (Mohr) 12:446
The Wrong Man (Hitchcock) 16:342-43, 346, 358
"Wrong Monday" (Piercy) 62:378
"Wrong Number" (Bukowski) 41:64
The Wrong Set, and Other Stories (Wilson) 2:470; 3:534
The Wrong Side of the Park (Mortimer) 28:284-85
"The Wrong Stop" (Calvino) 33:100; 73:33
"The Wrong Sun" (Coupland) 85:35, 39
"A Wrong Turning in American Poetry" (Bly) 38:50
The Wrong Way Down (Daly) 52:90
"Wrong Words" (Amis) 40:44
WSW (West South West) (Moure) 88:225-26, 230-31
Wu (Pa Chin)
   See Fog
"The Wub" (Dick)
   See "Beyond Lies the Wub"
"Wuden't Me" (Berry) 17:56
"Wunderkind" (McCullers) 12:433
Wünsche (Wellershoff) 46:435
Wunschkonzert (Request Concert) (Kroetz) 41:234, 236-38
Wunscholses Unglück (A Sorrow beyond Dreams: A Life Story) (Handke) 5:163, 165-67; 8:261, 263; 10:255-56, 258; 38:218-19, 221-24, 227
"Wunschzettel" (Weiss) 8:545
"Wu-Sang-Kuei" (Guillen) 79:229
"Wuthering Heights" (Plath) 51:345; 111:200, 202, 214
Wuthering Heights (Bunuel)
   See Abismos de pasion
The Wycherly Woman (Macdonald) 2:255; 14:334
"The Wykehamist" (Betjeman) 43:35
Wyndmere (Muske) 90:312-15
"Wyndmere, Wyndmere" (Muske) 90:313
Wyrds (Allen) 84:28
Wyst: Alastor 1716 (Vance) 35:421
"X" (Abbott) 48:6
"X" (Merrill) 8:382
"X" (Thesen) 56:415
The X Factor (Norton) 12:457, 468
X: Writings, '79-'82 (Cage) 41:85-6
Xaipe: Seventy-One Poems (Cummings) 15:163; 68:31, 42, 48, 52
Xala (Ousmane) 66:336, 341-42, 344-45
"Xanadu" (Thomas) 13:539; 107:315-19, 326
"Xavier Speaking" (Baxter) 45:51; 78:16
"Xeethra" (Smith) 43:424
Xenia (Montale) 7:224-25, 228, 231; 9:386-88; 18:340-41
"Xenia I" (Montale) 9:387-89
"Xenia II" (Montale) 9:387-8
Xénophiles (Breton) 54:30; 9:128
"Xerox" (Belitt) 22:54
"Xi" (Tolson) 105:242, 251
"Xiaohuolun shang" ("On a Small Steamboat") (Ding Ling) 68:58
Xiccarph (Smith) 43:418
"Xmas Coming" (Rexroth) 112:377
XPD (Deighton) 22:118-19; 46:129
"X-Ray" (Abse) 29:20
"X-Ray Photograph" (Hope) 51:227
Y and X (Olson) 29:330
"Y/Me" (Grayson) 38:211-12
Y pondrán esposas a las flores (Arrabal)
   See Et ils passèrent des menottes aux fleurs
"Ya no es posible" (Aleixandre) 9:12
"Yacht for Sale" (MacLeish) 68:287, 290
"Yaddo" (Rakosi) 47:347
"Yadkin Picnic" (Ammons) 57:50
"Yage" (Ginsberg) 109:325
The Yage Letters (Burroughs) 109:184, 187
"Yaikini" (Kenny) 87:241, 246
"Yajima Ryudo" (Shiga) 33:367
The Yakuza (Schrader) 26:389
The Yakuza (Towne) 87:360
Yankee Doodle (Linney) 51:263
Yankee Privateer (Norton) 12:456
"The Yanks Are Coming, in Five Breathless Colors" (Perelman) 49:265
Yanks Three Detroit Zero Top of the Seventh (Reynolds) 38:387
"Yánnina" (Merrill) 13:376, 381-82; 18:328
"Yaqzat al mumya'" ("The Awakening of the Mummy") (Mahfuz) 55:174

A Yard of Sun: A Summer Comedy (Fry) 2:143-44
"Yarrow" (Oates) 108:384
"Yase: September" (Snyder) 32:387
"The Yattering and Jack" (Barker) 52:51
Yawar fiesta (Arguedas) 10:8, 10; 18:7, 9-10
The Yawning Heights (Aksyonov) 37:13
The Yawning Heights (Zinoviev)
  See *Ziyayuschiye vysoty*
"Ye Olde Ivory Tower" (Perelman) 49:258
"Yea Tigers" (Souster) 5:395
Yea! Wildcats (Tunis) 12:598
"The Year" (Milosz) 82:295
"The Year 1905" (Pasternak)
  See "Devyatsat pyaty god"
A Year and a Day (Mayne) 12:404-05
Year Before Last (Boyle) 58:64-5
Year Five of the Algerian Revolution (Fanon)
  See *L'an V de la révolution algérienne*
A Year from Monday: New Lectures and Writings (Cage) 41:77-83, 85-6
A Year in Provence (Mayle) 89:143, 145-47, 149-54
A Year in the Dark: Journal of a Film Critic, 1968-1969 (Adler) 31:11, 13
"The Year of Getting to Know Us" (Canin) 55:36, 38-9
The Year of Living Dangerously (Koch) 42:260-62, 264-65, 268
The Year of Living Dangerously (Williamson) 56:437-38, 443
"The Year of Mourning" (Jeffers) 54:235
The Year of My Rebirth (Stuart) 8:507; 34:375
The Year of Silence (Bell) 102:2-3, 8
"The Year of the Big Spring Clean" (Aldiss) 40:17
The Year of the Century: 1876 (Brown) 47:37-8
"The Year of the Child" (Hayden) 37:156
"The Year of the Double Spring" (Swenson) 4:534; 106:338
Year of the Dragon (Stone) 73:365, 370, 382
The Year of the French (Flanagan) 25:163-67; 52:148, 151-55
"The Year of the Jackpot" (Heinlein) 55:304
"Year of the Pigeons" (Still) 49:365
The Year of the Raccoon (Kingman) 17:245
"The Year of the Sloes, for Ishi" (Muldoon) 72:279
The Year of the Unicorn (Norton) 12:468
"The Year of the Whale" (Brown) 5:78; 48:57
The Year of the Whale (Brown) 100:84
The Year of the Young Rebels (Spender) 41:422; 91:261
The Year One (Raine) 45:331, 333-34, 341
A Year or So with Edgar (Higgins) 18:233
"Yearning for My Mother" (Tanizaki)
  See "Haha no kouru ki"
"Yearning for the Day" (Aleixandre) 36:29
Yearning: Race, Gender, and Cultural Politics (hooks) 94:131, 145-50, 159
"Years" (Plath) 5:339; 9:426-27, 433; 111:175, 204
The Years (Haavikko)
  See *Vuodet*
The Years (Souster) 5:396; 14:504
The Years as Catches: First Poems, 1939-1946 (Duncan) 55:293-94
The Years Between (du Maurier) 59:286
"A Year's Changes" (Harrison) 33:198
"Year's End" (Hacker) 91:111
"Year's End" (Voigt) 54:430-31
"Year's End" (Wilbur) 53:401-02

"The Year's First Rain" (Clark) 38:121, 128
"The Years from You to Me" (Celan) 82:47
"The Years in Exile" (Metcalf) 37:300, 306
Years of Hope (Paustovsky)
  See *The Time of Great Expectations*
"Years of Indiscretion" (Ashbery) 13:33
The Years with Ross (Thurber) 5:436
"Yeats" (Plath) 5:345
Yeats (Bloom) 24:71; 103:19, 36, 39
Yeats (Tuohy) 37:430
"Yeats an Example?" (Heaney) 74:178
"Yeats in Civil War" (Boland) 113:93, 121
"Yeats in Dublin" (Watkins) 43:453
Yeats: The Man and the Masks (Ellmann) 50:308-09
"Yeats's Tower" (Watkins) 43:441
Yehuda (Levin) 7:206
"Yehuda Ha-Levi" (Amichai) 57:44
"Yehuda Halevi, Ibn Gabirol, Leah Goldberg meta" ("Leah Goldberg Died") (Amichai) 116:118
"Yeletov" (Shammas) 55:86
"Yellow" (Jacobsen) 48:195
Yellow Back Radio Broke-Down (Reed) 2:368-69; 3:424-25; 5:368-70; 6:448-50; 13:479; 32:359, 364; 60:300, 302, 305, 307-08, 311-12
"The Yellow Bird" (Abse) 29:13
"The Yellow Bird" (Williams) 15:579; 45:453, 456
"A Yellow Flower" (Cortazar)
  See "Una flor amarilla"
Yellow Flowers in the Antipodean Room (Frame) 2:141
  See *Yellow Flowers in the Antipodean Room*
Yellow for Peril, Black for Beautiful: Poems and a Play (Cassity) 42:95, 98
The Yellow Heart (Neruda)
  See *El corazón amarillo*
"The Yellow House" (MacEwen) 55:169
The Yellow House on the Corner (*House on the Corner*) (Dove) 50:152-53, 155; 81:132-34, 136-37, 143, 145, 151
Yellow Man (Endo)
  See *Kiiroi hito*
"Yellow Pages" (Raine) 103:179, 188
The Yellow Pages: Fifty-Nine Poems (Merrill) 6:323-24
"Yellow Pitcher Plant" (Gunn) 81:178, 188
A Yellow Raft in Blue Water (Dorris) 109:296-97, 299-301, 303, 306, 308-13
The Yellow Room (Hall) 1:137; 37:146
"The Yellow Rose" (Borges) 83:159
Yellow Submarine (Lennon and McCartney) 12:360, 365
"The Yellow Sugar" (Vollmann) 89:278
"Yellow Tent" (Graver) 70:51
"Yellow Trains" (Lively) 32:277
The Yellow Wind (Grossman) 67:57-64, 74
"Yellow Woman" (Silko) 23:409-10, 412; 74:321, 332-35, 338; 114:314
"Yellowjackets" (Komunyakaa) 94:241
"Yentl the Yeshiva Boy" (Singer) 6:511; 15:509; 38:416-17; 69:320
"Yer Blues" (Lennon and McCartney) 35:266
Yer demir gök bakir (*Iron Earth, Copper Sky*) (Kemal) 14:299-301
"Yes and No" (Grigson) 7:135
Yes from No-Man's-Land (Kops) 4:274
"Yes: I Mean So OK—Love" (Bronk) 10:74
"Yes, the Agency Can Handle That" (Fearing) 51:117
Yes Yes No No (Kushner) 81:204

The Yeshira (Grade)
  See *Tsemakh Atlas*
The Yeshiva (Grade) 10:246, 248-49
"Yesterday" (Lennon and McCartney) 12:359, 375; 35:278, 289, 293
"Yesterday" (Merwin) 45:274; 88:205
"Yesterday I Was Called Nigger" (Guillen)
  See "Ayer me dijeron negro"
Yesterday, Today, Tomorrow (De Sica) 20:91, 94
"Yesterday, Tomorrow, Always" (Derleth) 31:136
Yesterday We Saw Mermaids (Friesner) 70:332
"Yesterday's Light" 75:61
"Yesterday's Love" (Farrell) 66:129
Yesterday's Magic (Williams) 15:577
Yesterday's Spy (Deighton) 7:75-6
"Yesterday's Tomorrow" (Roberts) 14:463
Yesterday's Wine (Nelson) 17:304, 306
"Yester-Me, Yester-You, Yesterday" (Wonder) 12:655
Les yeux bleux, cheveux noir (*Blue Eyes, Black Hair*) (Duras) 68:85, 87-8, 99-100; 100:118, 127
Les yeux de la nuit (Woolrich) 77:395
"Les yeux de la statue" (Laye) 38:286
Les yeux et la memoire (*Eyes and Memory*) (Aragon) 22:38
"Yeux Glauques" (Pound) 48:287
Les yeux ouverts; entretiens avec Matthieu Galey (*With Open Eyes: Conversations with Matthieu Galey*) (Yourcenar) 38:457, 462, 464; 87:402-04, 419, 424, 433-34
"The Yglesias of Ignatius Livingstone Island" (Schaeffer) 22:370
"YgUDuh" (Cummings) 15:162
"Yiddishe Kopf" (Ginsberg) 109:328
"Yige nüren he yige nanren" ("A Woman and a Man") (Ding Ling) 68:59, 66-7
Yikigunishu (Kawabata) 107:107
Yin: New Poems (Kizer) 39:169-71; 80:186
"Yin Yang" (Mitchell) 12:438
Yksityisiä asioita (Haavikko) 34:170
Ylilääkäri (*The Superintendent*) (Haavikko) 34:173
"Ylla" (Bradbury) 42:38
Yo (Grade) 10:246
"Yo acuso" ("I Accuse") (Neruda) 62:327
Yo, el supremo (*I, the Supreme*) (Roa Bastos) 45:344, 347-51
Yo era un tonto (Alberti) 7:9
Yobgorgle (Pinkwater) 35:318-19
"Yodwigha, on a Red Couch, Among Lilies" (Plath) 111:201
"A yoga class" (Muske) 90:308
The Yogi and the Commissar and Other Essays (Koestler) 3:270-71; 33:230, 233
The Yogi of Cockroach Court (Waters) 88:331, 333-34, 359-60
Yojimbo (Kurosawa) 16:401, 403-06
The Yoknapatawpha Country (Brooks)
  See *William Faulkner: The Yoknapatawpha Country*
"Yoko" (Gunn) 18:204; 32:209
"Yom Kippur 1984" (Rich) 73:315
"Yonder Stands the Sinner" (Young) 17:572
Yonnondio: From the Thirties (Olsen) 4:385-87; 13:432; 114:194-96, 198, 201-03, 209, 211-12, 215, 220-29; 231-32, 235, 237
"York: In Memoriam W. H. Auden" ("Iork") (Brodsky) 36:81; 100:54

"Yosaku the Settler" (Ibuse)   22:227

"Yoshino: False Dawn of the Cherry Blossom" (Lieberman)   36:261

Yoshinokuzu (Arrowroot) (Tanizaki)   28:420-21

"You" (Borges)   13:110

"You" (Dubie)   36:133

"You" (Levine)   14:318

"You and I Are Disappearing" (Komunyakaa)   94:225, 231, 233, 240

"You and I Saw Hawks Exchanging Prey" (Wright)   3:544

You and Me (Lang)   20:206; 103:85

"You and the Boss" (Janowitz)   43:211-12

"You, Andrew Marvell" (MacLeish)   14:338; 68:272-73, 284, 286, 290-91, 294

"You Angel You" (Dylan)   4:150

"You Are" (Swenson)   106:337, 347-48

"You Are as Brave as Vincent Van Gogh" (Barthelme)   8:52

"You Are Forever" (Robinson)   21:350-51

You Are Happy (Atwood)   8:28-9; 13:44; 15:36; 25:63-4, 66-7; 84:64-5, 89

"You Are Not I" (Bowles)   53:36-7

You Are Not Poetry (Castellanos)
   See *Poesia no eres tú: Obra poética, 1948-1971*

You Are Now Entering the Human Heart (Frame)   66:144

"You Are the Sunshine of My Life" (Wonder)   12:657, 663

"You Are Welcome!" (Forester)   35:173

"You Are What You Own: A Notebook" (Adams)   46:21

"You Belong to Me" (Costello)   21:69

"You Belong to Me" (Simon)   26:411-12

You Bright and Risen Angels: A Cartoon (Vollmann)   89:275-76, 279-83, 286, 290-92, 298-304, 307, 310

"You Can Cry" (Levine)   33:274

"You Can Depend on Me" (Robinson)   21:350

"You Can Get It If You Really Want" (Cliff)   21:60, 63

"You Can Have It" (Levine)   33:271

"You Can Have It" (Oliver)   98:263

"You Can Leave" (Gaye)   26:134

"You Can Never Go Back" (Haldeman)   61:181

"You Can Start the Poetry Now, Or; News from Crazy Horse" (McGrath)   59:178, 181

"You Can Still Grow Flowers" (Greenberg)   7:134

"You Can't Always Get What You Want" (Jagger and Richard)   17:226, 236

"You Can't Be Any Poorer than Dead" (O'Connor)   15:413

"You Can't Be Wrong and Get Right" (Cliff)   21:63

"You Can't Do That" (Lennon)   35:274

You Can't Get There from Here (Hamner)   12:257-58

You Can't Get There from Here (Hood)   15:286; 28:189-91, 193-94

You Can't Get There from Here (Nash)   23:322

You Can't Keep a Good Woman Down (Walker)   103:357, 366-67, 369, 406-13, 422

"You Can't Rhumboogie in a Ball and Chain" (Fulton)   52:158-59

"You Can't Step into the Same Street Twice" (Dybek)   114:76

"You Can't Stop the Music" (Davies)   21:99

You Can't Take It with You (Capra)   16:155, 159-63

You Can't Take It with You (Hart and Kaufman)

38:260, 262, 265-66; 66:173-76, 178, 180, 182-86, 190-92

You Can't Take Twenty Dogs on a Date (Cavanna)   12:102

"You Could Drive a Person Crazy" (Sondheim)   30:387, 391

You Could Live If They Let You (Markfield)   8:380

You Didn't Even Try (Whalen)   29:444-45

"You Didn't Fit" (Musgrave)   54:341

You Don't Love Yourself (Sarraute)
   See *Tu ne t'aimes pas*

"You Don't Pull No Punches but You Don't Push the River" (Morrison)   21:236

"You, Dr. Martin" (Sexton)   53:313

You, Emperors, and Others: Poems, 1957-1960 (Warren)   4:578; 13:573, 575, 577; 39:265-66

"You Gave Me the Answer" (McCartney)   35:282-83

"You, Genoese Mariner" (Merwin)   5:285; 8:389

"You Gotta Be Crazy" (Pink Floyd)   35:311

"You Gotta Move" (Jagger and Richard)   17:224

"You Had to Go to Funerals" (Walker)   58:404

"You Have Left Your Lotus Pods on the Bus" (Bowles)   53:37

You Have Seen Their Faces (Caldwell)   8:124; 50:299, 301; 60:53, 60-1, 66

You Have to Draw the Line Somewhere (Harris)   12:261-62, 266

"You Haven't Done Nothin'" (Wonder)   12:658, 661

"You, Heavenly" (Bell)   8:66

"You Kissed Lilly" (Bukowski)   41:72

"You Know Charles" (Robison)   42:342

"You Know How to Turn On Those Lights" (Sainte-Marie)   17:431

"You Know I Can't Hear You When the Water's Running" (Anderson)   23:31

"You Know It Makes Sense" (Whalen)   29:447

"You Know Me" (MacEwen)   55:168

"You Lived in Glasgow" (Smith)   64:393

"You Love the Thunder" (Browne)   21:40

You Lovely People (Santos)   22:361-62, 365

"You Make It All Worthwhile" (Davies)   21:99

You Marry the Moon (Haavikko)   34:169

"You May Be Right" (Joel)   26:221

"You Must Meet My Wife" (Sondheim)   30:400

"You Must Remember This" (Coover)   46:121

You Must Remember This (Oates)   52:334-37; 108:374, 378, 390

"You mustn't show weakness" (Amichai)   116:97

"You Never Can Tell" (Berry)   17:54

You Only Live Once (Lang)   20:206, 208, 213-14

You Only Live Twice (Fleming)   30:138, 147-49

"You Pays Your Nickel" (Woolrich)   77:401

"You Really Got a Hold on Me" (Robinson)   21:347, 351

"You Really Got Me" (Davies)   21:89, 102

"You Rope You Tie Me" (Armatrading)   17:9-10

"You Shall above All Things Be Glad and Young" (Cummings)   68:44

"You Shattered" (Ungaretti)
   See "Tu ti spezzasti"

"You Shook Me" (Page and Plant)   12:482

"You Should Have Seen the Mess" (Spark)   5:400

"You Should Live So, Walden Pond" (Perelman)

49:258, 264

"You Speak No English" (Guillen)
   See "Tú no sabe inglé"

"You Still Believe in Me" (Wilson)   12:646

"You Sure Love to Ball" (Gaye)   26:133

You!: The Psychology of Surviving and Enhancing Your Social Life, Love Life, Sex Life, School Life, Home Life, Work Life, Emotional Life, Creative Life, Spiritual Life, Style of Life, Life (Gordon)   26:137-39

You, Too Are Guilty (Abe)
   See *Omaenimo tsumi ga aru*

"You, Too, Can Have a Body" (Scannell)   49:328

You Touched Me! (Williams)   71:360

"You Triflin' Skunk" ("The Triflin' Man") (Miller)   30:263

"You Wear It So Well" (Reed)   21:312-13

You Were Marvellous (Fenton)   32:167-68

"You Were Never Miss Brown to Me" (Williams)   89:321

"You Were Perfectly Fine" (Parker)   68:330, 335

"You Were Wearing" (Koch)   5:219; 44:243

"You Who Swim" (Updike)   23:476

You Will Forget Me (Breton and Soupault)
   See *Vous m'oublierez*

You Will Only Make Matters Worse (Cage)
   See *Diary: How to Improve the World*

You Would If You Loved Me (Gordon)   26:138-39

"You/Your" (Oates)   6:367

"You'll Accomp'ny Me" (Seger)   35:384-85

"You'll Never Be a Man" (Costello)   21:76

"You'll Never Get Away from Me" (Sondheim)   30:377

"You'll Never Know, Dear, How Much I Love You" (Updike)   5:449

"You'll Never See Me Again" (Woolrich)   77:389, 394

"You'll Take the High Road" (Brunner)   8:111

"Young" (Sexton)   53:318, 322, 324

Young Adolf (Bainbridge)   14:36-9; 22:45; 62:30-1

Young Adult Novel (Pinkwater)   35:318-20

Young American Writers (Kostelanetz)   28:212

Young Americans (Bowie)   17:62-4, 66, 68

Young Ames (Edmonds)   35:152, 156

The Young and Beautiful (Benson)   17:49-50

Young and Innocent (Hitchcock)   16:345

"Young and Innocent Days" (Davies)   21:91

The Young and the Damned (Bunuel)
   See *Los olvidados*

"The Young and the Old—Notes on a New History" (Lifton)   67:142

The Young and the Passionate (Fellini)
   See *I vitelloni*

"Young Archimedes" (Huxley)   3:256; 5:193; 11:281

The Young Assassins (Goytisolo)
   See *Juegos de manos*

"Young Bergdorf Goodman Brown" (Leyner)   92:292, 294

The Young Caesar (Warner)   45:435-36

"The Young Dancers" (Zaturenska)   6:586

"Young David" (Amichai)   9:22; 116:85, 87

"Young Edgcumbe" (Causley)   7:42

Young Entry (Keane)   31:230

Young Felix (Swinnerton)   31:422-23

"The Young Folks" (Salinger)   12:521

Young Frankenstein (Brooks)   12:77-80, 82

"The Young Girl" (Roethke)   101:330

"The Young Girl at the Ball" (Hope)   3:250

"Young Girls" (Souster) 14:501

"Young Girls Growing Up (1911)" (Justice) 102:277

"A Young Girl's Journal" (Aickman)
　See "Pages from a Young Girl's Diary"

The Young Girls of Wilko (Wajda) 16:584

"A Young Greek, Killed in the Wars" (Eberhart) 56:88

The Young Grizzly (Corcoran) 17:73

The Young Hemingway (Reynolds) 44:515-18

"A Young Highland Girl Studying Poetry" ("A Highland Girl Studying Poetry") (Smith) 64:387, 396-97

The Young Idea (Coward) 29:139

The Young in One Another's Arms (Rule) 27:418, 420-21

The Young Lady from Paris (Aiken) 35:20

The Young Landlords (Myers) 35:296-97

"Young Lions" (Jones) 76:65-6

The Young Lions (Shaw) 7:409-11, 413-14; 23:399-400; 34:368-70

Young Lonigan (Farrell) 1:98; 4:157, 159; 11:194; 66:112-13, 121, 131-32

The Young Lovers (Garrett) 51:145

Young Lust (Acker) 111:11

"The Young Man" (Gilchrist) 48:121

"Young Man Blues" (Townshend) 17:525

The Young Man From Atlanta (Foote) 91:113-18

"The Young Man from Kalgoorlie" (Bates) 46:56

Young Man in a Hurry: The Story of Cyrus W. Field (Latham) 12:323

Young Man in Chains (Mauriac)
　See *L'enfant chargé de chaines*

A Young Man in Search of Love (Singer) 11:499, 503-04; 23:422; 38:412; 69:303; 111:310

The Young Man Who Arrived Late (Oe)
　See *Okurete kita seinen*

"The Young Man with the Carnation" (Dinesen) 29:159, 161; 95:35, 51

The Young Manhood of Studs Lonigan (Farrell) 1:98; 4:157; 66:120, 127

Young Mark: The Story of a Venture (Almedingen) 12:3, 5-6

Young Martin Luther King (Childress)
　See *The Freedom Drum*

The Young May Moon (Newby) 2:311

"Young Men" (Scott) 43:370

Young Men and Fire (Maclean) 78:242, 243-44

"The Young Men Run" (Brooks) 49:38

"Young Men Waking at Daybreak" (Williams) 45:444

"Young Mothers I" (Olds) 85:285

Young Mr. Lincoln (Ford) 16:304, 310, 319

The Young One (Bunuel) 16:133, 136, 148

"The Young Park" (Koch) 44:249

Young Patullo (Stewart) 7:466

A Young Person's Guide to Ballet (Streatfeild) 21:412-13

The Young Pobble's Guide to His Toes (Ewart) 46:153-54

Young Razzle (Tunis) 12:596

The Young Rebecca: Writings of Rebecca West, 1911-17 (West) 31:459-60

"The Young Rector" (Nowlan) 15:398

Young Samurai (Mishima) 2:286

The Young Scoundrel (Coles) 67:180

Young Shoulders (Wain) 46:418-19

The Young Unicorns (L'Engle) 12:347-48

The Young Visitors (Wain) 46:414, 416, 418

"The Young Wife" (Walcott) 67:359, 361

A Young Wife's Tale (Sansom) 6:483

"A Young Woman in Green Lace" (Parker) 68:336

"Young Women" (Redgrove) 41:348

"Young Women in Rollers" (Dunn) 40:167

A Young World (De Sica) 20:94

Youngblood (Killens) 10:300

Youngblood Hawke (Wouk) 9:580; 38:448-49

Younger Brother (Ringwood) 48:330

"The Younger Sister's Clothes" (Kawabata) 107:107-08

The Youngest (Tindall) 7:473

The Youngest Science: Notes of a Medicine Watcher (Thomas) 35:412-14

"Younghusband" (Simmons) 43:414

"Youngsters" (Parra)
　See "Jóvenes"

"Your Attention Please" (Porter) 33:319, 322, 326

"Your Birthday in the California Mountains" (Rexroth) 112:386

"Your Body Is Stars Whose Million Glitter Here" (Spender) 41:419, 427

"Your Bright Baby Blues" (Browne) 21:39

"Your Errant Mom" (Robison) 98:307-08

"Your Faces, O My Sisters! Your Faces Filled of Light!" (Tiptree) 48:389

"Your Haploid Heart" (Tiptree) 48:389, 395-96

Your Hours Are Numbered (Cernuda)
　See *Con las horas contadas*

"Your House" (Akhmadulina)
　See "Tvoi dom"

"Your Impending Divorce" (Klappert) 57:259

"Your Kiss Is Sweet" (Wonder) 12:663

"Your Letter" (Armatrading) 17:10-11

Your Lover Just Called: Stories of Joan and Richard Maple (Updike)
　See *Too Far to Go: The Maples Stories*

"Your Morning Eagle Boy" (Jacobsen) 48:194

"Your Mother Should Know" (Lennon and McCartney) 12:362

Your Murderer (Aksyonov)
　See *Vash ubiytsa*

Your Native Land, Your Life (*Native Land*) (Rich) 73:314-18, 323, 325-26, 332; 76:211

"Your Own Private Thermidore" (Bernard) 59:46

Your Royal Hostage (Fraser) 107:50, 52

"Your Sightless Days" (Monette) 82:323, 332

Your Sins and Mine (Caldwell) 28:63-4

Your Skin (Hyde) 21:175

"Your Story" (De Marinis) 54:101

"Your Teeth Are Ivory Towers" (Empson) 33:142

"Your Time Is Gonna Come" (Page and Plant) 12:479

"Your Tiny Hand is Frozen" (Aickman) 57:2, 6

"Your Tired, Your Poor" (Mueller) 51:283-84

"Your Turn" (Sondheim) 30:390

Your Turn to Curtsy, My Turn to Bow (Goldman) 1:123; 48:128

"Your Way Home" (Williams) 42:443

"Your Wedding and You" (Keillor) 40:274

"Your Wound" (Pack) 13:438

"You're" (Plath) 9:428; 111:167

You're a Big Boy Now (Coppola) 16:231, 233, 236, 244-45

You're a Good Man, Charlie Brown (Schulz) 12:524

You're All Alone (Leiber) 25:310

"You're Dirt" (Reed) 21:316-17

"You're Gonna Love Tomorrow/Love Will See Us Through" (Sondheim) 30:400

"You're Gonna Make Me Lonesome When You Go" (Dylan) 77:173

You're Human Like the Rest of Them (Johnson) 9:303

You're in Love, Charlie Brown (Schulz) 12:527

"You're My Home" (Joel) 26:218

"You're So Vain" (Simon) 26:407-13

You're Something Else, Charlie Brown (Schulz) 12:524

"You're the One" (Simon) 26:411-12

"You're Ugly, Too" (Moore) 68:298, 300

"Yours" (Robison) 42:342; 98:310

"Youth" (Wright) 10:544

Youth (Ichikawa) 20:185

"Youth and Age on Beaulieu River, Hants" (Betjeman) 43:36

"Youth in an Austrian City" ("Youth in an Austrian Town") (Bachmann) 69:35-7

"Youth in an Austrian Town" (Bachmann)
　See "Youth in an Austrian City"

"Youth on Mars" (Abbott) 48:6

"Youth Stares at Minoan Sunset" (Warren) 18:535

The Youth Who Came in Late (Oe)
　See *Okurete kita seinen*

"Youthful Air" (p'Bitek) 96:286

"Youthful Truth-Seeker, Half-Naked, at Night, Running Down Beach South of San Francisco" (Warren) 39:272

Youthful Writings (Camus) 9:152

"Youth—Manhood—Middle Age" (Hall) 51:170

"You've Got Me on a String" (Ian) 21:189

"You've Got to Be Selfish" (Ferber) 93:139

You've Had Your Time (Burgess) 81:300-01, 303-07, 310

"Yowaki Utsuwa" ("The Weaker Sex") (Kawabata) 107:107

"Yo-Yo" (Davies) 21:107

Yr wylan deg (Roberts) 15:445

Yü (*Rain*) (Pa Chin) 18:372-73

Yukiguni (*Snow Country*) (Kawabata) 2:222-23; 5:207-08; 9:309, 312, 316; 18:280, 283, 285; 107:71-2, 98-101, 103-06, 108-12, 114

Yukinojo henge (*An Actor's Revenge*) (Ichikawa) 20:183

"Yume no ukihashi" ("The Bridge of Dreams"; "The Floating Bridge of Dreams") (Tanizaki) 8:510; 14:527; 28:420

Yurei wa koko ni iru (*Here Is a Ghost*) (Abe) 8:1

"Yurokon" (Harris) 25:217

Yusufçuk Yusuf (Kemal) 29:268

Yvonne, Princess of Burgundy (Gombrowicz)
　See *Iwona; Ksiezniczka Burgunda*

Yvor Winters: Uncollected Essays and Reviews (Winters) 32:465

"Z" (Merrill) 8:383

Z (Vassilikos) 4:551-52; 8:524-25

Zabriskie Point (Antonioni) 20:36-40

Zabriskie Point (Shepard) 48:490

"Zachaeus in the Leaves" (Watkins) 43:451

"Zadar" (Strand) 41:440

Zaduszki (*All Soul's Day*) (Konwicki) 117:282

"Zagrowsky Tells" (Paley) 37:339

"The Zahir" (Borges)
　See "El Zahir"

"El Zahir" ("The Zahir") (Borges) 2:76; 4:73; 6:90; 8:95, 97; 13:111-12; 48:39; 83:157,

166, 185-86
"Zahlen" ("Numbers") (Sachs) 98:337
"Zai heianzhong" ("In the Darkness") (Ding Ling) 68:55
"Zakhar-Kalita" ("Zakhar-the-Pouch") (Solzhenitsyn) 7:432
"Zakhar-the-Pouch" (Solzhenitsyn)
 See "Zakhar-Kalita"
"Zaklinanie" ("Incantation") (Akhmadulina) 53:13
Zalmen; or, The Madness of God (Wiesel)
 See *Zalmen; ou, La folie de Dieu*
Zalmen; ou, La folie de Dieu (*Zalmen; or, The Madness of God*) (Wiesel) 5:493; 37:452, 455
"Zambesi and Ranee" (Swenson) 106:340
Zami: A New Spelling of My Name (Lorde) 71:234-35, 237, 243
Zamolxe (*Zamolxes*) 75:64-5, 72
Zamolxes
 See *Zamolxe*
"Zamour; or, A Tale of Inheritance" (Goyen) 40:218
Zanth (Anthony) 35:37
"Zanzibar" (Joel) 26:217
The Zap Gun (Dick) 72:110, 121-22
Zap Number One (Crumb) 17:84-5
Zap Number Zero (Crumb) 17:84-5
"Zapatos" (Boyle) 90:48
Zapisi nekotorykh epizodov, sdelannye v gorode Goguleve Andreem Petrovichem Koviakinym (*Koviakin's Notes*; *Kovyakin's Diary*; *Kovyakin's Journal*; *A Record of Certain Episodes Made in the Town of Gogulev by Andrey Petrovich Kovyakin*) (Leonov) 92:237, 242, 256, 265, 275
Zappa in New York (Zappa) 17:592
Zapretnyi plod (Iskander)
 See *Trinadtsaty podvig Gerakla*
"Zaruthustra and the Youth" (Krleza)
 See "Zarutustra i mladic"
"Zarutustra i mladic" ("Zaruthustra and the Youth") (Krleza) 114:171
Zashchita Chika (Iskander) 47:198
Zastave (*The Banners*) (Krleza) 114:166, 177, 186, 188
Zastrozzi, the Master of Discipline (Walker) 61:423, 427
Zatovarennaia bochkotara (Aksyonov)
 See *The Tare of Barrels*
"Zauberspruch" (Celan) 82:52
Zavist' (*Envy*) (Olesha) 8:430, 432-33
Zazie dans le métro (*Zazie in the Metro*) (Queneau) 5:357-59, 362; 10:432; 42:330-31, 333
Zazie in the Metro (Queneau)
 See *Zazie dans le métro*
Zbabelci (*The Cowards*) (Skvorecky) 15:510; 39:225, 229; 69:326, 330, 334, 336, 339, 341-43, 346, 348-50, 352
A ZBC of Ezra Pound (Brooke-Rose) 40:106, 111
The Z-D Generation (Sanders) 53:309
Zdobycie wladzy (*The Seizure of Power*; *The Usurpers*) (Milosz) 22:305; 56:232
The Zebra-Striped Hearse (Macdonald) 2:255; 3:308; 14:334; 41:265-66, 270
Zee and Co. (O'Brien) 5:313; 116:192
Zeely (Hamilton) 26:147, 149, 153
"Zehn abendgedichte" (Jandl) 34:196
Zeichen im Sand (Sachs) 98:323
Zeit der Schuldlosen (Lenz) 27:252-53
"Die Zeit des Weltbildes" (Heidegger) 24:277

"Die Zeit vergeht" (Jandl) 34:197
Zeitgehöft (*Farmstead of Time*) (Celan) 53:73-4, 76, 81-2
"The Zeks as a Nation" (Solzhenitsyn) 7:440
Zelig (Allen) 52:48
"Zelzah: A Tale from Long Ago" (Mazer) 26:291
"Zemlia" (Pasternak) 18:389
Zemnoy prostor (*Spacious Earth*) (Pasternak) 18:383
Zen and the Art of Motorcycle Maintenance: An Inquiry into Values (Pirsig) 4:403-05; 6:420-21; 73:284-90, 292-96, 298-302, 307, 309
Zenia's Way (Polonsky) 92:402-03
"Zenith" (Le Guin) 45:216
"The Zenner Trophy" (Vidal) 33:407
"Zennor Cottages" (Watkins) 43:452
Zenyatta Mondatta (Police, The) 26:365
"The Zeppelin Factory" (Dove) 50:153; 81:139
"Zerelda" (Jiles) 58:276
Zerkalo (Tarkovsky) 75:382-85, 387-90, 392-95, 397, 401, 412
"Zero" (Gallagher) 63:118, 126
"Zero" (O'Hara) 42:327
"Zero and Then Some" (Ammons) 57:49-50, 52
Zero db (Bell) 102:4, 6
Zero Degree Writing (Barthes)
 See *Le degré zéro de l'écriture*
"Zero Gee" (Bova) 45:69
"Zero Hour" (Bradbury) 15:85
"Zero Hour" (Cardenal)
 See "La hora O"
Zero Hour (Gunnars) 69:268
Zero Hour and Other Documentary Poems (Cardenal) 31:76, 78-9
The Zero Stone (Norton) 12:458, 466-67
"Zeroing In" (Levertov) 66:252
Zert (*The Joke*) (Kundera) 4:276-78; 9:321-22; 19:266-68, 270; 32:257-62, 269, 272; 68:231-34, 236, 239-46, 261; 115:308, 311, 320-21, 347-49, 353, 356
"Zeta" (Tolson) 105:242-43, 254, 284
Zetland: By a Character Witness (Bellow) 33:69-70
Zettels Traum (Schmidt) 56:391-93, 395-96, 402
"Zeus over Redeye" (Hayden) 37:152
"Zhal', chto vas ne bylo s nami" (Aksyonov)
 See "Wish You Were Here"
Zhasnete svetla (*Put Out the Lights*; *Turn Off the Lights*; *Turn Out the Lights*) (Seifert) 34:257; 44:425; 93:319, 334-35, 342
Zhdu lyubvi ne verolomnoi 59:381
"Zhenia's Childhood" (Pasternak)
 See "Detstvo Luvers"
"Zhenshchina i more" (Yevtushenko) 13:620
"Zhivago and His Poems" (O'Hara) 78:347
"Zhivotut..." (Bagryana) 10:12
Zhizn i neobychainye prikliucheniia soldata Ivana Chonkina (*The Life and Extraordinary Adventures of Private Ivan Chonkin*) (Voinovich) 10:504-09; 49:374-82
Zhizn' i sud'ba (*Life and Fate*) (Grossman) 41:189-95; 59:368, 384, 388, 394
Zia (O'Dell) 30:274
Ziemia Ulro (*The Land of Ulro*) (Milosz) 31:269-71; 56:250; 82:274-75, 277, 280-81, 297, 299
The Zig Zag Walk (Logan) 5:254-55
"Zigeuner" (Coward) 1:65

Gli zii di Sicilia (*Sicilian Uncles*) (Sciascia) 8:473; 41:392
"Zillebeke Brook" (Blunden) 56:41
"Zima Junction" (Yevtushenko)
 See "Zima Station"
"Zima Station" (*Station Zima*; *Winter Station*; "Zima Junction") (Yevtushenko) 1:382; 3:547; 26:460, 469; 51:428, 430, 433
"Zimbabwe" (Marley) 17:273
Zimmerlautstärke (Kunze) 10:310
Zimmerschlacht (*Homefront*) (Walser) 27:461-62
"Lo zio acquativo" ("The Aquatic Uncle") (Calvino) 33:98
"Zion Train" (Marley) 17:273
Zip: A Novel of the Left and Right (Apple) 33:18-22
Zititai elpis (*Wanted: Hope*) (Samarakis) 5:381
Zivo meso (Popa) 19:375
Ziyayuschiye vysoty (*The Yawning Heights*) (Zinoviev) 19:485-90
"The Ziz" (Hollander) 8:300
Znaki zycia (*Signs of Life*) (Dabrowska) 15:169
Zniewolony umysl (*The Captive Mind*) (Milosz) 5:292; 11:376; 22:304-05, 308, 312; 31:263, 270; 56:232, 245, 250; 82:277-78, 280, 282, 289, 292-93, 297, 308, 311
The Zodiac (Dickey) 10:140-42; 15:174-75; 47:91-3, 95-7; 109:245, 264
"Zodiac 2000" (Ballard) 36:44
Zolotaja naš zelezka (Aksyonov) 22:27; 101:25
Zolotaya kareta (*The Golden Coach*) (Leonov) 92:247, 251, 255, 266, 270, 277
"Zombie" (Oates) 108:395-96
Zona sagrada (*Holy Place*; *The Sacred Zone*) (Fuentes) 8:222; 113:243
Zone of the Interior (Sigal) 7:425
"The Zonnebeke Road" (Blunden) 56:43
"The Zoo" (Smith) 8:491
Zoo (MacNeice) 53:234
"Zoo Celeste" (Huxley) 11:283
The Zoo Gang (Gallico) 2:147
"Zoo Keeper's Wife" (Plath) 5:345; 111:159, 171, 204
The Zoo Story (Albee) 1:5; 2:1, 3; 3:7; 5:10, 13; 9:2-6, 10; 11:13; 13:3-4; 25:33-5; 53:24, 26; 86:124; 113:3, 5-6, 15-16, 18, 21, 28, 30-1, 36, 40, 44-6, 51, 54
"Zooey" (Salinger) 1:295, 299; 3:444; 12:498, 502, 512-13
Zooman and the Sign (Fuller) 25:181-82
Zoot Allures (Zappa) 17:592
Zoot Suit (Valdez) 84:399-404, 406, 408, 413-17
El zorro de arriba y el zorro de abajo (Arguedas) 10:9; 18:8
Zorze wieczorne (*Evening Dawns*) (Konwicki) 117:284
Zothique (Smith) 43:417-18
Zothique (Vance) 35:428
"I zoungla" (Samarakis) 5:381-82
I zoungla (*The Jungle*) (Samarakis) 5:381
"Zov" ("Call") (Bagryana) 10:14
"Zovut na moreto" (Bagryana) 10:12
Zu den Akten (Eich) 15:204
"Zubby Sutra" (Harmon) 38:244
Zubr (*The Aurochs*; *Bison*) 59:388, 393
Zuckerman Bound: A Trilogy and an Epilogue (Roth) 47:357-59, 364; 86:260
Zuckerman Unbound (Roth) 31:337-38, 340-42, 345-46, 348; 47:357-58, 365; 86:256, 258

"Der Zug war pünktlich" ("The Train Was on Time") (Boell)   2:68; 9:108; 11:53, 55-6, 58; 27:55-9, 67; 39:292-95; 72:78-80, 100

Zulu Poems (Kunene)   85:160, 162, 164-65, 177-78

Zum Tee bei Dr. Borsig (*Tea with Dr. Borsig*) (Boell)   11:57

Zuma (Young)   17:575-76, 579, 582-83

Zuqaq al-Midaqq (*Midaq Alley*; *Zuqaq al-Midaqq*) (Mahfuz)   52:292, 29-300, 304; 55:181, 185, 188

Zuqaq al-Midaqq (Mahfuz)
  See *Zuqaq al-Midaqq*

"Zürich, the Stork Inn" (Celan)   53:76

Zvezda na morjaka (Bagryana)   10:14

Zvezdnyi bilet (Aksyonov)
  See *A Starry Ticket*

Zwei Ansichten (*Two Views*) (Johnson)   5:200-01; 10:283; 15:304; 40:268

"Die zwei Seelen" (Hildesheimer)   49:174

Zweiunddreig Zähne (Grass)   88:144

"Der Zwerg und die Puppe" ("The Dwarf and the Doll") (Boell)   27:66

Zwierzoczlekoupiór (*The Anthropos-Specter-Beast*) (Konwicki)   117:277, 285-87, 291

"Zygmunt" (Reading)   47:350